Economic Indicators Handbook

Fourth Edition

Economic Indicators Handbook

TIME SERIES • CONVERSIONS • DOCUMENTATION

Fourth Edition

Compiled and Edited by
Arsen J. Darnay

GALE

DETROIT • NEW YORK • LONDON

Arsen J. Darnay, *Editor*

Editorial Code & Data Inc. Staff

Sherae R. Carroll, *Data Entry*
Ken Muth, *Data Processing*

Gale Research Staff

Amanda Quick, *Developmental Editor*
Lawrence W. Baker, *Senior Developmental Editor*
Mary Beth Trimper, *Production Director*
Shanna P. Heilveil, *Production Assistant*
Cynthia Baldwin, *Art Director*
Pursuit Studios, *Cover Designers*

Gale Research
835 Penobscot Building
Detroit, Mi 48226-4094
ISBN 0-7876-1681-8
Printed in the United States of America

TABLE OF CONTENTS

INTRODUCTION

SUMMARY

Economic Indicators Handbook (EIH) is now in its fourth edition. It presents a wide range of statistical series commonly used for measuring the economy of the United States. Featured are national income and product accounts, including Gross National Product (GNP) and Gross Domestic Product (GDP); the composite indexes of leading, lagging, and coincident indicators and their subcomponents; other cyclic indicators; selected economic series; a comprehensive presentation of the Consumer Price Index (CPI) in the aggregate and for 27 cities; a substantial selection from Producer Price Index (PPI); and selected stock market indexes. *EIH* covers 266 series in this edition; most are shown with detailed subdivisions or in constant and actual dollars so that, in total, 801 tables are presented. In all cases where data were available, series begin with the earliest date for which statistics were collected or estimated by the government or other sources, ranging from 1864-67 for GNP, 1913 for the CPI, and the 1940s for most business cycle indicators. *EIH* also features descriptive text; each major category is introduced and brief explanations, including an indication of significance, are provided for each series. Texts and tables are thoroughly indexed.

NEW IN THE FOURTH EDITION

The fourth edition of *EIH* updates all series from their beginning to 1997. Some series were dropped because they have become obsolete. Others were added. Specific changes include the following:

- All series have been completely updated. Typically, two years of new data have been added to series that reach back to historical beginnings.

- The updated Gross Domestic Product (GDP) series, shown for the first time in the last edition, is now restated back to 1929 at the aggregate level.

- Gross National Product (GNP) is now presented from 1929 to 1997 in chained (1992) dollars. Historical GNP data are also shown. The series in 1987 constant dollars has been dropped.

- *EIH* now presents business cycle indicators as published by The Conference Board. Preparation of this series has been transferred by the U.S. Department of Commerce to this private-sector agency. The Leading, Coincident, and Lagging indicators have undergone change. These changes are reported for the first time.

- The new American Stock Exchange Composite Index is shown for the first time. The obsoleted Market Value Index has been dropped. A new table showing the sub-indices of the New York Stock Exchange has been added.

- All texts have been updated, to the extent necessary, to reflect changes in the series shown.

SCOPE

EIH presents statistical series grouped by major categories.

GNP and GDP. The fundamental measure of the U.S. economy—at least until the fall of 1991—has been GNP. For that reason, *EIH* begins with a presentation of aggregate GNP beginning with data for the 1869-1928 period and ending with data for 1997. This section is followed by a comprehensive presentation of GDP and all of its components, from 1929 to 1958 at the aggregate level and from 1959 through 1997 at the detailed level.

1995 was the year for one of the government's comprehensive, benchmark revisions of NIPA and thus of the GDP and its components. This edition continues to reflect those changes and presents summaries of what has changed in this Introduction and in chapter texts.

Constant dollar data have been replaced by chained dollar data in the NIPA accounts. This change is fully reflected in this edition and complete explanations for the changed indexes, and how they work, are incorporated.

Business Cycle Indicators. The federal government attempts to predict business cycles—recurring brief periods of decline in GNP/GDP followed by recovery and periods of growth—by using a number of economic series that lead the economy, coincide with it, or lag it (see Chapter 3). The composite indexes of leading, coincident, and lagging indicators are presented in full from the earliest period for which they are available; the series that make up these composite indexes are also presented. In this edition, for the first time, data prepared by The Conference Board, a not-for-profit business research organization, are presented. The Conference Board assumed the task of preparing these indicators under a contract with the U.S. Department of Commerce.

Cyclic Indicators. Not all series classified as cyclic in behavior are included in the leading, coincident, and lagging indexes. A selection of others is presented under headings of Employment; Production and Income; Consumption, Trade, Orders, and Deliveries; Fixed Capital Investment; Inventories and Inventory Investment; Prices, Costs, and Profits; and Money and Credit. The selection was based in part on a review of series normally published in the business press (hence indicating usage by the public) and editorial judgment.

Economic Series. Many statistical measures of the economy are not classified as cyclic in nature and are not used to *predict* but to *measure* economic activity. The series included in *EIH* were, again, selected because they are commonly reported in the press or, in the editor's opinion, provide interesting insight into the functioning of the economy. Series on GDP implicit deflators were added in the second edition.

Prices. Chapters 6 and 7 present consumer and producer price indexes in considerable detail. The CPI is shown for both "all urban consumers" and the "urban wage earners" categories. Furthermore, major subcomponents categories (food, apparel, housing, etc.) are shown. Data for 27 cities/metro areas are then presented in the same detail. All CPI data are shown back to the earliest year for which they were collected or estimated by the Department of Labor.

The Producer Price Index is presented in Chapter 7 for 120 major categories and subcategories in monthly format; annual average data are also shown.

Selected Stock Market Indexes. The final chapter shows selected index data from the American Stock Exchange, NASDAQ (National Association of Securities Dealers Automated Quotation system), and the New York Stock Exchange. Another stock index series, the Standard & Poor's 500 index—which is used by The Conference Board as a leading indicator—is presented in Chapter 3.

SOURCES

The information included in *EIH* came from the U.S. Department of Commerce, the U.S. Department of Labor, the American Stock Exchange, the National Association of Securities Dealers, and the New York Stock Exchange, and The Conference Board. With a few exceptions, data were obtained by special arrangement rather than by being extracted from published sources.

Most federal data series, of course, are built from multiple sources, public and private. The majority rely on surveys, some of which are voluntary and some of which, such as the quadrennial censuses of business, are mandated by law. GNP and GDP data; the indicator series built into the leading, coincident, and lagging indexes; and the CPI and PPI all require substantial statistical work by the federal agencies that prepare them. They are, in a very real sense, statistical "products" of the agencies (or consortia of agencies): they are built from a diverse number of statistical "raw materials" and the methods of constructing the final series are continuously being refined.

ORGANIZATION AND PRESENTATION

EIH is organized into eight chapters as follows:

Chapter 1 - Gross National Product   Chapter 5 - Economic Series
Chapter 2 - Gross Domestic Product   Chapter 6 - Consumer Price Index
Chapter 3 - Business Cycle Indicators   Chapter 7 - Producer Price Index
Chapter 4 - Cyclic Indicators   Chapter 8 - Stock Market Indexes

A keyword index holds references to text and table contents.

Each chapter begins with an introductory text. The subject to be covered in the chapter is outlined in general terms. A bibliography is provided. Chapters 1, 3, 4, and 5 are further subdivided. Each subdivision is separately introduced. Each series covered is separately discussed under its own heading in the chapter or section introductions.

STATISTICAL CONVENTIONS

Many statistical series presented in *EIH* make use of conventions which may be unfamiliar to the casual user. While most of these are discussed in context in the chapter and section notes, a general discussion of *Indexing, Base Periods, Constant and Current Dollars, Chained Dollars, Annualized Rates*, and *Seasonal Adjustments* is presented here.

Indexing. Statistical information in *EIH* is presented in the form of raw information (dollars, hours, weeks, etc.) or in the form of indexes. Index numbers are used to present information relative to data obtained for a specific period. A typical example is an index defined to have the value of 100 for the average outcome of a series in the year 1987. The following example illustrates the method used.

Year	Raw Value in Dollar	Index Value
1985	345	83.7
1986	356	86.4
1987	412	100.0
1988	436	105.8
1989	489	118.7

In the illustration above, 1987 is "the base period," discussed further below. It is assigned an arbitrary index value. In this case the value is 100, but it can be any number. Indexes of 10 or 50 are also commonly used, but 100 is the usual index base. The index for any year is calculated by the following formula:

(Current Year Raw Data / Base Year Raw Data) x 100.

Changes from one period to another may be calculated in index points or as a percent change. In the example above, the index point change between 1988 and 1989 is 12.9. The percentage change is 12.2, obtained by the formula:

((Current Index / Previous Index) - 1) x 100.

Measuring the percentage change between two index values produces the same result as measuring the percentage change in the raw data for the same periods.

Base Periods. Statistical series expressed as indexes or in constant dollars (see below) have base periods. A base period can be a day, a month, a year, or a range of years. The Consumer Price Index, for instance, is based on the 1982-1984 period; the average prices for these years are defined as 100.

The government periodically changes the base periods of indexes. The year chosen is typically the year of one of the quadrennial business censuses. The most recent such census was held in 1997. Many series are still expressed with a base of 1982 or 1987. Rebasing of a series (shifting to a more recent base period) is usually associated with a significant reworking of the statistical machinery which produces the numbers; hence there tends to be a time delaty between the most recent business census and the base period in use. For example, the Gross Domestic Product was rebased (to chained dollars) in 1995, three years following the 1992 economic censuses. Values based on the 1997 census are still years away (in 1998).

Constant and Current Dollars. The measurement of dollar-denominated values from one period to the next can produce inaccurate results, for some purposes, if changes due *only* to increasing or dropping prices are not taken into account. For this reason, many series are reported both in current dollars (also called "actual" dollars) and in constant dollars (also called "real" dollars). Constant dollars are current dollars that have been adjusted for the effects of inflation relative to a base period. Because a base period is used, people sometimes use phrases like "1982 dollars" or "1987 dollars." They mean constant dollars with a 1982 or a 1987 base year. The purchasing power of the dollar in the base year is arbitrarily defined as "real." And today's dollars are adjusted to that value by using series such as the Consumer Price Index and the Producer's Price Index. These indexes record changes in prices by surveying the actual prices charged for identical products and services two periods apart. If the same loaf of bread costs 89 cents in 1991 and 92 cents in 1992, inflation accounts for 3 cents: it took 3 cents more to get the same loaf in the second period. Constant dollar calculations, of course, use a wide range of representative products and services measured in a systematic manner across the nation.

Chained Dollars. A new measurement of national accounts (new in U.S. usage, at any rate), involves the calculation of chain-type indexes. An explanation of what these are and how they work is presented in this chapter under the heading of NIPA Revisions. In essence, chained dollar indexes work by averaging price changes in the prices of two adjacent periods and using the resulting change from one period to the next as the current dollar deflator. Chain-type indexes are definitely "in." They are used by the majority of other countries for national accounting. They have now been adopted by the Bureau of Economic Analysis for the same purpose. They are expected soon to be used by the Bureau of Labor Statistics as well in calculating the CPI and the PPI price indexes.

Annualized Rates. National production and income data—as well as some other series—report some figures quarterly at "annualized rates." This means that data developed for the quarter are multiplied by four to show what the year would be like if results in this quarter continued. The data, typically, are seasonally adjusted (see below) before they are expressed at annualized rates.

Seasonal Adjustments. Economic activity is by nature seasonal. More heating oil will be used in the winter, more people seek employment in the summer as college students come home. Retailers sell proportionally more goods in December than in other months. Many series are seasonally adjusted to take such fluctuations into account. Other series are shown as "not seasonally adjusted." Seasonal adjustments are made by statisticians in and out of government by using experience factors developed over time. Data are recalculated using these experience factors so that heavy fuel oil sales in the fall and winter are "distributed" evenly across the entire year.

NIPA Revisions

This edition of *EIH* reflects the 1995 comprehensive (benchmark) changes in the National Income and Product Accounts (NIPA), the source of the GDP and GNP reporting by the U.S. Department of Commerce. A new cycle of change is now in process and will be refelected in the next edition.

One major change in the last benchmark revision concerns the manner in which account measurements are translated from "current" into constant or "real" dollars. That change is discussed under the general heading of Indexing Changes. As in every major revision cycle, the government has again introduced a number of changes in the way it accounts for national income. These will be summarized in this section under the heading of Component Changes.

Indexing Changes

A significant change in the measurement of "real" GDP (and its components) was implemented as part of the comprehensive NIPA revisions of 1995. This change, in preparation for some years now, replaces measurement of GDP in fixed-year constant dollars with a measurement using chained-type indexes. A before and after presentation of the two approaches follows:

Fixed-Year Indexes

Calculating Fixed-Year Constant Dollars. Why does the government report GDP in both current (actual) dollars and in constant dollars? The answer is that Americans want to know whether or not GDP has grown or declined; we want to know the "real" change in the "quantity" of the GDP in order to know how the economy is doing. The current dollar measurement of GDP does not tell us what the *real* change is since the last quarter or year. The GDP may have grown in dollars, but how much of that growth is the result of price changes only (potatoes up by 13 cents a pound)? How much is due to increased output of goods and services (10 percent more potatoes were produced)? To see the "real" changes in the economy, we need to remove that portion of the change due only to changes in prices.

A simple way of doing this is to select one year as the base year for measurement and then to apply the prices that prevailed in the base year to the quantities produced in the current year:

Base year price per unit	95.00	1
Current year price per unit	135.00	2
Units produced in current year	15	3
Current dollar results (135 x 15)	2,025	4
Constant dollar results (95 x 15)	1,425	5

In the example above, current dollars of $2,025 are deflated to $1,425 in constant dollars by using base year prices and applying them to current year quantities.

For large aggregates like the GDP or its components, quantity measures (line 3 above) cannot be obtained conveniently. Instead, as the smallest subcomponents of GDP are added to GDP, price indexes are used to deflate current to constant dollars at the point where the characteristics of the component are still clearly visible, e.g., indexes are applied to Food Consumption Expenditures before the totals are added to Personal Consumption Expenditures.

Price indexes measure change in prices *only*, from one period to the next. Examples are the Consumer Price Index and the Producer Price Index, each of which is built up of many detailed categories. In the example above, the price index for the current year for our unnamed commodity is the current price per unit divided by the base year price per unit:

Price index in current year (135 / 95)	1.421	6
Constant dollar result (2,025 / 1.421)	1,425	7

The constant dollar result can be calculated by dividing current dollars by the index. Notice that line 5 and line 7 produce identical "deflated" values—one by using a price-quantity multiplication, the other by dividing current dollars by a price index.

The actual construction of GDP deflators must, of course, correctly blend many price indexes into a single number. This is done by applying weights to individual indexes. What percentage of total consumption is food? If that percentage is 5.5, the food index contributes only 5.5 percent to the deflator. Weights needed to create accurate deflators are obtained by surveys.

Pros and Cons of the Fixed-Year Measure. The fixed-year constant dollar measure is simple to calculate and is well understood by the public.

The chief disadvantage of the measure is that it distorts results the farther we move from the base year. Another way to put this is that moving the base period forward causes a lower growth rate when the new constant dollar GDP is calculated: "We thought we were growing at 3.5 percent a year; now they tell us it was only 3.3 percent."

This well-known effect, known as the "substitution bias," is due to the natural tendency of the price structure to change. On the whole, products and services that grow most are those with prices that grow least. The inverse is also true. Using the higher "old" prices and applying them to the larger "new" quantities artificially overstates real growth. When the base year is moved forward, the old high prices are replaced by the new low prices; these are applied to the lower old quantities. Now growth between the periods is artificially understated. The following example makes the point arithmetically:

	YEAR 1					YEAR 2				
	Total in Year 1 Dollars - D x E	Total in Year 2 Dollars - D x J	Total in Current Dollars - D x E	Quantity	Price	Total in Year 1 Dollars - I x E	Total in Year 2 Dollars - I x J	Total in Current Dollars - I x J	Quantity	Price
Apples	3.00	6.00	3.00	30	.10	2.00	4.00	4.00	20	.20
Oranges	2.00	2.50	2.00	10	.20	4.00	5.00	5.00	20	.25
Fruit	5.00	8.50	5.00			6.00	9.00	9.00		
Growth						1.20	1.06	1.80		
	A	B	C	D	E	F	G	H	I	J

In the above table, change between Years 1 and 2 in Year 1 dollars is 1.20 and in Year 2 dollars 1.06. These results are due to the shift in the price structure of this mini-economy.

Using either Year 1 or Year 2 dollars is legitimate, despite the obvious distortions. Neither index is more correct than the other. The only "real" measure is in current dollars—because, in reality, price-quantity relationships (including inflationary effects) are inseparable. Constant dollar measures are analytical attempts at isolating quantitative change and are always correct if calculated correctly.

But what if we took the two results above and averaged them? Would that get us closer to a more accurate, less biased measure? The answer is Yes. And that introduces the topic of chained indexes.

Chain-Type Indexes

Chain-type indexes are created by obtaining the geometrical mean of two growth calculations. The first growth value is obtained using Period 1 dollars for both Period 1 and Period 2. The second is obtained using Period 2 dollars in both periods. These are the rates shown in Columns F and G above. The periods must be adjacent (adjacent years, quarters, months). Using the example above, the calculation is:

> *chained growth value = square root of (1.20 x 1.06)*
> *chained growth value = 1.13*

In the example above, growth between Year 1 and Year 2 in chained dollars would be 13 percent (rather than 20 or 6 percent using one valuation period only). Year 2 results in chained dollars would be $5.56 (Year 1 result of $5 times the 1.13 calculated rate).

In more technical terminology, the annual change in real GDP is calculated using the Fisher Ideal Index formula, defined as the geometric mean of a Laspeyres and a Paasche index. Year 2 values in Year 1 prices (Column F) are the Laspeyres index; Year 2 values in Year 2 prices (Column G) are the Paasche index.

How a Chained Index is Created. To create a hypothetical chain-type index, growth rates for each period are calculated using the Fisher Ideal Index formula, as shown above. For a series of GDP (or component) measurements, this will produce individual growth rates of "real" GDP based on the price weights of the year and the year before, as shown below. Note, please, that the growth rates shown are not those between the current dollar values shown but between constant dollar expressions of these values. The actual step of moving from line 2 values to line 3 values is not illustrated.

	1989	1990	1991	1992	1993	1994	1
Assumed Current $ Values	555	580	719	741	778	708	2
Fisher Ideal growth rates (%)	-	13.0	21.1	5.0	4.0	-7.3	3

The percentages in line 3 are next expressed as multipliers by dividing the cells of line 3 by 100 and adding one (the result is shown in line 4 below). Next, the multipliers are "chained," i.e., multiplied together—hence the name of this type of index. Column A is multiplied by

Column B, and the result is placed back in Column B. Column B is then multiplied by Column C and the result placed back in Column C. And so on. Results are shown in line 5 below:

	A	B	C	D	E	F	
Expressed as multipliers	1.000	1.130	1.210	1.050	1.040	.927	4
Chained into Index	1.000	1.130	1.367	1.436	1.493	1.384	5

The chained values of line 5 can now be converted into an index of any desired base year. The method is to divide each cell's value by the base year value and to multiply the result by 100. In what follows, two indexes are created with base 1989 (line 6) and 1992 (line 7). Then the dollar values from line 2, above, will be translated into chained dollars of the base year (lines 8 and 9).

Index with 1989 Base	**100.0**	113.0	136.7	143.6	149.3	138.4	6
Index with 1992 Base	69.7	78.7	95.2	**100.0**	104.0	96.4	7
Chained (1989) Dollars	**555**	627	759	797	829	829	8
Chained (1992) Dollars	516	583	705	**741**	770	714	9

The chained dollar conversions are done by dividing the index with the appropriate base by 100 and multiplying the base year value (line 1 above) by the result.

Notice that the dollar magnitudes are different when expressed in different base year dollars. The growth relationships between the dollars, however, remain the same. The base year can be moved at will without affecting the growth relationships. Thus the growth from 1989 to 1990 in either chained (1989) dollars or chained (1992) dollars is 13 percent. Note, also, that as in the "old days," when fixed year constant dollars were used, so in chained dollar series, the base year's "current" dollars and "chained" dollars are identical.

In preparing this exposition, the author drew heavily on the wisdom presented in two papers in the *Survey of Current Business*. The first of these, by Allan H. Young, is titled "Alternative Measures of Change in Real Output and Prices," Volume 72, Number 4, April 1992, pp. 32-48. The second is by J. Steven Landefeld and Robert P. Parker, titled "Preview of the Comprehensive Revision of the National Income and Product Accounts: BEA's New Featured Measures of Output and Prices," Volume 75, Number 7, July 1995, pp. 31-38. Particularly useful was a note, appended to this article, written by Jack E. Triplett, titled

"Note on Calculating Output and Price Indexes." Whatever merits this presentation has are due largely to these experts. Whatever it lacks is due to the author's failure of grasp.

Component Changes

Comprehensive benchmark revisions of the National Income and Product Accounts take place at intervals of 5 years, roughly 3 years after the last complete economic census of the U.S. (last in 1992). In the past, benchmark revisions typically resulted in the movement of the "constant dollar" base year to the year of the most recent economic census. This time, "constant dollar" indexing has been retired in favor of the chain-type indexing of GDP and its components (see last subhead). Other important changes will be summarized below.

Changed Treatment of Government Investments. Until this revision, expenditures by government on structures and equipment (highways, schools, office buildings, motor vehicles, computers) were classified, along with other purchases, as Government Purchases, with their value assumed to be consumed in the year the expenditures were made. Analogous expenditures by the private sector were treated differently and classified as either "gross private domestic investment" or "net foreign investment." Beginning with the 1995 revisions, a new category of investment, "gross government investment," will be added. The depreciation associated with this investment will be shown as part of "government consumption expenditures," the new category that replaces "government purchases."

Changed Treatment of Depreciation. Successive NIPA revisions have attempted to approximate better the real character of depreciation. In the most recent revision, the government is abandoning a methodology based on straight-line depreciation and adopting a methodology which assumes that depreciation takes place at a constant percentage rate of the residual value of the depreciated object rather than a constant dollar amount. This change is based on a number of empirical studies conducted by the government. Detailed articles on this subject were promised by the BEA for 1996 in the *Survey of Current Business*.

Other Changes. New estimating procedures and new and revised data have been introduced. These changes include such items as the use of a new Input-Output table (1987), incorporation of the results of the 1991 Residential Finance Survey, incorporation of revised estimates of employer contributions to private health insurance, and other estimating and methodological changes.

To review in more detail all changes to the NIPA, it is suggested that the user consult the September 1995, November/December 1995, and the January/February 1996 issues of *Survey of Current Business*.

ACKNOWLEDGMENTS

Economic Indicators Handbook is based on the hard work and intellectual rigor of many individuals in government, academia, associations, and industry. Some of them took of their valuable time to help in the preparation of this book by providing data and patient explanations of sometimes very difficult concepts. In particular, the editor is indebted to the staff of The Conference Board; the staff of the Bureau of Economic Analysis, U.S. Department of Commerce; and staff of the Bureau of Labor Statistics, U.S. Department of Labor. The continuing cooperation of the Media Relations staff of the American Stock Exchange, the research staff of the New York Stock Exchange, and of the computer support folks at National Association of Securities Dealers Automated Quotation System (NASDAQ) is much appreciated.

COMMENTS AND SUGGESTIONS

Comments on *EIH* or suggestion for its improvement are always welcome. Although every effort is made to maintain accuracy, errors may occasionally occur; the editor will be grateful if these are called to his attention. Please contact:

Editor
Economic Indicators Handbook
Gale Research
835 Penobscot Building
Detroit, MI 48226-4094
Phone: (313) 961-2242 or (800) 347-GALE
Fax: (313) 961-6741

CHAPTER 1

GROSS NATIONAL PRODUCT

GROSS NATIONAL PRODUCT

The Gross National Product (GNP) is the sum of all purchases of goods and services by individuals and government; the value of gross domestic investment, including changes in business inventories; and exports less imports (net exports). GNP is thus a measure of the productivity of the nation. GNP can be summarized by the following formula:

GNP = Consumption + Investment + Government + Exports - Imports.

Only final purchases are measured to avoid double counting. The value of unfinished goods purchased by companies and not resold as finished product is reflected in changed business inventories.

GNP measures goods and services *produced by labor and property supplied by U.S. residents*. The labor and property may be located *in* the U.S. or abroad. Conversely, goods and services produced by foreign labor and property are excluded, even if located on U.S. soil. The next chapter covers Gross Domestic Product (GDP) which measures goods and services *produced by labor and property located in the U.S.* GDP has been selected by the U.S. Department of Commerce as the new measure of U.S. production, displacing GNP. However, since GNP accounting had been the dominant method until November 1991, GNP tables are provided here for retrospective reference.

Modern GNP reporting began in 1929 and is the product of a comprehensive statistical system (the National Income and Product Accounts, NIPA) managed by the Department of Commerce, Bureau of Economic Analysis (BEA). GNP estimates were extended back to 1909 based on limited statistical sources by the government; and estimates based on even less information have been made back to colonial times. Data in *EIH* are reported from 1929 forward when possible or from whatever year the Bureau of Economic Analysis, Department of Commerce, makes available. In this edition, for instance, data in the revised formats (1995 revisions) are presented back to 1959 only. *EIH* presents those data and also the earlier GNP series back to 1929 (1991 revisions).

GNP data are *estimates* based on a large number of surveys conducted by the federal government for other purposes or obtained from private industry or association sources. Precise measurement of economic activity on a scale such as that of the United States is virtually impossible; hence partial data, estimates, and statistical methods are necessary to approximate actual economic activity. During the years of the economic censuses, which recur at 5-year intervals, detailed data are collected for many GNP components which serve as "benchmarks" for estimates.

Presentation of Data

The first table is a summary of GNP for the period 1869-1928. Data were obtained, courtesy of the Bureau of Economic Analysis, for aggregate GNP for this period, in actual and in constant (1982) dollars.

The next table presents annual GNP data for the period 1929 through 1958 in current as well as chained 1992 dollars. This table is presented to provide continuity between the historical series and the officially published, complete GNP series which begins in 1959.

Two tables for the GNP by quarters, for the 1959-1997 period follow. The first is in current dollars, the second in chained 1992 dollars. Detailed component tables are not included because the government has

3

now completely shifted emphasis to Gross Domestic Product (GDP), and all data have been restated using GDP definitions.

Historical Data. The historical data are presented in decade averages for the 1869-1878 and the 1879-1888 periods and then annually thereafter to 1928. Data are shown in actual and in constant dollars, permitting the calculation of growth and decline rates year to year and the implicit price deflator. The implicit price deflator shows the relationship of prices, in a given year, as they compare to those of a base year—in this case 1982. The deflator is calculated by the formula:

(Actual Dollar Value / Constant Dollar Value) x 100.

With the implicit price deflator known, constant dollar value can be calculated, if unknown, by the formula:

(Current Dollar Value x 100) / Implicit Price Deflator.

And current value, if unknown, can be calculated from constant dollar value by the formula:

(Constant Dollar Value / 100) x Implicit Price Deflator.

Annual Data, 1929 through 1958. Not all of the GNP/GDP series are available in 1992 chained dollars back to 1929. Annual data are released by the Bureau of Economic Analysis in electronic format. Chained 1992 data for these early years are called "unpublished" by the BEA because components of the major series are of lower quality than aggregate series. For this reason, only annual totals are shown here. The data are presented here so that a continuous series from historical times to the present is available to the analyst.

Quarterly Data. Data for quarters, when available, represent seasonally adjusted, annualized quarterly estimates. This means that the results for the quarter are projected for the entire year; for example, if 2 million cars were sold in the quarter, the annual rate would be 8 million cars; therefore, the production value of 8 million cars is reflected in that quarter's estimate. Seasonal adjustments are made to reflect conditions that are due to well known, recurring, seasonal phenomena. For example, fuel oil consumption is known to be much higher in winter than in summer; fuel consumption, therefore, is increased in summer quarters and decreased in winter quarters to "smooth" the data. Each quarter, in other words, shows what GNP would be for the entire year if the conditions in that quarter, as adjusted, were to continue for the balance of the year.

Growth or decline between any two quarters is also annualized, showing a compounded growth rate reached by the formula:

(This Quarter / Last Quarter)^4 *- 1 x 100* = percent growth rate of GNP.

If this quarter is $4,118.9 billion and last quarter was $4,124.1 billion, the formula results in - 0.503 percent because the quarterly growth rate was compounded and annualized—rather than a rate of - 0.12 percent, which is the simple percentile difference between the two numbers.

Annual Data. Annual figures show final estimates for GNP. Since GNP estimates are revised as better and better data become available, data for recent years are subject to revision and results for the most recent year tend to be preliminary estimates. Annual growth or decline figures show simple percentile changes between the two years reached by the formula:

(This Year / Last Year) - 1 x 100.

If this year is $4,157.3 billion and last year was $4,117.7 billion, the growth is 0.96 percent.

GNP in Constant Dollars. Constant dollars (also referred to as "real" dollars) are used to measure GNP in order to account for inflationary or deflationary price changes; inflation is believed to come about because prices are raised in response to unusually high demand; deflation (a much rarer phenomenon) results when prices drop because demand is soft; in both cases, products or services sold remain unchanged; only prices change; constant dollar expression of GNP permits direct comparison of one period with another. In the 20-year period 1970 to 1989, for instance, GNP showed positive growth in every year in actual dollars; measured in constant dollars, the years 1970, 1974-75, 1980, 1982, and 1991 showed negative growth.

GNP in Chained (1992) Dollars. Beginning in 1995, the BEA has adopted a new indexing method to express "real" dollar values—values that remove the effect of inflation. Tables using this method of "normalization" are shown to be in "chained (1992) dollars." A full explanation of this method is presented in the Introduction under the subheading, *NIPA Changes, 1995*. In essence, the "chained dollar" measure is a more sensitive indicator of changes in the quantities of dollars reported. For purposes of analysis, they are essentially equivalent to the "constant dollar" indexing methods of the recent past. Thus values expressed in chained (1992) dollars normalize today's ("current") dollars in terms of 1992 purchasing power—but with greater accuracy.

GNP Revisions

Changes in GNP methodologies and allocation of items to national accounts are continuous. These changes typically involve (1) changes in the classification of certain items from one GNP account to another; for example, in 1985, railroad track replacement costs were shifted from business expenditures to investment; (2) the inclusion or exclusion of areas (e.g., Puerto Rico and U.S. territories were excluded from GNP in 1985); and (3) changes in methodology, especially for estimating categories not fully covered by surveys; for example, in 1985, improved adjustments were made for misreporting on tax returns, the so-called "underground economy adjustments." Major changes in recent decades were introduced in 1976, 1980, 1985, 1991, and 1995.

For a full discussion of the 1995 revisions, please consult the November/December 1995 issue of *Survey of Current Business* (reference 4 below). The major 1995 revision was completed early in 1997 and released April 30, 1997. The following are the major changes: (1) changes relating to the government's investment and contributions to retirement programs; (2) statistical changes, including (a) improved estimates of changes in output and prices; (b) new estimating procedures (especially for depreciation); (c) new and revised data from regular sources that become available less often than annually; (d) new and revised data from regular sources; and (e) updated seasonal factors for quarterly estimates.

These changes produce *increases* in current-dollar GNP—so that data for earlier years, in revised format, are higher. In other words, the comprehensive revisions of the national income accounts can, in effect, *revise financial history*.

For a bibliography of major and annual changes, see p. 23-30, reference 3, below, and Fall issues of the *Survey of Current Business* (reference 4).

Bibliography

1. Carnes, W. Stansbury and Stephen D. Slifer, *The Atlas of Economic Indicators*. Harper Collins, 1991.

2. U.S. Department of Commerce, Bureau of Economic Analysis. *GNP: An Overview of Source Data and Estimating Methods*. Methodology Paper Series MP-4. Washington, DC: U.S. Government Printing Office, September 1987.

3. U.S. Department of Commerce, Bureau of Economic Analysis. *An Introduction to National Economic Accounting*. Methodology Paper Series MP-1. Washington, DC: U.S. Government Printing Office, March 1985.

4. U.S. Department of Commerce, Bureau of Economic Analysis. *Survey of Current Business*. Superintendent of Documents, U.S. Government Printing Office, Washington, DC 20302.

Historical Gross National Product

1869-1928

Historial GNP estimates, 1869-1928, shown in billions of actual and constant 1982 dollars. 1869-78 and 1879-88 values are decade averages.

Year	Current Dollars (Billions)	Change from Previous Year - %	Constant 82 Dol. (Billions)	Change from Previous Year - %	Implicit Price Deflator 82=100	Year	Current Dollars (Billions)	Change from Previous Year - %	Constant 82 Dol. (Billions)	Change from Previous Year - %	Implicit Price Deflator 82=100
1869-78	7.7	-	84.6	-	9.102	1908	29.0	-8.8	366.4	-8.3	7.915
1879-88	11.7	-	154.5	-	7.573	1909	33.7	16.2	411.3	12.3	8.194
1889	13.1	-	179.5	-	7.298	1910	35.7	5.9	423.3	2.9	8.434
1890	13.7	4.6	192.8	7.4	7.106	1911	36.1	1.1	436.3	3.1	8.274
1891	14.1	2.9	201.6	4.6	6.994	1912	39.7	10.0	457.2	4.8	8.683
1892	15.0	6.4	220.7	9.5	6.797	1913	39.9	0.5	462.4	1.1	8.629
1893	14.4	-4.0	210.4	-4.7	6.844	1914	38.9	-2.5	444.4	-3.9	8.753
1894	13.2	-8.3	204.5	-2.8	6.455	1915	40.3	3.6	439.6	-1.1	9.167
1895	14.5	9.8	228.8	11.9	6.337	1916	48.6	20.6	472.8	7.6	10.279
1896	13.9	-4.1	223.7	-2.2	6.214	1917	60.7	24.9	481.7	1.9	12.601
1897	15.3	10.1	245.0	9.5	6.245	1918	76.8	26.5	570.0	18.3	13.474
1898	16.1	5.2	250.9	2.4	6.417	1919	84.7	10.3	528.3	-7.3	16.033
1899	18.2	13.0	273.7	9.1	6.650	1920	92.2	8.9	487.1	-7.8	18.928
1900	19.6	7.7	281.1	2.7	6.973	1921	70.2	-23.9	452.8	-7.0	15.504
1901	21.7	10.7	313.4	11.5	6.924	1922	74.8	6.6	519.6	14.8	14.396
1902	22.6	4.1	316.4	1.0	7.143	1923	85.9	14.8	576.9	11.0	14.890
1903	24.0	6.2	331.8	4.9	7.233	1924	85.5	-0.5	582.7	1.0	14.673
1904	24.0	0.0	328.2	-1.1	7.313	1925	94.0	9.9	625.0	7.3	15.040
1905	26.3	9.6	352.4	7.4	7.463	1926	97.9	4.1	662.3	6.0	14.782
1906	30.0	14.1	392.9	11.5	7.636	1927	95.8	-2.1	661.2	-0.2	14.489
1907	31.8	6.0	399.5	1.7	7.960	1928	97.7	2.0	667.7	1.0	14.632

Sources: National Bureau of Economic Research and U.S. Department of Commerce. Obtained as handwritten communication from Bureau of Economic Analysis.

Gross National Product - 1929-1958
(Billions of Current and Chained 1992 Dollars)

Annual GNP estimates, 1929-1958, in billions of current and in chained 1992 dollars. Changes from year to year are percentage changes.

Year	Current dollars	% Change	Chained 1992 dollars	% Change
1929	103.8	-	790.9	-
1930	91.1	-12.2	719.7	-9.0
1931	76.4	-16.1	674.0	-6.3
1932	58.6	-23.3	584.3	-13.3
1933	56.2	-4.1	577.3	-1.2
1934	65.9	17.3	641.1	11.1
1935	73.1	10.9	698.4	8.9
1936	83.6	14.4	790.0	13.1
1937	91.8	9.8	831.5	5.3
1938	85.9	-6.4	801.2	-3.6
1939	91.9	7.0	866.5	8.2
1940	101.2	10.1	941.2	8.6
1941	126.7	25.2	1,101.8	17.1
1942	161.6	27.5	1,308.9	18.8
1943	198.3	22.7	1,523.0	16.4
1944	219.7	10.8	1,644.7	8.0
1945	223.2	1.6	1,626.7	-1.1
1946	222.6	-0.3	1,447.7	-11.0
1947	244.6	9.9	1,430.7	-1.2
1948	269.7	10.3	1,491.0	4.2
1949	267.8	-0.7	1,479.8	-0.8
1950	294.6	10.0	1,611.3	8.9
1951	339.7	15.3	1,734.0	7.6
1952	358.6	5.6	1,798.7	3.7
1953	379.7	5.9	1,881.4	4.6
1954	381.3	0.4	1,868.2	-0.7
1955	415.1	8.9	2,001.1	7.1
1956	438.0	5.5	2,040.2	2.0
1957	461.0	5.3	2,078.5	1.9
1958	467.3	1.4	2,057.5	-1.0

Source: "National Income and Product Account Tables: Selected NIPA Tables," *Survey of Current Business*, November 1997, U.S. Department of Commerce, Bureau of Economic Analysis, National Income and Wealth Division. *Notes*: This table includes some series available only in electronic format. A dash (-) indicates no change.

Gross National Product - Actual Dollars

In billions of actual dollars and percent. Quarterly data are seasonally adjusted and annualized. Growth rates for quarters are compound annual growth rates; changes from year to year are percentage changes.

Year	1st Quarter	% Change	2nd Quarter	% Change	3rd Quarter	% Change	4th Quarter	% Change	TOTAL	% Change
1959	499.0	-	512.0	10.8	512.5	0.4	516.9	3.5	510.1	-
1960	530.3	10.8	529.2	-0.8	532.2	2.3	527.3	-3.6	529.8	3.9
1961	531.8	3.5	542.4	8.2	553.2	8.2	566.3	9.8	548.4	3.5
1962	579.0	9.3	586.9	5.6	594.1	5.0	597.7	2.4	589.4	7.5
1963	606.8	6.2	615.3	5.7	628.2	8.7	637.5	6.1	621.9	5.5
1964	654.5	11.1	663.4	5.6	674.3	6.7	679.9	3.4	668.0	7.4
1965	701.2	13.1	713.9	7.4	730.4	9.6	752.6	12.7	724.5	8.5
1966	775.6	12.8	785.2	5.0	798.6	7.0	812.5	7.1	793.0	9.5
1967	822.8	5.2	828.4	2.8	844.7	8.1	860.4	7.6	839.1	5.8
1968	886.4	12.6	911.0	11.6	926.4	6.9	943.1	7.4	916.7	9.2
1969	966.4	10.3	980.3	5.9	999.6	8.1	1,007.1	3.0	988.4	7.8
1970	1,020.2	5.3	1,036.2	6.4	1,054.4	7.2	1,057.4	1.1	1,042.0	5.4
1971	1,104.2	18.9	1,125.8	8.1	1,144.6	6.8	1,157.6	4.6	1,133.1	8.7
1972	1,198.5	14.9	1,232.6	11.9	1,256.9	8.1	1,295.9	13.0	1,246.0	10.0
1973	1,348.3	17.2	1,381.1	10.1	1,405.4	7.2	1,446.7	12.3	1,395.4	12.0
1974	1,463.7	4.8	1,499.1	10.0	1,527.2	7.7	1,560.3	9.0	1,512.6	8.4
1975	1,572.0	3.0	1,609.7	9.9	1,670.3	15.9	1,723.5	13.4	1,643.9	8.7
1976	1,783.3	14.6	1,814.8	7.3	1,847.8	7.5	1,898.5	11.4	1,836.1	11.7
1977	1,955.5	12.6	2,026.2	15.3	2,084.5	12.0	2,123.9	7.8	2,047.5	11.5
1978	2,170.1	9.0	2,292.8	24.6	2,355.3	11.4	2,435.5	14.3	2,313.5	13.0
1979	2,491.1	9.4	2,552.7	10.3	2,629.9	12.7	2,687.8	9.1	2,590.4	12.0
1980	2,761.2	11.4	2,756.2	-0.7	2,819.0	9.4	2,941.7	18.6	2,819.5	8.8
1981	3,073.6	19.2	3,102.4	3.8	3,202.1	13.5	3,224.4	2.8	3,150.6	11.7
1982	3,210.0	-1.8	3,267.1	7.3	3,288.4	2.6	3,327.3	4.8	3,273.2	3.9
1983	3,389.7	7.7	3,500.8	13.8	3,596.2	11.4	3,699.5	12.0	3,546.5	8.3
1984	3,822.7	14.0	3,911.9	9.7	3,974.5	6.6	4,025.0	5.2	3,933.5	10.9
1985	4,101.3	7.8	4,158.1	5.7	4,238.4	8.0	4,306.4	6.6	4,201.0	6.8
1986	4,376.6	6.7	4,398.2	2.0	4,456.7	5.4	4,508.7	4.7	4,435.1	5.6
1987	4,573.2	5.8	4,655.6	7.4	4,731.4	6.7	4,844.9	9.9	4,701.3	6.0
1988	4,914.2	5.8	5,013.5	8.3	5,105.3	7.5	5,217.5	9.1	5,062.6	7.7
1989	5,329.0	8.8	5,424.0	7.3	5,501.4	5.8	5,556.8	4.1	5,452.8	7.7
1990	5,681.6	9.3	5,767.6	6.2	5,796.6	2.0	5,813.8	1.2	5,764.9	5.7
1991	5,848.8	2.4	5,904.7	3.9	5,959.6	3.8	6,016.5	3.9	5,932.4	2.9
1992	6,138.3	8.3	6,212.2	4.9	6,281.1	4.5	6,390.5	7.2	6,255.5	5.4
1993	6,468.1	4.9	6,525.3	3.6	6,596.9	4.5	6,717.1	7.5	6,576.8	5.1
1994	6,811.2	5.7	6,920.3	6.6	6,992.3	4.2	7,096.8	6.1	6,955.2	5.8
1995	7,175.1	4.5	7,220.6	2.6	7,298.3	4.4	7,388.5	5.0	7,270.6	4.5
1996	7,475.3	4.8	7,610.5	7.4	7,669.1	3.1	7,796.1	6.8	7,637.7	5.0
1997	7,919.2	6.5	8,013.6	4.9	8,103.5	4.6	-	-	-	-

Source: The National Income and Product Accounts of the United States, 1959-97. Published on diskettes, September 1997, Bureau of Economic Analysis, U.S. Department of Commerce, Washington, D.C. - indicates that data are unavailable or zero.

Gross National Product - Chained (1992) Dollars

In billions of chained (1992) dollars and percent. Quarterly data are seasonally adjusted and annualized. Growth rates for quarters are compound annual growth rates; changes from year to year are percentage changes.

Year	1st Quarter	% Change	2nd Quarter	% Change	3rd Quarter	% Change	4th Quarter	% Change	TOTAL	% Change
1959	2,176.2	-	2,234.5	11.2	2,233.5	-0.2	2,243.9	1.9	2,222.0	-
1960	2,291.6	8.8	2,278.2	-2.3	2,281.6	0.6	2,252.7	-5.0	2,276.0	2.4
1961	2,266.8	2.5	2,306.3	7.2	2,347.1	7.3	2,395.9	8.6	2,329.1	2.3
1962	2,437.4	7.1	2,464.4	4.5	2,488.4	4.0	2,495.9	1.2	2,471.5	6.1
1963	2,526.9	5.1	2,555.5	4.6	2,604.0	7.8	2,622.9	2.9	2,577.3	4.3
1964	2,686.8	10.1	2,716.8	4.5	2,749.5	4.9	2,758.1	1.3	2,727.8	5.8
1965	2,830.0	10.8	2,868.2	5.5	2,918.9	7.3	2,988.6	9.9	2,901.4	6.4
1966	3,061.1	10.1	3,074.2	1.7	3,094.7	2.7	3,121.4	3.5	3,087.8	6.4
1967	3,145.9	3.2	3,147.7	0.2	3,174.4	3.4	3,197.5	2.9	3,166.4	2.5
1968	3,256.2	7.5	3,312.5	7.1	3,337.3	3.0	3,352.2	1.8	3,314.5	4.7
1969	3,402.8	6.2	3,410.3	0.9	3,428.5	2.2	3,411.4	-2.0	3,413.3	3.0
1970	3,406.0	-0.6	3,411.9	0.7	3,442.9	3.7	3,407.4	-4.1	3,417.1	0.1
1971	3,503.3	11.7	3,524.3	2.4	3,544.7	2.3	3,556.0	1.3	3,532.1	3.4
1972	3,627.9	8.3	3,710.7	9.4	3,751.2	4.4	3,815.3	7.0	3,726.3	5.5
1973	3,921.5	11.6	3,950.4	3.0	3,944.1	-0.6	3,984.4	4.2	3,950.1	6.0
1974	3,952.4	-3.2	3,964.3	1.2	3,917.6	-4.6	3,886.1	-3.2	3,930.2	-0.5
1975	3,827.3	-5.9	3,861.8	3.7	3,936.1	7.9	3,987.9	5.4	3,903.3	-0.7
1976	4,078.8	9.4	4,107.9	2.9	4,124.8	1.7	4,163.7	3.8	4,118.8	5.5
1977	4,219.4	5.5	4,302.2	8.1	4,371.2	6.6	4,365.0	-0.6	4,314.5	4.8
1978	4,388.6	2.2	4,546.1	15.1	4,591.1	4.0	4,649.0	5.1	4,543.7	5.3
1979	4,652.6	0.3	4,668.7	1.4	4,708.8	3.5	4,719.5	0.9	4,687.4	3.2
1980	4,743.0	2.0	4,625.6	-9.5	4,617.8	-0.7	4,696.6	7.0	4,670.8	-0.4
1981	4,787.7	8.0	4,742.6	-3.7	4,801.4	5.1	4,747.9	-4.4	4,769.9	2.1
1982	4,658.5	-7.3	4,682.9	2.1	4,651.1	-2.7	4,655.6	0.4	4,662.0	-2.3
1983	4,700.1	3.9	4,804.4	9.2	4,891.3	7.4	4,983.5	7.8	4,844.8	3.9
1984	5,092.6	9.0	5,172.4	6.4	5,209.5	2.9	5,237.5	2.2	5,178.0	6.9
1985	5,280.3	3.3	5,310.8	2.3	5,378.4	5.2	5,417.5	2.9	5,346.7	3.3
1986	5,481.1	4.8	5,480.1	-0.1	5,510.4	2.2	5,533.1	1.7	5,501.2	2.9
1987	5,568.7	2.6	5,628.7	4.4	5,676.0	3.4	5,759.6	6.0	5,658.2	2.9
1988	5,802.3	3.0	5,857.5	3.9	5,889.4	2.2	5,964.9	5.2	5,878.5	3.9
1989	6,023.1	4.0	6,065.5	2.8	6,101.8	2.4	6,112.3	0.7	6,075.7	3.4
1990	6,172.8	4.0	6,188.0	1.0	6,155.7	-2.1	6,111.3	-2.9	6,157.0	1.3
1991	6,074.3	-2.4	6,086.4	0.8	6,099.2	0.8	6,119.5	1.3	6,094.9	-1.0
1992	6,192.0	4.8	6,225.2	2.2	6,270.3	2.9	6,334.6	4.2	6,255.5	2.6
1993	6,351.3	1.1	6,375.9	1.6	6,415.3	2.5	6,489.7	4.7	6,408.0	2.4
1994	6,540.5	3.2	6,609.3	4.3	6,635.6	1.6	6,691.2	3.4	6,619.1	3.3
1995	6,711.3	1.2	6,721.0	0.6	6,758.3	2.2	6,804.2	2.7	6,748.7	2.0
1996	6,834.7	1.8	6,930.1	5.7	6,940.2	0.6	7,023.1	4.9	6,932.0	2.7
1997	7,091.8	4.0	7,144.4	3.0	7,198.8	3.1	-	-	-	-

Source: The National Income and Product Accounts of the United States, 1959-97. Published on diskettes, September 1997, Bureau of Economic Analysis, U.S. Department of Commerce, Washington, D.C. - indicates that data are unavailable or zero.

CHAPTER 2

GROSS DOMESTIC PRODUCT

GROSS DOMESTIC PRODUCT

In November 1995, the U.S. Department of Commerce's Bureau of Economic Analysis (BEA) introduced revisions to the National Income and Product Accounts (NIPA) which (1) changed the NIPA basing year for constant dollars from 1987 dollars to "chained (1992) dollars", (2) introduced new definitional changes, and (3) introduced a number of statistical changes. An earlier comprehensive revision, in 1991, had already shifted emphasis from the Gross National Product (GNP) to the Gross Domestic Product (GDP) as the principal measure of U.S. production. For more discussion of these issues, please see below and read the Introduction, the text accompanying the GNP chapter, and the November/December 1995 and January/February 1996 issues of the *Survey of Current Business* (reference 3).

The net effect of the 1995 NIPA revisions is that GDP is retrospectively *increased* and the accuracy of the GDP is improved by shifting from fixed base (1987) dollars to chained (1992) dollars to index quantitative changes in GDP and its components.

GDP versus GNP

The GDP and GNP differ in the following manner:

GNP measures goods and services produced by labor and property *supplied* by U.S. residents—wherever the goods and services are produced.

GDP measures goods and services produced by labor and property *located* in the U.S.—regardless of the nationality of the persons supplying the labor and property.

The difference between the two measures is *net factor income*; this is income produced by U.S. residents abroad less income produced by foreign residents in the United States. GNP is a better measure of *income* available to U.S. citizens by reason of their contribution to production. Savings are naturally expressed in relation to GNP; and estimating the availability of total resources (e.g., for education) is more appropriately made by looking at GNP.

GDP is a better measurement of *production* within the borders of the United States.

BEA's reasons for the shift may be summarized as follows:

1. GDP is the "appropriate measure for much of the short-term monitoring and analysis of the U.S. economy." It is "consistent in coverage with indicators such as employment, productivity, industry output, and investment in equipment and structures."

2. GDP is the measuring unit used by other countries; hence country-to-country comparisons will be easier. The U.S., in fact, is late in adopting the international System of National Accounts, the set of international guidelines for economic accounting.

3. The GDP measure makes quarterly estimates more accurate because BEA need not estimate factor income (which is received late and requires many adjustments for exchange rates, inflation, etc.) to obtain measures of the economy.

The 1995 Benchmark Revision

In January 1996, BEA released a comprehensive revision to the National Income and Product Accounts. These revisions were completed in early 1997 and released in April of that year. The 1995 revision (delayed in reaching the public by the "government shutdowns" of 1995) was the 10th comprehensive "benchmark" revision of NIPA. These revisions involve changes in definitions and classifications to reflect better the character of the U.S. economy and its evolving structure as well as statistical changes to incorporate new and revised data. A full discussion of the changes is beyond the scope of this book. Readers are referred to the November/December 1995 edition of *Survey of Current Business*, reference 3 in the Bibliography. Highlights follow:

> Government expenditures on certain classes of capital goods were recognized as an "investment".

> Government contributions to both civilian and military retirement programs were recognized.

> Fixed-year indexing (e.g. 1987=100) was replaced using chained (1992) dollar indexing to express "real" GDP changes from year to year. For a full discussion of this subject, see the Introduction.

> New estimating procedures, especially relating to depreciation, are used.

> Other statistical changes were made.

Presentation of Data

BEA has issued its revised GDP data from 1959 to 1997. The complete GDP series are shown for the 1959-1997 period only. Annual data from 1929 through and including 1958 are included in this edition for the first time.

The chapter consists of the 1929-1958 annual totals for GDP and 24 series shown in current and in chained (1992) dollars—a total of 49 tables. Explanatory texts are provided for subsections on Personal Consumption Expenditures, Gross Private Domestic Investment, Net Exports of Goods and Services, and Government Purchases.

Uses of GDP

Since 1991, the GDP is used as the instrument for measuring the output of the U.S. economy as a whole (its magnitude, growth, or decline) and to determine the economic processes or mechanisms which accounts for the national product (what proportion of it is accounted for by government spending, investment in structures and capital goods, by personal consumption expenditures—and subcategories of these such as durable goods, nondurable goods, services, etc.).

GDP, Business Cycles, and Markets. The best-known use of GDP is as an indicator of economic growth or decline. A sustained period of decline in real GDP is defined as a recession. A sustained period of growth is called an expansion. The period from the trough of a recession to the peak of an expansion is a business cycle. Various economic indicators, covered in this part of *EIH*, have in the past proved capable of predicting the onset of recessions and recoveries.

Since recession invariably means increased unemployment, dropping demand, and slowing production . . .

and rapid expansions can result in shortages and inflation, GDP is closely watched by government and private sector alike. Stock and bond market behavior is closely correlated with GDP's behavior as well: the stock market tends to rise and decline with GDP; the bond market behaves "counter cyclically," meaning that it rises when GDP drops and drops when GDP rises.

Bibliography

1. U.S. Department of Commerce. Bureau of Economic Analysis. *An Introduction to National Economic Accounting*. Methodology Paper Series MP-1. Washington, DC: U.S. Government Printing Office, March 1985.

2. U.S. Department of Commerce. Bureau of Economic Analysis. *GNP: An Overview of Source Data and Estimating Methods*. Methodology Paper Series MP-4. Washington, DC: U.S. Government Printing Office, September 1987.

3. U.S. Department of Commerce. Bureau of Economic Analysis. *Survey of Current Business*. Superintendent of Documents, U.S. Government Printing Office, Washington, DC 20302.

Gross Domestic Product - 1929-1958
(Billions of Current and Chained 1992 Dollars)

Annual GDP estimates, 1929-1958, in billions of current and in chained 1992 dollars. Changes from year to year are percentage changes.

Year	Current dollars	% Change	Chained 1992 dollars	% Change
1929	104.6	-	796.8	-
1930	91.8	-12.2	725.4	-9.0
1931	76.9	-16.2	678.5	-6.5
1932	58.9	-23.4	588.0	-13.3
1933	56.5	-4.1	580.3	-1.3
1934	66.1	17.0	643.7	10.9
1935	73.5	11.2	701.4	9.0
1936	83.9	14.1	792.4	13.0
1937	92.2	9.9	835.0	5.4
1938	86.3	-6.4	804.9	-3.6
1939	92.3	7.0	870.3	8.1
1940	101.6	10.1	944.2	8.5
1941	127.2	25.2	1,105.9	17.1
1942	162.1	27.4	1,312.7	18.7
1943	198.7	22.6	1,526.3	16.3
1944	220.2	10.8	1,648.2	8.0
1945	223.5	1.5	1,629.3	-1.1
1946	223.3	-0.1	1,452.0	-10.9
1947	245.8	10.1	1,437.0	-1.0
1948	271.2	10.3	1,498.8	4.3
1949	269.1	-0.8	1,486.8	-0.8
1950	296.1	10.0	1,619.1	8.9
1951	341.7	15.4	1,743.7	7.7
1952	360.7	5.6	1,809.0	3.7
1953	381.7	5.8	1,891.0	4.5
1954	383.4	0.4	1,878.6	-0.7
1955	417.7	8.9	2,012.9	7.1
1956	440.9	5.6	2,053.2	2.0
1957	464.2	5.3	2,092.4	1.9
1958	470.1	1.3	2,069.2	-1.1

Source: "National Income and Product Account Tables: Selected NIPA Tables," *Survey of Current Business*, November 1997, U.S. Department of Commerce, Bureau of Economic Analysis, National Income and Wealth Division. *Notes*: This table includes some series available only in electronic format. A dash (-) indicates no change.

Gross Domestic Product - Actual Dollars

In billions of actual dollars and percent. Quarterly data are seasonally adjusted and annualized. Growth rates for quarters are compound annual growth rates; changes from year to year are percentage changes.

Year	1st Quarter	% Change	2nd Quarter	% Change	3rd Quarter	% Change	4th Quarter	% Change	TOTAL	% Change
1959	496.3	-	509.3	10.9	509.6	0.2	513.8	3.3	507.2	-
1960	527.3	10.9	526.1	-0.9	529.0	2.2	523.9	-3.8	526.6	3.8
1961	528.1	3.2	538.9	8.4	549.6	8.2	562.6	9.8	544.8	3.5
1962	575.3	9.3	582.8	5.3	589.9	5.0	592.9	2.0	585.2	7.4
1963	602.2	6.4	610.9	5.9	623.7	8.6	632.8	6.0	617.4	5.5
1964	649.4	10.9	658.4	5.7	669.2	6.7	675.1	3.6	663.0	7.4
1965	695.6	12.7	708.2	7.4	725.0	9.8	747.7	13.1	719.1	8.5
1966	770.5	12.8	780.0	5.0	793.6	7.2	807.1	7.0	787.8	9.6
1967	817.5	5.3	823.3	2.9	838.9	7.8	854.7	7.7	833.6	5.8
1968	880.5	12.6	904.9	11.6	920.1	6.9	936.8	7.5	910.6	9.2
1969	960.0	10.3	974.1	6.0	993.6	8.3	1,001.0	3.0	982.2	7.9
1970	1,013.9	5.3	1,029.5	6.3	1,047.8	7.3	1,051.3	1.3	1,035.6	5.4
1971	1,096.8	18.5	1,117.7	7.8	1,137.3	7.2	1,149.8	4.5	1,125.4	8.7
1972	1,190.2	14.8	1,224.4	12.0	1,247.8	7.9	1,286.8	13.1	1,237.3	9.9
1973	1,337.5	16.7	1,369.4	9.9	1,391.4	6.6	1,432.3	12.3	1,382.6	11.7
1974	1,446.5	4.0	1,482.5	10.3	1,511.7	8.1	1,546.8	9.6	1,496.9	8.3
1975	1,560.3	3.5	1,597.8	10.0	1,657.1	15.7	1,707.3	12.7	1,630.6	8.9
1976	1,767.3	14.8	1,797.9	7.1	1,830.4	7.4	1,880.3	11.4	1,819.0	11.6
1977	1,934.4	12.0	2,005.1	15.4	2,063.2	12.1	2,104.7	8.3	2,026.9	11.4
1978	2,147.7	8.4	2,273.7	25.6	2,333.9	11.0	2,410.2	13.7	2,291.4	13.0
1979	2,464.5	9.3	2,522.3	9.7	2,592.8	11.7	2,650.4	9.2	2,557.5	11.6
1980	2,722.3	11.3	2,719.4	-0.4	2,783.4	9.8	2,911.8	19.8	2,784.2	8.9
1981	3,040.2	18.8	3,070.3	4.0	3,167.7	13.3	3,185.5	2.3	3,115.9	11.9
1982	3,178.6	-0.9	3,231.6	6.8	3,259.1	3.4	3,299.1	5.0	3,242.1	4.1
1983	3,361.0	7.7	3,469.2	13.5	3,563.3	11.3	3,664.6	11.9	3,514.5	8.4
1984	3,791.1	14.5	3,879.7	9.7	3,942.2	6.6	3,996.7	5.6	3,902.4	11.0
1985	4,081.2	8.7	4,134.8	5.4	4,221.4	8.6	4,285.3	6.2	4,180.7	7.1
1986	4,358.2	7.0	4,385.6	2.5	4,443.3	5.4	4,501.7	5.4	4,422.2	5.8
1987	4,565.7	5.8	4,645.1	7.1	4,722.6	6.8	4,835.9	9.9	4,692.3	6.1
1988	4,898.2	5.3	5,000.4	8.6	5,094.5	7.7	5,205.3	9.0	5,049.6	7.6
1989	5,316.8	8.8	5,413.2	7.5	5,486.9	5.6	5,537.8	3.8	5,438.7	7.7
1990	5,660.6	9.2	5,750.8	6.5	5,782.2	2.2	5,781.7	-0.0	5,743.8	5.6
1991	5,821.9	2.8	5,892.5	4.9	5,950.2	4.0	6,002.1	3.5	5,916.7	3.0
1992	6,121.8	8.2	6,201.2	5.3	6,271.7	4.6	6,383.1	7.3	6,244.4	5.5
1993	6,444.5	3.9	6,509.1	4.1	6,574.6	4.1	6,704.2	8.1	6,558.1	5.0
1994	6,794.3	5.5	6,911.4	7.1	6,986.5	4.4	7,095.7	6.4	6,947.0	5.9
1995	7,168.9	4.2	7,209.5	2.3	7,301.3	5.2	7,381.9	4.5	7,265.4	4.6
1996	7,467.5	4.7	7,607.7	7.7	7,676.0	3.6	7,792.9	6.2	7,636.0	5.1
1997	7,933.6	7.4	8,034.3	5.2	8,124.3	4.6	8,241.5	5.9	8,083.4	5.9

Source: "National Income and Product Account Tables: Selected NIPA Tables," *Survey of Current Business*, November 1997, U.S. Department of Commerce, Bureau of Economic Analysis, National Income and Wealth Division. Data for 1997 quarters downloaded from www.stat.usa.gov. A dash (-) indicates that no data are available.

Gross Domestic Product - Chained (1992) Dollars

In billions of chained (1992) dollars and percent. Quarterly data are seasonally adjusted and annualized. Growth rates for quarters are compound annual growth rates; changes from year to year are percentage changes.

Year	1st Quarter	% Change	2nd Quarter	% Change	3rd Quarter	% Change	4th Quarter	% Change	TOTAL	% Change
1959	2,165.0	-	2,223.3	11.2	2,221.4	-0.3	2,231.0	1.7	2,210.2	-
1960	2,279.2	8.9	2,265.5	-2.4	2,268.3	0.5	2,238.6	-5.1	2,262.9	2.4
1961	2,251.7	2.4	2,292.0	7.4	2,332.6	7.3	2,381.0	8.6	2,314.3	2.3
1962	2,422.6	7.2	2,448.0	4.3	2,471.9	4.0	2,476.7	0.8	2,454.8	6.1
1963	2,508.7	5.3	2,538.1	4.8	2,586.3	7.8	2,604.6	2.9	2,559.4	4.3
1964	2,666.7	9.9	2,697.5	4.7	2,729.6	4.8	2,739.7	1.5	2,708.4	5.8
1965	2,808.9	10.5	2,846.3	5.4	2,898.8	7.6	2,970.5	10.3	2,881.1	6.4
1966	3,042.4	10.0	3,055.5	1.7	3,076.5	2.8	3,102.4	3.4	3,069.2	6.5
1967	3,127.2	3.2	3,129.5	0.3	3,154.2	3.2	3,178.0	3.1	3,147.2	2.5
1968	3,236.2	7.5	3,292.1	7.1	3,316.1	2.9	3,331.2	1.8	3,293.9	4.7
1969	3,381.9	6.2	3,390.2	1.0	3,409.7	2.3	3,392.6	-2.0	3,393.6	3.0
1970	3,386.5	-0.7	3,391.6	0.6	3,423.0	3.8	3,389.4	-3.9	3,397.6	0.1
1971	3,481.4	11.3	3,500.9	2.3	3,523.8	2.6	3,533.8	1.1	3,510.0	3.3
1972	3,604.7	8.3	3,687.9	9.6	3,726.2	4.2	3,790.4	7.1	3,702.3	5.5
1973	3,892.2	11.2	3,919.0	2.8	3,907.1	-1.2	3,947.1	4.2	3,916.3	5.8
1974	3,908.1	-3.9	3,922.6	1.5	3,880.0	-4.3	3,854.1	-2.6	3,891.2	-0.6
1975	3,800.9	-5.4	3,835.2	3.7	3,907.0	7.7	3,952.5	4.7	3,873.9	-0.4
1976	4,044.6	9.7	4,072.2	2.8	4,088.5	1.6	4,126.4	3.8	4,082.9	5.4
1977	4,176.3	4.9	4,260.1	8.3	4,329.5	6.7	4,328.3	-0.1	4,273.6	4.7
1978	4,345.5	1.6	4,510.7	16.1	4,552.1	3.7	4,603.7	4.6	4,503.0	5.4
1979	4,605.7	0.2	4,615.6	0.9	4,644.9	2.6	4,656.2	1.0	4,630.6	2.8
1980	4,679.0	2.0	4,566.6	-9.3	4,562.3	-0.4	4,651.9	8.1	4,615.0	-0.3
1981	4,739.2	7.7	4,696.8	-3.5	4,753.0	4.9	4,693.8	-4.9	4,720.7	2.3
1982	4,615.9	-6.5	4,634.9	1.7	4,612.1	-2.0	4,618.3	0.5	4,620.3	-2.1
1983	4,663.0	3.9	4,763.6	8.9	4,849.0	7.4	4,939.2	7.7	4,803.7	4.0
1984	5,053.6	9.6	5,132.9	6.4	5,170.3	2.9	5,203.7	2.6	5,140.1	7.0
1985	5,257.3	4.2	5,283.7	2.0	5,359.6	5.9	5,393.6	2.6	5,323.5	3.6
1986	5,460.8	5.1	5,466.9	0.4	5,496.3	2.2	5,526.8	2.2	5,487.7	3.1
1987	5,561.8	2.6	5,618.0	4.1	5,667.4	3.6	5,750.6	6.0	5,649.5	2.9
1988	5,785.3	2.4	5,844.0	4.1	5,878.7	2.4	5,952.8	5.1	5,865.2	3.8
1989	6,011.0	4.0	6,055.6	3.0	6,088.0	2.2	6,093.5	0.4	6,062.0	3.4
1990	6,152.6	3.9	6,171.6	1.2	6,142.1	-1.9	6,079.0	-4.0	6,136.3	1.2
1991	6,047.5	-2.1	6,074.7	1.8	6,090.1	1.0	6,105.3	1.0	6,079.4	-0.9
1992	6,175.7	4.7	6,214.2	2.5	6,260.7	3.0	6,327.1	4.3	6,244.4	2.7
1993	6,327.9	0.1	6,359.9	2.0	6,393.5	2.1	6,476.9	5.3	6,389.6	2.3
1994	6,524.5	3.0	6,600.3	4.7	6,629.5	1.8	6,688.6	3.6	6,610.7	3.5
1995	6,703.7	0.9	6,708.8	0.3	6,759.2	3.0	6,796.5	2.2	6,742.1	2.0
1996	6,826.4	1.8	6,926.0	6.0	6,943.8	1.0	7,017.4	4.3	6,928.4	2.8
1997	7,101.6	4.9	7,159.6	3.3	7,214.0	3.1	7,290.3	4.3	7,191.4	3.8

Source: "National Income and Product Account Tables: Selected NIPA Tables," *Survey of Current Business*, November 1997, U.S. Department of Commerce, Bureau of Economic Analysis, National Income and Wealth Division. Data for 1997 quarters downloaded from www.stat.usa.gov. A dash (-) indicates that no data are available.

PERSONAL CONSUMPTION EXPENDITURES
Component of Gross Domestic Product

Personal Consumption Expenditures is the largest component of Gross Domestic Product (GDP). In 1996, it accounted for 68.0 percent of real GDP. The measure includes all expenditures by individuals on goods and services; goods are divided into durable and nondurable goods; services are reported as a single category.

The category is labeled "personal" consumption because it reflects all purchases by individuals. The category also incorporates goods and services that the private sector purchases in order to make final products. Paper clips purchased by an automobile producers, for instance, are accounted for in the ultimate price of cars sold to consumers. The measure excludes government purchases of goods and services and private purchases of goods (such as tooling) which are considered to be capital investments.

Note that Personal Consumption Expenditures do *not* include imported goods; these are measured as a separate category in the national accounts.

Sources for the data included in Personal Consumption Expenditures are many and varied. Typically, different sources are used for "benchmark" years (the years of the economic censuses), for other years, and for the most recent period in order to obtain the best and most accurate information. Where partial data only are available, estimates are made using a variety of procedures, including judgement based on trends.

All explanations are provided in this section, followed by tables showing Personal Consumption Expenditure totals and tables showing the subcomponents of the measure. Each item is shown in actual and in constant 1987 dollars.

Durable and Nondurable Goods

The Bureau of Economic Affairs bases its estimates on six distinct categories, each handled in a different way (reference 1). Most goods are based on census surveys in benchmark years and on annual and monthly retail surveys conducted in other years by the Census Bureau. Other distinct categories, using distinct estimating methodologies, are new trucks, new and used autos, gasoline and oil, and food furnished employees (including the military).

In 1996, durable goods accounted for 8.8 percent and nondurable goods for 20.7 percent of real GDP. Durable goods are products expected to last three years or longer; nondurables for a lesser time period.

Services

The category measures expenditures on services by individuals. The grouping of categories includes (1) rent paid for housing; (2) medical services; (3) expenditures on education from whatever sources; (4) financial, banking, brokerage services; (5) insurance, hospital expenses, religious activities, cable TV, utilities, and local transportation; (6) water and sanitary services; lotteries, (7) foreign travel by U.S. citizens less foreign visitors' spending in the U.S., and (8) a variety of other services, including repairs, tools, club memberships, etc. Estimating methods differ for each of these groupings.

The Services category of Personal Consumption Expenditures should not be viewed as equivalent to the "services" sector of the economy. The category includes rentals, insurance, banking, and financial services, which are classified elsewhere in the Standard Industrial Classification (SIC) system. And the category excludes services purchased by corporations and by government; services purchased by the private sector are "hidden" in the price of goods sold or services rendered; those purchased by government appear under the governmental category.

Presentation of Data

Data are shown from 1959 to 1997 in quarterly and in annual increments. Changes from one period to the next are shown. Changes from quarter to quarter are annualized, compounded growth rates as explained in the previous section on Gross National Product. Changes from year to year are simple percentile changes.

Analytical Uses

Personal consumption expenditures measure the allocation of individual resources between consumable products (food, clothing, etc.), durable goods (automobiles, appliances, etc.), and services (medical, entertainment, etc.) over time. As in all GDP series, significance appears when results for different periods are compared. Nondurable goods are the most essential; durable goods purchases can be deferred. Growth in one and decline in the other can thus signal a lack of consumer confidence. Strong growth in durables output, conversely, shows confidence in the future. The shift of expenditures from goods to services or from services to goods indicates, over time, changes in economic structure.

Gross Domestic Product

Personal consumption expenditures: Total - Actual Dollars

In billions of actual dollars and percent. Quarterly data are seasonally adjusted and annualized. Growth rates for quarters are compound annual growth rates; changes from year to year are percentage changes.

Year	1st Quarter	% Change	2nd Quarter	% Change	3rd Quarter	% Change	4th Quarter	% Change	TOTAL	% Change
1959	310.4	-	316.4	8.0	321.7	6.9	323.8	2.6	318.1	-
1960	327.3	4.4	333.2	7.4	333.1	-0.1	335.0	2.3	332.2	4.4
1961	335.7	0.8	340.6	6.0	343.5	3.4	350.7	8.7	342.6	3.1
1962	355.3	5.4	361.3	6.9	365.4	4.6	371.7	7.1	363.4	6.1
1963	375.1	3.7	379.4	4.7	386.4	7.6	391.1	5.0	383.0	5.4
1964	400.5	10.0	408.3	8.0	417.1	8.9	419.8	2.6	411.4	7.4
1965	430.6	10.7	437.8	6.9	447.2	8.9	461.5	13.4	444.3	8.0
1966	472.0	9.4	477.1	4.4	486.4	8.0	492.0	4.7	481.9	8.5
1967	496.8	4.0	506.2	7.8	513.7	6.1	521.2	6.0	509.5	5.7
1968	539.5	14.8	553.2	10.6	569.1	12.0	577.5	6.0	559.8	9.9
1969	588.8	8.1	599.4	7.4	609.2	6.7	621.1	8.0	604.7	8.0
1970	632.4	7.5	642.7	6.7	655.2	8.0	662.1	4.3	648.1	7.2
1971	681.6	12.3	695.8	8.6	708.2	7.3	724.5	9.5	702.5	8.4
1972	741.9	10.0	759.9	10.1	778.1	9.9	802.9	13.4	770.7	9.7
1973	827.2	12.7	842.1	7.4	860.8	9.2	876.1	7.3	851.6	10.5
1974	894.4	8.6	922.4	13.1	950.1	12.6	957.8	3.3	931.2	9.3
1975	982.7	10.8	1,012.4	12.6	1,046.3	14.1	1,075.1	11.5	1,029.1	10.5
1976	1,110.2	13.7	1,130.2	7.4	1,159.8	10.9	1,195.0	12.7	1,148.8	11.6
1977	1,230.7	12.5	1,259.1	9.6	1,290.3	10.3	1,328.1	12.2	1,277.1	11.2
1978	1,358.3	9.4	1,417.4	18.6	1,450.6	9.7	1,488.7	10.9	1,428.8	11.9
1979	1,529.3	11.4	1,563.9	9.4	1,617.4	14.4	1,663.5	11.9	1,593.5	11.5
1980	1,713.1	12.5	1,716.9	0.9	1,774.9	14.2	1,836.8	14.7	1,760.4	10.5
1981	1,890.3	12.2	1,923.5	7.2	1,967.4	9.4	1,983.9	3.4	1,941.3	10.3
1982	2,021.4	7.8	2,046.1	5.0	2,091.1	9.1	2,148.7	11.5	2,076.8	7.0
1983	2,185.0	6.9	2,257.2	13.9	2,316.8	11.0	2,374.7	10.4	2,283.4	9.9
1984	2,422.5	8.3	2,475.6	9.1	2,510.5	5.8	2,560.6	8.2	2,492.3	9.1
1985	2,623.8	10.2	2,673.4	7.8	2,742.3	10.7	2,779.6	5.6	2,704.8	8.5
1986	2,823.3	6.4	2,855.6	4.7	2,926.2	10.3	2,965.6	5.5	2,892.7	6.9
1987	3,002.4	5.1	3,070.0	9.3	3,134.2	8.6	3,171.3	4.8	3,094.5	7.0
1988	3,247.1	9.9	3,310.2	8.0	3,382.3	9.0	3,459.2	9.4	3,349.7	8.2
1989	3,506.1	5.5	3,569.7	7.5	3,627.3	6.6	3,676.1	5.5	3,594.8	7.3
1990	3,759.2	9.4	3,811.8	5.7	3,879.2	7.3	3,907.0	2.9	3,839.3	6.8
1991	3,910.7	0.4	3,961.0	5.2	4,001.6	4.2	4,027.1	2.6	3,975.1	3.5
1992	4,127.6	10.4	4,183.0	5.5	4,238.9	5.5	4,329.6	8.8	4,219.8	6.2
1993	4,365.4	3.3	4,428.1	5.9	4,488.6	5.6	4,554.9	6.0	4,459.2	5.7
1994	4,616.6	5.5	4,680.5	5.7	4,750.6	6.1	4,820.2	6.0	4,717.0	5.8
1995	4,871.7	4.3	4,934.8	5.3	4,990.6	4.6	5,033.8	3.5	4,957.7	5.1
1996	5,105.8	5.8	5,189.1	6.7	5,227.4	3.0	5,308.1	6.3	5,207.6	5.0
1997	5,405.7	7.6	5,432.1	2.0	5,527.4	7.2	5,589.3	4.6	5,488.6	5.4

Source: "National Income and Product Account Tables: Selected NIPA Tables," *Survey of Current Business*, November 1997, U.S. Department of Commerce, Bureau of Economic Analysis, National Income and Wealth Division. Data for 1997 quarters downloaded from www.stat.usa.gov. A dash (-) indicates that no data are available.

Gross Domestic Product
Personal consumption expenditures: Total - Chained (1992) Dollars

In billions of chained (1992) dollars and percent. Quarterly data are seasonally adjusted and annualized. Growth rates for quarters are compound annual growth rates; changes from year to year are percentage changes.

Year	1st Quarter	% Change	2nd Quarter	% Change	3rd Quarter	% Change	4th Quarter	% Change	TOTAL	% Change
1959	1,369.9	-	1,391.7	6.5	1,407.2	4.5	1,409.5	0.7	1,394.6	-
1960	1,422.5	3.7	1,439.6	4.9	1,433.5	-1.7	1,434.8	0.4	1,432.6	2.7
1961	1,434.2	-0.2	1,455.7	6.1	1,463.5	2.2	1,492.8	8.3	1,461.5	2.0
1962	1,508.4	4.2	1,526.7	4.9	1,539.6	3.4	1,560.6	5.6	1,533.8	4.9
1963	1,571.2	2.7	1,586.3	3.9	1,607.6	5.5	1,621.1	3.4	1,596.6	4.1
1964	1,653.6	8.3	1,683.1	7.3	1,713.9	7.5	1,718.6	1.1	1,692.3	6.0
1965	1,756.2	9.0	1,776.1	4.6	1,806.1	6.9	1,858.0	12.0	1,799.1	6.3
1966	1,885.6	6.1	1,890.9	1.1	1,912.4	4.6	1,919.1	1.4	1,902.0	5.7
1967	1,931.2	2.5	1,957.5	5.6	1,967.1	2.0	1,978.5	2.3	1,958.6	3.0
1968	2,025.1	9.8	2,056.4	6.3	2,095.1	7.7	2,104.4	1.8	2,070.2	5.7
1969	2,128.0	4.6	2,141.4	2.5	2,152.0	2.0	2,168.8	3.2	2,147.5	3.7
1970	2,182.3	2.5	2,192.9	2.0	2,211.6	3.5	2,204.6	-1.3	2,197.8	2.3
1971	2,246.5	7.8	2,266.5	3.6	2,283.9	3.1	2,321.1	6.7	2,279.5	3.7
1972	2,352.0	5.4	2,394.9	7.5	2,430.6	6.1	2,486.1	9.5	2,415.9	6.0
1973	2,530.4	7.3	2,527.5	-0.5	2,539.9	2.0	2,532.6	-1.1	2,532.6	4.8
1974	2,512.7	-3.1	2,522.7	1.6	2,532.4	1.5	2,490.9	-6.4	2,514.7	-0.7
1975	2,513.2	3.6	2,556.3	7.0	2,591.8	5.7	2,618.7	4.2	2,570.0	2.2
1976	2,674.2	8.8	2,697.9	3.6	2,724.4	4.0	2,760.8	5.5	2,714.3	5.6
1977	2,794.3	4.9	2,810.3	2.3	2,836.9	3.8	2,877.6	5.9	2,829.8	4.3
1978	2,893.1	2.2	2,954.6	8.8	2,968.2	1.9	2,990.6	3.1	2,951.6	4.3
1979	3,008.1	2.4	3,003.5	-0.6	3,028.7	3.4	3,040.2	1.5	3,020.2	2.3
1980	3,037.2	-0.4	2,968.8	-8.7	2,998.5	4.1	3,034.2	4.8	3,009.7	-0.3
1981	3,045.6	1.5	3,045.8	0.0	3,058.8	1.7	3,035.3	-3.0	3,046.4	1.2
1982	3,054.0	2.5	3,062.1	1.1	3,080.1	2.4	3,129.7	6.6	3,081.5	1.2
1983	3,156.5	3.5	3,220.0	8.3	3,267.1	6.0	3,318.6	6.5	3,240.6	5.2
1984	3,354.0	4.3	3,397.5	5.3	3,418.4	2.5	3,460.6	5.0	3,407.6	5.2
1985	3,511.2	6.0	3,540.8	3.4	3,602.1	7.1	3,612.1	1.1	3,566.5	4.7
1986	3,644.0	3.6	3,683.0	4.4	3,742.8	6.7	3,764.8	2.4	3,708.7	4.0
1987	3,765.7	0.1	3,814.0	5.2	3,852.9	4.1	3,856.5	0.4	3,822.3	3.1
1988	3,924.2	7.2	3,952.2	2.9	3,985.1	3.4	4,029.1	4.5	3,972.7	3.9
1989	4,032.8	0.4	4,047.4	1.5	4,083.2	3.6	4,095.0	1.2	4,064.6	2.3
1990	4,128.9	3.4	4,134.7	0.6	4,148.5	1.3	4,116.4	-3.1	4,132.2	1.7
1991	4,084.5	-3.1	4,110.0	2.5	4,119.5	0.9	4,109.1	-1.0	4,105.8	-0.6
1992	4,173.8	6.4	4,196.4	2.2	4,226.7	2.9	4,282.3	5.4	4,219.8	2.8
1993	4,286.8	0.4	4,322.8	3.4	4,366.6	4.1	4,398.0	2.9	4,343.6	2.9
1994	4,439.4	3.8	4,472.2	3.0	4,498.2	2.3	4,534.1	3.2	4,486.0	3.3
1995	4,551.3	1.5	4,583.5	2.9	4,612.9	2.6	4,633.5	1.8	4,595.3	2.4
1996	4,669.4	3.1	4,712.2	3.7	4,718.2	0.5	4,756.4	3.3	4,714.1	2.6
1997	4,818.1	5.3	4,829.4	0.9	4,896.2	5.6	4,935.0	3.2	4,869.7	3.3

Source: "National Income and Product Account Tables: Selected NIPA Tables," *Survey of Current Business*, November 1997, U.S. Department of Commerce, Bureau of Economic Analysis, National Income and Wealth Division. Data for 1997 quarters downloaded from www.stat.usa.gov. A dash (-) indicates that no data are available.

Gross Domestic Product

Personal consumption expenditures
Durable goods - Actual Dollars

In billions of actual dollars and percent. Quarterly data are seasonally adjusted and annualized. Growth rates for quarters are compound annual growth rates; changes from year to year are percentage changes.

Year	1st Quarter	% Change	2nd Quarter	% Change	3rd Quarter	% Change	4th Quarter	% Change	TOTAL	% Change
1959	41.5	-	43.2	17.4	44.1	8.6	41.8	-19.3	42.7	-
1960	43.2	14.1	44.1	8.6	43.6	-4.5	42.4	-10.6	43.3	1.4
1961	39.9	-21.6	40.9	10.4	42.1	12.3	44.2	21.5	41.8	-3.5
1962	45.2	9.4	46.4	11.0	46.9	4.4	48.9	18.2	46.9	12.2
1963	50.0	9.3	51.3	10.8	52.0	5.6	53.1	8.7	51.6	10.0
1964	55.2	16.8	56.6	10.5	58.4	13.3	56.4	-13.0	56.7	9.9
1965	61.9	45.1	61.7	-1.3	63.6	12.9	65.9	15.3	63.3	11.6
1966	68.9	19.5	66.3	-14.3	68.8	16.0	69.1	1.8	68.3	7.9
1967	67.6	-8.4	71.0	21.7	71.1	0.6	72.0	5.2	70.4	3.1
1968	77.1	31.5	79.1	10.8	83.3	23.0	83.6	1.4	80.8	14.8
1969	85.5	9.4	85.9	1.9	86.1	0.9	86.2	0.5	85.9	6.3
1970	84.9	-5.9	86.0	5.3	86.9	4.3	82.1	-20.3	85.0	-1.0
1971	92.7	62.5	95.5	12.6	97.8	10.0	101.5	16.0	96.9	14.0
1972	104.9	14.1	108.1	12.8	111.4	12.8	117.0	21.7	110.4	13.9
1973	125.2	31.1	124.1	-3.5	123.8	-1.0	121.1	-8.4	123.5	11.9
1974	118.9	-7.1	123.0	14.5	128.8	20.2	118.6	-28.1	122.3	-1.0
1975	123.2	16.4	128.3	17.6	138.0	33.8	144.4	19.9	133.5	9.2
1976	154.1	29.7	156.3	5.8	159.6	8.7	165.3	15.1	158.9	19.0
1977	173.6	21.6	178.7	12.3	183.0	10.0	189.0	13.8	181.1	14.0
1978	186.8	-4.6	204.4	43.4	204.8	0.8	209.8	10.1	201.4	11.2
1979	211.1	2.5	209.9	-2.3	218.4	17.2	216.3	-3.8	213.9	6.2
1980	219.4	5.9	199.2	-32.0	212.4	29.3	223.0	21.5	213.5	-0.2
1981	232.6	18.4	227.4	-8.6	238.4	20.8	223.6	-22.6	230.5	8.0
1982	233.2	18.3	235.6	4.2	238.1	4.3	250.1	21.7	239.3	3.8
1983	254.6	7.4	274.7	35.5	286.8	18.8	303.3	25.1	279.8	16.9
1984	315.0	16.3	324.4	12.5	324.9	0.6	336.0	14.4	325.1	16.2
1985	349.8	17.5	354.4	5.4	376.8	27.8	363.2	-13.7	361.1	11.1
1986	370.3	8.1	384.7	16.5	422.0	44.8	417.6	-4.1	398.7	10.4
1987	394.2	-20.6	413.8	21.4	434.7	21.8	424.1	-9.4	416.7	4.5
1988	444.2	20.3	448.2	3.7	447.1	-1.0	464.5	16.5	451.0	8.2
1989	462.5	-1.7	472.5	8.9	484.6	10.6	471.7	-10.2	472.8	4.8
1990	493.3	19.6	477.6	-12.1	473.2	-3.6	461.9	-9.2	476.5	0.8
1991	449.0	-10.7	452.7	3.3	462.0	8.5	457.3	-4.0	455.2	-4.5
1992	474.1	15.5	481.3	6.2	492.5	9.6	506.2	11.6	488.5	7.3
1993	506.4	0.2	524.2	14.8	537.2	10.3	553.1	12.4	530.2	8.5
1994	563.2	7.5	572.4	6.7	583.3	7.8	599.3	11.4	579.5	9.3
1995	596.9	-1.6	602.8	4.0	616.0	9.1	618.4	1.6	608.5	5.0
1996	626.7	5.5	638.6	7.8	634.5	-2.5	638.2	2.4	634.5	4.3
1997	658.4	13.3	644.5	-8.2	667.3	14.9	667.6	0.2	659.4	3.9

Source: "National Income and Product Account Tables: Selected NIPA Tables," *Survey of Current Business*, November 1997, U.S. Department of Commerce, Bureau of Economic Analysis, National Income and Wealth Division. Data for 1997 quarters downloaded from www.stat.usa.gov. A dash (-) indicates that no data are available.

Gross Domestic Product
Personal consumption expenditures
Durable goods - Chained (1992) Dollars

In billions of chained (1992) dollars and percent. Quarterly data are seasonally adjusted and annualized. Growth rates for quarters are compound annual growth rates; changes from year to year are percentage changes.

Year	1st Quarter	% Change	2nd Quarter	% Change	3rd Quarter	% Change	4th Quarter	% Change	TOTAL	% Change
1959	100.6	-	104.3	15.5	106.5	8.7	101.0	-19.1	103.1	-
1960	104.5	14.6	106.9	9.5	106.1	-3.0	103.2	-10.5	105.2	2.0
1961	97.1	-21.6	99.2	8.9	101.7	10.5	106.8	21.6	101.2	-3.8
1962	109.1	8.9	111.9	10.7	113.0	4.0	118.2	19.7	113.0	11.7
1963	120.7	8.7	123.4	9.3	124.9	5.0	127.0	6.9	124.0	9.7
1964	131.7	15.6	135.3	11.4	139.7	13.7	135.2	-12.3	135.5	9.3
1965	148.1	44.0	148.4	0.8	153.7	15.1	160.3	18.3	152.6	12.6
1966	168.0	20.6	161.0	-15.7	166.5	14.4	166.6	0.2	165.5	8.5
1967	163.3	-7.7	170.7	19.4	169.1	-3.7	169.4	0.7	168.1	1.6
1968	180.1	27.8	183.6	8.0	192.0	19.6	190.8	-2.5	186.6	11.0
1969	194.1	7.1	193.7	-0.8	193.2	-1.0	192.1	-2.3	193.3	3.6
1970	188.7	-6.9	190.7	4.3	191.3	1.3	177.6	-25.7	187.0	-3.3
1971	197.3	52.3	201.9	9.7	207.3	11.1	216.4	18.7	205.7	10.0
1972	221.7	10.2	227.2	10.3	233.2	11.0	245.3	22.4	231.9	12.7
1973	261.7	29.5	257.4	-6.4	255.4	-3.1	248.8	-9.9	255.8	10.3
1974	242.1	-10.3	244.3	3.7	246.4	3.5	220.0	-36.4	238.2	-6.9
1975	225.4	10.2	230.2	8.8	244.9	28.1	252.0	12.1	238.1	-0.0
1976	265.7	23.6	266.2	0.8	268.7	3.8	273.4	7.2	268.5	12.8
1977	284.7	17.6	291.9	10.5	295.9	5.6	301.0	7.1	293.4	9.3
1978	293.9	-9.1	316.3	34.2	311.4	-6.1	313.7	3.0	308.8	5.2
1979	310.5	-4.0	303.5	-8.7	311.9	11.5	303.3	-10.6	307.3	-0.5
1980	299.3	-5.2	265.8	-37.8	278.2	20.0	287.0	13.3	282.6	-8.0
1981	295.7	12.7	283.7	-15.3	292.8	13.5	271.2	-26.4	285.8	1.1
1982	280.5	14.4	281.4	1.3	283.3	2.7	296.7	20.3	285.5	-0.1
1983	299.9	4.4	322.7	34.1	334.9	16.0	352.1	22.2	327.4	14.7
1984	365.9	16.6	374.4	9.6	373.7	-0.7	385.8	13.6	374.9	14.5
1985	399.3	14.7	404.0	4.8	429.6	27.9	412.6	-14.9	411.4	9.7
1986	420.3	7.7	435.4	15.2	472.6	38.8	465.4	-6.0	448.4	9.0
1987	435.8	-23.1	453.5	17.3	472.1	17.4	458.3	-11.2	454.9	1.4
1988	480.9	21.2	482.6	1.4	477.9	-3.8	492.7	13.0	483.5	6.3
1989	488.4	-3.4	496.8	7.1	507.4	8.8	492.2	-11.5	496.2	2.6
1990	511.2	16.4	495.4	-11.8	490.4	-4.0	476.3	-11.0	493.3	-0.6
1991	458.6	-14.1	460.5	1.7	467.3	6.0	461.5	-4.9	462.0	-6.3
1992	476.1	13.3	481.1	4.3	491.9	9.3	505.0	11.1	488.5	5.7
1993	504.0	-0.8	519.3	12.7	529.9	8.4	542.1	9.5	523.8	7.2
1994	550.7	6.5	555.8	3.8	561.7	4.3	576.6	11.0	561.2	7.1
1995	572.2	-3.0	577.7	3.9	590.8	9.4	593.7	2.0	583.6	4.0
1996	600.7	4.8	614.8	9.7	611.9	-1.9	617.1	3.4	611.1	4.7
1997	637.8	14.1	629.0	-5.4	656.1	18.4	660.3	2.6	645.8	5.7

Source: "National Income and Product Account Tables: Selected NIPA Tables," *Survey of Current Business*, November 1997, U.S. Department of Commerce, Bureau of Economic Analysis, National Income and Wealth Division. Data for 1997 quarters downloaded from www.stat.usa.gov. A dash (-) indicates that no data are available.

Gross Domestic Product
Personal consumption expenditures
Nondurable goods - Actual Dollars

In billions of actual dollars and percent. Quarterly data are seasonally adjusted and annualized. Growth rates for quarters are compound annual growth rates; changes from year to year are percentage changes.

Year	1st Quarter	% Change	2nd Quarter	% Change	3rd Quarter	% Change	4th Quarter	% Change	TOTAL	% Change
1959	146.1	-	147.7	4.5	149.3	4.4	150.9	4.4	148.5	-
1960	150.8	-0.3	153.6	7.6	153.0	-1.6	153.9	2.4	152.9	3.0
1961	155.2	3.4	156.0	2.1	156.5	1.3	158.6	5.5	156.6	2.4
1962	160.6	5.1	161.9	3.3	163.4	3.8	165.3	4.7	162.8	4.0
1963	166.3	2.4	167.0	1.7	169.4	5.9	169.9	1.2	168.2	3.3
1964	174.1	10.3	177.3	7.6	181.0	8.6	182.3	2.9	178.7	6.2
1965	185.0	6.1	188.7	8.2	192.6	8.5	200.0	16.3	191.6	7.2
1966	204.3	8.9	208.0	7.4	211.0	5.9	211.7	1.3	208.8	9.0
1967	213.9	4.2	215.6	3.2	218.0	4.5	220.9	5.4	217.1	4.0
1968	228.1	13.7	233.3	9.4	239.4	10.9	242.0	4.4	235.7	8.6
1969	246.4	7.5	251.1	7.9	255.2	6.7	259.9	7.6	253.2	7.4
1970	266.2	10.1	269.8	5.5	273.7	5.9	278.4	7.0	272.0	7.4
1971	280.3	2.8	284.1	5.5	286.7	3.7	291.0	6.1	285.5	5.0
1972	295.9	6.9	304.3	11.8	311.5	9.8	320.5	12.1	308.0	7.9
1973	330.3	12.8	337.0	8.4	347.6	13.2	357.4	11.8	343.1	11.4
1974	369.1	13.8	380.3	12.7	391.7	12.5	396.7	5.2	384.5	12.1
1975	404.4	8.0	415.5	11.4	427.7	12.3	435.0	7.0	420.6	9.4
1976	445.3	9.8	452.6	6.7	462.4	8.9	472.4	8.9	458.2	8.9
1977	483.7	9.9	492.0	7.0	498.5	5.4	513.5	12.6	496.9	8.4
1978	524.1	8.5	542.6	14.9	558.1	11.9	574.9	12.6	549.9	10.7
1979	593.5	13.6	610.1	11.7	635.3	17.6	657.1	14.4	624.0	13.5
1980	679.2	14.1	686.0	4.1	698.9	7.7	717.8	11.3	695.5	11.5
1981	745.1	16.1	755.5	5.7	762.5	3.8	769.5	3.7	758.2	9.0
1982	775.5	3.2	777.8	1.2	792.2	7.6	801.9	5.0	786.8	3.8
1983	805.3	1.7	823.1	9.1	841.4	9.2	851.1	4.7	830.3	5.5
1984	865.4	6.9	882.7	8.2	888.6	2.7	897.5	4.1	883.6	6.4
1985	909.3	5.4	923.0	6.2	931.7	3.8	946.3	6.4	927.6	5.0
1986	956.1	4.2	949.4	-2.8	955.6	2.6	967.8	5.2	957.2	3.2
1987	992.9	10.8	1,010.4	7.2	1,020.7	4.1	1,031.9	4.5	1,014.0	5.9
1988	1,045.4	5.3	1,067.8	8.9	1,094.0	10.2	1,117.1	8.7	1,081.1	6.6
1989	1,132.3	5.6	1,159.6	10.0	1,173.6	4.9	1,189.8	5.6	1,163.8	7.6
1990	1,220.7	10.8	1,230.2	3.1	1,256.2	8.7	1,274.1	5.8	1,245.3	7.0
1991	1,268.3	-1.8	1,279.7	3.6	1,283.4	1.2	1,279.0	-1.4	1,277.6	2.6
1992	1,303.1	7.8	1,308.4	1.6	1,326.3	5.6	1,349.5	7.2	1,321.8	3.5
1993	1,354.4	1.5	1,366.3	3.6	1,373.9	2.2	1,388.0	4.2	1,370.7	3.7
1994	1,404.4	4.8	1,416.0	3.3	1,439.5	6.8	1,453.7	4.0	1,428.4	4.2
1995	1,462.7	2.5	1,472.4	2.7	1,480.4	2.2	1,487.8	2.0	1,475.8	3.3
1996	1,508.1	5.6	1,532.3	6.6	1,538.3	1.6	1,560.1	5.8	1,534.7	4.0
1997	1,587.4	7.2	1,578.9	-2.1	1,600.8	5.7	1,603.9	0.8	1,592.7	3.8

Source: "National Income and Product Account Tables: Selected NIPA Tables," *Survey of Current Business*, November 1997, U.S. Department of Commerce, Bureau of Economic Analysis, National Income and Wealth Division. Data for 1997 quarters downloaded from www.stat.usa.gov. A dash (-) indicates that no data are available.

Gross Domestic Product
Personal consumption expenditures
Nondurable goods - Chained (1992) Dollars

In billions of chained (1992) dollars and percent. Quarterly data are seasonally adjusted and annualized. Growth rates for quarters are compound annual growth rates; changes from year to year are percentage changes.

Year	1st Quarter	% Change	2nd Quarter	% Change	3rd Quarter	% Change	4th Quarter	% Change	TOTAL	% Change
1959	600.0	-	604.8	3.2	608.1	2.2	612.2	2.7	606.3	-
1960	612.1	-0.1	619.3	4.8	615.0	-2.7	615.4	0.3	615.4	1.5
1961	619.5	2.7	625.9	4.2	626.3	0.3	635.3	5.9	626.7	1.8
1962	640.7	3.4	643.9	2.0	648.7	3.0	652.7	2.5	646.5	3.2
1963	655.3	1.6	658.0	1.7	663.2	3.2	663.7	0.3	660.0	2.1
1964	676.3	7.8	688.8	7.6	701.3	7.5	703.7	1.4	692.5	4.9
1965	711.9	4.7	719.9	4.6	730.1	5.8	755.4	14.6	729.3	5.3
1966	762.4	3.8	769.0	3.5	774.2	2.7	771.2	-1.5	769.2	5.5
1967	777.3	3.2	781.0	1.9	781.5	0.3	785.8	2.2	781.4	1.6
1968	802.9	9.0	813.1	5.2	825.8	6.4	825.7	-0.0	816.9	4.5
1969	833.5	3.8	837.6	2.0	839.1	0.7	844.2	2.5	838.6	2.7
1970	853.1	4.3	854.9	0.8	860.7	2.7	867.5	3.2	859.1	2.4
1971	870.4	1.3	873.5	1.4	873.5	-	880.7	3.3	874.5	1.8
1972	886.2	2.5	908.0	10.2	920.7	5.7	936.7	7.1	912.9	4.4
1973	946.5	4.3	938.5	-3.3	945.3	2.9	941.3	-1.7	942.9	3.3
1974	929.5	-4.9	926.3	-1.4	927.5	0.5	914.6	-5.4	924.5	-2.0
1975	919.1	2.0	938.3	8.6	946.2	3.4	949.5	1.4	938.3	1.5
1976	968.4	8.2	981.6	5.6	990.1	3.5	999.1	3.7	984.8	5.0
1977	1,005.6	2.6	1,005.0	-0.2	1,006.5	0.6	1,024.4	7.3	1,010.4	2.6
1978	1,029.9	2.2	1,040.5	4.2	1,050.3	3.8	1,062.1	4.6	1,045.7	3.5
1979	1,066.7	1.7	1,061.6	-1.9	1,070.8	3.5	1,079.7	3.4	1,069.7	2.3
1980	1,076.1	-1.3	1,061.7	-5.2	1,058.6	-1.2	1,063.8	2.0	1,065.1	-0.4
1981	1,073.3	3.6	1,075.2	0.7	1,074.0	-0.4	1,074.6	0.2	1,074.3	0.9
1982	1,075.5	0.3	1,075.9	0.1	1,080.9	1.9	1,090.2	3.5	1,080.6	0.6
1983	1,095.4	1.9	1,104.7	3.4	1,120.0	5.7	1,129.5	3.4	1,112.4	2.9
1984	1,135.7	2.2	1,153.8	6.5	1,156.4	0.9	1,161.2	1.7	1,151.8	3.5
1985	1,167.7	2.3	1,175.0	2.5	1,181.5	2.2	1,189.3	2.7	1,178.3	2.3
1986	1,204.0	5.0	1,215.5	3.9	1,217.0	0.5	1,227.0	3.3	1,215.9	3.2
1987	1,233.3	2.1	1,240.6	2.4	1,239.8	-0.3	1,243.2	1.1	1,239.3	1.9
1988	1,254.9	3.8	1,266.8	3.8	1,281.0	4.6	1,294.8	4.4	1,274.4	2.8
1989	1,295.3	0.2	1,295.6	0.1	1,308.2	3.9	1,315.0	2.1	1,303.5	2.3
1990	1,319.2	1.3	1,316.9	-0.7	1,319.8	0.9	1,308.4	-3.4	1,316.1	1.0
1991	1,300.6	-2.4	1,308.0	2.3	1,307.1	-0.3	1,295.7	-3.4	1,302.9	-1.0
1992	1,314.4	5.9	1,312.0	-0.7	1,321.1	2.8	1,339.8	5.8	1,321.8	1.5
1993	1,337.5	-0.7	1,347.8	3.1	1,356.8	2.7	1,361.8	1.5	1,351.0	2.2
1994	1,378.4	5.0	1,385.5	2.1	1,393.2	2.2	1,402.5	2.7	1,389.9	2.9
1995	1,408.4	1.7	1,411.6	0.9	1,413.9	0.7	1,416.3	0.7	1,412.6	1.6
1996	1,422.5	1.8	1,431.6	2.6	1,433.9	0.6	1,441.2	2.1	1,432.3	1.4
1997	1,457.8	4.7	1,450.0	-2.1	1,465.5	4.3	1,464.1	-0.4	1,459.4	1.9

Source: "National Income and Product Account Tables: Selected NIPA Tables," *Survey of Current Business*, November 1997, U.S. Department of Commerce, Bureau of Economic Analysis, National Income and Wealth Division. Data for 1997 quarters downloaded from www.stat.usa.gov. A dash (-) indicates that no data are available.

Gross Domestic Product
Personal consumption expenditures
Services - Actual Dollars

In billions of actual dollars and percent. Quarterly data are seasonally adjusted and annualized. Growth rates for quarters are compound annual growth rates; changes from year to year are percentage changes.

Year	1st Quarter	% Change	2nd Quarter	% Change	3rd Quarter	% Change	4th Quarter	% Change	TOTAL	% Change
1959	122.8	-	125.5	9.1	128.4	9.6	131.1	8.7	127.0	-
1960	133.3	6.9	135.5	6.8	136.5	3.0	138.7	6.6	136.0	7.1
1961	140.6	5.6	143.7	9.1	144.9	3.4	147.9	8.5	144.3	6.1
1962	149.5	4.4	152.9	9.4	155.0	5.6	157.5	6.6	153.7	6.5
1963	158.8	3.3	161.1	5.9	165.0	10.0	168.0	7.5	163.2	6.2
1964	171.2	7.8	174.4	7.7	177.7	7.8	181.1	7.9	176.1	7.9
1965	183.7	5.9	187.4	8.3	191.0	7.9	195.7	10.2	189.4	7.6
1966	198.7	6.3	202.8	8.5	206.6	7.7	211.2	9.2	204.8	8.1
1967	215.3	8.0	219.6	8.2	224.5	9.2	228.3	6.9	222.0	8.4
1968	234.3	10.9	240.9	11.8	246.3	9.3	251.9	9.4	243.4	9.6
1969	256.9	8.2	262.4	8.8	267.9	8.7	275.0	11.0	265.5	9.1
1970	281.4	9.6	286.8	7.9	294.6	11.3	301.6	9.8	291.1	9.6
1971	308.6	9.6	316.1	10.1	323.7	10.0	332.1	10.8	320.1	10.0
1972	341.1	11.3	347.5	7.7	355.2	9.2	365.3	11.9	352.3	10.1
1973	371.6	7.1	381.0	10.5	389.4	9.1	397.6	8.7	384.9	9.3
1974	406.3	9.0	419.1	13.2	429.7	10.5	442.4	12.4	424.4	10.3
1975	455.1	12.0	468.6	12.4	480.6	10.6	495.7	13.2	475.0	11.9
1976	510.7	12.7	521.4	8.6	537.7	13.1	557.3	15.4	531.8	12.0
1977	573.4	12.1	588.3	10.8	608.8	14.7	625.5	11.4	599.0	12.6
1978	647.5	14.8	670.4	14.9	687.7	10.7	704.0	9.8	677.4	13.1
1979	724.7	12.3	743.9	11.0	763.7	11.1	790.1	14.6	755.6	11.5
1980	814.5	12.9	831.7	8.7	863.6	16.2	895.9	15.8	851.4	12.7
1981	912.6	7.7	940.6	12.8	966.6	11.5	990.8	10.4	952.6	11.9
1982	1,012.8	9.2	1,032.7	8.1	1,060.8	11.3	1,096.7	14.2	1,050.7	10.3
1983	1,125.1	10.8	1,159.4	12.8	1,188.5	10.4	1,220.2	11.1	1,173.3	11.7
1984	1,242.0	7.3	1,268.5	8.8	1,297.1	9.3	1,327.0	9.5	1,283.6	9.4
1985	1,364.7	11.9	1,395.9	9.5	1,433.8	11.3	1,470.1	10.5	1,416.1	10.3
1986	1,496.9	7.5	1,521.5	6.7	1,548.7	7.3	1,580.2	8.4	1,536.8	8.5
1987	1,615.2	9.2	1,645.8	7.8	1,678.9	8.3	1,715.3	9.0	1,663.8	8.3
1988	1,757.5	10.2	1,794.2	8.6	1,841.2	10.9	1,877.6	8.1	1,817.6	9.2
1989	1,911.4	7.4	1,937.6	5.6	1,969.1	6.7	2,014.5	9.5	1,958.1	7.7
1990	2,045.3	6.3	2,104.1	12.0	2,149.8	9.0	2,171.0	4.0	2,117.5	8.1
1991	2,193.5	4.2	2,228.6	6.6	2,256.3	5.1	2,290.7	6.2	2,242.3	5.9
1992	2,350.4	10.8	2,393.3	7.5	2,420.1	4.6	2,473.9	9.2	2,409.4	7.5
1993	2,504.6	5.1	2,537.6	5.4	2,577.4	6.4	2,613.8	5.8	2,558.4	6.2
1994	2,649.0	5.5	2,692.2	6.7	2,727.8	5.4	2,767.2	5.9	2,709.1	5.9
1995	2,812.2	6.7	2,859.6	6.9	2,894.2	4.9	2,927.5	4.7	2,873.4	6.1
1996	2,970.9	6.1	3,018.2	6.5	3,054.6	4.9	3,109.8	7.4	3,038.4	5.7
1997	3,159.9	6.6	3,208.7	6.3	3,259.3	6.5	3,317.9	7.4	3,236.5	6.5

Source: "National Income and Product Account Tables: Selected NIPA Tables," *Survey of Current Business*, November 1997, U.S. Department of Commerce, Bureau of Economic Analysis, National Income and Wealth Division. Data for 1997 quarters downloaded from www.stat.usa.gov. A dash (-) indicates that no data are available.

Gross Domestic Product
Personal consumption expenditures
Services - Chained (1992) Dollars

In billions of chained (1992) dollars and percent. Quarterly data are seasonally adjusted and annualized. Growth rates for quarters are compound annual growth rates; changes from year to year are percentage changes.

Year	1st Quarter	% Change	2nd Quarter	% Change	3rd Quarter	% Change	4th Quarter	% Change	TOTAL	% Change
1959	670.9	-	683.0	7.4	692.9	5.9	702.6	5.7	687.4	-
1960	711.0	4.9	717.3	3.6	717.1	-0.1	724.3	4.1	717.4	4.4
1961	731.5	4.0	744.7	7.4	748.3	1.9	761.5	7.2	746.5	4.1
1962	768.6	3.8	780.5	6.3	787.6	3.7	797.0	4.9	783.4	4.9
1963	801.2	2.1	810.1	4.5	826.0	8.1	837.3	5.6	818.7	4.5
1964	850.4	6.4	862.6	5.9	874.4	5.6	886.2	5.5	868.4	6.1
1965	894.6	3.8	907.5	5.9	919.8	5.5	936.3	7.4	914.6	5.3
1966	945.2	3.9	956.8	5.0	965.1	3.5	976.8	4.9	961.0	5.1
1967	989.7	5.4	1,002.0	5.1	1,015.6	5.5	1,023.0	2.9	1,007.6	4.8
1968	1,036.2	5.3	1,053.6	6.9	1,067.4	5.3	1,080.9	5.2	1,059.6	5.2
1969	1,092.5	4.4	1,104.1	4.3	1,115.5	4.2	1,130.8	5.6	1,110.8	4.8
1970	1,141.8	3.9	1,148.4	2.3	1,161.9	4.8	1,169.8	2.7	1,155.4	4.0
1971	1,179.7	3.4	1,191.0	3.9	1,201.3	3.5	1,219.5	6.2	1,197.9	3.7
1972	1,239.1	6.6	1,252.1	4.3	1,267.4	5.0	1,291.2	7.7	1,262.5	5.4
1973	1,302.7	3.6	1,316.5	4.3	1,325.3	2.7	1,333.0	2.3	1,319.4	4.5
1974	1,335.9	0.9	1,348.2	3.7	1,354.5	1.9	1,366.1	3.5	1,351.2	2.4
1975	1,377.6	3.4	1,395.2	5.2	1,402.5	2.1	1,418.0	4.5	1,398.3	3.5
1976	1,436.1	5.2	1,445.7	2.7	1,461.7	4.5	1,484.7	6.4	1,457.1	4.2
1977	1,497.2	3.4	1,504.8	2.0	1,527.1	6.1	1,543.6	4.4	1,518.2	4.2
1978	1,565.4	5.8	1,587.6	5.8	1,598.5	2.8	1,605.7	1.8	1,589.3	4.7
1979	1,625.0	4.9	1,636.8	2.9	1,641.5	1.2	1,656.2	3.6	1,639.8	3.2
1980	1,663.0	1.7	1,653.0	-2.4	1,672.8	4.9	1,694.0	5.2	1,670.7	1.9
1981	1,682.1	-2.8	1,697.6	3.7	1,700.8	0.8	1,703.9	0.7	1,696.1	1.5
1982	1,710.7	1.6	1,718.1	1.7	1,729.3	2.6	1,754.6	6.0	1,728.2	1.9
1983	1,773.4	4.4	1,801.6	6.5	1,819.1	3.9	1,841.8	5.1	1,809.0	4.7
1984	1,855.2	2.9	1,870.5	3.3	1,890.9	4.4	1,915.5	5.3	1,883.0	4.1
1985	1,945.2	6.3	1,962.8	3.7	1,989.3	5.5	2,011.8	4.6	1,977.3	5.0
1986	2,020.1	1.7	2,030.5	2.1	2,047.0	3.3	2,067.8	4.1	2,041.4	3.2
1987	2,097.0	5.8	2,118.5	4.2	2,138.0	3.7	2,154.1	3.0	2,126.9	4.2
1988	2,185.8	6.0	2,200.4	2.7	2,224.6	4.5	2,238.9	2.6	2,212.4	4.0
1989	2,247.0	1.5	2,252.2	0.9	2,264.4	2.2	2,285.8	3.8	2,262.3	2.3
1990	2,295.7	1.7	2,321.1	4.5	2,337.3	2.8	2,331.2	-1.0	2,321.3	2.6
1991	2,325.3	-1.0	2,341.5	2.8	2,345.0	0.6	2,352.0	1.2	2,341.0	0.8
1992	2,383.2	5.4	2,403.2	3.4	2,413.6	1.7	2,437.6	4.0	2,409.4	2.9
1993	2,445.3	1.3	2,455.9	1.7	2,480.0	4.0	2,494.4	2.3	2,468.9	2.5
1994	2,510.9	2.7	2,531.4	3.3	2,543.8	2.0	2,555.9	1.9	2,535.5	2.7
1995	2,571.2	2.4	2,594.5	3.7	2,608.7	2.2	2,623.8	2.3	2,599.6	2.5
1996	2,646.5	3.5	2,666.5	3.1	2,672.8	0.9	2,698.2	3.9	2,671.0	2.7
1997	2,723.9	3.9	2,749.8	3.9	2,776.1	3.9	2,811.0	5.1	2,765.2	3.5

Source: "National Income and Product Account Tables: Selected NIPA Tables," *Survey of Current Business*, November 1997, U.S. Department of Commerce, Bureau of Economic Analysis, National Income and Wealth Division. Data for 1997 quarters downloaded from www.stat.usa.gov. A dash (-) indicates that no data are available.

GROSS PRIVATE DOMESTIC INVESTMENT
Component of Gross Domestic Product

Gross Private Domestic Investment (GPDI) accounts for all expenditures on building and structures by corporations and individuals, all durable equipment ("capital goods") used in the production of goods and services (e.g., tooling, refineries, power plants, transmission lines, etc.), and change in business inventories. Excluded from this category are investments made by government (accounted for under *Government Purchases of Goods and Services*) and capital goods exports less imports (accounted for under *Net Exports of Goods and Services*).

The category is subdivided into Fixed Investment and Change in Business Inventories as follows:

> *Fixed Investment*
>   Nonresidential
>   Structures
>   Producers' durable equipment
>   Residential
> *Change in business inventories*
>   Nonfarm
>   Farm

GPDI represented 15.4 percent of real GDP in 1996, up substantially from the 1992 level (12.7 percent).

Fixed Investment

Nonresidential. Nonresidential fixed investment represents expenditures on permanent production facilities and equipment used by the private sector—the engine of economic activity. The category includes farm structures and farm machinery but excludes all investments made by government at all level, e.g., highways and bridges or government owned and operated production facilities. BEA estimates for the category are obtained under the headings of nonfarm buildings, public utilities, mining, other nonfarm structures, farm buildings, equipment except autos, and new and used autos; autos included in this category are used for business purposes; trucks are included under "equipment except autos." Each category has different sources of data and methods for obtaining estimates.

Residential. Residential fixed investments include permanent-site single-family housing units; multifamily housing units; mobile homes; and additions, alterations, and major replacements. Brokers commissions are also included under this category, as are purchases of capital equipment, used in production in a residential environment (e.g. a small printing press, apartment laundromat equipment, etc.).

Change in Business Inventories

Inventories are universally treated as capital investment—although not as fixed investment. Inventories "turn," meaning that stocks are withdrawn for use or sale while new stocks are added from purchases or production. For this reason, inventories, viewed as investments, are measured by comparing inventory levels at two points in time and measuring the change. The value can well be (1) negative if inventory levels have dropped from the first to the second period, (2) zero if no change took place, or (3) positive if inventory level has increased. Inventories may include finished goods (an automobile), work in process (an engine block), and raw materials in various stages (sheet steel, ingots). They may also be commodities like oil or gasoline stocks, grains or potatoes, or livestock.

The BEA subdivides the category into manufacturing and trade, other nonfarm industries, and farm; for each, different sources and estimating methods are used to arrive at quarterly and annual GDP estimates.

Presentation of Data

Data are shown from 1959 to 1997 in quarterly and in annual increments. Changes from one period to the next are shown for each category except Change in Business Inventories, which is already a change from one period to another. Changes from quarter to quarter are annualized, compounded growth rates as explained in the section on Gross National Product. Changes from year to year are simple percentile changes.

Analytical Uses

At the highest level of abstraction, GPDI is a measure, over time, of the relative proportion of national income that is reinvested to provide future productivity. A long-term decline in GPDI as a percentage of GDP indicates erosion of the nation's productive tooling and private infrastructure. A long-term growth in this measure may herald strong investment with benefits to be reaped in the future. The measure's chief limitation, for such analysis, is that it excludes public investment in infrastructure.

Change in business inventories can be used to evaluate the confidence of producers (signaled by inventory build-ups) or their vulnerability (unusually high inventories as the economy begins to decline). The measure will also reflect the likelihood of economic overheating (when inventories are low and demand is showing strong, sustained growth).

Gross Domestic Product
Gross private domestic investment: Total - Actual Dollars

In billions of actual dollars and percent. Quarterly data are seasonally adjusted and annualized. Growth rates for quarters are compound annual growth rates; changes from year to year are percentage changes.

Year	1st Quarter	% Change	2nd Quarter	% Change	3rd Quarter	% Change	4th Quarter	% Change	TOTAL	% Change
1959	76.7	-	82.7	35.2	76.3	-27.5	79.4	17.3	78.8	-
1960	89.1	58.6	79.4	-36.9	78.4	-4.9	68.1	-43.1	78.8	-
1961	70.1	12.3	75.4	33.8	82.2	41.3	84.0	9.1	77.9	-1.1
1962	89.3	27.7	87.9	-6.1	89.1	5.6	85.4	-15.6	87.9	12.8
1963	90.3	25.0	91.8	6.8	94.7	13.2	96.6	8.3	93.4	6.3
1964	100.6	17.6	100.4	-0.8	101.5	4.5	104.4	11.9	101.7	8.9
1965	115.8	51.4	115.8	-	119.1	11.9	121.3	7.6	118.0	16.0
1966	130.5	34.0	129.9	-1.8	129.4	-1.5	132.0	8.3	130.4	10.5
1967	127.7	-12.4	123.0	-13.9	128.5	19.1	133.0	14.8	128.0	-1.8
1968	135.7	8.4	141.9	19.6	138.7	-8.7	143.5	14.6	139.9	9.3
1969	154.7	35.1	154.4	-0.8	159.0	12.5	152.0	-16.5	155.0	10.8
1970	148.5	-8.9	151.1	7.2	153.8	7.3	147.6	-15.2	150.2	-3.1
1971	169.3	73.1	177.1	19.7	181.1	9.3	176.6	-9.6	176.0	17.2
1972	191.8	39.1	204.2	28.5	209.8	11.4	216.8	14.0	205.6	16.8
1973	232.9	33.2	242.4	17.3	240.3	-3.4	255.8	28.4	242.9	18.1
1974	241.2	-20.9	247.5	10.9	242.8	-7.4	251.0	14.2	245.6	1.1
1975	212.2	-48.9	211.2	-1.9	234.3	51.5	243.7	17.0	225.4	-8.2
1976	271.3	53.6	285.8	23.2	289.5	5.3	299.8	15.0	286.6	27.2
1977	321.3	31.9	353.2	46.0	373.8	25.5	378.0	4.6	356.6	24.4
1978	392.9	16.7	425.6	37.7	443.5	17.9	461.2	16.9	430.8	20.8
1979	471.1	8.9	482.4	9.9	486.4	3.4	483.5	-2.4	480.9	11.6
1980	493.0	8.1	449.8	-30.7	430.8	-15.9	490.1	67.5	465.9	-3.1
1981	549.9	58.5	534.7	-10.6	576.1	34.8	564.1	-8.1	556.2	19.4
1982	511.1	-32.6	514.1	2.4	509.3	-3.7	469.8	-27.6	501.1	-9.9
1983	481.3	10.2	526.0	42.7	561.7	30.0	619.4	47.9	547.1	9.2
1984	695.6	59.1	716.2	12.4	731.7	8.9	718.8	-6.9	715.6	30.8
1985	705.6	-7.1	711.2	3.2	706.3	-2.7	737.2	18.7	715.1	-0.1
1986	752.1	8.3	729.7	-11.4	699.4	-15.6	708.9	5.5	722.5	1.0
1987	729.6	12.2	732.3	1.5	734.0	0.9	792.8	36.1	747.2	3.4
1988	756.5	-17.1	767.3	5.8	776.5	4.9	795.5	10.2	773.9	3.6
1989	829.0	17.9	836.0	3.4	832.0	-1.9	819.9	-5.7	829.2	7.1
1990	822.7	1.4	835.0	6.1	804.7	-13.7	736.3	-29.9	799.7	-3.6
1991	723.5	-6.8	716.4	-3.9	744.1	16.4	760.7	9.2	736.2	-7.9
1992	755.2	-2.9	790.7	20.2	799.7	4.6	816.1	8.5	790.4	7.4
1993	854.3	20.1	857.4	1.5	872.8	7.4	920.3	23.6	876.2	10.9
1994	963.4	20.1	1,017.9	24.6	1,007.1	-4.2	1,043.1	15.1	1,007.9	15.0
1995	1,050.8	3.0	1,024.0	-9.8	1,028.8	1.9	1,049.1	8.1	1,038.2	3.0
1996	1,060.5	4.4	1,105.4	18.0	1,149.2	16.8	1,151.1	0.7	1,116.5	7.5
1997	1,193.6	15.6	1,242.0	17.2	1,250.2	2.7	1,264.5	4.7	1,237.6	10.8

Source: "National Income and Product Account Tables: Selected NIPA Tables," *Survey of Current Business*, November 1997, U.S. Department of Commerce, Bureau of Economic Analysis, National Income and Wealth Division. Data for 1997 quarters downloaded from www.stat.usa.gov. A dash (-) indicates that no data are available.

Gross Domestic Product

Gross private domestic investment: Total - Chained (1992) Dollars

In billions of chained (1992) dollars and percent. Quarterly data are seasonally adjusted and annualized. Growth rates for quarters are compound annual growth rates; changes from year to year are percentage changes.

Year	1st Quarter	% Change	2nd Quarter	% Change	3rd Quarter	% Change	4th Quarter	% Change	TOTAL	% Change
1959	260.4	-	285.4	44.3	265.3	-25.3	275.6	16.5	271.7	-
1960	304.3	48.6	271.7	-36.4	269.4	-3.3	236.6	-40.5	270.5	-0.4
1961	241.7	8.9	258.6	31.0	282.2	41.8	288.0	8.5	267.6	-1.1
1962	305.2	26.1	301.9	-4.3	306.5	6.2	295.0	-14.2	302.1	12.9
1963	313.1	26.9	316.2	4.0	327.4	14.9	329.7	2.8	321.6	6.5
1964	346.1	21.4	344.2	-2.2	349.1	5.8	353.9	5.6	348.3	8.3
1965	392.0	50.5	391.9	-0.4	400.9	9.8	404.2	3.3	397.2	14.0
1966	436.1	35.5	429.8	-5.7	426.7	-2.9	429.8	2.9	430.6	8.4
1967	415.7	-12.5	399.3	-14.9	411.5	12.8	420.6	9.1	411.8	-4.4
1968	425.2	4.4	442.9	17.7	430.1	-11.1	434.9	4.5	433.3	5.2
1969	463.3	28.8	458.9	-3.7	468.2	8.4	442.6	-20.1	458.3	5.8
1970	427.6	-12.9	427.3	-0.3	435.9	8.3	413.8	-18.8	426.1	-7.0
1971	465.0	59.5	480.6	14.1	484.1	2.9	470.0	-11.2	474.9	11.5
1972	502.4	30.6	533.3	27.0	542.4	7.0	549.1	5.0	531.8	12.0
1973	588.6	32.0	601.0	8.7	583.0	-11.5	609.2	19.2	595.5	12.0
1974	565.5	-25.8	561.0	-3.1	530.3	-20.2	529.2	-0.8	546.5	-8.2
1975	431.2	-55.9	419.9	-10.1	462.4	47.1	472.8	9.3	446.6	-18.3
1976	519.7	46.0	540.5	17.0	539.9	-0.4	549.6	7.4	537.4	20.3
1977	577.7	22.1	622.7	35.0	652.8	20.8	635.3	-10.3	622.1	15.8
1978	650.5	9.9	691.0	27.3	710.7	11.9	721.4	6.2	693.4	11.5
1979	717.8	-2.0	722.9	2.9	708.2	-7.9	690.1	-9.8	709.7	2.4
1980	689.6	-0.3	614.5	-36.9	570.7	-25.6	638.3	56.5	628.3	-11.5
1981	699.8	44.5	662.4	-19.7	704.5	28.0	677.1	-14.7	686.0	9.2
1982	605.8	-35.9	601.6	-2.7	593.7	-5.2	547.6	-27.6	587.2	-14.4
1983	563.9	12.4	617.7	44.0	661.4	31.4	725.3	44.6	642.1	9.3
1984	812.2	57.2	835.6	12.0	850.8	7.5	834.9	-7.3	833.4	29.8
1985	816.6	-8.5	821.1	2.2	816.0	-2.5	841.8	13.3	823.8	-1.2
1986	855.3	6.6	824.0	-13.9	781.3	-19.2	786.7	2.8	811.8	-1.5
1987	808.6	11.6	807.1	-0.7	806.3	-0.4	864.0	31.8	821.5	1.2
1988	817.8	-19.7	823.2	2.7	830.0	3.3	841.7	5.8	828.2	0.8
1989	870.5	14.4	873.1	1.2	864.0	-4.1	846.3	-7.9	863.5	4.3
1990	842.6	-1.7	853.4	5.2	817.9	-15.6	746.1	-30.8	815.0	-5.6
1991	725.1	-10.8	718.5	-3.6	745.8	16.1	763.2	9.7	738.1	-9.4
1992	758.2	-2.6	792.8	19.5	798.5	2.9	812.2	7.0	790.4	7.1
1993	845.5	17.4	846.1	0.3	858.6	6.0	904.0	22.9	863.6	9.3
1994	939.9	16.9	987.8	22.0	972.2	-6.2	1,003.0	13.3	975.7	13.0
1995	1,005.8	1.1	977.5	-10.8	982.0	1.9	1,000.8	7.9	991.5	1.6
1996	1,012.2	4.6	1,059.2	19.9	1,100.3	16.4	1,104.8	1.6	1,069.1	7.8
1997	1,149.2	17.1	1,197.1	17.7	1,204.6	2.5	1,217.9	4.5	1,192.2	11.5

Source: "National Income and Product Account Tables: Selected NIPA Tables," *Survey of Current Business*, November 1997, U.S. Department of Commerce, Bureau of Economic Analysis, National Income and Wealth Division. Data for 1997 quarters downloaded from www.stat.usa.gov. A dash (-) indicates that no data are available.

Gross Domestic Product
Gross private domestic investment
Fixed investment - Actual Dollars

In billions of actual dollars and percent. Quarterly data are seasonally adjusted and annualized. Growth rates for quarters are compound annual growth rates; changes from year to year are percentage changes.

Year	1st Quarter	% Change	2nd Quarter	% Change	3rd Quarter	% Change	4th Quarter	% Change	TOTAL	% Change
1959	72.3	-	74.9	15.2	76.1	6.6	75.1	-5.2	74.6	-
1960	77.8	15.2	76.3	-7.5	74.2	-10.6	73.8	-2.1	75.5	1.2
1961	72.7	-5.8	73.8	6.2	75.5	9.5	78.0	13.9	75.0	-0.7
1962	79.8	9.6	82.2	12.6	82.9	3.5	82.4	-2.4	81.8	9.1
1963	83.3	4.4	86.9	18.4	88.8	9.0	91.8	14.2	87.7	7.2
1964	95.0	14.7	95.6	2.6	97.2	6.9	99.0	7.6	96.7	10.3
1965	103.5	19.5	106.6	12.5	109.6	11.7	113.4	14.6	108.3	12.0
1966	117.0	13.3	117.4	1.4	117.3	-0.3	114.9	-7.9	116.7	7.8
1967	112.7	-7.4	116.2	13.0	118.1	6.7	123.3	18.8	117.6	0.8
1968	127.5	14.3	128.0	1.6	130.7	8.7	137.0	20.7	130.8	11.2
1969	142.7	17.7	144.8	6.0	148.3	10.0	146.2	-5.5	145.5	11.2
1970	146.5	0.8	146.5	-	148.6	5.9	150.6	5.5	148.1	1.8
1971	156.8	17.5	165.7	24.7	170.7	12.6	176.8	15.1	167.5	13.1
1972	187.2	25.7	191.7	10.0	195.8	8.8	208.1	27.6	195.7	16.8
1973	219.0	22.7	224.7	10.8	228.7	7.3	229.1	0.7	225.4	15.2
1974	228.0	-1.9	231.2	5.7	235.9	8.4	231.0	-8.1	231.5	2.7
1975	223.9	-11.7	225.9	3.6	234.4	15.9	242.6	14.7	231.7	0.1
1976	255.2	22.5	264.0	14.5	270.4	10.1	288.9	30.3	269.6	16.4
1977	306.4	26.5	330.2	34.9	341.8	14.8	355.7	17.3	333.5	23.7
1978	364.8	10.6	398.8	42.8	417.1	19.7	433.9	17.1	403.6	21.0
1979	446.8	12.4	455.1	7.6	474.9	18.6	479.2	3.7	464.0	15.0
1980	484.6	4.6	450.1	-25.6	464.6	13.5	494.8	28.6	473.5	2.0
1981	511.6	14.3	525.3	11.1	533.6	6.5	541.8	6.3	528.1	11.5
1982	531.5	-7.4	517.8	-9.9	505.0	-9.5	507.9	2.3	515.6	-2.4
1983	514.6	5.4	534.0	16.0	563.4	23.9	596.0	25.2	552.0	7.1
1984	616.0	14.1	645.4	20.5	659.3	8.9	671.6	7.7	648.1	17.4
1985	680.0	5.1	686.9	4.1	685.8	-0.6	702.8	10.3	688.9	6.3
1986	707.0	2.4	710.9	2.2	712.6	1.0	721.1	4.9	712.9	3.5
1987	705.3	-8.5	719.3	8.2	732.0	7.3	735.1	1.7	722.9	1.4
1988	744.3	5.1	760.9	9.2	766.8	3.1	780.3	7.2	763.1	5.6
1989	790.1	5.1	794.2	2.1	808.1	7.2	797.5	-5.1	797.5	4.5
1990	813.9	8.5	794.0	-9.4	791.2	-1.4	767.5	-11.5	791.6	-0.7
1991	739.7	-13.7	736.2	-1.9	738.6	1.3	739.5	0.5	738.5	-6.7
1992	755.4	8.9	780.5	14.0	788.1	4.0	809.7	11.4	783.4	6.1
1993	823.5	7.0	842.9	9.8	858.8	7.8	897.5	19.3	855.7	9.2
1994	911.0	6.2	941.7	14.2	956.9	6.6	977.0	8.7	946.6	10.6
1995	998.7	9.2	999.6	0.4	1,009.4	4.0	1,024.6	6.2	1,008.1	6.5
1996	1,049.4	10.0	1,082.0	13.0	1,112.0	11.6	1,119.2	2.6	1,090.7	8.2
1997	1,127.5	3.0	1,160.8	12.3	1,201.3	14.7	1,202.4	0.4	1,173.0	7.5

Source: "National Income and Product Account Tables: Selected NIPA Tables," *Survey of Current Business*, November 1997, U.S. Department of Commerce, Bureau of Economic Analysis, National Income and Wealth Division. Data for 1997 quarters downloaded from www.stat.usa.gov. A dash (-) indicates that no data are available.

Gross Domestic Product
Gross private domestic investment
Fixed investment - Chained (1992) Dollars

In billions of chained (1992) dollars and percent. Quarterly data are seasonally adjusted and annualized. Growth rates for quarters are compound annual growth rates; changes from year to year are percentage changes.

Year	1st Quarter	% Change	2nd Quarter	% Change	3rd Quarter	% Change	4th Quarter	% Change	TOTAL	% Change
1959	258.8	-	268.4	15.7	272.1	5.6	269.0	-4.5	267.1	-
1960	277.8	13.7	271.7	-8.5	264.2	-10.6	263.0	-1.8	269.2	0.8
1961	259.9	-4.6	263.2	5.2	269.6	10.1	278.7	14.2	267.9	-0.5
1962	284.5	8.6	293.6	13.4	295.9	3.2	294.1	-2.4	292.0	9.0
1963	297.2	4.3	310.5	19.1	318.4	10.6	328.5	13.3	313.7	7.4
1964	341.3	16.5	340.2	-1.3	345.5	6.4	347.7	2.6	343.7	9.6
1965	364.0	20.1	373.8	11.2	383.7	11.0	392.2	9.2	378.5	10.1
1966	406.8	15.7	401.2	-5.4	400.5	-0.7	387.7	-12.2	399.1	5.4
1967	378.3	-9.4	388.4	11.1	392.6	4.4	404.9	13.1	391.0	-2.0
1968	414.3	9.6	412.0	-2.2	417.9	5.9	428.1	10.1	418.1	6.9
1969	441.2	12.8	442.8	1.5	449.9	6.6	437.9	-10.2	442.9	5.9
1970	435.5	-2.2	425.6	-8.8	433.2	7.3	434.1	0.8	432.1	-2.4
1971	444.0	9.4	462.3	17.5	470.5	7.3	482.7	10.8	464.9	7.6
1972	504.7	19.5	513.6	7.2	519.2	4.4	543.6	20.2	520.3	11.9
1973	566.8	18.2	571.2	3.1	569.1	-1.5	562.7	-4.4	567.5	9.1
1974	549.4	-9.1	541.0	-6.0	530.9	-7.3	499.6	-21.6	530.2	-6.6
1975	467.8	-23.1	461.1	-5.6	473.0	10.7	482.2	8.0	471.0	-11.2
1976	502.4	17.8	510.6	6.7	515.5	3.9	541.9	22.1	517.6	9.9
1977	564.1	17.4	595.2	23.9	602.3	4.9	613.1	7.4	593.7	14.7
1978	616.6	2.3	660.2	31.4	676.8	10.4	689.5	7.7	660.8	11.3
1979	695.1	3.3	690.4	-2.7	702.6	7.3	694.1	-4.8	695.6	5.3
1980	685.5	-4.9	622.5	-32.0	629.3	4.4	656.3	18.3	648.4	-6.8
1981	660.7	2.7	662.6	1.2	661.5	-0.7	657.6	-2.3	660.6	1.9
1982	636.0	-12.5	612.8	-13.8	595.0	-11.1	597.7	1.8	610.4	-7.6
1983	608.4	7.4	633.4	17.5	668.9	24.4	706.1	24.2	654.2	7.2
1984	729.3	13.8	760.7	18.4	773.9	7.1	785.7	6.2	762.4	16.5
1985	792.9	3.7	800.1	3.7	794.9	-2.6	809.1	7.3	799.3	4.8
1986	809.3	0.1	806.6	-1.3	800.4	-3.0	803.9	1.8	805.0	0.7
1987	784.2	-9.4	797.7	7.1	809.5	6.0	806.3	-1.6	799.4	-0.7
1988	807.1	0.4	819.0	6.0	820.6	0.8	826.4	2.9	818.3	2.4
1989	831.9	2.7	830.9	-0.5	840.5	4.7	824.7	-7.3	832.0	1.7
1990	834.7	4.9	811.2	-10.8	803.1	-3.9	774.4	-13.5	805.8	-3.1
1991	742.6	-15.4	739.4	-1.7	741.0	0.9	742.0	0.5	741.3	-8.0
1992	758.3	9.1	782.4	13.3	787.3	2.5	805.8	9.7	783.4	5.7
1993	814.8	4.5	831.1	8.2	844.5	6.6	880.8	18.3	842.8	7.6
1994	887.8	3.2	913.2	11.9	922.7	4.2	938.5	7.0	915.5	8.6
1995	955.8	7.6	954.0	-0.8	962.3	3.5	976.3	5.9	962.1	5.1
1996	1,001.5	10.7	1,035.7	14.4	1,060.9	10.1	1,068.7	3.0	1,041.7	8.3
1997	1,079.0	3.9	1,111.4	12.6	1,149.3	14.4	1,149.6	0.1	1,122.3	7.7

Source: "National Income and Product Account Tables: Selected NIPA Tables," *Survey of Current Business*, November 1997, U.S. Department of Commerce, Bureau of Economic Analysis, National Income and Wealth Division. Data for 1997 quarters downloaded from www.stat.usa.gov. A dash (-) indicates that no data are available.

Gross Domestic Product
Gross private domestic investment
Fixed investment - Nonresidential - Actual Dollars

In billions of actual dollars and percent. Quarterly data are seasonally adjusted and annualized. Growth rates for quarters are compound annual growth rates; changes from year to year are percentage changes.

Year	1st Quarter	% Change	2nd Quarter	% Change	3rd Quarter	% Change	4th Quarter	% Change	TOTAL	% Change
1959	44.5	-	46.1	15.2	47.8	15.6	47.6	-1.7	46.5	-
1960	49.4	16.0	50.2	6.6	48.9	-10.0	48.5	-3.2	49.2	5.8
1961	47.4	-8.8	48.3	7.8	48.6	2.5	50.2	13.8	48.6	-1.2
1962	51.4	9.9	53.0	13.0	53.7	5.4	53.2	-3.7	52.8	8.6
1963	53.1	-0.7	54.7	12.6	56.3	12.2	58.1	13.4	55.6	5.3
1964	59.6	10.7	61.4	12.6	63.5	14.4	65.2	11.1	62.4	12.2
1965	69.7	30.6	72.4	16.4	75.3	17.0	78.9	20.5	74.1	18.8
1966	82.2	17.8	84.2	10.1	85.3	5.3	85.7	1.9	84.4	13.9
1967	84.3	-6.4	84.5	1.0	84.7	1.0	87.2	12.3	85.2	0.9
1968	90.6	16.5	89.9	-3.1	91.8	8.7	96.0	19.6	92.1	8.1
1969	99.5	15.4	101.4	7.9	105.1	15.4	105.6	1.9	102.9	11.7
1970	105.8	0.8	107.1	5.0	108.2	4.2	105.7	-8.9	106.7	3.7
1971	108.2	9.8	111.1	11.2	112.4	4.8	115.3	10.7	111.7	4.7
1972	120.6	19.7	123.5	10.0	126.3	9.4	133.8	26.0	126.1	12.9
1973	141.2	24.0	149.0	24.0	153.7	13.2	156.4	7.2	150.0	19.0
1974	159.0	6.8	163.7	12.4	168.5	12.3	171.0	6.1	165.6	10.4
1975	166.3	-10.5	166.0	-0.7	169.7	9.2	173.9	10.3	169.0	2.1
1976	179.1	12.5	183.4	10.0	189.8	14.7	196.4	14.7	187.2	10.8
1977	208.8	27.7	218.5	19.9	226.8	16.1	238.8	22.9	223.2	19.2
1978	243.8	8.6	268.2	46.5	281.3	21.0	294.8	20.6	272.0	21.9
1979	308.2	19.5	314.2	8.0	331.4	23.8	338.0	8.2	323.0	18.8
1980	350.0	15.0	338.9	-12.1	348.7	12.1	363.5	18.1	350.3	8.5
1981	379.7	19.1	396.4	18.8	413.4	18.3	432.2	19.5	405.4	15.7
1982	426.7	-5.0	415.0	-10.5	402.6	-11.4	395.1	-7.2	409.9	1.1
1983	383.7	-11.1	385.8	2.2	400.9	16.6	427.4	29.2	399.4	-2.6
1984	440.4	12.7	464.0	23.2	478.4	13.0	490.3	10.3	468.3	17.3
1985	496.6	5.2	504.1	6.2	498.2	-4.6	508.9	8.9	502.0	7.2
1986	502.4	-5.0	492.6	-7.6	488.6	-3.2	495.6	5.9	494.8	-1.4
1987	480.0	-12.0	490.1	8.7	504.6	12.4	506.8	1.8	495.4	0.1
1988	515.9	7.4	529.4	10.9	533.2	2.9	543.7	8.1	530.6	7.1
1989	553.0	7.0	562.0	6.7	579.0	12.7	570.9	-5.5	566.2	6.7
1990	581.2	7.4	571.6	-6.4	580.3	6.2	570.6	-6.5	575.9	1.7
1991	555.4	-10.2	550.2	-3.7	544.3	-4.2	539.2	-3.7	547.3	-5.0
1992	544.1	3.7	556.8	9.7	561.0	3.1	569.6	6.3	557.9	1.9
1993	580.5	7.9	598.8	13.2	606.4	5.2	630.6	16.9	604.1	8.3
1994	634.6	2.6	652.9	12.0	667.4	9.2	687.5	12.6	660.6	9.4
1995	710.9	14.3	722.5	6.7	725.4	1.6	733.1	4.3	723.0	9.4
1996	750.7	10.0	769.3	10.3	798.6	16.1	807.2	4.4	781.4	8.1
1997	811.3	2.0	836.3	12.9	872.0	18.2	862.3	-4.4	845.5	8.2

Source: "National Income and Product Account Tables: Selected NIPA Tables," *Survey of Current Business*, November 1997, U.S. Department of Commerce, Bureau of Economic Analysis, National Income and Wealth Division. Data for 1997 quarters downloaded from www.stat.usa.gov. A dash (-) indicates that no data are available.

Gross Domestic Product
Gross private domestic investment
Fixed investment - Nonresidential - Chained (1992) Dollars

In billions of chained (1992) dollars and percent. Quarterly data are seasonally adjusted and annualized. Growth rates for quarters are compound annual growth rates; changes from year to year are percentage changes.

Year	1st Quarter	% Change	2nd Quarter	% Change	3rd Quarter	% Change	4th Quarter	% Change	TOTAL	% Change
1959	141.2	-	146.5	15.9	151.6	14.7	151.4	-0.5	147.7	-
1960	156.7	14.8	158.7	5.2	154.6	-9.9	153.6	-2.6	155.9	5.6
1961	150.6	-7.6	153.2	7.1	154.5	3.4	159.8	14.4	154.5	-0.9
1962	163.3	9.1	168.6	13.6	170.8	5.3	169.2	-3.7	168.0	8.7
1963	168.7	-1.2	173.7	12.4	178.8	12.3	184.5	13.4	176.4	5.0
1964	189.4	11.1	194.1	10.3	200.6	14.1	204.5	8.0	197.1	11.7
1965	218.7	30.8	226.6	15.3	235.0	15.7	244.9	17.9	231.3	17.4
1966	255.6	18.7	259.3	5.9	262.0	4.2	260.8	-1.8	259.4	12.1
1967	255.0	-8.6	254.4	-0.9	253.4	-1.6	258.6	8.5	255.3	-1.6
1968	266.4	12.6	261.6	-7.0	264.9	5.1	272.7	12.3	266.4	4.3
1969	280.4	11.8	283.2	4.1	290.6	10.9	288.4	-3.0	285.6	7.2
1970	285.9	-3.4	284.3	-2.2	285.8	2.1	275.3	-13.9	282.8	-1.0
1971	277.9	3.8	281.8	5.7	282.3	0.7	287.7	7.9	282.4	-0.1
1972	297.6	14.5	302.5	6.8	307.3	6.5	323.6	23.0	307.7	9.0
1973	339.0	20.4	352.5	16.9	358.2	6.6	360.5	2.6	352.5	14.6
1974	360.2	-0.3	359.2	-1.1	354.5	-5.1	343.6	-11.7	354.4	0.5
1975	321.5	-23.4	312.8	-10.4	315.9	4.0	319.1	4.1	317.3	-10.5
1976	324.9	7.5	328.4	4.4	335.4	8.8	341.6	7.6	332.6	4.8
1977	357.6	20.1	367.8	11.9	374.6	7.6	387.1	14.0	371.8	11.8
1978	389.1	2.1	421.0	37.1	433.8	12.7	446.5	12.2	422.6	13.7
1979	456.8	9.6	455.9	-0.8	470.3	13.2	470.2	-0.1	463.3	9.6
1980	475.8	4.8	450.4	-19.7	454.1	3.3	464.3	9.3	461.1	-0.5
1981	471.3	6.2	479.5	7.1	490.7	9.7	501.4	9.0	485.7	5.3
1982	488.0	-10.3	469.6	-14.3	454.2	-12.5	445.5	-7.4	464.3	-4.4
1983	435.9	-8.3	440.6	4.4	459.2	18.0	490.0	29.7	456.4	-1.7
1984	505.5	13.3	530.8	21.6	546.3	12.2	558.8	9.5	535.4	17.3
1985	564.6	4.2	572.7	5.9	563.5	-6.3	572.9	6.8	568.4	6.2
1986	563.8	-6.2	548.0	-10.7	538.7	-6.6	543.4	3.5	548.5	-3.5
1987	526.2	-12.1	537.5	8.9	553.8	12.7	552.0	-1.3	542.4	-1.1
1988	556.1	3.0	567.1	8.2	568.0	0.6	572.9	3.5	566.0	4.4
1989	579.5	4.7	586.6	5.0	600.5	9.8	588.8	-7.6	588.8	4.0
1990	595.3	4.5	583.4	-7.8	588.1	3.3	573.9	-9.3	585.2	-0.6
1991	555.1	-12.5	550.9	-3.0	545.3	-4.0	539.5	-4.2	547.7	-6.4
1992	544.4	3.7	557.5	10.0	560.6	2.2	569.1	6.2	557.9	1.9
1993	577.8	6.3	595.1	12.5	602.3	4.9	625.6	16.4	600.2	7.6
1994	626.2	0.4	641.2	9.9	653.2	7.7	672.9	12.6	648.4	8.0
1995	695.7	14.3	705.4	5.7	708.2	1.6	716.8	4.9	706.5	9.0
1996	736.9	11.7	759.7	13.0	789.3	16.5	800.8	6.0	771.7	9.2
1997	808.9	4.1	837.0	14.6	874.5	19.2	866.5	-3.6	846.7	9.7

Source: "National Income and Product Account Tables: Selected NIPA Tables," *Survey of Current Business*, November 1997, U.S. Department of Commerce, Bureau of Economic Analysis, National Income and Wealth Division. Data for 1997 quarters downloaded from www.stat.usa.gov. A dash (-) indicates that no data are available.

Gross Domestic Product
Gross private domestic investment
Fixed investment - Nonresidential - Structures - Actual Dollars

In billions of actual dollars and percent. Quarterly data are seasonally adjusted and annualized. Growth rates for quarters are compound annual growth rates; changes from year to year are percentage changes.

Year	1st Quarter	% Change	2nd Quarter	% Change	3rd Quarter	% Change	4th Quarter	% Change	TOTAL	% Change
1959	17.4	-	18.0	14.5	18.6	14.0	18.5	-2.1	18.1	-
1960	19.4	20.9	19.5	2.1	19.4	-2.0	20.0	13.0	19.6	8.3
1961	19.9	-2.0	19.6	-5.9	19.7	2.1	19.6	-2.0	19.7	0.5
1962	20.0	8.4	20.8	17.0	21.4	12.0	20.9	-9.0	20.8	5.6
1963	20.2	-12.7	21.2	21.3	21.4	3.8	21.9	9.7	21.2	1.9
1964	22.4	9.4	23.4	19.1	24.3	16.3	24.8	8.5	23.7	11.8
1965	26.1	22.7	28.2	36.3	28.5	4.3	30.4	29.5	28.3	19.4
1966	31.1	9.5	31.2	1.3	31.9	9.3	31.2	-8.5	31.3	10.6
1967	31.7	6.6	30.9	-9.7	31.5	8.0	32.0	6.5	31.5	0.6
1968	33.1	14.5	33.2	1.2	33.2	-	34.8	20.7	33.6	6.7
1969	35.8	12.0	36.7	10.4	38.9	26.2	39.4	5.2	37.7	12.2
1970	39.5	1.0	40.3	8.4	40.6	3.0	40.8	2.0	40.3	6.9
1971	41.5	7.0	42.3	7.9	43.1	7.8	43.8	6.7	42.7	6.0
1972	45.8	19.6	46.6	7.2	47.3	6.1	49.0	15.2	47.2	10.5
1973	51.3	20.1	54.1	23.7	56.8	21.5	57.7	6.5	55.0	16.5
1974	59.0	9.3	61.3	16.5	61.4	0.7	63.2	12.3	61.2	11.3
1975	61.7	-9.2	60.4	-8.2	61.3	6.1	62.0	4.6	61.4	0.3
1976	64.1	14.3	65.1	6.4	66.7	10.2	67.8	6.8	65.9	7.3
1977	69.7	11.7	73.6	24.3	76.4	16.1	78.5	11.5	74.6	13.2
1978	79.2	3.6	88.6	56.6	95.8	36.7	102.0	28.5	91.4	22.5
1979	104.8	11.4	110.0	21.4	119.1	37.4	125.7	24.1	114.9	25.7
1980	130.3	15.5	129.8	-1.5	133.6	12.2	141.9	27.3	133.9	16.5
1981	147.5	16.7	158.3	32.7	166.8	23.3	185.7	53.6	164.6	22.9
1982	183.8	-4.0	179.6	-8.8	170.4	-19.0	166.2	-9.5	175.0	6.3
1983	156.7	-21.0	147.8	-20.9	151.0	8.9	155.5	12.5	152.7	-12.7
1984	164.5	25.2	174.4	26.3	181.0	16.0	184.2	7.3	176.0	15.3
1985	193.5	21.8	194.1	1.2	191.0	-6.2	194.6	7.8	193.3	9.8
1986	190.9	-7.4	173.9	-31.1	168.3	-12.3	170.1	4.3	175.8	-9.1
1987	165.4	-10.6	167.3	4.7	175.3	20.5	180.3	11.9	172.1	-2.1
1988	177.4	-6.3	182.5	12.0	181.9	-1.3	183.3	3.1	181.3	5.3
1989	188.3	11.4	188.0	-0.6	196.4	19.1	196.6	0.4	192.3	6.1
1990	201.9	11.2	202.4	1.0	203.5	2.2	195.4	-15.0	200.8	4.4
1991	192.3	-6.2	187.6	-9.4	176.1	-22.4	170.8	-11.5	181.7	-9.5
1992	171.6	1.9	170.4	-2.8	167.6	-6.4	167.1	-1.2	169.2	-6.9
1993	171.7	11.5	175.2	8.4	177.8	6.1	180.7	6.7	176.4	4.3
1994	175.4	-11.2	185.2	24.3	186.8	3.5	190.7	8.6	184.5	4.6
1995	197.7	15.5	201.1	7.1	202.8	3.4	200.7	-4.1	200.6	8.7
1996	205.7	10.3	210.6	9.9	217.7	14.2	227.0	18.2	215.2	7.3
1997	227.4	0.7	226.8	-1.1	232.9	11.2	233.7	1.4	230.2	7.0

Source: "National Income and Product Account Tables: Selected NIPA Tables," *Survey of Current Business*, November 1997, U.S. Department of Commerce, Bureau of Economic Analysis, National Income and Wealth Division. Data for 1997 quarters downloaded from www.stat.usa.gov. A dash (-) indicates that no data are available.

Gross Domestic Product
Gross private domestic investment
Fixed investment - Nonresidential - Structures - Chained (1992) Dollars

In billions of chained (1992) dollars and percent. Quarterly data are seasonally adjusted and annualized. Growth rates for quarters are compound annual growth rates; changes from year to year are percentage changes.

Year	1st Quarter	% Change	2nd Quarter	% Change	3rd Quarter	% Change	4th Quarter	% Change	TOTAL	% Change
1959	82.8	-	85.3	12.6	87.8	12.2	87.2	-2.7	85.8	-
1960	90.8	17.6	91.9	4.9	92.1	0.9	95.6	16.1	92.6	7.9
1961	95.2	-1.7	93.6	-6.6	93.6	-	93.1	-2.1	93.9	1.4
1962	94.8	7.5	98.2	15.1	100.9	11.5	98.4	-9.5	98.1	4.5
1963	95.0	-13.1	99.4	19.9	100.1	2.8	102.1	8.2	99.2	1.1
1964	104.8	11.0	108.4	14.5	111.9	13.6	112.8	3.3	109.5	10.4
1965	118.6	22.2	126.9	31.1	128.2	4.2	134.1	19.7	126.9	15.9
1966	137.3	9.9	134.6	-7.6	137.6	9.2	133.0	-12.7	135.6	6.9
1967	134.3	4.0	130.5	-10.8	131.8	4.0	132.1	0.9	132.2	-2.5
1968	134.7	8.1	133.5	-3.5	132.6	-2.7	135.4	8.7	134.1	1.4
1969	137.4	6.0	138.5	3.2	145.1	20.5	144.1	-2.7	141.3	5.4
1970	143.0	-3.0	141.5	-4.1	142.1	1.7	140.4	-4.7	141.7	0.3
1971	140.0	-1.1	139.7	-0.9	139.2	-1.4	138.8	-1.1	139.4	-1.6
1972	142.4	10.8	143.2	2.3	143.5	0.8	145.7	6.3	143.7	3.1
1973	150.5	13.8	155.2	13.1	158.7	9.3	157.3	-3.5	155.4	8.1
1974	156.4	-2.3	155.8	-1.5	149.1	-16.1	147.3	-4.7	152.2	-2.1
1975	139.8	-18.9	134.4	-14.6	135.3	2.7	135.4	0.3	136.2	-10.5
1976	139.1	11.4	138.6	-1.4	140.1	4.4	140.5	1.1	139.6	2.5
1977	141.8	3.8	146.3	13.3	148.3	5.6	149.2	2.4	146.4	4.9
1978	147.1	-5.5	159.8	39.3	168.3	23.0	174.3	15.0	162.3	10.9
1979	174.3	-	177.6	7.8	186.5	21.6	192.5	13.5	182.7	12.6
1980	195.8	7.0	191.1	-9.3	193.5	5.1	199.8	13.7	195.0	6.7
1981	198.6	-2.4	205.8	15.3	210.7	9.9	226.4	33.3	210.4	7.9
1982	219.2	-12.1	211.9	-12.7	200.9	-19.2	197.0	-7.5	207.2	-1.5
1983	189.0	-15.3	179.9	-17.9	184.2	9.9	189.9	13.0	185.7	-10.4
1984	200.8	25.0	210.8	21.5	217.4	13.1	219.9	4.7	212.2	14.3
1985	229.3	18.2	229.5	0.3	224.6	-8.3	227.6	5.5	227.8	7.4
1986	222.3	-9.0	201.4	-32.6	194.2	-13.6	195.2	2.1	203.3	-10.8
1987	190.0	-10.2	191.3	2.8	199.4	18.0	202.8	7.0	195.9	-3.6
1988	195.9	-12.9	199.1	6.7	196.4	-5.3	195.9	-1.0	196.8	0.5
1989	199.8	8.2	197.2	-5.1	204.6	15.9	203.2	-2.7	201.2	2.2
1990	206.5	6.7	205.5	-1.9	205.2	-0.6	196.0	-16.8	203.3	1.0
1991	192.2	-7.5	187.2	-10.0	175.5	-22.8	171.4	-9.0	181.6	-10.7
1992	172.7	3.1	171.0	-3.9	167.4	-8.2	165.6	-4.2	169.2	-6.8
1993	168.0	5.9	170.3	5.6	171.7	3.3	173.1	3.3	170.8	0.9
1994	166.3	-14.8	174.5	21.2	174.0	-1.1	175.0	2.3	172.5	1.0
1995	179.0	9.5	180.9	4.3	181.2	0.7	178.6	-5.6	179.9	4.3
1996	182.1	8.1	185.6	7.9	190.0	9.8	196.9	15.3	188.7	4.9
1997	195.9	-2.0	193.5	-4.8	196.7	6.8	195.3	-2.8	195.3	3.5

Source: "National Income and Product Account Tables: Selected NIPA Tables," *Survey of Current Business*, November 1997, U.S. Department of Commerce, Bureau of Economic Analysis, National Income and Wealth Division. Data for 1997 quarters downloaded from www.stat.usa.gov. A dash (-) indicates that no data are available.

Gross Domestic Product

Gross private domestic investment
Fixed investment - Nonresidential - Producers' durable equipment - Actual Dollars

In billions of actual dollars and percent. Quarterly data are seasonally adjusted and annualized. Growth rates for quarters are compound annual growth rates; changes from year to year are percentage changes.

Year	1st Quarter	% Change	2nd Quarter	% Change	3rd Quarter	% Change	4th Quarter	% Change	TOTAL	% Change
1959	27.1	-	28.1	15.6	29.1	15.0	29.1	-	28.3	-
1960	30.1	14.5	30.7	8.2	29.5	-14.7	28.4	-14.1	29.7	4.9
1961	27.5	-12.1	28.7	18.6	28.9	2.8	30.6	25.7	28.9	-2.7
1962	31.4	10.9	32.2	10.6	32.3	1.2	32.3	-	32.1	11.1
1963	32.9	7.6	33.5	7.5	34.9	17.8	36.2	15.8	34.4	7.2
1964	37.2	11.5	38.0	8.9	39.3	14.4	40.3	10.6	38.7	12.5
1965	43.5	35.7	44.3	7.6	46.8	24.6	48.5	15.3	45.8	18.3
1966	51.1	23.2	53.0	15.7	53.4	3.1	54.5	8.5	53.0	15.7
1967	52.7	-12.6	53.6	7.0	53.2	-3.0	55.3	16.7	53.7	1.3
1968	57.6	17.7	56.7	-6.1	58.6	14.1	61.3	19.7	58.5	8.9
1969	63.7	16.6	64.7	6.4	66.1	8.9	66.2	0.6	65.2	11.5
1970	66.4	1.2	66.8	2.4	67.6	4.9	64.9	-15.0	66.4	1.8
1971	66.7	11.6	68.8	13.2	69.3	2.9	71.5	13.3	69.1	4.1
1972	74.9	20.4	76.9	11.1	78.9	10.8	84.9	34.1	78.9	14.2
1973	89.9	25.7	94.9	24.2	96.8	8.3	98.6	7.6	95.1	20.5
1974	100.0	5.8	102.3	9.5	107.1	20.1	107.8	2.6	104.3	9.7
1975	104.6	-11.4	105.6	3.9	108.4	11.0	111.8	13.1	107.6	3.2
1976	115.0	12.0	118.3	12.0	123.1	17.2	128.6	19.1	121.2	12.6
1977	139.1	36.9	144.8	17.4	150.4	16.4	160.3	29.0	148.7	22.7
1978	164.5	10.9	179.6	42.1	185.6	14.0	192.8	16.4	180.6	21.5
1979	203.4	23.9	204.3	1.8	212.2	16.4	212.3	0.2	208.1	15.2
1980	219.7	14.7	209.1	-17.9	215.1	12.0	221.6	12.6	216.4	4.0
1981	232.1	20.3	238.1	10.7	246.6	15.1	246.5	-0.2	240.9	11.3
1982	242.9	-5.7	235.4	-11.8	232.2	-5.3	228.9	-5.6	234.9	-2.5
1983	227.0	-3.3	238.0	20.8	249.9	21.6	272.0	40.3	246.7	5.0
1984	275.9	5.9	289.6	21.4	297.5	11.4	306.1	12.1	292.3	18.5
1985	303.1	-3.9	310.0	9.4	307.2	-3.6	314.3	9.6	308.7	5.6
1986	311.5	-3.5	318.7	9.6	320.3	2.0	325.5	6.7	319.0	3.3
1987	314.6	-12.7	322.8	10.8	329.3	8.3	326.5	-3.4	323.3	1.3
1988	338.5	15.5	346.9	10.3	351.3	5.2	360.4	10.8	349.3	8.0
1989	364.7	4.9	374.0	10.6	382.5	9.4	374.3	-8.3	373.9	7.0
1990	379.3	5.5	369.2	-10.2	376.7	8.4	375.1	-1.7	375.1	0.3
1991	363.1	-12.2	362.6	-0.5	368.2	6.3	368.4	0.2	365.6	-2.5
1992	372.5	4.5	386.3	15.7	393.4	7.6	402.5	9.6	388.7	6.3
1993	408.9	6.5	423.6	15.2	428.6	4.8	449.9	21.4	427.7	10.0
1994	459.3	8.6	467.7	7.5	480.6	11.5	496.8	14.2	476.1	11.3
1995	513.2	13.9	521.4	6.5	522.6	0.9	532.4	7.7	522.4	9.7
1996	545.0	9.8	558.7	10.4	580.9	16.9	580.2	-0.5	566.2	8.4
1997	583.9	2.6	609.5	18.7	639.1	20.9	628.5	-6.5	615.2	8.7

Source: "National Income and Product Account Tables: Selected NIPA Tables," *Survey of Current Business*, November 1997, U.S. Department of Commerce, Bureau of Economic Analysis, National Income and Wealth Division. Data for 1997 quarters downloaded from www.stat.usa.gov. A dash (-) indicates that no data are available.

Gross Domestic Product
Gross private domestic investment
Fixed investment - Nonresidential - Producers' durable equipment - Chained (1992) Dollars

In billions of chained (1992) dollars and percent. Quarterly data are seasonally adjusted and annualized. Growth rates for quarters are compound annual growth rates; changes from year to year are percentage changes.

Year	1st Quarter	% Change	2nd Quarter	% Change	3rd Quarter	% Change	4th Quarter	% Change	TOTAL	% Change
1959	68.8	-	70.8	12.1	73.0	13.0	73.1	0.5	71.4	-
1960	75.6	14.4	76.8	6.5	73.7	-15.2	71.2	-12.9	74.3	4.1
1961	68.7	-13.3	71.7	18.6	72.7	5.7	77.1	26.5	72.5	-2.4
1962	79.0	10.2	81.4	12.7	81.7	1.5	81.8	0.5	81.0	11.7
1963	83.2	7.0	84.7	7.4	88.4	18.7	92.0	17.3	87.1	7.5
1964	94.4	10.9	96.2	7.8	99.5	14.4	102.1	10.9	98.1	12.6
1965	110.4	36.7	112.1	6.3	118.2	23.6	122.9	16.9	115.9	18.1
1966	129.7	24.0	134.3	15.0	134.7	1.2	136.5	5.5	133.8	15.4
1967	130.9	-15.4	132.7	5.6	131.0	-5.0	135.2	13.5	132.5	-1.0
1968	140.1	15.3	136.8	-9.1	140.2	10.3	145.0	14.4	140.5	6.0
1969	150.2	15.1	151.8	4.3	153.9	5.6	152.7	-3.1	152.2	8.3
1970	151.4	-3.4	150.9	-1.3	151.8	2.4	143.9	-19.2	149.5	-1.8
1971	146.3	6.8	149.9	10.2	150.7	2.2	155.7	13.9	150.7	0.8
1972	161.7	16.3	165.5	9.7	169.6	10.3	182.5	34.1	169.8	12.7
1973	192.7	24.3	201.4	19.3	203.8	4.9	207.0	6.4	201.2	18.5
1974	207.4	0.8	206.9	-1.0	207.9	1.9	199.4	-15.4	205.4	2.1
1975	185.0	-25.9	181.2	-8.0	183.3	4.7	186.1	6.3	183.9	-10.5
1976	188.6	5.5	192.2	7.9	197.4	11.3	202.7	11.2	195.2	6.1
1977	216.3	29.7	222.1	11.2	226.8	8.7	237.5	20.2	225.6	15.6
1978	241.0	6.0	260.3	36.1	265.2	7.7	272.1	10.8	259.6	15.1
1979	281.6	14.7	278.1	-4.9	284.1	8.9	279.0	-7.0	280.7	8.1
1980	281.5	3.6	261.5	-25.5	262.9	2.2	267.1	6.5	268.2	-4.5
1981	274.9	12.2	276.4	2.2	282.7	9.4	278.7	-5.5	278.2	3.7
1982	272.3	-8.9	261.2	-15.3	256.3	-7.3	251.5	-7.3	260.3	-6.4
1983	249.5	-3.1	262.5	22.5	276.5	23.1	301.1	40.6	272.4	4.6
1984	306.2	6.9	321.5	21.5	330.5	11.7	340.3	12.4	324.6	19.2
1985	337.3	-3.5	345.0	9.4	340.6	-5.0	346.9	7.6	342.4	5.5
1986	343.0	-4.4	347.2	5.0	344.8	-2.7	348.5	4.4	345.9	1.0
1987	336.7	-12.9	346.5	12.2	354.7	9.8	349.6	-5.6	346.9	0.3
1988	360.3	12.8	368.0	8.8	371.6	4.0	377.0	5.9	369.2	6.4
1989	379.7	2.9	389.4	10.6	395.9	6.8	385.6	-10.0	387.6	5.0
1990	388.8	3.4	377.8	-10.8	383.0	5.6	377.9	-5.2	381.9	-1.5
1991	362.9	-15.0	363.8	1.0	369.8	6.8	368.1	-1.8	366.2	-4.1
1992	371.7	4.0	386.4	16.8	393.1	7.1	403.5	11.0	388.7	6.1
1993	409.8	6.4	424.9	15.6	430.7	5.6	452.9	22.3	429.6	10.5
1994	460.6	7.0	467.3	5.9	480.0	11.3	499.1	16.9	476.8	11.0
1995	518.1	16.1	525.9	6.2	528.5	2.0	540.5	9.4	528.3	10.8
1996	557.4	13.1	577.1	14.9	602.9	19.1	606.7	2.5	586.0	10.9
1997	616.6	6.7	649.3	23.0	685.3	24.1	678.5	-3.9	657.4	12.2

Source: "National Income and Product Account Tables: Selected NIPA Tables," *Survey of Current Business*, November 1997, U.S. Department of Commerce, Bureau of Economic Analysis, National Income and Wealth Division. Data for 1997 quarters downloaded from www.stat.usa.gov. A dash (-) indicates that no data are available.

Gross Domestic Product
Gross private domestic investment
Fixed investment - Residential - Actual Dollars

In billions of actual dollars and percent. Quarterly data are seasonally adjusted and annualized. Growth rates for quarters are compound annual growth rates; changes from year to year are percentage changes.

Year	1st Quarter	% Change	2nd Quarter	% Change	3rd Quarter	% Change	4th Quarter	% Change	TOTAL	% Change
1959	27.8	-	28.8	15.2	28.3	-6.8	27.5	-10.8	28.1	-
1960	28.4	13.7	26.1	-28.7	25.3	-11.7	25.3	-	26.3	-6.4
1961	25.3	-	25.5	3.2	26.9	23.8	27.8	14.1	26.4	0.4
1962	28.4	8.9	29.2	11.8	29.2	-	29.1	-1.4	29.0	9.8
1963	30.2	16.0	32.2	29.2	32.5	3.8	33.7	15.6	32.1	10.7
1964	35.4	21.8	34.2	-12.9	33.7	-5.7	33.8	1.2	34.3	6.9
1965	33.9	1.2	34.2	3.6	34.3	1.2	34.5	2.4	34.2	-0.3
1966	34.8	3.5	33.2	-17.2	31.9	-14.8	29.2	-29.8	32.3	-5.6
1967	28.3	-11.8	31.6	55.5	33.4	24.8	36.0	35.0	32.4	0.3
1968	36.9	10.4	38.2	14.9	38.9	7.5	40.9	22.2	38.7	19.4
1969	43.2	24.5	43.4	1.9	43.2	-1.8	40.7	-21.2	42.6	10.1
1970	40.7	-	39.4	-12.2	40.4	10.5	45.0	53.9	41.4	-2.8
1971	48.6	36.0	54.6	59.3	58.3	30.0	61.5	23.8	55.8	34.8
1972	66.6	37.5	68.2	10.0	69.6	8.5	74.3	29.9	69.7	24.9
1973	77.9	20.8	75.8	-10.4	75.0	-4.2	72.7	-11.7	75.3	8.0
1974	69.0	-18.9	67.5	-8.4	67.4	-0.6	60.0	-37.2	66.0	-12.4
1975	57.7	-14.5	59.9	16.1	64.6	35.3	68.7	27.9	62.7	-5.0
1976	76.2	51.4	80.7	25.8	80.6	-0.5	92.5	73.5	82.5	31.6
1977	97.6	23.9	111.7	71.6	115.0	12.4	116.9	6.8	110.3	33.7
1978	121.1	15.2	130.5	34.9	135.8	17.3	139.1	10.1	131.6	19.3
1979	138.6	-1.4	140.9	6.8	143.5	7.6	141.2	-6.3	141.0	7.1
1980	134.5	-17.7	111.2	-53.3	115.9	18.0	131.3	64.7	123.2	-12.6
1981	132.0	2.1	128.9	-9.1	120.2	-24.4	109.6	-30.9	122.6	-0.5
1982	104.8	-16.4	102.8	-7.4	102.3	-1.9	112.8	47.8	105.7	-13.8
1983	130.9	81.4	148.2	64.3	162.6	44.9	168.5	15.3	152.5	44.3
1984	175.6	18.0	181.4	13.9	180.8	-1.3	181.3	1.1	179.8	17.9
1985	183.4	4.7	182.8	-1.3	187.7	11.2	193.9	13.9	186.9	3.9
1986	204.5	23.7	218.3	29.8	224.1	11.1	225.6	2.7	218.1	16.7
1987	225.3	-0.5	229.2	7.1	227.4	-3.1	228.4	1.8	227.6	4.4
1988	228.4	-	231.4	5.4	233.6	3.9	236.6	5.2	232.5	2.2
1989	237.2	1.0	232.2	-8.2	229.1	-5.2	226.6	-4.3	231.3	-0.5
1990	232.7	11.2	222.4	-16.6	210.9	-19.1	196.9	-24.0	215.7	-6.7
1991	184.3	-23.2	185.9	3.5	194.3	19.3	200.3	12.9	191.2	-11.4
1992	211.3	23.8	223.7	25.6	227.1	6.2	240.1	24.9	225.6	18.0
1993	243.0	4.9	244.1	1.8	252.4	14.3	266.8	24.8	251.6	11.5
1994	276.4	15.2	288.7	19.0	289.5	1.1	289.5	-	286.0	13.7
1995	287.8	-2.3	277.1	-14.1	284.0	10.3	291.4	10.8	285.1	-0.3
1996	298.8	10.6	312.7	19.9	313.5	1.0	312.0	-1.9	309.2	8.5
1997	316.2	5.5	324.6	11.1	329.3	5.9	340.1	13.8	327.6	5.9

Source: "National Income and Product Account Tables: Selected NIPA Tables," *Survey of Current Business*, November 1997, U.S. Department of Commerce, Bureau of Economic Analysis, National Income and Wealth Division. Data for 1997 quarters downloaded from www.stat.usa.gov. A dash (-) indicates that no data are available.

Gross Domestic Product

Gross private domestic investment

Fixed investment - Residential - Chained (1992) Dollars

In billions of chained (1992) dollars and percent. Quarterly data are seasonally adjusted and annualized. Growth rates for quarters are compound annual growth rates; changes from year to year are percentage changes.

Year	1st Quarter	% Change	2nd Quarter	% Change	3rd Quarter	% Change	4th Quarter	% Change	TOTAL	% Change
1959	129.9	-	134.5	14.9	132.0	-7.2	128.1	-11.3	131.1	-
1960	131.8	12.1	121.0	-29.0	117.3	-11.7	117.2	-0.3	121.8	-7.1
1961	117.6	1.4	118.0	1.4	124.4	23.5	128.6	14.2	122.2	0.3
1962	130.9	7.3	135.0	13.1	134.9	-0.3	134.7	-0.6	133.9	9.6
1963	139.6	15.4	149.6	31.9	152.4	7.7	157.0	12.6	149.6	11.7
1964	166.6	26.8	158.2	-18.7	155.6	-6.4	152.8	-7.0	158.3	5.8
1965	153.4	1.6	154.6	3.2	155.2	1.6	151.8	-8.5	153.7	-2.9
1966	155.2	9.3	142.8	-28.3	138.2	-12.3	123.7	-35.8	140.0	-8.9
1967	119.9	-11.7	133.6	54.2	140.3	21.6	148.4	25.2	135.6	-3.1
1968	149.3	2.4	153.1	10.6	155.9	7.5	157.8	5.0	154.0	13.6
1969	163.5	15.3	161.7	-4.3	160.5	-2.9	148.7	-26.3	158.6	3.0
1970	149.0	0.8	139.1	-24.0	146.4	22.7	161.9	49.6	149.1	-6.0
1971	170.6	23.3	187.8	46.8	197.0	21.1	204.6	16.3	190.0	27.4
1972	218.3	29.6	222.6	8.1	223.1	0.9	231.1	15.1	223.7	17.7
1973	238.8	14.0	226.6	-18.9	217.0	-15.9	206.8	-17.5	222.3	-0.6
1974	191.6	-26.3	183.2	-16.4	177.1	-12.7	153.9	-43.0	176.4	-20.6
1975	144.3	-22.7	147.4	8.9	157.7	31.0	164.6	18.7	153.5	-13.0
1976	181.4	47.5	186.6	12.0	183.6	-6.3	207.0	61.6	189.7	23.6
1977	212.8	11.7	236.6	52.8	236.4	-0.3	233.5	-4.8	229.8	21.1
1978	235.1	2.8	246.2	20.3	249.7	5.8	249.0	-1.1	245.0	6.6
1979	243.2	-9.0	238.9	-6.9	235.7	-5.3	226.4	-14.9	236.0	-3.7
1980	210.3	-25.6	169.9	-57.4	173.0	7.5	191.3	49.5	186.1	-21.1
1981	188.0	-6.7	180.8	-14.5	166.5	-28.1	149.6	-34.8	171.2	-8.0
1982	141.1	-20.9	136.5	-12.4	134.8	-4.9	147.8	44.5	140.1	-18.2
1983	170.8	78.3	192.9	62.7	210.5	41.8	216.3	11.5	197.6	41.0
1984	224.0	15.0	229.6	10.4	226.6	-5.1	225.5	-1.9	226.4	14.6
1985	226.9	2.5	225.7	-2.1	230.2	8.2	235.1	8.8	229.5	1.4
1986	245.1	18.1	259.2	25.1	262.5	5.2	261.2	-2.0	257.0	12.0
1987	258.8	-3.6	260.8	3.1	256.2	-6.9	254.7	-2.3	257.6	0.2
1988	251.3	-5.2	252.2	1.4	252.9	1.1	253.7	1.3	252.5	-2.0
1989	252.6	-1.7	244.3	-12.5	240.1	-6.7	236.0	-6.7	243.2	-3.7
1990	239.4	5.9	227.8	-18.0	214.9	-20.8	200.3	-24.5	220.6	-9.3
1991	187.4	-23.4	188.3	1.9	195.6	16.4	202.4	14.6	193.4	-12.3
1992	213.9	24.7	224.9	22.2	226.7	3.2	236.7	18.8	225.6	16.6
1993	237.0	0.5	236.1	-1.5	242.2	10.7	255.1	23.1	242.6	7.5
1994	261.3	10.1	271.5	16.6	269.4	-3.1	265.9	-5.1	267.0	10.1
1995	261.2	-6.9	250.4	-15.5	255.5	8.4	260.8	8.6	257.0	-3.7
1996	266.1	8.4	277.2	17.8	274.1	-4.4	271.1	-4.3	272.1	5.9
1997	273.3	3.3	278.2	7.4	280.1	2.8	287.1	10.4	279.7	2.8

Source: "National Income and Product Account Tables: Selected NIPA Tables," *Survey of Current Business*, November 1997, U.S. Department of Commerce, Bureau of Economic Analysis, National Income and Wealth Division. Data for 1997 quarters downloaded from www.stat.usa.gov. A dash (-) indicates that no data are available.

Gross Domestic Product
Gross private domestic investment
Change in business inventories - Actual Dollars

In billions of actual dollars. Quarterly data are seasonally adjusted and annualized.

Year	1st Quarter	2nd Quarter	3rd Quarter	4th Quarter	TOTAL
1959	4.4	7.8	0.2	4.3	4.2
1960	11.3	3.1	4.2	-5.7	3.2
1961	-2.6	1.6	6.7	6.0	2.9
1962	9.5	5.6	6.2	3.1	6.1
1963	7.0	4.9	5.9	4.8	5.7
1964	5.6	4.8	4.3	5.4	5.0
1965	12.3	9.2	9.5	7.8	9.7
1966	13.5	12.5	12.2	17.0	13.8
1967	15.0	6.8	10.4	9.7	10.5
1968	8.1	13.9	8.0	6.6	9.1
1969	12.0	9.7	10.7	5.8	9.5
1970	2.0	4.6	5.2	-3.1	2.2
1971	12.4	11.4	10.4	-0.2	8.5
1972	4.6	12.4	14.0	8.7	9.9
1973	13.9	17.6	11.6	26.7	17.5
1974	13.2	16.3	6.9	20.0	14.1
1975	-11.7	-14.7	-	1.2	-6.3
1976	16.0	21.8	19.1	10.9	16.9
1977	14.9	23.0	32.0	22.3	23.1
1978	28.1	26.9	26.4	27.4	27.2
1979	24.3	27.3	11.6	4.3	16.9
1980	8.4	-0.3	-33.8	-4.7	-7.6
1981	38.3	9.4	42.5	22.4	28.2
1982	-20.4	-3.8	4.3	-38.1	-14.5
1983	-33.3	-8.0	-1.7	23.4	-4.9
1984	79.5	70.7	72.4	47.2	67.5
1985	25.6	24.3	20.5	34.4	26.2
1986	45.1	18.8	-13.2	-12.2	9.6
1987	24.3	13.0	2.0	57.7	24.2
1988	12.2	6.4	9.7	15.2	10.9
1989	38.8	41.8	23.9	22.4	31.7
1990	8.8	41.0	13.6	-31.2	8.0
1991	-16.3	-19.8	5.5	21.3	-2.3
1992	-0.2	10.2	11.6	6.5	7.0
1993	30.7	14.5	14.0	22.9	20.5
1994	52.4	76.3	50.2	66.2	61.2
1995	52.1	24.5	19.4	24.5	30.1
1996	11.1	23.4	37.1	31.9	25.9
1997	66.1	81.1	48.9	62.1	64.6

Source: "National Income and Product Account Tables: Selected NIPA Tables," *Survey of Current Business*, November 1997, U.S. Department of Commerce, Bureau of Economic Analysis, National Income and Wealth Division. Data for 1997 quarters downloaded from www.stat.usa.gov. A dash (-) indicates that no data are available.

Gross Domestic Product
Gross private domestic investment
Change in business inventories - Chained (1992) Dollars

In billions of chained 1992 dollars. Quarterly data are seasonally adjusted and annualized.

Year	1st Quarter	2nd Quarter	3rd Quarter	4th Quarter	TOTAL
1959	10.9	23.7	3.5	14.6	13.2
1960	33.6	8.8	14.0	-14.3	10.5
1961	-7.0	4.6	20.0	16.7	8.6
1962	28.2	17.5	20.7	11.6	19.5
1963	25.0	15.4	19.0	11.8	17.8
1964	15.5	14.9	14.5	17.4	15.6
1965	38.2	29.1	29.0	24.7	30.3
1966	41.5	39.4	37.6	51.3	42.4
1967	46.1	23.5	30.6	27.9	32.0
1968	23.1	41.2	23.6	19.5	26.9
1969	33.9	28.7	29.7	15.5	27.0
1970	3.7	12.7	13.9	-8.7	5.4
1971	31.8	30.2	25.2	2.0	22.3
1972	12.1	33.1	35.6	18.2	24.7
1973	31.9	41.3	23.9	53.8	37.7
1974	23.7	25.8	9.4	34.6	23.4
1975	-23.2	-23.6	2.6	3.4	-10.2
1976	28.1	38.6	33.4	19.0	29.8
1977	24.9	38.9	59.0	32.3	38.8
1978	46.0	43.1	42.6	41.6	43.3
1979	35.3	39.6	15.1	3.5	23.4
1980	9.0	-1.7	-43.8	-4.4	-10.2
1981	44.3	11.5	50.0	26.8	33.1
1982	-21.9	-4.0	6.6	-43.0	-15.6
1983	-38.4	-9.7	-0.7	26.1	-5.7
1984	87.4	79.3	80.3	54.1	75.3
1985	29.5	27.2	25.4	38.5	30.2
1986	52.9	22.9	-16.3	-15.3	11.1
1987	29.7	14.8	1.4	59.8	26.4
1988	14.0	6.0	11.3	15.7	11.7
1989	41.2	43.8	25.4	22.8	33.3
1990	10.9	43.6	14.9	-27.8	10.4
1991	-17.1	-20.7	4.7	21.3	-3.0
1992	-0.5	11.0	12.0	5.6	7.0
1993	32.3	16.6	15.3	24.2	22.1
1994	53.1	75.9	49.7	63.6	60.6
1995	48.5	21.6	17.0	22.2	27.3
1996	8.0	21.3	37.9	32.9	25.0
1997	63.7	77.6	47.5	59.9	62.2

Source: "National Income and Product Account Tables: Selected NIPA Tables," *Survey of Current Business*, November 1997, U.S. Department of Commerce, Bureau of Economic Analysis, National Income and Wealth Division. Data for 1997 quarters downloaded from www.stat.usa.gov. A dash (-) indicates that no data are available.

NET EXPORTS OF GOODS AND SERVICES
Component of Gross Domestic Product

Net exports of goods and services—the trade balance—account for the United States' trade with the rest of the world. This measure presents exports less imports of all goods and services; hence it can be a negative value. The category is subdivided into Exports and Imports. BEA estimates are developed from three categories: (1) merchandise exports and imports, (2) receipts from abroad and payments made abroad, including investment earnings, and (3) receipts and payments for other services; federal purchases and sales abroad are included in this category.

Presentation of Data

Data are shown from 1959 to 1997 in quarterly and in annual increments. Changes from one period to the next are shown for Exports and Imports but not for Net Exports, which can and do exhibit negative values. Changes from quarter to quarter are annualized, compounded growth rates as explained in the section on Gross National Product. Changes from year to year are simple percentile changes.

Analytical Uses

Net exports are, generally, an indicator of the national vigor in trading with the rest of the world. The category measures the U.S. trade balance directly; the trade balance, in turn, has a direct impact on GDP. Indirectly, net exports reflect (1) the strength of the dollar, (2) U.S. vulnerability in commodity categories, and (3) U.S. competitiveness in manufacturing and services.

A positive net exports figure adds to GDP; a negative figure subtracts from GDP and, consequently, can contribute to or even cause negative GDP growth rate. In national product accounting, exports, manufactured domestically, are part of GDP; imports, manufactured elsewhere, and therefore in another nation's GDP, are taken from GDP.

The trade balance is significantly influenced by the strength of the dollar as measured against other currencies. When the dollar is strong relative to other currencies, it can buy more abroad; at the same time, dollar-denominated goods are more expensive abroad and discourage sales. The value of the dollar, however, is controlled in part by national and international policies and the relative performance of other economies rather than by pure market forces. A negative trade balance, therefore, does not invariably signal economic weakness.

The trade balance was negative in all but 2 of the 39 years in the 1959-1997 period. As an indicator of economic prospects, the fact that net exports are negative is not as meaningful as the trend: is the trade deficit growing or decreasing. A growing deficit may signal problems; a shrinking deficit may signal a stronger economy because the ratio of exports to imports is changing favorably.

Net exports indicate, indirectly, U.S. dependence on important commodities, e.g. petroleum. An artificial increase in the price of crude oil can produce large trade deficits and also increase prices domestically. Similarly, net exports are influenced by the competitiveness of other economies in selling their goods to us. In recent years attention has focused on Japan and China, for instance.

Gross Domestic Product

Net exports of goods and services - Actual Dollars

In billions of actual dollars. Quarterly data are seasonally adjusted and annualized.

Year	1st Quarter	2nd Quarter	3rd Quarter	4th Quarter	TOTAL
1959	-1.7	-2.5	-1.1	-1.4	-1.7
1960	0.9	1.7	3.0	4.0	2.4
1961	4.4	3.3	2.8	2.9	3.4
1962	2.3	3.2	2.9	1.5	2.4
1963	2.0	3.7	3.1	4.4	3.3
1964	5.9	4.9	5.4	5.7	5.5
1965	3.0	4.7	3.7	4.1	3.9
1966	3.2	2.0	0.8	1.5	1.9
1967	2.3	2.1	1.1	0.2	1.4
1968	-1.2	-0.6	-1.3	-1.9	-1.3
1969	-1.9	-1.8	-1.3	0.1	-1.2
1970	1.1	2.4	0.9	0.4	1.2
1971	0.8	-3.8	-3.1	-6.0	-3.0
1972	-8.6	-8.3	-7.9	-7.1	-8.0
1973	-4.4	-1.1	3.2	4.7	0.6
1974	4.3	-5.6	-9.1	-2.2	-3.1
1975	13.1	16.6	11.6	12.9	13.6
1976	4.2	-1.1	-5.0	-7.2	-2.3
1977	-21.6	-21.7	-21.1	-30.3	-23.7
1978	-39.3	-23.3	-24.6	-17.3	-26.1
1979	-19.2	-23.4	-24.4	-29.0	-24.0
1980	-37.2	-16.7	3.3	-8.9	-14.9
1981	-17.0	-16.4	-10.2	-16.3	-15.0
1982	-17.2	-5.0	-30.3	-29.7	-20.5
1983	-24.6	-45.5	-65.2	-71.3	-51.7
1984	-94.3	-103.5	-103.1	-107.1	-102.0
1985	-91.4	-114.7	-117.2	-133.6	-114.2
1986	-126.9	-128.8	-138.0	-132.3	-131.5
1987	-139.4	-144.7	-142.4	-142.0	-142.1
1988	-120.9	-103.3	-95.8	-104.2	-106.1
1989	-83.7	-81.2	-79.3	-77.5	-80.4
1990	-74.3	-60.3	-78.5	-72.0	-71.3
1991	-32.9	-12.3	-22.0	-14.8	-20.5
1992	-8.9	-29.0	-37.6	-42.7	-29.5
1993	-46.6	-57.5	-72.1	-66.6	-60.7
1994	-76.6	-87.9	-103.4	-95.6	-90.9
1995	-98.3	-105.4	-80.4	-60.1	-86.0
1996	-83.0	-93.8	-114.0	-88.6	-94.8
1997	-98.8	-88.7	-111.3	-87.9	-96.7

Source: "National Income and Product Account Tables: Selected NIPA Tables," *Survey of Current Business*, November 1997, U.S. Department of Commerce, Bureau of Economic Analysis, National Income and Wealth Division. Data for 1997 quarters downloaded from www.stat.usa.gov. A dash (-) indicates that no data are available.

Gross Domestic Product
Net exports of goods and services - Chained (1992) Dollars

In billions of chained 1992 dollars. Quarterly data are seasonally adjusted and annualized.

Year	1st Quarter	2nd Quarter	3rd Quarter	4th Quarter	TOTAL
1959	-33.7	-38.0	-33.6	-33.8	-34.8
1960	-27.3	-24.5	-19.1	-14.1	-21.3
1961	-13.0	-18.6	-21.8	-23.0	-19.1
1962	-27.0	-23.6	-25.4	-30.2	-26.5
1963	-27.0	-21.4	-23.7	-18.7	-22.7
1964	-12.8	-16.5	-16.6	-17.6	-15.9
1965	-26.9	-26.0	-28.7	-27.8	-27.4
1966	-33.2	-38.0	-46.3	-45.9	-40.9
1967	-46.6	-46.8	-50.4	-56.6	-50.1
1968	-64.4	-65.2	-68.9	-70.2	-67.2
1969	-65.1	-75.8	-74.8	-69.6	-71.3
1970	-65.6	-64.6	-64.3	-65.6	-65.0
1971	-64.3	-81.5	-78.1	-79.5	-75.8
1972	-95.6	-88.3	-85.7	-86.1	-88.9
1973	-81.2	-64.7	-55.9	-50.3	-63.0
1974	-34.1	-34.7	-41.1	-32.3	-35.6
1975	-6.8	2.5	-11.9	-12.7	-7.2
1976	-29.2	-38.3	-42.8	-49.2	-39.9
1977	-67.0	-63.2	-56.9	-69.9	-64.2
1978	-84.9	-59.6	-62.0	-55.6	-65.6
1979	-55.7	-56.1	-40.2	-29.1	-45.3
1980	-20.0	11.3	33.4	15.7	10.1
1981	8.3	9.5	5.5	-0.9	5.6
1982	-5.3	2.6	-26.5	-27.3	-14.1
1983	-29.8	-54.6	-78.0	-90.8	-63.3
1984	-115.5	-125.5	-130.5	-137.7	-127.3
1985	-127.3	-151.6	-152.6	-160.0	-147.9
1986	-149.7	-167.1	-173.9	-164.9	-163.9
1987	-161.2	-160.2	-152.2	-151.3	-156.2
1988	-125.9	-106.9	-110.6	-114.3	-114.4
1989	-88.7	-79.8	-84.5	-77.9	-82.7
1990	-67.1	-66.7	-71.2	-42.5	-61.9
1991	-24.3	-17.1	-29.8	-17.9	-22.3
1992	-14.8	-32.5	-30.8	-40.0	-29.5
1993	-54.7	-62.6	-83.1	-80.5	-70.2
1994	-97.6	-103.9	-111.1	-105.9	-104.6
1995	-113.5	-112.8	-92.9	-76.1	-98.8
1996	-100.8	-112.6	-138.9	-105.6	-114.4
1997	-126.3	-136.6	-164.1	-141.4	-142.1

Source: "National Income and Product Account Tables: Selected NIPA Tables," *Survey of Current Business*, November 1997, U.S. Department of Commerce, Bureau of Economic Analysis, National Income and Wealth Division. Data for 1997 quarters downloaded from www.stat.usa.gov. A dash (-) indicates that no data are available.

Gross Domestic Product

Net exports of goods and services
Exports: Total - Actual Dollars

In billions of actual dollars. Quarterly data are seasonally adjusted and annualized.

Year	1st Quarter	2nd Quarter	3rd Quarter	4th Quarter	TOTAL
1959	19.7	20.0	21.8	21.1	20.6
1960	24.2	25.2	25.9	25.8	25.3
1961	26.1	25.2	26.1	26.8	26.0
1962	26.6	28.1	28.0	27.0	27.4
1963	27.2	29.6	29.8	31.1	29.4
1964	32.9	32.6	33.9	35.0	33.6
1965	31.5	36.3	35.7	38.0	35.4
1966	38.2	38.2	39.0	40.4	38.9
1967	41.7	41.1	40.7	41.9	41.4
1968	43.2	44.8	47.0	46.2	45.3
1969	41.9	50.9	51.0	53.2	49.3
1970	54.7	57.6	57.3	58.3	57.0
1971	59.5	59.5	62.4	56.0	59.3
1972	63.5	63.1	66.2	72.1	66.2
1973	81.0	88.3	94.3	103.4	91.8
1974	114.6	123.8	124.5	134.4	124.3
1975	138.0	131.8	133.7	141.7	136.3
1976	143.1	146.0	150.9	155.4	148.9
1977	154.8	161.3	161.8	157.1	158.8
1978	164.0	185.6	190.5	204.5	186.1
1979	210.7	219.7	232.9	251.5	228.7
1980	267.1	275.9	282.5	290.3	278.9
1981	302.8	305.5	299.7	303.2	302.8
1982	292.3	294.2	279.0	265.1	282.6
1983	270.6	272.5	278.2	286.7	277.0
1984	293.7	303.0	306.5	309.2	303.1
1985	305.9	303.9	297.0	305.3	303.0
1986	312.2	314.5	320.5	335.4	320.7
1987	337.4	356.9	373.9	394.7	365.7
1988	421.1	442.1	456.2	469.3	447.2
1989	492.6	512.8	509.7	522.1	509.3
1990	541.6	554.8	555.5	577.3	557.3
1991	577.4	602.7	602.6	624.4	601.8
1992	632.4	635.9	640.2	649.1	639.4
1993	647.1	661.2	646.8	679.4	658.6
1994	678.5	710.1	732.6	763.7	721.2
1995	784.5	807.7	831.6	849.9	818.4
1996	850.2	865.0	863.7	904.6	870.9
1997	922.2	960.3	965.8	986.9	958.8

Source: "National Income and Product Account Tables: Selected NIPA Tables," *Survey of Current Business*, November 1997, U.S. Department of Commerce, Bureau of Economic Analysis, National Income and Wealth Division. Data for 1997 quarters downloaded from www.stat.usa.gov. A dash (-) indicates that no data are available.

Gross Domestic Product
Net exports of goods and services
Exports: Total - Chained (1992) Dollars

In billions of chained 1992 dollars. Quarterly data are seasonally adjusted and annualized.

Year	1st Quarter	2nd Quarter	3rd Quarter	4th Quarter	TOTAL
1959	68.6	70.1	75.8	72.9	71.9
1960	83.2	86.7	88.7	88.7	86.8
1961	89.3	85.0	88.6	90.1	88.3
1962	89.5	95.4	95.2	91.9	93.0
1963	92.1	100.6	101.3	106.0	100.0
1964	111.7	110.8	114.2	116.6	113.3
1965	102.5	118.7	116.6	124.7	115.6
1966	123.1	122.2	123.0	125.1	123.4
1967	127.0	125.6	124.4	127.3	126.1
1968	130.3	132.5	140.7	137.6	135.3
1969	123.2	149.5	147.7	150.4	142.7
1970	153.8	159.0	158.7	160.9	158.1
1971	159.6	159.4	168.1	149.7	159.2
1972	167.4	164.8	172.4	183.5	172.0
1973	200.3	209.0	210.3	218.8	209.6
1974	226.4	236.4	225.0	231.1	229.8
1975	230.5	220.9	224.7	236.7	228.2
1976	235.9	238.1	244.7	247.7	241.6
1977	243.8	250.1	252.2	243.6	247.4
1978	249.5	275.5	278.3	289.1	273.1
1979	288.9	289.7	299.7	317.8	299.0
1980	327.7	333.9	332.8	331.1	331.4
1981	336.7	338.9	331.4	334.1	335.3
1982	320.4	322.8	308.2	294.3	311.4
1983	298.9	299.8	304.3	310.2	303.3
1984	317.5	325.7	332.0	338.3	328.4
1985	338.7	337.3	332.0	341.4	337.3
1986	351.3	355.9	364.1	377.5	362.2
1987	377.7	393.5	411.1	425.7	402.0
1988	448.8	461.4	469.4	483.5	465.8
1989	502.0	522.0	521.3	535.5	520.2
1990	555.2	566.8	561.8	573.9	564.4
1991	572.3	600.3	603.6	623.5	599.9
1992	633.0	635.8	639.7	649.1	639.4
1993	647.2	660.1	646.3	679.1	658.2
1994	676.0	704.1	722.1	747.3	712.4
1995	760.4	777.4	802.4	824.6	791.2
1996	828.2	847.4	851.4	901.1	857.0
1997	922.7	962.5	973.0	999.3	964.4

Source: "National Income and Product Account Tables: Selected NIPA Tables," *Survey of Current Business*, November 1997, U.S. Department of Commerce, Bureau of Economic Analysis, National Income and Wealth Division. Data for 1997 quarters downloaded from www.stat.usa.gov. A dash (-) indicates that no data are available.

Gross Domestic Product
Net exports of goods and services
Exports - Goods - Actual Dollars

In billions of actual dollars. Quarterly data are seasonally adjusted and annualized.

Year	1st Quarter	2nd Quarter	3rd Quarter	4th Quarter	TOTAL
1959	15.6	15.9	17.5	16.9	16.5
1960	19.5	20.5	20.9	20.9	20.5
1961	21.2	20.1	21.0	21.5	20.9
1962	21.2	22.3	22.3	21.1	21.7
1963	21.3	23.4	23.8	24.9	23.3
1964	26.1	26.0	26.9	27.8	26.7
1965	24.4	28.8	27.9	30.1	27.8
1966	30.4	30.1	30.6	31.9	30.7
1967	32.5	32.3	31.6	32.3	32.2
1968	33.6	34.9	36.6	35.9	35.3
1969	31.6	39.9	39.5	42.0	38.3
1970	43.0	45.0	44.8	45.4	44.5
1971	45.9	45.7	48.4	42.2	45.6
1972	49.7	48.9	51.8	56.8	51.8
1973	64.4	70.9	75.6	84.8	73.9
1974	93.1	100.6	101.2	109.0	101.0
1975	112.0	105.9	107.1	113.4	109.6
1976	113.5	116.3	119.0	122.3	117.8
1977	121.3	126.2	126.1	121.0	123.7
1978	125.0	146.1	149.3	161.2	145.4
1979	167.0	175.7	188.0	205.4	184.0
1980	217.8	224.2	226.9	234.2	225.8
1981	242.2	242.0	234.2	238.0	239.1
1982	224.9	226.0	211.6	197.6	215.0
1983	200.7	202.8	207.4	218.3	207.3
1984	218.3	224.6	228.4	231.2	225.6
1985	225.7	223.5	217.4	222.4	222.2
1986	220.5	223.0	224.5	235.9	226.0
1987	234.3	248.7	264.2	283.0	257.5
1988	304.6	321.4	331.6	345.5	325.8
1989	359.3	377.8	370.2	379.4	371.7
1990	391.6	399.8	394.6	408.2	398.5
1991	414.8	428.8	423.9	438.1	426.4
1992	442.1	445.9	447.7	459.0	448.7
1993	451.2	462.2	447.9	477.7	459.7
1994	475.7	499.2	518.9	544.6	509.6
1995	560.7	578.6	591.1	605.1	583.9
1996	606.1	613.9	609.7	640.5	617.5
1997	656.2	690.0	691.1	711.1	687.1

Source: "National Income and Product Account Tables: Selected NIPA Tables," *Survey of Current Business*, November 1997, U.S. Department of Commerce, Bureau of Economic Analysis, National Income and Wealth Division. Data for 1997 quarters downloaded from www.stat.usa.gov. A dash (-) indicates that no data are available.

Gross Domestic Product
Net exports of goods and services
Exports - Goods - Chained (1992) Dollars

In billions of chained 1992 dollars. Quarterly data are seasonally adjusted and annualized.

Year	1st Quarter	2nd Quarter	3rd Quarter	4th Quarter	TOTAL
1959	48.8	50.2	55.2	52.7	51.7
1960	61.0	64.0	65.1	65.2	63.8
1961	65.6	61.2	64.4	65.5	64.2
1962	64.7	68.9	69.0	65.4	67.0
1963	65.7	72.5	73.8	77.2	72.3
1964	80.7	80.6	82.9	84.5	82.2
1965	72.1	85.6	82.9	89.9	82.6
1966	88.9	87.4	87.7	89.5	88.4
1967	89.2	89.1	87.7	89.2	88.8
1968	92.1	93.5	100.0	97.6	95.8
1969	84.4	106.9	104.2	107.8	100.8
1970	109.8	112.5	112.8	114.2	112.3
1971	112.1	111.9	119.9	103.7	111.9
1972	120.5	117.6	124.6	133.0	123.9
1973	145.1	152.2	151.9	160.3	152.4
1974	163.3	170.1	160.9	163.6	164.5
1975	162.8	155.2	158.1	166.5	160.7
1976	164.6	166.9	170.0	171.6	168.3
1977	168.2	172.5	174.2	167.0	170.5
1978	169.3	192.8	194.1	201.9	189.5
1979	202.0	203.6	213.0	229.1	211.9
1980	236.2	240.6	236.4	235.6	237.2
1981	237.6	237.5	230.1	233.8	234.7
1982	220.1	222.8	211.5	199.5	213.5
1983	202.5	203.9	207.3	215.4	207.3
1984	214.4	219.8	226.6	233.8	223.7
1985	231.9	231.6	228.6	234.9	231.7
1986	235.7	240.5	244.3	254.0	243.6
1987	251.1	261.9	278.0	290.9	270.5
1988	308.8	317.5	322.1	337.1	321.4
1989	347.2	365.6	361.1	372.9	361.7
1990	386.8	394.8	388.0	397.0	391.6
1991	403.3	419.8	420.0	433.7	419.2
1992	440.3	445.1	448.3	461.0	448.7
1993	454.1	465.3	452.0	483.5	463.7
1994	479.1	501.2	518.4	540.4	509.8
1995	550.4	565.7	580.4	599.1	573.9
1996	605.2	619.2	623.0	666.2	628.4
1997	686.2	725.8	731.8	759.4	725.8

Source: "National Income and Product Account Tables: Selected NIPA Tables," *Survey of Current Business*, November 1997, U.S. Department of Commerce, Bureau of Economic Analysis, National Income and Wealth Division. Data for 1997 quarters downloaded from www.stat.usa.gov. A dash (-) indicates that no data are available.

Gross Domestic Product

Net exports of goods and services
Exports - Services - Actual Dollars

In billions of actual dollars and percent. Quarterly data are seasonally adjusted and annualized. Growth rates for quarters are compound annual growth rates; changes from year to year are percentage changes.

Year	1st Quarter	% Change	2nd Quarter	% Change	3rd Quarter	% Change	4th Quarter	% Change	TOTAL	% Change
1959	4.1	-	4.1	-	4.3	21.0	4.3	-	4.2	-
1960	4.7	42.7	4.7	-	4.9	18.1	4.9	-	4.8	14.3
1961	4.9	-	5.1	17.4	5.2	8.1	5.2	-	5.1	6.2
1962	5.4	16.3	5.8	33.1	5.7	-6.7	5.9	14.8	5.7	11.8
1963	5.9	-	6.2	21.9	6.0	-12.3	6.3	21.6	6.1	7.0
1964	6.8	35.7	6.6	-11.3	6.9	19.5	7.1	12.1	6.9	13.1
1965	7.1	-	7.5	24.5	7.8	17.0	8.0	10.7	7.6	10.1
1966	7.8	-9.6	8.1	16.3	8.4	15.7	8.5	4.8	8.2	7.9
1967	9.2	37.2	8.9	-12.4	9.0	4.6	9.6	29.5	9.2	12.2
1968	9.6	-	9.9	13.1	10.3	17.2	10.3	-	10.0	8.7
1969	10.3	-	11.0	30.1	11.5	19.5	11.2	-10.0	11.0	10.0
1970	11.6	15.1	12.6	39.2	12.6	-	12.9	9.9	12.4	12.7
1971	13.6	23.5	13.8	6.0	13.9	2.9	13.8	-2.8	13.8	11.3
1972	13.8	-	14.2	12.1	14.3	2.8	15.3	31.0	14.4	4.3
1973	16.6	38.6	17.4	20.7	18.7	33.4	18.6	-2.1	17.8	23.6
1974	21.6	81.9	23.1	30.8	23.2	1.7	25.4	43.7	23.3	30.9
1975	26.0	9.8	25.9	-1.5	26.5	9.6	28.3	30.1	26.7	14.6
1976	29.6	19.7	29.7	1.4	31.9	33.1	33.1	15.9	31.1	16.5
1977	33.5	4.9	35.2	21.9	35.7	5.8	36.1	4.6	35.1	12.9
1978	38.9	34.8	39.5	6.3	41.2	18.4	43.3	22.0	40.7	16.0
1979	43.7	3.7	44.0	2.8	44.9	8.4	46.1	11.1	44.7	9.8
1980	49.3	30.8	51.7	20.9	55.6	33.8	56.1	3.6	53.2	19.0
1981	60.6	36.2	63.5	20.6	65.5	13.2	65.1	-2.4	63.7	19.7
1982	67.5	15.6	68.2	4.2	67.4	-4.6	67.5	0.6	67.6	6.1
1983	69.9	15.0	69.7	-1.1	70.8	6.5	68.4	-12.9	69.7	3.1
1984	75.4	47.7	78.4	16.9	78.1	-1.5	78.0	-0.5	77.5	11.2
1985	80.2	11.8	80.4	1.0	79.6	-3.9	82.9	17.6	80.8	4.3
1986	91.7	49.7	91.5	-0.9	96.0	21.2	99.5	15.4	94.7	17.2
1987	103.1	15.3	108.2	21.3	109.8	6.0	111.7	7.1	108.2	14.3
1988	116.5	18.3	120.7	15.2	124.5	13.2	123.9	-1.9	121.4	12.2
1989	133.3	34.0	135.0	5.2	139.5	14.0	142.7	9.5	137.6	13.3
1990	150.0	22.1	155.1	14.3	160.9	15.8	169.1	22.0	158.8	15.4
1991	162.7	-14.3	173.9	30.5	178.7	11.5	186.3	18.1	175.4	10.5
1992	190.3	8.9	190.0	-0.6	192.5	5.4	190.1	-4.9	190.7	8.7
1993	195.8	12.5	199.0	6.7	198.9	-0.2	201.7	5.8	198.9	4.3
1994	202.8	2.2	210.9	17.0	213.7	5.4	219.0	10.3	211.6	6.4
1995	223.9	9.3	229.2	9.8	240.5	21.2	244.7	7.2	234.6	10.9
1996	244.1	-1.0	251.1	12.0	254.0	4.7	264.2	17.1	253.3	8.0
1997	266.0	2.8	270.3	6.6	274.8	6.8	275.8	1.5	271.7	7.3

Source: "National Income and Product Account Tables: Selected NIPA Tables," *Survey of Current Business*, November 1997, U.S. Department of Commerce, Bureau of Economic Analysis, National Income and Wealth Division. Data for 1997 quarters downloaded from www.stat.usa.gov. A dash (-) indicates that no data are available.

Gross Domestic Product

Net exports of goods and services
Exports - Services - Chained (1992) Dollars

In billions of chained (1992) dollars and percent. Quarterly data are seasonally adjusted and annualized. Growth rates for quarters are compound annual growth rates; changes from year to year are percentage changes.

Year	1st Quarter	% Change	2nd Quarter	% Change	3rd Quarter	% Change	4th Quarter	% Change	TOTAL	% Change
1959	18.7	-	18.5	-4.2	18.8	6.6	18.7	-2.1	18.6	-
1960	20.0	30.8	20.3	6.1	21.2	18.9	21.1	-1.9	20.6	10.8
1961	21.2	1.9	22.1	18.1	22.2	1.8	22.5	5.5	22.0	6.8
1962	22.8	5.4	24.5	33.3	24.0	-7.9	24.8	14.0	24.0	9.1
1963	24.8	-	26.0	20.8	25.2	-11.8	26.2	16.8	25.5	6.3
1964	28.6	42.0	27.6	-13.3	28.7	16.9	29.4	10.1	28.6	12.2
1965	28.9	-6.6	30.6	25.7	31.6	13.7	32.2	7.8	30.8	7.7
1966	31.5	-8.4	32.5	13.3	33.2	8.9	33.3	1.2	32.6	5.8
1967	36.1	38.1	34.5	-16.6	34.8	3.5	36.5	21.0	35.5	8.9
1968	36.0	-5.4	36.9	10.4	38.3	16.1	37.8	-5.1	37.3	5.1
1969	37.8	-	39.7	21.7	41.2	16.0	39.7	-13.8	39.6	6.2
1970	41.2	16.0	44.0	30.1	43.2	-7.1	44.0	7.6	43.1	8.8
1971	45.2	11.4	45.3	0.9	45.3	-	44.3	-8.5	45.0	4.4
1972	43.7	-5.3	44.3	5.6	44.3	-	46.6	22.4	44.7	-0.7
1973	51.0	43.5	52.1	8.9	54.3	18.0	53.0	-9.2	52.6	17.7
1974	58.8	51.5	62.0	23.6	60.6	-8.7	64.9	31.5	61.6	17.1
1975	65.4	3.1	64.1	-7.7	64.8	4.4	68.2	22.7	65.6	6.5
1976	70.3	12.9	69.7	-3.4	74.0	27.1	75.7	9.5	72.5	10.5
1977	75.7	-	77.8	11.6	78.0	1.0	77.2	-4.0	77.2	6.5
1978	81.9	26.7	81.2	-3.4	83.1	9.7	85.9	14.2	83.0	7.5
1979	85.4	-2.3	84.0	-6.4	83.2	-3.8	82.9	-1.4	83.9	1.1
1980	85.6	13.7	87.5	9.2	92.5	24.9	91.4	-4.7	89.2	6.3
1981	96.1	22.2	99.3	14.0	100.4	4.5	98.4	-7.7	98.5	10.4
1982	100.7	9.7	99.9	-3.1	97.2	-10.4	96.3	-3.7	98.5	-
1983	98.0	7.3	97.1	-3.6	98.0	3.8	94.2	-14.6	96.8	-1.7
1984	104.8	53.2	107.7	11.5	106.3	-5.1	104.6	-6.2	105.9	9.4
1985	107.6	12.0	106.3	-4.7	103.9	-8.7	106.9	12.1	106.1	0.2
1986	117.4	45.5	116.8	-2.0	121.7	17.9	125.2	12.0	120.3	13.4
1987	128.9	12.4	134.0	16.8	134.8	2.4	136.0	3.6	133.4	10.9
1988	140.8	14.9	144.7	11.5	148.3	10.3	146.4	-5.0	145.0	8.7
1989	155.4	27.0	156.1	1.8	160.5	11.8	162.8	5.9	158.7	9.4
1990	168.6	15.0	172.2	8.8	174.3	5.0	177.3	7.1	173.1	9.1
1991	168.9	-17.6	180.6	30.7	183.8	7.3	189.8	13.7	180.8	4.4
1992	192.8	6.5	190.7	-4.3	191.3	1.3	188.2	-6.3	190.7	5.5
1993	193.1	10.8	194.8	3.6	194.2	-1.2	195.9	3.5	194.5	2.0
1994	197.0	2.3	203.1	13.0	204.1	2.0	207.5	6.8	202.9	4.3
1995	210.6	6.1	212.5	3.7	222.6	20.4	226.2	6.6	218.0	7.4
1996	224.0	-3.8	229.3	9.8	229.4	0.2	236.8	13.5	229.9	5.5
1997	238.9	3.6	240.8	3.2	245.0	7.2	245.1	0.2	242.5	5.5

Source: "National Income and Product Account Tables: Selected NIPA Tables," *Survey of Current Business*, November 1997, U.S. Department of Commerce, Bureau of Economic Analysis, National Income and Wealth Division. Data for 1997 quarters downloaded from www.stat.usa.gov. A dash (-) indicates that no data are available.

Gross Domestic Product
Net exports of goods and services
Imports: Total - Actual Dollars

In billions of actual dollars and percent. Quarterly data are seasonally adjusted and annualized. Growth rates for quarters are compound annual growth rates; changes from year to year are percentage changes.

Year	1st Quarter	% Change	2nd Quarter	% Change	3rd Quarter	% Change	4th Quarter	% Change	TOTAL	% Change
1959	21.4	-	22.5	22.2	22.9	7.3	22.5	-6.8	22.3	-
1960	23.3	15.0	23.5	3.5	22.9	-9.8	21.7	-19.4	22.8	2.2
1961	21.7	-	21.9	3.7	23.3	28.1	23.9	10.7	22.7	-0.4
1962	24.3	6.9	24.9	10.2	25.1	3.3	25.6	8.2	25.0	10.1
1963	25.2	-6.1	25.9	11.6	26.7	12.9	26.8	1.5	26.1	4.4
1964	27.0	3.0	27.7	10.8	28.4	10.5	29.3	13.3	28.1	7.7
1965	28.5	-10.5	31.7	53.1	32.0	3.8	33.9	26.0	31.5	12.1
1966	35.0	13.6	36.2	14.4	38.2	24.0	38.8	6.4	37.1	17.8
1967	39.4	6.3	39.0	-4.0	39.5	5.2	41.7	24.2	39.9	7.5
1968	44.4	28.5	45.4	9.3	48.2	27.0	48.2	-	46.6	16.8
1969	43.8	-31.8	52.7	109.6	52.4	-2.3	53.1	5.5	50.5	8.4
1970	53.5	3.0	55.2	13.3	56.4	9.0	57.9	11.1	55.8	10.5
1971	58.7	5.6	63.3	35.2	65.5	14.6	61.9	-20.2	62.3	11.6
1972	72.2	85.1	71.4	-4.4	74.1	16.0	79.2	30.5	74.2	19.1
1973	85.4	35.2	89.5	20.6	91.1	7.3	98.7	37.8	91.2	22.9
1974	110.3	56.0	129.4	89.4	133.6	13.6	136.6	9.3	127.5	39.8
1975	124.9	-30.1	115.2	-27.6	122.1	26.2	128.7	23.4	122.7	-3.8
1976	138.9	35.7	147.1	25.8	155.8	25.8	162.7	18.9	151.1	23.1
1977	176.4	38.2	183.0	15.8	182.9	-0.2	187.4	10.2	182.4	20.7
1978	203.3	38.5	208.8	11.3	215.1	12.6	221.8	13.1	212.3	16.4
1979	229.8	15.2	243.1	25.2	257.3	25.5	280.5	41.2	252.7	19.0
1980	304.3	38.5	292.6	-14.5	279.2	-17.1	299.2	31.9	293.8	16.3
1981	319.7	30.4	322.0	2.9	309.9	-14.2	319.4	12.8	317.8	8.2
1982	309.5	-11.8	299.1	-12.8	309.3	14.4	294.9	-17.4	303.2	-4.6
1983	295.3	0.5	318.0	34.5	343.4	36.0	358.0	18.1	328.6	8.4
1984	388.0	38.0	406.5	20.5	409.6	3.1	416.4	6.8	405.1	23.3
1985	397.3	-17.1	418.6	23.2	414.2	-4.1	438.9	26.1	417.2	3.0
1986	439.1	0.2	443.4	4.0	458.5	14.3	467.7	8.3	452.2	8.4
1987	476.9	8.1	501.6	22.4	516.4	12.3	536.7	16.7	507.9	12.3
1988	542.0	4.0	545.4	2.5	552.0	4.9	573.5	16.5	553.2	8.9
1989	576.3	2.0	594.0	12.9	589.0	-3.3	599.7	7.5	589.7	6.6
1990	615.9	11.3	615.1	-0.5	634.1	12.9	649.2	9.9	628.6	6.6
1991	610.3	-21.9	615.0	3.1	624.5	6.3	639.3	9.8	622.3	-1.0
1992	641.3	1.3	664.9	15.6	677.8	8.0	691.8	8.5	669.0	7.5
1993	693.7	1.1	718.7	15.2	718.9	0.1	746.0	16.0	719.3	7.5
1994	755.1	5.0	797.9	24.7	836.0	20.5	859.2	11.6	812.1	12.9
1995	882.8	11.4	913.1	14.5	912.0	-0.5	909.9	-0.9	904.5	11.4
1996	933.2	10.6	958.7	11.4	977.6	8.1	993.2	6.5	965.7	6.8
1997	1,021.0	11.7	1,049.0	11.4	1,077.1	11.2	1,074.8	-0.9	1,055.5	9.3

Source: "National Income and Product Account Tables: Selected NIPA Tables," *Survey of Current Business*, November 1997, U.S. Department of Commerce, Bureau of Economic Analysis, National Income and Wealth Division. Data for 1997 quarters downloaded from www.stat.usa.gov. A dash (-) indicates that no data are available.

Gross Domestic Product
Net exports of goods and services
Imports: Total - Chained (1992) Dollars

In billions of chained (1992) dollars and percent. Quarterly data are seasonally adjusted and annualized. Growth rates for quarters are compound annual growth rates; changes from year to year are percentage changes.

Year	1st Quarter	% Change	2nd Quarter	% Change	3rd Quarter	% Change	4th Quarter	% Change	TOTAL	% Change
1959	102.4	-	108.0	23.7	109.4	5.3	106.7	-9.5	106.6	-
1960	110.5	15.0	111.2	2.6	107.8	-11.7	102.7	-17.6	108.1	1.4
1961	102.3	-1.5	103.6	5.2	110.4	29.0	113.1	10.1	107.3	-0.7
1962	116.5	12.6	119.0	8.9	120.5	5.1	122.0	5.1	119.5	11.4
1963	119.1	-9.2	122.0	10.1	125.0	10.2	124.7	-1.0	122.7	2.7
1964	124.5	-0.6	127.4	9.6	130.8	11.1	134.2	10.8	129.2	5.3
1965	129.4	-13.6	144.7	56.4	145.3	1.7	152.5	21.3	143.0	10.7
1966	156.3	10.3	160.2	10.4	169.3	24.7	171.1	4.3	164.2	14.8
1967	173.6	6.0	172.4	-2.7	174.8	5.7	184.0	22.8	176.2	7.3
1968	194.7	25.4	197.7	6.3	209.6	26.3	207.8	-3.4	202.5	14.9
1969	188.3	-32.6	225.3	104.9	222.4	-5.1	220.0	-4.2	214.0	5.7
1970	219.4	-1.1	223.6	7.9	223.0	-1.1	226.5	6.4	223.1	4.3
1971	223.9	-4.5	240.9	34.0	246.1	8.9	229.2	-24.8	235.0	5.3
1972	263.0	73.4	253.1	-14.2	258.2	8.3	269.6	18.9	261.0	11.1
1973	281.5	18.9	273.7	-10.6	266.2	-10.5	269.1	4.4	272.6	4.4
1974	260.6	-12.0	271.1	17.1	266.1	-7.2	263.4	-4.0	265.3	-2.7
1975	237.3	-34.1	218.4	-28.3	236.6	37.7	249.3	23.3	235.4	-11.3
1976	265.2	28.1	276.5	18.2	287.5	16.9	296.8	13.6	281.5	19.6
1977	310.8	20.2	313.3	3.3	309.1	-5.3	313.4	5.7	311.6	10.7
1978	334.4	29.6	335.1	0.8	340.3	6.4	344.7	5.3	338.6	8.7
1979	344.6	-0.1	345.7	1.3	340.0	-6.4	346.9	8.4	344.3	1.7
1980	347.8	1.0	322.7	-25.9	299.4	-25.9	315.4	23.2	321.3	-6.7
1981	328.5	17.7	329.4	1.1	325.9	-4.2	334.9	11.5	329.7	2.6
1982	325.7	-10.5	320.2	-6.6	334.7	19.4	321.7	-14.7	325.5	-1.3
1983	328.8	9.1	354.5	35.1	382.2	35.1	401.0	21.2	366.6	12.6
1984	433.0	35.9	451.2	17.9	462.5	10.4	476.1	12.3	455.7	24.3
1985	466.0	-8.2	489.0	21.3	484.6	-3.6	501.3	14.5	485.2	6.5
1986	501.0	-0.2	523.0	18.8	538.1	12.1	542.3	3.2	526.1	8.4
1987	538.8	-2.6	553.7	11.5	563.2	7.0	577.0	10.2	558.2	6.1
1988	574.8	-1.5	568.3	-4.4	580.0	8.5	597.8	12.9	580.2	3.9
1989	590.7	-4.7	601.9	7.8	605.8	2.6	613.5	5.2	603.0	3.9
1990	622.3	5.9	633.5	7.4	633.0	-0.3	616.4	-10.1	626.3	3.9
1991	596.6	-12.2	617.4	14.7	633.4	10.8	641.4	5.1	622.2	-0.7
1992	647.8	4.1	668.3	13.3	670.5	1.3	689.1	11.6	669.0	7.5
1993	701.9	7.6	722.7	12.4	729.4	3.8	759.7	17.7	728.4	8.9
1994	773.6	7.5	808.0	19.0	833.2	13.1	853.2	10.0	817.0	12.2
1995	873.9	10.1	890.3	7.7	895.4	2.3	900.7	2.4	890.1	8.9
1996	929.0	13.2	960.0	14.0	990.2	13.2	1,006.6	6.8	971.5	9.1
1997	1,048.9	17.9	1,099.1	20.6	1,137.1	14.6	1,140.8	1.3	1,106.5	13.9

Source: "National Income and Product Account Tables: Selected NIPA Tables," *Survey of Current Business*, November 1997, U.S. Department of Commerce, Bureau of Economic Analysis, National Income and Wealth Division. Data for 1997 quarters downloaded from www.stat.usa.gov. A dash (-) indicates that no data are available.

Gross Domestic Product
Net exports of goods and services
Imports - Goods - Actual Dollars

In billions of actual dollars and percent. Quarterly data are seasonally adjusted and annualized. Growth rates for quarters are compound annual growth rates; changes from year to year are percentage changes.

Year	1st Quarter	% Change	2nd Quarter	% Change	3rd Quarter	% Change	4th Quarter	% Change	TOTAL	% Change
1959	14.5	-	15.5	30.6	15.8	8.0	15.4	-9.7	15.3	-
1960	15.7	8.0	15.9	5.2	15.1	-18.7	14.2	-21.8	15.2	-0.7
1961	14.1	-2.8	14.3	5.8	15.8	49.0	16.1	7.8	15.1	-0.7
1962	16.4	7.7	16.9	12.8	17.1	4.8	17.0	-2.3	16.9	11.9
1963	16.9	-2.3	17.6	17.6	18.2	14.3	18.2	-	17.7	4.7
1964	18.3	2.2	19.1	18.7	19.7	13.2	20.4	15.0	19.4	9.6
1965	19.6	-14.8	22.4	70.6	22.8	7.3	24.2	26.9	22.2	14.4
1966	24.9	12.1	25.6	11.7	27.2	27.4	27.7	7.6	26.3	18.5
1967	27.7	-	26.8	-12.4	27.0	3.0	29.5	42.5	27.8	5.7
1968	32.1	40.2	33.2	14.4	35.4	29.3	35.1	-3.3	33.9	21.9
1969	30.8	-40.7	39.1	159.7	38.5	-6.0	38.8	3.2	36.8	8.6
1970	39.3	5.3	40.1	8.4	41.2	11.4	42.8	16.5	40.9	11.1
1971	43.4	5.7	47.4	42.3	49.6	19.9	45.7	-27.9	46.6	13.9
1972	55.1	111.3	54.1	-7.1	57.3	25.8	61.3	31.0	56.9	22.1
1973	66.5	38.5	70.0	22.8	72.1	12.6	78.8	42.7	71.8	26.2
1974	88.8	61.3	106.4	106.1	110.6	16.7	112.3	6.3	104.5	45.5
1975	100.9	-34.8	92.3	-30.0	98.8	31.3	104.0	22.8	99.0	-5.3
1976	113.5	41.9	121.3	30.5	128.9	27.5	134.7	19.3	124.6	25.9
1977	147.6	44.2	153.2	16.1	153.2	-	156.6	9.2	152.6	22.5
1978	170.3	39.9	175.1	11.8	179.4	10.2	184.8	12.6	177.4	16.3
1979	192.2	17.0	204.1	27.2	216.8	27.3	238.1	45.5	212.8	20.0
1980	259.7	41.5	248.5	-16.2	234.1	-21.2	252.0	34.3	248.6	16.8
1981	270.2	32.2	271.8	2.4	260.5	-15.6	268.8	13.4	267.8	7.7
1982	257.6	-15.7	245.8	-17.1	257.2	19.9	241.5	-22.3	250.5	-6.5
1983	242.5	1.7	262.8	37.9	285.9	40.1	299.6	20.6	272.7	8.9
1984	322.5	34.3	337.9	20.5	339.9	2.4	345.0	6.1	336.3	23.3
1985	325.4	-20.9	344.4	25.5	340.5	-4.5	362.8	28.9	343.3	2.1
1986	357.7	-5.5	365.1	8.5	374.8	11.1	382.5	8.5	370.0	7.8
1987	389.5	7.5	409.1	21.7	422.8	14.1	437.7	14.9	414.8	12.1
1988	441.5	3.5	445.7	3.9	451.1	4.9	470.2	18.0	452.1	9.0
1989	473.0	2.4	490.3	15.5	483.1	-5.7	491.5	7.1	484.5	7.2
1990	500.4	7.4	497.4	-2.4	511.3	11.7	522.9	9.4	508.0	4.9
1991	488.3	-24.0	493.5	4.3	504.6	9.3	516.5	9.8	500.7	-1.4
1992	516.8	0.2	541.1	20.2	557.2	12.4	564.4	5.3	544.9	8.8
1993	570.8	4.6	593.2	16.6	592.8	-0.3	614.4	15.4	592.8	8.8
1994	622.4	5.3	663.8	29.4	699.2	23.1	721.7	13.5	676.8	14.2
1995	739.3	10.1	767.0	15.9	762.9	-2.1	761.0	-1.0	757.5	11.9
1996	778.4	9.5	802.9	13.2	820.2	8.9	834.6	7.2	809.0	6.8
1997	855.8	10.6	880.1	11.9	905.6	12.1	900.0	-2.5	885.4	9.4

Source: "National Income and Product Account Tables: Selected NIPA Tables," *Survey of Current Business*, November 1997, U.S. Department of Commerce, Bureau of Economic Analysis, National Income and Wealth Division. Data for 1997 quarters downloaded from www.stat.usa.gov. A dash (-) indicates that no data are available.

Gross Domestic Product
Net exports of goods and services
Imports - Goods - Chained (1992) Dollars

In billions of chained (1992) dollars and percent. Quarterly data are seasonally adjusted and annualized. Growth rates for quarters are compound annual growth rates; changes from year to year are percentage changes.

Year	1st Quarter	% Change	2nd Quarter	% Change	3rd Quarter	% Change	4th Quarter	% Change	TOTAL	% Change
1959	67.3	-	72.5	34.7	73.7	6.8	71.1	-13.4	71.1	-
1960	72.3	6.9	73.0	3.9	69.0	-20.2	65.7	-17.8	70.0	-1.5
1961	65.0	-4.2	66.2	7.6	73.3	50.3	75.0	9.6	69.9	-0.1
1962	77.7	15.2	80.1	12.9	81.6	7.7	81.4	-1.0	80.2	14.7
1963	80.4	-4.8	83.1	14.1	85.2	10.5	85.1	-0.5	83.5	4.1
1964	84.4	-3.2	87.4	15.0	90.6	15.5	93.5	13.4	89.0	6.6
1965	89.3	-16.8	103.3	79.1	104.3	3.9	109.4	21.0	101.6	14.2
1966	112.2	10.6	114.0	6.6	121.4	28.6	122.8	4.7	117.6	15.7
1967	123.0	0.7	119.6	-10.6	120.7	3.7	131.9	42.6	123.8	5.3
1968	142.4	35.9	145.8	9.9	155.9	30.7	153.3	-6.5	149.4	20.7
1969	133.6	-42.3	169.2	157.3	165.8	-7.8	161.6	-9.8	157.5	5.4
1970	161.9	0.7	163.2	3.3	162.6	-1.5	167.2	11.8	163.7	3.9
1971	166.4	-1.9	182.5	44.7	188.9	14.8	172.0	-31.3	177.4	8.4
1972	202.4	91.7	192.8	-17.7	201.0	18.1	210.2	19.6	201.6	13.6
1973	220.7	21.5	215.1	-9.8	212.2	-5.3	215.2	5.8	215.8	7.0
1974	205.5	-16.8	214.9	19.6	211.3	-6.5	207.5	-7.0	209.8	-2.8
1975	183.7	-38.6	168.0	-30.0	185.6	49.0	196.1	24.6	183.4	-12.6
1976	210.0	31.5	220.5	21.6	230.3	19.0	238.4	14.8	224.8	22.6
1977	251.3	23.5	253.2	3.1	250.3	-4.5	253.9	5.9	252.2	12.2
1978	271.4	30.6	272.3	1.3	276.0	5.5	279.4	5.0	274.8	9.0
1979	279.3	-0.1	280.7	2.0	275.6	-7.1	282.4	10.2	279.5	1.7
1980	282.8	0.6	261.0	-27.4	239.0	-29.7	252.3	24.2	258.7	-7.4
1981	262.6	17.4	263.4	1.2	260.9	-3.7	269.3	13.5	264.0	2.0
1982	259.4	-13.9	251.9	-11.1	266.1	24.5	252.1	-19.4	257.4	-2.5
1983	259.6	12.4	281.7	38.7	305.6	38.5	322.7	24.3	292.4	13.6
1984	346.3	32.6	360.6	17.6	368.0	8.5	377.5	10.7	363.1	24.2
1985	366.0	-11.6	387.6	25.8	386.9	-0.7	403.3	18.1	385.9	6.3
1986	400.5	-2.7	426.3	28.4	436.3	9.7	438.9	2.4	425.5	10.3
1987	431.4	-6.7	440.8	9.0	450.2	8.8	458.6	7.7	445.2	4.6
1988	457.1	-1.3	452.9	-3.6	463.7	9.9	479.0	13.9	463.2	4.0
1989	471.7	-6.0	482.4	9.4	485.2	2.3	491.4	5.2	482.7	4.2
1990	494.2	2.3	504.0	8.2	503.2	-0.6	487.9	-11.6	497.3	3.0
1991	472.2	-12.3	490.8	16.7	509.4	16.0	515.9	5.2	497.1	-0.0
1992	521.2	4.2	543.6	18.3	552.8	6.9	561.8	6.7	544.9	9.6
1993	578.7	12.6	597.8	13.9	603.1	3.6	628.3	17.8	602.0	10.5
1994	641.4	8.6	674.6	22.4	700.0	15.9	720.4	12.2	684.1	13.6
1995	733.5	7.5	751.4	10.1	753.6	1.2	758.2	2.5	749.2	9.5
1996	781.4	12.8	811.7	16.4	841.7	15.6	857.5	7.7	823.1	9.9
1997	891.3	16.7	938.4	22.9	972.7	15.4	973.9	0.5	944.1	14.7

Source: "National Income and Product Account Tables: Selected NIPA Tables," *Survey of Current Business*, November 1997, U.S. Department of Commerce, Bureau of Economic Analysis, National Income and Wealth Division. Data for 1997 quarters downloaded from www.stat.usa.gov. A dash (-) indicates that no data are available.

Gross Domestic Product
Net exports of goods and services
Imports - Services - Actual Dollars

In billions of actual dollars and percent. Quarterly data are seasonally adjusted and annualized. Growth rates for quarters are compound annual growth rates; changes from year to year are percentage changes.

Year	1st Quarter	% Change	2nd Quarter	% Change	3rd Quarter	% Change	4th Quarter	% Change	TOTAL	% Change
1959	6.9	-	7.0	5.9	7.1	5.8	7.1	-	7.0	-
1960	7.6	31.3	7.6	-	7.8	10.9	7.5	-14.5	7.6	8.6
1961	7.6	5.4	7.6	-	7.6	-	7.7	5.4	7.6	-
1962	7.9	10.8	8.0	5.2	8.0	-	8.5	27.4	8.1	6.6
1963	8.3	-9.1	8.3	-	8.6	15.3	8.5	-4.6	8.4	3.7
1964	8.6	4.8	8.6	-	8.7	4.7	8.9	9.5	8.7	3.6
1965	8.9	-	9.2	14.2	9.2	-	9.8	28.8	9.3	6.9
1966	10.1	12.8	10.6	21.3	11.0	16.0	11.1	3.7	10.7	15.1
1967	11.7	23.4	12.2	18.2	12.5	10.2	12.1	-12.2	12.2	14.0
1968	12.3	6.8	12.3	-	12.8	17.3	13.1	9.7	12.6	3.3
1969	13.0	-3.0	13.6	19.8	13.8	6.0	14.3	15.3	13.7	8.7
1970	14.2	-2.8	15.1	27.9	15.3	5.4	15.1	-5.1	14.9	8.8
1971	15.3	5.4	15.9	16.6	15.8	-2.5	16.2	10.5	15.8	6.0
1972	17.1	24.1	17.3	4.8	16.8	-11.1	17.9	28.9	17.3	9.5
1973	18.9	24.3	19.4	11.0	19.0	-8.0	19.9	20.3	19.3	11.6
1974	21.5	36.3	23.0	31.0	23.0	-	24.3	24.6	22.9	18.7
1975	24.0	-4.8	23.0	-15.7	23.3	5.3	24.7	26.3	23.7	3.5
1976	25.4	11.8	25.8	6.4	26.9	18.2	27.9	15.7	26.5	11.8
1977	28.8	13.5	29.9	16.2	29.7	-2.6	30.8	15.7	29.8	12.5
1978	32.9	30.2	33.7	10.1	35.7	25.9	37.1	16.6	34.8	16.8
1979	37.6	5.5	39.0	15.7	40.5	16.3	42.4	20.1	39.9	14.7
1980	44.7	23.5	44.1	-5.3	45.1	9.4	47.2	20.0	45.3	13.5
1981	49.5	21.0	50.2	5.8	49.4	-6.2	50.6	10.1	49.9	10.2
1982	51.9	10.7	53.3	11.2	52.1	-8.7	53.4	10.4	52.6	5.4
1983	52.7	-5.1	55.2	20.4	57.5	17.7	58.4	6.4	56.0	6.5
1984	65.5	58.2	68.6	20.3	69.7	6.6	71.3	9.5	68.8	22.9
1985	71.9	3.4	74.1	12.8	73.6	-2.7	76.0	13.7	73.9	7.4
1986	81.4	31.6	78.3	-14.4	83.8	31.2	85.3	7.4	82.2	11.2
1987	87.3	9.7	92.5	26.0	93.6	4.8	99.0	25.2	93.1	13.3
1988	100.5	6.2	99.7	-3.1	100.8	4.5	103.3	10.3	101.1	8.6
1989	103.3	-	103.8	2.0	105.9	8.3	108.1	8.6	105.3	4.2
1990	115.5	30.3	117.8	8.2	122.7	17.7	126.4	12.6	120.6	14.5
1991	122.1	-12.9	121.6	-1.6	119.9	-5.5	122.7	9.7	121.6	0.8
1992	124.5	6.0	123.8	-2.2	120.6	-9.9	127.4	24.5	124.1	2.1
1993	122.9	-13.4	125.4	8.4	126.1	2.3	131.6	18.6	126.5	1.9
1994	132.8	3.7	134.1	4.0	136.9	8.6	137.5	1.8	135.3	7.0
1995	143.5	18.6	146.1	7.4	149.1	8.5	149.0	-0.3	146.9	8.6
1996	154.8	16.5	155.8	2.6	157.5	4.4	158.6	2.8	156.7	6.7
1997	165.2	17.7	168.9	9.3	171.6	6.5	174.8	7.7	170.1	8.6

Source: "National Income and Product Account Tables: Selected NIPA Tables," *Survey of Current Business*, November 1997, U.S. Department of Commerce, Bureau of Economic Analysis, National Income and Wealth Division. Data for 1997 quarters downloaded from www.stat.usa.gov. A dash (-) indicates that no data are available.

Gross Domestic Product
Net exports of goods and services
Imports - Services - Chained (1992) Dollars

In billions of chained (1992) dollars and percent. Quarterly data are seasonally adjusted and annualized. Growth rates for quarters are compound annual growth rates; changes from year to year are percentage changes.

Year	1st Quarter	% Change	2nd Quarter	% Change	3rd Quarter	% Change	4th Quarter	% Change	TOTAL	% Change
1959	34.6	-	34.9	3.5	35.1	2.3	35.1	-	34.9	-
1960	37.8	34.5	37.7	-1.1	38.5	8.8	36.7	-17.4	37.7	8.0
1961	36.9	2.2	37.0	1.1	36.7	-3.2	37.5	9.0	37.0	-1.9
1962	38.3	8.8	38.3	-	38.4	1.0	40.0	17.7	38.8	4.9
1963	38.2	-16.8	38.3	1.1	39.2	9.7	39.0	-2.0	38.7	-0.3
1964	39.6	6.3	39.5	-1.0	39.6	1.0	40.1	5.1	39.7	2.6
1965	39.6	-4.9	40.8	12.7	40.5	-2.9	42.5	21.3	40.9	3.0
1966	43.5	9.7	45.6	20.8	47.3	15.8	47.7	3.4	46.0	12.5
1967	49.9	19.8	52.0	17.9	53.3	10.4	51.4	-13.5	51.7	12.4
1968	51.8	3.1	51.4	-3.1	53.2	14.8	54.0	6.2	52.6	1.7
1969	53.9	-0.7	55.7	14.0	56.2	3.6	57.9	12.7	55.9	6.3
1970	57.0	-6.1	59.9	22.0	59.8	-0.7	58.8	-6.5	58.8	5.2
1971	57.0	-11.7	58.0	7.2	57.0	-6.7	56.7	-2.1	57.2	-2.7
1972	60.2	27.1	60.0	-1.3	57.0	-18.5	59.3	17.1	59.1	3.3
1973	60.8	10.5	58.7	-13.1	53.8	-29.4	53.6	-1.5	56.7	-4.1
1974	55.1	11.7	56.1	7.5	54.5	-10.9	55.9	10.7	55.4	-2.3
1975	54.3	-11.0	51.3	-20.3	51.2	-0.8	53.4	18.3	52.5	-5.2
1976	55.0	12.5	55.5	3.7	56.7	8.9	57.7	7.2	56.2	7.0
1977	58.3	4.2	59.1	5.6	57.6	-9.8	58.4	5.7	58.4	3.9
1978	61.6	23.8	61.4	-1.3	62.9	10.1	64.0	7.2	62.5	7.0
1979	63.9	-0.6	63.6	-1.9	63.1	-3.1	62.9	-1.3	63.4	1.4
1980	63.4	3.2	60.6	-16.5	60.4	-1.3	63.0	18.4	61.8	-2.5
1981	65.8	19.0	65.9	0.6	64.7	-7.1	65.1	2.5	65.4	5.8
1982	66.4	8.2	69.3	18.6	68.9	-2.3	70.8	11.5	68.9	5.4
1983	70.0	-4.4	73.2	19.6	76.6	19.9	77.8	6.4	74.4	8.0
1984	86.7	54.2	90.7	19.8	94.9	19.8	99.3	19.9	92.9	24.9
1985	101.3	8.3	101.9	2.4	98.0	-14.5	97.8	-0.8	99.7	7.3
1986	100.7	12.4	95.9	-17.7	101.1	23.5	103.0	7.7	100.2	0.5
1987	107.4	18.2	113.1	23.0	113.1	-	118.8	21.7	113.1	12.9
1988	118.0	-2.7	115.6	-7.9	116.3	2.4	118.6	8.1	117.1	3.5
1989	119.1	1.7	119.3	0.7	120.6	4.4	122.0	4.7	120.2	2.6
1990	128.5	23.1	129.8	4.1	130.2	1.2	129.0	-3.6	129.4	7.7
1991	124.8	-12.4	126.8	6.6	124.1	-8.2	125.6	4.9	125.3	-3.2
1992	126.7	3.5	124.7	-6.2	117.7	-20.6	127.4	37.3	124.1	-1.0
1993	123.3	-12.3	124.9	5.3	126.3	4.6	131.4	17.2	126.5	1.9
1994	132.3	2.8	133.6	4.0	133.5	-0.3	133.2	-0.9	133.2	5.3
1995	140.7	24.5	139.3	-3.9	142.1	8.3	142.9	2.3	141.2	6.0
1996	147.8	14.4	148.8	2.7	149.3	1.4	150.0	1.9	149.0	5.5
1997	158.4	24.4	161.8	8.9	165.8	10.3	168.1	5.7	163.5	9.7

Source: "National Income and Product Account Tables: Selected NIPA Tables," *Survey of Current Business*, November 1997, U.S. Department of Commerce, Bureau of Economic Analysis, National Income and Wealth Division. Data for 1997 quarters downloaded from www.stat.usa.gov. A dash (-) indicates that no data are available.

GOVERNMENT CONSUMPTION EXPENDITURES AND GROSS INVESTMENT
Component of Gross Domestic Product

Government—federal, state, and local—represented nearly 18.2 percent of real GDP in 1996, down from 20.1 percent in 1992. The category includes purchases of durable and nondurable goods, expenditures on structures (such as highways and bridges), purchases of services, and compensation of government employees. This category *excludes* transfer payments such as entitlements, transactions in land, grants-in-aid, and financial transactions. The effect of these excluded budgetary items are accounted for in purchases made by those who receive the money. In constant dollars, state and local purchases account for well over half of the total (63.1 percent and growing), the federal government for the rest.

The category is divided as follows:

> *Federal*
> > National defense
> > Nondefense
>
> *State and local*

Estimates are prepared by BEA under four categories: (1) federal expenditures, derived from the *Budget of the United States* and other sources, with categories such as transfer payments removed; (2) state and local compensation, (3) state and local expenditures for structures, and (4) state and local purchases other than compensation and structures. Each category is governed by its own estimating procedures and analytical methodologies.

Presentation of Data

Data are shown from 1959 to 1997 in quarterly and in annual increments. Changes from one period to the next are shown for each category covered. Changes from quarter to quarter are annualized, compounded growth rates as explained in the section on Gross National Product. Changes from year to year are simple percentile changes.

Analytical Uses

The total category best depicts the importance of government as a customer and employer—in that it includes what governmental bodies purchase and what they pay. It is not a good measure of total governmental activity because it excludes money the government collects for redistribution in transfer payments. Government activity has shown sharp rise during periods of war.

Gross Domestic Product

Government consumption expenditures and gross investment: Total - Actual Dollars

In billions of actual dollars and percent. Quarterly data are seasonally adjusted and annualized. Growth rates for quarters are compound annual growth rates; changes from year to year are percentage changes.

Year	1st Quarter	% Change	2nd Quarter	% Change	3rd Quarter	% Change	4th Quarter	% Change	TOTAL	% Change
1959	110.9	-	112.6	6.3	112.6	-	111.9	-2.5	112.0	-
1960	110.0	-6.6	111.8	6.7	114.5	10.0	116.7	7.9	113.2	1.1
1961	117.8	3.8	119.7	6.6	121.0	4.4	124.9	13.5	120.9	6.8
1962	128.4	11.7	130.4	6.4	132.6	6.9	134.3	5.2	131.4	8.7
1963	134.7	1.2	135.9	3.6	139.5	11.0	140.7	3.5	137.7	4.8
1964	142.4	4.9	144.8	6.9	145.1	0.8	145.3	0.6	144.4	4.9
1965	146.2	2.5	149.9	10.5	155.0	14.3	160.9	16.1	153.0	6.0
1966	164.8	10.1	171.1	16.2	176.9	14.3	181.6	11.1	173.6	13.5
1967	190.8	21.9	191.9	2.3	195.6	7.9	200.3	10.0	194.6	12.1
1968	206.6	13.2	210.4	7.6	213.6	6.2	217.7	7.9	212.1	9.0
1969	218.4	1.3	222.0	6.8	226.7	8.7	227.8	2.0	223.8	5.5
1970	231.8	7.2	233.4	2.8	237.9	7.9	241.2	5.7	236.1	5.5
1971	245.1	6.6	248.7	6.0	251.1	3.9	254.6	5.7	249.9	5.8
1972	265.2	17.7	268.6	5.2	267.9	-1.0	274.1	9.6	268.9	7.6
1973	281.8	11.7	286.0	6.1	287.1	1.5	295.6	12.4	287.6	7.0
1974	306.6	15.7	318.2	16.0	328.0	12.9	340.1	15.6	323.2	12.4
1975	352.3	15.1	357.7	6.3	364.9	8.3	375.5	12.1	362.6	12.2
1976	381.7	6.8	383.0	1.4	386.0	3.2	392.8	7.2	385.9	6.4
1977	403.9	11.8	414.6	11.0	420.2	5.5	428.9	8.5	416.9	8.0
1978	435.8	6.6	453.9	17.7	464.4	9.6	477.5	11.8	457.9	9.8
1979	483.3	4.9	499.3	13.9	513.4	11.8	532.3	15.6	507.1	10.7
1980	553.4	16.8	569.5	12.2	574.5	3.6	593.8	14.1	572.8	13.0
1981	616.9	16.5	628.5	7.7	634.4	3.8	653.7	12.7	633.4	10.6
1982	663.4	6.1	676.3	8.0	689.1	7.8	710.3	12.9	684.8	8.1
1983	719.4	5.2	731.5	6.9	750.0	10.5	741.9	-4.3	735.7	7.4
1984	767.4	14.5	791.4	13.1	803.1	6.0	824.5	11.1	796.6	8.3
1985	843.1	9.3	864.8	10.7	890.0	12.2	902.1	5.6	875.0	9.8
1986	909.7	3.4	929.1	8.8	955.7	12.0	959.5	1.6	938.5	7.3
1987	973.2	5.8	987.4	6.0	996.8	3.9	1,013.8	7.0	992.8	5.8
1988	1,015.5	0.7	1,026.2	4.3	1,031.5	2.1	1,054.8	9.3	1,032.0	3.9
1989	1,065.3	4.0	1,088.7	9.1	1,107.0	6.9	1,119.4	4.6	1,095.1	6.1
1990	1,153.0	12.6	1,164.3	4.0	1,176.9	4.4	1,210.4	11.9	1,176.1	7.4
1991	1,220.6	3.4	1,227.4	2.2	1,226.5	-0.3	1,229.2	0.9	1,225.9	4.2
1992	1,247.9	6.2	1,256.4	2.8	1,270.7	4.6	1,280.0	3.0	1,263.8	3.1
1993	1,271.5	-2.6	1,281.2	3.1	1,285.3	1.3	1,295.5	3.2	1,283.4	1.6
1994	1,291.0	-1.4	1,300.8	3.1	1,332.3	10.0	1,328.0	-1.3	1,313.0	2.3
1995	1,344.7	5.1	1,356.0	3.4	1,362.2	1.8	1,359.2	-0.9	1,355.5	3.2
1996	1,384.2	7.6	1,407.0	6.8	1,413.5	1.9	1,422.3	2.5	1,406.7	3.8
1997	1,433.1	3.1	1,449.0	4.5	1,457.9	2.5	1,475.6	4.9	1,453.9	3.4

Source: "National Income and Product Account Tables: Selected NIPA Tables," *Survey of Current Business*, November 1997, U.S. Department of Commerce, Bureau of Economic Analysis, National Income and Wealth Division. Data for 1997 quarters downloaded from www.stat.usa.gov. A dash (-) indicates that no data are available.

Gross Domestic Product

Government consumption expenditures and gross investment: Total - Chained (1992) Dollars

In billions of chained (1992) dollars and percent. Quarterly data are seasonally adjusted and annualized. Growth rates for quarters are compound annual growth rates; changes from year to year are percentage changes.

Year	1st Quarter	% Change	2nd Quarter	% Change	3rd Quarter	% Change	4th Quarter	% Change	TOTAL	% Change
1959	610.2	-	621.1	7.3	624.2	2.0	618.5	-3.6	618.5	-
1960	605.5	-8.1	613.6	5.5	621.6	5.3	627.9	4.1	617.2	-0.2
1961	635.6	5.0	641.2	3.6	648.0	4.3	663.9	10.2	647.2	4.9
1962	674.8	6.7	682.4	4.6	691.4	5.4	695.4	2.3	686.0	6.0
1963	691.1	-2.5	694.5	2.0	713.3	11.3	708.6	-2.6	701.9	2.3
1964	712.5	2.2	721.4	5.1	714.9	-3.6	714.7	-0.1	715.9	2.0
1965	713.8	-0.5	728.4	8.4	746.3	10.2	761.7	8.5	737.6	3.0
1966	776.3	7.9	799.9	12.7	812.5	6.5	829.5	8.6	804.6	9.1
1967	864.3	17.9	860.2	-1.9	865.4	2.4	872.5	3.3	865.6	7.6
1968	887.3	7.0	892.2	2.2	893.6	0.6	896.6	1.3	892.4	3.1
1969	891.6	-2.2	890.8	-0.4	888.7	-0.9	878.8	-4.4	887.5	-0.5
1970	871.8	-3.1	863.2	-3.9	866.7	1.6	865.5	-0.6	866.8	-2.3
1971	856.4	-4.1	852.5	-1.8	848.8	-1.7	846.4	-1.1	851.0	-1.8
1972	858.8	6.0	859.9	0.5	848.4	-5.2	849.2	0.4	854.1	0.4
1973	854.6	2.6	852.3	-1.1	839.1	-6.1	847.7	4.2	848.4	-0.7
1974	857.5	4.7	866.9	4.5	861.8	-2.3	865.6	1.8	862.9	1.7
1975	875.7	4.7	871.6	-1.9	875.7	1.9	882.2	3.0	876.3	1.6
1976	886.1	1.8	876.8	-4.1	872.8	-1.8	871.5	-0.6	876.8	0.1
1977	878.1	3.1	887.6	4.4	887.4	-0.1	885.8	-0.7	884.7	0.9
1978	887.5	0.8	910.9	11.0	917.8	3.1	925.9	3.6	910.6	2.9
1979	916.2	-4.1	924.8	3.8	925.6	0.3	932.9	3.2	924.9	1.6
1980	946.5	6.0	948.3	0.8	936.4	-4.9	934.4	-0.9	941.4	1.8
1981	946.1	5.1	947.7	0.7	945.5	-0.9	951.7	2.6	947.7	0.7
1982	949.0	-1.1	954.7	2.4	961.2	2.8	975.5	6.1	960.1	1.3
1983	978.4	1.2	985.0	2.7	1,001.8	7.0	984.1	-6.9	987.3	2.8
1984	994.1	4.1	1,016.6	9.4	1,022.5	2.3	1,040.4	7.2	1,018.4	3.2
1985	1,053.2	5.0	1,072.8	7.7	1,095.7	8.8	1,098.9	1.2	1,080.1	6.1
1986	1,108.3	3.5	1,129.6	7.9	1,154.5	9.1	1,147.7	-2.3	1,135.0	5.1
1987	1,153.4	2.0	1,162.8	3.3	1,165.9	1.1	1,181.5	5.5	1,165.9	2.7
1988	1,172.5	-3.0	1,177.0	1.5	1,176.1	-0.3	1,198.1	7.7	1,180.9	1.3
1989	1,193.5	-1.5	1,211.1	6.0	1,222.6	3.9	1,228.4	1.9	1,213.9	2.8
1990	1,246.5	6.0	1,248.2	0.5	1,246.8	-0.4	1,259.9	4.3	1,250.4	3.0
1991	1,262.6	0.9	1,263.8	0.4	1,255.1	-2.7	1,250.7	-1.4	1,258.0	0.6
1992	1,258.5	2.5	1,257.5	-0.3	1,266.5	2.9	1,272.5	1.9	1,263.8	0.5
1993	1,250.1	-6.9	1,253.1	1.0	1,250.5	-0.8	1,254.7	1.4	1,252.1	-0.9
1994	1,241.9	-4.0	1,243.3	0.5	1,268.1	8.2	1,255.8	-3.8	1,252.3	0.0
1995	1,257.7	0.6	1,257.3	-0.1	1,255.0	-0.7	1,237.7	-5.4	1,251.9	-0.0
1996	1,243.2	1.8	1,265.1	7.2	1,261.5	-1.1	1,261.8	0.1	1,257.9	0.5
1997	1,260.5	-0.4	1,270.1	3.1	1,273.4	1.0	1,278.5	1.6	1,270.6	1.0

Source: "National Income and Product Account Tables: Selected NIPA Tables," *Survey of Current Business*, November 1997, U.S. Department of Commerce, Bureau of Economic Analysis, National Income and Wealth Division. Data for 1997 quarters downloaded from www.stat.usa.gov. A dash (-) indicates that no data are available.

Gross Domestic Product
Government consumption expenditures and gross investment
Federal: Total - Actual Dollars

In billions of actual dollars and percent. Quarterly data are seasonally adjusted and annualized. Growth rates for quarters are compound annual growth rates; changes from year to year are percentage changes.

Year	1st Quarter	% Change	2nd Quarter	% Change	3rd Quarter	% Change	4th Quarter	% Change	TOTAL	% Change
1959	66.2	-	67.8	10.0	67.7	-0.6	67.1	-3.5	67.2	-
1960	64.0	-17.2	64.5	3.2	66.2	11.0	67.7	9.4	65.6	-2.4
1961	67.1	-3.5	68.7	9.9	69.3	3.5	71.3	12.1	69.1	5.3
1962	74.5	19.2	75.9	7.7	77.3	7.6	78.1	4.2	76.5	10.7
1963	76.9	-6.0	77.3	2.1	79.1	9.6	79.0	-0.5	78.1	2.1
1964	79.4	2.0	80.1	3.6	79.4	-3.5	78.6	-4.0	79.4	1.7
1965	78.3	-1.5	79.9	8.4	82.4	13.1	86.5	21.4	81.8	3.0
1966	88.5	9.6	92.9	21.4	96.7	17.4	98.4	7.2	94.1	15.0
1967	105.1	30.1	105.0	-0.4	107.0	7.8	109.1	8.1	106.6	13.3
1968	112.4	12.7	113.1	2.5	114.2	3.9	115.5	4.6	113.8	6.8
1969	114.1	-4.8	114.8	2.5	117.6	10.1	116.7	-3.0	115.8	1.8
1970	117.1	1.4	115.5	-5.4	115.3	-0.7	115.7	1.4	115.9	0.1
1971	116.2	1.7	116.8	2.1	117.3	1.7	117.8	1.7	117.1	1.0
1972	125.2	27.6	127.3	6.9	123.1	-12.6	124.7	5.3	125.1	6.8
1973	128.3	12.1	129.1	2.5	126.0	-9.3	129.6	11.9	128.2	2.5
1974	133.7	13.3	137.2	10.9	140.9	11.2	147.8	21.1	139.9	9.1
1975	150.5	7.5	153.0	6.8	154.7	4.5	159.7	13.6	154.5	10.4
1976	159.3	-1.0	160.8	3.8	163.1	5.8	167.7	11.8	162.7	5.3
1977	172.7	12.5	177.8	12.3	179.5	3.9	183.7	9.7	178.4	9.6
1978	186.3	5.8	192.5	14.0	196.1	7.7	202.9	14.6	194.4	9.0
1979	206.5	7.3	212.0	11.1	216.0	7.8	225.6	19.0	215.0	10.6
1980	236.3	20.4	247.8	20.9	248.5	1.1	261.1	21.9	248.4	15.5
1981	271.3	16.6	282.8	18.1	285.4	3.7	296.9	17.1	284.1	14.4
1982	301.5	6.3	307.6	8.3	314.8	9.7	328.9	19.2	313.2	10.2
1983	334.5	7.0	343.8	11.6	355.5	14.3	344.0	-12.3	344.5	10.0
1984	358.1	17.4	372.6	17.2	373.3	0.8	386.3	14.7	372.6	8.2
1985	395.2	9.5	404.4	9.6	418.6	14.8	422.2	3.5	410.1	10.1
1986	418.6	-3.4	431.1	12.5	448.4	17.0	442.8	-4.9	435.2	6.1
1987	447.9	4.7	454.9	6.4	456.5	1.4	463.4	6.2	455.7	4.7
1988	456.3	-6.0	454.6	-1.5	453.5	-1.0	465.0	10.5	457.3	0.4
1989	465.5	0.4	476.5	9.8	484.9	7.2	482.0	-2.4	477.2	4.4
1990	496.4	12.5	500.1	3.0	501.2	0.9	516.7	13.0	503.6	5.5
1991	525.6	7.1	528.2	2.0	520.9	-5.4	515.5	-4.1	522.6	3.8
1992	521.8	5.0	523.2	1.1	532.0	6.9	535.0	2.3	528.0	1.0
1993	521.3	-9.9	517.8	-2.7	515.7	-1.6	518.5	2.2	518.3	-1.8
1994	506.9	-8.7	505.3	-1.3	520.4	12.5	508.3	-9.0	510.2	-1.6
1995	513.6	4.2	511.2	-1.9	512.9	1.3	500.6	-9.3	509.6	-0.1
1996	516.4	13.2	524.6	6.5	521.6	-2.3	517.6	-3.0	520.0	2.0
1997	516.1	-1.2	526.1	8.0	525.7	-0.3	531.1	4.2	524.7	0.9

Source: "National Income and Product Account Tables: Selected NIPA Tables," *Survey of Current Business*, November 1997, U.S. Department of Commerce, Bureau of Economic Analysis, National Income and Wealth Division. Data for 1997 quarters downloaded from www.stat.usa.gov. A dash (-) indicates that no data are available.

Gross Domestic Product
Government consumption expenditures and gross investment
Federal: Total - Chained (1992) Dollars

In billions of chained (1992) dollars and percent. Quarterly data are seasonally adjusted and annualized. Growth rates for quarters are compound annual growth rates; changes from year to year are percentage changes.

Year	1st Quarter	% Change	2nd Quarter	% Change	3rd Quarter	% Change	4th Quarter	% Change	TOTAL	% Change
1959	352.4	-	362.8	12.3	365.6	3.1	361.4	-4.5	360.5	-
1960	345.0	-17.0	347.1	2.5	351.1	4.7	354.5	3.9	349.4	-3.1
1961	353.6	-1.0	360.6	8.2	364.9	4.9	373.0	9.2	363.0	3.9
1962	386.2	14.9	391.7	5.8	397.0	5.5	398.0	1.0	393.2	8.3
1963	388.3	-9.4	388.8	0.5	399.5	11.5	390.5	-8.7	391.8	-0.4
1964	389.5	-1.0	391.6	2.2	381.7	-9.7	377.9	-3.9	385.2	-1.7
1965	374.2	-3.9	380.2	6.6	388.2	8.7	398.3	10.8	385.2	-
1966	407.7	9.8	428.1	21.6	436.6	8.2	444.2	7.1	429.1	11.4
1967	474.4	30.1	468.3	-5.0	471.8	3.0	472.3	0.4	471.7	9.9
1968	480.5	7.1	477.7	-2.3	473.6	-3.4	473.5	-0.1	476.3	1.0
1969	466.3	-5.9	462.5	-3.2	459.8	-2.3	451.0	-7.4	459.9	-3.4
1970	439.7	-9.7	428.5	-9.8	422.0	-5.9	418.3	-3.5	427.2	-7.1
1971	406.6	-10.7	399.7	-6.6	394.8	-4.8	386.8	-7.9	397.0	-7.1
1972	397.0	11.0	399.7	2.7	384.7	-14.2	379.3	-5.5	390.2	-1.7
1973	381.8	2.7	378.6	-3.3	360.6	-17.7	363.6	3.4	371.1	-4.9
1974	367.6	4.5	370.7	3.4	366.6	-4.4	370.4	4.2	368.8	-0.6
1975	368.5	-2.0	368.2	-0.3	366.9	-1.4	368.1	1.3	367.9	-0.2
1976	365.2	-3.1	364.4	-0.9	363.6	-0.9	363.8	0.2	364.3	-1.0
1977	366.0	2.4	372.3	7.1	372.2	-0.1	369.8	-2.6	370.1	1.6
1978	370.7	1.0	378.6	8.8	379.3	0.7	382.2	3.1	377.7	2.1
1979	381.3	-0.9	384.8	3.7	383.1	-1.8	384.0	0.9	383.3	1.5
1980	395.1	12.1	403.7	9.0	399.3	-4.3	399.2	-0.1	399.3	4.2
1981	406.7	7.7	418.4	12.0	418.1	-0.3	420.5	2.3	415.9	4.2
1982	420.2	-0.3	424.3	4.0	431.0	6.5	442.1	10.7	429.4	3.2
1983	444.6	2.3	452.5	7.3	465.1	11.6	448.4	-13.6	452.7	5.4
1984	450.8	2.2	465.9	14.1	463.1	-2.4	475.1	10.8	463.7	2.4
1985	482.3	6.2	491.5	7.9	505.2	11.6	503.4	-1.4	495.6	6.9
1986	500.1	-2.6	514.8	12.3	533.9	15.7	524.8	-6.6	518.4	4.6
1987	526.9	1.6	534.3	5.7	534.2	-0.1	542.2	6.1	534.4	3.1
1988	527.6	-10.3	522.2	-4.0	517.9	-3.3	530.6	10.2	524.6	-1.8
1989	521.4	-6.8	532.0	8.4	537.7	4.4	535.0	-2.0	531.5	1.3
1990	542.9	6.0	543.0	0.1	538.2	-3.5	543.5	4.0	541.9	2.0
1991	547.3	2.8	547.1	-0.1	536.3	-7.7	526.9	-6.8	539.4	-0.5
1992	525.1	-1.4	523.3	-1.4	529.6	4.9	534.0	3.4	528.0	-2.1
1993	512.1	-15.4	507.8	-3.3	501.5	-4.9	501.3	-0.2	505.7	-4.2
1994	487.2	-10.8	481.2	-4.8	496.4	13.2	481.7	-11.3	486.6	-3.8
1995	480.4	-1.1	474.9	-4.5	473.4	-1.3	452.6	-16.5	470.3	-3.3
1996	460.9	7.5	470.7	8.8	465.7	-4.2	459.6	-5.1	464.2	-1.3
1997	452.8	-5.8	460.1	6.6	458.8	-1.1	459.5	0.6	457.8	-1.4

Source: "National Income and Product Account Tables: Selected NIPA Tables," *Survey of Current Business*, November 1997, U.S. Department of Commerce, Bureau of Economic Analysis, National Income and Wealth Division. Data for 1997 quarters downloaded from www.stat.usa.gov. A dash (-) indicates that no data are available.

Gross Domestic Product

Government consumption expenditures and gross investment
Federal - National defense - Actual Dollars

In billions of actual dollars and percent. Quarterly data are seasonally adjusted and annualized. Growth rates for quarters are compound annual growth rates; changes from year to year are percentage changes.

Year	1st Quarter	% Change	2nd Quarter	% Change	3rd Quarter	% Change	4th Quarter	% Change	TOTAL	% Change
1959	56.1	-	55.6	-3.5	55.7	0.7	55.4	-2.1	55.7	-
1960	54.2	-8.4	54.2	-	55.2	7.6	55.8	4.4	54.9	-1.4
1961	56.6	5.9	57.3	5.0	57.6	2.1	59.3	12.3	57.7	5.1
1962	61.9	18.7	62.3	2.6	62.4	0.6	62.5	0.6	62.3	8.0
1963	62.0	-3.2	62.3	1.9	62.2	-0.6	62.4	1.3	62.2	-0.2
1964	62.0	-2.5	61.8	-1.3	61.2	-3.8	60.3	-5.8	61.3	-1.4
1965	59.5	-5.2	60.8	9.0	62.0	8.1	65.9	27.6	62.0	1.1
1966	68.0	13.4	71.4	21.6	75.9	27.7	78.5	14.4	73.4	18.4
1967	83.1	25.6	84.3	5.9	86.7	11.9	87.9	5.7	85.5	16.5
1968	90.9	14.4	92.1	5.4	92.0	-0.4	92.8	3.5	92.0	7.6
1969	91.1	-7.1	91.5	1.8	93.4	8.6	93.4	-	92.4	0.4
1970	92.6	-3.4	89.9	-11.2	89.9	-	90.1	0.9	90.6	-1.9
1971	90.1	-	88.5	-6.9	87.4	-4.9	88.8	6.6	88.7	-2.1
1972	94.0	25.6	95.3	5.6	91.2	-16.1	92.4	5.4	93.2	5.1
1973	94.9	11.3	95.8	3.8	92.4	-13.5	95.7	15.1	94.7	1.6
1974	97.7	8.6	102.0	18.8	101.9	-0.4	106.1	17.5	101.9	7.6
1975	108.6	9.8	109.9	4.9	111.0	4.1	114.2	12.0	110.9	8.8
1976	113.5	-2.4	115.0	5.4	116.8	6.4	119.2	8.5	116.1	4.7
1977	122.8	12.6	126.1	11.2	126.5	1.3	127.7	3.8	125.8	8.4
1978	130.2	8.1	134.4	13.5	136.9	7.7	140.9	12.2	135.6	7.8
1979	144.2	9.7	149.1	14.3	151.9	7.7	159.7	22.2	151.2	11.5
1980	166.7	18.7	171.4	11.8	174.2	6.7	184.6	26.1	174.2	15.2
1981	191.2	15.1	199.7	19.0	203.6	8.0	213.3	20.5	202.0	16.0
1982	219.0	11.1	227.8	17.1	233.7	10.8	243.3	17.5	230.9	14.3
1983	245.8	4.2	253.3	12.8	256.6	5.3	264.5	12.9	255.0	10.4
1984	275.5	17.7	280.8	7.9	281.1	0.4	293.4	18.7	282.7	10.9
1985	298.8	7.6	306.5	10.7	320.0	18.8	324.4	5.6	312.4	10.5
1986	320.2	-5.1	330.6	13.6	343.7	16.8	335.0	-9.7	332.4	6.4
1987	341.7	8.2	349.9	10.0	355.5	6.6	354.4	-1.2	350.4	5.4
1988	354.6	0.2	353.2	-1.6	351.5	-1.9	356.7	6.1	354.0	1.0
1989	352.8	-4.3	360.6	9.1	367.6	8.0	361.3	-6.7	360.6	1.9
1990	369.7	9.6	370.6	1.0	368.9	-1.8	383.3	16.6	373.1	3.5
1991	389.7	6.8	389.3	-0.4	382.1	-7.2	373.0	-9.2	383.5	2.8
1992	372.8	-0.2	374.1	1.4	380.9	7.5	375.3	-5.8	375.8	-2.0
1993	363.6	-11.9	361.7	-2.1	358.0	-4.0	359.4	1.6	360.7	-4.0
1994	344.9	-15.2	348.5	4.2	359.7	13.5	343.6	-16.7	349.2	-3.2
1995	346.3	3.2	348.1	2.1	347.3	-0.9	336.5	-11.9	344.6	-1.3
1996	348.4	14.9	357.3	10.6	354.8	-2.8	350.6	-4.7	352.8	2.4
1997	343.3	-8.1	350.6	8.8	352.1	1.7	357.1	5.8	350.8	-0.6

Source: "National Income and Product Account Tables: Selected NIPA Tables," *Survey of Current Business*, November 1997, U.S. Department of Commerce, Bureau of Economic Analysis, National Income and Wealth Division. Data for 1997 quarters downloaded from www.stat.usa.gov. A dash (-) indicates that no data are available.

Gross Domestic Product
Government consumption expenditures and gross investment
Federal - National defense - Chained (1992) Dollars

In billions of chained (1992) dollars and percent. Quarterly data are seasonally adjusted and annualized. Growth rates for quarters are compound annual growth rates; changes from year to year are percentage changes.

Year	1st Quarter	% Change	2nd Quarter	% Change	3rd Quarter	% Change	4th Quarter	% Change	TOTAL	% Change
1959	307.4	-	306.1	-1.7	309.8	4.9	306.9	-3.7	307.6	-
1960	300.8	-7.7	300.1	-0.9	302.6	3.4	301.6	-1.3	301.3	-2.0
1961	308.8	9.9	311.1	3.0	314.1	3.9	321.3	9.5	313.8	4.1
1962	332.5	14.7	333.5	1.2	332.0	-1.8	331.5	-0.6	332.4	5.9
1963	324.5	-8.2	325.4	1.1	326.5	1.4	319.6	-8.2	324.0	-2.5
1964	316.0	-4.4	314.6	-1.8	306.9	-9.4	302.2	-6.0	309.9	-4.4
1965	296.3	-7.6	300.7	6.1	303.7	4.1	314.4	14.9	303.8	-2.0
1966	326.0	15.6	342.8	22.3	355.4	15.5	368.5	15.6	348.2	14.6
1967	390.6	26.2	391.5	0.9	397.3	6.1	394.5	-2.8	393.5	13.0
1968	404.6	10.6	405.0	0.4	397.6	-7.1	396.4	-1.2	400.9	1.9
1969	387.9	-8.3	383.3	-4.7	380.0	-3.4	375.4	-4.8	381.6	-4.8
1970	363.1	-12.5	349.1	-14.6	343.9	-5.8	339.9	-4.6	349.0	-8.5
1971	328.5	-12.8	316.1	-14.3	307.2	-10.8	303.2	-5.1	313.7	-10.1
1972	307.5	5.8	309.1	2.1	294.7	-17.4	289.9	-6.4	300.3	-4.3
1973	291.3	1.9	288.8	-3.4	270.0	-23.6	274.5	6.8	281.2	-6.4
1974	273.9	-0.9	280.5	10.0	269.3	-15.0	270.5	1.8	273.5	-2.7
1975	271.2	1.0	270.1	-1.6	268.9	-1.8	268.7	-0.3	269.7	-1.4
1976	265.2	-5.1	265.2	-	265.0	-0.3	263.2	-2.7	264.7	-1.9
1977	265.5	3.5	269.9	6.8	268.1	-2.6	262.1	-8.7	266.4	0.6
1978	263.0	1.4	267.9	7.7	267.7	-0.3	268.5	1.2	266.7	0.1
1979	267.9	-0.9	272.1	6.4	271.0	-1.6	273.1	3.1	271.0	1.6
1980	279.8	10.2	279.2	-0.9	280.9	2.5	283.1	3.2	280.7	3.6
1981	287.3	6.1	295.9	12.5	298.6	3.7	302.2	4.9	296.0	5.5
1982	304.9	3.6	313.7	12.1	320.0	8.3	327.5	9.7	316.5	6.9
1983	326.8	-0.9	333.2	8.1	335.4	2.7	343.1	9.5	334.6	5.7
1984	342.8	-0.3	347.3	5.4	345.3	-2.3	356.9	14.1	348.1	4.0
1985	361.9	5.7	369.9	9.1	382.2	14.0	382.4	0.2	374.1	7.5
1986	379.0	-3.5	392.1	14.6	407.2	16.3	395.2	-11.3	393.4	5.2
1987	399.7	4.6	408.9	9.5	414.7	5.8	413.3	-1.3	409.2	4.0
1988	409.3	-3.8	405.6	-3.6	401.1	-4.4	406.1	5.1	405.5	-0.9
1989	394.4	-11.0	402.4	8.4	407.4	5.1	402.1	-5.1	401.6	-1.0
1990	404.1	2.0	402.8	-1.3	396.1	-6.5	403.1	7.3	401.5	-0.0
1991	408.4	5.4	405.0	-3.3	395.0	-9.5	381.7	-12.8	397.5	-1.0
1992	374.2	-7.6	373.3	-1.0	378.7	5.9	376.8	-2.0	375.8	-5.5
1993	359.2	-17.4	356.7	-2.8	351.1	-6.1	350.8	-0.3	354.4	-5.7
1994	335.1	-16.7	335.9	1.0	347.0	13.9	329.6	-18.6	336.9	-4.9
1995	328.7	-1.1	327.4	-1.6	324.0	-4.1	310.3	-15.9	322.6	-4.2
1996	314.9	6.1	323.2	11.0	319.4	-4.6	313.6	-7.1	317.8	-1.5
1997	303.9	-11.8	309.4	7.4	310.3	1.2	312.6	3.0	309.0	-2.8

Source: "National Income and Product Account Tables: Selected NIPA Tables," *Survey of Current Business*, November 1997, U.S. Department of Commerce, Bureau of Economic Analysis, National Income and Wealth Division. Data for 1997 quarters downloaded from www.stat.usa.gov. A dash (-) indicates that no data are available.

Gross Domestic Product
Government consumption expenditures and gross investment
Federal - Nondefense - Actual Dollars

In billions of actual dollars and percent. Quarterly data are seasonally adjusted and annualized. Growth rates for quarters are compound annual growth rates; changes from year to year are percentage changes.

Year	1st Quarter	% Change	2nd Quarter	% Change	3rd Quarter	% Change	4th Quarter	% Change	TOTAL	% Change
1959	10.1	-	12.2	112.9	12.0	-6.4	11.8	-6.5	11.5	-
1960	9.8	-52.4	10.3	22.0	11.0	30.1	11.9	37.0	10.8	-6.1
1961	10.5	-39.4	11.4	39.0	11.7	10.9	12.0	10.7	11.4	5.6
1962	12.6	21.6	13.6	35.7	14.9	44.1	15.5	17.1	14.2	24.6
1963	15.0	-12.3	14.9	-2.6	16.9	65.5	16.6	-6.9	15.9	12.0
1964	17.4	20.7	18.4	25.0	18.2	-4.3	18.4	4.5	18.1	13.8
1965	18.7	6.7	19.1	8.8	20.4	30.1	20.6	4.0	19.7	8.8
1966	20.5	-1.9	21.5	21.0	20.8	-12.4	19.9	-16.2	20.7	5.1
1967	22.0	49.4	20.6	-23.1	20.3	-5.7	21.2	18.9	21.0	1.4
1968	21.5	5.8	20.9	-10.7	22.2	27.3	22.6	7.4	21.8	3.8
1969	22.9	5.4	23.3	7.2	24.2	16.4	23.3	-14.1	23.4	7.3
1970	24.5	22.2	25.6	19.2	25.4	-3.1	25.6	3.2	25.3	8.1
1971	26.1	8.0	28.3	38.2	29.9	24.6	29.0	-11.5	28.3	11.9
1972	31.2	34.0	32.0	10.7	32.0	-	32.3	3.8	31.9	12.7
1973	33.3	13.0	33.3	-	33.6	3.7	33.8	2.4	33.5	5.0
1974	36.0	28.7	35.3	-7.6	39.0	49.0	41.7	30.7	38.0	13.4
1975	41.9	1.9	43.1	12.0	43.7	5.7	45.5	17.5	43.6	14.7
1976	45.8	2.7	45.9	0.9	46.3	3.5	48.6	21.4	46.6	6.9
1977	49.9	11.1	51.6	14.3	52.9	10.5	56.0	25.6	52.6	12.9
1978	56.1	0.7	58.2	15.8	59.2	7.1	62.0	20.3	58.9	12.0
1979	62.3	1.9	62.9	3.9	64.0	7.2	65.9	12.4	63.8	8.3
1980	69.6	24.4	76.4	45.2	74.3	-10.5	76.5	12.4	74.2	16.3
1981	80.1	20.2	83.2	16.4	81.8	-6.6	83.6	9.1	82.2	10.8
1982	82.5	-5.2	79.9	-12.0	81.1	6.1	85.6	24.1	82.3	0.1
1983	88.7	15.3	90.4	7.9	98.9	43.3	79.6	-58.0	89.4	8.6
1984	82.6	15.9	91.8	52.6	92.2	1.8	93.0	3.5	89.9	0.6
1985	96.4	15.4	97.9	6.4	98.6	2.9	97.8	-3.2	97.7	8.7
1986	98.5	2.9	100.5	8.4	104.7	17.8	107.7	12.0	102.9	5.3
1987	106.2	-5.5	105.0	-4.4	100.9	-14.7	109.0	36.2	105.3	2.3
1988	101.7	-24.2	101.4	-1.2	102.0	2.4	108.2	26.6	103.3	-1.9
1989	112.7	17.7	115.9	11.9	117.3	4.9	120.7	12.1	116.7	13.0
1990	126.7	21.4	129.5	9.1	132.3	8.9	133.3	3.1	130.4	11.7
1991	136.0	8.4	138.9	8.8	138.8	-0.3	142.6	11.4	139.1	6.7
1992	149.0	19.2	149.1	0.3	151.1	5.5	159.7	24.8	152.2	9.4
1993	157.7	-4.9	156.1	-4.0	157.7	4.2	159.1	3.6	157.7	3.6
1994	162.0	7.5	156.8	-12.2	160.7	10.3	164.7	10.3	161.0	2.1
1995	167.3	6.5	163.0	-9.9	165.5	6.3	164.1	-3.3	165.0	2.5
1996	168.0	9.9	167.3	-1.7	166.8	-1.2	167.0	0.5	167.3	1.4
1997	172.8	14.6	175.5	6.4	173.6	-4.3	174.0	0.9	174.0	4.0

Source: "National Income and Product Account Tables: Selected NIPA Tables," *Survey of Current Business*, November 1997, U.S. Department of Commerce, Bureau of Economic Analysis, National Income and Wealth Division. Data for 1997 quarters downloaded from www.stat.usa.gov. A dash (-) indicates that no data are available.

Gross Domestic Product

Government consumption expenditures and gross investment
Federal - Nondefense - Chained (1992) Dollars

In billions of chained (1992) dollars and percent. Quarterly data are seasonally adjusted and annualized. Growth rates for quarters are compound annual growth rates; changes from year to year are percentage changes.

Year	1st Quarter	% Change	2nd Quarter	% Change	3rd Quarter	% Change	4th Quarter	% Change	TOTAL	% Change
1959	51.2	-	62.3	119.2	61.6	-4.4	60.3	-8.2	58.8	-
1960	50.3	-51.6	53.0	23.3	54.4	11.0	58.6	34.6	54.1	-8.0
1961	51.2	-41.7	55.7	40.1	57.0	9.7	58.0	7.2	55.5	2.6
1962	60.2	16.1	64.4	31.0	70.6	44.4	71.9	7.6	66.8	20.4
1963	69.3	-13.7	68.9	-2.3	77.7	61.7	75.6	-10.4	72.9	9.1
1964	77.8	12.2	80.9	16.9	78.7	-10.4	79.3	3.1	79.2	8.6
1965	81.1	9.4	82.7	8.1	87.3	24.2	87.2	-0.5	84.6	6.8
1966	85.6	-7.1	89.4	19.0	86.1	-14.0	81.6	-19.3	85.7	1.3
1967	89.7	46.0	83.4	-25.3	81.5	-8.8	84.3	14.5	84.7	-1.2
1968	83.1	-5.6	80.2	-13.2	82.8	13.6	83.8	4.9	82.5	-2.6
1969	84.8	4.9	85.2	1.9	85.7	2.4	81.7	-17.4	84.3	2.2
1970	82.2	2.5	84.2	10.1	82.9	-6.0	82.9	-	83.0	-1.5
1971	82.3	-2.9	86.7	23.2	90.0	16.1	86.2	-15.8	86.3	4.0
1972	91.7	28.1	92.8	4.9	92.0	-3.4	91.2	-3.4	91.9	6.5
1973	92.1	4.0	91.5	-2.6	91.8	1.3	90.5	-5.5	91.5	-0.4
1974	94.8	20.4	91.7	-12.5	98.3	32.0	100.8	10.6	96.4	5.4
1975	98.3	-9.6	99.1	3.3	98.9	-0.8	100.2	5.4	99.1	2.8
1976	100.8	2.4	100.1	-2.7	99.5	-2.4	101.3	7.4	100.4	1.3
1977	101.3	-	103.2	7.7	104.8	6.3	108.1	13.2	104.3	3.9
1978	108.3	0.7	111.1	10.7	112.0	3.3	114.1	7.7	111.4	6.8
1979	113.7	-1.4	113.1	-2.1	112.6	-1.8	111.3	-4.5	112.7	1.2
1980	115.8	17.2	124.9	35.3	118.8	-18.2	116.6	-7.2	119.0	5.6
1981	119.8	11.4	122.9	10.8	120.0	-9.1	118.8	-3.9	120.4	1.2
1982	115.7	-10.0	111.0	-15.3	111.5	1.8	115.0	13.2	113.3	-5.9
1983	118.3	12.0	119.8	5.2	130.4	40.4	105.5	-57.2	118.5	4.6
1984	108.1	10.2	118.9	46.4	118.2	-2.3	118.5	1.0	115.9	-2.2
1985	120.8	8.0	122.0	4.0	123.3	4.3	121.2	-6.6	121.8	5.1
1986	121.2	-	122.9	5.7	126.8	13.3	129.8	9.8	125.2	2.8
1987	127.4	-7.2	125.4	-6.1	119.5	-17.5	128.9	35.4	125.3	0.1
1988	118.4	-28.8	116.7	-5.6	116.8	0.3	124.5	29.1	119.1	-4.9
1989	127.1	8.6	129.7	8.4	130.5	2.5	133.0	7.9	130.1	9.2
1990	138.9	19.0	140.4	4.4	142.2	5.2	140.5	-4.7	140.5	8.0
1991	139.0	-4.2	142.2	9.5	141.4	-2.2	145.3	11.5	142.0	1.1
1992	150.8	16.0	150.0	-2.1	150.9	2.4	157.1	17.5	152.2	7.2
1993	152.9	-10.3	151.1	-4.6	150.3	-2.1	150.4	0.3	151.2	-0.7
1994	151.9	4.0	145.1	-16.7	149.4	12.4	151.7	6.3	149.5	-1.1
1995	151.4	-0.8	147.3	-10.4	149.1	5.0	142.1	-17.5	147.5	-1.3
1996	145.7	10.5	147.2	4.2	146.0	-3.2	145.7	-0.8	146.1	-0.9
1997	148.5	7.9	150.2	4.7	148.0	-5.7	146.6	-3.7	148.3	1.5

Source: "National Income and Product Account Tables: Selected NIPA Tables," *Survey of Current Business*, November 1997, U.S. Department of Commerce, Bureau of Economic Analysis, National Income and Wealth Division. Data for 1997 quarters downloaded from www.stat.usa.gov. A dash (-) indicates that no data are available.

Gross Domestic Product
Government consumption expenditures and gross investment
State and local - Actual Dollars

In billions of actual dollars and percent. Quarterly data are seasonally adjusted and annualized. Growth rates for quarters are compound annual growth rates; changes from year to year are percentage changes.

Year	1st Quarter	% Change	2nd Quarter	% Change	3rd Quarter	% Change	4th Quarter	% Change	TOTAL	% Change
1959	44.7	-	44.9	1.8	44.9	-	44.8	-0.9	44.8	-
1960	46.0	11.2	47.3	11.8	48.2	7.8	49.0	6.8	47.6	6.3
1961	50.8	15.5	50.9	0.8	51.7	6.4	53.6	15.5	51.8	8.8
1962	53.9	2.3	54.5	4.5	55.3	6.0	56.2	6.7	55.0	6.2
1963	57.8	11.9	58.7	6.4	60.4	12.1	61.7	8.9	59.6	8.4
1964	62.9	8.0	64.6	11.3	65.7	7.0	66.7	6.2	65.0	9.1
1965	67.9	7.4	70.1	13.6	72.7	15.7	74.3	9.1	71.2	9.5
1966	76.3	11.2	78.2	10.3	80.2	10.6	83.3	16.4	79.5	11.7
1967	85.6	11.5	87.0	6.7	88.6	7.6	91.2	12.3	88.1	10.8
1968	94.2	13.8	97.3	13.8	99.5	9.4	102.3	11.7	98.3	11.6
1969	104.3	8.1	107.2	11.6	109.2	7.7	111.1	7.1	108.0	9.9
1970	114.7	13.6	117.9	11.6	122.5	16.5	125.5	10.2	120.2	11.3
1971	128.8	10.9	131.9	10.0	133.8	5.9	136.8	9.3	132.8	10.5
1972	140.0	9.7	141.3	3.8	144.7	10.0	149.4	13.6	143.8	8.3
1973	153.5	11.4	157.0	9.4	161.1	10.9	166.1	13.0	159.4	10.8
1974	172.9	17.4	181.0	20.1	187.1	14.2	192.3	11.6	183.3	15.0
1975	201.8	21.3	204.6	5.7	210.2	11.4	215.9	11.3	208.1	13.5
1976	222.3	12.4	222.2	-0.2	222.9	1.3	225.0	3.8	223.1	7.2
1977	231.2	11.5	236.8	10.0	240.7	6.8	245.2	7.7	238.5	6.9
1978	249.5	7.2	261.4	20.5	268.3	11.0	274.6	9.7	263.4	10.4
1979	276.8	3.2	287.3	16.1	297.4	14.8	306.6	13.0	292.0	10.9
1980	317.1	14.4	321.7	5.9	325.9	5.3	332.8	8.7	324.4	11.1
1981	345.6	16.3	345.7	0.1	348.9	3.8	356.8	9.4	349.2	7.6
1982	361.9	5.8	368.7	7.7	374.3	6.2	381.4	7.8	371.6	6.4
1983	384.8	3.6	387.7	3.0	394.5	7.2	397.9	3.5	391.2	5.3
1984	409.3	12.0	418.8	9.6	429.8	10.9	438.2	8.0	424.0	8.4
1985	448.0	9.3	460.4	11.5	471.4	9.9	479.9	7.4	464.9	9.6
1986	491.1	9.7	498.0	5.7	507.3	7.7	516.7	7.6	503.3	8.3
1987	525.3	6.8	532.6	5.7	540.4	6.0	550.4	7.6	537.2	6.7
1988	559.1	6.5	571.6	9.2	578.1	4.6	589.9	8.4	574.7	7.0
1989	599.9	7.0	612.1	8.4	622.1	6.7	637.4	10.2	617.9	7.5
1990	656.6	12.6	664.2	4.7	675.7	7.1	693.7	11.1	672.6	8.9
1991	695.0	0.8	699.2	2.4	705.5	3.7	713.6	4.7	703.4	4.6
1992	726.1	7.2	733.2	4.0	738.7	3.0	745.1	3.5	735.8	4.6
1993	750.1	2.7	763.4	7.3	769.6	3.3	777.0	3.9	765.0	4.0
1994	784.1	3.7	795.5	5.9	811.9	8.5	819.6	3.8	802.8	4.9
1995	831.1	5.7	844.8	6.8	849.3	2.1	858.6	4.5	846.0	5.4
1996	867.8	4.4	882.4	6.9	891.9	4.4	904.7	5.9	886.7	4.8
1997	917.0	5.6	923.0	2.6	932.3	4.1	944.4	5.3	929.2	4.8

Source: "National Income and Product Account Tables: Selected NIPA Tables," *Survey of Current Business*, November 1997, U.S. Department of Commerce, Bureau of Economic Analysis, National Income and Wealth Division. Data for 1997 quarters downloaded from www.stat.usa.gov. A dash (-) indicates that no data are available.

Gross Domestic Product

Government consumption expenditures and gross investment
State and local - Chained (1992) Dollars

In billions of chained (1992) dollars and percent. Quarterly data are seasonally adjusted and annualized. Growth rates for quarters are compound annual growth rates; changes from year to year are percentage changes.

Year	1st Quarter	% Change	2nd Quarter	% Change	3rd Quarter	% Change	4th Quarter	% Change	TOTAL	% Change
1959	256.9	-	257.1	0.3	257.3	0.3	255.9	-2.2	256.8	-
1960	259.9	6.4	266.0	9.7	270.0	6.2	273.0	4.5	267.2	4.0
1961	281.8	13.5	280.1	-2.4	282.6	3.6	290.5	11.7	283.8	6.2
1962	288.0	-3.4	290.0	2.8	293.6	5.1	296.7	4.3	292.1	2.9
1963	302.3	7.8	305.3	4.0	313.4	11.0	317.9	5.9	309.7	6.0
1964	322.9	6.4	329.9	9.0	333.6	4.6	337.3	4.5	330.9	6.8
1965	340.4	3.7	349.0	10.5	359.1	12.1	364.2	5.8	353.2	6.7
1966	369.4	5.8	372.3	3.2	376.3	4.4	385.8	10.5	375.9	6.4
1967	390.2	4.6	392.2	2.1	393.9	1.7	400.6	7.0	394.2	4.9
1968	407.1	6.6	414.9	7.9	420.4	5.4	423.6	3.1	416.5	5.7
1969	425.7	2.0	428.8	2.9	429.3	0.5	428.2	-1.0	428.0	2.8
1970	432.5	4.1	435.0	2.3	445.0	9.5	447.5	2.3	440.0	2.8
1971	450.0	2.3	453.1	2.8	454.3	1.1	460.0	5.1	454.4	3.3
1972	462.2	1.9	460.5	-1.5	464.3	3.3	470.8	5.7	464.5	2.2
1973	473.8	2.6	474.7	0.8	479.9	4.5	485.5	4.7	478.5	3.0
1974	491.3	4.9	497.6	5.2	496.7	-0.7	496.6	-0.1	495.6	3.6
1975	508.8	10.2	504.9	-3.0	510.5	4.5	515.9	4.3	510.0	2.9
1976	522.8	5.5	514.1	-6.5	511.0	-2.4	509.4	-1.2	514.3	0.8
1977	513.9	3.6	517.0	2.4	516.9	-0.1	517.7	0.6	516.4	0.4
1978	518.5	0.6	534.2	12.7	540.5	4.8	545.7	3.9	534.7	3.5
1979	536.8	-6.4	541.9	3.9	544.5	1.9	550.9	4.8	543.5	1.6
1980	553.2	1.7	546.1	-5.0	538.6	-5.4	536.6	-1.5	543.6	0.0
1981	540.7	3.1	530.3	-7.5	528.2	-1.6	532.0	2.9	532.8	-2.0
1982	529.6	-1.8	531.2	1.2	530.8	-0.3	533.8	2.3	531.4	-0.3
1983	534.1	0.2	532.7	-1.0	536.6	3.0	536.0	-0.4	534.9	0.7
1984	543.8	5.9	550.9	5.3	559.9	6.7	565.6	4.1	555.0	3.8
1985	571.1	3.9	581.5	7.5	590.5	6.3	595.6	3.5	584.7	5.4
1986	608.7	9.1	615.1	4.3	620.8	3.8	623.2	1.6	616.9	5.5
1987	626.8	2.3	628.8	1.3	632.0	2.1	639.6	4.9	631.8	2.4
1988	645.1	3.5	655.0	6.3	658.4	2.1	667.8	5.8	656.6	3.9
1989	672.3	2.7	679.4	4.3	685.1	3.4	693.7	5.1	682.6	4.0
1990	703.8	6.0	705.4	0.9	708.7	1.9	716.5	4.5	708.6	3.8
1991	715.5	-0.6	716.8	0.7	718.8	1.1	723.8	2.8	718.7	1.4
1992	733.5	5.5	734.2	0.4	736.9	1.5	738.5	0.9	735.8	2.4
1993	738.0	-0.3	745.3	4.0	749.1	2.1	753.4	2.3	746.4	1.4
1994	754.7	0.7	762.2	4.0	771.7	5.1	774.1	1.2	765.7	2.6
1995	777.3	1.7	782.3	2.6	781.5	-0.4	785.1	1.9	781.6	2.1
1996	782.4	-1.4	794.4	6.3	795.9	0.8	802.3	3.3	793.7	1.5
1997	807.7	2.7	810.1	1.2	814.7	2.3	819.0	2.1	812.9	2.4

Source: "National Income and Product Account Tables: Selected NIPA Tables," *Survey of Current Business*, November 1997, U.S. Department of Commerce, Bureau of Economic Analysis, National Income and Wealth Division. Data for 1997 quarters downloaded from www.stat.usa.gov. A dash (-) indicates that no data are available.

CHAPTER 3

BUSINESS CYCLE INDICATORS

BUSINESS CYCLE INDICATORS

The indexes of economic indicators, also called business cycle indicators, are used by government, industry, and other institutions to forecast tendencies in the national economy. They are composites of several statistical series which tend to signal *changes* in the economy's general direction. They are "business cycle indicators" because they can predict the beginnings and ends of periods of sustained growth; each such period is a single business cycle; each ends when economic growth stops, as measured by Gross Domestic Product (GDP), or shows negative growth.

Arthur F. Burns and Wesley C. Mitchell have described business cycles as follows:

> Business cycles are a type of fluctuation found in the aggregate economic activity of nations that organize their work mainly in business enterprises; a cycle consists of expansions occurring at about the same time in many economic activities, followed by similarly general recessions, contractions, and revivals which merge into the expansion phase of the next cycle; this sequence of changes is recurrent but not periodic; in duration business cycles vary from more than one year to ten or twelve years; they are not divisible into shorter cycles of similar character with amplitudes approximating their own. (Reference 2.)

History

Business cycle indicators were developed by the National Bureau of Economic Research, Inc. (NBER). The first list of cyclic indicators was published by Burns and Mitchell in 1938. Publication of the NBER's indicators by the U.S. Department of Commerce began in 1961. Commerce began to publish composite indexes of leading, coincident, and lagging indicators in 1968. Late in 1995, preparation of the series was transferred to The Conference Board, a New York-based, independent, not-for-profit business research organization. The current series are available from 1959 to the present time. The series have been revised from time to time. The most recent changes were introduced in December 1996 and December 1997. After changes are made, the indexes are restated in the new format for past years.

Characteristics of the Indexes

Three composite indexes are used to predict the peaks and troughs of business cycles—the highest points of growth and the bottoms of periods of decline. The composite index of *Leading Indicators* tends to signal a change (downturn or upturn) before the economy actually turns down or resumes growth. The composite index of *Coincident Indicators* tends to turn up or down at the same time as the economy. And the composite index of *Lagging Indicators* shows changes after they have already become visible.

A graphic presentation following this introductory text illustrates the relationships between the indicator series and Gross Domestic Product (GDP) for the period 1959-1995. The vertical rectangular areas indicate periods of recession as commonly defined.

Each composite index combines several component indexes which behave in the appropriate manner. For example, the composite index of leading indicators is formed of several other leading indicators. A composite of selected leading, coincident, or lagging indicators is used because, over time, it has been found that the composite index predicts more accurately than any one of the components taken alone. Revisions of the business cycle indicators have typically taken the form of removing and adding components and changing the relative weight assigned to each component in calculating the composite index. Components will be discussed in separate sections.

Presentation

Data for each of the composite indexes are presented in sequence. Each section begins with a discussion of the composite index and its components. Tables with the indexes follow. The composite indexes are shown in two formats: the actual index and change from previous month.

Format and Calculation

Data are presented, in most cases, for the years 1959 to 1997 and for each month of the year.

The composite indexes relate to a base year. The base year at present (1998) is 1992, with the value of 100. All other data points are calibrated to 1992. The 1992 base value, in turn, is produced by averaging the 1992 monthly values; for this reason, monthly values in 1992 will be very near 100. The significance of the composite indexes lies in month-to-month changes rather than in absolute value. A change is signalled when the index increases or decreases over a period of three or more months.

Values for the component indexes are shown in various formats (hours, weeks, dollars, percentages, index values). The formats are noted at the top of each component table.

Month-to-month percentage changes in the component series are used to construct the composite index. Calculation of each component's contribution is made by applying mathematical methods to minimize the tendency of volatile series to dominate the average and to standardize each series. These technical methods are described in the references. At present, each component contributes differentially to the composite index; that is to say, weighting factors are used. For example, the average weekly hours in manufacturing contributes 22.2 percent to the leading index. The index of consumer expectations contributes 1.7 percent. For details, see Reference 4.

Bibliography

1. Hertzberg, Marie P. and Barry A. Beckman, "Business Cycle Indicators: Revised Composite Indexes." U.S. Department of Commerce, Bureau of Economic Analysis. *Survey of Current Business*. January 1989, Superintendent of Documents, U.S. Government Printing Office, Washington, DC 20302.

2. *Measuring Business Cycles*. National Bureau of Economic Research, Inc., 1946.

3. U.S. Department of Commerce, Bureau of Economic Analysis. "Composite Indexes of Leading, Coincident, and Lagging Indicators," *Survey of Current Business*. November 1987, Superintendent of Documents, U.S. Government Printing Office, Washington, DC 20302.

4. *Leading Economic Indicators*. The Conference Board, 845 Third Avenue, New York, NY 10022-6679.

GDP and Economic Indicators: 1979-1997

(In Billions of chained 1992 dollars and Index)

Recession dates:

1980:
Peak - Jan 1980
Trough - July 1980

1981-1982:
Peak - July 1981
Trough - Nov 1982

1990-91:
Peak - July 1990
Trough - March 1991

Peak is the highest point reached by the expansion. Trough is the bottom of the recession.

Recessionary periods

Lagging Index

Leading Index

Coincident Index

Gross Domestic Product (Left Scale)

Index

120

110

100

90

80

70

60

Bil. 1992 $

7400

6900

6400

5900

5400

4900

4400

79 80 81 82 83 84 85 86 87 88 89 90 91 92 93 94 95 96 97

COMPOSITE INDEX OF LEADING INDICATORS

The composite index of leading indicators tends to signal the onset of a recession or a recovery some months before the economy actually registers the change. It is generally held that a change in the direction of the indicator must be sustained for at least three months before the indicator becomes predictive.

The "leading index" is accurate but fallible. All recessions have been accurately predicted by the index. But not all predictions based on the index have actually resulted in downturns or upturns. In 1950-51, 1966, and in 1984, the index showed obvious downturns which did not materialize. These "false signals" reflect the fact that the index components do not always measure economic factors completely; for example, service sector and international activity are not reflected in the index—although these sectors are increasingly important. The theoretical framework behind the index is also still in the process of development.

Components of the Leading Index

The index is a composite of 10 indicators, each of which is further discussed below:

>   Average weekly hours in manufacturing
>   Average weekly initial claims for unemployment insurance
>   Manufacturers' new orders, consumer goods and materials
>   Vendor performance, slow deliveries
>   Manufacturers' new orders, nondefense capital goods
>   Building permits for new private housing units
>   Index of stock prices, 500 common stocks
>   Money supply M2
>   Interest Rate Spread, 10-year Treasury bonds less federal funds
>   Consumer expectations

Average Weekly Hours in Manufacturing. The index is shown in hours worked by production or nonsupervisory workers. A decline in hours worked, if sustained over some period, signals a lower level of production; conversely, a sustained increase in hours shows pick-up in production. Data are always close to 40 hours per week because unemployed labor forces are drawn into the labor pool when demand increases—unless there is a labor shortage, as in the early months of 1945.

Average Weekly Initial Claims for Unemployment Insurance. Data are drawn from state unemployment program files and are a signal of increasing or decreasing layoffs—therefore an early signal of economic change.

Manufacturers' New Orders. The two series cover new orders in the consumer goods and materials industries and orders for capital goods in the nondefense industries. Since new orders represent future economic activity, the values (in millions of chained 1992 dollars, to remove inflationary bias) indicate future trends.

Vendor Performance. The index charts the percent of companies reporting late deliveries by vendors. Late deliveries are common when vendors are overbooked and have difficulty obtaining raw materials—a situation typically encountered in a strong economy. If late delivery percentages begin to rise in a recessionary economy, it signals the onset of an upturn—again only if the trend is sustained.

Building Permits for New Private Housing Units. The data are based on local building permits issued. Since permits must be obtained before building begins, this series predicts future housing starts and is thus a leading indicator. Increases in this index imply confidence that the economy will be strong, that money will be available for construction financing and house purchases.

Index of Stock Prices, 500 Common Stocks. This indicator is the Standard & Poor's 500 stock average index; it is an index to the 1941-1943 period, the average of which is expressed as 10. The index reflects stock price averages and is an indirect measure of investor confidence.

Money Supply M2. M2 is one of four monetary aggregates used by the Federal Reserve System to measure money supply. M1 is all currency, checking accounts, and other types of checkable deposits that can be turned into cash easily. M2 includes M1 and adds other liquid assets in the economy, including money market funds, money market deposit accounts, savings accounts, and small time deposits. M3 includes M2 plus large time deposits, institutional money market funds, and other less liquid assets. The fourth measure, labeled L (because it is *L*east under Federal Reserve control and *L*east liquid) includes M3 plus short-term Treasury securities, commercial paper, savings bonds, and bankers' acceptances. M2 is thus a measure of the money supply which includes some funds that are typically held for investment but not assets that are difficult to "liquefy."

M2 is used as a leading indicator because it tends to reach low points in its cycle approximately 12 months before Gross Domestic Product (GDP) reaches the bottom of its cycle. M2 thus serves as an early indicator of future GNP behavior.

Money supply, generally, affects the economy by influencing interest rates; these, in turn, can stimulate housing purchases and investments in capital goods. An increase in money supply usually results in low interest rates: there is more money to lend; a decline in money supply pushes interest rates up. In periods of high inflation, however, interest rates may not respond as just stated because lenders anticipate an inflationary devaluation of their funds and hence compensate by keeping interest rates high.

Interest Rate Spread, 10-year Treasury Bonds. The interest rate spread is the difference between the coupon rate of a bond (fixed interest) and the yield of the bond as traded in secondary markets. In effect this means that if bond prices are bid up, the yield is lowered—more is being paid for a fixed interest yield; conversely, if bond prices fall, yields increase. A positive spread implies confidence in the future; a negative spread implies lack of confidence. Bond prices thus fall in anticipation of expansionary periods and rise in expectation of deflationary periods.

Consumer Expectations. The index, based on surveys conducted by the University of Michigan, Survey Research Center, was added to the leading index in 1989. It is based on a monthly telephone survey of approximately 500 people in 48 states and the District of Columbia and combines the respondents' answers to questions about their expectations for the economy. The index is pegged to the first quarter of 1966, which is expressed as 100. The indicator, of course, measures consumer confidence. The index values, in themselves—while showing how attitudes have changed since 1966—are less valuable than changes month to month indicating a trend in consumer attitudes.

Sources and Revisions

Sources for the component series are largely drawn from federal sources, including the U.S. Department of Commerce, Bureau of Economic Analysis and Bureau of the Census; and U.S. Department of Labor, Bureau of Labor Statistics and Employment and Training Administration. Other sources are Standard & Poor's Corporation (Stock Index), McGraw-Hill Information Systems Company (contributor to Contracts and Orders for Plant and Equipment), National Association of Purchasing Management and Purchasing Management Association of Chicago (Vendor Performance), University of Michigan (Consumer Expectations), and others.

The composite index itself is constructed by The Conference Board, 845 Third Avenue, New York, NY 19922-6678. The Conference Board, a worldwide research and business membership group took over the preparation of the each index (leading, coincident, lagging) from the Bureau of Economic Analysis of the U.S. Department of Commerce in December 1995.

In the process of index preparation, mathematical operations are performed on the component data series to ensure that volatile series do not dominate the index. A volatile series may be one that fluctuates wildly month to month but shows less volatility when averaged over several months. Other smoothing and standardization methods are used as well.

The index was revised in December 1996 and again in December 1997.

Bibliography

1. Frumkin, Norman. *Guide to Economic Indicators*. M.E. Sharpe, Inc., 1990.

2. Green, George R. and Barry A. Beckman. "Business Cycle Indicators: Upcoming Revision of the Composite Indexes." U.S. Department of Commerce, Bureau of Economic Analysis. *Survey of Current Business*, October 1993. Superintendent of Documents, U.S. Government Printing Office, Washington, DC 20302.

3. Hertzberg, Marie P. and Barry A. Beckman. "Business Cycle Indicators: Revised Composite Indexes." U.S. Department of Commerce, Bureau of Economic Analysis. *Survey of Current Business*, January 1989. Superintendent of Documents, U.S. Government Printing Office, Washington, DC 20302.

4. U.S. Department of Commerce, Bureau of Economic Analysis. "Composite Indexes of Leading, Coincident, and Lagging Indicators." In *Survey of Current Business*, November 1987. Superintendent of Documents, U.S. Government Printing Office, Washington, DC 20302.

5. U.S. Department of Commerce, Bureau of Economic Analysis. *Survey of Current Business*. Superintendent of Documents, U.S. Government Printing Office, Washington, DC 20302.

6. *Leading Economic Indicators*. The Confenrence Board, 845 Third Avenue, New York, NY 10022-6679.

Composite Index of 10 Leading Indicators
(1992 = 100)

Year	Jan	Feb	Mar	Apr	May	Jun	Jul	Aug	Sep	Oct	Nov	Dec
1959	74.2	74.6	75.0	75.0	75.1	75.0	74.9	74.6	74.6	74.3	73.9	74.7
1960	74.5	74.1	73.6	73.7	73.8	73.8	73.8	74.0	73.9	73.8	73.7	73.8
1961	74.0	74.0	74.7	75.1	75.3	75.8	75.8	76.3	76.1	76.4	76.8	77.1
1962	77.1	77.4	77.4	77.3	77.0	76.7	77.0	77.0	77.2	77.3	77.7	77.8
1963	78.1	78.3	78.7	78.9	79.1	79.2	79.1	79.1	79.6	79.7	79.8	79.9
1964	80.2	80.4	80.6	80.8	81.1	81.2	81.5	81.7	81.9	81.9	82.1	82.3
1965	82.6	82.6	83.0	82.9	83.1	83.2	83.3	83.3	83.4	83.9	84.3	84.7
1966	84.6	84.7	85.1	84.9	84.5	84.2	84.0	83.8	83.7	83.4	83.3	83.2
1967	83.4	83.2	83.3	83.5	83.9	84.3	84.5	85.1	85.1	85.2	85.4	85.7
1968	85.6	85.9	86.1	85.6	85.7	85.9	86.2	85.9	86.4	86.9	87.1	87.1
1969	87.3	87.3	87.2	87.4	86.9	86.7	86.5	86.5	86.6	86.2	85.9	85.7
1970	85.2	84.7	84.5	83.9	84.3	84.5	84.4	84.6	84.5	84.4	84.4	85.4
1971	85.8	86.3	86.6	86.8	87.1	87.2	87.2	87.3	87.5	87.7	87.9	88.7
1972	89.2	89.6	89.8	89.9	89.9	90.0	90.4	91.1	91.5	91.7	92.0	92.3
1973	92.4	92.4	92.1	91.7	91.6	91.4	91.1	90.7	90.7	90.7	90.6	89.8
1974	89.6	89.2	89.5	88.8	88.7	88.2	87.8	87.1	86.1	85.7	84.9	84.1
1975	83.9	83.9	84.3	85.5	86.0	86.4	87.1	87.4	87.7	88.0	88.3	88.4
1976	89.4	90.1	90.1	90.1	90.4	90.4	90.7	90.8	91.0	90.9	91.2	91.8
1977	91.6	91.9	92.2	92.3	92.3	92.5	92.5	92.5	92.5	92.4	92.5	92.6
1978	92.0	92.3	92.4	92.9	92.8	92.8	92.6	92.7	92.9	93.0	92.4	92.1
1979	92.0	92.0	92.2	91.4	91.8	91.5	90.9	91.0	91.2	90.4	90.1	89.9
1980	90.1	90.2	88.3	87.0	87.2	88.3	89.1	89.8	90.5	90.8	90.8	90.1
1981	89.9	89.9	90.4	90.9	90.5	89.9	89.8	90.0	89.6	89.1	88.9	89.1
1982	88.9	89.0	88.7	89.1	89.2	89.1	89.5	89.4	90.0	90.3	90.6	91.2
1983	92.1	92.7	93.3	93.8	94.4	94.9	95.1	95.0	95.2	95.7	95.8	95.9
1984	96.4	96.6	96.5	96.5	96.6	96.2	96.2	95.8	95.7	95.8	96.1	96.5
1985	96.8	96.7	96.9	96.7	96.9	97.1	97.1	97.2	97.4	97.3	97.2	97.6
1986	97.7	97.7	97.8	98.1	98.3	98.5	98.5	98.6	98.7	99.0	99.0	99.3
1987	99.3	99.7	99.8	99.9	99.9	100.1	100.4	100.5	100.5	100.4	100.0	99.9
1988	99.8	100.2	100.5	100.3	100.4	100.8	100.3	100.3	100.2	100.3	100.2	100.3
1989	100.3	100.0	99.6	99.9	99.4	99.3	99.3	99.5	99.6	99.4	99.6	99.7
1990	100.0	99.6	99.9	99.7	99.7	99.7	99.6	99.1	98.8	98.2	97.9	98.0
1991	97.8	98.1	98.5	98.8	99.1	99.3	99.8	99.5	99.5	99.5	99.4	99.1
1992	99.4	99.7	99.9	99.9	100.0	99.9	99.9	99.9	99.9	100.1	100.4	101.0
1993	100.7	100.7	100.1	100.4	100.2	100.3	100.1	100.3	100.4	100.5	100.8	101.2
1994	101.2	101.0	101.5	101.4	101.4	101.4	101.2	101.5	101.4	101.5	101.6	101.6
1995	101.5	101.1	100.7	100.6	100.4	100.5	100.7	101.0	101.1	100.9	100.9	101.2
1996	100.5	101.4	101.6	101.8	102.1	102.3	102.3	102.4	102.5	102.5	102.6	102.7
1997	103.0	103.4	103.6	103.5	103.7	103.8	104.1	104.3	104.5	-	-	-

Source: The Conference Board. Primary source(s): The Conference Board, Inc., Economics Group, 845 Third Avenue, New York, NY 10022. A dash (-) indicates that data are not available or zero.

Composite Index of 10 Leading Indicators
Change in Index from Previous Month

Year	Jan	Feb	Mar	Apr	May	Jun	Jul	Aug	Sep	Oct	Nov	Dec
1959	-	+0.4	+0.4	-	+0.1	-0.1	-0.1	-0.3	-	-0.3	-0.4	+0.8
1960	-0.2	-0.4	-0.5	+0.1	+0.1	-	-	+0.2	-0.1	-0.1	-0.1	+0.1
1961	+0.2	-	+0.7	+0.4	+0.2	+0.5	-	+0.5	-0.2	+0.3	+0.4	+0.3
1962	-	+0.3	-	-0.1	-0.3	-0.3	+0.3	-	+0.2	+0.1	+0.4	+0.1
1963	+0.3	+0.2	+0.4	+0.2	+0.2	+0.1	-0.1	-	+0.5	+0.1	+0.1	+0.1
1964	+0.3	+0.2	+0.2	+0.2	+0.3	+0.1	+0.3	+0.2	+0.2	-	+0.2	+0.2
1965	+0.3	-	+0.4	-0.1	+0.2	+0.1	+0.1	-	+0.1	+0.5	+0.4	+0.4
1966	-0.1	+0.1	+0.4	-0.2	-0.4	-0.3	-0.2	-0.2	-0.1	-0.3	-0.1	-0.1
1967	+0.2	-0.2	+0.1	+0.2	+0.4	+0.4	+0.2	+0.6	-	+0.1	+0.2	+0.3
1968	-0.1	+0.3	+0.2	-0.5	+0.1	+0.2	+0.3	-0.3	+0.5	+0.5	+0.2	-
1969	+0.2	-	-0.1	+0.2	-0.5	-0.2	-0.2	-	+0.1	-0.4	-0.3	-0.2
1970	-0.5	-0.5	-0.2	-0.6	+0.4	+0.2	-0.1	+0.2	-0.1	-0.1	-	+1.0
1971	+0.4	+0.5	+0.3	+0.2	+0.3	+0.1	-	+0.1	+0.2	+0.2	+0.2	+0.8
1972	+0.5	+0.4	+0.2	+0.1	-	+0.1	+0.4	+0.7	+0.4	+0.2	+0.3	+0.3
1973	+0.1	-	-0.3	-0.4	-0.1	-0.2	-0.3	-0.4	-	-	-0.1	-0.8
1974	-0.2	-0.4	+0.3	-0.7	-0.1	-0.5	-0.4	-0.7	-1.0	-0.4	-0.8	-0.8
1975	-0.2	-	+0.4	+1.2	+0.5	+0.4	+0.7	+0.3	+0.3	+0.3	+0.3	+0.1
1976	+1.0	+0.7	-	-	+0.3	-	+0.3	+0.1	+0.2	-0.1	+0.3	+0.6
1977	-0.2	+0.3	+0.3	+0.1	-	+0.2	-	-	-	-0.1	+0.1	+0.1
1978	-0.6	+0.3	+0.1	+0.5	-0.1	-	-0.2	+0.1	+0.2	+0.1	-0.6	-0.3
1979	-0.1	-	+0.2	-0.8	+0.4	-0.3	-0.6	+0.1	+0.2	-0.8	-0.3	-0.2
1980	+0.2	+0.1	-1.9	-1.3	+0.2	+1.1	+0.8	+0.7	+0.7	+0.3	-	-0.7
1981	-0.2	-	+0.5	+0.5	-0.4	-0.6	-0.1	+0.2	-0.4	-0.5	-0.2	+0.2
1982	-0.2	+0.1	-0.3	+0.4	+0.1	-0.1	+0.4	-0.1	+0.6	+0.3	+0.3	+0.6
1983	+0.9	+0.6	+0.6	+0.5	+0.6	+0.5	+0.2	-0.1	+0.2	+0.5	+0.1	+0.1
1984	+0.5	+0.2	-0.1	-	+0.1	-0.4	-	-0.4	-0.1	+0.1	+0.3	+0.4
1985	+0.3	-0.1	+0.2	-0.2	+0.2	+0.2	-	+0.1	+0.2	-0.1	-0.1	+0.4
1986	+0.1	-	+0.1	+0.3	+0.2	+0.2	-	+0.1	+0.1	+0.3	-	+0.3
1987	-	+0.4	+0.1	+0.1	-	+0.2	+0.3	+0.1	-	-0.1	-0.4	-0.1
1988	-0.1	+0.4	+0.3	-0.2	+0.1	+0.4	-0.5	-	-0.1	+0.1	-0.1	+0.1
1989	-	-0.3	-0.4	+0.3	-0.5	-0.1	-	+0.2	+0.1	-0.2	+0.2	+0.1
1990	+0.3	-0.4	+0.3	-0.2	-	-	-0.1	-0.5	-0.3	-0.6	-0.3	+0.1
1991	-0.2	+0.3	+0.4	+0.3	+0.3	+0.2	+0.5	-0.3	-	-	-0.1	-0.3
1992	+0.3	+0.3	+0.2	-	+0.1	-0.1	-	-	-	+0.2	+0.3	+0.6
1993	-0.3	-	-0.6	+0.3	-0.2	+0.1	-0.2	+0.2	+0.1	+0.1	+0.3	+0.4
1994	-	-0.2	+0.5	-0.1	-	-	-0.2	+0.3	-0.1	+0.1	+0.1	-
1995	-0.1	-0.4	-0.4	-0.1	-0.2	+0.1	+0.2	+0.3	+0.1	-0.2	-	+0.3
1996	-0.7	+0.9	+0.2	+0.2	+0.3	+0.2	-	+0.1	+0.1	-	+0.1	+0.1
1997	+0.3	+0.4	+0.2	-0.1	+0.2	+0.1	+0.3	+0.2	+0.2	-	-	-

Source: The Conference Board. Primary source(s): The Conference Board, Inc., Economics Group, 845 Third Avenue, New York, NY 10022. A dash (-) indicates that data are not available or zero.

Average Weekly Hours, Manufacturing
(hours)

Year	Jan	Feb	Mar	Apr	May	Jun	Jul	Aug	Sep	Oct	Nov	Dec
1945	45.3	45.4	45.2	45.1	44.3	44.5	44.3	40.8	41.7	41.4	41.1	41.1
1946	40.8	40.4	40.5	40.4	39.9	39.8	39.8	40.5	40.5	40.3	40.2	40.5
1947	40.5	40.5	40.4	40.5	40.5	40.4	40.2	39.8	40.3	40.3	40.4	40.7
1948	40.4	40.2	40.4	40.4	40.2	40.2	40.1	40.0	39.6	39.7	39.7	39.5
1949	39.4	39.4	39.1	38.8	38.9	38.9	39.1	39.0	39.4	39.4	39.0	39.3
1950	39.6	39.7	39.7	40.1	40.2	40.5	40.8	41.1	40.8	40.9	40.9	40.8
1951	40.8	40.8	41.0	41.2	40.9	40.7	40.5	40.2	40.4	40.2	40.3	40.6
1952	40.7	40.7	40.6	40.1	40.4	40.5	40.1	40.5	41.0	41.1	41.0	41.1
1953	41.0	41.0	41.1	41.1	40.9	40.7	40.6	40.4	39.8	40.0	39.8	39.6
1954	39.5	39.7	39.5	39.4	39.5	39.6	39.6	39.7	39.5	39.6	40.1	40.0
1955	40.3	40.5	40.7	40.6	40.9	40.6	40.6	40.6	40.7	40.9	41.0	40.8
1956	40.8	40.6	40.4	40.6	40.2	40.1	40.2	40.2	40.4	40.5	40.4	40.5
1957	40.3	40.4	40.2	40.1	39.8	39.9	39.9	39.8	39.7	39.3	39.2	39.0
1958	38.8	38.6	38.7	38.6	38.8	39.0	39.2	39.4	39.6	39.5	39.8	39.8
1959	40.1	40.2	40.4	40.5	40.6	40.5	40.2	40.3	40.1	40.1	39.8	40.2
1960	40.5	40.1	39.9	39.7	40.0	39.8	39.8	39.7	39.4	39.6	39.2	38.4
1961	39.2	39.3	39.4	39.6	39.6	39.9	40.0	40.1	39.5	40.2	40.5	40.3
1962	40.0	40.3	40.5	40.7	40.5	40.4	40.4	40.3	40.5	40.2	40.3	40.2
1963	40.4	40.3	40.4	40.2	40.5	40.6	40.5	40.4	40.6	40.6	40.5	40.6
1964	40.1	40.6	40.6	40.8	40.7	40.7	40.8	40.9	40.5	40.6	40.8	41.1
1965	41.2	41.2	41.4	41.0	41.2	41.1	41.1	41.0	40.8	41.2	41.3	41.4
1966	41.4	41.6	41.5	41.5	41.4	41.4	41.2	41.4	41.3	41.3	41.2	40.9
1967	41.0	40.4	40.4	40.5	40.4	40.4	40.5	40.6	40.7	40.6	40.6	40.7
1968	40.3	40.9	40.7	40.0	40.9	40.9	40.8	40.7	40.9	40.9	40.8	40.7
1969	40.7	40.4	40.8	40.7	40.7	40.7	40.6	40.6	40.7	40.6	40.4	40.5
1970	40.4	40.2	40.1	39.9	39.8	39.9	40.0	39.8	39.3	39.5	39.5	39.5
1971	39.9	39.7	39.8	39.7	39.9	40.0	39.9	39.8	39.4	39.9	40.0	40.2
1972	40.2	40.4	40.4	40.7	40.5	40.6	40.5	40.6	40.6	40.7	40.8	40.5
1973	40.4	40.9	40.8	40.9	40.7	40.6	40.7	40.5	40.7	40.6	40.7	40.6
1974	40.5	40.4	40.4	39.3	40.3	40.2	40.2	40.2	40.0	40.0	39.5	39.3
1975	39.2	38.9	38.8	39.2	39.0	39.2	39.4	39.7	39.9	39.8	39.9	40.2
1976	40.5	40.3	40.2	39.6	40.3	40.2	40.3	40.1	39.8	40.0	40.1	40.0
1977	39.7	40.3	40.2	40.4	40.4	40.5	40.3	40.4	40.4	40.5	40.4	40.4
1978	39.6	39.9	40.5	40.8	40.4	40.5	40.6	40.5	40.6	40.5	40.6	40.6
1979	40.5	40.5	40.6	39.2	40.2	40.2	40.2	40.1	40.2	40.2	40.1	40.2
1980	40.0	40.1	39.8	39.5	39.3	39.2	39.1	39.4	39.6	39.8	40.0	40.3
1981	40.1	40.0	40.0	40.1	40.1	39.9	39.9	39.9	39.7	39.7	39.5	39.4
1982	38.0	39.6	39.1	38.9	39.0	39.1	39.2	39.0	39.0	38.9	39.1	39.1
1983	39.4	39.3	39.6	39.8	40.0	40.1	40.3	40.3	40.6	40.7	40.7	40.6
1984	40.7	41.1	40.7	40.9	40.7	40.7	40.6	40.5	40.5	40.5	40.5	40.6
1985	40.4	40.1	40.5	40.3	40.4	40.5	40.4	40.6	40.6	40.7	40.7	41.0
1986	40.8	40.6	40.8	40.6	40.7	40.6	40.6	40.8	40.7	40.6	40.8	40.9
1987	40.9	41.2	41.0	40.9	41.0	41.0	41.0	41.0	40.9	41.1	41.1	41.1
1988	41.1	41.0	41.0	40.8	41.0	41.0	41.0	40.9	40.9	41.0	41.1	40.9
1989	41.1	41.0	41.0	41.3	40.9	40.9	40.9	40.9	40.7	40.7	40.7	40.5
1990	40.7	40.7	40.8	40.8	40.9	40.9	40.8	40.7	40.8	40.6	40.4	40.6
1991	40.4	40.2	40.2	40.4	40.4	40.8	40.7	40.8	40.9	40.9	40.9	41.0
1992	40.8	41.0	41.0	41.0	41.1	41.1	41.1	41.1	41.0	41.1	41.2	41.2
1993	41.3	41.5	41.1	41.6	41.3	41.2	41.4	41.4	41.6	41.5	41.6	41.7
1994	41.7	41.2	42.0	41.9	42.0	42.0	42.0	42.0	41.9	42.1	42.1	42.1
1995	42.2	41.9	41.8	41.5	41.4	41.4	41.3	41.5	41.5	41.5	41.5	41.2
1996	40.1	41.4	41.3	41.5	41.6	41.7	41.6	41.7	41.7	41.7	41.7	42.0
1997	41.8	41.9	42.1	42.1	42.0	41.8	41.8	41.9	41.9	-	-	-

Source: The Conference Board. Primary source(s): U.S. Department of Labor, Bureau of Labor Statistics, Office of Employment and Unemployment Statistics, Division of Monthly Industry Employment Statistics, Washington, DC 20212. A dash (-) indicates that data are not available or zero.

Average Weekly Initial Claims, Unemployment Insurance
(Thousands)

Year	Jan	Feb	Mar	Apr	May	Jun	Jul	Aug	Sep	Oct	Nov	Dec
1945	16.0	26.0	28.3	33.9	43.8	70.4	72.3	362.4	378.1	249.9	221.7	186.7
1946	135.3	226.2	193.1	206.8	221.5	207.3	172.7	163.9	192.3	182.0	179.6	212.3
1947	122.3	174.9	186.6	208.5	236.8	220.2	231.0	194.4	180.6	164.6	173.1	173.3
1948	167.6	207.8	202.7	212.0	241.1	220.1	195.5	203.5	219.6	204.8	212.4	235.8
1949	287.6	307.0	335.7	382.2	379.4	361.2	342.2	388.0	322.2	388.8	346.6	300.3
1950	295.8	290.3	278.1	264.9	251.6	253.4	224.8	171.2	182.9	195.0	201.8	198.6
1951	175.3	182.8	167.3	200.7	200.2	210.3	238.0	255.6	243.7	235.2	211.8	215.0
1952	222.8	202.2	210.8	220.3	214.3	243.5	317.2	208.1	169.4	175.9	170.5	191.9
1953	176.3	178.5	189.8	180.5	199.5	196.1	208.1	230.2	240.2	252.4	300.1	281.7
1954	305.4	320.7	321.9	315.5	315.6	316.1	295.7	321.1	324.3	316.8	277.7	254.6
1955	258.0	241.3	229.6	229.6	224.0	223.8	224.2	235.0	205.2	225.8	216.9	215.7
1956	219.1	227.8	222.5	224.5	237.7	229.1	246.9	225.5	238.0	215.6	224.9	231.3
1957	244.0	226.3	221.1	241.1	245.6	247.6	268.8	236.5	307.5	303.7	322.8	357.7
1958	356.5	409.6	439.1	441.1	403.1	412.8	352.2	365.9	340.4	316.7	313.6	322.5
1959	294.1	286.2	259.7	246.1	248.0	259.4	265.5	293.5	273.0	313.1	353.6	277.2
1960	282.6	272.6	305.3	296.0	318.1	323.8	337.7	366.1	353.8	375.7	387.6	383.9
1961	396.0	432.6	381.5	383.8	360.5	336.2	350.9	318.0	331.8	306.4	306.8	298.5
1962	302.9	297.4	289.3	285.2	302.8	306.2	305.2	307.3	302.4	306.5	301.3	312.0
1963	311.9	303.1	289.6	295.5	289.7	285.7	283.9	291.9	287.2	284.4	278.3	303.4
1964	285.3	271.8	279.1	266.8	264.4	258.4	261.4	245.8	247.3	251.0	264.1	252.9
1965	244.7	249.9	239.0	239.2	225.2	226.0	232.4	249.7	219.9	210.3	214.0	208.0
1966	223.4	220.1	183.2	179.9	193.0	195.6	200.3	196.0	198.9	204.0	209.7	220.9
1967	208.7	252.0	247.6	263.6	234.7	221.7	232.1	211.6	215.3	216.6	199.4	214.7
1968	215.5	196.8	196.1	198.8	195.9	191.8	195.8	197.2	190.1	184.4	183.8	199.4
1969	194.2	194.7	185.3	182.3	181.6	191.1	200.3	198.6	194.0	199.5	206.8	219.5
1970	250.9	258.3	267.5	340.3	304.2	296.5	281.8	291.0	324.5	329.1	324.8	304.1
1971	297.5	283.5	293.3	284.4	292.2	290.0	296.8	324.7	304.4	296.7	286.6	267.6
1972	268.9	263.4	262.3	263.7	267.0	293.9	283.6	255.0	255.2	250.4	243.1	246.3
1973	228.3	220.5	227.2	238.5	235.5	240.0	242.3	254.1	247.4	241.3	255.7	290.5
1974	313.3	317.9	313.7	292.4	294.9	311.9	309.0	342.4	360.2	404.7	470.2	523.7
1975	560.6	541.0	546.3	516.4	496.3	495.0	449.0	451.1	444.9	417.6	396.8	373.9
1976	373.1	348.0	360.2	371.3	392.7	396.3	389.8	388.1	403.3	408.7	389.3	368.0
1977	407.1	450.3	356.9	371.3	379.6	357.4	364.1	366.7	361.5	361.5	353.0	357.4
1978	350.6	381.5	342.9	323.7	326.3	333.3	350.6	335.3	324.3	327.8	344.9	349.7
1979	357.2	359.8	358.6	415.2	343.3	365.0	379.1	387.3	384.8	401.7	417.9	430.8
1980	416.6	419.0	439.5	556.3	626.4	606.2	556.6	517.4	482.0	426.5	410.6	409.6
1981	413.7	428.3	407.2	408.8	416.8	432.4	434.5	443.5	476.9	493.3	511.3	534.8
1982	545.2	533.7	556.5	586.7	585.8	596.9	569.7	629.6	671.7	641.8	594.4	517.9
1983	492.8	488.7	479.3	497.0	468.1	435.1	404.3	435.9	409.1	399.5	385.1	369.8
1984	350.9	340.5	345.5	369.4	357.7	362.9	360.3	390.1	398.0	419.3	401.3	381.7
1985	375.7	388.3	382.2	398.0	393.9	394.6	379.4	403.3	406.1	400.7	392.0	386.0
1986	369.0	371.7	380.4	390.3	385.5	375.3	372.5	402.4	390.0	371.7	362.2	358.0
1987	354.0	346.9	332.8	333.5	331.7	326.5	323.8	314.7	299.6	295.0	306.1	325.8
1988	343.4	318.2	299.2	307.1	309.3	305.0	330.5	318.7	302.4	293.9	302.3	307.0
1989	294.9	313.5	314.9	302.5	317.4	334.3	338.0	330.6	335.7	361.3	344.5	371.8
1990	366.9	358.0	345.7	354.3	353.7	357.5	363.7	387.2	392.7	422.8	457.8	469.7
1991	457.8	491.1	500.8	466.2	437.9	424.6	411.2	425.4	422.4	426.9	447.5	463.0
1992	437.1	442.9	431.9	416.9	411.6	417.2	436.4	396.9	409.0	368.1	360.9	341.1
1993	344.2	336.6	353.0	347.1	343.8	345.0	350.6	336.9	336.9	350.5	340.9	324.4
1994	363.7	347.4	333.5	350.4	364.9	348.3	345.6	334.1	328.4	333.4	329.3	324.2
1995	331.3	337.0	339.3	352.9	373.5	375.9	374.3	351.5	358.9	365.8	375.6	362.5
1996	371.2	369.0	390.7	358.2	349.3	354.9	337.0	326.3	336.3	335.3	338.1	353.5
1997	329.5	310.5	311.4	336.4	323.7	338.9	304.9	326.0	308.8	-	-	-

Source: The Conference Board. Primary source(s): U.S. Department of Labor, Employment and Training Administration, Unemployment Insurance Services, Division of Actuarial Services, Washington, DC 20210. A dash (-) indicates that data are not available or zero.

Manufacturers' New Orders, Consumer Goods and Materials

(Millions of chained 1992 $)

Year	Jan	Feb	Mar	Apr	May	Jun	Jul	Aug	Sep	Oct	Nov	Dec
1959	55,748	59,687	60,676	59,564	57,902	58,045	56,520	53,833	53,579	53,443	52,262	56,717
1960	55,306	54,177	53,095	53,557	53,427	53,911	53,601	55,185	54,880	53,646	52,877	52,305
1961	50,214	49,696	53,377	55,166	56,363	57,821	55,635	58,915	58,182	58,267	60,853	62,532
1962	61,763	60,949	60,424	58,329	59,782	58,865	60,691	61,200	61,498	62,376	62,197	60,959
1963	62,520	64,455	65,143	67,365	65,631	64,512	67,146	63,416	64,816	67,338	67,325	67,442
1964	69,470	68,411	68,417	71,602	70,370	70,738	73,290	70,481	74,781	70,627	72,602	75,631
1965	76,532	76,636	77,687	77,551	77,183	77,857	80,145	80,384	75,152	78,688	81,572	83,246
1966	82,534	83,927	87,256	85,175	84,157	84,724	82,762	82,554	84,159	84,538	82,248	81,262
1967	80,669	79,667	78,832	79,921	81,172	82,009	81,388	85,559	82,340	80,957	83,901	89,759
1968	87,665	86,127	86,147	85,179	86,956	87,519	86,385	81,945	90,604	91,917	92,656	90,604
1969	91,193	91,110	90,858	90,795	90,680	90,608	91,422	91,625	93,281	92,612	88,906	88,968
1970	84,837	83,715	83,269	83,081	83,946	86,064	83,838	83,829	83,501	77,944	78,249	85,960
1971	87,894	87,898	88,307	85,801	85,448	84,854	85,945	88,827	87,329	87,736	89,951	92,436
1972	93,423	95,468	94,550	95,143	95,747	97,456	95,109	100,662	103,632	103,175	105,561	108,879
1973	111,845	113,909	114,386	110,066	111,282	109,293	109,337	108,139	107,366	109,475	111,258	107,286
1974	109,139	108,031	106,564	106,621	109,934	106,940	104,319	103,528	98,791	95,513	91,895	83,376
1975	81,643	80,808	77,029	79,902	80,594	81,250	85,310	87,327	87,789	88,528	87,905	89,171
1976	91,631	93,935	95,955	94,821	96,104	96,124	96,183	96,804	96,322	93,896	98,096	101,763
1977	101,819	102,506	107,151	103,615	104,472	105,466	105,534	106,650	106,585	105,992	108,518	109,147
1978	104,479	107,152	109,373	114,214	113,454	113,863	111,683	113,106	111,745	113,474	114,793	117,604
1979	114,932	112,458	115,344	110,793	111,875	111,887	108,253	105,308	106,465	104,849	103,219	102,238
1980	103,402	105,344	97,809	89,769	85,756	87,300	90,060	92,629	97,856	101,802	100,791	101,316
1981	95,329	99,954	99,476	101,516	102,538	102,253	100,756	97,429	95,300	92,021	90,032	89,022
1982	87,579	88,355	91,198	89,979	91,669	90,789	91,436	88,558	90,249	85,792	86,065	86,360
1983	91,478	93,118	93,156	94,611	97,545	100,526	101,956	103,587	103,513	107,407	108,384	110,025
1984	111,752	111,749	109,435	109,297	108,487	106,320	109,687	109,100	104,390	106,589	107,085	107,708
1985	109,611	107,065	107,230	107,242	109,297	108,480	108,395	109,654	110,029	109,803	109,750	109,138
1986	112,882	110,984	108,119	111,175	108,476	111,280	109,979	110,485	113,119	112,349	109,568	114,481
1987	110,448	117,183	117,730	116,317	115,510	117,780	119,480	116,112	118,530	119,583	119,047	118,975
1988	117,066	119,480	119,898	119,775	121,367	122,253	121,590	120,012	122,053	121,685	122,924	127,697
1989	126,547	125,146	120,949	123,401	120,552	120,547	114,866	120,234	121,020	117,444	119,897	118,904
1990	114,109	119,691	122,149	119,242	122,450	121,426	119,502	120,717	117,691	117,494	112,836	108,901
1991	110,105	109,972	106,400	113,001	115,288	112,795	119,260	117,412	119,045	117,625	118,143	113,876
1992	114,440	116,703	117,420	120,117	118,668	121,910	121,321	119,829	119,868	121,916	122,589	127,322
1993	125,048	127,128	124,708	123,954	122,260	124,150	123,065	122,487	125,981	126,996	128,378	130,111
1994	131,129	131,296	136,155	133,469	136,021	136,295	134,394	139,087	137,985	136,969	140,688	142,498
1995	143,080	140,937	140,567	137,171	137,266	137,543	137,345	139,751	138,567	140,055	139,134	139,198
1996	138,739	138,427	136,410	143,490	145,552	145,314	148,057	146,452	147,471	148,349	147,577	143,753
1997	149,145	151,109	149,430	151,505	150,926	152,967	153,805	157,233	155,619	-	-	-

Source: The Conference Board. Primary source(s): U.S. Department of Commerce, Bureau of the Census, Manufacturing and Construction Division, Manufacturers' Shipments, Inventories, and Orders Branch, Washington, DC 20233. F.W. Dodge; McGraw-Hill, Inc., Market Analysis Group, 24 Hartwell Avenue, Lexington, MA 02173. Deflators calculated by The Conference Board. A dash (-) indicates that data are not available or zero.

Vendor Performance, Slower Deliveries Diffusion Index

(Percent)

Year	Jan	Feb	Mar	Apr	May	Jun	Jul	Aug	Sep	Oct	Nov	Dec
1948	36.3	37.1	32.7	41.6	40.4	38.4	36.8	31.2	28.3	28.7	28.0	17.7
1949	16.6	13.1	12.4	16.2	15.5	15.0	22.4	33.0	39.9	46.1	51.5	52.2
1950	56.3	68.0	72.0	68.8	82.9	76.5	89.4	81.7	73.7	70.3	79.1	87.5
1951	88.7	93.3	85.1	65.7	45.0	36.7	32.2	32.0	46.4	47.2	34.9	33.6
1952	31.3	24.9	18.8	19.4	22.4	33.0	47.4	41.2	42.7	43.3	45.0	43.5
1953	41.5	41.8	41.8	38.6	35.1	33.3	28.5	26.5	23.2	20.7	20.2	21.8
1954	23.6	26.9	28.0	30.3	34.3	35.8	38.1	36.4	43.6	49.5	51.9	54.5
1955	60.6	67.2	68.5	71.9	68.7	65.7	67.0	64.3	66.3	66.5	64.9	61.4
1956	53.5	51.3	51.0	51.0	38.6	41.0	53.9	46.8	42.8	40.1	44.6	39.5
1957	36.3	31.2	26.3	28.9	30.0	30.0	36.8	30.8	28.8	32.6	27.8	27.3
1958	30.3	31.0	34.0	35.5	38.5	39.2	43.0	44.7	51.1	52.4	55.8	56.4
1959	61.8	67.3	66.3	64.8	63.0	63.7	59.1	57.4	57.5	58.5	54.6	53.7
1960	46.2	31.7	28.8	28.9	32.3	34.8	35.8	38.0	37.3	36.2	37.6	40.4
1961	39.2	41.1	42.1	47.5	47.9	49.3	49.4	50.6	50.7	52.4	51.1	55.8
1962	57.1	56.2	57.0	47.4	45.2	43.3	45.1	43.7	45.1	46.7	48.7	50.1
1963	50.4	51.0	54.9	58.2	56.4	56.3	43.6	48.5	49.7	47.4	48.7	47.6
1964	55.3	51.9	60.3	57.7	61.4	57.6	61.8	66.2	71.9	71.2	70.3	67.8
1965	68.5	68.1	65.9	69.4	68.9	69.3	65.1	65.4	61.2	59.1	65.1	73.5
1966	74.9	80.1	86.4	79.3	74.6	71.6	73.1	74.3	72.4	68.7	62.6	57.9
1967	48.2	49.9	38.0	36.9	34.4	36.5	40.9	44.8	46.5	51.1	51.4	49.9
1968	50.6	53.9	54.0	49.0	49.4	49.9	55.9	47.8	48.4	53.3	61.0	58.3
1969	63.6	60.1	60.5	63.9	64.9	67.0	65.7	70.3	68.9	66.8	64.1	66.8
1970	57.9	57.7	49.3	48.7	67.2	66.1	49.8	46.1	46.5	39.0	37.8	37.5
1971	39.8	44.2	45.0	48.9	49.4	47.9	47.4	49.7	48.9	50.9	50.9	53.3
1972	55.2	52.6	57.1	55.0	56.1	57.7	61.7	62.9	65.5	73.0	74.5	80.7
1973	83.7	85.2	87.5	86.7	86.6	85.6	85.2	86.7	90.1	88.7	96.8	92.8
1974	91.8	88.8	88.9	82.1	74.5	73.1	69.2	66.3	51.8	45.3	34.0	23.2
1975	19.5	15.9	17.3	21.7	22.7	24.9	28.7	35.1	43.8	44.8	46.8	41.2
1976	54.0	56.1	56.7	57.3	58.3	58.6	54.0	55.2	52.6	49.0	47.2	53.3
1977	55.3	65.1	49.6	54.6	55.4	53.3	58.3	53.5	56.7	53.6	56.3	57.1
1978	55.6	63.4	58.9	57.1	57.4	61.1	59.4	60.6	60.0	64.7	64.5	63.5
1979	66.4	64.0	66.7	75.6	63.7	61.4	57.4	52.9	50.7	46.9	46.8	42.2
1980	42.1	46.0	39.1	36.9	29.8	32.4	36.3	40.1	41.2	46.5	46.8	50.1
1981	49.7	48.5	48.7	51.2	50.2	47.9	44.9	49.6	45.9	37.7	40.5	41.2
1982	40.1	40.8	36.4	38.2	42.1	45.2	45.8	45.3	45.9	46.5	46.9	48.6
1983	46.7	49.9	50.8	52.7	51.9	56.8	58.9	60.2	60.7	62.8	67.5	62.1
1984	64.4	61.5	65.5	64.6	62.5	56.2	59.1	55.2	52.8	49.3	48.1	48.8
1985	50.4	48.6	46.7	46.1	48.0	47.1	45.7	46.6	49.5	50.0	48.5	49.3
1986	50.1	49.8	50.5	50.7	50.2	49.9	49.9	50.8	49.6	51.3	52.0	52.8
1987	51.5	51.2	51.9	52.8	54.0	56.8	58.9	60.3	61.5	62.2	64.9	62.7
1988	62.0	61.2	57.3	58.6	56.9	65.6	58.4	57.4	55.2	54.8	52.1	53.0
1989	53.9	54.0	52.5	52.2	49.1	46.5	46.1	44.0	43.9	43.3	42.5	43.5
1990	48.2	44.4	47.2	47.2	48.2	49.8	46.4	50.1	48.9	48.1	48.6	47.2
1991	44.4	44.7	43.9	45.0	46.0	47.1	49.6	48.3	48.8	50.2	50.1	49.4
1992	48.7	49.3	50.3	47.4	50.0	50.8	52.5	50.3	51.2	48.6	51.3	51.5
1993	52.3	51.7	52.7	52.8	51.5	50.4	51.0	51.8	51.3	50.7	50.9	51.5
1994	54.3	56.7	55.4	57.3	60.5	60.2	58.5	61.7	62.3	64.7	65.0	64.5
1995	62.2	60.2	57.0	56.3	53.7	51.6	51.7	49.4	50.1	48.4	45.6	47.2
1996	47.0	49.0	49.9	49.4	50.2	52.6	51.3	52.3	50.2	50.7	51.6	51.6
1997	48.5	51.3	53.6	53.4	55.2	54.6	55.3	55.8	55.2	-	-	-

Source: The Conference Board. Primary source(s): National Association of Purchasing Management, 2055 East Centennial Circle, P.O. Box 22160, Tempe, AZ 85285-2160. A dash (-) indicates that data are not available or zero.

Manufacturers' New Orders, Nondefense Capital Goods
(Millions of chained 1992 $)

Year	Jan	Feb	Mar	Apr	May	Jun	Jul	Aug	Sep	Oct	Nov	Dec
1959	9,717	10,014	11,347	10,326	10,815	11,088	11,215	10,348	11,283	10,864	10,156	10,932
1960	10,062	10,397	10,228	10,639	10,623	10,591	10,233	10,237	10,121	9,926	9,623	10,570
1961	10,114	10,165	10,174	10,089	9,844	10,417	10,898	11,400	10,759	10,866	11,237	10,656
1962	11,321	12,099	10,812	11,839	11,177	11,002	11,091	11,071	11,332	11,508	12,342	11,664
1963	11,866	12,195	12,379	12,416	12,953	12,336	12,453	12,891	13,104	13,141	12,798	13,383
1964	14,599	13,023	13,963	13,752	15,240	15,644	14,399	14,553	14,466	14,820	14,996	15,310
1965	15,248	14,999	16,252	16,068	15,639	16,161	16,424	15,953	16,512	17,001	17,338	18,553
1966	17,593	19,220	18,918	19,461	19,590	19,306	20,214	18,832	19,810	19,396	18,639	18,767
1967	15,976	16,866	16,983	17,151	17,499	18,006	18,347	18,716	17,809	17,994	18,171	19,051
1968	23,600	22,187	27,329	23,368	18,328	18,272	23,133	22,624	19,721	24,751	20,827	22,269
1969	24,044	26,873	23,554	28,751	23,784	23,321	23,582	24,251	26,639	22,482	23,162	20,978
1970	23,642	22,114	19,838	18,669	19,537	18,449	19,880	19,615	19,028	18,199	19,348	21,242
1971	20,544	21,790	21,130	20,710	20,103	23,216	18,735	21,191	22,691	20,311	21,323	22,276
1972	20,902	22,820	23,552	22,787	25,254	21,856	25,313	24,143	26,203	25,179	25,783	26,339
1973	26,489	28,182	28,816	29,903	29,220	28,468	29,843	30,172	29,927	32,323	32,525	31,570
1974	32,434	32,879	33,255	32,267	29,765	28,960	33,702	31,751	30,361	27,068	26,059	25,585
1975	26,247	23,546	21,481	23,889	21,955	21,591	24,073	23,709	22,732	23,127	23,032	21,893
1976	23,202	24,138	23,676	25,550	24,608	24,555	28,475	25,868	27,157	28,410	25,524	28,098
1977	27,395	26,666	26,723	27,420	27,485	30,012	27,958	28,406	30,731	30,655	29,301	31,083
1978	30,061	32,382	31,534	32,457	32,447	31,204	31,029	32,389	33,443	36,788	34,207	30,700
1979	33,956	37,315	39,938	33,170	33,559	33,922	32,859	32,768	32,927	33,416	31,353	31,195
1980	33,160	28,571	27,847	27,788	24,361	25,627	27,859	24,829	26,231	27,227	24,778	27,423
1981	29,621	25,400	28,607	29,625	27,143	27,570	28,296	28,122	26,787	26,659	26,017	23,026
1982	26,597	25,926	26,300	25,847	22,275	22,456	23,676	21,623	22,719	24,343	21,896	22,161
1983	23,343	19,537	21,493	23,042	22,723	24,414	22,580	23,705	25,913	27,559	24,713	24,611
1984	28,120	27,907	28,204	27,217	30,135	28,399	29,213	27,575	27,137	27,991	27,792	26,462
1985	27,411	30,916	29,280	26,694	27,104	28,938	27,765	28,723	30,280	29,963	26,699	31,454
1986	28,278	29,432	28,190	26,818	26,920	27,214	26,675	26,334	27,374	28,365	27,588	29,079
1987	28,103	27,660	26,821	28,503	30,655	30,507	32,131	28,881	28,876	30,250	30,484	33,008
1988	34,978	34,138	31,979	33,100	30,932	33,866	35,335	37,916	34,820	33,310	34,358	37,799
1989	37,691	35,285	34,832	36,430	33,962	36,292	38,183	31,933	31,620	31,257	34,442	39,949
1990	35,421	32,736	37,281	33,471	32,601	32,582	36,896	31,986	34,899	37,703	30,799	38,796
1991	33,856	33,606	31,621	28,693	28,016	27,813	37,126	30,564	29,754	30,286	34,194	27,359
1992	31,692	31,037	33,449	31,997	32,165	31,914	31,181	29,286	32,050	31,862	27,823	33,430
1993	28,864	32,965	29,617	31,486	30,462	33,063	29,175	30,975	29,747	31,242	33,007	33,271
1994	35,153	33,694	33,738	33,452	32,774	35,822	34,048	34,802	35,388	34,849	37,234	34,608
1995	37,582	37,784	38,028	36,478	39,715	37,983	35,607	36,845	41,648	38,360	41,286	44,122
1996	42,987	41,636	43,504	37,906	42,756	40,338	43,252	38,737	45,190	44,638	41,474	41,485
1997	43,325	44,460	42,798	42,052	42,499	45,370	45,564	45,978	46,781	-	-	-

Source: The Conference Board. Primary source(s): U.S. Department of Commerce, Bureau of the Census, Manufacturing and Construction Division, Manufacturers' Shipments, Inventories, and Orders Branch, Washington, DC 20233. F.W. Dodge; McGraw-Hill, Inc., Market Analysis Group, 24 Hartwell Avenue, Lexington, MA 02173. Deflators calculated by The Conference Board. A dash (-) indicates that data are not available or zero.

Building Permits for New Private Housing Units

(Thousands)

Year	Jan	Feb	Mar	Apr	May	Jun	Jul	Aug	Sep	Oct	Nov	Dec
1954	1,314	1,294	1,364	1,378	1,403	1,507	1,545	1,533	1,572	1,626	1,752	1,702
1955	1,759	1,946	1,667	1,713	1,723	1,626	1,632	1,576	1,552	1,519	1,386	1,380
1956	1,416	1,376	1,416	1,411	1,314	1,290	1,281	1,251	1,218	1,201	1,208	1,197
1957	1,115	1,172	1,182	1,117	1,167	1,192	1,111	1,187	1,191	1,175	1,141	1,150
1958	1,180	1,015	1,125	1,185	1,240	1,324	1,442	1,440	1,476	1,523	1,729	1,494
1959	1,478	1,542	1,611	1,539	1,513	1,490	1,452	1,465	1,411	1,358	1,298	1,394
1960	1,325	1,319	1,158	1,232	1,276	1,161	1,211	1,205	1,194	1,179	1,187	1,151
1961	1,176	1,166	1,212	1,214	1,246	1,297	1,313	1,405	1,331	1,361	1,396	1,408
1962	1,360	1,447	1,375	1,498	1,384	1,398	1,442	1,455	1,481	1,432	1,499	1,499
1963	1,457	1,415	1,468	1,504	1,576	1,571	1,542	1,529	1,650	1,652	1,585	1,661
1964	1,513	1,684	1,532	1,475	1,516	1,494	1,522	1,525	1,476	1,437	1,463	1,358
1965	1,475	1,383	1,414	1,356	1,409	1,448	1,444	1,458	1,432	1,493	1,525	1,535
1966	1,546	1,353	1,441	1,337	1,259	1,116	1,089	1,024	905	862	859	867
1967	1,125	1,025	1,078	1,171	1,215	1,321	1,330	1,389	1,445	1,446	1,465	1,486
1968	1,332	1,516	1,547	1,454	1,465	1,469	1,519	1,533	1,655	1,606	1,622	1,571
1969	1,649	1,689	1,624	1,627	1,502	1,525	1,444	1,489	1,427	1,374	1,346	1,306
1970	1,200	1,263	1,279	1,383	1,502	1,494	1,497	1,576	1,611	1,768	1,697	1,996
1971	1,857	1,794	1,988	1,973	2,229	2,151	2,338	2,265	2,255	2,289	2,349	2,410
1972	2,487	2,410	2,339	2,377	2,297	2,425	2,438	2,514	2,658	2,616	2,483	2,688
1973	2,523	2,473	2,291	2,120	2,145	2,278	2,021	2,010	1,894	1,569	1,557	1,431
1974	1,478	1,511	1,600	1,393	1,264	1,207	1,113	1,019	933	915	870	965
1975	807	810	788	962	1,016	1,051	1,133	1,105	1,182	1,217	1,233	1,212
1976	1,328	1,323	1,293	1,258	1,327	1,320	1,383	1,455	1,646	1,583	1,701	1,679
1977	1,607	1,734	1,844	1,844	1,853	1,946	1,874	1,978	1,860	1,953	1,969	1,949
1978	1,812	1,808	1,873	2,028	1,839	2,065	1,860	1,761	1,824	1,855	1,869	1,894
1979	1,521	1,553	1,791	1,663	1,754	1,708	1,598	1,657	1,705	1,542	1,329	1,306
1980	1,333	1,249	1,029	842	896	1,165	1,311	1,424	1,545	1,423	1,440	1,300
1981	1,272	1,249	1,232	1,239	1,221	1,017	974	926	882	762	779	829
1982	827	842	928	925	992	951	1,088	964	1,086	1,197	1,280	1,407
1983	1,485	1,532	1,536	1,630	1,738	1,842	1,869	1,784	1,651	1,787	1,737	1,694
1984	1,867	2,043	1,773	1,826	1,790	1,865	1,650	1,573	1,566	1,532	1,689	1,672
1985	1,706	1,709	1,775	1,711	1,757	1,764	1,745	1,859	1,970	1,792	1,739	1,844
1986	1,899	1,816	1,830	1,910	1,847	1,840	1,830	1,774	1,733	1,722	1,690	1,956
1987	1,737	1,736	1,752	1,646	1,542	1,565	1,558	1,553	1,556	1,488	1,498	1,383
1988	1,279	1,478	1,568	1,469	1,484	1,527	1,479	1,501	1,476	1,558	1,550	1,543
1989	1,507	1,422	1,248	1,415	1,420	1,359	1,319	1,371	1,351	1,403	1,382	1,462
1990	1,797	1,366	1,281	1,168	1,097	1,139	1,108	1,099	1,003	951	967	885
1991	808	877	937	942	1,019	991	1,000	970	1,001	1,019	1,012	1,091
1992	1,107	1,178	1,112	1,084	1,086	1,087	1,119	1,105	1,145	1,164	1,149	1,209
1993	1,210	1,180	1,086	1,135	1,143	1,162	1,207	1,264	1,286	1,323	1,395	1,502
1994	1,390	1,269	1,342	1,392	1,396	1,357	1,335	1,377	1,412	1,397	1,340	1,396
1995	1,282	1,254	1,226	1,259	1,271	1,305	1,354	1,386	1,421	1,400	1,430	1,442
1996	1,385	1,425	1,438	1,486	1,457	1,432	1,454	1,405	1,391	1,349	1,391	1,405
1997	1,395	1,438	1,457	1,442	1,432	1,402	1,414	1,397	1,445	-	-	-

Source: The Conference Board. Primary source(s): U.S. Department of Commerce, Bureau of the Census, Manufacturing and Construction Division, Building Permits Branch, Washington, DC 20233. A dash (-) indicates that data are not available or zero.

Index of Stock Prices, 500 Common Stocks

Not seasonally adjusted

(1941-43 = 10)

Year	Jan	Feb	Mar	Apr	May	Jun	Jul	Aug	Sep	Oct	Nov	Dec
1945	13.49	13.94	13.93	14.28	14.82	15.09	14.78	14.83	15.84	16.50	17.04	17.33
1946	18.02	18.07	17.53	18.66	18.70	18.58	18.05	17.70	15.09	14.75	14.69	15.13
1947	15.21	15.80	15.16	14.60	14.34	14.84	15.77	15.46	15.06	15.45	15.27	15.03
1948	14.83	14.10	14.30	15.40	16.15	16.82	16.42	15.94	15.76	16.19	15.29	15.19
1949	15.36	14.77	14.91	14.89	14.78	13.97	14.76	15.29	15.49	15.89	16.11	16.54
1950	16.88	17.21	17.35	17.84	18.44	18.74	17.38	18.43	19.08	19.87	19.83	19.75
1951	21.21	22.00	21.63	21.92	21.93	21.55	21.93	22.89	23.48	23.36	22.71	23.41
1952	24.19	23.75	23.81	23.74	23.73	24.38	25.08	25.18	24.78	24.26	25.03	26.04
1953	26.18	25.86	25.99	24.71	24.84	23.95	24.29	24.39	23.27	23.97	24.50	24.83
1954	25.46	26.02	26.57	27.63	28.73	28.96	30.13	30.73	31.45	32.18	33.44	34.97
1955	35.60	36.79	36.50	37.76	37.60	39.78	42.69	42.43	44.34	42.11	44.95	45.37
1956	44.15	44.43	47.49	48.05	46.54	46.27	48.78	48.49	46.84	46.24	45.76	46.44
1957	45.43	43.47	44.03	45.05	46.78	47.55	48.51	45.84	43.98	41.24	40.35	40.33
1958	41.12	41.26	42.11	42.34	43.70	44.75	45.98	47.70	48.96	50.95	52.50	53.49
1959	55.62	54.77	56.15	57.10	57.96	57.46	59.74	59.40	57.05	57.00	57.23	59.06
1960	58.03	55.78	55.02	55.73	55.22	57.26	55.84	56.51	54.81	53.73	55.47	56.80
1961	59.72	62.17	64.12	65.83	66.50	65.62	65.44	67.79	67.26	68.00	71.08	71.74
1962	69.07	70.22	70.29	68.05	62.99	55.63	56.97	58.52	58.00	56.17	60.04	62.64
1963	65.06	65.92	65.67	68.76	70.14	70.11	69.07	70.98	72.85	73.03	72.62	74.17
1964	76.45	77.39	78.80	79.94	80.72	80.24	83.22	82.00	83.41	84.85	85.44	83.96
1965	86.12	86.75	86.83	87.97	89.28	85.04	84.91	86.49	89.38	91.39	92.15	91.73
1966	93.32	92.69	88.88	91.60	86.78	86.06	85.84	80.65	77.81	77.13	80.99	81.33
1967	84.45	87.36	89.42	90.96	92.59	91.43	93.01	94.49	95.81	95.66	92.66	95.30
1968	95.04	90.75	89.09	95.67	97.87	100.53	100.30	98.11	101.34	103.76	105.40	106.48
1969	102.04	101.46	99.30	101.26	104.62	99.14	94.71	94.18	94.51	95.52	96.21	91.11
1970	90.31	87.16	88.65	85.95	76.06	75.59	75.72	77.92	82.58	84.37	84.28	90.05
1971	93.49	97.11	99.60	103.04	101.64	99.72	99.00	97.24	99.40	97.29	92.78	99.17
1972	103.30	105.24	107.69	108.81	107.65	108.01	107.21	111.01	109.39	109.56	115.05	117.50
1973	118.42	114.16	112.42	110.27	107.22	104.75	105.83	103.80	105.61	109.84	102.03	94.78
1974	96.11	93.45	97.44	92.46	89.67	89.79	82.82	76.03	68.12	69.44	71.74	67.07
1975	72.56	80.10	83.78	84.72	90.10	92.40	92.49	85.71	84.67	88.57	90.07	88.70
1976	96.86	100.64	101.08	101.93	101.16	101.77	104.20	103.29	105.45	101.89	101.19	104.66
1977	103.81	100.96	100.57	99.05	98.76	99.29	100.18	97.75	96.23	93.74	94.28	93.82
1978	90.25	88.98	88.82	92.71	97.41	97.66	97.19	103.92	103.86	100.58	94.71	96.11
1979	99.71	98.23	100.11	102.07	99.73	101.73	102.71	107.36	108.60	104.47	103.66	107.78
1980	110.87	115.34	104.69	102.97	107.69	114.55	119.83	123.50	126.51	130.22	135.65	133.48
1981	132.97	128.40	133.19	134.43	131.73	132.28	129.13	129.63	118.27	119.80	122.92	123.79
1982	117.28	114.50	110.84	116.31	116.35	109.70	109.38	109.65	122.43	132.66	138.10	139.37
1983	144.27	146.80	151.88	157.71	164.10	166.39	166.96	162.42	167.16	167.65	165.23	164.36
1984	166.39	157.25	157.44	157.60	156.55	153.12	151.08	164.42	166.11	164.82	166.27	164.48
1985	171.61	180.88	179.42	180.62	184.90	188.89	192.54	188.31	184.06	186.18	197.45	207.26
1986	208.19	219.37	232.33	237.98	238.46	245.30	240.18	245.00	238.27	237.36	245.09	248.61
1987	264.51	280.93	292.47	289.32	289.12	301.38	310.09	329.36	318.66	280.16	245.01	240.96
1988	250.48	258.13	265.74	262.61	256.12	270.68	269.05	263.73	267.97	277.40	271.02	276.51
1989	285.41	294.01	292.71	302.25	313.93	323.73	331.93	346.61	347.33	347.40	340.22	348.57
1990	339.97	330.45	338.47	338.18	350.25	360.39	360.03	330.75	315.41	307.12	315.29	328.75
1991	325.49	362.26	372.28	379.68	377.99	378.29	380.23	389.40	387.20	386.88	385.92	388.51
1992	416.08	412.56	407.36	407.41	414.81	408.27	415.05	417.93	418.48	412.50	422.84	435.64
1993	435.23	441.70	450.16	443.08	445.25	448.06	447.29	454.13	459.24	463.90	462.89	465.95
1994	472.99	471.58	463.81	447.23	450.90	454.83	451.40	464.24	466.96	463.81	461.01	455.19
1995	465.25	481.92	493.15	507.91	523.81	539.35	557.37	559.11	578.77	582.92	595.53	614.57
1996	614.42	649.54	647.07	647.17	661.23	668.50	644.07	662.68	674.88	701.45	735.67	743.25
1997	766.22	798.39	792.16	763.93	833.09	876.29	925.29	927.74	937.02	-	-	-

Source: The Conference Board. Primary source(s): Standard & Poor's Corporation, 25 Broadway, New York, NY 10004. A dash (-) indicates that data are not available or zero.

Money Supply M2
(Billions of chained 1992 $)

Year	Jan	Feb	Mar	Apr	May	Jun	Jul	Aug	Sep	Oct	Nov	Dec
1959	1,265.8	1,269.3	1,275.7	1,277.6	1,286.0	1,290.9	1,293.4	1,297.0	1,294.7	1,291.3	1,293.1	1,295.3
1960	1,298.0	1,296.7	1,299.7	1,297.3	1,299.8	1,305.4	1,310.6	1,320.4	1,325.5	1,328.4	1,330.1	1,336.0
1961	1,342.3	1,351.5	1,360.0	1,367.8	1,376.7	1,385.7	1,388.4	1,395.8	1,402.4	1,409.1	1,419.0	1,427.8
1962	1,436.3	1,443.2	1,453.7	1,461.1	1,467.9	1,475.1	1,482.2	1,488.3	1,489.5	1,500.5	1,510.2	1,522.8
1963	1,530.5	1,540.1	1,552.8	1,563.6	1,572.4	1,579.2	1,587.1	1,594.9	1,604.9	1,611.9	1,622.6	1,628.6
1964	1,632.9	1,641.3	1,649.5	1,656.7	1,666.5	1,676.6	1,686.4	1,699.1	1,710.8	1,718.4	1,727.6	1,736.7
1965	1,745.1	1,756.0	1,764.5	1,770.8	1,774.1	1,780.8	1,789.9	1,800.6	1,814.3	1,826.7	1,835.8	1,843.2
1966	1,852.3	1,855.2	1,860.9	1,863.5	1,863.9	1,863.7	1,857.6	1,857.5	1,862.6	1,859.4	1,861.9	1,868.7
1967	1,874.6	1,885.5	1,901.8	1,907.7	1,923.3	1,935.7	1,944.8	1,956.2	1,965.2	1,972.8	1,977.5	1,987.3
1968	1,986.5	1,990.4	1,994.4	1,997.7	2,003.2	2,010.7	2,016.0	2,022.1	2,030.9	2,037.4	2,048.4	2,061.4
1969	2,063.3	2,068.2	2,068.8	2,065.0	2,060.2	2,057.8	2,053.7	2,050.3	2,048.2	2,046.1	2,044.0	2,043.8
1970	2,041.3	2,022.6	2,020.7	2,013.9	2,018.0	2,024.6	2,029.5	2,042.8	2,054.5	2,061.3	2,068.3	2,077.3
1971	2,092.6	2,113.2	2,134.9	2,153.9	2,172.4	2,182.4	2,197.3	2,209.1	2,229.0	2,243.4	2,258.9	2,267.4
1972	2,282.8	2,298.8	2,320.1	2,331.6	2,342.4	2,358.2	2,380.8	2,402.1	2,422.1	2,443.9	2,458.2	2,476.7
1973	2,493.8	2,491.9	2,477.5	2,472.6	2,482.9	2,487.1	2,488.8	2,470.2	2,461.0	2,455.5	2,454.1	2,452.8
1974	2,443.2	2,427.3	2,417.2	2,409.2	2,390.8	2,380.6	2,373.9	2,355.8	2,343.6	2,340.5	2,337.6	2,330.6
1975	2,328.2	2,336.4	2,358.3	2,374.1	2,395.3	2,418.8	2,427.2	2,437.5	2,444.7	2,445.9	2,455.6	2,462.6
1976	2,478.2	2,507.6	2,525.4	2,544.6	2,560.3	2,560.5	2,567.4	2,581.8	2,595.7	2,615.9	2,632.2	2,648.8
1977	2,666.5	2,672.7	2,683.9	2,693.9	2,698.7	2,702.9	2,710.6	2,720.3	2,730.7	2,735.7	2,737.5	2,740.6
1978	2,743.6	2,740.7	2,737.6	2,733.0	2,730.3	2,727.9	2,726.0	2,730.0	2,740.5	2,735.6	2,734.1	2,733.0
1979	2,719.2	2,712.6	2,712.4	2,716.9	2,705.8	2,710.9	2,709.0	2,712.0	2,704.9	2,693.7	2,684.9	2,674.4
1980	2,659.3	2,652.0	2,632.8	2,617.7	2,612.7	2,627.0	2,633.7	2,641.7	2,640.0	2,640.3	2,640.3	2,628.5
1981	2,615.3	2,607.0	2,617.7	2,640.6	2,635.8	2,633.3	2,634.0	2,637.6	2,637.6	2,651.3	2,658.3	2,675.6
1982	2,685.1	2,681.5	2,694.9	2,718.8	2,719.3	2,715.2	2,711.1	2,727.4	2,739.6	2,741.8	2,751.9	2,778.4
1983	2,844.0	2,892.2	2,912.4	2,912.8	2,920.3	2,925.3	2,930.6	2,931.5	2,933.3	2,948.6	2,958.1	2,968.4
1984	2,978.2	2,993.9	3,008.1	3,019.1	3,032.2	3,040.8	3,044.6	3,043.0	3,055.9	3,066.2	3,090.7	3,119.5
1985	3,141.5	3,156.7	3,159.8	3,163.1	3,172.6	3,193.7	3,207.9	3,218.6	3,225.4	3,227.4	3,227.6	3,233.1
1986	3,233.4	3,247.9	3,281.7	3,316.6	3,342.6	3,355.5	3,377.4	3,396.6	3,408.4	3,427.7	3,438.7	3,463.3
1987	3,461.6	3,452.4	3,450.2	3,456.3	3,454.5	3,442.2	3,439.4	3,435.6	3,434.1	3,438.9	3,433.9	3,438.5
1988	3,457.5	3,480.5	3,491.8	3,498.5	3,502.8	3,501.3	3,496.8	3,489.2	3,476.9	3,475.1	3,481.9	3,478.8
1989	3,463.3	3,452.5	3,444.7	3,429.2	3,420.7	3,431.8	3,450.8	3,471.8	3,481.7	3,488.4	3,499.3	3,510.8
1990	3,501.0	3,499.6	3,494.5	3,494.3	3,480.4	3,479.0	3,477.7	3,473.6	3,466.0	3,447.2	3,444.3	3,448.8
1991	3,446.4	3,455.9	3,473.1	3,472.5	3,472.2	3,478.2	3,471.1	3,459.9	3,447.6	3,444.5	3,439.8	3,437.9
1992	3,435.6	3,445.7	3,438.1	3,427.1	3,418.5	3,404.6	3,392.8	3,407.8	3,399.3	3,399.6	3,397.6	3,391.8
1993	3,378.6	3,360.7	3,351.5	3,345.2	3,364.7	3,368.7	3,364.9	3,362.3	3,363.9	3,354.7	3,359.3	3,363.0
1994	3,366.2	3,357.6	3,351.1	3,353.7	3,349.7	3,330.1	3,326.0	3,311.1	3,303.9	3,296.9	3,292.5	3,289.8
1995	3,282.2	3,275.2	3,269.8	3,273.0	3,283.1	3,305.1	3,317.8	3,329.3	3,342.5	3,344.2	3,351.5	3,359.8
1996	3,364.5	3,370.0	3,388.1	3,387.2	3,382.9	3,393.4	3,390.1	3,397.7	3,400.9	3,400.9	3,413.8	3,429.7
1997	3,424.7	3,430.5	3,443.6	3,458.0	3,457.6	3,466.3	3,471.9	3,500.4	3,513.8	-	-	-

Source: The Conference Board. Primary source(s): Board of Governors of the Federal Reserve System (money supply), Division of Monetary Affairs, Money and Reserve Projections Section, Stop 59, Washington, DC 20551. Deflators are calculated by The Conference Board. A dash (-) indicates that data are not available or zero.

Interest Rate Spread, 10-Year Treasury Bonds Less Federal Funds

Year	Jan	Feb	Mar	Apr	May	Jun	Jul	Aug	Sep	Oct	Nov	Dec
1954	-	-	-	-	-	-	1.50	1.14	1.32	1.58	1.65	1.23
1955	1.22	1.36	1.33	1.32	1.33	1.14	1.22	1.01	0.79	0.64	0.54	0.48
1956	0.45	0.34	0.46	0.56	0.32	0.29	0.36	0.60	0.43	0.38	0.61	0.65
1957	0.62	0.34	0.45	0.48	0.60	0.80	0.94	0.69	0.45	0.47	0.44	0.23
1958	0.37	1.38	1.78	1.62	2.29	2.04	2.52	2.01	2.00	2.00	1.47	1.44
1959	1.54	1.53	1.19	1.16	1.41	0.95	0.93	0.93	0.92	0.55	0.53	0.70
1960	0.73	0.52	0.41	0.36	0.50	0.83	0.67	0.82	1.20	1.42	1.49	1.86
1961	2.39	1.24	1.72	2.29	1.73	2.15	2.75	2.04	2.10	1.66	1.33	1.73
1962	1.93	1.67	1.08	1.06	1.51	1.23	1.30	1.05	1.08	1.03	0.98	0.93
1963	0.91	0.92	0.95	1.07	0.93	1.00	1.00	0.51	0.60	0.61	0.64	0.75
1964	0.69	0.67	0.79	0.76	0.70	0.67	0.77	0.69	0.75	0.83	0.63	0.33
1965	0.29	0.23	0.17	0.11	0.11	0.17	0.11	0.13	0.28	0.27	0.35	0.30
1966	0.19	0.23	0.22	0.08	-0.12	-0.36	-0.28	-0.31	-0.22	-0.52	-0.60	-0.56
1967	-0.36	-0.37	0.01	0.54	0.91	1.04	1.37	1.38	1.31	1.60	1.62	1.19
1968	0.93	0.85	0.69	-0.12	-0.24	-0.35	-0.52	-0.61	-0.32	-0.33	-0.12	0.01
1969	-0.26	-0.42	-0.49	-1.24	-2.35	-2.33	-1.89	-2.50	-1.99	-1.90	-1.71	-1.32
1970	-1.19	-1.74	-0.69	-0.71	-0.03	0.24	0.25	0.92	1.10	1.13	1.24	1.49
1971	2.10	2.39	1.99	1.68	1.76	1.61	1.42	1.02	0.59	0.73	0.90	1.79
1972	2.45	2.79	2.24	2.02	1.86	1.65	1.56	1.41	1.68	1.44	1.22	1.03
1973	0.52	0.06	-0.38	-0.45	-0.99	-1.59	-3.27	-3.10	-3.69	-3.22	-3.30	-3.21
1974	-2.66	-2.01	-2.14	-3.00	-3.73	-4.39	-5.11	-3.97	-3.30	-2.16	-1.77	-1.10
1975	0.37	1.15	2.19	2.74	2.84	2.31	1.96	2.26	2.19	2.32	2.83	2.80
1976	2.87	3.02	2.89	2.74	2.61	2.38	2.52	2.48	2.34	2.39	2.34	2.22
1977	2.60	2.71	2.77	2.64	2.11	1.89	1.91	1.50	1.20	1.05	1.07	1.13
1978	1.26	1.25	1.25	1.26	0.99	0.86	0.83	0.37	-0.03	-0.32	-0.95	-1.02
1979	-0.97	-0.96	-0.97	-0.83	-0.99	-1.38	-1.52	-1.91	-2.10	-3.47	-2.53	-3.39
1980	-3.02	-1.72	-4.44	-6.14	-0.80	0.31	1.22	1.49	0.64	-1.06	-3.17	-6.06
1981	-6.51	-2.74	-1.58	-2.04	-4.42	-5.63	-4.76	-2.88	-0.55	0.07	0.08	1.35
1982	1.37	-0.35	-0.82	-1.07	-0.83	0.15	1.36	2.94	2.03	1.20	1.35	1.59
1983	1.78	2.21	1.74	1.60	1.75	1.87	2.01	2.29	2.20	2.06	2.35	2.36
1984	2.11	2.25	2.41	2.34	3.09	2.50	2.13	1.08	1.22	2.17	2.14	3.12
1985	3.03	3.01	3.28	3.16	2.88	2.63	2.43	2.43	2.45	2.25	1.73	0.99
1986	1.05	0.84	0.30	0.31	0.86	0.88	0.74	1.00	1.56	1.58	1.21	0.20
1987	0.65	1.15	1.12	1.65	1.76	1.67	1.87	2.03	2.20	2.23	2.17	2.22
1988	1.84	1.63	1.79	1.85	2.00	1.41	1.31	1.25	0.79	0.50	0.61	0.35
1989	-0.03	-0.19	-0.49	-0.66	-0.95	-1.25	-1.22	-0.88	-0.83	-0.83	-0.68	-0.61
1990	-0.02	0.23	0.31	0.53	0.58	0.19	0.32	0.62	0.69	0.61	0.58	0.77
1991	1.18	1.60	1.99	2.13	2.29	2.38	2.45	2.24	2.20	2.32	2.61	2.66
1992	3.00	3.28	3.56	3.75	3.57	3.50	3.59	3.29	3.20	3.49	3.78	3.85
1993	3.58	3.23	2.91	3.01	3.04	2.92	2.75	2.65	2.27	2.34	2.70	2.81
1994	2.70	2.72	3.14	3.41	3.17	2.85	3.04	2.77	2.73	2.98	2.67	2.36
1995	2.25	1.55	1.22	1.01	0.62	0.17	0.43	0.75	0.40	0.28	0.13	0.11
1996	0.09	0.59	0.96	1.29	1.50	1.64	1.47	1.42	1.53	1.29	0.89	1.01
1997	1.33	1.23	1.30	1.38	1.21	0.93	0.70	0.76	0.67	-	-	-

Source: The Conference Board. Primary source(s): Board of Governors of the Federal Reserve System, Division of Monetary Affairs, Washington, DC 20551. A dash (-) indicates that data are not available or zero.

Consumer Expectations
Not seasonally adjusted
(1966:I = 100)

Year	Jan	Feb	Mar	Apr	May	Jun	Jul	Aug	Sep	Oct	Nov	Dec
1952	-	-	-	-	-	-	-	-	-	-	92.4	93.4
1953	94.5	95.5	94.2	92.9	91.6	90.3	89.1	87.8	86.5	85.2	83.9	84.4
1954	84.8	85.3	85.6	85.8	86.1	86.7	87.3	87.9	88.5	89.1	89.7	91.4
1955	93.1	94.8	96.5	98.2	99.9	100.6	101.2	101.9	102.5	103.2	103.8	103.7
1956	103.6	103.6	103.5	103.4	103.3	103.9	104.6	105.2	105.2	105.2	105.2	103.7
1957	102.2	100.7	99.2	97.7	96.2	94.6	92.9	91.3	89.6	88.0	86.3	85.7
1958	85.2	84.6	84.0	83.5	82.9	84.8	86.6	88.5	90.4	92.2	94.1	94.7
1959	95.2	95.8	96.4	96.9	97.5	97.2	96.9	96.7	96.4	96.1	95.8	98.7
1960	101.7	104.6	102.6	100.6	98.6	98.2	97.9	97.5	96.1	94.8	93.4	93.9
1961	94.4	94.9	96.0	97.0	98.1	98.2	98.4	98.5	97.9	97.4	96.8	99.0
1962	101.2	103.4	101.1	98.8	96.5	95.5	94.4	93.4	95.3	97.3	99.2	99.4
1963	99.7	99.9	98.0	96.0	94.1	95.1	96.0	97.0	97.0	97.0	97.0	97.8
1964	98.6	99.4	98.7	97.9	97.2	97.8	98.5	99.1	99.8	100.4	101.1	101.7
1965	102.4	103.0	103.2	103.4	103.7	103.9	104.1	104.3	105.3	106.3	107.3	104.9
1966	102.4	100.0	98.7	97.3	96.0	94.2	92.5	90.7	90.5	90.4	90.2	92.3
1967	94.3	96.4	95.7	95.0	94.3	94.7	95.1	95.5	94.0	92.6	91.1	92.2
1968	93.2	94.3	92.8	91.4	89.9	89.8	89.7	89.6	90.3	90.9	91.6	93.7
1969	95.9	98.0	95.7	93.4	91.1	89.6	88.1	86.6	84.3	81.9	79.6	78.3
1970	77.1	75.8	74.3	72.7	71.2	72.7	74.2	75.7	74.2	72.8	71.3	72.8
1971	74.4	75.9	75.9	75.9	75.9	76.7	77.6	78.4	78.0	77.6	77.2	81.8
1972	86.3	90.9	88.0	85.1	82.2	85.2	88.3	91.3	90.1	89.0	87.8	83.0
1973	78.1	73.3	71.3	69.3	67.3	65.9	64.4	63.0	64.4	65.7	67.1	61.2
1974	55.3	49.4	54.2	59.1	63.9	61.8	59.7	57.6	55.5	53.3	51.2	50.8
1975	50.4	50.0	56.6	63.2	69.8	70.1	70.4	70.7	70.4	70.2	69.9	73.7
1976	77.4	81.2	80.6	80.1	79.5	81.5	83.5	85.5	85.6	85.8	85.9	85.3
1977	84.8	84.2	84.0	83.8	83.6	82.9	82.2	81.5	79.6	77.8	75.9	75.8
1978	75.7	77.2	69.5	71.1	73.0	68.1	72.0	67.0	69.8	71.7	62.8	53.8
1979	58.4	62.2	53.7	53.3	54.9	51.4	44.2	49.3	53.6	49.5	52.0	51.5
1980	54.1	54.9	44.3	44.4	45.3	53.0	53.4	59.6	67.2	68.9	76.2	59.7
1981	67.2	61.4	61.4	68.1	72.9	70.5	66.4	70.1	68.3	61.5	55.6	56.8
1982	62.9	58.7	53.1	61.1	62.0	60.1	57.6	60.9	66.9	70.4	71.0	67.9
1983	65.2	71.2	80.9	86.9	93.4	89.2	91.1	88.2	85.8	86.1	87.9	91.0
1984	97.0	93.2	97.7	91.4	90.6	89.8	91.9	93.7	96.4	91.6	91.5	87.9
1985	90.3	86.5	87.3	87.0	84.2	91.1	87.4	86.3	84.2	80.8	84.5	88.1
1986	85.3	87.8	86.9	88.5	87.5	90.3	88.5	85.9	81.3	87.1	81.6	78.3
1987	80.9	81.6	83.3	84.7	80.6	80.8	83.3	85.8	84.2	80.4	72.7	76.7
1988	80.9	81.9	85.2	82.4	87.3	85.7	82.3	88.8	89.5	87.0	86.3	85.5
1989	89.9	88.8	87.6	83.2	80.1	82.0	85.5	80.3	88.6	87.2	84.3	85.5
1990	83.4	81.3	81.3	83.9	79.3	76.6	77.3	62.9	58.8	50.9	52.8	53.7
1991	55.2	62.0	84.5	74.7	71.5	75.9	74.4	75.3	76.4	70.5	61.9	61.5
1992	59.1	61.8	70.3	70.5	71.2	70.7	67.6	69.5	67.4	67.5	78.2	89.5
1993	83.4	80.6	75.8	76.4	68.5	70.4	64.7	65.8	66.8	72.5	70.3	78.8
1994	86.4	83.5	85.1	82.6	84.2	82.7	78.5	80.8	83.5	85.1	84.8	88.8
1995	88.4	85.9	79.8	83.8	80.1	84.1	87.4	86.1	78.8	80.8	79.7	83.7
1996	78.7	77.8	86.2	83.0	79.2	84.0	86.5	87.3	90.1	89.9	93.9	91.8
1997	91.3	94.9	93.6	92.5	96.6	98.9	102.6	100.3	100.7	-	-	-

Source: The Conference Board. Primary source(s): University of Michigan, Surveys of Consumers, P.O. Box 1248, Ann Arbor, MI 48106-1248. Used by permission. A dash (-) indicates that data are not available or zero.

COMPOSITE INDEX OF COINCIDENT INDICATORS

The composite index of coincident indicators tends to *confirm* what the composite index of leading indicators has foreshadowed. In other words, the "coincident index" tends to decline just as the economy does (rather than before) and turns up as the economy turns up. As with the other composite indicators, a tendency signaled by this index must be sustained for at least three months before the indicator "confirms" a change in the economy's direction of growth or decline.

The coincident index is a fairly reliable indicator. In the 1948 to 1988 period, for instance, more than half of the turning points in the economy were marked exactly by the coincident index. With the exception of the 1957 peak, which the index showed six months too early, the rest of the turning points were indicated within three months of the actual turn.

Components of the Coincident Index

The index is a composite of 4 indicators, each of which is further discussed below:

> Employees on nonagricultural payrolls
> Personal income less transfer payments
> Index of industrial production
> Manufacturing and trade sales

Employees on Nonagricultural Payrolls. The index is shown in thousands of employees. Employment tends to drop during recessionary periods and increase with expansions. Before a recession or upturn takes place, producers tend to decrease or increase hours worked (hence Average Weekly Hours is part of the leading index). As the trend is confirmed, layoffs or hirings are reflected in actual employment totals. Total employment, of course, tends to grow over time. The significance of the index lies in month-to-month changes that show a pattern.

Personal Income Less Transfer Payments. Expressed in billions of chained 1992 dollars, this index measures all income except that derived from such sources as welfare, unemployment benefits, social security, medicaid, and the like, which are transfer payments. It includes dividends, rents, interest, and wages (the bulk). It is thus a good indicator of money now available to individuals from economic activities—which tends to shrink in recessions (while transfer payments may increase) and grow in periods of economic expansion.

Index of Industrial Production. This indicator, expressed as an index with 1992 as its base (1992 = 100), measures changes in the physical goods and power (rather than dollar sales) produced in mining, manufacturing, and utilities. Other sectors of the economy (construction, services, communications, trade, government, etc.) are, of course, indirectly reflected in this measure. Components of this index are measured and indexed; next, these indexes are weighted by their relative importance to the economy as measured by value added—the amount of value added to raw materials purchased by an industry through its own efforts. Industrial production reflects actual output; it does not signal future intent; therefore it serves well as a coincident indicator.

Manufacturing and Trade Sales. The index is reported in millions of chained 1992 dollars. It represents sales at all levels—production, wholesale, and retail. New orders signal future sales and are therefore indicators of future activity. The actual sales, as they are made, are an indicator of current activity; they drop or increase in cycle with the economy.

Sources and Revisions

The component series are drawn from federal sources, including the U.S. Department of Commerce, Bureau of Economic Analysis and Bureau of the Census; the U.S. Department of Labor, Bureau of Labor Statistics; and the Federal Reserve System.

The composite index itself is constructed by The Conference Board. In the process, mathematical operations are performed on the component data series to ensure that volatile series do not dominate the index. A volatile series may be one that fluctuates wildly month to month but shows less volatility when averaged over several months. Other smoothing and standardization methods are used as well.

The coincident index was last revised late in 1997. See Reference 6 for details.

Bibliography

1. Frumkin, Norman. *Guide to Economic Indicators*. M.E. Sharpe, Inc., 1990.

2. Green, George R. and Barry A. Beckman. "Business Cycle Indicators: Upcoming Revision of the Composite Indexes." U.S. Department of Commerce, Bureau of Economic Analysis. *Survey of Current Business*, October 1993. Superintendent of Documents, U.S. Government Printing Office, Washington, DC 20302.

3. Hertzberg, Marie P. and Barry A. Beckman. "Business Cycle Indicators: Revised Composite Indexes." U.S. Department of Commerce, Bureau of Economic Analysis. *Survey of Current Business*, January 1989. Superintendent of Documents, U.S. Government Printing Office, Washington, DC 20302.

4. U.S. Department of Commerce, Bureau of Economic Analysis. "Composite Indexes of Leading, Coincident, and Lagging Indicators." In *Survey of Current Business*, November 1987. Superintendent of Documents, U.S. Government Printing Office, Washington, DC 20302.

5. U.S. Department of Commerce, Bureau of Economic Analysis. *Survey of Current Business*. Superintendent of Documents, U.S. Government Printing Office, Washington, DC 20302.

6. *Leading Economic Indicators*. The Confenrence Board, 845 Third Avenue, New York, NY 10022-6679.

Composite Index of 4 Coincident Indicators
(1992 = 100)

Year	Jan	Feb	Mar	Apr	May	Jun	Jul	Aug	Sep	Oct	Nov	Dec
1959	40.9	41.1	41.5	41.8	42.2	42.3	42.1	41.6	41.6	41.6	41.8	42.6
1960	42.9	42.9	42.8	43.0	42.8	42.7	42.6	42.6	42.5	42.5	42.2	41.9
1961	41.9	41.9	42.1	42.2	42.5	42.8	42.9	43.2	43.3	43.6	44.0	44.2
1962	44.1	44.3	44.6	44.8	44.8	44.9	45.0	45.1	45.2	45.3	45.5	45.4
1963	45.5	45.7	45.9	46.1	46.2	46.4	46.5	46.6	46.8	47.0	47.0	47.3
1964	47.4	47.7	47.8	48.0	48.3	48.4	48.6	48.9	49.1	48.9	49.4	49.9
1965	50.0	50.2	50.6	50.8	51.0	51.2	51.5	51.7	51.9	52.4	52.7	53.1
1966	53.3	53.5	53.9	54.0	54.2	54.6	54.7	54.8	55.0	55.2	55.3	55.4
1967	55.7	55.5	55.6	55.7	55.7	55.9	56.0	56.3	56.4	56.4	57.0	57.4
1968	57.3	57.6	57.8	57.9	58.2	58.5	58.7	58.8	59.0	59.3	59.6	59.8
1969	59.8	60.1	60.4	60.5	60.6	60.9	61.1	61.3	61.4	61.6	61.4	61.5
1970	61.1	61.2	61.2	61.1	61.1	61.0	61.1	61.0	61.0	60.5	60.2	60.8
1971	61.1	61.1	61.2	61.4	61.6	61.7	61.7	61.8	62.1	62.2	62.5	62.9
1972	63.4	63.6	64.0	64.4	64.6	64.6	64.9	65.5	66.0	66.6	67.1	67.6
1973	67.7	68.1	68.2	68.3	68.5	68.7	68.9	68.8	69.2	69.8	70.2	70.0
1974	69.6	69.4	69.3	69.1	69.4	69.4	69.5	69.3	69.2	69.1	68.4	67.4
1975	66.8	66.3	65.8	65.9	66.0	66.2	66.4	67.0	67.2	67.5	67.7	68.0
1976	68.6	69.0	69.2	69.5	69.7	69.9	70.1	70.3	70.5	70.4	71.0	71.4
1977	71.5	71.8	72.3	72.6	73.0	73.4	73.7	73.9	74.3	74.5	74.9	75.1
1978	74.9	75.3	76.0	77.0	77.2	77.7	77.8	78.1	78.3	78.8	79.2	79.5
1979	79.4	79.7	80.3	79.7	80.2	80.3	80.2	80.3	80.2	80.4	80.5	80.6
1980	80.8	80.7	80.4	79.7	79.0	78.7	78.6	79.0	79.4	80.1	80.6	80.9
1981	81.0	81.0	81.0	80.8	80.8	81.0	81.4	81.4	81.2	80.9	80.6	80.3
1982	79.7	80.1	80.0	80.1	80.0	79.6	79.2	79.0	78.7	78.5	78.4	78.3
1983	78.7	78.6	79.1	79.4	79.9	80.4	80.9	80.8	81.9	82.4	82.8	83.4
1984	84.0	84.5	84.9	85.3	85.7	86.2	86.5	86.7	87.1	86.9	87.3	87.5
1985	87.6	87.8	88.2	88.3	88.5	88.5	88.5	88.9	89.1	89.2	89.4	89.7
1986	90.0	90.0	90.1	90.5	90.4	90.4	90.7	90.9	91.3	91.3	91.4	91.9
1987	91.6	92.4	92.6	92.8	93.0	93.3	93.6	93.8	94.0	94.7	94.8	95.5
1988	95.3	95.8	96.1	96.4	96.4	96.8	97.0	97.2	97.3	97.7	97.9	98.5
1989	98.8	98.8	99.0	99.2	99.0	99.0	98.8	99.2	99.0	99.0	99.4	99.6
1990	99.6	100.1	100.4	100.3	100.5	100.7	100.6	100.5	100.2	99.8	99.4	99.2
1991	98.5	98.3	98.1	98.4	98.6	98.8	98.8	98.8	99.0	99.0	99.0	98.9
1992	99.0	99.3	99.4	99.7	99.9	100.0	100.2	99.4	100.3	100.6	101.0	101.2
1993	101.4	101.6	101.3	101.6	101.9	102.0	102.1	102.4	102.7	103.0	103.3	103.7
1994	103.6	104.3	104.9	105.2	105.7	106.0	106.2	106.7	106.9	107.4	107.7	108.2
1995	108.5	108.6	108.7	108.7	108.7	109.1	109.1	109.6	109.8	109.9	110.2	110.6
1996	110.3	111.1	111.1	111.5	112.0	112.4	112.6	112.9	113.1	113.3	113.7	114.0
1997	114.3	114.9	115.2	115.4	115.6	116.1	116.5	116.7	117.0	-	-	-

Source: The Conference Board. Primary source(s): The Conference Board, Inc., Economics Group, 845 Third Avenue, New York, NY 10022. A dash (-) indicates that data are not available or zero.

Composite Index of 4 Coincident Indicators
Change in Index from Previous Month

Year	Jan	Feb	Mar	Apr	May	Jun	Jul	Aug	Sep	Oct	Nov	Dec
1959	-	+0.2	+0.4	+0.3	+0.4	+0.1	-0.2	-0.5	-	-	+0.2	+0.8
1960	+0.3	-	-0.1	+0.2	-0.2	-0.1	-0.1	-	-0.1	-	-0.3	-0.3
1961	-	-	+0.2	+0.1	+0.3	+0.3	+0.1	+0.3	+0.1	+0.3	+0.4	+0.2
1962	-0.1	+0.2	+0.3	+0.2	-	+0.1	+0.1	+0.1	+0.1	+0.1	+0.2	-0.1
1963	+0.1	+0.2	+0.2	+0.2	+0.1	+0.2	+0.1	+0.1	+0.2	+0.2	-	+0.3
1964	+0.1	+0.3	+0.1	+0.2	+0.3	+0.1	+0.2	+0.3	+0.2	-0.2	+0.5	+0.5
1965	+0.1	+0.2	+0.4	+0.2	+0.2	+0.2	+0.3	+0.2	+0.2	+0.5	+0.3	+0.4
1966	+0.2	+0.2	+0.4	+0.1	+0.2	+0.4	+0.1	+0.1	+0.2	+0.2	+0.1	+0.1
1967	+0.3	-0.2	+0.1	+0.1	-	+0.2	+0.1	+0.3	+0.1	-	+0.6	+0.4
1968	-0.1	+0.3	+0.2	+0.1	+0.3	+0.3	+0.3	+0.2	+0.1	+0.2	+0.3	+0.3
1969	-	+0.3	+0.3	+0.1	+0.1	+0.3	+0.2	+0.2	+0.1	+0.2	-0.2	+0.1
1970	-0.4	+0.1	-	-0.1	-	-0.1	+0.1	-0.1	-	-0.5	-0.3	+0.6
1971	+0.3	-	+0.1	+0.2	+0.2	+0.1	-	+0.1	+0.3	+0.1	+0.3	+0.4
1972	+0.5	+0.2	+0.4	+0.4	+0.2	-	+0.3	+0.6	+0.5	+0.6	+0.5	+0.5
1973	+0.1	+0.4	+0.1	+0.1	+0.2	+0.2	+0.2	-0.1	+0.4	+0.6	+0.4	-0.2
1974	-0.4	-0.2	-0.1	-0.2	+0.3	-	+0.1	-0.2	-0.1	-0.1	-0.7	-1.0
1975	-0.6	-0.5	-0.5	+0.1	+0.1	+0.2	+0.2	+0.6	+0.2	+0.3	+0.2	+0.3
1976	+0.6	+0.4	+0.2	+0.3	+0.2	+0.2	+0.2	+0.2	+0.2	-0.1	+0.6	+0.4
1977	+0.1	+0.3	+0.5	+0.3	+0.4	+0.4	+0.3	+0.2	+0.4	+0.2	+0.4	+0.2
1978	-0.2	+0.4	+0.7	+1.0	+0.2	+0.5	+0.1	+0.3	+0.2	+0.5	+0.4	+0.3
1979	-0.1	+0.3	+0.6	-0.6	+0.5	+0.1	-0.1	+0.1	-0.1	+0.2	+0.1	+0.1
1980	+0.2	-0.1	-0.3	-0.7	-0.7	-0.3	-0.1	+0.4	+0.4	+0.7	+0.5	+0.3
1981	+0.1	-	-	-0.2	-	+0.2	+0.4	-	-0.2	-0.3	-0.3	-0.3
1982	-0.6	+0.4	-0.1	+0.1	-0.1	-0.4	-0.4	-0.2	-0.3	-0.2	-0.1	-0.1
1983	+0.4	-0.1	+0.5	+0.3	+0.5	+0.5	+0.5	-0.1	+1.1	+0.5	+0.4	+0.6
1984	+0.6	+0.5	+0.4	+0.4	+0.4	+0.5	+0.3	+0.2	+0.4	-0.2	+0.4	+0.2
1985	+0.1	+0.2	+0.4	+0.1	+0.2	-	-	+0.4	+0.2	+0.1	+0.2	+0.3
1986	+0.3	-	+0.1	+0.4	-0.1	-	+0.3	+0.2	+0.4	-	+0.1	+0.5
1987	-0.3	+0.8	+0.2	+0.2	+0.2	+0.3	+0.3	+0.2	+0.2	+0.7	+0.1	+0.7
1988	-0.2	+0.5	+0.3	+0.3	-	+0.4	+0.2	+0.2	+0.1	+0.4	-	+0.2
1989	+0.3	-	+0.2	+0.2	-0.2	-	-0.2	+0.4	-0.2	-	+0.4	+0.2
1990	-	+0.5	+0.3	-0.1	+0.2	+0.2	-0.1	-0.1	-0.3	-0.4	-0.4	-0.2
1991	-0.7	-0.2	-0.2	+0.3	+0.2	+0.2	-	-	+0.2	-	-	-0.1
1992	+0.1	+0.3	+0.1	+0.3	+0.2	+0.1	+0.2	-0.8	+0.9	+0.3	+0.4	+0.2
1993	+0.2	+0.2	-0.3	+0.3	+0.3	+0.1	+0.1	+0.3	+0.3	+0.3	+0.3	+0.4
1994	-0.1	+0.7	+0.6	+0.3	+0.5	+0.3	+0.2	+0.5	+0.2	+0.5	+0.3	+0.5
1995	+0.3	+0.1	+0.1	-	-	+0.4	-	+0.5	+0.2	+0.1	+0.3	+0.4
1996	-0.3	+0.8	-	+0.4	+0.5	+0.4	+0.2	+0.3	+0.2	+0.2	+0.4	+0.3
1997	+0.3	+0.6	+0.3	+0.2	+0.2	+0.5	+0.4	+0.2	+0.3	-	-	-

Source: The Conference Board. Primary source(s): The Conference Board, Inc., Economics Group, 845 Third Avenue, New York, NY 10022. A dash (-) indicates that data are not available or zero.

Employees on Nonagricultural Payrolls
(Thousands)

Year	Jan	Feb	Mar	Apr	May	Jun	Jul	Aug	Sep	Oct	Nov	Dec
1945	41,767	41,770	41,715	41,276	41,120	40,899	40,609	40,298	38,356	38,436	38,799	39,009
1946	39,721	39,193	40,183	40,858	41,248	41,551	41,955	42,466	42,749	42,959	43,229	43,314
1947	43,497	43,578	43,621	43,501	43,544	43,685	43,682	43,784	44,001	44,176	44,313	44,519
1948	44,667	44,501	44,624	44,293	44,647	44,879	45,062	45,039	45,162	45,065	45,069	45,022
1949	44,624	44,417	44,136	44,112	43,814	43,592	43,418	43,479	43,699	42,805	43,142	43,491
1950	43,469	43,192	43,824	44,260	44,574	44,952	45,360	46,024	46,301	46,528	46,653	46,752
1951	47,230	47,531	47,794	47,760	47,805	47,913	47,925	47,794	47,748	47,825	48,027	48,122
1952	48,227	48,493	48,416	48,509	48,474	48,125	47,999	48,686	49,085	49,434	49,719	49,937
1953	50,045	50,273	50,382	50,314	50,358	50,389	50,382	50,271	50,226	50,108	49,825	49,625
1954	49,341	49,276	49,046	49,039	48,852	48,791	48,689	48,643	48,765	48,828	49,103	49,234
1955	49,354	49,523	49,851	50,104	50,404	50,693	50,811	50,929	51,103	51,323	51,507	51,714
1956	51,863	52,093	52,228	52,232	52,365	52,433	51,746	52,382	52,439	52,674	52,752	52,908
1957	52,808	53,003	53,062	53,053	52,996	52,941	52,972	52,913	52,816	52,663	52,482	52,307
1958	52,003	51,441	51,142	50,807	50,770	50,801	50,911	51,113	51,355	51,378	51,814	51,986
1959	52,408	52,568	52,883	53,132	53,422	53,584	53,663	53,220	53,257	53,196	53,509	54,040
1960	54,185	54,414	54,287	54,634	54,362	54,276	54,214	54,198	54,063	53,982	53,845	53,577
1961	53,534	53,380	53,510	53,462	53,677	53,916	54,027	54,222	54,285	54,376	54,622	54,744
1962	54,709	55,018	55,107	55,459	55,514	55,561	55,643	55,778	55,849	55,912	55,936	55,918
1963	55,935	56,055	56,153	56,454	56,513	56,563	56,688	56,823	56,962	57,152	57,126	57,252
1964	57,269	57,603	57,732	57,784	57,975	58,121	58,311	58,510	58,798	58,691	59,114	59,335
1965	59,398	59,683	59,864	60,124	60,363	60,595	60,860	61,085	61,367	61,578	61,882	62,230
1966	62,386	62,720	63,087	63,317	63,560	63,978	64,185	64,344	64,433	64,655	64,854	65,076
1967	65,215	65,208	65,338	65,323	65,478	65,654	65,831	65,964	66,089	66,111	66,591	66,776
1968	66,606	67,029	67,132	67,417	67,495	67,783	68,003	68,219	68,365	68,603	68,855	69,161
1969	69,272	69,542	69,791	69,948	70,180	70,498	70,668	70,799	70,833	70,993	70,941	71,127
1970	71,018	71,165	71,347	71,251	70,993	70,905	70,969	70,789	70,857	70,416	70,296	70,666
1971	70,718	70,657	70,746	70,936	71,129	71,163	71,219	71,220	71,527	71,532	71,734	71,996
1972	72,303	72,525	72,808	73,061	73,341	73,643	73,636	73,929	74,115	74,527	74,881	75,235
1973	75,474	75,908	76,137	76,312	76,516	76,738	76,758	77,018	77,164	77,502	77,833	77,992
1974	77,953	78,177	78,177	78,261	78,407	78,434	78,517	78,478	78,498	78,569	78,238	77,565
1975	77,145	76,742	76,419	76,298	76,459	76,388	76,626	76,980	77,188	77,499	77,619	77,915
1976	78,326	78,606	78,819	79,134	79,192	79,258	79,485	79,581	79,842	79,842	80,141	80,338
1977	80,517	80,794	81,221	81,610	81,977	82,381	82,760	82,974	83,431	83,661	84,031	84,271
1978	84,464	84,808	85,338	86,083	86,404	86,811	87,037	87,324	87,434	87,797	88,249	88,559
1979	88,728	88,985	89,426	89,363	89,681	89,955	90,019	90,159	90,149	90,360	90,466	90,617
1980	90,729	90,876	90,995	90,780	90,316	89,974	89,676	89,964	90,046	90,334	90,550	90,774
1981	91,003	91,095	91,206	91,219	91,142	91,285	91,410	91,320	91,191	91,216	91,014	90,831
1982	90,448	90,474	90,337	90,031	89,965	89,703	89,380	89,177	88,995	88,787	88,649	88,675
1983	88,826	88,758	88,946	89,211	89,497	89,886	90,313	89,973	91,088	91,408	91,727	92,110
1984	92,524	93,043	93,312	93,650	93,952	94,325	94,647	94,885	95,186	95,499	95,829	95,997
1985	96,249	96,397	96,734	96,896	97,163	97,280	97,465	97,696	97,878	98,098	98,286	98,500
1986	98,599	98,718	98,796	98,974	99,096	98,973	99,276	99,435	99,747	99,980	100,145	100,394
1987	100,543	100,772	101,005	101,367	101,564	101,713	102,047	102,266	102,430	102,980	103,200	103,544
1988	103,607	104,059	104,321	104,552	104,804	105,136	105,428	105,566	105,824	106,087	106,370	106,699
1989	106,991	107,243	107,447	107,654	107,737	107,840	107,965	108,024	108,197	108,300	108,583	108,698
1990	108,944	109,269	109,471	109,510	109,785	109,878	109,733	109,554	109,468	109,300	109,098	108,979
1991	108,756	108,498	108,339	108,147	108,138	108,209	108,139	108,215	108,212	108,220	108,123	108,138
1992	108,084	108,077	108,119	108,301	108,495	108,541	108,595	108,741	108,807	108,941	109,119	109,266
1993	109,516	109,852	109,757	110,071	110,386	110,550	110,759	110,983	111,220	111,541	111,795	112,050
1994	112,284	112,577	112,988	113,355	113,704	113,991	114,335	114,685	114,992	115,247	115,674	115,906
1995	116,234	116,517	116,694	116,891	116,855	117,064	117,142	117,465	117,636	117,775	117,951	118,120
1996	118,058	118,550	118,804	118,966	119,263	119,516	119,691	119,983	120,019	120,248	120,450	120,659
1997	120,909	121,162	121,344	121,671	121,834	122,056	122,440	122,480	122,695	-	-	-

Source: The Conference Board. Primary source(s): U.S. Department of Labor, Bureau of Labor Statistics, Office of Employment and Unemployment Statistics, Division of Monthly Industry Employment Statistics, Washington, DC 20212. A dash (-) indicates that data are not available or zero.

Personal Income Less Transfer Payments

(Annual Rate, Billions of chained 1992 $)

Year	Jan	Feb	Mar	Apr	May	Jun	Jul	Aug	Sep	Oct	Nov	Dec
1959	1,571.4	1,578.1	1,592.0	1,602.6	1,614.3	1,620.1	1,616.7	1,607.7	1,607.1	1,610.1	1,621.7	1,640.2
1960	1,648.8	1,647.9	1,647.0	1,653.2	1,656.6	1,655.1	1,655.8	1,653.0	1,653.4	1,658.9	1,648.8	1,636.6
1961	1,650.0	1,650.0	1,657.8	1,662.8	1,672.4	1,687.3	1,692.0	1,699.6	1,703.7	1,721.5	1,738.7	1,747.4
1962	1,743.1	1,750.9	1,762.2	1,771.9	1,775.5	1,780.9	1,788.9	1,790.8	1,792.5	1,795.3	1,805.7	1,814.6
1963	1,810.0	1,813.1	1,820.1	1,825.8	1,833.4	1,845.4	1,845.3	1,852.3	1,864.3	1,876.4	1,879.2	1,893.6
1964	1,893.6	1,910.4	1,918.9	1,930.6	1,942.3	1,951.3	1,960.3	1,976.5	1,984.9	1,987.4	2,000.3	2,020.5
1965	2,021.9	2,031.8	2,040.7	2,050.6	2,064.3	2,070.9	2,083.3	2,094.3	2,110.9	2,134.7	2,149.2	2,160.3
1966	2,163.0	2,172.2	2,181.9	2,182.7	2,189.9	2,204.7	2,213.9	2,219.9	2,225.0	2,236.6	2,244.6	2,241.6
1967	2,260.3	2,257.9	2,266.0	2,268.2	2,271.8	2,281.2	2,291.3	2,301.3	2,304.2	2,302.1	2,315.1	2,335.7
1968	2,337.7	2,355.1	2,366.2	2,374.3	2,390.5	2,401.7	2,416.2	2,424.0	2,435.3	2,443.4	2,452.6	2,462.1
1969	2,458.6	2,470.0	2,482.6	2,490.7	2,500.1	2,508.9	2,522.2	2,538.0	2,543.3	2,551.2	2,550.6	2,553.4
1970	2,543.0	2,543.7	2,549.6	2,552.0	2,552.6	2,545.4	2,553.9	2,558.5	2,558.3	2,542.2	2,539.4	2,545.1
1971	2,566.1	2,564.5	2,572.1	2,576.9	2,585.5	2,583.3	2,584.3	2,598.0	2,600.7	2,608.9	2,621.5	2,641.6
1972	2,656.8	2,669.7	2,681.3	2,694.5	2,704.2	2,681.2	2,738.2	2,772.8	2,789.9	2,825.9	2,849.0	2,867.8
1973	2,857.8	2,868.7	2,868.0	2,870.4	2,888.9	2,896.9	2,901.2	2,895.4	2,919.9	2,963.4	2,979.1	2,974.3
1974	2,934.0	2,907.6	2,882.2	2,855.2	2,859.6	2,863.9	2,878.9	2,866.4	2,859.5	2,864.0	2,833.3	2,815.6
1975	2,795.7	2,778.1	2,775.3	2,771.5	2,785.5	2,791.4	2,796.1	2,822.7	2,835.6	2,852.5	2,861.9	2,863.1
1976	2,882.6	2,901.1	2,914.3	2,929.1	2,939.6	2,939.2	2,951.3	2,961.4	2,967.3	2,969.9	2,997.1	3,005.7
1977	3,001.3	3,012.0	3,025.3	3,031.3	3,049.4	3,059.9	3,084.2	3,092.9	3,114.4	3,129.8	3,146.5	3,160.4
1978	3,153.7	3,173.0	3,202.2	3,238.4	3,244.3	3,264.3	3,267.0	3,281.6	3,295.2	3,322.8	3,333.3	3,353.7
1979	3,352.5	3,365.6	3,380.5	3,355.6	3,358.5	3,367.7	3,366.5	3,372.1	3,367.6	3,380.0	3,392.9	3,403.2
1980	3,404.9	3,391.0	3,373.6	3,339.1	3,317.1	3,319.3	3,308.3	3,317.2	3,328.5	3,374.1	3,400.4	3,424.4
1981	3,432.1	3,421.9	3,428.1	3,412.0	3,416.7	3,433.4	3,463.7	3,477.1	3,470.8	3,462.8	3,457.4	3,444.4
1982	3,422.1	3,431.4	3,435.2	3,471.7	3,475.5	3,453.3	3,421.1	3,416.4	3,403.4	3,402.6	3,401.5	3,413.4
1983	3,405.0	3,404.4	3,420.7	3,433.3	3,454.1	3,462.6	3,483.8	3,472.9	3,508.6	3,547.4	3,567.0	3,603.5
1984	3,629.5	3,666.4	3,691.2	3,719.6	3,727.7	3,760.9	3,786.8	3,813.4	3,845.7	3,811.2	3,835.4	3,860.2
1985	3,860.2	3,863.5	3,878.1	3,872.8	3,876.3	3,889.2	3,885.8	3,897.4	3,900.1	3,927.8	3,922.4	3,956.2
1986	3,951.0	3,969.0	4,004.3	4,006.3	4,006.6	4,008.4	4,018.8	4,032.5	4,032.1	4,026.3	4,033.9	4,051.2
1987	4,046.8	4,064.0	4,077.4	4,076.0	4,095.5	4,099.0	4,101.2	4,125.4	4,129.5	4,170.2	4,189.2	4,240.2
1988	4,205.5	4,227.9	4,233.7	4,248.0	4,247.0	4,258.8	4,271.9	4,273.1	4,278.0	4,298.0	4,298.5	4,327.1
1989	4,357.6	4,369.1	4,384.6	4,382.4	4,359.2	4,365.6	4,367.8	4,366.0	4,339.7	4,354.8	4,383.2	4,391.7
1990	4,398.7	4,419.2	4,423.3	4,447.8	4,433.4	4,440.2	4,455.2	4,427.4	4,423.2	4,379.4	4,374.0	4,381.8
1991	4,327.4	4,317.0	4,322.9	4,334.7	4,339.2	4,360.6	4,330.2	4,324.6	4,329.5	4,334.9	4,348.1	4,370.4
1992	4,355.8	4,380.8	4,376.7	4,386.1	4,398.2	4,406.3	4,396.7	4,275.4	4,393.9	4,419.9	4,451.5	4,443.0
1993	4,468.8	4,466.3	4,446.5	4,472.1	4,501.2	4,486.6	4,487.3	4,511.2	4,504.7	4,503.9	4,518.1	4,539.0
1994	4,511.1	4,557.4	4,572.0	4,586.9	4,615.5	4,605.8	4,612.3	4,613.8	4,634.9	4,675.3	4,674.2	4,694.6
1995	4,737.6	4,733.2	4,736.5	4,762.4	4,737.2	4,760.0	4,777.6	4,768.9	4,791.4	4,813.0	4,824.5	4,827.8
1996	4,826.0	4,865.0	4,869.8	4,876.6	4,889.0	4,938.9	4,913.7	4,937.1	4,962.4	4,937.6	4,958.7	4,991.0
1997	4,997.6	5,030.0	5,053.5	5,058.3	5,076.7	5,103.3	5,103.0	5,132.6	5,141.7	-	-	-

Source: The Conference Board. Primary source(s): U.S. Department of Commerce, Bureau of Economic Analysis, National Income and Wealth Division, BE-54, Washington, DC 20230. A dash (-) indicates that data are not available or zero.

Index of Industrial Production
(1992 = 100)

Year	Jan	Feb	Mar	Apr	May	Jun	Jul	Aug	Sep	Oct	Nov	Dec
1945	25.610	25.526	25.358	24.894	24.220	23.673	23.125	20.724	18.871	18.113	18.787	18.871
1946	17.818	16.933	18.702	18.365	17.691	18.787	19.418	20.134	20.514	20.893	21.019	21.145
1947	21.398	21.525	21.651	21.482	21.567	21.567	21.440	21.567	21.735	21.946	22.241	22.325
1948	22.451	22.493	22.241	22.283	22.662	22.957	22.957	22.872	22.704	22.872	22.578	22.367
1949	22.156	21.946	21.525	21.398	21.103	21.061	21.019	21.230	21.440	20.640	21.188	21.567
1950	21.946	22.030	22.746	23.504	24.052	24.768	25.568	26.369	26.200	26.369	26.326	26.790
1951	26.874	27.043	27.169	27.211	27.127	27.000	26.579	26.326	26.495	26.453	26.663	26.832
1952	27.127	27.295	27.380	27.127	26.874	26.621	26.200	27.885	28.896	29.191	29.780	29.949
1953	30.033	30.202	30.454	30.581	30.749	30.623	31.002	30.834	30.202	29.949	29.233	28.517
1954	28.306	28.390	28.222	28.053	28.222	28.306	28.348	28.306	28.348	28.685	29.149	29.528
1955	30.202	30.581	31.297	31.676	32.181	32.224	32.476	32.434	32.645	33.192	33.277	33.403
1956	33.614	33.319	33.319	33.571	33.277	32.982	31.971	33.277	34.035	34.330	34.035	34.540
1957	34.414	34.751	34.709	34.245	34.119	34.203	34.414	34.414	34.119	33.614	32.813	32.181
1958	31.592	30.918	30.539	30.033	30.328	31.128	31.592	32.224	32.518	32.898	33.866	33.908
1959	34.414	35.088	35.593	36.352	36.899	36.941	36.057	34.835	34.793	34.540	34.751	36.899
1960	37.868	37.531	37.194	36.899	36.857	36.394	36.267	36.225	35.846	35.804	35.299	34.625
1961	34.667	34.625	34.835	35.551	36.099	36.604	37.026	37.362	37.320	38.036	38.626	38.963
1962	38.626	39.258	39.469	39.553	39.511	39.427	39.806	39.848	40.100	40.143	40.311	40.311
1963	40.606	41.069	41.322	41.701	42.207	42.333	42.164	42.249	42.670	42.965	43.175	43.091
1964	43.470	43.765	43.765	44.481	44.734	44.860	45.155	45.450	45.618	44.987	46.377	46.924
1965	47.430	47.725	48.356	48.567	48.946	49.325	49.789	49.999	50.126	50.631	50.842	51.473
1966	51.979	52.316	53.032	53.116	53.622	53.874	54.169	54.211	54.717	55.096	54.717	54.843
1967	55.102	54.477	54.170	54.681	54.204	54.197	54.074	55.110	55.020	55.468	56.261	56.867
1968	56.806	57.010	57.188	57.271	57.913	58.126	58.037	58.199	58.419	58.535	59.292	59.479
1969	59.839	60.222	60.694	60.471	60.242	60.831	61.152	61.293	61.279	61.297	60.719	60.556
1970	59.435	59.396	59.318	59.166	59.097	58.906	59.050	58.945	58.539	57.368	57.020	58.330
1971	58.779	58.666	58.603	58.932	59.231	59.479	59.307	58.963	59.921	60.369	60.626	61.326
1972	62.687	63.119	63.639	64.657	64.505	64.713	64.616	65.496	66.215	67.166	67.969	68.615
1973	68.669	69.618	69.599	69.854	70.151	70.687	71.126	71.085	71.630	71.898	71.924	70.788
1974	69.808	69.535	69.852	69.722	70.538	70.757	70.430	70.184	70.476	69.965	67.957	65.131
1975	63.439	62.422	61.312	61.880	61.688	62.491	62.857	63.977	64.642	64.958	65.569	66.100
1976	66.815	68.002	67.836	68.099	68.877	68.923	69.329	69.726	69.952	70.191	71.361	71.929
1977	72.326	72.379	73.220	74.258	75.000	75.567	75.605	75.894	76.292	76.132	76.175	75.877
1978	75.622	75.631	76.392	78.991	79.033	79.905	80.140	80.339	80.737	81.146	81.611	81.913
1979	81.526	82.140	82.368	81.597	82.539	82.559	81.960	81.630	81.689	82.030	81.623	81.450
1980	81.830	81.892	81.868	80.271	78.283	77.291	76.795	77.696	78.846	79.413	80.695	81.095
1981	80.396	80.781	81.147	80.604	81.279	81.789	82.513	82.144	81.478	80.857	79.726	78.831
1982	77.562	79.235	78.681	77.938	77.341	77.083	76.450	76.046	75.488	74.863	74.664	74.050
1983	75.628	75.453	76.204	77.159	78.089	78.529	79.922	80.995	82.377	83.027	82.945	83.369
1984	85.102	84.968	85.906	86.362	86.859	87.251	87.426	87.415	87.294	86.885	86.956	86.567
1985	86.871	87.618	87.840	87.982	88.183	87.967	87.583	88.107	88.638	87.872	88.375	88.990
1986	89.568	88.928	88.032	88.705	88.508	88.204	88.490	88.739	88.656	89.454	89.898	90.727
1987	90.155	91.202	91.549	91.926	92.331	93.130	93.708	93.771	93.698	94.947	95.219	95.757
1988	95.835	96.134	96.162	96.718	96.766	96.798	97.444	97.961	97.617	97.896	98.618	99.134
1989	99.678	98.915	99.818	100.080	99.453	99.288	98.266	98.697	98.526	98.066	98.460	98.944
1990	98.455	98.964	99.443	98.874	99.292	99.291	99.219	99.392	99.519	98.981	97.677	97.117
1991	96.653	95.897	95.000	95.290	96.015	97.156	97.249	97.385	98.298	98.205	98.067	97.439
1992	97.487	98.136	98.924	99.630	100.012	99.726	100.419	100.055	100.507	101.281	101.876	101.948
1993	102.308	102.769	102.835	103.159	102.565	102.787	103.087	102.842	103.858	104.124	104.647	105.411
1994	105.709	106.238	106.963	107.419	108.081	108.611	109.142	109.183	109.259	109.943	110.596	111.553
1995	111.924	111.648	111.720	111.421	111.523	111.739	111.716	112.603	113.003	112.522	112.704	112.788
1996	112.361	113.782	113.241	114.284	114.782	115.466	115.495	115.848	115.978	116.231	117.216	117.697
1997	117.765	118.366	118.846	119.331	119.508	119.903	120.914	121.526	122.387	-	-	-

Source: The Conference Board. Primary source(s): Board of Governors of the Federal Reserve System, Division of Research and Statistics, Industrial Output Section, Stop 82, Washington, DC 20551. A dash (-) indicates that data are not available or zero.

Manufacturing and Trade Sales

(Millions of chained 1992 $)

Year	Jan	Feb	Mar	Apr	May	Jun	Jul	Aug	Sep	Oct	Nov	Dec
1959	198,740	201,548	204,077	206,542	209,348	210,020	208,572	204,132	203,672	203,835	203,593	209,993
1960	212,732	211,371	209,496	210,869	206,948	207,354	206,062	206,119	208,039	206,682	205,369	204,752
1961	199,598	200,746	203,918	203,531	205,923	209,723	208,117	212,874	214,327	216,353	219,364	220,479
1962	220,427	220,082	223,460	223,678	224,049	223,652	223,894	224,964	225,548	227,047	230,454	226,604
1963	228,003	232,268	233,110	235,494	233,736	236,530	239,246	236,600	237,539	240,614	238,866	242,702
1964	245,124	245,823	244,244	248,023	250,864	250,212	252,620	252,036	255,699	251,417	253,854	261,808
1965	262,179	261,451	267,358	268,247	266,486	266,234	270,423	270,693	267,156	274,296	278,239	280,053
1966	283,151	282,823	287,984	285,958	283,189	287,277	283,719	285,533	287,083	288,675	286,717	289,196
1967	289,620	288,476	290,595	290,398	290,166	292,290	290,481	294,414	295,313	293,267	301,189	307,885
1968	304,727	303,774	306,115	305,392	307,624	309,789	312,793	307,404	311,737	315,907	318,607	315,672
1969	315,684	316,169	317,449	318,716	318,551	318,282	318,408	321,858	323,402	327,123	322,631	322,042
1970	317,866	318,177	314,488	312,909	316,378	317,654	318,037	317,912	317,298	313,967	308,810	318,547
1971	321,609	323,325	324,625	326,525	328,111	332,618	328,725	330,876	333,835	334,040	339,743	342,884
1972	346,432	342,754	349,044	351,442	353,588	355,160	352,945	361,460	367,607	372,663	379,924	384,876
1973	389,753	390,379	388,714	387,189	385,935	385,327	390,146	383,033	385,003	394,924	401,260	395,841
1974	396,457	394,420	395,664	393,007	394,656	393,488	392,316	388,320	384,904	378,337	374,306	363,574
1975	362,572	360,187	349,742	352,855	352,792	355,974	358,049	362,133	362,956	363,349	362,658	366,469
1976	375,644	377,296	380,179	382,075	381,658	386,393	386,534	387,920	388,942	384,395	390,779	400,840
1977	398,288	403,713	408,652	408,069	408,332	411,941	413,003	413,697	415,188	418,129	420,105	425,682
1978	412,689	422,265	426,473	439,505	438,968	441,492	437,966	443,711	442,751	446,608	448,563	450,982
1979	446,085	444,084	456,903	444,673	454,427	449,784	448,916	449,636	447,050	445,678	445,853	444,570
1980	448,340	444,282	434,097	425,070	419,350	418,294	423,557	426,661	435,685	444,875	445,188	446,075
1981	448,597	446,863	442,418	442,814	439,552	438,460	439,363	437,541	434,467	428,533	425,214	419,705
1982	417,497	424,111	424,472	425,022	427,216	421,069	419,562	415,760	416,538	412,248	413,480	412,267
1983	420,075	418,312	425,408	425,403	431,897	442,998	442,635	441,948	448,766	453,601	458,398	466,831
1984	469,869	469,632	470,038	472,726	476,448	480,664	478,007	477,875	477,272	479,299	483,544	484,114
1985	483,282	484,552	488,788	488,159	493,647	485,627	486,814	495,565	497,018	491,809	495,632	493,728
1986	501,107	497,827	498,147	508,680	503,393	506,413	509,666	510,223	522,585	514,912	513,256	524,927
1987	508,040	526,425	526,319	525,197	524,141	526,710	531,013	528,605	535,122	534,019	532,227	537,526
1988	536,234	542,004	550,024	547,024	547,811	553,136	550,751	551,900	553,865	558,157	560,071	567,879
1989	567,857	561,442	557,759	563,021	559,979	558,200	552,058	568,053	563,289	557,954	562,338	563,683
1990	558,918	567,148	570,707	564,039	567,183	570,359	566,593	572,372	560,735	559,318	552,583	545,784
1991	540,299	544,370	541,995	552,190	556,120	554,330	561,965	559,761	562,025	562,033	561,685	553,230
1992	562,960	565,665	568,518	569,677	566,784	572,320	579,526	571,037	578,304	579,872	581,062	588,977
1993	590,675	589,309	586,076	587,741	588,943	594,310	590,970	594,487	599,211	601,917	604,857	607,652
1994	607,096	612,942	622,541	619,502	621,016	625,859	623,279	637,837	635,339	638,197	643,789	648,267
1995	650,231	648,684	647,125	641,825	646,019	651,575	643,824	655,128	655,962	655,887	660,792	666,037
1996	659,850	668,628	667,898	673,970	677,703	675,162	681,681	679,952	683,827	688,071	692,322	691,474
1997	699,604	710,177	708,333	708,783	706,142	715,192	723,662	718,798	-	-	-	-

Source: The Conference Board. Primary source(s): U.S. Department of Commerce (manufacturing and wholesalers sales; retail sales, deflator), Bureau of Economic Analysis, National Income and Wealth Division, BE-54, Washington, DC 20230 and U.S. Department of Commerce, Bureau of the Census, Services Division, Current Retail Inventories and Sales Branch, Washington, DC 20233. A dash (-) indicates that data are not available or zero.

COMPOSITE INDEX OF LAGGING INDICATORS

The composite index of lagging indicators turns down about 10 months after the economy turns down and turns up about six months after the economy has turned up. Thus it lags behind the economy. It is made up of components that have inertial tendencies—they change more slowly than the economy. The "lagging index," of course, also confirms the cyclical behaviour of the economy by moving in tandem with the leading and coincident indicators—at a lag in time.

The lagging index is also a somewhat uncertain indicator. At business cycle peaks, the lags range from 2 to 13 months; at business cycle troughs, the range is 4 to 15 months.

Components of the Lagging Index

The index is a composite of 7 indicators, each of which is further discussed below:

    Average duration of unemployment in weeks
    Ratio, manufacturing and trade inventories to sales
    Change in index of labor cost per unit of output in manufacturing
    Average prime rate charged by banks
    Commercial and industrial loans outstanding
    Ratio, consumer installment credit outstanding to personal income
    Change in consumer price index for services

Average Duration of Unemployment. The indicator is shown as number of weeks of unemployment. A recession is a sustained downturn in production after a sustained period of growth. The average duration of unemployment, therefore, will tend to be low at the start of a recession. The shrinking of the economy will cause this average to grow. As the economy turns up again, the average will be high; time has to pass until laid-off people are employed again and the average duration of unemployment drops. In this case, also, the indicator grows as the economy shrinks and declines as the economy grows.

Ratio, Manufacturing and Trade Inventories to Sales. The indicator is expressed as a ratio based on inventory and sales measures expressed in 1987 constant dollars. A ratio of 1.0 means that inventories and sales are identical. A high ratio indicates high inventories relative to sales. A low indicator tends to mean that inventories are depleted. A dropping ratio means that inventories are "selling out" while a climbing ratio means that sales are slowing. Manufacturers and merchants caught at the beginning of a recession with high inventories will be unable to sell them; therefore, the ratio will increase as the economy slumps. Conversely, in an expansionary period, the ratio will be dropping because producers cannot keep up with demand. In both cases, the indicator tends to move in the opposite direction of the economy—or in the same direction, but with a lag in time.

Change in Index of Labor Cost per Unit of Output in Manufacturing. The indicator is expressed in percent. Labor cost in manufacturing is in part a reflection of longer-term contractual arrangements between manufacturers and labor unions which are not subject to rapid adjustment as the economy changes. Even the compensation of non-union labor forces tends to lag behind economic events: managements avoid downward adjustments in wages to maintain morale and productivity and resist demands for increased pay in periods of growth. For these reasons, the index lags economic events. Recessionary forces cause the cost of labor to decline—slowly. In periods of upturn, labor cost rises slowly as well. Thus it is normal to have high wages at the start and during recessions and relatively low wages as the economy begins climbing to a new peak.

Average Prime Rate Charged by Banks. The indicator is shown as a percent of interest charged by major banks to their largest customers. Historically, the prime rate has tended to increase during recessions and to decrease during periods of expansion. At the onset of an economic downturn, the rate reflects the conditions of the previous expansion; as the recession deepens and demand for money slackens, the prime rate drops. The prime rate is strongly influenced by actions of the Federal Reserve System. The Federal Reserve's discount rate (interest charged to member banks for short-term borrowings) has an immediate effect on the prime rate; therefore, the behavior of this indicator is indirectly subject to alteration by government action.

Commercial and Industrial Loans Outstanding. The indicator is shown in millions of chained 1992 dollars. Business and industry assume debt in periods of growth and minimize debt in periods of decline. The total debt outstanding, however, reflects the business cycle at a lag in time; borrowers pay off debt over time and may be late in paying during economic turn-downs; they also contract new obligations later than the economy's upturn because both lenders and borrowers are more cautious after a recessionary period.

Ratio, Consumer Installment Credit Outstanding to Personal Income. The indicator is expressed as a percent. A high percentage indicates that consumer debt relative to income is high. A decline in personal income or an increase in consumer debt will cause the indicator to rise and, of course, an increase in personal income or decrease in debt will cause the ratio to decline. At the start of a recession, personal income tends to drop more rapidly than debt outstanding; this indicator, therefore, will increase as the economy decreases. Later, as debt is paid off and less is borrowed (because times are uncertain), the ratio will decrease just as the economy begins to expand again—the signature of a lagging indicator.

Change in Consumer Price Index for Services. The index is expressed as a percent; the data are "smoothed," meaning that data are arithmetically transformed to remove irregular short-term movements. Prices for services are less volatile than prices for food, fuel, and products. Hence this series is a good lagging indicator: it changes more slowly than the economy. More detailed presentations of the Consumer Price Index are provided later in this book.

Sources and Revisions

The component series are drawn from federal sources, including the U.S. Department of Commerce, Bureau of Economic Analysis and Bureau of the Census; the U.S. Department of Labor, Bureau of Labor Statistics; the Federal Reserve System; and the Federal Reserve Bank of New York.

The composite index itself is constructed by The Conference Board. In the process, mathematical operations are performed on the component data series to ensure that volatile series do not dominate the index. A volatile series may be one that fluctuates wildly month to month but shows less volatility when averaged over several months. Other smoothing and standardization methods are used as well.

The lagging index was last revised in 1997. See Reference 6 for details.

Bibliography

1. Frumkin, Norman. *Guide to Economic Indicators*. M.E. Sharpe, Inc., 1990.

2. Green, George R. and Barry A. Beckman. "Business Cycle Indicators: Upcoming Revision of the Composite Indexes." U.S. Department of Commerce, Bureau of Economic Analysis. *Survey of Current Business*, October 1993. Superintendent of Documents, U.S. Government Printing Office, Washington, DC 20302.

3. Hertzberg, Marie P. and Barry A. Beckman. "Business Cycle Indicators: Revised Composite Indexes." U.S. Department of Commerce, Bureau of Economic Analysis. *Survey of Current Business*, January 1989. Superintendent of Documents, U.S. Government Printing Office, Washington, DC 20302.

4. U.S. Department of Commerce, Bureau of Economic Analysis. "Composite Indexes of Leading, Coincident, and Lagging Indicators." In *Survey of Current Business*, November 1987. Superintendent of Documents, U.S. Government Printing Office, Washington, DC 20302.

5. U.S. Department of Commerce, Bureau of Economic Analysis. *Survey of Current Business*. Superintendent of Documents, U.S. Government Printing Office, Washington, DC 20302.

6. *Leading Economic Indicators*. The Confenrence Board, 845 Third Avenue, New York, NY 10022-6679.

Composite Index of 7 Lagging Indicators
(1992 = 100)

Year	Jan	Feb	Mar	Apr	May	Jun	Jul	Aug	Sep	Oct	Nov	Dec
1959	84.8	85.0	85.0	85.3	85.7	85.9	86.5	87.4	87.9	88.4	88.2	88.0
1960	87.5	88.0	88.3	88.3	89.1	89.4	89.5	89.4	89.2	89.1	89.1	89.4
1961	89.4	89.3	88.9	88.3	87.9	87.5	87.0	87.1	87.2	87.2	87.0	87.4
1962	87.9	87.7	88.0	88.1	88.3	88.6	88.7	88.9	88.9	89.0	89.1	89.3
1963	89.3	89.3	89.3	89.4	89.4	89.5	89.6	90.1	90.2	90.4	91.0	91.0
1964	90.7	90.9	91.1	91.4	91.1	91.2	91.2	91.7	91.8	92.3	91.9	92.0
1965	92.5	93.0	93.1	93.5	93.8	93.9	93.9	94.1	94.3	94.4	94.7	94.9
1966	95.1	95.6	95.7	96.2	96.6	97.0	97.3	97.5	97.5	97.3	97.9	97.8
1967	97.9	98.1	98.2	98.3	98.0	98.4	98.5	98.0	98.1	98.2	97.9	97.9
1968	97.8	98.1	98.3	98.5	98.8	99.0	98.8	99.3	99.3	99.2	99.4	99.8
1969	100.1	100.3	100.5	100.8	101.3	101.4	101.6	101.7	101.8	101.7	101.7	102.0
1970	102.4	102.4	102.5	102.1	101.8	101.9	101.2	101.3	100.9	100.8	100.5	99.8
1971	99.6	99.5	99.2	98.8	98.7	98.1	97.9	98.3	98.2	97.9	97.8	97.7
1972	96.4	96.2	96.6	96.7	97.0	97.1	97.2	96.8	96.6	96.7	96.6	96.6
1973	97.3	98.0	98.4	99.0	99.2	99.7	99.9	100.4	100.5	100.4	100.5	101.2
1974	101.7	101.8	101.8	102.3	102.7	102.7	103.0	103.3	103.8	103.9	104.1	104.5
1975	104.0	103.2	102.9	101.7	100.8	98.9	98.6	98.1	97.8	97.8	97.6	97.6
1976	97.5	97.4	97.3	97.2	96.9	96.7	96.6	96.6	96.6	96.8	96.9	96.8
1977	96.7	96.8	96.9	97.2	97.2	97.6	97.7	97.8	98.0	98.3	98.5	98.3
1978	99.0	99.1	99.4	99.0	99.4	99.7	100.1	100.2	100.4	100.6	101.2	101.4
1979	101.7	101.9	101.5	102.6	102.5	103.1	103.5	103.9	104.4	104.7	105.1	105.0
1980	104.9	105.1	106.1	106.7	106.1	105.2	103.4	102.4	101.5	101.1	101.1	101.7
1981	101.9	102.0	101.8	101.9	102.7	102.9	102.8	103.2	103.8	103.5	103.3	103.0
1982	103.0	102.1	101.8	101.8	101.5	101.6	101.5	101.3	100.9	100.3	99.5	98.6
1983	98.0	97.9	97.6	97.5	96.9	97.1	97.2	97.6	97.5	97.4	97.8	98.1
1984	98.1	98.9	99.4	99.8	100.4	100.8	101.5	101.9	102.2	102.6	102.6	102.8
1985	102.7	102.8	103.0	102.9	103.2	103.9	104.1	104.1	104.0	104.8	104.6	104.7
1986	104.6	104.7	105.2	104.5	104.7	104.7	104.5	104.5	103.8	104.5	104.4	104.0
1987	104.6	104.0	103.8	103.9	104.0	104.1	104.0	104.1	104.3	104.4	104.4	104.3
1988	104.7	104.5	104.6	104.8	104.9	105.2	105.0	105.1	105.0	105.3	105.4	105.5
1989	105.7	106.3	106.5	106.0	106.7	107.1	107.3	107.0	107.1	107.4	107.2	107.2
1990	106.7	106.6	106.7	106.7	106.6	106.7	106.8	106.5	106.5	106.5	106.5	106.3
1991	106.5	106.0	105.9	105.1	104.8	104.1	103.7	103.4	102.9	102.6	102.3	102.1
1992	101.3	100.9	100.7	100.4	100.1	99.8	99.4	100.2	99.5	99.2	99.4	99.0
1993	99.2	99.3	99.4	99.4	99.5	99.5	99.7	99.6	99.6	99.6	99.4	99.4
1994	99.8	99.3	99.2	99.3	99.6	100.0	100.1	100.4	100.7	100.9	101.5	101.7
1995	102.2	102.6	102.8	103.4	103.7	104.2	104.3	104.3	104.5	104.5	104.5	104.4
1996	104.6	104.4	104.5	104.5	104.6	104.5	104.7	104.8	104.8	104.7	104.7	104.8
1997	104.7	104.4	104.7	105.0	105.1	105.0	104.6	104.9	105.0	-	-	-

Source: The Conference Board. Primary source(s): The Conference Board, Inc., Economics Group, 845 Third Avenue, New York, NY 10022. A dash (-) indicates that data are not available or zero.

Composite Index of 7 Lagging Indicators
Change in Index from Previous Month

Year	Jan	Feb	Mar	Apr	May	Jun	Jul	Aug	Sep	Oct	Nov	Dec
1959	-	+0.2	-	+0.3	+0.4	+0.2	+0.6	+0.9	+0.5	+0.5	-0.2	-0.2
1960	-0.5	+0.5	+0.3	-	+0.8	+0.3	+0.1	-0.1	-0.2	-0.1	-	+0.3
1961	-	-0.1	-0.4	-0.6	-0.4	-0.4	-0.5	+0.1	+0.1	-	-0.2	+0.4
1962	+0.5	-0.2	+0.3	+0.1	+0.2	+0.3	+0.1	+0.2	-	+0.1	+0.1	+0.2
1963	-	-	-	+0.1	-	+0.1	+0.1	+0.5	+0.1	+0.2	+0.6	-
1964	-0.3	+0.2	+0.2	+0.3	-0.3	+0.1	-	+0.5	+0.1	+0.5	-0.4	+0.1
1965	+0.5	+0.5	+0.1	+0.4	+0.3	+0.1	-	+0.2	+0.2	+0.1	+0.3	+0.2
1966	+0.2	+0.5	+0.1	+0.5	+0.4	+0.4	+0.3	+0.2	-	-0.2	+0.6	-0.1
1967	+0.1	+0.2	+0.1	+0.1	-0.3	+0.4	+0.1	-0.5	+0.1	+0.1	-0.3	
1968	-0.1	+0.3	+0.2	+0.2	+0.3	+0.2	-0.2	+0.5	-	-0.1	+0.2	+0.4
1969	+0.3	+0.2	+0.2	+0.3	+0.5	+0.1	+0.2	+0.1	+0.1	-0.1	-	+0.3
1970	+0.4	-	+0.1	-0.4	-0.3	+0.1	-0.7	+0.1	-0.4	-0.1	-0.3	-0.7
1971	-0.2	-0.1	-0.3	-0.4	-0.1	-0.6	-0.2	+0.4	-0.1	-0.3	-0.1	-0.1
1972	-1.3	-0.2	+0.4	+0.1	+0.3	+0.1	+0.1	-0.4	-0.2	+0.1	-0.1	-
1973	+0.7	+0.7	+0.4	+0.6	+0.2	+0.5	+0.2	+0.5	+0.1	-0.1	+0.1	+0.7
1974	+0.5	+0.1	-	+0.5	+0.4	-	+0.3	+0.3	+0.5	+0.1	+0.2	+0.4
1975	-0.5	-0.8	-0.3	-1.2	-0.9	-1.9	-0.3	-0.5	-0.3	-	-0.2	-
1976	-0.1	-0.1	-0.1	-0.1	-0.3	-0.2	-0.1	-	-	+0.2	+0.1	-0.1
1977	-0.1	+0.1	+0.1	+0.3	-	+0.4	+0.1	+0.1	+0.2	+0.3	+0.2	-0.2
1978	+0.7	+0.1	+0.3	-0.4	+0.4	+0.3	+0.4	+0.1	+0.2	+0.2	+0.6	+0.2
1979	+0.3	+0.2	-0.4	+1.1	-0.1	+0.6	+0.4	+0.4	+0.5	+0.3	+0.4	-0.1
1980	-0.1	+0.2	+1.0	+0.6	-0.6	-0.9	-1.8	-1.0	-0.9	-0.4	-	+0.6
1981	+0.2	+0.1	-0.2	+0.1	+0.8	+0.2	-0.1	+0.4	+0.6	-0.3	-0.2	-0.3
1982	-	-0.9	-0.3	-	-0.3	+0.1	-0.1	-0.2	-0.4	-0.6	-0.8	-0.9
1983	-0.6	-0.1	-0.3	-0.1	-0.6	+0.2	+0.1	+0.4	-0.1	-0.1	+0.4	+0.3
1984	-	+0.8	+0.5	+0.4	+0.6	+0.4	+0.7	+0.4	+0.3	+0.4	-	+0.2
1985	-0.1	+0.1	+0.2	-0.1	+0.3	+0.7	+0.2	-	-0.1	+0.8	-0.2	+0.1
1986	-0.1	+0.1	+0.5	-0.7	+0.2	-	-0.2	-	-0.7	+0.7	-0.1	-0.4
1987	+0.6	-0.6	-0.2	+0.1	+0.1	+0.1	-0.1	+0.1	+0.2	+0.1	-	-0.1
1988	+0.4	-0.2	+0.1	+0.2	+0.1	+0.3	-0.2	+0.1	-0.1	+0.3	+0.1	+0.1
1989	+0.2	+0.6	+0.2	-0.5	+0.7	+0.4	+0.2	-0.3	+0.1	+0.3	-0.2	-
1990	-0.5	-0.1	+0.1	-	-0.1	+0.1	+0.1	-0.3	-	-	-	-0.2
1991	+0.2	-0.5	-0.1	-0.8	-0.3	-0.7	-0.4	-0.3	-0.5	-0.3	-0.3	-0.2
1992	-0.8	-0.4	-0.2	-0.3	-0.3	-0.3	-0.4	+0.8	-0.7	-0.3	+0.2	-0.4
1993	+0.2	+0.1	+0.1	-	+0.1	-	+0.2	-0.1	-	-	-0.2	-
1994	+0.4	-0.5	-0.1	+0.1	+0.3	+0.4	+0.1	+0.3	+0.3	+0.2	+0.6	+0.2
1995	+0.5	+0.4	+0.2	+0.6	+0.3	+0.5	+0.1	-	+0.2	-	-	-0.1
1996	+0.2	-0.2	+0.1	-	+0.1	-0.1	+0.2	+0.1	-	-0.1	-	+0.1
1997	-0.1	-0.3	+0.3	+0.3	+0.1	-0.1	-0.4	+0.3	+0.1	-	-	-

Source: The Conference Board. Primary source(s): The Conference Board, Inc., Economics Group, 845 Third Avenue, New York, NY 10022. A dash (-) indicates that data are not available or zero.

Average Duration of Unemployment in Weeks
(Weeks)

Year	Jan	Feb	Mar	Apr	May	Jun	Jul	Aug	Sep	Oct	Nov	Dec
1948	8.9	8.4	8.7	8.5	9.1	8.8	8.6	8.8	8.5	9.5	7.8	8.1
1949	8.2	8.3	8.3	8.8	9.1	10.0	10.8	11.0	11.7	10.9	11.6	11.8
1950	11.3	11.8	12.4	12.6	12.7	13.1	12.5	12.2	12.2	12.3	10.7	10.7
1951	10.6	10.8	10.1	10.6	9.9	8.7	9.2	9.1	9.1	8.9	9.7	9.3
1952	9.3	8.8	8.4	9.0	7.8	7.3	7.5	7.6	8.1	9.1	9.5	8.8
1953	9.3	8.4	8.5	7.8	7.9	8.2	7.9	8.0	7.1	7.2	7.9	8.0
1954	8.7	9.5	10.6	10.9	11.6	12.3	12.5	12.8	12.9	13.3	13.2	13.4
1955	13.4	14.2	13.4	14.3	14.4	13.4	13.8	12.3	11.7	11.5	11.3	12.0
1956	11.7	12.5	11.6	11.0	10.4	10.1	10.5	12.0	11.8	11.6	10.9	11.4
1957	10.4	10.7	10.8	10.6	10.4	10.2	10.1	10.5	9.8	11.1	10.4	10.4
1958	10.5	11.0	11.2	12.1	13.1	14.4	14.6	15.7	16.5	16.5	16.4	15.7
1959	16.3	15.5	15.3	14.9	14.7	14.9	14.3	13.7	13.7	12.9	13.1	13.1
1960	13.5	13.1	13.0	12.6	11.9	11.9	12.6	12.2	12.9	13.5	13.9	12.4
1961	13.7	13.6	14.1	15.5	15.6	16.2	17.3	17.0	16.1	15.9	17.0	15.8
1962	15.3	16.0	15.0	14.9	15.5	15.1	14.6	14.5	14.1	14.1	13.3	13.6
1963	13.8	14.1	14.5	14.5	14.5	14.0	14.0	13.9	14.2	13.9	13.3	13.3
1964	13.5	13.2	13.5	12.4	13.6	13.6	14.7	13.0	12.7	12.6	14.0	12.7
1965	12.2	12.6	12.0	11.4	11.1	11.6	11.6	11.9	11.9	12.1	11.7	11.4
1966	11.9	11.2	11.1	10.8	10.2	9.7	9.7	9.8	10.1	10.3	9.7	9.5
1967	9.3	9.2	8.9	8.8	8.7	8.3	8.3	8.9	8.4	8.7	8.9	8.6
1968	9.4	8.7	8.5	8.7	8.2	7.9	8.4	8.3	8.2	8.4	8.1	8.2
1969	8.1	7.9	7.9	7.9	7.9	7.7	7.8	7.9	8.0	7.6	8.0	8.0
1970	7.9	8.0	8.3	8.2	8.6	8.6	8.9	8.8	8.9	8.7	9.3	9.8
1971	10.5	10.4	10.6	10.9	11.2	11.6	11.5	11.5	11.9	12.6	12.0	11.5
1972	12.1	12.4	12.3	12.4	12.3	12.4	11.8	11.8	12.1	11.7	11.4	11.4
1973	11.0	10.5	10.6	10.0	10.1	9.6	9.6	9.8	9.4	10.2	9.9	9.5
1974	9.5	9.6	9.7	9.8	9.6	9.7	9.9	9.8	9.6	9.9	9.6	10.1
1975	10.7	11.7	11.8	12.9	13.4	15.3	15.0	15.6	16.1	15.4	16.6	16.5
1976	16.6	16.3	16.5	15.9	15.0	16.9	15.7	15.6	15.2	15.2	15.3	15.1
1977	15.2	14.7	14.5	14.4	14.9	14.4	14.3	13.9	14.0	13.7	13.6	13.6
1978	12.9	12.5	12.4	12.3	12.1	12.1	12.0	11.4	11.4	11.7	11.1	10.6
1979	11.1	11.2	11.7	11.0	11.1	10.4	10.3	10.6	10.5	10.5	10.6	10.8
1980	10.4	10.6	11.0	11.4	10.9	11.3	11.8	12.4	12.9	13.1	13.6	13.7
1981	14.3	14.1	14.0	13.9	13.6	13.7	13.8	14.4	13.6	13.5	13.1	13.1
1982	13.4	14.1	14.1	14.5	14.9	15.7	15.4	16.2	16.6	17.2	17.1	18.1
1983	19.4	19.2	19.4	19.5	20.5	20.8	21.2	20.0	20.2	20.2	19.7	19.2
1984	20.4	19.0	19.1	18.9	18.8	18.1	18.0	17.3	17.0	16.7	17.0	16.8
1985	15.9	15.9	16.1	16.4	15.3	15.5	15.5	15.3	15.3	15.3	15.7	15.1
1986	14.8	15.2	14.6	14.7	14.7	15.2	15.2	15.5	15.4	15.2	15.0	15.0
1987	14.9	14.7	14.9	14.8	14.9	14.9	14.2	14.4	14.2	14.0	14.0	14.2
1988	14.2	14.4	13.7	13.3	13.8	13.1	13.4	13.6	13.6	13.4	12.6	12.9
1989	12.6	12.4	12.3	12.5	12.0	11.1	11.8	11.4	11.5	11.9	11.7	11.6
1990	11.8	11.6	11.7	11.8	11.7	11.6	11.9	12.2	12.4	12.2	12.4	12.5
1991	12.2	12.7	12.9	13.5	12.9	13.7	13.8	13.9	14.0	14.4	14.8	15.4
1992	16.1	16.7	17.1	17.4	17.8	18.2	18.1	18.0	18.1	18.9	17.9	19.0
1993	18.3	18.2	17.6	17.6	17.5	17.8	17.7	18.0	18.1	18.1	18.6	18.3
1994	18.6	19.0	19.0	18.9	19.4	18.6	19.0	18.8	18.8	19.4	18.1	17.9
1995	17.1	17.1	17.2	17.4	16.9	15.7	16.5	16.2	16.3	16.2	16.5	16.4
1996	16.2	16.6	17.2	17.3	16.9	17.2	16.9	17.2	16.9	16.7	16.0	15.8
1997	16.0	16.0	15.3	15.2	15.1	15.1	16.6	15.9	16.0	-	-	-

Source: The Conference Board. Primary source(s): U.S. Department of Labor, Bureau of Labor Statistics, Office of Employment and Unemployment Statistics, Division of Labor Force Statistics, Washington, DC 20212. A dash (-) indicates that data are not available or zero.

Ratio, Manufacturing and Trade Inventories to Sales
(Chained 1992 $)

Year	Jan	Feb	Mar	Apr	May	Jun	Jul	Aug	Sep	Oct	Nov	Dec
1959	1.170	1.159	1.155	1.159	1.148	1.152	1.167	1.200	1.198	1.200	1.200	1.180
1960	1.180	1.199	1.221	1.211	1.240	1.239	1.250	1.252	1.247	1.251	1.260	1.247
1961	1.276	1.264	1.238	1.241	1.229	1.206	1.216	1.199	1.198	1.188	1.179	1.176
1962	1.188	1.196	1.187	1.186	1.194	1.202	1.205	1.208	1.212	1.209	1.193	1.216
1963	1.215	1.196	1.196	1.185	1.199	1.191	1.183	1.206	1.205	1.196	1.209	1.190
1964	1.188	1.188	1.199	1.188	1.178	1.185	1.177	1.186	1.178	1.197	1.194	1.166
1965	1.177	1.185	1.173	1.175	1.189	1.197	1.190	1.201	1.215	1.186	1.177	1.176
1966	1.174	1.188	1.179	1.195	1.221	1.217	1.242	1.250	1.249	1.257	1.280	1.280
1967	1.295	1.307	1.304	1.310	1.315	1.304	1.316	1.314	1.308	1.318	1.294	1.273
1968	1.295	1.301	1.292	1.304	1.304	1.298	1.290	1.327	1.305	1.301	1.293	1.307
1969	1.313	1.318	1.319	1.319	1.326	1.330	1.338	1.334	1.331	1.324	1.344	1.352
1970	1.367	1.368	1.385	1.401	1.382	1.381	1.389	1.398	1.397	1.410	1.436	1.388
1971	1.383	1.378	1.380	1.377	1.376	1.359	1.380	1.380	1.370	1.370	1.344	1.336
1972	1.328	1.341	1.319	1.316	1.317	1.312	1.321	1.303	1.290	1.278	1.259	1.244
1973	1.240	1.244	1.254	1.265	1.273	1.283	1.274	1.296	1.293	1.269	1.259	1.287
1974	1.289	1.298	1.303	1.315	1.318	1.329	1.335	1.344	1.363	1.396	1.419	1.475
1975	1.477	1.476	1.508	1.492	1.482	1.461	1.450	1.432	1.428	1.431	1.429	1.410
1976	1.380	1.381	1.376	1.376	1.384	1.378	1.385	1.383	1.391	1.414	1.395	1.365
1977	1.379	1.364	1.351	1.359	1.362	1.355	1.356	1.363	1.367	1.359	1.359	1.348
1978	1.396	1.370	1.369	1.340	1.347	1.344	1.358	1.346	1.352	1.347	1.350	1.351
1979	1.375	1.387	1.349	1.395	1.369	1.388	1.403	1.399	1.401	1.411	1.410	1.416
1980	1.411	1.425	1.461	1.502	1.522	1.522	1.501	1.485	1.451	1.419	1.417	1.417
1981	1.414	1.427	1.443	1.438	1.452	1.461	1.463	1.472	1.487	1.508	1.530	1.543
1982	1.542	1.504	1.506	1.509	1.488	1.516	1.526	1.536	1.532	1.544	1.526	1.523
1983	1.484	1.488	1.455	1.457	1.437	1.402	1.406	1.416	1.401	1.389	1.385	1.370
1984	1.368	1.384	1.398	1.404	1.409	1.403	1.422	1.440	1.449	1.454	1.449	1.452
1985	1.454	1.457	1.443	1.449	1.432	1.461	1.462	1.441	1.434	1.455	1.448	1.456
1986	1.435	1.454	1.462	1.440	1.452	1.445	1.438	1.435	1.394	1.415	1.421	1.380
1987	1.433	1.386	1.394	1.401	1.410	1.406	1.393	1.398	1.386	1.399	1.411	1.406
1988	1.410	1.400	1.382	1.393	1.392	1.384	1.391	1.395	1.395	1.386	1.385	1.375
1989	1.383	1.405	1.418	1.408	1.424	1.436	1.462	1.422	1.436	1.456	1.454	1.450
1990	1.458	1.436	1.434	1.456	1.459	1.451	1.469	1.452	1.484	1.487	1.508	1.521
1991	1.544	1.531	1.527	1.497	1.478	1.481	1.461	1.466	1.467	1.470	1.472	1.499
1992	1.468	1.458	1.451	1.450	1.454	1.445	1.430	1.455	1.435	1.431	1.430	1.412
1993	1.417	1.426	1.444	1.443	1.440	1.431	1.441	1.432	1.428	1.422	1.420	1.414
1994	1.419	1.411	1.391	1.402	1.411	1.406	1.418	1.391	1.399	1.400	1.392	1.390
1995	1.395	1.400	1.409	1.426	1.418	1.411	1.432	1.408	1.410	1.417	1.407	1.393
1996	1.411	1.393	1.390	1.384	1.375	1.380	1.374	1.379	1.373	1.370	1.365	1.367
1997	1.356	1.342	1.348	1.356	1.366	1.354	1.341	1.356	-	-	-	-

Source: The Conference Board. Primary source(s): U.S. Department of Commerce (manufacturing and trade sales and inventories; retail sales deflator), Bureau of Economic Analysis, National Income and Wealth Division, BE-54, Washington, DC 20230 and U.S. Department of Commerce, Bureau of the Census, Services Division, Current Retail Inventories and Sales Branch, Washington, DC 20233. A dash (-) indicates that data are not available or zero.

Change in Index of Labor Cost per Unit of Output, Manufacturing
(6-Month percent, Annual Rate)

Year	Jan	Feb	Mar	Apr	May	Jun	Jul	Aug	Sep	Oct	Nov	Dec
1946	-	-	-	-	-	-	17.9	8.9	10.4	-2.8	-12.1	-4.7
1947	-	2.1	4.2	7.9	10.1	7.0	6.3	4.9	7.6	6.9	4.1	7.5
1948	10.3	10.3	8.0	8.0	6.0	2.6	3.2	7.1	5.7	5.1	10.5	8.4
1949	5.7	2.5	-0.6	1.2	-1.2	-2.4	-3.0	-5.4	-4.8	-4.8	-7.8	-4.3
1950	-4.3	-2.5	-1.9	-4.3	-1.3	-5.0	-5.6	-5.6	-2.5	5.2	8.5	12.0
1951	12.7	16.9	16.7	14.2	11.3	12.6	16.5	15.0	12.3	7.1	7.1	7.0
1952	2.9	1.1	2.3	3.4	4.5	3.4	0.6	1.1	1.1	1.1	-2.7	-0.5
1953	2.2	2.2	2.2	2.8	3.4	2.2	2.2	0.6	-0.5	1.6	5.0	6.6
1954	7.2	7.8	8.4	5.5	2.2	-2.6	-3.1	-1.6	-4.2	-3.1	-1.1	-1.1
1955	-4.2	-4.7	-4.3	-6.3	-7.8	-5.8	-1.1	-1.1	1.1	1.7	5.6	2.8
1956	2.8	2.8	4.4	5.0	2.7	6.6	12.3	7.7	4.9	6.0	5.4	4.3
1957	-2.0	0.5	1.6	2.6	2.1	1.6	1.6	3.1	2.1	2.6	6.2	7.3
1958	8.9	10.0	11.6	9.3	3.5	-1.5	-2.4	-4.8	-5.3	-8.1	-6.3	-1.5
1959	-3.5	-4.0	-4.0	-3.5	-3.5	-3.0	2.0	5.7	6.7	10.0	10.0	1.0
1960	-4.0	-3.9	-2.4	-2.9	-1.5	6.7	7.8	5.1	2.5	2.5	3.0	2.0
1961	3.5	5.0	3.5	-	-2.4	-3.4	-5.7	-8.0	-7.6	-4.9	-4.9	-4.9
1962	-1.0	-0.5	1.0	3.0	3.6	5.7	1.5	2.0	1.0	-1.0	-2.0	-2.5
1963	-1.5	-2.5	-3.0	-4.9	-4.5	-4.0	-2.5	-2.0	-1.0	0.5	1.0	1.5
1964	-1.5	-	1.5	-	-	-1.0	0.5	0.5	-	1.0	-1.0	-2.0
1965	-3.0	-3.0	-6.0	-6.0	-4.1	-3.6	-3.6	-3.6	-1.0	0.5	1.6	-
1966	2.1	3.7	2.6	3.2	2.1	4.8	4.2	4.2	3.7	2.1	4.7	2.6
1967	3.6	2.0	4.1	3.6	2.0	4.1	4.6	3.5	1.5	1.0	-0.5	-1.0
1968	-0.5	2.0	3.0	6.1	6.1	6.6	6.0	3.4	4.9	4.4	3.9	3.9
1969	2.4	1.9	1.4	1.9	4.8	4.3	4.8	7.3	7.2	6.2	5.6	7.1
1970	10.9	8.4	8.4	7.4	5.5	5.0	0.9	2.2	0.4	1.3	2.2	-
1971	0.4	0.4	1.8	0.9	0.9	1.8	0.9	2.6	-2.2	-3.0	-3.4	-1.7
1972	-3.9	-3.8	0.9	0.4	2.2	0.9	3.6	0.9	0.4	1.8	-	-0.4
1973	1.7	3.5	4.4	6.6	6.6	6.6	5.2	3.9	3.0	2.5	4.7	9.9
1974	12.1	13.9	13.9	14.7	12.8	9.0	8.5	8.4	9.2	10.0	13.2	19.8
1975	20.4	20.2	23.8	18.6	16.7	7.2	3.5	2.8	-1.0	1.0	-0.3	2.1
1976	4.5	1.7	4.5	4.8	3.8	4.1	2.4	5.8	3.0	2.0	3.3	1.3
1977	1.3	3.0	2.6	2.6	3.3	5.3	6.7	3.6	5.6	7.9	7.5	7.8
1978	7.4	10.4	10.0	4.4	4.7	2.8	3.1	0.6	0.3	5.6	5.5	7.7
1979	8.9	9.2	9.5	10.3	8.7	8.4	8.9	10.3	10.9	8.4	10.7	12.4
1980	9.6	8.7	9.2	12.0	15.9	15.4	16.2	15.3	11.8	10.0	4.5	4.0
1981	5.5	3.5	6.0	6.7	7.0	6.4	3.4	8.4	8.3	9.2	11.2	12.1
1982	17.6	8.7	8.0	5.7	5.0	2.5	-0.9	4.0	3.3	3.6	2.2	4.0
1983	-1.1	-1.5	-3.2	-4.7	-5.8	-7.2	-4.3	-4.8	-4.6	-3.1	-0.9	0.9
1984	-1.1	0.7	1.8	2.0	0.2	-1.5	2.3	2.3	3.6	3.1	4.5	6.4
1985	6.1	2.9	4.9	0.9	-0.4	-0.9	-0.4	0.9	-2.6	4.6	2.9	2.8
1986	-1.1	0.2	5.1	-3.6	-0.6	-1.7	1.1	0.4	-3.8	1.5	-1.3	-3.2
1987	-0.6	-2.8	-1.3	-4.3	-2.0	-2.0	-4.7	-0.7	-0.9	-0.2	-0.7	0.4
1988	2.9	1.5	3.8	2.7	4.0	5.8	3.3	2.2	-0.2	5.5	1.5	-0.4
1989	-0.6	2.6	2.4	-2.7	0.6	1.5	4.6	1.5	1.1	6.8	4.1	3.9
1990	1.1	2.3	2.6	2.3	2.7	4.3	4.7	3.0	2.9	1.0	2.9	3.7
1991	4.6	5.9	7.1	6.0	5.2	1.4	1.0	1.2	-2.0	-1.6	-0.4	2.6
1992	1.0	0.4	0.8	0.2	-0.4	-1.2	-0.8	-	0.4	-0.6	-1.2	-1.2
1993	-1.2	-1.6	-1.6	0.8	1.8	1.4	2.4	3.4	3.5	2.0	1.4	1.0
1994	1.2	-1.4	-0.6	-1.6	-2.2	-1.6	-2.9	-1.2	-1.0	-	-0.2	-1.4
1995	-0.6	-0.6	-1.0	-0.2	-	0.8	1.8	0.2	-0.6	-	1.0	0.8
1996	-1.2	-	1.2	0.6	-	-	-	0.4	-0.2	-1.2	-2.0	-1.6
1997	-0.4	-1.4	-0.4	-0.2	0.6	-0.2	-2.0	-1.8	-2.6	-	-	-

Source: The Conference Board. Primary source(s): U.S. Department of Commerce (wages and salaries and supplements), Bureau of Economic Analysis, National Income and Wealth Division, BE-54, Washington, DC 20230 and Board of Governors of the Federal Reserve System (industrial production, manufacturing), Division of Research and Statistics, Industrial Output Section, Stop 82, Washington, DC 20551. A dash (-) indicates that data are not available or zero.

Average Prime Rate Charged by Banks
Not seasonally adjusted
(Percent)

Year	Jan	Feb	Mar	Apr	May	Jun	Jul	Aug	Sep	Oct	Nov	Dec
1949	2.0	2.0	2.0	2.0	2.0	2.0	2.0	2.0	2.0	2.0	2.0	2.0
1950	2.0	2.0	2.0	2.0	2.0	2.0	2.0	2.0	2.1	2.3	2.3	2.3
1951	2.4	2.5	2.5	2.5	2.5	2.5	2.5	2.5	2.5	2.6	2.8	2.8
1952	3.0	3.0	3.0	3.0	3.0	3.0	3.0	3.0	3.0	3.0	3.0	3.0
1953	3.0	3.0	3.0	3.0	3.3	3.3	3.3	3.3	3.3	3.3	3.3	3.3
1954	3.3	3.3	3.1	3.0	3.0	3.0	3.0	3.0	3.0	3.0	3.0	3.0
1955	3.0	3.0	3.0	3.0	3.0	3.0	3.0	3.2	3.3	3.4	3.5	3.5
1956	3.5	3.5	3.5	3.7	3.8	3.8	3.8	3.8	4.0	4.0	4.0	4.0
1957	4.0	4.0	4.0	4.0	4.0	4.0	4.0	4.4	4.5	4.5	4.5	4.5
1958	4.3	4.0	4.0	3.8	3.5	3.5	3.5	3.5	3.8	4.0	4.0	4.0
1959	4.0	4.0	4.0	4.0	4.2	4.5	4.5	4.5	5.0	5.0	5.0	5.0
1960	5.0	5.0	5.0	5.0	5.0	5.0	5.0	4.8	4.5	4.5	4.5	4.5
1961	4.5	4.5	4.5	4.5	4.5	4.5	4.5	4.5	4.5	4.5	4.5	4.5
1962	4.5	4.5	4.5	4.5	4.5	4.5	4.5	4.5	4.5	4.5	4.5	4.5
1963	4.5	4.5	4.5	4.5	4.5	4.5	4.5	4.5	4.5	4.5	4.5	4.5
1964	4.5	4.5	4.5	4.5	4.5	4.5	4.5	4.5	4.5	4.5	4.5	4.5
1965	4.5	4.5	4.5	4.5	4.5	4.5	4.5	4.5	4.5	4.5	4.5	4.9
1966	5.0	5.0	5.3	5.5	5.5	5.5	5.8	5.9	6.0	6.0	6.0	6.0
1967	6.0	5.8	5.7	5.5	5.5	5.5	5.5	5.5	5.5	5.5	5.7	6.0
1968	6.0	6.0	6.0	6.2	6.5	6.5	6.5	6.5	6.4	6.3	6.3	6.6
1969	6.9	7.0	7.2	7.5	7.5	8.2	8.5	8.5	8.5	8.5	8.5	8.5
1970	8.5	8.5	8.4	8.0	8.0	8.0	8.0	8.0	7.8	7.5	7.3	6.9
1971	6.3	5.9	5.4	5.3	5.5	5.5	5.9	6.0	6.0	5.9	5.5	5.5
1972	5.2	4.8	4.8	5.0	5.0	5.0	5.3	5.3	5.5	5.7	5.8	5.8
1973	6.0	6.0	6.3	6.6	7.0	7.5	8.3	9.2	9.9	9.9	9.8	9.8
1974	9.7	9.2	8.9	10.0	11.3	11.5	12.0	12.0	12.0	11.7	10.8	10.5
1975	10.1	9.0	7.9	7.5	7.4	7.1	7.2	7.7	7.9	8.0	7.5	7.3
1976	7.0	6.8	6.8	6.8	6.8	7.2	7.3	7.0	7.0	6.8	6.5	6.3
1977	6.3	6.3	6.3	6.3	6.4	6.8	6.8	6.8	7.1	7.5	7.8	7.8
1978	7.9	8.0	8.0	8.0	8.3	8.6	9.0	9.0	9.4	9.9	10.9	11.6
1979	11.7	11.7	11.7	11.7	11.7	11.6	11.5	11.9	12.9	14.4	15.6	15.3
1980	15.2	15.6	18.3	19.8	16.6	12.6	11.5	11.1	12.2	13.8	16.1	20.3
1981	20.2	19.4	18.0	17.2	19.6	20.0	20.4	20.5	20.1	18.5	16.8	15.8
1982	15.8	16.6	16.5	16.5	16.5	16.5	16.3	14.4	13.5	12.5	11.9	11.5
1983	11.2	11.0	10.5	10.5	10.5	10.5	10.5	10.9	11.0	11.0	11.0	11.0
1984	11.0	11.0	11.2	11.9	12.4	12.6	13.0	13.0	13.0	12.6	11.8	11.1
1985	10.6	10.5	10.5	10.5	10.3	9.8	9.5	9.5	9.5	9.5	9.5	9.5
1986	9.5	9.5	9.1	8.8	8.5	8.5	8.2	7.9	7.5	7.5	7.5	7.5
1987	7.5	7.5	7.5	7.8	8.1	8.3	8.3	8.3	8.7	9.1	8.8	8.8
1988	8.8	8.5	8.5	8.5	8.8	9.0	9.3	9.8	10.0	10.0	10.1	10.5
1989	10.5	10.9	11.5	11.5	11.5	11.1	11.0	10.5	10.5	10.5	10.5	10.5
1990	10.1	10.0	10.0	10.0	10.0	10.0	10.0	10.0	10.0	10.0	10.0	10.0
1991	9.5	9.1	9.0	9.0	8.5	8.5	8.5	8.5	8.2	8.0	7.6	7.2
1992	6.5	6.5	6.5	6.5	6.5	6.5	6.0	6.0	6.0	6.0	6.0	6.0
1993	6.0	6.0	6.0	6.0	6.0	6.0	6.0	6.0	6.0	6.0	6.0	6.0
1994	6.0	6.0	6.1	6.4	7.0	7.3	7.3	7.5	7.8	7.8	8.1	8.5
1995	8.5	9.0	9.0	9.0	9.0	9.0	8.8	8.8	8.8	8.8	8.8	8.6
1996	8.5	8.3	8.3	8.3	8.3	8.3	8.3	8.3	8.3	8.3	8.3	8.3
1997	8.3	8.3	8.3	8.5	8.5	8.5	8.5	8.5	8.5	-	-	-

Source: The Conference Board. Primary source(s): Board of Governors of the Federal Reserve System, Division of Monetary Affairs, Banking and Money Market Statistics Section, Stop 81, Washington, DC 20551. A dash (-) indicates that data are not available or zero.

Commercial and Industrial Loans Outstanding
(Millions of chained 1992 $)

Year	Jan	Feb	Mar	Apr	May	Jun	Jul	Aug	Sep	Oct	Nov	Dec
1959	126,167	126,103	127,129	128,119	130,149	131,863	131,553	133,268	133,729	134,641	135,256	136,089
1960	136,819	138,495	139,320	139,645	140,784	142,544	142,190	141,290	141,642	141,625	141,683	141,203
1961	141,020	140,772	141,474	141,437	141,090	140,812	140,763	141,158	141,361	141,362	141,647	142,265
1962	142,911	143,057	143,665	144,296	144,800	145,734	146,782	147,808	148,228	149,689	150,849	151,088
1963	151,035	151,234	151,853	152,707	153,169	153,326	153,558	154,030	155,252	157,003	159,894	161,681
1964	160,853	161,795	161,732	163,130	164,432	165,301	166,248	167,851	169,959	170,676	172,224	174,723
1965	177,828	182,041	185,585	187,914	191,571	193,079	194,278	198,476	202,379	205,082	208,073	209,925
1966	213,273	215,911	218,288	219,886	222,590	226,353	229,725	233,311	234,884	236,784	238,127	238,679
1967	240,843	242,560	245,052	246,545	247,556	249,407	249,997	248,402	248,768	249,906	251,020	253,977
1968	253,456	252,979	253,346	256,846	256,737	257,913	259,739	262,639	265,350	267,296	270,883	273,262
1969	279,236	281,509	284,861	291,010	294,028	297,028	297,364	300,921	304,023	306,386	307,508	309,606
1970	306,476	310,500	313,939	312,650	313,411	314,458	313,129	314,313	314,067	306,592	303,301	301,912
1971	300,699	302,056	301,895	297,342	298,671	294,188	290,828	295,275	300,749	297,015	295,914	293,047
1972	268,697	270,074	272,640	275,798	277,025	277,645	277,198	277,496	275,700	281,072	283,036	284,348
1973	290,150	300,080	304,257	306,975	309,533	313,920	317,111	319,537	318,027	319,577	320,533	320,435
1974	323,886	326,721	327,079	339,051	342,005	343,169	351,998	355,210	362,627	362,362	363,413	361,206
1975	361,279	356,824	351,985	346,567	338,021	329,901	325,371	321,016	315,896	311,280	307,181	305,694
1976	302,416	302,925	296,986	289,738	288,942	289,902	286,649	284,427	281,943	282,797	285,005	285,460
1977	284,426	285,426	284,870	284,889	285,137	286,321	284,506	286,217	286,577	287,960	288,701	289,623
1978	289,494	289,046	293,341	295,356	298,082	301,218	302,330	302,457	302,723	304,004	306,346	305,402
1979	308,971	311,513	313,123	321,173	322,968	326,904	330,968	335,446	341,256	339,635	335,398	337,893
1980	346,044	349,877	351,326	349,396	343,494	347,699	342,327	340,848	340,752	340,546	345,457	346,415
1981	346,374	343,466	338,282	342,968	350,346	355,489	359,561	365,088	368,752	371,125	374,309	377,611
1982	385,806	392,566	393,961	401,764	405,714	405,576	403,471	403,005	403,707	401,304	393,394	384,868
1983	388,590	388,051	388,547	380,396	372,889	372,586	370,469	370,704	369,121	366,745	367,617	373,005
1984	381,833	386,647	396,568	404,572	412,514	424,582	429,430	432,049	436,434	440,921	444,091	444,492
1985	443,111	444,805	445,922	445,380	447,859	444,689	447,067	447,639	444,738	448,620	450,931	451,587
1986	452,800	450,619	449,719	443,359	445,199	444,591	445,777	450,425	447,371	448,824	448,448	454,505
1987	461,339	457,505	454,456	452,647	450,729	450,381	447,864	442,477	444,600	446,154	443,369	445,992
1988	522,762	527,057	527,585	530,369	529,103	530,023	528,425	526,346	523,691	525,715	529,376	536,687
1989	540,283	547,832	546,752	545,773	555,233	556,542	556,995	561,953	559,969	559,514	560,807	561,985
1990	560,016	561,307	567,532	565,170	561,423	559,897	558,851	557,033	559,059	554,230	545,918	544,757
1991	542,144	533,257	533,736	526,628	519,796	516,095	511,498	499,954	492,754	487,893	484,545	477,632
1992	472,639	471,640	469,924	466,192	463,168	459,631	455,364	457,347	452,385	456,254	460,160	456,588
1993	455,182	453,838	448,615	449,196	453,257	454,121	455,729	453,795	452,153	448,584	447,104	447,860
1994	450,620	446,047	445,105	444,652	448,440	451,804	454,428	457,190	462,500	470,584	472,955	479,405
1995	484,908	493,170	497,197	505,939	506,672	511,050	513,043	515,613	517,858	521,116	517,242	523,895
1996	523,303	521,329	526,221	527,726	526,211	525,762	524,691	524,879	528,441	522,669	521,925	523,824
1997	527,216	527,532	530,320	530,747	533,711	541,370	544,042	547,135	556,017	-	-	-

Source: The Conference Board. Primary source(s): Board of Governors of the Federal Reserve System, Division of Monetary Affairs, Banking and Money Market Statistics Section, Stop 84, Washington, DC 20551 and Board of Governors of the Federal Reserve System, Capital Markets, Banking and Money Market Statistics Section, Stop 84, Washington, DC 20551. A dash (-) indicates that data are not available or zero.

Ratio, Consumer Installment Credit to Personal Income
(Percent)

Year	Jan	Feb	Mar	Apr	May	Jun	Jul	Aug	Sep	Oct	Nov	Dec
1946	3.84	4.01	4.08	4.23	4.31	4.36	4.38	4.58	4.80	4.86	5.02	5.08
1947	5.23	5.40	5.55	5.80	5.95	5.96	6.07	6.16	5.85	6.26	6.40	6.49
1948	6.56	6.72	6.83	6.95	7.01	7.01	7.11	7.12	7.25	7.25	7.31	7.50
1949	7.65	7.74	7.76	7.92	8.07	8.25	8.39	8.48	8.50	8.82	8.92	9.03
1950	8.80	8.82	8.80	9.12	9.33	9.53	9.74	9.84	9.94	9.83	9.76	9.52
1951	9.69	9.71	9.71	9.47	9.42	9.30	9.24	9.21	9.25	9.22	9.34	9.28
1952	9.38	9.37	9.42	9.52	9.70	9.87	10.06	9.90	9.95	10.11	10.35	10.45
1953	10.66	10.72	10.93	11.03	11.15	11.14	11.23	11.36	11.43	11.43	11.55	11.59
1954	11.69	11.51	11.53	11.61	11.64	11.66	11.70	11.63	11.62	11.59	11.60	11.66
1955	11.69	11.80	11.94	12.02	12.14	12.34	12.27	12.49	12.62	12.68	12.79	12.84
1956	12.86	12.92	13.09	12.99	13.14	13.09	13.13	13.07	13.08	12.96	13.12	13.05
1957	13.10	13.10	13.12	13.16	13.23	13.14	13.16	13.20	13.28	13.28	13.32	13.37
1958	13.41	13.39	13.25	13.22	13.20	13.07	12.83	12.86	12.84	12.81	12.73	12.75
1959	12.79	12.89	12.92	12.92	13.00	13.06	13.21	13.46	13.58	13.67	13.69	13.82
1960	13.77	13.86	13.97	14.06	14.11	14.18	14.22	14.27	14.33	14.31	14.41	14.51
1961	14.54	14.42	14.39	14.26	14.19	14.05	13.98	14.05	14.08	13.99	14.00	14.01
1962	14.05	14.06	14.05	14.11	14.25	14.30	14.30	14.40	14.43	14.49	14.55	14.59
1963	14.58	14.84	14.93	15.02	15.05	15.03	15.16	15.28	15.32	15.37	15.44	15.49
1964	15.57	15.60	15.79	15.80	15.90	15.92	15.97	16.00	16.09	16.16	16.13	16.14
1965	16.26	16.46	16.48	16.56	16.59	16.65	16.68	16.72	16.43	16.61	16.57	16.53
1966	16.66	16.67	16.65	16.64	16.65	16.59	16.53	16.47	16.35	16.27	16.23	16.25
1967	16.17	16.20	16.11	16.11	16.07	16.04	15.98	15.95	15.97	15.96	15.95	15.86
1968	15.76	15.66	15.67	15.65	15.61	15.59	15.63	15.60	15.63	15.70	15.72	15.79
1969	15.86	15.95	15.89	15.89	15.89	15.88	15.87	15.81	15.81	15.77	15.78	15.73
1970	15.79	15.76	15.67	15.32	15.40	15.48	15.21	15.17	15.14	15.14	15.07	15.03
1971	15.22	15.26	15.22	15.24	15.21	14.97	14.84	14.87	14.94	14.99	15.05	15.02
1972	14.91	14.81	14.93	14.99	15.06	15.32	15.10	15.02	15.02	14.85	14.80	14.90
1973	15.12	15.20	15.25	15.27	15.29	15.34	15.43	15.42	15.31	15.16	15.11	15.08
1974	15.20	15.25	15.26	15.31	15.23	15.16	15.02	15.00	14.91	14.76	14.77	14.69
1975	14.70	14.69	14.63	14.53	14.39	14.02	14.14	14.00	13.96	13.88	13.88	13.96
1976	13.93	13.92	13.99	14.04	14.01	14.04	13.98	13.96	14.01	14.11	14.09	14.16
1977	14.12	14.17	14.30	14.40	14.48	14.56	14.53	14.59	14.62	14.75	14.79	14.74
1978	14.86	14.89	14.94	14.89	14.99	15.13	15.16	15.22	15.25	15.19	15.29	15.27
1979	15.33	15.40	15.41	15.53	15.58	15.58	15.50	15.55	15.59	15.59	15.58	15.32
1980	15.07	15.05	15.00	14.91	14.74	14.53	14.32	14.22	14.05	13.86	13.72	13.63
1981	13.49	13.41	13.40	13.46	13.45	13.39	13.19	13.09	13.18	13.17	13.16	13.16
1982	13.19	13.11	13.12	13.00	12.96	12.99	12.97	12.97	13.00	12.94	12.93	13.01
1983	13.02	12.96	13.04	13.02	12.94	13.07	13.14	13.30	13.29	13.34	13.42	13.55
1984	13.52	13.62	13.70	13.72	13.99	14.11	14.17	14.23	14.24	14.49	14.55	14.69
1985	14.70	14.86	15.05	15.23	15.37	16.00	16.12	16.21	16.38	16.39	16.48	16.46
1986	16.54	16.62	16.65	16.77	16.85	16.87	16.88	16.90	17.00	17.23	17.18	17.14
1987	17.01	16.90	16.82	16.86	16.76	16.79	16.89	16.85	16.83	16.73	16.72	16.61
1988	16.76	16.76	16.78	16.79	16.85	16.83	16.77	16.82	16.78	16.74	16.78	16.91
1989	16.98	16.92	16.88	16.89	16.98	16.98	17.00	17.04	17.14	17.06	16.97	16.96
1990	16.83	16.74	16.65	16.53	16.56	16.52	16.49	16.50	16.40	16.48	16.45	16.25
1991	16.23	16.22	16.17	16.07	16.00	15.85	15.87	15.79	15.68	15.56	15.44	15.27
1992	15.23	15.12	15.07	14.95	14.86	14.78	14.76	15.16	14.73	14.60	14.54	14.06
1993	14.70	14.76	14.77	14.57	14.47	14.55	14.64	14.61	14.73	14.81	14.88	14.55
1994	15.27	15.21	15.31	15.27	15.36	15.53	15.58	15.75	15.86	15.92	16.06	16.15
1995	16.18	16.26	16.45	16.52	16.76	16.86	16.92	17.10	17.29	17.31	17.49	17.54
1996	17.57	17.59	17.68	17.74	17.77	17.70	17.90	17.92	17.84	17.94	17.90	17.77
1997	17.83	17.82	17.76	17.87	17.85	17.75	17.81	17.77	-	-	-	-

Source: The Conference Board. Primary source(s): Board of Governors of the Federal Reserve System (consumer installment credit), Publication Services, Stop 127, Washington, DC 20551 and U.S. Department of Commerce (personal income), Bureau of Economic Analysis, National Income and Wealth Division, BE-54, Washington, DC 20230. A dash (-) indicates that data are not available or zero.

Change in CPI for Services

(6-Month percent, Annual Rate)

Year	Jan	Feb	Mar	Apr	May	Jun	Jul	Aug	Sep	Oct	Nov	Dec
1956	-	-	-	-	-	-	1.9	2.9	3.9	2.9	3.9	3.9
1957	4.8	3.8	4.8	4.8	4.8	4.7	3.8	4.7	3.7	4.7	4.7	3.7
1958	4.6	4.6	3.7	3.7	3.6	3.6	3.6	2.7	3.6	2.7	1.8	1.8
1959	1.8	2.7	1.8	2.6	3.5	3.5	3.5	3.5	4.4	4.4	3.5	4.4
1960	3.5	3.4	3.4	2.6	3.4	2.5	3.4	2.5	2.5	2.5	2.5	2.5
1961	2.5	2.5	1.7	2.5	1.7	1.7	0.8	1.6	1.6	1.6	1.6	2.5
1962	2.5	1.6	2.5	1.6	2.4	1.6	2.4	2.4	1.6	1.6	1.6	1.6
1963	1.6	1.6	1.6	2.4	1.6	2.4	1.6	2.4	2.4	1.6	2.4	2.4
1964	2.4	1.6	1.6	2.4	1.6	1.6	1.6	1.6	1.6	1.6	2.3	1.5
1965	2.3	3.1	3.1	3.1	2.3	2.3	2.3	1.5	2.3	2.3	3.0	3.0
1966	3.0	3.0	3.0	3.8	3.8	4.5	5.3	5.3	6.0	5.2	5.9	5.2
1967	4.4	5.1	4.3	4.3	2.9	4.3	3.6	3.6	3.5	4.2	4.2	4.2
1968	4.9	4.9	5.6	4.9	5.6	5.5	6.2	6.9	6.1	6.8	6.8	6.7
1969	6.7	6.0	7.3	7.2	7.9	7.2	7.1	7.8	7.7	7.0	6.9	7.6
1970	8.2	8.1	8.7	9.3	9.2	9.2	8.5	8.4	7.1	7.1	7.0	7.0
1971	6.9	6.3	5.1	4.5	3.9	4.5	3.9	4.4	5.0	5.0	5.0	3.8
1972	4.4	3.8	3.8	3.8	3.8	3.7	3.2	3.2	3.2	3.2	3.2	3.1
1973	3.1	3.1	3.7	3.6	3.6	4.1	4.1	5.2	5.7	7.7	8.8	8.7
1974	9.8	9.2	9.6	8.0	8.9	9.9	10.8	12.3	12.6	13.6	12.9	12.8
1975	11.7	11.1	9.1	8.5	7.6	7.0	6.6	6.1	7.4	7.3	9.0	9.0
1976	10.7	10.6	10.1	9.6	7.4	7.3	6.4	6.4	6.8	7.1	7.9	7.9
1977	7.8	7.8	7.7	8.1	7.6	8.0	8.3	8.3	7.8	7.4	8.1	7.7
1978	7.2	7.6	7.9	8.6	8.5	9.2	9.5	9.8	10.4	10.3	10.6	9.5
1979	9.4	9.7	9.2	9.5	10.1	11.4	12.3	13.1	13.7	14.5	15.4	16.2
1980	16.9	17.0	18.7	19.4	19.1	20.4	15.3	12.2	9.8	9.1	9.2	8.3
1981	11.8	13.7	14.1	13.7	13.5	13.3	14.7	15.4	16.8	15.6	14.6	13.0
1982	10.6	9.1	6.2	7.1	7.0	7.7	7.6	8.0	7.8	6.4	4.2	0.8
1983	1.0	0.6	1.0	1.6	2.5	4.8	4.4	3.9	4.3	4.1	4.9	4.9
1984	5.1	5.7	5.7	5.6	5.2	5.2	5.6	5.5	5.7	5.5	5.5	5.6
1985	4.8	4.8	4.8	4.6	5.1	5.1	5.5	5.3	4.9	5.2	5.0	5.0
1986	5.1	5.1	5.7	5.6	4.9	5.4	4.7	4.6	4.3	4.1	4.2	3.5
1987	3.8	3.8	3.6	4.0	4.1	4.3	4.1	4.4	4.8	4.4	4.4	4.4
1988	4.7	4.3	4.2	4.5	4.5	4.8	4.4	4.8	5.1	4.9	5.0	4.8
1989	5.0	4.8	4.8	4.8	4.9	4.9	5.3	5.3	4.8	5.1	4.9	5.1
1990	4.9	4.9	5.8	5.6	5.4	6.0	6.1	6.9	6.4	6.2	6.3	5.5
1991	6.1	5.5	5.2	4.7	4.7	4.5	3.8	3.6	3.9	4.3	4.3	4.6
1992	4.4	4.1	4.0	4.0	3.8	3.5	3.4	3.5	3.2	3.6	3.9	3.9
1993	4.1	4.1	4.2	3.9	3.9	4.0	3.8	3.8	3.9	3.6	3.5	3.6
1994	3.3	3.6	3.6	3.4	3.1	2.9	3.0	3.1	2.9	3.0	3.2	3.0
1995	3.5	3.3	3.6	3.8	3.7	4.0	3.5	3.4	3.1	3.2	3.1	2.9
1996	3.1	3.2	3.2	3.0	3.3	3.4	3.5	3.3	3.5	3.4	3.3	3.4
1997	3.1	3.1	3.0	3.1	2.9	2.8	3.0	2.7	2.7	-	-	-

Source: The Conference Board. Primary source(s): U.S. Department of Labor, Bureau of Labor Statistics, Office of Prices and Living Conditions, Division of Consumer Prices and Price Indexes, Washington, DC 20212. A dash (-) indicates that data are not available or zero.

RATIO, COINCIDENT TO LAGGING INDEX

The composite indexes of coincident and the lagging indicators are used to create what is sometimes referred to as the "second" or the "best" leading indicator—the ratio of the coincident to the lagging index. The "coincident to lagging ratio" tends to signal changes in the economy's turning points (especially downturns) *sooner* than the leading index.

For example, in the 1970 recession the leading index signaled the downturn 8 months ahead of time, the ratio 13 months earlier. In other recessionary periods, similar results were noted: 1974-75, leading was 8, the ratio 11 months in advance of actual events; in 1980, leading was 15, the ratio 21; in 1982, leading was 2, the ratio was 9.

The ratio has been less predictive of turn-arounds. In 1970 it turned up as the economy turned up (acting as a coincident indicator), whereas the leading index gave a one-month warning; in 1974-1975, this pattern repeated; in 1980 and 1982, both the leading index and the ratio turned up 10 months ahead of the economy's actual turn-around.

The coincident to lagging ratio tends to work because of the manner in which its components—the coincident and the lagging indexes—behave. The lagging index tends to reflect the *past* of a business cycle, the coincident index its *present*. As the coincident index reaches a turning point, its rate of change tends to be smaller than that of the lagging indicator. If, for example, the economy is approaching a peak, monthly growth reflected in the coincident indicator will be small; meanwhile, the lagging indicator, which reflects events a few months back, will still be growing rapidly. The ratio between the two will, therefore, turn down, signaling a future decline in the economy as the peak is reached and passed. The process works in the same manner as a trough is reached: the composite index will decline less than the lagging index (which is still mirroring the earlier period of the recession); the consequence is an upturn in the ratio promising the start of an expansion soon.

Components of the Ratio

The ratio is expressed as an index with a 1992 base (1992 = 100) and is constructed by dividing the composite index value for a month by the lagging index value for the same month.

Bibliography

1. Carnes, W. Stansbury and Stephen D. Slifer. *The Atlas of Economic Indicators*. HarperCollins, 1991.

2. Frumkin, Norman. *Guide to Economic Indicators*. M.E. Sharpe, Inc., 1990.

3. *Leading Economic Indicators*. The Confenrence Board, 845 Third Avenue, New York, NY 10022-6679.

Ratio, Coincident Index to Lagging Index
(1992 = 100)

Year	Jan	Feb	Mar	Apr	May	Jun	Jul	Aug	Sep	Oct	Nov	Dec
1959	48.2	48.4	48.8	49.0	49.2	49.2	48.7	47.6	47.3	47.1	47.4	48.4
1960	49.0	48.7	48.5	48.7	48.0	47.8	47.6	47.7	47.6	47.7	47.4	46.9
1961	46.9	46.9	47.4	47.8	48.4	48.9	49.3	49.6	49.7	50.0	50.6	50.6
1962	50.2	50.5	50.7	50.9	50.7	50.7	50.7	50.7	50.8	50.9	51.1	50.8
1963	51.0	51.2	51.4	51.6	51.7	51.8	51.9	51.7	51.9	52.0	51.6	52.0
1964	52.3	52.5	52.5	52.5	53.0	53.1	53.3	53.3	53.5	53.0	53.8	54.2
1965	54.1	54.0	54.4	54.3	54.4	54.5	54.8	54.9	55.0	55.5	55.6	56.0
1966	56.0	56.0	56.3	56.1	56.1	56.3	56.2	56.2	56.4	56.7	56.5	56.6
1967	56.9	56.6	56.6	56.7	56.8	56.8	56.9	57.4	57.5	57.4	58.2	58.6
1968	58.6	58.7	58.8	58.8	58.9	59.1	59.4	59.2	59.4	59.8	60.0	59.9
1969	59.7	59.9	60.1	60.0	59.8	60.1	60.1	60.3	60.3	60.6	60.4	60.3
1970	59.7	59.8	59.7	59.8	60.0	59.9	60.4	60.2	60.5	60.0	59.9	60.9
1971	61.3	61.4	61.7	62.1	62.4	62.9	63.0	62.9	63.2	63.5	63.9	64.4
1972	65.8	66.1	66.3	66.6	66.6	66.5	66.8	67.7	68.3	68.9	69.5	70.0
1973	69.6	69.5	69.3	69.0	69.1	68.9	69.0	68.5	68.9	69.5	69.9	69.2
1974	68.4	68.2	68.1	67.5	67.6	67.6	67.5	67.1	66.7	66.5	65.7	64.5
1975	64.2	64.2	63.9	64.8	65.5	66.9	67.3	68.3	68.7	69.0	69.4	69.7
1976	70.4	70.8	71.1	71.5	71.9	72.3	72.6	72.8	73.0	72.7	73.3	73.8
1977	73.9	74.2	74.6	74.7	75.1	75.2	75.4	75.6	75.8	75.8	76.0	76.4
1978	75.7	76.0	76.5	77.8	77.7	77.9	77.7	77.9	78.0	78.3	78.3	78.4
1979	78.1	78.2	79.1	77.7	78.2	77.9	77.5	77.3	76.8	76.8	76.6	76.8
1980	77.0	76.8	75.8	74.7	74.5	74.8	76.0	77.1	78.2	79.2	79.7	79.5
1981	79.5	79.4	79.6	79.3	78.7	78.7	79.2	78.9	78.2	78.2	78.0	78.0
1982	77.4	78.5	78.6	78.7	78.8	78.3	78.0	78.0	78.0	78.3	78.8	79.4
1983	80.3	80.3	81.0	81.4	82.5	82.8	83.2	82.8	84.0	84.6	84.7	85.0
1984	85.6	85.4	85.4	85.5	85.4	85.5	85.2	85.1	85.2	84.7	85.1	85.1
1985	85.3	85.4	85.6	85.8	85.8	85.2	85.0	85.4	85.7	85.1	85.5	85.7
1986	86.0	86.0	85.6	86.6	86.3	86.3	86.8	87.0	88.0	87.4	87.5	88.4
1987	87.6	88.8	89.2	89.3	89.4	89.6	90.0	90.1	90.1	90.7	90.8	91.6
1988	91.0	91.7	91.9	92.0	91.9	92.0	92.4	92.5	92.7	92.8	92.9	93.4
1989	93.5	92.9	93.0	93.6	92.8	92.4	92.1	92.7	92.4	92.2	92.7	92.9
1990	93.3	93.9	94.1	94.0	94.3	94.4	94.2	94.4	94.1	93.7	93.3	93.3
1991	92.5	92.7	92.6	93.6	94.1	94.9	95.3	95.6	96.2	96.5	96.8	96.9
1992	97.7	98.4	98.7	99.3	99.8	100.2	100.8	99.2	100.8	101.4	101.6	102.2
1993	102.2	102.3	101.9	102.2	102.4	102.5	102.4	102.8	103.1	103.4	103.9	104.3
1994	103.8	105.0	105.7	105.9	106.1	106.0	106.1	106.3	106.2	106.4	106.1	106.4
1995	106.2	105.8	105.7	105.1	104.8	104.7	104.6	105.1	105.1	105.2	105.5	105.9
1996	105.4	106.4	106.3	106.7	107.1	107.6	107.5	107.7	107.9	108.2	108.6	108.8
1997	109.2	110.1	110.0	109.9	110.0	110.6	111.4	111.2	111.4	-	-	-

Source: The Conference Board. Primary source(s): The Conference Board, Inc., Economics Group, 845 Third Avenue, New York, NY 10022. A dash (-) indicates that data are not available or zero.

CHAPTER 4

CYCLIC INDICATORS

CYCLIC INDICATORS

The Business Cycle Indicators include, all told, 21 economic series which have been found, over time, to work well as indicators of cyclic change in the economy. In this section are presented 28 other economic series which are also considered cyclic indicators but are not part of the composite indexes of leading, coincident, and lagging indicators. They are grouped under seven headings:

Employment
Production and Income
Consumption, Trade, Orders, and Deliveries
Fixed Capital Investment
Inventories and Inventory Investment
Prices, Costs, and Profits
Money and Credit

A brief introduction to each of these sections provides a description of each series covered, the principal analytical uses of each series, and a listing of related series which are included under the Business Cycle Indicators heading.

Bibliography

1. Fischer, Stanley, Rudiger Dornbusch, and Richard Schmalensee. *Introduction to Macroeconomics*. McGraw-Hill Book Company, New York, 1988.

2. Fitch, Thomas P. *Dictionary of Banking Terms*. Barron's, New York, 1990.

3. Siegel, Barry N. *Money, Banking, and the Economy*. Academic Press, New York, 1982.

3. U.S. Department of Commerce, Bureau of Economic Analysis. *Survey of Current Business*. Superintendent of Documents, U.S. Government Printing Office, Washington, DC 20302.

INDICATORS OF EMPLOYMENT

In modern industrial economies, employment is the single most important indicator of economic well-being—and decline in employment a signal of economic woes. This section presents two series:

Unemployment rate
Number of persons unemployed

Related series, reported under Business Cycle Indicators, are:

Average weekly hours in manufacturing (Leading Index)
Average weekly initial claims for unemployment insurance (Leading Index)
Employment on nonagricultural payrolls (Coincident Index)
Average duration of unemployment in weeks (Lagging Index)

Unemployment Rate. Data are presented for persons unemployed 15 weeks and over as a percent of the work force. Data are shown from 1949 to 1997. The series behaves as a lagging indicator but is not part of the composite index of lagging indicators.

Number of Persons Unemployed. Data show total number of people unemployed in thousands from 1948 to 1997. The series is classified as a leading indicator at business cycle peaks, as a lagging indicator of business cycle troughs, and is unclassified overall.

Unemployment Rate, 15 Weeks and Over

(Percent)

Year	Jan	Feb	Mar	Apr	May	Jun	Jul	Aug	Sep	Oct	Nov	Dec
1949	0.5	0.6	0.7	0.8	1.0	1.2	1.4	1.5	1.6	1.6	1.7	1.6
1950	1.5	1.5	1.5	1.5	1.4	1.4	1.2	1.0	1.0	0.9	0.8	0.8
1951	0.7	0.6	0.6	0.5	0.4	0.4	0.4	0.4	0.4	0.4	0.5	0.4
1952	0.5	0.4	0.4	0.4	0.4	0.3	0.3	0.3	0.4	0.4	0.3	0.4
1953	0.4	0.3	0.3	0.3	0.3	0.3	0.3	0.3	0.3	0.3	0.4	0.5
1954	0.6	0.8	1.2	1.2	1.4	1.4	1.5	1.6	1.6	1.6	1.5	1.3
1955	1.4	1.3	1.3	1.3	1.1	1.0	1.0	0.8	0.9	0.9	0.9	0.9
1956	0.8	0.8	0.8	0.7	0.8	0.8	0.8	0.8	0.9	0.8	0.9	0.9
1957	0.8	0.8	0.8	0.8	0.8	0.8	0.8	0.8	0.8	1.0	1.0	1.1
1958	1.3	1.5	1.7	2.1	2.2	2.5	2.6	2.8	2.6	2.5	2.3	2.2
1959	2.1	1.9	1.8	1.5	1.4	1.4	1.3	1.3	1.3	1.3	1.4	1.3
1960	1.3	1.2	1.4	1.3	1.1	1.2	1.3	1.3	1.4	1.7	1.7	1.6
1961	1.9	2.0	2.1	2.3	2.4	2.3	2.6	2.3	2.2	2.1	2.0	1.9
1962	1.8	1.8	1.7	1.6	1.6	1.5	1.5	1.5	1.5	1.4	1.5	1.5
1963	1.6	1.6	1.5	1.5	1.6	1.5	1.5	1.6	1.5	1.5	1.5	1.4
1964	1.5	1.4	1.4	1.3	1.3	1.4	1.4	1.3	1.3	1.2	1.3	1.2
1965	1.1	1.2	1.1	1.1	1.0	1.1	0.9	1.0	1.0	0.9	0.9	0.9
1966	0.8	0.8	0.8	0.8	0.7	0.6	0.6	0.6	0.6	0.6	0.6	0.6
1967	0.6	0.6	0.6	0.6	0.5	0.5	0.5	0.6	0.6	0.6	0.6	0.6
1968	0.6	0.6	0.6	0.5	0.5	0.5	0.5	0.5	0.5	0.5	0.5	0.4
1969	0.4	0.4	0.4	0.5	0.5	0.5	0.5	0.5	0.5	0.5	0.5	0.5
1970	0.5	0.6	0.6	0.7	0.7	0.8	0.8	0.9	0.9	0.9	1.0	1.3
1971	1.3	1.3	1.3	1.4	1.4	1.4	1.5	1.5	1.5	1.5	1.5	1.5
1972	1.5	1.5	1.4	1.4	1.3	1.3	1.3	1.3	1.3	1.3	1.2	1.1
1973	1.1	1.0	1.0	0.9	0.9	0.9	0.8	0.9	0.9	0.9	0.9	0.8
1974	0.9	0.9	0.9	1.0	1.0	1.0	1.0	1.0	1.1	1.2	1.2	1.4
1975	1.7	2.0	2.2	2.6	2.8	3.0	3.1	3.0	3.1	2.9	3.0	3.0
1976	2.9	2.7	2.6	2.3	2.2	2.4	2.4	2.5	2.4	2.4	2.4	2.4
1977	2.3	2.2	2.1	2.0	2.0	1.9	1.9	1.8	1.9	1.8	1.8	1.7
1978	1.6	1.6	1.5	1.5	1.4	1.3	1.3	1.2	1.3	1.3	1.2	1.2
1979	1.2	1.2	1.3	1.2	1.2	1.1	1.1	1.1	1.1	1.2	1.2	1.2
1980	1.3	1.3	1.4	1.6	1.6	1.6	1.9	2.0	2.2	2.1	2.2	2.2
1981	2.2	2.2	2.1	2.0	2.0	2.1	2.0	2.1	2.1	2.1	2.1	2.2
1982	2.2	2.5	2.7	2.8	3.0	3.1	3.2	3.3	3.5	3.8	4.0	4.2
1983	4.2	4.2	4.2	3.9	4.1	4.0	3.9	3.6	3.4	3.3	3.1	3.0
1984	2.9	2.7	2.6	2.5	2.5	2.3	2.3	2.3	2.2	2.2	2.1	2.1
1985	2.0	2.1	2.1	2.1	2.0	2.0	2.0	2.0	1.9	2.0	1.9	1.9
1986	1.8	2.0	1.9	1.8	1.9	2.0	1.9	1.9	2.0	1.8	1.9	1.8
1987	1.8	1.8	1.7	1.8	1.8	1.7	1.6	1.6	1.6	1.5	1.5	1.5
1988	1.4	1.4	1.4	1.3	1.4	1.3	1.3	1.3	1.3	1.3	1.2	1.2
1989	1.2	1.1	1.1	1.1	1.1	1.0	1.2	1.0	1.1	1.1	1.1	1.1
1990	1.1	1.1	1.1	1.1	1.1	1.1	1.2	1.3	1.3	1.3	1.5	1.4
1991	1.5	1.6	1.7	1.7	1.8	2.0	1.9	2.0	2.0	2.1	2.1	2.3
1992	2.4	2.5	2.5	2.4	2.7	2.9	2.8	2.8	2.7	2.7	2.6	2.8
1993	2.6	2.5	2.4	2.3	2.4	2.4	2.4	2.3	2.4	2.3	2.3	2.3
1994	2.3	2.4	2.3	2.2	2.2	2.1	2.2	2.1	2.1	2.3	2.0	1.9
1995	1.8	1.8	1.7	1.8	1.9	1.7	1.8	1.8	1.8	1.7	1.8	1.8
1996	1.8	1.7	1.8	1.8	1.8	1.8	1.7	1.7	1.7	1.7	1.6	1.6
1997	1.6	1.6	1.5	1.5	1.5	1.5	1.6	1.5	1.6	-	-	-

Source: The Conference Board. Primary source(s): U.S. Department of Labor, Bureau of Labor Statistics, Office of Employment and Unemployment Statistics, Division of Labor Force Statistics, Washington, DC 20212. A dash (-) indicates that data are not available or zero.

Number of Persons Unemployed
(Thousands)

Year	Jan	Feb	Mar	Apr	May	Jun	Jul	Aug	Sep	Oct	Nov	Dec
1948	2,034	2,328	2,399	2,386	2,118	2,214	2,213	2,350	2,302	2,259	2,285	2,429
1949	2,596	2,849	3,030	3,260	3,707	3,776	4,111	4,193	4,049	4,916	3,996	4,063
1950	4,026	3,936	3,876	3,575	3,434	3,367	3,120	2,799	2,774	2,625	2,589	2,639
1951	2,305	2,117	2,125	1,919	1,856	1,995	1,950	1,933	2,067	2,194	2,178	1,960
1952	1,972	1,957	1,813	1,811	1,863	1,884	1,991	2,087	1,936	1,839	1,743	1,667
1953	1,839	1,636	1,647	1,723	1,596	1,607	1,660	1,665	1,821	1,974	2,211	2,818
1954	3,077	3,331	3,607	3,749	3,767	3,551	3,659	3,854	3,927	3,666	3,402	3,196
1955	3,157	2,969	2,918	3,049	2,747	2,701	2,632	2,784	2,678	2,830	2,780	2,761
1956	2,666	2,606	2,764	2,650	2,861	2,882	2,952	2,701	2,635	2,571	2,861	2,790
1957	2,796	2,622	2,509	2,600	2,710	2,856	2,796	2,747	2,943	3,020	3,454	3,476
1958	3,875	4,303	4,492	5,016	5,021	4,944	5,079	5,025	4,821	4,570	4,188	4,191
1959	4,068	3,965	3,801	3,571	3,479	3,429	3,528	3,588	3,775	3,910	4,003	3,653
1960	3,615	3,329	3,726	3,620	3,569	3,766	3,836	3,946	3,884	4,252	4,330	4,617
1961	4,671	4,832	4,853	4,893	5,003	4,885	4,928	4,682	4,676	4,573	4,295	4,177
1962	4,081	3,871	3,921	3,906	3,863	3,844	3,819	4,013	3,961	3,803	4,024	3,907
1963	4,074	4,238	4,072	4,055	4,217	3,977	4,051	3,878	3,957	3,987	4,151	3,975
1964	4,029	3,932	3,950	3,918	3,764	3,814	3,608	3,655	3,712	3,726	3,551	3,651
1965	3,572	3,730	3,510	3,595	3,432	3,387	3,301	3,254	3,216	3,143	3,073	3,031
1966	2,988	2,820	2,887	2,828	2,950	2,872	2,876	2,900	2,798	2,798	2,770	2,912
1967	2,968	2,915	2,889	2,895	2,929	2,992	2,944	2,945	2,958	3,143	3,066	3,018
1968	2,878	3,001	2,877	2,709	2,740	2,938	2,883	2,768	2,686	2,689	2,715	2,685
1969	2,718	2,692	2,712	2,758	2,713	2,816	2,868	2,856	3,040	3,049	2,856	2,884
1970	3,201	3,453	3,635	3,797	3,919	4,071	4,175	4,256	4,456	4,591	4,898	5,076
1971	4,986	4,903	4,987	4,959	4,996	4,949	5,035	5,134	5,042	4,954	5,161	5,154
1972	5,019	4,928	5,038	4,959	4,922	4,923	4,913	4,939	4,849	4,875	4,602	4,543
1973	4,326	4,452	4,394	4,459	4,329	4,363	4,305	4,305	4,350	4,144	4,396	4,489
1974	4,644	4,731	4,634	4,618	4,705	4,927	5,063	5,022	5,437	5,523	6,140	6,636
1975	7,501	7,520	7,978	8,210	8,433	8,220	8,127	7,928	7,923	7,897	7,794	7,744
1976	7,534	7,326	7,230	7,330	7,053	7,322	7,490	7,518	7,380	7,430	7,620	7,545
1977	7,280	7,443	7,307	7,059	6,911	7,134	6,829	6,925	6,751	6,763	6,815	6,386
1978	6,489	6,318	6,337	6,180	6,127	6,028	6,309	6,080	6,125	5,947	6,077	6,228
1979	6,109	6,173	6,109	6,069	5,840	5,959	5,996	6,320	6,190	6,296	6,238	6,325
1980	6,683	6,702	6,729	7,358	7,984	8,098	8,363	8,281	8,021	8,088	8,023	7,718
1981	8,071	8,051	7,982	7,869	8,174	8,098	7,863	8,036	8,230	8,646	9,029	9,267
1982	9,397	9,705	9,895	10,244	10,335	10,538	10,849	10,881	11,217	11,529	11,938	12,051
1983	11,534	11,545	11,408	11,268	11,154	11,246	10,548	10,623	10,282	9,887	9,499	9,331
1984	9,008	8,791	8,746	8,762	8,456	8,226	8,537	8,519	8,367	8,381	8,198	8,358
1985	8,423	8,321	8,339	8,395	8,302	8,460	8,513	8,196	8,248	8,298	8,128	8,138
1986	7,795	8,402	8,383	8,364	8,439	8,508	8,319	8,135	8,310	8,243	8,159	7,883
1987	7,892	7,865	7,862	7,542	7,574	7,398	7,268	7,261	7,102	7,227	7,035	6,936
1988	6,953	6,929	6,876	6,601	6,779	6,546	6,605	6,843	6,604	6,568	6,537	6,518
1989	6,682	6,359	6,205	6,468	6,375	6,577	6,495	6,511	6,590	6,630	6,725	6,667
1990	6,752	6,651	6,598	6,797	6,742	6,590	6,922	7,188	7,368	7,459	7,764	7,901
1991	8,015	8,265	8,586	8,439	8,736	8,692	8,586	8,666	8,722	8,842	8,931	9,198
1992	9,283	9,454	9,460	9,415	9,744	10,040	9,850	9,787	9,781	9,398	9,565	9,557
1993	9,325	9,183	9,056	9,110	9,149	9,121	8,930	8,763	8,714	8,750	8,542	8,477
1994	8,710	8,581	8,500	8,313	7,867	7,937	7,927	7,949	7,740	7,624	7,372	7,158
1995	7,432	7,203	7,201	7,590	7,358	7,445	7,496	7,517	7,523	7,329	7,409	7,354
1996	7,588	7,364	7,402	7,302	7,331	7,119	7,276	6,910	7,043	7,019	7,187	7,167
1997	7,268	7,205	7,144	6,714	6,534	6,836	6,583	6,677	6,752	-	-	-

Source: The Conference Board. Primary source(s): U.S. Department of Labor, Bureau of Labor Statistics, Office of Employment and Unemployment Statistics, Division of Labor Force Statistics, Washington, DC 20212. A dash (-) indicates that data are not available or zero.

INDICATORS OF PRODUCTION AND INCOME

Production and personal income are indicators of overall economic performance. They are cyclic indicators which tend to be coincident: they turn up or down as the economy does. This section presents four series:

> Personal income
> Wages and salaries
> Industrial Production in the U.S.
> Capacity utilization rate, all industry
> Capacity utilization rate, manufacturing

Related series, reported under Business Cycle Indicators, are:

> Index of industrial production (Coincident Index)
> Personal income less transfer payments (Coincident Index)

Personal Income. Data are reported for 1946 to 1997 in billions of dollars and billions of chained 1992 dollars. Monthly data are annualized, meaning that monthly survey results are multiplied by 12 months. Although not part of any composite index of economic indicators, personal income is viewed as a coincident cyclic indicator. The category includes all income received by individuals from any source, including dividends, rents, and transfer payments (welfare, social security, unemployment benefits, medicaid, etc.).

Wages and Salaries. Data are for wages and salaries in mining, manufacturing, and construction and are reported in billions of chained 1992 dollars. Monthly data are annualized, showing what would be annual results if the month's results were applied to the year as a whole. The series behaves as a coincident indicator overall but is not a component of a composite index.

Industrial Production in the U.S. Data shwon are for the 1945 through the 1997 period. The index of production is based on the year 1990 (1990=100). This data series is frequently used to compare U.S. to international production data.

Capacity Utilization Rate, All Industry. Data, for 1967 through 1997, are shown as percent of total capacity. The series can be used as a cyclic indicator (it is leading at the peak of the business cycle and coincident at the trough) and as an indicator of inflation. High rates of capacity utilization signal high rates of production and hence upward pressure on prices.

Capacity Utilization Rate, Manufacturing. Data are shown for 1948 through 1997 in percent. The series is a leading indicator at the peak and a coincident indicator at the trough of a cycle.

Personal Income
(Annual Rate, Billions of $)

Year	Jan	Feb	Mar	Apr	May	Jun	Jul	Aug	Sep	Oct	Nov	Dec
1946	169.2	168.8	172.0	173.5	175.1	176.7	181.4	182.5	179.0	183.1	183.6	185.8
1947	186.6	186.7	186.6	183.6	184.0	186.8	187.1	188.3	203.0	195.1	195.7	197.7
1948	201.4	201.0	204.2	205.1	206.9	210.9	211.5	213.9	214.1	214.9	213.5	210.8
1949	207.5	206.6	207.7	206.8	206.3	204.6	203.0	204.7	208.0	204.3	206.8	208.1
1950	216.6	219.7	224.9	220.4	221.0	222.1	226.4	230.6	232.8	236.2	238.5	244.1
1951	245.5	248.2	250.9	253.7	255.1	256.9	256.5	259.6	260.1	263.1	264.0	265.1
1952	263.3	267.2	267.7	267.2	270.1	271.6	270.5	278.0	280.9	282.2	281.6	283.8
1953	284.8	286.9	289.7	290.1	291.5	292.3	291.9	291.3	291.5	293.0	291.3	290.6
1954	290.7	291.8	290.9	289.6	290.4	290.6	291.0	292.5	294.2	296.2	299.0	300.1
1955	301.9	303.8	306.3	309.3	311.8	312.8	317.7	318.0	320.2	321.6	323.9	326.1
1956	327.0	328.9	330.4	333.7	334.5	336.8	335.8	340.3	342.7	346.2	346.3	348.2
1957	348.2	351.4	352.8	353.4	355.2	357.9	359.4	360.9	359.9	360.0	360.4	359.6
1958	359.5	359.1	361.0	360.4	361.8	363.8	370.2	370.0	372.0	372.7	377.2	379.0
1959	382.1	384.4	387.5	390.5	393.3	395.8	395.9	394.2	395.5	397.1	400.5	404.9
1960	406.1	406.7	407.4	410.4	411.7	412.0	412.9	413.3	414.3	416.1	415.6	413.4
1961	417.1	419.1	420.5	421.0	424.4	428.9	431.2	431.8	433.0	437.2	441.4	443.9
1962	443.1	446.1	449.8	452.6	453.8	455.4	457.4	458.8	461.2	462.5	465.0	466.9
1963	470.7	468.2	469.8	471.3	474.0	478.1	478.9	481.5	484.5	488.4	489.8	494.5
1964	497.4	499.8	502.3	505.6	508.6	511.4	514.5	518.8	521.8	522.8	526.6	532.8
1965	536.5	536.7	540.0	543.6	548.0	551.3	555.3	557.9	573.0	570.5	575.7	580.8
1966	582.6	587.6	591.7	593.5	596.3	601.2	605.0	610.5	615.9	620.5	625.4	626.7
1967	632.1	633.2	637.5	638.5	641.1	645.8	651.5	656.5	658.8	660.9	666.9	673.8
1968	678.2	685.8	693.8	699.4	705.9	711.3	717.6	723.5	728.8	734.4	739.5	743.6
1969	745.8	751.3	758.0	763.7	769.3	775.0	782.2	789.0	794.1	799.5	803.0	808.1
1970	808.8	812.9	817.0	835.1	831.5	832.1	838.9	843.8	849.6	850.7	853.1	859.6
1971	868.1	871.2	877.2	882.6	889.0	909.6	900.3	907.5	911.5	915.1	922.2	932.0
1972	940.2	951.1	956.7	960.9	966.5	961.2	983.0	998.1	1,007.2	1,028.8	1,043.0	1,050.5
1973	1,051.2	1,060.6	1,068.7	1,076.7	1,088.8	1,097.1	1,101.9	1,112.8	1,126.4	1,148.8	1,163.5	1,170.8
1974	1,170.1	1,174.5	1,177.9	1,180.6	1,193.9	1,204.6	1,223.2	1,231.1	1,240.9	1,253.5	1,251.8	1,257.4
1975	1,259.0	1,263.7	1,267.7	1,274.1	1,286.8	1,318.8	1,317.1	1,334.6	1,346.8	1,362.9	1,372.7	1,382.8
1976	1,398.3	1,408.5	1,415.5	1,424.8	1,434.2	1,442.0	1,460.1	1,472.0	1,482.3	1,490.3	1,511.8	1,524.6
1977	1,529.1	1,545.6	1,559.9	1,572.0	1,585.4	1,597.1	1,620.4	1,634.2	1,649.0	1,662.6	1,683.9	1,698.2
1978	1,705.3	1,723.0	1,748.0	1,776.7	1,794.7	1,814.1	1,832.2	1,850.0	1,865.6	1,893.2	1,909.8	1,930.4
1979	1,948.1	1,965.4	1,988.6	1,994.2	2,011.9	2,029.0	2,059.7	2,078.3	2,093.8	2,118.7	2,141.5	2,167.3
1980	2,197.3	2,210.4	2,221.9	2,218.0	2,224.8	2,241.9	2,277.4	2,299.3	2,330.3	2,372.0	2,401.9	2,433.2
1981	2,458.9	2,476.9	2,500.5	2,499.6	2,514.9	2,536.5	2,587.6	2,612.3	2,624.6	2,629.0	2,642.2	2,642.1
1982	2,641.5	2,658.5	2,667.7	2,700.6	2,719.4	2,725.0	2,729.2	2,733.7	2,737.3	2,755.4	2,771.9	2,784.0
1983	2,785.3	2,791.1	2,811.4	2,836.8	2,866.7	2,878.7	2,899.4	2,901.0	2,934.6	2,968.7	2,997.6	3,029.1
1984	3,058.6	3,096.2	3,124.5	3,156.9	3,167.3	3,199.2	3,225.5	3,258.1	3,288.3	3,274.7	3,300.0	3,316.6
1985	3,347.9	3,366.4	3,392.2	3,396.8	3,409.2	3,430.0	3,441.2	3,454.3	3,468.6	3,503.0	3,513.1	3,552.7
1986	3,569.5	3,584.5	3,608.4	3,608.3	3,620.7	3,637.2	3,658.0	3,672.4	3,687.8	3,690.8	3,704.7	3,727.7
1987	3,747.8	3,777.5	3,797.8	3,809.7	3,842.0	3,854.1	3,866.3	3,901.6	3,920.7	3,969.9	3,995.6	4,044.0
1988	4,039.3	4,063.7	4,088.8	4,117.5	4,130.3	4,157.4	4,188.7	4,204.7	4,228.7	4,263.1	4,275.9	4,315.8
1989	4,378.5	4,404.2	4,445.0	4,467.2	4,465.4	4,483.1	4,499.7	4,506.1	4,500.4	4,538.7	4,581.5	4,601.7
1990	4,655.5	4,692.7	4,719.0	4,759.1	4,761.9	4,794.2	4,824.2	4,828.9	4,860.4	4,854.5	4,862.1	4,886.6
1991	4,876.5	4,881.7	4,896.5	4,925.4	4,947.5	4,978.6	4,962.7	4,976.0	4,998.8	5,024.0	5,051.9	5,102.2
1992	5,125.9	5,171.9	5,185.6	5,213.0	5,237.6	5,258.5	5,269.7	5,140.3	5,290.0	5,339.6	5,371.7	5,566.6
1993	5,366.1	5,375.0	5,367.2	5,483.3	5,518.3	5,510.6	5,517.7	5,556.9	5,558.1	5,580.3	5,603.7	5,793.4
1994	5,562.0	5,628.0	5,658.9	5,740.4	5,776.6	5,782.8	5,811.5	5,834.2	5,868.5	5,928.8	5,937.6	5,972.0
1995	6,039.3	6,050.3	6,069.6	6,112.6	6,099.5	6,132.2	6,164.9	6,171.2	6,201.1	6,239.8	6,254.9	6,274.0
1996	6,311.0	6,371.1	6,396.0	6,424.7	6,446.8	6,512.4	6,504.9	6,538.9	6,582.0	6,575.6	6,615.2	6,664.4
1997	6,700.1	6,750.3	6,788.2	6,800.9	6,822.8	6,863.5	6,873.8	6,915.0	6,940.5	-	-	-

Source: The Conference Board. Primary source(s): U.S. Department of Commerce, Bureau of Economic Analysis, National Income and Wealth Division, BE-54, Washington, DC 20230. A dash (-) indicates that data are not available or zero.

Personal Income

(Annual Rate, Billions of chained 1992 $)

Year	Jan	Feb	Mar	Apr	May	Jun	Jul	Aug	Sep	Oct	Nov	Dec
1959	1,687.6	1,695.9	1,709.3	1,719.7	1,730.9	1,737.3	1,734.6	1,724.9	1,725.8	1,729.4	1,743.2	1,761.1
1960	1,767.6	1,767.4	1,768.6	1,774.7	1,778.4	1,779.0	1,779.5	1,778.2	1,780.6	1,786.0	1,778.0	1,767.9
1961	1,782.5	1,789.6	1,796.7	1,800.1	1,813.4	1,832.6	1,838.6	1,839.7	1,842.9	1,860.7	1,878.7	1,889.1
1962	1,885.6	1,893.0	1,905.8	1,914.0	1,917.5	1,923.2	1,932.6	1,935.5	1,935.6	1,942.8	1,951.8	1,960.3
1963	1,972.7	1,960.0	1,968.0	1,974.1	1,982.3	1,995.2	1,994.4	2,001.9	2,014.4	2,027.5	2,030.0	2,047.7
1964	2,055.1	2,063.1	2,072.3	2,085.2	2,096.9	2,106.2	2,115.7	2,132.3	2,141.2	2,143.6	2,155.9	2,178.3
1965	2,190.1	2,189.7	2,199.5	2,210.9	2,223.7	2,230.7	2,244.2	2,253.4	2,312.7	2,302.6	2,319.2	2,331.3
1966	2,335.8	2,346.3	2,356.7	2,356.6	2,364.3	2,377.9	2,387.1	2,399.5	2,413.1	2,425.4	2,439.7	2,438.9
1967	2,460.4	2,461.2	2,475.8	2,475.2	2,479.9	2,490.1	2,502.5	2,514.2	2,515.4	2,516.0	2,530.3	2,551.6
1968	2,555.9	2,573.5	2,595.1	2,608.1	2,624.0	2,635.9	2,651.6	2,662.9	2,674.1	2,683.4	2,693.4	2,703.9
1969	2,702.9	2,717.0	2,730.1	2,739.3	2,749.2	2,756.8	2,772.0	2,788.6	2,794.1	2,804.0	2,803.8	2,809.3
1970	2,800.2	2,803.8	2,811.0	2,858.7	2,836.8	2,830.5	2,841.9	2,849.6	2,855.8	2,844.9	2,840.8	2,849.7
1971	2,870.3	2,872.1	2,881.5	2,887.4	2,896.7	2,950.1	2,910.8	2,924.5	2,933.9	2,939.5	2,956.5	2,975.5
1972	2,990.5	3,012.8	3,026.1	3,034.2	3,045.8	3,023.4	3,081.4	3,119.0	3,134.4	3,195.1	3,229.6	3,242.9
1973	3,235.1	3,246.5	3,247.6	3,247.8	3,269.7	3,274.8	3,278.5	3,277.1	3,302.9	3,347.8	3,363.6	3,356.8
1974	3,325.3	3,298.9	3,272.2	3,258.1	3,263.7	3,266.9	3,294.1	3,280.5	3,274.3	3,283.1	3,255.6	3,247.1
1975	3,233.9	3,230.0	3,229.9	3,233.4	3,252.1	3,311.1	3,278.5	3,306.3	3,320.0	3,340.5	3,343.1	3,348.4
1976	3,373.5	3,392.8	3,404.2	3,417.7	3,422.8	3,426.0	3,449.6	3,457.8	3,462.2	3,461.0	3,494.0	3,503.4
1977	3,494.7	3,506.1	3,521.7	3,528.4	3,538.9	3,545.1	3,577.6	3,592.1	3,611.6	3,622.2	3,647.8	3,660.3
1978	3,652.6	3,671.2	3,701.3	3,731.8	3,740.3	3,754.4	3,769.8	3,786.0	3,796.2	3,824.2	3,836.8	3,856.5
1979	3,859.0	3,866.6	3,883.6	3,863.1	3,862.5	3,864.8	3,888.3	3,894.4	3,887.7	3,902.3	3,916.5	3,927.8
1980	3,938.3	3,920.0	3,895.1	3,863.5	3,844.9	3,850.3	3,880.4	3,884.9	3,903.6	3,945.6	3,965.3	3,994.5
1981	3,998.3	3,986.7	3,996.1	3,976.6	3,981.8	3,998.4	4,051.1	4,061.6	4,052.1	4,042.2	4,039.6	4,025.3
1982	4,001.3	4,015.0	4,021.7	4,068.4	4,070.9	4,049.8	4,031.2	4,027.5	4,020.1	4,023.0	4,035.2	4,047.9
1983	4,030.3	4,032.6	4,054.0	4,062.8	4,088.3	4,092.2	4,104.4	4,091.0	4,122.7	4,158.3	4,187.0	4,225.9
1984	4,250.4	4,285.2	4,311.8	4,340.9	4,347.6	4,381.2	4,406.0	4,435.0	4,464.7	4,433.9	4,459.6	4,474.6
1985	4,500.0	4,504.6	4,519.8	4,513.9	4,515.8	4,527.7	4,533.1	4,538.0	4,542.5	4,570.3	4,565.0	4,598.9
1986	4,603.4	4,623.0	4,664.6	4,668.9	4,671.6	4,673.9	4,693.0	4,700.2	4,700.2	4,695.8	4,703.0	4,722.3
1987	4,717.7	4,735.7	4,748.8	4,747.7	4,774.2	4,771.8	4,774.6	4,795.6	4,798.6	4,839.3	4,855.9	4,908.8
1988	4,891.1	4,915.3	4,927.7	4,936.1	4,932.7	4,942.4	4,955.2	4,957.1	4,959.4	4,980.3	4,981.7	5,010.7
1989	5,055.0	5,067.8	5,091.6	5,082.0	5,059.4	5,069.5	5,074.1	5,076.8	5,053.2	5,070.5	5,103.9	5,111.1
1990	5,136.6	5,155.7	5,158.3	5,181.8	5,167.9	5,178.3	5,193.8	5,163.7	5,163.8	5,124.9	5,121.9	5,138.9
1991	5,103.0	5,095.1	5,107.8	5,124.1	5,131.1	5,155.1	5,125.2	5,123.2	5,129.1	5,144.3	5,152.7	5,190.2
1992	5,198.4	5,230.4	5,227.5	5,241.0	5,254.6	5,263.6	5,255.1	5,138.7	5,260.7	5,289.1	5,312.7	5,498.1
1993	5,283.6	5,275.7	5,259.1	5,357.7	5,385.7	5,376.2	5,377.3	5,405.1	5,398.1	5,395.3	5,409.0	5,588.1
1994	5,363.4	5,411.9	5,426.9	5,495.8	5,522.2	5,511.9	5,519.3	5,522.1	5,542.3	5,585.6	5,584.2	5,609.9
1995	5,653.4	5,651.8	5,659.6	5,685.1	5,665.1	5,688.5	5,708.5	5,700.2	5,725.5	5,748.8	5,760.3	5,767.2
1996	5,785.8	5,826.5	5,834.7	5,842.8	5,853.9	5,905.8	5,880.6	5,904.5	5,929.2	5,903.5	5,926.9	5,960.9
1997	5,983.9	6,012.3	6,042.1	6,048.6	6,068.8	6,096.8	6,097.2	6,127.5	6,139.9	-	-	-

Source: The Conference Board. Primary source(s): U.S. Department of Commerce, Bureau of Economic Analysis, National Income and Wealth Division, BE-54, Washington, DC 20230. A dash (-) indicates that data are not available or zero.

Wages & Salaries in Mining, Manufacturing, Construction

(Annual Rate, Billions of chained 1992 $)

Year	Jan	Feb	Mar	Apr	May	Jun	Jul	Aug	Sep	Oct	Nov	Dec
1959	457.11	459.71	467.14	472.54	478.38	480.63	478.44	465.14	463.86	461.21	466.15	480.19
1960	487.07	487.58	484.47	482.59	483.81	480.17	477.08	473.69	469.76	470.42	464.18	455.45
1961	459.40	457.77	460.17	463.92	468.31	474.71	475.44	478.47	473.27	482.20	489.46	492.39
1962	490.24	494.37	498.70	504.51	502.82	502.97	505.33	504.53	505.73	504.50	506.62	507.18
1963	508.35	507.80	509.37	511.84	516.06	518.32	518.91	518.46	522.20	523.88	524.70	529.20
1964	524.73	533.74	537.17	540.69	542.58	544.45	547.33	551.98	555.62	547.80	556.37	565.42
1965	565.79	570.79	571.87	569.40	574.60	577.00	577.92	580.82	583.23	590.48	595.82	600.88
1966	603.40	610.14	614.58	619.83	621.71	627.70	627.75	631.62	632.76	634.78	635.08	633.16
1967	638.34	632.01	633.02	632.28	630.51	632.75	634.57	640.33	636.09	634.24	643.85	649.45
1968	648.96	657.82	658.69	661.16	666.50	667.04	668.80	668.38	673.30	677.07	681.45	684.34
1969	685.70	686.39	693.68	694.78	697.22	699.69	702.05	705.46	705.84	706.36	701.47	702.58
1970	696.24	694.65	697.08	688.40	680.29	681.68	682.61	679.13	667.56	654.45	650.01	661.05
1971	664.59	662.63	662.56	664.10	668.95	666.18	664.42	662.56	664.02	665.24	666.84	675.88
1972	681.30	687.70	693.98	697.22	699.29	700.18	696.53	704.05	708.60	717.11	722.39	726.07
1973	734.62	742.90	740.86	742.34	744.15	746.25	751.86	745.36	749.78	752.72	755.97	754.90
1974	748.85	745.45	738.68	736.29	739.44	739.02	735.47	734.91	731.70	729.43	707.40	698.28
1975	690.44	674.52	670.58	666.67	669.98	669.61	666.86	676.57	681.61	684.58	686.30	692.77
1976	704.00	707.70	711.38	714.58	716.45	714.43	717.76	720.68	719.40	717.15	726.16	727.29
1977	721.75	729.08	736.90	743.39	749.34	756.48	757.52	757.67	764.58	767.54	768.80	765.16
1978	760.16	766.41	777.95	793.74	792.78	798.02	801.41	802.23	806.82	810.81	818.47	823.29
1979	820.88	823.14	830.00	821.56	826.86	828.20	827.04	822.42	823.85	820.91	818.40	822.61
1980	815.34	812.94	807.46	797.09	786.51	781.08	770.50	780.26	783.80	790.79	798.05	803.92
1981	801.64	790.62	794.42	795.29	795.75	800.94	801.74	802.59	795.72	795.83	788.91	781.42
1982	776.63	777.18	773.21	767.26	764.96	757.06	749.01	742.98	735.64	726.23	721.18	722.19
1983	725.08	721.83	722.44	723.40	726.05	730.67	735.69	737.53	746.82	753.30	758.60	763.54
1984	770.15	776.30	778.04	784.06	786.25	792.78	794.86	797.55	797.00	796.82	800.57	805.04
1985	806.33	801.80	814.78	803.57	804.43	805.09	803.82	806.37	806.06	811.24	807.32	810.08
1986	807.20	804.27	814.02	809.36	807.56	803.14	803.38	806.06	802.32	809.94	804.59	806.32
1987	803.62	802.84	808.89	800.07	803.24	802.05	802.32	805.46	806.56	808.31	810.37	810.97
1988	816.62	820.81	831.32	827.06	826.80	828.72	829.17	825.38	826.82	836.10	829.88	827.69
1989	828.01	825.15	830.24	818.30	812.71	811.81	812.13	814.11	811.03	816.88	812.35	809.58
1990	803.90	813.01	813.15	811.93	807.65	807.38	804.44	796.55	794.06	785.02	776.17	777.15
1991	768.51	762.44	758.80	757.78	757.71	760.75	760.00	759.94	759.70	756.90	752.72	753.89
1992	748.34	749.59	751.63	752.21	753.94	753.33	751.12	753.97	748.63	747.97	749.38	793.71
1993	725.18	726.91	721.66	750.60	750.03	748.39	751.48	751.97	756.38	755.01	757.92	793.54
1994	753.40	752.74	758.38	769.64	773.37	773.78	775.64	775.75	779.33	782.34	785.20	787.76
1995	785.95	786.83	786.52	786.74	782.96	785.80	787.81	789.00	792.10	793.62	795.13	793.84
1996	789.45	802.49	797.85	807.12	809.51	814.17	812.08	816.56	816.41	814.57	817.11	823.51
1997	823.17	827.26	831.43	832.01	835.15	834.64	834.33	839.87	842.10	-	-	-

Source: The Conference Board. Primary source(s): U.S. Department of Commerce (wages and salaries), Bureau of Economic Analysis, National Income and Wealth Division, BE-54, Washington, DC 20230 and U.S. Department of Labor, Bureau of Labor Statistics, Office of Prices and Living Conditions, Division of Consumer Prices and Price Indexes, Washington, DC 20212. A dash (-) indicates that data are not available or zero.

Industrial Production in The U.S.
(1990 = 100)

Year	Jan	Feb	Mar	Apr	May	Jun	Jul	Aug	Sep	Oct	Nov	Dec
1945	25.9	25.8	25.7	25.2	24.5	23.9	23.4	21.0	19.1	18.3	19.0	19.1
1946	18.0	17.1	18.9	18.6	17.9	19.0	19.6	20.4	20.8	21.1	21.3	21.4
1947	21.6	21.8	21.9	21.7	21.8	21.8	21.7	21.8	22.0	22.2	22.5	22.6
1948	22.7	22.8	22.5	22.5	22.9	23.2	23.2	23.1	23.0	23.1	22.8	22.6
1949	22.4	22.2	21.8	21.6	21.3	21.3	21.3	21.5	21.7	20.9	21.4	21.8
1950	22.2	22.3	23.0	23.8	24.3	25.1	25.9	26.7	26.5	26.7	26.6	27.1
1951	27.2	27.4	27.5	27.5	27.4	27.3	26.9	26.6	26.8	26.8	27.0	27.1
1952	27.4	27.6	27.7	27.4	27.2	26.9	26.5	28.2	29.2	29.5	30.1	30.3
1953	30.4	30.6	30.8	30.9	31.1	31.0	31.4	31.2	30.6	30.3	29.6	28.8
1954	28.6	28.7	28.5	28.4	28.5	28.6	28.7	28.6	28.7	29.0	29.5	29.9
1955	30.6	30.9	31.7	32.0	32.6	32.6	32.9	32.8	33.0	33.6	33.7	33.8
1956	34.0	33.7	33.7	34.0	33.7	33.4	32.3	33.7	34.4	34.7	34.4	34.9
1957	34.8	35.2	35.1	34.6	34.5	34.6	34.8	34.8	34.5	34.0	33.2	32.6
1958	32.0	31.3	30.9	30.4	30.7	31.5	32.0	32.6	32.9	33.3	34.3	34.3
1959	34.8	35.5	36.0	36.8	37.3	37.4	36.5	35.2	35.2	34.9	35.2	37.3
1960	38.3	38.0	37.6	37.3	37.3	36.8	36.7	36.6	36.3	36.2	35.7	35.0
1961	35.1	35.0	35.2	36.0	36.5	37.0	37.5	37.8	37.8	38.5	39.1	39.4
1962	39.1	39.7	39.9	40.0	40.0	39.9	40.3	40.3	40.6	40.6	40.8	40.8
1963	41.1	41.5	41.8	42.2	42.7	42.8	42.7	42.7	43.2	43.5	43.7	43.6
1964	44.0	44.3	44.3	45.0	45.3	45.4	45.7	46.0	46.1	45.5	46.9	47.5
1965	48.0	48.3	48.9	49.1	49.5	49.9	50.4	50.6	50.7	51.2	51.4	52.1
1966	52.6	52.9	53.6	53.7	54.2	54.5	54.8	54.8	55.4	55.7	55.4	55.5
1967	55.7	55.1	54.8	55.3	54.8	54.8	54.7	55.8	55.7	56.1	56.9	57.5
1968	57.5	57.7	57.9	57.9	58.6	58.8	58.7	58.9	59.1	59.2	60.0	60.2
1969	60.5	60.9	61.4	61.2	60.9	61.5	61.9	62.0	62.0	62.0	61.4	61.3
1970	60.1	60.1	60.0	59.9	59.8	59.6	59.7	59.6	59.2	58.0	57.7	59.0
1971	59.5	59.3	59.3	59.6	59.9	60.2	60.0	59.6	60.6	61.1	61.3	62.0
1972	63.4	63.9	64.4	65.4	65.3	65.5	65.4	66.3	67.0	67.9	68.8	69.4
1973	69.5	70.4	70.4	70.7	71.0	71.5	72.0	71.9	72.5	72.7	72.8	71.6
1974	70.6	70.3	70.7	70.5	71.4	71.6	71.2	71.0	71.3	70.8	68.7	65.9
1975	64.2	63.1	62.0	62.6	62.4	63.2	63.6	64.7	65.4	65.7	66.3	66.9
1976	67.6	68.8	68.6	68.9	69.7	69.7	70.1	70.5	70.8	71.0	72.2	72.8
1977	73.2	73.2	74.1	75.1	75.9	76.4	76.5	76.8	77.2	77.0	77.1	76.8
1978	76.5	76.5	77.3	79.9	80.0	80.8	81.1	81.3	81.7	82.1	82.6	82.9
1979	82.5	83.1	83.3	82.5	83.5	83.5	82.9	82.6	82.6	83.0	82.6	82.4
1980	82.8	82.8	82.8	81.2	79.2	78.2	77.7	78.6	79.8	80.3	81.6	82.0
1981	81.3	81.7	82.1	81.5	82.2	82.7	83.5	83.1	82.4	81.8	80.7	79.7
1982	78.5	80.2	79.6	78.8	78.2	78.0	77.3	76.9	76.4	75.7	75.5	74.9
1983	76.5	76.3	77.1	78.1	79.0	79.4	80.9	81.9	83.3	84.0	83.9	84.3
1984	86.1	86.0	86.9	87.4	87.9	88.3	88.4	88.4	88.3	87.9	88.0	87.6
1985	87.9	88.6	88.9	89.0	89.2	89.0	88.6	89.1	89.7	88.9	89.4	90.0
1986	90.6	90.0	89.1	89.7	89.5	89.2	89.5	89.8	89.7	90.5	90.9	91.8
1987	91.2	92.3	92.6	93.0	93.4	94.2	94.8	94.9	94.8	96.0	96.3	96.9
1988	96.9	97.3	97.3	97.8	97.9	97.9	98.6	99.1	98.8	99.0	99.8	100.3
1989	100.8	100.1	101.0	101.2	100.6	100.4	99.4	99.8	99.7	99.2	99.6	100.1
1990	99.6	100.1	100.6	100.0	100.4	100.4	100.4	100.5	100.7	100.1	98.8	98.2
1991	97.8	97.0	96.1	96.4	97.1	98.3	98.4	98.5	99.4	99.3	99.2	98.6
1992	98.6	99.3	100.1	100.8	101.2	100.9	101.6	101.2	101.7	102.5	103.1	103.1
1993	103.5	104.0	104.0	104.4	103.8	104.0	104.3	104.0	105.1	105.3	105.9	106.6
1994	106.9	107.5	108.2	108.7	109.3	109.9	110.4	110.5	110.5	111.2	111.9	112.8
1995	113.2	112.9	113.0	112.7	112.8	113.0	113.0	113.9	114.3	113.8	114.0	114.1
1996	113.7	115.1	114.5	115.6	116.1	116.8	116.8	117.1	117.3	117.5	118.6	119.1
1997	119.2	119.8	120.2	120.7	120.9	121.3	121.8	122.9	123.8	-	-	-

Source: The Conference Board. Primary source(s): U.S. Department of Commerce, International Trade Administration, Office of Trade and Economic Analysis, Stop 2814B, Washington, DC 20230. A dash (-) indicates that data are not available or zero.

Capacity Utilization Rate, Total Industry
(Percent)

Year	Jan	Feb	Mar	Apr	May	Jun	Jul	Aug	Sep	Oct	Nov	Dec
1967	89.390	87.975	87.083	87.509	86.357	85.960	85.383	86.634	86.112	86.432	87.286	87.842
1968	87.380	87.341	87.262	87.040	87.666	87.640	87.160	87.059	87.047	86.879	87.661	87.597
1969	87.795	88.035	88.403	87.758	87.110	87.644	87.791	87.678	87.345	87.060	85.934	85.401
1970	83.538	83.218	82.846	82.371	82.015	81.493	81.436	81.036	80.227	78.377	77.661	79.199
1971	79.580	79.223	78.931	79.169	79.365	79.492	79.058	78.397	79.467	79.858	79.992	80.710
1972	82.287	82.631	83.087	84.192	83.770	83.815	83.473	84.393	85.101	86.101	86.908	87.511
1973	87.348	88.313	88.047	88.128	88.261	88.695	89.004	88.712	89.152	89.244	89.038	87.398
1974	85.946	85.357	85.494	85.085	85.829	85.844	85.200	84.657	84.763	83.905	81.264	77.661
1975	75.454	74.086	72.614	73.131	72.748	73.539	73.814	74.970	75.590	75.800	76.353	76.809
1976	77.471	78.668	78.298	78.425	79.142	79.017	79.304	79.579	79.659	79.754	80.902	81.366
1977	81.647	81.523	82.282	83.258	83.894	84.328	84.191	84.329	84.581	84.210	84.060	83.530
1978	83.038	82.826	83.433	86.036	85.844	86.550	86.572	86.553	86.745	86.947	87.206	87.288
1979	86.656	87.108	87.148	86.132	86.927	86.749	85.937	85.410	85.294	85.470	84.871	84.518
1980	84.733	84.615	84.407	82.583	80.365	79.175	78.510	79.273	80.285	80.699	81.834	82.069
1981	81.201	81.434	81.643	80.934	81.443	81.778	82.326	81.776	80.928	80.121	78.807	77.728
1982	76.303	77.787	77.081	76.189	75.440	75.021	74.247	73.694	72.993	72.229	71.875	71.122
1983	72.513	72.260	72.893	73.717	74.514	74.839	76.077	77.005	78.224	78.743	78.567	78.868
1984	80.368	80.065	80.770	81.019	81.305	81.491	81.482	81.300	81.016	80.464	80.357	79.824
1985	79.920	80.412	80.416	80.344	80.320	79.912	79.353	79.611	79.868	78.955	79.179	79.500
1986	79.842	79.157	78.247	78.732	78.447	78.071	78.222	78.343	78.173	78.784	79.083	79.723
1987	79.138	79.977	80.201	80.453	80.727	81.344	81.766	81.736	81.585	82.583	82.727	83.099
1988	83.082	83.265	83.211	83.611	83.569	83.510	83.982	84.339	83.953	84.100	84.626	84.971
1989	85.317	84.521	85.148	85.225	84.550	84.268	83.265	83.495	83.216	82.695	82.893	83.166
1990	82.628	82.936	83.216	82.618	82.842	82.715	82.530	82.545	82.521	81.943	80.731	80.136
1991	79.633	78.904	78.060	78.191	78.677	79.503	79.474	79.480	80.120	79.940	79.724	79.112
1992	79.035	79.430	79.935	80.375	80.551	80.191	80.625	80.211	80.452	80.950	81.303	81.239
1993	81.408	81.662	81.601	81.742	81.154	81.210	81.331	81.020	81.698	81.784	82.069	82.539
1994	82.609	82.825	83.190	83.342	83.651	83.855	84.064	83.894	83.750	84.070	84.362	84.883
1995	84.946	84.508	84.331	83.873	83.715	83.639	83.393	83.823	83.886	83.291	83.187	83.007
1996	82.449	83.244	82.600	83.108	83.215	83.452	83.225	83.228	83.069	82.996	83.441	83.521
1997	83.317	83.495	83.565	83.632	83.480	83.476	83.910	84.061	84.380	-	-	-

Source: The Conference Board. Primary source(s): Board of Governors of the Federal Reserve System, Division of Research and Statistics, Industrial Output Section, Stop 82, Washington, DC 20551. A dash (-) indicates that data are not available or zero.

Capacity Utilization Rate, Manufacturing

(Percent)

Year	Jan	Feb	Mar	Apr	May	Jun	Jul	Aug	Sep	Oct	Nov	Dec
1948	84.429	83.965	83.379	82.798	83.302	83.647	83.378	82.658	81.492	81.689	80.241	79.311
1949	77.944	76.884	75.887	74.165	73.184	73.084	73.129	73.608	74.804	71.683	72.019	73.625
1950	74.936	75.388	76.389	79.213	81.035	83.124	85.476	88.367	87.229	87.476	87.035	88.095
1951	88.330	88.292	88.383	88.203	87.353	86.642	84.869	83.641	83.746	83.058	83.559	83.907
1952	84.384	84.596	84.660	83.560	83.113	81.899	79.801	85.097	87.691	88.751	90.181	90.490
1953	90.548	91.104	91.426	91.498	91.694	90.659	90.979	90.564	88.326	87.195	84.741	82.308
1954	81.331	80.840	80.238	79.401	79.756	79.873	79.398	78.809	79.162	79.747	80.910	81.798
1955	83.491	84.133	85.769	86.705	87.862	87.646	87.659	87.332	87.458	88.367	88.265	89.026
1956	88.231	87.442	86.963	87.800	86.343	85.332	81.522	84.949	85.991	86.491	85.819	86.779
1957	86.151	86.998	86.414	84.997	84.214	84.577	84.317	84.162	83.186	81.395	79.411	77.549
1958	75.698	73.756	72.743	71.333	71.939	73.946	74.342	75.733	76.222	76.410	79.069	79.043
1959	80.197	81.443	82.477	83.992	84.916	84.769	82.980	79.468	79.049	78.154	78.505	83.568
1960	85.562	84.611	83.242	82.259	81.471	80.224	79.727	79.050	77.919	77.529	75.772	74.256
1961	74.109	73.512	73.864	75.383	76.356	77.324	78.109	78.978	78.156	79.553	80.766	81.604
1962	80.241	81.427	81.891	81.743	81.335	80.929	81.476	81.417	81.787	81.385	81.839	81.679
1963	81.945	82.378	82.624	83.458	83.951	83.940	83.345	83.501	83.823	84.307	84.295	84.009
1964	84.462	84.667	84.357	85.587	85.598	85.449	85.861	86.110	86.199	84.625	86.848	88.002
1965	88.599	88.723	89.277	89.287	89.449	89.458	90.297	89.851	89.559	89.789	89.648	90.514
1966	90.859	90.911	91.588	91.542	91.638	91.521	91.405	91.080	91.246	91.618	90.129	90.025
1967	89.842	88.395	87.516	87.656	86.611	86.069	85.307	86.492	86.064	86.370	87.535	88.004
1968	87.408	87.406	87.160	86.863	87.577	87.381	86.739	86.791	86.466	86.638	87.496	87.133
1969	87.304	87.671	88.001	87.298	86.616	86.812	87.112	86.904	86.460	86.224	85.008	84.239
1970	82.116	81.919	81.427	80.881	80.439	79.945	79.943	79.152	78.242	76.257	75.557	77.309
1971	77.743	77.581	77.222	77.429	77.753	77.750	77.685	76.571	77.924	78.884	78.976	79.510
1972	81.182	81.520	81.968	83.091	82.689	82.740	82.524	83.387	83.943	85.039	85.909	86.652
1973	86.607	87.567	87.502	87.493	87.576	87.921	88.146	87.994	88.243	88.524	88.469	86.573
1974	85.320	84.715	84.808	84.224	84.996	85.053	84.338	84.066	83.928	82.956	80.436	76.345
1975	73.895	72.262	70.516	71.126	70.836	71.726	72.280	73.336	74.098	74.475	74.917	75.512
1976	76.162	77.714	77.182	77.248	78.070	77.794	78.336	78.499	78.563	78.686	79.592	80.175
1977	80.588	80.552	81.384	82.344	82.903	83.296	83.151	83.639	83.512	83.225	83.218	83.359
1978	82.874	82.637	82.961	85.189	84.978	85.785	85.826	85.942	86.182	86.346	86.784	86.946
1979	86.393	86.739	86.855	85.332	86.374	86.256	85.558	84.528	84.290	84.476	83.632	83.337
1980	83.258	83.259	82.720	80.782	78.057	76.691	75.928	76.985	77.920	78.561	79.670	79.669
1981	78.976	79.241	79.269	79.252	79.629	79.333	79.631	78.837	78.033	76.982	75.617	74.242
1982	72.578	74.578	73.928	73.125	72.693	72.566	71.846	71.389	70.876	69.927	69.577	68.980
1983	70.611	70.833	71.750	72.459	73.368	73.868	74.845	75.587	77.160	77.554	77.682	77.529
1984	79.272	79.497	79.832	79.991	80.056	80.348	80.363	80.210	79.836	79.635	79.487	79.039
1985	78.869	79.077	79.344	79.227	79.375	78.893	78.333	78.766	78.800	77.920	78.521	78.194
1986	79.149	78.599	77.777	78.731	78.489	78.132	78.211	78.557	78.429	78.913	79.087	79.879
1987	79.124	80.229	80.267	80.555	80.666	81.368	81.791	81.527	81.526	82.484	82.750	83.141
1988	82.886	83.099	82.936	83.673	83.486	83.378	83.847	83.962	84.022	84.093	84.769	85.124
1989	85.716	84.536	85.037	84.949	84.210	84.060	82.979	83.102	82.699	82.077	82.206	82.151
1990	81.825	82.446	82.575	81.797	82.008	81.774	81.623	81.694	81.513	80.880	79.694	79.060
1991	78.249	77.561	76.632	76.783	77.175	78.138	78.207	78.256	79.027	78.870	78.576	78.071
1992	78.085	78.550	79.110	79.472	79.683	79.480	79.858	79.492	79.665	80.102	80.434	80.192
1993	80.665	80.795	80.743	81.024	80.485	80.357	80.489	80.077	80.854	80.904	81.201	81.732
1994	81.645	81.921	82.404	82.736	83.103	83.015	83.431	83.301	83.218	83.594	83.959	84.480
1995	84.584	84.026	83.878	83.355	83.026	82.959	82.583	82.879	83.176	82.582	82.211	82.048
1996	81.476	82.244	81.339	81.981	82.026	82.281	82.410	82.258	82.127	82.007	82.351	82.534
1997	82.357	82.606	82.664	82.594	82.414	82.489	82.946	83.281	83.354	-	-	-

Source: The Conference Board. Primary source(s): Board of Governors of the Federal Reserve System, Division of Research and Statistics, Industrial Output Section, Stop 82, Washington, DC 20551. A dash (-) indicates that data are not available or zero.

INDICATORS OF CONSUMPTION, TRADE, ORDERS, AND DELIVERIES

Consumption, trade, orders, and deliveries are indicators of the economy's general performance. They tend, on the whole, to be leading indicators. Included are two series:

  Manufacturers' new orders, durable goods
  Sales of retail stores

Related series, reported under Business Cycle Indicators, are:

  Manufacturers' new orders, consumer goods and materials (Leading Index)
  Vendor performance (Leading Index)
  Consumer expectations (Leading Index)
  Manufacturing and trade sales (Coincident Index)

Manufacturers' New Orders, Durable Goods. Orders are reported in billions of chained 1992 dollars from 1959 to 1997. New orders for consumer goods and materials are part of the leading index. This series is also considered to be a leading indicator overall but is not part of the composite index of leading indicators—most likely because orders for durable goods are less predictive than those for consumer goods and materials.

Sales of Retail Stores. The series shows data from 1959 to 1997 in millions of chained 1992 dollars. Retail sales are classified as leading indicators of the trough of business cycles but produce uncertain results at the peak of cycles. In other words, retail sales tend to grow somewhat earlier than the economy as a whole.

Manufacturers' New Orders, Durable Goods Industries
(Billions of chained 1992 $)

Year	Jan	Feb	Mar	Apr	May	Jun	Jul	Aug	Sep	Oct	Nov	Dec
1959	50,325	52,587	53,731	54,241	51,889	54,267	50,063	47,679	48,966	49,887	47,046	51,355
1960	49,384	49,286	48,803	48,285	48,838	49,780	48,139	51,132	50,912	47,238	47,416	48,052
1961	45,425	46,642	46,781	49,562	50,091	51,177	50,400	53,447	52,689	53,139	54,943	56,707
1962	56,559	56,959	55,342	54,574	54,780	54,454	55,233	54,937	57,422	58,614	57,223	60,277
1963	59,946	60,780	62,027	61,642	62,354	59,917	62,028	60,089	61,737	62,819	61,713	60,533
1964	67,318	64,809	64,299	66,817	66,705	67,137	70,128	64,455	68,446	67,348	66,840	70,298
1965	72,636	71,832	73,521	74,469	72,372	73,294	75,590	76,204	73,971	77,717	78,526	80,316
1966	82,721	82,258	85,670	83,835	82,606	84,616	82,534	80,639	86,577	83,686	80,681	80,246
1967	78,201	77,510	76,144	76,612	80,944	82,348	79,439	80,954	79,309	80,478	81,218	88,341
1968	83,037	83,145	86,481	82,769	81,183	82,211	81,767	81,228	85,806	89,559	85,912	85,177
1969	86,959	88,868	87,137	91,536	86,050	84,569	84,923	86,646	89,657	86,902	84,535	83,229
1970	79,503	78,610	76,295	74,385	76,452	77,736	76,683	76,084	76,170	69,863	70,683	78,355
1971	80,586	81,807	79,807	77,467	76,290	78,099	76,913	80,915	80,887	79,173	81,654	83,507
1972	84,909	86,416	86,165	86,734	88,104	88,323	86,370	90,694	95,947	94,008	96,137	100,503
1973	102,935	105,228	107,516	104,985	104,795	104,192	104,449	104,330	103,217	107,120	109,804	103,882
1974	108,330	107,286	104,828	104,728	107,976	105,020	105,785	107,654	99,808	92,521	90,146	81,772
1975	80,212	78,305	73,168	76,979	75,372	75,333	82,306	82,652	82,260	80,547	80,870	81,270
1976	84,073	87,700	90,803	90,106	89,836	91,044	93,577	92,569	92,725	92,244	94,398	99,129
1977	96,355	96,837	101,653	100,258	100,364	103,497	102,321	103,179	105,163	106,778	105,417	109,292
1978	102,129	105,614	110,207	113,266	113,669	114,448	111,606	114,598	116,528	120,045	119,353	117,413
1979	117,049	119,708	123,481	113,421	114,796	114,478	111,379	108,100	111,273	109,525	106,403	106,684
1980	111,221	110,335	105,283	97,943	89,797	92,722	100,046	97,862	106,119	108,433	104,174	107,773
1981	102,729	102,518	104,497	106,627	105,892	105,375	104,839	101,747	100,056	95,216	93,214	89,325
1982	93,346	93,120	96,139	93,864	90,529	90,205	91,385	87,087	89,257	87,886	84,862	91,312
1983	95,335	89,076	92,356	95,290	95,081	101,733	100,634	100,923	105,309	110,578	110,526	111,115
1984	113,308	114,521	119,330	110,040	112,689	109,101	113,525	112,509	108,688	109,365	114,481	110,978
1985	115,972	112,076	110,942	110,056	113,405	116,874	113,723	116,515	116,774	115,247	110,807	116,412
1986	119,207	116,887	115,758	113,469	112,120	112,839	114,675	110,950	116,505	113,766	113,704	117,690
1987	112,235	116,935	120,306	121,611	122,362	123,883	126,362	120,459	122,464	124,903	124,828	125,716
1988	127,344	128,333	127,035	126,916	128,322	131,305	130,298	131,235	130,803	131,886	130,333	142,556
1989	137,840	133,137	132,461	133,369	126,508	129,499	126,964	125,455	128,483	123,637	131,509	134,365
1990	124,132	127,473	135,286	127,815	131,843	129,062	131,545	127,635	128,358	130,431	118,207	123,065
1991	119,371	119,948	112,689	117,519	120,578	116,675	132,858	125,585	122,287	123,401	125,367	117,005
1992	122,286	122,119	124,851	127,538	125,520	128,465	125,546	123,739	125,779	128,360	126,031	135,341
1993	129,720	133,595	128,843	130,093	126,778	130,978	128,001	128,858	130,331	132,930	136,310	137,350
1994	142,447	139,110	141,204	140,936	142,594	146,007	142,187	146,114	147,726	146,542	151,425	154,538
1995	155,117	153,839	153,820	147,480	151,223	149,609	147,747	154,140	159,176	156,579	157,399	163,054
1996	161,980	157,883	161,460	160,176	166,939	165,857	168,251	162,757	170,448	170,592	169,344	166,016
1997	171,729	174,804	170,024	173,134	177,052	177,781	178,146	183,417	182,354	-	-	-

Source: The Conference Board. Primary source(s): U.S. Department of Commerce, Bureau of the Census, Manufacturing and Construction Division, Manufacturers' Shipments, Inventories, and Orders Branch, Washington, DC 20233. F.W. Dodge; McGraw-Hill, Inc., Market Analysis Group, 24 Hartwell Avenue, Lexington, MA 02173. Deflators calculated by The Conference Board. A dash (-) indicates that data are not available or zero.

Sales of Retail Stores
(Millions of chained 1992 $)

Year	Jan	Feb	Mar	Apr	May	Jun	Jul	Aug	Sep	Oct	Nov	Dec
1959	58,384	58,785	59,210	58,542	59,487	59,960	59,550	60,016	59,886	59,761	58,121	58,552
1960	59,882	59,636	59,889	61,521	59,927	60,326	59,708	59,714	59,842	60,035	59,636	58,989
1961	58,478	58,435	58,968	58,606	58,916	59,087	59,370	59,807	60,420	60,298	61,428	61,744
1962	61,764	61,657	62,978	62,708	63,511	62,918	63,558	63,496	64,294	64,425	64,943	65,017
1963	65,514	64,733	65,386	65,765	64,906	66,077	66,082	66,006	65,195	66,412	66,295	66,752
1964	66,553	68,006	67,888	68,181	69,559	69,350	69,543	71,097	71,849	69,206	69,074	72,822
1965	73,162	73,218	72,399	73,510	74,171	73,185	74,441	74,479	74,038	77,829	77,689	78,842
1966	78,394	78,348	79,176	78,412	76,317	77,597	78,205	78,176	77,763	78,504	78,117	79,030
1967	78,661	78,042	78,880	79,150	78,707	80,793	80,018	79,779	81,955	80,473	82,136	84,388
1968	82,370	83,166	84,941	84,557	84,732	86,021	86,861	87,625	85,370	87,341	89,178	87,782
1969	88,347	88,747	87,573	87,732	88,420	87,506	87,367	88,173	89,093	89,722	89,272	89,855
1970	89,639	89,771	88,899	89,507	90,548	91,076	91,655	91,420	91,323	91,711	89,298	91,535
1971	93,428	94,167	94,030	95,530	94,745	96,091	96,258	96,685	98,595	99,655	100,715	100,195
1972	99,717	100,169	102,704	102,884	103,883	104,521	104,695	105,393	106,763	108,267	108,687	110,606
1973	111,929	112,725	112,552	110,752	110,050	110,416	110,302	108,960	110,270	110,066	109,782	105,997
1974	106,285	105,534	105,772	106,392	106,465	105,940	107,013	108,746	105,041	103,239	102,034	99,918
1975	103,244	104,295	101,616	102,768	107,044	106,168	106,713	107,306	107,357	107,511	107,554	108,630
1976	111,225	110,502	111,192	113,098	111,651	113,674	114,004	112,954	112,310	113,362	113,650	116,503
1977	114,939	116,777	117,279	118,469	117,425	117,566	118,573	118,154	118,519	120,228	120,523	120,375
1978	117,564	119,981	122,294	124,401	124,128	125,370	123,814	124,761	124,756	125,987	127,070	127,981
1979	126,259	126,133	127,427	125,774	125,854	125,284	123,525	127,208	127,450	125,807	126,628	125,838
1980	126,900	124,639	121,242	118,830	118,255	119,282	120,929	121,027	120,293	122,394	122,468	121,848
1981	123,613	123,789	123,693	122,444	121,064	121,760	122,049	123,364	122,273	120,274	119,700	119,868
1982	118,005	120,881	119,776	120,628	121,240	118,331	120,001	119,461	121,050	122,144	123,956	124,042
1983	123,805	124,173	127,219	126,857	128,542	131,197	131,574	129,284	131,484	133,239	134,810	135,374
1984	137,933	137,472	136,187	138,394	139,292	141,129	138,693	137,625	139,198	139,528	142,003	141,259
1985	141,889	142,693	142,879	144,438	145,427	144,431	144,529	146,528	150,496	145,690	145,886	147,041
1986	148,125	147,554	148,324	150,452	152,182	151,811	152,542	153,880	162,310	155,738	154,749	161,012
1987	149,033	155,696	156,442	157,255	156,989	158,494	159,122	161,534	159,086	158,225	158,412	160,379
1988	160,754	161,934	164,242	162,624	163,802	164,090	163,740	164,324	162,975	165,935	166,913	167,610
1989	167,814	165,052	165,312	166,733	167,177	167,003	167,643	170,609	170,162	167,497	168,563	168,770
1990	171,864	169,969	170,008	169,149	168,127	169,479	169,545	169,237	168,429	167,012	167,416	164,116
1991	160,875	163,513	165,655	164,799	165,823	165,851	165,830	164,846	165,464	163,791	163,869	164,025
1992	167,975	168,650	167,371	167,306	168,254	168,203	168,851	169,606	170,739	173,202	172,945	174,306
1993	175,438	173,643	171,390	175,183	176,445	176,978	178,491	178,416	178,805	180,138	181,479	183,046
1994	181,880	184,800	187,521	186,518	185,773	186,847	186,262	188,504	188,776	191,374	191,250	190,887
1995	192,247	188,912	189,941	189,798	191,572	193,007	192,729	193,955	193,335	192,910	194,972	195,973
1996	195,136	198,447	198,585	198,428	200,106	199,383	199,727	199,702	200,909	202,012	201,181	201,982
1997	204,816	207,062	206,502	204,525	204,535	206,437	209,031	210,410	-	-	-	-

Source: The Conference Board. Primary source(s): U.S. Department of Commerce, Bureau of the Census, Services Division, Current Retail Inventories and Sales Branch, Washington, DC 20233 and U.S. Department of Commerce (deflator), Bureau of Economic Analysis, National Income and Wealth Division, BE-54, Washington, DC 20230. A dash (-) indicates that data are not available or zero.

INDICATORS OF FIXED CAPITAL INVESTMENT

Indicators of fixed capital investment cover business formations as well as expenditures on tooling and equipment and on buildings and housing. In the context of business cycles, the series reflect relative confidence in the future and hence tend to be leading indicators. Five series are presented:

> New business incorporations
> Contracts and orders for plant and equipment, current dollars
> New private housing units started

Related series, reported under Business Cycle Indicators, are:

> Manufacturers' new orders, nondefense capital goods (Leading Index)
> Building permits, new private housing units (Leading Index)

New Business Incorporations. Data show total incorporations from 1947 to 1996. New businesses are formed when entrepreneurs anticipate a strong economy and can obtain financing. The series, therefore, is classified as a leading indicator—although not included in the composite index of leading indicators.

Contracts and Orders for Plant and Equipment. Data are shown in billions of current dollars from 1947 to 1997. The series shows commitments to spend money on capital goods in the future—because payment will be made at a later date. The series, therefore, tends to predict future economic activity.

New Private Housing Units Started. Data are in thousands of units, by month, for 1946 through 1997. The composite index of leading indicators measures building permits issued—the first step in a cycle of construction. This series measures actual starts. Both series are leading indicators. Since the construction sector tends to be the first to slump and the first to revive, "housing starts" is a closely watched indicator series.

Number of New Business Incorporations
(number)

Year	Jan	Feb	Mar	Apr	May	Jun	Jul	Aug	Sep	Oct	Nov	Dec
1947	9,922	9,800	9,743	9,057	8,699	8,748	9,308	9,244	9,316	9,806	9,453	9,690
1948	9,380	8,329	8,349	8,396	8,064	8,210	8,168	7,439	7,483	7,349	7,241	7,054
1949	7,012	6,826	6,791	6,879	7,006	6,879	7,057	7,330	7,403	7,532	7,659	7,788
1950	7,830	8,275	8,078	8,132	8,403	8,394	7,898	7,684	7,092	7,176	7,059	7,007
1951	7,214	7,016	6,937	7,082	6,848	6,759	6,796	6,880	6,952	6,995	7,119	7,181
1952	7,080	7,214	7,348	7,499	7,441	7,700	7,683	8,065	8,259	8,341	8,265	8,096
1953	8,304	8,351	8,634	8,534	8,785	8,605	8,757	8,515	8,185	8,698	8,556	8,696
1954	8,638	8,937	9,155	9,276	9,158	9,436	9,772	9,882	10,085	10,730	11,212	11,604
1955	11,902	11,843	11,679	11,215	11,521	12,072	11,655	11,572	11,968	11,668	11,761	11,560
1956	11,620	12,449	11,591	11,888	12,245	11,999	11,851	11,707	11,193	11,925	11,186	11,139
1957	11,250	11,359	11,367	11,507	11,109	11,739	11,686	11,593	11,318	11,251	10,788	10,791
1958	11,042	11,049	11,042	10,636	11,752	12,032	12,504	13,644	13,933	13,669	14,599	15,577
1959	16,346	16,255	16,548	16,604	16,296	15,204	15,658	15,813	15,728	15,383	15,695	15,959
1960	16,561	15,274	15,233	15,280	15,176	15,630	15,828	15,114	15,112	15,035	14,264	14,097
1961	13,607	14,570	14,658	15,327	15,298	15,431	15,492	15,277	15,402	16,035	16,149	15,881
1962	15,599	15,758	15,670	15,372	15,245	14,947	15,171	15,056	15,249	14,892	14,951	14,985
1963	14,924	15,390	15,563	15,305	15,682	15,536	15,431	16,093	15,689	16,275	15,759	15,867
1964	15,993	16,326	15,917	16,132	16,473	16,282	16,550	15,692	16,948	16,728	16,804	17,021
1965	16,784	16,854	17,131	16,664	16,580	17,017	16,844	16,901	17,136	16,994	17,606	17,625
1966	18,087	17,451	17,266	17,057	16,644	16,577	16,074	16,343	15,764	16,233	16,206	16,583
1967	16,703	15,987	16,244	16,760	17,627	17,799	16,300	17,674	17,818	17,654	17,958	18,238
1968	18,061	18,041	18,538	18,663	18,723	18,839	19,407	19,947	20,582	21,093	20,890	20,619
1969	21,364	22,105	22,083	23,262	23,118	23,439	23,366	22,871	22,594	24,263	23,125	22,404
1970	22,196	22,968	21,346	21,829	21,874	21,796	21,614	21,796	22,181	21,712	22,217	22,272
1971	22,563	21,034	22,883	22,814	23,960	24,481	24,677	25,012	23,623	25,356	25,510	25,634
1972	25,270	25,084	26,231	26,630	26,270	26,175	26,789	26,365	27,168	27,529	26,234	27,699
1973	27,796	28,752	28,964	28,522	28,286	27,999	27,477	26,689	26,240	26,809	26,718	24,881
1974	26,511	27,056	26,458	29,071	27,562	25,785	27,790	26,495	26,313	25,404	25,555	25,003
1975	24,809	24,931	25,076	26,708	26,632	26,307	28,655	27,810	28,359	29,079	28,634	29,282
1976	29,613	29,772	31,000	30,808	28,784	31,420	31,037	31,301	31,921	32,160	33,183	33,124
1977	34,311	33,844	35,018	34,529	35,256	36,694	36,874	38,180	37,271	38,213	38,308	38,900
1978	36,414	39,434	37,847	39,585	39,059	39,860	40,152	41,007	41,553	41,437	41,423	42,179
1979	42,043	42,014	43,299	43,401	44,317	43,504	44,513	43,634	44,173	45,295	44,540	43,563
1980	44,230	44,175	43,359	42,240	42,710	40,648	43,621	44,255	45,746	45,945	46,750	47,840
1981	46,039	48,588	47,972	49,413	48,866	49,172	49,038	48,631	48,450	47,947	49,413	47,556
1982	43,330	47,234	46,899	46,876	46,995	45,936	44,525	46,981	45,552	45,530	48,474	57,507
1983	49,999	48,296	48,032	48,903	50,211	50,992	48,601	52,828	50,445	50,441	51,642	51,557
1984	52,674	53,535	53,075	53,298	50,736	53,884	53,211	52,025	52,646	52,587	53,838	53,558
1985	53,674	53,479	55,335	55,133	55,545	55,339	54,507	56,159	56,662	58,307	57,308	58,074
1986	57,636	59,114	58,870	59,156	57,747	57,446	57,717	56,299	57,942	57,120	56,652	65,691
1987	55,348	58,495	60,248	57,537	56,178	57,612	57,330	57,650	57,568	55,504	56,681	55,226
1988	56,108	56,475	60,655	54,670	58,046	55,620	56,915	59,730	55,915	56,529	54,553	58,592
1989	58,253	58,560	57,383	57,631	57,326	56,950	54,948	55,500	55,390	54,651	55,116	56,945
1990	59,141	56,325	56,172	55,000	53,616	53,784	52,142	52,958	52,176	51,899	51,429	52,060
1991	51,991	50,384	51,536	52,235	52,327	52,071	52,767	53,313	52,284	53,892	54,163	52,923
1992	58,141	55,092	57,449	54,474	48,688	58,730	56,942	51,245	59,179	52,492	55,392	61,695
1993	55,625	59,691	61,002	59,648	51,765	60,422	58,387	58,209	63,758	55,291	61,739	61,873
1994	61,978	60,680	64,058	58,992	58,528	63,097	56,380	64,844	64,564	67,909	64,542	62,908
1995	66,293	64,755	65,292	57,839	65,422	63,439	59,946	69,337	61,982	67,587	67,042	61,297
1996	69,438	69,709	60,556	67,454	68,269	61,602	73,208	62,229	62,593	-	-	-

Source: The Conference Board. Primary source(s): The Dunn & Bradstreet Corporation, Economic Analysis Department, 187 Danbury Road, Wilton, CT 06897. A dash (-) indicates that data are not available or zero.

Contracts and Orders for Plant and Equipment
(Billions of $)

Year	Jan	Feb	Mar	Apr	May	Jun	Jul	Aug	Sep	Oct	Nov	Dec
1959	3,092	3,188	3,733	3,353	3,459	3,537	3,610	3,224	3,634	3,502	3,295	3,493
1960	3,270	3,353	3,266	3,518	3,509	3,408	3,412	3,405	3,436	3,337	3,202	3,486
1961	3,485	3,403	3,246	3,274	3,223	3,408	3,487	3,667	3,429	3,506	3,719	3,429
1962	3,622	3,939	3,652	3,848	3,679	3,609	3,654	3,661	3,644	3,727	3,996	4,075
1963	3,795	3,909	3,880	3,975	4,361	3,991	3,958	4,074	4,196	4,275	4,497	4,565
1964	4,701	4,238	4,430	4,462	4,825	4,953	4,641	4,693	4,747	4,792	5,097	5,166
1965	4,890	4,927	5,216	5,247	5,178	5,097	5,267	5,082	5,492	5,510	5,450	5,823
1966	5,815	6,280	6,145	6,406	6,337	6,209	6,637	6,216	6,789	6,201	6,139	6,136
1967	5,299	5,688	5,815	5,701	5,879	6,106	6,053	6,264	6,091	6,194	6,216	6,398
1968	7,744	7,484	9,018	7,350	6,433	6,469	7,849	8,137	6,988	8,660	7,189	7,843
1969	8,992	8,999	7,962	9,245	8,510	8,050	8,243	8,364	9,240	8,239	8,058	8,011
1970	9,076	8,401	7,568	7,347	7,199	7,039	7,534	7,355	7,161	6,446	7,297	8,007
1971	7,800	8,414	8,280	8,188	7,771	8,879	7,237	8,463	8,561	7,662	8,246	8,460
1972	8,094	8,433	9,060	8,876	9,722	8,433	9,685	9,153	10,195	9,779	9,966	10,167
1973	10,349	11,061	10,995	11,135	11,532	11,686	12,061	12,528	11,957	13,291	13,281	12,576
1974	12,817	13,193	13,394	12,947	13,880	12,926	15,660	14,450	14,489	14,003	12,391	13,708
1975	12,423	11,572	10,890	12,825	12,913	12,828	12,206	13,735	11,460	11,399	11,261	10,835
1976	13,379	13,140	13,648	13,706	12,094	14,417	15,837	14,085	15,372	15,800	14,401	15,057
1977	14,975	15,124	14,569	15,874	17,444	17,412	15,548	17,498	18,955	16,753	16,732	19,095
1978	18,167	20,579	18,713	18,898	23,460	19,781	20,805	22,261	23,183	26,369	22,173	19,823
1979	23,459	25,316	27,862	25,304	23,647	24,071	24,435	23,396	24,246	25,055	24,859	24,579
1980	26,334	23,845	24,358	23,852	21,537	22,937	24,684	24,307	24,332	25,425	23,865	25,569
1981	27,487	23,971	26,685	28,454	25,759	26,684	26,351	25,297	24,850	25,704	24,360	23,814
1982	26,344	27,131	25,465	24,397	21,228	21,804	22,550	21,330	22,316	22,767	21,389	23,842
1983	22,001	20,383	21,475	23,144	24,262	24,088	22,184	23,923	25,288	26,618	24,671	23,899
1984	27,446	27,413	27,923	26,839	30,497	28,126	29,297	27,644	27,150	28,311	28,056	26,827
1985	27,843	30,612	29,886	27,713	28,357	29,130	28,825	29,117	30,994	31,126	27,817	31,384
1986	28,820	30,145	28,539	27,942	27,683	28,047	27,633	27,434	28,459	29,140	28,882	30,389
1987	29,259	28,692	28,518	29,750	31,190	32,211	33,466	30,651	30,538	31,947	31,938	34,731
1988	35,452	35,804	33,330	33,964	32,529	35,175	36,582	39,824	35,960	34,236	36,032	39,083
1989	40,749	37,343	37,459	39,388	36,623	39,145	41,023	35,517	36,238	35,062	37,769	44,633
1990	39,255	36,037	40,500	36,922	36,725	36,257	40,046	35,024	38,195	41,177	35,711	41,547
1991	36,787	37,048	34,853	33,636	31,771	30,441	40,488	34,237	33,061	33,950	36,925	30,762
1992	35,409	35,310	37,151	37,945	36,065	35,796	35,472	33,514	36,213	36,600	32,303	38,790
1993	33,360	36,754	34,402	36,149	34,572	38,299	34,273	35,645	34,523	36,588	38,607	38,444
1994	40,813	39,890	39,432	38,401	38,096	41,349	39,722	41,492	41,766	40,675	43,530	41,963
1995	44,832	45,262	45,194	43,275	47,301	45,064	42,421	44,100	49,170	45,785	49,408	51,595
1996	50,730	48,510	51,441	46,754	50,534	47,798	50,931	46,272	52,979	50,816	48,665	48,728
1997	55,312	51,417	49,186	49,625	49,363	52,712	53,331	53,109	54,353	-	-	-

Source: The Conference Board. Primary source(s): U.S. Department of Commerce, Bureau of the Census, Manufacturing and Construction Division, Manufacturers' Shipments, Inventories, and Orders Branch, Washington, DC 20233. F.W. Dodge; McGraw-Hill, Inc., Market Analysis Group, 24 Hartwell Avenue, Lexington, MA 02173. Deflators calculated by The Conference Board. A dash (-) indicates that data are not available or zero.

New Private Housing Units Started
(Annual Rate, Thousands)

Year	Jan	Feb	Mar	Apr	May	Jun	Jul	Aug	Sep	Oct	Nov	Dec
1946	1,040	1,085	1,167	1,057	1,028	985	972	1,007	958	974	957	991
1947	1,052	1,074	1,032	1,039	1,090	1,174	1,252	1,355	1,532	1,571	1,557	1,447
1948	1,385	1,200	1,379	1,501	1,450	1,441	1,419	1,329	1,303	1,190	1,196	1,218
1949	1,196	1,137	1,171	1,292	1,319	1,341	1,384	1,500	1,603	1,662	1,785	1,824
1950	1,883	1,834	1,976	1,945	2,052	2,042	2,051	2,121	1,821	1,605	1,561	1,900
1951	1,928	1,638	1,481	1,352	1,359	1,419	1,257	1,334	1,456	1,386	1,324	1,330
1952	1,388	1,516	1,483	1,412	1,408	1,353	1,438	1,443	1,483	1,513	1,475	1,476
1953	1,484	1,460	1,506	1,498	1,425	1,380	1,346	1,324	1,348	1,342	1,383	1,343
1954	1,358	1,417	1,411	1,433	1,412	1,498	1,559	1,563	1,618	1,610	1,730	1,807
1955	1,757	1,664	1,684	1,708	1,730	1,704	1,632	1,625	1,580	1,490	1,434	1,431
1956	1,441	1,444	1,401	1,408	1,375	1,325	1,289	1,313	1,234	1,266	1,212	1,184
1957	1,151	1,168	1,173	1,147	1,174	1,175	1,191	1,193	1,191	1,204	1,162	1,146
1958	1,170	1,107	1,108	1,154	1,191	1,236	1,337	1,374	1,451	1,472	1,593	1,598
1959	1,657	1,667	1,620	1,590	1,498	1,503	1,547	1,430	1,540	1,355	1,416	1,601
1960	1,460	1,503	1,109	1,289	1,271	1,247	1,197	1,344	1,097	1,246	1,246	1,063
1961	1,183	1,226	1,312	1,166	1,228	1,382	1,335	1,312	1,429	1,415	1,385	1,365
1962	1,361	1,278	1,443	1,524	1,483	1,404	1,450	1,517	1,324	1,533	1,622	1,564
1963	1,244	1,456	1,534	1,689	1,641	1,588	1,614	1,639	1,763	1,779	1,622	1,491
1964	1,603	1,820	1,517	1,448	1,467	1,550	1,562	1,569	1,455	1,524	1,486	1,484
1965	1,361	1,433	1,423	1,438	1,478	1,488	1,529	1,432	1,482	1,452	1,460	1,656
1966	1,370	1,378	1,394	1,352	1,265	1,194	1,086	1,119	1,046	843	961	990
1967	1,067	1,123	1,056	1,091	1,304	1,248	1,364	1,407	1,421	1,491	1,538	1,308
1968	1,380	1,520	1,466	1,554	1,408	1,405	1,512	1,495	1,556	1,569	1,630	1,548
1969	1,769	1,705	1,561	1,524	1,583	1,528	1,368	1,358	1,507	1,381	1,229	1,327
1970	1,085	1,305	1,319	1,264	1,290	1,385	1,517	1,399	1,534	1,580	1,647	1,893
1971	1,828	1,741	1,910	1,986	2,049	2,026	2,083	2,158	2,041	2,128	2,182	2,295
1972	2,494	2,390	2,334	2,249	2,221	2,254	2,252	2,382	2,481	2,485	2,421	2,366
1973	2,481	2,289	2,365	2,084	2,266	2,067	2,123	2,051	1,874	1,677	1,724	1,526
1974	1,451	1,752	1,555	1,607	1,426	1,513	1,316	1,142	1,150	1,070	1,026	975
1975	1,032	904	993	1,005	1,121	1,087	1,226	1,260	1,264	1,344	1,360	1,321
1976	1,367	1,538	1,421	1,395	1,459	1,495	1,401	1,550	1,720	1,629	1,641	1,804
1977	1,527	1,943	2,063	1,892	1,971	1,893	2,058	2,020	1,949	2,042	2,042	2,142
1978	1,718	1,738	2,032	2,197	2,075	2,070	2,092	1,996	1,970	1,981	2,094	2,044
1979	1,630	1,520	1,847	1,748	1,876	1,913	1,760	1,778	1,832	1,681	1,524	1,498
1980	1,341	1,350	1,047	1,051	927	1,196	1,269	1,436	1,471	1,523	1,510	1,482
1981	1,547	1,246	1,306	1,360	1,140	1,045	1,041	940	911	873	837	910
1982	843	866	931	917	1,025	902	1,166	1,046	1,144	1,173	1,372	1,303
1983	1,586	1,699	1,606	1,472	1,776	1,733	1,785	1,910	1,710	1,715	1,785	1,688
1984	1,897	2,260	1,663	1,851	1,774	1,843	1,732	1,586	1,698	1,590	1,689	1,612
1985	1,711	1,632	1,800	1,821	1,680	1,676	1,684	1,743	1,676	1,834	1,698	1,942
1986	1,972	1,848	1,876	1,933	1,854	1,847	1,782	1,807	1,687	1,681	1,623	1,833
1987	1,774	1,784	1,726	1,614	1,628	1,594	1,575	1,605	1,695	1,515	1,656	1,400
1988	1,271	1,473	1,532	1,573	1,421	1,478	1,467	1,493	1,492	1,522	1,569	1,563
1989	1,621	1,425	1,422	1,339	1,331	1,397	1,427	1,332	1,279	1,410	1,351	1,251
1990	1,551	1,437	1,289	1,248	1,212	1,177	1,171	1,115	1,110	1,014	1,145	969
1991	798	965	921	1,001	996	1,036	1,063	1,049	1,015	1,079	1,103	1,079
1992	1,176	1,250	1,297	1,099	1,214	1,145	1,139	1,226	1,186	1,244	1,214	1,227
1993	1,210	1,210	1,083	1,258	1,260	1,280	1,254	1,300	1,343	1,392	1,376	1,533
1994	1,272	1,337	1,564	1,465	1,526	1,409	1,439	1,450	1,474	1,450	1,511	1,455
1995	1,383	1,325	1,246	1,278	1,309	1,294	1,464	1,404	1,378	1,382	1,451	1,404
1996	1,444	1,520	1,429	1,522	1,476	1,488	1,492	1,515	1,470	1,407	1,486	1,353
1997	1,375	1,554	1,479	1,483	1,402	1,503	1,465	1,390	1,500	-	-	-

Source: The Conference Board. Primary source(s): U.S. Department of Commerce, Bureau of the Census, Manufacturing and Construction Division, Construction Starts Branch, Washington, DC 20233. A dash (-) indicates that data are not available or zero.

INDICATORS OF INVENTORIES AND INVENTORY INVESTMENT

Inventory levels tend to be leading indicators of economic activity. Inventories are built up in anticipation of sales; they stay high when sales do not materialize; they are depleted when the economy is growing rapidly, signaling overheating and the potential for inflation; they are "worked down" in anticipation of recession and built up in expectation of turn-arounds. Two series are shown:

> Change in business inventories
> Manufacturing trade inventories

Change in Business Inventories. The changes are reported quarterly for the 1947-1997 period in billions of chained 1992 dollars. The series is considered a leading indicator but is excluded from the composite index. See also the same category, stated in chained (1992) dollars as a component of GDP.

Manufacturing Trade Inventories. This series is presented for the 1959 to 1997 period in billions of chained 1992 dollars.

Change in Business Inventories

(Annual Rate, Billions of chained 1992 $)

Year	1st Quarter	2nd Quarter	3rd Quarter	4th Quarter
1947	-9.5	-5.1	-6.2	7.2
1948	14.0	22.1	23.3	16.0
1949	-0.3	-16.2	-6.2	-17.3
1950	6.7	10.0	13.5	43.3
1951	25.9	38.4	26.5	12.9
1952	14.6	-2.8	14.7	14.1
1953	11.9	10.6	6.4	-6.2
1954	-5.2	-9.4	-7.2	-2.5
1955	9.7	15.1	13.8	18.3
1956	16.7	12.5	9.5	8.9
1957	4.5	5.5	9.1	-7.2
1958	-9.3	-8.4	4.3	11.0
1959	10.9	23.7	3.5	14.6
1960	33.6	8.8	14.0	-14.3
1961	-7.0	4.6	20.0	16.7
1962	28.2	17.5	20.7	11.6
1963	25.0	15.4	19.0	11.8
1964	15.5	14.9	14.5	17.4
1965	38.2	29.1	29.0	24.7
1966	41.5	39.4	37.6	51.3
1967	46.1	23.5	30.6	27.9
1968	23.1	41.2	23.6	19.5
1969	33.9	28.7	29.7	15.5
1970	3.7	12.7	13.9	-8.7
1971	31.8	30.2	25.2	2.0
1972	12.1	33.1	35.6	18.2
1973	31.9	41.3	23.9	53.8
1974	23.7	25.8	9.4	34.6
1975	-23.2	-23.6	2.6	3.4
1976	28.1	38.6	33.4	19.0
1977	24.9	38.9	59.0	32.3
1978	46.0	43.1	42.6	41.6
1979	35.3	39.6	15.1	3.5
1980	9.0	-1.7	-43.8	-4.4
1981	44.3	11.5	50.0	26.8
1982	-21.9	-4.0	6.6	-43.0
1983	-38.4	-9.7	-0.7	26.1
1984	87.4	79.3	80.3	54.1
1985	29.5	27.2	25.4	38.5
1986	52.9	22.9	-16.3	-15.3
1987	29.7	14.8	1.4	59.8
1988	14.0	6.0	11.3	15.7
1989	41.2	43.8	25.4	22.8
1990	10.9	43.6	14.9	-27.8
1991	-17.1	-20.7	4.7	21.3
1992	-0.5	11.0	12.0	5.6
1993	32.3	16.6	15.3	24.2
1994	53.1	75.9	49.7	63.6
1995	48.5	21.6	17.0	22.2
1996	8.0	21.3	37.9	32.9
1997	63.7	77.6	51.5	-

Source: The Conference Board. Primary source(s): U.S. Department of Commerce, Bureau of Economic Analysis, National Income and Wealth Division, BE-54, Washington, DC 20230. A dash (-) indicates that data are not available or zero.

Manufacturing and Trade Inventories
(Billions of chained 1992 $)

Year	Jan	Feb	Mar	Apr	May	Jun	Jul	Aug	Sep	Oct	Nov	Dec
1959	232.47	233.60	235.81	239.47	240.27	242.00	243.39	244.87	244.10	244.62	244.36	247.84
1960	250.99	253.49	255.79	255.28	256.62	256.90	257.50	258.03	259.37	258.58	258.66	255.28
1961	254.76	253.81	252.55	252.55	252.98	252.91	253.13	255.22	256.78	256.98	258.62	259.32
1962	261.77	263.23	265.19	265.29	267.47	268.76	269.74	271.85	273.29	274.47	274.86	275.49
1963	276.97	277.88	278.78	279.08	280.25	281.67	283.02	285.27	286.21	287.72	288.82	288.90
1964	291.22	292.07	292.94	294.57	295.48	296.60	297.30	298.98	301.12	300.87	303.04	305.32
1965	308.48	309.70	313.63	315.16	316.85	318.76	321.82	325.21	324.64	325.26	327.36	329.28
1966	332.39	336.13	339.43	341.84	345.64	349.60	352.49	357.02	358.45	362.77	367.07	370.04
1967	375.09	377.02	379.02	380.51	381.53	381.11	382.42	386.78	386.26	386.51	389.64	391.85
1968	394.63	395.24	395.41	398.13	401.18	402.03	403.64	408.02	406.87	410.87	412.01	412.50
1969	414.38	416.72	418.71	420.39	422.38	423.33	426.02	429.44	430.45	433.07	433.78	435.43
1970	434.50	435.37	435.54	438.33	437.16	438.64	441.63	444.48	443.22	442.82	443.41	442.13
1971	444.68	445.44	448.14	449.78	451.38	451.90	453.51	456.58	457.20	457.74	456.69	458.26
1972	460.15	459.46	460.43	462.67	465.55	466.13	466.23	471.00	474.11	476.24	478.36	478.79
1973	483.18	485.81	487.46	489.72	491.35	494.36	497.14	496.46	497.96	501.01	505.20	509.38
1974	511.06	512.07	515.44	516.92	520.28	523.00	523.61	522.04	524.68	528.32	531.04	536.12
1975	535.42	531.81	527.34	526.52	522.79	519.94	519.05	518.48	518.37	520.02	518.08	516.82
1976	518.42	521.13	523.09	525.68	528.27	532.60	535.44	536.57	540.83	543.46	545.22	547.18
1977	549.13	550.52	552.00	554.51	556.33	558.05	560.23	563.75	567.61	568.28	570.98	573.68
1978	576.27	578.56	583.74	588.95	591.26	593.23	594.60	597.20	598.54	601.80	605.64	609.49
1979	613.19	615.88	616.54	620.13	622.27	624.42	629.65	629.21	626.51	628.86	628.60	629.34
1980	632.67	633.28	634.16	638.44	638.14	636.61	635.91	633.76	632.31	631.15	630.90	631.90
1981	634.33	637.49	638.45	636.69	638.43	640.45	642.91	643.87	646.07	646.07	650.43	647.77
1982	643.71	638.07	639.07	641.52	635.88	638.21	640.25	638.63	638.15	636.54	630.91	628.05
1983	623.48	622.55	619.15	619.74	620.49	621.08	622.17	625.72	628.77	630.23	634.81	639.54
1984	642.93	649.99	657.27	663.92	671.38	674.19	679.61	688.37	691.49	697.14	700.49	703.05
1985	702.79	705.98	705.35	707.16	706.96	709.27	711.76	714.18	712.84	715.72	717.74	718.66
1986	719.34	724.06	728.51	732.35	731.17	731.85	733.07	732.06	728.39	728.85	729.15	724.62
1987	727.92	729.48	733.54	735.82	738.81	740.34	739.68	738.93	741.68	747.18	751.13	755.85
1988	755.95	759.04	760.35	762.04	762.39	765.70	765.94	770.06	772.86	773.50	775.77	780.79
1989	785.59	788.56	790.76	792.84	797.44	801.82	806.85	808.03	808.83	812.29	817.62	817.57
1990	815.08	814.29	818.18	821.31	827.50	827.48	832.46	831.23	832.28	831.43	833.38	830.06
1991	834.00	833.42	827.37	826.54	822.10	821.19	820.92	820.51	824.29	825.94	826.78	829.15
1992	826.44	824.56	824.89	826.01	823.88	826.79	828.47	830.89	829.93	829.69	831.09	831.72
1993	837.13	840.64	846.14	848.26	848.24	850.46	851.31	851.51	855.76	855.67	859.14	859.11
1994	861.33	864.98	866.14	868.27	876.39	879.90	883.72	887.19	888.80	893.64	896.27	900.99
1995	906.89	908.26	911.73	915.19	916.08	919.46	921.68	922.33	925.13	929.50	929.52	928.09
1996	931.20	931.21	928.68	933.11	931.87	931.82	936.67	937.72	939.10	942.58	945.36	945.24
1997	948.55	953.34	955.06	961.32	964.29	968.57	970.61	974.50	-	-	-	-

Source: The Conference Board. Primary source(s): U.S. Department of Commerce, Bureau of Economic Analysis, National Income and Wealth Division, BE-54, Washington, DC 20230. A dash (-) indicates that data are not available or zero.

INDICATORS OF PRICES, COSTS, AND PROFITS

Prices, profits, and certain kinds of costs tend to react rapidly to changes in the economy—or anticipated changes. They tend, therefore, to be leading indicators. Some costs, however, most notably wages, are lagging indicators because institutional factors work against rapid response to changing circumstances. Four series are presented:

> Index of sensitive materials prices
> Corporate profits after tax
> Index of unit labor costs, all persons, business

Three related series, reported under Business Cycle Indicators, are:

> Index of stock prices (Leading Index)
> Index of labor cost per unit of output, manufacturing (Lagging Index)
> Consumer price index for services (Lagging Index)

Index of Sensitive Materials Prices. The index is based on 1992 (1992 = 100) and is available for 1959 through 1997. "Sensitive materials" are those most vital to a modern economy: metals, fibers, and minerals. Being raw materials (rather than finished components), they are purchased early in the production cycle and therefore can predict future economic behavior. A series showing *changes* in these prices is included in the composite index of leading indicators.

Corporate Profits after Tax. Data are available in billions of current dollars (1946-1997) and in billions of chainged 1992 dollars (1959-1997), on a quarterly, annualized basis. The series is classified as a leading indicator. The leading character of this series is explained by the fact that corporate profits tend to decline even as the economy is still reaching for a peak; the *rate* of economic growth slows before the economy turns around. Similarly, the rate of decline slows before a turn-around, with the consequence that profits improve before the economy as a whole reflects the shift.

Index of Unit Labor Costs, All Persons, Business. This lagging indicator is available in quarterly increments from 1947 to 1997; it is based on 1992 (1992 = 100). A similar index, for manufacturing only, is included in the composite index of lagging indicators. The lagging character of the index is explained by the fact that wage costs respond more slowly to economic cycles than do prices.

Economic Indicators Handbook, 4th Edition   **Cyclic Indicators**

Index of Sensitive Materials Prices
(1992 = 100)

Year	Jan	Feb	Mar	Apr	May	Jun	Jul	Aug	Sep	Oct	Nov	Dec
1959	30.56	30.74	31.30	31.61	31.97	32.26	32.13	32.28	32.54	32.70	32.61	32.91
1960	32.95	32.75	32.37	32.48	32.43	32.11	31.80	31.80	31.63	31.35	31.05	30.83
1961	30.74	31.06	31.55	31.75	31.76	31.19	31.24	31.48	31.41	31.16	30.54	31.08
1962	31.35	31.12	30.95	30.58	30.68	30.33	30.13	30.01	30.00	30.09	30.22	30.08
1963	30.17	30.01	29.96	29.79	29.93	30.19	30.55	30.52	30.29	30.64	31.02	31.15
1964	31.25	31.30	31.52	32.11	31.67	32.00	32.19	32.82	33.42	34.27	34.46	34.64
1965	34.00	34.01	34.17	34.71	35.26	35.21	35.28	35.62	35.62	35.58	35.52	35.73
1966	36.09	36.37	36.60	36.64	36.35	36.23	36.10	34.89	34.45	33.83	33.65	33.35
1967	33.34	32.85	32.26	31.68	31.63	31.99	31.86	31.64	31.79	31.63	31.65	31.98
1968	31.66	31.59	32.11	31.64	31.33	31.61	31.63	31.70	32.07	32.72	33.37	33.87
1969	34.58	35.20	35.53	35.82	35.82	36.04	36.31	37.10	37.75	37.51	37.77	37.97
1970	37.69	36.97	36.58	36.34	36.28	35.88	35.25	35.19	34.83	35.01	34.96	34.33
1971	33.92	33.96	34.34	34.91	34.23	34.14	34.40	34.73	35.12	35.15	35.30	35.46
1972	36.21	36.19	37.36	37.73	39.53	39.89	40.40	40.70	41.22	42.36	43.87	44.91
1973	46.33	48.46	50.24	51.86	52.39	54.54	56.18	58.82	58.81	59.84	61.73	66.78
1974	68.36	69.68	72.24	72.43	70.55	70.30	70.74	69.84	68.85	65.72	63.74	60.40
1975	58.68	57.61	56.82	57.40	58.07	56.00	55.70	57.44	60.00	59.71	59.70	60.59
1976	61.05	60.68	60.85	62.36	63.44	64.57	67.57	67.24	67.87	67.12	67.27	68.01
1977	68.54	69.26	71.36	70.80	70.58	68.94	69.32	70.11	70.11	70.29	70.02	71.48
1978	72.10	72.29	71.81	72.22	72.53	75.34	76.12	77.86	79.33	81.44	82.99	82.52
1979	83.60	85.92	88.97	92.02	93.77	95.14	96.39	95.45	94.78	98.20	99.74	100.60
1980	102.45	104.42	104.87	99.61	95.05	94.33	95.41	97.92	99.28	100.58	101.90	100.85
1981	98.62	95.97	96.68	97.84	98.13	98.02	98.68	98.90	95.87	94.42	92.47	91.12
1982	90.20	88.96	86.99	84.39	83.50	81.84	82.29	81.02	81.30	80.35	79.06	78.78
1983	80.00	82.59	83.23	83.73	84.79	86.24	87.40	89.93	90.89	92.48	94.57	95.92
1984	96.13	96.82	98.59	98.66	97.73	98.04	96.75	94.44	93.83	91.11	91.61	91.13
1985	89.13	88.10	87.72	87.24	86.53	84.80	84.02	83.19	82.37	81.92	81.26	81.32
1986	81.59	81.06	79.13	78.09	78.68	79.75	80.76	78.11	79.79	83.24	85.64	86.36
1987	87.54	86.65	86.88	88.78	92.14	93.26	95.21	97.10	98.17	99.39	98.19	99.63
1988	100.59	101.07	102.99	103.95	104.70	106.35	106.61	107.01	106.11	106.05	110.72	113.66
1989	115.79	118.36	119.76	117.97	116.89	115.69	114.50	113.31	113.60	114.41	112.11	109.14
1990	107.52	106.28	107.80	108.77	108.80	108.71	108.76	109.27	109.67	109.10	106.66	105.87
1991	105.00	102.82	100.95	99.95	99.48	98.99	99.12	97.84	96.41	96.41	97.04	97.33
1992	96.61	97.39	99.63	101.03	101.85	101.92	101.69	101.78	102.20	100.14	97.64	98.12
1993	99.05	98.98	97.42	95.59	94.53	94.38	94.40	94.23	93.92	95.09	95.97	97.56
1994	98.97	101.43	102.55	103.09	104.67	106.74	109.31	110.93	114.23	117.10	121.20	122.73
1995	124.85	123.43	123.75	124.73	124.85	125.06	124.22	122.16	120.93	120.83	120.75	117.97
1996	116.59	116.01	116.20	116.65	117.81	117.19	116.76	118.55	119.42	118.57	117.70	118.19
1997	119.94	120.95	120.98	119.13	120.50	120.68	120.85	122.47	122.40	-	-	-

Source: The Conference Board. Primary source(s): U.S. Department of Labor, Bureau of Labor Statistics, Office of Prices and Living Conditions, Division of Industrial Prices and Price Indexes, Washington, DC 20212 and Knight-Ridder Financial, 30 South Wacker Drive, Suite 1810, Chicago, IL 60606. A dash (-) indicates that data are not available or zero.

Corporate Profits After Tax

(Annual Rate, Billions of $)

Year	1st Quarter	2nd Quarter	3rd Quarter	4th Quarter
1946	10.8	13.9	18.1	20.5
1947	21.2	20.0	19.8	21.7
1948	22.9	24.1	23.7	23.0
1949	21.0	18.5	19.2	18.8
1950	19.3	23.0	28.0	30.8
1951	25.5	21.7	19.9	21.6
1952	20.9	20.0	20.1	22.1
1953	22.8	22.8	22.2	17.4
1954	20.0	20.6	22.0	23.7
1955	26.8	27.2	27.8	28.9
1956	28.1	28.7	27.4	29.0
1957	29.3	28.0	27.4	25.0
1958	21.4	21.8	24.3	27.7
1959	29.6	32.2	28.9	28.3
1960	31.1	28.7	27.5	26.5
1961	25.8	27.2	28.8	31.1
1962	31.7	31.7	32.7	33.5
1963	32.9	34.7	35.6	36.6
1964	39.7	39.6	40.6	40.1
1965	45.8	47.4	48.0	50.7
1966	51.8	51.9	51.5	50.5
1967	48.1	48.1	49.1	51.4
1968	49.9	51.0	51.2	52.7
1969	51.7	50.0	48.4	47.4
1970	44.7	44.4	44.9	42.1
1971	48.8	50.7	54.2	55.7
1972	59.4	60.1	62.8	68.3
1973	79.1	81.2	81.3	85.0
1974	89.0	91.2	97.1	86.8
1975	75.8	81.0	97.8	103.4
1976	108.5	109.4	110.0	110.3
1977	121.7	129.8	135.2	134.9
1978	137.8	154.3	158.3	168.1
1979	168.4	174.4	178.4	173.8
1980	174.6	144.9	151.6	155.3
1981	160.5	144.6	148.4	141.0
1982	113.9	116.3	113.5	111.0
1983	113.8	137.0	147.5	143.9
1984	156.8	157.2	145.3	141.3
1985	129.1	131.7	134.6	138.3
1986	112.5	113.1	115.7	123.0
1987	144.4	167.3	173.8	180.6
1988	201.0	217.1	220.3	231.0
1989	219.3	206.7	196.9	204.4
1990	221.7	232.2	233.9	237.1
1991	240.7	236.4	238.6	247.6
1992	267.2	275.2	240.4	270.6
1993	282.5	296.1	298.4	324.0
1994	312.1	342.5	361.6	377.7
1995	401.0	405.9	411.8	418.8
1996	438.7	450.0	447.5	454.0
1997	467.2	475.3	-	-

Source: The Conference Board. Primary source(s): U.S. Department of Commerce, Bureau of Economic Analysis, National Income and Wealth Division, BE-54, Washington, DC 20230. A dash (-) indicates that data are not available or zero.

Corporate Profits After Tax
(Annual Rate, Billions of 1992 $)

Year	1st Quarter	2nd Quarter	3rd Quarter	4th Quarter
1959	108.8	117.6	107.2	105.2
1960	114.2	106.4	102.6	98.9
1961	96.8	101.4	106.8	114.6
1962	116.2	116.6	119.7	122.0
1963	120.2	126.3	129.0	132.3
1964	142.7	142.4	145.7	143.7
1965	161.6	166.7	168.2	177.1
1966	179.9	178.6	176.2	171.2
1967	164.0	163.7	166.0	170.7
1968	166.2	168.1	167.5	170.2
1969	165.5	159.4	153.1	148.8
1970	139.0	135.9	135.8	126.6
1971	142.7	145.8	153.2	155.8
1972	164.2	165.3	170.9	183.0
1973	207.6	209.7	207.1	213.0
1974	218.0	216.4	221.8	192.3
1975	165.4	171.5	200.5	208.1
1976	216.5	217.0	215.8	213.9
1977	230.5	240.6	246.1	241.8
1978	243.0	265.1	267.8	279.0
1979	274.1	277.4	277.1	265.7
1980	261.1	216.2	220.5	221.2
1981	222.9	200.5	202.7	190.3
1982	155.9	156.5	151.8	148.8
1983	152.8	179.1	190.9	186.1
1984	199.8	198.7	184.1	178.9
1985	164.4	166.8	169.5	172.7
1986	144.0	145.5	147.5	154.2
1987	175.5	198.9	204.7	210.4
1988	231.1	246.4	248.1	257.1
1989	243.3	228.1	216.8	222.7
1990	238.4	246.7	245.6	245.8
1991	247.7	242.5	243.7	251.0
1992	269.1	275.9	239.9	268.6
1993	278.7	290.9	292.3	316.0
1994	302.9	330.8	346.9	360.9
1995	381.1	383.9	388.2	393.8
1996	410.5	420.3	416.1	420.7
1997	431.2	438.5	-	-

Source: The Conference Board. Primary source(s): U.S. Department of Commerce, Bureau of Economic Analysis, National Income and Wealth Division, BE-54, Washington, DC 20230. A dash (-) indicates that data are not available or zero.

Unit Labor Cost, All Persons, Business Sector

(1992 = 100)

Year	1st Quarter	2nd Quarter	3rd Quarter	4th Quarter
1947	20.0	20.0	20.1	20.6
1948	20.6	20.5	21.2	21.6
1949	21.2	20.8	20.5	20.8
1950	20.5	20.5	20.5	20.8
1951	21.6	22.0	21.8	22.1
1952	22.2	22.5	22.7	23.0
1953	23.0	23.1	23.4	23.4
1954	23.6	23.6	23.3	23.3
1955	22.9	23.0	23.1	23.5
1956	24.2	24.6	24.9	24.9
1957	25.3	25.5	25.4	25.6
1958	26.2	25.9	25.8	25.8
1959	25.9	25.7	25.9	26.1
1960	26.1	26.6	26.5	27.0
1961	27.0	26.7	26.5	26.5
1962	26.5	26.7	26.6	26.7
1963	26.6	26.6	26.4	26.7
1964	26.5	26.6	26.7	27.1
1965	26.9	27.0	26.7	26.6
1966	26.8	27.4	27.8	28.0
1967	28.0	28.3	28.6	28.8
1968	29.1	29.3	29.9	30.5
1969	30.6	31.4	32.0	32.8
1970	33.3	33.3	33.3	33.9
1971	33.6	34.0	34.2	34.8
1972	35.2	34.8	35.1	35.4
1973	35.8	36.4	37.6	38.1
1974	39.4	40.5	42.2	43.0
1975	43.7	43.7	43.8	44.7
1976	45.1	45.8	46.7	47.4
1977	48.0	48.6	49.1	50.5
1978	52.1	52.0	53.0	54.2
1979	56.2	57.4	58.8	60.4
1980	61.7	64.4	65.8	66.7
1981	67.3	69.3	69.8	71.8
1982	74.1	74.7	75.8	75.9
1983	76.0	75.5	75.7	76.2
1984	76.4	76.7	77.5	78.2
1985	78.8	79.5	79.5	80.7
1986	80.5	81.0	81.9	83.2
1987	84.2	84.4	85.0	86.0
1988	86.7	88.1	88.9	89.3
1989	89.3	89.4	90.0	91.1
1990	92.2	93.6	95.1	96.9
1991	97.4	97.9	98.6	99.3
1992	99.3	99.6	101.0	100.1
1993	101.7	102.7	103.0	102.3
1994	103.3	103.2	103.9	104.3
1995	105.6	106.1	106.7	107.0
1996	107.1	107.7	108.8	109.2
1997	109.9	110.0	-	-

Source: The Conference Board. Primary source(s): U.S. Department of Labor, Bureau of Labor Statistics, Office of Productivity and Technology, Division of Productivity Research, Washington, DC 20212. A dash (-) indicates that data are not available or zero.

INDICATORS OF MONEY AND CREDIT

This section presents 9 series commonly used to measure the relationships between the economy and money, expressed in measures of money supply, interest and other yields on investments, and credit. These indicators are leading, coincident, or lagging depending on the nature of the series. The series presented are:

> Free reserves
> Member bank borrowings from the Federal Reserve
> Federal funds rate
> Discount rate on new issues of 91-day Treasury bills
> Yield on new high-grade corporate bonds
> Yield on long-term Treasury bonds
> Yield on municipal bonds, 20-bond average
> Secondary market yields on FHA mortgages
> Commercial and industrial loans outstanding, current dollars

Three related series, reported under Business Cycle Indicators, are:

> Money supply M2 (Leading Index)
> Commercial and industrial loans (Lagging Index)
> Average prime rate charged by banks (Lagging Index)

Free Reserves. Data are for 1959 to 1997 in millions of dollars; data are not seasonally adjusted. Free reserves are funds held by banks that may be loaned out. Banks are required by the Federal Reserve System to hold reserves in a fixed ratio to their total deposits (the "reserve ratio"). Deposits in excess of the required reserve less borrowings from the Federal Reserve System, are "free" to be lent.

The series is a leading indicator at business cycle peaks. It is an "inverted" indicator: for cyclical analysis, changes from period to period are inverted; a growth is depicted as negative growth, a decline as a growth. A pattern of decreasing free reserves signals an increasing demand for money for purchases, that is, increasing economic activity; a pattern of increasing free reserves indicates the opposite—no demand for money. Thus by "inverting the sign" of this indicator, the right message is obtained. The series is undefined at cycle troughs and overall.

Member Bank Borrowings from the Federal Reserve. To some extent this series is the inverse of the previous series. Both are shown in millions of current dollars. Members of the Federal Reserve System may borrow from the Fed for short-term purposes paying the prevailing "discount rate" charged by each Federal Reserve bank. Banks borrow to satisfy immediate needs for cash, to maintain required reserve ratios, and to meet contingencies (such as, for instance, sudden withdrawals which exceed the bank's cash reserves). Member borrowings and free reserves move in tandem. With high free reserves on hand, banks borrow less.

The series is classified as a leading indicator of cycle peaks and as a lagging indicator of troughs. Before a business cycle peaks, growth will tend to slow and member borrowings therefore fall before the economy stops growing. On a resumption of growth, member borrowings will tend to lag because members have high levels of free reserves.

Federal Funds Rate. Shown for 1954 through 1997 as a percent. This is the interest rate charged in the interbank market for bank purchases of excess reserve balances. Excess reserves are bank money holdings that exceed minimum deposit requirements; excess reserves minus loans outstanding to the Fed are "free reserves" (see above). Therefore excess reserves are free reserves plus obligations outstanding to the Fed. These assets may be bought and sold in the federal funds market at an interest rate called the federal funds rate. Unlike the discount rate, the funds rate changes with each transaction.

The series is a leading indicator of cycle peaks and a lagging indicator of troughs; slowing demand for reserves as a business cycle draws to its close causes a drop in the funds rate; as the economy turns around, some time passes before bank demand for reserves causes the funds rate to rise again.

Discount Rate on New Issues of 91-Day Treasury Bills. Data are shown for 1946 through 1997 as a percent. Treasury bills are short-term securities issued by the Treasury; 91-day Treasury bills have the shortest maturities. The bills are purchased at prices below the face value (minimum $10,0000); the difference between face value and purchase price is the discount rate. The bills are sold at auction; hence the discount rate is set by market forces. The Federal Reserve usually buys or sells treasury bills to carry out its open market operations; purchases act to decrease money supply; sales act to increase money supply. The series acts as a coincident indicator of the peak of business cycles and as a lagging indicator of troughs.

Yield on New Issues of High-Grade Corporate Bonds. Data for 1946 through 1997 are shown as percent. Bonds are long-term debt instruments issued by corporations; high-grade "corporates" are bonds with high ratings for security based on the financial strength of the issuer. The yield percentage will tend to decline *after* a recessionary trend is well established and turn up *after* a recovery is clearly under way; hence the series is regarded as a lagging indicator of the business cycle.

Yield on Long-Term Treasury Bonds. Data for 1945 through 1997 are shown in percent. Long-term Treasury bonds are debt instruments sold by the U.S. Treasury with maturities of 10 years or more in denominations of $1,000. The series is a coincident indicator of business cycle peaks and a lagging indictor of troughs.

Yield on Municipal Bonds, 20-Bond Average. These instruments are governmental debt instruments sold by municipalities. Data are shown in percent from 1948 through 1997. The series is classified as a lagging indicator of the trough of business cycles; it is unclassified at the peak, indicating behavior that does not follow any discernible pattern. Since most municipal bond yields ("public purpose bonds") are tax exempt, yields will tend to rise in an expanding economy where tax shelters are more valuable than in a declining economy.

Secondary Market Yields on FHA Mortgages. Data are shown in percent from 1949 to 1997. The primary market for Federal Housing Administration (FHA) or other mortgages is that defined by the home buyer and the original mortgage lender. The lender can then sell the loan—at a discount, of course—to investors. This second transaction is the secondary market for mortgages. The original lender receives cash for lending (increases his/her liquidity); the investor obtains an asset. Government agencies buy the original mortgages, assemble them into mortgage pools, and sell them as collateralized mortgage obligations.

The series is a lagging indicator. Before mortgages can be resold, people have to buy homes and take out mortgages. The secondary market, therefore, will tend to "soften" after a downturn in the economy; although housing starts tend to lead an expansion, housing purchases come later and secondary mortgage operations even later than that—explaining the lagging character of this series.

Commercial and Industrial Loans Outstanding, Current Dollars. This series is shown for 1945 through 1997 in millions of current dollars. The same series, in chained 1992 dollars, is a lagging indicator—as is this series. Business and industry assume debt in periods of growth and minimize debt in periods of decline. The total debt outstanding, however, reflects the business cycle at a lag in time; borrowers pay off debt over time and may be late in paying during economic turn-downs; they also contract new obligations later than the economy's upturn because both lenders and borrowers are more cautious after a recessionary period.

Free Reserves
Not seasonally adjusted
(Millions of $)

Year	Jan	Feb	Mar	Apr	May	Jun	Jul	Aug	Sep	Oct	Nov	Dec
1959	-54	-51	-139	-261	-320	-523	-545	-542	-484	-466	-415	-435
1960	-373	-356	-218	-180	-51	46	122	246	412	495	610	669
1961	706	516	476	559	461	527	562	514	542	461	493	451
1962	536	434	383	420	456	371	442	405	409	414	437	312
1963	359	295	286	327	220	158	156	116	109	77	92	158
1964	166	111	108	141	94	107	113	106	86	77	8	142
1965	115	7	-45	-130	-161	-175	-175	-151	-144	-130	-80	-21
1966	-41	-135	-218	-282	-346	-351	-363	-368	-398	-401	-222	-193
1967	-7	5	214	204	276	246	303	284	253	206	226	147
1968	141	13	-322	-350	-381	-366	-176	-236	-143	-198	-237	-320
1969	-490	-581	-683	-836	-1,119	-1,081	-1,027	-982	-805	-987	-974	-833
1970	-785	-872	-735	-693	-811	-691	-1,194	-663	-356	-258	-181	-83
1971	-130	-78	-124	15	-65	-291	-639	-613	-306	-194	-147	56
1972	185	119	92	38	28	103	-45	-200	-329	-344	-254	-766
1973	-902	-1,396	-1,615	-1,488	-1,704	-1,626	-1,638	-1,968	-1,595	-1,208	-1,168	-994
1974	-886	-1,007	-1,180	-1,554	-1,772	-1,582	-1,709	-1,611	-1,472	-1,208	-887	-322
1975	-115	100	131	59	93	-10	-93	-4	-192	28	228	148
1976	173	147	172	111	95	87	101	107	139	125	185	221
1977	198	126	112	119	2	-115	-48	-861	-417	-1,096	-611	-379
1978	-217	-165	-129	-409	-993	-916	-1,120	-972	-867	-1,115	-481	-636
1979	-789	-764	-833	-742	-1,624	-1,197	-960	-863	-1,149	-1,750	-1,661	-1,031
1980	-990	-1,444	-2,538	-1,706	-97	131	142	-115	-964	-1,104	-1,539	-1,173
1981	-951	-933	-705	-1,161	-1,960	-1,692	-1,336	-1,048	-741	-465	-154	-169
1982	-902	-1,253	-886	-1,050	-582	-793	-327	-109	-430	68	-31	52
1983	176	132	-42	-128	10	-198	-368	-609	-428	-83	-370	-211
1984	-98	356	-246	-701	-2,381	-659	-287	-289	-153	-365	-73	273
1985	364	378	139	296	-48	376	222	320	30	176	-295	218
1986	848	688	635	497	557	642	507	319	252	366	596	846
1987	728	925	652	124	327	712	329	527	257	622	719	752
1988	592	957	642	496	583	367	116	382	220	545	610	575
1989	533	700	427	217	513	333	378	250	266	486	617	678
1990	603	76	687	672	503	238	385	68	291	455	742	1,361
1991	1,662	1,590	991	886	815	676	345	622	586	834	785	788
1992	771	990	939	1,049	845	684	681	684	707	931	939	1,032
1993	1,095	1,059	1,122	1,023	875	730	845	600	662	804	1,012	981
1994	1,375	1,070	912	1,027	715	772	649	535	573	424	759	959
1995	1,207	887	725	642	730	692	719	706	672	836	739	1,021
1996	1,447	816	1,116	1,029	733	764	697	627	670	707	821	1,269
1997	1,178	989	1,004	749	997	913	792	655	857	-	-	-

Source: The Conference Board. Primary source(s): Board of Governors of the Federal Reserve System, Division of Monetary Affairs, Money and Reserve Projections Section, Stop 59, Washington, DC 20551. A dash (-) indicates that data are not available or zero.

Member Bank Borrowings From Federal Reserve
Not seasonally adjusted
(Millions of $)

Year	Jan	Feb	Mar	Apr	May	Jun	Jul	Aug	Sep	Oct	Nov	Dec
1947	106	203	173	126	107	135	92	127	133	171	274	224
1948	143	244	270	111	144	100	95	87	128	111	118	134
1949	169	110	148	98	176	100	109	94	75	46	134	118
1950	35	123	128	101	80	68	123	164	96	67	145	142
1951	212	330	242	161	438	170	194	292	338	95	340	657
1952	210	365	307	367	563	579	1,077	1,032	683	1,048	1,532	1,593
1953	1,347	1,310	1,202	1,166	944	423	418	651	468	362	486	441
1954	100	293	189	139	155	146	65	115	67	82	164	246
1955	313	354	463	495	368	401	527	765	849	884	1,016	839
1956	807	799	993	1,060	971	769	738	898	792	715	744	688
1957	406	640	834	1,011	909	1,005	917	1,005	988	811	804	710
1958	451	242	138	130	119	142	109	252	476	425	486	557
1959	552	505	599	692	741	930	961	990	927	907	859	941
1960	887	810	641	606	496	434	379	296	215	167	133	74
1961	66	133	70	57	95	63	54	65	38	71	98	133
1962	87	68	89	72	61	102	92	125	81	63	120	260
1963	146	166	148	130	210	259	298	329	319	320	349	332
1964	274	286	278	211	260	268	263	315	345	321	400	264
1965	300	405	411	471	495	537	528	547	554	488	432	444
1966	420	482	560	637	687	707	741	735	769	734	607	532
1967	410	364	200	146	89	106	115	81	89	129	132	228
1968	246	373	659	685	741	694	527	565	504	443	545	746
1969	736	835	902	1,003	1,374	1,385	1,252	1,219	1,079	1,150	1,203	1,119
1970	959	1,080	898	845	968	881	1,360	837	600	463	415	332
1971	364	332	319	153	284	492	823	809	495	357	384	126
1972	21	33	98	118	111	100	238	388	541	555	608	1,050
1973	1,160	1,593	1,824	1,711	1,843	1,851	1,953	2,165	1,852	1,476	1,393	1,298
1974	1,051	1,191	1,314	1,736	2,590	3,006	3,301	3,336	3,282	1,813	1,252	727
1975	398	147	106	110	66	227	301	211	397	190	60	130
1976	78	81	54	44	115	127	133	100	62	94	72	53
1977	68	72	103	73	206	262	323	1,061	626	1,306	862	569
1978	484	406	328	557	1,212	1,094	1,317	1,140	1,060	1,277	703	868
1979	1,003	973	991	918	1,765	1,418	1,171	1,085	1,340	2,022	1,906	1,473
1980	1,241	1,655	2,823	2,455	1,018	379	395	658	1,311	1,310	2,060	1,690
1981	1,395	1,304	1,000	1,338	2,223	2,037	1,679	1,420	1,456	1,181	663	636
1982	1,517	1,789	1,555	1,568	1,117	1,205	691	515	933	477	621	634
1983	529	582	792	1,009	952	1,636	1,453	1,546	1,441	844	905	774
1984	715	567	952	1,234	2,988	3,300	5,924	8,017	7,242	6,017	4,617	3,186
1985	1,395	1,289	1,593	1,323	1,334	1,205	1,107	1,073	1,289	1,187	1,741	1,318
1986	770	884	761	893	876	803	741	872	1,008	841	752	827
1987	580	556	527	993	1,035	776	672	647	940	943	625	777
1988	1,082	396	1,752	2,993	2,578	3,083	3,440	3,241	2,839	2,299	2,861	1,716
1989	1,662	1,487	1,813	2,289	1,720	1,490	694	675	693	555	349	265
1990	440	1,448	2,124	1,628	1,335	881	757	927	624	410	230	326
1991	534	252	241	231	303	340	607	764	645	261	108	192
1992	233	77	91	90	155	229	284	251	287	143	104	124
1993	166	45	91	73	121	181	244	352	428	285	89	82
1994	73	70	55	124	200	333	458	469	487	380	249	209
1995	136	59	69	111	150	272	371	282	278	245	204	257
1996	38	35	21	91	127	386	368	334	368	287	214	155
1997	45	42	156	261	243	367	409	598	438	-	-	-

Source: The Conference Board. Primary source(s): Board of Governors of the Federal Reserve System, Division of Monetary Affairs, Money and Reserve Projections Section, Stop 59, Washington, DC 20551. A dash (-) indicates that data are not available or zero.

Federal Funds Rate
Not seasonally adjusted
(Percent)

Year	Jan	Feb	Mar	Apr	May	Jun	Jul	Aug	Sep	Oct	Nov	Dec
1954	-	-	-	-	-	-	0.80	1.22	1.06	0.85	0.83	1.28
1955	1.39	1.29	1.35	1.43	1.43	1.64	1.68	1.96	2.18	2.24	2.35	2.48
1956	2.45	2.50	2.50	2.62	2.75	2.71	2.75	2.73	2.95	2.96	2.88	2.94
1957	2.84	3.00	2.96	3.00	3.00	3.00	2.99	3.24	3.47	3.50	3.28	2.98
1958	2.72	1.67	1.20	1.26	0.63	0.93	0.68	1.53	1.76	1.80	2.27	2.42
1959	2.48	2.43	2.80	2.96	2.90	3.39	3.47	3.50	3.76	3.98	4.00	3.99
1960	3.99	3.97	3.84	3.92	3.85	3.32	3.23	2.98	2.60	2.47	2.44	1.98
1961	1.45	2.54	2.02	1.49	1.98	1.73	1.17	2.00	1.88	2.26	2.61	2.33
1962	2.15	2.37	2.85	2.78	2.36	2.68	2.71	2.93	2.90	2.90	2.94	2.93
1963	2.92	3.00	2.98	2.90	3.00	2.99	3.02	3.49	3.48	3.50	3.48	3.38
1964	3.48	3.48	3.43	3.47	3.50	3.50	3.42	3.50	3.45	3.36	3.52	3.85
1965	3.90	3.98	4.04	4.09	4.10	4.04	4.09	4.12	4.01	4.08	4.10	4.32
1966	4.42	4.60	4.65	4.67	4.90	5.17	5.30	5.53	5.40	5.53	5.76	5.40
1967	4.94	5.00	4.53	4.05	3.94	3.98	3.79	3.90	3.99	3.88	4.13	4.51
1968	4.60	4.71	5.05	5.76	6.11	6.07	6.02	6.03	5.78	5.91	5.82	6.02
1969	6.30	6.61	6.79	7.41	8.67	8.90	8.61	9.19	9.15	9.00	8.85	8.97
1970	8.98	8.98	7.76	8.10	7.94	7.60	7.21	6.61	6.29	6.20	5.60	4.90
1971	4.14	3.72	3.71	4.15	4.63	4.91	5.31	5.56	5.55	5.20	4.91	4.14
1972	3.50	3.29	3.83	4.17	4.27	4.46	4.55	4.80	4.87	5.04	5.06	5.33
1973	5.94	6.58	7.09	7.12	7.84	8.49	10.40	10.50	10.78	10.01	10.03	9.95
1974	9.65	8.97	9.35	10.51	11.31	11.93	12.92	12.01	11.34	10.06	9.45	8.53
1975	7.13	6.24	5.54	5.49	5.22	5.55	6.10	6.14	6.24	5.82	5.22	5.20
1976	4.87	4.77	4.84	4.82	5.29	5.48	5.31	5.29	5.25	5.02	4.95	4.65
1977	4.61	4.68	4.69	4.73	5.35	5.39	5.42	5.90	6.14	6.47	6.51	6.56
1978	6.70	6.78	6.79	6.89	7.36	7.60	7.81	8.04	8.45	8.96	9.76	10.03
1979	10.07	10.06	10.09	10.01	10.24	10.29	10.47	10.94	11.43	13.77	13.18	13.78
1980	13.82	14.13	17.19	17.61	10.98	9.47	9.03	9.61	10.87	12.81	15.85	18.90
1981	19.08	15.93	14.70	15.72	18.52	19.10	19.04	17.82	15.87	15.08	13.31	12.37
1982	13.22	14.78	14.68	14.94	14.45	14.15	12.59	10.12	10.31	9.71	9.20	8.95
1983	8.68	8.51	8.77	8.80	8.63	8.98	9.37	9.56	9.45	9.48	9.34	9.47
1984	9.56	9.59	9.91	10.29	10.32	11.06	11.23	11.64	11.30	9.99	9.43	8.38
1985	8.35	8.50	8.58	8.27	7.97	7.53	7.88	7.90	7.92	7.99	8.05	8.27
1986	8.14	7.86	7.48	6.99	6.85	6.92	6.56	6.17	5.89	5.85	6.04	6.91
1987	6.43	6.10	6.13	6.37	6.85	6.73	6.58	6.73	7.22	7.29	6.69	6.77
1988	6.83	6.58	6.58	6.87	7.09	7.51	7.75	8.01	8.19	8.30	8.35	8.76
1989	9.12	9.36	9.85	9.84	9.81	9.53	9.24	8.99	9.02	8.84	8.55	8.45
1990	8.23	8.24	8.28	8.26	8.18	8.29	8.15	8.13	8.20	8.11	7.81	7.31
1991	6.91	6.25	6.12	5.91	5.78	5.90	5.82	5.66	5.45	5.21	4.81	4.43
1992	4.03	4.06	3.98	3.73	3.82	3.76	3.25	3.30	3.22	3.10	3.09	2.92
1993	3.02	3.03	3.07	2.96	3.00	3.04	3.06	3.03	3.09	2.99	3.02	2.96
1994	3.05	3.25	3.34	3.56	4.01	4.25	4.26	4.47	4.73	4.76	5.29	5.45
1995	5.53	5.92	5.98	6.05	6.01	6.00	5.85	5.74	5.80	5.76	5.80	5.60
1996	5.56	5.22	5.31	5.22	5.24	5.27	5.40	5.22	5.30	5.24	5.31	5.29
1997	5.25	5.19	5.39	5.51	5.50	5.56	5.52	5.54	5.54	-	-	-

Source: The Conference Board. Primary source(s): Board of Governors of the Federal Reserve System, Division of Monetary Affairs, Banking and Money Market Statistics Section, Stop 81, Washington, DC 20551. A dash (-) indicates that data are not available or zero.

Discount Rate on New 91-Day Treasury Bills
Not seasonally adjusted
(Percent)

Year	Jan	Feb	Mar	Apr	May	Jun	Jul	Aug	Sep	Oct	Nov	Dec
1946	0.38	0.38	0.38	0.38	0.38	0.38	0.38	0.38	0.38	0.38	0.38	0.38
1947	0.38	0.38	0.38	0.38	0.38	0.38	0.64	0.74	0.79	0.84	0.92	0.95
1948	0.97	0.99	1.00	1.00	1.00	1.00	1.00	1.03	1.09	1.12	1.14	1.15
1949	1.16	1.16	1.16	1.16	1.15	1.16	0.98	1.02	1.06	1.04	1.06	1.10
1950	1.09	1.13	1.14	1.16	1.17	1.17	1.17	1.21	1.32	1.33	1.36	1.37
1951	1.39	1.39	1.42	1.52	1.58	1.50	1.59	1.64	1.65	1.61	1.61	1.73
1952	1.69	1.57	1.66	1.62	1.71	1.70	1.82	1.88	1.79	1.78	1.86	2.13
1953	2.04	2.02	2.08	2.18	2.20	2.23	2.10	2.09	1.88	1.40	1.43	1.63
1954	1.21	0.98	1.05	1.01	0.78	0.65	0.71	0.89	1.01	0.99	0.95	1.17
1955	1.26	1.18	1.34	1.62	1.49	1.43	1.62	1.88	2.09	2.26	2.23	2.56
1956	2.46	2.37	2.31	2.61	2.65	2.53	2.33	2.61	2.85	2.96	3.00	3.23
1957	3.21	3.17	3.14	3.11	3.04	3.32	3.17	3.40	3.58	3.59	3.34	3.10
1958	2.60	1.56	1.35	1.13	1.05	0.88	0.96	1.69	2.48	2.79	2.76	2.81
1959	2.84	2.71	2.85	2.96	2.85	3.25	3.24	3.36	4.00	4.12	4.21	4.57
1960	4.44	3.95	3.44	3.24	3.39	2.64	2.40	2.29	2.49	2.43	2.38	2.27
1961	2.30	2.41	2.42	2.33	2.29	2.36	2.27	2.40	2.30	2.35	2.46	2.62
1962	2.75	2.75	2.72	2.73	2.69	2.72	2.94	2.84	2.79	2.75	2.80	2.86
1963	2.91	2.92	2.90	2.91	2.92	2.99	3.14	3.32	3.38	3.45	3.52	3.52
1964	3.53	3.53	3.55	3.48	3.48	3.48	3.48	3.51	3.53	3.58	3.62	3.86
1965	3.83	3.93	3.94	3.93	3.89	3.81	3.83	3.84	3.91	4.03	4.08	4.36
1966	4.60	4.67	4.63	4.61	4.64	4.54	4.86	4.93	5.36	5.39	5.34	5.01
1967	4.76	4.55	4.29	3.85	3.64	3.48	4.31	4.27	4.45	4.59	4.76	5.01
1968	5.08	4.97	5.14	5.36	5.62	5.54	5.38	5.09	5.20	5.33	5.49	5.92
1969	6.18	6.16	6.08	6.15	6.08	6.49	7.00	7.01	7.13	7.04	7.19	7.72
1970	7.91	7.16	6.71	6.48	7.03	6.74	6.47	6.41	6.24	5.93	5.29	4.86
1971	4.49	3.77	3.32	3.78	4.14	4.70	5.40	5.08	4.67	4.49	4.19	4.02
1972	3.40	3.18	3.72	3.72	3.65	3.87	4.06	4.01	4.65	4.72	4.77	5.06
1973	5.31	5.56	6.05	6.29	6.35	7.19	8.01	8.67	8.48	7.15	7.87	7.36
1974	7.76	7.06	7.99	8.23	8.43	8.14	7.75	8.74	8.36	7.24	7.58	7.18
1975	6.49	5.58	5.54	5.69	5.32	5.19	6.16	6.46	6.38	6.08	5.47	5.50
1976	4.96	4.85	5.05	4.88	5.18	5.44	5.28	5.15	5.08	4.93	4.81	4.35
1977	4.60	4.66	4.61	4.54	4.94	5.00	5.15	5.50	5.77	6.19	6.16	6.06
1978	6.45	6.46	6.32	6.31	6.43	6.71	7.07	7.04	7.84	8.13	8.79	9.12
1979	9.35	9.26	9.46	9.49	9.58	9.05	9.26	9.45	10.18	11.47	11.87	12.07
1980	12.04	12.81	15.53	14.00	9.15	7.00	8.13	9.26	10.32	11.58	13.89	15.66
1981	14.72	14.91	13.48	13.63	16.29	14.56	14.70	15.61	14.95	13.87	11.27	10.93
1982	12.41	13.78	12.49	12.82	12.15	12.11	11.91	9.01	8.20	7.75	8.04	8.01
1983	7.81	8.13	8.30	8.25	8.18	8.82	9.12	9.38	9.05	8.71	8.71	8.96
1984	8.93	9.03	9.44	9.69	9.90	9.94	10.13	10.49	10.41	9.97	8.79	8.16
1985	7.76	8.22	8.56	7.99	7.56	7.01	7.05	7.18	7.08	7.17	7.20	7.07
1986	7.04	7.03	6.59	6.06	6.12	6.21	5.84	5.57	5.19	5.18	5.35	5.49
1987	5.45	5.59	5.56	5.76	5.75	5.69	5.78	6.00	6.32	6.40	5.81	5.80
1988	5.90	5.69	5.69	5.92	6.27	6.50	6.73	7.02	7.23	7.34	7.68	8.09
1989	8.29	8.48	8.83	8.70	8.40	8.22	7.92	7.91	7.72	7.59	7.65	7.64
1990	7.64	7.76	7.87	7.78	7.78	7.74	7.66	7.44	7.38	7.19	7.07	6.81
1991	6.30	5.95	5.91	5.67	5.51	5.60	5.58	5.39	5.25	5.03	4.60	4.12
1992	3.84	3.84	4.05	3.81	3.66	3.70	3.28	3.14	2.97	2.84	3.14	3.25
1993	3.06	2.95	2.97	2.89	2.96	3.10	3.05	3.05	2.96	3.04	3.12	3.08
1994	3.02	3.21	3.52	3.74	4.19	4.18	4.39	4.50	4.64	4.96	5.25	5.64
1995	5.81	5.80	5.73	5.67	5.70	5.50	5.47	5.41	5.26	5.30	5.35	5.16
1996	5.02	4.87	4.96	4.99	5.02	5.11	5.17	5.09	5.15	5.01	5.03	4.87
1997	5.05	5.00	5.14	5.17	5.13	4.92	5.07	5.13	4.97	-	-	-

Source: The Conference Board. Primary source(s): Board of Governors of the Federal Reserve System, Division of Monetary Affairs, Banking and Money Market Statistics Section, Stop 81, Washington, DC 20551. A dash (-) indicates that data are not available or zero.

Yield on New High-Grade Corporate Bonds
Not seasonally adjusted
(Percent)

Year	Jan	Feb	Mar	Apr	May	Jun	Jul	Aug	Sep	Oct	Nov	Dec
1946	2.56	2.38	2.46	2.27	2.47	2.45	2.48	2.06	2.75	2.70	2.49	2.70
1947	2.46	2.53	2.60	2.43	2.47	2.60	2.57	2.62	2.66	2.91	2.69	2.88
1948	2.97	2.85	2.99	2.81	2.86	2.93	2.80	2.83	2.86	2.99	2.96	3.15
1949	2.66	2.77	2.75	2.74	2.69	2.77	2.68	2.60	2.40	2.50	2.54	2.53
1950	2.60	2.58	2.57	2.40	2.58	2.63	2.55	2.61	2.70	2.64	2.63	2.75
1951	2.74	2.78	2.90	3.06	2.98	3.24	3.20	3.01	2.91	3.09	3.36	3.22
1952	3.08	2.94	3.14	3.09	3.25	3.09	3.11	3.08	3.14	3.16	3.07	3.04
1953	3.17	3.26	3.41	3.53	3.80	3.82	3.59	3.46	3.60	3.09	3.13	3.23
1954	3.00	2.88	2.74	2.88	2.90	2.91	2.94	2.94	3.01	2.84	2.94	2.87
1955	2.99	3.09	3.14	3.11	3.15	3.11	3.14	3.41	3.27	3.15	3.17	3.27
1956	3.20	3.07	3.25	3.55	3.48	3.56	3.56	4.02	3.96	3.94	4.29	4.26
1957	4.28	4.13	4.18	4.23	4.41	4.81	4.59	4.78	4.68	4.71	4.56	4.04
1958	3.62	3.73	3.88	3.67	3.66	3.61	3.85	4.39	4.56	4.48	4.35	4.44
1959	4.58	4.60	4.53	4.60	4.92	5.00	4.95	4.90	5.28	5.37	5.14	5.27
1960	5.34	5.24	4.98	4.97	4.95	4.91	4.79	4.65	4.64	4.75	4.82	4.94
1961	4.63	4.43	4.37	4.57	4.67	4.82	4.81	4.79	4.72	4.60	4.52	4.58
1962	4.56	4.53	4.41	4.37	4.32	4.30	4.41	4.39	4.28	4.26	4.23	4.28
1963	4.22	4.25	4.28	4.35	4.36	4.32	4.34	4.34	4.40	4.37	4.42	4.49
1964	4.50	4.39	4.45	4.48	4.48	4.50	4.44	4.44	4.49	4.49	4.48	4.49
1965	4.45	4.45	4.49	4.48	4.52	4.57	4.57	4.66	4.71	4.70	4.75	4.92
1966	4.93	5.09	5.33	5.38	5.55	5.67	5.81	6.04	6.14	6.04	6.11	5.98
1967	5.53	5.35	5.55	5.59	5.90	6.06	6.06	6.30	6.33	6.53	6.87	6.93
1968	6.57	6.57	6.80	6.79	7.00	7.02	6.91	6.54	6.69	6.88	7.00	7.28
1969	7.29	7.33	7.76	7.54	7.62	8.04	8.06	8.05	8.36	8.46	8.94	9.22
1970	9.00	8.84	9.00	9.09	9.53	9.70	9.09	9.08	9.00	9.14	8.97	8.13
1971	7.63	7.54	7.62	7.76	8.25	8.15	8.24	8.14	7.90	7.72	7.67	7.54
1972	7.36	7.57	7.53	7.77	7.61	7.63	7.72	7.59	7.72	7.66	7.46	7.50
1973	7.61	7.67	7.75	7.70	7.69	7.73	7.97	8.45	8.10	7.97	7.95	8.09
1974	8.32	8.21	8.60	9.04	9.39	9.59	10.18	10.30	10.44	10.29	9.22	9.47
1975	9.17	8.84	9.48	9.81	9.76	9.27	9.56	9.71	9.89	9.54	9.48	9.59
1976	8.97	8.71	8.73	8.68	9.00	8.90	8.76	8.59	8.37	8.25	8.17	7.90
1977	7.96	8.18	8.33	8.30	8.38	8.08	8.12	8.06	8.11	8.21	8.26	8.39
1978	8.70	8.70	8.70	8.88	9.00	9.15	9.27	8.83	8.78	9.14	9.30	9.30
1979	9.47	9.52	9.65	9.69	9.82	9.51	9.47	9.57	9.87	11.17	11.52	11.30
1980	11.65	13.23	14.08	13.36	11.61	11.12	11.48	12.31	12.74	13.17	14.10	14.38
1981	14.01	14.60	14.49	15.00	15.68	14.97	15.67	16.34	16.97	16.96	15.53	15.55
1982	16.34	16.35	15.72	15.62	15.37	15.96	15.75	14.64	13.78	12.63	11.89	12.15
1983	12.04	12.11	11.81	11.58	11.24	11.90	12.46	12.89	12.68	12.54	12.86	12.87
1984	12.65	12.80	13.36	13.64	14.41	14.49	14.25	13.54	13.37	13.02	12.40	12.47
1985	12.46	12.39	12.85	12.45	11.85	11.33	11.28	11.61	11.66	11.51	11.19	10.42
1986	10.33	9.76	8.95	8.71	9.09	9.39	9.11	9.03	9.28	9.29	8.99	8.87
1987	8.59	8.58	8.68	9.36	9.95	9.64	9.70	10.09	10.63	10.80	10.09	10.22
1988	9.81	9.43	9.68	9.92	10.25	10.08	10.12	10.27	10.03	9.86	9.98	10.05
1989	9.92	10.11	10.33	10.11	9.82	9.24	9.20	9.09	9.29	9.04	9.20	9.23
1990	9.56	9.68	9.79	10.02	9.97	9.69	9.72	10.05	10.17	10.09	9.79	9.55
1991	9.60	9.14	9.14	9.07	9.13	9.37	9.38	8.88	8.79	8.81	8.72	8.55
1992	8.36	8.63	8.62	8.59	8.57	8.45	8.19	7.96	7.99	8.17	8.25	8.12
1993	7.91	7.73	7.39	7.48	7.52	7.48	7.35	7.04	6.88	6.88	7.17	7.22
1994	7.16	7.27	7.64	7.95	8.17	8.16	8.30	8.25	8.48	8.76	8.89	8.66
1995	8.59	8.39	8.23	8.10	7.68	7.42	7.54	7.75	7.42	7.29	7.20	7.02
1996	7.00	7.14	7.57	7.81	7.87	8.00	7.97	7.68	7.84	7.69	7.43	7.45
1997	7.62	7.54	7.85	8.04	7.90	7.71	7.44	7.30	7.04	-	-	-

Source: The Conference Board. Primary source(s): U.S. Department of the Treasury, Office of Market Finance, Domestic Finance Division, Washington, DC 20220. A dash (-) indicates that data are not available or zero.

Yield on Long-Term Treasury Bonds
Not seasonally adjusted
(Percent)

Year	Jan	Feb	Mar	Apr	May	Jun	Jul	Aug	Sep	Oct	Nov	Dec
1945	2.44	2.38	2.40	2.39	2.39	2.35	2.34	2.36	2.37	2.35	2.33	2.33
1946	2.21	2.12	2.09	2.08	2.19	2.16	2.18	2.23	2.28	2.26	2.25	2.24
1947	2.21	2.21	2.19	2.19	2.19	2.22	2.25	2.24	2.24	2.27	2.36	2.39
1948	2.45	2.45	2.44	2.44	2.42	2.41	2.41	2.45	2.45	2.45	2.44	2.44
1949	2.42	2.39	2.38	2.38	2.38	2.38	2.27	2.24	2.22	2.22	2.20	2.19
1950	2.20	2.24	2.27	2.30	2.31	2.33	2.34	2.33	2.36	2.38	2.38	2.39
1951	2.39	2.40	2.47	2.56	2.63	2.65	2.63	2.57	2.56	2.61	2.66	2.70
1952	2.74	2.71	2.70	2.64	2.57	2.61	2.61	2.70	2.71	2.74	2.71	2.75
1953	2.80	2.83	2.89	2.97	3.12	3.13	3.04	3.05	3.01	2.87	2.86	2.79
1954	2.69	2.62	2.53	2.48	2.54	2.55	2.47	2.48	2.52	2.54	2.57	2.59
1955	2.68	2.77	2.78	2.82	2.81	2.82	2.91	2.95	2.92	2.87	2.89	2.91
1956	2.88	2.85	2.93	3.07	2.97	2.93	3.00	3.17	3.21	3.20	3.30	3.40
1957	3.34	3.22	3.26	3.32	3.40	3.58	3.60	3.63	3.66	3.73	3.57	3.30
1958	3.24	3.26	3.25	3.12	3.14	3.19	3.36	3.60	3.75	3.76	3.70	3.80
1959	3.90	3.92	3.92	4.01	4.08	4.09	4.11	4.10	4.26	4.11	4.12	4.27
1960	4.37	4.22	4.08	4.17	4.16	3.99	3.86	3.79	3.82	3.91	3.93	3.88
1961	3.89	3.81	3.78	3.80	3.73	3.88	3.90	4.00	4.02	3.98	3.98	4.06
1962	4.08	4.09	4.01	3.89	3.88	3.90	4.02	3.97	3.94	3.89	3.87	3.87
1963	3.88	3.92	3.93	3.97	3.97	4.00	4.01	3.99	4.04	4.07	4.10	4.14
1964	4.15	4.14	4.18	4.20	4.16	4.13	4.13	4.14	4.16	4.16	4.12	4.14
1965	4.14	4.16	4.15	4.15	4.14	4.14	4.15	4.19	4.25	4.27	4.34	4.43
1966	4.43	4.61	4.63	4.55	4.57	4.63	4.74	4.80	4.79	4.70	4.74	4.65
1967	4.40	4.47	4.45	4.51	4.76	4.86	4.86	4.95	4.99	5.18	5.44	5.36
1968	5.18	5.16	5.39	5.28	5.40	5.23	5.09	5.04	5.09	5.24	5.36	5.65
1969	5.74	5.86	6.05	5.84	5.85	6.06	6.07	6.02	6.32	6.27	6.51	6.81
1970	6.86	6.44	6.39	6.53	6.94	6.99	6.57	6.75	6.63	6.59	6.24	5.97
1971	5.91	5.84	5.71	5.75	5.96	5.94	5.91	5.78	5.56	5.46	5.44	5.62
1972	5.62	5.67	5.66	5.74	5.64	5.59	5.57	5.54	5.70	5.69	5.50	5.63
1973	5.94	6.14	6.20	6.11	6.22	6.32	6.53	6.81	6.42	6.26	6.31	6.35
1974	6.56	6.54	6.81	7.04	7.07	7.03	7.18	7.33	7.30	7.22	6.93	6.78
1975	6.68	6.61	6.73	7.03	6.99	6.86	6.89	7.06	7.29	7.29	7.21	7.17
1976	6.94	6.92	6.87	6.73	6.99	6.92	6.85	6.79	6.70	6.65	6.62	6.39
1977	6.68	7.15	7.20	7.13	7.17	6.99	6.97	7.00	6.94	7.08	7.14	7.23
1978	7.50	7.60	7.63	7.74	7.87	7.94	8.09	7.87	7.82	8.07	8.16	8.35
1979	8.43	8.43	8.45	8.44	8.55	8.32	8.35	8.42	8.68	9.44	9.80	9.59
1980	10.03	11.55	11.87	10.83	9.82	9.40	9.83	10.53	10.94	11.20	11.83	11.89
1981	11.65	12.23	12.15	12.62	12.96	12.39	13.05	13.78	14.14	14.13	12.68	12.88
1982	13.73	13.63	12.98	12.84	12.67	13.32	12.97	12.15	11.48	10.51	10.18	10.33
1983	10.37	10.60	10.34	10.19	10.21	10.64	11.10	11.42	11.26	11.21	11.32	11.44
1984	11.29	11.44	11.90	12.17	12.89	13.04	12.82	12.23	11.97	11.66	11.25	11.21
1985	11.15	11.35	11.78	11.42	10.96	10.36	10.51	10.59	10.67	10.56	10.08	9.59
1986	9.51	9.07	8.13	7.59	8.02	8.23	7.86	7.72	8.08	8.04	7.81	7.67
1987	7.60	7.69	7.62	8.31	8.79	8.63	8.70	8.97	9.58	9.61	8.99	9.12
1988	8.82	8.41	8.61	8.91	9.24	9.04	9.20	9.33	9.06	8.89	9.07	9.13
1989	9.07	9.16	9.33	9.18	8.95	8.40	8.19	8.26	8.31	8.15	8.03	8.02
1990	8.39	8.66	8.74	8.92	8.90	8.62	8.64	8.97	9.11	8.93	8.60	8.31
1991	8.33	8.12	8.38	8.29	8.33	8.54	8.50	8.17	7.96	7.88	7.83	7.58
1992	7.48	7.78	7.93	7.88	7.80	7.72	7.40	7.19	7.08	7.26	7.43	7.30
1993	7.17	6.89	6.65	6.64	6.68	6.55	6.34	6.18	5.94	5.90	6.25	6.27
1994	6.24	6.44	6.90	7.32	7.47	7.43	7.61	7.55	7.81	8.02	8.16	7.97
1995	7.93	7.69	7.52	7.41	6.99	6.59	6.71	6.90	6.63	6.43	6.31	6.11
1996	6.07	6.28	6.72	6.94	7.08	7.20	7.13	6.94	7.13	6.87	6.55	6.63
1997	6.89	6.76	7.03	7.18	7.00	6.82	6.55	6.64	6.54	-	-	-

Source: The Conference Board. Primary source(s): Board of Governors of the Federal Reserve System, Division of Monetary Affairs, Banking and Money Market Statistics Section, Stop 81, Washington, DC 20551. A dash (-) indicates that data are not available or zero.

Yield on Municipal Bonds, 20-Bond Average
Not seasonally adjusted
(Percent)

Year	Jan	Feb	Mar	Apr	May	Jun	Jul	Aug	Sep	Oct	Nov	Dec
1948	2.36	2.47	2.45	2.37	2.31	2.24	2.27	2.37	2.41	2.42	2.38	2.26
1949	2.16	2.20	2.18	2.14	2.14	2.20	2.16	2.12	2.14	2.16	2.12	2.09
1950	2.06	2.03	2.01	2.03	2.00	1.99	2.01	1.83	1.84	1.79	1.74	1.72
1951	1.61	1.58	1.74	1.94	2.00	2.19	2.15	2.02	2.01	2.06	2.05	2.09
1952	2.09	2.07	2.08	2.04	2.06	2.13	2.15	2.24	2.30	2.38	2.38	2.38
1953	2.43	2.55	2.65	2.65	2.78	2.99	2.98	2.90	2.90	2.75	2.62	2.60
1954	2.50	2.42	2.40	2.47	2.50	2.48	2.32	2.26	2.31	2.34	2.32	2.36
1955	2.40	2.44	2.44	2.41	2.38	2.41	2.54	2.60	2.58	2.51	2.46	2.57
1956	2.50	2.44	2.57	2.70	2.68	2.54	2.65	2.80	2.94	2.95	3.16	3.22
1957	3.18	3.00	3.10	3.13	3.27	3.41	3.40	3.54	3.54	3.42	3.37	3.04
1958	2.91	3.02	3.06	2.96	2.92	2.97	3.09	3.36	3.54	3.45	3.32	3.34
1959	3.42	3.36	3.30	3.39	3.58	3.72	3.71	3.58	3.78	3.62	3.55	3.68
1960	3.72	3.60	3.56	3.56	3.60	3.55	3.50	3.34	3.42	3.53	3.40	3.40
1961	3.40	3.31	3.45	3.50	3.43	3.52	3.52	3.52	3.53	3.43	3.41	3.47
1962	3.34	3.21	3.14	3.06	3.11	3.26	3.28	3.23	3.11	3.02	3.05	3.07
1963	3.10	3.15	3.05	3.10	3.11	3.21	3.21	3.13	3.20	3.20	3.30	3.28
1964	3.22	3.14	3.29	3.28	3.21	3.20	3.19	3.19	3.24	3.26	3.18	3.14
1965	3.07	3.09	3.18	3.16	3.17	3.25	3.28	3.24	3.35	3.40	3.46	3.54
1966	3.52	3.65	3.72	3.56	3.65	3.77	3.95	4.12	4.12	3.93	3.87	3.86
1967	3.55	3.52	3.55	3.60	3.89	3.96	4.02	3.99	4.12	4.30	4.34	4.43
1968	4.29	4.31	4.54	4.34	4.54	4.50	4.33	4.21	4.38	4.49	4.60	4.82
1969	4.85	4.98	5.26	5.19	5.33	5.76	5.75	6.00	6.26	6.09	6.31	6.82
1970	6.65	6.36	6.03	6.49	7.00	6.96	6.53	6.20	6.25	6.39	5.93	5.46
1971	5.36	5.23	5.17	5.37	5.91	5.95	6.06	5.82	5.37	5.06	5.20	5.21
1972	5.12	5.29	5.31	5.43	5.31	5.34	5.41	5.30	5.36	5.19	5.02	5.05
1973	5.05	5.13	5.29	5.15	5.15	5.18	5.40	5.48	5.10	5.05	5.18	5.12
1974	5.22	5.20	5.41	5.73	6.02	6.13	6.68	6.71	6.76	6.57	6.61	7.05
1975	6.82	6.39	6.74	6.95	6.97	6.95	7.07	7.17	7.44	7.39	7.43	7.31
1976	7.07	6.94	6.92	6.60	6.87	6.87	6.79	6.61	6.51	6.30	6.29	5.94
1977	5.87	5.89	5.89	5.73	5.75	5.62	5.63	5.62	5.51	5.64	5.49	5.57
1978	5.71	5.62	5.61	5.80	6.03	6.22	6.28	6.12	6.09	6.13	6.19	6.51
1979	6.47	6.31	6.33	6.29	6.25	6.13	6.13	6.20	6.52	7.08	7.30	7.22
1980	7.35	8.16	9.17	8.63	7.59	7.63	8.13	8.67	8.94	9.11	9.56	10.11
1981	9.66	10.10	10.16	10.62	10.78	10.67	11.14	12.26	12.92	12.83	11.89	12.90
1982	13.28	12.97	12.82	12.59	11.95	12.45	12.28	11.23	10.66	9.69	10.06	9.96
1983	9.50	9.58	9.20	9.05	9.11	9.52	9.53	9.72	9.58	9.66	9.75	9.89
1984	9.63	9.64	9.94	9.96	10.49	10.67	10.42	9.99	10.10	10.25	10.17	9.95
1985	9.51	9.65	9.77	9.42	9.01	8.69	8.81	9.08	9.27	9.08	8.54	8.43
1986	8.08	7.44	7.08	7.20	7.54	7.87	7.51	7.21	7.11	7.08	6.85	6.86
1987	6.61	6.61	6.66	7.55	8.00	7.79	7.72	7.81	8.26	8.70	7.95	7.96
1988	7.70	7.49	7.74	7.81	7.90	7.78	7.76	7.79	7.66	7.47	7.46	7.61
1989	7.35	7.44	7.59	7.49	7.25	7.02	6.96	7.06	7.26	7.22	7.14	6.98
1990	7.10	7.22	7.29	7.39	7.35	7.24	7.19	7.32	7.53	7.49	7.18	7.09
1991	7.08	6.91	7.10	7.02	6.95	7.13	7.05	6.90	6.80	6.68	6.73	6.69
1992	6.54	6.74	6.76	6.67	6.57	6.49	6.13	6.16	6.25	6.41	6.36	6.22
1993	6.16	5.86	5.85	5.76	5.73	5.63	5.57	5.45	5.29	5.25	5.47	5.35
1994	5.31	5.40	5.91	6.23	6.19	6.11	6.23	6.21	6.28	6.52	6.97	6.80
1995	6.53	6.22	6.10	6.02	5.95	5.84	5.92	6.06	5.91	5.80	5.64	5.45
1996	5.43	5.43	5.79	5.94	5.98	6.02	5.92	5.76	5.87	5.72	5.59	5.64
1997	5.72	5.63	5.76	5.88	5.70	5.53	5.35	5.41	5.39	-	-	-

Source: The Conference Board. Primary source(s): Board of Governors of the Federal Reserve System, Division of Monetary Affairs, Banking and Money Market Statistics Section, Stop 81, Washington, DC 20551. A dash (-) indicates that data are not available or zero.

Secondary Market Yields on FHA Mortgages
Not seasonally adjusted
(Percent)

Year	Jan	Feb	Mar	Apr	May	Jun	Jul	Aug	Sep	Oct	Nov	Dec
1949	4.35	4.35	4.35	4.35	4.34	4.35	4.34	4.34	4.32	4.32	4.32	4.32
1950	4.31	4.31	4.30	-	-	4.09	4.07	4.07	4.07	4.07	4.07	4.07
1951	4.07	4.07	4.12	4.19	4.27	4.29	4.31	4.31	4.30	4.27	4.27	4.26
1952	4.26	4.27	4.29	4.29	4.29	4.30	4.30	4.30	4.30	4.31	4.32	4.32
1953	4.34	4.34	4.34	-	-	4.67	4.74	4.82	4.86	4.82	4.81	4.78
1954	4.75	4.69	4.64	4.62	4.59	4.57	4.56	4.56	4.56	4.56	4.56	4.56
1955	4.56	4.56	4.59	4.60	4.63	4.63	4.64	4.67	4.70	4.73	4.75	4.73
1956	4.73	4.70	4.68	4.71	4.78	4.81	4.81	4.87	4.92	4.95	-	-
1957	-	5.36	5.35	5.35	5.32	5.35	5.38	-	-	5.63	5.63	5.62
1958	5.59	5.57	5.51	5.44	5.39	5.37	5.35	5.37	5.50	5.58	5.60	5.60
1959	5.60	5.59	5.58	5.59	5.64	5.71	5.75	5.81	-	-	6.23	6.23
1960	6.25	6.23	6.22	6.21	6.20	6.19	6.17	6.14	6.11	6.09	6.07	6.04
1961	6.02	5.86	5.80	5.77	-	-	5.68	5.68	5.69	5.70	5.70	5.69
1962	5.69	5.68	5.65	5.64	5.60	5.59	5.58	5.57	5.56	5.55	5.54	5.53
1963	5.52	5.48	5.47	5.46	5.45	5.45	5.45	5.45	5.45	5.45	5.45	5.45
1964	5.45	5.45	5.45	5.45	5.45	5.45	5.46	5.46	5.46	5.45	5.45	5.45
1965	5.45	5.45	5.45	5.45	5.45	5.44	5.44	5.45	5.46	5.49	5.51	5.62
1966	5.70	-	6.00	-	6.32	6.45	6.51	6.58	6.63	-	6.81	6.77
1967	6.62	6.46	6.35	6.29	6.44	6.51	6.53	6.60	6.63	6.65	6.77	6.81
1968	6.81	6.78	6.83	6.94	-	7.52	7.42	7.35	7.28	7.29	7.36	7.50
1969	-	7.99	8.05	8.06	8.06	8.35	8.36	8.36	8.40	8.48	8.48	8.62
1970	-	9.29	9.20	9.10	9.11	9.16	9.11	9.07	9.01	8.97	8.90	8.40
1971	-	-	7.32	7.37	7.75	7.89	7.97	7.92	7.84	7.75	7.62	7.59
1972	7.49	7.46	7.45	7.50	7.53	7.54	7.54	7.55	7.56	7.57	7.57	7.56
1973	7.55	7.56	7.63	7.73	7.79	7.89	8.19	-	9.18	8.97	8.86	8.78
1974	-	8.54	8.66	9.17	9.46	9.46	9.85	10.30	10.38	10.13	-	9.51
1975	8.99	8.84	8.69	-	9.16	9.06	9.13	9.32	9.74	9.53	9.41	9.32
1976	9.06	9.04	-	8.82	9.03	9.05	8.99	8.93	8.82	8.55	8.45	8.28
1977	8.45	8.55	8.65	8.64	-	8.77	8.77	8.77	8.74	8.81	8.81	8.96
1978	9.18	-	9.35	9.44	9.74	-	9.96	9.81	9.81	9.98	10.04	10.23
1979	10.24	10.24	10.26	-	10.61	10.49	10.46	10.58	11.37	-	12.41	12.24
1980	12.60	-	14.63	13.45	11.99	11.85	12.39	13.54	14.26	14.38	14.47	14.08
1981	14.23	14.79	15.04	15.91	16.33	16.31	16.76	17.96	18.55	17.43	15.98	16.43
1982	17.38	17.10	16.41	16.31	16.19	16.73	16.29	14.61	14.03	12.99	12.82	12.80
1983	12.87	12.65	12.68	12.50	12.41	12.96	14.23	13.78	13.55	13.23	13.23	13.25
1984	13.08	13.20	13.68	13.80	15.01	14.91	14.58	14.21	13.99	13.43	12.90	12.99
1985	13.01	13.27	13.43	12.97	12.28	11.89	12.12	11.99	12.04	11.87	11.28	10.70
1986	10.78	10.59	9.77	9.80	10.07	9.98	10.01	9.80	9.90	9.80	9.26	9.21
1987	8.79	8.81	8.94	10.02	10.61	10.33	10.38	10.55	11.22	10.90	10.76	10.63
1988	10.17	9.86	10.28	10.46	10.84	10.65	10.66	10.74	10.58	10.23	10.63	10.81
1989	10.69	10.88	11.16	10.88	10.55	10.08	9.61	9.95	9.94	9.73	9.69	9.72
1990	10.01	10.22	10.30	10.75	10.23	10.18	10.11	10.28	10.24	10.23	9.81	9.66
1991	9.58	9.57	9.61	9.61	9.62	9.71	9.59	9.14	9.06	8.71	8.69	8.10
1992	8.72	8.74	8.85	8.79	8.66	8.56	8.12	8.08	8.06	8.29	8.54	8.12
1993	8.04	7.55	7.57	7.56	7.59	7.52	7.51	7.02	7.03	7.08	7.51	7.52
1994	7.05	7.59	8.57	8.63	8.63	9.03	8.65	8.66	9.10	9.23	9.53	9.54
1995	9.10	9.05	8.60	8.56	8.03	8.00	8.09	8.03	8.03	7.61	7.51	7.52
1996	7.11	7.57	8.09	8.52	8.57	8.55	8.56	8.58	8.57	8.00	8.14	8.06
1997	8.06	8.06	8.08	8.55	8.56	8.05	8.02	7.61	8.02	-	-	-

Source: The Conference Board. Primary source(s): U.S. Department of Housing and Urban Development, Office of Housing-FHA Comptroller, Program Evaluation Division, Washington, DC 20410. A dash (-) indicates that data are not available or zero.

Commercial and Industrial Loans Outstanding
(Millions of $)

Year	Jan	Feb	Mar	Apr	May	Jun	Jul	Aug	Sep	Oct	Nov	Dec
1945	6,511	6,388	6,283	6,268	6,256	6,410	6,454	6,434	6,487	6,498	6,715	7,147
1946	7,364	7,430	7,621	7,864	8,047	8,211	8,614	9,074	9,443	9,863	10,134	10,260
1947	10,475	10,713	11,149	11,506	11,592	11,639	11,770	12,019	12,250	12,548	12,904	13,158
1948	13,417	13,358	13,371	13,473	13,834	14,065	14,385	14,507	14,461	14,356	14,196	14,087
1949	14,055	13,979	13,861	13,605	13,409	13,163	12,833	12,660	12,641	12,670	12,604	12,573
1950	12,677	12,764	12,763	12,849	12,936	13,242	13,619	14,057	14,696	15,027	15,462	15,986
1951	16,503	17,116	17,579	18,079	18,453	18,646	18,757	18,865	18,968	19,111	19,194	19,411
1952	19,632	19,641	19,761	19,742	19,809	19,969	20,141	20,190	20,381	20,650	21,031	21,133
1953	21,227	21,277	21,430	21,675	21,816	21,747	21,778	21,934	21,819	21,640	21,451	21,058
1954	21,000	21,064	21,036	20,967	20,811	20,650	20,651	19,804	19,753	19,718	19,955	20,314
1955	20,529	20,692	20,916	21,049	21,416	21,796	22,244	22,664	22,977	23,421	23,771	24,110
1956	24,515	24,686	25,414	25,932	26,448	26,799	27,145	27,418	27,778	27,858	28,199	28,395
1957	28,695	28,720	29,182	29,503	29,650	30,033	30,245	30,285	30,374	29,969	29,573	29,517
1958	29,171	28,835	28,728	28,554	28,168	28,079	28,039	27,941	28,122	28,215	28,342	28,496
1959	28,567	28,583	28,820	29,092	29,573	30,042	30,026	30,456	30,646	30,915	31,076	31,288
1960	31,433	31,870	32,093	32,293	32,591	33,011	32,993	32,840	32,956	32,996	33,118	33,018
1961	32,999	32,966	33,111	33,079	33,020	32,955	33,012	33,131	33,214	33,215	33,280	33,429
1962	33,582	33,712	33,907	34,121	34,269	34,509	34,740	35,038	35,318	35,635	35,939	35,986
1963	36,039	36,126	36,251	36,458	36,626	36,740	36,872	37,047	37,341	37,821	38,579	39,045
1964	38,931	39,195	39,201	39,554	39,882	40,137	40,428	40,839	41,418	41,625	42,068	42,737
1965	43,562	44,618	45,563	46,203	47,209	47,718	48,072	49,139	50,141	50,812	51,650	52,300
1966	53,195	54,071	54,805	55,377	56,139	57,228	58,223	59,360	59,950	60,578	61,043	61,332
1967	61,876	62,404	63,100	63,598	63,998	64,682	65,083	64,862	65,155	65,644	66,161	67,068
1968	67,254	67,415	67,732	68,877	69,067	69,598	70,294	71,359	72,318	73,153	74,374	75,150
1969	77,048	77,843	79,091	81,132	82,277	83,502	83,909	85,141	86,404	87,358	88,070	89,059
1970	88,521	90,023	91,243	91,333	91,864	92,444	92,433	93,072	93,435	91,680	91,082	91,069
1971	90,944	91,625	91,904	90,891	91,662	90,706	89,951	91,627	93,437	92,465	92,301	91,788
1972	84,478	85,260	86,195	87,342	87,906	88,268	88,429	88,800	88,593	90,502	91,408	92,111
1973	94,279	98,034	100,124	101,768	103,074	105,166	106,581	108,505	108,458	109,664	110,877	111,764
1974	113,967	116,322	117,738	122,857	125,111	126,537	130,706	133,304	137,429	138,352	139,734	139,873
1975	140,652	139,605	138,152	136,564	133,750	131,397	130,713	129,579	128,146	126,999	126,131	126,245
1976	125,349	125,758	123,490	120,789	121,069	122,018	121,328	121,083	120,710	121,770	123,317	124,225
1977	124,450	125,824	126,179	126,925	127,740	128,990	128,860	130,214	130,848	132,174	133,272	134,372
1978	135,158	135,658	138,536	140,620	143,029	145,547	146,937	147,792	148,769	150,501	152,486	152,870
1979	155,975	158,341	160,335	165,793	168,229	171,623	175,320	179,017	183,790	184,399	183,394	186,443
1980	193,068	197,288	200,406	200,583	198,756	202,454	200,910	201,732	203,417	204,727	209,253	211,014
1981	213,016	213,391	211,676	215,581	221,279	225,515	229,664	234,814	238,847	241,377	244,824	247,853
1982	254,693	259,934	261,328	266,688	271,022	272,899	273,160	273,540	274,885	274,856	270,235	264,699
1983	268,553	268,582	269,450	265,604	261,465	262,099	261,703	262,875	262,747	261,829	263,187	267,368
1984	274,768	279,364	287,370	294,220	300,525	310,036	314,375	317,394	321,437	325,648	328,615	329,459
1985	329,668	332,412	334,670	335,158	338,108	336,876	339,378	340,740	339,599	343,857	347,028	348,859
1986	351,101	349,392	347,888	342,642	345,052	345,978	347,464	351,931	351,008	352,769	353,255	358,781
1987	366,490	364,936	363,447	363,216	362,718	363,766	362,668	359,989	363,258	366,003	364,818	367,421
1988	431,717	435,744	437,771	442,415	443,032	445,844	446,681	446,456	446,531	450,009	454,371	462,256
1989	467,977	476,097	477,317	479,745	490,048	492,163	493,944	498,784	498,706	500,827	503,402	505,979
1990	507,561	510,900	519,202	519,069	517,319	518,371	519,085	520,914	526,207	524,986	518,228	518,014
1991	518,081	510,920	511,652	506,209	501,198	498,425	495,277	485,585	480,239	476,481	475,069	469,530
1992	466,043	466,360	466,157	463,705	461,668	459,183	456,626	457,488	454,906	460,606	465,271	462,275
1993	462,288	462,384	457,838	459,727	464,419	465,475	467,626	466,544	465,554	463,965	463,194	464,316
1994	467,305	463,858	464,131	464,444	469,099	474,005	478,484	483,031	489,721	499,495	502,889	510,348
1995	518,012	527,940	533,217	543,987	545,526	550,914	554,061	558,220	560,874	565,621	561,654	569,934
1996	570,801	570,058	576,840	580,282	579,510	579,767	580,396	581,279	586,624	582,170	582,533	585,643
1997	590,320	592,281	595,805	596,763	600,015	609,448	613,340	617,449	628,518	-	-	-

Source: The Conference Board. Primary source(s): Board of Governors of the Federal Reserve System, Division of Monetary Affairs, Banking and Money Market Statistics Section, Stop 84, Washington, DC 20551 and Board of Governors of the Federal Reserve System, Capital Markets, Banking and Money Market Statistics Section, Stop 84, Washington, DC 20551. A dash (-) indicates that data are not available or zero.

CHAPTER 5

ECONOMIC SERIES

ECONOMIC SERIES

The 21 series in this chapter are classified as "important economic measures" by the Department of Commerce. They are not cyclic indicators but measure other aspects of the economy. The series are grouped under four headings:

Savings
Producer Prices, Wages, and Productivity
Implicit Price Deflators for Gross Domestic Product Sectors
Labor and Employment
International Transactions

The section on implicit price deflators for GDP is a new feature of this edition aimed at providing better data to the user for calculating inflationary pressures on personal or institutional income.

A brief introduction to each of these sections provides a description of each series covered and some discussion of the analytical uses of each series.

Bibliography

1. Fischer, Stanley, Rudiger Dornbusch, and Richard Schmalensee. *Introduction to Macroeconomics*. McGraw-Hill Book Company, New York, 1988.

2. Fitch, Thomas P. *Dictionary of Banking Terms*. Barron's, New York, 1990.

3. Siegel, Barry N. *Money, Banking, and the Economy*. Academic Press, New York, 1982.

3. U.S. Department of Commerce, Bureau of Economic Analysis. *Survey of Current Business*. Superintendent of Documents, U.S. Government Printing Office, Washington, DC 20302.

INDICATORS OF SAVINGS

This section presents 5 series used to measure the nation's savings rate. The series presented are:

> Gross saving
> Business saving
> Personal saving
> Personal saving rate
> Government surplus or deficit

In the aggregate, savings taken as a total are an indirect indicator of the nation's capacity to invest in future productive facilities. Business and personal savings create the pool of capital available for new housing, infrastructure, tooling, factories, etc.—investment. These private sources of savings are diminished by government deficits and increased by foreign investment in the United States.

Gross Saving. Data for 1946 through 1997 are shown on a quarterly, annualized basis in billions of current dollars. The series is made up of personal savings plus business savings less (currently) government deficits at the federal, state, and local levels.

Business Saving. Presented as billions of current dollars for 1946 through 1997 in quarterly, annualized values, business savings is a complex category made up of the following components:

> Undistributed corporate profits
> Corporate capital consumption allowances
> Noncorporate capital consumption allowances
> Wage accruals less disbursements

Corporate profits are adjusted for inventory valuation changes and capital consumption adjustments. Noncorporate capital consumption allowances are also adjusted. The sum of these values combines into savings carried by the business sector from one period into another.

Personal Saving and **Personal Saving Rate.** Data for Personal saving are presented in the same format as Gross and Business saving; Personal saving rate is shown in percent. Personal saving is derived by deducting taxes from personal income, yielding disposable personal income (DPI); personal expenditures are deducted from DPI to obtain personal saving. Personal saving as a percent of DPI is the Personal saving rate. In the first quarter of 1993, this value was 3.4 percent; the highest rate shown in the data was the first quarter of 1946 (11.7%) and, more recently, in the 2nd quarter of 1975 (11.2%—after a recession). The saving rate rarely reaches double digits in the United States; in Japan and some European countries, a high double-digit saving rate is the rule rather than the exception.

Government Surplus or Deficit. Data show quarterly values, in billions of current dollars, for 1946 through 1997. In the early 1990s, the government has run large deficits; since deficits are financed from savings, deficits reduce total resources available for investment; the government competes with private users of capital for funds. However, if government deficits were erased by higher taxes, the net result would be largely the same: personal and business savings are income *net* of taxes; therefore higher taxes would also reduce gross savings.

Gross Saving
(Annual Rate, Billions of $)

Year	1st Quarter	2nd Quarter	3rd Quarter	4th Quarter
1946	33.1	38.7	40.8	42.8
1947	47.0	44.5	45.4	51.0
1948	56.5	59.8	59.0	59.2
1949	51.7	44.6	46.4	42.1
1950	49.0	56.9	63.5	74.9
1951	71.5	77.9	76.3	77.3
1952	78.0	71.6	74.0	76.5
1953	77.8	78.3	77.9	70.0
1954	72.3	72.2	73.2	78.3
1955	83.1	88.8	90.1	94.1
1956	97.1	98.8	102.7	103.3
1957	103.3	103.6	103.9	94.9
1958	90.3	85.8	93.1	101.9
1959	107.9	113.5	104.9	107.7
1960	120.1	112.7	113.1	107.6
1961	110.0	112.0	119.1	124.0
1962	126.3	125.7	127.7	127.6
1963	130.2	134.7	135.1	139.5
1964	141.6	141.8	145.6	152.1
1965	158.9	160.7	160.6	161.5
1966	169.1	169.9	169.3	176.2
1967	171.3	167.6	175.1	181.2
1968	179.0	184.7	185.3	191.3
1969	198.8	200.3	207.0	202.4
1970	196.5	199.7	199.2	193.7
1971	208.2	212.5	216.4	220.3
1972	229.7	235.7	246.1	264.0
1973	278.2	286.9	298.4	322.3
1974	303.5	300.9	300.2	300.4
1975	280.0	280.8	308.2	320.2
1976	336.2	341.3	341.0	341.5
1977	356.9	389.9	414.9	417.3
1978	431.0	471.5	487.3	517.7
1979	530.8	539.4	545.7	546.3
1980	549.1	526.4	531.7	581.5
1981	632.3	625.2	680.9	665.0
1982	612.0	648.0	602.9	554.3
1983	558.0	576.8	583.9	637.3
1984	712.0	746.7	778.1	766.0
1985	765.4	750.4	734.7	732.1
1986	773.4	725.8	684.0	695.9
1987	735.8	761.0	784.5	837.2
1988	838.1	873.7	892.4	899.8
1989	930.0	912.8	903.4	878.9
1990	894.9	939.2	893.5	884.6
1991	982.0	926.9	904.3	922.6
1992	920.3	914.0	899.9	883.0
1993	932.0	942.1	943.8	980.1
1994	1,062.4	1,065.5	1,071.0	1,118.0
1995	1,136.8	1,133.4	1,167.7	1,224.0
1996	1,215.9	1,256.3	1,295.9	1,303.0
1997	1,332.9	1,396.9	-	-

Source: The Conference Board. Primary source(s): U.S. Department of Commerce, Bureau of Economic Analysis, National Income and Wealth Division, BE-54, Washington, DC 20230. A dash (-) indicates that data are not available or zero.

Business Saving
(Annual Rate, Billions of $)

Year	1st Quarter	2nd Quarter	3rd Quarter	4th Quarter
1946	18.1	16.6	13.1	12.1
1947	9.5	3.7	7.6	5.9
1948	8.4	12.1	15.5	14.4
1949	10.4	8.1	8.6	7.7
1950	18.3	14.1	7.8	16.4
1951	11.9	21.4	20.9	20.3
1952	19.6	18.0	21.7	18.8
1953	19.1	21.3	20.6	21.1
1954	21.2	17.9	17.6	18.7
1955	17.0	18.1	19.9	19.8
1956	21.7	24.2	25.0	26.1
1957	24.8	26.6	26.4	25.0
1958	25.4	25.4	28.2	29.5
1959	26.0	27.1	22.7	24.9
1960	25.5	22.9	24.6	23.6
1961	26.7	27.4	30.9	31.7
1962	31.5	31.1	30.6	28.4
1963	28.8	28.9	28.2	32.2
1964	32.8	37.0	35.6	40.2
1965	35.6	36.5	42.5	40.1
1966	37.8	37.9	39.7	44.9
1967	49.9	47.3	50.5	51.8
1968	50.1	52.3	43.5	45.5
1969	40.2	43.5	54.0	54.0
1970	53.4	62.4	65.8	66.4
1971	68.3	73.9	71.7	65.6
1972	61.6	57.1	64.6	77.5
1973	76.3	88.0	91.2	110.6
1974	105.5	93.5	96.5	105.3
1975	92.9	130.6	102.0	105.6
1976	102.4	102.2	101.6	95.3
1977	83.5	92.8	103.2	109.3
1978	117.7	111.3	116.8	126.9
1979	135.5	136.0	134.1	139.3
1980	155.9	163.3	168.3	188.8
1981	192.0	182.7	220.9	233.3
1982	208.4	233.1	218.8	195.7
1983	185.3	165.5	169.6	183.8
1984	221.4	240.2	270.8	249.5
1985	215.5	248.6	189.3	212.0
1986	230.6	227.0	197.5	174.6
1987	209.7	140.1	158.4	211.3
1988	212.8	200.4	202.6	187.8
1989	225.1	198.1	184.0	190.4
1990	211.6	226.4	220.8	226.4
1991	243.8	259.6	255.0	279.4
1992	277.5	292.9	267.6	304.5
1993	218.6	269.0	239.0	267.6
1994	165.2	212.8	222.1	242.4
1995	279.2	245.4	243.8	249.9
1996	258.1	225.7	254.0	220.4
1997	215.9	247.0	211.1	-

Source: The Conference Board. Primary source(s): U.S. Department of Commerce, Bureau of Economic Analysis, National Income and Wealth Division, BE-54, Washington, DC 20230. A dash (-) indicates that data are not available or zero.

158

Personal Saving
(Annual Rate, Billions of $)

Year	1st Quarter	2nd Quarter	3rd Quarter	4th Quarter
1946	11.7	10.5	8.0	7.3
1947	5.7	2.2	4.4	3.3
1948	4.6	6.4	8.0	7.4
1949	5.5	4.3	4.5	4.0
1950	9.0	6.9	3.7	7.5
1951	5.3	9.3	9.0	8.6
1952	8.3	7.6	8.9	7.5
1953	7.5	8.2	8.0	8.1
1954	8.1	6.8	6.7	6.9
1955	6.2	6.5	7.0	6.8
1956	7.4	8.1	8.2	8.4
1957	7.9	8.4	8.2	7.8
1958	7.9	7.8	8.5	8.7
1959	7.6	7.7	6.5	7.0
1960	7.1	6.3	6.7	6.5
1961	7.2	7.3	8.1	8.1
1962	8.0	7.8	7.6	7.0
1963	7.0	6.9	6.6	7.4
1964	7.4	8.1	7.7	8.5
1965	7.5	7.5	8.5	7.8
1966	7.2	7.2	7.4	8.2
1967	8.9	8.3	8.7	8.8
1968	8.3	8.4	6.9	7.1
1969	6.2	6.6	7.9	7.8
1970	7.6	8.6	8.9	8.9
1971	8.9	9.4	9.0	8.1
1972	7.5	6.8	7.5	8.6
1973	8.2	9.2	9.3	10.9
1974	10.3	9.0	9.0	9.7
1975	8.4	11.2	8.7	8.8
1976	8.3	8.1	7.9	7.2
1977	6.2	6.7	7.2	7.4
1978	7.8	7.1	7.3	7.7
1979	7.9	7.8	7.5	7.5
1980	8.1	8.5	8.4	9.1
1981	9.0	8.4	9.8	10.2
1982	9.1	9.9	9.2	8.1
1983	7.6	6.6	6.6	7.0
1984	8.1	8.6	9.5	8.6
1985	7.4	8.3	6.3	6.9
1986	7.3	7.1	6.1	5.4
1987	6.3	4.2	4.7	6.1
1988	6.0	5.5	5.5	5.0
1989	5.9	5.1	4.7	4.8
1990	5.2	5.4	5.2	5.3
1991	5.7	6.0	5.8	6.3
1992	6.1	6.4	5.8	6.4
1993	4.6	5.6	4.9	5.4
1994	3.4	4.2	4.4	4.7
1995	5.3	4.6	4.5	4.6
1996	4.7	4.1	4.5	3.9
1997	3.7	4.2	3.6	-

Source: The Conference Board. Primary source(s): U.S. Department of Commerce, Bureau of Economic Analysis, National Income and Wealth Division, BE-54, Washington, DC 20230. A dash (-) indicates that data are not available or zero.

Personal Saving Rate
(Percent)

Year	1st Quarter	2nd Quarter	3rd Quarter	4th Quarter
1946	26.0	25.7	25.8	27.3
1947	28.4	32.5	33.0	34.3
1948	37.7	39.5	39.2	41.5
1949	41.5	39.9	40.9	37.4
1950	36.3	37.5	38.6	40.6
1951	37.5	41.9	46.2	45.2
1952	46.1	45.2	45.3	48.2
1953	48.7	47.7	47.8	45.9
1954	48.3	50.4	51.2	53.8
1955	56.7	58.4	57.7	59.3
1956	59.3	59.7	61.3	61.4
1957	63.5	63.9	64.5	63.5
1958	61.6	62.3	62.7	67.6
1959	70.0	72.9	70.2	71.4
1960	73.1	71.6	71.9	71.0
1961	70.5	73.6	74.7	76.5
1962	81.0	80.5	81.8	84.5
1963	84.7	86.7	87.6	88.8
1964	92.6	92.9	93.8	93.9
1965	100.9	102.5	103.5	106.3
1966	109.1	110.2	110.6	114.7
1967	113.0	112.9	115.0	118.9
1968	116.0	119.8	120.8	123.4
1969	124.5	124.5	125.4	123.0
1970	124.9	127.2	129.3	129.2
1971	140.9	144.4	149.5	155.6
1972	157.7	167.3	166.8	174.8
1973	178.9	179.3	185.0	187.1
1974	185.4	187.3	185.0	198.4
1975	215.2	230.2	244.6	253.7
1976	259.4	258.4	261.3	264.8
1977	275.8	297.2	312.7	310.9
1978	315.6	334.7	344.9	356.9
1979	355.5	365.1	375.4	380.7
1980	374.7	374.2	384.4	400.7
1981	424.1	434.9	457.9	462.8
1982	454.3	471.3	484.8	484.3
1983	497.8	515.1	525.9	549.5
1984	550.2	567.6	585.5	595.1
1985	591.7	594.7	617.2	600.4
1986	613.0	594.7	582.6	589.6
1987	612.4	639.1	660.4	667.5
1988	688.5	700.7	717.3	735.3
1989	701.3	716.7	748.3	734.5
1990	751.9	774.2	734.6	764.6
1991	804.3	789.9	786.2	798.2
1992	825.4	814.1	847.7	765.8
1993	913.8	840.9	868.4	833.5
1994	1,021.5	921.1	938.0	953.0
1995	941.3	961.8	999.3	1,026.4
1996	1,007.4	1,027.8	1,038.8	1,059.3
1997	1,067.7	1,081.8	-	-

Source: The Conference Board. Primary source(s): U.S. Department of Commerce, Bureau of Economic Analysis, National Income and Wealth Division, BE-54, Washington, DC 20230. A dash (-) indicates that data are not available or zero.

Government Surplus or Deficit
(Annual Rate, Billions of $)

Year	1st Quarter	2nd Quarter	3rd Quarter	4th Quarter
1946	-10.9	-3.7	1.9	3.3
1947	9.2	8.3	4.7	10.9
1948	10.4	8.2	4.3	3.4
1949	-0.2	-3.4	-3.1	-3.1
1950	-5.6	5.3	17.2	17.9
1951	22.1	14.8	10.1	11.1
1952	12.3	8.4	7.1	9.5
1953	10.0	9.3	9.4	3.0
1954	2.8	4.0	4.4	5.9
1955	9.5	12.8	11.8	14.9
1956	16.2	14.9	16.2	15.8
1957	15.1	13.1	13.0	6.4
1958	3.8	-1.3	0.9	4.8
1959	11.9	13.5	12.0	11.4
1960	21.5	18.2	16.7	12.8
1961	12.8	11.0	13.5	15.8
1962	13.8	14.0	15.4	14.8
1963	16.6	19.1	19.3	18.5
1964	16.1	11.9	16.2	18.0
1965	22.4	21.7	14.7	15.0
1966	22.1	21.8	19.1	16.6
1967	8.4	7.4	9.6	10.4
1968	13.0	12.5	21.0	22.4
1969	34.2	32.3	27.5	25.4
1970	19.7	7.0	2.8	-2.8
1971	-1.8	-6.5	-5.2	-1.0
1972	9.2	10.2	14.0	13.1
1973	22.9	19.3	22.2	24.5
1974	20.6	19.5	17.3	-3.2
1975	-27.9	-79.8	-38.4	-39.0
1976	-25.5	-19.3	-21.9	-18.4
1977	-2.3	-	-1.0	-2.8
1978	-2.2	25.6	26.0	34.4
1979	38.8	36.2	35.0	25.4
1980	17.2	-12.3	-22.2	-9.2
1981	15.1	6.4	1.3	-32.3
1982	-50.8	-56.5	-100.6	-125.7
1983	-125.0	-105.1	-112.1	-95.9
1984	-59.4	-60.9	-78.2	-78.0
1985	-41.8	-93.8	-71.9	-80.2
1986	-70.2	-95.9	-96.0	-68.3
1987	-86.2	-18.2	-34.1	-41.9
1988	-63.2	-27.3	-27.6	-23.3
1989	3.6	-1.9	-28.8	-46.1
1990	-68.6	-61.3	-61.9	-106.2
1991	-65.8	-123.0	-136.9	-155.0
1992	-182.6	-193.0	-215.5	-187.3
1993	-200.4	-167.9	-163.7	-120.9
1994	-124.3	-68.4	-89.2	-77.5
1995	-83.8	-73.9	-75.4	-52.4
1996	-49.5	2.8	3.1	23.3
1997	49.2	68.1	-	-

Source: The Conference Board. Primary source(s): U.S. Department of Commerce, Bureau of Economic Analysis, National Income and Wealth Division, BE-54, Washington, DC 20230. A dash (-) indicates that data are not available or zero.

INDICATORS OF PRODUCER PRICES, WAGES, AND PRODUCTIVITY

This section presents 9 series used to measure the nation's inflation rate, prices, and output. The series presented are:

Producer Price Index, crude materials
Producer Price Index, intermediate materials
Producer Price Index, capital equipment
Producer Price Index, finished consumer goods
Producer Price Index, finished goods
Producer Price Index, crude nonfood less energy
Producer Price Index, petroleum products
Index of output per hour, business sector
Index of output per hour, nonfarm business sector

Conspicuous by absence, perhaps, is the *Consumer Price Index*. It is presented in the next chapter in considerable detail. Similarly, much more detailed statistics are presented on the *Producer Price Index*, a summary of which is presented later in this section.

Producer Price Index Series. All seven tables are indexes based on 1982 (1982 = 100). Detailed PPI tables are presented in the next chapter. The tables included in this section are summary series showing broad categories. Production processes refine crude raw materials (ores, logs, crude oil) into intermediate products (steel, pulp, engine blocks); intermediate products are transformed into finished products (autos, writing paper, gasoline). The tables included follow price trends at each of these levels. The data are used in a variety of ways in macroeconomic analysis and in business planning. For example, note that the inflation rate shown by the PPI for crude and intermediate materials is substantially less than it is for finished goods; at lower levels of refinement and product differentiation, competitive forces are greater (the "stuff" handled is more of a commodity); as raw materials are formed into products, differentiation increases and opportunities for aggressive pricing are greater.

Indices of Output Per Hour. Data are shown from 1947 to 1997 in quarterly increments as an index based on 1992 (1992 = 100). These are indicators of national productivity. Output per hour reflects all inputs to the production process, including tooling, fuels, improved raw materials, degree of capacity utilization . . . *and* human effort, measured in time. The indicators, therefore, are influenced by the personal productivity of employees but also, more importantly in today's environment, by technology and therefore by the level of investment. Rising productivity means that more is produced, in absolute terms, by one hour of labor. It does not mean that employment is increasing; it may be decreasing as better machines take over human tasks. Rising productivity may also mean that the capital required per workplace is on the increase. The series, therefore, yield best results when viewed in concert with other series on wages, employment, capacity utilization, and investment.

Producer Price Index, Crude Materials
(1982 = 100)

Year	Jan	Feb	Mar	Apr	May	Jun	Jul	Aug	Sep	Oct	Nov	Dec
1947	-	-	-	30.7	30.5	30.6	31.1	31.6	32.4	33.6	33.8	35.3
1948	36.3	34.4	33.5	34.2	35.3	36.2	36.0	35.5	34.8	33.8	33.5	33.0
1949	32.0	31.0	30.7	30.2	30.1	29.7	29.2	29.2	29.5	29.5	29.7	29.7
1950	29.6	30.5	30.3	30.5	31.6	32.1	33.3	34.0	34.5	34.5	35.4	36.7
1951	38.1	39.6	39.1	39.1	38.5	38.1	36.7	36.2	35.9	36.7	36.4	36.5
1952	35.8	35.5	35.0	34.9	34.8	34.7	34.6	34.7	33.9	33.7	33.7	32.9
1953	32.6	32.4	32.5	31.6	31.9	31.4	32.4	31.7	32.0	31.4	31.2	31.7
1954	32.1	32.0	32.1	32.2	32.1	31.5	31.4	31.3	31.0	31.2	31.4	30.9
1955	31.1	31.0	30.7	30.9	30.1	30.7	30.4	30.1	30.5	30.4	29.4	29.5
1956	29.5	29.9	29.8	30.3	30.7	30.5	30.5	31.0	31.0	31.0	31.1	31.6
1957	31.3	31.0	30.8	30.8	30.7	31.5	32.0	32.1	31.2	31.0	31.1	31.5
1958	31.4	31.9	32.3	31.9	32.4	32.0	32.1	31.9	31.7	31.9	32.1	31.6
1959	31.6	31.4	31.5	31.7	31.5	31.3	31.0	30.7	30.9	30.7	30.5	30.4
1960	30.4	30.4	30.7	30.7	30.8	30.5	30.4	29.8	30.0	30.2	30.2	30.3
1961	30.4	30.5	30.3	30.2	29.9	29.4	29.7	30.5	30.2	30.3	30.2	30.6
1962	30.6	30.6	30.5	30.1	30.1	30.0	30.2	30.5	31.2	30.8	31.0	30.7
1963	30.3	30.0	29.5	29.7	29.6	29.9	30.0	29.9	29.8	30.0	30.2	29.4
1964	29.8	29.4	29.5	29.5	29.4	29.1	29.2	29.4	30.1	29.8	29.9	29.8
1965	29.5	29.9	30.0	30.4	30.8	31.6	31.2	31.5	31.4	31.7	32.1	32.7
1966	33.0	33.7	33.5	33.3	33.1	33.0	33.4	33.6	33.4	32.9	32.3	32.0
1967	32.2	31.5	31.1	30.7	31.1	31.4	31.3	31.3	31.2	31.3	31.1	31.5
1968	31.4	31.5	31.6	31.7	31.5	31.3	31.6	31.7	31.9	32.1	32.8	32.4
1969	32.6	32.3	32.7	33.1	34.0	34.5	34.1	34.4	34.4	34.8	35.2	35.1
1970	35.1	35.2	35.6	35.5	35.0	35.0	35.1	34.7	35.5	35.5	35.1	34.5
1971	34.8	35.9	35.4	36.0	36.0	36.2	35.9	35.8	35.7	36.4	37.0	37.2
1972	37.8	38.1	38.1	38.7	39.3	39.4	40.0	40.3	40.5	40.9	42.0	43.8
1973	45.0	47.1	49.3	50.1	52.5	55.0	52.5	64.1	60.9	58.5	59.0	59.1
1974	63.3	64.3	62.3	60.6	58.3	55.4	59.8	62.9	60.9	63.2	64.2	61.5
1975	59.6	57.9	57.1	59.5	61.2	61.5	62.4	63.0	64.5	65.1	64.4	64.0
1976	63.0	62.1	61.5	63.9	63.6	65.2	64.8	63.6	63.4	63.0	63.4	64.5
1977	64.3	65.7	66.6	68.3	67.6	65.5	64.7	63.9	63.7	64.0	65.4	66.4
1978	67.3	68.4	69.8	72.1	72.8	74.6	74.2	73.7	75.1	77.0	77.4	78.0
1979	80.1	82.1	83.8	84.4	84.7	85.6	86.5	85.5	87.9	88.8	90.0	91.2
1980	90.9	92.6	90.8	88.3	89.5	90.1	94.6	99.0	100.4	102.2	103.5	102.7
1981	103.4	104.2	103.8	104.2	103.8	104.9	105.0	104.0	102.7	101.2	99.7	98.8
1982	99.7	100.0	99.7	100.2	101.9	101.8	100.7	99.8	99.2	98.7	99.2	98.8
1983	98.8	100.0	100.5	101.2	100.9	100.5	99.5	102.2	103.3	103.2	102.3	103.5
1984	104.6	103.8	105.7	105.2	104.5	103.3	104.0	103.3	102.8	101.5	101.9	101.4
1985	99.9	99.4	97.6	96.7	95.8	95.2	94.9	92.9	91.8	94.1	95.7	95.5
1986	94.2	90.5	88.2	85.6	86.5	86.2	86.4	86.7	86.6	87.4	87.6	86.9
1987	89.3	90.2	90.5	92.5	93.8	94.5	95.6	96.5	96.0	95.8	95.1	94.9
1988	94.2	95.2	94.1	95.4	95.8	97.0	96.7	97.0	97.0	96.6	95.2	98.1
1989	102.0	101.7	102.9	104.1	104.5	103.2	103.5	101.2	102.5	102.7	103.5	105.1
1990	106.7	106.8	105.1	102.7	103.1	100.6	101.0	110.5	115.8	125.8	117.8	110.8
1991	113.3	104.1	100.5	100.2	100.9	99.2	99.4	99.1	98.4	100.8	100.7	98.2
1992	97.2	98.6	97.1	98.1	100.3	101.6	101.6	100.7	102.8	102.8	102.5	101.3
1993	101.7	101.3	101.9	103.4	105.8	103.9	101.5	100.7	101.2	103.7	102.9	101.4
1994	103.3	101.7	103.5	103.8	102.4	102.8	102.1	101.9	99.8	98.9	99.4	100.9
1995	101.6	102.5	101.9	103.4	102.5	103.0	102.0	100.4	102.5	102.5	104.0	106.3
1996	109.0	111.1	109.8	114.2	115.4	112.6	115.1	115.8	112.8	112.0	115.0	122.1
1997	126.7	116.2	107.3	107.9	110.2	106.8	106.7	107.4	108.0	-	-	-

Source: The Conference Board. Primary source(s): U.S. Department of Labor, Bureau of Labor Statistics, Office of Prices and Living Conditions, Division of Industrial Prices and Price Indexes, Washington, DC 20212. A dash (-) indicates that data are not available or zero.

Producer Price Index, Intermediate Materials
(1982 = 100)

Year	Jan	Feb	Mar	Apr	May	Jun	Jul	Aug	Sep	Oct	Nov	Dec
1947	-	-	-	23.1	23.0	23.1	23.2	23.3	23.7	23.9	24.2	24.5
1948	25.0	24.7	24.8	25.0	25.2	25.4	25.4	25.5	25.5	25.4	25.4	25.2
1949	25.1	24.9	24.7	24.4	24.3	24.1	24.1	23.9	23.8	23.8	23.7	23.7
1950	23.8	24.0	24.1	24.2	24.6	24.7	25.2	25.6	26.2	26.6	26.9	27.7
1951	28.5	28.7	28.8	28.8	28.8	28.7	28.4	28.0	27.9	27.9	27.9	27.8
1952	27.8	27.7	27.5	27.5	27.4	27.5	27.5	27.5	27.6	27.5	27.4	27.3
1953	27.4	27.4	27.5	27.5	27.7	27.8	28.0	27.9	27.8	27.8	27.8	27.8
1954	27.9	27.8	27.8	27.9	27.9	27.8	27.9	27.8	27.8	27.8	27.9	27.8
1955	27.9	28.0	28.0	28.0	28.1	28.2	28.4	28.5	28.7	28.9	28.9	29.0
1956	29.1	29.1	29.4	29.5	29.6	29.7	29.4	29.7	29.8	30.0	30.0	30.1
1957	30.2	30.3	30.3	30.3	30.2	30.3	30.3	30.4	30.4	30.3	30.4	30.4
1958	30.4	30.3	30.3	30.3	30.3	30.3	30.3	30.4	30.4	30.4	30.5	30.6
1959	30.6	30.7	30.7	30.8	30.9	30.9	30.9	30.8	30.8	30.8	30.9	30.8
1960	30.9	30.9	30.9	30.9	30.8	30.9	30.8	30.8	30.8	30.8	30.7	30.6
1961	30.7	30.7	30.7	30.7	30.6	30.5	30.5	30.5	30.5	30.4	30.5	30.6
1962	30.5	30.5	30.6	30.6	30.6	30.6	30.6	30.6	30.6	30.6	30.5	30.5
1963	30.5	30.5	30.5	30.4	30.7	30.7	30.7	30.7	30.7	30.8	30.8	30.8
1964	30.8	30.8	30.7	30.7	30.7	30.6	30.7	30.7	30.7	30.9	30.9	30.9
1965	30.9	30.9	31.0	31.0	31.1	31.2	31.2	31.3	31.3	31.3	31.4	31.4
1966	31.5	31.6	31.7	31.8	32.0	32.0	32.2	32.3	32.3	32.2	32.2	32.2
1967	32.2	32.1	32.1	32.1	32.1	32.2	32.2	32.2	32.3	32.3	32.4	32.6
1968	32.6	32.7	32.8	32.8	32.8	32.9	33.0	33.0	33.1	33.2	33.2	33.4
1969	33.6	33.7	33.9	33.8	33.9	34.0	34.0	34.2	34.2	34.4	34.6	34.7
1970	35.0	35.0	34.9	35.1	35.2	35.3	35.5	35.5	35.6	35.8	35.9	35.9
1971	36.0	36.1	36.3	36.3	36.5	36.7	36.9	37.2	37.2	37.1	37.2	37.4
1972	37.5	37.7	37.8	37.9	38.0	38.0	38.1	38.2	38.5	38.7	39.0	39.6
1973	39.8	40.4	41.1	41.3	42.2	43.0	42.3	43.5	43.0	43.4	43.8	44.8
1974	45.9	46.8	48.1	49.0	50.6	51.5	53.4	55.8	55.9	57.2	57.8	57.8
1975	58.0	57.8	57.4	57.5	57.3	57.3	57.5	58.0	58.2	58.8	59.0	59.2
1976	59.4	59.6	59.8	60.0	60.3	60.8	61.1	61.3	61.9	62.0	62.4	62.8
1977	63.0	63.3	63.9	64.4	64.9	64.9	65.1	65.4	65.7	65.8	66.3	66.6
1978	66.9	67.4	67.8	68.1	68.7	69.2	69.4	69.9	70.5	71.3	71.9	72.4
1979	73.1	73.7	74.6	75.7	76.6	77.5	78.7	79.8	81.1	82.4	83.2	84.0
1980	86.0	87.6	88.2	88.5	89.0	89.8	90.5	91.5	91.9	92.8	93.5	94.4
1981	95.6	96.1	97.1	98.3	98.7	99.0	99.2	99.7	99.7	99.8	99.9	100.0
1982	100.4	100.3	99.9	99.7	99.7	99.8	100.0	99.9	100.0	99.9	100.1	100.1
1983	99.8	100.0	99.7	99.5	99.8	100.2	100.5	100.9	101.6	101.7	101.8	101.9
1984	102.1	102.5	103.0	103.2	103.4	103.6	103.4	103.2	103.1	103.2	103.3	103.2
1985	103.1	102.8	102.7	102.9	103.2	102.6	102.3	102.3	102.2	102.3	102.5	102.9
1986	102.4	101.2	99.9	98.9	98.7	98.6	98.0	98.0	98.5	98.3	98.3	98.5
1987	99.0	99.8	99.9	100.3	100.8	101.4	101.9	102.4	102.6	103.1	103.5	103.8
1988	104.1	104.4	104.8	105.5	106.2	107.4	108.3	108.5	108.7	108.6	108.8	109.4
1989	110.8	111.3	111.9	112.5	112.6	112.5	112.2	111.8	112.1	112.2	112.0	112.2
1990	113.7	112.8	112.9	113.1	113.1	112.9	112.8	114.0	115.8	117.4	117.7	116.9
1991	116.9	115.9	114.7	114.2	114.1	113.9	113.6	113.8	114.0	114.0	114.1	114.0
1992	113.4	113.8	113.9	114.1	114.5	115.1	115.2	115.1	115.3	115.3	115.1	115.1
1993	115.5	115.9	116.3	116.6	116.2	116.3	116.3	116.2	116.3	116.5	116.5	116.3
1994	116.5	116.9	117.1	117.1	117.2	117.8	118.4	119.1	119.7	120.1	121.0	121.5
1995	122.8	123.7	124.2	124.9	125.2	125.5	125.6	125.7	125.5	125.5	125.3	125.5
1996	125.5	125.0	125.2	125.6	126.1	125.7	125.5	125.7	126.2	126.0	125.8	126.4
1997	126.6	126.4	125.9	125.5	125.3	125.3	125.1	125.2	125.6	-	-	-

Source: The Conference Board. Primary source(s): U.S. Department of Labor, Bureau of Labor Statistics, Office of Prices and Living Conditions, Division of Industrial Prices and Price Indexes, Washington, DC 20212. A dash (-) indicates that data are not available or zero.

Producer Price Index, Capital Equipment
(1982 = 100)

Year	Jan	Feb	Mar	Apr	May	Jun	Jul	Aug	Sep	Oct	Nov	Dec
1947	-	-	-	19.5	19.8	19.9	19.9	20.0	20.1	20.3	20.4	20.5
1948	20.6	20.7	20.8	20.9	21.0	21.3	21.7	22.1	22.3	22.5	22.5	22.6
1949	22.6	22.8	22.8	22.9	22.8	22.8	22.8	22.7	22.5	22.5	22.5	22.5
1950	22.5	22.5	22.5	22.7	22.8	22.8	23.0	23.4	23.7	23.9	24.1	24.8
1951	25.1	25.2	25.4	25.5	25.6	25.6	25.6	25.5	25.6	25.7	25.7	25.7
1952	25.7	25.9	25.9	25.9	26.0	26.0	26.1	25.9	25.9	25.9	25.9	25.9
1953	25.9	25.9	26.0	26.1	26.2	26.4	26.6	26.5	26.6	26.6	26.4	26.5
1954	26.6	26.6	26.6	26.7	26.7	26.7	26.7	26.7	26.7	26.7	26.7	26.8
1955	26.8	26.9	26.9	27.0	27.1	27.2	27.3	27.6	27.9	28.2	28.1	28.3
1956	28.4	28.6	28.8	29.1	29.2	29.3	29.4	29.6	30.1	30.3	30.6	30.6
1957	30.7	30.9	31.0	31.1	31.1	31.2	31.4	31.5	31.6	31.7	31.9	32.0
1958	32.0	32.0	32.0	32.1	32.1	32.1	32.1	32.1	32.1	32.1	32.3	32.4
1959	32.5	32.5	32.6	32.7	32.8	32.9	32.9	32.9	32.9	32.9	32.7	32.7
1960	32.8	32.8	32.9	32.8	32.8	32.8	32.9	32.9	32.6	32.8	32.8	32.8
1961	32.9	32.8	32.9	32.9	32.9	32.9	32.9	32.9	32.9	32.9	32.9	32.9
1962	32.9	32.9	33.0	33.0	33.0	33.0	33.0	33.0	33.0	33.0	33.0	33.0
1963	33.0	33.0	33.0	33.0	33.0	33.0	33.0	33.0	33.1	33.1	33.1	33.2
1964	33.1	33.2	33.3	33.3	33.4	33.4	33.5	33.5	33.5	33.5	33.5	33.5
1965	33.6	33.6	33.7	33.8	33.7	33.8	33.8	33.9	33.9	33.9	33.9	34.0
1966	34.0	34.1	34.2	34.3	34.5	34.6	34.7	34.8	34.9	35.0	35.2	35.3
1967	35.4	35.5	35.5	35.6	35.7	35.7	35.8	35.9	35.9	36.1	36.2	36.4
1968	36.5	36.6	36.6	36.8	37.0	37.0	37.1	37.2	37.3	37.4	37.5	37.5
1969	37.6	37.7	37.8	37.9	38.0	38.1	38.3	38.4	38.5	38.7	39.0	39.2
1970	39.3	39.4	39.6	39.7	39.8	39.9	40.0	40.2	40.3	40.8	41.0	41.1
1971	41.3	41.4	41.5	41.6	41.7	41.7	41.9	42.0	41.9	41.8	41.8	42.1
1972	42.3	42.5	42.6	42.7	42.8	42.8	42.9	42.9	43.0	42.8	42.9	43.0
1973	43.0	43.3	43.6	43.8	44.1	44.2	44.3	44.4	44.6	44.7	44.9	45.3
1974	45.8	46.2	46.8	47.4	48.7	49.7	50.7	52.1	53.1	54.2	55.0	55.5
1975	56.2	56.7	57.2	57.5	57.8	58.0	58.4	58.5	58.9	59.3	59.7	60.0
1976	60.4	60.7	61.1	61.3	61.5	61.8	62.1	62.5	62.9	63.1	63.4	64.0
1977	64.0	64.3	64.7	65.0	65.3	65.7	66.0	66.6	67.0	67.6	68.1	68.6
1978	68.8	69.1	69.6	69.9	70.5	71.0	71.5	72.0	72.6	72.8	73.5	74.0
1979	74.5	75.2	75.7	76.4	76.8	77.3	77.8	77.8	78.7	79.2	79.8	80.6
1980	81.7	82.3	83.1	84.4	84.6	85.1	86.2	87.0	87.5	88.8	89.3	89.7
1981	90.8	91.7	92.4	93.1	93.8	94.4	95.0	95.4	96.1	96.9	97.5	98.1
1982	98.6	98.2	98.7	99.0	99.5	100.0	100.3	100.7	101.0	101.1	101.3	101.9
1983	101.8	102.1	102.2	102.3	102.5	102.6	102.8	103.1	103.3	103.4	103.5	103.8
1984	104.1	104.5	104.6	105.3	105.1	105.2	105.5	105.6	105.9	105.6	105.8	105.6
1985	106.3	106.9	107.1	107.1	107.4	107.6	107.7	107.9	107.2	108.3	108.5	108.6
1986	108.6	108.7	108.9	109.2	109.3	109.6	109.7	109.8	109.7	110.6	110.8	110.9
1987	111.3	111.1	111.1	111.6	111.6	111.5	111.7	112.0	112.0	112.0	112.1	112.2
1988	112.8	113.0	113.2	113.5	113.8	114.0	114.4	114.9	115.2	115.5	115.7	116.1
1989	116.9	117.3	117.5	117.6	118.3	118.9	118.9	119.3	119.7	120.0	120.4	120.6
1990	121.0	121.4	121.8	122.1	122.1	122.5	122.9	123.3	123.8	124.1	124.5	124.8
1991	125.6	125.8	126.0	126.1	126.5	126.6	126.7	126.8	127.2	127.6	127.8	128.0
1992	128.2	128.3	128.6	129.0	129.0	129.0	129.1	129.4	129.4	129.7	129.9	130.1
1993	130.4	130.7	130.9	131.1	131.2	131.1	131.5	131.6	131.8	131.7	132.2	132.4
1994	132.9	133.1	133.3	133.7	134.1	134.2	134.4	134.6	135.0	134.3	134.5	134.9
1995	135.5	135.8	135.9	136.2	136.4	136.5	136.8	136.9	137.0	137.6	138.1	138.0
1996	138.0	138.0	138.1	138.1	138.1	138.3	138.3	138.5	138.7	138.5	138.5	138.5
1997	138.6	138.5	138.5	138.4	138.1	138.1	138.0	138.0	138.4	-	-	-

Source: The Conference Board. Primary source(s): U.S. Department of Labor, Bureau of Labor Statistics, Office of Prices and Living Conditions, Division of Industrial Prices and Price Indexes, Washington, DC 20212. A dash (-) indicates that data are not available or zero.

Producer Price Index, Finished Consumer Goods

(1982 = 100)

Year	Jan	Feb	Mar	Apr	May	Jun	Jul	Aug	Sep	Oct	Nov	Dec
1947	-	-	-	28.4	28.3	28.3	28.3	28.5	28.9	29.2	29.6	30.1
1948	30.7	30.5	30.5	30.7	30.9	31.0	31.1	31.2	31.0	30.9	30.6	30.4
1949	30.2	29.9	29.8	29.6	29.5	29.5	29.2	29.1	29.0	29.0	28.9	28.8
1950	28.8	28.9	28.9	28.9	29.1	29.2	29.8	30.4	30.7	30.8	31.1	31.7
1951	32.3	32.8	32.8	32.9	33.0	32.8	32.5	32.5	32.4	32.6	32.6	32.7
1952	32.5	32.5	32.5	32.4	32.3	32.2	32.4	32.4	32.2	32.1	32.0	31.7
1953	31.8	31.7	31.7	31.6	31.6	31.7	31.7	31.7	31.9	31.8	31.6	31.7
1954	31.9	31.7	31.7	31.9	31.9	31.7	31.8	31.7	31.5	31.5	31.6	31.5
1955	31.6	31.7	31.5	31.6	31.4	31.6	31.3	31.4	31.5	31.4	31.5	31.5
1956	31.5	31.5	31.7	31.7	32.0	32.1	32.0	32.0	32.2	32.2	32.4	32.5
1957	32.5	32.6	32.6	32.7	32.7	32.8	33.0	33.0	33.0	33.1	33.2	33.4
1958	33.5	33.5	33.9	33.7	33.8	33.7	33.6	33.6	33.6	33.5	33.5	33.5
1959	33.4	33.4	33.3	33.4	33.3	33.3	33.2	33.1	33.5	33.2	33.1	33.2
1960	33.2	33.2	33.5	33.6	33.6	33.6	33.7	33.7	33.7	33.9	34.0	33.9
1961	33.8	34.0	33.8	33.6	33.4	33.4	33.5	33.6	33.5	33.4	33.5	33.6
1962	33.7	33.8	33.7	33.6	33.6	33.5	33.5	33.7	34.0	33.7	33.7	33.6
1963	33.6	33.5	33.3	33.3	33.5	33.6	33.6	33.5	33.5	33.5	33.6	33.5
1964	33.7	33.5	33.5	33.5	33.5	33.5	33.6	33.6	33.6	33.6	33.6	33.6
1965	33.6	33.6	33.8	34.0	34.1	34.3	34.2	34.3	34.3	34.5	34.6	34.9
1966	34.9	35.2	35.3	35.4	35.2	35.1	35.2	35.7	35.8	35.7	35.6	35.5
1967	35.4	35.3	35.2	35.3	35.4	35.7	35.6	35.7	35.8	35.8	35.9	35.9
1968	35.9	36.1	36.2	36.4	36.4	36.5	36.6	36.7	36.9	37.0	37.0	37.0
1969	37.2	37.1	37.3	37.5	37.8	38.0	38.0	38.1	38.2	38.5	38.8	38.8
1970	39.0	38.9	39.0	39.0	38.9	39.0	39.0	39.0	39.4	39.3	39.5	39.4
1971	39.5	39.7	39.8	40.0	40.1	40.3	40.1	40.4	40.3	40.4	40.6	40.9
1972	40.7	40.9	40.9	40.9	41.1	41.4	41.6	41.7	42.0	41.9	42.1	42.6
1973	43.0	43.5	44.7	45.0	45.3	45.9	45.7	47.7	47.5	47.4	47.9	48.3
1974	49.6	50.7	51.1	51.5	52.0	51.8	53.2	54.1	54.6	55.6	56.7	56.6
1975	56.8	56.6	56.4	56.9	57.3	57.8	58.4	59.0	59.4	59.9	60.1	60.1
1976	59.9	59.6	59.6	60.0	60.0	60.1	60.3	60.4	60.5	60.9	61.4	61.9
1977	62.1	62.8	63.4	63.7	64.2	64.2	64.5	64.8	65.0	65.3	65.8	66.1
1978	66.4	66.9	67.3	68.2	68.6	69.3	69.9	69.9	70.6	71.0	71.5	72.5
1979	73.3	74.2	74.8	75.6	75.9	76.4	77.3	78.3	79.8	80.6	81.8	82.6
1980	83.9	85.2	86.1	86.7	87.1	87.9	89.4	90.5	90.8	91.3	92.0	92.4
1981	93.3	94.1	95.3	96.4	96.6	97.0	97.1	97.1	97.5	97.8	98.0	98.4
1982	99.0	99.0	98.8	98.9	98.8	99.8	100.1	100.5	100.7	101.0	101.4	101.7
1983	100.8	100.8	100.7	100.7	101.0	101.3	101.3	101.6	101.8	101.9	101.5	101.9
1984	102.7	103.1	103.6	103.5	103.5	103.4	103.6	103.3	103.2	103.1	103.4	103.5
1985	103.4	103.4	103.3	103.9	104.2	103.8	103.8	103.6	102.9	103.9	104.6	105.3
1986	104.6	102.8	101.0	100.3	101.0	101.2	100.2	100.7	100.9	101.5	101.4	101.5
1987	102.1	102.5	102.6	103.3	103.4	103.8	104.0	104.2	104.5	104.4	104.3	104.1
1988	104.6	104.4	104.7	105.2	105.4	105.7	106.6	107.1	107.3	107.5	107.9	108.3
1989	109.5	110.5	110.9	111.9	112.9	112.7	112.4	111.7	112.5	113.1	113.2	114.1
1990	116.9	116.7	116.3	116.1	116.3	116.3	116.6	118.2	120.0	121.5	122.3	121.4
1991	122.0	120.8	120.2	120.2	120.4	120.1	119.6	119.9	120.1	120.5	121.0	120.8
1992	120.4	120.8	120.8	120.9	121.4	121.9	121.9	121.9	122.3	122.8	122.6	122.7
1993	122.9	123.2	123.4	124.2	124.1	123.6	123.4	122.0	122.2	122.4	122.5	122.5
1994	122.5	122.9	122.9	122.8	122.6	122.8	123.4	124.1	123.6	123.2	124.0	124.6
1995	124.6	124.8	125.0	125.2	125.4	125.4	125.6	125.5	125.9	126.1	126.3	127.4
1996	127.6	127.5	128.4	128.7	128.9	129.4	129.4	129.4	129.9	130.3	131.0	132.1
1997	131.6	131.1	130.8	129.9	129.6	129.4	129.2	129.7	130.4	-	-	-

Source: The Conference Board. Primary source(s): U.S. Department of Labor, Bureau of Labor Statistics, Office of Prices and Living Conditions, Division of Industrial Prices and Price Indexes, Washington, DC 20212. A dash (-) indicates that data are not available or zero.

Producer Price Index, Finished Goods
(1982 = 100)

Year	Jan	Feb	Mar	Apr	May	Jun	Jul	Aug	Sep	Oct	Nov	Dec
1947	-	-	-	26.0	26.1	26.2	26.2	26.3	26.7	26.8	27.1	27.7
1948	28.1	27.9	28.0	28.1	28.4	28.6	28.8	28.9	28.8	28.7	28.5	28.5
1949	28.3	28.0	28.0	27.9	27.8	27.7	27.5	27.4	27.4	27.3	27.2	27.2
1950	27.2	27.2	27.3	27.3	27.5	27.6	28.0	28.6	28.9	29.0	29.4	30.0
1951	30.5	30.8	30.9	30.9	31.1	31.0	30.8	30.7	30.6	30.8	30.9	30.9
1952	30.8	30.7	30.9	30.7	30.7	30.7	30.8	30.7	30.6	30.5	30.4	30.2
1953	30.3	30.2	30.3	30.2	30.3	30.4	30.5	30.4	30.4	30.4	30.3	30.4
1954	30.5	30.4	30.4	30.6	30.6	30.4	30.5	30.4	30.3	30.2	30.3	30.3
1955	30.4	30.5	30.3	30.4	30.4	30.5	30.4	30.4	30.5	30.6	30.6	30.7
1956	30.7	30.8	30.9	31.0	31.2	31.4	31.3	31.4	31.6	31.8	31.9	31.9
1957	32.1	32.2	32.1	32.3	32.3	32.5	32.6	32.6	32.6	32.7	32.9	33.0
1958	33.2	33.2	33.4	33.2	33.2	33.3	33.2	33.2	33.2	33.2	33.2	33.1
1959	33.1	33.2	33.2	33.2	33.3	33.2	33.1	33.0	33.4	33.1	33.0	33.0
1960	33.1	33.1	33.4	33.4	33.4	33.4	33.5	33.4	33.4	33.7	33.7	33.6
1961	33.6	33.7	33.6	33.4	33.3	33.3	33.3	33.4	33.3	33.3	33.4	33.4
1962	33.5	33.6	33.5	33.5	33.4	33.4	33.4	33.5	33.8	33.6	33.6	33.5
1963	33.4	33.4	33.3	33.3	33.4	33.5	33.4	33.4	33.4	33.5	33.5	33.4
1964	33.5	33.5	33.4	33.5	33.5	33.5	33.5	33.6	33.6	33.6	33.6	33.6
1965	33.6	33.7	33.7	34.0	34.1	34.2	34.1	34.2	34.3	34.4	34.5	34.7
1966	34.7	35.0	35.0	35.1	35.1	34.9	35.1	35.4	35.6	35.5	35.5	35.4
1967	35.4	35.3	35.3	35.3	35.4	35.7	35.7	35.8	35.8	35.9	35.9	36.0
1968	36.1	36.2	36.3	36.5	36.5	36.6	36.7	36.8	37.0	37.0	37.1	37.1
1969	37.2	37.2	37.4	37.6	37.8	38.0	38.1	38.2	38.3	38.5	38.8	38.9
1970	39.1	39.0	39.1	39.1	39.1	39.2	39.2	39.2	39.6	39.6	39.8	39.8
1971	39.9	40.1	40.2	40.3	40.5	40.6	40.4	40.7	40.7	40.7	40.8	41.1
1972	41.0	41.3	41.3	41.3	41.5	41.7	41.8	42.0	42.2	42.0	42.3	42.7
1973	43.0	43.5	44.4	44.7	45.0	45.5	45.4	47.0	46.9	46.8	47.2	47.6
1974	48.8	49.7	50.2	50.7	51.3	51.3	52.7	53.7	54.3	55.3	56.4	56.4
1975	56.7	56.6	56.6	57.1	57.4	57.9	58.4	58.9	59.3	59.8	60.0	60.1
1976	60.0	59.9	60.0	60.3	60.4	60.5	60.7	60.9	61.1	61.4	61.9	62.4
1977	62.5	63.2	63.7	64.0	64.4	64.6	64.8	65.2	65.5	65.9	66.4	66.7
1978	67.0	67.5	67.8	68.6	69.1	69.7	70.3	70.4	71.1	71.4	72.0	72.8
1979	73.7	74.4	75.0	75.8	76.2	76.6	77.4	78.2	79.5	80.4	81.4	82.2
1980	83.4	84.6	85.5	86.2	86.6	87.3	88.7	89.7	90.1	90.8	91.4	91.8
1981	92.8	93.6	94.7	95.7	96.0	96.5	96.7	96.8	97.2	97.6	97.9	98.3
1982	98.9	98.8	98.8	99.0	99.0	99.8	100.2	100.6	100.7	101.0	101.4	101.8
1983	101.0	101.1	101.0	101.1	101.4	101.6	101.6	101.9	102.2	102.2	102.0	102.3
1984	103.0	103.4	103.8	103.9	103.8	103.8	104.0	103.8	103.8	103.6	104.0	104.0
1985	104.0	104.1	104.1	104.6	104.9	104.6	104.7	104.5	103.8	104.9	105.5	106.0
1986	105.5	104.1	102.8	102.3	102.8	103.1	102.3	102.7	102.9	103.5	103.4	103.6
1987	104.1	104.4	104.5	105.1	105.2	105.5	105.7	105.9	106.2	106.0	106.0	105.8
1988	106.4	106.3	106.6	107.0	107.2	107.5	108.4	108.8	109.0	109.2	109.6	110.0
1989	111.1	111.9	112.3	113.1	114.0	114.0	113.8	113.4	114.0	114.6	114.8	115.5
1990	117.7	117.6	117.5	117.4	117.5	117.6	117.9	119.2	120.7	121.9	122.6	122.0
1991	122.6	121.8	121.3	121.3	121.6	121.4	121.1	121.3	121.5	121.9	122.4	122.3
1992	122.0	122.3	122.4	122.5	122.9	123.4	123.3	123.4	123.7	124.2	124.1	124.2
1993	124.4	124.7	124.9	125.6	125.5	125.1	125.0	124.0	124.2	124.3	124.5	124.5
1994	124.7	125.0	125.1	125.1	125.0	125.2	125.7	126.3	126.0	125.5	126.2	126.8
1995	126.9	127.1	127.3	127.5	127.7	127.7	127.9	127.9	128.3	128.5	128.8	129.6
1996	129.7	129.7	130.4	130.6	130.8	131.2	131.2	131.6	132.0	132.5	132.7	133.4
1997	133.0	132.6	132.3	131.6	131.3	131.1	131.0	131.4	132.0	-	-	-

Source: The Conference Board. Primary source(s): U.S. Department of Labor, Bureau of Labor Statistics, Office of Prices and Living Conditions, Division of Industrial Prices and Price Indexes, Washington, DC 20212. A dash (-) indicates that data are not available or zero.

Producer Price Index, Crude Nonfood Less Energy
(1982 = 100)

Year	Jan	Feb	Mar	Apr	May	Jun	Jul	Aug	Sep	Oct	Nov	Dec
1974	86.3	86.5	88.3	89.7	83.8	82.9	84.2	85.5	82.5	80.6	77.6	71.6
1975	69.8	69.2	68.2	67.7	68.8	66.5	66.5	67.7	71.2	71.5	71.9	73.1
1976	72.4	73.8	74.5	78.1	80.6	82.8	87.3	84.1	84.4	82.2	81.8	81.1
1977	78.7	79.7	81.5	82.1	82.5	79.7	78.8	79.2	79.2	78.5	78.4	80.1
1978	80.3	80.6	80.3	82.2	84.6	87.4	89.6	90.4	92.3	94.7	96.3	96.8
1979	96.4	99.6	104.2	105.1	106.7	111.6	109.4	106.4	106.5	108.9	111.3	111.3
1980	112.6	115.3	111.7	109.9	107.2	106.1	109.6	112.4	116.2	118.2	119.8	119.3
1981	113.3	106.2	108.9	111.9	113.7	115.5	116.4	115.5	112.6	110.8	107.5	106.0
1982	101.2	100.7	100.0	101.1	102.2	101.0	101.4	100.0	98.9	97.7	96.3	95.9
1983	97.3	99.8	102.2	102.1	103.4	104.8	106.2	108.4	109.0	109.1	109.9	111.2
1984	111.5	113.8	114.8	115.1	115.7	114.1	112.0	109.6	110.5	108.5	107.7	107.3
1985	107.4	107.2	107.0	107.4	105.3	103.6	104.3	103.6	103.3	103.7	103.0	102.4
1986	103.6	103.5	103.8	103.9	104.1	104.7	105.3	99.7	100.3	102.0	102.8	104.1
1987	105.4	106.2	106.5	107.5	110.0	113.2	115.9	119.1	122.8	126.6	127.5	127.9
1988	129.4	131.7	133.0	132.1	130.7	131.1	133.2	134.3	133.3	133.6	136.0	137.6
1989	140.6	140.3	140.6	140.3	139.8	137.9	135.9	136.8	137.5	137.9	134.9	132.8
1990	132.7	131.6	133.9	137.0	138.0	137.3	138.0	140.1	139.9	138.4	135.7	133.8
1991	134.2	133.7	131.8	131.7	130.4	126.1	125.4	125.8	125.7	125.4	124.4	123.4
1992	123.4	125.2	127.7	128.4	129.1	128.8	129.6	130.4	130.4	128.9	128.2	130.5
1993	134.7	137.3	137.8	140.1	141.6	141.3	142.3	139.6	139.9	141.6	142.9	144.3
1994	148.2	151.8	152.6	152.4	150.8	151.9	155.3	157.8	159.4	160.4	165.7	169.3
1995	174.2	176.5	178.3	180.2	179.8	179.8	176.6	173.9	171.0	166.7	163.7	162.1
1996	162.2	161.9	158.5	156.4	157.5	154.7	152.2	152.9	153.7	153.5	153.2	153.2
1997	156.7	158.4	158.9	155.3	157.3	157.5	156.7	157.9	156.3	-	-	-

Source: The Conference Board. Primary source(s): U.S. Department of Labor, Bureau of Labor Statistics, Office of Prices and Living Conditions, Division of Industrial Prices and Price Indexes, Washington, DC 20212. A dash (-) indicates that data are not available or zero.

Producer Price Index, Petroleum Products
(1982 = 100)

Year	Jan	Feb	Mar	Apr	May	Jun	Jul	Aug	Sep	Oct	Nov	Dec
1967	13.1	13.2	13.2	13.1	13.2	13.1	13.1	13.4	13.3	13.1	13.0	12.9
1968	12.9	12.9	12.8	12.9	12.8	13.1	13.0	12.9	12.9	12.9	12.9	12.8
1969	12.9	12.9	13.1	13.1	13.0	13.1	13.1	13.1	13.0	13.2	13.2	13.2
1970	13.1	13.1	13.0	13.0	13.2	13.0	13.0	13.2	13.3	13.5	13.7	14.3
1971	14.3	14.1	13.9	13.7	14.0	13.9	14.0	14.1	14.2	14.3	14.3	14.2
1972	13.9	13.8	13.9	14.0	14.0	14.1	14.2	14.4	14.7	14.8	14.9	14.9
1973	14.8	15.6	15.8	16.0	16.3	16.6	16.9	16.9	17.2	17.7	18.7	20.2
1974	22.0	24.6	26.9	28.1	29.2	30.2	31.1	31.7	31.9	32.3	31.8	31.9
1975	32.0	31.6	31.7	31.8	32.1	32.9	33.6	34.9	35.6	36.1	36.7	36.6
1976	36.2	35.9	35.5	35.2	35.1	35.4	36.0	36.4	36.9	37.3	37.8	38.0
1977	38.5	39.2	40.1	40.7	41.0	41.0	40.8	40.5	40.5	40.9	41.3	41.5
1978	41.7	41.4	40.9	41.0	41.3	41.7	41.9	42.0	42.4	43.2	44.0	44.8
1979	45.8	46.3	47.2	49.6	52.4	55.5	58.6	62.8	67.1	70.3	72.3	73.6
1980	77.4	82.0	86.5	90.1	89.4	89.4	90.4	90.5	90.8	90.5	92.1	94.5
1981	97.6	101.6	108.0	112.1	110.1	108.8	106.3	105.5	105.2	105.0	104.9	105.0
1982	106.1	104.4	100.8	98.3	94.5	97.2	101.1	101.3	99.4	98.4	98.9	98.8
1983	95.4	91.7	87.4	87.0	87.7	90.1	89.6	90.0	90.7	90.6	89.2	88.7
1984	87.6	88.8	89.4	90.1	90.5	89.6	87.4	84.7	84.2	85.2	85.6	85.3
1985	84.0	81.6	81.5	86.0	87.9	82.6	81.3	80.5	80.7	81.5	83.0	85.7
1986	81.7	71.0	58.7	52.1	52.0	52.2	43.8	43.4	48.1	45.4	45.0	46.8
1987	52.4	55.7	54.4	54.8	54.2	56.3	58.3	61.4	58.7	59.4	59.1	57.5
1988	55.2	54.9	53.9	54.1	54.8	54.4	54.5	55.0	52.4	50.7	53.1	53.6
1989	56.0	57.5	59.3	65.2	65.9	65.0	61.8	57.1	60.4	61.8	60.9	63.2
1990	74.3	67.2	65.4	65.9	63.8	63.7	61.1	73.5	84.2	93.4	94.4	89.0
1991	81.4	74.6	66.0	64.6	65.2	65.0	62.1	65.6	65.3	64.1	66.8	65.5
1992	60.0	62.6	61.8	62.0	63.9	68.4	67.7	66.4	66.3	66.4	67.3	62.9
1993	64.2	65.5	66.7	65.3	64.0	62.8	61.3	59.5	59.3	61.2	60.9	54.0
1994	55.3	59.0	58.1	56.9	55.6	57.5	61.3	65.5	61.5	58.3	62.1	58.8
1995	60.6	60.7	61.3	62.9	63.2	62.7	60.7	60.6	59.8	58.0	58.4	61.1
1996	65.8	63.6	67.8	72.7	71.6	67.5	68.4	69.1	70.8	72.8	75.5	75.8
1997	77.4	75.8	72.2	67.6	64.8	64.2	63.9	67.2	67.1	-	-	-

Source: The Conference Board. Primary source(s): U.S. Department of Labor, Bureau of Labor Statistics, Office of Prices and Living Conditions, Division of Industrial Prices and Price Indexes, Washington, DC 20212. A dash (-) indicates that data are not available or zero.

Output per Hour, Business Sector
(1992 = 100)

Year	1st Quarter	2nd Quarter	3rd Quarter	4th Quarter
1947	32.9	33.8	33.9	34.3
1948	34.8	35.5	35.2	35.4
1949	35.3	35.5	36.5	36.6
1950	38.5	38.8	39.4	39.7
1951	39.5	39.8	41.0	40.8
1952	40.9	41.3	41.5	41.9
1953	42.6	43.1	43.2	43.0
1954	43.0	43.6	44.3	44.9
1955	45.6	46.0	45.9	45.5
1956	45.4	45.6	45.7	46.5
1957	46.8	46.8	47.4	47.8
1958	47.4	48.1	49.0	49.5
1959	50.0	50.4	50.8	50.9
1960	52.3	51.2	51.2	50.9
1961	51.5	53.2	53.8	54.5
1962	55.0	55.3	56.1	56.5
1963	57.0	57.3	58.5	58.7
1964	60.3	60.4	60.9	60.6
1965	61.7	61.8	63.1	64.1
1966	65.2	65.0	65.0	65.5
1967	66.2	66.7	66.7	66.9
1968	68.3	69.1	69.1	69.0
1969	69.2	69.2	69.3	69.1
1970	69.3	70.1	71.6	71.2
1971	73.3	73.4	74.2	73.4
1972	74.4	76.0	76.4	77.2
1973	78.9	78.7	77.9	78.2
1974	77.0	77.6	76.7	77.0
1975	78.2	79.6	80.6	80.6
1976	82.0	82.5	82.5	83.1
1977	83.5	83.7	84.7	83.8
1978	83.5	85.1	85.3	85.4
1979	84.6	84.6	84.5	84.2
1980	84.8	83.6	83.8	84.6
1981	85.9	85.3	86.4	85.2
1982	84.4	85.2	85.3	86.1
1983	86.7	88.1	88.3	88.8
1984	89.7	90.3	90.3	90.5
1985	90.8	91.0	92.4	92.5
1986	93.9	94.2	94.1	93.9
1987	93.4	93.9	93.9	94.6
1988	94.6	94.5	94.7	94.9
1989	95.0	95.5	95.6	95.7
1990	96.1	96.6	96.3	95.4
1991	95.9	96.7	97.1	97.5
1992	99.4	99.9	99.7	101.0
1993	100.1	99.7	99.9	101.0
1994	100.7	100.7	100.5	100.7
1995	100.2	100.4	100.6	101.1
1996	101.6	102.3	102.0	102.5
1997	102.9	103.6	-	-

Source: The Conference Board. Primary source(s): U.S. Department of Labor, Bureau of Labor Statistics, Office of Productivity and Technology, Division of Productivity Research, Washington, DC 20212. A dash (-) indicates that data are not available or zero.

Output per Hour, Nonfarm Business Sector
(1992 = 100)

Year	1st Quarter	2nd Quarter	3rd Quarter	4th Quarter
1947	38.2	39.3	38.4	39.9
1948	39.8	39.9	39.9	40.1
1949	40.5	40.9	42.0	41.7
1950	43.4	43.8	44.6	44.8
1951	44.7	44.8	45.8	45.8
1952	45.8	46.1	45.9	46.6
1953	46.9	47.1	47.4	47.2
1954	47.4	47.7	48.5	48.9
1955	49.9	50.1	50.3	50.0
1956	49.5	49.7	49.7	50.0
1957	50.6	50.5	51.3	51.3
1958	50.6	51.6	52.6	53.3
1959	53.7	54.4	54.3	54.3
1960	55.6	54.7	54.8	54.2
1961	54.9	56.3	57.1	57.8
1962	58.9	58.6	59.3	59.8
1963	60.2	60.7	61.8	61.9
1964	63.5	63.9	64.3	63.6
1965	64.6	65.1	66.1	67.2
1966	68.2	67.9	67.8	68.2
1967	68.8	69.1	69.4	69.6
1968	71.1	71.9	71.7	71.6
1969	72.2	71.6	71.5	71.2
1970	71.4	72.4	73.8	73.1
1971	75.3	75.6	76.2	75.4
1972	76.8	78.2	78.7	79.2
1973	81.3	81.0	80.5	79.9
1974	79.7	79.7	78.8	79.3
1975	80.0	81.4	82.4	82.3
1976	83.9	84.5	84.6	84.8
1977	85.3	85.9	86.6	85.4
1978	85.5	87.2	87.3	87.6
1979	86.5	86.4	86.2	86.0
1980	86.5	85.2	85.6	86.5
1981	87.6	86.5	87.4	86.2
1982	85.4	86.2	86.4	87.1
1983	88.1	89.9	90.6	90.8
1984	91.1	91.6	91.5	91.5
1985	91.7	91.8	92.8	93.0
1986	94.5	94.9	94.8	94.6
1987	94.0	94.6	94.4	95.0
1988	94.8	95.0	95.4	95.9
1989	95.4	95.7	95.9	96.1
1990	96.4	96.7	96.4	95.5
1991	96.1	96.8	97.3	97.6
1992	99.3	100.0	99.7	101.1
1993	100.1	99.6	100.0	100.8
1994	100.6	100.7	100.4	100.8
1995	100.3	100.5	100.8	101.2
1996	101.7	102.2	102.0	102.4
1997	102.8	103.5	-	-

Source: The Conference Board. Primary source(s): U.S. Department of Labor, Bureau of Labor Statistics, Office of Productivity and Technology, Division of Productivity Research, Washington, DC 20212. A dash (-) indicates that data are not available or zero.

PRICE INDEXES FOR GROSS DOMESTIC PRODUCT

The 12 series in this section show the functioning of inflation in the U.S. economy from 1959 through 1996.

Price indexes are presented for:

    Gross domestic product as a whole
    Busines sector
     Nonfarm business sector
      Nonfarm less housing
       Housing sector only
     Farms
    Households and institutions
     Private households
     Nonprofit institutions
    General government
     Federal government
     State and local government

Price Index versus Implicit Price Deflator

Before the 1995 revisions of the national income accounts, a special price index, known as the implicit price deflator (IPD), was used to derive GDP (or its components) in real dollars. The IPD reflects *both* changes in pricing and changes in the composition of GDP from one period to another. For this reason, the IPD was a superior tool for measuring inflation. That is now changing.

With the shift from constant dollar indexes to the chain-type price indexes, IPDs and chain-type price indexes are identical except for the most recent estimates (see Introduction for a full discussion). Both measures use the same weights to aggregate the detailed prices.

For these reasons, chain-type price indexes continue to be used in this edition of *EIH*.

Using the Indexes

The simplest explanation for these indexes is that they shows how inflation or deflation influence Gross Domestic Product and its major sectors. Using artificially simple numbers, if GDP in actual, current dollars was $1,000 in 1992 and $2,000 in 1994 and *no inflation in prices* had taken place in the 1992-1994 period, the chained price index for GDP in 1994 would be 100.0, i.e. the *same* as in the reference year. Therefore, the change between 1992 and 1994 was *real growth*.

Assume, however, that cumulative inflation in the period was 30%; this would mean that, in 1994, a person would have to spend $1.30 to have the same purchasing power as in 1992. The chained (1992) dollar value of the $2,000 GDP in 1994 would therefore be $1,538.46 (2000 / 1.30). The price index would be calculated as follows:

(2000 / 1538.46) x 100

This would produce an index of 130.0. The index, in other words, can be read as an indicator of inflation relative to the reference year—in this case 1992. The difference between any two years is the increase or decrease in prices between those years. In the example above, the *real growth* between 1992 and 1994 is only $538.46 rather than the apparent $1,000.

The price index for GDP is an indicator of *overall* inflation or deflation. Indexes are also provided for major sectors of GDP. Thus the user who wishes to calculate how she or he is doing relative to inflation would consult the table for private households; the business owner would consult the table for busines or for nonfarm business less housing.

An example showing the use of the Private Household table is presented below.

An Example. A person who got a job in January of 1989 paying $39,500 a year would like to calculate how he is doing in January 1996. The person now makes $45,000 a year, an increase of $5,500. Has this person gained or lost purchasing power?

The price index for the Private Households sector of GDP was 88.41 in the first quarter of 1989; it was 111.97 in the first quarter of 1996. The following formula provides the percent increase in prices between 1989 and 1996 in the index:

((Current Index / Previous Index) - 1) x 100.

The result is 26.65 percent. Multiplying the 1989 salary by 1.2665 produces $50,027. Therefore the person has not kept up with inflation. On the contrary, he has lost real purchasing power since 1989 despite an 11.4 percent increase in pay.

Price Indexes for Gross Domestic Product
Based on chained 1992 $

Year	1st Quarter	2nd Quarter	3rd Quarter	4th Quarter
1959	22.86	22.92	22.96	23.05
1960	23.10	23.21	23.32	23.44
1961	23.48	23.51	23.55	23.61
1962	23.73	23.80	23.86	23.96
1963	24.03	24.07	24.11	24.26
1964	24.33	24.41	24.53	24.64
1965	24.76	24.88	25.01	25.16
1966	25.30	25.50	25.82	26.03
1967	26.16	26.32	26.57	26.87
1968	27.19	27.50	27.75	28.12
1969	28.38	28.74	29.14	29.51
1970	29.92	30.36	30.60	31.02
1971	31.50	31.93	32.25	32.53
1972	33.01	33.23	33.50	33.93
1973	34.38	34.96	35.63	36.24
1974	36.98	37.79	38.93	40.14
1975	41.04	41.67	42.44	43.21
1976	43.68	44.17	44.78	45.56
1977	46.31	47.08	47.74	48.55
1978	49.39	50.43	51.32	52.37
1979	53.46	54.70	55.82	56.92
1980	58.25	59.59	60.93	62.57
1981	64.19	65.35	66.65	67.85
1982	68.85	69.71	70.69	71.46
1983	72.12	72.84	73.50	74.19
1984	75.00	75.62	76.25	76.82
1985	77.64	78.25	78.80	79.44
1986	79.81	80.26	80.81	81.44
1987	82.11	82.68	83.35	84.08
1988	84.69	85.56	86.67	87.46
1989	88.44	89.40	90.13	90.91
1990	92.01	93.20	94.19	95.14
1991	96.26	97.02	97.70	98.30
1992	99.14	99.81	100.17	100.88
1993	101.85	102.38	102.83	103.52
1994	104.16	104.74	105.39	106.07
1995	106.93	107.49	108.03	108.60
1996	109.35	109.86	110.59	111.10

Source: U.S. Department of Commerce, Bureau of Economic Analysis, National Income and Wealth Division. A dash (-) indicates that data are not available or zero.

Price Indexes for GDP
Business Sector
Based on chained 1992 $

Year	1st Quarter	2nd Quarter	3rd Quarter	4th Quarter
1959	25.30	25.36	25.38	25.46
1960	25.49	25.62	25.70	25.82
1961	25.86	25.86	25.89	25.94
1962	26.03	26.10	26.16	26.22
1963	26.26	26.28	26.33	26.43
1964	26.47	26.55	26.64	26.75
1965	26.88	27.00	27.10	27.21
1966	27.34	27.54	27.86	28.09
1967	28.19	28.33	28.58	28.83
1968	29.14	29.46	29.66	30.04
1969	30.29	30.67	30.99	31.35
1970	31.65	32.07	32.27	32.71
1971	33.08	33.51	33.83	34.06
1972	34.42	34.59	34.84	35.19
1973	35.61	36.20	36.89	37.50
1974	38.29	39.13	40.38	41.63
1975	42.56	43.16	43.97	44.68
1976	45.11	45.56	46.21	46.97
1977	47.73	48.51	49.17	49.91
1978	50.79	51.92	52.86	53.95
1979	55.05	56.36	57.50	58.57
1980	59.96	61.34	62.73	64.28
1981	65.96	67.17	68.60	69.72
1982	70.68	71.52	72.49	73.15
1983	73.77	74.44	75.06	75.73
1984	76.27	76.82	77.41	77.95
1985	78.66	79.29	79.82	80.42
1986	80.76	81.17	81.66	82.21
1987	82.79	83.29	83.96	84.68
1988	85.22	86.12	87.34	88.17
1989	89.09	90.11	90.79	91.55
1990	92.55	93.74	94.71	95.61
1991	96.69	97.37	98.00	98.55
1992	99.25	99.76	100.13	100.87
1993	101.76	102.33	102.73	103.42
1994	103.98	104.54	105.22	105.86
1995	106.66	107.16	107.65	108.03
1996	108.62	109.26	109.95	110.43

Source: U.S. Department of Commerce, Bureau of Economic Analysis, National Income and Wealth Division. A dash (-) indicates that data are not available or zero.

Price Indexes for GDP
Business Sector - Nonfarm
Based on chained 1992 $

Year	1st Quarter	2nd Quarter	3rd Quarter	4th Quarter
1959	24.82	24.89	24.93	25.03
1960	25.06	25.16	25.26	25.36
1961	25.41	25.45	25.45	25.45
1962	25.55	25.65	25.70	25.74
1963	25.80	25.84	25.88	26.00
1964	26.04	26.13	26.23	26.33
1965	26.45	26.50	26.62	26.69
1966	26.76	27.00	27.29	27.59
1967	27.72	27.89	28.14	28.40
1968	28.68	28.98	29.17	29.55
1969	29.83	30.14	30.45	30.76
1970	31.09	31.56	31.73	32.22
1971	32.57	32.99	33.32	33.50
1972	33.82	33.97	34.15	34.41
1973	34.64	35.02	35.44	36.22
1974	36.94	38.19	39.29	40.44
1975	41.69	42.36	43.05	43.72
1976	44.21	44.71	45.38	46.22
1977	46.93	47.74	48.41	49.25
1978	49.91	50.88	51.87	52.90
1979	53.87	55.24	56.45	57.60
1980	59.13	60.83	61.80	63.10
1981	65.00	66.37	67.92	69.23
1982	70.20	71.04	71.97	72.79
1983	73.20	73.75	74.37	74.96
1984	75.49	76.15	76.85	77.42
1985	78.21	78.97	79.64	80.15
1986	80.61	80.96	81.37	81.89
1987	82.52	83.03	83.75	84.49
1988	84.99	85.88	86.90	87.77
1989	88.66	89.75	90.47	91.21
1990	92.21	93.43	94.44	95.47
1991	96.64	97.26	97.96	98.50
1992	99.24	99.78	100.10	100.88
1993	101.84	102.34	102.69	103.36
1994	103.96	104.61	105.39	106.03
1995	106.88	107.35	107.73	108.04
1996	108.67	109.20	109.76	110.21

Source: U.S. Department of Commerce, Bureau of Economic Analysis, National Income and Wealth Division. A dash (-) indicates that data are not available or zero.

Price Indexes for GDP

Business Sector - Nonfarm Less Housing
Based on chained 1992 $

Year	1st Quarter	2nd Quarter	3rd Quarter	4th Quarter
1959	24.97	25.05	25.09	25.19
1960	25.21	25.32	25.41	25.51
1961	25.56	25.60	25.59	25.59
1962	25.69	25.79	25.83	25.88
1963	25.94	25.97	26.01	26.14
1964	26.18	26.27	26.38	26.47
1965	26.60	26.65	26.77	26.85
1966	26.91	27.16	27.48	27.80
1967	27.93	28.10	28.36	28.64
1968	28.94	29.25	29.44	29.84
1969	30.13	30.45	30.76	31.07
1970	31.41	31.90	32.06	32.56
1971	32.91	33.33	33.67	33.84
1972	34.17	34.31	34.49	34.74
1973	34.95	35.33	35.75	36.58
1974	37.36	38.73	39.90	41.12
1975	42.43	43.12	43.83	44.50
1976	44.97	45.46	46.14	47.00
1977	47.68	48.48	49.15	50.01
1978	50.68	51.71	52.74	53.79
1979	54.79	56.24	57.45	58.57
1980	60.19	61.99	62.92	64.17
1981	66.16	67.54	69.10	70.38
1982	71.33	72.20	73.08	73.84
1983	74.20	74.73	75.32	75.90
1984	76.40	77.01	77.67	78.21
1985	78.97	79.68	80.27	80.69
1986	81.09	81.35	81.69	82.16
1987	82.80	83.27	83.97	84.63
1988	85.09	86.00	87.03	87.89
1989	88.79	89.90	90.59	91.27
1990	92.27	93.47	94.42	95.51
1991	96.75	97.36	98.06	98.55
1992	99.27	99.79	100.09	100.85
1993	101.84	102.31	102.65	103.33
1994	103.88	104.54	105.33	105.94
1995	106.78	107.21	107.53	107.76
1996	108.36	108.88	109.40	109.82

Source: U.S. Department of Commerce, Bureau of Economic Analysis, National Income and Wealth Division. A dash (-) indicates that data are not available or zero.

Price Indexes for GDP
Business Sector - Nonfarm Housing
Based on chained 1992 $

Year	1st Quarter	2nd Quarter	3rd Quarter	4th Quarter
1959	23.76	23.75	23.76	23.88
1960	24.00	24.07	24.19	24.29
1961	24.35	24.42	24.47	24.54
1962	24.64	24.69	24.76	24.84
1963	24.89	24.95	25.01	25.09
1964	25.15	25.20	25.26	25.35
1965	25.39	25.45	25.54	25.59
1966	25.72	25.80	25.88	26.02
1967	26.12	26.25	26.37	26.48
1968	26.69	26.87	27.04	27.22
1969	27.43	27.68	27.97	28.23
1970	28.52	28.82	29.10	29.45
1971	29.85	30.25	30.53	30.75
1972	31.01	31.25	31.50	31.77
1973	32.24	32.60	32.92	33.28
1974	33.45	33.69	34.06	34.64
1975	35.44	35.92	36.47	37.15
1976	37.78	38.30	38.92	39.59
1977	40.62	41.45	42.21	42.90
1978	43.41	43.95	44.50	45.37
1979	46.02	46.76	47.92	49.30
1980	50.11	51.00	52.35	53.96
1981	55.12	56.35	57.81	59.41
1982	60.57	61.20	62.48	63.70
1983	64.56	65.26	66.09	66.81
1984	67.59	68.65	69.71	70.61
1985	71.51	72.74	74.14	75.46
1986	76.37	77.61	78.52	79.46
1987	80.14	80.92	81.84	83.21
1988	84.15	84.85	85.83	86.71
1989	87.55	88.49	89.46	90.73
1990	91.78	93.10	94.67	95.09
1991	95.69	96.36	97.09	98.06
1992	98.99	99.69	100.23	101.10
1993	101.88	102.53	103.03	103.63
1994	104.64	105.22	105.97	106.77
1995	107.71	108.58	109.46	110.47
1996	111.36	112.06	112.88	113.63

Source: U.S. Department of Commerce, Bureau of Economic Analysis, National Income and Wealth Division. A dash (-) indicates that data are not available or zero.

Price Indexes for GDP
Business Sector - Farms
Based on chained 1992 $

Year	1st Quarter	2nd Quarter	3rd Quarter	4th Quarter
1959	57.37	56.36	55.97	54.87
1960	55.08	56.63	55.57	56.97
1961	56.42	54.64	55.99	58.29
1962	58.15	56.80	57.67	58.47
1963	57.28	56.59	57.10	55.85
1964	55.90	55.48	55.05	56.20
1965	56.53	61.13	59.84	62.18
1966	66.40	64.20	66.31	61.75
1967	60.04	58.22	58.92	58.49
1968	60.22	62.06	62.79	63.60
1969	61.86	66.82	67.87	71.88
1970	69.38	67.00	68.54	65.92
1971	67.72	68.92	68.29	72.79
1972	75.03	76.50	81.78	89.33
1973	103.77	119.86	141.90	128.75
1974	135.24	103.97	116.79	125.46
1975	102.44	98.98	107.46	111.72
1976	107.65	105.01	104.02	99.06
1977	103.33	102.41	102.07	94.07
1978	113.14	125.17	122.17	127.69
1979	139.51	135.40	131.23	127.27
1980	117.64	93.75	124.89	144.47
1981	129.62	119.63	113.73	102.90
1982	103.46	104.75	109.52	98.30
1983	113.34	122.28	123.35	129.87
1984	131.23	123.13	115.28	113.81
1985	109.55	101.05	91.98	98.92
1986	90.93	95.05	101.54	104.62
1987	101.46	101.17	98.25	97.79
1988	100.80	102.49	118.69	116.49
1989	119.71	114.97	112.54	115.42
1990	115.85	115.27	113.06	105.55
1991	100.03	104.82	100.89	101.55
1992	99.63	98.45	101.79	100.13
1993	96.19	102.09	105.65	107.50
1994	105.65	99.80	93.29	94.23
1995	91.35	93.48	102.82	108.39
1996	105.84	114.23	125.11	128.16

Source: U.S. Department of Commerce, Bureau of Economic Analysis, National Income and Wealth Division. A dash (-) indicates that data are not available or zero.

Price Indexes for GDP
Households and Institutions
Based on chained 1992 $

Year	1st Quarter	2nd Quarter	3rd Quarter	4th Quarter
1959	11.48	11.63	11.91	12.24
1960	12.16	12.32	12.51	12.58
1961	12.65	12.75	12.82	12.95
1962	13.17	13.29	13.34	13.52
1963	13.73	13.87	13.90	14.00
1964	14.29	14.33	14.59	14.70
1965	14.58	14.95	15.24	15.63
1966	15.51	15.87	16.23	16.52
1967	16.72	16.95	17.16	17.49
1968	18.15	18.29	18.55	19.05
1969	19.49	19.92	20.44	21.23
1970	21.64	22.23	22.94	23.21
1971	23.68	24.06	24.26	24.79
1972	25.26	25.61	25.72	26.40
1973	27.01	27.48	27.97	28.67
1974	29.18	29.94	30.49	31.29
1975	31.67	31.90	32.35	33.23
1976	34.17	34.83	35.20	36.00
1977	36.04	36.81	37.65	38.65
1978	39.69	40.37	41.55	42.22
1979	43.15	43.91	44.97	46.04
1980	47.03	48.29	49.25	50.48
1981	51.67	52.90	54.11	55.05
1982	56.05	56.86	58.11	59.27
1983	60.22	61.21	62.59	63.88
1984	64.89	66.15	67.28	67.80
1985	68.39	68.88	69.71	70.18
1986	70.87	71.33	72.43	73.30
1987	74.72	76.46	78.07	80.02
1988	80.29	80.79	81.31	82.08
1989	83.20	83.97	85.21	86.45
1990	88.15	89.65	91.15	91.42
1991	92.65	94.16	95.21	96.47
1992	97.40	100.39	100.70	101.51
1993	101.96	101.77	102.19	102.91
1994	103.76	104.28	105.42	106.49
1995	107.53	108.50	109.03	109.93
1996	110.62	110.78	111.36	111.98

Source: U.S. Department of Commerce, Bureau of Economic Analysis, National Income and Wealth Division. A dash (-) indicates that data are not available or zero.

Price Indexes for GDP
Private Households
Based on chained 1992 $

Year	1st Quarter	2nd Quarter	3rd Quarter	4th Quarter
1959	18.66	18.68	19.58	20.01
1960	20.17	20.44	20.49	20.54
1961	20.59	20.65	20.64	20.79
1962	20.99	21.10	21.31	21.49
1963	21.57	21.66	21.65	21.70
1964	21.94	22.30	22.52	22.69
1965	22.89	23.23	23.63	23.93
1966	24.23	24.45	24.83	25.33
1967	25.30	25.42	25.58	26.18
1968	27.33	28.09	28.33	29.01
1969	29.59	29.91	30.29	31.07
1970	31.77	32.38	32.95	33.69
1971	34.12	34.45	34.88	35.18
1972	35.86	36.28	36.53	36.99
1973	38.07	38.88	39.15	39.85
1974	39.94	42.05	44.97	45.28
1975	45.43	45.28	46.02	47.60
1976	50.11	51.82	52.66	54.39
1977	55.89	56.33	56.68	56.72
1978	57.87	59.82	61.79	64.03
1979	65.80	67.34	68.69	70.05
1980	71.32	72.75	74.05	75.42
1981	76.82	78.23	79.83	81.19
1982	82.00	82.34	82.31	82.27
1983	82.22	82.55	82.54	82.73
1984	83.21	83.32	83.57	83.78
1985	84.09	84.38	84.41	84.68
1986	85.02	85.19	85.58	85.95
1987	86.21	86.15	86.56	86.64
1988	86.72	87.36	87.73	87.95
1989	88.41	88.77	88.84	89.02
1990	89.76	90.89	92.12	93.85
1991	94.96	95.93	96.71	97.89
1992	98.40	99.38	100.67	101.53
1993	101.81	102.53	103.69	104.66
1994	105.21	105.78	106.73	107.45
1995	108.57	109.05	109.75	111.09
1996	111.97	112.56	114.29	115.40

Source: U.S. Department of Commerce, Bureau of Economic Analysis, National Income and Wealth Division. A dash (-) indicates that data are not available or zero.

Price Indexes for GDP
Nonprofit Institutions
Based on chained 1992 $

Year	1st Quarter	2nd Quarter	3rd Quarter	4th Quarter
1959	10.96	11.15	11.32	11.64
1960	11.51	11.66	11.89	11.98
1961	12.05	12.18	12.27	12.40
1962	12.64	12.77	12.80	13.00
1963	13.24	13.40	13.45	13.56
1964	13.87	13.85	14.15	14.25
1965	14.07	14.47	14.76	15.18
1966	14.99	15.39	15.76	16.03
1967	16.28	16.54	16.77	17.07
1968	17.69	17.75	18.03	18.52
1969	18.97	19.43	19.98	20.79
1970	21.18	21.79	22.54	22.76
1971	23.25	23.65	23.83	24.39
1972	24.86	25.21	25.31	26.03
1973	26.61	27.06	27.57	28.29
1974	28.85	29.51	29.90	30.75
1975	31.14	31.40	31.83	32.68
1976	33.52	34.12	34.46	35.21
1977	35.15	35.95	36.84	37.92
1978	38.96	39.56	40.71	41.29
1979	42.18	42.90	43.95	45.01
1980	45.99	47.25	48.19	49.41
1981	50.60	51.82	53.02	53.94
1982	54.95	55.78	57.08	58.29
1983	59.28	60.30	61.74	63.08
1984	64.11	65.42	66.59	67.13
1985	67.73	68.23	69.09	69.57
1986	70.28	70.76	71.89	72.78
1987	74.25	76.07	77.73	79.75
1988	80.03	80.53	81.05	81.85
1989	82.99	83.78	85.07	86.35
1990	88.09	89.61	91.12	91.33
1991	92.56	94.09	95.15	96.42
1992	97.36	100.43	100.70	101.51
1993	101.96	101.74	102.13	102.84
1994	103.70	104.22	105.37	106.45
1995	107.50	108.47	109.00	109.89
1996	110.57	110.72	111.25	111.86

Source: U.S. Department of Commerce, Bureau of Economic Analysis, National Income and Wealth Division. A dash (-) indicates that data are not available or zero.

Price Indexes for GDP
General Government
Based on chained 1992 $

Year	1st Quarter	2nd Quarter	3rd Quarter	4th Quarter
1959	13.88	13.94	13.97	14.01
1960	14.17	14.19	14.44	14.53
1961	14.57	14.68	14.75	14.86
1962	15.05	15.08	15.15	15.40
1963	15.57	15.65	15.66	15.99
1964	16.15	16.25	16.41	16.50
1965	16.65	16.72	16.93	17.22
1966	17.43	17.60	17.87	17.99
1967	18.20	18.46	18.70	19.18
1968	19.46	19.71	20.18	20.48
1969	20.67	20.92	21.65	21.95
1970	22.85	23.28	23.60	23.94
1971	24.85	25.34	25.66	26.08
1972	27.12	27.49	27.91	28.62
1973	29.24	29.79	30.33	30.94
1974	31.45	32.08	32.83	33.91
1975	34.78	35.60	36.30	37.25
1976	37.83	38.45	38.93	39.78
1977	40.64	41.35	41.94	43.11
1978	43.67	44.28	44.82	45.72
1979	46.75	47.72	48.76	50.00
1980	51.08	52.23	53.37	55.67
1981	57.00	57.84	58.41	60.12
1982	61.35	62.35	63.27	64.58
1983	65.38	66.35	66.97	67.69
1984	70.05	70.87	71.68	72.43
1985	74.00	74.58	75.13	76.10
1986	76.59	77.23	78.03	79.13
1987	80.13	80.78	81.16	81.59
1988	82.75	83.54	84.15	84.67
1989	85.96	86.66	87.54	88.27
1990	89.88	90.89	91.92	93.38
1991	94.75	95.74	96.58	97.37
1992	99.02	99.95	100.31	100.72
1993	102.39	102.87	103.76	104.40
1994	105.48	106.23	106.52	107.34
1995	108.56	109.32	110.28	112.15
1996	114.07	113.75	114.89	115.62

Source: U.S. Department of Commerce, Bureau of Economic Analysis, National Income and Wealth Division. A dash (-) indicates that data are not available or zero.

Price Indexes for GDP
Federal Government
Based on chained 1992 $

Year	1st Quarter	2nd Quarter	3rd Quarter	4th Quarter
1959	13.65	13.69	13.70	13.71
1960	13.76	13.71	14.07	14.14
1961	14.12	14.15	14.13	14.17
1962	14.26	14.25	14.36	14.70
1963	14.85	14.89	14.87	15.31
1964	15.56	15.63	15.83	15.94
1965	16.02	16.09	16.34	16.79
1966	16.88	16.93	17.15	17.10
1967	17.06	17.26	17.40	18.07
1968	18.27	18.45	19.07	19.27
1969	19.33	19.39	20.38	20.53
1970	21.77	22.11	22.31	22.62
1971	23.92	24.45	24.75	25.49
1972	27.09	27.40	27.67	28.71
1973	29.33	29.79	30.44	31.37
1974	31.82	32.43	33.24	34.85
1975	35.73	36.31	36.89	38.30
1976	38.55	39.04	39.56	40.99
1977	42.04	42.62	42.87	44.65
1978	44.97	45.43	45.99	47.66
1979	48.51	49.13	49.80	52.20
1980	53.00	53.91	54.58	58.42
1981	59.45	60.03	60.47	63.35
1982	64.37	65.15	65.50	66.97
1983	67.37	68.27	68.52	68.90
1984	73.13	73.68	74.24	74.50
1985	76.65	76.75	76.91	78.14
1986	78.43	78.80	79.27	79.89
1987	81.26	81.31	81.23	81.28
1988	82.85	83.87	84.48	84.47
1989	86.74	87.09	87.40	87.04
1990	88.91	89.44	90.13	92.17
1991	94.10	95.13	95.90	96.52
1992	99.50	100.29	100.43	99.79
1993	102.80	102.60	103.78	104.46
1994	105.70	106.87	106.20	107.18
1995	109.26	109.58	110.75	114.56
1996	116.58	116.09	116.92	117.71

Source: U.S. Department of Commerce, Bureau of Economic Analysis, National Income and Wealth Division. A dash (-) indicates that data are not available or zero.

Price Indexes for GDP
State and Local Government
Based on chained 1992 $

Year	1st Quarter	2nd Quarter	3rd Quarter	4th Quarter
1959	13.91	14.00	14.04	14.13
1960	14.41	14.53	14.64	14.74
1961	14.85	15.07	15.23	15.42
1962	15.72	15.79	15.83	15.96
1963	16.17	16.28	16.33	16.52
1964	16.60	16.72	16.83	16.90
1965	17.12	17.19	17.36	17.50
1966	17.82	18.11	18.42	18.72
1967	19.19	19.52	19.84	20.13
1968	20.50	20.82	21.13	21.51
1969	21.83	22.27	22.75	23.18
1970	23.78	24.29	24.72	25.07
1971	25.65	26.08	26.43	26.60
1972	27.20	27.62	28.15	28.62
1973	29.24	29.84	30.30	30.69
1974	31.25	31.89	32.61	33.33
1975	34.19	35.18	35.95	36.62
1976	37.39	38.10	38.57	39.04
1977	39.78	40.58	41.38	42.16
1978	42.88	43.58	44.10	44.54
1979	45.67	46.85	48.13	48.67
1980	49.91	51.21	52.62	54.00
1981	55.52	56.50	57.15	58.17
1982	59.52	60.65	61.91	63.13
1983	64.17	65.18	66.03	66.95
1984	68.16	69.15	70.12	71.17
1985	72.39	73.26	74.06	74.86
1986	75.47	76.27	77.27	78.67
1987	79.44	80.45	81.11	81.77
1988	82.69	83.32	83.94	84.77
1989	85.49	86.41	87.60	88.96
1990	90.43	91.71	92.93	94.05
1991	95.10	96.08	96.95	97.83
1992	98.76	99.78	100.25	101.21
1993	102.17	103.02	103.75	104.37
1994	105.38	105.92	106.68	107.41
1995	108.21	109.18	110.04	111.02
1996	112.89	112.65	113.93	114.64

Source: U.S. Department of Commerce, Bureau of Economic Analysis, National Income and Wealth Division. A dash (-) indicates that data are not available or zero.

INDICATORS OF LABOR AND EMPLOYMENT

This section presents 3 indicators of employment and labor:

> Civilian labor force
> Civilian employment
> Civilian labor force participation
> > Males, 20 years and over
> > Females, 20 years and over
> > Both sexes, 16 to 19 years of age

Civilian Labor Force and **Civilian Employment**. The series are available from 1948 through 1997 and are shown in thousands. The two series are the source of unemployment data (number and rate) shown in the section on Other Cyclic Indicators. The labor force is defined as individuals working or actively seeking work. Civilian employment is that portion of the labor force which is now employed. The unemployment rate is calculated by the following formula:

(1-(Civilian Employment / Civilian Labor Force)) x 100

For January 1995, the labor force was 132,298,000 and employment was 124,766,000, indicating unemployment of 7,432,000. This number represents 5.6 percent of the labor force.

A certain level of unemployment is a "natural" phenomenon in a healthy economy. Some economists equate 3-4 percent unemployment with "full employment," on the basis that a certain small fraction of the labor force is, of necessity, in transition between jobs. At the peak of the 1961-1969 expansion (12/69), unemployment was at 3.5 percent; at the peak of the 1971-1973 expansion (10/73), unemployment stood at 4.6 percent. By contrast, at the trough of the 1970 recession (12/70), unemployment stood at 6.1 percent; during the 1974-1975 recession, unemployment reached nearly 9 percent (5/75).

Civilian Labor Force Participation. The three tables showing labor force participation extend from 1948 to 1997 and show participation in percent. In January 1991, for instance, 77.9 percent of males 20 years or older participated in the labor force. Base data—the number of people of the gender and age group overall—are derived from the censuses of population and estimates based on them. The participation values are based on estimates of the total labor force.

The values show interesting general patterns. Labor force participation for males has declined gradually from nearly 90 percent in the late 1940s to under 80 percent in recent times. Female labor force participation, however, which was just over 30 percent in the 1940s and 1950s, has just passed 60 percent in 1996. The participation of young people (16 to 19 years of age) has remained virtually unchanged since the 1940s—although it dipped somewhat in the 1950s and 1960s.

Underlying the labor participation numbers are complex economic and demographic forces, including efforts to maintain family income levels, the rise in the skill level demanded in the work place, the reduced role of manufacturing and the corresponding rise in the services sectors of the economy, and others.

Civilian Labor Force

(Thousands)

Year	Jan	Feb	Mar	Apr	May	Jun	Jul	Aug	Sep	Oct	Nov	Dec
1948	60,095	60,524	60,070	60,677	59,972	60,957	61,181	60,806	60,815	60,646	60,702	61,169
1949	60,771	61,057	61,073	61,007	61,259	60,948	61,301	61,590	61,633	62,185	62,005	61,908
1950	61,661	61,687	61,604	62,158	62,083	62,419	62,121	62,596	62,349	62,428	62,286	62,068
1951	61,941	61,778	62,526	61,808	62,044	61,615	62,106	61,927	61,780	62,204	62,014	62,457
1952	62,432	62,419	61,721	61,720	62,058	62,103	61,962	61,877	62,457	61,971	62,491	62,621
1953	63,439	63,520	63,657	63,167	62,615	63,063	63,057	62,816	62,727	62,867	62,949	62,795
1954	63,101	63,994	63,793	63,934	63,675	63,343	63,302	63,707	64,209	63,936	63,759	63,312
1955	63,910	63,696	63,882	64,564	64,381	64,482	65,145	65,581	65,628	65,821	66,037	66,445
1956	66,419	66,124	66,175	66,264	66,722	66,702	66,752	66,673	66,714	66,546	66,657	66,700
1957	66,428	66,879	66,913	66,647	66,695	67,052	67,336	66,706	67,064	67,066	67,123	67,398
1958	67,095	67,201	67,223	67,647	67,895	67,674	67,824	68,037	68,002	68,045	67,658	67,740
1959	67,936	67,649	68,068	68,339	68,178	68,278	68,539	68,432	68,545	68,821	68,533	68,994
1960	68,962	68,949	68,399	69,579	69,626	69,934	69,745	69,841	70,151	69,884	70,439	70,395
1961	70,447	70,420	70,703	70,267	70,452	70,878	70,536	70,534	70,217	70,492	70,376	70,077
1962	70,189	70,409	70,414	70,278	70,551	70,514	70,302	70,981	71,153	70,917	70,871	70,854
1963	71,146	71,262	71,423	71,697	71,832	71,626	71,956	71,786	72,131	72,281	72,418	72,188
1964	72,356	72,683	72,713	73,274	73,395	73,032	73,007	73,118	73,290	73,308	73,286	73,465
1965	73,569	73,857	73,949	74,228	74,466	74,412	74,761	74,616	74,502	74,838	74,797	75,093
1966	75,186	74,954	75,075	75,338	75,447	75,647	75,736	76,046	76,056	76,199	76,610	76,641
1967	76,639	76,521	76,328	76,777	76,773	77,270	77,464	77,712	77,812	78,194	78,191	78,491
1968	77,578	78,230	78,256	78,270	78,847	79,120	78,970	78,811	78,858	78,913	79,209	79,463
1969	79,523	80,019	80,079	80,281	80,125	80,696	80,827	81,106	81,290	81,494	81,397	81,624
1970	81,981	82,151	82,498	82,727	82,483	82,484	82,901	82,880	82,954	83,276	83,548	83,670
1971	83,850	83,603	83,575	83,946	84,135	83,706	84,340	84,673	84,731	84,872	85,458	85,625
1972	85,978	86,036	86,611	86,614	86,809	87,006	87,143	87,517	87,392	87,491	87,592	87,943
1973	87,487	88,364	88,846	89,018	88,977	89,548	89,604	89,509	89,838	90,131	90,716	90,890
1974	91,199	91,485	91,453	91,287	91,596	91,868	92,212	92,059	92,488	92,518	92,766	92,780
1975	93,128	92,776	93,165	93,399	93,884	93,575	94,021	94,162	94,202	94,267	94,250	94,409
1976	94,934	94,998	95,215	95,746	95,847	95,885	96,583	96,741	96,553	96,704	97,254	97,348
1977	97,208	97,785	98,115	98,330	98,665	99,093	98,913	99,366	99,453	99,815	100,576	100,491
1978	100,873	100,837	101,092	101,574	101,896	102,371	102,399	102,511	102,795	103,080	103,562	103,809
1979	104,057	104,502	104,589	104,172	104,171	104,638	105,002	105,096	105,530	105,700	105,812	106,258
1980	106,562	106,697	106,442	106,591	106,929	106,780	107,159	107,105	107,098	107,405	107,568	107,352
1981	108,026	108,242	108,553	108,925	109,222	108,396	108,556	108,725	108,294	109,024	109,236	108,912
1982	109,089	109,467	109,567	109,820	110,451	110,081	110,342	110,514	110,721	110,744	111,050	111,083
1983	110,695	110,634	110,587	110,828	110,796	111,879	111,756	112,231	112,298	111,926	112,228	112,327
1984	112,209	112,615	112,713	113,098	113,649	113,817	113,972	113,682	113,857	114,019	114,170	114,581
1985	114,725	114,876	115,328	115,331	115,234	114,965	115,320	115,291	115,905	116,145	116,135	116,354
1986	116,682	116,882	117,220	117,316	117,528	118,084	118,129	118,150	118,395	118,516	118,634	118,611
1987	118,845	119,122	119,270	119,336	120,008	119,644	119,902	120,318	120,011	120,509	120,540	120,729
1988	120,969	121,156	120,913	121,251	121,071	121,473	121,665	122,125	121,960	122,206	122,637	122,622
1989	123,390	123,135	123,227	123,565	123,474	123,995	123,967	124,166	123,944	124,211	124,637	124,497
1990	125,833	125,710	125,801	125,649	125,893	125,573	125,732	125,990	125,892	125,995	126,070	126,142
1991	125,955	126,020	126,238	126,548	126,176	126,331	126,154	126,150	126,650	126,642	126,701	126,664
1992	127,261	127,207	127,604	127,841	128,119	128,459	128,563	128,613	128,501	128,026	128,441	128,554
1993	128,400	128,458	128,598	128,584	129,264	129,411	129,397	129,619	129,268	129,573	129,711	129,941
1994	130,709	130,685	130,501	130,644	130,828	130,590	130,644	131,223	131,284	131,676	131,846	131,847
1995	132,198	132,140	132,271	132,613	131,935	131,978	132,300	132,246	132,450	132,564	132,533	132,422
1996	132,899	133,070	133,464	133,427	133,759	133,709	134,165	133,898	134,291	134,636	134,831	135,022
1997	135,848	135,634	136,319	136,098	136,173	136,200	136,290	136,480	136,467	-	-	-

Source: The Conference Board. Primary source(s): U.S. Department of Labor, Bureau of Labor Statistics, Office of Employment and Unemployment Statistics, Division of Labor Force Statistics, Washington, DC 20212. A dash (-) indicates that data are not available or zero.

Civilian Employment

(Thousands)

Year	Jan	Feb	Mar	Apr	May	Jun	Jul	Aug	Sep	Oct	Nov	Dec
1948	58,061	58,196	57,671	58,291	57,854	58,743	58,968	58,456	58,513	58,387	58,417	58,740
1949	58,175	58,208	58,043	57,747	57,552	57,172	57,190	57,397	57,584	57,269	58,009	57,845
1950	57,635	57,751	57,728	58,583	58,649	59,052	59,001	59,797	59,575	59,803	59,697	59,429
1951	59,636	59,661	60,401	59,889	60,188	59,620	60,156	59,994	59,713	60,010	59,836	60,497
1952	60,460	60,462	59,908	59,909	60,195	60,219	59,971	59,790	60,521	60,132	60,748	60,954
1953	61,600	61,884	62,010	61,444	61,019	61,456	61,397	61,151	60,906	60,893	60,738	59,977
1954	60,024	60,663	60,186	60,185	59,908	59,792	59,643	59,853	60,282	60,270	60,357	60,116
1955	60,753	60,727	60,964	61,515	61,634	61,781	62,513	62,797	62,950	62,991	63,257	63,684
1956	63,753	63,518	63,411	63,614	63,861	63,820	63,800	63,972	64,079	63,975	63,796	63,910
1957	63,632	64,257	64,404	64,047	63,985	64,196	64,540	63,959	64,121	64,046	63,669	63,922
1958	63,220	62,898	62,731	62,631	62,874	62,730	62,745	63,012	63,181	63,475	63,470	63,549
1959	63,868	63,684	64,267	64,768	64,699	64,849	65,011	64,844	64,770	64,911	64,530	65,341
1960	65,347	65,620	64,673	65,959	66,057	66,168	65,909	65,895	66,267	65,632	66,109	65,778
1961	65,776	65,588	65,850	65,374	65,449	65,993	65,608	65,852	65,541	65,919	66,081	65,900
1962	66,108	66,538	66,493	66,372	66,688	66,670	66,483	66,968	67,192	67,114	66,847	66,947
1963	67,072	67,024	67,351	67,642	67,615	67,649	67,905	67,908	68,174	68,294	68,267	68,213
1964	68,327	68,751	68,763	69,356	69,631	69,218	69,399	69,463	69,578	69,582	69,735	69,814
1965	69,997	70,127	70,439	70,633	71,034	71,025	71,460	71,362	71,286	71,695	71,724	72,062
1966	72,198	72,134	72,188	72,510	72,497	72,775	72,860	73,146	73,258	73,401	73,840	73,729
1967	73,671	73,606	73,439	73,882	73,844	74,278	74,520	74,767	74,854	75,051	75,125	75,473
1968	74,700	75,229	75,379	75,561	76,107	76,182	76,087	76,043	76,172	76,224	76,494	76,778
1969	76,805	77,327	77,367	77,523	77,412	77,880	77,959	78,250	78,250	78,445	78,541	78,740
1970	78,780	78,698	78,863	78,930	78,564	78,413	78,726	78,624	78,498	78,685	78,650	78,594
1971	78,864	78,700	78,588	78,987	79,139	78,757	79,305	79,539	79,689	79,918	80,297	80,471
1972	80,959	81,108	81,573	81,655	81,887	82,083	82,230	82,578	82,543	82,616	82,990	83,400
1973	83,161	83,912	84,452	84,559	84,648	85,185	85,299	85,204	85,488	85,987	86,320	86,401
1974	86,555	86,754	86,819	86,669	86,891	86,941	87,149	87,037	87,051	86,995	86,626	86,144
1975	85,627	85,256	85,187	85,189	85,451	85,355	85,894	86,234	86,279	86,370	86,456	86,665
1976	87,400	87,672	87,985	88,416	88,794	88,563	89,093	89,223	89,173	89,274	89,634	89,803
1977	89,928	90,342	90,808	91,271	91,754	91,959	92,084	92,441	92,702	93,052	93,761	94,105
1978	94,384	94,519	94,755	95,394	95,769	96,343	96,090	96,431	96,670	97,133	97,485	97,581
1979	97,948	98,329	98,480	98,103	98,331	98,679	99,006	98,776	99,340	99,404	99,574	99,933
1980	99,879	99,995	99,713	99,233	98,945	98,682	98,796	98,824	99,077	99,317	99,545	99,634
1981	99,955	100,191	100,571	101,056	101,048	100,298	100,693	100,689	100,064	100,378	100,207	99,645
1982	99,692	99,762	99,672	99,576	100,116	99,543	99,493	99,633	99,504	99,215	99,112	99,032
1983	99,161	99,089	99,179	99,560	99,642	100,633	101,208	101,608	102,016	102,039	102,729	102,996
1984	103,201	103,824	103,967	104,336	105,193	105,591	105,435	105,163	105,490	105,638	105,972	106,223
1985	106,302	106,555	106,989	106,936	106,932	106,503	106,807	107,095	107,657	107,047	108,007	108,216
1986	108,887	108,480	108,837	108,952	109,089	109,576	109,810	110,015	110,085	110,273	110,475	110,728
1987	110,953	111,257	111,408	111,794	112,434	112,246	112,634	113,057	112,909	113,282	113,505	113,793
1988	114,016	114,227	114,037	114,650	114,292	114,927	115,060	115,282	115,356	115,638	116,100	116,104
1989	116,708	116,776	117,022	117,097	117,099	117,418	117,472	117,655	117,354	117,581	117,912	117,830
1990	119,081	119,059	119,203	118,852	119,151	118,983	118,810	118,802	118,524	118,536	118,306	118,241
1991	117,940	117,755	117,652	118,109	117,440	117,639	117,568	117,484	117,928	117,800	117,770	117,466
1992	117,978	117,753	118,144	118,426	118,375	118,419	118,713	118,826	118,720	118,628	118,876	118,997
1993	119,075	119,275	119,542	119,474	120,115	120,290	120,467	120,856	120,554	120,823	121,169	121,464
1994	121,999	122,104	122,001	122,331	122,961	122,653	122,717	123,274	123,544	124,052	124,474	124,689
1995	124,766	124,937	125,070	125,023	124,577	124,533	124,804	124,729	124,927	125,235	125,124	125,068
1996	125,311	125,706	126,062	126,125	126,428	126,590	126,889	126,988	127,248	127,617	127,644	127,855
1997	128,580	128,430	129,175	129,384	129,639	129,364	129,708	129,804	129,715	-	-	-

Source: The Conference Board. Primary source(s): U.S. Department of Labor, Bureau of Labor Statistics, Office of Employment and Unemployment Statistics, Division of Labor Force Statistics, Washington, DC 20212. A dash (-) indicates that data are not available or zero.

Labor Force Participation Rate, Males 20 and Over
(Percent)

Year	Jan	Feb	Mar	Apr	May	Jun	Jul	Aug	Sep	Oct	Nov	Dec
1948	88.7	89.0	88.2	88.3	88.1	88.5	88.7	88.8	88.5	88.8	88.7	89.0
1949	88.5	88.5	88.5	88.4	88.4	88.4	88.2	88.7	88.6	89.5	88.7	88.7
1950	88.1	88.0	88.0	88.2	88.4	88.3	88.1	88.5	88.4	88.2	88.2	88.2
1951	88.0	88.4	88.8	88.3	88.4	88.4	88.2	88.4	88.2	88.6	88.4	88.7
1952	88.8	89.0	88.6	88.5	88.4	88.4	88.3	88.0	88.0	87.6	87.6	88.5
1953	88.3	88.6	88.7	88.2	88.0	88.0	88.1	87.9	87.6	87.6	88.0	87.8
1954	87.8	88.1	87.7	88.2	87.9	87.8	87.7	88.2	88.4	88.0	87.6	87.3
1955	87.4	87.2	87.4	87.5	87.4	87.2	87.6	87.6	87.6	87.6	87.7	87.8
1956	88.1	87.9	87.9	87.8	87.6	87.6	87.5	87.5	87.3	87.2	87.3	87.3
1957	87.0	87.2	87.2	87.1	87.0	87.3	87.1	86.7	86.9	86.6	86.5	86.6
1958	86.4	86.2	86.2	86.6	86.9	86.8	87.0	87.1	87.1	87.0	86.5	86.3
1959	86.2	86.0	86.3	86.4	86.2	86.1	86.6	86.3	86.5	86.4	86.3	86.5
1960	86.2	86.0	85.6	86.1	86.0	85.9	85.9	86.0	86.2	86.1	86.3	86.3
1961	86.1	85.8	85.9	85.8	85.9	85.8	85.6	85.6	85.5	85.5	85.5	85.3
1962	85.1	85.3	85.3	84.7	85.0	84.8	84.4	84.9	84.8	84.6	84.6	84.4
1963	84.3	84.3	84.4	84.4	84.3	84.3	84.5	84.3	84.3	84.2	84.3	84.2
1964	84.2	84.1	84.0	84.5	84.5	84.0	84.3	84.1	84.2	84.2	84.0	83.9
1965	84.1	84.1	84.1	84.1	84.3	83.8	83.9	83.8	83.6	83.6	83.5	83.6
1966	83.6	83.5	83.6	83.7	83.6	83.6	83.4	83.5	83.5	83.4	83.5	83.6
1967	83.7	83.5	83.3	83.5	83.4	83.5	83.5	83.4	83.2	83.4	83.3	83.4
1968	83.1	83.1	83.0	83.1	83.2	83.4	83.3	83.2	83.0	82.9	82.9	83.1
1969	82.9	83.1	83.0	82.8	82.7	82.7	82.7	82.9	82.9	82.8	82.5	82.6
1970	82.8	82.8	82.9	83.0	82.9	82.6	82.6	82.5	82.5	82.4	82.5	82.5
1971	82.3	82.0	81.9	82.2	82.3	82.0	82.1	82.1	82.0	81.7	81.9	81.9
1972	81.6	81.5	81.8	81.7	81.6	81.7	81.7	81.6	81.6	81.4	81.4	81.5
1973	81.2	81.4	81.6	81.4	81.2	81.2	81.3	81.1	81.0	81.1	81.3	81.4
1974	81.8	81.7	81.3	81.0	81.1	80.9	80.7	80.9	80.8	80.8	80.9	80.7
1975	80.6	80.4	80.4	80.5	80.7	80.2	80.4	80.4	80.2	80.0	79.9	79.6
1976	79.7	79.6	79.6	79.9	79.8	79.7	79.9	79.9	79.9	79.8	80.0	79.8
1977	79.6	79.8	79.7	79.6	79.6	79.8	79.6	79.7	79.4	79.8	79.9	80.0
1978	79.9	79.8	79.7	79.8	79.8	79.8	79.7	79.6	79.5	79.6	80.0	80.0
1979	80.1	80.3	79.9	79.8	79.5	79.7	79.8	79.7	79.8	79.7	79.5	79.5
1980	79.7	79.9	79.4	79.5	79.6	79.3	79.4	79.4	79.3	79.2	79.2	79.0
1981	79.1	79.1	79.3	79.3	79.5	78.9	78.9	78.9	78.7	78.7	78.7	78.6
1982	78.6	78.7	78.7	78.8	78.9	78.8	78.8	78.7	78.9	78.8	78.8	78.7
1983	78.2	78.2	78.2	78.3	78.3	78.7	78.7	78.7	78.6	78.4	78.5	78.3
1984	78.3	78.3	78.2	78.3	78.3	78.4	78.4	78.3	78.4	78.3	78.3	78.3
1985	78.1	78.0	78.1	78.2	78.1	78.0	77.9	78.0	78.2	78.3	78.1	78.0
1986	78.3	78.1	78.1	78.0	78.0	78.1	78.1	78.0	78.1	78.0	78.2	78.4
1987	78.2	78.1	78.1	78.0	78.2	78.0	78.0	78.0	77.9	78.0	78.0	77.8
1988	77.9	78.0	77.8	78.1	78.0	77.8	77.9	78.1	77.8	77.9	77.9	77.8
1989	78.1	78.1	78.1	78.2	77.9	78.2	78.1	78.0	77.8	78.0	78.0	78.0
1990	78.6	78.4	78.4	78.1	78.2	78.1	78.1	78.2	78.0	78.0	78.2	78.1
1991	77.9	77.8	78.0	78.1	77.7	77.8	77.7	77.6	77.7	77.4	77.5	77.3
1992	77.5	77.4	77.7	77.8	78.0	78.0	77.9	77.8	77.7	77.4	77.4	77.3
1993	77.3	77.2	77.3	77.2	77.4	77.5	77.5	77.5	77.1	77.2	77.0	76.9
1994	77.0	76.8	76.7	76.7	76.6	76.5	76.6	76.6	76.6	76.9	77.0	77.1
1995	77.2	77.0	77.0	77.0	76.7	76.6	76.5	76.4	76.5	76.4	76.4	76.3
1996	76.6	76.7	76.8	76.7	76.8	76.9	77.0	76.8	76.7	76.8	76.9	76.8
1997	77.1	76.9	77.1	77.1	76.9	77.0	77.0	77.0	76.8	-	-	-

Source: The Conference Board. Primary source(s): U.S. Department of Labor, Bureau of Labor Statistics, Office of Employment and Unemployment Statistics, Division of Labor Force Statistics, Washington, DC 20212. A dash (-) indicates that data are not available or zero.

Labor Force Participation Rate, Females 20 and Over
(Percent)

Year	Jan	Feb	Mar	Apr	May	Jun	Jul	Aug	Sep	Oct	Nov	Dec
1948	31.0	31.4	31.1	32.1	31.3	32.5	32.7	32.0	32.3	31.7	31.8	32.1
1949	31.7	32.1	31.9	31.9	32.3	32.2	32.9	32.7	32.5	32.7	32.9	32.7
1950	32.7	32.8	32.7	33.4	33.0	33.8	33.2	33.6	33.1	33.6	33.7	33.5
1951	33.7	33.6	34.3	33.8	34.1	33.6	34.5	33.9	33.8	34.2	34.1	34.5
1952	34.4	34.3	33.5	33.6	34.0	33.8	33.7	33.9	34.9	34.2	34.8	34.2
1953	34.6	34.2	34.5	34.0	33.4	34.1	34.1	33.7	33.7	34.0	33.6	33.2
1954	33.4	34.5	34.5	34.4	34.3	34.1	33.8	33.9	34.5	34.4	34.4	34.0
1955	34.5	34.4	34.3	35.1	34.7	35.0	35.5	36.0	35.9	36.0	36.0	36.4
1956	36.3	36.0	36.0	36.2	36.7	36.4	36.6	36.6	36.8	36.6	36.4	36.4
1957	36.2	36.7	36.5	36.2	36.3	36.4	36.9	36.4	36.5	36.6	36.6	36.9
1958	36.7	36.8	36.8	37.1	37.0	37.0	37.0	37.2	36.8	36.8	36.6	36.7
1959	37.0	36.7	37.0	37.1	37.1	37.2	37.1	36.9	36.9	37.3	37.0	37.2
1960	36.9	36.9	36.3	37.6	37.7	37.9	37.9	37.9	38.1	37.6	38.2	38.2
1961	38.1	38.4	38.5	37.9	38.1	38.4	38.0	37.7	37.5	37.9	37.6	37.5
1962	37.9	38.0	37.7	37.6	37.6	37.5	37.6	38.1	38.3	37.9	37.8	37.8
1963	38.0	38.2	38.2	38.4	38.4	38.2	38.3	38.1	38.4	38.6	38.7	38.5
1964	38.5	38.8	38.8	39.5	39.3	39.0	38.7	38.9	38.6	38.8	38.7	38.9
1965	39.0	39.2	39.2	39.2	39.2	39.7	39.7	39.6	39.3	39.4	39.5	39.6
1966	39.8	39.6	39.6	39.8	40.0	39.9	40.0	40.3	40.6	40.6	40.9	40.8
1967	40.7	40.5	40.4	40.8	40.8	40.9	41.0	41.1	41.4	41.7	41.6	41.8
1968	40.9	41.3	41.4	41.4	42.0	41.9	41.7	41.3	41.6	41.6	41.9	41.9
1969	42.0	42.4	42.4	42.6	42.5	42.8	42.7	42.8	42.8	42.9	42.8	42.9
1970	43.1	43.1	43.4	43.5	43.0	43.2	43.5	43.3	43.0	43.4	43.4	43.4
1971	43.6	43.3	43.2	43.2	43.2	43.0	43.0	43.2	43.4	43.5	43.8	43.8
1972	43.6	43.4	43.7	43.6	43.8	43.6	43.7	43.8	43.7	43.7	43.6	43.7
1973	43.6	44.0	44.1	44.3	44.3	44.5	44.5	44.5	44.6	44.6	44.9	44.8
1974	44.7	45.0	45.1	45.1	45.1	45.3	45.8	45.5	45.5	45.3	45.5	45.6
1975	45.9	45.6	45.9	46.0	46.0	46.0	46.1	46.2	46.1	46.3	46.2	46.3
1976	46.6	46.6	46.7	46.8	46.8	47.0	47.3	47.3	47.1	47.1	47.5	47.6
1977	47.4	47.6	47.9	48.0	48.2	48.1	48.0	48.1	48.5	48.3	48.8	48.7
1978	48.9	48.9	49.1	49.4	49.4	49.6	49.6	49.5	49.9	50.0	50.1	50.2
1979	50.1	50.3	50.5	50.2	50.2	50.3	50.6	50.8	50.8	50.9	51.0	51.2
1980	51.3	51.3	51.2	51.4	51.3	51.2	51.3	51.4	51.2	51.4	51.6	51.4
1981	51.8	51.9	52.1	52.2	52.4	52.2	52.2	52.1	51.7	52.3	52.4	52.2
1982	52.2	52.4	52.5	52.5	52.8	52.9	52.9	52.9	52.9	52.7	52.9	53.1
1983	53.0	53.0	52.9	52.8	52.8	53.1	53.0	53.3	53.5	53.2	53.3	53.3
1984	53.0	53.3	53.4	53.6	54.1	53.8	54.0	53.8	53.6	53.9	53.9	54.1
1985	54.3	54.5	54.8	54.7	54.5	54.5	54.4	54.5	54.8	54.8	54.9	55.1
1986	54.9	55.0	55.1	55.2	55.4	55.7	55.7	55.8	55.8	55.8	55.8	55.6
1987	55.7	55.8	56.0	56.0	56.2	56.2	56.3	56.4	56.3	56.5	56.5	56.6
1988	56.6	56.7	56.7	56.7	56.4	56.5	56.6	56.8	56.8	57.1	57.5	57.4
1989	57.7	57.5	57.5	57.6	57.6	57.5	57.7	57.6	57.7	57.6	58.0	57.8
1990	58.1	58.1	58.0	58.0	58.1	57.9	57.9	58.1	58.1	58.0	57.9	57.9
1991	57.8	57.9	57.8	58.1	58.0	58.0	57.8	57.8	58.0	58.1	58.0	58.0
1992	58.3	58.3	58.4	58.6	58.5	58.6	58.7	58.6	58.5	58.3	58.4	58.5
1993	58.3	58.2	58.2	58.3	58.6	58.7	58.5	58.6	58.5	58.6	58.7	59.0
1994	59.3	59.4	59.3	59.2	59.5	59.2	59.1	59.4	59.6	59.5	59.5	59.1
1995	59.3	59.4	59.3	59.7	59.3	59.1	59.6	59.5	59.5	59.7	59.6	59.3
1996	59.5	59.5	59.7	59.7	59.7	59.7	59.9	59.9	60.0	60.1	60.2	60.3
1997	60.4	60.2	60.6	60.4	60.5	60.5	60.4	60.6	60.6	-	-	-

Source: The Conference Board. Primary source(s): U.S. Department of Labor, Bureau of Labor Statistics, Office of Employment and Unemployment Statistics, Division of Labor Force Statistics, Washington, DC 20212. A dash (-) indicates that data are not available or zero.

Labor Force Participation Rate, 16-19 Years of Age
(Percent)

Year	Jan	Feb	Mar	Apr	May	Jun	Jul	Aug	Sep	Oct	Nov	Dec
1948	53.2	53.7	54.1	54.2	50.9	53.8	52.6	51.5	51.5	50.6	51.0	53.1
1949	52.8	53.7	54.5	53.0	53.4	49.8	50.3	51.7	53.1	52.5	52.9	52.6
1950	51.9	51.7	50.2	50.8	50.9	50.4	50.8	52.0	52.5	53.5	52.6	52.5
1951	51.4	51.0	53.3	50.9	52.6	51.3	52.6	53.0	52.7	52.4	51.9	52.9
1952	52.2	51.8	50.9	50.7	52.3	52.8	51.2	50.0	50.5	50.2	51.4	51.1
1953	52.4	54.0	53.1	51.8	49.5	50.9	49.5	49.6	49.1	48.2	48.9	49.2
1954	50.9	51.4	51.7	50.1	48.6	46.3	47.1	48.0	48.5	47.3	46.3	44.6
1955	46.8	45.4	46.3	47.3	47.6	46.7	48.4	49.6	50.5	51.1	52.7	53.4
1956	51.4	50.5	50.0	49.4	52.1	52.5	51.7	50.6	50.3	49.7	50.4	50.3
1957	49.5	49.8	50.6	49.5	49.4	50.2	50.2	48.4	49.3	49.3	49.4	49.3
1958	47.4	48.0	47.5	48.1	48.9	46.5	46.8	47.1	47.9	47.9	46.8	47.1
1959	47.5	46.7	46.7	47.7	46.2	46.0	46.3	46.6	46.9	46.6	46.3	47.4
1960	47.2	47.4	46.7	48.5	48.1	49.7	47.3	46.9	47.4	47.3	47.4	46.5
1961	47.4	46.7	47.6	46.0	45.8	47.8	47.1	48.0	46.4	46.4	47.4	45.6
1962	45.6	45.9	46.8	46.5	47.4	47.8	46.5	46.4	45.8	45.3	44.9	44.8
1963	45.4	45.1	44.8	45.3	46.2	44.6	45.0	44.8	45.7	45.8	44.8	43.9
1964	44.4	45.3	45.0	44.0	44.8	44.4	44.0	44.2	45.5	44.1	44.1	44.3
1965	43.0	43.7	44.1	45.3	45.6	44.0	46.3	45.5	46.5	47.8	47.1	48.1
1966	48.0	46.7	46.9	47.4	46.9	48.5	49.1	49.3	47.5	48.2	49.1	49.3
1967	48.3	48.2	47.5	47.6	47.2	48.8	49.0	49.5	48.3	48.7	48.3	48.3
1968	46.6	48.5	48.2	47.9	48.2	49.3	49.1	49.0	47.9	48.0	47.7	47.8
1969	47.7	47.8	48.3	48.7	47.5	49.6	50.0	50.0	50.5	50.9	50.9	50.4
1970	50.4	50.3	50.4	49.9	49.7	49.0	49.4	49.7	50.4	50.1	50.1	49.8
1971	50.0	49.9	49.3	49.7	49.4	47.5	50.5	50.5	49.3	49.7	50.5	50.6
1972	51.1	51.4	51.9	51.8	51.5	51.9	51.6	52.9	51.6	51.9	52.4	52.8
1973	50.8	52.9	53.5	53.7	53.2	54.5	53.3	53.2	54.3	54.8	55.1	55.1
1974	55.1	55.2	55.0	53.8	54.3	55.3	54.9	53.8	55.7	55.5	55.1	54.4
1975	54.9	54.1	54.1	53.6	54.7	53.8	54.1	53.8	54.1	53.5	53.2	53.8
1976	54.2	54.2	54.4	55.2	55.1	53.8	55.3	55.1	53.9	54.4	54.4	54.1
1977	54.2	55.2	55.5	55.7	55.6	57.0	56.1	57.2	55.9	56.5	57.2	56.3
1978	56.7	56.6	56.5	57.0	57.9	58.5	58.4	59.3	58.1	58.3	58.2	58.2
1979	58.5	58.6	58.4	57.9	57.3	58.0	57.7	56.8	57.8	57.5	57.7	58.3
1980	57.7	57.2	57.2	55.9	57.0	57.0	57.3	55.9	56.3	56.6	56.2	55.9
1981	56.7	56.6	56.4	57.0	56.3	54.0	54.5	55.2	54.8	55.0	55.2	53.8
1982	54.4	54.7	53.8	54.3	55.3	52.5	53.2	54.2	54.0	54.4	54.7	53.9
1983	53.7	52.7	52.5	52.6	52.2	55.2	53.8	55.1	53.8	53.0	53.6	53.8
1984	53.2	53.3	53.3	53.9	53.8	55.2	54.8	53.3	54.4	53.9	53.8	54.5
1985	55.0	54.9	55.3	54.7	55.0	53.0	55.5	53.4	54.1	54.5	54.3	54.1
1986	53.3	54.6	55.1	55.6	55.2	55.4	54.7	54.6	54.8	54.9	54.2	53.4
1987	54.0	54.8	54.4	54.4	55.3	53.7	54.1	56.2	54.3	55.1	54.6	55.4
1988	55.6	55.0	53.8	54.4	54.2	56.4	56.4	56.6	56.1	55.1	54.8	55.1
1989	55.6	54.8	54.5	55.5	55.5	57.0	56.1	57.4	55.6	56.3	56.5	55.8
1990	54.9	54.3	55.0	54.6	54.2	53.5	53.5	53.5	52.6	52.7	52.4	52.6
1991	52.6	52.2	52.5	52.0	51.7	51.4	50.8	50.6	50.8	51.5	51.4	51.2
1992	51.6	51.3	50.5	49.8	50.8	51.6	51.2	52.0	52.1	50.4	51.7	51.9
1993	51.2	51.9	51.7	51.2	52.2	51.0	51.7	51.8	51.3	51.1	51.5	51.1
1994	53.3	52.9	52.7	53.5	52.8	53.0	52.2	53.2	51.4	52.7	52.1	53.3
1995	53.7	53.8	54.4	54.1	53.3	54.1	53.4	53.9	53.2	52.7	52.6	52.9
1996	52.7	52.7	52.7	52.6	53.1	51.8	52.2	50.7	52.2	52.4	52.0	52.3
1997	51.9	52.8	52.9	52.1	52.2	51.0	51.4	50.5	50.7	-	-	-

Source: The Conference Board. Primary source(s): U.S. Department of Labor, Bureau of Labor Statistics, Office of Employment and Unemployment Statistics, Division of Labor Force Statistics, Washington, DC 20212. A dash (-) indicates that data are not available or zero.

INDICATORS OF INTERNATIONAL TRANSACTIONS

International trade has been a subject of concern and debate since the mid-1970s, when the U.S. trade balance turned negative and has continued negative since. As a percent of GDP, foreign trade has also grown. And with the rise of new industrial economies on the Asian rim of the Pacific, a world-wide competition for trade has intensified concerns. Negative trade balances have a direct impact on GDP; they are also, indirectly, a measure of U.S. competitiveness in world markets. The three tables included in this section present the basic facts about this phenomenon as seen from the U.S. vantage point. The tables are:

> Merchandise exports, adjusted annual rate, excluding military
> Merchandise imports, adjusted annual rate, excluding military
> Balance on merchandise trade

Merchandise Exports, Excluding Military. Data from 1960 to 1997 are shown in billions of current dollars. Data for each quarter are annualized; the sum of the four quarters, divided by 4, produces the annual value. Data exclude Department of Defense sales contracts (exports) and military grants. Military aid shipments and exports are excluded because, arising from government policy, such shipments would distort the market-based nature of the overall export business.

Merchandise Imports, Excluding Military. Data are also for 1960 to 1997 in billions of current dollars, annualized. Data exclude Department of Defense purchases (imports).

Balance on Merchandise Trade. Data are in billions of current dollars for 1960 to 1997. The values shown are merchandise exports less merchandise imports from the earlier tables, indicating to what extent the U.S. enjoyed a trade surplus (positive numbers) or a deficit (negative values).

Surplus or deficit in foreign trade has always played an important role in international relations. In pre-modern times, when gold was the standard of exchange, a trade deficit meant that a country lost some of its gold stock to another country; a surplus meant a gain in gold; for this reason, countries tried to maintain surpluses or, failing that, a balance between imports and exports. International trade has become much more complex since, but underlying concepts remain in force. Thus the purchasing power of the dollar has a direct influence on the trade deficit. A strong dollar (meaning a dollar expensive relative to other currencies) acts to diminish exports—because dollar-denominated goods are expensive elsewhere; importers are aided because their goods are relatively cheap in the U.S. market. Conversely, a weak dollar helps exports and impedes imports. The strong and weak dollar have other consequences as well: a strong dollar tends to reduce production but curbs inflation; a weak dollar is associated with high production but also with inflation. Needless to say, the weakening of foreign currencies, e.g., the Korea and Indonesian problems in 1997, also cause the dollar's value to increase.

A strong dollar in the 1985-to-current period was one of the causes of dramatically increasing trade deficits. The value of the dollar, in turn, reflects the strength of an economy relative to other economies and *perceptions* of this strength; perceptions are translated into policy and trading actions by others—which cause the value of the dollar to rise or fall. Public policy can influence—but cannot set—the value of the dollar.

The trade deficit has a negative impact on GDP growth because trade balance is part of GDP. The change from period to period is more important, in this context, than the absolute magnitude of the trade balance or its arithmetic sign. A shrinking deficit or a growing surplus will both translate into a positive signal for GDP.

Exports, imports, and the trade balance are subject to trade policies followed in the U.S. and in foreign countries. Therefore, ultimately, foreign trade data reflect pure market forces only indirectly.

Merchandise Exports
Adjusted Annual Rate, excluding military
(Billions of $)

Year	1st Quarter	2nd Quarter	3rd Quarter	4th Quarter
1960	18.7	19.7	20.1	20.1
1961	20.4	19.2	20.2	20.7
1962	20.3	21.3	21.3	20.1
1963	20.3	22.4	22.7	23.8
1964	25.0	24.8	25.7	26.5
1965	23.1	27.5	26.6	28.7
1966	29.0	28.7	29.2	30.4
1967	31.0	30.8	30.1	30.8
1968	32.0	33.3	35.0	34.2
1969	29.9	38.1	37.6	40.0
1970	41.0	43.0	42.7	43.2
1971	43.7	43.5	46.2	39.9
1972	47.3	46.5	49.4	54.3
1973	61.9	68.4	73.1	82.2
1974	90.5	98.0	98.5	106.3
1975	109.9	103.5	104.4	110.5
1976	110.3	113.0	116.2	119.4
1977	118.7	123.4	123.0	118.2
1978	121.9	142.7	146.1	157.6
1979	165.9	175.5	188.4	207.9
1980	216.9	223.9	223.3	232.9
1981	241.3	240.6	232.1	234.2
1982	220.7	221.4	208.4	194.2
1983	196.8	197.4	201.3	211.7
1984	212.0	218.5	223.6	225.7
1985	219.5	216.6	211.3	216.2
1986	214.1	227.3	222.6	229.3
1987	226.8	240.8	256.9	276.4
1988	302.6	318.2	323.8	336.4
1989	349.7	368.8	360.7	369.3
1990	381.2	390.3	385.4	400.4
1991	405.4	418.1	414.9	429.2
1992	433.4	436.1	438.4	453.6
1993	447.4	456.7	445.7	477.4
1994	473.5	492.1	510.5	533.4
1995	553.6	572.7	581.4	595.8
1996	600.2	613.6	603.1	631.4
1997	650.1	686.0	-	-

Source: The Conference Board. Primary source(s): U.S. Department of Commerce, Bureau of Economic Analysis, Balance of Payments Division, BE-58, Washington, DC 20230. A dash (-) indicates that data are not available or zero.

Merchandise Imports
Adjusted Annual Rate, excluding military
(Billions of $)

Year	1st Quarter	2nd Quarter	3rd Quarter	4th Quarter
1960	15.2	15.4	14.6	13.8
1961	13.6	13.8	15.2	15.6
1962	15.9	16.3	16.5	16.4
1963	16.3	16.9	17.5	17.5
1964	17.7	18.4	19.0	19.7
1965	18.8	21.7	22.1	23.4
1966	24.0	24.8	26.3	26.8
1967	26.8	25.9	26.1	28.6
1968	31.2	32.2	34.4	34.1
1969	29.8	38.1	37.5	37.8
1970	38.3	39.1	40.2	41.9
1971	42.4	46.5	48.7	44.8
1972	54.0	53.0	56.1	60.1
1973	65.1	68.7	70.7	77.5
1974	87.8	105.4	109.5	112.6
1975	99.9	91.3	97.9	103.5
1976	112.7	120.7	128.9	134.6
1977	146.3	152.3	152.0	157.0
1978	169.9	173.7	177.7	182.7
1979	190.3	203.1	216.0	238.6
1980	263.3	249.1	236.0	250.6
1981	268.0	268.7	257.6	265.9
1982	254.0	242.3	254.8	239.5
1983	239.0	259.1	281.5	296.0
1984	319.0	335.2	335.7	339.8
1985	321.3	338.3	335.6	357.2
1986	356.9	367.0	371.2	378.6
1987	384.1	402.6	417.6	434.7
1988	439.9	443.3	443.6	462.0
1989	465.9	483.6	475.5	484.4
1990	489.8	488.7	501.6	513.3
1991	480.6	482.8	493.9	506.6
1992	505.1	533.1	547.5	560.0
1993	564.3	590.3	591.7	611.5
1994	620.0	655.4	687.9	711.0
1995	731.2	763.0	752.7	750.9
1996	771.9	803.9	813.0	824.1
1997	849.3	873.6	-	-

Source: The Conference Board. Primary source(s): U.S. Department of Commerce, Bureau of Economic Analysis, Balance of Payments Division, BE-58, Washington, DC 20230. A dash (-) indicates that data are not available or zero.

Balance on Merchandise Trade
Adjusted Annual Rate
(Billions of $)

Year	1st Quarter	2nd Quarter	3rd Quarter	4th Quarter
1960	3.5	4.2	5.5	6.3
1961	6.8	5.5	4.9	5.1
1962	4.4	5.0	4.9	3.8
1963	4.0	5.5	5.2	6.2
1964	7.3	6.4	6.7	6.8
1965	4.2	5.8	4.5	5.3
1966	4.9	3.9	2.9	3.6
1967	4.2	4.9	4.0	2.1
1968	0.8	1.1	0.5	0.1
1969	0.1	-	0.1	2.2
1970	2.7	3.9	2.5	1.4
1971	1.3	-2.9	-2.5	-4.9
1972	-6.7	-6.5	-6.7	-5.8
1973	-3.2	-0.2	2.4	4.8
1974	2.6	-7.4	-11.0	-6.3
1975	10.0	12.1	6.5	7.0
1976	-2.4	-7.7	-12.6	-15.2
1977	-27.7	-28.8	-29.0	-38.8
1978	-48.1	-31.0	-31.6	-25.1
1979	-24.4	-27.6	-27.6	-30.7
1980	-46.3	-25.2	-12.7	-17.7
1981	-26.7	-28.2	-25.5	-31.7
1982	-33.4	-20.9	-46.4	-45.2
1983	-42.2	-61.8	-80.2	-84.2
1984	-107.0	-116.7	-112.1	-114.2
1985	-101.8	-121.6	-124.3	-140.9
1986	-142.7	-139.7	-148.6	-149.3
1987	-157.3	-161.8	-160.8	-158.4
1988	-137.2	-125.2	-119.8	-125.6
1989	-116.2	-114.8	-114.8	-115.1
1990	-108.6	-98.4	-116.2	-113.0
1991	-75.2	-64.7	-79.0	-77.4
1992	-71.8	-97.0	-109.2	-106.5
1993	-116.8	-133.5	-146.0	-134.1
1994	-146.5	-163.3	-177.4	-177.6
1995	-177.6	-190.2	-171.3	-155.1
1996	-171.7	-190.2	-210.0	-192.8
1997	-199.1	-187.6	-	-

Source: The Conference Board. Primary source(s): U.S. Department of Commerce, Bureau of Economic Analysis, Balance of Payments Division, BE-58, Washington, DC 20230. A dash (-) indicates that data are not available or zero.

CHAPTER 6

CONSUMER PRICE INDEX

CONSUMER PRICE INDEX

The Consumer Price Index (CPI) is the primary system for measuring price change in the United States in a consistent manner. The CPI, therefore, is the chief measure of inflation and the source of data for converting "current dollar" measurements and estimates into "constant" or "real dollar" values used in National Income and Product Accounts and in cyclic indicators of the economy. It is produced by the U.S. Department of Labor, Bureau of Labor Statistics (BLS), Division of Consumer Prices and Price Indexes.

General Concept

The CPI is based on obtaining the price of an *identical* "basket" of goods at two different points in time and measuring the difference. By way of illustration, consider the following simple case:

> A basket of goods is purchased in January 1975 containing a loaf of bread, a quart of milk, a pound of potatoes, a package of bacon, five pounds of flour and of sugar. The price is noted. It is $15.00.

> A year later, exactly the same items are purchased. This time the price is $18.00.

In this situation, inflation has been $3.00. Only the price has changed. It has increased by 20%.

Rather than dealing with actual dollar figures, we can express these relationships as an index. If 1975 is chosen as the base year and set to a value of 100, the 1976 value would be 120—showing a 20% inflation rate.

The system works in the same way if prices decrease. Assume that in 1977 the same basket of goods cost $12.00. This price is 20% lower than the price in the base year. The new 1977 index, therefore, would be 80. The change between 1976 and 1977 would be a 33.3% decrease:

$$((80 / 120) - 1) \times 100 = -33.3$$

These concepts underlie the CPI. The index measures the price of a "fixed market basket of goods and services" at monthly intervals. This is a hypothetical basket because it includes not only items one ordinarily buys in a store but also the costs of fuel, housing, transportation, and other services. A base period is selected; currently (1994) it is the average of 1982-1984. The price index is shown with reference to the base period, which is defined as 100.

Implementation of the Concept

In order to implement this concept in a useful manner, it is necessary, first, to determine the make-up of the "fixed market basket": what proportion of a family's budget is devoted to food, clothing, housing, etc. Since consumption patterns differ somewhat from region to region, it is also necessary to know how the market basket's contents change from place to place; fuel costs, typically, will be a lesser proportion of budgets in mild climates, for instance. BLS conducts surveys at regular intervals in selected urban areas to answer these questions. Consumer surveys are then used to change how the index is constructed and what weight or importance to give to each major component in the basket. From the beginning of the CPI, surveys of spending patterns have been followed by comprehensive revisions of the index.

The modern index is built by pricing goods and services in 94 primary sampling units in 91 geographical areas. Sampling units and geographical areas are selected using population census data to arrive at a representative sampling.

Raw data collected from sampling units are processed into geographical indexes and into a U.S. City average. Major components (food, apparel, housing, etc.) are combined by applying appropriate weights to produce a final consumer price index.

History and Revisions

The CPI was initiated during World War I as a tool for calculating cost-of-living adjustments in wages. The first surveys of consumption patterns were carried out by the Department of Labor from 1917-1919; periodic collection of prices began in 1919 by the Department's Bureau of Labor Statistics. Regular publication began in 1921, with indexes estimated back to 1913. The cycle of surveys and revisions began in 1934-36 (survey) and 1940 (index revision). Thereafter, major changes were introduced as follows:

> 1951 - adjustments to reflect immediate postwar changes
> 1953 - comprehensive postwar revisions, statistical overhaul
> 1964 - new expenditure weights reflecting single persons as well as families
> 1978 - changes in sample, data collection, inclusion of all urban consumers
> 1983 - changes in home ownership cost calculations for all urban consumers
> 1985 - changes in home ownership cost calculations for urban wage earners
> 1987 - improvements of sampling, data collection, processing, and estimation

The CPI was originally designed to measure the cost of living of urban wage earners and clerical workers (usually called CPI-W). A more encompassing category including all urban families (CPI-U) was introduced in 1978; CPI-U includes, in addition to CPI-W, professional and salaried workers, part-time workers, the self-employed, the unemployed, and retired people.

Sampling, Components, and Methods

Sampling Universe. CPI pricing data are collected in 91 urban areas; 21,000 retail and service establishments are sampled; these include supermarkets, department stores, filling stations, hospitals, and other establishments. Housing costs are collected from 40,000 tenants and on 20,000 owner-occupied housing units.

Product/Service Categories. Items/services to be priced are subdivided into 7 major product groups: food and beverages, fuels and utilities, household services and furnishings, apparel and upkeep, transportation, medical care, entertainment, and other commodities and services. These major groupings are made up of 69 expenditure classes (e.g. furniture and bedding) which, in turn, are divided into 207 item strata (bedroom furniture) and finally into 364 "entry level items" (mattresses and springs). Pricing on approximately 100,000 entry level items is conducted for the CPI on a regular basis.

Sampling Frequency. Food, fuel, and selected other items are priced monthly in all of the sample geographies. Most other goods and services are surveyed monthly in the five largest urban areas and bimonthly in all the others.

Basing Years. BLS provides data calculated with a base of 1967 and 1982-1984—in which data are expressed with 1967 values as 100 and the 1982-1984 averages as 100. The annual average index for 1982 is 95.6, for 1983 99.6 and for 1984 103.9. The sum of these index values is 300; divided by 3, we get the basing value of 100.

Measurement of Changes. Index movements from one month to the next are expressed as percent changes rather than as changes in index points. The following formula is used in the tables to show change from period to period:

((Current Index / Previous Index) - 1) x 100.

This formula can be used to calculate, for example, how the cost of living has changed between January 1990 and January 1991 without reference to the base year of the series. The U.S. average data for base 1982-1984 were as follows:

January 1990 - 127.4
January 1991 - 134.6

By applying the formula to these values, we get a percent change of 5.7.

The data for the same series but with a 1967 base are:

January 1990 - 381.5
January 1991 - 403.1

These values *also* produce a 5.7% change.

The meaning of the change for a person with a fixed income of $30,000 a year would be that his or her income in 1991 was 5.7% less than in 1990 due to inflation. The purchasing power of the income would be $28,290 in 1991.

Uses of the CPI

The CPI is the most widely used measure of inflation; consequently, it plays a role in economic measurement and in the setting of monetary and fiscal policy and is used widely as an indicator in all manner of institutions, public and private, for a range of activities, including wage settlements.

The CPI is used as a deflator of other economic series. Throughout *Economic Indicators Handbook*, references are made to current dollar and constant dollar presentations of data; the latter are also referred to as "real" dollars, meaning that inflation has been removed by use of a deflator. In the example above, the person with a fixed income of $30,000 had an income in 1991 of $30,000 in *current* dollars but only an income of $28,290 in *constant* or "real" dollars (in this case 1990 dollars).

The CPI is used for income adjustments. More than 3 million union workers are covered by contracts tied to CPI. The income of more than 60 million other people is affected by changes in CPI, including 38 million Social Security recipients, 3 million military and federal retirees and survivors, and about 19 million people receiving food stamps. Federal income tax indexing uses the CPI. There are also many uses of the CPI by the private sector.

Presentation and Limitations of Data

In the following tables, data are presented as follows:

U.S. City Average Data. These data are the overall CPI, calculated for all cities. *EIH* presents the following subsets of the data:

>   Annual Averages for all items and 7 subcategories, 1982-1984 basis
>   For all urban consumers
>   For urban wage earners and clerical workers

>   U.S. City Average for all items, monthly, 1982-1984 basis
>   All urban consumers
>   Urban wage earners and clerical workers

>   U.S. City Average for each of 7 subcategories of expenditure, 1982-1984 basis
>   Monthly for all urban consumers
>   Monthly for urban wage earners and clerical workers

Index values are shown from 1913 to 1993 as available. Percent change from one period to the next is precalculated and shown. In tables of annual averages, the comparison is between two rows in the same column; in monthly tables, the comparison is between two columns of the same row.

Limitations of the U.S. City Average Data. The CPI measures cost changes in urban areas and should not be applied to situations in other contexts. The index is based on a sample of consumer purchases rather than all consumer purchases; hence sampling errors are inherent in the series. The CPI cannot be used for demographic subgroups of the population, such as the elderly.

City/Urban Area Data. Following the U.S. City Average tables, data are presented for 27 cities/urban areas. The cities are ordered alphabetically. For each city, the following tables are presented:

>   Annual averages for all items and 7 subcategories, 1982-1984 basis
>   For all urban consumers
>   For urban wage earners and clerical workers

>   All items, monthly, 1982-1984 basis
>   All urban consumers
>   Urban wage earners and clerical workers

>   Seven tables of subcategories, 1982-1984 basis
>   Monthly for all urban consumers
>   Monthly for urban wage earners and clerical workers

Years and months of coverage for cities varies. For some, categories data are available back to 1913. In other cases, data start at a later date and are shown for the months in which data were collected. The tables, in fact, show how the frequency and timing of collections have changed over time.

Limitations of City/Urban Area Data. Is it more expensive to live in New York than in Los Angeles? *The CPI cannot be used to answer this question.* Cost of living comparisons *between* cities are not a legitimate use of the index. The CPI, in other words, cannot be used to determine "relative" cost of living. The index measures only changes in the cost of living *in* one urban area. The CPI is suitable for determining whether or not prices are rising faster in one city than in another; they do not measure absolute price levels between cities.

Bibliography

1. U.S. Department of Labor, Bureau of Labor Statistics. *BLS Handbook of Methods*, Bulletin 2285, 1987. Washington, DC.

U.S. CITY AVERAGE
Consumer Price Index - All Urban Consumers
Base 1982-1984 = 100
Annual Averages

For 1913-1997. Columns headed % show percentile change in the index from the previous period for which an index is available.

Year	All Items		Food & Beverage		Housing		Apparel & Upkeep		Trans- portation		Medical Care		Entertain- ment		Other Goods & Services	
	Index	%	Index	%	Index	%	Index	%	Index	%	Index	%	Index	%	Index	%
1913	9.9	-	-	-	-	-	14.9	-	-	-	-	-	-	-	-	-
1914	10.0	1.0	-	-	-	-	15.0	0.7	-	-	-	-	-	-	-	-
1915	10.1	1.0	-	-	-	-	15.3	2.0	-	-	-	-	-	-	-	-
1916	10.9	7.9	-	-	-	-	16.8	9.8	-	-	-	-	-	-	-	-
1917	12.8	17.4	-	-	-	-	20.2	20.2	-	-	-	-	-	-	-	-
1918	15.1	18.0	-	-	-	-	27.3	35.1	-	-	-	-	-	-	-	-
1919	17.3	14.6	-	-	-	-	36.2	32.6	-	-	-	-	-	-	-	-
1920	20.0	15.6	-	-	-	-	43.1	19.1	-	-	-	-	-	-	-	-
1921	17.9	-10.5	-	-	-	-	33.2	-23.0	-	-	-	-	-	-	-	-
1922	16.8	-6.1	-	-	-	-	27.0	-18.7	-	-	-	-	-	-	-	-
1923	17.1	1.8	-	-	-	-	27.1	0.4	-	-	-	-	-	-	-	-
1924	17.1	0.0	-	-	-	-	26.8	-1.1	-	-	-	-	-	-	-	-
1925	17.5	2.3	-	-	-	-	26.3	-1.9	-	-	-	-	-	-	-	-
1926	17.7	1.1	-	-	-	-	25.9	-1.5	-	-	-	-	-	-	-	-
1927	17.4	-1.7	-	-	-	-	25.3	-2.3	-	-	-	-	-	-	-	-
1928	17.1	-1.7	-	-	-	-	25.0	-1.2	-	-	-	-	-	-	-	-
1929	17.1	0.0	-	-	-	-	24.7	-1.2	-	-	-	-	-	-	-	-
1930	16.7	-2.3	-	-	-	-	24.2	-2.0	-	-	-	-	-	-	-	-
1931	15.2	-9.0	-	-	-	-	22.0	-9.1	-	-	-	-	-	-	-	-
1932	13.7	-9.9	-	-	-	-	19.5	-11.4	-	-	-	-	-	-	-	-
1933	13.0	-5.1	-	-	-	-	18.8	-3.6	-	-	-	-	-	-	-	-
1934	13.4	3.1	-	-	-	-	20.6	9.6	-	-	-	-	-	-	-	-
1935	13.7	2.2	-	-	-	-	20.8	1.0	14.2	-	10.2	-	-	-	-	-
1936	13.9	1.5	-	-	-	-	21.0	1.0	14.3	0.7	10.2	0.0	-	-	-	-
1937	14.4	3.6	-	-	-	-	22.0	4.8	14.5	1.4	10.3	1.0	-	-	-	-
1938	14.1	-2.1	-	-	-	-	21.9	-0.5	14.6	0.7	10.3	0.0	-	-	-	-
1939	13.9	-1.4	-	-	-	-	21.6	-1.4	14.3	-2.1	10.3	0.0	-	-	-	-
1940	14.0	0.7	-	-	-	-	21.8	0.9	14.2	-0.7	10.4	1.0	-	-	-	-
1941	14.7	5.0	-	-	-	-	22.8	4.6	14.7	3.5	10.4	0.0	-	-	-	-
1942	16.3	10.9	-	-	-	-	26.7	17.1	16.0	8.8	10.7	2.9	-	-	-	-
1943	17.3	6.1	-	-	-	-	27.8	4.1	15.9	-0.6	11.2	4.7	-	-	-	-
1944	17.6	1.7	-	-	-	-	29.8	7.2	15.9	0.0	11.6	3.6	-	-	-	-
1945	18.0	2.3	-	-	-	-	31.4	5.4	15.9	0.0	11.9	2.6	-	-	-	-
1946	19.5	8.3	-	-	-	-	34.4	9.6	16.7	5.0	12.5	5.0	-	-	-	-
1947	22.3	14.4	-	-	-	-	39.9	16.0	18.5	10.8	13.5	8.0	-	-	-	-
1948	24.1	8.1	-	-	-	-	42.5	6.5	20.6	11.4	14.4	6.7	-	-	-	-
1949	23.8	-1.2	-	-	-	-	40.8	-4.0	22.1	7.3	14.8	2.8	-	-	-	-
1950	24.1	1.3	-	-	-	-	40.3	-1.2	22.7	2.7	15.1	2.0	-	-	-	-
1951	26.0	7.9	-	-	-	-	43.9	8.9	24.1	6.2	15.9	5.3	-	-	-	-
1952	26.5	1.9	-	-	-	-	43.5	-0.9	25.7	6.6	16.7	5.0	-	-	-	-
1953	26.7	0.8	-	-	-	-	43.1	-0.9	26.5	3.1	17.3	3.6	-	-	-	-
1954	26.9	0.7	-	-	-	-	43.1	0.0	26.1	-1.5	17.8	2.9	-	-	-	-
1955	26.8	-0.4	-	-	-	-	42.9	-0.5	25.8	-1.1	18.2	2.2	-	-	-	-
1956	27.2	1.5	-	-	-	-	43.7	1.9	26.2	1.6	18.9	3.8	-	-	-	-
1957	28.1	3.3	-	-	-	-	44.5	1.8	27.7	5.7	19.7	4.2	-	-	-	-

[Continued]

U.S. City Average
Consumer Price Index - All Urban Consumers
Base 1982-1984 = 100
Annual Averages
[Continued]

For 1913-1997. Columns headed % show percentile change in the index from the previous period for which an index is available.

Year	All Items		Food & Beverage		Housing		Apparel & Upkeep		Trans-portation		Medical Care		Entertain-ment		Other Goods & Services	
	Index	%	Index	%	Index	%	Index	%	Index	%	Index	%	Index	%	Index	%
1958	28.9	2.8	-	-	-	-	44.6	0.2	28.6	3.2	20.6	4.6	-	-	-	-
1959	29.1	0.7	-	-	-	-	45.0	0.9	29.8	4.2	21.5	4.4	-	-	-	-
1960	29.6	1.7	-	-	-	-	45.7	1.6	29.8	0.0	22.3	3.7	-	-	-	-
1961	29.9	1.0	-	-	-	-	46.1	0.9	30.1	1.0	22.9	2.7	-	-	-	-
1962	30.2	1.0					46.3	0.4	30.8	2.3	23.5	2.6			-	-
1963	30.6	1.3	-	-	-	-	46.9	1.3	30.9	0.3	24.1	2.6	-	-	-	-
1964	31.0	1.3	-	-	-	-	47.3	0.9	31.4	1.6	24.6	2.1	-	-	-	-
1965	31.5	1.6	-	-	-	-	47.8	1.1	31.9	1.6	25.2	2.4	-	-	-	-
1966	32.4	2.9	-	-	-	-	49.0	2.5	32.3	1.3	26.3	4.4	-	-	-	-
1967	33.4	3.1	35.0	-	30.8	-	51.0	4.1	33.3	3.1	28.2	7.2	40.7	-	35.1	-
1968	34.8	4.2	36.2	3.4	32.0	3.9	53.7	5.3	34.3	3.0	29.9	6.0	43.0	5.7	36.9	5.1
1969	36.7	5.5	38.1	5.2	34.0	6.3	56.8	5.8	35.7	4.1	31.9	6.7	45.2	5.1	38.7	4.9
1970	38.8	5.7	40.1	5.2	36.4	7.1	59.2	4.2	37.5	5.0	34.0	6.6	47.5	5.1	40.9	5.7
1971	40.5	4.4	41.4	3.2	38.0	4.4	61.1	3.2	39.5	5.3	36.1	6.2	50.0	5.3	42.9	4.9
1972	41.8	3.2	43.1	4.1	39.4	3.7	62.3	2.0	39.9	1.0	37.3	3.3	51.5	3.0	44.7	4.2
1973	44.4	6.2	48.8	13.2	41.2	4.6	64.6	3.7	41.2	3.3	38.8	4.0	52.9	2.7	46.4	3.8
1974	49.3	11.0	55.5	13.7	45.8	11.2	69.4	7.4	45.8	11.2	42.4	9.3	56.9	7.6	49.8	7.3
1975	53.8	9.1	60.2	8.5	50.7	10.7	72.5	4.5	50.1	9.4	47.5	12.0	62.0	9.0	53.9	8.2
1976	56.9	5.8	62.1	3.2	53.8	6.1	75.2	3.7	55.1	10.0	52.0	9.5	65.1	5.0	57.0	5.8
1977	60.6	6.5	65.8	6.0	57.4	6.7	78.6	4.5	59.0	7.1	57.0	9.6	68.3	4.9	60.4	6.0
1978	65.2	7.6	72.2	9.7	62.4	8.7	81.4	3.6	61.7	4.6	61.8	8.4	71.9	5.3	64.3	6.5
1979	72.6	11.3	79.9	10.7	70.1	12.3	84.9	4.3	70.5	14.3	67.5	9.2	76.7	6.7	68.9	7.2
1980	82.4	13.5	86.7	8.5	81.1	15.7	90.9	7.1	83.1	17.9	74.9	11.0	83.6	9.0	75.2	9.1
1981	90.9	10.3	93.5	7.8	90.4	11.5	95.3	4.8	93.2	12.2	82.9	10.7	90.1	7.8	82.6	9.8
1982	96.5	6.2	97.3	4.1	96.9	7.2	97.8	2.6	97.0	4.1	92.5	11.6	96.0	6.5	91.1	10.3
1983	99.6	3.2	99.5	2.3	99.5	2.7	100.2	2.5	99.3	2.4	100.6	8.8	100.1	4.3	101.1	11.0
1984	103.9	4.3	103.2	3.7	103.6	4.1	102.1	1.9	103.7	4.4	106.8	6.2	103.8	3.7	107.9	6.7
1985	107.6	3.6	105.6	2.3	107.7	4.0	105.0	2.8	106.4	2.6	113.5	6.3	107.9	3.9	114.5	6.1
1986	109.6	1.9	109.1	3.3	110.9	3.0	105.9	0.9	102.3	-3.9	122.0	7.5	111.6	3.4	121.4	6.0
1987	113.6	3.6	113.5	4.0	114.2	3.0	110.6	4.4	105.4	3.0	130.1	6.6	115.3	3.3	128.5	5.8
1988	118.3	4.1	118.2	4.1	118.5	3.8	115.4	4.3	108.7	3.1	138.6	6.5	120.3	4.3	137.0	6.6
1989	124.0	4.8	124.9	5.7	123.0	3.8	118.6	2.8	114.1	5.0	149.3	7.7	126.5	5.2	147.7	7.8
1990	130.7	5.4	132.1	5.8	128.5	4.5	124.1	4.6	120.5	5.6	162.8	9.0	132.4	4.7	159.0	7.7
1991	136.2	4.2	136.8	3.6	133.6	4.0	128.7	3.7	123.8	2.7	177.0	8.7	138.4	4.5	171.6	7.9
1992	140.3	3.0	138.7	1.4	137.5	2.9	131.9	2.5	126.5	2.2	190.1	7.4	142.3	2.8	183.3	6.8
1993	144.5	3.0	141.6	2.1	141.2	2.7	133.7	1.4	130.4	3.1	201.4	5.9	145.8	2.5	192.9	5.2
1994	148.2	2.6	144.9	2.3	144.8	2.5	133.4	-0.2	134.3	3.0	211.0	4.8	150.1	2.9	198.5	2.9
1995	152.4	2.8	148.9	2.8	148.5	2.6	132.0	-1.0	139.1	3.6	220.5	4.5	153.9	2.5	206.9	4.2
1996	156.9	3.0	153.7	3.2	152.8	2.9	131.7	-0.2	143.0	2.8	228.2	3.5	159.1	3.4	215.4	4.1
1997	160.5	2.3	157.7	2.6	156.8	2.6	132.9	0.9	144.3	0.9	234.6	2.8	162.5	2.1	224.8	4.4

Source: U.S. Department of Labor, Bureau of Labor Statistics, Division of Consumer Prices and Price Indexes.

U.S. CITY AVERAGE
Consumer Price Index - Urban Wage Earners
Base 1982-1984 = 100
Annual Averages

For 1913-1997. Columns headed % show percentile change in the index from the previous period for which an index is available.

Year	All Items		Food & Beverage		Housing		Apparel & Upkeep		Trans- portation		Medical Care		Entertain- ment		Other Goods & Services	
	Index	%	Index	%	Index	%	Index	%	Index	%	Index	%	Index	%	Index	%
1913	10.0	-	-	-	-	-	15.0	-	-	-	-	-	-	-	-	-
1914	10.1	1.0	-	-	-	-	15.1	0.7	-	-	-	-	-	-	-	-
1915	10.2	1.0	-	-	-	-	15.4	2.0	-	-	-	-	-	-	-	-
1916	11.0	7.8	-	-	-	-	16.9	9.7	-	-	-	-	-	-	-	-
1917	12.9	17.3	-	-	-	-	20.3	20.1	-	-	-	-	-	-	-	-
1918	15.1	17.1	-	-	-	-	27.5	35.5	-	-	-	-	-	-	-	-
1919	17.4	15.2	-	-	-	-	36.4	32.4	-	-	-	-	-	-	-	-
1920	20.1	15.5	-	-	-	-	43.3	19.0	-	-	-	-	-	-	-	-
1921	18.0	-10.4	-	-	-	-	33.4	-22.9	-	-	-	-	-	-	-	-
1922	16.9	-6.1	-	-	-	-	27.2	-18.6	-	-	-	-	-	-	-	-
1923	17.2	1.8	-	-	-	-	27.2	0.0	-	-	-	-	-	-	-	-
1924	17.2	0.0	-	-	-	-	26.9	-1.1	-	-	-	-	-	-	-	-
1925	17.6	2.3	-	-	-	-	26.4	-1.9	-	-	-	-	-	-	-	-
1926	17.8	1.1	-	-	-	-	26.0	-1.5	-	-	-	-	-	-	-	-
1927	17.5	-1.7	-	-	-	-	25.5	-1.9	-	-	-	-	-	-	-	-
1928	17.2	-1.7	-	-	-	-	25.1	-1.6	-	-	-	-	-	-	-	-
1929	17.2	0.0	-	-	-	-	24.8	-1.2	-	-	-	-	-	-	-	-
1930	16.8	-2.3	-	-	-	-	24.3	-2.0	-	-	-	-	-	-	-	-
1931	15.3	-8.9	-	-	-	-	22.1	-9.1	-	-	-	-	-	-	-	-
1932	13.7	-10.5	-	-	-	-	19.6	-11.3	-	-	-	-	-	-	-	-
1933	13.0	-5.1	-	-	-	-	18.9	-3.6	-	-	-	-	-	-	-	-
1934	13.5	3.8	-	-	-	-	20.7	9.5	-	-	-	-	-	-	-	-
1935	13.8	2.2	-	-	-	-	20.9	1.0	14.1	-	10.2	-	-	-	-	-
1936	13.9	0.7	-	-	-	-	21.1	1.0	14.2	0.7	10.3	1.0	-	-	-	-
1937	14.4	3.6	-	-	-	-	22.1	4.7	14.5	2.1	10.4	1.0	-	-	-	-
1938	14.2	-1.4	-	-	-	-	22.0	-0.5	14.6	0.7	10.4	0.0	-	-	-	-
1939	14.0	-1.4	-	-	-	-	21.7	-1.4	14.2	-2.7	10.4	0.0	-	-	-	-
1940	14.1	0.7	-	-	-	-	21.9	0.9	14.1	-0.7	10.4	0.0	-	-	-	-
1941	14.8	5.0	-	-	-	-	23.0	5.0	14.6	3.5	10.5	1.0	-	-	-	-
1942	16.4	10.8	-	-	-	-	26.8	16.5	15.9	8.9	10.8	2.9	-	-	-	-
1943	17.4	6.1	-	-	-	-	28.0	4.5	15.8	-0.6	11.3	4.6	-	-	-	-
1944	17.7	1.7	-	-	-	-	30.0	7.1	15.8	0.0	11.6	2.7	-	-	-	-
1945	18.1	2.3	-	-	-	-	31.5	5.0	15.8	0.0	11.9	2.6	-	-	-	-
1946	19.6	8.3	-	-	-	-	34.6	9.8	16.6	5.1	12.6	5.9	-	-	-	-
1947	22.5	14.8	-	-	-	-	40.1	15.9	18.4	10.8	13.6	7.9	-	-	-	-
1948	24.2	7.6	-	-	-	-	42.7	6.5	20.4	10.9	14.5	6.6	-	-	-	-
1949	24.0	-0.8	-	-	-	-	41.0	-4.0	22.0	7.8	14.9	2.8	-	-	-	-
1950	24.2	0.8	-	-	-	-	40.5	-1.2	22.6	2.7	15.2	2.0	-	-	-	-
1951	26.1	7.9	-	-	-	-	44.1	8.9	24.0	6.2	15.9	4.6	-	-	-	-
1952	26.7	2.3	-	-	-	-	43.7	-0.9	25.6	6.7	16.8	5.7	-	-	-	-
1953	26.9	0.7	-	-	-	-	43.3	-0.9	26.3	2.7	17.4	3.6	-	-	-	-
1954	27.0	0.4	-	-	-	-	43.3	0.0	25.9	-1.5	17.9	2.9	-	-	-	-
1955	26.9	-0.4	-	-	-	-	43.1	-0.5	25.6	-1.2	18.3	2.2	-	-	-	-
1956	27.3	1.5	-	-	-	-	44.0	2.1	26.1	2.0	19.0	3.8	-	-	-	-
1957	28.3	3.7	-	-	-	-	44.7	1.6	27.6	5.7	19.8	4.2	-	-	-	-

[Continued]

U.S. City Average
Consumer Price Index - Urban Wage Earners
Base 1982-1984 = 100
Annual Averages
[Continued]

For 1913-1997. Columns headed % show percentile change in the index from the previous period for which an index is available.

Year	All Items		Food & Beverage		Housing		Apparel & Upkeep		Trans-portation		Medical Care		Entertain-ment		Other Goods & Services	
	Index	%	Index	%	Index	%	Index	%	Index	%	Index	%	Index	%	Index	%
1958	29.1	2.8	-	-	-	-	44.8	0.2	28.4	2.9	20.7	4.5	-	-	-	-
1959	29.3	0.7	-	-	-	-	45.2	0.9	29.6	4.2	21.6	4.3	-	-	-	-
1960	29.8	1.7	-	-	-	-	45.9	1.5	29.6	0.0	22.4	3.7	-	-	-	-
1961	30.1	1.0	-	-	-	-	46.3	0.9	30.0	1.4	23.0	2.7	-	-	-	-
1962	30.4	1.0	-	-	-	-	46.6	0.6	30.6	2.0	23.6	2.6	-	-	-	-
1963	30.8	1.3	-	-	-	-	47.1	1.1	30.8	0.7	24.2	2.5	-	-	-	-
1964	31.2	1.3	-	-	-	-	47.5	0.8	31.2	1.3	24.7	2.1	-	-	-	-
1965	31.7	1.6	-	-	-	-	48.0	1.1	31.7	1.6	25.3	2.4	-	-	-	-
1966	32.6	2.8	-	-	-	-	49.2	2.5	32.2	1.6	26.4	4.3	-	-	-	-
1967	33.6	3.1	35.0	-	31.1	-	51.2	4.1	33.1	2.8	28.3	7.2	41.3	-	35.4	-
1968	35.0	4.2	36.2	3.4	32.3	3.9	54.0	5.5	34.1	3.0	30.0	6.0	43.7	5.8	37.2	5.1
1969	36.9	5.4	38.0	5.0	34.3	6.2	57.1	5.7	35.5	4.1	32.1	7.0	45.9	5.0	39.1	5.1
1970	39.0	5.7	40.1	5.5	36.7	7.0	59.5	4.2	37.3	5.1	34.1	6.2	48.2	5.0	41.3	5.6
1971	40.7	4.4	41.3	3.0	38.3	4.4	61.4	3.2	39.2	5.1	36.3	6.5	50.8	5.4	43.3	4.8
1972	42.1	3.4	43.1	4.4	39.8	3.9	62.7	2.1	39.7	1.3	37.5	3.3	52.3	3.0	45.1	4.2
1973	44.7	6.2	48.8	13.2	41.5	4.3	65.0	3.7	41.0	3.3	39.0	4.0	53.7	2.7	46.9	4.0
1974	49.6	11.0	55.5	13.7	46.2	11.3	69.8	7.4	45.5	11.0	42.6	9.2	57.8	7.6	50.2	7.0
1975	54.1	9.1	60.2	8.5	51.1	10.6	72.9	4.4	49.8	9.5	47.7	12.0	62.9	8.8	54.4	8.4
1976	57.2	5.7	62.0	3.0	54.2	6.1	75.6	3.7	54.7	9.8	52.3	9.6	66.0	4.9	57.6	5.9
1977	60.9	6.5	65.7	6.0	57.9	6.8	79.0	4.5	58.6	7.1	57.3	9.6	69.3	5.0	60.9	5.7
1978	65.6	7.7	72.1	9.7	62.9	8.6	81.7	3.4	61.5	4.9	62.1	8.4	72.8	5.1	64.8	6.4
1979	73.1	11.4	79.9	10.8	70.7	12.4	85.2	4.3	70.4	14.5	68.0	9.5	77.6	6.6	69.4	7.1
1980	82.9	13.4	86.9	8.8	81.7	15.6	90.9	6.7	82.9	17.8	75.6	11.2	84.2	8.5	75.6	8.9
1981	91.4	10.3	93.6	7.7	91.1	11.5	95.6	5.2	93.0	12.2	83.5	10.4	90.5	7.5	82.5	9.1
1982	96.9	6.0	97.3	4.0	97.7	7.2	97.8	2.3	97.0	4.3	92.5	10.8	96.0	6.1	90.9	10.2
1983	99.8	3.0	99.5	2.3	100.0	2.4	100.2	2.5	99.2	2.3	100.5	8.6	100.2	4.4	101.3	11.4
1984	103.3	3.5	103.2	3.7	102.2	2.2	102.0	1.8	103.8	4.6	106.9	6.4	103.8	3.6	107.9	6.5
1985	106.9	3.5	105.5	2.2	106.6	4.3	105.0	2.9	106.4	2.5	113.6	6.3	107.5	3.6	114.2	5.8
1986	108.6	1.6	108.9	3.2	109.7	2.9	105.8	0.8	101.7	-4.4	122.0	7.4	111.0	3.3	120.9	5.9
1987	112.5	3.6	113.3	4.0	112.8	2.8	110.4	4.3	105.1	3.3	130.2	6.7	114.8	3.4	127.8	5.7
1988	117.0	4.0	117.9	4.1	116.8	3.5	114.9	4.1	108.3	3.0	139.0	6.8	119.7	4.3	136.5	6.8
1989	122.6	4.8	124.6	5.7	121.2	3.8	117.9	2.6	113.9	5.2	149.6	7.6	125.8	5.1	147.4	8.0
1990	129.0	5.2	131.8	5.8	126.4	4.3	123.1	4.4	120.1	5.4	162.7	8.8	131.4	4.5	158.9	7.8
1991	134.3	4.1	136.5	3.6	131.2	3.8	127.4	3.5	123.1	2.5	176.5	8.5	136.9	4.2	171.7	8.1
1992	138.2	2.9	138.3	1.3	135.0	2.9	130.7	2.6	125.8	2.2	189.6	7.4	140.8	2.8	183.3	6.8
1993	142.1	2.8	141.2	2.1	138.5	2.6	132.4	1.3	129.4	2.9	200.9	6.0	144.1	2.3	192.2	4.9
1994	145.6	2.5	144.4	2.3	142.0	2.5	132.2	-0.2	133.4	3.1	210.4	4.7	148.2	2.8	196.4	2.2
1995	149.8	2.9	148.3	2.7	145.4	2.4	130.9	-1.0	138.8	4.0	219.8	4.5	151.8	2.4	204.2	4.0
1996	154.1	2.9	153.2	3.3	149.6	2.9	130.9	0.0	142.8	2.9	227.6	3.5	156.8	3.3	212.2	3.9
1997	157.6	2.3	157.2	2.6	153.4	2.5	132.1	0.9	143.6	0.6	234.0	2.8	160.0	2.0	221.6	4.4

Source: U.S. Department of Labor, Bureau of Labor Statistics, Division of Consumer Prices and Price Indexes.

U.S. CITY AVERAGE
Consumer Price Index - All Urban Consumers
Base 1982-1984 = 100
All Items

For 1913-1997. Columns headed % show percentile change in the index from the previous period for which an index is available.

Year	Jan Index	%	Feb Index	%	Mar Index	%	Apr Index	%	May Index	%	Jun Index	%	Jul Index	%	Aug Index	%	Sep Index	%	Oct Index	%	Nov Index	%	Dec Index	%
1913	9.8	-	9.8	0.0	9.8	0.0	9.8	0.0	9.7	-1.0	9.8	1.0	9.9	1.0	9.9	0.0	10.0	1.0	10.0	0.0	10.1	1.0	10.0	-1.0
1914	10.0	0.0	9.9	-1.0	9.9	0.0	9.8	-1.0	9.9	1.0	9.9	0.0	10.0	1.0	10.2	2.0	10.2	0.0	10.1	-1.0	10.2	1.0	10.1	-1.0
1915	10.1	0.0	10.0	-1.0	9.9	-1.0	10.0	1.0	10.1	1.0	10.1	0.0	10.1	0.0	10.1	0.0	10.1	0.0	10.2	1.0	10.3	1.0	10.3	0.0
1916	10.4	1.0	10.4	0.0	10.5	1.0	10.6	1.0	10.7	0.9	10.8	0.9	10.8	0.0	10.9	0.9	11.1	1.8	11.3	1.8	11.5	1.8	11.6	0.9
1917	11.7	0.9	12.0	2.6	12.0	0.0	12.6	5.0	12.8	1.6	13.0	1.6	12.8	-1.5	13.0	1.6	13.3	2.3	13.5	1.5	13.5	0.0	13.7	1.5
1918	14.0	2.2	14.1	0.7	14.0	-0.7	14.2	1.4	14.5	2.1	14.7	1.4	15.1	2.7	15.4	2.0	15.7	1.9	16.0	1.9	16.3	1.9	16.5	1.2
1919	16.5	0.0	16.2	-1.8	16.4	1.2	16.7	1.8	16.9	1.2	16.9	0.0	17.4	3.0	17.7	1.7	17.8	0.6	18.1	1.7	18.5	2.2	18.9	2.2
1920	19.3	2.1	19.5	1.0	19.7	1.0	20.3	3.0	20.6	1.5	20.9	1.5	20.8	-0.5	20.3	-2.4	20.0	-1.5	19.9	-0.5	19.8	-0.5	19.4	-2.0
1921	19.0	-2.1	18.4	-3.2	18.3	-0.5	18.1	-1.1	17.7	-2.2	17.6	-0.6	17.7	0.6	17.7	0.0	17.5	-1.1	17.5	0.0	17.4	-0.6	17.3	-0.6
1922	16.9	-2.3	16.9	0.0	16.7	-1.2	16.7	0.0	16.7	0.0	16.7	0.0	16.8	0.6	16.6	-1.2	16.6	0.0	16.7	0.6	16.8	0.6	16.9	0.6
1923	16.8	-0.6	16.8	0.0	16.8	0.0	16.9	0.6	16.9	0.0	17.0	0.6	17.2	1.2	17.1	-0.6	17.2	0.6	17.3	0.6	17.3	0.0	17.3	0.0
1924	17.3	0.0	17.2	-0.6	17.1	-0.6	17.0	-0.6	17.0	0.0	17.0	0.0	17.1	0.6	17.0	-0.6	17.1	0.6	17.2	0.6	17.2	0.0	17.3	0.6
1925	17.3	0.0	17.2	-0.6	17.3	0.6	17.2	-0.6	17.3	0.6	17.5	1.2	17.7	1.1	17.7	0.0	17.7	0.0	17.7	0.0	18.0	1.7	17.9	-0.6
1926	17.9	0.0	17.9	0.0	17.8	-0.6	17.9	0.6	17.8	-0.6	17.7	-0.6	17.5	-1.1	17.4	-0.6	17.5	0.6	17.6	0.6	17.7	0.6	17.7	0.0
1927	17.5	-1.1	17.4	-0.6	17.3	-0.6	17.3	0.0	17.4	0.6	17.6	1.1	17.3	-1.7	17.2	-0.6	17.3	0.6	17.4	0.6	17.3	-0.6	17.3	0.0
1928	17.3	0.0	17.1	-1.2	17.1	0.0	17.1	0.0	17.2	0.6	17.1	-0.6	17.1	0.0	17.1	0.0	17.3	1.2	17.2	-0.6	17.2	0.0	17.1	-0.6
1929	17.1	0.0	17.1	0.0	17.0	-0.6	16.9	-0.6	17.0	0.6	17.1	0.6	17.3	1.2	17.3	0.0	17.3	0.0	17.3	0.0	17.3	0.0	17.2	-0.6
1930	17.1	-0.6	17.0	-0.6	16.9	-0.6	17.0	0.6	16.9	-0.6	16.8	-0.6	16.6	-1.2	16.5	-0.6	16.6	0.6	16.5	-0.6	16.4	-0.6	16.1	-1.8
1931	15.9	-1.2	15.7	-1.3	15.6	-0.6	15.5	-0.6	15.3	-1.3	15.1	-1.3	15.1	0.0	15.1	0.0	15.0	-0.7	14.9	-0.7	14.7	-1.3	14.6	-0.7
1932	14.3	-2.1	14.1	-1.4	14.0	-0.7	13.9	-0.7	13.7	-1.4	13.6	-0.7	13.6	0.0	13.5	-0.7	13.4	-0.7	13.3	-0.7	13.2	-0.8	13.1	-0.8
1933	12.9	-1.5	12.7	-1.6	12.6	-0.8	12.6	0.0	12.6	0.0	12.7	0.8	13.1	3.1	13.2	0.8	13.2	0.0	13.2	0.0	13.2	0.0	13.2	0.0
1934	13.2	0.0	13.3	0.8	13.3	0.0	13.3	0.0	13.3	0.0	13.4	0.8	13.4	0.0	13.4	0.0	13.6	1.5	13.5	-0.7	13.5	0.0	13.4	-0.7
1935	13.6	1.5	13.7	0.7	13.7	0.0	13.8	0.7	13.8	0.0	13.7	-0.7	13.7	0.0	13.7	0.0	13.7	0.0	13.7	0.0	13.8	0.7	13.8	0.0
1936	13.8	0.0	13.8	0.0	13.7	-0.7	13.7	0.0	13.7	0.0	13.8	0.7	13.9	0.7	14.0	0.7	14.0	0.0	14.0	0.0	14.0	0.0	14.0	0.0
1937	14.1	0.7	14.1	0.0	14.2	0.7	14.3	0.7	14.4	0.7	14.4	0.0	14.5	0.7	14.5	0.0	14.6	0.7	14.6	0.0	14.5	-0.7	14.4	-0.7
1938	14.2	-1.4	14.1	-0.7	14.1	0.0	14.2	0.7	14.1	-0.7	14.1	0.0	14.1	0.0	14.1	0.0	14.1	0.0	14.1	0.0	14.0	-0.7	14.0	0.0
1939	14.0	0.0	13.9	-0.7	13.9	0.0	13.8	-0.7	13.8	0.0	13.8	0.0	13.8	0.0	13.8	0.0	14.1	2.2	14.0	-0.7	14.0	0.0	14.0	0.0
1940	13.9	-0.7	14.0	0.7	14.0	0.0	14.0	0.0	14.0	0.0	14.1	0.7	14.0	-0.7	14.0	0.0	14.0	0.0	14.0	0.0	14.0	0.0	14.1	0.7
1941	14.1	0.0	14.1	0.0	14.2	0.7	14.3	0.7	14.4	0.7	14.7	2.1	14.7	0.0	14.9	1.4	15.1	1.3	15.3	1.3	15.4	0.7	15.5	0.6
1942	15.7	1.3	15.8	0.6	16.0	1.3	16.1	0.6	16.3	1.2	16.3	0.0	16.4	0.6	16.5	0.6	16.5	0.0	16.7	1.2	16.8	0.6	16.9	0.6
1943	16.9	0.0	16.9	0.0	17.2	1.8	17.4	1.2	17.5	0.6	17.5	0.0	17.4	-0.6	17.3	-0.6	17.4	0.6	17.4	0.0	17.4	0.0	17.4	0.0
1944	17.4	0.0	17.4	0.0	17.4	0.0	17.5	0.6	17.5	0.0	17.6	0.6	17.7	0.6	17.7	0.0	17.7	0.0	17.7	0.0	17.7	0.0	17.8	0.6
1945	17.8	0.0	17.8	0.0	17.8	0.0	17.8	0.0	17.9	0.6	18.1	1.1	18.1	0.0	18.1	0.0	18.1	0.0	18.1	0.0	18.1	0.0	18.2	0.6
1946	18.2	0.0	18.1	-0.5	18.3	1.1	18.4	0.5	18.5	0.5	18.7	1.1	19.8	5.9	20.2	2.0	20.4	1.0	20.8	2.0	21.3	2.4	21.5	0.9
1947	21.5	0.0	21.5	0.0	21.9	1.9	21.9	0.0	21.9	0.0	22.0	0.5	22.2	0.9	22.5	1.4	23.0	2.2	23.0	0.0	23.1	0.4	23.4	1.3
1948	23.7	1.3	23.5	-0.8	23.4	-0.4	23.8	1.7	23.9	0.4	24.1	0.8	24.4	1.2	24.5	0.4	24.5	0.0	24.4	-0.4	24.2	-0.8	24.1	-0.4
1949	24.0	-0.4	23.8	-0.8	23.8	0.0	23.9	0.4	23.8	-0.4	23.9	0.4	23.7	-0.8	23.8	0.4	23.9	0.4	23.7	-0.8	23.8	0.4	23.6	-0.8
1950	23.5	-0.4	23.5	0.0	23.6	0.4	23.6	0.0	23.7	0.4	23.8	0.4	24.1	1.3	24.3	0.8	24.4	0.4	24.6	0.8	24.7	0.4	25.0	1.2
1951	25.4	1.6	25.7	1.2	25.8	0.4	25.8	0.0	25.9	0.4	25.9	0.0	25.9	0.0	25.9	0.0	26.1	0.8	26.2	0.4	26.4	0.8	26.5	0.4
1952	26.5	0.0	26.3	-0.8	26.3	0.0	26.4	0.4	26.4	0.0	26.5	0.4	26.7	0.8	26.7	0.0	26.7	0.0	27.0	0.4	26.9	-0.4	26.9	0.0
1953	26.6	-0.4	26.5	-0.4	26.6	0.4	26.6	0.0	26.7	0.4	26.8	0.4	26.8	0.0	26.9	0.4	26.9	0.0	26.8	0.0	26.9	0.4	26.7	-0.4
1954	26.9	0.0	26.9	0.0	26.9	0.0	26.8	-0.4	26.9	0.4	26.9	0.0	26.9	0.0	26.9	0.0	26.8	-0.4	26.8	0.0	26.9	0.0	26.8	-0.4
1955	26.7	0.0	26.7	0.0	26.7	0.0	26.7	0.0	26.7	0.0	26.7	0.0	26.8	0.4	26.8	0.0	26.9	0.4	26.9	0.0	26.9	0.0	26.8	-0.4
1956	26.8	0.0	26.8	0.0	26.8	0.0	26.9	0.4	27.0	0.4	27.2	0.7	27.4	0.7	27.3	-0.4	27.4	0.4	27.5	0.4	27.5	0.0	27.6	0.4
1957	27.6	0.0	27.7	0.4	27.8	0.4	27.9	0.4	28.0	0.4	28.1	0.4	28.3	0.7	28.3	0.0	28.3	0.0	28.3	0.0	28.4	0.4	28.4	0.0

[Continued]

U.S. City Average
Consumer Price Index - All Urban Consumers
Base 1982-1984 = 100
All Items
[Continued]

For 1913-1997. Columns headed % show percentile change in the index from the previous period for which an index is available.

Year	Jan Index	%	Feb Index	%	Mar Index	%	Apr Index	%	May Index	%	Jun Index	%	Jul Index	%	Aug Index	%	Sep Index	%	Oct Index	%	Nov Index	%	Dec Index	%
1958	28.6	0.7	28.6	0.0	28.8	0.7	28.9	0.3	28.9	0.0	28.9	0.0	29.0	0.3	28.9	-0.3	28.9	0.0	28.9	0.0	29.0	0.3	28.9	-0.3
1959	29.0	0.3	28.9	-0.3	28.9	0.0	29.0	0.3	29.0	0.0	29.1	0.3	29.2	0.3	29.2	0.0	29.3	0.3	29.4	0.3	29.4	0.0	29.4	0.0
1960	29.3	-0.3	29.4	0.3	29.4	0.0	29.5	0.3	29.5	0.0	29.6	0.3	29.6	0.0	29.6	0.0	29.6	0.0	29.8	0.7	29.8	0.0	29.8	0.0
1961	29.8	0.0	29.8	0.0	29.8	0.0	29.8	0.0	29.8	0.0	29.8	0.0	30.0	0.7	29.9	-0.3	30.0	0.3	30.0	0.0	30.0	0.0	30.0	0.0
1962	30.0	0.0	30.1	0.3	30.1	0.0	30.2	0.3	30.2	0.0	30.2	0.0	30.3	0.3	30.3	0.0	30.4	0.3	30.4	0.0	30.4	0.0	30.4	0.0
1963	30.4	0.0	30.4	0.0	30.5	0.3	30.5	0.0	30.5	0.0	30.6	0.3	30.7	0.3	30.7	0.0	30.7	0.0	30.8	0.3	30.8	0.0	30.9	0.3
1964	30.9	0.0	30.9	0.0	30.9	0.0	30.9	0.0	30.9	0.0	31.0	0.3	31.1	0.3	31.0	-0.3	31.1	0.3	31.1	0.0	31.2	0.3	31.2	0.0
1965	31.2	0.0	31.2	0.0	31.3	0.3	31.4	0.3	31.4	0.0	31.6	0.6	31.6	0.0	31.6	0.0	31.6	0.0	31.7	0.3	31.7	0.0	31.8	0.3
1966	31.8	0.0	32.0	0.6	32.1	0.3	32.3	0.6	32.3	0.0	32.4	0.3	32.5	0.3	32.7	0.6	32.7	0.0	32.9	0.6	32.9	0.0	32.9	0.0
1967	32.9	0.0	32.9	0.0	33.0	0.3	33.1	0.3	33.2	0.3	33.3	0.3	33.4	0.3	33.5	0.3	33.6	0.3	33.7	0.3	33.8	0.3	33.9	0.3
1968	34.1	0.6	34.2	0.3	34.3	0.3	34.4	0.3	34.5	0.3	34.7	0.6	34.9	0.6	35.0	0.3	35.1	0.3	35.3	0.6	35.4	0.3	35.5	0.3
1969	35.6	0.3	35.8	0.6	36.1	0.8	36.3	0.6	36.4	0.3	36.6	0.5	36.8	0.5	37.0	0.5	37.1	0.3	37.3	0.5	37.5	0.5	37.7	0.5
1970	37.8	0.3	38.0	0.5	38.2	0.5	38.5	0.8	38.6	0.3	38.8	0.5	39.0	0.5	39.0	0.0	39.2	0.5	39.4	0.5	39.6	0.5	39.8	0.5
1971	39.8	0.0	39.9	0.3	40.0	0.3	40.1	0.2	40.3	0.5	40.6	0.7	40.7	0.2	40.8	0.2	40.8	0.0	40.9	0.2	40.9	0.0	41.1	0.5
1972	41.1	0.0	41.3	0.5	41.4	0.2	41.5	0.2	41.6	0.2	41.7	0.2	41.9	0.5	42.0	0.2	42.1	0.2	42.3	0.5	42.4	0.2	42.5	0.2
1973	42.6	0.2	42.9	0.7	43.3	0.9	43.6	0.7	43.9	0.7	44.2	0.7	44.3	0.2	45.1	1.8	45.2	0.2	45.6	0.9	45.9	0.7	46.2	0.7
1974	46.6	0.9	47.2	1.3	47.8	1.3	48.0	0.4	48.6	1.2	49.0	0.8	49.4	0.8	50.0	1.2	50.6	1.2	51.1	1.0	51.5	0.8	51.9	0.8
1975	52.1	0.4	52.5	0.8	52.7	0.4	52.9	0.4	53.2	0.6	53.6	0.8	54.2	1.1	54.3	0.2	54.6	0.6	54.9	0.5	55.3	0.7	55.5	0.4
1976	55.6	0.2	55.8	0.4	55.9	0.2	56.1	0.4	56.5	0.7	56.8	0.5	57.1	0.5	57.4	0.5	57.6	0.3	57.9	0.5	58.0	0.2	58.2	0.3
1977	58.5	0.5	59.1	1.0	59.5	0.7	60.0	0.8	60.3	0.5	60.7	0.7	61.0	0.5	61.2	0.3	61.4	0.3	61.6	0.3	61.9	0.5	62.1	0.3
1978	62.5	0.6	62.9	0.6	63.4	0.8	63.9	0.8	64.5	0.9	65.2	1.1	65.7	0.8	66.0	0.5	66.5	0.8	67.1	0.9	67.4	0.4	67.7	0.4
1979	68.3	0.9	69.1	1.2	69.8	1.0	70.6	1.1	71.5	1.3	72.3	1.1	73.1	1.1	73.8	1.0	74.6	1.1	75.2	0.8	75.9	0.9	76.7	1.1
1980	77.8	1.4	78.9	1.4	80.1	1.5	81.0	1.1	81.8	1.0	82.7	1.1	82.7	0.0	83.3	0.7	84.0	0.8	84.8	1.0	85.5	0.8	86.3	0.9
1981	87.0	0.8	87.9	1.0	88.5	0.7	89.1	0.7	89.8	0.8	90.6	0.9	91.6	1.1	92.3	0.8	93.2	1.0	93.4	0.2	93.7	0.3	94.0	0.3
1982	94.3	0.3	94.6	0.3	94.5	-0.1	94.9	0.4	95.8	0.9	97.0	1.3	97.5	0.5	97.7	0.2	97.9	0.2	98.2	0.3	98.0	-0.2	97.6	-0.4
1983	97.8	0.2	97.9	0.1	97.9	0.0	98.6	0.7	99.2	0.6	99.5	0.3	99.9	0.4	100.2	0.3	100.7	0.5	101.0	0.3	101.2	0.2	101.3	0.1
1984	101.9	0.6	102.4	0.5	102.6	0.2	103.1	0.5	103.4	0.3	103.7	0.3	104.1	0.4	104.5	0.4	105.0	0.5	105.3	0.3	105.3	0.0	105.3	0.0
1985	105.5	0.2	106.0	0.5	106.4	0.4	106.9	0.5	107.3	0.4	107.6	0.3	107.8	0.2	108.0	0.2	108.3	0.3	108.7	0.4	109.0	0.3	109.3	0.3
1986	109.6	0.3	109.3	-0.3	108.8	-0.5	108.6	-0.2	108.9	0.3	109.5	0.6	109.5	0.0	109.7	0.2	110.2	0.5	110.3	0.1	110.4	0.1	110.5	0.1
1987	111.2	0.6	111.6	0.4	112.1	0.4	112.7	0.5	113.1	0.4	113.5	0.4	113.8	0.3	114.4	0.5	115.0	0.5	115.3	0.3	115.4	0.1	115.4	0.0
1988	115.7	0.3	116.0	0.3	116.5	0.4	117.1	0.5	117.5	0.3	118.0	0.4	118.5	0.4	119.0	0.4	119.8	0.7	120.2	0.3	120.3	0.1	120.5	0.2
1989	121.1	0.5	121.6	0.4	122.3	0.6	123.1	0.7	123.8	0.6	124.1	0.2	124.4	0.2	124.6	0.2	125.0	0.3	125.6	0.5	125.9	0.2	126.1	0.2
1990	127.4	1.0	128.0	0.5	128.7	0.5	128.9	0.2	129.2	0.2	129.9	0.5	130.4	0.4	131.6	0.9	132.7	0.8	133.5	0.6	133.8	0.2	133.8	0.0
1991	134.6	0.6	134.8	0.1	135.0	0.1	135.2	0.1	135.6	0.3	136.0	0.3	136.2	0.1	136.6	0.3	137.2	0.4	137.4	0.1	137.8	0.3	137.9	0.1
1992	138.1	0.1	138.6	0.4	139.3	0.5	139.5	0.1	139.7	0.1	140.2	0.4	140.5	0.2	140.9	0.3	141.3	0.3	141.8	0.4	142.0	0.1	141.9	-0.1
1993	142.6	0.5	143.1	0.4	143.6	0.3	144.0	0.3	144.2	0.1	144.4	0.1	144.4	0.0	144.8	0.3	145.1	0.2	145.7	0.4	145.8	0.1	145.8	0.0
1994	146.2	0.3	146.7	0.3	147.2	0.3	147.4	0.1	147.5	0.1	148.0	0.3	148.4	0.3	149.0	0.4	149.4	0.3	149.5	0.1	149.7	0.1	149.7	0.0
1995	150.3	0.4	150.9	0.4	151.4	0.3	151.9	0.3	152.2	0.2	152.5	0.2	152.5	0.0	152.9	0.3	153.2	0.2	153.7	0.3	153.6	-0.1	153.5	-0.1
1996	154.4	0.6	154.9	0.3	155.7	0.5	156.3	0.4	156.6	0.2	156.7	0.1	157.0	0.2	157.3	0.2	157.8	0.3	158.3	0.3	158.6	0.2	158.6	0.0
1997	159.1	0.3	159.6	0.3	160.0	0.3	160.2	0.1	160.1	-0.1	160.3	0.1	160.5	0.1	160.8	0.2	161.2	0.2	161.6	0.2	161.5	-0.1	161.3	-0.1

Source: U.S. Department of Labor, Bureau of Labor Statistics, Division of Consumer Prices and Price Indexes.

U.S. CITY AVERAGE
Consumer Price Index - Urban Wage Earners
Base 1982-1984 = 100
All Items

For 1913-1997. Columns headed % show percentile change in the index from the previous period for which an index is available.

Year	Jan Index	%	Feb Index	%	Mar Index	%	Apr Index	%	May Index	%	Jun Index	%	Jul Index	%	Aug Index	%	Sep Index	%	Oct Index	%	Nov Index	%	Dec Index	%
1913	9.9	-	9.8	-1.0	9.8	0.0	9.9	1.0	9.8	-1.0	9.8	0.0	9.9	1.0	10.0	1.0	10.0	0.0	10.1	1.0	10.1	0.0	10.1	0.0
1914	10.1	0.0	10.0	-1.0	10.0	0.0	9.9	-1.0	9.9	0.0	10.0	1.0	10.1	1.0	10.2	1.0	10.3	1.0	10.2	-1.0	10.2	0.0	10.2	0.0
1915	10.2	0.0	10.1	-1.0	10.0	-1.0	10.1	1.0	10.1	0.0	10.2	1.0	10.2	0.0	10.2	0.0	10.2	0.0	10.3	1.0	10.4	1.0	10.4	0.0
1916	10.5	1.0	10.5	0.0	10.6	1.0	10.7	0.9	10.7	0.0	10.9	1.9	10.9	0.0	11.0	0.9	11.2	1.8	11.3	0.9	11.5	1.8	11.6	0.9
1917	11.8	1.7	12.0	1.7	12.1	0.8	12.6	4.1	12.9	2.4	13.0	0.8	12.9	-0.8	13.1	1.6	13.3	1.5	13.6	2.3	13.6	0.0	13.8	1.5
1918	14.0	1.4	14.2	1.4	14.1	-0.7	14.3	1.4	14.5	1.4	14.8	2.1	15.2	2.7	15.4	1.3	15.8	2.6	16.1	1.9	16.3	1.2	16.6	1.8
1919	16.6	0.0	16.2	-2.4	16.5	1.9	16.8	1.8	17.0	1.2	17.0	0.0	17.5	2.9	17.8	1.7	17.9	0.6	18.2	1.7	18.6	2.2	19.0	2.2
1920	19.4	2.1	19.6	1.0	19.8	1.0	20.4	3.0	20.7	1.5	21.0	1.4	20.9	-0.5	20.4	-2.4	20.1	-1.5	20.0	-0.5	19.9	-0.5	19.5	-2.0
1921	19.1	-2.1	18.5	-3.1	18.4	-0.5	18.2	-1.1	17.8	-2.2	17.7	-0.6	17.8	0.6	17.8	0.0	17.6	-1.1	17.6	0.0	17.5	-0.6	17.4	-0.6
1922	17.0	-2.3	17.0	0.0	16.8	-1.2	16.8	0.0	16.8	0.0	16.8	0.0	16.9	0.6	16.7	-1.2	16.7	0.0	16.8	0.6	16.9	0.6	17.0	0.6
1923	16.9	-0.6	16.9	0.0	16.9	0.0	17.0	0.6	17.0	0.0	17.1	0.6	17.3	1.2	17.2	-0.6	17.3	0.6	17.4	0.6	17.4	0.0	17.4	0.0
1924	17.4	0.0	17.3	-0.6	17.2	-0.6	17.1	-0.6	17.1	0.0	17.1	0.0	17.2	0.6	17.1	-0.6	17.2	0.6	17.3	0.6	17.3	0.0	17.4	0.6
1925	17.4	0.0	17.3	-0.6	17.4	0.6	17.3	-0.6	17.4	0.6	17.6	1.1	17.8	1.1	17.8	0.0	17.8	0.0	17.8	0.0	18.1	1.7	18.0	-0.6
1926	18.0	0.0	18.0	0.0	17.9	-0.6	18.0	0.6	17.9	-0.6	17.8	-0.6	17.6	-1.1	17.5	-0.6	17.6	0.6	17.7	0.6	17.8	0.6	17.8	0.0
1927	17.6	-1.1	17.5	-0.6	17.4	-0.6	17.4	0.0	17.5	0.6	17.7	1.1	17.4	-1.7	17.3	-0.6	17.4	0.6	17.5	0.6	17.4	-0.6	17.4	0.0
1928	17.4	0.0	17.2	-1.1	17.2	0.0	17.2	0.0	17.3	0.6	17.2	-0.6	17.2	0.0	17.2	0.0	17.4	1.2	17.3	-0.6	17.3	0.0	17.2	-0.6
1929	17.2	0.0	17.2	0.0	17.1	-0.6	17.0	-0.6	17.1	0.6	17.2	0.6	17.4	1.2	17.4	0.0	17.4	0.0	17.4	0.0	17.4	0.0	17.3	-0.6
1930	17.2	-0.6	17.1	-0.6	17.0	-0.6	17.1	0.6	17.0	-0.6	16.9	-0.6	16.7	-1.2	16.6	-0.6	16.7	0.6	16.6	-0.6	16.5	-0.6	16.2	-1.8
1931	16.0	-1.2	15.7	-1.9	15.6	-0.6	15.5	-0.6	15.4	-0.6	15.2	-1.3	15.2	0.0	15.1	-0.7	15.1	0.0	15.0	-0.7	14.8	-1.3	14.7	-0.7
1932	14.4	-2.0	14.2	-1.4	14.1	-0.7	14.0	-0.7	13.8	-1.4	13.7	-0.7	13.7	0.0	13.5	-1.5	13.5	0.0	13.4	-0.7	13.3	-0.7	13.2	-0.8
1933	13.0	-1.5	12.8	-1.5	12.7	-0.8	12.6	-0.8	12.7	0.8	12.8	0.8	13.2	3.1	13.3	0.8	13.3	0.0	13.3	0.0	13.3	0.0	13.2	-0.8
1934	13.3	0.8	13.4	0.8	13.4	0.0	13.4	0.0	13.4	0.0	13.4	0.0	13.4	0.0	13.4	0.0	13.5	0.7	13.7	1.5	13.6	-0.7	13.5	-0.7	13.5	0.0
1935	13.7	1.5	13.8	0.7	13.8	0.0	13.9	0.7	13.8	-0.7	13.8	0.0	13.7	-0.7	13.7	0.0	13.8	0.7	13.8	0.0	13.9	0.7	13.9	0.0
1936	13.9	0.0	13.8	-0.7	13.8	0.0	13.8	0.0	13.8	0.0	13.9	0.7	14.0	0.7	14.1	0.7	14.1	0.0	14.1	0.0	14.1	0.0	14.1	0.0
1937	14.2	0.7	14.2	0.0	14.3	0.7	14.4	0.7	14.4	0.0	14.5	0.7	14.5	0.0	14.6	0.7	14.7	0.7	14.6	-0.7	14.5	-0.7	14.5	0.0
1938	14.3	-1.4	14.2	-0.7	14.2	0.0	14.2	0.0	14.2	0.0	14.2	0.0	14.2	0.0	14.2	0.0	14.2	0.0	14.1	-0.7	14.1	0.0	14.1	0.0
1939	14.0	-0.7	14.0	0.0	13.9	-0.7	13.9	0.0	13.9	0.0	13.9	0.0	13.9	0.0	13.9	0.0	14.2	2.2	14.1	-0.7	14.1	0.0	14.0	-0.7
1940	14.0	0.0	14.1	0.7	14.1	0.0	14.1	0.0	14.1	0.0	14.1	0.0	14.1	0.0	14.1	0.0	14.1	0.0	14.1	0.0	14.1	0.0	14.2	0.7
1941	14.2	0.0	14.2	0.0	14.2	0.0	14.4	1.4	14.5	0.7	14.7	1.4	14.8	0.7	14.9	0.7	15.2	2.0	15.4	1.3	15.5	0.6	15.5	0.0
1942	15.7	1.3	15.9	1.3	16.1	1.3	16.2	0.6	16.3	0.6	16.4	0.6	16.5	0.6	16.6	0.6	16.6	0.0	16.8	1.2	16.9	0.6	17.0	0.6
1943	17.0	0.0	17.0	0.0	17.3	1.8	17.5	1.2	17.6	0.6	17.6	0.0	17.5	-0.6	17.4	-0.6	17.5	0.6	17.5	0.0	17.5	0.0	17.5	0.0
1944	17.5	0.0	17.5	0.0	17.5	0.0	17.6	0.6	17.6	0.0	17.7	0.6	17.8	0.6	17.8	0.0	17.8	0.0	17.8	0.0	17.8	0.0	17.9	0.6
1945	17.9	0.0	17.9	0.0	17.9	0.0	17.9	0.0	18.0	0.6	18.2	1.1	18.2	0.0	18.2	0.0	18.2	0.0	18.2	0.0	18.2	0.0	18.3	0.5
1946	18.3	0.0	18.2	-0.5	18.4	1.1	18.5	0.5	18.6	0.5	18.8	1.1	19.9	5.9	20.3	2.0	20.5	1.0	20.9	2.0	21.5	2.9	21.6	0.5
1947	21.6	0.0	21.6	0.0	22.1	2.3	22.1	0.0	22.0	-0.5	22.2	0.9	22.4	0.9	22.6	0.9	23.1	2.2	23.1	0.0	23.3	0.9	23.6	1.3
1948	23.8	0.8	23.6	-0.8	23.6	0.0	23.9	1.3	24.1	0.8	24.2	0.4	24.5	1.2	24.6	0.4	24.6	0.0	24.5	-0.4	24.4	-0.4	24.2	-0.8
1949	24.2	0.0	23.9	-1.2	24.0	0.4	24.0	0.0	24.0	0.0	24.0	0.0	23.8	-0.8	23.9	0.4	24.0	0.4	23.9	-0.4	23.9	0.0	23.8	-0.4
1950	23.7	-0.4	23.6	-0.4	23.7	0.4	23.7	0.0	23.8	0.4	24.0	0.8	24.2	0.8	24.4	0.8	24.6	0.8	24.7	0.4	24.8	0.4	25.1	1.2
1951	25.5	1.6	25.9	1.6	26.0	0.4	26.0	0.0	26.1	0.4	26.1	0.0	26.1	0.0	26.1	0.0	26.3	0.8	26.4	0.4	26.5	0.4	26.6	0.4
1952	26.6	0.0	26.5	-0.4	26.5	0.0	26.6	0.4	26.6	0.0	26.7	0.4	26.9	0.7	26.9	0.0	26.9	0.0	26.9	0.0	26.9	0.0	26.9	0.0
1953	26.8	-0.4	26.7	-0.4	26.7	0.0	26.8	0.4	26.8	0.0	26.9	0.4	27.0	0.4	27.1	0.4	27.1	0.0	27.2	0.4	27.1	-0.4	27.0	-0.4
1954	27.1	0.4	27.1	0.0	27.0	-0.4	27.0	0.0	27.1	0.4	27.1	0.0	27.1	0.0	27.1	0.0	27.0	-0.4	26.9	-0.4	27.0	0.4	26.9	-0.4
1955	26.9	0.0	26.9	0.0	26.9	0.0	26.9	0.0	26.9	0.0	26.9	0.0	27.0	0.4	26.9	-0.4	27.0	0.4	27.0	0.0	27.1	0.4	27.0	-0.4
1956	27.0	0.0	27.0	0.0	27.0	0.0	27.0	0.0	27.2	0.7	27.3	0.4	27.5	0.7	27.5	0.0	27.5	0.0	27.7	0.7	27.7	0.0	27.8	0.4
1957	27.8	0.0	27.9	0.4	28.0	0.4	28.1	0.4	28.1	0.0	28.3	0.7	28.4	0.4	28.5	0.4	28.5	0.0	28.5	0.0	28.6	0.4	28.6	0.0

[Continued]

U.S. City Average
Consumer Price Index - Urban Wage Earners
Base 1982-1984 = 100
All Items
[Continued]

For 1913-1997. Columns headed % show percentile change in the index from the previous period for which an index is available.

Year	Jan Index	%	Feb Index	%	Mar Index	%	Apr Index	%	May Index	%	Jun Index	%	Jul Index	%	Aug Index	%	Sep Index	%	Oct Index	%	Nov Index	%	Dec Index	%
1958	28.8	0.7	28.8	0.0	29.0	0.7	29.1	0.3	29.1	0.0	29.1	0.0	29.1	0.0	29.1	0.0	29.1	0.0	29.1	0.0	29.1	0.0	29.1	0.0
1959	29.1	0.0	29.1	0.0	29.1	0.0	29.1	0.0	29.2	0.3	29.3	0.3	29.4	0.3	29.3	-0.3	29.4	0.3	29.5	0.3	29.5	0.0	29.5	0.0
1960	29.5	0.0	29.5	0.0	29.5	0.0	29.7	0.7	29.7	0.0	29.8	0.3	29.8	0.0	29.8	0.0	29.8	0.0	29.9	0.3	30.0	0.3	30.0	0.0
1961	30.0	0.0	30.0	0.0	30.0	0.0	30.0	0.0	30.0	0.0	30.0	0.0	30.1	0.3	30.1	0.0	30.2	0.3	30.2	0.0	30.2	0.0	30.2	0.0
1962	30.2	0.0	30.2	0.0	30.3	0.3	30.4	0.3	30.4	0.0	30.4	0.0	30.4	0.0	30.4	0.0	30.6	0.7	30.6	0.0	30.6	0.0	30.6	0.0
1963	30.6	0.0	30.6	0.0	30.7	0.3	30.7	0.0	30.7	0.0	30.8	0.3	30.9	0.3	30.9	0.0	30.9	0.0	31.0	0.3	31.0	0.0	31.1	0.3
1964	31.1	0.0	31.1	0.0	31.1	0.0	31.1	0.0	31.1	0.0	31.2	0.3	31.3	0.3	31.2	-0.3	31.3	0.3	31.3	0.0	31.4	0.3	31.4	0.0
1965	31.4	0.0	31.4	0.0	31.5	0.3	31.6	0.3	31.6	0.0	31.8	0.6	31.8	0.0	31.8	0.0	31.8	0.0	31.9	0.3	31.9	0.0	32.0	0.3
1966	32.0	0.0	32.2	0.6	32.3	0.3	32.5	0.6	32.5	0.0	32.6	0.3	32.7	0.3	32.9	0.6	32.9	0.0	33.1	0.6	33.1	0.0	33.1	0.0
1967	33.1	0.0	33.1	0.0	33.2	0.3	33.3	0.3	33.4	0.3	33.5	0.3	33.6	0.3	33.7	0.3	33.8	0.3	33.9	0.3	34.0	0.3	34.1	0.3
1968	34.2	0.3	34.3	0.3	34.5	0.6	34.6	0.3	34.7	0.3	34.9	0.6	35.1	0.6	35.2	0.3	35.3	0.3	35.5	0.6	35.6	0.3	35.7	0.3
1969	35.8	0.3	36.0	0.6	36.3	0.8	36.5	0.6	36.6	0.3	36.8	0.5	37.0	0.5	37.2	0.5	37.3	0.3	37.5	0.5	37.7	0.5	37.9	0.5
1970	38.0	0.3	38.2	0.5	38.4	0.5	38.7	0.8	38.8	0.3	39.0	0.5	39.2	0.5	39.2	0.0	39.4	0.5	39.6	0.5	39.8	0.5	40.0	0.5
1971	40.0	0.0	40.1	0.2	40.2	0.2	40.4	0.5	40.6	0.5	40.8	0.5	40.9	0.2	41.0	0.2	41.0	0.0	41.1	0.2	41.2	0.2	41.3	0.2
1972	41.4	0.2	41.6	0.5	41.6	0.0	41.7	0.2	41.9	0.5	42.0	0.2	42.1	0.2	42.2	0.2	42.4	0.5	42.5	0.2	42.6	0.2	42.7	0.2
1973	42.9	0.5	43.2	0.7	43.6	0.9	43.9	0.7	44.1	0.5	44.4	0.7	44.5	0.2	45.4	2.0	45.5	0.2	45.9	0.9	46.2	0.7	46.5	0.6
1974	46.9	0.9	47.5	1.3	48.0	1.1	48.3	0.6	48.8	1.0	49.3	1.0	49.7	0.8	50.3	1.2	50.9	1.2	51.4	1.0	51.8	0.8	52.2	0.8
1975	52.4	0.4	52.8	0.8	53.0	0.4	53.2	0.4	53.5	0.6	53.9	0.7	54.5	1.1	54.7	0.4	54.9	0.4	55.3	0.7	55.6	0.5	55.8	0.4
1976	56.0	0.4	56.1	0.2	56.2	0.2	56.5	0.5	56.8	0.5	57.1	0.5	57.4	0.5	57.7	0.5	57.9	0.3	58.2	0.5	58.3	0.2	58.5	0.3
1977	58.9	0.7	59.5	1.0	59.8	0.5	60.3	0.8	60.6	0.5	61.0	0.7	61.3	0.5	61.5	0.3	61.8	0.5	61.9	0.2	62.2	0.5	62.5	0.5
1978	62.8	0.5	63.2	0.6	63.7	0.8	64.3	0.9	64.9	0.9	65.6	1.1	66.0	0.6	66.4	0.6	66.8	0.6	67.4	0.9	67.7	0.4	68.1	0.6
1979	68.7	0.9	69.5	1.2	70.3	1.2	71.1	1.1	71.9	1.1	72.8	1.3	73.7	1.2	74.4	0.9	75.1	0.9	75.7	0.8	76.4	0.9	77.2	1.0
1980	78.3	1.4	79.4	1.4	80.5	1.4	81.4	1.1	82.3	1.1	83.2	1.1	83.3	0.1	83.8	0.6	84.6	1.0	85.3	0.8	86.1	0.9	86.9	0.9
1981	87.5	0.7	88.5	1.1	89.0	0.6	89.6	0.7	90.3	0.8	91.1	0.9	92.2	1.2	92.8	0.7	93.7	1.0	93.9	0.2	94.1	0.2	94.4	0.3
1982	94.7	0.3	95.0	0.3	94.8	-0.2	95.2	0.4	96.2	1.1	97.4	1.2	98.0	0.6	98.2	0.2	98.3	0.1	98.6	0.3	98.4	-0.2	98.0	-0.4
1983	98.1	0.1	98.1	0.0	98.4	0.3	99.0	0.6	99.5	0.5	99.8	0.3	100.1	0.3	100.5	0.4	101.0	0.5	101.2	0.2	101.2	0.0	101.2	0.0
1984	101.6	0.4	101.8	0.2	101.8	0.0	102.1	0.3	102.5	0.4	102.8	0.3	103.2	0.4	104.2	1.0	104.8	0.6	104.8	0.0	104.7	-0.1	104.8	0.1
1985	104.9	0.1	105.4	0.5	105.9	0.5	106.3	0.4	106.7	0.4	107.0	0.3	107.1	0.1	107.3	0.2	107.6	0.3	107.9	0.3	108.3	0.4	108.6	0.3
1986	108.9	0.3	108.5	-0.4	107.9	-0.6	107.6	-0.3	107.9	0.3	108.4	0.5	108.4	0.0	108.6	0.2	109.1	0.5	109.1	0.0	109.2	0.1	109.3	0.1
1987	110.0	0.6	110.5	0.5	111.0	0.5	111.6	0.5	111.9	0.3	112.4	0.4	112.7	0.3	113.3	0.5	113.8	0.4	114.1	0.3	114.3	0.2	114.2	-0.1
1988	114.5	0.3	114.7	0.2	115.1	0.3	115.7	0.5	116.2	0.4	116.7	0.4	117.2	0.4	117.7	0.4	118.5	0.7	118.9	0.3	119.0	0.1	119.2	0.2
1989	119.7	0.4	120.2	0.4	120.8	0.5	121.8	0.8	122.5	0.6	122.8	0.2	123.2	0.3	123.2	0.0	123.6	0.3	124.2	0.5	124.4	0.2	124.6	0.2
1990	125.9	1.0	126.4	0.4	127.1	0.6	127.3	0.2	127.5	0.2	128.3	0.6	128.7	0.3	129.9	0.9	131.1	0.9	131.9	0.6	132.2	0.2	132.2	0.0
1991	132.8	0.5	132.8	0.0	133.0	0.2	133.3	0.2	133.8	0.4	134.1	0.2	134.3	0.1	134.6	0.2	135.2	0.4	135.4	0.1	135.8	0.3	135.9	0.1
1992	136.0	0.1	136.4	0.3	137.0	0.4	137.3	0.2	137.6	0.2	138.1	0.4	138.4	0.2	138.8	0.3	139.1	0.2	139.6	0.4	139.8	0.1	139.8	0.0
1993	140.3	0.4	140.7	0.3	141.1	0.3	141.6	0.4	141.9	0.2	142.0	0.1	142.1	0.1	142.4	0.2	142.6	0.1	143.3	0.5	143.4	0.1	143.3	-0.1
1994	143.6	0.2	144.0	0.3	144.4	0.3	144.7	0.2	144.9	0.1	145.4	0.3	145.8	0.3	146.5	0.5	146.9	0.3	147.0	0.1	147.3	0.2	147.2	-0.1
1995	147.8	0.4	148.3	0.3	148.7	0.3	149.3	0.4	149.6	0.2	149.9	0.2	149.9	0.0	150.2	0.2	150.6	0.3	151.0	0.3	150.9	-0.1	150.9	0.0
1996	151.7	0.5	152.2	0.3	152.9	0.5	153.6	0.5	154.0	0.3	154.1	0.1	154.3	0.1	154.5	0.1	155.1	0.4	155.5	0.3	155.9	0.3	155.9	0.0
1997	156.3	0.3	156.8	0.3	157.0	0.1	157.2	0.1	157.2	0.0	157.4	0.1	157.5	0.1	157.8	0.2	158.3	0.3	158.5	0.1	158.5	0.0	158.2	-0.2

Source: U.S. Department of Labor, Bureau of Labor Statistics, Division of Consumer Prices and Price Indexes.

U.S. City Average
Consumer Price Index - All Urban Consumers
Base 1982-1984 = 100
Food and Beverages

For 1967-1997. Columns headed % show percentile change in the index from the previous period for which an index is available.

Year	Jan Index	%	Feb Index	%	Mar Index	%	Apr Index	%	May Index	%	Jun Index	%	Jul Index	%	Aug Index	%	Sep Index	%	Oct Index	%	Nov Index	%	Dec Index	%
1967	34.8	-	34.7	-0.3	34.7	0.0	34.6	-0.3	34.6	0.0	34.9	0.9	35.2	0.9	35.4	0.6	35.2	-0.6	35.2	0.0	35.2	0.0	35.3	0.3
1968	35.6	0.8	35.7	0.3	35.8	0.3	36.0	0.6	36.1	0.3	36.2	0.3	36.4	0.6	36.6	0.5	36.6	0.0	36.7	0.3	36.6	-0.3	36.8	0.5
1969	37.0	0.5	37.0	0.0	37.2	0.5	37.4	0.5	37.5	0.3	38.0	1.3	38.4	1.1	38.6	0.5	38.7	0.3	38.6	-0.3	38.9	0.8	39.4	1.3
1970	39.6	0.5	39.8	0.5	39.8	0.0	40.0	0.5	40.1	0.2	40.2	0.2	40.4	0.5	40.4	0.0	40.4	0.0	40.4	0.0	40.2	-0.5	40.3	0.2
1971	40.4	0.2	40.5	0.2	40.9	1.0	41.2	0.7	41.3	0.2	41.6	0.7	41.8	0.5	41.9	0.2	41.6	-0.7	41.6	0.0	41.6	0.0	42.0	1.0
1972	42.0	0.0	42.6	1.4	42.7	0.2	42.7	0.0	42.7	0.0	42.9	0.5	43.3	0.9	43.4	0.2	43.5	0.2	43.5	0.0	43.7	0.5	43.9	0.5
1973	44.7	1.8	45.5	1.8	46.6	2.4	47.2	1.3	47.7	1.1	48.3	1.3	48.7	0.8	51.3	5.3	51.0	-0.6	51.0	0.0	51.6	1.2	52.0	0.8
1974	52.8	1.5	54.0	2.3	54.5	0.9	54.4	-0.2	54.8	0.7	55.0	0.4	55.1	0.2	55.9	1.5	56.7	1.4	57.1	0.7	57.6	0.9	58.3	1.2
1975	58.7	0.7	58.9	0.3	58.9	0.0	58.8	-0.2	59.0	0.3	59.9	1.5	61.2	2.2	61.1	-0.2	61.0	-0.2	61.4	0.7	61.6	0.3	61.9	0.5
1976	61.9	0.0	61.7	-0.3	61.3	-0.6	61.5	0.3	61.8	0.5	62.1	0.5	62.5	0.6	62.6	0.2	62.3	-0.5	62.4	0.2	62.2	-0.3	62.4	0.3
1977	62.9	0.8	64.3	2.2	64.6	0.5	65.3	1.1	65.6	0.5	66.2	0.9	66.5	0.5	66.7	0.3	66.5	-0.3	66.5	0.0	66.9	0.6	67.1	0.3
1978	68.1	1.5	69.0	1.3	69.8	1.2	70.9	1.6	71.8	1.3	72.9	1.5	73.4	0.7	73.5	0.1	73.6	0.1	74.0	0.5	74.3	0.4	74.9	0.8
1979	76.4	2.0	77.8	1.8	78.5	0.9	79.2	0.9	79.8	0.8	80.2	0.5	80.7	0.6	80.5	-0.2	80.8	0.4	81.2	0.5	81.5	0.4	82.4	1.1
1980	83.1	0.8	83.5	0.5	84.3	1.0	84.9	0.7	85.4	0.6	85.9	0.6	86.9	1.2	88.1	1.4	88.9	0.9	89.4	0.6	90.0	0.7	90.7	0.8
1981	91.4	0.8	92.2	0.9	92.7	0.5	92.9	0.2	92.8	-0.1	93.2	0.4	94.1	1.0	94.5	0.4	94.7	0.2	94.5	-0.2	94.4	-0.1	94.6	0.2
1982	95.7	1.2	96.5	-0.8	96.4	-0.1	96.7	0.3	97.3	0.6	98.0	0.7	98.2	0.2	97.9	-0.3	98.0	0.1	97.8	-0.2	97.6	-0.2	97.6	0.0
1983	98.2	0.6	98.5	0.3	99.1	0.6	99.6	0.5	99.7	0.1	99.6	-0.1	99.6	0.0	99.7	0.1	99.8	0.1	99.9	0.1	99.8	-0.1	100.2	0.4
1984	102.0	1.8	102.9	0.9	102.9	0.0	103.0	0.1	102.7	-0.3	102.9	0.2	103.3	0.4	103.9	0.6	103.7	-0.2	103.7	0.0	103.6	-0.1	104.0	0.4
1985	104.7	0.7	105.4	0.7	105.5	0.1	105.5	0.0	105.3	-0.2	105.4	0.1	105.5	0.1	105.6	0.1	105.7	0.1	105.8	0.1	106.2	0.4	106.9	0.7
1986	107.7	0.7	107.6	-0.1	107.7	0.1	107.9	0.2	108.2	0.3	108.3	0.1	109.2	0.8	110.0	0.7	110.2	0.2	110.4	0.2	110.7	0.3	110.9	0.2
1987	112.1	1.1	112.5	0.4	112.5	0.0	112.8	0.3	113.3	0.4	113.8	0.4	113.7	-0.1	113.8	0.1	114.2	0.4	114.3	0.1	114.3	0.0	114.8	0.4
1988	115.7	0.8	115.8	0.1	116.0	0.2	116.7	0.6	117.1	0.3	117.6	0.4	118.8	1.0	119.4	0.5	120.1	0.6	120.3	0.2	120.2	-0.1	120.6	0.3
1989	122.0	1.2	122.7	0.6	123.3	0.5	124.0	0.6	124.7	0.6	124.9	0.2	125.4	0.4	125.6	0.2	125.9	0.2	126.3	0.3	126.7	0.3	127.2	0.4
1990	130.0	2.2	130.9	0.7	131.2	0.2	131.0	-0.2	131.1	0.1	131.7	0.5	132.4	0.5	132.7	0.2	133.0	0.2	133.4	0.3	133.7	0.2	133.9	0.1
1991	135.9	1.5	136.0	0.1	136.3	0.2	137.2	0.7	137.3	0.1	137.7	0.3	137.1	-0.4	136.6	-0.4	136.7	0.1	136.5	-0.1	136.9	0.3	137.3	0.3
1992	137.9	0.4	138.1	0.1	138.8	0.5	138.8	0.0	138.3	-0.4	138.3	0.0	138.1	-0.1	138.8	0.5	139.3	0.4	139.2	-0.1	139.1	-0.1	139.5	0.3
1993	140.5	0.7	140.7	0.1	140.9	0.1	141.4	0.4	141.8	0.3	141.1	-0.5	141.1	0.0	141.5	0.3	141.8	0.2	142.3	0.4	142.6	0.2	143.3	0.5
1994	144.3	0.7	143.6	-0.5	143.9	0.2	144.0	0.1	144.1	0.1	144.2	0.1	144.8	0.4	145.3	0.3	145.6	0.2	145.6	0.0	145.9	0.2	147.2	0.9
1995	147.9	0.5	147.8	-0.1	147.9	0.1	148.9	0.7	148.7	-0.1	148.4	-0.2	148.6	0.1	148.9	0.2	149.4	0.3	149.8	0.3	149.8	0.0	150.3	0.3
1996	151.4	0.7	151.3	-0.1	152.1	0.5	152.7	0.4	152.5	-0.1	153.1	0.4	153.6	0.3	154.2	0.4	155.0	0.5	155.8	0.5	156.2	0.3	156.6	0.3
1997	156.9	0.2	156.9	0.0	157.1	0.1	157.1	0.0	157.1	0.0	157.1	0.0	157.5	0.3	158.1	0.4	158.4	0.2	158.7	0.2	158.9	0.1	159.1	0.1

Source: U.S. Department of Labor, Bureau of Labor Statistics, Division of Consumer Prices and Price Indexes.

U.S. City Average
Consumer Price Index - Urban Wage Earners
Base 1982-1984 = 100
Food and Beverages

For 1967-1997. Columns headed % show percentile change in the index from the previous period for which an index is available.

Year	Jan Index	%	Feb Index	%	Mar Index	%	Apr Index	%	May Index	%	Jun Index	%	Jul Index	%	Aug Index	%	Sep Index	%	Oct Index	%	Nov Index	%	Dec Index	%
1967	34.8	-	34.6	-0.6	34.6	0.0	34.5	-0.3	34.6	0.3	34.9	0.9	35.2	0.9	35.4	0.6	35.2	-0.6	35.1	-0.3	35.1	0.0	35.3	0.6
1968	35.5	0.6	35.7	0.6	35.8	0.3	35.9	0.3	36.0	0.3	36.1	0.3	36.4	0.8	36.6	0.5	36.5	-0.3	36.7	0.5	36.6	-0.3	36.8	0.5
1969	37.0	0.5	37.0	0.0	37.2	0.5	37.4	0.5	37.5	0.3	38.0	1.3	38.3	0.8	38.6	0.8	38.6	0.0	38.6	0.0	38.8	0.5	39.3	1.3
1970	39.6	0.8	39.8	0.5	39.8	0.0	39.9	0.3	40.1	0.5	40.2	0.2	40.4	0.5	40.4	0.0	40.4	0.0	40.3	-0.2	40.2	-0.2	40.3	0.2
1971	40.4	0.2	40.5	0.2	40.9	1.0	41.1	0.5	41.3	0.5	41.6	0.7	41.8	0.5	41.9	0.2	41.6	-0.7	41.5	-0.2	41.6	0.2	42.0	1.0
1972	42.0	0.0	42.6	1.4	42.7	0.2	42.7	0.0	42.7	0.0	42.9	0.5	43.3	0.9	43.4	0.2	43.5	0.2	43.5	0.0	43.7	0.5	43.9	0.5
1973	44.7	1.8	45.5	1.8	46.6	2.4	47.2	1.3	47.6	0.8	48.3	1.5	48.6	0.6	51.3	5.6	51.0	-0.6	51.0	0.0	51.5	1.0	52.0	1.0
1974	52.7	1.3	54.0	2.5	54.5	0.9	54.4	-0.2	54.7	0.6	55.0	0.5	55.1	0.2	55.9	1.5	56.7	1.4	57.0	0.5	57.6	1.1	58.2	1.0
1975	58.6	0.7	58.9	0.5	58.8	-0.2	58.8	0.0	59.0	0.3	59.8	1.4	61.1	2.2	61.0	-0.2	60.9	-0.2	61.3	0.7	61.5	0.3	61.9	0.7
1976	61.9	0.0	61.7	-0.3	61.3	-0.6	61.5	0.3	61.7	0.3	62.0	0.5	62.4	0.6	62.5	0.2	62.3	-0.3	62.3	0.0	62.1	-0.3	62.4	0.5
1977	62.9	0.8	64.2	2.1	64.5	0.5	65.3	1.2	65.5	0.3	66.2	1.1	66.5	0.5	66.7	0.3	66.5	-0.3	66.4	-0.2	66.8	0.6	67.1	0.4
1978	68.0	1.3	68.9	1.3	69.6	1.0	70.7	1.6	71.7	1.4	72.8	1.5	73.2	0.5	73.4	0.3	73.4	0.0	73.9	0.7	74.2	0.4	74.8	0.8
1979	76.3	2.0	77.8	2.0	78.7	1.2	79.2	0.6	79.8	0.8	80.1	0.4	80.7	0.7	80.5	-0.2	80.8	0.4	81.2	0.5	81.5	0.4	82.4	1.1
1980	83.1	0.8	83.5	0.5	84.3	1.0	85.0	0.8	85.5	0.6	86.1	0.7	87.1	1.2	88.3	1.4	89.2	1.0	89.7	0.6	90.4	0.8	91.0	0.7
1981	91.6	0.7	92.4	0.9	92.8	0.4	93.0	0.2	92.9	-0.1	93.3	0.4	94.2	1.0	94.6	0.4	94.7	0.1	94.6	-0.1	94.5	-0.1	94.6	0.1
1982	95.7	1.2	96.5	0.8	96.4	-0.1	96.7	0.3	97.3	0.6	98.0	0.7	98.3	0.3	97.9	-0.4	98.0	0.1	97.8	-0.2	97.7	-0.1	97.7	0.0
1983	98.2	0.5	98.6	0.4	99.1	0.5	99.6	0.5	99.8	0.2	99.6	-0.2	99.6	0.0	99.6	0.0	99.8	0.2	99.9	0.1	99.8	-0.1	100.2	0.4
1984	102.0	1.8	102.9	0.9	102.9	0.0	103.0	0.1	102.7	-0.3	102.9	0.2	103.2	0.3	103.8	0.6	103.6	-0.2	103.6	0.0	103.5	-0.1	103.8	0.3
1985	104.5	0.7	105.3	0.8	105.4	0.1	105.3	-0.1	105.1	-0.2	105.3	0.2	105.3	0.0	105.4	0.1	105.5	0.1	105.6	0.1	106.0	0.4	106.7	0.7
1986	107.5	0.7	107.5	0.0	107.5	0.0	107.8	0.3	108.0	0.2	108.1	0.1	109.0	0.8	109.9	0.8	110.1	0.2	110.2	0.1	110.5	0.3	110.7	0.2
1987	111.9	1.1	112.3	0.4	112.3	0.0	112.6	0.3	113.1	0.4	113.6	0.4	113.5	-0.1	113.6	0.1	114.0	0.4	114.1	0.1	114.1	0.0	114.5	0.4
1988	115.4	0.8	115.5	0.1	115.7	0.2	116.3	0.5	116.8	0.4	117.4	0.5	118.5	0.9	119.1	0.5	119.8	0.6	120.0	0.2	119.9	-0.1	120.3	0.3
1989	121.7	1.2	122.4	0.6	123.1	0.6	123.7	0.5	124.4	0.6	124.6	0.2	125.1	0.4	125.3	0.2	125.6	0.2	126.0	0.3	126.4	0.3	126.9	0.4
1990	129.7	2.2	130.6	0.7	130.9	0.2	130.7	-0.2	130.7	0.0	131.5	0.6	132.1	0.5	132.4	0.2	132.7	0.2	133.1	0.3	133.5	0.3	133.6	0.1
1991	135.6	1.5	135.7	0.1	136.1	0.3	136.9	0.6	137.0	0.1	137.4	0.3	136.8	-0.4	136.4	-0.3	136.5	0.1	136.2	-0.2	136.5	0.2	136.9	0.3
1992	137.4	0.4	137.8	0.3	138.4	0.4	138.5	0.1	137.9	-0.4	137.9	0.0	137.8	-0.1	138.5	0.5	138.9	0.3	138.8	-0.1	138.8	0.0	139.1	0.2
1993	140.1	0.7	140.2	0.1	140.5	0.2	140.9	0.3	141.4	0.4	140.8	-0.4	140.8	0.0	141.2	0.3	141.5	0.2	142.0	0.4	142.2	0.1	142.9	0.5
1994	143.8	0.6	143.2	-0.4	143.4	0.1	143.6	0.1	143.7	0.1	143.8	0.1	144.4	0.4	144.9	0.3	145.1	0.1	145.1	0.0	145.3	0.1	146.6	0.9
1995	147.2	0.4	147.3	0.1	147.3	0.0	148.3	0.7	148.1	-0.1	147.8	-0.2	148.0	0.1	148.3	0.2	148.9	0.4	149.3	0.3	149.3	0.0	149.8	0.3
1996	150.8	0.7	150.7	-0.1	151.5	0.5	152.2	0.5	151.9	-0.2	152.6	0.5	153.1	0.3	153.7	0.4	154.5	0.5	155.2	0.5	155.7	0.3	156.1	0.3
1997	156.4	0.2	156.4	0.0	156.5	0.1	156.5	0.0	156.6	0.1	156.6	0.0	157.0	0.3	157.6	0.4	157.8	0.1	158.1	0.2	158.3	0.1	158.5	0.1

Source: U.S. Department of Labor, Bureau of Labor Statistics, Division of Consumer Prices and Price Indexes.

U.S. City Average
Consumer Price Index - All Urban Consumers
Base 1982-1984 = 100
Housing

For 1967-1997. Columns headed % show percentile change in the index from the previous period for which an index is available.

Year	Jan Index	%	Feb Index	%	Mar Index	%	Apr Index	%	May Index	%	Jun Index	%	Jul Index	%	Aug Index	%	Sep Index	%	Oct Index	%	Nov Index	%	Dec Index	%
1967	30.5	-	30.5	0.0	30.5	0.0	30.6	0.3	30.7	0.3	30.7	0.0	30.8	0.3	30.9	0.3	30.9	0.0	31.0	0.3	31.1	0.3	31.2	0.3
1968	31.3	0.3	31.5	0.6	31.5	0.0	31.6	0.3	31.7	0.3	31.9	0.6	32.1	0.6	32.3	0.6	32.4	0.3	32.5	0.3	32.7	0.6	32.9	0.6
1969	32.9	0.0	33.1	0.6	33.4	0.9	33.6	0.6	33.8	0.6	33.9	0.3	34.1	0.6	34.3	0.6	34.5	0.6	34.6	0.3	34.8	0.6	35.0	0.6
1970	35.1	0.3	35.4	0.9	35.8	1.1	36.0	0.6	36.2	0.6	36.3	0.3	36.5	0.6	36.7	0.5	36.9	0.5	37.1	0.5	37.3	0.5	37.5	0.5
1971	37.5	0.0	37.5	0.0	37.4	-0.3	37.4	0.0	37.7	0.8	37.9	0.5	38.1	0.5	38.2	0.3	38.3	0.3	38.5	0.5	38.6	0.3	38.7	0.3
1972	38.9	0.5	39.0	0.3	39.1	0.3	39.2	0.3	39.3	0.3	39.4	0.3	39.5	0.3	39.7	0.5	39.8	0.3	39.8	0.0	39.9	0.3	40.1	0.5
1973	40.1	0.0	40.3	0.5	40.4	0.2	40.5	0.2	40.7	0.5	40.8	0.2	40.9	0.2	41.2	0.7	41.6	1.0	42.1	1.2	42.5	1.0	42.8	0.7
1974	43.3	1.2	43.7	0.9	44.1	0.9	44.5	0.9	44.9	0.9	45.4	1.1	45.9	1.1	46.5	1.3	47.1	1.3	47.6	1.1	48.1	1.1	48.6	1.0
1975	49.0	0.8	49.5	1.0	49.7	0.4	50.0	0.6	50.2	0.4	50.5	0.6	50.7	0.4	50.9	0.4	51.3	0.8	51.5	0.4	52.0	1.0	52.3	0.6
1976	52.6	0.6	52.7	0.2	53.0	0.6	53.1	0.2	53.3	0.4	53.5	0.4	53.9	0.7	54.1	0.4	54.4	0.6	54.6	0.4	54.8	0.4	55.1	0.5
1977	55.5	0.7	55.9	0.7	56.2	0.5	56.6	0.7	56.8	0.4	57.3	0.9	57.7	0.7	58.0	0.5	58.4	0.7	58.6	0.3	58.9	0.5	59.2	0.5
1978	59.7	0.8	60.0	0.5	60.6	1.0	61.1	0.8	61.6	0.8	62.2	1.0	62.8	1.0	63.2	0.6	63.9	1.1	64.5	0.9	64.9	0.6	65.1	0.3
1979	65.6	0.8	66.4	1.2	67.0	0.9	67.7	1.0	68.5	1.2	69.4	1.3	70.3	1.3	71.3	1.4	72.2	1.3	73.2	1.4	74.1	1.2	75.0	1.2
1980	76.2	1.6	77.1	1.2	78.4	1.7	79.4	1.3	80.6	1.5	82.1	1.9	81.6	-0.6	81.8	0.2	82.4	0.7	83.5	1.3	84.3	1.0	85.3	1.2
1981	85.9	0.7	86.5	0.7	87.0	0.6	87.7	0.8	88.8	1.3	90.0	1.4	91.5	1.7	92.3	0.9	93.5	1.3	93.5	0.0	93.7	0.2	94.0	0.3
1982	94.3	0.3	94.6	0.3	94.4	-0.2	95.3	1.0	96.6	1.4	97.8	1.2	98.3	0.5	98.6	0.3	98.4	-0.2	98.8	0.4	98.2	-0.6	97.4	-0.8
1983	97.9	0.5	98.1	0.2	98.1	0.0	98.6	0.5	99.1	0.5	99.5	0.4	99.9	0.4	100.0	0.1	100.5	0.5	100.6	0.1	100.7	0.1	100.8	0.1
1984	101.4	0.6	101.9	0.5	102.1	0.2	102.6	0.5	103.0	0.4	103.5	0.5	104.1	0.6	104.5	0.4	105.1	0.6	105.1	0.0	105.0	-0.1	105.1	0.1
1985	105.3	0.2	105.8	0.5	106.1	0.3	106.5	0.4	107.3	0.8	107.9	0.6	108.3	0.4	108.7	0.4	108.9	0.2	109.1	0.2	109.3	0.2	109.6	0.3
1986	109.9	0.3	109.8	-0.1	109.9	0.1	110.2	0.3	110.4	0.2	111.2	0.7	111.3	0.1	111.6	0.3	112.0	0.4	111.8	-0.2	111.4	-0.4	111.5	0.1
1987	112.0	0.4	112.4	0.4	112.8	0.4	113.2	0.4	113.6	0.4	114.3	0.6	114.7	0.3	115.4	0.6	115.6	0.2	115.5	-0.1	115.5	0.0	115.6	0.1
1988	116.2	0.5	116.6	0.3	117.0	0.3	117.3	0.3	117.7	0.3	118.6	0.8	119.1	0.4	119.5	0.3	119.9	0.3	119.9	0.0	119.9	0.0	120.2	0.3
1989	120.7	0.4	121.1	0.3	121.5	0.3	121.6	0.1	122.1	0.4	122.9	0.7	123.9	0.8	124.2	0.2	124.3	0.1	124.4	0.1	124.5	0.1	124.9	0.3
1990	125.9	0.8	126.1	0.2	126.8	0.6	126.8	0.0	127.1	0.2	128.3	0.9	129.2	0.7	130.2	0.8	130.5	0.2	130.6	0.1	130.4	-0.2	130.5	0.1
1991	131.8	1.0	132.4	0.5	132.6	0.2	132.5	-0.1	132.8	0.2	133.4	0.5	134.2	0.6	134.5	0.2	134.7	0.1	134.7	0.0	134.7	0.0	135.0	0.2
1992	135.7	0.5	136.1	0.3	136.6	0.4	136.5	-0.1	136.7	0.1	137.7	0.7	138.3	0.4	138.6	0.2	138.4	-0.1	138.5	0.1	138.5	0.0	138.5	0.0
1993	139.3	0.6	139.7	0.3	140.2	0.4	140.4	0.1	140.5	0.1	141.5	0.7	141.9	0.3	142.3	0.3	142.3	0.0	142.2	-0.1	142.0	-0.1	142.3	0.2
1994	142.9	0.4	143.7	0.6	144.1	0.3	143.9	-0.1	144.1	0.1	144.9	0.6	145.4	0.3	145.9	0.3	145.8	-0.1	145.7	-0.1	145.5	-0.1	145.4	-0.1
1995	146.4	0.7	147.0	0.4	147.4	0.3	147.4	0.0	147.6	0.1	148.5	0.6	149.2	0.5	149.6	0.3	149.5	-0.1	149.7	0.1	149.4	-0.2	149.7	0.2
1996	150.6	0.6	151.2	0.4	151.7	0.3	151.8	0.1	152.0	0.1	152.7	0.5	153.6	0.6	154.0	0.3	153.9	-0.1	154.0	0.1	153.9	-0.1	154.0	0.1
1997	155.1	0.7	155.8	0.5	155.9	0.1	155.8	-0.1	155.9	0.1	156.9	0.6	157.5	0.4	157.6	0.1	157.7	0.1	157.7	0.0	157.7	0.0	157.7	0.0

Source: U.S. Department of Labor, Bureau of Labor Statistics, Division of Consumer Prices and Price Indexes.

U.S. City Average
Consumer Price Index - Urban Wage Earners
Base 1982-1984 = 100
Housing

For 1967-1997. Columns headed % show percentile change in the index from the previous period for which an index is available.

Year	Jan Index	%	Feb Index	%	Mar Index	%	Apr Index	%	May Index	%	Jun Index	%	Jul Index	%	Aug Index	%	Sep Index	%	Oct Index	%	Nov Index	%	Dec Index	%
1967	30.7	-	30.8	0.3	30.8	0.0	30.9	0.3	31.0	0.3	31.0	0.0	31.1	0.3	31.1	0.0	31.2	0.3	31.3	0.3	31.3	0.0	31.5	0.6
1968	31.6	0.3	31.7	0.3	31.8	0.3	31.9	0.3	32.0	0.3	32.2	0.6	32.4	0.6	32.6	0.6	32.6	0.0	32.8	0.6	33.0	0.6	33.1	0.3
1969	33.2	0.3	33.4	0.6	33.7	0.9	33.9	0.6	34.1	0.6	34.2	0.3	34.4	0.6	34.6	0.6	34.8	0.6	34.9	0.3	35.1	0.6	35.3	0.6
1970	35.4	0.3	35.7	0.8	36.1	1.1	36.3	0.6	36.5	0.6	36.6	0.3	36.8	0.5	37.0	0.5	37.2	0.5	37.4	0.5	37.6	0.5	37.8	0.5
1971	37.8	0.0	37.8	0.0	37.7	-0.3	37.8	0.3	38.0	0.5	38.2	0.5	38.4	0.5	38.5	0.3	38.7	0.5	38.8	0.3	38.9	0.3	39.1	0.5
1972	39.2	0.3	39.3	0.3	39.4	0.3	39.5	0.3	39.6	0.3	39.7	0.3	39.9	0.5	40.0	0.3	40.1	0.2	40.2	0.2	40.3	0.2	40.4	0.2
1973	40.5	0.2	40.6	0.2	40.7	0.2	40.9	0.5	41.0	0.2	41.2	0.5	41.3	0.2	41.6	0.7	42.0	1.0	42.5	1.2	42.8	0.7	43.2	0.9
1974	43.7	1.2	44.1	0.9	44.5	0.9	44.8	0.7	45.3	1.1	45.8	1.1	46.3	1.1	46.9	1.3	47.5	1.3	48.0	1.1	48.5	1.0	49.0	1.0
1975	49.4	0.8	49.9	1.0	50.1	0.4	50.5	0.8	50.7	0.4	51.0	0.6	51.2	0.4	51.4	0.4	51.7	0.6	52.0	0.6	52.5	1.0	52.7	0.4
1976	53.0	0.6	53.2	0.4	53.4	0.4	53.5	0.2	53.7	0.4	54.0	0.6	54.3	0.6	54.6	0.6	54.9	0.5	55.1	0.4	55.3	0.4	55.5	0.4
1977	56.0	0.9	56.3	0.5	56.7	0.7	57.1	0.7	57.3	0.4	57.8	0.9	58.2	0.7	58.5	0.5	58.9	0.7	59.1	0.3	59.4	0.5	59.8	0.7
1978	60.2	0.7	60.6	0.7	61.1	0.8	61.5	0.7	62.1	1.0	62.7	1.0	63.2	0.8	63.6	0.6	64.3	1.1	64.9	0.9	65.3	0.6	65.6	0.5
1979	66.1	0.8	66.9	1.2	67.6	1.0	68.2	0.9	69.0	1.2	70.0	1.4	70.9	1.3	71.9	1.4	72.8	1.3	73.8	1.4	74.8	1.4	75.7	1.2
1980	76.8	1.5	77.8	1.3	79.0	1.5	80.1	1.4	81.3	1.5	82.9	2.0	82.3	-0.7	82.6	0.4	83.1	0.6	84.2	1.3	85.0	1.0	86.1	1.3
1981	86.7	0.7	87.2	0.6	87.6	0.5	88.3	0.8	89.5	1.4	90.7	1.3	92.2	1.7	93.1	1.0	94.3	1.3	94.2	-0.1	94.4	0.2	94.6	0.2
1982	94.9	0.3	95.3	0.4	95.1	-0.2	96.0	0.9	97.4	1.5	98.6	1.2	99.2	0.6	99.5	0.3	99.4	-0.1	99.8	0.4	99.3	-0.5	98.4	-0.9
1983	98.5	0.1	98.6	0.1	99.1	0.5	99.5	0.4	99.8	0.3	100.1	0.3	100.3	0.2	100.7	0.4	101.0	0.3	101.0	0.0	100.8	-0.2	100.7	-0.1
1984	100.8	0.1	100.7	-0.1	100.3	-0.4	100.2	-0.1	101.0	0.8	101.3	0.3	102.1	0.8	103.8	1.7	104.6	0.8	104.2	-0.4	103.9	-0.3	104.0	0.1
1985	104.3	0.3	104.7	0.4	105.0	0.3	105.4	0.4	106.3	0.9	106.8	0.5	107.2	0.4	107.5	0.3	107.8	0.3	107.9	0.1	108.2	0.3	108.4	0.2
1986	108.7	0.3	108.6	-0.1	108.7	0.1	109.0	0.3	109.2	0.2	110.0	0.7	110.1	0.1	110.4	0.3	110.8	0.4	110.4	-0.4	110.0	-0.4	110.2	0.2
1987	110.7	0.5	111.0	0.3	111.4	0.4	111.8	0.4	112.2	0.4	112.9	0.6	113.2	0.3	114.0	0.7	114.1	0.1	114.0	-0.1	113.9	-0.1	114.1	0.2
1988	114.6	0.4	115.0	0.3	115.4	0.3	115.6	0.2	116.0	0.3	116.9	0.8	117.4	0.4	117.8	0.3	118.2	0.3	118.2	0.0	118.3	0.1	118.5	0.2
1989	119.0	0.4	119.3	0.3	119.6	0.3	119.8	0.2	120.3	0.4	121.1	0.7	122.1	0.8	122.4	0.2	122.5	0.1	122.5	0.0	122.7	0.2	123.1	0.3
1990	123.9	0.6	124.1	0.2	124.7	0.5	124.7	0.0	125.1	0.3	126.2	0.9	127.0	0.6	127.9	0.7	128.3	0.3	128.3	0.0	128.2	-0.1	128.3	0.1
1991	129.4	0.9	130.0	0.5	130.2	0.2	130.1	-0.1	130.5	0.3	131.1	0.5	131.8	0.5	132.0	0.2	132.4	0.3	132.3	-0.1	132.4	0.1	132.7	0.2
1992	133.3	0.5	133.6	0.2	134.0	0.3	133.9	-0.1	134.1	0.1	135.1	0.7	135.7	0.4	135.9	0.1	135.8	-0.1	135.9	0.1	136.0	0.1	136.1	0.1
1993	136.7	0.4	137.0	0.2	137.4	0.3	137.7	0.2	137.9	0.1	138.8	0.7	139.1	0.2	139.5	0.3	139.7	0.1	139.6	-0.1	139.4	-0.1	139.7	0.2
1994	140.2	0.4	140.9	0.5	141.3	0.3	141.1	-0.1	141.3	0.1	142.1	0.6	142.5	0.3	143.0	0.4	143.0	0.0	142.8	-0.1	142.7	-0.1	142.7	0.0
1995	143.5	0.6	144.0	0.3	144.3	0.2	144.4	0.1	144.6	0.1	145.5	0.6	146.1	0.4	146.5	0.3	146.5	0.0	146.6	0.1	146.4	-0.1	146.7	0.2
1996	147.5	0.5	148.0	0.3	148.5	0.3	148.6	0.1	148.9	0.2	149.6	0.5	150.4	0.5	150.7	0.2	150.8	0.1	150.7	-0.1	150.7	0.0	151.0	0.2
1997	151.8	0.5	152.4	0.4	152.5	0.1	152.4	-0.1	152.6	0.1	153.6	0.7	154.1	0.3	154.2	0.1	154.4	0.1	154.4	0.0	154.5	0.1	154.4	-0.1

Source: U.S. Department of Labor, Bureau of Labor Statistics, Division of Consumer Prices and Price Indexes.

U.S. City Average
Consumer Price Index - All Urban Consumers
Base 1982-1984 = 100
Apparel and Upkeep

For 1913-1997. Columns headed % show percentile change in the index from the previous period for which an index is available.

Year	Jan Index	%	Feb Index	%	Mar Index	%	Apr Index	%	May Index	%	Jun Index	%	Jul Index	%	Aug Index	%	Sep Index	%	Oct Index	%	Nov Index	%	Dec Index	%
1913	-	-	-	-	-	-	-	-	-	-	-	-	-	-	-	-	-	-	-	-	-	-	-	-
1914	-	-	-	-	-	-	-	-	-	-	-	-	-	-	-	-	-	-	-	-	-	-	15.0	-
1915	-	-	-	-	-	-	-	-	-	-	-	-	-	-	-	-	-	-	-	-	-	-	15.6	4.0
1916	-	-	-	-	-	-	-	-	-	-	-	-	-	-	-	-	-	-	-	-	-	-	17.9	14.7
1917	-	-	-	-	-	-	-	-	-	-	-	-	-	-	-	-	-	-	-	-	-	-	22.2	24.0
1918	-	-	-	-	-	-	-	-	-	-	-	-	-	-	-	-	-	-	-	-	-	-	31.8	43.2
1919	-	-	-	-	-	-	-	-	-	-	34.4	8.2	-	-	-	-	-	-	-	-	-	-	42.6	23.8
1920	-	-	-	-	-	-	-	-	-	-	45.0	5.6	-	-	-	-	-	-	-	-	-	-	40.3	-10.4
1921	-	-	-	-	-	-	-	-	34.7	-13.9	-	-	-	-	-	-	30.0	-13.5	-	-	-	-	28.6	-4.7
1922	-	-	-	-	27.3	-4.5	-	-	-	-	26.8	-1.8	-	-	-	-	26.6	-0.7	-	-	-	-	26.6	0.0
1923	-	-	-	-	27.0	1.5	-	-	-	-	27.0	0.0	-	-	-	-	27.2	0.7	-	-	-	-	27.2	0.0
1924	-	-	-	-	27.1	-0.4	-	-	-	-	26.9	-0.7	-	-	-	-	26.6	-1.1	-	-	-	-	26.4	-0.8
1925	-	-	-	-	-	-	-	-	-	-	26.4	0.0	-	-	-	-	-	-	-	-	-	-	26.2	-0.8
1926	-	-	-	-	-	-	-	-	-	-	25.9	-1.1	-	-	-	-	-	-	-	-	-	-	25.7	-0.8
1927	-	-	-	-	-	-	-	-	-	-	25.4	-1.2	-	-	-	-	-	-	-	-	-	-	25.1	-1.2
1928	-	-	-	-	-	-	-	-	-	-	25.0	-0.4	-	-	-	-	-	-	-	-	-	-	24.9	-0.4
1929	-	-	-	-	-	-	-	-	-	-	24.7	-0.8	-	-	-	-	-	-	-	-	-	-	24.6	-0.4
1930	-	-	-	-	-	-	-	-	-	-	24.5	-0.4	-	-	-	-	-	-	-	-	-	-	23.5	-4.1
1931	-	-	-	-	-	-	-	-	-	-	22.2	-5.5	-	-	-	-	-	-	-	-	-	-	20.6	-7.2
1932	-	-	-	-	-	-	-	-	-	-	19.5	-5.3	-	-	-	-	-	-	-	-	-	-	18.6	-4.6
1933	-	-	-	-	-	-	-	-	-	-	18.2	-2.2	-	-	-	-	-	-	-	-	-	-	20.2	11.0
1934	-	-	-	-	-	-	-	-	-	-	20.7	2.5	-	-	-	-	-	-	-	-	20.7	0.0	-	-
1935	-	-	-	-	20.8	0.5	-	-	-	-	-	-	20.7	-0.5	-	-	-	-	20.9	1.0	-	-	-	-
1936	21.0	0.5	-	-	-	-	21.0	0.0	-	-	-	-	20.9	-0.5	-	-	21.0	0.5	-	-	-	-	21.3	1.4
1937	-	-	-	-	21.7	1.9	-	-	-	-	22.0	1.4	-	-	-	-	22.5	2.3	-	-	-	-	22.5	0.0
1938	-	-	-	-	22.1	-1.8	-	-	-	-	21.9	-0.9	-	-	-	-	21.7	-0.9	-	-	-	-	21.7	0.0
1939	-	-	-	-	21.6	-0.5	-	-	-	-	21.6	0.0	-	-	-	-	21.6	0.0	-	-	-	-	21.7	0.5
1940	-	-	-	-	21.9	0.9	-	-	-	-	21.8	-0.5	-	-	-	-	21.8	0.0	21.8	0.0	21.8	0.0	21.8	0.0
1941	21.6	-0.9	21.6	0.0	21.9	1.4	22.0	0.5	22.0	0.0	22.2	0.9	22.5	1.4	22.9	1.8	23.8	3.9	24.2	1.7	24.5	1.2	24.6	0.4
1942	24.9	1.2	25.5	2.4	26.6	4.3	27.2	2.3	27.1	-0.4	26.9	-0.7	26.9	0.0	26.9	0.0	27.1	0.7	27.1	0.0	27.1	0.0	27.1	0.0
1943	27.1	0.0	27.1	0.0	27.4	1.1	27.5	0.4	27.5	0.0	27.5	0.0	27.7	0.7	27.8	0.4	28.4	2.2	28.6	0.7	28.7	0.3	29.0	1.0
1944	29.0	0.0	29.1	0.3	29.4	1.0	29.5	0.3	29.5	0.0	29.7	0.7	29.7	0.0	30.0	1.0	30.3	1.0	30.4	0.3	30.5	0.3	30.6	0.3
1945	30.7	0.3	30.8	0.3	30.8	0.0	30.9	0.3	31.0	0.3	31.2	0.6	31.4	0.6	31.5	0.3	31.9	1.3	31.9	0.0	31.9	0.0	32.1	0.6
1946	32.2	0.3	32.3	0.3	32.9	1.9	33.2	0.9	33.4	0.6	33.7	0.9	34.1	1.2	34.6	1.5	35.6	2.9	36.1	1.4	36.7	1.7	37.9	3.3
1947	38.4	1.3	38.9	1.3	39.5	1.5	39.7	0.5	39.7	0.0	39.9	0.5	39.6	-0.8	39.9	0.8	40.3	1.0	40.6	0.7	40.8	0.5	41.0	0.5
1948	41.3	0.7	41.9	1.5	42.1	0.5	42.2	0.2	42.4	0.5	42.3	-0.2	42.3	0.0	42.9	1.4	43.1	0.5	43.3	0.5	43.2	-0.2	43.1	-0.2
1949	42.2	-2.1	41.9	-0.7	41.7	-0.5	41.3	-1.0	41.1	-0.5	40.9	-0.5	40.5	-1.0	40.2	-0.7	40.2	0.0	40.1	-0.2	40.0	-0.2	39.9	-0.2
1950	39.7	-0.5	39.7	0.0	39.8	0.3	39.7	-0.3	39.6	-0.3	39.6	0.0	39.6	0.0	39.9	0.8	40.7	2.0	41.4	1.7	41.7	0.7	42.0	0.7
1951	42.6	1.4	43.4	1.9	43.6	0.5	43.7	0.2	43.8	0.2	43.8	0.0	43.7	-0.2	43.7	0.0	44.9	2.7	44.9	0.0	44.6	-0.7	44.4	-0.4
1952	43.9	-1.1	43.9	0.0	43.7	-0.5	43.5	-0.5	43.5	0.0	43.4	-0.2	43.2	-0.5	43.1	-0.2	43.5	0.9	43.4	-0.2	43.2	-0.5	43.1	-0.2
1953	43.0	-0.2	43.0	0.0	43.0	0.0	43.0	0.0	43.1	0.2	43.1	0.0	43.1	0.0	43.0	-0.2	43.4	0.9	43.5	0.2	43.5	0.0	43.4	-0.2
1954	43.2	-0.5	43.1	-0.2	43.0	-0.2	42.9	-0.2	43.0	0.2	43.0	0.0	42.9	-0.2	42.8	-0.2	43.0	0.5	43.1	0.2	43.1	0.0	43.1	0.0
1955	42.7	-0.9	42.7	0.0	42.7	0.0	42.6	-0.2	42.7	0.2	42.7	0.0	42.7	0.0	42.8	0.2	43.2	0.9	43.2	0.0	43.3	0.2	43.3	0.0
1956	43.2	-0.2	43.4	0.5	43.4	0.0	43.5	0.2	43.5	0.0	43.5	0.0	43.6	0.2	43.7	0.2	44.1	0.9	44.3	0.5	44.4	0.2	44.4	0.0
1957	44.2	-0.5	44.1	-0.2	44.4	0.7	44.3	-0.2	44.4	0.2	44.4	0.0	44.4	0.0	44.4	0.0	44.7	0.7	44.9	0.4	45.0	0.2	44.8	-0.4

[Continued]

U.S. City Average
Consumer Price Index - All Urban Consumers
Base 1982-1984 = 100
Apparel and Upkeep
[Continued]

For 1913-1997. Columns headed % show percentile change in the index from the previous period for which an index is available.

Year	Jan Index	%	Feb Index	%	Mar Index	%	Apr Index	%	May Index	%	Jun Index	%	Jul Index	%	Aug Index	%	Sep Index	%	Oct Index	%	Nov Index	%	Dec Index	%
1958	44.6	-0.4	44.6	0.0	44.6	0.0	44.6	0.0	44.6	0.0	44.6	0.0	44.6	0.0	44.5	-0.2	44.7	0.4	44.8	0.2	45.0	0.4	44.9	-0.2
1959	44.6	-0.7	44.6	0.0	44.6	0.0	44.7	0.2	44.8	0.2	44.8	0.0	44.9	0.2	45.1	0.4	45.5	0.9	45.6	0.2	45.6	0.0	45.5	-0.2
1960	45.1	-0.9	45.3	0.4	45.4	0.2	45.5	0.2	45.5	0.0	45.5	0.0	45.6	0.2	45.7	0.2	46.1	0.9	46.3	0.4	46.2	-0.2	46.2	0.0
1961	45.8	-0.9	45.8	0.0	45.9	0.2	45.8	-0.2	45.9	0.2	45.8	-0.2	46.0	0.4	46.0	0.0	46.4	0.9	46.5	0.2	46.4	-0.2	46.4	0.0
1962	45.7	-1.5	45.9	0.4	46.1	0.4	46.1	0.0	46.1	0.0	46.2	0.2	46.2	0.0	46.1	-0.2	46.9	1.7	47.0	0.2	46.8	-0.4	46.7	-0.2
1963	46.4	-0.6	46.5	0.2	46.6	0.2	46.7	0.2	46.6	-0.2	46.7	0.2	46.7	0.0	46.8	0.2	47.2	0.9	47.4	0.4	47.5	0.2	47.5	0.0
1964	47.0	-1.1	47.0	0.0	47.1	0.2	47.2	0.2	47.3	0.2	47.3	0.0	47.2	-0.2	47.1	-0.2	47.4	0.6	47.5	0.2	47.6	0.2	47.7	0.2
1965	47.2	-1.0	47.3	0.2	47.4	0.2	47.5	0.2	47.8	0.6	47.8	0.0	47.5	-0.6	47.6	0.2	47.9	0.6	48.2	0.6	48.3	0.2	48.3	0.0
1966	48.0	-0.6	48.1	0.2	48.4	0.6	48.6	0.4	48.9	0.6	48.9	0.0	48.8	-0.2	48.8	0.0	49.5	1.4	49.9	0.8	50.1	0.4	50.2	0.2
1967	49.8	-0.8	50.1	0.6	50.4	0.6	50.5	0.2	50.9	0.8	50.9	0.0	50.8	-0.2	50.9	0.2	51.5	1.2	51.9	0.8	52.2	0.6	52.3	0.2
1968	51.8	-1.0	52.2	0.8	52.6	0.8	53.0	0.8	53.4	0.8	53.6	0.4	53.5	-0.2	53.8	0.6	54.7	1.7	55.2	0.9	55.5	0.5	55.6	0.2
1969	55.2	-0.7	55.4	0.4	55.9	0.9	56.2	0.5	56.6	0.7	56.8	0.4	56.7	-0.2	56.6	-0.2	57.6	1.8	58.1	0.9	58.4	0.5	58.5	0.2
1970	57.8	-1.2	58.1	0.5	58.4	0.5	58.6	0.3	59.0	0.7	59.1	0.2	58.8	-0.5	58.8	0.0	59.7	1.5	60.3	1.0	60.7	0.7	60.8	0.2
1971	60.0	-1.3	60.2	0.3	60.5	0.5	60.7	0.3	61.3	1.0	61.2	-0.2	60.8	-0.7	60.7	-0.2	61.5	1.3	62.0	0.8	62.1	0.2	62.1	0.0
1972	61.3	-1.3	61.5	0.3	61.8	0.5	62.1	0.5	62.5	0.6	62.2	-0.5	61.7	-0.8	61.6	-0.2	62.8	1.9	63.4	1.0	63.7	0.5	63.7	0.0
1973	62.7	-1.6	63.0	0.5	63.6	1.0	64.1	0.8	64.6	0.8	64.6	0.0	64.1	-0.8	64.5	0.6	65.4	1.4	66.1	1.1	66.5	0.6	66.5	0.0
1974	65.7	-1.2	66.5	1.2	67.4	1.4	68.1	1.0	68.8	1.0	69.2	0.6	69.0	-0.3	70.4	2.0	71.3	1.3	71.9	0.8	72.6	1.0	72.3	-0.4
1975	71.1	-1.7	71.5	0.6	71.8	0.4	72.0	0.3	72.3	0.4	72.1	-0.3	71.9	-0.3	72.5	0.8	73.2	1.0	73.7	0.7	74.2	0.7	74.0	-0.3
1976	73.1	-1.2	73.4	0.4	73.9	0.7	74.3	0.5	74.8	0.7	74.9	0.1	74.7	-0.3	75.5	1.1	76.6	1.5	76.9	0.4	77.4	0.7	77.4	0.0
1977	76.5	-1.2	76.9	0.5	77.3	0.5	77.6	0.4	78.2	0.8	78.5	0.4	78.2	-0.4	78.9	0.9	79.6	0.9	80.1	0.6	80.8	0.9	80.7	-0.1
1978	79.4	-1.6	78.8	-0.8	79.8	1.3	80.8	1.3	81.5	0.9	81.5	0.0	80.5	-1.2	81.4	1.1	82.5	1.4	83.3	1.0	83.7	0.5	83.2	-0.6
1979	81.9	-1.6	82.3	0.5	83.8	1.8	84.3	0.6	84.7	0.5	84.5	-0.2	83.8	-0.8	84.8	1.2	86.6	2.1	87.2	0.7	87.5	0.3	87.8	0.3
1980	87.2	-0.7	87.6	0.5	89.7	2.4	90.4	0.8	90.5	0.2	90.3	-0.2	89.8	-0.6	91.1	1.4	92.9	2.0	93.8	1.0	94.2	0.4	93.8	-0.4
1981	92.3	-1.6	92.8	0.5	94.4	1.7	95.0	0.6	95.0	0.0	94.7	-0.3	94.2	-0.5	95.5	1.4	97.2	1.8	97.6	0.4	97.5	-0.1	97.1	-0.4
1982	95.5	-1.6	95.8	0.3	97.4	1.7	97.8	0.4	97.6	-0.2	97.3	-0.3	96.7	-0.6	97.8	1.1	99.4	1.6	99.7	0.3	99.6	-0.1	98.7	-0.9
1983	97.4	-1.3	97.9	0.5	99.2	1.3	99.7	0.5	100.0	0.3	99.7	-0.3	99.4	-0.3	100.6	1.2	102.2	1.6	102.3	0.1	102.3	0.0	101.6	-0.7
1984	100.1	-1.5	100.0	-0.1	101.3	1.3	101.6	0.3	101.4	-0.2	100.6	-0.8	100.2	-0.4	102.0	1.8	104.1	2.1	104.9	0.8	104.6	-0.3	103.6	-1.0
1985	101.9	-1.6	102.9	1.0	104.7	1.7	105.0	0.3	104.7	-0.3	104.3	-0.4	103.4	-0.9	104.7	1.3	106.9	2.1	107.6	0.7	107.7	0.1	106.5	-1.1
1986	104.5	-1.9	104.1	-0.4	105.2	1.1	105.7	0.5	105.2	-0.5	104.3	-0.9	103.6	-0.7	105.5	1.8	108.1	2.5	108.7	0.6	108.6	-0.1	107.5	-1.0
1987	105.6	-1.8	106.2	0.6	109.7	3.3	111.5	1.6	111.1	-0.4	109.3	-1.6	107.3	-1.8	109.4	2.0	113.3	3.6	115.4	1.9	115.4	0.0	112.7	-2.3
1988	110.4	-2.0	110.2	-0.2	114.3	3.7	117.0	2.4	116.3	-0.6	114.6	-1.5	112.7	-1.7	112.6	-0.1	117.8	4.6	120.7	2.5	119.9	-0.7	118.0	-1.6
1989	115.3	-2.3	115.3	0.0	119.3	3.5	120.9	1.3	120.4	-0.4	117.8	-2.2	115.0	-2.4	115.0	0.0	120.0	4.3	122.7	2.2	122.1	-0.5	119.2	-2.4
1990	116.7	-2.1	120.4	3.2	125.4	4.2	126.7	1.0	125.5	-1.0	123.3	-1.8	120.8	-2.0	122.2	1.2	126.8	3.8	128.4	1.3	127.5	-0.7	125.3	-1.7
1991	123.8	-1.2	126.2	1.9	128.8	2.1	130.1	1.0	129.4	-0.5	126.9	-1.9	125.2	-1.3	127.6	1.9	131.3	2.9	132.7	1.1	132.9	0.2	129.6	-2.5
1992	127.9	-1.3	130.2	1.8	133.4	2.5	133.3	-0.1	133.1	-0.2	131.0	-1.6	129.2	-1.4	130.2	0.8	133.3	2.4	135.0	1.3	134.5	-0.4	131.4	-2.3
1993	129.7	-1.3	133.4	2.9	136.2	2.1	136.9	0.5	135.0	-1.4	131.9	-2.3	129.4	-1.9	131.9	1.9	134.6	2.0	136.1	1.1	136.2	0.1	132.6	-2.6
1994	130.4	-1.7	132.4	1.5	136.1	2.8	136.4	0.2	135.6	-0.6	133.8	-1.3	130.9	-2.2	131.1	0.2	134.2	2.4	135.2	0.7	134.2	-0.7	130.5	-2.8
1995	129.4	-0.8	131.1	1.3	134.4	2.5	134.8	0.3	133.4	-1.0	130.5	-2.2	128.3	-1.7	130.1	1.4	132.7	2.0	134.5	1.4	133.7	-0.6	130.6	-2.3
1996	130.0	-0.5	131.2	0.9	134.8	2.7	134.9	0.1	133.7	-0.9	130.8	-2.2	128.3	-1.9	128.1	-0.2	131.5	2.7	133.4	1.4	133.4	0.0	130.3	-2.3
1997	129.6	-0.5	131.9	1.8	134.5	2.0	136.1	1.2	135.3	-0.6	132.4	-2.1	130.2	-1.7	130.0	-0.2	133.0	2.3	134.9	1.4	134.7	-0.1	131.6	-2.3

Source: U.S. Department of Labor, Bureau of Labor Statistics, Division of Consumer Prices and Price Indexes.

U.S. City Average
Consumer Price Index - Urban Wage Earners
Base 1982-1984 = 100
Apparel and Upkeep

For 1913-1997. Columns headed % show percentile change in the index from the previous period for which an index is available.

Year	Jan Index	%	Feb Index	%	Mar Index	%	Apr Index	%	May Index	%	Jun Index	%	Jul Index	%	Aug Index	%	Sep Index	%	Oct Index	%	Nov Index	%	Dec Index	%
1913	-	-	-	-	-	-	-	-	-	-	-	-	-	-	-	-	-	-	-	-	-	-	-	-
1914	-	-	-	-	-	-	-	-	-	-	-	-	-	-	-	-	-	-	-	-	-	-	15.1	-
1915	-	-	-	-	-	-	-	-	-	-	-	-	-	-	-	-	-	-	-	-	-	-	15.7	4.0
1916	-	-	-	-	-	-	-	-	-	-	-	-	-	-	-	-	-	-	-	-	-	-	18.0	14.6
1917	-	-	-	-	-	-	-	-	-	-	-	-	-	-	-	-	-	-	-	-	-	-	22.3	23.9
1918	-	-	-	-	-	-	-	-	-	-	-	-	-	-	-	-	-	-	-	-	-	-	31.9	43.0
1919	-	-	-	-	-	-	-	-	-	-	34.6	8.5	-	-	-	-	-	-	-	-	-	-	42.8	23.7
1920	-	-	-	-	-	-	-	-	-	-	45.2	5.6	-	-	-	-	-	-	-	-	-	-	40.5	-10.4
1921	-	-	-	-	-	-	-	-	34.8	-14.1	-	-	-	-	-	-	30.1	-13.5	-	-	-	-	28.7	-4.7
1922	-	-	-	-	27.5	-4.2	-	-	-	-	26.9	-2.2	-	-	-	-	26.7	-0.7	-	-	-	-	26.7	0.0
1923	-	-	-	-	27.1	1.5	-	-	-	-	27.2	0.4	-	-	-	-	27.4	0.7	-	-	-	-	27.4	0.0
1924	-	-	-	-	27.3	-0.4	-	-	-	-	27.0	-1.1	-	-	-	-	26.7	-1.1	-	-	-	-	26.5	-0.7
1925	-	-	-	-	-	-	-	-	-	-	26.5	0.0	-	-	-	-	-	-	-	-	-	-	26.3	-0.8
1926	-	-	-	-	-	-	-	-	-	-	26.1	-0.8	-	-	-	-	-	-	-	-	-	-	25.8	-1.1
1927	-	-	-	-	-	-	-	-	-	-	25.5	-1.2	-	-	-	-	-	-	-	-	-	-	25.2	-1.2
1928	-	-	-	-	-	-	-	-	-	-	25.2	0.0	-	-	-	-	-	-	-	-	-	-	25.0	-0.8
1929	-	-	-	-	-	-	-	-	-	-	24.8	-0.8	-	-	-	-	-	-	-	-	-	-	24.7	-0.4
1930	-	-	-	-	-	-	-	-	-	-	24.6	-0.4	-	-	-	-	-	-	-	-	-	-	23.6	-4.1
1931	-	-	-	-	-	-	-	-	-	-	22.3	-5.5	-	-	-	-	-	-	-	-	-	-	20.7	-7.2
1932	-	-	-	-	-	-	-	-	-	-	19.6	-5.3	-	-	-	-	-	-	-	-	-	-	18.6	-5.1
1933	-	-	-	-	-	-	-	-	-	-	18.3	-1.6	-	-	-	-	-	-	-	-	-	-	20.3	10.9
1934	-	-	-	-	-	-	-	-	-	-	20.8	2.5	-	-	-	-	-	-	-	-	20.8	0.0	-	-
1935	-	-	-	-	20.9	0.5	-	-	-	-	-	-	20.8	-0.5	-	-	-	-	21.0	1.0	-	-	-	-
1936	21.1	0.5	-	-	-	-	21.1	0.0	-	-	-	-	21.0	-0.5	-	-	21.1	0.5	-	-	-	-	21.4	1.4
1937	-	-	-	-	21.8	1.9	-	-	-	-	22.1	1.4	-	-	-	-	22.6	2.3	-	-	-	-	22.6	0.0
1938	-	-	-	-	22.2	-1.8	-	-	-	-	22.0	-0.9	-	-	-	-	21.8	-0.9	-	-	-	-	21.8	0.0
1939	-	-	-	-	21.7	-0.5	-	-	-	-	21.7	0.0	-	-	-	-	21.7	0.0	-	-	-	-	21.8	0.5
1940	-	-	-	-	22.0	0.9	-	-	-	-	21.9	-0.5	-	-	-	-	21.9	0.0	21.9	0.0	21.9	0.0	21.9	0.0
1941	21.7	-0.9	21.7	0.0	22.0	1.4	22.1	0.5	22.1	0.0	22.3	0.9	22.6	1.3	23.1	2.2	23.9	3.5	24.3	1.7	24.6	1.2	24.7	0.4
1942	25.1	1.6	25.7	2.4	26.7	3.9	27.3	2.2	27.3	0.0	27.0	-1.1	27.0	0.0	27.0	0.0	27.2	0.7	27.2	0.0	27.2	0.0	27.2	0.0
1943	27.3	0.4	27.3	0.0	27.5	0.7	27.6	0.4	27.6	0.0	27.6	0.0	27.9	1.1	28.0	0.4	28.6	2.1	28.7	0.3	28.8	0.3	29.1	1.0
1944	29.1	0.0	29.2	0.3	29.5	1.0	29.6	0.3	29.7	0.3	29.8	0.3	29.8	0.0	30.1	1.0	30.5	1.3	30.6	0.3	30.6	0.0	30.8	0.7
1945	30.9	0.3	30.9	0.0	31.0	0.3	31.0	0.0	31.2	0.6	31.4	0.6	31.5	0.3	31.6	0.3	32.0	1.3	32.0	0.0	32.1	0.3	32.3	0.6
1946	32.3	0.0	32.5	0.6	33.0	1.5	33.3	0.9	33.6	0.9	33.9	0.9	34.2	0.9	34.8	1.8	35.8	2.9	36.3	1.4	36.9	1.7	38.1	3.3
1947	38.6	1.3	39.1	1.3	39.7	1.5	39.9	0.5	39.9	0.0	40.1	0.5	39.8	-0.7	40.1	0.8	40.5	1.0	40.8	0.7	41.0	0.5	41.2	0.5
1948	41.5	0.7	42.1	1.4	42.3	0.5	42.4	0.2	42.6	0.5	42.5	-0.2	42.5	0.0	43.1	1.4	43.3	0.5	43.5	0.5	43.4	-0.2	43.3	-0.2
1949	42.4	-2.1	42.1	-0.7	41.9	-0.5	41.5	-1.0	41.3	-0.5	41.1	-0.5	40.7	-1.0	40.4	-0.7	40.4	0.0	40.3	-0.2	40.2	-0.2	40.1	-0.2
1950	39.9	-0.5	39.9	0.0	40.0	0.3	39.9	-0.2	39.8	-0.3	39.8	0.0	39.8	0.0	40.1	0.8	40.9	2.0	41.6	1.7	41.9	0.7	42.2	0.7
1951	42.8	1.4	43.6	1.9	43.9	0.7	44.0	0.2	44.0	0.0	44.0	0.0	43.9	-0.2	44.0	0.2	45.1	2.5	45.1	0.0	44.8	-0.7	44.6	-0.4
1952	44.2	-0.9	44.1	-0.2	44.0	-0.2	43.7	-0.7	43.7	0.0	43.6	-0.2	43.4	-0.5	43.3	-0.2	43.6	0.9	43.7	0.2	43.7	0.0	43.6	-0.2
1953	43.2	-0.2	43.2	0.0	43.2	0.0	43.2	0.0	43.3	0.2	43.3	0.0	43.1	-0.2	43.0	-0.2	43.2	0.5	43.3	0.2	43.3	0.0	43.3	0.0
1954	43.4	-0.5	43.3	-0.2	43.2	-0.2	43.1	-0.2	43.2	0.2	42.9	0.0	42.9	0.0	43.0	0.0	43.4	0.9	43.4	0.0	43.5	0.2	43.5	0.0
1955	42.9	-0.9	42.9	0.0	42.9	0.0	42.8	-0.2	42.9	0.2	42.9	0.0	42.9	0.0	43.0	0.2	44.0	0.9	44.4	0.9	44.5	0.2	44.6	0.0
1956	43.4	-0.2	43.6	0.5	43.6	0.0	43.7	0.2	43.7	0.0	43.7	0.0	43.9	0.5	44.0	0.2	44.4	0.9	44.5	0.2	44.6	0.2	44.6	0.0
1957	44.4	-0.4	44.4	0.0	44.6	0.5	44.5	-0.2	44.6	0.2	44.6	0.0	44.6	0.0	44.6	0.0	44.9	0.7	45.1	0.4	45.2	0.2	45.0	-0.4

[Continued]

U.S. City Average
Consumer Price Index - Urban Wage Earners
Base 1982-1984 = 100
Apparel and Upkeep
[Continued]

For 1913-1997. Columns headed % show percentile change in the index from the previous period for which an index is available.

Year	Jan Index	%	Feb Index	%	Mar Index	%	Apr Index	%	May Index	%	Jun Index	%	Jul Index	%	Aug Index	%	Sep Index	%	Oct Index	%	Nov Index	%	Dec Index	%
1958	44.8	-0.4	44.8	0.0	44.8	0.0	44.8	0.0	44.8	0.0	44.8	0.0	44.8	0.0	44.7	-0.2	44.9	0.4	45.0	0.2	45.2	0.4	45.1	-0.2
1959	44.8	-0.7	44.8	0.0	44.8	0.0	44.9	0.2	45.0	0.2	45.0	0.0	45.1	0.2	45.3	0.4	45.7	0.9	45.8	0.2	45.8	0.0	45.7	-0.2
1960	45.3	-0.9	45.5	0.4	45.6	0.2	45.7	0.2	45.7	0.0	45.7	0.0	45.8	0.2	45.9	0.2	46.4	1.1	46.6	0.4	46.5	-0.2	46.4	-0.2
1961	46.0	-0.9	46.1	0.2	46.1	0.0	46.1	0.0	46.1	0.0	46.1	0.0	46.2	0.2	46.2	0.0	46.7	1.1	46.7	0.0	46.7	0.0	46.6	-0.2
1962	46.0	-1.3	46.1	0.2	46.4	0.7	46.4	0.0	46.4	0.0	46.5	0.2	46.5	0.0	46.3	-0.4	47.1	1.7	47.2	0.2	47.0	-0.4	46.9	-0.2
1963	46.6	-0.6	46.7	0.2	46.8	0.2	46.9	0.2	46.9	0.0	47.0	0.2	47.0	0.0	47.0	0.0	47.4	0.9	47.6	0.4	47.7	0.2	47.7	0.0
1964	47.2	-1.0	47.2	0.0	47.3	0.2	47.4	0.2	47.5	0.2	47.5	0.0	47.4	-0.2	47.3	-0.2	47.6	0.6	47.7	0.2	47.8	0.2	47.9	0.2
1965	47.4	-1.0	47.5	0.2	47.6	0.2	47.7	0.2	48.0	0.6	48.1	0.2	47.7	-0.8	47.8	0.2	48.2	0.8	48.5	0.6	48.6	0.2	48.6	0.0
1966	48.2	-0.8	48.4	0.4	48.6	0.4	48.9	0.6	49.1	0.4	49.2	0.2	49.1	-0.2	49.1	0.0	49.7	1.2	50.1	0.8	50.3	0.4	50.5	0.4
1967	50.0	-1.0	50.3	0.6	50.6	0.6	50.8	0.4	51.1	0.6	51.2	0.2	51.1	-0.2	51.1	0.0	51.7	1.2	52.2	1.0	52.4	0.4	52.5	0.2
1968	52.1	-0.8	52.4	0.6	52.9	1.0	53.2	0.6	53.7	0.9	53.9	0.4	53.8	-0.2	54.0	0.4	54.9	1.7	55.4	0.9	55.7	0.5	55.8	0.2
1969	55.4	-0.7	55.7	0.5	56.1	0.7	56.5	0.7	56.9	0.7	57.1	0.4	57.0	-0.2	56.9	-0.2	57.8	1.6	58.3	0.9	58.7	0.7	58.8	0.2
1970	58.1	-1.2	58.4	0.5	58.7	0.5	58.9	0.3	59.3	0.7	59.4	0.2	59.1	-0.5	59.1	0.0	60.0	1.5	60.6	1.0	61.0	0.7	61.1	0.2
1971	60.2	-1.5	60.5	0.5	60.8	0.5	61.0	0.3	61.6	1.0	61.5	-0.2	61.1	-0.7	61.0	-0.2	61.8	1.3	62.3	0.8	62.4	0.2	62.4	0.0
1972	61.6	-1.3	61.8	0.3	62.1	0.5	62.4	0.5	62.8	0.6	62.5	-0.5	62.0	-0.8	61.9	-0.2	63.1	1.9	63.7	1.0	64.0	0.5	64.0	0.0
1973	63.0	-1.6	63.3	0.5	63.9	0.9	64.4	0.8	64.9	0.8	65.0	0.2	64.4	-0.9	64.8	0.6	65.7	1.4	66.4	1.1	66.9	0.8	66.9	0.0
1974	66.0	-1.3	66.8	1.2	67.7	1.3	68.4	1.0	69.2	1.2	69.5	0.4	69.3	-0.3	70.7	2.0	71.7	1.4	72.3	0.8	72.9	0.8	72.7	-0.3
1975	71.4	-1.8	71.8	0.6	72.2	0.6	72.4	0.3	72.6	0.3	72.4	-0.3	72.3	-0.1	72.9	0.8	73.5	0.8	74.1	0.8	74.5	0.5	74.4	-0.1
1976	73.4	-1.3	73.8	0.5	74.3	0.7	74.6	0.4	75.2	0.8	75.3	0.1	75.0	-0.4	75.9	1.2	76.9	1.3	77.3	0.5	77.8	0.6	77.8	0.0
1977	76.8	-1.3	77.3	0.7	77.7	0.5	78.0	0.4	78.6	0.8	78.8	0.3	78.6	-0.3	79.3	0.9	80.0	0.9	80.5	0.6	81.2	0.9	81.0	-0.2
1978	79.6	-1.7	79.1	-0.6	79.9	1.0	81.0	1.4	81.8	1.0	81.9	0.1	81.0	-1.1	81.8	1.0	82.9	1.3	83.8	1.1	84.0	0.2	83.7	-0.4
1979	82.5	-1.4	82.8	0.4	84.1	1.6	84.7	0.7	84.9	0.2	84.7	-0.2	84.3	-0.5	85.1	0.9	86.7	1.9	87.5	0.9	87.8	0.3	87.8	0.0
1980	87.0	-0.9	87.9	1.0	89.7	2.0	90.2	0.6	90.6	0.4	90.2	-0.4	89.9	-0.3	91.1	1.3	92.9	2.0	93.6	0.8	93.9	0.3	93.7	-0.2
1981	92.6	-1.2	93.1	0.5	94.4	1.4	95.3	1.0	95.4	0.1	95.2	-0.2	95.0	-0.2	96.3	1.4	97.6	1.3	97.6	0.0	97.6	0.0	97.0	-0.6
1982	95.5	-1.5	96.0	0.5	97.6	1.7	97.9	0.3	97.6	-0.3	97.1	-0.5	96.7	-0.4	97.7	1.0	99.4	1.7	99.7	0.3	99.6	-0.1	98.8	-0.8
1983	97.3	-1.5	97.8	0.5	99.4	1.6	99.8	0.4	100.0	0.2	99.7	-0.3	99.4	-0.3	100.6	1.2	102.1	1.5	102.4	0.3	102.3	-0.1	101.5	-0.8
1984	100.0	-1.5	100.1	0.1	101.4	1.3	101.5	0.1	101.3	-0.2	100.5	-0.8	100.0	-0.5	101.9	1.9	104.1	2.2	104.9	0.8	104.6	-0.3	103.5	-1.1
1985	101.7	-1.7	102.8	1.1	104.6	1.8	105.0	0.4	104.6	-0.4	104.4	-0.2	103.4	-1.0	104.7	1.3	106.9	2.1	107.7	0.7	107.7	0.0	106.6	-1.0
1986	104.6	-1.9	104.0	-0.6	105.1	1.1	105.6	0.5	105.1	-0.5	104.0	-1.0	103.4	-0.6	105.5	2.0	108.1	2.5	108.6	0.5	108.3	-0.3	107.4	-0.8
1987	105.4	-1.9	106.0	0.6	109.5	3.3	111.4	1.7	110.9	-0.4	109.1	-1.6	107.1	-1.8	109.1	1.9	112.9	3.5	115.2	2.0	115.2	0.0	112.6	-2.3
1988	110.3	-2.0	110.0	-0.3	113.9	3.5	116.3	2.1	115.7	-0.5	114.1	-1.4	112.4	-1.5	112.2	-0.2	117.2	4.5	120.1	2.5	119.5	-0.5	117.6	-1.6
1989	114.8	-2.4	114.7	-0.1	118.4	3.2	120.0	1.4	119.4	-0.5	116.9	-2.1	114.4	-2.1	114.5	0.1	119.3	4.2	122.0	2.3	121.4	-0.5	118.5	-2.4
1990	116.1	-2.0	119.3	2.8	124.4	4.3	125.8	1.1	124.7	-0.9	122.4	-1.8	119.8	-2.1	121.3	1.3	125.7	3.6	127.1	1.1	126.5	-0.5	124.5	-1.6
1991	122.9	-1.3	124.8	1.5	127.5	2.2	128.8	1.0	127.9	-0.7	125.7	-1.7	124.1	-1.3	126.4	1.9	129.7	2.6	131.1	1.1	131.4	0.2	128.4	-2.3
1992	126.8	-1.2	128.8	1.6	132.1	2.6	132.1	0.0	131.8	-0.2	129.8	-1.5	128.1	-1.3	129.5	1.1	132.1	2.0	133.8	1.3	133.4	-0.3	130.4	-2.2
1993	128.4	-1.5	132.0	2.8	134.8	2.1	135.2	0.3	133.6	-1.2	130.7	-2.2	128.4	-1.8	130.5	1.6	133.3	2.1	135.1	1.4	135.0	-0.1	131.3	-2.7
1994	129.4	-1.4	131.4	1.5	134.7	2.5	135.0	0.2	134.3	-0.5	132.4	-1.4	129.8	-2.0	130.2	0.3	133.1	2.2	133.9	0.6	133.0	-0.7	129.3	-2.8
1995	128.3	-0.8	130.0	1.3	133.2	2.5	133.6	0.3	132.1	-1.1	129.6	-1.9	127.4	-1.7	129.1	1.3	131.6	1.9	133.4	1.4	132.5	-0.7	129.5	-2.3
1996	129.1	-0.3	130.2	0.9	133.9	2.8	134.2	0.2	133.2	-0.7	130.2	-2.3	127.9	-1.8	127.5	-0.3	130.6	2.4	132.4	1.4	132.4	0.0	129.3	-2.3
1997	128.7	-0.5	131.1	1.9	133.8	2.1	135.5	1.3	134.7	-0.6	131.8	-2.2	129.8	-1.5	129.4	-0.3	132.1	2.1	133.9	1.4	133.6	-0.2	130.3	-2.5

Source: U.S. Department of Labor, Bureau of Labor Statistics, Division of Consumer Prices and Price Indexes.

U.S. City Average
Consumer Price Index - All Urban Consumers
Base 1982-1984 = 100
Transportation

For 1935-1997. Columns headed % show percentile change in the index from the previous period for which an index is available.

Year	Jan Index	%	Feb Index	%	Mar Index	%	Apr Index	%	May Index	%	Jun Index	%	Jul Index	%	Aug Index	%	Sep Index	%	Oct Index	%	Nov Index	%	Dec Index	%
1935	-	-	-	-	14.2	-	-	-	-	-	-	-	14.3	0.7	-	-	-	-	14.1	-1.4	-	-	-	-
1936	14.1	0.0	-	-	-	-	14.3	1.4	-	-	-	-	14.3	0.0	-	-	14.3	0.0	-	-	-	-	14.3	0.0
1937	-	-	-	-	14.5	1.4	-	-	-	-	14.5	0.0	-	-	-	-	14.6	0.7	-	-	-	-	14.7	0.7
1938	-	-	-	-	14.7	0.0	-	-	-	-	14.7	0.0	-	-	-	-	14.7	0.0	-	-	-	-	14.4	-2.0
1939	-	-	-	-	14.3	-0.7	-	-	-	-	14.3	0.0	-	-	-	-	14.3	0.0	-	-	-	-	14.3	0.0
1940	-	-	-	-	14.3	0.0	-	-	-	-	14.1	-1.4	-	-	-	-	14.2	0.7	-	-	-	-	14.3	0.7
1941	-	-	-	-	14.3	0.0	-	-	-	-	14.6	2.1	-	-	-	-	14.8	1.4	-	-	-	-	15.4	4.1
1942	-	-	-	-	16.0	3.9	-	-	-	-	16.1	0.6	-	-	-	-	16.0	-0.6	-	-	-	-	16.0	0.0
1943	-	-	-	-	16.0	0.0	-	-	-	-	15.9	-0.6	-	-	-	-	15.9	0.0	-	-	-	-	15.9	0.0
1944	-	-	-	-	15.9	0.0	-	-	-	-	15.9	0.0	-	-	-	-	15.9	0.0	-	-	-	-	15.9	0.0
1945	-	-	-	-	15.9	0.0	-	-	-	-	15.9	0.0	-	-	-	-	15.9	0.0	-	-	-	-	15.9	0.0
1946	-	-	-	-	16.0	0.6	-	-	-	-	16.2	1.3	-	-	-	-	17.5	8.0	-	-	-	-	17.9	2.3
1947	17.9	0.0	17.9	0.0	18.1	1.1	18.2	0.6	18.3	0.5	18.3	0.0	18.4	0.5	18.5	0.5	18.7	1.1	18.9	1.1	19.0	0.5	19.2	1.1
1948	19.5	1.6	19.6	0.5	19.6	0.0	19.8	1.0	19.8	0.0	19.9	0.5	21.0	5.5	21.4	1.9	21.5	0.5	21.6	0.5	21.6	0.0	21.6	0.0
1949	21.6	0.0	21.8	0.9	21.9	0.5	22.0	0.5	22.1	0.5	22.0	-0.5	22.1	0.5	22.3	0.9	22.3	0.0	22.4	0.4	22.4	0.0	22.5	0.4
1950	22.5	0.0	22.4	-0.4	22.4	0.0	22.3	-0.4	22.4	0.4	22.4	0.0	22.7	1.3	22.9	0.9	23.0	0.4	22.9	-0.4	23.0	0.4	23.3	1.3
1951	23.4	0.4	23.6	0.9	23.8	0.8	23.9	0.4	24.0	0.4	24.0	0.0	24.0	0.0	24.2	0.8	24.4	0.8	24.6	0.8	24.9	1.2	24.9	0.0
1952	25.0	0.4	25.2	0.8	25.4	0.8	25.4	0.0	25.5	0.4	25.7	0.8	25.9	0.8	25.9	0.0	26.0	0.4	26.2	0.8	26.3	0.4	26.3	0.0
1953	26.4	0.4	26.3	-0.4	26.4	0.4	26.4	0.0	26.4	0.0	26.4	0.0	26.5	0.4	26.6	0.4	26.7	0.4	26.7	0.0	26.5	-0.7	26.3	-0.8
1954	26.6	1.1	26.4	-0.8	26.3	-0.4	26.3	0.0	26.3	0.0	26.3	0.0	25.8	-1.9	25.8	0.0	25.8	0.0	25.5	-1.2	26.0	2.0	25.9	-0.4
1955	26.0	0.4	26.0	0.0	25.9	-0.4	25.5	-1.5	25.6	0.4	25.6	0.0	25.6	0.0	25.6	0.0	25.5	-0.4	25.8	1.2	26.2	1.6	25.9	-1.1
1956	25.9	0.0	25.9	0.0	25.8	-0.4	25.8	0.0	25.9	0.4	25.9	0.0	26.0	0.4	26.2	0.8	26.2	0.0	27.0	3.1	27.1	0.4	27.1	0.0
1957	27.2	0.4	27.4	0.7	27.5	0.4	27.6	0.4	27.5	-0.4	27.5	0.0	27.7	0.7	27.7	0.0	27.7	0.0	27.7	0.0	28.5	2.9	28.3	-0.7
1958	28.2	-0.4	28.2	0.0	28.2	0.0	28.2	0.0	28.2	0.0	28.3	0.4	28.6	1.1	28.7	0.3	28.8	0.3	29.1	1.0	29.4	1.0	29.4	0.0
1959	29.4	0.0	29.4	0.0	29.5	0.3	29.6	0.3	29.6	0.0	29.7	0.3	29.8	0.3	29.9	0.3	29.8	-0.3	30.2	1.3	30.3	0.3	30.3	0.0
1960	30.1	-0.7	30.0	-0.3	29.8	-0.7	29.8	0.0	29.6	-0.7	29.7	0.3	29.7	0.0	29.8	0.3	29.5	-1.0	29.8	1.0	29.8	0.0	29.8	0.0
1961	29.8	0.0	29.8	0.0	29.7	-0.3	29.7	0.0	29.8	0.3	30.1	1.0	30.2	0.3	30.4	0.7	30.4	0.0	30.6	0.7	30.6	0.0	30.4	-0.7
1962	30.4	0.0	30.4	0.0	30.4	0.0	30.8	1.3	30.8	0.0	30.8	0.0	30.6	-0.6	30.8	0.7	30.9	0.3	31.0	0.3	31.1	0.3	31.0	-0.3
1963	30.6	-1.3	30.6	0.0	30.7	0.3	30.7	0.0	30.8	0.3	30.8	0.0	30.9	0.3	31.1	0.6	31.0	-0.3	31.3	1.0	31.3	0.0	31.3	0.0
1964	31.4	0.3	31.2	-0.6	31.3	0.3	31.3	0.0	31.3	0.0	31.3	0.0	31.4	0.3	31.4	0.0	31.3	-0.3	31.4	0.3	31.6	0.6	31.7	0.3
1965	31.9	0.6	31.7	-0.6	31.7	0.0	31.9	0.6	32.0	0.3	31.9	-0.3	32.0	0.3	31.9	-0.3	31.9	0.0	31.9	0.0	32.0	0.3	32.0	0.0
1966	31.9	-0.3	31.9	0.0	32.0	0.3	32.1	0.3	32.1	0.0	32.2	0.3	32.6	1.2	32.6	0.0	32.5	-0.3	32.8	0.9	32.9	0.3	32.7	-0.6
1967	32.5	-0.6	32.7	0.6	32.8	0.3	33.0	0.6	33.2	0.6	33.2	0.0	33.4	0.6	33.4	0.0	33.5	0.3	33.8	0.9	34.0	0.6	33.8	-0.6
1968	34.1	0.9	34.0	-0.3	34.2	0.6	34.2	0.0	34.2	0.0	34.4	0.6	34.4	0.0	34.4	0.0	34.3	-0.3	34.6	0.9	34.8	0.6	34.5	-0.9
1969	34.6	0.3	35.0	1.2	35.7	2.0	35.8	0.3	35.6	-0.6	35.8	0.6	35.7	-0.3	35.7	0.0	35.5	-0.6	36.1	1.7	36.1	0.0	36.3	0.6
1970	36.5	0.6	36.5	0.0	36.5	0.0	37.0	1.4	37.3	0.8	37.5	0.5	37.7	0.5	37.5	-0.5	37.6	0.3	38.3	1.9	38.6	0.8	38.9	0.8
1971	39.1	0.5	39.1	0.0	39.2	0.3	39.3	0.3	39.5	0.5	39.8	0.8	39.7	-0.3	39.7	0.0	39.5	-0.5	39.7	0.5	39.5	-0.5	39.4	-0.3
1972	39.6	0.5	39.4	-0.5	39.4	0.0	39.5	0.3	39.8	0.8	39.9	0.3	40.0	0.3	40.1	0.2	40.3	0.5	40.3	0.0	40.4	0.2	40.4	0.0
1973	40.3	-0.2	40.3	0.0	40.4	0.2	40.8	1.0	41.1	0.7	41.5	1.0	41.5	0.0	41.4	-0.2	41.2	-0.5	41.6	1.0	41.9	0.7	42.2	0.7
1974	42.6	0.9	43.0	0.9	43.9	2.1	44.5	1.4	45.4	2.0	46.2	1.8	46.8	1.3	47.0	0.4	47.3	0.6	47.5	0.4	47.7	0.4	47.7	0.0
1975	47.6	-0.2	47.7	0.2	48.2	1.0	48.6	0.8	49.0	0.8	49.8	1.6	50.8	2.0	51.1	0.6	51.7	1.2	51.9	0.4	52.4	1.0	52.4	0.0
1976	52.6	0.4	52.7	0.2	53.2	0.9	53.7	0.9	54.4	1.3	55.2	1.5	55.8	1.1	56.1	0.5	56.4	0.5	56.9	0.9	57.0	0.2	57.0	0.0
1977	57.3	0.5	57.6	0.5	58.1	0.9	58.8	1.2	59.3	0.9	59.6	0.5	59.6	0.0	59.5	-0.2	59.4	-0.2	59.4	0.0	59.5	0.2	59.5	0.0
1978	59.6	0.2	59.7	0.2	59.9	0.3	60.3	0.7	61.0	1.2	61.7	1.1	62.3	1.0	62.6	0.5	62.8	0.3	63.1	0.5	63.7	1.0	64.1	0.6
1979	64.5	0.6	65.1	0.9	65.9	1.2	67.5	2.4	69.1	2.4	70.7	2.3	72.1	2.0	73.1	1.4	73.7	0.8	74.1	0.5	74.8	0.9	75.8	1.3

[Continued]

U.S. City Average
Consumer Price Index - All Urban Consumers
Base 1982-1984 = 100
Transportation
[Continued]

For 1935-1997. Columns headed % show percentile change in the index from the previous period for which an index is available.

Year	Jan Index	%	Feb Index	%	Mar Index	%	Apr Index	%	May Index	%	Jun Index	%	Jul Index	%	Aug Index	%	Sep Index	%	Oct Index	%	Nov Index	%	Dec Index	%
1980	77.7	2.5	79.7	2.6	81.1	1.8	82.1	1.2	82.8	0.9	83.1	0.4	83.5	0.5	84.1	0.7	84.7	0.7	85.2	0.6	86.2	1.2	86.9	0.8
1981	88.1	1.4	90.1	2.3	91.0	1.0	91.6	0.7	92.4	0.9	93.1	0.8	94.0	1.0	94.4	0.4	94.9	0.5	95.6	0.7	96.2	0.6	96.4	0.2
1982	96.5	0.1	95.8	-0.7	94.9	-0.9	94.1	-0.8	95.0	1.0	97.4	2.5	98.5	1.1	98.6	0.1	98.3	-0.3	98.3	0.0	98.4	0.1	98.1	-0.3
1983	97.5	-0.6	96.5	-1.0	95.6	-0.9	97.3	1.8	98.6	1.3	99.3	0.7	100.0	0.7	100.6	0.6	101.0	0.4	101.5	0.5	101.9	0.4	101.9	0.0
1984	101.8	-0.1	101.7	-0.1	102.1	0.4	103.0	0.9	103.9	0.9	104.2	0.3	104.1	-0.1	104.1	0.0	104.4	0.3	105.0	0.6	105.2	0.2	105.1	-0.1
1985	104.7	-0.4	104.6	-0.1	105.4	0.8	106.5	1.0	106.9	0.4	107.1	0.2	107.1	0.0	106.7	-0.4	106.4	-0.3	106.8	0.4	107.5	0.7	107.8	0.3
1986	107.8	0.0	106.2	-1.5	103.0	-3.0	100.9	-2.0	101.7	0.8	102.7	1.0	101.4	-1.3	100.3	-1.1	100.5	0.2	100.7	0.2	101.2	0.5	101.4	0.2
1987	102.6	1.2	103.1	0.5	103.3	0.2	104.2	0.9	104.7	0.5	105.4	0.7	106.0	0.6	106.5	0.5	106.6	0.1	107.1	0.5	107.8	0.7	107.6	-0.2
1988	107.1	-0.5	106.8	-0.3	106.5	-0.3	107.2	0.7	108.1	0.8	108.5	0.4	108.9	0.4	109.6	0.6	109.7	0.1	110.0	0.3	110.7	0.6	110.8	0.1
1989	111.1	0.3	111.6	0.5	111.9	0.3	114.6	2.4	116.0	1.2	115.9	-0.1	115.4	-0.4	114.3	-1.0	113.7	-0.5	114.5	0.7	115.0	0.4	115.2	0.2
1990	117.2	1.7	117.1	-0.1	116.8	-0.3	117.3	0.4	117.7	0.3	118.2	0.4	118.4	0.2	120.6	1.9	123.0	2.0	125.8	2.3	126.9	0.9	127.2	0.2
1991	125.5	-1.3	123.7	-1.4	122.3	-1.1	122.2	-0.1	123.3	0.9	123.7	0.3	123.4	-0.2	123.8	0.3	123.8	0.0	124.0	0.2	125.0	0.8	125.3	0.2
1992	124.5	-0.6	124.1	-0.3	124.4	0.2	125.2	0.6	126.3	0.9	126.9	0.5	127.2	0.2	126.9	-0.2	126.8	-0.1	128.0	0.9	129.2	0.9	129.0	-0.2
1993	129.1	0.1	129.2	0.1	129.0	-0.2	129.4	0.3	130.2	0.6	130.3	0.1	130.3	0.0	130.2	-0.1	130.1	-0.1	131.8	1.3	132.6	0.6	132.1	-0.4
1994	131.6	-0.4	131.9	0.2	132.2	0.2	132.6	0.3	132.8	0.2	133.8	0.8	134.6	0.6	135.9	1.0	135.9	0.0	136.1	0.1	137.1	0.7	137.1	0.0
1995	137.3	0.1	137.5	0.1	138.0	0.4	139.1	0.8	140.3	0.9	141.1	0.6	140.1	-0.7	139.2	-0.6	138.8	-0.3	139.4	0.4	139.4	0.0	139.1	-0.2
1996	139.9	0.6	140.4	0.4	141.2	0.6	143.1	1.3	144.4	0.9	144.0	-0.3	143.5	-0.3	142.8	-0.5	143.2	0.3	143.9	0.5	144.8	0.6	145.2	0.3
1997	145.0	-0.1	144.8	-0.1	144.9	0.1	144.8	-0.1	144.4	-0.3	144.0	-0.3	143.7	-0.2	143.8	0.1	144.3	0.3	144.5	0.1	143.9	-0.4	143.2	-0.5

Source: U.S. Department of Labor, Bureau of Labor Statistics, Division of Consumer Prices and Price Indexes.

U.S. City Average
Consumer Price Index - Urban Wage Earners
Base 1982-1984 = 100
Transportation

For 1935-1997. Columns headed % show percentile change in the index from the previous period for which an index is available.

Year	Jan Index	%	Feb Index	%	Mar Index	%	Apr Index	%	May Index	%	Jun Index	%	Jul Index	%	Aug Index	%	Sep Index	%	Oct Index	%	Nov Index	%	Dec Index	%
1935	-	-	-	-	14.1	-	-	-	-	-	-	-	14.2	0.7	-	-	-	-	14.0	-1.4	-	-	-	-
1936	14.1	0.7	-	-	-	-	14.2	0.7	-	-	-	-	14.3	0.7	-	-	14.3	0.0	-	-	-	-	14.3	0.0
1937	-	-	-	-	14.4	0.7	-	-	-	-	14.4	0.0	-	-	-	-	14.5	0.7	-	-	-	-	14.6	0.7
1938	-	-	-	-	14.6	0.0	-	-	-	-	14.6	0.0	-	-	-	-	14.6	0.0	-	-	-	-	14.3	-2.1
1939	-	-	-	-	14.2	-0.7	-	-	-	-	14.2	0.0	-	-	-	-	14.3	0.7	-	-	-	-	14.2	-0.7
1940	-	-	-	-	14.2	0.0	-	-	-	-	14.1	-0.7	-	-	-	-	14.1	0.0	-	-	-	-	14.2	0.7
1941	-	-	-	-	14.3	0.7	-	-	-	-	14.6	2.1	-	-	-	-	14.7	0.7	-	-	-	-	15.3	4.1
1942	-	-	-	-	15.9	3.9	-	-	-	-	16.0	0.6	-	-	-	-	15.9	-0.6	-	-	-	-	15.9	0.0
1943	-	-	-	-	15.9	0.0	-	-	-	-	15.8	-0.6	-	-	-	-	15.8	0.0	-	-	-	-	15.8	0.0
1944	-	-	-	-	15.8	0.0	-	-	-	-	15.8	0.0	-	-	-	-	15.8	0.0	-	-	-	-	15.8	0.0
1945	-	-	-	-	15.8	0.0	-	-	-	-	15.8	0.0	-	-	-	-	15.8	0.0	-	-	-	-	15.8	0.0
1946	-	-	-	-	15.9	0.6	-	-	-	-	16.1	1.3	-	-	-	-	17.4	8.1	-	-	-	-	17.8	2.3
1947	17.8	0.0	17.8	0.0	18.0	1.1	18.1	0.6	18.2	0.6	18.2	0.0	18.3	0.5	18.4	0.5	18.6	1.1	18.8	1.1	18.9	0.5	19.1	1.1
1948	19.4	1.6	19.4	0.0	19.4	0.0	19.7	1.5	19.7	0.0	19.8	0.5	20.8	5.1	21.2	1.9	21.3	0.5	21.5	0.9	21.5	0.0	21.5	0.0
1949	21.5	0.0	21.7	0.9	21.8	0.5	21.9	0.5	22.0	0.5	21.9	-0.5	22.0	0.5	22.2	0.9	22.2	0.0	22.3	0.5	22.2	-0.4	22.4	0.9
1950	22.3	-0.4	22.3	0.0	22.2	-0.4	22.2	0.0	22.3	0.5	22.3	0.0	22.5	0.9	22.8	1.3	22.8	0.0	22.8	0.0	22.9	0.4	23.1	0.9
1951	23.2	0.4	23.5	1.3	23.7	0.9	23.7	0.0	23.8	0.4	23.8	0.0	23.8	0.0	24.0	0.8	24.2	0.8	24.4	0.8	24.7	1.2	24.7	0.0
1952	24.9	0.8	25.1	0.8	25.2	0.4	25.3	0.4	25.3	0.0	25.6	1.2	25.7	0.4	25.7	0.0	25.9	0.8	26.0	0.4	26.1	0.4	26.1	0.0
1953	26.2	0.4	26.1	-0.4	26.2	0.4	26.2	0.0	26.2	0.0	26.2	0.0	26.3	0.4	26.5	0.8	26.5	0.0	26.5	0.0	26.3	-0.8	26.1	-0.8
1954	26.4	1.1	26.2	-0.8	26.1	-0.4	26.1	0.0	26.1	0.0	26.1	0.0	25.7	-1.5	25.7	0.0	25.6	-0.4	25.3	-1.2	25.9	2.4	25.8	-0.4
1955	25.9	0.4	25.8	-0.4	25.8	0.0	25.4	-1.6	25.4	0.0	25.7	0.4	25.7	0.0	25.9	0.8	26.0	0.4	26.1	0.4	26.9	3.1	27.0	0.4	27.0	0.0
1956	25.7	-0.4	25.7	0.0	25.7	0.0	25.6	-0.4	25.7	0.4	27.4	0.0	27.5	0.4	27.6	0.4	27.6	0.0	27.5	-0.4	28.4	3.3	28.1	-1.1
1957	27.1	0.4	27.2	0.4	27.4	0.7	27.5	0.4	27.4	-0.4	27.4	0.0	27.5	0.4	27.6	0.4	27.6	0.0	27.5	-0.4	28.4	3.3	28.1	-1.1
1958	28.1	0.0	28.1	0.0	28.1	0.0	28.0	-0.4	28.1	0.4	28.1	0.0	28.4	1.1	28.6	0.7	28.6	0.0	28.9	1.0	29.3	1.4	29.2	-0.3
1959	29.2	0.0	29.2	0.0	29.3	0.3	29.4	0.3	29.4	0.0	29.5	0.3	29.6	0.3	29.7	0.3	29.6	-0.3	30.1	1.7	30.2	0.3	30.1	-0.3
1960	29.9	-0.7	29.9	0.0	29.7	-0.7	29.6	-0.3	29.5	-0.3	29.5	0.0	29.5	0.0	29.6	0.3	29.3	-1.0	29.6	1.0	29.7	0.3	29.7	0.0
1961	29.6	-0.3	29.6	0.0	29.5	-0.3	29.5	0.0	29.7	0.7	29.9	0.7	30.1	0.7	30.3	0.7	30.3	0.0	30.5	0.7	30.5	0.0	30.3	-0.7
1962	30.3	0.0	30.3	0.0	30.2	-0.3	30.6	1.3	30.6	0.0	30.6	0.0	30.5	-0.3	30.7	0.7	30.8	0.3	30.9	0.3	30.9	0.0	30.8	-0.3
1963	30.4	-1.3	30.5	0.3	30.5	0.0	30.5	0.0	30.7	0.7	30.7	0.0	30.8	0.3	30.9	0.3	30.8	-0.3	31.1	1.0	31.1	0.0	31.1	0.0
1964	31.2	0.3	31.0	-0.6	31.1	0.3	31.1	0.0	31.1	0.0	31.2	0.3	31.2	0.0	31.2	0.0	31.1	-0.3	31.2	0.3	31.4	0.6	31.5	0.3
1965	31.7	0.6	31.6	-0.3	31.6	0.0	31.7	0.3	31.8	0.3	31.7	-0.3	31.8	0.3	31.7	-0.3	31.7	0.0	31.7	0.0	31.8	0.3	31.9	0.3
1966	31.7	-0.6	31.7	0.0	31.8	0.3	32.0	0.6	32.0	0.0	32.0	0.0	32.4	1.3	32.4	0.0	32.4	0.0	32.6	0.6	32.7	0.3	32.5	-0.6
1967	32.4	-0.3	32.5	0.3	32.6	0.3	32.8	0.6	33.0	0.6	33.0	0.0	33.2	0.6	33.2	0.0	33.3	0.3	33.6	0.9	33.8	0.6	33.6	-0.6
1968	33.9	0.9	33.8	-0.3	34.0	0.6	34.0	0.0	34.0	0.0	34.2	0.6	34.2	0.0	34.2	0.0	34.1	-0.3	34.4	0.9	34.6	0.6	34.3	-0.9
1969	34.4	0.3	34.8	1.2	35.5	2.0	35.6	0.3	35.4	-0.6	35.6	0.6	35.5	-0.3	35.5	0.0	35.3	-0.6	35.9	1.7	35.9	0.0	36.1	0.6
1970	36.3	0.6	36.3	0.0	36.3	0.0	36.8	1.4	37.1	0.8	37.3	0.5	37.5	0.5	37.3	-0.5	37.4	0.3	38.1	1.9	38.4	0.8	38.7	0.8
1971	38.9	0.5	38.9	0.0	39.0	0.3	39.1	0.3	39.3	0.5	39.6	0.8	39.5	-0.3	39.5	0.0	39.2	-0.8	39.5	0.8	39.3	-0.5	39.2	-0.3
1972	39.3	0.3	39.1	-0.5	39.2	0.3	39.2	0.0	39.5	0.8	39.6	0.3	39.8	0.5	39.9	0.3	40.0	0.3	40.1	0.2	40.2	0.2	40.1	-0.2
1973	40.0	-0.2	40.1	0.2	40.2	0.2	40.6	1.0	40.9	0.7	41.2	0.7	41.3	0.2	41.2	-0.2	41.0	-0.5	41.3	0.7	41.6	0.7	41.9	0.7
1974	42.4	1.2	42.8	0.9	43.7	2.1	44.2	1.1	45.1	2.0	45.9	1.8	46.5	1.3	46.7	0.4	47.0	0.6	47.3	0.6	47.4	0.2	47.5	0.2
1975	47.4	-0.2	47.5	0.2	47.9	0.8	48.4	1.0	48.8	0.8	49.6	1.6	50.5	1.8	50.8	0.6	51.4	1.2	51.6	0.4	52.1	1.0	52.1	0.0
1976	52.3	0.4	52.4	0.2	52.9	1.0	53.4	0.9	54.1	1.3	54.9	1.5	55.4	0.9	55.7	0.5	56.1	0.7	56.5	0.7	56.7	0.4	56.7	0.0
1977	57.0	0.5	57.3	0.5	57.8	0.9	58.4	1.0	58.9	0.9	59.2	0.5	59.3	0.2	59.1	-0.3	59.0	-0.2	59.1	0.2	59.1	0.0	59.1	0.0
1978	59.2	0.2	59.4	0.3	59.5	0.2	60.0	0.8	60.7	1.2	61.5	1.3	62.1	1.0	62.4	0.5	62.6	0.3	62.9	0.5	63.5	1.0	63.9	0.6
1979	64.3	0.6	64.9	0.9	65.7	1.2	67.4	2.6	69.0	2.4	70.7	2.5	72.0	1.8	73.0	1.4	73.6	0.8	73.9	0.4	74.7	1.1	75.5	1.1

[Continued]

U.S. City Average
Consumer Price Index - Urban Wage Earners
Base 1982-1984 = 100
Transportation
[Continued]

For 1935-1997. Columns headed % show percentile change in the index from the previous period for which an index is available.

Year	Jan Index	%	Feb Index	%	Mar Index	%	Apr Index	%	May Index	%	Jun Index	%	Jul Index	%	Aug Index	%	Sep Index	%	Oct Index	%	Nov Index	%	Dec Index	%
1980	77.4	2.5	79.5	2.7	80.8	1.6	81.9	1.4	82.7	1.0	82.9	0.2	83.3	0.5	83.9	0.7	84.4	0.6	84.9	0.6	85.9	1.2	86.6	0.8
1981	87.9	1.5	90.0	2.4	90.8	0.9	91.4	0.7	92.3	1.0	92.9	0.7	93.9	1.1	94.3	0.4	94.8	0.5	95.6	0.8	96.2	0.6	96.4	0.2
1982	96.5	0.1	95.8	-0.7	94.8	-1.0	94.0	-0.8	95.0	1.1	97.4	2.5	98.5	1.1	98.6	0.1	98.2	-0.4	98.2	0.0	98.3	0.1	98.0	-0.3
1983	97.3	-0.7	96.3	-1.0	95.5	-0.8	97.1	1.7	98.4	1.3	99.1	0.7	99.9	0.8	100.6	0.7	101.1	0.5	101.5	0.4	101.9	0.4	101.9	0.0
1984	101.8	-0.1	101.8	0.0	102.2	0.4	103.2	1.0	104.1	0.9	104.4	0.3	104.3	-0.1	104.3	0.0	104.5	0.2	105.1	0.6	105.3	0.2	105.2	-0.1
1985	104.8	-0.4	104.6	-0.2	105.4	0.8	106.5	1.0	106.9	0.4	107.0	0.1	107.0	0.0	106.6	-0.4	106.2	-0.4	106.6	0.4	107.4	0.8	107.6	0.2
1986	107.5	-0.1	105.9	-1.5	102.6	-3.1	100.4	-2.1	101.2	0.8	102.1	0.9	100.8	-1.3	99.5	-1.3	99.8	0.3	100.0	0.2	100.6	0.6	100.6	0.0
1987	101.9	1.3	102.5	0.6	102.8	0.3	103.8	1.0	104.4	0.6	105.1	0.7	105.8	0.7	106.3	0.5	106.4	0.1	106.9	0.5	107.6	0.7	107.3	-0.3
1988	106.8	-0.5	106.4	-0.4	106.2	-0.2	106.8	0.6	107.8	0.9	108.2	0.4	108.6	0.4	109.4	0.7	109.4	0.0	109.8	0.4	110.3	0.5	110.4	0.1
1989	110.7	0.3	111.2	0.5	111.6	0.4	114.5	2.6	116.0	1.3	116.0	0.0	115.4	-0.5	114.2	-1.0	113.5	-0.6	114.3	0.7	114.6	0.3	114.8	0.2
1990	116.8	1.7	116.6	-0.2	116.2	-0.3	116.6	0.3	117.1	0.4	117.7	0.5	117.8	0.1	120.3	2.1	122.9	2.2	125.7	2.3	126.6	0.7	126.7	0.1
1991	124.7	-1.6	122.6	-1.7	121.2	-1.1	121.3	0.1	122.7	1.2	123.1	0.3	122.9	-0.2	123.2	0.2	123.3	0.1	123.4	0.1	124.5	0.9	124.5	0.0
1992	123.5	-0.8	122.9	-0.5	123.2	0.2	124.1	0.7	125.5	1.1	126.5	0.8	126.7	0.2	126.5	-0.2	126.5	0.0	127.5	0.8	128.5	0.8	128.2	-0.2
1993	128.0	-0.2	128.0	0.0	127.8	-0.2	128.4	0.5	129.2	0.6	129.5	0.2	129.4	-0.1	129.4	0.0	129.2	-0.2	131.0	1.4	131.6	0.5	130.8	-0.6
1994	130.2	-0.5	130.4	0.2	130.5	0.1	131.2	0.5	131.8	0.5	132.9	0.8	133.9	0.8	135.2	1.0	135.3	0.1	135.6	0.2	136.7	0.8	136.7	0.0
1995	136.9	0.1	137.1	0.1	137.6	0.4	138.7	0.8	140.1	1.0	140.8	0.5	139.8	-0.7	138.9	-0.6	138.5	-0.3	139.0	0.4	139.0	0.0	138.9	-0.1
1996	139.7	0.6	140.0	0.2	140.9	0.6	143.0	1.5	144.4	1.0	143.8	-0.4	143.3	-0.3	142.6	-0.5	142.9	0.2	143.5	0.4	144.5	0.7	144.8	0.2
1997	144.6	-0.1	144.4	-0.1	144.2	-0.1	144.2	0.0	143.8	-0.3	143.4	-0.3	142.9	-0.3	143.3	0.3	143.6	0.2	143.6	0.0	143.1	-0.3	142.4	-0.5

Source: U.S. Department of Labor, Bureau of Labor Statistics, Division of Consumer Prices and Price Indexes.

U.S. City Average
Consumer Price Index - All Urban Consumers
Base 1982-1984 = 100
Medical Care

For 1935-1997. Columns headed % show percentile change in the index from the previous period for which an index is available.

Year	Jan Index	%	Feb Index	%	Mar Index	%	Apr Index	%	May Index	%	Jun Index	%	Jul Index	%	Aug Index	%	Sep Index	%	Oct Index	%	Nov Index	%	Dec Index	%
1935	-	-	-	-	10.2	-	-	-	-	-	-	-	10.2	0.0	-	-	-	-	10.2	0.0	-	-	-	-
1936	10.2	0.0	-	-	-	-	10.2	0.0	-	-	-	-	10.2	0.0	-	-	10.2	0.0	-	-	-	-	10.2	0.0
1937	-	-	-	-	10.3	1.0	-	-	-	-	10.3	0.0	-	-	-	-	10.3	0.0	-	-	-	-	10.3	0.0
1938	-	-	-	-	10.3	0.0			-	-	10.3	0.0	-	-	-	-	10.3	0.0	-	-	-	-	10.3	0.0
1939	-	-	-	-	10.3	0.0			-	-	10.4	1.0	-	-	-	-	10.4	0.0	-	-	-	-	10.4	0.0
1940	-	-	-	-	10.4	0.0			-	-	10.3	-1.0	-	-	-	-	10.3	0.0	-	-	-	-	10.4	1.0
1941	-	-	-	-	10.4	0.0			-	-	10.4	0.0			-	-	10.4	0.0	-	-	-	-	10.5	1.0
1942	-	-	-	-	10.6	1.0			-	-	10.7	0.9			-	-	10.8	0.9			-	-	10.9	0.9
1943	-	-	-	-	11.1	1.8			-	-	11.2	0.9			-	-	11.4	1.8			-	-	11.4	0.0
1944	-	-	-	-	11.5	0.9			-	-	11.5	0.0			-	-	11.6	0.9			-	-	11.7	0.9
1945	-	-	-	-	11.8	0.9			-	-	11.9	0.8			-	-	11.9	0.0			-	-	12.0	0.8
1946	-	-	-	-	12.2	1.7			-	-	12.4	1.6			-	-	12.7	2.4			-	-	13.0	2.4
1947	13.2	1.5	13.3	0.8	13.3	0.0	13.4	0.8	13.5	0.7	13.5	0.0	13.5	0.0	13.6	0.7	13.7	0.7	13.8	0.7	13.8	0.0	13.9	0.7
1948	14.0	0.7	14.0	0.0	14.1	0.7	14.3	1.4	14.3	0.0	14.3	0.0	14.5	1.4	14.5	0.0	14.5	0.0	14.6	0.7	14.7	0.7	14.7	0.0
1949	14.8	0.7	14.8	0.0	14.8	0.0	14.8	0.0	14.8	0.0	14.8	0.0	14.8	0.0	14.9	0.7	14.9	0.0	14.9	0.0	14.9	0.0	14.9	0.0
1950	15.0	0.7	15.0	0.0	15.0	0.0	15.0	0.0	15.0	0.0	15.0	0.0	15.1	0.7	15.1	0.0	15.2	0.7	15.3	0.7	15.3	0.0	15.4	0.7
1951	15.5	0.6	15.5	0.0	15.7	1.3	15.7	0.0	15.8	0.6	15.8	0.0	15.8	0.0	15.9	0.6	15.9	0.0	16.0	0.6	16.1	0.6	16.3	1.2
1952	16.4	0.6	16.4	0.0	16.5	0.6	16.5	0.0	16.5	0.0	16.8	1.8	16.8	0.0	16.8	0.0	16.9	0.6	16.9	0.0	16.9	0.0	17.0	0.6
1953	17.0	0.0	17.0	0.0	17.0	0.0	17.1	0.6	17.2	0.6	17.3	0.6	17.3	0.0	17.4	0.6	17.5	0.6	17.5	0.0	17.6	0.6	17.6	0.0
1954	17.6	0.0	17.7	0.6	17.7	0.0	17.8	0.6	17.8	0.0	17.8	0.0	17.8	0.0	17.9	0.6	17.9	0.0	17.9	0.0	18.0	0.6	18.0	0.0
1955	18.0	0.0	18.1	0.6	18.1	0.0	18.1	0.0	18.2	0.6	18.2	0.0	18.2	0.0	18.2	0.0	18.3	0.5	18.4	0.5	18.5	0.5	18.6	0.5
1956	18.6	0.0	18.7	0.5	18.7	0.0	18.8	0.5	18.8	0.0	18.8	0.0	18.9	0.5	19.0	0.5	19.1	0.5	19.1	0.0	19.2	0.5	19.2	0.0
1957	19.3	0.5	19.3	0.0	19.5	1.0	19.5	0.0	19.6	0.5	19.7	0.5	19.7	0.0	19.8	0.5	19.8	0.0	19.9	0.5	20.0	0.5	20.1	0.5
1958	20.2	0.5	20.2	0.0	20.3	0.5	20.4	0.5	20.5	0.5	20.6	0.5	20.7	0.5	20.7	0.0	20.9	1.0	21.0	0.5	21.0	0.0	21.0	0.0
1959	21.1	0.5	21.2	0.5	21.3	0.5	21.3	0.0	21.4	0.5	21.5	0.5	21.5	0.0	21.6	0.5	21.7	0.5	21.7	0.0	21.8	0.5	21.8	0.0
1960	21.9	0.5	22.0	0.5	22.1	0.5	22.2	0.5	22.2	0.0	22.2	0.0	22.3	0.5	22.3	0.0	22.4	0.4	22.4	0.0	22.5	0.4	22.5	0.0
1961	22.6	0.4	22.7	0.4	22.7	0.0	22.8	0.4	22.9	0.4	22.9	0.0	23.0	0.4	23.0	0.0	23.1	0.4	23.1	0.0	23.1	0.0	23.2	0.4
1962	23.2	0.0	23.3	0.4	23.4	0.4	23.5	0.4	23.5	0.0	23.6	0.4	23.6	0.0	23.6	0.0	23.6	0.0	23.7	0.4	23.7	0.0	23.7	0.0
1963	23.8	0.4	23.9	0.4	23.9	0.0	24.0	0.4	24.0	0.0	24.1	0.4	24.2	0.4	24.2	0.0	24.2	0.0	24.2	0.0	24.3	0.4	24.3	0.0
1964	24.4	0.4	24.4	0.0	24.4	0.0	24.5	0.4	24.5	0.0	24.6	0.4	24.6	0.0	24.7	0.4	24.7	0.0	24.7	0.0	24.7	0.0	24.8	0.4
1965	24.8	0.0	24.9	0.4	25.0	0.4	25.1	0.4	25.1	0.0	25.2	0.4	25.3	0.4	25.3	0.0	25.3	0.0	25.3	0.0	25.4	0.4	25.5	0.4
1966	25.6	0.4	25.6	0.0	25.8	0.8	25.9	0.4	26.0	0.4	26.2	0.8	26.3	0.4	26.4	0.4	26.7	1.1	26.9	0.7	27.0	0.4	27.2	0.7
1967	27.4	0.7	27.5	0.4	27.7	0.7	27.8	0.4	28.0	0.7	28.1	0.4	28.2	0.4	28.3	0.4	28.5	0.7	28.6	0.4	28.8	0.7	28.9	0.3
1968	29.1	0.7	29.2	0.3	29.4	0.7	29.6	0.7	29.6	0.0	29.7	0.3	29.9	0.7	30.0	0.3	30.2	0.7	30.4	0.7	30.5	0.3	30.7	0.7
1969	30.9	0.7	31.2	1.0	31.4	0.6	31.6	0.6	31.8	0.6	32.0	0.6	32.1	0.3	32.3	0.6	32.5	0.6	32.3	-0.6	32.4	0.3	32.6	0.6
1970	32.7	0.3	33.0	0.9	33.3	0.9	33.5	0.6	33.7	0.6	33.9	0.6	34.2	0.9	34.3	0.3	34.5	0.6	34.6	0.3	34.7	0.3	35.0	0.9
1971	35.2	0.6	35.4	0.6	35.7	0.8	35.9	0.6	36.1	0.6	36.2	0.3	36.4	0.6	36.6	0.5	36.7	0.3	36.5	-0.5	36.5	0.0	36.6	0.3
1972	36.7	0.3	36.9	0.5	37.0	0.3	37.1	0.3	37.2	0.3	37.3	0.3	37.4	0.3	37.4	0.0	37.5	0.3	37.7	0.5	37.8	0.3	37.8	0.0
1973	38.0	0.5	38.1	0.3	38.2	0.3	38.3	0.3	38.5	0.5	38.6	0.3	38.7	0.3	38.7	0.0	38.9	0.5	39.6	1.8	39.7	0.3	39.8	0.3
1974	40.0	0.5	40.4	1.0	40.8	1.0	41.0	0.5	41.4	1.0	42.1	1.7	42.6	1.2	43.3	1.6	43.7	0.9	44.0	0.7	44.3	0.7	44.8	1.1
1975	45.3	1.1	45.9	1.3	46.3	0.9	46.7	0.9	47.0	0.6	47.3	0.6	47.8	1.1	48.1	0.6	48.5	0.8	48.8	0.6	48.8	0.0	49.2	0.8
1976	49.7	1.0	50.3	1.2	50.8	1.0	51.1	0.6	51.4	0.6	51.7	0.6	52.2	1.0	52.6	0.8	52.9	0.6	53.2	0.6	53.9	1.3	54.1	0.4
1977	54.6	0.9	55.1	0.9	55.6	0.9	56.1	0.9	56.4	0.5	56.8	0.7	57.3	0.9	57.7	0.7	58.1	0.7	58.3	0.3	58.6	0.5	58.9	0.5
1978	59.5	1.0	60.1	1.0	60.4	0.5	60.7	0.5	61.1	0.7	61.3	0.3	61.8	0.8	62.3	0.8	62.7	0.6	63.3	1.0	63.9	0.9	64.1	0.3
1979	65.0	1.4	65.5	0.8	65.9	0.6	66.2	0.5	66.5	0.5	66.9	0.6	67.5	0.9	68.1	0.9	68.6	0.7	69.2	0.9	69.8	0.9	70.6	1.1

[Continued]

U.S. City Average
Consumer Price Index - All Urban Consumers
Base 1982-1984 = 100
Medical Care
[Continued]

For 1935-1997. Columns headed % show percentile change in the index from the previous period for which an index is available.

Year	Jan Index	%	Feb Index	%	Mar Index	%	Apr Index	%	May Index	%	Jun Index	%	Jul Index	%	Aug Index	%	Sep Index	%	Oct Index	%	Nov Index	%	Dec Index	%
1980	71.5	1.3	72.6	1.5	73.3	1.0	73.8	0.7	74.2	0.5	74.5	0.4	75.1	0.8	75.6	0.7	76.2	0.8	76.8	0.8	77.3	0.7	77.6	0.4
1981	78.7	1.4	79.6	1.1	80.2	0.8	80.8	0.7	81.4	0.7	82.1	0.9	83.2	1.3	84.3	1.3	84.9	0.7	85.8	1.1	86.8	1.2	87.3	0.6
1982	88.2	1.0	89.0	0.9	89.8	0.9	90.6	0.9	91.2	0.7	91.9	0.8	92.9	1.1	93.8	1.0	94.6	0.9	95.4	0.8	96.3	0.9	96.9	0.6
1983	97.9	1.0	98.9	1.0	99.2	0.3	99.5	0.3	99.7	0.2	100.1	0.4	100.7	0.6	101.4	0.7	101.7	0.3	102.2	0.5	102.7	0.5	103.1	0.4
1984	104.0	0.9	105.1	1.1	105.4	0.3	105.8	0.4	106.1	0.3	106.4	0.3	107.1	0.7	107.5	0.4	107.9	0.4	108.5	0.6	109.1	0.6	109.4	0.3
1985	110.1	0.6	110.9	0.7	111.6	0.6	112.1	0.4	112.5	0.4	113.1	0.5	113.7	0.5	114.5	0.7	115.0	0.4	115.6	0.5	116.3	0.6	116.8	0.4
1986	117.7	0.8	118.9	1.0	119.9	0.8	120.5	0.5	121.0	0.4	121.6	0.5	122.4	0.7	123.2	0.7	123.8	0.5	124.5	0.6	125.2	0.6	125.8	0.5
1987	126.6	0.6	127.4	0.6	128.1	0.5	128.7	0.5	129.2	0.4	129.9	0.5	130.7	0.6	131.2	0.4	131.7	0.4	132.3	0.5	132.8	0.4	133.1	0.2
1988	134.4	1.0	135.5	0.8	136.3	0.6	136.9	0.4	137.5	0.4	138.2	0.5	139.3	0.8	139.9	0.4	140.4	0.4	141.2	0.6	141.8	0.4	142.3	0.4
1989	143.8	1.1	145.2	1.0	146.1	0.6	146.8	0.5	147.5	0.5	148.5	0.7	149.7	0.8	150.7	0.7	151.7	0.7	152.7	0.7	153.9	0.8	154.4	0.3
1990	155.9	1.0	157.5	1.0	158.7	0.8	159.8	0.7	160.8	0.6	161.9	0.7	163.5	1.0	165.0	0.9	165.8	0.5	167.1	0.8	168.4	0.8	169.2	0.5
1991	171.0	1.1	172.5	0.9	173.7	0.7	174.4	0.4	175.2	0.5	176.2	0.6	177.5	0.7	178.9	0.8	179.7	0.4	180.7	0.6	181.8	0.6	182.6	0.4
1992	184.3	0.9	186.2	1.0	187.3	0.6	188.1	0.4	188.7	0.3	189.4	0.4	190.7	0.7	191.5	0.4	192.3	0.4	193.3	0.5	194.3	0.5	194.7	0.2
1993	196.4	0.9	198.0	0.8	198.6	0.3	199.4	0.4	200.5	0.6	201.1	0.3	202.2	0.5	202.9	0.3	203.3	0.2	204.4	0.5	204.9	0.2	205.2	0.1
1994	206.4	0.6	207.7	0.6	208.3	0.3	209.2	0.4	209.7	0.2	210.4	0.3	211.5	0.5	212.2	0.3	212.8	0.3	214.0	0.6	214.7	0.3	215.3	0.3
1995	216.6	0.6	217.9	0.6	218.4	0.2	218.9	0.2	219.3	0.2	219.8	0.2	220.8	0.5	221.6	0.4	222.1	0.2	222.9	0.4	223.5	0.3	223.8	0.1
1996	225.2	0.6	226.2	0.4	226.6	0.2	227.0	0.2	227.4	0.2	227.8	0.2	228.7	0.4	229.2	0.2	229.4	0.1	230.1	0.3	230.5	0.2	230.6	0.0
1997	231.8	0.5	232.7	0.4	233.4	0.3	233.8	0.2	234.2	0.2	234.4	0.1	234.8	0.2	235.2	0.2	235.4	0.1	235.8	0.2	236.4	0.3	237.1	0.3

Source: U.S. Department of Labor, Bureau of Labor Statistics, Division of Consumer Prices and Price Indexes.

U.S. City Average
Consumer Price Index - Urban Wage Earners
Base 1982-1984 = 100
Medical Care

For 1935-1997. Columns headed % show percentile change in the index from the previous period for which an index is available.

Year	Jan Index	%	Feb Index	%	Mar Index	%	Apr Index	%	May Index	%	Jun Index	%	Jul Index	%	Aug Index	%	Sep Index	%	Oct Index	%	Nov Index	%	Dec Index	%
1935	-	-	-	-	10.2	-	-	-	-	-	-	-	10.2	0.0	-	-	-	-	10.2	0.0	-	-	-	-
1936	10.2	0.0	-	-	-	-	10.2	0.0	-	-	-	-	10.2	0.0	-	-	10.3	1.0	-	-	-	-	10.3	0.0
1937	-	-	-	-	10.4	1.0	-	-	-	-	10.4	0.0	-	-	-	-	10.4	0.0	-	-	-	-	10.4	0.0
1938	-	-	-	-	10.4	0.0	-	-	-	-	10.4	0.0	-	-	-	-	10.4	0.0	-	-	-	-	10.4	0.0
1939	-	-	-	-	10.4	0.0	-	-	-	-	10.4	0.0	-	-	-	-	10.4	0.0	-	-	-	-	10.4	0.0
1940	-	-	-	-	10.4	0.0	-	-	-	-	10.4	0.0			-	-	10.4	0.0					10.4	0.0
1941	-	-	-	-	10.4	0.0	-	-	-	-	10.4	0.0	-	-	-	-	10.5	1.0	-	-	-	-	10.6	1.0
1942	-	-	-	-	10.6	0.0	-	-	-	-	10.8	1.9	-	-	-	-	10.9	0.9	-	-	-	-	11.0	0.9
1943	-	-	-	-	11.2	1.8	-	-	-	-	11.3	0.9	-	-	-	-	11.4	0.9	-	-	-	-	11.5	0.9
1944	-	-	-	-	11.5	0.0	-	-	-	-	11.6	0.9	-	-	-	-	11.7	0.9	-	-	-	-	11.8	0.9
1945	-	-	-	-	11.8	0.0	-	-	-	-	11.9	0.8	-	-	-	-	11.9	0.0	-	-	-	-	12.1	1.7
1946	-	-	-	-	12.3	1.7	-	-	-	-	12.5	1.6	-	-	-	-	12.8	2.4	-	-	-	-	13.1	2.3
1947	13.3	1.5	13.3	0.0	13.4	0.8	13.5	0.7	13.5	0.0	13.6	0.7	13.6	0.0	13.6	0.0	13.8	1.5	13.8	0.0	13.9	0.7	13.9	0.0
1948	14.1	1.4	14.1	0.0	14.2	0.7	14.4	1.4	14.4	0.0	14.4	0.0	14.6	1.4	14.6	0.0	14.6	0.0	14.7	0.7	14.7	0.0	14.7	0.0
1949	14.8	0.7	14.8	0.0	14.9	0.7	14.9	0.0	14.9	0.0	14.9	0.0	14.9	0.0	14.9	0.0	15.0	0.7	14.9	-0.7	14.9	0.0	15.0	0.7
1950	15.1	0.7	15.1	0.0	15.1	0.0	15.1	0.0	15.1	0.0	15.1	0.0	15.1	0.0	15.2	0.7	15.3	0.7	15.3	0.0	15.4	0.7	15.5	0.6
1951	15.5	0.0	15.6	0.6	15.8	1.3	15.8	0.0	15.9	0.6	15.9	0.0	15.9	0.0	15.9	0.0	16.0	0.6	16.1	0.6	16.2	0.6	16.4	1.2
1952	16.4	0.0	16.4	0.0	16.6	1.2	16.6	0.0	16.6	0.0	16.9	1.8	16.9	0.0	16.9	0.0	17.0	0.6	17.0	0.0	17.0	0.0	17.1	0.6
1953	17.1	0.0	17.1	0.0	17.1	0.0	17.2	0.6	17.3	0.6	17.4	0.6	17.4	0.0	17.5	0.6	17.6	0.6	17.6	0.0	17.7	0.6	17.7	0.0
1954	17.7	0.0	17.8	0.6	17.8	0.0	17.9	0.6	17.9	0.0	17.9	0.0	17.9	0.0	18.0	0.6	18.0	0.0	18.0	0.0	18.1	0.6	18.1	0.0
1955	18.1	0.0	18.2	0.6	18.2	0.0	18.2	0.0	18.3	0.5	18.3	0.0	18.3	0.0	18.3	0.0	18.4	0.5	18.5	0.5	18.6	0.5	18.7	0.5
1956	18.7	0.0	18.8	0.5	18.8	0.0	18.9	0.5	18.9	0.0	18.9	0.0	19.0	0.5	19.1	0.5	19.2	0.5	19.2	0.0	19.3	0.5	19.3	0.0
1957	19.4	0.5	19.4	0.0	19.6	1.0	19.6	0.0	19.7	0.5	19.8	0.5	19.8	0.0	19.9	0.5	19.9	0.0	20.0	0.5	20.1	0.5	20.2	0.5
1958	20.3	0.5	20.3	0.0	20.4	0.5	20.5	0.5	20.6	0.5	20.7	0.5	20.8	0.5	20.8	0.0	21.0	1.0	21.1	0.5	21.1	0.0	21.1	0.0
1959	21.2	0.5	21.3	0.5	21.4	0.5	21.4	0.0	21.5	0.5	21.6	0.5	21.6	0.0	21.7	0.5	21.8	0.5	21.9	0.5	21.9	0.0	21.9	0.0
1960	22.0	0.5	22.2	0.9	22.2	0.0	22.3	0.5	22.3	0.0	22.4	0.4	22.4	0.0	22.4	0.0	22.5	0.4	22.6	0.4	22.6	0.0	22.6	0.0
1961	22.7	0.4	22.8	0.4	22.9	0.4	22.9	0.0	23.0	0.4	23.0	0.0	23.1	0.4	23.1	0.0	23.2	0.4	23.3	0.4	23.3	0.0	23.3	0.0
1962	23.3	0.0	23.4	0.4	23.5	0.4	23.6	0.4	23.6	0.0	23.7	0.4	23.7	0.0	23.7	0.0	23.8	0.4	23.8	0.0	23.8	0.0	23.9	0.4
1963	24.0	0.4	24.0	0.0	24.0	0.0	24.1	0.4	24.2	0.4	24.3	0.4	24.3	0.0	24.3	0.0	24.3	0.0	24.4	0.4	24.4	0.0	24.4	0.0
1964	24.5	0.4	24.5	0.0	24.6	0.4	24.7	0.4	24.7	0.0	24.7	0.0	24.7	0.0	24.8	0.4	24.8	0.0	24.8	0.0	24.9	0.4	24.9	0.0
1965	25.0	0.4	25.1	0.4	25.1	0.0	25.2	0.4	25.2	0.0	25.3	0.4	25.4	0.4	25.4	0.0	25.4	0.0	25.5	0.4	25.6	0.4	25.6	0.0
1966	25.7	0.4	25.8	0.4	26.0	0.8	26.0	0.0	26.2	0.8	26.3	0.4	26.4	0.4	26.6	0.8	26.8	0.8	27.0	0.7	27.2	0.7	27.3	0.4
1967	27.5	0.7	27.7	0.7	27.9	0.7	28.0	0.4	28.1	0.4	28.2	0.4	28.3	0.4	28.5	0.7	28.7	0.7	28.8	0.3	28.9	0.3	29.1	0.7
1968	29.2	0.3	29.4	0.7	29.6	0.7	29.7	0.3	29.8	0.3	29.9	0.3	30.0	0.3	30.1	0.3	30.3	0.7	30.5	0.7	30.7	0.7	30.9	0.7
1969	31.1	0.6	31.3	0.6	31.6	1.0	31.8	0.6	32.0	0.6	32.1	0.3	32.3	0.6	32.5	0.6	32.6	0.3	32.5	-0.3	32.6	0.3	32.8	0.6
1970	32.9	0.3	33.1	0.6	33.5	1.2	33.7	0.6	33.9	0.6	34.1	0.6	34.3	0.6	34.5	0.6	34.7	0.6	34.8	0.3	34.9	0.3	35.2	0.9
1971	35.4	0.6	35.6	0.6	35.9	0.8	36.1	0.6	36.3	0.6	36.4	0.3	36.6	0.5	36.8	0.5	36.9	0.3	36.7	-0.5	36.7	0.0	36.8	0.3
1972	36.9	0.3	37.1	0.5	37.2	0.3	37.3	0.3	37.4	0.3	37.5	0.3	37.6	0.3	37.6	0.0	37.7	0.3	37.9	0.5	38.0	0.3	38.0	0.0
1973	38.2	0.5	38.3	0.3	38.4	0.3	38.6	0.5	38.7	0.3	38.8	0.3	38.9	0.3	39.0	0.3	39.2	0.5	39.8	1.5	39.9	0.3	40.0	0.3
1974	40.3	0.7	40.6	0.7	41.0	1.0	41.2	0.5	41.7	1.2	42.3	1.4	42.9	1.4	43.5	1.4	43.9	0.9	44.2	0.7	44.6	0.9	45.0	0.9
1975	45.6	1.3	46.1	1.1	46.6	1.1	46.9	0.6	47.2	0.6	47.6	0.8	48.1	1.1	48.4	0.6	48.7	0.6	49.1	0.8	49.1	0.0	49.5	0.8
1976	50.0	1.0	50.6	1.2	51.1	1.0	51.4	0.6	51.7	0.6	52.0	0.6	52.5	1.0	52.9	0.8	53.2	0.6	53.5	0.6	54.2	1.3	54.4	0.4
1977	54.9	0.9	55.4	0.9	55.9	0.9	56.4	0.9	56.8	0.7	57.1	0.5	57.6	0.9	58.0	0.7	58.4	0.7	58.7	0.5	58.9	0.3	59.2	0.5
1978	59.8	1.0	60.4	1.0	60.7	0.5	61.0	0.5	61.4	0.7	61.7	0.5	62.1	0.6	62.6	0.8	63.1	0.8	63.7	1.0	64.2	0.8	64.5	0.5
1979	65.2	1.1	65.7	0.8	66.2	0.8	66.6	0.6	66.9	0.5	67.4	0.7	68.1	1.0	68.7	0.9	69.3	0.9	70.0	1.0	70.5	0.7	71.3	1.1

[Continued]

U.S. City Average
Consumer Price Index - Urban Wage Earners
Base 1982-1984 = 100
Medical Care
[Continued]

For 1935-1997. Columns headed % show percentile change in the index from the previous period for which an index is available.

Year	Jan Index	%	Feb Index	%	Mar Index	%	Apr Index	%	May Index	%	Jun Index	%	Jul Index	%	Aug Index	%	Sep Index	%	Oct Index	%	Nov Index	%	Dec Index	%
1980	72.2	1.3	73.2	1.4	73.9	1.0	74.5	0.8	75.0	0.7	75.3	0.4	75.8	0.7	76.4	0.8	77.1	0.9	77.7	0.8	78.2	0.6	78.6	0.5
1981	79.7	1.4	80.5	1.0	81.2	0.9	81.8	0.7	82.3	0.6	82.9	0.7	83.6	0.8	84.5	1.1	85.2	0.8	86.1	1.1	86.9	0.9	87.5	0.7
1982	88.3	0.9	89.1	0.9	89.9	0.9	90.6	0.8	91.2	0.7	91.9	0.8	92.9	1.1	93.8	1.0	94.5	0.7	95.3	0.8	96.2	0.9	96.8	0.6
1983	97.7	0.9	98.8	1.1	99.1	0.3	99.4	0.3	99.7	0.3	100.0	0.3	100.7	0.7	101.3	0.6	101.7	0.4	102.2	0.5	102.7	0.5	103.1	0.4
1984	104.0	0.9	105.1	1.1	105.5	0.4	105.8	0.3	106.2	0.4	106.5	0.3	107.1	0.6	107.6	0.5	107.9	0.3	108.6	0.6	109.2	0.6	109.5	0.3
1985	110.2	0.6	111.0	0.7	111.7	0.6	112.1	0.4	112.6	0.4	113.2	0.5	113.8	0.5	114.5	0.6	115.0	0.4	115.6	0.5	116.3	0.6	116.8	0.4
1986	117.8	0.9	118.9	0.9	119.9	0.8	120.5	0.5	121.0	0.4	121.6	0.5	122.4	0.7	123.1	0.6	123.7	0.5	124.5	0.6	125.0	0.4	125.7	0.6
1987	126.5	0.6	127.3	0.6	128.1	0.6	128.8	0.5	129.3	0.4	130.0	0.5	130.8	0.6	131.4	0.5	132.0	0.5	132.6	0.5	133.0	0.3	133.4	0.3
1988	134.6	0.9	135.8	0.9	136.5	0.5	137.1	0.4	137.8	0.5	138.5	0.5	139.6	0.8	140.3	0.5	140.8	0.4	141.7	0.6	142.2	0.4	142.8	0.4
1989	144.2	1.0	145.6	1.0	146.5	0.6	147.2	0.5	147.9	0.5	148.8	0.6	150.1	0.9	151.1	0.7	152.1	0.7	153.0	0.6	154.2	0.8	154.7	0.3
1990	156.1	0.9	157.6	1.0	158.8	0.8	159.8	0.6	160.8	0.6	161.8	0.6	163.3	0.9	164.7	0.9	165.5	0.5	166.8	0.8	168.1	0.8	168.8	0.4
1991	170.5	1.0	172.1	0.9	173.2	0.6	173.9	0.4	174.6	0.4	175.6	0.6	176.9	0.7	178.3	0.8	179.2	0.5	180.2	0.6	181.2	0.6	182.0	0.4
1992	183.7	0.9	185.7	1.1	186.8	0.6	187.6	0.4	188.2	0.3	188.9	0.4	190.2	0.7	191.2	0.5	191.9	0.4	193.0	0.6	193.8	0.4	194.3	0.3
1993	196.0	0.9	197.6	0.8	198.2	0.3	199.0	0.4	200.1	0.6	200.7	0.3	201.7	0.5	202.4	0.3	202.8	0.2	203.8	0.5	204.2	0.2	204.5	0.1
1994	205.8	0.6	207.0	0.6	207.7	0.3	208.6	0.4	209.1	0.2	209.7	0.3	210.8	0.5	211.5	0.3	212.0	0.2	213.4	0.7	214.0	0.3	214.6	0.3
1995	215.9	0.6	217.3	0.6	217.7	0.2	218.2	0.2	218.7	0.2	219.2	0.2	220.2	0.5	221.1	0.4	221.5	0.2	222.3	0.4	222.8	0.2	223.1	0.1
1996	224.5	0.6	225.6	0.5	226.0	0.2	226.4	0.2	226.8	0.2	227.3	0.2	228.2	0.4	228.5	0.1	228.8	0.1	229.4	0.3	229.9	0.2	230.1	0.1
1997	231.1	0.4	232.1	0.4	232.8	0.3	233.2	0.2	233.6	0.2	233.8	0.1	234.2	0.2	234.6	0.2	234.7	0.0	235.2	0.2	235.8	0.3	236.5	0.3

Source: U.S. Department of Labor, Bureau of Labor Statistics, Division of Consumer Prices and Price Indexes.

U.S. City Average
Consumer Price Index - All Urban Consumers
Base 1982-1984 = 100
Entertainment

For 1967-1997. Columns headed % show percentile change in the index from the previous period for which an index is available.

Year	Jan Index	%	Feb Index	%	Mar Index	%	Apr Index	%	May Index	%	Jun Index	%	Jul Index	%	Aug Index	%	Sep Index	%	Oct Index	%	Nov Index	%	Dec Index	%
1967	39.9	-	40.0	0.3	40.1	0.2	40.4	0.7	40.5	0.2	40.6	0.2	40.7	0.2	40.7	0.0	41.0	0.7	41.3	0.7	41.6	0.7	41.6	0.0
1968	41.9	0.7	42.1	0.5	42.3	0.5	42.7	0.9	42.8	0.2	43.0	0.5	43.1	0.2	43.3	0.5	43.5	0.5	43.7	0.5	43.9	0.5	44.0	0.2
1969	44.2	0.5	44.2	0.0	44.3	0.2	44.7	0.9	45.0	0.7	45.1	0.2	45.3	0.4	45.5	0.4	45.7	0.4	45.8	0.2	46.0	0.4	46.2	0.4
1970	46.4	0.4	46.5	0.2	46.7	0.4	46.9	0.4	47.1	0.4	47.3	0.4	47.6	0.6	47.9	0.6	48.1	0.4	48.4	0.6	48.6	0.4	48.8	0.4
1971	49.1	0.6	49.2	0.2	49.3	0.2	49.7	0.8	50.0	0.6	50.2	0.4	50.4	0.4	50.4	0.0	50.5	0.2	50.5	0.0	50.6	0.2	50.6	0.0
1972	50.8	0.4	50.9	0.2	51.0	0.2	51.3	0.6	51.4	0.2	51.6	0.4	51.7	0.2	51.7	0.0	51.8	0.2	51.9	0.2	51.9	0.0	51.9	0.0
1973	52.0	0.2	52.1	0.2	52.2	0.2	52.6	0.8	52.8	0.4	53.0	0.4	53.2	0.4	53.2	0.0	53.2	0.0	53.4	0.4	53.6	0.4	53.7	0.2
1974	54.1	0.7	54.4	0.6	54.7	0.6	55.2	0.9	56.1	1.6	57.0	1.6	57.5	0.9	57.8	0.5	58.5	1.2	58.7	0.3	59.2	0.9	59.7	0.8
1975	60.3	1.0	60.8	0.8	60.9	0.2	61.7	1.3	61.8	0.2	62.0	0.3	62.2	0.3	62.3	0.2	62.7	0.6	62.7	0.0	62.9	0.3	63.2	0.5
1976	63.6	0.6	63.7	0.2	64.0	0.5	64.3	0.5	64.8	0.8	65.1	0.5	65.3	0.3	65.4	0.2	65.7	0.5	66.0	0.5	66.3	0.5	66.5	0.3
1977	66.8	0.5	67.1	0.4	67.3	0.3	67.4	0.1	67.8	0.6	68.3	0.7	68.4	0.1	68.6	0.3	69.1	0.7	69.3	0.3	69.4	0.1	69.6	0.3
1978	70.0	0.6	70.4	0.6	70.9	0.7	71.5	0.8	71.7	0.3	71.7	0.0	72.1	0.6	72.2	0.1	72.6	0.6	73.0	0.6	73.1	0.1	73.6	0.7
1979	74.2	0.8	74.6	0.5	75.2	0.8	75.9	0.9	76.5	0.8	76.6	0.1	77.0	0.5	77.4	0.5	77.8	0.5	78.2	0.5	78.5	0.4	78.7	0.3
1980	79.5	1.0	80.5	1.3	81.7	1.5	82.4	0.9	83.0	0.7	83.6	0.7	84.1	0.6	84.7	0.7	85.4	0.8	85.9	0.6	86.0	0.1	86.3	0.3
1981	87.3	1.2	88.2	1.0	88.8	0.7	89.2	0.5	89.7	0.6	89.9	0.2	90.0	0.1	90.5	0.6	91.2	0.8	91.8	0.7	92.3	0.5	92.5	0.2
1982	93.3	0.9	94.1	0.9	94.8	0.7	95.2	0.4	95.4	0.2	95.9	0.5	96.3	0.4	96.6	0.3	97.0	0.4	97.8	0.8	97.7	-0.1	97.7	0.0
1983	98.3	0.6	99.0	0.7	99.6	0.6	99.6	0.0	99.7	0.1	99.9	0.2	100.1	0.2	100.4	0.3	100.8	0.4	101.4	0.6	101.6	0.2	101.6	0.0
1984	101.7	0.1	102.4	0.7	102.5	0.1	103.3	0.8	103.2	-0.1	103.6	0.4	103.9	0.3	104.4	0.5	104.7	0.3	105.2	0.5	105.4	0.2	105.9	0.5
1985	106.3	0.4	106.4	0.1	106.7	0.3	107.2	0.5	107.3	0.1	107.8	0.5	108.2	0.4	108.2	0.0	108.6	0.4	109.3	0.6	109.5	0.2	109.2	-0.3
1986	110.2	0.9	110.7	0.5	110.7	0.0	110.9	0.2	111.1	0.2	111.5	0.4	111.7	0.2	111.8	0.1	112.1	0.3	112.6	0.4	112.9	0.3	112.9	0.0
1987	113.3	0.4	113.5	0.2	113.9	0.4	114.5	0.5	114.8	0.3	114.9	0.1	115.4	0.4	115.6	0.2	116.1	0.4	116.9	0.7	117.3	0.3	117.4	0.1
1988	118.1	0.6	118.3	0.2	119.0	0.6	119.6	0.5	119.7	0.1	120.1	0.3	120.5	0.3	120.7	0.2	121.3	0.5	121.8	0.4	122.2	0.3	122.8	0.5
1989	123.8	0.8	124.3	0.4	124.7	0.3	125.4	0.6	125.5	0.1	126.2	0.6	126.9	0.6	127.3	0.3	127.8	0.4	128.4	0.5	128.6	0.2	129.1	0.4
1990	129.9	0.6	130.4	0.4	130.9	0.4	131.4	0.4	131.7	0.2	131.9	0.2	132.7	0.6	133.0	0.2	134.1	0.8	134.3	0.1	134.4	0.1	134.6	0.1
1991	135.5	0.7	136.2	0.5	136.7	0.4	137.7	0.7	137.8	0.1	138.1	0.2	138.6	0.4	139.2	0.4	140.2	0.7	140.5	0.2	140.4	-0.1	139.9	-0.4
1992	140.1	0.1	140.7	0.4	141.2	0.4	142.0	0.6	142.0	0.0	142.0	0.0	142.4	0.3	142.6	0.1	143.2	0.4	143.5	0.2	143.7	0.1	143.8	0.1
1993	144.3	0.3	144.5	0.1	144.8	0.2	145.3	0.3	145.0	-0.2	145.5	0.3	145.3	-0.1	145.8	0.3	146.6	0.5	147.3	0.5	147.7	0.3	147.8	0.1
1994	148.5	0.5	149.1	0.4	149.6	0.3	149.7	0.1	149.9	0.1	149.8	-0.1	150.2	0.3	150.2	0.0	150.7	0.3	151.0	0.2	151.6	0.4	151.2	-0.3
1995	152.1	0.6	152.5	0.3	152.6	0.1	153.3	0.5	153.6	0.2	153.2	-0.3	153.6	0.3	154.1	0.3	154.9	0.5	155.2	0.2	156.0	0.5	156.2	0.1
1996	157.0	0.5	158.3	0.8	158.4	0.1	158.6	0.1	158.8	0.1	159.0	0.1	159.0	0.0	159.2	0.1	159.8	0.4	160.1	0.2	160.7	0.4	160.8	0.1
1997	161.3	0.3	161.8	0.3	162.1	0.2	162.2	0.1	162.2	0.0	162.7	0.3	162.6	-0.1	163.0	0.2	163.0	0.0	163.1	0.1	162.9	-0.1	163.1	0.1

Source: U.S. Department of Labor, Bureau of Labor Statistics, Division of Consumer Prices and Price Indexes.

U.S. City Average

Consumer Price Index - Urban Wage Earners
Base 1982-1984 = 100
Entertainment

For 1967-1997. Columns headed % show percentile change in the index from the previous period for which an index is available.

Year	Jan Index	%	Feb Index	%	Mar Index	%	Apr Index	%	May Index	%	Jun Index	%	Jul Index	%	Aug Index	%	Sep Index	%	Oct Index	%	Nov Index	%	Dec Index	%
1967	40.5	-	40.6	0.2	40.7	0.2	41.0	0.7	41.1	0.2	41.2	0.2	41.3	0.2	41.3	0.0	41.6	0.7	41.9	0.7	42.2	0.7	42.3	0.2
1968	42.6	0.7	42.7	0.2	42.9	0.5	43.3	0.9	43.4	0.2	43.6	0.5	43.7	0.2	44.0	0.7	44.1	0.2	44.4	0.7	44.6	0.5	44.7	0.2
1969	44.8	0.2	44.8	0.0	45.0	0.4	45.4	0.9	45.7	0.7	45.8	0.2	46.0	0.4	46.2	0.4	46.4	0.4	46.5	0.2	46.7	0.4	46.9	0.4
1970	47.1	0.4	47.2	0.2	47.4	0.4	47.6	0.4	47.8	0.4	48.1	0.6	48.3	0.4	48.6	0.6	48.8	0.4	49.1	0.6	49.4	0.6	49.5	0.2
1971	49.8	0.6	49.9	0.2	50.0	0.2	50.5	1.0	50.7	0.4	51.0	0.6	51.1	0.2	51.2	0.2	51.3	0.2	51.3	0.0	51.4	0.2	51.4	0.0
1972	51.6	0.4	51.7	0.2	51.7	0.0	52.1	0.8	52.2	0.2	52.4	0.4	52.5	0.2	52.4	-0.2	52.6	0.4	52.7	0.2	52.7	0.0	52.7	0.0
1973	52.8	0.2	52.9	0.2	53.0	0.2	53.4	0.8	53.6	0.4	53.8	0.4	54.0	0.4	54.0	0.0	54.1	0.2	54.2	0.2	54.4	0.4	54.5	0.2
1974	54.9	0.7	55.2	0.5	55.5	0.5	56.0	0.9	56.9	1.6	57.8	1.6	58.4	1.0	58.7	0.5	59.4	1.2	59.6	0.3	60.1	0.8	60.6	0.8
1975	61.2	1.0	61.7	0.8	61.8	0.2	62.6	1.3	62.8	0.3	63.0	0.3	63.1	0.2	63.3	0.3	63.6	0.5	63.7	0.2	63.9	0.3	64.2	0.5
1976	64.5	0.5	64.7	0.3	65.0	0.5	65.2	0.3	65.7	0.8	66.1	0.6	66.3	0.3	66.4	0.2	66.7	0.5	67.0	0.4	67.3	0.4	67.5	0.3
1977	67.8	0.4	68.1	0.4	68.3	0.3	68.4	0.1	68.8	0.6	69.3	0.7	69.4	0.1	69.7	0.4	70.1	0.6	70.4	0.4	70.4	0.0	70.7	0.4
1978	71.0	0.4	71.8	1.1	71.9	0.1	72.4	0.7	72.6	0.3	72.5	-0.1	72.8	0.4	72.9	0.1	73.3	0.5	73.7	0.5	73.9	0.3	74.8	1.2
1979	75.2	0.5	75.4	0.3	76.0	0.8	76.7	0.9	77.3	0.8	77.5	0.3	77.9	0.5	78.1	0.3	78.6	0.6	79.1	0.6	79.3	0.3	79.5	0.3
1980	80.1	0.8	81.1	1.2	82.4	1.6	83.2	1.0	83.6	0.5	84.3	0.8	84.5	0.2	85.0	0.6	86.0	1.2	86.4	0.5	86.7	0.3	86.8	0.1
1981	87.7	1.0	88.8	1.3	89.3	0.6	89.7	0.4	90.0	0.3	90.2	0.2	90.4	0.2	90.9	0.6	91.5	0.7	92.3	0.9	92.7	0.4	92.7	0.0
1982	93.4	0.8	94.3	1.0	94.8	0.5	95.2	0.4	95.5	0.3	96.0	0.5	96.5	0.5	96.7	0.2	97.0	0.3	97.7	0.7	97.6	-0.1	97.7	0.1
1983	98.2	0.5	99.0	0.8	99.5	0.5	99.6	0.1	99.7	0.1	100.0	0.3	100.2	0.2	100.5	0.3	100.9	0.4	101.4	0.5	101.5	0.1	101.6	0.1
1984	101.7	0.1	102.4	0.7	102.5	0.1	103.2	0.7	103.1	-0.1	103.6	0.5	103.9	0.3	104.3	0.4	104.7	0.4	105.0	0.3	105.3	0.3	105.7	0.4
1985	106.0	0.3	106.2	0.2	106.3	0.1	106.9	0.6	107.0	0.1	107.5	0.5	107.8	0.3	107.8	0.0	108.1	0.3	108.7	0.6	109.0	0.3	108.7	-0.3
1986	109.7	0.9	110.1	0.4	110.1	0.0	110.3	0.2	110.5	0.2	110.9	0.4	111.2	0.3	111.2	0.0	111.6	0.4	112.0	0.4	112.4	0.4	112.5	0.1
1987	112.8	0.3	113.0	0.2	113.4	0.4	114.0	0.5	114.4	0.4	114.5	0.1	115.0	0.4	115.1	0.1	115.6	0.4	116.3	0.6	116.7	0.3	116.9	0.2
1988	117.4	0.4	117.6	0.2	118.2	0.5	118.9	0.6	119.0	0.1	119.4	0.3	119.8	0.3	120.1	0.3	120.6	0.4	121.2	0.5	121.7	0.4	122.2	0.4
1989	123.1	0.7	123.6	0.4	124.1	0.4	124.8	0.6	124.9	0.1	125.5	0.5	126.1	0.5	126.5	0.3	127.0	0.4	127.7	0.6	127.9	0.2	128.4	0.4
1990	129.1	0.5	129.5	0.3	130.0	0.4	130.6	0.5	130.8	0.2	131.0	0.2	131.7	0.5	132.1	0.3	132.9	0.6	133.1	0.2	133.2	0.1	133.3	0.1
1991	134.2	0.7	134.9	0.5	135.4	0.4	136.4	0.7	136.4	0.0	136.7	0.2	137.1	0.3	137.6	0.4	138.7	0.8	138.8	0.1	138.7	-0.1	138.4	-0.2
1992	138.6	0.1	139.1	0.4	139.7	0.4	140.5	0.6	140.5	0.0	140.5	0.0	141.0	0.4	141.2	0.1	141.6	0.3	141.9	0.2	142.2	0.2	142.2	0.0
1993	142.7	0.4	142.8	0.1	143.1	0.2	143.5	0.3	143.3	-0.1	143.8	0.3	143.7	-0.1	144.1	0.3	144.8	0.5	145.5	0.5	145.8	0.2	146.1	0.2
1994	146.7	0.4	147.1	0.3	147.7	0.4	147.8	0.1	148.1	0.2	148.0	-0.1	148.4	0.3	148.3	-0.1	148.6	0.2	149.0	0.3	149.6	0.4	149.2	-0.3
1995	150.1	0.6	150.4	0.2	150.6	0.1	151.3	0.5	151.5	0.1	151.2	-0.2	151.5	0.2	152.0	0.3	152.7	0.5	152.9	0.1	153.6	0.5	153.8	0.1
1996	154.7	0.6	156.0	0.8	156.1	0.1	156.3	0.1	156.5	0.1	156.7	0.1	156.7	0.0	157.0	0.2	157.4	0.3	157.8	0.3	158.3	0.3	158.4	0.1
1997	158.8	0.3	159.2	0.3	159.6	0.3	159.7	0.1	159.7	0.0	160.1	0.3	160.1	0.0	160.6	0.3	160.5	-0.1	160.6	0.1	160.3	-0.2	160.4	0.1

Source: U.S. Department of Labor, Bureau of Labor Statistics, Division of Consumer Prices and Price Indexes.

U.S. City Average
Consumer Price Index - All Urban Consumers
Base 1982-1984 = 100
Other Goods and Services

For 1967-1997. Columns headed % show percentile change in the index from the previous period for which an index is available.

Year	Jan Index	%	Feb Index	%	Mar Index	%	Apr Index	%	May Index	%	Jun Index	%	Jul Index	%	Aug Index	%	Sep Index	%	Oct Index	%	Nov Index	%	Dec Index	%
1967	34.4	-	34.5	0.3	34.5	0.0	34.6	0.3	34.7	0.3	34.8	0.3	35.0	0.6	35.3	0.9	35.5	0.6	35.6	0.3	35.8	0.6	35.9	0.3
1968	36.1	0.6	36.1	0.0	36.5	1.1	36.5	0.0	36.6	0.3	36.9	0.8	36.9	0.0	37.1	0.5	37.2	0.3	37.4	0.5	37.6	0.5	37.7	0.3
1969	37.8	0.3	37.8	0.0	38.0	0.5	38.1	0.3	38.2	0.3	38.5	0.8	38.8	0.8	39.0	0.5	39.3	0.8	39.4	0.3	39.7	0.8	39.8	0.3
1970	39.9	0.3	40.0	0.3	40.2	0.5	40.5	0.7	40.6	0.2	40.9	0.7	41.2	0.7	41.3	0.2	41.5	0.5	41.6	0.2	41.8	0.5	41.9	0.2
1971	42.2	0.7	42.2	0.0	42.3	0.2	42.4	0.2	42.5	0.2	42.6	0.2	42.9	0.7	43.1	0.5	43.5	0.9	43.6	0.2	43.6	0.0	43.7	0.2
1972	43.9	0.5	44.2	0.7	44.3	0.2	44.4	0.2	44.6	0.5	44.8	0.4	44.8	0.0	44.8	0.0	45.0	0.4	45.2	0.4	45.2	0.0	45.3	0.2
1973	45.4	0.2	45.5	0.2	45.8	0.7	46.0	0.4	46.2	0.4	46.4	0.4	46.5	0.2	46.6	0.2	46.9	0.6	47.1	0.4	47.4	0.6	47.5	0.2
1974	47.7	0.4	47.9	0.4	48.2	0.6	48.4	0.4	48.9	1.0	49.4	1.0	50.0	1.2	50.3	0.6	50.9	1.2	51.4	1.0	51.9	1.0	52.4	1.0
1975	52.7	0.6	53.1	0.8	53.3	0.4	53.5	0.4	53.6	0.2	53.7	0.2	53.9	0.4	54.0	0.2	54.4	0.7	54.7	0.6	54.9	0.4	55.3	0.7
1976	55.7	0.7	56.1	0.7	56.2	0.2	56.4	0.4	56.6	0.4	56.8	0.4	56.9	0.2	57.1	0.4	57.6	0.9	58.0	0.7	58.4	0.7	58.6	0.3
1977	59.0	0.7	59.2	0.3	59.3	0.2	59.5	0.3	59.7	0.3	60.0	0.5	60.2	0.3	60.4	0.3	61.1	1.2	61.7	1.0	62.1	0.6	62.3	0.3
1978	62.6	0.5	62.7	0.2	62.9	0.3	63.0	0.2	63.2	0.3	63.4	0.3	64.2	1.3	64.5	0.5	65.8	2.0	66.0	0.3	66.2	0.3	66.3	0.2
1979	66.8	0.8	67.3	0.7	67.6	0.4	67.7	0.1	68.0	0.4	68.2	0.3	68.4	0.3	69.1	1.0	70.7	2.3	70.9	0.3	71.1	0.3	71.5	0.6
1980	72.3	1.1	72.9	0.8	73.2	0.4	73.5	0.4	74.0	0.7	74.5	0.7	74.8	0.4	75.2	0.5	77.3	2.8	77.6	0.4	78.1	0.6	78.7	0.8
1981	79.3	0.8	79.7	0.5	80.2	0.6	80.6	0.5	81.4	1.0	81.8	0.5	82.2	0.5	82.6	0.5	85.2	3.1	86.0	0.9	86.2	0.2	86.5	0.3
1982	87.1	0.7	87.7	0.7	88.4	0.8	89.0	0.7	89.4	0.4	89.7	0.3	90.2	0.6	90.5	0.3	93.5	3.3	95.1	1.7	96.0	0.9	97.0	1.0
1983	98.1	1.1	98.7	0.6	98.8	0.1	99.3	0.5	99.4	0.1	99.7	0.3	100.8	1.1	101.3	0.5	103.2	1.9	104.0	0.8	104.5	0.5	104.7	0.2
1984	105.3	0.6	105.7	0.4	105.9	0.2	106.1	0.2	106.3	0.2	106.7	0.4	107.4	0.7	107.7	0.3	110.3	2.4	110.7	0.4	110.9	0.2	111.0	0.1
1985	111.9	0.8	112.3	0.4	112.6	0.3	112.8	0.2	113.0	0.2	113.2	0.2	113.9	0.6	114.3	0.4	116.8	2.2	117.4	0.5	117.5	0.1	118.0	0.4
1986	118.9	0.8	119.3	0.3	119.6	0.3	119.8	0.2	119.9	0.1	120.1	0.2	120.9	0.7	121.4	0.4	123.8	2.0	124.3	0.4	124.4	0.1	124.5	0.1
1987	125.5	0.8	126.1	0.5	126.3	0.2	126.6	0.2	126.9	0.2	127.2	0.2	128.0	0.6	128.5	0.4	131.1	2.0	131.6	0.4	131.8	0.2	132.1	0.2
1988	133.4	1.0	134.2	0.6	134.6	0.3	134.8	0.1	135.1	0.2	135.5	0.3	136.5	0.7	137.5	0.7	140.0	1.8	140.6	0.4	141.0	0.3	141.3	0.2
1989	143.4	1.5	144.1	0.5	144.4	0.2	144.7	0.2	145.4	0.5	146.3	0.6	147.3	0.7	148.7	1.0	151.2	1.7	151.8	0.4	151.9	0.1	152.9	0.7
1990	154.0	0.7	154.7	0.5	155.2	0.3	155.8	0.4	156.6	0.5	157.8	0.8	159.2	0.9	160.4	0.8	162.6	1.4	163.2	0.4	163.6	0.2	164.5	0.6
1991	166.5	1.2	167.4	0.5	167.9	0.3	168.8	0.5	169.1	0.2	170.0	0.5	170.8	0.5	172.2	0.8	175.8	2.1	176.2	0.2	176.9	0.4	177.6	0.4
1992	178.6	0.6	179.4	0.4	179.8	0.2	180.3	0.3	181.3	0.6	181.5	0.1	182.3	0.4	183.9	0.9	187.0	1.7	187.9	0.5	188.0	0.1	189.1	0.6
1993	191.0	1.0	191.5	0.3	192.0	0.3	192.4	0.2	193.2	0.4	193.1	-0.1	193.7	0.3	193.4	-0.2	193.1	-0.2	193.4	0.2	193.8	0.2	194.2	0.2
1994	195.1	0.5	195.2	0.1	195.5	0.2	196.4	0.5	197.1	0.4	197.6	0.3	198.0	0.2	199.4	0.7	201.4	1.0	201.9	0.2	202.3	0.2	202.4	0.0
1995	203.0	0.3	204.1	0.5	204.0	-0.0	204.3	0.1	204.9	0.3	205.3	0.2	205.7	0.2	207.7	1.0	210.2	1.2	210.7	0.2	211.2	0.2	211.1	-0.0
1996	212.0	0.4	212.6	0.3	213.0	0.2	213.3	0.1	214.1	0.4	214.0	-0.0	214.6	0.3	216.3	0.8	218.3	0.9	218.8	0.2	219.2	0.2	218.7	-0.2
1997	220.0	0.6	220.7	0.3	221.4	0.3	222.7	0.6	223.1	0.2	223.1	0.0	223.5	0.2	225.7	1.0	228.1	1.1	229.4	0.6	229.9	0.2	230.1	0.1

Source: U.S. Department of Labor, Bureau of Labor Statistics, Division of Consumer Prices and Price Indexes.

U.S. City Average
Consumer Price Index - Urban Wage Earners
Base 1982-1984 = 100
Other Goods and Services

For 1967-1997. Columns headed % show percentile change in the index from the previous period for which an index is available.

Year	Jan Index	%	Feb Index	%	Mar Index	%	Apr Index	%	May Index	%	Jun Index	%	Jul Index	%	Aug Index	%	Sep Index	%	Oct Index	%	Nov Index	%	Dec Index	%
1967	34.7	-	34.8	0.3	34.8	0.0	34.9	0.3	35.0	0.3	35.1	0.3	35.3	0.6	35.6	0.8	35.8	0.6	36.0	0.6	36.1	0.3	36.3	0.6
1968	36.4	0.3	36.4	0.0	36.8	1.1	36.8	0.0	36.9	0.3	37.2	0.8	37.3	0.3	37.4	0.3	37.6	0.5	37.8	0.5	37.9	0.3	38.1	0.5
1969	38.1	0.0	38.2	0.3	38.3	0.3	38.5	0.5	38.6	0.3	38.8	0.5	39.1	0.8	39.4	0.8	39.6	0.5	39.8	0.5	40.0	0.5	40.1	0.2
1970	40.3	0.5	40.4	0.2	40.5	0.2	40.8	0.7	41.0	0.5	41.3	0.7	41.5	0.5	41.7	0.5	41.8	0.2	42.0	0.5	42.2	0.5	42.3	0.2
1971	42.6	0.7	42.6	0.0	42.7	0.2	42.8	0.2	42.9	0.2	43.0	0.2	43.3	0.7	43.5	0.5	43.9	0.9	44.0	0.2	44.0	0.0	44.1	0.2
1972	44.3	0.5	44.6	0.7	44.7	0.2	44.8	0.2	45.0	0.4	45.2	0.4	45.2	0.0	45.2	0.0	45.5	0.7	45.6	0.2	45.6	0.0	45.7	0.2
1973	45.8	0.2	46.0	0.4	46.2	0.4	46.4	0.4	46.6	0.4	46.8	0.4	46.9	0.2	47.0	0.2	47.3	0.6	47.6	0.6	47.8	0.4	48.0	0.4
1974	48.1	0.2	48.4	0.6	48.6	0.4	48.9	0.6	49.3	0.8	49.9	1.2	50.4	1.0	50.8	0.8	51.4	1.2	51.9	1.0	52.4	1.0	52.8	0.8
1975	53.2	0.8	53.6	0.8	53.8	0.4	53.9	0.2	54.1	0.4	54.2	0.2	54.4	0.4	54.5	0.2	54.9	0.7	55.2	0.5	55.4	0.4	55.9	0.9
1976	56.2	0.5	56.6	0.7	56.7	0.2	57.0	0.5	57.1	0.2	57.3	0.4	57.4	0.2	57.7	0.5	58.2	0.9	58.5	0.5	58.9	0.7	59.1	0.3
1977	59.5	0.7	59.7	0.3	59.9	0.3	60.1	0.3	60.3	0.3	60.5	0.3	60.7	0.3	60.9	0.3	61.7	1.3	62.3	1.0	62.7	0.6	62.9	0.3
1978	63.1	0.3	63.4	0.5	63.5	0.2	63.7	0.3	63.9	0.3	64.2	0.5	65.0	1.2	65.2	0.3	66.2	1.5	66.4	0.3	66.6	0.3	66.6	0.0
1979	67.3	1.1	67.9	0.9	68.1	0.3	68.3	0.3	68.6	0.4	68.7	0.1	69.0	0.4	69.8	1.2	71.0	1.7	71.2	0.3	71.5	0.4	71.8	0.4
1980	72.9	1.5	73.5	0.8	73.7	0.3	74.0	0.4	74.5	0.7	75.0	0.7	75.3	0.4	75.7	0.5	77.5	2.4	77.8	0.4	78.2	0.5	78.9	0.9
1981	79.4	0.6	79.8	0.5	80.2	0.5	80.6	0.5	81.5	1.1	81.9	0.5	82.2	0.4	82.6	0.5	84.6	2.4	85.4	0.9	85.8	0.5	86.1	0.3
1982	86.7	0.7	87.4	0.8	88.2	0.9	88.8	0.7	89.3	0.6	89.5	0.2	90.0	0.6	90.5	0.6	93.0	2.8	94.7	1.8	95.8	1.2	96.9	1.1
1983	98.3	1.4	98.9	0.6	99.0	0.1	99.5	0.5	99.7	0.2	100.0	0.3	101.3	1.3	101.9	0.6	103.3	1.4	104.0	0.7	104.5	0.5	104.7	0.2
1984	105.4	0.7	105.8	0.4	106.0	0.2	106.3	0.3	106.4	0.1	106.9	0.5	107.7	0.7	108.0	0.3	110.0	1.9	110.3	0.3	110.6	0.3	110.6	0.0
1985	111.6	0.9	112.2	0.5	112.3	0.1	112.6	0.3	112.8	0.2	113.0	0.2	113.8	0.7	114.2	0.4	116.3	1.8	116.8	0.4	116.9	0.1	117.4	0.4
1986	118.5	0.9	118.9	0.3	119.2	0.3	119.4	0.2	119.6	0.2	119.7	0.1	120.7	0.8	121.2	0.4	122.9	1.4	123.4	0.4	123.5	0.1	123.6	0.1
1987	124.8	1.0	125.4	0.5	125.6	0.2	125.9	0.2	126.2	0.2	126.6	0.3	127.5	0.7	128.0	0.4	130.3	1.8	130.8	0.4	131.0	0.2	131.3	0.2
1988	132.7	1.1	133.6	0.7	134.0	0.3	134.2	0.1	134.5	0.2	135.0	0.4	136.3	1.0	137.2	0.7	139.3	1.5	139.9	0.4	140.3	0.3	140.6	0.2
1989	143.0	1.7	143.7	0.5	144.0	0.2	144.4	0.3	145.2	0.6	146.3	0.8	147.5	0.8	148.8	0.9	150.8	1.3	151.4	0.4	151.5	0.1	152.7	0.8
1990	153.9	0.8	154.6	0.5	155.1	0.3	155.7	0.4	156.3	0.4	157.8	1.0	159.4	1.0	160.5	0.7	162.4	1.2	162.8	0.2	163.4	0.4	164.4	0.6
1991	166.6	1.3	167.5	0.5	168.1	0.4	169.1	0.6	169.4	0.2	170.5	0.6	171.2	0.4	172.6	0.8	175.5	1.7	175.9	0.2	176.8	0.5	177.7	0.5
1992	178.6	0.5	179.4	0.4	179.7	0.2	180.3	0.3	181.6	0.7	181.8	0.1	182.7	0.5	184.2	0.8	186.7	1.4	187.7	0.5	187.7	0.0	189.0	0.7
1993	191.2	1.2	191.6	0.2	192.2	0.3	192.8	0.3	193.6	0.4	193.3	-0.2	193.8	0.3	192.7	-0.6	190.9	-0.9	191.1	0.1	191.6	0.3	192.0	0.2
1994	193.1	0.6	193.2	0.1	193.4	0.1	194.4	0.5	195.3	0.5	195.8	0.3	196.3	0.3	197.5	0.6	198.9	0.7	199.4	0.3	199.8	0.2	200.0	0.1
1995	200.5	0.3	201.5	0.5	201.4	-0.0	201.7	0.1	202.5	0.4	203.0	0.2	203.3	0.1	205.0	0.8	207.2	1.1	207.8	0.3	208.3	0.2	208.1	-0.1
1996	209.0	0.4	209.6	0.3	209.9	0.1	210.1	0.1	211.2	0.5	211.0	-0.1	211.6	0.3	213.0	0.7	214.7	0.8	215.3	0.3	215.8	0.2	215.2	-0.3
1997	216.7	0.7	217.4	0.3	218.0	0.3	219.8	0.8	220.2	0.2	219.9	-0.1	220.3	0.2	222.1	0.8	224.6	1.1	226.1	0.7	226.7	0.3	226.9	0.1

Source: U.S. Department of Labor, Bureau of Labor Statistics, Division of Consumer Prices and Price Indexes.

Anchorage, AK
Consumer Price Index - All Urban Consumers
Base 1982-1984 = 100
Annual Averages

For 1960-1997. Columns headed % show percentile change in the index from the previous period for which an index is available.

Year	All Items		Food & Beverage		Housing		Apparel & Upkeep		Trans-portation		Medical Care		Entertain-ment		Other Goods & Services	
	Index	%	Index	%	Index	%	Index	%	Index	%	Index	%	Index	%	Index	%
1960	-	-	-	-	-	-	-	-	-	-	-	-	-	-	-	-
1961	34.5	-	-	-	-	-	-	-	-	-	-	-	-	-	-	-
1962	34.7	0.6	-	-	-	-	-	-	-	-	-	-	-	-	-	-
1963	34.8	0.3	-	-	-	-	-	-	-	-	-	-	-	-	-	-
1964	35.0	0.6	-	-	-	-	-	-	-	-	-	-	-	-	-	-
1965	35.3	0.9	-	-	-	-	-	-	-	-	-	-	-	-	-	-
1966	36.3	2.8	-	-	-	-	-	-	-	-	-	-	-	-	-	-
1967	37.2	2.5	-	-	-	-	-	-	-	-	-	-	-	-	-	-
1968	38.1	2.4	-	-	-	-	-	-	-	-	-	-	-	-	-	-
1969	39.6	3.9	-	-	-	-	-	-	-	-	-	-	-	-	-	-
1970	41.1	3.8	-	-	-	-	-	-	-	-	-	-	-	-	-	-
1971	42.3	2.9	-	-	-	-	56.5	-	40.8	-	35.2	-	-	-	-	-
1972	43.4	2.6	-	-	-	-	58.3	3.2	40.9	0.2	35.8	1.7	-	-	-	-
1973	45.3	4.4	-	-	-	-	60.7	4.1	41.4	1.2	37.3	4.2	-	-	-	-
1974	50.2	10.8	-	-	-	-	64.7	6.6	44.9	8.5	41.5	11.3	-	-	-	-
1975	57.1	13.7	-	-	-	-	69.8	7.9	49.3	9.8	46.9	13.0	-	-	-	-
1976	61.5	7.7	64.2	-	62.6	-	74.1	6.2	54.9	11.4	52.6	12.2	64.4	-	63.8	-
1977	65.6	6.7	68.9	7.3	65.5	4.6	79.2	6.9	60.2	9.7	57.9	10.1	69.4	7.8	68.1	6.7
1978	70.2	7.0	75.9	10.2	69.7	6.4	79.7	0.6	64.5	7.1	63.4	9.5	72.6	4.6	71.7	5.3
1979	77.6	10.5	84.0	10.7	78.0	11.9	81.7	2.5	71.3	10.5	69.1	9.0	74.5	2.6	76.9	7.3
1980	85.5	10.2	89.7	6.8	85.9	10.1	89.7	9.8	82.2	15.3	78.8	14.0	79.0	6.0	83.1	8.1
1981	92.4	8.1	94.3	5.1	92.5	7.7	94.1	4.9	92.7	12.8	86.9	10.3	85.9	8.7	88.1	6.0
1982	97.4	5.4	97.2	3.1	98.2	6.2	96.6	2.7	96.8	4.4	94.8	9.1	94.7	10.2	93.2	5.8
1983	99.2	1.8	99.7	2.6	99.0	0.8	101.6	5.2	98.5	1.8	99.7	5.2	100.6	6.2	101.5	8.9
1984	103.3	4.1	103.2	3.5	102.7	3.7	101.7	0.1	104.6	6.2	105.5	5.8	104.6	4.0	105.3	3.7
1985	105.8	2.4	106.2	2.9	103.0	0.3	105.8	4.0	108.2	3.4	110.9	5.1	108.9	4.1	114.2	8.5
1986	107.8	1.9	110.8	4.3	102.6	-0.4	109.0	3.0	107.8	-0.4	127.8	15.2	112.4	3.2	123.2	7.9
1987	118.0	9.5	118.6	7.0	118.0	15.0	109.9	0.8	108.7	0.8	136.1	6.5	119.2	6.0	130.8	6.2
1988	123.7	4.8	124.8	5.2	125.1	6.0	107.4	-2.3	112.8	3.8	144.8	6.4	122.8	3.0	139.5	6.7
1989	130.6	5.6	132.1	5.8	131.8	5.4	114.0	6.1	116.5	3.3	155.8	7.6	129.5	5.5	151.9	8.9
1990	138.5	6.0	139.6	5.7	139.3	5.7	121.8	6.8	123.1	5.7	172.4	10.7	135.6	4.7	164.0	8.0
1991	144.8	4.5	144.3	3.4	145.7	4.6	124.5	2.2	127.9	3.9	186.6	8.2	140.8	3.8	177.2	8.0
1992	150.0	3.6	146.0	1.2	151.4	3.9	128.5	3.2	131.5	2.8	200.0	7.2	146.4	4.0	191.0	7.8
1993	154.5	3.0	149.0	2.1	155.5	2.7	129.3	0.6	137.7	4.7	209.1	4.6	149.8	2.3	200.1	4.8
1994	158.2	2.4	151.9	1.9	159.9	2.8	126.2	-2.4	141.8	3.0	217.6	4.1	154.0	2.8	204.9	2.4
1995	162.2	2.5	155.9	2.6	163.4	2.2	126.0	-0.2	145.9	2.9	226.8	4.2	158.8	3.1	213.5	4.2
1996	166.9	2.9	159.7	2.4	167.7	2.6	127.7	1.3	152.4	4.5	235.4	3.8	163.5	3.0	221.7	3.8
1997	144.8	-13.2	145.8	-8.7	129.4	-22.8	127.0	-0.5	147.0	-3.5	248.9	5.7	180.3	10.3	171.3	-22.7

Source: U.S. Department of Labor, Bureau of Labor Statistics, Division of Consumer Prices and Price Indexes. - indicates no data collected for period.

Anchorage, AK
Consumer Price Index - Urban Wage Earners
Base 1982-1984 = 100
Annual Averages

For 1960-1997. Columns headed % show percentile change in the index from the previous period for which an index is available.

Year	All Items		Food & Beverage		Housing		Apparel & Upkeep		Trans- portation		Medical Care		Entertain- ment		Other Goods & Services	
	Index	%	Index	%	Index	%	Index	%	Index	%	Index	%	Index	%	Index	%
1960	-	-	-	-	-	-	-	-	-	-	-	-	-	-	-	-
1961	35.4	-	-	-	-	-	-	-	-	-	-	-	-	-	-	-
1962	35.5	0.3	-	-	-	-	-	-	-	-	-	-	-	-	-	-
1963	35.7	0.6	-	-	-	-	-	-	-	-	-	-	-	-	-	-
1964	35.9	0.6	-	-	-	-	-	-	-	-	-	-	-	-	-	-
1965	36.2	0.8	-	-	-	-	-	-	-	-	-	-	-	-	-	-
1966	37.2	2.8	-	-	-	-	-	-	-	-	-	-	-	-	-	-
1967	38.2	2.7	-	-	-	-	-	-	-	-	-	-	-	-	-	-
1968	39.1	2.4	-	-	-	-	-	-	-	-	-	-	-	-	-	-
1969	40.7	4.1	-	-	-	-	-	-	-	-	-	-	-	-	-	-
1970	42.1	3.4	-	-	-	-	-	-	-	-	-	-	-	-	-	-
1971	43.4	3.1	-	-	-	-	57.1	-	40.4	-	36.2	-	-	-	-	-
1972	44.5	2.5	-	-	-	-	58.9	3.2	40.5	0.2	36.9	1.9	-	-	-	-
1973	46.4	4.3	-	-	-	-	61.4	4.2	41.0	1.2	38.4	4.1	-	-	-	-
1974	51.4	10.8	-	-	-	-	65.4	6.5	44.4	8.3	42.7	11.2	-	-	-	-
1975	58.5	13.8	-	-	-	-	70.5	7.8	48.8	9.9	48.3	13.1	-	-	-	-
1976	63.1	7.9	64.5	-	65.7	-	74.9	6.2	54.3	11.3	54.1	12.0	70.5	-	62.6	-
1977	67.2	6.5	69.3	7.4	68.8	4.7	80.0	6.8	59.6	9.8	59.7	10.4	76.0	7.8	66.9	6.9
1978	72.0	7.1	76.9	11.0	73.0	6.1	80.3	0.4	64.1	7.6	67.1	12.4	76.0	0.0	70.1	4.8
1979	79.0	9.7	86.1	12.0	80.5	10.3	81.6	1.6	71.2	11.1	72.8	8.5	77.0	1.3	75.0	7.0
1980	86.3	9.2	90.3	4.9	87.6	8.8	86.5	6.0	82.9	16.4	79.3	8.9	79.9	3.8	81.9	9.2
1981	92.9	7.6	94.2	4.3	93.9	7.2	92.6	7.1	93.4	12.7	86.8	9.5	86.2	7.9	86.4	5.5
1982	98.2	5.7	97.2	3.2	100.1	6.6	96.3	4.0	97.3	4.2	94.9	9.3	94.6	9.7	92.4	6.9
1983	98.9	0.7	99.7	2.6	98.2	-1.9	101.6	5.5	98.4	1.1	99.8	5.2	100.5	6.2	101.9	10.3
1984	102.9	4.0	103.2	3.5	101.6	3.5	102.1	0.5	104.3	6.0	105.3	5.5	105.0	4.5	105.7	3.7
1985	105.8	2.8	106.2	2.9	103.4	1.8	105.5	3.3	107.6	3.2	110.5	4.9	108.7	3.5	114.1	7.9
1986	107.7	1.8	110.9	4.4	103.1	-0.3	108.1	2.5	106.5	-1.0	125.3	13.4	112.5	3.5	123.2	8.0
1987	116.6	8.3	118.2	6.6	116.0	12.5	110.2	1.9	108.4	1.8	136.8	9.2	120.3	6.9	129.5	5.1
1988	121.8	4.5	124.3	5.2	122.5	5.6	106.3	-3.5	112.4	3.7	145.8	6.6	123.9	3.0	137.9	6.5
1989	128.6	5.6	131.7	6.0	129.0	5.3	112.5	5.8	116.1	3.3	157.0	7.7	130.3	5.2	150.7	9.3
1990	136.3	6.0	139.4	5.8	135.9	5.3	120.1	6.8	123.1	6.0	172.0	9.6	136.2	4.5	163.6	8.6
1991	142.1	4.3	144.0	3.3	141.6	4.2	122.1	1.7	127.8	3.8	186.2	8.3	141.3	3.7	177.5	8.5
1992	146.9	3.4	145.6	1.1	146.7	3.6	125.8	3.0	131.6	3.0	200.3	7.6	146.6	3.8	191.0	7.6
1993	151.1	2.9	148.6	2.1	150.6	2.7	126.2	0.3	137.4	4.4	209.0	4.3	149.5	2.0	200.4	4.9
1994	154.5	2.3	151.5	2.0	154.6	2.7	122.7	-2.8	141.6	3.1	217.9	4.3	153.5	2.7	204.8	2.2
1995	158.3	2.5	155.3	2.5	158.0	2.2	121.8	-0.7	146.0	3.1	227.6	4.5	158.1	3.0	213.1	4.1
1996	163.1	3.0	159.0	2.4	162.2	2.7	123.6	1.5	153.3	5.0	236.0	3.7	162.2	2.6	221.2	3.8
1997	144.5	-11.4	146.2	-8.1	129.3	-20.3	128.0	3.6	145.1	-5.3	241.0	2.1	189.1	16.6	169.3	-23.5

Source: U.S. Department of Labor, Bureau of Labor Statistics, Division of Consumer Prices and Price Indexes. - indicates no data collected for period.

Anchorage, AK
Consumer Price Index - All Urban Consumers
Base 1982-1984 = 100
All Items

For 1960-1997. Columns headed % show percentile change in the index from the previous period for which an index is available.

Year	Jan Index	%	Feb Index	%	Mar Index	%	Apr Index	%	May Index	%	Jun Index	%	Jul Index	%	Aug Index	%	Sep Index	%	Oct Index	%	Nov Index	%	Dec Index	%
1960	-	-	-	-	-	-	-	-	34.2	-	-	-	-	-	-	-	-	-	34.4	0.6	-	-	-	-
1961	-	-	-	-	-	-	-	-	34.4	0.0	-	-	-	-	-	-	-	-	34.8	1.2	-	-	-	-
1962	-	-	-	-	-	-	-	-	34.6	-0.6	-	-	-	-	-	-	-	-	34.7	0.3	-	-	-	-
1963	-	-	-	-	-	-	34.8	0.3	-	-	-	-	-	-	-	-	-	-	34.9	0.3	-	-	-	-
1964	-	-	-	-	-	-	34.8	-0.3	-	-	-	-	-	-	-	-	-	-	35.2	1.1	-	-	-	-
1965	-	-	-	-	-	-	35.3	0.3	-	-	-	-	-	-	-	-	-	-	35.3	0.0	-	-	-	-
1966	-	-	-	-	-	-	-	-	-	-	-	-	-	-	-	-	-	-	36.7	4.0	-	-	-	-
1967	-	-	-	-	-	-	-	-	-	-	-	-	-	-	-	-	-	-	37.5	2.2	-	-	-	-
1968	-	-	-	-	-	-	-	-	-	-	-	-	-	-	-	-	-	-	38.4	2.4	-	-	-	-
1969	38.9	1.3	-	-	-	-	39.5	1.5	-	-	-	-	39.6	0.3	-	-	-	-	40.2	1.5	-	-	-	-
1970	40.4	0.5	-	-	-	-	40.5	0.2	-	-	-	-	41.1	1.5	-	-	-	-	41.8	1.7	-	-	-	-
1971	41.8	0.0	-	-	-	-	41.8	0.0	-	-	-	-	42.3	1.2	-	-	-	-	42.8	1.2	-	-	-	-
1972	42.8	0.0	-	-	-	-	43.4	1.4	-	-	-	-	43.4	0.0	-	-	-	-	43.8	0.9	-	-	-	-
1973	43.6	-0.5	-	-	-	-	44.7	2.5	-	-	-	-	45.1	0.9	-	-	-	-	46.4	2.9	-	-	-	-
1974	47.1	1.5	-	-	-	-	48.7	3.4	-	-	-	-	50.3	3.3	-	-	-	-	52.5	4.4	-	-	-	-
1975	53.5	1.9	-	-	-	-	56.2	5.0	-	-	-	-	57.6	2.5	-	-	-	-	59.0	2.4	-	-	-	-
1976	59.5	0.8	-	-	-	-	60.6	1.8	-	-	-	-	61.8	2.0	-	-	-	-	62.8	1.6	-	-	-	-
1977	63.5	1.1	-	-	-	-	64.7	1.9	-	-	-	-	66.5	2.8	-	-	-	-	66.4	-0.2	-	-	-	-
1978	67.1	1.1	-	-	67.7	0.9	-	-	69.0	1.9	-	-	70.6	2.3	-	-	72.4	2.5	-	-	72.9	0.7	-	-
1979	74.2	1.8	-	-	75.3	1.5	-	-	76.2	1.2	-	-	77.7	2.0	-	-	79.9	2.8	-	-	80.1	0.3	-	-
1980	81.7	2.0	-	-	83.7	2.4	-	-	84.9	1.4	-	-	85.6	0.8	-	-	86.5	1.1	-	-	88.6	2.4	-	-
1981	90.0	1.6	-	-	90.3	0.3	-	-	91.6	1.4	-	-	92.2	0.7	-	-	93.9	1.8	-	-	95.0	1.2	-	-
1982	94.8	-0.2	-	-	97.4	2.7	-	-	98.8	1.4	-	-	98.8	0.0	-	-	98.7	-0.1	-	-	96.4	-2.3	-	-
1983	96.5	0.1	-	-	97.8	1.3	-	-	98.3	0.5	-	-	99.6	1.3	-	-	100.4	0.8	-	-	101.3	0.9	-	-
1984	101.7	0.4	-	-	102.8	1.1	-	-	103.1	0.3	-	-	103.2	0.1	-	-	104.1	0.9	-	-	104.0	-0.1	-	-
1985	104.3	0.3	-	-	104.9	0.6	-	-	104.5	-0.4	-	-	106.1	1.5	-	-	106.6	0.5	-	-	107.5	0.8	-	-
1986	107.6	0.1	-	-	109.1	1.4	-	-	108.2	-0.8	-	-	107.3	-0.8	-	-	107.2	-0.1	-	-	107.8	0.6	107.4	-0.4
1987	-	-	-	-	-	-	-	-	-	-	116.2	8.2	-	-	-	-	-	-	-	-	-	-	119.7	3.0
1988	-	-	-	-	-	-	-	-	-	-	122.1	2.0	-	-	-	-	-	-	-	-	-	-	125.3	2.6
1989	-	-	-	-	-	-	-	-	-	-	129.0	3.0	-	-	-	-	-	-	-	-	-	-	132.2	2.5
1990	-	-	-	-	-	-	-	-	-	-	136.4	3.2	-	-	-	-	-	-	-	-	-	-	140.7	3.2
1991	-	-	-	-	-	-	-	-	-	-	143.7	2.1	-	-	-	-	-	-	-	-	-	-	145.9	1.5
1992	-	-	-	-	-	-	-	-	-	-	148.7	1.9	-	-	-	-	-	-	-	-	-	-	151.4	1.8
1993	-	-	-	-	-	-	-	-	-	-	153.8	1.6	-	-	-	-	-	-	-	-	-	-	155.2	0.9
1994	-	-	-	-	-	-	-	-	-	-	157.4	1.4	-	-	-	-	-	-	-	-	-	-	159.0	1.0
1995	-	-	-	-	-	-	-	-	-	-	161.1	1.3	-	-	-	-	-	-	-	-	-	-	163.2	1.3
1996	-	-	-	-	-	-	-	-	-	-	166.0	1.7	-	-	-	-	-	-	-	-	-	-	167.9	1.1
1997	-	-	-	-	-	-	-	-	-	-	170.1	1.3	-	-	-	-	-	-	-	-	-	-	-	-

Source: U.S. Department of Labor, Bureau of Labor Statistics, Division of Consumer Prices and Price Indexes. - indicates no data collected for period.

Anchorage, AK
Consumer Price Index - Urban Wage Earners
Base 1982-1984 = 100
All Items

For 1960-1997. Columns headed % show percentile change in the index from the previous period for which an index is available.

Year	Jan Index	Jan %	Feb Index	Feb %	Mar Index	Mar %	Apr Index	Apr %	May Index	May %	Jun Index	Jun %	Jul Index	Jul %	Aug Index	Aug %	Sep Index	Sep %	Oct Index	Oct %	Nov Index	Nov %	Dec Index	Dec %
1960	-	-	-	-	-	-	-	-	35.1	-	-	-	-	-	-	-	-	-	35.3	0.6	-	-	-	-
1961	-	-	-	-	-	-	-	-	35.2	-0.3	-	-	-	-	-	-	-	-	35.7	1.4	-	-	-	-
1962	-	-	-	-	-	-	-	-	35.5	-0.6	-	-	-	-	-	-	-	-	35.5	0.0	-	-	-	-
1963	-	-	-	-	-	-	35.7	0.6	-	-	-	-	-	-	-	-	-	-	35.8	0.3	-	-	-	-
1964	-	-	-	-	-	-	35.7	-0.3	-	-	-	-	-	-	-	-	-	-	36.1	1.1	-	-	-	-
1965	-	-	-	-	-	-	36.2	0.3	-	-	-	-	-	-	-	-	-	-	36.2	0.0	-	-	-	-
1966	-	-	-	-	-	-	-	-	-	-	-	-	-	-	-	-	-	-	37.6	3.9	-	-	-	-
1967	-	-	-	-	-	-	-	-	-	-	-	-	-	-	-	-	-	-	38.4	2.1	-	-	-	-
1968	-	-	-	-	-	-	-	-	-	-	-	-	-	-	-	-	-	-	39.4	2.6	-	-	-	-
1969	39.8	1.0	-	-	-	-	40.5	1.8	-	-	-	-	40.6	0.2	-	-	-	-	41.2	1.5	-	-	-	-
1970	41.4	0.5	-	-	-	-	41.6	0.5	-	-	-	-	42.1	1.2	-	-	-	-	42.8	1.7	-	-	-	-
1971	42.8	0.0	-	-	-	-	42.9	0.2	-	-	-	-	43.4	1.2	-	-	-	-	43.9	1.2	-	-	-	-
1972	43.9	0.0	-	-	-	-	44.5	1.4	-	-	-	-	44.5	0.0	-	-	-	-	44.9	0.9	-	-	-	-
1973	44.7	-0.4	-	-	-	-	45.9	2.7	-	-	-	-	46.3	0.9	-	-	-	-	47.6	2.8	-	-	-	-
1974	48.3	1.5	-	-	-	-	49.9	3.3	-	-	-	-	51.6	3.4	-	-	-	-	53.9	4.5	-	-	-	-
1975	54.9	1.9	-	-	-	-	57.6	4.9	-	-	-	-	59.1	2.6	-	-	-	-	60.5	2.4	-	-	-	-
1976	61.0	0.8	-	-	-	-	62.1	1.8	-	-	-	-	63.4	2.1	-	-	-	-	64.4	1.6	-	-	-	-
1977	65.1	1.1	-	-	-	-	66.3	1.8	-	-	-	-	68.2	2.9	-	-	-	-	68.1	-0.1	-	-	-	-
1978	68.9	1.2	-	-	69.5	0.9	-	-	70.7	1.7	-	-	72.5	2.5	-	-	74.1	2.2	-	-	74.8	0.9	-	-
1979	75.8	1.3	-	-	77.0	1.6	-	-	77.8	1.0	-	-	79.3	1.9	-	-	81.0	2.1	-	-	81.4	0.5	-	-
1980	83.0	2.0	-	-	84.6	1.9	-	-	85.7	1.3	-	-	86.4	0.8	-	-	87.1	0.8	-	-	89.1	2.3	-	-
1981	90.3	1.3	-	-	90.8	0.6	-	-	92.3	1.7	-	-	92.9	0.7	-	-	94.5	1.7	-	-	95.8	1.4	-	-
1982	95.5	-0.3	-	-	97.8	2.4	-	-	99.1	1.3	-	-	99.6	0.5	-	-	99.5	-0.1	-	-	97.7	-1.8	-	-
1983	96.3	-1.4	-	-	97.6	1.3	-	-	97.9	0.3	-	-	98.9	1.0	-	-	100.2	1.3	-	-	101.4	1.2	-	-
1984	101.4	0.0	-	-	102.2	0.8	-	-	102.1	-0.1	-	-	102.5	0.4	-	-	104.1	1.6	-	-	104.1	0.0	-	-
1985	104.4	0.3	-	-	104.9	0.5	-	-	104.5	-0.4	-	-	106.0	1.4	-	-	106.5	0.5	-	-	107.6	1.0	-	-
1986	107.7	0.1	-	-	109.3	1.5	-	-	108.3	-0.9	-	-	107.0	-1.2	-	-	106.8	-0.2	-	-	107.5	0.7	107.2	-0.3
1987	-	-	-	-	-	-	-	-	-	-	114.8	7.1	-	-	-	-	-	-	-	-	-	-	118.2	3.0
1988	-	-	-	-	-	-	-	-	-	-	120.2	1.7	-	-	-	-	-	-	-	-	-	-	123.4	2.7
1989	-	-	-	-	-	-	-	-	-	-	127.0	2.9	-	-	-	-	-	-	-	-	-	-	130.2	2.5
1990	-	-	-	-	-	-	-	-	-	-	134.3	3.1	-	-	-	-	-	-	-	-	-	-	138.4	3.1
1991	-	-	-	-	-	-	-	-	-	-	141.0	1.9	-	-	-	-	-	-	-	-	-	-	143.2	1.6
1992	-	-	-	-	-	-	-	-	-	-	145.5	1.6	-	-	-	-	-	-	-	-	-	-	148.3	1.9
1993	-	-	-	-	-	-	-	-	-	-	150.5	1.5	-	-	-	-	-	-	-	-	-	-	151.7	0.8
1994	-	-	-	-	-	-	-	-	-	-	153.6	1.3	-	-	-	-	-	-	-	-	-	-	155.4	1.2
1995	-	-	-	-	-	-	-	-	-	-	157.3	1.2	-	-	-	-	-	-	-	-	-	-	159.4	1.3
1996	-	-	-	-	-	-	-	-	-	-	162.2	1.8	-	-	-	-	-	-	-	-	-	-	164.1	1.2
1997	-	-	-	-	-	-	-	-	-	-	166.0	1.2	-	-	-	-	-	-	-	-	-	-	-	-

Source: U.S. Department of Labor, Bureau of Labor Statistics, Division of Consumer Prices and Price Indexes. - indicates no data collected for period.

Anchorage, AK
Consumer Price Index - All Urban Consumers
Base 1982-1984 = 100
Food and Beverages

For 1976-1997. Columns headed % show percentile change in the index from the previous period for which an index is available.

Year	Jan Index	%	Feb Index	%	Mar Index	%	Apr Index	%	May Index	%	Jun Index	%	Jul Index	%	Aug Index	%	Sep Index	%	Oct Index	%	Nov Index	%	Dec Index	%
1976	63.2	-	-	-	-	-	63.4	0.3	-	-	-	-	64.4	1.6	-	-	-	-	64.8	0.6	-	-	-	-
1977	65.4	0.9	-	-	-	-	67.3	2.9	-	-	-	-	70.9	5.3	-	-	-	-	69.8	-1.6	-	-	-	-
1978	71.6	2.6	-	-	73.2	2.2	-	-	76.2	4.1	-	-	76.2	0.0	-	-	77.7	2.0	-	-	78.2	0.6	-	-
1979	80.6	3.1	-	-	82.7	2.6	-	-	82.7	0.0	-	-	84.5	2.2	-	-	85.7	1.4	-	-	86.2	0.6	-	-
1980	86.8	0.7	-	-	87.3	0.6	-	-	88.6	1.5	-	-	89.9	1.5	-	-	91.0	1.2	-	-	93.0	2.2	-	-
1981	92.9	-0.1	-	-	92.6	-0.3	-	-	93.1	0.5	-	-	94.6	1.6	-	-	95.7	1.2	-	-	96.0	0.3	-	-
1982	96.5	0.5	-	-	95.6	-0.9	-	-	96.7	1.2	-	-	98.2	1.6	-	-	97.8	-0.4	-	-	97.9	0.1	-	-
1983	97.8	-0.1	-	-	98.4	0.6	-	-	99.2	0.8	-	-	100.2	1.0	-	-	100.3	0.1	-	-	101.0	0.7	-	-
1984	102.2	1.2	-	-	102.9	0.7	-	-	103.3	0.4	-	-	103.2	-0.1	-	-	103.2	0.0	-	-	103.7	0.5	-	-
1985	103.8	0.1	-	-	104.5	0.7	-	-	105.1	0.6	-	-	106.5	1.3	-	-	107.1	0.6	-	-	108.6	1.4	-	-
1986	109.7	1.0	-	-	109.8	0.1	-	-	110.5	0.6	-	-	111.1	0.5	-	-	111.5	0.4	-	-	111.6	0.1	111.9	0.3
1987	-	-	-	-	-	-	-	-	-	-	117.3	4.8	-	-	-	-	-	-	-	-	-	-	119.9	2.2
1988	-	-	-	-	-	-	-	-	-	-	123.3	2.8	-	-	-	-	-	-	-	-	-	-	126.4	2.5
1989	-	-	-	-	-	-	-	-	-	-	131.0	3.6	-	-	-	-	-	-	-	-	-	-	133.2	1.7
1990	-	-	-	-	-	-	-	-	-	-	138.4	3.9	-	-	-	-	-	-	-	-	-	-	140.8	1.7
1991	-	-	-	-	-	-	-	-	-	-	144.7	2.8	-	-	-	-	-	-	-	-	-	-	143.9	-0.6
1992	-	-	-	-	-	-	-	-	-	-	145.7	1.3	-	-	-	-	-	-	-	-	-	-	146.2	0.3
1993	-	-	-	-	-	-	-	-	-	-	148.8	1.8	-	-	-	-	-	-	-	-	-	-	149.3	0.3
1994	-	-	-	-	-	-	-	-	-	-	151.2	1.3	-	-	-	-	-	-	-	-	-	-	152.7	1.0
1995	-	-	-	-	-	-	-	-	-	-	155.1	1.6	-	-	-	-	-	-	-	-	-	-	156.7	1.0
1996	-	-	-	-	-	-	-	-	-	-	158.7	1.3	-	-	-	-	-	-	-	-	-	-	160.6	1.2
1997	-	-	-	-	-	-	-	-	-	-	162.5	1.2	-	-	-	-	-	-	-	-	-	-	-	-

Source: U.S. Department of Labor, Bureau of Labor Statistics, Division of Consumer Prices and Price Indexes. - indicates no data collected for period.

Anchorage, AK
Consumer Price Index - Urban Wage Earners
Base 1982-1984 = 100
Food and Beverages

For 1976-1997. Columns headed % show percentile change in the index from the previous period for which an index is available.

Year	Jan Index	%	Feb Index	%	Mar Index	%	Apr Index	%	May Index	%	Jun Index	%	Jul Index	%	Aug Index	%	Sep Index	%	Oct Index	%	Nov Index	%	Dec Index	%
1976	63.6	-	-	-	-	-	63.7	0.2	-	-	-	-	64.8	1.7	-	-	-	-	65.2	0.6	-	-	-	-
1977	65.8	0.9	-	-	-	-	67.7	2.9	-	-	-	-	71.3	5.3	-	-	-	-	70.2	-1.5	-	-	-	-
1978	72.0	2.6	-	-	73.3	1.8	-	-	76.0	3.7	-	-	78.0	2.6	-	-	79.5	1.9	-	-	80.4	1.1	-	-
1979	81.6	1.5	-	-	84.9	4.0	-	-	85.5	0.7	-	-	86.8	1.5	-	-	88.0	1.4	-	-	88.3	0.3	-	-
1980	88.8	0.6	-	-	88.1	-0.8	-	-	89.2	1.2	-	-	90.6	1.6	-	-	91.3	0.8	-	-	93.0	1.9	-	-
1981	92.4	-0.6	-	-	92.2	-0.2	-	-	93.2	1.1	-	-	94.2	1.1	-	-	95.9	1.8	-	-	96.0	0.1	-	-
1982	96.4	0.4	-	-	95.6	-0.8	-	-	96.6	1.0	-	-	98.1	1.6	-	-	97.8	-0.3	-	-	97.9	0.1	-	-
1983	98.1	0.2	-	-	98.5	0.4	-	-	99.1	0.6	-	-	100.2	1.1	-	-	100.4	0.2	-	-	100.9	0.5	-	-
1984	102.1	1.2	-	-	102.9	0.8	-	-	103.3	0.4	-	-	103.3	0.0	-	-	103.3	0.0	-	-	103.8	0.5	-	-
1985	103.8	0.0	-	-	104.6	0.8	-	-	105.2	0.6	-	-	106.6	1.3	-	-	107.0	0.4	-	-	108.5	1.4	-	-
1986	109.6	1.0	-	-	110.0	0.4	-	-	110.5	0.5	-	-	111.1	0.5	-	-	111.6	0.5	-	-	111.8	0.2	111.9	0.1
1987	-	-	-	-	-	-	-	-	-	-	116.9	4.5	-	-	-	-	-	-	-	-	-	-	119.4	2.1
1988	-	-	-	-	-	-	-	-	-	-	122.7	2.8	-	-	-	-	-	-	-	-	-	-	125.9	2.6
1989	-	-	-	-	-	-	-	-	-	-	130.6	3.7	-	-	-	-	-	-	-	-	-	-	132.8	1.7
1990	-	-	-	-	-	-	-	-	-	-	138.1	4.0	-	-	-	-	-	-	-	-	-	-	140.6	1.8
1991	-	-	-	-	-	-	-	-	-	-	144.5	2.8	-	-	-	-	-	-	-	-	-	-	143.6	-0.6
1992	-	-	-	-	-	-	-	-	-	-	145.4	1.3	-	-	-	-	-	-	-	-	-	-	145.8	0.3
1993	-	-	-	-	-	-	-	-	-	-	148.3	1.7	-	-	-	-	-	-	-	-	-	-	148.8	0.3
1994	-	-	-	-	-	-	-	-	-	-	150.8	1.3	-	-	-	-	-	-	-	-	-	-	152.3	1.0
1995	-	-	-	-	-	-	-	-	-	-	154.5	1.4	-	-	-	-	-	-	-	-	-	-	156.1	1.0
1996	-	-	-	-	-	-	-	-	-	-	158.1	1.3	-	-	-	-	-	-	-	-	-	-	159.9	1.1
1997	-	-	-	-	-	-	-	-	-	-	161.6	1.1	-	-	-	-	-	-	-	-	-	-	-	-

Source: U.S. Department of Labor, Bureau of Labor Statistics, Division of Consumer Prices and Price Indexes. - indicates no data collected for period.

Anchorage, AK
Consumer Price Index - All Urban Consumers
Base 1982-1984 = 100
Housing

For 1976-1997. Columns headed % show percentile change in the index from the previous period for which an index is available.

Year	Jan Index	%	Feb Index	%	Mar Index	%	Apr Index	%	May Index	%	Jun Index	%	Jul Index	%	Aug Index	%	Sep Index	%	Oct Index	%	Nov Index	%	Dec Index	%
1976	61.0	-	-	-	-	-	61.7	1.1	-	-	-	-	62.8	1.8	-	-	-	-	63.7	1.4	-	-	-	-
1977	64.3	0.9	-	-	-	-	64.6	0.5	-	-	-	-	66.0	2.2	-	-	-	-	66.4	0.6	-	-	-	-
1978	66.6	0.3	-	-	66.9	0.5	-	-	67.5	0.9	-	-	70.1	3.9	-	-	72.5	3.4	-	-	73.0	0.7	-	-
1979	74.4	1.9	-	-	75.7	1.7	-	-	76.7	1.3	-	-	78.3	2.1	-	-	80.5	2.8	-	-	80.4	-0.1	-	-
1980	82.4	2.5	-	-	84.6	2.7	-	-	85.4	0.9	-	-	85.9	0.6	-	-	86.4	0.6	-	-	88.8	2.8	-	-
1981	90.8	2.3	-	-	90.7	-0.1	-	-	91.6	1.0	-	-	91.9	0.3	-	-	93.7	2.0	-	-	95.2	1.6	-	-
1982	94.4	-0.8	-	-	99.4	5.3	-	-	101.4	2.0	-	-	100.1	-1.3	-	-	99.6	-0.5	-	-	94.8	-4.8	-	-
1983	95.2	0.4	-	-	97.8	2.7	-	-	98.1	0.3	-	-	99.7	1.6	-	-	100.7	1.0	-	-	100.9	0.2	-	-
1984	101.7	0.8	-	-	102.9	1.2	-	-	103.0	0.1	-	-	102.2	-0.8	-	-	103.2	1.0	-	-	102.7	-0.5	-	-
1985	103.0	0.3	-	-	102.7	-0.3	-	-	101.4	-1.3	-	-	104.2	2.8	-	-	103.8	-0.4	-	-	103.2	-0.6	-	-
1986	103.3	0.1	-	-	105.8	2.4	-	-	105.5	-0.3	-	-	101.1	-4.2	-	-	100.2	-0.9	-	-	100.1	-0.1	100.1	0.0
1987	-	-	-	-	-	-	-	-	-	-	116.2	16.1	-	-	-	-	-	-	-	-	-	-	119.9	3.2
1988	-	-	-	-	-	-	-	-	-	-	123.7	3.2	-	-	-	-	-	-	-	-	-	-	126.6	2.3
1989	-	-	-	-	-	-	-	-	-	-	130.0	2.7	-	-	-	-	-	-	-	-	-	-	133.7	2.8
1990	-	-	-	-	-	-	-	-	-	-	137.4	2.8	-	-	-	-	-	-	-	-	-	-	141.2	2.8
1991	-	-	-	-	-	-	-	-	-	-	144.5	2.3	-	-	-	-	-	-	-	-	-	-	146.9	1.7
1992	-	-	-	-	-	-	-	-	-	-	150.2	2.2	-	-	-	-	-	-	-	-	-	-	152.6	1.6
1993	-	-	-	-	-	-	-	-	-	-	154.6	1.3	-	-	-	-	-	-	-	-	-	-	156.4	1.2
1994	-	-	-	-	-	-	-	-	-	-	159.1	1.7	-	-	-	-	-	-	-	-	-	-	160.6	0.9
1995	-	-	-	-	-	-	-	-	-	-	162.3	1.1	-	-	-	-	-	-	-	-	-	-	164.6	1.4
1996	-	-	-	-	-	-	-	-	-	-	166.9	1.4	-	-	-	-	-	-	-	-	-	-	168.5	1.0
1997	-	-	-	-	-	-	-	-	-	-	170.7	1.3	-	-	-	-	-	-	-	-	-	-	-	-

Source: U.S. Department of Labor, Bureau of Labor Statistics, Division of Consumer Prices and Price Indexes. - indicates no data collected for period.

Anchorage, AK
Consumer Price Index - Urban Wage Earners
Base 1982-1984 = 100
Housing

For 1976-1997. Columns headed % show percentile change in the index from the previous period for which an index is available.

Year	Jan Index	%	Feb Index	%	Mar Index	%	Apr Index	%	May Index	%	Jun Index	%	Jul Index	%	Aug Index	%	Sep Index	%	Oct Index	%	Nov Index	%	Dec Index	%
1976	64.1	-	-	-	-	-	64.8	1.1	-	-	-	-	66.0	1.9	-	-	-	-	66.9	1.4	-	-	-	-
1977	67.5	0.9	-	-	-	-	67.8	0.4	-	-	-	-	69.3	2.2	-	-	-	-	69.7	0.6	-	-	-	-
1978	69.9	0.3	-	-	70.3	0.6	-	-	70.9	0.9	-	-	73.3	3.4	-	-	75.6	3.1	-	-	76.2	0.8	-	-
1979	77.4	1.6	-	-	78.7	1.7	-	-	79.2	0.6	-	-	80.7	1.9	-	-	82.6	2.4	-	-	82.6	0.0	-	-
1980	84.3	2.1	-	-	86.3	2.4	-	-	87.3	1.2	-	-	87.6	0.3	-	-	87.9	0.3	-	-	90.3	2.7	-	-
1981	92.1	2.0	-	-	92.0	-0.1	-	-	93.1	1.2	-	-	93.3	0.2	-	-	95.0	1.8	-	-	96.8	1.9	-	-
1982	96.0	-0.8	-	-	100.8	5.0	-	-	103.0	2.2	-	-	102.3	-0.7	-	-	101.7	-0.6	-	-	97.6	-4.0	-	-
1983	94.5	-3.2	-	-	97.1	2.8	-	-	97.0	-0.1	-	-	98.1	1.1	-	-	99.9	1.8	-	-	101.1	1.2	-	-
1984	100.8	-0.3	-	-	101.4	0.6	-	-	100.4	-1.0	-	-	100.6	0.2	-	-	103.0	2.4	-	-	102.9	-0.1	-	-
1985	103.3	0.4	-	-	102.9	-0.4	-	-	101.5	-1.4	-	-	104.4	2.9	-	-	104.2	-0.2	-	-	103.8	-0.4	-	-
1986	103.6	-0.2	-	-	106.6	2.9	-	-	106.3	-0.3	-	-	101.7	-4.3	-	-	100.9	-0.8	-	-	100.4	-0.5	100.6	0.2
1987	-	-	-	-	-	-	-	-	-	-	114.2	13.5	-	-	-	-	-	-	-	-	-	-	117.8	3.2
1988	-	-	-	-	-	-	-	-	-	-	121.0	2.7	-	-	-	-	-	-	-	-	-	-	123.9	2.4
1989	-	-	-	-	-	-	-	-	-	-	127.1	2.6	-	-	-	-	-	-	-	-	-	-	131.0	3.1
1990	-	-	-	-	-	-	-	-	-	-	134.3	2.5	-	-	-	-	-	-	-	-	-	-	137.6	2.5
1991	-	-	-	-	-	-	-	-	-	-	140.3	2.0	-	-	-	-	-	-	-	-	-	-	142.9	1.9
1992	-	-	-	-	-	-	-	-	-	-	145.6	1.9	-	-	-	-	-	-	-	-	-	-	147.9	1.6
1993	-	-	-	-	-	-	-	-	-	-	149.9	1.4	-	-	-	-	-	-	-	-	-	-	151.4	1.0
1994	-	-	-	-	-	-	-	-	-	-	153.8	1.6	-	-	-	-	-	-	-	-	-	-	155.5	1.1
1995	-	-	-	-	-	-	-	-	-	-	157.0	1.0	-	-	-	-	-	-	-	-	-	-	159.1	1.3
1996	-	-	-	-	-	-	-	-	-	-	161.3	1.4	-	-	-	-	-	-	-	-	-	-	163.2	1.2
1997	-	-	-	-	-	-	-	-	-	-	165.0	1.1	-	-	-	-	-	-	-	-	-	-	-	-

Source: U.S. Department of Labor, Bureau of Labor Statistics, Division of Consumer Prices and Price Indexes. - indicates no data collected for period.

Anchorage, AK
Consumer Price Index - All Urban Consumers
Base 1982-1984 = 100
Apparel and Upkeep

For 1971-1997. Columns headed % show percentile change in the index from the previous period for which an index is available.

Year	Jan Index	%	Feb Index	%	Mar Index	%	Apr Index	%	May Index	%	Jun Index	%	Jul Index	%	Aug Index	%	Sep Index	%	Oct Index	%	Nov Index	%	Dec Index	%
1971	55.3	-	-	-	-	-	56.1	1.4	-	-	-	-	56.8	1.2	-	-	-	-	57.0	0.4	-	-	-	-
1972	56.7	-0.5	-	-	-	-	58.5	3.2	-	-	-	-	58.3	-0.3	-	-	-	-	59.0	1.2	-	-	-	-
1973	58.9	-0.2	-	-	-	-	59.9	1.7	-	-	-	-	61.1	2.0	-	-	-	-	62.1	1.6	-	-	-	-
1974	61.7	-0.6	-	-	-	-	62.8	1.8	-	-	-	-	64.9	3.3	-	-	-	-	67.4	3.9	-	-	-	-
1975	67.6	0.3	-	-	-	-	70.1	3.7	-	-	-	-	69.6	-0.7	-	-	-	-	71.2	2.3	-	-	-	-
1976	70.3	-1.3	-	-	-	-	72.3	2.8	-	-	-	-	73.5	1.7	-	-	-	-	77.4	5.3	-	-	-	-
1977	78.7	1.7	-	-	-	-	79.1	0.5	-	-	-	-	79.0	-0.1	-	-	-	-	80.3	1.6	-	-	-	-
1978	77.5	-3.5	-	-	78.2	0.9	-	-	80.1	2.4	-	-	79.1	-1.2	-	-	81.4	2.9	-	-	81.5	0.1	-	-
1979	79.6	-2.3	-	-	79.3	-0.4	-	-	79.7	0.5	-	-	78.9	-1.0	-	-	86.5	9.6	-	-	85.0	-1.7	-	-
1980	83.8	-1.4	-	-	86.4	3.1	-	-	88.4	2.3	-	-	91.7	3.7	-	-	92.1	0.4	-	-	93.5	1.5	-	-
1981	92.7	-0.9	-	-	94.3	1.7	-	-	95.0	0.7	-	-	91.5	-3.7	-	-	95.7	4.6	-	-	95.0	-0.7	-	-
1982	93.9	-1.2	-	-	93.9	0.0	-	-	96.3	2.6	-	-	96.7	0.4	-	-	99.0	2.4	-	-	99.4	0.4	-	-
1983	95.7	-3.7	-	-	101.5	6.1	-	-	101.9	0.4	-	-	102.4	0.5	-	-	102.3	-0.1	-	-	104.8	2.4	-	-
1984	100.8	-3.8	-	-	102.3	1.5	-	-	99.9	-2.3	-	-	101.5	1.6	-	-	104.7	3.2	-	-	107.6	-1.0	-	-
1985	100.4	-1.2	-	-	107.3	6.9	-	-	106.1	-1.1	-	-	103.2	-2.7	-	-	108.7	5.3	-	-	110.7	0.4	108.9	-1.6
1986	105.5	-2.0	-	-	110.2	4.5	-	-	107.7	-2.3	-	-	109.0	1.2	-	-	110.3	1.2	-	-	-	-	111.2	2.4
1987	-	-	-	-	-	-	-	-	-	-	108.6	-0.3	-	-	-	-	-	-	-	-	-	-	110.4	5.7
1988	-	-	-	-	-	-	-	-	-	-	104.4	-6.1	-	-	-	-	-	-	-	-	-	-	115.4	2.6
1989	-	-	-	-	-	-	-	-	-	-	112.5	1.9	-	-	-	-	-	-	-	-	-	-	123.4	2.6
1990	-	-	-	-	-	-	-	-	-	-	120.3	4.2	-	-	-	-	-	-	-	-	-	-	126.3	2.9
1991	-	-	-	-	-	-	-	-	-	-	122.8	-0.5	-	-	-	-	-	-	-	-	-	-	131.5	4.8
1992	-	-	-	-	-	-	-	-	-	-	125.5	-0.6	-	-	-	-	-	-	-	-	-	-	129.0	-0.5
1993	-	-	-	-	-	-	-	-	-	-	129.7	-1.4	-	-	-	-	-	-	-	-	-	-	124.9	-2.1
1994	-	-	-	-	-	-	-	-	-	-	127.6	-1.1	-	-	-	-	-	-	-	-	-	-	126.4	0.7
1995	-	-	-	-	-	-	-	-	-	-	125.5	0.5	-	-	-	-	-	-	-	-	-	-	127.3	-0.6
1996	-	-	-	-	-	-	-	-	-	-	128.1	1.3	-	-	-	-	-	-	-	-	-	-	-	-
1997	-	-	-	-	-	-	-	-	-	-	130.1	2.2	-	-	-	-	-	-	-	-	-	-	-	-

Source: U.S. Department of Labor, Bureau of Labor Statistics, Division of Consumer Prices and Price Indexes. - indicates no data collected for period.

Anchorage, AK
Consumer Price Index - Urban Wage Earners
Base 1982-1984 = 100
Apparel and Upkeep

For 1971-1997. Columns headed % show percentile change in the index from the previous period for which an index is available.

Year	Jan Index	%	Feb Index	%	Mar Index	%	Apr Index	%	May Index	%	Jun Index	%	Jul Index	%	Aug Index	%	Sep Index	%	Oct Index	%	Nov Index	%	Dec Index	%
1971	55.9	-	-	-	-	-	56.7	1.4	-	-	-	-	57.4	1.2	-	-	-	-	57.6	0.3	-	-	-	-
1972	57.3	-0.5	-	-	-	-	59.1	3.1	-	-	-	-	58.9	-0.3	-	-	-	-	59.7	1.4	-	-	-	-
1973	59.6	-0.2	-	-	-	-	60.5	1.5	-	-	-	-	61.8	2.1	-	-	-	-	62.8	1.6	-	-	-	-
1974	62.4	-0.6	-	-	-	-	63.5	1.8	-	-	-	-	65.6	3.3	-	-	-	-	68.2	4.0	-	-	-	-
1975	68.4	0.3	-	-	-	-	70.8	3.5	-	-	-	-	70.3	-0.7	-	-	-	-	71.9	2.3	-	-	-	-
1976	71.1	-1.1	-	-	-	-	73.0	2.7	-	-	-	-	74.3	1.8	-	-	-	-	78.2	5.2	-	-	-	-
1977	79.6	1.8	-	-	-	-	80.0	0.5	-	-	-	-	79.8	-0.2	-	-	-	-	81.2	1.8	-	-	-	-
1978	78.3	-3.6	-	-	78.9	0.8	-	-	80.5	2.0	-	-	80.0	-0.6	-	-	81.6	2.0	-	-	82.0	0.5	-	-
1979	81.1	-1.1	-	-	80.0	-1.4	-	-	80.0	0.0	-	-	80.7	0.9	-	-	84.0	4.1	-	-	83.5	-0.6	-	-
1980	83.1	-0.5	-	-	84.1	1.2	-	-	84.6	0.6	-	-	87.2	3.1	-	-	88.4	1.4	-	-	89.6	1.4	-	-
1981	91.6	2.2	-	-	92.3	0.8	-	-	92.3	0.0	-	-	90.9	-1.5	-	-	93.9	3.3	-	-	94.3	0.4	-	-
1982	92.7	-1.7	-	-	93.5	0.9	-	-	95.0	1.6	-	-	96.9	2.0	-	-	99.3	2.5	-	-	99.8	0.5	-	-
1983	95.7	-4.1	-	-	101.7	6.3	-	-	102.2	0.5	-	-	102.1	-0.1	-	-	102.6	0.5	-	-	104.2	1.6	-	-
1984	100.6	-3.5	-	-	101.8	1.2	-	-	100.2	-1.6	-	-	102.1	1.9	-	-	105.4	3.2	-	-	102.4	-2.8	-	-
1985	101.2	-1.2	-	-	106.5	5.2	-	-	105.8	-0.7	-	-	103.3	-2.4	-	-	108.4	4.9	-	-	106.9	-1.4	-	-
1986	105.0	-1.8	-	-	109.6	4.4	-	-	107.0	-2.4	-	-	108.2	1.1	-	-	108.9	0.6	-	-	109.4	0.5	108.2	-1.1
1987	-	-	-	-	-	-	-	-	-	-	109.4	1.1	-	-	-	-	-	-	-	-	-	-	111.1	1.6
1988	-	-	-	-	-	-	-	-	-	-	103.5	-6.8	-	-	-	-	-	-	-	-	-	-	109.1	5.4
1989	-	-	-	-	-	-	-	-	-	-	111.0	1.7	-	-	-	-	-	-	-	-	-	-	114.0	2.7
1990	-	-	-	-	-	-	-	-	-	-	118.5	3.9	-	-	-	-	-	-	-	-	-	-	121.7	2.7
1991	-	-	-	-	-	-	-	-	-	-	120.4	-1.1	-	-	-	-	-	-	-	-	-	-	123.8	2.8
1992	-	-	-	-	-	-	-	-	-	-	122.2	-1.3	-	-	-	-	-	-	-	-	-	-	129.4	5.9
1993	-	-	-	-	-	-	-	-	-	-	126.6	-2.2	-	-	-	-	-	-	-	-	-	-	125.7	-0.7
1994	-	-	-	-	-	-	-	-	-	-	124.4	-1.0	-	-	-	-	-	-	-	-	-	-	121.0	-2.7
1995	-	-	-	-	-	-	-	-	-	-	121.5	0.4	-	-	-	-	-	-	-	-	-	-	122.2	0.6
1996	-	-	-	-	-	-	-	-	-	-	124.3	1.7	-	-	-	-	-	-	-	-	-	-	122.9	-1.1
1997	-	-	-	-	-	-	-	-	-	-	126.0	2.5	-	-	-	-	-	-	-	-	-	-	-	-

Source: U.S. Department of Labor, Bureau of Labor Statistics, Division of Consumer Prices and Price Indexes. - indicates no data collected for period.

Anchorage, AK
Consumer Price Index - All Urban Consumers
Base 1982-1984 = 100
Transportation

For 1971-1997. Columns headed % show percentile change in the index from the previous period for which an index is available.

Year	Jan Index	Jan %	Feb Index	Feb %	Mar Index	Mar %	Apr Index	Apr %	May Index	May %	Jun Index	Jun %	Jul Index	Jul %	Aug Index	Aug %	Sep Index	Sep %	Oct Index	Oct %	Nov Index	Nov %	Dec Index	Dec %
1971	40.3	-	-	-	-	-	40.6	0.7	-	-	-	-	41.2	1.5	-	-	-	-	40.8	-1.0	-	-	-	-
1972	40.7	-0.2	-	-	-	-	40.6	-0.2	-	-	-	-	41.0	1.0	-	-	-	-	41.2	0.5	-	-	-	-
1973	41.0	-0.5	-	-	-	-	41.1	0.2	-	-	-	-	41.6	1.2	-	-	-	-	41.5	-0.2	-	-	-	-
1974	42.0	1.2	-	-	-	-	43.3	3.1	-	-	-	-	45.6	5.3	-	-	-	-	46.9	2.9	-	-	-	-
1975	46.8	-0.2	-	-	-	-	48.0	2.6	-	-	-	-	50.1	4.4	-	-	-	-	50.7	1.2	-	-	-	-
1976	51.5	1.6	-	-	-	-	53.8	4.5	-	-	-	-	55.4	3.0	-	-	-	-	57.0	2.9	-	-	-	-
1977	57.1	0.2	-	-	-	-	59.8	4.7	-	-	-	-	61.6	3.0	-	-	-	-	60.9	-1.1	-	-	-	-
1978	61.6	1.1	-	-	61.9	0.5	-	-	64.2	3.7	-	-	65.5	2.0	-	-	65.7	0.3	-	-	66.8	1.7	-	-
1979	67.3	0.7	-	-	67.7	0.6	-	-	69.7	3.0	-	-	72.1	3.4	-	-	73.9	2.5	-	-	74.9	1.4	-	-
1980	77.1	2.9	-	-	79.6	3.2	-	-	80.8	1.5	-	-	82.3	1.9	-	-	84.0	2.1	-	-	86.7	3.2	-	-
1981	87.7	1.2	-	-	89.7	2.3	-	-	92.1	2.7	-	-	93.6	1.6	-	-	95.0	1.5	-	-	96.0	1.1	-	-
1982	95.7	-0.3	-	-	95.8	0.1	-	-	95.8	0.0	-	-	97.3	1.6	-	-	97.8	0.5	-	-	98.1	0.3	-	-
1983	97.6	-0.5	-	-	95.8	-1.8	-	-	97.1	1.4	-	-	98.3	1.2	-	-	99.4	1.1	-	-	101.9	2.5	-	-
1984	101.6	-0.3	-	-	102.6	1.0	-	-	104.3	1.7	-	-	105.0	0.7	-	-	106.0	1.0	-	-	107.0	0.9	-	-
1985	107.2	0.2	-	-	107.4	0.2	-	-	107.6	0.2	-	-	107.5	-0.1	-	-	107.9	0.4	-	-	110.6	2.5	-	-
1986	111.1	0.5	-	-	110.8	-0.3	-	-	107.1	-3.3	-	-	105.5	-1.5	-	-	105.0	-0.5	-	-	108.1	3.0	107.9	-0.2
1987	-	-	-	-	-	-	-	-	-	-	106.9	-0.9	-	-	-	-	-	-	-	-	-	-	110.6	3.5
1988	-	-	-	-	-	-	-	-	-	-	111.5	0.8	-	-	-	-	-	-	-	-	-	-	114.0	2.2
1989	-	-	-	-	-	-	-	-	-	-	116.1	1.8	-	-	-	-	-	-	-	-	-	-	116.8	0.6
1990	-	-	-	-	-	-	-	-	-	-	119.6	2.4	-	-	-	-	-	-	-	-	-	-	126.5	5.8
1991	-	-	-	-	-	-	-	-	-	-	127.4	0.7	-	-	-	-	-	-	-	-	-	-	128.4	0.8
1992	-	-	-	-	-	-	-	-	-	-	129.8	1.1	-	-	-	-	-	-	-	-	-	-	133.1	2.5
1993	-	-	-	-	-	-	-	-	-	-	136.8	2.8	-	-	-	-	-	-	-	-	-	-	138.6	1.3
1994	-	-	-	-	-	-	-	-	-	-	140.5	1.4	-	-	-	-	-	-	-	-	-	-	143.2	1.9
1995	-	-	-	-	-	-	-	-	-	-	145.2	1.4	-	-	-	-	-	-	-	-	-	-	146.6	1.0
1996	-	-	-	-	-	-	-	-	-	-	151.2	3.1	-	-	-	-	-	-	-	-	-	-	153.7	1.7
1997	-	-	-	-	-	-	-	-	-	-	154.3	0.4	-	-	-	-	-	-	-	-	-	-	-	-

Source: U.S. Department of Labor, Bureau of Labor Statistics, Division of Consumer Prices and Price Indexes. - indicates no data collected for period.

Anchorage, AK
Consumer Price Index - Urban Wage Earners
Base 1982-1984 = 100
Transportation

For 1971-1997. Columns headed % show percentile change in the index from the previous period for which an index is available.

Year	Jan Index	%	Feb Index	%	Mar Index	%	Apr Index	%	May Index	%	Jun Index	%	Jul Index	%	Aug Index	%	Sep Index	%	Oct Index	%	Nov Index	%	Dec Index	%
1971	39.9	-	-	-	-	-	40.2	0.8	-	-	-	-	40.8	1.5	-	-	-	-	40.4	-1.0	-	-	-	-
1972	40.3	-0.2	-	-	-	-	40.2	-0.2	-	-	-	-	40.6	1.0	-	-	-	-	40.8	0.5	-	-	-	-
1973	40.6	-0.5	-	-	-	-	40.7	0.2	-	-	-	-	41.2	1.2	-	-	-	-	41.1	-0.2	-	-	-	-
1974	41.6	1.2	-	-	-	-	42.9	3.1	-	-	-	-	45.1	5.1	-	-	-	-	46.4	2.9	-	-	-	-
1975	46.3	-0.2	-	-	-	-	47.5	2.6	-	-	-	-	49.6	4.4	-	-	-	-	50.1	1.0	-	-	-	-
1976	51.0	1.8	-	-	-	-	53.2	4.3	-	-	-	-	54.8	3.0	-	-	-	-	56.4	2.9	-	-	-	-
1977	56.5	0.2	-	-	-	-	59.2	4.8	-	-	-	-	60.9	2.9	-	-	-	-	60.2	-1.1	-	-	-	-
1978	61.0	1.3	-	-	61.3	0.5	-	-	63.8	4.1	-	-	65.2	2.2	-	-	65.3	0.2	-	-	66.5	1.8	-	-
1979	66.9	0.6	-	-	67.4	0.7	-	-	69.5	3.1	-	-	72.0	3.6	-	-	73.8	2.5	-	-	74.7	1.2	-	-
1980	77.4	3.6	-	-	80.2	3.6	-	-	81.7	1.9	-	-	83.2	1.8	-	-	84.8	1.9	-	-	87.4	3.1	-	-
1981	88.3	1.0	-	-	90.3	2.3	-	-	92.9	2.9	-	-	94.5	1.7	-	-	95.8	1.4	-	-	96.8	1.0	-	-
1982	96.5	-0.3	-	-	96.5	0.0	-	-	96.2	-0.3	-	-	97.9	1.8	-	-	98.1	0.2	-	-	98.5	0.4	-	-
1983	97.7	-0.8	-	-	95.7	-2.0	-	-	96.8	1.1	-	-	98.2	1.4	-	-	99.3	1.1	-	-	101.7	2.4	-	-
1984	101.6	-0.1	-	-	102.3	0.7	-	-	104.0	1.7	-	-	104.7	0.7	-	-	105.5	0.8	-	-	106.5	0.9	-	-
1985	106.6	0.1	-	-	106.7	0.1	-	-	107.0	0.3	-	-	106.8	-0.2	-	-	107.2	0.4	-	-	110.1	2.7	-	-
1986	110.5	0.4	-	-	109.8	-0.6	-	-	105.7	-3.7	-	-	104.0	-1.6	-	-	103.5	-0.5	-	-	106.8	3.2	106.6	-0.2
1987	-	-	-	-	-	-	-	-	-	-	106.4	-0.2	-	-	-	-	-	-	-	-	-	-	110.5	3.9
1988	-	-	-	-	-	-	-	-	-	-	111.2	0.6	-	-	-	-	-	-	-	-	-	-	113.6	2.2
1989	-	-	-	-	-	-	-	-	-	-	115.7	1.8	-	-	-	-	-	-	-	-	-	-	116.6	0.8
1990	-	-	-	-	-	-	-	-	-	-	119.3	2.3	-	-	-	-	-	-	-	-	-	-	127.0	6.5
1991	-	-	-	-	-	-	-	-	-	-	127.2	0.2	-	-	-	-	-	-	-	-	-	-	128.4	0.9
1992	-	-	-	-	-	-	-	-	-	-	129.8	1.1	-	-	-	-	-	-	-	-	-	-	133.5	2.9
1993	-	-	-	-	-	-	-	-	-	-	136.4	2.2	-	-	-	-	-	-	-	-	-	-	138.4	1.5
1994	-	-	-	-	-	-	-	-	-	-	139.8	1.0	-	-	-	-	-	-	-	-	-	-	143.4	2.6
1995	-	-	-	-	-	-	-	-	-	-	145.3	1.3	-	-	-	-	-	-	-	-	-	-	146.8	1.0
1996	-	-	-	-	-	-	-	-	-	-	152.0	3.5	-	-	-	-	-	-	-	-	-	-	154.6	1.7
1997	-	-	-	-	-	-	-	-	-	-	155.0	0.3	-	-	-	-	-	-	-	-	-	-	-	-

Source: U.S. Department of Labor, Bureau of Labor Statistics, Division of Consumer Prices and Price Indexes. - indicates no data collected for period.

Anchorage, AK
Consumer Price Index - All Urban Consumers
Base 1982-1984 = 100
Medical Care

For 1971-1997. Columns headed % show percentile change in the index from the previous period for which an index is available.

Year	Jan Index	Jan %	Feb Index	Feb %	Mar Index	Mar %	Apr Index	Apr %	May Index	May %	Jun Index	Jun %	Jul Index	Jul %	Aug Index	Aug %	Sep Index	Sep %	Oct Index	Oct %	Nov Index	Nov %	Dec Index	Dec %
1971	34.4	-	-	-	-	-	35.0	1.7	-	-	-	-	35.1	0.3	-	-	-	-	35.5	1.1	-	-	-	-
1972	35.7	0.6	-	-	-	-	35.7	0.0	-	-	-	-	35.7	0.0	-	-	-	-	36.1	1.1	-	-	-	-
1973	36.2	0.3	-	-	-	-	36.5	0.8	-	-	-	-	37.3	2.2	-	-	-	-	38.3	2.7	-	-	-	-
1974	38.7	1.0	-	-	-	-	39.7	2.6	-	-	-	-	41.9	5.5	-	-	-	-	43.6	4.1	-	-	-	-
1975	44.7	2.5	-	-	-	-	45.6	2.0	-	-	-	-	47.0	3.1	-	-	-	-	48.3	2.8	-	-	-	-
1976	49.9	3.3	-	-	-	-	51.1	2.4	-	-	-	-	53.3	4.3	-	-	-	-	54.1	1.5	-	-	-	-
1977	55.4	2.4	-	-	-	-	57.0	2.9	-	-	-	-	58.1	1.9	-	-	-	-	59.0	1.5	-	-	-	-
1978	62.0	5.1	-	-	62.1	0.2	-	-	62.2	0.2	-	-	63.5	2.1	-	-	64.7	1.9	-	-	64.8	0.2	-	-
1979	67.9	4.8	-	-	67.6	-0.4	-	-	69.4	2.7	-	-	69.2	-0.3	-	-	69.4	0.3	-	-	69.8	0.6	-	-
1980	73.4	5.2	-	-	77.4	5.4	-	-	79.0	2.1	-	-	79.8	1.0	-	-	80.2	0.5	-	-	80.9	0.9	-	-
1981	82.7	2.2	-	-	84.7	2.4	-	-	87.2	3.0	-	-	87.7	0.6	-	-	87.5	-0.2	-	-	89.0	1.7	-	-
1982	92.9	4.4	-	-	92.9	0.0	-	-	93.6	0.8	-	-	95.2	1.7	-	-	96.1	0.9	-	-	96.7	0.6	-	-
1983	99.0	2.4	-	-	99.2	0.2	-	-	99.0	-0.2	-	-	99.6	0.6	-	-	100.0	0.4	-	-	100.0	0.0	-	-
1984	103.7	3.7	-	-	104.7	1.0	-	-	104.8	0.1	-	-	105.6	0.8	-	-	106.7	1.0	-	-	106.7	0.0	-	-
1985	107.2	0.5	-	-	108.5	1.2	-	-	108.8	0.3	-	-	112.8	3.7	-	-	112.9	0.1	-	-	113.5	0.5	-	-
1986	115.0	1.3	-	-	118.2	2.8	-	-	119.1	0.8	-	-	137.2	15.2	-	-	137.3	0.1	-	-	137.7	0.3	131.5	-4.5
1987	-	-	-	-	-	-	-	-	-	-	134.6	2.4	-	-	-	-	-	-	-	-	-	-	137.5	2.2
1988	-	-	-	-	-	-	-	-	-	-	142.6	3.7	-	-	-	-	-	-	-	-	-	-	146.9	3.0
1989	-	-	-	-	-	-	-	-	-	-	152.8	4.0	-	-	-	-	-	-	-	-	-	-	158.8	3.9
1990	-	-	-	-	-	-	-	-	-	-	168.6	6.2	-	-	-	-	-	-	-	-	-	-	176.2	4.5
1991	-	-	-	-	-	-	-	-	-	-	183.5	4.1	-	-	-	-	-	-	-	-	-	-	189.6	3.3
1992	-	-	-	-	-	-	-	-	-	-	197.8	4.3	-	-	-	-	-	-	-	-	-	-	202.2	2.2
1993	-	-	-	-	-	-	-	-	-	-	207.2	2.5	-	-	-	-	-	-	-	-	-	-	211.0	1.8
1994	-	-	-	-	-	-	-	-	-	-	215.5	2.1	-	-	-	-	-	-	-	-	-	-	219.7	1.9
1995	-	-	-	-	-	-	-	-	-	-	225.2	2.5	-	-	-	-	-	-	-	-	-	-	228.5	1.5
1996	-	-	-	-	-	-	-	-	-	-	232.7	1.8	-	-	-	-	-	-	-	-	-	-	238.0	2.3
1997	-	-	-	-	-	-	-	-	-	-	243.4	2.3	-	-	-	-	-	-	-	-	-	-	-	-

Source: U.S. Department of Labor, Bureau of Labor Statistics, Division of Consumer Prices and Price Indexes. - indicates no data collected for period.

Anchorage, AK
Consumer Price Index - Urban Wage Earners
Base 1982-1984 = 100
Medical Care

For 1971-1997. Columns headed % show percentile change in the index from the previous period for which an index is available.

Year	Jan Index	%	Feb Index	%	Mar Index	%	Apr Index	%	May Index	%	Jun Index	%	Jul Index	%	Aug Index	%	Sep Index	%	Oct Index	%	Nov Index	%	Dec Index	%
1971	35.4	-	-	-	-	-	36.1	2.0	-	-	-	-	36.1	0.0	-	-	-	-	36.6	1.4	-	-	-	-
1972	36.8	0.5	-	-	-	-	36.8	0.0	-	-	-	-	36.8	0.0	-	-	-	-	37.2	1.1	-	-	-	-
1973	37.3	0.3	-	-	-	-	37.6	0.8	-	-	-	-	38.4	2.1	-	-	-	-	39.5	2.9	-	-	-	-
1974	39.8	0.8	-	-	-	-	40.9	2.8	-	-	-	-	43.2	5.6	-	-	-	-	44.9	3.9	-	-	-	-
1975	46.1	2.7	-	-	-	-	47.0	2.0	-	-	-	-	48.4	3.0	-	-	-	-	49.8	2.9	-	-	-	-
1976	51.4	3.2	-	-	-	-	52.6	2.3	-	-	-	-	54.9	4.4	-	-	-	-	55.7	1.5	-	-	-	-
1977	57.0	2.3	-	-	-	-	58.8	3.2	-	-	-	-	59.9	1.9	-	-	-	-	60.7	1.3	-	-	-	-
1978	63.9	5.3	-	-	66.0	3.3	-	-	66.1	0.2	-	-	66.4	0.5	-	-	67.6	1.8	-	-	70.5	4.3	-	-
1979	72.7	3.1	-	-	72.3	-0.6	-	-	72.4	0.1	-	-	72.8	0.6	-	-	72.9	0.1	-	-	73.3	0.5	-	-
1980	75.0	2.3	-	-	77.5	3.3	-	-	79.0	1.9	-	-	80.4	1.8	-	-	80.9	0.6	-	-	80.9	0.0	-	-
1981	82.9	2.5	-	-	84.6	2.1	-	-	86.6	2.4	-	-	87.4	0.9	-	-	87.6	0.2	-	-	89.3	1.9	-	-
1982	92.7	3.8	-	-	92.8	0.1	-	-	93.7	1.0	-	-	95.3	1.7	-	-	96.4	1.2	-	-	97.0	0.6	-	-
1983	99.1	2.2	-	-	99.3	0.2	-	-	99.0	-0.3	-	-	99.8	0.8	-	-	100.3	0.5	-	-	100.3	0.0	-	-
1984	103.3	3.0	-	-	104.5	1.2	-	-	104.6	0.1	-	-	105.4	0.8	-	-	106.6	1.1	-	-	106.4	-0.2	-	-
1985	106.8	0.4	-	-	108.2	1.3	-	-	108.5	0.3	-	-	112.3	3.5	-	-	112.4	0.1	-	-	113.1	0.6	-	-
1986	114.4	1.1	-	-	117.8	3.0	-	-	118.7	0.8	-	-	132.8	11.9	-	-	132.8	0.0	-	-	133.3	0.4	128.4	-3.7
1987	-	-	-	-	-	-	-	-	-	-	135.0	5.1	-	-	-	-	-	-	-	-	-	-	138.6	2.7
1988	-	-	-	-	-	-	-	-	-	-	143.7	3.7	-	-	-	-	-	-	-	-	-	-	148.0	3.0
1989	-	-	-	-	-	-	-	-	-	-	154.0	4.1	-	-	-	-	-	-	-	-	-	-	160.0	3.9
1990	-	-	-	-	-	-	-	-	-	-	168.8	5.5	-	-	-	-	-	-	-	-	-	-	175.2	3.8
1991	-	-	-	-	-	-	-	-	-	-	182.8	4.3	-	-	-	-	-	-	-	-	-	-	189.7	3.8
1992	-	-	-	-	-	-	-	-	-	-	197.8	4.3	-	-	-	-	-	-	-	-	-	-	202.7	2.5
1993	-	-	-	-	-	-	-	-	-	-	207.3	2.3	-	-	-	-	-	-	-	-	-	-	210.8	1.7
1994	-	-	-	-	-	-	-	-	-	-	215.6	2.3	-	-	-	-	-	-	-	-	-	-	220.2	2.1
1995	-	-	-	-	-	-	-	-	-	-	226.0	2.6	-	-	-	-	-	-	-	-	-	-	229.1	1.4
1996	-	-	-	-	-	-	-	-	-	-	233.4	1.9	-	-	-	-	-	-	-	-	-	-	238.7	2.3
1997	-	-	-	-	-	-	-	-	-	-	243.7	2.1	-	-	-	-	-	-	-	-	-	-	-	-

Source: U.S. Department of Labor, Bureau of Labor Statistics, Division of Consumer Prices and Price Indexes. - indicates no data collected for period.

Anchorage, AK
Consumer Price Index - All Urban Consumers
Base 1982-1984 = 100
Entertainment

For 1976-1997. Columns headed % show percentile change in the index from the previous period for which an index is available.

Year	Jan Index	%	Feb Index	%	Mar Index	%	Apr Index	%	May Index	%	Jun Index	%	Jul Index	%	Aug Index	%	Sep Index	%	Oct Index	%	Nov Index	%	Dec Index	%
1976	60.6	-	-	-	-	-	64.3	6.1	-	-	-	-	64.6	0.5	-	-	-	-	66.0	2.2	-	-	-	-
1977	66.5	0.8	-	-	-	-	69.0	3.8	-	-	-	-	70.0	1.4	-	-	-	-	70.6	0.9	-	-	-	-
1978	70.2	-0.6	-	-	72.2	2.8	-	-	72.9	1.0	-	-	71.9	-1.4	-	-	74.1	3.1	-	-	73.6	-0.7	-	-
1979	73.7	0.1	-	-	73.8	0.1	-	-	73.3	-0.7	-	-	73.5	0.3	-	-	75.8	3.1	-	-	76.3	0.7	-	-
1980	77.5	1.6	-	-	78.8	1.7	-	-	81.7	3.7	-	-	76.4	-6.5	-	-	79.6	4.2	-	-	79.3	-0.4	-	-
1981	80.5	1.5	-	-	82.0	1.9	-	-	85.2	3.9	-	-	85.6	0.5	-	-	87.2	1.9	-	-	91.6	5.0	-	-
1982	92.8	1.3	-	-	92.6	-0.2	-	-	94.1	1.6	-	-	94.9	0.9	-	-	94.5	-0.4	-	-	97.8	3.5	-	-
1983	99.1	1.3	-	-	101.0	1.9	-	-	99.3	-1.7	-	-	99.7	0.4	-	-	101.4	1.7	-	-	102.6	1.2	-	-
1984	102.0	-0.6	-	-	103.4	1.4	-	-	103.4	0.0	-	-	105.5	2.0	-	-	106.5	0.9	-	-	106.0	-0.5	-	-
1985	106.4	0.4	-	-	108.6	2.1	-	-	106.9	-1.6	-	-	109.5	2.4	-	-	109.1	-0.4	-	-	112.2	2.8	-	-
1986	109.5	-2.4	-	-	111.4	1.7	-	-	110.2	-1.1	-	-	113.4	2.9	-	-	114.5	1.0	-	-	114.8	0.3	113.1	-1.5
1987	-	-	-	-	-	-	-	-	-	-	117.5	3.9	-	-	-	-	-	-	-	-	-	-	120.9	2.9
1988	-	-	-	-	-	-	-	-	-	-	121.6	0.6	-	-	-	-	-	-	-	-	-	-	124.1	2.1
1989	-	-	-	-	-	-	-	-	-	-	127.8	3.0	-	-	-	-	-	-	-	-	-	-	131.3	2.7
1990	-	-	-	-	-	-	-	-	-	-	134.4	2.4	-	-	-	-	-	-	-	-	-	-	136.8	1.8
1991	-	-	-	-	-	-	-	-	-	-	139.6	2.0	-	-	-	-	-	-	-	-	-	-	142.1	1.8
1992	-	-	-	-	-	-	-	-	-	-	145.4	2.3	-	-	-	-	-	-	-	-	-	-	147.5	1.4
1993	-	-	-	-	-	-	-	-	-	-	149.3	1.2	-	-	-	-	-	-	-	-	-	-	150.3	0.7
1994	-	-	-	-	-	-	-	-	-	-	152.9	1.7	-	-	-	-	-	-	-	-	-	-	155.1	1.4
1995	-	-	-	-	-	-	-	-	-	-	157.7	1.7	-	-	-	-	-	-	-	-	-	-	159.9	1.4
1996	-	-	-	-	-	-	-	-	-	-	163.0	1.9	-	-	-	-	-	-	-	-	-	-	164.1	0.7
1997	-	-	-	-	-	-	-	-	-	-	167.6	2.1	-	-	-	-	-	-	-	-	-	-	-	-

Source: U.S. Department of Labor, Bureau of Labor Statistics, Division of Consumer Prices and Price Indexes. - indicates no data collected for period.

Anchorage, AK
Consumer Price Index - Urban Wage Earners
Base 1982-1984 = 100
Entertainment

For 1976-1997. Columns headed % show percentile change in the index from the previous period for which an index is available.

Year	Jan Index	%	Feb Index	%	Mar Index	%	Apr Index	%	May Index	%	Jun Index	%	Jul Index	%	Aug Index	%	Sep Index	%	Oct Index	%	Nov Index	%	Dec Index	%
1976	66.4	-	-	-	-	-	70.4	6.0	-	-	-	-	70.7	0.4	-	-	-	-	72.3	2.3	-	-	-	-
1977	72.8	0.7	-	-	-	-	75.6	3.8	-	-	-	-	76.7	1.5	-	-	-	-	77.3	0.8	-	-	-	-
1978	76.9	-0.5	-	-	77.2	0.4	-	-	74.7	-3.2	-	-	74.9	0.3	-	-	76.2	1.7	-	-	76.1	-0.1	-	-
1979	76.6	0.7	-	-	76.6	0.0	-	-	76.1	-0.7	-	-	75.8	-0.4	-	-	77.6	2.4	-	-	78.6	1.3	-	-
1980	80.0	1.8	-	-	81.5	1.9	-	-	82.7	1.5	-	-	76.9	-7.0	-	-	78.9	2.6	-	-	79.6	0.9	-	-
1981	79.7	0.1	-	-	82.0	2.9	-	-	85.6	4.4	-	-	86.7	1.3	-	-	88.6	2.2	-	-	91.4	3.2	-	-
1982	92.8	1.5	-	-	92.4	-0.4	-	-	94.0	1.7	-	-	95.0	1.1	-	-	94.3	-0.7	-	-	97.5	3.4	-	-
1983	99.1	1.6	-	-	100.7	1.6	-	-	99.2	-1.5	-	-	99.7	0.5	-	-	101.1	1.4	-	-	102.3	1.2	-	-
1984	102.2	-0.1	-	-	103.4	1.2	-	-	103.6	0.2	-	-	106.2	2.5	-	-	107.0	0.8	-	-	106.3	-0.7	-	-
1985	106.4	0.1	-	-	108.3	1.8	-	-	106.9	-1.3	-	-	109.2	2.2	-	-	108.7	-0.5	-	-	111.9	2.9	-	-
1986	109.7	-2.0	-	-	110.8	1.0	-	-	110.1	-0.6	-	-	113.9	3.5	-	-	114.8	0.8	-	-	115.2	0.3	113.7	-1.3
1987	-	-	-	-	-	-	-	-	-	-	118.6	4.3	-	-	-	-	-	-	-	-	-	-	122.1	3.0
1988	-	-	-	-	-	-	-	-	-	-	122.5	0.3	-	-	-	-	-	-	-	-	-	-	125.2	2.2
1989	-	-	-	-	-	-	-	-	-	-	128.9	3.0	-	-	-	-	-	-	-	-	-	-	131.8	2.2
1990	-	-	-	-	-	-	-	-	-	-	134.9	2.4	-	-	-	-	-	-	-	-	-	-	137.4	1.9
1991	-	-	-	-	-	-	-	-	-	-	140.1	2.0	-	-	-	-	-	-	-	-	-	-	142.4	1.6
1992	-	-	-	-	-	-	-	-	-	-	145.8	2.4	-	-	-	-	-	-	-	-	-	-	147.3	1.0
1993	-	-	-	-	-	-	-	-	-	-	149.4	1.4	-	-	-	-	-	-	-	-	-	-	149.7	0.2
1994	-	-	-	-	-	-	-	-	-	-	152.1	1.6	-	-	-	-	-	-	-	-	-	-	154.9	1.8
1995	-	-	-	-	-	-	-	-	-	-	157.3	1.5	-	-	-	-	-	-	-	-	-	-	159.0	1.1
1996	-	-	-	-	-	-	-	-	-	-	161.7	1.7	-	-	-	-	-	-	-	-	-	-	162.7	0.6
1997	-	-	-	-	-	-	-	-	-	-	165.5	1.7	-	-	-	-	-	-	-	-	-	-	-	-

Source: U.S. Department of Labor, Bureau of Labor Statistics, Division of Consumer Prices and Price Indexes. - indicates no data collected for period.

Anchorage, AK
Consumer Price Index - All Urban Consumers
Base 1982-1984 = 100
Other Goods and Services

For 1976-1997. Columns headed % show percentile change in the index from the previous period for which an index is available.

Year	Jan Index	Jan %	Feb Index	Feb %	Mar Index	Mar %	Apr Index	Apr %	May Index	May %	Jun Index	Jun %	Jul Index	Jul %	Aug Index	Aug %	Sep Index	Sep %	Oct Index	Oct %	Nov Index	Nov %	Dec Index	Dec %
1976	60.9	-	-	-	-	-	63.2	3.8	-	-	-	-	63.8	0.9	-	-	-	-	65.0	1.9	-	-	-	-
1977	67.3	3.5	-	-	-	-	67.5	0.3	-	-	-	-	68.2	1.0	-	-	-	-	68.8	0.9	-	-	-	-
1978	69.5	1.0	-	-	70.0	0.7	-	-	71.1	1.6	-	-	71.5	0.6	-	-	73.3	2.5	-	-	73.5	0.3	-	-
1979	74.1	0.8	-	-	75.4	1.8	-	-	76.2	1.1	-	-	76.1	-0.1	-	-	78.8	3.5	-	-	78.9	0.1	-	-
1980	80.5	2.0	-	-	80.9	0.5	-	-	82.7	2.2	-	-	83.3	0.7	-	-	84.7	1.7	-	-	85.0	0.4	-	-
1981	86.3	1.5	-	-	85.9	-0.5	-	-	87.7	2.1	-	-	88.0	0.3	-	-	89.5	1.7	-	-	90.4	1.0	-	-
1982	89.9	-0.6	-	-	92.1	2.4	-	-	92.5	0.4	-	-	92.9	0.4	-	-	94.6	1.8	-	-	95.3	0.7	-	-
1983	98.1	2.9	-	-	99.3	1.2	-	-	100.9	1.6	-	-	102.5	1.6	-	-	103.2	0.7	-	-	103.8	0.6	-	-
1984	103.2	-0.6	-	-	104.6	1.4	-	-	105.1	0.5	-	-	105.5	0.4	-	-	106.7	1.1	-	-	105.4	-1.2	-	-
1985	108.4	2.8	-	-	110.9	2.3	-	-	111.3	0.4	-	-	112.0	0.6	-	-	118.0	5.4	-	-	121.8	3.2	-	-
1986	119.6	-1.8	-	-	121.0	1.2	-	-	121.7	0.6	-	-	121.9	0.2	-	-	126.5	3.8	-	-	126.6	0.1	126.9	0.2
1987	-	-	-	-	-	-	-	-	-	-	128.6	1.3	-	-	-	-	-	-	-	-	-	-	-	-
1988	-	-	-	-	-	-	-	-	-	-	137.3	6.8	-	-	-	-	-	-	-	-	-	-	-	-
1989	-	-	-	-	-	-	-	-	-	-	147.8	7.6	-	-	-	-	-	-	-	-	-	-	-	-
1990	-	-	-	-	-	-	-	-	-	-	160.6	8.7	-	-	-	-	-	-	-	-	-	-	-	-
1991	-	-	-	-	-	-	-	-	-	-	172.9	7.7	-	-	-	-	-	-	-	-	-	-	-	-
1992	-	-	-	-	-	-	-	-	-	-	188.0	8.7	-	-	-	-	-	-	-	-	-	-	-	-
1993	-	-	-	-	-	-	-	-	-	-	198.8	5.7	-	-	-	-	-	-	-	-	-	-	-	-
1994	-	-	-	-	-	-	-	-	-	-	202.6	1.9	-	-	-	-	-	-	-	-	-	-	-	-
1995	-	-	-	-	-	-	-	-	-	-	210.3	3.8	-	-	-	-	-	-	-	-	-	-	-	-
1996	-	-	-	-	-	-	-	-	-	-	219.7	4.5	-	-	-	-	-	-	-	-	-	-	-	-
1997	-	-	-	-	-	-	-	-	-	-	227.2	3.4	-	-	-	-	-	-	-	-	-	-	-	-

Source: U.S. Department of Labor, Bureau of Labor Statistics, Division of Consumer Prices and Price Indexes. - indicates no data collected for period.

Anchorage, AK
Consumer Price Index - Urban Wage Earners
Base 1982-1984 = 100
Other Goods and Services

For 1976-1997. Columns headed % show percentile change in the index from the previous period for which an index is available.

Year	Jan Index	%	Feb Index	%	Mar Index	%	Apr Index	%	May Index	%	Jun Index	%	Jul Index	%	Aug Index	%	Sep Index	%	Oct Index	%	Nov Index	%	Dec Index	%
1976	59.8	-	-	-	-	-	62.1	3.8	-	-	-	-	62.6	0.8	-	-	-	-	63.8	1.9	-	-	-	-
1977	66.0	3.4	-	-	-	-	66.3	0.5	-	-	-	-	67.0	1.1	-	-	-	-	67.5	0.7	-	-	-	-
1978	68.2	1.0	-	-	68.7	0.7	-	-	69.5	1.2	-	-	70.4	1.3	-	-	71.5	1.6	-	-	71.4	-0.1	-	-
1979	72.1	1.0	-	-	73.5	1.9	-	-	73.6	0.1	-	-	75.0	1.9	-	-	76.5	2.0	-	-	77.7	1.6	-	-
1980	78.8	1.4	-	-	80.3	1.9	-	-	82.1	2.2	-	-	82.6	0.6	-	-	82.5	-0.1	-	-	83.4	1.1	-	-
1981	84.8	1.7	-	-	83.9	-1.1	-	-	85.5	1.9	-	-	85.8	0.4	-	-	88.0	2.6	-	-	89.2	1.4	-	-
1982	88.7	-0.6	-	-	91.4	3.0	-	-	91.5	0.1	-	-	92.0	0.5	-	-	93.8	2.0	-	-	94.7	1.0	-	-
1983	98.0	3.5	-	-	99.2	1.2	-	-	101.2	2.0	-	-	103.1	1.9	-	-	104.0	0.9	-	-	104.5	0.5	-	-
1984	104.0	-0.5	-	-	105.4	1.3	-	-	106.0	0.6	-	-	106.5	0.5	-	-	106.4	-0.1	-	-	104.9	-1.4	-	-
1985	108.4	3.3	-	-	111.4	2.8	-	-	111.8	0.4	-	-	112.7	0.8	-	-	116.4	3.3	-	-	120.9	3.9	-	-
1986	120.0	-0.7	-	-	121.8	1.5	-	-	122.5	0.6	-	-	122.6	0.1	-	-	125.2	2.1	-	-	125.4	0.2	125.8	0.3
1987	-	-	-	-	-	-	-	-	-	-	127.3	1.2	-	-	-	-	-	-	-	-	-	-	-	-
1988	-	-	-	-	-	-	-	-	-	-	135.7	6.6	-	-	-	-	-	-	-	-	-	-	-	-
1989	-	-	-	-	-	-	-	-	-	-	146.6	8.0	-	-	-	-	-	-	-	-	-	-	-	-
1990	-	-	-	-	-	-	-	-	-	-	159.4	8.7	-	-	-	-	-	-	-	-	-	-	-	-
1991	-	-	-	-	-	-	-	-	-	-	173.2	8.7	-	-	-	-	-	-	-	-	-	-	-	-
1992	-	-	-	-	-	-	-	-	-	-	188.0	8.5	-	-	-	-	-	-	-	-	-	-	-	-
1993	-	-	-	-	-	-	-	-	-	-	199.0	5.9	-	-	-	-	-	-	-	-	-	-	-	-
1994	-	-	-	-	-	-	-	-	-	-	202.6	1.8	-	-	-	-	-	-	-	-	-	-	-	-
1995	-	-	-	-	-	-	-	-	-	-	209.8	3.6	-	-	-	-	-	-	-	-	-	-	-	-
1996	-	-	-	-	-	-	-	-	-	-	219.1	4.4	-	-	-	-	-	-	-	-	-	-	-	-
1997	-	-	-	-	-	-	-	-	-	-	228.1	4.1	-	-	-	-	-	-	-	-	-	-	-	-

Source: U.S. Department of Labor, Bureau of Labor Statistics, Division of Consumer Prices and Price Indexes. - indicates no data collected for period.

Atlanta, GA
Consumer Price Index - All Urban Consumers
Base 1982-1984 = 100
Annual Averages

For 1917-1997. Columns headed % show percentile change in the index from the previous period for which an index is available.

Year	All Items		Food & Beverage		Housing		Apparel & Upkeep		Trans- portation		Medical Care		Entertain- ment		Other Goods & Services	
	Index	%	Index	%	Index	%	Index	%	Index	%	Index	%	Index	%	Index	%
1917	-	-	-	-	-	-	-	-	-	-	-	-	-	-	-	-
1918	16.6	-	-	-	-	-	-	-	-	-	-	-	-	-	-	-
1919	19.3	16.3	-	-	-	-	-	-	-	-	-	-	-	-	-	-
1920	21.9	13.5	-	-	-	-	-	-	-	-	-	-	-	-	-	-
1921	19.0	-13.2	-	-	-	-	-	-	-	-	-	-	-	-	-	-
1922	17.5	-7.9	-	-	-	-	-	-	-	-	-	-	-	-	-	-
1923	17.6	0.6	-	-	-	-	-	-	-	-	-	-	-	-	-	-
1924	17.3	-1.7	-	-	-	-	-	-	-	-	-	-	-	-	-	-
1925	17.9	3.5	-	-	-	-	-	-	-	-	-	-	-	-	-	-
1926	18.1	1.1	-	-	-	-	-	-	-	-	-	-	-	-	-	-
1927	17.5	-3.3	-	-	-	-	-	-	-	-	-	-	-	-	-	-
1928	17.3	-1.1	-	-	-	-	-	-	-	-	-	-	-	-	-	-
1929	17.2	-0.6	-	-	-	-	-	-	-	-	-	-	-	-	-	-
1930	16.5	-4.1	-	-	-	-	-	-	-	-	-	-	-	-	-	-
1931	14.9	-9.7	-	-	-	-	-	-	-	-	-	-	-	-	-	-
1932	13.3	-10.7	-	-	-	-	-	-	-	-	-	-	-	-	-	-
1933	12.6	-5.3	-	-	-	-	-	-	-	-	-	-	-	-	-	-
1934	13.2	4.8	-	-	-	-	-	-	-	-	-	-	-	-	-	-
1935	13.5	2.3	-	-	-	-	-	-	-	-	-	-	-	-	-	-
1936	13.7	1.5	-	-	-	-	-	-	-	-	-	-	-	-	-	-
1937	14.1	2.9	-	-	-	-	-	-	-	-	-	-	-	-	-	-
1938	13.7	-2.8	-	-	-	-	-	-	-	-	-	-	-	-	-	-
1939	13.6	-0.7	-	-	-	-	-	-	-	-	-	-	-	-	-	-
1940	13.6	0.0	-	-	-	-	-	-	-	-	-	-	-	-	-	-
1941	14.4	5.9	-	-	-	-	-	-	-	-	-	-	-	-	-	-
1942	15.9	10.4	-	-	-	-	-	-	-	-	-	-	-	-	-	-
1943	17.0	6.9	-	-	-	-	-	-	-	-	-	-	-	-	-	-
1944	17.3	1.8	-	-	-	-	-	-	-	-	-	-	-	-	-	-
1945	17.9	3.5	-	-	-	-	-	-	-	-	-	-	-	-	-	-
1946	19.3	7.8	-	-	-	-	-	-	-	-	-	-	-	-	-	-
1947	22.3	15.5	-	-	-	-	-	-	20.4	-	15.2	-	-	-	-	-
1948	23.8	6.7	-	-	-	-	-	-	22.4	9.8	15.7	3.3	-	-	-	-
1949	23.8	0.0	-	-	-	-	-	-	24.1	7.6	16.1	2.5	-	-	-	-
1950	24.1	1.3	-	-	-	-	-	-	24.6	2.1	16.1	0.0	-	-	-	-
1951	26.4	9.5	-	-	-	-	-	-	26.4	7.3	16.9	5.0	-	-	-	-
1952	27.0	2.3	-	-	-	-	-	-	28.1	6.4	18.1	7.1	-	-	-	-
1953	27.3	1.1	-	-	-	-	42.2	-	28.9	2.8	18.5	2.2	-	-	-	-
1954	27.2	-0.4	-	-	-	-	42.4	0.5	28.0	-3.1	18.9	2.2	-	-	-	-
1955	27.1	-0.4	-	-	-	-	42.1	-0.7	27.5	-1.8	19.6	3.7	-	-	-	-
1956	27.5	1.5	-	-	-	-	42.9	1.9	28.2	2.5	20.2	3.1	-	-	-	-
1957	28.3	2.9	-	-	-	-	43.7	1.9	30.0	6.4	20.7	2.5	-	-	-	-
1958	29.0	2.5	-	-	-	-	44.3	1.4	31.3	4.3	21.4	3.4	-	-	-	-
1959	29.2	0.7	-	-	-	-	44.3	0.0	32.4	3.5	22.3	4.2	-	-	-	-
1960	29.6	1.4	-	-	-	-	45.0	1.6	32.0	-1.2	23.0	3.1	-	-	-	-
1961	29.7	0.3	-	-	-	-	45.1	0.2	32.4	1.3	23.2	0.9	-	-	-	-

[Continued]

250

Atlanta, GA
Consumer Price Index - All Urban Consumers
Base 1982-1984 = 100
Annual Averages
[Continued]

For 1917-1997. Columns headed % show percentile change in the index from the previous period for which an index is available.

Year	All Items		Food & Beverage		Housing		Apparel & Upkeep		Trans-portation		Medical Care		Entertain-ment		Other Goods & Services	
	Index	%	Index	%	Index	%	Index	%	Index	%	Index	%	Index	%	Index	%
1962	30.0	1.0	-	-	-	-	45.1	0.0	33.1	2.2	23.9	3.0	-	-	-	-
1963	30.3	1.0	-	-	-	-	46.1	2.2	33.8	2.1	24.2	1.3	-	-	-	-
1964	30.8	1.7	-	-	-	-	46.2	0.2	34.7	2.7	24.8	2.5	-	-	-	-
1965	31.2	1.3	-	-	-	-	46.7	1.1	34.6	-0.3	25.4	2.4	-	-	-	-
1966	32.2	3.2	-	-	-	-	48.9	4.7	34.6	0.0	26.7	5.1	-	-	-	-
1967	33.2	3.1	-	-	-	-	51.6	5.5	35.2	1.7	28.4	6.4	-	-	-	-
1968	34.5	3.9	-	-	-	-	53.8	4.3	36.1	2.6	30.3	6.7	-	-	-	-
1969	36.5	5.8	-	-	-	-	56.0	4.1	37.3	3.3	33.3	9.9	-	-	-	-
1970	38.6	5.8	-	-	-	-	58.4	4.3	38.2	2.4	35.8	7.5	-	-	-	-
1971	40.4	4.7	-	-	-	-	59.9	2.6	40.6	6.3	38.6	7.8	-	-	-	-
1972	41.6	3.0	-	-	-	-	61.3	2.3	39.8	-2.0	39.6	2.6	-	-	-	-
1973	44.3	6.5	-	-	-	-	63.8	4.1	41.1	3.3	41.5	4.8	-	-	-	-
1974	49.2	11.1	-	-	-	-	69.1	8.3	46.5	13.1	46.1	11.1	-	-	-	-
1975	53.6	8.9	-	-	-	-	71.6	3.6	50.4	8.4	52.1	13.0	-	-	-	-
1976	56.1	4.7	62.5	-	51.9	-	74.3	3.8	54.2	7.5	56.0	7.5	77.2	-	55.4	-
1977	59.6	6.2	65.9	5.4	55.2	6.4	79.5	7.0	57.3	5.7	60.7	8.4	80.3	4.0	58.5	5.6
1978	63.9	7.2	72.2	9.6	59.8	8.3	84.0	5.7	59.6	4.0	63.8	5.1	83.8	4.4	62.7	7.2
1979	70.5	10.3	79.5	10.1	65.9	10.2	87.6	4.3	69.5	16.6	68.1	6.7	85.6	2.1	68.9	9.9
1980	80.3	13.9	85.8	7.9	76.1	15.5	93.1	6.3	84.8	22.0	74.7	9.7	88.7	3.6	75.6	9.7
1981	90.2	12.3	93.1	8.5	87.7	15.2	96.2	3.3	94.9	11.9	82.3	10.2	94.6	6.7	84.1	11.2
1982	96.0	6.4	97.1	4.3	95.4	8.8	96.8	0.6	97.5	2.7	92.6	12.5	97.8	3.4	91.7	9.0
1983	99.9	4.1	99.8	2.8	100.0	4.8	100.5	3.8	99.4	1.9	101.2	9.3	98.0	0.2	100.5	9.6
1984	104.1	4.2	103.1	3.3	104.6	4.6	102.7	2.2	103.0	3.6	106.2	4.9	104.1	6.2	107.9	7.4
1985	108.9	4.6	106.1	2.9	109.9	5.1	111.7	8.8	106.7	3.6	112.9	6.3	111.4	7.0	113.0	4.7
1986	112.2	3.0	111.2	4.8	115.2	4.8	110.4	-1.2	102.9	-3.6	123.7	9.6	118.7	6.6	119.8	6.0
1987	116.8	4.1	112.1	0.8	118.4	2.8	107.7	-2.4	111.5	8.4	133.0	7.5	112.2	-5.5	135.9	13.4
1988	122.4	4.8	116.0	3.5	124.8	5.4	109.9	2.0	115.6	3.7	142.2	6.9	120.8	7.7	145.1	6.8
1989	128.3	4.8	124.2	7.1	130.8	4.8	99.4	-9.6	121.5	5.1	155.3	9.2	128.6	6.5	155.4	7.1
1990	135.8	5.8	131.2	5.6	138.7	6.0	101.4	2.0	127.7	5.1	167.4	7.8	133.5	3.8	171.9	10.6
1991	142.2	4.7	135.4	3.2	145.6	5.0	103.7	2.3	132.3	3.6	183.5	9.6	138.0	3.4	185.5	7.9
1992	146.6	3.1	137.6	1.6	149.6	2.7	106.5	2.7	136.1	2.9	196.6	7.1	144.4	4.6	195.8	5.6
1993	150.2	2.5	139.7	1.5	151.9	1.5	106.0	-0.5	139.5	2.5	211.6	7.6	147.5	2.1	210.7	7.6
1994	154.6	2.9	142.7	2.1	155.1	2.1	105.8	-0.2	144.0	3.2	223.9	5.8	160.3	8.7	222.2	5.5
1995	158.7	2.7	148.8	4.3	158.4	2.1	102.1	-3.5	148.7	3.3	232.5	3.8	166.7	4.0	227.1	2.2
1996	162.8	2.6	152.2	2.3	162.4	2.5	103.8	1.7	151.5	1.9	242.2	4.2	178.2	6.9	232.9	2.6
1997	158.9	-2.4	159.5	4.8	156.4	-3.7	137.0	32.0	132.5	-12.5	243.5	0.5	186.6	4.7	212.4	-8.8

Source: U.S. Department of Labor, Bureau of Labor Statistics, Division of Consumer Prices and Price Indexes. - indicates no data collected for period.

Atlanta, GA
Consumer Price Index - Urban Wage Earners
Base 1982-1984 = 100
Annual Averages

For 1917-1997. Columns headed % show percentile change in the index from the previous period for which an index is available.

Year	All Items		Food & Beverage		Housing		Apparel & Upkeep		Trans-portation		Medical Care		Entertain-ment		Other Goods & Services	
	Index	%	Index	%	Index	%	Index	%	Index	%	Index	%	Index	%	Index	%
1917	-	-	-	-	-	-	-	-	-	-	-	-	-	-	-	-
1918	16.6	-	-	-	-	-	-	-	-	-	-	-	-	-	-	-
1919	19.3	16.3	-	-	-	-	-	-	-	-	-	-	-	-	-	-
1920	21.8	13.0	-	-	-	-	-	-	-	-	-	-	-	-	-	-
1921	18.9	-13.3	-	-	-	-	-	-	-	-	-	-	-	-	-	-
1922	17.5	-7.4	-	-	-	-	-	-	-	-	-	-	-	-	-	-
1923	17.5	0.0	-	-	-	-	-	-	-	-	-	-	-	-	-	-
1924	17.3	-1.1	-	-	-	-	-	-	-	-	-	-	-	-	-	-
1925	17.8	2.9	-	-	-	-	-	-	-	-	-	-	-	-	-	-
1926	18.0	1.1	-	-	-	-	-	-	-	-	-	-	-	-	-	-
1927	17.5	-2.8	-	-	-	-	-	-	-	-	-	-	-	-	-	-
1928	17.3	-1.1	-	-	-	-	-	-	-	-	-	-	-	-	-	-
1929	17.2	-0.6	-	-	-	-	-	-	-	-	-	-	-	-	-	-
1930	16.5	-4.1	-	-	-	-	-	-	-	-	-	-	-	-	-	-
1931	14.8	-10.3	-	-	-	-	-	-	-	-	-	-	-	-	-	-
1932	13.2	-10.8	-	-	-	-	-	-	-	-	-	-	-	-	-	-
1933	12.6	-4.5	-	-	-	-	-	-	-	-	-	-	-	-	-	-
1934	13.2	4.8	-	-	-	-	-	-	-	-	-	-	-	-	-	-
1935	13.5	2.3	-	-	-	-	-	-	-	-	-	-	-	-	-	-
1936	13.7	1.5	-	-	-	-	-	-	-	-	-	-	-	-	-	-
1937	14.1	2.9	-	-	-	-	-	-	-	-	-	-	-	-	-	-
1938	13.7	-2.8	-	-	-	-	-	-	-	-	-	-	-	-	-	-
1939	13.6	-0.7	-	-	-	-	-	-	-	-	-	-	-	-	-	-
1940	13.6	0.0	-	-	-	-	-	-	-	-	-	-	-	-	-	-
1941	14.3	5.1	-	-	-	-	-	-	-	-	-	-	-	-	-	-
1942	15.9	11.2	-	-	-	-	-	-	-	-	-	-	-	-	-	-
1943	17.0	6.9	-	-	-	-	-	-	-	-	-	-	-	-	-	-
1944	17.3	1.8	-	-	-	-	-	-	-	-	-	-	-	-	-	-
1945	17.9	3.5	-	-	-	-	-	-	-	-	-	-	-	-	-	-
1946	19.2	7.3	-	-	-	-	-	-	-	-	-	-	-	-	-	-
1947	22.3	16.1	-	-	-	-	-	-	19.8	-	14.6	-	-	-	-	-
1948	23.7	6.3	-	-	-	-	-	-	21.8	10.1	15.1	3.4	-	-	-	-
1949	23.7	0.0	-	-	-	-	-	-	23.5	7.8	15.5	2.6	-	-	-	-
1950	24.0	1.3	-	-	-	-	-	-	24.0	2.1	15.5	0.0	-	-	-	-
1951	26.3	9.6	-	-	-	-	-	-	25.7	7.1	16.3	5.2	-	-	-	-
1952	27.0	2.7	-	-	-	-	-	-	27.4	6.6	17.4	6.7	-	-	-	-
1953	27.2	0.7	-	-	-	-	40.0	-	28.1	2.6	17.8	2.3	-	-	-	-
1954	27.1	-0.4	-	-	-	-	40.1	0.2	27.2	-3.2	18.2	2.2	-	-	-	-
1955	27.0	-0.4	-	-	-	-	39.9	-0.5	26.8	-1.5	18.8	3.3	-	-	-	-
1956	27.5	1.9	-	-	-	-	40.7	2.0	27.5	2.6	19.5	3.7	-	-	-	-
1957	28.2	2.5	-	-	-	-	41.5	2.0	29.2	6.2	19.9	2.1	-	-	-	-
1958	28.9	2.5	-	-	-	-	42.0	1.2	30.5	4.5	20.6	3.5	-	-	-	-
1959	29.1	0.7	-	-	-	-	42.0	0.0	31.5	3.3	21.5	4.4	-	-	-	-
1960	29.5	1.4	-	-	-	-	42.7	1.7	31.2	-1.0	22.1	2.8	-	-	-	-
1961	29.7	0.7	-	-	-	-	42.7	0.0	31.6	1.3	22.3	0.9	-	-	-	-

[Continued]

Atlanta, GA
Consumer Price Index - Urban Wage Earners
Base 1982-1984 = 100
Annual Averages
[Continued]

For 1917-1997. Columns headed % show percentile change in the index from the previous period for which an index is available.

Year	All Items		Food & Beverage		Housing		Apparel & Upkeep		Trans-portation		Medical Care		Entertain-ment		Other Goods & Services	
	Index	%	Index	%	Index	%	Index	%	Index	%	Index	%	Index	%	Index	%
1962	29.9	0.7	-	-	-	-	42.7	0.0	32.2	1.9	23.0	3.1	-	-	-	-
1963	30.2	1.0	-	-	-	-	43.7	2.3	32.9	2.2	23.3	1.3	-	-	-	-
1964	30.7	1.7	-	-	-	-	43.8	0.2	33.8	2.7	23.9	2.6			-	-
1965	31.1	1.3					44.3	1.1	33.7	-0.3	24.4	2.1	-	-	-	-
1966	32.1	3.2				-	46.4	4.7	33.7	0.0	25.7	5.3	-	-	-	-
1967	33.1	3.1	-	-	-	-	49.0	5.6	34.3	1.8	27.3	6.2	-	-	-	-
1968	34.4	3.9	-	-	-	-	51.0	4.1	35.1	2.3	29.1	6.6	-	-	-	-
1969	36.4	5.8	-	-	-	-	53.1	4.1	36.3	3.4	32.1	10.3	-	-	-	-
1970	38.5	5.8	-	-	-	-	55.3	4.1	37.2	2.5	34.5	7.5	-	-	-	-
1971	40.2	4.4	-	-	-	-	56.8	2.7	39.5	6.2	37.2	7.8	-	-	-	-
1972	41.5	3.2	-	-	-	-	58.1	2.3	38.8	-1.8	38.1	2.4	-	-	-	-
1973	44.2	6.5	-	-	-	-	60.5	4.1	40.0	3.1	40.0	5.0	-	-	-	-
1974	49.1	11.1	-	-	-	-	65.5	8.3	45.3	13.2	44.3	10.8	-	-	-	-
1975	53.5	9.0	-	-	-	-	67.9	3.7	49.0	8.2	50.2	13.3	-	-	-	-
1976	56.0	4.7	61.8	-	52.6	-	70.4	3.7	52.8	7.8	53.9	7.4	69.9	-	58.1	-
1977	59.4	6.1	65.2	5.5	56.0	6.5	75.3	7.0	55.8	5.7	58.4	8.3	72.6	3.9	61.3	5.5
1978	63.8	7.4	71.9	10.3	60.6	8.2	78.2	3.9	58.3	4.5	62.4	6.8	74.6	2.8	65.2	6.4
1979	71.0	11.3	79.4	10.4	67.0	10.6	84.4	7.9	69.0	18.4	68.1	9.1	75.6	1.3	70.2	7.7
1980	81.1	14.2	85.7	7.9	76.7	14.5	89.9	6.5	86.1	24.8	73.0	7.2	89.1	17.9	75.7	7.8
1981	90.8	12.0	93.2	8.8	87.9	14.6	95.9	6.7	96.0	11.5	81.8	12.1	98.9	11.0	83.6	10.4
1982	96.4	6.2	97.1	4.2	95.8	9.0	97.9	2.1	98.2	2.3	92.5	13.1	99.6	0.7	91.4	9.3
1983	100.1	3.8	99.9	2.9	100.7	5.1	100.0	2.1	99.5	1.3	101.3	9.5	94.9	-4.7	100.7	10.2
1984	103.5	3.4	103.0	3.1	103.6	2.9	102.1	2.1	102.3	2.8	106.3	4.9	105.5	11.2	107.9	7.1
1985	107.9	4.3	105.9	2.8	108.4	4.6	109.4	7.1	106.0	3.6	113.0	6.3	110.3	4.5	112.8	4.5
1986	110.8	2.7	111.0	4.8	113.1	4.3	108.2	-1.1	101.9	-3.9	124.0	9.7	118.2	7.2	119.7	6.1
1987	116.7	5.3	112.4	1.3	120.0	6.1	104.4	-3.5	110.8	8.7	132.7	7.0	110.6	-6.4	134.7	12.5
1988	122.2	4.7	116.5	3.6	126.3	5.2	106.0	1.5	115.1	3.9	141.5	6.6	118.8	7.4	144.3	7.1
1989	128.3	5.0	125.1	7.4	133.0	5.3	94.5	-10.8	121.6	5.6	154.0	8.8	126.1	6.1	153.8	6.6
1990	136.1	6.1	132.3	5.8	140.7	5.8	97.6	3.3	128.4	5.6	165.9	7.7	130.2	3.3	170.7	11.0
1991	142.2	4.5	136.5	3.2	147.5	4.8	99.0	1.4	132.8	3.4	180.9	9.0	134.7	3.5	184.3	8.0
1992	146.4	3.0	138.7	1.6	151.3	2.6	103.3	4.3	136.1	2.5	193.9	7.2	140.2	4.1	194.3	5.4
1993	150.1	2.5	140.9	1.6	153.8	1.7	104.7	1.4	139.2	2.3	208.8	7.7	142.6	1.7	208.5	7.3
1994	154.2	2.7	143.9	2.1	156.9	2.0	101.9	-2.7	144.0	3.4	220.5	5.6	155.7	9.2	218.2	4.7
1995	158.3	2.7	150.0	4.2	160.3	2.2	98.1	-3.7	149.5	3.8	228.5	3.6	162.2	4.2	222.2	1.8
1996	162.2	2.5	153.3	2.2	164.1	2.4	100.1	2.0	152.2	1.8	237.9	4.1	173.5	7.0	227.4	2.3
1997	156.5	-3.5	158.2	3.2	153.7	-6.3	132.4	32.3	130.3	-14.4	241.1	1.3	185.1	6.7	218.1	-4.1

Source: U.S. Department of Labor, Bureau of Labor Statistics, Division of Consumer Prices and Price Indexes. - indicates no data collected for period.

Atlanta, GA
Consumer Price Index - All Urban Consumers
Base 1982-1984 = 100
All Items

For 1917-1997. Columns headed % show percentile change in the index from the previous period for which an index is available.

Year	Jan Index	%	Feb Index	%	Mar Index	%	Apr Index	%	May Index	%	Jun Index	%	Jul Index	%	Aug Index	%	Sep Index	%	Oct Index	%	Nov Index	%	Dec Index	%
1917	-	-	-	-	-	-	-	-	-	-	-	-	-	-	-	-	-	-	-	-	-	-	15.2	-
1918	-	-	-	-	-	-	-	-	-	-	-	-	-	-	-	-	-	-	-	-	-	-	18.2	19.7
1919	-	-	-	-	-	-	-	-	-	-	18.9	3.8	-	-	-	-	-	-	-	-	-	-	20.8	10.1
1920	-	-	-	-	-	-	-	-	-	-	23.0	10.6	-	-	-	-	-	-	-	-	-	-	20.8	-9.6
1921	-	-	-	-	-	-	-	-	19.0	-8.7	-	-	-	-	-	-	18.5	-2.6	-	-	-	-	18.0	-2.7
1922	-	-	-	-	17.4	-3.3	-	-	-	-	17.5	0.6	-	-	-	-	17.4	-0.6	-	-	-	-	17.3	-0.6
1923	-	-	-	-	17.4	0.6	-	-	-	-	17.6	1.1	-	-	-	-	17.8	1.1	-	-	-	-	17.5	-1.7
1924	-	-	-	-	17.3	-1.1	-	-	-	-	17.3	0.0	-	-	-	-	17.3	0.0	-	-	-	-	17.3	0.0
1925	-	-	-	-	-	-	-	-	-	-	17.9	3.5	-	-	-	-	-	-	-	-	-	-	18.3	2.2
1926	-	-	-	-	-	-	-	-	-	-	18.0	-1.6	-	-	-	-	-	-	-	-	-	-	17.8	-1.1
1927	-	-	-	-	-	-	-	-	-	-	18.1	1.7	-	-	-	-	-	-	-	-	-	-	17.2	-5.0
1928	-	-	-	-	-	-	-	-	-	-	17.4	1.2	-	-	-	-	-	-	-	-	-	-	17.3	-0.6
1929	-	-	-	-	-	-	-	-	-	-	17.1	-1.2	-	-	-	-	-	-	-	-	-	-	17.1	0.0
1930	-	-	-	-	-	-	-	-	-	-	16.5	-3.5	-	-	-	-	-	-	-	-	-	-	15.8	-4.2
1931	-	-	-	-	-	-	-	-	-	-	14.8	-6.3	-	-	-	-	-	-	-	-	-	-	14.0	-5.4
1932	-	-	-	-	-	-	-	-	-	-	13.4	-4.3	-	-	-	-	-	-	-	-	-	-	12.6	-6.0
1933	-	-	-	-	-	-	-	-	-	-	12.5	-0.8	-	-	-	-	-	-	-	-	-	-	12.9	3.2
1934	-	-	-	-	-	-	-	-	-	-	13.1	1.6	-	-	-	-	-	-	-	-	13.4	2.3	-	-
1935	-	-	-	-	13.4	0.0	-	-	-	-	-	-	13.4	0.0	-	-	-	-	13.7	2.2	-	-	-	-
1936	13.8	0.7	-	-	-	-	13.5	-2.2	-	-	-	-	13.7	1.5	-	-	13.9	1.5	-	-	-	-	13.9	0.0
1937	-	-	-	-	14.0	0.7	-	-	-	-	14.1	0.7	-	-	-	-	14.3	1.4	-	-	-	-	14.1	-1.4
1938	-	-	-	-	13.8	-2.1	-	-	-	-	13.6	-1.4	-	-	-	-	13.8	1.5	-	-	-	-	13.8	0.0
1939	-	-	-	-	13.6	-1.4	-	-	-	-	13.5	-0.7	-	-	-	-	13.8	2.2	-	-	-	-	13.6	-1.4
1940	-	-	-	-	13.7	0.7	-	-	-	-	13.5	-1.5	-	-	-	-	13.6	0.7	-	-	-	-	13.8	1.5
1941	-	-	-	-	13.8	0.0	-	-	-	-	14.2	2.9	-	-	-	-	14.8	4.2	-	-	-	-	15.2	2.7
1942	-	-	-	-	15.7	3.3	-	-	-	-	15.9	1.3	-	-	-	-	16.1	1.3	-	-	-	-	16.4	1.9
1943	-	-	-	-	16.9	3.0	-	-	-	-	17.2	1.8	-	-	-	-	17.1	-0.6	-	-	-	-	17.1	0.0
1944	-	-	-	-	17.0	-0.6	-	-	-	-	17.3	1.8	-	-	-	-	17.5	1.2	-	-	-	-	17.7	1.1
1945	-	-	-	-	17.7	0.0	-	-	-	-	17.9	1.1	-	-	-	-	18.1	1.1	-	-	-	-	18.1	0.0
1946	-	-	-	-	18.1	0.0	-	-	-	-	18.4	1.7	-	-	-	-	20.2	9.8	-	-	-	-	21.4	5.9
1947	-	-	-	-	22.2	3.7	-	-	-	-	21.9	-1.4	-	-	22.3	1.8	-	-	-	-	23.1	3.6	-	-
1948	-	-	23.3	0.9	-	-	-	-	23.6	1.3	-	-	-	-	24.4	3.4	-	-	-	-	24.0	-1.6	-	-
1949	-	-	23.6	-1.7	-	-	-	-	23.7	0.4	-	-	-	-	24.0	1.3	-	-	-	-	23.8	-0.8	-	-
1950	-	-	23.4	-1.7	-	-	-	-	23.6	0.9	-	-	-	-	24.4	3.4	-	-	-	-	24.8	1.6	-	-
1951	-	-	25.8	4.0	-	-	-	-	26.5	2.7	-	-	-	-	26.5	0.0	-	-	-	-	26.9	1.5	-	-
1952	-	-	26.8	-0.4	-	-	-	-	26.7	-0.4	-	-	-	-	27.3	2.2	-	-	-	-	27.3	0.0	27.2	-0.4
1953	-	-	-	-	27.2	0.0	-	-	-	-	27.3	0.4	-	-	-	-	27.4	0.4	-	-	-	-	27.3	-0.4
1954	-	-	-	-	27.3	0.0	-	-	-	-	27.4	0.4	-	-	-	-	27.1	-1.1	-	-	-	-	27.0	-0.4
1955	-	-	-	-	26.9	-0.4	-	-	-	-	27.0	0.4	-	-	-	-	27.3	1.1	-	-	-	-	27.3	0.0
1956	-	-	-	-	27.2	-0.4	-	-	-	-	27.5	1.1	-	-	-	-	27.7	0.7	-	-	-	-	27.8	0.4
1957	-	-	-	-	28.1	1.1	-	-	-	-	28.2	0.4	-	-	-	-	28.5	1.1	-	-	-	-	28.5	0.0
1958	-	-	-	-	29.1	2.1	-	-	-	-	29.1	0.0	-	-	-	-	29.0	-0.3	-	-	-	-	29.0	0.0
1959	-	-	-	-	28.9	-0.3	-	-	-	-	29.2	1.0	-	-	-	-	29.3	0.3	-	-	-	-	29.4	0.3
1960	-	-	-	-	29.5	0.3	-	-	-	-	29.6	0.3	-	-	-	-	29.8	0.7	-	-	-	-	29.7	-0.3
1961	-	-	-	-	29.7	0.0	-	-	-	-	29.7	0.0	-	-	-	-	29.9	0.7	-	-	-	-	29.8	-0.3

[Continued]

Atlanta, GA
Consumer Price Index - All Urban Consumers
Base 1982-1984 = 100
All Items
[Continued]

For 1917-1997. Columns headed % show percentile change in the index from the previous period for which an index is available.

Year	Jan Index	%	Feb Index	%	Mar Index	%	Apr Index	%	May Index	%	Jun Index	%	Jul Index	%	Aug Index	%	Sep Index	%	Oct Index	%	Nov Index	%	Dec Index	%
1962	-	-	-	-	29.9	0.3	-	-	-	-	30.0	0.3	-	-	-	-	30.2	0.7	-	-	-	-	30.1	-0.3
1963	-	-	-	-	30.2	0.3	-	-	-	-	30.2	0.0	-	-	-	-	30.3	0.3	-	-	-	-	30.5	0.7
1964	-	-	-	-	30.7	0.7	-	-	-	-	30.6	-0.3	-	-	-	-	30.9	1.0	-	-	-	-	31.0	0.3
1965	-	-	-	-	31.0	0.0	-	-	-	-	31.1	0.3	-	-	-	-	31.2	0.3	-	-	-	-	31.5	1.0
1966	-	-	-	-	31.8	1.0	-	-	-	-	32.0	0.6	-	-	-	-	32.5	1.6	-	-	-	-	32.7	0.6
1967	-	-	-	-	32.9	0.6	-	-	-	-	33.1	0.6	-	-	-	-	33.3	0.6	-	-	-	-	33.7	1.2
1968	-	-	-	-	34.0	0.9	-	-	-	-	34.3	0.9	-	-	-	-	35.0	2.0	-	-	-	-	35.2	0.6
1969	-	-	-	-	36.0	2.3	-	-	-	-	36.4	1.1	-	-	-	-	37.1	1.9	-	-	-	-	37.5	1.1
1970	-	-	-	-	38.0	1.3	-	-	-	-	38.6	1.6	-	-	-	-	39.0	1.0	-	-	-	-	39.6	1.5
1971	-	-	-	-	39.9	0.8	-	-	-	-	40.6	1.8	-	-	-	-	40.5	-0.2	-	-	-	-	41.0	1.2
1972	-	-	-	-	41.1	0.2	-	-	-	-	41.4	0.7	-	-	-	-	42.1	1.7	-	-	-	-	42.3	0.5
1973	-	-	-	-	43.1	1.9	-	-	-	-	44.0	2.1	-	-	-	-	45.4	3.2	-	-	-	-	46.1	1.5
1974	-	-	-	-	47.8	3.7	-	-	-	-	48.8	2.1	-	-	-	-	50.6	3.7	-	-	-	-	51.7	2.2
1975	-	-	-	-	52.6	1.7	-	-	-	-	53.4	1.5	-	-	-	-	54.6	2.2	-	-	-	-	55.1	0.9
1976	-	-	-	-	55.2	0.2	-	-	-	-	55.9	1.3	-	-	-	-	56.9	1.8	-	-	-	-	57.0	0.2
1977	-	-	-	-	58.4	2.5	-	-	-	-	59.4	1.7	-	-	-	-	60.7	2.2	-	-	-	-	61.2	0.8
1978	-	-	61.7	0.8	-	-	62.5	1.3	-	-	63.6	1.8	-	-	64.7	1.7	-	-	65.9	1.9	-	-	65.9	0.0
1979	-	-	66.9	1.5	-	-	68.5	2.4	-	-	70.5	2.9	-	-	71.9	2.0	-	-	73.2	1.8	-	-	74.0	1.1
1980	-	-	76.4	3.2	-	-	78.0	2.1	-	-	80.3	2.9	-	-	81.7	1.7	-	-	83.0	1.6	-	-	85.7	3.3
1981	-	-	87.2	1.8	-	-	88.2	1.1	-	-	89.3	1.2	-	-	91.6	2.6	-	-	93.3	1.9	-	-	93.6	0.3
1982	-	-	92.8	-0.9	-	-	92.9	0.1	-	-	96.5	3.9	-	-	98.0	1.6	-	-	98.8	0.8	-	-	98.2	-0.6
1983	-	-	97.9	-0.3	-	-	98.7	0.8	-	-	100.2	1.5	-	-	100.8	0.6	-	-	100.9	0.1	-	-	101.9	1.0
1984	-	-	102.6	0.7	-	-	103.2	0.6	-	-	104.1	0.9	-	-	104.8	0.7	-	-	105.4	0.6	-	-	105.5	0.1
1985	-	-	107.0	1.4	-	-	107.6	0.6	-	-	108.8	1.1	-	-	109.9	1.0	-	-	110.4	0.5	-	-	111.2	0.7
1986	-	-	111.7	0.4	-	-	111.1	-0.5	-	-	112.2	1.0	-	-	112.4	0.2	-	-	112.7	0.3	-	-	113.5	0.7
1987	-	-	-	-	-	-	-	-	-	-	115.1	1.4	-	-	-	-	-	-	-	-	-	-	118.5	3.0
1988	-	-	-	-	-	-	-	-	-	-	120.2	1.4	-	-	-	-	-	-	-	-	-	-	124.6	3.7
1989	-	-	-	-	-	-	-	-	-	-	126.8	1.8	-	-	-	-	-	-	-	-	-	-	129.9	2.4
1990	-	-	-	-	-	-	-	-	-	-	133.5	2.8	-	-	-	-	-	-	-	-	-	-	138.2	3.5
1991	-	-	-	-	-	-	-	-	-	-	141.0	2.0	-	-	-	-	-	-	-	-	-	-	143.4	1.7
1992	-	-	-	-	-	-	-	-	-	-	145.4	1.4	-	-	-	-	-	-	-	-	-	-	147.7	1.6
1993	-	-	-	-	-	-	-	-	-	-	149.1	0.9	-	-	-	-	-	-	-	-	-	-	151.3	1.5
1994	-	-	-	-	-	-	-	-	-	-	153.3	1.3	-	-	-	-	-	-	-	-	-	-	156.0	1.8
1995	-	-	-	-	-	-	-	-	-	-	157.7	1.1	-	-	-	-	-	-	-	-	-	-	159.7	1.3
1996	-	-	-	-	-	-	-	-	-	-	161.6	1.2	-	-	-	-	-	-	-	-	-	-	164.1	1.5
1997	-	-	-	-	-	-	-	-	-	-	165.9	1.1	-	-	-	-	-	-	-	-	-	-	-	-

Source: U.S. Department of Labor, Bureau of Labor Statistics, Division of Consumer Prices and Price Indexes. - indicates no data collected for period.

Atlanta, GA
Consumer Price Index - Urban Wage Earners
Base 1982-1984 = 100
All Items

For 1917-1997. Columns headed % show percentile change in the index from the previous period for which an index is available.

Year	Jan Index	%	Feb Index	%	Mar Index	%	Apr Index	%	May Index	%	Jun Index	%	Jul Index	%	Aug Index	%	Sep Index	%	Oct Index	%	Nov Index	%	Dec Index	%
1917	-	-	-	-	-	-	-	-	-	-	-	-	-	-	-	-	-	-	-	-	-	-	15.1	-
1918	-	-	-	-	-	-	-	-	-	-	-	-	-	-	-	-	-	-	-	-	-	-	18.1	19.9
1919	-	-	-	-	-	-	-	-	-	-	18.9	4.4	-	-	-	-	-	-	-	-	-	-	20.7	9.5
1920	-	-	-	-	-	-	-	-	-	-	23.0	11.1	-	-	-	-	-	-	-	-	-	-	20.8	-9.6
1921	-	-	-	-	-	-	-	-	18.9	-9.1	-	-	-	-	-	-	18.4	-2.6	-	-	-	-	17.9	-2.7
1922	-	-	-	-	17.4	-2.8	-	-	-	-	17.5	0.6	-	-	-	-	17.3	-1.1	-	-	-	-	17.3	0.0
1923	-	-	-	-	17.3	0.0	-	-	-	-	17.5	1.2	-	-	-	-	17.8	1.7	-	-	-	-	17.5	-1.7
1924	-	-	-	-	17.2	-1.7	-	-	-	-	17.3	0.6	-	-	-	-	17.3	0.0	-	-	-	-	17.3	0.0
1925	-	-	-	-	-	-	-	-	-	-	17.8	2.9	-	-	-	-	-	-	-	-	-	-	18.2	2.2
1926	-	-	-	-	-	-	-	-	-	-	18.0	-1.1	-	-	-	-	-	-	-	-	-	-	17.7	-1.7
1927	-	-	-	-	-	-	-	-	-	-	18.1	2.3	-	-	-	-	-	-	-	-	-	-	17.2	-5.0
1928	-	-	-	-	-	-	-	-	-	-	17.3	0.6	-	-	-	-	-	-	-	-	-	-	17.3	0.0
1929	-	-	-	-	-	-	-	-	-	-	17.1	-1.2	-	-	-	-	-	-	-	-	-	-	17.1	0.0
1930	-	-	-	-	-	-	-	-	-	-	16.4	-4.1	-	-	-	-	-	-	-	-	-	-	15.7	-4.3
1931	-	-	-	-	-	-	-	-	-	-	14.8	-5.7	-	-	-	-	-	-	-	-	-	-	14.0	-5.4
1932	-	-	-	-	-	-	-	-	-	-	13.3	-5.0	-	-	-	-	-	-	-	-	-	-	12.6	-5.3
1933	-	-	-	-	-	-	-	-	-	-	12.5	-0.8	-	-	-	-	-	-	-	-	-	-	12.9	3.2
1934	-	-	-	-	-	-	-	-	-	-	13.1	1.6	-	-	-	-	-	-	-	-	13.3	1.5	-	-
1935	-	-	-	-	13.3	0.0	-	-	-	-	-	-	13.3	0.0	-	-	-	-	13.7	3.0	-	-	-	-
1936	13.7	0.0	-	-	-	-	13.5	-1.5	-	-	-	-	13.7	1.5	-	-	13.8	0.7	-	-	-	-	13.8	0.0
1937	-	-	-	-	14.0	1.4	-	-	-	-	14.1	0.7	-	-	-	-	14.3	1.4	-	-	-	-	14.1	-1.4
1938	-	-	-	-	13.7	-2.8	-	-	-	-	13.6	-0.7	-	-	-	-	13.7	0.7	-	-	-	-	13.7	0.0
1939	-	-	-	-	13.6	-0.7	-	-	-	-	13.4	-1.5	-	-	-	-	13.7	2.2	-	-	-	-	13.5	-1.5
1940	-	-	-	-	13.6	0.7	-	-	-	-	13.5	-0.7	-	-	-	-	13.6	0.7	-	-	-	-	13.7	0.7
1941	-	-	-	-	13.8	0.7	-	-	-	-	14.2	2.9	-	-	-	-	14.7	3.5	-	-	-	-	15.1	2.7
1942	-	-	-	-	15.6	3.3	-	-	-	-	15.8	1.3	-	-	-	-	16.1	1.9	-	-	-	-	16.3	1.2
1943	-	-	-	-	16.9	3.7	-	-	-	-	17.2	1.8	-	-	-	-	17.1	-0.6	-	-	-	-	17.0	-0.6
1944	-	-	-	-	16.9	-0.6	-	-	-	-	17.2	1.8	-	-	-	-	17.5	1.7	-	-	-	-	17.7	1.1
1945	-	-	-	-	17.7	0.0	-	-	-	-	17.8	0.6	-	-	-	-	18.1	1.7	-	-	-	-	18.0	-0.6
1946	-	-	-	-	18.1	0.6	-	-	-	-	18.4	1.7	-	-	-	-	20.1	9.2	-	-	-	-	21.4	6.5
1947	-	-	-	-	22.1	3.3	-	-	-	-	21.8	-1.4	-	-	22.3	2.3	-	-	-	-	23.0	3.1	-	-
1948	-	-	23.3	1.3	-	-	-	-	23.5	0.9	-	-	-	-	24.3	3.4	-	-	-	-	24.0	-1.2	-	-
1949	-	-	23.5	-2.1	-	-	-	-	23.6	0.4	-	-	-	-	23.9	1.3	-	-	-	-	23.7	-0.8	-	-
1950	-	-	23.4	-1.3	-	-	-	-	23.5	0.4	-	-	-	-	24.4	3.8	-	-	-	-	24.7	1.2	-	-
1951	-	-	25.7	4.0	-	-	-	-	26.4	2.7	-	-	-	-	26.5	0.4	-	-	-	-	26.9	1.5	-	-
1952	-	-	26.8	-0.4	-	-	-	-	26.6	-0.7	-	-	-	-	27.2	2.3	-	-	-	-	27.2	0.0	27.1	-0.4
1953	-	-	-	-	27.1	0.0	-	-	-	-	27.2	0.4	-	-	-	-	27.3	0.4	-	-	-	-	27.2	-0.4
1954	-	-	-	-	27.2	0.0	-	-	-	-	27.3	0.4	-	-	-	-	27.0	-1.1	-	-	-	-	26.9	-0.4
1955	-	-	-	-	26.8	-0.4	-	-	-	-	27.0	0.7	-	-	-	-	27.2	0.7	-	-	-	-	27.2	0.0
1956	-	-	-	-	27.1	-0.4	-	-	-	-	27.4	1.1	-	-	-	-	27.6	0.7	-	-	-	-	27.7	0.4
1957	-	-	-	-	28.0	1.1	-	-	-	-	28.1	0.4	-	-	-	-	28.4	1.1	-	-	-	-	28.4	0.0
1958	-	-	-	-	29.0	2.1	-	-	-	-	29.0	0.0	-	-	-	-	28.9	-0.3	-	-	-	-	28.9	0.0
1959	-	-	-	-	28.9	0.0	-	-	-	-	29.2	1.0	-	-	-	-	29.3	0.3	-	-	-	-	29.4	0.3
1960	-	-	-	-	29.4	0.0	-	-	-	-	29.5	0.3	-	-	-	-	29.7	0.7	-	-	-	-	29.7	0.0
1961	-	-	-	-	29.7	0.0	-	-	-	-	29.6	-0.3	-	-	-	-	29.8	0.7	-	-	-	-	29.7	-0.3

[Continued]

256

Atlanta, GA
Consumer Price Index - Urban Wage Earners
Base 1982-1984 = 100
All Items
[Continued]

For 1917-1997. Columns headed % show percentile change in the index from the previous period for which an index is available.

Year	Jan Index	%	Feb Index	%	Mar Index	%	Apr Index	%	May Index	%	Jun Index	%	Jul Index	%	Aug Index	%	Sep Index	%	Oct Index	%	Nov Index	%	Dec Index	%
1962	-	-	-	-	29.8	0.3	-	-	-	-	29.9	0.3	-	-	-	-	30.1	0.7	-	-	-	-	30.1	0.0
1963	-	-	-	-	30.2	0.3	-	-	-	-	30.2	0.0	-	-	-	-	30.3	0.3	-	-	-	-	30.4	0.3
1964	-	-	-	-	30.7	1.0	-	-	-	-	30.6	-0.3	-	-	-	-	30.8	0.7	-	-	-	-	30.9	0.3
1965	-	-	-	-	31.0	0.3	-	-	-	-	31.0	0.0	-	-	-	-	31.1	0.3	-	-	-	-	31.4	1.0
1966	-	-	-	-	31.7	1.0	-	-	-	-	31.9	0.6	-	-	-	-	32.4	1.6	-	-	-	-	32.6	0.6
1967	-	-	-	-	32.8	0.6	-	-	-	-	33.0	0.6	-	-	-	-	33.2	0.6	-	-	-	-	33.6	1.2
1968	-	-	-	-	33.9	0.9	-	-	-	-	34.2	0.9	-	-	-	-	34.9	2.0	-	-	-	-	35.1	0.6
1969	-	-	-	-	35.9	2.3	-	-	-	-	36.3	1.1	-	-	-	-	37.0	1.9	-	-	-	-	37.4	1.1
1970	-	-	-	-	37.9	1.3	-	-	-	-	38.5	1.6	-	-	-	-	38.9	1.0	-	-	-	-	39.5	1.5
1971	-	-	-	-	39.8	0.8	-	-	-	-	40.4	1.5	-	-	-	-	40.3	-0.2	-	-	-	-	40.8	1.2
1972	-	-	-	-	40.9	0.2	-	-	-	-	41.3	1.0	-	-	-	-	42.0	1.7	-	-	-	-	42.2	0.5
1973	-	-	-	-	43.0	1.9	-	-	-	-	43.9	2.1	-	-	-	-	45.3	3.2	-	-	-	-	45.9	1.3
1974	-	-	-	-	47.7	3.9	-	-	-	-	48.7	2.1	-	-	-	-	50.5	3.7	-	-	-	-	51.6	2.2
1975	-	-	-	-	52.4	1.6	-	-	-	-	53.2	1.5	-	-	-	-	54.5	2.4	-	-	-	-	55.0	0.9
1976	-	-	-	-	55.1	0.2	-	-	-	-	55.7	1.1	-	-	-	-	56.8	2.0	-	-	-	-	56.9	0.2
1977	-	-	-	-	58.2	2.3	-	-	-	-	59.2	1.7	-	-	-	-	60.5	2.2	-	-	-	-	61.0	0.8
1978	-	-	61.7	1.1	-	-	62.5	1.3	-	-	63.7	1.9	-	-	64.6	1.4	-	-	65.6	1.5	-	-	65.9	0.5
1979	-	-	67.0	1.7	-	-	68.9	2.8	-	-	70.9	2.9	-	-	72.4	2.1	-	-	73.9	2.1	-	-	75.1	1.6
1980	-	-	77.2	2.8	-	-	79.1	2.5	-	-	80.9	2.3	-	-	82.6	2.1	-	-	83.5	1.1	-	-	86.1	3.1
1981	-	-	88.1	2.3	-	-	88.9	0.9	-	-	90.2	1.5	-	-	92.0	2.0	-	-	93.6	1.7	-	-	94.0	0.4
1982	-	-	93.5	-0.5	-	-	93.6	0.1	-	-	96.9	3.5	-	-	98.3	1.4	-	-	98.8	0.5	-	-	98.5	-0.3
1983	-	-	98.2	-0.3	-	-	99.3	1.1	-	-	99.9	0.6	-	-	100.6	0.7	-	-	101.3	0.7	-	-	102.4	1.1
1984	-	-	102.4	0.0	-	-	102.3	-0.1	-	-	102.8	0.5	-	-	104.2	1.4	-	-	105.2	1.0	-	-	104.5	-0.7
1985	-	-	105.9	1.3	-	-	106.6	0.7	-	-	107.8	1.1	-	-	108.9	1.0	-	-	109.1	0.2	-	-	110.0	0.8
1986	-	-	110.6	0.5	-	-	109.7	-0.8	-	-	111.0	1.2	-	-	110.9	-0.1	-	-	111.1	0.2	-	-	111.7	0.5
1987	-	-	-	-	-	-	-	-	-	-	114.9	2.9	-	-	-	-	-	-	-	-	-	-	118.5	3.1
1988	-	-	-	-	-	-	-	-	-	-	120.0	1.3	-	-	-	-	-	-	-	-	-	-	124.4	3.7
1989	-	-	-	-	-	-	-	-	-	-	126.7	1.8	-	-	-	-	-	-	-	-	-	-	130.0	2.6
1990	-	-	-	-	-	-	-	-	-	-	133.6	2.8	-	-	-	-	-	-	-	-	-	-	138.5	3.7
1991	-	-	-	-	-	-	-	-	-	-	141.0	1.8	-	-	-	-	-	-	-	-	-	-	143.4	1.7
1992	-	-	-	-	-	-	-	-	-	-	145.2	1.3	-	-	-	-	-	-	-	-	-	-	147.6	1.7
1993	-	-	-	-	-	-	-	-	-	-	149.0	0.9	-	-	-	-	-	-	-	-	-	-	151.2	1.5
1994	-	-	-	-	-	-	-	-	-	-	152.8	1.1	-	-	-	-	-	-	-	-	-	-	155.6	1.8
1995	-	-	-	-	-	-	-	-	-	-	157.4	1.2	-	-	-	-	-	-	-	-	-	-	159.2	1.1
1996	-	-	-	-	-	-	-	-	-	-	161.0	1.1	-	-	-	-	-	-	-	-	-	-	163.4	1.5
1997	-	-	-	-	-	-	-	-	-	-	165.0	1.0	-	-	-	-	-	-	-	-	-	-	-	-

Source: U.S. Department of Labor, Bureau of Labor Statistics, Division of Consumer Prices and Price Indexes. - indicates no data collected for period.

Atlanta, GA
Consumer Price Index - All Urban Consumers
Base 1982-1984 = 100
Food and Beverages

For 1975-1997. Columns headed % show percentile change in the index from the previous period for which an index is available.

Year	Jan Index	%	Feb Index	%	Mar Index	%	Apr Index	%	May Index	%	Jun Index	%	Jul Index	%	Aug Index	%	Sep Index	%	Oct Index	%	Nov Index	%	Dec Index	%
1975	-	-	-	-	-	-	-	-	-	-	-	-	-	-	-	-	-	-	-	-	-	-	63.2	-
1976	-	-	-	-	62.1	-1.7	-	-	-	-	62.2	0.2	-	-	-	-	-	-	63.0	1.3	-	-	62.4	-1.0
1977	-	-	-	-	64.9	4.0	-	-	-	-	65.9	1.5	-	-	-	-	-	-	67.2	2.0	-	-	67.6	0.6
1978	-	-	69.0	2.1	-	-	70.2	1.7	-	-	73.1	4.1	-	-	73.8	1.0	-	-	74.0	0.3	-	-	74.9	1.2
1979	-	-	77.7	3.7	-	-	78.8	1.4	-	-	79.1	0.4	-	-	80.8	2.1	-	-	80.7	-0.1	-	-	81.6	1.1
1980	-	-	82.4	1.0	-	-	82.9	0.6	-	-	84.4	1.8	-	-	87.6	3.8	-	-	88.6	1.1	-	-	91.4	3.2
1981	-	-	92.2	0.9	-	-	92.2	0.0	-	-	92.5	0.3	-	-	93.5	1.1	-	-	94.1	0.6	-	-	95.0	1.0
1982	-	-	96.1	1.2	-	-	96.3	0.2	-	-	97.5	1.2	-	-	97.4	-0.1	-	-	97.7	0.3	-	-	98.2	0.5
1983	-	-	98.8	0.6	-	-	100.2	1.4	-	-	100.0	-0.2	-	-	99.9	-0.1	-	-	100.1	0.2	-	-	100.4	0.3
1984	-	-	103.4	3.0	-	-	102.7	-0.7	-	-	102.2	-0.5	-	-	103.8	1.6	-	-	103.5	-0.3	-	-	104.3	0.8
1985	-	-	106.2	1.8	-	-	105.5	-0.7	-	-	105.5	0.0	-	-	105.3	-0.2	-	-	106.3	0.9	-	-	108.6	2.2
1986	-	-	109.4	0.7	-	-	110.5	1.0	-	-	110.6	0.1	-	-	113.0	2.2	-	-	112.5	-0.4	-	-	112.1	-0.4
1987	-	-	-	-	-	-	-	-	-	-	111.2	-0.8	-	-	-	-	-	-	-	-	-	-	112.9	1.5
1988	-	-	-	-	-	-	-	-	-	-	114.4	1.3	-	-	-	-	-	-	-	-	-	-	117.6	2.8
1989	-	-	-	-	-	-	-	-	-	-	121.9	3.7	-	-	-	-	-	-	-	-	-	-	126.5	3.8
1990	-	-	-	-	-	-	-	-	-	-	130.1	2.8	-	-	-	-	-	-	-	-	-	-	132.4	1.8
1991	-	-	-	-	-	-	-	-	-	-	135.6	2.4	-	-	-	-	-	-	-	-	-	-	135.2	-0.3
1992	-	-	-	-	-	-	-	-	-	-	137.2	1.5	-	-	-	-	-	-	-	-	-	-	138.0	0.6
1993	-	-	-	-	-	-	-	-	-	-	139.6	1.2	-	-	-	-	-	-	-	-	-	-	139.7	0.1
1994	-	-	-	-	-	-	-	-	-	-	141.4	1.2	-	-	-	-	-	-	-	-	-	-	144.1	1.9
1995	-	-	-	-	-	-	-	-	-	-	148.3	2.9	-	-	-	-	-	-	-	-	-	-	149.3	0.7
1996	-	-	-	-	-	-	-	-	-	-	151.2	1.3	-	-	-	-	-	-	-	-	-	-	153.1	1.3
1997	-	-	-	-	-	-	-	-	-	-	154.2	0.7	-	-	-	-	-	-	-	-	-	-	-	-

Source: U.S. Department of Labor, Bureau of Labor Statistics, Division of Consumer Prices and Price Indexes. - indicates no data collected for period.

Atlanta, GA
Consumer Price Index - Urban Wage Earners
Base 1982-1984 = 100
Food and Beverages

For 1975-1997. Columns headed % show percentile change in the index from the previous period for which an index is available.

Year	Jan Index	%	Feb Index	%	Mar Index	%	Apr Index	%	May Index	%	Jun Index	%	Jul Index	%	Aug Index	%	Sep Index	%	Oct Index	%	Nov Index	%	Dec Index	%
1975	-	-	-	-	-	-	-	-	-	-	-	-	-	-	-	-	-	-	-	-	-	-	62.5	-
1976	-	-	-	-	61.4	-1.8	-	-	-	-	61.5	0.2	-	-	-	-	62.3	1.3	-	-	-	-	61.7	-1.0
1977	-	-	-	-	64.1	3.9	-	-	-	-	65.1	1.6	-	-	-	-	66.5	2.2	-	-	-	-	66.8	0.5
1978	-	-	68.3	2.2	-	-	70.1	2.6	-	-	72.8	3.9	-	-	73.8	1.4	-	-	73.7	-0.1	-	-	74.4	0.9
1979	-	-	77.4	4.0	-	-	78.7	1.7	-	-	79.1	0.5	-	-	80.5	1.8	-	-	80.7	0.2	-	-	81.6	1.1
1980	-	-	82.4	1.0	-	-	83.6	1.5	-	-	84.3	0.8	-	-	87.1	3.3	-	-	88.4	1.5	-	-	90.8	2.7
1981	-	-	91.9	1.2	-	-	92.6	0.8	-	-	93.1	0.5	-	-	93.7	0.6	-	-	94.2	0.5	-	-	94.8	0.6
1982	-	-	95.9	1.2	-	-	96.3	0.4	-	-	97.5	1.2	-	-	97.5	0.0	-	-	97.9	0.4	-	-	98.4	0.5
1983	-	-	98.9	0.5	-	-	100.3	1.4	-	-	100.1	-0.2	-	-	99.9	-0.2	-	-	100.1	0.2	-	-	100.4	0.3
1984	-	-	103.1	2.7	-	-	102.5	-0.6	-	-	102.3	-0.2	-	-	103.6	1.3	-	-	103.4	-0.2	-	-	104.2	0.8
1985	-	-	106.0	1.7	-	-	105.3	-0.7	-	-	105.4	0.1	-	-	105.2	-0.2	-	-	106.1	0.9	-	-	108.4	2.2
1986	-	-	109.2	0.7	-	-	110.3	1.0	-	-	110.3	0.0	-	-	112.9	2.4	-	-	112.5	-0.4	-	-	111.8	-0.6
1987	-	-	-	-	-	-	-	-	-	-	111.4	-0.4	-	-	-	-	-	-	-	-	-	-	113.3	1.7
1988	-	-	-	-	-	-	-	-	-	-	114.7	1.2	-	-	-	-	-	-	-	-	-	-	118.2	3.1
1989	-	-	-	-	-	-	-	-	-	-	122.8	3.9	-	-	-	-	-	-	-	-	-	-	127.4	3.7
1990	-	-	-	-	-	-	-	-	-	-	131.1	2.9	-	-	-	-	-	-	-	-	-	-	133.6	1.9
1991	-	-	-	-	-	-	-	-	-	-	136.7	2.3	-	-	-	-	-	-	-	-	-	-	136.4	-0.2
1992	-	-	-	-	-	-	-	-	-	-	138.2	1.3	-	-	-	-	-	-	-	-	-	-	139.3	0.8
1993	-	-	-	-	-	-	-	-	-	-	140.8	1.1	-	-	-	-	-	-	-	-	-	-	141.0	0.1
1994	-	-	-	-	-	-	-	-	-	-	142.6	1.1	-	-	-	-	-	-	-	-	-	-	145.3	1.9
1995	-	-	-	-	-	-	-	-	-	-	149.4	2.8	-	-	-	-	-	-	-	-	-	-	150.5	0.7
1996	-	-	-	-	-	-	-	-	-	-	152.4	1.3	-	-	-	-	-	-	-	-	-	-	154.3	1.2
1997	-	-	-	-	-	-	-	-	-	-	155.4	0.7	-	-	-	-	-	-	-	-	-	-	-	-

Source: U.S. Department of Labor, Bureau of Labor Statistics, Division of Consumer Prices and Price Indexes. - indicates no data collected for period.

Atlanta, GA
Consumer Price Index - All Urban Consumers
Base 1982-1984 = 100
Housing

For 1975-1997. Columns headed % show percentile change in the index from the previous period for which an index is available.

Year	Jan Index	%	Feb Index	%	Mar Index	%	Apr Index	%	May Index	%	Jun Index	%	Jul Index	%	Aug Index	%	Sep Index	%	Oct Index	%	Nov Index	%	Dec Index	%
1975	-	-	-	-	-	-	-	-	-	-	-	-	-	-	-	-	-	-	-	-	-	-	50.7	-
1976	-	-	-	-	51.2	1.0	-	-	-	-	51.8	1.2	-	-	-	-	52.5	1.4	-	-	-	-	52.8	0.6
1977	-	-	-	-	53.7	1.7	-	-	-	-	55.1	2.6	-	-	-	-	56.4	2.4	-	-	-	-	57.2	1.4
1978	-	-	57.6	0.7	-	-	58.5	1.6	-	-	59.2	1.2	-	-	60.4	2.0	-	-	62.2	3.0	-	-	62.0	-0.3
1979	-	-	62.3	0.5	-	-	63.5	1.9	-	-	66.0	3.9	-	-	66.9	1.4	-	-	68.9	3.0	-	-	69.6	1.0
1980	-	-	71.5	2.7	-	-	73.6	2.9	-	-	77.0	4.6	-	-	76.8	-0.3	-	-	78.4	2.1	-	-	82.4	5.1
1981	-	-	83.6	1.5	-	-	84.3	0.8	-	-	86.4	2.5	-	-	90.0	4.2	-	-	92.3	2.6	-	-	92.4	0.1
1982	-	-	90.7	-1.8	-	-	91.7	1.1	-	-	96.4	5.1	-	-	98.5	2.2	-	-	98.7	0.2	-	-	97.7	-1.0
1983	-	-	98.0	0.3	-	-	98.9	0.9	-	-	101.1	2.2	-	-	100.5	-0.6	-	-	100.2	-0.3	-	-	102.5	2.3
1984	-	-	102.7	0.2	-	-	103.4	0.7	-	-	105.3	1.8	-	-	106.0	0.7	-	-	105.4	-0.6	-	-	105.7	0.3
1985	-	-	107.4	1.6	-	-	108.4	0.9	-	-	110.2	1.7	-	-	111.6	1.3	-	-	111.2	-0.4	-	-	112.3	1.0
1986	-	-	112.7	0.4	-	-	114.1	1.2	-	-	116.1	1.8	-	-	116.3	0.2	-	-	115.9	-0.3	-	-	117.4	1.3
1987	-	-	-	-	-	-	-	-	-	-	116.4	-0.9	-	-	-	-	-	-	-	-	-	-	120.4	3.4
1988	-	-	-	-	-	-	-	-	-	-	121.8	1.2	-	-	-	-	-	-	-	-	-	-	127.8	4.9
1989	-	-	-	-	-	-	-	-	-	-	128.8	0.8	-	-	-	-	-	-	-	-	-	-	132.8	3.1
1990	-	-	-	-	-	-	-	-	-	-	136.2	2.6	-	-	-	-	-	-	-	-	-	-	141.1	3.6
1991	-	-	-	-	-	-	-	-	-	-	144.2	2.2	-	-	-	-	-	-	-	-	-	-	147.0	1.9
1992	-	-	-	-	-	-	-	-	-	-	148.5	1.0	-	-	-	-	-	-	-	-	-	-	150.7	1.5
1993	-	-	-	-	-	-	-	-	-	-	151.3	0.4	-	-	-	-	-	-	-	-	-	-	152.5	0.8
1994	-	-	-	-	-	-	-	-	-	-	153.7	0.8	-	-	-	-	-	-	-	-	-	-	156.5	1.8
1995	-	-	-	-	-	-	-	-	-	-	157.0	0.3	-	-	-	-	-	-	-	-	-	-	159.7	1.7
1996	-	-	-	-	-	-	-	-	-	-	161.3	1.0	-	-	-	-	-	-	-	-	-	-	163.5	1.4
1997	-	-	-	-	-	-	-	-	-	-	166.4	1.8	-	-	-	-	-	-	-	-	-	-	-	-

Source: U.S. Department of Labor, Bureau of Labor Statistics, Division of Consumer Prices and Price Indexes. - indicates no data collected for period.

Atlanta, GA
Consumer Price Index - Urban Wage Earners
Base 1982-1984 = 100
Housing

For 1975-1997. Columns headed % show percentile change in the index from the previous period for which an index is available.

Year	Jan Index	%	Feb Index	%	Mar Index	%	Apr Index	%	May Index	%	Jun Index	%	Jul Index	%	Aug Index	%	Sep Index	%	Oct Index	%	Nov Index	%	Dec Index	%
1975	-	-	-	-	-	-	-	-	-	-	-	-	-	-	-	-	-	-	-	-	-	-	51.3	-
1976	-	-	-	-	51.9	1.2	-	-	-	-	52.5	1.2	-	-	-	-	53.2	1.3	-	-	-	-	53.5	0.6
1977	-	-	-	-	54.5	1.9	-	-	-	-	55.8	2.4	-	-	-	-	57.2	2.5	-	-	-	-	58.0	1.4
1978	-	-	58.6	1.0	-	-	59.3	1.2	-	-	60.1	1.3	-	-	61.1	1.7	-	-	62.6	2.5	-	-	62.9	0.5
1979	-	-	63.3	0.6	-	-	64.6	2.1	-	-	67.3	4.2	-	-	68.0	1.0	-	-	69.8	2.6	-	-	70.7	1.3
1980	-	-	72.4	2.4	-	-	74.6	3.0	-	-	77.8	4.3	-	-	77.6	-0.3	-	-	78.4	1.0	-	-	82.4	5.1
1981	-	-	83.6	1.5	-	-	84.4	1.0	-	-	86.8	2.8	-	-	90.2	3.9	-	-	92.3	2.3	-	-	92.6	0.3
1982	-	-	91.2	-1.5	-	-	92.4	1.3	-	-	96.8	4.8	-	-	98.8	2.1	-	-	98.7	-0.1	-	-	98.0	-0.7
1983	-	-	99.0	1.0	-	-	100.2	1.2	-	-	100.3	0.1	-	-	100.7	0.4	-	-	101.7	1.0	-	-	103.8	2.1
1984	-	-	102.5	-1.3	-	-	101.7	-0.8	-	-	102.4	0.7	-	-	104.8	2.3	-	-	105.7	0.9	-	-	104.4	-1.2
1985	-	-	106.1	1.6	-	-	107.0	0.8	-	-	108.8	1.7	-	-	110.2	1.3	-	-	109.4	-0.7	-	-	110.4	0.9
1986	-	-	110.7	0.3	-	-	111.9	1.1	-	-	114.2	2.1	-	-	114.2	0.0	-	-	113.7	-0.4	-	-	115.3	1.4
1987	-	-	-	-	-	-	-	-	-	-	117.9	2.3	-	-	-	-	-	-	-	-	-	-	122.0	3.5
1988	-	-	-	-	-	-	-	-	-	-	123.3	1.1	-	-	-	-	-	-	-	-	-	-	129.4	4.9
1989	-	-	-	-	-	-	-	-	-	-	130.9	1.2	-	-	-	-	-	-	-	-	-	-	135.1	3.2
1990	-	-	-	-	-	-	-	-	-	-	138.3	2.4	-	-	-	-	-	-	-	-	-	-	143.1	3.5
1991	-	-	-	-	-	-	-	-	-	-	145.9	2.0	-	-	-	-	-	-	-	-	-	-	149.0	2.1
1992	-	-	-	-	-	-	-	-	-	-	150.2	0.8	-	-	-	-	-	-	-	-	-	-	152.4	1.5
1993	-	-	-	-	-	-	-	-	-	-	153.1	0.5	-	-	-	-	-	-	-	-	-	-	154.5	0.9
1994	-	-	-	-	-	-	-	-	-	-	155.5	0.6	-	-	-	-	-	-	-	-	-	-	158.3	1.8
1995	-	-	-	-	-	-	-	-	-	-	158.9	0.4	-	-	-	-	-	-	-	-	-	-	161.7	1.8
1996	-	-	-	-	-	-	-	-	-	-	163.0	0.8	-	-	-	-	-	-	-	-	-	-	165.2	1.3
1997	-	-	-	-	-	-	-	-	-	-	167.9	1.6	-	-	-	-	-	-	-	-	-	-	-	-

Source: U.S. Department of Labor, Bureau of Labor Statistics, Division of Consumer Prices and Price Indexes. - indicates no data collected for period.

Atlanta, GA
Consumer Price Index - All Urban Consumers
Base 1982-1984 = 100
Apparel and Upkeep

For 1952-1997. Columns headed % show percentile change in the index from the previous period for which an index is available.

Year	Jan Index	%	Feb Index	%	Mar Index	%	Apr Index	%	May Index	%	Jun Index	%	Jul Index	%	Aug Index	%	Sep Index	%	Oct Index	%	Nov Index	%	Dec Index	%
1952	-	-	-	-	-	-	-	-	-	-	-	-	-	-	-	-	-	-	-	-	42.1	-	-	-
1953	-	-	-	-	42.2	0.2	-	-	-	-	42.1	-0.2	-	-	-	-	42.5	1.0	-	-	-	-	42.2	-0.7
1954	-	-	-	-	42.5	0.7	-	-	-	-	42.6	0.2	-	-	-	-	42.2	-0.9	-	-	-	-	42.1	-0.2
1955	-	-	-	-	41.5	-1.4	-	-	-	-	42.1	1.4	-	-	-	-	42.5	1.0	-	-	-	-	42.5	0.0
1956	-	-	-	-	42.6	0.2	-	-	-	-	42.8	0.5	-	-	-	-	43.4	1.4	-	-	-	-	43.2	-0.5
1957	-	-	-	-	43.7	1.2	-	-	-	-	43.6	-0.2	-	-	-	-	44.1	1.1	-	-	-	-	44.1	0.0
1958	-	-	-	-	44.3	0.5	-	-	-	-	44.1	-0.5	-	-	-	-	44.3	0.5	-	-	-	-	44.3	0.0
1959	-	-	-	-	44.0	-0.7	-	-	-	-	44.0	0.0	-	-	-	-	44.4	0.9	-	-	-	-	44.7	0.7
1960	-	-	-	-	44.7	0.0	-	-	-	-	44.7	0.0	-	-	-	-	45.5	1.8	-	-	-	-	45.3	-0.4
1961	-	-	-	-	45.1	-0.4	-	-	-	-	45.1	0.0	-	-	-	-	45.0	-0.2	-	-	-	-	44.9	-0.2
1962	-	-	-	-	45.0	0.2	-	-	-	-	44.9	-0.2	-	-	-	-	45.2	0.7	-	-	-	-	45.5	0.7
1963	-	-	-	-	45.9	0.9	-	-	-	-	46.0	0.2	-	-	-	-	46.5	1.1	-	-	-	-	46.2	-0.6
1964	-	-	-	-	46.2	0.0	-	-	-	-	46.0	-0.4	-	-	-	-	46.2	0.4	-	-	-	-	46.3	0.2
1965	-	-	-	-	46.4	0.2	-	-	-	-	46.4	0.0	-	-	-	-	47.0	1.3	-	-	-	-	47.1	0.2
1966	-	-	-	-	47.8	1.5	-	-	-	-	48.4	1.3	-	-	-	-	50.0	3.3	-	-	-	-	50.8	1.6
1967	-	-	-	-	51.3	1.0	-	-	-	-	51.4	0.2	-	-	-	-	52.0	1.2	-	-	-	-	52.3	0.6
1968	-	-	-	-	53.3	1.9	-	-	-	-	53.4	0.2	-	-	-	-	54.3	1.7	-	-	-	-	55.0	1.3
1969	-	-	-	-	55.0	0.0	-	-	-	-	55.8	1.5	-	-	-	-	56.7	1.6	-	-	-	-	57.1	0.7
1970	-	-	-	-	57.8	1.2	-	-	-	-	57.9	0.2	-	-	-	-	59.0	1.9	-	-	-	-	59.4	0.7
1971	-	-	-	-	60.1	1.2	-	-	-	-	59.3	-1.3	-	-	-	-	60.2	1.5	-	-	-	-	60.2	0.0
1972	-	-	-	-	60.4	0.3	-	-	-	-	60.3	-0.2	-	-	-	-	62.6	3.8	-	-	-	-	62.6	0.0
1973	-	-	-	-	63.0	0.6	-	-	-	-	62.7	-0.5	-	-	-	-	65.0	3.7	-	-	-	-	65.4	0.6
1974	-	-	-	-	67.3	2.9	-	-	-	-	69.1	2.7	-	-	-	-	71.1	2.9	-	-	-	-	70.3	-1.1
1975	-	-	-	-	71.6	1.8	-	-	-	-	70.5	-1.5	-	-	-	-	72.7	3.1	-	-	-	-	72.4	-0.4
1976	-	-	-	-	73.1	1.0	-	-	-	-	72.8	-0.4	-	-	-	-	76.3	4.8	-	-	-	-	76.4	0.1
1977	-	-	-	-	78.7	3.0	-	-	-	-	77.0	-2.2	-	-	-	-	82.2	6.8	-	-	-	-	82.0	-0.2
1978	-	-	81.7	-0.4	-	-	83.8	2.6	-	-	83.6	-0.2	-	-	85.9	2.8	-	-	85.1	-0.9	-	-	84.4	-0.8
1979	-	-	85.0	0.7	-	-	86.8	2.1	-	-	88.0	1.4	-	-	88.8	0.9	-	-	89.0	0.2	-	-	89.4	0.4
1980	-	-	92.1	3.0	-	-	90.8	-1.4	-	-	92.1	1.4	-	-	94.1	2.2	-	-	96.0	2.0	-	-	95.0	-1.0
1981	-	-	94.1	-0.9	-	-	96.9	3.0	-	-	94.1	-2.9	-	-	99.6	5.8	-	-	96.5	-3.1	-	-	96.4	-0.1
1982	-	-	94.9	-1.6	-	-	93.9	-1.1	-	-	93.9	0.0	-	-	96.9	3.2	-	-	102.5	5.8	-	-	99.3	-3.1
1983	-	-	97.7	-1.6	-	-	93.8	-4.0	-	-	99.1	5.7	-	-	107.0	8.0	-	-	105.1	-1.8	-	-	101.0	-3.9
1984	-	-	98.4	-2.6	-	-	101.0	2.6	-	-	101.0	0.0	-	-	101.1	0.1	-	-	109.4	8.2	-	-	106.7	-2.5
1985	-	-	113.3	6.2	-	-	107.9	-4.8	-	-	109.1	1.1	-	-	114.0	4.5	-	-	116.9	2.5	-	-	109.5	-6.3
1986	-	-	108.0	-1.4	-	-	110.4	2.2	-	-	107.0	-3.1	-	-	107.9	0.8	-	-	115.8	7.3	-	-	114.4	-1.2
1987	-	-	-	-	-	-	-	-	-	-	105.5	-7.8	-	-	-	-	-	-	-	-	-	-	109.9	4.2
1988	-	-	-	-	-	-	-	-	-	-	108.4	-1.4	-	-	-	-	-	-	-	-	-	-	111.4	2.8
1989	-	-	-	-	-	-	-	-	-	-	104.2	-6.5	-	-	-	-	-	-	-	-	-	-	94.5	-9.3
1990	-	-	-	-	-	-	-	-	-	-	100.4	6.2	-	-	-	-	-	-	-	-	-	-	102.4	2.0
1991	-	-	-	-	-	-	-	-	-	-	103.9	1.5	-	-	-	-	-	-	-	-	-	-	103.6	-0.3
1992	-	-	-	-	-	-	-	-	-	-	106.6	2.9	-	-	-	-	-	-	-	-	-	-	106.3	-0.3
1993	-	-	-	-	-	-	-	-	-	-	105.3	-0.9	-	-	-	-	-	-	-	-	-	-	106.8	1.4
1994	-	-	-	-	-	-	-	-	-	-	106.2	-0.6	-	-	-	-	-	-	-	-	-	-	105.4	-0.8

[Continued]

Atlanta, GA
Consumer Price Index - All Urban Consumers
Base 1982-1984 = 100
Apparel and Upkeep
[Continued]

For 1952-1997. Columns headed % show percentile change in the index from the previous period for which an index is available.

Year	Jan		Feb		Mar		Apr		May		Jun		Jul		Aug		Sep		Oct		Nov		Dec	
	Index	%	Index	%	Index	%	Index	%	Index	%	Index	%	Index	%	Index	%	Index	%	Index	%	Index	%	Index	%
1995	-	-	-	-	-	-	-	-	-	-	102.9	-2.4	-	-	-	-	-	-	-	-	-	-	101.3	-1.6
1996	-	-	-	-	-	-	-	-	-	-	102.8	1.5	-	-	-	-	-	-	-	-	-	-	104.8	1.9
1997	-	-	-	-	-	-	-	-	-	-	102.5	-2.2	-	-	-	-	-	-	-	-	-	-	-	-

Source: U.S. Department of Labor, Bureau of Labor Statistics, Division of Consumer Prices and Price Indexes. - indicates no data collected for period.

Atlanta, GA
Consumer Price Index - Urban Wage Earners
Base 1982-1984 = 100
Apparel and Upkeep

For 1952-1997. Columns headed % show percentile change in the index from the previous period for which an index is available.

Year	Jan Index	%	Feb Index	%	Mar Index	%	Apr Index	%	May Index	%	Jun Index	%	Jul Index	%	Aug Index	%	Sep Index	%	Oct Index	%	Nov Index	%	Dec Index	%
1952	-	-	-	-	-	-	-	-	-	-	-	-	-	-	-	-	-	-	-	-	39.9	-	-	-
1953	-	-	-	-	40.0	0.3	-	-	-	-	39.9	-0.2	-	-	-	-	40.2	0.8	-	-	-	-	40.0	-0.5
1954	-	-	-	-	40.3	0.7	-	-	-	-	40.3	0.0	-	-	-	-	40.0	-0.7	-	-	-	-	39.9	-0.2
1955	-	-	-	-	39.3	-1.5	-	-	-	-	39.9	1.5	-	-	-	-	40.3	1.0	-	-	-	-	40.2	-0.2
1956	-	-	-	-	40.4	0.5	-	-	-	-	40.5	0.2	-	-	-	-	41.1	1.5	-	-	-	-	41.0	-0.2
1957	-	-	-	-	41.4	1.0	-	-	-	-	41.3	-0.2	-	-	-	-	41.8	1.2	-	-	-	-	41.8	0.0
1958	-	-	-	-	42.0	0.5	-	-	-	-	41.8	-0.5	-	-	-	-	42.0	0.5	-	-	-	-	42.0	0.0
1959	-	-	-	-	41.7	-0.7	-	-	-	-	41.7	0.0	-	-	-	-	42.1	1.0	-	-	-	-	42.4	0.7
1960	-	-	-	-	42.3	-0.2	-	-	-	-	42.4	0.2	-	-	-	-	43.1	1.7	-	-	-	-	43.0	-0.2
1961	-	-	-	-	42.8	-0.5	-	-	-	-	42.8	0.0	-	-	-	-	42.6	-0.5	-	-	-	-	42.5	-0.2
1962	-	-	-	-	42.6	0.2	-	-	-	-	42.5	-0.2	-	-	-	-	42.8	0.7	-	-	-	-	43.1	0.7
1963	-	-	-	-	43.5	0.9	-	-	-	-	43.6	0.2	-	-	-	-	44.1	1.1	-	-	-	-	43.8	-0.7
1964	-	-	-	-	43.8	0.0	-	-	-	-	43.6	-0.5	-	-	-	-	43.8	0.5	-	-	-	-	43.9	0.2
1965	-	-	-	-	44.0	0.2	-	-	-	-	44.0	0.0	-	-	-	-	44.5	1.1	-	-	-	-	44.6	0.2
1966	-	-	-	-	45.3	1.6	-	-	-	-	45.9	1.3	-	-	-	-	47.4	3.3	-	-	-	-	48.1	1.5
1967	-	-	-	-	48.7	1.2	-	-	-	-	48.8	0.2	-	-	-	-	49.3	1.0	-	-	-	-	49.6	0.6
1968	-	-	-	-	50.5	1.8	-	-	-	-	50.6	0.2	-	-	-	-	51.5	1.8	-	-	-	-	52.1	1.2
1969	-	-	-	-	52.1	0.0	-	-	-	-	52.9	1.5	-	-	-	-	53.8	1.7	-	-	-	-	54.1	0.6
1970	-	-	-	-	54.8	1.3	-	-	-	-	54.9	0.2	-	-	-	-	56.0	2.0	-	-	-	-	56.3	0.5
1971	-	-	-	-	57.0	1.2	-	-	-	-	56.2	-1.4	-	-	-	-	57.0	1.4	-	-	-	-	57.1	0.2
1972	-	-	-	-	57.3	0.4	-	-	-	-	57.2	-0.2	-	-	-	-	59.3	3.7	-	-	-	-	59.3	0.0
1973	-	-	-	-	59.7	0.7	-	-	-	-	59.4	-0.5	-	-	-	-	61.6	3.7	-	-	-	-	62.0	0.6
1974	-	-	-	-	63.8	2.9	-	-	-	-	65.5	2.7	-	-	-	-	67.4	2.9	-	-	-	-	66.7	-1.0
1975	-	-	-	-	67.9	1.8	-	-	-	-	66.8	-1.6	-	-	-	-	68.9	3.1	-	-	-	-	68.6	-0.4
1976	-	-	-	-	69.3	1.0	-	-	-	-	69.0	-0.4	-	-	-	-	72.4	4.9	-	-	-	-	72.5	0.1
1977	-	-	-	-	74.6	2.9	-	-	-	-	72.9	-2.3	-	-	-	-	77.9	6.9	-	-	-	-	77.7	-0.3
1978	-	-	77.3	-0.5	-	-	77.5	0.3	-	-	77.5	0.0	-	-	78.1	0.8	-	-	79.7	2.0	-	-	79.7	0.0
1979	-	-	79.3	-0.5	-	-	82.5	4.0	-	-	84.1	1.9	-	-	86.7	3.1	-	-	87.1	0.5	-	-	88.6	1.7
1980	-	-	86.5	-2.4	-	-	86.5	0.0	-	-	87.9	1.6	-	-	92.3	5.0	-	-	92.9	0.7	-	-	95.1	2.4
1981	-	-	93.4	-1.8	-	-	94.6	1.3	-	-	94.7	0.1	-	-	95.9	1.3	-	-	99.5	3.8	-	-	97.7	-1.8
1982	-	-	96.8	-0.9	-	-	95.5	-1.3	-	-	95.2	-0.3	-	-	98.4	3.4	-	-	102.6	4.3	-	-	99.8	-2.7
1983	-	-	97.5	-2.3	-	-	94.4	-3.2	-	-	98.5	4.3	-	-	105.3	6.9	-	-	104.4	-0.9	-	-	100.1	-4.1
1984	-	-	97.6	-2.5	-	-	100.6	3.1	-	-	101.2	0.6	-	-	101.4	0.2	-	-	108.6	7.1	-	-	104.1	-4.1
1985	-	-	110.8	6.4	-	-	106.0	-4.3	-	-	108.2	2.1	-	-	111.9	3.4	-	-	113.1	1.1	-	-	107.5	-5.0
1986	-	-	106.1	-1.3	-	-	108.9	2.6	-	-	105.6	-3.0	-	-	105.5	-0.1	-	-	112.7	6.8	-	-	111.2	-1.3
1987	-	-	-	-	-	-	-	-	-	-	102.0	-8.3	-	-	-	-	-	-	-	-	-	-	106.9	4.8
1988	-	-	-	-	-	-	-	-	-	-	105.4	-1.4	-	-	-	-	-	-	-	-	-	-	106.6	1.1
1989	-	-	-	-	-	-	-	-	-	-	99.1	-7.0	-	-	-	-	-	-	-	-	-	-	90.0	-9.2
1990	-	-	-	-	-	-	-	-	-	-	96.7	7.4	-	-	-	-	-	-	-	-	-	-	98.6	2.0
1991	-	-	-	-	-	-	-	-	-	-	99.1	0.5	-	-	-	-	-	-	-	-	-	-	98.9	-0.2
1992	-	-	-	-	-	-	-	-	-	-	103.3	4.4	-	-	-	-	-	-	-	-	-	-	103.4	0.1
1993	-	-	-	-	-	-	-	-	-	-	103.8	0.4	-	-	-	-	-	-	-	-	-	-	105.6	1.7
1994	-	-	-	-	-	-	-	-	-	-	102.4	-3.0	-	-	-	-	-	-	-	-	-	-	101.3	-1.1

[Continued]

Atlanta, GA
Consumer Price Index - Urban Wage Earners
Base 1982-1984 = 100
Apparel and Upkeep
[Continued]

For 1952-1997. Columns headed % show percentile change in the index from the previous period for which an index is available.

Year	Jan		Feb		Mar		Apr		May		Jun		Jul		Aug		Sep		Oct		Nov		Dec	
	Index	%	Index	%	Index	%	Index	%	Index	%	Index	%	Index	%	Index	%	Index	%	Index	%	Index	%	Index	%
1995	-	-	-	-	-	-	-	-	-	-	99.0	-2.3	-	-	-	-	-	-	-	-	-	-	97.3	-1.7
1996	-	-	-	-	-	-	-	-	-	-	98.4	1.1	-	-	-	-	-	-	-	-	-	-	101.9	3.6
1997	-	-	-	-	-	-	-	-	-	-	99.2	-2.6	-	-	-	-	-	-	-	-	-	-	-	-

Source: U.S. Department of Labor, Bureau of Labor Statistics, Division of Consumer Prices and Price Indexes. - indicates no data collected for period.

Atlanta, GA
Consumer Price Index - All Urban Consumers
Base 1982-1984 = 100
Transportation

For 1947-1997. Columns headed % show percentile change in the index from the previous period for which an index is available.

Year	Jan Index	%	Feb Index	%	Mar Index	%	Apr Index	%	May Index	%	Jun Index	%	Jul Index	%	Aug Index	%	Sep Index	%	Oct Index	%	Nov Index	%	Dec Index	%
1947	-	-	-	-	20.0	-	-	-	-	-	20.2	1.0	-	-	20.4	1.0	-	-	-	-	21.0	2.9	-	-
1948	-	-	21.5	2.4	-	-	-	-	22.0	2.3	-	-	-	-	23.1	5.0	-	-	-	-	23.1	0.0	-	-
1949	-	-	23.5	1.7	-	-	-	-	24.1	2.6	-	-	-	-	24.4	1.2	-	-	-	-	24.4	0.0	-	-
1950	-	-	24.4	0.0	-	-	-	-	24.4	0.0	-	-	-	-	24.8	1.6	-	-	-	-	25.0	0.8	-	-
1951	-	-	24.9	-0.4	-	-	-	-	26.6	6.8	-	-	-	-	26.6	0.0	-	-	-	-	27.2	2.3	-	-
1952	-	-	27.7	1.8	-	-	-	-	27.7	0.0	-	-	-	-	28.0	1.1	-	-	-	-	29.2	4.3	-	-
1953	-	-	-	-	29.1	-0.3	-	-	-	-	28.8	-1.0	-	-	-	-	28.8	0.0	-	-	-	-	28.8	0.0
1954	-	-	-	-	28.4	-1.4	-	-	-	-	28.4	0.0	-	-	-	-	26.8	-5.6	-	-	-	-	28.0	4.5
1955	-	-	-	-	27.5	-1.8	-	-	-	-	27.7	0.7	-	-	-	-	27.2	-1.8	-	-	-	-	27.7	1.8
1956	-	-	-	-	27.7	0.0	-	-	-	-	27.7	0.0	-	-	-	-	28.7	3.6	-	-	-	-	29.1	1.4
1957	-	-	-	-	30.2	3.8	-	-	-	-	29.8	-1.3	-	-	-	-	29.5	-1.0	-	-	-	-	31.0	5.1
1958	-	-	-	-	31.2	0.6	-	-	-	-	31.1	-0.3	-	-	-	-	31.2	0.3	-	-	-	-	32.2	3.2
1959	-	-	-	-	32.3	0.3	-	-	-	-	31.9	-1.2	-	-	-	-	32.5	1.9	-	-	-	-	33.1	1.8
1960	-	-	-	-	32.2	-2.7	-	-	-	-	32.0	-0.6	-	-	-	-	31.8	-0.6	-	-	-	-	31.4	-1.3
1961	-	-	-	-	32.1	2.2	-	-	-	-	32.6	1.6	-	-	-	-	32.5	-0.3	-	-	-	-	32.9	1.2
1962	-	-	-	-	32.4	-1.5	-	-	-	-	33.0	1.9	-	-	-	-	33.4	1.2	-	-	-	-	33.8	1.2
1963	-	-	-	-	33.5	-0.9	-	-	-	-	33.8	0.9	-	-	-	-	33.4	-1.2	-	-	-	-	34.8	4.2
1964	-	-	-	-	34.6	-0.6	-	-	-	-	34.5	-0.3	-	-	-	-	34.7	0.6	-	-	-	-	35.0	0.9
1965	-	-	-	-	35.0	0.0	-	-	-	-	34.0	-2.9	-	-	-	-	34.5	1.5	-	-	-	-	34.8	0.9
1966	-	-	-	-	34.4	-1.1	-	-	-	-	34.5	0.3	-	-	-	-	34.6	0.3	-	-	-	-	34.7	0.3
1967	-	-	-	-	34.7	0.0	-	-	-	-	35.2	1.4	-	-	-	-	35.5	0.9	-	-	-	-	35.9	1.1
1968	-	-	-	-	35.9	0.0	-	-	-	-	36.1	0.6	-	-	-	-	36.0	-0.3	-	-	-	-	36.5	1.4
1969	-	-	-	-	37.3	2.2	-	-	-	-	37.3	0.0	-	-	-	-	37.1	-0.5	-	-	-	-	37.6	1.3
1970	-	-	-	-	37.2	-1.1	-	-	-	-	38.1	2.4	-	-	-	-	38.4	0.8	-	-	-	-	40.1	4.4
1971	-	-	-	-	40.3	0.5	-	-	-	-	41.2	2.2	-	-	-	-	40.4	-1.9	-	-	-	-	40.7	0.7
1972	-	-	-	-	39.2	-3.7	-	-	-	-	39.5	0.8	-	-	-	-	40.1	1.5	-	-	-	-	40.4	0.7
1973	-	-	-	-	40.4	0.0	-	-	-	-	41.3	2.2	-	-	-	-	41.1	-0.5	-	-	-	-	42.2	2.7
1974	-	-	-	-	44.2	4.7	-	-	-	-	47.0	6.3	-	-	-	-	48.5	3.2	-	-	-	-	48.5	0.0
1975	-	-	-	-	48.6	0.2	-	-	-	-	50.4	3.7	-	-	-	-	51.5	2.2	-	-	-	-	52.2	1.4
1976	-	-	-	-	52.4	0.4	-	-	-	-	54.4	3.8	-	-	-	-	55.5	2.0	-	-	-	-	56.0	0.9
1977	-	-	-	-	56.5	0.9	-	-	-	-	57.9	2.5	-	-	-	-	57.5	-0.7	-	-	-	-	58.0	0.9
1978	-	-	57.9	-0.2	-	-	58.1	0.3	-	-	59.5	2.4	-	-	60.3	1.3	-	-	61.3	1.7	-	-	61.8	0.8
1979	-	-	63.0	1.9	-	-	66.3	5.2	-	-	69.4	4.7	-	-	72.3	4.2	-	-	73.8	2.1	-	-	75.6	2.4
1980	-	-	80.4	6.3	-	-	83.4	3.7	-	-	84.0	0.7	-	-	87.3	3.9	-	-	88.2	1.0	-	-	89.3	1.2
1981	-	-	92.5	3.6	-	-	94.4	2.1	-	-	95.2	0.8	-	-	95.1	-0.1	-	-	97.0	2.0	-	-	97.5	0.5
1982	-	-	96.4	-1.1	-	-	94.4	-2.1	-	-	98.3	4.1	-	-	99.2	0.9	-	-	98.7	-0.5	-	-	98.6	-0.1
1983	-	-	96.4	-2.2	-	-	97.9	1.6	-	-	99.5	1.6	-	-	100.6	1.1	-	-	101.3	0.7	-	-	101.8	0.5
1984	-	-	101.6	-0.2	-	-	102.7	1.1	-	-	103.3	0.6	-	-	103.1	-0.2	-	-	103.9	0.8	-	-	104.0	0.1
1985	-	-	103.3	-0.7	-	-	106.1	2.7	-	-	106.6	0.5	-	-	107.5	0.8	-	-	108.2	0.7	-	-	109.7	1.4
1986	-	-	108.4	-1.2	-	-	101.5	-6.4	-	-	103.3	1.8	-	-	100.6	-2.6	-	-	100.1	-0.5	-	-	101.0	0.9
1987	-	-	-	-	-	-	-	-	-	-	109.7	8.6	-	-	-	-	-	-	-	-	-	-	113.2	3.2
1988	-	-	-	-	-	-	-	-	-	-	114.6	1.2	-	-	-	-	-	-	-	-	-	-	116.6	1.7
1989	-	-	-	-	-	-	-	-	-	-	120.2	3.1	-	-	-	-	-	-	-	-	-	-	122.9	2.2
1990	-	-	-	-	-	-	-	-	-	-	125.4	2.0	-	-	-	-	-	-	-	-	-	-	130.0	3.7
1991	-	-	-	-	-	-	-	-	-	-	131.0	0.8	-	-	-	-	-	-	-	-	-	-	133.7	2.1

[Continued]

Atlanta, GA
Consumer Price Index - All Urban Consumers
Base 1982-1984 = 100
Transportation
[Continued]

For 1947-1997. Columns headed % show percentile change in the index from the previous period for which an index is available.

Year	Jan		Feb		Mar		Apr		May		Jun		Jul		Aug		Sep		Oct		Nov		Dec	
	Index	%	Index	%	Index	%	Index	%	Index	%	Index	%	Index	%	Index	%	Index	%	Index	%	Index	%	Index	%
1992	-	-	-	-	-	-	-	-	-	-	135.0	1.0	-	-	-	-	-	-	-	-	-	-	137.2	1.6
1993	-	-	-	-	-	-	-	-	-	-	138.5	0.9	-	-	-	-	-	-	-	-	-	-	140.5	1.4
1994	-	-	-	-	-	-	-	-	-	-	142.4	1.4	-	-	-	-	-	-	-	-	-	-	145.6	2.2
1995	-	-	-	-	-	-	-	-	-	-	148.5	2.0	-	-	-	-	-	-	-	-	-	-	149.0	0.3
1996	-	-	-	-	-	-	-	-	-	-	150.4	0.9	-	-	-	-	-	-	-	-	-	-	152.7	1.5
1997	-	-	-	-	-	-	-	-	-	-	153.1	0.3	-	-	-	-	-	-	-	-	-	-	-	-

Source: U.S. Department of Labor, Bureau of Labor Statistics, Division of Consumer Prices and Price Indexes. - indicates no data collected for period.

Atlanta, GA
Consumer Price Index - Urban Wage Earners
Base 1982-1984 = 100
Transportation

For 1947-1997. Columns headed % show percentile change in the index from the previous period for which an index is available.

Year	Jan Index	%	Feb Index	%	Mar Index	%	Apr Index	%	May Index	%	Jun Index	%	Jul Index	%	Aug Index	%	Sep Index	%	Oct Index	%	Nov Index	%	Dec Index	%
1947	-	-	-	-	19.5	-	-	-	-	-	19.6	0.5	-	-	19.9	1.5	-	-	-	-	20.4	2.5	-	-
1948	-	-	20.9	2.5	-	-	-	-	21.4	2.4	-	-	-	-	22.5	5.1	-	-	-	-	22.5	0.0	-	-
1949	-	-	22.9	1.8	-	-	-	-	23.5	2.6	-	-	-	-	23.8	1.3	-	-	-	-	23.8	0.0	-	-
1950	-	-	23.8	0.0	-	-	-	-	23.8	0.0	-	-	-	-	24.1	1.3	-	-	-	-	24.3	0.8	-	-
1951	-	-	24.3	0.0	-	-	-	-	25.9	6.6	-	-	-	-	25.9	0.0	-	-	-	-	26.5	2.3	-	-
1952	-	-	27.0	1.9	-	-	-	-	27.0	0.0	-	-	-	-	27.3	1.1	-	-	-	-	28.4	4.0	-	-
1953	-	-	-	-	28.3	-0.4	-	-	-	-	28.0	-1.1	-	-	-	-	28.0	0.0	-	-	-	-	28.0	0.0
1954	-	-	-	-	27.6	-1.4	-	-	-	-	27.6	0.0	-	-	-	-	26.0	-5.8	-	-	-	-	27.3	5.0
1955	-	-	-	-	26.8	-1.8	-	-	-	-	26.9	0.4	-	-	-	-	26.5	-1.5	-	-	-	-	27.0	1.9
1956	-	-	-	-	27.0	0.0	-	-	-	-	27.0	0.0	-	-	-	-	28.0	3.7	-	-	-	-	28.3	1.1
1957	-	-	-	-	29.4	3.9	-	-	-	-	29.0	-1.4	-	-	-	-	28.7	-1.0	-	-	-	-	30.2	5.2
1958	-	-	-	-	30.3	0.3	-	-	-	-	30.2	-0.3	-	-	-	-	30.4	0.7	-	-	-	-	31.3	3.0
1959	-	-	-	-	31.4	0.3	-	-	-	-	31.1	-1.0	-	-	-	-	31.6	1.6	-	-	-	-	32.2	1.9
1960	-	-	-	-	31.4	-2.5	-	-	-	-	31.2	-0.6	-	-	-	-	31.0	-0.6	-	-	-	-	30.6	-1.3
1961	-	-	-	-	31.3	2.3	-	-	-	-	31.7	1.3	-	-	-	-	31.7	0.0	-	-	-	-	32.0	0.9
1962	-	-	-	-	31.6	-1.2	-	-	-	-	32.1	1.6	-	-	-	-	32.5	1.2	-	-	-	-	32.9	1.2
1963	-	-	-	-	32.6	-0.9	-	-	-	-	32.9	0.9	-	-	-	-	32.5	-1.2	-	-	-	-	33.9	4.3
1964	-	-	-	-	33.7	-0.6	-	-	-	-	33.6	-0.3	-	-	-	-	33.8	0.6	-	-	-	-	34.1	0.9
1965	-	-	-	-	34.1	0.0	-	-	-	-	33.1	-2.9	-	-	-	-	33.6	1.5	-	-	-	-	33.9	0.9
1966	-	-	-	-	33.5	-1.2	-	-	-	-	33.6	0.3	-	-	-	-	33.7	0.3	-	-	-	-	33.8	0.3
1967	-	-	-	-	33.8	0.0	-	-	-	-	34.3	1.5	-	-	-	-	34.6	0.9	-	-	-	-	35.0	1.2
1968	-	-	-	-	34.9	-0.3	-	-	-	-	35.2	0.9	-	-	-	-	35.1	-0.3	-	-	-	-	35.5	1.1
1969	-	-	-	-	36.3	2.3	-	-	-	-	36.3	0.0	-	-	-	-	36.1	-0.6	-	-	-	-	36.6	1.4
1970	-	-	-	-	36.2	-1.1	-	-	-	-	37.1	2.5	-	-	-	-	37.4	0.8	-	-	-	-	39.0	4.3
1971	-	-	-	-	39.2	0.5	-	-	-	-	40.1	2.3	-	-	-	-	39.4	-1.7	-	-	-	-	39.7	0.8
1972	-	-	-	-	38.2	-3.8	-	-	-	-	38.5	0.8	-	-	-	-	39.0	1.3	-	-	-	-	39.3	0.8
1973	-	-	-	-	39.3	0.0	-	-	-	-	40.2	2.3	-	-	-	-	40.0	-0.5	-	-	-	-	41.1	2.8
1974	-	-	-	-	43.1	4.9	-	-	-	-	45.7	6.0	-	-	-	-	47.2	3.3	-	-	-	-	47.2	0.0
1975	-	-	-	-	47.3	0.2	-	-	-	-	49.1	3.8	-	-	-	-	50.1	2.0	-	-	-	-	50.8	1.4
1976	-	-	-	-	51.0	0.4	-	-	-	-	53.0	3.9	-	-	-	-	54.0	1.9	-	-	-	-	54.5	0.9
1977	-	-	-	-	55.0	0.9	-	-	-	-	56.3	2.4	-	-	-	-	56.0	-0.5	-	-	-	-	56.5	0.9
1978	-	-	56.6	0.2	-	-	56.8	0.4	-	-	58.0	2.1	-	-	58.9	1.6	-	-	59.9	1.7	-	-	60.5	1.0
1979	-	-	61.8	2.1	-	-	65.5	6.0	-	-	68.5	4.6	-	-	71.6	4.5	-	-	74.3	3.8	-	-	76.5	3.0
1980	-	-	81.0	5.9	-	-	84.5	4.3	-	-	84.7	0.2	-	-	89.3	5.4	-	-	89.9	0.7	-	-	90.8	1.0
1981	-	-	94.5	4.1	-	-	95.7	1.3	-	-	96.0	0.3	-	-	95.9	-0.1	-	-	97.5	1.7	-	-	98.5	1.0
1982	-	-	97.5	-1.0	-	-	95.1	-2.5	-	-	99.0	4.1	-	-	99.8	0.8	-	-	99.1	-0.7	-	-	98.9	-0.2
1983	-	-	96.5	-2.4	-	-	98.1	1.7	-	-	99.7	1.6	-	-	100.6	0.9	-	-	101.1	0.5	-	-	101.4	0.3
1984	-	-	101.2	-0.2	-	-	102.2	1.0	-	-	102.6	0.4	-	-	102.3	-0.3	-	-	103.0	0.7	-	-	103.1	0.1
1985	-	-	102.3	-0.8	-	-	105.2	2.8	-	-	105.9	0.7	-	-	107.1	1.1	-	-	107.7	0.6	-	-	109.4	1.6
1986	-	-	108.1	-1.2	-	-	100.6	-6.9	-	-	102.5	1.9	-	-	99.6	-2.8	-	-	98.7	-0.9	-	-	99.6	0.9
1987	-	-	-	-	-	-	-	-	-	-	108.8	9.2	-	-	-	-	-	-	-	-	-	-	112.7	3.6
1988	-	-	-	-	-	-	-	-	-	-	114.1	1.2	-	-	-	-	-	-	-	-	-	-	116.2	1.8
1989	-	-	-	-	-	-	-	-	-	-	120.1	3.4	-	-	-	-	-	-	-	-	-	-	123.2	2.6
1990	-	-	-	-	-	-	-	-	-	-	125.6	1.9	-	-	-	-	-	-	-	-	-	-	131.2	4.5
1991	-	-	-	-	-	-	-	-	-	-	131.3	0.1	-	-	-	-	-	-	-	-	-	-	134.3	2.3

[Continued]

Atlanta, GA
Consumer Price Index - Urban Wage Earners
Base 1982-1984 = 100
Transportation
[Continued]

For 1947-1997. Columns headed % show percentile change in the index from the previous period for which an index is available.

Year	Jan		Feb		Mar		Apr		May		Jun		Jul		Aug		Sep		Oct		Nov		Dec	
	Index	%	Index	%	Index	%	Index	%	Index	%	Index	%	Index	%	Index	%	Index	%	Index	%	Index	%	Index	%
1992	-	-	-	-	-	-	-	-	-	-	134.7	0.3	-	-	-	-	-	-	-	-	-	-	137.4	2.0
1993	-	-	-	-	-	-	-	-	-	-	138.2	0.6	-	-	-	-	-	-	-	-	-	-	140.3	1.5
1994	-	-	-	-	-	-	-	-	-	-	141.8	1.1	-	-	-	-	-	-	-	-	-	-	146.3	3.2
1995	-	-	-	-	-	-	-	-	-	-	149.3	2.1	-	-	-	-	-	-	-	-	-	-	149.7	0.3
1996	-	-	-	-	-	-	-	-	-	-	151.1	0.9	-	-	-	-	-	-	-	-	-	-	153.3	1.5
1997	-	-	-	-	-	-	-	-	-	-	153.8	0.3	-	-	-	-	-	-	-	-	-	-	-	-

Source: U.S. Department of Labor, Bureau of Labor Statistics, Division of Consumer Prices and Price Indexes. - indicates no data collected for period.

Atlanta, GA
Consumer Price Index - All Urban Consumers
Base 1982-1984 = 100
Medical Care

For 1947-1997. Columns headed % show percentile change in the index from the previous period for which an index is available.

Year	Jan Index	%	Feb Index	%	Mar Index	%	Apr Index	%	May Index	%	Jun Index	%	Jul Index	%	Aug Index	%	Sep Index	%	Oct Index	%	Nov Index	%	Dec Index	%
1947	-	-	-	-	15.1	-	-	-	-	-	15.1	0.0	-	-	15.3	1.3	-	-	-	-	15.3	0.0	-	-
1948	-	-	15.5	1.3	-	-	-	-	15.6	0.6	-	-	-	-	15.8	1.3	-	-	-	-	16.0	1.3	-	-
1949	-	-	16.1	0.6	-	-	-	-	16.1	0.0	-	-	-	-	16.1	0.0	-	-	-	-	16.1	0.0	-	-
1950	-	-	16.1	0.0	-	-	-	-	16.1	0.0	-	-	-	-	16.1	0.0	-	-	-	-	16.3	1.2	-	-
1951	-	-	16.6	1.8	-	-	-	-	17.0	2.4	-	-	-	-	17.0	0.0	-	-	-	-	17.1	0.6	-	-
1952	-	-	17.5	2.3	-	-	-	-	18.2	4.0	-	-	-	-	18.2	0.0	-	-	-	-	18.5	1.6	-	-
1953	-	-	-	-	18.5	0.0	-	-	-	-	18.6	0.5	-	-	-	-	18.4	-1.1	-	-	-	-	18.7	1.6
1954	-	-	-	-	18.9	1.1	-	-	-	-	18.9	0.0	-	-	-	-	19.0	0.5	-	-	-	-	19.0	0.0
1955	-	-	-	-	19.2	1.1	-	-	-	-	19.2	0.0	-	-	-	-	20.0	4.2	-	-	-	-	20.1	0.5
1956	-	-	-	-	20.1	0.0	-	-	-	-	20.3	1.0	-	-	-	-	20.2	-0.5	-	-	-	-	20.3	0.5
1957	-	-	-	-	20.7	2.0	-	-	-	-	20.7	0.0	-	-	-	-	20.8	0.5	-	-	-	-	20.9	0.5
1958	-	-	-	-	21.3	1.9	-	-	-	-	21.4	0.5	-	-	-	-	21.4	0.0	-	-	-	-	21.6	0.9
1959	-	-	-	-	21.6	0.0	-	-	-	-	22.6	4.6	-	-	-	-	22.6	0.0	-	-	-	-	22.8	0.9
1960	-	-	-	-	23.0	0.9	-	-	-	-	23.0	0.0	-	-	-	-	23.0	0.0	-	-	-	-	22.8	-0.9
1961	-	-	-	-	22.8	0.0	-	-	-	-	23.0	0.9	-	-	-	-	23.4	1.7	-	-	-	-	23.6	0.9
1962	-	-	-	-	23.8	0.8	-	-	-	-	23.9	0.4	-	-	-	-	23.9	0.0	-	-	-	-	23.9	0.0
1963	-	-	-	-	23.9	0.0	-	-	-	-	24.4	2.1	-	-	-	-	24.4	0.0	-	-	-	-	24.4	0.0
1964	-	-	-	-	24.6	0.8	-	-	-	-	24.7	0.4	-	-	-	-	25.0	1.2	-	-	-	-	25.1	0.4
1965	-	-	-	-	25.3	0.8	-	-	-	-	25.3	0.0	-	-	-	-	25.5	0.8	-	-	-	-	25.6	0.4
1966	-	-	-	-	26.1	2.0	-	-	-	-	26.6	1.9	-	-	-	-	27.3	2.6	-	-	-	-	27.4	0.4
1967	-	-	-	-	28.1	2.6	-	-	-	-	28.3	0.7	-	-	-	-	28.8	1.8	-	-	-	-	28.9	0.3
1968	-	-	-	-	29.7	2.8	-	-	-	-	30.0	1.0	-	-	-	-	30.8	2.7	-	-	-	-	31.4	1.9
1969	-	-	-	-	32.7	4.1	-	-	-	-	33.3	1.8	-	-	-	-	34.0	2.1	-	-	-	-	34.2	0.6
1970	-	-	-	-	35.1	2.6	-	-	-	-	35.9	2.3	-	-	-	-	36.2	0.8	-	-	-	-	36.9	1.9
1971	-	-	-	-	38.3	3.8	-	-	-	-	38.8	1.3	-	-	-	-	39.1	0.8	-	-	-	-	38.9	-0.5
1972	-	-	-	-	39.2	0.8	-	-	-	-	39.8	1.5	-	-	-	-	39.8	0.0	-	-	-	-	40.1	0.8
1973	-	-	-	-	40.4	0.7	-	-	-	-	41.5	2.7	-	-	-	-	42.3	1.9	-	-	-	-	42.9	1.4
1974	-	-	-	-	43.9	2.3	-	-	-	-	46.4	5.7	-	-	-	-	47.6	2.6	-	-	-	-	48.3	1.5
1975	-	-	-	-	51.3	6.2	-	-	-	-	51.8	1.0	-	-	-	-	53.5	3.3	-	-	-	-	53.7	0.4
1976	-	-	-	-	55.0	2.4	-	-	-	-	55.3	0.5	-	-	-	-	57.0	3.1	-	-	-	-	58.0	1.8
1977	-	-	-	-	59.9	3.3	-	-	-	-	60.9	1.7	-	-	-	-	61.7	1.3	-	-	-	-	61.7	0.0
1978	-	-	62.9	1.9	-	-	63.3	0.6	-	-	63.8	0.8	-	-	64.3	0.8	-	-	64.7	0.6	-	-	64.6	-0.2
1979	-	-	65.9	2.0	-	-	67.2	2.0	-	-	68.0	1.2	-	-	68.8	1.2	-	-	69.4	0.9	-	-	70.5	1.6
1980	-	-	71.5	1.4	-	-	72.1	0.8	-	-	75.0	4.0	-	-	76.4	1.9	-	-	77.0	0.8	-	-	78.3	1.7
1981	-	-	80.6	2.9	-	-	80.9	0.4	-	-	81.6	0.9	-	-	82.9	1.6	-	-	84.9	2.4	-	-	84.5	-0.5
1982	-	-	85.2	0.8	-	-	87.0	2.1	-	-	92.7	6.6	-	-	95.7	3.2	-	-	99.2	3.7	-	-	100.0	0.8
1983	-	-	100.9	0.9	-	-	101.1	0.2	-	-	101.2	0.1	-	-	101.1	-0.1	-	-	101.5	0.4	-	-	101.8	0.3
1984	-	-	103.5	1.7	-	-	104.6	1.1	-	-	106.0	1.3	-	-	107.3	1.2	-	-	108.8	1.4	-	-	109.0	0.2
1985	-	-	110.9	1.7	-	-	111.6	0.6	-	-	113.1	1.3	-	-	113.5	0.4	-	-	115.0	1.3	-	-	114.7	-0.3
1986	-	-	120.4	5.0	-	-	120.9	0.4	-	-	123.2	1.9	-	-	125.3	1.7	-	-	127.2	1.5	-	-	128.6	1.1
1987	-	-	-	-	-	-	-	-	-	-	131.0	1.9	-	-	-	-	-	-	-	-	-	-	135.1	3.1
1988	-	-	-	-	-	-	-	-	-	-	139.3	3.1	-	-	-	-	-	-	-	-	-	-	145.0	4.1
1989	-	-	-	-	-	-	-	-	-	-	150.3	3.7	-	-	-	-	-	-	-	-	-	-	160.3	6.7
1990	-	-	-	-	-	-	-	-	-	-	163.0	1.7	-	-	-	-	-	-	-	-	-	-	171.8	5.4
1991	-	-	-	-	-	-	-	-	-	-	179.5	4.5	-	-	-	-	-	-	-	-	-	-	187.4	4.4

[Continued]

Atlanta, GA
Consumer Price Index - All Urban Consumers
Base 1982-1984 = 100
Medical Care
[Continued]

For 1947-1997. Columns headed % show percentile change in the index from the previous period for which an index is available.

Year	Jan		Feb		Mar		Apr		May		Jun		Jul		Aug		Sep		Oct		Nov		Dec	
	Index	%	Index	%	Index	%	Index	%	Index	%	Index	%	Index	%	Index	%	Index	%	Index	%	Index	%	Index	%
1992	-	-	-	-	-	-	-	-	-	-	192.3	2.6	-	-	-	-	-	-	-	-	-	-	200.9	4.5
1993	-	-	-	-	-	-	-	-	-	-	206.9	3.0	-	-	-	-	-	-	-	-	-	-	216.2	4.5
1994	-	-	-	-	-	-	-	-	-	-	221.6	2.5	-	-	-	-	-	-	-	-	-	-	226.2	2.1
1995	-	-	-	-	-	-	-	-	-	-	229.6	1.5	-	-	-	-	-	-	-	-	-	-	235.4	2.5
1996	-	-	-	-	-	-	-	-	-	-	238.3	1.2	-	-	-	-	-	-	-	-	-	-	246.2	3.3
1997	-	-	-	-	-	-	-	-	-	-	246.7	0.2	-	-	-	-	-	-	-	-	-	-	-	-

Source: U.S. Department of Labor, Bureau of Labor Statistics, Division of Consumer Prices and Price Indexes. - indicates no data collected for period.

Atlanta, GA
Consumer Price Index - Urban Wage Earners
Base 1982-1984 = 100
Medical Care

For 1947-1997. Columns headed % show percentile change in the index from the previous period for which an index is available.

Year	Jan Index	%	Feb Index	%	Mar Index	%	Apr Index	%	May Index	%	Jun Index	%	Jul Index	%	Aug Index	%	Sep Index	%	Oct Index	%	Nov Index	%	Dec Index	%
1947	-	-	-	-	14.6	-	-	-	-	-	14.6	0.0	-	-	14.7	0.7	-	-	-	-	14.7	0.0	-	-
1948	-	-	14.9	1.4	-	-	-	-	15.0	0.7	-	-	-	-	15.2	1.3	-	-	-	-	15.4	1.3	-	-
1949	-	-	15.5	0.6	-	-	-	-	15.5	0.0	-	-	-	-	15.5	0.0	-	-	-	-	15.5	0.0	-	-
1950	-	-	15.5	0.0	-	-	-	-	15.5	0.0	-	-	-	-	15.5	0.0	-	-	-	-	15.6	0.6	-	-
1951	-	-	16.0	2.6	-	-	-	-	16.4	2.5	-	-	-	-	16.3	-0.6	-	-	-	-	16.4	0.6	-	-
1952	-	-	16.8	2.4	-	-	-	-	17.6	4.8	-	-	-	-	17.5	-0.6	-	-	-	-	17.8	1.7	-	-
1953	-	-	-	-	17.8	0.0	-	-	-	-	17.9	0.6	-	-	-	-	17.7	-1.1	-	-	-	-	18.0	1.7
1954	-	-	-	-	18.2	1.1	-	-	-	-	18.2	0.0	-	-	-	-	18.2	0.0	-	-	-	-	18.3	0.5
1955	-	-	-	-	18.5	1.1	-	-	-	-	18.5	0.0	-	-	-	-	19.2	3.8	-	-	-	-	19.4	1.0
1956	-	-	-	-	19.4	0.0	-	-	-	-	19.6	1.0	-	-	-	-	19.5	-0.5	-	-	-	-	19.6	0.5
1957	-	-	-	-	19.9	1.5	-	-	-	-	19.9	0.0	-	-	-	-	20.0	0.5	-	-	-	-	20.1	0.5
1958	-	-	-	-	20.5	2.0	-	-	-	-	20.6	0.5	-	-	-	-	20.6	0.0	-	-	-	-	20.8	1.0
1959	-	-	-	-	20.8	0.0	-	-	-	-	21.8	4.8	-	-	-	-	21.8	0.0	-	-	-	-	22.0	0.9
1960	-	-	-	-	22.1	0.5	-	-	-	-	22.1	0.0	-	-	-	-	22.2	0.5	-	-	-	-	21.9	-1.4
1961	-	-	-	-	21.9	0.0	-	-	-	-	22.2	1.4	-	-	-	-	22.6	1.8	-	-	-	-	22.7	0.4
1962	-	-	-	-	22.9	0.9	-	-	-	-	23.0	0.4	-	-	-	-	23.0	0.0	-	-	-	-	23.0	0.0
1963	-	-	-	-	23.0	0.0	-	-	-	-	23.5	2.2	-	-	-	-	23.5	0.0	-	-	-	-	23.5	0.0
1964	-	-	-	-	23.7	0.9	-	-	-	-	23.7	0.0	-	-	-	-	24.1	1.7	-	-	-	-	24.1	0.0
1965	-	-	-	-	24.3	0.8	-	-	-	-	24.4	0.4	-	-	-	-	24.5	0.4	-	-	-	-	24.6	0.4
1966	-	-	-	-	25.2	2.4	-	-	-	-	25.6	1.6	-	-	-	-	26.2	2.3	-	-	-	-	26.3	0.4
1967	-	-	-	-	27.0	2.7	-	-	-	-	27.2	0.7	-	-	-	-	27.7	1.8	-	-	-	-	27.9	0.7
1968	-	-	-	-	28.6	2.5	-	-	-	-	28.8	0.7	-	-	-	-	29.6	2.8	-	-	-	-	30.2	2.0
1969	-	-	-	-	31.5	4.3	-	-	-	-	32.0	1.6	-	-	-	-	32.7	2.2	-	-	-	-	32.9	0.6
1970	-	-	-	-	33.8	2.7	-	-	-	-	34.5	2.1	-	-	-	-	34.8	0.9	-	-	-	-	35.6	2.3
1971	-	-	-	-	36.9	3.7	-	-	-	-	37.3	1.1	-	-	-	-	37.6	0.8	-	-	-	-	37.5	-0.3
1972	-	-	-	-	37.7	0.5	-	-	-	-	38.3	1.6	-	-	-	-	38.3	0.0	-	-	-	-	38.6	0.8
1973	-	-	-	-	38.8	0.5	-	-	-	-	40.0	3.1	-	-	-	-	40.7	1.7	-	-	-	-	41.3	1.5
1974	-	-	-	-	42.2	2.2	-	-	-	-	44.6	5.7	-	-	-	-	45.8	2.7	-	-	-	-	46.5	1.5
1975	-	-	-	-	49.4	6.2	-	-	-	-	49.8	0.8	-	-	-	-	51.5	3.4	-	-	-	-	51.7	0.4
1976	-	-	-	-	52.9	2.3	-	-	-	-	53.2	0.6	-	-	-	-	54.8	3.0	-	-	-	-	55.8	1.8
1977	-	-	-	-	57.7	3.4	-	-	-	-	58.6	1.6	-	-	-	-	59.3	1.2	-	-	-	-	59.3	0.0
1978	-	-	60.4	1.9	-	-	61.8	2.3	-	-	62.3	0.8	-	-	63.1	1.3	-	-	63.6	0.8	-	-	64.4	1.3
1979	-	-	66.0	2.5	-	-	67.1	1.7	-	-	68.2	1.6	-	-	69.3	1.6	-	-	69.6	0.4	-	-	70.0	0.6
1980	-	-	70.7	1.0	-	-	70.8	0.1	-	-	72.3	2.1	-	-	74.1	2.5	-	-	75.0	1.2	-	-	76.5	2.0
1981	-	-	80.6	5.4	-	-	80.8	0.2	-	-	81.0	0.2	-	-	82.2	1.5	-	-	83.9	2.1	-	-	84.1	0.2
1982	-	-	84.8	0.8	-	-	86.6	2.1	-	-	92.7	7.0	-	-	95.5	3.0	-	-	99.2	3.9	-	-	100.0	0.8
1983	-	-	101.0	1.0	-	-	101.2	0.2	-	-	101.2	0.0	-	-	101.3	0.1	-	-	101.7	0.4	-	-	102.0	0.3
1984	-	-	103.6	1.6	-	-	104.7	1.1	-	-	106.0	1.2	-	-	107.3	1.2	-	-	108.7	1.3	-	-	109.0	0.3
1985	-	-	111.0	1.8	-	-	111.6	0.5	-	-	113.2	1.4	-	-	113.7	0.4	-	-	115.1	1.2	-	-	114.6	-0.4
1986	-	-	120.6	5.2	-	-	121.1	0.4	-	-	123.6	2.1	-	-	125.8	1.8	-	-	127.6	1.4	-	-	128.8	0.9
1987	-	-	-	-	-	-	-	-	-	-	130.7	1.5	-	-	-	-	-	-	-	-	-	-	134.6	3.0
1988	-	-	-	-	-	-	-	-	-	-	138.8	3.1	-	-	-	-	-	-	-	-	-	-	144.2	3.9
1989	-	-	-	-	-	-	-	-	-	-	149.4	3.6	-	-	-	-	-	-	-	-	-	-	158.6	6.2
1990	-	-	-	-	-	-	-	-	-	-	161.8	2.0	-	-	-	-	-	-	-	-	-	-	170.0	5.1
1991	-	-	-	-	-	-	-	-	-	-	177.2	4.2	-	-	-	-	-	-	-	-	-	-	184.7	4.2

[Continued]

Atlanta, GA
Consumer Price Index - Urban Wage Earners
Base 1982-1984 = 100
Medical Care
[Continued]

For 1947-1997. Columns headed % show percentile change in the index from the previous period for which an index is available.

Year	Jan Index	%	Feb Index	%	Mar Index	%	Apr Index	%	May Index	%	Jun Index	%	Jul Index	%	Aug Index	%	Sep Index	%	Oct Index	%	Nov Index	%	Dec Index	%
1992	-	-	-	-	-	-	-	-	-	-	189.5	2.6	-	-	-	-	-	-	-	-	-	-	198.3	4.6
1993	-	-	-	-	-	-	-	-	-	-	204.3	3.0	-	-	-	-	-	-	-	-	-	-	213.3	4.4
1994	-	-	-	-	-	-	-	-	-	-	218.3	2.3	-	-	-	-	-	-	-	-	-	-	222.7	2.0
1995	-	-	-	-	-	-	-	-	-	-	225.8	1.4	-	-	-	-	-	-	-	-	-	-	231.1	2.3
1996	-	-	-	-	-	-	-	-	-	-	234.0	1.3	-	-	-	-	-	-	-	-	-	-	241.9	3.4
1997	-	-	-	-	-	-	-	-	-	-	242.5	0.2	-	-	-	-	-	-	-	-	-	-	-	-

Source: U.S. Department of Labor, Bureau of Labor Statistics, Division of Consumer Prices and Price Indexes. - indicates no data collected for period.

Atlanta, GA
Consumer Price Index - All Urban Consumers
Base 1982-1984 = 100
Entertainment

For 1975-1997. Columns headed % show percentile change in the index from the previous period for which an index is available.

Year	Jan Index	%	Feb Index	%	Mar Index	%	Apr Index	%	May Index	%	Jun Index	%	Jul Index	%	Aug Index	%	Sep Index	%	Oct Index	%	Nov Index	%	Dec Index	%
1975	-	-	-	-	-	-	-	-	-	-	-	-	-	-	-	-	-	-	-	-	-	-	76.6	-
1976	-	-	-	-	76.2	-0.5	-	-	-	-	77.7	2.0	-	-	-	-	77.6	-0.1	-	-	-	-	77.8	0.3
1977	-	-	-	-	78.8	1.3	-	-	-	-	80.7	2.4	-	-	-	-	81.4	0.9	-	-	-	-	81.3	-0.1
1978	-	-	83.2	2.3	-	-	83.7	0.6	-	-	84.4	0.8	-	-	83.9	-0.6	-	-	85.2	1.5	-	-	82.5	-3.2
1979	-	-	84.7	2.7	-	-	87.2	3.0	-	-	86.3	-1.0	-	-	87.3	1.2	-	-	85.7	-1.8	-	-	82.0	-4.3
1980	-	-	85.1	3.8	-	-	85.5	0.5	-	-	86.1	0.7	-	-	94.3	9.5	-	-	92.3	-2.1	-	-	91.0	-1.4
1981	-	-	93.7	3.0	-	-	94.1	0.4	-	-	92.7	-1.5	-	-	94.8	2.3	-	-	97.8	3.2	-	-	95.8	-2.0
1982	-	-	101.0	5.4	-	-	94.3	-6.6	-	-	96.6	2.4	-	-	96.2	-0.4	-	-	101.3	5.3	-	-	98.1	-3.2
1983	-	-	95.4	-2.8	-	-	96.5	1.2	-	-	98.3	1.9	-	-	98.7	0.4	-	-	98.6	-0.1	-	-	101.9	3.3
1984	-	-	102.8	0.9	-	-	103.4	0.6	-	-	103.6	0.2	-	-	104.6	1.0	-	-	106.1	1.4	-	-	105.2	-0.8
1985	-	-	106.1	0.9	-	-	109.1	2.8	-	-	113.5	4.0	-	-	114.7	1.1	-	-	114.4	-0.3	-	-	113.0	-1.2
1986	-	-	116.8	3.4	-	-	117.7	0.8	-	-	120.0	2.0	-	-	119.5	-0.4	-	-	120.0	0.4	-	-	120.1	0.1
1987	-	-	-	-	-	-	-	-	-	-	111.0	-7.6	-	-	-	-	-	-	-	-	-	-	113.3	2.1
1988	-	-	-	-	-	-	-	-	-	-	117.5	3.7	-	-	-	-	-	-	-	-	-	-	124.1	5.6
1989	-	-	-	-	-	-	-	-	-	-	127.7	2.9	-	-	-	-	-	-	-	-	-	-	129.6	1.5
1990	-	-	-	-	-	-	-	-	-	-	132.8	2.5	-	-	-	-	-	-	-	-	-	-	134.1	1.0
1991	-	-	-	-	-	-	-	-	-	-	136.4	1.7	-	-	-	-	-	-	-	-	-	-	139.7	2.4
1992	-	-	-	-	-	-	-	-	-	-	142.9	2.3	-	-	-	-	-	-	-	-	-	-	145.8	2.0
1993	-	-	-	-	-	-	-	-	-	-	144.6	-0.8	-	-	-	-	-	-	-	-	-	-	150.4	4.0
1994	-	-	-	-	-	-	-	-	-	-	159.6	6.1	-	-	-	-	-	-	-	-	-	-	161.0	0.9
1995	-	-	-	-	-	-	-	-	-	-	164.2	2.0	-	-	-	-	-	-	-	-	-	-	169.2	3.0
1996	-	-	-	-	-	-	-	-	-	-	177.0	4.6	-	-	-	-	-	-	-	-	-	-	179.4	1.4
1997	-	-	-	-	-	-	-	-	-	-	181.8	1.3	-	-	-	-	-	-	-	-	-	-	-	-

Source: U.S. Department of Labor, Bureau of Labor Statistics, Division of Consumer Prices and Price Indexes. - indicates no data collected for period.

Atlanta, GA
Consumer Price Index - Urban Wage Earners
Base 1982-1984 = 100
Entertainment

For 1975-1997. Columns headed % show percentile change in the index from the previous period for which an index is available.

Year	Jan Index	%	Feb Index	%	Mar Index	%	Apr Index	%	May Index	%	Jun Index	%	Jul Index	%	Aug Index	%	Sep Index	%	Oct Index	%	Nov Index	%	Dec Index	%
1975	-	-	-	-			-	-					-	-	-	-	-	-	-	-	-	-	69.3	-
1976	-	-	-	-	69.0	-0.4	-	-			70.3	1.9	-	-	-	-	70.2	-0.1	-	-	-	-	70.4	0.3
1977	-	-	-	-	71.3	1.3	-	-			73.0	2.4	-	-	-	-	73.6	0.8	-	-	-	-	73.6	0.0
1978	-	-	74.7	1.5	-	-	74.3	-0.5	-	-	75.0	0.9	-	-	74.9	-0.1	-	-	75.1	0.3	-	-	73.5	-2.1
1979	-	-	72.7	-1.1	-	-	75.3	3.6	-	-	75.4	0.1	-	-	76.7	1.7	-	-	76.8	0.1	-	-	77.7	1.2
1980	-	-	89.6	15.3	-	-	89.8	0.2	-	-	90.9	1.2	-	-	90.0	-1.0	-	-	88.8	-1.3	-	-	88.5	-0.3
1981	-	-	99.9	12.9	-	-	99.5	-0.4	-	-	100.5	1.0	-	-	100.5	0.0	-	-	97.8	-2.7	-	-	97.4	-0.4
1982	-	-	102.1	4.8	-	-	96.9	-5.1	-	-	99.0	2.2	-	-	98.3	-0.7	-	-	101.0	2.7	-	-	101.5	0.5
1983	-	-	89.5	-11.8	-	-	90.8	1.5	-	-	95.1	4.7	-	-	95.6	0.5	-	-	95.1	-0.5	-	-	104.0	9.4
1984	-	-	104.9	0.9	-	-	104.9	0.0	-	-	105.0	0.1	-	-	105.7	0.7	-	-	108.0	2.2	-	-	104.8	-3.0
1985	-	-	105.4	0.6	-	-	109.0	3.4	-	-	112.5	3.2	-	-	113.5	0.9	-	-	113.4	-0.1	-	-	109.6	-3.4
1986	-	-	116.9	6.7	-	-	117.3	0.3	-	-	120.9	3.1	-	-	118.0	-2.4	-	-	119.3	1.1	-	-	119.3	0.0
1987	-	-	-	-	-	-	-	-	-	-	109.2	-8.5	-	-	-	-	-	-	-	-	-	-	111.9	2.5
1988	-	-	-	-	-	-	-	-	-	-	115.7	3.4	-	-	-	-	-	-	-	-	-	-	121.8	5.3
1989	-	-	-	-	-	-	-	-	-	-	125.2	2.8	-	-	-	-	-	-	-	-	-	-	127.0	1.4
1990	-	-	-	-	-	-	-	-	-	-	129.9	2.3	-	-	-	-	-	-	-	-	-	-	130.6	0.5
1991	-	-	-	-	-	-	-	-	-	-	133.1	1.9	-	-	-	-	-	-	-	-	-	-	136.2	2.3
1992	-	-	-	-	-	-	-	-	-	-	139.0	2.1	-	-	-	-	-	-	-	-	-	-	141.3	1.7
1993	-	-	-	-	-	-	-	-	-	-	140.0	-0.9	-	-	-	-	-	-	-	-	-	-	145.1	3.6
1994	-	-	-	-	-	-	-	-	-	-	155.1	6.9	-	-	-	-	-	-	-	-	-	-	156.3	0.8
1995	-	-	-	-	-	-	-	-	-	-	159.7	2.2	-	-	-	-	-	-	-	-	-	-	164.8	3.2
1996	-	-	-	-	-	-	-	-	-	-	172.1	4.4	-	-	-	-	-	-	-	-	-	-	174.9	1.6
1997	-	-	-	-	-	-	-	-	-	-	176.8	1.1	-	-	-	-	-	-	-	-	-	-	-	-

Source: U.S. Department of Labor, Bureau of Labor Statistics, Division of Consumer Prices and Price Indexes. - indicates no data collected for period.

Atlanta, GA
Consumer Price Index - All Urban Consumers
Base 1982-1984 = 100
Other Goods and Services

For 1975-1997. Columns headed % show percentile change in the index from the previous period for which an index is available.

Year	Jan Index	%	Feb Index	%	Mar Index	%	Apr Index	%	May Index	%	Jun Index	%	Jul Index	%	Aug Index	%	Sep Index	%	Oct Index	%	Nov Index	%	Dec Index	%
1975	-	-	-	-	-	-	-	-	-	-	-	-	-	-	-	-	-	-	-	-	-	-	54.7	-
1976	-	-	-	-	54.8	0.2	-	-	-	-	55.4	1.1	-	-	-	-	55.7	0.5	-	-	-	-	56.5	1.4
1977	-	-	-	-	57.1	1.1	-	-	-	-	58.1	1.8	-	-	-	-	59.5	2.4	-	-	-	-	60.5	1.7
1978	-	-	60.4	-0.2	-	-	61.1	1.2	-	-	61.8	1.1	-	-	63.8	3.2	-	-	65.2	2.2	-	-	65.3	0.2
1979	-	-	67.3	3.1	-	-	67.8	0.7	-	-	67.9	0.1	-	-	69.1	1.8	-	-	71.1	2.9	-	-	72.0	1.3
1980	-	-	73.8	2.5	-	-	74.1	0.4	-	-	75.3	1.6	-	-	75.6	0.4	-	-	77.8	2.9	-	-	79.2	1.8
1981	-	-	81.5	2.9	-	-	83.3	2.2	-	-	83.9	0.7	-	-	84.1	0.2	-	-	86.6	3.0	-	-	87.6	1.2
1982	-	-	87.9	0.3	-	-	90.0	2.4	-	-	91.0	1.1	-	-	91.9	1.0	-	-	95.2	3.6	-	-	96.6	1.5
1983	-	-	98.5	2.0	-	-	98.9	0.4	-	-	98.9	0.0	-	-	100.6	1.7	-	-	103.4	2.8	-	-	104.2	0.8
1984	-	-	106.2	1.9	-	-	106.0	-0.2	-	-	107.7	1.6	-	-	108.3	0.6	-	-	110.2	1.8	-	-	110.3	0.1
1985	-	-	111.7	1.3	-	-	111.3	-0.4	-	-	112.0	0.6	-	-	113.2	1.1	-	-	115.1	1.7	-	-	116.2	1.0
1986	-	-	118.3	1.8	-	-	119.0	0.6	-	-	118.5	-0.4	-	-	120.0	1.3	-	-	121.6	1.3	-	-	122.9	1.1
1987	-	-	-	-	-	-	-	-	-	-	134.0	9.0	-	-	-	-	-	-	-	-	-	-	-	-
1988	-	-	-	-	-	-	-	-	-	-	142.6	6.4	-	-	-	-	-	-	-	-	-	-	-	-
1989	-	-	-	-	-	-	-	-	-	-	153.0	7.3	-	-	-	-	-	-	-	-	-	-	-	-
1990	-	-	-	-	-	-	-	-	-	-	165.2	8.0	-	-	-	-	-	-	-	-	-	-	-	-
1991	-	-	-	-	-	-	-	-	-	-	182.9	10.7	-	-	-	-	-	-	-	-	-	-	-	-
1992	-	-	-	-	-	-	-	-	-	-	192.6	5.3	-	-	-	-	-	-	-	-	-	-	-	-
1993	-	-	-	-	-	-	-	-	-	-	205.9	6.9	-	-	-	-	-	-	-	-	-	-	-	-
1994	-	-	-	-	-	-	-	-	-	-	220.3	7.0	-	-	-	-	-	-	-	-	-	-	-	-
1995	-	-	-	-	-	-	-	-	-	-	225.5	2.4	-	-	-	-	-	-	-	-	-	-	-	-
1996	-	-	-	-	-	-	-	-	-	-	231.4	2.6	-	-	-	-	-	-	-	-	-	-	-	-
1997	-	-	-	-	-	-	-	-	-	-	239.4	3.5	-	-	-	-	-	-	-	-	-	-	-	-

Source: U.S. Department of Labor, Bureau of Labor Statistics, Division of Consumer Prices and Price Indexes. - indicates no data collected for period.

Atlanta, GA
Consumer Price Index - Urban Wage Earners
Base 1982-1984 = 100
Other Goods and Services

For 1975-1997. Columns headed % show percentile change in the index from the previous period for which an index is available.

Year	Jan Index	%	Feb Index	%	Mar Index	%	Apr Index	%	May Index	%	Jun Index	%	Jul Index	%	Aug Index	%	Sep Index	%	Oct Index	%	Nov Index	%	Dec Index	%
1975	-	-	-	-	-	-	-	-	-	-	-	-	-	-	-	-	-	-	-	-	-	-	57.3	-
1976	-	-	-	-	57.4	0.2	-	-	-	-	58.1	1.2	-	-	-	-	58.4	0.5	-	-	-	-	59.2	1.4
1977	-	-	-	-	59.8	1.0	-	-	-	-	60.9	1.8	-	-	-	-	62.4	2.5	-	-	-	-	63.3	1.4
1978	-	-	64.0	1.1	-	-	64.4	0.6	-	-	65.2	1.2	-	-	65.3	0.2	-	-	66.7	2.1	-	-	66.4	-0.4
1979	-	-	68.5	3.2	-	-	68.9	0.6	-	-	69.9	1.5	-	-	70.5	0.9	-	-	72.2	2.4	-	-	72.6	0.6
1980	-	-	74.1	2.1	-	-	74.4	0.4	-	-	75.1	0.9	-	-	75.5	0.5	-	-	77.7	2.9	-	-	79.0	1.7
1981	-	-	81.1	2.7	-	-	81.6	0.6	-	-	83.4	2.2	-	-	84.2	1.0	-	-	86.1	2.3	-	-	87.1	1.2
1982	-	-	87.4	0.3	-	-	89.6	2.5	-	-	90.9	1.5	-	-	91.7	0.9	-	-	94.9	3.5	-	-	96.5	1.7
1983	-	-	98.7	2.3	-	-	99.2	0.5	-	-	99.3	0.1	-	-	101.1	1.8	-	-	103.5	2.4	-	-	104.3	0.8
1984	-	-	106.7	2.3	-	-	106.3	-0.4	-	-	107.9	1.5	-	-	108.5	0.6	-	-	109.7	1.1	-	-	109.8	0.1
1985	-	-	111.4	1.5	-	-	111.3	-0.1	-	-	111.9	0.5	-	-	113.3	1.3	-	-	114.6	1.1	-	-	115.9	1.1
1986	-	-	118.5	2.2	-	-	119.5	0.8	-	-	118.6	-0.8	-	-	119.8	1.0	-	-	121.2	1.2	-	-	122.5	1.1
1987	-	-	-	-	-	-	-	-	-	-	132.8	8.4	-	-	-	-	-	-	-	-	-	-	-	-
1988	-	-	-	-	-	-	-	-	-	-	141.8	6.8	-	-	-	-	-	-	-	-	-	-	-	-
1989	-	-	-	-	-	-	-	-	-	-	151.6	6.9	-	-	-	-	-	-	-	-	-	-	-	-
1990	-	-	-	-	-	-	-	-	-	-	163.5	7.8	-	-	-	-	-	-	-	-	-	-	-	-
1991	-	-	-	-	-	-	-	-	-	-	182.2	11.4	-	-	-	-	-	-	-	-	-	-	-	-
1992	-	-	-	-	-	-	-	-	-	-	191.0	4.8	-	-	-	-	-	-	-	-	-	-	-	-
1993	-	-	-	-	-	-	-	-	-	-	204.6	7.1	-	-	-	-	-	-	-	-	-	-	-	-
1994	-	-	-	-	-	-	-	-	-	-	216.6	5.9	-	-	-	-	-	-	-	-	-	-	-	-
1995	-	-	-	-	-	-	-	-	-	-	221.0	2.0	-	-	-	-	-	-	-	-	-	-	-	-
1996	-	-	-	-	-	-	-	-	-	-	226.2	2.4	-	-	-	-	-	-	-	-	-	-	-	-
1997	-	-	-	-	-	-	-	-	-	-	233.6	3.3	-	-	-	-	-	-	-	-	-	-	-	-

Source: U.S. Department of Labor, Bureau of Labor Statistics, Division of Consumer Prices and Price Indexes. - indicates no data collected for period.

Baltimore, MD
Consumer Price Index - All Urban Consumers
Base 1982-1984 = 100
Annual Averages

For 1914-1997. Columns headed % show percentile change in the index from the previous period for which an index is available.

Year	All Items		Food & Beverage		Housing		Apparel & Upkeep		Trans- portation		Medical Care		Entertain- ment		Other Goods & Services	
	Index	%	Index	%	Index	%	Index	%	Index	%	Index	%	Index	%	Index	%
1914	-	-	-	-	-	-	-	-	-	-	-	-	-	-	-	-
1915	8.9	-	-	-	-	-	-	-	-	-	-	-	-	-	-	-
1916	9.7	9.0	-	-	-	-	-	-	-	-	-	-	-	-	-	-
1917	11.9	22.7	-	-	-	-	-	-	-	-	-	-	-	-	-	-
1918	14.3	20.2	-	-	-	-	-	-	-	-	-	-	-	-	-	-
1919	16.3	14.0	-	-	-	-	-	-	-	-	-	-	-	-	-	-
1920	18.3	12.3	-	-	-	-	-	-	-	-	-	-	-	-	-	-
1921	16.2	-11.5	-	-	-	-	-	-	-	-	-	-	-	-	-	-
1922	15.4	-4.9	-	-	-	-	-	-	-	-	-	-	-	-	-	-
1923	15.7	1.9	-	-	-	-	-	-	-	-	-	-	-	-	-	-
1924	15.7	0.0	-	-	-	-	-	-	-	-	-	-	-	-	-	-
1925	16.2	3.2	-	-	-	-	-	-	-	-	-	-	-	-	-	-
1926	16.4	1.2	-	-	-	-	-	-	-	-	-	-	-	-	-	-
1927	16.0	-2.4	-	-	-	-	-	-	-	-	-	-	-	-	-	-
1928	15.9	-0.6	-	-	-	-	-	-	-	-	-	-	-	-	-	-
1929	15.9	0.0	-	-	-	-	-	-	-	-	-	-	-	-	-	-
1930	15.6	-1.9	-	-	-	-	-	-	-	-	-	-	-	-	-	-
1931	14.4	-7.7	-	-	-	-	-	-	-	-	-	-	-	-	-	-
1932	13.1	-9.0	-	-	-	-	-	-	-	-	-	-	-	-	-	-
1933	12.5	-4.6	-	-	-	-	-	-	-	-	-	-	-	-	-	-
1934	13.0	4.0	-	-	-	-	-	-	-	-	-	-	-	-	-	-
1935	13.3	2.3	-	-	-	-	-	-	-	-	-	-	-	-	-	-
1936	13.4	0.8	-	-	-	-	-	-	-	-	-	-	-	-	-	-
1937	13.8	3.0	-	-	-	-	-	-	-	-	-	-	-	-	-	-
1938	13.5	-2.2	-	-	-	-	-	-	-	-	-	-	-	-	-	-
1939	13.4	-0.7	-	-	-	-	-	-	-	-	-	-	-	-	-	-
1940	13.5	0.7	-	-	-	-	-	-	-	-	-	-	-	-	-	-
1941	14.3	5.9	-	-	-	-	-	-	-	-	-	-	-	-	-	-
1942	16.0	11.9	-	-	-	-	-	-	-	-	-	-	-	-	-	-
1943	17.0	6.3	-	-	-	-	-	-	-	-	-	-	-	-	-	-
1944	17.3	1.8	-	-	-	-	-	-	-	-	-	-	-	-	-	-
1945	17.8	2.9	-	-	-	-	-	-	-	-	-	-	-	-	-	-
1946	19.2	7.9	-	-	-	-	-	-	-	-	-	-	-	-	-	-
1947	22.1	15.1	-	-	-	-	-	-	17.3	-	12.8	-	-	-	-	-
1948	23.8	7.7	-	-	-	-	-	-	18.8	8.7	13.3	3.9	-	-	-	-
1949	23.7	-0.4	-	-	-	-	-	-	21.8	16.0	13.4	0.8	-	-	-	-
1950	23.9	0.8	-	-	-	-	-	-	22.7	4.1	13.6	1.5	-	-	-	-
1951	25.6	7.1	-	-	-	-	-	-	24.2	6.6	14.8	8.8	-	-	-	-
1952	26.3	2.7	-	-	-	-	-	-	25.6	5.8	16.4	10.8	-	-	-	-
1953	26.6	1.1	-	-	-	-	38.1	-	26.9	5.1	17.4	6.1	-	-	-	-
1954	26.7	0.4	-	-	-	-	38.0	-0.3	26.6	-1.1	17.6	1.1	-	-	-	-
1955	26.7	0.0	-	-	-	-	37.9	-0.3	26.4	-0.8	17.8	1.1	-	-	-	-
1956	27.1	1.5	-	-	-	-	39.3	3.7	26.9	1.9	18.6	4.5	-	-	-	-
1957	28.1	3.7	-	-	-	-	40.1	2.0	28.5	5.9	19.1	2.7	-	-	-	-
1958	28.9	2.8	-	-	-	-	40.7	1.5	29.3	2.8	19.7	3.1	-	-	-	-

[Continued]

278

Baltimore, MD
Consumer Price Index - All Urban Consumers
Base 1982-1984 = 100
Annual Averages
[Continued]

For 1914-1997. Columns headed % show percentile change in the index from the previous period for which an index is available.

Year	All Items		Food & Beverage		Housing		Apparel & Upkeep		Trans-portation		Medical Care		Entertain-ment		Other Goods & Services	
	Index	%	Index	%	Index	%	Index	%	Index	%	Index	%	Index	%	Index	%
1959	29.4	1.7	-	-	-	-	41.6	2.2	31.1	6.1	21.0	6.6	-	-	-	-
1960	29.8	1.4	-	-	-	-	42.2	1.4	30.9	-0.6	22.2	5.7	-	-	-	-
1961	30.1	1.0	-	-	-	-	42.9	1.7	31.4	1.6	23.2	4.5	-	-	-	-
1962	30.3	0.7	-	-	-	-	43.2	0.7	31.4	0.0	23.7	2.2	-	-	-	-
1963	30.8	1.7	-	-	-	-	43.6	0.9	32.0	1.9	25.2	6.3	-	-	-	-
1964	31.1	1.0	-	-	-	-	43.5	-0.2	32.8	2.5	25.8	2.4	-	-	-	-
1965	31.6	1.6	-	-	-	-	44.1	1.4	33.3	1.5	26.4	2.3	-	-	-	-
1966	32.7	3.5	-	-	-	-	45.4	2.9	33.6	0.9	27.5	4.2	-	-	-	-
1967	33.4	2.1	-	-	-	-	47.5	4.6	34.3	2.1	29.8	8.4	-	-	-	-
1968	34.8	4.2	-	-	-	-	49.7	4.6	35.5	3.5	31.5	5.7	-	-	-	-
1969	36.9	6.0	-	-	-	-	53.7	8.0	37.4	5.4	33.6	6.7	-	-	-	-
1970	39.1	6.0	-	-	-	-	56.6	5.4	38.5	2.9	36.7	9.2	-	-	-	-
1971	41.3	5.6	-	-	-	-	58.6	3.5	40.3	4.7	40.5	10.4	-	-	-	-
1972	42.2	2.2	-	-	-	-	58.8	0.3	40.0	-0.7	42.5	4.9	-	-	-	-
1973	45.1	6.9	-	-	-	-	62.0	5.4	41.3	3.2	44.4	4.5	-	-	-	-
1974	51.0	13.1	-	-	-	-	67.1	8.2	46.1	11.6	49.2	10.8	-	-	-	-
1975	55.2	8.2	-	-	-	-	70.1	4.5	50.2	8.9	53.8	9.3	-	-	-	-
1976	58.1	5.3	63.9	-	55.1	-	73.2	4.4	54.5	8.6	57.5	6.9	66.9	-	57.2	-
1977	62.2	7.1	67.9	6.3	59.8	8.5	77.2	5.5	57.7	5.9	61.9	7.7	69.7	4.2	60.3	5.4
1978	66.7	7.2	74.3	9.4	64.9	8.5	80.6	4.4	60.1	4.2	65.7	6.1	72.5	4.0	64.4	6.8
1979	73.0	9.4	81.2	9.3	70.4	8.5	83.2	3.2	68.9	14.6	72.2	9.9	76.6	5.7	69.5	7.9
1980	83.7	14.7	87.9	8.3	82.8	17.6	93.3	12.1	82.3	19.4	79.2	9.7	83.5	9.0	75.8	9.1
1981	91.5	9.3	94.0	6.9	91.2	10.1	96.7	3.6	92.0	11.8	85.0	7.3	90.0	7.8	82.5	8.8
1982	95.6	4.5	96.5	2.7	95.5	4.7	98.2	1.6	96.0	4.3	94.0	10.6	94.4	4.9	89.6	8.6
1983	99.9	4.5	99.5	3.1	99.6	4.3	100.5	2.3	99.8	4.0	100.6	7.0	101.5	7.5	101.2	12.9
1984	104.5	4.6	104.0	4.5	104.8	5.2	101.3	0.8	104.3	4.5	105.4	4.8	104.2	2.7	109.2	7.9
1985	108.2	3.5	107.1	3.0	108.3	3.3	106.3	4.9	107.3	2.9	111.9	6.2	109.3	4.9	114.1	4.5
1986	110.9	2.5	112.0	4.6	111.1	2.6	110.8	4.2	104.5	-2.6	121.8	8.8	113.9	4.2	120.3	5.4
1987	114.2	3.0	116.8	4.3	112.6	1.4	119.7	8.0	106.9	2.3	127.9	5.0	118.9	4.4	127.1	5.7
1988	119.3	4.5	121.8	4.3	116.2	3.2	130.1	8.7	111.5	4.3	134.7	5.3	122.8	3.3	138.9	9.3
1989	124.5	4.4	129.2	6.1	120.0	3.3	127.8	-1.8	116.9	4.8	145.6	8.1	128.7	4.8	149.2	7.4
1990	130.8	5.1	136.9	6.0	125.2	4.3	128.1	0.2	122.8	5.0	158.4	8.8	138.3	7.5	158.5	6.2
1991	136.4	4.3	140.6	2.7	131.0	4.6	132.9	3.7	125.5	2.2	171.9	8.5	143.8	4.0	172.8	9.0
1992	140.1	2.7	142.4	1.3	133.3	1.8	135.2	1.7	128.5	2.4	184.4	7.3	149.3	3.8	188.2	8.9
1993	143.1	2.1	144.3	1.3	135.6	1.7	135.9	0.5	129.7	0.9	198.7	7.8	152.6	2.2	198.1	5.3
1994	146.9	2.7	149.7	3.7	138.4	2.1	135.3	-0.4	132.8	2.4	218.1	9.8	154.7	1.4	199.7	0.8
1995	150.7	2.6	154.5	3.2	140.7	1.7	130.5	-3.5	138.4	4.2	230.0	5.5	160.6	3.8	207.3	3.8
1996	154.2	2.3	158.8	2.8	143.7	2.1	132.8	1.8	140.3	1.4	237.4	3.2	167.2	4.1	213.9	3.2
1997	-	-	-	-	-	-	-	-	-	-	-	-	-	-	-	-

Source: U.S. Department of Labor, Bureau of Labor Statistics, Division of Consumer Prices and Price Indexes. - indicates no data collected for period.

Baltimore, MD
Consumer Price Index - Urban Wage Earners
Base 1982-1984 = 100
Annual Averages

For 1914-1997. Columns headed % show percentile change in the index from the previous period for which an index is available.

Year	All Items		Food & Beverage		Housing		Apparel & Upkeep		Trans-portation		Medical Care		Entertain-ment		Other Goods & Services	
	Index	%	Index	%	Index	%	Index	%	Index	%	Index	%	Index	%	Index	%
1914	-	-	-	-	-	-	-	-	-	-	-	-	-	-	-	-
1915	8.9	-	-	-	-	-	-	-	-	-	-	-	-	-	-	-
1916	9.7	9.0	-	-	-	-	-	-	-	-	-	-	-	-	-	-
1917	11.9	22.7	-	-	-	-	-	-	-	-	-	-	-	-	-	-
1918	14.4	21.0	-	-	-	-	-	-	-	-	-	-	-	-	-	-
1919	16.3	13.2	-	-	-	-	-	-	-	-	-	-	-	-	-	-
1920	18.3	12.3	-	-	-	-	-	-	-	-	-	-	-	-	-	-
1921	16.3	-10.9	-	-	-	-	-	-	-	-	-	-	-	-	-	-
1922	15.4	-5.5	-	-	-	-	-	-	-	-	-	-	-	-	-	-
1923	15.8	2.6	-	-	-	-	-	-	-	-	-	-	-	-	-	-
1924	15.8	0.0	-	-	-	-	-	-	-	-	-	-	-	-	-	-
1925	16.2	2.5	-	-	-	-	-	-	-	-	-	-	-	-	-	-
1926	16.4	1.2	-	-	-	-	-	-	-	-	-	-	-	-	-	-
1927	16.0	-2.4	-	-	-	-	-	-	-	-	-	-	-	-	-	-
1928	15.9	-0.6	-	-	-	-	-	-	-	-	-	-	-	-	-	-
1929	15.9	0.0	-	-	-	-	-	-	-	-	-	-	-	-	-	-
1930	15.7	-1.3	-	-	-	-	-	-	-	-	-	-	-	-	-	-
1931	14.5	-7.6	-	-	-	-	-	-	-	-	-	-	-	-	-	-
1932	13.1	-9.7	-	-	-	-	-	-	-	-	-	-	-	-	-	-
1933	12.5	-4.6	-	-	-	-	-	-	-	-	-	-	-	-	-	-
1934	13.0	4.0	-	-	-	-	-	-	-	-	-	-	-	-	-	-
1935	13.4	3.1	-	-	-	-	-	-	-	-	-	-	-	-	-	-
1936	13.5	0.7	-	-	-	-	-	-	-	-	-	-	-	-	-	-
1937	13.8	2.2	-	-	-	-	-	-	-	-	-	-	-	-	-	-
1938	13.6	-1.4	-	-	-	-	-	-	-	-	-	-	-	-	-	-
1939	13.5	-0.7	-	-	-	-	-	-	-	-	-	-	-	-	-	-
1940	13.5	0.0	-	-	-	-	-	-	-	-	-	-	-	-	-	-
1941	14.4	6.7	-	-	-	-	-	-	-	-	-	-	-	-	-	-
1942	16.0	11.1	-	-	-	-	-	-	-	-	-	-	-	-	-	-
1943	17.1	6.9	-	-	-	-	-	-	-	-	-	-	-	-	-	-
1944	17.3	1.2	-	-	-	-	-	-	-	-	-	-	-	-	-	-
1945	17.9	3.5	-	-	-	-	-	-	-	-	-	-	-	-	-	-
1946	19.3	7.8	-	-	-	-	-	-	-	-	-	-	-	-	-	-
1947	22.2	15.0	-	-	-	-	-	-	17.2	-	13.7	-	-	-	-	-
1948	23.9	7.7	-	-	-	-	-	-	18.7	8.7	14.2	3.6	-	-	-	-
1949	23.8	-0.4	-	-	-	-	-	-	21.7	16.0	14.3	0.7	-	-	-	-
1950	24.0	0.8	-	-	-	-	-	-	22.5	3.7	14.5	1.4	-	-	-	-
1951	25.7	7.1	-	-	-	-	-	-	24.0	6.7	15.7	8.3	-	-	-	-
1952	26.4	2.7	-	-	-	-	-	-	25.5	6.3	17.5	11.5	-	-	-	-
1953	26.7	1.1	-	-	-	-	39.0	-	26.7	4.7	18.5	5.7	-	-	-	-
1954	26.8	0.4	-	-	-	-	38.9	-0.3	26.5	-0.7	18.7	1.1	-	-	-	-
1955	26.8	0.0	-	-	-	-	38.8	-0.3	26.2	-1.1	18.9	1.1	-	-	-	-
1956	27.2	1.5	-	-	-	-	40.2	3.6	26.7	1.9	19.7	4.2	-	-	-	-
1957	28.2	3.7	-	-	-	-	41.1	2.2	28.4	6.4	20.3	3.0	-	-	-	-
1958	29.0	2.8	-	-	-	-	41.6	1.2	29.1	2.5	20.9	3.0	-	-	-	-

[Continued]

Baltimore, MD
Consumer Price Index - Urban Wage Earners
Base 1982-1984 = 100
Annual Averages
[Continued]

For 1914-1997. Columns headed % show percentile change in the index from the previous period for which an index is available.

Year	All Items		Food & Beverage		Housing		Apparel & Upkeep		Trans- portation		Medical Care		Entertain- ment		Other Goods & Services	
	Index	%	Index	%	Index	%	Index	%	Index	%	Index	%	Index	%	Index	%
1959	29.5	1.7	-	-	-	-	42.5	2.2	30.9	6.2	22.3	6.7	-	-	-	-
1960	29.9	1.4	-	-	-	-	43.2	1.6	30.7	-0.6	23.6	5.8	-	-	-	-
1961	30.2	1.0	-	-	-	-	43.9	1.6	31.2	1.6	24.7	4.7	-	-	-	-
1962	30.4	0.7	-	-	-	-	44.2	0.7	31.2	0.0	25.2	2.0	-	-	-	-
1963	30.9	1.6	-	-	-	-	44.6	0.9	31.8	1.9	26.7	6.0	-	-	-	-
1964	31.2	1.0	-	-	-	-	44.6	0.0	32.6	2.5	27.4	2.6	-	-	-	-
1965	31.7	1.6	-	-	-	-	45.1	1.1	33.1	1.5	28.1	2.6	-	-	-	-
1966	32.8	3.5	-	-	-	-	46.5	3.1	33.4	0.9	29.3	4.3	-	-	-	-
1967	33.5	2.1	-	-	-	-	48.6	4.5	34.1	2.1	31.7	8.2	-	-	-	-
1968	34.9	4.2	-	-	-	-	50.8	4.5	35.2	3.2	33.4	5.4	-	-	-	-
1969	37.1	6.3	-	-	-	-	54.9	8.1	37.1	5.4	35.7	6.9	-	-	-	-
1970	39.2	5.7	-	-	-	-	57.9	5.5	38.3	3.2	39.0	9.2	-	-	-	-
1971	41.4	5.6	-	-	-	-	60.0	3.6	40.0	4.4	43.0	10.3	-	-	-	-
1972	42.4	2.4	-	-	-	-	60.2	0.3	39.7	-0.7	45.1	4.9	-	-	-	-
1973	45.3	6.8	-	-	-	-	63.4	5.3	41.1	3.5	47.2	4.7	-	-	-	-
1974	51.1	12.8	-	-	-	-	68.7	8.4	45.8	11.4	52.3	10.8	-	-	-	-
1975	55.4	8.4	-	-	-	-	71.7	4.4	49.9	9.0	57.1	9.2	-	-	-	-
1976	58.3	5.2	63.8	-	55.5	-	74.9	4.5	54.1	8.4	61.1	7.0	66.5	-	58.7	-
1977	62.4	7.0	67.8	6.3	60.2	8.5	79.0	5.5	57.3	5.9	65.8	7.7	69.3	4.2	61.9	5.5
1978	67.0	7.4	73.9	9.0	65.5	8.8	82.4	4.3	59.8	4.4	70.0	6.4	72.0	3.9	65.2	5.3
1979	73.4	9.6	80.4	8.8	71.9	9.8	83.9	1.8	68.0	13.7	76.0	8.6	76.6	6.4	69.2	6.1
1980	83.6	13.9	87.7	9.1	83.5	16.1	91.3	8.8	80.6	18.5	81.1	6.7	83.1	8.5	75.8	9.5
1981	91.8	9.8	93.7	6.8	92.6	10.9	95.9	5.0	91.0	12.9	85.7	5.7	89.1	7.2	83.0	9.5
1982	95.9	4.5	96.5	3.0	96.5	4.2	97.6	1.8	95.5	4.9	94.0	9.7	95.7	7.4	89.5	7.8
1983	99.8	4.1	99.5	3.1	99.4	3.0	100.7	3.2	99.7	4.4	100.6	7.0	101.2	5.7	101.3	13.2
1984	104.3	4.5	104.0	4.5	104.0	4.6	101.7	1.0	104.8	5.1	105.4	4.8	103.1	1.9	109.2	7.8
1985	108.3	3.8	107.1	3.0	108.7	4.5	106.6	4.8	107.6	2.7	111.9	6.2	108.2	4.9	114.1	4.5
1986	110.5	2.0	111.9	4.5	111.3	2.4	110.1	3.3	104.2	-3.2	122.0	9.0	112.8	4.3	120.2	5.3
1987	113.8	3.0	116.6	4.2	112.5	1.1	119.1	8.2	107.2	2.9	127.6	4.6	118.1	4.7	126.7	5.4
1988	118.9	4.5	121.7	4.4	116.0	3.1	128.9	8.2	112.3	4.8	134.1	5.1	123.0	4.1	138.1	9.0
1989	124.1	4.4	128.8	5.8	120.0	3.4	126.0	-2.2	117.7	4.8	143.9	7.3	129.2	5.0	148.2	7.3
1990	130.1	4.8	136.4	5.9	124.9	4.1	125.5	-0.4	123.6	5.0	156.1	8.5	139.0	7.6	157.2	6.1
1991	135.6	4.2	140.2	2.8	130.5	4.5	130.9	4.3	125.9	1.9	169.4	8.5	145.9	5.0	172.1	9.5
1992	139.5	2.9	142.1	1.4	132.6	1.6	135.5	3.5	129.1	2.5	181.3	7.0	151.6	3.9	189.7	10.2
1993	142.3	2.0	143.8	1.2	134.7	1.6	135.9	0.3	130.0	0.7	196.0	8.1	155.0	2.2	199.4	5.1
1994	145.9	2.5	149.1	3.7	137.7	2.2	133.5	-1.8	133.4	2.6	214.1	9.2	158.1	2.0	199.5	0.1
1995	149.7	2.6	153.7	3.1	139.7	1.5	127.5	-4.5	139.5	4.6	225.4	5.3	164.1	3.8	207.0	3.8
1996	153.1	2.3	158.1	2.9	142.5	2.0	128.4	0.7	141.4	1.4	232.8	3.3	171.5	4.5	214.0	3.4
1997	-	-	-	-	-	-	-	-	-	-	-	-	-	-	-	-

Source: U.S. Department of Labor, Bureau of Labor Statistics, Division of Consumer Prices and Price Indexes. - indicates no data collected for period.

Baltimore, MD
Consumer Price Index - All Urban Consumers
Base 1982-1984 = 100
All Items

For 1914-1997. Columns headed % show percentile change in the index from the previous period for which an index is available.

Year	Jan Index	%	Feb Index	%	Mar Index	%	Apr Index	%	May Index	%	Jun Index	%	Jul Index	%	Aug Index	%	Sep Index	%	Oct Index	%	Nov Index	%	Dec Index	%
1914	-	-	-	-	-	-	-	-	-	-	-	-	-	-	-	-	-	-	-	-	-	-	9.0	-
1915	-	-	-	-	-	-	-	-	-	-	-	-	-	-	-	-	-	-	-	-	-	-	9.0	0.0
1916	-	-	-	-	-	-	-	-	-	-	-	-	-	-	-	-	-	-	-	-	-	-	10.4	15.6
1917	-	-	-	-	-	-	-	-	-	-	-	-	-	-	-	-	-	-	-	-	-	-	12.9	24.0
1918	-	-	-	-	-	-	-	-	-	-	-	-	-	-	-	-	-	-	-	-	-	-	15.7	21.7
1919	-	-	-	-	-	-	-	-	-	-	15.9	1.3	-	-	-	-	-	-	-	-	-	-	17.3	8.8
1920	-	-	-	-	-	-	-	-	-	-	19.2	11.0	-	-	-	-	-	-	-	-	-	-	17.5	-8.9
1921	-	-	-	-	-	-	-	-	16.1	-8.0	-	-	-	-	-	-	16.1	0.0	-	-	-	-	15.7	-2.5
1922	-	-	-	-	15.4	-1.9	-	-	-	-	15.4	0.0	-	-	-	-	15.2	-1.3	-	-	-	-	15.5	2.0
1923	-	-	-	-	15.5	0.0	-	-	-	-	15.8	1.9	-	-	-	-	16.0	1.3	-	-	-	-	15.9	-0.6
1924	-	-	-	-	15.7	-1.3	-	-	-	-	15.8	0.6	-	-	-	-	15.7	-0.6	-	-	-	-	15.8	0.6
1925	-	-	-	-	-	-	-	-	-	-	16.2	2.5	-	-	-	-	-	-	-	-	-	-	16.6	2.5
1926	-	-	-	-	-	-	-	-	-	-	16.4	-1.2	-	-	-	-	-	-	-	-	-	-	16.3	-0.6
1927	-	-	-	-	-	-	-	-	-	-	16.2	-0.6	-	-	-	-	-	-	-	-	-	-	15.9	-1.9
1928	-	-	-	-	-	-	-	-	-	-	15.9	0.0	-	-	-	-	-	-	-	-	-	-	15.7	-1.3
1929	-	-	-	-	-	-	-	-	-	-	15.8	0.6	-	-	-	-	-	-	-	-	-	-	15.9	0.6
1930	-	-	-	-	-	-	-	-	-	-	15.8	-0.6	-	-	-	-	-	-	-	-	-	-	15.2	-3.8
1931	-	-	-	-	-	-	-	-	-	-	14.3	-5.9	-	-	-	-	-	-	-	-	-	-	13.9	-2.8
1932	-	-	-	-	-	-	-	-	-	-	13.0	-6.5	-	-	-	-	-	-	-	-	-	-	12.6	-3.1
1933	-	-	-	-	-	-	-	-	-	-	12.2	-3.2	-	-	-	-	-	-	-	-	-	-	12.8	4.9
1934	-	-	-	-	-	-	-	-	-	-	12.9	0.8	-	-	-	-	-	-	-	-	13.1	1.6	-	-
1935	-	-	-	-	13.2	0.8	-	-	-	-	-	-	13.3	0.8	-	-	-	-	13.3	0.0	-	-	13.4	-1.5
1936	13.5	1.5	-	-	-	-	13.4	-0.7	-	-	-	-	13.4	0.0	-	-	13.6	1.5	-	-	-	-	13.8	-0.7
1937	-	-	-	-	13.7	2.2	-	-	-	-	13.7	0.0	-	-	-	-	13.9	1.5	-	-	-	-	13.5	0.0
1938	-	-	-	-	13.5	-2.2	-	-	-	-	13.5	0.0	-	-	-	-	13.5	0.0	-	-	-	-	13.3	-2.2
1939	-	-	-	-	13.4	-0.7	-	-	-	-	13.4	0.0	-	-	-	-	13.6	1.5	-	-	-	-	13.6	0.7
1940	-	-	-	-	13.4	0.8	-	-	-	-	13.6	1.5	-	-	-	-	13.5	-0.7	13.5	0.0	13.5	0.0	13.6	0.7
1941	13.6	0.0	13.6	0.0	13.7	0.7	13.8	0.7	14.0	1.4	14.3	2.1	14.4	0.7	14.5	0.7	14.8	2.1	14.9	0.7	15.0	0.7	15.2	1.3
1942	15.4	1.3	15.5	0.6	15.7	1.3	15.8	0.6	15.9	0.6	16.1	1.3	16.0	-0.6	16.1	0.6	16.2	0.6	16.3	0.6	16.3	0.0	16.5	1.2
1943	16.6	0.6	16.6	0.0	16.9	1.8	17.1	1.2	17.4	1.8	17.4	0.0	17.1	-1.7	17.0	-0.6	17.1	0.6	17.2	0.6	17.0	-1.2	17.1	0.6
1944	17.1	0.0	17.0	-0.6	17.1	0.6	17.1	0.0	17.2	0.6	17.3	0.6	17.4	0.6	17.4	0.0	17.3	-0.6	17.4	0.6	17.5	0.6	17.5	0.0
1945	17.6	0.6	17.6	0.0	17.6	0.0	17.6	0.0	17.8	1.1	18.0	1.1	18.0	0.0	18.0	0.0	18.0	0.0	17.9	-0.6	17.9	0.0	18.0	0.6
1946	18.0	0.0	17.8	-1.1	17.9	0.6	18.1	1.1	18.1	0.0	18.4	1.7	19.4	5.4	19.9	2.6	20.1	1.0	20.5	2.0	21.0	2.4	21.1	0.5
1947	21.2	0.5	21.1	-0.5	21.7	2.8	21.7	0.0	21.6	-0.5	21.8	0.9	-	-	-	-	22.8	4.6	-	-	-	-	23.3	2.2
1948	-	-	-	-	23.2	-0.4	-	-	-	-	23.9	3.0	-	-	-	-	24.4	2.1	-	-	-	-	23.7	-2.9
1949	-	-	-	-	23.7	0.0	-	-	-	-	23.8	0.4	-	-	-	-	23.8	0.0	-	-	-	-	23.4	-1.7
1950	-	-	-	-	23.4	0.0	-	-	-	-	23.6	0.9	-	-	-	-	24.4	3.4	-	-	-	-	24.7	1.2
1951	-	-	-	-	25.4	2.8	-	-	-	-	25.6	0.8	-	-	-	-	25.7	0.4	-	-	-	-	26.1	1.6
1952	-	-	-	-	26.1	0.0	-	-	-	-	26.2	0.4	-	-	-	-	26.7	1.9	-	-	-	-	26.5	-0.7
1953	-	-	-	-	26.5	0.0	-	-	-	-	26.7	0.8	-	-	-	-	26.7	0.0	-	-	-	-	26.6	-0.4
1954	-	-	-	-	26.6	0.0	-	-	-	-	26.8	0.8	-	-	-	-	26.7	-0.4	-	-	-	-	26.6	-0.4
1955	-	-	-	-	26.7	0.4	-	-	-	-	26.7	0.0	-	-	-	-	26.8	0.4	-	-	-	-	26.9	0.4
1956	-	-	-	-	26.7	-0.7	-	-	-	-	27.1	1.5	-	-	-	-	27.3	0.7	-	-	-	-	27.7	1.5
1957	-	-	-	-	27.8	0.4	-	-	-	-	28.2	1.4	-	-	-	-	28.3	0.4	-	-	-	-	28.4	0.4
1958	-	-	-	-	28.8	1.4	-	-	-	-	29.0	0.7	-	-	-	-	29.0	0.0	-	-	-	-	29.1	0.3

[Continued]

Baltimore, MD
Consumer Price Index - All Urban Consumers
Base 1982-1984 = 100
All Items
[Continued]

For 1914-1997. Columns headed % show percentile change in the index from the previous period for which an index is available.

Year	Jan Index	%	Feb Index	%	Mar Index	%	Apr Index	%	May Index	%	Jun Index	%	Jul Index	%	Aug Index	%	Sep Index	%	Oct Index	%	Nov Index	%	Dec Index	%
1959	-	-	-	-	29.4	1.0	-	-	-	-	29.4	0.0	-	-	-	-	29.6	0.7	-	-	-	-	29.5	-0.3
1960	-	-	-	-	29.6	0.3	-	-	-	-	29.8	0.7	-	-	-	-	29.9	0.3	-	-	-	-	30.0	0.3
1961	-	-	-	-	30.1	0.3	-	-	-	-	30.1	0.0	-	-	-	-	30.1	0.0	-	-	-	-	30.1	0.0
1962	-	-	-	-	30.1	0.0	-	-	-	-	30.2	0.3	-	-	-	-	30.5	1.0	-	-	-	-	30.4	-0.3
1963	-	-	-	-	30.6	0.7	-	-	-	-	30.8	0.7	-	-	-	-	30.8	0.0	-	-	-	-	31.0	0.6
1964	-	-	-	-	31.0	0.0	-	-	-	-	31.1	0.3	-	-	-	-	31.1	0.0	-	-	-	-	31.3	0.6
1965	-	-	-	-	31.2	-0.3	-	-	-	-	31.7	1.6	-	-	-	-	31.7	0.0	-	-	-	-	31.9	0.6
1966	-	-	-	-	32.4	1.6	-	-	-	-	32.7	0.9	-	-	-	-	32.9	0.6	-	-	-	-	33.0	0.3
1967	-	-	-	-	33.1	0.3	-	-	-	-	33.3	0.6	-	-	-	-	33.9	1.8	-	-	-	-	33.8	-0.3
1968	-	-	-	-	34.2	1.2	-	-	-	-	34.7	1.5	-	-	-	-	35.2	1.4	-	-	-	-	35.7	1.4
1969	-	-	-	-	36.2	1.4	-	-	-	-	36.8	1.7	-	-	-	-	37.5	1.9	-	-	-	-	38.0	1.3
1970	-	-	-	-	38.4	1.1	-	-	-	-	39.0	1.6	-	-	-	-	39.5	1.3	-	-	-	-	40.4	2.3
1971	-	-	-	-	40.8	1.0	-	-	-	-	41.3	1.2	-	-	-	-	41.6	0.7	-	-	-	-	41.8	0.5
1972	-	-	-	-	41.8	0.0	-	-	-	-	42.0	0.5	-	-	-	-	42.7	1.7	-	-	-	-	42.8	0.2
1973	-	-	-	-	44.1	3.0	-	-	-	-	44.7	1.4	-	-	-	-	46.0	2.9	-	-	-	-	47.0	2.2
1974	-	-	-	-	49.2	4.7	-	-	-	-	50.6	2.8	-	-	-	-	52.6	4.0	-	-	-	-	53.5	1.7
1975	-	-	-	-	54.5	1.9	-	-	-	-	55.1	1.1	-	-	-	-	56.0	1.6	-	-	-	-	56.3	0.5
1976	-	-	-	-	57.0	1.2	-	-	-	-	58.1	1.9	-	-	-	-	59.0	1.5	-	-	-	-	59.6	1.0
1977	-	-	-	-	60.9	2.2	-	-	-	-	62.1	2.0	-	-	-	-	63.1	1.6	-	-	-	-	63.8	1.1
1978	-	-	-	-	65.4	2.5	-	-	66.2	1.2	-	-	67.5	2.0	-	-	68.0	0.7	-	-	67.9	-0.1	-	-
1979	68.3	0.6	-	-	69.9	2.3	-	-	72.0	3.0	-	-	73.9	2.6	-	-	75.2	1.8	-	-	76.0	1.1	-	-
1980	78.4	3.2	-	-	81.9	4.5	-	-	83.3	1.7	-	-	84.4	1.3	-	-	85.3	1.1	-	-	86.4	1.3	-	-
1981	88.4	2.3	-	-	90.4	2.3	-	-	90.0	-0.4	-	-	91.1	1.2	-	-	93.6	2.7	-	-	93.9	0.3	-	-
1982	94.3	0.4	-	-	94.3	0.0	-	-	94.8	0.5	-	-	95.7	0.9	-	-	96.7	1.0	-	-	97.0	0.3	-	-
1983	97.4	0.4	-	-	97.9	0.5	-	-	99.1	1.2	-	-	100.4	1.3	-	-	101.3	0.9	-	-	101.9	0.6	-	-
1984	102.8	0.9	-	-	103.8	1.0	-	-	104.1	0.3	-	-	104.7	0.6	-	-	105.8	1.1	-	-	105.4	-0.4	-	-
1985	105.4	0.0	-	-	107.2	1.7	-	-	108.0	0.7	-	-	108.3	0.3	-	-	109.5	1.1	-	-	109.4	-0.1	-	-
1986	111.0	1.5	-	-	110.7	-0.3	-	-	110.0	-0.6	-	-	110.4	0.4	-	-	111.7	1.2	-	-	111.5	-0.2	-	-
1987	111.7	0.2	-	-	112.3	0.5	-	-	113.7	1.2	-	-	115.0	1.1	-	-	115.7	0.6	-	-	115.7	0.0	-	-
1988	116.8	1.0	-	-	117.7	0.8	-	-	117.8	0.1	-	-	119.9	1.8	-	-	121.3	1.2	-	-	121.2	-0.1	-	-
1989	121.3	0.1	-	-	122.8	1.2	-	-	124.1	1.1	-	-	124.9	0.6	-	-	125.9	0.8	-	-	126.6	0.6	-	-
1990	127.9	1.0	-	-	129.3	1.1	-	-	129.0	-0.2	-	-	130.2	0.9	-	-	132.9	2.1	-	-	133.9	0.8	-	-
1991	134.3	0.3	-	-	135.1	0.6	-	-	135.4	0.2	-	-	136.5	0.8	-	-	138.2	1.2	-	-	137.8	-0.3	-	-
1992	138.0	0.1	-	-	138.7	0.5	-	-	139.5	0.6	-	-	140.6	0.8	-	-	141.9	0.9	-	-	141.1	-0.6	-	-
1993	142.0	0.6	-	-	142.6	0.4	-	-	142.8	0.1	-	-	143.7	0.6	-	-	143.6	-0.1	-	-	143.4	-0.1	-	-
1994	143.8	0.3	-	-	145.0	0.8	-	-	145.8	0.6	-	-	148.2	1.6	-	-	148.6	0.3	-	-	148.6	0.0	-	-
1995	148.7	0.1	-	-	150.3	1.1	-	-	150.4	0.1	-	-	151.5	0.7	-	-	151.8	0.2	-	-	151.1	-0.5	-	-
1996	151.6	0.3	-	-	153.0	0.9	-	-	153.9	0.6	-	-	155.7	1.2	-	-	155.4	-0.2	-	-	154.8	-0.4	-	-
1997	155.8	0.6	-	-	157.1	0.8	-	-	155.5	-1.0	156.2	0.5	156.9	0.4	-	-	156.7	-0.1	-	-	156.0	-0.4	-	-

Source: U.S. Department of Labor, Bureau of Labor Statistics, Division of Consumer Prices and Price Indexes. - indicates no data collected for period.

Baltimore, MD
Consumer Price Index - Urban Wage Earners
Base 1982-1984 = 100
All Items

For 1914-1997. Columns headed % show percentile change in the index from the previous period for which an index is available.

Year	Jan Index	%	Feb Index	%	Mar Index	%	Apr Index	%	May Index	%	Jun Index	%	Jul Index	%	Aug Index	%	Sep Index	%	Oct Index	%	Nov Index	%	Dec Index	%
1914	-	-	-	-	-	-	-	-	-	-	-	-	-	-	-	-	-	-	-	-	-	-	9.0	-
1915	-	-	-	-	-	-	-	-	-	-	-	-	-	-	-	-	-	-	-	-	-	-	9.0	0.0
1916	-	-	-	-	-	-	-	-	-	-	-	-	-	-	-	-	-	-	-	-	-	-	10.4	15.6
1917	-	-	-	-	-	-	-	-	-	-	-	-	-	-	-	-	-	-	-	-	-	-	12.9	24.0
1918	-	-	-	-	-	-	-	-	-	-	-	-	-	-	-	-	-	-	-	-	-	-	15.8	22.5
1919	-	-	-	-	-	-	-	-	-	-	16.0	1.3	-	-	-	-	-	-	-	-	-	-	17.3	8.1
1920	-	-	-	-	-	-	-	-	-	-	19.3	11.6	-	-	-	-	-	-	-	-	-	-	17.5	-9.3
1921	-	-	-	-	-	-	-	-	16.1	-8.0	-	-	-	-	-	-	16.1	0.0	-	-	-	-	15.8	-1.9
1922	-	-	-	-	15.4	-2.5	-	-	-	-	15.4	0.0	-	-	-	-	15.3	-0.6	-	-	-	-	15.5	1.3
1923	-	-	-	-	15.5	0.0	-	-	-	-	15.9	2.6	-	-	-	-	16.0	0.6	-	-	-	-	15.9	-0.6
1924	-	-	-	-	15.8	-0.6	-	-	-	-	15.8	0.0	-	-	-	-	15.8	0.0	-	-	-	-	15.9	0.6
1925	-	-	-	-	-	-	-	-	-	-	16.2	1.9	-	-	-	-	-	-	-	-	-	-	16.6	2.5
1926	-	-	-	-	-	-	-	-	-	-	16.5	-0.6	-	-	-	-	-	-	-	-	-	-	16.4	-0.6
1927	-	-	-	-	-	-	-	-	-	-	16.3	-0.6	-	-	-	-	-	-	-	-	-	-	15.9	-2.5
1928	-	-	-	-	-	-	-	-	-	-	15.9	0.0	-	-	-	-	-	-	-	-	-	-	15.8	-0.6
1929	-	-	-	-	-	-	-	-	-	-	15.9	0.6	-	-	-	-	-	-	-	-	-	-	16.0	0.6
1930	-	-	-	-	-	-	-	-	-	-	15.8	-1.2	-	-	-	-	-	-	-	-	-	-	15.2	-3.8
1931	-	-	-	-	-	-	-	-	-	-	14.4	-5.3	-	-	-	-	-	-	-	-	-	-	14.0	-2.8
1932	-	-	-	-	-	-	-	-	-	-	13.0	-7.1	-	-	-	-	-	-	-	-	-	-	12.6	-3.1
1933	-	-	-	-	-	-	-	-	-	-	12.3	-2.4	-	-	-	-	-	-	-	-	-	-	12.9	4.9
1934	-	-	-	-	-	-	-	-	-	-	13.0	0.8	-	-	-	-	-	-	-	-	13.1	0.8	-	-
1935	-	-	-	-	13.3	1.5	-	-	-	-	-	-	13.3	0.0	-	-	-	-	13.4	0.8	-	-	-	-
1936	13.5	0.7	-	-	-	-	13.4	-0.7	-	-	-	-	13.5	0.7	-	-	13.6	0.7	-	-	-	-	13.5	-0.7
1937	-	-	-	-	13.7	1.5	-	-	-	-	13.8	0.7	-	-	-	-	14.0	1.4	-	-	-	-	13.8	-1.4
1938	-	-	-	-	13.6	-1.4	-	-	-	-	13.6	0.0	-	-	-	-	13.6	0.0	-	-	-	-	13.6	0.0
1939	-	-	-	-	13.5	-0.7	-	-	-	-	13.5	0.0	-	-	-	-	13.6	0.7	-	-	-	-	13.4	-1.5
1940	-	-	-	-	13.5	0.7	-	-	-	-	13.6	0.7	-	-	-	-	13.6	0.0	13.5	-0.7	13.5	0.0	13.6	0.7
1941	13.7	0.7	13.7	0.0	13.7	0.0	13.9	1.5	14.1	1.4	14.3	1.4	14.5	1.4	14.6	0.7	14.9	2.1	15.0	0.7	15.1	0.7	15.2	0.7
1942	15.4	1.3	15.6	1.3	15.8	1.3	15.9	0.6	16.0	0.6	16.1	0.6	16.1	0.0	16.1	0.0	16.2	0.6	16.4	1.2	16.4	0.0	16.5	0.6
1943	16.6	0.6	16.6	0.0	17.0	2.4	17.2	1.2	17.4	1.2	17.4	0.0	17.1	-1.7	17.0	-0.6	17.1	0.6	17.2	0.6	17.0	-1.2	17.1	0.6
1944	17.1	0.0	17.0	-0.6	17.1	0.6	17.2	0.6	17.2	0.0	17.3	0.6	17.4	0.6	17.5	0.6	17.4	-0.6	17.4	0.0	17.6	1.1	17.6	0.0
1945	17.6	0.0	17.7	0.6	17.6	-0.6	17.7	0.6	17.8	0.6	18.0	1.1	18.1	0.6	18.0	-0.6	18.0	0.0	18.0	0.0	17.9	-0.6	18.0	0.6
1946	18.0	0.0	17.9	-0.6	18.0	0.6	18.2	1.1	18.2	0.0	18.5	1.6	19.5	5.4	20.0	2.6	20.1	0.5	20.5	2.0	21.1	2.9	21.1	0.0
1947	21.2	0.5	21.2	0.0	21.7	2.4	21.8	0.5	21.7	-0.5	21.9	0.9	-	-	-	-	22.8	4.1	-	-	-	-	23.3	2.2
1948	-	-	-	-	23.3	0.0	-	-	-	-	24.0	3.0	-	-	-	-	24.5	2.1	-	-	-	-	23.8	-2.9
1949	-	-	-	-	23.8	0.0	-	-	-	-	23.9	0.4	-	-	-	-	23.9	0.0	-	-	-	-	23.5	-1.7
1950	-	-	-	-	23.4	-0.4	-	-	-	-	23.6	0.9	-	-	-	-	24.5	3.8	-	-	-	-	24.8	1.2
1951	-	-	-	-	25.5	2.8	-	-	-	-	25.7	0.8	-	-	-	-	25.8	0.4	-	-	-	-	26.2	1.6
1952	-	-	-	-	26.2	0.0	-	-	-	-	26.3	0.4	-	-	-	-	26.8	1.9	-	-	-	-	26.6	-0.7
1953	-	-	-	-	26.6	0.0	-	-	-	-	26.8	0.8	-	-	-	-	26.8	0.0	-	-	-	-	26.7	-0.4
1954	-	-	-	-	26.7	0.0	-	-	-	-	26.9	0.7	-	-	-	-	26.8	-0.4	-	-	-	-	26.7	-0.4
1955	-	-	-	-	26.8	0.4	-	-	-	-	26.8	0.0	-	-	-	-	26.9	0.4	-	-	-	-	27.0	0.4
1956	-	-	-	-	26.8	-0.7	-	-	-	-	27.2	1.5	-	-	-	-	27.4	0.7	-	-	-	-	27.8	1.5
1957	-	-	-	-	27.9	0.4	-	-	-	-	28.2	1.1	-	-	-	-	28.3	0.4	-	-	-	-	28.4	0.4
1958	-	-	-	-	28.9	1.8	-	-	-	-	29.1	0.7	-	-	-	-	29.1	0.0	-	-	-	-	29.2	0.3

[Continued]

Baltimore, MD
Consumer Price Index - Urban Wage Earners
Base 1982-1984 = 100
All Items
[Continued]

For 1914-1997. Columns headed % show percentile change in the index from the previous period for which an index is available.

Year	Jan		Feb		Mar		Apr		May		Jun		Jul		Aug		Sep		Oct		Nov		Dec	
	Index	%	Index	%	Index	%	Index	%	Index	%	Index	%	Index	%	Index	%	Index	%	Index	%	Index	%	Index	%
1959	-	-	-	-	29.5	1.0	-	-	-	-	29.5	0.0	-	-	-	-	29.7	0.7	-	-	-	-	29.6	-0.3
1960	-	-	-	-	29.7	0.3	-	-	-	-	29.9	0.7	-	-	-	-	30.0	0.3	-	-	-	-	30.1	0.3
1961	-	-	-	-	30.2	0.3	-	-	-	-	30.2	0.0	-	-	-	-	30.2	0.0	-	-	-	-	30.2	0.0
1962	-	-	-	-	30.2	0.0	-	-	-	-	30.3	0.3	-	-	-	-	30.6	1.0	-	-	-	-	30.5	-0.3
1963	-	-	-	-	30.7	0.7	-	-	-	-	30.9	0.7	-	-	-	-	30.9	0.0	-	-	-	-	31.1	0.6
1964	-	-	-	-	31.1	0.0	-	-	-	-	31.2	0.3	-	-	-	-	31.2	0.0	-	-	-	-	31.4	0.6
1965	-	-	-	-	31.3	-0.3	-	-	-	-	31.8	1.6	-	-	-	-	31.8	0.0	-	-	-	-	32.0	0.6
1966	-	-	-	-	32.5	1.6	-	-	-	-	32.8	0.9	-	-	-	-	33.0	0.6	-	-	-	-	33.1	0.3
1967	-	-	-	-	33.2	0.3	-	-	-	-	33.4	0.6	-	-	-	-	34.0	1.8	-	-	-	-	33.9	-0.3
1968	-	-	-	-	34.3	1.2	-	-	-	-	34.9	1.7	-	-	-	-	35.4	1.4	-	-	-	-	35.8	1.1
1969	-	-	-	-	36.3	1.4	-	-	-	-	37.0	1.9	-	-	-	-	37.7	1.9	-	-	-	-	38.1	1.1
1970	-	-	-	-	38.6	1.3	-	-	-	-	39.1	1.3	-	-	-	-	39.7	1.5	-	-	-	-	40.5	2.0
1971	-	-	-	-	41.0	1.2	-	-	-	-	41.4	1.0	-	-	-	-	41.7	0.7	-	-	-	-	42.0	0.7
1972	-	-	-	-	41.9	-0.2	-	-	-	-	42.1	0.5	-	-	-	-	42.8	1.7	-	-	-	-	42.9	0.2
1973	-	-	-	-	44.2	3.0	-	-	-	-	44.8	1.4	-	-	-	-	46.1	2.9	-	-	-	-	47.2	2.4
1974	-	-	-	-	49.4	4.7	-	-	-	-	50.8	2.8	-	-	-	-	52.8	3.9	-	-	-	-	53.7	1.7
1975	-	-	-	-	54.6	1.7	-	-	-	-	55.2	1.1	-	-	-	-	56.2	1.8	-	-	-	-	56.5	0.5
1976	-	-	-	-	57.2	1.2	-	-	-	-	58.3	1.9	-	-	-	-	59.2	1.5	-	-	-	-	59.8	1.0
1977	-	-	-	-	61.1	2.2	-	-	-	-	62.3	2.0	-	-	-	-	63.3	1.6	-	-	-	-	64.0	1.1
1978	-	-	-	-	65.6	2.5	-	-	66.6	1.5	-	-	67.7	1.7	-	-	68.2	0.7	-	-	68.1	-0.1	-	-
1979	68.8	1.0	-	-	70.6	2.6	-	-	72.5	2.7	-	-	74.3	2.5	-	-	75.4	1.5	-	-	76.5	1.5	-	-
1980	78.7	2.9	-	-	81.8	3.9	-	-	83.1	1.6	-	-	84.1	1.2	-	-	84.9	1.0	-	-	86.3	1.6	-	-
1981	88.1	2.1	-	-	90.3	2.5	-	-	90.1	-0.2	-	-	91.8	1.9	-	-	94.5	2.9	-	-	94.2	-0.3	-	-
1982	94.7	0.5	-	-	94.7	0.0	-	-	95.2	0.5	-	-	96.3	1.2	-	-	96.9	0.6	-	-	97.2	0.3	-	-
1983	97.2	0.0	-	-	99.0	1.9	-	-	99.5	0.5	-	-	99.8	0.3	-	-	100.5	0.7	-	-	101.4	0.9	-	-
1984	101.9	0.5	-	-	103.1	1.2	-	-	103.8	0.7	-	-	104.5	0.7	-	-	106.1	1.5	-	-	105.7	-0.4	-	-
1985	105.7	0.0	-	-	107.4	1.6	-	-	108.1	0.7	-	-	108.5	0.4	-	-	109.5	0.9	-	-	109.5	0.0	-	-
1986	111.1	1.5	-	-	110.5	-0.5	-	-	109.6	-0.8	-	-	110.0	0.4	-	-	111.0	0.9	-	-	110.8	-0.2	-	-
1987	111.1	0.3	-	-	111.8	0.6	-	-	113.2	1.3	-	-	114.7	1.3	-	-	115.5	0.7	-	-	115.3	-0.2	-	-
1988	116.2	0.8	-	-	117.3	0.9	-	-	117.4	0.1	-	-	119.7	2.0	-	-	121.0	1.1	-	-	120.8	-0.2	-	-
1989	120.9	0.1	-	-	122.3	1.2	-	-	123.7	1.1	-	-	124.6	0.7	-	-	125.4	0.6	-	-	126.0	0.5	-	-
1990	127.2	1.0	-	-	128.6	1.1	-	-	128.3	-0.2	-	-	129.5	0.9	-	-	132.3	2.2	-	-	133.2	0.7	-	-
1991	133.7	0.4	-	-	134.1	0.3	-	-	134.4	0.2	-	-	135.8	1.0	-	-	137.5	1.3	-	-	137.0	-0.4	-	-
1992	137.3	0.2	-	-	137.9	0.4	-	-	138.9	0.7	-	-	140.2	0.9	-	-	141.4	0.9	-	-	140.6	-0.6	-	-
1993	141.3	0.5	-	-	141.8	0.4	-	-	142.1	0.2	-	-	143.0	0.6	-	-	142.8	-0.1	-	-	142.5	-0.2	-	-
1994	142.7	0.1	-	-	144.2	1.1	-	-	144.9	0.5	-	-	147.3	1.7	-	-	147.8	0.3	-	-	147.6	-0.1	-	-
1995	147.7	0.1	-	-	149.1	0.9	-	-	149.4	0.2	-	-	150.5	0.7	-	-	150.8	0.2	-	-	149.9	-0.6	-	-
1996	150.3	0.3	-	-	151.8	1.0	-	-	152.8	0.7	-	-	154.6	1.2	-	-	154.4	-0.1	-	-	153.6	-0.5	-	-
1997	154.6	0.7	-	-	155.9	0.8	-	-	154.3	-1.0	155.0	0.5	155.6	0.4	-	-	155.6	0.0	-	-	154.6	-0.6	-	-

Source: U.S. Department of Labor, Bureau of Labor Statistics, Division of Consumer Prices and Price Indexes. - indicates no data collected for period.

Baltimore, MD
Consumer Price Index - All Urban Consumers
Base 1982-1984 = 100
Food and Beverages

For 1975-1997. Columns headed % show percentile change in the index from the previous period for which an index is available.

Year	Jan Index	%	Feb Index	%	Mar Index	%	Apr Index	%	May Index	%	Jun Index	%	Jul Index	%	Aug Index	%	Sep Index	%	Oct Index	%	Nov Index	%	Dec Index	%
1975	-	-	-	-	-	-	-	-	-	-	-	-	-	-	-	-	-	-	-	-	-	-	63.2	-
1976	-	-	-	-	63.0	-0.3	-	-	-	-	64.1	1.7	-	-	-	-	64.6	0.8	-	-	-	-	64.3	-0.5
1977	-	-	-	-	66.6	3.6	-	-	-	-	68.4	2.7	-	-	-	-	69.1	1.0	-	-	-	-	69.2	0.1
1978	-	-	-	-	72.0	4.0	-	-	74.0	2.8	-	-	76.6	3.5	-	-	75.5	-1.4	-	-	75.8	0.4	-	-
1979	78.4	3.4	-	-	80.1	2.2	-	-	80.7	0.7	-	-	81.9	1.5	-	-	82.4	0.6	-	-	82.3	-0.1	-	-
1980	84.3	2.4	-	-	85.2	1.1	-	-	86.2	1.2	-	-	87.8	1.9	-	-	90.1	2.6	-	-	91.3	1.3	-	-
1981	93.1	2.0	-	-	94.8	1.8	-	-	93.2	-1.7	-	-	93.5	0.3	-	-	94.2	0.7	-	-	94.3	0.1	-	-
1982	95.2	1.0	-	-	95.3	0.1	-	-	96.5	1.3	-	-	97.6	1.1	-	-	97.5	-0.1	-	-	96.3	-1.2	-	-
1983	96.9	0.6	-	-	98.3	1.4	-	-	100.3	2.0	-	-	99.9	-0.4	-	-	99.7	-0.2	-	-	100.6	0.9	-	-
1984	102.9	2.3	-	-	103.6	0.7	-	-	104.2	0.6	-	-	104.2	0.0	-	-	104.3	0.1	-	-	104.2	-0.1	-	-
1985	105.2	1.0	-	-	107.3	2.0	-	-	106.7	-0.6	-	-	107.5	0.7	-	-	106.9	-0.6	-	-	107.8	0.8	-	-
1986	110.5	2.5	-	-	110.2	-0.3	-	-	110.1	-0.1	-	-	112.1	1.8	-	-	113.9	1.6	-	-	114.1	0.2	-	-
1987	115.6	1.3	-	-	115.1	-0.4	-	-	116.2	1.0	-	-	117.0	0.7	-	-	118.0	0.9	-	-	118.0	0.0	-	-
1988	118.8	0.7	-	-	119.7	0.8	-	-	121.1	1.2	-	-	123.1	1.7	-	-	123.2	0.1	-	-	123.5	0.2	-	-
1989	125.5	1.6	-	-	127.4	1.5	-	-	129.0	1.3	-	-	129.7	0.5	-	-	129.3	-0.3	-	-	131.5	1.7	-	-
1990	135.7	3.2	-	-	135.8	0.1	-	-	134.9	-0.7	-	-	137.3	1.8	-	-	137.6	0.2	-	-	138.9	0.9	-	-
1991	140.2	0.9	-	-	140.9	0.5	-	-	140.5	-0.3	-	-	141.3	0.6	-	-	140.3	-0.7	-	-	139.8	-0.4	-	-
1992	141.6	1.3	-	-	142.5	0.6	-	-	141.9	-0.4	-	-	141.8	-0.1	-	-	143.5	1.2	-	-	142.8	-0.5	-	-
1993	143.6	0.6	-	-	144.3	0.5	-	-	143.9	-0.3	-	-	144.0	0.1	-	-	143.8	-0.1	-	-	145.2	1.0	-	-
1994	148.4	2.2	-	-	148.5	0.1	-	-	149.3	0.5	-	-	151.3	1.3	-	-	148.6	-1.8	-	-	151.1	1.7	-	-
1995	151.6	0.3	-	-	153.2	1.1	-	-	154.2	0.7	-	-	153.3	-0.6	-	-	157.8	2.9	-	-	155.8	-1.3	-	-
1996	156.5	0.4	-	-	156.6	0.1	-	-	157.8	0.8	-	-	160.7	1.8	-	-	159.1	-1.0	-	-	161.1	1.3	-	-
1997	161.3	0.1	-	-	161.7	0.2	-	-	159.6	-1.3	160.8	0.8	160.3	-0.3	-	-	159.9	-0.2	-	-	161.9	1.3	-	-

Source: U.S. Department of Labor, Bureau of Labor Statistics, Division of Consumer Prices and Price Indexes. - indicates no data collected for period.

Baltimore, MD
Consumer Price Index - Urban Wage Earners
Base 1982-1984 = 100
Food and Beverages

For 1975-1997. Columns headed % show percentile change in the index from the previous period for which an index is available.

Year	Jan Index	%	Feb Index	%	Mar Index	%	Apr Index	%	May Index	%	Jun Index	%	Jul Index	%	Aug Index	%	Sep Index	%	Oct Index	%	Nov Index	%	Dec Index	%
1975	-	-	-	-	-	-	-	-	-	-	-	-	-	-	-	-	-	-	-	-	-	-	63.1	-
1976	-	-	-	-	63.0	-0.2	-	-	-	-	64.0	1.6	-	-	-	-	64.5	0.8	-	-	-	-	64.2	-0.5
1977	-	-	-	-	66.5	3.6	-	-	-	-	68.3	2.7	-	-	-	-	69.0	1.0	-	-	-	-	69.1	0.1
1978	-	-	-	-	71.9	4.1	-	-	73.9	2.8	-	-	75.5	2.2	-	-	74.9	-0.8	-	-	75.3	0.5	-	-
1979	77.7	3.2	-	-	79.8	2.7	-	-	80.0	0.3	-	-	80.8	1.0	-	-	80.9	0.1	-	-	82.0	1.4	-	-
1980	83.8	2.2	-	-	85.3	1.8	-	-	85.9	0.7	-	-	87.0	1.3	-	-	90.4	3.9	-	-	91.5	1.2	-	-
1981	92.7	1.3	-	-	94.3	1.7	-	-	92.9	-1.5	-	-	92.9	0.0	-	-	94.5	1.7	-	-	94.5	0.0	-	-
1982	95.1	0.6	-	-	95.3	0.2	-	-	96.5	1.3	-	-	97.7	1.2	-	-	97.4	-0.3	-	-	96.4	-1.0	-	-
1983	97.0	0.6	-	-	98.3	1.3	-	-	100.4	2.1	-	-	99.9	-0.5	-	-	99.7	-0.2	-	-	100.5	0.8	-	-
1984	102.9	2.4	-	-	103.6	0.7	-	-	104.3	0.7	-	-	104.3	0.0	-	-	104.4	0.1	-	-	104.2	-0.2	-	-
1985	105.3	1.1	-	-	107.3	1.9	-	-	106.8	-0.5	-	-	107.4	0.6	-	-	106.9	-0.5	-	-	107.7	0.7	-	-
1986	110.5	2.6	-	-	110.3	-0.2	-	-	110.1	-0.2	-	-	111.8	1.5	-	-	113.7	1.7	-	-	113.9	0.2	-	-
1987	115.5	1.4	-	-	114.8	-0.6	-	-	115.9	1.0	-	-	116.7	0.7	-	-	118.0	1.1	-	-	118.0	0.0	-	-
1988	118.8	0.7	-	-	119.7	0.8	-	-	121.1	1.2	-	-	122.9	1.5	-	-	123.0	0.1	-	-	123.2	0.2	-	-
1989	125.2	1.6	-	-	127.0	1.4	-	-	128.6	1.3	-	-	129.4	0.6	-	-	128.9	-0.4	-	-	131.0	1.6	-	-
1990	135.2	3.2	-	-	135.3	0.1	-	-	134.6	-0.5	-	-	136.9	1.7	-	-	137.2	0.2	-	-	138.4	0.9	-	-
1991	139.9	1.1	-	-	140.5	0.4	-	-	139.9	-0.4	-	-	141.0	0.8	-	-	140.1	-0.6	-	-	139.5	-0.4	-	-
1992	141.2	1.2	-	-	142.3	0.8	-	-	141.5	-0.6	-	-	141.5	0.0	-	-	143.0	1.1	-	-	142.5	-0.3	-	-
1993	143.2	0.5	-	-	143.8	0.4	-	-	143.4	-0.3	-	-	143.5	0.1	-	-	143.4	-0.1	-	-	144.6	0.8	-	-
1994	147.9	2.3	-	-	148.1	0.1	-	-	148.7	0.4	-	-	150.7	1.3	-	-	148.1	-1.7	-	-	150.3	1.5	-	-
1995	150.8	0.3	-	-	152.3	1.0	-	-	153.4	0.7	-	-	152.8	-0.4	-	-	156.9	2.7	-	-	155.1	-1.1	-	-
1996	155.7	0.4	-	-	156.1	0.3	-	-	157.0	0.6	-	-	159.9	1.8	-	-	158.4	-0.9	-	-	160.5	1.3	-	-
1997	160.5	0.0	-	-	161.0	0.3	-	-	159.2	-1.1	160.2	0.6	159.8	-0.2	-	-	159.5	-0.2	-	-	161.2	1.1	-	-

Source: U.S. Department of Labor, Bureau of Labor Statistics, Division of Consumer Prices and Price Indexes. - indicates no data collected for period.

Baltimore, MD
Consumer Price Index - All Urban Consumers
Base 1982-1984 = 100
Housing

For 1975-1997. Columns headed % show percentile change in the index from the previous period for which an index is available.

Year	Jan Index	%	Feb Index	%	Mar Index	%	Apr Index	%	May Index	%	Jun Index	%	Jul Index	%	Aug Index	%	Sep Index	%	Oct Index	%	Nov Index	%	Dec Index	%
1975	-	-	-	-	-	-	-	-	-	-	-	-	-	-	-	-	-	-	-	-	-	-	52.8	-
1976	-	-	-	-	53.7	1.7	-	-	-	-	54.6	1.7	-	-	-	-	56.1	2.7	-	-	-	-	57.3	2.1
1977	-	-	-	-	58.2	1.6	-	-	-	-	59.0	1.4	-	-	-	-	61.0	3.4	-	-	-	-	62.4	2.3
1978	-	-	-	-	64.1	2.7	-	-	64.0	-0.2	-	-	65.9	3.0	-	-	66.5	0.9	-	-	65.2	-2.0	-	-
1979	65.2	0.0	-	-	66.3	1.7	-	-	69.3	4.5	-	-	72.1	4.0	-	-	73.3	1.7	-	-	73.7	0.5	-	-
1980	76.5	3.8	-	-	81.2	6.1	-	-	82.8	2.0	-	-	84.0	1.4	-	-	83.9	-0.1	-	-	85.3	1.7	-	-
1981	87.9	3.0	-	-	89.6	1.9	-	-	88.5	-1.2	-	-	90.1	1.8	-	-	94.9	5.3	-	-	94.6	-0.3	-	-
1982	95.2	0.6	-	-	94.2	-1.1	-	-	95.2	1.1	-	-	95.4	0.2	-	-	95.9	0.5	-	-	96.9	1.0	-	-
1983	97.4	0.5	-	-	97.7	0.3	-	-	98.3	0.6	-	-	100.6	2.3	-	-	101.4	0.8	-	-	100.9	-0.5	-	-
1984	103.3	2.4	-	-	104.0	0.7	-	-	104.1	0.1	-	-	105.2	1.1	-	-	106.7	1.4	-	-	105.1	-1.5	-	-
1985	105.5	0.4	-	-	107.1	1.5	-	-	108.0	0.8	-	-	108.6	0.6	-	-	110.3	1.6	-	-	109.0	-1.2	-	-
1986	110.7	1.6	-	-	110.8	0.1	-	-	110.3	-0.5	-	-	111.0	0.6	-	-	112.6	1.4	-	-	111.5	-1.0	-	-
1987	111.4	-0.1	-	-	110.9	-0.4	-	-	113.1	2.0	-	-	113.5	0.4	-	-	113.0	-0.4	-	-	112.8	-0.2	-	-
1988	114.9	1.9	-	-	115.1	0.2	-	-	115.0	-0.1	-	-	117.1	1.8	-	-	117.5	0.3	-	-	116.8	-0.6	-	-
1989	117.4	0.5	-	-	117.8	0.3	-	-	118.9	0.9	-	-	121.3	2.0	-	-	122.1	0.7	-	-	121.4	-0.6	-	-
1990	123.1	1.4	-	-	123.6	0.4	-	-	123.8	0.2	-	-	126.1	1.9	-	-	127.1	0.8	-	-	126.7	-0.3	-	-
1991	127.6	0.7	-	-	130.2	2.0	-	-	129.6	-0.5	-	-	131.9	1.8	-	-	134.0	1.6	-	-	131.9	-1.6	-	-
1992	131.9	0.0	-	-	131.7	-0.2	-	-	132.4	0.5	-	-	135.3	2.2	-	-	135.1	-0.1	-	-	132.8	-1.7	-	-
1993	134.1	1.0	-	-	134.5	0.3	-	-	134.2	-0.2	-	-	137.1	2.2	-	-	137.3	0.1	-	-	135.6	-1.2	-	-
1994	136.5	0.7	-	-	137.8	1.0	-	-	137.0	-0.6	-	-	141.0	2.9	-	-	139.9	-0.8	-	-	138.0	-1.4	-	-
1995	137.7	-0.2	-	-	139.4	1.2	-	-	138.9	-0.4	-	-	143.4	3.2	-	-	143.0	-0.3	-	-	140.6	-1.7	-	-
1996	142.1	1.1	-	-	142.4	0.2	-	-	142.5	0.1	-	-	146.1	2.5	-	-	145.5	-0.4	-	-	143.1	-1.6	-	-
1997	144.4	0.9	-	-	145.3	0.6	-	-	143.9	-1.0	144.8	0.6	147.8	2.1	-	-	146.9	-0.6	-	-	144.7	-1.5	-	-

Source: U.S. Department of Labor, Bureau of Labor Statistics, Division of Consumer Prices and Price Indexes. - indicates no data collected for period.

Baltimore, MD
Consumer Price Index - Urban Wage Earners
Base 1982-1984 = 100
Housing

For 1975-1997. Columns headed % show percentile change in the index from the previous period for which an index is available.

Year	Jan Index	Jan %	Feb Index	Feb %	Mar Index	Mar %	Apr Index	Apr %	May Index	May %	Jun Index	Jun %	Jul Index	Jul %	Aug Index	Aug %	Sep Index	Sep %	Oct Index	Oct %	Nov Index	Nov %	Dec Index	Dec %
1975	-	-	-	-	-	-	-	-	-	-	-	-	-	-	-	-	-	-	-	-	-	-	53.2	-
1976	-	-	-	-	54.2	1.9	-	-	-	-	55.0	1.5	-	-	-	-	56.6	2.9	-	-	-	-	57.7	1.9
1977	-	-	-	-	58.7	1.7	-	-	-	-	59.5	1.4	-	-	-	-	61.5	3.4	-	-	-	-	62.9	2.3
1978	-	-	-	-	64.6	2.7	-	-	64.9	0.5	-	-	66.4	2.3	-	-	67.1	1.1	-	-	66.0	-1.6	-	-
1979	66.3	0.5	-	-	68.1	2.7	-	-	70.8	4.0	-	-	73.5	3.8	-	-	74.7	1.6	-	-	75.3	0.8	-	-
1980	78.0	3.6	-	-	81.9	5.0	-	-	83.7	2.2	-	-	84.9	1.4	-	-	84.1	-0.9	-	-	85.6	1.8	-	-
1981	88.1	2.9	-	-	90.4	2.6	-	-	89.4	-1.1	-	-	92.4	3.4	-	-	97.4	5.4	-	-	95.7	-1.7	-	-
1982	96.2	0.5	-	-	95.4	-0.8	-	-	96.3	0.9	-	-	96.7	0.4	-	-	96.7	0.0	-	-	97.7	1.0	-	-
1983	97.0	-0.7	-	-	100.5	3.6	-	-	99.5	-1.0	-	-	99.1	-0.4	-	-	99.5	0.4	-	-	99.9	0.4	-	-
1984	100.8	0.9	-	-	102.2	1.4	-	-	103.0	0.8	-	-	104.4	1.4	-	-	107.1	2.6	-	-	105.6	-1.4	-	-
1985	105.9	0.3	-	-	107.5	1.5	-	-	108.2	0.7	-	-	108.9	0.6	-	-	110.8	1.7	-	-	109.6	-1.1	-	-
1986	111.3	1.6	-	-	111.1	-0.2	-	-	110.5	-0.5	-	-	111.2	0.6	-	-	112.7	1.3	-	-	111.4	-1.2	-	-
1987	111.3	-0.1	-	-	110.7	-0.5	-	-	113.0	2.1	-	-	113.5	0.4	-	-	113.1	-0.4	-	-	112.6	-0.4	-	-
1988	114.5	1.7	-	-	114.8	0.3	-	-	114.7	-0.1	-	-	117.0	2.0	-	-	117.4	0.3	-	-	116.7	-0.6	-	-
1989	117.3	0.5	-	-	117.6	0.3	-	-	118.8	1.0	-	-	121.5	2.3	-	-	122.1	0.5	-	-	121.3	-0.7	-	-
1990	122.8	1.2	-	-	123.3	0.4	-	-	123.5	0.2	-	-	126.0	2.0	-	-	126.8	0.6	-	-	126.2	-0.5	-	-
1991	127.2	0.8	-	-	129.5	1.8	-	-	128.8	-0.5	-	-	131.4	2.0	-	-	133.6	1.7	-	-	131.2	-1.8	-	-
1992	131.4	0.2	-	-	131.2	-0.2	-	-	131.6	0.3	-	-	134.8	2.4	-	-	134.3	-0.4	-	-	131.8	-1.9	-	-
1993	133.0	0.9	-	-	133.2	0.2	-	-	133.2	0.0	-	-	136.5	2.5	-	-	136.8	0.2	-	-	134.8	-1.5	-	-
1994	135.7	0.7	-	-	137.1	1.0	-	-	136.3	-0.6	-	-	140.4	3.0	-	-	139.6	-0.6	-	-	137.1	-1.8	-	-
1995	136.8	-0.2	-	-	138.2	1.0	-	-	137.7	-0.4	-	-	142.5	3.5	-	-	142.3	-0.1	-	-	139.5	-2.0	-	-
1996	140.8	0.9	-	-	141.1	0.2	-	-	141.3	0.1	-	-	145.1	2.7	-	-	144.7	-0.3	-	-	141.7	-2.1	-	-
1997	143.1	1.0	-	-	144.1	0.7	-	-	142.6	-1.0	143.6	0.7	146.6	2.1	-	-	146.1	-0.3	-	-	143.5	-1.8	-	-

Source: U.S. Department of Labor, Bureau of Labor Statistics, Division of Consumer Prices and Price Indexes. - indicates no data collected for period.

Baltimore, MD
Consumer Price Index - All Urban Consumers
Base 1982-1984 = 100
Apparel and Upkeep

For 1952-1997. Columns headed % show percentile change in the index from the previous period for which an index is available.

Year	Jan Index	%	Feb Index	%	Mar Index	%	Apr Index	%	May Index	%	Jun Index	%	Jul Index	%	Aug Index	%	Sep Index	%	Oct Index	%	Nov Index	%	Dec Index	%
1952	-	-	-	-	-	-	-	-	-	-	-	-	-	-	-	-	-	-	-	-	-	-	37.9	-
1953	-	-	-	-	38.0	0.3	-	-	-	-	38.4	1.1	-	-	-	-	38.2	-0.5	-	-	-	-	37.8	-1.0
1954	-	-	-	-	37.8	0.0	-	-	-	-	37.8	0.0	-	-	-	-	38.2	1.1	-	-	-	-	38.0	-0.5
1955	-	-	-	-	37.8	-0.5	-	-	-	-	37.9	0.3	-	-	-	-	37.8	-0.3	-	-	-	-	38.3	1.3
1956	-	-	-	-	38.8	1.3	-	-	-	-	39.3	1.3	-	-	-	-	39.8	1.3	-	-	-	-	39.7	-0.3
1957	-	-	-	-	39.6	-0.3	-	-	-	-	40.0	1.0	-	-	-	-	40.8	2.0	-	-	-	-	40.5	-0.7
1958	-	-	-	-	40.7	0.5	-	-	-	-	40.7	0.0	-	-	-	-	40.8	0.2	-	-	-	-	40.3	-1.2
1959	-	-	-	-	41.3	2.5	-	-	-	-	41.4	0.2	-	-	-	-	42.1	1.7	-	-	-	-	41.9	-0.5
1960	-	-	-	-	42.1	0.5	-	-	-	-	41.9	-0.5	-	-	-	-	42.6	1.7	-	-	-	-	42.4	-0.5
1961	-	-	-	-	43.0	1.4	-	-	-	-	42.9	-0.2	-	-	-	-	43.0	0.2	-	-	-	-	42.8	-0.5
1962	-	-	-	-	42.9	0.2	-	-	-	-	42.9	0.0	-	-	-	-	43.5	1.4	-	-	-	-	43.5	0.0
1963	-	-	-	-	43.5	0.0	-	-	-	-	43.6	0.2	-	-	-	-	43.6	0.0	-	-	-	-	43.6	0.0
1964	-	-	-	-	43.3	-0.7	-	-	-	-	43.5	0.5	-	-	-	-	43.6	0.2	-	-	-	-	43.8	0.5
1965	-	-	-	-	43.6	-0.5	-	-	-	-	44.1	1.1	-	-	-	-	44.4	0.7	-	-	-	-	44.5	0.2
1966	-	-	-	-	45.1	1.3	-	-	-	-	45.4	0.7	-	-	-	-	45.6	0.4	-	-	-	-	46.0	0.9
1967	-	-	-	-	46.9	2.0	-	-	-	-	47.4	1.1	-	-	-	-	48.2	1.7	-	-	-	-	48.0	-0.4
1968	-	-	-	-	48.6	1.2	-	-	-	-	49.5	1.9	-	-	-	-	50.5	2.0	-	-	-	-	51.0	1.0
1969	-	-	-	-	52.3	2.5	-	-	-	-	53.5	2.3	-	-	-	-	54.9	2.6	-	-	-	-	55.3	0.7
1970	-	-	-	-	55.7	0.7	-	-	-	-	56.3	1.1	-	-	-	-	57.1	1.4	-	-	-	-	58.3	2.1
1971	-	-	-	-	58.6	0.5	-	-	-	-	57.8	-1.4	-	-	-	-	59.2	2.4	-	-	-	-	59.0	-0.3
1972	-	-	-	-	59.0	0.0	-	-	-	-	58.1	-1.5	-	-	-	-	59.1	1.7	-	-	-	-	58.9	-0.3
1973	-	-	-	-	60.5	2.7	-	-	-	-	61.4	1.5	-	-	-	-	63.4	3.3	-	-	-	-	64.3	1.4
1974	-	-	-	-	65.6	2.0	-	-	-	-	66.7	1.7	-	-	-	-	68.4	2.5	-	-	-	-	69.3	1.3
1975	-	-	-	-	70.0	1.0	-	-	-	-	69.7	-0.4	-	-	-	-	70.7	1.4	-	-	-	-	70.4	-0.4
1976	-	-	-	-	72.0	2.3	-	-	-	-	73.0	1.4	-	-	-	-	74.3	1.8	-	-	-	-	75.0	0.9
1977	-	-	-	-	75.9	1.2	-	-	-	-	77.3	1.8	-	-	-	-	78.3	1.3	-	-	-	-	78.3	0.0
1978	-	-	-	-	81.0	3.4	-	-	83.4	3.0	-	-	76.5	-8.3	-	-	82.1	7.3	-	-	81.9	-0.2	-	-
1979	77.5	-5.4	-	-	83.2	7.4	-	-	84.2	1.2	-	-	80.4	-4.5	-	-	85.1	5.8	-	-	86.9	2.1	-	-
1980	85.0	-2.2	-	-	92.5	8.8	-	-	94.2	1.8	-	-	93.3	-1.0	-	-	95.3	2.1	-	-	97.2	2.0	-	-
1981	94.6	-2.7	-	-	98.5	4.1	-	-	98.2	-0.3	-	-	96.2	-2.0	-	-	96.5	0.3	-	-	96.5	0.0	-	-
1982	92.4	-4.2	-	-	98.7	6.8	-	-	99.1	0.4	-	-	95.5	-3.6	-	-	100.9	5.7	-	-	101.2	0.3	-	-
1983	98.4	-2.8	-	-	99.0	0.6	-	-	101.6	2.6	-	-	101.4	-0.2	-	-	99.3	-2.1	-	-	103.2	3.9	-	-
1984	99.4	-3.7	-	-	101.7	2.3	-	-	101.5	-0.2	-	-	98.5	-3.0	-	-	103.6	5.2	-	-	103.2	-0.4	-	-
1985	98.2	-4.8	-	-	106.5	8.5	-	-	106.6	0.1	-	-	103.9	-2.5	-	-	111.2	7.0	-	-	109.3	-1.7	-	-
1986	106.9	-2.2	-	-	111.5	4.3	-	-	112.3	0.7	-	-	108.5	-3.4	-	-	112.6	3.8	-	-	112.9	0.3	-	-
1987	106.2	-5.9	-	-	120.4	13.4	-	-	120.2	-0.2	-	-	123.0	2.3	-	-	124.4	1.1	-	-	121.2	-2.6	-	-
1988	118.0	-2.6	-	-	129.2	9.5	-	-	123.0	-4.8	-	-	133.1	8.2	-	-	140.1	5.3	-	-	136.0	-2.9	-	-
1989	124.2	-8.7	-	-	136.1	9.6	-	-	130.1	-4.4	-	-	123.1	-5.4	-	-	129.4	5.1	-	-	127.2	-1.7	-	-
1990	112.2	-11.8	-	-	136.6	21.7	-	-	130.9	-4.2	-	-	118.1	-9.8	-	-	137.3	16.3	-	-	130.0	-5.3	-	-
1991	129.2	-0.6	-	-	135.6	5.0	-	-	134.4	-0.9	-	-	129.7	-3.5	-	-	134.4	3.6	-	-	133.8	-0.4	-	-
1992	129.9	-2.9	-	-	142.4	9.6	-	-	140.3	-1.5	-	-	128.4	-8.5	-	-	136.7	6.5	-	-	133.7	-2.2	-	-
1993	130.7	-2.2	-	-	140.3	7.3	-	-	141.9	1.1	-	-	133.6	-5.8	-	-	137.4	2.8	-	-	133.1	-3.1	-	-
1994	124.7	-6.3	-	-	134.7	8.0	-	-	140.6	4.4	-	-	132.9	-5.5	-	-	139.9	5.3	-	-	137.1	-2.0	-	-

[Continued]

Baltimore, MD
Consumer Price Index - All Urban Consumers
Base 1982-1984 = 100
Apparel and Upkeep
[Continued]

For 1952-1997. Columns headed % show percentile change in the index from the previous period for which an index is available.

Year	Jan		Feb		Mar		Apr		May		Jun		Jul		Aug		Sep		Oct		Nov		Dec	
	Index	%	Index	%	Index	%	Index	%	Index	%	Index	%	Index	%	Index	%	Index	%	Index	%	Index	%	Index	%
1995	132.8	-3.1	-	-	140.1	5.5	-	-	136.1	-2.9	-	-	127.4	-6.4	-	-	124.1	-2.6	-	-	126.3	1.8	-	-
1996	119.1	-5.7	-	-	138.7	16.5	-	-	137.2	-1.1	-	-	132.9	-3.1	-	-	132.9	0.0	-	-	133.5	0.5	-	-
1997	130.9	-1.9	-	-	137.2	4.8	-	-	137.2	0.0	135.4	-1.3	134.0	-1.0	-	-	130.7	-2.5	-	-	129.3	-1.1	-	-

Source: U.S. Department of Labor, Bureau of Labor Statistics, Division of Consumer Prices and Price Indexes. - indicates no data collected for period.

Baltimore, MD
Consumer Price Index - Urban Wage Earners
Base 1982-1984 = 100
Apparel and Upkeep

For 1952-1997. Columns headed % show percentile change in the index from the previous period for which an index is available.

Year	Jan Index	%	Feb Index	%	Mar Index	%	Apr Index	%	May Index	%	Jun Index	%	Jul Index	%	Aug Index	%	Sep Index	%	Oct Index	%	Nov Index	%	Dec Index	%
1952	-	-	-	-	-	-	-	-	-	-	-	-	-	-	-	-	-	-	-	-	-	-	38.8	-
1953	-	-	-	-	38.9	0.3	-	-	-	-	39.3	1.0	-	-	-	-	39.1	-0.5	-	-	-	-	38.7	-1.0
1954	-	-	-	-	38.7	0.0	-	-	-	-	38.7	0.0	-	-	-	-	39.1	1.0	-	-	-	-	38.9	-0.5
1955	-	-	-	-	38.7	-0.5	-	-	-	-	38.8	0.3	-	-	-	-	38.7	-0.3	-	-	-	-	39.2	1.3
1956	-	-	-	-	39.6	1.0	-	-	-	-	40.2	1.5	-	-	-	-	40.8	1.5	-	-	-	-	40.7	-0.2
1957	-	-	-	-	40.5	-0.5	-	-	-	-	40.9	1.0	-	-	-	-	41.8	2.2	-	-	-	-	41.4	-1.0
1958	-	-	-	-	41.6	0.5	-	-	-	-	41.6	0.0	-	-	-	-	41.8	0.5	-	-	-	-	41.3	-1.2
1959	-	-	-	-	42.2	2.2	-	-	-	-	42.3	0.2	-	-	-	-	43.0	1.7	-	-	-	-	42.9	-0.2
1960	-	-	-	-	43.0	0.2	-	-	-	-	42.9	-0.2	-	-	-	-	43.6	1.6	-	-	-	-	43.4	-0.5
1961	-	-	-	-	44.0	1.4	-	-	-	-	43.9	-0.2	-	-	-	-	44.0	0.2	-	-	-	-	43.8	-0.5
1962	-	-	-	-	43.9	0.2	-	-	-	-	43.9	0.0	-	-	-	-	44.6	1.6	-	-	-	-	44.5	-0.2
1963	-	-	-	-	44.6	0.2	-	-	-	-	44.6	0.0	-	-	-	-	44.6	0.0	-	-	-	-	44.6	0.0
1964	-	-	-	-	44.3	-0.7	-	-	-	-	44.5	0.5	-	-	-	-	44.7	0.4	-	-	-	-	44.8	0.2
1965	-	-	-	-	44.7	-0.2	-	-	-	-	45.1	0.9	-	-	-	-	45.4	0.7	-	-	-	-	45.5	0.2
1966	-	-	-	-	46.1	1.3	-	-	-	-	46.5	0.9	-	-	-	-	46.7	0.4	-	-	-	-	47.0	0.6
1967	-	-	-	-	48.0	2.1	-	-	-	-	48.5	1.0	-	-	-	-	49.3	1.6	-	-	-	-	49.1	-0.4
1968	-	-	-	-	49.8	1.4	-	-	-	-	50.7	1.8	-	-	-	-	51.7	2.0	-	-	-	-	52.2	1.0
1969	-	-	-	-	53.5	2.5	-	-	-	-	54.8	2.4	-	-	-	-	56.1	2.4	-	-	-	-	56.6	0.9
1970	-	-	-	-	57.0	0.7	-	-	-	-	57.6	1.1	-	-	-	-	58.5	1.6	-	-	-	-	59.7	2.1
1971	-	-	-	-	60.0	0.5	-	-	-	-	59.2	-1.3	-	-	-	-	60.5	2.2	-	-	-	-	60.3	-0.3
1972	-	-	-	-	60.4	0.2	-	-	-	-	59.5	-1.5	-	-	-	-	60.4	1.5	-	-	-	-	60.3	-0.2
1973	-	-	-	-	62.0	2.8	-	-	-	-	62.8	1.3	-	-	-	-	64.9	3.3	-	-	-	-	65.7	1.2
1974	-	-	-	-	67.1	2.1	-	-	-	-	68.3	1.8	-	-	-	-	70.0	2.5	-	-	-	-	70.9	1.3
1975	-	-	-	-	71.6	1.0	-	-	-	-	71.3	-0.4	-	-	-	-	72.3	1.4	-	-	-	-	72.1	-0.3
1976	-	-	-	-	73.7	2.2	-	-	-	-	74.7	1.4	-	-	-	-	76.0	1.7	-	-	-	-	76.8	1.1
1977	-	-	-	-	77.6	1.0	-	-	-	-	79.1	1.9	-	-	-	-	80.1	1.3	-	-	-	-	80.1	0.0
1978	-	-	-	-	82.9	3.5	-	-	83.8	1.1	-	-	80.5	-3.9	-	-	82.9	3.0	-	-	83.2	0.4	-	-
1979	80.2	-3.6	-	-	83.9	4.6	-	-	85.6	2.0	-	-	81.9	-4.3	-	-	85.2	4.0	-	-	85.5	0.4	-	-
1980	85.4	-0.1	-	-	90.9	6.4	-	-	91.3	0.4	-	-	90.4	-1.0	-	-	92.9	2.8	-	-	94.4	1.6	-	-
1981	95.0	0.6	-	-	96.7	1.8	-	-	97.0	0.3	-	-	94.9	-2.2	-	-	96.4	1.6	-	-	95.9	-0.5	-	-
1982	92.5	-3.5	-	-	98.4	6.4	-	-	98.9	0.5	-	-	95.5	-3.4	-	-	99.4	4.1	-	-	99.7	0.3	-	-
1983	98.0	-1.7	-	-	99.5	1.5	-	-	102.0	2.5	-	-	101.1	-0.9	-	-	99.1	-2.0	-	-	103.5	4.4	-	-
1984	100.8	-2.6	-	-	101.7	0.9	-	-	102.1	0.4	-	-	99.0	-3.0	-	-	103.7	4.7	-	-	103.5	-0.2	-	-
1985	99.0	-4.3	-	-	107.1	8.2	-	-	106.9	-0.2	-	-	105.2	-1.6	-	-	110.5	5.0	-	-	109.0	-1.4	-	-
1986	106.8	-2.0	-	-	111.0	3.9	-	-	111.6	0.5	-	-	107.8	-3.4	-	-	110.8	2.8	-	-	112.0	1.1	-	-
1987	105.9	-5.4	-	-	120.2	13.5	-	-	119.5	-0.6	-	-	122.7	2.7	-	-	124.3	1.3	-	-	119.5	-3.9	-	-
1988	116.0	-2.9	-	-	128.2	10.5	-	-	120.6	-5.9	-	-	133.0	10.3	-	-	139.0	4.5	-	-	135.4	-2.6	-	-
1989	122.0	-9.9	-	-	135.1	10.7	-	-	127.8	-5.4	-	-	120.5	-5.7	-	-	127.7	6.0	-	-	126.0	-1.3	-	-
1990	110.6	-12.2	-	-	133.6	20.8	-	-	128.3	-4.0	-	-	115.8	-9.7	-	-	134.6	16.2	-	-	126.7	-5.9	-	-
1991	126.1	-0.5	-	-	133.3	5.7	-	-	131.6	-1.3	-	-	127.0	-3.5	-	-	133.8	5.4	-	-	132.6	-0.9	-	-
1992	129.0	-2.7	-	-	141.9	10.0	-	-	140.2	-1.2	-	-	128.3	-8.5	-	-	137.4	7.1	-	-	135.8	-1.2	-	-
1993	131.6	-3.1	-	-	141.0	7.1	-	-	142.3	0.9	-	-	133.2	-6.4	-	-	138.3	3.8	-	-	131.7	-4.8	-	-
1994	121.2	-8.0	-	-	134.1	10.6	-	-	139.0	3.7	-	-	131.6	-5.3	-	-	138.2	5.0	-	-	134.6	-2.6	-	-

[Continued]

Baltimore, MD
Consumer Price Index - Urban Wage Earners
Base 1982-1984 = 100
Apparel and Upkeep
[Continued]

For 1952-1997. Columns headed % show percentile change in the index from the previous period for which an index is available.

Year	Jan		Feb		Mar		Apr		May		Jun		Jul		Aug		Sep		Oct		Nov		Dec	
	Index	%	Index	%	Index	%	Index	%	Index	%	Index	%	Index	%	Index	%	Index	%	Index	%	Index	%	Index	%
1995	130.4	-3.1	-	-	137.4	5.4	-	-	133.6	-2.8	-	-	123.9	-7.3	-	-	120.9	-2.4	-	-	122.7	1.5	-	-
1996	115.6	-5.8	-	-	133.8	15.7	-	-	131.8	-1.5	-	-	128.2	-2.7	-	-	128.8	0.5	-	-	129.2	0.3	-	-
1997	128.0	-0.9	-	-	133.3	4.1	-	-	132.6	-0.5	131.5	-0.8	130.2	-1.0	-	-	126.6	-2.8	-	-	124.3	-1.8	-	-

Source: U.S. Department of Labor, Bureau of Labor Statistics, Division of Consumer Prices and Price Indexes. - indicates no data collected for period.

Baltimore, MD
Consumer Price Index - All Urban Consumers
Base 1982-1984 = 100
Transportation

For 1947-1997. Columns headed % show percentile change in the index from the previous period for which an index is available.

Year	Jan Index	%	Feb Index	%	Mar Index	%	Apr Index	%	May Index	%	Jun Index	%	Jul Index	%	Aug Index	%	Sep Index	%	Oct Index	%	Nov Index	%	Dec Index	%
1947	16.9	-	16.8	-0.6	16.8	0.0	17.0	1.2	17.0	0.0	17.0	0.0	-	-	-	-	17.8	4.7	-	-	-	-	17.9	0.6
1948	-	-	-	-	18.4	2.8	-	-	-	-	18.4	0.0	-	-	-	-	19.5	6.0	-	-	-	-	19.6	0.5
1949	-	-	-	-	22.0	12.2	-	-	-	-	22.1	0.5	-	-	-	-	22.1	0.0	-	-	-	-	22.0	-0.5
1950	-	-	-	-	22.0	0.0	-	-	-	-	21.9	-0.5	-	-	-	-	23.7	8.2	-	-	-	-	23.7	0.0
1951	-	-	-	-	23.9	0.8	-	-	-	-	23.9	0.0	-	-	-	-	24.5	2.5	-	-	-	-	24.7	0.8
1952	-	-	-	-	24.9	0.8	-	-	-	-	24.9	0.0	-	-	-	-	26.7	7.2	-	-	-	-	26.7	0.0
1953	-	-	-	-	26.7	0.0	-	-	-	-	26.8	0.4	-	-	-	-	27.1	1.1	-	-	-	-	27.0	-0.4
1954	-	-	-	-	26.7	-1.1	-	-	-	-	26.7	0.0	-	-	-	-	26.2	-1.9	-	-	-	-	26.9	2.7
1955	-	-	-	-	26.4	-1.9	-	-	-	-	26.5	0.4	-	-	-	-	26.2	-1.1	-	-	-	-	26.2	0.0
1956	-	-	-	-	26.4	0.8	-	-	-	-	26.5	0.4	-	-	-	-	27.1	2.3	-	-	-	-	28.1	3.7
1957	-	-	-	-	28.5	1.4	-	-	-	-	28.4	-0.4	-	-	-	-	28.6	0.7	-	-	-	-	29.1	1.7
1958	-	-	-	-	28.9	-0.7	-	-	-	-	28.6	-1.0	-	-	-	-	29.4	2.8	-	-	-	-	30.8	4.8
1959	-	-	-	-	30.8	0.0	-	-	-	-	30.9	0.3	-	-	-	-	31.2	1.0	-	-	-	-	31.5	1.0
1960	-	-	-	-	31.3	-0.6	-	-	-	-	30.9	-1.3	-	-	-	-	30.5	-1.3	-	-	-	-	30.8	1.0
1961	-	-	-	-	31.0	0.6	-	-	-	-	31.4	1.3	-	-	-	-	31.8	1.3	-	-	-	-	31.7	-0.3
1962	-	-	-	-	31.5	-0.6	-	-	-	-	30.9	-1.9	-	-	-	-	31.5	1.9	-	-	-	-	31.6	0.3
1963	-	-	-	-	31.7	0.3	-	-	-	-	32.0	0.9	-	-	-	-	32.2	0.6	-	-	-	-	32.6	1.2
1964	-	-	-	-	32.5	-0.3	-	-	-	-	32.9	1.2	-	-	-	-	32.8	-0.3	-	-	-	-	33.2	1.2
1965	-	-	-	-	33.3	0.3	-	-	-	-	33.2	-0.3	-	-	-	-	33.3	0.3	-	-	-	-	33.6	0.9
1966	-	-	-	-	33.5	-0.3	-	-	-	-	33.7	0.6	-	-	-	-	33.7	0.0	-	-	-	-	33.7	0.0
1967	-	-	-	-	33.9	0.6	-	-	-	-	34.2	0.9	-	-	-	-	34.4	0.6	-	-	-	-	34.9	1.5
1968	-	-	-	-	34.9	0.0	-	-	-	-	35.4	1.4	-	-	-	-	35.5	0.3	-	-	-	-	36.4	2.5
1969	-	-	-	-	37.2	2.2	-	-	-	-	37.6	1.1	-	-	-	-	37.3	-0.8	-	-	-	-	37.8	1.3
1970	-	-	-	-	37.7	-0.3	-	-	-	-	38.6	2.4	-	-	-	-	38.5	-0.3	-	-	-	-	39.8	3.4
1971	-	-	-	-	39.8	0.0	-	-	-	-	40.7	2.3	-	-	-	-	40.4	-0.7	-	-	-	-	40.3	-0.2
1972	-	-	-	-	39.5	-2.0	-	-	-	-	39.8	0.8	-	-	-	-	40.3	1.3	-	-	-	-	40.4	0.2
1973	-	-	-	-	40.7	0.7	-	-	-	-	41.5	2.0	-	-	-	-	41.4	-0.2	-	-	-	-	42.3	2.2
1974	-	-	-	-	44.3	4.7	-	-	-	-	46.3	4.5	-	-	-	-	47.7	3.0	-	-	-	-	48.2	1.0
1975	-	-	-	-	48.7	1.0	-	-	-	-	50.1	2.9	-	-	-	-	51.2	2.2	-	-	-	-	51.6	0.8
1976	-	-	-	-	52.8	2.3	-	-	-	-	54.9	4.0	-	-	-	-	55.6	1.3	-	-	-	-	56.0	0.7
1977	-	-	-	-	56.9	1.6	-	-	-	-	58.5	2.8	-	-	-	-	58.1	-0.7	-	-	-	-	58.0	-0.2
1978	-	-	-	-	58.2	0.3	-	-	59.4	2.1	-	-	60.5	1.9	-	-	60.9	0.7	-	-	62.3	2.3	-	-
1979	63.0	1.1	-	-	64.3	2.1	-	-	66.9	4.0	-	-	70.2	4.9	-	-	71.6	2.0	-	-	73.8	3.1	-	-
1980	76.8	4.1	-	-	80.6	4.9	-	-	81.7	1.4	-	-	83.1	1.7	-	-	84.0	1.1	-	-	85.0	1.2	-	-
1981	87.1	2.5	-	-	90.1	3.4	-	-	91.6	1.7	-	-	93.1	1.6	-	-	93.3	0.2	-	-	94.6	1.4	-	-
1982	95.5	1.0	-	-	94.4	-1.2	-	-	94.1	-0.3	-	-	97.3	3.4	-	-	97.3	0.0	-	-	96.9	-0.4	-	-
1983	97.4	0.5	-	-	96.4	-1.0	-	-	98.1	1.8	-	-	99.8	1.7	-	-	102.4	2.6	-	-	103.2	0.8	-	-
1984	102.7	-0.5	-	-	103.2	0.5	-	-	103.8	0.6	-	-	104.8	1.0	-	-	105.1	0.3	-	-	105.5	0.4	-	-
1985	105.2	-0.3	-	-	105.9	0.7	-	-	107.7	1.7	-	-	107.7	0.0	-	-	107.5	-0.2	-	-	108.7	1.1	-	-
1986	110.0	1.2	-	-	106.8	-2.9	-	-	103.5	-3.1	-	-	103.0	-0.5	-	-	102.5	-0.5	-	-	102.8	0.3	-	-
1987	104.1	1.3	-	-	104.5	0.4	-	-	105.3	0.8	-	-	108.2	2.8	-	-	108.5	0.3	-	-	109.3	0.7	-	-
1988	110.1	0.7	-	-	109.5	-0.5	-	-	110.6	1.0	-	-	111.3	0.6	-	-	112.4	1.0	-	-	113.9	1.3	-	-
1989	114.1	0.2	-	-	114.8	0.6	-	-	117.9	2.7	-	-	117.5	-0.3	-	-	117.0	-0.4	-	-	118.6	1.4	-	-
1990	121.2	2.2	-	-	119.9	-1.1	-	-	119.5	-0.3	-	-	120.4	0.8	-	-	124.6	3.5	-	-	129.8	4.2	-	-
1991	128.0	-1.4	-	-	123.1	-3.8	-	-	124.4	1.1	-	-	124.5	0.1	-	-	125.7	1.0	-	-	127.4	1.4	-	-

[Continued]

Baltimore, MD
Consumer Price Index - All Urban Consumers
Base 1982-1984 = 100
Transportation
[Continued]

For 1947-1997. Columns headed % show percentile change in the index from the previous period for which an index is available.

Year	Jan Index	Jan %	Feb Index	Feb %	Mar Index	Mar %	Apr Index	Apr %	May Index	May %	Jun Index	Jun %	Jul Index	Jul %	Aug Index	Aug %	Sep Index	Sep %	Oct Index	Oct %	Nov Index	Nov %	Dec Index	Dec %
1992	127.1	-0.2	-	-	126.7	-0.3	-	-	127.7	0.8	-	-	129.0	1.0	-	-	129.0	0.0	-	-	130.8	1.4	-	-
1993	130.2	-0.5	-	-	129.0	-0.9	-	-	129.8	0.6	-	-	129.5	-0.2	-	-	128.6	-0.7	-	-	131.0	1.9	-	-
1994	129.7	-1.0	-	-	129.4	-0.2	-	-	130.4	0.8	-	-	132.7	1.8	-	-	135.2	1.9	-	-	137.3	1.6	-	-
1995	138.3	0.7	-	-	138.6	0.2	-	-	139.1	0.4	-	-	138.7	-0.3	-	-	136.7	-1.4	-	-	139.1	1.8	-	-
1996	139.2	0.1	-	-	138.9	-0.2	-	-	141.7	2.0	-	-	140.7	-0.7	-	-	140.0	-0.5	-	-	140.4	0.3	-	-
1997	142.2	1.3	-	-	143.3	0.8	-	-	141.4	-1.3	142.1	0.5	140.2	-1.3	-	-	141.2	0.7	-	-	139.9	-0.9	-	-

Source: U.S. Department of Labor, Bureau of Labor Statistics, Division of Consumer Prices and Price Indexes. - indicates no data collected for period.

Baltimore, MD
Consumer Price Index - Urban Wage Earners
Base 1982-1984 = 100
Transportation

For 1947-1997. Columns headed % show percentile change in the index from the previous period for which an index is available.

Year	Jan Index	%	Feb Index	%	Mar Index	%	Apr Index	%	May Index	%	Jun Index	%	Jul Index	%	Aug Index	%	Sep Index	%	Oct Index	%	Nov Index	%	Dec Index	%
1947	16.8	-	16.7	-0.6	16.7	0.0	16.9	1.2	16.9	0.0	16.9	0.0	-	-	-	-	17.7	4.7	-	-	-	-	17.8	0.6
1948	-	-	-	-	18.3	2.8	-	-	-	-	18.3	0.0	-	-	-	-	19.4	6.0	-	-	-	-	19.5	0.5
1949	-	-	-	-	21.9	12.3	-	-	-	-	21.9	0.0	-	-	-	-	21.9	0.0	-	-	-	-	21.9	0.0
1950	-	-	-	-	21.9	0.0	-	-	-	-	21.7	-0.9	-	-	-	-	23.5	8.3	-	-	-	-	23.6	0.4
1951	-	-	-	-	23.7	0.4	-	-	-	-	23.8	0.4	-	-	-	-	24.3	2.1	-	-	-	-	24.6	1.2
1952	-	-	-	-	24.8	0.8	-	-	-	-	24.8	0.0	-	-	-	-	26.6	7.3	-	-	-	-	26.6	0.0
1953	-	-	-	-	26.5	-0.4	-	-	-	-	26.7	0.8	-	-	-	-	26.9	0.7	-	-	-	-	26.8	-0.4
1954	-	-	-	-	26.6	-0.7	-	-	-	-	26.5	-0.4	-	-	-	-	26.0	-1.9	-	-	-	-	26.7	2.7
1955	-	-	-	-	26.3	-1.5	-	-	-	-	26.3	0.0	-	-	-	-	26.1	-0.8	-	-	-	-	26.0	-0.4
1956	-	-	-	-	26.3	1.2	-	-	-	-	26.4	0.4	-	-	-	-	26.9	1.9	-	-	-	-	27.9	3.7
1957	-	-	-	-	28.3	1.4	-	-	-	-	28.2	-0.4	-	-	-	-	28.4	0.7	-	-	-	-	28.9	1.8
1958	-	-	-	-	28.8	-0.3	-	-	-	-	28.5	-1.0	-	-	-	-	29.3	2.8	-	-	-	-	30.6	4.4
1959	-	-	-	-	30.6	0.0	-	-	-	-	30.7	0.3	-	-	-	-	31.0	1.0	-	-	-	-	31.3	1.0
1960	-	-	-	-	31.1	-0.6	-	-	-	-	30.7	-1.3	-	-	-	-	30.3	-1.3	-	-	-	-	30.6	1.0
1961	-	-	-	-	30.8	0.7	-	-	-	-	31.2	1.3	-	-	-	-	31.6	1.3	-	-	-	-	31.5	-0.3
1962	-	-	-	-	31.3	-0.6	-	-	-	-	30.7	-1.9	-	-	-	-	31.3	2.0	-	-	-	-	31.4	0.3
1963	-	-	-	-	31.5	0.3	-	-	-	-	31.8	1.0	-	-	-	-	32.0	0.6	-	-	-	-	32.4	1.3
1964	-	-	-	-	32.3	-0.3	-	-	-	-	32.7	1.2	-	-	-	-	32.6	-0.3	-	-	-	-	33.0	1.2
1965	-	-	-	-	33.1	0.3	-	-	-	-	33.0	-0.3	-	-	-	-	33.1	0.3	-	-	-	-	33.4	0.9
1966	-	-	-	-	33.3	-0.3	-	-	-	-	33.5	0.6	-	-	-	-	33.5	0.0	-	-	-	-	33.5	0.0
1967	-	-	-	-	33.7	0.6	-	-	-	-	34.0	0.9	-	-	-	-	34.2	0.6	-	-	-	-	34.7	1.5
1968	-	-	-	-	34.7	0.0	-	-	-	-	35.2	1.4	-	-	-	-	35.3	0.3	-	-	-	-	36.2	2.5
1969	-	-	-	-	37.0	2.2	-	-	-	-	37.4	1.1	-	-	-	-	37.1	-0.8	-	-	-	-	37.5	1.1
1970	-	-	-	-	37.5	0.0	-	-	-	-	38.4	2.4	-	-	-	-	38.3	-0.3	-	-	-	-	39.6	3.4
1971	-	-	-	-	39.6	0.0	-	-	-	-	40.4	2.0	-	-	-	-	40.1	-0.7	-	-	-	-	40.0	-0.2
1972	-	-	-	-	39.3	-1.7	-	-	-	-	39.5	0.5	-	-	-	-	40.0	1.3	-	-	-	-	40.1	0.2
1973	-	-	-	-	40.5	1.0	-	-	-	-	41.3	2.0	-	-	-	-	41.2	-0.2	-	-	-	-	42.1	2.2
1974	-	-	-	-	44.0	4.5	-	-	-	-	46.0	4.5	-	-	-	-	47.4	3.0	-	-	-	-	47.9	1.1
1975	-	-	-	-	48.5	1.3	-	-	-	-	49.8	2.7	-	-	-	-	50.9	2.2	-	-	-	-	51.3	0.8
1976	-	-	-	-	52.5	2.3	-	-	-	-	54.6	4.0	-	-	-	-	55.2	1.1	-	-	-	-	55.6	0.7
1977	-	-	-	-	56.6	1.8	-	-	-	-	58.2	2.8	-	-	-	-	57.8	-0.7	-	-	-	-	57.6	-0.3
1978	-	-	-	-	57.9	0.5	-	-	59.1	2.1	-	-	60.4	2.2	-	-	60.8	0.7	-	-	61.5	1.2	-	-
1979	62.2	1.1	-	-	63.5	2.1	-	-	66.2	4.3	-	-	69.2	4.5	-	-	70.7	2.2	-	-	72.7	2.8	-	-
1980	75.2	3.4	-	-	78.7	4.7	-	-	79.8	1.4	-	-	81.2	1.8	-	-	82.1	1.1	-	-	84.1	2.4	-	-
1981	86.0	2.3	-	-	89.0	3.5	-	-	90.1	1.2	-	-	92.1	2.2	-	-	92.6	0.5	-	-	94.0	1.5	-	-
1982	94.7	0.7	-	-	93.7	-1.1	-	-	93.4	-0.3	-	-	96.9	3.7	-	-	97.0	0.1	-	-	96.7	-0.3	-	-
1983	97.1	0.4	-	-	96.1	-1.0	-	-	97.9	1.9	-	-	99.9	2.0	-	-	102.4	2.5	-	-	103.4	1.0	-	-
1984	102.9	-0.5	-	-	103.4	0.5	-	-	104.5	1.1	-	-	105.4	0.9	-	-	105.7	0.3	-	-	106.0	0.3	-	-
1985	105.8	-0.2	-	-	106.3	0.5	-	-	107.9	1.5	-	-	107.9	0.0	-	-	107.7	-0.2	-	-	108.7	0.9	-	-
1986	109.8	1.0	-	-	106.8	-2.7	-	-	103.2	-3.4	-	-	102.8	-0.4	-	-	102.2	-0.6	-	-	102.4	0.2	-	-
1987	103.7	1.3	-	-	104.4	0.7	-	-	105.5	1.1	-	-	108.9	3.2	-	-	109.4	0.5	-	-	109.9	0.5	-	-
1988	110.8	0.8	-	-	110.5	-0.3	-	-	111.3	0.7	-	-	112.3	0.9	-	-	113.4	1.0	-	-	114.5	1.0	-	-
1989	114.7	0.2	-	-	115.3	0.5	-	-	118.9	3.1	-	-	118.5	-0.3	-	-	117.8	-0.6	-	-	119.4	1.4	-	-
1990	122.0	2.2	-	-	120.5	-1.2	-	-	120.2	-0.2	-	-	120.9	0.6	-	-	125.6	3.9	-	-	131.0	4.3	-	-
1991	128.6	-1.8	-	-	123.2	-4.2	-	-	124.7	1.2	-	-	125.0	0.2	-	-	126.4	1.1	-	-	127.9	1.2	-	-

[Continued]

Baltimore, MD
Consumer Price Index - Urban Wage Earners
Base 1982-1984 = 100
Transportation

[Continued]

For 1947-1997. Columns headed % show percentile change in the index from the previous period for which an index is available.

Year	Jan		Feb		Mar		Apr		May		Jun		Jul		Aug		Sep		Oct		Nov		Dec	
	Index	%	Index	%	Index	%	Index	%	Index	%	Index	%	Index	%	Index	%	Index	%	Index	%	Index	%	Index	%
1992	127.3	-0.5	-	-	126.6	-0.5	-	-	128.2	1.3	-	-	130.1	1.5	-	-	130.1	0.0	-	-	131.7	1.2	-	-
1993	130.9	-0.6	-	-	129.3	-1.2	-	-	130.2	0.7	-	-	129.8	-0.3	-	-	128.8	-0.8	-	-	131.4	2.0	-	-
1994	130.1	-1.0	-	-	129.6	-0.4	-	-	131.0	1.1	-	-	133.2	1.7	-	-	136.0	2.1	-	-	138.2	1.6	-	-
1995	139.0	0.6	-	-	139.5	0.4	-	-	140.5	0.7	-	-	140.2	-0.2	-	-	138.1	-1.5	-	-	139.7	1.2	-	-
1996	140.0	0.2	-	-	139.8	-0.1	-	-	143.3	2.5	-	-	142.2	-0.8	-	-	141.3	-0.6	-	-	141.3	0.0	-	-
1997	143.0	1.2	-	-	144.1	0.8	-	-	142.1	-1.4	142.9	0.6	140.7	-1.5	-	-	141.9	0.9	-	-	140.3	-1.1	-	-

Source: U.S. Department of Labor, Bureau of Labor Statistics, Division of Consumer Prices and Price Indexes. - indicates no data collected for period.

Baltimore, MD
Consumer Price Index - All Urban Consumers
Base 1982-1984 = 100
Medical Care

For 1947-1997. Columns headed % show percentile change in the index from the previous period for which an index is available.

Year	Jan Index	%	Feb Index	%	Mar Index	%	Apr Index	%	May Index	%	Jun Index	%	Jul Index	%	Aug Index	%	Sep Index	%	Oct Index	%	Nov Index	%	Dec Index	%
1947	12.5	-	12.6	0.8	12.6	0.0	12.6	0.0	12.7	0.8	12.8	0.8	-	-	-	-	13.1	2.3	-	-	-	-	13.2	0.8
1948	-	-	-	-	13.2	0.0	-	-	-	-	13.4	1.5	-	-	-	-	13.4	0.0	-	-	-	-	13.4	0.0
1949	-	-	-	-	13.4	0.0	-	-	-	-	13.4	0.0	-	-	-	-	13.4	0.0	-	-	-	-	13.5	0.7
1950	-	-	-	-	13.6	0.7	-	-	-	-	13.6	0.0	-	-	-	-	13.7	0.7	-	-	-	-	13.8	0.7
1951	-	-	-	-	14.3	3.6	-	-	-	-	14.9	4.2	-	-	-	-	14.9	0.0	-	-	-	-	15.9	6.7
1952	-	-	-	-	16.4	3.1	-	-	-	-	16.5	0.6	-	-	-	-	16.5	0.0	-	-	-	-	16.5	0.0
1953	-	-	-	-	17.4	5.5	-	-	-	-	17.4	0.0	-	-	-	-	17.5	0.6	-	-	-	-	17.5	0.0
1954	-	-	-	-	17.6	0.6	-	-	-	-	17.6	0.0	-	-	-	-	17.6	0.0	-	-	-	-	17.6	0.0
1955	-	-	-	-	17.7	0.6	-	-	-	-	17.7	0.0	-	-	-	-	17.8	0.6	-	-	-	-	18.0	1.1
1956	-	-	-	-	18.0	0.0	-	-	-	-	18.8	4.4	-	-	-	-	18.9	0.5	-	-	-	-	19.0	0.5
1957	-	-	-	-	19.1	0.5	-	-	-	-	19.1	0.0	-	-	-	-	19.1	0.0	-	-	-	-	19.1	0.0
1958	-	-	-	-	19.3	1.0	-	-	-	-	19.6	1.6	-	-	-	-	19.7	0.5	-	-	-	-	20.6	4.6
1959	-	-	-	-	20.7	0.5	-	-	-	-	20.9	1.0	-	-	-	-	21.0	0.5	-	-	-	-	21.8	3.8
1960	-	-	-	-	22.0	0.9	-	-	-	-	22.1	0.5	-	-	-	-	22.3	0.9	-	-	-	-	23.0	3.1
1961	-	-	-	-	23.2	0.9	-	-	-	-	23.2	0.0	-	-	-	-	23.3	0.4	-	-	-	-	23.4	0.4
1962	-	-	-	-	23.6	0.9	-	-	-	-	23.7	0.4	-	-	-	-	23.9	0.8	-	-	-	-	23.9	0.0
1963	-	-	-	-	25.0	4.6	-	-	-	-	25.3	1.2	-	-	-	-	25.4	0.4	-	-	-	-	25.5	0.4
1964	-	-	-	-	25.6	0.4	-	-	-	-	25.8	0.8	-	-	-	-	25.9	0.4	-	-	-	-	26.1	0.8
1965	-	-	-	-	26.2	0.4	-	-	-	-	26.3	0.4	-	-	-	-	26.6	1.1	-	-	-	-	26.8	0.8
1966	-	-	-	-	27.0	0.7	-	-	-	-	27.5	1.9	-	-	-	-	27.9	1.5	-	-	-	-	28.2	1.1
1967	-	-	-	-	29.5	4.6	-	-	-	-	29.7	0.7	-	-	-	-	30.3	2.0	-	-	-	-	30.5	0.7
1968	-	-	-	-	31.3	2.6	-	-	-	-	31.4	0.3	-	-	-	-	31.9	1.6	-	-	-	-	32.0	0.3
1969	-	-	-	-	33.0	3.1	-	-	-	-	33.2	0.6	-	-	-	-	34.5	3.9	-	-	-	-	34.5	0.0
1970	-	-	-	-	35.8	3.8	-	-	-	-	36.4	1.7	-	-	-	-	37.3	2.5	-	-	-	-	38.5	3.2
1971	-	-	-	-	39.5	2.6	-	-	-	-	40.3	2.0	-	-	-	-	41.7	3.5	-	-	-	-	41.6	-0.2
1972	-	-	-	-	41.8	0.5	-	-	-	-	42.4	1.4	-	-	-	-	43.1	1.7	-	-	-	-	43.4	0.7
1973	-	-	-	-	43.7	0.7	-	-	-	-	43.9	0.5	-	-	-	-	44.6	1.6	-	-	-	-	46.3	3.8
1974	-	-	-	-	46.9	1.3	-	-	-	-	49.5	5.5	-	-	-	-	50.7	2.4	-	-	-	-	51.4	1.4
1975	-	-	-	-	53.1	3.3	-	-	-	-	53.8	1.3	-	-	-	-	54.6	1.5	-	-	-	-	54.7	0.2
1976	-	-	-	-	56.0	2.4	-	-	-	-	58.0	3.6	-	-	-	-	58.1	0.2	-	-	-	-	59.4	2.2
1977	-	-	-	-	61.3	3.2	-	-	-	-	61.9	1.0	-	-	-	-	62.5	1.0	-	-	-	-	63.1	1.0
1978	-	-	-	-	64.3	1.9	-	-	65.0	1.1	-	-	66.1	1.7	-	-	66.7	0.9	-	-	67.6	1.3	-	-
1979	68.5	1.3	-	-	70.4	2.8	-	-	70.8	0.6	-	-	72.0	1.7	-	-	74.3	3.2	-	-	75.3	1.3	-	-
1980	76.1	1.1	-	-	77.5	1.8	-	-	79.6	2.7	-	-	79.0	-0.8	-	-	80.3	1.6	-	-	81.0	0.9	-	-
1981	81.4	0.5	-	-	83.2	2.2	-	-	84.3	1.3	-	-	85.1	0.9	-	-	87.1	2.4	-	-	86.8	-0.3	-	-
1982	89.3	2.9	-	-	91.4	2.4	-	-	92.7	1.4	-	-	94.0	1.4	-	-	96.8	3.0	-	-	97.5	0.7	-	-
1983	98.7	1.2	-	-	99.2	0.5	-	-	99.5	0.3	-	-	101.2	1.7	-	-	101.6	0.4	-	-	102.9	1.3	-	-
1984	102.7	-0.2	-	-	103.5	0.8	-	-	104.2	0.7	-	-	106.8	2.5	-	-	106.3	-0.5	-	-	107.3	0.9	-	-
1985	108.1	0.7	-	-	109.0	0.8	-	-	110.5	1.4	-	-	111.6	1.0	-	-	113.7	1.9	-	-	115.6	1.7	-	-
1986	118.2	2.2	-	-	119.7	1.3	-	-	121.3	1.3	-	-	122.6	1.1	-	-	123.7	0.9	-	-	123.5	-0.2	-	-
1987	125.4	1.5	-	-	124.5	-0.7	-	-	126.0	1.2	-	-	127.9	1.5	-	-	130.6	2.1	-	-	131.7	0.8	-	-
1988	130.8	-0.7	-	-	133.3	1.9	-	-	134.2	0.7	-	-	133.9	-0.2	-	-	136.8	2.2	-	-	137.1	0.2	-	-
1989	139.8	2.0	-	-	140.9	0.8	-	-	142.3	1.0	-	-	143.4	0.8	-	-	151.0	5.3	-	-	153.5	1.7	-	-
1990	150.3	-2.1	-	-	152.3	1.3	-	-	157.1	3.2	-	-	159.8	1.7	-	-	161.2	0.9	-	-	165.2	2.5	-	-
1991	167.4	1.3	-	-	167.2	-0.1	-	-	170.7	2.1	-	-	172.7	1.2	-	-	172.7	0.0	-	-	177.5	2.8	-	-

[Continued]

Baltimore, MD
Consumer Price Index - All Urban Consumers
Base 1982-1984 = 100
Medical Care
[Continued]

For 1947-1997. Columns headed % show percentile change in the index from the previous period for which an index is available.

Year	Jan Index	%	Feb Index	%	Mar Index	%	Apr Index	%	May Index	%	Jun Index	%	Jul Index	%	Aug Index	%	Sep Index	%	Oct Index	%	Nov Index	%	Dec Index	%
1992	181.2	2.1	-	-	179.9	-0.7	-	-	178.8	-0.6	-	-	185.2	3.6	-	-	187.4	1.2	-	-	190.6	1.7	-	-
1993	193.8	1.7	-	-	194.3	0.3	-	-	196.0	0.9	-	-	197.7	0.9	-	-	203.0	2.7	-	-	204.5	0.7	-	-
1994	206.0	0.7	-	-	209.3	1.6	-	-	216.0	3.2	-	-	222.0	2.8	-	-	222.1	0.0	-	-	227.6	2.5	-	-
1995	227.6	0.0	-	-	229.0	0.6	-	-	231.0	0.9	-	-	229.8	-0.5	-	-	230.1	0.1	-	-	231.0	0.4	-	-
1996	233.2	1.0	-	-	234.8	0.7	-	-	236.0	0.5	-	-	238.2	0.9	-	-	240.2	0.8	-	-	240.5	0.1	-	-
1997	238.7	-0.7	-	-	239.4	0.3	-	-	236.8	-1.1	238.0	0.5	235.6	-1.0	-	-	234.9	-0.3	-	-	239.3	1.9	-	-

Source: U.S. Department of Labor, Bureau of Labor Statistics, Division of Consumer Prices and Price Indexes. - indicates no data collected for period.

Baltimore, MD
Consumer Price Index - Urban Wage Earners
Base 1982-1984 = 100
Medical Care

For 1947-1997. Columns headed % show percentile change in the index from the previous period for which an index is available.

Year	Jan Index	%	Feb Index	%	Mar Index	%	Apr Index	%	May Index	%	Jun Index	%	Jul Index	%	Aug Index	%	Sep Index	%	Oct Index	%	Nov Index	%	Dec Index	%
1947	13.3	-	13.3	0.0	13.4	0.8	13.4	0.0	13.5	0.7	13.6	0.7	-	-	-	-	13.9	2.2	-	-	-	-	14.0	0.7
1948	-	-	-	-	14.1	0.7	-	-	-	-	14.2	0.7	-	-	-	-	14.2	0.0	-	-	-	-	14.2	0.0
1949	-	-	-	-	14.3	0.7	-	-	-	-	14.3	0.0	-	-	-	-	14.3	0.0	-	-	-	-	14.3	0.0
1950	-	-	-	-	14.4	0.7	-	-	-	-	14.5	0.7	-	-	-	-	14.5	0.0	-	-	-	-	14.6	0.7
1951	-	-	-	-	15.1	3.4	-	-	-	-	15.8	4.6	-	-	-	-	15.8	0.0	-	-	-	-	16.9	7.0
1952	-	-	-	-	17.4	3.0	-	-	-	-	17.5	0.6	-	-	-	-	17.5	0.0	-	-	-	-	17.6	0.6
1953	-	-	-	-	18.5	5.1	-	-	-	-	18.5	0.0	-	-	-	-	18.6	0.5	-	-	-	-	18.6	0.0
1954	-	-	-	-	18.7	0.5	-	-	-	-	18.7	0.0	-	-	-	-	18.7	0.0	-	-	-	-	18.7	0.0
1955	-	-	-	-	18.8	0.5	-	-	-	-	18.8	0.0	-	-	-	-	18.9	0.5	-	-	-	-	19.1	1.1
1956	-	-	-	-	19.1	0.0	-	-	-	-	20.0	4.7	-	-	-	-	20.1	0.5	-	-	-	-	20.2	0.5
1957	-	-	-	-	20.3	0.5	-	-	-	-	20.3	0.0	-	-	-	-	20.3	0.0	-	-	-	-	20.3	0.0
1958	-	-	-	-	20.5	1.0	-	-	-	-	20.8	1.5	-	-	-	-	20.9	0.5	-	-	-	-	21.9	4.8
1959	-	-	-	-	22.0	0.5	-	-	-	-	22.2	0.9	-	-	-	-	22.3	0.5	-	-	-	-	23.2	4.0
1960	-	-	-	-	23.3	0.4	-	-	-	-	23.4	0.4	-	-	-	-	23.7	1.3	-	-	-	-	24.5	3.4
1961	-	-	-	-	24.6	0.4	-	-	-	-	24.7	0.4	-	-	-	-	24.7	0.0	-	-	-	-	24.9	0.8
1962	-	-	-	-	25.1	0.8	-	-	-	-	25.2	0.4	-	-	-	-	25.4	0.8	-	-	-	-	25.4	0.0
1963	-	-	-	-	26.5	4.3	-	-	-	-	26.9	1.5	-	-	-	-	27.0	0.4	-	-	-	-	27.1	0.4
1964	-	-	-	-	27.2	0.4	-	-	-	-	27.4	0.7	-	-	-	-	27.5	0.4	-	-	-	-	27.7	0.7
1965	-	-	-	-	27.9	0.7	-	-	-	-	27.9	0.0	-	-	-	-	28.3	1.4	-	-	-	-	28.5	0.7
1966	-	-	-	-	28.7	0.7	-	-	-	-	29.2	1.7	-	-	-	-	29.6	1.4	-	-	-	-	29.9	1.0
1967	-	-	-	-	31.3	4.7	-	-	-	-	31.6	1.0	-	-	-	-	32.2	1.9	-	-	-	-	32.4	0.6
1968	-	-	-	-	33.2	2.5	-	-	-	-	33.4	0.6	-	-	-	-	33.9	1.5	-	-	-	-	34.0	0.3
1969	-	-	-	-	35.0	2.9	-	-	-	-	35.3	0.9	-	-	-	-	36.6	3.7	-	-	-	-	36.7	0.3
1970	-	-	-	-	38.0	3.5	-	-	-	-	38.7	1.8	-	-	-	-	39.6	2.3	-	-	-	-	40.9	3.3
1971	-	-	-	-	42.0	2.7	-	-	-	-	42.8	1.9	-	-	-	-	44.3	3.5	-	-	-	-	44.2	-0.2
1972	-	-	-	-	44.4	0.5	-	-	-	-	45.0	1.4	-	-	-	-	45.7	1.6	-	-	-	-	46.1	0.9
1973	-	-	-	-	46.5	0.9	-	-	-	-	46.6	0.2	-	-	-	-	47.4	1.7	-	-	-	-	49.2	3.8
1974	-	-	-	-	49.8	1.2	-	-	-	-	52.6	5.6	-	-	-	-	53.9	2.5	-	-	-	-	54.6	1.3
1975	-	-	-	-	56.4	3.3	-	-	-	-	57.2	1.4	-	-	-	-	58.0	1.4	-	-	-	-	58.1	0.2
1976	-	-	-	-	59.5	2.4	-	-	-	-	61.6	3.5	-	-	-	-	61.7	0.2	-	-	-	-	63.1	2.3
1977	-	-	-	-	65.2	3.3	-	-	-	-	65.8	0.9	-	-	-	-	66.4	0.9	-	-	-	-	67.0	0.9
1978	-	-	-	-	68.4	2.1	-	-	69.6	1.8	-	-	70.1	0.7	-	-	71.3	1.7	-	-	71.9	0.8	-	-
1979	72.4	0.7	-	-	74.7	3.2	-	-	74.3	-0.5	-	-	75.9	2.2	-	-	78.2	3.0	-	-	78.7	0.6	-	-
1980	79.3	0.8	-	-	80.5	1.5	-	-	82.2	2.1	-	-	81.0	-1.5	-	-	81.4	0.5	-	-	81.6	0.2	-	-
1981	81.8	0.2	-	-	84.4	3.2	-	-	85.3	1.1	-	-	85.6	0.4	-	-	87.4	2.1	-	-	87.8	0.5	-	-
1982	89.6	2.1	-	-	91.5	2.1	-	-	92.6	1.2	-	-	93.9	1.4	-	-	96.8	3.1	-	-	97.5	0.7	-	-
1983	98.7	1.2	-	-	99.2	0.5	-	-	99.3	0.1	-	-	101.1	1.8	-	-	101.6	0.5	Oct		102.8	1.2	-	-
1984	102.6	-0.2	-	-	103.5	0.9	-	-	104.2	0.7	-	-	106.9	2.6	-	-	106.4	-0.5	-		107.4	0.9	-	-
1985	108.2	0.7	-	-	109.0	0.7	-	-	110.7	1.6	-	-	111.7	0.9	-	-	113.9	2.0	-		115.6	1.5	-	-
1986	118.5	2.5	-	-	120.0	1.3	-	-	121.6	1.3	-	-	122.7	0.9	-	-	123.7	0.8	-		123.5	-0.2	-	-
1987	124.7	1.0	-	-	124.4	-0.2	-	-	125.8	1.1	-	-	127.5	1.4	-	-	130.3	2.2	-		131.4	0.8	-	-
1988	130.6	-0.6	-	-	132.5	1.5	-	-	133.6	0.8	-	-	133.4	-0.1	-	-	135.9	1.9	-		136.5	0.4	-	-
1989	139.1	1.9	-	-	140.0	0.6	-	-	141.1	0.8	-	-	142.4	0.9	-	-	148.2	4.1	-		150.4	1.5	-	-
1990	148.1	-1.5	-	-	150.3	1.5	-	-	155.2	3.3	-	-	157.5	1.5	-	-	158.7	0.8	-		162.9	2.6	-	-
1991	164.8	1.2	-	-	165.3	0.3	-	-	168.0	1.6	-	-	170.1	1.3	-	-	170.1	0.0	-		174.9	2.8	-	-

[Continued]

Baltimore, MD
Consumer Price Index - Urban Wage Earners
Base 1982-1984 = 100
Medical Care
[Continued]

For 1947-1997. Columns headed % show percentile change in the index from the previous period for which an index is available.

Year	Jan Index	%	Feb Index	%	Mar Index	%	Apr Index	%	May Index	%	Jun Index	%	Jul Index	%	Aug Index	%	Sep Index	%	Oct Index	%	Nov Index	%	Dec Index	%
1992	178.2	1.9	-	-	176.3	-1.1	-	-	175.8	-0.3	-	-	182.2	3.6	-	-	184.3	1.2	-	-	187.8	1.9	-	-
1993	191.0	1.7	-	-	191.6	0.3	-	-	193.0	0.7	-	-	195.0	1.0	-	-	200.3	2.7	-	-	201.8	0.7	-	-
1994	203.4	0.8	-	-	206.5	1.5	-	-	212.0	2.7	-	-	217.2	2.5	-	-	217.8	0.3	-	-	223.0	2.4	-	-
1995	223.0	0.0	-	-	224.4	0.6	-	-	226.4	0.9	-	-	225.3	-0.5	-	-	225.4	0.0	-	-	226.5	0.5	-	-
1996	229.0	1.1	-	-	230.5	0.7	-	-	231.6	0.5	-	-	233.6	0.9	-	-	235.3	0.7	-	-	235.5	0.1	-	-
1997	233.4	-0.9	-	-	234.2	0.3	-	-	231.1	-1.3	232.6	0.6	229.6	-1.3	-	-	229.0	-0.3	-	-	233.4	1.9	-	-

Source: U.S. Department of Labor, Bureau of Labor Statistics, Division of Consumer Prices and Price Indexes. - indicates no data collected for period.

Baltimore, MD
Consumer Price Index - All Urban Consumers
Base 1982-1984 = 100
Entertainment

For 1975-1997. Columns headed % show percentile change in the index from the previous period for which an index is available.

Year	Jan Index	%	Feb Index	%	Mar Index	%	Apr Index	%	May Index	%	Jun Index	%	Jul Index	%	Aug Index	%	Sep Index	%	Oct Index	%	Nov Index	%	Dec Index	%
1975	-	-	-	-	-	-	-	-	-	-	-	-	-	-	-	-	-	-	-	-	-	-	65.5	-
1976	-	-	-	-	65.7	0.3	-	-	-	-	66.8	1.7	-	-	-	-	67.6	1.2	-	-	-	-	68.0	0.6
1977	-	-	-	-	68.8	1.2	-	-	-	-	69.6	1.2	-	-	-	-	70.5	1.3	-	-	-	-	70.9	0.6
1978	-	-	-	-	71.5	0.8	-	-	72.6	1.5	-	-	72.5	-0.1	-	-	73.0	0.7	-	-	73.8	1.1	-	-
1979	74.5	0.9	-	-	76.5	2.7	-	-	77.0	0.7	-	-	75.9	-1.4	-	-	76.2	0.4	-	-	77.8	2.1	-	-
1980	81.4	4.6	-	-	82.2	1.0	-	-	82.4	0.2	-	-	83.5	1.3	-	-	85.1	1.9	-	-	84.7	-0.5	-	-
1981	87.7	3.5	-	-	89.4	1.9	-	-	89.8	0.4	-	-	89.9	0.1	-	-	90.5	0.7	-	-	91.8	1.4	-	-
1982	91.5	-0.3	-	-	94.3	3.1	-	-	91.8	-2.7	-	-	92.6	0.9	-	-	97.1	4.9	-	-	97.2	0.1	-	-
1983	98.5	1.3	-	-	101.8	3.4	-	-	102.2	0.4	-	-	101.1	-1.1	-	-	102.5	1.4	-	-	102.5	0.0	-	-
1984	99.2	-3.2	-	-	103.4	4.2	-	-	104.3	0.9	-	-	104.5	0.2	-	-	105.1	0.6	-	-	106.8	1.6	-	-
1985	106.1	-0.7	-	-	107.6	1.4	-	-	109.8	2.0	-	-	109.6	-0.2	-	-	110.8	1.1	-	-	110.4	-0.4	-	-
1986	111.9	1.4	-	-	112.4	0.4	-	-	114.1	1.5	-	-	113.1	-0.9	-	-	114.8	1.5	-	-	115.8	0.9	-	-
1987	117.1	1.1	-	-	118.4	1.1	-	-	118.9	0.4	-	-	118.8	-0.1	-	-	119.0	0.2	-	-	119.9	0.8	-	-
1988	121.7	1.5	-	-	120.0	-1.4	-	-	121.1	0.9	-	-	122.8	1.4	-	-	125.5	2.2	-	-	124.7	-0.6	-	-
1989	125.3	0.5	-	-	126.7	1.1	-	-	128.4	1.3	-	-	129.0	0.5	-	-	126.5	-1.9	-	-	133.1	5.2	-	-
1990	137.9	3.6	-	-	138.1	0.1	-	-	137.2	-0.7	-	-	137.6	0.3	-	-	138.0	0.3	-	-	140.5	1.8	-	-
1991	140.2	-0.2	-	-	142.3	1.5	-	-	142.6	0.2	-	-	142.3	-0.2	-	-	145.9	2.5	-	-	147.6	1.2	-	-
1992	147.7	0.1	-	-	148.6	0.6	-	-	149.4	0.5	-	-	150.3	0.6	-	-	150.4	0.1	-	-	148.3	-1.4	-	-
1993	152.1	2.6	-	-	152.5	0.3	-	-	151.9	-0.4	-	-	152.7	0.5	-	-	154.4	1.1	-	-	152.1	-1.5	-	-
1994	153.0	0.6	-	-	152.2	-0.5	-	-	153.0	0.5	-	-	154.7	1.1	-	-	158.1	2.2	-	-	156.1	-1.3	-	-
1995	158.6	1.6	-	-	157.4	-0.8	-	-	159.7	1.5	-	-	159.1	-0.4	-	-	163.6	2.8	-	-	163.7	0.1	-	-
1996	163.7	0.0	-	-	166.0	1.4	-	-	166.5	0.3	-	-	167.1	0.4	-	-	169.5	1.4	-	-	168.6	-0.5	-	-
1997	171.5	1.7	-	-	171.7	0.1	-	-	168.8	-1.7	170.6	1.1	170.6	0.0	-	-	169.2	-0.8	-	-	169.9	0.4	-	-

Source: U.S. Department of Labor, Bureau of Labor Statistics, Division of Consumer Prices and Price Indexes. - indicates no data collected for period.

Baltimore, MD
Consumer Price Index - Urban Wage Earners
Base 1982-1984 = 100
Entertainment

For 1975-1997. Columns headed % show percentile change in the index from the previous period for which an index is available.

Year	Jan Index	%	Feb Index	%	Mar Index	%	Apr Index	%	May Index	%	Jun Index	%	Jul Index	%	Aug Index	%	Sep Index	%	Oct Index	%	Nov Index	%	Dec Index	%
1975	-	-	-	-	-	-			-				-				-		-		-		65.1	-
1976	-	-	-	-	65.3	0.3			-		66.4	1.7	-				67.2	1.2	-		-		67.6	0.6
1977	-	-	-	-	68.4	1.2			-		69.2	1.2	-				70.1	1.3	-		-		70.4	0.4
1978	-	-	-	-	71.1	1.0			72.7	2.3	-		71.4	-1.8			72.8	2.0	-		72.5	-0.4	-	
1979	75.4	4.0	-	-	76.3	1.2			76.4	0.1	-		76.8	0.5			76.3	-0.7	-		77.6	1.7	-	
1980	79.8	2.8	-	-	81.9	2.6			83.0	1.3	-		83.4	0.5			85.0	1.9	-		84.4	-0.7	-	
1981	85.0	0.7	-	-	87.2	2.6			87.3	0.1	-		89.2	2.2			90.2	1.1	-		93.6	3.8	-	
1982	93.3	-0.3	-	-	96.3	3.2			93.6	-2.8	-		94.2	0.6			97.8	3.8	-		97.7	-0.1	-	
1983	98.6	0.9	-	-	101.8	3.2			102.5	0.7	-		100.7	-1.8			101.8	1.1	-		101.9	0.1	-	
1984	98.2	-3.6	-	-	102.5	4.4			103.0	0.5	-		103.1	0.1			104.2	1.1	-		106.1	1.8	-	
1985	105.6	-0.5	-	-	106.8	1.1			108.8	1.9	-		108.4	-0.4			109.5	1.0	-		109.0	-0.5	-	
1986	110.9	1.7	-	-	110.9	0.0			113.1	2.0	-		112.6	-0.4			113.4	0.7	-		114.6	1.1	-	
1987	115.5	0.8	-	-	117.0	1.3			118.1	0.9	-		118.2	0.1			118.6	0.3	-		119.6	0.8	-	
1988	121.3	1.4	-	-	120.4	-0.7			121.7	1.1	-		122.4	0.6			125.4	2.5	-		125.4	0.0	-	
1989	126.0	0.5	-	-	127.3	1.0			129.0	1.3	-		129.9	0.7			126.5	-2.6	-		133.8	5.8	-	
1990	138.1	3.2	-	-	138.6	0.4			137.6	-0.7	-		138.0	0.3			138.7	0.5	-		142.1	2.5	-	
1991	142.0	-0.1	-	-	144.1	1.5			144.6	0.3	-		144.7	0.1			147.8	2.1	-		150.3	1.7	-	
1992	150.1	-0.1	-	-	151.1	0.7			151.9	0.5	-		152.5	0.4			152.7	0.1	-		150.6	-1.4	-	
1993	153.9	2.2	-	-	154.6	0.5			154.1	-0.3	-		154.9	0.5			156.9	1.3	-		154.9	-1.3	-	
1994	156.0	0.7	-	-	155.6	-0.3			156.4	0.5	-		158.7	1.5			161.5	1.8	-		159.2	-1.4	-	
1995	161.8	1.6	-	-	160.6	-0.7			163.2	1.6	-		162.6	-0.4			167.5	3.0	-		167.5	0.0	-	
1996	167.7	0.1	-	-	169.9	1.3			170.7	0.5	-		171.5	0.5			174.1	1.5	-		173.2	-0.5	-	
1997	176.1	1.7	-	-	176.3	0.1			174.2	-1.2	175.5	0.7	176.0	0.3			173.8	-1.2	-		174.1	0.2	-	

Source: U.S. Department of Labor, Bureau of Labor Statistics, Division of Consumer Prices and Price Indexes. - indicates no data collected for period.

Baltimore, MD
Consumer Price Index - All Urban Consumers
Base 1982-1984 = 100
Other Goods and Services

For 1975-1997. Columns headed % show percentile change in the index from the previous period for which an index is available.

Year	Jan Index	%	Feb Index	%	Mar Index	%	Apr Index	%	May Index	%	Jun Index	%	Jul Index	%	Aug Index	%	Sep Index	%	Oct Index	%	Nov Index	%	Dec Index	%
1975	-	-	-	-	-	-	-	-	-	-	-	-	-	-	-	-	-	-	-	-	-	-	56.2	-
1976	-	-	-	-	56.7	0.9	-	-	-	-	57.0	0.5	-	-	-	-	57.4	0.7	-	-	-	-	58.7	2.3
1977	-	-	-	-	59.1	0.7	-	-	-	-	60.4	2.2	-	-	-	-	61.2	1.3	-	-	-	-	61.8	1.0
1978	-	-	-	-	62.2	0.6	-	-	62.8	1.0	-	-	65.0	3.5	-	-	66.2	1.8	-	-	67.2	1.5	-	-
1979	66.7	-0.7	-	-	69.2	3.7	-	-	69.3	0.1	-	-	68.9	-0.6	-	-	70.5	2.3	-	-	70.7	0.3	-	-
1980	72.1	2.0	-	-	73.2	1.5	-	-	75.0	2.5	-	-	75.6	0.8	-	-	78.2	3.4	-	-	78.5	0.4	-	-
1981	79.3	1.0	-	-	79.7	0.5	-	-	82.1	3.0	-	-	83.2	1.3	-	-	83.1	-0.1	-	-	85.9	3.4	-	-
1982	86.3	0.5	-	-	86.8	0.6	-	-	87.1	0.3	-	-	87.2	0.1	-	-	92.7	6.3	-	-	94.9	2.4	-	-
1983	96.8	2.0	-	-	98.5	1.8	-	-	99.4	0.9	-	-	101.9	2.5	-	-	102.7	0.8	-	-	105.6	2.8	-	-
1984	107.3	1.6	-	-	108.6	1.2	-	-	107.7	-0.8	-	-	107.7	0.0	-	-	110.6	2.7	-	-	112.0	1.3	-	-
1985	112.0	0.0	-	-	112.7	0.6	-	-	112.9	0.2	-	-	113.9	0.9	-	-	115.6	1.5	-	-	116.2	0.5	-	-
1986	117.0	0.7	-	-	118.2	1.0	-	-	119.8	1.4	-	-	120.6	0.7	-	-	121.7	0.9	-	-	122.8	0.9	-	-
1987	122.7	-0.1	-	-	122.5	-0.2	-	-	122.7	0.2	-	-	125.2	2.0	-	-	132.4	5.8	-	-	134.0	1.2	-	-
1988	134.4	0.3	-	-	136.0	1.2	-	-	136.0	0.0	-	-	137.3	1.0	-	-	142.7	3.9	-	-	144.2	1.1	-	-
1989	144.7	0.3	-	-	144.9	0.1	-	-	147.6	1.9	-	-	148.8	0.8	-	-	153.3	3.0	-	-	153.2	-0.1	-	-
1990	155.7	1.6	-	-	155.7	0.0	-	-	154.8	-0.6	-	-	158.7	2.5	-	-	161.8	2.0	-	-	161.8	0.0	-	-
1991	165.3	2.2	-	-	166.2	0.5	-	-	170.5	2.6	-	-	174.2	2.2	-	-	178.5	2.5	-	-	178.5	0.0	-	-
1992	178.9	0.2	-	-	179.0	0.1	-	-	187.5	4.7	-	-	187.8	0.2	-	-	195.0	3.8	-	-	196.3	0.7	-	-
1993	199.2	1.5	-	-	199.0	-0.1	-	-	199.9	0.5	-	-	201.6	0.9	-	-	194.2	-3.7	-	-	195.3	0.6	-	-
1994	196.9	0.8	-	-	197.2	0.2	-	-	198.2	0.5	-	-	199.0	0.4	-	-	202.7	1.9	-	-	202.7	0.0	-	-
1995	204.2	0.7	-	-	205.3	0.5	-	-	206.8	0.7	-	-	207.5	0.3	-	-	209.2	0.8	-	-	209.5	0.1	-	-
1996	210.1	0.3	-	-	210.6	0.2	-	-	212.1	0.7	-	-	213.7	0.8	-	-	217.1	1.6	-	-	217.2	0.0	-	-
1997	219.9	1.2	-	-	222.7	1.3	-	-	221.7	-0.4	221.7	0.0	222.9	0.5	-	-	228.1	2.3	-	-	228.3	0.1	-	-

Source: U.S. Department of Labor, Bureau of Labor Statistics, Division of Consumer Prices and Price Indexes. - indicates no data collected for period.

Baltimore, MD
Consumer Price Index - Urban Wage Earners
Base 1982-1984 = 100
Other Goods and Services

For 1975-1997. Columns headed % show percentile change in the index from the previous period for which an index is available.

Year	Jan Index	%	Feb Index	%	Mar Index	%	Apr Index	%	May Index	%	Jun Index	%	Jul Index	%	Aug Index	%	Sep Index	%	Oct Index	%	Nov Index	%	Dec Index	%
1975	-	-	-	-	-	-			-	-			-	-	-	-	-	-			-	-	57.7	-
1976	-	-	-	-	58.1	0.7			-	-	58.5	0.7	-	-			58.9	0.7			-	-	60.3	2.4
1977	-	-	-	-	60.6	0.5			-	-	61.9	2.1	-	-			62.8	1.5	-	-	-	-	63.4	1.0
1978	-	-	-	-	63.8	0.6	-	-	63.6	-0.3	-	-	65.6	3.1	-	-	66.5	1.4	-	-	67.4	1.4	-	-
1979	67.2	-0.3	-	-	69.2	3.0	-	-	69.1	-0.1	-	-	68.3	-1.2	-	-	69.9	2.3	-	-	70.4	0.7	-	-
1980	72.0	2.3	-	-	73.1	1.5	-	-	74.1	1.4	-	-	76.5	3.2	-	-	78.2	2.2	-	-	79.2	1.3	-	-
1981	79.0	-0.3	-	-	80.7	2.2	-	-	83.4	3.3	-	-	84.0	0.7	-	-	83.7	-0.4	-	-	85.1	1.7	-	-
1982	86.2	1.3	-	-	87.0	0.9	-	-	87.3	0.3	-	-	87.3	0.0	-	-	92.1	5.5	-	-	94.5	2.6	-	-
1983	97.0	2.6	-	-	98.5	1.5	-	-	99.4	0.9	-	-	102.0	2.6	-	-	102.7	0.7	-	-	105.6	2.8	-	-
1984	107.4	1.7	-	-	108.6	1.1	-	-	107.8	-0.7	-	-	108.0	0.2	-	-	110.6	2.4	-	-	111.7	1.0	-	-
1985	111.8	0.1	-	-	112.8	0.9	-	-	112.9	0.1	-	-	114.1	1.1	-	-	115.7	1.4	-	-	116.0	0.3	-	-
1986	117.1	0.9	-	-	118.2	0.9	-	-	119.6	1.2	-	-	120.7	0.9	-	-	121.5	0.7	-	-	122.4	0.7	-	-
1987	122.4	0.0	-	-	122.4	0.0	-	-	122.8	0.3	-	-	125.5	2.2	-	-	131.8	5.0	-	-	132.8	0.8	-	-
1988	133.5	0.5	-	-	135.2	1.3	-	-	135.2	0.0	-	-	137.0	1.3	-	-	142.2	3.8	-	-	143.1	0.6	-	-
1989	143.9	0.6	-	-	144.3	0.3	-	-	146.7	1.7	-	-	148.2	1.0	-	-	151.8	2.4	-	-	151.6	-0.1	-	-
1990	154.3	1.8	-	-	154.3	0.0	-	-	153.5	-0.5	-	-	157.7	2.7	-	-	160.5	1.8	-	-	160.5	0.0	-	-
1991	164.6	2.6	-	-	165.5	0.5	-	-	169.6	2.5	-	-	174.0	2.6	-	-	177.8	2.2	-	-	177.8	0.0	-	-
1992	178.9	0.6	-	-	179.0	0.1	-	-	189.8	6.0	-	-	190.2	0.2	-	-	196.9	3.5	-	-	197.7	0.4	-	-
1993	201.8	2.1	-	-	201.5	-0.1	-	-	202.6	0.5	-	-	203.9	0.6	-	-	193.5	-5.1	-	-	194.5	0.5	-	-
1994	196.6	1.1	-	-	197.1	0.3	-	-	198.4	0.7	-	-	199.1	0.4	-	-	202.1	1.5	-	-	202.0	-0.0	-	-
1995	204.1	1.0	-	-	204.7	0.3	-	-	206.7	1.0	-	-	207.3	0.3	-	-	208.7	0.7	-	-	209.0	0.1	-	-
1996	209.9	0.4	-	-	210.8	0.4	-	-	211.9	0.5	-	-	214.1	1.0	-	-	217.3	1.5	-	-	217.6	0.1	-	-
1997	220.5	1.3	-	-	224.2	1.7	-	-	222.9	-0.6	222.8	-0.0	224.1	0.6	-	-	228.9	2.1	-	-	229.1	0.1	-	-

Source: U.S. Department of Labor, Bureau of Labor Statistics, Division of Consumer Prices and Price Indexes. - indicates no data collected for period.

Boston, MA
Consumer Price Index - All Urban Consumers
Base 1982-1984 = 100
Annual Averages

For 1914-1997. Columns headed % show percentile change in the index from the previous period for which an index is available.

Year	All Items		Food & Beverage		Housing		Apparel & Upkeep		Trans- portation		Medical Care		Entertain- ment		Other Goods & Services	
	Index	%	Index	%	Index	%	Index	%	Index	%	Index	%	Index	%	Index	%
1914	-	-	-	-	-	-	-	-	-	-	-	-	-	-	-	-
1915	10.5	-	-	-	-	-	-	-	-	-	-	-	-	-	-	-
1916	11.3	7.6	-	-	-	-	-	-	-	-	-	-	-	-	-	-
1917	13.3	17.7	-	-	-	-	-	-	-	-	-	-	-	-	-	-
1918	15.7	18.0	-	-	-	-	-	-	-	-	-	-	-	-	-	-
1919	18.0	14.6	-	-	-	-	-	-	-	-	-	-	-	-	-	-
1920	20.6	14.4	-	-	-	-	-	-	-	-	-	-	-	-	-	-
1921	18.3	-11.2	-	-	-	-	-	-	-	-	-	-	-	-	-	-
1922	17.0	-7.1	-	-	-	-	-	-	-	-	-	-	-	-	-	-
1923	17.4	2.4	-	-	-	-	-	-	-	-	-	-	-	-	-	-
1924	17.4	0.0	-	-	-	-	-	-	-	-	-	-	-	-	-	-
1925	17.9	2.9	-	-	-	-	-	-	-	-	-	-	-	-	-	-
1926	18.2	1.7	-	-	-	-	-	-	-	-	-	-	-	-	-	-
1927	17.9	-1.6	-	-	-	-	-	-	-	-	-	-	-	-	-	-
1928	17.7	-1.1	-	-	-	-	-	-	-	-	-	-	-	-	-	-
1929	17.8	0.6	-	-	-	-	-	-	-	-	-	-	-	-	-	-
1930	17.3	-2.8	-	-	-	-	-	-	-	-	-	-	-	-	-	-
1931	15.8	-8.7	-	-	-	-	-	-	-	-	-	-	-	-	-	-
1932	14.2	-10.1	-	-	-	-	-	-	-	-	-	-	-	-	-	-
1933	13.6	-4.2	-	-	-	-	-	-	-	-	-	-	-	-	-	-
1934	14.1	3.7	-	-	-	-	-	-	-	-	-	-	-	-	-	-
1935	14.3	1.4	-	-	-	-	-	-	-	-	-	-	-	-	-	-
1936	14.3	0.0	-	-	-	-	-	-	-	-	-	-	-	-	-	-
1937	14.8	3.5	-	-	-	-	-	-	-	-	-	-	-	-	-	-
1938	14.3	-3.4	-	-	-	-	-	-	-	-	-	-	-	-	-	-
1939	14.1	-1.4	-	-	-	-	-	-	-	-	-	-	-	-	-	-
1940	14.3	1.4	-	-	-	-	-	-	-	-	-	-	-	-	-	-
1941	14.9	4.2	-	-	-	-	-	-	-	-	-	-	-	-	-	-
1942	16.5	10.7	-	-	-	-	-	-	-	-	-	-	-	-	-	-
1943	17.4	5.5	-	-	-	-	-	-	-	-	-	-	-	-	-	-
1944	17.6	1.1	-	-	-	-	-	-	-	-	-	-	-	-	-	-
1945	17.9	1.7	-	-	-	-	-	-	-	-	-	-	-	-	-	-
1946	19.4	8.4	-	-	-	-	-	-	-	-	-	-	-	-	-	-
1947	22.1	13.9	-	-	-	-	-	-	16.4	-	13.4	-	-	-	-	-
1948	23.9	8.1	-	-	-	-	-	-	16.9	3.0	14.3	6.7	-	-	-	-
1949	23.6	-1.3	-	-	-	-	-	-	18.6	10.1	15.1	5.6	-	-	-	-
1950	23.9	1.3	-	-	-	-	-	-	20.6	10.8	15.7	4.0	-	-	-	-
1951	25.5	6.7	-	-	-	-	-	-	21.2	2.9	16.3	3.8	-	-	-	-
1952	26.0	2.0	-	-	-	-	-	-	22.6	6.6	17.2	5.5	-	-	-	-
1953	26.1	0.4	-	-	-	-	39.4	-	23.5	4.0	17.6	2.3	-	-	-	-
1954	26.3	0.8	-	-	-	-	39.1	-0.8	23.6	0.4	17.7	0.6	-	-	-	-
1955	26.4	0.4	-	-	-	-	39.2	0.3	23.2	-1.7	17.9	1.1	-	-	-	-
1956	27.1	2.7	-	-	-	-	39.8	1.5	24.0	3.4	19.0	6.1	-	-	-	-
1957	28.1	3.7	-	-	-	-	40.5	1.8	25.0	4.2	20.8	9.5	-	-	-	-
1958	28.9	2.8	-	-	-	-	41.1	1.5	25.8	3.2	22.2	6.7	-	-	-	-

[Continued]

Boston, MA
Consumer Price Index - All Urban Consumers
Base 1982-1984 = 100
Annual Averages
[Continued]

For 1914-1997. Columns headed % show percentile change in the index from the previous period for which an index is available.

Year	All Items		Food & Beverage		Housing		Apparel & Upkeep		Trans-portation		Medical Care		Entertain-ment		Other Goods & Services	
	Index	%	Index	%	Index	%	Index	%	Index	%	Index	%	Index	%	Index	%
1959	29.1	0.7	-	-	-	-	40.8	-0.7	26.4	2.3	22.8	2.7	-	-	-	-
1960	29.8	2.4	-	-	-	-	42.0	2.9	25.8	-2.3	23.2	1.8	-	-	-	-
1961	30.2	1.3	-	-	-	-	42.4	1.0	26.2	1.6	23.9	3.0	-	-	-	-
1962	30.8	2.0	-	-	-	-	43.0	1.4	28.2	7.6	24.8	3.8	-	-	-	-
1963	31.4	1.9	-	-	-	-	43.3	0.7	28.3	0.4	25.3	2.0	-	-	-	-
1964	31.9	1.6	-	-	-	-	43.6	0.7	28.5	0.7	26.1	3.2	-	-	-	-
1965	32.5	1.9	-	-	-	-	43.9	0.7	29.2	2.5	27.1	3.8	-	-	-	-
1966	33.6	3.4	-	-	-	-	45.0	2.5	29.9	2.4	28.2	4.1	-	-	-	-
1967	34.4	2.4	-	-	-	-	46.5	3.3	30.6	2.3	30.1	6.7	-	-	-	-
1968	35.8	4.1	-	-	-	-	49.3	6.0	31.6	3.3	32.5	8.0	-	-	-	-
1969	37.8	5.6	-	-	-	-	52.1	5.7	33.5	6.0	35.1	8.0	-	-	-	-
1970	40.2	6.3	-	-	-	-	54.6	4.8	34.9	4.2	37.4	6.6	-	-	-	-
1971	42.2	5.0	-	-	-	-	56.6	3.7	36.6	4.9	39.2	4.8	-	-	-	-
1972	43.7	3.6	-	-	-	-	57.8	2.1	36.6	0.0	40.5	3.3	-	-	-	-
1973	46.3	5.9	-	-	-	-	59.8	3.5	37.6	2.7	41.8	3.2	-	-	-	-
1974	51.2	10.6	-	-	-	-	64.1	7.2	41.0	9.0	44.8	7.2	-	-	-	-
1975	55.8	9.0	-	-	-	-	68.3	6.6	47.0	14.6	50.1	11.8	-	-	-	-
1976	60.0	7.5	67.0	-	56.3	-	71.5	4.7	59.3	26.2	53.4	6.6	64.6	-	56.4	-
1977	63.1	5.2	69.7	4.0	59.5	5.7	73.2	2.4	63.4	6.9	57.8	8.2	66.2	2.5	59.4	5.3
1978	66.4	5.2	75.3	8.0	63.1	6.1	78.7	7.5	63.0	-0.6	62.0	7.3	69.2	4.5	62.5	5.2
1979	73.2	10.2	83.2	10.5	69.9	10.8	84.9	7.9	69.4	10.2	69.5	12.1	75.6	9.2	67.4	7.8
1980	82.6	12.8	89.1	7.1	80.5	15.2	89.5	5.4	82.7	19.2	76.9	10.6	83.3	10.2	73.6	9.2
1981	91.8	11.1	94.3	5.8	92.0	14.3	93.8	4.8	94.1	13.8	83.7	8.8	89.9	7.9	81.0	10.1
1982	95.5	4.0	96.6	2.4	94.6	2.8	97.4	3.8	98.3	4.5	92.6	10.6	96.3	7.1	90.5	11.7
1983	99.8	4.5	99.1	2.6	100.3	6.0	99.8	2.5	99.2	0.9	98.8	6.7	100.2	4.0	100.1	10.6
1984	104.7	4.9	104.2	5.1	105.0	4.7	102.7	2.9	102.5	3.3	108.6	9.9	103.5	3.3	109.4	9.3
1985	109.4	4.5	108.6	4.2	109.1	3.9	106.1	3.3	105.3	2.7	120.5	11.0	109.8	6.1	118.9	8.7
1986	112.2	2.6	113.7	4.7	111.6	2.3	108.3	2.1	101.6	-3.5	131.8	9.4	114.6	4.4	128.8	8.3
1987	117.1	4.4	119.4	5.0	116.8	4.7	115.8	6.9	103.3	1.7	139.2	5.6	119.4	4.2	136.0	5.6
1988	124.2	6.1	124.4	4.2	123.7	5.9	125.8	8.6	108.3	4.8	152.1	9.3	127.0	6.4	147.1	8.2
1989	131.3	5.7	132.2	6.3	131.3	6.1	125.1	-0.6	113.7	5.0	165.3	8.7	133.6	5.2	157.9	7.3
1990	138.9	5.8	138.6	4.8	137.0	4.3	138.2	10.5	119.7	5.3	181.6	9.9	144.2	7.9	173.4	9.8
1991	145.0	4.4	142.5	2.8	140.9	2.8	144.6	4.6	125.5	4.8	202.7	11.6	152.2	5.5	188.4	8.7
1992	148.6	2.5	143.3	0.6	143.5	1.8	145.1	0.3	129.1	2.9	224.2	10.6	155.0	1.8	197.9	5.0
1993	152.9	2.9	146.3	2.1	146.4	2.0	157.6	8.6	132.5	2.6	239.0	6.6	160.1	3.3	202.6	2.4
1994	154.9	1.3	150.0	2.5	147.9	1.0	146.8	-6.9	135.0	1.9	251.1	5.1	163.9	2.4	206.6	2.0
1995	158.6	2.4	153.6	2.4	151.6	2.5	143.7	-2.1	137.1	1.6	266.1	6.0	167.4	2.1	213.3	3.2
1996	163.3	3.0	157.7	2.7	157.2	3.7	142.9	-0.6	139.5	1.8	280.8	5.5	169.7	1.4	220.2	3.2
1997	-	-	-	-	-	-	-	-	-	-	-	-	-	-	-	-

Source: U.S. Department of Labor, Bureau of Labor Statistics, Division of Consumer Prices and Price Indexes. - indicates no data collected for period.

Boston, MA
Consumer Price Index - Urban Wage Earners
Base 1982-1984 = 100
Annual Averages

For 1914-1997. Columns headed % show percentile change in the index from the previous period for which an index is available.

Year	All Items		Food & Beverage		Housing		Apparel & Upkeep		Trans- portation		Medical Care		Entertain- ment		Other Goods & Services	
	Index	%	Index	%	Index	%	Index	%	Index	%	Index	%	Index	%	Index	%
1914	-	-	-	-	-	-	-	-	-	-	-	-	-	-	-	-
1915	10.5	-	-	-	-	-	-	-	-	-	-	-	-	-	-	-
1916	11.3	7.6	-	-	-	-	-	-	-	-	-	-	-	-	-	-
1917	13.4	18.6	-	-	-	-	-	-	-	-	-	-	-	-	-	-
1918	15.8	17.9	-	-	-	-	-	-	-	-	-	-	-	-	-	-
1919	18.1	14.6	-	-	-	-	-	-	-	-	-	-	-	-	-	-
1920	20.8	14.9	-	-	-	-	-	-	-	-	-	-	-	-	-	-
1921	18.4	-11.5	-	-	-	-	-	-	-	-	-	-	-	-	-	-
1922	17.1	-7.1	-	-	-	-	-	-	-	-	-	-	-	-	-	-
1923	17.5	2.3	-	-	-	-	-	-	-	-	-	-	-	-	-	-
1924	17.5	0.0	-	-	-	-	-	-	-	-	-	-	-	-	-	-
1925	18.0	2.9	-	-	-	-	-	-	-	-	-	-	-	-	-	-
1926	18.3	1.7	-	-	-	-	-	-	-	-	-	-	-	-	-	-
1927	18.0	-1.6	-	-	-	-	-	-	-	-	-	-	-	-	-	-
1928	17.8	-1.1	-	-	-	-	-	-	-	-	-	-	-	-	-	-
1929	17.9	0.6	-	-	-	-	-	-	-	-	-	-	-	-	-	-
1930	17.4	-2.8	-	-	-	-	-	-	-	-	-	-	-	-	-	-
1931	15.9	-8.6	-	-	-	-	-	-	-	-	-	-	-	-	-	-
1932	14.3	-10.1	-	-	-	-	-	-	-	-	-	-	-	-	-	-
1933	13.7	-4.2	-	-	-	-	-	-	-	-	-	-	-	-	-	-
1934	14.2	3.6	-	-	-	-	-	-	-	-	-	-	-	-	-	-
1935	14.4	1.4	-	-	-	-	-	-	-	-	-	-	-	-	-	-
1936	14.4	0.0	-	-	-	-	-	-	-	-	-	-	-	-	-	-
1937	14.8	2.8	-	-	-	-	-	-	-	-	-	-	-	-	-	-
1938	14.4	-2.7	-	-	-	-	-	-	-	-	-	-	-	-	-	-
1939	14.2	-1.4	-	-	-	-	-	-	-	-	-	-	-	-	-	-
1940	14.4	1.4	-	-	-	-	-	-	-	-	-	-	-	-	-	-
1941	15.0	4.2	-	-	-	-	-	-	-	-	-	-	-	-	-	-
1942	16.6	10.7	-	-	-	-	-	-	-	-	-	-	-	-	-	-
1943	17.5	5.4	-	-	-	-	-	-	-	-	-	-	-	-	-	-
1944	17.7	1.1	-	-	-	-	-	-	-	-	-	-	-	-	-	-
1945	18.0	1.7	-	-	-	-	-	-	-	-	-	-	-	-	-	-
1946	19.5	8.3	-	-	-	-	-	-	-	-	-	-	-	-	-	-
1947	22.2	13.8	-	-	-	-	-	-	16.4	-	13.6	-	-	-	-	-
1948	24.0	8.1	-	-	-	-	-	-	16.9	3.0	14.5	6.6	-	-	-	-
1949	23.7	-1.2	-	-	-	-	-	-	18.5	9.5	15.3	5.5	-	-	-	-
1950	24.0	1.3	-	-	-	-	-	-	20.5	10.8	16.0	4.6	-	-	-	-
1951	25.6	6.7	-	-	-	-	-	-	21.2	3.4	16.5	3.1	-	-	-	-
1952	26.2	2.3	-	-	-	-	-	-	22.6	6.6	17.4	5.5	-	-	-	-
1953	26.3	0.4	-	-	-	-	39.7	-	23.4	3.5	17.9	2.9	-	-	-	-
1954	26.4	0.4	-	-	-	-	39.4	-0.8	23.6	0.9	18.0	0.6	-	-	-	-
1955	26.5	0.4	-	-	-	-	39.5	0.3	23.1	-2.1	18.1	0.6	-	-	-	-
1956	27.3	3.0	-	-	-	-	40.1	1.5	24.0	3.9	19.3	6.6	-	-	-	-
1957	28.2	3.3	-	-	-	-	40.8	1.7	24.9	3.8	21.1	9.3	-	-	-	-
1958	29.1	3.2	-	-	-	-	41.4	1.5	25.7	3.2	22.6	7.1	-	-	-	-

[Continued]

308

Boston, MA
Consumer Price Index - Urban Wage Earners
Base 1982-1984 = 100
Annual Averages
[Continued]

For 1914-1997. Columns headed % show percentile change in the index from the previous period for which an index is available.

Year	All Items		Food & Beverage		Housing		Apparel & Upkeep		Trans-portation		Medical Care		Entertain-ment		Other Goods & Services	
	Index	%	Index	%	Index	%	Index	%	Index	%	Index	%	Index	%	Index	%
1959	29.3	0.7	-	-	-	-	41.1	-0.7	26.3	2.3	23.1	2.2	-	-	-	-
1960	29.9	2.0	-	-	-	-	42.4	3.2	25.7	-2.3	23.5	1.7	-	-	-	-
1961	30.3	1.3	-	-	-	-	42.7	0.7	26.2	1.9	24.3	3.4	-	-	-	-
1962	31.0	2.3	-	-	-	-	43.3	1.4	28.1	7.3	25.1	3.3	-	-	-	-
1963	31.6	1.9	-	-	-	-	43.7	0.9	28.2	0.4	25.7	2.4	-	-	-	-
1964	32.1	1.6	-	-	-	-	43.9	0.5	28.4	0.7	26.5	3.1	-	-	-	-
1965	32.7	1.9	-	-	-	-	44.3	0.9	29.1	2.5	27.5	3.8	-	-	-	-
1966	33.8	3.4	-	-	-	-	45.3	2.3	29.8	2.4	28.6	4.0	-	-	-	-
1967	34.6	2.4	-	-	-	-	46.8	3.3	30.6	2.7	30.5	6.6	-	-	-	-
1968	36.0	4.0	-	-	-	-	49.7	6.2	31.5	2.9	33.0	8.2	-	-	-	-
1969	38.1	5.8	-	-	-	-	52.5	5.6	33.4	6.0	35.6	7.9	-	-	-	-
1970	40.4	6.0	-	-	-	-	55.0	4.8	34.8	4.2	38.0	6.7	-	-	-	-
1971	42.5	5.2	-	-	-	-	57.1	3.8	36.5	4.9	39.8	4.7	-	-	-	-
1972	44.0	3.5	-	-	-	-	58.2	1.9	36.5	0.0	41.1	3.3	-	-	-	-
1973	46.6	5.9	-	-	-	-	60.2	3.4	37.5	2.7	42.4	3.2	-	-	-	-
1974	51.4	10.3	-	-	-	-	64.6	7.3	40.9	9.1	45.4	7.1	-	-	-	-
1975	56.1	9.1	-	-	-	-	68.8	6.5	46.9	14.7	50.8	11.9	-	-	-	-
1976	60.4	7.7	67.6	-	56.2	-	72.0	4.7	59.2	26.2	54.2	6.7	67.0	-	57.1	-
1977	63.5	5.1	70.3	4.0	59.4	5.7	73.7	2.4	63.2	6.8	58.7	8.3	68.5	2.2	60.2	5.4
1978	66.7	5.0	75.8	7.8	63.0	6.1	78.2	6.1	62.9	-0.5	62.8	7.0	70.7	3.2	63.3	5.1
1979	73.5	10.2	83.3	9.9	70.1	11.3	82.6	5.6	70.0	11.3	69.4	10.5	77.0	8.9	68.1	7.6
1980	83.0	12.9	89.6	7.6	81.3	16.0	86.8	5.1	83.4	19.1	76.4	10.1	83.4	8.3	73.7	8.2
1981	92.2	11.1	94.6	5.6	93.2	14.6	92.9	7.0	94.0	12.7	83.8	9.7	89.6	7.4	81.1	10.0
1982	95.9	4.0	96.5	2.0	95.4	2.4	98.0	5.5	98.4	4.7	92.3	10.1	96.2	7.4	90.3	11.3
1983	99.7	4.0	99.1	2.7	100.2	5.0	100.2	2.2	99.1	0.7	98.8	7.0	100.3	4.3	100.1	10.9
1984	104.3	4.6	104.4	5.3	104.2	4.0	101.8	1.6	102.5	3.4	108.9	10.2	103.6	3.3	109.6	9.5
1985	109.3	4.8	108.4	3.8	109.6	5.2	104.8	2.9	105.1	2.5	119.3	9.6	109.2	5.4	119.1	8.7
1986	111.8	2.3	113.1	4.3	111.9	2.1	107.0	2.1	101.1	-3.8	130.6	9.5	114.1	4.5	128.8	8.1
1987	117.1	4.7	118.9	5.1	116.8	4.4	121.3	13.4	103.7	2.6	138.8	6.3	117.8	3.2	136.0	5.6
1988	124.1	6.0	123.8	4.1	123.5	5.7	132.6	9.3	109.2	5.3	151.4	9.1	125.3	6.4	147.0	8.1
1989	131.5	6.0	131.5	6.2	131.0	6.1	134.0	1.1	115.6	5.9	163.9	8.3	133.0	6.1	158.6	7.9
1990	138.8	5.6	137.9	4.9	136.0	3.8	146.9	9.6	122.0	5.5	179.7	9.6	144.5	8.6	174.3	9.9
1991	144.6	4.2	141.6	2.7	139.6	2.6	153.1	4.2	128.3	5.2	199.7	11.1	152.8	5.7	189.6	8.8
1992	148.0	2.4	142.4	0.6	142.0	1.7	153.2	0.1	131.9	2.8	219.9	10.1	155.5	1.8	200.0	5.5
1993	152.1	2.8	145.4	2.1	144.9	2.0	165.9	8.3	134.9	2.3	234.6	6.7	161.2	3.7	203.8	1.9
1994	153.8	1.1	148.7	2.3	146.4	1.0	152.2	-8.3	137.7	2.1	245.7	4.7	165.1	2.4	204.9	0.5
1995	157.4	2.3	152.1	2.3	150.0	2.5	150.7	-1.0	140.1	1.7	259.9	5.8	169.9	2.9	211.1	3.0
1996	162.2	3.0	156.2	2.7	155.5	3.7	150.5	-0.1	143.0	2.1	273.9	5.4	171.7	1.1	218.4	3.5
1997	-	-	-	-	-	-	-	-	-	-	-	-	-	-	-	-

Source: U.S. Department of Labor, Bureau of Labor Statistics, Division of Consumer Prices and Price Indexes. - indicates no data collected for period.

Boston, MA
Consumer Price Index - All Urban Consumers
Base 1982-1984 = 100
All Items

For 1914-1997. Columns headed % show percentile change in the index from the previous period for which an index is available.

Year	Jan Index	%	Feb Index	%	Mar Index	%	Apr Index	%	May Index	%	Jun Index	%	Jul Index	%	Aug Index	%	Sep Index	%	Oct Index	%	Nov Index	%	Dec Index	%
1914	-	-	-	-	-	-	-	-	-	-	-	-	-	-	-	-	-	-	-	-	-	-	10.5	-
1915	-	-	-	-	-	-	-	-	-	-	-	-	-	-	-	-	-	-	-	-	-	-	10.7	1.9
1916	-	-	-	-	-	-	-	-	-	-	-	-	-	-	-	-	-	-	-	-	-	-	12.1	13.1
1917	-	-	-	-	-	-	-	-	-	-	-	-	-	-	-	-	-	-	-	-	-	-	14.2	17.4
1918	-	-	-	-	-	-	-	-	-	-	-	-	-	-	-	-	-	-	-	-	-	-	17.3	21.8
1919	-	-	-	-	-	-	-	-	-	-	17.4	0.6	-	-	-	-	-	-	-	-	-	-	19.5	12.1
1920	-	-	-	-	-	-	-	-	-	-	21.5	10.3	-	-	-	-	-	-	-	-	-	-	20.2	-6.0
1921	-	-	-	-	-	-	-	-	18.0	-10.9	-	-	-	-	-	-	18.0	0.0	-	-	-	-	17.8	-1.1
1922	-	-	-	-	16.9	-5.1	-	-	-	-	16.8	-0.6	-	-	-	-	16.9	0.6	-	-	-	-	17.3	2.4
1923	-	-	-	-	17.1	-1.2	-	-	-	-	17.1	0.0	-	-	-	-	17.6	2.9	-	-	-	-	17.8	1.1
1924	-	-	-	-	17.3	-2.8	-	-	-	-	17.2	-0.6	-	-	-	-	17.5	1.7	-	-	-	-	17.6	0.6
1925	-	-	-	-	-	-	-	-	-	-	17.5	-0.6	-	-	-	-	-	-	-	-	-	-	18.5	5.7
1926	-	-	-	-	-	-	-	-	-	-	18.1	-2.2	-	-	-	-	-	-	-	-	-	-	18.2	0.6
1927	-	-	-	-	-	-	-	-	-	-	18.0	-1.1	-	-	-	-	-	-	-	-	-	-	18.0	0.0
1928	-	-	-	-	-	-	-	-	-	-	17.5	-2.8	-	-	-	-	-	-	-	-	-	-	17.8	1.7
1929	-	-	-	-	-	-	-	-	-	-	17.5	-1.7	-	-	-	-	-	-	-	-	-	-	17.8	1.7
1930	-	-	-	-	-	-	-	-	-	-	17.4	-2.2	-	-	-	-	-	-	-	-	-	-	16.9	-2.9
1931	-	-	-	-	-	-	-	-	-	-	15.7	-7.1	-	-	-	-	-	-	-	-	-	-	15.3	-2.5
1932	-	-	-	-	-	-	-	-	-	-	14.1	-7.8	-	-	-	-	-	-	-	-	-	-	13.8	-2.1
1933	-	-	-	-	-	-	-	-	-	-	13.4	-2.9	-	-	-	-	-	-	-	-	-	-	13.9	3.7
1934	-	-	-	-	-	-	-	-	-	-	14.1	1.4	-	-	-	-	-	-	-	-	14.2	0.7	-	-
1935	-	-	-	-	14.5	2.1	-	-	-	-	-	-	14.2	-2.1	-	-	-	-	14.3	0.7	-	-	-	-
1936	14.4	0.7	-	-	-	-	14.3	-0.7	-	-	-	-	14.5	1.4	-	-	14.5	0.0	-	-	-	-	14.3	-1.4
1937	-	-	-	-	14.6	2.1	-	-	-	-	14.8	1.4	-	-	-	-	15.1	2.0	-	-	-	-	14.7	-2.6
1938	-	-	-	-	14.3	-2.7	-	-	-	-	14.3	0.0	-	-	-	-	14.3	0.0	-	-	-	-	14.2	-0.7
1939	-	-	-	-	14.1	-0.7	-	-	-	-	14.0	-0.7	-	-	-	-	14.3	2.1	-	-	-	-	14.1	-1.4
1940	-	-	-	-	14.3	1.4	-	-	-	-	14.4	0.7	-	-	-	-	14.3	-0.7	14.2	-0.7	14.2	0.0	14.3	0.7
1941	14.3	0.0	14.3	0.0	14.3	0.0	14.5	1.4	14.6	0.7	14.8	1.4	15.0	1.4	15.1	0.7	15.3	1.3	15.4	0.7	15.7	1.9	15.6	-0.6
1942	15.8	1.3	16.0	1.3	16.1	0.6	16.1	0.0	16.3	1.2	16.4	0.6	16.7	1.8	16.6	-0.6	16.8	1.2	17.0	1.2	17.1	0.6	17.1	0.0
1943	17.1	0.0	17.1	0.0	17.4	1.8	17.5	0.6	17.6	0.6	17.5	-0.6	17.3	-1.1	17.3	0.0	17.3	0.0	17.5	1.2	17.4	-0.6	17.4	0.0
1944	17.4	0.0	17.3	-0.6	17.3	0.0	17.5	1.2	17.5	0.0	17.5	0.0	17.6	0.6	17.7	0.6	17.8	0.6	17.6	-1.1	17.7	0.6	17.8	0.6
1945	17.8	0.0	17.8	0.0	17.7	-0.6	17.7	0.0	17.8	0.6	18.1	1.7	18.1	0.0	18.1	0.0	18.0	-0.6	17.9	-0.6	18.0	0.6	18.0	0.0
1946	18.1	0.6	18.0	-0.6	18.1	0.6	18.2	0.6	18.2	0.0	18.4	1.1	19.8	7.6	20.2	2.0	20.4	1.0	20.8	2.0	21.1	1.4	21.3	0.9
1947	21.4	0.5	21.3	-0.5	21.7	1.9	21.5	-0.9	21.4	-0.5	21.7	1.4	21.9	0.9	22.3	1.8	22.9	2.7	22.7	-0.9	22.8	0.4	23.2	1.8
1948	23.5	1.3	23.3	-0.9	23.2	-0.4	23.6	1.7	23.7	0.4	24.0	1.3	24.3	1.2	24.4	0.4	24.4	0.0	24.3	-0.4	24.1	-0.8	23.8	-1.2
1949	23.7	-0.4	23.3	-1.7	23.5	0.9	23.5	0.0	23.5	0.0	23.6	0.4	23.5	-0.4	23.7	0.9	23.9	0.8	23.7	-0.8	23.7	0.0	23.5	-0.8
1950	23.4	-0.4	23.3	-0.4	23.5	0.9	23.5	0.0	23.5	0.0	23.8	1.3	24.0	0.8	24.2	0.8	24.2	0.0	24.4	0.8	24.4	0.0	24.6	0.8
1951	25.0	1.6	25.3	1.2	25.3	0.0	25.3	0.0	25.4	0.4	25.4	0.0	25.5	0.4	25.5	0.0	25.6	0.4	25.8	0.8	25.9	0.4	26.0	0.4
1952	25.9	-0.4	25.8	-0.4	25.8	0.0	25.8	0.0	25.9	0.4	26.0	0.4	26.4	1.5	26.4	0.0	26.3	-0.4	26.3	0.0	26.1	-0.8	26.0	-0.4
1953	26.0	0.0	-	-	-	-	25.9	-0.4	-	-	-	-	26.2	1.2	-	-	-	-	26.3	0.8	-	-	-	-
1954	26.1	-1.1	-	-	-	-	26.1	0.0	-	-	-	-	26.4	1.1	-	-	-	-	26.3	-0.4	-	-	-	-
1955	26.2	-0.4	-	-	-	-	26.3	0.4	-	-	-	-	26.4	0.4	-	-	-	-	26.5	0.4	-	-	-	-
1956	26.6	0.4	-	-	-	-	26.7	0.4	-	-	-	-	27.3	2.2	-	-	-	-	27.7	1.5	-	-	-	-
1957	27.6	-0.4	-	-	-	-	27.9	1.1	-	-	-	-	28.3	1.4	-	-	-	-	28.3	0.0	-	-	-	-
1958	28.6	1.1	-	-	-	-	28.9	1.0	-	-	-	-	29.1	0.7	-	-	-	-	29.1	0.0	-	-	-	-

[Continued]

Boston, MA
Consumer Price Index - All Urban Consumers
Base 1982-1984 = 100
All Items
[Continued]

For 1914-1997. Columns headed % show percentile change in the index from the previous period for which an index is available.

Year	Jan Index	%	Feb Index	%	Mar Index	%	Apr Index	%	May Index	%	Jun Index	%	Jul Index	%	Aug Index	%	Sep Index	%	Oct Index	%	Nov Index	%	Dec Index	%
1959	29.1	0.0	-	-	-	-	29.0	-0.3	-	-	-	-	29.1	0.3	-	-	-	-	29.4	1.0	-	-	-	-
1960	29.3	-0.3	-	-	-	-	29.8	1.7	-	-	-	-	29.8	0.0	-	-	-	-	29.9	0.3	-	-	-	-
1961	30.0	0.3	-	-	-	-	30.1	0.3	-	-	-	-	30.2	0.3	-	-	-	-	30.3	0.3	-	-	-	-
1962	30.5	0.7	-	-	-	-	30.8	1.0	-	-	-	-	30.8	0.0	-	-	-	-	31.1	1.0	-	-	-	-
1963	31.2	0.3	-	-	-	-	31.4	0.6	-	-	-	-	31.5	0.3	-	-	-	-	31.6	0.3	-	-	-	-
1964	31.6	0.0	-	-	-	-	31.8	0.6	-	-	-	-	31.9	0.3	-	-	-	-	32.1	0.6	-	-	-	-
1965	32.2	0.3	-	-	-	-	32.4	0.6	-	-	-	-	32.6	0.6	-	-	-	-	32.6	0.0	-	-	-	-
1966	32.7	0.3	-	-	-	-	33.5	2.4	-	-	-	-	33.6	0.3	-	-	-	-	34.0	1.2	-	-	-	-
1967	34.1	0.3	-	-	-	-	34.1	0.0	-	-	-	-	34.4	0.9	-	-	-	-	34.7	0.9	-	-	-	-
1968	35.0	0.9	-	-	-	-	35.5	1.4	-	-	-	-	35.8	0.8	-	-	-	-	36.4	1.7	-	-	-	-
1969	36.7	0.8	-	-	-	-	37.3	1.6	-	-	-	-	37.9	1.6	-	-	-	-	38.7	2.1	-	-	-	-
1970	39.1	1.0	-	-	-	-	39.6	1.3	-	-	-	-	40.0	1.0	-	-	-	-	41.1	2.8	-	-	-	-
1971	41.5	1.0	-	-	-	-	41.8	0.7	-	-	-	-	42.2	1.0	-	-	-	-	42.8	1.4	-	-	-	-
1972	42.9	0.2	-	-	-	-	43.4	1.2	-	-	-	-	43.7	0.7	-	-	-	-	44.3	1.4	-	-	-	-
1973	44.6	0.7	-	-	-	-	45.6	2.2	-	-	-	-	46.1	1.1	-	-	-	-	47.7	3.5	-	-	-	-
1974	48.9	2.5	-	-	-	-	50.0	2.2	-	-	-	-	51.5	3.0	-	-	-	-	52.6	2.1	-	-	-	-
1975	53.8	2.3	-	-	-	-	54.7	1.7	-	-	-	-	56.1	2.6	-	-	-	-	56.7	1.1	-	-	-	-
1976	59.1	4.2	-	-	-	-	59.3	0.3	-	-	-	-	60.3	1.7	-	-	-	-	60.6	0.5	-	-	-	-
1977	61.6	1.7	-	-	-	-	62.5	1.5	-	-	-	-	63.5	1.6	-	-	-	-	63.9	0.6	-	-	-	-
1978	64.5	0.9	-	-	64.8	0.5	-	-	65.6	1.2	-	-	66.4	1.2	-	-	67.4	1.5	-	-	68.7	1.9	-	-
1979	69.4	1.0	-	-	70.6	1.7	-	-	72.1	2.1	-	-	73.7	2.2	-	-	75.0	1.8	-	-	76.6	2.1	-	-
1980	78.2	2.1	-	-	80.6	3.1	-	-	81.5	1.1	-	-	82.9	1.7	-	-	84.1	1.4	-	-	85.6	1.8	-	-
1981	88.2	3.0	-	-	90.2	2.3	-	-	90.7	0.6	-	-	91.6	1.0	-	-	93.9	2.5	-	-	94.3	0.4	-	-
1982	94.3	0.0	-	-	92.8	-1.6	-	-	93.8	1.1	-	-	96.1	2.5	-	-	97.3	1.2	-	-	98.1	0.8	-	-
1983	98.7	0.6	-	-	98.6	-0.1	-	-	99.1	0.5	-	-	99.7	0.6	-	-	100.2	0.5	-	-	101.4	1.2	-	-
1984	102.3	0.9	-	-	103.9	1.6	-	-	104.3	0.4	-	-	104.9	0.6	-	-	105.8	0.9	-	-	105.9	0.1	-	-
1985	106.5	0.6	-	-	108.2	1.6	-	-	108.4	0.2	-	-	109.3	0.8	-	-	110.5	1.1	-	-	112.0	1.4	-	-
1986	112.5	0.4	-	-	111.8	-0.6	-	-	111.0	-0.7	-	-	111.3	0.3	-	-	112.9	1.4	-	-	113.3	0.4	-	-
1987	114.6	1.1	-	-	115.9	1.1	-	-	115.3	-0.5	-	-	116.3	0.9	-	-	119.5	2.8	-	-	119.9	0.3	-	-
1988	120.1	0.2	-	-	122.1	1.7	-	-	123.1	0.8	-	-	123.8	0.6	-	-	126.2	1.9	-	-	127.4	1.0	-	-
1989	129.0	1.3	-	-	129.7	0.5	-	-	130.5	0.6	-	-	130.3	-0.2	-	-	132.2	1.5	-	-	134.3	1.6	-	-
1990	136.0	1.3	-	-	136.3	0.2	-	-	136.6	0.2	-	-	137.6	0.7	-	-	141.3	2.7	-	-	143.7	1.7	-	-
1991	143.8	0.1	-	-	143.9	0.1	-	-	143.5	-0.3	-	-	145.1	1.1	-	-	146.3	0.8	-	-	146.6	0.2	-	-
1992	146.3	-0.2	-	-	147.9	1.1	-	-	147.5	-0.3	-	-	148.9	0.9	-	-	149.4	0.3	-	-	150.4	0.7	-	-
1993	151.9	1.0	-	-	154.1	1.4	-	-	151.9	-1.4	-	-	152.5	0.4	-	-	152.0	-0.3	-	-	154.5	1.6	-	-
1994	153.6	-0.6	-	-	155.0	0.9	-	-	153.6	-0.9	-	-	153.9	0.2	-	-	155.7	1.2	-	-	156.7	0.6	-	-
1995	158.0	0.8	-	-	158.4	0.3	-	-	157.7	-0.4	-	-	157.8	0.1	-	-	158.6	0.5	-	-	160.3	1.1	-	-
1996	162.2	1.2	-	-	162.8	0.4	-	-	161.8	-0.6	-	-	162.0	0.1	-	-	163.5	0.9	-	-	166.3	1.7	-	-
1997	167.7	0.8	-	-	168.1	0.2	-	-	166.7	-0.8	167.5	0.5	167.1	-0.2	-	-	167.8	0.4	-	-	169.4	1.0	-	-

Source: U.S. Department of Labor, Bureau of Labor Statistics, Division of Consumer Prices and Price Indexes. - indicates no data collected for period.

Boston, MA
Consumer Price Index - Urban Wage Earners
Base 1982-1984 = 100
All Items

For 1914-1997. Columns headed % show percentile change in the index from the previous period for which an index is available.

Year	Jan Index	%	Feb Index	%	Mar Index	%	Apr Index	%	May Index	%	Jun Index	%	Jul Index	%	Aug Index	%	Sep Index	%	Oct Index	%	Nov Index	%	Dec Index	%
1914	-	-	-	-	-	-	-	-	-	-	-	-	-	-	-	-	-	-	-	-	-	-	10.6	-
1915	-	-	-	-	-	-	-	-	-	-	-	-	-	-	-	-	-	-	-	-	-	-	10.7	0.9
1916	-	-	-	-	-	-	-	-	-	-	-	-	-	-	-	-	-	-	-	-	-	-	12.1	13.1
1917	-	-	-	-	-	-	-	-	-	-	-	-	-	-	-	-	-	-	-	-	-	-	14.3	18.2
1918	-	-	-	-	-	-	-	-	-	-	-	-	-	-	-	-	-	-	-	-	-	-	17.4	21.7
1919	-	-	-	-	-	-	-	-	-	-	17.5	0.6	-	-	-	-	-	-	-	-	-	-	19.6	12.0
1920	-	-	-	-	-	-	-	-	-	-	21.6	10.2	-	-	-	-	-	-	-	-	-	-	20.3	-6.0
1921	-	-	-	-	-	-	-	-	18.1	-10.8	-	-	-	-	-	-	18.1	0.0	-	-	-	-	17.9	-1.1
1922	-	-	-	-	17.0	-5.0	-	-	-	-	16.8	-1.2	-	-	-	-	17.0	1.2	-	-	-	-	17.4	2.4
1923	-	-	-	-	17.2	-1.1	-	-	-	-	17.2	0.0	-	-	-	-	17.7	2.9	-	-	-	-	17.9	1.1
1924	-	-	-	-	17.4	-2.8	-	-	-	-	17.3	-0.6	-	-	-	-	17.6	1.7	-	-	-	-	17.7	0.6
1925	-	-	-	-	-	-	-	-	-	-	17.6	-0.6	-	-	-	-	-	-	-	-	-	-	18.6	5.7
1926	-	-	-	-	-	-	-	-	-	-	18.2	-2.2	-	-	-	-	-	-	-	-	-	-	18.3	0.5
1927	-	-	-	-	-	-	-	-	-	-	18.1	-1.1	-	-	-	-	-	-	-	-	-	-	18.1	0.0
1928	-	-	-	-	-	-	-	-	-	-	17.6	-2.8	-	-	-	-	-	-	-	-	-	-	17.9	1.7
1929	-	-	-	-	-	-	-	-	-	-	17.6	-1.7	-	-	-	-	-	-	-	-	-	-	17.9	1.7
1930	-	-	-	-	-	-	-	-	-	-	17.5	-2.2	-	-	-	-	-	-	-	-	-	-	17.0	-2.9
1931	-	-	-	-	-	-	-	-	-	-	15.8	-7.1	-	-	-	-	-	-	-	-	-	-	15.4	-2.5
1932	-	-	-	-	-	-	-	-	-	-	14.2	-7.8	-	-	-	-	-	-	-	-	-	-	13.9	-2.1
1933	-	-	-	-	-	-	-	-	-	-	13.5	-2.9	-	-	-	-	-	-	-	-	-	-	13.9	3.0
1934	-	-	-	-	-	-	-	-	-	-	14.2	2.2	-	-	-	-	-	-	-	-	14.3	0.7	-	-
1935	-	-	-	-	14.5	1.4	-	-	-	-	-	-	14.3	-1.4	-	-	-	-	14.4	0.7	-	-	-	-
1936	14.5	0.7	-	-	-	-	14.4	-0.7	-	-	-	-	14.6	1.4	-	-	14.5	-0.7	-	-	-	-	14.4	-0.7
1937	-	-	-	-	14.7	2.1	-	-	-	-	14.8	0.7	-	-	-	-	15.2	2.7	-	-	-	-	14.8	-2.6
1938	-	-	-	-	14.4	-2.7	-	-	-	-	14.4	0.0	-	-	-	-	14.4	0.0	-	-	-	-	14.3	-0.7
1939	-	-	-	-	14.2	-0.7	-	-	-	-	14.1	-0.7	-	-	-	-	14.4	2.1	-	-	-	-	14.2	-1.4
1940	-	-	-	-	14.4	1.4	-	-	-	-	14.5	0.7	-	-	-	-	14.4	-0.7	14.3	-0.7	14.3	0.0	14.4	0.7
1941	14.4	0.0	14.4	0.0	14.4	0.0	14.6	1.4	14.7	0.7	14.8	0.7	15.1	2.0	15.2	0.7	15.4	1.3	15.5	0.6	15.7	1.3	15.6	-0.6
1942	15.8	1.3	16.1	1.9	16.2	0.6	16.2	0.0	16.4	1.2	16.5	0.6	16.7	1.2	16.7	0.0	16.8	0.6	17.1	1.8	17.2	0.6	17.2	0.0
1943	17.2	0.0	17.2	0.0	17.5	1.7	17.6	0.6	17.7	0.6	17.6	-0.6	17.4	-1.1	17.4	0.0	17.4	0.0	17.6	1.1	17.5	-0.6	17.5	0.0
1944	17.5	0.0	17.4	-0.6	17.4	0.0	17.6	1.1	17.6	0.0	17.6	0.0	17.7	0.6	17.8	0.6	17.9	0.6	17.7	-1.1	17.8	0.6	17.9	0.6
1945	17.9	0.0	17.9	0.0	17.8	-0.6	17.8	0.0	17.9	0.6	18.2	1.7	18.2	0.0	18.2	0.0	18.1	-0.5	18.0	-0.6	18.1	0.6	18.1	0.0
1946	18.2	0.6	18.1	-0.5	18.2	0.6	18.3	0.5	18.3	0.0	18.5	1.1	19.9	7.6	20.3	2.0	20.5	1.0	21.0	2.4	21.2	1.0	21.5	1.4
1947	21.6	0.5	21.4	-0.9	21.8	1.9	21.7	-0.5	21.6	-0.5	21.8	0.9	22.0	0.9	22.4	1.8	23.0	2.7	22.8	-0.9	23.0	0.9	23.3	1.3
1948	23.7	1.7	23.4	-1.3	23.4	0.0	23.7	1.3	23.8	0.4	24.1	1.3	24.5	1.7	24.5	0.0	24.6	0.4	24.4	-0.8	24.2	-0.8	23.9	-1.2
1949	23.8	-0.4	23.5	-1.3	23.6	0.4	23.6	0.0	23.6	0.0	23.7	0.4	23.7	0.0	23.8	0.4	24.0	0.8	23.8	-0.8	23.8	0.0	23.7	-0.4
1950	23.5	-0.8	23.5	0.0	23.6	0.4	23.6	0.0	23.7	0.4	24.0	1.3	24.2	0.8	24.4	0.8	24.4	0.0	24.6	0.8	24.6	0.0	24.8	0.8
1951	25.1	1.2	25.4	1.2	25.4	0.0	25.4	0.0	25.5	0.4	25.6	0.4	25.6	0.0	25.7	0.4	25.7	0.0	25.9	0.8	26.1	0.8	26.2	0.4
1952	26.1	-0.4	25.9	-0.8	25.9	0.0	25.9	0.0	26.1	0.8	26.1	0.0	26.5	1.5	26.5	0.0	26.4	-0.4	26.4	0.0	26.3	-0.4	26.2	-0.4
1953	26.1	-0.4	-	-	-	-	26.1	0.0	-	-	-	-	26.4	1.1	-	-	-	-	26.5	0.4	-	-	-	-
1954	26.3	-0.8	-	-	-	-	26.3	0.0	-	-	-	-	26.5	0.8	-	-	-	-	26.5	0.0	-	-	-	-
1955	26.3	-0.8	-	-	-	-	26.4	0.4	-	-	-	-	26.5	0.4	-	-	-	-	26.7	0.8	-	-	-	-
1956	26.7	0.0	-	-	-	-	26.8	0.4	-	-	-	-	27.5	2.6	-	-	-	-	27.8	1.1	-	-	-	-
1957	27.7	-0.4	-	-	-	-	28.0	1.1	-	-	-	-	28.4	1.4	-	-	-	-	28.4	0.0	-	-	-	-
1958	28.8	1.4	-	-	-	-	29.0	0.7	-	-	-	-	29.2	0.7	-	-	-	-	29.2	0.0	-	-	-	-

[Continued]

Boston, MA
Consumer Price Index - Urban Wage Earners
Base 1982-1984 = 100
All Items
[Continued]

For 1914-1997. Columns headed % show percentile change in the index from the previous period for which an index is available.

Year	Jan Index	%	Feb Index	%	Mar Index	%	Apr Index	%	May Index	%	Jun Index	%	Jul Index	%	Aug Index	%	Sep Index	%	Oct Index	%	Nov Index	%	Dec Index	%
1959	29.2	0.0	-	-	-	-	29.2	0.0	-	-	-	-	29.3	0.3	-	-	-	-	29.5	0.7	-	-	-	-
1960	29.4	-0.3	-	-	-	-	29.9	1.7	-	-	-	-	30.0	0.3	-	-	-	-	30.1	0.3	-	-	-	-
1961	30.1	0.0	-	-	-	-	30.3	0.7	-	-	-	-	30.4	0.3	-	-	-	-	30.4	0.0	-	-	-	-
1962	30.7	1.0	-	-	-	-	30.9	0.7	-	-	-	-	31.0	0.3	-	-	-	-	31.2	0.6	-	-	-	-
1963	31.4	0.6	-	-	-	-	31.6	0.6	-	-	-	-	31.7	0.3	-	-	-	-	31.8	0.3	-	-	-	-
1964	31.8	0.0	-	-	-	-	31.9	0.3	-	-	-	-	32.1	0.6	-	-	-	-	32.2	0.3	-	-	-	-
1965	32.4	0.6	-	-	-	-	32.6	0.6	-	-	-	-	32.8	0.6	-	-	-	-	32.8	0.0	-	-	-	-
1966	32.9	0.3	-	-	-	-	33.7	2.4	-	-	-	-	33.8	0.3	-	-	-	-	34.2	1.2	-	-	-	-
1967	34.3	0.3	-	-	-	-	34.3	0.0	-	-	-	-	34.6	0.9	-	-	-	-	34.9	0.9	-	-	-	-
1968	35.2	0.9	-	-	-	-	35.7	1.4	-	-	-	-	36.0	0.8	-	-	-	-	36.6	1.7	-	-	-	-
1969	37.0	1.1	-	-	-	-	37.5	1.4	-	-	-	-	38.2	1.9	-	-	-	-	38.9	1.8	-	-	-	-
1970	39.3	1.0	-	-	-	-	39.8	1.3	-	-	-	-	40.3	1.3	-	-	-	-	41.3	2.5	-	-	-	-
1971	41.8	1.2	-	-	-	-	42.1	0.7	-	-	-	-	42.5	1.0	-	-	-	-	43.0	1.2	-	-	-	-
1972	43.2	0.5	-	-	-	-	43.7	1.2	-	-	-	-	43.9	0.5	-	-	-	-	44.6	1.6	-	-	-	-
1973	44.9	0.7	-	-	-	-	45.8	2.0	-	-	-	-	46.4	1.3	-	-	-	-	48.0	3.4	-	-	-	-
1974	49.1	2.3	-	-	-	-	50.2	2.2	-	-	-	-	51.8	3.2	-	-	-	-	52.9	2.1	-	-	-	-
1975	54.1	2.3	-	-	-	-	55.0	1.7	-	-	-	-	56.4	2.5	-	-	-	-	57.0	1.1	-	-	-	-
1976	59.5	4.4	-	-	-	-	59.7	0.3	-	-	-	-	60.6	1.5	-	-	-	-	60.9	0.5	-	-	-	-
1977	61.9	1.6	-	-	-	-	62.8	1.5	-	-	-	-	63.8	1.6	-	-	-	-	64.2	0.6	-	-	-	-
1978	64.9	1.1	-	-	65.0	0.2	-	-	65.8	1.2	-	-	66.7	1.4	-	-	67.6	1.3	-	-	68.9	1.9	-	-
1979	69.4	0.7	-	-	70.7	1.9	-	-	72.2	2.1	-	-	73.9	2.4	-	-	75.4	2.0	-	-	77.0	2.1	-	-
1980	78.5	1.9	-	-	81.0	3.2	-	-	81.9	1.1	-	-	83.3	1.7	-	-	84.6	1.6	-	-	86.2	1.9	-	-
1981	88.5	2.7	-	-	90.6	2.4	-	-	91.2	0.7	-	-	92.2	1.1	-	-	94.7	2.7	-	-	94.9	0.2	-	-
1982	94.6	-0.3	-	-	93.3	-1.4	-	-	94.1	0.9	-	-	96.4	2.4	-	-	97.8	1.5	-	-	98.4	0.6	-	-
1983	98.4	0.0	-	-	98.6	0.2	-	-	98.9	0.3	-	-	99.9	1.0	-	-	100.1	0.2	-	-	101.4	1.3	-	-
1984	102.1	0.7	-	-	103.2	1.1	-	-	104.1	0.9	-	-	104.1	0.0	-	-	105.6	1.4	-	-	106.0	0.4	-	-
1985	106.5	0.5	-	-	108.0	1.4	-	-	108.4	0.4	-	-	109.2	0.7	-	-	110.5	1.2	-	-	111.8	1.2	-	-
1986	112.3	0.4	-	-	111.5	-0.7	-	-	110.5	-0.9	-	-	111.0	0.5	-	-	112.5	1.4	-	-	112.8	0.3	-	-
1987	114.5	1.5	-	-	115.8	1.1	-	-	115.2	-0.5	-	-	116.4	1.0	-	-	119.5	2.7	-	-	119.9	0.3	-	-
1988	120.2	0.3	-	-	121.8	1.3	-	-	123.1	1.1	-	-	123.7	0.5	-	-	126.1	1.9	-	-	127.4	1.0	-	-
1989	128.9	1.2	-	-	129.7	0.6	-	-	130.6	0.7	-	-	130.8	0.2	-	-	132.6	1.4	-	-	134.7	1.6	-	-
1990	136.0	1.0	-	-	136.5	0.4	-	-	136.8	0.2	-	-	137.4	0.4	-	-	140.9	2.5	-	-	143.5	1.8	-	-
1991	143.3	-0.1	-	-	143.3	0.0	-	-	143.4	0.1	-	-	144.7	0.9	-	-	145.8	0.8	-	-	146.2	0.3	-	-
1992	146.1	-0.1	-	-	147.2	0.8	-	-	146.8	-0.3	-	-	148.2	1.0	-	-	148.7	0.3	-	-	150.0	0.9	-	-
1993	151.1	0.7	-	-	154.0	1.9	-	-	151.4	-1.7	-	-	151.6	0.1	-	-	151.0	-0.4	-	-	153.4	1.6	-	-
1994	152.5	-0.6	-	-	153.5	0.7	-	-	152.2	-0.8	-	-	152.9	0.5	-	-	154.7	1.2	-	-	155.8	0.7	-	-
1995	157.0	0.8	-	-	156.9	-0.1	-	-	156.5	-0.3	-	-	156.6	0.1	-	-	157.4	0.5	-	-	159.3	1.2	-	-
1996	161.1	1.1	-	-	161.7	0.4	-	-	160.8	-0.6	-	-	160.9	0.1	-	-	162.1	0.7	-	-	165.4	2.0	-	-
1997	166.6	0.7	-	-	166.8	0.1	-	-	165.6	-0.7	166.3	0.4	165.8	-0.3	-	-	166.2	0.2	-	-	167.8	1.0	-	-

Source: U.S. Department of Labor, Bureau of Labor Statistics, Division of Consumer Prices and Price Indexes. - indicates no data collected for period.

Boston, MA
Consumer Price Index - All Urban Consumers
Base 1982-1984 = 100
Food and Beverages

For 1976-1997. Columns headed % show percentile change in the index from the previous period for which an index is available.

Year	Jan Index	%	Feb Index	%	Mar Index	%	Apr Index	%	May Index	%	Jun Index	%	Jul Index	%	Aug Index	%	Sep Index	%	Oct Index	%	Nov Index	%	Dec Index	%
1976	66.9	-	-	-	-	-	66.6	-0.4	-	-	-	-	67.6	1.5	-	-	-	-	67.0	-0.9	-	-	-	-
1977	66.8	-0.3	-	-	-	-	69.0	3.3	-	-	-	-	70.8	2.6	-	-	-	-	70.6	-0.3	-	-	-	-
1978	71.5	1.3	-	-	72.7	1.7	-	-	74.6	2.6	-	-	76.5	2.5	-	-	77.1	0.8	-	-	77.4	0.4	-	-
1979	78.7	1.7	-	-	81.0	2.9	-	-	83.7	3.3	-	-	85.7	2.4	-	-	84.1	-1.9	-	-	84.1	0.0	-	-
1980	86.2	2.5	-	-	87.4	1.4	-	-	87.6	0.2	-	-	89.6	2.3	-	-	90.2	0.7	-	-	91.6	1.6	-	-
1981	94.4	3.1	-	-	94.6	0.2	-	-	94.2	-0.4	-	-	94.4	0.2	-	-	93.8	-0.6	-	-	94.1	0.3	-	-
1982	95.9	1.9	-	-	95.9	0.0	-	-	96.5	0.6	-	-	97.2	0.7	-	-	97.1	-0.1	-	-	96.8	-0.3	-	-
1983	97.4	0.6	-	-	99.1	1.7	-	-	98.6	-0.5	-	-	99.5	0.9	-	-	99.2	-0.3	-	-	100.0	0.8	-	-
1984	102.2	2.2	-	-	103.8	1.6	-	-	104.0	0.2	-	-	104.4	0.4	-	-	105.0	0.6	-	-	104.9	-0.1	-	-
1985	106.6	1.6	-	-	107.7	1.0	-	-	107.8	0.1	-	-	109.2	1.3	-	-	109.0	-0.2	-	-	110.1	1.0	-	-
1986	111.9	1.6	-	-	110.8	-1.0	-	-	112.2	1.3	-	-	114.1	1.7	-	-	116.2	1.8	-	-	115.4	-0.7	-	-
1987	119.3	3.4	-	-	118.4	-0.8	-	-	119.0	0.5	-	-	119.4	0.3	-	-	120.2	0.7	-	-	119.7	-0.4	-	-
1988	122.0	1.9	-	-	120.8	-1.0	-	-	123.5	2.2	-	-	124.8	1.1	-	-	127.3	2.0	-	-	126.4	-0.7	-	-
1989	128.1	1.3	-	-	130.2	1.6	-	-	131.5	1.0	-	-	133.5	1.5	-	-	133.8	0.2	-	-	133.9	0.1	-	-
1990	137.1	2.4	-	-	138.3	0.9	-	-	138.0	-0.2	-	-	138.3	0.2	-	-	139.4	0.8	-	-	139.5	0.1	-	-
1991	142.2	1.9	-	-	141.3	-0.6	-	-	143.2	1.3	-	-	143.0	-0.1	-	-	141.9	-0.8	-	-	142.9	0.7	-	-
1992	143.5	0.4	-	-	143.7	0.1	-	-	142.4	-0.9	-	-	143.1	0.5	-	-	143.3	0.1	-	-	143.5	0.1	-	-
1993	145.4	1.3	-	-	145.2	-0.1	-	-	146.3	0.8	-	-	146.7	0.3	-	-	146.6	-0.1	-	-	146.9	0.2	-	-
1994	148.0	0.7	-	-	149.4	0.9	-	-	148.6	-0.5	-	-	149.8	0.8	-	-	151.4	1.1	-	-	150.8	-0.4	-	-
1995	155.0	2.8	-	-	153.1	-1.2	-	-	154.0	0.6	-	-	152.5	-1.0	-	-	153.4	0.6	-	-	153.7	0.2	-	-
1996	156.0	1.5	-	-	157.6	1.0	-	-	156.9	-0.4	-	-	157.4	0.3	-	-	158.4	0.6	-	-	159.1	0.4	-	-
1997	159.2	0.1	-	-	160.1	0.6	-	-	159.6	-0.3	159.7	0.1	160.3	0.4	-	-	160.8	0.3	-	-	161.2	0.2	-	-

Source: U.S. Department of Labor, Bureau of Labor Statistics, Division of Consumer Prices and Price Indexes. - indicates no data collected for period.

Boston, MA
Consumer Price Index - Urban Wage Earners
Base 1982-1984 = 100
Food and Beverages

For 1976-1997. Columns headed % show percentile change in the index from the previous period for which an index is available.

Year	Jan Index	Jan %	Feb Index	Feb %	Mar Index	Mar %	Apr Index	Apr %	May Index	May %	Jun Index	Jun %	Jul Index	Jul %	Aug Index	Aug %	Sep Index	Sep %	Oct Index	Oct %	Nov Index	Nov %	Dec Index	Dec %
1976	67.5	-	-	-	-	-	67.2	-0.4	-	-	-	-	68.1	1.3	-	-	-	-	67.5	-0.9	-	-	-	-
1977	67.4	-0.1	-	-	-	-	69.7	3.4	-	-	-	-	71.4	2.4	-	-	-	-	71.2	-0.3	-	-	-	-
1978	72.1	1.3	-	-	73.3	1.7	-	-	74.9	2.2	-	-	77.6	3.6	-	-	77.5	-0.1	-	-	78.0	0.6	-	-
1979	78.6	0.8	-	-	81.3	3.4	-	-	83.5	2.7	-	-	85.8	2.8	-	-	84.0	-2.1	-	-	84.6	0.7	-	-
1980	86.1	1.8	-	-	87.7	1.9	-	-	88.6	1.0	-	-	90.1	1.7	-	-	90.9	0.9	-	-	92.2	1.4	-	-
1981	94.3	2.3	-	-	95.2	1.0	-	-	94.7	-0.5	-	-	94.7	0.0	-	-	94.4	-0.3	-	-	94.2	-0.2	-	-
1982	95.6	1.5	-	-	95.7	0.1	-	-	96.3	0.6	-	-	97.3	1.0	-	-	97.2	-0.1	-	-	96.7	-0.5	-	-
1983	97.2	0.5	-	-	99.0	1.9	-	-	98.6	-0.4	-	-	99.6	1.0	-	-	99.2	-0.4	-	-	99.9	0.7	-	-
1984	102.3	2.4	-	-	104.1	1.8	-	-	104.2	0.1	-	-	104.8	0.6	-	-	104.9	0.1	-	-	104.7	-0.2	-	-
1985	106.5	1.7	-	-	107.7	1.1	-	-	107.6	-0.1	-	-	109.1	1.4	-	-	108.7	-0.4	-	-	109.4	0.6	-	-
1986	111.3	1.7	-	-	110.3	-0.9	-	-	111.4	1.0	-	-	113.8	2.2	-	-	115.9	1.8	-	-	114.7	-1.0	-	-
1987	119.1	3.8	-	-	117.9	-1.0	-	-	118.2	0.3	-	-	118.8	0.5	-	-	119.6	0.7	-	-	119.0	-0.5	-	-
1988	121.3	1.9	-	-	120.1	-1.0	-	-	123.0	2.4	-	-	124.4	1.1	-	-	126.9	2.0	-	-	125.7	-0.9	-	-
1989	127.5	1.4	-	-	129.5	1.6	-	-	130.8	1.0	-	-	133.0	1.7	-	-	133.1	0.1	-	-	132.9	-0.2	-	-
1990	136.2	2.5	-	-	137.4	0.9	-	-	137.2	-0.1	-	-	137.7	0.4	-	-	138.9	0.9	-	-	138.8	-0.1	-	-
1991	141.3	1.8	-	-	140.4	-0.6	-	-	142.5	1.5	-	-	142.1	-0.3	-	-	141.2	-0.6	-	-	142.1	0.6	-	-
1992	142.6	0.4	-	-	142.8	0.1	-	-	141.6	-0.8	-	-	142.0	0.3	-	-	142.4	0.3	-	-	142.5	0.1	-	-
1993	144.6	1.5	-	-	144.4	-0.1	-	-	145.3	0.6	-	-	145.9	0.4	-	-	145.7	-0.1	-	-	145.9	0.1	-	-
1994	147.0	0.8	-	-	148.3	0.9	-	-	147.4	-0.6	-	-	148.6	0.8	-	-	150.1	1.0	-	-	149.2	-0.6	-	-
1995	153.6	2.9	-	-	151.6	-1.3	-	-	152.4	0.5	-	-	150.8	-1.0	-	-	152.0	0.8	-	-	152.1	0.1	-	-
1996	154.4	1.5	-	-	155.9	1.0	-	-	155.5	-0.3	-	-	156.1	0.4	-	-	157.0	0.6	-	-	157.6	0.4	-	-
1997	157.8	0.1	-	-	158.4	0.4	-	-	157.9	-0.3	158.1	0.1	158.8	0.4	-	-	159.0	0.1	-	-	159.4	0.3	-	-

Source: U.S. Department of Labor, Bureau of Labor Statistics, Division of Consumer Prices and Price Indexes. - indicates no data collected for period.

315

Boston, MA
Consumer Price Index - All Urban Consumers
Base 1982-1984 = 100
Housing

For 1976-1997. Columns headed % show percentile change in the index from the previous period for which an index is available.

Year	Jan Index	%	Feb Index	%	Mar Index	%	Apr Index	%	May Index	%	Jun Index	%	Jul Index	%	Aug Index	%	Sep Index	%	Oct Index	%	Nov Index	%	Dec Index	%
1976	55.2	-	-	-	-	-	55.6	0.7	-	-	-	-	56.4	1.4	-	-	-	-	56.7	0.5	-	-	-	-
1977	58.7	3.5	-	-	-	-	58.9	0.3	-	-	-	-	59.8	1.5	-	-	-	-	60.0	0.3	-	-	-	-
1978	61.2	2.0	-	-	61.9	1.1	-	-	62.1	0.3	-	-	62.9	1.3	-	-	63.6	1.1	-	-	65.4	2.8	-	-
1979	67.1	2.6	-	-	67.4	0.4	-	-	67.9	0.7	-	-	69.2	1.9	-	-	71.7	3.6	-	-	74.1	3.3	-	-
1980	75.6	2.0	-	-	78.4	3.7	-	-	79.3	1.1	-	-	81.0	2.1	-	-	82.0	1.2	-	-	83.4	1.7	-	-
1981	87.8	5.3	-	-	90.0	2.5	-	-	90.1	0.1	-	-	91.7	1.8	-	-	95.5	4.1	-	-	95.2	-0.3	-	-
1982	94.1	-1.2	-	-	89.6	-4.8	-	-	91.7	2.3	-	-	95.2	3.8	-	-	97.1	2.0	-	-	98.6	1.5	-	-
1983	100.1	1.5	-	-	98.8	-1.3	-	-	99.3	0.5	-	-	99.7	0.4	-	-	100.8	1.1	-	-	102.5	1.7	-	-
1984	103.1	0.6	-	-	104.0	0.9	-	-	104.3	0.3	-	-	105.5	1.2	-	-	106.1	0.6	-	-	106.4	0.3	-	-
1985	106.9	0.5	-	-	107.6	0.7	-	-	107.6	0.0	-	-	109.4	1.7	-	-	110.1	0.6	-	-	112.2	1.9	-	-
1986	111.8	-0.4	-	-	111.4	-0.4	-	-	110.1	-1.2	-	-	110.2	0.1	-	-	112.4	2.0	-	-	113.5	1.0	-	-
1987	114.2	0.6	-	-	115.3	1.0	-	-	114.7	-0.5	-	-	116.1	1.2	-	-	119.1	2.6	-	-	119.9	0.7	-	-
1988	119.8	-0.1	-	-	121.0	1.0	-	-	122.9	1.6	-	-	123.9	0.8	-	-	125.5	1.3	-	-	126.6	0.9	-	-
1989	130.0	2.7	-	-	130.5	0.4	-	-	129.2	-1.0	-	-	129.7	0.4	-	-	132.8	2.4	-	-	134.1	1.0	-	-
1990	136.0	1.4	-	-	135.4	-0.4	-	-	134.4	-0.7	-	-	136.4	1.5	-	-	137.4	0.7	-	-	140.9	2.5	-	-
1991	142.3	1.0	-	-	142.3	0.0	-	-	139.4	-2.0	-	-	140.6	0.9	-	-	140.7	0.1	-	-	140.7	0.0	-	-
1992	140.9	0.1	-	-	143.9	2.1	-	-	142.0	-1.3	-	-	144.1	1.5	-	-	143.7	-0.3	-	-	145.5	1.3	-	-
1993	146.7	0.8	-	-	147.1	0.3	-	-	144.8	-1.6	-	-	146.0	0.8	-	-	145.4	-0.4	-	-	148.1	1.9	-	-
1994	147.0	-0.7	-	-	148.1	0.7	-	-	145.8	-1.6	-	-	147.1	0.9	-	-	148.1	0.7	-	-	150.2	1.4	-	-
1995	151.7	1.0	-	-	153.1	0.9	-	-	149.4	-2.4	-	-	149.9	0.3	-	-	151.0	0.7	-	-	153.4	1.6	-	-
1996	157.1	2.4	-	-	157.3	0.1	-	-	154.7	-1.7	-	-	155.5	0.5	-	-	156.3	0.5	-	-	160.6	2.8	-	-
1997	163.1	1.6	-	-	164.4	0.8	-	-	160.4	-2.4	162.5	1.3	161.9	-0.4	-	-	161.4	-0.3	-	-	163.4	1.2	-	-

Source: U.S. Department of Labor, Bureau of Labor Statistics, Division of Consumer Prices and Price Indexes. - indicates no data collected for period.

Boston, MA
Consumer Price Index - Urban Wage Earners
Base 1982-1984 = 100
Housing

For 1976-1997. Columns headed % show percentile change in the index from the previous period for which an index is available.

Year	Jan Index	%	Feb Index	%	Mar Index	%	Apr Index	%	May Index	%	Jun Index	%	Jul Index	%	Aug Index	%	Sep Index	%	Oct Index	%	Nov Index	%	Dec Index	%
1976	55.1	-	-	-	-	-	55.5	0.7	-	-	-	-	56.3	1.4	-	-	-	-	56.6	0.5	-	-	-	-
1977	58.6	3.5	-	-	-	-	58.8	0.3	-	-	-	-	59.7	1.5	-	-	-	-	59.9	0.3	-	-	-	-
1978	61.1	2.0	-	-	61.8	1.1	-	-	61.9	0.2	-	-	62.8	1.5	-	-	63.7	1.4	-	-	65.5	2.8	-	-
1979	67.1	2.4	-	-	67.4	0.4	-	-	68.1	1.0	-	-	69.5	2.1	-	-	71.9	3.5	-	-	74.4	3.5	-	-
1980	76.2	2.4	-	-	79.2	3.9	-	-	80.1	1.1	-	-	81.7	2.0	-	-	82.7	1.2	-	-	84.6	2.3	-	-
1981	88.9	5.1	-	-	91.0	2.4	-	-	91.3	0.3	-	-	93.5	2.4	-	-	97.1	3.9	-	-	96.2	-0.9	-	-
1982	95.1	-1.1	-	-	90.2	-5.2	-	-	92.5	2.5	-	-	96.1	3.9	-	-	98.0	2.0	-	-	99.6	1.6	-	-
1983	99.8	0.2	-	-	98.7	-1.1	-	-	98.8	0.1	-	-	100.3	1.5	-	-	100.5	0.2	-	-	102.6	2.1	-	-
1984	102.6	0.0	-	-	102.3	-0.3	-	-	103.8	1.5	-	-	103.3	-0.5	-	-	105.9	2.5	-	-	106.9	0.9	-	-
1985	107.4	0.5	-	-	108.0	0.6	-	-	108.1	0.1	-	-	109.9	1.7	-	-	110.5	0.5	-	-	112.6	1.9	-	-
1986	112.4	-0.2	-	-	111.8	-0.5	-	-	110.3	-1.3	-	-	110.4	0.1	-	-	112.5	1.9	-	-	113.6	1.0	-	-
1987	114.0	0.4	-	-	115.4	1.2	-	-	114.8	-0.5	-	-	116.1	1.1	-	-	119.1	2.6	-	-	120.1	0.8	-	-
1988	119.7	-0.3	-	-	120.8	0.9	-	-	122.8	1.7	-	-	123.6	0.7	-	-	125.2	1.3	-	-	126.6	1.1	-	-
1989	129.6	2.4	-	-	130.1	0.4	-	-	128.7	-1.1	-	-	129.5	0.6	-	-	132.5	2.3	-	-	134.1	1.2	-	-
1990	135.3	0.9	-	-	134.8	-0.4	-	-	133.6	-0.9	-	-	135.2	1.2	-	-	136.1	0.7	-	-	140.0	2.9	-	-
1991	140.6	0.4	-	-	140.5	-0.1	-	-	138.1	-1.7	-	-	139.1	0.7	-	-	139.5	0.3	-	-	139.9	0.3	-	-
1992	139.6	-0.2	-	-	142.2	1.9	-	-	140.4	-1.3	-	-	142.5	1.5	-	-	142.1	-0.3	-	-	144.5	1.7	-	-
1993	145.4	0.6	-	-	145.5	0.1	-	-	143.5	-1.4	-	-	144.2	0.5	-	-	143.9	-0.2	-	-	147.2	2.3	-	-
1994	145.7	-1.0	-	-	146.4	0.5	-	-	144.5	-1.3	-	-	145.4	0.6	-	-	146.5	0.8	-	-	149.0	1.7	-	-
1995	150.2	0.8	-	-	151.1	0.6	-	-	147.8	-2.2	-	-	148.1	0.2	-	-	149.3	0.8	-	-	152.1	1.9	-	-
1996	155.5	2.2	-	-	155.7	0.1	-	-	153.0	-1.7	-	-	153.7	0.5	-	-	154.5	0.5	-	-	159.1	3.0	-	-
1997	161.5	1.5	-	-	162.4	0.6	-	-	158.5	-2.4	160.6	1.3	159.7	-0.6	-	-	159.1	-0.4	-	-	161.7	1.6	-	-

Source: U.S. Department of Labor, Bureau of Labor Statistics, Division of Consumer Prices and Price Indexes. - indicates no data collected for period.

Boston, MA
Consumer Price Index - All Urban Consumers
Base 1982-1984 = 100
Apparel and Upkeep

For 1952-1997. Columns headed % show percentile change in the index from the previous period for which an index is available.

Year	Jan Index	Jan %	Feb Index	Feb %	Mar Index	Mar %	Apr Index	Apr %	May Index	May %	Jun Index	Jun %	Jul Index	Jul %	Aug Index	Aug %	Sep Index	Sep %	Oct Index	Oct %	Nov Index	Nov %	Dec Index	Dec %
1952	-		-		-		-		-		-		-		-		-		39.6	-	-		-	
1953	39.2	-1.0	-		-		39.5	0.8	-		-		39.5	0.0	-		-		39.6	0.3	-		-	
1954	38.6	-2.5	-		-		38.8	0.5	-		-		39.1	0.8	-		-		39.9	2.0	-		-	
1955	39.0	-2.3	-		-		39.3	0.8	-		-		39.1	-0.5	-		-		39.5	1.0	-		-	
1956	39.0	-1.3	-		-		39.6	1.5	-		-		39.7	0.3	-		-		40.6	2.3	-		-	
1957	39.7	-2.2	-		-		40.5	2.0	-		-		40.3	-0.5	-		-		41.1	2.0	-		-	
1958	40.8	-0.7	-		-		40.9	0.2	-		-		41.2		-		-		41.8	1.5	-		-	
1959	40.3	-3.6	-		-		40.3	0.0	-		-		40.7	1.0	-		-		41.7	2.5	-		-	
1960	41.3	-1.0	-		-		41.9	1.5	-		-		42.3	1.0	-		-		42.6	0.7	-		-	
1961	42.1	-1.2	-		-		42.0	-0.2	-		-		42.3	0.7	-		-		43.0	1.7	-		-	
1962	41.9	-2.6	-		-		43.0	2.6	-		-		43.1	0.2	-		-		43.7	1.4	-		-	
1963	43.0	-1.6	-		-		43.3	0.7	-		-		43.0	-0.7	-		-		44.1	2.6	-		-	
1964	43.0	-2.5	-		-		43.8	1.9	-		-		43.5	-0.7	-		-		44.1	1.4	-		-	
1965	43.2	-2.0	-		-		43.7	1.2	-		-		44.0	0.7	-		-		44.5	1.1	-		-	
1966	44.4	-0.2	-		-		44.9	1.1	-		-		44.6	-0.7	-		-		45.9	2.9	-		-	
1967	45.3	-1.3	-		-		46.3	2.2	-		-		46.3	0.0	-		-		47.5	2.6	-		-	
1968	46.9	-1.3	-		-		49.3	5.1	-		-		48.8	-1.0	-		-		51.0	4.5	-		-	
1969	50.4	-1.2	-		-		51.4	2.0	-		-		51.4	0.0	-		-		54.4	5.8	-		-	
1970	52.6	-3.3	-		-		54.9	4.4	-		-		53.7	-2.2	-		-		56.5	5.2	-		-	
1971	55.4	-1.9	-		-		56.6	2.2	-		-		56.2	-0.7	-		-		57.9	3.0	-		-	
1972	56.7	-2.1	-		-		57.2	0.9	-		-		57.3	0.2	-		-		59.5	3.8	-		-	
1973	58.1	-2.4	-		-		59.6	2.6	-		-		59.2	-0.7	-		-		61.3	3.5	-		-	
1974	60.7	-1.0	-		-		63.4	4.4	-		-		63.8	0.6	-		-		66.6	4.4	-		-	
1975	66.0	-0.9	-		-		67.5	2.3	-		-		67.6	0.1	-		-		70.4	4.1	-		-	
1976	70.6	0.3	-		-		71.2	0.8	-		-		71.1	-0.1	-		-		72.7	2.3	-		-	
1977	71.4	-1.8	-		-		72.5	1.5	-		-		72.0	-0.7	-		-		75.6	5.0	-		-	
1978	74.8	-1.1	-		76.9	2.8	-		79.4	3.3	-		76.2	-4.0	-		81.2	6.6	-		83.0	2.2	-	
1979	78.7	-5.2	-		84.6	7.5	-		84.6	0.0	-		83.7	-1.1	-		88.0	5.1	-		88.1	0.1	-	
1980	85.7	-2.7	-		88.4	3.2	-		88.8	0.5	-		87.2	-1.8	-		92.5	6.1	-		93.2	0.8	-	
1981	90.6	-2.8	-		95.3	5.2	-		93.4	-2.0	-		92.3	-1.2	-		95.6	3.6	-		95.6	0.0	-	
1982	92.5	-3.2	-		97.0	4.9	-		95.8	-1.2	-		95.9	0.1	-		101.0	5.3	-		100.6	-0.4	-	
1983	99.3	-1.3	-		101.3	2.0	-		100.8	-0.5	-		99.8	-1.0	-		98.4	-1.4	-		99.8	1.4	-	
1984	98.7	-1.1	-		103.3	4.7	-		102.9	-0.4	-		101.0	-1.8	-		106.2	5.1	-		103.8	-2.3	-	
1985	100.7	-3.0	-		106.8	6.1	-		107.1	0.3	-		101.7	-5.0	-		110.4	8.6	-		108.8	-1.4	-	
1986	106.2	-2.4	-		108.4	2.1	-		107.8	-0.6	-		106.6	-1.1	-		111.2	4.3	-		108.5	-2.4	-	
1987	107.4	-1.0	-		122.6	14.2	-		112.4	-8.3	-		110.3	-1.9	-		123.4	11.9	-		117.8	-4.5	-	
1988	112.6	-4.4	-		134.7	19.6	-		128.4	-4.7	-		118.9	-7.4	-		126.7	6.6	-		130.8	3.2	-	
1989	124.6	-4.7	-		121.4	-2.6	-		126.3	4.0	-		117.6	-6.9	-		121.5	3.3	-		137.5	13.2	-	
1990	132.0	-4.0	-		129.7	-1.7	-		135.2	4.2	-		124.7	-7.8	-		154.6	24.0	-		152.5	-1.4	-	
1991	135.6	-11.1	-		139.3	2.7	-		140.8	1.1	-		138.1	-1.9	-		157.9	14.3	-		154.1	-2.4	-	
1992	144.5	-6.2	-		142.5	-1.4	-		142.7	0.1	-		141.4	-0.9	-		152.7	8.0	-		145.8	-4.5	-	
1993	148.6	1.9	-		182.1	22.5	-		155.8	-14.4	-		150.1	-3.7	-		151.4	0.9	-		158.0	4.4	-	
1994	149.9	-5.1	-		156.2	4.2	-		153.3	-1.9	-		140.1	-8.6	-		144.7	3.3	-		139.6	-3.5	-	

[Continued]

Boston, MA
Consumer Price Index - All Urban Consumers
Base 1982-1984 = 100
Apparel and Upkeep
[Continued]

For 1952-1997. Columns headed % show percentile change in the index from the previous period for which an index is available.

Year	Jan		Feb		Mar		Apr		May		Jun		Jul		Aug		Sep		Oct		Nov		Dec	
	Index	%	Index	%	Index	%	Index	%	Index	%	Index	%	Index	%	Index	%	Index	%	Index	%	Index	%	Index	%
1995	139.0	-0.4	-	-	142.3	2.4	-	-	145.5	2.2	-	-	145.5	0.0	-	-	145.8	0.2	-	-	144.3	-1.0	-	-
1996	138.5	-4.0	-	-	145.2	4.8	-	-	142.0	-2.2	-	-	138.1	-2.7	-	-	145.2	5.1	-	-	146.9	1.2	-	-
1997	144.3	-1.8	-	-	141.1	-2.2	-	-	146.8	4.0	143.7	-2.1	140.1	-2.5	-	-	143.7	2.6	-	-	147.6	2.7	-	-

Source: U.S. Department of Labor, Bureau of Labor Statistics, Division of Consumer Prices and Price Indexes. - indicates no data collected for period.

Boston, MA
Consumer Price Index - Urban Wage Earners
Base 1982-1984 = 100
Apparel and Upkeep

For 1952-1997. Columns headed % show percentile change in the index from the previous period for which an index is available.

Year	Jan Index	%	Feb Index	%	Mar Index	%	Apr Index	%	May Index	%	Jun Index	%	Jul Index	%	Aug Index	%	Sep Index	%	Oct Index	%	Nov Index	%	Dec Index	%
1952	-	-	-	-	-	-	-	-	-	-	-	-	-	-	-	-	-	-	39.9	-	-	-	-	-
1953	39.4	-1.3	-	-	-	-	39.8	1.0	-	-	-	-	39.8	0.0	-	-	-	-	39.9	0.3	-	-	-	-
1954	38.9	-2.5	-	-	-	-	39.1	0.5	-	-	-	-	39.4	0.8	-	-	-	-	40.1	1.8	-	-	-	-
1955	39.3	-2.0	-	-	-	-	39.6	0.8	-	-	-	-	39.4	-0.5	-	-	-	-	39.8	1.0	-	-	-	-
1956	39.3	-1.3	-	-	-	-	39.9	1.5	-	-	-	-	40.0	0.3	-	-	-	-	40.9	2.3	-	-	-	-
1957	40.0	-2.2	-	-	-	-	40.8	2.0	-	-	-	-	40.6	-0.5	-	-	-	-	41.4	2.0	-	-	-	-
1958	41.1	-0.7	-	-	-	-	41.2	0.2	-	-	-	-	41.5	0.7	-	-	-	-	42.1	1.4	-	-	-	-
1959	40.6	-3.6	-	-	-	-	40.6	0.0	-	-	-	-	41.0	1.0	-	-	-	-	42.0	2.4	-	-	-	-
1960	41.6	-1.0	-	-	-	-	42.2	1.4	-	-	-	-	42.6	0.9	-	-	-	-	42.9	0.7	-	-	-	-
1961	42.4	-1.2	-	-	-	-	42.4	0.0	-	-	-	-	42.6	0.5	-	-	-	-	43.3	1.6	-	-	-	-
1962	42.3	-2.3	-	-	-	-	43.3	2.4	-	-	-	-	43.4	0.2	-	-	-	-	44.0	1.4	-	-	-	-
1963	43.3	-1.6	-	-	-	-	43.6	0.7	-	-	-	-	43.3	-0.7	-	-	-	-	44.4	2.5	-	-	-	-
1964	43.3	-2.5	-	-	-	-	44.1	1.8	-	-	-	-	43.8	-0.7	-	-	-	-	44.4	1.4	-	-	-	-
1965	43.6	-1.8	-	-	-	-	44.0	0.9	-	-	-	-	44.3	0.7	-	-	-	-	44.8	1.1	-	-	-	-
1966	44.7	-0.2	-	-	-	-	45.3	1.3	-	-	-	-	44.9	-0.9	-	-	-	-	46.2	2.9	-	-	-	-
1967	45.7	-1.1	-	-	-	-	46.7	2.2	-	-	-	-	46.7	0.0	-	-	-	-	47.9	2.6	-	-	-	-
1968	47.2	-1.5	-	-	-	-	49.7	5.3	-	-	-	-	49.1	-1.2	-	-	-	-	51.3	4.5	-	-	-	-
1969	50.7	-1.2	-	-	-	-	51.8	2.2	-	-	-	-	51.8	0.0	-	-	-	-	54.8	5.8	-	-	-	-
1970	53.0	-3.3	-	-	-	-	55.3	4.3	-	-	-	-	54.1	-2.2	-	-	-	-	57.0	5.4	-	-	-	-
1971	55.8	-2.1	-	-	-	-	57.0	2.2	-	-	-	-	56.6	-0.7	-	-	-	-	58.4	3.2	-	-	-	-
1972	57.2	-2.1	-	-	-	-	57.7	0.9	-	-	-	-	57.7	0.0	-	-	-	-	59.9	3.8	-	-	-	-
1973	58.5	-2.3	-	-	-	-	60.0	2.6	-	-	-	-	59.6	-0.7	-	-	-	-	61.8	3.7	-	-	-	-
1974	61.1	-1.1	-	-	-	-	63.9	4.6	-	-	-	-	64.3	0.6	-	-	-	-	67.1	4.4	-	-	-	-
1975	66.5	-0.9	-	-	-	-	68.0	2.3	-	-	-	-	68.1	0.1	-	-	-	-	70.9	4.1	-	-	-	-
1976	71.2	0.4	-	-	-	-	71.7	0.7	-	-	-	-	71.6	-0.1	-	-	-	-	73.3	2.4	-	-	-	-
1977	72.0	-1.8	-	-	-	-	73.0	1.4	-	-	-	-	72.5	-0.7	-	-	-	-	76.1	5.0	-	-	-	-
1978	75.4	-0.9	-	-	76.3	1.2	-	-	79.2	3.8	-	-	75.9	-4.2	-	-	81.4	7.2	-	-	80.9	-0.6	-	-
1979	77.2	-4.6	-	-	80.8	4.7	-	-	82.0	1.5	-	-	79.7	-2.8	-	-	87.7	10.0	-	-	86.8	-1.0	-	-
1980	83.0	-4.4	-	-	85.5	3.0	-	-	85.2	-0.4	-	-	84.4	-0.9	-	-	90.3	7.0	-	-	91.4	1.2	-	-
1981	87.6	-4.2	-	-	93.9	7.2	-	-	93.1	-0.9	-	-	89.6	-3.8	-	-	95.9	7.0	-	-	96.3	0.4	-	-
1982	92.2	-4.3	-	-	99.4	7.8	-	-	95.8	-3.6	-	-	95.9	0.1	-	-	102.3	6.7	-	-	101.0	-1.3	-	-
1983	98.5	-2.5	-	-	103.9	5.5	-	-	102.2	-1.6	-	-	99.2	-2.9	-	-	98.4	-0.8	-	-	99.0	0.6	-	-
1984	97.7	-1.3	-	-	101.9	4.3	-	-	101.6	-0.3	-	-	100.3	-1.3	-	-	105.8	5.5	-	-	103.4	-2.3	-	-
1985	99.6	-3.7	-	-	105.4	5.8	-	-	104.8	-0.6	-	-	100.0	-4.6	-	-	110.0	10.0	-	-	107.9	-1.9	-	-
1986	104.4	-3.2	-	-	107.8	3.3	-	-	106.2	-1.5	-	-	105.2	-0.9	-	-	110.1	4.7	-	-	107.2	-2.6	-	-
1987	112.2	4.7	-	-	127.6	13.7	-	-	115.9	-9.2	-	-	115.7	-0.2	-	-	130.1	12.4	-	-	124.3	-4.5	-	-
1988	120.9	-2.7	-	-	139.3	15.2	-	-	134.6	-3.4	-	-	125.9	-6.5	-	-	134.1	6.5	-	-	138.4	3.2	-	-
1989	130.5	-5.7	-	-	128.6	-1.5	-	-	134.9	4.9	-	-	126.8	-6.0	-	-	132.6	4.6	-	-	148.3	11.8	-	-
1990	141.4	-4.7	-	-	139.5	-1.3	-	-	147.3	5.6	-	-	134.5	-8.7	-	-	158.8	18.1	-	-	159.7	0.6	-	-
1991	143.7	-10.0	-	-	151.4	5.4	-	-	151.5	0.1	-	-	149.4	-1.4	-	-	162.6	8.8	-	-	157.7	-3.0	-	-
1992	154.2	-2.2	-	-	149.8	-2.9	-	-	150.1	0.2	-	-	149.1	-0.7	-	-	161.3	8.2	-	-	155.1	-3.8	-	-
1993	153.9	-0.8	-	-	202.4	31.5	-	-	164.3	-18.8	-	-	155.2	-5.5	-	-	157.8	1.7	-	-	163.1	3.4	-	-
1994	154.4	-5.3	-	-	157.5	2.0	-	-	156.5	-0.6	-	-	148.3	-5.2	-	-	152.1	2.6	-	-	146.7	-3.6	-	-

[Continued]

Boston, MA
Consumer Price Index - Urban Wage Earners
Base 1982-1984 = 100
Apparel and Upkeep
[Continued]

For 1952-1997. Columns headed % show percentile change in the index from the previous period for which an index is available.

Year	Jan		Feb		Mar		Apr		May		Jun		Jul		Aug		Sep		Oct		Nov		Dec	
	Index	%	Index	%	Index	%	Index	%	Index	%	Index	%	Index	%	Index	%	Index	%	Index	%	Index	%	Index	%
1995	146.5	-0.1	-	-	148.5	1.4	-	-	151.8	2.2	-	-	152.8	0.7	-	-	152.5	-0.2	-	-	151.9	-0.4	-	-
1996	147.4	-3.0	-	-	152.2	3.3	-	-	149.9	-1.5	-	-	146.0	-2.6	-	-	151.8	4.0	-	-	154.5	1.8	-	-
1997	152.7	-1.2	-	-	146.9	-3.8	-	-	157.0	6.9	151.9	-3.2	148.7	-2.1	-	-	150.4	1.1	-	-	150.9	0.3	-	-

Source: U.S. Department of Labor, Bureau of Labor Statistics, Division of Consumer Prices and Price Indexes. - indicates no data collected for period.

Boston, MA
Consumer Price Index - All Urban Consumers
Base 1982-1984 = 100
Transportation

For 1947-1997. Columns headed % show percentile change in the index from the previous period for which an index is available.

Year	Jan Index	%	Feb Index	%	Mar Index	%	Apr Index	%	May Index	%	Jun Index	%	Jul Index	%	Aug Index	%	Sep Index	%	Oct Index	%	Nov Index	%	Dec Index	%
1947	16.2	-	16.2	0.0	16.3	0.6	16.3	0.0	16.3	0.0	16.4	0.6	16.4	0.0	16.5	0.6	16.6	0.6	16.6	0.0	16.6	0.0	16.6	0.0
1948	16.7	0.6	16.8	0.6	16.8	0.0	16.8	0.0	16.8	0.0	16.8	0.0	16.9	0.6	17.1	1.2	17.1	0.0	17.1	0.0	17.1	0.0	17.1	0.0
1949	17.1	0.0	17.2	0.6	17.2	0.0	17.3	0.6	17.3	0.0	17.3	0.0	17.3	0.0	20.4	17.9	20.4	0.0	20.4	0.0	20.4	0.0	20.5	0.5
1950	20.5	0.0	20.4	-0.5	20.4	0.0	20.4	0.0	20.5	0.5	20.5	0.0	20.6	0.5	20.6	0.0	20.7	0.5	20.7	0.0	20.7	0.0	20.8	0.5
1951	20.8	0.0	20.8	0.0	20.8	0.0	20.8	0.0	20.8	0.0	20.8	0.0	20.8	0.0	21.6	3.8	21.6	0.0	21.8	0.9	21.9	0.5	21.9	0.0
1952	22.0	0.5	22.3	1.4	22.3	0.0	22.3	0.0	22.3	0.0	22.3	0.0	23.0	3.1	23.0	0.0	23.1	0.4	23.1	0.0	23.1	0.0	23.1	0.0
1953	23.2	0.4	-	-	-	-	23.5	1.3	-	-	-	-	23.7	0.9	-	-	-	-	23.7	0.0	-	-	-	-
1954	23.4	-1.3	-	-	-	-	24.4	4.3	-	-	-	-	23.7	-2.9	-	-	-	-	23.0	-3.0	-	-	-	-
1955	23.2	0.9	-	-	-	-	23.2	0.0	-	-	-	-	22.9	-1.3	-	-	-	-	23.5	2.6	-	-	-	-
1956	23.5	0.0	-	-	-	-	23.6	0.4	-	-	-	-	23.5	-0.4	-	-	-	-	25.1	6.8	-	-	-	-
1957	24.7	-1.6	-	-	-	-	24.9	0.8	-	-	-	-	25.0	0.4	-	-	-	-	25.2	0.8	-	-	-	-
1958	25.4	0.8	-	-	-	-	25.9	2.0	-	-	-	-	25.8	-0.4	-	-	-	-	25.7	-0.4	-	-	-	-
1959	26.5	3.1	-	-	-	-	26.4	-0.4	-	-	-	-	26.4	0.0	-	-	-	-	26.4	0.0	-	-	-	-
1960	25.7	-2.7	-	-	-	-	25.7	0.0	-	-	-	-	25.9	0.8	-	-	-	-	25.9	0.0	-	-	-	-
1961	25.6	-1.2	-	-	-	-	26.0	1.6	-	-	-	-	26.4	1.5	-	-	-	-	26.2	-0.8	-	-	-	-
1962	28.1	7.3	-	-	-	-	28.3	0.7	-	-	-	-	28.0	-1.1	-	-	-	-	28.3	1.1	-	-	-	-
1963	28.0	-1.1	-	-	-	-	28.3	1.1	-	-	-	-	28.5	0.7	-	-	-	-	28.3	-0.7	-	-	-	-
1964	28.4	0.4	-	-	-	-	28.3	-0.4	-	-	-	-	28.6	1.1	-	-	-	-	28.3	-1.0	-	-	-	-
1965	28.9	2.1	-	-	-	-	29.0	0.3	-	-	-	-	29.2	0.7	-	-	-	-	29.5	1.0	-	-	-	-
1966	29.3	-0.7	-	-	-	-	29.9	2.0	-	-	-	-	30.1	0.7	-	-	-	-	30.1	0.0	-	-	-	-
1967	30.1	0.0	-	-	-	-	30.4	1.0	-	-	-	-	30.7	1.0	-	-	-	-	30.9	0.7	-	-	-	-
1968	31.2	1.0	-	-	-	-	31.5	1.0	-	-	-	-	31.5	0.0	-	-	-	-	31.7	0.6	-	-	-	-
1969	32.9	3.8	-	-	-	-	33.6	2.1	-	-	-	-	33.6	0.0	-	-	-	-	33.6	0.0	-	-	-	-
1970	33.7	0.3	-	-	-	-	34.0	0.9	-	-	-	-	34.5	1.5	-	-	-	-	36.3	5.2	-	-	-	-
1971	36.6	0.8	-	-	-	-	36.2	-1.1	-	-	-	-	36.9	1.9	-	-	-	-	36.7	-0.5	-	-	-	-
1972	36.5	-0.5	-	-	-	-	36.3	-0.5	-	-	-	-	36.5	0.6	-	-	-	-	37.0	1.4	-	-	-	-
1973	37.0	0.0	-	-	-	-	37.1	0.3	-	-	-	-	37.8	1.9	-	-	-	-	37.8	0.0	-	-	-	-
1974	38.6	2.1	-	-	-	-	39.8	3.1	-	-	-	-	42.0	5.5	-	-	-	-	42.3	0.7	-	-	-	-
1975	42.8	1.2	-	-	-	-	45.1	5.4	-	-	-	-	47.0	4.2	-	-	-	-	47.6	1.3	-	-	-	-
1976	57.8	21.4	-	-	-	-	58.1	0.5	-	-	-	-	59.8	2.9	-	-	-	-	60.2	0.7	-	-	-	-
1977	62.2	3.3	-	-	-	-	63.3	1.8	-	-	-	-	63.9	0.9	-	-	-	-	63.6	-0.5	-	-	-	-
1978	63.7	0.2	-	-	61.2	-3.9	-	-	62.2	1.6	-	-	63.3	1.8	-	-	63.6	0.5	-	-	64.2	0.9	-	-
1979	63.6	-0.9	-	-	64.8	1.9	-	-	68.0	4.9	-	-	70.9	4.3	-	-	72.1	1.7	-	-	74.0	2.6	-	-
1980	76.6	3.5	-	-	80.5	5.1	-	-	81.8	1.6	-	-	83.5	2.1	-	-	84.7	1.4	-	-	86.3	1.9	-	-
1981	87.6	1.5	-	-	91.3	4.2	-	-	94.0	3.0	-	-	94.5	0.5	-	-	96.6	2.2	-	-	98.0	1.4	-	-
1982	97.6	-0.4	-	-	97.0	-0.6	-	-	96.1	-0.9	-	-	99.3	3.3	-	-	99.8	0.5	-	-	99.7	-0.1	-	-
1983	98.7	-1.0	-	-	97.2	-1.5	-	-	98.5	1.3	-	-	99.6	1.1	-	-	100.1	0.5	-	-	100.5	0.4	-	-
1984	100.7	0.2	-	-	101.8	1.1	-	-	102.9	1.1	-	-	103.0	0.1	-	-	103.0	0.0	-	-	103.1	0.1	-	-
1985	102.9	-0.2	-	-	104.3	1.4	-	-	105.4	1.1	-	-	105.7	0.3	-	-	105.7	0.0	-	-	106.8	1.0	-	-
1986	106.9	0.1	-	-	103.8	-2.9	-	-	100.5	-3.2	-	-	100.5	0.0	-	-	99.4	-1.1	-	-	100.1	0.7	-	-
1987	101.4	1.3	-	-	100.6	-0.8	-	-	101.8	1.2	-	-	103.4	1.6	-	-	104.9	1.5	-	-	106.8	1.8	-	-
1988	106.1	-0.7	-	-	105.5	-0.6	-	-	106.2	0.7	-	-	107.9	1.6	-	-	109.6	1.6	-	-	112.8	2.9	-	-
1989	112.5	-0.3	-	-	113.5	0.9	-	-	115.8	2.0	-	-	112.6	-2.8	-	-	112.6	0.0	-	-	114.6	1.8	-	-
1990	115.7	1.0	-	-	116.1	0.3	-	-	117.1	0.9	-	-	117.3	0.2	-	-	122.3	4.3	-	-	127.4	4.2	-	-
1991	125.3	-1.6	-	-	123.0	-1.8	-	-	124.3	1.1	-	-	125.7	1.1	-	-	126.2	0.4	-	-	127.8	1.3	-	-

[Continued]

Boston, MA
Consumer Price Index - All Urban Consumers
Base 1982-1984 = 100
Transportation
[Continued]

For 1947-1997. Columns headed % show percentile change in the index from the previous period for which an index is available.

Year	Jan		Feb		Mar		Apr		May		Jun		Jul		Aug		Sep		Oct		Nov		Dec	
	Index	%	Index	%	Index	%	Index	%	Index	%	Index	%	Index	%	Index	%	Index	%	Index	%	Index	%	Index	%
1992	127.2	-0.5	-	-	128.6	1.1	-	-	129.1	0.4	-	-	129.9	0.6	-	-	128.9	-0.8	-	-	129.8	0.7	-	-
1993	131.9	1.6	-	-	132.4	0.4	-	-	132.1	-0.2	-	-	132.2	0.1	-	-	131.4	-0.6	-	-	134.4	2.3	-	-
1994	133.4	-0.7	-	-	134.1	0.5	-	-	132.5	-1.2	-	-	134.6	1.6	-	-	136.8	1.6	-	-	137.9	0.8	-	-
1995	137.1	-0.6	-	-	135.9	-0.9	-	-	137.5	1.2	-	-	137.4	-0.1	-	-	136.4	-0.7	-	-	137.7	1.0	-	-
1996	138.7	0.7	-	-	137.1	-1.2	-	-	139.6	1.8	-	-	139.1	-0.4	-	-	140.2	0.8	-	-	141.4	0.9	-	-
1997	142.3	0.6	-	-	141.6	-0.5	-	-	140.2	-1.0	141.2	0.7	140.5	-0.5	-	-	142.1	1.1	-	-	142.8	0.5	-	-

Source: U.S. Department of Labor, Bureau of Labor Statistics, Division of Consumer Prices and Price Indexes. - indicates no data collected for period.

Boston, MA
Consumer Price Index - Urban Wage Earners
Base 1982-1984 = 100
Transportation

For 1947-1997. Columns headed % show percentile change in the index from the previous period for which an index is available.

Year	Jan Index	%	Feb Index	%	Mar Index	%	Apr Index	%	May Index	%	Jun Index	%	Jul Index	%	Aug Index	%	Sep Index	%	Oct Index	%	Nov Index	%	Dec Index	%
1947	16.2	-	16.2	0.0	16.2	0.0	16.3	0.6	16.3	0.0	16.3	0.0	16.4	0.6	16.4	0.0	16.5	0.6	16.5	0.0	16.5	0.0	16.6	0.6
1948	16.7	0.6	16.7	0.0	16.8	0.6	16.7	-0.6	16.8	0.6	16.8	0.0	16.9	0.6	17.0	0.6	17.1	0.6	17.1	0.0	17.1	0.0	17.1	0.0
1949	17.1	0.0	17.2	0.6	17.2	0.0	17.2	0.0	17.2	0.0	17.2	0.0	17.2	0.0	20.4	18.6	20.4	0.0	20.4	0.0	20.4	0.0	20.4	0.0
1950	20.4	0.0	20.4	0.0	20.4	0.0	20.4	0.0	20.4	0.0	20.5	0.5	20.5	0.0	20.6	0.5	20.6	0.0	20.6	0.0	20.6	0.0	20.7	0.5
1951	20.7	0.0	20.7	0.0	20.8	0.5	20.8	0.0	20.8	0.0	20.8	0.0	20.7	-0.5	21.5	3.9	21.5	0.0	21.8	1.4	21.9	0.5	21.9	0.0
1952	21.9	0.0	22.2	1.4	22.3	0.5	22.3	0.0	22.3	0.0	22.2	-0.4	23.0	3.6	23.0	0.0	23.0	0.0	23.0	0.0	23.0	0.0	23.0	0.0
1953	23.1	0.4	-	-	-	-	23.4	1.3	-	-	-	-	23.6	0.9	-	-	23.6	0.0	-	-	-	-	-	-
1954	23.4	-0.8	-	-	-	-	24.3	3.8	-	-	-	-	23.7	-2.5	-	-	22.9	-3.4	-	-	-	-	-	-
1955	23.1	0.9	-	-	-	-	23.1	0.0	-	-	-	-	22.9	-0.9	-	-	23.4	2.2	-	-	-	-	-	-
1956	23.4	0.0	-	-	-	-	23.5	0.4	-	-	-	-	23.4	-0.4	-	-	25.1	7.3	-	-	-	-	-	-
1957	24.7	-1.6	-	-	-	-	24.8	0.4	-	-	-	-	24.9	0.4	-	-	25.2	1.2	-	-	-	-	-	-
1958	25.4	0.8	-	-	-	-	25.8	1.6	-	-	-	-	25.7	-0.4	-	-	25.6	-0.4	-	-	-	-	-	-
1959	26.4	3.1	-	-	-	-	26.4	0.0	-	-	-	-	26.4	0.0	-	-	26.3	-0.4	-	-	-	-	-	-
1960	25.6	-2.7	-	-	-	-	25.7	0.4	-	-	-	-	25.8	0.4	-	-	25.8	0.0	-	-	-	-	-	-
1961	25.5	-1.2	-	-	-	-	25.9	1.6	-	-	-	-	26.3	1.5	-	-	-	-	26.1	-0.8	-	-	-	-
1962	28.0	7.3	-	-	-	-	28.3	1.1	-	-	-	-	27.9	-1.4	-	-	-	-	28.2	1.1	-	-	-	-
1963	27.9	-1.1	-	-	-	-	28.2	1.1	-	-	-	-	28.4	0.7	-	-	-	-	28.2	-0.7	-	-	-	-
1964	28.3	0.4	-	-	-	-	28.2	-0.4	-	-	-	-	28.6	1.4	-	-	-	-	28.2	-1.4	-	-	-	-
1965	28.9	2.5	-	-	-	-	28.9	0.0	-	-	-	-	29.1	0.7	-	-	-	-	29.4	1.0	-	-	-	-
1966	29.2	-0.7	-	-	-	-	29.9	2.4	-	-	-	-	30.0	0.3	-	-	-	-	30.0	0.0	-	-	-	-
1967	30.1	0.3	-	-	-	-	30.3	0.7	-	-	-	-	30.7	1.3	-	-	-	-	30.9	0.7	-	-	-	-
1968	31.2	1.0	-	-	-	-	31.4	0.6	-	-	-	-	31.4	0.0	-	-	-	-	31.6	0.6	-	-	-	-
1969	32.8	3.8	-	-	-	-	33.6	2.4	-	-	-	-	33.5	-0.3	-	-	-	-	33.5	0.0	-	-	-	-
1970	33.6	0.3	-	-	-	-	33.9	0.9	-	-	-	-	34.5	1.8	-	-	-	-	36.2	4.9	-	-	-	-
1971	36.6	1.1	-	-	-	-	36.1	-1.4	-	-	-	-	36.8	1.9	-	-	-	-	36.6	-0.5	-	-	-	-
1972	36.4	-0.5	-	-	-	-	36.2	-0.5	-	-	-	-	36.4	0.6	-	-	-	-	36.9	1.4	-	-	-	-
1973	36.9	0.0	-	-	-	-	37.1	0.5	-	-	-	-	37.7	1.6	-	-	-	-	37.8	0.3	-	-	-	-
1974	38.5	1.9	-	-	-	-	39.7	3.1	-	-	-	-	41.9	5.5	-	-	-	-	42.2	0.7	-	-	-	-
1975	42.7	1.2	-	-	-	-	45.0	5.4	-	-	-	-	46.9	4.2	-	-	-	-	47.5	1.3	-	-	-	-
1976	57.6	21.3	-	-	-	-	57.9	0.5	-	-	-	-	59.7	3.1	-	-	-	-	60.1	0.7	-	-	-	-
1977	62.1	3.3	-	-	-	-	63.2	1.8	-	-	-	-	63.7	0.8	-	-	-	-	63.4	-0.5	-	-	-	-
1978	63.6	0.3	-	-	60.9	-4.2	-	-	62.1	2.0	-	-	63.0	1.4	-	-	63.4	0.6	-	-	64.3	1.4	-	-
1979	63.8	-0.8	-	-	65.2	2.2	-	-	68.4	4.9	-	-	71.6	4.7	-	-	72.9	1.8	-	-	74.6	2.3	-	-
1980	77.3	3.6	-	-	81.1	4.9	-	-	82.3	1.5	-	-	84.6	2.8	-	-	85.4	0.9	-	-	86.7	1.5	-	-
1981	88.0	1.5	-	-	90.8	3.2	-	-	93.0	2.4	-	-	94.3	1.4	-	-	96.9	2.8	-	-	98.4	1.5	-	-
1982	97.9	-0.5	-	-	97.3	-0.6	-	-	96.2	-1.1	-	-	99.3	3.2	-	-	99.8	0.5	-	-	99.6	-0.2	-	-
1983	98.6	-1.0	-	-	97.1	-1.5	-	-	98.4	1.3	-	-	99.5	1.1	-	-	100.1	0.6	-	-	100.6	0.5	-	-
1984	100.6	0.0	-	-	101.8	1.2	-	-	103.0	1.2	-	-	102.9	-0.1	-	-	102.9	0.0	-	-	103.2	0.3	-	-
1985	103.0	-0.2	-	-	104.2	1.2	-	-	105.3	1.1	-	-	105.5	0.2	-	-	105.3	-0.2	-	-	106.4	1.0	-	-
1986	106.6	0.2	-	-	103.3	-3.1	-	-	100.0	-3.2	-	-	100.0	0.0	-	-	98.9	-1.1	-	-	99.5	0.6	-	-
1987	100.8	1.3	-	-	100.4	-0.4	-	-	101.9	1.5	-	-	103.8	1.9	-	-	105.9	2.0	-	-	107.7	1.7	-	-
1988	107.3	-0.4	-	-	106.4	-0.8	-	-	107.0	0.6	-	-	108.7	1.6	-	-	110.6	1.7	-	-	113.9	3.0	-	-
1989	113.6	-0.3	-	-	115.3	1.5	-	-	117.9	2.3	-	-	114.8	-2.6	-	-	114.6	-0.2	-	-	116.5	1.7	-	-
1990	117.4	0.8	-	-	117.8	0.3	-	-	118.7	0.8	-	-	119.1	0.3	-	-	125.6	5.5	-	-	131.0	4.3	-	-
1991	127.9	-2.4	-	-	124.9	-2.3	-	-	127.4	2.0	-	-	128.7	1.0	-	-	129.6	0.7	-	-	130.7	0.8	-	-

[Continued]

Boston, MA
Consumer Price Index - Urban Wage Earners
Base 1982-1984 = 100
Transportation
[Continued]

For 1947-1997. Columns headed % show percentile change in the index from the previous period for which an index is available.

Year	Jan Index	%	Feb Index	%	Mar Index	%	Apr Index	%	May Index	%	Jun Index	%	Jul Index	%	Aug Index	%	Sep Index	%	Oct Index	%	Nov Index	%	Dec Index	%
1992	130.5	-0.2	-	-	130.8	0.2	-	-	131.5	0.5	-	-	133.0	1.1	-	-	132.2	-0.6	-	-	132.7	0.4	-	-
1993	134.6	1.4	-	-	134.9	0.2	-	-	134.6	-0.2	-	-	134.7	0.1	-	-	133.7	-0.7	-	-	136.5	2.1	-	-
1994	135.6	-0.7	-	-	136.2	0.4	-	-	134.9	-1.0	-	-	137.2	1.7	-	-	140.0	2.0	-	-	141.2	0.9	-	-
1995	140.0	-0.8	-	-	138.4	-1.1	-	-	140.2	1.3	-	-	140.8	0.4	-	-	139.8	-0.7	-	-	141.1	0.9	-	-
1996	141.9	0.6	-	-	140.3	-1.1	-	-	143.4	2.2	-	-	142.9	-0.3	-	-	143.5	0.4	-	-	145.2	1.2	-	-
1997	146.2	0.7	-	-	145.4	-0.5	-	-	143.6	-1.2	144.8	0.8	143.5	-0.9	-	-	145.4	1.3	-	-	145.5	0.1	-	-

Source: U.S. Department of Labor, Bureau of Labor Statistics, Division of Consumer Prices and Price Indexes. - indicates no data collected for period.

Boston, MA
Consumer Price Index - All Urban Consumers
Base 1982-1984 = 100
Medical Care

For 1947-1997. Columns headed % show percentile change in the index from the previous period for which an index is available.

Year	Jan Index	%	Feb Index	%	Mar Index	%	Apr Index	%	May Index	%	Jun Index	%	Jul Index	%	Aug Index	%	Sep Index	%	Oct Index	%	Nov Index	%	Dec Index	%
1947	13.3	-	13.3	0.0	13.4	0.8	13.4	0.0	13.4	0.0	13.4	0.0	13.3	-0.7	13.3	0.0	13.4	0.8	13.4	0.0	13.4	0.0	13.4	0.0
1948	13.8	3.0	13.8	0.0	14.3	3.6	14.4	0.7	14.5	0.7	14.3	-1.4	14.3	0.0	14.4	0.7	14.4	0.0	14.4	0.0	14.4	0.0	14.4	0.0
1949	14.8	2.8	14.8	0.0	14.9	0.7	14.9	0.0	14.9	0.0	15.0	0.7	15.3	2.0	15.3	0.0	15.4	0.7	15.4	0.0	15.4	0.0	15.4	0.0
1950	15.6	1.3	15.6	0.0	15.7	0.6	15.7	0.0	15.7	0.0	15.7	0.0	15.7	0.0	15.7	0.0	15.7	0.0	15.7	0.0	15.8	0.6	16.0	1.3
1951	16.1	0.6	16.1	0.0	16.2	0.6	16.2	0.0	16.2	0.0	16.3	0.6	16.3	0.0	16.3	0.0	16.2	-0.6	16.3	0.6	16.3	0.0	16.7	2.5
1952	16.8	0.6	16.8	0.0	16.8	0.0	16.9	0.6	16.9	0.0	17.1	1.2	17.2	0.6	17.2	0.0	17.5	1.7	17.5	0.0	17.5	0.0	17.5	0.0
1953	17.6	0.6	-	-	-	-	17.6	0.0	-	-	-	-	17.6	0.0	-	-	-	-	17.7	0.6	-	-	-	-
1954	17.7	0.0	-	-	-	-	17.7	0.0	-	-	-	-	17.7	0.0	-	-	-	-	17.7	0.0	-	-	-	-
1955	17.7	0.0	-	-	-	-	17.7	0.0	-	-	-	-	17.8	0.6	-	-	-	-	18.0	1.1	-	-	-	-
1956	18.3	1.7	-	-	-	-	18.3	0.0	-	-	-	-	19.5	6.6	-	-	-	-	19.6	0.5	-	-	-	-
1957	19.7	0.5	-	-	-	-	20.1	2.0	-	-	-	-	21.2	5.5	-	-	-	-	21.2	0.0	-	-	-	-
1958	22.0	3.8	-	-	-	-	22.1	0.5	-	-	-	-	22.3	0.9	-	-	-	-	22.4	0.4	-	-	-	-
1959	22.6	0.9	-	-	-	-	22.7	0.4	-	-	-	-	22.7	0.0	-	-	-	-	22.9	0.9	-	-	-	-
1960	23.0	0.4	-	-	-	-	23.1	0.4	-	-	-	-	23.2	0.4	-	-	-	-	23.3	0.4	-	-	-	-
1961	23.7	1.7	-	-	-	-	23.8	0.4	-	-	-	-	23.9	0.4	-	-	-	-	24.1	0.8	-	-	-	-
1962	24.5	1.7	-	-	-	-	24.8	1.2	-	-	-	-	24.8	0.0	-	-	-	-	24.9	0.4	-	-	-	-
1963	24.9	0.0	-	-	-	-	25.3	1.6	-	-	-	-	25.3	0.0	-	-	-	-	25.5	0.8	-	-	-	-
1964	25.6	0.4	-	-	-	-	25.9	1.2	-	-	-	-	25.9	0.0	-	-	-	-	26.5	2.3	-	-	-	-
1965	26.8	1.1	-	-	-	-	26.8	0.0	-	-	-	-	27.1	1.1	-	-	-	-	27.3	0.7	-	-	-	-
1966	27.4	0.4	-	-	-	-	27.9	1.8	-	-	-	-	28.0	0.4	-	-	-	-	28.8	2.9	-	-	-	-
1967	29.3	1.7	-	-	-	-	29.3	0.0	-	-	-	-	29.9	2.0	-	-	-	-	31.0	3.7	-	-	-	-
1968	31.7	2.3	-	-	-	-	31.8	0.3	-	-	-	-	32.2	1.3	-	-	-	-	33.6	4.3	-	-	-	-
1969	34.2	1.8	-	-	-	-	34.5	0.9	-	-	-	-	34.9	1.2	-	-	-	-	36.0	3.2	-	-	-	-
1970	36.5	1.4	-	-	-	-	36.8	0.8	-	-	-	-	37.2	1.1	-	-	-	-	38.5	3.5	-	-	-	-
1971	38.8	0.8	-	-	-	-	39.2	1.0	-	-	-	-	39.4	0.5	-	-	-	-	39.2	-0.5	-	-	-	-
1972	40.0	2.0	-	-	-	-	40.4	1.0	-	-	-	-	40.5	0.2	-	-	-	-	40.9	1.0	-	-	-	-
1973	41.2	0.7	-	-	-	-	41.4	0.5	-	-	-	-	41.6	0.5	-	-	-	-	42.5	2.2	-	-	-	-
1974	42.8	0.7	-	-	-	-	43.3	1.2	-	-	-	-	44.7	3.2	-	-	-	-	46.6	4.3	-	-	-	-
1975	47.9	2.8	-	-	-	-	49.2	2.7	-	-	-	-	50.2	2.0	-	-	-	-	51.9	3.4	-	-	-	-
1976	51.6	-0.6	-	-	-	-	51.8	0.4	-	-	-	-	53.9	4.1	-	-	-	-	54.9	1.9	-	-	-	-
1977	56.2	2.4	-	-	-	-	56.9	1.2	-	-	-	-	57.9	1.8	-	-	-	-	59.2	2.2	-	-	-	-
1978	59.4	0.3	-	-	59.8	0.7	-	-	-	-	60.6	1.3	61.5	1.5	-	-	62.8	2.1	-	-	66.1	5.3	-	-
1979	66.9	1.2	-	-	67.7	1.2	-	-	-	-	68.2	0.7	69.8	2.3	-	-	70.2	0.6	-	-	72.1	2.7	-	-
1980	74.3	3.1	-	-	74.9	0.8	-	-	-	-	76.6	2.3	76.4	-0.3	-	-	76.5	0.1	-	-	80.9	5.8	-	-
1981	81.6	0.9	-	-	82.0	0.5	-	-	82.3	0.4	-	-	82.7	0.5	-	-	83.4	0.8	-	-	88.0	5.5	-	-
1982	90.3	2.6	-	-	90.6	0.3	-	-	91.4	0.9	-	-	93.2	2.0	-	-	93.4	0.2	-	-	95.1	1.8	-	-
1983	96.9	1.9	-	-	96.6	-0.3	-	-	96.9	0.3	-	-	98.3	1.4	-	-	100.3	2.0	-	-	102.1	1.8	-	-
1984	104.2	2.1	-	-	106.7	2.4	-	-	107.8	1.0	-	-	109.4	1.5	-	-	109.1	-0.3	-	-	112.2	2.8	-	-
1985	112.2	0.0	-	-	119.7	6.7	-	-	121.5	1.5	-	-	121.6	0.1	-	-	120.9	-0.6	-	-	123.5	2.2	-	-
1986	126.5	2.4	-	-	130.2	2.9	-	-	131.9	1.3	-	-	132.9	0.8	-	-	133.8	0.7	-	-	133.5	-0.2	-	-
1987	135.0	1.1	-	-	137.7	2.0	-	-	138.5	0.6	-	-	138.7	0.1	-	-	139.4	0.5	-	-	143.3	2.8	-	-
1988	146.2	2.0	-	-	149.3	2.1	-	-	150.7	0.9	-	-	153.4	1.8	-	-	155.0	1.0	-	-	154.9	-0.1	-	-
1989	157.7	1.8	-	-	160.3	1.6	-	-	164.3	2.5	-	-	166.4	1.3	-	-	169.3	1.7	-	-	170.1	0.5	-	-
1990	173.2	1.8	-	-	177.9	2.7	-	-	181.7	2.1	-	-	182.3	0.3	-	-	182.7	0.2	-	-	187.5	2.6	-	-
1991	189.7	1.2	-	-	198.4	4.6	-	-	201.8	1.7	-	-	205.4	1.8	-	-	204.6	-0.4	-	-	210.4	2.8	-	-

[Continued]

Boston, MA
Consumer Price Index - All Urban Consumers
Base 1982-1984 = 100
Medical Care
[Continued]

For 1947-1997. Columns headed % show percentile change in the index from the previous period for which an index is available.

Year	Jan		Feb		Mar		Apr		May		Jun		Jul		Aug		Sep		Oct		Nov		Dec	
	Index	%	Index	%	Index	%	Index	%	Index	%	Index	%	Index	%	Index	%	Index	%	Index	%	Index	%	Index	%
1992	213.8	1.6	-	-	218.6	2.2	-	-	223.9	2.4	-	-	223.9	0.0	-	-	227.4	1.6	-	-	232.5	2.2	-	-
1993	233.9	0.6	-	-	232.7	-0.5	-	-	237.7	2.1	-	-	240.1	1.0	-	-	240.2	0.0	-	-	246.1	2.5	-	-
1994	247.3	0.5	-	-	249.3	0.8	-	-	250.4	0.4	-	-	250.2	-0.1	-	-	251.8	0.6	-	-	255.0	1.3	-	-
1995	257.9	1.1	-	-	262.7	1.9	-	-	265.1	0.9	-	-	266.7	0.6	-	-	265.9	-0.3	-	-	273.9	3.0	-	-
1996	275.2	0.5	-	-	278.5	1.2	-	-	278.5	0.0	-	-	279.8	0.5	-	-	282.3	0.9	-	-	286.5	1.5	-	-
1997	291.4	1.7	-	-	289.8	-0.5	-	-	292.0	0.8	291.2	-0.3	292.8	0.5	-	-	291.8	-0.3	-	-	298.2	2.2	-	-

Source: U.S. Department of Labor, Bureau of Labor Statistics, Division of Consumer Prices and Price Indexes. - indicates no data collected for period.

Boston, MA
Consumer Price Index - Urban Wage Earners
Base 1982-1984 = 100
Medical Care

For 1947-1997. Columns headed % show percentile change in the index from the previous period for which an index is available.

Year	Jan Index	%	Feb Index	%	Mar Index	%	Apr Index	%	May Index	%	Jun Index	%	Jul Index	%	Aug Index	%	Sep Index	%	Oct Index	%	Nov Index	%	Dec Index	%
1947	13.5	-	13.5	0.0	13.6	0.7	13.6	0.0	13.6	0.0	13.6	0.0	13.5	-0.7	13.5	0.0	13.6	0.7	13.6	0.0	13.6	0.0	13.6	0.0
1948	14.0	2.9	14.0	0.0	14.5	3.6	14.7	1.4	14.7	0.0	14.5	-1.4	14.5	0.0	14.6	0.7	14.6	0.0	14.6	0.0	14.6	0.0	14.6	0.0
1949	15.0	2.7	15.0	0.0	15.1	0.7	15.1	0.0	15.1	0.0	15.2	0.7	15.5	2.0	15.6	0.6	15.6	0.0	15.6	0.0	15.6	0.0	15.6	0.0
1950	15.8	1.3	15.8	0.0	15.9	0.6	15.9	0.0	15.9	0.0	16.0	0.6	16.0	0.0	16.0	0.0	16.0	0.0	16.0	0.0	16.0	0.0	16.2	1.3
1951	16.3	0.6	16.3	0.0	16.5	1.2	16.5	0.0	16.5	0.0	16.5	0.0	16.5	0.0	16.5	0.0	16.5	0.0	16.5	0.0	16.6	0.6	17.0	2.4
1952	17.1	0.6	17.1	0.0	17.1	0.0	17.1	0.0	17.1	0.0	17.3	1.2	17.4	0.6	17.4	0.0	17.7	1.7	17.7	0.0	17.7	0.0	17.8	0.6
1953	17.8	0.0	-	-	-	-	17.8	0.0	-	-	-	-	17.9	0.6	-	-	-	-	18.0	0.6	-	-	-	-
1954	18.0	0.0	-	-	-	-	18.0	0.0	-	-	-	-	18.0	0.0	-	-	-	-	18.0	0.0	-	-	-	-
1955	18.0	0.0	-	-	-	-	18.0	0.0	-	-	-	-	18.1	0.6	-	-	-	-	18.3	1.1	-	-	-	-
1956	18.6	1.6	-	-	-	-	18.6	0.0	-	-	-	-	19.8	6.5	-	-	-	-	19.9	0.5	-	-	-	-
1957	20.0	0.5	-	-	-	-	20.4	2.0	-	-	-	-	21.5	5.4	-	-	-	-	21.6	0.5	-	-	-	-
1958	22.3	3.2	-	-	-	-	22.4	0.4	-	-	-	-	22.6	0.9	-	-	-	-	22.7	0.4	-	-	-	-
1959	23.0	1.3	-	-	-	-	23.0	0.0	-	-	-	-	23.1	0.4	-	-	-	-	23.2	0.4	-	-	-	-
1960	23.3	0.4	-	-	-	-	23.4	0.4	-	-	-	-	23.5	0.4	-	-	-	-	23.6	0.4	-	-	-	-
1961	24.1	2.1	-	-	-	-	24.1	0.0	-	-	-	-	24.3	0.8	-	-	-	-	24.4	0.4	-	-	-	-
1962	24.9	2.0	-	-	-	-	25.1	0.8	-	-	-	-	25.1	0.0	-	-	-	-	25.2	0.4	-	-	-	-
1963	25.3	0.4	-	-	-	-	25.7	1.6	-	-	-	-	25.7	0.0	-	-	-	-	25.9	0.8	-	-	-	-
1964	26.0	0.4	-	-	-	-	26.3	1.2	-	-	-	-	26.3	0.0	-	-	-	-	26.9	2.3	-	-	-	-
1965	27.2	1.1	-	-	-	-	27.2	0.0	-	-	-	-	27.5	1.1	-	-	-	-	27.7	0.7	-	-	-	-
1966	27.8	0.4	-	-	-	-	28.3	1.8	-	-	-	-	28.4	0.4	-	-	-	-	29.2	2.8	-	-	-	-
1967	29.8	2.1	-	-	-	-	29.8	0.0	-	-	-	-	30.4	2.0	-	-	-	-	31.4	3.3	-	-	-	-
1968	32.1	2.2	-	-	-	-	32.3	0.6	-	-	-	-	32.7	1.2	-	-	-	-	34.1	4.3	-	-	-	-
1969	34.7	1.8	-	-	-	-	35.0	0.9	-	-	-	-	35.4	1.1	-	-	-	-	36.5	3.1	-	-	-	-
1970	37.0	1.4	-	-	-	-	37.4	1.1	-	-	-	-	37.8	1.1	-	-	-	-	39.0	3.2	-	-	-	-
1971	39.4	1.0	-	-	-	-	39.7	0.8	-	-	-	-	40.0	0.8	-	-	-	-	39.8	-0.5	-	-	-	-
1972	40.6	2.0	-	-	-	-	41.0	1.0	-	-	-	-	41.1	0.2	-	-	-	-	41.5	1.0	-	-	-	-
1973	41.8	0.7	-	-	-	-	42.0	0.5	-	-	-	-	42.2	0.5	-	-	-	-	43.2	2.4	-	-	-	-
1974	43.4	0.5	-	-	-	-	44.0	1.4	-	-	-	-	45.3	3.0	-	-	-	-	47.3	4.4	-	-	-	-
1975	48.6	2.7	-	-	-	-	49.9	2.7	-	-	-	-	50.9	2.0	-	-	-	-	52.7	3.5	-	-	-	-
1976	52.4	-0.6	-	-	-	-	52.6	0.4	-	-	-	-	54.7	4.0	-	-	-	-	55.7	1.8	-	-	-	-
1977	57.0	2.3	-	-	-	-	57.8	1.4	-	-	-	-	58.7	1.6	-	-	-	-	60.1	2.4	-	-	-	-
1978	60.3	0.3	-	-	61.2	1.5	-	-	61.9	1.1	-	-	62.0	0.2	-	-	63.9	3.1	-	-	65.8	3.0	-	-
1979	66.7	1.4	-	-	67.3	0.9	-	-	68.2	1.3	-	-	69.8	2.3	-	-	69.9	0.1	-	-	72.5	3.7	-	-
1980	73.6	1.5	-	-	74.4	1.1	-	-	77.0	3.5	-	-	75.6	-1.8	-	-	76.1	0.7	-	-	79.7	4.7	-	-
1981	80.5	1.0	-	-	81.9	1.7	-	-	83.9	2.4	-	-	82.8	-1.3	-	-	83.5	0.8	-	-	87.7	5.0	-	-
1982	89.8	2.4	-	-	90.3	0.6	-	-	91.2	1.0	-	-	93.0	2.0	-	-	93.1	0.1	-	-	94.6	1.6	-	-
1983	96.6	2.1	-	-	96.4	-0.2	-	-	96.7	0.3	-	-	98.4	1.8	-	-	100.5	2.1	-	-	102.3	1.8	-	-
1984	104.9	2.5	-	-	107.2	2.2	-	-	108.3	1.0	-	-	109.8	1.4	-	-	109.5	-0.3	-	-	112.0	2.3	-	-
1985	111.8	-0.2	-	-	118.1	5.6	-	-	119.9	1.5	-	-	120.5	0.5	-	-	120.0	-0.4	-	-	122.4	2.0	-	-
1986	125.1	2.2	-	-	128.8	3.0	-	-	130.6	1.4	-	-	131.7	0.8	-	-	132.8	0.8	-	-	132.7	-0.1	-	-
1987	134.6	1.4	-	-	137.1	1.9	-	-	138.2	0.8	-	-	138.2	0.0	-	-	139.3	0.8	-	-	142.8	2.5	-	-
1988	145.7	2.0	-	-	148.5	1.9	-	-	150.2	1.1	-	-	152.6	1.6	-	-	154.0	0.9	-	-	154.5	0.3	-	-
1989	157.1	1.7	-	-	159.5	1.5	-	-	162.7	2.0	-	-	164.5	1.1	-	-	167.7	1.9	-	-	168.4	0.4	-	-
1990	171.3	1.7	-	-	175.8	2.6	-	-	180.0	2.4	-	-	180.7	0.4	-	-	181.1	0.2	-	-	185.3	2.3	-	-
1991	187.4	1.1	-	-	194.9	4.0	-	-	198.9	2.1	-	-	202.5	1.8	-	-	201.9	-0.3	-	-	207.1	2.6	-	-

[Continued]

Boston, MA
Consumer Price Index - Urban Wage Earners
Base 1982-1984 = 100
Medical Care
[Continued]

For 1947-1997. Columns headed % show percentile change in the index from the previous period for which an index is available.

Year	Jan Index	%	Feb Index	%	Mar Index	%	Apr Index	%	May Index	%	Jun Index	%	Jul Index	%	Aug Index	%	Sep Index	%	Oct Index	%	Nov Index	%	Dec Index	%
1992	210.2	1.5	-	-	214.4	2.0	-	-	219.1	2.2	-	-	219.1	0.0	-	-	223.7	2.1	-	-	228.4	2.1	-	-
1993	229.5	0.5	-	-	228.7	-0.3	-	-	233.8	2.2	-	-	236.1	1.0	-	-	236.1	0.0	-	-	240.4	1.8	-	-
1994	241.7	0.5	-	-	243.8	0.9	-	-	245.1	0.5	-	-	245.1	0.0	-	-	246.5	0.6	-	-	249.3	1.1	-	-
1995	252.1	1.1	-	-	256.7	1.8	-	-	258.9	0.9	-	-	260.8	0.7	-	-	260.1	-0.3	-	-	267.0	2.7	-	-
1996	268.3	0.5	-	-	271.8	1.3	-	-	272.1	0.1	-	-	273.3	0.4	-	-	275.2	0.7	-	-	279.2	1.5	-	-
1997	283.6	1.6	-	-	281.8	-0.6	-	-	284.3	0.9	283.4	-0.3	285.1	0.6	-	-	284.3	-0.3	-	-	290.0	2.0	-	-

Source: U.S. Department of Labor, Bureau of Labor Statistics, Division of Consumer Prices and Price Indexes. - indicates no data collected for period.

Boston, MA
Consumer Price Index - All Urban Consumers
Base 1982-1984 = 100
Entertainment

For 1976-1997. Columns headed % show percentile change in the index from the previous period for which an index is available.

Year	Jan Index	%	Feb Index	%	Mar Index	%	Apr Index	%	May Index	%	Jun Index	%	Jul Index	%	Aug Index	%	Sep Index	%	Oct Index	%	Nov Index	%	Dec Index	%
1976	63.7	-	-	-	-	-	64.0	0.5	-	-	-	-	64.8	1.3	-	-	-	-	65.4	0.9	-	-	-	-
1977	65.5	0.2	-	-	-	-	65.4	-0.2	-	-	-	-	66.6	1.8	-	-	-	-	66.7	0.2	-	-	-	-
1978	67.1	0.6	-	-	68.3	1.8	-	-	69.0	1.0	-	-	68.4	-0.9	-	-	68.7	0.4	-	-	72.6	5.7	-	-
1979	72.4	-0.3	-	-	73.5	1.5	-	-	75.6	2.9	-	-	76.0	0.5	-	-	76.5	0.7	-	-	78.1	2.1	-	-
1980	79.9	2.3	-	-	80.7	1.0	-	-	83.3	3.2	-	-	83.7	0.5	-	-	84.4	0.8	-	-	85.7	1.5	-	-
1981	87.0	1.5	-	-	88.7	2.0	-	-	88.8	0.1	-	-	90.1	1.5	-	-	91.1	1.1	-	-	91.9	0.9	-	-
1982	92.9	1.1	-	-	93.8	1.0	-	-	96.4	2.8	-	-	96.6	0.2	-	-	97.9	1.3	-	-	98.4	0.5	-	-
1983	99.0	0.6	-	-	99.3	0.3	-	-	100.8	1.5	-	-	101.3	0.5	-	-	100.5	-0.8	-	-	100.0	-0.5	-	-
1984	101.8	1.8	-	-	103.8	2.0	-	-	103.2	-0.6	-	-	103.6	0.4	-	-	104.1	0.5	-	-	103.0	-1.1	-	-
1985	107.4	4.3	-	-	110.1	2.5	-	-	107.4	-2.5	-	-	109.4	1.9	-	-	111.0	1.5	-	-	111.0	0.0	-	-
1986	117.0	5.4	-	-	114.0	-2.6	-	-	114.7	0.6	-	-	112.9	-1.6	-	-	113.4	0.4	-	-	115.2	1.6	-	-
1987	118.5	2.9	-	-	118.1	-0.3	-	-	116.9	-1.0	-	-	119.4	2.1	-	-	121.5	1.8	-	-	120.7	-0.7	-	-
1988	122.9	1.8	-	-	127.9	4.1	-	-	125.9	-1.6	-	-	127.5	1.3	-	-	127.9	0.3	-	-	128.2	0.2	-	-
1989	128.9	0.5	-	-	128.9	0.0	-	-	132.5	2.8	-	-	135.4	2.2	-	-	137.0	1.2	-	-	136.7	-0.2	-	-
1990	137.7	0.7	-	-	141.2	2.5	-	-	143.7	1.8	-	-	145.4	1.2	-	-	148.4	2.1	-	-	146.3	-1.4	-	-
1991	147.5	0.8	-	-	148.5	0.7	-	-	150.7	1.5	-	-	156.3	3.7	-	-	156.7	0.3	-	-	152.3	-2.8	-	-
1992	152.8	0.3	-	-	152.8	0.0	-	-	154.0	0.8	-	-	155.9	1.2	-	-	156.3	0.3	-	-	156.9	0.4	-	-
1993	156.9	0.0	-	-	157.7	0.5	-	-	159.5	1.1	-	-	159.5	0.0	-	-	161.9	1.5	-	-	163.5	1.0	-	-
1994	162.3	-0.7	-	-	161.7	-0.4	-	-	163.6	1.2	-	-	164.2	0.4	-	-	165.1	0.5	-	-	165.7	0.4	-	-
1995	166.3	0.4	-	-	166.0	-0.2	-	-	167.1	0.7	-	-	168.4	0.8	-	-	167.0	-0.8	-	-	169.3	1.4	-	-
1996	168.5	-0.5	-	-	169.6	0.7	-	-	168.5	-0.6	-	-	168.2	-0.2	-	-	171.2	1.8	-	-	171.3	0.1	-	-
1997	172.9	0.9	-	-	173.7	0.5	-	-	176.8	1.8	174.6	-1.2	174.7	0.1	-	-	175.7	0.6	-	-	176.4	0.4	-	-

Source: U.S. Department of Labor, Bureau of Labor Statistics, Division of Consumer Prices and Price Indexes. - indicates no data collected for period.

Boston, MA
Consumer Price Index - Urban Wage Earners
Base 1982-1984 = 100
Entertainment

For 1976-1997. Columns headed % show percentile change in the index from the previous period for which an index is available.

Year	Jan Index	%	Feb Index	%	Mar Index	%	Apr Index	%	May Index	%	Jun Index	%	Jul Index	%	Aug Index	%	Sep Index	%	Oct Index	%	Nov Index	%	Dec Index	%
1976	66.0	-	-	-	-	-	66.3	0.5	-	-	-	-	67.1	1.2	-	-	-	-	67.8	1.0	-	-	-	-
1977	67.8	0.0	-	-	-	-	67.7	-0.1	-	-	-	-	69.0	1.9	-	-	-	-	69.1	0.1	-	-	-	-
1978	69.5	0.6	-	-	70.2	1.0	-	-	70.8	0.9	-	-	68.8	-2.8	-	-	69.0	0.3	-	-	74.6	8.1	-	-
1979	74.9	0.4	-	-	75.6	0.9	-	-	76.4	1.1	-	-	77.3	1.2	-	-	77.8	0.6	-	-	79.1	1.7	-	-
1980	79.6	0.6	-	-	81.8	2.8	-	-	83.2	1.7	-	-	83.5	0.4	-	-	84.4	1.1	-	-	86.1	2.0	-	-
1981	86.6	0.6	-	-	88.3	2.0	-	-	89.0	0.8	-	-	89.4	0.4	-	-	90.7	1.5	-	-	92.2	1.7	-	-
1982	93.0	0.9	-	-	93.7	0.8	-	-	96.5	3.0	-	-	96.1	-0.4	-	-	97.8	1.8	-	-	98.5	0.7	-	-
1983	98.9	0.4	-	-	99.2	0.3	-	-	100.8	1.6	-	-	101.2	0.4	-	-	100.4	-0.8	-	-	100.3	-0.1	-	-
1984	102.1	1.8	-	-	103.2	1.1	-	-	103.4	0.2	-	-	103.9	0.5	-	-	104.1	0.2	-	-	103.4	-0.7	-	-
1985	107.3	3.8	-	-	109.0	1.6	-	-	107.5	-1.4	-	-	109.0	1.4	-	-	109.9	0.8	-	-	110.6	0.6	-	-
1986	116.0	4.9	-	-	113.7	-2.0	-	-	114.4	0.6	-	-	112.4	-1.7	-	-	112.9	0.4	-	-	114.4	1.3	-	-
1987	117.2	2.4	-	-	116.8	-0.3	-	-	115.1	-1.5	-	-	118.3	2.8	-	-	120.0	1.4	-	-	118.9	-0.9	-	-
1988	120.5	1.3	-	-	125.2	3.9	-	-	124.8	-0.3	-	-	126.2	1.1	-	-	125.8	-0.3	-	-	127.4	1.3	-	-
1989	127.8	0.3	-	-	127.7	-0.1	-	-	131.6	3.1	-	-	135.1	2.7	-	-	136.7	1.2	-	-	136.5	-0.1	-	-
1990	137.6	0.8	-	-	140.8	2.3	-	-	144.1	2.3	-	-	146.6	1.7	-	-	149.0	1.6	-	-	146.2	-1.9	-	-
1991	148.1	1.3	-	-	150.0	1.3	-	-	152.2	1.5	-	-	155.7	2.3	-	-	156.1	0.3	-	-	153.4	-1.7	-	-
1992	153.3	-0.1	-	-	153.3	0.0	-	-	154.9	1.0	-	-	156.7	1.2	-	-	156.6	-0.1	-	-	157.1	0.3	-	-
1993	157.1	0.0	-	-	158.4	0.8	-	-	160.3	1.2	-	-	161.9	1.0	-	-	164.0	1.3	-	-	164.3	0.2	-	-
1994	163.0	-0.8	-	-	162.1	-0.6	-	-	164.1	1.2	-	-	166.3	1.3	-	-	166.6	0.2	-	-	167.3	0.4	-	-
1995	169.1	1.1	-	-	168.4	-0.4	-	-	169.8	0.8	-	-	171.3	0.9	-	-	168.8	-1.5	-	-	171.5	1.6	-	-
1996	170.7	-0.5	-	-	172.4	1.0	-	-	170.9	-0.9	-	-	170.4	-0.3	-	-	172.5	1.2	-	-	172.5	0.0	-	-
1997	174.2	1.0	-	-	175.7	0.9	-	-	177.7	1.1	176.0	-1.0	175.3	-0.4	-	-	175.3	0.0	-	-	176.5	0.7	-	-

Source: U.S. Department of Labor, Bureau of Labor Statistics, Division of Consumer Prices and Price Indexes. - indicates no data collected for period.

Boston, MA
Consumer Price Index - All Urban Consumers
Base 1982-1984 = 100
Other Goods and Services

For 1976-1997. Columns headed % show percentile change in the index from the previous period for which an index is available.

Year	Jan Index	%	Feb Index	%	Mar Index	%	Apr Index	%	May Index	%	Jun Index	%	Jul Index	%	Aug Index	%	Sep Index	%	Oct Index	%	Nov Index	%	Dec Index	%
1976	55.1	-	-	-	-	-	55.6	0.9	-	-	-	-	56.3	1.3	-	-	-	-	57.2	1.6	-	-	-	-
1977	58.3	1.9	-	-	-	-	58.6	0.5	-	-	-	-	59.1	0.9	-	-	-	-	60.7	2.7	-	-	-	-
1978	60.8	0.2	-	-	60.9	0.2	-	-	61.1	0.3	-	-	62.1	1.6	-	-	64.3	3.5	-	-	64.6	0.5	-	-
1979	64.6	0.0	-	-	65.3	1.1	-	-	65.9	0.9	-	-	66.7	1.2	-	-	69.8	4.6	-	-	70.4	0.9	-	-
1980	71.0	0.9	-	-	71.5	0.7	-	-	72.1	0.8	-	-	72.9	1.1	-	-	75.9	4.1	-	-	76.5	0.8	-	-
1981	77.4	1.2	-	-	78.4	1.3	-	-	79.3	1.1	-	-	81.0	2.1	-	-	83.5	3.1	-	-	84.7	1.4	-	-
1982	85.4	0.8	-	-	89.5	4.8	-	-	89.9	0.4	-	-	89.9	0.0	-	-	92.2	2.6	-	-	93.7	1.6	-	-
1983	94.7	1.1	-	-	99.0	4.5	-	-	99.5	0.5	-	-	100.4	0.9	-	-	101.4	1.0	-	-	103.4	2.0	-	-
1984	104.3	0.9	-	-	107.7	3.3	-	-	108.0	0.3	-	-	108.4	0.4	-	-	112.7	4.0	-	-	113.1	0.4	-	-
1985	113.2	0.1	-	-	114.7	1.3	-	-	115.7	0.9	-	-	116.0	0.3	-	-	124.4	7.2	-	-	126.1	1.4	-	-
1986	126.7	0.5	-	-	127.4	0.6	-	-	126.8	-0.5	-	-	127.3	0.4	-	-	131.0	2.9	-	-	132.1	0.8	-	-
1987	132.3	0.2	-	-	132.7	0.3	-	-	132.7	0.0	-	-	133.2	0.4	-	-	141.3	6.1	-	-	141.6	0.2	-	-
1988	142.3	0.5	-	-	144.0	1.2	-	-	144.2	0.1	-	-	145.1	0.6	-	-	152.0	4.8	-	-	152.3	0.2	-	-
1989	153.9	1.1	-	-	154.8	0.6	-	-	156.2	0.9	-	-	159.2	1.9	-	-	159.2	0.0	-	-	161.1	1.2	-	-
1990	166.3	3.2	-	-	167.8	0.9	-	-	168.4	0.4	-	-	175.4	4.2	-	-	180.1	2.7	-	-	178.0	-1.2	-	-
1991	183.1	2.9	-	-	182.3	-0.4	-	-	182.7	0.2	-	-	191.9	5.0	-	-	194.0	1.1	-	-	193.5	-0.3	-	-
1992	194.5	0.5	-	-	192.9	-0.8	-	-	196.1	1.7	-	-	200.4	2.2	-	-	199.8	-0.3	-	-	201.5	0.9	-	-
1993	202.7	0.6	-	-	202.2	-0.2	-	-	202.1	-0.0	-	-	205.5	1.7	-	-	202.2	-1.6	-	-	200.6	-0.8	-	-
1994	203.0	1.2	-	-	205.3	1.1	-	-	204.7	-0.3	-	-	204.8	0.0	-	-	209.3	2.2	-	-	210.7	0.7	-	-
1995	209.5	-0.6	-	-	209.0	-0.2	-	-	211.4	1.1	-	-	212.0	0.3	-	-	217.7	2.7	-	-	218.2	0.2	-	-
1996	217.8	-0.2	-	-	218.3	0.2	-	-	218.8	0.2	-	-	218.7	-0.0	-	-	221.0	1.1	-	-	225.5	2.0	-	-
1997	223.8	-0.8	-	-	226.2	1.1	-	-	227.6	0.6	226.3	-0.6	228.6	1.0	-	-	232.6	1.7	-	-	233.0	0.2	-	-

Source: U.S. Department of Labor, Bureau of Labor Statistics, Division of Consumer Prices and Price Indexes. - indicates no data collected for period.

Boston, MA
Consumer Price Index - Urban Wage Earners
Base 1982-1984 = 100
Other Goods and Services

For 1976-1997. Columns headed % show percentile change in the index from the previous period for which an index is available.

Year	Jan Index	%	Feb Index	%	Mar Index	%	Apr Index	%	May Index	%	Jun Index	%	Jul Index	%	Aug Index	%	Sep Index	%	Oct Index	%	Nov Index	%	Dec Index	%
1976	55.9	-	-	-	-	-	56.4	0.9	-	-	-	-	57.1	1.2	-	-	-	-	58.0	1.6	-	-	-	-
1977	59.1	1.9	-	-	-	-	59.4	0.5	-	-	-	-	59.9	0.8	-	-	-	-	61.5	2.7	-	-	-	-
1978	61.6	0.2	-	-	61.7	0.2	-	-	61.9	0.3	-	-	62.9	1.6	-	-	65.0	3.3	-	-	65.5	0.8	-	-
1979	65.3	-0.3	-	-	66.3	1.5	-	-	66.6	0.5	-	-	67.6	1.5	-	-	70.3	4.0	-	-	70.8	0.7	-	-
1980	71.6	1.1	-	-	72.0	0.6	-	-	71.9	-0.1	-	-	73.1	1.7	-	-	75.8	3.7	-	-	76.5	0.9	-	-
1981	77.1	0.8	-	-	78.8	2.2	-	-	79.5	0.9	-	-	81.2	2.1	-	-	83.4	2.7	-	-	84.7	1.6	-	-
1982	85.1	0.5	-	-	89.4	5.1	-	-	89.7	0.3	-	-	89.7	0.0	-	-	92.0	2.6	-	-	93.6	1.7	-	-
1983	94.6	1.1	-	-	99.0	4.7	-	-	99.5	0.5	-	-	100.4	0.9	-	-	101.3	0.9	-	-	103.5	2.2	-	-
1984	104.4	0.9	-	-	107.9	3.4	-	-	108.2	0.3	-	-	108.7	0.5	-	-	112.8	3.8	-	-	113.2	0.4	-	-
1985	113.3	0.1	-	-	114.9	1.4	-	-	116.0	1.0	-	-	116.3	0.3	-	-	124.6	7.1	-	-	126.2	1.3	-	-
1986	126.8	0.5	-	-	127.5	0.6	-	-	126.9	-0.5	-	-	127.4	0.4	-	-	130.9	2.7	-	-	132.1	0.9	-	-
1987	132.5	0.3	-	-	133.0	0.4	-	-	133.0	0.0	-	-	133.9	0.7	-	-	140.5	4.9	-	-	140.7	0.1	-	-
1988	141.6	0.6	-	-	143.6	1.4	-	-	144.1	0.3	-	-	145.2	0.8	-	-	151.9	4.6	-	-	152.3	0.3	-	-
1989	154.1	1.2	-	-	154.7	0.4	-	-	156.4	1.1	-	-	160.6	2.7	-	-	160.3	-0.2	-	-	162.3	1.2	-	-
1990	167.5	3.2	-	-	170.1	1.6	-	-	170.2	0.1	-	-	176.9	3.9	-	-	180.3	1.9	-	-	176.7	-2.0	-	-
1991	183.7	4.0	-	-	182.4	-0.7	-	-	183.0	0.3	-	-	193.0	5.5	-	-	195.4	1.2	-	-	196.4	0.5	-	-
1992	197.7	0.7	-	-	195.0	-1.4	-	-	199.1	2.1	-	-	203.2	2.1	-	-	200.3	-1.4	-	-	203.2	1.4	-	-
1993	205.0	0.9	-	-	205.8	0.4	-	-	205.6	-0.1	-	-	208.3	1.3	-	-	200.6	-3.7	-	-	198.5	-1.0	-	-
1994	201.5	1.5	-	-	204.3	1.4	-	-	203.2	-0.5	-	-	203.2	0.0	-	-	207.0	1.9	-	-	209.0	1.0	-	-
1995	207.5	-0.7	-	-	205.8	-0.8	-	-	209.4	1.7	-	-	209.7	0.1	-	-	215.8	2.9	-	-	216.4	0.3	-	-
1996	215.9	-0.2	-	-	216.5	0.3	-	-	216.8	0.1	-	-	215.6	-0.6	-	-	218.2	1.2	-	-	225.6	3.4	-	-
1997	222.9	-1.2	-	-	226.4	1.6	-	-	228.6	1.0	226.5	-0.9	229.5	1.3	-	-	233.5	1.7	-	-	234.5	0.4	-	-

Source: U.S. Department of Labor, Bureau of Labor Statistics, Division of Consumer Prices and Price Indexes. - indicates no data collected for period.

Buffalo, NY
Consumer Price Index - All Urban Consumers
Base 1982-1984 = 100
Annual Averages

For 1963-1997. Columns headed % show percentile change in the index from the previous period for which an index is available.

Year	All Items		Food & Beverage		Housing		Apparel & Upkeep		Trans- portation		Medical Care		Entertain- ment		Other Goods & Services	
	Index	%	Index	%	Index	%	Index	%	Index	%	Index	%	Index	%	Index	%
1963	-	-	-	-	-	-	-	-	-	-	-	-	-	-	-	-
1964	32.6	-	-	-	-	-	40.4	-	32.8	-	29.9	-	-	-	-	-
1965	33.4	2.5	-	-	-	-	41.8	3.5	34.1	4.0	30.7	2.7	-	-	-	-
1966	34.5	3.3	-	-	-	-	43.2	3.3	34.9	2.3	32.4	5.5	-	-	-	-
1967	35.5	2.9	-	-	-	-	45.3	4.9	35.8	2.6	34.4	6.2	-	-	-	-
1968	37.1	4.5	-	-	-	-	48.3	6.6	36.7	2.5	35.7	3.8	-	-	-	-
1969	38.9	4.9	-	-	-	-	51.6	6.8	38.1	3.8	37.5	5.0	-	-	-	-
1970	41.2	5.9	-	-	-	-	53.3	3.3	40.0	5.0	39.7	5.9	-	-	-	-
1971	43.2	4.9	-	-	-	-	55.8	4.7	41.8	4.5	42.1	6.0	-	-	-	-
1972	44.9	3.9	-	-	-	-	57.1	2.3	42.2	1.0	43.4	3.1	-	-	-	-
1973	47.8	6.5	-	-	-	-	61.0	6.8	43.9	4.0	44.8	3.2	-	-	-	-
1974	53.0	10.9	-	-	-	-	66.0	8.2	48.7	10.9	48.9	9.2	-	-	-	-
1975	57.4	8.3	-	-	-	-	69.8	5.8	52.7	8.2	53.4	9.2	-	-	-	-
1976	60.5	5.4	63.4	-	59.5	-	73.2	4.9	57.7	9.5	57.9	8.4	62.9	-	58.1	-
1977	64.4	6.4	66.9	5.5	63.5	6.7	79.0	7.9	61.3	6.2	62.6	8.1	66.3	5.4	60.7	4.5
1978	68.4	6.2	72.8	8.8	67.0	5.5	82.2	4.1	64.3	4.9	68.2	8.9	70.5	6.3	63.4	4.4
1979	74.9	9.5	80.0	9.9	73.0	9.0	86.1	4.7	73.8	14.8	73.1	7.2	72.1	2.3	66.9	5.5
1980	83.5	11.5	86.8	8.5	81.7	11.9	91.1	5.8	86.5	17.2	78.4	7.3	78.8	9.3	72.6	8.5
1981	91.3	9.3	94.2	8.5	89.5	9.5	93.8	3.0	95.6	10.5	85.7	9.3	88.1	11.8	81.7	12.5
1982	94.7	3.7	97.5	3.5	92.5	3.4	97.7	4.2	97.5	2.0	91.5	6.8	94.0	6.7	90.7	11.0
1983	100.9	6.5	99.8	2.4	102.2	10.5	100.4	2.8	99.5	2.1	100.9	10.3	100.6	7.0	101.0	11.4
1984	104.4	3.5	102.6	2.8	105.3	3.0	101.9	1.5	103.0	3.5	107.6	6.6	105.5	4.9	108.3	7.2
1985	108.6	4.0	105.8	3.1	110.2	4.7	108.3	6.3	105.2	2.1	113.0	5.0	111.5	5.7	116.6	7.7
1986	109.6	0.9	108.5	2.6	112.4	2.0	111.4	2.9	98.4	-6.5	119.8	6.0	114.6	2.8	125.5	7.6
1987	113.0	3.1	112.1	3.3	114.8	2.1	117.9	5.8	99.8	1.4	127.6	6.5	122.7	7.1	132.3	5.4
1988	117.4	3.9	116.7	4.1	120.1	4.6	125.8	6.7	101.0	1.2	131.9	3.4	125.1	2.0	139.5	5.4
1989	121.6	3.6	125.8	7.8	125.0	4.1	109.4	-13.0	103.2	2.2	141.9	7.6	132.2	5.7	147.7	5.9
1990	127.7	5.0	131.5	4.5	132.0	5.6	107.6	-1.6	109.1	5.7	151.7	6.9	142.8	8.0	155.0	4.9
1991	133.4	4.5	136.0	3.4	139.4	5.6	112.0	4.1	112.2	2.8	159.0	4.8	148.2	3.8	164.6	6.2
1992	137.9	3.4	137.1	0.8	146.2	4.9	111.3	-0.6	114.0	1.6	166.5	4.7	155.7	5.1	180.0	9.4
1993	142.7	3.5	139.3	1.6	152.1	4.0	112.6	1.2	117.5	3.1	172.4	3.5	167.4	7.5	190.9	6.1
1994	146.8	2.9	143.1	2.7	155.9	2.5	118.7	5.4	120.9	2.9	174.5	1.2	177.7	6.2	194.5	1.9
1995	151.5	3.2	147.1	2.8	159.6	2.4	116.9	-1.5	127.8	5.7	181.8	4.2	187.9	5.7	203.7	4.7
1996	157.1	3.7	153.0	4.0	165.5	3.7	119.0	1.8	132.4	3.6	187.3	3.0	197.1	4.9	212.7	4.4
1997	160.5	2.2	158.2	3.4	169.6	2.5	119.2	0.2	133.0	0.5	192.6	2.8	197.4	0.2	223.2	4.9

Source: U.S. Department of Labor, Bureau of Labor Statistics, Division of Consumer Prices and Price Indexes. - indicates no data collected for period.

Buffalo, NY
Consumer Price Index - Urban Wage Earners
Base 1982-1984 = 100
Annual Averages

For 1963-1997. Columns headed % show percentile change in the index from the previous period for which an index is available.

Year	All Items		Food & Beverage		Housing		Apparel & Upkeep		Trans- portation		Medical Care		Entertain- ment		Other Goods & Services	
	Index	%	Index	%	Index	%	Index	%	Index	%	Index	%	Index	%	Index	%
1963	-	-	-	-	-	-	-	-	-	-	-	-	-	-	-	-
1964	33.0	-	-	-	-	-	41.8	-	32.6	-	29.4	-	-	-	-	-
1965	33.8	2.4	-	-	-	-	43.2	3.3	33.8	3.7	30.2	2.7	-	-	-	-
1966	35.0	3.6	-	-	-	-	44.7	3.5	34.7	2.7	31.8	5.3	-	-	-	-
1967	35.9	2.6	-	-	-	-	46.9	4.9	35.5	2.3	33.8	6.3	-	-	-	-
1968	37.5	4.5	-	-	-	-	50.0	6.6	36.5	2.8	35.1	3.8	-	-	-	-
1969	39.4	5.1	-	-	-	-	53.4	6.8	37.8	3.6	36.8	4.8	-	-	-	-
1970	41.7	5.8	-	-	-	-	55.2	3.4	39.7	5.0	39.0	6.0	-	-	-	-
1971	43.7	4.8	-	-	-	-	57.8	4.7	41.5	4.5	41.3	5.9	-	-	-	-
1972	45.5	4.1	-	-	-	-	59.1	2.2	41.9	1.0	42.6	3.1	-	-	-	-
1973	48.4	6.4	-	-	-	-	63.2	6.9	43.6	4.1	44.0	3.3	-	-	-	-
1974	53.7	11.0	-	-	-	-	68.3	8.1	48.4	11.0	48.0	9.1	-	-	-	-
1975	58.1	8.2	-	-	-	-	72.3	5.9	52.3	8.1	52.5	9.4	-	-	-	-
1976	61.3	5.5	64.3	-	60.3	-	75.7	4.7	57.3	9.6	56.9	8.4	67.2	-	61.0	-
1977	65.3	6.5	68.0	5.8	64.4	6.8	81.7	7.9	60.8	6.1	61.5	8.1	70.9	5.5	63.7	4.4
1978	69.3	6.1	73.9	8.7	68.1	5.7	84.8	3.8	64.0	5.3	67.0	8.9	72.3	2.0	66.7	4.7
1979	76.0	9.7	81.3	10.0	73.9	8.5	87.3	2.9	73.8	15.3	72.2	7.8	72.6	0.4	70.9	6.3
1980	84.3	10.9	87.8	8.0	82.4	11.5	90.0	3.1	86.0	16.5	79.0	9.4	79.3	9.2	76.7	8.2
1981	92.0	9.1	94.5	7.6	90.3	9.6	93.4	3.8	95.5	11.0	85.6	8.4	87.4	10.2	83.8	9.3
1982	95.2	3.5	97.6	3.3	93.0	3.0	97.6	4.5	97.4	2.0	91.7	7.1	94.3	7.9	90.7	8.2
1983	101.3	6.4	99.7	2.2	103.8	11.6	100.3	2.8	99.4	2.1	100.7	9.8	100.6	6.7	101.3	11.7
1984	103.5	2.2	102.7	3.0	103.2	-0.6	102.0	1.7	103.1	3.7	107.6	6.9	105.2	4.6	107.9	6.5
1985	105.1	1.5	106.0	3.2	101.4	-1.7	107.9	5.8	105.0	1.8	112.9	4.9	110.3	4.8	115.2	6.8
1986	105.7	0.6	108.7	2.5	103.5	2.1	111.0	2.9	97.3	-7.3	119.3	5.7	113.8	3.2	123.7	7.4
1987	109.0	3.1	112.1	3.1	105.8	2.2	118.1	6.4	99.3	2.1	126.8	6.3	122.0	7.2	130.4	5.4
1988	113.2	3.9	116.7	4.1	110.5	4.4	126.3	6.9	100.5	1.2	131.0	3.3	124.6	2.1	137.8	5.7
1989	117.3	3.6	125.7	7.7	115.1	4.2	109.9	-13.0	103.0	2.5	141.3	7.9	131.1	5.2	146.3	6.2
1990	123.2	5.0	131.4	4.5	121.6	5.6	107.7	-2.0	109.2	6.0	150.4	6.4	141.7	8.1	154.1	5.3
1991	128.8	4.5	135.7	3.3	128.7	5.8	112.0	4.0	112.3	2.8	158.1	5.1	146.8	3.6	164.5	6.7
1992	133.1	3.3	137.0	1.0	135.1	5.0	111.5	-0.4	113.9	1.4	165.9	4.9	154.3	5.1	180.4	9.7
1993	137.6	3.4	139.1	1.5	140.4	3.9	112.0	0.4	116.9	2.6	172.6	4.0	165.8	7.5	192.4	6.7
1994	141.5	2.8	142.9	2.7	143.7	2.4	118.4	5.7	120.6	3.2	174.8	1.3	176.1	6.2	195.9	1.8
1995	146.3	3.4	146.8	2.7	146.8	2.2	115.9	-2.1	129.2	7.1	181.9	4.1	186.4	5.8	205.3	4.8
1996	151.8	3.8	152.7	4.0	152.1	3.6	118.3	2.1	134.1	3.8	186.8	2.7	196.1	5.2	214.3	4.4
1997	155.2	2.2	157.9	3.4	155.6	2.3	118.9	0.5	135.1	0.7	192.6	3.1	195.7	-0.2	226.2	5.6

Source: U.S. Department of Labor, Bureau of Labor Statistics, Division of Consumer Prices and Price Indexes. - indicates no data collected for period.

Buffalo, NY
Consumer Price Index - All Urban Consumers
Base 1982-1984 = 100
All Items

For 1963-1997. Columns headed % show percentile change in the index from the previous period for which an index is available.

Year	Jan Index	%	Feb Index	%	Mar Index	%	Apr Index	%	May Index	%	Jun Index	%	Jul Index	%	Aug Index	%	Sep Index	%	Oct Index	%	Nov Index	%	Dec Index	%
1963	-	-	-	-	-	-	-	-	-	-	-	-	-	-	-	-	-	-	-	-	32.3	-	-	-
1964	-	-	32.3	0.0	-	-	-	-	32.5	0.6	-	-	-	-	32.7	0.6	-	-	-	-	32.9	0.6	-	-
1965	-	-	33.0	0.3	-	-	-	-	33.2	0.6	-	-	-	-	33.5	0.9	-	-	-	-	33.8	0.9	-	-
1966	-	-	34.1	0.9	-	-	-	-	34.4	0.9	-	-	-	-	34.7	0.9	-	-	-	-	34.9	0.6	-	-
1967	-	-	35.0	0.3	-	-	-	-	35.3	0.9	-	-	-	-	35.6	0.8	-	-	-	-	35.9	0.8	-	-
1968	-	-	36.2	0.8	-	-	-	-	36.9	1.9	-	-	-	-	37.3	1.1	-	-	-	-	37.7	1.1	-	-
1969	-	-	37.8	0.3	-	-	-	-	38.8	2.6	-	-	-	-	39.1	0.8	-	-	-	-	39.7	1.5	-	-
1970	-	-	40.4	1.8	-	-	-	-	41.0	1.5	-	-	-	-	41.3	0.7	-	-	-	-	42.1	1.9	-	-
1971	-	-	42.4	0.7	-	-	-	-	43.0	1.4	-	-	-	-	43.5	1.2	-	-	-	-	43.6	0.2	-	-
1972	-	-	44.3	1.6	-	-	-	-	44.7	0.9	-	-	-	-	45.0	0.7	-	-	-	-	45.6	1.3	-	-
1973	-	-	46.2	1.3	-	-	-	-	47.2	2.2	-	-	-	-	48.4	2.5	-	-	-	-	49.1	1.4	-	-
1974	-	-	51.1	4.1	-	-	-	-	52.3	2.3	-	-	-	-	53.7	2.7	-	-	-	-	55.0	2.4	-	-
1975	-	-	55.9	1.6	-	-	-	-	56.9	1.8	-	-	-	-	58.0	1.9	-	-	-	-	58.8	1.4	-	-
1976	-	-	59.3	0.9	-	-	-	-	60.0	1.2	-	-	-	-	61.0	1.7	-	-	-	-	61.6	1.0	-	-
1977	-	-	62.9	2.1	-	-	-	-	64.3	2.2	-	-	-	-	64.8	0.8	-	-	-	-	65.7	1.4	-	-
1978	-	-	66.5	1.2	-	-	67.0	0.8	-	-	68.3	1.9	-	-	69.0	1.0	-	-	70.2	1.7	-	-	70.8	0.9
1979	-	-	72.0	1.7	-	-	73.3	1.8	-	-	74.2	1.2	-	-	76.1	2.6	-	-	77.5	1.8	-	-	78.4	1.2
1980	-	-	80.8	3.1	-	-	82.9	2.6	-	-	83.5	0.7	-	-	84.0	0.6	-	-	85.0	1.2	-	-	87.4	2.8
1981	-	-	89.1	1.9	-	-	90.3	1.3	-	-	91.2	1.0	-	-	92.3	1.2	-	-	93.1	0.9	-	-	93.7	0.6
1982	-	-	92.2	-1.6	-	-	91.6	-0.7	-	-	94.2	2.8	-	-	94.9	0.7	-	-	98.3	3.6	-	-	98.5	0.2
1983	-	-	99.4	0.9	-	-	100.2	0.8	-	-	100.8	0.6	-	-	101.4	0.6	-	-	102.3	0.9	-	-	102.2	-0.1
1984	-	-	103.0	0.8	-	-	103.9	0.9	-	-	103.7	-0.2	-	-	104.4	0.7	-	-	105.0	0.6	-	-	107.6	2.5
1985	-	-	106.8	-0.7	-	-	108.3	1.4	-	-	109.0	0.6	-	-	108.7	-0.3	-	-	109.7	0.9	-	-	109.9	0.2
1986	-	-	110.0	0.1	-	-	109.2	-0.7	-	-	109.5	0.3	-	-	109.0	-0.5	-	-	109.7	0.6	-	-	110.4	0.6
1987	-	-	-	-	-	-	-	-	-	-	111.8	1.3	-	-	-	-	-	-	-	-	-	-	114.2	2.1
1988	-	-	-	-	-	-	-	-	-	-	115.9	1.5	-	-	-	-	-	-	-	-	-	-	118.9	2.6
1989	-	-	-	-	-	-	-	-	-	-	120.7	1.5	-	-	-	-	-	-	-	-	-	-	122.4	1.4
1990	-	-	-	-	-	-	-	-	-	-	125.8	2.8	-	-	-	-	-	-	-	-	-	-	129.7	3.1
1991	-	-	-	-	-	-	-	-	-	-	132.7	2.3	-	-	-	-	-	-	-	-	-	-	134.1	1.1
1992	-	-	-	-	-	-	-	-	-	-	136.0	1.4	-	-	-	-	-	-	-	-	-	-	139.8	2.8
1993	-	-	-	-	-	-	-	-	-	-	141.2	1.0	-	-	-	-	-	-	-	-	-	-	144.2	2.1
1994	-	-	-	-	-	-	-	-	-	-	145.7	1.0	-	-	-	-	-	-	-	-	-	-	147.8	1.4
1995	-	-	-	-	-	-	-	-	-	-	150.3	1.7	-	-	-	-	-	-	-	-	-	-	152.7	1.6
1996	-	-	-	-	-	-	-	-	-	-	156.2	2.3	-	-	-	-	-	-	-	-	-	-	158.0	1.2
1997	-	-	-	-	-	-	-	-	-	-	159.9	1.2	-	-	-	-	-	-	-	-	-	-	-	-

Source: U.S. Department of Labor, Bureau of Labor Statistics, Division of Consumer Prices and Price Indexes. - indicates no data collected for period.

Buffalo, NY
Consumer Price Index - Urban Wage Earners
Base 1982-1984 = 100
All Items

For 1963-1997. Columns headed % show percentile change in the index from the previous period for which an index is available.

Year	Jan Index	%	Feb Index	%	Mar Index	%	Apr Index	%	May Index	%	Jun Index	%	Jul Index	%	Aug Index	%	Sep Index	%	Oct Index	%	Nov Index	%	Dec Index	%
1963	-	-	-		-	-	-	-	-		-		-		-		-		-		32.7	-	-	-
1964	-	-	32.7	0.0	-	-	-	-	32.9	0.6	-	-	-	-	33.1	0.6	-	-	-	-	33.4	0.9	-	-
1965	-	-	33.5	0.3	-	-	-	-	33.7	0.6	-	-	-	-	34.0	0.9	-	-	-	-	34.2	0.6	-	-
1966	-	-	34.6	1.2	-	-	-	-	34.8	0.6	-	-	-	-	35.2	1.1	-	-	-	-	35.3	0.3	-	-
1967	-	-	35.4	0.3	-	-	-	-	35.8	1.1	-	-	-	-	36.1	0.8	-	-	-	-	36.3	0.6	-	-
1968	-	-	36.7	1.1	-	-	-	-	37.3	1.6	-	-	-	-	37.8	1.3	-	-	-	-	38.2	1.1	-	-
1969	-	-	38.3	0.3	-	-	-	-	39.3	2.6	-	-	-	-	39.6	0.8	-	-	-	-	40.3	1.8	-	-
1970	-	-	40.9	1.5	-	-	-	-	41.5	1.5	-	-	-	-	41.8	0.7	-	-	-	-	42.6	1.9	-	-
1971	-	-	43.0	0.9	-	-	-	-	43.6	1.4	-	-	-	-	44.1	1.1	-	-	-	-	44.2	0.2	-	-
1972	-	-	44.9	1.6	-	-	-	-	45.3	0.9	-		-	-	45.5	0.4	-	-	-	-	46.2	1.5	-	-
1973	-	-	46.8	1.3	-	-	-	-	47.8	2.1	-	-	-	-	49.1	2.7	-	-	-	-	49.8	1.4	-	-
1974	-	-	51.8	4.0	-	-	-	-	53.0	2.3	-	-	-	-	54.4	2.6	-	-	-	-	55.7	2.4	-	-
1975	-	-	56.6	1.6	-	-	-	-	57.6	1.8	-	-	-	-	58.7	1.9	-	-	-	-	59.5	1.4	-	-
1976	-	-	60.0	0.8	-	-	-	-	60.7	1.2	-	-	-	-	61.8	1.8	-	-	-	-	62.4	1.0	-	-
1977	-	-	63.7	2.1	-	-	-	-	65.1	2.2	-		-	-	65.6	0.8	-	-	-	-	66.5	1.4	-	-
1978	-	-	67.3	1.2	-	-	67.9	0.9	-	-	69.3	2.1	-	-	69.9	0.9	-	-	71.0	1.6	-	-	71.6	0.8
1979	-	-	72.9	1.8	-	-	74.4	2.1	-	-	75.3	1.2	-	-	77.3	2.7	-	-	78.5	1.6	-	-	79.3	1.0
1980	-	-	81.8	3.2	-	-	83.8	2.4	-	-	84.3	0.6	-	-	84.6	0.4	-	-	85.5	1.1	-	-	88.1	3.0
1981	-	-	89.7	1.8	-	-	90.8	1.2	-	-	92.0	1.3	-	-	93.2	1.3	-	-	93.8	0.6	-	-	94.3	0.5
1982	-	-	92.7	-1.7	-	-	92.1	-0.6	-	-	94.8	2.9	-	-	95.3	0.5	-	-	98.5	3.4	-	-	98.8	0.3
1983	-	-	99.3	0.5	-	-	100.0	0.7	-	-	101.7	1.7	-	-	102.4	0.7	-	-	103.0	0.6	-	-	102.6	-0.4
1984	-	-	102.7	0.1	-	-	102.9	0.2	-	-	103.2	0.3	-	-	103.6	0.4	-	-	104.9	1.3	-	-	104.1	-0.8
1985	-	-	103.5	-0.6	-	-	104.8	1.3	-	-	105.5	0.7	-	-	105.2	-0.3	-	-	106.1	0.9	-	-	106.3	0.2
1986	-	-	106.2	-0.1	-	-	105.1	-1.0	-	-	105.6	0.5	-	-	105.0	-0.6	-	-	105.7	0.7	-	-	106.3	0.6
1987	-	-	-	-	-	-	-	-	-	-	107.8	1.4	-	-	-	-	-	-	-	-	-	-	110.2	2.2
1988	-	-	-	-	-	-	-	-	-	-	111.7	1.4	-	-	-	-	-	-	-	-	-	-	114.6	2.6
1989	-	-	-	-	-	-	-	-	-	-	116.5	1.7	-	-	-	-	-	-	-	-	-	-	118.2	1.5
1990	-	-	-	-	-	-	-	-	-	-	121.2	2.5	-	-	-	-	-	-	-	-	-	-	125.2	3.3
1991	-	-	-	-	-	-	-	-	-	-	128.0	2.2	-	-	-	-	-	-	-	-	-	-	129.6	1.3
1992	-	-	-	-	-	-	-	-	-	-	131.2	1.2	-	-	-	-	-	-	-	-	-	-	135.0	2.9
1993	-	-	-	-	-	-	-	-	-	-	136.1	0.8	-	-	-	-	-	-	-	-	-	-	139.1	2.2
1994	-	-	-	-	-	-	-	-	-	-	140.4	0.9	-	-	-	-	-	-	-	-	-	-	142.7	1.6
1995	-	-	-	-	-	-	-	-	-	-	145.0	1.6	-	-	-	-	-	-	-	-	-	-	147.6	1.8
1996	-	-	-	-	-	-	-	-	-	-	150.9	2.2	-	-	-	-	-	-	-	-	-	-	152.7	1.2
1997	-	-	-	-	-	-	-	-	-	-	154.5	1.2	-	-	-	-	-	-	-	-	-	-	-	-

Source: U.S. Department of Labor, Bureau of Labor Statistics, Division of Consumer Prices and Price Indexes. - indicates no data collected for period.

Buffalo, NY
Consumer Price Index - All Urban Consumers
Base 1982-1984 = 100
Food and Beverages

For 1975-1997. Columns headed % show percentile change in the index from the previous period for which an index is available.

Year	Jan Index	%	Feb Index	%	Mar Index	%	Apr Index	%	May Index	%	Jun Index	%	Jul Index	%	Aug Index	%	Sep Index	%	Oct Index	%	Nov Index	%	Dec Index	%
1975	-	-	-	-	-	-	-	-	-	-	-	-	-	-	-	-	-	-	-	-	62.5	-	-	-
1976	-	-	63.3	1.3	-	-	-	-	62.7	-0.9	-	-	-	-	63.7	1.6	-	-	-	-	63.4	-0.5	-	-
1977	-	-	66.0	4.1	-	-	-	-	66.7	1.1	-	-	-	-	67.4	1.0	-	-	-	-	67.8	0.6	-	-
1978	-	-	69.8	2.9	-	-	71.3	2.1	-	-	74.3	4.2	-	-	73.8	-0.7	-	-	74.2	0.5	-	-	75.1	1.2
1979	-	-	77.6	3.3	-	-	79.8	2.8	-	-	80.7	1.1	-	-	80.1	-0.7	-	-	81.1	1.2	-	-	82.5	1.7
1980	-	-	83.7	1.5	-	-	84.3	0.7	-	-	86.2	2.3	-	-	87.6	1.6	-	-	89.8	2.5	-	-	91.6	2.0
1981	-	-	93.4	2.0	-	-	94.1	0.7	-	-	94.1	0.0	-	-	94.9	0.9	-	-	94.4	-0.5	-	-	94.9	0.5
1982	-	-	96.5	1.7	-	-	96.6	0.1	-	-	99.0	2.5	-	-	98.0	-1.0	-	-	97.9	-0.1	-	-	97.8	-0.1
1983	-	-	99.2	1.4	-	-	99.6	0.4	-	-	100.5	0.9	-	-	100.0	-0.5	-	-	99.7	-0.3	-	-	100.9	1.2
1984	-	-	103.2	2.3	-	-	103.3	0.1	-	-	102.4	-0.9	-	-	102.7	0.3	-	-	102.4	-0.3	-	-	102.2	-0.2
1985	-	-	104.9	2.6	-	-	106.9	1.9	-	-	106.2	-0.7	-	-	105.5	-0.7	-	-	105.8	0.3	-	-	106.7	0.9
1986	-	-	107.3	0.6	-	-	106.9	-0.4	-	-	107.6	0.7	-	-	109.9	2.1	-	-	110.1	0.2	-	-	110.2	0.1
1987	-	-	-	-	-	-	-	-	-	-	111.7	1.4	-	-	-	-	-	-	-	-	-	-	112.6	0.8
1988	-	-	-	-	-	-	-	-	-	-	114.7	1.9	-	-	-	-	-	-	-	-	-	-	118.8	3.6
1989	-	-	-	-	-	-	-	-	-	-	123.7	4.1	-	-	-	-	-	-	-	-	-	-	127.9	3.4
1990	-	-	-	-	-	-	-	-	-	-	130.9	2.3	-	-	-	-	-	-	-	-	-	-	132.2	1.0
1991	-	-	-	-	-	-	-	-	-	-	136.2	3.0	-	-	-	-	-	-	-	-	-	-	135.9	-0.2
1992	-	-	-	-	-	-	-	-	-	-	136.3	0.3	-	-	-	-	-	-	-	-	-	-	138.0	1.2
1993	-	-	-	-	-	-	-	-	-	-	137.6	-0.3	-	-	-	-	-	-	-	-	-	-	140.9	2.4
1994	-	-	-	-	-	-	-	-	-	-	143.3	1.7	-	-	-	-	-	-	-	-	-	-	142.9	-0.3
1995	-	-	-	-	-	-	-	-	-	-	146.6	2.6	-	-	-	-	-	-	-	-	-	-	147.5	0.6
1996	-	-	-	-	-	-	-	-	-	-	151.8	2.9	-	-	-	-	-	-	-	-	-	-	154.1	1.5
1997	-	-	-	-	-	-	-	-	-	-	157.8	2.4	-	-	-	-	-	-	-	-	-	-	-	-

Source: U.S. Department of Labor, Bureau of Labor Statistics, Division of Consumer Prices and Price Indexes. - indicates no data collected for period.

Buffalo, NY
Consumer Price Index - Urban Wage Earners
Base 1982-1984 = 100
Food and Beverages

For 1975-1997. Columns headed % show percentile change in the index from the previous period for which an index is available.

Year	Jan Index	%	Feb Index	%	Mar Index	%	Apr Index	%	May Index	%	Jun Index	%	Jul Index	%	Aug Index	%	Sep Index	%	Oct Index	%	Nov Index	%	Dec Index	%
1975	-	-	-		-	-	-		-		-		-	-	-		-	-			63.5	-	-	-
1976	-	-	64.3	1.3	-	-	-	-	63.7	-0.9	-	-	-	-	64.7	1.6	-	-	-	-	64.4	-0.5	-	-
1977	-	-	67.0	4.0	-	-	-	-	67.7	1.0	-	-	-	-	68.5	1.2	-	-	-	-	68.8	0.4	-	-
1978	-	-	70.9	3.1	-	-	72.4	2.1	-	-	75.2	3.9	-	-	75.1	-0.1	-	-	75.4	0.4	-	-	76.1	0.9
1979	-	-	78.5	3.2	-	-	81.5	3.8	-	-	82.2	0.9	-	-	82.1	-0.1	-	-	82.4	0.4	-	-	83.0	0.7
1980	-	-	84.5	1.8	-	-	85.5	1.2	-	-	87.2	2.0	-	-	88.6	1.6	-	-	90.8	2.5	-	-	92.6	2.0
1981	-	-	94.0	1.5	-	-	94.0	0.0	-	-	94.5	0.5	-	-	95.4	1.0	-	-	94.6	-0.8	-	-	95.2	0.6
1982	-	-	96.5	1.4	-	-	96.8	0.3	-	-	99.3	2.6	-	-	98.0	-1.3	-	-	97.9	-0.1	-	-	97.9	0.0
1983	-	-	99.2	1.3	-	-	99.3	0.1	-	-	100.5	1.2	-	-	99.9	-0.6	-	-	99.6	-0.3	-	-	100.7	1.1
1984	-	-	103.3	2.6	-	-	103.5	0.2	-	-	102.3	-1.2	-	-	102.6	0.3	-	-	102.4	-0.2	-	-	102.3	-0.1
1985	-	-	105.0	2.6	-	-	107.1	2.0	-	-	106.4	-0.7	-	-	105.6	-0.8	-	-	106.1	0.5	-	-	106.9	0.8
1986	-	-	107.5	0.6	-	-	107.0	-0.5	-	-	107.6	0.6	-	-	110.5	2.7	-	-	110.3	-0.2	-	-	110.0	-0.3
1987	-	-	-	-	-	-	-	-	-	-	111.7	1.5	-	-	-	-	-	-	-	-	-	-	112.6	0.8
1988	-	-	-	-	-	-	-	-	-	-	114.7	1.9	-	-	-	-	-	-	-	-	-	-	118.7	3.5
1989	-	-	-	-	-	-	-	-	-	-	123.6	4.1	-	-	-	-	-	-	-	-	-	-	127.7	3.3
1990	-	-	-	-	-	-	-	-	-	-	130.7	2.3	-	-	-	-	-	-	-	-	-	-	132.1	1.1
1991	-	-	-	-	-	-	-	-	-	-	135.7	2.7	-	-	-	-	-	-	-	-	-		135.6	-0.1
1992	-	-	-	-	-	-	-	-	-	-	136.1	0.4	-	-	-	-	-	-	-	-	-		137.8	1.2
1993	-	-	-	-	-	-	-	-	-	-	137.4	-0.3	-	-	-	-	-	-	-	-	-		140.7	2.4
1994	-	-	-	-	-	-	-	-	-	-	143.2	1.8	-	-	-	-	-	-	-	-	-		142.7	-0.3
1995	-	-	-	-	-	-	-	-	-	-	146.3	2.5	-	-	-	-	-	-	-	-	-		147.3	0.7
1996	-	-	-	-	-	-	-	-	-	-	151.6	2.9	-	-	-	-	-	-	-	-	-		153.8	1.5
1997	-	-	-	-	-	-	-	-	-	-	157.5	2.4	-	-	-	-	-	-	-	-	-	-	-	-

Source: U.S. Department of Labor, Bureau of Labor Statistics, Division of Consumer Prices and Price Indexes. - indicates no data collected for period.

Buffalo, NY
Consumer Price Index - All Urban Consumers
Base 1982-1984 = 100
Housing

For 1975-1997: Columns headed % show percentile change in the index from the previous period for which an index is available.

Year	Jan Index	%	Feb Index	%	Mar Index	%	Apr Index	%	May Index	%	Jun Index	%	Jul Index	%	Aug Index	%	Sep Index	%	Oct Index	%	Nov Index	%	Dec Index	%
1975	-	-	-	-	-	-	-	-	-	-	-	-	-	-	-	-	-	-	-	-	57.8	-	-	-
1976	-	-	58.1	0.5	-	-	-	-	58.7	1.0	-	-	-	-	60.1	2.4	-	-	-	-	60.7	1.0	-	-
1977	-	-	62.0	2.1	-	-	-	-	63.5	2.4	-	-	-	-	63.8	0.5	-	-	-	-	65.0	1.9	-	-
1978	-	-	65.4	0.6	-	-	65.7	0.5	-	-	66.2	0.8	-	-	67.3	1.7	-	-	69.1	2.7	-	-	69.7	0.9
1979	-	-	70.9	1.7	-	-	71.2	0.4	-	-	71.4	0.3	-	-	73.8	3.4	-	-	75.7	2.6	-	-	76.6	1.2
1980	-	-	79.0	3.1	-	-	82.2	4.1	-	-	82.3	0.1	-	-	81.4	-1.1	-	-	81.7	0.4	-	-	86.0	5.3
1981	-	-	86.9	1.0	-	-	87.4	0.6	-	-	89.4	2.3	-	-	91.1	1.9	-	-	91.7	0.7	-	-	92.5	0.9
1982	-	-	87.9	-5.0	-	-	87.0	-1.0	-	-	91.0	4.6	-	-	92.5	1.6	-	-	99.1	7.1	-	-	99.4	0.3
1983	-	-	101.5	2.1	-	-	102.0	0.5	-	-	102.0	0.0	-	-	102.7	0.7	-	-	103.5	0.8	-	-	102.5	-1.0
1984	-	-	102.7	0.2	-	-	104.0	1.3	-	-	104.1	0.1	-	-	105.3	1.2	-	-	105.5	0.2	-	-	112.6	6.7
1985	-	-	108.7	-3.5	-	-	109.3	0.6	-	-	110.4	1.0	-	-	110.1	-0.3	-	-	111.3	1.1	-	-	110.9	-0.4
1986	-	-	111.9	0.9	-	-	113.3	1.3	-	-	113.2	-0.1	-	-	111.7	-1.3	-	-	112.0	0.3	-	-	112.7	0.6
1987	-	-	-	-	-	-	-	-	-	-	113.1	0.4	-	-	-	-	-	-	-	-	-	-	116.5	3.0
1988	-	-	-	-	-	-	-	-	-	-	118.4	1.6	-	-	-	-	-	-	-	-	-	-	121.8	2.9
1989	-	-	-	-	-	-	-	-	-	-	123.6	1.5	-	-	-	-	-	-	-	-	-	-	126.4	2.3
1990	-	-	-	-	-	-	-	-	-	-	130.2	3.0	-	-	-	-	-	-	-	-	-	-	133.8	2.8
1991	-	-	-	-	-	-	-	-	-	-	138.2	3.3	-	-	-	-	-	-	-	-	-	-	140.7	1.8
1992	-	-	-	-	-	-	-	-	-	-	144.2	2.5	-	-	-	-	-	-	-	-	-	-	148.1	2.7
1993	-	-	-	-	-	-	-	-	-	-	150.6	1.7	-	-	-	-	-	-	-	-	-	-	153.7	2.1
1994	-	-	-	-	-	-	-	-	-	-	155.1	0.9	-	-	-	-	-	-	-	-	-	-	156.7	1.0
1995	-	-	-	-	-	-	-	-	-	-	158.5	1.1	-	-	-	-	-	-	-	-	-	-	160.7	1.4
1996	-	-	-	-	-	-	-	-	-	-	164.4	2.3	-	-	-	-	-	-	-	-	-	-	166.7	1.4
1997	-	-	-	-	-	-	-	-	-	-	168.7	1.2	-	-	-	-	-	-	-	-	-	-	-	-

Source: U.S. Department of Labor, Bureau of Labor Statistics, Division of Consumer Prices and Price Indexes. - indicates no data collected for period.

Buffalo, NY
Consumer Price Index - Urban Wage Earners
Base 1982-1984 = 100
Housing

For 1975-1997. Columns headed % show percentile change in the index from the previous period for which an index is available.

Year	Jan Index	%	Feb Index	%	Mar Index	%	Apr Index	%	May Index	%	Jun Index	%	Jul Index	%	Aug Index	%	Sep Index	%	Oct Index	%	Nov Index	%	Dec Index	%
1975	-	-	-		-	-	-		-		-	-	-	-	-		-	-	-	-	58.6	-	-	-
1976	-	-	58.9	0.5	-	-	-	-	59.5	1.0	-	-	-	-	61.0	2.5	-	-	-	-	61.6	1.0	-	-
1977	-	-	62.8	1.9	-	-	-	-	64.3	2.4	-	-	-	-	64.7	0.6	-	-	-	-	65.9	1.9	-	-
1978	-	-	66.3	0.6	-	-	66.5	0.3	-	-	67.2	1.1	-	-	68.4	1.8	-	-	70.3	2.8	-	-	71.0	1.0
1979	-	-	72.1	1.5	-	-	72.1	0.0	-	-	72.0	-0.1	-	-	74.6	3.6	-	-	76.6	2.7	-	-	77.6	1.3
1980	-	-	80.2	3.4	-	-	83.0	3.5	-	-	82.7	-0.4	-	-	81.9	-1.0	-	-	82.1	0.2	-	-	86.7	5.6
1981	-	-	87.4	0.8	-	-	88.0	0.7	-	-	90.1	2.4	-	-	92.2	2.3	-	-	92.6	0.4	-	-	93.5	1.0
1982	-	-	88.2	-5.7	-	-	87.2	-1.1	-	-	91.5	4.9	-	-	92.9	1.5	-	-	99.9	7.5	-	-	100.2	0.3
1983	-	-	101.7	1.5	-	-	102.0	0.3	-	-	104.8	2.7	-	-	105.5	0.7	-	-	105.6	0.1	-	-	103.7	-1.8
1984	-	-	102.2	-1.4	-	-	101.5	-0.7	-	-	103.0	1.5	-	-	103.6	0.6	-	-	105.7	2.0	-	-	103.6	-2.0
1985	-	-	100.1	-3.4	-	-	100.7	0.6	-	-	101.6	0.9	-	-	101.4	-0.2	-	-	102.4	1.0	-	-	102.2	-0.2
1986	-	-	103.0	0.8	-	-	104.3	1.3	-	-	104.2	-0.1	-	-	102.8	-1.3	-	-	103.1	0.3	-	-	104.0	0.9
1987	-	-	-	-	-	-	-	-	-	-	104.4	0.4	-	-	-	-	-	-	-	-	-	-	107.4	2.9
1988	-	-	-	-	-	-	-	-	-	-	108.9	1.4	-	-	-	-	-	-	-	-	-	-	112.1	2.9
1989	-	-	-	-	-	-	-	-	-	-	113.9	1.6	-	-	-	-	-	-	-	-	-	-	116.4	2.2
1990	-	-	-	-	-	-	-	-	-	-	120.0	3.1	-	-	-	-	-	-	-	-	-	-	123.2	2.7
1991	-	-	-	-	-	-	-	-	-	-	127.5	3.5	-	-	-	-	-	-	-	-	-	-	129.9	1.9
1992	-	-	-	-	-	-	-	-	-	-	133.4	2.7	-	-	-	-	-	-	-	-	-	-	136.9	2.6
1993	-	-	-	-	-	-	-	-	-	-	139.0	1.5	-	-	-	-	-	-	-	-	-	-	141.9	2.1
1994	-	-	-	-	-	-	-	-	-	-	143.0	0.8	-	-	-	-	-	-	-	-	-	-	144.4	1.0
1995	-	-	-	-	-	-	-	-	-	-	145.9	1.0	-	-	-	-	-	-	-	-	-	-	147.8	1.3
1996	-	-	-	-	-	-	-	-	-	-	151.0	2.2	-	-	-	-	-	-	-	-	-	-	153.1	1.4
1997	-	-	-	-	-	-	-	-	-	-	154.8	1.1	-	-	-	-	-	-	-	-	-	-	-	-

Source: U.S. Department of Labor, Bureau of Labor Statistics, Division of Consumer Prices and Price Indexes. - indicates no data collected for period.

Buffalo, NY
Consumer Price Index - All Urban Consumers
Base 1982-1984 = 100
Apparel and Upkeep

For 1963-1997. Columns headed % show percentile change in the index from the previous period for which an index is available.

Year	Jan Index	%	Feb Index	%	Mar Index	%	Apr Index	%	May Index	%	Jun Index	%	Jul Index	%	Aug Index	%	Sep Index	%	Oct Index	%	Nov Index	%	Dec Index	%
1963	-	-	-	-	-	-	-	-	-	-	-	-	-	-	-	-	-	-	-	-	40.0	-	-	-
1964	-	-	40.1	0.2	-	-	-	-	40.0	-0.2	-	-	-	-	40.4	1.0	-	-	-	-	40.9	1.2	-	-
1965	-	-	41.2	0.7	-	-	-	-	41.6	1.0	-	-	-	-	41.9	0.7	-	-	-	-	42.4	1.2	-	-
1966	-	-	42.8	0.9	-	-	-	-	43.3	1.2	-	-	-	-	43.1	-0.5	-	-	-	-	43.8	1.6	-	-
1967	-	-	44.4	1.4	-	-	-	-	45.4	2.3	-	-	-	-	45.2	-0.4	-	-	-	-	46.1	2.0	-	-
1968	-	-	46.8	1.5	-	-	-	-	48.2	3.0	-	-	-	-	48.9	1.5	-	-	-	-	49.5	1.2	-	-
1969	-	-	48.9	-1.2	-	-	-	-	51.9	6.1	-	-	-	-	52.0	0.2	-	-	-	-	53.9	3.7	-	-
1970	-	-	52.5	-2.6	-	-	-	-	53.1	1.1	-	-	-	-	52.5	-1.1	-	-	-	-	55.1	5.0	-	-
1971	-	-	54.7	-0.7	-	-	-	-	56.6	3.5	-	-	-	-	55.5	-1.9	-	-	-	-	56.5	1.8	-	-
1972	-	-	55.4	-1.9	-	-	-	-	57.8	4.3	-	-	-	-	56.2	-2.8	-	-	-	-	58.9	4.8	-	-
1973	-	-	60.1	2.0	-	-	-	-	60.5	0.7	-	-	-	-	61.6	1.8	-	-	-	-	61.9	0.5	-	-
1974	-	-	63.1	1.9	-	-	-	-	65.0	3.0	-	-	-	-	67.0	3.1	-	-	-	-	68.9	2.8	-	-
1975	-	-	68.5	-0.6	-	-	-	-	68.9	0.6	-	-	-	-	70.1	1.7	-	-	-	-	71.8	2.4	-	-
1976	-	-	70.6	-1.7	-	-	-	-	73.8	4.5	-	-	-	-	73.0	-1.1	-	-	-	-	75.1	2.9	-	-
1977	-	-	75.1	0.0	-	-	-	-	79.2	5.5	-	-	-	-	80.0	1.0	-	-	-	-	81.8	2.3	-	-
1978	-	-	80.3	-1.8	-	-	81.1	1.0	-	-	81.0	-0.1	-	-	83.2	2.7	-	-	84.4	1.4	-	-	84.0	-0.5
1979	-	-	82.2	-2.1	-	-	84.8	3.2	-	-	83.8	-1.2	-	-	88.6	5.7	-	-	90.3	1.9	-	-	88.0	-2.5
1980	-	-	88.1	0.1	-	-	89.1	1.1	-	-	90.0	1.0	-	-	94.2	4.7	-	-	94.4	0.2	-	-	91.7	-2.9
1981	-	-	91.1	-0.7	-	-	93.7	2.9	-	-	93.6	-0.1	-	-	93.9	0.3	-	-	95.5	1.7	-	-	96.0	0.5
1982	-	-	95.8	-0.2	-	-	97.3	1.6	-	-	97.3	0.0	-	-	98.2	0.9	-	-	99.7	1.5	-	-	98.2	-1.5
1983	-	-	96.3	-1.9	-	-	100.9	4.8	-	-	100.4	-0.5	-	-	100.5	0.1	-	-	103.4	2.9	-	-	102.1	-1.3
1984	-	-	101.5	-0.6	-	-	101.1	-0.4	-	-	99.9	-1.2	-	-	101.1	1.2	-	-	103.9	2.8	-	-	104.8	0.9
1985	-	-	103.5	-1.2	-	-	110.0	6.3	-	-	109.6	-0.4	-	-	107.1	-2.3	-	-	111.1	3.7	-	-	109.3	-1.6
1986	-	-	108.2	-1.0	-	-	113.6	5.0	-	-	109.2	-3.9	-	-	112.6	3.1	-	-	111.5	-1.0	-	-	115.0	3.1
1987	-	-	-	-	-	-	-	-	-	-	116.7	1.5	-	-	-	-	-	-	-	-	-	-	119.1	2.1
1988	-	-	-	-	-	-	-	-	-	-	123.5	3.7	-	-	-	-	-	-	-	-	-	-	128.1	3.7
1989	-	-	-	-	-	-	-	-	-	-	113.8	-11.2	-	-	-	-	-	-	-	-	-	-	105.1	-7.6
1990	-	-	-	-	-	-	-	-	-	-	106.1	1.0	-	-	-	-	-	-	-	-	-	-	109.1	2.8
1991	-	-	-	-	-	-	-	-	-	-	109.5	0.4	-	-	-	-	-	-	-	-	-	-	114.5	4.6
1992	-	-	-	-	-	-	-	-	-	-	106.0	-7.4	-	-	-	-	-	-	-	-	-	-	116.7	10.1
1993	-	-	-	-	-	-	-	-	-	-	111.3	-4.6	-	-	-	-	-	-	-	-	-	-	113.9	2.3
1994	-	-	-	-	-	-	-	-	-	-	116.3	2.1	-	-	-	-	-	-	-	-	-	-	121.2	4.2
1995	-	-	-	-	-	-	-	-	-	-	115.9	-4.4	-	-	-	-	-	-	-	-	-	-	117.9	1.7
1996	-	-	-	-	-	-	-	-	-	-	119.0	0.9	-	-	-	-	-	-	-	-	-	-	119.0	0.0
1997	-	-	-	-	-	-	-	-	-	-	119.6	0.5	-	-	-	-	-	-	-	-	-	-	-	-

Source: U.S. Department of Labor, Bureau of Labor Statistics, Division of Consumer Prices and Price Indexes. - indicates no data collected for period.

Buffalo, NY
Consumer Price Index - Urban Wage Earners
Base 1982-1984 = 100
Apparel and Upkeep

For 1963-1997. Columns headed % show percentile change in the index from the previous period for which an index is available.

Year	Jan Index	%	Feb Index	%	Mar Index	%	Apr Index	%	May Index	%	Jun Index	%	Jul Index	%	Aug Index	%	Sep Index	%	Oct Index	%	Nov Index	%	Dec Index	%
1963	-	-	-	-	-	-	-	-	-	-	-	-	-	-	-	-	-	-	-	-	41.4	-	-	-
1964	-	-	41.5	0.2	-	-	-	-	41.4	-0.2	-	-	-	-	41.8	1.0	-	-	-	-	42.4	1.4	-	-
1965	-	-	42.6	0.5	-	-	-	-	43.0	0.9	-	-	-	-	43.4	0.9	-	-	-	-	43.9	1.2	-	-
1966	-	-	44.3	0.9	-	-	-	-	44.8	1.1	-	-	-	-	44.6	-0.4	-	-	-	-	45.3	1.6	-	-
1967	-	-	46.0	1.5	-	-	-	-	47.0	2.2	-	-	-	-	46.8	-0.4	-	-	-	-	47.7	1.9	-	-
1968	-	-	48.5	1.7	-	-	-	-	49.9	2.9	-	-	-	-	50.6	1.4	-	-	-	-	51.2	1.2	-	-
1969	-	-	50.6	-1.2	-	-	-	-	53.7	6.1	-	-	-	-	53.8	0.2	-	-	-	-	55.8	3.7	-	-
1970	-	-	54.3	-2.7	-	-	-	-	55.0	1.3	-	-	-	-	54.3	-1.3	-	-	-	-	57.1	5.2	-	-
1971	-	-	56.6	-0.9	-	-	-	-	58.6	3.5	-	-	-	-	57.4	-2.0	-	-	-	-	58.5	1.9	-	-
1972	-	-	57.4	-1.9	-	-	-	-	59.8	4.2	-	-	-	-	58.1	-2.8	-	-	-	-	61.0	5.0	-	-
1973	-	-	62.2	2.0	-	-	-	-	62.6	0.6	-	-	-	-	63.7	1.8	-	-	-	-	64.1	0.6	-	-
1974	-	-	65.4	2.0	-	-	-	-	67.3	2.9	-	-	-	-	69.4	3.1	-	-	-	-	71.3	2.7	-	-
1975	-	-	70.9	-0.6	-	-	-	-	71.4	0.7	-	-	-	-	72.5	1.5	-	-	-	-	74.4	2.6	-	-
1976	-	-	73.1	-1.7	-	-	-	-	76.4	4.5	-	-	-	-	75.6	-1.0	-	-	-	-	77.8	2.9	-	-
1977	-	-	77.7	-0.1	-	-	-	-	82.0	5.5	-	-	-	-	82.8	1.0	-	-	-	-	84.6	2.2	-	-
1978	-	-	83.1	-1.8	-	-	85.6	3.0	-	-	85.4	-0.2	-	-	84.5	-1.1	-	-	85.2	0.8	-	-	85.3	0.1
1979	-	-	84.4	-1.1	-	-	86.9	3.0	-	-	85.1	-2.1	-	-	89.1	4.7	-	-	90.5	1.6	-	-	88.9	-1.8
1980	-	-	88.6	-0.3	-	-	89.4	0.9	-	-	90.5	1.2	-	-	90.7	0.2	-	-	90.5	-0.2	-	-	90.8	0.3
1981	-	-	88.1	-3.0	-	-	92.8	5.3	-	-	93.8	1.1	-	-	95.0	1.3	-	-	96.4	1.5	-	-	95.4	-1.0
1982	-	-	95.6	0.2	-	-	97.3	1.8	-	-	96.9	-0.4	-	-	98.1	1.2	-	-	100.0	1.9	-	-	98.8	-1.2
1983	-	-	96.8	-2.0	-	-	100.2	3.5	-	-	100.1	-0.1	-	-	99.6	-0.5	-	-	104.0	4.4	-	-	102.2	-1.7
1984	-	-	101.5	-0.7	-	-	101.7	0.2	-	-	99.5	-2.2	-	-	100.7	1.2	-	-	104.6	3.9	-	-	105.1	0.5
1985	-	-	104.6	-0.5	-	-	108.4	3.6	-	-	108.7	0.3	-	-	107.5	-1.1	-	-	110.2	2.5	-	-	109.0	-1.1
1986	-	-	107.9	-1.0	-	-	112.6	4.4	-	-	109.0	-3.2	-	-	111.9	2.7	-	-	110.9	-0.9	-	-	115.6	4.2
1987	-	-	-	-	-	-	-	-	-	-	117.0	1.2	-	-	-	-	-	-	-	-	-	-	119.3	2.0
1988	-	-	-	-	-	-	-	-	-	-	124.4	4.3	-	-	-	-	-	-	-	-	-	-	128.1	3.0
1989	-	-	-	-	-	-	-	-	-	-	114.4	-10.7	-	-	-	-	-	-	-	-	-	-	105.5	-7.8
1990	-	-	-	-	-	-	-	-	-	-	105.9	0.4	-	-	-	-	-	-	-	-	-	-	109.5	3.4
1991	-	-	-	-	-	-	-	-	-	-	109.2	-0.3	-	-	-	-	-	-	-	-	-	-	114.8	5.1
1992	-	-	-	-	-	-	-	-	-	-	106.2	-7.5	-	-	-	-	-	-	-	-	-	-	116.8	10.0
1993	-	-	-	-	-	-	-	-	-	-	110.0	-5.8	-	-	-	-	-	-	-	-	-	-	113.9	3.5
1994	-	-	-	-	-	-	-	-	-	-	115.8	1.7	-	-	-	-	-	-	-	-	-	-	121.0	4.5
1995	-	-	-	-	-	-	-	-	-	-	114.6	-5.3	-	-	-	-	-	-	-	-	-	-	117.2	2.3
1996	-	-	-	-	-	-	-	-	-	-	118.5	1.1	-	-	-	-	-	-	-	-	-	-	118.2	-0.3
1997	-	-	-	-	-	-	-	-	-	-	118.9	0.6	-	-	-	-	-	-	-	-	-	-	-	-

Source: U.S. Department of Labor, Bureau of Labor Statistics, Division of Consumer Prices and Price Indexes. - indicates no data collected for period.

Buffalo, NY
Consumer Price Index - All Urban Consumers
Base 1982-1984 = 100
Transportation

For 1963-1997. Columns headed % show percentile change in the index from the previous period for which an index is available.

Year	Jan Index	%	Feb Index	%	Mar Index	%	Apr Index	%	May Index	%	Jun Index	%	Jul Index	%	Aug Index	%	Sep Index	%	Oct Index	%	Nov Index	%	Dec Index	%
1963	-	-	-	-	-	-	-	-	-	-	-	-	-	-	-	-	-	-	-	-	32.9	-	-	-
1964	-	-	32.5	-1.2	-	-	-	-	33.0	1.5	-	-	-	-	32.6	-1.2	-	-	-	-	33.1	1.5	-	-
1965	-	-	33.6	1.5	-	-	-	-	34.1	1.5	-	-	-	-	34.3	0.6	-	-	-	-	34.3	0.0	-	-
1966	-	-	34.5	0.6	-	-	-	-	34.8	0.9	-	-	-	-	35.1	0.9	-	-	-	-	35.2	0.3	-	-
1967	-	-	35.4	0.6	-	-	-	-	35.7	0.8	-	-	-	-	35.7	0.0	-	-	-	-	36.3	1.7	-	-
1968	-	-	36.4	0.3	-	-	-	-	36.6	0.5	-	-	-	-	36.8	0.5	-	-	-	-	37.1	0.8	-	-
1969	-	-	37.4	0.8	-	-	-	-	38.0	1.6	-	-	-	-	38.1	0.3	-	-	-	-	38.8	1.8	-	-
1970	-	-	39.3	1.3	-	-	-	-	39.8	1.3	-	-	-	-	39.8	0.0	-	-	-	-	40.9	2.8	-	-
1971	-	-	41.8	2.2	-	-	-	-	41.8	0.0	-	-	-	-	42.3	1.2	-	-	-	-	41.3	-2.4	-	-
1972	-	-	41.2	-0.2	-	-	-	-	42.3	2.7	-	-	-	-	42.3	0.0	-	-	-	-	42.8	1.2	-	-
1973	-	-	43.1	0.7	-	-	-	-	43.7	1.4	-	-	-	-	44.2	1.1	-	-	-	-	44.7	1.1	-	-
1974	-	-	46.1	3.1	-	-	-	-	48.6	5.4	-	-	-	-	50.0	2.9	-	-	-	-	50.3	0.6	-	-
1975	-	-	50.7	0.8	-	-	-	-	51.8	2.2	-	-	-	-	53.5	3.3	-	-	-	-	54.7	2.2	-	-
1976	-	-	55.2	0.9	-	-	-	-	57.2	3.6	-	-	-	-	58.7	2.6	-	-	-	-	59.7	1.7	-	-
1977	-	-	59.9	0.3	-	-	-	-	61.3	2.3	-	-	-	-	61.6	0.5	-	-	-	-	62.1	0.8	-	-
1978	-	-	62.1	0.0	-	-	62.5	0.6	-	-	64.3	2.9	-	-	65.2	1.4	-	-	66.0	1.2	-	-	66.4	0.6
1979	-	-	67.4	1.5	-	-	69.9	3.7	-	-	73.7	5.4	-	-	77.2	4.7	-	-	78.3	1.4	-	-	79.6	1.7
1980	-	-	84.3	5.9	-	-	86.1	2.1	-	-	86.4	0.3	-	-	87.4	1.2	-	-	88.4	1.1	-	-	89.1	0.8
1981	-	-	93.0	4.4	-	-	95.4	2.6	-	-	95.7	0.3	-	-	96.3	0.6	-	-	97.5	1.2	-	-	97.9	0.4
1982	-	-	96.9	-1.0	-	-	94.8	-2.2	-	-	97.5	2.8	-	-	98.2	0.7	-	-	99.0	0.8	-	-	99.0	0.0
1983	-	-	96.6	-2.4	-	-	97.2	0.6	-	-	99.1	2.0	-	-	100.8	1.7	-	-	101.9	1.1	-	-	102.0	0.1
1984	-	-	101.6	-0.4	-	-	102.6	1.0	-	-	103.5	0.9	-	-	103.1	-0.4	-	-	103.8	0.7	-	-	103.9	0.1
1985	-	-	103.1	-0.8	-	-	104.6	1.5	-	-	105.9	1.2	-	-	105.6	-0.3	-	-	105.9	0.3	-	-	106.5	0.6
1986	-	-	104.4	-2.0	-	-	97.4	-6.7	-	-	99.2	1.8	-	-	95.0	-4.2	-	-	95.9	0.9	-	-	96.5	0.6
1987	-	-	-	-	-	-	-	-	-	-	98.4	2.0	-	-	-	-	-	-	-	-	-	-	101.1	2.7
1988	-	-	-	-	-	-	-	-	-	-	100.9	-0.2	-	-	-	-	-	-	-	-	-	-	101.2	0.3
1989	-	-	-	-	-	-	-	-	-	-	103.1	1.9	-	-	-	-	-	-	-	-	-	-	103.4	0.3
1990	-	-	-	-	-	-	-	-	-	-	105.8	2.3	-	-	-	-	-	-	-	-	-	-	112.4	6.2
1991	-	-	-	-	-	-	-	-	-	-	112.6	0.2	-	-	-	-	-	-	-	-	-	-	111.9	-0.6
1992	-	-	-	-	-	-	-	-	-	-	112.7	0.7	-	-	-	-	-	-	-	-	-	-	115.2	2.2
1993	-	-	-	-	-	-	-	-	-	-	116.7	1.3	-	-	-	-	-	-	-	-	-	-	118.3	1.4
1994	-	-	-	-	-	-	-	-	-	-	118.9	0.5	-	-	-	-	-	-	-	-	-	-	123.0	3.4
1995	-	-	-	-	-	-	-	-	-	-	126.4	2.8	-	-	-	-	-	-	-	-	-	-	129.3	2.3
1996	-	-	-	-	-	-	-	-	-	-	132.1	2.2	-	-	-	-	-	-	-	-	-	-	132.8	0.5
1997	-	-	-	-	-	-	-	-	-	-	133.2	0.3	-	-	-	-	-	-	-	-	-	-	-	-

Source: U.S. Department of Labor, Bureau of Labor Statistics, Division of Consumer Prices and Price Indexes. - indicates no data collected for period.

Buffalo, NY
Consumer Price Index - Urban Wage Earners
Base 1982-1984 = 100
Transportation

For 1963-1997. Columns headed % show percentile change in the index from the previous period for which an index is available.

Year	Jan Index	%	Feb Index	%	Mar Index	%	Apr Index	%	May Index	%	Jun Index	%	Jul Index	%	Aug Index	%	Sep Index	%	Oct Index	%	Nov Index	%	Dec Index	%
1963	-	-	-	-	-	-	-	-	-	-	-	-	-	-	-	-	-	-	-	-	32.7	-	-	-
1964	-	-	32.3	-1.2	-	-	-	-	32.8	1.5	-	-	-	-	32.4	-1.2	-	-	-	-	32.8	1.2	-	-
1965	-	-	33.4	1.8	-	-	-	-	33.8	1.2	-	-	-	-	34.0	0.6	-	-	-	-	34.1	0.3	-	-
1966	-	-	34.3	0.6	-	-	-	-	34.5	0.6	-	-	-	-	34.9	1.2	-	-	-	-	34.9	0.0	-	-
1967	-	-	35.2	0.9	-	-	-	-	35.5	0.9	-	-	-	-	35.4	-0.3	-	-	-	-	36.0	1.7	-	-
1968	-	-	36.1	0.3	-	-	-	-	36.3	0.6	-	-	-	-	36.5	0.6	-	-	-	-	36.8	0.8	-	-
1969	-	-	37.2	1.1	-	-	-	-	37.7	1.3	-	-	-	-	37.8	0.3	-	-	-	-	38.5	1.9	-	-
1970	-	-	39.0	1.3	-	-	-	-	39.5	1.3	-	-	-	-	39.5	0.0	-	-	-	-	40.6	2.8	-	-
1971	-	-	41.5	2.2	-	-	-	-	41.5	0.0	-	-	-	-	42.0	1.2	-	-	-	-	41.0	-2.4	-	-
1972	-	-	40.9	-0.2	-	-	-	-	42.0	2.7	-	-	-	-	42.0	0.0	-	-	-	-	42.5	1.2	-	-
1973	-	-	42.8	0.7	-	-	-	-	43.4	1.4	-	-	-	-	43.9	1.2	-	-	-	-	44.3	0.9	-	-
1974	-	-	45.8	3.4	-	-	-	-	48.2	5.2	-	-	-	-	49.7	3.1	-	-	-	-	50.0	0.6	-	-
1975	-	-	50.3	0.6	-	-	-	-	51.5	2.4	-	-	-	-	53.1	3.1	-	-	-	-	54.3	2.3	-	-
1976	-	-	54.8	0.9	-	-	-	-	56.8	3.6	-	-	-	-	58.3	2.6	-	-	-	-	59.2	1.5	-	-
1977	-	-	59.5	0.5	-	-	-	-	60.9	2.4	-	-	-	-	61.2	0.5	-	-	-	-	61.7	0.8	-	-
1978	-	-	61.7	0.0	-	-	62.1	0.6	-	-	64.1	3.2	-	-	65.2	1.7	-	-	65.7	0.8	-	-	66.0	0.5
1979	-	-	67.3	2.0	-	-	69.9	3.9	-	-	73.9	5.7	-	-	77.5	4.9	-	-	78.1	0.8	-	-	79.3	1.5
1980	-	-	83.7	5.5	-	-	86.1	2.9	-	-	85.8	-0.3	-	-	86.8	1.2	-	-	87.8	1.2	-	-	88.6	0.9
1981	-	-	92.9	4.9	-	-	95.1	2.4	-	-	95.8	0.7	-	-	96.0	0.2	-	-	97.6	1.7	-	-	98.0	0.4
1982	-	-	96.8	-1.2	-	-	94.6	-2.3	-	-	97.4	3.0	-	-	98.2	0.8	-	-	98.9	0.7	-	-	98.9	0.0
1983	-	-	96.4	-2.5	-	-	96.9	0.5	-	-	99.1	2.3	-	-	100.9	1.8	-	-	102.0	1.1	-	-	102.2	0.2
1984	-	-	101.7	-0.5	-	-	102.8	1.1	-	-	103.7	0.9	-	-	103.3	-0.4	-	-	103.8	0.5	-	-	103.9	0.1
1985	-	-	103.0	-0.9	-	-	104.4	1.4	-	-	105.8	1.3	-	-	105.4	-0.4	-	-	105.7	0.3	-	-	106.3	0.6
1986	-	-	103.9	-2.3	-	-	96.3	-7.3	-	-	98.1	1.9	-	-	93.4	-4.8	-	-	94.4	1.1	-	-	94.9	0.5
1987	-	-	-	-	-	-	-	-	-	-	97.8	3.1	-	-	-	-	-	-	-	-	-	-	100.9	3.2
1988	-	-	-	-	-	-	-	-	-	-	100.4	-0.5	-	-	-	-	-	-	-	-	-	-	100.7	0.3
1989	-	-	-	-	-	-	-	-	-	-	102.7	2.0	-	-	-	-	-	-	-	-	-	-	103.3	0.6
1990	-	-	-	-	-	-	-	-	-	-	105.4	2.0	-	-	-	-	-	-	-	-	-	-	113.0	7.2
1991	-	-	-	-	-	-	-	-	-	-	112.6	-0.4	-	-	-	-	-	-	-	-	-	-	112.0	-0.5
1992	-	-	-	-	-	-	-	-	-	-	112.5	0.4	-	-	-	-	-	-	-	-	-	-	115.2	2.4
1993	-	-	-	-	-	-	-	-	-	-	115.9	0.6	-	-	-	-	-	-	-	-	-	-	117.9	1.7
1994	-	-	-	-	-	-	-	-	-	-	117.9	0.0	-	-	-	-	-	-	-	-	-	-	123.2	4.5
1995	-	-	-	-	-	-	-	-	-	-	127.4	3.4	-	-	-	-	-	-	-	-	-	-	131.0	2.8
1996	-	-	-	-	-	-	-	-	-	-	133.7	2.1	-	-	-	-	-	-	-	-	-	-	134.6	0.7
1997	-	-	-	-	-	-	-	-	-	-	135.1	0.4	-	-	-	-	-	-	-	-	-	-	-	-

Source: U.S. Department of Labor, Bureau of Labor Statistics, Division of Consumer Prices and Price Indexes. - indicates no data collected for period.

Buffalo, NY
Consumer Price Index - All Urban Consumers
Base 1982-1984 = 100
Medical Care

For 1963-1997. Columns headed % show percentile change in the index from the previous period for which an index is available.

Year	Jan Index	%	Feb Index	%	Mar Index	%	Apr Index	%	May Index	%	Jun Index	%	Jul Index	%	Aug Index	%	Sep Index	%	Oct Index	%	Nov Index	%	Dec Index	%
1963	-	-	-	-	-	-	-	-	-	-	-	-	-	-	-	-	-	-	-	-	29.5	-	-	-
1964	-	-	29.6	0.3	-	-	-	-	29.7	0.3	-	-	-	-	29.9	0.7	-	-	-	-	30.5	2.0	-	-
1965	-	-	30.5	0.0	-	-	-	-	30.5	0.0	-	-	-	-	30.7	0.7	-	-	-	-	31.0	1.0	-	-
1966	-	-	31.4	1.3	-	-	-	-	32.0	1.9	-	-	-	-	32.8	2.5	-	-	-	-	33.3	1.5	-	-
1967	-	-	33.8	1.5	-	-	-	-	34.1	0.9	-	-	-	-	34.6	1.5	-	-	-	-	35.1	1.4	-	-
1968	-	-	35.4	0.9	-	-	-	-	35.4	0.0	-	-	-	-	35.9	1.4	-	-	-	-	36.3	1.1	-	-
1969	-	-	36.8	1.4	-	-	-	-	37.4	1.6	-	-	-	-	37.7	0.8	-	-	-	-	38.0	0.8	-	-
1970	-	-	38.8	2.1	-	-	-	-	39.6	2.1	-	-	-	-	40.0	1.0	-	-	-	-	40.6	1.5	-	-
1971	-	-	41.2	1.5	-	-	-	-	41.8	1.5	-	-	-	-	42.6	1.9	-	-	-	-	42.6	0.0	-	-
1972	-	-	43.1	1.2	-	-	-	-	43.3	0.5	-	-	-	-	43.4	0.2	-	-	-	-	43.6	0.5	-	-
1973	-	-	44.2	1.4	-	-	-	-	44.6	0.9	-	-	-	-	44.8	0.4	-	-	-	-	45.5	1.6	-	-
1974	-	-	47.3	4.0	-	-	-	-	48.1	1.7	-	-	-	-	49.6	3.1	-	-	-	-	50.5	1.8	-	-
1975	-	-	52.1	3.2	-	-	-	-	53.0	1.7	-	-	-	-	53.9	1.7	-	-	-	-	54.6	1.3	-	-
1976	-	-	56.6	3.7	-	-	-	-	57.3	1.2	-	-	-	-	58.5	2.1	-	-	-	-	59.0	0.9	-	-
1977	-	-	61.9	4.9	-	-	-	-	62.2	0.5	-	-	-	-	63.1	1.4	-	-	-	-	64.0	1.4	-	-
1978	-	-	67.2	5.0	-	-	67.5	0.4	-	-	68.2	1.0	-	-	68.4	0.3	-	-	69.0	0.9	-	-	70.1	1.6
1979	-	-	71.9	2.6	-	-	72.0	0.1	-	-	73.2	1.7	-	-	73.9	1.0	-	-	74.3	0.5	-	-	74.8	0.7
1980	-	-	76.7	2.5	-	-	77.5	1.0	-	-	77.8	0.4	-	-	78.8	1.3	-	-	79.7	1.1	-	-	81.3	2.0
1981	-	-	83.5	2.7	-	-	84.7	1.4	-	-	85.6	1.1	-	-	86.5	1.1	-	-	87.5	1.2	-	-	87.8	0.3
1982	-	-	89.9	2.4	-	-	90.8	1.0	-	-	91.3	0.6	-	-	91.5	0.2	-	-	92.2	0.8	-	-	94.9	2.9
1983	-	-	99.2	4.5	-	-	100.3	1.1	-	-	100.5	0.2	-	-	101.7	1.2	-	-	102.6	0.9	-	-	103.0	0.4
1984	-	-	106.4	3.3	-	-	107.6	1.1	-	-	107.8	0.2	-	-	107.9	0.1	-	-	108.5	0.6	-	-	109.2	0.6
1985	-	-	111.1	1.7	-	-	111.6	0.5	-	-	112.7	1.0	-	-	114.2	1.3	-	-	114.9	0.6	-	-	115.2	0.3
1986	-	-	116.6	1.2	-	-	117.3	0.6	-	-	119.2	1.6	-	-	121.5	1.9	-	-	122.6	0.9	-	-	123.4	0.7
1987	-	-	-	-	-	-	-	-	-	-	126.7	2.7	-	-	-	-	-	-	-	-	-	-	128.6	1.5
1988	-	-	-	-	-	-	-	-	-	-	129.9	1.0	-	-	-	-	-	-	-	-	-	-	134.0	3.2
1989	-	-	-	-	-	-	-	-	-	-	140.4	4.8	-	-	-	-	-	-	-	-	-	-	143.4	2.1
1990	-	-	-	-	-	-	-	-	-	-	150.0	4.6	-	-	-	-	-	-	-	-	-	-	153.4	2.3
1991	-	-	-	-	-	-	-	-	-	-	157.7	2.8	-	-	-	-	-	-	-	-	-	-	160.4	1.7
1992	-	-	-	-	-	-	-	-	-	-	165.5	3.2	-	-	-	-	-	-	-	-	-	-	167.4	1.1
1993	-	-	-	-	-	-	-	-	-	-	171.8	2.6	-	-	-	-	-	-	-	-	-	-	173.0	0.7
1994	-	-	-	-	-	-	-	-	-	-	172.9	-0.1	-	-	-	-	-	-	-	-	-	-	176.1	1.9
1995	-	-	-	-	-	-	-	-	-	-	180.1	2.3	-	-	-	-	-	-	-	-	-	-	183.5	1.9
1996	-	-	-	-	-	-	-	-	-	-	186.0	1.4	-	-	-	-	-	-	-	-	-	-	188.6	1.4
1997	-	-	-	-	-	-	-	-	-	-	192.0	1.8	-	-	-	-	-	-	-	-	-	-	-	-

Source: U.S. Department of Labor, Bureau of Labor Statistics, Division of Consumer Prices and Price Indexes. - indicates no data collected for period.

Buffalo, NY
Consumer Price Index - Urban Wage Earners
Base 1982-1984 = 100
Medical Care

For 1963-1997. Columns headed % show percentile change in the index from the previous period for which an index is available.

Year	Jan Index	%	Feb Index	%	Mar Index	%	Apr Index	%	May Index	%	Jun Index	%	Jul Index	%	Aug Index	%	Sep Index	%	Oct Index	%	Nov Index	%	Dec Index	%
1963	-	-	-	-	-	-	-	-	-	-	-	-	-	-	-	-	-	-	-	-	29.0	-	-	-
1964	-	-	29.1	0.3	-	-	-	-	29.2	0.3	-	-	-	-	29.4	0.7	-	-	-	-	30.0	2.0	-	-
1965	-	-	30.0	0.0	-	-	-	-	30.0	0.0	-	-	-	-	30.1	0.3	-	-	-	-	30.5	1.3	-	-
1966	-	-	30.8	1.0	-	-	-	-	31.5	2.3	-	-	-	-	32.2	2.2	-	-	-	-	32.7	1.6	-	-
1967	-	-	33.2	1.5	-	-	-	-	33.5	0.9	-	-	-	-	34.0	1.5	-	-	-	-	34.5	1.5	-	-
1968	-	-	34.8	0.9	-	-	-	-	34.8	0.0	-	-	-	-	35.2	1.1	-	-	-	-	35.7	1.4	-	-
1969	-	-	36.1	1.1	-	-	-	-	36.8	1.9	-	-	-	-	37.1	0.8	-	-	-	-	37.3	0.5	-	-
1970	-	-	38.1	2.1	-	-	-	-	38.9	2.1	-	-	-	-	39.3	1.0	-	-	-	-	39.9	1.5	-	-
1971	-	-	40.4	1.3	-	-	-	-	41.1	1.7	-	-	-	-	41.9	1.9	-	-	-	-	41.8	-0.2	-	-
1972	-	-	42.4	1.4	-	-	-	-	42.5	0.2	-	-	-	-	42.6	0.2	-	-	-	-	42.8	0.5	-	-
1973	-	-	43.4	1.4	-	-	-	-	43.8	0.9	-	-	-	-	44.0	0.5	-	-	-	-	44.7	1.6	-	-
1974	-	-	46.4	3.8	-	-	-	-	47.3	1.9	-	-	-	-	48.7	3.0	-	-	-	-	49.6	1.8	-	-
1975	-	-	51.2	3.2	-	-	-	-	52.1	1.8	-	-	-	-	52.9	1.5	-	-	-	-	53.6	1.3	-	-
1976	-	-	55.6	3.7	-	-	-	-	56.3	1.3	-	-	-	-	57.5	2.1	-	-	-	-	58.0	0.9	-	-
1977	-	-	60.8	4.8	-	-	-	-	61.1	0.5	-	-	-	-	62.0	1.5	-	-	-	-	62.9	1.5	-	-
1978	-	-	66.0	4.9	-	-	66.2	0.3	-	-	67.1	1.4	-	-	67.4	0.4	-	-	67.5	0.1	-	-	69.2	2.5
1979	-	-	71.1	2.7	-	-	71.1	0.0	-	-	72.2	1.5	-	-	72.9	1.0	-	-	73.2	0.4	-	-	73.6	0.5
1980	-	-	76.8	4.3	-	-	77.9	1.4	-	-	79.0	1.4	-	-	79.4	0.5	-	-	81.2	2.3	-	-	81.8	0.7
1981	-	-	83.1	1.6	-	-	84.6	1.8	-	-	85.2	0.7	-	-	86.2	1.2	-	-	87.7	1.7	-	-	88.3	0.7
1982	-	-	90.3	2.3	-	-	91.1	0.9	-	-	91.6	0.5	-	-	91.8	0.2	-	-	92.5	0.8	-	-	94.8	2.5
1983	-	-	99.0	4.4	-	-	100.1	1.1	-	-	100.4	0.3	-	-	101.6	1.2	-	-	102.5	0.9	-	-	103.0	0.5
1984	-	-	106.3	3.2	-	-	107.5	1.1	-	-	107.7	0.2	-	-	107.8	0.1	-	-	108.4	0.6	-	-	109.1	0.6
1985	-	-	111.1	1.8	-	-	111.5	0.4	-	-	112.5	0.9	-	-	114.1	1.4	-	-	114.8	0.6	-	-	115.0	0.2
1986	-	-	116.2	1.0	-	-	116.9	0.6	-	-	118.8	1.6	-	-	120.9	1.8	-	-	121.9	0.8	-	-	122.7	0.7
1987	-	-	-	-	-	-	-	-	-	-	125.9	2.6	-	-	-	-	-	-	-	-	-	-	127.8	1.5
1988	-	-	-	-	-	-	-	-	-	-	128.6	0.6	-	-	-	-	-	-	-	-	-	-	133.4	3.7
1989	-	-	-	-	-	-	-	-	-	-	140.0	4.9	-	-	-	-	-	-	-	-	-	-	142.6	1.9
1990	-	-	-	-	-	-	-	-	-	-	148.8	4.3	-	-	-	-	-	-	-	-	-	-	152.0	2.2
1991	-	-	-	-	-	-	-	-	-	-	156.7	3.1	-	-	-	-	-	-	-	-	-	-	159.6	1.9
1992	-	-	-	-	-	-	-	-	-	-	164.9	3.3	-	-	-	-	-	-	-	-	-	-	167.0	1.3
1993	-	-	-	-	-	-	-	-	-	-	171.7	2.8	-	-	-	-	-	-	-	-	-	-	173.5	1.0
1994	-	-	-	-	-	-	-	-	-	-	173.2	-0.2	-	-	-	-	-	-	-	-	-	-	176.3	1.8
1995	-	-	-	-	-	-	-	-	-	-	180.4	2.3	-	-	-	-	-	-	-	-	-	-	183.4	1.7
1996	-	-	-	-	-	-	-	-	-	-	185.7	1.3	-	-	-	-	-	-	-	-	-	-	188.0	1.2
1997	-	-	-	-	-	-	-	-	-	-	191.6	1.9	-	-	-	-	-	-	-	-	-	-	-	-

Source: U.S. Department of Labor, Bureau of Labor Statistics, Division of Consumer Prices and Price Indexes. - indicates no data collected for period.

Buffalo, NY
Consumer Price Index - All Urban Consumers
Base 1982-1984 = 100
Entertainment

For 1975-1997. Columns headed % show percentile change in the index from the previous period for which an index is available.

Year	Jan Index	%	Feb Index	%	Mar Index	%	Apr Index	%	May Index	%	Jun Index	%	Jul Index	%	Aug Index	%	Sep Index	%	Oct Index	%	Nov Index	%	Dec Index	%
1975	-	-	-	-	-	-	-	-	-	-	-	-	-	-	-	-	-	-	-	-	62.4	-	-	-
1976	-	-	62.3	-0.2	-	-	-	-	62.6	0.5	-	-	-	-	62.5	-0.2	-	-	-	-	64.2	2.7	-	-
1977	-	-	64.8	0.9	-	-	-	-	66.5	2.6	-	-	-	-	66.3	-0.3	-	-	-	-	67.7	2.1	-	-
1978	-	-	68.9	1.8	-	-	68.7	-0.3	-	-	70.6	2.8	-	-	69.8	-1.1	-	-	72.8	4.3	-	-	73.8	1.4
1979	-	-	72.8	-1.4	-	-	73.3	0.7	-	-	70.0	-4.5	-	-	70.2	0.3	-	-	72.8	3.7	-	-	73.1	0.4
1980	-	-	73.7	0.8	-	-	77.6	5.3	-	-	77.5	-0.1	-	-	78.9	1.8	-	-	82.6	4.7	-	-	85.5	3.5
1981	-	-	87.7	2.6	-	-	88.5	0.9	-	-	86.5	-2.3	-	-	86.6	0.1	-	-	90.0	3.9	-	-	90.6	0.7
1982	-	-	92.5	2.1	-	-	93.1	0.6	-	-	91.4	-1.8	-	-	93.5	2.3	-	-	97.7	4.5	-	-	97.5	-0.2
1983	-	-	99.6	2.2	-	-	100.0	0.4	-	-	100.6	0.6	-	-	99.4	-1.2	-	-	102.4	3.0	-	-	102.6	0.2
1984	-	-	103.7	1.1	-	-	105.8	2.0	-	-	101.9	-3.7	-	-	105.0	3.0	-	-	109.2	4.0	-	-	108.8	-0.4
1985	-	-	109.7	0.8	-	-	111.1	1.3	-	-	111.7	0.5	-	-	112.6	0.8	-	-	112.3	-0.3	-	-	112.8	0.4
1986	-	-	113.2	0.4	-	-	114.1	0.8	-	-	111.6	-2.2	-	-	112.4	0.7	-	-	118.6	5.5	-	-	119.2	0.5
1987	-	-	-	-	-	-	-	-	-	-	121.9	2.3	-	-	-	-	-	-	-	-	-	-	123.5	1.3
1988	-	-	-	-	-	-	-	-	-	-	123.5	0.0	-	-	-	-	-	-	-	-	-	-	126.7	2.6
1989	-	-	-	-	-	-	-	-	-	-	130.8	3.2	-	-	-	-	-	-	-	-	-	-	133.7	2.2
1990	-	-	-	-	-	-	-	-	-	-	140.5	5.1	-	-	-	-	-	-	-	-	-	-	145.1	3.3
1991	-	-	-	-	-	-	-	-	-	-	146.8	1.2	-	-	-	-	-	-	-	-	-	-	149.5	1.8
1992	-	-	-	-	-	-	-	-	-	-	152.9	2.3	-	-	-	-	-	-	-	-	-	-	158.5	3.7
1993	-	-	-	-	-	-	-	-	-	-	162.9	2.8	-	-	-	-	-	-	-	-	-	-	172.0	5.6
1994	-	-	-	-	-	-	-	-	-	-	176.0	2.3	-	-	-	-	-	-	-	-	-	-	179.4	1.9
1995	-	-	-	-	-	-	-	-	-	-	186.3	3.8	-	-	-	-	-	-	-	-	-	-	189.5	1.7
1996	-	-	-	-	-	-	-	-	-	-	196.2	3.5	-	-	-	-	-	-	-	-	-	-	198.1	1.0
1997	-	-	-	-	-	-	-	-	-	-	195.8	-1.2	-	-	-	-	-	-	-	-	-	-	-	-

Source: U.S. Department of Labor, Bureau of Labor Statistics, Division of Consumer Prices and Price Indexes. - indicates no data collected for period.

Buffalo, NY
Consumer Price Index - Urban Wage Earners
Base 1982-1984 = 100
Entertainment

For 1975-1997. Columns headed % show percentile change in the index from the previous period for which an index is available.

Year	Jan Index	%	Feb Index	%	Mar Index	%	Apr Index	%	May Index	%	Jun Index	%	Jul Index	%	Aug Index	%	Sep Index	%	Oct Index	%	Nov Index	%	Dec Index	%
1975	-	-	-	-	-	-	-	-	-	-	-	-	-	-	-	-	-	-	-	-	66.7	-	-	-
1976	-	-	66.6	-0.1	-	-	-	-	66.9	0.5	-	-	-	-	66.8	-0.1	-	-	-	-	68.6	2.7	-	-
1977	-	-	69.2	0.9	-	-	-	-	71.0	2.6	-	-	-	-	70.9	-0.1	-	-	-	-	72.3	2.0	-	-
1978	-	-	73.6	1.8	-	-	72.6	-1.4	-	-	70.7	-2.6	-	-	69.5	-1.7	-	-	73.7	6.0	-	-	74.3	0.8
1979	-	-	73.2	-1.5	-	-	73.8	0.8	-	-	70.3	-4.7	-	-	70.3	0.0	-	-	73.5	4.6	-	-	74.4	1.2
1980	-	-	75.8	1.9	-	-	78.2	3.2	-	-	78.9	0.9	-	-	79.4	0.6	-	-	82.0	3.3	-	-	83.6	2.0
1981	-	-	85.2	1.9	-	-	86.6	1.6	-	-	86.8	0.2	-	-	87.4	0.7	-	-	89.9	2.9	-	-	90.4	0.6
1982	-	-	92.4	2.2	-	-	93.1	0.8	-	-	92.1	-1.1	-	-	94.5	2.6	-	-	97.6	3.3	-	-	97.4	-0.2
1983	-	-	99.6	2.3	-	-	100.1	0.5	-	-	100.3	0.2	-	-	100.5	0.2	-	-	101.9	1.4	-	-	102.4	0.5
1984	-	-	103.6	1.2	-	-	105.5	1.8	-	-	101.9	-3.4	-	-	105.3	3.3	-	-	108.4	2.9	-	-	107.7	-0.6
1985	-	-	108.5	0.7	-	-	109.9	1.3	-	-	110.6	0.6	-	-	111.4	0.7	-	-	110.9	-0.4	-	-	111.3	0.4
1986	-	-	111.8	0.4	-	-	112.7	0.8	-	-	110.9	-1.6	-	-	111.9	0.9	-	-	118.4	5.8	-	-	118.9	0.4
1987	-	-	-	-	-	-	-	-	-	-	121.2	1.9	-	-	-	-	-	-	-	-	-	-	122.9	1.4
1988	-	-	-	-	-	-	-	-	-	-	123.0	0.1	-	-	-	-	-	-	-	-	-	-	126.1	2.5
1989	-	-	-	-	-	-	-	-	-	-	129.8	2.9	-	-	-	-	-	-	-	-	-	-	132.4	2.0
1990	-	-	-	-	-	-	-	-	-	-	139.4	5.3	-	-	-	-	-	-	-	-	-	-	144.0	3.3
1991	-	-	-	-	-	-	-	-	-	-	145.5	1.0	-	-	-	-	-	-	-	-	-	-	148.0	1.7
1992	-	-	-	-	-	-	-	-	-	-	151.6	2.4	-	-	-	-	-	-	-	-	-	-	157.1	3.6
1993	-	-	-	-	-	-	-	-	-	-	161.5	2.8	-	-	-	-	-	-	-	-	-	-	170.1	5.3
1994	-	-	-	-	-	-	-	-	-	-	174.2	2.4	-	-	-	-	-	-	-	-	-	-	177.9	2.1
1995	-	-	-	-	-	-	-	-	-	-	184.7	3.8	-	-	-	-	-	-	-	-	-	-	188.1	1.8
1996	-	-	-	-	-	-	-	-	-	-	195.1	3.7	-	-	-	-	-	-	-	-	-	-	197.1	1.0
1997	-	-	-	-	-	-	-	-	-	-	194.2	-1.5	-	-	-	-	-	-	-	-	-	-	-	-

Source: U.S. Department of Labor, Bureau of Labor Statistics, Division of Consumer Prices and Price Indexes. - indicates no data collected for period.

Buffalo, NY
Consumer Price Index - All Urban Consumers
Base 1982-1984 = 100
Other Goods and Services

For 1975-1997. Columns headed % show percentile change in the index from the previous period for which an index is available.

Year	Jan Index	%	Feb Index	%	Mar Index	%	Apr Index	%	May Index	%	Jun Index	%	Jul Index	%	Aug Index	%	Sep Index	%	Oct Index	%	Nov Index	%	Dec Index	%
1975	-	-	-	-	-	-	-	-	-	-	-	-	-	-	-	-	-	-	-	-	55.9	-	-	-
1976	-	-	56.9	1.8	-	-	-	-	57.6	1.2	-	-	-	-	58.3	1.2	-	-	-	-	59.6	2.2	-	-
1977	-	-	60.1	0.8	-	-	-	-	60.1	0.0	-	-	-	-	60.4	0.5	-	-	-	-	62.1	2.8	-	-
1978	-	-	62.3	0.3	-	-	62.5	0.3	-	-	62.8	0.5	-	-	63.9	1.8	-	-	64.7	1.3	-	-	64.8	0.2
1979	-	-	65.5	1.1	-	-	65.9	0.6	-	-	66.3	0.6	-	-	67.5	1.8	-	-	68.3	1.2	-	-	69.0	1.0
1980	-	-	70.4	2.0	-	-	70.7	0.4	-	-	72.3	2.3	-	-	73.2	1.2	-	-	74.7	2.0	-	-	76.3	2.1
1981	-	-	77.6	1.7	-	-	79.4	2.3	-	-	81.6	2.8	-	-	82.1	0.6	-	-	86.1	4.9	-	-	86.2	0.1
1982	-	-	88.7	2.9	-	-	90.2	1.7	-	-	90.0	-0.2	-	-	89.0	-1.1	-	-	93.1	4.6	-	-	95.9	3.0
1983	-	-	97.7	1.9	-	-	100.2	2.6	-	-	100.5	0.3	-	-	101.7	1.2	-	-	103.8	2.1	-	-	104.3	0.5
1984	-	-	105.9	1.5	-	-	107.8	1.8	-	-	107.5	-0.3	-	-	109.8	2.1	-	-	110.3	0.5	-	-	109.7	-0.5
1985	-	-	113.0	3.0	-	-	114.2	1.1	-	-	116.0	1.6	-	-	116.7	0.6	-	-	121.0	3.7	-	-	121.6	0.5
1986	-	-	122.6	0.8	-	-	123.3	0.6	-	-	124.7	1.1	-	-	126.7	1.6	-	-	128.7	1.6	-	-	129.1	0.3
1987	-	-	-	-	-	-	-	-	-	-	130.7	1.2	-	-	-	-	-	-	-	-	-	-	-	-
1988	-	-	-	-	-	-	-	-	-	-	137.5	5.2	-	-	-	-	-	-	-	-	-	-	-	-
1989	-	-	-	-	-	-	-	-	-	-	144.8	5.3	-	-	-	-	-	-	-	-	-	-	-	-
1990	-	-	-	-	-	-	-	-	-	-	151.8	4.8	-	-	-	-	-	-	-	-	-	-	-	-
1991	-	-	-	-	-	-	-	-	-	-	163.5	7.7	-	-	-	-	-	-	-	-	-	-	-	-
1992	-	-	-	-	-	-	-	-	-	-	175.6	7.4	-	-	-	-	-	-	-	-	-	-	-	-
1993	-	-	-	-	-	-	-	-	-	-	189.1	7.7	-	-	-	-	-	-	-	-	-	-	-	-
1994	-	-	-	-	-	-	-	-	-	-	193.4	2.3	-	-	-	-	-	-	-	-	-	-	-	-
1995	-	-	-	-	-	-	-	-	-	-	199.6	3.2	-	-	-	-	-	-	-	-	-	-	-	-
1996	-	-	-	-	-	-	-	-	-	-	211.2	5.8	-	-	-	-	-	-	-	-	-	-	-	-
1997	-	-	-	-	-	-	-	-	-	-	218.7	3.6	-	-	-	-	-	-	-	-	-	-	-	-

Source: U.S. Department of Labor, Bureau of Labor Statistics, Division of Consumer Prices and Price Indexes. - indicates no data collected for period.

Buffalo, NY
Consumer Price Index - Urban Wage Earners
Base 1982-1984 = 100
Other Goods and Services

For 1975-1997. Columns headed % show percentile change in the index from the previous period for which an index is available.

Year	Jan Index	%	Feb Index	%	Mar Index	%	Apr Index	%	May Index	%	Jun Index	%	Jul Index	%	Aug Index	%	Sep Index	%	Oct Index	%	Nov Index	%	Dec Index	%
1975	-	-	-	-	-	-	-	-			-	-	-	-	-	-	-	-	-	-	58.7	-	-	-
1976	-	-	59.8	1.9	-	-	-	-	60.5	1.2	-	-	-	-	61.2	1.2	-	-	-	-	62.5	2.1	-	-
1977	-	-	63.0	0.8	-	-	-	-	63.1	0.2	-	-	-	-	63.4	0.5	-	-	-	-	65.2	2.8	-	-
1978	-	-	65.4	0.3	-	-	66.2	1.2	-	-	65.9	-0.5	-	-	67.3	2.1	-	-	67.7	0.6	-	-	68.2	0.7
1979	-	-	69.1	1.3	-	-	70.2	1.6	-	-	70.4	0.3	-	-	71.4	1.4	-	-	72.2	1.1	-	-	73.0	1.1
1980	-	-	74.9	2.6	-	-	74.5	-0.5	-	-	76.8	3.1	-	-	77.8	1.3	-	-	77.6	-0.3	-	-	80.0	3.1
1981	-	-	81.1	1.4	-	-	81.9	1.0	-	-	83.5	2.0	-	-	84.0	0.6	-	-	87.5	4.2	-	-	86.5	-1.1
1982	-	-	88.7	2.5	-	-	90.2	1.7	-	-	90.1	-0.1	-	-	89.2	-1.0	-	-	92.8	4.0	-	-	95.9	3.3
1983	-	-	97.8	2.0	-	-	100.7	3.0	-	-	100.8	0.1	-	-	102.3	1.5	-	-	103.9	1.6	-	-	104.4	0.5
1984	-	-	106.0	1.5	-	-	107.3	1.2	-	-	107.1	-0.2	-	-	109.2	2.0	-	-	110.1	0.8	-	-	109.3	-0.7
1985	-	-	112.3	2.7	-	-	113.0	0.6	-	-	114.6	1.4	-	-	115.2	0.5	-	-	119.3	3.6	-	-	119.6	0.3
1986	-	-	120.7	0.9	-	-	121.5	0.7	-	-	123.0	1.2	-	-	125.1	1.7	-	-	126.9	1.4	-	-	127.2	0.2
1987	-	-	-	-	-	-	-	-	-	-	128.7	1.2	-	-	-	-	-	-	-	-	-	-	-	-
1988	-	-	-	-	-	-	-	-	-	-	135.7	5.4	-	-	-	-	-	-	-	-	-	-	-	-
1989	-	-	-	-	-	-	-	-	-	-	142.9	5.3	-	-	-	-	-	-	-	-	-	-	-	-
1990	-	-	-	-	-	-	-	-	-	-	151.1	5.7	-	-	-	-	-	-	-	-	-	-	-	-
1991	-	-	-	-	-	-	-	-	-	-	163.0	7.9	-	-	-	-	-	-	-	-	-	-	-	-
1992	-	-	-	-	-	-	-	-	-	-	175.3	7.5	-	-	-	-	-	-	-	-	-	-	-	-
1993	-	-	-	-	-	-	-	-	-	-	190.7	8.8	-	-	-	-	-	-	-	-	-	-	-	-
1994	-	-	-	-	-	-	-	-	-	-	194.8	2.1	-	-	-	-	-	-	-	-	-	-	-	-
1995	-	-	-	-	-	-	-	-	-	-	201.0	3.2	-	-	-	-	-	-	-	-	-	-	-	-
1996	-	-	-	-	-	-	-	-	-	-	212.5	5.7	-	-	-	-	-	-	-	-	-	-	-	-
1997	-	-	-	-	-	-	-	-	-	-	221.2	4.1	-	-	-	-	-	-	-	-	-	-	-	-

Source: U.S. Department of Labor, Bureau of Labor Statistics, Division of Consumer Prices and Price Indexes. - indicates no data collected for period.

Chicago, IL-NW IN
Consumer Price Index - All Urban Consumers
Base 1982-1984 = 100
Annual Averages

For 1914-1997. Columns headed % show percentile change in the index from the previous period for which an index is available.

Year	All Items		Food & Beverage		Housing		Apparel & Upkeep		Trans-portation		Medical Care		Entertain-ment		Other Goods & Services	
	Index	%	Index	%	Index	%	Index	%	Index	%	Index	%	Index	%	Index	%
1914	-	-	-	-	-	-	-	-	-	-	-	-	-	-	-	-
1915	10.1	-	-	-	-	-	-	-	-	-	-	-	-	-	-	-
1916	10.9	7.9	-	-	-	-	-	-	-	-	-	-	-	-	-	-
1917	12.9	18.3	-	-	-	-	-	-	-	-	-	-	-	-	-	-
1918	14.9	15.5	-	-	-	-	-	-	-	-	-	-	-	-	-	-
1919	17.3	16.1	-	-	-	-	-	-	-	-	-	-	-	-	-	-
1920	19.8	14.5	-	-	-	-	-	-	-	-	-	-	-	-	-	-
1921	18.0	-9.1	-	-	-	-	-	-	-	-	-	-	-	-	-	-
1922	17.0	-5.6	-	-	-	-	-	-	-	-	-	-	-	-	-	-
1923	17.4	2.4	-	-	-	-	-	-	-	-	-	-	-	-	-	-
1924	17.7	1.7	-	-	-	-	-	-	-	-	-	-	-	-	-	-
1925	18.2	2.8	-	-	-	-	-	-	-	-	-	-	-	-	-	-
1926	18.3	0.5	-	-	-	-	-	-	-	-	-	-	-	-	-	-
1927	17.9	-2.2	-	-	-	-	-	-	-	-	-	-	-	-	-	-
1928	17.7	-1.1	-	-	-	-	-	-	-	-	-	-	-	-	-	-
1929	17.6	-0.6	-	-	-	-	-	-	-	-	-	-	-	-	-	-
1930	17.2	-2.3	-	-	-	-	-	-	-	-	-	-	-	-	-	-
1931	15.6	-9.3	-	-	-	-	-	-	-	-	-	-	-	-	-	-
1932	13.7	-12.2	-	-	-	-	-	-	-	-	-	-	-	-	-	-
1933	12.6	-8.0	-	-	-	-	-	-	-	-	-	-	-	-	-	-
1934	12.8	1.6	-	-	-	-	-	-	-	-	-	-	-	-	-	-
1935	13.4	4.7	-	-	-	-	-	-	-	-	-	-	-	-	-	-
1936	13.5	0.7	-	-	-	-	-	-	-	-	-	-	-	-	-	-
1937	14.2	5.2	-	-	-	-	-	-	-	-	-	-	-	-	-	-
1938	13.9	-2.1	-	-	-	-	-	-	-	-	-	-	-	-	-	-
1939	13.7	-1.4	-	-	-	-	-	-	-	-	-	-	-	-	-	-
1940	13.8	0.7	-	-	-	-	-	-	-	-	-	-	-	-	-	-
1941	14.5	5.1	-	-	-	-	-	-	-	-	-	-	-	-	-	-
1942	16.0	10.3	-	-	-	-	-	-	-	-	-	-	-	-	-	-
1943	16.9	5.6	-	-	-	-	-	-	-	-	-	-	-	-	-	-
1944	17.1	1.2	-	-	-	-	-	-	-	-	-	-	-	-	-	-
1945	17.5	2.3	-	-	-	-	-	-	-	-	-	-	-	-	-	-
1946	19.0	8.6	-	-	-	-	-	-	-	-	-	-	-	-	-	-
1947	22.1	16.3	-	-	-	-	-	-	17.5	-	12.1	-	-	-	-	-
1948	24.0	8.6	-	-	-	-	-	-	20.2	15.4	12.9	6.6	-	-	-	-
1949	24.0	0.0	-	-	-	-	-	-	22.0	8.9	13.5	4.7	-	-	-	-
1950	24.2	0.8	-	-	-	-	-	-	22.6	2.7	13.7	1.5	-	-	-	-
1951	26.1	7.9	-	-	-	-	-	-	23.9	5.8	14.5	5.8	-	-	-	-
1952	26.7	2.3	-	-	-	-	-	-	26.0	8.8	14.9	2.8	-	-	-	-
1953	26.9	0.7	-	-	-	-	52.4	-	26.6	2.3	15.5	4.0	-	-	-	-
1954	27.4	1.9	-	-	-	-	52.7	0.6	26.4	-0.8	15.9	2.6	-	-	-	-
1955	27.5	0.4	-	-	-	-	52.3	-0.8	26.2	-0.8	16.6	4.4	-	-	-	-
1956	27.9	1.5	-	-	-	-	54.0	3.3	26.7	1.9	17.6	6.0	-	-	-	-
1957	28.8	3.2	-	-	-	-	54.8	1.5	28.4	6.4	18.3	4.0	-	-	-	-
1958	29.7	3.1	-	-	-	-	55.0	0.4	30.0	5.6	19.4	6.0	-	-	-	-

[Continued]

Chicago, IL-NW IN
Consumer Price Index - All Urban Consumers
Base 1982-1984 = 100
Annual Averages
[Continued]

For 1914-1997. Columns headed % show percentile change in the index from the previous period for which an index is available.

Year	All Items		Food & Beverage		Housing		Apparel & Upkeep		Trans-portation		Medical Care		Entertain-ment		Other Goods & Services	
	Index	%	Index	%	Index	%	Index	%	Index	%	Index	%	Index	%	Index	%
1959	29.9	0.7	-	-	-	-	55.5	0.9	31.0	3.3	20.3	4.6	-	-	-	-
1960	30.4	1.7	-	-	-	-	56.4	1.6	31.1	0.3	21.5	5.9	-	-	-	-
1961	30.5	0.3	-	-	-	-	56.0	-0.7	30.9	-0.6	22.0	2.3	-	-	-	-
1962	30.8	1.0	-	-	-	-	55.8	-0.4	31.5	1.9	22.7	3.2	-	-	-	-
1963	31.1	1.0	-	-	-	-	56.0	0.4	31.7	0.6	24.3	7.0	-	-	-	-
1964	31.3	0.6	-	-	-	-	56.2	0.4	31.8	0.3	24.7	1.6	-	-	-	-
1965	31.7	1.3	-	-	-	-	56.8	1.1	32.6	2.5	25.1	1.6	-	-	-	-
1966	32.6	2.8	-	-	-	-	58.3	2.6	32.6	0.0	25.9	3.2	-	-	-	-
1967	33.5	2.8	-	-	-	-	60.6	3.9	33.5	2.8	28.0	8.1	-	-	-	-
1968	34.9	4.2	-	-	-	-	63.8	5.3	35.0	4.5	29.6	5.7	-	-	-	-
1969	36.8	5.4	-	-	-	-	66.9	4.9	37.2	6.3	31.4	6.1	-	-	-	-
1970	38.9	5.7	-	-	-	-	68.6	2.5	39.7	6.7	33.5	6.7	-	-	-	-
1971	40.4	3.9	-	-	-	-	71.1	3.6	42.1	6.0	35.9	7.2	-	-	-	-
1972	41.6	3.0	-	-	-	-	72.5	2.0	41.7	-1.0	36.8	2.5	-	-	-	-
1973	44.2	6.3	-	-	-	-	76.0	4.8	42.9	2.9	38.3	4.1	-	-	-	-
1974	48.9	10.6	-	-	-	-	80.4	5.8	47.2	10.0	42.0	9.7	-	-	-	-
1975	52.8	8.0	-	-	-	-	82.7	2.9	50.9	7.8	47.3	12.6	-	-	-	-
1976	55.3	4.7	64.2	-	48.5	-	83.7	1.2	56.1	10.2	52.8	11.6	61.7	-	58.0	-
1977	58.8	6.3	67.9	5.8	51.5	6.2	86.2	3.0	60.8	8.4	58.0	9.8	64.6	4.7	62.2	7.2
1978	63.8	8.5	75.8	11.6	57.3	11.3	88.0	2.1	63.1	3.8	62.1	7.1	68.0	5.3	65.8	5.8
1979	71.8	12.5	83.8	10.6	66.1	15.4	90.5	2.8	71.7	13.6	67.6	8.9	75.7	11.3	69.7	5.9
1980	82.2	14.5	91.2	8.8	77.4	17.1	95.6	5.6	85.0	18.5	76.3	12.9	84.9	12.2	76.1	9.2
1981	90.0	9.5	96.4	5.7	85.6	10.6	96.4	0.8	95.6	12.5	84.3	10.5	92.4	8.8	84.5	11.0
1982	96.2	6.9	98.7	2.4	94.7	10.6	97.7	1.3	98.3	2.8	92.1	9.3	98.4	6.5	91.9	8.8
1983	100.0	4.0	99.4	0.7	100.6	6.2	100.2	2.6	99.0	0.7	101.1	9.8	99.6	1.2	100.5	9.4
1984	103.8	3.8	102.0	2.6	104.7	4.1	102.1	1.9	102.7	3.7	106.8	5.6	102.1	2.5	107.6	7.1
1985	107.7	3.8	104.2	2.2	109.6	4.7	106.0	3.8	105.3	2.5	112.8	5.6	105.1	2.9	115.1	7.0
1986	110.0	2.1	108.9	4.5	112.9	3.0	103.9	-2.0	101.2	-3.9	120.1	6.5	109.9	4.6	124.2	7.9
1987	114.5	4.1	113.2	3.9	116.3	3.0	109.2	5.1	106.1	4.8	129.2	7.6	116.0	5.6	129.6	4.3
1988	119.0	3.9	117.1	3.4	120.7	3.8	116.6	6.8	107.6	1.4	138.0	6.8	122.3	5.4	138.0	6.5
1989	125.0	5.0	122.5	4.6	126.4	4.7	118.1	1.3	112.1	4.2	149.2	8.1	131.6	7.6	153.1	10.9
1990	131.7	5.4	130.3	6.4	131.4	4.0	124.3	5.2	118.7	5.9	163.0	9.2	139.2	5.8	164.3	7.3
1991	137.0	4.0	135.5	4.0	136.4	3.8	125.3	0.8	121.2	2.1	177.9	9.1	145.9	4.8	179.0	8.9
1992	141.1	3.0	139.2	2.7	139.9	2.6	126.2	0.7	123.2	1.7	190.7	7.2	149.4	2.4	192.0	7.3
1993	145.4	3.0	143.1	2.8	143.3	2.4	131.1	3.9	126.2	2.4	203.1	6.5	153.9	3.0	202.5	5.5
1994	148.6	2.2	147.0	2.7	144.8	1.0	131.0	-0.1	130.3	3.2	213.2	5.0	160.0	4.0	208.8	3.1
1995	153.3	3.2	151.3	2.9	150.6	4.0	126.3	-3.6	135.1	3.7	223.3	4.7	160.9	0.6	216.8	3.8
1996	157.4	2.7	156.1	3.2	155.1	3.0	120.6	-4.5	139.9	3.6	229.4	2.7	167.2	3.9	222.4	2.6
1997	161.7	2.7	160.5	2.8	160.2	3.3	122.3	1.4	140.2	0.2	235.5	2.7	175.3	4.8	233.3	4.9

Source: U.S. Department of Labor, Bureau of Labor Statistics, Division of Consumer Prices and Price Indexes. - indicates no data collected for period.

Chicago, IL-NW IN
Consumer Price Index - Urban Wage Earners
Base 1982-1984 = 100
Annual Averages

For 1914-1997. Columns headed % show percentile change in the index from the previous period for which an index is available.

Year	All Items		Food & Beverage		Housing		Apparel & Upkeep		Trans-portation		Medical Care		Entertain-ment		Other Goods & Services	
	Index	%	Index	%	Index	%	Index	%	Index	%	Index	%	Index	%	Index	%
1914	-	-	-	-	-	-	-	-	-	-	-	-	-	-	-	-
1915	10.2	-	-	-	-	-	-	-	-	-	-	-	-	-	-	-
1916	11.1	8.8	-	-	-	-	-	-	-	-	-	-	-	-	-	-
1917	13.1	18.0	-	-	-	-	-	-	-	-	-	-	-	-	-	-
1918	15.2	16.0	-	-	-	-	-	-	-	-	-	-	-	-	-	-
1919	17.6	15.8	-	-	-	-	-	-	-	-	-	-	-	-	-	-
1920	20.2	14.8	-	-	-	-	-	-	-	-	-	-	-	-	-	-
1921	18.3	-9.4	-	-	-	-	-	-	-	-	-	-	-	-	-	-
1922	17.3	-5.5	-	-	-	-	-	-	-	-	-	-	-	-	-	-
1923	17.7	2.3	-	-	-	-	-	-	-	-	-	-	-	-	-	-
1924	18.0	1.7	-	-	-	-	-	-	-	-	-	-	-	-	-	-
1925	18.5	2.8	-	-	-	-	-	-	-	-	-	-	-	-	-	-
1926	18.6	0.5	-	-	-	-	-	-	-	-	-	-	-	-	-	-
1927	18.2	-2.2	-	-	-	-	-	-	-	-	-	-	-	-	-	-
1928	18.0	-1.1	-	-	-	-	-	-	-	-	-	-	-	-	-	-
1929	17.9	-0.6	-	-	-	-	-	-	-	-	-	-	-	-	-	-
1930	17.5	-2.2	-	-	-	-	-	-	-	-	-	-	-	-	-	-
1931	15.9	-9.1	-	-	-	-	-	-	-	-	-	-	-	-	-	-
1932	13.9	-12.6	-	-	-	-	-	-	-	-	-	-	-	-	-	-
1933	12.8	-7.9	-	-	-	-	-	-	-	-	-	-	-	-	-	-
1934	13.0	1.6	-	-	-	-	-	-	-	-	-	-	-	-	-	-
1935	13.6	4.6	-	-	-	-	-	-	-	-	-	-	-	-	-	-
1936	13.7	0.7	-	-	-	-	-	-	-	-	-	-	-	-	-	-
1937	14.4	5.1	-	-	-	-	-	-	-	-	-	-	-	-	-	-
1938	14.2	-1.4	-	-	-	-	-	-	-	-	-	-	-	-	-	-
1939	13.9	-2.1	-	-	-	-	-	-	-	-	-	-	-	-	-	-
1940	14.1	1.4	-	-	-	-	-	-	-	-	-	-	-	-	-	-
1941	14.7	4.3	-	-	-	-	-	-	-	-	-	-	-	-	-	-
1942	16.2	10.2	-	-	-	-	-	-	-	-	-	-	-	-	-	-
1943	17.2	6.2	-	-	-	-	-	-	-	-	-	-	-	-	-	-
1944	17.4	1.2	-	-	-	-	-	-	-	-	-	-	-	-	-	-
1945	17.8	2.3	-	-	-	-	-	-	-	-	-	-	-	-	-	-
1946	19.4	9.0	-	-	-	-	-	-	-	-	-	-	-	-	-	-
1947	22.4	15.5	-	-	-	-	-	-	17.2	-	11.9	-	-	-	-	-
1948	24.4	8.9	-	-	-	-	-	-	19.9	15.7	12.7	6.7	-	-	-	-
1949	24.4	0.0	-	-	-	-	-	-	21.6	8.5	13.3	4.7	-	-	-	-
1950	24.7	1.2	-	-	-	-	-	-	22.3	3.2	13.5	1.5	-	-	-	-
1951	26.6	7.7	-	-	-	-	-	-	23.5	5.4	14.3	5.9	-	-	-	-
1952	27.2	2.3	-	-	-	-	-	-	25.6	8.9	14.7	2.8	-	-	-	-
1953	27.4	0.7	-	-	-	-	50.8	-	26.2	2.3	15.2	3.4	-	-	-	-
1954	27.9	1.8	-	-	-	-	51.1	0.6	26.0	-0.8	15.6	2.6	-	-	-	-
1955	28.0	0.4	-	-	-	-	50.7	-0.8	25.7	-1.2	16.3	4.5	-	-	-	-
1956	28.4	1.4	-	-	-	-	52.3	3.2	26.2	1.9	17.3	6.1	-	-	-	-
1957	29.3	3.2	-	-	-	-	53.1	1.5	27.9	6.5	18.0	4.0	-	-	-	-
1958	30.2	3.1	-	-	-	-	53.3	0.4	29.5	5.7	19.1	6.1	-	-	-	-

[Continued]

354

Chicago, IL-NW IN
Consumer Price Index - Urban Wage Earners
Base 1982-1984 = 100
Annual Averages
[Continued]

For 1914-1997. Columns headed % show percentile change in the index from the previous period for which an index is available.

Year	All Items		Food & Beverage		Housing		Apparel & Upkeep		Trans-portation		Medical Care		Entertain-ment		Other Goods & Services	
	Index	%	Index	%	Index	%	Index	%	Index	%	Index	%	Index	%	Index	%
1959	30.4	0.7	-	-	-	-	53.8	0.9	30.5	3.4	20.0	4.7	-	-	-	-
1960	30.9	1.6	-	-	-	-	54.7	1.7	30.6	0.3	21.1	5.5	-	-	-	-
1961	31.1	0.6	-	-	-	-	54.3	-0.7	30.4	-0.7	21.6	2.4	-	-	-	-
1962	31.4	1.0	-	-	-	-	54.1	-0.4	31.0	2.0	22.4	3.7	-	-	-	-
1963	31.7	1.0	-	-	-	-	54.3	0.4	31.2	0.6	23.9	6.7	-	-	-	-
1964	31.8	0.3	-	-	-	-	54.5	0.4	31.3	0.3	24.3	1.7	-	-	-	-
1965	32.2	1.3	-	-	-	-	55.1	1.1	32.0	2.2	24.7	1.6	-	-	-	-
1966	33.2	3.1	-	-	-	-	56.5	2.5	32.1	0.3	25.5	3.2	-	-	-	-
1967	34.0	2.4	-	-	-	-	58.7	3.9	33.0	2.8	27.5	7.8	-	-	-	-
1968	35.5	4.4	-	-	-	-	61.8	5.3	34.5	4.5	29.1	5.8	-	-	-	-
1969	37.4	5.4	-	-	-	-	64.8	4.9	36.6	6.1	30.9	6.2	-	-	-	-
1970	39.6	5.9	-	-	-	-	66.5	2.6	39.1	6.8	33.0	6.8	-	-	-	-
1971	41.1	3.8	-	-	-	-	68.9	3.6	41.4	5.9	35.3	7.0	-	-	-	-
1972	42.3	2.9	-	-	-	-	70.3	2.0	41.0	-1.0	36.2	2.5	-	-	-	-
1973	44.9	6.1	-	-	-	-	73.7	4.8	42.2	2.9	37.7	4.1	-	-	-	-
1974	49.7	10.7	-	-	-	-	77.9	5.7	46.4	10.0	41.3	9.5	-	-	-	-
1975	53.7	8.0	-	-	-	-	80.2	3.0	50.1	8.0	46.5	12.6	-	-	-	-
1976	56.2	4.7	65.2	-	50.7	-	81.1	1.1	55.2	10.2	51.9	11.6	54.6	-	59.6	-
1977	59.8	6.4	69.0	5.8	53.8	6.1	83.5	3.0	59.8	8.3	57.1	10.0	57.2	4.8	63.9	7.2
1978	64.8	8.4	76.3	10.6	59.6	10.8	86.8	4.0	62.1	3.8	61.3	7.4	59.7	4.4	68.1	6.6
1979	72.9	12.5	84.5	10.7	68.4	14.8	89.7	3.3	71.1	14.5	67.5	10.1	67.1	12.4	71.8	5.4
1980	83.5	14.5	92.3	9.2	79.8	16.7	94.9	5.8	84.5	18.8	76.9	13.9	77.4	15.4	78.1	8.8
1981	91.4	9.5	96.3	4.3	88.3	10.7	95.9	1.1	95.5	13.0	84.4	9.8	88.1	13.8	84.9	8.7
1982	97.7	6.9	98.7	2.5	97.9	10.9	97.9	2.1	98.7	3.4	92.1	9.1	97.4	10.6	91.9	8.2
1983	100.4	2.8	99.4	0.7	101.6	3.8	100.0	2.1	98.8	0.1	101.0	9.7	99.9	2.6	100.6	9.5
1984	101.9	1.5	102.0	2.6	100.6	-1.0	102.2	2.2	102.4	3.6	106.8	5.7	102.8	2.9	107.5	6.9
1985	105.1	3.1	104.2	2.2	103.9	3.3	105.6	3.3	104.8	2.3	112.7	5.5	105.8	2.9	115.2	7.2
1986	106.8	1.6	109.0	4.6	106.9	2.9	104.1	-1.4	99.8	-4.8	119.9	6.4	110.9	4.8	124.8	8.3
1987	111.1	4.0	113.3	3.9	109.7	2.6	109.4	5.1	104.3	4.5	128.9	7.5	118.0	6.4	130.3	4.4
1988	115.3	3.8	117.2	3.4	113.6	3.6	116.1	6.1	106.3	1.9	138.4	7.4	124.2	5.3	138.5	6.3
1989	121.2	5.1	122.6	4.6	118.9	4.7	117.6	1.3	111.0	4.4	150.4	8.7	132.9	7.0	153.6	10.9
1990	127.8	5.4	130.4	6.4	123.8	4.1	124.5	5.9	117.2	5.6	164.3	9.2	140.0	5.3	166.2	8.2
1991	132.9	4.0	135.7	4.1	128.4	3.7	125.6	0.9	119.3	1.8	179.4	9.2	146.0	4.3	182.4	9.7
1992	136.7	2.9	139.2	2.6	131.7	2.6	125.9	0.2	121.2	1.6	192.4	7.2	149.5	2.4	195.9	7.4
1993	140.9	3.1	143.3	2.9	135.0	2.5	130.5	3.7	124.0	2.3	205.6	6.9	153.7	2.8	207.0	5.7
1994	144.0	2.2	147.2	2.7	136.3	1.0	130.0	-0.4	128.4	3.5	215.9	5.0	159.4	3.7	211.3	2.1
1995	148.4	3.1	151.6	3.0	141.4	3.7	125.1	-3.8	133.5	4.0	227.0	5.1	160.1	0.4	217.3	2.8
1996	152.4	2.7	156.3	3.1	145.7	3.0	119.6	-4.4	138.1	3.4	234.0	3.1	165.9	3.6	221.2	1.8
1997	156.2	2.5	160.7	2.8	150.4	3.2	119.6	0.0	137.6	-0.4	240.2	2.6	173.8	4.8	232.4	5.1

Source: U.S. Department of Labor, Bureau of Labor Statistics, Division of Consumer Prices and Price Indexes. - indicates no data collected for period.

Chicago, IL-NW IN
Consumer Price Index - All Urban Consumers
Base 1982-1984 = 100
All Items

For 1914-1997. Columns headed % show percentile change in the index from the previous period for which an index is available.

Year	Jan Index	Jan %	Feb Index	Feb %	Mar Index	Mar %	Apr Index	Apr %	May Index	May %	Jun Index	Jun %	Jul Index	Jul %	Aug Index	Aug %	Sep Index	Sep %	Oct Index	Oct %	Nov Index	Nov %	Dec Index	Dec %
1914	-	-	-	-	-	-	-	-	-	-	-	-	-	-	-	-	-	-	-	-	-	-	10.0	-
1915	-	-	-	-	-	-	-	-	-	-	-	-	-	-	-	-	-	-	-	-	-	-	10.2	2.0
1916	-	-	-	-	-	-	-	-	-	-	-	-	-	-	-	-	-	-	-	-	-	-	11.6	13.7
1917	-	-	-	-	-	-	-	-	-	-	-	-	-	-	-	-	-	-	-	-	-	-	13.5	16.4
1918	-	-	-	-	-	-	-	-	-	-	-	-	-	-	-	-	-	-	-	-	-	-	16.3	20.7
1919	-	-	-	-	-	-	-	-	-	-	16.6	1.8	-	-	-	-	-	-	-	-	-	-	18.9	13.9
1920	-	-	-	-	-	-	-	-	-	-	20.8	10.1	-	-	-	-	-	-	-	-	-	-	18.9	-9.1
1921	-	-	-	-	-	-	-	-	17.9	-5.3	-	-	-	-	-	-	17.8	-0.6	-	-	-	-	17.5	-1.7
1922	-	-	-	-	-	-	-	-	16.9	-3.4	17.0	0.6	-	-	-	-	17.0	0.0	-	-	-	-	17.1	0.6
1923	-	-	-	-	17.2	0.6	-	-	-	-	17.3	0.6	-	-	-	-	17.7	2.3	-	-	-	-	17.7	0.0
1924	-	-	-	-	17.6	-0.6	-	-	-	-	17.7	0.6	-	-	-	-	17.8	0.6	-	-	-	-	17.9	0.6
1925	-	-	-	-	-	-	-	-	-	-	18.2	1.7	-	-	-	-	-	-	-	-	-	-	18.6	2.2
1926	-	-	-	-	-	-	-	-	-	-	18.3	-1.6	-	-	-	-	-	-	-	-	-	-	18.3	0.0
1927	-	-	-	-	-	-	-	-	-	-	18.3	0.0	-	-	-	-	-	-	-	-	-	-	17.8	-2.7
1928	-	-	-	-	-	-	-	-	-	-	17.6	-1.1	-	-	-	-	-	-	-	-	-	-	17.7	0.6
1929	-	-	-	-	-	-	-	-	-	-	17.6	-0.6	-	-	-	-	-	-	-	-	-	-	17.7	0.6
1930	-	-	-	-	-	-	-	-	-	-	17.4	-1.7	-	-	-	-	-	-	-	-	-	-	16.6	-4.6
1931	-	-	-	-	-	-	-	-	-	-	15.6	-6.0	-	-	-	-	-	-	-	-	-	-	14.9	-4.5
1932	-	-	-	-	-	-	-	-	-	-	13.6	-8.7	-	-	-	-	-	-	-	-	-	-	12.9	-5.1
1933	-	-	-	-	-	-	-	-	-	-	12.4	-3.9	-	-	-	-	-	-	-	-	-	-	12.7	2.4
1934	-	-	-	-	-	-	-	-	-	-	12.7	0.0	-	-	-	-	-	-	-	-	12.8	0.8	-	-
1935	-	-	-	-	13.3	3.9	-	-	-	-	-	-	13.4	0.8	-	-	-	-	13.4	0.0	-	-	-	-
1936	13.4	0.0	-	-	-	-	13.3	-0.7	-	-	-	-	13.6	2.3	-	-	13.8	1.5	-	-	-	-	13.7	-0.7
1937	-	-	-	-	13.9	1.5	-	-	-	-	14.2	2.2	-	-	-	-	14.4	1.4	-	-	-	-	14.2	-1.4
1938	-	-	-	-	13.9	-2.1	-	-	-	-	14.0	0.7	-	-	-	-	14.0	0.0	-	-	-	-	13.8	-1.4
1939	-	-	-	-	13.7	-0.7	-	-	-	-	13.6	-0.7	-	-	-	-	13.8	1.5	-	-	-	-	13.7	-0.7
1940	-	-	-	-	13.7	0.0	-	-	-	-	13.9	1.5	-	-	-	-	13.8	-0.7	13.8	0.0	13.8	0.0	13.9	0.7
1941	13.9	0.0	13.9	0.0	13.9	0.0	14.1	1.4	14.2	0.7	14.4	1.4	14.6	1.4	14.7	0.7	15.0	2.0	15.1	0.7	15.2	0.7	15.2	0.0
1942	15.4	1.3	15.4	0.0	15.6	1.3	15.8	1.3	16.0	1.3	16.0	0.0	16.0	0.0	16.1	0.6	16.1	0.0	16.3	1.2	16.4	0.6	16.4	0.0
1943	16.4	0.0	16.5	0.6	16.8	1.8	16.9	0.6	17.1	1.2	17.0	-0.6	16.8	-1.2	16.9	0.6	17.0	0.6	17.0	0.0	16.9	-0.6	16.9	0.0
1944	16.8	-0.6	16.8	0.0	16.8	0.0	17.0	1.2	17.0	0.0	17.1	0.6	17.3	1.2	17.3	0.0	17.3	0.0	17.3	0.0	17.3	0.0	17.3	0.0
1945	17.3	0.0	17.3	0.0	17.3	0.0	17.3	0.0	17.6	1.7	17.6	0.0	17.6	0.0	17.6	0.0	17.5	-0.6	17.5	0.0	17.5	0.0	17.6	0.6
1946	17.6	0.0	17.6	0.0	17.6	0.0	17.8	1.1	17.9	0.6	18.0	0.6	19.4	7.8	19.8	2.1	20.0	1.0	20.6	3.0	21.0	1.9	21.1	0.5
1947	21.1	0.0	21.0	-0.5	21.5	2.4	21.4	-0.5	21.5	0.5	21.8	1.4	22.0	0.9	22.4	1.8	23.1	3.1	23.0	-0.4	23.1	0.4	23.4	1.3
1948	23.5	0.4	23.2	-1.3	23.2	0.0	23.7	2.2	24.0	1.3	24.2	0.8	24.5	1.2	24.6	0.4	24.7	0.4	24.5	-0.8	24.2	-1.2	24.1	-0.4
1949	24.0	-0.4	23.8	-0.8	24.0	0.8	24.1	0.4	24.0	-0.4	24.2	0.8	23.9	-1.2	24.0	0.4	24.2	0.8	24.0	-0.8	24.1	0.4	23.8	-1.2
1950	23.7	-0.4	23.7	0.0	23.8	0.4	23.7	-0.4	24.0	1.3	24.0	0.0	24.3	1.2	24.5	0.8	24.6	0.4	24.7	0.4	24.8	0.4	25.2	1.6
1951	25.5	1.2	25.9	1.6	25.9	0.0	26.0	0.4	26.0	0.0	26.1	0.4	26.2	0.4	26.2	0.0	26.3	0.4	26.5	0.8	26.7	0.8	26.6	-0.4
1952	26.6	0.0	26.3	-1.1	26.4	0.4	26.5	0.4	26.7	0.8	26.8	0.4	26.9	0.4	27.0	0.4	27.2	0.0	26.9	0.0	26.9	0.0	26.8	-0.4
1953	26.7	-0.4	26.6	-0.4	26.6	0.0	26.7	0.4	26.8	0.4	26.9	0.4	27.0	0.4	27.2	0.7	27.2	0.0	27.4	0.7	27.2	-0.7	27.2	0.0
1954	27.2	0.0	27.2	0.0	27.2	0.0	27.2	0.0	27.4	0.7	27.4	0.0	27.6	0.7	27.5	-0.4	27.4	-0.4	27.4	0.0	27.5	0.4	27.3	-0.7
1955	27.3	0.0	27.4	0.4	27.3	-0.4	27.3	0.0	27.4	0.4	27.4	0.0	27.6	0.7	27.7	0.4	27.8	0.4	27.8	0.0	27.8	0.0	27.7	-0.4
1956	27.6	-0.4	27.6	0.0	27.5	-0.4	27.6	0.4	27.7	0.4	27.9	0.7	28.2	1.1	28.0	-0.7	28.1	0.4	28.3	0.7	28.3	0.0	28.3	0.0
1957	28.3	0.0	28.4	0.4	28.4	0.0	28.5	0.4	28.6	0.4	28.7	0.3	29.0	1.0	29.0	0.0	29.1	0.3	29.2	0.3	29.4	0.7	29.4	0.0
1958	29.5	0.3	29.5	0.0	29.7	0.7	29.7	0.0	29.7	0.0	29.8	0.3	29.8	0.0	29.7	-0.3	29.8	0.3	29.8	0.0	29.8	0.0	29.7	-0.3

[Continued]

Chicago, IL-NW IN
Consumer Price Index - All Urban Consumers
Base 1982-1984 = 100
All Items
[Continued]

For 1914-1997. Columns headed % show percentile change in the index from the previous period for which an index is available.

Year	Jan Index	%	Feb Index	%	Mar Index	%	Apr Index	%	May Index	%	Jun Index	%	Jul Index	%	Aug Index	%	Sep Index	%	Oct Index	%	Nov Index	%	Dec Index	%
1959	29.7	0.0	29.7	0.0	29.7	0.0	29.8	0.3	29.8	0.0	29.9	0.3	30.0	0.3	30.0	0.0	30.2	0.7	30.2	0.0	30.2	0.0	30.2	0.0
1960	30.1	-0.3	30.2	0.3	30.2	0.0	30.3	0.3	30.3	0.0	30.4	0.3	30.5	0.3	30.4	-0.3	30.5	0.3	30.5	0.0	30.5	0.0	30.5	0.0
1961	30.5	0.0	30.5	0.0	30.4	-0.3	30.4	0.0	30.4	0.0	30.3	-0.3	30.6	1.0	30.6	0.0	30.6	0.0	30.7	0.3	30.6	-0.3	30.6	0.0
1962	30.6	0.0	30.8	0.7	30.8	0.0	30.9	0.3	30.8	-0.3	30.8	0.0	30.8	0.0	30.8	0.0	31.0	0.6	30.9	-0.3	30.9	0.0	30.9	0.0
1963	31.0	0.3	31.0	0.0	31.1	0.3	31.1	0.0	31.0	-0.3	31.1	0.3	31.3	0.6	31.2	-0.3	31.2	0.0	31.2	0.0	31.2	0.0	31.3	0.3
1964	31.2	-0.3	31.1	-0.3	31.1	0.0	31.1	0.0	31.2	0.3	31.3	0.3	31.4	0.3	31.3	-0.3	31.3	0.0	31.4	0.3	31.4	0.0	31.4	0.0
1965	31.4	0.0	31.4	0.0	31.4	0.0	31.5	0.3	31.6	0.3	31.8	0.6	31.7	-0.3	31.7	0.0	31.8	0.3	31.9	0.3	31.9	0.0	32.1	0.6
1966	32.0	-0.3	32.2	0.6	32.4	0.6	32.4	0.0	32.5	0.3	32.6	0.3	32.6	0.0	32.8	0.6	33.0	0.6	33.0	0.0	33.0	0.0	33.1	0.3
1967	32.9	-0.6	33.1	0.6	33.1	0.0	33.1	0.0	33.2	0.3	33.3	0.3	33.5	0.6	33.7	0.6	33.9	0.6	33.9	0.0	34.0	0.3	34.1	0.3
1968	34.1	0.0	34.3	0.6	34.5	0.6	34.6	0.3	34.7	0.3	34.8	0.3	35.0	0.6	35.1	0.3	35.3	0.6	35.4	0.3	35.4	0.0	35.6	0.6
1969	35.8	0.6	35.9	0.3	36.2	0.8	36.3	0.3	36.4	0.3	36.7	0.8	36.9	0.5	37.2	0.8	37.5	0.8	37.4	-0.3	37.6	0.5	37.8	0.5
1970	38.0	0.5	38.1	0.3	38.3	0.5	38.4	0.3	38.6	0.5	38.8	0.5	39.0	0.5	39.2	0.5	39.4	0.5	39.6	0.5	39.7	0.3	39.9	0.5
1971	39.9	0.0	40.0	0.3	40.1	0.2	40.2	0.2	40.4	0.5	40.5	0.2	40.5	0.0	40.7	0.5	40.7	0.0	40.7	0.0	40.8	0.2	40.9	0.2
1972	40.9	0.0	41.2	0.7	41.2	0.0	41.3	0.2	41.4	0.2	41.6	0.5	41.6	0.0	41.8	0.5	41.9	0.2	42.0	0.2	42.1	0.2	42.2	0.2
1973	42.3	0.2	42.7	0.9	43.2	1.2	43.5	0.7	43.8	0.7	44.1	0.7	44.0	-0.2	45.0	2.3	45.1	0.2	45.4	0.7	45.6	0.4	45.8	0.4
1974	46.4	1.3	47.1	1.5	47.6	1.1	47.8	0.4	48.2	0.8	48.7	1.0	48.9	0.4	49.5	1.2	49.9	0.8	50.4	1.0	50.8	0.8	51.3	1.0
1975	51.3	0.0	51.7	0.8	52.1	0.8	52.2	0.2	52.0	-0.4	52.4	0.8	53.0	1.1	53.3	0.6	53.4	0.2	53.7	0.6	53.8	0.2	54.0	0.4
1976	53.7	-0.6	54.1	0.7	54.2	0.2	54.5	0.6	54.8	0.6	55.2	0.7	55.5	0.5	55.8	0.5	56.1	0.5	56.3	0.4	56.4	0.2	56.6	0.4
1977	56.7	0.2	57.3	1.1	57.7	0.7	58.2	0.9	58.4	0.3	58.6	0.3	59.0	0.7	59.3	0.5	59.7	0.7	59.8	0.2	60.0	0.3	60.2	0.3
1978	61.1	1.5	61.7	1.0	62.4	1.1	62.7	0.5	63.3	1.0	63.7	0.6	64.1	0.6	64.1	0.0	64.9	1.2	65.4	0.8	66.3	1.4	66.5	0.3
1979	66.8	0.5	67.8	1.5	69.2	2.1	69.9	1.0	70.3	0.6	71.5	1.7	72.8	1.8	73.2	0.5	74.1	1.2	74.2	0.1	75.6	1.9	76.4	1.1
1980	77.1	0.9	77.9	1.0	78.8	1.2	80.4	2.0	81.4	1.2	83.1	2.1	82.6	-0.6	82.1	-0.6	83.7	1.9	84.9	1.4	87.0	2.5	87.1	0.1
1981	86.7	-0.5	86.9	0.2	86.9	0.0	88.3	1.6	88.5	0.2	90.1	1.8	91.3	1.3	92.3	1.1	92.7	0.4	92.4	-0.3	92.7	0.3	91.7	-1.1
1982	92.2	0.5	92.0	-0.2	92.5	0.5	93.8	1.4	96.3	2.7	97.7	1.5	98.1	0.4	98.1	0.0	98.4	0.3	98.5	0.1	98.5	0.0	98.1	-0.4
1983	98.4	0.3	98.3	-0.1	98.3	0.0	98.8	0.5	99.2	0.4	99.9	0.7	100.3	0.4	101.0	0.7	101.4	0.4	101.2	-0.2	101.7	0.5	101.7	0.0
1984	102.2	0.5	102.1	-0.1	102.3	0.2	102.7	0.4	102.8	0.1	103.7	0.9	104.0	0.3	104.9	0.9	105.5	0.6	105.1	-0.4	105.1	0.0	105.1	0.0
1985	105.5	0.4	106.0	0.5	106.2	0.2	106.8	0.6	107.0	0.2	108.5	1.4	108.6	0.1	109.1	0.5	109.2	0.1	108.0	-1.1	108.5	0.5	109.1	0.6
1986	109.2	0.1	109.3	0.1	108.4	-0.8	108.3	-0.1	108.5	0.2	110.6	1.9	110.8	0.2	110.9	0.1	111.8	0.8	110.0	-1.6	110.9	0.8	110.8	-0.1
1987	111.9	1.0	111.9	0.0	112.3	0.4	112.8	0.4	113.3	0.4	115.5	1.9	115.9	0.3	116.7	0.7	117.1	0.3	115.1	-1.7	115.7	0.5	115.7	0.0
1988	115.3	-0.3	116.6	1.1	116.9	0.3	117.1	0.2	117.0	-0.1	118.9	1.6	119.8	0.8	120.1	0.3	122.0	1.6	121.6	-0.3	121.0	-0.5	121.3	0.2
1989	121.5	0.2	122.2	0.6	123.0	0.7	123.6	0.5	123.9	0.2	125.7	1.5	126.4	0.6	126.4	0.0	127.1	0.6	126.8	-0.2	126.7	-0.1	126.5	-0.2
1990	128.1	1.3	129.2	0.9	129.5	0.2	130.4	0.7	130.4	0.0	131.7	1.0	132.0	0.2	133.2	0.9	133.8	0.5	133.3	-0.4	134.2	0.7	134.6	0.3
1991	135.1	0.4	135.5	0.3	136.2	0.5	136.1	-0.1	136.8	0.5	137.3	0.4	137.3	0.0	137.6	0.2	138.3	0.5	138.0	-0.2	138.0	0.0	138.3	0.2
1992	138.9	0.4	139.2	0.2	139.7	0.4	139.8	0.1	140.5	0.5	141.2	0.5	141.4	0.1	141.9	0.4	142.7	0.6	142.1	-0.4	142.4	0.2	142.9	0.4
1993	143.2	0.2	143.6	0.3	144.1	0.3	144.7	0.4	145.7	0.7	145.6	-0.1	145.5	-0.1	146.1	0.4	146.7	0.4	147.2	0.3	146.4	-0.5	146.1	-0.2
1994	146.5	0.3	146.8	0.2	147.6	0.5	147.9	0.2	147.6	-0.2	148.1	0.3	148.3	0.1	149.8	1.0	150.2	0.3	149.4	-0.5	150.4	0.7	150.5	0.1
1995	151.8	0.9	152.3	0.3	152.6	0.2	153.1	0.3	153.0	-0.1	153.5	0.3	153.6	0.1	153.8	0.1	154.0	0.1	154.3	0.2	154.0	-0.2	153.8	-0.1
1996	154.6	0.5	155.2	0.4	156.3	0.7	156.4	0.1	156.9	0.3	157.6	0.4	157.7	0.1	158.1	0.3	158.3	0.1	158.8	0.3	159.4	0.4	159.7	0.2
1997	160.4	0.4	161.1	0.4	161.0	-0.1	160.9	-0.1	161.1	0.1	161.7	0.4	161.7	0.0	162.5	0.5	162.1	-0.2	162.5	0.2	162.9	0.2	162.8	-0.1

Source: U.S. Department of Labor, Bureau of Labor Statistics, Division of Consumer Prices and Price Indexes. - indicates no data collected for period.

Chicago, IL-NW IN
Consumer Price Index - Urban Wage Earners
Base 1982-1984 = 100
All Items

For 1914-1997. Columns headed % show percentile change in the index from the previous period for which an index is available.

Year	Jan Index	%	Feb Index	%	Mar Index	%	Apr Index	%	May Index	%	Jun Index	%	Jul Index	%	Aug Index	%	Sep Index	%	Oct Index	%	Nov Index	%	Dec Index	%
1914	-	-	-	-	-	-	-	-	-	-	-	-	-	-	-	-	-	-	-	-	-	-	10.1	-
1915	-	-	-	-	-	-	-	-	-	-	-	-	-	-	-	-	-	-	-	-	-	-	10.4	3.0
1916	-	-	-	-	-	-	-	-	-	-	-	-	-	-	-	-	-	-	-	-	-	-	11.8	13.5
1917	-	-	-	-	-	-	-	-	-	-	-	-	-	-	-	-	-	-	-	-	-	-	13.7	16.1
1918	-	-	-	-	-	-	-	-	-	-	-	-	-	-	-	-	-	-	-	-	-	-	16.6	21.2
1919	-	-	-	-	-	-	-	-	-	-	16.9	1.8	-	-	-	-	-	-	-	-	-	-	19.2	13.6
1920	-	-	-	-	-	-	-	-	-	-	21.2	10.4	-	-	-	-	-	-	-	-	-	-	19.2	-9.4
1921	-	-	-	-	-	-	-	-	18.2	-5.2	-	-	-	-	-	-	18.1	-0.5	-	-	-	-	17.8	-1.7
1922	-	-	-	-	-	-	-	-	17.2	-3.4	17.3	0.6	-	-	-	-	17.3	0.0	-	-	-	-	17.4	0.6
1923	-	-	-	-	17.5	0.6	-	-	-	-	17.6	0.6	-	-	-	-	18.0	2.3	-	-	-	-	18.0	0.0
1924	-	-	-	-	17.9	-0.6	-	-	-	-	18.0	0.6	-	-	-	-	18.1	0.6	-	-	-	-	18.2	0.6
1925	-	-	-	-	-	-	-	-	-	-	18.5	1.6	-	-	-	-	-	-	-	-	-	-	18.9	2.2
1926	-	-	-	-	-	-	-	-	-	-	18.7	-1.1	-	-	-	-	-	-	-	-	-	-	18.6	-0.5
1927	-	-	-	-	-	-	-	-	-	-	18.6	0.0	-	-	-	-	-	-	-	-	-	-	18.1	-2.7
1928	-	-	-	-	-	-	-	-	-	-	17.9	-1.1	-	-	-	-	-	-	-	-	-	-	18.0	0.6
1929	-	-	-	-	-	-	-	-	-	-	17.9	-0.6	-	-	-	-	-	-	-	-	-	-	18.0	0.6
1930	-	-	-	-	-	-	-	-	-	-	17.7	-1.7	-	-	-	-	-	-	-	-	-	-	16.9	-4.5
1931	-	-	-	-	-	-	-	-	-	-	15.8	-6.5	-	-	-	-	-	-	-	-	-	-	15.2	-3.8
1932	-	-	-	-	-	-	-	-	-	-	13.8	-9.2	-	-	-	-	-	-	-	-	-	-	13.1	-5.1
1933	-	-	-	-	-	-	-	-	-	-	12.6	-3.8	-	-	-	-	-	-	-	-	-	-	12.9	2.4
1934	-	-	-	-	-	-	-	-	-	-	12.9	0.0	-	-	-	-	-	-	-	-	13.0	0.8	-	-
1935	-	-	-	-	13.6	4.6	-	-	-	-	-	-	13.6	0.0	-	-	-	-	13.6	0.0	-	-	-	-
1936	13.7	0.7	-	-	-	-	13.5	-1.5	-	-	-	-	13.8	2.2	-	-	14.0	1.4	-	-	-	-	13.9	-0.7
1937	-	-	-	-	14.1	1.4	-	-	-	-	14.4	2.1	-	-	-	-	14.6	1.4	-	-	-	-	14.4	-1.4
1938	-	-	-	-	14.1	-2.1	-	-	-	-	14.3	1.4	-	-	-	-	14.3	0.0	-	-	-	-	14.1	-1.4
1939	-	-	-	-	13.9	-1.4	-	-	-	-	13.8	-0.7	-	-	-	-	14.1	2.2	-	-	-	-	13.9	-1.4
1940	-	-	-	-	13.9	0.0	-	-	-	-	14.1	1.4	-	-	-	-	14.1	0.0	14.1	0.0	14.0	-0.7	14.1	0.7
1941	14.1	0.0	14.1	0.0	14.2	0.7	14.3	0.7	14.4	0.7	14.6	1.4	14.8	1.4	14.9	0.7	15.3	2.7	15.4	0.7	15.5	0.6	15.4	-0.6
1942	15.7	1.9	15.7	0.0	15.9	1.3	16.1	1.3	16.2	0.6	16.2	0.0	16.2	0.0	16.4	1.2	16.4	0.0	16.6	1.2	16.7	0.6	16.7	0.0
1943	16.7	0.0	16.8	0.6	17.1	1.8	17.2	0.6	17.4	1.2	17.3	-0.6	17.1	-1.2	17.2	0.6	17.3	0.6	17.3	0.0	17.2	-0.6	17.2	0.0
1944	17.1	-0.6	17.1	0.0	17.1	0.0	17.3	1.2	17.3	0.0	17.4	0.6	17.6	1.1	17.6	0.0	17.6	0.0	17.6	0.0	17.6	0.0	17.6	0.0
1945	17.6	0.0	17.6	0.0	17.6	0.0	17.6	0.0	17.9	1.7	17.9	0.0	17.9	0.0	17.9	0.0	17.8	-0.6	17.8	0.0	17.8	0.0	17.9	0.6
1946	17.9	0.0	17.9	0.0	17.9	0.0	18.1	1.1	18.2	0.6	18.3	0.5	19.7	7.7	20.2	2.5	20.4	1.0	20.9	2.5	21.3	1.9	21.4	0.5
1947	21.4	0.0	21.3	-0.5	21.8	2.3	21.8	0.0	21.9	0.5	22.1	0.9	22.4	1.4	22.7	1.3	23.5	3.5	23.4	-0.4	23.5	0.4	23.8	1.3
1948	23.9	0.4	23.6	-1.3	23.6	0.0	24.1	2.1	24.4	1.2	24.7	1.2	25.0	1.2	25.0	0.0	25.1	0.4	24.9	-0.8	24.6	-1.2	24.5	-0.4
1949	24.4	-0.4	24.2	-0.8	24.4	0.8	24.5	0.4	24.4	-0.4	24.6	0.8	24.3	-1.2	24.4	0.4	24.6	0.8	24.4	-0.8	24.5	0.4	24.2	-1.2
1950	24.1	-0.4	24.1	0.0	24.2	0.4	24.1	-0.4	24.4	1.2	24.4	0.0	24.8	1.6	25.0	0.8	25.1	0.4	25.2	0.4	25.2	0.0	25.6	1.6
1951	25.9	1.2	26.3	1.5	26.4	0.4	26.4	0.0	26.5	0.4	26.5	0.0	26.7	0.8	26.7	0.0	26.8	0.4	27.0	0.7	27.1	0.4	27.1	0.0
1952	27.1	0.0	26.8	-1.1	26.9	0.4	26.9	0.0	27.2	1.1	27.3	0.4	27.3	0.0	27.4	0.4	27.3	-0.4	27.3	0.0	27.4	0.4	27.2	-0.7
1953	27.2	0.0	27.1	-0.4	27.0	-0.4	27.2	0.7	27.2	0.0	27.4	0.7	27.5	0.4	27.6	0.4	27.7	0.4	27.9	0.7	27.7	-0.7	27.7	0.0
1954	27.7	0.0	27.7	0.0	27.7	0.0	27.7	0.0	27.9	0.7	27.9	0.0	28.1	0.7	28.0	-0.4	27.9	-0.4	27.9	0.0	28.0	0.4	27.8	-0.7
1955	27.8	0.0	27.9	0.4	27.8	-0.4	27.8	0.0	27.9	0.4	27.9	0.0	28.1	0.7	28.2	0.4	28.3	0.4	28.3	0.0	28.3	0.0	28.2	-0.4
1956	28.1	-0.4	28.1	0.0	28.0	-0.4	28.1	0.4	28.2	0.4	28.4	0.7	28.7	1.1	28.5	-0.7	28.6	0.4	28.8	0.7	28.8	0.0	28.8	0.0
1957	28.8	0.0	28.9	0.3	28.9	0.0	29.0	0.3	29.0	0.0	29.2	0.7	29.5	1.0	29.5	0.0	29.6	0.3	29.7	0.3	29.9	0.7	29.9	0.0
1958	30.0	0.3	30.0	0.0	30.2	0.7	30.2	0.0	30.2	0.0	30.3	0.3	30.3	0.0	30.2	-0.3	30.3	0.3	30.3	0.0	30.3	0.0	30.2	-0.3

[Continued]

Chicago, IL-NW IN
Consumer Price Index - Urban Wage Earners
Base 1982-1984 = 100
All Items
[Continued]

For 1914-1997. Columns headed % show percentile change in the index from the previous period for which an index is available.

Year	Jan Index	%	Feb Index	%	Mar Index	%	Apr Index	%	May Index	%	Jun Index	%	Jul Index	%	Aug Index	%	Sep Index	%	Oct Index	%	Nov Index	%	Dec Index	%
1959	30.2	0.0	30.2	0.0	30.2	0.0	30.3	0.3	30.3	0.0	30.4	0.3	30.5	0.3	30.5	0.0	30.7	0.7	30.7	0.0	30.7	0.0	30.7	0.0
1960	30.6	-0.3	30.7	0.3	30.7	0.0	30.8	0.3	30.8	0.0	30.9	0.3	31.0	0.3	31.0	0.0	31.0	0.0	31.1	0.3	31.0	-0.3	31.1	0.3
1961	31.0	-0.3	31.0	0.0	31.0	0.0	30.9	-0.3	30.9	0.0	30.8	-0.3	31.1	1.0	31.1	0.0	31.2	0.3	31.2	0.0	31.1	-0.3	31.1	0.0
1962	31.2	0.3	31.3	0.3	31.3	0.0	31.4	0.3	31.4	0.0	31.3	-0.3	31.3	0.0	31.3	0.0	31.5	0.6	31.5	0.0	31.5	0.0	31.4	-0.3
1963	31.5	0.3	31.5	0.0	31.6	0.3	31.6	0.0	31.6	0.0	31.6	0.0	31.9	0.9	31.8	-0.3	31.8	0.0	31.8	0.0	31.7	-0.3	31.8	0.3
1964	31.7	-0.3	31.7	0.0	31.7	0.0	31.7	0.0	31.7	0.0	31.8	0.3	31.9	0.3	31.9	0.0	31.9	0.0	31.9	0.0	31.9	0.0	31.9	0.0
1965	31.9	0.0	31.9	0.0	32.0	0.3	32.0	0.0	32.1	0.3	32.3	0.6	32.3	0.0	32.3	0.0	32.4	0.3	32.4	0.0	32.5	0.3	32.6	0.3
1966	32.6	0.0	32.8	0.6	32.9	0.3	32.9	0.0	33.0	0.3	33.2	0.6	33.1	-0.3	33.4	0.9	33.5	0.3	33.6	0.3	33.5	-0.3	33.6	0.3
1967	33.5	-0.3	33.6	0.3	33.7	0.3	33.6	-0.3	33.7	0.3	33.8	0.3	34.1	0.9	34.3	0.6	34.5	0.6	34.5	0.0	34.6	0.3	34.7	0.3
1968	34.7	0.0	34.9	0.6	35.1	0.6	35.2	0.3	35.3	0.3	35.4	0.3	35.7	0.8	35.8	0.3	35.9	0.3	36.0	0.3	36.1	0.3	36.3	0.6
1969	36.4	0.3	36.5	0.3	36.8	0.8	36.9	0.3	37.0	0.3	37.4	1.1	37.6	0.5	37.8	0.5	38.1	0.8	38.0	-0.3	38.3	0.8	38.4	0.3
1970	38.7	0.8	38.7	0.0	38.9	0.5	39.0	0.3	39.3	0.8	39.4	0.3	39.7	0.8	39.9	0.5	40.1	0.5	40.3	0.5	40.4	0.2	40.6	0.5
1971	40.6	0.0	40.7	0.2	40.8	0.2	40.9	0.2	41.1	0.5	41.2	0.2	41.2	0.0	41.4	0.5	41.4	0.0	41.4	0.0	41.5	0.2	41.6	0.2
1972	41.6	0.0	41.9	0.7	41.9	0.0	42.0	0.2	42.1	0.2	42.3	0.5	42.4	0.2	42.6	0.5	42.7	0.2	42.7	0.0	42.8	0.2	42.9	0.2
1973	43.0	0.2	43.4	0.9	43.9	1.2	44.2	0.7	44.5	0.7	44.8	0.7	44.7	-0.2	45.8	2.5	45.8	0.0	46.2	0.9	46.3	0.2	46.6	0.6
1974	47.2	1.3	47.9	1.5	48.4	1.0	48.7	0.6	49.0	0.6	49.6	1.2	49.8	0.4	50.4	1.2	50.7	0.6	51.3	1.2	51.7	0.8	52.2	1.0
1975	52.2	0.0	52.6	0.8	53.0	0.8	53.1	0.2	52.9	-0.4	53.3	0.8	53.9	1.1	54.2	0.6	54.3	0.2	54.7	0.7	54.7	0.0	54.9	0.4
1976	54.7	-0.4	55.0	0.5	55.2	0.4	55.5	0.5	55.7	0.4	56.1	0.7	56.4	0.5	56.8	0.7	57.0	0.4	57.3	0.5	57.4	0.2	57.6	0.3
1977	57.7	0.2	58.3	1.0	58.7	0.7	59.2	0.9	59.4	0.3	59.6	0.3	60.1	0.8	60.4	0.5	60.8	0.7	60.9	0.2	61.1	0.3	61.3	0.3
1978	62.1	1.3	62.6	0.8	63.2	1.0	63.5	0.5	64.1	0.9	64.7	0.9	65.2	0.8	65.0	-0.3	65.7	1.1	66.5	1.2	67.3	1.2	67.6	0.4
1979	68.0	0.6	68.9	1.3	70.2	1.9	70.9	1.0	71.4	0.7	72.6	1.7	73.8	1.7	74.3	0.7	75.1	1.1	75.5	0.5	76.8	1.7	77.6	1.0
1980	78.3	0.9	79.2	1.1	80.1	1.1	81.7	2.0	82.7	1.2	84.4	2.1	84.1	-0.4	83.6	-0.6	85.0	1.7	86.1	1.3	88.2	2.4	88.2	0.0
1981	87.9	-0.3	88.1	0.2	88.2	0.1	89.6	1.6	89.9	0.3	91.2	1.4	92.5	1.4	93.5	1.1	93.9	0.4	94.1	0.2	94.4	0.3	93.4	-1.1
1982	93.9	0.5	93.8	-0.1	94.1	0.3	95.3	1.3	97.7	2.5	99.3	1.6	99.7	0.4	99.6	-0.1	99.7	0.1	99.8	0.1	99.8	0.0	99.4	-0.4
1983	99.7	0.3	99.2	-0.5	99.2	0.0	100.0	0.8	100.4	0.4	100.7	0.3	100.9	0.2	101.3	0.4	101.8	0.5	100.3	-1.5	100.7	0.4	100.2	-0.5
1984	101.6	1.4	101.1	-0.5	100.9	-0.2	100.9	0.0	101.0	0.1	101.5	0.5	101.8	0.3	102.6	0.8	103.6	1.0	102.8	-0.8	103.0	0.2	102.7	-0.3
1985	103.0	0.3	103.5	0.5	103.8	0.3	104.3	0.5	104.5	0.2	105.9	1.3	105.9	0.0	106.3	0.4	106.3	0.0	105.2	-1.0	105.9	0.7	106.4	0.5
1986	106.5	0.1	106.5	0.0	105.5	-0.9	105.2	-0.3	105.4	0.2	107.5	2.0	107.6	0.1	107.7	0.1	108.4	0.6	106.7	-1.6	107.6	0.8	107.5	-0.1
1987	108.7	1.1	108.6	-0.1	109.0	0.4	109.5	0.5	109.9	0.4	112.0	1.9	112.4	0.4	113.2	0.7	113.6	0.4	111.7	-1.7	112.2	0.4	112.2	0.0
1988	111.9	-0.3	112.9	0.9	113.2	0.3	113.3	0.1	113.3	0.0	115.2	1.7	116.2	0.9	116.4	0.2	118.2	1.5	117.8	-0.3	117.4	-0.3	117.7	0.3
1989	117.9	0.2	118.4	0.4	119.1	0.6	119.8	0.6	120.1	0.3	121.8	1.4	122.6	0.7	122.5	-0.1	123.1	0.5	122.9	-0.2	122.9	0.0	122.8	-0.1
1990	124.4	1.3	125.4	0.8	125.6	0.2	126.5	0.7	126.5	0.0	127.9	1.1	128.0	0.1	129.3	1.0	129.9	0.5	129.4	-0.4	130.3	0.7	130.7	0.3
1991	131.1	0.3	131.5	0.3	132.0	0.4	132.1	0.1	132.7	0.5	133.1	0.3	133.2	0.1	133.4	0.2	133.9	0.4	133.6	-0.2	133.8	0.1	134.1	0.2
1992	134.4	0.2	134.7	0.2	135.2	0.4	135.4	0.1	136.2	0.6	136.9	0.5	137.0	0.1	137.5	0.4	138.3	0.6	137.7	-0.4	138.2	0.4	138.5	0.2
1993	138.9	0.3	139.1	0.1	139.5	0.3	140.3	0.6	141.4	0.8	141.2	-0.1	141.1	-0.1	141.6	0.4	142.1	0.4	142.6	0.4	141.8	-0.6	141.7	-0.1
1994	142.0	0.2	142.3	0.2	143.0	0.5	143.3	0.2	143.1	-0.1	143.6	0.3	143.7	0.1	145.1	1.0	145.4	0.2	144.6	-0.6	145.7	0.8	145.8	0.1
1995	147.1	0.9	147.5	0.3	147.8	0.2	148.3	0.3	148.2	-0.1	148.5	0.2	148.7	0.1	148.8	0.1	149.0	0.1	149.2	0.1	149.0	-0.1	149.0	0.0
1996	149.7	0.5	150.2	0.3	151.3	0.7	151.5	0.1	151.9	0.3	152.6	0.5	152.7	0.1	152.9	0.1	153.2	0.2	153.7	0.3	154.4	0.5	154.6	0.1
1997	155.3	0.5	155.9	0.4	155.6	-0.2	155.3	-0.2	155.5	0.1	156.0	0.3	156.0	0.0	156.7	0.4	156.4	-0.2	156.9	0.3	157.2	0.2	157.3	0.1

Source: U.S. Department of Labor, Bureau of Labor Statistics, Division of Consumer Prices and Price Indexes. - indicates no data collected for period.

Chicago, IL-NW IN
Consumer Price Index - All Urban Consumers
Base 1982-1984 = 100
Food and Beverages

For 1976-1997. Columns headed % show percentile change in the index from the previous period for which an index is available.

Year	Jan Index	%	Feb Index	%	Mar Index	%	Apr Index	%	May Index	%	Jun Index	%	Jul Index	%	Aug Index	%	Sep Index	%	Oct Index	%	Nov Index	%	Dec Index	%
1976	63.6	-	63.7	0.2	63.3	-0.6	64.0	1.1	63.7	-0.5	64.4	1.1	64.9	0.8	65.0	0.2	64.7	-0.5	64.9	0.3	64.5	-0.6	64.4	-0.2
1977	64.7	0.5	65.9	1.9	66.5	0.9	67.3	1.2	67.3	0.0	67.9	0.9	68.6	1.0	69.0	0.6	69.4	0.6	69.5	0.1	69.4	-0.1	70.0	0.9
1978	71.8	2.6	72.8	1.4	73.5	1.0	74.4	1.2	75.1	0.9	76.0	1.2	76.4	0.5	77.0	0.8	77.4	0.5	77.5	0.1	78.4	1.2	78.6	0.3
1979	80.0	1.8	81.2	1.5	82.3	1.4	82.9	0.7	83.7	1.0	83.9	0.2	84.7	1.0	84.1	-0.7	84.3	0.2	85.0	0.8	86.1	1.3	87.0	1.0
1980	86.8	-0.2	87.6	0.9	88.8	1.4	89.5	0.8	90.1	0.7	90.2	0.1	91.4	1.3	92.7	1.4	93.5	0.9	94.1	0.6	94.5	0.4	95.0	0.5
1981	95.6	0.6	96.2	0.6	96.3	0.1	95.9	-0.4	95.4	-0.5	96.2	0.8	96.5	0.3	97.1	0.6	96.9	-0.2	97.1	0.2	96.7	-0.4	96.7	0.0
1982	97.5	0.8	97.6	0.1	97.4	-0.2	98.5	1.1	99.4	0.9	99.9	0.5	99.5	-0.4	99.1	-0.4	98.9	-0.2	98.9	0.0	98.7	-0.2	98.8	0.1
1983	99.7	0.9	99.7	0.0	99.6	-0.1	99.8	0.2	99.4	-0.4	99.3	-0.1	98.5	-0.8	98.4	-0.1	99.3	0.9	99.3	0.0	99.8	0.5	99.5	-0.3
1984	101.8	2.3	102.7	0.9	102.2	-0.5	102.0	-0.2	101.7	-0.3	101.4	-0.3	102.0	0.6	102.5	0.5	102.1	-0.4	102.0	-0.1	101.2	-0.8	101.9	0.7
1985	102.6	0.7	104.0	1.4	104.1	0.1	103.5	-0.6	103.2	-0.3	104.1	0.9	103.8	-0.3	104.0	0.2	104.3	0.3	104.4	0.1	105.6	1.1	107.0	1.3
1986	106.9	-0.1	107.9	0.9	107.7	-0.2	107.8	0.1	107.4	-0.4	108.5	1.0	109.3	0.7	110.4	1.0	110.1	-0.3	109.1	-0.9	111.1	1.8	110.9	-0.2
1987	113.1	2.0	112.7	-0.4	112.0	-0.6	112.9	0.8	112.7	-0.2	113.6	0.8	113.2	-0.4	113.5	0.3	113.7	0.2	113.5	-0.2	113.7	0.2	113.7	0.0
1988	114.4	0.6	114.9	0.4	115.0	0.1	115.2	0.2	115.8	0.5	116.1	0.3	117.9	1.6	118.8	0.8	119.3	0.4	119.2	-0.1	118.9	-0.3	119.3	0.3
1989	120.7	1.2	121.5	0.7	121.5	0.0	122.7	1.0	122.3	-0.3	122.3	0.0	122.7	0.3	122.4	-0.2	122.9	0.4	123.2	0.2	123.6	0.3	124.2	0.5
1990	128.0	3.1	128.7	0.5	129.0	0.2	128.9	-0.1	129.1	0.2	129.8	0.5	131.3	1.2	131.0	-0.2	131.3	0.2	131.1	-0.2	132.2	0.8	132.9	0.5
1991	134.7	1.4	134.8	0.1	135.3	0.4	136.0	0.5	136.5	0.4	136.2	-0.2	136.0	-0.1	134.8	-0.9	135.5	0.5	134.6	-0.7	135.6	0.7	135.9	0.2
1992	136.6	0.5	137.7	0.8	138.8	0.8	139.1	0.2	139.8	0.5	138.9	-0.6	138.8	-0.1	139.2	0.3	140.4	0.9	139.6	-0.6	140.2	0.4	140.8	0.4
1993	142.5	1.2	140.8	-1.2	142.2	1.0	141.9	-0.2	143.3	1.0	142.7	-0.4	142.9	0.1	143.1	0.1	143.3	0.1	144.3	0.7	144.4	0.1	145.6	0.8
1994	147.2	1.1	146.4	-0.5	147.0	0.4	147.4	0.3	146.8	-0.4	145.9	-0.6	146.2	0.2	147.2	0.7	147.2	0.0	147.5	0.2	147.3	-0.1	147.6	0.2
1995	150.2	1.8	151.4	0.8	151.3	-0.1	151.7	0.3	150.9	-0.5	150.8	-0.1	151.2	0.3	150.9	-0.2	150.6	-0.2	151.4	0.5	152.3	0.6	152.9	0.4
1996	153.3	0.3	153.1	-0.1	154.2	0.7	154.8	0.4	154.0	-0.5	155.6	1.0	156.1	0.3	156.5	0.3	157.5	0.6	158.4	0.6	159.3	0.6	160.2	0.6
1997	160.2	0.0	159.5	-0.4	159.7	0.1	159.0	-0.4	159.6	0.4	159.6	0.0	160.3	0.4	160.5	0.1	160.3	-0.1	161.8	0.9	161.8	0.0	163.1	0.8

Source: U.S. Department of Labor, Bureau of Labor Statistics, Division of Consumer Prices and Price Indexes. - indicates no data collected for period.

Chicago, IL-NW IN
Consumer Price Index - Urban Wage Earners
Base 1982-1984 = 100
Food and Beverages

For 1976-1997. Columns headed % show percentile change in the index from the previous period for which an index is available.

Year	Jan Index	%	Feb Index	%	Mar Index	%	Apr Index	%	May Index	%	Jun Index	%	Jul Index	%	Aug Index	%	Sep Index	%	Oct Index	%	Nov Index	%	Dec Index	%
1976	64.6	-	64.6	0.0	64.2	-0.6	64.9	1.1	64.7	-0.3	65.3	0.9	65.9	0.9	66.0	0.2	65.6	-0.6	65.9	0.5	65.5	-0.6	65.4	-0.2
1977	65.7	0.5	66.9	1.8	67.5	0.9	68.3	1.2	68.3	0.0	68.9	0.9	69.6	1.0	70.1	0.7	70.4	0.4	70.6	0.3	70.5	-0.1	71.1	0.9
1978	72.6	2.1	73.1	0.7	73.6	0.7	74.7	1.5	75.5	1.1	76.5	1.3	77.1	0.8	77.5	0.5	78.0	0.6	78.4	0.5	79.1	0.9	79.3	0.3
1979	81.1	2.3	81.9	1.0	83.3	1.7	83.7	0.5	84.4	0.8	84.6	0.2	85.2	0.7	84.4	-0.9	84.7	0.4	85.9	1.4	86.8	1.0	87.6	0.9
1980	87.9	0.3	88.4	0.6	89.7	1.5	90.5	0.9	91.5	1.1	91.7	0.2	93.0	1.4	93.6	0.6	94.8	1.3	95.0	0.2	95.8	0.8	95.4	-0.4
1981	95.5	0.1	95.9	0.4	95.9	0.0	96.0	0.1	95.4	-0.6	96.2	0.8	96.5	0.3	96.9	0.4	96.8	-0.1	97.1	0.3	96.6	-0.5	96.7	0.1
1982	97.5	0.8	97.6	0.1	97.3	-0.3	98.5	1.2	99.4	0.9	99.8	0.4	99.5	-0.3	99.1	-0.4	98.8	-0.3	98.7	-0.1	98.7	0.0	98.8	0.1
1983	99.6	0.8	99.7	0.1	99.6	-0.1	99.7	0.1	99.4	-0.3	99.3	-0.1	98.5	-0.8	98.4	-0.1	99.3	0.9	99.5	0.2	99.8	0.3	99.7	-0.1
1984	101.9	2.2	102.7	0.8	102.2	-0.5	102.1	-0.1	101.8	-0.3	101.5	-0.3	101.9	0.4	102.5	0.6	102.0	-0.5	101.9	-0.1	101.3	-0.6	102.0	0.7
1985	102.6	0.6	104.0	1.4	104.1	0.1	103.6	-0.5	103.2	-0.4	104.1	0.9	103.7	-0.4	103.9	0.2	104.3	0.4	104.5	0.2	105.7	1.1	106.9	1.1
1986	107.0	0.1	107.9	0.8	107.8	-0.1	107.9	0.1	107.5	-0.4	108.6	1.0	109.4	0.7	110.5	1.0	110.2	-0.3	109.2	-0.9	111.3	1.9	110.9	-0.4
1987	113.2	2.1	112.8	-0.4	112.1	-0.6	113.0	0.8	112.8	-0.2	113.7	0.8	113.3	-0.4	113.6	0.3	113.8	0.2	113.6	-0.2	113.8	0.2	113.8	0.0
1988	114.5	0.6	114.9	0.3	115.1	0.2	115.3	0.2	115.9	0.5	116.1	0.2	118.0	1.6	118.9	0.8	119.4	0.4	119.3	-0.1	119.0	-0.3	119.4	0.3
1989	120.8	1.2	121.5	0.6	121.5	0.0	122.7	1.0	122.3	-0.3	122.4	0.1	122.8	0.3	122.5	-0.2	123.1	0.5	123.3	0.2	123.7	0.3	124.3	0.5
1990	128.3	3.2	128.8	0.4	129.1	0.2	129.1	0.0	129.2	0.1	130.0	0.6	131.4	1.1	131.2	-0.2	131.5	0.2	131.2	-0.2	132.4	0.9	133.0	0.5
1991	134.8	1.4	134.9	0.1	135.5	0.4	136.2	0.5	136.7	0.4	136.4	-0.2	136.2	-0.1	135.0	-0.9	135.7	0.5	134.7	-0.7	135.8	0.8	135.9	0.1
1992	136.6	0.5	137.7	0.8	138.9	0.9	139.2	0.2	139.8	0.4	139.0	-0.6	138.8	-0.1	139.2	0.3	140.4	0.9	139.7	-0.5	140.3	0.4	140.9	0.4
1993	142.6	1.2	140.9	-1.2	142.3	1.0	142.1	-0.1	143.4	0.9	142.8	-0.4	143.1	0.2	143.3	0.1	143.5	0.1	144.5	0.7	144.7	0.1	145.9	0.8
1994	147.4	1.0	146.5	-0.6	147.3	0.5	147.6	0.2	147.0	-0.4	146.1	-0.6	146.4	0.2	147.4	0.7	147.4	0.0	147.7	0.2	147.4	-0.2	147.8	0.3
1995	150.5	1.8	151.7	0.8	151.6	-0.1	151.9	0.2	151.1	-0.5	151.0	-0.1	151.4	0.3	151.1	-0.2	150.9	-0.1	151.7	0.5	152.6	0.6	153.2	0.4
1996	153.5	0.2	153.3	-0.1	154.4	0.7	155.0	0.4	154.0	-0.6	155.8	1.2	156.3	0.3	156.7	0.3	157.7	0.6	158.7	0.6	159.6	0.6	160.6	0.6
1997	160.5	-0.1	159.7	-0.5	160.0	0.2	159.3	-0.4	159.8	0.3	159.9	0.1	160.5	0.4	160.7	0.1	160.5	-0.1	162.0	0.9	162.0	0.0	163.4	0.9

Source: U.S. Department of Labor, Bureau of Labor Statistics, Division of Consumer Prices and Price Indexes. - indicates no data collected for period.

Chicago, IL-NW IN
Consumer Price Index - All Urban Consumers
Base 1982-1984 = 100
Housing

For 1976-1997. Columns headed % show percentile change in the index from the previous period for which an index is available.

Year	Jan Index	%	Feb Index	%	Mar Index	%	Apr Index	%	May Index	%	Jun Index	%	Jul Index	%	Aug Index	%	Sep Index	%	Oct Index	%	Nov Index	%	Dec Index	%
1976	47.5	-	47.6	0.2	47.8	0.4	47.9	0.2	48.1	0.4	48.3	0.4	48.6	0.6	48.8	0.4	49.1	0.6	49.3	0.4	49.3	0.0	49.9	1.2
1977	50.0	0.2	50.4	0.8	50.5	0.2	50.9	0.8	51.0	0.2	51.0	0.0	51.6	1.2	51.9	0.6	52.4	1.0	52.6	0.4	52.9	0.6	53.0	0.2
1978	54.2	2.3	55.0	1.5	56.1	2.0	56.2	0.2	56.6	0.7	57.0	0.7	57.5	0.9	57.0	-0.9	58.2	2.1	58.9	1.2	60.1	2.0	60.3	0.3
1979	60.3	0.0	61.5	2.0	63.3	2.9	64.1	1.3	63.8	-0.5	65.6	2.8	67.2	2.4	68.0	1.2	68.9	1.3	68.6	-0.4	70.6	2.9	71.1	0.7
1980	71.5	0.6	72.0	0.7	72.3	0.4	74.6	3.2	76.2	2.1	79.6	4.5	78.1	-1.9	76.2	-2.4	78.7	3.3	80.7	2.5	84.3	4.5	84.1	-0.2
1981	81.8	-2.7	81.4	-0.5	81.0	-0.5	83.3	2.8	83.6	0.4	86.3	3.2	88.0	2.0	89.3	1.5	89.4	0.1	88.5	-1.0	88.8	0.3	86.3	-2.8
1982	87.5	1.4	87.2	-0.3	88.8	1.8	91.0	2.5	95.6	5.1	97.1	1.6	98.0	0.9	97.9	-0.1	98.5	0.6	98.5	0.0	98.5	0.0	97.8	-0.7
1983	98.2	0.4	98.6	0.4	98.8	0.2	99.1	0.3	99.4	0.3	101.5	2.1	102.1	0.6	102.4	0.3	102.2	-0.2	100.8	-1.4	101.8	1.0	102.3	0.5
1984	102.5	0.2	102.1	-0.4	102.5	0.4	103.0	0.5	103.0	0.0	105.1	2.0	105.0	-0.1	106.7	1.6	107.8	1.0	106.1	-1.6	106.2	0.1	106.3	0.1
1985	107.1	0.8	107.2	0.1	106.8	-0.4	107.6	0.7	108.1	0.5	111.6	3.2	111.7	0.1	113.2	1.3	113.3	0.1	109.4	-3.4	109.2	-0.2	109.6	0.4
1986	110.3	0.6	110.5	0.2	110.4	-0.1	111.3	0.8	111.0	-0.3	115.5	4.1	116.0	0.4	116.1	0.1	117.1	0.9	112.1	-4.3	112.7	0.5	112.1	-0.5
1987	113.1	0.9	113.3	0.2	113.3	0.0	113.9	0.5	114.1	0.2	118.7	4.0	119.6	0.8	120.3	0.6	120.6	0.2	115.4	-4.3	116.6	1.0	117.0	0.3
1988	115.7	-1.1	118.0	2.0	118.0	0.0	118.1	0.1	118.1	0.0	121.9	3.2	122.7	0.7	122.1	-0.5	124.6	2.0	123.7	-0.7	122.3	-1.1	123.1	0.7
1989	123.1	0.0	123.8	0.6	124.2	0.3	124.2	0.0	124.5	0.2	128.2	3.0	128.9	0.5	128.8	-0.1	129.9	0.9	126.9	-2.3	126.9	0.0	127.2	0.2
1990	128.0	0.6	129.2	0.9	129.3	0.1	130.2	0.7	129.6	-0.5	133.2	2.8	133.4	0.2	134.3	0.7	134.2	-0.1	130.8	-2.5	131.7	0.7	132.5	0.6
1991	134.2	1.3	134.3	0.1	135.8	1.1	134.9	-0.7	136.1	0.9	137.6	1.1	138.3	0.5	137.9	-0.3	137.7	-0.1	137.0	-0.5	135.6	-1.0	137.4	1.3
1992	138.9	1.1	138.3	-0.4	138.2	-0.1	138.2	0.0	139.1	0.7	141.4	1.7	140.7	-0.5	140.6	-0.1	141.6	0.7	139.5	-1.5	140.5	0.7	141.8	0.9
1993	141.8	0.0	141.3	-0.4	141.0	-0.2	142.5	1.1	142.9	0.3	144.3	1.0	143.3	-0.7	144.3	0.7	145.2	0.6	145.6	0.3	143.4	-1.5	143.4	0.0
1994	143.2	-0.1	143.2	0.0	143.6	0.3	144.2	0.4	144.1	-0.1	145.3	0.8	144.7	-0.4	145.4	0.5	145.9	0.3	144.2	-1.2	146.4	1.5	147.9	1.0
1995	149.2	0.9	149.1	-0.1	149.1	0.0	149.7	0.4	149.9	0.1	150.7	0.5	151.7	0.7	151.9	0.1	151.3	-0.4	151.3	0.0	151.4	0.1	152.1	0.5
1996	152.4	0.2	153.0	0.4	153.8	0.5	154.1	0.2	154.5	0.3	155.8	0.8	155.9	0.1	156.8	0.6	156.2	-0.4	156.3	0.1	156.0	-0.2	156.9	0.6
1997	158.6	1.1	159.2	0.4	158.7	-0.3	157.7	-0.6	158.1	0.3	159.7	1.0	160.1	0.3	161.0	0.6	161.4	0.2	161.8	0.2	163.2	0.9	162.3	-0.6

Source: U.S. Department of Labor, Bureau of Labor Statistics, Division of Consumer Prices and Price Indexes. - indicates no data collected for period.

Chicago, IL-NW IN
Consumer Price Index - Urban Wage Earners
Base 1982-1984 = 100
Housing

For 1976-1997. Columns headed % show percentile change in the index from the previous period for which an index is available.

Year	Jan Index	%	Feb Index	%	Mar Index	%	Apr Index	%	May Index	%	Jun Index	%	Jul Index	%	Aug Index	%	Sep Index	%	Oct Index	%	Nov Index	%	Dec Index	%
1976	49.6	-	49.7	0.2	50.0	0.6	50.1	0.2	50.3	0.4	50.5	0.4	50.7	0.4	51.0	0.6	51.3	0.6	51.5	0.4	51.5	0.0	52.1	1.2
1977	52.3	0.4	52.7	0.8	52.8	0.2	53.2	0.8	53.3	0.2	53.3	0.0	53.9	1.1	54.2	0.6	54.7	0.9	54.9	0.4	55.3	0.7	55.4	0.2
1978	56.6	2.2	57.4	1.4	58.5	1.9	58.5	0.0	59.0	0.9	59.4	0.7	60.0	1.0	59.1	-1.5	60.3	2.0	61.3	1.7	62.4	1.8	62.9	0.8
1979	62.8	-0.2	63.9	1.8	65.7	2.8	66.3	0.9	66.1	-0.3	67.9	2.7	69.5	2.4	70.3	1.2	71.2	1.3	71.0	-0.3	73.0	2.8	73.4	0.5
1980	73.8	0.5	74.3	0.7	74.9	0.8	77.0	2.8	78.6	2.1	82.1	4.5	80.6	-1.8	78.7	-2.4	81.1	3.0	82.9	2.2	86.4	4.2	86.5	0.1
1981	84.3	-2.5	83.8	-0.6	83.4	-0.5	85.8	2.9	86.2	0.5	88.9	3.1	90.7	2.0	92.1	1.5	92.3	0.2	91.4	-1.0	91.8	0.4	89.2	-2.8
1982	90.4	1.3	90.2	-0.2	91.8	1.8	94.0	2.4	98.8	5.1	100.5	1.7	101.4	0.9	101.2	-0.2	101.8	0.6	101.8	0.0	101.7	-0.1	101.0	-0.7
1983	101.6	0.6	101.1	-0.5	101.3	0.2	102.1	0.8	102.5	0.4	103.2	0.7	103.4	0.2	103.0	-0.4	103.3	0.3	99.1	-4.1	99.6	0.5	98.8	-0.8
1984	101.4	2.6	100.1	-1.3	99.4	-0.7	99.0	-0.4	98.9	-0.1	99.9	1.0	100.0	0.1	101.3	1.3	103.3	2.0	100.7	-2.5	101.6	0.9	100.9	-0.7
1985	101.5	0.6	101.7	0.2	101.3	-0.4	102.0	0.7	102.4	0.4	106.0	3.5	106.1	0.1	107.4	1.2	107.5	0.1	103.6	-3.6	103.5	-0.1	103.9	0.4
1986	104.5	0.6	104.7	0.2	104.4	-0.3	105.3	0.9	105.0	-0.3	109.4	4.2	110.1	0.6	110.3	0.2	111.0	0.6	105.9	-4.6	106.5	0.6	105.9	-0.6
1987	106.8	0.8	107.0	0.2	106.9	-0.1	107.3	0.4	107.5	0.2	112.0	4.2	112.8	0.7	113.6	0.7	113.8	0.2	108.7	-4.5	109.8	1.0	110.3	0.5
1988	109.1	-1.1	111.2	1.9	110.9	-0.3	111.0	0.1	111.0	0.0	114.7	3.3	115.6	0.8	114.8	-0.7	117.2	2.1	116.4	-0.7	115.3	-0.9	116.1	0.7
1989	116.0	-0.1	116.6	0.5	116.7	0.1	116.7	0.0	117.0	0.3	120.7	3.2	121.3	0.5	121.3	0.0	122.3	0.8	119.3	-2.5	119.6	0.3	119.8	0.2
1990	120.6	0.7	121.7	0.9	121.7	0.0	122.7	0.8	122.1	-0.5	125.5	2.8	125.7	0.2	126.6	0.7	126.7	0.1	123.2	-2.8	124.1	0.7	125.0	0.7
1991	126.4	1.1	126.5	0.1	127.8	1.0	127.0	-0.6	128.0	0.8	129.4	1.1	130.2	0.6	129.7	-0.4	129.6	-0.1	128.8	-0.6	127.6	-0.9	129.5	1.5
1992	130.7	0.9	130.1	-0.5	129.9	-0.2	130.0	0.1	130.9	0.7	133.0	1.6	132.4	-0.5	132.2	-0.2	133.3	0.8	131.4	-1.4	132.5	0.8	133.7	0.9
1993	133.8	0.1	133.3	-0.4	132.8	-0.4	134.3	1.1	134.7	0.3	135.9	0.9	135.0	-0.7	135.9	0.7	136.7	0.6	137.2	0.4	135.1	-1.5	135.3	0.1
1994	135.1	-0.1	134.9	-0.1	135.3	0.3	135.8	0.4	135.5	-0.2	136.8	1.0	136.0	-0.6	136.7	0.5	137.2	0.4	135.6	-1.2	137.7	1.5	139.3	1.2
1995	140.4	0.8	140.3	-0.1	140.2	-0.1	140.7	0.4	140.8	0.1	141.4	0.4	142.2	0.6	142.4	0.1	142.0	-0.3	142.0	0.0	142.2	0.1	142.7	0.4
1996	143.2	0.4	143.7	0.3	144.5	0.6	144.8	0.2	145.1	0.2	146.2	0.8	146.3	0.1	147.1	0.5	146.8	-0.2	146.8	0.0	146.7	-0.1	147.6	0.6
1997	149.2	1.1	149.7	0.3	149.2	-0.3	148.1	-0.7	148.3	0.1	149.8	1.0	150.2	0.3	151.0	0.5	151.5	0.3	151.9	0.3	153.3	0.9	152.6	-0.5

Source: U.S. Department of Labor, Bureau of Labor Statistics, Division of Consumer Prices and Price Indexes. - indicates no data collected for period.

Chicago, IL-NW IN
Consumer Price Index - All Urban Consumers
Base 1982-1984 = 100
Apparel and Upkeep

For 1952-1997. Columns headed % show percentile change in the index from the previous period for which an index is available.

Year	Jan Index	%	Feb Index	%	Mar Index	%	Apr Index	%	May Index	%	Jun Index	%	Jul Index	%	Aug Index	%	Sep Index	%	Oct Index	%	Nov Index	%	Dec Index	%
1952	-	-	-	-	-	-	-	-	-	-	-	-	-	-	-	-	-	-	-	-	-	-	52.2	-
1953	51.8	-0.8	51.9	0.2	52.0	0.2	52.1	0.2	52.3	0.4	52.4	0.2	52.4	0.0	52.6	0.4	53.1	1.0	53.1	0.0	53.1	0.0	52.9	-0.4
1954	52.9	0.0	52.9	0.0	53.0	0.2	52.9	-0.2	52.9	0.0	52.9	0.0	52.9	0.0	52.4	-0.9	52.5	0.2	52.4	-0.2	52.3	-0.2	52.2	-0.2
1955	51.4	-1.5	51.6	0.4	51.7	0.2	51.3	-0.8	51.4	0.2	51.5	0.2	52.1	1.2	52.3	0.4	53.3	1.9	53.4	0.2	53.7	0.6	53.4	-0.6
1956	53.4	0.0	53.4	0.0	53.5	0.2	53.6	0.2	53.5	-0.2	53.5	0.0	53.8	0.6	54.1	0.6	54.5	0.7	54.8	0.6	54.6	-0.4	54.8	0.4
1957	53.9	-1.6	54.1	0.4	54.7	1.1	54.6	-0.2	54.6	0.0	54.8	0.4	54.7	-0.2	54.8	0.2	55.7	1.6	55.6	-0.2	55.4	-0.4	55.4	0.0
1958	54.9	-0.9	54.8	-0.2	54.8	0.0	54.7	-0.2	54.7	0.0	54.9	0.4	55.2	0.5	54.8	-0.7	55.4	1.1	55.3	-0.2	55.4	0.2	55.1	-0.5
1959	54.8	-0.5	54.6	-0.4	54.5	-0.2	54.9	0.7	55.1	0.4	54.9	-0.4	55.4	0.9	55.6	0.4	56.6	1.8	56.6	0.0	56.6	0.0	56.6	0.0
1960	56.0	-1.1	56.1	0.2	56.2	0.2	55.7	-0.9	56.0	0.5	56.0	0.0	56.4	0.7	56.6	0.4	56.7	0.2	56.8	0.2	56.7	-0.2	56.9	0.4
1961	56.0	-1.6	56.0	0.0	56.0	0.0	56.0	0.0	55.8	-0.4	55.5	-0.5	55.8	0.5	55.5	-0.5	56.7	2.2	56.6	-0.2	56.4	-0.4	56.4	0.0
1962	55.4	-1.8	55.3	-0.2	55.6	0.5	55.5	-0.2	55.6	0.2	55.5	-0.2	55.7	0.4	55.4	-0.5	56.3	1.6	56.3	0.0	56.3	0.0	56.4	0.2
1963	55.6	-1.4	55.7	0.2	55.8	0.2	55.9	0.2	55.8	-0.2	55.4	-0.7	55.7	0.5	55.5	-0.4	56.9	2.5	57.0	0.2	56.6	-0.7	56.8	0.4
1964	55.4	-2.5	55.8	0.7	56.4	1.1	56.4	0.0	56.4	0.0	56.3	-0.2	56.1	-0.4	55.7	-0.7	56.7	1.8	56.6	-0.2	56.4	-0.4	56.5	0.2
1965	56.0	-0.9	55.8	-0.4	56.3	0.9	56.4	0.2	56.9	0.9	57.0	0.2	56.1	-1.6	56.4	0.5	57.5	2.0	57.7	0.3	57.7	0.0	57.9	0.3
1966	56.8	-1.9	56.7	-0.2	58.0	2.3	57.8	-0.3	58.1	0.5	58.3	0.3	57.4	-1.5	57.9	0.9	59.7	3.1	59.7	0.0	59.4	-0.5	59.7	0.5
1967	59.1	-1.0	59.2	0.2	59.7	0.8	59.8	0.2	60.3	0.8	60.4	0.2	59.8	-1.0	60.3	0.8	61.7	2.3	61.9	0.3	62.1	0.3	62.3	0.3
1968	60.5	-2.9	61.2	1.2	62.8	2.6	63.2	0.6	63.9	1.1	64.0	0.2	63.2	-1.2	63.4	0.3	65.2	2.8	65.7	0.8	65.8	0.2	65.9	0.2
1969	64.1	-2.7	65.7	2.5	66.3	0.9	66.0	-0.5	66.6	0.9	67.0	0.6	66.6	-0.6	65.2	-2.1	68.6	5.2	68.5	-0.1	68.9	0.6	68.8	-0.1
1970	66.2	-3.8	66.8	0.9	68.2	2.1	67.6	-0.9	68.7	1.6	68.3	-0.6	67.1	-1.8	67.9	1.2	71.0	4.6	70.7	-0.4	70.7	0.0	70.4	-0.4
1971	68.1	-3.3	69.8	2.5	70.7	1.3	70.5	-0.3	71.1	0.9	71.3	0.3	69.7	-2.2	70.3	0.9	72.9	3.7	72.8	-0.1	73.0	0.3	73.0	0.0
1972	70.4	-3.6	72.0	2.3	72.4	0.6	72.1	-0.4	72.2	0.1	72.1	-0.1	70.2	-2.6	70.4	0.3	74.3	5.5	74.3	0.0	74.7	0.5	74.7	0.0
1973	73.0	-2.3	74.1	1.5	76.1	2.7	76.1	0.0	76.5	0.5	76.2	-0.4	74.7	-2.0	75.5	1.1	77.5	2.6	77.3	-0.3	77.8	0.6	77.5	-0.4
1974	75.5	-2.6	77.2	2.3	78.4	1.6	79.3	1.1	79.6	0.4	80.1	0.6	79.0	-1.4	82.3	4.2	82.6	0.4	82.9	0.4	83.7	1.0	83.7	0.0
1975	81.0	-3.2	81.5	0.6	82.7	1.5	82.9	0.2	82.6	-0.4	82.1	-0.6	81.6	-0.6	82.7	1.3	84.3	1.9	84.1	-0.2	84.1	0.0	83.5	-0.7
1976	80.9	-3.1	82.0	1.4	82.6	0.7	82.2	-0.5	83.0	1.0	83.6	0.7	82.7	-1.1	84.2	1.8	86.0	2.1	85.6	-0.5	85.9	0.4	85.7	-0.2
1977	83.0	-3.2	84.1	1.3	85.4	1.5	85.3	-0.1	85.3	0.0	86.4	1.3	85.9	-0.6	87.0	1.3	88.7	2.0	87.3	-1.6	88.0	0.8	87.8	-0.2
1978	85.2	-3.0	85.0	-0.2	86.4	1.6	87.9	1.7	88.6	0.8	88.4	-0.2	87.7	-0.8	88.8	1.3	89.5	0.8	89.5	0.0	90.2	0.8	88.8	-1.6
1979	87.5	-1.5	88.2	0.8	90.4	2.5	89.6	-0.9	90.2	0.7	89.4	-0.9	89.9	0.6	89.3	-0.7	91.9	2.9	91.9	0.0	93.5	1.7	93.8	0.3
1980	93.7	-0.1	93.0	-0.7	95.1	2.3	94.8	-0.3	94.2	-0.6	95.2	1.1	95.5	0.3	96.2	0.7	97.4	1.2	97.9	0.5	98.3	0.4	95.8	-2.5
1981	93.1	-2.8	93.0	-0.1	94.4	1.5	94.9	0.5	95.1	0.2	94.0	-1.2	94.1	0.1	99.0	5.2	100.8	1.8	99.9	-0.9	100.8	0.9	98.1	-2.7
1982	95.6	-2.5	96.9	1.4	95.7	-1.2	97.2	1.6	98.7	1.5	97.8	-0.9	94.3	-3.6	99.3	5.3	100.5	1.2	99.8	-0.7	99.2	-0.6	97.4	-1.8
1983	96.4	-1.0	95.6	-0.8	98.6	3.1	97.9	-0.7	99.0	1.1	96.8	-2.2	97.4	0.6	102.2	4.9	104.7	2.4	104.7	0.0	106.0	1.2	103.5	-2.4
1984	99.0	-4.3	96.5	-2.5	98.7	2.3	99.7	1.0	100.4	0.7	98.8	-1.6	102.4	3.6	104.9	2.4	106.1	1.1	106.1	0.0	107.8	1.6	104.7	-2.9
1985	100.7	-3.8	103.8	3.1	105.7	1.8	106.7	0.9	105.7	-0.9	104.9	-0.8	105.6	0.7	106.4	0.8	108.4	1.9	108.3	-0.1	108.6	0.3	106.9	-1.6
1986	102.5	-4.1	102.4	-0.1	101.1	-1.3	100.2	-0.9	100.3	0.1	99.3	-1.0	101.1	1.8	105.0	3.9	109.4	4.2	109.4	0.0	108.6	-0.7	107.0	-1.5
1987	104.4	-2.4	102.7	-1.6	108.0	5.2	107.6	-0.4	108.6	0.9	106.7	-1.7	105.1	-1.5	112.7	7.2	114.3	1.4	114.2	-0.1	114.5	0.3	112.0	-2.2
1988	111.1	-0.8	112.2	1.0	115.8	3.2	115.3	-0.4	113.6	-1.5	115.6	1.8	114.7	-0.8	116.8	1.8	122.8	5.1	121.1	-1.4	120.4	-0.6	119.8	-0.5
1989	114.1	-4.8	112.3	-1.6	119.3	6.2	117.8	-1.3	116.0	-1.5	113.5	-2.2	118.1	4.1	119.6	1.3	120.5	0.8	124.8	3.6	123.2	-1.3	117.5	-4.6
1990	114.5	-2.6	121.4	6.0	126.1	3.9	129.4	2.6	129.4	0.0	123.0	-4.9	119.8	-2.6	123.5	3.1	126.7	2.6	126.6	-0.1	127.9	1.0	122.8	-4.0
1991	116.5	-5.1	124.1	6.5	127.1	2.4	128.9	1.4	125.2	-2.9	122.3	-2.3	119.6	-2.2	127.1	6.3	128.8	1.3	129.5	0.5	130.0	0.4	124.0	-4.6
1992	120.8	-2.6	126.5	4.7	129.3	2.2	124.7	-3.6	124.5	-0.2	123.5	-0.8	124.7	1.0	132.3	6.1	130.8	-1.1	129.4	-1.1	125.2	-3.2	123.1	-1.7
1993	121.2	-1.5	133.3	10.0	137.0	2.8	133.4	-2.6	133.9	0.4	126.6	-5.5	128.2	1.3	134.0	4.5	134.3	0.2	133.9	-0.3	131.9	-1.5	125.8	-4.6
1994	126.6	0.6	132.4	4.6	136.5	3.1	133.1	-2.5	129.0	-3.1	128.6	-0.3	126.5	-1.6	135.1	6.8	134.2	-0.7	131.8	-1.8	132.0	0.2	126.0	-4.5

[Continued]

Chicago, IL-NW IN
Consumer Price Index - All Urban Consumers
Base 1982-1984 = 100
Apparel and Upkeep
[Continued]

For 1952-1997. Columns headed % show percentile change in the index from the previous period for which an index is available.

Year	Jan Index	%	Feb Index	%	Mar Index	%	Apr Index	%	May Index	%	Jun Index	%	Jul Index	%	Aug Index	%	Sep Index	%	Oct Index	%	Nov Index	%	Dec Index	%
1995	125.3	-0.6	128.2	2.3	130.1	1.5	130.0	-0.1	126.6	-2.6	123.8	-2.2	121.6	-1.8	124.2	2.1	131.0	5.5	131.4	0.3	125.4	-4.6	118.5	-5.5
1996	120.8	1.9	124.5	3.1	127.7	2.6	122.1	-4.4	122.1	0.0	118.0	-3.4	118.4	0.3	118.8	0.3	119.2	0.3	119.8	0.5	120.6	0.7	115.4	-4.3
1997	116.9	1.3	124.0	6.1	124.8	0.6	131.5	5.4	127.5	-3.0	124.6	-2.3	120.4	-3.4	122.2	1.5	120.0	-1.8	118.4	-1.3	119.7	1.1	117.9	-1.5

Source: U.S. Department of Labor, Bureau of Labor Statistics, Division of Consumer Prices and Price Indexes. - indicates no data collected for period.

Chicago, IL-NW IN
Consumer Price Index - Urban Wage Earners
Base 1982-1984 = 100
Apparel and Upkeep

For 1952-1997. Columns headed % show percentile change in the index from the previous period for which an index is available.

Year	Jan Index	%	Feb Index	%	Mar Index	%	Apr Index	%	May Index	%	Jun Index	%	Jul Index	%	Aug Index	%	Sep Index	%	Oct Index	%	Nov Index	%	Dec Index	%
1952	-	-	-	-	-	-	-	-	-	-	-	-	-	-	-	-	-	-	-	-	-	-	50.6	-
1953	50.2	-0.8	50.3	0.2	50.4	0.2	50.5	0.2	50.7	0.4	50.8	0.2	50.8	0.0	51.0	0.4	51.4	0.8	51.4	0.0	51.5	0.2	51.3	-0.4
1954	51.2	-0.2	51.3	0.2	51.4	0.2	51.3	-0.2	51.3	0.0	51.3	0.0	51.3	0.0	50.8	-1.0	50.9	0.2	50.8	-0.2	50.7	-0.2	50.6	-0.2
1955	49.8	-1.6	50.0	0.4	50.1	0.2	49.7	-0.8	49.8	0.2	50.0	0.4	50.5	1.0	50.7	0.4	51.7	2.0	51.7	0.0	52.0	0.6	51.8	-0.4
1956	51.8	0.0	51.7	-0.2	51.9	0.4	52.0	0.2	51.8	-0.4	51.8	0.0	52.2	0.8	52.4	0.4	52.8	0.8	53.1	0.6	52.9	-0.4	53.1	0.4
1957	52.2	-1.7	52.4	0.4	53.0	1.1	52.9	-0.2	52.9	0.0	53.1	0.4	53.0	-0.2	53.1	0.2	54.0	1.7	53.9	-0.2	53.7	-0.4	53.7	0.0
1958	53.2	-0.9	53.1	-0.2	53.1	0.0	53.0	-0.2	53.0	0.0	53.2	0.4	53.5	0.6	53.1	-0.7	53.7	1.1	53.6	-0.2	53.7	0.2	53.4	-0.6
1959	53.1	-0.6	52.9	-0.4	52.8	-0.2	53.2	0.8	53.4	0.4	53.2	-0.4	53.7	0.9	53.9	0.4	54.8	1.7	54.8	0.0	54.8	0.0	54.8	0.0
1960	54.2	-1.1	54.4	0.4	54.5	0.2	54.0	-0.9	54.3	0.6	54.2	-0.2	54.7	0.9	54.8	0.2	55.0	0.4	55.1	0.2	55.0	-0.2	55.1	0.2
1961	54.3	-1.5	54.2	-0.2	54.2	0.0	54.2	0.0	54.1	-0.2	53.8	-0.6	54.1	0.6	53.8	-0.6	54.9	2.0	54.8	-0.2	54.7	-0.2	54.7	0.0
1962	53.7	-1.8	53.6	-0.2	53.9	0.6	53.8	-0.2	53.9	0.2	53.8	-0.2	53.9	0.2	53.7	-0.4	54.6	1.7	54.6	0.0	54.5	-0.2	54.7	0.4
1963	53.9	-1.5	53.9	0.0	54.1	0.4	54.2	0.2	54.1	-0.2	53.7	-0.7	54.0	0.6	53.8	-0.4	55.1	2.4	55.2	0.2	54.9	-0.5	55.1	0.4
1964	53.7	-2.5	54.1	0.7	54.7	1.1	54.7	0.0	54.7	0.0	54.5	-0.4	54.4	-0.2	54.0	-0.7	54.9	1.7	54.9	0.0	54.7	-0.4	54.8	0.2
1965	54.2	-1.1	54.1	-0.2	54.5	0.7	54.7	0.4	55.1	0.7	55.2	0.2	54.4	-1.4	54.7	0.6	55.7	1.8	55.9	0.4	55.9	0.0	56.1	0.4
1966	55.1	-1.8	55.0	-0.2	56.2	2.2	56.1	-0.2	56.3	0.4	56.5	0.4	55.6	-1.6	56.1	0.9	57.8	3.0	57.8	0.0	57.6	-0.3	57.9	0.5
1967	57.2	-1.2	57.4	0.3	57.8	0.7	57.9	0.2	58.4	0.9	58.6	0.3	58.0	-1.0	58.5	0.9	59.8	2.2	60.0	0.3	60.2	0.3	60.3	0.2
1968	58.6	-2.8	59.3	1.2	60.9	2.7	61.3	0.7	61.9	1.0	62.0	0.2	61.2	-1.3	61.5	0.5	63.2	2.8	63.7	0.8	63.8	0.2	63.9	0.2
1969	62.2	-2.7	63.6	2.3	64.2	0.9	64.0	-0.3	64.5	0.8	65.0	0.8	64.6	-0.6	63.2	-2.2	66.5	5.2	66.4	-0.2	66.7	0.5	66.7	0.0
1970	64.2	-3.7	64.7	0.8	66.1	2.2	65.5	-0.9	66.6	1.7	66.2	-0.6	65.0	-1.8	65.8	1.2	68.8	4.6	68.6	-0.3	68.5	-0.1	68.3	-0.3
1971	66.0	-3.4	67.6	2.4	68.5	1.3	68.3	-0.3	68.9	0.9	69.1	0.3	67.5	-2.3	68.1	0.9	70.7	3.8	70.6	-0.1	70.8	0.3	70.7	-0.1
1972	68.3	-3.4	69.7	2.0	70.2	0.7	69.9	-0.4	70.0	0.1	69.9	-0.1	68.0	-2.7	68.2	0.3	72.0	5.6	72.0	0.0	72.4	0.6	72.4	0.0
1973	70.8	-2.2	71.9	1.6	73.7	2.5	73.8	0.1	74.1	0.4	73.8	-0.4	72.4	-1.9	73.2	1.1	75.1	2.6	74.9	-0.3	75.4	0.7	75.1	-0.4
1974	73.1	-2.7	74.8	2.3	76.0	1.6	76.9	1.2	77.1	0.3	77.7	0.8	76.5	-1.5	79.8	4.3	80.1	0.4	80.3	0.2	81.1	1.0	81.1	0.0
1975	78.5	-3.2	79.0	0.6	80.2	1.5	80.4	0.2	80.1	-0.4	79.6	-0.6	79.1	-0.6	80.2	1.4	81.7	1.9	81.5	-0.2	81.5	0.0	80.9	-0.7
1976	78.4	-3.1	79.5	1.4	80.1	0.8	79.7	-0.5	80.4	0.9	81.0	0.7	80.1	-1.1	81.6	1.9	83.4	2.2	82.9	-0.6	83.2	0.4	83.1	-0.1
1977	80.5	-3.1	81.5	1.2	82.8	1.6	82.7	-0.1	82.7	0.0	83.8	1.3	83.3	-0.6	84.3	1.2	85.9	1.9	84.6	-1.5	85.3	0.8	85.1	-0.2
1978	84.4	-0.8	84.6	0.2	84.5	-0.1	86.4	2.2	86.2	-0.2	86.9	0.8	86.9	0.0	86.6	-0.3	87.9	1.5	89.3	1.6	89.6	0.3	88.2	-1.6
1979	85.7	-2.8	87.9	2.6	89.4	1.7	88.8	-0.7	88.9	0.1	88.2	-0.8	88.5	0.3	88.6	0.1	91.8	3.6	91.9	0.1	93.6	1.8	93.3	-0.3
1980	91.5	-1.9	93.0	1.6	93.6	0.6	93.3	-0.3	94.4	1.2	95.7	1.4	95.5	-0.2	96.1	0.6	95.9	-0.2	97.6	1.8	97.0	-0.6	95.1	-2.0
1981	92.2	-3.0	90.8	-1.5	91.8	1.1	93.2	1.5	94.0	0.9	93.2	-0.9	94.9	1.8	99.0	4.3	101.4	2.4	100.7	-0.7	100.7	0.0	98.5	-2.2
1982	96.0	-2.5	97.2	1.2	95.4	-1.9	97.2	1.9	99.1	2.0	98.1	-1.0	95.0	-3.2	98.7	3.9	100.4	1.7	100.0	-0.4	99.3	-0.7	97.6	-1.7
1983	96.2	-1.4	94.9	-1.4	98.1	3.4	97.5	-0.6	98.7	1.2	96.6	-2.1	97.2	0.6	101.8	4.7	104.6	2.8	104.6	0.0	106.0	1.3	103.6	-2.3
1984	98.6	-4.8	96.4	-2.2	99.0	2.7	99.5	0.5	100.4	0.9	99.4	-1.0	101.9	2.5	105.0	3.0	106.5	1.4	106.3	-0.2	108.2	1.8	105.0	-3.0
1985	100.5	-4.3	103.3	2.8	105.4	2.0	106.2	0.8	105.6	-0.6	104.5	-1.0	104.5	0.0	105.3	0.8	108.5	3.0	108.1	-0.4	108.2	0.1	107.0	-1.1
1986	102.9	-3.8	103.1	0.2	101.4	-1.6	100.6	-0.8	100.8	0.2	99.9	-0.9	101.2	1.3	104.7	3.5	109.4	4.5	109.4	0.0	108.7	-0.6	107.3	-1.3
1987	104.5	-2.6	102.9	-1.5	108.4	5.3	108.8	0.4	109.1	0.3	107.2	-1.7	105.5	-1.6	112.3	6.4	113.9	1.4	114.8	0.8	114.0	-0.7	111.9	-1.8
1988	110.5	-1.3	110.8	0.3	115.0	3.8	114.7	-0.3	112.1	-2.3	115.2	2.8	114.6	-0.5	115.8	1.0	122.9	6.1	121.2	-1.4	120.3	-0.7	119.8	-0.4
1989	114.0	-4.8	112.0	-1.8	118.8	6.1	117.9	-0.8	115.1	-2.4	113.2	-1.7	117.4	3.7	118.2	0.7	119.3	0.9	124.5	4.4	122.8	-1.4	117.7	-4.2
1990	114.3	-2.9	121.4	6.2	126.4	4.1	130.4	3.2	130.0	-0.3	123.8	-4.8	120.1	-3.0	123.6	2.9	126.9	2.7	126.6	-0.2	127.8	0.9	123.1	-3.7
1991	117.1	-4.9	125.6	7.3	128.0	1.9	130.2	1.7	126.0	-3.2	122.7	-2.6	120.3	-2.0	126.8	5.4	128.1	1.0	129.1	0.8	130.2	0.9	123.6	-5.1
1992	120.0	-2.9	125.6	4.7	129.2	2.9	125.8	-2.6	125.2	-0.5	123.9	-1.0	124.4	0.4	132.3	6.4	130.2	-1.6	128.7	-1.2	124.1	-3.6	121.3	-2.3
1993	119.3	-1.6	131.1	9.9	135.4	3.3	133.0	-1.8	134.1	0.8	126.9	-5.4	128.5	1.3	133.2	3.7	134.2	0.8	133.7	-0.4	131.6	-1.6	125.5	-4.6
1994	125.9	0.3	132.9	5.6	136.4	2.6	132.6	-2.8	128.8	-2.9	128.4	-0.3	126.5	-1.5	133.0	5.1	132.2	-0.6	129.5	-2.0	129.9	0.3	124.3	-4.3

[Continued]

Chicago, IL-NW IN
Consumer Price Index - Urban Wage Earners
Base 1982-1984 = 100
Apparel and Upkeep
[Continued]

For 1952-1997. Columns headed % show percentile change in the index from the previous period for which an index is available.

Year	Jan Index	%	Feb Index	%	Mar Index	%	Apr Index	%	May Index	%	Jun Index	%	Jul Index	%	Aug Index	%	Sep Index	%	Oct Index	%	Nov Index	%	Dec Index	%
1995	124.3	0.0	126.6	1.9	128.9	1.8	128.6	-0.2	125.3	-2.6	122.0	-2.6	120.7	-1.1	124.0	2.7	129.6	4.5	129.7	0.1	123.8	-4.5	117.5	-5.1
1996	120.6	2.6	122.8	1.8	125.8	2.4	120.8	-4.0	120.7	-0.1	117.1	-3.0	118.6	1.3	117.8	-0.7	118.4	0.5	118.5	0.1	119.8	1.1	114.0	-4.8
1997	115.8	1.6	121.8	5.2	122.7	0.7	127.7	4.1	123.7	-3.1	121.6	-1.7	118.2	-2.8	118.7	0.4	117.3	-1.2	116.4	-0.8	116.6	0.2	115.2	-1.2

Source: U.S. Department of Labor, Bureau of Labor Statistics, Division of Consumer Prices and Price Indexes. - indicates no data collected for period.

Chicago, IL-NW IN
Consumer Price Index - All Urban Consumers
Base 1982-1984 = 100
Transportation

For 1947-1997. Columns headed % show percentile change in the index from the previous period for which an index is available.

Year	Jan Index	%	Feb Index	%	Mar Index	%	Apr Index	%	May Index	%	Jun Index	%	Jul Index	%	Aug Index	%	Sep Index	%	Oct Index	%	Nov Index	%	Dec Index	%
1947	16.8	-	16.8	0.0	16.8	0.0	17.1	1.8	17.4	1.8	17.4	0.0	17.4	0.0	17.5	0.6	17.7	1.1	18.1	2.3	18.2	0.6	18.3	0.5
1948	18.6	1.6	18.6	0.0	18.6	0.0	18.6	0.0	19.3	3.8	19.3	0.0	21.2	9.8	21.5	1.4	21.6	0.5	21.6	0.0	21.6	0.0	21.6	0.0
1949	21.6	0.0	21.7	0.5	21.7	0.0	21.7	0.0	21.7	0.0	21.7	0.0	21.7	0.0	21.7	0.0	21.7	0.0	22.9	5.5	22.9	0.0	22.8	-0.4
1950	22.8	0.0	22.7	-0.4	22.6	-0.4	22.4	-0.9	22.4	0.0	22.4	0.0	22.5	0.4	22.8	1.3	22.6	-0.9	22.6	0.0	22.7	0.4	22.9	0.9
1951	22.9	0.0	23.0	0.4	23.3	1.3	23.3	0.0	23.3	0.0	23.3	0.0	23.8	2.1	24.6	3.4	24.8	0.8	24.9	0.4	25.1	0.8	24.4	-2.8
1952	25.2	3.3	25.3	0.4	25.3	0.0	25.3	0.0	25.4	0.4	26.5	4.3	26.5	0.0	26.6	0.4	26.6	0.0	26.6	0.0	26.6	0.0	26.6	0.0
1953	26.8	0.8	26.7	-0.4	26.7	0.0	26.6	-0.4	26.5	-0.4	26.6	0.4	26.7	0.4	26.7	0.0	26.6	-0.4	26.5	-0.4	26.4	-0.4	26.4	0.0
1954	26.6	0.8	26.4	-0.8	26.4	0.0	26.3	-0.4	26.6	1.1	26.7	0.4	26.6	-0.4	26.5	-0.4	26.5	0.0	25.4	-4.2	26.7	5.1	26.5	-0.7
1955	26.6	0.4	26.4	-0.8	26.5	0.4	25.8	-2.6	25.9	0.4	25.9	0.0	25.9	0.0	26.0	0.4	26.0	0.0	26.3	1.2	26.5	0.8	26.1	-1.5
1956	26.0	-0.4	26.1	0.4	26.0	-0.4	26.1	0.4	26.2	0.4	26.2	0.0	26.6	1.5	26.6	0.0	26.6	0.0	27.8	4.5	27.8	0.0	27.7	-0.4
1957	28.0	1.1	27.7	-1.1	27.8	0.4	27.8	0.0	27.7	-0.4	27.7	0.0	28.7	3.6	28.9	0.7	28.6	-1.0	28.5	-0.3	29.6	3.9	30.0	1.4
1958	30.1	0.3	29.7	-1.3	29.5	-0.7	29.4	-0.3	29.5	0.3	29.7	0.7	29.6	-0.3	29.8	0.7	29.8	0.0	30.4	2.0	30.6	0.7	30.9	1.0
1959	30.8	-0.3	30.7	-0.3	30.8	0.3	30.8	0.0	30.7	-0.3	30.6	-0.3	30.9	1.0	30.9	0.0	30.9	0.0	31.5	1.9	31.7	0.6	31.9	0.6
1960	31.5	-1.3	31.4	-0.3	31.2	-0.6	31.0	-0.6	30.8	-0.6	30.9	0.3	31.0	0.3	31.1	0.3	31.0	-0.3	31.4	1.3	31.2	-0.6	31.0	-0.6
1961	30.8	-0.6	30.7	-0.3	30.3	-1.3	30.5	0.7	30.5	0.0	30.2	-1.0	31.2	3.3	31.4	0.6	31.3	-0.3	31.8	1.6	31.3	-1.6	31.1	-0.6
1962	31.2	0.3	31.4	0.6	31.4	0.0	31.8	1.3	31.8	0.0	31.3	-1.6	31.0	-1.0	30.8	-0.6	31.8	3.2	31.8	0.0	31.8	0.0	31.7	-0.3
1963	31.4	-0.9	31.5	0.3	31.8	1.0	31.7	-0.3	32.0	0.9	31.9	-0.3	31.9	0.0	31.8	-0.3	31.5	-0.9	31.9	1.3	31.6	-0.9	31.9	0.9
1964	31.5	-1.3	31.4	-0.3	31.3	-0.3	31.3	0.0	31.8	1.6	31.9	0.3	32.1	0.6	32.0	-0.3	31.7	-0.9	31.9	0.6	32.2	0.9	32.2	0.0
1965	32.4	0.6	32.3	-0.3	32.4	0.3	32.7	0.9	32.8	0.3	32.7	-0.3	32.7	0.0	32.5	-0.6	32.3	-0.6	32.6	0.9	32.6	0.0	32.7	0.3
1966	32.4	-0.9	32.4	0.0	32.4	0.0	32.5	0.3	32.5	0.0	32.6	0.3	32.6	0.0	32.8	0.6	32.8	0.0	32.9	0.3	32.9	0.0	32.7	-0.6
1967	32.6	-0.3	33.0	1.2	33.0	0.0	33.1	0.3	33.3	0.6	33.3	0.0	33.5	0.6	33.5	0.0	33.8	0.9	33.9	0.3	34.8	2.7	34.6	-0.6
1968	34.7	0.3	34.7	0.0	34.9	0.6	35.0	0.3	34.9	-0.3	35.0	0.3	35.0	0.0	35.0	0.0	34.9	-0.3	35.2	0.9	35.3	0.3	36.0	2.0
1969	36.2	0.6	36.5	0.8	37.2	1.9	37.4	0.5	37.1	-0.8	37.3	0.5	37.3	0.0	37.3	0.0	37.2	-0.3	37.7	1.3	37.8	0.3	38.0	0.5
1970	38.4	1.1	38.1	-0.8	38.1	0.0	38.7	1.6	38.9	0.5	39.1	0.5	40.3	3.1	40.3	0.0	40.0	-0.7	41.2	3.0	41.7	1.2	42.0	0.7
1971	41.9	-0.2	42.2	0.7	42.0	-0.5	42.0	0.0	42.5	1.2	42.0	-1.2	42.3	0.7	42.5	0.5	42.2	-0.7	41.9	-0.7	41.8	-0.2	42.0	0.5
1972	41.5	-1.2	40.9	-1.4	40.9	0.0	41.2	0.7	41.6	1.0	41.5	-0.2	41.9	1.0	42.1	0.5	42.1	0.0	42.0	-0.2	42.1	0.2	42.1	0.0
1973	41.8	-0.7	41.8	0.0	42.0	0.5	42.4	1.0	42.9	1.2	43.2	0.7	43.2	0.0	43.0	-0.5	42.9	-0.2	43.5	1.4	43.6	0.2	44.0	0.9
1974	44.5	1.1	44.6	0.2	45.3	1.6	45.7	0.9	46.7	2.2	47.4	1.5	48.1	1.5	48.4	0.6	48.6	0.4	48.8	0.4	49.0	0.4	49.0	0.0
1975	48.5	-1.0	48.5	0.0	49.0	1.0	49.4	0.8	49.8	0.8	50.5	1.4	51.6	2.2	52.4	1.6	52.6	0.4	52.7	0.2	52.9	0.4	52.8	-0.2
1976	52.6	-0.4	53.4	1.5	53.8	0.7	54.3	0.9	55.4	2.0	56.2	1.4	56.7	0.9	57.2	0.9	57.8	1.0	58.3	0.9	58.9	1.0	58.8	-0.2
1977	59.0	0.3	59.6	1.0	60.0	0.7	60.9	1.5	61.4	0.8	61.6	0.3	61.5	-0.2	61.4	-0.2	61.0	-0.7	61.1	0.2	61.0	-0.2	61.2	0.3
1978	61.3	0.2	61.3	0.0	61.3	0.0	61.5	0.3	62.4	1.5	63.2	1.3	63.5	0.5	63.9	0.6	63.9	0.0	64.6	1.1	65.0	0.6	65.4	0.6
1979	66.0	0.9	66.5	0.8	67.2	1.1	68.6	2.1	69.9	1.9	71.5	2.3	72.7	1.7	73.8	1.5	74.7	1.2	75.7	1.3	76.3	0.8	77.4	1.4
1980	79.8	3.1	81.2	1.8	83.1	2.3	84.7	1.9	85.5	0.9	85.4	-0.1	85.2	-0.2	85.7	0.6	86.2	0.6	86.6	0.5	88.1	1.7	88.8	0.8
1981	91.1	2.6	92.5	1.5	93.4	1.0	93.6	0.2	94.4	0.9	95.0	0.6	96.6	1.7	96.7	0.1	97.3	0.6	98.3	1.0	98.9	0.6	99.2	0.3
1982	98.7	-0.5	97.7	-1.0	96.7	-1.0	96.3	-0.4	96.9	0.6	99.6	2.8	100.1	0.5	99.8	-0.3	98.6	-1.2	98.9	0.3	98.8	-0.1	98.0	-0.8
1983	97.4	-0.6	96.4	-1.0	95.4	-1.0	97.0	1.7	98.2	1.2	98.4	0.2	99.3	0.9	100.7	1.4	100.6	-0.1	101.6	1.0	101.8	0.2	101.3	-0.5
1984	101.3	0.0	100.9	-0.4	101.5	0.6	102.2	0.7	102.6	0.4	103.0	0.4	103.2	0.2	103.0	-0.2	103.0	0.0	103.8	0.8	103.8	0.0	103.6	-0.2
1985	103.6	0.0	103.3	-0.3	104.2	0.9	105.3	1.1	106.1	0.8	106.0	-0.1	106.3	0.3	105.7	-0.6	104.7	-0.9	105.3	0.6	106.6	1.2	106.6	0.0
1986	106.1	-0.5	104.8	-1.2	101.3	-3.3	99.2	-2.1	100.8	1.6	101.9	1.1	99.9	-2.0	98.9	-1.0	99.0	0.1	99.7	0.7	100.7	1.0	101.9	1.2
1987	103.4	1.5	103.3	-0.1	104.0	0.7	104.6	0.6	105.9	1.2	106.5	0.6	107.2	0.7	107.2	0.0	107.1	-0.1	108.1	0.9	108.1	0.0	107.7	-0.4
1988	107.0	-0.6	107.1	0.1	107.0	-0.1	107.5	0.5	106.6	-0.8	107.1	0.5	107.1	0.0	108.1	0.9	108.3	0.2	108.1	-0.2	109.0	0.8	108.6	-0.4
1989	109.3	0.6	109.5	0.2	109.9	0.4	112.1	2.0	113.7	1.4	114.0	0.3	112.8	-1.1	111.9	-0.8	111.6	-0.3	113.9	2.1	113.1	-0.7	113.1	0.0
1990	116.6	3.1	115.4	-1.0	114.3	-1.0	115.5	1.0	115.9	0.3	116.6	0.6	116.1	-0.4	118.9	2.4	119.8	0.8	124.5	3.9	125.3	0.6	125.5	0.2
1991	123.5	-1.6	121.7	-1.5	120.0	-1.4	119.3	-0.6	121.1	1.5	121.1	0.0	120.4	-0.6	120.4	0.0	120.6	0.2	121.1	0.4	122.5	1.2	122.1	-0.3

[Continued]

Chicago, IL-NW IN
Consumer Price Index - All Urban Consumers
Base 1982-1984 = 100
Transportation
[Continued]

For 1947-1997. Columns headed % show percentile change in the index from the previous period for which an index is available.

Year	Jan		Feb		Mar		Apr		May		Jun		Jul		Aug		Sep		Oct		Nov		Dec	
	Index	%	Index	%	Index	%	Index	%	Index	%	Index	%	Index	%	Index	%	Index	%	Index	%	Index	%	Index	%
1992	121.9	-0.2	120.7	-1.0	120.6	-0.1	121.9	1.1	123.1	1.0	123.2	0.1	123.6	0.3	122.6	-0.8	122.8	0.2	125.6	2.3	126.3	0.6	125.6	-0.6
1993	124.9	-0.6	125.0	0.1	124.8	-0.2	126.2	1.1	127.4	1.0	126.8	-0.5	126.6	-0.2	125.4	-0.9	125.6	0.2	127.0	1.1	127.7	0.6	126.6	-0.9
1994	125.7	-0.7	126.7	0.8	126.9	0.2	128.1	0.9	128.5	0.3	129.9	1.1	131.9	1.5	133.3	1.1	133.4	0.1	132.7	-0.5	133.7	0.8	133.0	-0.5
1995	133.2	0.2	133.0	-0.2	134.6	1.2	135.2	0.4	136.1	0.7	138.0	1.4	136.3	-1.2	135.2	-0.8	134.8	-0.3	135.9	0.8	134.8	-0.8	134.3	-0.4
1996	136.0	1.3	136.4	0.3	138.3	1.4	139.6	0.9	142.3	1.9	141.4	-0.6	140.2	-0.8	139.6	-0.4	139.6	0.0	140.3	0.5	142.5	1.6	142.9	0.3
1997	141.9	-0.7	142.0	0.1	141.5	-0.4	140.6	-0.6	141.2	0.4	140.0	-0.8	139.6	-0.3	139.8	0.1	139.6	-0.1	139.5	-0.1	138.6	-0.6	138.6	0.0

Source: U.S. Department of Labor, Bureau of Labor Statistics, Division of Consumer Prices and Price Indexes. - indicates no data collected for period.

Chicago, IL-NW IN
Consumer Price Index - Urban Wage Earners
Base 1982-1984 = 100
Transportation

For 1947-1997. Columns headed % show percentile change in the index from the previous period for which an index is available.

Year	Jan Index	%	Feb Index	%	Mar Index	%	Apr Index	%	May Index	%	Jun Index	%	Jul Index	%	Aug Index	%	Sep Index	%	Oct Index	%	Nov Index	%	Dec Index	%
1947	16.5	-	16.5	0.0	16.6	0.6	16.8	1.2	17.2	2.4	17.2	0.0	17.2	0.0	17.3	0.6	17.5	1.2	17.8	1.7	17.9	0.6	18.0	0.6
1948	18.3	1.7	18.3	0.0	18.3	0.0	18.3	0.0	19.0	3.8	19.0	0.0	20.9	10.0	21.1	1.0	21.2	0.5	21.2	0.0	21.2	0.0	21.2	0.0
1949	21.2	0.0	21.3	0.5	21.3	0.0	21.4	0.5	21.4	0.0	21.3	-0.5	21.3	0.0	21.3	0.0	21.3	0.0	22.5	5.6	22.5	0.0	22.4	-0.4
1950	22.4	0.0	22.4	0.0	22.3	-0.4	22.0	-1.3	22.0	0.0	22.1	0.5	22.1	0.0	22.4	1.4	22.3	-0.4	22.3	0.0	22.3	0.0	22.5	0.9
1951	22.5	0.0	22.6	0.4	23.0	1.8	23.0	0.0	23.0	0.0	23.0	0.0	23.4	1.7	24.2	3.4	24.4	0.8	24.5	0.4	24.7	0.8	24.0	-2.8
1952	24.7	2.9	24.9	0.8	24.9	0.0	24.9	0.0	24.9	0.0	26.1	4.8	26.1	0.0	26.1	0.0	26.1	0.0	26.1	0.0	26.1	0.0	26.1	0.0
1953	26.3	0.8	26.3	0.0	26.2	-0.4	26.2	0.0	26.1	-0.4	26.2	0.4	26.3	0.4	26.3	0.0	26.2	-0.4	26.1	-0.4	26.0	-0.4	26.0	0.0
1954	26.2	0.8	26.0	-0.8	26.0	0.0	25.9	-0.4	26.2	1.2	26.3	0.4	26.2	-0.4	26.1	-0.4	26.1	0.0	25.0	-4.2	26.2	4.8	26.1	-0.4
1955	26.2	0.4	26.0	-0.8	26.0	0.0	25.3	-2.7	25.5	0.8	25.5	0.0	25.4	-0.4	25.5	0.4	25.5	0.0	25.9	1.6	26.1	0.8	25.7	-1.5
1956	25.6	-0.4	25.6	0.0	25.5	-0.4	25.6	0.4	25.8	0.8	25.8	0.0	26.1	1.2	26.2	0.4	26.2	0.0	27.3	4.2	27.3	0.0	27.3	0.0
1957	27.5	0.7	27.3	-0.7	27.4	0.4	27.3	-0.4	27.2	-0.4	27.2	0.0	28.3	4.0	28.4	0.4	28.1	-1.1	28.0	-0.4	29.2	4.3	29.5	1.0
1958	29.6	0.3	29.2	-1.4	29.0	-0.7	29.0	0.0	29.0	0.0	29.2	0.7	29.1	-0.3	29.3	0.7	29.4	0.3	29.9	1.7	30.1	0.7	30.4	1.0
1959	30.3	-0.3	30.2	-0.3	30.3	0.3	30.3	0.0	30.2	-0.3	30.1	-0.3	30.4	1.0	30.4	0.0	30.4	0.0	31.0	2.0	31.2	0.6	31.3	0.3
1960	30.9	-1.3	30.9	0.0	30.7	-0.6	30.5	-0.7	30.3	-0.7	30.4	0.3	30.5	0.3	30.6	0.3	30.5	-0.3	30.8	1.0	30.7	-0.3	30.5	-0.7
1961	30.3	-0.7	30.2	-0.3	29.8	-1.3	30.0	0.7	30.0	0.0	29.7	-1.0	30.7	3.4	30.8	0.3	30.8	0.0	31.3	1.6	30.8	-1.6	30.5	-1.0
1962	30.7	0.7	30.8	0.3	30.9	0.3	31.3	1.3	31.3	0.0	30.8	-1.6	30.5	-1.0	30.3	-0.7	31.2	3.0	31.3	0.3	31.2	-0.3	31.2	0.0
1963	30.8	-1.3	30.9	0.3	31.3	1.3	31.2	-0.3	31.5	1.0	31.4	-0.3	31.4	0.0	31.3	-0.3	31.0	-1.0	31.4	1.3	31.0	-1.3	31.3	1.0
1964	31.0	-1.0	30.8	-0.6	30.8	0.0	30.7	-0.3	31.3	2.0	31.4	0.3	31.6	0.6	31.4	-0.6	31.2	-0.6	31.4	0.6	31.6	0.6	31.6	0.0
1965	31.9	0.9	31.8	-0.3	31.8	0.0	32.2	1.3	32.2	0.0	32.2	0.0	32.2	0.0	32.0	-0.6	31.8	-0.6	32.1	0.9	32.1	0.0	32.2	0.3
1966	31.9	-0.9	31.9	0.0	31.8	-0.3	31.9	0.3	32.0	0.3	32.1	0.3	32.1	0.0	32.3	0.6	32.2	-0.3	32.3	0.3	32.3	0.0	32.2	-0.3
1967	32.1	-0.3	32.4	0.9	32.5	0.3	32.6	0.3	32.7	0.3	32.8	0.3	32.9	0.3	33.0	0.3	33.3	0.9	33.3	0.0	34.2	2.7	34.1	-0.3
1968	34.2	0.3	34.2	0.0	34.3	0.3	34.4	0.3	34.3	-0.3	34.4	0.3	34.5	0.3	34.4	-0.3	34.4	0.0	34.6	0.6	34.7	0.3	35.4	2.0
1969	35.6	0.6	35.9	0.8	36.6	1.9	36.8	0.5	36.5	-0.8	36.7	0.5	36.7	0.0	36.7	0.0	36.6	-0.3	37.1	1.4	37.1	0.0	37.4	0.8
1970	37.8	1.1	37.5	-0.8	37.4	-0.3	38.0	1.6	38.2	0.5	38.4	0.5	39.6	3.1	39.6	0.0	39.4	-0.5	40.5	2.8	41.0	1.2	41.3	0.7
1971	41.2	-0.2	41.5	0.7	41.3	-0.5	41.3	0.0	41.8	1.2	41.3	-1.2	41.6	0.7	41.8	0.5	41.5	-0.7	41.2	-0.7	41.1	-0.2	41.3	0.5
1972	40.8	-1.2	40.2	-1.5	40.2	0.0	40.5	0.7	40.9	1.0	40.8	-0.2	41.2	1.0	41.4	0.5	41.4	0.0	41.3	-0.2	41.4	0.2	41.4	0.0
1973	41.1	-0.7	41.1	0.0	41.3	0.5	41.7	1.0	42.2	1.2	42.5	0.7	42.5	0.0	42.3	-0.5	42.2	-0.2	42.8	1.4	42.9	0.2	43.3	0.9
1974	43.8	1.2	43.8	0.0	44.6	1.8	45.0	0.9	45.9	2.0	46.6	1.5	47.3	1.5	47.6	0.6	47.8	0.4	48.0	0.4	48.2	0.4	48.2	0.0
1975	47.7	-1.0	47.7	0.0	48.2	1.0	48.6	0.8	49.0	0.8	49.7	1.4	50.8	2.2	51.6	1.6	51.8	0.4	51.8	0.0	52.1	0.6	52.0	-0.2
1976	51.7	-0.6	52.6	1.7	52.9	0.6	53.4	0.9	54.5	2.1	55.3	1.5	55.8	0.9	56.2	0.7	56.9	1.2	57.3	0.7	57.9	1.0	57.8	-0.2
1977	58.1	0.5	58.6	0.9	59.0	0.7	59.9	1.5	60.4	0.8	60.6	0.3	60.5	-0.2	60.4	-0.2	60.0	-0.7	60.1	0.2	60.0	-0.2	60.2	0.3
1978	60.3	0.2	60.3	0.0	60.4	0.2	60.5	0.2	61.2	1.2	62.0	1.3	62.4	0.6	62.7	0.5	62.8	0.2	63.6	1.3	63.9	0.5	64.4	0.8
1979	65.0	0.9	65.6	0.9	66.4	1.2	67.8	2.1	69.3	2.2	71.0	2.5	72.4	2.0	73.6	1.7	74.4	1.1	75.1	0.9	76.0	1.2	77.0	1.3
1980	79.1	2.7	80.6	1.9	82.3	2.1	84.2	2.3	84.8	0.7	84.9	0.1	85.0	0.1	85.3	0.4	85.5	0.2	85.8	0.4	87.6	2.1	88.0	0.5
1981	90.7	3.1	92.2	1.7	93.0	0.9	93.9	1.0	94.5	0.6	94.9	0.4	96.4	1.6	96.6	0.2	97.2	0.6	98.4	1.2	98.9	0.5	99.7	0.8
1982	99.3	-0.4	98.1	-1.2	97.2	-0.9	96.5	-0.7	97.3	0.8	100.1	2.9	100.6	0.5	100.3	-0.3	98.9	-1.4	99.2	0.3	99.0	-0.2	98.0	-1.0
1983	97.3	-0.7	96.1	-1.2	95.2	-0.9	96.8	1.7	98.0	1.2	98.2	0.2	99.1	0.9	100.7	1.6	100.5	-0.2	101.5	1.0	101.7	0.2	101.2	-0.5
1984	101.1	-0.1	100.8	-0.3	101.2	0.4	102.1	0.9	102.4	0.3	102.8	0.4	103.0	0.2	102.7	-0.3	102.8	0.1	103.6	0.8	103.6	0.0	103.3	-0.3
1985	103.2	-0.1	102.9	-0.3	103.9	1.0	104.8	0.9	105.6	0.8	105.5	-0.1	105.7	0.2	105.1	-0.6	103.9	-1.1	104.6	0.7	106.0	1.3	106.0	0.0
1986	105.3	-0.7	103.9	-1.3	100.0	-3.8	97.8	-2.2	99.4	1.6	100.5	1.1	98.3	-2.2	97.3	-1.0	97.3	0.0	98.1	0.8	99.2	1.1	100.1	0.9
1987	101.9	1.8	101.7	-0.2	102.4	0.7	102.9	0.5	104.0	1.1	104.7	0.7	105.3	0.6	105.3	0.0	105.3	0.0	106.3	0.9	106.0	-0.3	105.7	-0.3
1988	105.2	-0.5	105.3	0.1	105.1	-0.2	105.3	0.2	105.4	0.1	105.9	0.5	106.1	0.2	107.2	1.0	107.4	-0.2	107.2	-0.2	107.9	0.7	107.6	-0.3
1989	108.1	0.5	108.3	0.2	108.6	0.3	111.0	2.2	112.7	1.5	113.1	0.4	111.9	-1.1	110.9	-0.9	110.4	-0.5	112.8	2.2	112.0	-0.7	112.0	0.0
1990	115.4	3.0	114.4	-0.9	112.9	-1.3	114.0	1.0	114.4	0.4	115.1	0.6	114.5	-0.5	117.5	2.6	118.3	0.7	122.8	3.8	123.4	0.5	123.5	0.1
1991	121.4	-1.7	119.6	-1.5	117.8	-1.5	117.5	-0.3	119.3	1.5	119.4	0.1	118.6	-0.7	118.8	0.2	118.8	0.0	119.4	0.5	120.6	1.0	120.1	-0.4

[Continued]

Chicago, IL-NW IN
Consumer Price Index - Urban Wage Earners
Base 1982-1984 = 100
Transportation
[Continued]

For 1947-1997. Columns headed % show percentile change in the index from the previous period for which an index is available.

Year	Jan		Feb		Mar		Apr		May		Jun		Jul		Aug		Sep		Oct		Nov		Dec	
	Index	%	Index	%	Index	%	Index	%	Index	%	Index	%	Index	%	Index	%	Index	%	Index	%	Index	%	Index	%
1992	119.6	-0.4	118.5	-0.9	118.3	-0.2	119.5	1.0	121.2	1.4	121.8	0.5	121.8	0.0	121.0	-0.7	121.4	0.3	123.6	1.8	124.3	0.6	123.6	-0.6
1993	122.8	-0.6	122.9	0.1	122.6	-0.2	123.9	1.1	125.3	1.1	124.9	-0.3	124.4	-0.4	123.4	-0.8	123.4	0.0	124.9	1.2	125.4	0.4	124.4	-0.8
1994	123.5	-0.7	124.4	0.7	124.5	0.1	125.7	1.0	126.7	0.8	128.2	1.2	129.9	1.3	131.4	1.2	131.5	0.1	131.0	-0.4	132.0	0.8	131.5	-0.4
1995	131.5	0.0	131.5	0.0	132.6	0.8	133.5	0.7	134.7	0.9	136.1	1.0	134.6	-1.1	133.6	-0.7	133.2	-0.3	134.0	0.6	133.1	-0.7	133.3	0.2
1996	134.6	1.0	134.7	0.1	136.5	1.3	138.0	1.1	140.2	1.6	139.6	-0.4	138.4	-0.9	137.6	-0.6	137.7	0.1	138.4	0.5	140.4	1.4	140.5	0.1
1997	139.8	-0.5	139.5	-0.2	138.7	-0.6	137.9	-0.6	138.4	0.4	137.6	-0.6	136.8	-0.6	137.3	0.4	136.9	-0.3	136.6	-0.2	135.8	-0.6	135.7	-0.1

Source: U.S. Department of Labor, Bureau of Labor Statistics, Division of Consumer Prices and Price Indexes. - indicates no data collected for period.

Chicago, IL-NW IN
Consumer Price Index - All Urban Consumers
Base 1982-1984 = 100
Medical Care

For 1947-1997. Columns headed % show percentile change in the index from the previous period for which an index is available.

Year	Jan Index	%	Feb Index	%	Mar Index	%	Apr Index	%	May Index	%	Jun Index	%	Jul Index	%	Aug Index	%	Sep Index	%	Oct Index	%	Nov Index	%	Dec Index	%
1947	11.7	-	11.7	0.0	11.9	1.7	12.0	0.8	12.1	0.8	12.2	0.8	12.2	0.0	12.4	1.6	12.4	0.0	12.4	0.0	12.4	0.0	12.5	0.8
1948	12.7	1.6	12.7	0.0	12.7	0.0	12.8	0.8	12.9	0.8	12.9	0.0	12.9	0.0	13.0	0.8	13.0	0.0	13.0	0.0	13.3	2.3	13.3	0.0
1949	13.4	0.8	13.4	0.0	13.6	1.5	13.6	0.0	13.6	0.0	13.6	0.0	13.6	0.0	13.6	0.0	13.5	-0.7	13.5	0.0	13.5	0.0	13.5	0.0
1950	13.5	0.0	13.5	0.0	13.5	0.0	13.5	0.0	13.5	0.0	13.5	0.0	13.5	0.0	13.6	0.7	14.2	4.4	14.2	0.0	14.2	0.0	14.3	0.7
1951	14.3	0.0	14.3	0.0	14.4	0.7	14.5	0.7	14.5	0.0	14.5	0.0	14.5	0.0	14.5	0.0	14.7	1.4	14.7	0.0	14.8	0.7	14.8	0.0
1952	14.8	0.0	14.8	0.0	14.9	0.7	14.9	0.0	14.9	0.0	14.9	0.0	14.9	0.0	14.9	0.0	14.9	0.0	14.9	0.0	14.9	0.0	15.0	0.7
1953	15.0	0.0	15.0	0.0	15.0	0.0	15.4	2.7	15.4	0.0	15.4	0.0	15.6	1.3	15.6	0.0	15.6	0.0	15.7	0.6	15.8	0.6	15.8	0.0
1954	15.8	0.0	15.8	0.0	15.8	0.0	15.8	0.0	15.8	0.0	15.8	0.0	15.8	0.0	15.8	0.0	15.8	0.0	16.2	2.5	16.2	0.0	16.2	0.0
1955	16.4	1.2	16.4	0.0	16.4	0.0	16.5	0.6	16.5	0.0	16.5	0.0	16.5	0.0	16.5	0.0	16.5	0.0	16.6	0.6	17.2	3.6	17.2	0.0
1956	17.4	1.2	17.4	0.0	17.4	0.0	17.6	1.1	17.6	0.0	17.5	-0.6	17.6	0.6	17.6	0.0	17.6	0.0	17.7	0.6	17.8	0.6	17.8	0.0
1957	17.9	0.6	17.9	0.0	18.0	0.6	18.2	1.1	18.2	0.0	18.2	0.0	18.2	0.0	18.2	0.0	18.2	0.0	18.8	3.3	18.9	0.5	18.9	0.0
1958	19.3	2.1	19.3	0.0	19.3	0.0	19.4	0.5	19.4	0.0	19.4	0.0	19.4	0.0	19.4	0.0	19.4	0.0	19.5	0.5	19.5	0.0	19.5	0.0
1959	19.5	0.0	20.1	3.1	20.1	0.0	20.4	1.5	20.4	0.0	20.4	0.0	20.4	0.0	20.4	0.0	20.4	0.0	20.4	0.0	20.5	0.5	20.6	0.5
1960	20.7	0.5	21.5	3.9	21.5	0.0	21.6	0.5	21.6	0.0	21.6	0.0	21.4	-0.9	21.4	0.0	21.4	0.0	21.4	0.0	21.7	1.4	21.7	0.0
1961	21.9	0.9	21.9	0.0	21.9	0.0	21.9	0.0	21.9	0.0	21.9	0.0	21.9	0.0	21.9	0.0	21.9	0.0	22.3	1.8	22.3	0.0	22.3	0.0
1962	22.6	1.3	22.6	0.0	22.6	0.0	22.7	0.4	22.7	0.0	22.7	0.0	22.7	0.0	22.7	0.0	22.7	0.0	22.9	0.9	22.9	0.0	22.9	0.0
1963	24.1	5.2	24.1	0.0	24.1	0.0	24.2	0.4	24.3	0.4	24.3	0.0	24.4	0.4	24.4	0.0	24.4	0.0	24.5	0.4	24.5	0.0	24.5	0.0
1964	24.6	0.4	24.6	0.0	24.6	0.0	24.6	0.0	24.6	0.0	24.6	0.0	24.8	0.8	24.8	0.0	24.7	-0.4	24.8	0.4	24.9	0.4	24.9	0.0
1965	24.9	0.0	25.0	0.4	25.0	0.0	25.0	0.0	25.0	0.0	25.1	0.4	25.2	0.4	25.2	0.0	25.2	0.0	25.3	0.4	25.3	0.0	25.4	0.4
1966	25.5	0.4	25.6	0.4	25.6	0.0	25.6	0.0	25.7	0.4	25.8	0.4	25.9	0.4	26.0	0.4	26.3	1.2	26.4	0.4	26.5	0.4	26.7	0.8
1967	26.9	0.7	27.0	0.4	27.5	1.9	27.5	0.0	27.7	0.7	27.8	0.4	28.1	1.1	28.3	0.7	28.6	1.1	28.6	0.0	28.7	0.3	28.8	0.3
1968	29.0	0.7	29.3	1.0	29.4	0.3	29.6	0.7	29.5	-0.3	29.5	0.0	29.5	0.0	29.6	0.3	29.7	0.3	29.8	0.3	30.1	1.0	30.3	0.7
1969	30.4	0.3	30.6	0.7	30.7	0.3	31.3	2.0	31.4	0.3	31.5	0.3	31.5	0.0	31.6	0.3	32.0	1.3	31.9	-0.3	32.1	0.6	32.1	0.0
1970	32.3	0.6	32.5	0.6	33.0	1.5	33.1	0.3	33.2	0.3	33.2	0.0	33.3	0.3	33.8	1.5	34.2	1.2	34.5	0.9	34.6	0.3	34.8	0.6
1971	35.2	1.1	35.6	1.1	35.7	0.3	35.7	0.0	35.9	0.6	36.0	0.3	36.1	0.3	36.3	0.6	36.3	0.0	36.0	-0.8	36.0	0.0	36.1	0.3
1972	36.2	0.3	36.4	0.6	36.4	0.0	36.5	0.3	36.7	0.5	36.7	0.0	36.8	0.3	36.9	0.3	36.9	0.0	37.2	0.8	37.4	0.5	37.4	0.0
1973	37.6	0.5	37.6	0.0	37.8	0.5	37.8	0.0	38.0	0.5	38.0	0.0	38.2	0.5	38.2	0.0	38.6	1.0	39.2	1.6	39.3	0.3	39.3	0.0
1974	39.7	1.0	40.1	1.0	40.4	0.7	40.4	0.0	41.0	1.5	42.1	2.7	42.3	0.5	42.7	0.9	43.2	1.2	43.5	0.7	43.9	0.9	44.4	1.1
1975	45.0	1.4	45.3	0.7	45.8	1.1	45.9	0.2	46.2	0.7	47.0	1.7	47.7	1.5	48.3	1.3	48.7	0.8	49.2	1.0	48.8	-0.8	49.3	1.0
1976	49.7	0.8	50.6	1.8	51.5	1.8	51.8	0.6	52.2	0.8	52.5	0.6	53.2	1.3	53.5	0.6	54.0	0.9	54.3	0.6	54.8	0.9	55.1	0.5
1977	55.7	1.1	56.5	1.4	56.7	0.4	57.1	0.7	57.4	0.5	57.9	0.9	58.3	0.7	58.6	0.5	59.1	0.9	59.5	0.7	59.6	0.2	59.7	0.2
1978	60.4	1.2	60.7	0.5	60.9	0.3	61.3	0.7	61.5	0.3	61.6	-0.2	62.2	1.0	62.1	-0.2	62.3	0.3	63.6	2.1	64.4	1.3	64.5	0.2
1979	65.4	1.4	65.4	0.0	65.5	0.2	65.9	0.6	67.1	1.8	67.1	0.0	68.4	1.9	68.5	0.1	68.6	0.1	68.7	0.1	69.0	0.4	71.5	3.6
1980	72.8	1.8	73.8	1.4	74.3	0.7	75.8	2.0	76.3	0.7	76.5	0.3	77.2	0.9	77.5	0.4	77.6	0.1	77.8	0.3	77.8	0.0	78.6	1.0
1981	80.1	1.9	80.7	0.7	81.2	0.6	82.8	2.0	83.1	0.4	84.6	1.8	84.9	0.4	86.1	1.4	86.2	0.1	86.6	0.5	87.0	0.5	88.0	1.1
1982	87.9	-0.1	88.8	1.0	89.3	0.6	90.2	1.0	90.6	0.4	91.8	1.3	93.0	1.3	93.3	0.3	93.5	0.2	94.3	0.9	95.7	1.5	97.2	1.6
1983	98.7	1.5	99.4	0.7	99.8	0.4	100.2	0.4	100.3	0.1	100.8	0.5	101.4	0.6	101.4	0.0	102.4	1.0	102.6	0.2	102.7	0.1	103.1	0.4
1984	104.6	1.5	105.1	0.5	105.1	0.0	105.1	0.0	105.0	-0.1	106.8	1.7	107.8	0.9	107.6	-0.2	107.7	0.1	108.8	1.0	108.9	0.1	109.3	0.4
1985	109.9	0.5	110.0	0.1	111.4	1.3	111.7	0.3	112.3	0.5	112.6	0.3	112.7	0.1	113.3	0.5	114.6	1.1	114.7	0.1	115.1	0.3	115.2	0.1
1986	116.3	1.0	117.1	0.7	118.0	0.8	118.7	0.6	119.2	0.4	119.5	0.3	121.0	1.3	121.1	0.1	122.0	0.7	122.6	0.5	122.7	0.1	123.1	0.3
1987	124.4	1.1	125.7	1.0	125.9	0.2	126.3	0.3	127.6	1.0	129.4	1.4	130.6	0.9	130.9	0.2	132.0	0.8	132.3	0.2	132.7	0.3	132.9	0.2
1988	134.2	1.0	134.8	0.4	135.6	0.6	135.9	0.2	136.4	0.4	137.4	0.7	139.9	1.8	139.5	-0.3	140.4	0.6	140.9	0.4	140.5	-0.3	140.8	0.2
1989	142.1	0.9	143.7	1.1	144.7	0.7	144.9	0.1	146.0	0.8	147.2	0.8	150.2	2.0	152.1	1.3	153.9	1.2	155.2	0.8	155.3	0.1	155.6	0.2
1990	156.2	0.4	157.6	0.9	158.9	0.8	160.2	0.8	161.5	0.8	162.0	0.3	164.3	1.4	165.3	0.6	166.8	0.9	167.4	0.4	168.0	0.4	168.2	0.1
1991	170.2	1.2	172.9	1.6	175.0	1.2	175.7	0.4	176.4	0.4	176.9	0.3	179.2	1.3	179.7	0.3	181.3	0.9	181.3	0.0	183.0	0.9	183.7	0.4

[Continued]

Chicago, IL-NW IN
Consumer Price Index - All Urban Consumers
Base 1982-1984 = 100
Medical Care
[Continued]

For 1947-1997. Columns headed % show percentile change in the index from the previous period for which an index is available.

Year	Jan Index	%	Feb Index	%	Mar Index	%	Apr Index	%	May Index	%	Jun Index	%	Jul Index	%	Aug Index	%	Sep Index	%	Oct Index	%	Nov Index	%	Dec Index	%
1992	185.1	0.8	186.9	1.0	189.4	1.3	189.5	0.1	189.9	0.2	190.2	0.2	191.3	0.6	191.7	0.2	193.1	0.7	192.9	-0.1	194.0	0.6	194.7	0.4
1993	198.4	1.9	199.3	0.5	200.5	0.6	201.0	0.2	202.1	0.5	203.1	0.5	204.8	0.8	205.3	0.2	205.3	0.0	205.4	0.0	205.7	0.1	206.2	0.2
1994	209.6	1.6	210.8	0.6	211.1	0.1	211.1	0.0	211.6	0.2	212.9	0.6	214.5	0.8	214.2	-0.1	215.0	0.4	215.2	0.1	215.5	0.1	217.0	0.7
1995	220.8	1.8	221.7	0.4	221.9	0.1	222.3	0.2	223.2	0.4	222.6	-0.3	223.7	0.5	224.5	0.4	224.5	0.0	225.2	0.3	225.4	0.1	224.2	-0.5
1996	227.3	1.4	227.9	0.3	228.1	0.1	228.1	0.0	228.3	0.1	229.3	0.4	230.7	0.6	229.5	-0.5	230.0	0.2	231.3	0.6	231.0	-0.1	231.7	0.3
1997	233.4	0.7	234.2	0.3	234.4	0.1	234.7	0.1	235.3	0.3	235.6	0.1	236.6	0.4	235.6	-0.4	235.2	-0.2	236.8	0.7	236.7	-0.0	237.0	0.1

Source: U.S. Department of Labor, Bureau of Labor Statistics, Division of Consumer Prices and Price Indexes. - indicates no data collected for period.

Chicago, IL-NW IN
Consumer Price Index - Urban Wage Earners
Base 1982-1984 = 100
Medical Care

For 1947-1997. Columns headed % show percentile change in the index from the previous period for which an index is available.

Year	Jan Index	%	Feb Index	%	Mar Index	%	Apr Index	%	May Index	%	Jun Index	%	Jul Index	%	Aug Index	%	Sep Index	%	Oct Index	%	Nov Index	%	Dec Index	%
1947	11.5	-	11.5	0.0	11.7	1.7	11.8	0.9	11.9	0.8	12.0	0.8	12.0	0.0	12.2	1.7	12.2	0.0	12.2	0.0	12.2	0.0	12.3	0.8
1948	12.5	1.6	12.5	0.0	12.5	0.0	12.6	0.8	12.7	0.8	12.7	0.0	12.7	0.0	12.8	0.8	12.8	0.0	12.8	0.0	13.1	2.3	13.1	0.0
1949	13.2	0.8	13.2	0.0	13.4	1.5	13.4	0.0	13.4	0.0	13.3	-0.7	13.3	0.0	13.3	0.0	13.3	0.0	13.3	0.0	13.2	-0.8	13.2	0.0
1950	13.2	0.0	13.2	0.0	13.3	0.8	13.3	0.0	13.3	0.0	13.3	0.0	13.3	0.0	13.3	0.0	14.0	5.3	14.0	0.0	14.0	0.0	14.1	0.7
1951	14.1	0.0	14.1	0.0	14.2	0.7	14.3	0.7	14.3	0.0	14.3	0.0	14.3	0.0	14.3	0.0	14.4	0.7	14.4	0.0	14.6	1.4	14.6	0.0
1952	14.6	0.0	14.6	0.0	14.6	0.0	14.7	0.7	14.7	0.0	14.7	0.0	14.7	0.0	14.7	0.0	14.7	0.0	14.7	0.0	14.7	0.0	14.8	0.7
1953	14.8	0.0	14.8	0.0	14.8	0.0	15.1	2.0	15.2	0.7	15.2	0.0	15.3	0.7	15.3	0.0	15.3	0.0	15.5	1.3	15.5	0.0	15.5	0.0
1954	15.5	0.0	15.5	0.0	15.5	0.0	15.5	0.0	15.5	0.0	15.5	0.0	15.5	0.0	15.5	0.0	15.5	0.0	16.0	3.2	16.0	0.0	16.0	0.0
1955	16.1	0.6	16.1	0.0	16.1	0.0	16.2	0.6	16.2	0.0	16.3	0.6	16.3	0.0	16.3	0.0	16.3	0.0	16.3	0.0	16.9	3.7	16.9	0.0
1956	17.1	1.2	17.1	0.0	17.1	0.0	17.3	1.2	17.3	0.0	17.3	0.0	17.3	0.0	17.3	0.0	17.3	0.0	17.4	0.6	17.5	0.6	17.5	0.0
1957	17.6	0.6	17.6	0.0	17.7	0.6	17.9	1.1	17.9	0.0	17.9	0.0	17.9	0.0	17.9	0.0	17.9	0.0	18.5	3.4	18.6	0.5	18.6	0.0
1958	19.0	2.2	19.0	0.0	19.0	0.0	19.0	0.0	19.0	0.0	19.0	0.0	19.0	0.0	19.0	0.0	19.1	0.5	19.2	0.5	19.2	0.0	19.2	0.0
1959	19.2	0.0	19.7	2.6	19.7	0.0	20.1	2.0	20.1	0.0	20.1	0.0	20.1	0.0	20.1	0.0	20.1	0.0	20.1	0.0	20.1	0.0	20.2	0.5
1960	20.3	0.5	21.2	4.4	21.2	0.0	21.3	0.5	21.3	0.0	21.3	0.0	21.1	-0.9	21.1	0.0	21.1	0.0	21.3	0.9	21.3	0.0	21.3	0.0
1961	21.5	0.9	21.5	0.0	21.5	0.0	21.5	0.0	21.6	0.5	21.6	0.0	21.5	-0.5	21.5	0.0	21.5	0.0	21.9	1.9	21.9	0.0	21.9	0.0
1962	22.2	1.4	22.2	0.0	22.2	0.0	22.3	0.5	22.3	0.0	22.3	0.0	22.4	0.4	22.4	0.0	22.4	0.0	22.6	0.9	22.6	0.0	22.6	0.0
1963	23.7	4.9	23.7	0.0	23.7	0.0	23.9	0.8	23.9	0.0	23.9	0.0	24.0	0.4	24.0	0.0	24.0	0.0	24.1	0.4	24.1	0.0	24.1	0.0
1964	24.2	0.4	24.2	0.0	24.2	0.0	24.2	0.0	24.2	0.0	24.2	0.0	24.4	0.8	24.4	0.0	24.3	-0.4	24.4	0.4	24.5	0.4	24.5	0.0
1965	24.5	0.0	24.6	0.4	24.6	0.0	24.6	0.0	24.6	0.0	24.7	0.4	24.8	0.4	24.8	0.0	24.8	0.0	24.9	0.4	24.9	0.0	25.0	0.4
1966	25.1	0.4	25.1	0.0	25.1	0.0	25.2	0.4	25.3	0.4	25.3	0.0	25.5	0.8	25.5	0.0	25.8	1.2	25.9	0.4	26.1	0.8	26.3	0.8
1967	26.4	0.4	26.6	0.8	27.0	1.5	27.1	0.4	27.2	0.4	27.4	0.7	27.6	0.7	27.8	0.7	28.1	1.1	28.1	0.0	28.2	0.4	28.4	0.7
1968	28.5	0.4	28.8	1.1	29.0	0.7	29.1	0.3	29.0	-0.3	29.0	0.0	29.1	0.3	29.1	0.0	29.2	0.3	29.3	0.3	29.6	1.0	29.9	1.0
1969	29.9	0.0	30.1	0.7	30.2	0.3	30.8	2.0	30.9	0.3	31.0	0.3	31.0	0.0	31.1	0.3	31.5	1.3	31.4	-0.3	31.6	0.6	31.6	0.0
1970	31.8	0.6	32.0	0.6	32.5	1.6	32.6	0.3	32.7	0.3	32.7	0.0	32.8	0.3	33.2	1.2	33.7	1.5	33.9	0.6	34.0	0.3	34.3	0.9
1971	34.6	0.9	35.0	1.2	35.2	0.6	35.2	0.0	35.4	0.6	35.4	0.0	35.6	0.6	35.7	0.3	35.7	0.0	35.4	-0.8	35.4	0.0	35.5	0.3
1972	35.7	0.6	35.8	0.3	35.9	0.3	35.9	0.0	36.1	0.6	36.1	0.0	36.2	0.3	36.3	0.3	36.3	0.0	36.6	0.8	36.8	0.5	36.8	0.0
1973	37.0	0.5	37.0	0.0	37.2	0.5	37.2	0.0	37.4	0.5	37.4	0.0	37.6	0.5	37.6	0.0	37.9	0.8	38.6	1.8	38.7	0.3	38.7	0.0
1974	39.0	0.8	39.4	1.0	39.8	1.0	39.8	0.0	40.3	1.3	41.5	3.0	41.6	0.2	42.0	1.0	42.5	1.2	42.8	0.7	43.2	0.9	43.7	1.2
1975	44.3	1.4	44.6	0.7	45.1	1.1	45.2	0.2	45.5	0.7	46.3	1.8	46.9	1.3	47.5	1.3	47.9	0.8	48.4	1.0	48.0	-0.8	48.5	1.0
1976	48.9	0.8	49.8	1.8	50.7	1.8	51.0	0.6	51.4	0.8	51.7	0.6	52.4	1.4	52.6	0.4	53.2	1.1	53.4	0.4	53.9	0.9	54.2	0.6
1977	54.8	1.1	55.6	1.5	55.7	0.2	56.2	0.9	56.5	0.5	57.0	0.9	57.4	0.7	57.7	0.5	58.1	0.7	58.5	0.7	58.6	0.2	58.8	0.3
1978	59.2	0.7	59.5	0.5	59.8	0.5	60.3	0.8	60.6	0.5	60.8	0.3	61.5	1.2	61.5	0.0	61.6	0.2	62.9	2.1	63.9	1.6	64.2	0.5
1979	65.3	1.7	65.4	0.2	65.7	0.5	66.0	0.5	66.7	1.1	66.7	0.0	67.7	1.5	67.9	0.3	68.4	0.7	69.2	1.2	69.4	0.3	72.1	3.9
1980	73.9	2.5	74.6	0.9	74.7	0.1	76.1	1.9	76.7	0.8	76.5	-0.3	77.7	1.6	77.9	0.3	78.3	0.5	78.6	0.4	78.8	0.3	79.2	0.5
1981	80.6	1.8	81.5	1.1	81.9	0.5	82.9	1.2	83.6	0.8	84.4	1.0	84.8	0.5	84.8	0.0	85.8	1.2	86.3	0.6	87.6	1.5	88.1	0.6
1982	87.9	-0.2	88.8	1.0	89.3	0.6	90.1	0.9	90.6	0.6	91.8	1.3	93.0	1.3	93.3	0.3	93.4	0.1	94.3	1.0	95.6	1.4	97.1	1.6
1983	98.6	1.5	99.3	0.7	99.8	0.5	100.1	0.3	100.3	0.2	100.8	0.5	101.4	0.6	101.4	0.0	102.4	1.0	102.6	0.2	102.7	0.1	103.2	0.5
1984	104.7	1.5	105.2	0.5	105.2	0.0	105.2	0.0	105.1	-0.1	106.8	1.6	107.8	0.9	107.5	-0.3	107.7	0.2	108.7	0.9	108.9	0.2	109.2	0.3
1985	109.8	0.5	109.9	0.1	111.3	1.3	111.5	0.2	112.2	0.6	112.5	0.3	112.6	0.1	113.2	0.5	114.5	1.1	114.6	0.1	115.0	0.3	115.2	0.2
1986	116.2	0.9	117.0	0.7	117.8	0.7	118.5	0.6	119.1	0.5	119.3	0.2	120.8	1.3	120.8	0.0	121.8	0.8	122.3	0.4	122.4	0.1	122.8	0.3
1987	124.0	1.0	125.3	1.0	125.5	0.2	125.9	0.3	127.2	1.0	128.8	1.3	130.3	1.2	130.6	0.2	131.8	0.9	132.1	0.2	132.4	0.2	132.7	0.2
1988	134.1	1.1	134.9	0.6	135.5	0.4	136.1	0.4	136.6	0.4	137.4	0.6	140.4	2.2	140.1	-0.2	141.0	0.6	141.5	0.4	141.2	-0.2	141.5	0.2
1989	142.9	1.0	144.8	1.3	145.7	0.6	145.8	0.1	147.1	0.9	148.2	0.7	151.6	2.3	153.2	1.1	155.5	1.5	156.7	0.8	156.7	0.0	157.0	0.2
1990	157.5	0.3	158.8	0.8	159.8	0.6	161.4	1.0	162.7	0.8	163.1	0.2	165.8	1.7	166.6	0.5	168.2	1.0	168.6	0.2	169.2	0.4	169.3	0.1
1991	171.6	1.4	174.6	1.7	176.5	1.1	176.8	0.2	177.7	0.5	178.1	0.2	180.6	1.4	181.2	0.3	182.9	0.9	182.8	-0.1	184.8	1.1	185.5	0.4

[Continued]

Chicago, IL-NW IN
Consumer Price Index - Urban Wage Earners
Base 1982-1984 = 100
Medical Care
[Continued]

For 1947-1997. Columns headed % show percentile change in the index from the previous period for which an index is available.

Year	Jan Index	%	Feb Index	%	Mar Index	%	Apr Index	%	May Index	%	Jun Index	%	Jul Index	%	Aug Index	%	Sep Index	%	Oct Index	%	Nov Index	%	Dec Index	%
1992	186.9	0.8	188.6	0.9	190.7	1.1	190.8	0.1	191.2	0.2	191.7	0.3	193.0	0.7	193.5	0.3	195.2	0.9	194.9	-0.2	195.8	0.5	196.7	0.5
1993	200.7	2.0	201.7	0.5	202.9	0.6	203.4	0.2	204.4	0.5	205.3	0.4	207.4	1.0	207.9	0.2	207.9	0.0	208.0	0.0	208.3	0.1	208.7	0.2
1994	212.4	1.8	213.4	0.5	213.6	0.1	213.6	0.0	214.1	0.2	215.5	0.7	217.3	0.8	217.1	-0.1	217.8	0.3	217.9	0.0	218.3	0.2	219.9	0.7
1995	223.9	1.8	225.1	0.5	225.2	0.0	225.7	0.2	226.6	0.4	226.1	-0.2	227.4	0.6	228.4	0.4	228.4	0.0	229.1	0.3	229.3	0.1	228.3	-0.4
1996	231.5	1.4	232.3	0.3	232.5	0.1	232.7	0.1	232.7	0.0	233.8	0.5	235.3	0.6	234.2	-0.5	234.8	0.3	236.1	0.6	235.8	-0.1	236.7	0.4
1997	238.3	0.7	239.0	0.3	239.3	0.1	239.5	0.1	240.1	0.3	240.4	0.1	241.5	0.5	240.3	-0.5	239.9	-0.2	241.4	0.6	241.4	0.0	241.8	0.2

Source: U.S. Department of Labor, Bureau of Labor Statistics, Division of Consumer Prices and Price Indexes. - indicates no data collected for period.

Chicago, IL-NW IN
Consumer Price Index - All Urban Consumers
Base 1982-1984 = 100
Entertainment

For 1976-1997. Columns headed % show percentile change in the index from the previous period for which an index is available.

Year	Jan Index	%	Feb Index	%	Mar Index	%	Apr Index	%	May Index	%	Jun Index	%	Jul Index	%	Aug Index	%	Sep Index	%	Oct Index	%	Nov Index	%	Dec Index	%
1976	60.3	-	60.5	0.3	61.3	1.3	61.6	0.5	61.8	0.3	61.6	-0.3	61.8	0.3	61.9	0.2	62.0	0.2	62.5	0.8	62.8	0.5	62.8	0.0
1977	63.8	1.6	63.8	0.0	64.5	1.1	63.9	-0.9	64.3	0.6	64.3	0.0	64.2	-0.2	64.6	0.6	64.6	0.0	65.2	0.9	65.7	0.8	66.0	0.5
1978	66.7	1.1	67.0	0.4	67.2	0.3	67.4	0.3	67.4	0.0	67.2	-0.3	67.7	0.7	67.9	0.3	68.7	1.2	69.2	0.7	69.6	0.6	69.7	0.1
1979	70.4	1.0	71.8	2.0	73.1	1.8	72.9	-0.3	75.7	3.8	75.7	0.0	77.0	1.7	77.2	0.3	77.6	0.5	78.3	0.9	79.0	0.9	80.3	1.6
1980	80.2	-0.1	82.8	3.2	83.8	1.2	84.0	0.2	84.0	0.0	84.3	0.4	84.9	0.7	85.6	0.8	87.1	1.8	87.5	0.5	87.2	-0.3	87.6	0.5
1981	90.3	3.1	90.4	0.1	89.6	-0.9	91.6	2.2	91.7	0.1	92.1	0.4	92.2	0.1	93.1	1.0	94.4	1.4	93.2	-1.3	94.2	1.1	96.0	1.9
1982	97.1	1.1	97.5	0.4	97.0	-0.5	98.2	1.2	97.3	-0.9	98.0	0.7	98.8	0.8	98.7	-0.1	99.8	1.1	100.6	0.8	97.9	-2.7	99.6	1.7
1983	100.0	0.4	98.8	-1.2	98.6	-0.2	99.3	0.7	99.0	-0.3	99.3	0.3	99.7	0.4	99.2	-0.5	100.4	1.2	100.0	-0.4	100.2	0.2	100.2	0.0
1984	100.5	0.3	100.7	0.2	100.7	0.0	100.7	0.0	100.8	0.1	101.8	1.0	101.3	-0.5	102.0	0.7	104.3	2.3	104.4	0.1	103.1	-1.2	104.3	1.2
1985	104.5	0.2	105.7	1.1	105.2	-0.5	106.7	1.4	106.3	-0.4	105.5	-0.8	105.8	0.3	105.5	-0.3	103.2	-2.2	103.5	0.3	104.5	1.0	104.9	0.4
1986	107.6	2.6	108.2	0.6	108.5	0.3	108.6	0.1	108.2	-0.4	108.2	0.0	109.7	1.4	107.9	-1.6	111.4	3.2	112.8	1.3	113.8	0.9	113.3	-0.4
1987	114.1	0.7	113.9	-0.2	115.6	1.5	116.0	0.3	115.6	-0.3	115.6	0.0	116.3	0.6	115.3	-0.9	116.6	1.1	117.4	0.7	117.5	0.1	118.1	0.5
1988	118.9	0.7	119.0	0.1	120.3	1.1	121.1	0.7	120.3	-0.7	121.3	0.8	122.0	0.6	123.1	0.9	124.0	0.7	125.5	1.2	126.2	0.6	125.8	-0.3
1989	126.9	0.9	128.7	1.4	130.3	1.2	130.5	0.2	130.3	-0.2	132.4	1.6	133.3	0.7	131.3	-1.5	132.7	1.1	134.3	1.2	135.2	0.7	133.2	-1.5
1990	136.0	2.1	136.8	0.6	137.7	0.7	137.8	0.1	139.2	1.0	138.3	-0.6	139.0	0.5	139.9	0.6	140.3	0.3	141.2	0.6	141.3	0.1	142.5	0.8
1991	144.8	1.6	144.6	-0.1	144.4	-0.1	144.7	0.2	145.8	0.8	147.0	0.8	144.4	-1.8	146.5	1.5	148.4	1.3	147.1	-0.9	147.0	-0.1	146.2	-0.5
1992	147.3	0.8	146.9	-0.3	148.0	0.7	148.7	0.5	148.3	-0.3	148.1	-0.1	151.5	2.3	150.7	-0.5	151.3	0.4	151.2	-0.1	150.7	-0.3	150.3	-0.3
1993	151.0	0.5	152.7	1.1	152.9	0.1	153.9	0.7	152.4	-1.0	155.2	1.8	153.9	-0.8	153.4	-0.3	155.2	1.2	154.7	-0.3	154.8	0.1	156.6	1.2
1994	158.4	1.1	157.2	-0.8	159.0	1.1	159.6	0.4	160.3	0.4	158.9	-0.9	159.8	0.6	161.4	1.0	162.7	0.8	163.1	0.2	162.1	-0.6	157.9	-2.6
1995	159.1	0.8	160.2	0.7	160.0	-0.1	160.6	0.4	160.4	-0.1	160.0	-0.2	160.4	0.2	162.7	1.4	162.6	-0.1	160.4	-1.4	162.0	1.0	162.4	0.2
1996	162.0	-0.2	163.6	1.0	162.8	-0.5	162.0	-0.5	162.9	0.6	167.7	2.9	167.9	0.1	170.5	1.5	170.3	-0.1	171.3	0.6	172.2	0.5	172.6	0.2
1997	172.0	-0.3	172.5	0.3	173.1	0.3	174.0	0.5	172.8	-0.7	182.2	5.4	181.9	-0.2	184.2	1.3	173.4	-5.9	173.4	0.0	171.8	-0.9	172.2	0.2

Source: U.S. Department of Labor, Bureau of Labor Statistics, Division of Consumer Prices and Price Indexes. - indicates no data collected for period.

Chicago, IL-NW IN
Consumer Price Index - Urban Wage Earners
Base 1982-1984 = 100
Entertainment

For 1976-1997. Columns headed % show percentile change in the index from the previous period for which an index is available.

Year	Jan Index	%	Feb Index	%	Mar Index	%	Apr Index	%	May Index	%	Jun Index	%	Jul Index	%	Aug Index	%	Sep Index	%	Oct Index	%	Nov Index	%	Dec Index	%
1976	53.4	-	53.5	0.2	54.3	1.5	54.6	0.6	54.7	0.2	54.5	-0.4	54.7	0.4	54.8	0.2	54.9	0.2	55.3	0.7	55.6	0.5	55.6	0.0
1977	56.5	1.6	56.5	0.0	57.1	1.1	56.6	-0.9	56.9	0.5	56.9	0.0	56.9	0.0	57.2	0.5	57.2	0.0	57.8	1.0	58.2	0.7	58.4	0.3
1978	58.8	0.7	59.4	1.0	59.4	0.0	59.3	-0.2	59.4	0.2	59.0	-0.7	59.6	1.0	59.7	0.2	60.1	0.7	60.4	0.5	60.9	0.8	60.8	-0.2
1979	60.9	0.2	61.8	1.5	63.3	2.4	63.3	0.0	66.5	5.1	68.3	2.7	69.3	1.5	69.5	0.3	69.5	0.0	70.3	1.2	71.0	1.0	72.3	1.8
1980	71.8	-0.7	74.1	3.2	74.7	0.8	75.0	0.4	75.3	0.4	76.9	2.1	76.8	-0.1	77.4	0.8	78.3	1.2	82.2	5.0	82.8	0.7	83.1	0.4
1981	84.9	2.2	85.4	0.6	84.6	-0.9	86.1	1.8	86.6	0.6	85.9	-0.8	86.4	0.6	87.5	1.3	86.8	-0.8	93.2	7.4	94.8	1.7	95.0	0.2
1982	96.4	1.5	96.4	0.0	96.0	-0.4	97.0	1.0	95.9	-1.1	96.8	0.9	97.7	0.9	97.6	-0.1	98.9	1.3	99.5	0.6	97.4	-2.1	98.9	1.5
1983	99.3	0.4	99.0	-0.3	98.9	-0.1	99.7	0.8	99.3	-0.4	99.8	0.5	100.0	0.2	99.5	-0.5	100.9	1.4	100.5	-0.4	100.7	0.2	100.8	0.1
1984	101.1	0.3	101.2	0.1	101.0	-0.2	101.4	0.4	101.5	0.1	102.4	0.9	101.8	-0.6	102.6	0.8	105.4	2.7	105.4	0.0	104.0	-1.3	105.3	1.3
1985	106.2	0.9	106.7	0.5	105.9	-0.7	107.5	1.5	107.2	-0.3	106.1	-1.0	106.4	0.3	106.1	-0.3	103.0	-2.9	103.5	0.5	105.0	1.4	105.5	0.5
1986	108.9	3.2	109.2	0.3	109.5	0.3	109.7	0.2	109.0	-0.6	109.0	0.0	110.5	1.4	108.4	-1.9	112.6	3.9	114.4	1.6	115.4	0.9	114.7	-0.6
1987	115.6	0.8	115.4	-0.2	117.5	1.8	118.0	0.4	117.9	-0.1	117.6	-0.3	118.3	0.6	117.4	-0.8	118.7	1.1	119.5	0.7	119.6	0.1	120.3	0.6
1988	120.9	0.5	121.1	0.2	122.4	1.1	123.2	0.7	122.6	-0.5	123.6	0.8	123.9	0.2	124.9	0.8	125.4	0.4	127.0	1.3	127.9	0.7	127.5	-0.3
1989	128.5	0.8	130.4	1.5	132.0	1.2	132.2	0.2	132.2	0.0	133.3	0.8	134.1	0.6	132.5	-1.2	134.0	1.1	135.3	1.0	136.2	0.7	134.3	-1.4
1990	137.0	2.0	137.6	0.4	138.6	0.7	139.0	0.3	140.1	0.8	139.1	-0.7	139.6	0.4	140.8	0.9	141.1	0.2	142.1	0.7	142.1	0.0	143.3	0.8
1991	145.1	1.3	144.9	-0.1	144.5	-0.3	145.2	0.5	146.0	0.6	147.0	0.7	143.8	-2.2	146.4	1.8	148.5	1.4	147.0	-1.0	147.0	0.0	146.2	-0.5
1992	147.3	0.8	146.9	-0.3	147.9	0.7	148.9	0.7	148.4	-0.3	148.2	-0.1	151.8	2.4	151.0	-0.5	151.6	0.4	151.1	-0.3	150.4	-0.5	150.0	-0.3
1993	150.9	0.6	152.4	1.0	152.6	0.1	153.7	0.7	152.2	-1.0	155.2	2.0	153.9	-0.8	153.3	-0.4	155.0	1.1	154.3	-0.5	154.4	0.1	156.2	1.2
1994	157.8	1.0	156.3	-1.0	158.1	1.2	158.7	0.4	159.6	0.6	158.3	-0.8	159.3	0.6	160.7	0.9	162.3	1.0	162.6	0.2	161.7	-0.6	157.0	-2.9
1995	158.7	1.1	159.6	0.6	159.5	-0.1	160.1	0.4	159.4	-0.4	158.8	-0.4	159.4	0.4	161.9	1.6	161.7	-0.1	159.5	-1.4	161.1	1.0	161.5	0.2
1996	160.9	-0.4	162.7	1.1	161.9	-0.5	160.8	-0.7	162.0	0.7	166.8	3.0	166.2	-0.4	169.4	1.9	168.7	-0.4	169.8	0.7	170.5	0.4	171.4	0.5
1997	170.5	-0.5	171.1	0.4	171.6	0.3	172.4	0.5	171.4	-0.6	180.3	5.2	180.2	-0.1	182.6	1.3	172.2	-5.7	172.3	0.1	170.2	-1.2	170.9	0.4

Source: U.S. Department of Labor, Bureau of Labor Statistics, Division of Consumer Prices and Price Indexes. - indicates no data collected for period.

Chicago, IL-NW IN
Consumer Price Index - All Urban Consumers
Base 1982-1984 = 100
Other Goods and Services

For 1976-1997. Columns headed % show percentile change in the index from the previous period for which an index is available.

Year	Jan Index	%	Feb Index	%	Mar Index	%	Apr Index	%	May Index	%	Jun Index	%	Jul Index	%	Aug Index	%	Sep Index	%	Oct Index	%	Nov Index	%	Dec Index	%
1976	56.7	-	56.9	0.4	57.2	0.5	57.3	0.2	57.4	0.2	57.8	0.7	57.8	0.0	57.9	0.2	58.6	1.2	59.0	0.7	59.8	1.4	59.9	0.2
1977	60.5	1.0	60.2	-0.5	60.8	1.0	61.0	0.3	61.2	0.3	61.4	0.3	62.0	1.0	62.2	0.3	63.5	2.1	64.3	1.3	64.3	0.0	64.4	0.2
1978	64.7	0.5	64.6	-0.2	64.3	-0.5	64.4	0.2	65.3	1.4	65.1	-0.3	65.7	0.9	65.4	-0.5	67.8	3.7	67.5	-0.4	67.4	-0.1	67.1	-0.4
1979	68.1	1.5	68.2	0.1	69.1	1.3	68.2	-1.3	69.0	1.2	68.5	-0.7	69.2	1.0	68.5	-1.0	71.5	4.4	71.3	-0.3	72.0	1.0	72.8	1.1
1980	72.8	0.0	73.6	1.1	74.1	0.7	74.4	0.4	74.7	0.4	75.8	1.5	75.6	-0.3	75.8	0.3	78.0	2.9	78.6	0.8	79.7	1.4	80.1	0.5
1981	80.5	0.5	81.1	0.7	81.5	0.5	82.8	1.6	84.0	1.4	84.2	0.2	84.4	0.2	84.9	0.6	87.2	2.7	87.7	0.6	87.8	0.1	88.4	0.7
1982	88.5	0.1	89.2	0.8	89.6	0.4	90.0	0.4	89.9	-0.1	90.4	0.6	90.6	0.2	90.7	0.1	94.7	4.4	95.3	0.6	96.5	1.3	97.0	0.5
1983	98.3	1.3	98.6	0.3	98.8	0.2	98.8	0.0	98.8	0.0	99.3	0.5	99.5	0.2	100.0	0.5	102.9	2.9	103.6	0.7	103.6	0.0	104.1	0.5
1984	104.9	0.8	105.8	0.9	105.8	0.0	105.6	-0.2	105.9	0.3	106.8	0.8	107.3	0.5	107.8	0.5	109.6	1.7	110.5	0.8	110.6	0.1	110.6	0.0
1985	112.2	1.4	113.3	1.0	113.1	-0.2	113.1	0.0	113.5	0.4	113.7	0.2	113.9	0.2	113.5	-0.4	117.5	3.5	117.8	0.3	118.1	0.3	121.4	2.8
1986	122.2	0.7	122.8	0.5	123.1	0.2	123.2	0.1	122.8	-0.3	123.1	0.2	124.5	1.1	124.0	-0.4	125.7	1.4	126.5	0.6	126.3	-0.2	126.4	0.1
1987	127.7	1.0	128.2	0.4	128.2	0.0	128.4	0.2	129.2	0.6	129.4	0.2	129.9	0.4	130.5	0.5	130.7	0.2	131.0	0.2	131.2	0.2	131.2	0.0
1988	132.6	1.1	134.9	1.7	135.4	0.4	135.6	0.1	135.6	0.0	135.8	0.1	136.8	0.7	137.7	0.7	142.7	3.6	143.1	0.3	143.2	0.1	143.0	-0.1
1989	144.7	1.2	147.2	1.7	147.9	0.5	148.0	0.1	148.6	0.4	152.5	2.6	155.1	1.7	156.8	1.1	157.9	0.7	158.7	0.5	159.0	0.2	160.3	0.8
1990	159.7	-0.4	160.7	0.6	161.1	0.2	161.5	0.2	162.2	0.4	162.8	0.4	163.1	0.2	164.3	0.7	167.0	1.6	167.8	0.5	170.2	1.4	171.3	0.6
1991	172.8	0.9	174.1	0.8	174.6	0.3	175.9	0.7	175.4	-0.3	175.5	0.1	177.3	1.0	178.3	0.6	184.9	3.7	185.5	0.3	187.0	0.8	186.8	-0.1
1992	186.7	-0.1	188.0	0.7	187.7	-0.2	188.7	0.5	189.9	0.6	189.4	-0.3	191.3	1.0	194.4	1.6	196.2	0.9	196.7	0.3	196.8	0.1	197.6	0.4
1993	198.2	0.3	196.4	-0.9	198.5	1.1	198.5	0.0	204.0	2.8	201.8	-1.1	204.5	1.3	204.8	0.1	206.6	0.9	204.9	-0.8	205.7	0.4	206.1	0.2
1994	206.6	0.2	205.4	-0.6	206.0	0.3	206.3	0.1	206.6	0.1	205.9	-0.3	207.3	0.7	209.0	0.8	211.9	1.4	213.4	0.7	213.5	0.0	214.0	0.2
1995	214.4	0.2	215.2	0.4	214.6	-0.3	214.7	0.0	214.9	0.1	216.1	0.6	216.6	0.2	217.1	0.2	219.3	1.0	219.4	0.0	219.5	0.0	219.6	0.0
1996	219.2	-0.2	219.4	0.1	219.9	0.2	219.7	-0.1	220.5	0.4	221.3	0.4	221.9	0.3	221.6	-0.1	225.0	1.5	226.5	0.7	226.8	0.1	226.4	-0.2
1997	227.0	0.3	229.0	0.9	228.9	-0.0	231.0	0.9	232.4	0.6	230.9	-0.6	231.4	0.2	234.5	1.3	237.7	1.4	238.1	0.2	238.3	0.1	240.1	0.8

Source: U.S. Department of Labor, Bureau of Labor Statistics, Division of Consumer Prices and Price Indexes. - indicates no data collected for period.

Chicago, IL-NW IN
Consumer Price Index - Urban Wage Earners
Base 1982-1984 = 100
Other Goods and Services

For 1976-1997. Columns headed % show percentile change in the index from the previous period for which an index is available.

Year	Jan Index	%	Feb Index	%	Mar Index	%	Apr Index	%	May Index	%	Jun Index	%	Jul Index	%	Aug Index	%	Sep Index	%	Oct Index	%	Nov Index	%	Dec Index	%
1976	58.2	-	58.5	0.5	58.8	0.5	58.9	0.2	59.0	0.2	59.4	0.7	59.3	-0.2	59.5	0.3	60.2	1.2	60.6	0.7	61.5	1.5	61.6	0.2
1977	62.2	1.0	61.9	-0.5	62.4	0.8	62.7	0.5	62.9	0.3	63.1	0.3	63.7	1.0	63.9	0.3	65.2	2.0	66.0	1.2	66.1	0.2	66.2	0.2
1978	66.3	0.2	66.5	0.3	66.5	0.0	67.2	1.1	67.2	0.0	67.7	0.7	68.5	1.2	68.7	0.3	69.6	1.3	69.8	0.3	69.9	0.1	70.0	0.1
1979	70.6	0.9	71.1	0.7	71.3	0.3	71.2	-0.1	71.2	0.0	70.9	-0.4	71.0	0.1	71.1	0.1	72.5	2.0	72.6	0.1	73.3	1.0	74.0	1.0
1980	74.9	1.2	75.7	1.1	76.0	0.4	76.4	0.5	77.0	0.8	78.2	1.6	78.3	0.1	78.4	0.1	80.0	2.0	80.2	0.2	80.9	0.9	81.2	0.4
1981	81.7	0.6	82.1	0.5	82.4	0.4	82.8	0.5	83.7	1.1	83.3	-0.5	84.1	1.0	85.4	1.5	87.7	2.7	88.2	0.6	88.3	0.1	88.4	0.1
1982	88.5	0.1	89.3	0.9	89.8	0.6	90.3	0.6	90.1	-0.2	90.6	0.6	90.8	0.2	90.9	0.1	94.1	3.5	94.9	0.9	96.3	1.5	96.9	0.6
1983	98.6	1.8	99.0	0.4	99.2	0.2	99.2	0.0	99.2	0.0	99.8	0.6	100.0	0.2	100.6	0.6	102.2	1.6	103.1	0.9	103.0	-0.1	103.6	0.6
1984	104.6	1.0	105.6	1.0	105.6	0.0	105.5	-0.1	105.9	0.4	106.7	0.8	107.4	0.7	108.0	0.6	109.4	1.3	110.4	0.9	110.5	0.1	110.5	0.0
1985	112.5	1.8	113.7	1.1	113.4	-0.3	113.5	0.1	113.8	0.3	114.1	0.3	114.3	0.2	114.0	-0.3	116.8	2.5	117.1	0.3	117.5	0.3	121.5	3.4
1986	122.7	1.0	123.3	0.5	123.8	0.4	123.9	0.1	123.4	-0.4	123.8	0.3	125.6	1.5	125.1	-0.4	126.0	0.7	126.8	0.6	126.6	-0.2	126.7	0.1
1987	128.1	1.1	128.6	0.4	128.5	-0.1	128.8	0.2	129.7	0.7	129.9	0.2	130.6	0.5	131.3	0.5	131.7	0.3	132.0	0.2	132.3	0.2	132.4	0.1
1988	134.5	1.6	135.6	0.8	136.1	0.4	136.4	0.2	136.5	0.1	136.7	0.1	138.2	1.1	138.9	0.5	141.9	2.2	142.4	0.4	142.6	0.1	142.5	-0.1
1989	144.8	1.6	146.6	1.2	147.5	0.6	147.6	0.1	148.1	0.3	152.3	2.8	156.2	2.6	158.6	1.5	158.7	0.1	159.9	0.8	160.2	0.2	162.2	1.2
1990	161.0	-0.7	162.5	0.9	163.0	0.3	163.3	0.2	164.3	0.6	165.3	0.6	165.6	0.2	166.7	0.7	168.5	1.1	169.3	0.5	171.9	1.5	173.5	0.9
1991	175.5	1.2	177.2	1.0	177.8	0.3	179.6	1.0	179.0	-0.3	179.8	0.4	181.7	1.1	182.6	0.5	187.4	2.6	187.7	0.2	190.1	1.3	189.9	-0.1
1992	189.8	-0.1	191.1	0.7	190.7	-0.2	192.6	1.0	194.0	0.7	193.4	-0.3	196.1	1.4	199.4	1.7	200.2	0.4	200.7	0.2	201.0	0.1	202.1	0.5
1993	203.1	0.5	200.5	-1.3	202.4	0.9	202.8	0.2	210.6	3.8	207.6	-1.4	210.8	1.5	210.7	-0.0	209.9	-0.4	207.6	-1.1	208.7	0.5	209.2	0.2
1994	209.7	0.2	208.4	-0.6	209.1	0.3	209.4	0.1	209.6	0.1	208.9	-0.3	210.1	0.6	211.6	0.7	213.5	0.9	214.7	0.6	214.9	0.1	215.5	0.3
1995	215.3	-0.1	216.2	0.4	215.2	-0.5	215.3	0.0	215.9	0.3	217.5	0.7	217.8	0.1	217.8	0.0	218.9	0.5	219.0	0.0	219.2	0.1	219.2	0.0
1996	218.3	-0.4	218.4	0.0	218.9	0.2	218.8	-0.0	219.8	0.5	220.7	0.4	221.1	0.2	219.8	-0.6	223.3	1.6	225.2	0.9	225.5	0.1	224.8	-0.3
1997	225.7	0.4	227.8	0.9	227.4	-0.2	230.6	1.4	232.2	0.7	229.7	-1.1	231.0	0.6	233.3	1.0	236.5	1.4	237.0	0.2	237.3	0.1	240.5	1.3

Source: U.S. Department of Labor, Bureau of Labor Statistics, Division of Consumer Prices and Price Indexes. - indicates no data collected for period.

Cincinnati, OH-KY-IN
Consumer Price Index - All Urban Consumers
Base 1982-1984 = 100
Annual Averages

For 1917-1997. Columns headed % show percentile change in the index from the previous period for which an index is available.

Year	All Items		Food & Beverage		Housing		Apparel & Upkeep		Trans- portation		Medical Care		Entertain- ment		Other Goods & Services	
	Index	%	Index	%	Index	%	Index	%	Index	%	Index	%	Index	%	Index	%
1917	-	-	-	-	-	-	-	-	-	-	-	-	-	-	-	-
1918	14.5	-	-	-	-	-	-	-	-	-	-	-	-	-	-	-
1919	16.9	16.6	-	-	-	-	-	-	-	-	-	-	-	-	-	-
1920	19.3	14.2	-	-	-	-	-	-	-	-	-	-	-	-	-	-
1921	16.5	-14.5													-	-
1922	15.5	-6.1														
1923	15.9	2.6	-	-												
1924	16.0	0.6														
1925	16.8	5.0														
1926	17.1	1.8	-	-												
1927	16.8	-1.8														
1928	16.7	-0.6														
1929	16.9	1.2	-	-					-	-	-	-	-	-	-	-
1930	16.7	-1.2														
1931	15.1	-9.6	-	-											-	-
1932	13.3	-11.9	-	-												
1933	12.8	-3.8	-	-	-	-										
1934	13.3	3.9	-	-	-	-										
1935	13.7	3.0	-	-	-	-										
1936	13.9	1.5	-	-	-	-										
1937	14.3	2.9	-	-	-	-										
1938	14.0	-2.1	-	-												
1939	13.7	-2.1	-	-												
1940	13.8	0.7	-	-	-	-										
1941	14.5	5.1	-	-							-	-	-	-	-	-
1942	16.2	11.7	-	-												
1943	17.1	5.6	-	-												
1944	17.5	2.3	-	-							-	-	-	-	-	-
1945	17.8	1.7	-	-							-	-	-	-	-	-
1946	19.3	8.4							-	-	-	-	-	-	-	-
1947	22.4	16.1							20.6	-	11.8	-	-	-	-	-
1948	24.1	7.6							23.3	13.1	13.1	11.0	-	-	-	-
1949	23.7	-1.7					-	-	25.1	7.7	13.4	2.3	-	-	-	-
1950	23.9	0.8	-	-	-	-	-	-	25.6	2.0	13.5	0.7	-	-	-	-
1951	25.8	7.9	-	-	-	-	-	-	27.5	7.4	13.8	2.2	-	-	-	-
1952	26.3	1.9	-	-	-	-	-	-	29.2	6.2	14.9	8.0	-	-	-	-
1953	26.7	1.5	-	-	-	-	37.5	-	30.0	2.7	15.6	4.7	-	-	-	-
1954	26.7	0.0	-	-	-	-	37.2	-0.8	29.2	-2.7	16.0	2.6	-	-	-	-
1955	26.6	-0.4	-	-	-	-	37.6	1.1	28.2	-3.4	16.5	3.1	-	-	-	-
1956	27.1	1.9	-	-	-	-	38.5	2.4	28.4	0.7	17.5	6.1	-	-	-	-
1957	28.0	3.3	-	-	-	-	38.8	0.8	30.1	6.0	18.0	2.9			-	-
1958	28.6	2.1	-	-	-	-	39.1	0.8	30.8	2.3	19.1	6.1			-	-
1959	28.8	0.7	-	-	-	-	39.5	1.0	32.8	6.5	19.6	2.6	-	-	-	-
1960	29.1	1.0	-	-	-	-	40.1	1.5	33.1	0.9	20.0	2.0	-	-	-	-
1961	29.2	0.3	-	-	-	-	40.3	0.5	33.1	0.0	20.6	3.0	-	-	-	-

[Continued]

Cincinnati, OH-KY-IN
Consumer Price Index - All Urban Consumers
Base 1982-1984 = 100
Annual Averages
[Continued]

For 1917-1997. Columns headed % show percentile change in the index from the previous period for which an index is available.

Year	All Items Index	%	Food & Beverage Index	%	Housing Index	%	Apparel & Upkeep Index	%	Trans-portation Index	%	Medical Care Index	%	Entertain-ment Index	%	Other Goods & Services Index	%
1962	29.5	1.0	-	-	-	-	40.6	0.7	33.8	2.1	21.1	2.4	-	-	-	-
1963	29.8	1.0	-	-	-	-	41.0	1.0	34.0	0.6	21.8	3.3	-	-	-	-
1964	30.3	1.7	-	-	-	-	41.5	1.2	34.5	1.5	22.4	2.8	-	-	-	-
1965	30.5	0.7	-	-	-	-	41.8	0.7	34.5	0.0	23.9	6.7	-	-	-	-
1966	31.4	3.0	-	-	-	-	43.3	3.6	35.1	1.7	24.9	4.2	-	-	-	-
1967	32.3	2.9	-	-	-	-	45.0	3.9	35.9	2.3	26.7	7.2	-	-	-	-
1968	33.9	5.0	-	-	-	-	48.1	6.9	37.7	5.0	28.7	7.5	-	-	-	-
1969	35.5	4.7	-	-	-	-	51.2	6.4	38.8	2.9	31.1	8.4	-	-	-	-
1970	37.4	5.4	-	-	-	-	53.5	4.5	40.7	4.9	32.7	5.1	-	-	-	-
1971	39.0	4.3	-	-	-	-	55.0	2.8	43.0	5.7	35.2	7.6	-	-	-	-
1972	40.3	3.3	-	-	-	-	55.3	0.5	44.4	3.3	36.4	3.4	-	-	-	-
1973	42.7	6.0	-	-	-	-	57.6	4.2	44.3	-0.2	38.4	5.5	-	-	-	-
1974	47.3	10.8	-	-	-	-	61.6	6.9	47.7	7.7	42.4	10.4	-	-	-	-
1975	51.8	9.5	-	-	-	-	64.6	4.9	51.7	8.4	47.2	11.3	-	-	-	-
1976	55.0	6.2	60.1	-	50.8	-	68.8	6.5	56.0	8.3	52.6	11.4	67.1	-	55.8	-
1977	58.9	7.1	64.3	7.0	54.5	7.3	72.3	5.1	60.0	7.1	58.9	12.0	68.9	2.7	59.2	6.1
1978	64.3	9.2	71.1	10.6	60.4	10.8	77.7	7.5	62.5	4.2	65.5	11.2	72.5	5.2	62.7	5.9
1979	72.3	12.4	79.1	11.3	69.1	14.4	82.1	5.7	71.5	14.4	72.6	10.8	77.1	6.3	67.6	7.8
1980	82.1	13.6	85.9	8.6	80.1	15.9	89.1	8.5	84.1	17.6	79.2	9.1	83.7	8.6	74.2	9.8
1981	87.9	7.1	93.2	8.5	84.2	5.1	93.4	4.8	93.8	11.5	85.9	8.5	87.5	4.5	81.6	10.0
1982	94.9	8.0	97.0	4.1	93.6	11.2	97.6	4.5	97.3	3.7	93.6	9.0	94.8	8.3	90.1	10.4
1983	100.8	6.2	99.2	2.3	102.1	9.1	100.6	3.1	99.7	2.5	100.2	7.1	100.7	6.2	101.5	12.7
1984	104.3	3.5	103.8	4.6	104.2	2.1	101.7	1.1	103.0	3.3	106.3	6.1	104.5	3.8	108.4	6.8
1985	106.6	2.2	104.6	0.8	106.8	2.5	103.4	1.7	106.0	2.9	112.0	5.4	99.8	-4.5	115.5	6.5
1986	107.6	0.9	107.2	2.5	108.6	1.7	105.5	2.0	99.7	-5.9	117.7	5.1	103.8	4.0	120.9	4.7
1987	114.5	6.4	113.2	5.6	116.3	7.1	109.2	3.5	106.1	6.4	129.2	9.8	116.0	11.8	129.6	7.2
1988	119.0	3.9	117.1	3.4	120.7	3.8	116.6	6.8	107.6	1.4	138.0	6.8	122.3	5.4	138.0	6.5
1989	125.0	5.0	122.5	4.6	126.4	4.7	118.1	1.3	112.1	4.2	149.2	8.1	131.6	7.6	153.1	10.9
1990	131.7	5.4	130.3	6.4	131.4	4.0	124.3	5.2	118.7	5.9	163.0	9.2	139.2	5.8	164.3	7.3
1991	137.0	4.0	135.5	4.0	136.4	3.8	125.3	0.8	121.2	2.1	177.9	9.1	145.9	4.8	179.0	8.9
1992	141.1	3.0	139.2	2.7	139.9	2.6	126.2	0.7	123.2	1.7	190.7	7.2	149.4	2.4	192.0	7.3
1993	145.4	3.0	143.1	2.8	143.3	2.4	131.1	3.9	126.2	2.4	203.1	6.5	153.9	3.0	202.5	5.5
1994	148.6	2.2	147.0	2.7	144.8	1.0	131.0	-0.1	130.3	3.2	213.2	5.0	160.0	4.0	208.8	3.1
1995	153.3	3.2	151.3	2.9	150.6	4.0	126.3	-3.6	135.1	3.7	223.3	4.7	160.9	0.6	216.8	3.8
1996	157.4	2.7	156.1	3.2	155.1	3.0	120.6	-4.5	139.9	3.6	229.4	2.7	167.2	3.9	222.4	2.6
1997	-	-	-	-	-	-	-	-	-	-	-	-	-	-	-	-

Source: U.S. Department of Labor, Bureau of Labor Statistics, Division of Consumer Prices and Price Indexes. - indicates no data collected for period.

Cincinnati, OH-KY-IN
Consumer Price Index - Urban Wage Earners
Base 1982-1984 = 100
Annual Averages

For 1917-1997. Columns headed % show percentile change in the index from the previous period for which an index is available.

Year	All Items		Food & Beverage		Housing		Apparel & Upkeep		Transportation		Medical Care		Entertainment		Other Goods & Services	
	Index	%	Index	%	Index	%	Index	%	Index	%	Index	%	Index	%	Index	%
1917	-	-	-	-	-	-	-	-	-	-	-	-	-	-	-	-
1918	14.6	-	-	-	-	-	-	-	-	-	-	-	-	-	-	-
1919	17.0	16.4	-	-	-	-	-	-	-	-	-	-	-	-	-	-
1920	19.5	14.7	-	-	-	-	-	-	-	-	-	-	-	-	-	-
1921	16.7	-14.4	-	-	-	-	-	-	-	-	-	-	-	-	-	-
1922	15.7	-6.0	-	-	-	-	-	-	-	-	-	-	-	-	-	-
1923	16.0	1.9	-	-	-	-	-	-	-	-	-	-	-	-	-	-
1924	16.1	0.6	-	-	-	-	-	-	-	-	-	-	-	-	-	-
1925	17.0	5.6	-	-	-	-	-	-	-	-	-	-	-	-	-	-
1926	17.2	1.2	-	-	-	-	-	-	-	-	-	-	-	-	-	-
1927	16.9	-1.7	-	-	-	-	-	-	-	-	-	-	-	-	-	-
1928	16.8	-0.6	-	-	-	-	-	-	-	-	-	-	-	-	-	-
1929	17.0	1.2	-	-	-	-	-	-	-	-	-	-	-	-	-	-
1930	16.8	-1.2	-	-	-	-	-	-	-	-	-	-	-	-	-	-
1931	15.2	-9.5	-	-	-	-	-	-	-	-	-	-	-	-	-	-
1932	13.4	-11.8	-	-	-	-	-	-	-	-	-	-	-	-	-	-
1933	12.9	-3.7	-	-	-	-	-	-	-	-	-	-	-	-	-	-
1934	13.4	3.9	-	-	-	-	-	-	-	-	-	-	-	-	-	-
1935	13.8	3.0	-	-	-	-	-	-	-	-	-	-	-	-	-	-
1936	14.0	1.4	-	-	-	-	-	-	-	-	-	-	-	-	-	-
1937	14.4	2.9	-	-	-	-	-	-	-	-	-	-	-	-	-	-
1938	14.1	-2.1	-	-	-	-	-	-	-	-	-	-	-	-	-	-
1939	13.8	-2.1	-	-	-	-	-	-	-	-	-	-	-	-	-	-
1940	13.9	0.7	-	-	-	-	-	-	-	-	-	-	-	-	-	-
1941	14.6	5.0	-	-	-	-	-	-	-	-	-	-	-	-	-	-
1942	16.3	11.6	-	-	-	-	-	-	-	-	-	-	-	-	-	-
1943	17.2	5.5	-	-	-	-	-	-	-	-	-	-	-	-	-	-
1944	17.6	2.3	-	-	-	-	-	-	-	-	-	-	-	-	-	-
1945	18.0	2.3	-	-	-	-	-	-	-	-	-	-	-	-	-	-
1946	19.4	7.8	-	-	-	-	-	-	-	-	-	-	-	-	-	-
1947	22.6	16.5	-	-	-	-	-	-	20.8	-	11.3	-	-	-	-	-
1948	24.3	7.5	-	-	-	-	-	-	23.5	13.0	12.4	9.7	-	-	-	-
1949	23.9	-1.6	-	-	-	-	-	-	25.4	8.1	12.8	3.2	-	-	-	-
1950	24.1	0.8	-	-	-	-	-	-	25.9	2.0	12.8	0.0	-	-	-	-
1951	25.9	7.5	-	-	-	-	-	-	27.7	6.9	13.2	3.1	-	-	-	-
1952	26.5	2.3	-	-	-	-	-	-	29.5	6.5	14.2	7.6	-	-	-	-
1953	26.9	1.5	-	-	-	-	36.4	-	30.3	2.7	14.9	4.9	-	-	-	-
1954	26.9	0.0	-	-	-	-	36.2	-0.5	29.5	-2.6	15.2	2.0	-	-	-	-
1955	26.8	-0.4	-	-	-	-	36.5	0.8	28.5	-3.4	15.7	3.3	-	-	-	-
1956	27.3	1.9	-	-	-	-	37.4	2.5	28.7	0.7	16.7	6.4	-	-	-	-
1957	28.2	3.3	-	-	-	-	37.7	0.8	30.4	5.9	17.2	3.0	-	-	-	-
1958	28.8	2.1	-	-	-	-	37.9	0.5	31.1	2.3	18.2	5.8	-	-	-	-
1959	29.0	0.7	-	-	-	-	38.3	1.1	33.2	6.8	18.7	2.7	-	-	-	-
1960	29.3	1.0	-	-	-	-	38.9	1.6	33.4	0.6	19.0	1.6	-	-	-	-
1961	29.4	0.3	-	-	-	-	39.1	0.5	33.5	0.3	19.6	3.2	-	-	-	-

[Continued]

382

Cincinnati, OH-KY-IN
Consumer Price Index - Urban Wage Earners
Base 1982-1984 = 100
Annual Averages
[Continued]

For 1917-1997. Columns headed % show percentile change in the index from the previous period for which an index is available.

Year	All Items		Food & Beverage		Housing		Apparel & Upkeep		Trans-portation		Medical Care		Entertain-ment		Other Goods & Services	
	Index	%	Index	%	Index	%	Index	%	Index	%	Index	%	Index	%	Index	%
1962	29.7	1.0	-	-	-	-	39.4	0.8	34.1	1.8	20.1	2.6	-	-	-	-
1963	30.0	1.0	-	-	-	-	39.8	1.0	34.3	0.6	20.8	3.5	-	-	-	-
1964	30.5	1.7	-	-	-	-	40.3	1.3	34.8	1.5	21.4	2.9	-	-	-	-
1965	30.7	0.7	-	-	-	-	40.6	0.7	34.9	0.3	22.7	6.1	-	-	-	-
1966	31.6	2.9	-	-	-	-	42.0	3.4	35.5	1.7	23.8	4.8	-	-	-	-
1967	32.5	2.8	-	-	-	-	43.7	4.0	36.2	2.0	25.4	6.7	-	-	-	-
1968	34.1	4.9	-	-	-	-	46.7	6.9	38.1	5.2	27.4	7.9	-	-	-	-
1969	35.7	4.7	-	-	-	-	49.7	6.4	39.2	2.9	29.7	8.4	-	-	-	-
1970	37.6	5.3	-	-	-	-	52.0	4.6	41.1	4.8	31.2	5.1	-	-	-	-
1971	39.3	4.5	-	-	-	-	53.4	2.7	43.5	5.8	33.5	7.4	-	-	-	-
1972	40.6	3.3	-	-	-	-	53.7	0.6	44.8	3.0	34.7	3.6	-	-	-	-
1973	43.0	5.9	-	-	-	-	55.9	4.1	44.7	-0.2	36.6	5.5	-	-	-	-
1974	47.6	10.7	-	-	-	-	59.8	7.0	48.2	7.8	40.4	10.4	-	-	-	-
1975	52.2	9.7	-	-	-	-	62.7	4.8	52.2	8.3	45.0	11.4	-	-	-	-
1976	55.4	6.1	59.8	-	51.7	-	66.8	6.5	56.5	8.2	50.1	11.3	69.7	-	55.6	-
1977	59.3	7.0	64.1	7.2	55.5	7.4	70.2	5.1	60.6	7.3	56.1	12.0	71.6	2.7	59.0	6.1
1978	64.9	9.4	71.1	10.9	61.7	11.2	75.8	8.0	63.0	4.0	62.0	10.5	75.5	5.4	63.1	6.9
1979	73.3	12.9	79.7	12.1	70.8	14.7	81.0	6.9	72.0	14.3	70.2	13.2	78.3	3.7	68.3	8.2
1980	83.2	13.5	86.3	8.3	82.4	16.4	86.6	6.9	84.5	17.4	78.2	11.4	83.9	7.2	74.6	9.2
1981	89.2	7.2	92.9	7.6	86.3	4.7	93.1	7.5	94.0	11.2	85.6	9.5	88.5	5.5	82.3	10.3
1982	96.4	8.1	97.2	4.6	96.5	11.8	97.5	4.7	97.4	3.6	93.5	9.2	95.2	7.6	90.2	9.6
1983	100.8	4.6	99.2	2.1	102.0	5.7	100.9	3.5	99.7	2.4	100.2	7.2	100.7	5.8	101.7	12.7
1984	102.8	2.0	103.6	4.4	101.5	-0.5	101.6	0.7	102.9	3.2	106.3	6.1	104.0	3.3	108.2	6.4
1985	105.2	2.3	104.3	0.7	104.6	3.1	102.5	0.9	105.7	2.7	112.0	5.4	96.8	-6.9	114.7	6.0
1986	105.8	0.6	106.8	2.4	106.3	1.6	104.5	2.0	99.7	-5.7	117.4	4.8	100.3	3.6	119.9	4.5
1987	111.1	5.0	113.3	6.1	109.7	3.2	109.4	4.7	104.3	4.6	128.9	9.8	118.0	17.6	130.3	8.7
1988	115.3	3.8	117.2	3.4	113.6	3.6	116.1	6.1	106.3	1.9	138.4	7.4	124.2	5.3	138.5	6.3
1989	121.2	5.1	122.6	4.6	118.9	4.7	117.6	1.3	111.0	4.4	150.4	8.7	132.9	7.0	153.6	10.9
1990	127.8	5.4	130.4	6.4	123.8	4.1	124.5	5.9	117.2	5.6	164.3	9.2	140.0	5.3	166.2	8.2
1991	132.9	4.0	135.7	4.1	128.4	3.7	125.6	0.9	119.3	1.8	179.4	9.2	146.0	4.3	182.4	9.7
1992	136.7	2.9	139.2	2.6	131.7	2.6	125.9	0.2	121.2	1.6	192.4	7.2	149.5	2.4	195.9	7.4
1993	140.9	3.1	143.3	2.9	135.0	2.5	130.5	3.7	124.0	2.3	205.6	6.9	153.7	2.8	207.0	5.7
1994	144.0	2.2	147.2	2.7	136.3	1.0	130.0	-0.4	128.4	3.5	215.9	5.0	159.4	3.7	211.3	2.1
1995	148.4	3.1	151.6	3.0	141.4	3.7	125.1	-3.8	133.5	4.0	227.0	5.1	160.1	0.4	217.3	2.8
1996	152.4	2.7	156.3	3.1	145.7	3.0	119.6	-4.4	138.1	3.4	234.0	3.1	165.9	3.6	221.2	1.8
1997	-	-	-	-	-	-	-	-	-	-	-	-	-	-	-	-

Source: U.S. Department of Labor, Bureau of Labor Statistics, Division of Consumer Prices and Price Indexes. - indicates no data collected for period.

Cincinnati, OH-KY-IN
Consumer Price Index - All Urban Consumers
Base 1982-1984 = 100
All Items

For 1917-1997. Columns headed % show percentile change in the index from the previous period for which an index is available.

Year	Jan Index	%	Feb Index	%	Mar Index	%	Apr Index	%	May Index	%	Jun Index	%	Jul Index	%	Aug Index	%	Sep Index	%	Oct Index	%	Nov Index	%	Dec Index	%
1917	-	-	-	-	-	-	-	-	-	-	-	-	-	-	-	-	-	-	-	-	-	-	13.5	-
1918	-	-	-	-	-	-	-	-	-	-	-	-	-	-	-	-	-	-	-	-	-	-	15.7	16.3
1919	-	-	-	-	-	-	-	-	-	-	16.5	5.1	-	-	-	-	-	-	-	-	-	-	18.2	10.3
1920	-	-	-	-	-	-	-	-	-	-	20.4	12.1	-	-	-	-	-	-	-	-	-	-	18.3	-10.3
1921	-	-	-	-	-	-	-	-	16.6	-9.3	-	-	-	-	-	-	16.4	-1.2	-	-	-	-	15.8	-3.7
1922	-	-	-	-	15.4	-2.5	-	-	-	-	15.7	1.9	-	-	-	-	15.4	-1.9	-	-	-	-	15.5	0.6
1923	-	-	-	-	15.7	1.3	-	-	-	-	16.0	1.9	-	-	-	-	16.1	0.6	-	-	-	-	16.0	-0.6
1924	-	-	-	-	16.1	0.6	-	-	-	-	16.1	0.0	-	-	-	-	16.1	0.0	-	-	-	-	16.1	0.0
1925	-	-	-	-	-	-	-	-	-	-	17.0	5.6	-	-	-	-	-	-	-	-	-	-	17.1	0.6
1926	-	-	-	-	-	-	-	-	-	-	17.1	0.0	-	-	-	-	-	-	-	-	-	-	17.0	-0.6
1927	-	-	-	-	-	-	-	-	-	-	17.4	2.4	-	-	-	-	-	-	-	-	-	-	16.6	-4.6
1928	-	-	-	-	-	-	-	-	-	-	16.7	0.6	-	-	-	-	-	-	-	-	-	-	16.6	-0.6
1929	-	-	-	-	-	-	-	-	-	-	16.8	1.2	-	-	-	-	-	-	-	-	-	-	17.0	1.2
1930	-	-	-	-	-	-	-	-	-	-	16.7	-1.8	-	-	-	-	-	-	-	-	-	-	16.0	-4.2
1931	-	-	-	-	-	-	-	-	-	-	15.0	-6.3	-	-	-	-	-	-	-	-	-	-	14.4	-4.0
1932	-	-	-	-	-	-	-	-	-	-	13.3	-7.6	-	-	-	-	-	-	-	-	-	-	12.8	-3.8
1933	-	-	-	-	-	-	-	-	-	-	12.6	-1.6	-	-	-	-	-	-	-	-	-	-	12.9	2.4
1934	-	-	-	-	-	-	-	-	-	-	13.2	2.3	-	-	-	-	-	-	-	-	13.3	0.8	-	-
1935	-	-	-	-	13.7	3.0	-	-	-	-	-	-	13.7	0.0	-	-	-	-	13.8	0.7	-	-	-	-
1936	13.8	0.0	-	-	-	-	13.6	-1.4	-	-	-	-	14.0	2.9	-	-	14.1	0.7	-	-	-	-	13.9	-1.4
1937	-	-	-	-	14.3	2.9	-	-	-	-	14.3	0.0	-	-	-	-	14.5	1.4	-	-	-	-	14.3	-1.4
1938	-	-	-	-	14.0	-2.1	-	-	-	-	14.0	0.0	-	-	-	-	14.0	0.0	-	-	-	-	13.8	-1.4
1939	-	-	-	-	13.6	-1.4	-	-	-	-	13.5	-0.7	-	-	-	-	13.8	2.2	-	-	-	-	13.6	-1.4
1940	-	-	-	-	13.7	0.7	-	-	-	-	13.7	0.0	-	-	-	-	13.9	1.5	13.8	-0.7	13.8	0.0	13.8	0.0
1941	13.8	0.0	13.8	0.0	14.0	1.4	14.1	0.7	14.2	0.7	14.4	1.4	14.5	0.7	14.8	2.1	15.0	1.4	15.3	2.0	15.4	0.7	15.3	-0.6
1942	15.5	1.3	15.7	1.3	15.9	1.3	16.0	0.6	16.1	0.6	16.2	0.6	16.2	0.0	16.3	0.6	16.4	0.6	16.6	1.2	16.6	0.0	16.7	0.6
1943	16.6	-0.6	16.7	0.6	16.9	1.2	17.1	1.2	17.2	0.6	17.3	0.6	17.3	0.0	17.3	0.0	17.2	-0.6	17.3	0.6	17.2	-0.6	17.3	0.6
1944	17.2	-0.6	17.1	-0.6	17.1	0.0	17.4	1.8	17.3	-0.6	17.6	1.7	17.6	0.0	17.6	0.0	17.6	0.0	17.5	-0.6	17.6	0.6	17.6	0.0
1945	17.6	0.0	17.6	0.0	17.6	0.0	17.6	0.0	17.8	1.1	18.0	1.1	18.0	0.0	18.0	0.0	17.9	-0.6	18.0	0.6	-	-	18.0	0.0
1946	18.0	0.0	17.9	-0.6	18.0	0.6	18.1	0.6	18.2	0.6	18.4	1.1	19.5	6.0	20.0	2.6	20.2	1.0	20.4	1.0	21.3	4.4	21.2	-0.5
1947	21.2	0.0	21.3	0.5	21.8	2.3	21.9	0.5	21.8	-0.5	22.1	1.4	22.4	1.4	22.6	0.9	23.1	2.2	23.3	0.9	23.3	0.0	23.7	1.7
1948	23.9	0.8	23.7	-0.8	23.6	-0.4	23.8	0.8	24.0	0.8	24.2	0.8	24.5	1.2	24.5	0.0	24.6	0.4	24.5	-0.4	24.2	-1.2	24.0	-0.8
1949	24.0	0.0	23.7	-1.2	23.8	0.4	23.8	0.0	23.6	-0.8	23.8	0.8	23.6	-0.8	23.6	0.0	23.8	0.8	23.6	-0.8	23.5	-0.4	23.4	-0.4
1950	23.4	0.0	23.3	-0.4	23.4	0.4	23.3	-0.4	23.6	1.3	23.7	0.4	23.9	0.8	24.2	1.3	24.4	0.8	24.5	0.4	24.5	0.0	24.8	1.2
1951	25.3	2.0	25.5	0.8	25.6	0.4	25.7	0.4	25.7	0.0	25.7	0.0	25.8	0.4	25.7	-0.4	26.0	1.2	26.0	0.0	26.1	0.4	26.1	0.0
1952	26.2	0.4	26.0	-0.8	26.0	0.0	26.2	0.8	26.3	0.4	26.4	0.4	26.5	0.4	26.5	0.0	26.5	0.0	26.5	0.0	26.3	-0.8	26.3	0.0
1953	-	-	-	-	26.3	0.0	-	-	-	-	26.8	1.9	-	-	-	-	27.0	0.7	-	-	-	-	26.8	-0.7
1954	-	-	-	-	26.7	-0.4	-	-	-	-	26.7	0.0	-	-	-	-	26.7	0.0	-	-	-	-	26.5	-0.7
1955	-	-	-	-	26.5	0.0	-	-	-	-	26.6	0.4	-	-	-	-	26.6	0.0	-	-	-	-	26.7	0.4
1956	-	-	-	-	26.7	0.0	-	-	-	-	27.2	1.9	-	-	-	-	27.4	0.7	-	-	-	-	27.5	0.4
1957	-	-	-	-	27.6	0.4	-	-	-	-	28.0	1.4	-	-	-	-	28.3	1.1	-	-	-	-	28.3	0.0
1958	-	-	-	-	28.6	1.1	-	-	-	-	28.7	0.3	-	-	-	-	28.7	0.0	-	-	-	-	28.6	-0.3
1959	-	-	-	-	28.6	0.0	-	-	-	-	28.8	0.7	-	-	-	-	28.9	0.3	-	-	-	-	29.0	0.3
1960	-	-	-	-	28.9	-0.3	-	-	-	-	29.2	1.0	-	-	-	-	29.2	0.0	-	-	-	-	29.2	0.0
1961	-	-	-	-	29.2	0.0	-	-	-	-	29.2	0.0	-	-	-	-	29.3	0.3	-	-	-	-	29.2	-0.3

[Continued]

Cincinnati, OH-KY-IN
Consumer Price Index - All Urban Consumers
Base 1982-1984 = 100
All Items
[Continued]

For 1917-1997. Columns headed % show percentile change in the index from the previous period for which an index is available.

Year	Jan Index	%	Feb Index	%	Mar Index	%	Apr Index	%	May Index	%	Jun Index	%	Jul Index	%	Aug Index	%	Sep Index	%	Oct Index	%	Nov Index	%	Dec Index	%
1962	-	-	-	-	29.4	0.7	-	-	-	-	29.4	0.0	-	-	-	-	29.7	1.0	-	-	-	-	29.6	-0.3
1963	-	-	-	-	29.8	0.7	-	-	-	-	29.8	0.0	-	-	-	-	29.9	0.3	-	-	-	-	29.9	0.0
1964	-	-	-	-	30.1	0.7	-	-	-	-	30.2	0.3	-	-	-	-	30.5	1.0	-	-	-	-	30.4	-0.3
1965	-	-	-	-	30.4	0.0	-	-	-	-	30.6	0.7	-	-	-	-	30.5	-0.3	-	-	-	-	30.7	0.7
1966	-	-	-	-	31.1	1.3	-	-	-	-	31.4	1.0	-	-	-	-	31.8	1.3	-	-	-	-	31.7	-0.3
1967	-	-	-	-	31.8	0.3	-	-	-	-	32.2	1.3	-	-	-	-	32.7	1.6	-	-	-	-	33.0	0.9
1968	-	-	-	-	33.4	1.2	-	-	-	-	33.8	1.2	-	-	-	-	34.3	1.5	-	-	-	-	34.5	0.6
1969	-	-	-	-	34.9	1.2	-	-	-	-	35.5	1.7	-	-	-	-	35.7	0.6	-	-	-	-	36.4	2.0
1970	-	-	-	-	36.8	1.1	-	-	-	-	37.4	1.6	-	-	-	-	37.7	0.8	-	-	-	-	38.3	1.6
1971	-	-	-	-	38.7	1.0	-	-	-	-	39.0	0.8	-	-	-	-	39.2	0.5	-	-	-	-	39.4	0.5
1972	-	-	-	-	39.8	1.0	-	-	-	-	40.3	1.3	-	-	-	-	40.8	1.2	-	-	-	-	40.9	0.2
1973	-	-	-	-	41.9	2.4	-	-	-	-	42.3	1.0	-	-	-	-	43.4	2.6	-	-	-	-	44.1	1.6
1974	-	-	-	-	45.7	3.6	-	-	-	-	47.1	3.1	-	-	-	-	48.6	3.2	-	-	-	-	49.7	2.3
1975	-	-	-	-	50.4	1.4	-	-	-	-	51.9	3.0	-	-	-	-	53.0	2.1	-	-	-	-	53.2	0.4
1976	-	-	-	-	54.0	1.5	-	-	-	-	54.9	1.7	-	-	-	-	55.6	1.3	-	-	-	-	56.4	1.4
1977	-	-	-	-	57.8	2.5	-	-	-	-	58.8	1.7	-	-	-	-	59.9	1.9	-	-	-	-	60.3	0.7
1978	-	-	-	-	62.1	3.0	-	-	63.8	2.7	-	-	64.7	1.4	-	-	65.8	1.7	-	-	66.9	1.7	-	-
1979	68.3	2.1	-	-	69.7	2.0	-	-	71.6	2.7	-	-	72.7	1.5	-	-	74.0	1.8	-	-	75.4	1.9	-	-
1980	77.4	2.7	-	-	80.1	3.5	-	-	81.3	1.5	-	-	83.0	2.1	-	-	84.0	1.2	-	-	84.7	0.8	-	-
1981	85.5	0.9	-	-	86.0	0.6	-	-	87.8	2.1	-	-	88.3	0.6	-	-	88.9	0.7	-	-	89.4	0.6	-	-
1982	92.3	3.2	-	-	92.1	-0.2	-	-	93.3	1.3	-	-	94.8	1.6	-	-	97.0	2.3	-	-	98.3	1.3	-	-
1983	98.9	0.6	-	-	99.4	0.5	-	-	100.6	1.2	-	-	101.0	0.4	-	-	101.7	0.7	-	-	102.4	0.7	-	-
1984	102.9	0.5	-	-	103.4	0.5	-	-	104.0	0.6	-	-	104.5	0.5	-	-	105.1	0.6	-	-	105.2	0.1	-	-
1985	105.1	-0.1	-	-	106.1	1.0	-	-	106.8	0.7	-	-	106.7	-0.1	-	-	106.6	-0.1	-	-	107.7	1.0	-	-
1986	107.7	0.0	-	-	106.5	-1.1	-	-	107.3	0.8	-	-	107.4	0.1	-	-	107.6	0.2	-	-	108.4	0.7	-	-
1987	-	-	-	-	-	-	-	-	-	-	112.9	4.2	-	-	-	-	-	-	-	-	-	-	116.0	2.7
1988	-	-	-	-	-	-	-	-	-	-	117.0	0.9	-	-	-	-	-	-	-	-	-	-	121.0	3.4
1989	-	-	-	-	-	-	-	-	-	-	123.3	1.9	-	-	-	-	-	-	-	-	-	-	126.7	2.8
1990	-	-	-	-	-	-	-	-	-	-	129.9	2.5	-	-	-	-	-	-	-	-	-	-	133.5	2.8
1991	-	-	-	-	-	-	-	-	-	-	136.2	2.0	-	-	-	-	-	-	-	-	-	-	137.9	1.2
1992	-	-	-	-	-	-	-	-	-	-	139.9	1.5	-	-	-	-	-	-	-	-	-	-	142.2	1.6
1993	-	-	-	-	-	-	-	-	-	-	144.5	1.6	-	-	-	-	-	-	-	-	-	-	146.3	1.2
1994	-	-	-	-	-	-	-	-	-	-	147.4	0.8	-	-	-	-	-	-	-	-	-	-	149.8	1.6
1995	-	-	-	-	-	-	-	-	-	-	152.7	1.9	-	-	-	-	-	-	-	-	-	-	153.9	0.8
1996	-	-	-	-	-	-	-	-	-	-	156.2	1.5	-	-	-	-	-	-	-	-	-	-	158.7	1.6
1997	-	-	-	-	-	-	-	-	-	-	161.0	1.4	-	-	-	-	-	-	-	-	-	-	-	-

Source: U.S. Department of Labor, Bureau of Labor Statistics, Division of Consumer Prices and Price Indexes. - indicates no data collected for period.

Cincinnati, OH-KY-IN
Consumer Price Index - Urban Wage Earners
Base 1982-1984 = 100
All Items

For 1917-1997. Columns headed % show percentile change in the index from the previous period for which an index is available.

Year	Jan Index	%	Feb Index	%	Mar Index	%	Apr Index	%	May Index	%	Jun Index	%	Jul Index	%	Aug Index	%	Sep Index	%	Oct Index	%	Nov Index	%	Dec Index	%
1917	-	-	-	-	-	-	-	-	-	-	-	-	-	-	-	-	-	-	-	-	-	-	13.6	-
1918	-	-	-	-	-	-	-	-	-	-	-	-	-	-	-	-	-	-	-	-	-	-	15.8	16.2
1919	-	-	-	-	-	-	-	-	-	-	16.6	5.1	-	-	-	-	-	-	-	-	-	-	18.4	10.8
1920	-	-	-	-	-	-	-	-	-	-	20.6	12.0	-	-	-	-	-	-	-	-	-	-	18.4	-10.7
1921	-	-	-	-	-	-	-	-	16.8	-8.7	-	-	-	-	-	-	16.5	-1.8	-	-	-	-	15.9	-3.6
1922	-	-	-	-	15.6	-1.9	-	-	-	-	15.8	1.3	-	-	-	-	15.6	-1.3	-	-	-	-	15.6	0.0
1923	-	-	-	-	15.8	1.3	-	-	-	-	16.1	1.9	-	-	-	-	16.2	0.6	-	-	-	-	16.1	-0.6
1924	-	-	-	-	16.2	0.6	-	-	-	-	16.2	0.0	-	-	-	-	16.2	0.0	-	-	-	-	16.2	0.0
1925	-	-	-	-	-	-	-	-	-	-	17.1	5.6	-	-	-	-	-	-	-	-	-	-	17.2	0.6
1926	-	-	-	-	-	-	-	-	-	-	17.2	0.0	-	-	-	-	-	-	-	-	-	-	17.1	-0.6
1927	-	-	-	-	-	-	-	-	-	-	17.5	2.3	-	-	-	-	-	-	-	-	-	-	16.7	-4.6
1928	-	-	-	-	-	-	-	-	-	-	16.8	0.6	-	-	-	-	-	-	-	-	-	-	16.7	-0.6
1929	-	-	-	-	-	-	-	-	-	-	17.0	1.8	-	-	-	-	-	-	-	-	-	-	17.1	0.6
1930	-	-	-	-	-	-	-	-	-	-	16.9	-1.2	-	-	-	-	-	-	-	-	-	-	16.1	-4.7
1931	-	-	-	-	-	-	-	-	-	-	15.1	-6.2	-	-	-	-	-	-	-	-	-	-	14.5	-4.0
1932	-	-	-	-	-	-	-	-	-	-	13.4	-7.6	-	-	-	-	-	-	-	-	-	-	12.9	-3.7
1933	-	-	-	-	-	-	-	-	-	-	12.7	-1.6	-	-	-	-	-	-	-	-	-	-	13.0	2.4
1934	-	-	-	-	-	-	-	-	-	-	13.3	2.3	-	-	-	-	-	-	-	-	13.4	0.8	-	-
1935	-	-	-	-	13.8	3.0	-	-	-	-	-	-	13.8	0.0	-	-	-	-	13.9	0.7	-	-	-	-
1936	13.9	0.0	-	-	-	-	13.7	-1.4	-	-	-	-	14.1	2.9	-	-	14.2	0.7	-	-	-	-	14.0	-1.4
1937	-	-	-	-	14.4	2.9	-	-	-	-	14.4	0.0	-	-	-	-	14.6	1.4	-	-	-	-	14.4	-1.4
1938	-	-	-	-	14.1	-2.1	-	-	-	-	14.1	0.0	-	-	-	-	14.1	0.0	-	-	-	-	13.9	-1.4
1939	-	-	-	-	13.7	-1.4	-	-	-	-	13.6	-0.7	-	-	-	-	13.9	2.2	-	-	-	-	13.7	-1.4
1940	-	-	-	-	13.8	0.7	-	-	-	-	13.8	0.0	-	-	-	-	14.0	1.4	13.9	-0.7	13.9	0.0	13.9	0.0
1941	13.9	0.0	13.9	0.0	14.1	1.4	14.2	0.7	14.3	0.7	14.5	1.4	14.6	0.7	14.9	2.1	15.1	1.3	15.4	2.0	15.5	0.6	15.4	-0.6
1942	15.7	1.9	15.8	0.6	16.0	1.3	16.1	0.6	16.2	0.6	16.3	0.6	16.3	0.0	16.4	0.6	16.5	0.6	16.7	1.2	16.7	0.0	16.8	0.6
1943	16.8	0.0	16.8	0.0	17.1	1.8	17.2	0.6	17.3	0.6	17.4	0.6	17.4	0.0	17.4	0.0	17.3	-0.6	17.4	0.6	17.3	-0.6	17.4	0.6
1944	17.3	-0.6	17.2	-0.6	17.2	0.0	17.5	1.7	17.4	-0.6	17.7	1.7	17.8	0.6	17.7	-0.6	17.7	0.0	17.6	-0.6	17.7	0.6	17.7	0.0
1945	17.8	0.6	17.7	-0.6	17.7	0.0	17.8	0.6	17.9	0.6	18.1	1.1	18.2	0.6	18.1	-0.5	18.0	-0.6	18.1	0.6	-	-	18.2	0.6
1946	18.2	0.0	18.1	-0.5	18.1	0.0	18.2	0.6	18.4	1.1	18.5	0.5	19.7	6.5	20.1	2.0	20.4	1.5	20.5	0.5	21.4	4.4	21.4	0.0
1947	21.3	-0.5	21.5	0.9	22.0	2.3	22.0	0.0	22.0	0.0	22.2	0.9	22.5	1.4	22.8	1.3	23.3	2.2	23.5	0.9	23.5	0.0	23.9	1.7
1948	24.0	0.4	23.9	-0.4	23.8	-0.4	24.0	0.8	24.2	0.8	24.4	0.8	24.7	1.2	24.7	0.0	24.8	0.4	24.6	-0.8	24.4	-0.8	24.2	-0.8
1949	24.2	0.0	23.9	-1.2	24.0	0.4	24.0	0.0	23.8	-0.8	24.0	0.8	23.7	-1.2	23.7	0.0	24.0	1.3	23.7	-1.2	23.7	0.0	23.6	-0.4
1950	23.6	0.0	23.5	-0.4	23.6	0.4	23.5	-0.4	23.8	1.3	23.9	0.4	24.0	0.4	24.3	1.2	24.5	0.8	24.6	0.4	24.6	0.0	25.0	1.6
1951	25.5	2.0	25.7	0.8	25.8	0.4	25.8	0.0	25.8	0.0	25.9	0.4	26.0	0.4	25.9	-0.4	26.1	0.8	26.2	0.4	26.3	0.4	26.3	0.0
1952	26.4	0.4	26.2	-0.8	26.2	0.0	26.4	0.8	26.5	0.4	26.6	0.4	26.7	0.4	26.7	0.0	26.7	0.0	26.7	0.0	26.5	-0.7	26.5	0.0
1953	-	-	-	-	26.5	0.0	-	-	-	-	27.0	1.9	-	-	-	-	27.1	0.4	-	-	-	-	27.0	-0.4
1954	-	-	-	-	26.9	-0.4	-	-	-	-	26.9	0.0	-	-	-	-	26.9	0.0	-	-	-	-	26.7	-0.7
1955	-	-	-	-	26.7	0.0	-	-	-	-	26.8	0.4	-	-	-	-	26.8	0.0	-	-	-	-	26.9	0.4
1956	-	-	-	-	26.9	0.0	-	-	-	-	27.4	1.9	-	-	-	-	27.6	0.7	-	-	-	-	27.7	0.4
1957	-	-	-	-	27.8	0.4	-	-	-	-	28.2	1.4	-	-	-	-	28.5	1.1	-	-	-	-	28.5	0.0
1958	-	-	-	-	28.8	1.1	-	-	-	-	28.9	0.3	-	-	-	-	28.9	0.0	-	-	-	-	28.8	-0.3
1959	-	-	-	-	28.8	0.0	-	-	-	-	29.0	0.7	-	-	-	-	29.1	0.3	-	-	-	-	29.2	0.3
1960	-	-	-	-	29.1	-0.3	-	-	-	-	29.4	1.0	-	-	-	-	29.4	0.0	-	-	-	-	29.4	0.0
1961	-	-	-	-	29.4	0.0	-	-	-	-	29.4	0.0	-	-	-	-	29.5	0.3	-	-	-	-	29.4	-0.3

[Continued]

Cincinnati, OH-KY-IN
Consumer Price Index - Urban Wage Earners
Base 1982-1984 = 100
All Items
[Continued]

For 1917-1997. Columns headed % show percentile change in the index from the previous period for which an index is available.

Year	Jan Index	%	Feb Index	%	Mar Index	%	Apr Index	%	May Index	%	Jun Index	%	Jul Index	%	Aug Index	%	Sep Index	%	Oct Index	%	Nov Index	%	Dec Index	%
1962	-	-	-	-	29.6	0.7	-	-	-	-	29.6	0.0	-	-	-	-	29.9	1.0	-	-	-	-	29.8	-0.3
1963	-	-	-	-	30.0	0.7	-	-	-	-	30.0	0.0	-	-	-	-	30.1	0.3	-	-	-	-	30.1	0.0
1964	-	-	-	-	30.3	0.7	-	-	-	-	30.4	0.3	-	-	-	-	30.7	1.0	-	-	-	-	30.7	0.0
1965	-	-	-	-	30.6	-0.3	-	-	-	-	30.8	0.7	-	-	-	-	30.7	-0.3	-	-	-	-	30.9	0.7
1966	-	-	-	-	31.3	1.3	-	-	-	-	31.6	1.0	-	-	-	-	32.0	1.3	-	-	-	-	31.9	-0.3
1967	-	-	-	-	32.0	0.3	-	-	-	-	32.4	1.3	-	-	-	-	32.9	1.5	-	-	-	-	33.3	1.2
1968	-	-	-	-	33.6	0.9	-	-	-	-	34.0	1.2	-	-	-	-	34.5	1.5	-	-	-	-	34.7	0.6
1969	-	-	-	-	35.2	1.4	-	-	-	-	35.7	1.4	-	-	-	-	36.0	0.8	-	-	-	-	36.6	1.7
1970	-	-	-	-	37.0	1.1	-	-	-	-	37.6	1.6	-	-	-	-	38.0	1.1	-	-	-	-	38.6	1.6
1971	-	-	-	-	39.0	1.0	-	-	-	-	39.3	0.8	-	-	-	-	39.5	0.5	-	-	-	-	39.7	0.5
1972	-	-	-	-	40.0	0.8	-	-	-	-	40.5	1.3	-	-	-	-	41.1	1.5	-	-	-	-	41.2	0.2
1973	-	-	-	-	42.2	2.4	-	-	-	-	42.6	0.9	-	-	-	-	43.7	2.6	-	-	-	-	44.5	1.8
1974	-	-	-	-	46.0	3.4	-	-	-	-	47.4	3.0	-	-	-	-	48.9	3.2	-	-	-	-	50.0	2.2
1975	-	-	-	-	50.7	1.4	-	-	-	-	52.3	3.2	-	-	-	-	53.3	1.9	-	-	-	-	53.6	0.6
1976	-	-	-	-	54.4	1.5	-	-	-	-	55.3	1.7	-	-	-	-	56.0	1.3	-	-	-	-	56.8	1.4
1977	-	-	-	-	58.2	2.5	-	-	-	-	59.2	1.7	-	-	-	-	60.3	1.9	-	-	-	-	60.8	0.8
1978	-	-	-	-	62.6	3.0	-	-	64.3	2.7	-	-	65.4	1.7	-	-	66.3	1.4	-	-	67.5	1.8	-	-
1979	69.1	2.4	-	-	70.5	2.0	-	-	72.6	3.0	-	-	73.7	1.5	-	-	75.1	1.9	-	-	76.7	2.1	-	-
1980	78.4	2.2	-	-	81.3	3.7	-	-	82.3	1.2	-	-	84.3	2.4	-	-	85.2	1.1	-	-	85.7	0.6	-	-
1981	86.7	1.2	-	-	87.1	0.5	-	-	88.9	2.1	-	-	89.9	1.1	-	-	90.2	0.3	-	-	90.8	0.7	-	-
1982	93.8	3.3	-	-	93.5	-0.3	-	-	94.8	1.4	-	-	96.3	1.6	-	-	98.5	2.3	-	-	99.9	1.4	-	-
1983	99.3	-0.6	-	-	100.1	0.8	-	-	100.7	0.6	-	-	100.2	-0.5	-	-	101.3	1.1	-	-	102.8	1.5	-	-
1984	102.0	-0.8	-	-	102.1	0.1	-	-	101.6	-0.5	-	-	102.3	0.7	-	-	104.4	2.1	-	-	103.9	-0.5	-	-
1985	103.8	-0.1	-	-	104.8	1.0	-	-	105.4	0.6	-	-	105.2	-0.2	-	-	105.0	-0.2	-	-	106.1	1.0	-	-
1986	106.1	0.0	-	-	104.7	-1.3	-	-	105.7	1.0	-	-	105.7	0.0	-	-	105.7	0.0	-	-	106.6	0.9	-	-
1987	-	-	-	-	-	-	-	-	-	-	109.6	2.8	-	-	-	-	-	-	-	-	-	-	112.6	2.7
1988	-	-	-	-	-	-	-	-	-	-	113.3	0.6	-	-	-	-	-	-	-	-	-	-	117.3	3.5
1989	-	-	-	-	-	-	-	-	-	-	119.5	1.9	-	-	-	-	-	-	-	-	-	-	122.8	2.8
1990	-	-	-	-	-	-	-	-	-	-	126.1	2.7	-	-	-	-	-	-	-	-	-	-	129.6	2.8
1991	-	-	-	-	-	-	-	-	-	-	132.1	1.9	-	-	-	-	-	-	-	-	-	-	133.7	1.2
1992	-	-	-	-	-	-	-	-	-	-	135.5	1.3	-	-	-	-	-	-	-	-	-	-	137.9	1.8
1993	-	-	-	-	-	-	-	-	-	-	140.1	1.6	-	-	-	-	-	-	-	-	-	-	141.8	1.2
1994	-	-	-	-	-	-	-	-	-	-	142.9	0.8	-	-	-	-	-	-	-	-	-	-	145.1	1.5
1995	-	-	-	-	-	-	-	-	-	-	147.9	1.9	-	-	-	-	-	-	-	-	-	-	149.0	0.7
1996	-	-	-	-	-	-	-	-	-	-	151.2	1.5	-	-	-	-	-	-	-	-	-	-	153.6	1.6
1997	-	-	-	-	-	-	-	-	-	-	155.6	1.3	-	-	-	-	-	-	-	-	-	-	-	-

Source: U.S. Department of Labor, Bureau of Labor Statistics, Division of Consumer Prices and Price Indexes. - indicates no data collected for period.

Cincinnati, OH-KY-IN
Consumer Price Index - All Urban Consumers
Base 1982-1984 = 100
Food and Beverages

For 1975-1997. Columns headed % show percentile change in the index from the previous period for which an index is available.

Year	Jan Index	Jan %	Feb Index	Feb %	Mar Index	Mar %	Apr Index	Apr %	May Index	May %	Jun Index	Jun %	Jul Index	Jul %	Aug Index	Aug %	Sep Index	Sep %	Oct Index	Oct %	Nov Index	Nov %	Dec Index	Dec %
1975	-	-	-	-	-	-	-	-	-	-	-	-	-	-	-	-	-	-	-	-	-	-	59.1	-
1976	-	-	-	-	59.2	0.2	-	-	-	-	60.2	1.7	-	-	-	-	60.7	0.8	-	-	-	-	60.7	0.0
1977	-	-	-	-	63.0	3.8	-	-	-	-	64.5	2.4	-	-	-	-	65.5	1.6	-	-	-	-	66.0	0.8
1978	-	-	-	-	68.5	3.8	-	-	70.4	2.8	-	-	72.7	3.3	-	-	72.4	-0.4	-	-	73.5	1.5	-	-
1979	75.6	2.9	-	-	77.5	2.5	-	-	79.5	2.6	-	-	79.7	0.3	-	-	79.9	0.3	-	-	80.8	1.1	-	-
1980	82.2	1.7	-	-	83.5	1.6	-	-	84.7	1.4	-	-	85.8	1.3	-	-	87.9	2.4	-	-	89.1	1.4	-	-
1981	91.4	2.6	-	-	92.5	1.2	-	-	93.1	0.6	-	-	93.2	0.1	-	-	94.0	0.9	-	-	93.8	-0.2	-	-
1982	95.2	1.5	-	-	95.3	0.1	-	-	96.6	1.4	-	-	98.4	1.9	-	-	98.1	-0.3	-	-	97.7	-0.4	-	-
1983	97.7	0.0	-	-	99.0	1.3	-	-	99.5	0.5	-	-	99.2	-0.3	-	-	98.8	-0.4	-	-	99.7	0.9	-	-
1984	102.4	2.7	-	-	103.5	1.1	-	-	103.9	0.4	-	-	103.7	-0.2	-	-	104.7	1.0	-	-	104.5	-0.2	-	-
1985	104.1	-0.4	-	-	105.4	1.2	-	-	105.1	-0.3	-	-	104.4	-0.7	-	-	104.1	-0.3	-	-	104.4	0.3	-	-
1986	105.0	0.6	-	-	105.2	0.2	-	-	106.0	0.8	-	-	107.8	1.7	-	-	109.0	1.1	-	-	109.2	0.2	-	-
1987	-	-	-	-	-	-	-	-	-	-	112.8	3.3	-	-	-	-	-	-	-	-	-	-	113.6	0.7
1988	-	-	-	-	-	-	-	-	-	-	115.2	1.4	-	-	-	-	-	-	-	-	-	-	118.9	3.2
1989	-	-	-	-	-	-	-	-	-	-	121.8	2.4	-	-	-	-	-	-	-	-	-	-	123.2	1.1
1990	-	-	-	-	-	-	-	-	-	-	128.9	4.6	-	-	-	-	-	-	-	-	-	-	131.6	2.1
1991	-	-	-	-	-	-	-	-	-	-	135.6	3.0	-	-	-	-	-	-	-	-	-	-	135.4	-0.1
1992	-	-	-	-	-	-	-	-	-	-	138.5	2.3	-	-	-	-	-	-	-	-	-	-	139.8	0.9
1993	-	-	-	-	-	-	-	-	-	-	142.2	1.7	-	-	-	-	-	-	-	-	-	-	143.9	1.2
1994	-	-	-	-	-	-	-	-	-	-	146.8	2.0	-	-	-	-	-	-	-	-	-	-	147.2	0.3
1995	-	-	-	-	-	-	-	-	-	-	151.1	2.6	-	-	-	-	-	-	-	-	-	-	151.6	0.3
1996	-	-	-	-	-	-	-	-	-	-	154.2	1.7	-	-	-	-	-	-	-	-	-	-	158.0	2.5
1997	-	-	-	-	-	-	-	-	-	-	159.6	1.0	-	-	-	-	-	-	-	-	-	-	-	-

Source: U.S. Department of Labor, Bureau of Labor Statistics, Division of Consumer Prices and Price Indexes. - indicates no data collected for period.

Cincinnati, OH-KY-IN
Consumer Price Index - Urban Wage Earners
Base 1982-1984 = 100
Food and Beverages

For 1975-1997. Columns headed % show percentile change in the index from the previous period for which an index is available.

Year	Jan Index	%	Feb Index	%	Mar Index	%	Apr Index	%	May Index	%	Jun Index	%	Jul Index	%	Aug Index	%	Sep Index	%	Oct Index	%	Nov Index	%	Dec Index	%
1975	-	-	-	-	-	-	-	-	-	-	-	-	-	-	-	-	-	-	-	-	-	-	58.9	-
1976	-	-	-	-	59.0	0.2	-	-	-	-	60.0	1.7	-	-	-	-	60.4	0.7	-	-	-	-	60.4	0.0
1977	-	-	-	-	62.7	3.8	-	-	-	-	64.3	2.6	-	-	-	-	65.3	1.6	-	-	-	-	65.8	0.8
1978	-	-	-	-	68.3	3.8	-	-	70.6	3.4	-	-	72.6	2.8	-	-	72.3	-0.4	-	-	73.7	1.9	-	-
1979	76.1	3.3	-	-	77.8	2.2	-	-	80.3	3.2	-	-	80.5	0.2	-	-	80.8	0.4	-	-	81.5	0.9	-	-
1980	82.2	0.9	-	-	83.8	1.9	-	-	85.0	1.4	-	-	86.4	1.6	-	-	88.6	2.5	-	-	89.3	0.8	-	-
1981	91.5	2.5	-	-	92.2	0.8	-	-	92.6	0.4	-	-	92.9	0.3	-	-	93.7	0.9	-	-	93.8	0.1	-	-
1982	95.6	1.9	-	-	95.7	0.1	-	-	96.9	1.3	-	-	98.4	1.5	-	-	98.2	-0.2	-	-	97.8	-0.4	-	-
1983	97.8	0.0	-	-	99.2	1.4	-	-	99.7	0.5	-	-	99.2	-0.5	-	-	98.8	-0.4	-	-	99.7	0.9	-	-
1984	102.3	2.6	-	-	103.3	1.0	-	-	103.7	0.4	-	-	103.3	-0.4	-	-	104.4	1.1	-	-	104.1	-0.3	-	-
1985	104.0	-0.1	-	-	105.3	1.3	-	-	104.8	-0.5	-	-	104.0	-0.8	-	-	103.8	-0.2	-	-	104.1	0.3	-	-
1986	104.7	0.6	-	-	105.0	0.3	-	-	105.7	0.7	-	-	107.4	1.6	-	-	108.4	0.9	-	-	108.8	0.4	-	-
1987	-	-	-	-	-	-	-	-	-	-	113.0	3.9	-	-	-	-	-	-	-	-	-	-	113.7	0.6
1988	-	-	-	-	-	-	-	-	-	-	115.3	1.4	-	-	-	-	-	-	-	-	-	-	119.0	3.2
1989	-	-	-	-	-	-	-	-	-	-	121.9	2.4	-	-	-	-	-	-	-	-	-	-	123.3	1.1
1990	-	-	-	-	-	-	-	-	-	-	129.1	4.7	-	-	-	-	-	-	-	-	-	-	131.8	2.1
1991	-	-	-	-	-	-	-	-	-	-	135.8	3.0	-	-	-	-	-	-	-	-	-	-	135.6	-0.1
1992	-	-	-	-	-	-	-	-	-	-	138.5	2.1	-	-	-	-	-	-	-	-	-	-	139.9	1.0
1993	-	-	-	-	-	-	-	-	-	-	142.4	1.8	-	-	-	-	-	-	-	-	-	-	144.2	1.3
1994	-	-	-	-	-	-	-	-	-	-	147.0	1.9	-	-	-	-	-	-	-	-	-	-	147.4	0.3
1995	-	-	-	-	-	-	-	-	-	-	151.3	2.6	-	-	-	-	-	-	-	-	-	-	151.8	0.3
1996	-	-	-	-	-	-	-	-	-	-	154.3	1.6	-	-	-	-	-	-	-	-	-	-	158.3	2.6
1997	-	-	-	-	-	-	-	-	-	-	159.9	1.0	-	-	-	-	-	-	-	-	-	-	-	-

Source: U.S. Department of Labor, Bureau of Labor Statistics, Division of Consumer Prices and Price Indexes. - indicates no data collected for period.

Cincinnati, OH-KY-IN
Consumer Price Index - All Urban Consumers
Base 1982-1984 = 100
Housing

For 1975-1997. Columns headed % show percentile change in the index from the previous period for which an index is available.

Year	Jan Index	%	Feb Index	%	Mar Index	%	Apr Index	%	May Index	%	Jun Index	%	Jul Index	%	Aug Index	%	Sep Index	%	Oct Index	%	Nov Index	%	Dec Index	%
1975	-	-	-	-	-	-	-	-	-	-	-	-	-	-	-	-	-	-	-	-	-	-	49.3	-
1976	-	-	-	-	50.2	1.8	-	-	-	-	50.6	0.8	-	-	-	-	51.0	0.8	-	-	-	-	52.5	2.9
1977	-	-	-	-	53.3	1.5	-	-	-	-	54.2	1.7	-	-	-	-	55.4	2.2	-	-	-	-	56.2	1.4
1978	-	-	-	-	58.0	3.2	-	-	59.9	3.3	-	-	60.4	0.8	-	-	62.2	3.0	-	-	63.5	2.1	-	-
1979	64.7	1.9	-	-	66.6	2.9	-	-	68.1	2.3	-	-	69.2	1.6	-	-	70.5	1.9	-	-	72.7	3.1	-	-
1980	74.7	2.8	-	-	78.1	4.6	-	-	79.3	1.5	-	-	82.2	3.7	-	-	82.1	-0.1	-	-	82.5	0.5	-	-
1981	82.2	-0.4	-	-	81.2	-1.2	-	-	84.7	4.3	-	-	85.4	0.8	-	-	84.6	-0.9	-	-	85.2	0.7	-	-
1982	90.0	5.6	-	-	89.4	-0.7	-	-	91.6	2.5	-	-	92.7	1.2	-	-	96.6	4.2	-	-	99.3	2.8	-	-
1983	99.6	0.3	-	-	101.1	1.5	-	-	102.4	1.3	-	-	102.6	0.2	-	-	103.1	0.5	-	-	103.0	-0.1	-	-
1984	103.3	0.3	-	-	103.6	0.3	-	-	104.0	0.4	-	-	104.6	0.6	-	-	104.6	0.0	-	-	104.7	0.1	-	-
1985	105.7	1.0	-	-	106.2	0.5	-	-	106.7	0.5	-	-	107.4	0.7	-	-	106.7	-0.7	-	-	107.4	0.7	-	-
1986	107.8	0.4	-	-	108.5	0.6	-	-	109.1	0.6	-	-	109.3	0.2	-	-	107.3	-1.8	-	-	109.1	1.7	-	-
1987	-	-	-	-	-	-	-	-	-	-	114.4	4.9	-	-	-	-	-	-	-	-	-	-	118.3	3.4
1988	-	-	-	-	-	-	-	-	-	-	118.3	0.0	-	-	-	-	-	-	-	-	-	-	123.1	4.1
1989	-	-	-	-	-	-	-	-	-	-	124.7	1.3	-	-	-	-	-	-	-	-	-	-	128.1	2.7
1990	-	-	-	-	-	-	-	-	-	-	129.9	1.4	-	-	-	-	-	-	-	-	-	-	132.8	2.2
1991	-	-	-	-	-	-	-	-	-	-	135.5	2.0	-	-	-	-	-	-	-	-	-	-	137.3	1.3
1992	-	-	-	-	-	-	-	-	-	-	139.0	1.2	-	-	-	-	-	-	-	-	-	-	140.8	1.3
1993	-	-	-	-	-	-	-	-	-	-	142.3	1.1	-	-	-	-	-	-	-	-	-	-	144.2	1.3
1994	-	-	-	-	-	-	-	-	-	-	143.9	-0.2	-	-	-	-	-	-	-	-	-	-	145.8	1.3
1995	-	-	-	-	-	-	-	-	-	-	149.6	2.6	-	-	-	-	-	-	-	-	-	-	151.6	1.3
1996	-	-	-	-	-	-	-	-	-	-	153.9	1.5	-	-	-	-	-	-	-	-	-	-	156.4	1.6
1997	-	-	-	-	-	-	-	-	-	-	158.7	1.5	-	-	-	-	-	-	-	-	-	-	-	-

Source: U.S. Department of Labor, Bureau of Labor Statistics, Division of Consumer Prices and Price Indexes. - indicates no data collected for period.

Cincinnati, OH-KY-IN
Consumer Price Index - Urban Wage Earners
Base 1982-1984 = 100
Housing

For 1975-1997. Columns headed % show percentile change in the index from the previous period for which an index is available.

Year	Jan Index	%	Feb Index	%	Mar Index	%	Apr Index	%	May Index	%	Jun Index	%	Jul Index	%	Aug Index	%	Sep Index	%	Oct Index	%	Nov Index	%	Dec Index	%
1975	-	-	-	-	-	-	-	-	-	-	-	-	-	-	-	-	-	-	-	-	-	-	50.2	-
1976	-	-	-	-	51.1	1.8	-	-	-	-	51.5	0.8	-	-	-	-	51.9	0.8	-	-	-	-	53.5	3.1
1977	-	-	-	-	54.3	1.5	-	-	-	-	55.2	1.7	-	-	-	-	56.5	2.4	-	-	-	-	57.2	1.2
1978	-	-	-	-	59.1	3.3	-	-	61.0	3.2	-	-	61.7	1.1	-	-	63.3	2.6	-	-	65.0	2.7	-	-
1979	66.2	1.8	-	-	68.3	3.2	-	-	69.9	2.3	-	-	71.0	1.6	-	-	72.3	1.8	-	-	74.8	3.5	-	-
1980	76.9	2.8	-	-	80.5	4.7	-	-	81.5	1.2	-	-	84.5	3.7	-	-	84.3	-0.2	-	-	84.7	0.5	-	-
1981	84.4	-0.4	-	-	83.2	-1.4	-	-	86.6	4.1	-	-	87.7	1.3	-	-	86.7	-1.1	-	-	87.5	0.9	-	-
1982	92.7	5.9	-	-	91.9	-0.9	-	-	94.3	2.6	-	-	95.5	1.3	-	-	99.7	4.4	-	-	102.7	3.0	-	-
1983	100.5	-2.1	-	-	102.3	1.8	-	-	102.3	0.0	-	-	100.7	-1.6	-	-	102.0	1.3	-	-	104.1	2.1	-	-
1984	101.4	-2.6	-	-	101.0	-0.4	-	-	99.1	-1.9	-	-	100.4	1.3	-	-	103.9	3.5	-	-	102.7	-1.2	-	-
1985	103.7	1.0	-	-	104.2	0.5	-	-	104.5	0.3	-	-	105.2	0.7	-	-	104.4	-0.8	-	-	105.2	0.8	-	-
1986	105.6	0.4	-	-	106.3	0.7	-	-	107.0	0.7	-	-	107.0	0.0	-	-	104.8	-2.1	-	-	106.8	1.9	-	-
1987	-	-	-	-	-	-	-	-	-	-	107.9	1.0	-	-	-	-	-	-	-	-	-	-	111.5	3.3
1988	-	-	-	-	-	-	-	-	-	-	111.3	-0.2	-	-	-	-	-	-	-	-	-	-	115.9	4.1
1989	-	-	-	-	-	-	-	-	-	-	117.3	1.2	-	-	-	-	-	-	-	-	-	-	120.6	2.8
1990	-	-	-	-	-	-	-	-	-	-	122.4	1.5	-	-	-	-	-	-	-	-	-	-	125.2	2.3
1991	-	-	-	-	-	-	-	-	-	-	127.5	1.8	-	-	-	-	-	-	-	-	-	-	129.2	1.3
1992	-	-	-	-	-	-	-	-	-	-	130.8	1.2	-	-	-	-	-	-	-	-	-	-	132.6	1.4
1993	-	-	-	-	-	-	-	-	-	-	134.1	1.1	-	-	-	-	-	-	-	-	-	-	135.9	1.3
1994	-	-	-	-	-	-	-	-	-	-	135.6	-0.2	-	-	-	-	-	-	-	-	-	-	137.1	1.1
1995	-	-	-	-	-	-	-	-	-	-	140.6	2.6	-	-	-	-	-	-	-	-	-	-	142.3	1.2
1996	-	-	-	-	-	-	-	-	-	-	144.6	1.6	-	-	-	-	-	-	-	-	-	-	146.9	1.6
1997	-	-	-	-	-	-	-	-	-	-	149.1	1.5	-	-	-	-	-	-	-	-	-	-	-	-

Source: U.S. Department of Labor, Bureau of Labor Statistics, Division of Consumer Prices and Price Indexes. - indicates no data collected for period.

Cincinnati, OH-KY-IN

Consumer Price Index - All Urban Consumers
Base 1982-1984 = 100

Apparel and Upkeep

For 1952-1997. Columns headed % show percentile change in the index from the previous period for which an index is available.

Year	Jan Index	%	Feb Index	%	Mar Index	%	Apr Index	%	May Index	%	Jun Index	%	Jul Index	%	Aug Index	%	Sep Index	%	Oct Index	%	Nov Index	%	Dec Index	%
1952	-	-	-	-	-	-	-	-	-	-	-	-	-	-	-	-	-	-	-	-	-	-	36.9	-
1953	-	-	-	-	37.1	0.5	-	-	-	-	37.7	1.6	-	-	-	-	37.8	0.3	-	-	-	-	37.4	-1.1
1954	-	-	-	-	37.1	-0.8	-	-	-	-	37.0	-0.3	-	-	-	-	37.5	1.4	-	-	-	-	37.2	-0.8
1955	-	-	-	-	37.3	0.3	-	-	-	-	37.2	-0.3	-	-	-	-	38.0	2.2	-	-	-	-	38.1	0.3
1956	-	-	-	-	38.6	1.3	-	-	-	-	38.4	-0.5	-	-	-	-	38.8	1.0	-	-	-	-	38.7	-0.3
1957	-	-	-	-	38.6	-0.3	-	-	-	-	38.6	0.0	-	-	-	-	39.4	2.1	-	-	-	-	38.9	-1.3
1958	-	-	-	-	39.0	0.3	-	-	-	-	38.7	-0.8	-	-	-	-	39.3	1.6	-	-	-	-	39.3	0.0
1959	-	-	-	-	39.3	0.0	-	-	-	-	39.3	0.0	-	-	-	-	39.7	1.0	-	-	-	-	39.7	0.0
1960	-	-	-	-	39.8	0.3	-	-	-	-	40.1	0.8	-	-	-	-	40.6	1.2	-	-	-	-	40.2	-1.0
1961	-	-	-	-	40.2	0.0	-	-	-	-	39.9	-0.7	-	-	-	-	40.6	1.8	-	-	-	-	40.5	-0.2
1962	-	-	-	-	40.5	0.0	-	-	-	-	40.5	0.0	-	-	-	-	40.9	1.0	-	-	-	-	40.8	-0.2
1963	-	-	-	-	40.9	0.2	-	-	-	-	40.7	-0.5	-	-	-	-	41.3	1.5	-	-	-	-	41.2	-0.2
1964	-	-	-	-	41.3	0.2	-	-	-	-	41.4	0.2	-	-	-	-	41.9	1.2	-	-	-	-	41.4	-1.2
1965	-	-	-	-	41.5	0.2	-	-	-	-	41.5	0.0	-	-	-	-	42.1	1.4	-	-	-	-	42.1	0.0
1966	-	-	-	-	42.7	1.4	-	-	-	-	43.3	1.4	-	-	-	-	44.0	1.6	-	-	-	-	44.0	0.0
1967	-	-	-	-	44.4	0.9	-	-	-	-	44.3	-0.2	-	-	-	-	45.7	3.2	-	-	-	-	46.0	0.7
1968	-	-	-	-	46.9	2.0	-	-	-	-	47.3	0.9	-	-	-	-	49.8	5.3	-	-	-	-	49.9	0.2
1969	-	-	-	-	50.3	0.8	-	-	-	-	50.9	1.2	-	-	-	-	52.3	2.8	-	-	-	-	52.3	0.0
1970	-	-	-	-	52.8	1.0	-	-	-	-	53.1	0.6	-	-	-	-	54.1	1.9	-	-	-	-	54.9	1.5
1971	-	-	-	-	55.2	0.5	-	-	-	-	54.7	-0.9	-	-	-	-	55.2	0.9	-	-	-	-	54.9	-0.5
1972	-	-	-	-	54.6	-0.5	-	-	-	-	54.7	0.2	-	-	-	-	55.9	2.2	-	-	-	-	56.2	0.5
1973	-	-	-	-	56.7	0.9	-	-	-	-	56.8	0.2	-	-	-	-	58.5	3.0	-	-	-	-	59.1	1.0
1974	-	-	-	-	59.8	1.2	-	-	-	-	60.8	1.7	-	-	-	-	63.5	4.4	-	-	-	-	63.7	0.3
1975	-	-	-	-	64.0	0.5	-	-	-	-	63.3	-1.1	-	-	-	-	65.6	3.6	-	-	-	-	66.1	0.8
1976	-	-	-	-	68.0	2.9	-	-	-	-	67.9	-0.1	-	-	-	-	70.6	4.0	-	-	-	-	70.0	-0.8
1977	-	-	-	-	71.1	1.6	-	-	-	-	71.1	0.0	-	-	-	-	73.9	3.9	-	-	-	-	74.7	1.1
1978	-	-	-	-	75.8	1.5	-	-	78.7	3.8	-	-	76.7	-2.5	-	-	78.9	2.9	-	-	80.0	1.4	-	-
1979	80.3	0.4	-	-	78.0	-2.9	-	-	83.1	6.5	-	-	81.5	-1.9	-	-	84.4	3.6	-	-	83.5	-1.1	-	-
1980	86.2	3.2	-	-	88.8	3.0	-	-	88.5	-0.3	-	-	85.2	-3.7	-	-	92.9	9.0	-	-	92.4	-0.5	-	-
1981	89.5	-3.1	-	-	94.7	5.8	-	-	91.5	-3.4	-	-	88.8	-3.0	-	-	97.7	10.0	-	-	96.9	-0.8	-	-
1982	94.3	-2.7	-	-	98.4	4.3	-	-	96.7	-1.7	-	-	95.5	-1.2	-	-	100.4	5.1	-	-	98.9	-1.5	-	-
1983	101.1	2.2	-	-	100.9	-0.2	-	-	98.6	-2.3	-	-	99.5	0.9	-	-	102.6	3.1	-	-	102.1	-0.5	-	-
1984	97.3	-4.7	-	-	101.5	4.3	-	-	102.7	1.2	-	-	101.8	-0.9	-	-	104.4	2.6	-	-	101.6	-2.7	-	-
1985	101.7	0.1	-	-	103.6	1.9	-	-	102.7	-0.9	-	-	98.0	-4.6	-	-	105.4	7.6	-	-	108.6	3.0	-	-
1986	103.3	-4.9	-	-	103.8	0.5	-	-	102.7	-1.1	-	-	101.7	-1.0	-	-	111.3	9.4	-	-	109.3	-1.8	-	-
1987	-	-	-	-	-	-	-	-	-	-	106.4	-2.7	-	-	-	-	-	-	-	-	-	-	112.1	5.4
1988	-	-	-	-	-	-	-	-	-	-	113.9	1.6	-	-	-	-	-	-	-	-	-	-	119.3	4.7
1989	-	-	-	-	-	-	-	-	-	-	115.5	-3.2	-	-	-	-	-	-	-	-	-	-	120.6	4.4
1990	-	-	-	-	-	-	-	-	-	-	124.0	2.8	-	-	-	-	-	-	-	-	-	-	124.6	0.5
1991	-	-	-	-	-	-	-	-	-	-	124.0	-0.5	-	-	-	-	-	-	-	-	-	-	126.5	2.0
1992	-	-	-	-	-	-	-	-	-	-	124.9	-1.3	-	-	-	-	-	-	-	-	-	-	127.6	2.2
1993	-	-	-	-	-	-	-	-	-	-	130.9	2.6	-	-	-	-	-	-	-	-	-	-	131.4	0.4
1994	-	-	-	-	-	-	-	-	-	-	131.0	-0.3	-	-	-	-	-	-	-	-	-	-	130.9	-0.1

[Continued]

Cincinnati, OH-KY-IN
Consumer Price Index - All Urban Consumers
Base 1982-1984 = 100
Apparel and Upkeep
[Continued]

For 1952-1997. Columns headed % show percentile change in the index from the previous period for which an index is available.

Year	Jan Index	%	Feb Index	%	Mar Index	%	Apr Index	%	May Index	%	Jun Index	%	Jul Index	%	Aug Index	%	Sep Index	%	Oct Index	%	Nov Index	%	Dec Index	%
1995	-	-	-	-	-	-	-	-	-	-	127.3	-2.8	-	-	-	-	-	-	-	-	-	-	125.4	-1.5
1996	-	-	-	-	-	-	-	-	-	-	122.5	-2.3	-	-	-	-	-	-	-	-	-	-	118.7	-3.1
1997	-	-	-	-	-	-	-	-	-	-	124.9	5.2	-	-	-	-	-	-	-	-	-	-	-	-

Source: U.S. Department of Labor, Bureau of Labor Statistics, Division of Consumer Prices and Price Indexes. - indicates no data collected for period.

Cincinnati, OH-KY-IN
Consumer Price Index - Urban Wage Earners
Base 1982-1984 = 100
Apparel and Upkeep

For 1952-1997. Columns headed % show percentile change in the index from the previous period for which an index is available.

Year	Jan Index	%	Feb Index	%	Mar Index	%	Apr Index	%	May Index	%	Jun Index	%	Jul Index	%	Aug Index	%	Sep Index	%	Oct Index	%	Nov Index	%	Dec Index	%
1952	-	-	-	-	-	-	-	-	-	-	-	-	-	-	-	-	-	-	-	-	-	-	35.8	-
1953	-	-	-	-	36.1	0.8	-	-	-	-	36.6	1.4	-	-	-	-	36.7	0.3	-	-	-	-	36.3	-1.1
1954	-	-	-	-	36.1	-0.6	-	-	-	-	35.9	-0.6	-	-	-	-	36.4	1.4	-	-	-	-	36.1	-0.8
1955	-	-	-	-	36.2	0.3	-	-	-	-	36.1	-0.3	-	-	-	-	36.9	2.2	-	-	-	-	37.0	0.3
1956	-	-	-	-	37.5	1.4	-	-	-	-	37.2	-0.8	-	-	-	-	37.6	1.1	-	-	-	-	37.6	0.0
1957	-	-	-	-	37.5	-0.3	-	-	-	-	37.5	0.0	-	-	-	-	38.2	1.9	-	-	-	-	37.8	-1.0
1958	-	-	-	-	37.9	0.3	-	-	-	-	37.5	-1.1	-	-	-	-	38.2	1.9	-	-	-	-	38.2	0.0
1959	-	-	-	-	38.2	0.0	-	-	-	-	38.2	0.0	-	-	-	-	38.6	1.0	-	-	-	-	38.5	-0.3
1960	-	-	-	-	38.7	0.5	-	-	-	-	38.9	0.5	-	-	-	-	39.4	1.3	-	-	-	-	39.0	-1.0
1961	-	-	-	-	39.0	0.0	-	-	-	-	38.8	-0.5	-	-	-	-	39.4	1.5	-	-	-	-	39.3	-0.3
1962	-	-	-	-	39.3	0.0	-	-	-	-	39.3	0.0	-	-	-	-	39.7	1.0	-	-	-	-	39.6	-0.3
1963	-	-	-	-	39.7	0.3	-	-	-	-	39.6	-0.3	-	-	-	-	40.1	1.3	-	-	-	-	40.0	-0.2
1964	-	-	-	-	40.1	0.2	-	-	-	-	40.2	0.2	-	-	-	-	40.6	1.0	-	-	-	-	40.2	-1.0
1965	-	-	-	-	40.3	0.2	-	-	-	-	40.3	0.0	-	-	-	-	40.9	1.5	-	-	-	-	40.9	0.0
1966	-	-	-	-	41.4	1.2	-	-	-	-	42.0	1.4	-	-	-	-	42.7	1.7	-	-	-	-	42.7	0.0
1967	-	-	-	-	43.1	0.9	-	-	-	-	43.1	0.0	-	-	-	-	44.4	3.0	-	-	-	-	44.7	0.7
1968	-	-	-	-	45.5	1.8	-	-	-	-	46.0	1.1	-	-	-	-	48.4	5.2	-	-	-	-	48.4	0.0
1969	-	-	-	-	48.9	1.0	-	-	-	-	49.4	1.0	-	-	-	-	50.8	2.8	-	-	-	-	50.8	0.0
1970	-	-	-	-	51.3	1.0	-	-	-	-	51.5	0.4	-	-	-	-	52.6	2.1	-	-	-	-	53.3	1.3
1971	-	-	-	-	53.6	0.6	-	-	-	-	53.1	-0.9	-	-	-	-	53.6	0.9	-	-	-	-	53.3	-0.6
1972	-	-	-	-	53.0	-0.6	-	-	-	-	53.1	0.2	-	-	-	-	54.3	2.3	-	-	-	-	54.6	0.6
1973	-	-	-	-	55.1	0.9	-	-	-	-	55.1	0.0	-	-	-	-	56.8	3.1	-	-	-	-	57.4	1.1
1974	-	-	-	-	58.0	1.0	-	-	-	-	59.1	1.9	-	-	-	-	61.7	4.4	-	-	-	-	61.9	0.3
1975	-	-	-	-	62.1	0.3	-	-	-	-	61.5	-1.0	-	-	-	-	63.7	3.6	-	-	-	-	64.2	0.8
1976	-	-	-	-	66.0	2.8	-	-	-	-	66.0	0.0	-	-	-	-	68.5	3.8	-	-	-	-	67.9	-0.9
1977	-	-	-	-	69.1	1.8	-	-	-	-	69.1	0.0	-	-	-	-	71.7	3.8	-	-	-	-	72.5	1.1
1978	-	-	-	-	73.6	1.5	-	-	76.3	3.7	-	-	74.8	-2.0	-	-	77.7	3.9	-	-	77.6	-0.1	-	-
1979	79.5	2.4	-	-	76.6	-3.6	-	-	82.2	7.3	-	-	80.2	-2.4	-	-	83.6	4.2	-	-	83.4	-0.2	-	-
1980	81.9	-1.8	-	-	84.7	3.4	-	-	83.9	-0.9	-	-	85.5	1.9	-	-	90.9	6.3	-	-	91.1	0.2	-	-
1981	88.1	-3.3	-	-	92.7	5.2	-	-	91.2	-1.6	-	-	92.0	0.9	-	-	97.2	5.7	-	-	96.2	-1.0	-	-
1982	93.6	-2.7	-	-	97.7	4.4	-	-	96.8	-0.9	-	-	95.8	-1.0	-	-	100.9	5.3	-	-	99.1	-1.8	-	-
1983	100.2	1.1	-	-	101.7	1.5	-	-	98.6	-3.0	-	-	99.2	0.6	-	-	103.5	4.3	-	-	102.5	-1.0	-	-
1984	98.6	-3.8	-	-	101.7	3.1	-	-	102.3	0.6	-	-	100.8	-1.5	-	-	104.2	3.4	-	-	101.2	-2.9	-	-
1985	101.3	0.1	-	-	103.2	1.9	-	-	101.7	-1.5	-	-	97.2	-4.4	-	-	104.9	7.9	-	-	106.6	1.6	-	-
1986	101.9	-4.4	-	-	102.6	0.7	-	-	101.7	-0.9	-	-	102.6	0.9	-	-	109.5	6.7	-	-	108.2	-1.2	-	-
1987	-	-	-	-	-	-	-	-	-	-	106.8	-1.3	-	-	-	-	-	-	-	-	-	-	112.1	5.0
1988	-	-	-	-	-	-	-	-	-	-	113.1	0.9	-	-	-	-	-	-	-	-	-	-	119.1	5.3
1989	-	-	-	-	-	-	-	-	-	-	115.2	-3.3	-	-	-	-	-	-	-	-	-	-	120.0	4.2
1990	-	-	-	-	-	-	-	-	-	-	124.4	3.7	-	-	-	-	-	-	-	-	-	-	124.7	0.2
1991	-	-	-	-	-	-	-	-	-	-	124.9	0.2	-	-	-	-	-	-	-	-	-	-	126.4	1.2
1992	-	-	-	-	-	-	-	-	-	-	125.0	-1.1	-	-	-	-	-	-	-	-	-	-	126.8	1.4
1993	-	-	-	-	-	-	-	-	-	-	130.0	2.5	-	-	-	-	-	-	-	-	-	-	131.1	0.8
1994	-	-	-	-	-	-	-	-	-	-	130.8	-0.2	-	-	-	-	-	-	-	-	-	-	129.2	-1.2

[Continued]

Cincinnati, OH-KY-IN
Consumer Price Index - Urban Wage Earners
Base 1982-1984 = 100
Apparel and Upkeep
[Continued]

For 1952-1997. Columns headed % show percentile change in the index from the previous period for which an index is available.

Year	Jan		Feb		Mar		Apr		May		Jun		Jul		Aug		Sep		Oct		Nov		Dec	
	Index	%	Index	%	Index	%	Index	%	Index	%	Index	%	Index	%	Index	%	Index	%	Index	%	Index	%	Index	%
1995	-	-	-	-	-	-	-	-	-	-	126.0	-2.5	-	-	-	-	-	-	-	-	-	-	124.2	-1.4
1996	-	-	-	-	-	-	-	-	-	-	121.3	-2.3	-	-	-	-	-	-	-	-	-	-	117.9	-2.8
1997	-	-	-	-	-	-	-	-	-	-	122.2	3.6	-	-	-	-	-	-	-	-	-	-	-	-

Source: U.S. Department of Labor, Bureau of Labor Statistics, Division of Consumer Prices and Price Indexes. - indicates no data collected for period.

Cincinnati, OH-KY-IN
Consumer Price Index - All Urban Consumers
Base 1982-1984 = 100
Transportation

For 1947-1997. Columns headed % show percentile change in the index from the previous period for which an index is available.

Year	Jan Index	%	Feb Index	%	Mar Index	%	Apr Index	%	May Index	%	Jun Index	%	Jul Index	%	Aug Index	%	Sep Index	%	Oct Index	%	Nov Index	%	Dec Index	%
1947	19.8	-	19.8	0.0	20.2	2.0	20.2	0.0	20.2	0.0	20.2	0.0	20.5	1.5	20.5	0.0	21.0	2.4	21.0	0.0	21.9	4.3	22.1	0.9
1948	22.2	0.5	22.2	0.0	22.2	0.0	22.2	0.0	22.2	0.0	22.7	2.3	23.8	4.8	24.2	1.7	24.3	0.4	24.3	0.0	24.3	0.0	24.3	0.0
1949	24.3	0.0	24.6	1.2	25.2	2.4	25.3	0.4	25.3	0.0	25.2	-0.4	25.2	0.0	25.2	0.0	25.2	0.0	25.2	0.0	25.2	0.0	25.1	-0.4
1950	25.1	0.0	25.1	0.0	25.1	0.0	24.9	-0.8	25.6	2.8	25.6	0.0	25.7	0.4	26.0	1.2	26.0	0.0	26.0	0.0	26.0	0.0	26.1	0.4
1951	26.7	2.3	26.7	0.0	27.0	1.1	27.0	0.0	27.0	0.0	27.0	0.0	27.0	0.0	27.4	1.5	28.1	2.6	28.3	0.7	28.6	1.1	28.6	0.0
1952	28.6	0.0	28.9	1.0	28.9	0.0	28.8	-0.3	29.4	2.1	29.4	0.0	29.4	0.0	29.4	0.0	29.4	0.0	29.4	0.0	29.4	0.0	29.4	0.0
1953	-		-		30.0	2.0	-		-		29.9	-0.3	-		-		30.2	1.0	-		-		30.0	-0.7
1954	-		-		29.4	-2.0	-		-		29.1	-1.0	-		-		29.2	0.3	-		-		28.4	-2.7
1955	-		-		28.5	0.4	-		-		28.3	-0.7	-		-		27.7	-2.1	-		-		28.1	1.4
1956	-		-		27.8	-1.1	-		-		28.1	1.1	-		-		28.5	1.4	-		-		29.5	3.5
1957	-		-		29.7	0.7	-		-		29.9	0.7	-		-		30.4	1.7	-		-		30.7	1.0
1958	-		-		30.4	-1.0	-		-		30.4	0.0	-		-		30.6	0.7	-		-		32.1	4.9
1959	-		-		32.5	1.2	-		-		32.8	0.9	-		-		32.7	-0.3	-		-		34.1	4.3
1960	-		-		33.5	-1.8	-		-		32.9	-1.8	-		-		32.8	-0.3	-		-		32.8	0.0
1961	-		-		32.8	0.0	-		-		33.3	1.5	-		-		33.6	0.9	-		-		32.9	-2.1
1962	-		-		33.8	2.7	-		-		33.8	0.0	-		-		33.9	0.3	-		-		33.8	-0.3
1963	-		-		33.9	0.3	-		-		33.8	-0.3	-		-		34.0	0.6	-		-		34.2	0.6
1964	-		-		34.4	0.6	-		-		34.4	0.0	-		-		34.5	0.3	-		-		34.5	0.0
1965	-		-		34.3	-0.6	-		-		34.5	0.6	-		-		34.6	0.3	-		-		34.8	0.6
1966	-		-		34.7	-0.3	-		-		35.1	1.2	-		-		35.5	1.1	-		-		35.3	-0.6
1967	-		-		35.1	-0.6	-		-		35.6	1.4	-		-		36.2	1.7	-		-		37.2	2.8
1968	-		-		37.4	0.5	-		-		37.9	1.3	-		-		37.9	0.0	-		-		37.6	-0.8
1969	-		-		38.9	3.5	-		-		38.9	0.0	-		-		38.5	-1.0	-		-		39.4	2.3
1970	-		-		39.0	-1.0	-		-		40.8	4.6	-		-		41.1	0.7	-		-		42.9	4.4
1971	-		-		42.3	-1.4	-		-		43.3	2.4	-		-		43.1	-0.5	-		-		43.6	1.2
1972	-		-		42.7	-2.1	-		-		44.5	4.2	-		-		45.6	2.5	-		-		45.2	-0.9
1973	-		-		45.5	0.7	-		-		43.8	-3.7	-		-		43.6	-0.5	-		-		43.8	0.5
1974	-		-		45.1	3.0	-		-		48.4	7.3	-		-		49.6	2.5	-		-		49.6	0.0
1975	-		-		49.7	0.2	-		-		51.7	4.0	-		-		53.3	3.1	-		-		53.2	-0.2
1976	-		-		53.2	0.0	-		-		56.5	6.2	-		-		57.5	1.8	-		-		58.2	1.2
1977	-		-		59.4	2.1	-		-		60.9	2.5	-		-		60.2	-1.1	-		-		60.1	-0.2
1978	-		-		60.7	1.0	-		61.7	1.6	-		62.9	1.9	-		63.5	1.0	-		64.5	1.6	-	
1979	65.2	1.1	-		66.4	1.8	-		69.6	4.8	-		72.6	4.3	-		75.1	3.4	-		76.5	1.9	-	
1980	79.0	3.3	-		81.3	2.9	-		83.6	2.8	-		85.0	1.7	-		86.1	1.3	-		87.2	1.3	-	
1981	89.8	3.0	-		92.2	2.7	-		93.5	1.4	-		94.0	0.5	-		95.0	1.1	-		96.3	1.4	-	
1982	97.2	0.9	-		95.4	-1.9	-		95.2	-0.2	-		98.8	3.8	-		98.5	-0.3	-		98.4	-0.1	-	
1983	98.0	-0.4	-		95.8	-2.2	-		99.1	3.4	-		100.0	0.9	-		101.4	1.4	-		102.6	1.2	-	
1984	101.8	-0.8	-		101.7	-0.1	-		102.9	1.2	-		103.2	0.3	-		103.7	0.5	-		104.8	1.1	-	
1985	103.3	-1.4	-		104.8	1.5	-		107.2	2.3	-		107.1	-0.1	-		105.4	-1.6	-		107.6	2.1	-	
1986	106.8	-0.7	-		98.4	-7.9	-		100.4	2.0	-		97.8	-2.6	-		98.0	0.2	-		98.7	0.7	-	
1987	-		-		-		-		-		104.6	6.0	-		-		-		-		-		107.6	2.9
1988	-		-		-		-		-		107.1	-0.5	-		-		-		-		-		108.2	1.0
1989	-		-		-		-		-		111.4	3.0	-		-		-		-		-		112.7	1.2
1990	-		-		-		-		-		115.7	2.7	-		-		-		-		-		121.7	5.2
1991	-		-		-		-		-		121.1	-0.5	-		-		-		-		-		121.2	0.1

[Continued]

Cincinnati, OH-KY-IN
Consumer Price Index - All Urban Consumers
Base 1982-1984 = 100
Transportation
[Continued]

For 1947-1997. Columns headed % show percentile change in the index from the previous period for which an index is available.

Year	Jan		Feb		Mar		Apr		May		Jun		Jul		Aug		Sep		Oct		Nov		Dec	
	Index	%	Index	%	Index	%	Index	%	Index	%	Index	%	Index	%	Index	%	Index	%	Index	%	Index	%	Index	%
1992	-	-	-	-	-	-	-	-	-	-	121.9	0.6	-	-	-	-	-	-	-	-	-	-	124.4	2.1
1993	-	-	-	-	-	-	-	-	-	-	125.9	1.2	-	-	-	-	-	-	-	-	-	-	126.5	0.5
1994	-	-	-	-	-	-	-	-	-	-	127.6	0.9	-	-	-	-	-	-	-	-	-	-	133.0	4.2
1995	-	-	-	-	-	-	-	-	-	-	135.0	1.5	-	-	-	-	-	-	-	-	-	-	135.2	0.1
1996	-	-	-	-	-	-	-	-	-	-	139.0	2.8	-	-	-	-	-	-	-	-	-	-	140.9	1.4
1997	-	-	-	-	-	-	-	-	-	-	141.2	0.2	-	-	-	-	-	-	-	-	-	-	-	-

Source: U.S. Department of Labor, Bureau of Labor Statistics, Division of Consumer Prices and Price Indexes. - indicates no data collected for period.

Cincinnati, OH-KY-IN
Consumer Price Index - Urban Wage Earners
Base 1982-1984 = 100
Transportation

For 1947-1997. Columns headed % show percentile change in the index from the previous period for which an index is available.

Year	Jan Index	%	Feb Index	%	Mar Index	%	Apr Index	%	May Index	%	Jun Index	%	Jul Index	%	Aug Index	%	Sep Index	%	Oct Index	%	Nov Index	%	Dec Index	%
1947	20.0	-	20.0	0.0	20.4	2.0	20.4	0.0	20.4	0.0	20.4	0.0	20.7	1.5	20.8	0.5	21.2	1.9	21.2	0.0	22.1	4.2	22.3	0.9
1948	22.5	0.9	22.5	0.0	22.5	0.0	22.5	0.0	22.5	0.0	22.9	1.8	24.0	4.8	24.4	1.7	24.6	0.8	24.6	0.0	24.6	0.0	24.6	0.0
1949	24.6	0.0	24.8	0.8	25.4	2.4	25.5	0.4	25.5	0.0	25.5	0.0	25.4	-0.4	25.5	0.4	25.5	0.0	25.5	0.0	25.5	0.0	25.4	-0.4
1950	25.3	-0.4	25.3	0.0	25.3	0.0	25.2	-0.4	25.8	2.4	25.9	0.4	26.0	0.4	26.3	1.2	26.3	0.0	26.3	0.0	26.3	0.0	26.3	0.0
1951	26.9	2.3	27.0	0.4	27.3	1.1	27.3	0.0	27.3	0.0	27.3	0.0	27.3	0.0	27.6	1.1	28.4	2.9	28.6	0.7	28.9	1.0	28.9	0.0
1952	28.9	0.0	29.2	1.0	29.2	0.0	29.1	-0.3	29.7	2.1	29.7	0.0	29.7	0.0	29.7	0.0	29.7	0.0	29.7	0.0	29.7	0.0	29.7	0.0
1953	-		-		30.3	2.0	-		-		30.2	-0.3	-		-		30.5	1.0	-		-		30.3	-0.7
1954	-		-		29.7	-2.0	-		-		29.4	-1.0	-		-		29.5	0.3	-		-		28.7	-2.7
1955	-		-		28.8	0.3	-		-		28.6	-0.7	-		-		28.0	-2.1	-		-		28.4	1.4
1956	-		-		28.1	-1.1	-		-		28.4	1.1	-		-		28.8	1.4	-		-		29.8	3.5
1957	-		-		30.0	0.7	-		-		30.2	0.7	-		-		30.7	1.7	-		-		31.0	1.0
1958	-		-		30.7	-1.0	-		-		30.7	0.0	-		-		30.9	0.7	-		-		32.4	4.9
1959	-		-		32.8	1.2	-		-		33.2	1.2	-		-		33.0	-0.6	-		-		34.4	4.2
1960	-		-		33.8	-1.7	-		-		33.3	-1.5	-		-		33.1	-0.6	-		-		33.2	0.3
1961	-		-		33.2	0.0	-		-		33.6	1.2	-		-		33.9	0.9	-		-		33.2	-2.1
1962	-		-		34.1	2.7	-		-		34.2	0.3	-		-		34.2	0.0	-		-		34.2	0.0
1963	-		-		34.2	0.0	-		-		34.2	0.0	-		-		34.3	0.3	-		-		34.5	0.6
1964	-		-		34.7	0.6	-		-		34.8	0.3	-		-		34.9	0.3	-		-		35.1	0.3
1965	-		-		34.6	-0.6	-		-		34.8	0.6	-		-		35.0	0.6	-		-		35.6	-0.6
1966	-		-		35.1	0.0	-		-		35.5	1.1	-		-		35.8	0.8	-		-		37.6	2.7
1967	-		-		35.4	-0.6	-		-		36.0	1.7	-		-		36.6	1.7	-		-		38.0	-0.8
1968	-		-		37.8	0.5	-		-		38.3	1.3	-		-		38.3	0.0	-		-		39.8	2.3
1969	-		-		39.3	3.4	-		-		39.3	0.0	-		-		38.9	-1.0	-		-		43.3	4.3
1970	-		-		39.4	-1.0	-		-		41.2	4.6	-		-		41.5	0.7	-		-		44.1	1.4
1971	-		-		42.8	-1.2	-		-		43.7	2.1	-		-		43.5	-0.5	-		-		45.6	-1.1
1972	-		-		43.2	-2.0	-		-		45.0	4.2	-		-		46.1	2.4	-		-		44.2	0.5
1973	-		-		46.0	0.9	-		-		44.3	-3.7	-		-		44.0	-0.7	-		-		50.1	0.0
1974	-		-		45.6	3.2	-		-		48.9	7.2	-		-		50.1	2.5	-		-		53.8	0.0
1975	-		-		50.2	0.2	-		-		52.2	4.0	-		-		53.8	3.1	-		-		58.8	1.2
1976	-		-		53.7	-0.2	-		-		57.1	6.3	-		-		58.1	1.8	-		-		60.7	-0.2
1977	-		-		60.0	2.0	-		-		61.5	2.5	-		-		60.8	-1.1	-		-		-	
1978	-		-		61.3	1.0	-		62.3	1.6	-		63.7	2.2	-		63.9	0.3	-		65.1	1.9	-	
1979	65.8	1.1	-		67.0	1.8	-		70.2	4.8	-		73.1	4.1	-		75.5	3.3	-		77.0	2.0	-	
1980	79.6	3.4	-		82.2	3.3	-		83.9	2.1	-		85.6	2.0	-		86.0	0.5	-		87.0	1.2	-	
1981	89.7	3.1	-		92.6	3.2	-		93.6	1.1	-		94.6	1.1	-		95.3	0.7	-		96.4	1.2	-	
1982	97.3	0.9	-		95.6	-1.7	-		95.4	-0.2	-		98.9	3.7	-		98.5	-0.4	-		98.5	0.0	-	
1983	98.2	-0.3	-		96.1	-2.1	-		99.1	3.1	-		99.9	0.8	-		101.3	1.4	-		102.6	1.3	-	
1984	101.7	-0.9	-		101.6	-0.1	-		102.8	1.2	-		103.0	0.2	-		103.5	0.5	-		104.6	1.1	-	
1985	103.1	-1.4	-		104.6	1.5	-		106.9	2.2	-		106.7	-0.2	-		105.0	-1.6	-		107.3	2.2	-	
1986	106.5	-0.7	-		98.4	-7.6	-		100.4	2.0	-		97.7	-2.7	-		97.9	0.2	-		98.7	0.8	-	
1987	-		-		-		-		-		102.9	4.3	-		-		-		-		-		105.7	2.7
1988	-		-		-		-		-		105.4	-0.3	-		-		-		-		-		107.2	1.7
1989	-		-		-		-		-		110.3	2.9	-		-		-		-		-		111.7	1.3
1990	-		-		-		-		-		114.4	2.4	-		-		-		-		-		120.0	4.9
1991	-		-		-		-		-		119.2	-0.7	-		-		-		-		-		119.4	0.2

[Continued]

Cincinnati, OH-KY-IN
Consumer Price Index - Urban Wage Earners
Base 1982-1984 = 100
Transportation
[Continued]

For 1947-1997. Columns headed % show percentile change in the index from the previous period for which an index is available.

Year	Jan		Feb		Mar		Apr		May		Jun		Jul		Aug		Sep		Oct		Nov		Dec	
	Index	%	Index	%	Index	%	Index	%	Index	%	Index	%	Index	%	Index	%	Index	%	Index	%	Index	%	Index	%
1992	-	-	-	-	-	-	-	-	-	-	119.8	0.3	-	-	-	-	-	-	-	-	-	-	122.6	2.3
1993	-	-	-	-	-	-	-	-	-	-	123.7	0.9	-	-	-	-	-	-	-	-	-	-	124.3	0.5
1994	-	-	-	-	-	-	-	-	-	-	125.5	1.0	-	-	-	-	-	-	-	-	-	-	131.2	4.5
1995	-	-	-	-	-	-	-	-	-	-	133.3	1.6	-	-	-	-	-	-	-	-	-	-	133.6	0.2
1996	-	-	-	-	-	-	-	-	-	-	137.3	2.8	-	-	-	-	-	-	-	-	-	-	138.8	1.1
1997	-	-	-	-	-	-	-	-	-	-	138.7	-0.1	-	-	-	-	-	-	-	-	-	-	-	-

Source: U.S. Department of Labor, Bureau of Labor Statistics, Division of Consumer Prices and Price Indexes. - indicates no data collected for period.

Cincinnati, OH-KY-IN
Consumer Price Index - All Urban Consumers
Base 1982-1984 = 100
Medical Care

For 1947-1997. Columns headed % show percentile change in the index from the previous period for which an index is available.

Year	Jan Index	%	Feb Index	%	Mar Index	%	Apr Index	%	May Index	%	Jun Index	%	Jul Index	%	Aug Index	%	Sep Index	%	Oct Index	%	Nov Index	%	Dec Index	%
1947	11.3	-	11.3	0.0	11.3	0.0	11.4	0.9	11.6	1.8	11.7	0.9	12.1	3.4	12.2	0.8	12.2	0.0	12.3	0.8	12.3	0.0	12.4	0.8
1948	12.8	3.2	12.7	-0.8	12.7	0.0	13.1	3.1	13.1	0.0	13.1	0.0	13.2	0.8	13.2	0.0	13.2	0.0	13.2	0.0	13.2	0.0	13.2	0.0
1949	13.2	0.0	13.2	0.0	13.4	1.5	13.4	0.0	13.4	0.0	13.5	0.7	13.5	0.0	13.5	0.0	13.5	0.0	13.5	0.0	13.5	0.0	13.5	0.0
1950	13.5	0.0	13.5	0.0	13.5	0.0	13.5	0.0	13.5	0.0	13.5	0.0	13.5	0.0	13.5	0.0	13.5	0.0	13.5	0.0	13.5	0.0	13.6	0.7
1951	13.6	0.0	13.6	0.0	13.7	0.7	13.7	0.0	13.7	0.0	13.8	0.7	13.8	0.0	13.8	0.0	13.9	0.7	13.9	0.0	13.9	0.0	14.6	5.0
1952	14.6	0.0	14.7	0.7	14.9	1.4	14.9	0.0	14.9	0.0	14.9	0.0	15.0	0.7	15.0	0.0	15.0	0.0	15.0	0.0	15.0	0.0	15.0	0.0
1953	-	-	-	-	15.5	3.3	-	-	-	-	15.5	0.0	-	-	-	-	15.7	1.3	-	-	-	-	15.9	1.3
1954	-	-	-	-	15.9	0.0	-	-	-	-	15.9	0.0	-	-	-	-	15.9	0.0	-	-	-	-	16.1	1.3
1955	-	-	-	-	16.3	1.2	-	-	-	-	16.3	0.0	-	-	-	-	16.3	0.0	-	-	-	-	17.5	7.4
1956	-	-	-	-	17.5	0.0	-	-	-	-	17.5	0.0	-	-	-	-	17.5	0.0	-	-	-	-	17.6	0.6
1957	-	-	-	-	17.8	1.1	-	-	-	-	17.9	0.6	-	-	-	-	17.9	0.0	-	-	-	-	19.0	6.1
1958	-	-	-	-	19.0	0.0	-	-	-	-	19.0	0.0	-	-	-	-	19.0	0.0	-	-	-	-	19.4	2.1
1959	-	-	-	-	19.3	-0.5	-	-	-	-	19.7	2.1	-	-	-	-	19.7	0.0	-	-	-	-	19.7	0.0
1960	-	-	-	-	19.8	0.5	-	-	-	-	19.8	0.0	-	-	-	-	20.0	1.0	-	-	-	-	20.4	2.0
1961	-	-	-	-	20.5	0.5	-	-	-	-	20.6	0.5	-	-	-	-	20.7	0.5	-	-	-	-	20.7	0.0
1962	-	-	-	-	20.7	0.0	-	-	-	-	20.8	0.5	-	-	-	-	21.5	3.4	-	-	-	-	21.5	0.0
1963	-	-	-	-	21.7	0.9	-	-	-	-	21.9	0.9	-	-	-	-	21.9	0.0	-	-	-	-	21.9	0.0
1964	-	-	-	-	22.2	1.4	-	-	-	-	22.3	0.5	-	-	-	-	22.3	0.0	-	-	-	-	23.5	5.4
1965	-	-	-	-	23.6	0.4	-	-	-	-	23.9	1.3	-	-	-	-	23.9	0.0	-	-	-	-	24.2	1.3
1966	-	-	-	-	24.6	1.7	-	-	-	-	24.9	1.2	-	-	-	-	25.1	0.8	-	-	-	-	25.6	2.0
1967	-	-	-	-	26.5	3.5	-	-	-	-	26.6	0.4	-	-	-	-	27.0	1.5	-	-	-	-	27.4	1.5
1968	-	-	-	-	28.5	4.0	-	-	-	-	28.7	0.7	-	-	-	-	29.0	1.0	-	-	-	-	29.4	1.4
1969	-	-	-	-	30.8	4.8	-	-	-	-	31.2	1.3	-	-	-	-	31.7	1.6	-	-	-	-	31.7	0.0
1970	-	-	-	-	32.3	1.9	-	-	-	-	32.6	0.9	-	-	-	-	32.9	0.9	-	-	-	-	33.6	2.1
1971	-	-	-	-	35.0	4.2	-	-	-	-	35.4	1.1	-	-	-	-	35.6	0.6	-	-	-	-	35.4	-0.6
1972	-	-	-	-	36.4	2.8	-	-	-	-	36.5	0.3	-	-	-	-	36.5	0.0	-	-	-	-	36.9	1.1
1973	-	-	-	-	38.0	3.0	-	-	-	-	38.3	0.8	-	-	-	-	38.5	0.5	-	-	-	-	39.7	3.1
1974	-	-	-	-	41.4	4.3	-	-	-	-	42.0	1.4	-	-	-	-	43.3	3.1	-	-	-	-	44.4	2.5
1975	-	-	-	-	46.5	4.7	-	-	-	-	47.1	1.3	-	-	-	-	48.0	1.9	-	-	-	-	48.4	0.8
1976	-	-	-	-	51.6	6.6	-	-	-	-	52.3	1.4	-	-	-	-	53.6	2.5	-	-	-	-	55.1	2.8
1977	-	-	-	-	58.2	5.6	-	-	-	-	58.8	1.0	-	-	-	-	60.0	2.0	-	-	-	-	60.2	0.3
1978	-	-	-	-	63.3	5.1	-	-	64.5	1.9	-	-	65.4	1.4	-	-	68.1	4.1	-	-	68.2	0.1	-	-
1979	71.6	5.0	-	-	72.1	0.7	-	-	71.8	-0.4	-	-	72.1	0.4	-	-	73.0	1.2	-	-	73.9	1.2	-	-
1980	76.6	3.7	-	-	78.5	2.5	-	-	78.6	0.1	-	-	79.6	1.3	-	-	80.1	0.6	-	-	80.6	0.6	-	-
1981	82.0	1.7	-	-	83.2	1.5	-	-	83.9	0.8	-	-	87.3	4.1	-	-	88.1	0.9	-	-	88.7	0.7	-	-
1982	91.4	3.0	-	-	91.8	0.4	-	-	92.7	1.0	-	-	93.8	1.2	-	-	95.0	1.3	-	-	94.9	-0.1	-	-
1983	98.5	3.8	-	-	98.9	0.4	-	-	99.4	0.5	-	-	100.6	1.2	-	-	100.5	-0.1	-	-	101.7	1.2	-	-
1984	104.2	2.5	-	-	104.5	0.3	-	-	105.1	0.6	-	-	107.1	1.9	-	-	107.8	0.7	-	-	107.7	-0.1	-	-
1985	109.2	1.4	-	-	110.4	1.1	-	-	111.5	1.0	-	-	112.2	0.6	-	-	113.2	0.9	-	-	114.3	1.0	-	-
1986	115.1	0.7	-	-	115.8	0.6	-	-	116.3	0.4	-	-	119.0	2.3	-	-	118.8	-0.2	-	-	119.1	0.3	-	-
1987	-	-	-	-	-	-	-	-	-	-	126.5	6.2	-	-	-	-	-	-	-	-	-	-	131.9	4.3
1988	-	-	-	-	-	-	-	-	-	-	135.7	2.9	-	-	-	-	-	-	-	-	-	-	140.3	3.4
1989	-	-	-	-	-	-	-	-	-	-	144.8	3.2	-	-	-	-	-	-	-	-	-	-	153.7	6.1
1990	-	-	-	-	-	-	-	-	-	-	159.4	3.7	-	-	-	-	-	-	-	-	-	-	166.7	4.6
1991	-	-	-	-	-	-	-	-	-	-	174.5	4.7	-	-	-	-	-	-	-	-	-	-	181.4	4.0

[Continued]

Cincinnati, OH-KY-IN
Consumer Price Index - All Urban Consumers
Base 1982-1984 = 100
Medical Care
[Continued]

For 1947-1997. Columns headed % show percentile change in the index from the previous period for which an index is available.

Year	Jan Index	%	Feb Index	%	Mar Index	%	Apr Index	%	May Index	%	Jun Index	%	Jul Index	%	Aug Index	%	Sep Index	%	Oct Index	%	Nov Index	%	Dec Index	%
1992	-	-	-	-	-	-	-	-	-	-	188.5	3.9	-	-	-	-	-	-	-	-	-	-	193.0	2.4
1993	-	-	-	-	-	-	-	-	-	-	200.7	4.0	-	-	-	-	-	-	-	-	-	-	205.5	2.4
1994	-	-	-	-	-	-	-	-	-	-	211.2	2.8	-	-	-	-	-	-	-	-	-	-	215.2	1.9
1995	-	-	-	-	-	-	-	-	-	-	222.1	3.2	-	-	-	-	-	-	-	-	-	-	224.6	1.1
1996	-	-	-	-	-	-	-	-	-	-	228.2	1.6	-	-	-	-	-	-	-	-	-	-	230.7	1.1
1997	-	-	-	-	-	-	-	-	-	-	234.6	1.7	-	-	-	-	-	-	-	-	-	-	-	-

Source: U.S. Department of Labor, Bureau of Labor Statistics, Division of Consumer Prices and Price Indexes. - indicates no data collected for period.

Cincinnati, OH-KY-IN
Consumer Price Index - Urban Wage Earners
Base 1982-1984 = 100
Medical Care

For 1947-1997. Columns headed % show percentile change in the index from the previous period for which an index is available.

Year	Jan Index	Jan %	Feb Index	Feb %	Mar Index	Mar %	Apr Index	Apr %	May Index	May %	Jun Index	Jun %	Jul Index	Jul %	Aug Index	Aug %	Sep Index	Sep %	Oct Index	Oct %	Nov Index	Nov %	Dec Index	Dec %
1947	10.8	-	10.8	0.0	10.8	0.0	10.9	0.9	11.0	0.9	11.2	1.8	11.5	2.7	11.6	0.9	11.7	0.9	11.7	0.0	11.7	0.0	11.8	0.9
1948	12.2	3.4	12.1	-0.8	12.1	0.0	12.4	2.5	12.4	0.0	12.5	0.8	12.5	0.0	12.5	0.0	12.6	0.8	12.6	0.0	12.6	0.0	12.6	0.0
1949	12.6	0.0	12.6	0.0	12.7	0.8	12.8	0.8	12.8	0.0	12.8	0.0	12.8	0.0	12.8	0.0	12.8	0.0	12.8	0.0	12.8	0.0	12.8	0.0
1950	12.8	0.0	12.8	0.0	12.8	0.0	12.8	0.0	12.8	0.0	12.8	0.0	12.8	0.0	12.8	0.0	12.8	0.0	12.8	0.0	12.8	0.0	13.0	1.6
1951	13.0	0.0	13.0	0.0	13.0	0.0	13.1	0.8	13.1	0.0	13.1	0.0	13.1	0.0	13.1	0.0	13.3	1.5	13.3	0.0	13.3	0.0	13.9	4.5
1952	13.9	0.0	14.0	0.7	14.2	1.4	14.2	0.0	14.2	0.0	14.2	0.0	14.3	0.7	14.3	0.0	14.3	0.0	14.3	0.0	14.3	0.0	14.3	0.0
1953	-	-	-	-	14.7	2.8	-	-	-	-	14.8	0.7	-	-	-	-	15.0	1.4	-	-	-	-	15.2	1.3
1954	-	-	-	-	15.2	0.0	-	-	-	-	15.2	0.0	-	-	-	-	15.2	0.0	-	-	-	-	15.4	1.3
1955	-	-	-	-	15.5	0.6	-	-	-	-	15.5	0.0	-	-	-	-	15.5	0.0	-	-	-	-	16.7	7.7
1956	-	-	-	-	16.7	0.0	-	-	-	-	16.7	0.0	-	-	-	-	16.7	0.0	-	-	-	-	16.7	0.0
1957	-	-	-	-	17.0	1.8	-	-	-	-	17.0	0.0	-	-	-	-	17.1	0.6	-	-	-	-	18.1	5.8
1958	-	-	-	-	18.1	0.0	-	-	-	-	18.1	0.0	-	-	-	-	18.1	0.0	-	-	-	-	18.5	2.2
1959	-	-	-	-	18.4	-0.5	-	-	-	-	18.7	1.6	-	-	-	-	18.8	0.5	-	-	-	-	18.8	0.0
1960	-	-	-	-	18.9	0.5	-	-	-	-	18.9	0.0	-	-	-	-	19.1	1.1	-	-	-	-	19.5	2.1
1961	-	-	-	-	19.6	0.5	-	-	-	-	19.7	0.5	-	-	-	-	19.7	0.0	-	-	-	-	19.7	0.0
1962	-	-	-	-	19.7	0.0	-	-	-	-	19.8	0.5	-	-	-	-	20.5	3.5	-	-	-	-	20.5	0.0
1963	-	-	-	-	20.7	1.0	-	-	-	-	20.9	1.0	-	-	-	-	20.9	0.0	-	-	-	-	20.9	0.0
1964	-	-	-	-	21.2	1.4	-	-	-	-	21.2	0.0	-	-	-	-	21.2	0.0	-	-	-	-	22.4	5.7
1965	-	-	-	-	22.5	0.4	-	-	-	-	22.7	0.9	-	-	-	-	22.8	0.4	-	-	-	-	23.1	1.3
1966	-	-	-	-	23.5	1.7	-	-	-	-	23.7	0.9	-	-	-	-	23.9	0.8	-	-	-	-	24.4	2.1
1967	-	-	-	-	25.2	3.3	-	-	-	-	25.3	0.4	-	-	-	-	25.7	1.6	-	-	-	-	26.1	1.6
1968	-	-	-	-	27.2	4.2	-	-	-	-	27.3	0.4	-	-	-	-	27.6	1.1	-	-	-	-	28.0	1.4
1969	-	-	-	-	29.4	5.0	-	-	-	-	29.8	1.4	-	-	-	-	30.2	1.3	-	-	-	-	30.2	0.0
1970	-	-	-	-	30.8	2.0	-	-	-	-	31.0	0.6	-	-	-	-	31.3	1.0	-	-	-	-	32.1	2.6
1971	-	-	-	-	33.4	4.0	-	-	-	-	33.7	0.9	-	-	-	-	33.9	0.6	-	-	-	-	33.7	-0.6
1972	-	-	-	-	34.7	3.0	-	-	-	-	34.8	0.3	-	-	-	-	34.8	0.0	-	-	-	-	35.1	0.9
1973	-	-	-	-	36.2	3.1	-	-	-	-	36.5	0.8	-	-	-	-	36.7	0.5	-	-	-	-	37.8	3.0
1974	-	-	-	-	39.5	4.5	-	-	-	-	40.0	1.3	-	-	-	-	41.3	3.2	-	-	-	-	42.3	2.4
1975	-	-	-	-	44.3	4.7	-	-	-	-	44.8	1.1	-	-	-	-	45.8	2.2	-	-	-	-	46.1	0.7
1976	-	-	-	-	49.2	6.7	-	-	-	-	49.9	1.4	-	-	-	-	51.1	2.4	-	-	-	-	52.5	2.7
1977	-	-	-	-	55.4	5.5	-	-	-	-	56.1	1.3	-	-	-	-	57.2	2.0	-	-	-	-	57.4	0.3
1978	-	-	-	-	60.3	5.1	-	-	60.6	0.5	-	-	63.3	4.5	-	-	63.4	0.2	-	-	63.9	0.8	-	-
1979	68.2	6.7	-	-	68.5	0.4	-	-	69.8	1.9	-	-	70.5	1.0	-	-	71.2	1.0	-	-	71.5	0.4	-	-
1980	75.0	4.9	-	-	77.1	2.8	-	-	77.6	0.6	-	-	78.8	1.5	-	-	79.2	0.5	-	-	79.7	0.6	-	-
1981	82.0	2.9	-	-	82.6	0.7	-	-	83.4	1.0	-	-	86.6	3.8	-	-	87.8	1.4	-	-	88.8	1.1	-	-
1982	91.4	2.9	-	-	91.7	0.3	-	-	92.7	1.1	-	-	93.8	1.2	-	-	95.0	1.3	-	-	94.9	-0.1	-	-
1983	98.3	3.6	-	-	98.8	0.5	-	-	99.4	0.6	-	-	100.7	1.3	-	-	100.5	-0.2	-	-	101.8	1.3	-	-
1984	104.3	2.5	-	-	104.6	0.3	-	-	105.2	0.6	-	-	107.1	1.8	-	-	107.8	0.7	-	-	107.6	-0.2	-	-
1985	109.2	1.5	-	-	110.4	1.1	-	-	111.5	1.0	-	-	112.2	0.6	-	-	113.1	0.8	-	-	114.2	1.0	-	-
1986	114.9	0.6	-	-	115.6	0.6	-	-	116.0	0.3	-	-	118.7	2.3	-	-	118.5	-0.2	-	-	118.8	0.3	-	-
1987	-	-	-	-	-	-	-	-	-	-	126.1	6.1	-	-	-	-	-	-	-	-	-	-	131.7	4.4
1988	-	-	-	-	-	-	-	-	-	-	135.8	3.1	-	-	-	-	-	-	-	-	-	-	141.0	3.8
1989	-	-	-	-	-	-	-	-	-	-	145.8	3.4	-	-	-	-	-	-	-	-	-	-	155.1	6.4
1990	-	-	-	-	-	-	-	-	-	-	160.6	3.5	-	-	-	-	-	-	-	-	-	-	168.0	4.6
1991	-	-	-	-	-	-	-	-	-	-	175.9	4.7	-	-	-	-	-	-	-	-	-	-	183.0	4.0

[Continued]

Cincinnati, OH-KY-IN
Consumer Price Index - Urban Wage Earners
Base 1982-1984 = 100
Medical Care
[Continued]

For 1947-1997. Columns headed % show percentile change in the index from the previous period for which an index is available.

Year	Jan Index	%	Feb Index	%	Mar Index	%	Apr Index	%	May Index	%	Jun Index	%	Jul Index	%	Aug Index	%	Sep Index	%	Oct Index	%	Nov Index	%	Dec Index	%
1992	-		-		-		-		-		190.0	3.8	-		-		-		-		-		194.9	2.6
1993	-		-		-		-		-		203.1	4.2	-		-		-		-		-		208.0	2.4
1994	-		-		-		-		-		213.8	2.8	-		-		-		-		-		218.1	2.0
1995	-		-		-		-		-		225.4	3.3	-		-		-		-		-		228.5	1.4
1996	-		-		-		-		-		232.6	1.8	-		-		-		-		-		235.5	1.2
1997	-		-		-		-		-		239.4	1.7	-		-		-		-		-		-	

Source: U.S. Department of Labor, Bureau of Labor Statistics, Division of Consumer Prices and Price Indexes. - indicates no data collected for period.

Cincinnati, OH-KY-IN
Consumer Price Index - All Urban Consumers
Base 1982-1984 = 100
Entertainment

For 1975-1997. Columns headed % show percentile change in the index from the previous period for which an index is available.

Year	Jan Index	%	Feb Index	%	Mar Index	%	Apr Index	%	May Index	%	Jun Index	%	Jul Index	%	Aug Index	%	Sep Index	%	Oct Index	%	Nov Index	%	Dec Index	%
1975	-	-	-	-	-	-	-	-	-	-	-	-	-	-	-	-	-	-	-	-	-	-	65.3	-
1976	-	-	-	-	66.5	1.8	-	-	-	-	67.1	0.9	-	-	-	-	67.7	0.9	-	-	-	-	67.6	-0.1
1977	-	-	-	-	68.4	1.2	-	-	-	-	68.6	0.3	-	-	-	-	69.6	1.5	-	-	-	-	69.8	0.3
1978	-	-	-	-	71.7	2.7	-	-	73.1	2.0	-	-	72.7	-0.5	-	-	73.0	0.4	-	-	73.2	0.3	-	-
1979	74.2	1.4	-	-	76.1	2.6	-	-	77.1	1.3	-	-	78.1	1.3	-	-	78.3	0.3	-	-	77.4	-1.1	-	-
1980	78.0	0.8	-	-	83.6	7.2	-	-	84.6	1.2	-	-	83.1	-1.8	-	-	84.8	2.0	-	-	86.1	1.5	-	-
1981	86.6	0.6	-	-	88.1	1.7	-	-	86.1	-2.3	-	-	86.4	0.3	-	-	88.0	1.9	-	-	88.0	0.0	-	-
1982	93.2	5.9	-	-	93.5	0.3	-	-	93.5	0.0	-	-	94.4	1.0	-	-	95.6	1.3	-	-	97.3	1.8	-	-
1983	99.7	2.5	-	-	100.1	0.4	-	-	99.7	-0.4	-	-	99.7	0.0	-	-	101.2	1.5	-	-	102.8	1.6	-	-
1984	103.3	0.5	-	-	102.6	-0.7	-	-	103.4	0.8	-	-	105.5	2.0	-	-	106.2	0.7	-	-	106.7	0.5	-	-
1985	99.8	-6.5	-	-	100.4	0.6	-	-	100.0	-0.4	-	-	98.0	-2.0	-	-	98.7	0.7	-	-	101.6	2.9	-	-
1986	101.7	0.1	-	-	102.1	0.4	-	-	104.3	2.2	-	-	104.2	-0.1	-	-	104.7	0.5	-	-	104.7	0.0	-	-
1987	-	-	-	-	-	-	-	-	-	-	115.1	9.9	-	-	-	-	-	-	-	-	-	-	116.9	1.6
1988	-	-	-	-	-	-	-	-	-	-	120.2	2.8	-	-	-	-	-	-	-	-	-	-	124.4	3.5
1989	-	-	-	-	-	-	-	-	-	-	129.9	4.4	-	-	-	-	-	-	-	-	-	-	133.3	2.6
1990	-	-	-	-	-	-	-	-	-	-	137.6	3.2	-	-	-	-	-	-	-	-	-	-	140.7	2.3
1991	-	-	-	-	-	-	-	-	-	-	145.2	3.2	-	-	-	-	-	-	-	-	-	-	146.6	1.0
1992	-	-	-	-	-	-	-	-	-	-	147.9	0.9	-	-	-	-	-	-	-	-	-	-	151.0	2.1
1993	-	-	-	-	-	-	-	-	-	-	153.0	1.3	-	-	-	-	-	-	-	-	-	-	154.8	1.2
1994	-	-	-	-	-	-	-	-	-	-	158.9	2.6	-	-	-	-	-	-	-	-	-	-	161.2	1.4
1995	-	-	-	-	-	-	-	-	-	-	160.1	-0.7	-	-	-	-	-	-	-	-	-	-	161.8	1.1
1996	-	-	-	-	-	-	-	-	-	-	163.5	1.1	-	-	-	-	-	-	-	-	-	-	170.8	4.5
1997	-	-	-	-	-	-	-	-	-	-	174.4	2.1	-	-	-	-	-	-	-	-	-	-	-	-

Source: U.S. Department of Labor, Bureau of Labor Statistics, Division of Consumer Prices and Price Indexes. - indicates no data collected for period.

Cincinnati, OH-KY-IN
Consumer Price Index - Urban Wage Earners
Base 1982-1984 = 100
Entertainment

For 1975-1997. Columns headed % show percentile change in the index from the previous period for which an index is available.

Year	Jan Index	%	Feb Index	%	Mar Index	%	Apr Index	%	May Index	%	Jun Index	%	Jul Index	%	Aug Index	%	Sep Index	%	Oct Index	%	Nov Index	%	Dec Index	%
1975	-	-	-	-	-	-	-	-	-	-	-	-	-	-	-	-	-	-	-	-	-	-	67.8	-
1976	-	-	-	-	69.1	1.9	-	-	-	-	69.8	1.0	-	-	-	-	70.4	0.9	-	-	-	-	70.2	-0.3
1977	-	-	-	-	71.1	1.3	-	-	-	-	71.2	0.1	-	-	-	-	72.3	1.5	-	-	-	-	72.6	0.4
1978	-	-	-	-	74.5	2.6	-	-	75.2	0.9	-	-	76.1	1.2	-	-	76.6	0.7	-	-	76.7	0.1	-	-
1979	77.1	0.5	-	-	77.6	0.6	-	-	78.3	0.9	-	-	78.8	0.6	-	-	79.0	0.3	-	-	78.4	-0.8	-	-
1980	79.4	1.3	-	-	83.5	5.2	-	-	85.1	1.9	-	-	83.3	-2.1	-	-	84.7	1.7	-	-	85.7	1.2	-	-
1981	86.7	1.2	-	-	88.0	1.5	-	-	87.8	-0.2	-	-	88.0	0.2	-	-	89.5	1.7	-	-	89.4	-0.1	-	-
1982	93.8	4.9	-	-	94.0	0.2	-	-	94.0	0.0	-	-	94.6	0.6	-	-	96.0	1.5	-	-	97.6	1.7	-	-
1983	99.7	2.2	-	-	100.0	0.3	-	-	99.9	-0.1	-	-	100.0	0.1	-	-	101.3	1.3	-	-	102.6	1.3	-	-
1984	103.2	0.6	-	-	102.6	-0.6	-	-	103.0	0.4	-	-	105.1	2.0	-	-	105.7	0.6	-	-	106.1	0.4	-	-
1985	97.7	-7.9	-	-	98.2	0.5	-	-	97.9	-0.3	-	-	94.5	-3.5	-	-	95.2	0.7	-	-	97.7	2.6	-	-
1986	97.7	0.0	-	-	97.8	0.1	-	-	101.4	3.7	-	-	101.2	-0.2	-	-	101.2	0.0	-	-	101.3	0.1	-	-
1987	-	-	-	-	-	-	-	-	-	-	117.0	15.5	-	-	-	-	-	-	-	-	-	-	119.0	1.7
1988	-	-	-	-	-	-	-	-	-	-	122.3	2.8	-	-	-	-	-	-	-	-	-	-	126.1	3.1
1989	-	-	-	-	-	-	-	-	-	-	131.4	4.2	-	-	-	-	-	-	-	-	-	-	134.4	2.3
1990	-	-	-	-	-	-	-	-	-	-	138.6	3.1	-	-	-	-	-	-	-	-	-	-	141.5	2.1
1991	-	-	-	-	-	-	-	-	-	-	145.5	2.8	-	-	-	-	-	-	-	-	-	-	146.5	0.7
1992	-	-	-	-	-	-	-	-	-	-	147.9	1.0	-	-	-	-	-	-	-	-	-	-	151.0	2.1
1993	-	-	-	-	-	-	-	-	-	-	152.8	1.2	-	-	-	-	-	-	-	-	-	-	154.5	1.1
1994	-	-	-	-	-	-	-	-	-	-	158.1	2.3	-	-	-	-	-	-	-	-	-	-	160.6	1.6
1995	-	-	-	-	-	-	-	-	-	-	159.4	-0.7	-	-	-	-	-	-	-	-	-	-	160.9	0.9
1996	-	-	-	-	-	-	-	-	-	-	162.5	1.0	-	-	-	-	-	-	-	-	-	-	169.3	4.2
1997	-	-	-	-	-	-	-	-	-	-	172.9	2.1	-	-	-	-	-	-	-	-	-	-	-	-

Source: U.S. Department of Labor, Bureau of Labor Statistics, Division of Consumer Prices and Price Indexes. - indicates no data collected for period.

Cincinnati, OH-KY-IN
Consumer Price Index - All Urban Consumers
Base 1982-1984 = 100
Other Goods and Services

For 1975-1997. Columns headed % show percentile change in the index from the previous period for which an index is available.

Year	Jan Index	%	Feb Index	%	Mar Index	%	Apr Index	%	May Index	%	Jun Index	%	Jul Index	%	Aug Index	%	Sep Index	%	Oct Index	%	Nov Index	%	Dec Index	%
1975	-	-	-	-	-	-	-	-	-	-	-	-	-	-	-	-	-	-	-	-	-	-	54.7	-
1976	-	-	-	-	55.4	1.3	-	-	-	-	55.3	-0.2	-	-	-	-	56.0	1.3	-	-	-	-	57.7	3.0
1977	-	-	-	-	57.9	0.3	-	-	-	-	58.6	1.2	-	-	-	-	60.6	3.4	-	-	-	-	60.8	0.3
1978	-	-	-	-	61.7	1.5	-	-	61.8	0.2	-	-	62.8	1.6	-	-	64.2	2.2	-	-	63.6	-0.9	-	-
1979	65.2	2.5	-	-	65.7	0.8	-	-	66.3	0.9	-	-	66.9	0.9	-	-	69.6	4.0	-	-	70.3	1.0	-	-
1980	71.5	1.7	-	-	72.4	1.3	-	-	73.3	1.2	-	-	73.8	0.7	-	-	75.6	2.4	-	-	77.0	1.9	-	-
1981	78.9	2.5	-	-	79.0	0.1	-	-	80.3	1.6	-	-	80.8	0.6	-	-	84.1	4.1	-	-	84.9	1.0	-	-
1982	86.3	1.6	-	-	87.6	1.5	-	-	88.1	0.6	-	-	87.8	-0.3	-	-	92.1	4.9	-	-	96.0	4.2	-	-
1983	98.0	2.1	-	-	99.1	1.1	-	-	100.0	0.9	-	-	101.5	1.5	-	-	102.3	0.8	-	-	105.7	3.3	-	-
1984	107.0	1.2	-	-	107.5	0.5	-	-	106.7	-0.7	-	-	108.5	1.7	-	-	109.5	0.9	-	-	109.8	0.3	-	-
1985	111.3	1.4	-	-	113.6	2.1	-	-	114.5	0.8	-	-	115.9	1.2	-	-	117.6	1.5	-	-	118.1	0.4	-	-
1986	119.0	0.8	-	-	119.2	0.2	-	-	119.7	0.4	-	-	120.4	0.6	-	-	122.7	1.9	-	-	123.0	0.2	-	-
1987	-	-	-	-	-	-	-	-	-	-	128.5	4.5	-	-	-	-	-	-	-	-	-	-	-	-
1988	-	-	-	-	-	-	-	-	-	-	135.0	5.1	-	-	-	-	-	-	-	-	-	-	-	-
1989	-	-	-	-	-	-	-	-	-	-	148.2	9.8	-	-	-	-	-	-	-	-	-	-	-	-
1990	-	-	-	-	-	-	-	-	-	-	161.3	8.8	-	-	-	-	-	-	-	-	-	-	-	-
1991	-	-	-	-	-	-	-	-	-	-	174.7	8.3	-	-	-	-	-	-	-	-	-	-	-	-
1992	-	-	-	-	-	-	-	-	-	-	188.4	7.8	-	-	-	-	-	-	-	-	-	-	-	-
1993	-	-	-	-	-	-	-	-	-	-	199.6	5.9	-	-	-	-	-	-	-	-	-	-	-	-
1994	-	-	-	-	-	-	-	-	-	-	206.1	3.3	-	-	-	-	-	-	-	-	-	-	-	-
1995	-	-	-	-	-	-	-	-	-	-	215.0	4.3	-	-	-	-	-	-	-	-	-	-	-	-
1996	-	-	-	-	-	-	-	-	-	-	220.0	2.3	-	-	-	-	-	-	-	-	-	-	-	-
1997	-	-	-	-	-	-	-	-	-	-	229.9	4.5	-	-	-	-	-	-	-	-	-	-	-	-

Source: U.S. Department of Labor, Bureau of Labor Statistics, Division of Consumer Prices and Price Indexes. - indicates no data collected for period.

Cincinnati, OH-KY-IN
Consumer Price Index - Urban Wage Earners
Base 1982-1984 = 100
Other Goods and Services

For 1975-1997. Columns headed % show percentile change in the index from the previous period for which an index is available.

Year	Jan Index	%	Feb Index	%	Mar Index	%	Apr Index	%	May Index	%	Jun Index	%	Jul Index	%	Aug Index	%	Sep Index	%	Oct Index	%	Nov Index	%	Dec Index	%
1975	-	-	-	-	-	-	-	-	-	-	-	-	-	-	-	-	-	-	-	-	-	-	54.5	-
1976	-	-	-	-	55.2	1.3	-	-	-	-	55.1	-0.2	-	-	-	-	55.8	1.3	-	-	-	-	57.5	3.0
1977	-	-	-	-	57.7	0.3	-	-	-	-	58.4	1.2	-	-	-	-	60.4	3.4	-	-	-	-	60.6	0.3
1978	-	-	-	-	61.5	1.5	-	-	62.5	1.6	-	-	63.4	1.4	-	-	64.4	1.6	-	-	64.4	0.0	-	-
1979	66.4	3.1	-	-	67.3	1.4	-	-	66.4	-1.3	-	-	67.4	1.5	-	-	69.9	3.7	-	-	71.0	1.6	-	-
1980	72.1	1.5	-	-	73.0	1.2	-	-	73.7	1.0	-	-	74.5	1.1	-	-	75.7	1.6	-	-	76.9	1.6	-	-
1981	79.5	3.4	-	-	80.0	0.6	-	-	81.2	1.5	-	-	81.7	0.6	-	-	84.5	3.4	-	-	85.1	0.7	-	-
1982	86.2	1.3	-	-	87.7	1.7	-	-	88.2	0.6	-	-	87.9	-0.3	-	-	92.1	4.8	-	-	95.9	4.1	-	-
1983	98.2	2.4	-	-	99.3	1.1	-	-	100.2	0.9	-	-	102.1	1.9	-	-	102.4	0.3	-	-	105.6	3.1	-	-
1984	107.0	1.3	-	-	107.5	0.5	-	-	106.6	-0.8	-	-	108.6	1.9	-	-	109.1	0.5	-	-	109.2	0.1	-	-
1985	110.9	1.6	-	-	112.7	1.6	-	-	113.7	0.9	-	-	115.3	1.4	-	-	116.8	1.3	-	-	117.2	0.3	-	-
1986	118.2	0.9	-	-	118.3	0.1	-	-	118.9	0.5	-	-	119.6	0.6	-	-	121.5	1.6	-	-	121.6	0.1	-	-
1987	-	-	-	-	-	-	-	-	-	-	128.9	6.0	-	-	-	-	-	-	-	-	-	-	-	-
1988	-	-	-	-	-	-	-	-	-	-	136.0	5.5	-	-	-	-	-	-	-	-	-	-	-	-
1989	-	-	-	-	-	-	-	-	-	-	147.8	8.7	-	-	-	-	-	-	-	-	-	-	-	-
1990	-	-	-	-	-	-	-	-	-	-	163.2	10.4	-	-	-	-	-	-	-	-	-	-	-	-
1991	-	-	-	-	-	-	-	-	-	-	178.2	9.2	-	-	-	-	-	-	-	-	-	-	-	-
1992	-	-	-	-	-	-	-	-	-	-	191.9	7.7	-	-	-	-	-	-	-	-	-	-	-	-
1993	-	-	-	-	-	-	-	-	-	-	204.5	6.6	-	-	-	-	-	-	-	-	-	-	-	-
1994	-	-	-	-	-	-	-	-	-	-	209.2	2.3	-	-	-	-	-	-	-	-	-	-	-	-
1995	-	-	-	-	-	-	-	-	-	-	215.9	3.2	-	-	-	-	-	-	-	-	-	-	-	-
1996	-	-	-	-	-	-	-	-	-	-	219.2	1.5	-	-	-	-	-	-	-	-	-	-	-	-
1997	-	-	-	-	-	-	-	-	-	-	228.9	4.4	-	-	-	-	-	-	-	-	-	-	-	-

Source: U.S. Department of Labor, Bureau of Labor Statistics, Division of Consumer Prices and Price Indexes. - indicates no data collected for period.

Cleveland, OH
Consumer Price Index - All Urban Consumers
Base 1982-1984 = 100
Annual Averages

For 1914-1997. Columns headed % show percentile change in the index from the previous period for which an index is available.

Year	All Items		Food & Beverage		Housing		Apparel & Upkeep		Trans-portation		Medical Care		Entertain-ment		Other Goods & Services	
	Index	%	Index	%	Index	%	Index	%	Index	%	Index	%	Index	%	Index	%
1914	-	-	-	-	-	-	-	-	-	-	-	-	-	-	-	-
1915	8.7	-	-	-	-	-	-	-	-	-	-	-	-	-	-	-
1916	9.4	8.0	-	-	-	-	-	-	-	-	-	-	-	-	-	-
1917	11.4	21.3	-	-	-	-	-	-	-	-	-	-	-	-	-	-
1918	13.2	15.8	-	-	-	-	-	-	-	-	-	-	-	-	-	-
1919	15.5	17.4	-	-	-	-	-	-	-	-	-	-	-	-	-	-
1920	18.3	18.1	-	-	-	-	-	-	-	-	-	-	-	-	-	-
1921	16.6	-9.3	-	-	-	-	-	-	-	-	-	-	-	-	-	-
1922	15.1	-9.0	-	-	-	-	-	-	-	-	-	-	-	-	-	-
1923	15.7	4.0	-	-	-	-	-	-	-	-	-	-	-	-	-	-
1924	15.7	0.0	-	-	-	-	-	-	-	-	-	-	-	-	-	-
1925	16.0	1.9	-	-	-	-	-	-	-	-	-	-	-	-	-	-
1926	16.1	0.6	-	-	-	-	-	-	-	-	-	-	-	-	-	-
1927	15.8	-1.9	-	-	-	-	-	-	-	-	-	-	-	-	-	-
1928	15.6	-1.3	-	-	-	-	-	-	-	-	-	-	-	-	-	-
1929	15.5	-0.6	-	-	-	-	-	-	-	-	-	-	-	-	-	-
1930	15.2	-1.9	-	-	-	-	-	-	-	-	-	-	-	-	-	-
1931	13.7	-9.9	-	-	-	-	-	-	-	-	-	-	-	-	-	-
1932	12.4	-9.5	-	-	-	-	-	-	-	-	-	-	-	-	-	-
1933	11.8	-4.8	-	-	-	-	-	-	-	-	-	-	-	-	-	-
1934	12.2	3.4	-	-	-	-	-	-	-	-	-	-	-	-	-	-
1935	12.7	4.1	-	-	-	-	-	-	-	-	-	-	-	-	-	-
1936	12.8	0.8	-	-	-	-	-	-	-	-	-	-	-	-	-	-
1937	13.4	4.7	-	-	-	-	-	-	-	-	-	-	-	-	-	-
1938	13.3	-0.7	-	-	-	-	-	-	-	-	-	-	-	-	-	-
1939	13.2	-0.8	-	-	-	-	-	-	-	-	-	-	-	-	-	-
1940	13.2	0.0	-	-	-	-	-	-	-	-	-	-	-	-	-	-
1941	14.0	6.1	-	-	-	-	-	-	-	-	-	-	-	-	-	-
1942	15.5	10.7	-	-	-	-	-	-	-	-	-	-	-	-	-	-
1943	16.6	7.1	-	-	-	-	-	-	-	-	-	-	-	-	-	-
1944	16.9	1.8	-	-	-	-	-	-	-	-	-	-	-	-	-	-
1945	17.2	1.8	-	-	-	-	-	-	-	-	-	-	-	-	-	-
1946	18.5	7.6	-	-	-	-	-	-	-	-	-	-	-	-	-	-
1947	21.2	14.6	-	-	-	-	-	-	18.9	-	10.6	-	-	-	-	-
1948	23.0	8.5	-	-	-	-	-	-	21.8	15.3	11.2	5.7	-	-	-	-
1949	22.6	-1.7	-	-	-	-	-	-	23.1	6.0	11.7	4.5	-	-	-	-
1950	22.8	0.9	-	-	-	-	-	-	23.1	0.0	11.8	0.9	-	-	-	-
1951	24.6	7.9	-	-	-	-	-	-	24.6	6.5	12.6	6.8	-	-	-	-
1952	25.2	2.4	-	-	-	-	-	-	26.0	5.7	13.3	5.6	-	-	-	-
1953	25.4	0.8	-	-	-	-	44.1	-	26.3	1.2	13.8	3.8	-	-	-	-
1954	25.7	1.2	-	-	-	-	44.1	0.0	25.8	-1.9	14.5	5.1	-	-	-	-
1955	25.7	0.0	-	-	-	-	43.8	-0.7	25.6	-0.8	15.1	4.1	-	-	-	-
1956	26.2	1.9	-	-	-	-	44.8	2.3	26.7	4.3	16.1	6.6	-	-	-	-
1957	27.2	3.8	-	-	-	-	45.5	1.6	28.5	6.7	16.7	3.7	-	-	-	-
1958	27.8	2.2	-	-	-	-	45.9	0.9	29.0	1.8	17.1	2.4	-	-	-	-

[Continued]

408

Cleveland, OH
Consumer Price Index - All Urban Consumers
Base 1982-1984 = 100
Annual Averages
[Continued]

For 1914-1997. Columns headed % show percentile change in the index from the previous period for which an index is available.

Year	All Items		Food & Beverage		Housing		Apparel & Upkeep		Trans- portation		Medical Care		Entertain- ment		Other Goods & Services	
	Index	%	Index	%	Index	%	Index	%	Index	%	Index	%	Index	%	Index	%
1959	27.9	0.4	-	-	-	-	46.2	0.7	30.1	3.8	18.7	9.4	-	-	-	-
1960	28.3	1.4	-	-	-	-	46.4	0.4	30.3	0.7	19.3	3.2	-	-	-	-
1961	28.5	0.7	-	-	-	-	46.8	0.9	31.0	2.3	20.7	7.3	-	-	-	-
1962	28.6	0.4	-	-	-	-	47.0	0.4	31.4	1.3	20.8	0.5	-	-	-	-
1963	28.9	1.0	-	-	-	-	47.7	1.5	31.5	0.3	21.9	5.3	-	-	-	-
1964	29.1	0.7	-	-	-	-	47.9	0.4	32.1	1.9	22.5	2.7	-	-	-	-
1965	29.6	1.7	-	-	-	-	48.3	0.8	32.6	1.6	23.2	3.1	-	-	-	-
1966	30.3	2.4	-	-	-	-	49.8	3.1	32.9	0.9	23.7	2.2	-	-	-	-
1967	31.2	3.0	-	-	-	-	51.3	3.0	33.9	3.0	25.2	6.3	-	-	-	-
1968	33.0	5.8	-	-	-	-	54.4	6.0	35.5	4.7	27.3	8.3	-	-	-	-
1969	34.9	5.8	-	-	-	-	57.6	5.9	37.0	4.2	30.5	11.7	-	-	-	-
1970	37.2	6.6	-	-	-	-	60.4	4.9	39.5	6.8	32.9	7.9	-	-	-	-
1971	38.3	3.0	-	-	-	-	62.4	3.3	42.2	6.8	35.2	7.0	-	-	-	-
1972	39.5	3.1	-	-	-	-	63.5	1.8	42.7	1.2	36.2	2.8	-	-	-	-
1973	41.8	5.8	-	-	-	-	66.5	4.7	44.1	3.3	38.0	5.0	-	-	-	-
1974	46.1	10.3	-	-	-	-	72.6	9.2	49.4	12.0	41.3	8.7	-	-	-	-
1975	50.2	8.9	-	-	-	-	74.4	2.5	52.1	5.5	46.0	11.4	-	-	-	-
1976	52.7	5.0	63.1	-	46.2	-	76.2	2.4	54.4	4.4	50.6	10.0	67.3	-	58.3	-
1977	56.3	6.8	66.4	5.2	49.7	7.6	80.5	5.6	57.8	6.3	56.7	12.1	70.6	4.9	61.8	6.0
1978	60.5	7.5	72.1	8.6	53.6	7.8	82.1	2.0	60.8	5.2	61.9	9.2	74.8	5.9	65.9	6.6
1979	68.5	13.2	79.6	10.4	63.0	17.5	84.5	2.9	69.2	13.8	66.0	6.6	78.7	5.2	71.1	7.9
1980	78.9	15.2	85.6	7.5	75.9	20.5	89.4	5.8	80.9	16.9	72.7	10.2	83.6	6.2	76.7	7.9
1981	87.2	10.5	93.2	8.9	83.8	10.4	95.0	6.3	92.0	13.7	81.2	11.7	88.6	6.0	84.9	10.7
1982	94.0	7.8	96.3	3.3	92.3	10.1	99.5	4.7	96.9	5.3	91.5	12.7	95.7	8.0	92.8	9.3
1983	101.2	7.7	99.8	3.6	102.6	11.2	99.3	-0.2	99.5	2.7	101.2	10.6	100.3	4.8	100.6	8.4
1984	104.8	3.6	103.9	4.1	105.1	2.4	101.3	2.0	103.6	4.1	107.4	6.1	104.1	3.8	106.7	6.1
1985	107.8	2.9	106.2	2.2	108.5	3.2	104.1	2.8	105.6	1.9	111.9	4.2	107.0	2.8	111.5	4.5
1986	109.4	1.5	107.6	1.3	111.8	3.0	102.4	-1.6	101.2	-4.2	122.3	9.3	114.2	6.7	117.0	4.9
1987	112.7	3.0	111.3	3.4	114.0	2.0	108.5	6.0	103.9	2.7	128.5	5.1	115.8	1.4	123.8	5.8
1988	116.7	3.5	116.4	4.6	117.8	3.3	105.8	-2.5	107.3	3.3	134.9	5.0	119.9	3.5	133.1	7.5
1989	122.7	5.1	124.0	6.5	122.7	4.2	111.4	5.3	113.0	5.3	143.5	6.4	127.0	5.9	141.0	5.9
1990	129.0	5.1	130.6	5.3	127.7	4.1	117.8	5.7	119.4	5.7	156.6	9.1	133.6	5.2	149.6	6.1
1991	134.2	4.0	135.4	3.7	132.5	3.8	121.9	3.5	123.1	3.1	171.7	9.6	138.6	3.7	160.1	7.0
1992	136.8	1.9	136.1	0.5	135.8	2.5	122.2	0.2	124.1	0.8	178.6	4.0	139.6	0.7	170.2	6.3
1993	140.3	2.6	139.7	2.6	139.0	2.4	125.1	2.4	125.0	0.7	187.2	4.8	143.2	2.6	180.3	5.9
1994	144.4	2.9	144.4	3.4	142.4	2.4	128.8	3.0	128.6	2.9	195.8	4.6	149.4	4.3	184.3	2.2
1995	147.9	2.4	148.9	3.1	145.1	1.9	127.1	-1.3	133.1	3.5	202.6	3.5	153.1	2.5	190.0	3.1
1996	152.0	2.8	154.2	3.6	148.6	2.4	128.8	1.3	138.5	4.1	209.4	3.4	155.8	1.8	193.0	1.6
1997	-	-	-	-	-	-	-	-	-	-	-	-	-	-	-	-

Source: U.S. Department of Labor, Bureau of Labor Statistics, Division of Consumer Prices and Price Indexes. - indicates no data collected for period.

Cleveland, OH
Consumer Price Index - Urban Wage Earners
Base 1982-1984 = 100
Annual Averages

For 1914-1997. Columns headed % show percentile change in the index from the previous period for which an index is available.

Year	All Items		Food & Beverage		Housing		Apparel & Upkeep		Trans-portation		Medical Care		Entertain-ment		Other Goods & Services	
	Index	%	Index	%	Index	%	Index	%	Index	%	Index	%	Index	%	Index	%
1914	-	-	-	-	-	-	-	-	-	-	-	-	-	-	-	-
1915	8.9	-	-	-	-	-	-	-	-	-	-	-	-	-	-	-
1916	9.7	9.0	-	-	-	-	-	-	-	-	-	-	-	-	-	-
1917	11.6	19.6	-	-	-	-	-	-	-	-	-	-	-	-	-	-
1918	13.6	17.2	-	-	-	-	-	-	-	-	-	-	-	-	-	-
1919	15.9	16.9	-	-	-	-	-	-	-	-	-	-	-	-	-	-
1920	18.8	18.2	-	-	-	-	-	-	-	-	-	-	-	-	-	-
1921	17.0	-9.6	-	-	-	-	-	-	-	-	-	-	-	-	-	-
1922	15.5	-8.8	-	-	-	-	-	-	-	-	-	-	-	-	-	-
1923	16.1	3.9	-	-	-	-	-	-	-	-	-	-	-	-	-	-
1924	16.1	0.0	-	-	-	-	-	-	-	-	-	-	-	-	-	-
1925	16.4	1.9	-	-	-	-	-	-	-	-	-	-	-	-	-	-
1926	16.5	0.6	-	-	-	-	-	-	-	-	-	-	-	-	-	-
1927	16.2	-1.8	-	-	-	-	-	-	-	-	-	-	-	-	-	-
1928	16.0	-1.2	-	-	-	-	-	-	-	-	-	-	-	-	-	-
1929	15.9	-0.6	-	-	-	-	-	-	-	-	-	-	-	-	-	-
1930	15.6	-1.9	-	-	-	-	-	-	-	-	-	-	-	-	-	-
1931	14.0	-10.3	-	-	-	-	-	-	-	-	-	-	-	-	-	-
1932	12.7	-9.3	-	-	-	-	-	-	-	-	-	-	-	-	-	-
1933	12.1	-4.7	-	-	-	-	-	-	-	-	-	-	-	-	-	-
1934	12.5	3.3	-	-	-	-	-	-	-	-	-	-	-	-	-	-
1935	13.0	4.0	-	-	-	-	-	-	-	-	-	-	-	-	-	-
1936	13.2	1.5	-	-	-	-	-	-	-	-	-	-	-	-	-	-
1937	13.7	3.8	-	-	-	-	-	-	-	-	-	-	-	-	-	-
1938	13.6	-0.7	-	-	-	-	-	-	-	-	-	-	-	-	-	-
1939	13.5	-0.7	-	-	-	-	-	-	-	-	-	-	-	-	-	-
1940	13.5	0.0	-	-	-	-	-	-	-	-	-	-	-	-	-	-
1941	14.3	5.9	-	-	-	-	-	-	-	-	-	-	-	-	-	-
1942	15.9	11.2	-	-	-	-	-	-	-	-	-	-	-	-	-	-
1943	17.0	6.9	-	-	-	-	-	-	-	-	-	-	-	-	-	-
1944	17.3	1.8	-	-	-	-	-	-	-	-	-	-	-	-	-	-
1945	17.6	1.7	-	-	-	-	-	-	-	-	-	-	-	-	-	-
1946	19.0	8.0	-	-	-	-	-	-	-	-	-	-	-	-	-	-
1947	21.7	14.2	-	-	-	-	-	-	19.1	-	10.4	-	-	-	-	-
1948	23.6	8.8	-	-	-	-	-	-	22.0	15.2	11.0	5.8	-	-	-	-
1949	23.2	-1.7	-	-	-	-	-	-	23.4	6.4	11.5	4.5	-	-	-	-
1950	23.4	0.9	-	-	-	-	-	-	23.4	0.0	11.6	0.9	-	-	-	-
1951	25.3	8.1	-	-	-	-	-	-	24.9	6.4	12.4	6.9	-	-	-	-
1952	25.9	2.4	-	-	-	-	-	-	26.3	5.6	13.1	5.6	-	-	-	-
1953	26.1	0.8	-	-	-	-	42.7	-	26.6	1.1	13.6	3.8	-	-	-	-
1954	26.3	0.8	-	-	-	-	42.7	0.0	26.1	-1.9	14.3	5.1	-	-	-	-
1955	26.4	0.4	-	-	-	-	42.5	-0.5	25.9	-0.8	14.9	4.2	-	-	-	-
1956	26.9	1.9	-	-	-	-	43.4	2.1	27.0	4.2	15.8	6.0	-	-	-	-
1957	27.9	3.7	-	-	-	-	44.1	1.6	28.9	7.0	16.4	3.8	-	-	-	-
1958	28.5	2.2	-	-	-	-	44.5	0.9	29.4	1.7	16.8	2.4	-	-	-	-

[Continued]

410

Cleveland, OH
Consumer Price Index - Urban Wage Earners
Base 1982-1984 = 100
Annual Averages
[Continued]

For 1914-1997. Columns headed % show percentile change in the index from the previous period for which an index is available.

Year	All Items		Food & Beverage		Housing		Apparel & Upkeep		Trans- portation		Medical Care		Entertain- ment		Other Goods & Services	
	Index	%	Index	%	Index	%	Index	%	Index	%	Index	%	Index	%	Index	%
1959	28.6	0.4	-	-	-	-	44.8	0.7	30.4	3.4	18.4	9.5	-	-	-	-
1960	29.0	1.4	-	-	-	-	45.0	0.4	30.7	1.0	19.0	3.3	-	-	-	-
1961	29.3	1.0	-	-	-	-	45.4	0.9	31.3	2.0	20.3	6.8	-	-	-	-
1962	29.3	0.0	-	-	-	-	45.6	0.4	31.8	1.6	20.4	0.5	-	-	-	-
1963	29.7	1.4	-	-	-	-	46.3	1.5	31.9	0.3	21.5	5.4	-	-	-	-
1964	29.8	0.3	-	-	-	-	46.4	0.2	32.5	1.9	22.2	3.3	-	-	-	-
1965	30.3	1.7	-	-	-	-	46.8	0.9	33.0	1.5	22.8	2.7	-	-	-	-
1966	31.1	2.6	-	-	-	-	48.3	3.2	33.3	0.9	23.3	2.2	-	-	-	-
1967	32.0	2.9	-	-	-	-	49.8	3.1	34.3	3.0	24.7	6.0	-	-	-	-
1968	33.9	5.9	-	-	-	-	52.8	6.0	36.0	5.0	26.8	8.5	-	-	-	-
1969	35.8	5.6	-	-	-	-	55.9	5.9	37.5	4.2	30.0	11.9	-	-	-	-
1970	38.2	6.7	-	-	-	-	58.6	4.8	40.0	6.7	32.4	8.0	-	-	-	-
1971	39.3	2.9	-	-		-	60.5	3.2	42.7	6.8	34.6	6.8	-	-	-	-
1972	40.5	3.1	-	-	-	-	61.6	1.8	43.3	1.4	35.6	2.9	-	-	-	-
1973	42.9	5.9	-	-	-	-	64.5	4.7	44.6	3.0	37.3	4.8	-	-	-	-
1974	47.3	10.3	-	-	-	-	70.4	9.1	50.0	12.1	40.7	9.1	-	-	-	-
1975	51.5	8.9	-	-	-	-	72.2	2.6	52.7	5.4	45.3	11.3	-	-	-	-
1976	54.1	5.0	62.3	-	48.1	-	73.9	2.4	55.1	4.6	49.8	9.9	67.2	-	57.2	-
1977	57.8	6.8	65.6	5.3	51.8	7.7	78.1	5.7	58.5	6.2	55.8	12.0	70.6	5.1	60.6	5.9
1978	62.2	7.6	72.1	9.9	55.9	7.9	80.7	3.3	61.7	5.5	61.2	9.7	73.9	4.7	64.6	6.6
1979	70.6	13.5	80.4	11.5	65.3	16.8	83.6	3.6	70.6	14.4	66.5	8.7	78.2	5.8	69.8	8.0
1980	81.1	14.9	86.9	8.1	78.7	20.5	87.0	4.1	82.2	16.4	73.7	10.8	84.2	7.7	76.1	9.0
1981	89.2	10.0	94.0	8.2	86.8	10.3	93.2	7.1	92.4	12.4	81.4	10.4	89.3	6.1	84.3	10.8
1982	95.9	7.5	96.5	2.7	95.9	10.5	99.2	6.4	96.7	4.7	91.7	12.7	95.3	6.7	92.5	9.7
1983	101.1	5.4	99.9	3.5	102.4	6.8	99.3	0.1	99.6	3.0	101.1	10.3	100.1	5.0	100.7	8.9
1984	103.0	1.9	103.6	3.7	101.7	-0.7	101.5	2.2	103.7	4.1	107.1	5.9	104.6	4.5	106.8	6.1
1985	103.8	0.8	105.9	2.2	100.7	-1.0	105.0	3.4	105.6	1.8	111.5	4.1	107.4	2.7	111.2	4.1
1986	105.0	1.2	107.3	1.3	103.8	3.1	103.5	-1.4	100.1	-5.2	121.6	9.1	114.9	7.0	116.9	5.1
1987	108.0	2.9	110.9	3.4	105.7	1.8	109.2	5.5	102.1	2.0	127.9	5.2	116.0	1.0	124.7	6.7
1988	111.8	3.5	115.9	4.5	109.3	3.4	106.2	-2.7	105.4	3.2	134.1	4.8	120.6	4.0	134.8	8.1
1989	117.3	4.9	123.5	6.6	113.5	3.8	110.7	4.2	110.7	5.0	142.1	6.0	126.3	4.7	143.4	6.4
1990	123.0	4.9	130.2	5.4	117.9	3.9	117.0	5.7	116.6	5.3	154.6	8.8	130.6	3.4	150.7	5.1
1991	127.8	3.9	134.9	3.6	122.2	3.6	121.3	3.7	120.0	2.9	168.7	9.1	134.5	3.0	162.2	7.6
1992	130.3	2.0	135.7	0.6	125.4	2.6	122.4	0.9	120.8	0.7	175.6	4.1	136.2	1.3	173.3	6.8
1993	133.3	2.3	139.3	2.7	128.2	2.2	124.2	1.5	121.7	0.7	184.0	4.8	139.5	2.4	183.9	6.1
1994	137.0	2.8	143.9	3.3	131.1	2.3	127.5	2.7	125.3	3.0	192.3	4.5	144.9	3.9	186.3	1.3
1995	140.2	2.3	148.4	3.1	133.3	1.7	125.2	-1.8	129.8	3.6	199.2	3.6	148.4	2.4	191.3	2.7
1996	144.3	2.9	153.7	3.6	137.1	2.9	126.2	0.8	134.5	3.6	206.6	3.7	151.5	2.1	193.2	1.0
1997	-	-	-	-	-	-	-	-	-	-	-	-	-	-	-	-

Source: U.S. Department of Labor, Bureau of Labor Statistics, Division of Consumer Prices and Price Indexes. - indicates no data collected for period.

Cleveland, OH
Consumer Price Index - All Urban Consumers
Base 1982-1984 = 100
All Items

For 1914-1997. Columns headed % show percentile change in the index from the previous period for which an index is available.

Year	Jan Index	%	Feb Index	%	Mar Index	%	Apr Index	%	May Index	%	Jun Index	%	Jul Index	%	Aug Index	%	Sep Index	%	Oct Index	%	Nov Index	%	Dec Index	%
1914	-	-	-	-	-	-	-	-	-	-	-	-	-	-	-	-	-	-	-	-	-	-	8.7	-
1915	-	-	-	-	-	-	-	-	-	-	-	-	-	-	-	-	-	-	-	-	-	-	8.8	1.1
1916	-	-	-	-	-	-	-	-	-	-	-	-	-	-	-	-	-	-	-	-	-	-	10.1	14.8
1917	-	-	-	-	-	-	-	-	-	-	-	-	-	-	-	-	-	-	-	-	-	-	12.0	18.8
1918	-	-	-	-	-	-	-	-	-	-	-	-	-	-	-	-	-	-	-	-	-	-	14.4	20.0
1919	-	-	-	-	-	-	-	-	-	-	15.1	4.9	-	-	-	-	-	-	-	-	-	-	16.9	11.9
1920	-	-	-	-	-	-	-	-	-	-	19.0	12.4	-	-	-	-	-	-	-	-	-	-	18.0	-5.3
1921	-	-	-	-	-	-	-	-	16.6	-7.8	-	-	-	-	-	-	16.2	-2.4	-	-	-	-	15.9	-1.9
1922	-	-	-	-	15.0	-5.7	-	-	-	-	15.1	0.7	-	-	-	-	14.9	-1.3	-	-	-	-	15.3	2.7
1923	-	-	-	-	15.4	0.7	-	-	-	-	15.8	2.6	-	-	-	-	16.0	1.3	-	-	-	-	15.9	-0.6
1924	-	-	-	-	15.7	-1.3	-	-	-	-	15.6	-0.6	-	-	-	-	15.7	0.6	-	-	-	-	15.7	0.0
1925	-	-	-	-	-	-	-	-	-	-	16.1	2.5	-	-	-	-	-	-	-	-	-	-	16.2	0.6
1926	-	-	-	-	-	-	-	-	-	-	16.2	0.0	-	-	-	-	-	-	-	-	-	-	16.1	-0.6
1927	-	-	-	-	-	-	-	-	-	-	16.1	0.0	-	-	-	-	-	-	-	-	-	-	15.7	-2.5
1928	-	-	-	-	-	-	-	-	-	-	15.7	0.0	-	-	-	-	-	-	-	-	-	-	15.5	-1.3
1929	-	-	-	-	-	-	-	-	-	-	15.6	0.6	-	-	-	-	-	-	-	-	-	-	15.4	-1.3
1930	-	-	-	-	-	-	-	-	-	-	15.4	0.0	-	-	-	-	-	-	-	-	-	-	14.6	-5.2
1931	-	-	-	-	-	-	-	-	-	-	13.6	-6.8	-	-	-	-	-	-	-	-	-	-	13.1	-3.7
1932	-	-	-	-	-	-	-	-	-	-	12.5	-4.6	-	-	-	-	-	-	-	-	-	-	11.8	-5.6
1933	-	-	-	-	-	-	-	-	-	-	11.6	-1.7	-	-	-	-	-	-	-	-	-	-	12.0	3.4
1934	-	-	-	-	-	-	-	-	-	-	12.2	1.7	-	-	-	-	-	-	-	-	12.2	0.0	-	-
1935	-	-	-	-	12.7	4.1	-	-	-	-	-	-	12.7	0.0	-	-	-	-	12.7	0.0	-	-	-	-
1936	12.7	0.0	-	-	-	-	12.6	-0.8	-	-	-	-	12.9	2.4	-	-	13.1	1.6	-	-	-	-	12.9	-1.5
1937	-	-	-	-	13.1	1.6	-	-	-	-	13.4	2.3	-	-	-	-	13.6	1.5	-	-	-	-	13.4	-1.5
1938	-	-	-	-	13.2	-1.5	-	-	-	-	13.3	0.8	-	-	-	-	13.3	0.0	-	-	-	-	13.2	-0.8
1939	-	-	-	-	13.2	0.0	-	-	-	-	13.2	0.0	-	-	-	-	13.3	0.8	-	-	-	-	13.2	-0.8
1940	-	-	-	-	13.2	0.0	-	-	-	-	13.3	0.8	-	-	-	-	13.4	0.8	13.3	-0.7	13.2	-0.8	13.3	0.8
1941	13.3	0.0	13.4	0.8	13.4	0.0	13.5	0.7	13.6	0.7	13.9	2.2	14.0	0.7	14.2	1.4	14.5	2.1	14.6	0.7	14.8	1.4	14.8	0.0
1942	15.0	1.4	15.0	0.0	15.3	2.0	15.4	0.7	15.5	0.6	15.6	0.6	15.6	0.0	15.5	-0.6	15.6	0.6	15.9	1.9	15.9	0.0	16.1	1.3
1943	16.1	0.0	16.2	0.6	16.4	1.2	16.5	0.6	16.7	1.2	16.9	1.2	16.7	-1.2	16.7	0.0	16.8	0.6	16.8	0.0	16.8	0.0	16.8	0.0
1944	16.7	-0.6	16.7	0.0	16.7	0.0	16.9	1.2	16.9	0.0	16.9	0.0	17.1	1.2	17.1	0.0	17.1	0.0	17.0	-0.6	17.1	0.6	16.9	-1.2
1945	17.0	0.6	17.0	0.0	17.0	0.0	17.0	0.0	17.3	1.8	17.3	0.0	17.3	0.0	17.3	0.0	17.2	-0.6	17.3	0.6	17.3	0.0	17.3	0.0
1946	17.3	0.0	17.3	0.0	17.3	0.0	17.4	0.6	17.5	0.6	17.8	1.7	18.8	5.6	19.3	2.7	19.3	0.0	19.6	1.6	20.2	3.1	20.5	1.5
1947	20.4	-0.5	20.4	0.0	20.9	2.5	20.9	0.0	20.8	-0.5	21.0	1.0	-	-	21.4	1.9	-	-	-	-	21.9	2.3	-	-
1948	-	-	22.5	2.7	-	-	-	-	22.8	1.3	-	-	-	-	23.6	3.5	-	-	-	-	23.1	-2.1	-	-
1949	-	-	22.7	-1.7	-	-	-	-	22.6	-0.4	-	-	-	-	22.6	0.0	-	-	-	-	22.4	-0.9	-	-
1950	-	-	22.2	-0.9	-	-	-	-	22.3	0.5	-	-	-	-	23.1	3.6	-	-	-	-	23.5	1.7	-	-
1951	-	-	24.3	3.4	-	-	-	-	24.6	1.2	-	-	-	-	24.7	0.4	-	-	-	-	25.1	1.6	-	-
1952	-	-	25.1	0.0	-	-	-	-	25.2	0.4	-	-	-	-	25.4	0.8	-	-	-	-	25.3	-0.4	-	-
1953	-	-	25.0	-1.2	-	-	-	-	25.3	1.2	-	-	-	-	25.6	1.2	-	-	-	-	25.7	0.4	-	-
1954	-	-	25.7	0.0	-	-	-	-	25.7	0.0	-	-	-	-	25.7	0.0	-	-	-	-	25.7	0.0	-	-
1955	-	-	25.6	-0.4	-	-	-	-	25.7	0.4	-	-	-	-	25.8	0.4	-	-	-	-	25.9	0.4	-	-
1956	-	-	25.8	-0.4	-	-	-	-	26.1	1.2	-	-	-	-	26.5	1.5	-	-	-	-	26.7	0.8	-	-
1957	-	-	26.8	0.4	-	-	-	-	27.1	1.1	-	-	-	-	27.3	0.7	-	-	-	-	27.5	0.7	-	-
1958	-	-	27.7	0.7	-	-	-	-	27.8	0.4	-	-	-	-	27.8	0.0	-	-	-	-	27.7	-0.4	-	-

[Continued]

Cleveland, OH
Consumer Price Index - All Urban Consumers
Base 1982-1984 = 100
All Items
[Continued]

For 1914-1997. Columns headed % show percentile change in the index from the previous period for which an index is available.

Year	Jan Index	%	Feb Index	%	Mar Index	%	Apr Index	%	May Index	%	Jun Index	%	Jul Index	%	Aug Index	%	Sep Index	%	Oct Index	%	Nov Index	%	Dec Index	%
1959	-	-	27.8	0.4	-	-	-	-	27.9	0.4	-	-	-	-	28.0	0.4	-	-	-	-	28.1	0.4	-	-
1960	-	-	28.1	0.0	-	-	-	-	28.3	0.7	-	-	-	-	28.4	0.4	-	-	-	-	28.5	0.4	-	-
1961	-	-	28.6	0.4	-	-	-	-	28.5	-0.3	-	-	-	-	28.6	0.4	-	-	-	-	28.5	-0.3	-	-
1962	-	-	28.5	0.0	-	-	-	-	28.6	0.4	-	-	-	-	28.7	0.3	-	-	-	-	28.7	0.0	-	-
1963	-	-	28.8	0.3	-	-	-	-	28.8	0.0	-	-	-	-	29.1	1.0	-	-	-	-	29.0	-0.3	-	-
1964	-	-	29.1	0.3	-	-	-	-	28.9	-0.7	-	-	-	-	29.1	0.7	-	-	-	-	29.3	0.7	-	-
1965	-	-	29.3	0.0	-	-	-	-	29.5	0.7	-	-	-	-	29.6	0.3	-	-	-	-	29.8	0.7	-	-
1966	-	-	29.9	0.3	-	-	-	-	30.3	1.3	-	-	-	-	30.5	0.7	-	-	-	-	30.6	0.3	-	-
1967	-	-	30.8	0.7	-	-	-	-	30.9	0.3	-	-	-	-	31.3	1.3	-	-	-	-	31.7	1.3	-	-
1968	-	-	32.5	2.5	-	-	-	-	32.9	1.2	-	-	-	-	33.2	0.9	-	-	-	-	33.7	1.5	-	-
1969	-	-	34.0	0.9	-	-	-	-	34.6	1.8	-	-	-	-	35.2	1.7	-	-	-	-	35.8	1.7	-	-
1970	-	-	36.6	2.2	-	-	-	-	37.1	1.4	-	-	-	-	37.5	1.1	-	-	-	-	37.9	1.1	-	-
1971	-	-	37.9	0.0	-	-	-	-	38.1	0.5	-	-	-	-	38.4	0.8	-	-	-	-	38.8	1.0	-	-
1972	-	-	39.3	1.3	-	-	-	-	39.4	0.3	-	-	-	-	39.4	0.0	-	-	-	-	39.9	1.3	-	-
1973	-	-	40.5	1.5	-	-	-	-	41.4	2.2	-	-	-	-	42.4	2.4	-	-	-	-	42.9	1.2	-	-
1974	-	-	44.3	3.3	-	-	-	-	45.6	2.9	-	-	-	-	46.8	2.6	-	-	-	-	47.7	1.9	-	-
1975	-	-	49.2	3.1	-	-	-	-	49.8	1.2	-	-	-	-	50.7	1.8	-	-	-	-	51.3	1.2	-	-
1976	-	-	51.5	0.4	-	-	-	-	52.1	1.2	-	-	-	-	53.2	2.1	-	-	-	-	54.0	1.5	-	-
1977	-	-	55.1	2.0	-	-	-	-	56.1	1.8	-	-	-	-	56.5	0.7	-	-	-	-	57.5	1.8	-	-
1978	-	-	58.2	1.2	-	-	59.4	2.1	-	-	59.6	0.3	-	-	60.8	2.0	-	-	62.4	2.6	-	-	64.2	2.9
1979	-	-	65.6	2.2	-	-	67.1	2.3	-	-	68.6	2.2	-	-	69.1	0.7	-	-	70.1	1.4	-	-	72.6	3.6
1980	-	-	76.0	4.7	-	-	77.2	1.6	-	-	78.0	1.0	-	-	79.2	1.5	-	-	82.6	4.3	-	-	83.2	0.7
1981	-	-	85.3	2.5	-	-	84.9	-0.5	-	-	89.0	4.8	-	-	88.8	-0.2	-	-	88.3	-0.6	-	-	87.9	-0.5
1982	-	-	89.2	1.5	-	-	89.4	0.2	-	-	92.9	3.9	-	-	97.4	4.8	-	-	98.8	1.4	-	-	99.1	0.3
1983	-	-	99.5	0.4	-	-	99.7	0.2	-	-	101.2	1.5	-	-	101.8	0.6	-	-	103.2	1.4	-	-	102.6	-0.6
1984	-	-	103.3	0.7	-	-	103.9	0.6	-	-	105.1	1.2	-	-	105.3	0.2	-	-	106.1	0.8	-	-	106.0	-0.1
1985	-	-	106.2	0.2	-	-	106.9	0.7	-	-	108.1	1.1	-	-	108.6	0.5	-	-	108.8	0.2	-	-	108.8	0.0
1986	-	-	109.3	0.5	-	-	108.3	-0.9	-	-	109.4	1.0	-	-	110.1	0.6	-	-	109.9	-0.2	110.1	0.2	109.8	-0.3
1987	110.1	0.3	-	-	111.4	1.2	-	-	111.6	0.2	-	-	112.8	1.1	-	-	114.7	1.7	-	-	114.5	-0.2	-	-
1988	113.9	-0.5	-	-	115.1	1.1	-	-	116.6	1.3	-	-	117.6	0.9	-	-	117.6	0.0	-	-	118.0	0.3	-	-
1989	118.9	0.8	-	-	121.5	2.2	-	-	122.8	1.1	-	-	124.4	1.3	-	-	123.7	-0.6	-	-	123.4	-0.2	-	-
1990	125.0	1.3	-	-	127.4	1.9	-	-	128.1	0.5	-	-	128.8	0.5	-	-	131.1	1.8	-	-	131.7	0.5	-	-
1991	131.9	0.2	-	-	133.2	1.0	-	-	134.3	0.8	-	-	133.9	-0.3	-	-	135.4	1.1	-	-	135.7	0.2	-	-
1992	136.2	0.4	-	-	136.3	0.1	-	-	136.1	-0.1	-	-	137.1	0.7	-	-	137.9	0.6	-	-	137.1	-0.6	-	-
1993	137.5	0.3	-	-	138.8	0.9	-	-	139.6	0.6	-	-	140.9	0.9	-	-	141.7	0.6	-	-	142.1	0.3	-	-
1994	142.4	0.2	-	-	143.3	0.6	-	-	143.7	0.3	-	-	143.7	0.0	-	-	146.3	1.8	-	-	146.0	-0.2	-	-
1995	146.6	0.4	-	-	147.3	0.5	-	-	147.4	0.1	-	-	148.1	0.5	-	-	149.0	0.6	-	-	148.2	-0.5	-	-
1996	149.0	0.5	-	-	150.9	1.3	-	-	151.8	0.6	-	-	152.1	0.2	-	-	153.5	0.9	-	-	153.8	0.2	-	-
1997	153.8	0.0	-	-	155.4	1.0	-	-	155.6	0.1	155.1	-0.3	156.3	0.8	-	-	157.3	0.6	-	-	157.1	-0.1	-	-

Source: U.S. Department of Labor, Bureau of Labor Statistics, Division of Consumer Prices and Price Indexes. - indicates no data collected for period.

Cleveland, OH
Consumer Price Index - Urban Wage Earners
Base 1982-1984 = 100
All Items

For 1914-1997. Columns headed % show percentile change in the index from the previous period for which an index is available.

Year	Jan Index	%	Feb Index	%	Mar Index	%	Apr Index	%	May Index	%	Jun Index	%	Jul Index	%	Aug Index	%	Sep Index	%	Oct Index	%	Nov Index	%	Dec Index	%
1914	-	-	-	-	-	-	-	-	-	-	-	-	-	-	-	-	-	-	-	-	-	-	8.9	-
1915	-	-	-	-	-	-	-	-	-	-	-	-	-	-	-	-	-	-	-	-	-	-	9.1	2.2
1916	-	-	-	-	-	-	-	-	-	-	-	-	-	-	-	-	-	-	-	-	-	-	10.4	14.3
1917	-	-	-	-	-	-	-	-	-	-	-	-	-	-	-	-	-	-	-	-	-	-	12.4	19.2
1918	-	-	-	-	-	-	-	-	-	-	-	-	-	-	-	-	-	-	-	-	-	-	14.8	19.4
1919	-	-	-	-	-	-	-	-	-	-	15.5	4.7	-	-	-	-	-	-	-	-	-	-	17.3	11.6
1920	-	-	-	-	-	-	-	-	-	-	19.5	12.7	-	-	-	-	-	-	-	-	-	-	18.5	-5.1
1921	-	-	-	-	-	-	-	-	17.0	-8.1	-	-	-	-	-	-	16.6	-2.4	-	-	-	-	16.3	-1.8
1922	-	-	-	-	15.4	-5.5	-	-	-	-	15.5	0.6	-	-	-	-	15.3	-1.3	-	-	-	-	15.7	2.6
1923	-	-	-	-	15.7	0.0	-	-	-	-	16.2	3.2	-	-	-	-	16.4	1.2	-	-	-	-	16.3	-0.6
1924	-	-	-	-	16.1	-1.2	-	-	-	-	16.0	-0.6	-	-	-	-	16.1	0.6	-	-	-	-	16.1	0.0
1925	-	-	-	-	-	-	-	-	-	-	16.5	2.5	-	-	-	-	-	-	-	-	-	-	16.6	0.6
1926	-	-	-	-	-	-	-	-	-	-	16.6	0.0	-	-	-	-	-	-	-	-	-	-	16.5	-0.6
1927	-	-	-	-	-	-	-	-	-	-	16.5	0.0	-	-	-	-	-	-	-	-	-	-	16.1	-2.4
1928	-	-	-	-	-	-	-	-	-	-	16.1	0.0	-	-	-	-	-	-	-	-	-	-	15.9	-1.2
1929	-	-	-	-	-	-	-	-	-	-	16.0	0.6	-	-	-	-	-	-	-	-	-	-	15.8	-1.2
1930	-	-	-	-	-	-	-	-	-	-	15.8	0.0	-	-	-	-	-	-	-	-	-	-	15.0	-5.1
1931	-	-	-	-	-	-	-	-	-	-	14.0	-6.7	-	-	-	-	-	-	-	-	-	-	13.4	-4.3
1932	-	-	-	-	-	-	-	-	-	-	12.8	-4.5	-	-	-	-	-	-	-	-	-	-	12.1	-5.5
1933	-	-	-	-	-	-	-	-	-	-	11.9	-1.7	-	-	-	-	-	-	-	-	-	-	12.3	3.4
1934	-	-	-	-	-	-	-	-	-	-	12.5	1.6	-	-	-	-	-	-	-	-	12.5	0.0	-	-
1935	-	-	-	-	13.0	4.0	-	-	-	-	-	-	13.0	0.0	-	-	-	-	13.1	0.8	-	-	-	-
1936	13.0	-0.8	-	-	-	-	13.0	0.0	-	-	-	-	13.2	1.5	-	-	13.4	1.5	-	-	-	-	13.2	-1.5
1937	-	-	-	-	13.5	2.3	-	-	-	-	13.8	2.2	-	-	-	-	14.0	1.4	-	-	-	-	13.8	-1.4
1938	-	-	-	-	13.5	-2.2	-	-	-	-	13.6	0.7	-	-	-	-	13.6	0.0	-	-	-	-	13.6	0.0
1939	-	-	-	-	13.5	-0.7	-	-	-	-	13.5	0.0	-	-	-	-	13.6	0.7	-	-	-	-	13.5	-0.7
1940	-	-	-	-	13.5	0.0	-	-	-	-	13.6	0.7	-	-	-	-	13.7	0.7	13.6	-0.7	13.5	-0.7	13.7	1.5
1941	13.7	0.0	13.7	0.0	13.8	0.7	13.9	0.7	14.0	0.7	14.2	1.4	14.3	0.7	14.6	2.1	14.8	1.4	15.0	1.4	15.1	0.7	15.2	0.7
1942	15.4	1.3	15.4	0.0	15.7	1.9	15.8	0.6	15.9	0.6	16.0	0.6	16.0	0.0	15.9	-0.6	16.0	0.6	16.3	1.9	16.4	0.6	16.5	0.6
1943	16.5	0.0	16.6	0.6	16.8	1.2	16.9	0.6	17.2	1.8	17.3	0.6	17.2	-0.6	17.2	0.0	17.2	0.0	17.2	0.0	17.2	0.0	17.2	0.0
1944	17.2	0.0	17.2	0.0	17.2	0.0	17.3	0.6	17.3	0.0	17.3	0.0	17.5	1.2	17.5	0.0	17.5	0.0	17.5	0.0	17.5	0.0	17.3	-1.1
1945	17.4	0.6	17.4	0.0	17.4	0.0	17.5	0.6	17.7	1.1	17.7	0.0	17.7	0.0	17.7	0.0	17.6	-0.6	17.7	0.6	17.7	0.0	17.8	0.6
1946	17.7	-0.6	17.7	0.0	17.7	0.0	17.8	0.6	18.0	1.1	18.2	1.1	19.3	6.0	19.7	2.1	19.8	0.5	20.1	1.5	20.7	3.0	21.0	1.4
1947	21.0	0.0	21.0	0.0	21.4	1.9	21.4	0.0	21.4	0.0	21.6	0.9	-	-	22.0	1.9	-	-	-	-	22.5	2.3	-	-
1948	-	-	23.1	2.7	-	-	-	-	23.4	1.3	-	-	-	-	24.2	3.4	-	-	-	-	23.7	-2.1	-	-
1949	-	-	23.2	-2.1	-	-	-	-	23.1	-0.4	-	-	-	-	23.2	0.4	-	-	-	-	23.0	-0.9	-	-
1950	-	-	22.8	-0.9	-	-	-	-	22.9	0.4	-	-	-	-	23.7	3.5	-	-	-	-	24.1	1.7	-	-
1951	-	-	24.9	3.3	-	-	-	-	25.2	1.2	-	-	-	-	25.3	0.4	-	-	-	-	25.7	1.6	-	-
1952	-	-	25.7	0.0	-	-	-	-	25.8	0.4	-	-	-	-	26.0	0.8	-	-	-	-	25.9	-0.4	-	-
1953	-	-	25.7	-0.8	-	-	-	-	25.9	0.8	-	-	-	-	26.3	1.5	-	-	-	-	26.4	0.4	-	-
1954	-	-	26.3	-0.4	-	-	-	-	26.3	0.0	-	-	-	-	26.3	0.0	-	-	-	-	26.3	0.0	-	-
1955	-	-	26.2	-0.4	-	-	-	-	26.3	0.4	-	-	-	-	26.5	0.8	-	-	-	-	26.5	0.0	-	-
1956	-	-	26.4	-0.4	-	-	-	-	26.8	1.5	-	-	-	-	27.2	1.5	-	-	-	-	27.4	0.7	-	-
1957	-	-	27.5	0.4	-	-	-	-	27.8	1.1	-	-	-	-	28.0	0.7	-	-	-	-	28.2	0.7	-	-
1958	-	-	28.4	0.7	-	-	-	-	28.5	0.4	-	-	-	-	28.5	0.0	-	-	-	-	28.4	-0.4	-	-

[Continued]

Cleveland, OH
Consumer Price Index - Urban Wage Earners
Base 1982-1984 = 100
All Items
[Continued]

For 1914-1997. Columns headed % show percentile change in the index from the previous period for which an index is available.

Year	Jan Index	%	Feb Index	%	Mar Index	%	Apr Index	%	May Index	%	Jun Index	%	Jul Index	%	Aug Index	%	Sep Index	%	Oct Index	%	Nov Index	%	Dec Index	%
1959	-	-	28.5	0.4	-	-	-	-	28.6	0.4	-	-	-	-	28.7	0.3	-	-	-	-	28.9	0.7	-	-
1960	-	-	28.8	-0.3	-	-	-	-	29.0	0.7	-	-	-	-	29.1	0.3	-	-	-	-	29.2	0.3	-	-
1961	-	-	29.3	0.3	-	-	-	-	29.2	-0.3	-	-	-	-	29.4	0.7	-	-	-	-	29.2	-0.7	-	-
1962	-	-	29.2	0.0	-	-	-	-	29.3	0.3	-	-	-	-	29.4	0.3	-	-	-	-	29.4	0.0	-	-
1963	-	-	29.6	0.7	-	-	-	-	29.6	0.0	-	-	-	-	29.8	0.7	-	-	-	-	29.8	0.0	-	-
1964	-	-	29.8	0.0	-	-	-	-	29.6	-0.7	-	-	-	-	29.8	0.7	-	-	-	-	30.0	0.7	-	-
1965	-	-	30.1	0.3	-	-	-	-	30.3	0.7	-	-	-	-	30.4	0.3	-	-	-	-	30.6	0.7	-	-
1966	-	-	30.6	0.0	-	-	-	-	31.1	1.6	-	-	-	-	31.2	0.3	-	-	-	-	31.4	0.6	-	-
1967	-	-	31.6	0.6	-	-	-	-	31.7	0.3	-	-	-	-	32.1	1.3	-	-	-	-	32.5	1.2	-	-
1968	-	-	33.4	2.8	-	-	-	-	33.8	1.2	-	-	-	-	34.0	0.6	-	-	-	-	34.5	1.5	-	-
1969	-	-	34.9	1.2	-	-	-	-	35.5	1.7	-	-	-	-	36.1	1.7	-	-	-	-	36.7	1.7	-	-
1970	-	-	37.5	2.2	-	-	-	-	38.1	1.6	-	-	-	-	38.4	0.8	-	-	-	-	38.8	1.0	-	-
1971	-	-	38.9	0.3	-	-	-	-	39.0	0.3	-	-	-	-	39.4	1.0	-	-	-	-	39.8	1.0	-	-
1972	-	-	40.3	1.3	-	-	-	-	40.4	0.2	-	-	-	-	40.4	0.0	-	-	-	-	40.9	1.2	-	-
1973	-	-	41.6	1.7	-	-	-	-	42.5	2.2	-	-	-	-	43.5	2.4	-	-	-	-	44.0	1.1	-	-
1974	-	-	45.5	3.4	-	-	-	-	46.8	2.9	-	-	-	-	48.0	2.6	-	-	-	-	49.0	2.1	-	-
1975	-	-	50.5	3.1	-	-	-	-	51.0	1.0	-	-	-	-	52.0	2.0	-	-	-	-	52.6	1.2	-	-
1976	-	-	52.8	0.4	-	-	-	-	53.4	1.1	-	-	-	-	54.6	2.2	-	-	-	-	55.4	1.5	-	-
1977	-	-	56.5	2.0	-	-	-	-	57.6	1.9	-	-	-	-	58.0	0.7	-	-	-	-	59.0	1.7	-	-
1978	-	-	59.7	1.2	-	-	61.0	2.2	-	-	61.5	0.8	-	-	62.7	2.0	-	-	64.2	2.4	-	-	65.9	2.6
1979	-	-	67.5	2.4	-	-	69.2	2.5	-	-	70.8	2.3	-	-	71.2	0.6	-	-	72.2	1.4	-	-	74.6	3.3
1980	-	-	78.1	4.7	-	-	79.5	1.8	-	-	80.2	0.9	-	-	81.4	1.5	-	-	84.6	3.9	-	-	85.4	0.9
1981	-	-	87.7	2.7	-	-	87.1	-0.7	-	-	90.8	4.2	-	-	90.6	-0.2	-	-	90.3	-0.3	-	-	90.0	-0.3
1982	-	-	91.2	1.3	-	-	91.4	0.2	-	-	95.0	3.9	-	-	99.4	4.6	-	-	100.5	1.1	-	-	100.8	0.3
1983	-	-	100.3	-0.5	-	-	100.9	0.6	-	-	101.3	0.4	-	-	101.6	0.3	-	-	101.5	-0.1	-	-	100.7	-0.8
1984	-	-	101.8	1.1	-	-	102.6	0.8	-	-	103.0	0.4	-	-	105.0	1.9	-	-	103.8	-1.1	-	-	102.0	-1.7
1985	-	-	102.3	0.3	-	-	103.0	0.7	-	-	104.1	1.1	-	-	104.7	0.6	-	-	104.7	0.0	-	-	104.8	0.1
1986	-	-	105.1	0.3	-	-	103.8	-1.2	-	-	105.0	1.2	-	-	105.6	0.6	-	-	105.4	-0.2	105.5	0.1	105.3	-0.2
1987	105.6	0.3	-	-	106.7	1.0	-	-	107.0	0.3	-	-	108.1	1.0	-	-	109.9	1.7	-	-	109.9	0.0	-	-
1988	109.3	-0.5	-	-	110.2	0.8	-	-	111.7	1.4	-	-	112.6	0.8	-	-	112.7	0.1	-	-	113.0	0.3	-	-
1989	113.8	0.7	-	-	116.2	2.1	-	-	117.7	1.3	-	-	118.8	0.9	-	-	118.2	-0.5	-	-	118.0	-0.2	-	-
1990	119.5	1.3	-	-	121.5	1.7	-	-	122.1	0.5	-	-	122.7	0.5	-	-	125.0	1.9	-	-	125.8	0.6	-	-
1991	125.8	0.0	-	-	126.8	0.8	-	-	127.8	0.8	-	-	127.4	-0.3	-	-	129.0	1.3	-	-	129.3	0.2	-	-
1992	129.6	0.2	-	-	129.7	0.1	-	-	129.6	-0.1	-	-	130.5	0.7	-	-	131.3	0.6	-	-	130.8	-0.4	-	-
1993	130.8	0.0	-	-	131.8	0.8	-	-	132.7	0.7	-	-	133.9	0.9	-	-	134.6	0.5	-	-	135.1	0.4	-	-
1994	135.1	0.0	-	-	135.7	0.4	-	-	136.1	0.3	-	-	136.3	0.1	-	-	138.9	1.9	-	-	138.8	-0.1	-	-
1995	139.0	0.1	-	-	139.7	0.5	-	-	139.9	0.1	-	-	140.3	0.3	-	-	141.3	0.7	-	-	140.6	-0.5	-	-
1996	141.5	0.6	-	-	143.1	1.1	-	-	144.0	0.6	-	-	144.3	0.2	-	-	145.8	1.0	-	-	146.2	0.3	-	-
1997	146.2	0.0	-	-	147.5	0.9	-	-	147.8	0.2	147.3	-0.3	148.2	0.6	-	-	149.2	0.7	-	-	149.1	-0.1	-	-

Source: U.S. Department of Labor, Bureau of Labor Statistics, Division of Consumer Prices and Price Indexes. - indicates no data collected for period.

Cleveland, OH
Consumer Price Index - All Urban Consumers
Base 1982-1984 = 100
Food and Beverages

For 1975-1997. Columns headed % show percentile change in the index from the previous period for which an index is available.

Year	Jan Index	%	Feb Index	%	Mar Index	%	Apr Index	%	May Index	%	Jun Index	%	Jul Index	%	Aug Index	%	Sep Index	%	Oct Index	%	Nov Index	%	Dec Index	%
1975	-	-	-	-	-	-	-	-	-	-	-	-	-	-	-	-	-	-	-	-	62.1	-	-	-
1976	-	-	62.1	0.0	-	-	-	-	63.0	1.4	-	-	-	-	63.2	0.3	-	-	-	-	63.7	0.8	-	-
1977	-	-	65.4	2.7	-	-	-	-	67.6	3.4	-	-	-	-	65.2	-3.6	-	-	-	-	67.4	3.4	-	-
1978	-	-	69.4	3.0	-	-	70.5	1.6	-	-	72.9	3.4	-	-	73.1	0.3	-	-	73.6	0.7	-	-	74.9	1.8
1979	-	-	77.9	4.0	-	-	79.4	1.9	-	-	79.8	0.5	-	-	80.2	0.5	-	-	80.6	0.5	-	-	81.4	1.0
1980	-	-	83.2	2.2	-	-	83.7	0.6	-	-	83.5	-0.2	-	-	86.6	3.7	-	-	89.0	2.8	-	-	89.5	0.6
1981	-	-	91.8	2.6	-	-	91.9	0.1	-	-	94.2	2.5	-	-	94.0	-0.2	-	-	94.4	0.4	-	-	94.2	-0.2
1982	-	-	95.4	1.3	-	-	95.5	0.1	-	-	96.7	1.3	-	-	96.7	0.0	-	-	97.1	0.4	-	-	97.2	0.1
1983	-	-	98.7	1.5	-	-	99.3	0.6	-	-	99.4	0.1	-	-	100.3	0.9	-	-	100.9	0.6	-	-	101.2	0.3
1984	-	-	103.6	2.4	-	-	103.2	-0.4	-	-	103.3	0.1	-	-	104.2	0.9	-	-	104.7	0.5	-	-	105.3	0.6
1985	-	-	107.0	1.6	-	-	106.2	-0.7	-	-	105.4	-0.8	-	-	106.0	0.6	-	-	106.1	0.1	-	-	106.5	0.4
1986	-	-	107.0	0.5	-	-	106.9	-0.1	-	-	106.3	-0.6	-	-	108.2	1.8	-	-	108.7	0.5	108.9	0.2	109.4	0.5
1987	110.6	1.1	-	-	110.7	0.1	-	-	110.9	0.2	-	-	110.6	-0.3	-	-	111.7	1.0	-	-	112.7	0.9	-	-
1988	113.3	0.5	-	-	114.8	1.3	-	-	114.2	-0.5	-	-	116.4	1.9	-	-	118.8	2.1	-	-	118.9	0.1	-	-
1989	121.0	1.8	-	-	121.8	0.7	-	-	123.3	1.2	-	-	124.9	1.3	-	-	125.4	0.4	-	-	125.6	0.2	-	-
1990	128.9	2.6	-	-	129.9	0.8	-	-	128.8	-0.8	-	-	131.2	1.9	-	-	131.5	0.2	-	-	131.6	0.1	-	-
1991	134.8	2.4	-	-	135.3	0.4	-	-	136.6	1.0	-	-	135.5	-0.8	-	-	134.8	-0.5	-	-	134.8	0.0	-	-
1992	136.4	1.2	-	-	136.4	0.0	-	-	136.4	0.0	-	-	134.9	-1.1	-	-	136.8	1.4	-	-	135.8	-0.7	-	-
1993	137.1	1.0	-	-	138.2	0.8	-	-	139.2	0.7	-	-	139.1	-0.1	-	-	141.5	1.7	-	-	141.9	0.3	-	-
1994	142.9	0.7	-	-	141.9	-0.7	-	-	143.7	1.3	-	-	143.6	-0.1	-	-	146.0	1.7	-	-	146.7	0.5	-	-
1995	149.1	1.6	-	-	146.9	-1.5	-	-	148.4	1.0	-	-	148.7	0.2	-	-	149.5	0.5	-	-	150.7	0.8	-	-
1996	150.7	0.0	-	-	151.6	0.6	-	-	153.4	1.2	-	-	153.9	0.3	-	-	156.3	1.6	-	-	157.5	0.8	-	-
1997	157.7	0.1	-	-	156.8	-0.6	-	-	157.5	0.4	157.3	-0.1	157.7	0.3	-	-	158.4	0.4	-	-	159.4	0.6	-	-

Source: U.S. Department of Labor, Bureau of Labor Statistics, Division of Consumer Prices and Price Indexes. - indicates no data collected for period.

Cleveland, OH
Consumer Price Index - Urban Wage Earners
Base 1982-1984 = 100
Food and Beverages

For 1975-1997. Columns headed % show percentile change in the index from the previous period for which an index is available.

Year	Jan Index	%	Feb Index	%	Mar Index	%	Apr Index	%	May Index	%	Jun Index	%	Jul Index	%	Aug Index	%	Sep Index	%	Oct Index	%	Nov Index	%	Dec Index	%
1975	-	-	-	-	-	-	-	-	-	-	-	-	-	-	-	-	-	-	-	-	61.4	-	-	-
1976	-	-	61.4	0.0	-	-	-	-	62.2	1.3	-	-	-	-	62.5	0.5	-	-	-	-	62.9	0.6	-	-
1977	-	-	64.6	2.7	-	-	-	-	66.8	3.4	-	-	-	-	64.4	-3.6	-	-	-	-	66.6	3.4	-	-
1978	-	-	68.5	2.9	-	-	70.0	2.2	-	-	73.3	4.7	-	-	73.7	0.5	-	-	73.8	0.1	-	-	75.3	2.0
1979	-	-	78.4	4.1	-	-	80.3	2.4	-	-	80.8	0.6	-	-	80.9	0.1	-	-	81.2	0.4	-	-	83.0	2.2
1980	-	-	84.1	1.3	-	-	84.9	1.0	-	-	84.6	-0.4	-	-	88.1	4.1	-	-	90.1	2.3	-	-	91.5	1.6
1981	-	-	93.2	1.9	-	-	93.5	0.3	-	-	94.3	0.9	-	-	94.4	0.1	-	-	94.8	0.4	-	-	94.3	-0.5
1982	-	-	95.4	1.2	-	-	95.7	0.3	-	-	96.9	1.3	-	-	96.8	-0.1	-	-	97.4	0.6	-	-	97.6	0.2
1983	-	-	99.0	1.4	-	-	99.5	0.5	-	-	99.5	0.0	-	-	100.3	0.8	-	-	100.8	0.5	-	-	101.0	0.2
1984	-	-	103.3	2.3	-	-	102.9	-0.4	-	-	103.1	0.2	-	-	104.1	1.0	-	-	104.5	0.4	-	-	105.0	0.5
1985	-	-	106.7	1.6	-	-	106.0	-0.7	-	-	105.1	-0.8	-	-	105.8	0.7	-	-	105.9	0.1	-	-	106.2	0.3
1986	-	-	106.6	0.4	-	-	106.6	0.0	-	-	106.0	-0.6	-	-	107.9	1.8	-	-	108.3	0.4	108.6	0.3	109.0	0.4
1987	110.2	1.1	-	-	110.2	0.0	-	-	110.5	0.3	-	-	110.3	-0.2	-	-	111.4	1.0	-	-	112.3	0.8	-	-
1988	112.8	0.4	-	-	114.3	1.3	-	-	113.7	-0.5	-	-	115.9	1.9	-	-	118.3	2.1	-	-	118.4	0.1	-	-
1989	120.5	1.8	-	-	121.3	0.7	-	-	122.8	1.2	-	-	124.4	1.3	-	-	124.9	0.4	-	-	125.2	0.2	-	-
1990	128.5	2.6	-	-	129.5	0.8	-	-	128.4	-0.8	-	-	130.8	1.9	-	-	131.2	0.3	-	-	131.3	0.1	-	-
1991	134.4	2.4	-	-	134.9	0.4	-	-	136.2	1.0	-	-	135.1	-0.8	-	-	134.3	-0.6	-	-	134.3	0.0	-	-
1992	136.0	1.3	-	-	136.0	0.0	-	-	135.8	-0.1	-	-	134.3	-1.1	-	-	136.3	1.5	-	-	135.4	-0.7	-	-
1993	136.7	1.0	-	-	137.8	0.8	-	-	138.7	0.7	-	-	138.6	-0.1	-	-	141.0	1.7	-	-	141.4	0.3	-	-
1994	142.4	0.7	-	-	141.4	-0.7	-	-	143.3	1.3	-	-	143.1	-0.1	-	-	145.4	1.6	-	-	146.2	0.6	-	-
1995	148.5	1.6	-	-	146.3	-1.5	-	-	147.8	1.0	-	-	148.1	0.2	-	-	148.9	0.5	-	-	150.2	0.9	-	-
1996	150.2	0.0	-	-	151.2	0.7	-	-	152.9	1.1	-	-	153.4	0.3	-	-	155.8	1.6	-	-	157.0	0.8	-	-
1997	157.2	0.1	-	-	156.3	-0.6	-	-	156.9	0.4	156.8	-0.1	157.1	0.2	-	-	157.9	0.5	-	-	158.9	0.6	-	-

Source: U.S. Department of Labor, Bureau of Labor Statistics, Division of Consumer Prices and Price Indexes. - indicates no data collected for period.

Cleveland, OH
Consumer Price Index - All Urban Consumers
Base 1982-1984 = 100
Housing

For 1975-1997. Columns headed % show percentile change in the index from the previous period for which an index is available.

Year	Jan Index	%	Feb Index	%	Mar Index	%	Apr Index	%	May Index	%	Jun Index	%	Jul Index	%	Aug Index	%	Sep Index	%	Oct Index	%	Nov Index	%	Dec Index	%
1975	-	-	-	-	-	-	-	-	-	-	-	-	-	-	-	-	-	-	-	-	45.1	-	-	-
1976	-	-	45.0	-0.2	-	-	-	-	45.2	0.4	-	-	-	-	46.8	3.5	-	-	-	-	47.4	1.3	-	-
1977	-	-	48.5	2.3	-	-	-	-	48.9	0.8	-	-	-	-	50.5	3.3	-	-	-	-	50.9	0.8	-	-
1978	-	-	51.1	0.4	-	-	52.7	3.1	-	-	51.8	-1.7	-	-	53.4	3.1	-	-	55.9	4.7	-	-	58.6	4.8
1979	-	-	59.7	1.9	-	-	61.5	3.0	-	-	63.7	3.6	-	-	63.3	-0.6	-	-	63.9	0.9	-	-	67.7	5.9
1980	-	-	72.5	7.1	-	-	73.8	1.8	-	-	75.2	1.9	-	-	75.6	0.5	-	-	80.7	6.7	-	-	80.6	-0.1
1981	-	-	82.4	2.2	-	-	80.4	-2.4	-	-	87.4	8.7	-	-	86.2	-1.4	-	-	84.1	-2.4	-	-	82.6	-1.8
1982	-	-	84.4	2.2	-	-	84.8	0.5	-	-	90.2	6.4	-	-	97.9	8.5	-	-	100.3	2.5	-	-	100.7	0.4
1983	-	-	101.1	0.4	-	-	101.0	-0.1	-	-	103.7	2.7	-	-	102.9	-0.8	-	-	104.7	1.7	-	-	102.8	-1.8
1984	-	-	102.7	-0.1	-	-	104.1	1.4	-	-	105.9	1.7	-	-	105.8	-0.1	-	-	106.9	1.0	-	-	106.0	-0.8
1985	-	-	106.3	0.3	-	-	106.3	0.0	-	-	110.4	3.9	-	-	110.6	0.2	-	-	109.4	-1.1	-	-	108.9	-0.5
1986	-	-	110.0	1.0	-	-	110.9	0.8	-	-	112.7	1.6	-	-	113.9	1.1	-	-	112.2	-1.5	112.5	0.3	111.7	-0.7
1987	111.3	-0.4	-	-	113.1	1.6	-	-	112.9	-0.2	-	-	115.1	1.9	-	-	115.8	0.6	-	-	114.8	-0.9	-	-
1988	114.5	-0.3	-	-	116.3	1.6	-	-	117.7	1.2	-	-	119.2	1.3	-	-	118.5	-0.6	-	-	119.3	0.7	-	-
1989	120.6	1.1	-	-	121.4	0.7	-	-	121.4	0.0	-	-	125.4	3.3	-	-	124.3	-0.9	-	-	122.5	-1.4	-	-
1990	123.7	1.0	-	-	125.6	1.5	-	-	126.9	1.0	-	-	128.5	1.3	-	-	130.7	1.7	-	-	129.2	-1.1	-	-
1991	129.7	0.4	-	-	131.2	1.2	-	-	132.3	0.8	-	-	132.8	0.4	-	-	133.9	0.8	-	-	133.4	-0.4	-	-
1992	136.0	1.9	-	-	134.1	-1.4	-	-	134.1	0.0	-	-	137.8	2.8	-	-	137.3	-0.4	-	-	135.1	-1.6	-	-
1993	136.7	1.2	-	-	138.5	1.3	-	-	137.3	-0.9	-	-	139.7	1.7	-	-	141.3	1.1	-	-	139.9	-1.0	-	-
1994	140.2	0.2	-	-	142.2	1.4	-	-	142.5	0.2	-	-	143.2	0.5	-	-	143.6	0.3	-	-	142.1	-1.0	-	-
1995	143.8	1.2	-	-	143.8	0.0	-	-	143.2	-0.4	-	-	146.6	2.4	-	-	147.0	0.3	-	-	145.7	-0.9	-	-
1996	145.7	0.0	-	-	148.0	1.6	-	-	147.8	-0.1	-	-	150.0	1.5	-	-	150.1	0.1	-	-	148.8	-0.9	-	-
1997	149.7	0.6	-	-	152.3	1.7	-	-	151.8	-0.3	151.7	-0.1	154.7	2.0	-	-	154.5	-0.1	-	-	154.4	-0.1	-	-

Source: U.S. Department of Labor, Bureau of Labor Statistics, Division of Consumer Prices and Price Indexes. - indicates no data collected for period.

Cleveland, OH
Consumer Price Index - Urban Wage Earners
Base 1982-1984 = 100
Housing

For 1975-1997. Columns headed % show percentile change in the index from the previous period for which an index is available.

Year	Jan Index	Jan %	Feb Index	Feb %	Mar Index	Mar %	Apr Index	Apr %	May Index	May %	Jun Index	Jun %	Jul Index	Jul %	Aug Index	Aug %	Sep Index	Sep %	Oct Index	Oct %	Nov Index	Nov %	Dec Index	Dec %
1975	-	-	-	-	-	-	-	-	-	-	-	-	-	-	-	-	-	-	-	-	47.0	-	-	-
1976	-	-	46.9	-0.2	-	-	-	-	47.1	0.4	-	-	-	-	48.8	3.6	-	-	-	-	49.4	1.2	-	-
1977	-	-	50.6	2.4	-	-	-	-	50.9	0.6	-	-	-	-	52.6	3.3	-	-	-	-	53.1	1.0	-	-
1978	-	-	53.2	0.2	-	-	55.0	3.4	-	-	54.0	-1.8	-	-	55.7	3.1	-	-	58.3	4.7	-	-	60.9	4.5
1979	-	-	62.1	2.0	-	-	63.8	2.7	-	-	66.2	3.8	-	-	65.8	-0.6	-	-	66.3	0.8	-	-	70.2	5.9
1980	-	-	75.3	7.3	-	-	77.0	2.3	-	-	77.9	1.2	-	-	78.4	0.6	-	-	83.6	6.6	-	-	83.6	0.0
1981	-	-	85.5	2.3	-	-	83.3	-2.6	-	-	90.7	8.9	-	-	89.2	-1.7	-	-	87.2	-2.2	-	-	85.8	-1.6
1982	-	-	87.7	2.2	-	-	88.2	0.6	-	-	94.0	6.6	-	-	102.0	8.5	-	-	104.0	2.0	-	-	104.4	0.4
1983	-	-	102.9	-1.4	-	-	103.6	0.7	-	-	103.5	-0.1	-	-	102.6	-0.9	-	-	101.3	-1.3	-	-	99.3	-2.0
1984	-	-	100.3	1.0	-	-	102.0	1.7	-	-	101.6	-0.4	-	-	105.6	3.9	-	-	102.3	-3.1	-	-	98.1	-4.1
1985	-	-	98.6	0.5	-	-	98.6	0.0	-	-	102.6	4.1	-	-	102.9	0.3	-	-	101.4	-1.5	-	-	101.0	-0.4
1986	-	-	102.1	1.1	-	-	102.8	0.7	-	-	104.7	1.8	-	-	105.8	1.1	-	-	104.2	-1.5	104.3	0.1	103.5	-0.8
1987	103.3	-0.2	-	-	104.9	1.5	-	-	104.8	-0.1	-	-	106.7	1.8	-	-	107.5	0.7	-	-	106.5	-0.9	-	-
1988	106.3	-0.2	-	-	108.0	1.6	-	-	109.2	1.1	-	-	110.5	1.2	-	-	109.9	-0.5	-	-	110.4	0.5	-	-
1989	111.6	1.1	-	-	112.2	0.5	-	-	112.4	0.2	-	-	115.7	2.9	-	-	115.1	-0.5	-	-	113.3	-1.6	-	-
1990	114.4	1.0	-	-	116.0	1.4	-	-	117.1	0.9	-	-	118.6	1.3	-	-	120.6	1.7	-	-	119.3	-1.1	-	-
1991	119.7	0.3	-	-	120.9	1.0	-	-	121.8	0.7	-	-	122.3	0.4	-	-	123.8	1.2	-	-	123.2	-0.5	-	-
1992	125.6	1.9	-	-	123.8	-1.4	-	-	123.9	0.1	-	-	127.1	2.6	-	-	126.6	-0.4	-	-	125.0	-1.3	-	-
1993	126.2	1.0	-	-	127.7	1.2	-	-	126.7	-0.8	-	-	128.8	1.7	-	-	130.1	1.0	-	-	129.3	-0.6	-	-
1994	129.1	-0.2	-	-	130.6	1.2	-	-	130.9	0.2	-	-	131.7	0.6	-	-	132.3	0.5	-	-	131.0	-1.0	-	-
1995	132.3	1.0	-	-	132.2	-0.1	-	-	131.7	-0.4	-	-	134.6	2.2	-	-	135.1	0.4	-	-	133.8	-1.0	-	-
1996	134.3	0.4	-	-	136.3	1.5	-	-	136.3	0.0	-	-	138.4	1.5	-	-	138.7	0.2	-	-	137.6	-0.8	-	-
1997	138.4	0.6	-	-	140.6	1.6	-	-	140.3	-0.2	140.1	-0.1	142.9	2.0	-	-	142.7	-0.1	-	-	142.6	-0.1	-	-

Source: U.S. Department of Labor, Bureau of Labor Statistics, Division of Consumer Prices and Price Indexes. - indicates no data collected for period.

Cleveland, OH
Consumer Price Index - All Urban Consumers
Base 1982-1984 = 100
Apparel and Upkeep

For 1952-1997. Columns headed % show percentile change in the index from the previous period for which an index is available.

Year	Jan Index	%	Feb Index	%	Mar Index	%	Apr Index	%	May Index	%	Jun Index	%	Jul Index	%	Aug Index	%	Sep Index	%	Oct Index	%	Nov Index	%	Dec Index	%
1952	-	-	-	-	-	-	-	-	-	-	-	-	-	-	-	-	-	-	-	-	43.7	-	-	-
1953	-	-	43.3	-0.9	-	-	-	-	44.4	2.5	-	-	-	-	44.2	-0.5	-	-	-	-	44.2	0.0	-	-
1954	-	-	44.1	-0.2	-	-	-	-	44.1	0.0	-	-	-	-	44.1	0.0	-	-	-	-	44.0	-0.2	-	-
1955	-	-	43.8	-0.5	-	-	-	-	43.8	0.0	-	-	-	-	43.7	-0.2	-	-	-	-	44.1	0.9	-	-
1956	-	-	44.2	0.2	-	-	-	-	44.6	0.9	-	-	-	-	45.0	0.9	-	-	-	-	45.3	0.7	-	-
1957	-	-	45.0	-0.7	-	-	-	-	45.4	0.9	-	-	-	-	45.5	0.2	-	-	-	-	45.8	0.7	-	-
1958	-	-	45.9	0.2	-	-	-	-	46.0	0.2	-	-	-	-	45.9	-0.2	-	-	-	-	45.9	0.0	-	-
1959	-	-	46.0	0.2	-	-	-	-	46.2	0.4	-	-	-	-	46.3	0.2	-	-	-	-	46.4	0.2	-	-
1960	-	-	46.4	0.0	-	-	-	-	46.3	-0.2	-	-	-	-	46.4	0.2	-	-	-	-	46.5	0.2	-	-
1961	-	-	46.5	0.0	-	-	-	-	46.7	0.4	-	-	-	-	46.9	0.4	-	-	-	-	47.0	0.2	-	-
1962	-	-	46.9	-0.2	-	-	-	-	47.1	0.4	-	-	-	-	46.9	-0.4	-	-	-	-	47.1	0.4	-	-
1963	-	-	47.3	0.4	-	-	-	-	47.8	1.1	-	-	-	-	48.1	0.6	-	-	-	-	47.7	-0.8	-	-
1964	-	-	47.8	0.2	-	-	-	-	48.0	0.4	-	-	-	-	47.7	-0.6	-	-	-	-	48.0	0.6	-	-
1965	-	-	47.9	-0.2	-	-	-	-	48.6	1.5	-	-	-	-	48.0	-1.2	-	-	-	-	48.5	1.0	-	-
1966	-	-	48.8	0.6	-	-	-	-	49.9	2.3	-	-	-	-	49.8	-0.2	-	-	-	-	50.4	1.2	-	-
1967	-	-	50.5	0.2	-	-	-	-	51.1	1.2	-	-	-	-	50.8	-0.6	-	-	-	-	52.7	3.7	-	-
1968	-	-	53.5	1.5	-	-	-	-	54.0	0.9	-	-	-	-	54.6	1.1	-	-	-	-	55.7	2.0	-	-
1969	-	-	56.1	0.7	-	-	-	-	57.3	2.1	-	-	-	-	57.7	0.7	-	-	-	-	59.3	2.8	-	-
1970	-	-	59.4	0.2	-	-	-	-	60.4	1.7	-	-	-	-	60.3	-0.2	-	-	-	-	61.4	1.8	-	-
1971	-	-	61.4	0.0	-	-	-	-	62.8	2.3	-	-	-	-	62.4	-0.6	-	-	-	-	63.0	1.0	-	-
1972	-	-	62.9	-0.2	-	-	-	-	63.5	1.0	-	-	-	-	63.4	-0.2	-	-	-	-	64.2	1.3	-	-
1973	-	-	64.2	0.0	-	-	-	-	65.7	2.3	-	-	-	-	66.6	1.4	-	-	-	-	69.3	4.1	-	-
1974	-	-	70.6	1.9	-	-	-	-	71.5	1.3	-	-	-	-	73.2	2.4	-	-	-	-	75.6	3.3	-	-
1975	-	-	74.0	-2.1	-	-	-	-	74.4	0.5	-	-	-	-	74.2	-0.3	-	-	-	-	74.9	0.9	-	-
1976	-	-	74.5	-0.5	-	-	-	-	75.3	1.1	-	-	-	-	76.3	1.3	-	-	-	-	78.6	3.0	-	-
1977	-	-	78.1	-0.6	-	-	-	-	79.7	2.0	-	-	-	-	81.4	2.1	-	-	-	-	82.8	1.7	-	-
1978	-	-	81.0	-2.2	-	-	80.2	-1.0	-	-	81.3	1.4	-	-	83.6	2.8	-	-	84.0	0.5	-	-	82.9	-1.3
1979	-	-	83.5	0.7	-	-	82.4	-1.3	-	-	81.4	-1.2	-	-	85.5	5.0	-	-	87.6	2.5	-	-	88.2	0.7
1980	-	-	87.7	-0.6	-	-	88.7	1.1	-	-	87.6	-1.2	-	-	90.4	3.2	-	-	91.6	1.3	-	-	91.4	-0.2
1981	-	-	93.2	2.0	-	-	96.1	3.1	-	-	94.6	-1.6	-	-	95.2	0.6	-	-	95.0	-0.2	-	-	97.3	2.4
1982	-	-	98.0	0.7	-	-	97.5	-0.5	-	-	98.4	0.9	-	-	102.1	3.8	-	-	101.6	-0.5	-	-	99.7	-1.9
1983	-	-	100.6	0.9	-	-	97.6	-3.0	-	-	98.7	1.1	-	-	99.1	0.4	-	-	99.9	0.8	-	-	99.5	-0.4
1984	-	-	101.2	1.7	-	-	98.4	-2.8	-	-	101.2	2.8	-	-	102.9	1.7	-	-	102.2	-0.7	-	-	102.8	0.6
1985	-	-	101.9	-0.9	-	-	103.2	1.3	-	-	101.5	-1.6	-	-	106.5	4.9	-	-	107.8	1.2	-	-	103.8	-3.7
1986	-	-	104.1	0.3	-	-	100.9	-3.1	-	-	99.3	-1.6	-	-	105.1	5.8	-	-	104.2	-0.9	103.1	-1.1	98.5	-4.5
1987	97.8	-0.7	-	-	105.5	7.9	-	-	104.0	-1.4	-	-	105.0	1.0	-	-	121.3	15.5	-	-	115.3	-4.9	-	-
1988	106.7	-7.5	-	-	111.0	4.0	-	-	111.8	0.7	-	-	108.0	-3.4	-	-	101.0	-6.5	-	-	100.1	-0.9	-	-
1989	91.9	-8.2	-	-	119.5	30.0	-	-	120.5	0.8	-	-	114.6	-4.9	-	-	111.2	-3.0	-	-	108.7	-2.2	-	-
1990	102.6	-5.6	-	-	128.8	25.5	-	-	127.6	-0.9	-	-	115.4	-9.6	-	-	115.5	0.1	-	-	115.0	-0.4	-	-
1991	112.8	-1.9	-	-	125.1	10.9	-	-	122.7	-1.9	-	-	115.2	-6.1	-	-	126.1	9.5	-	-	127.4	1.0	-	-
1992	121.0	-5.0	-	-	128.2	6.0	-	-	122.7	-4.3	-	-	116.8	-4.8	-	-	124.9	6.9	-	-	120.7	-3.4	-	-
1993	116.4	-3.6	-	-	119.7	2.8	-	-	126.7	5.8	-	-	127.2	0.4	-	-	129.3	1.7	-	-	128.6	-0.5	-	-
1994	126.9	-1.3	-	-	128.8	1.5	-	-	127.3	-1.2	-	-	116.3	-8.6	-	-	141.6	21.8	-	-	132.9	-6.1	-	-

[Continued]

Cleveland, OH
Consumer Price Index - All Urban Consumers
Base 1982-1984 = 100
Apparel and Upkeep
[Continued]

For 1952-1997. Columns headed % show percentile change in the index from the previous period for which an index is available.

Year	Jan Index	%	Feb Index	%	Mar Index	%	Apr Index	%	May Index	%	Jun Index	%	Jul Index	%	Aug Index	%	Sep Index	%	Oct Index	%	Nov Index	%	Dec Index	%
1995	124.2	-6.5	-	-	136.5	9.9	-	-	129.9	-4.8	-	-	122.5	-5.7	-	-	126.3	3.1	-	-	123.9	-1.9	-	-
1996	120.9	-2.4	-	-	132.2	9.3	-	-	133.7	1.1	-	-	124.1	-7.2	-	-	133.2	7.3	-	-	128.7	-3.4	-	-
1997	121.6	-5.5	-	-	128.9	6.0	-	-	128.6	-0.2	126.6	-1.6	124.7	-1.5	-	-	131.9	5.8	-	-	129.4	-1.9	-	-

Source: U.S. Department of Labor, Bureau of Labor Statistics, Division of Consumer Prices and Price Indexes. - indicates no data collected for period.

Cleveland, OH
Consumer Price Index - Urban Wage Earners
Base 1982-1984 = 100
Apparel and Upkeep

For 1952-1997. Columns headed % show percentile change in the index from the previous period for which an index is available.

Year	Jan Index	%	Feb Index	%	Mar Index	%	Apr Index	%	May Index	%	Jun Index	%	Jul Index	%	Aug Index	%	Sep Index	%	Oct Index	%	Nov Index	%	Dec Index	%
1952	-	-	-	-	-	-	-	-	-	-	-	-	-	-	-	-	-	-	-	-	42.4	-	-	-
1953	-	-	42.0	-0.9	-	-	-	-	43.0	2.4	-	-	-	-	42.9	-0.2	-	-	-	-	42.9	0.0	-	-
1954	-	-	42.8	-0.2	-	-	-	-	42.8	0.0	-	-	-	-	42.7	-0.2	-	-	-	-	42.6	-0.2	-	-
1955	-	-	42.4	-0.5	-	-	-	-	42.5	0.2	-	-	-	-	42.4	-0.2	-	-	-	-	42.7	0.7	-	-
1956	-	-	42.9	0.5	-	-	-	-	43.2	0.7	-	-	-	-	43.6	0.9	-	-	-	-	44.0	0.9	-	-
1957	-	-	43.6	-0.9	-	-	-	-	44.0	0.9	-	-	-	-	44.1	0.2	-	-	-	-	44.4	0.7	-	-
1958	-	-	44.5	0.2	-	-	-	-	44.6	0.2	-	-	-	-	44.5	-0.2	-	-	-	-	44.5	0.0	-	-
1959	-	-	44.6	0.2	-	-	-	-	44.8	0.4	-	-	-	-	44.9	0.2	-	-	-	-	45.0	0.2	-	-
1960	-	-	45.0	0.0	-	-	-	-	44.9	-0.2	-	-	-	-	45.0	0.2	-	-	-	-	45.1	0.2	-	-
1961	-	-	45.1	0.0	-	-	-	-	45.3	0.4	-	-	-	-	45.5	0.4	-	-	-	-	45.6	0.2	-	-
1962	-	-	45.5	-0.2	-	-	-	-	45.7	0.4	-	-	-	-	45.5	-0.4	-	-	-	-	45.7	0.4	-	-
1963	-	-	45.9	0.4	-	-	-	-	46.4	1.1	-	-	-	-	46.7	0.6	-	-	-	-	46.2	-1.1	-	-
1964	-	-	46.3	0.2	-	-	-	-	46.6	0.6	-	-	-	-	46.2	-0.9	-	-	-	-	46.5	0.6	-	-
1965	-	-	46.4	-0.2	-	-	-	-	47.2	1.7	-	-	-	-	46.6	-1.3	-	-	-	-	47.1	1.1	-	-
1966	-	-	47.3	0.4	-	-	-	-	48.4	2.3	-	-	-	-	48.3	-0.2	-	-	-	-	48.9	1.2	-	-
1967	-	-	49.0	0.2	-	-	-	-	49.6	1.2	-	-	-	-	49.3	-0.6	-	-	-	-	51.1	3.7	-	-
1968	-	-	51.8	1.4	-	-	-	-	52.3	1.0	-	-	-	-	53.0	1.3	-	-	-	-	54.0	1.9	-	-
1969	-	-	54.4	0.7	-	-	-	-	55.6	2.2	-	-	-	-	56.0	0.7	-	-	-	-	57.5	2.7	-	-
1970	-	-	57.6	0.2	-	-	-	-	58.6	1.7	-	-	-	-	58.5	-0.2	-	-	-	-	59.6	1.9	-	-
1971	-	-	59.6	0.0	-	-	-	-	60.9	2.2	-	-	-	-	60.5	-0.7	-	-	-	-	61.1	1.0	-	-
1972	-	-	61.1	0.0	-	-	-	-	61.6	0.8	-	-	-	-	61.5	-0.2	-	-	-	-	62.3	1.3	-	-
1973	-	-	62.2	-0.2	-	-	-	-	63.7	2.4	-	-	-	-	64.6	1.4	-	-	-	-	67.2	4.0	-	-
1974	-	-	68.5	1.9	-	-	-	-	69.3	1.2	-	-	-	-	71.0	2.5	-	-	-	-	73.3	3.2	-	-
1975	-	-	71.8	-2.0	-	-	-	-	72.2	0.6	-	-	-	-	72.0	-0.3	-	-	-	-	72.7	1.0	-	-
1976	-	-	72.3	-0.6	-	-	-	-	73.0	1.0	-	-	-	-	74.0	1.4	-	-	-	-	76.3	3.1	-	-
1977	-	-	75.8	-0.7	-	-	-	-	77.3	2.0	-	-	-	-	79.0	2.2	-	-	-	-	80.4	1.8	-	-
1978	-	-	78.5	-2.4	-	-	79.5	1.3	-	-	79.9	0.5	-	-	81.2	1.6	-	-	82.9	2.1	-	-	83.1	0.2
1979	-	-	83.6	0.6	-	-	83.2	-0.5	-	-	81.5	-2.0	-	-	83.3	2.2	-	-	85.3	2.4	-	-	85.7	0.5
1980	-	-	85.5	-0.2	-	-	86.9	1.6	-	-	85.3	-1.8	-	-	86.7	1.6	-	-	89.1	2.8	-	-	89.9	0.9
1981	-	-	91.1	1.3	-	-	92.8	1.9	-	-	92.3	-0.5	-	-	92.3	0.0	-	-	95.3	3.3	-	-	97.5	2.3
1982	-	-	97.6	0.1	-	-	97.3	-0.3	-	-	98.3	1.0	-	-	101.8	3.6	-	-	101.3	-0.5	-	-	99.7	-1.6
1983	-	-	101.0	1.3	-	-	97.7	-3.3	-	-	98.6	0.9	-	-	99.2	0.6	-	-	100.0	0.8	-	-	99.3	-0.7
1984	-	-	101.8	2.5	-	-	98.3	-3.4	-	-	101.4	3.2	-	-	103.4	2.0	-	-	102.7	-0.7	-	-	102.1	-0.6
1985	-	-	102.6	0.5	-	-	103.9	1.3	-	-	102.2	-1.6	-	-	107.8	5.5	-	-	109.1	1.2	-	-	105.3	-3.5
1986	-	-	104.9	-0.4	-	-	102.1	-2.7	-	-	100.5	-1.6	-	-	106.4	5.9	-	-	105.8	-0.6	103.8	-1.9	99.7	-3.9
1987	98.2	-1.5	-	-	105.9	7.8	-	-	104.6	-1.2	-	-	105.8	1.1	-	-	121.8	15.1	-	-	116.6	-4.3	-	-
1988	107.3	-8.0	-	-	111.5	3.9	-	-	112.4	0.8	-	-	108.4	-3.6	-	-	101.3	-6.5	-	-	100.0	-1.3	-	-
1989	92.0	-8.0	-	-	118.5	28.8	-	-	119.8	1.1	-	-	114.0	-4.8	-	-	109.9	-3.6	-	-	107.9	-1.8	-	-
1990	102.2	-5.3	-	-	127.3	24.6	-	-	126.3	-0.8	-	-	114.2	-9.6	-	-	115.2	0.9	-	-	114.7	-0.4	-	-
1991	112.2	-2.2	-	-	124.2	10.7	-	-	121.9	-1.9	-	-	114.9	-5.7	-	-	125.7	9.4	-	-	127.1	1.1	-	-
1992	120.9	-4.9	-	-	128.4	6.2	-	-	122.9	-4.3	-	-	116.7	-5.0	-	-	125.7	7.7	-	-	121.2	-3.6	-	-
1993	116.9	-3.5	-	-	119.5	2.2	-	-	125.3	4.9	-	-	126.3	0.8	-	-	128.0	1.3	-	-	127.2	-0.6	-	-
1994	125.9	-1.0	-	-	127.4	1.2	-	-	126.4	-0.8	-	-	115.5	-8.6	-	-	140.0	21.2	-	-	131.2	-6.3	-	-

[Continued]

Cleveland, OH
Consumer Price Index - Urban Wage Earners
Base 1982-1984 = 100
Apparel and Upkeep
[Continued]

For 1952-1997. Columns headed % show percentile change in the index from the previous period for which an index is available.

Year	Jan Index	%	Feb Index	%	Mar Index	%	Apr Index	%	May Index	%	Jun Index	%	Jul Index	%	Aug Index	%	Sep Index	%	Oct Index	%	Nov Index	%	Dec Index	%
1995	122.3	-6.8	-	-	134.3	9.8	-	-	127.7	-4.9	-	-	120.6	-5.6	-	-	124.8	3.5	-	-	122.6	-1.8	-	-
1996	118.5	-3.3	-	-	129.6	9.4	-	-	131.4	1.4	-	-	121.8	-7.3	-	-	130.1	6.8	-	-	125.7	-3.4	-	-
1997	119.7	-4.8	-	-	125.5	4.8	-	-	125.7	0.2	123.8	-1.5	121.7	-1.7	-	-	129.0	6.0	-	-	126.1	-2.2	-	-

Source: U.S. Department of Labor, Bureau of Labor Statistics, Division of Consumer Prices and Price Indexes. - indicates no data collected for period.

Cleveland, OH
Consumer Price Index - All Urban Consumers
Base 1982-1984 = 100
Transportation

For 1947-1997. Columns headed % show percentile change in the index from the previous period for which an index is available.

Year	Jan Index	%	Feb Index	%	Mar Index	%	Apr Index	%	May Index	%	Jun Index	%	Jul Index	%	Aug Index	%	Sep Index	%	Oct Index	%	Nov Index	%	Dec Index	%
1947	18.3	-	18.3	0.0	18.6	1.6	18.7	0.5	18.6	-0.5	18.6	0.0	-	-	18.9	1.6	-	-	-	-	19.5	3.2	-	-
1948	-	-	20.7	6.2	-	-	-	-	20.8	0.5	-	-	-	-	22.8	9.6	-	-	-	-	22.9	0.4	-	-
1949	-	-	23.1	0.9	-	-	-	-	23.2	0.4	-	-	-	-	23.1	-0.4	-	-	-	-	23.1	0.0	-	-
1950	-	-	22.8	-1.3	-	-	-	-	22.7	-0.4	-	-	-	-	23.4	3.1	-	-	-	-	23.5	0.4	-	-
1951	-	-	23.7	0.9	-	-	-	-	23.9	0.8	-	-	-	-	24.9	4.2	-	-	-	-	25.6	2.8	-	-
1952	-	-	26.0	1.6	-	-	-	-	26.0	0.0	-	-	-	-	26.0	0.0	-	-	-	-	26.0	0.0	-	-
1953	-	-	26.1	0.4	-	-	-	-	26.2	0.4	-	-	-	-	26.6	1.5	-	-	-	-	26.4	-0.8	-	-
1954	-	-	26.1	-1.1	-	-	-	-	26.0	-0.4	-	-	-	-	25.0	-3.8	-	-	-	-	25.9	3.6	-	-
1955	-	-	25.4	-1.9	-	-	-	-	25.0	-1.6	-	-	-	-	25.4	1.6	-	-	-	-	26.5	4.3	-	-
1956	-	-	26.0	-1.9	-	-	-	-	26.1	0.4	-	-	-	-	26.7	2.3	-	-	-	-	27.8	4.1	-	-
1957	-	-	28.1	1.1	-	-	-	-	28.1	0.0	-	-	-	-	28.6	1.8	-	-	-	-	29.4	2.8	-	-
1958	-	-	28.7	-2.4	-	-	-	-	28.9	0.7	-	-	-	-	29.0	0.3	-	-	-	-	29.4	1.4	-	-
1959	-	-	29.6	0.7	-	-	-	-	29.7	0.3	-	-	-	-	30.3	2.0	-	-	-	-	30.7	1.3	-	-
1960	-	-	30.4	-1.0	-	-	-	-	30.2	-0.7	-	-	-	-	30.1	-0.3	-	-	-	-	30.5	1.3	-	-
1961	-	-	30.5	0.0	-	-	-	-	30.6	0.3	-	-	-	-	31.3	2.3	-	-	-	-	31.4	0.3	-	-
1962	-	-	31.1	-1.0	-	-	-	-	31.4	1.0	-	-	-	-	31.5	0.3	-	-	-	-	31.5	0.0	-	-
1963	-	-	31.3	-0.6	-	-	-	-	31.3	0.0	-	-	-	-	31.6	1.0	-	-	-	-	31.9	0.9	-	-
1964	-	-	31.9	0.0	-	-	-	-	32.0	0.3	-	-	-	-	32.0	0.0	-	-	-	-	32.4	1.3	-	-
1965	-	-	32.5	0.3	-	-	-	-	32.8	0.9	-	-	-	-	32.5	-0.9	-	-	-	-	32.7	0.6	-	-
1966	-	-	32.5	-0.6	-	-	-	-	33.0	1.5	-	-	-	-	32.9	-0.3	-	-	-	-	33.2	0.9	-	-
1967	-	-	33.2	0.0	-	-	-	-	33.4	0.6	-	-	-	-	34.0	1.8	-	-	-	-	34.9	2.6	-	-
1968	-	-	35.2	0.9	-	-	-	-	35.3	0.3	-	-	-	-	35.6	0.8	-	-	-	-	36.3	2.0	-	-
1969	-	-	35.9	-1.1	-	-	-	-	37.0	3.1	-	-	-	-	37.1	0.3	-	-	-	-	38.0	2.4	-	-
1970	-	-	38.4	1.1	-	-	-	-	38.8	1.0	-	-	-	-	39.2	1.0	-	-	-	-	41.9	6.9	-	-
1971	-	-	42.1	0.5	-	-	-	-	42.3	0.5	-	-	-	-	42.4	0.2	-	-	-	-	42.1	-0.7	-	-
1972	-	-	42.4	0.7	-	-	-	-	42.8	0.9	-	-	-	-	42.9	0.2	-	-	-	-	42.9	0.0	-	-
1973	-	-	43.1	0.5	-	-	-	-	44.0	2.1	-	-	-	-	44.2	0.5	-	-	-	-	44.8	1.4	-	-
1974	-	-	47.2	5.4	-	-	-	-	49.9	5.7	-	-	-	-	50.2	0.6	-	-	-	-	50.7	1.0	-	-
1975	-	-	50.7	0.0	-	-	-	-	51.9	2.4	-	-	-	-	53.5	3.1	-	-	-	-	52.1	-2.6	-	-
1976	-	-	52.2	0.2	-	-	-	-	53.7	2.9	-	-	-	-	55.5	3.4	-	-	-	-	56.2	1.3	-	-
1977	-	-	56.4	0.4	-	-	-	-	57.9	2.7	-	-	-	-	58.0	0.2	-	-	-	-	58.7	1.2	-	-
1978	-	-	58.8	0.2	-	-	59.6	1.4	-	-	60.9	2.2	-	-	61.8	1.5	-	-	62.1	0.5	-	-	62.8	1.1
1979	-	-	64.3	2.4	-	-	66.6	3.6	-	-	68.8	3.3	-	-	71.1	3.3	-	-	72.7	2.3	-	-	74.4	2.3
1980	-	-	77.4	4.0	-	-	79.5	2.7	-	-	80.7	1.5	-	-	82.4	2.1	-	-	82.9	0.6	-	-	85.4	3.0
1981	-	-	88.4	3.5	-	-	90.1	1.9	-	-	91.4	1.4	-	-	93.4	2.2	-	-	95.3	2.0	-	-	96.2	0.9
1982	-	-	95.1	-1.1	-	-	94.2	-0.9	-	-	97.2	3.2	-	-	99.1	2.0	-	-	98.0	-1.1	-	-	98.4	0.4
1983	-	-	96.0	-2.4	-	-	97.1	1.1	-	-	98.9	1.9	-	-	101.3	2.4	-	-	102.5	1.2	-	-	102.5	0.0
1984	-	-	101.8	-0.7	-	-	102.7	0.9	-	-	104.3	1.6	-	-	103.8	-0.5	-	-	104.8	1.0	-	-	104.7	-0.1
1985	-	-	103.5	-1.1	-	-	106.0	2.4	-	-	106.1	0.1	-	-	105.4	-0.7	-	-	106.2	0.8	-	-	107.2	0.9
1986	-	-	105.0	-2.1	-	-	99.5	-5.2	-	-	101.7	2.2	-	-	99.0	-2.7	-	-	99.6	0.6	100.3	0.7	100.9	0.6
1987	102.3	1.4	-	-	101.9	-0.4	-	-	103.0	1.1	-	-	104.5	1.5	-	-	104.7	0.2	-	-	106.4	1.6	-	-
1988	105.5	-0.8	-	-	103.7	-1.7	-	-	107.6	3.8	-	-	107.8	0.2	-	-	109.1	1.2	-	-	109.4	0.3	-	-
1989	109.3	-0.1	-	-	110.5	1.1	-	-	116.1	5.1	-	-	113.8	-2.0	-	-	111.9	-1.7	-	-	114.3	2.1	-	-
1990	117.0	2.4	-	-	114.7	-2.0	-	-	116.1	1.2	-	-	116.5	0.3	-	-	122.5	5.2	-	-	128.1	4.6	-	-
1991	123.9	-3.3	-	-	121.6	-1.9	-	-	122.7	0.9	-	-	123.1	0.3	-	-	123.1	0.0	-	-	124.7	1.3	-	-

[Continued]

Cleveland, OH
Consumer Price Index - All Urban Consumers
Base 1982-1984 = 100
Transportation
[Continued]

For 1947-1997. Columns headed % show percentile change in the index from the previous period for which an index is available.

Year	Jan Index	%	Feb Index	%	Mar Index	%	Apr Index	%	May Index	%	Jun Index	%	Jul Index	%	Aug Index	%	Sep Index	%	Oct Index	%	Nov Index	%	Dec Index	%
1992	122.0	-2.2	-	-	123.1	0.9	-	-	124.4	1.1	-	-	124.9	0.4	-	-	123.7	-1.0	-	-	126.6	2.3	-	-
1993	122.8	-3.0	-	-	123.3	0.4	-	-	125.9	2.1	-	-	126.1	0.2	-	-	124.7	-1.1	-	-	126.5	1.4	-	-
1994	125.5	-0.8	-	-	125.8	0.2	-	-	127.2	1.1	-	-	129.6	1.9	-	-	130.0	0.3	-	-	132.1	1.6	-	-
1995	131.0	-0.8	-	-	132.2	0.9	-	-	135.7	2.6	-	-	133.5	-1.6	-	-	133.7	0.1	-	-	131.5	-1.6	-	-
1996	134.0	1.9	-	-	136.0	1.5	-	-	138.8	2.1	-	-	138.1	-0.5	-	-	138.7	0.4	-	-	143.2	3.2	-	-
1997	142.1	-0.8	-	-	142.5	0.3	-	-	142.5	0.0	142.2	-0.2	140.1	-1.5	-	-	142.5	1.7	-	-	141.1	-1.0	-	-

Source: U.S. Department of Labor, Bureau of Labor Statistics, Division of Consumer Prices and Price Indexes. - indicates no data collected for period.

Cleveland, OH
Consumer Price Index - Urban Wage Earners
Base 1982-1984 = 100
Transportation

For 1947-1997. Columns headed % show percentile change in the index from the previous period for which an index is available.

Year	Jan Index	%	Feb Index	%	Mar Index	%	Apr Index	%	May Index	%	Jun Index	%	Jul Index	%	Aug Index	%	Sep Index	%	Oct Index	%	Nov Index	%	Dec Index	%
1947	18.6	-	18.6	0.0	18.8	1.1	18.9	0.5	18.8	-0.5	18.8	0.0	-	-	19.1	1.6	-	-	-	-	19.7	3.1	-	-
1948	-	-	20.9	6.1	-	-	-	-	21.0	0.5	-	-	-	-	23.1	10.0	-	-	-	-	23.1	0.0	-	-
1949	-	-	23.4	1.3	-	-	-	-	23.4	0.0	-	-	-	-	23.4	0.0	-	-	-	-	23.4	0.0	-	-
1950	-	-	23.1	-1.3	-	-	-	-	23.0	-0.4	-	-	-	-	23.7	3.0	-	-	-	-	23.8	0.4	-	-
1951	-	-	24.0	0.8	-	-	-	-	24.2	0.8	-	-	-	-	25.2	4.1	-	-	-	-	26.0	3.2	-	-
1952	-	-	26.3	1.2	-	-	-	-	26.3	0.0	-	-	-	-	26.3	0.0	-	-	-	-	26.4	0.4	-	-
1953	-	-	26.5	0.4	-	-	-	-	26.5	0.0	-	-	-	-	26.9	1.5	-	-	-	-	26.7	-0.7	-	-
1954	-	-	26.5	-0.7	-	-	-	-	26.4	-0.4	-	-	-	-	25.3	-4.2	-	-	-	-	26.2	3.6	-	-
1955	-	-	25.7	-1.9	-	-	-	-	25.3	-1.6	-	-	-	-	25.7	1.6	-	-	-	-	26.8	4.3	-	-
1956	-	-	26.3	-1.9	-	-	-	-	26.4	0.4	-	-	-	-	27.0	2.3	-	-	-	-	28.1	4.1	-	-
1957	-	-	28.4	1.1	-	-	-	-	28.4	0.0	-	-	-	-	28.9	1.8	-	-	-	-	29.7	2.8	-	-
1958	-	-	29.1	-2.0	-	-	-	-	29.2	0.3	-	-	-	-	29.3	0.3	-	-	-	-	29.8	1.7	-	-
1959	-	-	30.0	0.7	-	-	-	-	30.0	0.0	-	-	-	-	30.7	2.3	-	-	-	-	31.1	1.3	-	-
1960	-	-	30.7	-1.3	-	-	-	-	30.6	-0.3	-	-	-	-	30.5	-0.3	-	-	-	-	30.8	1.0	-	-
1961	-	-	30.9	0.3	-	-	-	-	31.0	0.3	-	-	-	-	31.7	2.3	-	-	-	-	31.8	0.3	-	-
1962	-	-	31.5	-0.9	-	-	-	-	31.8	1.0	-	-	-	-	31.9	0.3	-	-	-	-	31.9	0.0	-	-
1963	-	-	31.7	-0.6	-	-	-	-	31.7	0.0	-	-	-	-	32.0	0.9	-	-	-	-	32.3	0.9	-	-
1964	-	-	32.3	0.0	-	-	-	-	32.4	0.3	-	-	-	-	32.4	0.0	-	-	-	-	32.8	1.2	-	-
1965	-	-	32.9	0.3	-	-	-	-	33.2	0.9	-	-	-	-	32.9	-0.9	-	-	-	-	33.1	0.6	-	-
1966	-	-	32.9	-0.6	-	-	-	-	33.4	1.5	-	-	-	-	33.3	-0.3	-	-	-	-	33.6	0.9	-	-
1967	-	-	33.6	0.0	-	-	-	-	33.8	0.6	-	-	-	-	34.4	1.8	-	-	-	-	35.4	2.9	-	-
1968	-	-	35.6	0.6	-	-	-	-	35.7	0.3	-	-	-	-	36.0	0.8	-	-	-	-	36.7	1.9	-	-
1969	-	-	36.4	-0.8	-	-	-	-	37.5	3.0	-	-	-	-	37.6	0.3	-	-	-	-	38.5	2.4	-	-
1970	-	-	38.9	1.0	-	-	-	-	39.2	0.8	-	-	-	-	39.7	1.3	-	-	-	-	42.4	6.8	-	-
1971	-	-	42.6	0.5	-	-	-	-	42.8	0.5	-	-	-	-	42.9	0.2	-	-	-	-	42.6	-0.7	-	-
1972	-	-	42.9	0.7	-	-	-	-	43.3	0.9	-	-	-	-	43.5	0.5	-	-	-	-	43.4	-0.2	-	-
1973	-	-	43.6	0.5	-	-	-	-	44.5	2.1	-	-	-	-	44.7	0.4	-	-	-	-	45.3	1.3	-	-
1974	-	-	47.8	5.5	-	-	-	-	50.5	5.6	-	-	-	-	50.8	0.6	-	-	-	-	51.4	1.2	-	-
1975	-	-	51.3	-0.2	-	-	-	-	52.6	2.5	-	-	-	-	54.2	3.0	-	-	-	-	52.8	-2.6	-	-
1976	-	-	52.9	0.2	-	-	-	-	54.3	2.6	-	-	-	-	56.2	3.5	-	-	-	-	56.9	1.2	-	-
1977	-	-	57.1	0.4	-	-	-	-	58.6	2.6	-	-	-	-	58.7	0.2	-	-	-	-	59.5	1.4	-	-
1978	-	-	59.5	0.0	-	-	60.3	1.3	-	-	61.9	2.7	-	-	62.9	1.6	-	-	62.9	0.0	-	-	63.5	1.0
1979	-	-	65.5	3.1	-	-	68.1	4.0	-	-	70.5	3.5	-	-	72.7	3.1	-	-	74.4	2.3	-	-	75.5	1.5
1980	-	-	79.0	4.6	-	-	80.6	2.0	-	-	82.3	2.1	-	-	83.7	1.7	-	-	84.1	0.5	-	-	86.0	2.3
1981	-	-	89.6	4.2	-	-	90.9	1.5	-	-	91.6	0.8	-	-	93.7	2.3	-	-	95.3	1.7	-	-	95.9	0.6
1982	-	-	94.7	-1.3	-	-	93.6	-1.2	-	-	97.0	3.6	-	-	99.1	2.2	-	-	98.2	-0.9	-	-	98.5	0.3
1983	-	-	96.0	-2.5	-	-	97.1	1.1	-	-	99.2	2.2	-	-	101.4	2.2	-	-	102.5	1.1	-	-	102.5	0.0
1984	-	-	101.8	-0.7	-	-	102.8	1.0	-	-	104.5	1.7	-	-	104.0	-0.5	-	-	104.8	0.8	-	-	104.6	-0.2
1985	-	-	103.3	-1.2	-	-	106.1	2.7	-	-	106.2	0.1	-	-	105.4	-0.8	-	-	105.9	0.5	-	-	107.1	1.1
1986	-	-	104.4	-2.5	-	-	98.3	-5.8	-	-	100.7	2.4	-	-	97.6	-3.1	-	-	98.1	0.5	98.8	0.7	99.4	0.6
1987	100.6	1.2	-	-	100.2	-0.4	-	-	101.3	1.1	-	-	102.6	1.3	-	-	102.6	0.0	-	-	104.5	1.9	-	-
1988	103.8	-0.7	-	-	101.9	-1.8	-	-	105.5	3.5	-	-	105.6	0.1	-	-	107.0	1.3	-	-	107.5	0.5	-	-
1989	107.4	-0.1	-	-	108.5	1.0	-	-	113.7	4.8	-	-	111.4	-2.0	-	-	109.5	-1.7	-	-	112.1	2.4	-	-
1990	114.6	2.2	-	-	112.2	-2.1	-	-	113.6	1.2	-	-	114.0	0.4	-	-	119.3	4.6	-	-	124.4	4.3	-	-
1991	120.7	-3.0	-	-	118.6	-1.7	-	-	119.7	0.9	-	-	120.1	0.3	-	-	120.0	-0.1	-	-	121.4	1.2	-	-

[Continued]

Cleveland, OH
Consumer Price Index - Urban Wage Earners
Base 1982-1984 = 100
Transportation
[Continued]

For 1947-1997. Columns headed % show percentile change in the index from the previous period for which an index is available.

Year	Jan		Feb		Mar		Apr		May		Jun		Jul		Aug		Sep		Oct		Nov		Dec	
	Index	%	Index	%	Index	%	Index	%	Index	%	Index	%	Index	%	Index	%	Index	%	Index	%	Index	%	Index	%
1992	118.8	-2.1	-	-	119.6	0.7	-	-	121.0	1.2	-	-	121.6	0.5	-	-	120.6	-0.8	-	-	123.1	2.1	-	-
1993	119.6	-2.8	-	-	119.7	0.1	-	-	122.4	2.3	-	-	122.8	0.3	-	-	121.7	-0.9	-	-	123.4	1.4	-	-
1994	122.3	-0.9	-	-	122.4	0.1	-	-	123.9	1.2	-	-	126.3	1.9	-	-	126.7	0.3	-	-	129.0	1.8	-	-
1995	128.0	-0.8	-	-	129.0	0.8	-	-	132.2	2.5	-	-	130.2	-1.5	-	-	130.3	0.1	-	-	128.5	-1.4	-	-
1996	130.8	1.8	-	-	132.5	1.3	-	-	134.8	1.7	-	-	134.2	-0.4	-	-	134.7	0.4	-	-	138.6	2.9	-	-
1997	137.8	-0.6	-	-	137.9	0.1	-	-	138.1	0.1	137.7	-0.3	135.6	-1.5	-	-	138.0	1.8	-	-	136.9	-0.8	-	-

Source: U.S. Department of Labor, Bureau of Labor Statistics, Division of Consumer Prices and Price Indexes. - indicates no data collected for period.

Cleveland, OH
Consumer Price Index - All Urban Consumers
Base 1982-1984 = 100
Medical Care

For 1947-1997. Columns headed % show percentile change in the index from the previous period for which an index is available.

Year	Jan Index	%	Feb Index	%	Mar Index	%	Apr Index	%	May Index	%	Jun Index	%	Jul Index	%	Aug Index	%	Sep Index	%	Oct Index	%	Nov Index	%	Dec Index	%
1947	10.5	-	10.5	0.0	10.5	0.0	10.5	0.0	10.5	0.0	10.5	0.0	-	-	10.5	0.0	-	-	-	-	10.9	3.8	-	-
1948	-	-	11.0	0.9	-	-	-	-	11.2	1.8	-	-	-	-	11.2	0.0	-	-	-	-	11.5	2.7	-	-
1949	-	-	11.6	0.9	-	-	-	-	11.6	0.0	-	-	-	-	11.7	0.9	-	-	-	-	11.8	0.9	-	-
1950	-	-	11.8	0.0	-	-	-	-	11.8	0.0	-	-	-	-	11.7	-0.8	-	-	-	-	11.9	1.7	-	-
1951	-	-	12.2	2.5	-	-	-	-	12.6	3.3	-	-	-	-	12.6	0.0	-	-	-	-	13.2	4.8	-	-
1952	-	-	13.2	0.0	-	-	-	-	13.3	0.8	-	-	-	-	13.4	0.8	-	-	-	-	13.3	-0.7	-	-
1953	-	-	13.4	0.8	-	-	-	-	13.4	0.0	-	-	-	-	14.2	6.0	-	-	-	-	14.2	0.0	-	-
1954	-	-	14.4	1.4	-	-	-	-	14.5	0.7	-	-	-	-	14.5	0.0	-	-	-	-	14.6	0.7	-	-
1955	-	-	14.6	0.0	-	-	-	-	15.3	4.8	-	-	-	-	15.3	0.0	-	-	-	-	15.4	0.7	-	-
1956	-	-	15.4	0.0	-	-	-	-	16.3	5.8	-	-	-	-	16.3	0.0	-	-	-	-	16.3	0.0	-	-
1957	-	-	16.4	0.6	-	-	-	-	16.7	1.8	-	-	-	-	16.8	0.6	-	-	-	-	16.8	0.0	-	-
1958	-	-	17.0	1.2	-	-	-	-	17.1	0.6	-	-	-	-	17.1	0.0	-	-	-	-	17.2	0.6	-	-
1959	-	-	18.6	8.1	-	-	-	-	18.7	0.5	-	-	-	-	18.8	0.5	-	-	-	-	19.0	1.1	-	-
1960	-	-	19.0	0.0	-	-	-	-	19.3	1.6	-	-	-	-	19.4	0.5	-	-	-	-	19.4	0.0	-	-
1961	-	-	20.7	6.7	-	-	-	-	20.8	0.5	-	-	-	-	20.6	-1.0	-	-	-	-	20.7	0.5	-	-
1962	-	-	20.7	0.0	-	-	-	-	20.8	0.5	-	-	-	-	20.8	0.0	-	-	-	-	20.8	0.0	-	-
1963	-	-	20.8	0.0	-	-	-	-	22.1	6.3	-	-	-	-	22.2	0.5	-	-	-	-	22.3	0.5	-	-
1964	-	-	22.4	0.4	-	-	-	-	22.5	0.4	-	-	-	-	22.5	0.0	-	-	-	-	22.7	0.9	-	-
1965	-	-	23.1	1.8	-	-	-	-	23.2	0.4	-	-	-	-	23.2	0.0	-	-	-	-	23.3	0.4	-	-
1966	-	-	23.5	0.9	-	-	-	-	23.6	0.4	-	-	-	-	23.7	0.4	-	-	-	-	24.2	2.1	-	-
1967	-	-	24.4	0.8	-	-	-	-	25.1	2.9	-	-	-	-	25.4	1.2	-	-	-	-	25.7	1.2	-	-
1968	-	-	26.4	2.7	-	-	-	-	26.9	1.9	-	-	-	-	27.2	1.1	-	-	-	-	28.5	4.8	-	-
1969	-	-	29.4	3.2	-	-	-	-	30.3	3.1	-	-	-	-	31.2	3.0	-	-	-	-	31.4	0.6	-	-
1970	-	-	32.3	2.9	-	-	-	-	32.8	1.5	-	-	-	-	33.4	1.8	-	-	-	-	33.3	-0.3	-	-
1971	-	-	34.2	2.7	-	-	-	-	34.9	2.0	-	-	-	-	36.1	3.4	-	-	-	-	35.8	-0.8	-	-
1972	-	-	35.7	-0.3	-	-	-	-	36.0	0.8	-	-	-	-	36.5	1.4	-	-	-	-	36.8	0.8	-	-
1973	-	-	37.4	1.6	-	-	-	-	37.7	0.8	-	-	-	-	37.9	0.5	-	-	-	-	38.6	1.8	-	-
1974	-	-	40.2	4.1	-	-	-	-	40.7	1.2	-	-	-	-	41.9	2.9	-	-	-	-	42.4	1.2	-	-
1975	-	-	45.5	7.3	-	-	-	-	46.1	1.3	-	-	-	-	45.8	-0.7	-	-	-	-	46.9	2.4	-	-
1976	-	-	49.5	5.5	-	-	-	-	50.2	1.4	-	-	-	-	50.9	1.4	-	-	-	-	51.9	2.0	-	-
1977	-	-	55.0	6.0	-	-	-	-	56.4	2.5	-	-	-	-	57.4	1.8	-	-	-	-	58.3	1.6	-	-
1978	-	-	61.0	4.6	-	-	61.2	0.3	-	-	61.9	1.1	-	-	62.4	0.8	-	-	62.7	0.5	-	-	63.2	0.8
1979	-	-	64.7	2.4	-	-	65.0	0.5	-	-	66.0	1.5	-	-	66.3	0.5	-	-	66.8	0.8	-	-	68.6	2.7
1980	-	-	71.9	4.8	-	-	71.6	-0.4	-	-	72.1	0.7	-	-	73.4	1.8	-	-	73.9	0.7	-	-	74.9	1.4
1981	-	-	79.7	6.4	-	-	80.6	1.1	-	-	81.3	0.9	-	-	82.1	1.0	-	-	82.1	0.0	-	-	83.4	1.6
1982	-	-	87.9	5.4	-	-	90.8	3.3	-	-	91.4	0.7	-	-	92.5	1.2	-	-	94.1	1.7	-	-	95.0	1.0
1983	-	-	99.8	5.1	-	-	101.3	1.5	-	-	101.5	0.2	-	-	101.9	0.4	-	-	101.7	-0.2	-	-	102.7	1.0
1984	-	-	106.6	3.8	-	-	107.3	0.7	-	-	108.1	0.7	-	-	107.8	-0.3	-	-	107.8	0.0	-	-	108.1	0.3
1985	-	-	110.4	2.1	-	-	111.1	0.6	-	-	111.5	0.4	-	-	112.0	0.4	-	-	112.5	0.4	-	-	116.0	3.1
1986	-	-	119.0	2.6	-	-	119.9	0.8	-	-	123.5	3.0	-	-	124.1	0.5	-	-	124.4	0.2	124.9	0.4	124.8	-0.1
1987	127.4	2.1	-	-	127.7	0.2	-	-	128.0	0.2	-	-	127.7	-0.2	-	-	129.4	1.3	-	-	129.8	0.3	-	-
1988	132.4	2.0	-	-	132.9	0.4	-	-	133.1	0.2	-	-	133.8	0.5	-	-	137.7	2.9	-	-	137.5	-0.1	-	-
1989	140.1	1.9	-	-	141.1	0.7	-	-	141.7	0.4	-	-	144.3	1.8	-	-	144.6	0.2	-	-	146.6	1.4	-	-
1990	150.2	2.5	-	-	151.7	1.0	-	-	153.4	1.1	-	-	158.5	3.3	-	-	159.4	0.6	-	-	162.8	2.1	-	-
1991	166.0	2.0	-	-	168.8	1.7	-	-	171.4	1.5	-	-	171.9	0.3	-	-	174.2	1.3	-	-	175.1	0.5	-	-

[Continued]

Cleveland, OH
Consumer Price Index - All Urban Consumers
Base 1982-1984 = 100
Medical Care
[Continued]

For 1947-1997. Columns headed % show percentile change in the index from the previous period for which an index is available.

Year	Jan Index	%	Feb Index	%	Mar Index	%	Apr Index	%	May Index	%	Jun Index	%	Jul Index	%	Aug Index	%	Sep Index	%	Oct Index	%	Nov Index	%	Dec Index	%
1992	176.5	0.8	-	-	177.8	0.7	-	-	178.5	0.4	-	-	179.0	0.3	-	-	178.4	-0.3	-	-	179.0	0.3	-	-
1993	185.5	3.6	-	-	185.1	-0.2	-	-	186.0	0.5	-	-	188.0	1.1	-	-	188.2	0.1	-	-	188.9	0.4	-	-
1994	192.6	2.0	-	-	195.3	1.4	-	-	194.5	-0.4	-	-	194.7	0.1	-	-	197.7	1.5	-	-	197.6	-0.1	-	-
1995	201.2	1.8	-	-	202.6	0.7	-	-	201.9	-0.3	-	-	202.4	0.2	-	-	202.4	0.0	-	-	203.3	0.4	-	-
1996	208.0	2.3	-	-	209.0	0.5	-	-	209.6	0.3	-	-	210.0	0.2	-	-	209.6	-0.2	-	-	209.8	0.1	-	-
1997	210.2	0.2	-	-	211.1	0.4	-	-	210.5	-0.3	210.8	0.1	212.3	0.7	-	-	212.2	-0.0	-	-	212.5	0.1	-	-

Source: U.S. Department of Labor, Bureau of Labor Statistics, Division of Consumer Prices and Price Indexes. - indicates no data collected for period.

Cleveland, OH
Consumer Price Index - Urban Wage Earners
Base 1982-1984 = 100
Medical Care

For 1947-1997. Columns headed % show percentile change in the index from the previous period for which an index is available.

Year	Jan Index	%	Feb Index	%	Mar Index	%	Apr Index	%	May Index	%	Jun Index	%	Jul Index	%	Aug Index	%	Sep Index	%	Oct Index	%	Nov Index	%	Dec Index	%
1947	10.3	-	10.3	0.0	10.3	0.0	10.3	0.0	10.3	0.0	10.3	0.0	-	-	10.4	1.0	-	-	-	-	10.8	3.8	-	-
1948	-	-	10.8	0.0	-	-	-	-	11.0	1.9	-	-	-	-	11.0	0.0	-	-	-	-	11.4	3.6	-	-
1949	-	-	11.4	0.0	-	-	-	-	11.4	0.0	-	-	-	-	11.5	0.9	-	-	-	-	11.6	0.9	-	-
1950	-	-	11.6	0.0	-	-	-	-	11.6	0.0	-	-	-	-	11.5	-0.9	-	-	-	-	11.7	1.7	-	-
1951	-	-	12.0	2.6	-	-	-	-	12.4	3.3	-	-	-	-	12.4	0.0	-	-	-	-	13.0	4.8	-	-
1952	-	-	13.0	0.0	-	-	-	-	13.0	0.0	-	-	-	-	13.1	0.8	-	-	-	-	13.1	0.0	-	-
1953	-	-	13.1	0.0	-	-	-	-	13.2	0.8	-	-	-	-	13.9	5.3	-	-	-	-	14.0	0.7	-	-
1954	-	-	14.2	1.4	-	-	-	-	14.2	0.0	-	-	-	-	14.2	0.0	-	-	-	-	14.4	1.4	-	-
1955	-	-	14.4	0.0	-	-	-	-	15.0	4.2	-	-	-	-	15.0	0.0	-	-	-	-	15.2	1.3	-	-
1956	-	-	15.2	0.0	-	-	-	-	16.0	5.3	-	-	-	-	16.1	0.6	-	-	-	-	16.1	0.0	-	-
1957	-	-	16.2	0.6	-	-	-	-	16.4	1.2	-	-	-	-	16.6	1.2	-	-	-	-	16.6	0.0	-	-
1958	-	-	16.8	1.2	-	-	-	-	16.8	0.0	-	-	-	-	16.8	0.0	-	-	-	-	16.9	0.6	-	-
1959	-	-	18.3	8.3	-	-	-	-	18.4	0.5	-	-	-	-	18.5	0.5	-	-	-	-	18.7	1.1	-	-
1960	-	-	18.7	0.0	-	-	-	-	19.0	1.6	-	-	-	-	19.1	0.5	-	-	-	-	19.1	0.0	-	-
1961	-	-	20.4	6.8	-	-	-	-	20.4	0.0	-	-	-	-	20.3	-0.5	-	-	-	-	20.3	0.0	-	-
1962	-	-	20.4	0.5	-	-	-	-	20.4	0.0	-	-	-	-	20.4	0.0	-	-	-	-	20.4	0.0	-	-
1963	-	-	20.5	0.5	-	-	-	-	21.8	6.3	-	-	-	-	21.9	0.5	-	-	-	-	21.9	0.0	-	-
1964	-	-	22.0	0.5	-	-	-	-	22.1	0.5	-	-	-	-	22.1	0.0	-	-	-	-	22.3	0.9	-	-
1965	-	-	22.7	1.8	-	-	-	-	22.8	0.4	-	-	-	-	22.8	0.0	-	-	-	-	22.9	0.4	-	-
1966	-	-	23.1	0.9	-	-	-	-	23.2	0.4	-	-	-	-	23.3	0.4	-	-	-	-	23.8	2.1	-	-
1967	-	-	24.0	0.8	-	-	-	-	24.7	2.9	-	-	-	-	25.0	1.2	-	-	-	-	25.2	0.8	-	-
1968	-	-	26.0	3.2	-	-	-	-	26.5	1.9	-	-	-	-	26.7	0.8	-	-	-	-	28.1	5.2	-	-
1969	-	-	28.9	2.8	-	-	-	-	29.8	3.1	-	-	-	-	30.7	3.0	-	-	-	-	30.8	0.3	-	-
1970	-	-	31.8	3.2	-	-	-	-	32.2	1.3	-	-	-	-	32.9	2.2	-	-	-	-	32.7	-0.6	-	-
1971	-	-	33.6	2.8	-	-	-	-	34.3	2.1	-	-	-	-	35.5	3.5	-	-	-	-	35.2	-0.8	-	-
1972	-	-	35.1	-0.3	-	-	-	-	35.4	0.9	-	-	-	-	35.9	1.4	-	-	-	-	36.2	0.8	-	-
1973	-	-	36.8	1.7	-	-	-	-	37.1	0.8	-	-	-	-	37.3	0.5	-	-	-	-	38.0	1.9	-	-
1974	-	-	39.5	3.9	-	-	-	-	40.0	1.3	-	-	-	-	41.2	3.0	-	-	-	-	41.7	1.2	-	-
1975	-	-	44.8	7.4	-	-	-	-	45.4	1.3	-	-	-	-	45.1	-0.7	-	-	-	-	46.1	2.2	-	-
1976	-	-	48.7	5.6	-	-	-	-	49.3	1.2	-	-	-	-	50.0	1.4	-	-	-	-	51.0	2.0	-	-
1977	-	-	54.1	6.1	-	-	-	-	55.4	2.4	-	-	-	-	56.4	1.8	-	-	-	-	57.3	1.6	-	-
1978	-	-	60.0	4.7	-	-	60.1	0.2	-	-	61.0	1.5	-	-	61.4	0.7	-	-	62.4	1.6	-	-	63.4	1.6
1979	-	-	65.0	2.5	-	-	65.2	0.3	-	-	65.9	1.1	-	-	67.1	1.8	-	-	67.8	1.0	-	-	69.5	2.5
1980	-	-	72.6	4.5	-	-	72.7	0.1	-	-	73.6	1.2	-	-	74.5	1.2	-	-	74.5	0.0	-	-	75.6	1.5
1981	-	-	80.6	6.6	-	-	80.8	0.2	-	-	80.9	0.1	-	-	81.8	1.1	-	-	82.7	1.1	-	-	83.9	1.5
1982	-	-	88.2	5.1	-	-	91.0	3.2	-	-	91.6	0.7	-	-	92.7	1.2	-	-	94.3	1.7	-	-	95.2	1.0
1983	-	-	100.0	5.0	-	-	101.3	1.3	-	-	101.5	0.2	-	-	101.7	0.2	-	-	101.6	-0.1	-	-	102.5	0.9
1984	-	-	106.4	3.8	-	-	107.1	0.7	-	-	107.9	0.7	-	-	107.5	-0.4	-	-	107.6	0.1	-	-	107.8	0.2
1985	-	-	110.0	2.0	-	-	110.6	0.5	-	-	111.0	0.4	-	-	111.6	0.5	-	-	112.0	0.4	-	-	115.3	2.9
1986	-	-	118.4	2.7	-	-	119.3	0.8	-	-	122.8	2.9	-	-	123.4	0.5	-	-	123.7	0.2	124.2	0.4	124.1	-0.1
1987	126.7	2.1	-	-	127.0	0.2	-	-	127.4	0.3	-	-	127.1	-0.2	-	-	128.8	1.3	-	-	129.0	0.2	-	-
1988	131.6	2.0	-	-	132.1	0.4	-	-	132.4	0.2	-	-	133.1	0.5	-	-	136.8	2.8	-	-	136.6	-0.1	-	-
1989	139.1	1.8	-	-	140.0	0.6	-	-	140.6	0.4	-	-	142.8	1.6	-	-	143.1	0.2	-	-	144.9	1.3	-	-
1990	148.3	2.3	-	-	149.6	0.9	-	-	151.0	0.9	-	-	156.8	3.8	-	-	157.5	0.4	-	-	160.8	2.1	-	-
1991	163.5	1.7	-	-	165.9	1.5	-	-	168.3	1.4	-	-	168.7	0.2	-	-	171.3	1.5	-	-	172.1	0.5	-	-

[Continued]

Cleveland, OH
Consumer Price Index - Urban Wage Earners
Base 1982-1984 = 100
Medical Care
[Continued]

For 1947-1997. Columns headed % show percentile change in the index from the previous period for which an index is available.

Year	Jan Index	%	Feb Index	%	Mar Index	%	Apr Index	%	May Index	%	Jun Index	%	Jul Index	%	Aug Index	%	Sep Index	%	Oct Index	%	Nov Index	%	Dec Index	%
1992	173.5	0.8	-	-	174.6	0.6	-	-	175.6	0.6	-	-	176.2	0.3	-	-	175.6	-0.3	-	-	176.1	0.3	-	-
1993	182.2	3.5	-	-	181.9	-0.2	-	-	182.7	0.4	-	-	185.0	1.3	-	-	185.0	0.0	-	-	185.7	0.4	-	-
1994	189.1	1.8	-	-	191.9	1.5	-	-	191.1	-0.4	-	-	191.3	0.1	-	-	194.4	1.6	-	-	194.1	-0.2	-	-
1995	197.5	1.8	-	-	198.8	0.7	-	-	198.5	-0.2	-	-	199.1	0.3	-	-	199.2	0.1	-	-	200.3	0.6	-	-
1996	205.0	2.3	-	-	206.0	0.5	-	-	206.6	0.3	-	-	207.1	0.2	-	-	206.9	-0.1	-	-	207.2	0.1	-	-
1997	207.4	0.1	-	-	208.7	0.6	-	-	208.2	-0.2	208.3	0.0	209.9	0.8	-	-	209.7	-0.1	-	-	209.9	0.1	-	-

Source: U.S. Department of Labor, Bureau of Labor Statistics, Division of Consumer Prices and Price Indexes. - indicates no data collected for period.

Cleveland, OH
Consumer Price Index - All Urban Consumers
Base 1982-1984 = 100
Entertainment

For 1975-1997. Columns headed % show percentile change in the index from the previous period for which an index is available.

Year	Jan Index	%	Feb Index	%	Mar Index	%	Apr Index	%	May Index	%	Jun Index	%	Jul Index	%	Aug Index	%	Sep Index	%	Oct Index	%	Nov Index	%	Dec Index	%
1975	-	-	-	-	-	-	-	-	-	-	-	-	-	-	-	-	-	-	-	-	65.8	-	-	-
1976	-	-	65.9	0.2	-	-	-	-	66.6	1.1	-	-	-	-	67.6	1.5	-	-	-	-	68.9	1.9	-	-
1977	-	-	69.8	1.3	-	-	-	-	70.5	1.0	-	-	-	-	70.3	-0.3	-	-	-	-	71.8	2.1	-	-
1978	-	-	73.2	1.9	-	-	74.0	1.1	-	-	73.6	-0.5	-	-	74.3	1.0	-	-	76.7	3.2	-	-	78.2	2.0
1979	-	-	77.9	-0.4	-	-	78.5	0.8	-	-	76.4	-2.7	-	-	77.8	1.8	-	-	80.8	3.9	-	-	81.5	0.9
1980	-	-	81.9	0.5	-	-	82.5	0.7	-	-	82.2	-0.4	-	-	84.2	2.4	-	-	85.9	2.0	-	-	86.4	0.6
1981	-	-	86.8	0.5	-	-	87.9	1.3	-	-	88.2	0.3	-	-	87.4	-0.9	-	-	90.8	3.9	-	-	91.7	1.0
1982	-	-	95.2	3.8	-	-	94.7	-0.5	-	-	95.1	0.4	-	-	95.8	0.7	-	-	97.3	1.6	-	-	97.2	-0.1
1983	-	-	98.9	1.7	-	-	98.7	-0.2	-	-	98.9	0.2	-	-	99.4	0.5	-	-	103.8	4.4	-	-	103.7	-0.1
1984	-	-	104.0	0.3	-	-	104.4	0.4	-	-	103.8	-0.6	-	-	102.4	-1.3	-	-	104.3	1.9	-	-	105.8	1.4
1985	-	-	104.1	-1.6	-	-	105.8	1.6	-	-	105.0	-0.8	-	-	106.5	1.4	-	-	111.0	4.2	-	-	110.7	-0.3
1986	-	-	113.7	2.7	-	-	113.7	0.0	-	-	113.9	0.2	-	-	114.1	0.2	-	-	116.5	2.1	114.5	-1.7	115.1	0.5
1987	114.5	-0.5	-	-	115.3	0.7	-	-	116.4	1.0	-	-	116.2	-0.2	-	-	116.1	-0.1	-	-	116.0	-0.1	-	-
1988	116.5	0.4	-	-	119.5	2.6	-	-	121.8	1.9	-	-	122.8	0.8	-	-	118.8	-3.3	-	-	117.1	-1.4	-	-
1989	128.0	9.3	-	-	126.8	-0.9	-	-	120.3	-5.1	-	-	129.3	7.5	-	-	128.4	-0.7	-	-	128.6	0.2	-	-
1990	131.7	2.4	-	-	132.9	0.9	-	-	132.7	-0.2	-	-	134.9	1.7	-	-	135.2	0.2	-	-	133.4	-1.3	-	-
1991	135.7	1.7	-	-	136.6	0.7	-	-	139.2	1.9	-	-	136.5	-1.9	-	-	142.5	4.4	-	-	140.1	-1.7	-	-
1992	139.8	-0.2	-	-	142.1	1.6	-	-	137.0	-3.6	-	-	138.5	1.1	-	-	139.7	0.9	-	-	140.4	0.5	-	-
1993	141.1	0.5	-	-	140.9	-0.1	-	-	142.9	1.4	-	-	140.2	-1.9	-	-	140.1	-0.1	-	-	151.2	7.9	-	-
1994	152.1	0.6	-	-	151.3	-0.5	-	-	152.0	0.5	-	-	145.0	-4.6	-	-	144.3	-0.5	-	-	152.2	5.5	-	-
1995	151.4	-0.5	-	-	154.1	1.8	-	-	150.2	-2.5	-	-	150.5	0.2	-	-	155.2	3.1	-	-	156.0	0.5	-	-
1996	155.9	-0.1	-	-	154.3	-1.0	-	-	154.6	0.2	-	-	154.8	0.1	-	-	157.1	1.5	-	-	157.6	0.3	-	-
1997	158.1	0.3	-	-	157.7	-0.3	-	-	158.4	0.4	158.2	-0.1	159.3	0.7	-	-	158.6	-0.4	-	-	158.2	-0.3	-	-

Source: U.S. Department of Labor, Bureau of Labor Statistics, Division of Consumer Prices and Price Indexes. - indicates no data collected for period.

Cleveland, OH
Consumer Price Index - Urban Wage Earners
Base 1982-1984 = 100
Entertainment

For 1975-1997. Columns headed % show percentile change in the index from the previous period for which an index is available.

Year	Jan Index	%	Feb Index	%	Mar Index	%	Apr Index	%	May Index	%	Jun Index	%	Jul Index	%	Aug Index	%	Sep Index	%	Oct Index	%	Nov Index	%	Dec Index	%
1975	-	-	-	-	-	-	-	-	-	-	-	-	-	-	-	-	-	-	-	-	65.7	-	-	-
1976	-	-	65.9	0.3	-	-	-	-	66.5	0.9	-	-	-	-	67.5	1.5	-	-	-	-	68.9	2.1	-	-
1977	-	-	69.7	1.2	-	-	-	-	70.5	1.1	-	-	-	-	70.2	-0.4	-	-	-	-	71.8	2.3	-	-
1978	-	-	73.2	1.9	-	-	73.9	1.0	-	-	73.0	-1.2	-	-	73.5	0.7	-	-	74.9	1.9	-	-	76.2	1.7
1979	-	-	76.7	0.7	-	-	76.8	0.1	-	-	76.2	-0.8	-	-	78.0	2.4	-	-	80.9	3.7	-	-	81.6	0.9
1980	-	-	83.1	1.8	-	-	83.4	0.4	-	-	83.3	-0.1	-	-	84.3	1.2	-	-	86.0	2.0	-	-	86.5	0.6
1981	-	-	87.4	1.0	-	-	88.6	1.4	-	-	89.3	0.8	-	-	88.7	-0.7	-	-	90.8	2.4	-	-	92.3	1.7
1982	-	-	94.8	2.7	-	-	94.4	-0.4	-	-	94.8	0.4	-	-	95.5	0.7	-	-	96.9	1.5	-	-	96.6	-0.3
1983	-	-	98.6	2.1	-	-	98.4	-0.2	-	-	98.6	0.2	-	-	99.4	0.8	-	-	103.7	4.3	-	-	103.8	0.1
1984	-	-	104.2	0.4	-	-	104.9	0.7	-	-	104.4	-0.5	-	-	103.4	-1.0	-	-	105.0	1.5	-	-	106.1	1.0
1985	-	-	105.0	-1.0	-	-	106.4	1.3	-	-	105.2	-1.1	-	-	106.8	1.5	-	-	111.4	4.3	-	-	111.2	-0.2
1986	-	-	114.4	2.9	-	-	114.4	0.0	-	-	114.6	0.2	-	-	114.7	0.1	-	-	117.3	2.3	115.1	-1.9	115.6	0.4
1987	114.6	-0.9	-	-	115.4	0.7	-	-	116.6	1.0	-	-	116.0	-0.5	-	-	116.4	0.3	-	-	116.6	0.2	-	-
1988	117.0	0.3	-	-	120.1	2.6	-	-	122.6	2.1	-	-	123.5	0.7	-	-	119.7	-3.1	-	-	118.3	-1.2	-	-
1989	127.2	7.5	-	-	126.5	-0.6	-	-	120.0	-5.1	-	-	128.4	7.0	-	-	127.8	-0.5	-	-	127.8	0.0	-	-
1990	128.6	0.6	-	-	129.8	0.9	-	-	130.0	0.2	-	-	131.9	1.5	-	-	132.0	0.1	-	-	130.1	-1.4	-	-
1991	132.5	1.8	-	-	132.7	0.2	-	-	135.0	1.7	-	-	132.4	-1.9	-	-	138.1	4.3	-	-	135.7	-1.7	-	-
1992	135.0	-0.5	-	-	138.2	2.4	-	-	133.7	-3.3	-	-	135.1	1.0	-	-	136.9	1.3	-	-	137.3	0.3	-	-
1993	137.9	0.4	-	-	136.7	-0.9	-	-	137.9	0.9	-	-	137.2	-0.5	-	-	137.3	0.1	-	-	147.7	7.6	-	-
1994	147.2	-0.3	-	-	146.1	-0.7	-	-	147.2	0.8	-	-	140.5	-4.6	-	-	140.1	-0.3	-	-	148.3	5.9	-	-
1995	146.8	-1.0	-	-	149.8	2.0	-	-	145.3	-3.0	-	-	145.8	0.3	-	-	150.3	3.1	-	-	151.4	0.7	-	-
1996	151.3	-0.1	-	-	149.5	-1.2	-	-	150.2	0.5	-	-	150.3	0.1	-	-	153.2	1.9	-	-	154.0	0.5	-	-
1997	154.0	0.0	-	-	153.4	-0.4	-	-	153.9	0.3	153.8	-0.1	154.6	0.5	-	-	153.6	-0.6	-	-	153.2	-0.3	-	-

Source: U.S. Department of Labor, Bureau of Labor Statistics, Division of Consumer Prices and Price Indexes. - indicates no data collected for period.

Cleveland, OH
Consumer Price Index - All Urban Consumers
Base 1982-1984 = 100
Other Goods and Services

For 1975-1997. Columns headed % show percentile change in the index from the previous period for which an index is available.

Year	Jan Index	%	Feb Index	%	Mar Index	%	Apr Index	%	May Index	%	Jun Index	%	Jul Index	%	Aug Index	%	Sep Index	%	Oct Index	%	Nov Index	%	Dec Index	%
1975	-	-	-	-	-	-	-	-	-	-	-	-	-	-	-	-	-	-	-	-	56.3	-	-	-
1976	-	-	57.2	1.6	-	-	-	-	57.4	0.3	-	-	-	-	58.5	1.9	-	-	-	-	60.2	2.9	-	-
1977	-	-	60.6	0.7	-	-	-	-	61.5	1.5	-	-	-	-	61.6	0.2	-	-	-	-	63.3	2.8	-	-
1978	-	-	64.3	1.6	-	-	64.9	0.9	-	-	65.1	0.3	-	-	65.7	0.9	-	-	67.4	2.6	-	-	69.3	2.8
1979	-	-	69.7	0.6	-	-	69.7	0.0	-	-	69.9	0.3	-	-	70.8	1.3	-	-	73.9	4.4	-	-	73.6	-0.4
1980	-	-	74.9	1.8	-	-	75.4	0.7	-	-	75.5	0.1	-	-	76.1	0.8	-	-	79.4	4.3	-	-	80.9	1.9
1981	-	-	82.7	2.2	-	-	83.3	0.7	-	-	84.6	1.6	-	-	85.3	0.8	-	-	86.8	1.8	-	-	88.2	1.6
1982	-	-	90.3	2.4	-	-	91.5	1.3	-	-	90.6	-1.0	-	-	92.2	1.8	-	-	96.4	4.6	-	-	97.8	1.5
1983	-	-	99.1	1.3	-	-	99.1	0.0	-	-	99.6	0.5	-	-	100.7	1.1	-	-	102.9	2.2	-	-	103.5	0.6
1984	-	-	104.8	1.3	-	-	104.9	0.1	-	-	105.3	0.4	-	-	107.3	1.9	-	-	109.4	2.0	-	-	109.8	0.4
1985	-	-	109.4	-0.4	-	-	109.9	0.5	-	-	110.1	0.2	-	-	112.2	1.9	-	-	114.4	2.0	-	-	114.3	-0.1
1986	-	-	115.9	1.4	-	-	115.8	-0.1	-	-	116.2	0.3	-	-	117.1	0.8	-	-	119.2	1.8	119.1	-0.1	119.5	0.3
1987	120.9	1.2	-	-	120.7	-0.2	-	-	121.7	0.8	-	-	122.8	0.9	-	-	126.7	3.2	-	-	128.0	1.0	-	-
1988	129.4	1.1	-	-	129.3	-0.1	-	-	131.5	1.7	-	-	134.4	2.2	-	-	135.2	0.6	-	-	136.7	1.1	-	-
1989	137.3	0.4	-	-	137.4	0.1	-	-	139.4	1.5	-	-	140.2	0.6	-	-	144.9	3.4	-	-	144.9	0.0	-	-
1990	145.7	0.6	-	-	147.4	1.2	-	-	148.9	1.0	-	-	148.6	-0.2	-	-	152.0	2.3	-	-	152.5	0.3	-	-
1991	154.9	1.6	-	-	156.5	1.0	-	-	157.7	0.8	-	-	159.5	1.1	-	-	163.8	2.7	-	-	165.4	1.0	-	-
1992	166.1	0.4	-	-	167.5	0.8	-	-	168.5	0.6	-	-	168.6	0.1	-	-	173.9	3.1	-	-	174.1	0.1	-	-
1993	177.0	1.7	-	-	178.3	0.7	-	-	179.3	0.6	-	-	183.4	2.3	-	-	180.8	-1.4	-	-	181.3	0.3	-	-
1994	183.3	1.1	-	-	183.7	0.2	-	-	179.4	-2.3	-	-	183.5	2.3	-	-	187.7	2.3	-	-	186.9	-0.4	-	-
1995	187.9	0.5	-	-	188.0	0.1	-	-	188.2	0.1	-	-	189.0	0.4	-	-	191.6	1.4	-	-	192.9	0.7	-	-
1996	198.7	3.0	-	-	191.1	-3.8	-	-	190.2	-0.5	-	-	190.9	0.4	-	-	193.8	1.5	-	-	193.7	-0.1	-	-
1997	197.2	1.8	-	-	199.3	1.1	-	-	205.0	2.9	201.2	-1.9	206.3	2.5	-	-	207.1	0.4	-	-	209.5	1.2	-	-

Source: U.S. Department of Labor, Bureau of Labor Statistics, Division of Consumer Prices and Price Indexes. - indicates no data collected for period.

Cleveland, OH
Consumer Price Index - Urban Wage Earners
Base 1982-1984 = 100
Other Goods and Services

For 1975-1997. Columns headed % show percentile change in the index from the previous period for which an index is available.

Year	Jan Index	%	Feb Index	%	Mar Index	%	Apr Index	%	May Index	%	Jun Index	%	Jul Index	%	Aug Index	%	Sep Index	%	Oct Index	%	Nov Index	%	Dec Index	%
1975	-	-	-	-	-	-	-	-	-	-	-	-	-	-	-	-	-	-	-	-	55.2	-	-	-
1976	-	-	56.1	1.6	-	-	-	-	56.3	0.4	-	-	-	-	57.4	2.0	-	-	-	-	59.1	3.0	-	-
1977	-	-	59.5	0.7	-	-	-	-	60.3	1.3	-	-	-	-	60.4	0.2	-	-	-	-	62.1	2.8	-	-
1978	-	-	63.1	1.6	-	-	63.2	0.2	-	-	63.9	1.1	-	-	64.8	1.4	-	-	66.6	2.8	-	-	67.6	1.5
1979	-	-	68.1	0.7	-	-	68.5	0.6	-	-	68.9	0.6	-	-	69.7	1.2	-	-	72.3	3.7	-	-	72.3	0.0
1980	-	-	74.0	2.4	-	-	74.9	1.2	-	-	75.4	0.7	-	-	76.1	0.9	-	-	78.6	3.3	-	-	79.5	1.1
1981	-	-	82.4	3.6	-	-	83.1	0.8	-	-	84.8	2.0	-	-	84.2	-0.7	-	-	85.7	1.8	-	-	87.9	2.6
1982	-	-	89.8	2.2	-	-	91.4	1.8	-	-	90.6	-0.9	-	-	91.9	1.4	-	-	95.9	4.4	-	-	97.7	1.9
1983	-	-	99.1	1.4	-	-	99.3	0.2	-	-	99.8	0.5	-	-	101.2	1.4	-	-	102.9	1.7	-	-	103.6	0.7
1984	-	-	105.3	1.6	-	-	105.5	0.2	-	-	106.0	0.5	-	-	107.4	1.3	-	-	108.9	1.4	-	-	109.3	0.4
1985	-	-	109.2	-0.1	-	-	109.7	0.5	-	-	109.9	0.2	-	-	112.0	1.9	-	-	113.9	1.7	-	-	113.8	-0.1
1986	-	-	115.6	1.6	-	-	115.5	-0.1	-	-	115.9	0.3	-	-	117.2	1.1	-	-	119.3	1.8	119.4	0.1	119.7	0.3
1987	121.3	1.3	-	-	121.2	-0.1	-	-	122.1	0.7	-	-	123.9	1.5	-	-	127.9	3.2	-	-	129.2	1.0	-	-
1988	130.8	1.2	-	-	130.6	-0.2	-	-	133.1	1.9	-	-	136.1	2.3	-	-	137.1	0.7	-	-	139.0	1.4	-	-
1989	139.7	0.5	-	-	139.7	0.0	-	-	141.9	1.6	-	-	143.0	0.8	-	-	147.2	2.9	-	-	147.3	0.1	-	-
1990	146.7	-0.4	-	-	148.5	1.2	-	-	150.4	1.3	-	-	149.4	-0.7	-	-	153.0	2.4	-	-	153.6	0.4	-	-
1991	156.5	1.9	-	-	158.4	1.2	-	-	159.5	0.7	-	-	161.6	1.3	-	-	166.2	2.8	-	-	168.2	1.2	-	-
1992	168.8	0.4	-	-	170.1	0.8	-	-	171.4	0.8	-	-	171.4	0.0	-	-	177.4	3.5	-	-	177.6	0.1	-	-
1993	181.3	2.1	-	-	181.6	0.2	-	-	182.8	0.7	-	-	187.6	2.6	-	-	184.3	-1.8	-	-	184.5	0.1	-	-
1994	186.5	1.1	-	-	186.9	0.2	-	-	180.2	-3.6	-	-	185.2	2.8	-	-	189.6	2.4	-	-	188.6	-0.5	-	-
1995	189.4	0.4	-	-	189.4	0.0	-	-	189.1	-0.2	-	-	189.9	0.4	-	-	192.7	1.5	-	-	194.3	0.8	-	-
1996	201.4	3.7	-	-	191.5	-4.9	-	-	189.8	-0.9	-	-	190.4	0.3	-	-	193.8	1.8	-	-	193.5	-0.2	-	-
1997	197.8	2.2	-	-	200.6	1.4	-	-	207.1	3.2	202.7	-2.1	207.8	2.5	-	-	208.3	0.2	-	-	211.2	1.4	-	-

Source: U.S. Department of Labor, Bureau of Labor Statistics, Division of Consumer Prices and Price Indexes. - indicates no data collected for period.

Dallas-Fort Worth, TX
Consumer Price Index - All Urban Consumers
Base 1982-1984 = 100
Annual Averages

For 1963-1997. Columns headed % show percentile change in the index from the previous period for which an index is available.

Year	All Items Index	%	Food & Beverage Index	%	Housing Index	%	Apparel & Upkeep Index	%	Trans-portation Index	%	Medical Care Index	%	Entertain-ment Index	%	Other Goods & Services Index	%
1963	-	-	-	-	-	-	-	-	-	-	-	-	-	-	-	-
1964	29.5	-	-	-	-	-	45.4	-	31.3	-	24.5	-	-	-	-	-
1965	29.9	1.4	-	-	-	-	45.2	-0.4	31.6	1.0	25.0	2.0	-	-	-	-
1966	31.0	3.7	-	-	-	-	46.7	3.3	32.3	2.2	26.4	5.6	-	-	-	-
1967	31.9	2.9	-	-	-	-	48.7	4.3	33.3	3.1	28.3	7.2	-	-	-	-
1968	33.3	4.4	-	-	-	-	51.4	5.5	34.4	3.3	30.0	6.0	-	-	-	-
1969	35.5	6.6	-	-	-	-	54.8	6.6	35.6	3.5	32.4	8.0	-	-	-	-
1970	37.6	5.9	-	-	-	-	57.4	4.7	36.9	3.7	34.8	7.4	-	-	-	-
1971	38.7	2.9	-	-	-	-	57.6	0.3	39.1	6.0	36.4	4.6	-	-	-	-
1972	39.8	2.8	-	-	-	-	59.2	2.8	39.9	2.0	37.2	2.2	-	-	-	-
1973	42.1	5.8	-	-	-	-	62.6	5.7	41.1	3.0	38.7	4.0	-	-	-	-
1974	46.3	10.0	-	-	-	-	66.6	6.4	47.4	15.3	41.8	8.0	-	-	-	-
1975	50.4	8.9	-	-	-	-	68.8	3.3	52.1	9.9	46.0	10.0	-	-	-	-
1976	53.5	6.2	59.0	-	48.1	-	70.9	3.1	56.7	8.8	50.1	8.9	67.2	-	55.9	-
1977	57.4	7.3	63.7	8.0	51.7	7.5	74.8	5.5	61.0	7.6	55.2	10.2	69.5	3.4	59.5	6.4
1978	61.8	7.7	69.5	9.1	56.8	9.9	78.9	5.5	62.8	3.0	59.6	8.0	69.9	0.6	63.4	6.6
1979	69.7	12.8	78.1	12.4	65.3	15.0	83.6	6.0	71.9	14.5	62.9	5.5	73.6	5.3	68.8	8.5
1980	81.5	16.9	85.4	9.3	79.3	21.4	88.9	6.3	86.3	20.0	69.9	11.1	82.4	12.0	76.1	10.6
1981	90.8	11.4	92.4	8.2	90.1	13.6	95.0	6.9	95.5	10.7	80.3	14.9	87.2	5.8	84.0	10.4
1982	96.0	5.7	96.1	4.0	96.4	7.0	97.2	2.3	97.4	2.0	91.9	14.4	93.1	6.8	91.9	9.4
1983	99.7	3.9	99.6	3.6	99.6	3.3	99.7	2.6	99.2	1.8	101.2	10.1	99.6	7.0	100.9	9.8
1984	104.3	4.6	104.3	4.7	104.0	4.4	103.1	3.4	103.4	4.2	107.0	5.7	107.2	7.6	107.3	6.3
1985	108.2	3.7	107.1	2.7	107.3	3.2	107.7	4.5	107.2	3.7	113.9	6.4	114.0	6.3	112.5	4.8
1986	109.9	1.6	111.2	3.8	109.9	2.4	107.6	-0.1	101.1	-5.7	126.7	11.2	115.8	1.6	119.5	6.2
1987	112.9	2.7	115.9	4.2	109.5	-0.4	114.5	6.4	103.5	2.4	134.2	5.9	122.0	5.4	128.8	7.8
1988	116.1	2.8	120.1	3.6	109.8	0.3	123.1	7.5	108.0	4.3	141.9	5.7	127.3	4.3	135.2	5.0
1989	119.5	2.9	125.4	4.4	111.6	1.6	124.5	1.1	110.8	2.6	150.9	6.3	132.7	4.2	146.1	8.1
1990	125.1	4.7	131.1	4.5	114.3	2.4	137.5	10.4	117.2	5.8	161.9	7.3	137.5	3.6	156.3	7.0
1991	130.8	4.6	136.3	4.0	118.6	3.8	151.7	10.3	120.7	3.0	174.8	8.0	142.4	3.6	163.7	4.7
1992	133.9	2.4	138.3	1.5	121.8	2.7	151.3	-0.3	123.4	2.2	188.3	7.7	142.0	-0.3	170.5	4.2
1993	137.3	2.5	139.0	0.5	125.3	2.9	147.8	-2.3	128.9	4.5	196.8	4.5	144.0	1.4	180.5	5.9
1994	141.2	2.8	142.2	2.3	129.0	3.0	148.2	0.3	134.5	4.3	205.6	4.5	147.1	2.2	181.0	0.3
1995	144.9	2.6	145.6	2.4	132.1	2.4	147.8	-0.3	139.4	3.6	216.9	5.5	150.3	2.2	185.7	2.6
1996	148.8	2.7	152.8	4.9	135.5	2.6	141.9	-4.0	142.1	1.9	224.6	3.6	162.8	8.3	195.6	5.3
1997	151.4	1.7	157.0	2.7	138.8	2.4	137.2	-3.3	142.9	0.6	225.3	0.3	168.9	3.7	205.6	5.1

Source: U.S. Department of Labor, Bureau of Labor Statistics, Division of Consumer Prices and Price Indexes. - indicates no data collected for period.

Dallas-Fort Worth, TX
Consumer Price Index - Urban Wage Earners
Base 1982-1984 = 100
Annual Averages

For 1963-1997. Columns headed % show percentile change in the index from the previous period for which an index is available.

Year	All Items		Food & Beverage		Housing		Apparel & Upkeep		Trans- portation		Medical Care		Entertain- ment		Other Goods & Services	
	Index	%	Index	%	Index	%	Index	%	Index	%	Index	%	Index	%	Index	%
1963	-	-	-	-	-	-	-	-	-	-	-	-	-	-	-	-
1964	30.0	-	-	-	-	-	47.9	-	31.3	-	24.9	-	-	-	-	-
1965	30.4	1.3	-	-	-	-	47.7	-0.4	31.6	1.0	25.4	2.0	-	-	-	-
1966	31.5	3.6	-	-	-	-	49.3	3.4	32.3	2.2	26.8	5.5	-	-	-	-
1967	32.4	2.9	-	-	-	-	51.4	4.3	33.3	3.1	28.7	7.1	-	-	-	-
1968	33.9	4.6	-	-	-	-	54.3	5.6	34.5	3.6	30.5	6.3	-	-	-	-
1969	36.1	6.5	-	-	-	-	57.9	6.6	35.6	3.2	32.9	7.9	-	-	-	-
1970	38.2	5.8	-	-	-	-	60.6	4.7	37.0	3.9	35.4	7.6	-	-	-	-
1971	39.3	2.9	-	-	-	-	60.9	0.5	39.1	5.7	37.0	4.5	-	-	-	-
1972	40.5	3.1	-	-	-	-	62.5	2.6	39.9	2.0	37.8	2.2	-	-	-	-
1973	42.8	5.7	-	-	-	-	66.1	5.8	41.1	3.0	39.3	4.0	-	-	-	-
1974	47.1	10.0	-	-	-	-	70.4	6.5	47.4	15.3	42.4	7.9	-	-	-	-
1975	51.3	8.9	-	-	-	-	72.7	3.3	52.1	9.9	46.8	10.4	-	-	-	-
1976	54.4	6.0	58.5	-	48.7	-	74.8	2.9	56.7	8.8	50.9	8.8	71.8	-	58.6	-
1977	58.4	7.4	63.2	8.0	52.4	7.6	78.9	5.5	61.0	7.6	56.1	10.2	74.3	3.5	62.4	6.5
1978	62.9	7.7	69.2	9.5	57.6	9.9	82.5	4.6	63.0	3.3	60.6	8.0	74.5	0.3	66.5	6.6
1979	70.9	12.7	77.9	12.6	66.1	14.8	87.3	5.8	72.3	14.8	65.2	7.6	76.7	3.0	71.7	7.8
1980	82.4	16.2	84.9	9.0	79.8	20.7	94.6	8.4	86.7	19.9	72.1	10.6	82.4	7.4	79.4	10.7
1981	91.5	11.0	92.2	8.6	90.5	13.4	98.9	4.5	96.4	11.2	81.2	12.6	87.6	6.3	84.4	6.3
1982	96.4	5.4	96.2	4.3	97.0	7.2	97.5	-1.4	97.6	1.2	91.7	12.9	93.6	6.8	91.6	8.5
1983	99.4	3.1	99.6	3.5	99.0	2.1	99.4	1.9	99.3	1.7	101.2	10.4	99.6	6.4	101.3	10.6
1984	104.2	4.8	104.2	4.6	104.0	5.1	103.0	3.6	103.2	3.9	107.1	5.8	106.8	7.2	107.1	5.7
1985	108.1	3.7	106.9	2.6	107.8	3.7	109.2	6.0	106.9	3.6	114.3	6.7	112.8	5.6	111.8	4.4
1986	109.4	1.2	110.8	3.6	110.3	2.3	109.3	0.1	100.5	-6.0	127.5	11.5	114.5	1.5	118.7	6.2
1987	112.6	2.9	115.6	4.3	109.8	-0.5	115.1	5.3	104.2	3.7	135.5	6.3	120.6	5.3	126.3	6.4
1988	115.8	2.8	119.7	3.5	110.1	0.3	123.1	7.0	108.5	4.1	143.5	5.9	126.0	4.5	132.6	5.0
1989	119.3	3.0	124.9	4.3	111.8	1.5	122.8	-0.2	111.8	3.0	153.2	6.8	131.6	4.4	143.3	8.1
1990	124.5	4.4	130.6	4.6	114.3	2.2	130.9	6.6	118.1	5.6	164.5	7.4	135.6	3.0	153.7	7.3
1991	129.6	4.1	135.7	3.9	118.7	3.8	138.7	6.0	121.6	3.0	177.7	8.0	140.7	3.8	161.8	5.3
1992	133.1	2.7	137.5	1.3	121.4	2.3	141.5	2.0	126.2	3.8	192.1	8.1	140.1	-0.4	168.7	4.3
1993	137.0	2.9	138.2	0.5	124.6	2.6	143.0	1.1	132.8	5.2	200.8	4.5	141.7	1.1	178.2	5.6
1994	140.5	2.6	141.0	2.0	128.3	3.0	140.3	-1.9	138.1	4.0	209.2	4.2	144.9	2.3	177.7	-0.3
1995	144.6	2.9	144.2	2.3	131.5	2.5	141.7	1.0	144.1	4.3	221.5	5.9	147.3	1.7	182.1	2.5
1996	148.9	3.0	151.5	5.1	134.6	2.4	138.5	-2.3	147.1	2.1	228.7	3.3	160.3	8.8	191.9	5.4
1997	151.4	1.7	155.8	2.8	137.8	2.4	133.0	-4.0	147.7	0.4	229.7	0.4	166.1	3.6	201.3	4.9

Source: U.S. Department of Labor, Bureau of Labor Statistics, Division of Consumer Prices and Price Indexes. - indicates no data collected for period.

Dallas-Fort Worth, TX
Consumer Price Index - All Urban Consumers
Base 1982-1984 = 100
All Items

For 1963-1997. Columns headed % show percentile change in the index from the previous period for which an index is available.

Year	Jan Index	%	Feb Index	%	Mar Index	%	Apr Index	%	May Index	%	Jun Index	%	Jul Index	%	Aug Index	%	Sep Index	%	Oct Index	%	Nov Index	%	Dec Index	%
1963	-		-		-		-		-		-		-		-		-		-		29.5	-	-	
1964	-		29.4	-0.3	-		-		29.6	0.7	-		-		29.5	-0.3	-		-		29.7	0.7	-	
1965	-		29.5	-0.7	-		-		29.8	1.0	-		-		30.0	0.7	-		-		30.3	1.0	-	
1966	-		30.5	0.7	-		-		30.9	1.3	-		-		31.1	0.6	-		-		31.4	1.0	-	
1967	-		31.6	0.6	-		-		31.7	0.3	-		-		32.1	1.3	-		-		32.2	0.3	-	
1968	-		32.5	0.9	-		-		33.2	2.2	-		-		33.5	0.9	-		-		34.0	1.5	-	
1969	-		34.4	1.2	-		-		35.2	2.3	-		-		35.7	1.4	-		-		36.5	2.2	-	
1970	-		37.0	1.4	-		-		37.5	1.4	-		-		37.8	0.8	-		-		37.9	0.3	-	
1971	-		38.2	0.8	-		-		38.4	0.5	-		-		39.1	1.8	-		-		39.0	-0.3	-	
1972	-		39.4	1.0	-		-		39.7	0.8	-		-		40.0	0.8	-		-		40.1	0.2	-	
1973	-		40.7	1.5	-		-		41.6	2.2	-		-		42.6	2.4	-		-		43.2	1.4	-	
1974	-		44.5	3.0	-		-		45.6	2.5	-		-		47.0	3.1	-		-		48.2	2.6	-	
1975	-		49.1	1.9	-		-		49.7	1.2	-		-		51.2	3.0	-		-		51.8	1.2	-	
1976	-		52.2	0.8	-		-		53.0	1.5	-		-		53.9	1.7	-		-		54.7	1.5	-	
1977	-		55.9	2.2	-		-		57.2	2.3	-		-		58.1	1.6	-		-		58.6	0.9	-	
1978	-		59.5	1.5	-		60.3	1.3	-		61.7	2.3	-		62.9	1.9	-		63.7	1.3	-		64.3	0.9
1979	-		65.6	2.0	-		67.3	2.6	-		69.3	3.0	-		71.1	2.6	-		72.7	2.3	-		74.6	2.6
1980	-		77.0	3.2	-		80.1	4.0	-		81.7	2.0	-		82.4	0.9	-		84.4	2.4	-		85.9	1.8
1981	-		87.5	1.9	-		89.1	1.8	-		91.2	2.4	-		91.9	0.8	-		93.2	1.4	-		94.1	1.0
1982	-		93.6	-0.5	-		94.7	1.2	-		97.2	2.6	-		97.0	-0.2	-		97.8	0.8	-		96.7	-1.1
1983	-		97.1	0.4	-		98.4	1.3	-		100.1	1.7	-		100.7	0.6	-		101.5	0.8	-		101.2	-0.3
1984	-		102.9	1.7	-		103.3	0.4	-		103.8	0.5	-		105.1	1.3	-		106.4	1.2	-		105.4	-0.9
1985	-		106.2	0.8	-		107.0	0.8	-		108.3	1.2	-		109.5	1.1	-		109.6	0.1	-		109.8	0.2
1986	-		110.6	0.7	-		108.8	-1.6	-		109.9	1.0	-		110.4	0.5	-		110.3	-0.1	-		109.3	-0.9
1987	-		110.9	1.5	-		112.2	1.2	-		112.9	0.6	-		113.5	0.5	-		114.9	1.2	-		113.9	-0.9
1988	-		114.0	0.1	-		115.4	1.2	-		115.6	0.2	-		117.2	1.4	-		117.9	0.6	-		117.2	-0.6
1989	-		117.5	0.3	-		118.7	1.0	-		120.0	1.1	-		120.0	0.0	-		121.4	1.2	-		120.5	-0.7
1990	-		122.2	1.4	-		122.9	0.6	-		123.8	0.7	-		126.0	1.8	-		129.5	2.8	-		128.4	-0.8
1991	-		129.4	0.8	-		129.5	0.1	-		130.1	0.5	-		131.1	0.8	-		133.6	1.9	-		132.0	-1.2
1992	-		132.4	0.3	-		132.5	0.1	-		134.2	1.3	-		134.4	0.1	-		136.1	1.3	-		134.6	-1.1
1993	-		135.4	0.6	-		137.0	1.2	-		136.2	-0.6	-		138.1	1.4	-		139.6	1.1	-		138.8	-0.6
1994	-		139.2	0.3	-		140.3	0.8	-		141.4	0.8	-		142.2	0.6	-		142.8	0.4	-		141.9	-0.6
1995	-		143.3	1.0	-		145.0	1.2	-		144.4	-0.4	-		145.1	0.5	-		146.8	1.2	-		145.5	-0.9
1996	-		146.2	0.5	-		148.5	1.6	-		149.4	0.6	-		149.5	0.1	-		150.7	0.8	-		150.0	-0.5
1997	-		150.7	0.5	-		150.6	-0.1	-		151.4	0.5	-		151.2	-0.1	-		152.8	1.1	-		152.5	-0.2

Source: U.S. Department of Labor, Bureau of Labor Statistics, Division of Consumer Prices and Price Indexes. - indicates no data collected for period.

Dallas-Fort Worth, TX
Consumer Price Index - Urban Wage Earners
Base 1982-1984 = 100
All Items

For 1963-1997. Columns headed % show percentile change in the index from the previous period for which an index is available.

Year	Jan Index	%	Feb Index	%	Mar Index	%	Apr Index	%	May Index	%	Jun Index	%	Jul Index	%	Aug Index	%	Sep Index	%	Oct Index	%	Nov Index	%	Dec Index	%
1963	-	-	-	-	-	-	-	-	-	-	-	-	-	-	-	-	-	-	-	-	30.0	-	-	-
1964	-	-	29.9	-0.3	-	-	-	-	30.1	0.7	-	-	-	-	30.0	-0.3	-	-	-	-	30.2	0.7	-	-
1965	-	-	30.0	-0.7	-	-	-	-	30.3	1.0	-	-	-	-	30.5	0.7	-	-	-	-	30.8	1.0	-	-
1966	-	-	31.0	0.6	-	-	-	-	31.4	1.3	-	-	-	-	31.7	1.0	-	-	-	-	31.9	0.6	-	-
1967	-	-	32.1	0.6	-	-	-	-	32.2	0.3	-	-	-	-	32.7	1.6	-	-	-	-	32.7	0.0	-	-
1968	-	-	33.1	1.2	-	-	-	-	33.8	2.1	-	-	-	-	34.1	0.9	-	-	-	-	34.6	1.5	-	-
1969	-	-	35.0	1.2	-	-	-	-	35.8	2.3	-	-	-	-	36.4	1.7	-	-	-	-	37.1	1.9	-	-
1970	-	-	37.7	1.6	-	-	-	-	38.1	1.1	-	-	-	-	38.5	1.0	-	-	-	-	38.6	0.3	-	-
1971	-	-	38.8	0.5	-	-	-	-	39.0	0.5	-	-	-	-	39.8	2.1	-	-	-	-	39.7	-0.3	-	-
1972	-	-	40.1	1.0	-	-	-	-	40.4	0.7	-	-	-	-	40.7	0.7	-	-	-	-	40.8	0.2	-	-
1973	-	-	41.4	1.5	-	-	-	-	42.4	2.4	-	-	-	-	43.4	2.4	-	-	-	-	44.0	1.4	-	-
1974	-	-	45.3	3.0	-	-	-	-	46.4	2.4	-	-	-	-	47.8	3.0	-	-	-	-	49.1	2.7	-	-
1975	-	-	49.9	1.6	-	-	-	-	50.5	1.2	-	-	-	-	52.1	3.2	-	-	-	-	52.7	1.2	-	-
1976	-	-	53.1	0.8	-	-	-	-	53.9	1.5	-	-	-	-	54.8	1.7	-	-	-	-	55.7	1.6	-	-
1977	-	-	56.8	2.0	-	-	-	-	58.2	2.5	-	-	-	-	59.2	1.7	-	-	-	-	59.6	0.7	-	-
1978	-	-	60.5	1.5	-	-	61.5	1.7	-	-	62.7	2.0	-	-	64.0	2.1	-	-	64.9	1.4	-	-	65.2	0.5
1979	-	-	66.9	2.6	-	-	68.6	2.5	-	-	70.7	3.1	-	-	72.3	2.3	-	-	73.9	2.2	-	-	75.7	2.4
1980	-	-	78.1	3.2	-	-	80.9	3.6	-	-	82.5	2.0	-	-	83.5	1.2	-	-	85.3	2.2	-	-	87.0	2.0
1981	-	-	88.5	1.7	-	-	89.8	1.5	-	-	92.1	2.6	-	-	92.5	0.4	-	-	93.7	1.3	-	-	94.4	0.7
1982	-	-	94.0	-0.4	-	-	94.9	1.0	-	-	97.4	2.6	-	-	97.4	0.0	-	-	98.1	0.7	-	-	97.1	-1.0
1983	-	-	96.7	-0.4	-	-	97.8	1.1	-	-	99.3	1.5	-	-	100.2	0.9	-	-	102.1	1.9	-	-	101.7	-0.4
1984	-	-	103.0	1.3	-	-	102.6	-0.4	-	-	103.4	0.8	-	-	105.3	1.8	-	-	106.4	1.0	-	-	105.4	-0.9
1985	-	-	106.0	0.6	-	-	106.9	0.8	-	-	108.2	1.2	-	-	109.3	1.0	-	-	109.4	0.1	-	-	109.7	0.3
1986	-	-	110.4	0.6	-	-	108.3	-1.9	-	-	109.4	1.0	-	-	110.0	0.5	-	-	109.8	-0.2	-	-	108.6	-1.1
1987	-	-	110.6	1.8	-	-	111.7	1.0	-	-	112.6	0.8	-	-	113.3	0.6	-	-	114.7	1.2	-	-	113.8	-0.8
1988	-	-	113.8	0.0	-	-	114.8	0.9	-	-	115.4	0.5	-	-	117.0	1.4	-	-	117.7	0.6	-	-	117.0	-0.6
1989	-	-	117.2	0.2	-	-	118.6	1.2	-	-	120.0	1.2	-	-	119.8	-0.2	-	-	121.1	1.1	-	-	120.1	-0.8
1990	-	-	121.3	1.0	-	-	122.2	0.7	-	-	123.2	0.8	-	-	125.4	1.8	-	-	128.8	2.7	-	-	127.8	-0.8
1991	-	-	128.1	0.2	-	-	128.2	0.1	-	-	129.4	0.9	-	-	129.9	0.4	-	-	131.8	1.5	-	-	130.9	-0.7
1992	-	-	131.2	0.2	-	-	131.5	0.2	-	-	133.5	1.5	-	-	134.0	0.4	-	-	135.4	1.0	-	-	134.1	-1.0
1993	-	-	134.8	0.5	-	-	136.3	1.1	-	-	136.5	0.1	-	-	138.0	1.1	-	-	139.1	0.8	-	-	138.6	-0.4
1994	-	-	138.1	-0.4	-	-	139.3	0.9	-	-	140.6	0.9	-	-	141.6	0.7	-	-	142.4	0.6	-	-	141.7	-0.5
1995	-	-	142.7	0.7	-	-	144.5	1.3	-	-	144.4	-0.1	-	-	144.8	0.3	-	-	146.5	1.2	-	-	145.4	-0.8
1996	-	-	145.9	0.3	-	-	148.6	1.9	-	-	149.6	0.7	-	-	149.5	-0.1	-	-	150.7	0.8	-	-	150.2	-0.3
1997	-	-	150.8	0.4	-	-	150.4	-0.3	-	-	151.4	0.7	-	-	151.1	-0.2	-	-	152.8	1.1	-	-	152.7	-0.1

Source: U.S. Department of Labor, Bureau of Labor Statistics, Division of Consumer Prices and Price Indexes. - indicates no data collected for period.

Dallas-Fort Worth, TX
Consumer Price Index - All Urban Consumers
Base 1982-1984 = 100
Food and Beverages

For 1975-1997. Columns headed % show percentile change in the index from the previous period for which an index is available.

Year	Jan Index	%	Feb Index	%	Mar Index	%	Apr Index	%	May Index	%	Jun Index	%	Jul Index	%	Aug Index	%	Sep Index	%	Oct Index	%	Nov Index	%	Dec Index	%
1975	-	-	-	-	-	-	-	-	-	-	-	-	-	-	-	-	-	-	-	-	58.8	-	-	-
1976	-	-	58.7	-0.2	-	-	-	-	58.6	-0.2	-	-	-	-	59.3	1.2	-	-	-	-	59.2	-0.2	-	-
1977	-	-	62.3	5.2	-	-	-	-	63.4	1.8	-	-	-	-	64.5	1.7	-	-	-	-	64.9	0.6	-	-
1978	-	-	66.5	2.5	-	-	67.5	1.5	-	-	69.6	3.1	-	-	70.4	1.1	-	-	71.6	1.7	-	-	73.8	3.1
1979	-	-	75.8	2.7	-	-	77.2	1.8	-	-	78.3	1.4	-	-	78.2	-0.1	-	-	79.6	1.8	-	-	81.4	2.3
1980	-	-	81.9	0.6	-	-	82.9	1.2	-	-	84.5	1.9	-	-	86.3	2.1	-	-	88.8	2.9	-	-	90.0	1.4
1981	-	-	91.0	1.1	-	-	92.3	1.4	-	-	92.3	0.0	-	-	92.9	0.7	-	-	93.3	0.4	-	-	93.2	-0.1
1982	-	-	94.6	1.5	-	-	95.3	0.7	-	-	96.4	1.2	-	-	96.7	0.3	-	-	96.9	0.2	-	-	97.7	0.8
1983	-	-	98.3	0.6	-	-	99.3	1.0	-	-	99.4	0.1	-	-	99.7	0.3	-	-	100.9	1.2	-	-	100.9	0.0
1984	-	-	103.5	2.6	-	-	104.2	0.7	-	-	104.1	-0.1	-	-	105.0	0.9	-	-	104.7	-0.3	-	-	105.4	0.7
1985	-	-	106.3	0.9	-	-	107.0	0.7	-	-	107.5	0.5	-	-	106.9	-0.6	-	-	107.0	0.1	-	-	109.0	1.9
1986	-	-	110.0	0.9	-	-	110.1	0.1	-	-	110.6	0.5	-	-	111.9	1.2	-	-	112.6	0.6	-	-	112.8	0.2
1987	-	-	115.6	2.5	-	-	114.5	-1.0	-	-	116.2	1.5	-	-	116.1	-0.1	-	-	117.3	1.0	-	-	116.9	-0.3
1988	-	-	117.5	0.5	-	-	118.3	0.7	-	-	119.9	1.4	-	-	120.8	0.8	-	-	122.4	1.3	-	-	123.1	0.6
1989	-	-	124.4	1.1	-	-	124.8	0.3	-	-	124.9	0.1	-	-	125.3	0.3	-	-	126.6	1.0	-	-	127.9	1.0
1990	-	-	129.6	1.3	-	-	130.7	0.8	-	-	130.5	-0.2	-	-	131.5	0.8	-	-	132.0	0.4	-	-	134.1	1.6
1991	-	-	134.7	0.4	-	-	135.5	0.6	-	-	138.2	2.0	-	-	136.6	-1.2	-	-	135.6	-0.7	-	-	138.0	1.8
1992	-	-	139.6	1.2	-	-	138.6	-0.7	-	-	137.2	-1.0	-	-	138.1	0.7	-	-	138.6	0.4	-	-	137.9	-0.5
1993	-	-	138.1	0.1	-	-	139.3	0.9	-	-	139.1	-0.1	-	-	138.3	-0.6	-	-	137.6	-0.5	-	-	142.5	3.6
1994	-	-	140.2	-1.6	-	-	141.4	0.9	-	-	142.3	0.6	-	-	143.3	0.7	-	-	142.8	-0.3	-	-	143.9	0.8
1995	-	-	144.1	0.1	-	-	145.7	1.1	-	-	144.1	-1.1	-	-	145.5	1.0	-	-	146.8	0.9	-	-	148.2	1.0
1996	-	-	149.8	1.1	-	-	151.8	1.3	-	-	152.5	0.5	-	-	152.7	0.1	-	-	155.8	2.0	-	-	156.0	0.1
1997	-	-	155.7	-0.2	-	-	155.3	-0.3	-	-	157.1	1.2	-	-	157.4	0.2	-	-	158.1	0.4	-	-	159.6	0.9

Source: U.S. Department of Labor, Bureau of Labor Statistics, Division of Consumer Prices and Price Indexes. - indicates no data collected for period.

Dallas-Fort Worth, TX
Consumer Price Index - Urban Wage Earners
Base 1982-1984 = 100
Food and Beverages

For 1975-1997. Columns headed % show percentile change in the index from the previous period for which an index is available.

Year	Jan Index	%	Feb Index	%	Mar Index	%	Apr Index	%	May Index	%	Jun Index	%	Jul Index	%	Aug Index	%	Sep Index	%	Oct Index	%	Nov Index	%	Dec Index	%
1975	-	-	-	-	-	-	-	-	-	-	-	-	-	-	-	-	-	-	-	-	58.3	-	-	-
1976	-	-	58.2	-0.2	-	-	-	-	58.1	-0.2	-	-	-	-	58.8	1.2	-	-	-	-	58.7	-0.2	-	-
1977	-	-	61.8	5.3	-	-	-	-	62.9	1.8	-	-	-	-	64.0	1.7	-	-	-	-	64.4	0.6	-	-
1978	-	-	65.9	2.3	-	-	67.8	2.9	-	-	69.0	1.8	-	-	70.0	1.4	-	-	71.9	2.7	-	-	72.5	0.8
1979	-	-	75.9	4.7	-	-	77.2	1.7	-	-	78.3	1.4	-	-	77.9	-0.5	-	-	79.4	1.9	-	-	80.7	1.6
1980	-	-	81.4	0.9	-	-	82.5	1.4	-	-	83.6	1.3	-	-	86.2	3.1	-	-	88.5	2.7	-	-	89.8	1.5
1981	-	-	90.3	0.6	-	-	91.1	0.9	-	-	92.1	1.1	-	-	93.7	1.7	-	-	93.6	-0.1	-	-	93.3	-0.3
1982	-	-	94.7	1.5	-	-	95.3	0.6	-	-	96.5	1.3	-	-	96.8	0.3	-	-	97.0	0.2	-	-	97.9	0.9
1983	-	-	98.3	0.4	-	-	99.2	0.9	-	-	99.5	0.3	-	-	99.7	0.2	-	-	100.9	1.2	-	-	100.8	-0.1
1984	-	-	103.5	2.7	-	-	104.2	0.7	-	-	104.0	-0.2	-	-	104.8	0.8	-	-	104.5	-0.3	-	-	105.3	0.8
1985	-	-	106.1	0.8	-	-	106.8	0.7	-	-	107.2	0.4	-	-	106.6	-0.6	-	-	106.5	-0.1	-	-	108.8	2.2
1986	-	-	109.6	0.7	-	-	109.6	0.0	-	-	110.2	0.5	-	-	111.7	1.4	-	-	112.3	0.5	-	-	112.4	0.1
1987	-	-	115.2	2.5	-	-	114.2	-0.9	-	-	115.8	1.4	-	-	115.8	0.0	-	-	116.9	0.9	-	-	116.6	-0.3
1988	-	-	117.1	0.4	-	-	117.9	0.7	-	-	119.5	1.4	-	-	120.4	0.8	-	-	122.0	1.3	-	-	122.7	0.6
1989	-	-	123.9	1.0	-	-	124.2	0.2	-	-	124.4	0.2	-	-	124.7	0.2	-	-	126.0	1.0	-	-	127.5	1.2
1990	-	-	129.1	1.3	-	-	130.0	0.7	-	-	129.8	-0.2	-	-	131.0	0.9	-	-	131.5	0.4	-	-	133.7	1.7
1991	-	-	134.2	0.4	-	-	135.1	0.7	-	-	137.7	1.9	-	-	136.0	-1.2	-	-	135.0	-0.7	-	-	137.1	1.6
1992	-	-	138.9	1.3	-	-	137.8	-0.8	-	-	136.3	-1.1	-	-	137.1	0.6	-	-	137.8	0.5	-	-	137.1	-0.5
1993	-	-	137.5	0.3	-	-	138.6	0.8	-	-	138.4	-0.1	-	-	137.6	-0.6	-	-	137.0	-0.4	-	-	141.4	3.2
1994	-	-	139.0	-1.7	-	-	140.4	1.0	-	-	141.0	0.4	-	-	141.8	0.6	-	-	141.4	-0.3	-	-	142.6	0.8
1995	-	-	142.6	0.0	-	-	144.5	1.3	-	-	142.7	-1.2	-	-	144.0	0.9	-	-	145.4	1.0	-	-	146.9	1.0
1996	-	-	148.8	1.3	-	-	150.5	1.1	-	-	151.1	0.4	-	-	151.3	0.1	-	-	154.6	2.2	-	-	155.0	0.3
1997	-	-	154.5	-0.3	-	-	154.3	-0.1	-	-	155.8	1.0	-	-	156.0	0.1	-	-	156.9	0.6	-	-	158.5	1.0

Source: U.S. Department of Labor, Bureau of Labor Statistics, Division of Consumer Prices and Price Indexes. - indicates no data collected for period.

Dallas-Fort Worth, TX

Consumer Price Index - All Urban Consumers
Base 1982-1984 = 100

Housing

For 1975-1997. Columns headed % show percentile change in the index from the previous period for which an index is available.

Year	Jan Index	%	Feb Index	%	Mar Index	%	Apr Index	%	May Index	%	Jun Index	%	Jul Index	%	Aug Index	%	Sep Index	%	Oct Index	%	Nov Index	%	Dec Index	%
1975	-	-	-	-	-	-	-	-	-	-	-	-	-	-	-	-	-	-	-	-	46.0	-	-	-
1976	-	-	47.0	2.2	-	-	-	-	47.7	1.5	-	-	-	-	48.4	1.5	-	-	-	-	49.4	2.1	-	-
1977	-	-	50.0	1.2	-	-	-	-	51.4	2.8	-	-	-	-	52.4	1.9	-	-	-	-	53.0	1.1	-	-
1978	-	-	54.3	2.5	-	-	55.3	1.8	-	-	56.7	2.5	-	-	58.2	2.6	-	-	59.0	1.4	-	-	58.9	-0.2
1979	-	-	60.4	2.5	-	-	62.0	2.6	-	-	64.8	4.5	-	-	66.9	3.2	-	-	69.3	3.6	-	-	71.3	2.9
1980	-	-	73.6	3.2	-	-	77.7	5.6	-	-	80.2	3.2	-	-	80.1	-0.1	-	-	82.7	3.2	-	-	85.0	2.8
1981	-	-	86.1	1.3	-	-	87.6	1.7	-	-	90.8	3.7	-	-	91.0	0.2	-	-	92.9	2.1	-	-	94.5	1.7
1982	-	-	92.5	-2.1	-	-	95.9	3.7	-	-	98.5	2.7	-	-	97.4	-1.1	-	-	98.4	1.0	-	-	95.8	-2.6
1983	-	-	96.7	0.9	-	-	97.9	1.2	-	-	101.3	3.5	-	-	101.0	-0.3	-	-	101.3	0.3	-	-	100.7	-0.6
1984	-	-	103.0	2.3	-	-	102.8	-0.2	-	-	104.0	1.2	-	-	105.3	1.3	-	-	106.3	0.9	-	-	103.4	-2.7
1985	-	-	105.0	1.5	-	-	105.6	0.6	-	-	107.9	2.2	-	-	110.0	1.9	-	-	109.1	-0.8	-	-	107.7	-1.3
1986	-	-	109.7	1.9	-	-	109.8	0.1	-	-	111.3	1.4	-	-	111.6	0.3	-	-	110.0	-1.4	-	-	107.1	-2.6
1987	-	-	108.0	0.8	-	-	109.1	1.0	-	-	109.7	0.5	-	-	110.5	0.7	-	-	111.4	0.8	-	-	108.9	-2.2
1988	-	-	107.9	-0.9	-	-	109.2	1.2	-	-	109.4	0.2	-	-	111.9	2.3	-	-	111.2	-0.6	-	-	109.2	-1.8
1989	-	-	110.3	1.0	-	-	109.7	-0.5	-	-	112.4	2.5	-	-	112.9	0.4	-	-	113.7	0.7	-	-	111.2	-2.2
1990	-	-	111.6	0.4	-	-	112.2	0.5	-	-	114.0	1.6	-	-	116.1	1.8	-	-	118.3	1.9	-	-	114.8	-3.0
1991	-	-	116.8	1.7	-	-	117.1	0.3	-	-	117.8	0.6	-	-	119.1	1.1	-	-	121.9	2.4	-	-	120.3	-1.3
1992	-	-	118.4	-1.6	-	-	119.0	0.5	-	-	123.9	4.1	-	-	124.9	0.8	-	-	123.2	-1.4	-	-	121.7	-1.2
1993	-	-	123.9	1.8	-	-	123.7	-0.2	-	-	123.6	-0.1	-	-	127.6	3.2	-	-	128.1	0.4	-	-	126.1	-1.6
1994	-	-	126.6	0.4	-	-	128.5	1.5	-	-	129.5	0.8	-	-	130.1	0.5	-	-	131.0	0.7	-	-	128.9	-1.6
1995	-	-	131.6	2.1	-	-	131.5	-0.1	-	-	131.5	0.0	-	-	132.6	0.8	-	-	133.8	0.9	-	-	132.3	-1.1
1996	-	-	132.2	-0.1	-	-	134.1	1.4	-	-	136.2	1.6	-	-	137.5	1.0	-	-	138.1	0.4	-	-	136.1	-1.4
1997	-	-	137.9	1.3	-	-	136.7	-0.9	-	-	139.0	1.7	-	-	138.2	-0.6	-	-	141.5	2.4	-	-	140.5	-0.7

Source: U.S. Department of Labor, Bureau of Labor Statistics, Division of Consumer Prices and Price Indexes. - indicates no data collected for period.

Dallas-Fort Worth, TX
Consumer Price Index - Urban Wage Earners
Base 1982-1984 = 100
Housing

For 1975-1997. Columns headed % show percentile change in the index from the previous period for which an index is available.

Year	Jan Index	%	Feb Index	%	Mar Index	%	Apr Index	%	May Index	%	Jun Index	%	Jul Index	%	Aug Index	%	Sep Index	%	Oct Index	%	Nov Index	%	Dec Index	%
1975	-	-	-	-	-	-	-	-	-	-	-	-	-	-	-	-	-	-	-	-	46.6	-	-	-
1976	-	-	47.6	2.1	-	-	-	-	48.3	1.5	-	-	-	-	49.1	1.7	-	-	-	-	50.0	1.8	-	-
1977	-	-	50.6	1.2	-	-	-	-	52.1	3.0	-	-	-	-	53.0	1.7	-	-	-	-	53.7	1.3	-	-
1978	-	-	55.0	2.4	-	-	56.1	2.0	-	-	57.5	2.5	-	-	59.0	2.6	-	-	59.8	1.4	-	-	59.6	-0.3
1979	-	-	61.2	2.7	-	-	62.8	2.6	-	-	65.6	4.5	-	-	67.7	3.2	-	-	70.1	3.5	-	-	72.0	2.7
1980	-	-	74.1	2.9	-	-	78.3	5.7	-	-	80.8	3.2	-	-	80.6	-0.2	-	-	82.9	2.9	-	-	85.5	3.1
1981	-	-	86.6	1.3	-	-	87.9	1.5	-	-	91.2	3.8	-	-	91.3	0.1	-	-	93.2	2.1	-	-	95.1	2.0
1982	-	-	93.1	-2.1	-	-	96.4	3.5	-	-	99.2	2.9	-	-	98.1	-1.1	-	-	99.2	1.1	-	-	96.5	-2.7
1983	-	-	95.8	-0.7	-	-	96.6	0.8	-	-	99.1	2.6	-	-	99.8	0.7	-	-	102.4	2.6	-	-	101.8	-0.6
1984	-	-	103.3	1.5	-	-	101.5	-1.7	-	-	102.9	1.4	-	-	105.8	2.8	-	-	106.9	1.0	-	-	104.0	-2.7
1985	-	-	105.4	1.3	-	-	105.9	0.5	-	-	108.4	2.4	-	-	110.5	1.9	-	-	109.7	-0.7	-	-	108.1	-1.5
1986	-	-	110.1	1.9	-	-	110.0	-0.1	-	-	111.8	1.6	-	-	112.1	0.3	-	-	110.3	-1.6	-	-	107.1	-2.9
1987	-	-	108.2	1.0	-	-	109.1	0.8	-	-	110.3	1.1	-	-	111.1	0.7	-	-	111.9	0.7	-	-	109.0	-2.6
1988	-	-	108.2	-0.7	-	-	109.4	1.1	-	-	110.0	0.5	-	-	112.2	2.0	-	-	111.6	-0.5	-	-	109.4	-2.0
1989	-	-	110.2	0.7	-	-	109.8	-0.4	-	-	112.7	2.6	-	-	113.2	0.4	-	-	114.0	0.7	-	-	111.3	-2.4
1990	-	-	111.3	0.0	-	-	112.2	0.8	-	-	113.9	1.5	-	-	116.1	1.9	-	-	118.7	2.2	-	-	114.4	-3.6
1991	-	-	117.1	2.4	-	-	117.1	0.0	-	-	118.0	0.8	-	-	119.4	1.2	-	-	122.1	2.3	-	-	120.0	-1.7
1992	-	-	118.6	-1.2	-	-	118.9	0.3	-	-	123.2	3.6	-	-	124.3	0.9	-	-	122.8	-1.2	-	-	121.1	-1.4
1993	-	-	123.1	1.7	-	-	122.6	-0.4	-	-	123.2	0.5	-	-	126.7	2.8	-	-	127.8	0.9	-	-	125.4	-1.9
1994	-	-	125.8	0.3	-	-	127.6	1.4	-	-	128.9	1.0	-	-	129.7	0.6	-	-	130.5	0.6	-	-	128.3	-1.7
1995	-	-	130.8	1.9	-	-	130.8	0.0	-	-	131.4	0.5	-	-	132.2	0.6	-	-	133.3	0.8	-	-	131.6	-1.3
1996	-	-	131.0	-0.5	-	-	133.1	1.6	-	-	135.5	1.8	-	-	136.5	0.7	-	-	137.0	0.4	-	-	135.3	-1.2
1997	-	-	137.1	1.3	-	-	135.3	-1.3	-	-	138.3	2.2	-	-	137.1	-0.9	-	-	140.6	2.6	-	-	139.6	-0.7

Source: U.S. Department of Labor, Bureau of Labor Statistics, Division of Consumer Prices and Price Indexes. - indicates no data collected for period.

Dallas-Fort Worth, TX
Consumer Price Index - All Urban Consumers
Base 1982-1984 = 100
Apparel and Upkeep

For 1963-1997. Columns headed % show percentile change in the index from the previous period for which an index is available.

Year	Jan Index	%	Feb Index	%	Mar Index	%	Apr Index	%	May Index	%	Jun Index	%	Jul Index	%	Aug Index	%	Sep Index	%	Oct Index	%	Nov Index	%	Dec Index	%
1963	-	-	-	-	-	-	-	-	-	-	-	-	-	-	-	-	-	-	-	-	45.6	-	-	-
1964	-	-	45.6	0.0	-	-	-	-	45.5	-0.2	-	-	-	-	45.1	-0.9	-	-	-	-	45.5	0.9	-	-
1965	-	-	45.0	-1.1	-	-	-	-	45.2	0.4	-	-	-	-	44.8	-0.9	-	-	-	-	45.6	1.8	-	-
1966	-	-	45.7	0.2	-	-	-	-	46.6	2.0	-	-	-	-	46.5	-0.2	-	-	-	-	47.9	3.0	-	-
1967	-	-	48.2	0.6	-	-	-	-	48.6	0.8	-	-	-	-	48.8	0.4	-	-	-	-	49.0	0.4	-	-
1968	-	-	49.6	1.2	-	-	-	-	51.4	3.6	-	-	-	-	51.8	0.8	-	-	-	-	52.9	2.1	-	-
1969	-	-	53.3	0.8	-	-	-	-	54.6	2.4	-	-	-	-	54.8	0.4	-	-	-	-	56.7	3.5	-	-
1970	-	-	57.6	1.6	-	-	-	-	57.3	-0.5	-	-	-	-	57.7	0.7	-	-	-	-	57.1	-1.0	-	-
1971	-	-	56.9	-0.4	-	-	-	-	57.7	1.4	-	-	-	-	58.2	0.9	-	-	-	-	57.6	-1.0	-	-
1972	-	-	58.4	1.4	-	-	-	-	59.1	1.2	-	-	-	-	59.2	0.2	-	-	-	-	60.3	1.9	-	-
1973	-	-	61.1	1.3	-	-	-	-	62.4	2.1	-	-	-	-	63.1	1.1	-	-	-	-	63.9	1.3	-	-
1974	-	-	65.2	2.0	-	-	-	-	66.1	1.4	-	-	-	-	67.0	1.4	-	-	-	-	68.3	1.9	-	-
1975	-	-	68.2	-0.1	-	-	-	-	68.1	-0.1	-	-	-	-	69.3	1.8	-	-	-	-	69.6	0.4	-	-
1976	-	-	69.4	-0.3	-	-	-	-	70.7	1.9	-	-	-	-	71.0	0.4	-	-	-	-	72.2	1.7	-	-
1977	-	-	72.9	1.0	-	-	-	-	73.5	0.8	-	-	-	-	76.0	3.4	-	-	-	-	76.7	0.9	-	-
1978	-	-	77.1	0.5	-	-	78.1	1.3	-	-	78.0	-0.1	-	-	79.8	2.3	-	-	80.3	0.6	-	-	81.6	1.6
1979	-	-	81.5	-0.1	-	-	83.4	2.3	-	-	82.2	-1.4	-	-	84.5	2.8	-	-	85.2	0.8	-	-	85.6	0.5
1980	-	-	86.8	1.4	-	-	88.2	1.6	-	-	87.3	-1.0	-	-	89.7	2.7	-	-	92.6	3.2	-	-	90.1	-2.7
1981	-	-	91.6	1.7	-	-	93.1	1.6	-	-	93.5	0.4	-	-	98.0	4.8	-	-	99.5	1.5	-	-	96.2	-3.3
1982	-	-	98.6	2.5	-	-	97.6	-1.0	-	-	97.6	0.0	-	-	96.2	-1.4	-	-	96.6	0.4	-	-	96.8	0.2
1983	-	-	98.4	1.7	-	-	101.1	2.7	-	-	98.6	-2.5	-	-	99.9	1.3	-	-	100.7	0.8	-	-	100.1	-0.6
1984	-	-	103.3	3.2	-	-	102.8	-0.5	-	-	99.6	-3.1	-	-	101.0	1.4	-	-	107.0	5.9	-	-	106.8	-0.2
1985	-	-	106.2	-0.6	-	-	105.8	-0.4	-	-	106.4	0.6	-	-	108.7	2.2	-	-	110.8	1.9	-	-	108.5	-2.1
1986	-	-	107.0	-1.4	-	-	106.2	-0.7	-	-	106.6	0.4	-	-	109.2	2.4	-	-	109.7	0.5	-	-	106.5	-2.9
1987	-	-	108.2	1.6	-	-	117.5	8.6	-	-	114.9	-2.2	-	-	113.9	-0.9	-	-	118.5	4.0	-	-	116.5	-1.7
1988	-	-	117.4	0.8	-	-	125.1	6.6	-	-	120.0	-4.1	-	-	123.0	2.5	-	-	128.8	4.7	-	-	126.7	-1.6
1989	-	-	118.4	-6.6	-	-	130.0	9.8	-	-	122.8	-5.5	-	-	124.6	1.5	-	-	126.1	1.2	-	-	124.9	-1.0
1990	-	-	133.6	7.0	-	-	136.1	1.9	-	-	133.0	-2.3	-	-	137.7	3.5	-	-	146.2	6.2	-	-	142.7	-2.4
1991	-	-	149.8	5.0	-	-	154.1	2.9	-	-	146.9	-4.7	-	-	150.6	2.5	-	-	166.3	10.4	-	-	142.8	-14.1
1992	-	-	157.5	10.3	-	-	152.4	-3.2	-	-	147.6	-3.1	-	-	144.5	-2.1	-	-	157.9	9.3	-	-	149.9	-5.1
1993	-	-	144.3	-3.7	-	-	161.5	11.9	-	-	142.8	-11.6	-	-	139.7	-2.2	-	-	153.9	10.2	-	-	143.3	-6.9
1994	-	-	148.0	3.3	-	-	147.6	-0.3	-	-	151.2	2.4	-	-	147.8	-2.2	-	-	149.3	1.0	-	-	146.2	-2.1
1995	-	-	145.6	-0.4	-	-	154.6	6.2	-	-	147.8	-4.4	-	-	145.0	-1.9	-	-	149.5	3.1	-	-	143.7	-3.9
1996	-	-	141.8	-1.3	-	-	149.4	5.4	-	-	141.4	-5.4	-	-	140.5	-0.6	-	-	139.7	-0.6	-	-	136.9	-2.0
1997	-	-	135.9	-0.7	-	-	139.8	2.9	-	-	137.3	-1.8	-	-	135.4	-1.4	-	-	138.4	2.2	-	-	136.5	-1.4

Source: U.S. Department of Labor, Bureau of Labor Statistics, Division of Consumer Prices and Price Indexes. - indicates no data collected for period.

Dallas-Fort Worth, TX
Consumer Price Index - Urban Wage Earners
Base 1982-1984 = 100
Apparel and Upkeep

For 1963-1997. Columns headed % show percentile change in the index from the previous period for which an index is available.

Year	Jan Index	%	Feb Index	%	Mar Index	%	Apr Index	%	May Index	%	Jun Index	%	Jul Index	%	Aug Index	%	Sep Index	%	Oct Index	%	Nov Index	%	Dec Index	%
1963	-	-	-	-	-	-	-	-	-	-	-	-	-	-	-	-	-	-	-	-	48.1	-	-	-
1964	-	-	48.1	0.0	-	-	-	-	48.0	-0.2	-	-	-	-	47.6	-0.8	-	-	-	-	48.0	0.8	-	-
1965	-	-	47.5	-1.0	-	-	-	-	47.7	0.4	-	-	-	-	47.3	-0.8	-	-	-	-	48.1	1.7	-	-
1966	-	-	48.3	0.4	-	-	-	-	49.2	1.9	-	-	-	-	49.1	-0.2	-	-	-	-	50.6	3.1	-	-
1967	-	-	50.9	0.6	-	-	-	-	51.3	0.8	-	-	-	-	51.5	0.4	-	-	-	-	51.7	0.4	-	-
1968	-	-	52.4	1.4	-	-	-	-	54.3	3.6	-	-	-	-	54.7	0.7	-	-	-	-	55.8	2.0	-	-
1969	-	-	56.3	0.9	-	-	-	-	57.7	2.5	-	-	-	-	57.9	0.3	-	-	-	-	59.9	3.5	-	-
1970	-	-	60.8	1.5	-	-	-	-	60.5	-0.5	-	-	-	-	60.9	0.7	-	-	-	-	60.3	-1.0	-	-
1971	-	-	60.1	-0.3	-	-	-	-	60.9	1.3	-	-	-	-	61.4	0.8	-	-	-	-	60.8	-1.0	-	-
1972	-	-	61.7	1.5	-	-	-	-	62.4	1.1	-	-	-	-	62.5	0.2	-	-	-	-	63.7	1.9	-	-
1973	-	-	64.6	1.4	-	-	-	-	65.9	2.0	-	-	-	-	66.6	1.1	-	-	-	-	67.5	1.4	-	-
1974	-	-	68.8	1.9	-	-	-	-	69.8	1.5	-	-	-	-	70.7	1.3	-	-	-	-	72.1	2.0	-	-
1975	-	-	72.1	0.0	-	-	-	-	72.0	-0.1	-	-	-	-	73.1	1.5	-	-	-	-	73.5	0.5	-	-
1976	-	-	73.2	-0.4	-	-	-	-	74.7	2.0	-	-	-	-	74.9	0.3	-	-	-	-	76.3	1.9	-	-
1977	-	-	76.9	0.8	-	-	-	-	77.6	0.9	-	-	-	-	80.2	3.4	-	-	-	-	81.0	1.0	-	-
1978	-	-	81.5	0.6	-	-	80.5	-1.2	-	-	80.7	0.2	-	-	84.3	4.5	-	-	84.3	0.0	-	-	85.0	0.8
1979	-	-	85.8	0.9	-	-	86.2	0.5	-	-	85.7	-0.6	-	-	88.6	3.4	-	-	89.2	0.7	-	-	89.2	0.0
1980	-	-	90.9	1.9	-	-	93.1	2.4	-	-	94.1	1.1	-	-	96.2	2.2	-	-	97.5	1.4	-	-	98.1	0.6
1981	-	-	98.6	0.5	-	-	99.9	1.3	-	-	100.9	1.0	-	-	99.5	-1.4	-	-	98.2	-1.3	-	-	95.7	-2.5
1982	-	-	98.4	2.8	-	-	97.4	-1.0	-	-	97.3	-0.1	-	-	97.2	-0.1	-	-	97.6	0.4	-	-	97.3	-0.3
1983	-	-	98.6	1.3	-	-	100.8	2.2	-	-	98.4	-2.4	-	-	98.9	0.5	-	-	101.2	2.3	-	-	99.3	-1.9
1984	-	-	103.9	4.6	-	-	102.3	-1.5	-	-	100.1	-2.2	-	-	100.7	0.6	-	-	106.3	5.6	-	-	106.9	0.6
1985	-	-	106.3	-0.6	-	-	107.8	1.4	-	-	108.7	0.8	-	-	110.1	1.3	-	-	112.9	2.5	-	-	110.1	-2.5
1986	-	-	107.7	-2.2	-	-	107.7	0.0	-	-	107.8	0.1	-	-	111.8	3.7	-	-	111.7	-0.1	-	-	108.5	-2.9
1987	-	-	110.6	1.9	-	-	118.2	6.9	-	-	113.8	-3.7	-	-	113.3	-0.4	-	-	119.1	5.1	-	-	117.9	-1.0
1988	-	-	118.8	0.8	-	-	124.1	4.5	-	-	119.6	-3.6	-	-	122.5	2.4	-	-	129.0	5.3	-	-	127.1	-1.5
1989	-	-	118.3	-6.9	-	-	129.7	9.6	-	-	121.0	-6.7	-	-	121.1	0.1	-	-	123.6	2.1	-	-	121.9	-1.4
1990	-	-	125.9	3.3	-	-	131.1	4.1	-	-	127.4	-2.8	-	-	131.2	3.0	-	-	137.2	4.6	-	-	135.8	-1.0
1991	-	-	138.1	1.7	-	-	142.9	3.5	-	-	138.4	-3.1	-	-	134.8	-2.6	-	-	146.4	8.6	-	-	130.5	-10.9
1992	-	-	143.7	10.1	-	-	142.3	-1.0	-	-	139.2	-2.2	-	-	135.8	-2.4	-	-	148.6	9.4	-	-	142.5	-4.1
1993	-	-	139.4	-2.2	-	-	155.9	11.8	-	-	142.5	-8.6	-	-	134.8	-5.4	-	-	145.3	7.8	-	-	139.6	-3.9
1994	-	-	138.7	-0.6	-	-	140.6	1.4	-	-	142.8	1.6	-	-	139.2	-2.5	-	-	142.2	2.2	-	-	138.2	-2.8
1995	-	-	137.2	-0.7	-	-	147.3	7.4	-	-	142.9	-3.0	-	-	137.8	-3.6	-	-	145.1	5.3	-	-	140.3	-3.3
1996	-	-	137.2	-2.2	-	-	146.0	6.4	-	-	138.8	-4.9	-	-	137.8	-0.7	-	-	136.1	-1.2	-	-	133.1	-2.2
1997	-	-	130.8	-1.7	-	-	135.4	3.5	-	-	132.3	-2.3	-	-	130.0	-1.7	-	-	135.6	4.3	-	-	134.0	-1.2

Source: U.S. Department of Labor, Bureau of Labor Statistics, Division of Consumer Prices and Price Indexes. - indicates no data collected for period.

Dallas-Fort Worth, TX
Consumer Price Index - All Urban Consumers
Base 1982-1984 = 100
Transportation

For 1963-1997. Columns headed % show percentile change in the index from the previous period for which an index is available.

Year	Jan Index	%	Feb Index	%	Mar Index	%	Apr Index	%	May Index	%	Jun Index	%	Jul Index	%	Aug Index	%	Sep Index	%	Oct Index	%	Nov Index	%	Dec Index	%
1963	-	-	-	-	-	-	-	-	-	-	-	-	-	-	-	-	-	-	-	-	31.5	-	-	-
1964	-	-	30.7	-2.5	-	-	-	-	31.9	3.9	-	-	-	-	30.6	-4.1	-	-	-	-	31.9	4.2	-	-
1965	-	-	30.1	-5.6	-	-	-	-	31.9	6.0	-	-	-	-	32.0	0.3	-	-	-	-	32.2	0.6	-	-
1966	-	-	31.7	-1.6	-	-	-	-	32.3	1.9	-	-	-	-	32.4	0.3	-	-	-	-	32.7	0.9	-	-
1967	-	-	32.6	-0.3	-	-	-	-	33.1	1.5	-	-	-	-	33.8	2.1	-	-	-	-	33.6	-0.6	-	-
1968	-	-	33.6	0.0	-	-	-	-	34.5	2.7	-	-	-	-	34.8	0.9	-	-	-	-	34.9	0.3	-	-
1969	-	-	34.8	-0.3	-	-	-	-	35.5	2.0	-	-	-	-	35.6	0.3	-	-	-	-	36.4	2.2	-	-
1970	-	-	35.9	-1.4	-	-	-	-	36.8	2.5	-	-	-	-	37.3	1.4	-	-	-	-	37.4	0.3	-	-
1971	-	-	38.5	2.9	-	-	-	-	38.7	0.5	-	-	-	-	39.9	3.1	-	-	-	-	39.5	-1.0	-	-
1972	-	-	39.2	-0.8	-	-	-	-	40.2	2.6	-	-	-	-	40.4	0.5	-	-	-	-	39.8	-1.5	-	-
1973	-	-	39.6	-0.5	-	-	-	-	41.1	3.8	-	-	-	-	41.4	0.7	-	-	-	-	42.0	1.4	-	-
1974	-	-	43.9	4.5	-	-	-	-	47.0	7.1	-	-	-	-	49.2	4.7	-	-	-	-	49.6	0.8	-	-
1975	-	-	49.6	0.0	-	-	-	-	51.1	3.0	-	-	-	-	53.7	5.1	-	-	-	-	54.0	0.6	-	-
1976	-	-	53.6	-0.7	-	-	-	-	56.1	4.7	-	-	-	-	57.7	2.9	-	-	-	-	59.2	2.6	-	-
1977	-	-	59.4	0.3	-	-	-	-	61.5	3.5	-	-	-	-	61.7	0.3	-	-	-	-	61.3	-0.6	-	-
1978	-	-	61.0	-0.5	-	-	61.4	0.7	-	-	62.6	2.0	-	-	63.4	1.3	-	-	64.4	1.6	-	-	65.0	0.9
1979	-	-	66.1	1.7	-	-	68.9	4.2	-	-	72.3	4.9	-	-	74.4	2.9	-	-	75.4	1.3	-	-	77.8	3.2
1980	-	-	83.3	7.1	-	-	86.2	3.5	-	-	86.6	0.5	-	-	87.6	1.2	-	-	88.1	0.6	-	-	88.6	0.6
1981	-	-	92.3	4.2	-	-	95.1	3.0	-	-	96.5	1.5	-	-	96.5	0.0	-	-	97.2	0.7	-	-	97.6	0.4
1982	-	-	97.2	-0.4	-	-	93.8	-3.5	-	-	98.0	4.5	-	-	99.1	1.1	-	-	98.4	-0.7	-	-	97.9	-0.5
1983	-	-	95.6	-2.3	-	-	97.3	1.8	-	-	99.4	2.2	-	-	100.6	1.2	-	-	102.0	1.4	-	-	101.5	-0.5
1984	-	-	100.7	-0.8	-	-	101.7	1.0	-	-	102.4	0.7	-	-	104.8	2.3	-	-	105.9	1.0	-	-	105.6	-0.3
1985	-	-	104.9	-0.7	-	-	106.5	1.5	-	-	107.6	1.0	-	-	108.0	0.4	-	-	108.6	0.6	-	-	108.7	0.1
1986	-	-	107.9	-0.7	-	-	99.2	-8.1	-	-	100.2	1.0	-	-	98.7	-1.5	-	-	99.2	0.5	-	-	98.7	-0.5
1987	-	-	101.2	2.5	-	-	101.0	-0.2	-	-	103.2	2.2	-	-	104.7	1.5	-	-	105.8	1.1	-	-	107.2	1.3
1988	-	-	107.2	0.0	-	-	106.6	-0.6	-	-	108.2	1.5	-	-	108.4	0.2	-	-	108.8	0.4	-	-	109.0	0.2
1989	-	-	108.9	-0.1	-	-	109.5	0.6	-	-	112.6	2.8	-	-	110.4	-2.0	-	-	111.9	1.4	-	-	112.1	0.2
1990	-	-	113.9	1.6	-	-	113.1	-0.7	-	-	114.1	0.9	-	-	116.6	2.2	-	-	123.6	6.0	-	-	125.3	1.4
1991	-	-	121.0	-3.4	-	-	118.3	-2.2	-	-	119.5	1.0	-	-	120.8	1.1	-	-	121.1	0.2	-	-	123.1	1.7
1992	-	-	121.3	-1.5	-	-	122.4	0.9	-	-	123.0	0.5	-	-	122.9	-0.1	-	-	126.1	2.6	-	-	125.6	-0.4
1993	-	-	125.5	-0.1	-	-	126.1	0.5	-	-	127.9	1.4	-	-	130.4	2.0	-	-	132.1	1.3	-	-	133.1	0.8
1994	-	-	132.8	-0.2	-	-	133.1	0.2	-	-	133.3	0.2	-	-	135.7	1.8	-	-	136.4	0.5	-	-	136.5	0.1
1995	-	-	137.4	0.7	-	-	140.3	2.1	-	-	140.6	0.2	-	-	139.7	-0.6	-	-	140.9	0.9	-	-	138.3	-1.8
1996	-	-	139.6	0.9	-	-	141.9	1.6	-	-	143.5	1.1	-	-	141.2	-1.6	-	-	143.3	1.5	-	-	145.0	1.2
1997	-	-	144.1	-0.6	-	-	143.9	-0.1	-	-	143.3	-0.4	-	-	143.1	-0.1	-	-	141.6	-1.0	-	-	140.0	-1.1

Source: U.S. Department of Labor, Bureau of Labor Statistics, Division of Consumer Prices and Price Indexes. - indicates no data collected for period.

Dallas-Fort Worth, TX
Consumer Price Index - Urban Wage Earners
Base 1982-1984 = 100
Transportation

For 1963-1997. Columns headed % show percentile change in the index from the previous period for which an index is available.

Year	Jan Index	%	Feb Index	%	Mar Index	%	Apr Index	%	May Index	%	Jun Index	%	Jul Index	%	Aug Index	%	Sep Index	%	Oct Index	%	Nov Index	%	Dec Index	%
1963	-	-	-	-	-	-	-	-	-	-	-	-	-	-	-	-	-	-	-	-	31.5	-	-	-
1964	-	-	30.8	-2.2	-	-	-	-	31.9	3.6	-	-	-	-	30.7	-3.8	-	-	-	-	32.0	4.2	-	-
1965	-	-	30.2	-5.6	-	-	-	-	31.9	5.6	-	-	-	-	32.1	0.6	-	-	-	-	32.2	0.3	-	-
1966	-	-	31.7	-1.6	-	-	-	-	32.3	1.9	-	-	-	-	32.4	0.3	-	-	-	-	32.8	1.2	-	-
1967	-	-	32.6	-0.6	-	-	-	-	33.1	1.5	-	-	-	-	33.9	2.4	-	-	-	-	33.6	-0.9	-	-
1968	-	-	33.7	0.3	-	-	-	-	34.5	2.4	-	-	-	-	34.8	0.9	-	-	-	-	35.0	0.6	-	-
1969	-	-	34.8	-0.6	-	-	-	-	35.6	2.3	-	-	-	-	35.6	0.0	-	-	-	-	36.4	2.2	-	-
1970	-	-	36.0	-1.1	-	-	-	-	36.9	2.5	-	-	-	-	37.3	1.1	-	-	-	-	37.5	0.5	-	-
1971	-	-	38.5	2.7	-	-	-	-	38.8	0.8	-	-	-	-	39.9	2.8	-	-	-	-	39.5	-1.0	-	-
1972	-	-	39.2	-0.8	-	-	-	-	40.2	2.6	-	-	-	-	40.4	0.5	-	-	-	-	39.9	-1.2	-	-
1973	-	-	39.6	-0.8	-	-	-	-	41.2	4.0	-	-	-	-	41.4	0.5	-	-	-	-	42.0	1.4	-	-
1974	-	-	43.9	4.5	-	-	-	-	47.0	7.1	-	-	-	-	49.3	4.9	-	-	-	-	49.7	0.8	-	-
1975	-	-	49.6	-0.2	-	-	-	-	51.1	3.0	-	-	-	-	53.7	5.1	-	-	-	-	54.0	0.6	-	-
1976	-	-	53.7	-0.6	-	-	-	-	56.1	4.5	-	-	-	-	57.7	2.9	-	-	-	-	59.2	2.6	-	-
1977	-	-	59.5	0.5	-	-	-	-	61.6	3.5	-	-	-	-	61.7	0.2	-	-	-	-	61.3	-0.6	-	-
1978	-	-	61.0	-0.5	-	-	61.5	0.8	-	-	62.7	2.0	-	-	63.7	1.6	-	-	64.6	1.4	-	-	65.3	1.1
1979	-	-	66.4	1.7	-	-	69.3	4.4	-	-	72.7	4.9	-	-	75.0	3.2	-	-	75.7	0.9	-	-	78.1	3.2
1980	-	-	83.8	7.3	-	-	86.5	3.2	-	-	86.7	0.2	-	-	87.8	1.3	-	-	88.7	1.0	-	-	89.4	0.8
1981	-	-	93.3	4.4	-	-	95.6	2.5	-	-	97.7	2.2	-	-	97.5	-0.2	-	-	98.6	1.1	-	-	98.0	-0.6
1982	-	-	97.5	-0.5	-	-	94.0	-3.6	-	-	98.2	4.5	-	-	99.3	1.1	-	-	98.6	-0.7	-	-	98.0	-0.6
1983	-	-	95.6	-2.4	-	-	97.4	1.9	-	-	99.4	2.1	-	-	100.6	1.2	-	-	102.0	1.4	-	-	101.4	-0.6
1984	-	-	100.6	-0.8	-	-	101.5	0.9	-	-	102.3	0.8	-	-	104.6	2.2	-	-	105.7	1.1	-	-	105.3	-0.4
1985	-	-	104.5	-0.8	-	-	106.2	1.6	-	-	107.3	1.0	-	-	107.6	0.3	-	-	108.3	0.7	-	-	108.4	0.1
1986	-	-	107.6	-0.7	-	-	98.7	-8.3	-	-	99.7	1.0	-	-	98.1	-1.6	-	-	98.4	0.3	-	-	97.8	-0.6
1987	-	-	101.1	3.4	-	-	101.8	0.7	-	-	104.3	2.5	-	-	106.0	1.6	-	-	106.8	0.8	-	-	107.8	0.9
1988	-	-	107.7	-0.1	-	-	106.9	-0.7	-	-	108.4	1.4	-	-	109.2	0.7	-	-	109.5	0.3	-	-	109.5	0.0
1989	-	-	109.2	-0.3	-	-	110.8	1.5	-	-	114.3	3.2	-	-	111.9	-2.1	-	-	112.9	0.9	-	-	112.6	-0.3
1990	-	-	114.4	1.6	-	-	113.5	-0.8	-	-	115.0	1.3	-	-	117.7	2.3	-	-	125.0	6.2	-	-	126.2	1.0
1991	-	-	120.9	-4.2	-	-	118.5	-2.0	-	-	120.6	1.8	-	-	122.0	1.2	-	-	122.9	0.7	-	-	124.4	1.2
1992	-	-	121.8	-2.1	-	-	123.4	1.3	-	-	126.5	2.5	-	-	127.5	0.8	-	-	129.8	1.8	-	-	129.5	-0.2
1993	-	-	128.3	-0.9	-	-	129.5	0.9	-	-	132.1	2.0	-	-	135.1	2.3	-	-	136.9	1.3	-	-	136.6	-0.2
1994	-	-	135.0	-1.2	-	-	135.5	0.4	-	-	136.8	1.0	-	-	139.8	2.2	-	-	141.3	1.1	-	-	141.8	0.4
1995	-	-	142.3	0.4	-	-	144.5	1.5	-	-	145.4	0.6	-	-	144.5	-0.6	-	-	145.0	0.3	-	-	143.2	-1.2
1996	-	-	143.9	0.5	-	-	147.6	2.6	-	-	148.7	0.7	-	-	146.5	-1.5	-	-	148.3	1.2	-	-	149.5	0.8
1997	-	-	149.0	-0.3	-	-	148.5	-0.3	-	-	148.0	-0.3	-	-	147.9	-0.1	-	-	146.6	-0.9	-	-	144.9	-1.2

Source: U.S. Department of Labor, Bureau of Labor Statistics, Division of Consumer Prices and Price Indexes. - indicates no data collected for period.

Dallas-Fort Worth, TX
Consumer Price Index - All Urban Consumers
Base 1982-1984 = 100
Medical Care

For 1963-1997. Columns headed % show percentile change in the index from the previous period for which an index is available.

Year	Jan Index	%	Feb Index	%	Mar Index	%	Apr Index	%	May Index	%	Jun Index	%	Jul Index	%	Aug Index	%	Sep Index	%	Oct Index	%	Nov Index	%	Dec Index	%
1963	-	-	-	-	-	-	-	-	-	-	-	-	-	-	-	-	-	-	-	-	24.1	-	-	-
1964	-	-	24.4	1.2	-	-	-	-	24.5	0.4	-	-	-	-	24.5	0.0	-	-	-	-	24.5	0.0	-	-
1965	-	-	24.8	1.2	-	-	-	-	25.0	0.8	-	-	-	-	25.0	0.0	-	-	-	-	25.2	0.8	-	-
1966	-	-	25.8	2.4	-	-	-	-	26.3	1.9	-	-	-	-	26.6	1.1	-	-	-	-	26.9	1.1	-	-
1967	-	-	28.0	4.1	-	-	-	-	28.0	0.0	-	-	-	-	28.3	1.1	-	-	-	-	28.8	1.8	-	-
1968	-	-	29.5	2.4	-	-	-	-	30.0	1.7	-	-	-	-	30.0	0.0	-	-	-	-	30.5	1.7	-	-
1969	-	-	31.7	3.9	-	-	-	-	32.2	1.6	-	-	-	-	32.6	1.2	-	-	-	-	32.9	0.9	-	-
1970	-	-	34.2	4.0	-	-	-	-	34.8	1.8	-	-	-	-	35.1	0.9	-	-	-	-	35.1	0.0	-	-
1971	-	-	36.1	2.8	-	-	-	-	36.5	1.1	-	-	-	-	36.7	0.5	-	-	-	-	36.4	-0.8	-	-
1972	-	-	36.9	1.4	-	-	-	-	37.1	0.5	-	-	-	-	37.2	0.3	-	-	-	-	37.5	0.8	-	-
1973	-	-	38.2	1.9	-	-	-	-	38.6	1.0	-	-	-	-	38.5	-0.3	-	-	-	-	39.5	2.6	-	-
1974	-	-	40.2	1.8	-	-	-	-	40.9	1.7	-	-	-	-	42.4	3.7	-	-	-	-	43.4	2.4	-	-
1975	-	-	44.6	2.8	-	-	-	-	45.4	1.8	-	-	-	-	46.8	3.1	-	-	-	-	47.2	0.9	-	-
1976	-	-	48.5	2.8	-	-	-	-	48.8	0.6	-	-	-	-	50.7	3.9	-	-	-	-	52.3	3.2	-	-
1977	-	-	53.3	1.9	-	-	-	-	54.8	2.8	-	-	-	-	55.8	1.8	-	-	-	-	57.0	2.2	-	-
1978	-	-	58.3	2.3	-	-	58.9	1.0	-	-	59.8	1.5	-	-	60.0	0.3	-	-	60.4	0.7	-	-	61.1	1.2
1979	-	-	61.3	0.3	-	-	62.2	1.5	-	-	62.4	0.3	-	-	63.5	1.8	-	-	63.6	0.2	-	-	65.2	2.5
1980	-	-	66.5	2.0	-	-	69.0	3.8	-	-	69.7	1.0	-	-	71.9	3.2	-	-	71.8	-0.1	-	-	72.4	0.8
1981	-	-	74.1	2.3	-	-	75.6	2.0	-	-	79.4	5.0	-	-	83.3	4.9	-	-	85.5	2.6	-	-	87.4	2.2
1982	-	-	89.2	2.1	-	-	90.3	1.2	-	-	91.6	1.4	-	-	92.2	0.7	-	-	94.2	2.2	-	-	96.0	1.9
1983	-	-	98.8	2.9	-	-	100.9	2.1	-	-	100.8	-0.1	-	-	102.3	1.5	-	-	102.3	0.0	-	-	104.1	1.8
1984	-	-	105.4	1.2	-	-	106.0	0.6	-	-	106.5	0.5	-	-	107.4	0.8	-	-	108.5	1.0	-	-	109.3	0.7
1985	-	-	110.5	1.1	-	-	111.3	0.7	-	-	112.1	0.7	-	-	114.7	2.3	-	-	116.1	1.2	-	-	122.1	5.2
1986	-	-	123.7	1.3	-	-	125.3	1.3	-	-	126.0	0.6	-	-	127.5	1.2	-	-	129.2	1.3	-	-	130.6	1.1
1987	-	-	130.3	-0.2	-	-	134.0	2.8	-	-	134.3	0.2	-	-	135.4	0.8	-	-	135.3	-0.1	-	-	137.9	1.9
1988	-	-	141.6	2.7	-	-	140.7	-0.6	-	-	140.9	0.1	-	-	141.6	0.5	-	-	142.9	0.9	-	-	145.7	2.0
1989	-	-	148.2	1.7	-	-	148.7	0.3	-	-	149.8	0.7	-	-	151.9	1.4	-	-	154.4	1.6	-	-	154.4	0.0
1990	-	-	156.4	1.3	-	-	156.9	0.3	-	-	162.1	3.3	-	-	163.7	1.0	-	-	167.3	2.2	-	-	168.2	0.5
1991	-	-	170.4	1.3	-	-	170.9	0.3	-	-	174.3	2.0	-	-	176.3	1.1	-	-	179.0	1.5	-	-	180.8	1.0
1992	-	-	182.7	1.1	-	-	185.7	1.6	-	-	187.7	1.1	-	-	188.9	0.6	-	-	193.8	2.6	-	-	194.1	0.2
1993	-	-	193.5	-0.3	-	-	194.0	0.3	-	-	196.7	1.4	-	-	197.9	0.6	-	-	199.7	0.9	-	-	200.6	0.5
1994	-	-	202.1	0.7	-	-	203.7	0.8	-	-	204.5	0.4	-	-	205.3	0.4	-	-	209.6	2.1	-	-	210.8	0.6
1995	-	-	212.8	0.9	-	-	216.2	1.6	-	-	215.6	-0.3	-	-	218.6	1.4	-	-	220.4	0.8	-	-	220.3	-0.0
1996	-	-	224.9	2.1	-	-	225.5	0.3	-	-	228.0	1.1	-	-	223.4	-2.0	-	-	224.1	0.3	-	-	222.6	-0.7
1997	-	-	222.6	0.0	-	-	224.1	0.7	-	-	224.2	0.0	-	-	226.7	1.1	-	-	227.3	0.3	-	-	228.1	0.4

Source: U.S. Department of Labor, Bureau of Labor Statistics, Division of Consumer Prices and Price Indexes. - indicates no data collected for period.

Dallas-Fort Worth, TX
Consumer Price Index - Urban Wage Earners
Base 1982-1984 = 100
Medical Care

For 1963-1997. Columns headed % show percentile change in the index from the previous period for which an index is available.

Year	Jan Index	%	Feb Index	%	Mar Index	%	Apr Index	%	May Index	%	Jun Index	%	Jul Index	%	Aug Index	%	Sep Index	%	Oct Index	%	Nov Index	%	Dec Index	%
1963	-	-	-	-	-	-	-	-	24.9	-	-	-	-	-	-	-	-	-	-	-	24.5	-	-	-
1964	-	-	24.8	1.2	-	-	-	-	24.9	0.4	-	-	-	-	24.9	0.0	-	-	-	-	24.9	0.0	-	-
1965	-	-	25.2	1.2	-	-	-	-	25.4	0.8	-	-	-	-	25.4	0.0	-	-	-	-	25.6	0.8	-	-
1966	-	-	26.2	2.3	-	-	-	-	26.8	2.3	-	-	-	-	27.0	0.7	-	-	-	-	27.3	1.1	-	-
1967	-	-	28.4	4.0	-	-	-	-	28.5	0.4	-	-	-	-	28.8	1.1	-	-	-	-	29.3	1.7	-	-
1968	-	-	30.0	2.4	-	-	-	-	30.5	1.7	-	-	-	-	30.5	0.0	-	-	-	-	31.0	1.6	-	-
1969	-	-	32.2	3.9	-	-	-	-	32.8	1.9	-	-	-	-	33.2	1.2	-	-	-	-	33.5	0.9	-	-
1970	-	-	34.8	3.9	-	-	-	-	35.4	1.7	-	-	-	-	35.7	0.8	-	-	-	-	35.6	-0.3	-	-
1971	-	-	36.7	3.1	-	-	-	-	37.1	1.1	-	-	-	-	37.3	0.5	-	-	-	-	37.0	-0.8	-	-
1972	-	-	37.6	1.6	-	-	-	-	37.7	0.3	-	-	-	-	37.8	0.3	-	-	-	-	38.2	1.1	-	-
1973	-	-	38.8	1.6	-	-	-	-	39.2	1.0	-	-	-	-	39.2	0.0	-	-	-	-	40.1	2.3	-	-
1974	-	-	40.9	2.0	-	-	-	-	41.6	1.7	-	-	-	-	43.1	3.6	-	-	-	-	44.1	2.3	-	-
1975	-	-	45.3	2.7	-	-	-	-	46.2	2.0	-	-	-	-	47.6	3.0	-	-	-	-	48.0	0.8	-	-
1976	-	-	49.3	2.7	-	-	-	-	49.6	0.6	-	-	-	-	51.5	3.8	-	-	-	-	53.2	3.3	-	-
1977	-	-	54.1	1.7	-	-	-	-	55.7	3.0	-	-	-	-	56.7	1.8	-	-	-	-	57.9	2.1	-	-
1978	-	-	59.2	2.2	-	-	59.9	1.2	-	-	60.1	0.3	-	-	60.9	1.3	-	-	61.7	1.3	-	-	63.1	2.3
1979	-	-	63.1	0.0	-	-	64.5	2.2	-	-	65.1	0.9	-	-	66.1	1.5	-	-	66.0	-0.2	-	-	67.3	2.0
1980	-	-	68.2	1.3	-	-	70.2	2.9	-	-	71.1	1.3	-	-	74.6	4.9	-	-	74.5	-0.1	-	-	76.0	2.0
1981	-	-	76.8	1.1	-	-	77.6	1.0	-	-	80.4	3.6	-	-	83.3	3.6	-	-	84.8	1.8	-	-	87.0	2.6
1982	-	-	88.8	2.1	-	-	90.1	1.5	-	-	91.3	1.3	-	-	92.0	0.8	-	-	94.1	2.3	-	-	95.9	1.9
1983	-	-	98.8	3.0	-	-	101.0	2.2	-	-	100.7	-0.3	-	-	102.3	1.6	-	-	102.3	0.0	-	-	104.2	1.9
1984	-	-	105.7	1.4	-	-	106.1	0.4	-	-	106.6	0.5	-	-	107.6	0.9	-	-	108.7	1.0	-	-	109.6	0.8
1985	-	-	110.8	1.1	-	-	111.6	0.7	-	-	112.3	0.6	-	-	115.1	2.5	-	-	116.6	1.3	-	-	122.9	5.4
1986	-	-	124.5	1.3	-	-	126.0	1.2	-	-	126.8	0.6	-	-	128.4	1.3	-	-	130.1	1.3	-	-	131.5	1.1
1987	-	-	131.4	-0.1	-	-	135.1	2.8	-	-	135.5	0.3	-	-	136.8	1.0	-	-	136.8	0.0	-	-	139.8	2.2
1988	-	-	143.1	2.4	-	-	142.0	-0.8	-	-	142.4	0.3	-	-	143.4	0.7	-	-	144.4	0.7	-	-	148.1	2.6
1989	-	-	150.6	1.7	-	-	151.0	0.3	-	-	152.2	0.8	-	-	154.2	1.3	-	-	156.5	1.5	-	-	156.8	0.2
1990	-	-	158.8	1.3	-	-	159.3	0.3	-	-	164.7	3.4	-	-	166.6	1.2	-	-	170.1	2.1	-	-	170.8	0.4
1991	-	-	172.9	1.2	-	-	174.0	0.6	-	-	177.2	1.8	-	-	179.5	1.3	-	-	182.4	1.6	-	-	183.7	0.7
1992	-	-	185.7	1.1	-	-	189.5	2.0	-	-	191.9	1.3	-	-	193.1	0.6	-	-	198.1	2.6	-	-	198.0	-0.1
1993	-	-	197.2	-0.4	-	-	197.6	0.2	-	-	200.9	1.7	-	-	202.1	0.6	-	-	203.8	0.8	-	-	204.7	0.4
1994	-	-	205.9	0.6	-	-	207.4	0.7	-	-	207.9	0.2	-	-	208.8	0.4	-	-	213.3	2.2	-	-	214.6	0.6
1995	-	-	216.5	0.9	-	-	220.9	2.0	-	-	220.3	-0.3	-	-	223.3	1.4	-	-	225.3	0.9	-	-	225.1	-0.1
1996	-	-	229.0	1.7	-	-	229.4	0.2	-	-	232.0	1.1	-	-	226.5	-2.4	-	-	227.8	0.6	-	-	228.0	0.1
1997	-	-	227.7	-0.1	-	-	228.6	0.4	-	-	228.8	0.1	-	-	230.6	0.8	-	-	231.5	0.4	-	-	232.2	0.3

Source: U.S. Department of Labor, Bureau of Labor Statistics, Division of Consumer Prices and Price Indexes. - indicates no data collected for period.

Dallas-Fort Worth, TX
Consumer Price Index - All Urban Consumers
Base 1982-1984 = 100
Entertainment

For 1975-1997. Columns headed % show percentile change in the index from the previous period for which an index is available.

Year	Jan Index	%	Feb Index	%	Mar Index	%	Apr Index	%	May Index	%	Jun Index	%	Jul Index	%	Aug Index	%	Sep Index	%	Oct Index	%	Nov Index	%	Dec Index	%
1975	-	-	-	-	-	-	-	-	-	-	-	-	-	-	-	-	-	-	-	-	64.6	-	-	-
1976	-	-	65.3	1.1	-	-	-	-	67.2	2.9	-	-	-	-	67.8	0.9	-	-	-	-	68.5	1.0	-	-
1977	-	-	68.5	0.0	-	-	-	-	69.7	1.8	-	-	-	-	70.8	1.6	-	-	-	-	69.1	-2.4	-	-
1978	-	-	68.8	-0.4	-	-	68.4	-0.6	-	-	70.5	3.1	-	-	70.5	0.0	-	-	70.6	0.1	-	-	70.9	0.4
1979	-	-	71.8	1.3	-	-	72.3	0.7	-	-	72.9	0.8	-	-	74.1	1.6	-	-	75.4	1.8	-	-	76.5	1.5
1980	-	-	77.3	1.0	-	-	81.4	5.3	-	-	83.2	2.2	-	-	84.5	1.6	-	-	84.8	0.4	-	-	85.8	1.2
1981	-	-	86.4	0.7	-	-	86.0	-0.5	-	-	86.9	1.0	-	-	87.6	0.8	-	-	88.6	1.1	-	-	88.5	-0.1
1982	-	-	90.7	2.5	-	-	90.7	0.0	-	-	93.2	2.8	-	-	93.3	0.1	-	-	97.0	4.0	-	-	95.7	-1.3
1983	-	-	98.2	2.6	-	-	97.4	-0.8	-	-	98.2	0.8	-	-	101.2	3.1	-	-	102.4	1.2	-	-	102.1	-0.3
1984	-	-	104.4	2.3	-	-	106.2	1.7	-	-	106.4	0.2	-	-	106.8	0.4	-	-	110.0	3.0	-	-	111.9	1.7
1985	-	-	114.3	2.1	-	-	114.1	-0.2	-	-	112.5	-1.4	-	-	114.7	2.0	-	-	114.5	-0.2	-	-	115.0	0.4
1986	-	-	113.5	-1.3	-	-	114.4	0.8	-	-	115.7	1.1	-	-	115.6	-0.1	-	-	117.6	1.7	-	-	119.3	1.4
1987	-	-	120.8	1.3	-	-	121.8	0.8	-	-	121.8	0.0	-	-	122.2	0.3	-	-	124.8	2.1	-	-	121.4	-2.7
1988	-	-	124.0	2.1	-	-	128.4	3.5	-	-	127.9	-0.4	-	-	128.7	0.6	-	-	129.2	0.4	-	-	127.4	-1.4
1989	-	-	128.5	0.9	-	-	133.8	4.1	-	-	134.7	0.7	-	-	131.8	-2.2	-	-	134.3	1.9	-	-	135.3	0.7
1990	-	-	134.6	-0.5	-	-	138.4	2.8	-	-	137.8	-0.4	-	-	136.6	-0.9	-	-	139.8	2.3	-	-	138.7	-0.8
1991	-	-	142.4	2.7	-	-	142.6	0.1	-	-	142.5	-0.1	-	-	143.7	0.8	-	-	142.0	-1.2	-	-	142.1	0.1
1992	-	-	142.1	0.0	-	-	142.9	0.6	-	-	141.6	-0.9	-	-	140.9	-0.5	-	-	141.7	0.6	-	-	143.4	1.2
1993	-	-	144.1	0.5	-	-	142.6	-1.0	-	-	143.5	0.6	-	-	143.7	0.1	-	-	145.8	1.5	-	-	145.1	-0.5
1994	-	-	147.1	1.4	-	-	145.6	-1.0	-	-	147.1	1.0	-	-	148.6	1.0	-	-	147.6	-0.7	-	-	147.2	-0.3
1995	-	-	145.7	-1.0	-	-	145.6	-0.1	-	-	148.2	1.8	-	-	151.6	2.3	-	-	155.8	2.8	-	-	157.7	1.2
1996	-	-	161.0	2.1	-	-	161.5	0.3	-	-	162.9	0.9	-	-	162.9	0.0	-	-	163.5	0.4	-	-	167.1	2.2
1997	-	-	168.0	0.5	-	-	169.8	1.1	-	-	167.5	-1.4	-	-	169.6	1.3	-	-	168.2	-0.8	-	-	171.4	1.9

Source: U.S. Department of Labor, Bureau of Labor Statistics, Division of Consumer Prices and Price Indexes. - indicates no data collected for period.

Dallas-Fort Worth, TX
Consumer Price Index - Urban Wage Earners
Base 1982-1984 = 100
Entertainment

For 1975-1997. Columns headed % show percentile change in the index from the previous period for which an index is available.

Year	Jan Index	%	Feb Index	%	Mar Index	%	Apr Index	%	May Index	%	Jun Index	%	Jul Index	%	Aug Index	%	Sep Index	%	Oct Index	%	Nov Index	%	Dec Index	%
1975	-	-	-	-	-	-	-	-	-	-	-	-	-	-	-	-	-	-	-	-	69.0	-	-	-
1976	-	-	69.8	1.2	-	-	-	-	71.8	2.9	-	-	-	-	72.5	1.0	-	-	-	-	73.3	1.1	-	-
1977	-	-	73.3	0.0	-	-	-	-	74.5	1.6	-	-	-	-	75.7	1.6	-	-	-	-	73.9	-2.4	-	-
1978	-	-	73.6	-0.4	-	-	74.3	1.0	-	-	74.8	0.7	-	-	74.5	-0.4	-	-	74.7	0.3	-	-	75.3	0.8
1979	-	-	75.7	0.5	-	-	75.9	0.3	-	-	75.4	-0.7	-	-	76.4	1.3	-	-	79.3	3.8	-	-	78.7	-0.8
1980	-	-	79.8	1.4	-	-	80.3	0.6	-	-	82.8	3.1	-	-	84.0	1.4	-	-	84.3	0.4	-	-	84.9	0.7
1981	-	-	86.4	1.8	-	-	87.1	0.8	-	-	87.4	0.3	-	-	87.9	0.6	-	-	89.0	1.3	-	-	89.1	0.1
1982	-	-	91.4	2.6	-	-	91.4	0.0	-	-	93.7	2.5	-	-	93.8	0.1	-	-	97.0	3.4	-	-	96.3	-0.7
1983	-	-	98.2	2.0	-	-	97.5	-0.7	-	-	98.2	0.7	-	-	101.1	3.0	-	-	102.1	1.0	-	-	101.7	-0.4
1984	-	-	104.2	2.5	-	-	105.9	1.6	-	-	106.5	0.6	-	-	106.5	0.0	-	-	109.4	2.7	-	-	110.5	1.0
1985	-	-	113.3	2.5	-	-	113.1	-0.2	-	-	111.1	-1.8	-	-	113.5	2.2	-	-	113.2	-0.3	-	-	113.7	0.4
1986	-	-	112.5	-1.1	-	-	113.3	0.7	-	-	114.2	0.8	-	-	114.3	0.1	-	-	116.1	1.6	-	-	117.4	1.1
1987	-	-	119.4	1.7	-	-	120.2	0.7	-	-	120.2	0.0	-	-	120.7	0.4	-	-	123.2	2.1	-	-	120.5	-2.2
1988	-	-	122.9	2.0	-	-	126.8	3.2	-	-	126.6	-0.2	-	-	127.5	0.7	-	-	127.5	0.0	-	-	126.1	-1.1
1989	-	-	127.3	1.0	-	-	132.7	4.2	-	-	133.7	0.8	-	-	130.9	-2.1	-	-	133.2	1.8	-	-	134.1	0.7
1990	-	-	133.2	-0.7	-	-	136.3	2.3	-	-	135.6	-0.5	-	-	134.8	-0.6	-	-	137.9	2.3	-	-	136.7	-0.9
1991	-	-	140.6	2.9	-	-	140.9	0.2	-	-	140.8	-0.1	-	-	142.0	0.9	-	-	140.2	-1.3	-	-	140.5	0.2
1992	-	-	140.5	0.0	-	-	141.2	0.5	-	-	139.6	-1.1	-	-	138.6	-0.7	-	-	139.6	0.7	-	-	141.3	1.2
1993	-	-	142.0	0.5	-	-	140.4	-1.1	-	-	140.7	0.2	-	-	141.0	0.2	-	-	143.7	1.9	-	-	143.0	-0.5
1994	-	-	145.2	1.5	-	-	143.4	-1.2	-	-	145.1	1.2	-	-	146.5	1.0	-	-	145.1	-1.0	-	-	144.8	-0.2
1995	-	-	142.6	-1.5	-	-	142.7	0.1	-	-	144.5	1.3	-	-	148.6	2.8	-	-	152.9	2.9	-	-	154.9	1.3
1996	-	-	158.8	2.5	-	-	159.2	0.3	-	-	160.4	0.8	-	-	160.5	0.1	-	-	161.0	0.3	-	-	164.7	2.3
1997	-	-	165.5	0.5	-	-	167.1	1.0	-	-	164.5	-1.6	-	-	167.2	1.6	-	-	165.1	-1.3	-	-	167.7	1.6

Source: U.S. Department of Labor, Bureau of Labor Statistics, Division of Consumer Prices and Price Indexes. - indicates no data collected for period.

Dallas-Fort Worth, TX
Consumer Price Index - All Urban Consumers
Base 1982-1984 = 100
Other Goods and Services

For 1975-1997. Columns headed % show percentile change in the index from the previous period for which an index is available.

Year	Jan Index	%	Feb Index	%	Mar Index	%	Apr Index	%	May Index	%	Jun Index	%	Jul Index	%	Aug Index	%	Sep Index	%	Oct Index	%	Nov Index	%	Dec Index	%
1975	-	-	-	-	-	-	-	-	-	-	-	-	-	-	-	-	-	-	-	-	54.4	-	-	-
1976	-	-	54.8	0.7	-	-	-	-	55.5	1.3	-	-	-	-	55.8	0.5	-	-	-	-	57.5	3.0	-	-
1977	-	-	58.2	1.2	-	-	-	-	59.2	1.7	-	-	-	-	59.9	1.2	-	-	-	-	60.9	1.7	-	-
1978	-	-	61.6	1.1	-	-	61.9	0.5	-	-	61.9	0.0	-	-	64.6	4.4	-	-	65.5	1.4	-	-	66.1	0.9
1979	-	-	67.7	2.4	-	-	67.7	0.0	-	-	67.4	-0.4	-	-	69.0	2.4	-	-	70.5	2.2	-	-	71.6	1.6
1980	-	-	74.1	3.5	-	-	74.6	0.7	-	-	75.0	0.5	-	-	75.1	0.1	-	-	79.2	5.5	-	-	81.2	2.5
1981	-	-	81.3	0.1	-	-	82.9	2.0	-	-	83.3	0.5	-	-	84.6	1.6	-	-	86.5	2.2	-	-	86.8	0.3
1982	-	-	87.9	1.3	-	-	89.5	1.8	-	-	90.7	1.3	-	-	92.5	2.0	-	-	96.1	3.9	-	-	97.2	1.1
1983	-	-	98.3	1.1	-	-	99.5	1.2	-	-	100.3	0.8	-	-	101.9	1.6	-	-	103.4	1.5	-	-	103.5	0.1
1984	-	-	104.9	1.4	-	-	106.2	1.2	-	-	107.0	0.8	-	-	107.2	0.2	-	-	109.8	2.4	-	-	110.1	0.3
1985	-	-	110.1	0.0	-	-	111.0	0.8	-	-	111.2	0.2	-	-	112.5	1.2	-	-	115.7	2.8	-	-	116.0	0.3
1986	-	-	117.0	0.9	-	-	116.7	-0.3	-	-	116.5	-0.2	-	-	120.7	3.6	-	-	122.6	1.6	-	-	126.3	3.0
1987	-	-	128.2	1.5	-	-	128.6	0.3	-	-	127.4	-0.9	-	-	127.3	-0.1	-	-	130.7	2.7	-	-	131.9	0.9
1988	-	-	131.8	-0.1	-	-	133.2	1.1	-	-	134.5	1.0	-	-	135.1	0.4	-	-	138.6	2.6	-	-	139.8	0.9
1989	-	-	143.2	2.4	-	-	144.9	1.2	-	-	144.8	-0.1	-	-	146.0	0.8	-	-	150.5	3.1	-	-	149.9	-0.4
1990	-	-	153.8	2.6	-	-	153.9	0.1	-	-	155.1	0.8	-	-	158.2	2.0	-	-	159.2	0.6	-	-	160.3	0.7
1991	-	-	160.9	0.4	-	-	162.1	0.7	-	-	164.4	1.4	-	-	164.7	0.2	-	-	164.4	-0.2	-	-	167.9	2.1
1992	-	-	170.2	1.4	-	-	169.5	-0.4	-	-	169.4	-0.1	-	-	168.8	-0.4	-	-	173.5	2.8	-	-	172.9	-0.3
1993	-	-	178.4	3.2	-	-	179.9	0.8	-	-	184.9	2.8	-	-	184.7	-0.1	-	-	177.6	-3.8	-	-	178.8	0.7
1994	-	-	179.3	0.3	-	-	179.8	0.3	-	-	182.8	1.7	-	-	182.8	0.0	-	-	180.1	-1.5	-	-	181.9	1.0
1995	-	-	182.2	0.2	-	-	183.5	0.7	-	-	184.5	0.5	-	-	186.9	1.3	-	-	189.1	1.2	-	-	189.8	0.4
1996	-	-	192.2	1.3	-	-	192.6	0.2	-	-	193.5	0.5	-	-	199.2	2.9	-	-	200.0	0.4	-	-	198.6	-0.7
1997	-	-	202.8	2.1	-	-	203.4	0.3	-	-	203.2	-0.1	-	-	205.3	1.0	-	-	208.6	1.6	-	-	214.6	2.9

Source: U.S. Department of Labor, Bureau of Labor Statistics, Division of Consumer Prices and Price Indexes. - indicates no data collected for period.

Dallas-Fort Worth, TX
Consumer Price Index - Urban Wage Earners
Base 1982-1984 = 100
Other Goods and Services

For 1975-1997. Columns headed % show percentile change in the index from the previous period for which an index is available.

Year	Jan Index	%	Feb Index	%	Mar Index	%	Apr Index	%	May Index	%	Jun Index	%	Jul Index	%	Aug Index	%	Sep Index	%	Oct Index	%	Nov Index	%	Dec Index	%
1975	-	-	-	-	-	-	-	-	-	-	-	-	-	-	-	-	-	-	-	-	57.0	-	-	-
1976	-	-	57.4	0.7	-	-	-	-	58.2	1.4	-	-	-	-	58.5	0.5	-	-	-	-	60.2	2.9	-	-
1977	-	-	61.0	1.3	-	-	-	-	62.1	1.8	-	-	-	-	62.8	1.1	-	-	-	-	63.8	1.6	-	-
1978	-	-	64.5	1.1	-	-	65.4	1.4	-	-	65.6	0.3	-	-	67.8	3.4	-	-	68.2	0.6	-	-	68.6	0.6
1979	-	-	70.0	2.0	-	-	70.2	0.3	-	-	70.5	0.4	-	-	71.8	1.8	-	-	73.8	2.8	-	-	75.3	2.0
1980	-	-	77.6	3.1	-	-	78.0	0.5	-	-	78.9	1.2	-	-	79.2	0.4	-	-	82.0	3.5	-	-	83.0	1.2
1981	-	-	84.1	1.3	-	-	83.8	-0.4	-	-	84.1	0.4	-	-	83.7	-0.5	-	-	85.3	1.9	-	-	86.4	1.3
1982	-	-	87.3	1.0	-	-	89.1	2.1	-	-	90.4	1.5	-	-	92.3	2.1	-	-	95.8	3.8	-	-	97.5	1.8
1983	-	-	98.5	1.0	-	-	100.2	1.7	-	-	101.0	0.8	-	-	102.5	1.5	-	-	103.5	1.0	-	-	103.7	0.2
1984	-	-	104.8	1.1	-	-	106.1	1.2	-	-	107.1	0.9	-	-	107.3	0.2	-	-	109.3	1.9	-	-	109.6	0.3
1985	-	-	109.8	0.2	-	-	110.4	0.5	-	-	110.3	-0.1	-	-	112.1	1.6	-	-	114.6	2.2	-	-	114.9	0.3
1986	-	-	116.3	1.2	-	-	115.9	-0.3	-	-	115.5	-0.3	-	-	120.5	4.3	-	-	121.9	1.2	-	-	124.5	2.1
1987	-	-	125.8	1.0	-	-	126.3	0.4	-	-	124.9	-1.1	-	-	124.8	-0.1	-	-	127.8	2.4	-	-	129.3	1.2
1988	-	-	129.0	-0.2	-	-	130.7	1.3	-	-	132.3	1.2	-	-	132.9	0.5	-	-	135.8	2.2	-	-	137.2	1.0
1989	-	-	141.3	3.0	-	-	142.1	0.6	-	-	141.9	-0.1	-	-	143.2	0.9	-	-	147.3	2.9	-	-	146.6	-0.5
1990	-	-	150.9	2.9	-	-	151.1	0.1	-	-	152.3	0.8	-	-	155.9	2.4	-	-	156.8	0.6	-	-	158.2	0.9
1991	-	-	158.9	0.4	-	-	160.4	0.9	-	-	162.2	1.1	-	-	162.6	0.2	-	-	162.2	-0.2	-	-	166.3	2.5
1992	-	-	168.6	1.4	-	-	167.8	-0.5	-	-	167.6	-0.1	-	-	166.8	-0.5	-	-	171.5	2.8	-	-	170.8	-0.4
1993	-	-	176.4	3.3	-	-	178.0	0.9	-	-	183.0	2.8	-	-	182.9	-0.1	-	-	174.4	-4.6	-	-	175.9	0.9
1994	-	-	176.4	0.3	-	-	177.0	0.3	-	-	179.5	1.4	-	-	179.4	-0.1	-	-	176.4	-1.7	-	-	178.2	1.0
1995	-	-	178.5	0.2	-	-	180.0	0.8	-	-	181.0	0.6	-	-	183.4	1.3	-	-	185.5	1.1	-	-	186.4	0.5
1996	-	-	188.8	1.3	-	-	189.2	0.2	-	-	190.2	0.5	-	-	195.3	2.7	-	-	195.9	0.3	-	-	194.1	-0.9
1997	-	-	198.7	2.4	-	-	199.5	0.4	-	-	198.9	-0.3	-	-	200.7	0.9	-	-	203.6	1.4	-	-	210.8	3.5

Source: U.S. Department of Labor, Bureau of Labor Statistics, Division of Consumer Prices and Price Indexes. - indicates no data collected for period.

Denver-Boulder, CO
Consumer Price Index - All Urban Consumers
Base 1982-1984 = 100
Annual Averages

For 1964-1997. Columns headed % show percentile change in the index from the previous period for which an index is available.

Year	All Items		Food & Beverage		Housing		Apparel & Upkeep		Trans-portation		Medical Care		Entertain-ment		Other Goods & Services	
	Index	%	Index	%	Index	%	Index	%	Index	%	Index	%	Index	%	Index	%
1964	28.3	-	-	-	-	-	-	-	-	-	-	-	-	-	-	-
1965	28.8	1.8	-	-	-	-	-	-	-	-	-	-	-	-	-	-
1966	29.7	3.1	-	-	-	-	-	-	-	-	-	-	-	-	-	-
1967	30.0	1.0	-	-	-	-	-	-	-	-	-	-	-	-	-	-
1968	30.7	2.3	-	-	-	-	-	-	-	-	-	-	-	-	-	-
1969	32.0	4.2	-	-	-	-	-	-	-	-	-	-	-	-	-	-
1970	34.5	7.8	-	-	-	-	-	-	-	-	-	-	-	-	-	-
1971	35.9	4.1	-	-	-	-	64.3	-	37.9	-	36.5	-	-	-	-	-
1972	37.0	3.1	-	-	-	-	66.1	2.8	37.8	-0.3	37.6	3.0	-	-	-	-
1973	39.6	7.0	-	-	-	-	68.8	4.1	39.6	4.8	39.0	3.7	-	-	-	-
1974	43.9	10.9	-	-	-	-	74.3	8.0	44.0	11.1	42.6	9.2	-	-	-	-
1975	48.4	10.3	-	-	-	-	78.6	5.8	48.3	9.8	47.4	11.3	-	-	-	-
1976	51.1	5.6	63.8	-	44.4	-	83.1	5.7	52.4	8.5	51.0	7.6	57.8	-	52.2	-
1977	55.4	8.4	68.9	8.0	48.6	9.5	88.0	5.9	56.3	7.4	55.8	9.4	61.5	6.4	56.6	8.4
1978	60.6	9.4	74.9	8.7	54.6	12.3	90.2	2.5	59.8	6.2	60.7	8.8	66.1	7.5	60.8	7.4
1979	70.0	15.5	82.8	10.5	65.6	20.1	92.1	2.1	70.3	17.6	66.2	9.1	72.2	9.2	64.8	6.6
1980	78.4	12.0	86.1	4.0	74.7	13.9	95.6	3.8	82.4	17.2	73.7	11.3	79.7	10.4	72.2	11.4
1981	87.2	11.2	93.2	8.2	84.7	13.4	96.4	0.8	91.7	11.3	81.0	9.9	85.9	7.8	80.9	12.0
1982	95.1	9.1	96.1	3.1	94.8	11.9	101.2	5.0	96.3	5.0	91.1	12.5	94.2	9.7	89.4	10.5
1983	100.5	5.7	99.6	3.6	100.9	6.4	98.8	-2.4	100.1	3.9	100.9	10.8	101.8	8.1	101.5	13.5
1984	104.3	3.8	104.3	4.7	104.1	3.2	100.0	1.2	103.6	3.5	108.0	7.0	104.1	2.3	109.1	7.5
1985	107.1	2.7	106.1	1.7	106.8	2.6	102.6	2.6	105.9	2.2	115.1	6.6	104.4	0.3	115.5	5.9
1986	107.9	0.7	107.2	1.0	108.2	1.3	102.8	0.2	100.9	-4.7	124.0	7.7	106.7	2.2	124.1	7.4
1987	112.7	4.4	111.3	3.8	114.0	5.4	108.5	5.5	103.9	3.0	128.5	3.6	115.8	8.5	123.8	-0.2
1988	116.7	3.5	116.4	4.6	117.8	3.3	105.8	-2.5	107.3	3.3	134.9	5.0	119.9	3.5	133.1	7.5
1989	122.7	5.1	124.0	6.5	122.7	4.2	111.4	5.3	113.0	5.3	143.5	6.4	127.0	5.9	141.0	5.9
1990	129.0	5.1	130.6	5.3	127.7	4.1	117.8	5.7	119.4	5.7	156.6	9.1	133.6	5.2	149.6	6.1
1991	134.2	4.0	135.4	3.7	132.5	3.8	121.9	3.5	123.1	3.1	171.7	9.6	138.6	3.7	160.1	7.0
1992	136.8	1.9	136.1	0.5	135.8	2.5	122.2	0.2	124.1	0.8	178.6	4.0	139.6	0.7	170.2	6.3
1993	140.3	2.6	139.7	2.6	139.0	2.4	125.1	2.4	125.0	0.7	187.2	4.8	143.2	2.6	180.3	5.9
1994	144.4	2.9	144.4	3.4	142.4	2.4	128.8	3.0	128.6	2.9	195.8	4.6	149.4	4.3	184.3	2.2
1995	147.9	2.4	148.9	3.1	145.1	1.9	127.1	-1.3	133.1	3.5	202.6	3.5	153.1	2.5	190.0	3.1
1996	152.0	2.8	154.2	3.6	148.6	2.4	128.8	1.3	138.5	4.1	209.4	3.4	155.8	1.8	193.0	1.6
1997	158.1	4.0	148.0	-4.0	147.7	-0.6	104.0	-19.3	165.6	19.6	265.8	26.9	155.2	-0.4	212.8	10.3

Source: U.S. Department of Labor, Bureau of Labor Statistics, Division of Consumer Prices and Price Indexes. - indicates no data collected for period.

Denver-Boulder, CO
Consumer Price Index - Urban Wage Earners
Base 1982-1984 = 100
Annual Averages

For 1964-1997. Columns headed % show percentile change in the index from the previous period for which an index is available.

Year	All Items		Food & Beverage		Housing		Apparel & Upkeep		Trans-portation		Medical Care		Entertain-ment		Other Goods & Services	
	Index	%	Index	%	Index	%	Index	%	Index	%	Index	%	Index	%	Index	%
1964	28.4	-	-	-	-	-	-	-	-	-	-	-	-	-	-	-
1965	28.8	1.4	-	-	-	-	-	-	-	-	-	-	-	-	-	-
1966	29.7	3.1	-	-	-	-	-	-	-	-	-	-	-	-	-	-
1967	30.0	1.0	-	-	-	-	-	-	-	-	-	-	-	-	-	-
1968	30.8	2.7	-	-	-	-	-	-	-	-	-	-	-	-	-	-
1969	32.1	4.2	-	-	-	-	-	-	-	-	-	-	-	-	-	-
1970	34.5	7.5	-	-	-	-	-	-	-	-	-	-	-	-	-	-
1971	35.9	4.1	-	-	-	-	56.2	-	37.6	-	36.9	-	-	-	-	-
1972	37.1	3.3	-	-	-	-	57.9	3.0	37.5	-0.3	38.0	3.0	-	-	-	-
1973	39.6	6.7	-	-	-	-	60.2	4.0	39.3	4.8	39.4	3.7	-	-	-	-
1974	44.0	11.1	-	-	-	-	65.0	8.0	43.6	10.9	43.1	9.4	-	-	-	-
1975	48.5	10.2	-	-	-	-	68.8	5.8	48.0	10.1	47.8	10.9	-	-	-	-
1976	51.2	5.6	61.7	-	45.2	-	72.7	5.7	51.9	8.1	51.6	7.9	60.7	-	52.3	-
1977	55.5	8.4	66.6	7.9	49.5	9.5	77.0	5.9	55.9	7.7	56.4	9.3	64.6	6.4	56.8	8.6
1978	61.0	9.9	72.9	9.5	55.7	12.5	81.7	6.1	59.1	5.7	61.9	9.8	68.4	5.9	60.7	6.9
1979	70.9	16.2	80.3	10.2	67.5	21.2	88.3	8.1	69.8	18.1	66.4	7.3	73.2	7.0	65.6	8.1
1980	79.9	12.7	85.1	6.0	77.2	14.4	94.2	6.7	82.4	18.1	73.5	10.7	81.6	11.5	72.1	9.9
1981	88.9	11.3	92.9	9.2	87.5	13.3	95.4	1.3	91.8	11.4	81.6	11.0	87.3	7.0	80.3	11.4
1982	97.1	9.2	96.2	3.6	98.2	12.2	100.4	5.2	96.8	5.4	90.9	11.4	94.0	7.7	88.9	10.7
1983	99.8	2.8	99.6	3.5	99.5	1.3	99.0	-1.4	100.0	3.3	101.1	11.2	102.0	8.5	101.8	14.5
1984	103.2	3.4	104.2	4.6	102.3	2.8	100.6	1.6	103.3	3.3	108.0	6.8	104.0	2.0	109.3	7.4
1985	105.9	2.6	106.1	1.8	105.4	3.0	102.4	1.8	105.9	2.5	115.1	6.6	103.1	-0.9	115.4	5.6
1986	106.3	0.4	106.9	0.8	106.6	1.1	101.3	-1.1	100.6	-5.0	124.1	7.8	104.4	1.3	124.1	7.5
1987	108.0	1.6	110.9	3.7	105.7	-0.8	109.2	7.8	102.1	1.5	127.9	3.1	116.0	11.1	124.7	0.5
1988	111.8	3.5	115.9	4.5	109.3	3.4	106.2	-2.7	105.4	3.2	134.1	4.8	120.6	4.0	134.8	8.1
1989	117.3	4.9	123.5	6.6	113.5	3.8	110.7	4.2	110.7	5.0	142.1	6.0	126.3	4.7	143.4	6.4
1990	123.0	4.9	130.2	5.4	117.9	3.9	117.0	5.7	116.6	5.3	154.6	8.8	130.6	3.4	150.7	5.1
1991	127.8	3.9	134.9	3.6	122.2	3.6	121.3	3.7	120.0	2.9	168.7	9.1	134.5	3.0	162.2	7.6
1992	130.3	2.0	135.7	0.6	125.4	2.6	122.4	0.9	120.8	0.7	175.6	4.1	136.2	1.3	173.3	6.8
1993	133.3	2.3	139.3	2.7	128.2	2.2	124.2	1.5	121.7	0.7	184.0	4.8	139.5	2.4	183.9	6.1
1994	137.0	2.8	143.9	3.3	131.1	2.3	127.5	2.7	125.3	3.0	192.3	4.5	144.9	3.9	186.3	1.3
1995	140.2	2.3	148.4	3.1	133.3	1.7	125.2	-1.8	129.8	3.6	199.2	3.6	148.4	2.4	191.3	2.7
1996	144.3	2.9	153.7	3.6	137.1	2.9	126.2	0.8	134.5	3.6	206.6	3.7	151.5	2.1	193.2	1.0
1997	153.6	6.4	147.0	-4.4	143.9	5.0	102.3	-18.9	163.9	21.9	264.6	28.1	144.6	-4.6	206.8	7.0

Source: U.S. Department of Labor, Bureau of Labor Statistics, Division of Consumer Prices and Price Indexes. - indicates no data collected for period.

Denver-Boulder, CO
Consumer Price Index - All Urban Consumers
Base 1982-1984 = 100
All Items

For 1964-1997. Columns headed % show percentile change in the index from the previous period for which an index is available.

Year	Jan Index	%	Feb Index	%	Mar Index	%	Apr Index	%	May Index	%	Jun Index	%	Jul Index	%	Aug Index	%	Sep Index	%	Oct Index	%	Nov Index	%	Dec Index	%
1964	28.2	-	-	-	-	-	28.0	-0.7	-	-	-	-	28.5	1.8	-	-	-	-	28.5	0.0	-	-	-	-
1965	28.5	0.0	-	-	-	-	28.6	0.4	-	-	-	-	28.9	1.0	-	-	-	-	28.9	0.0	-	-	-	-
1966	29.2	1.0	-	-	-	-	29.6	1.4	-	-	-	-	29.7	0.3	-	-	-	-	29.9	0.7	-	-	-	-
1967	29.7	-0.7	-	-	-	-	29.7	0.0	-	-	-	-	30.1	1.3	-	-	-	-	30.2	0.3	-	-	-	-
1968	30.4	0.7	-	-	-	-	30.7	1.0	-	-	-	-	30.7	0.0	-	-	-	-	30.9	0.7	-	-	-	-
1969	31.1	0.6	-	-	-	-	31.6	1.6	-	-	-	-	32.0	1.3	-	-	-	-	32.7	2.2	-	-	-	-
1970	33.0	0.9	-	-	-	-	33.9	2.7	-	-	-	-	34.9	2.9	-	-	-	-	35.2	0.9	-	-	-	-
1971	35.3	0.3	-	-	-	-	35.5	0.6	-	-	-	-	36.0	1.4	-	-	-	-	36.3	0.8	-	-	-	-
1972	36.3	0.0	-	-	-	-	36.9	1.7	-	-	-	-	37.0	0.3	-	-	-	-	37.4	1.1	-	-	-	-
1973	37.8	1.1	-	-	-	-	39.0	3.2	-	-	-	-	39.6	1.5	-	-	-	-	40.6	2.5	-	-	-	-
1974	41.5	2.2	-	-	-	-	42.7	2.9	-	-	-	-	44.1	3.3	-	-	-	-	45.6	3.4	-	-	-	-
1975	46.9	2.9	-	-	-	-	47.6	1.5	-	-	-	-	48.7	2.3	-	-	-	-	49.3	1.2	-	-	-	-
1976	49.7	0.8	-	-	-	-	50.4	1.4	-	-	-	-	51.4	2.0	-	-	-	-	51.9	1.0	-	-	-	-
1977	52.7	1.5	-	-	-	-	54.8	4.0	-	-	-	-	55.8	1.8	-	-	-	-	56.6	1.4	-	-	-	-
1978	57.7	1.9	-	-	58.5	1.4	-	-	59.5	1.7	-	-	60.7	2.0	-	-	62.1	2.3	-	-	63.4	2.1	-	-
1979	64.8	2.2	-	-	66.9	3.2	-	-	69.3	3.6	-	-	70.9	2.3	-	-	72.2	1.8	-	-	73.7	2.1	-	-
1980	74.2	0.7	-	-	76.5	3.1	-	-	77.4	1.2	-	-	78.5	1.4	-	-	80.2	2.2	-	-	81.5	1.6	-	-
1981	83.2	2.1	-	-	84.4	1.4	-	-	86.4	2.4	-	-	88.2	2.1	-	-	89.6	1.6	-	-	89.3	-0.3	-	-
1982	91.6	2.6	-	-	92.7	1.2	-	-	94.0	1.4	-	-	95.9	2.0	-	-	97.3	1.5	-	-	97.8	0.5	-	-
1983	98.2	0.4	-	-	98.8	0.6	-	-	100.4	1.6	-	-	100.7	0.3	-	-	101.8	1.1	-	-	101.9	0.1	-	-
1984	103.0	1.1	-	-	103.5	0.5	-	-	103.9	0.4	-	-	104.9	1.0	-	-	105.4	0.5	-	-	104.8	-0.6	-	-
1985	105.1	0.3	-	-	106.5	1.3	-	-	106.8	0.3	-	-	108.0	1.1	-	-	107.4	-0.6	-	-	107.8	0.4	-	-
1986	109.3	1.4	-	-	106.7	-2.4	-	-	106.8	0.1	-	-	107.5	0.7	-	-	108.8	1.2	-	-	108.3	-0.5	108.4	0.1
1987	-	-	-	-	-	-	-	-	-	-	111.2	2.6	-	-	-	-	-	-	-	-	-	-	114.1	2.6
1988	-	-	-	-	-	-	-	-	-	-	115.5	1.2	-	-	-	-	-	-	-	-	-	-	117.8	2.0
1989	-	-	-	-	-	-	-	-	-	-	121.5	3.1	-	-	-	-	-	-	-	-	-	-	123.9	2.0
1990	-	-	-	-	-	-	-	-	-	-	127.1	2.6	-	-	-	-	-	-	-	-	-	-	130.8	2.9
1991	-	-	-	-	-	-	-	-	-	-	133.3	1.9	-	-	-	-	-	-	-	-	-	-	135.2	1.4
1992	-	-	-	-	-	-	-	-	-	-	136.3	0.8	-	-	-	-	-	-	-	-	-	-	137.4	0.8
1993	-	-	-	-	-	-	-	-	-	-	138.9	1.1	-	-	-	-	-	-	-	-	-	-	141.7	2.0
1994	-	-	-	-	-	-	-	-	-	-	143.2	1.1	-	-	-	-	-	-	-	-	-	-	145.6	1.7
1995	-	-	-	-	-	-	-	-	-	-	147.2	1.1	-	-	-	-	-	-	-	-	-	-	148.5	0.9
1996	-	-	-	-	-	-	-	-	-	-	150.8	1.5	-	-	-	-	-	-	-	-	-	-	153.3	1.7
1997	-	-	-	-	-	-	-	-	-	-	155.1	1.2	-	-	-	-	-	-	-	-	-	-	-	-

Source: U.S. Department of Labor, Bureau of Labor Statistics, Division of Consumer Prices and Price Indexes. - indicates no data collected for period.

Denver-Boulder, CO
Consumer Price Index - Urban Wage Earners
Base 1982-1984 = 100
All Items

For 1964-1997. Columns headed % show percentile change in the index from the previous period for which an index is available.

Year	Jan Index	%	Feb Index	%	Mar Index	%	Apr Index	%	May Index	%	Jun Index	%	Jul Index	%	Aug Index	%	Sep Index	%	Oct Index	%	Nov Index	%	Dec Index	%
1964	28.2	-	-	-	-	-	28.1	-0.4	-	-	-	-	28.5	1.4	-	-	-	-	28.5	0.0	-	-	-	-
1965	28.6	0.4	-	-	-	-	28.6	0.0	-	-	-	-	29.0	1.4	-	-	-	-	29.0	0.0	-	-	-	-
1966	29.2	0.7	-	-	-	-	29.7	1.7	-	-	-	-	29.8	0.3	-	-	-	-	30.0	0.7	-	-	-	-
1967	29.8	-0.7	-	-	-	-	29.8	0.0	-	-	-	-	30.1	1.0	-	-	-	-	30.3	0.7	-	-	-	-
1968	30.5	0.7	-	-	-	-	30.7	0.7	-	-	-	-	30.7	0.0	-	-	-	-	31.0	1.0	-	-	-	-
1969	31.1	0.3	-	-	-	-	31.7	1.9	-	-	-	-	32.1	1.3	-	-	-	-	32.8	2.2	-	-	-	-
1970	33.1	0.9	-	-	-	-	34.0	2.7	-	-	-	-	35.0	2.9	-	-	-	-	35.3	0.9	-	-	-	-
1971	35.4	0.3	-	-	-	-	35.6	0.6	-	-	-	-	36.1	1.4	-	-	-	-	36.4	0.8	-	-	-	-
1972	36.4	0.0	-	-	-	-	36.9	1.4	-	-	-	-	37.0	0.3	-	-	-	-	37.5	1.4	-	-	-	-
1973	37.8	0.8	-	-	-	-	39.1	3.4	-	-	-	-	39.7	1.5	-	-	-	-	40.7	2.5	-	-	-	-
1974	41.6	2.2	-	-	-	-	42.8	2.9	-	-	-	-	44.2	3.3	-	-	-	-	45.6	3.2	-	-	-	-
1975	47.0	3.1	-	-	-	-	47.7	1.5	-	-	-	-	48.8	2.3	-	-	-	-	49.4	1.2	-	-	-	-
1976	49.8	0.8	-	-	-	-	50.4	1.2	-	-	-	-	51.5	2.2	-	-	-	-	52.0	1.0	-	-	-	-
1977	52.8	1.5	-	-	-	-	54.9	4.0	-	-	-	-	55.9	1.8	-	-	-	-	56.7	1.4	-	-	-	-
1978	57.8	1.9	-	-	58.8	1.7	-	-	59.9	1.9	-	-	61.0	1.8	-	-	62.5	2.5	-	-	64.0	2.4	-	-
1979	65.5	2.3	-	-	67.6	3.2	-	-	70.1	3.7	-	-	71.9	2.6	-	-	73.2	1.8	-	-	74.7	2.0	-	-
1980	75.4	0.9	-	-	77.9	3.3	-	-	78.8	1.2	-	-	79.9	1.4	-	-	81.6	2.1	-	-	83.1	1.8	-	-
1981	84.8	2.0	-	-	85.9	1.3	-	-	88.1	2.6	-	-	90.1	2.3	-	-	91.4	1.4	-	-	91.0	-0.4	-	-
1982	93.3	2.5	-	-	94.6	1.4	-	-	96.0	1.5	-	-	98.0	2.1	-	-	99.5	1.5	-	-	99.9	0.4	-	-
1983	97.3	-2.6	-	-	98.2	0.9	-	-	99.7	1.5	-	-	99.7	0.0	-	-	101.3	1.6	-	-	101.7	0.4	-	-
1984	101.0	-0.7	-	-	102.7	1.7	-	-	102.4	-0.3	-	-	104.3	1.9	-	-	104.0	-0.3	-	-	103.7	-0.3	-	-
1985	104.0	0.3	-	-	105.4	1.3	-	-	105.7	0.3	-	-	106.9	1.1	-	-	106.1	-0.7	-	-	106.4	0.3	-	-
1986	107.9	1.4	-	-	105.2	-2.5	-	-	105.2	0.0	-	-	105.9	0.7	-	-	107.3	1.3	-	-	106.7	-0.6	106.7	0.0
1987	-	-	-	-	-	-	-	-	-	-	106.6	-0.1	-	-	-	-	-	-	-	-	-	-	109.4	2.6
1988	-	-	-	-	-	-	-	-	-	-	110.7	1.2	-	-	-	-	-	-	-	-	-	-	112.9	2.0
1989	-	-	-	-	-	-	-	-	-	-	116.3	3.0	-	-	-	-	-	-	-	-	-	-	118.4	1.8
1990	-	-	-	-	-	-	-	-	-	-	121.3	2.4	-	-	-	-	-	-	-	-	-	-	124.8	2.9
1991	-	-	-	-	-	-	-	-	-	-	126.9	1.7	-	-	-	-	-	-	-	-	-	-	128.7	1.4
1992	-	-	-	-	-	-	-	-	-	-	129.7	0.8	-	-	-	-	-	-	-	-	-	-	130.9	0.9
1993	-	-	-	-	-	-	-	-	-	-	132.0	0.8	-	-	-	-	-	-	-	-	-	-	134.6	2.0
1994	-	-	-	-	-	-	-	-	-	-	135.7	0.8	-	-	-	-	-	-	-	-	-	-	138.2	1.8
1995	-	-	-	-	-	-	-	-	-	-	139.6	1.0	-	-	-	-	-	-	-	-	-	-	140.8	0.9
1996	-	-	-	-	-	-	-	-	-	-	143.1	1.6	-	-	-	-	-	-	-	-	-	-	145.6	1.7
1997	-	-	-	-	-	-	-	-	-	-	147.3	1.2	-	-	-	-	-	-	-	-	-	-	-	-

Source: U.S. Department of Labor, Bureau of Labor Statistics, Division of Consumer Prices and Price Indexes. - indicates no data collected for period.

Denver-Boulder, CO
Consumer Price Index - All Urban Consumers
Base 1982-1984 = 100
Food and Beverages

For 1976-1997. Columns headed % show percentile change in the index from the previous period for which an index is available.

Year	Jan Index	%	Feb Index	%	Mar Index	%	Apr Index	%	May Index	%	Jun Index	%	Jul Index	%	Aug Index	%	Sep Index	%	Oct Index	%	Nov Index	%	Dec Index	%
1976	63.3	-	-	-	-	-	62.7	-0.9	-	-	-	-	64.1	2.2	-	-	-	-	64.3	0.3	-	-	-	-
1977	65.7	2.2	-	-	-	-	69.2	5.3	-	-	-	-	70.1	1.3	-	-	-	-	68.8	-1.9	-	-	-	-
1978	70.8	2.9	-	-	72.4	2.3	-	-	74.7	3.2	-	-	76.1	1.9	-	-	76.2	0.1	-	-	77.2	1.3	-	-
1979	80.2	3.9	-	-	82.4	2.7	-	-	83.4	1.2	-	-	84.1	0.8	-	-	83.0	-1.3	-	-	83.6	0.7	-	-
1980	81.9	-2.0	-	-	82.6	0.9	-	-	84.3	2.1	-	-	86.1	2.1	-	-	89.3	3.7	-	-	90.1	0.9	-	-
1981	90.8	0.8	-	-	92.0	1.3	-	-	92.9	1.0	-	-	94.2	1.4	-	-	94.6	0.4	-	-	93.9	-0.7	-	-
1982	94.9	1.1	-	-	95.6	0.7	-	-	95.9	0.3	-	-	96.5	0.6	-	-	96.5	0.0	-	-	96.7	0.2	-	-
1983	97.1	0.4	-	-	98.2	1.1	-	-	100.2	2.0	-	-	99.8	-0.4	-	-	100.2	0.4	-	-	100.7	0.5	-	-
1984	102.7	2.0	-	-	104.3	1.6	-	-	104.0	-0.3	-	-	104.8	0.8	-	-	104.9	0.1	-	-	104.5	-0.4	-	-
1985	104.9	0.4	-	-	107.4	2.4	-	-	105.9	-1.4	-	-	106.9	0.9	-	-	105.5	-1.3	-	-	105.5	0.0	-	-
1986	107.8	2.2	-	-	107.3	-0.5	-	-	105.5	-1.7	-	-	106.0	0.5	-	-	108.5	2.4	-	-	108.1	-0.4	108.1	0.0
1987	-	-	-	-	-	-	-	-	-	-	110.7	2.4	-	-	-	-	-	-	-	-	-	-	111.9	1.1
1988	-	-	-	-	-	-	-	-	-	-	114.4	2.2	-	-	-	-	-	-	-	-	-	-	118.4	3.5
1989	-	-	-	-	-	-	-	-	-	-	122.4	3.4	-	-	-	-	-	-	-	-	-	-	125.6	2.6
1990	-	-	-	-	-	-	-	-	-	-	129.4	3.0	-	-	-	-	-	-	-	-	-	-	131.7	1.8
1991	-	-	-	-	-	-	-	-	-	-	135.6	3.0	-	-	-	-	-	-	-	-	-	-	135.1	-0.4
1992	-	-	-	-	-	-	-	-	-	-	136.3	0.9	-	-	-	-	-	-	-	-	-	-	136.0	-0.2
1993	-	-	-	-	-	-	-	-	-	-	138.3	1.7	-	-	-	-	-	-	-	-	-	-	141.2	2.1
1994	-	-	-	-	-	-	-	-	-	-	142.9	1.2	-	-	-	-	-	-	-	-	-	-	145.9	2.1
1995	-	-	-	-	-	-	-	-	-	-	148.1	1.5	-	-	-	-	-	-	-	-	-	-	149.8	1.1
1996	-	-	-	-	-	-	-	-	-	-	152.2	1.6	-	-	-	-	-	-	-	-	-	-	156.2	2.6
1997	-	-	-	-	-	-	-	-	-	-	157.3	0.7	-	-	-	-	-	-	-	-	-	-	-	-

Source: U.S. Department of Labor, Bureau of Labor Statistics, Division of Consumer Prices and Price Indexes. - indicates no data collected for period.

Denver-Boulder, CO
Consumer Price Index - Urban Wage Earners
Base 1982-1984 = 100
Food and Beverages

For 1976-1997. Columns headed % show percentile change in the index from the previous period for which an index is available.

Year	Jan Index	%	Feb Index	%	Mar Index	%	Apr Index	%	May Index	%	Jun Index	%	Jul Index	%	Aug Index	%	Sep Index	%	Oct Index	%	Nov Index	%	Dec Index	%
1976	61.2	-	-	-	-	-	60.7	-0.8	-	-	-	-	62.0	2.1	-	-	-	-	62.2	0.3	-	-	-	-
1977	63.5	2.1	-	-	-	-	67.0	5.5	-	-	-	-	67.8	1.2	-	-	-	-	66.6	-1.8	-	-	-	-
1978	68.4	2.7	-	-	70.7	3.4	-	-	72.9	3.1	-	-	73.7	1.1	-	-	74.1	0.5	-	-	75.3	1.6	-	-
1979	78.0	3.6	-	-	79.5	1.9	-	-	80.3	1.0	-	-	81.4	1.4	-	-	80.3	-1.4	-	-	81.6	1.6	-	-
1980	80.8	-1.0	-	-	81.8	1.2	-	-	83.5	2.1	-	-	85.4	2.3	-	-	88.1	3.2	-	-	88.7	0.7	-	-
1981	90.1	1.6	-	-	91.5	1.6	-	-	92.1	0.7	-	-	93.9	2.0	-	-	94.1	0.2	-	-	94.2	0.1	-	-
1982	95.0	0.8	-	-	95.6	0.6	-	-	96.0	0.4	-	-	96.7	0.7	-	-	96.7	0.0	-	-	96.8	0.1	-	-
1983	97.2	0.4	-	-	98.3	1.1	-	-	100.1	1.8	-	-	99.8	-0.3	-	-	100.1	0.3	-	-	100.7	0.6	-	-
1984	102.6	1.9	-	-	104.1	1.5	-	-	103.8	-0.3	-	-	104.7	0.9	-	-	105.0	0.3	-	-	104.6	-0.4	-	-
1985	104.9	0.3	-	-	107.4	2.4	-	-	105.8	-1.5	-	-	106.8	0.9	-	-	105.5	-1.2	-	-	105.4	-0.1	-	-
1986	107.7	2.2	-	-	106.9	-0.7	-	-	105.1	-1.7	-	-	105.6	0.5	-	-	108.2	2.5	-	-	107.9	-0.3	107.8	-0.1
1987	-	-	-	-	-	-	-	-	-	-	110.3	2.3	-	-	-	-	-	-	-	-	-	-	111.5	1.1
1988	-	-	-	-	-	-	-	-	-	-	113.9	2.2	-	-	-	-	-	-	-	-	-	-	117.9	3.5
1989	-	-	-	-	-	-	-	-	-	-	121.9	3.4	-	-	-	-	-	-	-	-	-	-	125.2	2.7
1990	-	-	-	-	-	-	-	-	-	-	129.0	3.0	-	-	-	-	-	-	-	-	-	-	131.4	1.9
1991	-	-	-	-	-	-	-	-	-	-	135.2	2.9	-	-	-	-	-	-	-	-	-	-	134.6	-0.4
1992	-	-	-	-	-	-	-	-	-	-	135.8	0.9	-	-	-	-	-	-	-	-	-	-	135.5	-0.2
1993	-	-	-	-	-	-	-	-	-	-	137.9	1.8	-	-	-	-	-	-	-	-	-	-	140.7	2.0
1994	-	-	-	-	-	-	-	-	-	-	142.4	1.2	-	-	-	-	-	-	-	-	-	-	145.3	2.0
1995	-	-	-	-	-	-	-	-	-	-	147.5	1.5	-	-	-	-	-	-	-	-	-	-	149.2	1.2
1996	-	-	-	-	-	-	-	-	-	-	151.7	1.7	-	-	-	-	-	-	-	-	-	-	155.7	2.6
1997	-	-	-	-	-	-	-	-	-	-	156.8	0.7	-	-	-	-	-	-	-	-	-	-	-	-

Source: U.S. Department of Labor, Bureau of Labor Statistics, Division of Consumer Prices and Price Indexes. - indicates no data collected for period.

Denver-Boulder, CO
Consumer Price Index - All Urban Consumers
Base 1982-1984 = 100
Housing

For 1976-1997. Columns headed % show percentile change in the index from the previous period for which an index is available.

Year	Jan Index	%	Feb Index	%	Mar Index	%	Apr Index	%	May Index	%	Jun Index	%	Jul Index	%	Aug Index	%	Sep Index	%	Oct Index	%	Nov Index	%	Dec Index	%
1976	43.1	-	-	-	-	-	43.8	1.6	-	-	-	-	44.8	2.3	-	-	-	-	44.9	0.2	-	-	-	-
1977	45.6	1.6	-	-	-	-	47.9	5.0	-	-	-	-	48.8	1.9	-	-	-	-	50.3	3.1	-	-	-	-
1978	51.4	2.2	-	-	52.5	2.1	-	-	53.1	1.1	-	-	54.3	2.3	-	-	56.2	3.5	-	-	58.1	3.4	-	-
1979	59.7	2.8	-	-	61.7	3.4	-	-	64.6	4.7	-	-	66.7	3.3	-	-	68.1	2.1	-	-	70.1	2.9	-	-
1980	70.4	0.4	-	-	73.0	3.7	-	-	73.6	0.8	-	-	74.8	1.6	-	-	76.3	2.0	-	-	77.9	2.1	-	-
1981	80.1	2.8	-	-	80.7	0.7	-	-	83.7	3.7	-	-	86.2	3.0	-	-	87.9	2.0	-	-	87.0	-1.0	-	-
1982	90.3	3.8	-	-	92.0	1.9	-	-	93.8	2.0	-	-	95.9	2.2	-	-	97.7	1.9	-	-	98.1	0.4	-	-
1983	99.4	1.3	-	-	100.6	1.2	-	-	101.0	0.4	-	-	100.5	-0.5	-	-	101.7	1.2	-	-	101.0	-0.7	-	-
1984	103.2	2.2	-	-	102.7	-0.5	-	-	102.9	0.2	-	-	105.5	2.5	-	-	105.5	0.0	-	-	104.3	-1.1	-	-
1985	105.9	1.5	-	-	106.1	0.2	-	-	106.1	0.0	-	-	107.9	1.7	-	-	106.6	-1.2	-	-	107.4	0.8	-	-
1986	110.6	3.0	-	-	107.3	-3.0	-	-	107.7	0.4	-	-	108.1	0.4	-	-	108.2	0.1	-	-	107.6	-0.6	108.2	0.6
1987	-	-	-	-	-	-	-	-	-	-	112.7	4.2	-	-	-	-	-	-	-	-	-	-	115.2	2.2
1988	-	-	-	-	-	-	-	-	-	-	116.6	1.2	-	-	-	-	-	-	-	-	-	-	119.1	2.1
1989	-	-	-	-	-	-	-	-	-	-	121.5	2.0	-	-	-	-	-	-	-	-	-	-	123.9	2.0
1990	-	-	-	-	-	-	-	-	-	-	125.8	1.5	-	-	-	-	-	-	-	-	-	-	129.6	3.0
1991	-	-	-	-	-	-	-	-	-	-	131.3	1.3	-	-	-	-	-	-	-	-	-	-	133.6	1.8
1992	-	-	-	-	-	-	-	-	-	-	134.9	1.0	-	-	-	-	-	-	-	-	-	-	136.6	1.3
1993	-	-	-	-	-	-	-	-	-	-	137.8	0.9	-	-	-	-	-	-	-	-	-	-	140.3	1.8
1994	-	-	-	-	-	-	-	-	-	-	141.9	1.1	-	-	-	-	-	-	-	-	-	-	143.0	0.8
1995	-	-	-	-	-	-	-	-	-	-	143.8	0.6	-	-	-	-	-	-	-	-	-	-	146.4	1.8
1996	-	-	-	-	-	-	-	-	-	-	147.5	0.8	-	-	-	-	-	-	-	-	-	-	149.6	1.4
1997	-	-	-	-	-	-	-	-	-	-	151.7	1.4	-	-	-	-	-	-	-	-	-	-	-	-

Source: U.S. Department of Labor, Bureau of Labor Statistics, Division of Consumer Prices and Price Indexes. - indicates no data collected for period.

Denver-Boulder, CO
Consumer Price Index - Urban Wage Earners
Base 1982-1984 = 100
Housing

For 1976-1997. Columns headed % show percentile change in the index from the previous period for which an index is available.

Year	Jan Index	%	Feb Index	%	Mar Index	%	Apr Index	%	May Index	%	Jun Index	%	Jul Index	%	Aug Index	%	Sep Index	%	Oct Index	%	Nov Index	%	Dec Index	%
1976	43.8	-	-	-	-	-	44.6	1.8	-	-	-	-	45.6	2.2	-	-	-	-	45.8	0.4	-	-	-	-
1977	46.4	1.3	-	-	-	-	48.8	5.2	-	-	-	-	49.7	1.8	-	-	-	-	51.2	3.0	-	-	-	-
1978	52.4	2.3	-	-	53.5	2.1	-	-	54.2	1.3	-	-	55.4	2.2	-	-	57.5	3.8	-	-	59.4	3.3	-	-
1979	61.2	3.0	-	-	63.4	3.6	-	-	66.5	4.9	-	-	68.7	3.3	-	-	70.1	2.0	-	-	72.2	3.0	-	-
1980	72.6	0.6	-	-	75.4	3.9	-	-	76.0	0.8	-	-	77.1	1.4	-	-	78.8	2.2	-	-	80.6	2.3	-	-
1981	82.8	2.7	-	-	83.2	0.5	-	-	86.6	4.1	-	-	89.1	2.9	-	-	90.8	1.9	-	-	89.8	-1.1	-	-
1982	93.3	3.9	-	-	95.3	2.1	-	-	97.2	2.0	-	-	99.5	2.4	-	-	101.4	1.9	-	-	101.6	0.2	-	-
1983	97.3	-4.2	-	-	98.6	1.3	-	-	99.6	1.0	-	-	98.8	-0.8	-	-	101.1	2.3	-	-	101.1	0.0	-	-
1984	99.7	-1.4	-	-	101.8	2.1	-	-	100.9	-0.9	-	-	104.3	3.4	-	-	103.1	-1.2	-	-	102.8	-0.3	-	-
1985	104.5	1.7	-	-	104.6	0.1	-	-	104.7	0.1	-	-	106.3	1.5	-	-	105.1	-1.1	-	-	105.9	0.8	-	-
1986	109.0	2.9	-	-	105.6	-3.1	-	-	106.1	0.5	-	-	106.6	0.5	-	-	106.7	0.1	-	-	106.1	-0.6	106.7	0.6
1987	-	-	-	-	-	-	-	-	-	-	104.6	-2.0	-	-	-	-	-	-	-	-	-	-	106.9	2.2
1988	-	-	-	-	-	-	-	-	-	-	108.2	1.2	-	-	-	-	-	-	-	-	-	-	110.4	2.0
1989	-	-	-	-	-	-	-	-	-	-	112.4	1.8	-	-	-	-	-	-	-	-	-	-	114.6	2.0
1990	-	-	-	-	-	-	-	-	-	-	116.2	1.4	-	-	-	-	-	-	-	-	-	-	119.6	2.9
1991	-	-	-	-	-	-	-	-	-	-	121.0	1.2	-	-	-	-	-	-	-	-	-	-	123.4	2.0
1992	-	-	-	-	-	-	-	-	-	-	124.6	1.0	-	-	-	-	-	-	-	-	-	-	126.2	1.3
1993	-	-	-	-	-	-	-	-	-	-	127.1	0.7	-	-	-	-	-	-	-	-	-	-	129.4	1.8
1994	-	-	-	-	-	-	-	-	-	-	130.4	0.8	-	-	-	-	-	-	-	-	-	-	131.7	1.0
1995	-	-	-	-	-	-	-	-	-	-	132.2	0.4	-	-	-	-	-	-	-	-	-	-	134.5	1.7
1996	-	-	-	-	-	-	-	-	-	-	136.0	1.1	-	-	-	-	-	-	-	-	-	-	138.2	1.6
1997	-	-	-	-	-	-	-	-	-	-	140.1	1.4	-	-	-	-	-	-	-	-	-	-	-	-

Source: U.S. Department of Labor, Bureau of Labor Statistics, Division of Consumer Prices and Price Indexes. - indicates no data collected for period.

Denver-Boulder, CO
Consumer Price Index - All Urban Consumers
Base 1982-1984 = 100
Apparel and Upkeep

For 1971-1997. Columns headed % show percentile change in the index from the previous period for which an index is available.

Year	Jan Index	%	Feb Index	%	Mar Index	%	Apr Index	%	May Index	%	Jun Index	%	Jul Index	%	Aug Index	%	Sep Index	%	Oct Index	%	Nov Index	%	Dec Index	%
1971	62.3	-	-	-	-	-	63.5	1.9	-	-	-	-	63.3	-0.3	-	-	-	-	66.9	5.7	-	-	-	-
1972	65.3	-2.4	-	-	-	-	66.2	1.4	-	-	-	-	65.4	-1.2	-	-	-	-	67.6	3.4	-	-	-	-
1973	65.6	-3.0	-	-	-	-	68.4	4.3	-	-	-	-	68.2	-0.3	-	-	-	-	71.2	4.4	-	-	-	-
1974	71.2	0.0	-	-	-	-	73.1	2.7	-	-	-	-	74.3	1.6	-	-	-	-	77.3	4.0	-	-	-	-
1975	75.8	-1.9	-	-	-	-	77.2	1.8	-	-	-	-	78.0	1.0	-	-	-	-	82.1	5.3	-	-	-	-
1976	79.9	-2.7	-	-	-	-	82.5	3.3	-	-	-	-	82.5	0.0	-	-	-	-	86.0	4.2	-	-	-	-
1977	83.8	-2.6	-	-	-	-	87.6	4.5	-	-	-	-	87.8	0.2	-	-	-	-	91.1	3.8	-	-	-	-
1978	89.0	-2.3	-	-	86.7	-2.6	-	-	90.3	4.2	-	-	90.9	0.7	-	-	93.4	2.8	-	-	91.4	-2.1	-	-
1979	86.7	-5.1	-	-	92.2	6.3	-	-	92.3	0.1	-	-	90.2	-2.3	-	-	94.7	5.0	-	-	95.7	1.1	-	-
1980	91.3	-4.6	-	-	96.3	5.5	-	-	95.1	-1.2	-	-	94.6	-0.5	-	-	97.7	3.3	-	-	98.0	0.3	-	-
1981	94.4	-3.7	-	-	97.2	3.0	-	-	96.0	-1.2	-	-	95.0	-1.0	-	-	98.1	3.3	-	-	96.9	-1.2	-	-
1982	97.2	0.3	-	-	102.4	5.3	-	-	102.5	0.1	-	-	99.1	-3.3	-	-	102.8	3.7	-	-	103.1	0.3	-	-
1983	97.8	-5.1	-	-	100.6	2.9	-	-	98.0	-2.6	-	-	96.6	-1.4	-	-	99.6	3.1	-	-	100.6	1.0	-	-
1984	97.4	-3.2	-	-	100.3	3.0	-	-	100.4	0.1	-	-	96.6	-3.8	-	-	102.2	5.8	-	-	102.5	0.3	-	-
1985	99.1	-3.3	-	-	103.8	4.7	-	-	104.5	0.7	-	-	102.1	-2.3	-	-	103.6	1.5	-	-	102.5	-1.1	-	-
1986	98.7	-3.7	-	-	101.6	2.9	-	-	102.5	0.9	-	-	100.8	-1.7	-	-	107.1	6.3	-	-	105.5	-1.5	103.1	-2.3
1987	-	-	-	-	-	-	-	-	-	-	103.0	-0.1	-	-	-	-	-	-	-	-	-	-	114.0	10.7
1988	-	-	-	-	-	-	-	-	-	-	109.9	-3.6	-	-	-	-	-	-	-	-	-	-	101.7	-7.5
1989	-	-	-	-	-	-	-	-	-	-	112.4	10.5	-	-	-	-	-	-	-	-	-	-	110.5	-1.7
1990	-	-	-	-	-	-	-	-	-	-	120.6	9.1	-	-	-	-	-	-	-	-	-	-	115.1	-4.6
1991	-	-	-	-	-	-	-	-	-	-	120.4	4.6	-	-	-	-	-	-	-	-	-	-	123.4	2.5
1992	-	-	-	-	-	-	-	-	-	-	123.6	0.2	-	-	-	-	-	-	-	-	-	-	120.8	-2.3
1993	-	-	-	-	-	-	-	-	-	-	121.8	0.8	-	-	-	-	-	-	-	-	-	-	128.3	5.3
1994	-	-	-	-	-	-	-	-	-	-	126.8	-1.2	-	-	-	-	-	-	-	-	-	-	130.8	3.2
1995	-	-	-	-	-	-	-	-	-	-	130.0	-0.6	-	-	-	-	-	-	-	-	-	-	124.1	-4.5
1996	-	-	-	-	-	-	-	-	-	-	129.2	4.1	-	-	-	-	-	-	-	-	-	-	128.4	-0.6
1997	-	-	-	-	-	-	-	-	-	-	126.6	-1.4	-	-	-	-	-	-	-	-	-	-	-	-

Source: U.S. Department of Labor, Bureau of Labor Statistics, Division of Consumer Prices and Price Indexes. - indicates no data collected for period.

Denver-Boulder, CO
Consumer Price Index - Urban Wage Earners
Base 1982-1984 = 100
Apparel and Upkeep

For 1971-1997. Columns headed % show percentile change in the index from the previous period for which an index is available.

Year	Jan Index	%	Feb Index	%	Mar Index	%	Apr Index	%	May Index	%	Jun Index	%	Jul Index	%	Aug Index	%	Sep Index	%	Oct Index	%	Nov Index	%	Dec Index	%
1971	54.5	-	-	-	-	-	55.5	1.8	-	-	-	-	55.4	-0.2	-	-	-	-	58.6	5.8	-	-	-	-
1972	57.1	-2.6	-	-	-	-	57.9	1.4	-	-	-	-	57.2	-1.2	-	-	-	-	59.2	3.5	-	-	-	-
1973	57.3	-3.2	-	-	-	-	59.8	4.4	-	-	-	-	59.6	-0.3	-	-	-	-	62.3	4.5	-	-	-	-
1974	62.3	0.0	-	-	-	-	63.9	2.6	-	-	-	-	65.0	1.7	-	-	-	-	67.6	4.0	-	-	-	-
1975	66.3	-1.9	-	-	-	-	67.6	2.0	-	-	-	-	68.3	1.0	-	-	-	-	71.8	5.1	-	-	-	-
1976	69.9	-2.6	-	-	-	-	72.2	3.3	-	-	-	-	72.2	0.0	-	-	-	-	75.2	4.2	-	-	-	-
1977	73.3	-2.5	-	-	-	-	76.7	4.6	-	-	-	-	76.8	0.1	-	-	-	-	79.7	3.8	-	-	-	-
1978	77.9	-2.3	-	-	78.1	0.3	-	-	82.0	5.0	-	-	82.1	0.1	-	-	85.7	4.4	-	-	83.6	-2.5	-	-
1979	82.2	-1.7	-	-	86.5	5.2	-	-	87.5	1.2	-	-	87.4	-0.1	-	-	92.8	6.2	-	-	91.6	-1.3	-	-
1980	90.2	-1.5	-	-	96.4	6.9	-	-	93.6	-2.9	-	-	91.9	-1.8	-	-	96.4	4.9	-	-	96.2	-0.2	-	-
1981	92.3	-4.1	-	-	94.4	2.3	-	-	93.6	-0.8	-	-	95.4	1.9	-	-	98.7	3.5	-	-	97.0	-1.7	-	-
1982	96.6	-0.4	-	-	102.2	5.8	-	-	101.2	-1.0	-	-	97.8	-3.4	-	-	102.3	4.6	-	-	102.5	0.2	-	-
1983	97.7	-4.7	-	-	100.1	2.5	-	-	97.7	-2.4	-	-	96.7	-1.0	-	-	100.0	3.4	-	-	101.6	1.6	-	-
1984	97.9	-3.6	-	-	101.3	3.5	-	-	100.8	-0.5	-	-	97.0	-3.8	-	-	102.6	5.8	-	-	103.4	0.8	-	-
1985	100.2	-3.1	-	-	103.6	3.4	-	-	104.1	0.5	-	-	102.3	-1.7	-	-	103.1	0.8	-	-	101.6	-1.5	-	-
1986	98.2	-3.3	-	-	100.4	2.2	-	-	101.0	0.6	-	-	99.1	-1.9	-	-	105.9	6.9	-	-	103.5	-2.3	100.9	-2.5
1987	-	-	-	-	-	-	-	-	-	-	103.5	2.6	-	-	-	-	-	-	-	-	-	-	114.8	10.9
1988	-	-	-	-	-	-	-	-	-	-	110.5	-3.7	-	-	-	-	-	-	-	-	-	-	101.8	-7.9
1989	-	-	-	-	-	-	-	-	-	-	111.8	9.8	-	-	-	-	-	-	-	-	-	-	109.6	-2.0
1990	-	-	-	-	-	-	-	-	-	-	119.5	9.0	-	-	-	-	-	-	-	-	-	-	114.5	-4.2
1991	-	-	-	-	-	-	-	-	-	-	119.6	4.5	-	-	-	-	-	-	-	-	-	-	123.1	2.9
1992	-	-	-	-	-	-	-	-	-	-	123.7	0.5	-	-	-	-	-	-	-	-	-	-	121.2	-2.0
1993	-	-	-	-	-	-	-	-	-	-	121.4	0.2	-	-	-	-	-	-	-	-	-	-	127.1	4.7
1994	-	-	-	-	-	-	-	-	-	-	125.7	-1.1	-	-	-	-	-	-	-	-	-	-	129.4	2.9
1995	-	-	-	-	-	-	-	-	-	-	127.9	-1.2	-	-	-	-	-	-	-	-	-	-	122.5	-4.2
1996	-	-	-	-	-	-	-	-	-	-	126.7	3.4	-	-	-	-	-	-	-	-	-	-	125.7	-0.8
1997	-	-	-	-	-	-	-	-	-	-	123.8	-1.5	-	-	-	-	-	-	-	-	-	-	-	-

Source: U.S. Department of Labor, Bureau of Labor Statistics, Division of Consumer Prices and Price Indexes. - indicates no data collected for period.

Denver-Boulder, CO
Consumer Price Index - All Urban Consumers
Base 1982-1984 = 100
Transportation

For 1971-1997. Columns headed % show percentile change in the index from the previous period for which an index is available.

Year	Jan Index	%	Feb Index	%	Mar Index	%	Apr Index	%	May Index	%	Jun Index	%	Jul Index	%	Aug Index	%	Sep Index	%	Oct Index	%	Nov Index	%	Dec Index	%
1971	38.0	-	-	-	-	-	38.0	0.0	-	-	-	-	37.8	-0.5	-	-	-	-	38.1	0.8	-	-	-	-
1972	37.1	-2.6	-	-	-	-	37.6	1.3	-	-	-	-	38.0	1.1	-	-	-	-	38.4	1.1	-	-	-	-
1973	38.0	-1.0	-	-	-	-	39.5	3.9	-	-	-	-	40.4	2.3	-	-	-	-	39.5	-2.2	-	-	-	-
1974	41.3	4.6	-	-	-	-	42.7	3.4	-	-	-	-	45.0	5.4	-	-	-	-	45.4	0.9	-	-	-	-
1975	45.9	1.1	-	-	-	-	47.0	2.4	-	-	-	-	49.3	4.9	-	-	-	-	49.8	1.0	-	-	-	-
1976	49.7	-0.2	-	-	-	-	50.8	2.2	-	-	-	-	53.2	4.7	-	-	-	-	53.9	1.3	-	-	-	-
1977	55.1	2.2	-	-	-	-	55.8	1.3	-	-	-	-	56.9	2.0	-	-	-	-	56.7	-0.4	-	-	-	-
1978	57.6	1.6	-	-	57.9	0.5	-	-	58.5	1.0	-	-	60.4	3.2	-	-	61.3	1.5	-	-	61.9	1.0	-	-
1979	63.3	2.3	-	-	65.2	3.0	-	-	68.9	5.7	-	-	71.6	3.9	-	-	73.7	2.9	-	-	75.1	1.9	-	-
1980	77.6	3.3	-	-	80.5	3.7	-	-	82.1	2.0	-	-	83.0	1.1	-	-	84.0	1.2	-	-	85.0	1.2	-	-
1981	87.0	2.4	-	-	89.7	3.1	-	-	91.1	1.6	-	-	92.7	1.8	-	-	93.5	0.9	-	-	94.7	1.3	-	-
1982	94.6	-0.1	-	-	94.0	-0.6	-	-	94.0	0.0	-	-	97.6	3.8	-	-	98.2	0.6	-	-	98.8	0.6	-	-
1983	97.0	-1.8	-	-	95.1	-2.0	-	-	99.6	4.7	-	-	101.5	1.9	-	-	102.7	1.2	-	-	103.3	0.6	-	-
1984	102.0	-1.3	-	-	102.6	0.6	-	-	104.1	1.5	-	-	103.8	-0.3	-	-	104.5	0.7	-	-	104.7	0.2	-	-
1985	102.5	-2.1	-	-	104.4	1.9	-	-	106.7	2.2	-	-	107.2	0.5	-	-	106.6	-0.6	-	-	107.2	0.6	-	-
1986	106.3	-0.8	-	-	98.8	-7.1	-	-	99.5	0.7	-	-	100.1	0.6	-	-	101.6	1.5	-	-	101.0	-0.6	100.3	-0.7
1987	-	-	-	-	-	-	-	-	-	-	102.6	2.3	-	-	-	-	-	-	-	-	-	-	105.3	2.6
1988	-	-	-	-	-	-	-	-	-	-	105.8	0.5	-	-	-	-	-	-	-	-	-	-	108.9	2.9
1989	-	-	-	-	-	-	-	-	-	-	112.3	3.1	-	-	-	-	-	-	-	-	-	-	113.6	1.2
1990	-	-	-	-	-	-	-	-	-	-	115.9	2.0	-	-	-	-	-	-	-	-	-	-	123.0	6.1
1991	-	-	-	-	-	-	-	-	-	-	122.7	-0.2	-	-	-	-	-	-	-	-	-	-	123.5	0.7
1992	-	-	-	-	-	-	-	-	-	-	123.4	-0.1	-	-	-	-	-	-	-	-	-	-	124.9	1.2
1993	-	-	-	-	-	-	-	-	-	-	124.3	-0.5	-	-	-	-	-	-	-	-	-	-	125.7	1.1
1994	-	-	-	-	-	-	-	-	-	-	126.5	0.6	-	-	-	-	-	-	-	-	-	-	130.7	3.3
1995	-	-	-	-	-	-	-	-	-	-	133.2	1.9	-	-	-	-	-	-	-	-	-	-	132.9	-0.2
1996	-	-	-	-	-	-	-	-	-	-	136.6	2.8	-	-	-	-	-	-	-	-	-	-	140.3	2.7
1997	-	-	-	-	-	-	-	-	-	-	142.2	1.4	-	-	-	-	-	-	-	-	-	-	-	-

Source: U.S. Department of Labor, Bureau of Labor Statistics, Division of Consumer Prices and Price Indexes. - indicates no data collected for period.

Denver-Boulder, CO
Consumer Price Index - Urban Wage Earners
Base 1982-1984 = 100
Transportation

For 1971-1997. Columns headed % show percentile change in the index from the previous period for which an index is available.

Year	Jan Index	%	Feb Index	%	Mar Index	%	Apr Index	%	May Index	%	Jun Index	%	Jul Index	%	Aug Index	%	Sep Index	%	Oct Index	%	Nov Index	%	Dec Index	%
1971	37.7	-	-	-	-	-	37.7	0.0	-	-	-	-	37.5	-0.5	-	-	-	-	37.8	0.8	-	-	-	-
1972	36.8	-2.6	-	-	-	-	37.3	1.4	-	-	-	-	37.7	1.1	-	-	-	-	38.1	1.1	-	-	-	-
1973	37.7	-1.0	-	-	-	-	39.2	4.0	-	-	-	-	40.1	2.3	-	-	-	-	39.2	-2.2	-	-	-	-
1974	40.9	4.3	-	-	-	-	42.3	3.4	-	-	-	-	44.6	5.4	-	-	-	-	45.0	0.9	-	-	-	-
1975	45.6	1.3	-	-	-	-	46.6	2.2	-	-	-	-	48.9	4.9	-	-	-	-	49.4	1.0	-	-	-	-
1976	49.3	-0.2	-	-	-	-	50.4	2.2	-	-	-	-	52.8	4.8	-	-	-	-	53.5	1.3	-	-	-	-
1977	54.6	2.1	-	-	-	-	55.4	1.5	-	-	-	-	56.5	2.0	-	-	-	-	56.2	-0.5	-	-	-	-
1978	57.1	1.6	-	-	57.2	0.2	-	-	58.1	1.6	-	-	59.4	2.2	-	-	60.2	1.3	-	-	61.3	1.8	-	-
1979	62.4	1.8	-	-	64.6	3.5	-	-	68.5	6.0	-	-	71.3	4.1	-	-	73.5	3.1	-	-	74.8	1.8	-	-
1980	77.4	3.5	-	-	80.3	3.7	-	-	82.2	2.4	-	-	83.1	1.1	-	-	83.8	0.8	-	-	85.1	1.6	-	-
1981	86.8	2.0	-	-	89.6	3.2	-	-	90.9	1.5	-	-	92.7	2.0	-	-	93.8	1.2	-	-	95.1	1.4	-	-
1982	95.0	-0.1	-	-	94.7	-0.3	-	-	94.3	-0.4	-	-	98.1	4.0	-	-	98.8	0.7	-	-	99.3	0.5	-	-
1983	97.1	-2.2	-	-	95.1	-2.1	-	-	99.6	4.7	-	-	101.4	1.8	-	-	102.6	1.2	-	-	103.0	0.4	-	-
1984	101.5	-1.5	-	-	102.3	0.8	-	-	103.7	1.4	-	-	103.5	-0.2	-	-	104.2	0.7	-	-	104.3	0.1	-	-
1985	102.0	-2.2	-	-	104.0	2.0	-	-	106.7	2.6	-	-	107.3	0.6	-	-	106.8	-0.5	-	-	107.3	0.5	-	-
1986	106.3	-0.9	-	-	98.6	-7.2	-	-	99.1	0.5	-	-	99.8	0.7	-	-	101.1	1.3	-	-	100.6	-0.5	99.9	-0.7
1987	-	-	-	-	-	-	-	-	-	-	100.9	1.0	-	-	-	-	-	-	-	-	-	-	103.3	2.4
1988	-	-	-	-	-	-	-	-	-	-	103.9	0.6	-	-	-	-	-	-	-	-	-	-	106.8	2.8
1989	-	-	-	-	-	-	-	-	-	-	110.2	3.2	-	-	-	-	-	-	-	-	-	-	111.3	1.0
1990	-	-	-	-	-	-	-	-	-	-	113.4	1.9	-	-	-	-	-	-	-	-	-	-	119.8	5.6
1991	-	-	-	-	-	-	-	-	-	-	119.6	-0.2	-	-	-	-	-	-	-	-	-	-	120.4	0.7
1992	-	-	-	-	-	-	-	-	-	-	120.0	-0.3	-	-	-	-	-	-	-	-	-	-	121.6	1.3
1993	-	-	-	-	-	-	-	-	-	-	120.8	-0.7	-	-	-	-	-	-	-	-	-	-	122.6	1.5
1994	-	-	-	-	-	-	-	-	-	-	123.2	0.5	-	-	-	-	-	-	-	-	-	-	127.5	3.5
1995	-	-	-	-	-	-	-	-	-	-	129.9	1.9	-	-	-	-	-	-	-	-	-	-	129.7	-0.2
1996	-	-	-	-	-	-	-	-	-	-	133.0	2.5	-	-	-	-	-	-	-	-	-	-	136.1	2.3
1997	-	-	-	-	-	-	-	-	-	-	137.7	1.2	-	-	-	-	-	-	-	-	-	-	-	-

Source: U.S. Department of Labor, Bureau of Labor Statistics, Division of Consumer Prices and Price Indexes. - indicates no data collected for period.

Denver-Boulder, CO
Consumer Price Index - All Urban Consumers
Base 1982-1984 = 100
Medical Care

For 1971-1997. Columns headed % show percentile change in the index from the previous period for which an index is available.

Year	Jan Index	%	Feb Index	%	Mar Index	%	Apr Index	%	May Index	%	Jun Index	%	Jul Index	%	Aug Index	%	Sep Index	%	Oct Index	%	Nov Index	%	Dec Index	%
1971	35.4	-	-	-	-	-	36.1	2.0	-	-	-	-	37.1	2.8	-	-	-	-	36.9	-0.5	-	-	-	-
1972	37.2	0.8	-	-	-	-	37.3	0.3	-	-	-	-	37.5	0.5	-	-	-	-	38.0	1.3	-	-	-	-
1973	38.1	0.3	-	-	-	-	38.5	1.0	-	-	-	-	38.8	0.8	-	-	-	-	39.7	2.3	-	-	-	-
1974	40.7	2.5	-	-	-	-	41.2	1.2	-	-	-	-	43.2	4.9	-	-	-	-	43.7	1.2	-	-	-	-
1975	45.7	4.6	-	-	-	-	46.7	2.2	-	-	-	-	47.6	1.9	-	-	-	-	48.3	1.5	-	-	-	-
1976	49.1	1.7	-	-	-	-	50.3	2.4	-	-	-	-	51.1	1.6	-	-	-	-	52.2	2.2	-	-	-	-
1977	53.3	2.1	-	-	-	-	54.6	2.4	-	-	-	-	56.2	2.9	-	-	-	-	57.3	2.0	-	-	-	-
1978	58.9	2.8	-	-	59.5	1.0	-	-	60.3	1.3	-	-	60.4	0.2	-	-	61.4	1.7	-	-	62.5	1.8	-	-
1979	63.3	1.3	-	-	64.1	1.3	-	-	65.7	2.5	-	-	66.1	0.6	-	-	67.2	1.7	-	-	68.5	1.9	-	-
1980	71.6	4.5	-	-	72.3	1.0	-	-	73.0	1.0	-	-	73.0	0.0	-	-	74.3	1.8	-	-	76.0	2.3	-	-
1981	78.4	3.2	-	-	78.8	0.5	-	-	79.4	0.8	-	-	80.1	0.9	-	-	82.4	2.9	-	-	84.3	2.3	-	-
1982	87.5	3.8	-	-	88.2	0.8	-	-	88.9	0.8	-	-	91.8	3.3	-	-	93.2	1.5	-	-	94.5	1.4	-	-
1983	97.4	3.1	-	-	99.0	1.6	-	-	99.4	0.4	-	-	102.4	3.0	-	-	102.5	0.1	-	-	102.8	0.3	-	-
1984	106.4	3.5	-	-	107.2	0.8	-	-	107.4	0.2	-	-	108.0	0.6	-	-	108.2	0.2	-	-	109.4	1.1	-	-
1985	110.8	1.3	-	-	112.5	1.5	-	-	113.2	0.6	-	-	115.9	2.4	-	-	117.6	1.5	-	-	118.5	0.8	-	-
1986	119.9	1.2	-	-	121.2	1.1	-	-	123.2	1.7	-	-	125.7	2.0	-	-	126.4	0.6	-	-	125.7	-0.6	126.1	0.3
1987	-		-		-		-		-		127.7	1.3	-		-		-		-		-		129.4	1.3
1988	-		-		-		-		-		132.9	2.7	-		-		-		-		-		136.9	3.0
1989	-		-		-		-		-		141.3	3.2	-		-		-		-		-		145.7	3.1
1990	-		-		-		-		-		152.4	4.6	-		-		-		-		-		160.9	5.6
1991	-		-		-		-		-		169.2	5.2	-		-		-		-		-		174.1	2.9
1992	-		-		-		-		-		177.8	2.1	-		-		-		-		-		179.3	0.8
1993	-		-		-		-		-		185.7	3.6	-		-		-		-		-		188.7	1.6
1994	-		-		-		-		-		194.3	3.0	-		-		-		-		-		197.2	1.5
1995	-		-		-		-		-		202.0	2.4	-		-		-		-		-		203.2	0.6
1996	-		-		-		-		-		209.0	2.9	-		-		-		-		-		209.8	0.4
1997	-		-		-		-		-		210.8	0.5	-		-		-		-		-		-	

Source: U.S. Department of Labor, Bureau of Labor Statistics, Division of Consumer Prices and Price Indexes. - indicates no data collected for period.

Denver-Boulder, CO
Consumer Price Index - Urban Wage Earners
Base 1982-1984 = 100
Medical Care

For 1971-1997. Columns headed % show percentile change in the index from the previous period for which an index is available.

Year	Jan Index	%	Feb Index	%	Mar Index	%	Apr Index	%	May Index	%	Jun Index	%	Jul Index	%	Aug Index	%	Sep Index	%	Oct Index	%	Nov Index	%	Dec Index	%
1971	35.8	-	-	-	-	-	36.5	2.0	-	-	-	-	37.5	2.7	-	-	-	-	37.3	-0.5	-	-	-	-
1972	37.6	0.8	-	-	-	-	37.7	0.3	-	-	-	-	37.9	0.5	-	-	-	-	38.4	1.3	-	-	-	-
1973	38.5	0.3	-	-	-	-	38.9	1.0	-	-	-	-	39.2	0.8	-	-	-	-	40.1	2.3	-	-	-	-
1974	41.1	2.5	-	-	-	-	41.7	1.5	-	-	-	-	43.7	4.8	-	-	-	-	44.1	0.9	-	-	-	-
1975	46.2	4.8	-	-	-	-	47.2	2.2	-	-	-	-	48.1	1.9	-	-	-	-	48.8	1.5	-	-	-	-
1976	49.6	1.6	-	-	-	-	50.8	2.4	-	-	-	-	51.7	1.8	-	-	-	-	52.7	1.9	-	-	-	-
1977	53.9	2.3	-	-	-	-	55.1	2.2	-	-	-	-	56.8	3.1	-	-	-	-	57.9	1.9	-	-	-	-
1978	59.5	2.8	-	-	60.3	1.3	-	-	61.4	1.8	-	-	62.1	1.1	-	-	62.9	1.3	-	-	64.0	1.7	-	-
1979	64.4	0.6	-	-	65.6	1.9	-	-	65.7	0.2	-	-	65.9	0.3	-	-	67.0	1.7	-	-	68.5	2.2	-	-
1980	70.0	2.2	-	-	71.5	2.1	-	-	72.3	1.1	-	-	73.0	1.0	-	-	75.6	3.6	-	-	76.2	0.8	-	-
1981	79.2	3.9	-	-	79.5	0.4	-	-	81.0	1.9	-	-	81.5	0.6	-	-	82.4	1.1	-	-	83.9	1.8	-	-
1982	86.9	3.6	-	-	87.8	1.0	-	-	88.6	0.9	-	-	91.6	3.4	-	-	93.1	1.6	-	-	94.5	1.5	-	-
1983	97.4	3.1	-	-	99.0	1.6	-	-	99.5	0.5	-	-	102.7	3.2	-	-	102.8	0.1	-	-	103.2	0.4	-	-
1984	106.5	3.2	-	-	107.3	0.8	-	-	107.5	0.2	-	-	108.0	0.5	-	-	108.2	0.2	-	-	109.4	1.1	-	-
1985	110.7	1.2	-	-	112.5	1.6	-	-	113.2	0.6	-	-	115.9	2.4	-	-	117.6	1.5	-	-	118.7	0.9	-	-
1986	120.0	1.1	-	-	121.2	1.0	-	-	123.3	1.7	-	-	125.9	2.1	-	-	126.6	0.6	-	-	126.1	-0.4	126.5	0.3
1987	-	-	-	-	-	-	-	-	-	-	127.1	0.5	-	-	-	-	-	-	-	-	-	-	128.7	1.3
1988	-	-	-	-	-	-	-	-	-	-	132.1	2.6	-	-	-	-	-	-	-	-	-	-	136.0	3.0
1989	-	-	-	-	-	-	-	-	-	-	140.2	3.1	-	-	-	-	-	-	-	-	-	-	144.1	2.8
1990	-	-	-	-	-	-	-	-	-	-	150.3	4.3	-	-	-	-	-	-	-	-	-	-	158.9	5.7
1991	-	-	-	-	-	-	-	-	-	-	166.3	4.7	-	-	-	-	-	-	-	-	-	-	171.1	2.9
1992	-	-	-	-	-	-	-	-	-	-	174.8	2.2	-	-	-	-	-	-	-	-	-	-	176.5	1.0
1993	-	-	-	-	-	-	-	-	-	-	182.5	3.4	-	-	-	-	-	-	-	-	-	-	185.6	1.7
1994	-	-	-	-	-	-	-	-	-	-	190.9	2.9	-	-	-	-	-	-	-	-	-	-	193.8	1.5
1995	-	-	-	-	-	-	-	-	-	-	198.4	2.4	-	-	-	-	-	-	-	-	-	-	200.0	0.8
1996	-	-	-	-	-	-	-	-	-	-	206.0	3.0	-	-	-	-	-	-	-	-	-	-	207.1	0.5
1997	-	-	-	-	-	-	-	-	-	-	208.3	0.6	-	-	-	-	-	-	-	-	-	-	-	-

Source: U.S. Department of Labor, Bureau of Labor Statistics, Division of Consumer Prices and Price Indexes. - indicates no data collected for period.

Denver-Boulder, CO
Consumer Price Index - All Urban Consumers
Base 1982-1984 = 100
Entertainment

For 1976-1997. Columns headed % show percentile change in the index from the previous period for which an index is available.

Year	Jan Index	%	Feb Index	%	Mar Index	%	Apr Index	%	May Index	%	Jun Index	%	Jul Index	%	Aug Index	%	Sep Index	%	Oct Index	%	Nov Index	%	Dec Index	%
1976	56.6	-	-	-	-	-	57.6	1.8	-	-	-	-	57.8	0.3	-	-	-	-	58.0	0.3	-	-	-	-
1977	59.4	2.4	-	-	-	-	60.8	2.4	-	-	-	-	61.8	1.6	-	-	-	-	62.6	1.3	-	-	-	-
1978	63.1	0.8	-	-	64.5	2.2	-	-	65.9	2.2	-	-	66.6	1.1	-	-	66.9	0.5	-	-	68.3	2.1	-	-
1979	69.0	1.0	-	-	71.1	3.0	-	-	71.6	0.7	-	-	72.8	1.7	-	-	73.2	0.5	-	-	73.8	0.8	-	-
1980	75.8	2.7	-	-	78.1	3.0	-	-	79.0	1.2	-	-	80.4	1.8	-	-	80.6	0.2	-	-	82.3	2.1	-	-
1981	82.9	0.7	-	-	83.9	1.2	-	-	86.4	3.0	-	-	87.1	0.8	-	-	86.5	-0.7	-	-	87.2	0.8	-	-
1982	89.5	2.6	-	-	88.1	-1.6	-	-	93.8	6.5	-	-	96.6	3.0	-	-	97.8	1.2	-	-	97.1	-0.7	-	-
1983	99.1	2.1	-	-	99.8	0.7	-	-	102.2	2.4	-	-	102.6	0.4	-	-	102.8	0.2	-	-	103.0	0.2	-	-
1984	103.5	0.5	-	-	104.8	1.3	-	-	105.7	0.9	-	-	105.7	0.0	-	-	104.8	-0.9	-	-	100.4	-4.2	-	-
1985	101.7	1.3	-	-	103.0	1.3	-	-	104.6	1.6	-	-	107.2	2.5	-	-	105.6	-1.5	-	-	103.2	-2.3	-	-
1986	105.2	1.9	-	-	105.3	0.1	-	-	105.6	0.3	-	-	107.4	1.7	-	-	108.5	1.0	-	-	107.3	-1.1	107.9	0.6
1987	-	-	-	-	-	-	-	-	-	-	115.6	7.1	-	-	-	-	-	-	-	-	-	-	116.1	0.4
1988	-	-	-	-	-	-	-	-	-	-	119.8	3.2	-	-	-	-	-	-	-	-	-	-	120.0	0.2
1989	-	-	-	-	-	-	-	-	-	-	125.1	4.2	-	-	-	-	-	-	-	-	-	-	129.0	3.1
1990	-	-	-	-	-	-	-	-	-	-	132.7	2.9	-	-	-	-	-	-	-	-	-	-	134.6	1.4
1991	-	-	-	-	-	-	-	-	-	-	137.2	1.9	-	-	-	-	-	-	-	-	-	-	140.0	2.0
1992	-	-	-	-	-	-	-	-	-	-	139.5	-0.4	-	-	-	-	-	-	-	-	-	-	139.7	0.1
1993	-	-	-	-	-	-	-	-	-	-	141.6	1.4	-	-	-	-	-	-	-	-	-	-	144.8	2.3
1994	-	-	-	-	-	-	-	-	-	-	151.2	4.4	-	-	-	-	-	-	-	-	-	-	147.7	-2.3
1995	-	-	-	-	-	-	-	-	-	-	151.8	2.8	-	-	-	-	-	-	-	-	-	-	154.3	1.6
1996	-	-	-	-	-	-	-	-	-	-	154.8	0.3	-	-	-	-	-	-	-	-	-	-	156.8	1.3
1997	-	-	-	-	-	-	-	-	-	-	158.2	0.9	-	-	-	-	-	-	-	-	-	-	-	-

Source: U.S. Department of Labor, Bureau of Labor Statistics, Division of Consumer Prices and Price Indexes. - indicates no data collected for period.

Denver-Boulder, CO
Consumer Price Index - Urban Wage Earners
Base 1982-1984 = 100
Entertainment

For 1976-1997. Columns headed % show percentile change in the index from the previous period for which an index is available.

Year	Jan Index	%	Feb Index	%	Mar Index	%	Apr Index	%	May Index	%	Jun Index	%	Jul Index	%	Aug Index	%	Sep Index	%	Oct Index	%	Nov Index	%	Dec Index	%
1976	59.4	-	-	-	-	-	60.5	1.9	-	-	-	-	60.7	0.3	-	-	-	-	60.9	0.3	-	-	-	-
1977	62.4	2.5	-	-	-	-	63.8	2.2	-	-	-	-	64.9	1.7	-	-	-	-	65.8	1.4	-	-	-	-
1978	66.3	0.8	-	-	67.1	1.2	-	-	68.3	1.8	-	-	68.2	-0.1	-	-	68.6	0.6	-	-	70.5	2.8	-	-
1979	70.8	0.4	-	-	72.8	2.8	-	-	72.5	-0.4	-	-	73.3	1.1	-	-	73.8	0.7	-	-	74.7	1.2	-	-
1980	77.0	3.1	-	-	79.4	3.1	-	-	81.4	2.5	-	-	82.9	1.8	-	-	82.0	-1.1	-	-	85.0	3.7	-	-
1981	85.2	0.2	-	-	86.9	2.0	-	-	89.3	2.8	-	-	89.2	-0.1	-	-	86.8	-2.7	-	-	85.7	-1.3	-	-
1982	88.0	2.7	-	-	85.9	-2.4	-	-	94.5	10.0	-	-	97.3	3.0	-	-	98.4	1.1	-	-	97.4	-1.0	-	-
1983	99.4	2.1	-	-	99.9	0.5	-	-	102.3	2.4	-	-	102.9	0.6	-	-	103.0	0.1	-	-	103.2	0.2	-	-
1984	103.7	0.5	-	-	105.1	1.4	-	-	106.1	1.0	-	-	106.0	-0.1	-	-	104.9	-1.0	-	-	98.9	-5.7	-	-
1985	100.4	1.5	-	-	101.8	1.4	-	-	103.3	1.5	-	-	107.1	3.7	-	-	103.9	-3.0	-	-	101.3	-2.5	-	-
1986	103.1	1.8	-	-	103.6	0.5	-	-	103.7	0.1	-	-	105.7	1.9	-	-	105.6	-0.1	-	-	104.2	-1.3	104.9	0.7
1987	-	-	-	-	-	-	-	-	-	-	115.7	10.3	-	-	-	-	-	-	-	-	-	-	116.4	0.6
1988	-	-	-	-	-	-	-	-	-	-	120.4	3.4	-	-	-	-	-	-	-	-	-	-	120.8	0.3
1989	-	-	-	-	-	-	-	-	-	-	124.6	3.1	-	-	-	-	-	-	-	-	-	-	128.0	2.7
1990	-	-	-	-	-	-	-	-	-	-	129.7	1.3	-	-	-	-	-	-	-	-	-	-	131.4	1.3
1991	-	-	-	-	-	-	-	-	-	-	133.4	1.5	-	-	-	-	-	-	-	-	-	-	135.6	1.6
1992	-	-	-	-	-	-	-	-	-	-	135.6	0.0	-	-	-	-	-	-	-	-	-	-	136.7	0.8
1993	-	-	-	-	-	-	-	-	-	-	137.4	0.5	-	-	-	-	-	-	-	-	-	-	141.5	3.0
1994	-	-	-	-	-	-	-	-	-	-	146.3	3.4	-	-	-	-	-	-	-	-	-	-	143.5	-1.9
1995	-	-	-	-	-	-	-	-	-	-	147.2	2.6	-	-	-	-	-	-	-	-	-	-	149.6	1.6
1996	-	-	-	-	-	-	-	-	-	-	150.2	0.4	-	-	-	-	-	-	-	-	-	-	152.8	1.7
1997	-	-	-	-	-	-	-	-	-	-	153.8	0.7	-	-	-	-	-	-	-	-	-	-	-	-

Source: U.S. Department of Labor, Bureau of Labor Statistics, Division of Consumer Prices and Price Indexes. - indicates no data collected for period.

Denver-Boulder, CO
Consumer Price Index - All Urban Consumers
Base 1982-1984 = 100
Other Goods and Services

For 1976-1997. Columns headed % show percentile change in the index from the previous period for which an index is available.

Year	Jan Index	%	Feb Index	%	Mar Index	%	Apr Index	%	May Index	%	Jun Index	%	Jul Index	%	Aug Index	%	Sep Index	%	Oct Index	%	Nov Index	%	Dec Index	%
1976	50.6	-	-	-	-	-	51.9	2.6	-	-	-	-	52.3	0.8	-	-	-	-	52.8	1.0	-	-	-	-
1977	54.0	2.3	-	-	-	-	54.7	1.3	-	-	-	-	57.1	4.4	-	-	-	-	59.0	3.3	-	-	-	-
1978	59.8	1.4	-	-	60.5	1.2	-	-	60.2	-0.5	-	-	60.2	0.0	-	-	61.2	1.7	-	-	61.9	1.1	-	-
1979	62.7	1.3	-	-	63.7	1.6	-	-	64.0	0.5	-	-	63.3	-1.1	-	-	66.2	4.6	-	-	67.1	1.4	-	-
1980	69.1	3.0	-	-	70.5	2.0	-	-	71.1	0.9	-	-	71.1	0.0	-	-	73.9	3.9	-	-	75.4	2.0	-	-
1981	76.4	1.3	-	-	79.4	3.9	-	-	81.2	2.3	-	-	80.0	-1.5	-	-	82.4	3.0	-	-	83.6	1.5	-	-
1982	85.7	2.5	-	-	87.0	1.5	-	-	87.0	0.0	-	-	88.9	2.2	-	-	90.6	1.9	-	-	94.4	4.2	-	-
1983	96.8	2.5	-	-	98.9	2.2	-	-	99.4	0.5	-	-	101.2	1.8	-	-	103.5	2.3	-	-	106.5	2.9	-	-
1984	107.7	1.1	-	-	108.0	0.3	-	-	108.4	0.4	-	-	108.7	0.3	-	-	109.4	0.6	-	-	111.2	1.6	-	-
1985	113.2	1.8	-	-	114.1	0.8	-	-	114.7	0.5	-	-	114.1	-0.5	-	-	116.9	2.5	-	-	118.3	1.2	-	-
1986	118.8	0.4	-	-	121.7	2.4	-	-	121.2	-0.4	-	-	123.2	1.7	-	-	127.3	3.3	-	-	129.3	1.6	129.3	0.0
1987	-	-	-	-	-	-	-	-	-	-	121.3	-6.2	-	-	-	-	-	-	-	-	-	-	-	-
1988	-	-	-	-	-	-	-	-	-	-	130.5	7.6	-	-	-	-	-	-	-	-	-	-	-	-
1989	-	-	-	-	-	-	-	-	-	-	138.3	6.0	-	-	-	-	-	-	-	-	-	-	-	-
1990	-	-	-	-	-	-	-	-	-	-	147.6	6.7	-	-	-	-	-	-	-	-	-	-	-	-
1991	-	-	-	-	-	-	-	-	-	-	156.8	6.2	-	-	-	-	-	-	-	-	-	-	-	-
1992	-	-	-	-	-	-	-	-	-	-	167.6	6.9	-	-	-	-	-	-	-	-	-	-	-	-
1993	-	-	-	-	-	-	-	-	-	-	178.7	6.6	-	-	-	-	-	-	-	-	-	-	-	-
1994	-	-	-	-	-	-	-	-	-	-	182.1	1.9	-	-	-	-	-	-	-	-	-	-	-	-
1995	-	-	-	-	-	-	-	-	-	-	188.1	3.3	-	-	-	-	-	-	-	-	-	-	-	-
1996	-	-	-	-	-	-	-	-	-	-	192.7	2.4	-	-	-	-	-	-	-	-	-	-	-	-
1997	-	-	-	-	-	-	-	-	-	-	201.2	4.4	-	-	-	-	-	-	-	-	-	-	-	-

Source: U.S. Department of Labor, Bureau of Labor Statistics, Division of Consumer Prices and Price Indexes. - indicates no data collected for period.

Denver-Boulder, CO
Consumer Price Index - Urban Wage Earners
Base 1982-1984 = 100
Other Goods and Services

For 1976-1997. Columns headed % show percentile change in the index from the previous period for which an index is available.

Year	Jan Index	%	Feb Index	%	Mar Index	%	Apr Index	%	May Index	%	Jun Index	%	Jul Index	%	Aug Index	%	Sep Index	%	Oct Index	%	Nov Index	%	Dec Index	%
1976	50.8	-	-	-	-	-	52.0	2.4	-	-	-	-	52.4	0.8	-	-	-	-	53.0	1.1	-	-	-	-
1977	54.1	2.1	-	-	-	-	54.9	1.5	-	-	-	-	57.2	4.2	-	-	-	-	59.1	3.3	-	-	-	-
1978	59.9	1.4	-	-	60.2	0.5	-	-	60.3	0.2	-	-	60.7	0.7	-	-	60.6	-0.2	-	-	61.8	2.0	-	-
1979	63.0	1.9	-	-	64.8	2.9	-	-	65.0	0.3	-	-	65.2	0.3	-	-	67.0	2.8	-	-	66.6	-0.6	-	-
1980	69.5	4.4	-	-	70.5	1.4	-	-	70.9	0.6	-	-	70.8	-0.1	-	-	73.0	3.1	-	-	76.1	4.2	-	-
1981	78.0	2.5	-	-	78.8	1.0	-	-	80.5	2.2	-	-	79.2	-1.6	-	-	81.3	2.7	-	-	82.3	1.2	-	-
1982	85.1	3.4	-	-	86.8	2.0	-	-	86.5	-0.3	-	-	88.5	2.3	-	-	89.9	1.6	-	-	93.8	4.3	-	-
1983	96.7	3.1	-	-	99.0	2.4	-	-	99.8	0.8	-	-	102.1	2.3	-	-	103.7	1.6	-	-	106.5	2.7	-	-
1984	108.1	1.5	-	-	108.4	0.3	-	-	108.6	0.2	-	-	109.3	0.6	-	-	109.5	0.2	-	-	110.7	1.1	-	-
1985	113.4	2.4	-	-	114.2	0.7	-	-	114.9	0.6	-	-	113.8	-1.0	-	-	116.7	2.5	-	-	117.9	1.0	-	-
1986	118.7	0.7	-	-	121.7	2.5	-	-	121.1	-0.5	-	-	123.4	1.9	-	-	127.9	3.6	-	-	129.3	1.1	129.3	0.0
1987	-	-	-	-	-	-	-	-	-	-	121.7	-5.9	-	-	-	-	-	-	-	-	-	-	-	-
1988	-	-	-	-	-	-	-	-	-	-	131.9	8.4	-	-	-	-	-	-	-	-	-	-	-	-
1989	-	-	-	-	-	-	-	-	-	-	140.7	6.7	-	-	-	-	-	-	-	-	-	-	-	-
1990	-	-	-	-	-	-	-	-	-	-	148.8	5.8	-	-	-	-	-	-	-	-	-	-	-	-
1991	-	-	-	-	-	-	-	-	-	-	158.5	6.5	-	-	-	-	-	-	-	-	-	-	-	-
1992	-	-	-	-	-	-	-	-	-	-	170.3	7.4	-	-	-	-	-	-	-	-	-	-	-	-
1993	-	-	-	-	-	-	-	-	-	-	182.4	7.1	-	-	-	-	-	-	-	-	-	-	-	-
1994	-	-	-	-	-	-	-	-	-	-	184.4	1.1	-	-	-	-	-	-	-	-	-	-	-	-
1995	-	-	-	-	-	-	-	-	-	-	189.3	2.7	-	-	-	-	-	-	-	-	-	-	-	-
1996	-	-	-	-	-	-	-	-	-	-	193.3	2.1	-	-	-	-	-	-	-	-	-	-	-	-
1997	-	-	-	-	-	-	-	-	-	-	202.7	4.9	-	-	-	-	-	-	-	-	-	-	-	-

Source: U.S. Department of Labor, Bureau of Labor Statistics, Division of Consumer Prices and Price Indexes. - indicates no data collected for period.

Detroit, MI
Consumer Price Index - All Urban Consumers
Base 1982-1984 = 100
Annual Averages

For 1914-1997. Columns headed % show percentile change in the index from the previous period for which an index is available.

Year	All Items		Food & Beverage		Housing		Apparel & Upkeep		Trans- portation		Medical Care		Entertain- ment		Other Goods & Services	
	Index	%	Index	%	Index	%	Index	%	Index	%	Index	%	Index	%	Index	%
1914	-	-	-	-	-	-	-	-	-	-	-	-	-	-	-	-
1915	9.8	-	-	-	-	-	-	-	-	-	-	-	-	-	-	-
1916	10.8	10.2	-	-	-	-	-	-	-	-	-	-	-	-	-	-
1917	13.3	23.1	-	-	-	-	-	-	-	-	-	-	-	-	-	-
1918	15.7	18.0	-	-	-	-	-	-	-	-	-	-	-	-	-	-
1919	18.2	15.9	-	-	-	-	-	-	-	-	-	-	-	-	-	-
1920	21.8	19.8	-	-	-	-	-	-	-	-	-	-	-	-	-	-
1921	19.0	-12.8	-	-	-	-	-	-	-	-	-	-	-	-	-	-
1922	17.4	-8.4	-	-	-	-	-	-	-	-	-	-	-	-	-	-
1923	18.0	3.4	-	-	-	-	-	-	-	-	-	-	-	-	-	-
1924	18.0	0.0	-	-	-	-	-	-	-	-	-	-	-	-	-	-
1925	18.2	1.1	-	-	-	-	-	-	-	-	-	-	-	-	-	-
1926	18.3	0.5	-	-	-	-	-	-	-	-	-	-	-	-	-	-
1927	17.9	-2.2	-	-	-	-	-	-	-	-	-	-	-	-	-	-
1928	17.5	-2.2	-	-	-	-	-	-	-	-	-	-	-	-	-	-
1929	17.6	0.6	-	-	-	-	-	-	-	-	-	-	-	-	-	-
1930	16.9	-4.0	-	-	-	-	-	-	-	-	-	-	-	-	-	-
1931	14.8	-12.4	-	-	-	-	-	-	-	-	-	-	-	-	-	-
1932	12.8	-13.5	-	-	-	-	-	-	-	-	-	-	-	-	-	-
1933	12.1	-5.5	-	-	-	-	-	-	-	-	-	-	-	-	-	-
1934	12.8	5.8	-	-	-	-	-	-	-	-	-	-	-	-	-	-
1935	13.4	4.7	-	-	-	-	-	-	-	-	-	-	-	-	-	-
1936	13.8	3.0	-	-	-	-	-	-	-	-	-	-	-	-	-	-
1937	14.7	6.5	-	-	-	-	-	-	-	-	-	-	-	-	-	-
1938	14.4	-2.0	-	-	-	-	-	-	-	-	-	-	-	-	-	-
1939	14.0	-2.8	-	-	-	-	-	-	-	-	-	-	-	-	-	-
1940	14.1	0.7	-	-	-	-	-	-	-	-	-	-	-	-	-	-
1941	15.0	6.4	-	-	-	-	-	-	-	-	-	-	-	-	-	-
1942	16.7	11.3	-	-	-	-	-	-	-	-	-	-	-	-	-	-
1943	17.5	4.8	-	-	-	-	-	-	-	-	-	-	-	-	-	-
1944	17.8	1.7	-	-	-	-	-	-	-	-	-	-	-	-	-	-
1945	18.3	2.8	-	-	-	-	-	-	-	-	-	-	-	-	-	-
1946	19.9	8.7	-	-	-	-	-	-	-	-	-	-	-	-	-	-
1947	22.7	14.1	-	-	-	-	-	-	19.7	-	11.8	-	-	-	-	-
1948	24.5	7.9	-	-	-	-	-	-	22.2	12.7	12.3	4.2	-	-	-	-
1949	24.2	-1.2	-	-	-	-	-	-	23.4	5.4	12.6	2.4	-	-	-	-
1950	24.6	1.7	-	-	-	-	-	-	23.7	1.3	12.8	1.6	-	-	-	-
1951	26.5	7.7	-	-	-	-	-	-	24.7	4.2	13.4	4.7	-	-	-	-
1952	27.1	2.3	-	-	-	-	-	-	26.4	6.9	14.1	5.2	-	-	-	-
1953	27.6	1.8	-	-	-	-	52.1	-	27.5	4.2	14.7	4.3	-	-	-	-
1954	27.7	0.4	-	-	-	-	51.9	-0.4	26.3	-4.4	15.3	4.1	-	-	-	-
1955	27.7	0.0	-	-	-	-	51.8	-0.2	26.6	1.1	16.3	6.5	-	-	-	-
1956	28.2	1.8	-	-	-	-	52.6	1.5	27.5	3.4	17.4	6.7	-	-	-	-
1957	29.0	2.8	-	-	-	-	53.2	1.1	28.9	5.1	18.0	3.4	-	-	-	-
1958	29.4	1.4	-	-	-	-	53.0	-0.4	29.0	0.3	18.5	2.8	-	-	-	-

[Continued]

472

Detroit, MI
Consumer Price Index - All Urban Consumers
Base 1982-1984 = 100
Annual Averages
[Continued]

For 1914-1997. Columns headed % show percentile change in the index from the previous period for which an index is available.

Year	All Items		Food & Beverage		Housing		Apparel & Upkeep		Trans- portation		Medical Care		Entertain- ment		Other Goods & Services	
	Index	%	Index	%	Index	%	Index	%	Index	%	Index	%	Index	%	Index	%
1959	29.4	0.0	-	-	-	-	53.9	1.7	30.1	3.8	19.3	4.3	-	-	-	-
1960	29.7	1.0	-	-	-	-	54.4	0.9	30.2	0.3	19.6	1.6	-	-	-	-
1961	29.8	0.3	-	-	-	-	55.2	1.5	29.7	-1.7	20.6	5.1	-	-	-	-
1962	29.9	0.3	-	-	-	-	55.5	0.5	30.3	2.0	21.2	2.9	-	-	-	-
1963	30.2	1.0	-	-	-	-	56.1	1.1	30.4	0.3	22.3	5.2	-	-	-	-
1964	30.4	0.7	-	-	-	-	56.8	1.2	30.7	1.0	23.2	4.0	-	-	-	-
1965	31.2	2.6	-	-	-	-	57.7	1.6	32.0	4.2	23.8	2.6	-	-	-	-
1966	32.5	4.2	-	-	-	-	59.0	2.3	32.8	2.5	25.1	5.5	-	-	-	-
1967	33.6	3.4	-	-	-	-	60.6	2.7	33.5	2.1	26.9	7.2	-	-	-	-
1968	35.1	4.5	-	-	-	-	63.2	4.3	34.9	4.2	28.7	6.7	-	-	-	-
1969	37.2	6.0	-	-	-	-	66.0	4.4	36.0	3.2	30.8	7.3	-	-	-	-
1970	39.5	6.2	-	-	-	-	67.9	2.9	36.9	2.5	33.5	8.8	-	-	-	-
1971	40.9	3.5	-	-	-	-	70.0	3.1	38.4	4.1	36.1	7.8	-	-	-	-
1972	42.5	3.9	-	-	-	-	71.7	2.4	39.1	1.8	38.0	5.3	-	-	-	-
1973	45.2	6.4	-	-	-	-	74.1	3.3	41.5	6.1	40.0	5.3	-	-	-	-
1974	50.1	10.8	-	-	-	-	80.2	8.2	46.5	12.0	43.8	9.5	-	-	-	-
1975	53.9	7.6	-	-	-	-	83.6	4.2	50.0	7.5	50.4	15.1	-	-	-	-
1976	56.8	5.4	63.8	-	52.3	-	86.0	2.9	53.7	7.4	56.3	11.7	73.5	-	57.5	-
1977	60.7	6.9	67.6	6.0	55.8	6.7	88.9	3.4	58.6	9.1	63.2	12.3	75.7	3.0	61.3	6.6
1978	65.3	7.6	74.5	10.2	60.3	8.1	89.7	0.9	62.0	5.8	67.7	7.1	80.0	5.7	65.8	7.3
1979	73.6	12.7	82.2	10.3	70.3	16.6	89.7	0.0	70.4	13.5	73.9	9.2	82.8	3.5	70.2	6.7
1980	85.3	15.9	88.9	8.2	85.5	21.6	94.3	5.1	82.8	17.6	80.1	8.4	87.8	6.0	75.1	7.0
1981	93.2	9.3	95.8	7.8	93.4	9.2	96.4	2.2	93.8	13.3	86.1	7.5	92.3	5.1	81.8	8.9
1982	97.0	4.1	99.3	3.7	96.3	3.1	98.3	2.0	97.9	4.4	93.2	8.2	97.0	5.1	91.8	12.2
1983	99.8	2.9	99.3	0.0	100.4	4.3	101.0	2.7	98.5	0.6	98.3	5.5	101.2	4.3	102.0	11.1
1984	103.2	3.4	101.4	2.1	103.3	2.9	100.8	-0.2	103.6	5.2	108.5	10.4	101.8	0.6	106.2	4.1
1985	106.8	3.5	103.2	1.8	107.5	4.1	102.6	1.8	106.6	2.9	116.4	7.3	106.6	4.7	111.6	5.1
1986	108.3	1.4	107.3	4.0	109.8	2.1	103.3	0.7	103.2	-3.2	125.0	7.4	108.6	1.9	114.6	2.7
1987	111.7	3.1	110.5	3.0	113.0	2.9	108.0	4.5	105.3	2.0	132.9	6.3	112.1	3.2	120.4	5.1
1988	116.1	3.9	114.7	3.8	116.1	2.7	115.2	6.7	109.5	4.0	140.2	5.5	114.7	2.3	130.0	8.0
1989	122.3	5.3	120.8	5.3	121.2	4.4	122.7	6.5	117.0	6.8	147.1	4.9	120.5	5.1	137.9	6.1
1990	128.6	5.2	126.5	4.7	126.4	4.3	127.9	4.2	124.0	6.0	159.8	8.6	128.1	6.3	147.5	7.0
1991	133.1	3.5	131.1	3.6	128.6	1.7	131.8	3.0	129.3	4.3	171.0	7.0	132.7	3.6	160.7	8.9
1992	135.9	2.1	133.4	1.8	131.8	2.5	129.9	-1.4	129.9	0.5	181.6	6.2	130.7	-1.5	173.8	8.2
1993	139.6	2.7	135.2	1.3	134.4	2.0	137.9	6.2	132.5	2.0	190.9	5.1	137.7	5.4	183.5	5.6
1994	144.0	3.2	138.7	2.6	137.6	2.4	136.1	-1.3	138.6	4.6	199.7	4.6	145.7	5.8	197.1	7.4
1995	148.6	3.2	143.6	3.5	140.6	2.2	136.9	0.6	143.6	3.6	209.2	4.8	150.5	3.3	210.8	7.0
1996	152.5	2.6	147.9	3.0	145.5	3.5	131.7	-3.8	148.0	3.1	213.7	2.2	154.8	2.9	217.5	3.2
1997	156.3	2.5	151.4	2.4	149.9	3.0	135.2	2.7	149.0	0.7	214.1	0.2	160.3	3.6	228.4	5.0

Source: U.S. Department of Labor, Bureau of Labor Statistics, Division of Consumer Prices and Price Indexes. - indicates no data collected for period.

Detroit, MI
Consumer Price Index - Urban Wage Earners
Base 1982-1984 = 100
Annual Averages

For 1914-1997. Columns headed % show percentile change in the index from the previous period for which an index is available.

Year	All Items		Food & Beverage		Housing		Apparel & Upkeep		Trans- portation		Medical Care		Entertain- ment		Other Goods & Services	
	Index	%	Index	%	Index	%	Index	%	Index	%	Index	%	Index	%	Index	%
1914	-	-	-	-	-	-	-	-	-	-	-	-	-	-	-	-
1915	9.8	-	-	-	-	-	-	-	-	-	-	-	-	-	-	-
1916	10.9	11.2	-	-	-	-	-	-	-	-	-	-	-	-	-	-
1917	13.4	22.9	-	-	-	-	-	-	-	-	-	-	-	-	-	-
1918	15.8	17.9	-	-	-	-	-	-	-	-	-	-	-	-	-	-
1919	18.4	16.5	-	-	-	-	-	-	-	-	-	-	-	-	-	-
1920	22.0	19.6	-	-	-	-	-	-	-	-	-	-	-	-	-	-
1921	19.2	-12.7	-	-	-	-	-	-	-	-	-	-	-	-	-	-
1922	17.6	-8.3	-	-	-	-	-	-	-	-	-	-	-	-	-	-
1923	18.2	3.4	-	-	-	-	-	-	-	-	-	-	-	-	-	-
1924	18.2	0.0	-	-	-	-	-	-	-	-	-	-	-	-	-	-
1925	18.4	1.1	-	-	-	-	-	-	-	-	-	-	-	-	-	-
1926	18.5	0.5	-	-	-	-	-	-	-	-	-	-	-	-	-	-
1927	18.0	-2.7	-	-	-	-	-	-	-	-	-	-	-	-	-	-
1928	17.7	-1.7	-	-	-	-	-	-	-	-	-	-	-	-	-	-
1929	17.7	0.0	-	-	-	-	-	-	-	-	-	-	-	-	-	-
1930	17.0	-4.0	-	-	-	-	-	-	-	-	-	-	-	-	-	-
1931	14.9	-12.4	-	-	-	-	-	-	-	-	-	-	-	-	-	-
1932	12.9	-13.4	-	-	-	-	-	-	-	-	-	-	-	-	-	-
1933	12.2	-5.4	-	-	-	-	-	-	-	-	-	-	-	-	-	-
1934	12.9	5.7	-	-	-	-	-	-	-	-	-	-	-	-	-	-
1935	13.5	4.7	-	-	-	-	-	-	-	-	-	-	-	-	-	-
1936	14.0	3.7	-	-	-	-	-	-	-	-	-	-	-	-	-	-
1937	14.8	5.7	-	-	-	-	-	-	-	-	-	-	-	-	-	-
1938	14.6	-1.4	-	-	-	-	-	-	-	-	-	-	-	-	-	-
1939	14.2	-2.7	-	-	-	-	-	-	-	-	-	-	-	-	-	-
1940	14.2	0.0	-	-	-	-	-	-	-	-	-	-	-	-	-	-
1941	15.1	6.3	-	-	-	-	-	-	-	-	-	-	-	-	-	-
1942	16.8	11.3	-	-	-	-	-	-	-	-	-	-	-	-	-	-
1943	17.7	5.4	-	-	-	-	-	-	-	-	-	-	-	-	-	-
1944	18.0	1.7	-	-	-	-	-	-	-	-	-	-	-	-	-	-
1945	18.4	2.2	-	-	-	-	-	-	-	-	-	-	-	-	-	-
1946	20.1	9.2	-	-	-	-	-	-	-	-	-	-	-	-	-	-
1947	22.9	13.9	-	-	-	-	-	-	20.5	-	12.0	-	-	-	-	-
1948	24.7	7.9	-	-	-	-	-	-	23.0	12.2	12.5	4.2	-	-	-	-
1949	24.4	-1.2	-	-	-	-	-	-	24.3	5.7	12.8	2.4	-	-	-	-
1950	24.8	1.6	-	-	-	-	-	-	24.6	1.2	13.1	2.3	-	-	-	-
1951	26.8	8.1	-	-	-	-	-	-	25.6	4.1	13.6	3.8	-	-	-	-
1952	27.4	2.2	-	-	-	-	-	-	27.4	7.0	14.3	5.1	-	-	-	-
1953	27.8	1.5	-	-	-	-	53.0	-	28.5	4.0	14.9	4.2	-	-	-	-
1954	27.9	0.4	-	-	-	-	52.9	-0.2	27.3	-4.2	15.5	4.0	-	-	-	-
1955	27.9	0.0	-	-	-	-	52.7	-0.4	27.6	1.1	16.6	7.1	-	-	-	-
1956	28.5	2.2	-	-	-	-	53.5	1.5	28.5	3.3	17.7	6.6	-	-	-	-
1957	29.3	2.8	-	-	-	-	54.2	1.3	30.0	5.3	18.3	3.4	-	-	-	-
1958	29.7	1.4	-	-	-	-	54.0	-0.4	30.1	0.3	18.9	3.3	-	-	-	-

[Continued]

Detroit, MI
Consumer Price Index - Urban Wage Earners
Base 1982-1984 = 100
Annual Averages

[Continued]

For 1914-1997. Columns headed % show percentile change in the index from the previous period for which an index is available.

Year	All Items		Food & Beverage		Housing		Apparel & Upkeep		Transportation		Medical Care		Entertainment		Other Goods & Services	
	Index	%	Index	%	Index	%	Index	%	Index	%	Index	%	Index	%	Index	%
1959	29.7	0.0	-	-	-	-	54.8	1.5	31.3	4.0	19.6	3.7	-	-	-	-
1960	29.9	0.7	-	-	-	-	55.4	1.1	31.3	0.0	20.0	2.0	-	-	-	-
1961	30.1	0.7	-	-	-	-	56.2	1.4	30.8	-1.6	21.0	5.0	-	-	-	-
1962	30.2	0.3	-	-	-	-	56.5	0.5	31.5	2.3	21.6	2.9	-	-	-	-
1963	30.5	1.0	-	-	-	-	57.1	1.1	31.6	0.3	22.7	5.1	-	-	-	-
1964	30.7	0.7	-	-	-	-	57.9	1.4	31.8	0.6	23.6	4.0	-	-	-	-
1965	31.4	2.3	-	-	-	-	58.8	1.6	33.2	4.4	24.2	2.5	-	-	-	-
1966	32.8	4.5	-	-	-	-	60.1	2.2	34.0	2.4	25.6	5.8	-	-	-	-
1967	34.0	3.7	-	-	-	-	61.7	2.7	34.8	2.4	27.4	7.0	-	-	-	-
1968	35.4	4.1	-	-	-	-	64.3	4.2	36.2	4.0	29.2	6.6	-	-	-	-
1969	37.6	6.2	-	-	-	-	67.2	4.5	37.4	3.3	31.4	7.5	-	-	-	-
1970	39.9	6.1	-	-	-	-	69.1	2.8	38.2	2.1	34.1	8.6	-	-	-	-
1971	41.3	3.5	-	-	-	-	71.3	3.2	39.9	4.5	36.8	7.9	-	-	-	-
1972	42.8	3.6	-	-	-	-	73.0	2.4	40.5	1.5	38.8	5.4	-	-	-	-
1973	45.7	6.8	-	-	-	-	75.4	3.3	43.0	6.2	40.7	4.9	-	-	-	-
1974	50.6	10.7	-	-	-	-	81.7	8.4	48.3	12.3	44.6	9.6	-	-	-	-
1975	54.4	7.5	-	-	-	-	85.1	4.2	51.9	7.5	51.4	15.2	-	-	-	-
1976	57.3	5.3	63.2	-	52.5	-	87.6	2.9	55.8	7.5	57.4	11.7	77.0	-	55.5	-
1977	61.3	7.0	66.9	5.9	56.0	6.7	90.5	3.3	60.8	9.0	64.4	12.2	79.3	3.0	59.1	6.5
1978	65.9	7.5	74.2	10.9	60.3	7.7	93.7	3.5	64.1	5.4	69.1	7.3	83.1	4.8	63.0	6.6
1979	74.3	12.7	82.2	10.8	70.3	16.6	93.6	-0.1	72.7	13.4	75.8	9.7	86.0	3.5	67.3	6.8
1980	85.6	15.2	88.7	7.9	85.2	21.2	97.7	4.4	84.5	16.2	81.3	7.3	90.9	5.7	73.5	9.2
1981	92.7	8.3	95.7	7.9	92.6	8.7	97.3	-0.4	93.1	10.2	86.8	6.8	92.7	2.0	80.5	9.5
1982	96.7	4.3	99.4	3.9	95.7	3.3	98.4	1.1	97.8	5.0	93.5	7.7	97.3	5.0	91.7	13.9
1983	101.1	4.6	99.2	-0.2	103.4	8.0	100.8	2.4	98.5	0.7	98.5	5.3	101.1	3.9	102.1	11.3
1984	102.2	1.1	101.4	2.2	100.9	-2.4	100.8	0.0	103.6	5.2	108.1	9.7	101.6	0.5	106.2	4.0
1985	104.5	2.3	102.9	1.5	102.7	1.8	103.5	2.7	106.7	3.0	115.6	6.9	106.5	4.8	111.5	5.0
1986	105.8	1.2	106.9	3.9	104.9	2.1	105.5	1.9	103.2	-3.3	123.6	6.9	109.3	2.6	114.1	2.3
1987	109.1	3.1	110.2	3.1	108.0	3.0	111.3	5.5	105.5	2.2	131.3	6.2	112.9	3.3	120.0	5.2
1988	113.3	3.8	114.2	3.6	110.9	2.7	119.1	7.0	109.5	3.8	139.6	6.3	115.5	2.3	130.1	8.4
1989	119.4	5.4	120.3	5.3	115.7	4.3	125.9	5.7	117.0	6.8	146.9	5.2	121.4	5.1	137.4	5.6
1990	125.6	5.2	126.1	4.8	120.7	4.3	131.8	4.7	124.1	6.1	159.1	8.3	128.8	6.1	147.3	7.2
1991	129.8	3.3	130.7	3.6	122.8	1.7	134.9	2.4	129.2	4.1	169.7	6.7	133.4	3.6	160.3	8.8
1992	132.1	1.8	133.1	1.8	125.7	2.4	133.3	-1.2	129.7	0.4	180.0	6.1	130.8	-1.9	170.0	6.1
1993	135.4	2.5	134.8	1.3	128.1	1.9	140.6	5.5	132.4	2.1	189.3	5.2	137.9	5.4	175.8	3.4
1994	139.5	3.0	138.4	2.7	131.0	2.3	138.9	-1.2	138.6	4.7	197.4	4.3	146.0	5.9	186.7	6.2
1995	143.9	3.2	143.4	3.6	133.8	2.1	139.0	0.1	143.7	3.7	207.1	4.9	150.8	3.3	201.9	8.1
1996	147.7	2.6	147.6	2.9	138.2	3.3	134.6	-3.2	148.1	3.1	212.0	2.4	155.0	2.8	209.1	3.6
1997	151.0	2.2	151.1	2.4	142.2	2.9	137.9	2.5	149.0	0.6	212.3	0.1	160.0	3.2	218.9	4.7

Source: U.S. Department of Labor, Bureau of Labor Statistics, Division of Consumer Prices and Price Indexes. - indicates no data collected for period.

Detroit, MI
Consumer Price Index - All Urban Consumers
Base 1982-1984 = 100
All Items

For 1914-1997. Columns headed % show percentile change in the index from the previous period for which an index is available.

Year	Jan Index	%	Feb Index	%	Mar Index	%	Apr Index	%	May Index	%	Jun Index	%	Jul Index	%	Aug Index	%	Sep Index	%	Oct Index	%	Nov Index	%	Dec Index	%
1914	-	-	-	-	-	-	-	-	-	-	-	-	-	-	-	-	-	-	-	-	-	-	9.7	-
1915	-	-	-	-	-	-	-	-	-	-	-	-	-	-	-	-	-	-	-	-	-	-	10.1	4.1
1916	-	-	-	-	-	-	-	-	-	-	-	-	-	-	-	-	-	-	-	-	-	-	11.7	15.8
1917	-	-	-	-	-	-	-	-	-	-	-	-	-	-	-	-	-	-	-	-	-	-	14.3	22.2
1918	-	-	-	-	-	-	-	-	-	-	-	-	-	-	-	-	-	-	-	-	-	-	17.0	18.9
1919	-	-	-	-	-	-	-	-	-	-	17.8	4.7	-	-	-	-	-	-	-	-	-	-	19.9	11.8
1920	-	-	-	-	-	-	-	-	-	-	22.9	15.1	-	-	-	-	-	-	-	-	-	-	21.2	-7.4
1921	-	-	-	-	-	-	-	-	19.0	-10.4	-	-	-	-	-	-	18.5	-2.6	-	-	-	-	17.9	-3.2
1922	-	-	-	-	17.3	-3.4	-	-	-	-	17.4	0.6	-	-	-	-	17.3	-0.6	-	-	-	-	17.5	1.2
1923	-	-	-	-	17.7	1.1	-	-	-	-	18.0	1.7	-	-	-	-	18.4	2.2	-	-	-	-	18.2	-1.1
1924	-	-	-	-	18.1	-0.5	-	-	-	-	18.1	0.0	-	-	-	-	17.9	-1.1	-	-	-	-	17.9	0.0
1925	-	-	-	-	-	-	-	-	-	-	18.3	2.2	-	-	-	-	-	-	-	-	-	-	18.6	1.6
1926	-	-	-	-	-	-	-	-	-	-	18.4	-1.1	-	-	-	-	-	-	-	-	-	-	18.2	-1.1
1927	-	-	-	-	-	-	-	-	-	-	18.2	0.0	-	-	-	-	-	-	-	-	-	-	17.7	-2.7
1928	-	-	-	-	-	-	-	-	-	-	17.4	-1.7	-	-	-	-	-	-	-	-	-	-	17.4	0.0
1929	-	-	-	-	-	-	-	-	-	-	17.6	1.1	-	-	-	-	-	-	-	-	-	-	17.5	-0.6
1930	-	-	-	-	-	-	-	-	-	-	17.2	-1.7	-	-	-	-	-	-	-	-	-	-	15.9	-7.6
1931	-	-	-	-	-	-	-	-	-	-	14.8	-6.9	-	-	-	-	-	-	-	-	-	-	13.9	-6.1
1932	-	-	-	-	-	-	-	-	-	-	12.9	-7.2	-	-	-	-	-	-	-	-	-	-	12.1	-6.2
1933	-	-	-	-	-	-	-	-	-	-	11.7	-3.3	-	-	-	-	-	-	-	-	-	-	12.3	5.1
1934	-	-	-	-	-	-	-	-	-	-	12.8	4.1	-	-	-	-	-	-	-	-	12.8	0.0	-	-
1935	-	-	-	-	13.3	3.9	-	-	-	-	-	-	13.4	0.8	-	-	-	-	13.4	0.0	-	-	-	-
1936	13.6	1.5	-	-	-	-	13.6	0.0	-	-	-	-	14.0	2.9	-	-	14.1	0.7	-	-	-	-	14.0	-0.7
1937	-	-	-	-	14.4	2.9	-	-	-	-	14.8	2.8	-	-	-	-	14.9	0.7	-	-	-	-	15.0	0.7
1938	-	-	-	-	14.6	-2.7	-	-	-	-	14.5	-0.7	-	-	-	-	14.3	-1.4	-	-	-	-	14.2	-0.7
1939	-	-	-	-	14.0	-1.4	-	-	-	-	13.9	-0.7	-	-	-	-	14.1	1.4	-	-	-	-	14.0	-0.7
1940	-	-	-	-	14.1	0.7	-	-	-	-	14.2	0.7	-	-	-	-	14.1	-0.7	14.1	0.0	14.1	0.0	14.2	0.7
1941	14.2	0.0	14.3	0.7	14.4	0.7	14.6	1.4	14.6	0.0	15.0	2.7	15.0	0.0	15.1	0.7	15.4	2.0	15.7	1.9	15.8	0.6	15.9	0.6
1942	16.1	1.3	16.2	0.6	16.5	1.9	16.7	1.2	16.7	0.0	16.7	0.0	16.7	0.0	16.6	-0.6	16.7	0.6	16.9	1.2	17.0	0.6	17.1	0.6
1943	17.1	0.0	17.2	0.6	17.5	1.7	17.6	0.6	17.9	1.7	17.9	0.0	17.8	-0.6	17.5	-1.7	17.5	0.0	17.6	0.6	17.5	-0.6	17.7	1.1
1944	17.6	-0.6	17.5	-0.6	17.5	0.0	17.7	1.1	17.7	0.0	17.8	0.6	18.0	1.1	18.0	0.0	18.0	0.0	17.9	-0.6	17.9	0.0	18.0	0.6
1945	18.0	0.0	18.0	0.0	18.0	0.0	18.0	0.0	18.2	1.1	18.4	1.1	18.4	0.0	18.5	0.5	18.4	-0.5	18.4	0.0	18.5	0.5	18.5	0.0
1946	18.6	0.5	18.6	0.0	18.6	0.0	18.8	1.1	19.0	1.1	19.2	1.1	20.4	6.2	20.5	0.5	20.7	1.0	21.0	1.4	21.4	1.9	21.6	0.9
1947	21.6	0.0	21.6	0.0	22.1	2.3	22.1	0.0	22.1	0.0	22.4	1.4	22.6	0.9	23.0	1.8	23.2	0.9	23.6	1.7	23.5	-0.4	23.9	1.7
1948	24.1	0.8	23.9	-0.8	23.8	-0.4	24.3	2.1	24.5	0.8	24.7	0.8	24.9	0.8	24.9	0.0	24.8	-0.4	24.7	-0.4	24.5	-0.8	24.5	0.0
1949	24.3	-0.8	24.2	-0.4	24.2	0.0	24.2	0.0	24.3	0.4	24.3	0.0	24.1	-0.8	24.1	0.0	24.1	0.0	23.9	-0.8	24.1	0.8	24.0	-0.4
1950	23.9	-0.4	23.8	-0.4	24.0	0.8	24.0	0.0	24.2	0.8	24.4	0.8	24.6	0.8	24.7	0.4	25.0	1.2	25.2	0.8	25.3	0.4	25.5	0.8
1951	25.9	1.6	26.2	1.2	26.3	0.4	26.3	0.0	26.3	0.0	26.5	0.8	26.5	0.0	26.5	0.0	26.6	0.4	26.7	0.4	26.9	0.7	27.0	0.4
1952	27.0	0.0	26.8	-0.7	26.8	0.0	27.0	0.7	27.0	0.0	27.0	0.0	27.2	0.7	27.3	0.4	27.2	-0.4	27.4	0.7	27.4	0.0	27.6	0.7
1953	27.5	-0.4	27.3	-0.7	27.4	0.4	27.4	0.0	27.5	0.4	27.7	0.7	27.8	0.4	27.8	0.0	27.8	0.0	27.9	0.4	27.7	-0.7	27.7	0.0
1954	27.8	0.4	27.7	-0.4	27.7	0.0	27.7	0.0	27.8	0.4	27.8	0.0	27.9	0.4	27.7	-0.7	27.6	-0.4	27.6	0.0	27.8	0.7	27.6	-0.7
1955	27.6	0.0	27.6	0.0	27.6	0.0	27.6	0.0	27.7	0.4	27.7	0.0	27.7	0.0	27.7	0.0	27.8	0.4	27.7	-0.4	27.7	0.0	28.6	0.0
1956	27.6	-0.4	27.7	0.4	27.8	0.4	27.9	0.4	28.0	0.4	28.2	0.7	28.6	1.4	28.4	-0.7	28.4	0.0	28.5	0.4	28.6	0.4	28.6	0.0
1957	28.6	0.0	28.7	0.3	28.7	0.0	28.8	0.3	29.0	0.7	29.1	0.3	29.2	0.3	29.2	0.0	29.2	0.0	29.1	-0.3	29.3	0.7	29.3	0.0
1958	29.4	0.3	29.4	0.0	29.5	0.3	29.5	0.0	29.5	0.0	29.5	0.0	29.5	0.0	29.4	-0.3	29.4	0.0	29.3	-0.3	29.3	0.0	29.3	0.0

[Continued]

Detroit, MI
Consumer Price Index - All Urban Consumers
Base 1982-1984 = 100
All Items
[Continued]

For 1914-1997. Columns headed % show percentile change in the index from the previous period for which an index is available.

Year	Jan Index	%	Feb Index	%	Mar Index	%	Apr Index	%	May Index	%	Jun Index	%	Jul Index	%	Aug Index	%	Sep Index	%	Oct Index	%	Nov Index	%	Dec Index	%
1959	29.3	0.0	29.3	0.0	29.2	-0.3	29.3	0.3	29.3	0.0	29.3	0.0	29.5	0.7	29.4	-0.3	29.6	0.7	29.7	0.3	29.5	-0.7	29.5	0.0
1960	29.3	-0.7	29.4	0.3	29.4	0.0	29.5	0.3	29.5	0.0	29.7	0.7	29.9	0.7	29.8	-0.3	29.8	0.0	29.8	0.0	29.8	0.0	29.9	0.3
1961	30.0	0.3	30.0	0.0	29.9	-0.3	29.8	-0.3	29.8	0.0	29.9	0.3	29.8	-0.3	29.9	0.3	29.7	-0.7	29.8	0.3	29.7	-0.3	29.5	-0.7
1962	29.6	0.3	29.9	1.0	29.9	0.0	29.9	0.0	29.9	0.0	29.8	-0.3	29.8	0.0	29.9	0.3	30.1	0.7	30.1	0.0	30.0	-0.3	30.0	0.0
1963	30.0	0.0	30.0	0.0	30.0	0.0	29.9	-0.3	30.0	0.3	30.3	1.0	30.4	0.3	30.6	0.7	30.2	-1.3	30.3	0.3	30.4	0.3	30.3	-0.3
1964	30.4	0.3	30.2	-0.7	30.3	0.3	30.4	0.3	30.2	-0.7	30.3	0.3	30.5	0.7	30.5	0.0	30.6	0.3	30.7	0.3	30.6	-0.3	30.7	0.3
1965	30.7	0.0	30.6	-0.3	30.7	0.3	30.9	0.7	31.1	0.6	31.3	0.6	31.3	0.0	31.3	0.0	31.3	0.0	31.5	0.6	31.5	0.0	31.6	0.3
1966	31.7	0.3	31.9	0.6	32.1	0.6	32.3	0.6	32.4	0.3	32.6	0.6	32.6	0.0	32.8	0.6	32.8	0.0	33.0	0.6	33.0	0.0	33.2	0.6
1967	33.2	0.0	33.2	0.0	33.5	0.9	33.5	0.0	33.5	0.0	33.6	0.3	33.7	0.3	33.7	0.0	33.7	0.0	33.8	0.3	34.0	0.6	34.1	0.3
1968	34.1	0.0	34.3	0.6	34.6	0.9	34.7	0.3	34.8	0.3	35.1	0.9	35.2	0.3	35.3	0.3	35.5	0.6	35.6	0.3	35.8	0.6	35.9	0.3
1969	36.0	0.3	36.1	0.3	36.6	1.4	36.8	0.5	37.0	0.5	37.3	0.8	37.4	0.3	37.6	0.5	37.6	0.0	37.8	0.5	38.0	0.5	38.3	0.8
1970	38.4	0.3	38.7	0.8	39.0	0.8	39.2	0.5	39.5	0.8	39.6	0.3	39.7	0.3	39.6	-0.3	39.8	0.5	40.1	0.8	40.3	0.5	40.2	-0.2
1971	40.5	0.7	40.4	-0.2	40.4	0.0	40.4	0.0	40.7	0.7	41.0	0.7	41.0	0.0	41.3	0.7	41.3	0.0	41.3	0.0	41.5	0.5	41.6	0.2
1972	41.8	0.5	42.0	0.5	42.1	0.2	42.1	0.0	42.2	0.2	42.4	0.5	42.6	0.5	42.7	0.2	42.8	0.2	42.8	0.0	42.9	0.2	43.2	0.7
1973	43.2	0.0	43.6	0.9	44.1	1.1	44.5	0.9	44.9	0.9	45.0	0.2	45.0	0.0	46.0	2.2	46.2	0.4	46.4	0.4	46.8	0.9	47.1	0.6
1974	47.6	1.1	48.4	1.7	48.7	0.6	48.9	0.4	49.3	0.8	49.9	1.2	50.3	0.8	50.8	1.0	51.3	1.0	51.7	0.8	52.2	1.0	52.5	0.6
1975	52.3	-0.4	52.7	0.8	52.8	0.2	53.1	0.6	53.2	0.2	53.7	0.9	54.1	0.7	54.3	0.4	54.8	0.9	54.9	0.2	55.1	0.4	55.4	0.5
1976	55.7	0.5	55.8	0.2	55.7	-0.2	56.0	0.5	56.3	0.5	56.5	0.4	56.9	0.7	57.1	0.4	57.6	0.9	57.7	0.2	58.0	0.5	58.2	0.3
1977	58.5	0.5	58.9	0.7	59.5	1.0	60.2	1.2	60.3	0.2	60.9	1.0	61.4	0.8	61.4	0.0	61.5	0.2	61.6	0.2	62.1	0.8	62.0	-0.2
1978	62.2	0.3	62.4	0.3	63.4	1.6	64.0	0.9	64.7	1.1	65.4	1.1	65.5	0.2	65.9	0.6	66.5	0.9	67.6	1.7	68.0	0.6	68.0	0.0
1979	69.0	1.5	70.2	1.7	71.2	1.4	71.7	0.7	72.0	0.4	72.5	0.7	73.8	1.8	74.8	1.4	75.3	0.7	76.4	1.5	77.8	1.8	78.5	0.9
1980	79.8	1.7	80.9	1.4	81.7	1.0	83.5	2.2	83.6	0.1	86.4	3.3	85.4	-1.2	85.8	0.5	87.3	1.7	88.9	1.8	89.6	0.8	90.7	1.2
1981	90.3	-0.4	90.9	0.7	90.2	-0.8	91.6	1.6	92.6	1.1	94.4	1.9	95.2	0.8	95.4	0.2	95.6	0.2	94.7	-0.9	94.1	-0.6	93.6	-0.5
1982	94.5	1.0	93.5	-1.1	93.6	0.1	95.4	1.9	96.2	0.8	97.3	1.1	98.4	1.1	98.5	0.1	99.2	0.7	99.3	0.1	99.6	0.3	98.4	-1.2
1983	98.4	0.0	98.3	-0.1	98.4	0.1	99.2	0.8	99.2	0.0	99.8	0.6	100.4	0.6	100.5	0.1	100.7	0.2	100.3	-0.4	100.9	0.6	101.0	0.1
1984	101.4	0.4	102.0	0.6	102.3	0.3	102.8	0.5	102.8	0.0	103.0	0.2	103.5	0.5	103.6	0.1	104.8	1.2	104.9	0.1	103.9	-1.0	104.0	0.1
1985	104.6	0.6	105.5	0.9	106.1	0.6	106.2	0.1	106.3	0.1	106.6	0.3	107.0	0.4	107.0	0.0	107.8	0.7	107.6	-0.2	108.7	1.0	108.7	0.0
1986	108.7	0.0	108.6	-0.1	107.7	-0.8	107.3	-0.4	108.2	0.8	108.0	-0.2	107.1	-0.8	108.7	1.5	108.0	-0.6	109.1	1.0	109.4	0.3	109.2	-0.2
1987	-	-	110.2	0.9	-	-	111.2	0.9	-	-	111.1	-0.1	-	-	112.2	1.0	-	-	114.1	1.7	-	-	112.6	-1.3
1988	-	-	113.7	1.0	-	-	114.4	0.6	-	-	115.4	0.9	-	-	117.6	1.9	-	-	118.6	0.9	-	-	118.3	-0.3
1989	-	-	120.1	1.5	-	-	121.7	1.3	-	-	122.1	0.3	-	-	122.2	0.1	-	-	124.6	2.0	-	-	124.4	-0.2
1990	-	-	126.1	1.4	-	-	126.9	0.6	-	-	127.7	0.6	-	-	129.4	1.3	-	-	131.8	1.9	-	-	131.2	-0.5
1991	-	-	132.2	0.8	-	-	131.7	-0.4	-	-	133.5	1.4	-	-	133.2	-0.2	-	-	134.6	1.1	-	-	134.0	-0.4
1992	-	-	134.9	0.7	-	-	135.3	0.3	-	-	135.5	0.1	-	-	135.8	0.2	-	-	137.5	1.3	-	-	137.1	-0.3
1993	-	-	138.3	0.9	-	-	138.7	0.3	-	-	139.1	0.3	-	-	139.9	0.6	-	-	141.9	1.4	-	-	140.2	-1.2
1994	-	-	141.7	1.1	-	-	142.6	0.6	-	-	144.8	1.5	-	-	145.3	0.3	-	-	145.7	0.3	-	-	145.5	-0.1
1995	-	-	147.3	1.2	-	-	148.1	0.5	-	-	148.3	0.1	-	-	148.8	0.3	-	-	149.8	0.7	-	-	150.3	0.3
1996	-	-	151.3	0.7	-	-	152.3	0.7	-	-	151.9	-0.3	-	-	152.7	0.5	-	-	153.8	0.7	-	-	154.3	0.3
1997	-	-	155.4	0.7	-	-	156.0	0.4	-	-	155.0	-0.6	-	-	156.9	1.2	-	-	157.9	0.6	-	-	157.1	-0.5

Source: U.S. Department of Labor, Bureau of Labor Statistics, Division of Consumer Prices and Price Indexes. - indicates no data collected for period.

Detroit, MI
Consumer Price Index - Urban Wage Earners
Base 1982-1984 = 100
All Items

For 1914-1997. Columns headed % show percentile change in the index from the previous period for which an index is available.

Year	Jan Index	%	Feb Index	%	Mar Index	%	Apr Index	%	May Index	%	Jun Index	%	Jul Index	%	Aug Index	%	Sep Index	%	Oct Index	%	Nov Index	%	Dec Index	%
1914	-	-	-	-	-	-	-	-	-	-	-	-	-	-	-	-	-	-	-	-	-	-	9.8	-
1915	-	-	-	-	-	-	-	-	-	-	-	-	-	-	-	-	-	-	-	-	-	-	10.2	4.1
1916	-	-	-	-	-	-	-	-	-	-	-	-	-	-	-	-	-	-	-	-	-	-	11.8	15.7
1917	-	-	-	-	-	-	-	-	-	-	-	-	-	-	-	-	-	-	-	-	-	-	14.4	22.0
1918	-	-	-	-	-	-	-	-	-	-	-	-	-	-	-	-	-	-	-	-	-	-	17.2	19.4
1919	-	-	-	-	-	-	-	-	-	-	17.9	4.1	-	-	-	-	-	-	-	-	-	-	20.1	12.3
1920	-	-	-	-	-	-	-	-	-	-	23.2	15.4	-	-	-	-	-	-	-	-	-	-	21.4	-7.8
1921	-	-	-	-	-	-	-	-	19.2	-10.3	-	-	-	-	-	-	18.6	-3.1	-	-	-	-	18.1	-2.7
1922	-	-	-	-	17.5	-3.3	-	-	-	-	17.6	0.6	-	-	-	-	17.5	-0.6	-	-	-	-	17.7	1.1
1923	-	-	-	-	17.9	1.1	-	-	-	-	18.2	1.7	-	-	-	-	18.5	1.6	-	-	-	-	18.4	-0.5
1924	-	-	-	-	18.3	-0.5	-	-	-	-	18.3	0.0	-	-	-	-	18.1	-1.1	-	-	-	-	18.1	0.0
1925	-	-	-	-	-	-	-	-	-	-	18.4	1.7	-	-	-	-	-	-	-	-	-	-	18.8	2.2
1926	-	-	-	-	-	-	-	-	-	-	18.6	-1.1	-	-	-	-	-	-	-	-	-	-	18.3	-1.6
1927	-	-	-	-	-	-	-	-	-	-	18.4	0.5	-	-	-	-	-	-	-	-	-	-	17.8	-3.3
1928	-	-	-	-	-	-	-	-	-	-	17.6	-1.1	-	-	-	-	-	-	-	-	-	-	17.6	0.0
1929	-	-	-	-	-	-	-	-	-	-	17.8	1.1	-	-	-	-	-	-	-	-	-	-	17.7	-0.6
1930	-	-	-	-	-	-	-	-	-	-	17.3	-2.3	-	-	-	-	-	-	-	-	-	-	16.1	-6.9
1931	-	-	-	-	-	-	-	-	-	-	14.9	-7.5	-	-	-	-	-	-	-	-	-	-	14.0	-6.0
1932	-	-	-	-	-	-	-	-	-	-	13.0	-7.1	-	-	-	-	-	-	-	-	-	-	12.2	-6.2
1933	-	-	-	-	-	-	-	-	-	-	11.8	-3.3	-	-	-	-	-	-	-	-	-	-	12.4	5.1
1934	-	-	-	-	-	-	-	-	-	-	12.9	4.0	-	-	-	-	-	-	-	-	12.9	0.0	-	-
1935	-	-	-	-	13.4	3.9	-	-	-	-	-	-	13.5	0.7	-	-	-	-	13.5	0.0	-	-	-	-
1936	13.7	1.5	-	-	-	-	13.7	0.0	-	-	-	-	14.1	2.9	-	-	14.2	0.7	-	-	-	-	14.1	-0.7
1937	-	-	-	-	14.6	3.5	-	-	-	-	14.9	2.1	-	-	-	-	15.1	1.3	-	-	-	-	15.1	0.0
1938	-	-	-	-	14.8	-2.0	-	-	-	-	14.6	-1.4	-	-	-	-	14.4	-1.4	-	-	-	-	14.3	-0.7
1939	-	-	-	-	14.2	-0.7	-	-	-	-	14.1	-0.7	-	-	-	-	14.2	0.7	-	-	-	-	14.2	0.0
1940	-	-	-	-	14.2	0.0	-	-	-	-	14.3	0.7	-	-	-	-	14.3	0.0	14.3	0.0	14.3	0.0	14.3	0.0
1941	14.4	0.7	14.4	0.0	14.5	0.7	14.7	1.4	14.7	0.0	15.1	2.7	15.2	0.7	15.3	0.7	15.6	2.0	15.9	1.9	16.0	0.6	16.0	0.0
1942	16.3	1.9	16.4	0.6	16.6	1.2	16.8	1.2	16.9	0.6	16.8	-0.6	16.8	0.0	16.8	0.0	16.8	0.0	17.0	1.2	17.1	0.6	17.2	0.6
1943	17.2	0.0	17.4	1.2	17.6	1.1	17.8	1.1	18.1	1.7	18.0	-0.6	17.9	-0.6	17.7	-1.1	17.7	0.0	17.8	0.6	17.7	-0.6	17.8	0.6
1944	17.8	0.0	17.7	-0.6	17.7	0.0	17.8	0.6	17.9	0.6	18.0	0.6	18.2	1.1	18.1	-0.5	18.1	0.0	18.1	0.0	18.1	0.0	18.1	0.0
1945	18.1	0.0	18.1	0.0	18.1	0.0	18.2	0.6	18.4	1.1	18.6	1.1	18.6	0.0	18.7	0.5	18.6	-0.5	18.6	0.0	18.6	0.0	18.7	0.5
1946	18.8	0.5	18.8	0.0	18.8	0.0	19.0	1.1	19.1	0.5	19.4	1.6	20.5	5.7	20.7	1.0	20.8	0.5	21.2	1.9	21.6	1.9	21.8	0.9
1947	21.8	0.0	21.8	0.0	22.3	2.3	22.3	0.0	22.3	0.0	22.6	1.3	22.9	1.3	23.2	1.3	23.4	0.9	23.8	1.7	23.8	0.0	24.1	1.3
1948	24.3	0.8	24.1	-0.8	24.0	-0.4	24.5	2.1	24.7	0.8	24.9	0.8	25.1	0.8	25.1	0.0	25.0	-0.4	24.9	-0.4	24.7	-0.8	24.7	0.0
1949	24.5	-0.8	24.4	-0.4	24.4	0.0	24.4	0.0	24.5	0.4	24.5	0.0	24.3	-0.8	24.3	0.0	24.3	0.0	24.1	-0.8	24.3	0.8	24.2	-0.4
1950	24.1	-0.4	24.0	-0.4	24.2	0.8	24.2	0.0	24.4	0.8	24.7	1.2	24.9	0.8	25.0	0.4	25.2	0.8	25.4	0.8	25.5	0.4	25.7	0.8
1951	26.1	1.6	26.4	1.1	26.6	0.8	26.5	-0.4	26.6	0.4	26.8	0.8	26.8	0.0	26.8	0.0	26.8	0.0	27.0	0.7	27.2	0.7	27.2	0.0
1952	27.2	0.0	27.1	-0.4	27.1	0.0	27.2	0.4	27.2	0.0	27.3	0.4	27.5	0.7	27.6	0.4	27.5	-0.4	27.7	0.7	27.6	-0.4	27.8	0.7
1953	27.7	-0.4	27.6	-0.4	27.6	0.0	27.6	0.0	27.7	0.4	27.9	0.7	28.0	0.4	28.0	0.0	28.0	0.0	28.1	0.4	27.9	-0.7	27.9	0.0
1954	28.0	0.4	27.9	-0.4	27.9	0.0	27.9	0.0	28.0	0.4	28.1	0.4	28.1	0.0	28.0	-0.4	27.8	-0.7	27.8	0.0	28.0	0.7	27.8	-0.7
1955	27.8	0.0	27.9	0.4	27.9	0.0	27.8	-0.4	27.9	0.4	27.9	0.0	28.0	0.4	27.9	-0.4	28.0	0.4	27.9	-0.4	28.0	0.4	27.9	-0.4
1956	27.9	0.0	27.9	0.0	28.0	0.4	28.1	0.4	28.3	0.7	28.5	0.7	28.8	1.1	28.7	-0.3	28.7	0.0	28.8	0.3	28.9	0.3	28.8	-0.3
1957	28.9	0.3	29.0	0.3	29.0	0.0	29.1	0.3	29.2	0.3	29.4	0.7	29.5	0.3	29.5	0.0	29.4	-0.3	29.4	0.0	29.6	0.7	29.5	-0.3
1958	29.6	0.3	29.6	0.0	29.7	0.3	29.8	0.3	29.8	0.0	29.7	-0.3	29.8	0.3	29.6	-0.7	29.7	0.3	29.5	-0.7	29.6	0.3	29.5	-0.3

[Continued]

Detroit, MI
Consumer Price Index - Urban Wage Earners
Base 1982-1984 = 100
All Items
[Continued]

For 1914-1997. Columns headed % show percentile change in the index from the previous period for which an index is available.

Year	Jan Index	%	Feb Index	%	Mar Index	%	Apr Index	%	May Index	%	Jun Index	%	Jul Index	%	Aug Index	%	Sep Index	%	Oct Index	%	Nov Index	%	Dec Index	%
1959	29.5	0.0	29.5	0.0	29.5	0.0	29.6	0.3	29.6	0.0	29.6	0.0	29.8	0.7	29.6	-0.7	29.9	1.0	29.9	0.0	29.7	-0.7	29.7	0.0
1960	29.6	-0.3	29.7	0.3	29.7	0.0	29.7	0.0	29.8	0.3	30.0	0.7	30.2	0.7	30.1	-0.3	30.0	-0.3	30.1	0.3	30.1	0.0	30.2	0.3
1961	30.3	0.3	30.3	0.0	30.2	-0.3	30.1	-0.3	30.1	0.0	30.2	0.3	30.1	-0.3	30.2	0.3	29.9	-1.0	30.0	0.3	30.0	0.0	29.8	-0.7
1962	29.9	0.3	30.2	1.0	30.2	0.0	30.2	0.0	30.2	0.0	30.1	-0.3	30.1	0.0	30.2	0.3	30.4	0.7	30.4	0.0	30.3	-0.3	30.3	0.0
1963	30.3	0.0	30.3	0.0	30.3	0.0	30.2	-0.3	30.3	0.3	30.6	1.0	30.7	0.3	30.9	0.7	30.5	-1.3	30.6	0.3	30.7	0.3	30.6	-0.3
1964	30.7	0.3	30.5	-0.7	30.6	0.3	30.7	0.3	30.5	-0.7	30.6	0.3	30.8	0.7	30.8	0.0	30.9	0.3	31.0	0.3	30.9	-0.3	31.0	0.3
1965	31.0	0.0	30.9	-0.3	31.0	0.3	31.2	0.6	31.3	0.3	31.6	1.0	31.6	0.0	31.6	0.0	31.6	0.0	31.7	0.3	31.8	0.3	31.9	0.3
1966	32.0	0.3	32.2	0.6	32.4	0.6	32.6	0.6	32.7	0.3	32.9	0.6	32.9	0.0	33.1	0.6	33.1	0.0	33.3	0.6	33.3	0.0	33.5	0.6
1967	33.5	0.0	33.5	0.0	33.8	0.9	33.9	0.3	33.9	0.0	33.9	0.0	34.0	0.3	34.1	0.3	34.1	0.0	34.1	0.0	34.3	0.6	34.4	0.3
1968	34.5	0.3	34.7	0.6	34.9	0.6	35.0	0.3	35.1	0.3	35.4	0.9	35.5	0.3	35.7	0.6	35.8	0.3	36.0	0.6	36.1	0.3	36.2	0.3
1969	36.3	0.3	36.5	0.6	37.0	1.4	37.1	0.3	37.3	0.5	37.6	0.8	37.7	0.3	38.0	0.8	38.0	0.0	38.2	0.5	38.4	0.5	38.6	0.5
1970	38.7	0.3	39.1	1.0	39.3	0.5	39.5	0.5	39.9	1.0	40.0	0.3	40.0	0.0	40.0	0.0	40.2	0.5	40.5	0.7	40.7	0.5	40.6	-0.2
1971	40.8	0.5	40.7	-0.2	40.8	0.2	40.8	0.0	41.0	0.5	41.4	1.0	41.4	0.0	41.7	0.7	41.7	0.0	41.7	0.0	41.9	0.5	42.0	0.2
1972	42.2	0.5	42.4	0.5	42.4	0.0	42.4	0.0	42.6	0.5	42.8	0.5	43.0	0.5	43.1	0.2	43.2	0.2	43.2	0.0	43.3	0.2	43.6	0.7
1973	43.6	0.0	44.0	0.9	44.5	1.1	45.0	1.1	45.3	0.7	45.4	0.2	45.4	0.0	46.4	2.2	46.6	0.4	46.8	0.4	47.2	0.9	47.5	0.6
1974	48.0	1.1	48.8	1.7	49.2	0.8	49.4	0.4	49.7	0.6	50.4	1.4	50.7	0.6	51.2	1.0	51.7	1.0	52.2	1.0	52.7	1.0	53.0	0.6
1975	52.8	-0.4	53.1	0.6	53.3	0.4	53.5	0.4	53.7	0.4	54.2	0.9	54.6	0.7	54.8	0.4	55.3	0.9	55.4	0.2	55.6	0.4	55.9	0.5
1976	56.3	0.7	56.3	0.0	56.2	-0.2	56.5	0.5	56.8	0.5	57.0	0.4	57.4	0.7	57.6	0.3	58.2	1.0	58.2	0.0	58.6	0.7	58.8	0.3
1977	59.0	0.3	59.5	0.8	60.0	0.8	60.8	1.3	60.9	0.2	61.5	1.0	62.0	0.8	62.0	0.0	62.1	0.2	62.2	0.2	62.6	0.6	62.6	0.0
1978	62.8	0.3	63.1	0.5	63.8	1.1	64.4	0.9	65.2	1.2	66.1	1.4	66.1	0.0	66.6	0.8	67.3	1.1	68.1	1.2	68.5	0.6	68.6	0.1
1979	69.6	1.5	70.9	1.9	71.8	1.3	72.4	0.8	72.7	0.4	73.2	0.7	74.6	1.9	75.6	1.3	75.9	0.4	77.0	1.4	78.4	1.8	78.8	0.5
1980	80.3	1.9	81.5	1.5	82.3	1.0	84.2	2.3	84.5	0.4	86.9	2.8	85.6	-1.5	86.2	0.7	87.5	1.5	88.8	1.5	89.5	0.8	90.1	0.7
1981	89.8	-0.3	90.1	0.3	89.5	-0.7	91.0	1.7	92.1	1.2	93.7	1.7	94.7	1.1	94.8	0.1	95.1	0.3	94.5	-0.6	93.8	-0.7	93.4	-0.4
1982	94.3	1.0	93.3	-1.1	93.4	0.1	95.2	1.9	96.0	0.8	97.1	1.1	98.2	1.1	98.2	0.0	98.9	0.7	98.9	0.0	99.2	0.3	98.0	-1.2
1983	97.8	-0.2	97.5	-0.3	98.4	0.9	100.2	1.8	101.5	1.3	102.1	0.6	103.2	1.1	103.1	-0.1	103.4	0.3	101.5	-1.8	102.5	1.0	102.3	-0.2
1984	104.5	2.2	103.5	-1.0	102.8	-0.7	101.4	-1.4	101.3	-0.1	100.8	-0.5	101.3	0.5	101.5	0.2	102.3	0.8	102.8	0.5	101.8	-1.0	101.9	0.1
1985	102.3	0.4	103.2	0.9	103.9	0.7	104.0	0.1	104.1	0.1	104.4	0.3	104.7	0.3	104.7	0.0	105.4	0.7	105.2	-0.2	106.3	1.0	106.3	0.0
1986	106.4	0.1	106.0	-0.4	105.0	-0.9	104.6	-0.4	105.6	1.0	105.3	-0.3	104.4	-0.9	106.2	1.7	105.4	-0.8	106.5	1.0	106.9	0.4	106.6	-0.3
1987	-	-	107.5	0.8	-	-	108.6	1.0	-	-	108.6	0.0	-	-	109.6	0.9	-	-	111.3	1.6	-	-	109.8	-1.3
1988	-	-	110.9	1.0	-	-	111.9	0.9	-	-	112.7	0.7	-	-	114.6	1.7	-	-	115.6	0.9	-	-	115.7	0.1
1989	-	-	117.3	1.4	-	-	119.0	1.4	-	-	119.3	0.3	-	-	119.2	-0.1	-	-	121.5	1.9	-	-	121.4	-0.1
1990	-	-	123.2	1.5	-	-	123.9	0.6	-	-	124.7	0.6	-	-	126.5	1.4	-	-	128.7	1.7	-	-	128.1	-0.5
1991	-	-	128.9	0.6	-	-	128.3	-0.5	-	-	130.1	1.4	-	-	130.2	0.1	-	-	131.1	0.7	-	-	130.6	-0.4
1992	-	-	131.3	0.5	-	-	131.7	0.3	-	-	131.8	0.1	-	-	132.0	0.2	-	-	133.5	1.1	-	-	133.1	-0.3
1993	-	-	134.4	1.0	-	-	134.6	0.1	-	-	135.1	0.4	-	-	135.7	0.4	-	-	137.5	1.3	-	-	135.7	-1.3
1994	-	-	137.0	1.0	-	-	137.9	0.7	-	-	140.2	1.7	-	-	141.0	0.6	-	-	141.1	0.1	-	-	141.0	-0.1
1995	-	-	142.7	1.2	-	-	143.6	0.6	-	-	143.7	0.1	-	-	144.0	0.2	-	-	145.0	0.7	-	-	145.5	0.3
1996	-	-	146.5	0.7	-	-	147.6	0.8	-	-	147.1	-0.3	-	-	148.0	0.6	-	-	148.8	0.5	-	-	149.4	0.4
1997	-	-	150.3	0.6	-	-	151.0	0.5	-	-	149.8	-0.8	-	-	151.6	1.2	-	-	152.4	0.5	-	-	151.7	-0.5

Source: U.S. Department of Labor, Bureau of Labor Statistics, Division of Consumer Prices and Price Indexes. - indicates no data collected for period.

Detroit, MI
Consumer Price Index - All Urban Consumers
Base 1982-1984 = 100
Food and Beverages

For 1976-1997. Columns headed % show percentile change in the index from the previous period for which an index is available.

Year	Jan Index	%	Feb Index	%	Mar Index	%	Apr Index	%	May Index	%	Jun Index	%	Jul Index	%	Aug Index	%	Sep Index	%	Oct Index	%	Nov Index	%	Dec Index	%
1976	63.8	-	63.8	0.0	63.1	-1.1	63.5	0.6	63.9	0.6	63.9	0.0	64.3	0.6	64.0	-0.5	63.7	-0.5	63.6	-0.2	64.0	0.6	64.5	0.8
1977	64.8	0.5	65.9	1.7	65.8	-0.2	66.9	1.7	67.2	0.4	68.2	1.5	68.5	0.4	68.6	0.1	68.1	-0.7	68.4	0.4	69.2	1.2	69.2	0.0
1978	70.5	1.9	71.2	1.0	72.0	1.1	73.0	1.4	74.0	1.4	75.3	1.8	76.0	0.9	75.7	-0.4	75.9	0.3	76.2	0.4	76.8	0.8	77.6	1.0
1979	79.5	2.4	80.8	1.6	81.3	0.6	81.9	0.7	82.4	0.6	82.5	0.1	82.9	0.5	81.9	-1.2	82.4	0.6	82.9	0.6	83.3	0.5	84.2	1.1
1980	86.0	2.1	86.1	0.1	86.7	0.7	86.9	0.2	87.8	1.0	88.5	0.8	89.4	1.0	90.4	1.1	90.1	-0.3	90.6	0.6	92.1	1.7	92.8	0.8
1981	93.5	0.8	94.9	1.5	94.8	-0.1	95.1	0.3	95.3	0.2	95.4	0.1	96.1	0.7	96.1	0.0	96.6	0.5	96.7	0.1	97.3	0.6	97.4	0.1
1982	98.2	0.8	99.1	0.9	98.9	-0.2	99.1	0.2	99.3	0.2	100.1	0.8	100.2	0.1	99.5	-0.7	99.7	0.2	99.3	-0.4	99.6	0.3	99.2	-0.4
1983	99.7	0.5	100.1	0.4	100.8	0.7	100.7	-0.1	100.2	-0.5	99.9	-0.3	99.6	-0.3	99.3	-0.3	98.4	-0.9	97.1	-1.3	97.5	0.4	98.0	0.5
1984	100.2	2.2	101.1	0.9	101.1	0.0	102.1	1.0	101.6	-0.5	101.3	-0.3	102.1	0.8	101.9	-0.2	101.6	-0.3	101.0	-0.6	100.8	-0.2	101.8	1.0
1985	102.0	0.2	102.9	0.9	103.4	0.5	103.3	-0.1	103.1	-0.2	102.9	-0.2	103.1	0.2	102.5	-0.6	102.4	-0.1	103.3	0.9	104.3	1.0	104.8	0.5
1986	104.7	-0.1	105.3	0.6	105.8	0.5	105.7	-0.1	106.3	0.6	106.4	0.1	107.5	1.0	108.9	1.3	108.6	-0.3	109.3	0.6	109.5	0.2	109.2	-0.3
1987	-		109.7	0.5	-		109.4	-0.3	-		111.4	1.8	-		110.8	-0.5	-		111.5	0.6	-		110.9	-0.5
1988	-		112.3	1.3	-		113.0	0.6	-		114.4	1.2	-		115.5	1.0	-		116.9	1.2	-		117.8	0.8
1989	-		119.4	1.4	-		120.5	0.9	-		120.3	-0.2	-		121.2	0.7	-		121.5	0.2	-		123.0	1.2
1990	-		125.3	1.9	-		125.4	0.1	-		126.5	0.9	-		127.6	0.9	-		127.7	0.1	-		127.9	0.2
1991	-		129.0	0.9	-		130.3	1.0	-		131.6	1.0	-		131.6	0.0	-		132.6	0.8	-		133.0	0.3
1992	-		133.6	0.5	-		133.4	-0.1	-		132.9	-0.4	-		133.5	0.5	-		133.5	0.0	-		134.0	0.4
1993	-		134.1	0.1	-		134.2	0.1	-		135.1	0.7	-		135.8	0.5	-		136.8	0.7	-		136.1	-0.5
1994	-		136.4	0.2	-		136.9	0.4	-		138.9	1.5	-		140.1	0.9	-		139.7	-0.3	-		141.9	1.6
1995	-		142.8	0.6	-		143.1	0.2	-		143.5	0.3	-		143.9	0.3	-		144.2	0.2	-		144.9	0.5
1996	-		145.7	0.6	-		146.6	0.6	-		146.0	-0.4	-		149.2	2.2	-		150.4	0.8	-		151.2	0.5
1997	-		150.9	-0.2	-		151.0	0.1	-		151.2	0.1	-		151.9	0.5	-		151.8	-0.1	-		152.2	0.3

Source: U.S. Department of Labor, Bureau of Labor Statistics, Division of Consumer Prices and Price Indexes. - indicates no data collected for period.

Detroit, MI
Consumer Price Index - Urban Wage Earners
Base 1982-1984 = 100
Food and Beverages

For 1976-1997. Columns headed % show percentile change in the index from the previous period for which an index is available.

Year	Jan Index	%	Feb Index	%	Mar Index	%	Apr Index	%	May Index	%	Jun Index	%	Jul Index	%	Aug Index	%	Sep Index	%	Oct Index	%	Nov Index	%	Dec Index	%
1976	63.2	-	63.1	-0.2	62.5	-1.0	62.9	0.6	63.2	0.5	63.2	0.0	63.6	0.6	63.4	-0.3	63.0	-0.6	62.9	-0.2	63.3	0.6	63.9	0.9
1977	64.2	0.5	65.2	1.6	65.2	0.0	66.2	1.5	66.6	0.6	67.5	1.4	67.8	0.4	67.9	0.1	67.4	-0.7	67.7	0.4	68.5	1.2	68.5	0.0
1978	70.0	2.2	70.8	1.1	71.4	0.8	72.5	1.5	73.5	1.4	75.2	2.3	76.0	1.1	75.9	-0.1	76.0	0.1	75.7	-0.4	76.5	1.1	77.3	1.0
1979	79.2	2.5	80.5	1.6	81.5	1.2	81.8	0.4	82.2	0.5	82.4	0.2	83.2	1.0	82.0	-1.4	82.4	0.5	83.0	0.7	83.3	0.4	84.3	1.2
1980	85.8	1.8	86.0	0.2	86.6	0.7	86.7	0.1	87.6	1.0	88.3	0.8	89.1	0.9	89.9	0.9	90.0	0.1	90.5	0.6	91.5	1.1	92.2	0.8
1981	92.9	0.8	94.2	1.4	94.3	0.1	95.1	0.8	95.3	0.2	95.6	0.3	96.4	0.8	96.3	-0.1	97.0	0.7	96.9	-0.1	97.4	0.5	97.3	-0.1
1982	98.3	1.0	99.0	0.7	98.9	-0.1	99.2	0.3	99.4	0.2	100.2	0.8	100.4	0.2	99.7	-0.7	99.9	0.2	99.4	-0.5	99.6	0.2	99.1	-0.5
1983	99.7	0.6	100.1	0.4	100.8	0.7	100.7	-0.1	100.2	-0.5	99.8	-0.4	99.5	-0.3	99.2	-0.3	98.3	-0.9	97.1	-1.2	97.4	0.3	97.9	0.5
1984	100.1	2.2	101.2	1.1	101.0	-0.2	102.1	1.1	101.5	-0.6	101.3	-0.2	102.0	0.7	102.1	0.1	101.7	-0.4	100.9	-0.8	100.6	-0.3	101.9	1.3
1985	101.8	-0.1	102.8	1.0	103.2	0.4	103.0	-0.2	102.9	-0.1	102.7	-0.2	102.9	0.2	102.2	-0.7	102.1	-0.1	102.9	0.8	104.0	1.1	104.5	0.5
1986	104.4	-0.1	104.7	0.3	105.5	0.8	105.3	-0.2	106.0	0.7	106.1	0.1	107.0	0.8	108.5	1.4	108.1	-0.4	109.0	0.8	109.1	0.1	109.0	-0.1
1987	-	-	109.5	0.5	-	-	109.1	-0.4	-	-	111.1	1.8	-	-	110.5	-0.5	-	-	111.2	0.6	-	-	110.4	-0.7
1988	-	-	112.0	1.4	-	-	112.5	0.4	-	-	113.9	1.2	-	-	115.0	1.0	-	-	116.4	1.2	-	-	117.3	0.8
1989	-	-	119.0	1.4	-	-	120.1	0.9	-	-	119.9	-0.2	-	-	120.8	0.8	-	-	121.0	0.2	-	-	122.7	1.4
1990	-	-	125.0	1.9	-	-	125.0	0.0	-	-	126.1	0.9	-	-	127.2	0.9	-	-	127.2	0.0	-	-	127.4	0.2
1991	-	-	128.6	0.9	-	-	129.9	1.0	-	-	131.2	1.0	-	-	131.1	-0.1	-	-	132.3	0.9	-	-	132.7	0.3
1992	-	-	133.3	0.5	-	-	133.0	-0.2	-	-	132.6	-0.3	-	-	133.1	0.4	-	-	133.0	-0.1	-	-	133.6	0.5
1993	-	-	133.7	0.1	-	-	133.8	0.1	-	-	134.7	0.7	-	-	135.3	0.4	-	-	136.4	0.8	-	-	135.7	-0.5
1994	-	-	136.0	0.2	-	-	136.5	0.4	-	-	138.6	1.5	-	-	139.9	0.9	-	-	139.5	-0.3	-	-	141.8	1.6
1995	-	-	142.5	0.5	-	-	142.8	0.2	-	-	143.2	0.3	-	-	143.6	0.3	-	-	144.0	0.3	-	-	144.8	0.6
1996	-	-	145.5	0.5	-	-	146.4	0.6	-	-	145.7	-0.5	-	-	149.0	2.3	-	-	149.9	0.6	-	-	151.0	0.7
1997	-	-	150.6	-0.3	-	-	150.6	0.0	-	-	150.9	0.2	-	-	151.6	0.5	-	-	151.5	-0.1	-	-	151.9	0.3

Source: U.S. Department of Labor, Bureau of Labor Statistics, Division of Consumer Prices and Price Indexes. - indicates no data collected for period.

481

Detroit, MI
Consumer Price Index - All Urban Consumers
Base 1982-1984 = 100
Housing

For 1976-1997. Columns headed % show percentile change in the index from the previous period for which an index is available.

Year	Jan Index	%	Feb Index	%	Mar Index	%	Apr Index	%	May Index	%	Jun Index	%	Jul Index	%	Aug Index	%	Sep Index	%	Oct Index	%	Nov Index	%	Dec Index	%
1976	51.2	-	51.2	0.0	51.2	0.0	51.2	0.0	51.5	0.6	51.8	0.6	52.2	0.8	52.6	0.8	53.7	2.1	53.4	-0.6	53.7	0.6	53.9	0.4
1977	54.1	0.4	54.4	0.6	55.1	1.3	55.6	0.9	55.2	-0.7	55.7	0.9	56.6	1.6	56.2	-0.7	56.4	0.4	56.4	0.0	56.9	0.9	56.9	0.0
1978	57.1	0.4	57.1	0.0	58.4	2.3	58.8	0.7	59.4	1.0	60.3	1.5	60.0	-0.5	60.6	1.0	61.8	2.0	63.2	2.3	63.6	0.6	63.4	-0.3
1979	64.4	1.6	66.3	3.0	67.7	2.1	67.7	0.0	67.6	-0.1	68.1	0.7	70.2	3.1	71.7	2.1	72.2	0.7	74.1	2.6	76.6	3.4	77.3	0.9
1980	78.5	1.6	79.8	1.7	80.5	0.9	83.2	3.4	82.6	-0.7	88.0	6.5	86.1	-2.2	85.9	-0.2	87.7	2.1	90.4	3.1	90.5	0.1	92.8	2.5
1981	91.2	-1.7	91.0	-0.2	88.9	-2.3	91.1	2.5	92.3	1.3	96.2	4.2	96.7	0.5	97.2	0.5	97.0	-0.2	94.3	-2.8	92.7	-1.7	91.8	-1.0
1982	93.2	1.5	90.8	-2.6	91.1	0.3	95.0	4.3	95.5	0.5	96.7	1.3	98.0	1.3	98.2	0.2	99.4	1.2	99.6	0.2	100.0	0.4	98.0	-2.0
1983	98.5	0.5	98.3	-0.2	98.3	0.0	100.3	2.0	99.6	-0.7	101.5	1.9	102.1	0.6	101.5	-0.6	101.3	-0.2	101.1	-0.2	101.5	0.4	101.5	0.0
1984	101.5	0.0	101.8	0.3	102.3	0.5	102.5	0.2	102.6	0.1	103.2	0.6	103.8	0.6	103.9	0.1	105.5	1.5	105.5	0.0	102.8	-2.6	103.5	0.7
1985	105.8	2.2	106.0	0.2	106.7	0.7	106.6	-0.1	106.8	0.2	107.8	0.9	107.8	0.0	107.3	-0.5	109.2	1.8	107.5	-1.6	109.3	1.7	109.1	-0.2
1986	109.6	0.5	110.6	0.9	109.6	-0.9	109.9	0.3	110.6	0.6	109.7	-0.8	107.5	-2.0	110.8	3.1	108.8	-1.8	110.5	1.6	110.2	-0.3	110.0	-0.2
1987	-	-	112.5	2.3	-	-	112.8	0.3	-	-	112.2	-0.5	-	-	114.1	1.7	-	-	114.7	0.5	-	-	112.4	-2.0
1988	-	-	115.0	2.3	-	-	114.2	-0.7	-	-	115.4	1.1	-	-	118.6	2.8	-	-	117.9	-0.6	-	-	116.7	-1.0
1989	-	-	119.6	2.5	-	-	119.5	-0.1	-	-	120.5	0.8	-	-	121.9	1.2	-	-	124.0	1.7	-	-	123.5	-0.4
1990	-	-	123.8	0.2	-	-	125.0	1.0	-	-	126.5	1.2	-	-	127.9	1.1	-	-	128.7	0.6	-	-	127.2	-1.2
1991	-	-	129.1	1.5	-	-	125.8	-2.6	-	-	129.9	3.3	-	-	128.9	-0.8	-	-	129.8	0.7	-	-	128.8	-0.8
1992	-	-	130.7	1.5	-	-	130.7	0.0	-	-	131.9	0.9	-	-	132.5	0.5	-	-	133.3	0.6	-	-	133.0	-0.2
1993	-	-	133.4	0.3	-	-	132.1	-1.0	-	-	133.9	1.4	-	-	135.0	0.8	-	-	137.0	1.5	-	-	135.6	-1.0
1994	-	-	136.4	0.6	-	-	136.7	0.2	-	-	137.6	0.7	-	-	138.3	0.5	-	-	138.8	0.4	-	-	138.5	-0.2
1995	-	-	139.1	0.4	-	-	139.3	0.1	-	-	140.2	0.6	-	-	141.2	0.7	-	-	142.1	0.6	-	-	143.1	0.7
1996	-	-	144.2	0.8	-	-	144.9	0.5	-	-	145.1	0.1	-	-	146.3	0.8	-	-	146.5	0.1	-	-	147.0	0.3
1997	-	-	148.8	1.2	-	-	149.4	0.4	-	-	148.9	-0.3	-	-	149.9	0.7	-	-	152.0	1.4	-	-	151.5	-0.3

Source: U.S. Department of Labor, Bureau of Labor Statistics, Division of Consumer Prices and Price Indexes. - indicates no data collected for period.

Detroit, MI
Consumer Price Index - Urban Wage Earners
Base 1982-1984 = 100
Housing

For 1976-1997. Columns headed % show percentile change in the index from the previous period for which an index is available.

Year	Jan Index	%	Feb Index	%	Mar Index	%	Apr Index	%	May Index	%	Jun Index	%	Jul Index	%	Aug Index	%	Sep Index	%	Oct Index	%	Nov Index	%	Dec Index	%
1976	51.4	-	51.4	0.0	51.3	-0.2	51.4	0.2	51.7	0.6	52.0	0.6	52.3	0.6	52.7	0.8	53.9	2.3	53.6	-0.6	53.9	0.6	54.0	0.2
1977	54.3	0.6	54.5	0.4	55.2	1.3	55.7	0.9	55.4	-0.5	55.8	0.7	56.8	1.8	56.4	-0.7	56.6	0.4	56.6	0.0	57.0	0.7	57.0	0.0
1978	57.2	0.4	57.4	0.3	58.4	1.7	58.8	0.7	59.6	1.4	60.4	1.3	60.0	-0.7	60.6	1.0	61.8	2.0	63.2	2.3	63.4	0.3	63.1	-0.5
1979	64.2	1.7	66.3	3.3	67.7	2.1	67.9	0.3	67.7	-0.3	68.1	0.6	70.2	3.1	71.8	2.3	72.3	0.7	73.8	2.1	76.4	3.5	77.1	0.9
1980	78.3	1.6	79.6	1.7	80.2	0.8	82.8	3.2	82.3	-0.6	87.7	6.6	85.6	-2.4	85.5	-0.1	87.2	2.0	89.7	2.9	90.2	0.6	92.4	2.4
1981	90.7	-1.8	90.1	-0.7	87.9	-2.4	90.2	2.6	91.6	1.6	95.1	3.8	95.9	0.8	96.3	0.4	96.1	-0.2	93.8	-2.4	92.0	-1.9	91.1	-1.0
1982	92.5	1.5	90.0	-2.7	90.4	0.4	94.4	4.4	94.9	0.5	96.1	1.3	97.5	1.5	97.6	0.1	98.8	1.2	99.0	0.2	99.5	0.5	97.4	-2.1
1983	97.1	-0.3	96.5	-0.6	98.4	2.0	102.2	3.9	104.6	2.3	106.1	1.4	107.8	1.6	107.1	-0.6	107.5	0.4	103.6	-3.6	105.0	1.4	104.7	-0.3
1984	108.9	4.0	105.2	-3.4	103.6	-1.5	99.5	-4.0	99.2	-0.3	98.3	-0.9	99.1	0.8	99.2	0.1	99.8	0.6	100.8	1.0	98.7	-2.1	99.1	0.4
1985	101.2	2.1	101.3	0.1	102.0	0.7	101.9	-0.1	102.0	0.1	102.9	0.9	103.0	0.1	102.5	-0.5	104.3	1.8	102.6	-1.6	104.4	1.8	104.3	-0.1
1986	104.7	0.4	105.5	0.8	104.7	-0.8	105.1	0.4	105.6	0.5	104.7	-0.9	102.7	-1.9	105.9	3.1	103.9	-1.9	105.6	1.6	105.3	-0.3	105.1	-0.2
1987	-	-	107.4	2.2	-	-	107.7	0.3	-	-	107.4	-0.3	-	-	109.0	1.5	-	-	109.6	0.6	-	-	107.4	-2.0
1988	-	-	109.8	2.2	-	-	109.1	-0.6	-	-	110.3	1.1	-	-	112.9	2.4	-	-	112.5	-0.4	-	-	111.7	-0.7
1989	-	-	114.2	2.2	-	-	114.1	-0.1	-	-	114.9	0.7	-	-	116.3	1.2	-	-	118.2	1.6	-	-	118.1	-0.1
1990	-	-	118.3	0.2	-	-	119.4	0.9	-	-	120.9	1.3	-	-	122.1	1.0	-	-	123.0	0.7	-	-	121.5	-1.2
1991	-	-	123.3	1.5	-	-	119.7	-2.9	-	-	123.9	3.5	-	-	123.1	-0.6	-	-	123.9	0.6	-	-	123.0	-0.7
1992	-	-	124.7	1.4	-	-	124.6	-0.1	-	-	125.9	1.0	-	-	126.3	0.3	-	-	127.1	0.6	-	-	126.9	-0.2
1993	-	-	127.2	0.2	-	-	125.9	-1.0	-	-	127.7	1.4	-	-	128.6	0.7	-	-	130.6	1.6	-	-	129.4	-0.9
1994	-	-	129.9	0.4	-	-	130.2	0.2	-	-	131.0	0.6	-	-	131.6	0.5	-	-	132.2	0.5	-	-	131.9	-0.2
1995	-	-	132.4	0.4	-	-	132.6	0.2	-	-	133.5	0.7	-	-	134.3	0.6	-	-	135.1	0.6	-	-	136.1	0.7
1996	-	-	137.1	0.7	-	-	137.6	0.4	-	-	137.9	0.2	-	-	139.0	0.8	-	-	139.1	0.1	-	-	139.7	0.4
1997	-	-	141.2	1.1	-	-	141.7	0.4	-	-	141.3	-0.3	-	-	142.1	0.6	-	-	144.0	1.3	-	-	143.7	-0.2

Source: U.S. Department of Labor, Bureau of Labor Statistics, Division of Consumer Prices and Price Indexes. - indicates no data collected for period.

Detroit, MI
Consumer Price Index - All Urban Consumers
Base 1982-1984 = 100
Apparel and Upkeep

For 1952-1997. Columns headed % show percentile change in the index from the previous period for which an index is available.

Year	Jan Index	%	Feb Index	%	Mar Index	%	Apr Index	%	May Index	%	Jun Index	%	Jul Index	%	Aug Index	%	Sep Index	%	Oct Index	%	Nov Index	%	Dec Index	%
1952	-	-	-	-	-	-	-	-	-	-	-	-	-	-	-	-	-	-	-	-	-	-	51.7	-
1953	51.7	0.0	51.8	0.2	51.9	0.2	52.0	0.2	52.2	0.4	52.2	0.0	52.2	0.0	52.1	-0.2	52.1	0.0	52.3	0.4	52.2	-0.2	52.1	-0.2
1954	52.0	-0.2	52.1	0.2	51.9	-0.4	51.9	0.0	51.9	0.0	52.1	0.4	52.1	0.0	51.9	-0.4	52.1	0.4	51.9	-0.4	51.9	0.0	51.9	0.0
1955	51.9	0.0	51.9	0.0	51.9	0.0	51.7	-0.4	51.7	0.0	51.8	0.2	51.9	0.2	51.7	-0.4	51.9	0.4	51.6	-0.6	51.7	0.2	51.8	0.2
1956	51.7	-0.2	52.0	0.6	52.1	0.2	52.4	0.6	52.3	-0.2	52.3	0.0	52.5	0.4	52.9	0.8	53.3	0.8	53.3	0.0	53.2	-0.2	52.9	-0.6
1957	53.1	0.4	53.2	0.2	53.2	0.0	53.3	0.2	53.4	0.2	53.2	-0.4	53.0	-0.4	53.1	0.2	53.3	0.4	53.2	-0.2	53.3	0.2	53.2	-0.2
1958	52.7	-0.9	52.7	0.0	52.8	0.2	52.9	0.2	52.8	-0.2	52.8	0.0	52.8	0.0	52.9	0.2	53.3	0.8	53.4	0.2	53.4	0.0	53.6	0.4
1959	53.5	-0.2	53.2	-0.6	53.5	0.6	53.6	0.2	53.6	0.0	53.6	0.0	53.3	-0.6	53.7	0.8	54.6	1.7	55.0	0.7	54.5	-0.9	54.5	0.0
1960	54.1	-0.7	54.0	-0.2	53.8	-0.4	53.8	0.0	54.1	0.6	54.2	0.2	54.3	0.2	54.2	-0.2	55.1	1.7	55.1	0.0	55.1	0.0	55.0	-0.2
1961	55.4	0.7	55.5	0.2	55.3	-0.4	55.3	0.0	55.1	-0.4	55.0	-0.2	54.8	-0.4	54.9	0.2	55.2	0.5	55.5	0.5	55.3	-0.4	55.5	0.4
1962	55.1	-0.7	55.4	0.5	55.4	0.0	55.4	0.0	55.5	0.2	55.6	0.2	55.4	-0.4	55.6	0.4	55.9	0.5	55.9	0.0	55.8	-0.2	55.3	-0.9
1963	55.3	0.0	55.6	0.5	55.4	-0.4	55.7	0.5	55.7	0.0	55.9	0.4	55.8	-0.2	56.2	0.7	56.7	0.9	56.6	-0.2	56.9	0.5	56.8	-0.2
1964	56.1	-1.2	56.4	0.5	56.9	0.9	56.9	0.0	56.8	-0.2	56.8	0.0	56.8	0.0	56.8	0.0	57.2	0.7	57.3	0.2	57.2	-0.2	57.4	0.3
1965	56.8	-1.0	57.2	0.7	57.6	0.7	58.1	0.9	57.9	-0.3	58.1	0.3	57.7	-0.7	57.6	-0.2	58.1	0.9	58.1	0.0	58.1	0.0	58.3	0.3
1966	57.6	-1.2	57.9	0.5	58.4	0.9	58.8	0.7	58.8	0.0	58.8	0.0	58.4	-0.7	58.9	0.9	59.9	1.7	60.0	0.2	60.1	0.2	60.2	0.2
1967	59.9	-0.5	60.1	0.3	60.6	0.8	60.6	0.0	60.7	0.2	60.7	0.0	59.8	-1.5	60.1	0.5	61.0	1.5	61.3	0.5	61.3	0.0	61.3	0.0
1968	60.3	-1.6	61.3	1.7	62.2	1.5	62.2	0.0	63.0	1.3	63.0	0.0	62.5	-0.8	63.4	1.4	64.6	1.9	65.1	0.8	65.6	0.8	65.7	0.2
1969	64.8	-1.4	65.6	1.2	65.8	0.3	65.6	-0.3	65.7	0.2	65.7	0.0	65.0	-1.1	65.2	0.3	67.1	2.9	67.1	0.0	67.1	0.0	67.2	0.1
1970	66.0	-1.8	67.1	1.7	68.9	2.7	67.6	-1.9	67.4	-0.3	67.7	0.4	67.1	-0.9	66.8	-0.4	68.8	3.0	68.9	0.1	69.1	0.3	68.6	-0.7
1971	66.8	-2.6	69.6	4.2	70.0	0.6	69.3	-1.0	70.1	1.2	70.0	-0.1	69.6	-0.6	69.9	0.4	70.5	0.9	71.4	1.3	71.6	0.3	71.0	-0.8
1972	69.4	-2.3	70.9	2.2	70.8	-0.1	71.0	0.3	71.6	0.8	71.1	-0.7	70.8	-0.4	71.3	0.7	72.8	2.1	73.4	0.8	73.6	0.3	73.2	-0.5
1973	71.1	-2.9	72.9	2.5	73.9	1.4	74.4	0.7	74.2	-0.3	73.9	-0.4	72.2	-2.3	73.8	2.2	75.3	2.0	76.0	0.9	75.8	-0.3	75.9	0.1
1974	74.2	-2.2	76.2	2.7	77.5	1.7	78.3	1.0	78.7	0.5	79.6	1.1	79.4	-0.3	83.9	5.7	84.5	0.7	83.4	-1.3	83.7	0.4	83.1	-0.7
1975	82.0	-1.3	81.5	-0.6	83.1	2.0	82.9	-0.2	82.8	-0.1	83.6	1.0	83.6	0.0	83.7	0.1	84.5	1.0	85.1	0.7	85.1	0.0	84.9	-0.2
1976	84.6	-0.4	85.2	0.7	85.4	0.2	86.2	0.9	85.3	-1.0	85.1	-0.2	85.0	-0.1	85.9	1.1	87.1	1.4	87.8	0.8	87.6	-0.2	87.5	-0.1
1977	87.0	-0.6	87.8	0.9	88.1	0.3	88.3	0.2	88.0	-0.3	89.2	1.4	89.0	-0.2	89.4	0.4	89.7	0.3	90.0	0.3	90.4	0.4	89.9	-0.6
1978	87.0	-3.2	86.5	-0.6	87.9	1.6	89.6	1.9	91.1	1.7	91.0	-0.1	88.1	-3.2	91.1	3.4	90.3	-0.9	91.9	1.8	91.6	-0.3	90.5	-1.2
1979	87.7	-3.1	87.3	-0.5	89.5	2.5	89.5	0.0	89.9	0.4	88.1	-2.0	88.2	0.1	91.6	3.9	92.1	0.5	91.9	-0.2	91.6	-0.3	89.7	-2.1
1980	89.1	-0.7	89.7	0.7	93.4	4.1	95.5	2.2	95.0	-0.5	93.3	-1.8	93.6	0.3	94.2	0.6	97.0	3.0	96.8	-0.2	98.1	1.3	96.2	-1.9
1981	95.1	-1.1	95.6	0.5	96.8	1.3	97.6	0.8	98.4	0.8	96.5	-1.9	97.0	0.5	95.4	-1.6	96.7	1.4	97.7	1.0	96.1	-1.6	94.3	-1.9
1982	92.7	-1.7	95.2	2.7	96.2	1.1	96.5	0.3	96.5	0.0	93.4	-3.2	98.3	5.2	100.0	1.7	104.8	4.8	103.7	-1.0	103.1	-0.6	99.2	-3.8
1983	96.2	-3.0	99.2	3.1	99.0	-0.2	99.7	0.7	101.1	1.4	99.4	-1.7	99.9	0.5	103.1	3.2	105.4	2.2	104.3	-1.0	104.3	0.0	100.0	-4.1
1984	96.7	-3.3	101.9	5.4	101.6	-0.3	98.8	-2.8	99.3	0.5	99.9	0.6	100.3	0.4	99.8	-0.5	105.7	5.9	103.4	-2.2	102.3	-1.1	99.1	-3.1
1985	93.1	-6.1	99.1	6.4	100.3	1.2	100.5	0.2	101.3	0.8	100.0	-1.3	101.3	1.3	105.3	3.9	108.6	3.1	107.1	-1.4	108.8	1.6	106.0	-2.6
1986	102.0	-3.8	103.1	1.1	102.9	-0.2	102.3	-0.6	101.9	-0.4	100.2	-1.7	98.4	-1.8	103.4	5.1	106.4	2.9	106.9	0.5	106.5	-0.4	105.2	-1.2
1987	-	-	103.0	-2.1	-	-	109.8	6.6	-	-	104.6	-4.7	-	-	104.0	-0.6	-	-	116.8	12.3	-	-	111.8	-4.3
1988	-	-	108.8	-2.7	-	-	118.5	8.9	-	-	111.3	-6.1	-	-	113.2	1.7	-	-	122.8	8.5	-	-	118.5	-3.5
1989	-	-	119.6	0.9	-	-	126.2	5.5	-	-	121.1	-4.0	-	-	118.8	-1.9	-	-	128.8	8.4	-	-	122.8	-4.7
1990	-	-	126.7	3.2	-	-	131.0	3.4	-	-	122.9	-6.2	-	-	127.8	4.0	-	-	131.4	2.8	-	-	129.0	-1.8
1991	-	-	129.6	0.5	-	-	134.1	3.5	-	-	130.0	-3.1	-	-	131.7	1.3	-	-	137.0	4.0	-	-	128.4	-6.3
1992	-	-	131.7	2.6	-	-	133.4	1.3	-	-	127.4	-4.5	-	-	127.8	0.3	-	-	130.1	1.8	-	-	129.6	-0.4
1993	-	-	134.8	4.0	-	-	144.1	6.9	-	-	134.2	-6.9	-	-	138.3	3.1	-	-	144.0	4.1	-	-	133.0	-7.6
1994	-	-	139.7	5.0	-	-	142.4	1.9	-	-	138.9	-2.5	-	-	130.9	-5.8	-	-	135.3	3.4	-	-	128.2	-5.2

[Continued]

Detroit, MI
Consumer Price Index - All Urban Consumers
Base 1982-1984 = 100
Apparel and Upkeep
[Continued]

For 1952-1997. Columns headed % show percentile change in the index from the previous period for which an index is available.

Year	Jan Index	%	Feb Index	%	Mar Index	%	Apr Index	%	May Index	%	Jun Index	%	Jul Index	%	Aug Index	%	Sep Index	%	Oct Index	%	Nov Index	%	Dec Index	%
1995	-	-	139.6	8.9	-	-	139.2	-0.3	-	-	132.8	-4.6	-	-	139.0	4.7	-	-	137.3	-1.2	-	-	135.7	-1.2
1996	-	-	136.1	0.3	-	-	137.0	0.7	-	-	131.3	-4.2	-	-	127.4	-3.0	-	-	130.5	2.4	-	-	125.6	-3.8
1997	-	-	137.8	9.7	-	-	142.1	3.1	-	-	128.2	-9.8	-	-	137.5	7.3	-	-	136.1	-1.0	-	-	130.8	-3.9

Source: U.S. Department of Labor, Bureau of Labor Statistics, Division of Consumer Prices and Price Indexes. - indicates no data collected for period.

Detroit, MI
Consumer Price Index - Urban Wage Earners
Base 1982-1984 = 100
Apparel and Upkeep

For 1952-1997. Columns headed % show percentile change in the index from the previous period for which an index is available.

Year	Jan Index	%	Feb Index	%	Mar Index	%	Apr Index	%	May Index	%	Jun Index	%	Jul Index	%	Aug Index	%	Sep Index	%	Oct Index	%	Nov Index	%	Dec Index	%
1952	-	-	-	-	-	-	-	-	-	-	-	-	-	-	-	-	-	-	-	-	-	-	52.6	-
1953	52.7	0.2	52.7	0.0	52.9	0.4	52.9	0.0	53.1	0.4	53.2	0.2	53.1	-0.2	53.1	0.0	53.1	0.0	53.2	0.2	53.1	-0.2	53.0	-0.2
1954	52.9	-0.2	53.0	0.2	52.8	-0.4	52.8	0.0	52.8	0.0	53.0	0.4	53.0	0.0	52.8	-0.4	53.0	0.4	52.9	-0.2	52.8	-0.2	52.8	0.0
1955	52.8	0.0	52.8	0.0	52.9	0.2	52.7	-0.4	52.7	0.0	52.7	0.0	52.8	0.2	52.6	-0.4	52.8	0.4	52.5	-0.6	52.6	0.2	52.7	0.2
1956	52.7	0.0	52.9	0.4	53.1	0.4	53.3	0.4	53.2	-0.2	53.2	0.0	53.4	0.4	53.9	0.9	54.3	0.7	54.2	-0.2	54.2	0.0	53.9	-0.6
1957	54.1	0.4	54.2	0.2	54.2	0.0	54.2	0.0	54.4	0.4	54.2	-0.4	53.9	-0.6	54.0	0.2	54.3	0.6	54.2	-0.2	54.3	0.2	54.2	-0.2
1958	53.7	-0.9	53.7	0.0	53.7	0.0	53.9	0.4	53.7	-0.4	53.7	0.0	53.7	0.0	53.9	0.4	54.2	0.6	54.4	0.4	54.4	0.0	54.5	0.2
1959	54.5	0.0	54.2	-0.6	54.5	0.6	54.5	0.0	54.6	0.2	54.5	-0.2	54.2	-0.6	54.7	0.9	55.6	1.6	56.0	0.7	55.5	-0.9	55.5	0.0
1960	55.0	-0.9	55.0	0.0	54.8	-0.4	54.8	0.0	55.0	0.4	55.2	0.4	55.3	0.2	55.2	-0.2	56.1	1.6	56.1	0.0	56.1	0.0	56.0	-0.2
1961	56.4	0.7	56.5	0.2	56.3	-0.4	56.3	0.0	56.1	-0.4	56.0	-0.2	55.8	-0.4	55.9	0.2	56.2	0.5	56.5	0.5	56.3	-0.4	56.5	0.4
1962	56.1	-0.7	56.4	0.5	56.4	0.0	56.4	0.0	56.5	0.2	56.6	0.2	56.4	-0.4	56.6	0.4	56.9	0.5	56.9	0.0	56.8	-0.2	56.3	-0.9
1963	56.3	0.0	56.6	0.5	56.4	-0.4	56.7	0.5	56.8	0.2	56.9	0.2	56.8	-0.2	57.2	0.7	57.7	0.9	57.6	-0.2	57.9	0.5	57.8	-0.2
1964	57.1	-1.2	57.4	0.5	57.9	0.9	57.9	0.0	57.9	0.0	57.8	-0.2	57.8	0.0	57.8	0.0	58.2	0.7	58.3	0.2	58.2	-0.2	58.4	0.3
1965	57.8	-1.0	58.2	0.7	58.7	0.9	59.1	0.7	58.9	-0.3	59.1	0.3	58.7	-0.7	58.7	0.0	59.2	0.9	59.2	0.0	59.2	0.0	59.3	0.2
1966	58.6	-1.2	58.9	0.5	59.5	1.0	59.8	0.5	59.8	0.0	59.8	0.0	59.5	-0.5	60.0	0.8	61.0	1.7	61.1	0.2	61.2	0.2	61.3	0.2
1967	61.0	-0.5	61.2	0.3	61.7	0.8	61.7	0.0	61.8	0.2	61.8	0.0	60.9	-1.5	61.1	0.3	62.1	1.6	62.4	0.5	62.4	0.0	62.4	0.0
1968	61.4	-1.6	62.4	1.6	63.3	1.4	63.3	0.0	64.1	1.3	64.2	0.2	63.7	-0.8	64.6	1.4	65.8	1.9	66.3	0.8	66.8	0.8	66.9	0.1
1969	65.9	-1.5	66.8	1.4	67.0	0.3	66.8	-0.3	66.9	0.1	66.9	0.0	66.1	-1.2	66.4	0.5	68.3	2.9	68.3	0.0	68.4	0.1	68.4	0.0
1970	67.2	-1.8	68.3	1.6	70.1	2.6	68.8	-1.9	68.7	-0.1	68.9	0.3	68.3	-0.9	68.0	-0.4	70.0	2.9	70.1	0.1	70.4	0.4	69.8	-0.9
1971	68.0	-2.6	70.8	4.1	71.3	0.7	70.6	-1.0	71.4	1.1	71.3	-0.1	70.9	-0.6	71.2	0.4	71.7	0.7	72.7	1.4	72.9	0.3	72.2	-1.0
1972	70.6	-2.2	72.2	2.3	72.1	-0.1	72.3	0.3	72.9	0.8	72.4	-0.7	72.1	-0.4	72.6	0.7	74.1	2.1	74.8	0.9	74.9	0.1	74.5	-0.5
1973	72.4	-2.8	74.2	2.5	75.2	1.3	75.7	0.7	75.6	-0.1	75.3	-0.4	73.5	-2.4	75.1	2.2	76.6	2.0	77.4	1.0	77.2	-0.3	77.2	0.0
1974	75.5	-2.2	77.5	2.6	78.9	1.8	79.7	1.0	80.1	0.5	81.0	1.1	80.9	-0.1	85.4	5.6	86.1	0.8	84.9	-1.4	85.3	0.5	84.6	-0.8
1975	83.5	-1.3	83.0	-0.6	84.6	1.9	84.4	-0.2	84.3	-0.1	85.1	0.9	85.1	0.0	85.2	0.1	86.0	0.9	86.6	0.7	86.6	0.0	86.4	-0.2
1976	86.1	-0.3	86.7	0.7	87.0	0.3	87.8	0.9	86.8	-1.1	86.7	-0.1	86.5	-0.2	87.4	1.0	88.7	1.5	89.4	0.8	89.1	-0.3	89.1	0.0
1977	88.6	-0.6	89.4	0.9	89.7	0.3	89.9	0.2	89.6	-0.3	90.8	1.3	90.6	-0.2	91.0	0.4	91.3	0.3	91.7	0.4	92.0	0.3	91.6	-0.4
1978	87.0	-5.0	87.5	0.6	87.9	0.5	90.5	3.0	93.5	3.3	95.2	1.8	92.5	-2.8	98.4	6.4	98.2	-0.2	98.0	-0.2	98.4	0.4	97.5	-0.9
1979	93.0	-4.6	92.5	-0.5	94.0	1.6	94.0	0.0	93.8	-0.2	90.8	-3.2	89.5	-1.4	95.9	7.2	96.1	0.2	95.9	-0.2	95.6	-0.3	92.0	-3.8
1980	92.4	0.4	96.6	4.5	99.4	2.9	100.4	1.0	102.6	2.2	94.1	-8.3	95.6	1.6	95.3	-0.3	96.7	1.5	100.1	3.5	100.9	0.8	97.9	-3.0
1981	97.2	-0.7	96.8	-0.4	98.6	1.9	99.4	0.8	99.4	0.0	97.7	-1.7	98.9	1.2	95.2	-3.7	97.1	2.0	97.5	0.4	95.7	-1.8	94.1	-1.7
1982	94.2	0.1	96.5	2.4	97.4	0.9	97.8	0.4	97.9	0.1	94.1	-3.9	99.1	5.3	99.5	0.4	104.3	4.8	101.4	-2.8	101.0	-0.4	97.6	-3.4
1983	95.3	-2.4	99.2	4.1	99.7	0.5	100.1	0.4	101.9	1.8	100.6	-1.3	100.4	-0.2	102.7	2.3	104.1	1.4	103.4	-0.7	103.7	0.3	98.4	-5.1
1984	95.1	-3.4	102.7	8.0	103.0	0.3	99.9	-3.0	100.3	0.4	100.5	0.2	98.8	-1.7	100.1	1.3	105.7	5.6	103.7	-1.9	101.3	-2.3	98.8	-2.5
1985	91.9	-7.0	98.6	7.3	101.2	2.6	101.4	0.2	102.2	0.8	102.0	-0.2	102.9	0.9	106.7	3.7	109.6	2.7	108.6	-0.9	110.6	1.8	106.7	-3.5
1986	105.2	-1.4	104.5	-0.7	104.0	-0.5	103.3	-0.7	102.8	-0.5	100.5	-2.2	98.3	-2.2	108.3	10.2	110.1	1.7	110.9	0.7	109.4	-1.4	108.2	-1.1
1987	-	-	105.9	-2.1	-	-	114.8	8.4	-	-	107.8	-6.1	-	-	107.6	-0.2	-	-	118.9	10.5	-	-	114.5	-3.7
1988	-	-	112.9	-1.4	-	-	123.0	8.9	-	-	115.4	-6.2	-	-	117.2	1.6	-	-	125.6	7.2	-	-	122.8	-2.2
1989	-	-	123.4	0.5	-	-	129.8	5.2	-	-	124.8	-3.9	-	-	121.1	-3.0	-	-	131.7	8.8	-	-	125.6	-4.6
1990	-	-	130.1	3.6	-	-	134.3	3.2	-	-	126.8	-5.6	-	-	133.4	5.2	-	-	135.7	1.7	-	-	132.3	-2.5
1991	-	-	132.5	0.2	-	-	135.4	2.2	-	-	131.5	-2.9	-	-	137.1	4.3	-	-	140.6	2.6	-	-	132.5	-5.8
1992	-	-	134.8	1.7	-	-	135.9	0.8	-	-	130.3	-4.1	-	-	131.3	0.8	-	-	134.0	2.1	-	-	134.0	0.0
1993	-	-	139.2	3.9	-	-	146.1	5.0	-	-	136.0	-6.9	-	-	140.4	3.2	-	-	146.9	4.6	-	-	135.7	-7.6
1994	-	-	141.7	4.4	-	-	144.2	1.8	-	-	140.9	-2.3	-	-	135.0	-4.2	-	-	139.2	3.1	-	-	131.8	-5.3

[Continued]

Detroit, MI
Consumer Price Index - Urban Wage Earners
Base 1982-1984 = 100
Apparel and Upkeep
[Continued]

For 1952-1997. Columns headed % show percentile change in the index from the previous period for which an index is available.

Year	Jan		Feb		Mar		Apr		May		Jun		Jul		Aug		Sep		Oct		Nov		Dec	
	Index	%	Index	%	Index	%	Index	%	Index	%	Index	%	Index	%	Index	%	Index	%	Index	%	Index	%	Index	%
1995	-	-	142.0	7.7	-	-	142.1	0.1	-	-	134.3	-5.5	-	-	140.3	4.5	-	-	139.2	-0.8	-	-	137.9	-0.9
1996	-	-	138.8	0.7	-	-	140.8	1.4	-	-	133.9	-4.9	-	-	131.6	-1.7	-	-	132.3	0.5	-	-	127.7	-3.5
1997	-	-	140.3	9.9	-	-	146.2	4.2	-	-	130.0	-11.1	-	-	140.7	8.2	-	-	138.7	-1.4	-	-	133.4	-3.8

Source: U.S. Department of Labor, Bureau of Labor Statistics, Division of Consumer Prices and Price Indexes. - indicates no data collected for period.

Detroit, MI
Consumer Price Index - All Urban Consumers
Base 1982-1984 = 100
Transportation

For 1947-1997. Columns headed % show percentile change in the index from the previous period for which an index is available.

Year	Jan Index	%	Feb Index	%	Mar Index	%	Apr Index	%	May Index	%	Jun Index	%	Jul Index	%	Aug Index	%	Sep Index	%	Oct Index	%	Nov Index	%	Dec Index	%
1947	19.2	-	19.3	0.5	19.4	0.5	19.5	0.5	19.5	0.0	19.5	0.0	19.5	0.0	19.8	1.5	20.1	1.5	20.1	0.0	20.3	1.0	20.7	2.0
1948	20.7	0.0	20.7	0.0	20.7	0.0	21.8	5.3	21.8	0.0	22.0	0.9	22.6	2.7	23.0	1.8	23.1	0.4	23.1	0.0	23.1	0.0	23.1	0.0
1949	23.1	0.0	23.4	1.3	23.4	0.0	23.5	0.4	23.5	0.0	23.4	-0.4	23.4	0.0	23.4	0.0	23.4	0.0	23.4	0.0	23.4	0.0	23.4	0.0
1950	23.4	0.0	23.4	0.0	23.4	0.0	23.4	0.0	23.8	1.7	23.9	0.4	23.9	0.0	23.7	-0.8	23.8	0.4	23.7	-0.4	23.8	0.4	23.8	0.0
1951	23.8	0.0	23.8	0.0	24.1	1.3	24.1	0.0	24.1	0.0	24.6	2.1	24.8	0.8	24.8	0.0	25.1	1.2	25.5	1.6	25.9	1.6	25.9	0.0
1952	25.9	0.0	25.9	0.0	26.1	0.8	26.1	0.0	26.1	0.0	26.1	0.0	26.1	0.0	26.5	1.5	26.6	0.4	27.4	3.0	27.4	0.0	27.4	0.0
1953	27.4	0.0	27.4	0.0	27.3	-0.4	27.4	0.4	27.4	0.0	27.6	0.7	27.8	0.7	27.8	0.0	27.7	-0.4	27.6	-0.4	27.5	-0.4	26.7	-2.9
1954	27.3	2.2	26.5	-2.9	26.4	-0.4	26.3	-0.4	26.3	0.0	26.0	-1.1	26.1	0.4	25.7	-1.5	25.7	0.0	26.4	0.4	26.7	1.1	26.7	-2.2
1955	26.6	-0.4	26.4	-0.8	26.4	0.0	26.3	-0.4	26.3	0.0	26.7	1.5	26.6	-0.4	26.3	-1.1	26.4	0.4	26.7	1.1	27.2	1.9	27.2	0.0
1956	27.1	-0.4	27.1	0.0	27.0	-0.4	27.2	0.7	27.2	0.0	27.1	-0.4	27.5	1.5	27.6	0.4	27.5	-0.4	28.0	1.8	28.3	1.1	28.3	0.0
1957	28.6	1.1	28.5	-0.3	28.7	0.7	28.6	-0.3	28.8	0.7	28.8	0.0	28.8	0.0	28.9	0.3	28.7	-0.7	28.6	-0.3	30.0	4.9	29.7	-1.0
1958	29.3	-1.3	28.6	-2.4	28.6	0.0	28.5	-0.3	28.3	-0.7	28.7	1.4	28.7	0.0	29.2	1.7	29.3	0.3	29.2	-0.3	29.4	0.7	29.7	1.0
1959	29.8	0.3	29.5	-1.0	29.8	1.0	30.1	1.0	30.0	-0.3	29.1	-3.0	30.4	4.5	30.3	-0.3	30.7	1.3	30.7	0.0	30.5	-0.7	30.6	0.3
1960	29.9	-2.3	30.2	1.0	29.8	-1.3	29.3	-1.7	29.5	0.7	30.6	3.7	30.6	0.0	30.7	0.3	30.3	-1.3	30.4	0.3	30.4	0.0	30.0	-1.3
1961	30.2	0.7	30.1	-0.3	29.5	-2.0	29.1	-1.4	29.5	1.4	29.2	-1.0	28.9	-1.0	30.5	5.5	29.8	-2.3	30.1	1.0	30.2	0.3	28.7	-5.0
1962	29.0	1.0	30.6	5.5	30.6	0.0	31.0	1.3	29.8	-3.9	29.9	0.3	29.3	-2.0	30.3	3.4	30.8	1.7	31.0	0.6	30.4	-1.9	31.1	2.3
1963	30.6	-1.6	30.4	-0.7	30.6	0.7	29.5	-3.6	30.4	3.1	30.2	-0.7	30.3	0.3	31.4	3.6	29.7	-5.4	30.5	2.7	31.0	1.6	30.7	-1.0
1964	30.9	0.7	29.7	-3.9	30.3	2.0	30.3	0.0	29.8	-1.7	30.2	1.3	30.7	1.7	31.0	1.0	31.2	0.6	31.6	1.3	31.1	-1.6	31.3	0.6
1965	31.8	1.6	31.2	-1.9	31.1	-0.3	31.8	2.3	32.3	1.6	32.2	-0.3	32.2	0.0	32.0	-0.6	32.0	0.0	32.2	0.6	32.4	0.6	32.4	0.0
1966	32.5	0.3	32.3	-0.6	32.7	1.2	32.9	0.6	32.9	0.0	32.9	0.0	32.8	-0.3	32.9	0.3	32.6	-0.9	33.0	1.2	33.1	0.3	33.0	-0.3
1967	33.0	0.0	33.2	0.6	33.4	0.6	33.6	0.6	33.6	0.0	33.5	-0.3	33.5	0.0	33.4	-0.3	33.5	0.3	33.6	0.3	34.0	1.2	34.1	0.3
1968	34.4	0.9	34.4	0.0	34.9	1.5	34.9	0.0	35.0	0.3	35.1	0.3	35.0	-0.3	34.9	-0.3	34.8	-0.3	35.1	0.9	35.3	0.6	35.1	-0.6
1969	35.0	-0.3	35.4	1.1	36.6	3.4	36.5	-0.3	36.6	0.3	36.7	0.3	35.7	-2.7	36.7	2.8	35.6	-3.0	36.1	1.4	35.8	-0.8	36.0	0.6
1970	36.1	0.3	36.9	2.2	35.4	-4.1	36.5	3.1	37.2	1.9	36.4	-2.2	36.5	0.3	35.8	-1.9	36.0	0.6	38.7	7.5	38.9	0.5	37.8	-2.8
1971	39.5	4.5	38.1	-3.5	37.8	-0.8	38.1	0.8	38.7	1.6	38.8	0.3	37.8	-2.6	38.9	2.9	38.2	-1.8	38.2	0.0	38.6	1.0	38.4	-0.5
1972	39.1	1.8	39.2	0.3	38.8	-1.0	38.7	-0.3	38.7	0.0	39.2	1.3	39.1	-0.3	39.2	0.3	39.0	-0.5	39.2	0.5	39.2	0.0	39.6	1.0
1973	39.6	0.0	40.4	2.0	40.5	0.2	41.2	1.7	41.5	0.7	41.9	1.0	41.9	0.0	41.8	-0.2	41.5	-0.7	42.0	1.2	42.3	0.7	42.9	1.4
1974	43.4	1.2	43.9	1.2	45.2	3.0	45.9	1.5	46.3	0.9	47.1	1.7	47.5	0.8	47.6	0.2	47.8	0.4	47.9	0.2	47.9	0.0	47.9	0.0
1975	47.9	0.0	47.9	0.0	48.4	1.0	48.7	0.6	49.0	0.6	50.0	2.0	51.1	2.2	51.1	0.0	51.3	0.4	51.6	0.6	51.6	0.0	51.6	0.0
1976	51.8	0.4	51.8	0.0	51.9	0.2	52.3	0.8	53.1	1.5	53.8	1.3	54.2	0.7	54.4	0.4	54.8	0.7	55.1	0.5	55.8	1.3	55.9	0.2
1977	56.0	0.2	56.3	0.5	57.4	2.0	58.4	1.7	59.0	1.0	59.3	0.5	59.4	0.2	59.6	0.3	59.5	-0.2	59.5	0.0	59.5	0.0	59.5	0.0
1978	59.6	0.2	59.7	0.2	60.3	1.0	60.6	0.5	61.6	1.7	62.2	1.0	62.7	0.8	62.8	0.2	62.9	0.2	63.8	1.4	64.1	0.5	64.2	0.2
1979	65.3	1.7	65.8	0.8	66.3	0.8	68.0	2.6	68.9	1.3	70.3	2.0	71.5	1.7	72.5	1.4	73.1	0.8	74.0	1.2	74.4	0.5	75.3	1.2
1980	77.1	2.4	78.5	1.8	79.8	1.7	81.2	1.8	82.1	1.1	82.8	0.9	81.5	-1.6	83.2	2.1	85.2	2.4	86.4	1.4	87.9	1.7	87.7	-0.2
1981	88.9	1.4	90.0	1.2	91.1	1.2	92.0	1.0	93.1	1.2	93.3	0.2	95.4	2.3	95.4	0.0	95.4	0.0	96.8	1.5	97.1	0.3	97.0	-0.1
1982	97.4	0.4	96.2	-1.2	95.7	-0.5	95.4	-0.3	96.7	1.4	99.1	2.5	99.8	0.7	99.9	0.1	98.5	-1.4	98.6	0.1	98.6	0.0	98.4	-0.2
1983	97.3	-1.1	96.4	-0.9	96.1	-0.3	96.4	0.3	97.6	1.2	97.5	-0.1	98.7	1.2	99.6	0.9	100.2	0.6	100.3	0.1	101.2	0.9	101.0	-0.2
1984	101.1	0.1	101.4	0.3	102.0	0.6	103.1	1.1	103.6	0.5	103.5	-0.1	103.4	-0.1	103.4	0.0	104.5	1.1	106.0	1.4	106.1	0.1	105.3	-0.8
1985	104.6	-0.7	105.4	0.8	106.1	0.7	106.5	0.4	106.5	0.0	106.6	0.1	106.7	0.1	107.1	0.4	106.0	-1.0	107.2	1.1	107.9	0.7	108.3	0.4
1986	108.0	-0.3	106.0	-1.9	102.7	-3.1	101.2	-1.5	103.5	2.3	103.9	0.4	102.3	-1.5	101.7	-0.6	100.8	-0.9	102.2	1.4	103.6	1.4	103.1	-0.5
1987	-		102.9	-0.2	-		104.2	1.3	-		104.9	0.7	-		106.4	1.4	-		107.8	1.3	-		106.7	-1.0
1988	-		105.5	-1.1	-		106.8	1.2	-		110.3	3.3	-		111.3	0.9	-		111.7	0.4	-		112.8	1.0
1989	-		113.7	0.8	-		117.9	3.7	-		119.0	0.9	-		116.0	-2.5	-		118.4	2.1	-		118.3	-0.1
1990	-		120.5	1.9	-		120.2	-0.2	-		121.7	1.2	-		124.1	2.0	-		130.4	5.1	-		130.5	0.1
1991	-		128.3	-1.7	-		129.2	0.7	-		129.8	0.5	-		128.9	-0.7	-		129.1	0.2	-		130.9	1.4

[Continued]

Detroit, MI
Consumer Price Index - All Urban Consumers
Base 1982-1984 = 100
Transportation
[Continued]

For 1947-1997. Columns headed % show percentile change in the index from the previous period for which an index is available.

Year	Jan		Feb		Mar		Apr		May		Jun		Jul		Aug		Sep		Oct		Nov		Dec	
	Index	%	Index	%	Index	%	Index	%	Index	%	Index	%	Index	%	Index	%	Index	%	Index	%	Index	%	Index	%
1992	-	-	128.5	-1.8	-	-	130.0	1.2	-	-	130.1	0.1	-	-	128.6	-1.2	-	-	132.1	2.7	-	-	130.3	-1.4
1993	-	-	131.8	1.2	-	-	131.7	-0.1	-	-	132.7	0.8	-	-	132.7	0.0	-	-	134.4	1.3	-	-	132.6	-1.3
1994	-	-	134.9	1.7	-	-	136.3	1.0	-	-	139.9	2.6	-	-	142.2	1.6	-	-	140.4	-1.3	-	-	140.1	-0.2
1995	-	-	142.0	1.4	-	-	144.9	2.0	-	-	145.5	0.4	-	-	141.8	-2.5	-	-	144.4	1.8	-	-	143.8	-0.4
1996	-	-	145.1	0.9	-	-	147.6	1.7	-	-	148.5	0.6	-	-	147.0	-1.0	-	-	149.4	1.6	-	-	152.5	2.1
1997	-	-	148.4	-2.7	-	-	147.7	-0.5	-	-	148.7	0.7	-	-	149.5	0.5	-	-	150.4	0.6	-	-	148.2	-1.5

Source: U.S. Department of Labor, Bureau of Labor Statistics, Division of Consumer Prices and Price Indexes. - indicates no data collected for period.

Detroit, MI
Consumer Price Index - Urban Wage Earners
Base 1982-1984 = 100
Transportation

For 1947-1997. Columns headed % show percentile change in the index from the previous period for which an index is available.

Year	Jan Index	%	Feb Index	%	Mar Index	%	Apr Index	%	May Index	%	Jun Index	%	Jul Index	%	Aug Index	%	Sep Index	%	Oct Index	%	Nov Index	%	Dec Index	%
1947	19.9	-	20.0	0.5	20.1	0.5	20.2	0.5	20.2	0.0	20.2	0.0	20.2	0.0	20.5	1.5	20.9	2.0	20.9	0.0	21.1	1.0	21.5	1.9
1948	21.5	0.0	21.5	0.0	21.5	0.0	22.6	5.1	22.6	0.0	22.8	0.9	23.4	2.6	23.9	2.1	24.0	0.4	24.0	0.0	24.0	0.0	24.0	0.0
1949	24.0	0.0	24.3	1.2	24.3	0.0	24.4	0.4	24.4	0.0	24.3	-0.4	24.3	0.0	24.3	0.0	24.3	0.0	24.3	0.0	24.3	0.0	24.3	0.0
1950	24.3	0.0	24.3	0.0	24.3	0.0	24.3	0.0	24.7	1.6	24.8	0.4	24.8	0.0	24.6	-0.8	24.7	0.4	24.6	-0.4	24.7	0.4	24.7	0.0
1951	24.7	0.0	24.7	0.0	25.0	1.2	25.1	0.4	25.1	0.0	25.5	1.6	25.8	1.2	25.8	0.0	26.1	1.2	26.5	1.5	26.8	1.1	26.8	0.0
1952	26.8	0.0	26.9	0.4	27.0	0.4	27.0	0.0	27.0	0.0	27.0	0.0	27.0	0.0	27.5	1.9	27.6	0.4	28.4	2.9	28.4	0.0	28.4	0.0
1953	28.5	0.4	28.4	-0.4	28.4	0.0	28.4	0.0	28.4	0.0	28.6	0.7	28.8	0.7	28.8	0.0	28.7	-0.3	28.6	-0.3	28.5	-0.3	27.7	-2.8
1954	28.4	2.5	27.5	-3.2	27.4	-0.4	27.3	-0.4	27.3	-0.4	27.0	-1.1	27.0	0.0	26.7	-1.1	26.7	0.0	26.7	0.0	28.3	6.0	27.7	-2.1
1955	27.6	-0.4	27.4	-0.7	27.4	0.0	27.3	-0.4	27.3	0.0	27.7	1.5	27.6	-0.4	27.3	-1.1	27.4	0.4	27.7	1.1	28.2	1.8	28.3	0.4
1956	28.2	-0.4	28.1	-0.4	28.1	0.0	28.2	0.4	28.3	0.4	28.2	-0.4	28.5	1.1	28.6	0.4	28.6	0.0	29.0	1.4	29.4	1.4	29.4	0.0
1957	29.7	1.0	29.6	-0.3	29.8	0.7	29.7	-0.3	29.9	0.7	29.9	0.0	29.9	0.0	30.0	0.3	29.8	-0.7	29.7	-0.3	31.1	4.7	30.8	-1.0
1958	30.5	-1.0	29.7	-2.6	29.7	0.0	29.5	-0.7	29.4	-0.3	29.8	1.4	29.8	0.0	30.3	1.7	30.4	0.3	30.3	-0.3	30.5	0.7	30.8	1.0
1959	30.9	0.3	30.6	-1.0	30.9	1.0	31.3	1.3	31.1	-0.6	30.2	-2.9	31.6	4.6	31.4	-0.6	31.8	1.3	31.8	0.0	31.6	-0.6	31.8	0.6
1960	31.0	-2.5	31.4	1.3	30.9	-1.6	30.5	-1.3	30.6	0.3	31.8	3.9	31.8	0.0	31.8	0.0	31.4	-1.3	31.5	0.3	31.5	0.0	31.1	-1.3
1961	31.4	1.0	31.2	-0.6	30.6	-1.9	30.2	-1.3	30.7	1.7	30.3	-1.3	30.0	-1.0	31.6	5.3	30.9	-2.2	31.3	1.3	31.3	0.0	29.8	-4.8
1962	30.1	1.0	31.8	5.6	31.8	0.0	32.2	1.3	30.9	-4.0	31.0	0.3	30.4	-1.9	31.5	3.6	32.0	1.6	32.2	0.6	31.6	-1.9	32.3	2.2
1963	31.8	-1.5	31.5	-0.9	31.8	1.0	30.6	-3.8	31.5	2.9	31.3	-0.6	31.4	0.3	32.5	3.5	30.8	-5.2	31.7	2.9	32.2	1.6	31.9	-0.9
1964	32.0	0.3	30.8	-3.8	31.4	1.9	31.4	0.0	30.9	-1.6	31.3	1.3	31.8	1.6	32.2	1.3	32.3	0.3	32.7	1.2	32.3	-1.2	32.4	0.3
1965	33.0	1.9	32.3	-2.1	32.2	-0.3	33.0	2.5	33.5	1.5	33.4	-0.3	33.4	0.0	33.2	-0.6	33.2	0.0	33.4	0.6	33.6	0.6	33.6	0.0
1966	33.7	0.3	33.5	-0.6	34.0	1.5	34.2	0.6	34.1	-0.3	34.1	0.0	34.0	-0.3	34.1	0.3	33.8	-0.9	34.2	1.2	34.4	0.6	34.2	-0.6
1967	34.2	0.0	34.5	0.9	34.7	0.6	34.9	0.6	34.8	-0.3	34.8	0.0	34.7	-0.3	34.7	0.0	34.7	0.0	34.9	0.6	35.3	1.1	35.4	0.3
1968	35.7	0.8	35.7	0.0	36.2	1.4	36.2	0.0	36.3	0.3	36.4	0.3	36.3	-0.3	36.2	-0.3	36.1	-0.3	36.4	0.8	36.6	0.5	36.4	-0.5
1969	36.3	-0.3	36.8	1.4	38.0	3.3	37.9	-0.3	38.0	0.3	38.1	0.3	37.0	-2.9	38.0	2.7	37.0	-2.6	37.4	1.1	37.1	-0.8	37.3	0.5
1970	37.4	0.3	38.3	2.4	36.7	-4.2	37.9	3.3	38.6	1.8	37.8	-2.1	37.8	0.0	37.2	-1.6	37.3	0.3	40.1	7.5	40.4	0.7	39.2	-3.0
1971	41.0	4.6	39.5	-3.7	39.3	-0.5	39.6	0.8	40.1	1.3	40.3	0.5	39.2	-2.7	40.4	3.1	39.7	-1.7	39.7	0.0	40.1	1.0	39.9	-0.5
1972	40.6	1.8	40.7	0.2	40.2	-1.2	40.1	-0.2	40.2	0.2	40.6	1.0	40.5	-0.2	40.7	0.5	40.5	-0.5	40.6	0.2	40.7	0.2	41.1	1.0
1973	41.1	0.0	41.9	1.9	42.0	0.2	42.7	1.7	43.1	0.9	43.4	0.7	43.5	0.2	43.4	-0.2	43.1	-0.7	43.6	1.2	43.9	0.7	44.5	1.4
1974	45.0	1.1	45.6	1.3	46.9	2.9	47.6	1.5	48.0	0.8	48.8	1.7	49.2	0.8	49.4	0.4	49.6	0.4	49.7	0.2	49.7	0.0	49.7	0.0
1975	49.7	0.0	49.7	0.0	50.3	1.2	50.5	0.4	50.8	0.6	51.9	2.2	53.0	2.1	53.0	0.0	53.2	0.4	53.5	0.6	53.5	0.0	53.5	0.0
1976	53.7	0.4	53.7	0.0	53.8	0.2	54.3	0.9	55.1	1.5	55.9	1.5	56.2	0.5	56.4	0.4	56.8	0.7	57.2	0.7	57.9	1.2	58.0	0.2
1977	58.2	0.3	58.4	0.3	59.5	1.9	60.6	1.8	61.2	1.0	61.5	0.5	61.6	0.1	61.8	0.3	61.7	-0.2	61.7	0.0	61.8	0.2	61.8	0.0
1978	61.8	0.0	62.0	0.3	62.3	0.5	62.7	0.6	63.6	1.4	64.2	0.9	64.6	0.6	64.8	0.3	64.9	0.2	65.8	1.4	66.0	0.3	66.2	0.3
1979	67.5	2.0	68.0	0.7	68.6	0.9	70.1	2.2	71.1	1.4	72.6	2.1	74.2	2.2	75.0	1.1	74.9	-0.1	76.4	2.0	76.6	0.3	77.1	0.7
1980	79.1	2.6	80.4	1.6	81.7	1.6	84.3	3.2	85.3	1.2	85.5	0.2	83.4	-2.5	85.6	2.6	87.4	2.1	86.9	-0.6	88.1	1.4	86.9	-1.4
1981	88.0	1.3	89.3	1.5	90.0	0.8	90.9	1.0	92.4	1.7	92.6	0.2	94.3	1.8	94.5	0.2	95.2	0.7	96.4	1.3	96.9	0.5	97.0	0.1
1982	97.3	0.3	96.2	-1.1	95.7	-0.5	95.3	-0.4	96.6	1.4	99.1	2.6	99.8	0.7	99.8	0.0	98.5	-1.3	98.6	0.1	98.6	0.0	98.5	-0.1
1983	97.3	-1.2	96.4	-0.9	96.1	-0.3	96.4	0.3	97.7	1.3	97.6	-0.1	98.7	1.1	99.6	0.9	100.2	0.6	100.3	0.1	101.2	0.9	101.0	-0.2
1984	101.1	0.1	101.4	0.3	102.0	0.6	103.1	1.1	103.6	0.5	103.5	-0.1	103.4	-0.1	103.4	0.0	104.5	1.1	106.0	1.4	106.0	0.0	105.3	-0.7
1985	104.6	-0.7	105.5	0.9	106.1	0.6	106.6	0.5	106.6	0.0	106.7	0.1	106.9	0.2	107.3	0.4	106.1	-1.1	107.3	1.1	108.1	0.7	108.4	0.3
1986	108.1	-0.3	106.0	-1.9	102.6	-3.2	101.1	-1.5	103.5	2.4	103.9	0.4	102.3	-1.5	101.6	-0.7	100.8	-0.8	102.1	1.3	103.5	1.4	103.0	-0.5
1987	-		102.9	-0.1	-		104.3	1.4	-		105.0	0.7	-		106.6	1.5	-		108.1	1.4	-		106.9	-1.1
1988	-		105.6	-1.2	-		107.0	1.3	-		110.2	3.0	-		111.4	1.1	-		111.7	0.3	-		112.8	1.0
1989	-		113.6	0.7	-		118.0	3.9	-		119.2	1.0	-		116.0	-2.7	-		118.3	2.0	-		118.1	-0.2
1990	-		120.5	2.0	-		120.1	-0.3	-		121.7	1.3	-		124.2	2.1	-		130.7	5.2	-		130.6	-0.1
1991	-		128.1	-1.9	-		129.0	0.7	-		129.7	0.5	-		128.8	-0.7	-		129.0	0.2	-		130.7	1.3

[Continued]

Detroit, MI
Consumer Price Index - Urban Wage Earners
Base 1982-1984 = 100
Transportation
[Continued]

For 1947-1997. Columns headed % show percentile change in the index from the previous period for which an index is available.

Year	Jan Index	%	Feb Index	%	Mar Index	%	Apr Index	%	May Index	%	Jun Index	%	Jul Index	%	Aug Index	%	Sep Index	%	Oct Index	%	Nov Index	%	Dec Index	%
1992	-	-	128.2	-1.9	-	-	129.8	1.2	-	-	129.9	0.1	-	-	128.4	-1.2	-	-	131.9	2.7	-	-	130.1	-1.4
1993	-	-	131.6	1.2	-	-	131.6	0.0	-	-	132.7	0.8	-	-	132.6	-0.1	-	-	134.3	1.3	-	-	132.4	-1.4
1994	-	-	134.7	1.7	-	-	136.1	1.0	-	-	139.7	2.6	-	-	142.3	1.9	-	-	140.4	-1.3	-	-	140.1	-0.2
1995	-	-	142.0	1.4	-	-	145.1	2.2	-	-	145.8	0.5	-	-	141.9	-2.7	-	-	144.5	1.8	-	-	143.8	-0.5
1996	-	-	145.2	1.0	-	-	147.8	1.8	-	-	148.7	0.6	-	-	147.1	-1.1	-	-	149.6	1.7	-	-	152.7	2.1
1997	-	-	148.5	-2.8	-	-	147.7	-0.5	-	-	148.7	0.7	-	-	149.5	0.5	-	-	150.3	0.5	-	-	148.0	-1.5

Source: U.S. Department of Labor, Bureau of Labor Statistics, Division of Consumer Prices and Price Indexes. - indicates no data collected for period.

Detroit, MI
Consumer Price Index - All Urban Consumers
Base 1982-1984 = 100
Medical Care

For 1947-1997. Columns headed % show percentile change in the index from the previous period for which an index is available.

Year	Jan Index	%	Feb Index	%	Mar Index	%	Apr Index	%	May Index	%	Jun Index	%	Jul Index	%	Aug Index	%	Sep Index	%	Oct Index	%	Nov Index	%	Dec Index	%
1947	11.5	-	11.6	0.9	11.7	0.9	11.7	0.0	11.8	0.9	11.8	0.0	11.8	0.0	11.8	0.0	12.0	1.7	12.0	0.0	12.0	0.0	12.0	0.0
1948	12.1	0.8	12.1	0.0	12.2	0.8	12.2	0.0	12.2	0.0	12.2	0.0	12.2	0.0	12.3	0.8	12.4	0.8	12.4	0.0	12.4	0.0	12.4	0.0
1949	12.4	0.0	12.5	0.8	12.5	0.0	12.5	0.0	12.5	0.0	12.5	0.0	12.5	0.0	12.6	0.8	12.7	0.8	12.7	0.0	12.7	0.0	12.7	0.0
1950	12.7	0.0	12.8	0.8	12.8	0.0	12.8	0.0	12.8	0.0	12.8	0.0	12.8	0.0	12.8	0.0	12.8	0.0	12.9	0.8	12.9	0.0	12.9	0.0
1951	12.9	0.0	12.9	0.0	13.0	0.8	13.0	0.0	13.0	0.0	13.5	3.8	13.6	0.7	13.6	0.0	13.6	0.0	13.6	0.0	13.6	0.0	13.8	1.5
1952	13.7	-0.7	13.7	0.0	14.0	2.2	14.0	0.0	14.0	0.0	14.1	0.7	14.1	0.0	14.1	0.0	14.2	0.7	14.3	0.7	14.3	0.0	14.3	0.0
1953	14.3	0.0	14.3	0.0	14.3	0.0	14.3	0.0	14.8	3.5	14.8	0.0	14.8	0.0	14.9	0.7	14.8	-0.7	14.9	0.7	14.9	0.0	14.9	0.0
1954	14.9	0.0	15.0	0.7	15.0	0.0	15.0	0.0	15.2	1.3	15.2	0.0	15.2	0.0	15.2	0.0	15.5	2.0	15.5	0.0	15.6	0.6	15.6	0.0
1955	15.6	0.0	16.2	3.8	16.2	0.0	16.2	0.0	16.2	0.0	16.2	0.0	16.2	0.0	16.2	0.0	16.2	0.0	16.2	0.0	16.8	3.7	16.8	0.0
1956	16.8	0.0	16.8	0.0	17.4	3.6	17.4	0.0	17.4	0.0	17.4	0.0	17.4	0.0	17.5	0.6	17.5	0.0	17.5	0.0	17.6	0.6	17.6	0.0
1957	17.7	0.6	17.9	1.1	17.9	0.0	17.9	0.0	17.9	0.0	17.9	0.0	17.9	0.0	17.9	0.0	17.9	0.0	17.9	0.0	18.5	3.4	18.5	0.0
1958	18.5	0.0	18.4	-0.5	18.5	0.5	18.5	0.0	18.5	0.0	18.5	0.0	18.5	0.0	18.6	0.5	18.6	0.0	18.6	0.0	18.7	0.5	18.7	0.0
1959	18.7	0.0	19.3	3.2	19.3	0.0	19.3	0.0	19.3	0.0	19.3	0.0	19.3	0.0	19.3	0.0	19.3	0.0	19.3	0.0	19.3	0.0	19.3	0.0
1960	19.3	0.0	19.4	0.5	19.4	0.0	19.4	0.0	19.5	0.5	19.5	0.0	19.8	1.5	19.9	0.5	19.9	0.0	19.9	0.0	19.9	0.0	19.9	0.0
1961	20.0	0.5	20.0	0.0	20.0	0.0	20.0	0.0	20.0	0.0	20.9	4.5	21.0	0.5	21.0	0.0	21.0	0.0	21.0	0.0	21.0	0.0	21.0	0.0
1962	20.9	-0.5	21.0	0.5	21.1	0.5	21.1	0.0	21.3	0.9	21.3	0.0	21.3	0.0	21.3	0.0	21.3	0.0	21.3	0.0	21.3	0.0	21.3	0.0
1963	21.3	0.0	21.4	0.5	21.4	0.0	21.4	0.0	21.5	0.5	22.9	6.5	22.9	0.0	22.9	0.0	22.9	0.0	22.9	0.0	23.0	0.4	23.0	0.0
1964	23.0	0.0	23.0	0.0	23.2	0.9	23.2	0.0	23.2	0.0	23.2	0.0	23.2	0.0	23.2	0.0	23.2	0.0	23.1	-0.4	23.3	0.9	23.3	0.0
1965	23.4	0.4	23.4	0.0	23.7	1.3	23.7	0.0	23.8	0.4	23.8	0.0	23.8	0.0	24.0	0.8	23.9	-0.4	23.9	0.0	23.9	0.0	23.9	0.0
1966	24.3	1.7	24.4	0.4	24.8	1.6	24.8	-0.0	24.9	0.4	25.1	0.8	25.2	0.4	25.3	0.4	25.5	0.8	25.6	0.4	25.9	1.2	26.1	0.8
1967	26.2	0.4	26.3	0.4	26.6	1.1	26.5	-0.4	26.6	0.4	26.7	0.4	26.8	0.4	26.8	0.0	27.3	1.9	27.3	0.0	27.7	1.5	27.8	0.4
1968	28.1	1.1	28.3	0.7	28.6	1.1	28.6	0.0	28.7	0.3	28.5	-0.7	28.5	0.0	28.6	0.4	28.8	0.7	29.0	0.7	29.0	0.0	29.4	1.4
1969	29.8	1.4	30.0	0.7	30.3	1.0	30.5	0.7	30.7	0.7	30.9	0.7	31.0	0.3	31.2	0.6	31.5	1.0	31.0	-1.6	31.2	0.6	31.4	0.6
1970	31.9	1.6	32.3	1.3	32.9	1.9	33.1	0.6	33.2	0.3	33.3	0.3	33.6	0.9	34.0	1.2	34.2	0.6	34.2	0.0	34.4	0.6	34.6	0.6
1971	35.1	1.4	35.4	0.9	35.5	0.3	35.6	0.3	35.7	0.3	36.0	0.8	36.2	0.6	36.4	0.6	36.7	0.8	36.6	-0.3	36.7	0.3	37.0	0.8
1972	37.5	1.4	37.6	0.3	37.7	0.3	37.8	0.3	37.8	0.0	38.0	0.5	38.0	0.0	38.2	0.5	38.2	0.0	38.6	1.0	38.6	0.0	38.6	0.0
1973	38.7	0.3	38.8	0.3	39.4	1.5	39.5	0.3	39.7	0.5	39.8	0.3	39.9	0.3	40.0	0.3	40.4	1.0	40.8	1.0	41.2	1.0	41.2	0.0
1974	41.5	0.7	42.0	1.2	42.2	0.5	42.4	0.5	42.9	1.2	43.3	0.9	43.8	1.2	44.5	1.6	45.3	1.8	45.6	0.7	46.0	0.9	46.1	0.2
1975	47.4	2.8	48.5	2.3	48.6	0.2	49.2	1.2	49.4	0.4	49.8	0.8	50.6	1.6	51.6	2.0	52.1	1.0	52.5	0.8	52.4	-0.2	52.7	0.6
1976	54.1	2.7	54.6	0.9	54.8	0.4	55.0	0.4	55.5	0.9	55.6	0.2	57.1	2.7	57.3	0.4	57.3	0.0	57.6	0.5	58.5	1.6	58.5	0.0
1977	59.0	0.9	59.1	0.2	60.5	2.4	61.6	1.8	62.7	1.8	63.4	1.1	63.8	0.6	65.1	2.0	65.4	0.5	65.5	0.2	65.9	0.6	65.8	-0.2
1978	65.8	0.0	66.3	0.8	66.8	0.8	67.2	0.6	67.4	0.3	67.4	0.0	67.5	0.1	67.6	0.1	67.7	0.1	69.5	2.7	69.5	0.0	70.3	1.2
1979	71.7	2.0	72.1	0.6	72.2	0.1	73.0	1.1	72.6	-0.5	73.4	1.1	74.0	0.8	74.2	0.3	74.4	0.3	74.9	0.7	75.8	1.2	78.0	2.9
1980	78.1	0.1	78.2	0.1	78.6	0.5	79.3	0.9	79.4	0.1	79.7	0.4	80.4	0.9	80.0	-0.5	80.9	1.1	81.7	1.0	82.3	0.7	82.4	0.1
1981	83.2	1.0	84.4	1.4	84.7	0.4	85.2	0.6	85.8	0.7	86.0	0.2	86.3	0.3	86.3	0.0	87.1	0.9	88.0	1.0	88.1	0.1	88.3	0.2
1982	89.2	1.0	90.1	1.0	91.0	1.0	91.6	0.7	92.7	1.2	92.7	0.0	93.8	1.2	94.6	0.9	95.5	1.0	95.8	0.3	95.8	0.0	95.8	0.0
1983	96.2	0.4	96.1	-0.1	96.8	0.7	96.7	-0.1	96.5	-0.2	96.3	-0.2	97.9	1.7	98.9	1.0	98.9	0.0	99.4	0.5	101.2	1.8	105.1	3.9
1984	105.8	0.7	106.5	0.7	106.9	0.4	107.7	0.7	107.7	0.0	107.7	0.0	108.9	1.1	109.4	0.5	109.9	0.5	110.0	0.1	110.5	0.5	110.6	0.1
1985	111.4	0.7	113.1	1.5	114.2	1.0	114.5	0.3	115.2	0.6	115.2	0.0	117.1	1.6	117.7	0.5	118.7	0.8	119.2	0.4	120.1	0.8	120.3	0.2
1986	121.7	1.2	122.0	0.2	122.7	0.6	123.0	0.2	123.6	0.5	124.1	0.4	126.5	1.9	126.6	0.1	126.8	0.2	127.2	0.3	127.4	0.2	128.2	0.6
1987	-	-	130.2	1.6	-	-	131.6	1.1	-	-	132.9	1.0	-	-	134.3	1.1	-	-	134.9	0.4	-	-	135.3	0.3
1988	-	-	138.6	2.4	-	-	138.5	-0.1	-	-	137.5	-0.7	-	-	142.7	3.8	-	-	142.1	-0.4	-	-	143.8	1.2
1989	-	-	142.9	-0.6	-	-	145.0	1.5	-	-	146.2	0.8	-	-	149.5	2.3	-	-	149.9	0.3	-	-	150.8	0.6
1990	-	-	154.7	2.6	-	-	156.5	1.2	-	-	158.9	1.5	-	-	163.7	3.0	-	-	163.9	0.1	-	-	164.6	0.4
1991	-	-	168.4	2.3	-	-	167.9	-0.3	-	-	169.5	1.0	-	-	173.0	2.1	-	-	174.4	0.8	-	-	175.6	0.7

[Continued]

Detroit, MI
Consumer Price Index - All Urban Consumers
Base 1982-1984 = 100
Medical Care
[Continued]

For 1947-1997. Columns headed % show percentile change in the index from the previous period for which an index is available.

Year	Jan Index	%	Feb Index	%	Mar Index	%	Apr Index	%	May Index	%	Jun Index	%	Jul Index	%	Aug Index	%	Sep Index	%	Oct Index	%	Nov Index	%	Dec Index	%
1992	-	-	179.2	2.1	-	-	180.9	0.9	-	-	181.0	0.1	-	-	182.1	0.6	-	-	184.2	1.2	-	-	184.6	0.2
1993	-	-	188.6	2.2	-	-	191.3	1.4	-	-	191.0	-0.2	-	-	191.6	0.3	-	-	192.3	0.4	-	-	192.5	0.1
1994	-	-	195.3	1.5	-	-	199.0	1.9	-	-	200.0	0.5	-	-	200.0	0.0	-	-	203.1	1.6	-	-	203.9	0.4
1995	-	-	206.2	1.1	-	-	208.8	1.3	-	-	209.8	0.5	-	-	209.9	0.0	-	-	210.0	0.0	-	-	212.8	1.3
1996	-	-	216.4	1.7	-	-	214.7	-0.8	-	-	213.8	-0.4	-	-	213.1	-0.3	-	-	212.2	-0.4	-	-	211.7	-0.2
1997	-	-	213.9	1.0	-	-	213.5	-0.2	-	-	213.7	0.1	-	-	213.7	0.0	-	-	214.8	0.5	-	-	216.1	0.6

Source: U.S. Department of Labor, Bureau of Labor Statistics, Division of Consumer Prices and Price Indexes. - indicates no data collected for period.

Detroit, MI
Consumer Price Index - Urban Wage Earners
Base 1982-1984 = 100
Medical Care

For 1947-1997. Columns headed % show percentile change in the index from the previous period for which an index is available.

Year	Jan Index	%	Feb Index	%	Mar Index	%	Apr Index	%	May Index	%	Jun Index	%	Jul Index	%	Aug Index	%	Sep Index	%	Oct Index	%	Nov Index	%	Dec Index	%
1947	11.7	-	11.8	0.9	11.9	0.8	12.0	0.8	12.0	0.0	12.1	0.8	12.1	0.0	12.1	0.0	12.2	0.8	12.2	0.0	12.2	0.0	12.2	0.0
1948	12.4	1.6	12.4	0.0	12.4	0.0	12.5	0.8	12.5	0.0	12.5	0.0	12.5	0.0	12.6	0.8	12.6	0.0	12.6	0.0	12.6	0.0	12.6	0.0
1949	12.6	0.0	12.7	0.8	12.8	0.8	12.8	0.0	12.8	0.0	12.8	0.0	12.8	0.0	12.8	0.0	12.9	0.8	12.9	0.0	13.0	0.8	13.0	0.0
1950	13.0	0.0	13.0	0.0	13.0	0.0	13.0	0.0	13.0	0.0	13.1	0.8	13.1	0.0	13.1	0.0	13.1	0.0	13.1	0.0	13.2	0.8	13.2	0.0
1951	13.2	0.0	13.2	0.0	13.3	0.8	13.3	0.0	13.3	0.0	13.8	3.8	13.8	0.0	13.8	0.0	13.8	0.0	13.9	0.7	13.9	0.0	14.1	1.4
1952	14.0	-0.7	14.0	0.0	14.3	2.1	14.3	0.0	14.3	0.0	14.4	0.7	14.4	0.0	14.4	0.0	14.5	0.7	14.6	0.7	14.6	0.0	14.6	0.0
1953	14.5	-0.7	14.6	0.7	14.6	0.0	14.6	0.0	15.1	3.4	15.1	0.0	15.1	0.0	15.1	0.0	15.1	0.0	15.1	0.0	15.2	0.7	15.2	0.0
1954	15.2	0.0	15.2	0.0	15.2	0.0	15.2	0.0	15.5	2.0	15.5	0.0	15.5	0.0	15.8	1.9	15.8	0.0	15.8	0.0	15.9	0.6	15.9	0.0
1955	15.9	0.0	16.5	3.8	16.5	0.0	16.5	0.0	16.5	0.0	16.5	0.0	16.5	0.0	16.5	0.0	16.5	0.0	16.5	0.0	17.1	3.6	17.1	0.0
1956	17.1	0.0	17.1	0.0	17.7	3.5	17.7	0.0	17.7	0.0	17.8	0.6	17.8	0.0	17.9	0.6	17.9	0.0	17.8	-0.6	17.9	0.6	17.9	0.0
1957	18.0	0.6	18.3	1.7	18.3	0.0	18.3	0.0	18.2	-0.5	18.2	0.0	18.2	0.0	18.3	0.5	18.3	0.0	18.3	0.0	18.8	2.7	18.8	0.0
1958	18.8	0.0	18.8	0.0	18.8	0.0	18.8	0.0	18.8	0.0	18.9	0.5	18.9	0.0	19.0	0.5	19.0	0.0	19.0	0.0	19.1	0.5	19.1	0.0
1959	19.1	0.0	19.7	3.1	19.7	0.0	19.7	0.0	19.7	0.0	19.7	0.0	19.7	0.0	19.7	0.0	19.7	0.0	19.7	0.0	19.7	0.0	19.7	0.0
1960	19.7	0.0	19.8	0.5	19.8	0.0	19.8	0.0	19.9	0.5	19.9	0.0	20.2	1.5	20.2	0.0	20.2	0.0	20.3	0.5	20.3	0.0	20.3	0.0
1961	20.3	0.0	20.4	0.5	20.4	0.0	20.3	-0.5	20.4	0.5	21.3	4.4	21.4	0.5	21.4	0.0	21.4	0.0	21.4	0.0	21.4	0.0	21.4	0.0
1962	21.3	-0.5	21.4	0.5	21.5	0.5	21.5	0.0	21.7	0.9	21.7	0.0	21.7	0.0	21.7	0.0	21.7	0.0	21.7	0.0	21.7	0.0	21.7	0.0
1963	21.7	0.0	21.8	0.5	21.9	0.5	21.9	0.0	21.9	0.0	23.3	6.4	23.3	0.0	23.3	0.0	23.3	0.0	23.3	0.0	23.4	0.4	23.4	0.0
1964	23.4	0.0	23.5	0.4	23.6	0.4	23.6	0.0	23.6	0.0	23.6	0.0	23.6	0.0	23.7	0.4	23.6	-0.4	23.6	0.0	23.7	0.4	23.7	0.0
1965	23.9	0.8	23.9	0.0	24.1	0.8	24.2	0.4	24.2	0.0	24.3	0.4	24.3	0.0	24.5	0.8	24.4	-0.4	24.4	0.0	24.4	0.0	24.4	0.0
1966	24.8	1.6	24.9	0.4	25.3	1.6	25.3	0.0	25.4	0.4	25.6	0.8	25.6	0.0	25.7	0.4	26.0	1.2	26.1	0.4	26.4	1.1	26.6	0.8
1967	26.7	0.4	26.8	0.4	27.1	1.1	27.0	-0.4	27.1	0.4	27.3	0.7	27.3	0.0	27.3	0.0	27.8	1.8	27.9	0.4	28.2	1.1	28.4	0.7
1968	28.7	1.1	28.8	0.3	29.1	1.0	29.2	0.3	29.3	0.3	29.1	-0.7	29.1	0.0	29.1	0.0	29.3	0.7	29.6	1.0	29.6	0.0	30.0	1.4
1969	30.3	1.0	30.6	1.0	30.9	1.0	31.1	0.6	31.3	0.6	31.5	0.6	31.6	0.3	31.8	0.6	32.1	0.9	31.6	-1.6	31.8	0.6	32.0	0.6
1970	32.5	1.6	32.9	1.2	33.5	1.8	33.8	0.9	33.9	0.3	34.0	0.3	34.2	0.6	34.6	1.2	34.8	0.6	34.8	0.0	35.1	0.9	35.3	0.6
1971	35.8	1.4	36.1	0.8	36.1	0.0	36.3	0.6	36.4	0.3	36.7	0.8	36.9	0.5	37.1	0.5	37.4	0.8	37.3	-0.3	37.4	0.3	37.7	0.8
1972	38.2	1.3	38.4	0.5	38.5	0.3	38.5	0.0	38.5	0.0	38.7	0.5	38.7	0.0	38.9	0.5	38.9	0.0	39.3	1.0	39.3	0.0	39.3	0.0
1973	39.4	0.3	39.5	0.3	40.1	1.5	40.3	0.5	40.4	0.2	40.6	0.5	40.7	0.2	40.8	0.2	41.2	1.0	41.6	1.0	42.0	1.0	42.0	0.0
1974	42.3	0.7	42.8	1.2	43.0	0.5	43.2	0.5	43.7	1.2	44.1	0.9	44.6	1.1	45.4	1.8	46.1	1.5	46.5	0.9	46.9	0.9	47.0	0.2
1975	48.3	2.8	49.4	2.3	49.6	0.4	50.2	1.2	50.4	0.4	50.8	0.8	51.6	1.6	52.6	1.9	53.1	1.0	53.5	0.8	53.4	-0.2	53.7	0.6
1976	55.2	2.8	55.6	0.7	55.9	0.5	56.0	0.2	56.5	0.9	56.7	0.4	58.2	2.6	58.4	0.3	58.4	0.0	58.7	0.5	59.6	1.5	59.6	0.0
1977	60.1	0.8	60.3	0.3	61.6	2.2	62.8	1.9	63.9	1.8	64.6	1.1	65.1	0.8	66.3	1.8	66.7	0.6	66.7	0.0	67.2	0.7	67.1	-0.1
1978	67.2	0.1	67.4	0.3	67.7	0.4	68.4	1.0	68.4	0.0	68.4	0.0	68.4	0.0	68.5	0.1	69.7	1.8	71.5	2.6	71.7	0.3	71.8	0.1
1979	72.9	1.5	72.8	-0.1	73.3	0.7	75.0	2.3	75.3	0.4	75.8	0.7	76.3	0.7	76.6	0.4	76.8	0.3	77.4	0.8	78.1	0.9	79.1	1.3
1980	79.1	0.0	79.2	0.1	79.4	0.3	80.9	1.9	81.4	0.6	81.6	0.2	81.7	0.1	81.6	-0.1	82.1	0.6	82.6	0.6	82.8	0.2	83.4	0.7
1981	84.5	1.3	85.4	1.1	85.9	0.6	86.0	0.1	86.2	0.2	86.6	0.5	86.8	0.2	87.2	0.5	87.7	0.6	88.2	0.6	88.7	0.6	88.6	-0.1
1982	89.6	1.1	90.4	0.9	91.4	1.1	91.9	0.5	93.0	1.2	93.0	0.0	94.0	1.1	94.7	0.7	95.7	1.1	96.0	0.3	95.9	-0.1	95.9	0.0
1983	96.4	0.5	96.3	-0.1	96.9	0.6	96.9	0.0	96.7	-0.2	96.6	-0.1	98.2	1.7	99.0	0.8	99.0	0.0	99.6	0.6	101.2	1.6	104.8	3.6
1984	105.4	0.6	106.2	0.8	106.6	0.4	107.2	0.6	107.3	0.1	107.4	0.1	108.5	1.0	108.9	0.4	109.5	0.6	109.6	0.1	110.2	0.5	110.3	0.1
1985	111.0	0.6	112.6	1.4	113.6	0.9	113.8	0.2	114.6	0.7	114.5	-0.1	116.2	1.5	116.8	0.5	117.7	0.8	118.2	0.4	119.0	0.7	119.3	0.3
1986	120.4	0.9	120.8	0.3	121.4	0.5	121.8	0.3	122.4	0.5	122.9	0.4	125.0	1.7	125.0	0.0	125.2	0.2	125.8	0.5	125.9	0.1	126.7	0.6
1987	-		128.5	1.4	-		130.1	1.2	-		131.3	0.9	-		132.7	1.1	-		133.1	0.3	-		133.9	0.6
1988	-		137.7	2.8	-		137.7	0.0	-		136.5	-0.9	-		142.5	4.4	-		141.9	-0.4	-		143.4	1.1
1989	-		142.9	-0.3	-		144.7	1.3	-		145.9	0.8	-		149.4	2.4	-		149.7	0.2	-		150.5	0.5
1990	-		154.2	2.5	-		155.9	1.1	-		158.0	1.3	-		163.1	3.2	-		163.2	0.1	-		163.6	0.2
1991	-		167.7	2.5	-		166.8	-0.5	-		168.1	0.8	-		171.4	2.0	-		172.8	0.8	-		174.1	0.8

[Continued]

Detroit, MI
Consumer Price Index - Urban Wage Earners
Base 1982-1984 = 100
Medical Care
[Continued]

For 1947-1997. Columns headed % show percentile change in the index from the previous period for which an index is available.

Year	Jan		Feb		Mar		Apr		May		Jun		Jul		Aug		Sep		Oct		Nov		Dec	
	Index	%	Index	%	Index	%	Index	%	Index	%	Index	%	Index	%	Index	%	Index	%	Index	%	Index	%	Index	%
1992	-	-	177.6	2.0	-	-	179.3	1.0	-	-	179.5	0.1	-	-	180.4	0.5	-	-	182.7	1.3	-	-	182.9	0.1
1993	-	-	187.1	2.3	-	-	189.8	1.4	-	-	189.5	-0.2	-	-	190.0	0.3	-	-	190.7	0.4	-	-	190.7	0.0
1994	-	-	193.3	1.4	-	-	196.8	1.8	-	-	197.7	0.5	-	-	197.6	-0.1	-	-	200.7	1.6	-	-	201.3	0.3
1995	-	-	204.1	1.4	-	-	206.4	1.1	-	-	207.7	0.6	-	-	207.8	0.0	-	-	208.1	0.1	-	-	210.7	1.2
1996	-	-	214.7	1.9	-	-	213.0	-0.8	-	-	212.2	-0.4	-	-	211.6	-0.3	-	-	210.7	-0.4	-	-	209.8	-0.4
1997	-	-	211.9	1.0	-	-	211.7	-0.1	-	-	212.0	0.1	-	-	212.2	0.1	-	-	213.0	0.4	-	-	214.4	0.7

Source: U.S. Department of Labor, Bureau of Labor Statistics, Division of Consumer Prices and Price Indexes. - indicates no data collected for period.

Detroit, MI
Consumer Price Index - All Urban Consumers
Base 1982-1984 = 100
Entertainment

For 1976-1997. Columns headed % show percentile change in the index from the previous period for which an index is available.

Year	Jan Index	%	Feb Index	%	Mar Index	%	Apr Index	%	May Index	%	Jun Index	%	Jul Index	%	Aug Index	%	Sep Index	%	Oct Index	%	Nov Index	%	Dec Index	%
1976	72.1	-	72.4	0.4	72.9	0.7	73.5	0.8	73.6	0.1	73.0	-0.8	73.2	0.3	73.0	-0.3	74.2	1.6	74.3	0.1	74.5	0.3	74.8	0.4
1977	74.9	0.1	74.9	0.0	75.1	0.3	75.0	-0.1	75.2	0.3	75.2	0.0	75.4	0.3	75.7	0.4	76.5	1.1	76.3	-0.3	76.8	0.7	77.3	0.7
1978	77.5	0.3	77.7	0.3	78.3	0.8	79.9	2.0	79.9	0.0	79.5	-0.5	80.0	0.6	81.0	1.3	81.2	0.2	81.2	0.0	81.4	0.2	82.0	0.7
1979	82.2	0.2	82.7	0.6	81.3	-1.7	83.3	2.5	84.2	1.1	84.6	0.5	83.8	-0.9	83.0	-1.0	81.4	-1.9	82.5	1.4	82.9	0.5	81.7	-1.4
1980	84.2	3.1	85.9	2.0	87.4	1.7	87.8	0.5	88.0	0.2	88.8	0.9	88.1	-0.8	87.8	-0.3	88.9	1.3	89.3	0.4	88.9	-0.4	88.9	0.0
1981	89.3	0.4	89.8	0.6	91.4	1.8	93.2	2.0	93.6	0.4	93.4	-0.2	93.4	0.0	92.5	-1.0	91.8	-0.8	93.0	1.3	92.6	-0.4	93.3	0.8
1982	93.1	-0.2	95.3	2.4	96.2	0.9	94.9	-1.4	95.5	0.6	94.9	-0.6	97.7	3.0	98.1	0.4	98.2	0.1	100.1	1.9	100.0	-0.1	100.0	0.0
1983	101.5	1.5	101.9	0.4	100.9	-1.0	100.6	-0.3	100.2	-0.4	100.9	0.7	101.2	0.3	101.8	0.6	100.8	-1.0	101.7	0.9	101.4	-0.3	101.2	-0.2
1984	101.6	0.4	101.4	-0.2	101.2	-0.2	102.2	1.0	100.2	-2.0	101.1	0.9	101.8	0.7	103.1	1.3	103.3	0.2	102.5	-0.8	101.8	-0.7	101.7	-0.1
1985	104.0	2.3	107.0	2.9	106.7	-0.3	106.3	-0.4	106.1	-0.2	105.6	-0.5	106.9	1.2	105.8	-1.0	108.5	2.6	107.0	-1.4	107.5	0.5	107.4	-0.1
1986	108.1	0.7	108.3	0.2	109.7	1.3	107.5	-2.0	106.9	-0.6	107.4	0.5	107.0	-0.4	108.6	1.5	111.1	2.3	108.1	-2.7	109.7	1.5	110.5	0.7
1987	-		110.1	-0.4	-		112.3	2.0	-		110.0	-2.0	-		113.1	2.8	-		113.6	0.4	-		114.3	0.6
1988	-		112.7	-1.4	-		113.2	0.4	-		114.1	0.8	-		115.2	1.0	-		115.8	0.5	-		118.0	1.9
1989	-		118.8	0.7	-		119.9	0.9	-		119.5	-0.3	-		119.8	0.3	-		122.5	2.3	-		124.1	1.3
1990	-		128.2	3.3	-		127.7	-0.4	-		126.8	-0.7	-		126.8	0.0	-		129.6	2.2	-		131.6	1.5
1991	-		133.0	1.1	-		135.0	1.5	-		134.6	-0.3	-		134.3	-0.2	-		129.6	-3.5	-		129.2	-0.3
1992	-		130.5	1.0	-		130.3	-0.2	-		131.0	0.5	-		130.2	-0.6	-		131.5	1.0	-		131.4	-0.1
1993	-		134.0	2.0	-		136.2	1.6	-		137.5	1.0	-		138.6	0.8	-		140.4	1.3	-		142.0	1.1
1994	-		143.8	1.3	-		145.5	1.2	-		146.7	0.8	-		147.3	0.4	-		145.9	-1.0	-		146.3	0.3
1995	-		147.9	1.1	-		150.4	1.7	-		148.3	-1.4	-		151.7	2.3	-		152.7	0.7	-		154.0	0.9
1996	-		153.4	-0.4	-		153.5	0.1	-		152.1	-0.9	-		154.8	1.8	-		158.6	2.5	-		157.0	-1.0
1997	-		159.6	1.7	-		159.0	-0.4	-		159.7	0.4	-		162.1	1.5	-		160.3	-1.1	-		162.3	1.2

Source: U.S. Department of Labor, Bureau of Labor Statistics, Division of Consumer Prices and Price Indexes. - indicates no data collected for period.

Detroit, MI
Consumer Price Index - Urban Wage Earners
Base 1982-1984 = 100
Entertainment

For 1976-1997. Columns headed % show percentile change in the index from the previous period for which an index is available.

Year	Jan Index	%	Feb Index	%	Mar Index	%	Apr Index	%	May Index	%	Jun Index	%	Jul Index	%	Aug Index	%	Sep Index	%	Oct Index	%	Nov Index	%	Dec Index	%
1976	75.6	-	75.8	0.3	76.3	0.7	77.0	0.9	77.1	0.1	76.5	-0.8	76.7	0.3	76.5	-0.3	77.8	1.7	77.9	0.1	78.0	0.1	78.4	0.5
1977	78.4	0.0	78.5	0.1	78.6	0.1	78.5	-0.1	78.8	0.4	78.8	0.0	79.0	0.3	79.3	0.4	80.2	1.1	80.0	-0.2	80.4	0.5	81.0	0.7
1978	81.1	0.1	81.6	0.6	82.2	0.7	84.0	2.2	83.4	-0.7	82.3	-1.3	82.8	0.6	83.0	0.2	83.2	0.2	83.3	0.1	84.7	1.7	85.3	0.7
1979	85.7	0.5	86.1	0.5	84.7	-1.6	86.7	2.4	87.6	1.0	88.1	0.6	87.8	-0.3	86.3	-1.7	84.6	-2.0	84.9	0.4	85.6	0.8	84.6	-1.2
1980	86.9	2.7	88.6	2.0	91.0	2.7	91.5	0.5	91.5	0.0	92.4	1.0	92.7	0.3	91.9	-0.9	91.8	-0.1	92.3	0.5	92.0	-0.3	88.6	-3.7
1981	88.9	0.3	89.4	0.6	91.6	2.5	93.7	2.3	94.1	0.4	93.6	-0.5	94.1	0.5	93.3	-0.9	93.1	-0.2	93.4	0.3	93.2	-0.2	93.4	0.2
1982	93.2	-0.2	95.3	2.3	96.2	0.9	95.2	-1.0	95.8	0.6	95.4	-0.4	98.2	2.9	98.5	0.3	98.6	0.1	100.3	1.7	100.3	0.0	100.4	0.1
1983	101.7	1.3	102.1	0.4	100.7	-1.4	100.3	-0.4	100.0	-0.3	100.7	0.7	101.4	0.7	101.8	0.4	100.8	-1.0	101.5	0.7	101.1	-0.4	101.1	0.0
1984	101.5	0.4	101.3	-0.2	101.3	0.0	102.2	0.9	100.1	-2.1	100.7	0.6	101.5	0.8	102.8	1.3	103.0	0.2	102.3	-0.7	101.7	-0.6	101.4	-0.3
1985	103.5	2.1	106.9	3.3	106.8	-0.1	106.3	-0.5	105.7	-0.6	105.0	-0.7	106.4	1.3	105.4	-0.9	108.9	3.3	107.6	-1.2	108.1	0.5	107.9	-0.2
1986	108.7	0.7	108.8	0.1	110.3	1.4	108.0	-2.1	107.5	-0.5	107.9	0.4	107.2	-0.6	109.2	1.9	113.1	3.6	108.9	-3.7	110.3	1.3	111.3	0.9
1987	-		110.9	-0.4	-		113.3	2.2	-		110.6	-2.4	-		114.0	3.1	-		114.5	0.4	-		115.2	0.6
1988	-		113.8	-1.2	-		114.3	0.4	-		114.5	0.2	-		115.9	1.2	-		116.6	0.6	-		119.0	2.1
1989	-		119.9	0.8	-		121.1	1.0	-		120.5	-0.5	-		120.8	0.2	-		123.3	2.1	-		124.4	0.9
1990	-		129.0	3.7	-		128.3	-0.5	-		127.5	-0.6	-		127.4	-0.1	-		130.5	2.4	-		132.2	1.3
1991	-		133.8	1.2	-		136.1	1.7	-		135.5	-0.4	-		135.0	-0.4	-		129.9	-3.8	-		129.4	-0.4
1992	-		130.6	0.9	-		130.5	-0.1	-		131.3	0.6	-		130.1	-0.9	-		131.5	1.1	-		131.4	-0.1
1993	-		133.9	1.9	-		136.1	1.6	-		138.0	1.4	-		139.0	0.7	-		141.0	1.4	-		142.4	1.0
1994	-		144.0	1.1	-		145.7	1.2	-		147.0	0.9	-		147.5	0.3	-		146.3	-0.8	-		146.7	0.3
1995	-		148.2	1.0	-		150.9	1.8	-		148.5	-1.6	-		151.9	2.3	-		153.1	0.8	-		154.4	0.8
1996	-		154.0	-0.3	-		153.8	-0.1	-		152.2	-1.0	-		155.0	1.8	-		158.5	2.3	-		157.2	-0.8
1997	-		159.2	1.3	-		158.9	-0.2	-		159.4	0.3	-		161.7	1.4	-		160.1	-1.0	-		162.0	1.2

Source: U.S. Department of Labor, Bureau of Labor Statistics, Division of Consumer Prices and Price Indexes. - indicates no data collected for period.

Detroit, MI
Consumer Price Index - All Urban Consumers
Base 1982-1984 = 100
Other Goods and Services

For 1976-1997. Columns headed % show percentile change in the index from the previous period for which an index is available.

Year	Jan Index	%	Feb Index	%	Mar Index	%	Apr Index	%	May Index	%	Jun Index	%	Jul Index	%	Aug Index	%	Sep Index	%	Oct Index	%	Nov Index	%	Dec Index	%
1976	56.5	-	56.5	0.0	56.7	0.4	57.1	0.7	57.2	0.2	57.3	0.2	57.3	0.0	57.7	0.7	57.8	0.2	58.4	1.0	58.7	0.5	58.8	0.2
1977	59.2	0.7	59.4	0.3	59.6	0.3	60.8	2.0	60.9	0.2	60.9	0.0	61.4	0.8	61.5	0.2	62.3	1.3	63.2	1.4	63.4	0.3	63.5	0.2
1978	63.5	0.0	64.0	0.8	64.1	0.2	64.4	0.5	64.9	0.8	65.5	0.9	66.3	1.2	66.0	-0.5	67.5	2.3	67.7	0.3	67.7	0.0	67.7	0.0
1979	68.6	1.3	68.8	0.3	69.2	0.6	69.2	0.0	69.2	0.0	69.2	0.0	69.7	0.7	70.5	1.1	71.8	1.8	71.9	0.1	71.7	-0.3	71.9	0.3
1980	72.7	1.1	73.2	0.7	73.3	0.1	73.5	0.3	74.1	0.8	74.5	0.5	74.7	0.3	75.3	0.8	77.5	2.9	77.1	-0.5	77.5	0.5	77.7	0.3
1981	77.9	0.3	79.4	1.9	80.0	0.8	80.2	0.2	80.7	0.6	80.9	0.2	81.3	0.5	81.3	0.0	84.9	4.4	85.0	0.1	85.0	0.0	85.3	0.4
1982	85.6	0.4	86.6	1.2	87.4	0.9	87.6	0.2	90.9	3.8	91.0	0.1	91.5	0.5	91.4	-0.1	96.0	5.0	97.2	1.2	97.6	0.4	98.7	1.1
1983	100.4	1.7	100.1	-0.3	100.5	0.4	100.9	0.4	101.4	0.5	101.5	0.1	101.9	0.4	101.5	-0.4	103.6	2.1	103.6	0.0	104.1	0.5	104.5	0.4
1984	105.7	1.1	105.1	-0.6	104.9	-0.2	105.1	0.2	105.0	-0.1	105.0	0.0	105.8	0.8	106.0	0.2	108.3	2.2	108.1	-0.2	107.7	-0.4	107.8	0.1
1985	109.3	1.4	109.6	0.3	109.4	-0.2	109.8	0.4	110.5	0.6	110.8	0.3	111.8	0.9	112.0	0.2	114.3	2.1	114.4	0.1	114.0	-0.3	113.7	-0.3
1986	114.2	0.4	112.5	-1.5	112.4	-0.1	112.4	0.0	112.8	0.4	112.7	-0.1	114.4	1.5	115.6	1.0	116.6	0.9	116.6	0.0	117.6	0.9	117.3	-0.3
1987	-	-	117.5	0.2	-	-	118.2	0.6	-	-	119.2	0.8	-	-	119.7	0.4	-	-	124.7	4.2	-	-	125.0	0.2
1988	-	-	128.3	2.6	-	-	127.8	-0.4	-	-	128.3	0.4	-	-	129.8	1.2	-	-	134.1	3.3	-	-	134.4	0.2
1989	-	-	135.4	0.7	-	-	135.5	0.1	-	-	137.4	1.4	-	-	137.6	0.1	-	-	141.6	2.9	-	-	142.0	0.3
1990	-	-	144.0	1.4	-	-	143.9	-0.1	-	-	146.5	1.8	-	-	146.6	0.1	-	-	152.7	4.2	-	-	154.3	1.0
1991	-	-	156.2	1.2	-	-	157.3	0.7	-	-	158.3	0.6	-	-	159.6	0.8	-	-	168.3	5.5	-	-	167.9	-0.2
1992	-	-	168.8	0.5	-	-	168.8	0.0	-	-	170.4	0.9	-	-	175.8	3.2	-	-	181.8	3.4	-	-	180.6	-0.7
1993	-	-	183.7	1.7	-	-	183.7	0.0	-	-	184.1	0.2	-	-	181.8	-1.2	-	-	183.8	1.1	-	-	184.9	0.6
1994	-	-	184.3	-0.3	-	-	185.1	0.4	-	-	201.0	8.6	-	-	202.6	0.8	-	-	207.4	2.4	-	-	208.2	0.4
1995	-	-	208.8	0.3	-	-	207.5	-0.6	-	-	209.1	0.8	-	-	212.0	1.4	-	-	214.2	1.0	-	-	214.9	0.3
1996	-	-	215.0	0.0	-	-	215.8	0.4	-	-	216.5	0.3	-	-	220.7	1.9	-	-	219.5	-0.5	-	-	218.8	-0.3
1997	-	-	222.2	1.6	-	-	225.6	1.5	-	-	223.8	-0.8	-	-	233.2	4.2	-	-	234.7	0.6	-	-	235.0	0.1

Source: U.S. Department of Labor, Bureau of Labor Statistics, Division of Consumer Prices and Price Indexes. - indicates no data collected for period.

Detroit, MI
Consumer Price Index - Urban Wage Earners
Base 1982-1984 = 100
Other Goods and Services

For 1976-1997. Columns headed % show percentile change in the index from the previous period for which an index is available.

Year	Jan Index	%	Feb Index	%	Mar Index	%	Apr Index	%	May Index	%	Jun Index	%	Jul Index	%	Aug Index	%	Sep Index	%	Oct Index	%	Nov Index	%	Dec Index	%
1976	54.5	-	54.5	0.0	54.7	0.4	55.0	0.5	55.1	0.2	55.2	0.2	55.3	0.2	55.6	0.5	55.8	0.4	56.3	0.9	56.6	0.5	56.7	0.2
1977	57.1	0.7	57.3	0.4	57.5	0.3	58.6	1.9	58.7	0.2	58.7	0.0	59.2	0.9	59.3	0.2	60.1	1.3	61.0	1.5	61.2	0.3	61.2	0.0
1978	61.5	0.5	61.8	0.5	61.4	-0.6	61.8	0.7	61.9	0.2	62.4	0.8	63.3	1.4	63.0	-0.5	64.6	2.5	64.5	-0.2	64.8	0.5	65.0	0.3
1979	66.1	1.7	66.4	0.5	66.3	-0.2	66.1	-0.3	66.1	0.0	66.1	0.0	66.5	0.6	67.7	1.8	69.0	1.9	69.2	0.3	69.0	-0.3	69.6	0.9
1980	71.2	2.3	72.0	1.1	71.8	-0.3	72.0	0.3	72.7	1.0	73.5	1.1	73.2	-0.4	73.9	1.0	75.1	1.6	75.0	-0.1	75.7	0.9	75.9	0.3
1981	76.1	0.3	78.0	2.5	77.9	-0.1	78.5	0.8	79.4	1.1	79.5	0.1	80.3	1.0	80.4	0.1	83.3	3.6	83.9	0.7	84.4	0.6	84.8	0.5
1982	85.2	0.5	86.2	1.2	87.0	0.9	87.2	0.2	91.2	4.6	91.2	0.0	91.7	0.5	91.6	-0.1	95.6	4.4	97.0	1.5	97.4	0.4	98.9	1.5
1983	100.6	1.7	100.3	-0.3	100.8	0.5	101.1	0.3	101.5	0.4	101.7	0.2	102.3	0.6	101.8	-0.5	103.5	1.7	103.5	0.0	104.0	0.5	104.4	0.4
1984	105.8	1.3	105.2	-0.6	105.0	-0.2	105.1	0.1	105.1	0.0	105.1	0.0	105.9	0.8	106.2	0.3	108.1	1.8	107.8	-0.3	107.4	-0.4	107.5	0.1
1985	109.3	1.7	109.5	0.2	109.3	-0.2	109.7	0.4	110.5	0.7	110.8	0.3	111.9	1.0	112.1	0.2	113.9	1.6	114.0	0.1	113.6	-0.4	113.2	-0.4
1986	113.8	0.5	111.9	-1.7	111.8	-0.1	111.8	0.0	112.2	0.4	112.2	0.0	114.1	1.7	115.4	1.1	115.9	0.4	115.9	0.0	117.0	0.9	116.7	-0.3
1987	-	-	116.9	0.2	-	-	118.0	0.9	-	-	119.3	1.1	-	-	120.0	0.6	-	-	123.7	3.1	-	-	124.1	0.3
1988	-	-	128.7	3.7	-	-	128.0	-0.5	-	-	128.5	0.4	-	-	130.7	1.7	-	-	133.2	1.9	-	-	133.7	0.4
1989	-	-	134.8	0.8	-	-	135.0	0.1	-	-	137.7	2.0	-	-	138.0	0.2	-	-	140.2	1.6	-	-	140.7	0.4
1990	-	-	143.5	2.0	-	-	143.6	0.1	-	-	147.1	2.4	-	-	147.2	0.1	-	-	151.6	3.0	-	-	154.0	1.6
1991	-	-	156.4	1.6	-	-	158.0	1.0	-	-	159.6	1.0	-	-	161.3	1.1	-	-	164.9	2.2	-	-	164.5	-0.2
1992	-	-	165.7	0.7	-	-	165.7	0.0	-	-	167.9	1.3	-	-	172.6	2.8	-	-	176.0	2.0	-	-	174.3	-1.0
1993	-	-	178.6	2.5	-	-	178.6	0.0	-	-	179.2	0.3	-	-	174.5	-2.6	-	-	171.2	-1.9	-	-	172.6	0.8
1994	-	-	171.2	-0.8	-	-	171.9	0.4	-	-	193.7	12.7	-	-	195.4	0.9	-	-	196.7	0.7	-	-	197.5	0.4
1995	-	-	198.1	0.3	-	-	198.7	0.3	-	-	200.4	0.9	-	-	203.9	1.7	-	-	206.0	1.0	-	-	206.7	0.3
1996	-	-	206.9	0.1	-	-	207.9	0.5	-	-	209.0	0.5	-	-	212.1	1.5	-	-	210.4	-0.8	-	-	209.3	-0.5
1997	-	-	212.8	1.7	-	-	217.6	2.3	-	-	215.0	-1.2	-	-	222.5	3.5	-	-	224.4	0.9	-	-	225.2	0.4

Source: U.S. Department of Labor, Bureau of Labor Statistics, Division of Consumer Prices and Price Indexes. - indicates no data collected for period.

Honolulu, HI
Consumer Price Index - All Urban Consumers
Base 1982-1984 = 100
Annual Averages

For 1963-1997. Columns headed % show percentile change in the index from the previous period for which an index is available.

Year	All Items		Food & Beverage		Housing		Apparel & Upkeep		Trans-portation		Medical Care		Entertain-ment		Other Goods & Services	
	Index	%	Index	%	Index	%	Index	%	Index	%	Index	%	Index	%	Index	%
1963	-	-	-	-	-	-	-	-	-	-	-	-	-	-	-	-
1964	33.7	-	-	-	-	-	46.7	-	37.7	-	25.1	-	-	-	-	-
1965	34.4	2.1	-	-	-	-	47.1	0.9	37.7	0.0	25.8	2.8	-	-	-	-
1966	35.3	2.6	-	-	-	-	47.9	1.7	37.8	0.3	26.6	3.1	-	-	-	-
1967	36.3	2.8	-	-	-	-	48.8	1.9	38.7	2.4	28.3	6.4	-	-	-	-
1968	37.7	3.9	-	-	-	-	50.7	3.9	40.1	3.6	29.9	5.7	-	-	-	-
1969	39.4	4.5	-	-	-	-	53.4	5.3	41.5	3.5	32.0	7.0	-	-	-	-
1970	41.5	5.3	-	-	-	-	56.2	5.2	43.4	4.6	33.5	4.7	-	-	-	-
1971	43.2	4.1	-	-	-	-	57.4	2.1	46.7	7.6	35.2	5.1	-	-	-	-
1972	44.6	3.2	-	-	-	-	58.9	2.6	47.6	1.9	36.0	2.3	-	-	-	-
1973	46.6	4.5	-	-	-	-	60.6	2.9	48.0	0.8	37.7	4.7	-	-	-	-
1974	51.5	10.5	-	-	-	-	65.1	7.4	52.3	9.0	41.5	10.1	-	-	-	-
1975	56.3	9.3	-	-	-	-	69.0	6.0	56.8	8.6	46.6	12.3	-	-	-	-
1976	59.1	5.0	59.7	-	59.2	-	71.6	3.8	59.5	4.8	51.5	10.5	63.6	-	53.8	-
1977	62.1	5.1	62.8	5.2	61.6	4.1	74.3	3.8	61.8	3.9	57.4	11.5	66.3	4.2	57.5	6.9
1978	66.9	7.7	69.0	9.9	66.0	7.1	78.8	6.1	66.0	6.8	62.5	8.9	69.0	4.1	61.4	6.8
1979	74.3	11.1	77.7	12.6	74.0	12.1	83.9	6.5	73.4	11.2	67.5	8.0	72.8	5.5	66.5	8.3
1980	83.0	11.7	84.2	8.4	83.2	12.4	89.8	7.0	86.6	18.0	73.1	8.3	78.2	7.4	73.3	10.2
1981	91.7	10.5	92.6	10.0	92.3	10.9	94.5	5.2	95.7	10.5	81.8	11.9	87.2	11.5	81.5	11.2
1982	97.2	6.0	96.9	4.6	98.0	6.2	98.4	4.1	99.0	3.4	91.6	12.0	95.7	9.7	92.0	12.9
1983	99.3	2.2	99.5	2.7	98.9	0.9	101.4	3.0	98.2	-0.8	101.1	10.4	100.0	4.5	101.4	10.2
1984	103.5	4.2	103.6	4.1	103.1	4.2	100.2	-1.2	102.9	4.8	107.3	6.1	104.3	4.3	106.6	5.1
1985	106.8	3.2	107.8	4.1	106.0	2.8	99.6	-0.6	104.9	1.9	113.2	5.5	111.9	7.3	112.5	5.5
1986	109.4	2.4	110.0	2.0	108.4	2.3	99.8	0.2	105.2	0.3	122.3	8.0	113.2	1.2	119.6	6.3
1987	111.5	1.9	112.0	1.8	114.3	5.4	111.4	11.6	101.5	-3.5	119.3	-2.5	107.7	-4.9	129.0	7.9
1988	115.9	3.9	115.8	3.4	118.4	3.6	121.0	8.6	103.1	1.6	128.4	7.6	111.3	3.3	139.0	7.8
1989	120.8	4.2	121.1	4.6	122.1	3.1	121.2	0.2	110.0	6.7	139.3	8.5	113.7	2.2	146.9	5.7
1990	126.2	4.5	128.1	5.8	126.0	3.2	126.0	4.0	115.2	4.7	150.8	8.3	118.7	4.4	156.6	6.6
1991	132.2	4.8	135.2	5.5	132.2	4.9	125.4	-0.5	119.1	3.4	159.5	5.8	124.0	4.5	169.8	8.4
1992	137.1	3.7	135.4	0.1	137.7	4.2	124.2	-1.0	123.1	3.4	174.3	9.3	130.0	4.8	182.0	7.2
1993	142.1	3.6	138.1	2.0	142.8	3.7	123.2	-0.8	128.5	4.4	185.5	6.4	133.1	2.4	194.9	7.1
1994	147.0	3.4	141.5	2.5	148.0	3.6	122.5	-0.6	134.2	4.4	201.7	8.7	130.2	-2.2	201.1	3.2
1995	151.0	2.7	146.6	3.6	152.2	2.8	121.4	-0.9	137.5	2.5	213.2	5.7	128.7	-1.2	207.1	3.0
1996	154.7	2.5	151.9	3.6	154.4	1.4	123.2	1.5	141.6	3.0	220.1	3.2	130.7	1.6	216.6	4.6
1997	171.9	11.1	159.2	4.8	177.1	14.7	117.3	-4.8	166.2	17.4	217.3	-1.3	147.9	13.2	239.0	10.3

Source: U.S. Department of Labor, Bureau of Labor Statistics, Division of Consumer Prices and Price Indexes. - indicates no data collected for period.

Honolulu, HI
Consumer Price Index - Urban Wage Earners
Base 1982-1984 = 100
Annual Averages

For 1963-1997. Columns headed % show percentile change in the index from the previous period for which an index is available.

Year	All Items		Food & Beverage		Housing		Apparel & Upkeep		Trans-portation		Medical Care		Entertain-ment		Other Goods & Services	
	Index	%	Index	%	Index	%	Index	%	Index	%	Index	%	Index	%	Index	%
1963	-	-	-	-	-	-	-	-	-	-	-	-	-	-	-	-
1964	33.3	-	-	-	-	-	45.2	-	37.8	-	24.6	-	-	-	-	-
1965	33.9	1.8	-	-	-	-	45.6	0.9	37.7	-0.3	25.3	2.8	-	-	-	-
1966	34.8	2.7	-	-	-	-	46.3	1.5	37.8	0.3	26.1	3.2	-	-	-	-
1967	35.8	2.9	-	-	-	-	47.2	1.9	38.7	2.4	27.7	6.1	-	-	-	-
1968	37.2	3.9	-	-	-	-	49.0	3.8	40.2	3.9	29.3	5.8	-	-	-	-
1969	38.8	4.3	-	-	-	-	51.7	5.5	41.5	3.2	31.3	6.8	-	-	-	-
1970	40.9	5.4	-	-	-	-	54.4	5.2	43.5	4.8	32.8	4.8	-	-	-	-
1971	42.6	4.2	-	-	-	-	55.6	2.2	46.7	7.4	34.5	5.2	-	-	-	-
1972	44.0	3.3	-	-	-	-	56.9	2.3	47.6	1.9	35.3	2.3	-	-	-	-
1973	45.9	4.3	-	-	-	-	58.6	3.0	48.0	0.8	36.9	4.5	-	-	-	-
1974	50.8	10.7	-	-	-	-	63.0	7.5	52.3	9.0	40.7	10.3	-	-	-	-
1975	55.5	9.3	-	-	-	-	66.7	5.9	56.9	8.8	45.6	12.0	-	-	-	-
1976	58.3	5.0	58.8	-	58.1	-	69.3	3.9	59.5	4.6	50.4	10.5	60.7	-	54.8	-
1977	61.2	5.0	61.9	5.3	60.4	4.0	71.9	3.8	61.9	4.0	56.2	11.5	63.2	4.1	58.5	6.8
1978	65.9	7.7	68.0	9.9	64.6	7.0	75.3	4.7	65.9	6.5	61.8	10.0	67.4	6.6	61.9	5.8
1979	73.2	11.1	76.4	12.4	72.2	11.8	79.9	6.1	73.5	11.5	66.3	7.3	73.5	9.1	66.9	8.1
1980	81.9	11.9	83.5	9.3	80.4	11.4	91.4	14.4	86.6	17.8	72.3	9.0	79.9	8.7	72.8	8.8
1981	90.5	10.5	92.3	10.5	89.0	10.7	95.3	4.3	96.2	11.1	81.9	13.3	87.4	9.4	81.1	11.4
1982	96.0	6.1	96.8	4.9	94.9	6.6	98.3	3.1	99.1	3.0	92.0	12.3	95.4	9.2	91.6	12.9
1983	99.8	4.0	99.5	2.8	100.1	5.5	101.4	3.2	98.1	-1.0	101.1	9.9	100.0	4.8	101.7	11.0
1984	104.3	4.5	103.7	4.2	104.9	4.8	100.3	-1.1	102.8	4.8	106.9	5.7	104.6	4.6	106.6	4.8
1985	107.9	3.5	108.3	4.4	108.6	3.5	99.4	-0.9	104.7	1.8	112.6	5.3	111.9	7.0	112.5	5.5
1986	110.3	2.2	110.8	2.3	111.0	2.2	100.1	0.7	104.7	0.0	121.1	7.5	113.1	1.1	119.1	5.9
1987	114.1	3.4	111.9	1.0	119.0	7.2	113.0	12.9	102.5	-2.1	120.6	-0.4	107.8	-4.7	128.4	7.8
1988	118.6	3.9	115.8	3.5	123.2	3.5	123.2	9.0	104.3	1.8	129.9	7.7	112.0	3.9	139.2	8.4
1989	123.5	4.1	120.9	4.4	126.9	3.0	123.5	0.2	110.9	6.3	141.4	8.9	115.0	2.7	147.6	6.0
1990	128.9	4.4	128.0	5.9	130.9	3.2	127.4	3.2	116.0	4.6	152.3	7.7	119.7	4.1	157.5	6.7
1991	135.0	4.7	135.1	5.5	137.2	4.8	128.1	0.5	119.3	2.8	160.7	5.5	125.4	4.8	171.6	9.0
1992	139.8	3.6	135.3	0.1	143.0	4.2	126.2	-1.5	123.9	3.9	175.3	9.1	130.9	4.4	184.3	7.4
1993	144.8	3.6	138.0	2.0	148.3	3.7	125.9	-0.2	129.5	4.5	186.2	6.2	133.6	2.1	196.6	6.7
1994	149.4	3.2	141.5	2.5	153.6	3.6	125.0	-0.7	134.6	3.9	202.1	8.5	131.2	-1.8	201.2	2.3
1995	153.5	2.7	146.6	3.6	157.9	2.8	125.4	0.3	137.8	2.4	213.3	5.5	129.2	-1.5	206.7	2.7
1996	157.0	2.3	151.9	3.6	160.0	1.3	127.8	1.9	141.2	2.5	219.5	2.9	130.9	1.3	216.2	4.6
1997	172.2	9.7	159.2	4.8	179.7	12.3	119.0	-6.9	163.8	16.0	221.6	1.0	148.8	13.7	239.8	10.9

Source: U.S. Department of Labor, Bureau of Labor Statistics, Division of Consumer Prices and Price Indexes. - indicates no data collected for period.

Honolulu, HI
Consumer Price Index - All Urban Consumers
Base 1982-1984 = 100
All Items

For 1963-1997. Columns headed % show percentile change in the index from the previous period for which an index is available.

Year	Jan Index	%	Feb Index	%	Mar Index	%	Apr Index	%	May Index	%	Jun Index	%	Jul Index	%	Aug Index	%	Sep Index	%	Oct Index	%	Nov Index	%	Dec Index	%
1963	-	-	-	-	-	-	-	-	-	-	-	-	-	-	-	-	-	-	-	-	-	-	33.7	-
1964	-	-	-	-	33.9	0.6	-	-	-	-	33.6	-0.9	-	-	-	-	33.7	0.3	-	-	-	-	34.0	0.9
1965	-	-	-	-	34.2	0.6	-	-	-	-	34.2	0.0	-	-	-	-	34.4	0.6	-	-	-	-	34.9	1.5
1966	-	-	-	-	35.1	0.6	-	-	-	-	35.2	0.3	-	-	-	-	35.6	1.1	-	-	-	-	35.9	0.8
1967	-	-	-	-	35.9	0.0	-	-	-	-	36.2	0.8	-	-	-	-	36.5	0.8	-	-	-	-	37.0	1.4
1968	-	-	-	-	37.3	0.8	-	-	-	-	37.6	0.8	-	-	-	-	38.0	1.1	-	-	-	-	38.4	1.1
1969	-	-	-	-	38.9	1.3	-	-	-	-	39.3	1.0	-	-	-	-	39.8	1.3	-	-	-	-	40.3	1.3
1970	-	-	-	-	41.1	2.0	-	-	-	-	41.6	1.2	-	-	-	-	41.7	0.2	-	-	-	-	42.0	0.7
1971	-	-	-	-	42.4	1.0	-	-	-	-	43.0	1.4	-	-	-	-	44.0	2.3	-	-	-	-	44.0	0.0
1972	-	-	-	-	44.5	1.1	-	-	-	-	44.4	-0.2	-	-	-	-	44.7	0.7	-	-	-	-	45.2	1.1
1973	-	-	-	-	45.8	1.3	-	-	-	-	46.3	1.1	-	-	-	-	47.1	1.7	-	-	-	-	48.2	2.3
1974	-	-	-	-	50.0	3.7	-	-	-	-	51.3	2.6	-	-	-	-	52.9	3.1	-	-	-	-	53.9	1.9
1975	-	-	-	-	55.2	2.4	-	-	-	-	56.0	1.4	-	-	-	-	57.2	2.1	-	-	-	-	58.0	1.4
1976	-	-	-	-	58.5	0.9	-	-	-	-	59.0	0.9	-	-	-	-	59.6	1.0	-	-	-	-	60.1	0.8
1977	-	-	-	-	61.1	1.7	-	-	-	-	61.9	1.3	-	-	-	-	63.0	1.8	-	-	-	-	63.5	0.8
1978	-	-	64.7	1.9	-	-	65.9	1.9	-	-	66.8	1.4	-	-	67.4	0.9	-	-	68.6	1.8	-	-	69.5	1.3
1979	-	-	71.3	2.6	-	-	72.9	2.2	-	-	74.2	1.8	-	-	75.3	1.5	-	-	76.5	1.6	-	-	78.0	2.0
1980	-	-	80.2	2.8	-	-	82.6	3.0	-	-	82.6	0.0	-	-	83.6	1.2	-	-	85.2	1.9	-	-	85.8	0.7
1981	-	-	88.4	3.0	-	-	90.8	2.7	-	-	91.8	1.1	-	-	93.2	1.5	-	-	94.2	1.1	-	-	93.8	-0.4
1982	-	-	95.2	1.5	-	-	95.6	0.4	-	-	97.7	2.2	-	-	97.9	0.2	-	-	100.0	2.1	-	-	98.0	-2.0
1983	-	-	98.2	0.2	-	-	99.1	0.9	-	-	98.6	-0.5	-	-	99.3	0.7	-	-	100.4	1.1	-	-	101.1	0.7
1984	-	-	102.0	0.9	-	-	102.9	0.9	-	-	103.4	0.5	-	-	103.9	0.5	-	-	104.4	0.5	-	-	105.3	0.9
1985	-	-	106.3	0.9	-	-	106.3	0.0	-	-	106.6	0.3	-	-	106.9	0.3	-	-	107.4	0.5	-	-	108.4	0.9
1986	-	-	109.4	0.9	-	-	108.6	-0.7	-	-	108.7	0.1	-	-	109.5	0.7	-	-	109.8	0.3	-	-	110.9	1.0
1987	-	-	-	-	-	-	-	-	-	-	110.1	-0.7	-	-	-	-	-	-	-	-	-	-	113.0	2.6
1988	-	-	-	-	-	-	-	-	-	-	114.5	1.3	-	-	-	-	-	-	-	-	-	-	117.2	2.4
1989	-	-	-	-	-	-	-	-	-	-	120.3	2.6	-	-	-	-	-	-	-	-	-	-	121.2	0.7
1990	-	-	-	-	-	-	-	-	-	-	123.9	2.2	-	-	-	-	-	-	-	-	-	-	128.6	3.8
1991	-	-	-	-	-	-	-	-	-	-	131.0	1.9	-	-	-	-	-	-	-	-	-	-	133.5	1.9
1992	-	-	-	-	-	-	-	-	-	-	135.9	1.8	-	-	-	-	-	-	-	-	-	-	138.2	1.7
1993	-	-	-	-	-	-	-	-	-	-	140.5	1.7	-	-	-	-	-	-	-	-	-	-	143.7	2.3
1994	-	-	-	-	-	-	-	-	-	-	146.0	1.6	-	-	-	-	-	-	-	-	-	-	147.9	1.3
1995	-	-	-	-	-	-	-	-	-	-	150.6	1.8	-	-	-	-	-	-	-	-	-	-	151.5	0.6
1996	-	-	-	-	-	-	-	-	-	-	153.7	1.5	-	-	-	-	-	-	-	-	-	-	155.6	1.2
1997	-	-	-	-	-	-	-	-	-	-	157.6	1.3	-	-	-	-	-	-	-	-	-	-	-	-

Source: U.S. Department of Labor, Bureau of Labor Statistics, Division of Consumer Prices and Price Indexes. - indicates no data collected for period.

Honolulu, HI
Consumer Price Index - Urban Wage Earners
Base 1982-1984 = 100
All Items

For 1963-1997. Columns headed % show percentile change in the index from the previous period for which an index is available.

Year	Jan Index	%	Feb Index	%	Mar Index	%	Apr Index	%	May Index	%	Jun Index	%	Jul Index	%	Aug Index	%	Sep Index	%	Oct Index	%	Nov Index	%	Dec Index	%
1963	-	-	-	-	-	-	-	-	-	-	-	-	-	-	-	-	-	-	-	-	-	-	33.2	-
1964	-	-	-	-	33.4	0.6	-	-	-	-	33.1	-0.9	-	-	-	-	33.3	0.6	-	-	-	-	33.5	0.6
1965	-	-	-	-	33.7	0.6	-	-	-	-	33.7	0.0	-	-	-	-	33.9	0.6	-	-	-	-	34.4	1.5
1966	-	-	-	-	34.6	0.6	-	-	-	-	34.6	0.0	-	-	-	-	35.0	1.2	-	-	-	-	35.4	1.1
1967	-	-	-	-	35.4	0.0	-	-	-	-	35.7	0.8	-	-	-	-	36.0	0.8	-	-	-	-	36.4	1.1
1968	-	-	-	-	36.8	1.1	-	-	-	-	37.0	0.5	-	-	-	-	37.4	1.1	-	-	-	-	37.8	1.1
1969	-	-	-	-	38.4	1.6	-	-	-	-	38.7	0.8	-	-	-	-	39.2	1.3	-	-	-	-	39.7	1.3
1970	-	-	-	-	40.5	2.0	-	-	-	-	40.9	1.0	-	-	-	-	41.1	0.5	-	-	-	-	41.4	0.7
1971	-	-	-	-	41.8	1.0	-	-	-	-	42.4	1.4	-	-	-	-	43.4	2.4	-	-	-	-	43.3	-0.2
1972	-	-	-	-	43.8	1.2	-	-	-	-	43.7	-0.2	-	-	-	-	44.1	0.9	-	-	-	-	44.5	0.9
1973	-	-	-	-	45.1	1.3	-	-	-	-	45.6	1.1	-	-	-	-	46.4	1.8	-	-	-	-	47.5	2.4
1974	-	-	-	-	49.3	3.8	-	-	-	-	50.5	2.4	-	-	-	-	52.1	3.2	-	-	-	-	53.2	2.1
1975	-	-	-	-	54.4	2.3	-	-	-	-	55.2	1.5	-	-	-	-	56.4	2.2	-	-	-	-	57.2	1.4
1976	-	-	-	-	57.7	0.9	-	-	-	-	58.1	0.7	-	-	-	-	58.7	1.0	-	-	-	-	59.2	0.9
1977	-	-	-	-	60.2	1.7	-	-	-	-	61.0	1.3	-	-	-	-	62.1	1.8	-	-	-	-	62.6	0.8
1978	-	-	63.5	1.4	-	-	64.9	2.2	-	-	65.9	1.5	-	-	66.6	1.1	-	-	67.5	1.4	-	-	68.4	1.3
1979	-	-	70.2	2.6	-	-	71.6	2.0	-	-	72.9	1.8	-	-	74.2	1.8	-	-	75.6	1.9	-	-	77.1	2.0
1980	-	-	79.2	2.7	-	-	81.8	3.3	-	-	81.6	-0.2	-	-	82.1	0.6	-	-	83.6	1.8	-	-	84.8	1.4
1981	-	-	87.2	2.8	-	-	89.6	2.8	-	-	90.8	1.3	-	-	91.8	1.1	-	-	92.7	1.0	-	-	92.8	0.1
1982	-	-	94.1	1.4	-	-	94.6	0.5	-	-	96.3	1.8	-	-	96.5	0.2	-	-	98.3	1.9	-	-	97.0	-1.3
1983	-	-	98.4	1.4	-	-	99.1	0.7	-	-	97.9	-1.2	-	-	99.6	1.7	-	-	102.3	2.7	-	-	103.2	0.9
1984	-	-	101.8	-1.4	-	-	103.4	1.6	-	-	104.1	0.7	-	-	105.1	1.0	-	-	105.4	0.3	-	-	106.5	1.0
1985	-	-	107.5	0.9	-	-	107.4	-0.1	-	-	107.5	0.1	-	-	107.8	0.3	-	-	108.4	0.6	-	-	109.5	1.0
1986	-	-	110.4	0.8	-	-	109.5	-0.8	-	-	109.7	0.2	-	-	110.4	0.6	-	-	110.5	0.1	-	-	111.9	1.3
1987	-	-	-	-	-	-	-	-	-	-	112.6	0.6	-	-	-	-	-	-	-	-	-	-	115.6	2.7
1988	-	-	-	-	-	-	-	-	-	-	117.2	1.4	-	-	-	-	-	-	-	-	-	-	120.1	2.5
1989	-	-	-	-	-	-	-	-	-	-	123.1	2.5	-	-	-	-	-	-	-	-	-	-	124.0	0.7
1990	-	-	-	-	-	-	-	-	-	-	126.3	1.9	-	-	-	-	-	-	-	-	-	-	131.6	4.2
1991	-	-	-	-	-	-	-	-	-	-	133.6	1.5	-	-	-	-	-	-	-	-	-	-	136.3	2.0
1992	-	-	-	-	-	-	-	-	-	-	138.4	1.5	-	-	-	-	-	-	-	-	-	-	141.2	2.0
1993	-	-	-	-	-	-	-	-	-	-	143.3	1.5	-	-	-	-	-	-	-	-	-	-	146.4	2.2
1994	-	-	-	-	-	-	-	-	-	-	148.4	1.4	-	-	-	-	-	-	-	-	-	-	150.5	1.4
1995	-	-	-	-	-	-	-	-	-	-	153.0	1.7	-	-	-	-	-	-	-	-	-	-	153.9	0.6
1996	-	-	-	-	-	-	-	-	-	-	156.2	1.5	-	-	-	-	-	-	-	-	-	-	157.9	1.1
1997	-	-	-	-	-	-	-	-	-	-	159.8	1.2	-	-	-	-	-	-	-	-	-	-	-	-

Source: U.S. Department of Labor, Bureau of Labor Statistics, Division of Consumer Prices and Price Indexes. - indicates no data collected for period.

Honolulu, HI
Consumer Price Index - All Urban Consumers
Base 1982-1984 = 100
Food and Beverages

For 1975-1997. Columns headed % show percentile change in the index from the previous period for which an index is available.

Year	Jan Index	%	Feb Index	%	Mar Index	%	Apr Index	%	May Index	%	Jun Index	%	Jul Index	%	Aug Index	%	Sep Index	%	Oct Index	%	Nov Index	%	Dec Index	%
1975	-	-	-	-	-	-	-	-	-	-	-	-	-	-	-	-	-	-	-	-	-	-	59.4	-
1976	-	-	-	-	59.5	0.2	-	-	-	-	59.6	0.2	-	-	-	-	-	-	59.5	-0.2	-	-	60.5	1.7
1977	-	-	-	-	61.8	2.1	-	-	-	-	62.6	1.3	-	-	-	-	63.8	1.9	-	-	-	-	64.4	0.9
1978	-	-	65.9	2.3	-	-	67.6	2.6	-	-	69.2	2.4	-	-	70.0	1.2	-	-	71.2	1.7	-	-	72.3	1.5
1979	-	-	74.6	3.2	-	-	76.5	2.5	-	-	78.3	2.4	-	-	78.4	0.1	-	-	79.5	1.4	-	-	80.6	1.4
1980	-	-	81.6	1.2	-	-	83.0	1.7	-	-	83.3	0.4	-	-	85.1	2.2	-	-	86.5	1.6	-	-	87.8	1.5
1981	-	-	90.8	3.4	-	-	92.2	1.5	-	-	92.7	0.5	-	-	93.5	0.9	-	-	94.2	0.7	-	-	93.8	-0.4
1982	-	-	96.1	2.5	-	-	96.2	0.1	-	-	96.9	0.7	-	-	97.3	0.4	-	-	97.7	0.4	-	-	98.3	0.6
1983	-	-	98.8	0.5	-	-	99.6	0.8	-	-	99.4	-0.2	-	-	99.8	0.4	-	-	100.0	0.2	-	-	99.6	-0.4
1984	-	-	101.4	1.8	-	-	102.2	0.8	-	-	103.6	1.4	-	-	104.5	0.9	-	-	104.6	0.1	-	-	107.3	2.6
1985	-	-	108.1	0.7	-	-	108.2	0.1	-	-	107.6	-0.6	-	-	107.5	-0.1	-	-	106.9	-0.6	-	-	108.6	1.6
1986	-	-	108.7	0.1	-	-	107.9	-0.7	-	-	110.1	2.0	-	-	109.7	-0.4	-	-	111.7	1.8	-	-	113.0	1.2
1987	-	-	-	-	-	-	-	-	-	-	112.0	-0.9	-	-	-	-	-	-	-	-	-	-	111.9	-0.1
1988	-	-	-	-	-	-	-	-	-	-	114.3	2.1	-	-	-	-	-	-	-	-	-	-	117.3	2.6
1989	-	-	-	-	-	-	-	-	-	-	120.1	2.4	-	-	-	-	-	-	-	-	-	-	122.0	1.6
1990	-	-	-	-	-	-	-	-	-	-	126.2	3.4	-	-	-	-	-	-	-	-	-	-	130.0	3.0
1991	-	-	-	-	-	-	-	-	-	-	134.8	3.7	-	-	-	-	-	-	-	-	-	-	135.7	0.7
1992	-	-	-	-	-	-	-	-	-	-	135.6	-0.1	-	-	-	-	-	-	-	-	-	-	135.3	-0.2
1993	-	-	-	-	-	-	-	-	-	-	137.0	1.3	-	-	-	-	-	-	-	-	-	-	139.2	1.6
1994	-	-	-	-	-	-	-	-	-	-	140.0	0.6	-	-	-	-	-	-	-	-	-	-	143.1	2.2
1995	-	-	-	-	-	-	-	-	-	-	145.7	1.8	-	-	-	-	-	-	-	-	-	-	147.4	1.2
1996	-	-	-	-	-	-	-	-	-	-	150.5	2.1	-	-	-	-	-	-	-	-	-	-	153.2	1.8
1997	-	-	-	-	-	-	-	-	-	-	154.4	0.8	-	-	-	-	-	-	-	-	-	-	-	-

Source: U.S. Department of Labor, Bureau of Labor Statistics, Division of Consumer Prices and Price Indexes. - indicates no data collected for period.

Honolulu, HI
Consumer Price Index - Urban Wage Earners
Base 1982-1984 = 100
Food and Beverages

For 1975-1997. Columns headed % show percentile change in the index from the previous period for which an index is available.

Year	Jan Index	%	Feb Index	%	Mar Index	%	Apr Index	%	May Index	%	Jun Index	%	Jul Index	%	Aug Index	%	Sep Index	%	Oct Index	%	Nov Index	%	Dec Index	%
1975	-	-	-	-	-	-	-	-	-	-	-	-	-	-	-	-	-	-	-	-	-	-	58.5	-
1976	-	-	-	-	58.7	0.3	-	-	-	-	58.7	0.0	-	-	-	-	58.6	-0.2	-	-	-	-	59.6	1.7
1977	-	-	-	-	60.8	2.0	-	-	-	-	61.7	1.5	-	-	-	-	62.8	1.8	-	-	-	-	63.5	1.1
1978	-	-	64.6	1.7	-	-	66.7	3.3	-	-	68.7	3.0	-	-	69.3	0.9	-	-	69.8	0.7	-	-	70.7	1.3
1979	-	-	74.0	4.7	-	-	75.5	2.0	-	-	76.2	0.9	-	-	76.9	0.9	-	-	78.3	1.8	-	-	79.8	1.9
1980	-	-	80.8	1.3	-	-	82.3	1.9	-	-	82.6	0.4	-	-	84.0	1.7	-	-	85.6	1.9	-	-	87.6	2.3
1981	-	-	90.5	3.3	-	-	91.9	1.5	-	-	92.2	0.3	-	-	93.0	0.9	-	-	93.6	0.6	-	-	94.0	0.4
1982	-	-	96.5	2.7	-	-	96.3	-0.2	-	-	96.7	0.4	-	-	96.9	0.2	-	-	97.4	0.5	-	-	98.2	0.8
1983	-	-	98.8	0.6	-	-	99.6	0.8	-	-	99.3	-0.3	-	-	99.8	0.5	-	-	99.8	0.0	-	-	99.8	0.0
1984	-	-	101.8	2.0	-	-	102.5	0.7	-	-	103.3	0.8	-	-	104.3	1.0	-	-	104.3	0.0	-	-	108.4	3.9
1985	-	-	109.1	0.6	-	-	108.6	-0.5	-	-	107.7	-0.8	-	-	107.9	0.2	-	-	107.3	-0.6	-	-	109.2	1.8
1986	-	-	109.6	0.4	-	-	108.9	-0.6	-	-	111.0	1.9	-	-	110.1	-0.8	-	-	112.5	2.2	-	-	114.1	1.4
1987	-	-	-	-	-	-	-	-	-	-	111.9	-1.9	-	-	-	-	-	-	-	-	-	-	111.8	-0.1
1988	-	-	-	-	-	-	-	-	-	-	114.4	2.3	-	-	-	-	-	-	-	-	-	-	117.1	2.4
1989	-	-	-	-	-	-	-	-	-	-	119.9	2.4	-	-	-	-	-	-	-	-	-	-	121.9	1.7
1990	-	-	-	-	-	-	-	-	-	-	126.0	3.4	-	-	-	-	-	-	-	-	-	-	130.0	3.2
1991	-	-	-	-	-	-	-	-	-	-	134.7	3.6	-	-	-	-	-	-	-	-	-	-	135.5	0.6
1992	-	-	-	-	-	-	-	-	-	-	135.4	-0.1	-	-	-	-	-	-	-	-	-	-	135.3	-0.1
1993	-	-	-	-	-	-	-	-	-	-	136.8	1.1	-	-	-	-	-	-	-	-	-	-	139.1	1.7
1994	-	-	-	-	-	-	-	-	-	-	139.9	0.6	-	-	-	-	-	-	-	-	-	-	143.1	2.3
1995	-	-	-	-	-	-	-	-	-	-	145.7	1.8	-	-	-	-	-	-	-	-	-	-	147.5	1.2
1996	-	-	-	-	-	-	-	-	-	-	150.6	2.1	-	-	-	-	-	-	-	-	-	-	153.2	1.7
1997	-	-	-	-	-	-	-	-	-	-	154.4	0.8	-	-	-	-	-	-	-	-	-	-	-	-

Source: U.S. Department of Labor, Bureau of Labor Statistics, Division of Consumer Prices and Price Indexes. - indicates no data collected for period.

Honolulu, HI
Consumer Price Index - All Urban Consumers
Base 1982-1984 = 100
Housing

For 1975-1997. Columns headed % show percentile change in the index from the previous period for which an index is available.

Year	Jan Index	%	Feb Index	%	Mar Index	%	Apr Index	%	May Index	%	Jun Index	%	Jul Index	%	Aug Index	%	Sep Index	%	Oct Index	%	Nov Index	%	Dec Index	%
1975	-	-	-	-	-	-	-	-	-	-	-	-	-	-	-	-	-	-	-	-	-	-	58.6	-
1976	-	-	-	-	58.6	0.0	-	-	-	-	59.1	0.9	-	-	-	-	59.8	1.2	-	-	-	-	59.7	-0.2
1977	-	-	-	-	60.7	1.7	-	-	-	-	61.3	1.0	-	-	-	-	62.5	2.0	-	-	-	-	62.8	0.5
1978	-	-	63.7	1.4	-	-	65.0	2.0	-	-	65.9	1.4	-	-	66.2	0.5	-	-	67.9	2.6	-	-	68.7	1.2
1979	-	-	70.9	3.2	-	-	72.8	2.7	-	-	73.9	1.5	-	-	75.1	1.6	-	-	76.3	1.6	-	-	77.7	1.8
1980	-	-	80.3	3.3	-	-	83.7	4.2	-	-	83.2	-0.6	-	-	83.2	0.0	-	-	85.3	2.5	-	-	85.7	0.5
1981	-	-	88.3	3.0	-	-	91.8	4.0	-	-	93.0	1.3	-	-	94.4	1.5	-	-	94.8	0.4	-	-	93.8	-1.1
1982	-	-	95.3	1.6	-	-	95.7	0.4	-	-	99.3	3.8	-	-	98.7	-0.6	-	-	102.2	3.5	-	-	97.8	-4.3
1983	-	-	98.0	0.2	-	-	99.1	1.1	-	-	97.8	-1.3	-	-	98.2	0.4	-	-	100.0	1.8	-	-	101.7	1.7
1984	-	-	101.7	0.0	-	-	102.9	1.2	-	-	103.0	0.1	-	-	103.1	0.1	-	-	104.1	1.0	-	-	104.2	0.1
1985	-	-	105.6	1.3	-	-	105.4	-0.2	-	-	106.3	0.9	-	-	105.4	-0.8	-	-	106.1	0.7	-	-	108.1	1.9
1986	-	-	108.4	0.3	-	-	108.1	-0.3	-	-	107.2	-0.8	-	-	109.4	2.1	-	-	108.3	-1.0	-	-	109.6	1.2
1987	-	-	-	-	-	-	-	-	-	-	112.4	2.6	-	-	-	-	-	-	-	-	-	-	116.2	3.4
1988	-	-	-	-	-	-	-	-	-	-	117.3	0.9	-	-	-	-	-	-	-	-	-	-	119.5	1.9
1989	-	-	-	-	-	-	-	-	-	-	121.8	1.9	-	-	-	-	-	-	-	-	-	-	122.5	0.6
1990	-	-	-	-	-	-	-	-	-	-	123.6	0.9	-	-	-	-	-	-	-	-	-	-	128.5	4.0
1991	-	-	-	-	-	-	-	-	-	-	131.0	1.9	-	-	-	-	-	-	-	-	-	-	133.3	1.8
1992	-	-	-	-	-	-	-	-	-	-	136.4	2.3	-	-	-	-	-	-	-	-	-	-	139.1	2.0
1993	-	-	-	-	-	-	-	-	-	-	140.9	1.3	-	-	-	-	-	-	-	-	-	-	144.7	2.7
1994	-	-	-	-	-	-	-	-	-	-	147.5	1.9	-	-	-	-	-	-	-	-	-	-	148.4	0.6
1995	-	-	-	-	-	-	-	-	-	-	152.1	2.5	-	-	-	-	-	-	-	-	-	-	152.4	0.2
1996	-	-	-	-	-	-	-	-	-	-	154.1	1.1	-	-	-	-	-	-	-	-	-	-	154.6	0.3
1997	-	-	-	-	-	-	-	-	-	-	156.1	1.0	-	-	-	-	-	-	-	-	-	-	-	-

Source: U.S. Department of Labor, Bureau of Labor Statistics, Division of Consumer Prices and Price Indexes. - indicates no data collected for period.

Honolulu, HI
Consumer Price Index - Urban Wage Earners
Base 1982-1984 = 100
Housing

For 1975-1997. Columns headed % show percentile change in the index from the previous period for which an index is available.

Year	Jan Index	%	Feb Index	%	Mar Index	%	Apr Index	%	May Index	%	Jun Index	%	Jul Index	%	Aug Index	%	Sep Index	%	Oct Index	%	Nov Index	%	Dec Index	%
1975	-	-	-	-	-	-	-	-	-	-	-	-	-	-	-	-	-	-	-	-	-	-	57.4	-
1976	-	-	-	-	57.5	0.2	-	-	-	-	57.9	0.7	-	-	-	-	58.7	1.4	-	-	-	-	58.5	-0.3
1977	-	-	-	-	59.5	1.7	-	-	-	-	60.1	1.0	-	-	-	-	61.3	2.0	-	-	-	-	61.6	0.5
1978	-	-	62.2	1.0	-	-	63.5	2.1	-	-	64.4	1.4	-	-	65.0	0.9	-	-	66.4	2.2	-	-	67.5	1.7
1979	-	-	68.9	2.1	-	-	70.6	2.5	-	-	71.9	1.8	-	-	73.4	2.1	-	-	74.5	1.5	-	-	76.1	2.1
1980	-	-	77.7	2.1	-	-	81.5	4.9	-	-	80.8	-0.9	-	-	79.9	-1.1	-	-	81.4	1.9	-	-	82.6	1.5
1981	-	-	84.8	2.7	-	-	88.4	4.2	-	-	90.0	1.8	-	-	91.0	1.1	-	-	91.4	0.4	-	-	90.8	-0.7
1982	-	-	92.3	1.7	-	-	92.8	0.5	-	-	96.0	3.4	-	-	95.5	-0.5	-	-	98.8	3.5	-	-	95.1	-3.7
1983	-	-	98.2	3.3	-	-	99.2	1.0	-	-	96.3	-2.9	-	-	98.9	2.7	-	-	104.8	6.0	-	-	106.4	1.5
1984	-	-	101.1	-5.0	-	-	104.1	3.0	-	-	105.0	0.9	-	-	106.2	1.1	-	-	106.7	0.5	-	-	106.7	0.0
1985	-	-	108.2	1.4	-	-	108.2	0.0	-	-	108.9	0.6	-	-	107.9	-0.9	-	-	108.7	0.7	-	-	110.7	1.8
1986	-	-	111.0	0.3	-	-	110.7	-0.3	-	-	109.7	-0.9	-	-	112.2	2.3	-	-	110.5	-1.5	-	-	112.1	1.4
1987	-	-	-	-	-	-	-	-	-	-	117.1	4.5	-	-	-	-	-	-	-	-	-	-	120.9	3.2
1988	-	-	-	-	-	-	-	-	-	-	122.1	1.0	-	-	-	-	-	-	-	-	-	-	124.4	1.9
1989	-	-	-	-	-	-	-	-	-	-	126.6	1.8	-	-	-	-	-	-	-	-	-	-	127.3	0.6
1990	-	-	-	-	-	-	-	-	-	-	128.4	0.9	-	-	-	-	-	-	-	-	-	-	133.4	3.9
1991	-	-	-	-	-	-	-	-	-	-	136.1	2.0	-	-	-	-	-	-	-	-	-	-	138.4	1.7
1992	-	-	-	-	-	-	-	-	-	-	141.5	2.2	-	-	-	-	-	-	-	-	-	-	144.4	2.0
1993	-	-	-	-	-	-	-	-	-	-	146.3	1.3	-	-	-	-	-	-	-	-	-	-	150.2	2.7
1994	-	-	-	-	-	-	-	-	-	-	153.1	1.9	-	-	-	-	-	-	-	-	-	-	154.0	0.6
1995	-	-	-	-	-	-	-	-	-	-	157.7	2.4	-	-	-	-	-	-	-	-	-	-	158.1	0.3
1996	-	-	-	-	-	-	-	-	-	-	159.8	1.1	-	-	-	-	-	-	-	-	-	-	160.3	0.3
1997	-	-	-	-	-	-	-	-	-	-	161.9	1.0	-	-	-	-	-	-	-	-	-	-	-	-

Source: U.S. Department of Labor, Bureau of Labor Statistics, Division of Consumer Prices and Price Indexes. - indicates no data collected for period.

Honolulu, HI
Consumer Price Index - All Urban Consumers
Base 1982-1984 = 100
Apparel and Upkeep

For 1963-1997. Columns headed % show percentile change in the index from the previous period for which an index is available.

Year	Jan Index	%	Feb Index	%	Mar Index	%	Apr Index	%	May Index	%	Jun Index	%	Jul Index	%	Aug Index	%	Sep Index	%	Oct Index	%	Nov Index	%	Dec Index	%
1963	-	-	-	-	-	-	-	-	-	-	-	-	-	-	-	-	-	-	-	-	-	-	46.2	-
1964	-	-	-	-	46.4	0.4	-	-	-	-	46.4	0.0	-	-	-	-	47.1	1.5	-	-	-	-	47.0	-0.2
1965	-	-	-	-	46.8	-0.4	-	-	-	-	47.3	1.1	-	-	-	-	47.1	-0.4	-	-	-	-	47.4	0.6
1966	-	-	-	-	47.6	0.4	-	-	-	-	48.1	1.1	-	-	-	-	48.1	0.0	-	-	-	-	48.1	0.0
1967	-	-	-	-	48.2	0.2	-	-	-	-	48.8	1.2	-	-	-	-	49.3	1.0	-	-	-	-	49.5	0.4
1968	-	-	-	-	50.0	1.0	-	-	-	-	50.2	0.4	-	-	-	-	51.5	2.6	-	-	-	-	51.8	0.6
1969	-	-	-	-	52.5	1.4	-	-	-	-	53.5	1.9	-	-	-	-	54.0	0.9	-	-	-	-	54.4	0.7
1970	-	-	-	-	54.7	0.6	-	-	-	-	56.0	2.4	-	-	-	-	57.7	3.0	-	-	-	-	57.5	-0.3
1971	-	-	-	-	57.3	-0.3	-	-	-	-	56.9	-0.7	-	-	-	-	57.5	1.1	-	-	-	-	58.2	1.2
1972	-	-	-	-	58.8	1.0	-	-	-	-	58.8	0.0	-	-	-	-	59.1	0.5	-	-	-	-	58.9	-0.3
1973	-	-	-	-	59.9	1.7	-	-	-	-	59.8	-0.2	-	-	-	-	61.5	2.8	-	-	-	-	62.3	1.3
1974	-	-	-	-	63.6	2.1	-	-	-	-	64.7	1.7	-	-	-	-	66.6	2.9	-	-	-	-	67.2	0.9
1975	-	-	-	-	68.5	1.9	-	-	-	-	68.9	0.6	-	-	-	-	69.6	1.0	-	-	-	-	69.7	0.1
1976	-	-	-	-	70.9	1.7	-	-	-	-	71.7	1.1	-	-	-	-	72.6	1.3	-	-	-	-	72.3	-0.4
1977	-	-	-	-	73.9	2.2	-	-	-	-	73.9	0.0	-	-	-	-	74.7	1.1	-	-	-	-	75.9	1.6
1978	-	-	77.1	1.6	-	-	77.8	0.9	-	-	77.5	-0.4	-	-	80.5	3.9	-	-	80.2	-0.4	-	-	80.8	0.7
1979	-	-	83.1	2.8	-	-	82.5	-0.7	-	-	84.3	2.2	-	-	84.5	0.2	-	-	84.6	0.1	-	-	85.4	0.9
1980	-	-	88.2	3.3	-	-	88.5	0.3	-	-	88.6	0.1	-	-	91.6	3.4	-	-	92.0	0.4	-	-	91.6	-0.4
1981	-	-	93.2	1.7	-	-	93.0	-0.2	-	-	92.9	-0.1	-	-	94.6	1.8	-	-	97.5	3.1	-	-	96.8	-0.7
1982	-	-	97.4	0.6	-	-	98.2	0.8	-	-	99.0	0.8	-	-	98.1	-0.9	-	-	99.1	1.0	-	-	99.3	0.2
1983	-	-	100.4	1.1	-	-	101.9	1.5	-	-	100.4	-1.5	-	-	102.1	1.7	-	-	102.6	0.5	-	-	102.0	-0.6
1984	-	-	103.1	1.1	-	-	101.8	-1.3	-	-	101.0	-0.8	-	-	97.5	-3.5	-	-	97.7	0.2	-	-	99.2	1.5
1985	-	-	99.6	0.4	-	-	98.7	-0.9	-	-	98.4	-0.3	-	-	99.7	1.3	-	-	101.4	1.7	-	-	99.9	-1.5
1986	-	-	100.7	0.8	-	-	100.4	-0.3	-	-	96.4	-4.0	-	-	99.3	3.0	-	-	100.9	1.6	-	-	101.8	0.9
1987	-	-	-	-	-	-	-	-	-	-	107.8	5.9	-	-	-	-	-	-	-	-	-	-	115.0	6.7
1988	-	-	-	-	-	-	-	-	-	-	118.1	2.7	-	-	-	-	-	-	-	-	-	-	123.9	4.9
1989	-	-	-	-	-	-	-	-	-	-	123.4	-0.4	-	-	-	-	-	-	-	-	-	-	119.1	3.5
1990	-	-	-	-	-	-	-	-	-	-	120.7	1.3	-	-	-	-	-	-	-	-	-	-	131.4	8.9
1991	-	-	-	-	-	-	-	-	-	-	124.1	-5.6	-	-	-	-	-	-	-	-	-	-	126.7	2.1
1992	-	-	-	-	-	-	-	-	-	-	123.6	-2.4	-	-	-	-	-	-	-	-	-	-	124.7	0.9
1993	-	-	-	-	-	-	-	-	-	-	120.5	-3.4	-	-	-	-	-	-	-	-	-	-	125.8	4.4
1994	-	-	-	-	-	-	-	-	-	-	121.3	-3.6	-	-	-	-	-	-	-	-	-	-	123.7	2.0
1995	-	-	-	-	-	-	-	-	-	-	119.6	-3.3	-	-	-	-	-	-	-	-	-	-	123.2	3.0
1996	-	-	-	-	-	-	-	-	-	-	122.8	-0.3	-	-	-	-	-	-	-	-	-	-	123.6	0.7
1997	-	-	-	-	-	-	-	-	-	-	126.4	2.3	-	-	-	-	-	-	-	-	-	-	-	-

Source: U.S. Department of Labor, Bureau of Labor Statistics, Division of Consumer Prices and Price Indexes. - indicates no data collected for period.

Honolulu, HI
Consumer Price Index - Urban Wage Earners
Base 1982-1984 = 100
Apparel and Upkeep

For 1963-1997. Columns headed % show percentile change in the index from the previous period for which an index is available.

Year	Jan Index	%	Feb Index	%	Mar Index	%	Apr Index	%	May Index	%	Jun Index	%	Jul Index	%	Aug Index	%	Sep Index	%	Oct Index	%	Nov Index	%	Dec Index	%
1963	-	-	-	-	-	-	-	-	-	-	-	-	-	-	-	-	-	-	-	-	-	-	44.6	-
1964	-	-	-	-	44.9	0.7	-	-	-	-	44.9	0.0	-	-	-	-	45.6	1.6	-	-	-	-	45.5	-0.2
1965	-	-	-	-	45.3	-0.4	-	-	-	-	45.8	1.1	-	-	-	-	45.5	-0.7	-	-	-	-	45.9	0.9
1966	-	-	-	-	46.0	0.2	-	-	-	-	46.5	1.1	-	-	-	-	46.5	0.0	-	-	-	-	46.5	0.0
1967	-	-	-	-	46.6	0.2	-	-	-	-	47.2	1.3	-	-	-	-	47.7	1.1	-	-	-	-	47.9	0.4
1968	-	-	-	-	48.4	1.0	-	-	-	-	48.6	0.4	-	-	-	-	49.8	2.5	-	-	-	-	50.1	0.6
1969	-	-	-	-	50.7	1.2	-	-	-	-	51.8	2.2	-	-	-	-	52.2	0.8	-	-	-	-	52.6	0.8
1970	-	-	-	-	53.0	0.8	-	-	-	-	54.2	2.3	-	-	-	-	55.8	3.0	-	-	-	-	55.6	-0.4
1971	-	-	-	-	55.5	-0.2	-	-	-	-	55.0	-0.9	-	-	-	-	55.6	1.1	-	-	-	-	56.3	1.3
1972	-	-	-	-	56.9	1.1	-	-	-	-	56.8	-0.2	-	-	-	-	57.2	0.7	-	-	-	-	57.0	-0.3
1973	-	-	-	-	58.0	1.8	-	-	-	-	57.9	-0.2	-	-	-	-	59.5	2.8	-	-	-	-	60.2	1.2
1974	-	-	-	-	61.5	2.2	-	-	-	-	62.6	1.8	-	-	-	-	64.4	2.9	-	-	-	-	65.0	0.9
1975	-	-	-	-	66.2	1.8	-	-	-	-	66.7	0.8	-	-	-	-	67.3	0.9	-	-	-	-	67.5	0.3
1976	-	-	-	-	68.5	1.5	-	-	-	-	69.3	1.2	-	-	-	-	70.2	1.3	-	-	-	-	69.9	-0.4
1977	-	-	-	-	71.5	2.3	-	-	-	-	71.5	0.0	-	-	-	-	72.2	1.0	-	-	-	-	73.5	1.8
1978	-	-	73.4	-0.1	-	-	74.4	1.4	-	-	73.9	-0.7	-	-	75.9	2.7	-	-	77.6	2.2	-	-	77.6	0.0
1979	-	-	78.9	1.7	-	-	78.0	-1.1	-	-	79.1	1.4	-	-	79.8	0.9	-	-	82.4	3.3	-	-	82.6	0.2
1980	-	-	90.8	9.9	-	-	92.3	1.7	-	-	90.2	-2.3	-	-	92.0	2.0	-	-	92.6	0.7	-	-	93.5	1.0
1981	-	-	94.8	1.4	-	-	94.7	-0.1	-	-	95.0	0.3	-	-	95.3	0.3	-	-	96.2	0.9	-	-	96.7	0.5
1982	-	-	97.1	0.4	-	-	98.0	0.9	-	-	98.8	0.8	-	-	97.9	-0.9	-	-	99.1	1.2	-	-	99.8	0.7
1983	-	-	100.5	0.7	-	-	101.8	1.3	-	-	100.3	-1.5	-	-	101.8	1.5	-	-	102.4	0.6	-	-	102.0	-0.4
1984	-	-	103.0	1.0	-	-	102.3	-0.7	-	-	100.3	-2.0	-	-	97.5	-2.8	-	-	98.5	1.0	-	-	99.6	1.1
1985	-	-	100.1	0.5	-	-	98.0	-2.1	-	-	97.6	-0.4	-	-	99.3	1.7	-	-	101.9	2.6	-	-	99.9	-2.0
1986	-	-	100.4	0.5	-	-	100.2	-0.2	-	-	97.1	-3.1	-	-	99.6	2.6	-	-	101.4	1.8	-	-	102.8	1.4
1987	-	-	-	-	-	-	-	-	-	-	109.7	6.7	-	-	-	-	-	-	-	-	-	-	116.3	6.0
1988	-	-	-	-	-	-	-	-	-	-	120.5	3.6	-	-	-	-	-	-	-	-	-	-	125.9	4.5
1989	-	-	-	-	-	-	-	-	-	-	125.9	0.0	-	-	-	-	-	-	-	-	-	-	121.1	-3.8
1990	-	-	-	-	-	-	-	-	-	-	120.9	-0.2	-	-	-	-	-	-	-	-	-	-	133.8	10.7
1991	-	-	-	-	-	-	-	-	-	-	126.0	-5.8	-	-	-	-	-	-	-	-	-	-	130.3	3.4
1992	-	-	-	-	-	-	-	-	-	-	125.1	-4.0	-	-	-	-	-	-	-	-	-	-	127.4	1.8
1993	-	-	-	-	-	-	-	-	-	-	123.8	-2.8	-	-	-	-	-	-	-	-	-	-	128.0	3.4
1994	-	-	-	-	-	-	-	-	-	-	123.4	-3.6	-	-	-	-	-	-	-	-	-	-	126.6	2.6
1995	-	-	-	-	-	-	-	-	-	-	122.8	-3.0	-	-	-	-	-	-	-	-	-	-	127.9	4.2
1996	-	-	-	-	-	-	-	-	-	-	127.7	-0.2	-	-	-	-	-	-	-	-	-	-	127.9	0.2
1997	-	-	-	-	-	-	-	-	-	-	131.8	3.0	-	-	-	-	-	-	-	-	-	-	-	-

Source: U.S. Department of Labor, Bureau of Labor Statistics, Division of Consumer Prices and Price Indexes. - indicates no data collected for period.

Honolulu, HI
Consumer Price Index - All Urban Consumers
Base 1982-1984 = 100
Transportation

For 1963-1997. Columns headed % show percentile change in the index from the previous period for which an index is available.

Year	Jan Index	%	Feb Index	%	Mar Index	%	Apr Index	%	May Index	%	Jun Index	%	Jul Index	%	Aug Index	%	Sep Index	%	Oct Index	%	Nov Index	%	Dec Index	%
1963	-	-	-	-	-	-	-	-	-	-	-	-	-	-	-	-	-	-	-	-	-	-	38.4	-
1964	-	-	-	-	38.0	-1.0	-	-	-	-	37.4	-1.6	-	-	-	-	37.4	0.0	-	-	-	-	38.0	1.6
1965	-	-	-	-	37.9	-0.3	-	-	-	-	37.5	-1.1	-	-	-	-	37.6	0.3	-	-	-	-	37.7	0.3
1966	-	-	-	-	37.5	-0.5	-	-	-	-	37.7	0.5	-	-	-	-	37.8	0.3	-	-	-	-	38.6	2.1
1967	-	-	-	-	38.4	-0.5	-	-	-	-	38.6	0.5	-	-	-	-	38.6	0.0	-	-	-	-	39.6	2.6
1968	-	-	-	-	40.1	1.3	-	-	-	-	40.0	-0.2	-	-	-	-	40.0	0.0	-	-	-	-	40.8	2.0
1969	-	-	-	-	41.7	2.2	-	-	-	-	41.5	-0.5	-	-	-	-	41.2	-0.7	-	-	-	-	42.2	2.4
1970	-	-	-	-	42.8	1.4	-	-	-	-	43.6	1.9	-	-	-	-	43.6	0.0	-	-	-	-	44.6	2.3
1971	-	-	-	-	45.7	2.5	-	-	-	-	47.7	4.4	-	-	-	-	47.2	-1.0	-	-	-	-	47.1	-0.2
1972	-	-	-	-	47.5	0.8	-	-	-	-	47.8	0.6	-	-	-	-	47.7	-0.2	-	-	-	-	47.7	0.0
1973	-	-	-	-	47.9	0.4	-	-	-	-	47.9	0.0	-	-	-	-	47.7	-0.4	-	-	-	-	48.7	2.1
1974	-	-	-	-	50.8	4.3	-	-	-	-	52.6	3.5	-	-	-	-	53.3	1.3	-	-	-	-	54.2	1.7
1975	-	-	-	-	55.2	1.8	-	-	-	-	57.1	3.4	-	-	-	-	58.1	1.8	-	-	-	-	58.0	-0.2
1976	-	-	-	-	58.7	1.2	-	-	-	-	59.3	1.0	-	-	-	-	60.0	1.2	-	-	-	-	60.9	1.5
1977	-	-	-	-	61.2	0.5	-	-	-	-	62.3	1.8	-	-	-	-	61.9	-0.6	-	-	-	-	62.6	1.1
1978	-	-	63.8	1.9	-	-	64.9	1.7	-	-	66.0	1.7	-	-	66.7	1.1	-	-	67.3	0.9	-	-	68.3	1.5
1979	-	-	68.6	0.4	-	-	70.5	2.8	-	-	72.8	3.3	-	-	74.7	2.6	-	-	76.5	2.4	-	-	79.9	4.4
1980	-	-	83.5	4.5	-	-	85.8	2.8	-	-	86.1	0.3	-	-	88.2	2.4	-	-	88.8	0.7	-	-	89.6	0.9
1981	-	-	92.5	3.2	-	-	94.7	2.4	-	-	95.9	1.3	-	-	97.1	1.3	-	-	97.6	0.5	-	-	98.3	0.7
1982	-	-	98.0	-0.3	-	-	97.6	-0.4	-	-	98.6	1.0	-	-	100.2	1.6	-	-	100.2	0.0	-	-	99.2	-1.0
1983	-	-	97.2	-2.0	-	-	96.6	-0.6	-	-	96.8	0.2	-	-	98.4	1.7	-	-	100.0	1.6	-	-	100.7	0.7
1984	-	-	101.2	0.5	-	-	101.8	0.6	-	-	103.2	1.4	-	-	104.0	0.8	-	-	103.9	-0.1	-	-	103.8	-0.1
1985	-	-	104.0	0.2	-	-	104.3	0.3	-	-	104.3	0.0	-	-	105.2	0.9	-	-	105.8	0.6	-	-	106.2	0.4
1986	-	-	108.1	1.8	-	-	104.6	-3.2	-	-	105.2	0.6	-	-	103.8	-1.3	-	-	103.5	-0.3	-	-	106.0	2.4
1987	-	-	-	-	-	-	-	-	-	-	100.1	-5.6	-	-	-	-	-	-	-	-	-	-	103.0	2.9
1988	-	-	-	-	-	-	-	-	-	-	101.7	-1.3	-	-	-	-	-	-	-	-	-	-	104.4	2.7
1989	-	-	-	-	-	-	-	-	-	-	110.0	5.4	-	-	-	-	-	-	-	-	-	-	110.1	0.1
1990	-	-	-	-	-	-	-	-	-	-	112.9	2.5	-	-	-	-	-	-	-	-	-	-	117.4	4.0
1991	-	-	-	-	-	-	-	-	-	-	117.7	0.3	-	-	-	-	-	-	-	-	-	-	120.6	2.5
1992	-	-	-	-	-	-	-	-	-	-	122.1	1.2	-	-	-	-	-	-	-	-	-	-	124.1	1.6
1993	-	-	-	-	-	-	-	-	-	-	127.3	2.6	-	-	-	-	-	-	-	-	-	-	129.7	1.9
1994	-	-	-	-	-	-	-	-	-	-	132.6	2.2	-	-	-	-	-	-	-	-	-	-	135.8	2.4
1995	-	-	-	-	-	-	-	-	-	-	137.8	1.5	-	-	-	-	-	-	-	-	-	-	137.2	-0.4
1996	-	-	-	-	-	-	-	-	-	-	139.9	2.0	-	-	-	-	-	-	-	-	-	-	143.2	2.4
1997	-	-	-	-	-	-	-	-	-	-	144.5	0.9	-	-	-	-	-	-	-	-	-	-	-	-

Source: U.S. Department of Labor, Bureau of Labor Statistics, Division of Consumer Prices and Price Indexes. - indicates no data collected for period.

Honolulu, HI
Consumer Price Index - Urban Wage Earners
Base 1982-1984 = 100
Transportation

For 1963-1997. Columns headed % show percentile change in the index from the previous period for which an index is available.

Year	Jan Index	%	Feb Index	%	Mar Index	%	Apr Index	%	May Index	%	Jun Index	%	Jul Index	%	Aug Index	%	Sep Index	%	Oct Index	%	Nov Index	%	Dec Index	%
1963	-	-	-	-	-	-	-	-	-	-	-	-	-	-	-	-	-	-	-	-	-	-	38.5	-
1964	-	-	-	-	38.0	-1.3	-	-	-	-	37.4	-1.6	-	-	-	-	37.4	0.0	-	-	-	-	38.0	1.6
1965	-	-	-	-	37.9	-0.3	-	-	-	-	37.5	-1.1	-	-	-	-	37.6	0.3	-	-	-	-	37.7	0.3
1966	-	-	-	-	37.5	-0.5	-	-	-	-	37.8	0.8	-	-	-	-	37.8	0.0	-	-	-	-	38.6	2.1
1967	-	-	-	-	38.5	-0.3	-	-	-	-	38.6	0.3	-	-	-	-	38.7	0.3	-	-	-	-	39.7	2.6
1968	-	-	-	-	40.1	1.0	-	-	-	-	40.1	0.0	-	-	-	-	40.0	-0.2	-	-	-	-	40.9	2.3
1969	-	-	-	-	41.7	2.0	-	-	-	-	41.5	-0.5	-	-	-	-	41.2	-0.7	-	-	-	-	42.2	2.4
1970	-	-	-	-	42.8	1.4	-	-	-	-	43.6	1.9	-	-	-	-	43.6	0.0	-	-	-	-	44.6	2.3
1971	-	-	-	-	45.7	2.5	-	-	-	-	47.7	4.4	-	-	-	-	47.2	-1.0	-	-	-	-	47.1	-0.2
1972	-	-	-	-	47.6	1.1	-	-	-	-	47.8	0.4	-	-	-	-	47.7	-0.2	-	-	-	-	47.7	0.0
1973	-	-	-	-	48.0	0.6	-	-	-	-	47.9	-0.2	-	-	-	-	47.7	-0.4	-	-	-	-	48.7	2.1
1974	-	-	-	-	50.9	4.5	-	-	-	-	52.6	3.3	-	-	-	-	53.4	1.5	-	-	-	-	54.3	1.7
1975	-	-	-	-	55.3	1.8	-	-	-	-	57.2	3.4	-	-	-	-	58.2	1.7	-	-	-	-	58.0	-0.3
1976	-	-	-	-	58.7	1.2	-	-	-	-	59.3	1.0	-	-	-	-	60.1	1.3	-	-	-	-	60.9	1.3
1977	-	-	-	-	61.2	0.5	-	-	-	-	62.3	1.8	-	-	-	-	61.9	-0.6	-	-	-	-	62.6	1.1
1978	-	-	63.8	1.9	-	-	64.9	1.7	-	-	66.0	1.7	-	-	66.6	0.9	-	-	67.2	0.9	-	-	68.1	1.3
1979	-	-	68.6	0.7	-	-	70.5	2.8	-	-	73.0	3.5	-	-	75.0	2.7	-	-	76.7	2.3	-	-	79.8	4.0
1980	-	-	83.4	4.5	-	-	86.0	3.1	-	-	86.2	0.2	-	-	88.0	2.1	-	-	88.9	1.0	-	-	90.0	1.2
1981	-	-	92.9	3.2	-	-	95.3	2.6	-	-	96.5	1.3	-	-	97.7	1.2	-	-	98.4	0.7	-	-	98.9	0.5
1982	-	-	98.4	-0.5	-	-	97.9	-0.5	-	-	98.8	0.9	-	-	100.3	1.5	-	-	100.3	0.0	-	-	99.1	-1.2
1983	-	-	97.1	-2.0	-	-	96.4	-0.7	-	-	96.7	0.3	-	-	98.4	1.8	-	-	99.9	1.5	-	-	100.7	0.8
1984	-	-	101.2	0.5	-	-	101.7	0.5	-	-	103.1	1.4	-	-	103.9	0.8	-	-	103.9	0.0	-	-	103.7	-0.2
1985	-	-	103.9	0.2	-	-	104.1	0.2	-	-	104.1	0.0	-	-	105.0	0.9	-	-	105.6	0.6	-	-	106.0	0.4
1986	-	-	107.9	1.8	-	-	104.1	-3.5	-	-	104.7	0.6	-	-	103.2	-1.4	-	-	102.8	-0.4	-	-	105.1	2.2
1987	-	-	-	-	-	-	-	-	-	-	100.9	-4.0	-	-	-	-	-	-	-	-	-	-	104.1	3.2
1988	-	-	-	-	-	-	-	-	-	-	102.9	-1.2	-	-	-	-	-	-	-	-	-	-	105.7	2.7
1989	-	-	-	-	-	-	-	-	-	-	110.9	4.9	-	-	-	-	-	-	-	-	-	-	110.8	-0.1
1990	-	-	-	-	-	-	-	-	-	-	113.3	2.3	-	-	-	-	-	-	-	-	-	-	118.7	4.8
1991	-	-	-	-	-	-	-	-	-	-	117.7	-0.8	-	-	-	-	-	-	-	-	-	-	120.9	2.7
1992	-	-	-	-	-	-	-	-	-	-	122.2	1.1	-	-	-	-	-	-	-	-	-	-	125.6	2.8
1993	-	-	-	-	-	-	-	-	-	-	128.3	2.1	-	-	-	-	-	-	-	-	-	-	130.6	1.8
1994	-	-	-	-	-	-	-	-	-	-	132.7	1.6	-	-	-	-	-	-	-	-	-	-	136.6	2.9
1995	-	-	-	-	-	-	-	-	-	-	138.3	1.2	-	-	-	-	-	-	-	-	-	-	137.4	-0.7
1996	-	-	-	-	-	-	-	-	-	-	140.1	2.0	-	-	-	-	-	-	-	-	-	-	142.3	1.6
1997	-	-	-	-	-	-	-	-	-	-	143.1	0.6	-	-	-	-	-	-	-	-	-	-	-	-

Source: U.S. Department of Labor, Bureau of Labor Statistics, Division of Consumer Prices and Price Indexes. - indicates no data collected for period.

Honolulu, HI
Consumer Price Index - All Urban Consumers
Base 1982-1984 = 100
Medical Care

For 1963-1997. Columns headed % show percentile change in the index from the previous period for which an index is available.

Year	Jan Index	%	Feb Index	%	Mar Index	%	Apr Index	%	May Index	%	Jun Index	%	Jul Index	%	Aug Index	%	Sep Index	%	Oct Index	%	Nov Index	%	Dec Index	%
1963	-	-	-	-	-	-	-	-	-	-	-	-	-	-	-	-	-	-	-	-	-	-	24.7	-
1964	-	-	-	-	25.0	1.2	-	-	-	-	25.1	0.4	-	-	-	-	25.2	0.4	-	-	-	-	25.3	0.4
1965	-	-	-	-	25.7	1.6	-	-	-	-	25.8	0.4	-	-	-	-	26.0	0.8	-	-	-	-	26.1	0.4
1966	-	-	-	-	26.3	0.8	-	-	-	-	26.5	0.8	-	-	-	-	26.8	1.1	-	-	-	-	27.4	2.2
1967	-	-	-	-	27.7	1.1	-	-	-	-	28.3	2.2	-	-	-	-	28.6	1.1	-	-	-	-	29.0	1.4
1968	-	-	-	-	29.3	1.0	-	-	-	-	29.8	1.7	-	-	-	-	30.3	1.7	-	-	-	-	30.7	1.3
1969	-	-	-	-	31.3	2.0	-	-	-	-	32.1	2.6	-	-	-	-	32.6	1.6	-	-	-	-	32.5	-0.3
1970	-	-	-	-	32.6	0.3	-	-	-	-	33.5	2.8	-	-	-	-	33.8	0.9	-	-	-	-	34.5	2.1
1971	-	-	-	-	35.0	1.4	-	-	-	-	35.2	0.6	-	-	-	-	35.6	1.1	-	-	-	-	35.6	0.0
1972	-	-	-	-	35.7	0.3	-	-	-	-	35.8	0.3	-	-	-	-	36.2	1.1	-	-	-	-	36.7	1.4
1973	-	-	-	-	37.1	1.1	-	-	-	-	37.5	1.1	-	-	-	-	38.0	1.3	-	-	-	-	38.7	1.8
1974	-	-	-	-	39.4	1.8	-	-	-	-	41.7	5.8	-	-	-	-	43.1	3.4	-	-	-	-	43.6	1.2
1975	-	-	-	-	45.5	4.4	-	-	-	-	46.5	2.2	-	-	-	-	47.6	2.4	-	-	-	-	48.1	1.1
1976	-	-	-	-	50.1	4.2	-	-	-	-	50.8	1.4	-	-	-	-	52.9	4.1	-	-	-	-	54.1	2.3
1977	-	-	-	-	55.6	2.8	-	-	-	-	56.7	2.0	-	-	-	-	59.3	4.6	-	-	-	-	59.7	0.7
1978	-	-	61.5	3.0	-	-	62.2	1.1	-	-	62.4	0.3	-	-	62.6	0.3	-	-	62.6	0.0	-	-	64.8	3.5
1979	-	-	66.1	2.0	-	-	66.9	1.2	-	-	67.1	0.3	-	-	68.2	1.6	-	-	68.4	0.3	-	-	69.2	1.2
1980	-	-	69.9	1.0	-	-	72.7	4.0	-	-	72.6	-0.1	-	-	74.1	2.1	-	-	75.5	1.9	-	-	75.3	-0.3
1981	-	-	76.9	2.1	-	-	79.3	3.1	-	-	81.1	2.3	-	-	84.1	3.7	-	-	85.8	2.0	-	-	86.4	0.7
1982	-	-	86.8	0.5	-	-	90.6	4.4	-	-	91.4	0.9	-	-	92.6	1.3	-	-	95.0	2.6	-	-	95.9	0.9
1983	-	-	98.6	2.8	-	-	100.4	1.8	-	-	100.6	0.2	-	-	103.3	2.7	-	-	102.5	-0.8	-	-	102.6	0.1
1984	-	-	105.2	2.5	-	-	106.9	1.6	-	-	107.0	0.1	-	-	108.5	1.4	-	-	108.6	0.1	-	-	109.3	0.6
1985	-	-	110.4	1.0	-	-	111.1	0.6	-	-	111.5	0.4	-	-	115.4	3.5	-	-	116.0	0.5	-	-	116.7	0.6
1986	-	-	120.0	2.8	-	-	120.4	0.3	-	-	121.2	0.7	-	-	124.6	2.8	-	-	125.2	0.5	-	-	124.5	-0.6
1987	-	-	-	-	-	-	-	-	-	-	117.8	-5.4	-	-	-	-	-	-	-	-	-	-	120.9	2.6
1988	-	-	-	-	-	-	-	-	-	-	127.4	5.4	-	-	-	-	-	-	-	-	-	-	129.4	1.6
1989	-	-	-	-	-	-	-	-	-	-	137.2	6.0	-	-	-	-	-	-	-	-	-	-	141.5	3.1
1990	-	-	-	-	-	-	-	-	-	-	149.5	5.7	-	-	-	-	-	-	-	-	-	-	152.1	1.7
1991	-	-	-	-	-	-	-	-	-	-	157.3	3.4	-	-	-	-	-	-	-	-	-	-	161.8	2.9
1992	-	-	-	-	-	-	-	-	-	-	172.5	6.6	-	-	-	-	-	-	-	-	-	-	176.1	2.1
1993	-	-	-	-	-	-	-	-	-	-	183.0	3.9	-	-	-	-	-	-	-	-	-	-	188.0	2.7
1994	-	-	-	-	-	-	-	-	-	-	196.6	4.6	-	-	-	-	-	-	-	-	-	-	206.8	5.2
1995	-	-	-	-	-	-	-	-	-	-	212.1	2.6	-	-	-	-	-	-	-	-	-	-	214.3	1.0
1996	-	-	-	-	-	-	-	-	-	-	218.3	1.9	-	-	-	-	-	-	-	-	-	-	222.0	1.7
1997	-	-	-	-	-	-	-	-	-	-	228.0	2.7	-	-	-	-	-	-	-	-	-	-		

Source: U.S. Department of Labor, Bureau of Labor Statistics, Division of Consumer Prices and Price Indexes. - indicates no data collected for period.

Honolulu, HI
Consumer Price Index - Urban Wage Earners
Base 1982-1984 = 100
Medical Care

For 1963-1997. Columns headed % show percentile change in the index from the previous period for which an index is available.

Year	Jan Index	%	Feb Index	%	Mar Index	%	Apr Index	%	May Index	%	Jun Index	%	Jul Index	%	Aug Index	%	Sep Index	%	Oct Index	%	Nov Index	%	Dec Index	%
1963	-	-	-	-	-	-	-	-	-	-	-	-	-	-	-	-	-	-	-	-	-	-	24.2	-
1964	-	-	-	-	24.5	1.2	-	-	-	-	24.5	0.0	-	-	-	-	24.7	0.8	-	-	-	-	24.8	0.4
1965	-	-	-	-	25.1	1.2	-	-	-	-	25.2	0.4	-	-	-	-	25.4	0.8	-	-	-	-	25.6	0.8
1966	-	-	-	-	25.7	0.4	-	-	-	-	26.0	1.2	-	-	-	-	26.2	0.8	-	-	-	-	26.8	2.3
1967	-	-	-	-	27.1	1.1	-	-	-	-	27.7	2.2	-	-	-	-	28.0	1.1	-	-	-	-	28.4	1.4
1968	-	-	-	-	28.7	1.1	-	-	-	-	29.2	1.7	-	-	-	-	29.7	1.7	-	-	-	-	30.1	1.3
1969	-	-	-	-	30.7	2.0	-	-	-	-	31.4	2.3	-	-	-	-	32.0	1.9	-	-	-	-	31.8	-0.6
1970	-	-	-	-	32.0	0.6	-	-	-	-	32.8	2.5	-	-	-	-	33.1	0.9	-	-	-	-	33.8	2.1
1971	-	-	-	-	34.2	1.2	-	-	-	-	34.5	0.9	-	-	-	-	34.8	0.9	-	-	-	-	34.9	0.3
1972	-	-	-	-	35.0	0.3	-	-	-	-	35.1	0.3	-	-	-	-	35.4	0.9	-	-	-	-	36.0	1.7
1973	-	-	-	-	36.3	0.8	-	-	-	-	36.7	1.1	-	-	-	-	37.3	1.6	-	-	-	-	37.9	1.6
1974	-	-	-	-	38.6	1.8	-	-	-	-	40.9	6.0	-	-	-	-	42.2	3.2	-	-	-	-	42.7	1.2
1975	-	-	-	-	44.6	4.4	-	-	-	-	45.6	2.2	-	-	-	-	46.6	2.2	-	-	-	-	47.1	1.1
1976	-	-	-	-	49.0	4.0	-	-	-	-	49.7	1.4	-	-	-	-	51.8	4.2	-	-	-	-	53.0	2.3
1977	-	-	-	-	54.4	2.6	-	-	-	-	55.5	2.0	-	-	-	-	58.1	4.7	-	-	-	-	58.5	0.7
1978	-	-	60.4	3.2	-	-	61.9	2.5	-	-	62.0	0.2	-	-	62.2	0.3	-	-	62.2	0.0	-	-	63.4	1.9
1979	-	-	64.8	2.2	-	-	65.3	0.8	-	-	66.4	1.7	-	-	66.3	-0.2	-	-	67.7	2.1	-	-	68.5	1.2
1980	-	-	68.9	0.6	-	-	71.0	3.0	-	-	71.3	0.4	-	-	73.7	3.4	-	-	75.5	2.4	-	-	75.2	-0.4
1981	-	-	76.8	2.1	-	-	78.8	2.6	-	-	81.8	3.8	-	-	84.5	3.3	-	-	85.8	1.5	-	-	86.7	1.0
1982	-	-	87.1	0.5	-	-	90.8	4.2	-	-	91.7	1.0	-	-	93.1	1.5	-	-	95.5	2.6	-	-	96.5	1.0
1983	-	-	99.0	2.6	-	-	100.5	1.5	-	-	100.6	0.1	-	-	103.1	2.5	-	-	102.3	-0.8	-	-	102.4	0.1
1984	-	-	105.0	2.5	-	-	106.6	1.5	-	-	106.7	0.1	-	-	108.0	1.2	-	-	108.0	0.0	-	-	108.7	0.6
1985	-	-	109.9	1.1	-	-	110.6	0.6	-	-	111.0	0.4	-	-	114.6	3.2	-	-	115.2	0.5	-	-	116.0	0.7
1986	-	-	119.0	2.6	-	-	119.4	0.3	-	-	120.2	0.7	-	-	123.1	2.4	-	-	123.7	0.5	-	-	123.2	-0.4
1987	-	-	-	-	-	-	-	-	-	-	118.9	-3.5	-	-	-	-	-	-	-	-	-	-	122.3	2.9
1988	-	-	-	-	-	-	-	-	-	-	128.8	5.3	-	-	-	-	-	-	-	-	-	-	131.0	1.7
1989	-	-	-	-	-	-	-	-	-	-	139.3	6.3	-	-	-	-	-	-	-	-	-	-	143.5	3.0
1990	-	-	-	-	-	-	-	-	-	-	151.1	5.3	-	-	-	-	-	-	-	-	-	-	153.5	1.6
1991	-	-	-	-	-	-	-	-	-	-	158.5	3.3	-	-	-	-	-	-	-	-	-	-	163.0	2.8
1992	-	-	-	-	-	-	-	-	-	-	173.6	6.5	-	-	-	-	-	-	-	-	-	-	177.0	2.0
1993	-	-	-	-	-	-	-	-	-	-	183.7	3.8	-	-	-	-	-	-	-	-	-	-	188.6	2.7
1994	-	-	-	-	-	-	-	-	-	-	196.9	4.4	-	-	-	-	-	-	-	-	-	-	207.4	5.3
1995	-	-	-	-	-	-	-	-	-	-	212.3	2.4	-	-	-	-	-	-	-	-	-	-	214.3	0.9
1996	-	-	-	-	-	-	-	-	-	-	217.8	1.6	-	-	-	-	-	-	-	-	-	-	221.2	1.6
1997	-	-	-	-	-	-	-	-	-	-	228.2	3.2	-	-	-	-	-	-	-	-	-	-	-	-

Source: U.S. Department of Labor, Bureau of Labor Statistics, Division of Consumer Prices and Price Indexes. - indicates no data collected for period.

Honolulu, HI
Consumer Price Index - All Urban Consumers
Base 1982-1984 = 100
Entertainment

For 1975-1997. Columns headed % show percentile change in the index from the previous period for which an index is available.

Year	Jan Index	%	Feb Index	%	Mar Index	%	Apr Index	%	May Index	%	Jun Index	%	Jul Index	%	Aug Index	%	Sep Index	%	Oct Index	%	Nov Index	%	Dec Index	%
1975	-	-	-	-	-	-	-	-	-	-	-	-	-	-	-	-	-	-	-	-	-	-	61.5	-
1976	-	-	-	-	62.3	1.3	-	-	-	-	63.5	1.9	-	-	-	-	65.0	2.4	-	-	-	-	64.9	-0.2
1977	-	-	-	-	65.7	1.2	-	-	-	-	66.6	1.4	-	-	-	-	66.6	0.0	-	-	-	-	66.9	0.5
1978	-	-	67.9	1.5	-	-	68.6	1.0	-	-	69.2	0.9	-	-	69.9	1.0	-	-	69.1	-1.1	-	-	69.9	1.2
1979	-	-	70.6	1.0	-	-	71.7	1.6	-	-	73.0	1.8	-	-	73.4	0.5	-	-	74.6	1.6	-	-	74.6	0.0
1980	-	-	76.4	2.4	-	-	77.3	1.2	-	-	77.9	0.8	-	-	78.7	1.0	-	-	79.9	1.5	-	-	80.1	0.3
1981	-	-	83.7	4.5	-	-	85.2	1.8	-	-	87.2	2.3	-	-	87.4	0.2	-	-	91.0	4.1	-	-	92.0	1.1
1982	-	-	96.0	4.3	-	-	95.3	-0.7	-	-	95.5	0.2	-	-	97.1	1.7	-	-	95.7	-1.4	-	-	95.8	0.1
1983	-	-	99.5	3.9	-	-	99.6	0.1	-	-	100.5	0.9	-	-	100.7	0.2	-	-	100.5	-0.2	-	-	99.9	-0.6
1984	-	-	101.7	1.8	-	-	103.9	2.2	-	-	103.8	-0.1	-	-	105.1	1.3	-	-	104.8	-0.3	-	-	109.1	4.1
1985	-	-	109.9	0.7	-	-	111.0	1.0	-	-	112.5	1.4	-	-	113.7	1.1	-	-	113.5	-0.2	-	-	111.5	-1.8
1986	-	-	115.7	3.8	-	-	115.9	0.2	-	-	116.1	0.2	-	-	110.7	-4.7	-	-	111.1	0.4	-	-	109.3	-1.6
1987	-	-	-	-	-	-	-	-	-	-	107.9	-1.3	-	-	-	-	-	-	-	-	-	-	107.5	-0.4
1988	-	-	-	-	-	-	-	-	-	-	109.8	2.1	-	-	-	-	-	-	-	-	-	-	112.9	2.8
1989	-	-	-	-	-	-	-	-	-	-	113.1	0.2	-	-	-	-	-	-	-	-	-	-	114.3	1.1
1990	-	-	-	-	-	-	-	-	-	-	117.5	2.8	-	-	-	-	-	-	-	-	-	-	119.9	2.0
1991	-	-	-	-	-	-	-	-	-	-	122.5	2.2	-	-	-	-	-	-	-	-	-	-	125.5	2.4
1992	-	-	-	-	-	-	-	-	-	-	129.5	3.2	-	-	-	-	-	-	-	-	-	-	130.6	0.8
1993	-	-	-	-	-	-	-	-	-	-	131.4	0.6	-	-	-	-	-	-	-	-	-	-	134.8	2.6
1994	-	-	-	-	-	-	-	-	-	-	135.0	0.1	-	-	-	-	-	-	-	-	-	-	125.5	-7.0
1995	-	-	-	-	-	-	-	-	-	-	127.9	1.9	-	-	-	-	-	-	-	-	-	-	129.5	1.3
1996	-	-	-	-	-	-	-	-	-	-	130.7	0.9	-	-	-	-	-	-	-	-	-	-	130.8	0.1
1997	-	-	-	-	-	-	-	-	-	-	138.8	6.1	-	-	-	-	-	-	-	-	-	-	-	-

Source: U.S. Department of Labor, Bureau of Labor Statistics, Division of Consumer Prices and Price Indexes. - indicates no data collected for period.

Honolulu, HI
Consumer Price Index - Urban Wage Earners
Base 1982-1984 = 100
Entertainment

For 1975-1997. Columns headed % show percentile change in the index from the previous period for which an index is available.

Year	Jan Index	%	Feb Index	%	Mar Index	%	Apr Index	%	May Index	%	Jun Index	%	Jul Index	%	Aug Index	%	Sep Index	%	Oct Index	%	Nov Index	%	Dec Index	%
1975	-	-	-	-	-	-	-	-	-	-	-	-	-	-	-	-	-	-	-	-	-	-	58.7	-
1976	-	-	-	-	59.4	1.2	-	-	-	-	60.6	2.0	-	-	-	-	62.0	2.3	-	-	-	-	61.9	-0.2
1977	-	-	-	-	62.7	1.3	-	-	-	-	63.5	1.3	-	-	-	-	63.6	0.2	-	-	-	-	63.9	0.5
1978	-	-	66.5	4.1	-	-	66.6	0.2	-	-	67.4	1.2	-	-	68.3	1.3	-	-	68.2	-0.1	-	-	68.6	0.6
1979	-	-	70.9	3.4	-	-	71.5	0.8	-	-	72.8	1.8	-	-	75.6	3.8	-	-	75.9	0.4	-	-	75.9	0.0
1980	-	-	78.4	3.3	-	-	78.6	0.3	-	-	79.9	1.7	-	-	80.2	0.4	-	-	81.4	1.5	-	-	82.4	1.2
1981	-	-	84.1	2.1	-	-	85.8	2.0	-	-	87.3	1.7	-	-	87.3	0.0	-	-	90.7	3.9	-	-	91.5	0.9
1982	-	-	95.8	4.7	-	-	94.9	-0.9	-	-	95.1	0.2	-	-	97.0	2.0	-	-	95.3	-1.8	-	-	95.5	0.2
1983	-	-	99.6	4.3	-	-	99.5	-0.1	-	-	100.4	0.9	-	-	100.8	0.4	-	-	100.6	-0.2	-	-	100.1	-0.5
1984	-	-	102.1	2.0	-	-	104.2	2.1	-	-	104.0	-0.2	-	-	105.3	1.3	-	-	105.2	-0.1	-	-	109.0	3.6
1985	-	-	110.0	0.9	-	-	111.1	1.0	-	-	112.6	1.4	-	-	113.6	0.9	-	-	113.4	-0.2	-	-	111.5	-1.7
1986	-	-	115.2	3.3	-	-	115.5	0.3	-	-	115.8	0.3	-	-	111.0	-4.1	-	-	111.3	0.3	-	-	109.4	-1.7
1987	-	-	-	-	-	-	-	-	-	-	108.0	-1.3	-	-	-	-	-	-	-	-	-	-	107.7	-0.3
1988	-	-	-	-	-	-	-	-	-	-	110.2	2.3	-	-	-	-	-	-	-	-	-	-	113.8	3.3
1989	-	-	-	-	-	-	-	-	-	-	114.6	0.7	-	-	-	-	-	-	-	-	-	-	115.5	0.8
1990	-	-	-	-	-	-	-	-	-	-	118.4	2.5	-	-	-	-	-	-	-	-	-	-	121.0	2.2
1991	-	-	-	-	-	-	-	-	-	-	124.1	2.6	-	-	-	-	-	-	-	-	-	-	126.8	2.2
1992	-	-	-	-	-	-	-	-	-	-	130.2	2.7	-	-	-	-	-	-	-	-	-	-	131.6	1.1
1993	-	-	-	-	-	-	-	-	-	-	131.7	0.1	-	-	-	-	-	-	-	-	-	-	135.4	2.8
1994	-	-	-	-	-	-	-	-	-	-	136.4	0.7	-	-	-	-	-	-	-	-	-	-	126.0	-7.6
1995	-	-	-	-	-	-	-	-	-	-	128.5	2.0	-	-	-	-	-	-	-	-	-	-	130.0	1.2
1996	-	-	-	-	-	-	-	-	-	-	131.1	0.8	-	-	-	-	-	-	-	-	-	-	130.7	-0.3
1997	-	-	-	-	-	-	-	-	-	-	138.8	6.2	-	-	-	-	-	-	-	-	-	-	-	-

Source: U.S. Department of Labor, Bureau of Labor Statistics, Division of Consumer Prices and Price Indexes. - indicates no data collected for period.

Honolulu, HI
Consumer Price Index - All Urban Consumers
Base 1982-1984 = 100
Other Goods and Services

For 1975-1997. Columns headed % show percentile change in the index from the previous period for which an index is available.

Year	Jan Index	%	Feb Index	%	Mar Index	%	Apr Index	%	May Index	%	Jun Index	%	Jul Index	%	Aug Index	%	Sep Index	%	Oct Index	%	Nov Index	%	Dec Index	%
1975	-	-	-	-	-	-	-	-	-	-	-	-	-	-	-	-	-	-	-	-	-	-	52.6	-
1976	-	-	-	-	53.3	1.3	-	-	-	-	53.5	0.4	-	-	-	-	54.2	1.3	-	-	-	-	55.3	2.0
1977	-	-	-	-	56.1	1.4	-	-	-	-	56.8	1.2	-	-	-	-	58.8	3.5	-	-	-	-	59.6	1.4
1978	-	-	59.9	0.5	-	-	60.3	0.7	-	-	61.1	1.3	-	-	61.9	1.3	-	-	62.9	1.6	-	-	63.1	0.3
1979	-	-	64.6	2.4	-	-	65.1	0.8	-	-	65.6	0.8	-	-	66.2	0.9	-	-	68.7	3.8	-	-	70.6	2.8
1980	-	-	71.3	1.0	-	-	70.4	-1.3	-	-	72.4	2.8	-	-	73.6	1.7	-	-	77.0	4.6	-	-	76.9	-0.1
1981	-	-	78.3	1.8	-	-	78.7	0.5	-	-	79.1	0.5	-	-	82.3	4.0	-	-	86.3	4.9	-	-	87.2	1.0
1982	-	-	87.5	0.3	-	-	90.1	3.0	-	-	91.0	1.0	-	-	91.1	0.1	-	-	96.3	5.7	-	-	99.2	3.0
1983	-	-	98.1	-1.1	-	-	101.4	3.4	-	-	102.0	0.6	-	-	101.8	-0.2	-	-	103.0	1.2	-	-	103.1	0.1
1984	-	-	104.6	1.5	-	-	104.9	0.3	-	-	105.5	0.6	-	-	107.7	2.1	-	-	109.1	1.3	-	-	109.1	0.0
1985	-	-	111.0	1.7	-	-	110.8	-0.2	-	-	111.2	0.4	-	-	113.3	1.9	-	-	114.9	1.4	-	-	115.0	0.1
1986	-	-	115.6	0.5	-	-	117.3	1.5	-	-	117.4	0.1	-	-	120.3	2.5	-	-	124.3	3.3	-	-	124.9	0.5
1987	-	-	-	-	-	-	-	-	-	-	126.3	1.1	-	-	-	-	-	-	-	-	-	-	-	-
1988	-	-	-	-	-	-	-	-	-	-	136.5	8.1	-	-	-	-	-	-	-	-	-	-	-	-
1989	-	-	-	-	-	-	-	-	-	-	145.0	6.2	-	-	-	-	-	-	-	-	-	-	-	-
1990	-	-	-	-	-	-	-	-	-	-	153.6	5.9	-	-	-	-	-	-	-	-	-	-	-	-
1991	-	-	-	-	-	-	-	-	-	-	166.6	8.5	-	-	-	-	-	-	-	-	-	-	-	-
1992	-	-	-	-	-	-	-	-	-	-	177.6	6.6	-	-	-	-	-	-	-	-	-	-	-	-
1993	-	-	-	-	-	-	-	-	-	-	194.2	9.3	-	-	-	-	-	-	-	-	-	-	-	-
1994	-	-	-	-	-	-	-	-	-	-	198.2	2.1	-	-	-	-	-	-	-	-	-	-	-	-
1995	-	-	-	-	-	-	-	-	-	-	205.0	3.4	-	-	-	-	-	-	-	-	-	-	-	-
1996	-	-	-	-	-	-	-	-	-	-	213.0	3.9	-	-	-	-	-	-	-	-	-	-	-	-
1997	-	-	-	-	-	-	-	-	-	-	221.4	3.9	-	-	-	-	-	-	-	-	-	-	-	-

Source: U.S. Department of Labor, Bureau of Labor Statistics, Division of Consumer Prices and Price Indexes. - indicates no data collected for period.

Honolulu, HI
Consumer Price Index - Urban Wage Earners
Base 1982-1984 = 100
Other Goods and Services

For 1975-1997. Columns headed % show percentile change in the index from the previous period for which an index is available.

Year	Jan Index	%	Feb Index	%	Mar Index	%	Apr Index	%	May Index	%	Jun Index	%	Jul Index	%	Aug Index	%	Sep Index	%	Oct Index	%	Nov Index	%	Dec Index	%
1975	-	-	-	-	-	-	-	-	-	-	-	-	-	-	-	-	-	-	-	-	-	-	53.5	-
1976	-	-	-	-	54.3	1.5	-	-	-	-	54.4	0.2	-	-	-	-	55.1	1.3	-	-	-	-	56.3	2.2
1977	-	-	-	-	57.1	1.4	-	-	-	-	57.8	1.2	-	-	-	-	59.8	3.5	-	-	-	-	60.6	1.3
1978	-	-	60.4	-0.3	-	-	60.8	0.7	-	-	61.3	0.8	-	-	62.4	1.8	-	-	63.5	1.8	-	-	63.6	0.2
1979	-	-	65.2	2.5	-	-	65.5	0.5	-	-	66.4	1.4	-	-	67.1	1.1	-	-	69.3	3.3	-	-	69.7	0.6
1980	-	-	70.6	1.3	-	-	70.4	-0.3	-	-	72.1	2.4	-	-	73.1	1.4	-	-	75.9	3.8	-	-	76.8	1.2
1981	-	-	77.5	0.9	-	-	78.4	1.2	-	-	79.9	1.9	-	-	80.7	1.0	-	-	86.3	6.9	-	-	86.7	0.5
1982	-	-	87.0	0.3	-	-	89.8	3.2	-	-	90.4	0.7	-	-	90.5	0.1	-	-	96.0	6.1	-	-	99.5	3.6
1983	-	-	98.5	-1.0	-	-	101.9	3.5	-	-	102.3	0.4	-	-	102.3	0.0	-	-	103.1	0.8	-	-	103.2	0.1
1984	-	-	104.7	1.5	-	-	105.1	0.4	-	-	105.5	0.4	-	-	107.8	2.2	-	-	109.1	1.2	-	-	109.0	-0.1
1985	-	-	111.2	2.0	-	-	110.9	-0.3	-	-	111.3	0.4	-	-	113.4	1.9	-	-	114.7	1.1	-	-	114.7	0.0
1986	-	-	115.5	0.7	-	-	117.0	1.3	-	-	117.1	0.1	-	-	120.2	2.6	-	-	123.2	2.5	-	-	123.9	0.6
1987	-	-	-	-	-	-	-	-	-	-	125.5	1.3	-	-	-	-	-	-	-	-	-	-	-	-
1988	-	-	-	-	-	-	-	-	-	-	136.5	8.8	-	-	-	-	-	-	-	-	-	-	-	-
1989	-	-	-	-	-	-	-	-	-	-	145.6	6.7	-	-	-	-	-	-	-	-	-	-	-	-
1990	-	-	-	-	-	-	-	-	-	-	154.3	6.0	-	-	-	-	-	-	-	-	-	-	-	-
1991	-	-	-	-	-	-	-	-	-	-	168.4	9.1	-	-	-	-	-	-	-	-	-	-	-	-
1992	-	-	-	-	-	-	-	-	-	-	179.6	6.7	-	-	-	-	-	-	-	-	-	-	-	-
1993	-	-	-	-	-	-	-	-	-	-	196.7	9.5	-	-	-	-	-	-	-	-	-	-	-	-
1994	-	-	-	-	-	-	-	-	-	-	198.5	0.9	-	-	-	-	-	-	-	-	-	-	-	-
1995	-	-	-	-	-	-	-	-	-	-	204.7	3.1	-	-	-	-	-	-	-	-	-	-	-	-
1996	-	-	-	-	-	-	-	-	-	-	212.9	4.0	-	-	-	-	-	-	-	-	-	-	-	-
1997	-	-	-	-	-	-	-	-	-	-	220.9	3.8	-	-	-	-	-	-	-	-	-	-	-	-

Source: U.S. Department of Labor, Bureau of Labor Statistics, Division of Consumer Prices and Price Indexes. - indicates no data collected for period.

Houston, TX
Consumer Price Index - All Urban Consumers
Base 1982-1984 = 100
Annual Averages

For 1914-1997. Columns headed % show percentile change in the index from the previous period for which an index is available.

Year	All Items		Food & Beverage		Housing		Apparel & Upkeep		Trans-portation		Medical Care		Entertain-ment		Other Goods & Services	
	Index	%	Index	%	Index	%	Index	%	Index	%	Index	%	Index	%	Index	%
1914	-	-	-	-	-	-	-	-	-	-	-	-	-	-	-	-
1915	9.4	-	-	-	-	-	-	-	-	-	-	-	-	-	-	-
1916	10.1	7.4	-	-	-	-	-	-	-	-	-	-	-	-	-	-
1917	12.4	22.8	-	-	-	-	-	-	-	-	-	-	-	-	-	-
1918	14.5	16.9	-	-	-	-	-	-	-	-	-	-	-	-	-	-
1919	16.9	16.6	-	-	-	-	-	-	-	-	-	-	-	-	-	-
1920	19.2	13.6	-	-	-	-	-	-	-	-	-	-	-	-	-	-
1921	17.0	-11.5	-	-	-	-	-	-	-	-	-	-	-	-	-	-
1922	15.9	-6.5	-	-	-	-	-	-	-	-	-	-	-	-	-	-
1923	15.9	0.0	-	-	-	-	-	-	-	-	-	-	-	-	-	-
1924	15.8	-0.6	-	-	-	-	-	-	-	-	-	-	-	-	-	-
1925	16.2	2.5	-	-	-	-	-	-	-	-	-	-	-	-	-	-
1926	16.0	-1.2	-	-	-	-	-	-	-	-	-	-	-	-	-	-
1927	15.7	-1.9	-	-	-	-	-	-	-	-	-	-	-	-	-	-
1928	15.6	-0.6	-	-	-	-	-	-	-	-	-	-	-	-	-	-
1929	15.7	0.6	-	-	-	-	-	-	-	-	-	-	-	-	-	-
1930	15.3	-2.5	-	-	-	-	-	-	-	-	-	-	-	-	-	-
1931	13.9	-9.2	-	-	-	-	-	-	-	-	-	-	-	-	-	-
1932	12.3	-11.5	-	-	-	-	-	-	-	-	-	-	-	-	-	-
1933	11.8	-4.1	-	-	-	-	-	-	-	-	-	-	-	-	-	-
1934	12.3	4.2	-	-	-	-	-	-	-	-	-	-	-	-	-	-
1935	12.7	3.3	-	-	-	-	-	-	-	-	-	-	-	-	-	-
1936	12.8	0.8	-	-	-	-	-	-	-	-	-	-	-	-	-	-
1937	13.3	3.9	-	-	-	-	-	-	-	-	-	-	-	-	-	-
1938	13.3	0.0	-	-	-	-	-	-	-	-	-	-	-	-	-	-
1939	13.2	-0.8	-	-	-	-	-	-	-	-	-	-	-	-	-	-
1940	13.2	0.0	-	-	-	-	-	-	-	-	-	-	-	-	-	-
1941	13.8	4.5	-	-	-	-	-	-	-	-	-	-	-	-	-	-
1942	15.2	10.1	-	-	-	-	-	-	-	-	-	-	-	-	-	-
1943	16.0	5.3	-	-	-	-	-	-	-	-	-	-	-	-	-	-
1944	16.2	1.3	-	-	-	-	-	-	-	-	-	-	-	-	-	-
1945	16.6	2.5	-	-	-	-	-	-	-	-	-	-	-	-	-	-
1946	17.9	7.8	-	-	-	-	-	-	-	-	-	-	-	-	-	-
1947	21.0	17.3	-	-	-	-	-	-	20.8	-	14.5	-	-	-	-	-
1948	22.7	8.1	-	-	-	-	-	-	23.2	11.5	14.9	2.8	-	-	-	-
1949	22.7	0.0	-	-	-	-	-	-	24.7	6.5	15.2	2.0	-	-	-	-
1950	23.4	3.1	-	-	-	-	-	-	25.7	4.0	15.6	2.6	-	-	-	-
1951	25.2	7.7	-	-	-	-	-	-	28.0	8.9	15.9	1.9	-	-	-	-
1952	25.5	1.2	-	-	-	-	-	-	28.5	1.8	16.8	5.7	-	-	-	-
1953	25.8	1.2	-	-	-	-	36.1	-	29.0	1.8	17.5	4.2	-	-	-	-
1954	25.8	0.0	-	-	-	-	36.0	-0.3	28.6	-1.4	17.7	1.1	-	-	-	-
1955	25.7	-0.4	-	-	-	-	36.0	0.0	28.3	-1.0	18.4	4.0	-	-	-	-
1956	26.1	1.6	-	-	-	-	36.7	1.9	28.9	2.1	18.9	2.7	-	-	-	-
1957	26.9	3.1	-	-	-	-	37.6	2.5	30.9	6.9	19.2	1.6	-	-	-	-
1958	27.3	1.5	-	-	-	-	38.3	1.9	31.5	1.9	19.7	2.6	-	-	-	-

[Continued]

518

Houston, TX
Consumer Price Index - All Urban Consumers
Base 1982-1984 = 100
Annual Averages
[Continued]

For 1914-1997. Columns headed % show percentile change in the index from the previous period for which an index is available.

Year	All Items		Food & Beverage		Housing		Apparel & Upkeep		Trans-portation		Medical Care		Entertain-ment		Other Goods & Services	
	Index	%	Index	%	Index	%	Index	%	Index	%	Index	%	Index	%	Index	%
1959	27.6	1.1	-	-	-	-	38.7	1.0	33.0	4.8	20.0	1.5	-	-	-	-
1960	27.8	0.7	-	-	-	-	38.7	0.0	32.9	-0.3	20.5	2.5	-	-	-	-
1961	28.0	0.7	-	-	-	-	38.9	0.5	33.1	0.6	20.8	1.5	-	-	-	-
1962	28.5	1.8	-	-	-	-	40.0	2.8	34.2	3.3	21.0	1.0	-	-	-	-
1963	28.8	1.1	-	-	-	-	40.5	1.3	33.5	-2.0	21.6	2.9	-	-	-	-
1964	29.2	1.4	-	-	-	-	40.8	0.7	34.3	2.4	22.2	2.8	-	-	-	-
1965	29.6	1.4	-	-	-	-	40.8	0.0	34.2	-0.3	22.8	2.7	-	-	-	-
1966	30.4	2.7	-	-	-	-	41.5	1.7	34.8	1.8	23.4	2.6	-	-	-	-
1967	31.2	2.6	-	-	-	-	42.2	1.7	36.0	3.4	24.9	6.4	-	-	-	-
1968	32.5	4.2	-	-	-	-	44.6	5.7	37.1	3.1	26.2	5.2	-	-	-	-
1969	34.6	6.5	-	-	-	-	48.1	7.8	38.4	3.5	28.5	8.8	-	-	-	-
1970	36.4	5.2	-	-	-	-	50.6	5.2	39.1	1.8	30.6	7.4	-	-	-	-
1971	37.7	3.6	-	-	-	-	51.5	1.8	40.8	4.3	32.4	5.9	-	-	-	-
1972	39.0	3.4	-	-	-	-	53.1	3.1	41.4	1.5	33.7	4.0	-	-	-	-
1973	41.2	5.6	-	-	-	-	55.1	3.8	42.2	1.9	35.0	3.9	-	-	-	-
1974	46.1	11.9	-	-	-	-	60.3	9.4	47.3	12.1	37.9	8.3	-	-	-	-
1975	51.4	11.5	-	-	-	-	64.2	6.5	51.9	9.7	43.2	14.0	-	-	-	-
1976	55.3	7.6	58.5	-	53.0	-	68.0	5.9	56.3	8.5	48.0	11.1	61.3	-	56.3	-
1977	59.3	7.2	61.6	5.3	57.4	8.3	72.0	5.9	60.5	7.5	54.2	12.9	64.0	4.4	59.8	6.2
1978	64.9	9.4	67.8	10.1	64.4	12.2	76.9	6.8	62.8	3.8	59.4	9.6	65.7	2.7	65.5	9.5
1979	73.5	13.3	76.8	13.3	73.6	14.3	83.1	8.1	72.3	15.1	65.1	9.6	70.1	6.7	71.7	9.5
1980	82.7	12.5	83.8	9.1	82.7	12.4	89.1	7.2	85.6	18.4	72.2	10.9	79.7	13.7	79.3	10.6
1981	91.0	10.0	91.8	9.5	91.2	10.3	95.6	7.3	94.8	10.7	80.0	10.8	86.4	8.4	85.3	7.6
1982	97.3	6.9	96.4	5.0	99.8	9.4	98.4	2.9	97.7	3.1	90.7	13.4	92.8	7.4	91.8	7.6
1983	100.0	2.8	99.3	3.0	100.3	0.5	99.8	1.4	99.1	1.4	101.1	11.5	103.1	11.1	101.0	10.0
1984	102.7	2.7	104.3	5.0	99.9	-0.4	101.9	2.1	103.3	4.2	108.1	6.9	104.1	1.0	107.2	6.1
1985	104.9	2.1	105.0	0.7	100.2	0.3	104.4	2.5	106.2	2.8	116.8	8.0	111.9	7.5	112.5	4.9
1986	103.9	-1.0	107.3	2.2	98.1	-2.1	106.1	1.6	99.2	-6.6	123.5	5.7	114.5	2.3	118.6	5.4
1987	106.5	2.5	111.8	4.2	97.0	-1.1	113.6	7.1	102.5	3.3	130.4	5.6	118.5	3.5	124.8	5.2
1988	109.5	2.8	116.2	3.9	98.0	1.0	121.1	6.6	104.5	2.0	136.7	4.8	124.5	5.1	131.2	5.1
1989	114.1	4.2	121.7	4.7	100.5	2.6	123.9	2.3	109.2	4.5	148.0	8.3	133.8	7.5	138.5	5.6
1990	120.6	5.7	128.7	5.8	104.8	4.3	132.5	6.9	116.0	6.2	161.2	8.9	134.9	0.8	152.1	9.8
1991	125.1	3.7	131.6	2.3	109.5	4.5	134.8	1.7	119.6	3.1	177.7	10.2	139.6	3.5	157.7	3.7
1992	129.1	3.2	130.8	-0.6	113.2	3.4	135.8	0.7	122.9	2.8	193.6	8.9	146.4	4.9	172.1	9.1
1993	133.4	3.3	132.4	1.2	116.8	3.2	142.1	4.6	128.2	4.3	200.8	3.7	153.2	4.6	180.8	5.1
1994	137.9	3.4	137.5	3.9	120.4	3.1	146.7	3.2	132.9	3.7	204.6	1.9	157.4	2.7	187.6	3.8
1995	139.8	1.4	140.2	2.0	121.1	0.6	138.3	-5.7	137.0	3.1	217.7	6.4	157.3	-0.1	193.4	3.1
1996	142.7	2.1	142.9	1.9	123.9	2.3	137.7	-0.4	140.4	2.5	222.6	2.3	160.4	2.0	197.6	2.2
1997	145.4	1.9	147.7	3.4	126.1	1.8	142.1	3.2	141.4	0.7	228.4	2.6	161.6	0.7	197.7	0.1

Source: U.S. Department of Labor, Bureau of Labor Statistics, Division of Consumer Prices and Price Indexes. - indicates no data collected for period.

Houston, TX
Consumer Price Index - Urban Wage Earners
Base 1982-1984 = 100
Annual Averages

For 1914-1997. Columns headed % show percentile change in the index from the previous period for which an index is available.

Year	All Items		Food & Beverage		Housing		Apparel & Upkeep		Trans-portation		Medical Care		Entertain-ment		Other Goods & Services	
	Index	%	Index	%	Index	%	Index	%	Index	%	Index	%	Index	%	Index	%
1914	-	-	-	-	-	-	-	-	-	-	-	-	-	-	-	-
1915	9.5	-	-	-	-	-	-	-	-	-	-	-	-	-	-	-
1916	10.1	6.3	-	-	-	-	-	-	-	-	-	-	-	-	-	-
1917	12.5	23.8	-	-	-	-	-	-	-	-	-	-	-	-	-	-
1918	14.5	16.0	-	-	-	-	-	-	-	-	-	-	-	-	-	-
1919	17.0	17.2	-	-	-	-	-	-	-	-	-	-	-	-	-	-
1920	19.3	13.5	-	-	-	-	-	-	-	-	-	-	-	-	-	-
1921	17.1	-11.4	-	-	-	-	-	-	-	-	-	-	-	-	-	-
1922	16.0	-6.4	-	-	-	-	-	-	-	-	-	-	-	-	-	-
1923	16.0	0.0	-	-	-	-	-	-	-	-	-	-	-	-	-	-
1924	15.9	-0.6	-	-	-	-	-	-	-	-	-	-	-	-	-	-
1925	16.2	1.9	-	-	-	-	-	-	-	-	-	-	-	-	-	-
1926	16.1	-0.6	-	-	-	-	-	-	-	-	-	-	-	-	-	-
1927	15.8	-1.9	-	-	-	-	-	-	-	-	-	-	-	-	-	-
1928	15.6	-1.3	-	-	-	-	-	-	-	-	-	-	-	-	-	-
1929	15.7	0.6	-	-	-	-	-	-	-	-	-	-	-	-	-	-
1930	15.4	-1.9	-	-	-	-	-	-	-	-	-	-	-	-	-	-
1931	13.9	-9.7	-	-	-	-	-	-	-	-	-	-	-	-	-	-
1932	12.4	-10.8	-	-	-	-	-	-	-	-	-	-	-	-	-	-
1933	11.8	-4.8	-	-	-	-	-	-	-	-	-	-	-	-	-	-
1934	12.4	5.1	-	-	-	-	-	-	-	-	-	-	-	-	-	-
1935	12.8	3.2	-	-	-	-	-	-	-	-	-	-	-	-	-	-
1936	12.9	0.8	-	-	-	-	-	-	-	-	-	-	-	-	-	-
1937	13.4	3.9	-	-	-	-	-	-	-	-	-	-	-	-	-	-
1938	13.3	-0.7	-	-	-	-	-	-	-	-	-	-	-	-	-	-
1939	13.2	-0.8	-	-	-	-	-	-	-	-	-	-	-	-	-	-
1940	13.3	0.8	-	-	-	-	-	-	-	-	-	-	-	-	-	-
1941	13.8	3.8	-	-	-	-	-	-	-	-	-	-	-	-	-	-
1942	15.3	10.9	-	-	-	-	-	-	-	-	-	-	-	-	-	-
1943	16.1	5.2	-	-	-	-	-	-	-	-	-	-	-	-	-	-
1944	16.3	1.2	-	-	-	-	-	-	-	-	-	-	-	-	-	-
1945	16.6	1.8	-	-	-	-	-	-	-	-	-	-	-	-	-	-
1946	18.0	8.4	-	-	-	-	-	-	-	-	-	-	-	-	-	-
1947	21.1	17.2	-	-	-	-	-	-	20.7	-	13.9	-	-	-	-	-
1948	22.8	8.1	-	-	-	-	-	-	23.2	12.1	14.2	2.2	-	-	-	-
1949	22.8	0.0	-	-	-	-	-	-	24.6	6.0	14.6	2.8	-	-	-	-
1950	23.5	3.1	-	-	-	-	-	-	25.6	4.1	14.9	2.1	-	-	-	-
1951	25.3	7.7	-	-	-	-	-	-	27.9	9.0	15.3	2.7	-	-	-	-
1952	25.7	1.6	-	-	-	-	-	-	28.4	1.8	16.1	5.2	-	-	-	-
1953	26.0	1.2	-	-	-	-	36.8	-	28.9	1.8	16.8	4.3	-	-	-	-
1954	25.9	-0.4	-	-	-	-	36.7	-0.3	28.5	-1.4	17.0	1.2	-	-	-	-
1955	25.8	-0.4	-	-	-	-	36.7	0.0	28.1	-1.4	17.7	4.1	-	-	-	-
1956	26.2	1.6	-	-	-	-	37.4	1.9	28.8	2.5	18.2	2.8	-	-	-	-
1957	27.0	3.1	-	-	-	-	38.3	2.4	30.8	6.9	18.4	1.1	-	-	-	-
1958	27.5	1.9	-	-	-	-	39.1	2.1	31.3	1.6	18.8	2.2	-	-	-	-

[Continued]

Houston, TX
Consumer Price Index - Urban Wage Earners
Base 1982-1984 = 100
Annual Averages
[Continued]

For 1914-1997. Columns headed % show percentile change in the index from the previous period for which an index is available.

Year	All Items		Food & Beverage		Housing		Apparel & Upkeep		Trans-portation		Medical Care		Entertain-ment		Other Goods & Services	
	Index	%	Index	%	Index	%	Index	%	Index	%	Index	%	Index	%	Index	%
1959	27.7	0.7	-	-	-	-	39.5	1.0	32.8	4.8	19.2	2.1	-	-	-	-
1960	27.9	0.7	-	-	-	-	39.4	-0.3	32.8	0.0	19.6	2.1	-	-	-	-
1961	28.1	0.7	-	-	-	-	39.6	0.5	32.9	0.3	19.9	1.5	-	-	-	-
1962	28.6	1.8	-	-	-	-	40.8	3.0	34.0	3.3	20.2	1.5	-	-	-	-
1963	28.9	1.0	-	-	-	-	41.3	1.2	33.4	-1.8	20.7	2.5	-	-	-	-
1964	29.4	1.7	-	-	-	-	41.6	0.7	34.2	2.4	21.3	2.9	-	-	-	-
1965	29.7	1.0	-	-	-	-	41.6	0.0	34.1	-0.3	21.8	2.3	-	-	-	-
1966	30.5	2.7	-	-	-	-	42.3	1.7	34.7	1.8	22.5	3.2	-	-	-	-
1967	31.3	2.6	-	-	-	-	43.0	1.7	35.9	3.5	23.9	6.2	-	-	-	-
1968	32.7	4.5	-	-	-	-	45.4	5.6	36.9	2.8	25.1	5.0	-	-	-	-
1969	34.8	6.4	-	-	-	-	49.1	8.1	38.3	3.8	27.4	9.2	-	-	-	-
1970	36.6	5.2	-	-	-	-	51.6	5.1	39.0	1.8	29.3	6.9	-	-	-	-
1971	37.9	3.6	-	-	-	-	52.5	1.7	40.6	4.1	31.0	5.8	-	-	-	-
1972	39.2	3.4	-	-	-	-	54.1	3.0	41.2	1.5	32.3	4.2	-	-	-	-
1973	41.5	5.9	-	-	-	-	56.2	3.9	42.0	1.9	33.6	4.0	-	-	-	-
1974	46.3	11.6	-	-	-	-	61.4	9.3	47.1	12.1	36.4	8.3	-	-	-	-
1975	51.7	11.7	-	-	-	-	65.5	6.7	51.7	9.8	41.4	13.7	-	-	-	-
1976	55.6	7.5	59.5	-	53.0	-	69.3	5.8	56.0	8.3	46.0	11.1	63.1	-	56.2	-
1977	59.6	7.2	62.6	5.2	57.4	8.3	73.4	5.9	60.2	7.5	51.9	12.8	65.8	4.3	59.6	6.0
1978	65.1	9.2	68.6	9.6	64.3	12.0	78.5	6.9	62.7	4.2	57.0	9.8	67.9	3.2	64.7	8.6
1979	73.4	12.7	77.0	12.2	72.7	13.1	85.3	8.7	72.1	15.0	64.7	13.5	71.6	5.4	70.6	9.1
1980	82.1	11.9	83.8	8.8	81.4	12.0	90.3	5.9	84.3	16.9	71.7	10.8	79.0	10.3	78.5	11.2
1981	90.3	10.0	91.6	9.3	90.0	10.6	96.4	6.8	93.4	10.8	79.6	11.0	85.2	7.8	84.6	7.8
1982	96.9	7.3	96.4	5.2	98.7	9.7	98.5	2.2	97.1	4.0	90.5	13.7	91.3	7.2	91.7	8.4
1983	100.1	3.3	99.4	3.1	100.4	1.7	99.8	1.3	99.0	2.0	101.2	11.8	104.0	13.9	101.0	10.1
1984	103.1	3.0	104.2	4.8	100.8	0.4	101.8	2.0	103.9	4.9	108.3	7.0	104.8	0.8	107.3	6.2
1985	104.6	1.5	104.8	0.6	100.1	-0.7	104.2	2.4	106.7	2.7	117.0	8.0	112.6	7.4	112.4	4.8
1986	103.6	-1.0	107.3	2.4	98.0	-2.1	105.7	1.4	100.3	-6.0	123.7	5.7	115.7	2.8	117.4	4.4
1987	106.4	2.7	111.7	4.1	96.5	-1.5	112.7	6.6	104.7	4.4	130.9	5.8	120.0	3.7	123.0	4.8
1988	109.7	3.1	116.1	3.9	97.5	1.0	121.1	7.5	107.1	2.3	137.7	5.2	126.3	5.2	130.4	6.0
1989	114.4	4.3	121.7	4.8	100.2	2.8	124.0	2.4	111.9	4.5	149.3	8.4	135.7	7.4	139.1	6.7
1990	120.9	5.7	128.8	5.8	104.5	4.3	132.8	7.1	118.7	6.1	162.3	8.7	136.6	0.7	152.8	9.8
1991	125.3	3.6	131.7	2.3	109.4	4.7	133.9	0.8	122.1	2.9	178.9	10.2	141.2	3.4	157.7	3.2
1992	128.9	2.9	131.0	-0.5	113.3	3.6	134.4	0.4	125.2	2.5	195.3	9.2	148.3	5.0	171.5	8.8
1993	133.0	3.2	132.6	1.2	117.2	3.4	138.9	3.3	129.4	3.4	202.9	3.9	156.2	5.3	179.6	4.7
1994	137.4	3.3	137.7	3.8	120.7	3.0	145.4	4.7	134.0	3.6	206.6	1.8	160.3	2.6	185.1	3.1
1995	139.4	1.5	140.3	1.9	121.2	0.4	137.6	-5.4	138.6	3.4	219.5	6.2	161.3	0.6	190.0	2.6
1996	142.0	1.9	143.1	2.0	123.8	2.1	136.8	-0.6	142.2	2.6	224.6	2.3	164.7	2.1	189.4	-0.3
1997	144.5	1.8	148.0	3.4	126.0	1.8	141.2	3.2	142.9	0.5	230.5	2.6	166.0	0.8	186.8	-1.4

Source: U.S. Department of Labor, Bureau of Labor Statistics, Division of Consumer Prices and Price Indexes. - indicates no data collected for period.

Houston, TX
Consumer Price Index - All Urban Consumers
Base 1982-1984 = 100
All Items

For 1914-1997. Columns headed % show percentile change in the index from the previous period for which an index is available.

Year	Jan Index	%	Feb Index	%	Mar Index	%	Apr Index	%	May Index	%	Jun Index	%	Jul Index	%	Aug Index	%	Sep Index	%	Oct Index	%	Nov Index	%	Dec Index	%
1914	-	-	-	-	-	-	-	-	-	-	-	-	-	-	-	-	-	-	-	-	-	-	9.5	-
1915	-	-	-	-	-	-	-	-	-	-	-	-	-	-	-	-	-	-	-	-	-	-	9.5	0.0
1916	-	-	-	-	-	-	-	-	-	-	-	-	-	-	-	-	-	-	-	-	-	-	10.9	14.7
1917	-	-	-	-	-	-	-	-	-	-	-	-	-	-	-	-	-	-	-	-	-	-	13.2	21.1
1918	-	-	-	-	-	-	-	-	-	-	-	-	-	-	-	-	-	-	-	-	-	-	15.9	20.5
1919	-	-	-	-	-	-	-	-	-	-	16.4	3.1	-	-	-	-	-	-	-	-	-	-	18.5	12.8
1920	-	-	-	-	-	-	-	-	-	-	19.7	6.5	-	-	-	-	-	-	-	-	-	-	18.9	-4.1
1921	-	-	-	-	-	-	-	-	16.9	-10.6	-	-	-	-	-	-	16.6	-1.8	-	-	-	-	16.4	-1.2
1922	-	-	-	-	15.9	-3.0	-	-	-	-	15.8	-0.6	-	-	-	-	15.7	-0.6	-	-	-	-	15.9	1.3
1923	-	-	-	-	15.7	-1.3	-	-	-	-	15.9	1.3	-	-	-	-	16.0	0.6	-	-	-	-	16.1	0.6
1924	-	-	-	-	15.9	-1.2	-	-	-	-	15.6	-1.9	-	-	-	-	15.8	1.3	-	-	-	-	16.0	1.3
1925	-	-	-	-	-	-	-	-	-	-	16.1	0.6	-	-	-	-	-	-	-	-	-	-	16.4	1.9
1926	-	-	-	-	-	-	-	-	-	-	16.0	-2.4	-	-	-	-	-	-	-	-	-	-	16.0	0.0
1927	-	-	-	-	-	-	-	-	-	-	15.7	-1.9	-	-	-	-	-	-	-	-	-	-	15.8	0.6
1928	-	-	-	-	-	-	-	-	-	-	15.5	-1.9	-	-	-	-	-	-	-	-	-	-	15.6	0.6
1929	-	-	-	-	-	-	-	-	-	-	15.6	0.0	-	-	-	-	-	-	-	-	-	-	15.8	1.3
1930	-	-	-	-	-	-	-	-	-	-	15.4	-2.5	-	-	-	-	-	-	-	-	-	-	14.7	-4.5
1931	-	-	-	-	-	-	-	-	-	-	13.8	-6.1	-	-	-	-	-	-	-	-	-	-	13.4	-2.9
1932	-	-	-	-	-	-	-	-	-	-	12.3	-8.2	-	-	-	-	-	-	-	-	-	-	11.7	-4.9
1933	-	-	-	-	-	-	-	-	-	-	11.6	-0.9	-	-	-	-	-	-	-	-	-	-	12.1	4.3
1934	-	-	-	-	-	-	-	-	-	-	12.2	0.8	-	-	-	-	-	-	-	-	12.6	3.3	-	-
1935	-	-	-	-	12.8	1.6	-	-	-	-	-	-	12.6	-1.6	-	-	-	-	12.7	0.8	-	-	-	-
1936	12.8	0.8	-	-	-	-	12.6	-1.6	-	-	-	-	12.9	2.4	-	-	13.0	0.8	-	-	-	-	13.0	0.0
1937	-	-	-	-	13.3	2.3	-	-	-	-	13.3	0.0	-	-	-	-	13.5	1.5	-	-	-	-	13.5	0.0
1938	-	-	-	-	13.3	-1.5	-	-	-	-	13.2	-0.8	-	-	-	-	13.3	0.8	-	-	-	-	13.3	0.0
1939	-	-	-	-	13.1	-1.5	-	-	-	-	13.1	0.0	-	-	-	-	13.3	1.5	-	-	-	-	13.2	-0.8
1940	-	-	-	-	13.2	0.0	-	-	-	-	13.2	0.0	-	-	-	-	13.2	0.0	13.3	0.8	13.3	0.0	13.3	0.0
1941	13.3	0.0	13.3	0.0	13.3	0.0	13.5	1.5	13.5	0.0	13.6	0.7	13.7	0.7	13.8	0.7	14.1	2.2	14.4	2.1	14.5	0.7	14.6	0.7
1942	14.7	0.7	14.9	1.4	15.1	1.3	15.1	0.0	15.2	0.7	15.1	-0.7	15.3	1.3	15.4	0.7	15.5	0.6	15.5	0.0	15.5	0.0	15.6	0.6
1943	15.7	0.6	15.8	0.6	16.2	2.5	16.2	0.0	16.3	0.6	16.1	-1.2	16.0	-0.6	15.9	-0.6	16.1	1.3	16.1	0.0	16.1	0.0	16.1	0.0
1944	16.1	0.0	16.1	0.0	16.0	-0.6	16.1	0.6	16.2	0.6	16.2	0.0	16.3	0.6	16.3	0.0	16.3	0.0	16.3	0.0	16.2	-0.6	16.3	0.6
1945	16.4	0.6	16.3	-0.6	16.3	0.0	16.4	0.6	16.5	0.6	16.6	0.6	16.7	0.6	16.7	0.0	16.7	0.0	16.6	-0.6	16.6	0.0	16.7	0.6
1946	16.6	-0.6	16.6	0.0	16.7	0.6	16.8	0.6	16.8	0.0	17.1	1.8	17.9	4.7	18.4	2.8	18.7	1.6	18.9	1.1	19.7	4.2	20.0	1.5
1947	20.2	1.0	20.2	0.0	20.6	2.0	20.8	1.0	20.7	-0.5	20.7	0.0	20.8	0.5	21.0	1.0	21.3	1.4	21.5	0.9	21.8	1.4	22.2	1.8
1948	22.4	0.9	22.4	0.0	22.4	0.0	22.5	0.4	22.5	0.0	22.7	0.9	22.9	0.9	23.1	0.9	23.1	0.0	23.0	-0.4	22.9	-0.4	22.9	0.0
1949	22.8	-0.4	22.5	-1.3	22.5	0.0	22.6	0.4	22.5	-0.4	22.5	0.0	22.5	0.0	22.6	0.4	22.7	0.4	22.8	0.4	23.0	0.9	23.0	0.0
1950	22.9	-0.4	22.9	0.0	23.0	0.4	22.9	-0.4	22.9	0.0	23.0	0.4	23.2	0.9	23.6	1.7	23.8	0.8	23.8	0.0	23.9	0.4	24.3	1.7
1951	24.8	2.1	25.0	0.8	25.1	0.4	25.2	0.4	25.2	0.0	25.1	-0.4	25.2	0.4	25.2	0.0	25.3	0.4	25.4	0.4	25.5	0.4	25.6	0.4
1952	25.5	-0.4	25.4	-0.4	25.4	0.0	25.4	0.0	25.4	0.0	25.4	0.0	25.5	0.4	25.6	0.4	25.5	-0.4	25.7	0.8	25.7	0.0	25.8	0.4
1953	-	-	25.7	-0.4	-	-	-	-	25.8	0.4	-	-	-	-	25.8	0.0	-	-	-	-	25.9	0.4	-	-
1954	-	-	25.9	0.0	-	-	-	-	25.8	-0.4	-	-	-	-	25.8	0.0	-	-	-	-	25.8	0.0	-	-
1955	-	-	25.6	-0.8	-	-	-	-	25.5	-0.4	-	-	-	-	25.5	0.0	-	-	-	-	25.8	1.2	-	-
1956	-	-	25.8	0.0	-	-	-	-	25.8	0.0	-	-	-	-	26.1	1.2	-	-	-	-	26.5	1.5	-	-
1957	-	-	26.7	0.8	-	-	-	-	26.8	0.4	-	-	-	-	27.0	0.7	-	-	-	-	27.1	0.4	-	-
1958	-	-	27.1	0.0	-	-	-	-	27.4	1.1	-	-	-	-	27.4	0.0	-	-	-	-	27.5	0.4	-	-

[Continued]

Houston, TX
Consumer Price Index - All Urban Consumers
Base 1982-1984 = 100
All Items
[Continued]

For 1914-1997. Columns headed % show percentile change in the index from the previous period for which an index is available.

Year	Jan Index	%	Feb Index	%	Mar Index	%	Apr Index	%	May Index	%	Jun Index	%	Jul Index	%	Aug Index	%	Sep Index	%	Oct Index	%	Nov Index	%	Dec Index	%
1959	-	-	27.4	-0.4	-	-	-	-	27.4	0.0	-	-	-	-	27.6	0.7	-	-	-	-	27.7	0.4	-	-
1960	-	-	27.8	0.4	-	-	-	-	27.7	-0.4	-	-	-	-	27.9	0.7	-	-	-	-	28.0	0.4	-	-
1961	-	-	27.7	-1.1	-	-	-	-	27.9	0.7	-	-	-	-	27.9	0.0	-	-	-	-	28.3	1.4	-	-
1962	-	-	28.5	0.7	-	-	-	-	28.5	0.0	-	-	-	-	28.5	0.0	-	-	-	-	28.5	0.0	-	-
1963	-	-	28.6	0.4	-	-	-	-	28.5	-0.3	-	-	-	-	28.9	1.4	-	-	-	-	29.1	0.7	-	-
1964	-	-	29.2	0.3	-	-	-	-	29.1	-0.3	-	-	-	-	29.2	0.3	-	-	-	-	29.2	0.0	-	-
1965	-	-	29.3	0.3	-	-	29.4	0.3	-	-	-	-	29.6	0.7	-	-	-	-	29.8	0.7	-	-	-	-
1966	30.0	0.7	-	-	-	-	30.2	0.7	-	-	-	-	30.4	0.7	-	-	-	-	30.6	0.7	-	-	-	-
1967	30.8	0.7	-	-	-	-	31.0	0.6	-	-	-	-	31.1	0.3	-	-	-	-	31.5	1.3	-	-	-	-
1968	31.8	1.0	-	-	-	-	32.1	0.9	-	-	-	-	32.5	1.2	-	-	-	-	33.0	1.5	-	-	-	-
1969	33.6	1.8	-	-	-	-	34.2	1.8	-	-	-	-	34.6	1.2	-	-	-	-	35.4	2.3	-	-	-	-
1970	35.7	0.8	-	-	-	-	36.2	1.4	-	-	-	-	36.4	0.6	-	-	-	-	36.8	1.1	-	-	-	-
1971	37.2	1.1	-	-	-	-	37.3	0.3	-	-	-	-	37.8	1.3	-	-	-	-	38.2	1.1	-	-	-	-
1972	38.4	0.5	-	-	-	-	38.9	1.3	-	-	-	-	39.0	0.3	-	-	-	-	39.4	1.0	-	-	-	-
1973	39.7	0.8	-	-	-	-	40.7	2.5	-	-	-	-	41.0	0.7	-	-	-	-	42.5	3.7	-	-	-	-
1974	43.4	2.1	-	-	-	-	44.6	2.8	-	-	-	-	46.1	3.4	-	-	-	-	48.1	4.3	-	-	-	-
1975	49.7	3.3	-	-	-	-	50.3	1.2	-	-	-	-	51.8	3.0	-	-	-	-	52.6	1.5	-	-	-	-
1976	53.7	2.1	-	-	-	-	54.3	1.1	-	-	-	-	55.2	1.7	-	-	-	-	56.7	2.7	-	-	-	-
1977	57.2	0.9	-	-	-	-	58.8	2.8	-	-	-	-	59.7	1.5	-	-	-	-	60.1	0.7	-	-	-	-
1978	61.3	2.0	-	-	-	-	63.3	3.3	-	-	64.7	2.2	-	-	65.9	1.9	-	-	67.0	1.7	-	-	68.5	2.2
1979	-	-	69.9	2.0	-	-	71.1	1.7	-	-	73.4	3.2	-	-	75.0	2.2	-	-	76.1	1.5	-	-	77.5	1.8
1980	-	-	79.8	3.0	-	-	81.3	1.9	-	-	83.1	2.2	-	-	83.7	0.7	-	-	84.9	1.4	-	-	85.7	0.9
1981	-	-	87.8	2.5	-	-	89.3	1.7	-	-	91.3	2.2	-	-	91.9	0.7	-	-	93.5	1.7	-	-	94.4	1.0
1982	-	-	94.8	0.4	-	-	95.1	0.3	-	-	97.9	2.9	-	-	99.3	1.4	-	-	99.0	-0.3	-	-	99.2	0.2
1983	-	-	98.9	-0.3	-	-	98.7	-0.2	-	-	100.2	1.5	-	-	101.0	0.8	-	-	101.1	0.1	-	-	100.0	-1.1
1984	-	-	100.9	0.9	-	-	101.5	0.6	-	-	103.0	1.5	-	-	103.5	0.5	-	-	104.3	0.8	-	-	103.9	-0.4
1985	-	-	104.0	0.1	-	-	104.5	0.5	-	-	105.3	0.8	-	-	105.4	0.1	-	-	105.3	-0.1	-	-	105.0	-0.3
1986	-	-	105.1	0.1	-	-	102.9	-2.1	-	-	103.9	1.0	-	-	103.8	-0.1	-	-	104.1	0.3	-	-	103.2	-0.9
1987	-	-	104.4	1.2	-	-	106.4	1.9	-	-	106.5	0.1	-	-	107.3	0.8	-	-	108.0	0.7	-	-	107.3	-0.6
1988	-	-	108.0	0.7	-	-	108.2	0.2	-	-	109.4	1.1	-	-	110.3	0.8	-	-	111.1	0.7	-	-	111.3	0.2
1989	-	-	112.7	1.3	-	-	113.2	0.4	-	-	114.1	0.8	-	-	114.4	0.3	-	-	115.7	1.1	-	-	115.5	-0.2
1990	-	-	118.7	2.8	-	-	118.3	-0.3	-	-	119.7	1.2	-	-	121.5	1.5	-	-	124.0	2.1	-	-	123.0	-0.8
1991	-	-	124.3	1.1	-	-	123.5	-0.6	-	-	124.9	1.1	-	-	124.8	-0.1	-	-	127.3	2.0	-	-	127.0	-0.2
1992	-	-	127.0	0.0	-	-	128.7	1.3	-	-	129.4	0.5	-	-	129.9	0.4	-	-	130.8	0.7	-	-	129.3	-1.1
1993	-	-	131.7	1.9	-	-	131.8	0.1	-	-	132.9	0.8	-	-	133.0	0.1	-	-	136.6	2.7	-	-	136.5	-0.1
1994	-	-	137.0	0.4	-	-	136.8	-0.1	-	-	137.4	0.4	-	-	139.2	1.3	-	-	139.3	0.1	-	-	137.8	-1.1
1995	-	-	139.3	1.1	-	-	138.0	-0.9	-	-	139.9	1.4	-	-	140.1	0.1	-	-	141.6	1.1	-	-	140.9	-0.5
1996	-	-	141.5	0.4	-	-	143.1	1.1	-	-	142.8	-0.2	-	-	142.8	0.0	-	-	143.2	0.3	-	-	143.6	0.3
1997	-	-	144.5	0.6	-	-	145.2	0.5	-	-	144.8	-0.3	-	-	145.4	0.4	-	-	147.3	1.3	-	-	145.6	-1.2

Source: U.S. Department of Labor, Bureau of Labor Statistics, Division of Consumer Prices and Price Indexes. - indicates no data collected for period.

Houston, TX
Consumer Price Index - Urban Wage Earners
Base 1982-1984 = 100
All Items

For 1914-1997. Columns headed % show percentile change in the index from the previous period for which an index is available.

Year	Jan Index	%	Feb Index	%	Mar Index	%	Apr Index	%	May Index	%	Jun Index	%	Jul Index	%	Aug Index	%	Sep Index	%	Oct Index	%	Nov Index	%	Dec Index	%
1914	-	-	-	-	-	-	-	-	-	-	-	-	-	-	-	-	-	-	-	-	-	-	9.6	-
1915	-	-	-	-	-	-	-	-	-	-	-	-	-	-	-	-	-	-	-	-	-	-	9.5	-1.0
1916	-	-	-	-	-	-	-	-	-	-	-	-	-	-	-	-	-	-	-	-	-	-	10.9	14.7
1917	-	-	-	-	-	-	-	-	-	-	-	-	-	-	-	-	-	-	-	-	-	-	13.3	22.0
1918	-	-	-	-	-	-	-	-	-	-	-	-	-	-	-	-	-	-	-	-	-	-	16.0	20.3
1919	-	-	-	-	-	-	-	-	-	-	16.4	2.5	-	-	-	-	-	-	-	-	-	-	18.6	13.4
1920	-	-	-	-	-	-	-	-	-	-	19.8	6.5	-	-	-	-	-	-	-	-	-	-	19.0	-4.0
1921	-	-	-	-	-	-	-	-	17.0	-10.5	-	-	-	-	-	-	16.6	-2.4	-	-	-	-	16.4	-1.2
1922	-	-	-	-	16.0	-2.4	-	-	-	-	15.9	-0.6	-	-	-	-	15.8	-0.6	-	-	-	-	16.0	1.3
1923	-	-	-	-	15.8	-1.2	-	-	-	-	15.9	0.6	-	-	-	-	16.0	0.6	-	-	-	-	16.2	1.3
1924	-	-	-	-	16.0	-1.2	-	-	-	-	15.7	-1.9	-	-	-	-	15.9	1.3	-	-	-	-	16.0	0.6
1925	-	-	-	-	-	-	-	-	-	-	16.2	1.3	-	-	-	-	-	-	-	-	-	-	16.4	1.2
1926	-	-	-	-	-	-	-	-	-	-	16.0	-2.4	-	-	-	-	-	-	-	-	-	-	16.1	0.6
1927	-	-	-	-	-	-	-	-	-	-	15.8	-1.9	-	-	-	-	-	-	-	-	-	-	15.9	0.6
1928	-	-	-	-	-	-	-	-	-	-	15.5	-2.5	-	-	-	-	-	-	-	-	-	-	15.7	1.3
1929	-	-	-	-	-	-	-	-	-	-	15.6	-0.6	-	-	-	-	-	-	-	-	-	-	15.9	1.9
1930	-	-	-	-	-	-	-	-	-	-	15.4	-3.1	-	-	-	-	-	-	-	-	-	-	14.7	-4.5
1931	-	-	-	-	-	-	-	-	-	-	13.9	-5.4	-	-	-	-	-	-	-	-	-	-	13.5	-2.9
1932	-	-	-	-	-	-	-	-	-	-	12.3	-8.9	-	-	-	-	-	-	-	-	-	-	11.7	-4.9
1933	-	-	-	-	-	-	-	-	-	-	11.7	0.0	-	-	-	-	-	-	-	-	-	-	12.1	3.4
1934	-	-	-	-	-	-	-	-	-	-	12.2	0.8	-	-	-	-	-	-	-	-	12.6	3.3	-	-
1935	-	-	-	-	12.8	1.6	-	-	-	-	-	-	12.7	-0.8	-	-	-	-	12.7	0.0	-	-	13.1	0.0
1936	12.8	0.8	-	-	-	-	12.7	-0.8	-	-	-	-	12.9	1.6	-	-	13.1	1.6	-	-	-	-	13.1	0.0
1937	-	-	-	-	13.3	1.5	-	-	-	-	13.3	0.0	-	-	-	-	13.6	2.3	-	-	-	-	13.5	-0.7
1938	-	-	-	-	13.4	-0.7	-	-	-	-	13.3	-0.7	-	-	-	-	13.3	0.0	-	-	-	-	13.3	0.0
1939	-	-	-	-	13.2	-0.8	-	-	-	-	13.2	0.0	-	-	-	-	13.3	0.8	-	-	-	-	13.3	0.0
1940	-	-	-	-	13.2	-0.8	-	-	-	-	13.2	0.0	-	-	-	-	13.3	0.8	13.4	0.8	13.4	0.0	13.4	0.0
1941	13.4	0.0	13.4	0.0	13.4	0.0	13.6	1.5	13.6	0.0	13.6	0.0	13.8	1.5	13.9	0.7	14.2	2.2	14.5	2.1	14.6	0.7	14.7	0.7
1942	14.8	0.7	15.0	1.4	15.2	1.3	15.2	0.0	15.3	0.7	15.2	-0.7	15.4	1.3	15.4	0.0	15.5	0.6	15.6	0.6	15.6	0.0	15.7	0.6
1943	15.7	0.0	15.9	1.3	16.2	1.9	16.3	0.6	16.4	0.6	16.2	-1.2	16.1	-0.6	16.0	-0.6	16.2	1.3	16.2	0.0	16.2	0.0	16.2	0.0
1944	16.2	0.0	16.2	0.0	16.1	-0.6	16.2	0.6	16.3	0.6	16.2	-0.6	16.4	1.2	16.4	0.0	16.4	0.0	16.4	0.0	16.3	-0.6	16.4	0.6
1945	16.4	0.0	16.4	0.0	16.4	0.0	16.5	0.6	16.6	0.6	16.7	0.6	16.8	0.6	16.8	0.0	16.8	0.0	16.7	-0.6	16.7	0.0	16.8	0.6
1946	16.7	-0.6	16.7	0.0	16.8	0.6	16.9	0.6	16.9	0.0	17.2	1.8	18.0	4.7	18.5	2.8	18.8	1.6	19.0	1.1	19.8	4.2	20.1	1.5
1947	20.3	1.0	20.3	0.0	20.7	2.0	20.9	1.0	20.8	-0.5	20.8	0.0	20.9	0.5	21.1	1.0	21.4	1.4	21.6	0.9	21.9	1.4	22.3	1.8
1948	22.5	0.9	22.5	0.0	22.5	0.0	22.7	0.9	22.7	0.0	22.8	0.4	23.0	0.9	23.2	0.9	23.2	0.0	23.2	0.0	23.0	-0.9	23.0	0.0
1949	22.9	-0.4	22.6	-1.3	22.6	0.0	22.7	0.4	22.7	0.0	22.7	0.0	22.7	0.0	22.7	0.0	22.8	0.4	22.9	0.4	23.1	0.9	23.1	0.0
1950	23.1	0.0	23.0	-0.4	23.1	0.4	23.0	-0.4	23.0	0.0	23.1	0.4	23.3	0.9	23.7	1.7	23.9	0.8	23.9	0.0	24.0	0.4	24.4	1.7
1951	25.0	2.5	25.1	0.4	25.3	0.8	25.3	0.0	25.3	0.0	25.3	0.0	25.3	0.0	25.3	0.0	25.5	0.8	25.5	0.0	25.6	0.4	25.8	0.8
1952	25.7	-0.4	25.5	-0.8	25.5	0.0	25.6	0.4	25.5	-0.4	25.6	0.4	25.6	0.0	25.8	0.8	25.7	-0.4	25.8	0.4	25.8	0.0	25.9	0.4
1953	-	-	25.8	-0.4	-	-	-	-	26.0	0.8	-	-	-	-	26.0	0.0	-	-	-	-	26.1	0.4	-	-
1954	-	-	26.0	-0.4	-	-	-	-	25.9	-0.4	-	-	-	-	25.9	0.0	-	-	-	-	25.9	0.0	-	-
1955	-	-	25.7	-0.8	-	-	-	-	25.7	0.0	-	-	-	-	25.7	0.0	-	-	-	-	25.9	0.8	-	-
1956	-	-	25.9	0.0	-	-	-	-	26.0	0.4	-	-	-	-	26.3	1.2	-	-	-	-	26.6	1.1	-	-
1957	-	-	26.8	0.8	-	-	-	-	26.9	0.4	-	-	-	-	27.1	0.7	-	-	-	-	27.2	0.4	-	-
1958	-	-	27.2	0.0	-	-	-	-	27.5	1.1	-	-	-	-	27.5	0.0	-	-	-	-	27.6	0.4	-	-

[Continued]

Houston, TX
Consumer Price Index - Urban Wage Earners
Base 1982-1984 = 100
All Items
[Continued]

For 1914-1997. Columns headed % show percentile change in the index from the previous period for which an index is available.

Year	Jan Index	%	Feb Index	%	Mar Index	%	Apr Index	%	May Index	%	Jun Index	%	Jul Index	%	Aug Index	%	Sep Index	%	Oct Index	%	Nov Index	%	Dec Index	%
1959	-	-	27.6	0.0	-	-	-	-	27.6	0.0	-	-	-	-	27.7	0.4	-	-	-	-	27.9	0.7	-	-
1960	-	-	27.9	0.0	-	-	-	-	27.8	-0.4	-	-	-	-	28.0	0.7	-	-	-	-	28.1	0.4	-	-
1961	-	-	27.8	-1.1	-	-	-	-	28.0	0.7	-	-	-	-	28.1	0.4	-	-	-	-	28.5	1.4	-	-
1962	-	-	28.6	0.4	-	-	-	-	28.7	0.3	-	-	-	-	28.6	-0.3	-	-	-	-	28.6	0.0	-	-
1963	-	-	28.8	0.7	-	-	-	-	28.6	-0.7	-	-	-	-	29.1	1.7	-	-	-	-	29.2	0.3	-	-
1964	-	-	29.4	0.7	-	-	-	-	29.3	-0.3	-	-	-	-	29.4	0.3	-	-	-	-	29.4	0.0	-	-
1965	-	-	29.4	0.0	-	-	29.5	0.3	-	-	-	-	29.7	0.7	-	-	-	-	29.9	0.7	-	-	-	-
1966	30.1	0.7	-	-	-	-	30.4	1.0	-	-	-	-	30.6	0.7	-	-	-	-	30.8	0.7	-	-	-	-
1967	31.0	0.6	-	-	-	-	31.1	0.3	-	-	-	-	31.3	0.6	-	-	-	-	31.6	1.0	-	-	-	-
1968	32.0	1.3	-	-	-	-	32.3	0.9	-	-	-	-	32.7	1.2	-	-	-	-	33.2	1.5	-	-	-	-
1969	33.7	1.5	-	-	-	-	34.4	2.1	-	-	-	-	34.8	1.2	-	-	-	-	35.6	2.3	-	-	-	-
1970	35.8	0.6	-	-	-	-	36.4	1.7	-	-	-	-	36.6	0.5	-	-	-	-	36.9	0.8	-	-	-	-
1971	37.4	1.4	-	-	-	-	37.4	0.0	-	-	-	-	38.0	1.6	-	-	-	-	38.4	1.1	-	-	-	-
1972	38.6	0.5	-	-	-	-	39.1	1.3	-	-	-	-	39.2	0.3	-	-	-	-	39.6	1.0	-	-	-	-
1973	39.9	0.8	-	-	-	-	40.9	2.5	-	-	-	-	41.2	0.7	-	-	-	-	42.7	3.6	-	-	-	-
1974	43.6	2.1	-	-	-	-	44.8	2.8	-	-	-	-	46.4	3.6	-	-	-	-	48.3	4.1	-	-	-	-
1975	49.9	3.3	-	-	-	-	50.6	1.4	-	-	-	-	52.0	2.8	-	-	-	-	52.9	1.7	-	-	-	-
1976	54.0	2.1	-	-	-	-	54.5	0.9	-	-	-	-	55.5	1.8	-	-	-	-	57.0	2.7	-	-	-	-
1977	57.5	0.9	-	-	-	-	59.1	2.8	-	-	-	-	60.0	1.5	-	-	-	-	60.4	0.7	-	-	-	-
1978	61.6	2.0	-	-	-	-	63.6	3.2	-	-	65.0	2.2	-	-	66.1	1.7	-	-	67.0	1.4	-	-	68.4	2.1
1979	-	-	69.9	2.2	-	-	71.3	2.0	-	-	73.5	3.1	-	-	74.9	1.9	-	-	75.8	1.2	-	-	77.1	1.7
1980	-	-	78.9	2.3	-	-	80.6	2.2	-	-	82.3	2.1	-	-	83.2	1.1	-	-	84.4	1.4	-	-	85.3	1.1
1981	-	-	87.0	2.0	-	-	88.7	2.0	-	-	90.7	2.3	-	-	91.4	0.8	-	-	92.7	1.4	-	-	93.6	1.0
1982	-	-	94.1	0.5	-	-	94.7	0.6	-	-	97.4	2.9	-	-	98.8	1.4	-	-	98.7	-0.1	-	-	99.0	0.3
1983	-	-	99.4	0.4	-	-	99.5	0.1	-	-	100.2	0.7	-	-	100.8	0.6	-	-	101.0	0.2	-	-	99.6	-1.4
1984	-	-	101.4	1.8	-	-	101.8	0.4	-	-	103.2	1.4	-	-	104.5	1.3	-	-	104.8	0.3	-	-	103.7	-1.0
1985	-	-	103.7	0.0	-	-	104.3	0.6	-	-	105.0	0.7	-	-	105.1	0.1	-	-	105.0	-0.1	-	-	104.7	-0.3
1986	-	-	104.7	0.0	-	-	102.7	-1.9	-	-	103.7	1.0	-	-	103.6	-0.1	-	-	103.9	0.3	-	-	102.9	-1.0
1987	-	-	104.3	1.4	-	-	106.1	1.7	-	-	106.4	0.3	-	-	107.1	0.7	-	-	108.1	0.9	-	-	107.4	-0.6
1988	-	-	108.1	0.7	-	-	108.1	0.0	-	-	109.4	1.2	-	-	110.6	1.1	-	-	111.4	0.7	-	-	111.4	0.0
1989	-	-	112.9	1.3	-	-	113.5	0.5	-	-	114.5	0.9	-	-	114.9	0.3	-	-	115.8	0.8	-	-	115.8	0.0
1990	-	-	118.9	2.7	-	-	118.6	-0.3	-	-	120.0	1.2	-	-	121.9	1.6	-	-	124.7	2.3	-	-	123.4	-1.0
1991	-	-	124.4	0.8	-	-	123.6	-0.6	-	-	125.2	1.3	-	-	124.9	-0.2	-	-	127.4	2.0	-	-	127.2	-0.2
1992	-	-	126.9	-0.2	-	-	128.4	1.2	-	-	129.2	0.6	-	-	129.8	0.5	-	-	130.7	0.7	-	-	129.2	-1.1
1993	-	-	131.3	1.6	-	-	131.3	0.0	-	-	132.4	0.8	-	-	132.7	0.2	-	-	136.1	2.6	-	-	136.0	-0.1
1994	-	-	136.3	0.2	-	-	136.2	-0.1	-	-	137.0	0.6	-	-	138.8	1.3	-	-	139.0	0.1	-	-	137.8	-0.9
1995	-	-	138.9	0.8	-	-	137.6	-0.9	-	-	139.5	1.4	-	-	139.8	0.2	-	-	140.9	0.8	-	-	140.5	-0.3
1996	-	-	140.8	0.2	-	-	142.3	1.1	-	-	142.2	-0.1	-	-	142.2	0.0	-	-	142.5	0.2	-	-	143.0	0.4
1997	-	-	143.6	0.4	-	-	144.1	0.3	-	-	144.1	0.0	-	-	144.9	0.6	-	-	146.3	1.0	-	-	144.5	-1.2

Source: U.S. Department of Labor, Bureau of Labor Statistics, Division of Consumer Prices and Price Indexes. - indicates no data collected for period.

Houston, TX
Consumer Price Index - All Urban Consumers
Base 1982-1984 = 100
Food and Beverages

For 1976-1997. Columns headed % show percentile change in the index from the previous period for which an index is available.

Year	Jan Index	%	Feb Index	%	Mar Index	%	Apr Index	%	May Index	%	Jun Index	%	Jul Index	%	Aug Index	%	Sep Index	%	Oct Index	%	Nov Index	%	Dec Index	%
1976	58.0	-	-	-	-	-	57.7	-0.5	-	-	-	-	58.9	2.1	-	-	-	-	59.0	0.2	-	-	-	-
1977	59.3	0.5	-	-	-	-	61.3	3.4	-	-	-	-	62.3	1.6	-	-	-	-	62.0	-0.5	-	-	-	-
1978	63.5	2.4	-	-	-	-	66.0	3.9	-	-	68.1	3.2	-	-	68.7	0.9	-	-	70.0	1.9	-	-	71.7	2.4
1979	-	-	74.7	4.2	-	-	75.7	1.3	-	-	77.2	2.0	-	-	77.8	0.8	-	-	78.0	0.3	-	-	79.5	1.9
1980	-	-	80.8	1.6	-	-	81.8	1.2	-	-	82.2	0.5	-	-	84.7	3.0	-	-	87.3	3.1	-	-	88.1	0.9
1981	-	-	89.9	2.0	-	-	90.9	1.1	-	-	91.7	0.9	-	-	93.2	1.6	-	-	93.3	0.1	-	-	93.3	0.0
1982	-	-	94.6	1.4	-	-	95.2	0.6	-	-	96.7	1.6	-	-	97.6	0.9	-	-	97.5	-0.1	-	-	97.8	0.3
1983	-	-	98.3	0.5	-	-	99.0	0.7	-	-	99.7	0.7	-	-	100.0	0.3	-	-	99.8	-0.2	-	-	99.7	-0.1
1984	-	-	104.0	4.3	-	-	104.2	0.2	-	-	104.3	0.1	-	-	104.6	0.3	-	-	104.6	0.0	-	-	105.4	0.8
1985	-	-	105.4	0.0	-	-	104.6	-0.8	-	-	104.6	0.0	-	-	105.0	0.4	-	-	104.6	-0.4	-	-	105.8	1.1
1986	-	-	106.4	0.6	-	-	106.3	-0.1	-	-	106.7	0.4	-	-	107.8	1.0	-	-	108.4	0.6	-	-	109.3	0.8
1987	-	-	111.4	1.9	-	-	111.2	-0.2	-	-	111.8	0.5	-	-	111.6	-0.2	-	-	113.1	1.3	-	-	112.5	-0.5
1988	-	-	113.9	1.2	-	-	114.3	0.4	-	-	114.6	0.3	-	-	117.8	2.8	-	-	119.6	1.5	-	-	118.2	-1.2
1989	-	-	121.7	3.0	-	-	121.7	0.0	-	-	121.8	0.1	-	-	121.1	-0.6	-	-	121.8	0.6	-	-	123.5	1.4
1990	-	-	127.9	3.6	-	-	127.1	-0.6	-	-	128.6	1.2	-	-	129.5	0.7	-	-	131.3	1.4	-	-	129.2	-1.6
1991	-	-	132.2	2.3	-	-	132.3	0.1	-	-	130.9	-1.1	-	-	131.4	0.4	-	-	131.7	0.2	-	-	131.5	-0.2
1992	-	-	132.7	0.9	-	-	132.2	-0.4	-	-	129.9	-1.7	-	-	129.6	-0.2	-	-	129.7	0.1	-	-	130.4	0.5
1993	-	-	132.2	1.4	-	-	128.9	-2.5	-	-	130.2	1.0	-	-	133.4	2.5	-	-	134.9	1.1	-	-	136.5	1.2
1994	-	-	135.9	-0.4	-	-	137.3	1.0	-	-	137.1	-0.1	-	-	138.0	0.7	-	-	137.7	-0.2	-	-	139.7	1.5
1995	-	-	139.7	0.0	-	-	140.7	0.7	-	-	139.7	-0.7	-	-	140.1	0.3	-	-	140.5	0.3	-	-	141.0	0.4
1996	-	-	140.6	-0.3	-	-	140.9	0.2	-	-	141.8	0.6	-	-	144.5	1.9	-	-	144.9	0.3	-	-	145.9	0.7
1997	-	-	146.8	0.6	-	-	146.3	-0.3	-	-	147.3	0.7	-	-	148.3	0.7	-	-	149.4	0.7	-	-	149.0	-0.3

Source: U.S. Department of Labor, Bureau of Labor Statistics, Division of Consumer Prices and Price Indexes. - indicates no data collected for period.

Houston, TX
Consumer Price Index - Urban Wage Earners
Base 1982-1984 = 100
Food and Beverages

For 1976-1997. Columns headed % show percentile change in the index from the previous period for which an index is available.

Year	Jan Index	%	Feb Index	%	Mar Index	%	Apr Index	%	May Index	%	Jun Index	%	Jul Index	%	Aug Index	%	Sep Index	%	Oct Index	%	Nov Index	%	Dec Index	%
1976	59.0	-	-	-	-	-	58.7	-0.5	-	-	-	-	59.9	2.0	-	-	-	-	60.0	0.2	-	-	-	-
1977	60.3	0.5	-	-	-	-	62.3	3.3	-	-	-	-	63.3	1.6	-	-	-	-	63.1	-0.3	-	-	-	-
1978	64.6	2.4	-	-	-	-	67.1	3.9	-	-	69.3	3.3	-	-	69.4	0.1	-	-	70.4	1.4	-	-	72.0	2.3
1979	-	-	74.9	4.0	-	-	76.1	1.6	-	-	77.2	1.4	-	-	77.9	0.9	-	-	78.4	0.6	-	-	79.5	1.4
1980	-	-	80.1	0.8	-	-	81.8	2.1	-	-	82.6	1.0	-	-	84.8	2.7	-	-	87.3	2.9	-	-	88.5	1.4
1981	-	-	90.0	1.7	-	-	90.6	0.7	-	-	91.1	0.6	-	-	92.9	2.0	-	-	93.0	0.1	-	-	93.1	0.1
1982	-	-	94.6	1.6	-	-	95.3	0.7	-	-	96.7	1.5	-	-	97.6	0.9	-	-	97.6	0.0	-	-	97.9	0.3
1983	-	-	98.5	0.6	-	-	99.1	0.6	-	-	99.6	0.5	-	-	99.9	0.3	-	-	99.7	-0.2	-	-	99.7	0.0
1984	-	-	104.2	4.5	-	-	104.2	0.0	-	-	104.2	0.0	-	-	104.4	0.2	-	-	104.5	0.1	-	-	105.3	0.8
1985	-	-	105.1	-0.2	-	-	104.5	-0.6	-	-	104.5	0.0	-	-	104.8	0.3	-	-	104.5	-0.3	-	-	105.8	1.2
1986	-	-	106.3	0.5	-	-	106.4	0.1	-	-	106.7	0.3	-	-	107.7	0.9	-	-	108.5	0.7	-	-	109.3	0.7
1987	-	-	111.3	1.8	-	-	111.0	-0.3	-	-	111.6	0.5	-	-	111.4	-0.2	-	-	113.1	1.5	-	-	112.4	-0.6
1988	-	-	113.7	1.2	-	-	114.1	0.4	-	-	114.5	0.4	-	-	117.8	2.9	-	-	119.6	1.5	-	-	118.1	-1.3
1989	-	-	121.7	3.0	-	-	121.7	0.0	-	-	121.7	0.0	-	-	121.0	-0.6	-	-	121.8	0.7	-	-	123.6	1.5
1990	-	-	128.1	3.6	-	-	127.3	-0.6	-	-	128.7	1.1	-	-	129.6	0.7	-	-	131.4	1.4	-	-	129.4	-1.5
1991	-	-	132.2	2.2	-	-	132.4	0.2	-	-	130.9	-1.1	-	-	131.5	0.5	-	-	131.9	0.3	-	-	131.8	-0.1
1992	-	-	133.0	0.9	-	-	132.4	-0.5	-	-	130.0	-1.8	-	-	129.8	-0.2	-	-	129.8	0.0	-	-	130.4	0.5
1993	-	-	132.2	1.4	-	-	129.1	-2.3	-	-	130.3	0.9	-	-	133.6	2.5	-	-	135.2	1.2	-	-	136.9	1.3
1994	-	-	136.3	-0.4	-	-	137.6	1.0	-	-	137.4	-0.1	-	-	138.1	0.5	-	-	137.8	-0.2	-	-	139.8	1.5
1995	-	-	139.7	-0.1	-	-	140.7	0.7	-	-	139.7	-0.7	-	-	140.2	0.4	-	-	140.6	0.3	-	-	141.2	0.4
1996	-	-	140.8	-0.3	-	-	141.0	0.1	-	-	141.8	0.6	-	-	144.8	2.1	-	-	145.2	0.3	-	-	146.3	0.8
1997	-	-	147.1	0.5	-	-	146.7	-0.3	-	-	147.5	0.5	-	-	148.5	0.7	-	-	149.5	0.7	-	-	149.4	-0.1

Source: U.S. Department of Labor, Bureau of Labor Statistics, Division of Consumer Prices and Price Indexes. - indicates no data collected for period.

Houston, TX
Consumer Price Index - All Urban Consumers
Base 1982-1984 = 100
Housing

For 1976-1997. Columns headed % show percentile change in the index from the previous period for which an index is available.

Year	Jan Index	%	Feb Index	%	Mar Index	%	Apr Index	%	May Index	%	Jun Index	%	Jul Index	%	Aug Index	%	Sep Index	%	Oct Index	%	Nov Index	%	Dec Index	%
1976	51.2	-	-	-	-	-	52.0	1.6	-	-	-	-	52.9	1.7	-	-	-	-	54.7	3.4	-	-	-	-
1977	55.3	1.1	-	-	-	-	56.7	2.5	-	-	-	-	57.8	1.9	-	-	-	-	58.2	0.7	-	-	-	-
1978	60.0	3.1	-	-	-	-	62.3	3.8	-	-	64.2	3.0	-	-	66.0	2.8	-	-	66.9	1.4	-	-	69.0	3.1
1979	-	-	70.0	1.4	-	-	70.5	0.7	-	-	73.5	4.3	-	-	75.3	2.4	-	-	76.7	1.9	-	-	78.1	1.8
1980	-	-	79.2	1.4	-	-	80.8	2.0	-	-	84.1	4.1	-	-	84.0	-0.1	-	-	84.8	1.0	-	-	85.4	0.7
1981	-	-	86.7	1.5	-	-	88.7	2.3	-	-	91.8	3.5	-	-	92.4	0.7	-	-	94.6	2.4	-	-	95.8	1.3
1982	-	-	96.4	0.6	-	-	97.6	1.2	-	-	100.8	3.3	-	-	102.8	2.0	-	-	101.5	-1.3	-	-	100.9	-0.6
1983	-	-	99.7	-1.2	-	-	98.3	-1.4	-	-	101.2	3.0	-	-	102.2	1.0	-	-	101.4	-0.8	-	-	98.8	-2.6
1984	-	-	98.4	-0.4	-	-	99.1	0.7	-	-	101.7	2.6	-	-	100.1	-1.6	-	-	101.0	0.9	-	-	99.2	-1.8
1985	-	-	100.0	0.8	-	-	100.0	0.0	-	-	101.1	1.1	-	-	101.0	-0.1	-	-	100.4	-0.6	-	-	98.4	-2.0
1986	-	-	99.2	0.8	-	-	97.6	-1.6	-	-	98.9	1.3	-	-	98.9	0.0	-	-	98.3	-0.6	-	-	95.2	-3.2
1987	-	-	94.8	-0.4	-	-	98.3	3.7	-	-	97.5	-0.8	-	-	97.9	0.4	-	-	97.5	-0.4	-	-	95.9	-1.6
1988	-	-	96.6	0.7	-	-	97.7	1.1	-	-	98.8	1.1	-	-	98.8	0.0	-	-	98.0	-0.8	-	-	99.3	1.3
1989	-	-	100.0	0.7	-	-	99.0	-1.0	-	-	100.6	1.6	-	-	101.7	1.1	-	-	101.8	0.1	-	-	100.4	-1.4
1990	-	-	103.1	2.7	-	-	102.8	-0.3	-	-	104.7	1.8	-	-	106.6	1.8	-	-	107.2	0.6	-	-	105.8	-1.3
1991	-	-	107.6	1.7	-	-	108.0	0.4	-	-	110.2	2.0	-	-	109.8	-0.4	-	-	111.4	1.5	-	-	111.0	-0.4
1992	-	-	109.9	-1.0	-	-	112.7	2.5	-	-	114.6	1.7	-	-	113.9	-0.6	-	-	115.4	1.3	-	-	113.3	-1.8
1993	-	-	114.7	1.2	-	-	114.7	0.0	-	-	117.5	2.4	-	-	117.2	-0.3	-	-	119.0	1.5	-	-	119.3	0.3
1994	-	-	119.9	0.5	-	-	119.0	-0.8	-	-	119.9	0.8	-	-	122.7	2.3	-	-	121.7	-0.8	-	-	119.5	-1.8
1995	-	-	122.3	2.3	-	-	116.5	-4.7	-	-	121.5	4.3	-	-	122.2	0.6	-	-	123.7	1.2	-	-	120.6	-2.5
1996	-	-	122.8	1.8	-	-	123.4	0.5	-	-	124.2	0.6	-	-	124.8	0.5	-	-	125.7	0.7	-	-	123.0	-2.1
1997	-	-	124.9	1.5	-	-	126.0	0.9	-	-	125.7	-0.2	-	-	126.4	0.6	-	-	128.5	1.7	-	-	126.0	-1.9

Source: U.S. Department of Labor, Bureau of Labor Statistics, Division of Consumer Prices and Price Indexes. - indicates no data collected for period.

Houston, TX
Consumer Price Index - Urban Wage Earners
Base 1982-1984 = 100
Housing

For 1976-1997. Columns headed % show percentile change in the index from the previous period for which an index is available.

Year	Jan Index	Jan %	Feb Index	Feb %	Mar Index	Mar %	Apr Index	Apr %	May Index	May %	Jun Index	Jun %	Jul Index	Jul %	Aug Index	Aug %	Sep Index	Sep %	Oct Index	Oct %	Nov Index	Nov %	Dec Index	Dec %
1976	51.2	-	-	-	-	-	52.0	1.6	-	-	-	-	52.9	1.7	-	-	-	-	54.8	3.6	-	-	-	-
1977	55.3	0.9	-	-	-	-	56.7	2.5	-	-	-	-	57.9	2.1	-	-	-	-	58.3	0.7	-	-	-	-
1978	60.1	3.1	-	-	-	-	62.3	3.7	-	-	64.1	2.9	-	-	65.8	2.7	-	-	66.4	0.9	-	-	68.4	3.0
1979	-	-	69.3	1.3	-	-	69.9	0.9	-	-	72.7	4.0	-	-	74.3	2.2	-	-	75.4	1.5	-	-	76.8	1.9
1980	-	-	77.7	1.2	-	-	79.4	2.2	-	-	82.5	3.9	-	-	82.7	0.2	-	-	83.5	1.0	-	-	84.2	0.8
1981	-	-	85.2	1.2	-	-	87.5	2.7	-	-	90.7	3.7	-	-	91.3	0.7	-	-	93.3	2.2	-	-	94.2	1.0
1982	-	-	94.9	0.7	-	-	96.6	1.8	-	-	99.8	3.3	-	-	101.6	1.8	-	-	100.6	-1.0	-	-	100.2	-0.4
1983	-	-	100.8	0.6	-	-	100.3	-0.5	-	-	101.0	0.7	-	-	101.3	0.3	-	-	101.0	-0.3	-	-	97.8	-3.2
1984	-	-	99.7	1.9	-	-	99.7	0.0	-	-	101.9	2.2	-	-	102.8	0.9	-	-	102.4	-0.4	-	-	99.0	-3.3
1985	-	-	100.0	1.0	-	-	99.9	-0.1	-	-	101.0	1.1	-	-	100.9	-0.1	-	-	100.3	-0.6	-	-	98.2	-2.1
1986	-	-	98.9	0.7	-	-	97.4	-1.5	-	-	98.8	1.4	-	-	98.7	-0.1	-	-	98.2	-0.5	-	-	94.9	-3.4
1987	-	-	94.5	-0.4	-	-	97.6	3.3	-	-	97.2	-0.4	-	-	97.1	-0.1	-	-	97.2	0.1	-	-	95.8	-1.4
1988	-	-	96.1	0.3	-	-	97.0	0.9	-	-	98.1	1.1	-	-	98.2	0.1	-	-	97.6	-0.6	-	-	98.7	1.1
1989	-	-	99.3	0.6	-	-	98.5	-0.8	-	-	100.3	1.8	-	-	101.6	1.3	-	-	101.4	-0.2	-	-	100.2	-1.2
1990	-	-	102.2	2.0	-	-	102.4	0.2	-	-	104.5	2.1	-	-	106.4	1.8	-	-	107.2	0.8	-	-	105.6	-1.5
1991	-	-	107.4	1.7	-	-	107.9	0.5	-	-	110.5	2.4	-	-	109.8	-0.6	-	-	111.1	1.2	-	-	111.3	0.2
1992	-	-	109.6	-1.5	-	-	112.6	2.7	-	-	114.7	1.9	-	-	114.2	-0.4	-	-	115.7	1.3	-	-	113.6	-1.8
1993	-	-	114.9	1.1	-	-	115.1	0.2	-	-	118.0	2.5	-	-	117.8	-0.2	-	-	119.4	1.4	-	-	119.7	0.3
1994	-	-	119.9	0.2	-	-	118.9	-0.8	-	-	120.1	1.0	-	-	123.0	2.4	-	-	122.2	-0.7	-	-	120.1	-1.7
1995	-	-	122.3	1.8	-	-	116.4	-4.8	-	-	121.6	4.5	-	-	122.5	0.7	-	-	123.6	0.9	-	-	121.0	-2.1
1996	-	-	122.7	1.4	-	-	122.8	0.1	-	-	124.3	1.2	-	-	125.0	0.6	-	-	125.7	0.6	-	-	123.2	-2.0
1997	-	-	124.3	0.9	-	-	125.5	1.0	-	-	126.0	0.4	-	-	126.9	0.7	-	-	128.2	1.0	-	-	125.7	-2.0

Source: U.S. Department of Labor, Bureau of Labor Statistics, Division of Consumer Prices and Price Indexes. - indicates no data collected for period.

Houston, TX
Consumer Price Index - All Urban Consumers
Base 1982-1984 = 100
Apparel and Upkeep

For 1952-1997. Columns headed % show percentile change in the index from the previous period for which an index is available.

Year	Jan Index	%	Feb Index	%	Mar Index	%	Apr Index	%	May Index	%	Jun Index	%	Jul Index	%	Aug Index	%	Sep Index	%	Oct Index	%	Nov Index	%	Dec Index	%
1952	-	-	-	-	-	-	-	-	-	-	-	-	-	-	-	-	-	-	-	-	-	-	36.1	-
1953	-	-	36.0	-0.3	-	-	-	-	36.0	0.0	-	-	-	-	35.9	-0.3	-	-	-	-	36.4	1.4	-	-
1954	-	-	36.0	-1.1	-	-	-	-	36.0	0.0	-	-	-	-	36.1	0.3	-	-	-	-	36.1	0.0	-	-
1955	-	-	35.9	-0.6	-	-	-	-	36.1	0.6	-	-	-	-	35.8	-0.8	-	-	-	-	36.1	0.8	-	-
1956	-	-	36.4	0.8	-	-	-	-	36.2	-0.5	-	-	-	-	36.7	1.4	-	-	-	-	37.6	2.5	-	-
1957	-	-	37.2	-1.1	-	-	-	-	37.6	1.1	-	-	-	-	37.6	0.0	-	-	-	-	38.2	1.6	-	-
1958	-	-	38.3	0.3	-	-	-	-	38.4	0.3	-	-	-	-	38.3	-0.3	-	-	-	-	38.4	0.3	-	-
1959	-	-	38.7	0.8	-	-	-	-	38.6	-0.3	-	-	-	-	38.8	0.5	-	-	-	-	38.8	0.0	-	-
1960	-	-	38.2	-1.5	-	-	-	-	38.8	1.6	-	-	-	-	38.9	0.3	-	-	-	-	38.8	-0.3	-	-
1961	-	-	38.6	-0.5	-	-	-	-	38.8	0.5	-	-	-	-	38.7	-0.3	-	-	-	-	39.6	2.3	-	-
1962	-	-	39.7	0.3	-	-	-	-	40.0	0.8	-	-	-	-	40.2	0.5	-	-	-	-	40.3	0.2	-	-
1963	-	-	40.4	0.2	-	-	-	-	40.3	-0.2	-	-	-	-	40.8	1.2	-	-	-	-	40.6	-0.5	-	-
1964	-	-	41.0	1.0	-	-	-	-	40.7	-0.7	-	-	-	-	40.7	0.0	-	-	-	-	40.7	0.0	-	-
1965	-	-	40.2	-1.2	-	-	41.0	2.0	-	-	-	-	40.8	-0.5	-	-	-	-	41.3	1.2	-	-	-	-
1966	41.0	-0.7	-	-	-	-	41.4	1.0	-	-	-	-	41.6	0.5	-	-	-	-	42.0	1.0	-	-	-	-
1967	41.2	-1.9	-	-	-	-	41.9	1.7	-	-	-	-	42.0	0.2	-	-	-	-	43.2	2.9	-	-	-	-
1968	43.1	-0.2	-	-	-	-	43.9	1.9	-	-	-	-	44.3	0.9	-	-	-	-	46.0	3.8	-	-	-	-
1969	46.5	1.1	-	-	-	-	47.3	1.7	-	-	-	-	47.7	0.8	-	-	-	-	50.1	5.0	-	-	-	-
1970	49.7	-0.8	-	-	-	-	50.2	1.0	-	-	-	-	50.1	-0.2	-	-	-	-	52.2	4.2	-	-	-	-
1971	50.8	-2.7	-	-	-	-	51.4	1.2	-	-	-	-	50.8	-1.2	-	-	-	-	52.7	3.7	-	-	-	-
1972	52.3	-0.8	-	-	-	-	53.2	1.7	-	-	-	-	52.0	-2.3	-	-	-	-	54.4	4.6	-	-	-	-
1973	53.1	-2.4	-	-	-	-	55.1	3.8	-	-	-	-	53.5	-2.9	-	-	-	-	57.3	7.1	-	-	-	-
1974	57.6	0.5	-	-	-	-	59.3	3.0	-	-	-	-	60.5	2.0	-	-	-	-	62.2	2.8	-	-	-	-
1975	61.8	-0.6	-	-	-	-	63.3	2.4	-	-	-	-	64.3	1.6	-	-	-	-	66.3	3.1	-	-	-	-
1976	65.7	-0.9	-	-	-	-	67.4	2.6	-	-	-	-	66.9	-0.7	-	-	-	-	70.4	5.2	-	-	-	-
1977	70.0	-0.6	-	-	-	-	71.6	2.3	-	-	-	-	71.6	0.0	-	-	-	-	74.0	3.4	-	-	-	-
1978	72.8	-1.6	-	-	-	-	75.7	4.0	-	-	76.6	1.2	-	-	78.0	1.8	-	-	79.9	2.4	-	-	79.7	-0.3
1979	-	-	80.6	1.1	-	-	82.8	2.7	-	-	82.4	-0.5	-	-	83.2	1.0	-	-	85.1	2.3	-	-	86.0	1.1
1980	-	-	88.3	2.7	-	-	88.3	0.0	-	-	87.8	-0.6	-	-	89.4	1.8	-	-	91.6	2.5	-	-	90.7	-1.0
1981	-	-	93.4	3.0	-	-	94.8	1.5	-	-	95.0	0.2	-	-	95.5	0.5	-	-	97.8	2.4	-	-	99.5	1.7
1982	-	-	98.6	-0.9	-	-	98.6	0.0	-	-	97.5	-1.1	-	-	98.0	0.5	-	-	98.7	0.7	-	-	98.7	0.0
1983	-	-	101.5	2.8	-	-	100.0	-1.5	-	-	98.0	-2.0	-	-	98.8	0.8	-	-	100.3	1.5	-	-	100.6	0.3
1984	-	-	100.3	-0.3	-	-	100.8	0.5	-	-	102.1	1.3	-	-	102.1	0.0	-	-	102.6	0.5	-	-	104.0	1.4
1985	-	-	104.2	0.2	-	-	104.4	0.2	-	-	103.8	-0.6	-	-	104.2	0.4	-	-	104.9	0.7	-	-	105.5	0.6
1986	-	-	106.1	0.6	-	-	106.6	0.5	-	-	104.6	-1.9	-	-	107.6	2.9	-	-	105.7	-1.8	-	-	106.1	0.4
1987	-	-	107.9	1.7	-	-	112.8	4.5	-	-	111.6	-1.1	-	-	115.4	3.4	-	-	118.4	2.6	-	-	118.3	-0.1
1988	-	-	121.3	2.5	-	-	117.4	-3.2	-	-	122.0	3.9	-	-	121.1	-0.7	-	-	125.3	3.5	-	-	119.9	-4.3
1989	-	-	122.7	2.3	-	-	126.7	3.3	-	-	121.0	-4.5	-	-	122.0	0.8	-	-	127.5	4.5	-	-	124.9	-2.0
1990	-	-	136.9	9.6	-	-	130.0	-5.0	-	-	133.3	2.5	-	-	132.5	-0.6	-	-	134.9	1.8	-	-	128.6	-4.7
1991	-	-	138.2	7.5	-	-	133.3	-3.5	-	-	135.3	1.5	-	-	129.7	-4.1	-	-	138.8	7.0	-	-	135.0	-2.7
1992	-	-	137.1	1.6	-	-	135.8	-0.9	-	-	134.4	-1.0	-	-	141.4	5.2	-	-	137.8	-2.5	-	-	126.1	-8.5
1993	-	-	140.4	11.3	-	-	142.4	1.4	-	-	137.8	-3.2	-	-	132.2	-4.1	-	-	155.4	17.5	-	-	151.3	-2.6
1994	-	-	153.8	1.7	-	-	149.1	-3.1	-	-	145.3	-2.5	-	-	144.1	-0.8	-	-	147.3	2.2	-	-	136.8	-7.1

[Continued]

Houston, TX
Consumer Price Index - All Urban Consumers
Base 1982-1984 = 100
Apparel and Upkeep

[Continued]

For 1952-1997. Columns headed % show percentile change in the index from the previous period for which an index is available.

Year	Jan Index	%	Feb Index	%	Mar Index	%	Apr Index	%	May Index	%	Jun Index	%	Jul Index	%	Aug Index	%	Sep Index	%	Oct Index	%	Nov Index	%	Dec Index	%
1995	-	-	139.1	1.7	-	-	140.9	1.3	-	-	131.5	-6.7	-	-	134.0	1.9	-	-	138.4	3.3	-	-	149.1	7.7
1996	-	-	138.0	-7.4	-	-	142.1	3.0	-	-	131.4	-7.5	-	-	135.3	3.0	-	-	133.9	-1.0	-	-	145.0	8.3
1997	-	-	140.4	-3.2	-	-	142.1	1.2	-	-	138.0	-2.9	-	-	139.9	1.4	-	-	147.8	5.6	-	-	144.4	-2.3

Source: U.S. Department of Labor, Bureau of Labor Statistics, Division of Consumer Prices and Price Indexes. - indicates no data collected for period.

Houston, TX
Consumer Price Index - Urban Wage Earners
Base 1982-1984 = 100
Apparel and Upkeep

For 1952-1997. Columns headed % show percentile change in the index from the previous period for which an index is available.

Year	Jan Index	%	Feb Index	%	Mar Index	%	Apr Index	%	May Index	%	Jun Index	%	Jul Index	%	Aug Index	%	Sep Index	%	Oct Index	%	Nov Index	%	Dec Index	%
1952	-	-	-	-	-	-	-	-	-	-	-	-	-	-	-	-	-	-	-	-	-	-	36.8	-
1953	-	-	36.7	-0.3	-	-	-	-	36.7	0.0	-	-	-	-	36.6	-0.3	-	-	-	-	37.1	1.4	-	-
1954	-	-	36.7	-1.1	-	-	-	-	36.7	0.0	-	-	-	-	36.8	0.3	-	-	-	-	36.8	0.0	-	-
1955	-	-	36.6	-0.5	-	-	-	-	36.8	0.5	-	-	-	-	36.4	-1.1	-	-	-	-	36.8	1.1	-	-
1956	-	-	37.1	0.8	-	-	-	-	36.9	-0.5	-	-	-	-	37.4	1.4	-	-	-	-	38.3	2.4	-	-
1957	-	-	37.9	-1.0	-	-	-	-	38.3	1.1	-	-	-	-	38.3	0.0	-	-	-	-	38.9	1.6	-	-
1958	-	-	39.1	0.5	-	-	-	-	39.1	0.0	-	-	-	-	39.0	-0.3	-	-	-	-	39.2	0.5	-	-
1959	-	-	39.4	0.5	-	-	-	-	39.3	-0.3	-	-	-	-	39.5	0.5	-	-	-	-	39.5	0.0	-	-
1960	-	-	38.9	-1.5	-	-	-	-	39.5	1.5	-	-	-	-	39.6	0.3	-	-	-	-	39.5	-0.3	-	-
1961	-	-	39.4	-0.3	-	-	-	-	39.5	0.3	-	-	-	-	39.4	-0.3	-	-	-	-	40.3	2.3	-	-
1962	-	-	40.4	0.2	-	-	-	-	40.8	1.0	-	-	-	-	40.9	0.2	-	-	-	-	41.1	0.5	-	-
1963	-	-	41.2	0.2	-	-	-	-	41.1	-0.2	-	-	-	-	41.6	1.2	-	-	-	-	41.4	-0.5	-	-
1964	-	-	41.8	1.0	-	-	-	-	41.4	-1.0	-	-	-	-	41.5	0.2	-	-	-	-	41.5	0.0	-	-
1965	-	-	41.0	-1.2	-	-	41.7	1.7	-	-	-	-	41.6	-0.2	-	-	-	-	42.0	1.0	-	-	-	-
1966	41.8	-0.5	-	-	-	-	42.2	1.0	-	-	-	-	42.3	0.2	-	-	-	-	42.8	1.2	-	-	-	-
1967	42.0	-1.9	-	-	-	-	42.7	1.7	-	-	-	-	42.8	0.2	-	-	-	-	44.0	2.8	-	-	-	-
1968	43.9	-0.2	-	-	-	-	44.8	2.1	-	-	-	-	45.1	0.7	-	-	-	-	46.9	4.0	-	-	-	-
1969	47.3	0.9	-	-	-	-	48.2	1.9	-	-	-	-	48.6	0.8	-	-	-	-	51.0	4.9	-	-	-	-
1970	50.6	-0.8	-	-	-	-	51.2	1.2	-	-	-	-	51.0	-0.4	-	-	-	-	53.2	4.3	-	-	-	-
1971	51.8	-2.6	-	-	-	-	52.4	1.2	-	-	-	-	51.7	-1.3	-	-	-	-	53.7	3.9	-	-	-	-
1972	53.3	-0.7	-	-	-	-	54.3	1.9	-	-	-	-	53.0	-2.4	-	-	-	-	55.5	4.7	-	-	-	-
1973	54.1	-2.5	-	-	-	-	56.1	3.7	-	-	-	-	54.5	-2.9	-	-	-	-	58.4	7.2	-	-	-	-
1974	58.7	0.5	-	-	-	-	60.5	3.1	-	-	-	-	61.7	2.0	-	-	-	-	63.4	2.8	-	-	-	-
1975	63.0	-0.6	-	-	-	-	64.5	2.4	-	-	-	-	65.5	1.6	-	-	-	-	67.6	3.2	-	-	-	-
1976	67.0	-0.9	-	-	-	-	68.6	2.4	-	-	-	-	68.2	-0.6	-	-	-	-	71.8	5.3	-	-	-	-
1977	71.4	-0.6	-	-	-	-	72.9	2.1	-	-	-	-	72.9	0.0	-	-	-	-	75.4	3.4	-	-	-	-
1978	74.1	-1.7	-	-	-	-	77.2	4.2	-	-	78.4	1.6	-	-	79.4	1.3	-	-	81.1	2.1	-	-	81.9	1.0
1979	-	-	83.1	1.5	-	-	85.3	2.6	-	-	84.4	-1.1	-	-	85.3	1.1	-	-	87.0	2.0	-	-	88.2	1.4
1980	-	-	89.2	1.1	-	-	89.7	0.6	-	-	89.4	-0.3	-	-	90.8	1.6	-	-	91.5	0.8	-	-	92.2	0.8
1981	-	-	94.6	2.6	-	-	95.8	1.3	-	-	95.2	-0.6	-	-	96.7	1.6	-	-	98.5	1.9	-	-	99.0	0.5
1982	-	-	98.3	-0.7	-	-	98.5	0.2	-	-	97.9	-0.6	-	-	98.2	0.3	-	-	98.8	0.6	-	-	99.2	0.4
1983	-	-	101.3	2.1	-	-	100.0	-1.3	-	-	98.0	-2.0	-	-	98.8	0.8	-	-	100.3	1.5	-	-	100.8	0.5
1984	-	-	100.4	-0.4	-	-	100.4	0.0	-	-	102.0	1.6	-	-	101.9	-0.1	-	-	102.7	0.8	-	-	103.8	1.1
1985	-	-	103.8	0.0	-	-	104.1	0.3	-	-	103.8	-0.3	-	-	104.1	0.3	-	-	104.7	0.6	-	-	105.3	0.6
1986	-	-	105.8	0.5	-	-	106.3	0.5	-	-	104.5	-1.7	-	-	106.9	2.3	-	-	105.5	-1.3	-	-	105.3	-0.2
1987	-	-	107.4	2.0	-	-	111.7	4.0	-	-	110.7	-0.9	-	-	114.7	3.6	-	-	117.2	2.2	-	-	117.6	0.3
1988	-	-	120.9	2.8	-	-	117.0	-3.2	-	-	122.1	4.4	-	-	121.2	-0.7	-	-	125.6	3.6	-	-	120.5	-4.1
1989	-	-	123.1	2.2	-	-	126.7	2.9	-	-	121.9	-3.8	-	-	122.0	0.1	-	-	126.8	3.9	-	-	124.8	-1.6
1990	-	-	137.4	10.1	-	-	130.7	-4.9	-	-	133.5	2.1	-	-	133.2	-0.2	-	-	134.8	1.2	-	-	127.8	-5.2
1991	-	-	137.1	7.3	-	-	132.7	-3.2	-	-	134.7	1.5	-	-	128.2	-4.8	-	-	137.9	7.6	-	-	134.2	-2.7
1992	-	-	136.4	1.6	-	-	134.7	-1.2	-	-	133.0	-1.3	-	-	139.2	4.7	-	-	136.5	-1.9	-	-	124.6	-8.7
1993	-	-	137.3	10.2	-	-	138.7	1.0	-	-	134.1	-3.3	-	-	130.2	-2.9	-	-	151.7	16.5	-	-	147.2	-3.0
1994	-	-	152.2	3.4	-	-	147.8	-2.9	-	-	144.3	-2.4	-	-	143.2	-0.8	-	-	146.1	2.0	-	-	136.1	-6.8

[Continued]

Houston, TX
Consumer Price Index - Urban Wage Earners
Base 1982-1984 = 100
Apparel and Upkeep

[Continued]

For 1952-1997. Columns headed % show percentile change in the index from the previous period for which an index is available.

Year	Jan Index	%	Feb Index	%	Mar Index	%	Apr Index	%	May Index	%	Jun Index	%	Jul Index	%	Aug Index	%	Sep Index	%	Oct Index	%	Nov Index	%	Dec Index	%
1995	-	-	139.0	2.1	-	-	139.8	0.6	-	-	132.2	-5.4	-	-	133.9	1.3	-	-	137.8	2.9	-	-	145.7	5.7
1996	-	-	138.4	-5.0	-	-	141.4	2.2	-	-	130.3	-7.9	-	-	134.5	3.2	-	-	132.4	-1.6	-	-	143.7	8.5
1997	-	-	139.3	-3.1	-	-	141.3	1.4	-	-	137.9	-2.4	-	-	140.0	1.5	-	-	146.4	4.6	-	-	142.1	-2.9

Source: U.S. Department of Labor, Bureau of Labor Statistics, Division of Consumer Prices and Price Indexes. - indicates no data collected for period.

Houston, TX
Consumer Price Index - All Urban Consumers
Base 1982-1984 = 100
Transportation

For 1947-1997. Columns headed % show percentile change in the index from the previous period for which an index is available.

Year	Jan Index	%	Feb Index	%	Mar Index	%	Apr Index	%	May Index	%	Jun Index	%	Jul Index	%	Aug Index	%	Sep Index	%	Oct Index	%	Nov Index	%	Dec Index	%
1947	19.9	-	20.1	1.0	20.2	0.5	20.4	1.0	20.5	0.5	20.5	0.0	20.6	0.5	20.8	1.0	21.0	1.0	21.4	1.9	21.9	2.3	22.0	0.5
1948	22.6	2.7	22.7	0.4	22.7	0.0	22.7	0.0	22.7	0.0	22.8	0.4	23.2	1.8	23.7	2.2	23.8	0.4	23.9	0.4	24.0	0.4	24.0	0.0
1949	24.0	0.0	24.3	1.2	24.3	0.0	24.4	0.4	24.4	0.0	24.3	-0.4	25.0	2.9	25.0	0.0	25.0	0.0	25.1	0.4	25.2	0.4	25.2	0.0
1950	25.3	0.4	25.3	0.0	25.3	0.0	25.3	0.0	25.5	0.8	25.5	0.0	25.6	0.4	25.7	0.4	25.7	0.0	25.7	0.0	25.7	0.0	27.2	5.8
1951	27.3	0.4	27.5	0.7	27.8	1.1	27.7	-0.4	27.7	0.0	27.9	0.7	27.9	0.0	27.9	0.0	28.2	1.1	28.2	0.0	28.6	1.4	28.6	0.0
1952	28.0	-2.1	28.4	1.4	28.4	0.0	28.4	0.0	28.4	0.0	28.4	0.0	28.4	0.0	28.4	0.0	28.4	0.0	29.2	2.8	29.2	0.0	29.2	0.0
1953	-	-	29.0	-0.7	-	-	-	-	29.0	0.0	-	-	-	-	29.1	0.3	-	-	-	-	29.0	-0.3	-	-
1954	-	-	28.7	-1.0	-	-	-	-	28.6	-0.3	-	-	-	-	28.2	-1.4	-	-	-	-	28.8	2.1	-	-
1955	-	-	28.3	-1.7	-	-	-	-	27.9	-1.4	-	-	-	-	27.8	-0.4	-	-	-	-	28.9	4.0	-	-
1956	-	-	28.7	-0.7	-	-	-	-	28.5	-0.7	-	-	-	-	28.9	1.4	-	-	-	-	29.7	2.8	-	-
1957	-	-	30.3	2.0	-	-	-	-	30.8	1.7	-	-	-	-	31.1	1.0	-	-	-	-	31.8	2.3	-	-
1958	-	-	29.0	-8.8	-	-	-	-	31.5	8.6	-	-	-	-	32.4	2.9	-	-	-	-	32.7	0.9	-	-
1959	-	-	32.5	-0.6	-	-	-	-	32.9	1.2	-	-	-	-	33.2	0.9	-	-	-	-	33.4	0.6	-	-
1960	-	-	33.7	0.9	-	-	-	-	31.4	-6.8	-	-	-	-	33.6	7.0	-	-	-	-	33.4	-0.6	-	-
1961	-	-	31.5	-5.7	-	-	-	-	33.4	6.0	-	-	-	-	32.6	-2.4	-	-	-	-	34.7	6.4	-	-
1962	-	-	34.6	-0.3	-	-	-	-	34.6	0.0	-	-	-	-	34.2	-1.2	-	-	-	-	33.2	-2.9	-	-
1963	-	-	33.9	2.1	-	-	-	-	32.4	-4.4	-	-	-	-	33.8	4.3	-	-	-	-	34.3	1.5	-	-
1964	-	-	34.0	-0.9	-	-	-	-	34.5	1.5	-	-	-	-	34.4	-0.3	-	-	-	-	34.6	0.6	-	-
1965	-	-	33.8	-2.3	-	-	34.1	0.9	-	-	-	-	34.0	-0.3	-	-	-	-	34.6	1.8	-	-	-	-
1966	34.6	0.0	-	-	-	-	34.6	0.0	-	-	-	-	35.0	1.2	-	-	-	-	35.0	0.0	-	-	-	-
1967	35.4	1.1	-	-	-	-	35.7	0.8	-	-	-	-	35.9	0.6	-	-	-	-	36.7	2.2	-	-	-	-
1968	36.7	0.0	-	-	-	-	37.0	0.8	-	-	-	-	37.0	0.0	-	-	-	-	37.3	0.8	-	-	-	-
1969	37.7	1.1	-	-	-	-	38.4	1.9	-	-	-	-	38.3	-0.3	-	-	-	-	38.8	1.3	-	-	-	-
1970	38.6	-0.5	-	-	-	-	39.0	1.0	-	-	-	-	38.9	-0.3	-	-	-	-	39.0	0.3	-	-	-	-
1971	41.3	5.9	-	-	-	-	40.8	-1.2	-	-	-	-	40.3	-1.2	-	-	-	-	40.8	1.2	-	-	-	-
1972	41.1	0.7	-	-	-	-	41.7	1.5	-	-	-	-	41.7	0.0	-	-	-	-	41.0	-1.7	-	-	-	-
1973	41.1	0.2	-	-	-	-	41.9	1.9	-	-	-	-	42.3	1.0	-	-	-	-	42.4	0.2	-	-	-	-
1974	43.9	3.5	-	-	-	-	45.9	4.6	-	-	-	-	48.0	4.6	-	-	-	-	49.6	3.3	-	-	-	-
1975	49.1	-1.0	-	-	-	-	50.4	2.6	-	-	-	-	52.9	5.0	-	-	-	-	53.4	0.9	-	-	-	-
1976	54.1	1.3	-	-	-	-	54.6	0.9	-	-	-	-	56.5	3.5	-	-	-	-	58.3	3.2	-	-	-	-
1977	58.6	0.5	-	-	-	-	60.4	3.1	-	-	-	-	61.3	1.5	-	-	-	-	60.7	-1.0	-	-	-	-
1978	61.1	0.7	-	-	-	-	61.6	0.8	-	-	62.5	1.5	-	-	63.3	1.3	-	-	64.1	1.3	-	-	65.1	1.6
1979	-	-	66.1	1.5	-	-	68.9	4.2	-	-	72.5	5.2	-	-	75.3	3.9	-	-	76.0	0.9	-	-	77.9	2.5
1980	-	-	82.8	6.3	-	-	85.4	3.1	-	-	86.1	0.8	-	-	86.6	0.6	-	-	87.0	0.5	-	-	88.2	1.4
1981	-	-	92.0	4.3	-	-	93.7	1.8	-	-	95.3	1.7	-	-	95.1	-0.2	-	-	97.0	2.0	-	-	97.9	0.9
1982	-	-	96.8	-1.1	-	-	93.9	-3.0	-	-	98.3	4.7	-	-	99.2	0.9	-	-	98.8	-0.4	-	-	99.2	0.4
1983	-	-	96.7	-2.5	-	-	97.3	0.6	-	-	98.8	1.5	-	-	99.9	1.1	-	-	101.1	1.2	-	-	100.9	-0.2
1984	-	-	100.2	-0.7	-	-	101.4	1.2	-	-	102.5	1.1	-	-	105.3	2.7	-	-	106.1	0.8	-	-	105.7	-0.4
1985	-	-	104.0	-1.6	-	-	105.7	1.6	-	-	106.9	1.1	-	-	106.8	-0.1	-	-	106.7	-0.1	-	-	107.1	0.4
1986	-	-	105.2	-1.8	-	-	97.2	-7.6	-	-	99.1	2.0	-	-	96.6	-2.5	-	-	97.7	1.1	-	-	97.3	-0.4
1987	-	-	100.3	3.1	-	-	101.3	1.0	-	-	102.8	1.5	-	-	103.9	1.1	-	-	104.3	0.4	-	-	104.2	-0.1
1988	-	-	102.9	-1.2	-	-	102.9	0.0	-	-	104.2	1.3	-	-	105.2	1.0	-	-	106.1	0.9	-	-	106.4	0.3
1989	-	-	106.9	0.5	-	-	108.5	1.5	-	-	110.3	1.7	-	-	109.1	-1.1	-	-	110.0	0.8	-	-	111.4	1.3
1990	-	-	112.8	1.3	-	-	112.5	-0.3	-	-	113.1	0.5	-	-	114.4	1.1	-	-	122.1	6.7	-	-	124.3	1.8
1991	-	-	120.1	-3.4	-	-	115.4	-3.9	-	-	118.4	2.6	-	-	118.3	-0.1	-	-	122.0	3.1	-	-	123.2	1.0

[Continued]

Houston, TX
Consumer Price Index - All Urban Consumers
Base 1982-1984 = 100
Transportation
[Continued]

For 1947-1997. Columns headed % show percentile change in the index from the previous period for which an index is available.

Year	Jan Index	%	Feb Index	%	Mar Index	%	Apr Index	%	May Index	%	Jun Index	%	Jul Index	%	Aug Index	%	Sep Index	%	Oct Index	%	Nov Index	%	Dec Index	%
1992	-	-	121.0	-1.8	-	-	122.0	0.8	-	-	123.0	0.8	-	-	123.1	0.1	-	-	124.3	1.0	-	-	124.3	0.0
1993	-	-	124.8	0.4	-	-	127.2	1.9	-	-	127.8	0.5	-	-	128.8	0.8	-	-	131.2	1.9	-	-	130.9	-0.2
1994	-	-	130.6	-0.2	-	-	131.0	0.3	-	-	132.2	0.9	-	-	134.5	1.7	-	-	134.9	0.3	-	-	135.4	0.4
1995	-	-	135.9	0.4	-	-	136.7	0.6	-	-	139.0	1.7	-	-	136.6	-1.7	-	-	137.8	0.9	-	-	135.9	-1.4
1996	-	-	137.6	1.3	-	-	141.4	2.8	-	-	141.4	0.0	-	-	140.3	-0.8	-	-	140.5	0.1	-	-	143.0	1.8
1997	-	-	142.2	-0.6	-	-	143.2	0.7	-	-	141.4	-1.3	-	-	140.9	-0.4	-	-	141.0	0.1	-	-	139.0	-1.4

Source: U.S. Department of Labor, Bureau of Labor Statistics, Division of Consumer Prices and Price Indexes. - indicates no data collected for period.

Houston, TX
Consumer Price Index - Urban Wage Earners
Base 1982-1984 = 100
Transportation

For 1947-1997. Columns headed % show percentile change in the index from the previous period for which an index is available.

Year	Jan Index	%	Feb Index	%	Mar Index	%	Apr Index	%	May Index	%	Jun Index	%	Jul Index	%	Aug Index	%	Sep Index	%	Oct Index	%	Nov Index	%	Dec Index	%
1947	19.8	-	20.1	1.5	20.1	0.0	20.3	1.0	20.4	0.5	20.4	0.0	20.5	0.5	20.7	1.0	21.0	1.4	21.3	1.4	21.8	2.3	21.9	0.5
1948	22.5	2.7	22.6	0.4	22.6	0.0	22.6	0.0	22.6	0.0	22.7	0.4	23.2	2.2	23.7	2.2	23.7	0.0	23.8	0.4	23.9	0.4	23.9	0.0
1949	23.9	0.0	24.2	1.3	24.2	0.0	24.3	0.4	24.3	0.0	24.2	-0.4	24.9	2.9	24.9	0.0	24.9	0.0	25.0	0.4	25.1	0.4	25.1	0.0
1950	25.2	0.4	25.2	0.0	25.2	0.0	25.2	0.0	25.4	0.8	25.4	0.0	25.5	0.4	25.6	0.4	25.6	0.0	25.6	0.0	25.6	0.0	27.1	5.9
1951	27.2	0.4	27.4	0.7	27.7	1.1	27.6	-0.4	27.6	0.0	27.8	0.7	27.8	0.0	27.8	0.0	28.1	1.1	28.1	0.0	28.5	1.4	28.5	0.0
1952	27.9	-2.1	28.2	1.1	28.2	0.0	28.2	0.0	28.2	0.0	28.2	0.0	28.2	0.0	28.2	0.0	28.3	0.4	29.0	2.5	29.0	0.0	29.0	0.0
1953	-		28.9	-0.3	-		-		28.9	0.0	-		-		29.0	0.3	-		-		28.9	-0.3	-	
1954	-		28.6	-1.0	-		-		28.5	-0.3	-		-		28.1	-1.4	-		-		28.7	2.1	-	
1955	-		28.2	-1.7	-		-		27.8	-1.4	-		-		27.7	-0.4	-		-		28.8	4.0	-	
1956	-		28.6	-0.7	-		-		28.4	-0.7	-		-		28.8	1.4	-		-		29.6	2.8	-	
1957	-		30.1	1.7	-		-		30.7	2.0	-		-		30.9	0.7	-		-		31.7	2.6	-	
1958	-		28.9	-8.8	-		-		31.4	8.7	-		-		32.2	2.5	-		-		32.6	1.2	-	
1959	-		32.4	-0.6	-		-		32.8	1.2	-		-		33.0	0.6	-		-		33.2	0.6	-	
1960	-		33.6	1.2	-		-		31.3	-6.8	-		-		33.5	7.0	-		-		33.2	-0.9	-	
1961	-		31.4	-5.4	-		-		33.2	5.7	-		-		32.5	-2.1	-		-		34.5	6.2	-	
1962	-		34.4	-0.3	-		-		34.5	0.3	-		-		34.1	-1.2	-		-		33.0	-3.2	-	
1963	-		33.8	2.4	-		-		32.3	-4.4	-		-		33.6	4.0	-		-		34.1	1.5	-	
1964	-		33.9	-0.6	-		-		34.3	1.2	-		-		34.2	-0.3	-		-		34.4	0.6	-	
1965	-		33.6	-2.3	-		34.0	1.2	-		-		33.9	-0.3	-		-		34.5	1.8	-		-	
1966	34.4	-0.3	-		-		34.5	0.3	-		-		34.9	1.2	-		-		34.9	0.0	-		-	
1967	35.2	0.9	-		-		35.6	1.1	-		-		35.7	0.3	-		-		36.6	2.5	-		-	
1968	36.6	0.0	-		-		36.8	0.5	-		-		36.9	0.3	-		-		37.1	0.5	-		-	
1969	37.5	1.1	-		-		38.3	2.1	-		-		38.2	-0.3	-		-		38.7	1.3	-		-	
1970	38.5	-0.5	-		-		38.8	0.8	-		-		38.8	0.0	-		-		38.9	0.3	-		-	
1971	41.1	5.7	-		-		40.6	-1.2	-		-		40.1	-1.2	-		-		40.6	1.2	-		-	
1972	41.0	1.0	-		-		41.5	1.2	-		-		41.5	0.0	-		-		40.8	-1.7	-		-	
1973	41.0	0.5	-		-		41.7	1.7	-		-		42.1	1.0	-		-		42.2	0.2	-		-	
1974	43.8	3.8	-		-		45.7	4.3	-		-		47.8	4.6	-		-		49.4	3.3	-		-	
1975	48.9	-1.0	-		-		50.2	2.7	-		-		52.7	5.0	-		-		53.2	0.9	-		-	
1976	53.9	1.3	-		-		54.4	0.9	-		-		56.2	3.3	-		-		58.1	3.4	-		-	
1977	58.4	0.5	-		-		60.2	3.1	-		-		61.1	1.5	-		-		60.4	-1.1	-		-	
1978	60.8	0.7	-		-		61.3	0.8	-		62.5	2.0	-		63.4	1.4	-		64.1	1.1	-		65.2	1.7
1979	-		66.2	1.5	-		69.2	4.5	-		72.7	5.1	-		75.0	3.2	-		75.4	0.5	-		77.1	2.3
1980	-		81.5	5.7	-		83.9	2.9	-		84.8	1.1	-		85.2	0.5	-		85.8	0.7	-		86.9	1.3
1981	-		90.4	4.0	-		92.2	2.0	-		93.9	1.8	-		94.2	0.3	-		95.4	1.3	-		97.0	1.7
1982	-		95.9	-1.1	-		93.5	-2.5	-		97.8	4.6	-		98.7	0.9	-		98.3	-0.4	-		98.7	0.4
1983	-		96.5	-2.2	-		97.1	0.6	-		98.6	1.5	-		99.8	1.2	-		101.2	1.4	-		101.2	0.0
1984	-		100.6	-0.6	-		102.1	1.5	-		103.3	1.2	-		106.0	2.6	-		106.8	0.8	-		106.4	-0.4
1985	-		104.8	-1.5	-		106.3	1.4	-		107.3	0.9	-		107.2	-0.1	-		107.2	0.0	-		107.5	0.3
1986	-		105.7	-1.7	-		98.5	-6.8	-		100.1	1.6	-		97.9	-2.2	-		98.9	1.0	-		98.5	-0.4
1987	-		102.2	3.8	-		103.4	1.2	-		105.0	1.5	-		106.2	1.1	-		107.0	0.8	-		106.7	-0.3
1988	-		105.5	-1.1	-		105.2	-0.3	-		106.6	1.3	-		108.0	1.3	-		108.7	0.6	-		109.0	0.3
1989	-		109.4	0.4	-		111.4	1.8	-		113.3	1.7	-		112.0	-1.1	-		112.6	0.5	-		113.9	1.2
1990	-		115.3	1.2	-		115.0	-0.3	-		115.6	0.5	-		117.1	1.3	-		125.4	7.1	-		127.5	1.7
1991	-		122.3	-4.1	-		117.6	-3.8	-		121.0	2.9	-		120.8	-0.2	-		124.6	3.1	-		125.6	0.8

[Continued]

Houston, TX
Consumer Price Index - Urban Wage Earners
Base 1982-1984 = 100
Transportation
[Continued]

For 1947-1997. Columns headed % show percentile change in the index from the previous period for which an index is available.

Year	Jan Index	%	Feb Index	%	Mar Index	%	Apr Index	%	May Index	%	Jun Index	%	Jul Index	%	Aug Index	%	Sep Index	%	Oct Index	%	Nov Index	%	Dec Index	%
1992	-	-	123.0	-2.1	-	-	123.9	0.7	-	-	125.6	1.4	-	-	125.8	0.2	-	-	126.5	0.6	-	-	126.5	0.0
1993	-	-	126.1	-0.3	-	-	128.5	1.9	-	-	129.4	0.7	-	-	130.1	0.5	-	-	132.3	1.7	-	-	131.5	-0.6
1994	-	-	130.9	-0.5	-	-	131.6	0.5	-	-	133.4	1.4	-	-	135.9	1.9	-	-	136.6	0.5	-	-	137.4	0.6
1995	-	-	137.7	0.2	-	-	138.3	0.4	-	-	140.5	1.6	-	-	138.5	-1.4	-	-	138.9	0.3	-	-	137.7	-0.9
1996	-	-	139.1	1.0	-	-	143.2	2.9	-	-	143.5	0.2	-	-	142.0	-1.0	-	-	142.6	0.4	-	-	144.8	1.5
1997	-	-	144.0	-0.6	-	-	144.0	0.0	-	-	142.7	-0.9	-	-	142.8	0.1	-	-	142.4	-0.3	-	-	140.5	-1.3

Source: U.S. Department of Labor, Bureau of Labor Statistics, Division of Consumer Prices and Price Indexes. - indicates no data collected for period.

Houston, TX
Consumer Price Index - All Urban Consumers
Base 1982-1984 = 100
Medical Care

For 1947-1997. Columns headed % show percentile change in the index from the previous period for which an index is available.

Year	Jan Index	%	Feb Index	%	Mar Index	%	Apr Index	%	May Index	%	Jun Index	%	Jul Index	%	Aug Index	%	Sep Index	%	Oct Index	%	Nov Index	%	Dec Index	%
1947	14.1	-	14.2	0.7	14.2	0.0	14.3	0.7	14.5	1.4	14.6	0.7	14.5	-0.7	14.5	0.0	14.6	0.7	14.7	0.7	14.7	0.0	14.7	0.0
1948	14.7	0.0	14.7	0.0	14.9	1.4	14.8	-0.7	14.8	0.0	14.9	0.7	14.9	0.0	14.9	0.0	14.9	0.0	14.9	0.0	14.9	0.0	14.9	0.0
1949	15.1	1.3	15.1	0.0	15.1	0.0	15.1	0.0	15.2	0.7	15.3	0.7	15.3	0.0	15.3	0.0	15.3	0.0	15.3	0.0	15.2	-0.7	15.5	2.0
1950	15.5	0.0	15.5	0.0	15.5	0.0	15.5	0.0	15.5	0.0	15.5	0.0	15.5	0.0	15.6	0.6	15.6	0.0	15.6	0.0	15.6	0.0	15.6	0.0
1951	15.6	0.0	15.6	0.0	15.8	1.3	15.8	0.0	15.8	0.0	15.8	0.0	15.8	0.0	15.8	0.0	15.8	0.0	16.6	5.1	16.6	0.0	16.7	0.6
1952	16.6	-0.6	16.6	0.0	16.6	0.0	16.7	0.6	16.7	0.0	16.7	0.0	16.7	0.0	16.7	0.0	16.7	0.0	16.7	0.0	16.7	0.0	17.4	4.2
1953	-	-	17.4	0.0	-	-	-	-	17.6	1.1	-	-	-	-	17.6	0.0	-	-	-	-	17.7	0.6	-	-
1954	-	-	17.7	0.0	-	-	-	-	17.7	0.0	-	-	-	-	17.8	0.6	-	-	-	-	17.8	0.0	-	-
1955	-	-	17.8	0.0	-	-	-	-	18.5	3.9	-	-	-	-	18.5	0.0	-	-	-	-	18.9	2.2	-	-
1956	-	-	18.9	0.0	-	-	-	-	18.8	-0.5	-	-	-	-	19.0	1.1	-	-	-	-	19.1	0.5	-	-
1957	-	-	19.3	1.0	-	-	-	-	19.2	-0.5	-	-	-	-	19.1	-0.5	-	-	-	-	19.2	0.5	-	-
1958	-	-	19.6	2.1	-	-	-	-	19.6	0.0	-	-	-	-	19.6	0.0	-	-	-	-	19.8	1.0	-	-
1959	-	-	19.8	0.0	-	-	-	-	20.1	1.5	-	-	-	-	20.1	0.0	-	-	-	-	20.1	0.0	-	-
1960	-	-	20.3	1.0	-	-	-	-	20.6	1.5	-	-	-	-	20.6	0.0	-	-	-	-	20.6	0.0	-	-
1961	-	-	20.6	0.0	-	-	-	-	20.8	1.0	-	-	-	-	20.8	0.0	-	-	-	-	20.9	0.5	-	-
1962	-	-	20.9	0.0	-	-	-	-	21.0	0.5	-	-	-	-	21.0	0.0	-	-	-	-	21.2	1.0	-	-
1963	-	-	21.5	1.4	-	-	-	-	21.6	0.5	-	-	-	-	21.6	0.0	-	-	-	-	21.8	0.9	-	-
1964	-	-	22.0	0.9	-	-	-	-	22.2	0.9	-	-	-	-	22.2	0.0	-	-	-	-	22.2	0.0	-	-
1965	-	-	22.5	1.4	-	-	22.7	0.9	-	-	-	-	22.8	0.4	-	-	-	-	22.9	0.4	-	-	-	-
1966	23.0	0.4	-	-	-	-	23.1	0.4	-	-	-	-	23.3	0.9	-	-	-	-	23.9	2.6	-	-	-	-
1967	24.4	2.1	-	-	-	-	24.7	1.2	-	-	-	-	24.8	0.4	-	-	-	-	25.2	1.6	-	-	-	-
1968	25.7	2.0	-	-	-	-	25.8	0.4	-	-	-	-	26.1	1.2	-	-	-	-	26.7	2.3	-	-	-	-
1969	27.6	3.4	-	-	-	-	28.3	2.5	-	-	-	-	28.5	0.7	-	-	-	-	29.1	2.1	-	-	-	-
1970	29.8	2.4	-	-	-	-	30.5	2.3	-	-	-	-	30.6	0.3	-	-	-	-	30.8	0.7	-	-	-	-
1971	31.5	2.3	-	-	-	-	31.9	1.3	-	-	-	-	33.0	3.4	-	-	-	-	32.7	-0.9	-	-	-	-
1972	32.8	0.3	-	-	-	-	33.6	2.4	-	-	-	-	33.6	0.0	-	-	-	-	34.1	1.5	-	-	-	-
1973	34.4	0.9	-	-	-	-	34.7	0.9	-	-	-	-	34.8	0.3	-	-	-	-	35.6	2.3	-	-	-	-
1974	36.3	2.0	-	-	-	-	36.5	0.6	-	-	-	-	38.3	4.9	-	-	-	-	39.2	2.3	-	-	-	-
1975	40.6	3.6	-	-	-	-	42.0	3.4	-	-	-	-	43.6	3.8	-	-	-	-	45.0	3.2	-	-	-	-
1976	45.5	1.1	-	-	-	-	46.7	2.6	-	-	-	-	48.0	2.8	-	-	-	-	49.8	3.8	-	-	-	-
1977	51.3	3.0	-	-	-	-	53.5	4.3	-	-	-	-	54.4	1.7	-	-	-	-	55.5	2.0	-	-	-	-
1978	57.4	3.4	-	-	-	-	58.5	1.9	-	-	59.1	1.0	-	-	60.0	1.5	-	-	61.0	1.7	-	-	61.4	0.7
1979	-	-	63.0	2.6	-	-	63.9	1.4	-	-	64.5	0.9	-	-	65.3	1.2	-	-	67.6	3.5	-	-	67.9	0.4
1980	-	-	69.7	2.7	-	-	71.0	1.9	-	-	71.8	1.1	-	-	72.2	0.6	-	-	74.3	2.9	-	-	76.0	2.3
1981	-	-	76.7	0.9	-	-	77.6	1.2	-	-	80.2	3.4	-	-	80.9	0.9	-	-	82.8	2.3	-	-	84.1	1.6
1982	-	-	85.6	1.8	-	-	87.4	2.1	-	-	88.9	1.7	-	-	92.2	3.7	-	-	95.3	3.4	-	-	98.6	3.5
1983	-	-	100.2	1.6	-	-	101.7	1.5	-	-	101.4	-0.3	-	-	101.7	0.3	-	-	101.5	-0.2	-	-	100.9	-0.6
1984	-	-	104.2	3.3	-	-	105.0	0.8	-	-	108.8	3.6	-	-	109.7	0.8	-	-	111.4	1.5	-	-	112.5	1.0
1985	-	-	113.9	1.2	-	-	115.9	1.8	-	-	116.5	0.5	-	-	117.7	1.0	-	-	118.8	0.9	-	-	119.5	0.6
1986	-	-	120.8	1.1	-	-	121.8	0.8	-	-	123.5	1.4	-	-	124.5	0.8	-	-	125.6	0.9	-	-	126.4	0.6
1987	-	-	127.3	0.7	-	-	128.6	1.0	-	-	129.9	1.0	-	-	132.2	1.8	-	-	132.9	0.5	-	-	133.5	0.5
1988	-	-	134.7	0.9	-	-	135.6	0.7	-	-	136.5	0.7	-	-	136.0	-0.4	-	-	138.9	2.1	-	-	140.6	1.2
1989	-	-	144.0	2.4	-	-	145.7	1.2	-	-	148.3	1.8	-	-	149.9	1.1	-	-	151.1	0.8	-	-	152.2	0.7
1990	-	-	153.7	1.0	-	-	158.1	2.9	-	-	158.5	0.3	-	-	163.9	3.4	-	-	168.0	2.5	-	-	169.1	0.7
1991	-	-	170.4	0.8	-	-	173.8	2.0	-	-	174.9	0.6	-	-	180.3	3.1	-	-	185.1	2.7	-	-	186.0	0.5

[Continued]

Houston, TX
Consumer Price Index - All Urban Consumers
Base 1982-1984 = 100
Medical Care
[Continued]

For 1947-1997. Columns headed % show percentile change in the index from the previous period for which an index is available.

Year	Jan		Feb		Mar		Apr		May		Jun		Jul		Aug		Sep		Oct		Nov		Dec	
	Index	%	Index	%	Index	%	Index	%	Index	%	Index	%	Index	%	Index	%	Index	%	Index	%	Index	%	Index	%
1992	-	-	190.7	2.5	-	-	192.2	0.8	-	-	194.5	1.2	-	-	195.1	0.3	-	-	195.7	0.3	-	-	196.1	0.2
1993	-	-	200.4	2.2	-	-	201.3	0.4	-	-	200.8	-0.2	-	-	200.8	0.0	-	-	201.9	0.5	-	-	201.2	-0.3
1994	-	-	200.9	-0.1	-	-	202.1	0.6	-	-	204.7	1.3	-	-	204.6	-0.0	-	-	208.5	1.9	-	-	208.7	0.1
1995	-	-	213.2	2.2	-	-	217.3	1.9	-	-	218.7	0.6	-	-	220.1	0.6	-	-	219.5	-0.3	-	-	220.6	0.5
1996	-	-	221.5	0.4	-	-	225.3	1.7	-	-	226.5	0.5	-	-	221.7	-2.1	-	-	220.4	-0.6	-	-	220.5	0.0
1997	-	-	226.0	2.5	-	-	228.2	1.0	-	-	228.0	-0.1	-	-	229.3	0.6	-	-	229.6	0.1	-	-	232.7	1.4

Source: U.S. Department of Labor, Bureau of Labor Statistics, Division of Consumer Prices and Price Indexes. - indicates no data collected for period.

Houston, TX
Consumer Price Index - Urban Wage Earners
Base 1982-1984 = 100
Medical Care

For 1947-1997. Columns headed % show percentile change in the index from the previous period for which an index is available.

Year	Jan Index	%	Feb Index	%	Mar Index	%	Apr Index	%	May Index	%	Jun Index	%	Jul Index	%	Aug Index	%	Sep Index	%	Oct Index	%	Nov Index	%	Dec Index	%
1947	13.5	-	13.6	0.7	13.6	0.0	13.7	0.7	13.9	1.5	14.0	0.7	13.9	-0.7	13.9	0.0	14.0	0.7	14.1	0.7	14.1	0.0	14.1	0.0
1948	14.1	0.0	14.1	0.0	14.3	1.4	14.2	-0.7	14.2	0.0	14.2	0.0	14.3	0.7	14.3	0.0	14.3	0.0	14.3	0.0	14.3	0.0	14.3	0.0
1949	14.4	0.7	14.4	0.0	14.4	0.0	14.5	0.7	14.6	0.7	14.7	0.7	14.6	-0.7	14.6	0.0	14.6	0.0	14.6	0.0	14.6	0.0	14.9	2.1
1950	14.9	0.0	14.9	0.0	14.9	0.0	14.9	0.0	14.9	0.0	14.9	0.0	14.9	0.0	14.9	0.0	15.0	0.7	15.0	0.0	15.0	0.0	15.0	0.0
1951	15.0	0.0	15.0	0.0	15.1	0.7	15.1	0.0	15.1	0.0	15.1	0.0	15.1	0.0	15.1	0.0	15.1	0.0	15.9	5.3	15.9	0.0	16.0	0.6
1952	15.9	-0.6	15.9	0.0	15.9	0.0	16.0	0.6	16.0	0.0	16.0	0.0	16.0	0.0	16.0	0.0	16.0	0.0	16.0	0.0	16.0	0.0	16.7	4.4
1953	-		16.7	0.0	-		-		16.8	0.6	-		-		16.8	0.0	-		-		17.0	1.2	-	
1954	-		17.0	0.0	-		-		17.0	0.0	-		-		17.1	0.6	-		-		17.1	0.0	-	
1955	-		17.1	0.0	-		-		17.7	3.5	-		-		17.8	0.6	-		-		18.1	1.7	-	
1956	-		18.2	0.6	-		-		18.0	-1.1	-		-		18.2	1.1	-		-		18.3	0.5	-	
1957	-		18.5	1.1	-		-		18.4	-0.5	-		-		18.3	-0.5	-		-		18.4	0.5	-	
1958	-		18.8	2.2	-		-		18.8	0.0	-		-		18.8	0.0	-		-		19.0	1.1	-	
1959	-		19.0	0.0	-		-		19.3	1.6	-		-		19.2	-0.5	-		-		19.2	0.0	-	
1960	-		19.4	1.0	-		-		19.7	1.5	-		-		19.7	0.0	-		-		19.8	0.5	-	
1961	-		19.7	-0.5	-		-		19.9	1.0	-		-		19.9	0.0	-		-		20.0	0.5	-	
1962	-		20.0	0.0	-		-		20.2	1.0	-		-		20.2	0.0	-		-		20.4	1.0	-	
1963	-		20.6	1.0	-		-		20.7	0.5	-		-		20.7	0.0	-		-		20.9	1.0	-	
1964	-		21.1	1.0	-		-		21.3	0.9	-		-		21.3	0.0	-		-		21.3	0.0	-	
1965	-		21.6	1.4	-		21.8	0.9	-		-		21.9	0.5	-		-		22.0	0.5	-		-	
1966	22.1	0.5	-		-		22.1	0.0	-		-		22.3	0.9	-		-		22.9	2.7	-		-	
1967	23.4	2.2	-		-		23.6	0.9	-		-		23.8	0.8	-		-		24.2	1.7	-		-	
1968	24.7	2.1	-		-		24.8	0.4	-		-		25.0	0.8	-		-		25.6	2.4	-		-	
1969	26.4	3.1	-		-		27.1	2.7	-		-		27.3	0.7	-		-		27.9	2.2	-		-	
1970	28.6	2.5	-		-		29.2	2.1	-		-		29.4	0.7	-		-		29.5	0.3	-		-	
1971	30.2	2.4	-		-		30.6	1.3	-		-		31.6	3.3	-		-		31.4	-0.6	-		-	
1972	31.5	0.3	-		-		32.2	2.2	-		-		32.2	0.0	-		-		32.7	1.6	-		-	
1973	33.0	0.9	-		-		33.3	0.9	-		-		33.4	0.3	-		-		34.1	2.1	-		-	
1974	34.8	2.1	-		-		35.0	0.6	-		-		36.7	4.9	-		-		37.6	2.5	-		-	
1975	38.9	3.5	-		-		40.3	3.6	-		-		41.8	3.7	-		-		43.2	3.3	-		-	
1976	43.6	0.9	-		-		44.8	2.8	-		-		46.1	2.9	-		-		47.8	3.7	-		-	
1977	49.2	2.9	-		-		51.3	4.3	-		-		52.2	1.8	-		-		53.2	1.9	-		-	
1978	55.0	3.4	-		-		56.1	2.0	-		56.3	0.4	-		57.8	2.7	-		58.4	1.0	-		59.0	1.0
1979	-		62.2	5.4	-		63.5	2.1	-		64.8	2.0	-		65.4	0.9	-		66.9	2.3	-		67.7	1.2
1980	-		68.6	1.3	-		70.5	2.8	-		70.6	0.1	-		72.9	3.3	-		74.0	1.5	-		75.4	1.9
1981	-		76.4	1.3	-		77.5	1.4	-		79.8	3.0	-		80.5	0.9	-		81.7	1.5	-		83.7	2.4
1982	-		85.3	1.9	-		87.1	2.1	-		88.6	1.7	-		92.1	4.0	-		95.3	3.5	-		98.8	3.7
1983	-		100.4	1.6	-		101.9	1.5	-		101.5	-0.4	-		101.7	0.2	-		101.3	-0.4	-		100.8	-0.5
1984	-		104.2	3.4	-		105.0	0.8	-		109.0	3.8	-		109.9	0.8	-		111.6	1.5	-		112.7	1.0
1985	-		114.2	1.3	-		116.2	1.8	-		116.8	0.5	-		117.9	0.9	-		119.0	0.9	-		119.6	0.5
1986	-		121.0	1.2	-		122.0	0.8	-		123.7	1.4	-		124.7	0.8	-		125.8	0.9	-		126.6	0.6
1987	-		127.6	0.8	-		129.0	1.1	-		130.4	1.1	-		132.7	1.8	-		133.4	0.5	-		134.3	0.7
1988	-		135.5	0.9	-		136.4	0.7	-		137.4	0.7	-		137.1	-0.2	-		140.1	2.2	-		141.8	1.2
1989	-		145.3	2.5	-		147.0	1.2	-		149.6	1.8	-		151.3	1.1	-		152.4	0.7	-		153.5	0.7
1990	-		154.7	0.8	-		159.3	3.0	-		159.5	0.1	-		165.0	3.4	-		169.2	2.5	-		170.3	0.7
1991	-		171.4	0.6	-		174.9	2.0	-		175.9	0.6	-		181.5	3.2	-		186.7	2.9	-		187.6	0.5

[Continued]

Houston, TX
Consumer Price Index - Urban Wage Earners
Base 1982-1984 = 100
Medical Care
[Continued]

For 1947-1997. Columns headed % show percentile change in the index from the previous period for which an index is available.

Year	Jan Index	%	Feb Index	%	Mar Index	%	Apr Index	%	May Index	%	Jun Index	%	Jul Index	%	Aug Index	%	Sep Index	%	Oct Index	%	Nov Index	%	Dec Index	%
1992	-	-	192.4	2.6	-	-	193.8	0.7	-	-	196.1	1.2	-	-	196.7	0.3	-	-	197.5	0.4	-	-	197.9	0.2
1993	-	-	202.3	2.2	-	-	203.3	0.5	-	-	202.9	-0.2	-	-	202.9	0.0	-	-	203.9	0.5	-	-	203.2	-0.3
1994	-	-	202.9	-0.1	-	-	204.0	0.5	-	-	206.7	1.3	-	-	206.5	-0.1	-	-	210.5	1.9	-	-	210.8	0.1
1995	-	-	215.3	2.1	-	-	218.9	1.7	-	-	220.4	0.7	-	-	221.9	0.7	-	-	221.0	-0.4	-	-	222.4	0.6
1996	-	-	223.3	0.4	-	-	227.2	1.7	-	-	228.5	0.6	-	-	223.9	-2.0	-	-	222.5	-0.6	-	-	222.6	0.0
1997	-	-	227.9	2.4	-	-	230.0	0.9	-	-	229.9	-0.0	-	-	231.3	0.6	-	-	231.8	0.2	-	-	235.0	1.4

Source: U.S. Department of Labor, Bureau of Labor Statistics, Division of Consumer Prices and Price Indexes. - indicates no data collected for period.

Houston, TX
Consumer Price Index - All Urban Consumers
Base 1982-1984 = 100
Entertainment

For 1976-1997. Columns headed % show percentile change in the index from the previous period for which an index is available.

Year	Jan Index	%	Feb Index	%	Mar Index	%	Apr Index	%	May Index	%	Jun Index	%	Jul Index	%	Aug Index	%	Sep Index	%	Oct Index	%	Nov Index	%	Dec Index	%
1976	59.9	-	-	-	-	-	60.6	1.2	-	-	-	-	61.7	1.8	-	-	-	-	61.8	0.2	-	-	-	-
1977	63.1	2.1	-	-	-	-	63.3	0.3	-	-	-	-	64.5	1.9	-	-	-	-	64.4	-0.2	-	-	-	-
1978	64.8	0.6	-	-	-	-	65.8	1.5	-	-	64.5	-2.0	-	-	65.2	1.1	-	-	66.7	2.3	-	-	67.7	1.5
1979	-	-	68.9	1.8	-	-	69.6	1.0	-	-	69.8	0.3	-	-	70.2	0.6	-	-	71.5	1.9	-	-	71.7	0.3
1980	-	-	78.4	9.3	-	-	79.2	1.0	-	-	80.2	1.3	-	-	81.2	1.2	-	-	80.8	-0.5	-	-	81.2	0.5
1981	-	-	87.3	7.5	-	-	86.5	-0.9	-	-	86.2	-0.3	-	-	86.2	0.0	-	-	86.8	0.7	-	-	86.9	0.1
1982	-	-	88.5	1.8	-	-	89.9	1.6	-	-	94.7	5.3	-	-	94.2	-0.5	-	-	95.9	1.8	-	-	95.9	0.0
1983	-	-	102.2	6.6	-	-	102.4	0.2	-	-	103.8	1.4	-	-	105.3	1.4	-	-	104.4	-0.9	-	-	102.1	-2.2
1984	-	-	102.6	0.5	-	-	102.8	0.2	-	-	101.9	-0.9	-	-	105.1	3.1	-	-	105.5	0.4	-	-	108.4	2.7
1985	-	-	109.5	1.0	-	-	112.2	2.5	-	-	113.3	1.0	-	-	113.6	0.3	-	-	111.9	-1.5	-	-	111.7	-0.2
1986	-	-	112.2	0.4	-	-	114.6	2.1	-	-	115.3	0.6	-	-	114.8	-0.4	-	-	115.4	0.5	-	-	116.0	0.5
1987	-	-	116.9	0.8	-	-	117.4	0.4	-	-	118.2	0.7	-	-	118.7	0.4	-	-	121.0	1.9	-	-	120.2	-0.7
1988	-	-	124.5	3.6	-	-	123.3	-1.0	-	-	123.6	0.2	-	-	123.4	-0.2	-	-	125.6	1.8	-	-	129.1	2.8
1989	-	-	128.4	-0.5	-	-	132.5	3.2	-	-	137.2	3.5	-	-	136.3	-0.7	-	-	135.8	-0.4	-	-	133.6	-1.6
1990	-	-	134.2	0.4	-	-	134.8	0.4	-	-	132.8	-1.5	-	-	135.8	2.3	-	-	136.1	0.2	-	-	136.2	0.1
1991	-	-	137.4	0.9	-	-	139.4	1.5	-	-	139.8	0.3	-	-	139.7	-0.1	-	-	141.2	1.1	-	-	141.2	0.0
1992	-	-	143.2	1.4	-	-	144.7	1.0	-	-	145.0	0.2	-	-	147.4	1.7	-	-	150.6	2.2	-	-	149.8	-0.5
1993	-	-	152.9	2.1	-	-	152.2	-0.5	-	-	153.4	0.8	-	-	150.8	-1.7	-	-	158.7	5.2	-	-	151.8	-4.3
1994	-	-	156.6	3.2	-	-	155.7	-0.6	-	-	159.0	2.1	-	-	162.4	2.1	-	-	159.3	-1.9	-	-	151.0	-5.2
1995	-	-	150.3	-0.5	-	-	154.6	2.9	-	-	158.2	2.3	-	-	161.0	1.8	-	-	161.8	0.5	-	-	160.5	-0.8
1996	-	-	162.9	1.5	-	-	162.8	-0.1	-	-	159.8	-1.8	-	-	158.9	-0.6	-	-	158.1	-0.5	-	-	159.8	1.1
1997	-	-	160.9	0.7	-	-	161.3	0.2	-	-	163.2	1.2	-	-	162.3	-0.6	-	-	161.5	-0.5	-	-	161.0	-0.3

Source: U.S. Department of Labor, Bureau of Labor Statistics, Division of Consumer Prices and Price Indexes. - indicates no data collected for period.

Houston, TX
Consumer Price Index - Urban Wage Earners
Base 1982-1984 = 100
Entertainment

For 1976-1997. Columns headed % show percentile change in the index from the previous period for which an index is available.

Year	Jan Index	%	Feb Index	%	Mar Index	%	Apr Index	%	May Index	%	Jun Index	%	Jul Index	%	Aug Index	%	Sep Index	%	Oct Index	%	Nov Index	%	Dec Index	%
1976	61.7	-	-	-	-	-	62.4	1.1	-	-	-	-	63.5	1.8	-	-	-	-	63.7	0.3	-	-	-	-
1977	64.9	1.9	-	-	-	-	65.2	0.5	-	-	-	-	66.4	1.8	-	-	-	-	66.3	-0.2	-	-	-	-
1978	66.7	0.6	-	-	-	-	67.7	1.5	-	-	67.0	-1.0	-	-	67.7	1.0	-	-	68.9	1.8	-	-	70.2	1.9
1979	-	-	69.9	-0.4	-	-	72.7	4.0	-	-	71.3	-1.9	-	-	71.4	0.1	-	-	72.5	1.5	-	-	72.8	0.4
1980	-	-	76.1	4.5	-	-	76.4	0.4	-	-	77.9	2.0	-	-	81.2	4.2	-	-	82.8	2.0	-	-	82.4	-0.5
1981	-	-	84.9	3.0	-	-	85.9	1.2	-	-	86.4	0.6	-	-	84.5	-2.2	-	-	85.0	0.6	-	-	85.0	0.0
1982	-	-	86.5	1.8	-	-	88.5	2.3	-	-	93.6	5.8	-	-	92.8	-0.9	-	-	94.3	1.6	-	-	94.3	0.0
1983	-	-	103.2	9.4	-	-	103.3	0.1	-	-	104.5	1.2	-	-	106.6	2.0	-	-	105.0	-1.5	-	-	103.3	-1.6
1984	-	-	103.8	0.5	-	-	103.8	0.0	-	-	101.8	-1.9	-	-	105.9	4.0	-	-	106.2	0.3	-	-	108.6	2.3
1985	-	-	109.8	1.1	-	-	112.9	2.8	-	-	113.9	0.9	-	-	114.1	0.2	-	-	113.1	-0.9	-	-	112.9	-0.2
1986	-	-	113.3	0.4	-	-	115.1	1.6	-	-	116.3	1.0	-	-	116.3	0.0	-	-	116.9	0.5	-	-	117.6	0.6
1987	-	-	118.4	0.7	-	-	118.9	0.4	-	-	119.7	0.7	-	-	120.2	0.4	-	-	122.5	1.9	-	-	121.6	-0.7
1988	-	-	126.3	3.9	-	-	124.9	-1.1	-	-	125.3	0.3	-	-	125.1	-0.2	-	-	127.5	1.9	-	-	130.9	2.7
1989	-	-	130.0	-0.7	-	-	134.3	3.3	-	-	139.3	3.7	-	-	138.3	-0.7	-	-	138.1	-0.1	-	-	135.3	-2.0
1990	-	-	135.9	0.4	-	-	136.6	0.5	-	-	134.6	-1.5	-	-	137.5	2.2	-	-	137.9	0.3	-	-	137.9	0.0
1991	-	-	139.2	0.9	-	-	141.0	1.3	-	-	141.4	0.3	-	-	141.4	0.0	-	-	142.8	1.0	-	-	142.7	-0.1
1992	-	-	144.4	1.2	-	-	146.1	1.2	-	-	146.4	0.2	-	-	149.0	1.8	-	-	153.8	3.2	-	-	152.8	-0.7
1993	-	-	155.8	2.0	-	-	155.1	-0.4	-	-	156.3	0.8	-	-	153.7	-1.7	-	-	161.9	5.3	-	-	154.7	-4.4
1994	-	-	159.4	3.0	-	-	158.4	-0.6	-	-	161.6	2.0	-	-	165.3	2.3	-	-	161.9	-2.1	-	-	155.5	-4.0
1995	-	-	153.5	-1.3	-	-	158.3	3.1	-	-	162.0	2.3	-	-	165.4	2.1	-	-	166.0	0.4	-	-	165.2	-0.5
1996	-	-	167.1	1.2	-	-	167.0	-0.1	-	-	164.2	-1.7	-	-	163.2	-0.6	-	-	162.4	-0.5	-	-	164.1	1.0
1997	-	-	165.5	0.9	-	-	165.5	0.0	-	-	167.5	1.2	-	-	166.7	-0.5	-	-	165.8	-0.5	-	-	165.3	-0.3

Source: U.S. Department of Labor, Bureau of Labor Statistics, Division of Consumer Prices and Price Indexes. - indicates no data collected for period.

Houston, TX
Consumer Price Index - All Urban Consumers
Base 1982-1984 = 100
Other Goods and Services

For 1976-1997. Columns headed % show percentile change in the index from the previous period for which an index is available.

Year	Jan Index	%	Feb Index	%	Mar Index	%	Apr Index	%	May Index	%	Jun Index	%	Jul Index	%	Aug Index	%	Sep Index	%	Oct Index	%	Nov Index	%	Dec Index	%
1976	55.4	-	-	-	-	-	56.1	1.3	-	-	-	-	56.1	0.0	-	-	-	-	56.8	1.2	-	-	-	-
1977	58.5	3.0	-	-	-	-	59.2	1.2	-	-	-	-	59.3	0.2	-	-	-	-	60.8	2.5	-	-	-	-
1978	62.6	3.0	-	-	-	-	64.0	2.2	-	-	64.6	0.9	-	-	66.1	2.3	-	-	68.0	2.9	-	-	68.7	1.0
1979	-	-	69.9	1.7	-	-	71.0	1.6	-	-	71.2	0.3	-	-	71.6	0.6	-	-	73.2	2.2	-	-	74.8	2.2
1980	-	-	76.8	2.7	-	-	78.1	1.7	-	-	78.9	1.0	-	-	79.6	0.9	-	-	81.7	2.6	-	-	82.9	1.5
1981	-	-	83.6	0.8	-	-	84.3	0.8	-	-	85.4	1.3	-	-	85.7	0.4	-	-	87.1	1.6	-	-	86.8	-0.3
1982	-	-	88.0	1.4	-	-	89.6	1.8	-	-	91.3	1.9	-	-	92.6	1.4	-	-	94.6	2.2	-	-	97.6	3.2
1983	-	-	99.8	2.3	-	-	99.6	-0.2	-	-	100.4	0.8	-	-	101.1	0.7	-	-	103.3	2.2	-	-	103.1	-0.2
1984	-	-	105.2	2.0	-	-	105.6	0.4	-	-	106.0	0.4	-	-	108.3	2.2	-	-	109.6	1.2	-	-	110.2	0.5
1985	-	-	111.0	0.7	-	-	111.1	0.1	-	-	111.5	0.4	-	-	112.1	0.5	-	-	115.2	2.8	-	-	115.2	0.0
1986	-	-	116.3	1.0	-	-	117.2	0.8	-	-	117.2	0.0	-	-	119.0	1.5	-	-	122.1	2.6	-	-	121.2	-0.7
1987	-	-	123.4	1.8	-	-	123.2	-0.2	-	-	123.6	0.3	-	-	124.3	0.6	-	-	127.8	2.8	-	-	128.1	0.2
1988	-	-	129.3	0.9	-	-	128.7	-0.5	-	-	130.1	1.1	-	-	133.1	2.3	-	-	133.6	0.4	-	-	133.5	-0.1
1989	-	-	134.5	0.7	-	-	135.0	0.4	-	-	134.4	-0.4	-	-	137.7	2.5	-	-	146.5	6.4	-	-	146.0	-0.3
1990	-	-	147.2	0.8	-	-	150.1	2.0	-	-	151.4	0.9	-	-	156.6	3.4	-	-	156.6	0.0	-	-	152.4	-2.7
1991	-	-	155.3	1.9	-	-	157.5	1.4	-	-	157.2	-0.2	-	-	159.0	1.1	-	-	160.7	1.1	-	-	157.6	-1.9
1992	-	-	161.7	2.6	-	-	168.9	4.5	-	-	172.6	2.2	-	-	176.8	2.4	-	-	178.8	1.1	-	-	179.0	0.1
1993	-	-	180.7	0.9	-	-	181.0	0.2	-	-	179.8	-0.7	-	-	179.3	-0.3	-	-	181.3	1.1	-	-	184.0	1.5
1994	-	-	184.6	0.3	-	-	186.6	1.1	-	-	186.8	0.1	-	-	187.9	0.6	-	-	191.3	1.8	-	-	189.9	-0.7
1995	-	-	188.5	-0.7	-	-	191.9	1.8	-	-	192.6	0.4	-	-	192.5	-0.1	-	-	198.5	3.1	-	-	198.7	0.1
1996	-	-	200.5	0.9	-	-	202.1	0.8	-	-	202.1	0.0	-	-	192.9	-4.6	-	-	193.9	0.5	-	-	192.8	-0.6
1997	-	-	195.4	1.3	-	-	194.0	-0.7	-	-	197.1	1.6	-	-	197.7	0.3	-	-	203.5	2.9	-	-	200.6	-1.4

Source: U.S. Department of Labor, Bureau of Labor Statistics, Division of Consumer Prices and Price Indexes. - indicates no data collected for period.

Houston, TX
Consumer Price Index - Urban Wage Earners
Base 1982-1984 = 100
Other Goods and Services

For 1976-1997. Columns headed % show percentile change in the index from the previous period for which an index is available.

Year	Jan Index	%	Feb Index	%	Mar Index	%	Apr Index	%	May Index	%	Jun Index	%	Jul Index	%	Aug Index	%	Sep Index	%	Oct Index	%	Nov Index	%	Dec Index	%
1976	55.3	-	-	-	-	-	55.9	1.1	-	-	-	-	56.0	0.2	-	-	-	-	56.6	1.1	-	-	-	-
1977	58.3	3.0	-	-	-	-	59.0	1.2	-	-	-	-	59.1	0.2	-	-	-	-	60.7	2.7	-	-	-	-
1978	62.4	2.8	-	-	-	-	63.8	2.2	-	-	64.5	1.1	-	-	64.8	0.5	-	-	67.0	3.4	-	-	66.2	-1.2
1979	-	-	69.2	4.5	-	-	70.5	1.9	-	-	69.8	-1.0	-	-	71.1	1.9	-	-	71.6	0.7	-	-	73.1	2.1
1980	-	-	76.3	4.4	-	-	77.1	1.0	-	-	79.1	2.6	-	-	78.4	-0.9	-	-	80.8	3.1	-	-	81.1	0.4
1981	-	-	81.3	0.2	-	-	82.5	1.5	-	-	85.7	3.9	-	-	85.9	0.2	-	-	86.7	0.9	-	-	87.0	0.3
1982	-	-	88.2	1.4	-	-	89.9	1.9	-	-	90.8	1.0	-	-	92.1	1.4	-	-	94.2	2.3	-	-	97.7	3.7
1983	-	-	100.1	2.5	-	-	99.9	-0.2	-	-	100.3	0.4	-	-	101.1	0.8	-	-	103.1	2.0	-	-	102.9	-0.2
1984	-	-	105.0	2.0	-	-	105.5	0.5	-	-	106.2	0.7	-	-	108.6	2.3	-	-	109.9	1.2	-	-	110.5	0.5
1985	-	-	111.4	0.8	-	-	111.5	0.1	-	-	111.6	0.1	-	-	112.2	0.5	-	-	114.5	2.0	-	-	114.1	-0.3
1986	-	-	115.2	1.0	-	-	116.3	1.0	-	-	116.3	0.0	-	-	118.3	1.7	-	-	120.4	1.8	-	-	119.5	-0.7
1987	-	-	121.4	1.6	-	-	121.2	-0.2	-	-	121.8	0.5	-	-	122.6	0.7	-	-	126.3	3.0	-	-	126.4	0.1
1988	-	-	127.9	1.2	-	-	127.1	-0.6	-	-	128.9	1.4	-	-	133.2	3.3	-	-	133.7	0.4	-	-	133.7	0.0
1989	-	-	135.1	1.0	-	-	135.7	0.4	-	-	134.7	-0.7	-	-	139.6	3.6	-	-	146.8	5.2	-	-	146.0	-0.5
1990	-	-	147.4	1.0	-	-	150.4	2.0	-	-	151.7	0.9	-	-	158.3	4.4	-	-	158.1	-0.1	-	-	152.2	-3.7
1991	-	-	155.5	2.2	-	-	157.6	1.4	-	-	157.4	-0.1	-	-	158.6	0.8	-	-	161.3	1.7	-	-	157.0	-2.7
1992	-	-	162.3	3.4	-	-	166.7	2.7	-	-	171.7	3.0	-	-	176.3	2.7	-	-	178.8	1.4	-	-	179.0	0.1
1993	-	-	181.2	1.2	-	-	181.5	0.2	-	-	179.3	-1.2	-	-	176.4	-1.6	-	-	178.4	1.1	-	-	181.6	1.8
1994	-	-	182.3	0.4	-	-	184.7	1.3	-	-	184.8	0.1	-	-	185.4	0.3	-	-	188.2	1.5	-	-	186.2	-1.1
1995	-	-	185.1	-0.6	-	-	188.5	1.8	-	-	189.6	0.6	-	-	189.3	-0.2	-	-	194.9	3.0	-	-	194.9	0.0
1996	-	-	194.3	-0.3	-	-	196.1	0.9	-	-	195.8	-0.2	-	-	182.0	-7.0	-	-	183.2	0.7	-	-	181.5	-0.9
1997	-	-	184.6	1.7	-	-	182.6	-1.1	-	-	186.7	2.2	-	-	187.5	0.4	-	-	192.7	2.8	-	-	188.4	-2.2

Source: U.S. Department of Labor, Bureau of Labor Statistics, Division of Consumer Prices and Price Indexes. - indicates no data collected for period.

Kansas City, MO-KS
Consumer Price Index - All Urban Consumers
Base 1982-1984 = 100
Annual Averages

For 1917-1997. Columns headed % show percentile change in the index from the previous period for which an index is available.

Year	All Items		Food & Beverage		Housing		Apparel & Upkeep		Trans-portation		Medical Care		Entertain-ment		Other Goods & Services	
	Index	%	Index	%	Index	%	Index	%	Index	%	Index	%	Index	%	Index	%
1917	-	-	-	-	-	-	-	-	-	-	-	-	-	-	-	-
1918	16.1	-	-	-	-	-	-	-	-	-	-	-	-	-	-	-
1919	18.5	14.9	-	-	-	-	-	-	-	-	-	-	-	-	-	-
1920	21.7	17.3	-	-	-	-	-	-	-	-	-	-	-	-	-	-
1921	19.2	-11.5	-	-	-	-	-	-	-	-	-	-	-	-	-	-
1922	17.5	-8.9	-	-	-	-	-	-	-	-	-	-	-	-	-	-
1923	17.4	-0.6	-	-	-	-	-	-	-	-	-	-	-	-	-	-
1924	17.3	-0.6	-	-	-	-	-	-	-	-	-	-	-	-	-	-
1925	17.5	1.2	-	-	-	-	-	-	-	-	-	-	-	-	-	-
1926	17.5	0.0	-	-	-	-	-	-	-	-	-	-	-	-	-	-
1927	17.0	-2.9	-	-	-	-	-	-	-	-	-	-	-	-	-	-
1928	16.7	-1.8	-	-	-	-	-	-	-	-	-	-	-	-	-	-
1929	16.8	0.6	-	-	-	-	-	-	-	-	-	-	-	-	-	-
1930	16.5	-1.8	-	-	-	-	-	-	-	-	-	-	-	-	-	-
1931	15.5	-6.1	-	-	-	-	-	-	-	-	-	-	-	-	-	-
1932	13.9	-10.3	-	-	-	-	-	-	-	-	-	-	-	-	-	-
1933	13.3	-4.3	-	-	-	-	-	-	-	-	-	-	-	-	-	-
1934	13.7	3.0	-	-	-	-	-	-	-	-	-	-	-	-	-	-
1935	14.0	2.2	-	-	-	-	-	-	-	-	-	-	-	-	-	-
1936	14.1	0.7	-	-	-	-	-	-	-	-	-	-	-	-	-	-
1937	14.6	3.5	-	-	-	-	-	-	-	-	-	-	-	-	-	-
1938	14.3	-2.1	-	-	-	-	-	-	-	-	-	-	-	-	-	-
1939	14.1	-1.4	-	-	-	-	-	-	-	-	-	-	-	-	-	-
1940	14.0	-0.7	-	-	-	-	-	-	-	-	-	-	-	-	-	-
1941	14.7	5.0	-	-	-	-	-	-	-	-	-	-	-	-	-	-
1942	16.3	10.9	-	-	-	-	-	-	-	-	-	-	-	-	-	-
1943	17.3	6.1	-	-	-	-	-	-	-	-	-	-	-	-	-	-
1944	17.6	1.7	-	-	-	-	-	-	-	-	-	-	-	-	-	-
1945	18.1	2.8	-	-	-	-	-	-	-	-	-	-	-	-	-	-
1946	19.3	6.6	-	-	-	-	-	-	-	-	-	-	-	-	-	-
1947	21.9	13.5	-	-	-	-	-	-	18.2	-	11.0	-	-	-	-	-
1948	23.6	7.8	-	-	-	-	-	-	20.2	11.0	11.9	8.2	-	-	-	-
1949	23.3	-1.3	-	-	-	-	-	-	21.5	6.4	12.2	2.5	-	-	-	-
1950	23.7	1.7	-	-	-	-	-	-	21.9	1.9	12.4	1.6	-	-	-	-
1951	25.5	7.6	-	-	-	-	-	-	23.2	5.9	13.0	4.8	-	-	-	-
1952	26.3	3.1	-	-	-	-	-	-	25.4	9.5	13.7	5.4	-	-	-	-
1953	26.4	0.4	-	-	-	-	39.2	-	26.0	2.4	14.0	2.2	-	-	-	-
1954	26.5	0.4	-	-	-	-	38.9	-0.8	25.2	-3.1	15.6	11.4	-	-	-	-
1955	26.5	0.0	-	-	-	-	38.9	0.0	25.0	-0.8	15.9	1.9	-	-	-	-
1956	26.9	1.5	-	-	-	-	39.4	1.3	25.4	1.6	16.6	4.4	-	-	-	-
1957	27.8	3.3	-	-	-	-	40.3	2.3	27.6	8.7	17.7	6.6	-	-	-	-
1958	28.5	2.5	-	-	-	-	40.4	0.2	29.1	5.4	19.0	7.3	-	-	-	-
1959	28.9	1.4	-	-	-	-	40.7	0.7	30.6	5.2	20.0	5.3	-	-	-	-
1960	29.3	1.4	-	-	-	-	41.7	2.5	30.6	0.0	20.3	1.5	-	-	-	-
1961	29.6	1.0	-	-	-	-	42.0	0.7	30.6	0.0	21.1	3.9	-	-	-	-

[Continued]

546

Kansas City, MO-KS
Consumer Price Index - All Urban Consumers
Base 1982-1984 = 100
Annual Averages
[Continued]

For 1917-1997. Columns headed % show percentile change in the index from the previous period for which an index is available.

Year	All Items		Food & Beverage		Housing		Apparel & Upkeep		Trans-portation		Medical Care		Entertain-ment		Other Goods & Services	
	Index	%	Index	%	Index	%	Index	%	Index	%	Index	%	Index	%	Index	%
1962	30.1	1.7	-	-	-	-	42.0	0.0	31.3	2.3	21.5	1.9	-	-	-	-
1963	30.4	1.0	-	-	-	-	42.6	1.4	31.3	0.0	21.7	0.9	-	-	-	-
1964	31.2	2.6	-	-	-	-	43.6	2.3	31.6	1.0	22.8	5.1	-	-	-	-
1965	32.2	3.2	-	-	-	-	44.5	2.1	33.8	7.0	24.0	5.3	-	-	-	-
1966	33.0	2.5	-	-	-	-	45.7	2.7	34.5	2.1	25.3	5.4	-	-	-	-
1967	33.7	2.1	-	-	-	-	47.3	3.5	34.7	0.6	27.2	7.5			-	-
1968	35.0	3.9	-	-	-	-	50.8	7.4	35.5	2.3	28.9	6.3	-	-	-	-
1969	36.9	5.4	-	-	-	-	54.4	7.1	37.2	4.8	30.4	5.2	-	-	-	-
1970	39.0	5.7	-	-	-	-	57.4	5.5	38.2	2.7	31.8	4.6	-	-	-	-
1971	40.6	4.1	-	-	-	-	58.9	2.6	41.0	7.3	33.8	6.3	-	-	-	-
1972	41.8	3.0	-	-	-	-	60.3	2.4	41.0	0.0	35.1	3.8			-	-
1973	43.9	5.0	-	-	-	-	61.8	2.5	42.6	3.9	36.7	4.6	-	-	-	-
1974	48.6	10.7	-	-	-	-	65.7	6.3	47.3	11.0	40.1	9.3	-	-	-	-
1975	53.2	9.5	-	-	-	-	69.0	5.0	51.5	8.9	43.6	8.7	-	-	-	-
1976	56.1	5.5	62.9	-	52.7	-	70.7	2.5	55.5	7.8	47.3	8.5	65.3	-	57.7	-
1977	60.0	7.0	67.0	6.5	56.6	7.4	77.0	8.9	59.2	6.7	51.8	9.5	68.3	4.6	61.4	6.4
1978	64.6	7.7	74.6	11.3	61.5	8.7	79.0	2.6	62.1	4.9	56.7	9.5	70.9	3.8	64.7	5.4
1979	73.8	14.2	82.6	10.7	72.1	17.2	84.3	6.7	72.3	16.4	63.7	12.3	74.2	4.7	69.9	8.0
1980	83.6	13.3	89.6	8.5	82.7	14.7	87.6	3.9	85.0	17.6	70.9	11.3	83.1	12.0	76.7	9.7
1981	90.5	8.3	95.0	6.0	89.5	8.2	92.3	5.4	93.2	9.6	79.7	12.4	90.4	8.8	84.5	10.2
1982	95.0	5.0	97.5	2.6	93.8	4.8	95.7	3.7	97.5	4.6	91.0	14.2	95.8	6.0	91.3	8.0
1983	100.5	5.8	99.2	1.7	101.2	7.9	101.8	6.4	99.5	2.1	101.1	11.1	99.9	4.3	100.6	10.2
1984	104.5	4.0	103.3	4.1	105.0	3.8	102.5	0.7	103.0	3.5	107.8	6.6	104.3	4.4	108.1	7.5
1985	107.7	3.1	106.0	2.6	107.6	2.5	105.0	2.4	106.5	3.4	111.7	3.6	107.0	2.6	115.7	7.0
1986	108.7	0.9	109.5	3.3	109.4	1.7	107.0	1.9	100.0	-6.1	117.7	5.4	111.0	3.7	125.5	8.5
1987	113.1	4.0	112.8	3.0	113.6	3.8	109.7	2.5	102.9	2.9	123.4	4.8	123.6	11.4	134.9	7.5
1988	117.4	3.8	115.8	2.7	118.3	4.1	113.1	3.1	107.2	4.2	130.8	6.0	124.2	0.5	141.6	5.0
1989	121.6	3.6	119.9	3.5	119.6	1.1	119.7	5.8	112.2	4.7	142.0	8.6	132.0	6.3	152.3	7.6
1990	126.0	3.6	127.5	6.3	121.8	1.8	116.5	-2.7	116.2	3.6	156.8	10.4	142.0	7.6	159.6	4.8
1991	131.2	4.1	130.9	2.7	125.4	3.0	124.7	7.0	119.2	2.6	173.5	10.7	149.3	5.1	175.7	10.1
1992	134.3	2.4	132.9	1.5	127.2	1.4	124.8	0.1	121.8	2.2	183.8	5.9	154.0	3.1	189.4	7.8
1993	138.1	2.8	137.7	3.6	130.4	2.5	125.3	0.4	124.7	2.4	195.6	6.4	152.5	-1.0	196.7	3.9
1994	141.3	2.3	140.2	1.8	133.1	2.1	123.3	-1.6	128.1	2.7	202.9	3.7	160.5	5.2	203.5	3.5
1995	145.3	2.8	144.6	3.1	136.7	2.7	125.8	2.0	133.4	4.1	208.5	2.8	160.4	-0.1	208.4	2.4
1996	151.6	4.3	154.1	6.6	142.4	4.2	129.6	3.0	137.6	3.1	212.2	1.8	169.1	5.4	221.4	6.2
1997	155.8	2.8	160.0	3.8	146.1	2.6	133.4	2.9	140.7	2.3	210.0	-1.0	171.0	1.1	237.8	7.4

Source: U.S. Department of Labor, Bureau of Labor Statistics, Division of Consumer Prices and Price Indexes. - indicates no data collected for period.

Kansas City, MO-KS
Consumer Price Index - Urban Wage Earners
Base 1982-1984 = 100
Annual Averages

For 1917-1997. Columns headed % show percentile change in the index from the previous period for which an index is available.

Year	All Items		Food & Beverage		Housing		Apparel & Upkeep		Transportation		Medical Care		Entertainment		Other Goods & Services	
	Index	%	Index	%	Index	%	Index	%	Index	%	Index	%	Index	%	Index	%
1917	-	-	-	-	-	-	-	-	-	-	-	-	-	-	-	-
1918	16.3	-	-	-	-	-	-	-	-	-	-	-	-	-	-	-
1919	18.7	14.7	-	-	-	-	-	-	-	-	-	-	-	-	-	-
1920	22.0	17.6	-	-	-	-	-	-	-	-	-	-	-	-	-	-
1921	19.4	-11.8	-	-	-	-	-	-	-	-	-	-	-	-	-	-
1922	17.7	-8.8	-	-	-	-	-	-	-	-	-	-	-	-	-	-
1923	17.7	0.0	-	-	-	-	-	-	-	-	-	-	-	-	-	-
1924	17.5	-1.1	-	-	-	-	-	-	-	-	-	-	-	-	-	-
1925	17.8	1.7	-	-	-	-	-	-	-	-	-	-	-	-	-	-
1926	17.8	0.0	-	-	-	-	-	-	-	-	-	-	-	-	-	-
1927	17.2	-3.4	-	-	-	-	-	-	-	-	-	-	-	-	-	-
1928	16.9	-1.7	-	-	-	-	-	-	-	-	-	-	-	-	-	-
1929	17.0	0.6	-	-	-	-	-	-	-	-	-	-	-	-	-	-
1930	16.7	-1.8	-	-	-	-	-	-	-	-	-	-	-	-	-	-
1931	15.7	-6.0	-	-	-	-	-	-	-	-	-	-	-	-	-	-
1932	14.1	-10.2	-	-	-	-	-	-	-	-	-	-	-	-	-	-
1933	13.4	-5.0	-	-	-	-	-	-	-	-	-	-	-	-	-	-
1934	13.9	3.7	-	-	-	-	-	-	-	-	-	-	-	-	-	-
1935	14.2	2.2	-	-	-	-	-	-	-	-	-	-	-	-	-	-
1936	14.3	0.7	-	-	-	-	-	-	-	-	-	-	-	-	-	-
1937	14.8	3.5	-	-	-	-	-	-	-	-	-	-	-	-	-	-
1938	14.5	-2.0	-	-	-	-	-	-	-	-	-	-	-	-	-	-
1939	14.3	-1.4	-	-	-	-	-	-	-	-	-	-	-	-	-	-
1940	14.2	-0.7	-	-	-	-	-	-	-	-	-	-	-	-	-	-
1941	14.9	4.9	-	-	-	-	-	-	-	-	-	-	-	-	-	-
1942	16.5	10.7	-	-	-	-	-	-	-	-	-	-	-	-	-	-
1943	17.5	6.1	-	-	-	-	-	-	-	-	-	-	-	-	-	-
1944	17.8	1.7	-	-	-	-	-	-	-	-	-	-	-	-	-	-
1945	18.3	2.8	-	-	-	-	-	-	-	-	-	-	-	-	-	-
1946	19.6	7.1	-	-	-	-	-	-	-	-	-	-	-	-	-	-
1947	22.2	13.3	-	-	-	-	-	-	18.1	-	11.0	-	-	-	-	-
1948	23.9	7.7	-	-	-	-	-	-	20.1	11.0	11.9	8.2	-	-	-	-
1949	23.7	-0.8	-	-	-	-	-	-	21.3	6.0	12.2	2.5	-	-	-	-
1950	24.0	1.3	-	-	-	-	-	-	21.8	2.3	12.4	1.6	-	-	-	-
1951	25.8	7.5	-	-	-	-	-	-	23.0	5.5	13.0	4.8	-	-	-	-
1952	26.6	3.1	-	-	-	-	-	-	25.2	9.6	13.7	5.4	-	-	-	-
1953	26.7	0.4	-	-	-	-	40.5	-	25.8	2.4	14.0	2.2	-	-	-	-
1954	26.9	0.7	-	-	-	-	40.1	-1.0	25.1	-2.7	15.6	11.4	-	-	-	-
1955	26.9	0.0	-	-	-	-	40.1	0.0	24.9	-0.8	15.9	1.9	-	-	-	-
1956	27.3	1.5	-	-	-	-	40.6	1.2	25.3	1.6	16.6	4.4	-	-	-	-
1957	28.2	3.3	-	-	-	-	41.5	2.2	27.4	8.3	17.7	6.6	-	-	-	-
1958	28.8	2.1	-	-	-	-	41.6	0.2	28.9	5.5	19.0	7.3	-	-	-	-
1959	29.3	1.7	-	-	-	-	42.0	1.0	30.4	5.2	20.0	5.3	-	-	-	-
1960	29.7	1.4	-	-	-	-	43.0	2.4	30.4	0.0	20.3	1.5	-	-	-	-
1961	30.0	1.0	-	-	-	-	43.3	0.7	30.4	0.0	21.1	3.9	-	-	-	-

[Continued]

548

Kansas City, MO-KS
Consumer Price Index - Urban Wage Earners
Base 1982-1984 = 100
Annual Averages
[Continued]

For 1917-1997. Columns headed % show percentile change in the index from the previous period for which an index is available.

Year	All Items		Food & Beverage		Housing		Apparel & Upkeep		Trans- portation		Medical Care		Entertain- ment		Other Goods & Services	
	Index	%	Index	%	Index	%	Index	%	Index	%	Index	%	Index	%	Index	%
1962	30.5	1.7	-	-	-	-	43.3	0.0	31.1	2.3	21.5	1.9	-	-	-	-
1963	30.8	1.0	-	-	-	-	43.9	1.4	31.1	0.0	21.7	0.9	-	-	-	-
1964	31.6	2.6	-	-	-	-	45.0	2.5	31.4	1.0	22.8	5.1	-	-	-	-
1965	32.6	3.2	-	-	-	-	45.9	2.0	33.6	7.0	24.0	5.3	-	-	-	-
1966	33.4	2.5	-	-	-	-	47.1	2.6	34.3	2.1	25.3	5.4	-	-	-	-
1967	34.1	2.1	-	-	-	-	48.8	3.6	34.5	0.6	27.2	7.5	-	-	-	-
1968	35.5	4.1	-	-	-	-	52.4	7.4	35.3	2.3	28.9	6.3	-	-	-	-
1969	37.4	5.4	-	-	-	-	56.1	7.1	36.9	4.5	30.4	5.2	-	-	-	-
1970	39.5	5.6	-	-	-	-	59.2	5.5	38.0	3.0	31.8	4.6	-	-	-	-
1971	41.1	4.1	-	-	-	-	60.7	2.5	40.8	7.4	33.8	6.3	-	-	-	-
1972	42.3	2.9	-	-	-	-	62.2	2.5	40.8	0.0	35.1	3.8			-	-
1973	44.5	5.2	-	-	-	-	63.7	2.4	42.4	3.9	36.7	4.6	-	-	-	-
1974	49.2	10.6	-	-	-	-	67.8	6.4	47.0	10.8	40.1	9.3	-	-	-	-
1975	53.9	9.6	-	-	-	-	71.1	4.9	51.2	8.9	43.6	8.7	-	-	-	-
1976	56.8	5.4	63.7	-	53.8	-	72.9	2.5	55.2	7.8	47.3	8.5	61.9	-	57.9	-
1977	60.9	7.2	67.8	6.4	57.8	7.4	79.4	8.9	58.8	6.5	51.8	9.5	64.7	4.5	61.6	6.4
1978	65.5	7.6	75.0	10.6	62.9	8.8	82.1	3.4	61.7	4.9	56.4	8.9	66.8	3.2	65.1	5.7
1979	74.4	13.6	82.0	9.3	73.2	16.4	84.4	2.8	72.2	17.0	63.9	13.3	71.1	6.4	71.4	9.7
1980	84.1	13.0	89.1	8.7	83.4	13.9	87.0	3.1	85.0	17.7	71.3	11.6	82.4	15.9	78.6	10.1
1981	91.2	8.4	94.7	6.3	90.3	8.3	92.3	6.1	93.7	10.2	79.2	11.1	90.4	9.7	84.9	8.0
1982	95.7	4.9	97.5	3.0	94.9	5.1	95.8	3.8	97.5	4.1	91.0	14.9	95.6	5.8	91.2	7.4
1983	101.3	5.9	99.3	1.8	103.2	8.7	102.2	6.7	99.5	2.1	101.1	11.1	100.0	4.6	100.7	10.4
1984	103.0	1.7	103.2	3.9	102.0	-1.2	102.1	-0.1	103.1	3.6	107.9	6.7	104.4	4.4	108.0	7.2
1985	105.7	2.6	105.8	2.5	103.5	1.5	105.7	3.5	106.5	3.3	111.8	3.6	107.0	2.5	115.5	6.9
1986	106.1	0.4	109.4	3.4	105.2	1.6	106.7	0.9	99.2	-6.9	117.6	5.2	110.6	3.4	125.3	8.5
1987	110.2	3.9	112.7	3.0	109.0	3.6	110.4	3.5	101.2	2.0	123.8	5.3	122.8	11.0	134.6	7.4
1988	114.4	3.8	115.8	2.8	113.4	4.0	114.2	3.4	105.5	4.2	131.6	6.3	123.1	0.2	141.4	5.1
1989	118.5	3.6	119.8	3.5	114.8	1.2	120.3	5.3	109.9	4.2	143.0	8.7	130.5	6.0	153.1	8.3
1990	122.4	3.3	127.4	6.3	117.0	1.9	116.8	-2.9	112.6	2.5	157.6	10.2	140.4	7.6	160.1	4.6
1991	127.4	4.1	131.0	2.8	120.2	2.7	125.6	7.5	115.9	2.9	173.7	10.2	147.6	5.1	176.8	10.4
1992	130.4	2.4	132.7	1.3	121.9	1.4	125.1	-0.4	119.1	2.8	184.2	6.0	152.7	3.5	191.3	8.2
1993	134.3	3.0	137.8	3.8	125.1	2.6	126.1	0.8	122.2	2.6	196.7	6.8	152.1	-0.4	198.5	3.8
1994	137.5	2.4	140.2	1.7	127.7	2.1	124.2	-1.5	126.1	3.2	203.9	3.7	160.4	5.5	205.5	3.5
1995	141.7	3.1	144.6	3.1	131.0	2.6	126.8	2.1	131.8	4.5	209.0	2.5	160.0	-0.2	210.9	2.6
1996	147.7	4.2	154.2	6.6	136.4	4.1	131.3	3.5	135.6	2.9	213.2	2.0	168.8	5.5	223.9	6.2
1997	151.5	2.6	160.1	3.8	139.9	2.6	133.2	1.4	137.8	1.6	211.5	-0.8	170.5	1.0	240.5	7.4

Source: U.S. Department of Labor, Bureau of Labor Statistics, Division of Consumer Prices and Price Indexes. - indicates no data collected for period.

Kansas City, MO-KS
Consumer Price Index - All Urban Consumers
Base 1982-1984 = 100
All Items

For 1917-1997. Columns headed % show percentile change in the index from the previous period for which an index is available.

Year	Jan Index	%	Feb Index	%	Mar Index	%	Apr Index	%	May Index	%	Jun Index	%	Jul Index	%	Aug Index	%	Sep Index	%	Oct Index	%	Nov Index	%	Dec Index	%
1917	-	-	-	-	-	-	-	-	-	-	-	-	-	-	-	-	-	-	-	-	-	-	14.8	-
1918	-	-	-	-	-	-	-	-	-	-	-	-	-	-	-	-	-	-	-	-	-	-	17.6	18.9
1919	-	-	-	-	-	-	-	-	-	-	17.7	0.6	-	-	-	-	-	-	-	-	-	-	20.4	15.3
1920	-	-	-	-	-	-	-	-	-	-	22.8	11.8	-	-	-	-	-	-	-	-	-	-	20.7	-9.2
1921	-	-	-	-	-	-	-	-	19.1	-7.7	-	-	-	-	-	-	18.7	-2.1	-	-	-	-	18.5	-1.1
1922	-	-	-	-	17.4	-5.9	-	-	-	-	17.4	0.0	-	-	-	-	17.3	-0.6	-	-	-	-	17.4	0.6
1923	-	-	-	-	17.4	0.0	-	-	-	-	17.4	0.0	-	-	-	-	17.5	0.6	-	-	-	-	17.5	0.0
1924	-	-	-	-	17.4	-0.6	-	-	-	-	17.2	-1.1	-	-	-	-	17.1	-0.6	-	-	-	-	17.3	1.2
1925	-	-	-	-	-	-	-	-	-	-	17.5	1.2	-	-	-	-	-	-	-	-	-	-	17.8	1.7
1926	-	-	-	-	-	-	-	-	-	-	17.7	-0.6	-	-	-	-	-	-	-	-	-	-	17.4	-1.7
1927	-	-	-	-	-	-	-	-	-	-	17.3	-0.6	-	-	-	-	-	-	-	-	-	-	16.7	-3.5
1928	-	-	-	-	-	-	-	-	-	-	16.7	0.0	-	-	-	-	-	-	-	-	-	-	16.7	0.0
1929	-	-	-	-	-	-	-	-	-	-	16.6	-0.6	-	-	-	-	-	-	-	-	-	-	16.8	1.2
1930	-	-	-	-	-	-	-	-	-	-	16.6	-1.2	-	-	-	-	-	-	-	-	-	-	16.1	-3.0
1931	-	-	-	-	-	-	-	-	-	-	15.5	-3.7	-	-	-	-	-	-	-	-	-	-	14.9	-3.9
1932	-	-	-	-	-	-	-	-	-	-	13.8	-7.4	-	-	-	-	-	-	-	-	-	-	13.5	-2.2
1933	-	-	-	-	-	-	-	-	-	-	13.2	-2.2	-	-	-	-	-	-	-	-	-	-	13.4	1.5
1934	-	-	-	-	-	-	-	-	-	-	13.6	1.5	-	-	-	-	-	-	-	-	13.8	1.5	-	-
1935	-	-	-	-	13.9	0.7	-	-	-	-	-	-	13.8	-0.7	-	-	-	-	13.9	0.7	-	-	-	-
1936	14.1	1.4	-	-	-	-	13.9	-1.4	-	-	-	-	14.1	1.4	-	-	14.3	1.4	-	-	-	-	14.2	-0.7
1937	-	-	-	-	14.5	2.1	-	-	-	-	14.7	1.4	-	-	-	-	14.8	0.7	-	-	-	-	14.6	-1.4
1938	-	-	-	-	14.4	-1.4	-	-	-	-	14.3	-0.7	-	-	-	-	14.3	0.0	-	-	-	-	14.2	-0.7
1939	-	-	-	-	14.1	-0.7	-	-	-	-	14.1	0.0	-	-	-	-	14.3	1.4	-	-	-	-	14.1	-1.4
1940	-	-	-	-	14.0	-0.7	-	-	-	-	14.0	0.0	-	-	-	-	13.9	-0.7	13.9	0.0	14.0	0.7	14.0	0.0
1941	14.0	0.0	14.0	0.0	14.1	0.7	14.3	1.4	14.3	0.0	14.5	1.4	14.5	0.0	14.7	1.4	15.1	2.7	15.3	1.3	15.4	0.7	15.5	0.6
1942	15.6	0.6	15.8	1.3	16.1	1.9	16.2	0.6	16.3	0.6	16.3	0.0	16.2	-0.6	16.4	1.2	16.3	-0.6	16.6	1.8	16.7	0.6	16.8	0.6
1943	16.8	0.0	16.9	0.6	17.2	1.8	17.4	1.2	17.4	0.0	17.4	0.0	17.2	-1.1	17.2	0.0	17.3	0.6	17.4	0.6	17.4	0.0	17.4	0.0
1944	17.4	0.0	17.4	0.0	17.4	0.0	17.5	0.6	17.6	0.6	17.6	0.0	17.7	0.6	17.6	-0.6	17.7	0.6	17.7	0.0	17.7	0.0	17.8	0.6
1945	17.8	0.0	17.8	0.0	17.8	0.0	17.9	0.6	18.0	0.6	18.1	0.6	18.2	0.6	18.2	0.0	18.1	-0.5	18.1	0.0	18.2	0.6	18.3	0.5
1946	18.3	0.0	18.2	-0.5	18.2	0.0	18.3	0.5	18.4	0.5	18.5	0.5	19.5	5.4	20.1	3.1	20.1	0.0	20.3	1.0	21.0	3.4	21.0	0.0
1947	21.1	0.5	21.2	0.5	21.5	1.4	21.6	0.5	21.5	-0.5	21.4	-0.5	21.5	0.5	-	-	-	-	22.6	5.1	-	-	-	-
1948	23.2	2.7	-	-	-	-	23.3	0.4	-	-	-	-	23.8	2.1	-	-	-	-	24.0	0.8	-	-	-	-
1949	23.6	-1.7	-	-	-	-	23.4	-0.8	-	-	-	-	23.3	-0.4	-	-	-	-	23.2	-0.4	-	-	-	-
1950	23.1	-0.4	-	-	-	-	23.3	0.9	-	-	-	-	23.8	2.1	-	-	-	-	24.1	1.3	-	-	-	-
1951	25.0	3.7	-	-	-	-	25.5	2.0	-	-	-	-	25.6	0.4	-	-	-	-	25.7	0.4	-	-	-	-
1952	26.0	1.2	-	-	-	-	26.1	0.4	-	-	-	-	26.4	1.1	-	-	-	-	26.4	0.0	-	-	-	-
1953	26.2	-0.8	-	-	-	-	26.2	0.0	-	-	-	-	26.4	0.8	-	-	-	-	26.5	0.4	-	-	-	-
1954	26.4	-0.4	-	-	-	-	26.5	0.4	-	-	-	-	26.5	0.0	-	-	-	-	26.5	0.0	-	-	-	-
1955	26.4	-0.4	-	-	-	-	26.4	0.0	-	-	-	-	26.6	0.8	-	-	-	-	26.6	0.0	-	-	-	-
1956	26.5	-0.4	-	-	-	-	26.7	0.8	-	-	-	-	27.0	1.1	-	-	-	-	27.3	1.1	-	-	-	-
1957	27.5	0.7	-	-	-	-	27.6	0.4	-	-	-	-	27.9	1.1	-	-	-	-	28.0	0.4	-	-	-	-
1958	28.1	0.4	-	-	-	-	28.4	1.1	-	-	-	-	28.6	0.7	-	-	-	-	28.7	0.3	-	-	-	-
1959	28.6	-0.3	-	-	-	-	28.8	0.7	-	-	-	-	28.9	0.3	-	-	-	-	29.1	0.7	-	-	-	-
1960	29.1	0.0	-	-	-	-	29.0	-0.3	-	-	-	-	29.3	1.0	-	-	-	-	29.4	0.3	-	-	-	-
1961	29.3	-0.3	-	-	-	-	29.7	1.4	-	-	-	-	29.8	0.3	-	-	-	-	29.7	-0.3	-	-	-	-

[Continued]

Kansas City, MO-KS
Consumer Price Index - All Urban Consumers
Base 1982-1984 = 100
All Items
[Continued]

For 1917-1997. Columns headed % show percentile change in the index from the previous period for which an index is available.

Year	Jan Index	%	Feb Index	%	Mar Index	%	Apr Index	%	May Index	%	Jun Index	%	Jul Index	%	Aug Index	%	Sep Index	%	Oct Index	%	Nov Index	%	Dec Index	%
1962	29.8	0.3	-	-	-	-	30.0	0.7	-	-	-	-	30.1	0.3	-	-	-	-	30.4	1.0	-	-	-	-
1963	30.0	-1.3	-	-	-	-	30.2	0.7	-	-	-	-	30.4	0.7	-	-	-	-	30.8	1.3	-	-	-	-
1964	30.8	0.0	-	-	-	-	30.9	0.3	-	-	-	-	31.3	1.3	-	-	-	-	31.4	0.3	-	-	-	-
1965	31.6	0.6	-	-	-	-	31.8	0.6	-	-	32.3	1.6	-	-	-	-	32.4	0.3	-	-	-	-	32.5	0.3
1966	-	-	-	-	32.7	0.6	-	-	-	-	33.0	0.9	-	-	-	-	33.2	0.6	-	-	-	-	33.3	0.3
1967	-	-	-	-	33.4	0.3	-	-	-	-	33.3	-0.3	-	-	-	-	34.1	2.4	-	-	-	-	34.1	0.0
1968	-	-	-	-	34.5	1.2	-	-	-	-	35.2	2.0	-	-	-	-	35.3	0.3	-	-	-	-	35.6	0.8
1969	-	-	-	-	36.3	2.0	-	-	-	-	37.0	1.9	-	-	-	-	37.3	0.8	-	-	-	-	37.8	1.3
1970	-	-	-	-	38.2	1.1	-	-	-	-	39.1	2.4	-	-	-	-	39.3	0.5	-	-	-	-	40.1	2.0
1971	-	-	-	-	40.1	0.0	-	-	-	-	40.6	1.2	-	-	-	-	40.9	0.7	-	-	-	-	40.9	0.0
1972	-	-	-	-	41.2	0.7	-	-	-	-	41.7	1.2	-	-	-	-	42.3	1.4	-	-	-	-	42.3	0.0
1973	-	-	-	-	42.9	1.4	-	-	-	-	43.7	1.9	-	-	-	-	44.6	2.1	-	-	-	-	45.3	1.6
1974	-	-	-	-	46.7	3.1	-	-	-	-	48.3	3.4	-	-	-	-	49.9	3.3	-	-	-	-	51.4	3.0
1975	-	-	-	-	52.1	1.4	-	-	-	-	52.9	1.5	-	-	-	-	54.0	2.1	-	-	-	-	54.9	1.7
1976	-	-	-	-	55.0	0.2	-	-	-	-	55.9	1.6	-	-	-	-	56.8	1.6	-	-	-	-	57.5	1.2
1977	-	-	-	-	58.9	2.4	-	-	-	-	60.3	2.4	-	-	-	-	60.8	0.8	-	-	-	-	61.5	1.2
1978	-	-	61.9	0.7	-	-	63.6	2.7	-	-	64.7	1.7	-	-	65.4	1.1	-	-	66.3	1.4	-	-	67.0	1.1
1979	-	-	68.9	2.8	-	-	71.2	3.3	-	-	73.9	3.8	-	-	75.6	2.3	-	-	77.4	2.4	-	-	78.7	1.7
1980	-	-	80.4	2.2	-	-	82.1	2.1	-	-	83.5	1.7	-	-	84.5	1.2	-	-	85.8	1.5	-	-	87.3	1.7
1981	-	-	88.2	1.0	-	-	89.4	1.4	-	-	91.1	1.9	-	-	91.4	0.3	-	-	91.8	0.4	-	-	92.1	0.3
1982	-	-	92.9	0.9	-	-	92.3	-0.6	-	-	94.8	2.7	-	-	96.0	1.3	-	-	97.4	1.5	-	-	97.9	0.5
1983	-	-	98.4	0.5	-	-	99.7	1.3	-	-	100.2	0.5	-	-	101.5	1.3	-	-	102.1	0.6	-	-	102.0	-0.1
1984	-	-	103.2	1.2	-	-	104.1	0.9	-	-	104.7	0.6	-	-	104.8	0.1	-	-	105.8	1.0	-	-	105.6	-0.2
1985	-	-	105.9	0.3	-	-	107.7	1.7	-	-	107.8	0.1	-	-	108.1	0.3	-	-	108.8	0.6	-	-	108.4	-0.4
1986	-	-	108.1	-0.3	-	-	108.0	-0.1	-	-	108.7	0.6	-	-	109.1	0.4	-	-	109.0	-0.1	-	-	109.3	0.3
1987	-	-	-	-	-	-	-	-	-	-	111.5	2.0	-	-	-	-	-	-	-	-	-	-	114.6	2.8
1988	-	-	-	-	-	-	-	-	-	-	116.3	1.5	-	-	-	-	-	-	-	-	-	-	118.4	1.8
1989	-	-	-	-	-	-	-	-	-	-	120.6	1.9	-	-	-	-	-	-	-	-	-	-	122.6	1.7
1990	-	-	-	-	-	-	-	-	-	-	124.3	1.4	-	-	-	-	-	-	-	-	-	-	127.7	2.7
1991	-	-	-	-	-	-	-	-	-	-	130.2	2.0	-	-	-	-	-	-	-	-	-	-	132.3	1.6
1992	-	-	-	-	-	-	-	-	-	-	133.4	0.8	-	-	-	-	-	-	-	-	-	-	135.2	1.3
1993	-	-	-	-	-	-	-	-	-	-	137.5	1.7	-	-	-	-	-	-	-	-	-	-	138.7	0.9
1994	-	-	-	-	-	-	-	-	-	-	140.6	1.4	-	-	-	-	-	-	-	-	-	-	141.9	0.9
1995	-	-	-	-	-	-	-	-	-	-	144.3	1.7	-	-	-	-	-	-	-	-	-	-	146.3	1.4
1996	-	-	-	-	-	-	-	-	-	-	150.6	2.9	-	-	-	-	-	-	-	-	-	-	152.6	1.3
1997	-	-	-	-	-	-	-	-	-	-	155.2	1.7	-	-	-	-	-	-	-	-	-	-	-	-

Source: U.S. Department of Labor, Bureau of Labor Statistics, Division of Consumer Prices and Price Indexes. - indicates no data collected for period.

Kansas City, MO-KS

Consumer Price Index - Urban Wage Earners
Base 1982-1984 = 100
All Items

For 1917-1997. Columns headed % show percentile change in the index from the previous period for which an index is available.

Year	Jan Index	%	Feb Index	%	Mar Index	%	Apr Index	%	May Index	%	Jun Index	%	Jul Index	%	Aug Index	%	Sep Index	%	Oct Index	%	Nov Index	%	Dec Index	%
1917	-	-	-	-	-	-	-	-	-	-	-	-	-	-	-	-	-	-	-	-	-	-	15.0	-
1918	-	-	-	-	-	-	-	-	-	-	-	-	-	-	-	-	-	-	-	-	-	-	17.8	18.7
1919	-	-	-	-	-	-	-	-	-	-	18.0	1.1	-	-	-	-	-	-	-	-	-	-	20.7	15.0
1920	-	-	-	-	-	-	-	-	-	-	23.1	11.6	-	-	-	-	-	-	-	-	-	-	21.0	-9.1
1921	-	-	-	-	-	-	-	-	19.4	-7.6	-	-	-	-	-	-	19.0	-2.1	-	-	-	-	18.7	-1.6
1922	-	-	-	-	17.7	-5.3	-	-	-	-	17.7	0.0	-	-	-	-	17.5	-1.1	-	-	-	-	17.6	0.6
1923	-	-	-	-	17.6	0.0	-	-	-	-	17.6	0.0	-	-	-	-	17.8	1.1	-	-	-	-	17.8	0.0
1924	-	-	-	-	17.6	-1.1	-	-	-	-	17.4	-1.1	-	-	-	-	17.4	0.0	-	-	-	-	17.5	0.6
1925	-	-	-	-	-	-	-	-	-	-	17.8	1.7	-	-	-	-	-	-	-	-	-	-	18.0	1.1
1926	-	-	-	-	-	-	-	-	-	-	17.9	-0.6	-	-	-	-	-	-	-	-	-	-	17.6	-1.7
1927	-	-	-	-	-	-	-	-	-	-	17.6	0.0	-	-	-	-	-	-	-	-	-	-	17.0	-3.4
1928	-	-	-	-	-	-	-	-	-	-	17.0	0.0	-	-	-	-	-	-	-	-	-	-	16.9	-0.6
1929	-	-	-	-	-	-	-	-	-	-	16.9	0.0	-	-	-	-	-	-	-	-	-	-	17.0	0.6
1930	-	-	-	-	-	-	-	-	-	-	16.8	-1.2	-	-	-	-	-	-	-	-	-	-	16.3	-3.0
1931	-	-	-	-	-	-	-	-	-	-	15.7	-3.7	-	-	-	-	-	-	-	-	-	-	15.1	-3.8
1932	-	-	-	-	-	-	-	-	-	-	14.0	-7.3	-	-	-	-	-	-	-	-	-	-	13.7	-2.1
1933	-	-	-	-	-	-	-	-	-	-	13.4	-2.2	-	-	-	-	-	-	-	-	-	-	13.5	0.7
1934	-	-	-	-	-	-	-	-	-	-	13.8	2.2	-	-	-	-	-	-	-	-	14.0	1.4	-	-
1935	-	-	-	-	14.1	0.7	-	-	-	-	-	-	14.0	-0.7	-	-	-	-	14.1	0.7	-	-	-	-
1936	14.3	1.4	-	-	-	-	14.1	-1.4	-	-	-	-	14.3	1.4	-	-	14.5	1.4	-	-	-	-	14.4	-0.7
1937	-	-	-	-	14.7	2.1	-	-	-	-	14.9	1.4	-	-	-	-	15.0	0.7	-	-	-	-	14.8	-1.3
1938	-	-	-	-	14.6	-1.4	-	-	-	-	14.5	-0.7	-	-	-	-	14.5	0.0	-	-	-	-	14.4	-0.7
1939	-	-	-	-	14.3	-0.7	-	-	-	-	14.3	0.0	-	-	-	-	14.5	1.4	-	-	-	-	14.3	-1.4
1940	-	-	-	-	14.2	-0.7	-	-	-	-	14.2	0.0	-	-	-	-	14.1	-0.7	14.1	0.0	14.2	0.7	14.2	0.0
1941	14.2	0.0	14.2	0.0	14.3	0.7	14.5	1.4	14.5	0.0	14.7	1.4	14.7	0.0	14.9	1.4	15.3	2.7	15.5	1.3	15.6	0.6	15.7	0.6
1942	15.8	0.6	16.0	1.3	16.3	1.9	16.4	0.6	16.5	0.6	16.5	0.0	16.5	0.0	16.6	0.6	16.6	0.0	16.8	1.2	16.9	0.6	17.0	0.6
1943	17.0	0.0	17.2	1.2	17.4	1.2	17.6	1.1	17.7	0.6	17.6	-0.6	17.4	-1.1	17.4	0.0	17.5	0.6	17.6	0.6	17.6	0.0	17.7	0.6
1944	17.6	-0.6	17.6	0.0	17.6	0.0	17.8	1.1	17.8	0.0	17.8	0.0	18.0	1.1	17.9	-0.6	18.0	0.6	17.9	-0.6	18.0	0.6	18.0	0.0
1945	18.1	0.6	18.1	0.0	18.1	0.0	18.2	0.6	18.3	0.5	18.4	0.5	18.4	0.0	18.5	0.5	18.4	-0.5	18.4	0.0	18.4	0.0	18.5	0.5
1946	18.5	0.0	18.4	-0.5	18.5	0.5	18.6	0.5	18.6	0.0	18.7	0.5	19.7	5.3	20.3	3.0	20.4	0.5	20.5	0.5	21.3	3.9	21.3	0.0
1947	21.4	0.5	21.5	0.5	21.8	1.4	21.8	0.0	21.8	0.0	21.6	-0.9	21.8	0.9	-	-	-	-	22.9	5.0	-	-	-	-
1948	23.5	2.6	-	-	-	-	23.7	0.9	-	-	-	-	24.1	1.7	-	-	-	-	24.3	0.8	-	-	-	-
1949	24.0	-1.2	-	-	-	-	23.8	-0.8	-	-	-	-	23.6	-0.8	-	-	-	-	23.5	-0.4	-	-	-	-
1950	23.4	-0.4	-	-	-	-	23.6	0.9	-	-	-	-	24.1	2.1	-	-	-	-	24.4	1.2	-	-	-	-
1951	25.4	4.1	-	-	-	-	25.8	1.6	-	-	-	-	25.9	0.4	-	-	-	-	26.0	0.4	-	-	-	-
1952	26.3	1.2	-	-	-	-	26.5	0.8	-	-	-	-	26.8	1.1	-	-	-	-	26.8	0.0	-	-	-	-
1953	26.6	-0.7	-	-	-	-	26.6	0.0	-	-	-	-	26.8	0.8	-	-	-	-	26.9	0.4	-	-	-	-
1954	26.7	-0.7	-	-	-	-	26.9	0.7	-	-	-	-	26.9	0.0	-	-	-	-	26.9	0.0	-	-	-	-
1955	26.8	-0.4	-	-	-	-	26.8	0.0	-	-	-	-	26.9	0.4	-	-	-	-	27.0	0.4	-	-	-	-
1956	26.9	-0.4	-	-	-	-	27.1	0.7	-	-	-	-	27.3	0.7	-	-	-	-	27.6	1.1	-	-	-	-
1957	27.8	0.7	-	-	-	-	28.0	0.7	-	-	-	-	28.3	1.1	-	-	-	-	28.3	0.0	-	-	-	-
1958	28.4	0.4	-	-	-	-	28.7	1.1	-	-	-	-	29.0	1.0	-	-	-	-	29.0	0.0	-	-	-	-
1959	28.9	-0.3	-	-	-	-	29.2	1.0	-	-	-	-	29.3	0.3	-	-	-	-	29.5	0.7	-	-	-	-
1960	29.5	0.0	-	-	-	-	29.4	-0.3	-	-	-	-	29.7	1.0	-	-	-	-	29.8	0.3	-	-	-	-
1961	29.7	-0.3	-	-	-	-	30.1	1.3	-	-	-	-	30.2	0.3	-	-	-	-	30.1	-0.3	-	-	-	-

[Continued]

Kansas City, MO-KS
Consumer Price Index - Urban Wage Earners
Base 1982-1984 = 100
All Items
[Continued]

For 1917-1997. Columns headed % show percentile change in the index from the previous period for which an index is available.

Year	Jan Index	%	Feb Index	%	Mar Index	%	Apr Index	%	May Index	%	Jun Index	%	Jul Index	%	Aug Index	%	Sep Index	%	Oct Index	%	Nov Index	%	Dec Index	%
1962	30.2	0.3	-	-	-	-	30.4	0.7	-	-	-	-	30.5	0.3	-	-	-	-	30.8	1.0	-	-	-	-
1963	30.4	-1.3	-	-	-	-	30.6	0.7	-	-	-	-	30.8	0.7	-	-	-	-	31.3	1.6	-	-	-	-
1964	31.2	-0.3	-	-	-	-	31.3	0.3	-	-	-	-	31.7	1.3	-	-	-	-	31.8	0.3	-	-	-	-
1965	32.0	0.6	-	-	-	-	32.2	0.6	-	-	32.8	1.9	-	-	-	-	32.9	0.3	-	-	-	-	32.9	0.0
1966	-	-	-	-	33.1	0.6	-	-	-	-	33.5	1.2	-	-	-	-	33.7	0.6	-	-	-	-	33.7	0.0
1967	-	-	-	-	33.9	0.6	-	-	-	-	33.8	-0.3	-	-	-	-	34.5	2.1	-	-	-	-	34.6	0.3
1968	-	-	-	-	35.0	1.2	-	-	-	-	35.7	2.0	-	-	-	-	35.8	0.3	-	-	-	-	36.1	0.8
1969	-	-	-	-	36.8	1.9	-	-	-	-	37.5	1.9	-	-	-	-	37.8	0.8	-	-	-	-	38.3	1.3
1970	-	-	-	-	38.7	1.0	-	-	-	-	39.7	2.6	-	-	-	-	39.8	0.3	-	-	-	-	40.6	2.0
1971	-	-	-	-	40.7	0.2	-	-	-	-	41.2	1.2	-	-	-	-	41.5	0.7	-	-	-	-	41.4	-0.2
1972	-	-	-	-	41.8	1.0	-	-	-	-	42.3	1.2	-	-	-	-	42.8	1.2	-	-	-	-	42.8	0.0
1973	-	-	-	-	43.5	1.6	-	-	-	-	44.3	1.8	-	-	-	-	45.2	2.0	-	-	-	-	45.9	1.5
1974	-	-	-	-	47.3	3.1	-	-	-	-	48.9	3.4	-	-	-	-	50.5	3.3	-	-	-	-	52.1	3.2
1975	-	-	-	-	52.8	1.3	-	-	-	-	53.7	1.7	-	-	-	-	54.7	1.9	-	-	-	-	55.6	1.6
1976	-	-	-	-	55.8	0.4	-	-	-	-	56.6	1.4	-	-	-	-	57.6	1.8	-	-	-	-	58.3	1.2
1977	-	-	-	-	59.7	2.4	-	-	-	-	61.1	2.3	-	-	-	-	61.6	0.8	-	-	-	-	62.4	1.3
1978	-	-	62.9	0.8	-	-	64.4	2.4	-	-	65.6	1.9	-	-	66.3	1.1	-	-	67.3	1.5	-	-	67.9	0.9
1979	-	-	69.7	2.7	-	-	72.0	3.3	-	-	74.5	3.5	-	-	76.1	2.1	-	-	77.8	2.2	-	-	79.3	1.9
1980	-	-	80.8	1.9	-	-	82.7	2.4	-	-	84.1	1.7	-	-	85.1	1.2	-	-	86.3	1.4	-	-	87.8	1.7
1981	-	-	88.8	1.1	-	-	90.2	1.6	-	-	91.8	1.8	-	-	92.2	0.4	-	-	92.6	0.4	-	-	92.8	0.2
1982	-	-	93.5	0.8	-	-	92.9	-0.6	-	-	95.6	2.9	-	-	96.8	1.3	-	-	98.1	1.3	-	-	98.5	0.4
1983	-	-	98.6	0.1	-	-	100.2	1.6	-	-	101.8	1.6	-	-	102.2	0.4	-	-	103.7	1.5	-	-	102.4	-1.3
1984	-	-	101.2	-1.2	-	-	102.3	1.1	-	-	102.4	0.1	-	-	103.9	1.5	-	-	105.0	1.1	-	-	103.8	-1.1
1985	-	-	103.9	0.1	-	-	105.7	1.7	-	-	106.0	0.3	-	-	106.2	0.2	-	-	106.8	0.6	-	-	106.4	-0.4
1986	-	-	105.8	-0.6	-	-	105.4	-0.4	-	-	106.3	0.9	-	-	106.5	0.2	-	-	106.2	-0.3	-	-	106.6	0.4
1987	-	-	-	-	-	-	-	-	-	-	108.6	1.9	-	-	-	-	-	-	-	-	-	-	111.7	2.9
1988	-	-	-	-	-	-	-	-	-	-	113.3	1.4	-	-	-	-	-	-	-	-	-	-	115.5	1.9
1989	-	-	-	-	-	-	-	-	-	-	117.6	1.8	-	-	-	-	-	-	-	-	-	-	119.4	1.5
1990	-	-	-	-	-	-	-	-	-	-	120.8	1.2	-	-	-	-	-	-	-	-	-	-	124.0	2.6
1991	-	-	-	-	-	-	-	-	-	-	126.2	1.8	-	-	-	-	-	-	-	-	-	-	128.5	1.8
1992	-	-	-	-	-	-	-	-	-	-	129.4	0.7	-	-	-	-	-	-	-	-	-	-	131.4	1.5
1993	-	-	-	-	-	-	-	-	-	-	133.5	1.6	-	-	-	-	-	-	-	-	-	-	135.0	1.1
1994	-	-	-	-	-	-	-	-	-	-	136.9	1.4	-	-	-	-	-	-	-	-	-	-	138.1	0.9
1995	-	-	-	-	-	-	-	-	-	-	140.9	2.0	-	-	-	-	-	-	-	-	-	-	142.6	1.2
1996	-	-	-	-	-	-	-	-	-	-	146.8	2.9	-	-	-	-	-	-	-	-	-	-	148.7	1.3
1997	-	-	-	-	-	-	-	-	-	-	151.0	1.5	-	-	-	-	-	-	-	-	-	-	-	-

Source: U.S. Department of Labor, Bureau of Labor Statistics, Division of Consumer Prices and Price Indexes. - indicates no data collected for period.

Kansas City, MO-KS
Consumer Price Index - All Urban Consumers
Base 1982-1984 = 100
Food and Beverages

For 1975-1997. Columns headed % show percentile change in the index from the previous period for which an index is available.

Year	Jan Index	%	Feb Index	%	Mar Index	%	Apr Index	%	May Index	%	Jun Index	%	Jul Index	%	Aug Index	%	Sep Index	%	Oct Index	%	Nov Index	%	Dec Index	%
1975	-	-	-	-	-	-	-	-	-	-	-	-	-	-	-	-	-	-	-	-	-	-	63.9	-
1976	-	-	-	-	62.7	-1.9	-	-	-	-	62.2	-0.8	-	-	-	-	63.4	1.9	-	-	-	-	63.2	-0.3
1977	-	-	-	-	65.6	3.8	-	-	-	-	67.7	3.2	-	-	-	-	68.0	0.4	-	-	-	-	68.5	0.7
1978	-	-	70.5	2.9	-	-	72.7	3.1	-	-	75.6	4.0	-	-	76.1	0.7	-	-	76.9	1.1	-	-	78.1	1.6
1979	-	-	81.3	4.1	-	-	82.3	1.2	-	-	82.6	0.4	-	-	83.1	0.6	-	-	83.3	0.2	-	-	84.9	1.9
1980	-	-	86.5	1.9	-	-	88.3	2.1	-	-	89.2	1.0	-	-	90.4	1.3	-	-	91.8	1.5	-	-	93.4	1.7
1981	-	-	95.0	1.7	-	-	95.5	0.5	-	-	93.5	-2.1	-	-	95.0	1.6	-	-	95.5	0.5	-	-	95.9	0.4
1982	-	-	96.9	1.0	-	-	96.2	-0.7	-	-	98.4	2.3	-	-	98.3	-0.1	-	-	98.1	-0.2	-	-	97.9	-0.2
1983	-	-	98.6	0.7	-	-	98.8	0.2	-	-	99.6	0.8	-	-	99.1	-0.5	-	-	99.8	0.7	-	-	99.6	-0.2
1984	-	-	102.6	3.0	-	-	103.2	0.6	-	-	102.6	-0.6	-	-	103.5	0.9	-	-	104.6	1.1	-	-	104.5	-0.1
1985	-	-	105.8	1.2	-	-	106.5	0.7	-	-	106.1	-0.4	-	-	105.7	-0.4	-	-	105.8	0.1	-	-	106.7	0.9
1986	-	-	107.9	1.1	-	-	108.6	0.6	-	-	109.0	0.4	-	-	110.8	1.7	-	-	110.7	-0.1	-	-	111.1	0.4
1987	-	-	-	-	-	-	-	-	-	-	112.7	1.4	-	-	-	-	-	-	-	-	-	-	112.9	0.2
1988	-	-	-	-	-	-	-	-	-	-	114.7	1.6	-	-	-	-	-	-	-	-	-	-	116.9	1.9
1989	-	-	-	-	-	-	-	-	-	-	118.8	1.6	-	-	-	-	-	-	-	-	-	-	120.9	1.8
1990	-	-	-	-	-	-	-	-	-	-	127.0	5.0	-	-	-	-	-	-	-	-	-	-	127.9	0.7
1991	-	-	-	-	-	-	-	-	-	-	131.1	2.5	-	-	-	-	-	-	-	-	-	-	130.8	-0.2
1992	-	-	-	-	-	-	-	-	-	-	130.7	-0.1	-	-	-	-	-	-	-	-	-	-	135.1	3.4
1993	-	-	-	-	-	-	-	-	-	-	137.4	1.7	-	-	-	-	-	-	-	-	-	-	138.1	0.5
1994	-	-	-	-	-	-	-	-	-	-	138.8	0.5	-	-	-	-	-	-	-	-	-	-	141.6	2.0
1995	-	-	-	-	-	-	-	-	-	-	142.8	0.8	-	-	-	-	-	-	-	-	-	-	146.5	2.6
1996	-	-	-	-	-	-	-	-	-	-	151.7	3.5	-	-	-	-	-	-	-	-	-	-	156.6	3.2
1997	-	-	-	-	-	-	-	-	-	-	158.8	1.4	-	-	-	-	-	-	-	-	-	-	-	-

Source: U.S. Department of Labor, Bureau of Labor Statistics, Division of Consumer Prices and Price Indexes. - indicates no data collected for period.

Kansas City, MO-KS
Consumer Price Index - Urban Wage Earners
Base 1982-1984 = 100
Food and Beverages

For 1975-1997. Columns headed % show percentile change in the index from the previous period for which an index is available.

Year	Jan Index	%	Feb Index	%	Mar Index	%	Apr Index	%	May Index	%	Jun Index	%	Jul Index	%	Aug Index	%	Sep Index	%	Oct Index	%	Nov Index	%	Dec Index	%
1975	-	-	-	-	-	-	-	-	-	-	-	-	-	-	-	-	-	-	-	-	-	-	64.7	-
1976	-	-	-	-	63.4	-2.0	-	-	-	-	63.0	-0.6	-	-	-	-	64.2	1.9	-	-	-	-	63.9	-0.5
1977	-	-	-	-	66.4	3.9	-	-	-	-	68.6	3.3	-	-	-	-	68.8	0.3	-	-	-	-	69.3	0.7
1978	-	-	71.0	2.5	-	-	73.0	2.8	-	-	76.1	4.2	-	-	76.5	0.5	-	-	77.2	0.9	-	-	78.6	1.8
1979	-	-	81.0	3.1	-	-	81.8	1.0	-	-	81.9	0.1	-	-	82.2	0.4	-	-	82.4	0.2	-	-	83.9	1.8
1980	-	-	85.7	2.1	-	-	87.4	2.0	-	-	88.3	1.0	-	-	90.0	1.9	-	-	91.9	2.1	-	-	93.3	1.5
1981	-	-	94.2	1.0	-	-	94.8	0.6	-	-	93.6	-1.3	-	-	94.9	1.4	-	-	95.9	1.1	-	-	95.9	0.0
1982	-	-	96.8	0.9	-	-	96.1	-0.7	-	-	98.4	2.4	-	-	98.5	0.1	-	-	98.1	-0.4	-	-	97.9	-0.2
1983	-	-	98.8	0.9	-	-	99.0	0.2	-	-	99.6	0.6	-	-	99.3	-0.3	-	-	99.8	0.5	-	-	99.6	-0.2
1984	-	-	102.5	2.9	-	-	103.1	0.6	-	-	102.5	-0.6	-	-	103.4	0.9	-	-	104.5	1.1	-	-	104.3	-0.2
1985	-	-	105.4	1.1	-	-	106.2	0.8	-	-	105.9	-0.3	-	-	105.6	-0.3	-	-	105.6	0.0	-	-	106.6	0.9
1986	-	-	107.9	1.2	-	-	108.5	0.6	-	-	108.7	0.2	-	-	110.7	1.8	-	-	110.7	0.0	-	-	111.1	0.4
1987	-	-	-	-	-	-	-	-	-	-	112.5	1.3	-	-	-	-	-	-	-	-	-	-	112.9	0.4
1988	-	-	-	-	-	-	-	-	-	-	114.7	1.6	-	-	-	-	-	-	-	-	-	-	116.9	1.9
1989	-	-	-	-	-	-	-	-	-	-	118.8	1.6	-	-	-	-	-	-	-	-	-	-	120.9	1.8
1990	-	-	-	-	-	-	-	-	-	-	126.9	5.0	-	-	-	-	-	-	-	-	-	-	127.9	0.8
1991	-	-	-	-	-	-	-	-	-	-	131.0	2.4	-	-	-	-	-	-	-	-	-	-	131.0	0.0
1992	-	-	-	-	-	-	-	-	-	-	130.4	-0.5	-	-	-	-	-	-	-	-	-	-	135.1	3.6
1993	-	-	-	-	-	-	-	-	-	-	137.3	1.6	-	-	-	-	-	-	-	-	-	-	138.2	0.7
1994	-	-	-	-	-	-	-	-	-	-	138.7	0.4	-	-	-	-	-	-	-	-	-	-	141.6	2.1
1995	-	-	-	-	-	-	-	-	-	-	142.7	0.8	-	-	-	-	-	-	-	-	-	-	146.5	2.7
1996	-	-	-	-	-	-	-	-	-	-	151.8	3.6	-	-	-	-	-	-	-	-	-	-	156.6	3.2
1997	-	-	-	-	-	-	-	-	-	-	158.9	1.5	-	-	-	-	-	-	-	-	-	-	-	-

Source: U.S. Department of Labor, Bureau of Labor Statistics, Division of Consumer Prices and Price Indexes. - indicates no data collected for period.

Kansas City, MO-KS
Consumer Price Index - All Urban Consumers
Base 1982-1984 = 100
Housing

For 1975-1997. Columns headed % show percentile change in the index from the previous period for which an index is available.

Year	Jan Index	%	Feb Index	%	Mar Index	%	Apr Index	%	May Index	%	Jun Index	%	Jul Index	%	Aug Index	%	Sep Index	%	Oct Index	%	Nov Index	%	Dec Index	%
1975	-	-	-	-	-	-	-	-	-	-	-	-	-	-	-	-	-	-	-	-	-	-	51.2	-
1976	-	-	-	-	51.6	0.8	-	-	-	-	52.5	1.7	-	-	-	-	53.4	1.7	-	-	-	-	54.4	1.9
1977	-	-	-	-	55.3	1.7	-	-	-	-	56.6	2.4	-	-	-	-	57.5	1.6	-	-	-	-	58.4	1.6
1978	-	-	58.8	0.7	-	-	60.9	3.6	-	-	61.7	1.3	-	-	62.2	0.8	-	-	63.0	1.3	-	-	63.2	0.3
1979	-	-	65.3	3.3	-	-	68.5	4.9	-	-	72.2	5.4	-	-	74.4	3.0	-	-	77.3	3.9	-	-	78.6	1.7
1980	-	-	79.3	0.9	-	-	80.6	1.6	-	-	83.0	3.0	-	-	83.8	1.0	-	-	85.2	1.7	-	-	86.6	1.6
1981	-	-	86.3	-0.3	-	-	88.0	2.0	-	-	91.5	4.0	-	-	91.0	-0.5	-	-	90.5	-0.5	-	-	90.5	0.0
1982	-	-	91.6	1.2	-	-	89.9	-1.9	-	-	93.1	3.6	-	-	94.5	1.5	-	-	97.1	2.8	-	-	98.4	1.3
1983	-	-	99.6	1.2	-	-	100.7	1.1	-	-	100.7	0.0	-	-	102.9	2.2	-	-	101.9	-1.0	-	-	102.2	0.3
1984	-	-	103.3	1.1	-	-	104.3	1.0	-	-	106.0	1.6	-	-	106.1	0.1	-	-	105.7	-0.4	-	-	105.8	0.1
1985	-	-	106.1	0.3	-	-	107.3	1.1	-	-	108.1	0.7	-	-	108.6	0.5	-	-	108.7	0.1	-	-	107.1	-1.5
1986	-	-	108.0	0.8	-	-	109.3	1.2	-	-	109.2	-0.1	-	-	111.3	1.9	-	-	109.5	-1.6	-	-	110.3	0.7
1987	-	-	-	-	-	-	-	-	-	-	112.2	1.7	-	-	-	-	-	-	-	-	-	-	114.9	2.4
1988	-	-	-	-	-	-	-	-	-	-	117.9	2.6	-	-	-	-	-	-	-	-	-	-	118.7	0.7
1989	-	-	-	-	-	-	-	-	-	-	119.6	0.8	-	-	-	-	-	-	-	-	-	-	119.7	0.1
1990	-	-	-	-	-	-	-	-	-	-	121.3	1.3	-	-	-	-	-	-	-	-	-	-	122.4	0.9
1991	-	-	-	-	-	-	-	-	-	-	124.5	1.7	-	-	-	-	-	-	-	-	-	-	126.3	1.4
1992	-	-	-	-	-	-	-	-	-	-	126.8	0.4	-	-	-	-	-	-	-	-	-	-	127.6	0.6
1993	-	-	-	-	-	-	-	-	-	-	129.3	1.3	-	-	-	-	-	-	-	-	-	-	131.6	1.8
1994	-	-	-	-	-	-	-	-	-	-	132.4	0.6	-	-	-	-	-	-	-	-	-	-	133.8	1.1
1995	-	-	-	-	-	-	-	-	-	-	135.0	0.9	-	-	-	-	-	-	-	-	-	-	138.3	2.4
1996	-	-	-	-	-	-	-	-	-	-	141.3	2.2	-	-	-	-	-	-	-	-	-	-	143.5	1.6
1997	-	-	-	-	-	-	-	-	-	-	145.1	1.1	-	-	-	-	-	-	-	-	-	-	-	-

Source: U.S. Department of Labor, Bureau of Labor Statistics, Division of Consumer Prices and Price Indexes. - indicates no data collected for period.

Kansas City, MO-KS
Consumer Price Index - Urban Wage Earners
Base 1982-1984 = 100
Housing

For 1975-1997. Columns headed % show percentile change in the index from the previous period for which an index is available.

Year	Jan Index	%	Feb Index	%	Mar Index	%	Apr Index	%	May Index	%	Jun Index	%	Jul Index	%	Aug Index	%	Sep Index	%	Oct Index	%	Nov Index	%	Dec Index	%
1975	-	-	-	-	-	-	-	-	-	-	-	-	-	-	-	-	-	-	-	-	-	-	52.2	-
1976	-	-	-	-	52.7	1.0	-	-	-	-	53.6	1.7	-	-	-	-	54.5	1.7	-	-	-	-	55.5	1.8
1977	-	-	-	-	56.4	1.6	-	-	-	-	57.8	2.5	-	-	-	-	58.7	1.6	-	-	-	-	59.6	1.5
1978	-	-	60.2	1.0	-	-	62.3	3.5	-	-	63.1	1.3	-	-	63.6	0.8	-	-	64.5	1.4	-	-	64.7	0.3
1979	-	-	66.8	3.2	-	-	69.8	4.5	-	-	73.4	5.2	-	-	75.4	2.7	-	-	78.1	3.6	-	-	79.6	1.9
1980	-	-	79.5	-0.1	-	-	81.1	2.0	-	-	83.8	3.3	-	-	84.6	1.0	-	-	85.8	1.4	-	-	87.3	1.7
1981	-	-	87.0	-0.3	-	-	88.8	2.1	-	-	92.2	3.8	-	-	91.9	-0.3	-	-	91.4	-0.5	-	-	91.4	0.0
1982	-	-	92.5	1.2	-	-	90.8	-1.8	-	-	94.2	3.7	-	-	95.7	1.6	-	-	98.2	2.6	-	-	99.8	1.6
1983	-	-	100.0	0.2	-	-	101.9	1.9	-	-	104.5	2.6	-	-	104.2	-0.3	-	-	106.0	1.7	-	-	103.4	-2.5
1984	-	-	99.3	-4.0	-	-	100.7	1.4	-	-	100.9	0.2	-	-	104.3	3.4	-	-	104.4	0.1	-	-	101.9	-2.4
1985	-	-	102.1	0.2	-	-	103.2	1.1	-	-	104.1	0.9	-	-	104.6	0.5	-	-	104.6	0.0	-	-	103.0	-1.5
1986	-	-	104.0	1.0	-	-	105.0	1.0	-	-	104.9	-0.1	-	-	107.1	2.1	-	-	105.1	-1.9	-	-	106.0	0.9
1987	-	-	-	-	-	-	-	-	-	-	107.8	1.7	-	-	-	-	-	-	-	-	-	-	110.3	2.3
1988	-	-	-	-	-	-	-	-	-	-	113.0	2.4	-	-	-	-	-	-	-	-	-	-	113.8	0.7
1989	-	-	-	-	-	-	-	-	-	-	114.8	0.9	-	-	-	-	-	-	-	-	-	-	114.8	0.0
1990	-	-	-	-	-	-	-	-	-	-	116.5	1.5	-	-	-	-	-	-	-	-	-	-	117.5	0.9
1991	-	-	-	-	-	-	-	-	-	-	119.4	1.6	-	-	-	-	-	-	-	-	-	-	121.0	1.3
1992	-	-	-	-	-	-	-	-	-	-	121.5	0.4	-	-	-	-	-	-	-	-	-	-	122.3	0.7
1993	-	-	-	-	-	-	-	-	-	-	123.9	1.3	-	-	-	-	-	-	-	-	-	-	126.3	1.9
1994	-	-	-	-	-	-	-	-	-	-	127.1	0.6	-	-	-	-	-	-	-	-	-	-	128.3	0.9
1995	-	-	-	-	-	-	-	-	-	-	129.5	0.9	-	-	-	-	-	-	-	-	-	-	132.6	2.4
1996	-	-	-	-	-	-	-	-	-	-	135.3	2.0	-	-	-	-	-	-	-	-	-	-	137.5	1.6
1997	-	-	-	-	-	-	-	-	-	-	138.9	1.0	-	-	-	-	-	-	-	-	-	-	-	-

Source: U.S. Department of Labor, Bureau of Labor Statistics, Division of Consumer Prices and Price Indexes. - indicates no data collected for period.

Kansas City, MO-KS
Consumer Price Index - All Urban Consumers
Base 1982-1984 = 100
Apparel and Upkeep

For 1952-1997. Columns headed % show percentile change in the index from the previous period for which an index is available.

Year	Jan Index	Jan %	Feb Index	Feb %	Mar Index	Mar %	Apr Index	Apr %	May Index	May %	Jun Index	Jun %	Jul Index	Jul %	Aug Index	Aug %	Sep Index	Sep %	Oct Index	Oct %	Nov Index	Nov %	Dec Index	Dec %
1952	-	-	-	-	-	-	-	-	-	-	-	-	-	-	-	-	-	-	39.3	-	-	-	-	-
1953	39.2	-0.3	-	-	-	-	39.2	0.0	-	-	-	-	39.4	0.5	-	-	-	-	39.3	-0.3	-	-	-	-
1954	39.0	-0.8	-	-	-	-	38.8	-0.5	-	-	-	-	38.8	0.0	-	-	-	-	39.1	0.8	-	-	-	-
1955	38.5	-1.5	-	-	-	-	38.6	0.3	-	-	-	-	38.6	0.0	-	-	-	-	39.4	2.1	-	-	-	-
1956	39.1	-0.8	-	-	-	-	39.1	0.0	-	-	-	-	39.2	0.3	-	-	-	-	39.7	1.3	-	-	-	-
1957	40.5	2.0	-	-	-	-	40.2	-0.7	-	-	-	-	39.9	-0.7	-	-	-	-	40.6	1.8	-	-	-	-
1958	40.0	-1.5	-	-	-	-	40.4	1.0	-	-	-	-	40.2	-0.5	-	-	-	-	40.8	1.5	-	-	-	-
1959	40.3	-1.2	-	-	-	-	40.5	0.5	-	-	-	-	40.5	0.0	-	-	-	-	41.4	2.2	-	-	-	-
1960	40.8	-1.4	-	-	-	-	41.6	2.0	-	-	-	-	42.0	1.0	-	-	-	-	42.2	0.5	-	-	-	-
1961	41.6	-1.4	-	-	-	-	41.9	0.7	-	-	-	-	42.1	0.5	-	-	-	-	42.5	1.0	-	-	-	-
1962	41.9	-1.4	-	-	-	-	41.8	-0.2	-	-	-	-	41.4	-1.0	-	-	-	-	43.0	3.9	-	-	-	-
1963	41.8	-2.8	-	-	-	-	42.2	1.0	-	-	-	-	42.1	-0.2	-	-	-	-	43.8	4.0	-	-	-	-
1964	43.1	-1.6	-	-	-	-	43.3	0.5	-	-	-	-	43.3	0.0	-	-	-	-	44.4	2.5	-	-	-	-
1965	43.6	-1.8	-	-	-	-	43.6	0.0	-	-	44.4	1.8	-	-	-	-	45.3	2.0	-	-	-	-	45.4	0.2
1966	-	-	-	-	45.0	-0.9	-	-	-	-	45.8	1.8	-	-	-	-	46.0	0.4	-	-	-	-	46.0	0.0
1967	-	-	-	-	46.3	0.7	-	-	-	-	46.7	0.9	-	-	-	-	48.6	4.1	-	-	-	-	48.6	0.0
1968	-	-	-	-	49.3	1.4	-	-	-	-	50.4	2.2	-	-	-	-	52.4	4.0	-	-	-	-	52.6	0.4
1969	-	-	-	-	53.1	1.0	-	-	-	-	54.2	2.1	-	-	-	-	55.6	2.6	-	-	-	-	55.8	0.4
1970	-	-	-	-	56.4	1.1	-	-	-	-	57.0	1.1	-	-	-	-	58.3	2.3	-	-	-	-	58.7	0.7
1971	-	-	-	-	58.6	-0.2	-	-	-	-	58.3	-0.5	-	-	-	-	59.8	2.6	-	-	-	-	58.9	-1.5
1972	-	-	-	-	59.7	1.4	-	-	-	-	59.9	0.3	-	-	-	-	61.5	2.7	-	-	-	-	61.1	-0.7
1973	-	-	-	-	61.2	0.2	-	-	-	-	61.6	0.7	-	-	-	-	62.6	1.6	-	-	-	-	62.3	-0.5
1974	-	-	-	-	63.6	2.1	-	-	-	-	64.9	2.0	-	-	-	-	68.2	5.1	-	-	-	-	68.3	0.1
1975	-	-	-	-	69.5	1.8	-	-	-	-	68.5	-1.4	-	-	-	-	69.5	1.5	-	-	-	-	68.3	-1.7
1976	-	-	-	-	69.5	1.8	-	-	-	-	71.0	2.2	-	-	-	-	73.2	3.1	-	-	-	-	73.0	-0.3
1977	-	-	-	-	75.9	4.0	-	-	-	-	76.3	0.5	-	-	-	-	78.8	3.3	-	-	-	-	79.0	0.3
1978	-	-	75.6	-4.3	-	-	79.2	4.8	-	-	78.1	-1.4	-	-	80.3	2.8	-	-	80.2	-0.1	-	-	81.0	1.0
1979	-	-	84.0	3.7	-	-	83.2	-1.0	-	-	83.1	-0.1	-	-	86.4	4.0	-	-	86.6	0.2	-	-	83.1	-4.0
1980	-	-	84.5	1.7	-	-	87.5	3.6	-	-	85.7	-2.1	-	-	87.9	2.6	-	-	91.1	3.6	-	-	91.1	0.0
1981	-	-	91.8	0.8	-	-	91.7	-0.1	-	-	91.1	-0.7	-	-	93.5	2.6	-	-	95.3	1.9	-	-	90.2	-5.4
1982	-	-	92.6	2.7	-	-	96.3	4.0	-	-	95.3	-1.0	-	-	97.8	2.6	-	-	96.1	-1.7	-	-	97.6	1.6
1983	-	-	98.6	1.0	-	-	102.6	4.1	-	-	101.3	-1.3	-	-	101.4	0.1	-	-	105.6	4.1	-	-	102.6	-2.8
1984	-	-	102.8	0.2	-	-	104.2	1.4	-	-	100.2	-3.8	-	-	101.9	1.7	-	-	104.0	2.1	-	-	102.0	-1.9
1985	-	-	104.8	2.7	-	-	108.1	3.1	-	-	102.8	-4.9	-	-	104.1	1.3	-	-	106.5	2.3	-	-	104.0	-2.3
1986	-	-	108.7	4.5	-	-	111.0	2.1	-	-	107.9	-2.8	-	-	106.2	-1.6	-	-	106.0	-0.2	-	-	101.4	-4.3
1987	-	-	-	-	-	-	-	-	-	-	104.8	3.4	-	-	-	-	-	-	-	-	-	-	114.6	9.4
1988	-	-	-	-	-	-	-	-	-	-	111.3	-2.9	-	-	-	-	-	-	-	-	-	-	115.0	3.3
1989	-	-	-	-	-	-	-	-	-	-	114.2	-0.7	-	-	-	-	-	-	-	-	-	-	125.1	9.5
1990	-	-	-	-	-	-	-	-	-	-	113.8	-9.0	-	-	-	-	-	-	-	-	-	-	119.3	4.8
1991	-	-	-	-	-	-	-	-	-	-	121.0	1.4	-	-	-	-	-	-	-	-	-	-	128.4	6.1
1992	-	-	-	-	-	-	-	-	-	-	125.3	-2.4	-	-	-	-	-	-	-	-	-	-	124.2	-0.9
1993	-	-	-	-	-	-	-	-	-	-	126.2	1.6	-	-	-	-	-	-	-	-	-	-	124.5	-1.3
1994	-	-	-	-	-	-	-	-	-	-	129.4	3.9	-	-	-	-	-	-	-	-	-	-	117.1	-9.5

[Continued]

Kansas City, MO-KS
Consumer Price Index - All Urban Consumers
Base 1982-1984 = 100
Apparel and Upkeep
[Continued]

For 1952-1997. Columns headed % show percentile change in the index from the previous period for which an index is available.

Year	Jan		Feb		Mar		Apr		May		Jun		Jul		Aug		Sep		Oct		Nov		Dec	
	Index	%	Index	%	Index	%	Index	%	Index	%	Index	%	Index	%	Index	%	Index	%	Index	%	Index	%	Index	%
1995	-	-	-	-	-	-	-	-	-	-	128.1	9.4	-	-	-	-	-	-	-	-	-	-	123.6	-3.5
1996	-	-	-	-	-	-	-	-	-	-	134.3	8.7	-	-	-	-	-	-	-	-	-	-	124.8	-7.1
1997	-	-	-	-	-	-	-	-	-	-	135.1	8.3	-	-	-	-	-	-	-	-	-	-	-	-

Source: U.S. Department of Labor, Bureau of Labor Statistics, Division of Consumer Prices and Price Indexes. - indicates no data collected for period.

Kansas City, MO-KS
Consumer Price Index - Urban Wage Earners
Base 1982-1984 = 100
Apparel and Upkeep

For 1952-1997. Columns headed % show percentile change in the index from the previous period for which an index is available.

Year	Jan Index	%	Feb Index	%	Mar Index	%	Apr Index	%	May Index	%	Jun Index	%	Jul Index	%	Aug Index	%	Sep Index	%	Oct Index	%	Nov Index	%	Dec Index	%
1952	-	-	-	-	-	-	-	-	-	-	-	-	-	-	-	-	-	-	40.6	-	-	-	-	-
1953	40.5	-0.2	-	-	-	-	40.4	-0.2	-	-	-	-	40.6	0.5	-	-	-	-	40.5	-0.2	-	-	-	-
1954	40.3	-0.5	-	-	-	-	40.0	-0.7	-	-	-	-	40.0	0.0	-	-	-	-	40.3	0.7	-	-	-	-
1955	39.7	-1.5	-	-	-	-	39.8	0.3	-	-	-	-	39.8	0.0	-	-	-	-	40.6	2.0	-	-	-	-
1956	40.3	-0.7	-	-	-	-	40.3	0.0	-	-	-	-	40.5	0.5	-	-	-	-	41.0	1.2	-	-	-	-
1957	41.8	2.0	-	-	-	-	41.5	-0.7	-	-	-	-	41.1	-1.0	-	-	-	-	41.9	1.9	-	-	-	-
1958	41.3	-1.4	-	-	-	-	41.6	0.7	-	-	-	-	41.5	-0.2	-	-	-	-	42.1	1.4	-	-	-	-
1959	41.5	-1.4	-	-	-	-	41.8	0.7	-	-	-	-	41.7	-0.2	-	-	-	-	42.7	2.4	-	-	-	-
1960	42.1	-1.4	-	-	-	-	42.9	1.9	-	-	-	-	43.3	0.9	-	-	-	-	43.5	0.5	-	-	-	-
1961	42.9	-1.4	-	-	-	-	43.2	0.7	-	-	-	-	43.4	0.5	-	-	-	-	43.8	0.9	-	-	-	-
1962	43.2	-1.4	-	-	-	-	43.1	-0.2	-	-	-	-	42.7	-0.9	-	-	-	-	44.3	3.7	-	-	-	-
1963	43.1	-2.7	-	-	-	-	43.5	0.9	-	-	-	-	43.4	-0.2	-	-	-	-	45.2	4.1	-	-	-	-
1964	44.4	-1.8	-	-	-	-	44.7	0.7	-	-	-	-	44.7	0.0	-	-	-	-	45.8	2.5	-	-	-	-
1965	45.0	-1.7	-	-	-	-	45.0	0.0	-	-	45.7	1.6	-	-	-	-	46.8	2.4	-	-	-	-	46.9	0.2
1966	-	-	-	-	46.4	-1.1	-	-	-	-	47.2	1.7	-	-	-	-	47.4	0.4	-	-	-	-	47.4	0.0
1967	-	-	-	-	47.7	0.6	-	-	-	-	48.1	0.8	-	-	-	-	50.1	4.2	-	-	-	-	50.1	0.0
1968	-	-	-	-	50.8	1.4	-	-	-	-	52.0	2.4	-	-	-	-	54.0	3.8	-	-	-	-	54.3	0.6
1969	-	-	-	-	54.7	0.7	-	-	-	-	55.9	2.2	-	-	-	-	57.3	2.5	-	-	-	-	57.5	0.3
1970	-	-	-	-	58.1	1.0	-	-	-	-	58.8	1.2	-	-	-	-	60.1	2.2	-	-	-	-	60.5	0.7
1971	-	-	-	-	60.4	-0.2	-	-	-	-	60.1	-0.5	-	-	-	-	61.6	2.5	-	-	-	-	60.7	-1.5
1972	-	-	-	-	61.6	1.5	-	-	-	-	61.7	0.2	-	-	-	-	63.4	2.8	-	-	-	-	63.0	-0.6
1973	-	-	-	-	63.1	0.2	-	-	-	-	63.6	0.8	-	-	-	-	64.5	1.4	-	-	-	-	64.2	-0.5
1974	-	-	-	-	65.6	2.2	-	-	-	-	66.9	2.0	-	-	-	-	70.3	5.1	-	-	-	-	70.5	0.3
1975	-	-	-	-	71.7	1.7	-	-	-	-	70.6	-1.5	-	-	-	-	71.7	1.6	-	-	-	-	70.5	-1.7
1976	-	-	-	-	71.7	1.7	-	-	-	-	73.2	2.1	-	-	-	-	75.5	3.1	-	-	-	-	75.3	-0.3
1977	-	-	-	-	78.3	4.0	-	-	-	-	78.7	0.5	-	-	-	-	81.3	3.3	-	-	-	-	81.5	0.2
1978	-	-	81.1	-0.5	-	-	82.2	1.4	-	-	79.9	-2.8	-	-	82.2	2.9	-	-	83.8	1.9	-	-	84.0	0.2
1979	-	-	84.3	0.4	-	-	84.9	0.7	-	-	82.7	-2.6	-	-	85.1	2.9	-	-	85.1	0.0	-	-	84.6	-0.6
1980	-	-	85.6	1.2	-	-	87.0	1.6	-	-	85.4	-1.8	-	-	86.5	1.3	-	-	89.7	3.7	-	-	88.8	-1.0
1981	-	-	91.6	3.2	-	-	92.8	1.3	-	-	91.7	-1.2	-	-	93.8	2.3	-	-	94.4	0.6	-	-	89.8	-4.9
1982	-	-	91.9	2.3	-	-	96.7	5.2	-	-	95.0	-1.8	-	-	98.4	3.6	-	-	96.6	-1.8	-	-	98.2	1.7
1983	-	-	98.8	0.6	-	-	102.8	4.0	-	-	101.6	-1.2	-	-	102.6	1.0	-	-	105.7	3.0	-	-	102.6	-2.9
1984	-	-	102.9	0.3	-	-	103.6	0.7	-	-	98.4	-5.0	-	-	101.2	2.8	-	-	104.2	3.0	-	-	102.1	-2.0
1985	-	-	104.5	2.4	-	-	108.5	3.8	-	-	104.1	-4.1	-	-	104.9	0.8	-	-	107.7	2.7	-	-	105.5	-2.0
1986	-	-	107.4	1.8	-	-	110.5	2.9	-	-	108.2	-2.1	-	-	106.4	-1.7	-	-	105.2	-1.1	-	-	101.8	-3.2
1987	-	-	-	-	-	-	-	-	-	-	105.6	3.7	-	-	-	-	-	-	-	-	-	-	115.3	9.2
1988	-	-	-	-	-	-	-	-	-	-	112.3	-2.6	-	-	-	-	-	-	-	-	-	-	116.2	3.5
1989	-	-	-	-	-	-	-	-	-	-	115.0	-1.0	-	-	-	-	-	-	-	-	-	-	125.6	9.2
1990	-	-	-	-	-	-	-	-	-	-	114.0	-9.2	-	-	-	-	-	-	-	-	-	-	119.6	4.9
1991	-	-	-	-	-	-	-	-	-	-	121.5	1.6	-	-	-	-	-	-	-	-	-	-	129.7	6.7
1992	-	-	-	-	-	-	-	-	-	-	125.1	-3.5	-	-	-	-	-	-	-	-	-	-	125.0	-0.1
1993	-	-	-	-	-	-	-	-	-	-	126.1	0.9	-	-	-	-	-	-	-	-	-	-	126.2	0.1
1994	-	-	-	-	-	-	-	-	-	-	131.4	4.1	-	-	-	-	-	-	-	-	-	-	117.1	-10.9

[Continued]

Kansas City, MO-KS
Consumer Price Index - Urban Wage Earners
Base 1982-1984 = 100
Apparel and Upkeep
[Continued]

For 1952-1997. Columns headed % show percentile change in the index from the previous period for which an index is available.

Year	Jan		Feb		Mar		Apr		May		Jun		Jul		Aug		Sep		Oct		Nov		Dec	
	Index	%	Index	%	Index	%	Index	%	Index	%	Index	%	Index	%	Index	%	Index	%	Index	%	Index	%	Index	%
1995	-	-	-	-	-	-	-	-	-	-	129.3	10.4	-	-	-	-	-	-	-	-	-	-	124.3	-3.9
1996	-	-	-	-	-	-	-	-	-	-	136.5	9.8	-	-	-	-	-	-	-	-	-	-	126.0	-7.7
1997	-	-	-	-	-	-	-	-	-	-	135.5	7.5	-	-	-	-	-	-	-	-	-	-	-	-

Source: U.S. Department of Labor, Bureau of Labor Statistics, Division of Consumer Prices and Price Indexes. - indicates no data collected for period.

Kansas City, MO-KS
Consumer Price Index - All Urban Consumers
Base 1982-1984 = 100
Transportation

For 1947-1997. Columns headed % show percentile change in the index from the previous period for which an index is available.

Year	Jan Index	%	Feb Index	%	Mar Index	%	Apr Index	%	May Index	%	Jun Index	%	Jul Index	%	Aug Index	%	Sep Index	%	Oct Index	%	Nov Index	%	Dec Index	%
1947	17.7	-	17.7	0.0	17.7	0.0	18.0	1.7	18.0	0.0	18.0	0.0	18.1	0.6	-	-	-	-	18.7	3.3	-	-	-	-
1948	19.5	4.3	-	-	-	-	19.6	0.5	-	-	-	-	20.1	2.6	-	-	-	-	21.1	5.0	-	-	-	-
1949	21.1	0.0	-	-	-	-	21.5	1.9	-	-	-	-	21.3	-0.9	-	-	-	-	21.6	1.4	-	-	-	-
1950	21.7	0.5	-	-	-	-	21.7	0.0	-	-	-	-	22.3	2.8	-	-	-	-	21.9	-1.8	-	-	-	-
1951	22.5	2.7	-	-	-	-	22.9	1.8	-	-	-	-	23.1	0.9	-	-	-	-	23.6	2.2	-	-	-	-
1952	23.9	1.3	-	-	-	-	25.3	5.9	-	-	-	-	25.7	1.6	-	-	-	-	26.0	1.2	-	-	-	-
1953	26.1	0.4	-	-	-	-	26.0	-0.4	-	-	-	-	26.0	0.0	-	-	-	-	26.1	0.4	-	-	-	-
1954	25.1	-3.8	-	-	-	-	25.9	3.2	-	-	-	-	25.0	-3.5	-	-	-	-	24.8	-0.8	-	-	-	-
1955	25.1	1.2	-	-	-	-	24.6	-2.0	-	-	-	-	25.1	2.0	-	-	-	-	25.4	1.2	-	-	-	-
1956	25.0	-1.6	-	-	-	-	25.5	2.0	-	-	-	-	24.5	-3.9	-	-	-	-	26.1	6.5	-	-	-	-
1957	27.1	3.8	-	-	-	-	27.4	1.1	-	-	-	-	27.6	0.7	-	-	-	-	27.7	0.4	-	-	-	-
1958	28.1	1.4	-	-	-	-	28.4	1.1	-	-	-	-	29.7	4.6	-	-	-	-	30.1	1.3	-	-	-	-
1959	29.4	-2.3	-	-	-	-	30.6	4.1	-	-	-	-	30.7	0.3	-	-	-	-	31.2	1.6	-	-	-	-
1960	30.9	-1.0	-	-	-	-	29.8	-3.6	-	-	-	-	30.9	3.7	-	-	-	-	31.0	0.3	-	-	-	-
1961	30.0	-3.2	-	-	-	-	30.8	2.7	-	-	-	-	31.0	0.6	-	-	-	-	30.3	-2.3	-	-	-	-
1962	31.0	2.3	-	-	-	-	31.7	2.3	-	-	-	-	30.6	-3.5	-	-	-	-	31.9	4.2	-	-	-	-
1963	30.6	-4.1	-	-	-	-	31.3	2.3	-	-	-	-	30.9	-1.3	-	-	-	-	32.2	4.2	-	-	-	-
1964	31.5	-2.2	-	-	-	-	31.4	-0.3	-	-	-	-	31.7	1.0	-	-	-	-	31.4	-0.9	-	-	-	-
1965	32.8	4.5	-	-	-	-	33.0	0.6	-	-	34.5	4.5	-	-	-	-	34.3	-0.6	-	-	-	-	34.1	-0.6
1966	-	-	-	-	34.1	0.0	-	-	-	-	34.7	1.8	-	-	-	-	34.6	-0.3	-	-	-	-	34.8	0.6
1967	-	-	-	-	34.9	0.3	-	-	-	-	33.6	-3.7	-	-	-	-	35.5	5.7	-	-	-	-	34.8	-2.0
1968	-	-	-	-	35.0	0.6	-	-	-	-	36.7	4.9	-	-	-	-	35.0	-4.6	-	-	-	-	35.8	2.3
1969	-	-	-	-	37.6	5.0	-	-	-	-	37.5	-0.3	-	-	-	-	36.6	-2.4	-	-	-	-	37.7	3.0
1970	-	-	-	-	36.7	-2.7	-	-	-	-	38.5	4.9	-	-	-	-	37.9	-1.6	-	-	-	-	41.1	8.4
1971	-	-	-	-	41.0	-0.2	-	-	-	-	41.7	1.7	-	-	-	-	40.9	-1.9	-	-	-	-	40.2	-1.7
1972	-	-	-	-	40.0	-0.5	-	-	-	-	41.3	3.2	-	-	-	-	41.7	1.0	-	-	-	-	41.8	0.2
1973	-	-	-	-	42.1	0.7	-	-	-	-	42.9	1.9	-	-	-	-	42.6	-0.7	-	-	-	-	43.4	1.9
1974	-	-	-	-	45.4	4.6	-	-	-	-	47.7	5.1	-	-	-	-	48.8	2.3	-	-	-	-	49.3	1.0
1975	-	-	-	-	49.5	0.4	-	-	-	-	51.1	3.2	-	-	-	-	53.1	3.9	-	-	-	-	53.7	1.1
1976	-	-	-	-	53.7	0.0	-	-	-	-	55.8	3.9	-	-	-	-	56.4	1.1	-	-	-	-	57.5	2.0
1977	-	-	-	-	58.6	1.9	-	-	-	-	59.9	2.2	-	-	-	-	59.2	-1.2	-	-	-	-	59.9	1.2
1978	-	-	59.9	0.0	-	-	60.2	0.5	-	-	62.0	3.0	-	-	62.8	1.3	-	-	64.0	1.9	-	-	65.1	1.7
1979	-	-	65.9	1.2	-	-	69.3	5.2	-	-	73.0	5.3	-	-	75.1	2.9	-	-	75.8	0.9	-	-	78.1	3.0
1980	-	-	82.0	5.0	-	-	85.0	3.7	-	-	85.1	0.1	-	-	85.7	0.7	-	-	86.3	0.7	-	-	88.2	2.2
1981	-	-	90.9	3.1	-	-	92.2	1.4	-	-	93.4	1.3	-	-	93.6	0.2	-	-	94.6	1.1	-	-	96.5	2.0
1982	-	-	95.6	-0.9	-	-	95.0	-0.6	-	-	98.7	3.9	-	-	99.3	0.6	-	-	98.9	-0.4	-	-	97.8	-1.1
1983	-	-	96.1	-1.7	-	-	97.8	1.8	-	-	99.6	1.8	-	-	100.6	1.0	-	-	102.3	1.7	-	-	101.7	-0.6
1984	-	-	101.4	-0.3	-	-	102.4	1.0	-	-	103.6	1.2	-	-	102.5	-1.1	-	-	104.6	2.0	-	-	104.3	-0.3
1985	-	-	102.9	-1.3	-	-	106.9	3.9	-	-	107.6	0.7	-	-	106.9	-0.7	-	-	107.7	0.7	-	-	107.6	-0.1
1986	-	-	102.5	-4.7	-	-	98.5	-3.9	-	-	101.7	3.2	-	-	97.7	-3.9	-	-	98.7	1.0	-	-	98.9	0.2
1987	-	-	-	-	-	-	-	-	-	-	101.0	2.1	-	-	-	-	-	-	-	-	-	-	104.7	3.7
1988	-	-	-	-	-	-	-	-	-	-	105.5	0.8	-	-	-	-	-	-	-	-	-	-	108.8	3.1
1989	-	-	-	-	-	-	-	-	-	-	112.0	2.9	-	-	-	-	-	-	-	-	-	-	112.4	0.4
1990	-	-	-	-	-	-	-	-	-	-	112.8	0.4	-	-	-	-	-	-	-	-	-	-	119.5	5.9
1991	-	-	-	-	-	-	-	-	-	-	118.5	-0.8	-	-	-	-	-	-	-	-	-	-	119.9	1.2

[Continued]

Kansas City, MO-KS
Consumer Price Index - All Urban Consumers
Base 1982-1984 = 100
Transportation
[Continued]

For 1947-1997. Columns headed % show percentile change in the index from the previous period for which an index is available.

Year	Jan		Feb		Mar		Apr		May		Jun		Jul		Aug		Sep		Oct		Nov		Dec	
	Index	%	Index	%	Index	%	Index	%	Index	%	Index	%	Index	%	Index	%	Index	%	Index	%	Index	%	Index	%
1992	-	-	-	-	-	-	-	-	-	-	120.9	0.8	-	-	-	-	-	-	-	-	-	-	122.8	1.6
1993	-	-	-	-	-	-	-	-	-	-	124.6	1.5	-	-	-	-	-	-	-	-	-	-	124.7	0.1
1994	-	-	-	-	-	-	-	-	-	-	126.6	1.5	-	-	-	-	-	-	-	-	-	-	129.6	2.4
1995	-	-	-	-	-	-	-	-	-	-	133.3	2.9	-	-	-	-	-	-	-	-	-	-	133.5	0.2
1996	-	-	-	-	-	-	-	-	-	-	136.6	2.3	-	-	-	-	-	-	-	-	-	-	138.6	1.5
1997	-	-	-	-	-	-	-	-	-	-	141.1	1.8	-	-	-	-	-	-	-	-	-	-	-	-

Source: U.S. Department of Labor, Bureau of Labor Statistics, Division of Consumer Prices and Price Indexes. - indicates no data collected for period.

Kansas City, MO-KS
Consumer Price Index - Urban Wage Earners
Base 1982-1984 = 100
Transportation

For 1947-1997. Columns headed % show percentile change in the index from the previous period for which an index is available.

Year	Jan Index	%	Feb Index	%	Mar Index	%	Apr Index	%	May Index	%	Jun Index	%	Jul Index	%	Aug Index	%	Sep Index	%	Oct Index	%	Nov Index	%	Dec Index	%
1947	17.6	-	17.6	0.0	17.6	0.0	17.9	1.7	17.9	0.0	17.9	0.0	18.0	0.6	-	-	-	-	18.5	2.8	-	-	-	-
1948	19.4	4.9	-	-	-	-	19.5	0.5	-	-	-	-	20.0	2.6	-	-	-	-	21.0	5.0	-	-	-	-
1949	21.0	0.0	-	-	-	-	21.4	1.9	-	-	-	-	21.2	-0.9	-	-	-	-	21.5	1.4	-	-	-	-
1950	21.6	0.5	-	-	-	-	21.6	0.0	-	-	-	-	22.1	2.3	-	-	-	-	21.7	-1.8	-	-	-	-
1951	22.3	2.8	-	-	-	-	22.8	2.2	-	-	-	-	23.0	0.9	-	-	-	-	23.5	2.2	-	-	-	-
1952	23.7	0.9	-	-	-	-	25.2	6.3	-	-	-	-	25.5	1.2	-	-	-	-	25.8	1.2	-	-	-	-
1953	25.9	0.4	-	-	-	-	25.8	-0.4	-	-	-	-	25.9	0.4	-	-	-	-	25.9	0.0	-	-	-	-
1954	25.0	-3.5	-	-	-	-	25.7	2.8	-	-	-	-	24.9	-3.1	-	-	-	-	24.6	-1.2	-	-	-	-
1955	25.0	1.6	-	-	-	-	24.5	-2.0	-	-	-	-	24.9	1.6	-	-	-	-	25.2	1.2	-	-	-	-
1956	24.8	-1.6	-	-	-	-	25.3	2.0	-	-	-	-	24.3	-4.0	-	-	-	-	26.0	7.0	-	-	-	-
1957	27.0	3.8	-	-	-	-	27.3	1.1	-	-	-	-	27.4	0.4	-	-	-	-	27.5	0.4	-	-	-	-
1958	27.9	1.5	-	-	-	-	28.2	1.1	-	-	-	-	29.5	4.6	-	-	-	-	29.9	1.4	-	-	-	-
1959	29.2	-2.3	-	-	-	-	30.4	4.1	-	-	-	-	30.6	0.7	-	-	-	-	31.0	1.3	-	-	-	-
1960	30.7	-1.0	-	-	-	-	29.6	-3.6	-	-	-	-	30.7	3.7	-	-	-	-	30.8	0.3	-	-	-	-
1961	29.8	-3.2	-	-	-	-	30.6	2.7	-	-	-	-	30.8	0.7	-	-	-	-	30.2	-1.9	-	-	-	-
1962	30.8	2.0	-	-	-	-	31.5	2.3	-	-	-	-	30.5	-3.2	-	-	-	-	31.7	3.9	-	-	-	-
1963	30.4	-4.1	-	-	-	-	31.2	2.6	-	-	-	-	30.7	-1.6	-	-	-	-	32.0	4.2	-	-	-	-
1964	31.3	-2.2	-	-	-	-	31.3	0.0	-	-	-	-	31.5	0.6	-	-	-	-	31.2	-1.0	-	-	-	-
1965	32.6	4.5	-	-	-	-	32.8	0.6	-	-	34.3	4.6	-	-	-	-	34.1	-0.6	-	-	-	-	33.9	-0.6
1966	-	-	-	-	33.9	0.0	-	-	-	-	34.5	1.8	-	-	-	-	34.4	-0.3	-	-	-	-	34.6	0.6
1967	-	-	-	-	34.7	0.3	-	-	-	-	33.4	-3.7	-	-	-	-	35.3	5.7	-	-	-	-	34.6	-2.0
1968	-	-	-	-	34.8	0.6	-	-	-	-	36.5	4.9	-	-	-	-	34.8	-4.7	-	-	-	-	35.6	2.3
1969	-	-	-	-	37.4	5.1	-	-	-	-	37.3	-0.3	-	-	-	-	36.4	-2.4	-	-	-	-	37.5	3.0
1970	-	-	-	-	36.5	-2.7	-	-	-	-	38.3	4.9	-	-	-	-	37.6	-1.8	-	-	-	-	40.9	8.8
1971	-	-	-	-	40.8	-0.2	-	-	-	-	41.5	1.7	-	-	-	-	40.7	-1.9	-	-	-	-	39.9	-2.0
1972	-	-	-	-	39.8	-0.3	-	-	-	-	41.0	3.0	-	-	-	-	41.4	1.0	-	-	-	-	41.5	0.2
1973	-	-	-	-	41.8	0.7	-	-	-	-	42.7	2.2	-	-	-	-	42.4	-0.7	-	-	-	-	43.1	1.7
1974	-	-	-	-	45.1	4.6	-	-	-	-	47.5	5.3	-	-	-	-	48.6	2.3	-	-	-	-	49.0	0.8
1975	-	-	-	-	49.2	0.4	-	-	-	-	50.8	3.3	-	-	-	-	52.8	3.9	-	-	-	-	53.3	0.9
1976	-	-	-	-	53.4	0.2	-	-	-	-	55.5	3.9	-	-	-	-	56.1	1.1	-	-	-	-	57.2	2.0
1977	-	-	-	-	58.2	1.7	-	-	-	-	59.6	2.4	-	-	-	-	58.8	-1.3	-	-	-	-	59.5	1.2
1978	-	-	59.4	-0.2	-	-	59.6	0.3	-	-	61.5	3.2	-	-	62.4	1.5	-	-	63.7	2.1	-	-	64.8	1.7
1979	-	-	65.6	1.2	-	-	69.2	5.5	-	-	72.9	5.3	-	-	75.1	3.0	-	-	75.8	0.9	-	-	78.2	3.2
1980	-	-	82.1	5.0	-	-	85.2	3.8	-	-	85.3	0.1	-	-	85.6	0.4	-	-	86.2	0.7	-	-	88.1	2.2
1981	-	-	91.2	3.5	-	-	92.9	1.9	-	-	94.1	1.3	-	-	94.3	0.2	-	-	95.3	1.1	-	-	96.6	1.4
1982	-	-	95.6	-1.0	-	-	94.7	-0.9	-	-	98.7	4.2	-	-	99.4	0.7	-	-	98.9	-0.5	-	-	97.8	-1.1
1983	-	-	95.9	-1.9	-	-	97.7	1.9	-	-	99.6	1.9	-	-	100.7	1.1	-	-	102.3	1.6	-	-	101.6	-0.7
1984	-	-	101.3	-0.3	-	-	102.5	1.2	-	-	103.7	1.2	-	-	102.5	-1.2	-	-	104.7	2.1	-	-	104.4	-0.3
1985	-	-	102.8	-1.5	-	-	107.0	4.1	-	-	107.8	0.7	-	-	107.0	-0.7	-	-	107.6	0.6	-	-	107.5	-0.1
1986	-	-	102.1	-5.0	-	-	97.5	-4.5	-	-	101.0	3.6	-	-	96.6	-4.4	-	-	97.7	1.1	-	-	97.8	0.1
1987	-	-	-	-	-	-	-	-	-	-	99.4	1.6	-	-	-	-	-	-	-	-	-	-	103.0	3.6
1988	-	-	-	-	-	-	-	-	-	-	104.0	1.0	-	-	-	-	-	-	-	-	-	-	107.1	3.0
1989	-	-	-	-	-	-	-	-	-	-	109.8	2.5	-	-	-	-	-	-	-	-	-	-	110.1	0.3
1990	-	-	-	-	-	-	-	-	-	-	110.0	-0.1	-	-	-	-	-	-	-	-	-	-	115.2	4.7
1991	-	-	-	-	-	-	-	-	-	-	114.9	-0.3	-	-	-	-	-	-	-	-	-	-	116.8	1.7

[Continued]

Kansas City, MO-KS
Consumer Price Index - Urban Wage Earners
Base 1982-1984 = 100
Transportation
[Continued]

For 1947-1997. Columns headed % show percentile change in the index from the previous period for which an index is available.

Year	Jan		Feb		Mar		Apr		May		Jun		Jul		Aug		Sep		Oct		Nov		Dec	
	Index	%	Index	%	Index	%	Index	%	Index	%	Index	%	Index	%	Index	%	Index	%	Index	%	Index	%	Index	%
1992	-	-	-	-	-	-	-	-	-	-	117.9	0.9	-	-	-	-	-	-	-	-	-	-	120.2	2.0
1993	-	-	-	-	-	-	-	-	-	-	121.8	1.3	-	-	-	-	-	-	-	-	-	-	122.6	0.7
1994	-	-	-	-	-	-	-	-	-	-	124.5	1.5	-	-	-	-	-	-	-	-	-	-	127.7	2.6
1995	-	-	-	-	-	-	-	-	-	-	131.8	3.2	-	-	-	-	-	-	-	-	-	-	131.9	0.1
1996	-	-	-	-	-	-	-	-	-	-	134.8	2.2	-	-	-	-	-	-	-	-	-	-	136.5	1.3
1997	-	-	-	-	-	-	-	-	-	-	138.4	1.4	-	-	-	-	-	-	-	-	-	-	-	-

Source: U.S. Department of Labor, Bureau of Labor Statistics, Division of Consumer Prices and Price Indexes. - indicates no data collected for period.

Kansas City, MO-KS
Consumer Price Index - All Urban Consumers
Base 1982-1984 = 100
Medical Care

For 1947-1997. Columns headed % show percentile change in the index from the previous period for which an index is available.

Year	Jan Index	%	Feb Index	%	Mar Index	%	Apr Index	%	May Index	%	Jun Index	%	Jul Index	%	Aug Index	%	Sep Index	%	Oct Index	%	Nov Index	%	Dec Index	%
1947	10.8	-	10.9	0.9	10.9	0.0	11.0	0.9	11.0	0.0	11.0	0.0	11.0	0.0	-	-	-	-	11.1	0.9	-	-	-	-
1948	11.5	3.6	-	-	-	-	11.9	3.5	-	-	-	-	11.9	0.0	-	-	-	-	12.1	1.7	-	-	-	-
1949	12.1	0.0	-	-	-	-	12.1	0.0	-	-	-	-	12.2	0.8	-	-	-	-	12.2	0.0	-	-	-	-
1950	12.2	0.0	-	-	-	-	12.3	0.8	-	-	-	-	12.3	0.0	-	-	-	-	12.7	3.3	-	-	-	-
1951	12.8	0.8	-	-	-	-	12.9	0.8	-	-	-	-	13.0	0.8	-	-	-	-	13.1	0.8	-	-	-	-
1952	13.3	1.5	-	-	-	-	13.4	0.8	-	-	-	-	13.9	3.7	-	-	-	-	13.9	0.0	-	-	-	-
1953	13.9	0.0	-	-	-	-	14.0	0.7	-	-	-	-	14.0	0.0	-	-	-	-	14.0	0.0	-	-	-	-
1954	14.0	0.0	-	-	-	-	15.8	12.9	-	-	-	-	15.9	0.6	-	-	-	-	15.9	0.0	-	-	-	-
1955	15.9	0.0	-	-	-	-	15.9	0.0	-	-	-	-	16.0	0.6	-	-	-	-	16.0	0.0	-	-	-	-
1956	16.0	0.0	-	-	-	-	16.2	1.3	-	-	-	-	16.2	0.0	-	-	-	-	17.5	8.0	-	-	-	-
1957	17.5	0.0	-	-	-	-	17.6	0.6	-	-	-	-	17.6	0.0	-	-	-	-	17.8	1.1	-	-	-	-
1958	17.9	0.6	-	-	-	-	17.9	0.0	-	-	-	-	19.9	11.2	-	-	-	-	19.9	0.0	-	-	-	-
1959	19.9	0.0	-	-	-	-	19.9	0.0	-	-	-	-	20.0	0.5	-	-	-	-	20.0	0.0	-	-	-	-
1960	20.1	0.5	-	-	-	-	20.2	0.5	-	-	-	-	20.5	1.5	-	-	-	-	20.4	-0.5	-	-	-	-
1961	20.4	0.0	-	-	-	-	21.2	3.9	-	-	-	-	21.1	-0.5	-	-	-	-	21.3	0.9	-	-	-	-
1962	21.4	0.5	-	-	-	-	21.4	0.0	-	-	-	-	21.5	0.5	-	-	-	-	21.6	0.5	-	-	-	-
1963	21.6	0.0	-	-	-	-	21.6	0.0	-	-	-	-	21.7	0.5	-	-	-	-	21.8	0.5	-	-	-	-
1964	21.8	0.0	-	-	-	-	22.0	0.9	-	-	-	-	23.5	6.8	-	-	-	-	23.5	0.0	-	-	-	-
1965	23.5	0.0	-	-	-	-	23.7	0.9	-	-	23.8	0.4	-	-	-	-	24.2	1.7	-	-	-	-	24.4	0.8
1966	-	-	-	-	25.2	3.3	-	-	-	-	25.4	0.8	-	-	-	-	25.5	0.4	-	-	-	-	25.7	0.8
1967	-	-	-	-	26.9	4.7	-	-	-	-	27.1	0.7	-	-	-	-	27.6	1.8	-	-	-	-	27.6	0.0
1968	-	-	-	-	28.7	4.0	-	-	-	-	29.0	1.0	-	-	-	-	29.1	0.3	-	-	-	-	29.6	1.7
1969	-	-	-	-	30.0	1.4	-	-	-	-	30.5	1.7	-	-	-	-	30.8	1.0	-	-	-	-	30.9	0.3
1970	-	-	-	-	31.2	1.0	-	-	-	-	31.7	1.6	-	-	-	-	32.1	1.3	-	-	-	-	32.7	1.9
1971	-	-	-	-	33.2	1.5	-	-	-	-	33.7	1.5	-	-	-	-	34.5	2.4	-	-	-	-	34.4	-0.3
1972	-	-	-	-	34.7	0.9	-	-	-	-	35.0	0.9	-	-	-	-	35.2	0.6	-	-	-	-	35.8	1.7
1973	-	-	-	-	36.4	1.7	-	-	-	-	36.5	0.3	-	-	-	-	36.7	0.5	-	-	-	-	37.7	2.7
1974	-	-	-	-	39.1	3.7	-	-	-	-	39.9	2.0	-	-	-	-	41.1	3.0	-	-	-	-	41.6	1.2
1975	-	-	-	-	43.3	4.1	-	-	-	-	43.3	0.0	-	-	-	-	44.0	1.6	-	-	-	-	44.9	2.0
1976	-	-	-	-	46.3	3.1	-	-	-	-	47.3	2.2	-	-	-	-	47.6	0.6	-	-	-	-	49.5	4.0
1977	-	-	-	-	51.1	3.2	-	-	-	-	51.7	1.2	-	-	-	-	52.5	1.5	-	-	-	-	53.3	1.5
1978	-	-	54.2	1.7	-	-	55.2	1.8	-	-	56.4	2.2	-	-	56.9	0.9	-	-	59.3	4.2	-	-	59.7	0.7
1979	-	-	61.8	3.5	-	-	62.8	1.6	-	-	63.4	1.0	-	-	63.9	0.8	-	-	65.3	2.2	-	-	66.6	2.0
1980	-	-	68.7	3.2	-	-	69.9	1.7	-	-	70.6	1.0	-	-	71.5	1.3	-	-	73.1	2.2	-	-	73.5	0.5
1981	-	-	77.7	5.7	-	-	78.2	0.6	-	-	79.0	1.0	-	-	80.2	1.5	-	-	82.5	2.9	-	-	83.2	0.8
1982	-	-	85.7	3.0	-	-	89.4	4.3	-	-	89.8	0.4	-	-	93.1	3.7	-	-	96.1	3.2	-	-	95.2	-0.9
1983	-	-	98.6	3.6	-	-	99.6	1.0	-	-	100.0	0.4	-	-	102.3	2.3	-	-	103.8	1.5	-	-	104.9	1.1
1984	-	-	107.0	2.0	-	-	108.0	0.9	-	-	107.5	-0.5	-	-	107.6	0.1	-	-	108.9	1.2	-	-	109.0	0.1
1985	-	-	109.4	0.4	-	-	109.9	0.5	-	-	111.0	1.0	-	-	113.2	2.0	-	-	113.5	0.3	-	-	114.5	0.9
1986	-	-	115.6	1.0	-	-	116.5	0.8	-	-	116.9	0.3	-	-	119.1	1.9	-	-	118.9	-0.2	-	-	120.9	1.7
1987	-	-	-	-	-	-	-	-	-	-	123.1	1.8	-	-	-	-	-	-	-	-	-	-	123.6	0.4
1988	-	-	-	-	-	-	-	-	-	-	128.8	4.2	-	-	-	-	-	-	-	-	-	-	132.9	3.2
1989	-	-	-	-	-	-	-	-	-	-	138.3	4.1	-	-	-	-	-	-	-	-	-	-	145.6	5.3
1990	-	-	-	-	-	-	-	-	-	-	152.8	4.9	-	-	-	-	-	-	-	-	-	-	160.8	5.2
1991	-	-	-	-	-	-	-	-	-	-	172.4	7.2	-	-	-	-	-	-	-	-	-	-	174.5	1.2

[Continued]

Kansas City, MO-KS
Consumer Price Index - All Urban Consumers
Base 1982-1984 = 100
Medical Care
[Continued]

For 1947-1997. Columns headed % show percentile change in the index from the previous period for which an index is available.

Year	Jan		Feb		Mar		Apr		May		Jun		Jul		Aug		Sep		Oct		Nov		Dec	
	Index	%	Index	%	Index	%	Index	%	Index	%	Index	%	Index	%	Index	%	Index	%	Index	%	Index	%	Index	%
1992	-	-	-	-	-	-	-	-	-	-	181.7	4.1	-	-	-	-	-	-	-	-	-	-	185.9	2.3
1993	-	-	-	-	-	-	-	-	-	-	195.5	5.2	-	-	-	-	-	-	-	-	-	-	195.8	0.2
1994	-	-	-	-	-	-	-	-	-	-	200.7	2.5	-	-	-	-	-	-	-	-	-	-	205.2	2.2
1995	-	-	-	-	-	-	-	-	-	-	207.8	1.3	-	-	-	-	-	-	-	-	-	-	209.1	0.6
1996	-	-	-	-	-	-	-	-	-	-	212.0	1.4	-	-	-	-	-	-	-	-	-	-	212.4	0.2
1997	-	-	-	-	-	-	-	-	-	-	210.9	-0.7	-	-	-	-	-	-	-	-	-	-	-	-

Source: U.S. Department of Labor, Bureau of Labor Statistics, Division of Consumer Prices and Price Indexes. - indicates no data collected for period.

Kansas City, MO-KS
Consumer Price Index - Urban Wage Earners
Base 1982-1984 = 100
Medical Care

For 1947-1997. Columns headed % show percentile change in the index from the previous period for which an index is available.

Year	Jan Index	%	Feb Index	%	Mar Index	%	Apr Index	%	May Index	%	Jun Index	%	Jul Index	%	Aug Index	%	Sep Index	%	Oct Index	%	Nov Index	%	Dec Index	%
1947	10.8	-	10.9	0.9	10.9	0.0	11.0	0.9	11.0	0.0	11.0	0.0	11.0	0.0	-	-	-	-	11.1	0.9	-	-	-	-
1948	11.5	3.6	-	-	-	-	11.9	3.5	-	-	-	-	11.9	0.0	-	-	-	-	12.1	1.7	-	-	-	-
1949	12.1	0.0	-	-	-	-	12.1	0.0	-	-	-	-	12.2	0.8	-	-	-	-	12.2	0.0	-	-	-	-
1950	12.2	0.0	-	-	-	-	12.3	0.8	-	-	-	-	12.3	0.0	-	-	-	-	12.7	3.3	-	-	-	-
1951	12.8	0.8	-	-	-	-	12.9	0.8	-	-	-	-	13.0	0.8	-	-	-	-	13.1	0.8	-	-	-	-
1952	13.3	1.5	-	-	-	-	13.4	0.8	-	-	-	-	13.9	3.7	-	-	-	-	13.9	0.0	-	-	-	-
1953	13.9	0.0	-	-	-	-	14.0	0.7	-	-	-	-	14.0	0.0	-	-	-	-	14.0	0.0	-	-	-	-
1954	14.0	0.0	-	-	-	-	15.8	12.9	-	-	-	-	15.9	0.6	-	-	-	-	15.9	0.0	-	-	-	-
1955	15.9	0.0	-	-	-	-	15.9	0.0	-	-	-	-	16.0	0.6	-	-	-	-	16.0	0.0	-	-	-	-
1956	16.0	0.0	-	-	-	-	16.2	1.3	-	-	-	-	16.2	0.0	-	-	-	-	17.5	8.0	-	-	-	-
1957	17.5	0.0	-	-	-	-	17.6	0.6	-	-	-	-	17.6	0.0	-	-	-	-	17.8	1.1	-	-	-	-
1958	17.9	0.6	-	-	-	-	17.9	0.0	-	-	-	-	19.9	11.2	-	-	-	-	19.9	0.0	-	-	-	-
1959	19.9	0.0	-	-	-	-	19.9	0.0	-	-	-	-	20.0	0.5	-	-	-	-	20.0	0.0	-	-	-	-
1960	20.1	0.5	-	-	-	-	20.2	0.5	-	-	-	-	20.5	1.5	-	-	-	-	20.4	-0.5	-	-	-	-
1961	20.4	0.0	-	-	-	-	21.2	3.9	-	-	-	-	21.1	-0.5	-	-	-	-	21.3	0.9	-	-	-	-
1962	21.4	0.5	-	-	-	-	21.4	0.0	-	-	-	-	21.5	0.5	-	-	-	-	21.6	0.5	-	-	-	-
1963	21.6	0.0	-	-	-	-	21.6	0.0	-	-	-	-	21.7	0.5	-	-	-	-	21.8	0.5	-	-	-	-
1964	21.8	0.0	-	-	-	-	22.0	0.9	-	-	-	-	23.5	6.8	-	-	-	-	23.5	0.0	-	-	-	-
1965	23.5	0.0	-	-	-	-	23.7	0.9	-	-	23.8	0.4	-	-	-	-	24.2	1.7	-	-	-	-	24.4	0.8
1966	-	-	-	-	25.1	2.9	-	-	-	-	25.4	1.2	-	-	-	-	25.5	0.4	-	-	-	-	25.7	0.8
1967	-	-	-	-	26.9	4.7	-	-	-	-	27.1	0.7	-	-	-	-	27.6	1.8	-	-	-	-	27.6	0.0
1968	-	-	-	-	28.7	4.0	-	-	-	-	29.0	1.0	-	-	-	-	29.1	0.3	-	-	-	-	29.6	1.7
1969	-	-	-	-	30.0	1.4	-	-	-	-	30.5	1.7	-	-	-	-	30.8	1.0	-	-	-	-	30.9	0.3
1970	-	-	-	-	31.2	1.0	-	-	-	-	31.7	1.6	-	-	-	-	32.1	1.3	-	-	-	-	32.7	1.9
1971	-	-	-	-	33.2	1.5	-	-	-	-	33.6	1.2	-	-	-	-	34.5	2.7	-	-	-	-	34.4	-0.3
1972	-	-	-	-	34.7	0.9	-	-	-	-	35.0	0.9	-	-	-	-	35.2	0.6	-	-	-	-	35.8	1.7
1973	-	-	-	-	36.4	1.7	-	-	-	-	36.5	0.3	-	-	-	-	36.7	0.5	-	-	-	-	37.7	2.7
1974	-	-	-	-	39.1	3.7	-	-	-	-	39.9	2.0	-	-	-	-	41.1	3.0	-	-	-	-	41.6	1.2
1975	-	-	-	-	43.3	4.1	-	-	-	-	43.3	0.0	-	-	-	-	44.0	1.6	-	-	-	-	44.9	2.0
1976	-	-	-	-	46.3	3.1	-	-	-	-	47.3	2.2	-	-	-	-	47.6	0.6	-	-	-	-	49.5	4.0
1977	-	-	-	-	51.1	3.2	-	-	-	-	51.7	1.2	-	-	-	-	52.5	1.5	-	-	-	-	53.3	1.5
1978	-	-	54.2	1.7	-	-	55.0	1.5	-	-	56.3	2.4	-	-	56.8	0.9	-	-	58.4	2.8	-	-	59.3	1.5
1979	-	-	61.8	4.2	-	-	62.8	1.6	-	-	63.7	1.4	-	-	64.1	0.6	-	-	65.7	2.5	-	-	67.1	2.1
1980	-	-	67.8	1.0	-	-	69.9	3.1	-	-	70.2	0.4	-	-	72.8	3.7	-	-	74.2	1.9	-	-	74.7	0.7
1981	-	-	77.0	3.1	-	-	77.3	0.4	-	-	78.1	1.0	-	-	79.8	2.2	-	-	81.9	2.6	-	-	83.3	1.7
1982	-	-	85.9	3.1	-	-	89.5	4.2	-	-	89.9	0.4	-	-	93.0	3.4	-	-	95.9	3.1	-	-	95.0	-0.9
1983	-	-	98.4	3.6	-	-	99.5	1.1	-	-	100.1	0.6	-	-	102.3	2.2	-	-	103.7	1.4	-	-	104.9	1.2
1984	-	-	107.0	2.0	-	-	108.0	0.9	-	-	107.6	-0.4	-	-	107.7	0.1	-	-	109.1	1.3	-	-	109.2	0.1
1985	-	-	109.6	0.4	-	-	110.0	0.4	-	-	111.1	1.0	-	-	113.2	1.9	-	-	113.5	0.3	-	-	114.5	0.9
1986	-	-	115.6	1.0	-	-	116.4	0.7	-	-	116.8	0.3	-	-	119.0	1.9	-	-	118.8	-0.2	-	-	120.7	1.6
1987	-	-	-	-	-	-	-	-	-	-	123.4	2.2	-	-	-	-	-	-	-	-	-	-	124.2	0.6
1988	-	-	-	-	-	-	-	-	-	-	129.3	4.1	-	-	-	-	-	-	-	-	-	-	133.9	3.6
1989	-	-	-	-	-	-	-	-	-	-	139.4	4.1	-	-	-	-	-	-	-	-	-	-	146.5	5.1
1990	-	-	-	-	-	-	-	-	-	-	153.8	5.0	-	-	-	-	-	-	-	-	-	-	161.3	4.9
1991	-	-	-	-	-	-	-	-	-	-	172.7	7.1	-	-	-	-	-	-	-	-	-	-	174.7	1.2

[Continued]

Kansas City, MO-KS
Consumer Price Index - Urban Wage Earners
Base 1982-1984 = 100
Medical Care
[Continued]

For 1947-1997. Columns headed % show percentile change in the index from the previous period for which an index is available.

Year	Jan		Feb		Mar		Apr		May		Jun		Jul		Aug		Sep		Oct		Nov		Dec	
	Index	%	Index	%	Index	%	Index	%	Index	%	Index	%	Index	%	Index	%	Index	%	Index	%	Index	%	Index	%
1992	-	-	-	-	-	-	-	-	-	-	182.1	4.2	-	-	-	-	-	-	-	-	-	-	186.4	2.4
1993	-	-	-	-	-	-	-	-	-	-	196.7	5.5	-	-	-	-	-	-	-	-	-	-	196.7	0.0
1994	-	-	-	-	-	-	-	-	-	-	201.7	2.5	-	-	-	-	-	-	-	-	-	-	206.1	2.2
1995	-	-	-	-	-	-	-	-	-	-	208.4	1.1	-	-	-	-	-	-	-	-	-	-	209.6	0.6
1996	-	-	-	-	-	-	-	-	-	-	212.9	1.6	-	-	-	-	-	-	-	-	-	-	213.4	0.2
1997	-	-	-	-	-	-	-	-	-	-	212.3	-0.5	-	-	-	-	-	-	-	-	-	-	-	-

Source: U.S. Department of Labor, Bureau of Labor Statistics, Division of Consumer Prices and Price Indexes. - indicates no data collected for period.

Kansas City, MO-KS
Consumer Price Index - All Urban Consumers
Base 1982-1984 = 100
Entertainment

For 1975-1997. Columns headed % show percentile change in the index from the previous period for which an index is available.

Year	Jan Index	%	Feb Index	%	Mar Index	%	Apr Index	%	May Index	%	Jun Index	%	Jul Index	%	Aug Index	%	Sep Index	%	Oct Index	%	Nov Index	%	Dec Index	%
1975	-	-	-	-	-	-	-	-	-	-	-	-	-	-	-	-	-	-	-	-	-	-	63.6	-
1976	-	-	-	-	64.0	0.6	-	-	-	-	65.2	1.9	-	-	-	-	66.4	1.8	-	-	-	-	66.4	0.0
1977	-	-	-	-	66.9	0.8	-	-	-	-	68.0	1.6	-	-	-	-	69.6	2.4	-	-	-	-	69.5	-0.1
1978	-	-	69.9	0.6	-	-	70.9	1.4	-	-	70.0	-1.3	-	-	71.0	1.4	-	-	72.0	1.4	-	-	72.2	0.3
1979	-	-	73.3	1.5	-	-	73.0	-0.4	-	-	73.6	0.8	-	-	74.2	0.8	-	-	76.2	2.7	-	-	76.4	0.3
1980	-	-	79.7	4.3	-	-	80.7	1.3	-	-	81.1	0.5	-	-	85.8	5.8	-	-	86.0	0.2	-	-	88.4	2.8
1981	-	-	88.9	0.6	-	-	89.1	0.2	-	-	90.2	1.2	-	-	90.4	0.2	-	-	92.0	1.8	-	-	92.7	0.8
1982	-	-	94.6	2.0	-	-	94.7	0.1	-	-	95.4	0.7	-	-	96.6	1.3	-	-	97.2	0.6	-	-	97.4	0.2
1983	-	-	99.2	1.8	-	-	98.9	-0.3	-	-	98.7	-0.2	-	-	100.9	2.2	-	-	101.3	0.4	-	-	101.7	0.4
1984	-	-	102.8	1.1	-	-	103.5	0.7	-	-	104.0	0.5	-	-	105.0	1.0	-	-	105.8	0.8	-	-	105.7	-0.1
1985	-	-	106.8	1.0	-	-	107.0	0.2	-	-	106.9	-0.1	-	-	106.9	0.0	-	-	107.6	0.7	-	-	107.0	-0.6
1986	-	-	108.1	1.0	-	-	109.3	1.1	-	-	110.4	1.0	-	-	110.6	0.2	-	-	114.4	3.4	-	-	114.8	0.3
1987	-	-	-	-	-	-	-	-	-	-	120.8	5.2	-	-	-	-	-	-	-	-	-	-	126.4	4.6
1988	-	-	-	-	-	-	-	-	-	-	123.3	-2.5	-	-	-	-	-	-	-	-	-	-	125.2	1.5
1989	-	-	-	-	-	-	-	-	-	-	129.9	3.8	-	-	-	-	-	-	-	-	-	-	134.1	3.2
1990	-	-	-	-	-	-	-	-	-	-	136.6	1.9	-	-	-	-	-	-	-	-	-	-	147.4	7.9
1991	-	-	-	-	-	-	-	-	-	-	147.3	-0.1	-	-	-	-	-	-	-	-	-	-	151.4	2.8
1992	-	-	-	-	-	-	-	-	-	-	154.5	2.0	-	-	-	-	-	-	-	-	-	-	153.5	-0.6
1993	-	-	-	-	-	-	-	-	-	-	152.4	-0.7	-	-	-	-	-	-	-	-	-	-	152.5	0.1
1994	-	-	-	-	-	-	-	-	-	-	159.6	4.7	-	-	-	-	-	-	-	-	-	-	161.5	1.2
1995	-	-	-	-	-	-	-	-	-	-	161.9	0.2	-	-	-	-	-	-	-	-	-	-	159.0	-1.8
1996	-	-	-	-	-	-	-	-	-	-	167.4	5.3	-	-	-	-	-	-	-	-	-	-	170.7	2.0
1997	-	-	-	-	-	-	-	-	-	-	171.7	0.6	-	-	-	-	-	-	-	-	-	-	-	-

Source: U.S. Department of Labor, Bureau of Labor Statistics, Division of Consumer Prices and Price Indexes. - indicates no data collected for period.

Kansas City, MO-KS
Consumer Price Index - Urban Wage Earners
Base 1982-1984 = 100
Entertainment

For 1975-1997. Columns headed % show percentile change in the index from the previous period for which an index is available.

Year	Jan Index	%	Feb Index	%	Mar Index	%	Apr Index	%	May Index	%	Jun Index	%	Jul Index	%	Aug Index	%	Sep Index	%	Oct Index	%	Nov Index	%	Dec Index	%
1975	-	-	-	-	-	-	-	-	-	-	-	-	-	-	-	-	-	-	-	-	-	-	60.3	-
1976	-	-	-	-	60.7	0.7	-	-	-	-	61.8	1.8	-	-	-	-	62.9	1.8	-	-	-	-	62.9	0.0
1977	-	-	-	-	63.4	0.8	-	-	-	-	64.5	1.7	-	-	-	-	65.9	2.2	-	-	-	-	65.9	0.0
1978	-	-	66.3	0.6	-	-	66.8	0.8	-	-	66.6	-0.3	-	-	67.3	1.1	-	-	67.4	0.1	-	-	66.8	-0.9
1979	-	-	68.6	2.7	-	-	68.7	0.1	-	-	70.0	1.9	-	-	70.9	1.3	-	-	75.3	6.2	-	-	75.3	0.0
1980	-	-	78.7	4.5	-	-	80.8	2.7	-	-	81.8	1.2	-	-	85.0	3.9	-	-	84.3	-0.8	-	-	86.8	3.0
1981	-	-	87.5	0.8	-	-	90.1	3.0	-	-	90.8	0.8	-	-	91.4	0.7	-	-	91.8	0.4	-	-	92.5	0.8
1982	-	-	94.5	2.2	-	-	94.4	-0.1	-	-	95.2	0.8	-	-	96.5	1.4	-	-	97.1	0.6	-	-	97.3	0.2
1983	-	-	99.2	2.0	-	-	98.9	-0.3	-	-	98.9	0.0	-	-	100.9	2.0	-	-	101.3	0.4	-	-	101.7	0.4
1984	-	-	103.1	1.4	-	-	103.7	0.6	-	-	104.1	0.4	-	-	105.0	0.9	-	-	105.7	0.7	-	-	106.0	0.3
1985	-	-	106.9	0.8	-	-	106.9	0.0	-	-	106.9	0.0	-	-	106.8	-0.1	-	-	107.5	0.7	-	-	107.2	-0.3
1986	-	-	108.4	1.1	-	-	109.4	0.9	-	-	110.5	1.0	-	-	110.7	0.2	-	-	112.8	1.9	-	-	113.6	0.7
1987	-	-	-	-	-	-	-	-	-	-	119.9	5.5	-	-	-	-	-	-	-	-	-	-	125.7	4.8
1988	-	-	-	-	-	-	-	-	-	-	122.1	-2.9	-	-	-	-	-	-	-	-	-	-	124.1	1.6
1989	-	-	-	-	-	-	-	-	-	-	128.7	3.7	-	-	-	-	-	-	-	-	-	-	132.4	2.9
1990	-	-	-	-	-	-	-	-	-	-	134.9	1.9	-	-	-	-	-	-	-	-	-	-	145.9	8.2
1991	-	-	-	-	-	-	-	-	-	-	145.2	-0.5	-	-	-	-	-	-	-	-	-	-	150.0	3.3
1992	-	-	-	-	-	-	-	-	-	-	152.9	1.9	-	-	-	-	-	-	-	-	-	-	152.5	-0.3
1993	-	-	-	-	-	-	-	-	-	-	151.9	-0.4	-	-	-	-	-	-	-	-	-	-	152.2	0.2
1994	-	-	-	-	-	-	-	-	-	-	159.5	4.8	-	-	-	-	-	-	-	-	-	-	161.4	1.2
1995	-	-	-	-	-	-	-	-	-	-	161.7	0.2	-	-	-	-	-	-	-	-	-	-	158.4	-2.0
1996	-	-	-	-	-	-	-	-	-	-	167.3	5.6	-	-	-	-	-	-	-	-	-	-	170.2	1.7
1997	-	-	-	-	-	-	-	-	-	-	171.2	0.6	-	-	-	-	-	-	-	-	-	-	-	-

Source: U.S. Department of Labor, Bureau of Labor Statistics, Division of Consumer Prices and Price Indexes. - indicates no data collected for period.

Kansas City, MO-KS
Consumer Price Index - All Urban Consumers
Base 1982-1984 = 100
Other Goods and Services

For 1975-1997. Columns headed % show percentile change in the index from the previous period for which an index is available.

Year	Jan Index	%	Feb Index	%	Mar Index	%	Apr Index	%	May Index	%	Jun Index	%	Jul Index	%	Aug Index	%	Sep Index	%	Oct Index	%	Nov Index	%	Dec Index	%
1975	-	-	-	-	-	-	-	-	-	-	-	-	-	-	-	-	-	-	-	-	-	-	56.2	-
1976	-	-	-	-	56.9	1.2	-	-	-	-	57.3	0.7	-	-	-	-	58.1	1.4	-	-	-	-	59.4	2.2
1977	-	-	-	-	60.1	1.2	-	-	-	-	61.0	1.5	-	-	-	-	62.6	2.6	-	-	-	-	63.0	0.6
1978	-	-	62.7	-0.5	-	-	64.2	2.4	-	-	63.9	-0.5	-	-	65.2	2.0	-	-	66.4	1.8	-	-	66.7	0.5
1979	-	-	67.7	1.5	-	-	67.9	0.3	-	-	69.9	2.9	-	-	70.4	0.7	-	-	71.9	2.1	-	-	73.2	1.8
1980	-	-	74.7	2.0	-	-	75.0	0.4	-	-	76.0	1.3	-	-	77.0	1.3	-	-	79.0	2.6	-	-	80.4	1.8
1981	-	-	81.6	1.5	-	-	81.7	0.1	-	-	84.2	3.1	-	-	85.1	1.1	-	-	87.9	3.3	-	-	88.5	0.7
1982	-	-	89.1	0.7	-	-	89.8	0.8	-	-	88.9	-1.0	-	-	90.5	1.8	-	-	95.5	5.5	-	-	95.9	0.4
1983	-	-	97.6	1.8	-	-	99.0	1.4	-	-	99.1	0.1	-	-	100.9	1.8	-	-	104.5	3.6	-	-	104.9	0.4
1984	-	-	105.7	0.8	-	-	106.4	0.7	-	-	107.3	0.8	-	-	107.7	0.4	-	-	111.4	3.4	-	-	111.9	0.4
1985	-	-	113.2	1.2	-	-	112.9	-0.3	-	-	112.5	-0.4	-	-	115.5	2.7	-	-	121.0	4.8	-	-	121.7	0.6
1986	-	-	122.4	0.6	-	-	123.0	0.5	-	-	123.8	0.7	-	-	125.5	1.4	-	-	129.8	3.4	-	-	130.3	0.4
1987	-	-	-	-	-	-	-	-	-	-	132.5	1.7	-	-	-	-	-	-	-	-	-	-	-	-
1988	-	-	-	-	-	-	-	-	-	-	139.5	5.3	-	-	-	-	-	-	-	-	-	-	-	-
1989	-	-	-	-	-	-	-	-	-	-	150.2	7.7	-	-	-	-	-	-	-	-	-	-	-	-
1990	-	-	-	-	-	-	-	-	-	-	157.5	4.9	-	-	-	-	-	-	-	-	-	-	-	-
1991	-	-	-	-	-	-	-	-	-	-	171.5	8.9	-	-	-	-	-	-	-	-	-	-	-	-
1992	-	-	-	-	-	-	-	-	-	-	187.8	9.5	-	-	-	-	-	-	-	-	-	-	-	-
1993	-	-	-	-	-	-	-	-	-	-	194.7	3.7	-	-	-	-	-	-	-	-	-	-	-	-
1994	-	-	-	-	-	-	-	-	-	-	202.3	3.9	-	-	-	-	-	-	-	-	-	-	-	-
1995	-	-	-	-	-	-	-	-	-	-	205.9	1.8	-	-	-	-	-	-	-	-	-	-	-	-
1996	-	-	-	-	-	-	-	-	-	-	218.1	5.9	-	-	-	-	-	-	-	-	-	-	-	-
1997	-	-	-	-	-	-	-	-	-	-	233.4	7.0	-	-	-	-	-	-	-	-	-	-	-	-

Source: U.S. Department of Labor, Bureau of Labor Statistics, Division of Consumer Prices and Price Indexes. - indicates no data collected for period.

Kansas City, MO-KS
Consumer Price Index - Urban Wage Earners
Base 1982-1984 = 100
Other Goods and Services

For 1975-1997. Columns headed % show percentile change in the index from the previous period for which an index is available.

Year	Jan Index	%	Feb Index	%	Mar Index	%	Apr Index	%	May Index	%	Jun Index	%	Jul Index	%	Aug Index	%	Sep Index	%	Oct Index	%	Nov Index	%	Dec Index	%
1975	-	-	-	-	-	-	-	-	-	-	-	-	-	-	-	-	-	-	-	-	-	-	56.4	-
1976	-	-	-	-	57.1	1.2	-	-	-	-	57.5	0.7	-	-	-	-	58.3	1.4	-	-	-	-	59.6	2.2
1977	-	-	-	-	60.3	1.2	-	-	-	-	61.3	1.7	-	-	-	-	62.8	2.4	-	-	-	-	63.3	0.8
1978	-	-	64.1	1.3	-	-	64.3	0.3	-	-	64.4	0.2	-	-	65.4	1.6	-	-	66.7	2.0	-	-	66.6	-0.1
1979	-	-	68.4	2.7	-	-	69.7	1.9	-	-	72.0	3.3	-	-	72.3	0.4	-	-	73.6	1.8	-	-	74.3	1.0
1980	-	-	76.5	3.0	-	-	76.4	-0.1	-	-	78.0	2.1	-	-	79.4	1.8	-	-	81.0	2.0	-	-	82.2	1.5
1981	-	-	83.2	1.2	-	-	81.5	-2.0	-	-	84.7	3.9	-	-	85.7	1.2	-	-	87.7	2.3	-	-	88.2	0.6
1982	-	-	88.8	0.7	-	-	89.8	1.1	-	-	88.7	-1.2	-	-	90.6	2.1	-	-	95.6	5.5	-	-	95.9	0.3
1983	-	-	97.5	1.7	-	-	99.3	1.8	-	-	99.3	0.0	-	-	101.5	2.2	-	-	104.3	2.8	-	-	104.7	0.4
1984	-	-	105.7	1.0	-	-	106.5	0.8	-	-	107.5	0.9	-	-	108.0	0.5	-	-	110.9	2.7	-	-	111.4	0.5
1985	-	-	113.0	1.4	-	-	112.6	-0.4	-	-	112.1	-0.4	-	-	115.8	3.3	-	-	120.6	4.1	-	-	121.3	0.6
1986	-	-	122.2	0.7	-	-	122.8	0.5	-	-	123.8	0.8	-	-	125.9	1.7	-	-	129.3	2.7	-	-	129.8	0.4
1987	-	-	-	-	-	-	-	-	-	-	132.1	1.8	-	-	-	-	-	-	-	-	-	-	-	-
1988	-	-	-	-	-	-	-	-	-	-	139.4	5.5	-	-	-	-	-	-	-	-	-	-	-	-
1989	-	-	-	-	-	-	-	-	-	-	150.9	8.2	-	-	-	-	-	-	-	-	-	-	-	-
1990	-	-	-	-	-	-	-	-	-	-	158.3	4.9	-	-	-	-	-	-	-	-	-	-	-	-
1991	-	-	-	-	-	-	-	-	-	-	172.7	9.1	-	-	-	-	-	-	-	-	-	-	-	-
1992	-	-	-	-	-	-	-	-	-	-	189.9	10.0	-	-	-	-	-	-	-	-	-	-	-	-
1993	-	-	-	-	-	-	-	-	-	-	196.8	3.6	-	-	-	-	-	-	-	-	-	-	-	-
1994	-	-	-	-	-	-	-	-	-	-	204.6	4.0	-	-	-	-	-	-	-	-	-	-	-	-
1995	-	-	-	-	-	-	-	-	-	-	208.4	1.9	-	-	-	-	-	-	-	-	-	-	-	-
1996	-	-	-	-	-	-	-	-	-	-	220.8	6.0	-	-	-	-	-	-	-	-	-	-	-	-
1997	-	-	-	-	-	-	-	-	-	-	236.2	7.0	-	-	-	-	-	-	-	-	-	-	-	-

Source: U.S. Department of Labor, Bureau of Labor Statistics, Division of Consumer Prices and Price Indexes. - indicates no data collected for period.

Los Angeles, CA
Consumer Price Index - All Urban Consumers
Base 1982-1984 = 100
Annual Averages

For 1914-1997. Columns headed % show percentile change in the index from the previous period for which an index is available.

Year	All Items		Food & Beverage		Housing		Apparel & Upkeep		Trans- portation		Medical Care		Entertain- ment		Other Goods & Services	
	Index	%	Index	%	Index	%	Index	%	Index	%	Index	%	Index	%	Index	%
1914	-	-	-	-	-	-	-	-	-	-	-	-	-	-	-	-
1915	10.0	-	-	-	-	-	-	-	-	-	-	-	-	-	-	-
1916	10.5	5.0	-	-	-	-	-	-	-	-	-	-	-	-	-	-
1917	12.1	15.2	-	-	-	-	-	-	-	-	-	-	-	-	-	-
1918	14.4	19.0	-	-	-	-	-	-	-	-	-	-	-	-	-	-
1919	17.0	18.1	-	-	-	-	-	-	-	-	-	-	-	-	-	-
1920	19.9	17.1	-	-	-	-	-	-	-	-	-	-	-	-	-	-
1921	18.6	-6.5	-	-	-	-	-	-	-	-	-	-	-	-	-	-
1922	18.1	-2.7	-	-	-	-	-	-	-	-	-	-	-	-	-	-
1923	18.3	1.1	-	-	-	-	-	-	-	-	-	-	-	-	-	-
1924	18.4	0.5	-	-	-	-	-	-	-	-	-	-	-	-	-	-
1925	18.4	0.0	-	-	-	-	-	-	-	-	-	-	-	-	-	-
1926	17.9	-2.7	-	-	-	-	-	-	-	-	-	-	-	-	-	-
1927	17.6	-1.7	-	-	-	-	-	-	-	-	-	-	-	-	-	-
1928	17.3	-1.7	-	-	-	-	-	-	-	-	-	-	-	-	-	-
1929	17.3	0.0	-	-	-	-	-	-	-	-	-	-	-	-	-	-
1930	16.7	-3.5	-	-	-	-	-	-	-	-	-	-	-	-	-	-
1931	15.1	-9.6	-	-	-	-	-	-	-	-	-	-	-	-	-	-
1932	13.6	-9.9	-	-	-	-	-	-	-	-	-	-	-	-	-	-
1933	12.8	-5.9	-	-	-	-	-	-	-	-	-	-	-	-	-	-
1934	12.9	0.8	-	-	-	-	-	-	-	-	-	-	-	-	-	-
1935	13.3	3.1	-	-	-	-	-	-	-	-	-	-	-	-	-	-
1936	13.5	1.5	-	-	-	-	-	-	-	-	-	-	-	-	-	-
1937	14.2	5.2	-	-	-	-	-	-	-	-	-	-	-	-	-	-
1938	14.0	-1.4	-	-	-	-	-	-	-	-	-	-	-	-	-	-
1939	13.9	-0.7	-	-	-	-	-	-	-	-	-	-	-	-	-	-
1940	13.9	0.0	-	-	-	-	-	-	-	-	-	-	-	-	-	-
1941	14.7	5.8	-	-	-	-	-	-	-	-	-	-	-	-	-	-
1942	16.5	12.2	-	-	-	-	-	-	-	-	-	-	-	-	-	-
1943	17.3	4.8	-	-	-	-	-	-	-	-	-	-	-	-	-	-
1944	17.6	1.7	-	-	-	-	-	-	-	-	-	-	-	-	-	-
1945	18.1	2.8	-	-	-	-	-	-	-	-	-	-	-	-	-	-
1946	19.5	7.7	-	-	-	-	-	-	-	-	-	-	-	-	-	-
1947	22.0	12.8	-	-	-	-	-	-	17.9	-	13.4	-	-	-	-	-
1948	23.6	7.3	-	-	-	-	-	-	19.8	10.6	14.2	6.0	-	-	-	-
1949	23.6	0.0	-	-	-	-	-	-	21.0	6.1	14.7	3.5	-	-	-	-
1950	23.7	0.4	-	-	-	-	-	-	20.7	-1.4	15.0	2.0	-	-	-	-
1951	25.7	8.4	-	-	-	-	-	-	21.6	4.3	15.9	6.0	-	-	-	-
1952	26.5	3.1	-	-	-	-	-	-	23.8	10.2	16.5	3.8	-	-	-	-
1953	26.7	0.8	-	-	-	-	48.7	-	24.8	4.2	16.9	2.4	-	-	-	-
1954	26.7	0.0	-	-	-	-	48.9	0.4	24.6	-0.8	17.3	2.4	-	-	-	-
1955	26.7	0.0	-	-	-	-	48.9	0.0	24.4	-0.8	17.4	0.6	-	-	-	-
1956	27.1	1.5	-	-	-	-	49.8	1.8	24.8	1.6	17.9	2.9	-	-	-	-
1957	28.0	3.3	-	-	-	-	50.9	2.2	25.8	4.0	18.4	2.8	-	-	-	-
1958	28.9	3.2	-	-	-	-	51.0	0.2	26.5	2.7	19.9	8.2	-	-	-	-

[Continued]

Los Angeles, CA

Consumer Price Index - All Urban Consumers
Base 1982-1984 = 100
Annual Averages

[Continued]

For 1914-1997. Columns headed % show percentile change in the index from the previous period for which an index is available.

Year	All Items		Food & Beverage		Housing		Apparel & Upkeep		Trans-portation		Medical Care		Entertain-ment		Other Goods & Services	
	Index	%	Index	%	Index	%	Index	%	Index	%	Index	%	Index	%	Index	%
1959	29.4	1.7	-	-	-	-	51.6	1.2	27.8	4.9	20.8	4.5	-	-	-	-
1960	30.0	2.0	-	-	-	-	52.8	2.3	28.0	0.7	21.4	2.9	-	-	-	-
1961	30.3	1.0	-	-	-	-	52.9	0.2	28.9	3.2	21.6	0.9	-	-	-	-
1962	30.7	1.3	-	-	-	-	53.0	0.2	29.9	3.5	22.3	3.2	-	-	-	-
1963	31.1	1.3	-	-	-	-	53.7	1.3	29.9	0.0	22.7	1.8	-	-	-	-
1964	31.7	1.9	-	-	-	-	54.5	1.5	31.1	4.0	23.2	2.2	-	-	-	-
1965	32.4	2.2	-	-	-	-	55.0	0.9	31.7	1.9	23.7	2.2	-	-	-	-
1966	33.0	1.9	-	-	-	-	55.9	1.6	31.9	0.6	24.6	3.8	-	-	-	-
1967	33.8	2.4	-	-	-	-	58.1	3.9	32.3	1.3	26.4	7.3	-	-	-	-
1968	35.2	4.1	-	-	-	-	61.2	5.3	33.3	3.1	27.8	5.3	-	-	-	-
1969	36.8	4.5	-	-	-	-	63.6	3.9	34.3	3.0	29.5	6.1	-	-	-	-
1970	38.7	5.2	-	-	-	-	66.5	4.6	35.4	3.2	31.6	7.1	-	-	-	-
1971	40.1	3.6	-	-	-	-	68.5	3.0	37.1	4.8	33.2	5.1	-	-	-	-
1972	41.4	3.2	-	-	-	-	69.7	1.8	38.0	2.4	33.9	2.1	-	-	-	-
1973	43.7	5.6	-	-	-	-	71.5	2.6	39.8	4.7	35.6	5.0	-	-	-	-
1974	48.2	10.3	-	-	-	-	76.7	7.3	44.5	11.8	39.0	9.6	-	-	-	-
1975	53.3	10.6	-	-	-	-	79.2	3.3	49.3	10.8	43.7	12.1	-	-	-	-
1976	56.9	6.8	60.5	-	54.4	-	80.9	2.1	54.2	9.9	49.3	12.8	70.5	-	57.3	-
1977	60.8	6.9	64.7	6.9	58.4	7.4	84.1	4.0	58.1	7.2	53.9	9.3	73.2	3.8	60.6	5.8
1978	65.3	7.4	71.6	10.7	63.2	8.2	85.8	2.0	60.6	4.3	58.6	8.7	74.4	1.6	65.1	7.4
1979	72.3	10.7	79.2	10.6	69.9	10.6	89.0	3.7	70.3	16.0	64.6	10.2	78.6	5.6	69.2	6.3
1980	83.7	15.8	85.7	8.2	83.7	19.7	98.3	10.4	82.5	17.4	72.7	12.5	85.7	9.0	76.4	10.4
1981	91.9	9.8	92.5	7.9	92.4	10.4	101.5	3.3	91.3	10.7	82.0	12.8	93.1	8.6	83.9	9.8
1982	97.3	5.9	96.8	4.6	97.8	5.8	98.9	-2.6	97.5	6.8	94.1	14.8	97.6	4.8	92.0	9.7
1983	99.1	1.8	100.1	3.4	98.3	0.5	99.7	0.8	98.8	1.3	100.7	7.0	99.8	2.3	101.2	10.0
1984	103.6	4.5	103.1	3.0	103.9	5.7	101.3	1.6	103.7	5.0	105.2	4.5	102.6	2.8	106.8	5.5
1985	108.4	4.6	105.5	2.3	109.7	5.6	105.1	3.8	107.5	3.7	112.9	7.3	106.9	4.2	115.3	8.0
1986	111.9	3.2	108.7	3.0	116.1	5.8	106.9	1.7	105.2	-2.1	120.9	7.1	109.0	2.0	122.3	6.1
1987	116.7	4.3	113.2	4.1	121.0	4.2	112.5	5.2	108.9	3.5	129.5	7.1	111.2	2.0	127.9	4.6
1988	122.1	4.6	117.2	3.5	126.6	4.6	114.3	1.6	113.8	4.5	139.6	7.8	115.4	3.8	139.9	9.4
1989	128.3	5.1	124.0	5.8	131.7	4.0	118.8	3.9	119.6	5.1	149.8	7.3	120.9	4.8	155.3	11.0
1990	135.9	5.9	130.9	5.6	139.3	5.8	126.4	6.4	126.5	5.8	163.3	9.0	125.4	3.7	166.3	7.1
1991	141.4	4.0	136.6	4.4	144.9	4.0	130.9	3.6	126.6	0.1	178.2	9.1	135.4	8.0	179.9	8.2
1992	146.5	3.6	140.9	3.1	148.6	2.6	133.2	1.8	133.0	5.1	192.4	8.0	134.1	-1.0	197.1	9.6
1993	150.3	2.6	145.1	3.0	150.4	1.2	131.6	-1.2	137.5	3.4	206.6	7.4	135.8	1.3	211.9	7.5
1994	152.3	1.3	148.5	2.3	151.0	0.4	129.6	-1.5	140.5	2.2	215.2	4.2	137.2	1.0	218.0	2.9
1995	154.6	1.5	153.4	3.3	152.2	0.8	126.7	-2.2	142.3	1.3	221.8	3.1	141.3	3.0	225.6	3.5
1996	157.5	1.9	157.8	2.9	154.1	1.2	126.0	-0.6	144.3	1.4	228.9	3.2	145.8	3.2	232.8	3.2
1997	160.0	1.6	163.2	3.4	156.6	1.6	121.0	-4.0	145.2	0.6	232.0	1.4	147.6	1.2	240.7	3.4

Source: U.S. Department of Labor, Bureau of Labor Statistics, Division of Consumer Prices and Price Indexes. - indicates no data collected for period.

Los Angeles, CA
Consumer Price Index - Urban Wage Earners
Base 1982-1984 = 100
Annual Averages

For 1914-1997. Columns headed % show percentile change in the index from the previous period for which an index is available.

Year	All Items		Food & Beverage		Housing		Apparel & Upkeep		Trans- portation		Medical Care		Entertain- ment		Other Goods & Services	
	Index	%	Index	%	Index	%	Index	%	Index	%	Index	%	Index	%	Index	%
1914	-	-	-	-	-	-	-	-	-	-	-	-	-	-	-	-
1915	9.9	-	-	-	-	-	-	-	-	-	-	-	-	-	-	-
1916	10.5	6.1	-	-	-	-	-	-	-	-	-	-	-	-	-	-
1917	12.1	15.2	-	-	-	-	-	-	-	-	-	-	-	-	-	-
1918	14.4	19.0	-	-	-	-	-	-	-	-	-	-	-	-	-	-
1919	17.0	18.1	-	-	-	-	-	-	-	-	-	-	-	-	-	-
1920	19.9	17.1	-	-	-	-	-	-	-	-	-	-	-	-	-	-
1921	18.6	-6.5	-	-	-	-	-	-	-	-	-	-	-	-	-	-
1922	18.1	-2.7	-	-	-	-	-	-	-	-	-	-	-	-	-	-
1923	18.3	1.1	-	-	-	-	-	-	-	-	-	-	-	-	-	-
1924	18.4	0.5	-	-	-	-	-	-	-	-	-	-	-	-	-	-
1925	18.4	0.0	-	-	-	-	-	-	-	-	-	-	-	-	-	-
1926	17.9	-2.7	-	-	-	-	-	-	-	-	-	-	-	-	-	-
1927	17.6	-1.7	-	-	-	-	-	-	-	-	-	-	-	-	-	-
1928	17.3	-1.7	-	-	-	-	-	-	-	-	-	-	-	-	-	-
1929	17.3	0.0	-	-	-	-	-	-	-	-	-	-	-	-	-	-
1930	16.7	-3.5	-	-	-	-	-	-	-	-	-	-	-	-	-	-
1931	15.1	-9.6	-	-	-	-	-	-	-	-	-	-	-	-	-	-
1932	13.6	-9.9	-	-	-	-	-	-	-	-	-	-	-	-	-	-
1933	12.8	-5.9	-	-	-	-	-	-	-	-	-	-	-	-	-	-
1934	12.9	0.8	-	-	-	-	-	-	-	-	-	-	-	-	-	-
1935	13.3	3.1	-	-	-	-	-	-	-	-	-	-	-	-	-	-
1936	13.5	1.5	-	-	-	-	-	-	-	-	-	-	-	-	-	-
1937	14.2	5.2	-	-	-	-	-	-	-	-	-	-	-	-	-	-
1938	14.0	-1.4	-	-	-	-	-	-	-	-	-	-	-	-	-	-
1939	13.9	-0.7	-	-	-	-	-	-	-	-	-	-	-	-	-	-
1940	13.9	0.0	-	-	-	-	-	-	-	-	-	-	-	-	-	-
1941	14.7	5.8	-	-	-	-	-	-	-	-	-	-	-	-	-	-
1942	16.5	12.2	-	-	-	-	-	-	-	-	-	-	-	-	-	-
1943	17.3	4.8	-	-	-	-	-	-	-	-	-	-	-	-	-	-
1944	17.6	1.7	-	-	-	-	-	-	-	-	-	-	-	-	-	-
1945	18.1	2.8	-	-	-	-	-	-	-	-	-	-	-	-	-	-
1946	19.5	7.7	-	-	-	-	-	-	-	-	-	-	-	-	-	-
1947	22.0	12.8	-	-	-	-	-	-	17.8	-	13.6	-	-	-	-	-
1948	23.6	7.3	-	-	-	-	-	-	19.7	10.7	14.4	5.9	-	-	-	-
1949	23.6	0.0	-	-	-	-	-	-	20.9	6.1	14.9	3.5	-	-	-	-
1950	23.7	0.4	-	-	-	-	-	-	20.6	-1.4	15.2	2.0	-	-	-	-
1951	25.7	8.4	-	-	-	-	-	-	21.5	4.4	16.1	5.9	-	-	-	-
1952	26.5	3.1	-	-	-	-	-	-	23.7	10.2	16.7	3.7	-	-	-	-
1953	26.7	0.8	-	-	-	-	48.9	-	24.6	3.8	17.2	3.0	-	-	-	-
1954	26.7	0.0	-	-	-	-	49.1	0.4	24.4	-0.8	17.5	1.7	-	-	-	-
1955	26.7	0.0	-	-	-	-	49.1	0.0	24.3	-0.4	17.6	0.6	-	-	-	-
1956	27.1	1.5	-	-	-	-	50.0	1.8	24.6	1.2	18.2	3.4	-	-	-	-
1957	28.0	3.3	-	-	-	-	51.1	2.2	25.6	4.1	18.7	2.7	-	-	-	-
1958	28.9	3.2	-	-	-	-	51.2	0.2	26.3	2.7	20.2	8.0	-	-	-	-

[Continued]

Los Angeles, CA
Consumer Price Index - Urban Wage Earners
Base 1982-1984 = 100
Annual Averages

[Continued]

For 1914-1997. Columns headed % show percentile change in the index from the previous period for which an index is available.

Year	All Items		Food & Beverage		Housing		Apparel & Upkeep		Trans-portation		Medical Care		Entertain-ment		Other Goods & Services	
	Index	%	Index	%	Index	%	Index	%	Index	%	Index	%	Index	%	Index	%
1959	29.4	1.7	-	-	-	-	51.8	1.2	27.7	5.3	21.1	4.5	-	-	-	-
1960	29.9	1.7	-	-	-	-	53.0	2.3	27.8	0.4	21.7	2.8	-	-	-	-
1961	30.3	1.3	-	-	-	-	53.1	0.2	28.7	3.2	22.0	1.4	-	-	-	-
1962	30.7	1.3	-	-	-	-	53.2	0.2	29.7	3.5	22.7	3.2	-	-	-	-
1963	31.1	1.3	-	-	-	-	53.9	1.3	29.8	0.3	23.0	1.3	-	-	-	-
1964	31.7	1.9	-	-	-	-	54.7	1.5	30.9	3.7	23.6	2.6	-	-	-	-
1965	32.4	2.2	-	-	-	-	55.2	0.9	31.6	2.3	24.0	1.7	-	-	-	-
1966	33.0	1.9	-	-	-	-	56.1	1.6	31.7	0.3	24.9	3.8	-	-	-	-
1967	33.8	2.4	-	-	-	-	58.3	3.9	32.1	1.3	26.8	7.6	-	-	-	-
1968	35.2	4.1	-	-	-	-	61.4	5.3	33.1	3.1	28.2	5.2	-	-	-	-
1969	36.8	4.5	-	-	-	-	63.9	4.1	34.1	3.0	29.9	6.0	-	-	-	-
1970	38.7	5.2	-	-	-	-	66.7	4.4	35.2	3.2	32.1	7.4	-	-	-	-
1971	40.1	3.6	-	-	-	-	68.8	3.1	36.9	4.8	33.7	5.0	-	-	-	-
1972	41.4	3.2	-	-	-	-	69.9	1.6	37.8	2.4	34.5	2.4	-	-	-	-
1973	43.7	5.6	-	-	-	-	71.8	2.7	39.6	4.8	36.1	4.6	-	-	-	-
1974	48.2	10.3	-	-	-	-	76.9	7.1	44.2	11.6	39.5	9.4	-	-	-	-
1975	53.3	10.6	-	-	-	-	79.5	3.4	49.1	11.1	44.4	12.4	-	-	-	-
1976	56.8	6.6	59.4	-	54.5	-	81.2	2.1	53.9	9.8	50.1	12.8	77.4	-	57.0	-
1977	60.8	7.0	63.5	6.9	58.5	7.3	84.4	3.9	57.8	7.2	54.7	9.2	80.3	3.7	60.2	5.6
1978	65.1	7.1	70.0	10.2	63.3	8.2	87.1	3.2	60.3	4.3	59.0	7.9	80.2	-0.1	64.3	6.8
1979	72.8	11.8	78.0	11.4	70.6	11.5	91.5	5.1	70.5	16.9	65.3	10.7	83.4	4.0	68.6	6.7
1980	84.7	16.3	85.2	9.2	85.3	20.8	97.3	6.3	83.2	18.0	74.0	13.3	90.8	8.9	75.3	9.8
1981	93.1	9.9	92.2	8.2	94.8	11.1	100.7	3.5	92.0	10.6	83.5	12.8	94.4	4.0	82.9	10.1
1982	98.5	5.8	96.8	5.0	100.4	5.9	99.0	-1.7	97.8	6.3	94.1	12.7	97.6	3.4	91.7	10.6
1983	99.3	0.8	100.2	3.5	99.0	-1.4	99.6	0.6	98.6	0.8	100.7	7.0	99.8	2.3	101.7	10.9
1984	102.2	2.9	103.1	2.9	100.6	1.6	101.4	1.8	103.5	5.0	105.2	4.5	102.6	2.8	106.7	4.9
1985	106.5	4.2	105.4	2.2	106.2	5.6	105.0	3.6	107.0	3.4	112.9	7.3	106.6	3.9	113.7	6.6
1986	109.5	2.8	108.5	2.9	112.3	5.7	107.2	2.1	103.9	-2.9	120.7	6.9	108.4	1.7	120.7	6.2
1987	114.0	4.1	113.0	4.1	117.0	4.2	111.9	4.4	107.0	3.0	129.0	6.9	110.5	1.9	126.4	4.7
1988	119.0	4.4	117.1	3.6	122.3	4.5	114.0	1.9	111.4	4.1	139.1	7.8	114.6	3.7	137.6	8.9
1989	124.9	5.0	123.9	5.8	127.1	3.9	118.8	4.2	116.6	4.7	148.7	6.9	120.0	4.7	154.9	12.6
1990	131.9	5.6	131.0	5.7	134.1	5.5	126.1	6.1	122.2	4.8	161.5	8.6	124.4	3.7	166.1	7.2
1991	137.1	3.9	136.8	4.4	139.6	4.1	130.8	3.7	122.5	0.2	175.7	8.8	134.1	7.8	179.1	7.8
1992	142.0	3.6	141.4	3.4	143.0	2.4	133.6	2.1	128.6	5.0	190.0	8.1	134.4	0.2	194.2	8.4
1993	145.2	2.3	145.6	3.0	144.8	1.3	132.4	-0.9	132.5	3.0	203.9	7.3	136.4	1.5	204.6	5.4
1994	147.0	1.2	148.8	2.2	145.4	0.4	130.0	-1.8	135.7	2.4	211.7	3.8	137.5	0.8	207.4	1.4
1995	149.4	1.6	153.5	3.2	146.4	0.7	126.8	-2.5	138.4	2.0	218.8	3.4	142.1	3.3	213.9	3.1
1996	152.1	1.8	158.0	2.9	148.2	1.2	126.0	-0.6	140.6	1.6	226.4	3.5	145.8	2.6	220.4	3.0
1997	154.3	1.4	163.3	3.4	150.6	1.6	120.9	-4.0	141.0	0.3	229.4	1.3	147.4	1.1	227.3	3.1

Source: U.S. Department of Labor, Bureau of Labor Statistics, Division of Consumer Prices and Price Indexes. - indicates no data collected for period.

Los Angeles, CA
Consumer Price Index - All Urban Consumers
Base 1982-1984 = 100
All Items

For 1914-1997. Columns headed % show percentile change in the index from the previous period for which an index is available.

Year	Jan Index	Jan %	Feb Index	Feb %	Mar Index	Mar %	Apr Index	Apr %	May Index	May %	Jun Index	Jun %	Jul Index	Jul %	Aug Index	Aug %	Sep Index	Sep %	Oct Index	Oct %	Nov Index	Nov %	Dec Index	Dec %
1914	-	-	-	-	-	-	-	-	-	-	-	-	-	-	-	-	-	-	-	-	-	-	10.2	-
1915	-	-	-	-	-	-	-	-	-	-	-	-	-	-	-	-	-	-	-	-	-	-	10.1	-1.0
1916	-	-	-	-	-	-	-	-	-	-	-	-	-	-	-	-	-	-	-	-	-	-	11.0	8.9
1917	-	-	-	-	-	-	-	-	-	-	-	-	-	-	-	-	-	-	-	-	-	-	13.0	18.2
1918	-	-	-	-	-	-	-	-	-	-	-	-	-	-	-	-	-	-	-	-	-	-	15.8	21.5
1919	-	-	-	-	-	-	-	-	-	-	16.4	3.8	-	-	-	-	-	-	-	-	-	-	18.6	13.4
1920	-	-	-	-	-	-	-	-	-	-	20.4	9.7	-	-	-	-	-	-	-	-	-	-	19.9	-2.5
1921	-	-	-	-	-	-	-	-	18.5	-7.0	-	-	-	-	-	-	18.3	-1.1	-	-	-	-	18.4	0.5
1922	-	-	-	-	18.2	-1.1	-	-	-	-	18.1	-0.5	-	-	-	-	18.0	-0.6	-	-	-	-	18.1	0.6
1923	-	-	-	-	18.0	-0.6	-	-	-	-	18.3	1.7	-	-	-	-	18.5	1.1	-	-	-	-	18.6	0.5
1924	-	-	-	-	18.5	-0.5	-	-	-	-	18.3	-1.1	-	-	-	-	18.4	0.5	-	-	-	-	18.2	-1.1
1925	-	-	-	-	-	-	-	-	-	-	18.5	1.6	-	-	-	-	-	-	-	-	-	-	18.5	0.0
1926	-	-	-	-	-	-	-	-	-	-	17.8	-3.8	-	-	-	-	-	-	-	-	-	-	17.8	0.0
1927	-	-	-	-	-	-	-	-	-	-	17.8	0.0	-	-	-	-	-	-	-	-	-	-	17.5	-1.7
1928	-	-	-	-	-	-	-	-	-	-	17.2	-1.7	-	-	-	-	-	-	-	-	-	-	17.4	1.2
1929	-	-	-	-	-	-	-	-	-	-	17.2	-1.1	-	-	-	-	-	-	-	-	-	-	17.2	0.0
1930	-	-	-	-	-	-	-	-	-	-	16.7	-2.9	-	-	-	-	-	-	-	-	-	-	16.0	-4.2
1931	-	-	-	-	-	-	-	-	-	-	14.9	-6.9	-	-	-	-	-	-	-	-	-	-	14.6	-2.0
1932	-	-	-	-	-	-	-	-	-	-	13.6	-6.8	-	-	-	-	-	-	-	-	-	-	13.1	-3.7
1933	-	-	-	-	-	-	-	-	-	-	12.5	-4.6	-	-	-	-	-	-	-	-	-	-	13.0	4.0
1934	-	-	-	-	-	-	-	-	-	-	12.9	-0.8	-	-	-	-	-	-	-	-	13.3	3.1	-	-
1935	-	-	-	-	13.6	2.3	-	-	-	-	-	-	13.2	-2.9	-	-	-	-	13.1	-0.8	-	-	-	-
1936	13.4	2.3	-	-	-	-	13.2	-1.5	-	-	-	-	13.4	1.5	-	-	13.7	2.2	-	-	-	-	13.7	0.0
1937	-	-	-	-	14.3	4.4	-	-	-	-	14.2	-0.7	-	-	-	-	14.4	1.4	-	-	-	-	14.3	-0.7
1938	-	-	-	-	14.0	-2.1	-	-	-	-	14.0	0.0	-	-	-	-	14.0	0.0	-	-	-	-	14.1	0.7
1939	-	-	-	-	14.0	-0.7	-	-	-	-	13.8	-1.4	-	-	-	-	14.1	2.2	-	-	-	-	13.9	-1.4
1940	-	-	-	-	13.9	0.0	-	-	-	-	13.9	0.0	-	-	-	-	14.0	0.7	14.0	0.0	14.1	0.7	14.1	0.0
1941	14.2	0.7	14.0	-1.4	14.1	0.7	14.3	1.4	14.4	0.7	14.6	1.4	14.6	0.0	14.7	0.7	15.0	2.0	15.2	1.3	15.3	0.7	15.5	1.3
1942	15.7	1.3	15.8	0.6	16.1	1.9	16.2	0.6	16.3	0.6	16.4	0.6	16.6	1.2	16.8	1.2	16.8	0.0	17.0	1.2	17.1	0.6	17.1	0.0
1943	17.1	0.0	17.0	-0.6	17.2	1.2	17.4	1.2	17.4	0.0	17.4	0.0	17.3	-0.6	17.2	-0.6	17.3	0.6	17.4	0.6	17.5	0.6	17.5	0.0
1944	17.4	-0.6	17.4	0.0	17.4	0.0	17.4	0.0	17.6	1.1	17.5	-0.6	17.5	0.0	17.6	0.6	17.7	0.6	17.8	0.6	17.8	0.0	17.9	0.6
1945	17.9	0.0	17.8	-0.6	17.9	0.6	18.0	0.6	18.0	0.0	18.0	0.0	18.1	0.6	18.1	0.0	18.3	1.1	18.3	0.0	18.4	0.5	18.5	0.5
1946	18.4	-0.5	18.4	0.0	18.4	0.0	18.5	0.5	18.6	0.5	18.8	1.1	19.7	4.8	20.0	1.5	20.1	0.5	20.5	2.0	21.4	4.4	21.4	0.0
1947	21.5	0.5	21.6	0.5	21.7	0.5	21.8	0.5	21.8	0.0	21.7	-0.5	21.8	0.5	21.9	0.5	22.4	2.3	22.4	0.0	22.8	1.8	23.0	0.9
1948	23.3	1.3	23.4	0.4	23.3	-0.4	23.5	0.9	23.5	0.0	23.5	0.0	23.7	0.9	23.8	0.4	23.8	0.0	23.9	0.4	24.0	0.4	24.1	0.4
1949	24.1	0.0	23.9	-0.8	23.9	0.0	23.9	0.0	23.7	-0.8	23.6	-0.4	23.4	-0.8	23.4	0.0	23.4	0.0	23.3	-0.4	23.4	0.4	23.2	-0.9
1950	23.4	0.9	23.3	-0.4	23.4	0.4	23.4	0.0	23.4	0.0	23.4	0.0	23.5	0.4	23.8	1.3	23.9	0.4	24.1	0.8	24.3	0.8	24.6	1.2
1951	25.0	1.6	25.5	2.0	25.7	0.8	25.7	0.0	25.7	0.0	25.7	0.0	25.8	0.4	25.8	0.0	25.9	0.4	25.9	0.0	26.2	1.2	26.3	0.4
1952	26.3	0.0	26.3	0.0	26.4	0.4	26.4	0.0	26.4	0.0	26.5	0.4	26.5	0.0	26.5	0.0	26.5	0.0	26.8	0.0	26.6	0.4	26.7	-0.4
1953	26.6	0.0	26.5	-0.4	26.6	0.4	26.7	0.4	26.6	-0.4	26.6	0.0	26.7	0.4	26.6	0.0	26.6	0.0	26.5	-0.4	26.5	0.0	10.2	-0.4
1954	27.0	1.1	26.9	-0.4	26.8	-0.4	26.7	-0.4	26.7	0.0	26.7	0.0	26.5	-0.7	26.6	-0.4	26.8	0.8	26.8	0.0	26.8	0.0	26.8	0.0
1955	26.6	0.0	26.5	-0.4	26.6	0.4	26.4	-0.8	26.6	0.8	26.6	0.0	26.7	0.4	26.6	-0.4	26.8	0.8	26.8	0.0	26.8	0.0	26.8	0.0
1956	26.8	0.0	26.7	-0.4	26.8	0.4	26.8	0.0	27.0	0.7	27.1	0.4	27.2	0.4	27.1	-0.4	27.2	0.4	27.3	0.4	27.5	0.7	27.6	0.4
1957	27.6	0.0	27.8	0.7	27.8	0.0	27.8	0.0	27.9	0.4	27.9	0.0	28.0	0.4	28.0	0.0	28.2	0.7	28.2	0.0	28.4	0.7	28.4	0.0
1958	28.6	0.7	28.6	0.0	28.8	0.7	29.0	0.7	28.9	-0.3	28.9	0.0	29.0	0.3	28.9	-0.3	29.1	0.7	29.1	0.0	29.2	0.3	29.2	0.0

[Continued]

Los Angeles, CA
Consumer Price Index - All Urban Consumers
Base 1982-1984 = 100
All Items
[Continued]

For 1914-1997. Columns headed % show percentile change in the index from the previous period for which an index is available.

Year	Jan Index	%	Feb Index	%	Mar Index	%	Apr Index	%	May Index	%	Jun Index	%	Jul Index	%	Aug Index	%	Sep Index	%	Oct Index	%	Nov Index	%	Dec Index	%
1959	29.2	0.0	29.2	0.0	29.2	0.0	29.2	0.0	29.3	0.3	29.3	0.0	29.4	0.3	29.4	0.0	29.5	0.3	29.7	0.7	29.7	0.0	29.8	0.3
1960	29.8	0.0	29.7	-0.3	29.9	0.7	30.0	0.3	30.0	0.0	29.9	-0.3	29.9	0.0	29.8	-0.3	30.0	0.7	30.1	0.3	30.1	0.0	30.3	0.7
1961	30.3	0.0	30.3	0.0	30.2	-0.3	30.3	0.3	30.3	0.0	30.3	0.0	30.3	0.0	30.3	0.0	30.3	0.0	30.4	0.3	30.5	0.3	30.5	0.0
1962	30.4	-0.3	30.4	0.0	30.5	0.3	30.6	0.3	30.8	0.7	30.8	0.0	30.7	-0.3	30.7	0.0	30.9	0.7	30.9	0.0	30.8	-0.3	30.9	0.3
1963	30.9	0.0	31.0	0.3	31.0	0.0	31.1	0.3	31.0	-0.3	30.9	-0.3	31.1	0.6	31.2	0.3	31.2	0.0	31.4	0.6	31.4	0.0	31.3	-0.3
1964	31.5	0.6	31.4	-0.3	31.6	0.6	31.6	0.0	31.6	0.0	31.6	0.0	31.6	0.0	31.7	0.3	31.6	-0.3	32.0	1.3	32.0	0.0	32.1	0.3
1965	32.1	0.0	32.2	0.3	32.3	0.3	32.4	0.3	32.4	0.0	32.5	0.3	32.4	-0.3	32.1	-0.9	32.5	1.2	32.4	-0.3	32.5	0.3	32.6	0.3
1966	32.5	-0.3	32.6	0.3	32.7	0.3	32.9	0.6	32.9	0.0	33.0	0.3	33.1	0.3	33.0	-0.3	33.3	0.9	33.4	0.3	33.5	0.3	33.5	0.0
1967	33.3	-0.6	33.3	0.0	33.2	-0.3	33.5	0.9	33.6	0.3	33.7	0.3	33.8	0.3	34.1	0.9	34.3	0.6	34.2	-0.3	34.5	0.9	34.5	0.0
1968	34.7	0.6	34.7	0.0	34.9	0.6	34.9	0.0	34.8	-0.3	35.1	0.9	35.2	0.3	35.3	0.3	35.3	0.0	35.6	0.8	35.7	0.3	35.7	0.0
1969	35.9	0.6	36.0	0.3	36.5	1.4	36.5	0.0	36.5	0.0	36.8	0.8	37.0	0.5	37.1	0.3	37.3	0.5	37.4	0.3	37.4	0.0	37.7	0.8
1970	37.8	0.3	37.9	0.3	38.0	0.3	38.4	1.1	38.5	0.3	38.6	0.3	38.9	0.8	38.7	-0.5	39.2	1.3	39.3	0.3	39.3	0.0	39.5	0.5
1971	39.5	0.0	39.3	-0.5	39.6	0.8	39.5	-0.3	40.0	1.3	40.2	0.5	40.3	0.2	40.4	0.2	40.6	0.5	40.7	0.2	40.6	-0.2	40.6	0.0
1972	40.6	0.0	40.7	0.2	41.0	0.7	41.0	0.0	41.1	0.2	41.2	0.2	41.5	0.7	41.6	0.2	41.9	0.7	41.9	0.0	42.1	0.5	42.1	0.0
1973	42.2	0.2	42.5	0.7	42.8	0.7	43.0	0.5	43.1	0.2	43.5	0.9	43.7	0.5	44.3	1.4	44.4	0.2	44.8	0.9	45.2	0.9	45.4	0.4
1974	45.8	0.9	46.1	0.7	46.6	1.1	47.0	0.9	47.5	1.1	47.9	0.8	48.4	1.0	49.0	1.2	49.8	1.6	49.8	0.0	50.3	1.0	50.8	1.0
1975	51.0	0.4	51.5	1.0	52.2	1.4	52.7	1.0	53.1	0.8	53.0	-0.2	53.5	0.9	53.7	0.4	54.3	1.1	54.7	0.7	55.0	0.5	55.4	0.7
1976	55.7	0.5	55.4	-0.5	55.5	0.2	55.5	0.0	56.3	1.4	56.5	0.4	57.1	1.1	57.4	0.5	57.8	0.7	58.0	0.3	58.3	0.5	58.5	0.3
1977	59.2	1.2	59.7	0.8	59.8	0.2	60.2	0.7	60.4	0.3	60.8	0.7	61.1	0.5	61.1	0.0	61.5	0.7	61.5	0.0	61.9	0.7	62.4	0.8
1978	62.8	0.6	63.1	0.5	63.4	0.5	64.2	1.3	64.8	0.9	65.5	1.1	65.8	0.5	66.0	0.3	66.8	1.2	66.9	0.1	67.1	0.3	66.7	-0.6
1979	67.6	1.3	68.3	1.0	69.0	1.0	70.3	1.9	71.4	1.6	72.1	1.0	72.7	0.8	73.6	1.2	74.7	1.5	75.1	0.5	75.9	1.1	77.2	1.7
1980	78.7	1.9	80.4	2.2	81.7	1.6	82.8	1.3	84.3	1.8	84.7	0.5	84.2	-0.6	83.7	-0.6	84.5	1.0	85.5	1.2	86.5	1.2	87.6	1.3
1981	87.8	0.2	88.5	0.8	89.1	0.7	89.9	0.9	90.5	0.7	90.7	0.2	92.1	1.5	93.0	1.0	94.5	1.6	95.2	0.7	95.3	0.1	95.5	0.2
1982	96.7	1.3	96.6	-0.1	96.9	0.3	97.0	0.1	97.2	0.2	98.2	1.0	97.9	-0.3	97.9	0.0	97.5	-0.4	98.0	0.5	97.6	-0.4	96.6	-1.0
1983	96.7	0.1	97.1	0.4	97.2	0.1	98.0	0.8	98.8	0.8	99.4	0.6	99.7	0.3	99.9	0.2	100.3	0.4	100.5	0.2	100.4	-0.1	100.8	0.4
1984	101.2	0.4	101.6	0.4	101.8	0.2	102.5	0.7	103.4	0.9	103.4	0.0	103.5	0.1	104.5	1.0	105.0	0.5	105.5	0.5	105.5	0.0	105.3	-0.2
1985	105.9	0.6	106.3	0.4	106.5	0.2	106.9	0.4	108.0	1.0	108.1	0.1	108.8	0.6	109.6	0.7	109.6	0.0	110.4	0.7	110.0	-0.4	110.4	0.4
1986	110.6	0.2	110.5	-0.1	111.1	0.5	110.6	-0.5	111.5	0.8	112.1	0.5	112.0	-0.1	112.0	0.0	113.3	1.2	113.8	0.4	113.0	-0.7	112.7	-0.3
1987	113.4	0.6	114.7	1.1	115.5	0.7	116.0	0.4	116.8	0.7	116.5	-0.3	116.5	0.0	117.3	0.7	118.0	0.6	118.6	0.5	118.2	-0.3	118.5	0.3
1988	118.9	0.3	119.7	0.7	120.6	0.8	121.1	0.4	122.0	0.7	122.0	0.0	122.1	0.1	122.6	0.4	123.4	0.7	124.0	0.5	124.1	0.1	124.2	0.1
1989	124.6	0.3	125.5	0.7	126.2	0.6	127.2	0.8	128.3	0.9	128.7	0.3	129.0	0.2	128.9	-0.1	130.1	0.9	130.0	-0.1	130.0	0.0	130.6	0.5
1990	132.1	1.1	133.6	1.1	134.5	0.7	134.2	-0.2	134.6	0.3	135.0	0.3	135.6	0.4	136.3	0.5	137.7	1.0	138.7	0.7	138.9	0.1	139.2	0.2
1991	140.0	0.6	139.9	-0.1	139.7	-0.1	140.7	0.7	140.8	0.1	140.8	0.0	141.5	0.5	141.7	0.1	142.6	0.6	142.9	0.2	143.5	0.4	143.1	-0.3
1992	144.3	0.8	144.9	0.4	145.5	0.4	145.8	0.2	146.0	0.1	146.2	0.1	146.7	0.3	146.9	0.1	147.4	0.3	148.4	0.7	148.2	-0.1	148.2	0.0
1993	149.2	0.7	150.0	0.5	149.8	-0.1	149.9	0.1	150.1	0.1	149.7	-0.3	149.8	0.1	149.9	0.1	150.2	0.2	150.9	0.5	151.6	0.5	151.9	0.2
1994	152.2	0.2	152.2	0.0	152.5	0.2	152.0	-0.3	151.4	-0.4	151.3	-0.1	151.7	0.3	152.0	0.2	152.7	0.5	153.4	0.5	152.9	-0.3	153.4	0.3
1995	154.3	0.6	154.5	0.1	154.6	0.1	154.7	0.1	155.1	0.3	154.8	-0.2	154.5	-0.2	154.4	-0.1	154.6	0.1	155.2	0.4	154.4	-0.5	154.6	0.1
1996	155.7	0.7	156.2	0.3	157.3	0.7	157.7	0.3	157.5	-0.1	156.7	-0.5	157.6	0.6	157.3	-0.2	158.2	0.6	158.8	0.4	158.4	-0.3	158.3	-0.1
1997	159.1	0.5	159.2	0.1	159.8	0.4	159.9	0.1	159.5	-0.3	159.4	-0.1	159.5	0.1	159.7	0.1	160.5	0.5	161.1	0.4	160.7	-0.2	161.2	0.3

Source: U.S. Department of Labor, Bureau of Labor Statistics, Division of Consumer Prices and Price Indexes. - indicates no data collected for period.

Los Angeles, CA
Consumer Price Index - Urban Wage Earners
Base 1982-1984 = 100
All Items

For 1914-1997. Columns headed % show percentile change in the index from the previous period for which an index is available.

Year	Jan Index	%	Feb Index	%	Mar Index	%	Apr Index	%	May Index	%	Jun Index	%	Jul Index	%	Aug Index	%	Sep Index	%	Oct Index	%	Nov Index	%	Dec Index	%
1914	-	-	-	-	-	-	-	-	-	-	-	-	-	-	-	-	-	-	-	-	-	-	10.2	-
1915	-	-	-	-	-	-	-	-	-	-	-	-	-	-	-	-	-	-	-	-	-	-	10.0	-2.0
1916	-	-	-	-	-	-	-	-	-	-	-	-	-	-	-	-	-	-	-	-	-	-	11.0	10.0
1917	-	-	-	-	-	-	-	-	-	-	-	-	-	-	-	-	-	-	-	-	-	-	13.0	18.2
1918	-	-	-	-	-	-	-	-	-	-	-	-	-	-	-	-	-	-	-	-	-	-	15.8	21.5
1919	-	-	-	-	-	-	-	-	-	-	16.4	3.8	-	-	-	-	-	-	-	-	-	-	18.6	13.4
1920	-	-	-	-	-	-	-	-	-	-	20.4	9.7	-	-	-	-	-	-	-	-	-	-	19.9	-2.5
1921	-	-	-	-	-	-	-	-	18.5	-7.0	-	-	-	-	-	-	18.3	-1.1	-	-	-	-	18.4	0.5
1922	-	-	-	-	18.2	-1.1	-	-	-	-	18.1	-0.5	-	-	-	-	18.0	-0.6	-	-	-	-	18.1	0.6
1923	-	-	-	-	18.0	-0.6	-	-	-	-	18.3	1.7	-	-	-	-	18.5	1.1	-	-	-	-	18.6	0.5
1924	-	-	-	-	18.5	-0.5	-	-	-	-	18.3	-1.1	-	-	-	-	18.4	0.5	-	-	-	-	18.2	-1.1
1925	-	-	-	-	-	-	-	-	-	-	18.5	1.6	-	-	-	-	-	-	-	-	-	-	18.5	0.0
1926	-	-	-	-	-	-	-	-	-	-	17.8	-3.8	-	-	-	-	-	-	-	-	-	-	17.8	0.0
1927	-	-	-	-	-	-	-	-	-	-	17.8	0.0	-	-	-	-	-	-	-	-	-	-	17.5	-1.7
1928	-	-	-	-	-	-	-	-	-	-	17.2	-1.7	-	-	-	-	-	-	-	-	-	-	17.4	1.2
1929	-	-	-	-	-	-	-	-	-	-	17.2	-1.1	-	-	-	-	-	-	-	-	-	-	17.2	0.0
1930	-	-	-	-	-	-	-	-	-	-	16.7	-2.9	-	-	-	-	-	-	-	-	-	-	16.0	-4.2
1931	-	-	-	-	-	-	-	-	-	-	14.9	-6.9	-	-	-	-	-	-	-	-	-	-	14.6	-2.0
1932	-	-	-	-	-	-	-	-	-	-	13.6	-6.8	-	-	-	-	-	-	-	-	-	-	13.1	-3.7
1933	-	-	-	-	-	-	-	-	-	-	12.5	-4.6	-	-	-	-	-	-	-	-	-	-	13.0	4.0
1934	-	-	-	-	-	-	-	-	-	-	12.9	-0.8	-	-	-	-	-	-	-	-	13.3	3.1	-	-
1935	-	-	-	-	13.6	2.3	-	-	-	-	-	-	13.2	-2.9	-	-	-	-	13.1	-0.8	-	-	-	-
1936	13.4	2.3	-	-	-	-	13.2	-1.5	-	-	-	-	13.4	1.5	-	-	13.7	2.2	-	-	-	-	13.7	0.0
1937	-	-	-	-	14.3	4.4	-	-	-	-	14.2	-0.7	-	-	-	-	14.4	1.4	-	-	-	-	14.3	-0.7
1938	-	-	-	-	14.0	-2.1	-	-	-	-	14.0	0.0	-	-	-	-	14.0	0.0	-	-	-	-	14.1	0.7
1939	-	-	-	-	14.0	-0.7	-	-	-	-	13.8	-1.4	-	-	-	-	14.1	2.2	-	-	-	-	13.9	-1.4
1940	-	-	-	-	13.9	0.0	-	-	-	-	13.9	0.0	-	-	-	-	14.0	0.7	14.0	0.0	14.1	0.7	14.1	0.0
1941	14.2	0.7	14.0	-1.4	14.1	0.7	14.3	1.4	14.4	0.7	14.6	1.4	14.6	0.0	14.7	0.7	15.0	2.0	15.2	1.3	15.3	0.7	15.5	1.3
1942	15.7	1.3	15.8	0.6	16.1	1.9	16.2	0.6	16.3	0.6	16.4	0.6	16.6	1.2	16.7	0.6	16.8	0.6	17.0	1.2	17.1	0.6	17.1	0.0
1943	17.1	0.0	17.0	-0.6	17.2	1.2	17.4	1.2	17.4	0.0	17.4	0.0	17.3	-0.6	17.2	-0.6	17.3	0.6	17.4	0.6	17.5	0.6	17.5	0.0
1944	17.4	-0.6	17.4	0.0	17.4	0.0	17.4	0.0	17.6	1.1	17.5	-0.6	17.5	0.0	17.6	0.6	17.7	0.6	17.8	0.6	17.8	0.0	17.9	0.6
1945	17.9	0.0	17.8	-0.6	17.9	0.6	18.0	0.6	18.0	0.0	18.0	0.0	18.1	0.6	18.1	0.0	18.3	1.1	18.3	0.0	18.4	0.5	18.5	0.5
1946	18.4	-0.5	18.4	0.0	18.4	0.0	18.5	0.5	18.6	0.5	18.8	1.1	19.7	4.8	20.0	1.5	20.1	0.5	20.5	2.0	21.4	4.4	21.4	0.0
1947	21.5	0.5	21.6	0.5	21.7	0.5	21.8	0.5	21.8	0.0	21.7	-0.5	21.8	0.5	21.9	0.5	22.4	2.3	22.4	0.0	22.8	1.8	23.0	0.9
1948	23.2	0.9	23.3	0.4	23.2	-0.4	23.5	1.3	23.5	0.0	23.5	0.0	23.7	0.9	23.8	0.4	23.8	0.0	23.9	0.4	24.0	0.4	24.1	0.4
1949	24.1	0.0	23.9	-0.8	23.9	0.0	23.9	0.0	23.7	-0.8	23.6	-0.4	23.3	-1.3	23.3	0.0	23.3	0.0	23.3	0.0	23.3	0.0	23.2	-0.4
1950	23.4	0.9	23.3	-0.4	23.3	0.0	23.4	0.4	23.4	0.0	23.3	-0.4	23.5	0.9	23.8	1.3	23.9	0.4	24.1	0.8	24.3	0.8	24.6	1.2
1951	25.0	1.6	25.4	1.6	25.6	0.8	25.6	0.0	25.7	0.4	25.7	0.0	25.8	0.4	25.8	0.0	25.9	0.4	25.9	0.0	26.2	1.2	26.3	0.4
1952	26.3	0.0	26.3	0.0	26.4	0.4	26.4	0.0	26.4	0.0	26.5	0.4	26.5	0.0	26.5	0.0	26.5	0.0	26.5	0.0	26.6	0.4	26.6	0.0
1953	26.6	0.0	26.5	-0.4	26.6	0.4	26.7	0.4	26.6	-0.4	26.6	0.0	26.7	0.4	26.7	0.0	26.8	0.4	26.8	0.0	26.8	0.0	26.7	-0.4
1954	27.0	1.1	26.9	-0.4	26.8	-0.4	26.7	-0.4	26.7	0.0	26.7	0.0	26.5	-0.7	26.6	0.4	26.6	0.0	26.5	-0.4	26.5	0.0	26.6	0.4
1955	26.6	0.0	26.5	-0.4	26.6	0.4	26.4	-0.8	26.6	0.8	26.6	0.0	26.7	0.4	26.6	-0.4	26.8	0.8	26.8	0.0	26.8	0.0	26.8	0.0
1956	26.8	0.0	26.7	-0.4	26.8	0.4	26.8	0.0	27.0	0.7	27.1	0.4	27.2	0.4	27.1	-0.4	27.2	0.4	27.3	0.4	27.5	0.7	27.5	0.0
1957	27.6	0.4	27.8	0.7	27.8	0.0	27.8	0.0	27.9	0.4	27.9	0.0	27.9	0.0	28.0	0.4	28.2	0.7	28.2	0.0	28.4	0.7	28.4	0.0
1958	28.6	0.7	28.6	0.0	28.8	0.7	29.0	0.7	28.9	-0.3	28.9	0.0	29.0	0.3	28.9	-0.3	29.1	0.7	29.1	0.0	29.2	0.3	29.2	0.0

[Continued]

Los Angeles, CA
Consumer Price Index - Urban Wage Earners
Base 1982-1984 = 100
All Items
[Continued]

For 1914-1997. Columns headed % show percentile change in the index from the previous period for which an index is available.

Year	Jan Index	%	Feb Index	%	Mar Index	%	Apr Index	%	May Index	%	Jun Index	%	Jul Index	%	Aug Index	%	Sep Index	%	Oct Index	%	Nov Index	%	Dec Index	%
1959	29.2	0.0	29.2	0.0	29.2	0.0	29.2	0.0	29.3	0.3	29.3	0.0	29.4	0.3	29.4	0.0	29.5	0.3	29.6	0.3	29.7	0.3	29.7	0.0
1960	29.8	0.3	29.7	-0.3	29.8	0.3	30.0	0.7	29.9	-0.3	29.9	0.0	29.9	0.0	29.8	-0.3	29.9	0.3	30.1	0.7	30.1	0.0	30.3	0.7
1961	30.3	0.0	30.3	0.0	30.2	-0.3	30.3	0.3	30.3	0.0	30.3	0.0	30.3	0.0	30.3	0.0	30.3	0.0	30.4	0.3	30.5	0.3	30.5	0.0
1962	30.4	-0.3	30.4	0.0	30.5	0.3	30.6	0.3	30.8	0.7	30.8	0.0	30.7	-0.3	30.7	0.0	30.9	0.7	30.9	0.0	30.8	-0.3	30.9	0.3
1963	30.9	0.0	31.0	0.3	31.0	0.0	31.1	0.3	31.0	-0.3	30.9	-0.3	31.1	0.6	31.2	0.3	31.2	0.0	31.4	0.6	31.4	0.0	31.3	-0.3
1964	31.5	0.6	31.4	-0.3	31.6	0.6	31.6	0.0	31.6	0.0	31.6	0.0	31.6	0.0	31.7	0.3	31.6	-0.3	31.9	0.9	32.0	0.3	32.0	0.0
1965	32.1	0.3	32.2	0.3	32.3	0.3	32.4	0.3	32.4	0.0	32.5	0.3	32.4	-0.3	32.1	-0.9	32.5	1.2	32.4	-0.3	32.5	0.3	32.6	0.3
1966	32.5	-0.3	32.6	0.3	32.7	0.3	32.9	0.6	32.9	0.0	33.0	0.3	33.1	0.3	33.0	-0.3	33.3	0.9	33.4	0.3	33.5	0.3	33.5	0.0
1967	33.3	-0.6	33.3	0.0	33.2	-0.3	33.5	0.9	33.6	0.3	33.7	0.3	33.8	0.3	34.0	0.6	34.3	0.9	34.2	-0.3	34.5	0.9	34.5	0.0
1968	34.7	0.6	34.7	0.0	34.9	0.6	34.9	0.0	34.8	-0.3	35.1	0.9	35.2	0.3	35.3	0.3	35.3	0.0	35.6	0.8	35.7	0.3	35.7	0.0
1969	35.9	0.6	36.0	0.3	36.4	1.1	36.5	0.3	36.5	0.0	36.8	0.8	37.0	0.5	37.1	0.3	37.3	0.5	37.4	0.3	37.4	0.0	37.7	0.8
1970	37.8	0.3	37.9	0.3	38.0	0.3	38.4	1.1	38.5	0.3	38.5	0.0	38.9	1.0	38.6	-0.8	39.2	1.6	39.3	0.3	39.3	0.0	39.5	0.5
1971	39.5	0.0	39.3	-0.5	39.6	0.8	39.5	-0.3	40.0	1.3	40.2	0.5	40.3	0.2	40.4	0.2	40.6	0.5	40.7	0.2	40.6	-0.2	40.6	0.0
1972	40.6	0.0	40.7	0.2	41.0	0.7	41.0	0.0	41.0	0.0	41.1	0.2	41.5	1.0	41.6	0.2	41.9	0.7	41.9	0.0	42.1	0.5	42.1	0.0
1973	42.2	0.2	42.5	0.7	42.8	0.7	42.9	0.2	43.1	0.5	43.5	0.9	43.7	0.5	44.3	1.4	44.4	0.2	44.8	0.9	45.2	0.9	45.4	0.4
1974	45.7	0.7	46.1	0.9	46.6	1.1	47.0	0.9	47.5	1.1	47.8	0.6	48.4	1.3	49.0	1.2	49.7	1.4	49.8	0.2	50.3	1.0	50.8	1.0
1975	51.0	0.4	51.5	1.0	52.2	1.4	52.7	1.0	53.1	0.8	53.0	-0.2	53.5	0.9	53.7	0.4	54.3	1.1	54.6	0.6	55.0	0.7	55.4	0.7
1976	55.7	0.5	55.4	-0.5	55.5	0.2	55.5	0.0	56.3	1.4	56.5	0.4	57.1	1.1	57.4	0.5	57.8	0.7	58.0	0.3	58.2	0.3	58.5	0.5
1977	59.1	1.0	59.7	1.0	59.8	0.2	60.2	0.7	60.4	0.3	60.7	0.5	61.0	0.5	61.1	0.2	61.4	0.5	61.4	0.0	61.9	0.8	62.4	0.8
1978	62.8	0.6	63.2	0.6	63.3	0.2	63.9	0.9	64.7	1.3	65.3	0.9	65.7	0.6	65.9	0.3	66.6	1.1	66.7	0.2	66.8	0.1	66.7	-0.1
1979	67.6	1.3	68.5	1.3	69.2	1.0	70.7	2.2	71.9	1.7	72.6	1.0	73.4	1.1	74.3	1.2	75.5	1.6	75.8	0.4	76.4	0.8	77.8	1.8
1980	79.5	2.2	81.2	2.1	82.5	1.6	83.8	1.6	85.5	2.0	85.7	0.2	85.1	-0.7	84.6	-0.6	85.3	0.8	86.3	1.2	87.4	1.3	88.7	1.5
1981	88.9	0.2	89.7	0.9	90.2	0.6	91.1	1.0	91.6	0.5	91.9	0.3	93.5	1.7	94.3	0.9	95.7	1.5	96.4	0.7	96.5	0.1	96.7	0.2
1982	98.0	1.3	97.9	-0.1	98.2	0.3	98.2	0.0	98.3	0.1	99.4	1.1	99.1	-0.3	99.1	0.0	98.7	-0.4	99.1	0.4	98.7	-0.4	97.5	-1.2
1983	97.5	0.0	98.2	0.7	98.0	-0.2	98.2	0.2	98.8	0.6	98.8	0.0	99.2	0.4	99.4	0.2	100.4	1.0	101.2	0.8	100.8	-0.4	101.5	0.7
1984	100.8	-0.7	101.2	0.4	100.8	-0.4	101.1	0.3	102.6	1.5	102.7	0.1	101.6	-1.1	103.2	1.6	102.9	-0.3	102.4	-0.5	102.9	0.5	103.7	0.8
1985	104.3	0.6	104.6	0.3	104.8	0.2	105.3	0.5	106.3	0.9	106.3	0.0	106.9	0.6	107.6	0.7	107.5	-0.1	108.3	0.7	108.0	-0.3	108.3	0.3
1986	108.6	0.3	108.4	-0.2	108.8	0.4	108.3	-0.5	109.2	0.8	109.8	0.5	109.6	-0.2	109.5	-0.1	110.6	1.0	111.1	0.5	110.4	-0.6	110.1	-0.3
1987	110.8	0.6	112.1	1.2	112.8	0.6	113.3	0.4	114.1	0.7	113.8	-0.3	113.8	0.0	114.6	0.7	115.2	0.5	115.8	0.5	115.4	-0.3	115.7	0.3
1988	115.9	0.2	116.6	0.6	117.5	0.8	118.0	0.4	118.9	0.8	118.9	0.0	119.0	0.1	119.5	0.4	120.3	0.7	121.0	0.6	120.9	-0.1	121.1	0.2
1989	121.4	0.2	122.3	0.7	122.9	0.5	124.0	0.9	125.0	0.8	125.3	0.2	125.7	0.3	125.5	-0.2	126.5	0.8	126.5	0.0	126.4	-0.1	127.0	0.5
1990	128.5	1.2	129.8	1.0	130.5	0.5	130.2	-0.2	130.7	0.4	131.1	0.3	131.6	0.4	132.3	0.5	133.5	0.9	134.5	0.7	134.8	0.2	135.2	0.3
1991	135.8	0.4	135.5	-0.2	135.3	-0.1	136.3	0.7	136.5	0.1	136.4	-0.1	137.3	0.7	137.4	0.1	138.2	0.6	138.5	0.2	139.0	0.4	138.6	-0.3
1992	139.6	0.7	140.3	0.5	141.0	0.5	141.3	0.2	141.4	0.1	141.8	0.3	142.2	0.3	142.4	0.1	142.8	0.3	143.6	0.6	143.5	-0.1	143.5	0.0
1993	144.4	0.6	145.0	0.4	144.8	-0.1	144.9	0.1	145.1	0.1	144.8	-0.2	144.8	0.0	144.9	0.1	145.0	0.1	145.7	0.5	146.4	0.5	146.7	0.2
1994	146.8	0.1	146.9	0.1	147.0	0.1	146.6	-0.3	146.2	-0.3	146.1	-0.1	146.5	0.3	146.8	0.2	147.3	0.3	148.0	0.5	147.7	-0.2	148.1	0.3
1995	149.0	0.6	149.2	0.1	149.3	0.1	149.5	0.1	149.8	0.2	149.7	-0.1	149.3	-0.3	149.2	-0.1	149.3	0.1	149.9	0.4	149.2	-0.5	149.4	0.1
1996	150.4	0.7	150.9	0.3	151.9	0.7	152.4	0.3	152.3	-0.1	151.5	-0.5	152.3	0.5	151.9	-0.3	152.7	0.5	153.2	0.3	152.9	-0.2	152.7	-0.1
1997	153.6	0.6	153.6	0.0	154.2	0.4	154.3	0.1	154.0	-0.2	153.8	-0.1	153.8	0.0	154.0	0.1	154.7	0.5	155.4	0.5	154.9	-0.3	155.3	0.3

Source: U.S. Department of Labor, Bureau of Labor Statistics, Division of Consumer Prices and Price Indexes. - indicates no data collected for period.

Los Angeles, CA
Consumer Price Index - All Urban Consumers
Base 1982-1984 = 100
Food and Beverages

For 1976-1997. Columns headed % show percentile change in the index from the previous period for which an index is available.

Year	Jan Index	%	Feb Index	%	Mar Index	%	Apr Index	%	May Index	%	Jun Index	%	Jul Index	%	Aug Index	%	Sep Index	%	Oct Index	%	Nov Index	%	Dec Index	%
1976	60.6	-	59.8	-1.3	59.5	-0.5	59.5	0.0	60.2	1.2	60.4	0.3	61.0	1.0	61.0	0.0	60.6	-0.7	60.7	0.2	61.0	0.5	61.5	0.8
1977	62.3	1.3	62.9	1.0	63.3	0.6	63.9	0.9	64.3	0.6	64.9	0.9	65.2	0.5	65.4	0.3	65.5	0.2	65.7	0.3	66.1	0.6	66.6	0.8
1978	67.6	1.5	68.4	1.2	69.2	1.2	70.7	2.2	71.1	0.6	72.2	1.5	72.3	0.1	72.6	0.4	73.1	0.7	73.7	0.8	73.8	0.1	74.6	1.1
1979	75.9	1.7	77.2	1.7	77.9	0.9	79.0	1.4	79.9	1.1	79.6	-0.4	79.2	-0.5	79.1	-0.1	79.7	0.8	80.3	0.8	80.9	0.7	82.0	1.4
1980	82.5	0.6	82.4	-0.1	83.4	1.2	84.1	0.8	84.5	0.5	84.9	0.5	85.6	0.8	86.9	1.5	88.3	1.6	88.3	0.0	88.7	0.5	89.2	0.6
1981	89.7	0.6	91.3	1.8	91.9	0.7	92.2	0.3	92.3	0.1	92.4	0.1	92.7	0.3	93.4	0.8	93.4	0.0	93.5	0.1	93.1	-0.4	93.9	0.9
1982	95.0	1.2	95.4	0.4	95.7	0.3	95.8	0.1	96.5	0.7	96.7	0.2	97.6	0.9	97.5	-0.1	97.5	0.0	98.2	0.7	98.4	0.2	97.8	-0.6
1983	98.9	1.1	99.2	0.3	100.1	0.9	100.5	0.4	101.1	0.6	100.2	-0.9	100.0	-0.2	99.9	-0.1	99.9	0.0	100.4	0.5	100.1	-0.3	100.8	0.7
1984	102.3	1.5	102.6	0.3	102.9	0.3	102.6	-0.3	102.3	-0.3	102.0	-0.3	102.9	0.9	103.6	0.7	103.6	0.0	103.7	0.1	104.1	0.4	104.2	0.1
1985	105.0	0.8	105.2	0.2	104.8	-0.4	104.9	0.1	105.4	0.5	105.4	0.0	104.8	-0.6	105.2	0.4	105.5	0.3	105.9	0.4	106.8	0.8	107.9	1.0
1986	108.3	0.4	107.8	-0.5	107.8	0.0	107.7	-0.1	108.1	0.4	108.4	0.3	108.4	0.0	108.9	0.5	108.8	-0.1	109.3	0.5	110.3	0.9	110.5	0.2
1987	112.3	1.6	113.7	1.2	112.8	-0.8	112.9	0.1	113.6	0.6	113.0	-0.5	112.8	-0.2	113.2	0.4	113.4	0.2	113.6	0.2	113.3	-0.3	114.0	0.6
1988	114.6	0.5	114.8	0.2	115.4	0.5	116.0	0.5	116.2	0.2	116.2	0.0	117.8	1.4	118.8	0.8	118.8	0.0	119.1	0.3	119.1	0.0	120.0	0.8
1989	121.5	1.3	122.2	0.6	122.8	0.5	123.6	0.7	124.1	0.4	123.5	-0.5	123.6	0.1	124.1	0.4	124.6	0.4	125.2	0.5	126.1	0.7	126.8	0.6
1990	129.6	2.2	130.9	1.0	130.6	-0.2	130.1	-0.4	130.4	0.2	130.5	0.1	130.6	0.1	130.7	0.1	131.0	0.2	131.5	0.4	132.5	0.8	132.7	0.2
1991	135.9	2.4	135.6	-0.2	135.7	0.1	137.4	1.3	137.0	-0.3	137.3	0.2	136.9	-0.3	135.8	-0.8	135.6	-0.1	136.3	0.5	137.3	0.7	138.0	0.5
1992	139.4	1.0	139.5	0.1	141.1	1.1	140.9	-0.1	139.6	-0.9	140.3	0.5	140.1	-0.1	141.0	0.6	142.2	0.9	142.7	0.4	142.3	-0.3	142.2	-0.1
1993	144.2	1.4	143.4	-0.6	143.9	0.3	144.6	0.5	145.4	0.6	144.9	-0.3	144.3	-0.4	144.3	0.0	145.1	0.6	146.2	0.8	146.4	0.1	148.6	1.5
1994	149.0	0.3	147.7	-0.9	147.8	0.1	147.1	-0.5	146.7	-0.3	147.0	0.2	147.6	0.4	147.7	0.1	148.7	0.7	149.9	0.8	150.1	0.1	153.1	2.0
1995	153.4	0.2	152.7	-0.5	152.7	0.0	153.8	0.7	152.8	-0.7	152.8	0.0	152.2	-0.4	152.7	0.3	153.2	0.3	154.7	1.0	154.5	-0.1	154.8	0.2
1996	154.8	0.0	155.4	0.4	157.0	1.0	156.9	-0.1	156.3	-0.4	156.4	0.1	157.2	0.5	157.6	0.3	158.7	0.7	160.0	0.8	161.0	0.6	162.0	0.6
1997	163.8	1.1	162.4	-0.9	163.3	0.6	163.0	-0.2	161.6	-0.9	162.6	0.6	161.9	-0.4	163.3	0.9	163.4	0.1	164.2	0.5	164.4	0.1	164.8	0.2

Source: U.S. Department of Labor, Bureau of Labor Statistics, Division of Consumer Prices and Price Indexes. - indicates no data collected for period.

Los Angeles, CA
Consumer Price Index - Urban Wage Earners
Base 1982-1984 = 100
Food and Beverages

For 1976-1997. Columns headed % show percentile change in the index from the previous period for which an index is available.

Year	Jan Index	%	Feb Index	%	Mar Index	%	Apr Index	%	May Index	%	Jun Index	%	Jul Index	%	Aug Index	%	Sep Index	%	Oct Index	%	Nov Index	%	Dec Index	%
1976	59.5	-	58.7	-1.3	58.4	-0.5	58.5	0.2	59.1	1.0	59.3	0.3	59.9	1.0	59.9	0.0	59.5	-0.7	59.7	0.3	59.9	0.3	60.4	0.8
1977	61.2	1.3	61.8	1.0	62.1	0.5	62.8	1.1	63.1	0.5	63.8	1.1	64.1	0.5	64.3	0.3	64.3	0.0	64.5	0.3	64.9	0.6	65.4	0.8
1978	66.5	1.7	67.4	1.4	67.7	0.4	68.9	1.8	69.6	1.0	70.4	1.1	70.7	0.4	70.9	0.3	71.4	0.7	71.8	0.6	71.7	-0.1	72.6	1.3
1979	73.9	1.8	75.3	1.9	76.6	1.7	77.5	1.2	78.1	0.8	78.4	0.4	78.3	-0.1	78.3	0.0	79.0	0.9	79.5	0.6	79.7	0.3	80.9	1.5
1980	81.3	0.5	81.4	0.1	82.3	1.1	83.5	1.5	83.9	0.5	84.3	0.5	85.1	0.9	86.4	1.5	88.0	1.9	87.9	-0.1	88.7	0.9	89.1	0.5
1981	89.6	0.6	90.8	1.3	91.5	0.8	91.8	0.3	91.5	-0.3	92.2	0.8	92.5	0.3	93.3	0.9	93.1	-0.2	92.9	-0.2	92.8	-0.1	93.7	1.0
1982	94.9	1.3	95.4	0.5	95.7	0.3	95.9	0.2	96.4	0.5	96.6	0.2	97.4	0.8	97.4	0.0	97.3	-0.1	98.1	0.8	98.3	0.2	97.8	-0.5
1983	98.9	1.1	99.3	0.4	100.2	0.9	100.6	0.4	101.2	0.6	100.3	-0.9	100.0	-0.3	100.0	0.0	99.9	-0.1	100.5	0.6	100.2	-0.3	100.9	0.7
1984	102.4	1.5	102.8	0.4	103.1	0.3	102.7	-0.4	102.3	-0.4	102.0	-0.3	102.9	0.9	103.5	0.6	103.5	0.0	103.6	0.1	103.9	0.3	104.1	0.2
1985	104.8	0.7	105.0	0.2	104.7	-0.3	104.8	0.1	105.2	0.4	105.2	0.0	104.6	-0.6	105.0	0.4	105.3	0.3	105.7	0.4	106.6	0.9	107.6	0.9
1986	108.1	0.5	107.6	-0.5	107.6	0.0	107.6	0.0	107.8	0.2	108.1	0.3	108.1	0.0	108.5	0.4	108.5	0.0	109.1	0.6	110.1	0.9	110.3	0.2
1987	112.0	1.5	113.4	1.3	112.5	-0.8	112.7	0.2	113.4	0.6	112.7	-0.6	112.6	-0.1	113.1	0.4	113.2	0.1	113.5	0.3	113.2	-0.3	113.9	0.6
1988	114.3	0.4	114.6	0.3	115.2	0.5	115.9	0.6	116.1	0.2	116.1	0.0	117.7	1.4	118.7	0.8	118.6	-0.1	119.0	0.3	119.0	0.0	119.9	0.8
1989	121.3	1.2	122.0	0.6	122.6	0.5	123.4	0.7	123.9	0.4	123.3	-0.5	123.5	0.2	124.1	0.5	124.6	0.4	125.1	0.4	126.1	0.8	126.9	0.6
1990	129.6	2.1	130.9	1.0	130.7	-0.2	130.2	-0.4	130.4	0.2	130.6	0.2	130.8	0.2	130.9	0.1	131.1	0.2	131.6	0.4	132.6	0.8	132.8	0.2
1991	136.0	2.4	135.7	-0.2	136.0	0.2	137.6	1.2	137.2	-0.3	137.5	0.2	137.2	-0.2	136.2	-0.7	135.9	-0.2	136.7	0.6	137.5	0.6	138.2	0.5
1992	139.6	1.0	139.8	0.1	141.6	1.3	141.4	-0.1	140.0	-1.0	140.7	0.5	140.6	-0.1	141.4	0.6	142.5	0.8	143.1	0.4	142.8	-0.2	142.7	-0.1
1993	144.6	1.3	143.8	-0.6	144.3	0.3	145.0	0.5	145.9	0.6	145.5	-0.3	144.8	-0.5	144.9	0.1	145.7	0.6	146.8	0.8	146.9	0.1	149.0	1.4
1994	149.4	0.3	148.2	-0.8	148.1	-0.1	147.4	-0.5	147.0	-0.3	147.4	0.3	147.9	0.3	148.0	0.1	148.9	0.6	149.9	0.7	150.0	0.1	153.1	2.1
1995	153.4	0.2	152.8	-0.4	152.9	0.1	153.8	0.6	152.9	-0.6	153.0	0.1	152.3	-0.5	152.9	0.4	153.3	0.3	154.8	1.0	154.7	-0.1	155.0	0.2
1996	155.0	0.0	155.7	0.5	157.3	1.0	157.1	-0.1	156.6	-0.3	156.7	0.1	157.4	0.4	158.0	0.4	159.0	0.6	160.2	0.8	161.1	0.6	162.1	0.6
1997	163.8	1.0	162.5	-0.8	163.3	0.5	163.0	-0.2	161.7	-0.8	162.6	0.6	162.0	-0.4	163.3	0.8	163.3	0.0	164.2	0.6	164.4	0.1	164.9	0.3

Source: U.S. Department of Labor, Bureau of Labor Statistics, Division of Consumer Prices and Price Indexes. - indicates no data collected for period.

Los Angeles, CA
Consumer Price Index - All Urban Consumers
Base 1982-1984 = 100
Housing

For 1976-1997. Columns headed % show percentile change in the index from the previous period for which an index is available.

Year	Jan Index	%	Feb Index	%	Mar Index	%	Apr Index	%	May Index	%	Jun Index	%	Jul Index	%	Aug Index	%	Sep Index	%	Oct Index	%	Nov Index	%	Dec Index	%
1976	53.9	-	53.2	-1.3	53.1	-0.2	52.9	-0.4	53.9	1.9	53.8	-0.2	54.4	1.1	54.7	0.6	55.4	1.3	55.7	0.5	55.7	0.0	56.0	0.5
1977	57.1	2.0	57.5	0.7	57.5	0.0	57.8	0.5	58.0	0.3	58.1	0.2	58.6	0.9	58.5	-0.2	59.1	1.0	58.8	-0.5	59.6	1.4	60.5	1.5
1978	60.9	0.7	61.2	0.5	61.4	0.3	62.2	1.3	62.9	1.1	63.5	1.0	63.8	0.5	64.0	0.3	65.1	1.7	65.0	-0.2	64.9	-0.2	63.7	-1.8
1979	64.7	1.6	65.6	1.4	66.1	0.8	67.4	2.0	68.6	1.8	69.4	1.2	70.1	1.0	71.3	1.7	72.6	1.8	73.0	0.6	74.1	1.5	75.9	2.4
1980	77.7	2.4	79.6	2.4	81.2	2.0	82.7	1.8	85.6	3.5	86.2	0.7	84.7	-1.7	83.0	-2.0	83.4	0.5	85.2	2.2	86.6	1.6	88.4	2.1
1981	88.4	0.0	88.6	0.2	88.8	0.2	89.6	0.9	90.4	0.9	90.3	-0.1	92.3	2.2	93.4	1.2	96.2	3.0	97.0	0.8	96.7	-0.3	96.7	0.0
1982	97.9	1.2	97.5	-0.4	98.3	0.8	98.4	0.1	98.3	-0.1	99.4	1.1	98.1	-1.3	98.0	-0.1	97.5	-0.5	97.8	0.3	97.0	-0.8	95.3	-1.8
1983	95.4	0.1	96.6	1.3	96.5	-0.1	97.0	0.5	97.8	0.8	98.4	0.6	98.7	0.3	99.1	0.4	100.2	1.1	100.4	0.2	100.0	-0.4	99.9	-0.1
1984	99.9	0.0	101.2	1.3	101.5	0.3	102.2	0.7	103.7	1.5	104.3	0.6	104.7	0.4	105.8	1.1	106.3	0.5	106.1	-0.2	105.6	-0.5	105.3	-0.3
1985	106.6	1.2	107.0	0.4	106.4	-0.6	106.6	0.2	109.1	2.3	108.4	-0.6	110.6	2.0	112.7	1.9	112.3	-0.4	113.5	1.1	111.7	-1.6	111.6	-0.1
1986	111.6	0.0	112.6	0.9	114.9	2.0	114.0	-0.8	115.4	1.2	115.9	0.4	116.9	0.9	117.2	0.3	120.0	2.4	120.4	0.3	117.5	-2.4	116.8	-0.6
1987	116.7	-0.1	118.3	1.4	119.5	1.0	120.4	0.8	121.6	1.0	120.7	-0.7	121.1	0.3	122.2	0.9	122.8	0.5	123.6	0.7	122.7	-0.7	122.9	0.2
1988	123.0	0.1	124.5	1.2	125.2	0.6	125.4	0.2	126.8	1.1	126.6	-0.2	126.4	-0.2	127.1	0.6	128.2	0.9	128.7	0.4	128.9	0.2	128.9	0.0
1989	128.7	-0.2	129.2	0.4	128.8	-0.3	128.6	-0.2	130.4	1.4	131.7	1.0	133.0	1.0	133.0	0.0	134.6	1.2	134.5	-0.1	134.0	-0.4	134.3	0.2
1990	135.8	1.1	136.7	0.7	138.1	1.0	137.1	-0.7	137.8	0.5	138.5	0.5	139.9	1.0	140.8	0.6	141.5	0.5	142.0	0.4	141.3	-0.5	141.5	0.1
1991	142.8	0.9	143.4	0.4	143.9	0.3	144.7	0.6	144.5	-0.1	144.4	-0.1	145.4	0.7	145.6	0.1	146.0	0.3	145.9	-0.1	146.3	0.3	146.1	-0.1
1992	147.0	0.6	147.7	0.5	147.9	0.1	147.9	0.0	148.1	0.1	148.8	0.5	149.0	0.1	149.3	0.2	149.2	-0.1	149.5	0.2	149.4	-0.1	148.9	-0.3
1993	149.9	0.7	150.8	0.6	150.0	-0.5	150.4	0.3	150.6	0.1	150.6	0.0	150.7	0.1	150.7	0.0	149.8	-0.6	150.2	0.3	150.4	0.1	151.0	0.4
1994	151.5	0.3	151.9	0.3	151.6	-0.2	150.8	-0.5	150.7	-0.1	150.6	-0.1	151.2	0.4	151.4	0.1	151.2	-0.1	151.2	0.0	150.9	-0.9	150.4	0.3
1995	151.3	0.6	152.0	0.5	152.0	0.0	151.6	-0.3	152.5	0.6	153.0	0.3	152.4	-0.4	152.5	0.1	152.7	0.1	152.7	0.0	150.9	-1.2	152.4	1.0
1996	153.1	0.5	153.4	0.2	153.4	0.0	153.6	0.1	153.4	-0.1	152.2	-0.8	154.4	1.4	154.6	0.1	155.4	0.5	155.6	0.1	155.1	-0.3	154.9	-0.1
1997	155.4	0.3	155.6	0.1	155.5	-0.1	155.2	-0.2	156.1	0.6	156.4	0.2	156.9	0.3	156.7	-0.1	157.1	0.3	157.9	0.5	157.7	-0.1	158.8	0.7

Source: U.S. Department of Labor, Bureau of Labor Statistics, Division of Consumer Prices and Price Indexes. - indicates no data collected for period.

Los Angeles, CA
Consumer Price Index - Urban Wage Earners
Base 1982-1984 = 100
Housing

For 1976-1997. Columns headed % show percentile change in the index from the previous period for which an index is available.

Year	Jan Index	%	Feb Index	%	Mar Index	%	Apr Index	%	May Index	%	Jun Index	%	Jul Index	%	Aug Index	%	Sep Index	%	Oct Index	%	Nov Index	%	Dec Index	%
1976	54.0	-	53.3	-1.3	53.1	-0.4	53.0	-0.2	54.0	1.9	53.9	-0.2	54.5	1.1	54.8	0.6	55.4	1.1	55.8	0.7	55.8	0.0	56.0	0.4
1977	57.2	2.1	57.6	0.7	57.5	-0.2	57.9	0.7	58.0	0.2	58.2	0.3	58.6	0.7	58.6	0.0	59.1	0.9	58.9	-0.3	59.7	1.4	60.6	1.5
1978	61.0	0.7	61.3	0.5	61.6	0.5	62.3	1.1	62.9	1.0	63.5	1.0	63.9	0.6	64.1	0.3	65.1	1.6	64.9	-0.3	64.8	-0.2	63.8	-1.5
1979	64.9	1.7	65.9	1.5	66.5	0.9	68.0	2.3	69.4	2.1	70.1	1.0	70.8	1.0	72.3	2.1	73.7	1.9	74.0	0.4	75.1	1.5	76.9	2.4
1980	79.2	3.0	81.2	2.5	82.9	2.1	84.4	1.8	87.6	3.8	88.1	0.6	86.4	-1.9	84.6	-2.1	84.7	0.1	86.6	2.2	88.2	1.8	90.3	2.4
1981	90.3	0.0	90.4	0.1	90.7	0.3	91.7	1.1	92.5	0.9	92.4	-0.1	95.1	2.9	96.2	1.2	99.1	3.0	99.9	0.8	99.5	-0.4	99.6	0.1
1982	100.9	1.3	100.3	-0.6	101.1	0.8	101.2	0.1	101.0	-0.2	102.2	1.2	100.7	-1.5	100.6	-0.1	100.0	-0.6	100.3	0.3	99.3	-1.0	97.4	-1.9
1983	97.3	-0.1	98.9	1.6	98.4	-0.5	97.6	-0.8	97.9	0.3	97.3	-0.6	97.7	0.4	98.0	0.3	100.3	2.3	101.7	1.4	100.9	-0.8	101.4	0.5
1984	99.1	-2.3	100.2	1.1	99.2	-1.0	99.1	-0.1	101.6	2.5	102.3	0.7	100.2	-2.1	102.8	2.6	101.6	-1.2	99.2	-2.4	100.2	1.0	102.0	1.8
1985	103.2	1.2	103.6	0.4	103.0	-0.6	103.2	0.2	105.8	2.5	104.9	-0.9	107.0	2.0	109.1	2.0	108.7	-0.4	109.8	1.0	108.1	-1.5	107.9	-0.2
1986	107.9	0.0	108.9	0.9	111.2	2.1	110.3	-0.8	111.7	1.3	112.2	0.4	113.1	0.8	113.4	0.3	116.1	2.4	116.5	0.3	113.6	-2.5	113.0	-0.5
1987	112.9	-0.1	114.4	1.3	115.4	0.9	116.3	0.8	117.6	1.1	116.7	-0.8	117.1	0.3	118.2	0.9	118.7	0.4	119.4	0.6	118.6	-0.7	118.9	0.3
1988	118.9	0.0	120.1	1.0	121.0	0.7	121.1	0.1	122.5	1.2	122.3	-0.2	122.1	-0.2	122.6	0.4	123.9	1.1	124.5	0.5	124.5	0.0	124.5	0.0
1989	124.2	-0.2	124.7	0.4	124.2	-0.4	124.1	-0.1	125.8	1.4	127.0	1.0	128.4	1.1	128.3	-0.1	129.7	1.1	129.7	0.0	129.1	-0.5	129.4	0.2
1990	130.9	1.2	131.7	0.6	133.0	1.0	132.0	-0.8	132.8	0.6	133.4	0.5	134.8	1.0	135.5	0.5	136.2	0.5	136.8	0.4	136.1	-0.5	136.3	0.1
1991	137.5	0.9	138.1	0.4	138.5	0.3	139.4	0.6	139.2	-0.1	139.1	-0.1	140.1	0.7	140.2	0.1	140.7	0.4	140.7	0.0	141.0	0.2	140.7	-0.2
1992	141.4	0.5	142.2	0.6	142.4	0.1	142.4	0.0	142.5	0.1	143.2	0.5	143.3	0.1	143.6	0.2	143.5	-0.1	143.9	0.3	143.8	-0.1	143.4	-0.3
1993	144.4	0.7	145.1	0.5	144.3	-0.6	144.7	0.3	144.9	0.1	144.9	0.0	144.9	0.0	145.0	0.1	144.1	-0.6	144.5	0.3	144.9	0.3	145.4	0.3
1994	145.8	0.3	146.3	0.3	145.9	-0.3	145.1	-0.5	145.1	0.0	144.9	-0.1	145.6	0.5	145.8	0.1	145.5	-0.2	145.4	-0.1	144.3	-0.8	144.7	0.3
1995	145.5	0.6	146.2	0.5	146.1	-0.1	145.9	-0.1	146.7	0.5	147.3	0.4	146.6	-0.5	146.7	0.1	147.0	0.2	146.9	-0.1	145.1	-1.2	146.8	1.2
1996	147.4	0.4	147.5	0.1	147.6	0.1	147.8	0.1	147.6	-0.1	146.5	-0.7	148.5	1.4	148.7	0.1	149.4	0.5	149.5	0.1	149.2	-0.2	149.0	-0.1
1997	149.3	0.2	149.5	0.1	149.5	0.0	149.2	-0.2	150.2	0.7	150.6	0.3	151.0	0.3	150.6	-0.3	151.1	0.3	151.8	0.5	151.7	-0.1	152.8	0.7

Source: U.S. Department of Labor, Bureau of Labor Statistics, Division of Consumer Prices and Price Indexes. - indicates no data collected for period.

Los Angeles, CA
Consumer Price Index - All Urban Consumers
Base 1982-1984 = 100
Apparel and Upkeep

For 1952-1997. Columns headed % show percentile change in the index from the previous period for which an index is available.

Year	Jan Index	%	Feb Index	%	Mar Index	%	Apr Index	%	May Index	%	Jun Index	%	Jul Index	%	Aug Index	%	Sep Index	%	Oct Index	%	Nov Index	%	Dec Index	%
1952	-	-	-	-	-	-	-	-	-	-	-	-	-	-	-	-	-	-	-	-	-	-	49.2	-
1953	48.9	-0.6	48.9	0.0	48.7	-0.4	48.6	-0.2	48.6	0.0	48.5	-0.2	48.7	0.4	48.4	-0.6	48.9	1.0	48.8	-0.2	48.8	0.0	48.9	0.2
1954	48.7	-0.4	48.9	0.4	49.0	0.2	48.7	-0.6	48.5	-0.4	48.9	0.8	48.8	-0.2	48.7	-0.2	49.3	1.2	49.3	0.0	49.2	-0.2	49.2	0.0
1955	48.8	-0.8	48.9	0.2	48.7	-0.4	48.7	0.0	48.8	0.2	48.7	-0.2	48.8	0.2	48.8	0.0	49.2	0.8	49.2	0.0	49.0	-0.4	49.2	0.4
1956	49.1	-0.2	49.3	0.4	49.4	0.2	49.3	-0.2	49.8	1.0	49.8	0.0	49.9	0.2	49.8	-0.2	50.5	1.4	50.5	0.0	50.5	0.0	50.6	0.2
1957	50.4	-0.4	50.5	0.2	50.7	0.4	50.7	0.0	50.8	0.2	50.8	0.0	50.8	0.0	50.6	-0.4	51.3	1.4	51.2	-0.2	51.3	0.2	51.3	0.0
1958	51.0	-0.6	51.4	0.8	51.1	-0.6	50.9	-0.4	50.9	0.0	50.6	-0.6	50.8	0.4	50.6	-0.4	51.0	0.8	51.0	0.0	51.1	0.2	51.0	-0.2
1959	51.0	0.0	51.0	0.0	51.0	0.0	51.0	0.0	51.3	0.6	51.0	-0.6	51.6	1.2	51.4	-0.4	52.2	1.6	52.4	0.4	52.6	0.4	52.6	0.0
1960	52.5	-0.2	52.7	0.4	52.7	0.0	52.9	0.4	52.9	0.0	52.6	-0.6	52.7	0.2	52.6	-0.2	52.9	0.6	53.0	0.2	53.0	0.0	53.0	0.0
1961	52.7	-0.6	53.1	0.8	53.1	0.0	52.7	-0.8	53.0	0.6	52.7	-0.6	53.1	0.8	52.8	-0.6	53.0	0.4	52.9	-0.2	52.9	0.0	53.0	0.2
1962	52.7	-0.6	52.7	0.0	52.8	0.2	52.6	-0.4	52.7	0.2	52.7	0.0	52.8	0.2	52.5	-0.6	53.7	2.3	53.6	-0.2	53.6	0.0	53.7	0.2
1963	53.5	-0.4	53.5	0.0	53.6	0.2	53.4	-0.4	53.6	0.4	53.4	-0.4	53.5	0.2	53.6	0.2	54.1	0.9	54.1	0.0	54.1	0.0	54.5	0.7
1964	53.8	-1.3	54.3	0.9	54.4	0.2	54.5	0.2	54.5	0.0	54.6	0.2	54.6	0.0	54.4	-0.4	54.6	0.4	54.6	0.0	54.6	0.0	54.8	0.4
1965	54.6	-0.4	55.0	0.7	55.1	0.2	55.1	0.0	55.3	0.4	55.4	0.2	54.7	-1.3	54.5	-0.4	54.9	0.7	55.0	0.2	55.2	0.4	55.0	-0.4
1966	55.1	0.2	55.4	0.5	55.3	-0.2	55.5	0.4	55.9	0.7	55.9	0.0	55.7	-0.4	55.5	-0.4	56.6	2.0	56.4	-0.4	56.7	0.5	57.0	0.5
1967	56.4	-1.1	57.0	1.1	57.0	0.0	57.1	0.2	57.4	0.5	57.6	0.3	57.7	0.2	58.7	1.7	59.5	1.4	59.4	-0.2	59.6	0.3	59.6	0.0
1968	59.2	-0.7	59.8	1.0	60.4	1.0	60.4	0.0	60.6	0.3	60.8	0.3	61.2	0.7	61.2	0.0	62.2	1.6	62.5	0.5	62.5	0.0	63.0	0.8
1969	62.5	-0.8	62.9	0.6	63.1	0.3	62.7	-0.6	63.2	0.8	63.4	0.3	63.5	0.2	63.1	-0.6	64.6	2.4	64.6	0.0	64.9	0.5	65.1	0.3
1970	64.9	-0.3	65.4	0.8	65.7	0.5	66.0	0.5	66.7	1.1	66.8	0.1	66.3	-0.7	66.1	-0.3	67.2	1.7	67.2	0.0	67.7	0.7	67.9	0.3
1971	67.1	-1.2	67.5	0.6	67.7	0.3	67.7	0.0	68.8	1.6	68.9	0.1	68.9	0.0	68.5	-0.6	69.6	1.6	69.3	-0.4	69.3	0.0	69.1	-0.3
1972	68.6	-0.7	68.9	0.4	69.7	1.2	69.8	0.1	69.8	0.0	69.7	-0.1	69.2	-0.7	69.0	-0.3	70.3	1.9	70.3	0.0	70.3	0.0	70.6	0.4
1973	69.3	-1.8	69.7	0.6	71.2	2.2	71.0	-0.3	71.3	0.4	71.4	0.1	71.0	-0.6	71.6	0.8	73.0	2.0	72.6	-0.5	72.7	0.1	72.8	0.1
1974	71.8	-1.4	73.0	1.7	75.0	2.7	75.8	1.1	76.9	1.5	77.1	0.3	76.9	-0.3	78.3	1.8	79.0	0.9	78.6	-0.5	79.2	0.8	78.6	-0.8
1975	77.6	-1.3	78.0	0.5	78.0	0.0	78.5	0.6	79.1	0.8	79.4	0.4	78.6	-1.0	79.7	1.4	80.6	1.1	80.7	0.1	80.2	-0.6	80.1	-0.1
1976	79.0	-1.4	79.1	0.1	80.5	1.8	79.9	-0.7	80.7	1.0	80.5	-0.2	79.8	-0.9	81.4	2.0	82.3	1.1	82.2	-0.1	82.3	0.1	82.8	0.6
1977	82.8	0.0	83.7	1.1	84.0	0.4	83.7	-0.4	83.9	0.2	83.6	-0.4	82.7	-1.1	83.4	0.8	84.3	1.1	85.3	1.2	85.7	0.5	86.1	0.5
1978	86.2	0.1	85.0	-1.4	85.1	0.1	84.7	-0.5	85.5	0.9	85.5	0.0	85.4	-0.1	85.8	0.5	86.2	0.5	86.2	0.0	87.2	1.2	87.3	0.1
1979	85.9	-1.6	86.4	0.6	87.3	1.0	88.6	1.5	88.8	0.2	89.5	0.8	87.6	-2.1	88.0	0.5	90.7	3.1	90.5	-0.2	92.5	2.2	91.9	-0.6
1980	94.6	2.9	97.2	2.7	98.5	1.3	98.3	-0.2	97.8	-0.5	98.3	0.5	98.0	-0.3	98.4	0.4	99.0	0.6	99.7	0.7	100.1	0.4	99.7	-0.4
1981	97.7	-2.0	98.4	0.7	101.0	2.6	102.1	1.1	103.0	0.9	102.7	-0.3	101.6	-1.1	101.9	0.3	102.8	0.9	102.6	-0.2	102.8	0.2	101.5	-1.3
1982	99.9	-1.6	101.7	1.8	100.6	-1.1	99.5	-1.1	99.0	-0.5	98.6	-0.4	97.9	-0.7	97.7	-0.2	97.3	-0.4	97.9	0.6	98.8	0.9	98.1	-0.7
1983	95.3	-2.9	98.0	2.8	98.1	0.1	98.6	0.5	98.4	-0.2	99.9	1.5	99.9	0.0	101.7	1.8	102.0	0.3	101.8	-0.2	101.7	-0.1	101.2	-0.5
1984	101.3	0.1	101.2	-0.1	100.1	-1.1	100.5	0.4	100.3	-0.2	98.0	-2.3	97.7	-0.3	103.0	5.4	104.0	1.0	104.4	0.4	103.5	-0.9	102.3	-1.2
1985	99.8	-2.4	103.7	3.9	104.4	0.7	103.3	-1.1	103.5	0.2	104.3	0.8	103.0	-1.2	105.8	2.7	108.7	2.7	108.0	-0.6	108.0	0.0	108.4	0.4
1986	107.3	-1.0	106.4	-0.8	106.8	0.4	106.6	-0.2	105.9	-0.7	106.4	0.5	106.3	-0.1	105.9	-0.4	108.0	2.0	107.7	-0.3	108.4	0.6	107.3	-1.0
1987	109.6	2.1	108.8	-0.7	114.3	5.1	111.6	-2.4	112.2	0.5	113.5	1.2	110.1	-3.0	113.5	3.1	115.1	1.4	113.9	-1.0	113.1	-0.7	113.8	0.6
1988	113.2	-0.5	114.1	0.8	118.5	3.9	116.7	-1.5	117.6	0.8	115.9	-1.4	113.8	-1.8	109.7	-3.6	110.5	0.7	113.3	2.5	114.1	0.7	113.9	-0.2
1989	111.7	-1.9	114.1	2.1	122.0	6.9	122.1	0.1	122.7	0.5	120.3	-2.0	117.1	-2.7	116.8	-0.3	120.3	3.0	119.4	-0.7	119.3	-0.1	119.4	0.1
1990	119.3	-0.1	128.3	7.5	129.6	1.0	130.4	0.6	129.2	-0.9	126.3	-2.2	123.1	-2.5	122.3	-0.6	125.7	2.8	127.4	1.4	127.7	0.2	127.3	-0.3
1991	127.5	0.2	129.1	1.3	129.2	0.1	132.8	2.8	130.2	-2.0	125.2	-3.8	128.2	2.4	130.2	1.6	136.3	4.7	136.2	-0.1	136.1	-0.1	130.3	-4.3
1992	132.7	1.8	135.2	1.9	136.9	1.3	136.3	-0.4	136.0	-0.2	130.4	-4.1	130.8	0.3	132.0	0.9	131.8	-0.2	134.6	2.1	131.6	-2.2	129.5	-1.6
1993	128.9	-0.5	134.7	4.5	135.7	0.7	133.7	-1.5	129.8	-2.9	127.8	-1.5	127.4	-0.3	130.7	2.6	134.9	3.2	131.9	-2.2	133.9	1.5	130.2	-2.8
1994	129.1	-0.8	131.0	1.5	133.2	1.7	133.8	0.5	131.3	-1.9	125.0	-4.8	122.4	-2.1	123.7	1.1	132.2	6.9	133.3	0.8	132.3	-0.8	128.0	-3.3

[Continued]

Los Angeles, CA
Consumer Price Index - All Urban Consumers
Base 1982-1984 = 100
Apparel and Upkeep

[Continued]

For 1952-1997. Columns headed % show percentile change in the index from the previous period for which an index is available.

Year	Jan Index	%	Feb Index	%	Mar Index	%	Apr Index	%	May Index	%	Jun Index	%	Jul Index	%	Aug Index	%	Sep Index	%	Oct Index	%	Nov Index	%	Dec Index	%
1995	129.7	1.3	130.5	0.6	131.0	0.4	129.1	-1.5	128.8	-0.2	123.7	-4.0	128.0	3.5	123.8	-3.3	124.7	0.7	125.9	1.0	125.2	-0.6	120.1	-4.1
1996	126.8	5.6	127.4	0.5	134.0	5.2	130.0	-3.0	125.8	-3.2	124.4	-1.1	122.6	-1.4	122.0	-0.5	125.0	2.5	129.9	3.9	125.2	-3.6	118.6	-5.3
1997	122.3	3.1	122.2	-0.1	124.5	1.9	125.1	0.5	123.6	-1.2	121.4	-1.8	119.2	-1.8	117.0	-1.8	119.4	2.1	120.7	1.1	118.8	-1.6	117.4	-1.2

Source: U.S. Department of Labor, Bureau of Labor Statistics, Division of Consumer Prices and Price Indexes. - indicates no data collected for period.

Los Angeles, CA
Consumer Price Index - Urban Wage Earners
Base 1982-1984 = 100
Apparel and Upkeep

For 1952-1997. Columns headed % show percentile change in the index from the previous period for which an index is available.

Year	Jan Index	%	Feb Index	%	Mar Index	%	Apr Index	%	May Index	%	Jun Index	%	Jul Index	%	Aug Index	%	Sep Index	%	Oct Index	%	Nov Index	%	Dec Index	%
1952	-	-	-	-	-	-	-	-	-	-	-	-	-	-	-	-	-	-	-	-	-	-	49.4	-
1953	49.1	-0.6	49.1	0.0	48.9	-0.4	48.8	-0.2	48.8	0.0	48.7	-0.2	48.8	0.2	48.6	-0.4	49.1	1.0	49.0	-0.2	49.0	0.0	49.1	0.2
1954	48.9	-0.4	49.1	0.4	49.1	0.0	48.9	-0.4	48.7	-0.4	49.1	0.8	49.0	-0.2	48.8	-0.4	49.5	1.4	49.5	0.0	49.4	-0.2	49.4	0.0
1955	49.0	-0.8	49.1	0.2	48.9	-0.4	48.8	-0.2	49.0	0.4	48.8	-0.4	49.0	0.4	49.0	0.0	49.4	0.8	49.4	0.0	49.2	-0.4	49.4	0.4
1956	49.3	-0.2	49.5	0.4	49.5	0.0	49.5	0.0	50.0	1.0	50.0	0.0	50.1	0.2	50.0	-0.2	50.7	1.4	50.7	0.0	50.7	0.0	50.8	0.2
1957	50.6	-0.4	50.7	0.2	50.9	0.4	50.9	0.0	51.0	0.2	50.9	-0.2	51.0	0.2	50.8	-0.4	51.5	1.4	51.4	-0.2	51.5	0.2	51.5	0.0
1958	51.2	-0.6	51.6	0.8	51.3	-0.6	51.1	-0.4	51.1	0.0	50.8	-0.6	50.9	0.2	50.8	-0.2	51.2	0.8	51.2	0.0	51.3	0.2	51.2	-0.2
1959	51.2	0.0	51.2	0.0	51.2	0.0	51.2	0.0	51.5	0.6	51.2	-0.6	51.8	1.2	51.6	-0.4	52.4	1.6	52.6	0.4	52.8	0.4	52.8	0.0
1960	52.7	-0.2	52.9	0.4	52.9	0.0	53.1	0.4	53.1	0.0	52.8	-0.6	52.9	0.2	52.8	-0.2	53.1	0.6	53.2	0.2	53.2	0.0	53.2	0.0
1961	52.9	-0.6	53.3	0.8	53.3	0.0	52.9	-0.8	53.2	0.6	52.9	-0.6	53.3	0.8	53.0	-0.6	53.2	0.4	53.1	-0.2	53.1	0.0	53.2	0.2
1962	52.9	-0.6	52.9	0.0	53.0	0.2	52.8	-0.4	52.9	0.2	52.9	0.0	53.0	0.2	52.7	-0.6	53.9	2.3	53.8	-0.2	53.8	0.0	53.9	0.2
1963	53.7	-0.4	53.7	0.0	53.8	0.2	53.6	-0.4	53.8	0.4	53.6	-0.4	53.7	0.2	53.8	0.2	54.3	0.9	54.3	0.0	54.3	0.0	54.7	0.7
1964	54.0	-1.3	54.5	0.9	54.6	0.2	54.7	0.2	54.7	0.0	54.8	0.2	54.8	0.0	54.6	-0.4	54.8	0.4	54.8	0.0	54.8	0.0	55.0	0.4
1965	54.8	-0.4	55.2	0.7	55.3	0.2	55.3	0.0	55.5	0.4	55.6	0.2	54.9	-1.3	54.7	-0.4	55.1	0.7	55.2	0.2	55.4	0.4	55.2	-0.4
1966	55.3	0.2	55.6	0.5	55.5	-0.2	55.7	0.4	56.1	0.7	56.1	0.0	55.9	-0.4	55.7	-0.4	56.8	2.0	56.7	-0.2	56.9	0.4	57.2	0.5
1967	56.6	-1.0	57.2	1.1	57.2	0.0	57.4	0.3	57.6	0.3	57.8	0.3	57.9	0.2	58.9	1.7	59.7	1.4	59.6	-0.2	59.8	0.3	59.8	0.0
1968	59.4	-0.7	60.0	1.0	60.6	1.0	60.6	0.0	60.9	0.5	61.0	0.2	61.4	0.7	61.4	0.0	62.4	1.6	62.8	0.6	62.7	-0.2	63.2	0.8
1969	62.8	-0.6	63.1	0.5	63.3	0.3	63.0	-0.5	63.5	0.8	63.7	0.3	63.7	0.0	63.3	-0.6	64.9	2.5	64.9	0.0	65.2	0.5	65.3	0.2
1970	65.2	-0.2	65.6	0.6	65.9	0.5	66.2	0.5	67.0	1.2	67.1	0.1	66.6	-0.7	66.4	-0.3	67.5	1.7	67.5	0.0	67.9	0.6	68.1	0.3
1971	67.4	-1.0	67.8	0.6	68.0	0.3	68.0	0.0	69.0	1.5	69.2	0.3	69.1	-0.1	68.7	-0.6	69.8	1.6	69.6	-0.3	69.5	-0.1	69.4	-0.1
1972	68.9	-0.7	69.2	0.4	69.9	1.0	70.1	0.3	70.1	0.0	69.9	-0.3	69.4	-0.7	69.2	-0.3	70.6	2.0	70.6	0.0	70.6	0.0	70.8	0.3
1973	69.6	-1.7	69.9	0.4	71.5	2.3	71.2	-0.4	71.5	0.4	71.7	0.3	71.3	-0.6	71.9	0.8	73.3	1.9	72.9	-0.5	73.0	0.1	73.0	0.0
1974	72.0	-1.4	73.3	1.8	75.3	2.7	76.1	1.1	77.2	1.4	77.3	0.1	77.2	-0.1	78.6	1.8	79.3	0.9	78.9	-0.5	79.4	0.6	78.9	-0.6
1975	77.9	-1.3	78.3	0.5	78.3	0.0	78.7	0.5	79.4	0.9	79.7	0.4	78.9	-1.0	80.0	1.4	80.9	1.1	81.0	0.1	80.5	-0.6	80.4	-0.1
1976	79.3	-1.4	79.4	0.1	80.8	1.8	80.2	-0.7	81.0	1.0	80.8	-0.2	80.1	-0.9	81.7	2.0	82.6	1.1	82.5	-0.1	82.6	0.1	83.1	0.6
1977	83.1	0.0	84.1	1.2	84.3	0.2	84.1	-0.2	84.2	0.1	83.9	-0.4	83.0	-1.1	83.7	0.8	84.6	1.1	85.6	1.2	86.0	0.5	86.4	-0.5
1978	85.5	-1.0	85.2	-0.4	85.6	0.5	85.7	0.1	86.6	1.1	87.7	1.3	86.1	-1.8	87.0	1.0	88.2	1.4	88.1	-0.1	89.7	1.8	89.5	-0.2
1979	89.1	-0.4	90.1	1.1	90.1	0.0	90.8	0.8	90.8	0.0	91.5	0.8	90.2	-1.4	91.2	1.1	93.2	2.2	93.8	0.6	93.8	0.0	93.7	-0.1
1980	95.5	1.9	96.8	1.4	98.2	1.4	97.8	-0.4	96.8	-1.0	96.9	0.1	96.7	-0.2	97.0	0.3	97.3	0.3	97.2	-0.1	98.7	1.5	99.3	0.6
1981	96.9	-2.4	98.7	1.9	99.3	0.6	100.6	1.3	101.1	0.5	100.7	-0.4	100.6	-0.1	101.8	1.2	102.4	0.6	101.9	-0.5	102.7	0.8	101.8	-0.9
1982	99.9	-1.9	101.8	1.9	100.7	-1.1	99.6	-1.1	99.1	-0.5	98.7	-0.4	98.2	-0.5	97.8	-0.4	97.6	-0.2	97.9	0.3	98.9	1.0	98.2	-0.7
1983	95.2	-3.1	97.9	2.8	97.9	0.0	98.5	0.6	98.2	-0.3	99.8	1.6	100.1	0.3	101.7	1.6	101.9	0.2	101.6	-0.3	101.5	-0.1	101.2	-0.3
1984	101.1	-0.1	101.0	-0.1	100.2	-0.8	100.8	0.6	100.3	-0.5	97.9	-2.4	97.7	-0.2	102.8	5.2	103.8	1.0	104.6	0.8	103.6	-1.0	102.2	-1.4
1985	100.0	-2.2	103.5	3.5	104.3	0.8	103.0	-1.2	103.3	0.3	104.0	0.7	102.8	-1.2	105.9	3.0	108.4	2.4	107.9	-0.5	108.0	0.1	108.6	0.6
1986	107.7	-0.8	106.8	-0.8	106.9	0.1	106.9	0.0	106.3	-0.6	106.9	0.6	106.5	-0.4	105.9	-0.6	108.2	2.2	108.1	-0.1	108.6	0.5	107.5	-1.0
1987	109.0	1.4	108.5	-0.5	113.7	4.8	111.0	-2.4	111.3	0.3	113.1	1.6	109.9	-2.8	113.1	2.9	114.4	1.1	113.3	-1.0	112.6	-0.6	113.4	0.7
1988	112.5	-0.8	113.8	1.2	116.6	2.5	115.5	-0.9	116.3	0.7	114.7	-1.4	113.1	-1.4	109.9	-2.8	111.1	1.1	114.2	2.8	115.2	0.9	115.1	-0.1
1989	112.1	-2.6	114.3	2.0	120.7	5.6	121.2	0.4	121.9	0.6	119.8	-1.7	117.2	-2.2	117.2	0.0	120.6	2.9	120.1	-0.4	120.0	-0.1	119.9	-0.1
1990	120.1	0.2	127.4	6.1	128.8	1.1	129.7	0.7	128.6	-0.8	125.7	-2.3	122.7	-2.4	122.2	-0.4	125.2	2.5	127.2	1.6	127.7	0.4	127.5	-0.2
1991	127.3	-0.2	128.6	1.0	128.8	0.2	132.8	3.1	129.9	-2.2	125.1	-3.7	128.5	2.7	130.4	1.5	135.8	4.1	135.9	0.1	136.2	0.2	130.4	-4.3
1992	132.4	1.5	135.7	2.5	137.3	1.2	136.2	-0.8	135.9	-0.2	131.2	-3.5	131.8	0.5	132.4	0.5	132.1	-0.2	135.2	2.3	132.4	-2.1	130.4	-1.5
1993	129.5	-0.7	134.9	4.2	136.2	1.0	134.1	-1.5	130.3	-2.8	128.6	-1.3	128.1	-0.4	131.7	2.8	136.0	3.3	132.8	-2.4	135.0	1.7	131.2	-2.8
1994	130.2	-0.8	132.1	1.5	133.6	1.1	134.1	0.4	131.3	-2.1	125.4	-4.5	123.2	-1.8	124.9	1.4	132.2	5.8	133.2	0.8	132.2	-0.8	127.7	-3.4

[Continued]

Los Angeles, CA
Consumer Price Index - Urban Wage Earners
Base 1982-1984 = 100
Apparel and Upkeep
[Continued]

For 1952-1997. Columns headed % show percentile change in the index from the previous period for which an index is available.

Year	Jan Index	%	Feb Index	%	Mar Index	%	Apr Index	%	May Index	%	Jun Index	%	Jul Index	%	Aug Index	%	Sep Index	%	Oct Index	%	Nov Index	%	Dec Index	%
1995	129.7	1.6	130.3	0.5	131.3	0.8	129.6	-1.3	129.0	-0.5	124.0	-3.9	127.8	3.1	124.0	-3.0	124.5	0.4	126.3	1.4	125.1	-1.0	120.4	-3.8
1996	126.7	5.2	127.8	0.9	133.5	4.5	129.8	-2.8	125.7	-3.2	124.4	-1.0	123.3	-0.9	122.2	-0.9	125.1	2.4	129.9	3.8	125.3	-3.5	118.2	-5.7
1997	122.0	3.2	122.3	0.2	124.4	1.7	125.0	0.5	123.9	-0.9	121.3	-2.1	119.4	-1.6	117.1	-1.9	118.9	1.5	120.6	1.4	119.0	-1.3	117.0	-1.7

Source: U.S. Department of Labor, Bureau of Labor Statistics, Division of Consumer Prices and Price Indexes. - indicates no data collected for period.

Los Angeles, CA
Consumer Price Index - All Urban Consumers
Base 1982-1984 = 100
Transportation

For 1947-1997. Columns headed % show percentile change in the index from the previous period for which an index is available.

Year	Jan Index	%	Feb Index	%	Mar Index	%	Apr Index	%	May Index	%	Jun Index	%	Jul Index	%	Aug Index	%	Sep Index	%	Oct Index	%	Nov Index	%	Dec Index	%
1947	17.3	-	17.5	1.2	17.5	0.0	17.7	1.1	17.6	-0.6	17.6	0.0	18.0	2.3	18.1	0.6	18.3	1.1	18.4	0.5	18.4	0.0	18.4	0.0
1948	19.2	4.3	19.2	0.0	19.2	0.0	19.3	0.5	19.2	-0.5	19.2	0.0	20.1	4.7	20.4	1.5	20.5	0.5	20.5	0.0	20.5	0.0	20.6	0.5
1949	20.6	0.0	21.0	1.9	20.9	-0.5	21.0	0.5	21.0	0.0	21.0	0.0	21.0	0.0	21.0	0.0	21.0	0.0	21.0	0.0	21.0	0.0	21.0	0.0
1950	21.0	0.0	20.9	-0.5	20.7	-1.0	20.5	-1.0	20.5	0.0	20.5	0.0	20.6	0.5	20.7	0.5	20.7	0.0	20.8	0.5	20.9	0.5	21.0	0.5
1951	21.0	0.0	21.3	1.4	21.5	0.9	21.5	0.0	21.5	0.0	21.5	0.0	21.6	0.5	21.6	0.0	21.8	0.9	22.0	0.9	22.3	1.4	22.3	0.0
1952	22.2	-0.4	23.5	5.9	23.5	0.0	23.5	0.0	23.7	0.9	23.7	0.0	24.2	2.1	24.2	0.0	24.2	0.0	24.2	0.0	24.4	0.8	24.4	0.0
1953	24.6	0.8	24.6	0.0	24.9	1.2	24.9	0.0	24.8	-0.4	24.8	0.0	25.0	0.8	25.1	0.4	24.9	-0.8	25.0	0.4	24.9	-0.4	24.1	-3.2
1954	25.2	4.6	25.1	-0.4	25.0	-0.4	24.9	-0.4	24.9	0.0	24.6	-1.2	23.7	-3.7	23.9	0.8	24.1	0.8	23.6	-2.1	24.7	4.7	24.7	0.0
1955	24.7	0.0	24.7	0.0	24.9	0.8	23.9	-4.0	24.2	1.3	24.0	-0.8	24.0	0.0	24.0	0.0	24.1	0.4	24.3	0.8	24.9	2.5	24.7	-0.8
1956	24.5	-0.8	24.4	-0.4	24.5	0.4	24.2	-1.2	24.6	1.7	24.6	0.0	25.0	1.6	24.7	-1.2	24.7	0.0	25.3	2.4	25.5	0.8	25.6	0.4
1957	25.5	-0.4	25.9	1.6	25.9	0.0	25.9	0.0	26.1	0.8	25.9	-0.8	25.9	0.0	25.4	-1.9	25.7	1.2	25.7	0.0	26.0	1.2	25.7	-1.2
1958	25.6	-0.4	26.0	1.6	26.0	0.0	26.2	0.8	26.3	0.4	26.2	-0.4	26.7	1.9	26.8	0.4	26.9	0.4	26.8	-0.4	27.1	1.1	27.1	0.0
1959	27.2	0.4	27.5	1.1	27.5	0.0	27.7	0.7	27.8	0.4	27.7	-0.4	27.6	-0.4	27.9	1.1	27.7	-0.7	28.3	2.2	28.5	0.7	28.5	0.0
1960	28.1	-1.4	27.9	-0.7	28.3	1.4	28.2	-0.4	28.0	-0.7	28.0	0.0	27.9	-0.4	27.8	-0.4	27.6	-0.7	27.9	1.1	27.9	0.0	28.2	1.1
1961	28.6	1.4	28.6	0.0	27.9	-2.4	27.9	0.0	28.1	0.7	29.3	4.3	29.3	0.0	29.5	0.7	29.2	-1.0	29.2	0.0	29.6	1.4	29.6	0.0
1962	29.3	-1.0	29.2	-0.3	29.3	0.3	29.6	1.0	30.0	1.4	30.2	0.7	30.1	-0.3	30.2	0.3	30.1	-0.3	30.3	0.7	30.2	-0.3	30.2	0.0
1963	29.8	-1.3	29.9	0.3	29.7	-0.7	30.0	1.0	29.8	-0.7	29.1	-2.3	29.1	0.0	30.2	3.8	30.1	-0.3	30.7	2.0	30.8	0.3	29.6	-3.9
1964	31.3	5.7	29.8	-4.8	31.0	4.0	31.1	0.3	31.0	-0.3	31.3	1.0	30.5	-2.6	31.1	2.0	30.5	-1.9	31.3	-1.6	32.0	2.2	32.0	0.0
1965	31.6	-0.6	31.6	0.0	31.6	0.0	31.9	0.9	31.9	0.0	31.8	-0.3	32.0	0.6	31.1	-2.8	31.8	2.3	32.5	0.6	32.7	0.6	32.2	-1.5
1966	31.0	-3.1	31.3	1.0	31.5	0.6	31.9	1.3	31.6	-0.9	31.8	0.6	32.4	1.9	31.3	-3.4	32.3	3.2	32.5	0.6	33.5	3.4	32.3	-3.6
1967	31.6	-1.9	31.5	-0.3	31.2	-1.0	32.3	3.5	32.4	0.3	32.4	0.0	32.4	0.0	32.5	0.3	33.2	2.2	32.4	-2.4	34.0	1.2	32.8	-3.5
1968	33.3	3.1	33.3	0.0	33.6	0.9	32.9	-2.1	32.8	-0.3	33.7	2.7	33.3	-1.2	33.6	0.9	32.9	-2.1	33.6	2.1	33.8	-3.4	34.9	3.3
1969	33.6	2.4	33.6	0.0	34.6	3.0	34.3	-0.9	33.6	-2.0	34.5	2.7	34.5	0.0	34.3	-0.6	34.2	-0.3	35.0	2.3	35.0	-0.8	37.1	1.6
1970	34.4	-1.4	33.9	-1.5	33.9	0.0	35.5	4.7	35.0	-1.4	34.7	-0.9	36.0	3.7	34.7	-3.6	36.4	4.9	36.8	1.1	36.5	-0.8	37.1	1.6
1971	36.8	-0.8	36.2	-1.6	37.5	3.6	36.5	-2.7	36.8	0.8	37.1	0.8	37.1	0.0	37.5	1.1	37.5	0.0	37.9	1.1	37.3	-1.6	37.1	-0.5
1972	37.0	-0.3	36.3	-1.9	37.5	3.3	37.4	-0.3	37.8	1.1	37.3	-1.3	38.1	2.1	38.2	0.3	38.9	1.8	39.1	0.5	39.2	0.3	39.2	0.0
1973	38.8	-1.0	38.9	0.3	39.0	0.3	39.4	1.0	39.7	0.8	40.0	0.8	40.4	1.0	40.2	-0.5	39.9	-0.7	40.1	0.5	40.5	1.0	40.5	0.0
1974	41.3	2.0	41.8	1.2	42.7	2.2	43.3	1.4	44.0	1.6	44.9	2.0	45.4	1.1	45.6	0.4	45.8	0.4	45.9	0.2	46.3	0.9	46.5	0.4
1975	46.6	0.2	46.8	0.4	47.1	0.6	47.9	1.7	48.5	1.3	49.4	1.9	50.4	2.0	50.8	0.8	50.8	0.0	51.4	1.2	51.4	0.0	51.2	-0.4
1976	51.3	0.2	51.4	0.2	51.7	0.6	52.3	1.2	53.0	1.3	53.8	1.5	55.3	2.8	55.7	0.7	56.2	0.9	56.6	0.7	56.7	0.2	56.6	-0.2
1977	56.7	0.2	57.0	0.5	57.3	0.5	57.9	1.0	58.3	0.7	58.8	0.9	59.2	0.7	58.9	-0.5	58.7	-0.3	58.5	-0.3	58.2	-0.5	58.1	-0.2
1978	58.2	0.2	58.6	0.7	58.7	0.2	58.9	0.3	59.8	1.5	60.5	1.2	61.1	1.0	61.3	0.3	61.7	0.7	62.1	0.6	62.8	1.1	63.0	0.3
1979	63.4	0.6	63.9	0.8	65.0	1.7	67.4	3.7	69.1	2.5	70.3	1.7	71.8	2.1	73.4	2.2	74.3	1.2	74.4	0.1	74.7	0.4	75.8	1.5
1980	77.8	2.6	80.3	3.2	81.3	1.2	82.2	1.1	82.3	0.1	82.0	-0.4	82.3	0.4	82.8	0.6	83.9	1.3	84.2	0.4	85.0	1.0	85.4	0.5
1981	86.1	0.8	87.9	2.1	88.6	0.8	89.7	1.2	90.5	0.9	91.3	0.9	92.3	1.1	92.3	0.0	92.8	0.5	94.2	1.5	94.8	0.6	94.9	0.1
1982	97.1	2.3	96.7	-0.4	95.8	-0.9	95.5	-0.3	96.1	0.6	98.2	2.2	99.1	0.9	99.0	-0.1	98.5	-0.5	98.8	0.3	98.2	-0.6	96.8	-1.4
1983	96.4	-0.4	94.7	-1.8	94.1	-0.6	96.7	2.8	98.5	1.9	100.1	1.6	100.9	0.8	100.9	0.0	100.6	-0.3	100.4	-0.2	100.3	-0.1	102.0	1.7
1984	102.2	0.2	101.0	-1.2	101.1	0.1	103.1	2.0	104.9	1.7	104.6	-0.3	103.1	-1.4	103.4	0.3	103.4	0.0	105.6	2.1	106.1	0.5	106.1	0.0
1985	105.6	-0.5	105.2	-0.4	106.5	1.2	108.4	1.8	108.3	-0.1	108.8	0.5	108.6	-0.2	107.4	-1.1	106.7	-0.7	107.5	0.7	108.0	0.5	108.6	0.6
1986	108.9	0.3	107.2	-1.6	105.3	-1.8	104.6	-0.7	105.6	1.0	106.8	1.1	104.6	-2.1	103.2	-1.3	103.4	0.2	104.3	0.9	104.3	0.0	104.0	-0.3
1987	105.3	1.3	106.9	1.5	107.8	0.8	108.4	0.6	108.9	0.5	109.1	0.2	108.9	-0.2	109.5	0.6	109.6	0.1	110.8	1.1	110.9	0.1	110.7	-0.2
1988	111.0	0.3	110.6	-0.4	110.8	0.2	112.9	1.9	114.1	1.1	114.7	0.5	114.6	-0.1	115.5	0.8	115.4	-0.1	115.5	0.1	115.0	-0.4	115.0	0.0
1989	114.6	-0.3	116.0	1.2	117.5	1.3	121.9	3.7	122.7	0.7	122.8	0.1	121.8	-0.8	120.3	-1.2	119.1	-1.0	119.0	-0.1	119.0	0.0	120.0	0.8
1990	121.4	1.2	122.3	0.7	123.2	0.7	123.5	0.2	123.9	0.3	125.1	1.0	125.3	0.2	127.1	1.4	129.0	1.5	131.5	1.9	132.5	0.8	133.6	0.8
1991	129.9	-2.8	127.1	-2.2	124.2	-2.3	123.8	-0.3	125.8	1.6	126.2	0.3	126.2	0.0	126.4	0.2	126.4	0.0	126.6	0.2	127.4	0.6	128.6	0.9

[Continued]

Los Angeles, CA
Consumer Price Index - All Urban Consumers
Base 1982-1984 = 100
Transportation
[Continued]

For 1947-1997. Columns headed % show percentile change in the index from the previous period for which an index is available.

Year	Jan Index	%	Feb Index	%	Mar Index	%	Apr Index	%	May Index	%	Jun Index	%	Jul Index	%	Aug Index	%	Sep Index	%	Oct Index	%	Nov Index	%	Dec Index	%
1992	129.3	0.5	129.6	0.2	130.1	0.4	130.6	0.4	132.3	1.3	132.7	0.3	134.6	1.4	133.8	-0.6	134.5	0.5	135.5	0.7	136.1	0.4	137.0	0.7
1993	137.5	0.4	137.9	0.3	137.7	-0.1	136.6	-0.8	137.0	0.3	136.4	-0.4	136.9	0.4	135.9	-0.7	136.7	0.6	138.2	1.1	139.6	1.0	139.4	-0.1
1994	139.0	-0.3	139.0	0.0	140.3	0.9	139.2	-0.8	137.9	-0.9	139.5	1.2	140.4	0.6	141.3	0.6	140.9	-0.3	142.5	1.1	142.9	0.3	142.6	-0.2
1995	143.3	0.5	142.3	-0.7	142.8	0.4	143.5	0.5	144.2	0.5	143.4	-0.6	142.2	-0.8	142.0	-0.1	140.9	-0.8	141.6	0.5	141.5	-0.1	140.1	-1.0
1996	141.2	0.8	142.2	0.7	143.7	1.1	146.5	1.9	148.6	1.4	146.9	-1.1	145.9	-0.7	144.5	-1.0	144.0	-0.3	143.0	-0.7	142.2	-0.6	143.4	0.8
1997	143.1	-0.2	143.8	0.5	146.0	1.5	146.7	0.5	145.0	-1.2	144.1	-0.6	144.5	0.3	145.1	0.4	147.1	1.4	146.3	-0.5	145.2	-0.8	144.9	-0.2

Source: U.S. Department of Labor, Bureau of Labor Statistics, Division of Consumer Prices and Price Indexes. - indicates no data collected for period.

Los Angeles, CA
Consumer Price Index - Urban Wage Earners
Base 1982-1984 = 100
Transportation

For 1947-1997. Columns headed % show percentile change in the index from the previous period for which an index is available.

Year	Jan Index	%	Feb Index	%	Mar Index	%	Apr Index	%	May Index	%	Jun Index	%	Jul Index	%	Aug Index	%	Sep Index	%	Oct Index	%	Nov Index	%	Dec Index	%
1947	17.2	-	17.4	1.2	17.4	0.0	17.6	1.1	17.5	-0.6	17.5	0.0	17.9	2.3	18.0	0.6	18.2	1.1	18.3	0.5	18.3	0.0	18.3	0.0
1948	19.1	4.4	19.1	0.0	19.1	0.0	19.2	0.5	19.1	-0.5	19.1	0.0	20.0	4.7	20.3	1.5	20.3	0.0	20.3	0.0	20.3	0.0	20.5	1.0
1949	20.5	0.0	20.9	2.0	20.8	-0.5	20.9	0.5	20.9	0.0	20.9	0.0	20.9	0.0	20.9	0.0	20.9	0.0	20.9	0.0	20.9	0.0	20.9	0.0
1950	20.9	0.0	20.8	-0.5	20.6	-1.0	20.4	-1.0	20.4	0.0	20.4	0.0	20.4	0.0	20.6	1.0	20.6	0.0	20.7	-0.5	20.8	0.5	20.9	0.5
1951	20.9	0.0	21.2	1.4	21.4	0.9	21.4	0.0	21.4	0.0	21.4	0.0	21.4	0.0	21.4	0.0	21.7	1.4	21.9	0.9	22.1	0.9	22.1	0.0
1952	22.1	0.0	23.4	5.9	23.4	0.0	23.4	0.0	23.6	0.9	23.6	0.0	24.0	1.7	24.0	0.0	24.1	0.4	24.1	0.0	24.3	0.8	24.3	0.0
1953	24.5	0.8	24.4	-0.4	24.8	1.6	24.7	-0.4	24.6	-0.4	24.6	0.0	24.9	1.2	24.9	0.0	24.8	-0.4	24.8	0.0	24.8	0.0	24.0	-3.2
1954	25.1	4.6	25.0	-0.4	24.8	-0.8	24.7	-0.4	24.8	0.4	24.5	-1.2	23.5	-4.1	23.8	1.3	23.9	0.4	23.5	-1.7	24.6	4.7	24.6	0.0
1955	24.6	0.0	24.6	0.0	24.8	0.8	23.8	-4.0	24.1	1.3	23.8	-1.2	23.9	0.4	23.8	-0.4	23.9	0.4	24.2	1.3	24.7	2.1	24.6	-0.4
1956	24.4	-0.8	24.2	-0.8	24.4	0.8	24.1	-1.2	24.4	1.2	24.4	0.0	24.9	2.0	24.6	-1.2	24.6	0.0	25.2	2.4	25.4	0.8	25.4	0.0
1957	25.4	0.0	25.8	1.6	25.7	-0.4	25.8	0.4	25.9	0.4	25.8	-0.4	25.7	-0.4	25.3	-1.6	25.6	1.2	25.6	0.0	25.9	1.2	25.6	-1.2
1958	25.5	-0.4	25.8	1.2	25.9	0.4	26.0	0.4	26.1	0.4	26.1	0.0	26.5	1.5	26.6	0.4	26.7	0.4	26.7	0.0	26.9	0.7	27.0	0.4
1959	27.1	0.4	27.4	1.1	27.4	0.0	27.5	0.4	27.6	0.4	27.6	0.0	27.5	-0.4	27.8	1.1	27.5	-1.1	28.1	2.2	28.3	0.7	28.3	0.0
1960	27.9	-1.4	27.7	-0.7	28.2	1.8	28.1	-0.4	27.9	-0.7	27.8	-0.4	27.8	0.0	27.7	-0.4	27.5	-0.7	27.7	0.7	27.8	0.4	28.1	1.1
1961	28.4	1.1	28.5	0.4	27.7	-2.8	27.7	0.0	28.0	1.1	29.1	3.9	29.1	0.0	29.3	0.7	29.1	-0.7	29.1	0.0	29.5	1.4	29.4	-0.3
1962	29.2	-0.7	29.0	-0.7	29.1	0.3	29.5	1.4	29.8	1.0	30.0	0.7	30.0	0.0	30.0	0.0	29.9	-0.3	30.1	0.7	30.0	-0.3	30.0	0.0
1963	29.6	-1.3	29.7	0.3	29.5	-0.7	29.9	1.4	29.6	-1.0	29.0	-2.0	29.0	0.0	30.0	3.4	30.0	0.0	30.5	1.7	30.6	0.3	29.4	-3.9
1964	31.2	6.1	29.6	-5.1	30.9	4.4	30.9	0.0	30.9	0.0	31.1	0.6	30.4	-2.3	30.9	1.6	30.3	-1.9	31.2	3.0	31.6	1.3	31.6	0.0
1965	31.5	-0.3	31.5	0.0	31.4	-0.3	31.7	1.0	31.8	0.3	31.6	-0.6	31.8	0.6	30.9	-2.8	31.6	2.3	31.2	-1.3	31.8	1.9	31.8	0.0
1966	30.8	-3.1	31.1	1.0	31.3	0.6	31.8	1.6	31.4	-1.3	31.6	0.6	32.2	1.9	31.1	-3.4	32.1	3.2	32.3	0.6	32.5	0.6	32.0	-1.5
1967	31.4	-1.9	31.3	-0.3	31.0	-1.0	32.1	3.5	32.2	0.3	32.2	0.0	32.2	0.0	32.3	0.3	33.0	2.2	32.2	-2.4	33.4	3.7	32.1	-3.9
1968	33.2	3.4	33.1	-0.3	33.4	0.9	32.7	-2.1	32.6	-0.3	33.5	2.8	33.1	-1.2	33.5	1.2	32.7	-2.4	33.4	2.1	33.8	1.2	32.6	-3.6
1969	33.5	2.8	33.5	0.0	34.5	3.0	34.1	-1.2	33.4	-2.1	34.4	3.0	34.4	0.0	34.1	-0.9	34.0	-0.3	34.8	2.4	33.6	-3.4	34.7	3.3
1970	34.2	-1.4	33.7	-1.5	33.7	0.0	35.3	4.7	34.8	-1.4	34.5	-0.9	35.8	3.8	34.5	-3.6	36.2	4.9	36.6	1.1	36.3	-0.8	36.9	1.7
1971	36.6	-0.8	36.0	-1.6	37.3	3.6	36.3	-2.7	36.6	0.8	36.9	0.8	36.9	0.0	37.2	0.8	37.3	0.3	37.7	1.1	37.1	-1.6	36.9	-0.5
1972	36.8	-0.3	36.1	-1.9	37.2	3.0	37.2	0.0	37.6	1.1	37.1	-1.3	37.9	2.2	38.0	0.3	38.7	1.8	38.9	0.5	39.0	0.3	39.0	0.0
1973	38.6	-1.0	38.7	0.3	38.8	0.3	39.2	1.0	39.5	0.8	39.8	0.8	40.1	0.8	39.9	-0.5	39.7	-0.5	39.9	0.5	40.3	1.0	40.3	0.0
1974	41.1	2.0	41.5	1.0	42.5	2.4	43.1	1.4	43.8	1.6	44.6	1.8	45.1	1.1	45.4	0.7	45.6	0.4	45.7	0.2	46.1	0.9	46.2	0.2
1975	46.3	0.2	46.5	0.4	46.9	0.9	47.7	1.7	48.2	1.0	49.1	1.9	50.1	2.0	50.5	0.8	50.5	0.0	51.1	1.2	51.1	0.0	50.9	-0.4
1976	51.0	0.2	51.2	0.4	51.4	0.4	52.0	1.2	52.7	1.3	53.5	1.5	55.0	2.8	55.4	0.7	55.9	0.9	56.3	0.7	56.4	0.2	56.3	-0.2
1977	56.4	0.2	56.7	0.5	57.0	0.5	57.6	1.1	58.0	0.7	58.5	0.9	58.9	0.7	58.6	-0.5	58.4	-0.3	58.2	-0.3	57.9	-0.5	57.8	-0.2
1978	58.0	0.3	58.0	0.0	58.3	0.5	58.7	0.7	59.5	1.4	60.3	1.3	60.9	1.0	61.2	0.5	61.5	0.5	61.9	0.7	62.7	1.3	63.0	0.5
1979	63.4	0.6	63.9	0.8	65.0	1.7	67.6	4.0	69.4	2.7	70.6	1.7	72.3	2.4	73.8	2.1	74.5	0.9	74.4	-0.1	75.0	0.8	76.1	1.5
1980	77.9	2.4	80.8	3.7	82.0	1.5	83.5	1.8	83.5	0.0	83.3	-0.2	83.3	0.0	83.8	0.6	84.4	0.7	84.6	0.2	85.4	0.9	85.8	0.5
1981	86.6	0.9	88.4	2.1	89.1	0.8	90.6	1.7	91.5	1.0	92.4	1.0	93.3	1.0	93.0	-0.3	93.0	0.0	94.9	2.0	95.5	0.6	95.5	0.0
1982	97.6	2.2	97.0	-0.6	96.2	-0.8	95.7	-0.5	96.3	0.6	98.7	2.5	99.6	0.9	99.6	0.0	99.0	-0.6	99.1	0.1	98.2	-0.9	96.8	-1.4
1983	96.2	-0.6	94.6	-1.7	93.9	-0.7	96.4	2.7	98.3	2.0	100.0	1.7	100.8	0.8	100.8	0.0	100.4	-0.4	100.1	-0.3	100.1	0.0	101.8	1.7
1984	101.9	0.1	100.8	-1.1	101.0	0.2	103.0	2.0	104.9	1.8	104.5	-0.4	102.9	-1.5	103.1	0.2	103.4	0.3	105.5	2.0	105.9	0.4	105.8	-0.1
1985	105.3	-0.5	104.8	-0.5	106.2	1.3	108.1	1.8	107.9	-0.2	108.4	0.5	108.2	-0.2	106.9	-1.2	106.0	-0.8	106.8	0.8	107.4	0.6	107.8	0.4
1986	108.0	0.2	106.2	-1.7	104.3	-1.8	103.5	-0.8	104.4	0.9	105.6	1.1	103.3	-2.2	101.7	-1.5	101.8	0.1	102.5	0.7	102.7	0.2	102.4	-0.3
1987	103.4	1.0	105.1	1.6	105.9	0.8	106.6	0.7	107.1	0.5	107.3	0.2	107.1	-0.2	107.6	0.5	107.6	0.0	108.9	1.2	109.0	0.1	108.8	-0.2
1988	109.0	0.2	108.7	-0.3	108.8	0.1	110.6	1.7	111.8	1.1	112.2	0.4	111.9	-0.3	112.8	0.8	112.9	0.1	113.2	0.3	112.5	-0.6	112.6	0.1
1989	112.1	-0.4	113.5	1.2	114.8	1.1	119.0	3.7	119.7	0.6	119.7	0.0	118.7	-0.8	117.1	-1.3	116.0	-0.9	115.8	-0.2	115.6	-0.2	116.7	1.0
1990	117.9	1.0	118.5	0.5	119.0	0.4	119.3	0.3	119.6	0.3	120.7	0.9	121.1	0.3	122.8	1.4	124.5	1.4	126.6	1.7	127.6	0.8	128.5	0.7
1991	125.1	-2.6	122.4	-2.2	119.8	-2.1	119.6	-0.2	121.7	1.8	122.2	0.4	122.2	0.0	122.5	0.2	122.8	0.2	123.0	0.2	123.6	0.5	124.6	0.8

[Continued]

Los Angeles, CA
Consumer Price Index - Urban Wage Earners
Base 1982-1984 = 100
Transportation
[Continued]

For 1947-1997. Columns headed % show percentile change in the index from the previous period for which an index is available.

Year	Jan		Feb		Mar		Apr		May		Jun		Jul		Aug		Sep		Oct		Nov		Dec	
	Index	%	Index	%	Index	%	Index	%	Index	%	Index	%	Index	%	Index	%	Index	%	Index	%	Index	%	Index	%
1992	125.1	0.4	125.4	0.2	125.7	0.2	126.3	0.5	128.0	1.3	128.8	0.6	129.9	0.9	129.6	-0.2	130.0	0.3	130.9	0.7	131.7	0.6	132.2	0.4
1993	132.4	0.2	132.7	0.2	132.5	-0.2	131.7	-0.6	131.9	0.2	131.7	-0.2	132.0	0.2	131.4	-0.5	131.9	0.4	133.5	1.2	134.5	0.7	134.0	-0.4
1994	133.7	-0.2	133.4	-0.2	134.4	0.7	134.0	-0.3	133.7	-0.2	135.1	1.0	135.9	0.6	136.6	0.5	136.4	-0.1	137.9	1.1	138.6	0.5	138.4	-0.1
1995	138.7	0.2	138.1	-0.4	138.5	0.3	139.1	0.4	139.8	0.5	139.4	-0.3	138.4	-0.7	138.0	-0.3	137.3	-0.5	138.0	0.5	138.0	0.0	137.1	-0.7
1996	137.8	0.5	138.6	0.6	139.7	0.8	142.6	2.1	144.7	1.5	143.0	-1.2	142.2	-0.6	140.6	-1.1	140.1	-0.4	139.3	-0.6	138.6	-0.5	139.4	0.6
1997	139.5	0.1	140.1	0.4	141.8	1.2	142.6	0.6	141.0	-1.1	140.0	-0.7	140.0	0.0	141.0	0.7	142.6	1.1	142.1	-0.4	140.9	-0.8	140.5	-0.3

Source: U.S. Department of Labor, Bureau of Labor Statistics, Division of Consumer Prices and Price Indexes. - indicates no data collected for period.

Los Angeles, CA
Consumer Price Index - All Urban Consumers
Base 1982-1984 = 100
Medical Care

For 1947-1997. Columns headed % show percentile change in the index from the previous period for which an index is available.

Year	Jan Index	%	Feb Index	%	Mar Index	%	Apr Index	%	May Index	%	Jun Index	%	Jul Index	%	Aug Index	%	Sep Index	%	Oct Index	%	Nov Index	%	Dec Index	%
1947	13.3	-	13.3	0.0	13.3	0.0	13.4	0.8	13.3	-0.7	13.3	0.0	13.3	0.0	13.3	0.0	13.4	0.8	13.6	1.5	13.6	0.0	13.6	0.0
1948	13.7	0.7	13.7	0.0	13.7	0.0	14.0	2.2	14.0	0.0	14.1	0.7	14.4	2.1	14.4	0.0	14.5	0.7	14.6	0.7	14.6	0.0	14.6	0.0
1949	14.7	0.7	14.7	0.0	14.7	0.0	14.7	0.0	14.7	0.0	14.7	0.0	14.7	0.0	14.7	0.0	14.7	0.0	14.7	0.0	14.7	0.0	14.7	0.0
1950	14.7	0.0	14.8	0.7	14.8	0.0	14.8	0.0	14.8	0.0	14.8	0.0	14.8	0.0	14.8	0.0	15.3	3.4	15.4	0.7	15.4	0.0	15.7	1.9
1951	15.7	0.0	15.7	0.0	15.9	1.3	15.9	0.0	15.9	0.0	15.9	0.0	16.0	0.6	16.0	0.0	16.0	0.0	16.0	0.0	16.0	0.0	16.0	0.0
1952	16.1	0.6	16.1	0.0	16.1	0.0	16.1	0.0	16.1	0.0	16.7	3.7	16.7	0.0	16.7	0.0	16.7	0.0	16.7	0.0	16.7	0.0	16.7	0.0
1953	16.7	0.0	16.7	0.0	16.7	0.0	16.9	1.2	16.9	0.0	16.9	0.0	16.9	0.0	17.0	0.6	17.0	0.0	17.1	0.6	17.1	0.0	17.1	0.0
1954	17.1	0.0	17.1	0.0	17.1	0.0	17.3	1.2	17.3	0.0	17.3	0.0	17.3	0.0	17.3	0.0	17.3	0.0	17.3	0.0	17.3	0.0	17.3	0.0
1955	17.3	0.0	17.3	0.0	17.3	0.0	17.1	-1.2	17.1	0.0	17.1	0.0	17.5	2.3	17.5	0.0	17.5	0.0	17.5	0.0	17.5	0.0	17.6	0.6
1956	17.8	1.1	17.8	0.0	17.8	0.0	17.9	0.6	17.9	0.0	17.9	0.0	17.9	0.0	18.0	0.6	18.0	0.0	18.1	0.6	18.1	0.0	18.0	-0.6
1957	18.3	1.7	18.3	0.0	18.3	0.0	18.3	0.0	18.3	0.0	18.4	0.5	18.4	0.0	18.5	0.5	18.5	0.0	18.5	0.0	18.5	0.0	18.6	0.5
1958	18.9	1.6	18.9	0.0	18.9	0.0	19.3	2.1	19.3	0.0	20.3	5.2	20.3	0.0	20.4	0.5	20.4	0.0	20.5	0.5	20.5	0.0	20.5	0.0
1959	20.6	0.5	20.6	0.0	20.6	0.0	20.6	0.0	20.7	0.5	20.7	0.0	20.7	0.0	20.7	0.0	20.7	0.0	21.1	1.9	21.1	0.0	21.1	0.0
1960	21.1	0.0	21.1	0.0	21.1	0.0	21.3	0.9	21.3	0.0	21.3	0.0	21.5	0.9	21.5	0.0	21.5	0.0	21.6	0.5	21.6	0.0	21.6	0.0
1961	21.6	0.0	21.6	0.0	21.6	0.0	21.6	0.0	21.6	0.0	21.6	0.0	21.6	0.0	21.7	0.5	21.7	0.0	21.7	0.0	21.7	0.0	21.7	0.0
1962	21.7	0.0	21.7	0.0	22.3	2.8	22.4	0.4	22.4	0.0	22.4	0.0	22.5	0.4	22.4	-0.4	22.4	0.0	22.4	0.0	22.4	0.0	22.4	0.0
1963	22.5	0.4	22.5	0.0	22.5	0.0	22.6	0.4	22.7	0.4	22.7	0.0	22.7	0.0	22.7	0.0	22.7	0.0	22.9	0.9	22.9	0.0	22.9	0.0
1964	23.0	0.4	23.1	0.4	23.1	0.0	23.2	0.4	23.2	0.0	23.2	0.0	23.3	0.4	23.3	0.0	23.3	0.0	23.5	0.9	23.5	0.0	23.4	-0.4
1965	23.4	0.0	23.5	0.4	23.5	0.0	23.6	0.4	23.7	0.4	23.7	0.0	23.7	0.0	23.7	0.0	23.7	0.0	23.7	0.0	23.8	0.4	23.8	0.0
1966	23.9	0.4	24.0	0.4	24.0	0.0	24.2	0.8	24.1	-0.4	24.2	0.4	24.3	0.4	24.3	0.0	25.2	3.7	25.4	0.8	25.5	0.4	25.7	0.8
1967	25.7	0.0	25.7	0.0	25.8	0.4	26.0	0.8	26.3	1.2	26.4	0.4	26.6	0.8	26.6	0.0	26.7	0.4	26.8	0.4	26.9	0.4	27.0	0.4
1968	27.2	0.7	27.3	0.4	27.3	0.0	27.5	0.7	27.8	1.1	27.8	0.0	28.0	0.7	28.1	0.4	28.1	0.0	28.2	0.4	28.3	0.4	28.5	0.7
1969	28.6	0.4	28.8	0.7	28.9	0.3	29.3	1.4	29.4	0.3	29.5	0.3	29.6	0.3	29.8	0.7	29.9	0.3	29.8	-0.3	30.0	0.7	30.4	1.3
1970	30.4	0.0	30.7	1.0	31.0	1.0	31.6	1.9	31.8	0.6	31.8	0.0	31.9	0.3	32.0	0.3	32.0	0.0	31.9	-0.3	31.9	0.0	32.1	0.6
1971	32.1	0.0	32.2	0.3	32.4	0.6	33.2	2.5	33.4	0.6	33.5	0.3	33.6	0.3	33.6	0.0	33.7	0.3	33.4	-0.9	33.4	0.0	33.4	0.0
1972	33.5	0.3	33.6	0.3	33.6	0.0	33.7	0.3	33.7	0.0	33.8	0.3	34.1	0.9	34.1	0.0	34.2	0.3	34.4	0.6	34.3	-0.3	34.5	0.6
1973	34.6	0.3	34.7	0.3	35.0	0.9	35.2	0.6	35.3	0.3	35.4	0.3	35.6	0.6	35.8	0.6	35.9	0.3	36.6	1.9	36.6	0.0	36.6	0.0
1974	36.9	0.8	37.2	0.8	37.5	0.8	37.6	0.3	38.4	2.1	38.8	1.0	39.3	1.3	39.8	1.3	40.0	0.5	40.3	0.7	40.9	1.5	41.1	0.5
1975	41.3	0.5	42.1	1.9	42.4	0.7	42.9	1.2	43.3	0.9	43.6	0.7	43.9	0.7	44.3	0.9	44.5	0.5	44.8	0.7	45.5	1.6	46.1	1.3
1976	46.4	0.7	47.7	2.8	47.9	0.4	48.3	0.8	48.9	1.2	49.3	0.8	49.7	0.8	50.1	0.8	50.3	0.4	50.6	0.6	51.3	1.4	51.3	0.0
1977	51.6	0.6	52.4	1.6	52.6	0.4	53.0	0.8	53.2	0.4	53.6	0.8	54.1	0.9	54.5	0.7	54.9	0.7	55.3	0.7	55.5	0.4	55.6	0.2
1978	56.0	0.7	56.3	0.5	56.4	0.2	56.6	0.4	58.2	2.8	58.4	0.3	58.7	0.5	60.0	2.2	60.2	0.3	60.6	0.7	61.1	0.8	61.1	0.0
1979	62.1	1.6	62.3	0.3	62.6	0.5	62.7	0.2	63.6	1.4	64.1	0.8	65.2	1.7	65.1	-0.2	66.2	1.7	66.6	0.6	66.8	0.3	67.7	1.3
1980	68.3	0.9	70.4	3.1	70.8	0.6	72.5	2.4	72.5	0.0	72.5	0.0	73.4	1.2	73.2	-0.3	73.6	0.5	74.7	1.5	75.2	0.7	75.3	0.1
1981	76.2	1.2	77.0	1.0	77.2	0.3	77.9	0.9	78.2	0.4	78.7	0.6	84.5	7.4	85.1	0.7	85.5	0.5	85.5	0.0	88.7	3.7	89.2	0.6
1982	90.0	0.9	90.1	0.1	90.6	0.6	91.6	1.1	92.6	1.1	94.4	1.9	94.8	0.4	95.9	1.2	97.1	1.3	96.9	-0.2	97.5	0.6	97.7	0.2
1983	99.3	1.6	99.6	0.3	99.7	0.1	100.2	0.5	100.2	0.0	101.0	0.8	101.6	0.6	101.2	-0.4	101.2	0.0	101.3	0.1	101.6	0.3	101.6	0.0
1984	103.2	1.6	103.3	0.1	103.6	0.3	104.0	0.4	104.5	0.5	104.5	0.0	105.6	1.1	106.1	0.5	106.0	-0.1	107.0	0.9	107.1	0.1	107.4	0.3
1985	110.1	2.5	110.5	0.4	111.1	0.5	111.2	0.1	111.3	0.1	112.2	0.8	112.8	0.5	113.7	0.8	114.6	0.8	115.1	0.4	115.7	0.5	116.4	0.6
1986	117.0	0.5	118.1	0.9	118.9	0.7	119.4	0.4	119.7	0.3	120.2	0.4	120.7	0.4	121.7	0.8	121.9	0.2	123.0	0.9	124.5	1.2	125.3	0.6
1987	126.6	1.0	127.2	0.5	127.6	0.3	128.1	0.4	128.1	0.0	129.3	0.9	129.6	0.2	130.2	0.5	130.6	0.3	131.7	0.8	132.3	0.5	132.6	0.2
1988	135.5	2.2	136.5	0.7	137.3	0.6	137.4	0.1	137.9	0.4	139.1	0.9	139.6	0.4	140.8	0.9	141.6	0.6	143.1	1.1	143.0	-0.1	143.1	0.1
1989	145.0	1.3	145.2	0.1	146.1	0.6	147.4	0.9	148.0	0.4	149.1	0.7	150.6	1.0	151.5	0.6	152.5	0.7	152.9	0.3	154.2	0.9	154.6	0.3
1990	157.0	1.6	158.2	0.8	159.0	0.5	160.0	0.6	160.8	0.5	161.7	0.6	163.6	1.2	164.0	0.2	165.9	1.2	168.5	1.6	170.1	0.9	170.4	0.2
1991	172.9	1.5	172.9	0.0	174.7	1.0	174.9	0.1	176.1	0.7	177.6	0.9	180.1	1.4	179.9	-0.1	180.4	0.3	181.0	0.3	183.4	1.3	184.2	0.4

[Continued]

Los Angeles, CA
Consumer Price Index - All Urban Consumers
Base 1982-1984 = 100
Medical Care
[Continued]

For 1947-1997. Columns headed % show percentile change in the index from the previous period for which an index is available.

Year	Jan Index	%	Feb Index	%	Mar Index	%	Apr Index	%	May Index	%	Jun Index	%	Jul Index	%	Aug Index	%	Sep Index	%	Oct Index	%	Nov Index	%	Dec Index	%
1992	186.5	1.2	187.8	0.7	188.7	0.5	189.5	0.4	190.8	0.7	191.9	0.6	193.5	0.8	193.9	0.2	194.6	0.4	197.0	1.2	196.7	-0.2	197.9	0.6
1993	199.0	0.6	202.3	1.7	201.9	-0.2	202.6	0.3	207.2	2.3	207.0	-0.1	207.3	0.1	207.8	0.2	208.8	0.5	211.3	1.2	211.4	0.0	212.0	0.3
1994	212.7	0.3	213.3	0.3	213.4	0.0	214.0	0.3	214.2	0.1	214.4	0.1	215.7	0.6	216.0	0.1	216.2	0.1	216.5	0.1	217.6	0.5	217.8	0.1
1995	219.1	0.6	219.6	0.2	220.7	0.5	220.4	-0.1	220.9	0.2	222.1	0.5	221.8	-0.1	222.3	0.2	222.3	0.0	223.5	0.5	224.1	0.3	224.2	0.0
1996	226.3	0.9	226.5	0.1	227.7	0.5	228.8	0.5	228.9	0.0	229.3	0.2	229.5	0.1	229.3	-0.1	229.4	0.0	229.9	0.2	230.1	0.1	230.5	0.2
1997	231.7	0.5	231.8	0.0	231.9	0.0	231.5	-0.2	231.2	-0.1	231.4	0.1	232.0	0.3	232.0	0.0	231.9	-0.0	232.4	0.2	232.9	0.2	232.7	-0.1

Source: U.S. Department of Labor, Bureau of Labor Statistics, Division of Consumer Prices and Price Indexes. - indicates no data collected for period.

Los Angeles, CA
Consumer Price Index - Urban Wage Earners
Base 1982-1984 = 100
Medical Care

For 1947-1997. Columns headed % show percentile change in the index from the previous period for which an index is available.

Year	Jan Index	%	Feb Index	%	Mar Index	%	Apr Index	%	May Index	%	Jun Index	%	Jul Index	%	Aug Index	%	Sep Index	%	Oct Index	%	Nov Index	%	Dec Index	%
1947	13.5	-	13.5	0.0	13.5	0.0	13.6	0.7	13.5	-0.7	13.5	0.0	13.5	0.0	13.5	0.0	13.6	0.7	13.8	1.5	13.8	0.0	13.8	0.0
1948	13.9	0.7	13.9	0.0	13.9	0.0	14.2	2.2	14.2	0.0	14.3	0.7	14.6	2.1	14.6	0.0	14.7	0.7	14.8	0.7	14.8	0.0	14.8	0.0
1949	14.9	0.7	14.9	0.0	14.9	0.0	14.9	0.0	14.9	0.0	14.9	0.0	14.9	0.0	14.9	0.0	15.0	0.7	15.0	0.0	15.0	0.0	15.0	0.0
1950	15.0	0.0	15.0	0.0	15.0	0.0	15.0	0.0	15.0	0.0	15.0	0.0	15.0	0.0	15.0	0.0	15.5	3.3	15.6	0.6	15.7	0.6	16.0	1.9
1951	16.0	0.0	16.0	0.0	16.2	1.3	16.2	0.0	16.2	0.0	16.2	0.0	16.2	0.0	16.2	0.0	16.2	0.0	16.2	0.0	16.2	0.0	16.2	0.0
1952	16.3	0.6	16.3	0.0	16.4	0.6	16.4	0.0	16.4	0.0	16.9	3.0	16.9	0.0	16.9	0.0	16.9	0.0	16.9	0.0	16.9	0.0	16.9	0.0
1953	16.9	0.0	16.9	0.0	16.9	0.0	17.1	1.2	17.2	0.6	17.2	0.0	17.2	0.0	17.2	0.0	17.2	0.0	17.3	0.6	17.3	0.0	17.4	0.6
1954	17.3	-0.6	17.3	0.0	17.4	0.6	17.5	0.6	17.5	0.0	17.5	0.0	17.6	0.6	17.6	0.0	17.6	0.0	17.6	0.0	17.6	0.0	17.6	0.0
1955	17.6	0.0	17.6	0.0	17.6	0.0	17.4	-1.1	17.4	0.0	17.4	0.0	17.8	2.3	17.8	0.0	17.8	0.0	17.8	0.0	17.8	0.0	17.9	0.6
1956	18.1	1.1	18.1	0.0	18.1	0.0	18.1	0.0	18.2	0.6	18.2	0.0	18.2	0.0	18.2	0.0	18.3	0.5	18.3	0.0	18.3	0.0	18.3	0.0
1957	18.5	1.1	18.5	0.0	18.5	0.0	18.6	0.5	18.6	0.0	18.6	0.0	18.7	0.5	18.7	0.0	18.7	0.0	18.7	0.0	18.8	0.5	18.9	0.5
1958	19.2	1.6	19.2	0.0	19.2	0.0	19.6	2.1	19.6	0.0	20.6	5.1	20.6	0.0	20.7	0.5	20.7	0.0	20.9	1.0	20.9	0.0	20.9	0.0
1959	20.9	0.0	20.9	0.0	20.9	0.0	20.9	0.0	21.0	0.5	21.0	0.0	21.0	0.0	21.0	0.0	21.0	0.0	21.4	1.9	21.4	0.0	21.4	0.0
1960	21.4	0.0	21.4	0.0	21.4	0.0	21.6	0.9	21.6	0.0	21.6	0.0	21.8	0.9	21.8	0.0	21.8	0.0	21.9	0.5	21.9	0.0	21.9	0.0
1961	21.9	0.0	21.9	0.0	21.9	0.0	21.9	0.0	21.9	0.0	22.0	0.5	22.0	0.0	22.0	0.0	22.1	0.5	22.1	0.0	22.1	0.0	22.1	0.0
1962	22.0	-0.5	22.0	0.0	22.7	3.2	22.8	0.4	22.8	0.0	22.8	0.0	22.8	0.0	22.8	0.0	22.8	0.0	22.8	0.0	22.8	0.0	22.8	0.0
1963	22.9	0.4	22.9	0.0	22.9	0.0	23.0	0.4	23.0	0.0	23.0	0.0	23.1	0.4	23.1	0.0	23.0	-0.4	23.2	0.9	23.2	0.0	23.2	0.0
1964	23.3	0.4	23.4	0.4	23.4	0.0	23.6	0.9	23.6	0.0	23.6	0.0	23.7	0.4	23.7	0.0	23.6	-0.4	23.8	0.9	23.8	0.0	23.8	0.0
1965	23.8	0.0	23.8	0.0	23.9	0.4	24.0	0.4	24.0	0.0	24.0	0.0	24.1	0.4	24.1	0.0	24.0	-0.4	24.1	0.4	24.1	0.0	24.2	0.4
1966	24.2	0.0	24.3	0.4	24.4	0.4	24.5	0.4	24.5	0.0	24.6	0.4	24.6	0.0	24.7	0.4	25.6	3.6	25.8	0.8	25.9	0.4	26.1	0.8
1967	26.1	0.0	26.1	0.0	26.2	0.4	26.4	0.8	26.7	1.1	26.8	0.4	27.0	0.7	27.0	0.0	27.2	0.7	27.2	0.0	27.3	0.4	27.4	0.4
1968	27.6	0.7	27.7	0.4	27.7	0.0	28.0	1.1	28.2	0.7	28.2	0.0	28.4	0.7	28.5	0.4	28.5	0.0	28.6	0.4	28.7	0.3	28.9	0.7
1969	29.0	0.3	29.2	0.7	29.3	0.3	29.7	1.4	29.9	0.7	30.0	0.3	30.0	0.0	30.2	0.7	30.3	0.3	30.2	-0.3	30.4	0.7	30.8	1.3
1970	30.9	0.3	31.2	1.0	31.5	1.0	32.1	1.9	32.2	0.3	32.3	0.3	32.4	0.3	32.5	0.3	32.5	0.0	32.3	-0.6	32.4	0.3	32.5	0.3
1971	32.6	0.3	32.7	0.3	32.9	0.6	33.7	2.4	33.9	0.6	34.0	0.3	34.1	0.3	34.1	0.0	34.2	0.3	34.0	-0.6	34.0	0.0	34.0	0.0
1972	34.0	0.0	34.1	0.3	34.1	0.0	34.2	0.3	34.2	0.0	34.4	0.6	34.6	0.6	34.6	0.0	34.7	0.3	34.9	0.6	34.9	0.0	35.0	0.3
1973	35.1	0.3	35.3	0.6	35.5	0.6	35.7	0.6	35.8	0.3	35.9	0.3	36.1	0.6	36.3	0.6	36.4	0.3	37.1	1.9	37.1	0.0	37.1	0.0
1974	37.4	0.8	37.7	0.8	38.1	1.1	38.2	0.3	38.9	1.8	39.3	1.0	39.9	1.5	40.4	1.3	40.6	0.5	40.9	0.7	41.5	1.5	41.7	0.5
1975	41.9	0.5	42.7	1.9	43.0	0.7	43.5	1.2	43.9	0.9	44.2	0.7	44.5	0.7	45.0	1.1	45.2	0.4	45.5	0.7	46.2	1.5	46.8	1.3
1976	47.1	0.6	48.4	2.8	48.6	0.4	49.0	0.8	49.7	1.4	50.1	0.8	50.4	0.6	50.9	1.0	51.0	0.2	51.4	0.8	52.1	1.4	52.1	0.0
1977	52.4	0.6	53.2	1.5	53.4	0.4	53.8	0.7	54.0	0.4	54.4	0.7	54.9	0.9	55.3	0.7	55.7	0.7	56.1	0.7	56.4	0.5	56.4	0.0
1978	56.8	0.7	57.1	0.5	57.2	0.2	57.4	0.3	58.7	2.3	58.7	0.0	59.1	0.7	59.8	1.2	60.2	0.7	60.8	1.0	61.4	1.0	61.2	-0.3
1979	62.3	1.8	62.5	0.3	62.7	0.3	62.8	0.2	63.6	1.3	64.1	0.8	66.0	3.0	66.8	1.2	67.7	1.3	67.8	0.1	68.1	0.4	68.6	0.7
1980	69.3	1.0	70.4	1.6	70.6	0.3	72.6	2.8	73.9	1.8	73.7	-0.3	74.5	1.1	74.7	0.3	75.4	0.9	76.4	1.3	77.8	1.8	78.3	0.6
1981	79.0	0.9	80.7	2.2	81.0	0.4	81.5	0.6	81.9	0.5	82.8	1.1	83.7	1.1	84.3	0.7	85.3	1.2	85.2	-0.1	87.7	2.9	89.3	1.8
1982	90.0	0.8	90.2	0.2	90.8	0.7	91.8	1.1	92.8	1.1	94.5	1.8	94.9	0.4	95.9	1.1	97.0	1.1	96.7	-0.3	97.4	0.7	97.5	0.1
1983	99.2	1.7	99.4	0.2	99.7	0.3	100.2	0.5	100.3	0.1	101.1	0.8	101.6	0.5	101.2	-0.4	101.2	0.0	101.3	0.1	101.5	0.2	101.6	0.1
1984	103.1	1.5	103.2	0.1	103.6	0.4	104.1	0.5	104.6	0.5	104.6	0.0	105.5	0.9	106.1	0.6	105.8	-0.3	107.0	1.1	107.1	0.1	107.3	0.2
1985	110.0	2.5	110.5	0.5	111.1	0.5	111.2	0.1	111.4	0.2	112.2	0.7	112.8	0.5	113.7	0.8	114.5	0.7	115.0	0.4	115.7	0.6	116.4	0.6
1986	117.0	0.5	118.1	0.9	118.8	0.6	119.2	0.3	119.6	0.3	120.0	0.3	120.5	0.4	121.5	0.8	121.7	0.2	122.8	0.9	124.1	1.1	124.9	0.6
1987	126.1	1.0	126.7	0.5	127.1	0.3	127.7	0.5	127.6	-0.1	128.9	1.0	129.1	0.2	129.8	0.5	130.3	0.4	131.2	0.7	131.8	0.5	132.1	0.2
1988	135.1	2.3	136.2	0.8	137.0	0.6	136.9	-0.1	137.4	0.4	138.8	1.0	139.3	0.4	140.3	0.7	140.9	0.4	142.5	1.1	142.2	-0.2	142.3	0.1
1989	144.2	1.3	144.4	0.1	145.3	0.6	146.5	0.8	147.2	0.5	148.2	0.7	149.4	0.8	150.1	0.5	151.4	0.9	151.8	0.3	153.0	0.8	153.4	0.3
1990	155.8	1.6	156.9	0.7	157.5	0.4	158.6	0.7	159.3	0.4	160.2	0.6	161.4	0.7	161.7	0.2	163.6	1.2	166.3	1.7	168.5	1.3	168.7	0.1
1991	170.9	1.3	170.6	-0.2	172.2	0.9	172.3	0.1	173.5	0.7	175.3	1.0	177.7	1.4	177.5	-0.1	178.0	0.3	178.2	0.1	180.9	1.5	181.6	0.4

[Continued]

Los Angeles, CA
Consumer Price Index - Urban Wage Earners
Base 1982-1984 = 100
Medical Care
[Continued]

For 1947-1997. Columns headed % show percentile change in the index from the previous period for which an index is available.

Year	Jan Index	%	Feb Index	%	Mar Index	%	Apr Index	%	May Index	%	Jun Index	%	Jul Index	%	Aug Index	%	Sep Index	%	Oct Index	%	Nov Index	%	Dec Index	%
1992	183.7	1.2	185.2	0.8	186.2	0.5	186.9	0.4	188.3	0.7	189.4	0.6	191.2	1.0	191.8	0.3	192.6	0.4	194.6	1.0	194.2	-0.2	195.5	0.7
1993	196.6	0.6	199.6	1.5	199.4	-0.1	200.1	0.4	204.8	2.3	204.3	-0.2	204.7	0.2	205.1	0.2	206.0	0.4	208.5	1.2	208.3	-0.1	208.9	0.3
1994	209.6	0.3	210.0	0.2	210.0	0.0	210.8	0.4	210.8	0.0	211.1	0.1	212.1	0.5	212.4	0.1	212.6	0.1	213.0	0.2	214.1	0.5	214.2	0.0
1995	215.6	0.7	216.0	0.2	217.5	0.7	217.1	-0.2	217.6	0.2	219.0	0.6	219.3	0.1	219.7	0.2	219.6	-0.0	220.8	0.5	221.5	0.3	221.6	0.0
1996	223.7	0.9	223.9	0.1	225.1	0.5	226.2	0.5	226.3	0.0	226.9	0.3	227.1	0.1	226.9	-0.1	227.0	0.0	227.7	0.3	227.7	0.0	228.3	0.3
1997	229.2	0.4	229.4	0.1	229.5	0.0	229.1	-0.2	228.8	-0.1	228.8	0.0	229.5	0.3	229.3	-0.1	228.9	-0.2	229.9	0.4	230.5	0.3	230.3	-0.1

Source: U.S. Department of Labor, Bureau of Labor Statistics, Division of Consumer Prices and Price Indexes. - indicates no data collected for period.

Los Angeles, CA
Consumer Price Index - All Urban Consumers
Base 1982-1984 = 100
Entertainment

For 1976-1997. Columns headed % show percentile change in the index from the previous period for which an index is available.

Year	Jan Index	%	Feb Index	%	Mar Index	%	Apr Index	%	May Index	%	Jun Index	%	Jul Index	%	Aug Index	%	Sep Index	%	Oct Index	%	Nov Index	%	Dec Index	%
1976	68.9	-	69.4	0.7	69.6	0.3	70.1	0.7	70.2	0.1	70.2	0.0	71.2	1.4	70.8	-0.6	71.1	0.4	70.7	-0.6	71.8	1.6	72.0	0.3
1977	72.1	0.1	73.1	1.4	73.2	0.1	73.4	0.3	72.7	-1.0	72.8	0.1	72.9	0.1	73.6	1.0	73.5	-0.1	73.3	-0.3	73.4	0.1	73.8	0.5
1978	71.9	-2.6	73.8	2.6	74.6	1.1	76.3	2.3	76.0	-0.4	74.3	-2.2	74.6	0.4	72.6	-2.7	74.4	2.5	75.1	0.9	73.8	-1.7	75.4	2.2
1979	76.2	1.1	75.6	-0.8	77.4	2.4	77.6	0.3	78.1	0.6	78.5	0.5	79.0	0.6	79.3	0.4	79.8	0.6	79.8	0.0	80.9	1.4	81.3	0.5
1980	81.9	0.7	82.9	1.2	84.1	1.4	83.7	-0.5	84.1	0.5	84.8	0.8	85.9	1.3	87.0	1.3	88.7	2.0	88.3	-0.5	88.5	0.2	89.1	0.7
1981	91.2	2.4	91.0	-0.2	92.1	1.2	91.7	-0.4	92.7	1.1	92.1	-0.6	92.0	-0.1	94.7	2.9	95.1	0.4	94.7	-0.4	94.9	0.2	95.5	0.6
1982	96.2	0.7	96.9	0.7	98.3	1.4	99.4	1.1	99.2	-0.2	98.5	-0.7	97.5	-1.0	96.8	-0.7	96.4	-0.4	97.0	0.6	97.1	0.1	98.4	1.3
1983	98.4	0.0	100.0	1.6	101.0	1.0	99.8	-1.2	99.1	-0.7	99.4	0.3	98.7	-0.7	99.2	0.5	99.1	-0.1	100.7	1.6	100.4	-0.3	102.1	1.7
1984	101.7	-0.4	102.7	1.0	102.3	-0.4	102.3	0.0	102.1	-0.2	102.5	0.4	102.0	-0.5	102.3	0.3	103.1	0.8	103.3	0.2	103.6	0.3	103.0	-0.6
1985	104.1	1.1	104.0	-0.1	105.7	1.6	105.7	0.0	105.3	-0.4	107.9	2.5	107.7	-0.2	108.1	0.4	108.1	0.0	108.8	0.6	108.6	-0.2	108.4	-0.2
1986	108.4	0.0	108.5	0.1	108.1	-0.4	108.3	0.2	109.3	0.9	109.8	0.5	109.6	-0.2	109.5	-0.1	108.4	-1.0	108.7	0.3	109.9	1.1	109.8	-0.1
1987	110.1	0.3	110.1	0.0	109.9	-0.2	110.9	0.9	110.3	-0.5	110.8	0.5	111.4	0.5	110.9	-0.4	111.6	0.6	111.9	0.3	112.9	0.9	113.0	0.1
1988	113.1	0.1	114.0	0.8	114.3	0.3	114.9	0.5	114.9	0.0	114.7	-0.2	115.4	0.6	115.9	0.4	116.0	0.1	116.7	0.6	117.4	0.6	117.3	-0.1
1989	118.2	0.8	118.7	0.4	118.5	-0.2	119.8	1.1	120.1	0.3	120.7	0.5	121.0	0.2	121.1	0.1	123.1	1.7	122.9	-0.2	123.1	0.2	123.5	0.3
1990	122.5	-0.8	123.1	0.5	123.8	0.6	124.1	0.2	124.0	-0.1	124.0	0.0	125.5	1.2	123.6	-1.5	128.8	4.2	128.2	-0.5	128.3	0.1	128.6	0.2
1991	130.5	1.5	131.1	0.5	131.1	0.0	133.7	2.0	134.8	0.8	135.4	0.4	137.2	1.3	138.7	1.1	138.5	-0.1	140.9	1.7	139.9	-0.7	133.3	-4.7
1992	133.8	0.4	133.8	0.0	134.1	0.2	134.9	0.6	134.8	-0.1	132.9	-1.4	133.5	0.5	133.2	-0.2	134.0	0.6	134.6	0.4	134.3	-0.2	135.1	0.6
1993	135.9	0.6	135.5	-0.3	135.7	0.1	135.4	-0.2	134.1	-1.0	133.0	-0.8	133.9	0.7	135.0	0.8	136.0	0.7	137.7	1.2	138.9	0.9	138.8	-0.1
1994	139.4	0.4	138.0	-1.0	138.1	0.1	138.5	0.3	138.3	-0.1	136.6	-1.2	136.6	0.0	135.1	-1.1	134.9	-0.1	136.4	1.1	137.1	0.5	137.0	-0.1
1995	140.6	2.6	140.9	0.2	141.2	0.2	141.8	0.4	140.9	-0.6	139.7	-0.9	140.2	0.4	139.6	-0.4	140.2	0.4	142.6	1.7	143.9	0.9	143.6	-0.2
1996	145.8	1.5	146.0	0.1	147.0	0.7	146.8	-0.1	144.7	-1.4	144.8	0.1	145.2	0.3	144.5	-0.5	145.4	0.6	144.7	-0.5	146.6	1.3	147.9	0.9
1997	148.5	0.4	148.4	-0.1	148.6	0.1	148.4	-0.1	148.1	-0.2	147.1	-0.7	146.3	-0.5	146.5	0.1	147.0	0.3	146.7	-0.2	147.9	0.8	148.0	0.1

Source: U.S. Department of Labor, Bureau of Labor Statistics, Division of Consumer Prices and Price Indexes. - indicates no data collected for period.

Los Angeles, CA
Consumer Price Index - Urban Wage Earners
Base 1982-1984 = 100
Entertainment

For 1976-1997. Columns headed % show percentile change in the index from the previous period for which an index is available.

Year	Jan Index	%	Feb Index	%	Mar Index	%	Apr Index	%	May Index	%	Jun Index	%	Jul Index	%	Aug Index	%	Sep Index	%	Oct Index	%	Nov Index	%	Dec Index	%
1976	75.6	-	76.2	0.8	76.4	0.3	76.9	0.7	77.0	0.1	77.0	0.0	78.2	1.6	77.8	-0.5	78.1	0.4	77.7	-0.5	78.8	1.4	79.1	0.4
1977	79.2	0.1	80.2	1.3	80.4	0.2	80.6	0.2	79.8	-1.0	80.0	0.3	80.0	0.0	80.8	1.0	80.7	-0.1	80.5	-0.2	80.5	0.0	81.0	0.6
1978	81.5	0.6	83.3	2.2	79.2	-4.9	78.8	-0.5	80.7	2.4	79.4	-1.6	79.9	0.6	78.7	-1.5	79.6	1.1	80.1	0.6	78.9	-1.5	81.4	3.2
1979	82.0	0.7	81.3	-0.9	81.2	-0.1	81.4	0.2	83.4	2.5	84.0	0.7	85.1	1.3	81.6	-4.1	84.7	3.8	84.7	0.0	85.1	0.5	86.7	1.9
1980	87.7	1.2	88.0	0.3	88.8	0.9	89.4	0.7	89.6	0.2	90.5	1.0	90.6	0.1	90.7	0.1	93.0	2.5	93.3	0.3	94.0	0.8	94.3	0.3
1981	94.1	-0.2	94.0	-0.1	94.6	0.6	92.9	-1.8	93.7	0.9	93.6	-0.1	93.8	0.2	94.7	1.0	95.6	1.0	95.3	-0.3	95.6	0.3	95.6	0.0
1982	96.2	0.6	96.9	0.7	98.2	1.3	99.4	1.2	99.1	-0.3	98.4	-0.7	97.7	-0.7	96.9	-0.8	96.3	-0.6	96.7	0.4	96.9	0.2	98.2	1.3
1983	98.2	0.0	99.9	1.7	100.9	1.0	99.7	-1.2	99.1	-0.6	99.5	0.4	98.8	-0.7	99.3	0.5	99.1	-0.2	100.6	1.5	100.4	-0.2	101.9	1.5
1984	101.8	-0.1	102.7	0.9	102.4	-0.3	102.3	-0.1	102.1	-0.2	102.5	0.4	102.1	-0.4	102.4	0.3	103.2	0.8	103.3	0.1	103.6	0.3	103.2	-0.4
1985	104.2	1.0	104.0	-0.2	105.5	1.4	105.6	0.1	105.2	-0.4	107.5	2.2	107.3	-0.2	107.8	0.5	107.7	-0.1	108.3	0.6	108.3	0.0	107.9	-0.4
1986	108.0	0.1	108.0	0.0	107.6	-0.4	107.7	0.1	108.8	1.0	109.2	0.4	109.0	-0.2	108.9	-0.1	107.7	-1.1	108.0	0.3	109.2	1.1	109.1	-0.1
1987	109.3	0.2	109.5	0.2	109.1	-0.4	110.2	1.0	109.5	-0.6	110.2	0.6	110.6	0.4	110.5	-0.1	111.2	0.6	110.8	-0.4	111.9	1.0	112.6	0.6
1988	112.5	-0.1	112.7	0.2	113.1	0.4	113.7	0.5	114.2	0.4	114.0	-0.2	114.8	0.7	115.3	0.4	115.5	0.2	116.2	0.6	116.4	0.2	116.4	0.0
1989	117.3	0.8	118.0	0.6	117.6	-0.3	118.9	1.1	119.3	0.3	119.8	0.4	120.3	0.4	120.4	0.1	122.1	1.4	121.8	-0.2	122.1	0.2	122.6	0.4
1990	121.8	-0.7	122.3	0.4	122.8	0.4	123.3	0.4	123.3	0.0	123.4	0.1	124.5	0.9	123.8	-0.6	127.3	2.8	126.8	-0.4	126.8	0.0	127.1	0.2
1991	129.1	1.6	129.4	0.2	129.4	0.0	132.3	2.2	133.1	0.6	134.1	0.8	136.7	1.9	137.1	0.3	137.6	0.4	139.4	1.3	138.5	-0.6	132.2	-4.5
1992	132.6	0.3	132.6	0.0	133.5	0.7	134.2	0.5	134.2	0.0	134.2	0.0	134.9	0.5	134.4	-0.4	135.0	0.4	135.6	0.4	135.3	-0.2	136.2	0.7
1993	136.5	0.2	135.8	-0.5	136.6	0.6	136.3	-0.2	134.8	-1.1	134.2	-0.4	134.9	0.5	135.6	0.5	136.2	0.4	137.9	1.2	138.9	0.7	138.8	-0.1
1994	139.2	0.3	137.9	-0.9	138.5	0.4	138.8	0.2	139.1	0.2	137.1	-1.4	137.4	0.2	135.8	-1.2	134.2	-1.2	137.2	2.2	137.4	0.1	137.5	0.1
1995	141.7	3.1	141.9	0.1	142.1	0.1	143.2	0.8	142.4	-0.6	141.3	-0.8	140.9	-0.3	140.3	-0.4	141.0	0.5	142.7	1.2	144.3	1.1	143.3	-0.7
1996	146.0	1.9	146.0	0.0	147.1	0.8	146.6	-0.3	145.1	-1.0	145.3	0.1	145.5	0.1	144.5	-0.7	145.2	0.5	144.5	-0.5	146.2	1.2	147.6	1.0
1997	147.9	0.2	147.1	-0.5	148.2	0.7	148.1	-0.1	147.8	-0.2	146.7	-0.7	146.9	0.1	146.9	0.0	147.1	0.1	146.8	-0.2	146.7	-0.1	148.0	0.9

Source: U.S. Department of Labor, Bureau of Labor Statistics, Division of Consumer Prices and Price Indexes. - indicates no data collected for period.

Los Angeles, CA
Consumer Price Index - All Urban Consumers
Base 1982-1984 = 100
Other Goods and Services

For 1976-1997. Columns headed % show percentile change in the index from the previous period for which an index is available.

Year	Jan Index	%	Feb Index	%	Mar Index	%	Apr Index	%	May Index	%	Jun Index	%	Jul Index	%	Aug Index	%	Sep Index	%	Oct Index	%	Nov Index	%	Dec Index	%
1976	55.9	-	55.9	0.0	56.5	1.1	56.6	0.2	56.8	0.4	57.3	0.9	57.4	0.2	57.4	0.0	57.8	0.7	58.3	0.9	58.9	1.0	59.2	0.5
1977	59.3	0.2	59.5	0.3	59.7	0.3	59.8	0.2	59.7	-0.2	60.1	0.7	60.3	0.3	60.3	0.0	61.5	2.0	62.1	1.0	62.0	-0.2	62.5	0.8
1978	63.4	1.4	63.6	0.3	63.4	-0.3	63.9	0.8	63.9	0.0	64.9	1.6	65.0	0.2	65.5	0.8	67.0	2.3	66.9	-0.1	66.8	-0.1	66.7	-0.1
1979	67.3	0.9	68.1	1.2	67.8	-0.4	68.5	1.0	68.0	-0.7	68.2	0.3	68.9	1.0	69.9	1.5	71.1	1.7	71.3	0.3	70.5	-1.1	71.3	1.1
1980	72.5	1.7	74.6	2.9	74.5	-0.1	75.6	1.5	76.0	0.5	76.1	0.1	76.1	0.0	76.4	0.4	78.2	2.4	78.5	0.4	78.6	0.1	79.3	0.9
1981	79.4	0.1	80.0	0.8	81.1	1.4	82.4	1.6	82.8	0.5	84.1	1.6	84.5	0.5	85.5	1.2	86.4	1.1	86.6	0.2	87.2	0.7	87.1	-0.1
1982	87.6	0.6	89.1	1.7	90.2	1.2	91.1	1.0	90.0	-1.2	90.3	0.3	91.5	1.3	92.1	0.7	92.9	0.9	94.8	2.0	97.2	2.5	97.8	0.6
1983	98.8	1.0	100.0	1.2	100.4	0.4	100.4	0.0	100.6	0.2	100.7	0.1	101.7	1.0	101.5	-0.2	102.1	0.6	102.6	0.5	102.6	0.0	102.5	-0.1
1984	103.3	0.8	103.9	0.6	103.8	-0.1	104.0	0.2	103.4	-0.6	103.3	-0.1	105.2	1.8	105.2	0.0	112.4	6.8	112.4	0.0	112.4	0.0	112.2	-0.2
1985	112.3	0.1	113.6	1.2	114.2	0.5	114.0	-0.2	113.9	-0.1	115.0	1.0	115.2	0.2	115.8	0.5	116.5	0.6	117.4	-0.8	117.2	-0.2	118.1	0.8
1986	120.4	1.9	121.0	0.5	120.6	-0.3	121.4	0.7	121.7	0.2	122.3	0.5	121.2	-0.9	122.8	1.3	123.8	0.8	124.4	0.5	124.0	-0.3	123.3	-0.6
1987	124.1	0.6	124.9	0.6	125.0	0.1	125.4	0.3	126.4	0.8	126.6	0.2	126.7	0.1	127.4	0.6	131.4	3.1	131.5	0.1	132.0	0.4	133.4	1.1
1988	134.0	0.4	136.1	1.6	137.6	1.1	138.3	0.5	137.7	-0.4	138.3	0.4	139.0	0.5	139.9	0.6	143.4	2.5	144.6	0.8	144.8	0.1	145.1	0.2
1989	151.5	4.4	152.9	0.9	152.6	-0.2	152.9	0.2	152.6	-0.2	152.9	0.2	153.6	0.5	155.3	1.1	159.8	2.9	159.5	-0.2	158.8	-0.4	160.9	1.3
1990	161.6	0.4	163.3	1.1	162.5	-0.5	164.4	1.2	165.1	0.4	165.7	0.4	165.2	-0.3	165.9	0.4	169.2	2.0	170.3	0.7	170.7	0.2	171.6	0.5
1991	173.9	1.3	174.2	0.2	175.2	0.6	176.1	0.5	176.3	0.1	176.7	0.2	177.6	0.5	179.0	0.8	186.9	4.4	187.8	0.5	187.3	-0.3	188.2	0.5
1992	189.9	0.9	190.6	0.4	190.3	-0.2	195.7	2.8	195.6	-0.1	195.9	0.2	195.8	-0.1	195.8	0.0	199.3	1.8	204.3	2.5	205.6	0.6	206.4	0.4
1993	209.7	1.6	209.7	0.0	209.7	0.0	210.7	0.5	210.8	0.0	211.0	0.1	212.4	0.7	210.9	-0.7	213.2	1.1	213.3	0.0	215.4	1.0	216.2	0.4
1994	216.1	-0.0	216.7	0.3	216.1	-0.3	217.1	0.5	216.8	-0.1	217.0	0.1	217.2	0.1	217.7	0.2	219.7	0.9	220.9	0.5	220.3	-0.3	220.7	0.2
1995	222.1	0.6	224.3	1.0	222.8	-0.7	223.7	0.4	224.8	0.5	224.8	0.0	225.3	0.2	227.2	0.8	228.1	0.4	227.7	-0.2	228.4	0.3	228.5	0.0
1996	228.9	0.2	229.8	0.4	230.1	0.1	231.0	0.4	229.8	-0.5	231.7	0.8	232.2	0.2	231.1	-0.5	235.4	1.9	238.2	1.2	239.1	0.4	236.8	-1.0
1997	238.2	0.6	239.7	0.6	239.0	-0.3	240.2	0.5	239.7	-0.2	238.0	-0.7	238.1	0.0	240.9	1.2	242.2	0.5	245.1	1.2	243.0	-0.9	244.3	0.5

Source: U.S. Department of Labor, Bureau of Labor Statistics, Division of Consumer Prices and Price Indexes. - indicates no data collected for period.

Los Angeles, CA
Consumer Price Index - Urban Wage Earners
Base 1982-1984 = 100
Other Goods and Services

For 1976-1997. Columns headed % show percentile change in the index from the previous period for which an index is available.

Year	Jan Index	%	Feb Index	%	Mar Index	%	Apr Index	%	May Index	%	Jun Index	%	Jul Index	%	Aug Index	%	Sep Index	%	Oct Index	%	Nov Index	%	Dec Index	%
1976	55.6	-	55.6	0.0	56.2	1.1	56.3	0.2	56.4	0.2	57.0	1.1	57.1	0.2	57.1	0.0	57.4	0.5	57.9	0.9	58.6	1.2	58.8	0.3
1977	59.0	0.3	59.1	0.2	59.3	0.3	59.4	0.2	59.4	0.0	59.7	0.5	59.9	0.3	59.9	0.0	61.1	2.0	61.7	1.0	61.6	-0.2	62.1	0.8
1978	62.7	1.0	63.2	0.8	63.4	0.3	62.9	-0.8	63.3	0.6	64.0	1.1	64.8	1.3	64.9	0.2	65.6	1.1	65.8	0.3	65.6	-0.3	65.3	-0.5
1979	66.7	2.1	67.3	0.9	67.4	0.1	67.8	0.6	68.0	0.3	68.1	0.1	68.7	0.9	69.2	0.7	69.9	1.0	70.1	0.3	69.6	-0.7	70.6	1.4
1980	72.2	2.3	73.5	1.8	73.6	0.1	74.5	1.2	75.3	1.1	74.6	-0.9	74.6	0.0	75.5	1.2	77.2	2.3	77.1	-0.1	77.3	0.3	78.6	1.7
1981	79.4	1.0	79.9	0.6	80.1	0.3	81.8	2.1	81.9	0.1	82.6	0.9	82.9	0.4	83.8	1.1	85.3	1.8	84.9	-0.5	85.7	0.9	86.3	0.7
1982	86.8	0.6	88.4	1.8	89.6	1.4	90.7	1.2	89.5	-1.3	89.9	0.4	91.1	1.3	91.8	0.8	92.5	0.8	94.6	2.3	97.1	2.6	97.8	0.7
1983	99.0	1.2	100.3	1.3	100.8	0.5	100.8	0.0	101.0	0.2	101.2	0.2	102.3	1.1	102.2	-0.1	102.8	0.6	103.2	0.4	103.3	0.1	103.0	-0.3
1984	103.9	0.9	104.6	0.7	104.5	-0.1	104.7	0.2	104.0	-0.7	103.9	-0.1	105.9	1.9	105.9	0.0	110.8	4.6	110.9	0.1	110.9	0.0	110.6	-0.3
1985	110.7	0.1	112.1	1.3	112.8	0.6	112.6	-0.2	112.5	-0.1	113.4	0.8	113.3	-0.1	114.2	0.8	114.8	0.5	115.8	0.9	115.5	-0.3	116.5	0.9
1986	118.9	2.1	119.6	0.6	119.1	-0.4	119.9	0.7	120.2	0.3	120.7	0.4	119.7	-0.8	121.4	1.4	122.1	0.6	122.7	0.5	122.4	-0.2	121.7	-0.6
1987	122.7	0.8	123.6	0.7	123.8	0.2	124.1	0.2	125.0	0.7	125.2	0.2	125.3	0.1	126.0	0.6	129.8	3.0	129.9	0.1	130.4	0.4	131.1	0.5
1988	131.9	0.6	133.6	1.3	135.1	1.1	135.9	0.6	135.1	-0.6	135.8	0.5	136.7	0.7	137.5	0.6	141.1	2.6	142.6	1.1	142.7	0.1	143.1	0.3
1989	151.0	5.5	152.7	1.1	152.4	-0.2	152.7	0.2	152.3	-0.3	152.5	0.1	153.4	0.6	155.3	1.2	159.4	2.6	159.0	-0.3	158.0	-0.6	160.5	1.6
1990	161.1	0.4	163.0	1.2	162.3	-0.4	164.3	1.2	164.9	0.4	165.8	0.5	165.3	-0.3	166.1	0.5	168.9	1.7	169.7	0.5	170.2	0.3	171.2	0.6
1991	173.7	1.5	173.8	0.1	174.8	0.6	175.6	0.5	175.9	0.2	176.5	0.3	177.6	0.6	179.3	1.0	184.8	3.1	185.4	0.3	185.2	-0.1	186.2	0.5
1992	188.1	1.0	189.1	0.5	188.5	-0.3	193.3	2.5	193.3	0.0	193.8	0.3	193.8	0.0	193.4	-0.2	195.8	1.2	199.0	1.6	200.4	0.7	201.5	0.5
1993	203.9	1.2	204.0	0.0	204.0	0.0	205.2	0.6	205.2	0.0	205.8	0.3	207.5	0.8	205.0	-1.2	202.1	-1.4	202.2	0.0	204.8	1.3	205.9	0.5
1994	205.8	-0.0	206.9	0.5	206.0	-0.4	207.3	0.6	206.9	-0.2	206.6	-0.1	206.8	0.1	206.8	0.0	208.0	0.6	209.4	0.7	208.6	-0.4	209.2	0.3
1995	210.6	0.7	212.6	0.9	211.4	-0.6	212.1	0.3	213.1	0.5	213.2	0.0	213.8	0.3	215.3	0.7	216.3	0.5	215.7	-0.3	216.6	0.4	216.6	0.0
1996	217.0	0.2	218.0	0.5	218.3	0.1	219.0	0.3	217.3	-0.8	219.6	1.1	220.4	0.4	218.5	-0.9	221.5	1.4	225.0	1.6	226.2	0.5	223.7	-1.1
1997	225.2	0.7	227.0	0.8	225.8	-0.5	227.4	0.7	226.8	-0.3	224.6	-1.0	224.6	0.0	227.7	1.4	228.2	0.2	231.4	1.4	228.7	-1.2	230.5	0.8

Source: U.S. Department of Labor, Bureau of Labor Statistics, Division of Consumer Prices and Price Indexes. - indicates no data collected for period.

Miami, FL
Consumer Price Index - All Urban Consumers
Base 1982-1984 = 100
Annual Averages

For 1977-1997. Columns headed % show percentile change in the index from the previous period for which an index is available.

Year	All Items		Food & Beverage		Housing		Apparel & Upkeep		Trans-portation		Medical Care		Entertain-ment		Other Goods & Services	
	Index	%	Index	%	Index	%	Index	%	Index	%	Index	%	Index	%	Index	%
1977	-	-	-	-	-	-	-	-	-	-	-	-	-	-	-	-
1978	64.8	-	69.8	-	62.9	-	77.6	-	59.6	-	61.4	-	80.2	-	63.7	-
1979	71.2	9.9	78.6	12.6	68.5	8.9	81.2	4.6	67.1	12.6	68.9	12.2	85.0	6.0	69.1	8.5
1980	81.1	13.9	84.7	7.8	80.8	18.0	87.0	7.1	78.5	17.0	75.6	9.7	89.6	5.4	76.2	10.3
1981	90.5	11.6	91.3	7.8	92.0	13.9	91.9	5.6	88.8	13.1	81.9	8.3	95.1	6.1	84.7	11.2
1982	96.7	6.9	96.8	6.0	97.8	6.3	98.2	6.9	94.8	6.8	93.8	14.5	98.4	3.5	93.1	9.9
1983	99.9	3.3	99.5	2.8	99.7	1.9	100.1	1.9	100.2	5.7	101.0	7.7	100.4	2.0	100.0	7.4
1984	103.5	3.6	103.6	4.1	102.6	2.9	101.7	1.6	105.0	4.8	105.1	4.1	101.3	0.9	106.9	6.9
1985	106.5	2.9	104.4	0.8	105.7	3.0	105.7	3.9	108.3	3.1	109.2	3.9	104.5	3.2	113.3	6.0
1986	107.9	1.3	107.1	2.6	107.0	1.2	109.0	3.1	103.7	-4.2	117.4	7.5	107.9	3.3	121.8	7.5
1987	111.8	3.6	113.0	5.5	108.7	1.6	115.6	6.1	106.6	2.8	126.6	7.8	113.7	5.4	128.3	5.3
1988	116.8	4.5	118.7	5.0	113.1	4.0	123.5	6.8	110.7	3.8	134.6	6.3	115.9	1.9	133.6	4.1
1989	121.5	4.0	125.6	5.8	116.2	2.7	131.3	6.3	114.8	3.7	140.5	4.4	117.8	1.6	139.8	4.6
1990	128.0	5.3	134.3	6.9	120.4	3.6	135.6	3.3	121.6	5.9	151.8	8.0	121.0	2.7	153.2	9.6
1991	132.3	3.4	137.7	2.5	123.7	2.7	140.4	3.5	126.0	3.6	162.8	7.2	126.4	4.5	161.5	5.4
1992	134.5	1.7	140.6	2.1	126.2	2.0	138.8	-1.1	127.8	1.4	172.3	5.8	124.6	-1.4	160.5	-0.6
1993	139.1	3.4	146.9	4.5	130.4	3.3	140.1	0.9	131.9	3.2	181.9	5.6	129.5	3.9	162.5	1.2
1994	143.6	3.2	152.7	3.9	135.2	3.7	143.5	2.4	135.3	2.6	188.1	3.4	134.4	3.8	162.8	0.2
1995	148.9	3.7	157.1	2.9	139.9	3.5	147.0	2.4	139.8	3.3	203.0	7.9	140.4	4.5	169.7	4.2
1996	153.7	3.2	161.4	2.7	145.1	3.7	146.0	-0.7	144.3	3.2	214.4	5.6	146.1	4.1	175.0	3.1
1997	-	-	-	-	-	-	-	-	-	-	-	-	-	-	-	-

Source: U.S. Department of Labor, Bureau of Labor Statistics, Division of Consumer Prices and Price Indexes. - indicates no data collected for period.

Miami, FL
Consumer Price Index - Urban Wage Earners
Base 1982-1984 = 100
Annual Averages

For 1977-1997. Columns headed % show percentile change in the index from the previous period for which an index is available.

Year	All Items		Food & Beverage		Housing		Apparel & Upkeep		Trans- portation		Medical Care		Entertain- ment		Other Goods & Services	
	Index	%	Index	%	Index	%	Index	%	Index	%	Index	%	Index	%	Index	%
1977	-	-	-	-	-	-	-	-	-	-	-	-	-	-	-	-
1978	64.5	-	68.6	-	62.9	-	76.0	-	59.4	-	61.9	-	75.7	-	66.0	-
1979	71.3	10.5	78.3	14.1	68.3	8.6	80.2	5.5	67.5	13.6	67.8	9.5	81.4	7.5	71.3	8.0
1980	81.4	14.2	85.4	9.1	80.4	17.7	86.7	8.1	79.5	17.8	74.3	9.6	88.1	8.2	77.3	8.4
1981	90.5	11.2	91.6	7.3	92.1	14.6	91.7	5.8	89.6	12.7	79.8	7.4	94.6	7.4	84.4	9.2
1982	96.8	7.0	96.9	5.8	98.1	6.5	97.8	6.7	94.9	5.9	93.7	17.4	98.5	4.1	93.1	10.3
1983	99.9	3.2	99.5	2.7	99.6	1.5	100.0	2.2	100.3	5.7	101.3	8.1	100.5	2.0	100.1	7.5
1984	103.3	3.4	103.6	4.1	102.2	2.6	102.2	2.2	104.8	4.5	105.0	3.7	101.0	0.5	106.9	6.8
1985	106.4	3.0	104.3	0.7	106.0	3.7	106.0	3.7	107.9	3.0	108.7	3.5	105.2	4.2	112.4	5.1
1986	107.4	0.9	107.5	3.1	107.3	1.2	109.6	3.4	102.3	-5.2	116.6	7.3	108.4	3.0	120.8	7.5
1987	111.1	3.4	113.0	5.1	109.0	1.6	115.7	5.6	105.1	2.7	125.8	7.9	114.3	5.4	126.8	5.0
1988	115.9	4.3	118.5	4.9	113.4	4.0	122.8	6.1	109.0	3.7	133.1	5.8	116.2	1.7	132.6	4.6
1989	120.3	3.8	126.3	6.6	116.2	2.5	129.7	5.6	112.6	3.3	139.0	4.4	118.8	2.2	138.9	4.8
1990	126.2	4.9	134.8	6.7	120.2	3.4	133.3	2.8	118.3	5.1	150.7	8.4	122.1	2.8	151.5	9.1
1991	130.4	3.3	137.8	2.2	123.3	2.6	139.7	4.8	122.6	3.6	161.7	7.3	127.6	4.5	159.7	5.4
1992	132.6	1.7	139.7	1.4	125.7	1.9	138.3	-1.0	125.3	2.2	171.5	6.1	125.5	-1.6	157.7	-1.3
1993	137.3	3.5	145.8	4.4	129.8	3.3	140.8	1.8	130.1	3.8	181.0	5.5	130.2	3.7	159.0	0.8
1994	141.5	3.1	151.3	3.8	134.4	3.5	145.5	3.3	133.5	2.6	185.5	2.5	135.1	3.8	157.2	-1.1
1995	146.9	3.8	155.7	2.9	139.2	3.6	149.4	2.7	138.9	4.0	200.0	7.8	141.9	5.0	163.4	3.9
1996	151.8	3.3	160.5	3.1	144.5	3.8	147.9	-1.0	143.2	3.1	211.7	5.8	148.4	4.6	167.7	2.6
1997	-	-	-	-	-	-	-	-	-	-	-	-	-	-	-	-

Source: U.S. Department of Labor, Bureau of Labor Statistics, Division of Consumer Prices and Price Indexes. - indicates no data collected for period.

Miami, FL
Consumer Price Index - All Urban Consumers
Base 1982-1984 = 100
All Items

For 1977-1997. Columns headed % show percentile change in the index from the previous period for which an index is available.

Year	Jan Index	%	Feb Index	%	Mar Index	%	Apr Index	%	May Index	%	Jun Index	%	Jul Index	%	Aug Index	%	Sep Index	%	Oct Index	%	Nov Index	%	Dec Index	%
1977	-	-	-	-	-	-	-	-	-	-	-	-	-	-	-	-	-	-	-	-	62.0	-	-	-
1978	62.5	0.8	-	-	63.4	1.4	-	-	63.8	0.6	-	-	65.1	2.0	-	-	66.1	1.5	-	-	66.6	0.8	-	-
1979	67.6	1.5	-	-	69.0	2.1	-	-	69.8	1.2	-	-	71.8	2.9	-	-	72.8	1.4	-	-	74.1	1.8	-	-
1980	76.5	3.2	-	-	79.2	3.5	-	-	80.5	1.6	-	-	82.9	3.0	-	-	82.6	-0.4	-	-	83.1	0.6	-	-
1981	85.2	2.5	-	-	86.9	2.0	-	-	88.8	2.2	-	-	90.6	2.0	-	-	93.2	2.9	-	-	95.3	2.3	-	-
1982	96.3	1.0	-	-	96.2	-0.1	-	-	96.6	0.4	-	-	96.2	-0.4	-	-	96.8	0.6	-	-	97.3	0.5	-	-
1983	98.0	0.7	-	-	98.6	0.6	-	-	98.9	0.3	-	-	99.8	0.9	-	-	101.1	1.3	-	-	101.7	0.6	-	-
1984	102.4	0.7	-	-	102.7	0.3	-	-	103.2	0.5	-	-	103.6	0.4	-	-	104.2	0.6	-	-	104.4	0.2	-	-
1985	104.6	0.2	-	-	105.5	0.9	-	-	106.1	0.6	-	-	106.3	0.2	-	-	107.6	1.2	-	-	107.9	0.3	-	-
1986	108.3	0.4	-	-	108.3	0.0	-	-	107.3	-0.9	-	-	106.2	-1.0	-	-	108.1	1.8	-	-	109.1	0.9	-	-
1987	109.9	0.7	-	-	110.7	0.7	-	-	111.1	0.4	-	-	112.0	0.8	-	-	112.5	0.4	-	-	113.8	1.2	-	-
1988	114.5	0.6	-	-	115.1	0.5	-	-	116.2	1.0	-	-	116.8	0.5	-	-	118.8	1.7	-	-	118.3	-0.4	-	-
1989	120.0	1.4	-	-	119.8	-0.2	-	-	120.9	0.9	-	-	121.6	0.6	-	-	122.9	1.1	-	-	123.0	0.1	-	-
1990	124.6	1.3	-	-	125.1	0.4	-	-	126.4	1.0	-	-	128.7	1.8	-	-	130.1	1.1	-	-	131.2	0.8	-	-
1991	131.5	0.2	-	-	132.0	0.4	-	-	132.0	0.0	-	-	132.0	0.0	-	-	132.1	0.1	-	-	133.5	1.1	-	-
1992	133.7	0.1	-	-	134.5	0.6	-	-	133.7	-0.6	-	-	133.8	0.1	-	-	134.6	0.6	-	-	135.9	1.0	-	-
1993	137.8	1.4	-	-	139.2	1.0	-	-	139.0	-0.1	-	-	139.0	0.0	-	-	139.2	0.1	-	-	139.8	0.4	-	-
1994	141.0	0.9	-	-	143.5	1.8	-	-	143.3	-0.1	-	-	143.4	0.1	-	-	144.5	0.8	-	-	144.5	0.0	-	-
1995	147.3	1.9	-	-	148.7	1.0	-	-	148.6	-0.1	-	-	148.3	-0.2	-	-	148.9	0.4	-	-	150.2	0.9	-	-
1996	152.0	1.2	-	-	152.4	0.3	-	-	152.6	0.1	-	-	152.4	-0.1	-	-	154.6	1.4	-	-	156.4	1.2	-	-
1997	158.1	1.1	-	-	158.5	0.3	-	-	157.9	-0.4	158.2	0.2	157.9	-0.2	-	-	158.5	0.4	-	-	159.5	0.6	-	-

Source: U.S. Department of Labor, Bureau of Labor Statistics, Division of Consumer Prices and Price Indexes. - indicates no data collected for period.

Miami, FL
Consumer Price Index - Urban Wage Earners
Base 1982-1984 = 100
All Items

For 1977-1997. Columns headed % show percentile change in the index from the previous period for which an index is available.

Year	Jan Index	%	Feb Index	%	Mar Index	%	Apr Index	%	May Index	%	Jun Index	%	Jul Index	%	Aug Index	%	Sep Index	%	Oct Index	%	Nov Index	%	Dec Index	%
1977	-		-	-			-	-	-				-		-	-	-		-	-	61.6	-	-	-
1978	61.9	0.5	-	-	63.0	1.8	-	-	63.6	1.0	-	-	65.0	2.2	-	-	65.9	1.4	-	-	66.4	0.8	-	-
1979	67.2	1.2	-	-	69.2	3.0	-	-	70.0	1.2	-	-	72.0	2.9	-	-	73.1	1.5	-	-	74.2	1.5	-	-
1980	76.9	3.6	-	-	79.3	3.1	-	-	80.6	1.6	-	-	82.9	2.9	-	-	83.0	0.1	-	-	83.5	0.6	-	-
1981	85.4	2.3	-	-	87.2	2.1	-	-	89.1	2.2	-	-	90.7	1.8	-	-	92.9	2.4	-	-	95.2	2.5	-	-
1982	96.3	1.2	-	-	96.3	0.0	-	-	96.6	0.3	-	-	96.6	0.0	-	-	96.9	0.3	-	-	97.3	0.4	-	-
1983	98.0	0.7	-	-	98.3	0.3	-	-	99.3	1.0	-	-	100.2	0.9	-	-	101.1	0.9	-	-	101.5	0.4	-	-
1984	102.1	0.6	-	-	102.4	0.3	-	-	102.9	0.5	-	-	103.4	0.5	-	-	104.5	1.1	-	-	104.4	-0.1	-	-
1985	104.5	0.1	-	-	105.4	0.9	-	-	106.0	0.6	-	-	106.3	0.3	-	-	107.4	1.0	-	-	107.7	0.3	-	-
1986	108.1	0.4	-	-	107.8	-0.3	-	-	106.7	-1.0	-	-	105.6	-1.0	-	-	107.4	1.7	-	-	108.4	0.9	-	-
1987	109.3	0.8	-	-	109.9	0.5	-	-	110.3	0.4	-	-	111.3	0.9	-	-	111.8	0.4	-	-	113.1	1.2	-	-
1988	113.8	0.6	-	-	114.3	0.4	-	-	115.1	0.7	-	-	116.0	0.8	-	-	117.8	1.6	-	-	117.2	-0.5	-	-
1989	118.8	1.4	-	-	118.7	-0.1	-	-	120.0	1.1	-	-	120.6	0.5	-	-	121.4	0.7	-	-	121.5	0.1	-	-
1990	123.2	1.4	-	-	123.4	0.2	-	-	124.6	1.0	-	-	126.7	1.7	-	-	128.2	1.2	-	-	129.3	0.9	-	-
1991	129.8	0.4	-	-	130.1	0.2	-	-	130.2	0.1	-	-	130.2	0.0	-	-	130.2	0.0	-	-	131.4	0.9	-	-
1992	131.7	0.2	-	-	132.3	0.5	-	-	131.6	-0.5	-	-	132.0	0.3	-	-	132.8	0.6	-	-	134.2	1.1	-	-
1993	135.9	1.3	-	-	137.1	0.9	-	-	137.2	0.1	-	-	137.2	0.0	-	-	137.5	0.2	-	-	138.0	0.4	-	-
1994	138.7	0.5	-	-	141.1	1.7	-	-	141.2	0.1	-	-	141.4	0.1	-	-	142.5	0.8	-	-	142.7	0.1	-	-
1995	145.3	1.8	-	-	146.6	0.9	-	-	146.8	0.1	-	-	146.5	-0.2	-	-	146.9	0.3	-	-	148.2	0.9	-	-
1996	150.0	1.2	-	-	150.3	0.2	-	-	151.0	0.5	-	-	150.8	-0.1	-	-	152.6	1.2	-	-	154.6	1.3	-	-
1997	156.0	0.9	-	-	156.2	0.1	-	-	155.6	-0.4	155.9	0.2	155.5	-0.3	-	-	156.1	0.4	-	-	157.0	0.6	-	-

Source: U.S. Department of Labor, Bureau of Labor Statistics, Division of Consumer Prices and Price Indexes. - indicates no data collected for period.

Miami, FL
Consumer Price Index - All Urban Consumers
Base 1982-1984 = 100
Food and Beverages

For 1977-1997. Columns headed % show percentile change in the index from the previous period for which an index is available.

Year	Jan Index	%	Feb Index	%	Mar Index	%	Apr Index	%	May Index	%	Jun Index	%	Jul Index	%	Aug Index	%	Sep Index	%	Oct Index	%	Nov Index	%	Dec Index	%
1977	-	-	-	-	-	-	-	-	-	-	-	-	-	-	-	-	-	-	-	-	65.1	-	-	-
1978	65.9	1.2	-	-	67.5	2.4	-	-	69.2	2.5	-	-	71.0	2.6	-	-	71.1	0.1	-	-	72.1	1.4	-	-
1979	74.9	3.9	-	-	76.9	2.7	-	-	78.3	1.8	-	-	79.9	2.0	-	-	80.2	0.4	-	-	80.1	-0.1	-	-
1980	81.4	1.6	-	-	82.0	0.7	-	-	82.7	0.9	-	-	84.8	2.5	-	-	87.2	2.8	-	-	88.3	1.3	-	-
1981	89.4	1.2	-	-	89.6	0.2	-	-	89.8	0.2	-	-	91.1	1.4	-	-	92.8	1.9	-	-	93.9	1.2	-	-
1982	94.9	1.1	-	-	95.8	0.9	-	-	96.9	1.1	-	-	97.8	0.9	-	-	97.8	0.0	-	-	97.0	-0.8	-	-
1983	97.9	0.9	-	-	98.9	1.0	-	-	99.1	0.2	-	-	99.0	-0.1	-	-	100.2	1.2	-	-	100.8	0.6	-	-
1984	104.0	3.2	-	-	104.2	0.2	-	-	102.6	-1.5	-	-	103.2	0.6	-	-	103.5	0.3	-	-	104.3	0.8	-	-
1985	104.1	-0.2	-	-	105.2	1.1	-	-	103.5	-1.6	-	-	104.4	0.9	-	-	104.1	-0.3	-	-	104.7	0.6	-	-
1986	106.3	1.5	-	-	106.9	0.6	-	-	106.9	0.0	-	-	103.1	-3.6	-	-	108.3	5.0	-	-	110.0	1.6	-	-
1987	110.7	0.6	-	-	112.2	1.4	-	-	113.9	1.5	-	-	113.6	-0.3	-	-	113.4	-0.2	-	-	113.5	0.1	-	-
1988	114.8	1.1	-	-	116.9	1.8	-	-	117.6	0.6	-	-	118.4	0.7	-	-	121.1	2.3	-	-	121.7	0.5	-	-
1989	122.3	0.5	-	-	123.0	0.6	-	-	124.0	0.8	-	-	126.7	2.2	-	-	126.4	-0.2	-	-	128.5	1.7	-	-
1990	134.1	4.4	-	-	134.1	0.0	-	-	132.4	-1.3	-	-	134.2	1.4	-	-	134.4	0.1	-	-	136.1	1.3	-	-
1991	136.0	-0.1	-	-	137.7	1.2	-	-	137.7	0.0	-	-	138.0	0.2	-	-	138.2	0.1	-	-	138.1	-0.1	-	-
1992	138.7	0.4	-	-	140.5	1.3	-	-	138.9	-1.1	-	-	139.9	0.7	-	-	142.0	1.5	-	-	142.2	0.1	-	-
1993	144.9	1.9	-	-	145.7	0.6	-	-	146.1	0.3	-	-	145.9	-0.1	-	-	147.6	1.2	-	-	149.3	1.2	-	-
1994	151.8	1.7	-	-	151.7	-0.1	-	-	152.1	0.3	-	-	152.3	0.1	-	-	152.8	0.3	-	-	154.6	1.2	-	-
1995	156.2	1.0	-	-	156.4	0.1	-	-	157.0	0.4	-	-	156.8	-0.1	-	-	157.6	0.5	-	-	157.9	0.2	-	-
1996	158.9	0.6	-	-	159.2	0.2	-	-	159.4	0.1	-	-	161.6	1.4	-	-	163.6	1.2	-	-	164.4	0.5	-	-
1997	163.9	-0.3	-	-	165.3	0.9	-	-	166.0	0.4	165.3	-0.4	166.2	0.5	-	-	165.6	-0.4	-	-	166.5	0.5	-	-

Source: U.S. Department of Labor, Bureau of Labor Statistics, Division of Consumer Prices and Price Indexes. - indicates no data collected for period.

Miami, FL
Consumer Price Index - Urban Wage Earners
Base 1982-1984 = 100
Food and Beverages

For 1977-1997. Columns headed % show percentile change in the index from the previous period for which an index is available.

Year	Jan Index	%	Feb Index	%	Mar Index	%	Apr Index	%	May Index	%	Jun Index	%	Jul Index	%	Aug Index	%	Sep Index	%	Oct Index	%	Nov Index	%	Dec Index	%
1977	-	-	-	-	-	-	-	-	68.2	-	-	-	-	-	-	-	-	-	-	-	63.0	-	-	-
1978	63.5	0.8	-	-	66.1	4.1	-	-	68.2	3.2	-	-	69.8	2.3	-	-	70.5	1.0	-	-	71.5	1.4	-	-
1979	73.1	2.2	-	-	77.1	5.5	-	-	78.2	1.4	-	-	79.3	1.4	-	-	79.7	0.5	-	-	80.2	0.6	-	-
1980	81.8	2.0	-	-	82.7	1.1	-	-	83.7	1.2	-	-	85.5	2.2	-	-	88.1	3.0	-	-	88.5	0.5	-	-
1981	89.5	1.1	-	-	89.8	0.3	-	-	90.0	0.2	-	-	91.8	2.0	-	-	93.8	2.2	-	-	93.6	-0.2	-	-
1982	94.7	1.2	-	-	95.6	1.0	-	-	97.0	1.5	-	-	98.2	1.2	-	-	98.2	0.0	-	-	97.0	-1.2	-	-
1983	97.8	0.8	-	-	99.0	1.2	-	-	99.2	0.2	-	-	99.2	0.0	-	-	100.2	1.0	-	-	100.5	0.3	-	-
1984	103.8	3.3	-	-	104.0	0.2	-	-	102.6	-1.3	-	-	103.1	0.5	-	-	103.6	0.5	-	-	104.3	0.7	-	-
1985	103.9	-0.4	-	-	105.1	1.2	-	-	103.4	-1.6	-	-	104.3	0.9	-	-	104.0	-0.3	-	-	104.6	0.6	-	-
1986	106.3	1.6	-	-	107.0	0.7	-	-	107.2	0.2	-	-	104.2	-2.8	-	-	108.7	4.3	-	-	110.4	1.6	-	-
1987	111.4	0.9	-	-	112.4	0.9	-	-	113.8	1.2	-	-	113.6	-0.2	-	-	113.1	-0.4	-	-	113.1	0.0	-	-
1988	114.2	1.0	-	-	116.5	2.0	-	-	116.9	0.3	-	-	118.2	1.1	-	-	121.4	2.7	-	-	121.9	0.4	-	-
1989	122.7	0.7	-	-	123.5	0.7	-	-	124.9	1.1	-	-	127.5	2.1	-	-	126.9	-0.5	-	-	128.9	1.6	-	-
1990	135.5	5.1	-	-	135.7	0.1	-	-	132.8	-2.1	-	-	134.1	1.0	-	-	134.2	0.1	-	-	136.4	1.6	-	-
1991	136.3	-0.1	-	-	138.1	1.3	-	-	138.2	0.1	-	-	138.4	0.1	-	-	138.0	-0.3	-	-	137.3	-0.5	-	-
1992	138.0	0.5	-	-	139.9	1.4	-	-	137.9	-1.4	-	-	138.7	0.6	-	-	141.2	1.8	-	-	141.0	-0.1	-	-
1993	143.7	1.9	-	-	144.8	0.8	-	-	145.2	0.3	-	-	144.5	-0.5	-	-	146.4	1.3	-	-	148.5	1.4	-	-
1994	150.1	1.1	-	-	150.5	0.3	-	-	151.1	0.4	-	-	150.8	-0.2	-	-	151.3	0.3	-	-	152.5	0.8	-	-
1995	155.1	1.7	-	-	155.1	0.0	-	-	155.6	0.3	-	-	155.2	-0.3	-	-	156.0	0.5	-	-	156.4	0.3	-	-
1996	157.4	0.6	-	-	157.8	0.3	-	-	158.4	0.4	-	-	160.9	1.6	-	-	163.1	1.4	-	-	163.9	0.5	-	-
1997	163.0	-0.5	-	-	164.3	0.8	-	-	165.0	0.4	164.3	-0.4	165.0	0.4	-	-	164.6	-0.2	-	-	165.7	0.7	-	-

Source: U.S. Department of Labor, Bureau of Labor Statistics, Division of Consumer Prices and Price Indexes. - indicates no data collected for period.

Miami, FL
Consumer Price Index - All Urban Consumers
Base 1982-1984 = 100
Housing

For 1977-1997. Columns headed % show percentile change in the index from the previous period for which an index is available.

Year	Jan Index	%	Feb Index	%	Mar Index	%	Apr Index	%	May Index	%	Jun Index	%	Jul Index	%	Aug Index	%	Sep Index	%	Oct Index	%	Nov Index	%	Dec Index	%
1977	-	-	-	-	-	-	-	-	-	-	-	-	-	-	-	-	-	-	-	-	60.6	-	-	-
1978	61.0	0.7	-	-	62.0	1.6	-	-	61.7	-0.5	-	-	63.2	2.4	-	-	64.4	1.9	-	-	64.5	0.2	-	-
1979	65.1	0.9	-	-	66.4	2.0	-	-	66.3	-0.2	-	-	68.8	3.8	-	-	69.8	1.5	-	-	71.8	2.9	-	-
1980	74.7	4.0	-	-	78.8	5.5	-	-	80.6	2.3	-	-	84.4	4.7	-	-	82.1	-2.7	-	-	81.9	-0.2	-	-
1981	84.8	3.5	-	-	86.7	2.2	-	-	89.8	3.6	-	-	92.3	2.8	-	-	95.7	3.7	-	-	99.2	3.7	-	-
1982	99.9	0.7	-	-	99.2	-0.7	-	-	98.7	-0.5	-	-	95.8	-2.9	-	-	96.7	0.9	-	-	96.7	0.0	-	-
1983	98.2	1.6	-	-	99.4	1.2	-	-	98.8	-0.6	-	-	99.7	0.9	-	-	100.6	0.9	-	-	100.8	0.2	-	-
1984	101.1	0.3	-	-	101.2	0.1	-	-	102.5	1.3	-	-	102.9	0.4	-	-	103.9	1.0	-	-	103.2	-0.7	-	-
1985	103.7	0.5	-	-	104.0	0.3	-	-	105.2	1.2	-	-	105.2	0.0	-	-	107.9	2.6	-	-	107.2	-0.6	-	-
1986	106.7	-0.5	-	-	107.6	0.8	-	-	106.8	-0.7	-	-	106.0	-0.7	-	-	107.3	1.2	-	-	107.6	0.3	-	-
1987	108.1	0.5	-	-	108.0	-0.1	-	-	106.9	-1.0	-	-	108.3	1.3	-	-	109.3	0.9	-	-	110.8	1.4	-	-
1988	111.8	0.9	-	-	111.1	-0.6	-	-	112.9	1.6	-	-	113.6	0.6	-	-	114.9	1.1	-	-	113.4	-1.3	-	-
1989	115.2	1.6	-	-	115.0	-0.2	-	-	115.2	0.2	-	-	116.5	1.1	-	-	117.9	1.2	-	-	117.2	-0.6	-	-
1990	116.7	-0.4	-	-	116.1	-0.5	-	-	119.6	3.0	-	-	123.3	3.1	-	-	123.1	-0.2	-	-	122.3	-0.6	-	-
1991	122.3	0.0	-	-	122.5	0.2	-	-	123.0	0.4	-	-	124.2	1.0	-	-	123.7	-0.4	-	-	125.4	1.4	-	-
1992	126.0	0.5	-	-	126.6	0.5	-	-	126.2	-0.3	-	-	125.7	-0.4	-	-	125.1	-0.5	-	-	127.0	1.5	-	-
1993	128.5	1.2	-	-	130.3	1.4	-	-	129.8	-0.4	-	-	130.5	0.5	-	-	131.2	0.5	-	-	131.1	-0.1	-	-
1994	133.0	1.4	-	-	134.3	1.0	-	-	134.9	0.4	-	-	135.3	0.3	-	-	136.1	0.6	-	-	136.0	-0.1	-	-
1995	138.5	1.8	-	-	139.1	0.4	-	-	138.4	-0.5	-	-	139.0	0.4	-	-	140.6	1.2	-	-	142.6	1.4	-	-
1996	143.8	0.8	-	-	144.5	0.5	-	-	143.5	-0.7	-	-	144.5	0.7	-	-	145.7	0.8	-	-	147.0	0.9	-	-
1997	149.7	1.8	-	-	150.3	0.4	-	-	149.6	-0.5	149.9	0.2	149.8	-0.1	-	-	149.8	0.0	-	-	151.6	1.2	-	-

Source: U.S. Department of Labor, Bureau of Labor Statistics, Division of Consumer Prices and Price Indexes. - indicates no data collected for period.

Miami, FL
Consumer Price Index - Urban Wage Earners
Base 1982-1984 = 100
Housing

For 1977-1997. Columns headed % show percentile change in the index from the previous period for which an index is available.

Year	Jan Index	%	Feb Index	%	Mar Index	%	Apr Index	%	May Index	%	Jun Index	%	Jul Index	%	Aug Index	%	Sep Index	%	Oct Index	%	Nov Index	%	Dec Index	%
1977	-	-	-	-	-	-	-	-	-	-	-	-	-	-	-	-	-	-	-	-	60.6	-	-	-
1978	60.9	0.5	-	-	62.0	1.8	-	-	61.6	-0.6	-	-	63.2	2.6	-	-	64.2	1.6	-	-	64.4	0.3	-	-
1979	65.1	1.1	-	-	66.3	1.8	-	-	66.3	0.0	-	-	68.7	3.6	-	-	69.7	1.5	-	-	71.5	2.6	-	-
1980	74.4	4.1	-	-	78.3	5.2	-	-	80.0	2.2	-	-	84.1	5.1	-	-	81.7	-2.9	-	-	81.7	0.0	-	-
1981	84.6	3.5	-	-	86.6	2.4	-	-	89.9	3.8	-	-	92.3	2.7	-	-	95.7	3.7	-	-	99.5	4.0	-	-
1982	100.4	0.9	-	-	99.7	-0.7	-	-	99.1	-0.6	-	-	96.0	-3.1	-	-	96.9	0.9	-	-	97.0	0.1	-	-
1983	97.9	0.9	-	-	98.4	0.5	-	-	99.6	1.2	-	-	100.4	0.8	-	-	100.4	0.0	-	-	100.4	0.0	-	-
1984	100.6	0.2	-	-	100.4	-0.2	-	-	101.8	1.4	-	-	102.4	0.6	-	-	104.5	2.1	-	-	103.3	-1.1	-	-
1985	103.9	0.6	-	-	104.4	0.5	-	-	105.6	1.1	-	-	105.6	0.0	-	-	108.2	2.5	-	-	107.5	-0.6	-	-
1986	107.0	-0.5	-	-	107.9	0.8	-	-	107.0	-0.8	-	-	106.1	-0.8	-	-	107.5	1.3	-	-	107.9	0.4	-	-
1987	108.4	0.5	-	-	108.3	-0.1	-	-	107.1	-1.1	-	-	108.6	1.4	-	-	109.5	0.8	-	-	111.1	1.5	-	-
1988	112.2	1.0	-	-	111.4	-0.7	-	-	113.0	1.4	-	-	113.8	0.7	-	-	115.3	1.3	-	-	113.7	-1.4	-	-
1989	115.3	1.4	-	-	114.9	-0.3	-	-	115.4	0.4	-	-	116.7	1.1	-	-	117.7	0.9	-	-	117.1	-0.5	-	-
1990	116.7	-0.3	-	-	116.0	-0.6	-	-	119.3	2.8	-	-	122.9	3.0	-	-	122.8	-0.1	-	-	122.0	-0.7	-	-
1991	122.0	0.0	-	-	122.2	0.2	-	-	122.6	0.3	-	-	123.8	1.0	-	-	123.4	-0.3	-	-	125.0	1.3	-	-
1992	125.6	0.5	-	-	126.2	0.5	-	-	125.6	-0.5	-	-	125.3	-0.2	-	-	124.6	-0.6	-	-	126.5	1.5	-	-
1993	127.9	1.1	-	-	129.6	1.3	-	-	129.3	-0.2	-	-	129.9	0.5	-	-	130.6	0.5	-	-	130.3	-0.2	-	-
1994	132.2	1.5	-	-	133.5	1.0	-	-	134.2	0.5	-	-	134.4	0.1	-	-	135.2	0.6	-	-	135.5	0.2	-	-
1995	137.5	1.5	-	-	138.1	0.4	-	-	137.7	-0.3	-	-	138.3	0.4	-	-	140.0	1.2	-	-	142.0	1.4	-	-
1996	143.1	0.8	-	-	143.5	0.3	-	-	143.1	-0.3	-	-	144.1	0.7	-	-	145.0	0.6	-	-	146.6	1.1	-	-
1997	148.8	1.5	-	-	149.1	0.2	-	-	148.7	-0.3	148.9	0.1	149.0	0.1	-	-	149.0	0.0	-	-	150.7	1.1	-	-

Source: U.S. Department of Labor, Bureau of Labor Statistics, Division of Consumer Prices and Price Indexes. - indicates no data collected for period.

Miami, FL
Consumer Price Index - All Urban Consumers
Base 1982-1984 = 100
Apparel and Upkeep

For 1977-1997. Columns headed % show percentile change in the index from the previous period for which an index is available.

Year	Jan Index	%	Feb Index	%	Mar Index	%	Apr Index	%	May Index	%	Jun Index	%	Jul Index	%	Aug Index	%	Sep Index	%	Oct Index	%	Nov Index	%	Dec Index	%
1977	-	-	-	-	-	-	-	-	-	-	-	-	-	-	-	-	-	-	-	-	74.8	-	-	-
1978	75.6	1.1	-	-	77.2	2.1	-	-	77.1	-0.1	-	-	77.6	0.6	-	-	78.7	1.4	-	-	78.9	0.3	-	-
1979	78.7	-0.3	-	-	79.8	1.4	-	-	80.3	0.6	-	-	81.5	1.5	-	-	82.2	0.9	-	-	83.7	1.8	-	-
1980	82.3	-1.7	-	-	86.0	4.5	-	-	87.2	1.4	-	-	87.8	0.7	-	-	88.0	0.2	-	-	88.8	0.9	-	-
1981	90.9	2.4	-	-	89.8	-1.2	-	-	90.3	0.6	-	-	92.3	2.2	-	-	93.2	1.0	-	-	93.6	0.4	-	-
1982	95.7	2.2	-	-	97.6	2.0	-	-	98.3	0.7	-	-	99.4	1.1	-	-	97.0	-2.4	-	-	100.3	3.4	-	-
1983	99.0	-1.3	-	-	99.8	0.8	-	-	99.2	-0.6	-	-	100.6	1.4	-	-	99.9	-0.7	-	-	102.2	2.3	-	-
1984	99.8	-2.3	-	-	100.6	0.8	-	-	101.8	1.2	-	-	102.0	0.2	-	-	102.7	0.7	-	-	102.7	0.0	-	-
1985	101.5	-1.2	-	-	104.9	3.3	-	-	104.5	-0.4	-	-	104.7	0.2	-	-	107.5	2.7	-	-	108.8	1.2	-	-
1986	109.5	0.6	-	-	108.5	-0.9	-	-	108.6	0.1	-	-	108.5	-0.1	-	-	108.6	0.1	-	-	110.4	1.7	-	-
1987	110.5	0.1	-	-	114.8	3.9	-	-	117.1	2.0	-	-	116.3	-0.7	-	-	115.8	-0.4	-	-	117.3	1.3	-	-
1988	119.0	1.4	-	-	121.7	2.3	-	-	121.4	-0.2	-	-	122.4	0.8	-	-	126.2	3.1	-	-	127.1	0.7	-	-
1989	131.0	3.1	-	-	129.0	-1.5	-	-	129.3	0.2	-	-	125.2	-3.2	-	-	138.0	10.2	-	-	135.8	-1.6	-	-
1990	130.4	-4.0	-	-	136.6	4.8	-	-	132.1	-3.3	-	-	134.9	2.1	-	-	138.6	2.7	-	-	139.5	0.6	-	-
1991	135.6	-2.8	-	-	143.6	5.9	-	-	142.3	-0.9	-	-	137.1	-3.7	-	-	140.6	2.6	-	-	142.2	1.1	-	-
1992	140.4	-1.3	-	-	140.7	0.2	-	-	138.8	-1.4	-	-	134.2	-3.3	-	-	144.2	7.5	-	-	134.8	-6.5	-	-
1993	139.4	3.4	-	-	148.9	6.8	-	-	144.5	-3.0	-	-	139.0	-3.8	-	-	137.5	-1.1	-	-	134.1	-2.5	-	-
1994	127.5	-4.9	-	-	154.9	21.5	-	-	149.1	-3.7	-	-	143.7	-3.6	-	-	144.4	0.5	-	-	136.6	-5.4	-	-
1995	148.2	8.5	-	-	158.9	7.2	-	-	150.2	-5.5	-	-	139.8	-6.9	-	-	142.1	1.6	-	-	142.4	0.2	-	-
1996	149.8	5.2	-	-	149.7	-0.1	-	-	145.4	-2.9	-	-	131.7	-9.4	-	-	146.8	11.5	-	-	149.6	1.9	-	-
1997	163.0	9.0	-	-	152.6	-6.4	-	-	151.1	-1.0	154.4	2.2	148.7	-3.7	-	-	153.3	3.1	-	-	155.3	1.3	-	-

Source: U.S. Department of Labor, Bureau of Labor Statistics, Division of Consumer Prices and Price Indexes. - indicates no data collected for period.

Miami, FL
Consumer Price Index - Urban Wage Earners
Base 1982-1984 = 100
Apparel and Upkeep

For 1977-1997. Columns headed % show percentile change in the index from the previous period for which an index is available.

Year	Jan Index	%	Feb Index	%	Mar Index	%	Apr Index	%	May Index	%	Jun Index	%	Jul Index	%	Aug Index	%	Sep Index	%	Oct Index	%	Nov Index	%	Dec Index	%
1977	-	-	-	-	-	-	-	-	-	-	-	-	-	-	-	-	-	-	-	-	74.5	-	-	-
1978	74.8	0.4	-	-	74.9	0.1	-	-	75.3	0.5	-	-	76.3	1.3	-	-	76.7	0.5	-	-	77.3	0.8	-	-
1979	76.9	-0.5	-	-	79.5	3.4	-	-	79.4	-0.1	-	-	80.1	0.9	-	-	81.6	1.9	-	-	82.5	1.1	-	-
1980	82.8	0.4	-	-	84.0	1.4	-	-	85.7	2.0	-	-	86.6	1.1	-	-	89.2	3.0	-	-	90.1	1.0	-	-
1981	90.7	0.7	-	-	91.2	0.6	-	-	91.5	0.3	-	-	91.3	-0.2	-	-	91.5	0.2	-	-	93.0	1.6	-	-
1982	95.1	2.3	-	-	97.1	2.1	-	-	97.9	0.8	-	-	99.2	1.3	-	-	96.5	-2.7	-	-	100.0	3.6	-	-
1983	98.9	-1.1	-	-	99.2	0.3	-	-	99.2	0.0	-	-	100.6	1.4	-	-	99.9	-0.7	-	-	101.9	2.0	-	-
1984	100.0	-1.9	-	-	100.9	0.9	-	-	102.4	1.5	-	-	102.8	0.4	-	-	103.4	0.6	-	-	103.5	0.1	-	-
1985	102.0	-1.4	-	-	105.5	3.4	-	-	104.7	-0.8	-	-	104.7	0.0	-	-	108.0	3.2	-	-	109.1	1.0	-	-
1986	110.0	0.8	-	-	109.0	-0.9	-	-	109.5	0.5	-	-	109.2	-0.3	-	-	109.1	-0.1	-	-	110.6	1.4	-	-
1987	110.8	0.2	-	-	114.9	3.7	-	-	117.1	1.9	-	-	116.1	-0.9	-	-	115.9	-0.2	-	-	117.2	1.1	-	-
1988	118.8	1.4	-	-	121.8	2.5	-	-	121.0	-0.7	-	-	122.5	1.2	-	-	124.5	1.6	-	-	125.6	0.9	-	-
1989	129.2	2.9	-	-	127.5	-1.3	-	-	127.9	0.3	-	-	123.4	-3.5	-	-	136.7	10.8	-	-	133.9	-2.0	-	-
1990	128.6	-4.0	-	-	134.3	4.4	-	-	129.6	-3.5	-	-	132.3	2.1	-	-	137.3	3.8	-	-	136.4	-0.7	-	-
1991	134.5	-1.4	-	-	142.4	5.9	-	-	141.3	-0.8	-	-	137.2	-2.9	-	-	139.9	2.0	-	-	141.8	1.4	-	-
1992	140.5	-0.9	-	-	140.5	0.0	-	-	138.0	-1.8	-	-	132.7	-3.8	-	-	143.5	8.1	-	-	134.9	-6.0	-	-
1993	139.5	3.4	-	-	147.7	5.9	-	-	145.6	-1.4	-	-	140.1	-3.8	-	-	139.5	-0.4	-	-	134.9	-3.3	-	-
1994	129.0	-4.4	-	-	157.0	21.7	-	-	150.6	-4.1	-	-	145.8	-3.2	-	-	146.8	0.7	-	-	139.0	-5.3	-	-
1995	150.5	8.3	-	-	162.5	8.0	-	-	152.5	-6.2	-	-	142.7	-6.4	-	-	145.1	1.7	-	-	142.8	-1.6	-	-
1996	151.6	6.2	-	-	151.3	-0.2	-	-	147.9	-2.2	-	-	133.7	-9.6	-	-	148.8	11.3	-	-	151.0	1.5	-	-
1997	165.4	9.5	-	-	155.0	-6.3	-	-	153.4	-1.0	156.8	2.2	151.4	-3.4	-	-	156.4	3.3	-	-	158.2	1.2	-	-

Source: U.S. Department of Labor, Bureau of Labor Statistics, Division of Consumer Prices and Price Indexes. - indicates no data collected for period.

Miami, FL
Consumer Price Index - All Urban Consumers
Base 1982-1984 = 100
Transportation

For 1977-1997. Columns headed % show percentile change in the index from the previous period for which an index is available.

Year	Jan Index	%	Feb Index	%	Mar Index	%	Apr Index	%	May Index	%	Jun Index	%	Jul Index	%	Aug Index	%	Sep Index	%	Oct Index	%	Nov Index	%	Dec Index	%
1977	-	-	-	-	-	-	-	-	-	-	-	-	-	-	-	-	-	-	-	-	58.0	-	-	-
1978	58.0	0.0	-	-	58.2	0.3	-	-	58.5	0.5	-	-	60.0	2.6	-	-	60.6	1.0	-	-	61.6	1.7	-	-
1979	62.2	1.0	-	-	63.4	1.9	-	-	66.0	4.1	-	-	68.5	3.8	-	-	69.5	1.5	-	-	70.0	0.7	-	-
1980	74.0	5.7	-	-	76.8	3.8	-	-	77.9	1.4	-	-	79.2	1.7	-	-	79.7	0.6	-	-	81.3	2.0	-	-
1981	83.0	2.1	-	-	86.8	4.6	-	-	88.4	1.8	-	-	89.8	1.6	-	-	90.5	0.8	-	-	91.8	1.4	-	-
1982	93.0	1.3	-	-	92.6	-0.4	-	-	93.4	0.9	-	-	96.1	2.9	-	-	96.0	-0.1	-	-	96.7	0.7	-	-
1983	96.9	0.2	-	-	96.6	-0.3	-	-	98.8	2.3	-	-	100.4	1.6	-	-	103.2	2.8	-	-	103.8	0.6	-	-
1984	103.1	-0.7	-	-	103.7	0.6	-	-	105.1	1.4	-	-	105.4	0.3	-	-	105.6	0.2	-	-	106.5	0.9	-	-
1985	106.1	-0.4	-	-	106.9	0.8	-	-	108.8	1.8	-	-	109.1	0.3	-	-	108.6	-0.5	-	-	109.3	0.6	-	-
1986	109.5	0.2	-	-	105.5	-3.7	-	-	102.5	-2.8	-	-	102.2	-0.3	-	-	101.4	-0.8	-	-	102.2	0.8	-	-
1987	104.0	1.8	-	-	104.8	0.8	-	-	106.2	1.3	-	-	107.0	0.8	-	-	107.3	0.3	-	-	109.3	1.9	-	-
1988	108.8	-0.5	-	-	109.0	0.2	-	-	109.8	0.7	-	-	110.7	0.8	-	-	112.2	1.4	-	-	112.3	0.1	-	-
1989	113.9	1.4	-	-	113.5	-0.4	-	-	116.3	2.5	-	-	115.9	-0.3	-	-	113.7	-1.9	-	-	114.3	0.5	-	-
1990	118.8	3.9	-	-	118.4	-0.3	-	-	119.8	1.2	-	-	119.0	-0.7	-	-	123.0	3.4	-	-	128.2	4.2	-	-
1991	129.4	0.9	-	-	126.2	-2.5	-	-	126.4	0.2	-	-	124.3	-1.7	-	-	124.4	0.1	-	-	126.3	1.5	-	-
1992	125.6	-0.6	-	-	125.5	-0.1	-	-	126.7	1.0	-	-	128.7	1.6	-	-	127.8	-0.7	-	-	131.3	2.7	-	-
1993	131.7	0.3	-	-	130.9	-0.6	-	-	131.7	0.6	-	-	132.0	0.2	-	-	130.7	-1.0	-	-	134.1	2.6	-	-
1994	133.8	-0.2	-	-	134.6	0.6	-	-	134.3	-0.2	-	-	135.3	0.7	-	-	136.0	0.5	-	-	137.1	0.8	-	-
1995	138.0	0.7	-	-	138.9	0.7	-	-	141.7	2.0	-	-	141.6	-0.1	-	-	138.0	-2.5	-	-	140.1	1.5	-	-
1996	141.4	0.9	-	-	141.1	-0.2	-	-	145.3	3.0	-	-	144.3	-0.7	-	-	144.0	-0.2	-	-	148.3	3.0	-	-
1997	146.8	-1.0	-	-	148.9	1.4	-	-	146.7	-1.5	147.5	0.5	146.7	-0.5	-	-	147.6	0.6	-	-	146.6	-0.7	-	-

Source: U.S. Department of Labor, Bureau of Labor Statistics, Division of Consumer Prices and Price Indexes. - indicates no data collected for period.

<h2 style="text-align:center">Miami, FL</h2>

Consumer Price Index - Urban Wage Earners
Base 1982-1984 = 100
Transportation

For 1977-1997. Columns headed % show percentile change in the index from the previous period for which an index is available.

Year	Jan Index	%	Feb Index	%	Mar Index	%	Apr Index	%	May Index	%	Jun Index	%	Jul Index	%	Aug Index	%	Sep Index	%	Oct Index	%	Nov Index	%	Dec Index	%
1977	-	-	-	-	-	-	-	-	-	-	-	-	-	-	-	-	-	-	-	-	57.6	-	-	-
1978	57.6	0.0	-	-	57.7	0.2	-	-	58.4	1.2	-	-	59.8	2.4	-	-	60.5	1.2	-	-	61.2	1.2	-	-
1979	62.0	1.3	-	-	63.5	2.4	-	-	66.4	4.6	-	-	69.0	3.9	-	-	70.0	1.4	-	-	70.5	0.7	-	-
1980	75.0	6.4	-	-	77.6	3.5	-	-	79.0	1.8	-	-	80.0	1.3	-	-	81.0	1.3	-	-	82.4	1.7	-	-
1981	84.4	2.4	-	-	88.0	4.3	-	-	89.4	1.6	-	-	90.1	0.8	-	-	91.0	1.0	-	-	92.6	1.8	-	-
1982	93.5	1.0	-	-	93.0	-0.5	-	-	93.1	0.1	-	-	96.2	3.3	-	-	96.1	-0.1	-	-	96.8	0.7	-	-
1983	97.4	0.6	-	-	96.6	-0.8	-	-	98.8	2.3	-	-	100.5	1.7	-	-	103.4	2.9	-	-	103.7	0.3	-	-
1984	102.9	-0.8	-	-	103.5	0.6	-	-	104.9	1.4	-	-	105.2	0.3	-	-	105.4	0.2	-	-	106.1	0.7	-	-
1985	105.7	-0.4	-	-	106.5	0.8	-	-	108.4	1.8	-	-	108.7	0.3	-	-	108.2	-0.5	-	-	108.8	0.6	-	-
1986	109.0	0.2	-	-	104.5	-4.1	-	-	101.0	-3.3	-	-	100.6	-0.4	-	-	99.9	-0.7	-	-	100.7	0.8	-	-
1987	102.0	1.3	-	-	103.0	1.0	-	-	104.7	1.7	-	-	105.8	1.1	-	-	105.9	0.1	-	-	107.8	1.8	-	-
1988	107.4	-0.4	-	-	107.5	0.1	-	-	108.1	0.6	-	-	109.0	0.8	-	-	110.3	1.2	-	-	110.4	0.1	-	-
1989	112.0	1.4	-	-	111.6	-0.4	-	-	114.0	2.2	-	-	113.7	-0.3	-	-	111.6	-1.8	-	-	112.0	0.4	-	-
1990	115.9	3.5	-	-	115.3	-0.5	-	-	116.6	1.1	-	-	116.0	-0.5	-	-	119.7	3.2	-	-	124.1	3.7	-	-
1991	125.1	0.8	-	-	122.3	-2.2	-	-	122.9	0.5	-	-	121.3	-1.3	-	-	121.5	0.2	-	-	123.1	1.3	-	-
1992	122.3	-0.6	-	-	121.9	-0.3	-	-	123.8	1.6	-	-	126.5	2.2	-	-	126.3	-0.2	-	-	129.2	2.3	-	-
1993	129.5	0.2	-	-	128.6	-0.7	-	-	129.6	0.8	-	-	130.3	0.5	-	-	129.6	-0.5	-	-	132.3	2.1	-	-
1994	131.5	-0.6	-	-	131.6	0.1	-	-	132.1	0.4	-	-	133.7	1.2	-	-	134.8	0.8	-	-	136.1	1.0	-	-
1995	137.0	0.7	-	-	137.5	0.4	-	-	140.7	2.3	-	-	140.6	-0.1	-	-	137.4	-2.3	-	-	139.4	1.5	-	-
1996	140.7	0.9	-	-	140.2	-0.4	-	-	144.5	3.1	-	-	143.3	-0.8	-	-	143.1	-0.1	-	-	146.6	2.4	-	-
1997	145.3	-0.9	-	-	146.7	1.0	-	-	144.8	-1.3	145.5	0.5	144.3	-0.8	-	-	144.9	0.4	-	-	144.2	-0.5	-	-

Source: U.S. Department of Labor, Bureau of Labor Statistics, Division of Consumer Prices and Price Indexes. - indicates no data collected for period.

Miami, FL
Consumer Price Index - All Urban Consumers
Base 1982-1984 = 100
Medical Care

For 1977-1997. Columns headed % show percentile change in the index from the previous period for which an index is available.

Year	Jan Index	%	Feb Index	%	Mar Index	%	Apr Index	%	May Index	%	Jun Index	%	Jul Index	%	Aug Index	%	Sep Index	%	Oct Index	%	Nov Index	%	Dec Index	%
1977	-	-	-	-	-	-	-	-	-	-	-	-	-	-	-	-	-	-	-	-	57.9	-	-	-
1978	59.3	2.4	-	-	59.5	0.3	-	-	60.3	1.3	-	-	60.6	0.5	-	-	63.0	4.0	-	-	64.4	2.2	-	-
1979	65.2	1.2	-	-	67.4	3.4	-	-	67.5	0.1	-	-	68.4	1.3	-	-	70.5	3.1	-	-	72.3	2.6	-	-
1980	74.6	3.2	-	-	75.5	1.2	-	-	75.6	0.1	-	-	75.4	-0.3	-	-	75.8	0.5	-	-	75.7	-0.1	-	-
1981	77.8	2.8	-	-	79.1	1.7	-	-	80.2	1.4	-	-	81.6	1.7	-	-	84.6	3.7	-	-	85.6	1.2	-	-
1982	87.8	2.6	-	-	89.1	1.5	-	-	92.0	3.3	-	-	95.1	3.4	-	-	96.5	1.5	-	-	99.8	3.4	-	-
1983	99.7	-0.1	-	-	100.0	0.3	-	-	100.0	0.0	-	-	101.0	1.0	-	-	101.5	0.5	-	-	102.9	1.4	-	-
1984	103.9	1.0	-	-	105.0	1.1	-	-	105.0	0.0	-	-	105.0	0.0	-	-	104.8	-0.2	-	-	106.3	1.4	-	-
1985	107.0	0.7	-	-	108.6	1.5	-	-	108.4	-0.2	-	-	108.7	0.3	-	-	109.7	0.9	-	-	111.2	1.4	-	-
1986	113.4	2.0	-	-	115.4	1.8	-	-	115.6	0.2	-	-	116.0	0.3	-	-	120.1	3.5	-	-	121.1	0.8	-	-
1987	122.9	1.5	-	-	123.7	0.7	-	-	124.8	0.9	-	-	128.4	2.9	-	-	127.7	-0.5	-	-	130.2	2.0	-	-
1988	131.4	0.9	-	-	133.3	1.4	-	-	134.0	0.5	-	-	134.4	0.3	-	-	136.1	1.3	-	-	136.7	0.4	-	-
1989	137.9	0.9	-	-	137.9	0.0	-	-	140.5	1.9	-	-	140.9	0.3	-	-	141.7	0.6	-	-	142.6	0.6	-	-
1990	143.3	0.5	-	-	145.0	1.2	-	-	150.1	3.5	-	-	153.5	2.3	-	-	156.4	1.9	-	-	158.3	1.2	-	-
1991	159.7	0.9	-	-	160.4	0.4	-	-	161.8	0.9	-	-	163.1	0.8	-	-	162.9	-0.1	-	-	166.7	2.3	-	-
1992	169.6	1.7	-	-	171.0	0.8	-	-	171.7	0.4	-	-	171.2	-0.3	-	-	171.3	0.1	-	-	176.4	3.0	-	-
1993	179.2	1.6	-	-	180.1	0.5	-	-	182.0	1.1	-	-	183.1	0.6	-	-	183.1	0.0	-	-	182.7	-0.2	-	-
1994	184.7	1.1	-	-	185.2	0.3	-	-	187.0	1.0	-	-	186.4	-0.3	-	-	190.7	2.3	-	-	191.6	0.5	-	-
1995	196.6	2.6	-	-	200.1	1.8	-	-	201.7	0.8	-	-	204.3	1.3	-	-	204.9	0.3	-	-	206.2	0.6	-	-
1996	212.8	3.2	-	-	213.6	0.4	-	-	214.9	0.6	-	-	214.6	-0.1	-	-	216.3	0.8	-	-	214.0	-1.1	-	-
1997	215.1	0.5	-	-	219.1	1.9	-	-	219.6	0.2	218.3	-0.6	220.1	0.8	-	-	219.6	-0.2	-	-	220.5	0.4	-	-

Source: U.S. Department of Labor, Bureau of Labor Statistics, Division of Consumer Prices and Price Indexes. - indicates no data collected for period.

Miami, FL
Consumer Price Index - Urban Wage Earners
Base 1982-1984 = 100
Medical Care

For 1977-1997. Columns headed % show percentile change in the index from the previous period for which an index is available.

Year	Jan Index	%	Feb Index	%	Mar Index	%	Apr Index	%	May Index	%	Jun Index	%	Jul Index	%	Aug Index	%	Sep Index	%	Oct Index	%	Nov Index	%	Dec Index	%
1977	-	-	-	-	-	-	-	-	-	-	-	-	-	-	-	-	-	-	-	-	58.2	-	-	-
1978	59.3	1.9	-	-	59.5	0.3	-	-	61.9	4.0	-	-	62.2	0.5	-	-	63.4	1.9	-	-	64.0	0.9	-	-
1979	64.7	1.1	-	-	65.5	1.2	-	-	65.8	0.5	-	-	66.8	1.5	-	-	70.4	5.4	-	-	71.4	1.4	-	-
1980	73.5	2.9	-	-	74.3	1.1	-	-	74.2	-0.1	-	-	74.0	-0.3	-	-	74.4	0.5	-	-	74.8	0.5	-	-
1981	76.0	1.6	-	-	77.1	1.4	-	-	77.5	0.5	-	-	79.5	2.6	-	-	80.7	1.5	-	-	85.4	5.8	-	-
1982	87.6	2.6	-	-	89.1	1.7	-	-	91.9	3.1	-	-	94.7	3.0	-	-	96.1	1.5	-	-	99.9	4.0	-	-
1983	100.0	0.1	-	-	100.4	0.4	-	-	100.4	0.0	-	-	101.3	0.9	-	-	101.8	0.5	-	-	103.0	1.2	-	-
1984	103.9	0.9	-	-	104.9	1.0	-	-	104.9	0.0	-	-	104.9	0.0	-	-	104.6	-0.3	-	-	106.0	1.3	-	-
1985	106.5	0.5	-	-	108.1	1.5	-	-	108.0	-0.1	-	-	108.2	0.2	-	-	109.2	0.9	-	-	110.6	1.3	-	-
1986	112.5	1.7	-	-	114.6	1.9	-	-	114.8	0.2	-	-	115.3	0.4	-	-	119.4	3.6	-	-	120.4	0.8	-	-
1987	122.2	1.5	-	-	123.0	0.7	-	-	124.2	1.0	-	-	127.6	2.7	-	-	126.9	-0.5	-	-	129.0	1.7	-	-
1988	130.4	1.1	-	-	131.8	1.1	-	-	132.6	0.6	-	-	132.8	0.2	-	-	134.5	1.3	-	-	134.8	0.2	-	-
1989	136.2	1.0	-	-	136.4	0.1	-	-	138.9	1.8	-	-	139.3	0.3	-	-	140.5	0.9	-	-	141.5	0.7	-	-
1990	142.1	0.4	-	-	143.7	1.1	-	-	149.0	3.7	-	-	152.2	2.1	-	-	155.6	2.2	-	-	157.3	1.1	-	-
1991	158.7	0.9	-	-	159.4	0.4	-	-	160.8	0.9	-	-	162.0	0.7	-	-	161.8	-0.1	-	-	165.4	2.2	-	-
1992	168.3	1.8	-	-	169.9	1.0	-	-	170.9	0.6	-	-	171.0	0.1	-	-	170.8	-0.1	-	-	175.6	2.8	-	-
1993	178.5	1.7	-	-	179.5	0.6	-	-	181.4	1.1	-	-	182.0	0.3	-	-	181.8	-0.1	-	-	181.6	-0.1	-	-
1994	182.6	0.6	-	-	182.8	0.1	-	-	184.0	0.7	-	-	183.6	-0.2	-	-	188.1	2.5	-	-	189.2	0.6	-	-
1995	193.6	2.3	-	-	196.9	1.7	-	-	198.6	0.9	-	-	201.3	1.4	-	-	202.1	0.4	-	-	203.4	0.6	-	-
1996	210.0	3.2	-	-	210.9	0.4	-	-	211.9	0.5	-	-	211.8	-0.0	-	-	213.5	0.8	-	-	211.7	-0.8	-	-
1997	212.0	0.1	-	-	216.1	1.9	-	-	216.5	0.2	215.3	-0.6	217.0	0.8	-	-	216.5	-0.2	-	-	218.0	0.7	-	-

Source: U.S. Department of Labor, Bureau of Labor Statistics, Division of Consumer Prices and Price Indexes. - indicates no data collected for period.

Miami, FL
Consumer Price Index - All Urban Consumers
Base 1982-1984 = 100
Entertainment

For 1977-1997. Columns headed % show percentile change in the index from the previous period for which an index is available.

Year	Jan Index	%	Feb Index	%	Mar Index	%	Apr Index	%	May Index	%	Jun Index	%	Jul Index	%	Aug Index	%	Sep Index	%	Oct Index	%	Nov Index	%	Dec Index	%
1977	-	-	-	-	-	-	-	-	-	-	-	-	-	-	-	-	-	-	-	-	77.8	-	-	-
1978	78.2	0.5	-	-	78.0	-0.3	-	-	79.5	1.9	-	-	80.9	1.8	-	-	81.3	0.5	-	-	82.0	0.9	-	-
1979	83.2	1.5	-	-	84.4	1.4	-	-	84.9	0.6	-	-	84.8	-0.1	-	-	85.9	1.3	-	-	86.0	0.1	-	-
1980	87.3	1.5	-	-	88.1	0.9	-	-	88.3	0.2	-	-	88.7	0.5	-	-	91.6	3.3	-	-	92.3	0.8	-	-
1981	92.3	0.0	-	-	93.6	1.4	-	-	96.3	2.9	-	-	94.1	-2.3	-	-	95.6	1.6	-	-	97.8	2.3	-	-
1982	97.2	-0.6	-	-	97.5	0.3	-	-	98.1	0.6	-	-	98.3	0.2	-	-	98.7	0.4	-	-	99.9	1.2	-	-
1983	99.8	-0.1	-	-	100.7	0.9	-	-	101.0	0.3	-	-	99.4	-1.6	-	-	99.8	0.4	-	-	101.3	1.5	-	-
1984	101.2	-0.1	-	-	101.8	0.6	-	-	100.9	-0.9	-	-	101.0	0.1	-	-	100.2	-0.8	-	-	102.0	1.8	-	-
1985	102.7	0.7	-	-	103.1	0.4	-	-	104.8	1.6	-	-	104.1	-0.7	-	-	104.6	0.5	-	-	106.6	1.9	-	-
1986	107.0	0.4	-	-	108.4	1.3	-	-	106.5	-1.8	-	-	106.3	-0.2	-	-	106.8	0.5	-	-	111.2	4.1	-	-
1987	113.2	1.8	-	-	112.6	-0.5	-	-	113.2	0.5	-	-	113.5	0.3	-	-	114.4	0.8	-	-	114.9	0.4	-	-
1988	115.2	0.3	-	-	116.8	1.4	-	-	118.1	1.1	-	-	116.2	-1.6	-	-	116.8	0.5	-	-	112.0	-4.1	-	-
1989	116.0	3.6	-	-	117.0	0.9	-	-	117.6	0.5	-	-	118.0	0.3	-	-	118.5	0.4	-	-	119.0	0.4	-	-
1990	119.6	0.5	-	-	118.9	-0.6	-	-	119.3	0.3	-	-	122.3	2.5	-	-	122.1	-0.2	-	-	122.1	0.0	-	-
1991	127.3	4.3	-	-	128.8	1.2	-	-	123.1	-4.4	-	-	127.0	3.2	-	-	126.4	-0.5	-	-	126.3	-0.1	-	-
1992	126.1	-0.2	-	-	127.8	1.3	-	-	122.1	-4.5	-	-	122.4	0.2	-	-	122.4	0.0	-	-	125.6	2.6	-	-
1993	130.4	3.8	-	-	131.3	0.7	-	-	130.1	-0.9	-	-	128.2	-1.5	-	-	128.4	0.2	-	-	128.5	0.1	-	-
1994	132.1	2.8	-	-	133.9	1.4	-	-	132.9	-0.7	-	-	134.8	1.4	-	-	135.2	0.3	-	-	135.6	0.3	-	-
1995	140.5	3.6	-	-	140.1	-0.3	-	-	140.2	0.1	-	-	139.1	-0.8	-	-	141.1	1.4	-	-	141.1	0.0	-	-
1996	142.5	1.0	-	-	144.6	1.5	-	-	144.6	0.0	-	-	143.8	-0.6	-	-	145.4	1.1	-	-	152.7	5.0	-	-
1997	155.1	1.6	-	-	153.4	-1.1	-	-	152.6	-0.5	153.5	0.6	152.8	-0.5	-	-	154.0	0.8	-	-	155.3	0.8	-	-

Source: U.S. Department of Labor, Bureau of Labor Statistics, Division of Consumer Prices and Price Indexes. - indicates no data collected for period.

Miami, FL
Consumer Price Index - Urban Wage Earners
Base 1982-1984 = 100
Entertainment

For 1977-1997. Columns headed % show percentile change in the index from the previous period for which an index is available.

Year	Jan Index	%	Feb Index	%	Mar Index	%	Apr Index	%	May Index	%	Jun Index	%	Jul Index	%	Aug Index	%	Sep Index	%	Oct Index	%	Nov Index	%	Dec Index	%
1977	-	-	-	-	-	-	-	-	-	-	-	-	-	-	-	-	-	-	-	-	73.1	-	-	-
1978	73.6	0.7	-	-	73.8	0.3	-	-	75.0	1.6	-	-	76.4	1.9	-	-	76.7	0.4	-	-	77.9	1.6	-	-
1979	77.9	0.0	-	-	80.6	3.5	-	-	81.5	1.1	-	-	81.2	-0.4	-	-	82.3	1.4	-	-	83.1	1.0	-	-
1980	84.9	2.2	-	-	86.9	2.4	-	-	86.4	-0.6	-	-	87.2	0.9	-	-	90.6	3.9	-	-	91.1	0.6	-	-
1981	91.5	0.4	-	-	92.3	0.9	-	-	95.9	3.9	-	-	93.7	-2.3	-	-	94.9	1.3	-	-	98.1	3.4	-	-
1982	97.3	-0.8	-	-	97.7	0.4	-	-	98.4	0.7	-	-	98.5	0.1	-	-	98.7	0.2	-	-	99.9	1.2	-	-
1983	99.7	-0.2	-	-	101.0	1.3	-	-	101.3	0.3	-	-	99.4	-1.9	-	-	100.0	0.6	-	-	100.9	0.9	-	-
1984	100.9	0.0	-	-	101.9	1.0	-	-	100.8	-1.1	-	-	100.5	-0.3	-	-	100.2	-0.3	-	-	101.6	1.4	-	-
1985	102.9	1.3	-	-	103.2	0.3	-	-	105.2	1.9	-	-	104.8	-0.4	-	-	106.1	1.2	-	-	107.6	1.4	-	-
1986	107.7	0.1	-	-	108.8	1.0	-	-	107.2	-1.5	-	-	107.0	-0.2	-	-	106.7	-0.3	-	-	111.8	4.8	-	-
1987	113.8	1.8	-	-	113.2	-0.5	-	-	113.6	0.4	-	-	113.9	0.3	-	-	115.2	1.1	-	-	115.5	0.3	-	-
1988	115.9	0.3	-	-	117.4	1.3	-	-	118.2	0.7	-	-	116.7	-1.3	-	-	117.0	0.3	-	-	111.9	-4.4	-	-
1989	116.9	4.5	-	-	118.0	0.9	-	-	118.5	0.4	-	-	119.0	0.4	-	-	119.5	0.4	-	-	120.0	0.4	-	-
1990	120.6	0.5	-	-	119.8	-0.7	-	-	120.1	0.3	-	-	123.6	2.9	-	-	123.6	0.0	-	-	123.2	-0.3	-	-
1991	128.5	4.3	-	-	129.6	0.9	-	-	123.8	-4.5	-	-	128.6	3.9	-	-	127.9	-0.5	-	-	127.4	-0.4	-	-
1992	127.0	-0.3	-	-	128.7	1.3	-	-	122.9	-4.5	-	-	123.7	0.7	-	-	123.6	-0.1	-	-	126.2	2.1	-	-
1993	131.0	3.8	-	-	132.3	1.0	-	-	131.2	-0.8	-	-	128.9	-1.8	-	-	129.1	0.2	-	-	128.6	-0.4	-	-
1994	132.5	3.0	-	-	134.3	1.4	-	-	133.2	-0.8	-	-	135.8	2.0	-	-	136.1	0.2	-	-	136.6	0.4	-	-
1995	142.0	4.0	-	-	141.3	-0.5	-	-	141.5	0.1	-	-	140.3	-0.8	-	-	143.1	2.0	-	-	142.9	-0.1	-	-
1996	144.4	1.0	-	-	146.6	1.5	-	-	146.6	0.0	-	-	145.9	-0.5	-	-	147.7	1.2	-	-	155.9	5.6	-	-
1997	158.3	1.5	-	-	156.4	-1.2	-	-	155.8	-0.4	156.6	0.5	156.0	-0.4	-	-	156.9	0.6	-	-	158.4	1.0	-	-

Source: U.S. Department of Labor, Bureau of Labor Statistics, Division of Consumer Prices and Price Indexes. - indicates no data collected for period.

Miami, FL
Consumer Price Index - All Urban Consumers
Base 1982-1984 = 100
Other Goods and Services

For 1977-1997. Columns headed % show percentile change in the index from the previous period for which an index is available.

Year	Jan Index	%	Feb Index	%	Mar Index	%	Apr Index	%	May Index	%	Jun Index	%	Jul Index	%	Aug Index	%	Sep Index	%	Oct Index	%	Nov Index	%	Dec Index	%
1977	-	-	-	-	-	-	-	-	-	-	-	-	-	-	-	-	-	-	-	-	61.5	-	-	-
1978	61.5	0.0	-	-	62.3	1.3	-	-	63.1	1.3	-	-	63.4	0.5	-	-	65.6	3.5	-	-	65.5	-0.2	-	-
1979	65.7	0.3	-	-	66.1	0.6	-	-	67.5	2.1	-	-	68.4	1.3	-	-	72.2	5.6	-	-	72.5	0.4	-	-
1980	74.2	2.3	-	-	74.4	0.3	-	-	74.9	0.7	-	-	75.7	1.1	-	-	78.2	3.3	-	-	78.3	0.1	-	-
1981	79.6	1.7	-	-	81.3	2.1	-	-	82.0	0.9	-	-	84.1	2.6	-	-	89.5	6.4	-	-	89.3	-0.2	-	-
1982	90.0	0.8	-	-	90.3	0.3	-	-	91.4	1.2	-	-	92.0	0.7	-	-	96.1	4.5	-	-	97.0	-0.9	-	-
1983	97.5	0.5	-	-	97.1	-0.4	-	-	97.3	0.2	-	-	99.4	2.2	-	-	102.7	3.3	-	-	104.2	1.5	-	-
1984	105.4	1.2	-	-	105.7	0.3	-	-	105.8	0.1	-	-	106.5	0.7	-	-	108.2	1.6	-	-	108.8	0.6	-	-
1985	109.6	0.7	-	-	111.5	1.7	-	-	112.2	0.6	-	-	112.5	0.3	-	-	116.3	3.4	-	-	116.0	-0.3	-	-
1986	117.3	1.1	-	-	119.8	2.1	-	-	120.4	0.5	-	-	120.4	0.0	-	-	125.3	4.1	-	-	125.4	0.1	-	-
1987	125.9	0.4	-	-	126.0	0.1	-	-	126.2	0.2	-	-	128.1	1.5	-	-	131.2	2.4	-	-	131.2	0.0	-	-
1988	131.3	0.1	-	-	131.8	0.4	-	-	132.0	0.2	-	-	132.0	0.0	-	-	136.5	3.4	-	-	136.7	0.1	-	-
1989	137.6	0.7	-	-	137.6	0.0	-	-	138.4	0.6	-	-	138.4	0.0	-	-	143.1	3.4	-	-	142.4	-0.5	-	-
1990	143.7	0.9	-	-	149.9	4.3	-	-	150.2	0.2	-	-	154.1	2.6	-	-	158.8	3.0	-	-	158.2	-0.4	-	-
1991	161.0	1.8	-	-	161.9	0.6	-	-	160.9	-0.6	-	-	160.5	-0.2	-	-	162.2	1.1	-	-	162.3	0.1	-	-
1992	162.1	-0.1	-	-	162.0	-0.1	-	-	158.0	-2.5	-	-	158.0	0.0	-	-	160.4	1.5	-	-	162.4	1.2	-	-
1993	162.8	0.2	-	-	162.8	0.0	-	-	163.0	0.1	-	-	163.3	0.2	-	-	162.8	-0.3	-	-	160.3	-1.5	-	-
1994	163.4	1.9	-	-	162.5	-0.6	-	-	160.0	-1.5	-	-	160.9	0.6	-	-	164.7	2.4	-	-	164.8	0.1	-	-
1995	166.5	1.0	-	-	167.4	0.5	-	-	166.9	-0.3	-	-	169.6	1.6	-	-	173.1	2.1	-	-	173.1	0.0	-	-
1996	173.2	0.1	-	-	173.5	0.2	-	-	171.9	-0.9	-	-	174.4	1.5	-	-	177.8	1.9	-	-	178.2	0.2	-	-
1997	177.9	-0.2	-	-	178.4	0.3	-	-	179.7	0.7	178.8	-0.5	180.0	0.7	-	-	185.1	2.8	-	-	184.7	-0.2	-	-

Source: U.S. Department of Labor, Bureau of Labor Statistics, Division of Consumer Prices and Price Indexes. - indicates no data collected for period.

Miami, FL
Consumer Price Index - Urban Wage Earners
Base 1982-1984 = 100
Other Goods and Services

For 1977-1997. Columns headed % show percentile change in the index from the previous period for which an index is available.

Year	Jan Index	%	Feb Index	%	Mar Index	%	Apr Index	%	May Index	%	Jun Index	%	Jul Index	%	Aug Index	%	Sep Index	%	Oct Index	%	Nov Index	%	Dec Index	%
1977	-	-	-	-	-	-	-	-	-	-	-	-	-	-	-	-	-	-	-	-	64.0	-	-	-
1978	63.9	-0.2	-	-	64.5	0.9	-	-	65.6	1.7	-	-	65.9	0.5	-	-	67.8	2.9	-	-	67.5	-0.4	-	-
1979	67.8	0.4	-	-	68.7	1.3	-	-	69.9	1.7	-	-	70.4	0.7	-	-	74.1	5.3	-	-	74.7	0.8	-	-
1980	76.0	1.7	-	-	75.9	-0.1	-	-	76.8	1.2	-	-	77.2	0.5	-	-	78.5	1.7	-	-	78.6	0.1	-	-
1981	80.2	2.0	-	-	81.3	1.4	-	-	82.1	1.0	-	-	83.1	1.2	-	-	88.4	6.4	-	-	88.9	0.6	-	-
1982	90.0	1.2	-	-	90.4	0.4	-	-	91.9	1.7	-	-	92.8	1.0	-	-	95.3	2.7	-	-	96.4	1.2	-	-
1983	97.1	0.7	-	-	97.1	0.0	-	-	97.4	0.3	-	-	100.3	3.0	-	-	101.8	1.5	-	-	104.5	2.7	-	-
1984	105.5	1.0	-	-	105.9	0.4	-	-	105.9	0.0	-	-	106.9	0.9	-	-	107.6	0.7	-	-	108.3	0.7	-	-
1985	109.4	1.0	-	-	110.4	0.9	-	-	111.3	0.8	-	-	111.6	0.3	-	-	115.2	3.2	-	-	114.9	-0.3	-	-
1986	116.3	1.2	-	-	119.2	2.5	-	-	119.7	0.4	-	-	119.9	0.2	-	-	123.9	3.3	-	-	123.7	-0.2	-	-
1987	124.4	0.6	-	-	124.6	0.2	-	-	124.9	0.2	-	-	126.5	1.3	-	-	129.4	2.3	-	-	129.4	0.0	-	-
1988	130.2	0.6	-	-	130.9	0.5	-	-	131.1	0.2	-	-	131.3	0.2	-	-	135.2	3.0	-	-	135.5	0.2	-	-
1989	136.6	0.8	-	-	136.6	0.0	-	-	137.8	0.9	-	-	137.8	0.0	-	-	142.0	3.0	-	-	141.1	-0.6	-	-
1990	142.6	1.1	-	-	147.9	3.7	-	-	148.3	0.3	-	-	153.8	3.7	-	-	156.5	1.8	-	-	155.7	-0.5	-	-
1991	159.5	2.4	-	-	160.8	0.8	-	-	159.4	-0.9	-	-	158.9	-0.3	-	-	159.7	0.5	-	-	159.8	0.1	-	-
1992	160.8	0.6	-	-	160.7	-0.1	-	-	154.6	-3.8	-	-	154.6	0.0	-	-	156.3	1.1	-	-	159.2	1.9	-	-
1993	160.1	0.6	-	-	160.1	0.0	-	-	160.3	0.1	-	-	160.4	0.1	-	-	158.9	-0.9	-	-	154.8	-2.6	-	-
1994	158.0	2.1	-	-	156.7	-0.8	-	-	154.9	-1.1	-	-	155.6	0.5	-	-	158.7	2.0	-	-	158.8	0.1	-	-
1995	160.3	0.9	-	-	161.3	0.6	-	-	160.8	-0.3	-	-	163.5	1.7	-	-	166.5	1.8	-	-	166.5	0.0	-	-
1996	166.1	-0.2	-	-	166.4	0.2	-	-	164.7	-1.0	-	-	167.3	1.6	-	-	170.2	1.7	-	-	170.7	0.3	-	-
1997	170.4	-0.2	-	-	171.0	0.4	-	-	172.8	1.1	171.6	-0.7	172.8	0.7	-	-	177.5	2.7	-	-	176.9	-0.3	-	-

Source: U.S. Department of Labor, Bureau of Labor Statistics, Division of Consumer Prices and Price Indexes. - indicates no data collected for period.

Milwaukee, WI
Consumer Price Index - All Urban Consumers
Base 1982-1984 = 100
Annual Averages

For 1935-1997. Columns headed % show percentile change in the index from the previous period for which an index is available.

Year	All Items		Food & Beverage		Housing		Apparel & Upkeep		Trans-portation		Medical Care		Entertain-ment		Other Goods & Services	
	Index	%	Index	%	Index	%	Index	%	Index	%	Index	%	Index	%	Index	%
1935	13.4	-	-	-	-	-	-	-	-	-	-	-	-	-	-	-
1936	13.6	1.5	-	-	-	-	-	-	-	-	-	-	-	-	-	-
1937	14.2	4.4	-	-	-	-	-	-	-	-	-	-	-	-	-	-
1938	13.8	-2.8	-	-	-	-	-	-	-	-	-	-	-	-	-	-
1939	13.5	-2.2	-	-	-	-	-	-	-	-	-	-	-	-	-	-
1940	13.5	0.0	-	-	-	-	-	-	-	-	-	-	-	-	-	-
1941	14.2	5.2	-	-	-	-	-	-	-	-	-	-	-	-	-	-
1942	15.7	10.6	-	-	-	-	-	-	-	-	-	-	-	-	-	-
1943	16.6	5.7	-	-	-	-	-	-	-	-	-	-	-	-	-	-
1944	16.9	1.8	-	-	-	-	-	-	-	-	-	-	-	-	-	-
1945	17.3	2.4	-	-	-	-	-	-	-	-	-	-	-	-	-	-
1946	18.6	7.5	-	-	-	-	-	-	-	-	-	-	-	-	-	-
1947	21.7	16.7	-	-	-	-	-	-	20.3	-	12.8	-	-	-	-	-
1948	23.4	7.8	-	-	-	-	-	-	21.9	7.9	13.6	6.3	-	-	-	-
1949	23.1	-1.3	-	-	-	-	-	-	22.8	4.1	14.2	4.4	-	-	-	-
1950	23.9	3.5	-	-	-	-	-	-	23.2	1.8	14.9	4.9	-	-	-	-
1951	26.2	9.6	-	-	-	-	-	-	24.8	6.9	16.5	10.7	-	-	-	-
1952	27.0	3.1	-	-	-	-	-	-	26.2	5.6	17.3	4.8	-	-	-	-
1953	27.1	0.4	-	-	-	-	39.6	-	27.1	3.4	17.9	3.5	-	-	-	-
1954	27.1	0.0	-	-	-	-	39.5	-0.3	26.8	-1.1	19.0	6.1	-	-	-	-
1955	27.1	0.0	-	-	-	-	39.3	-0.5	26.5	-1.1	19.5	2.6	-	-	-	-
1956	27.5	1.5	-	-	-	-	40.3	2.5	27.2	2.6	19.9	2.1	-	-	-	-
1957	28.4	3.3	-	-	-	-	40.9	1.5	28.4	4.4	21.4	7.5	-	-	-	-
1958	28.8	1.4	-	-	-	-	40.9	0.0	28.9	1.8	22.1	3.3	-	-	-	-
1959	28.8	0.0	-	-	-	-	41.3	1.0	29.8	3.1	22.5	1.8	-	-	-	-
1960	29.2	1.4	-	-	-	-	41.8	1.2	29.5	-1.0	23.1	2.7	-	-	-	-
1961	29.4	0.7	-	-	-	-	42.0	0.5	29.8	1.0	23.2	0.4	-	-	-	-
1962	29.8	1.4	-	-	-	-	42.2	0.5	30.8	3.4	23.4	0.9	-	-	-	-
1963	30.1	1.0	-	-	-	-	42.2	0.0	31.0	0.6	23.9	2.1	-	-	-	-
1964	30.4	1.0	-	-	-	-	42.8	1.4	31.1	0.3	24.4	2.1	-	-	-	-
1965	31.0	2.0	-	-	-	-	43.5	1.6	32.2	3.5	25.3	3.7	-	-	-	-
1966	31.7	2.3	-	-	-	-	44.2	1.6	32.4	0.6	26.7	5.5	-	-	-	-
1967	32.4	2.2	-	-	-	-	45.8	3.6	32.9	1.5	28.8	7.9	-	-	-	-
1968	33.5	3.4	-	-	-	-	47.7	4.1	33.2	0.9	30.4	5.6	-	-	-	-
1969	35.5	6.0	-	-	-	-	51.7	8.4	35.0	5.4	32.6	7.2	-	-	-	-
1970	37.5	5.6	-	-	-	-	55.9	8.1	36.4	4.0	34.3	5.2	-	-	-	-
1971	38.9	3.7	-	-	-	-	56.9	1.8	38.5	5.8	36.3	5.8	-	-	-	-
1972	40.1	3.1	-	-	-	-	58.1	2.1	39.2	1.8	36.9	1.7	-	-	-	-
1973	42.6	6.2	-	-	-	-	60.9	4.8	41.4	5.6	38.6	4.6	-	-	-	-
1974	46.7	9.6	-	-	-	-	64.9	6.6	46.0	11.1	42.4	9.8	-	-	-	-
1975	50.8	8.8	-	-	-	-	70.0	7.9	49.9	8.5	47.1	11.1	-	-	-	-
1976	54.1	6.5	63.4	-	47.4	-	74.2	6.0	53.5	7.2	52.6	11.7	61.8	-	59.9	-
1977	57.6	6.5	66.9	5.5	50.9	7.4	77.5	4.4	57.0	6.5	57.3	8.9	68.4	10.7	63.1	5.3
1978	62.3	8.2	73.4	9.7	55.9	9.8	78.3	1.0	60.5	6.1	61.9	8.0	72.2	5.6	66.5	5.4
1979	70.8	13.6	81.6	11.2	65.2	16.6	82.2	5.0	70.5	16.5	69.3	12.0	77.9	7.9	70.5	6.0

[Continued]

Milwaukee, WI
Consumer Price Index - All Urban Consumers
Base 1982-1984 = 100
Annual Averages
[Continued]

For 1935-1997. Columns headed % show percentile change in the index from the previous period for which an index is available.

Year	All Items		Food & Beverage		Housing		Apparel & Upkeep		Trans- portation		Medical Care		Entertain- ment		Other Goods & Services	
	Index	%	Index	%	Index	%	Index	%	Index	%	Index	%	Index	%	Index	%
1980	81.4	15.0	87.2	6.9	78.2	19.9	87.5	6.4	83.2	18.0	77.9	12.4	84.4	8.3	75.7	7.4
1981	90.7	11.4	94.9	8.8	88.3	12.9	92.3	5.5	93.5	12.4	86.7	11.3	92.1	9.1	83.2	9.9
1982	95.9	5.7	98.5	3.8	94.0	6.5	96.9	5.0	98.5	5.3	93.7	8.1	95.8	4.0	92.4	11.1
1983	100.2	4.5	99.6	1.1	100.7	7.1	101.8	5.1	99.0	0.5	100.6	7.4	100.3	4.7	100.8	9.1
1984	103.8	3.6	101.9	2.3	105.1	4.4	101.3	-0.5	102.5	3.5	105.7	5.1	103.9	3.6	106.8	6.0
1985	107.0	3.1	105.7	3.7	108.5	3.2	103.4	2.1	103.9	1.4	109.3	3.4	109.6	5.5	113.1	5.9
1986	107.4	0.4	107.9	2.1	109.5	0.9	105.1	1.6	98.7	-5.0	114.6	4.8	110.3	0.6	121.6	7.5
1987	114.2	6.3	116.8	8.2	112.6	2.8	119.7	13.9	106.9	8.3	127.9	11.6	118.9	7.8	127.1	4.5
1988	119.3	4.5	121.8	4.3	116.2	3.2	130.1	8.7	111.5	4.3	134.7	5.3	122.8	3.3	138.9	9.3
1989	124.5	4.4	129.2	6.1	120.0	3.3	127.8	-1.8	116.9	4.8	145.6	8.1	128.7	4.8	149.2	7.4
1990	130.8	5.1	136.9	6.0	125.2	4.3	128.1	0.2	122.8	5.0	158.4	8.8	138.3	7.5	158.5	6.2
1991	136.4	4.3	140.6	2.7	131.0	4.6	132.9	3.7	125.5	2.2	171.9	8.5	143.8	4.0	172.8	9.0
1992	140.1	2.7	142.4	1.3	133.3	1.8	135.2	1.7	128.5	2.4	184.4	7.3	149.3	3.8	188.2	8.9
1993	143.1	2.1	144.3	1.3	135.6	1.7	135.9	0.5	129.7	0.9	198.7	7.8	152.6	2.2	198.1	5.3
1994	146.9	2.7	149.7	3.7	138.4	2.1	135.3	-0.4	132.8	2.4	218.1	9.8	154.7	1.4	199.7	0.8
1995	150.7	2.6	154.5	3.2	140.7	1.7	130.5	-3.5	138.4	4.2	230.0	5.5	160.6	3.8	207.3	3.8
1996	154.2	2.3	158.8	2.8	143.7	2.1	132.8	1.8	140.3	1.4	237.4	3.2	167.2	4.1	213.9	3.2
1997	157.7	2.3	154.5	-2.7	156.1	8.6	122.9	-7.5	143.7	2.4	230.5	-2.9	140.1	-16.2	225.6	5.5

Source: U.S. Department of Labor, Bureau of Labor Statistics, Division of Consumer Prices and Price Indexes. - indicates no data collected for period.

Milwaukee, WI
Consumer Price Index - Urban Wage Earners
Base 1982-1984 = 100
Annual Averages

For 1935-1997. Columns headed % show percentile change in the index from the previous period for which an index is available.

Year	All Items		Food & Beverage		Housing		Apparel & Upkeep		Trans-portation		Medical Care		Entertain-ment		Other Goods & Services	
	Index	%	Index	%	Index	%	Index	%	Index	%	Index	%	Index	%	Index	%
1935	12.9	-	-	-	-	-	-	-	-	-	-	-	-	-	-	-
1936	13.2	2.3	-	-	-	-	-	-	-	-	-	-	-	-	-	-
1937	13.7	3.8	-	-	-	-	-	-	-	-	-	-	-	-	-	-
1938	13.4	-2.2	-	-	-	-	-	-	-	-	-	-	-	-	-	-
1939	13.0	-3.0	-	-	-	-	-	-	-	-	-	-	-	-	-	-
1940	13.0	0.0	-	-	-	-	-	-	-	-	-	-	-	-	-	-
1941	13.7	5.4														
1942	15.1	10.2														
1943	16.0	6.0	-	-	-	-	-	-								
1944	16.3	1.9	-	-	-	-	-	-								
1945	16.7	2.5	-	-	-	-	-	-								
1946	18.0	7.8	-	-	-	-	-	-								
1947	20.9	16.1	-	-	-	-	-	-	20.5	-	13.0	-				
1948	22.6	8.1	-	-	-	-	-	-	22.1	7.8	13.8	6.2				
1949	22.4	-0.9	-	-	-	-	-	-	23.1	4.5	14.4	4.3				
1950	23.1	3.1	-	-	-	-	-	-	23.5	1.7	15.0	4.2				
1951	25.3	9.5	-	-	-	-	-	-	25.1	6.8	16.6	10.7	-	-	-	-
1952	26.1	3.2	-	-	-	-	-	-	26.5	5.6	17.5	5.4	-	-	-	-
1953	26.2	0.4	-	-	-	-	40.5	-	27.4	3.4	18.1	3.4	-	-	-	-
1954	26.2	0.0	-	-	-	-	40.4	-0.2	27.1	-1.1	19.2	6.1	-	-	-	-
1955	26.2	0.0	-	-	-	-	40.2	-0.5	26.8	-1.1	19.7	2.6	-	-	-	-
1956	26.6	1.5	-	-	-	-	41.2	2.5	27.5	2.6	20.1	2.0	-	-	-	-
1957	27.5	3.4	-	-	-	-	41.8	1.5	28.7	4.4	21.6	7.5	-	-	-	-
1958	27.8	1.1	-	-	-	-	41.8	0.0	29.2	1.7	22.3	3.2	-	-	-	-
1959	27.8	0.0	-	-	-	-	42.2	1.0	30.1	3.1	22.8	2.2	-	-	-	-
1960	28.2	1.4	-	-	-	-	42.7	1.2	29.9	-0.7	23.3	2.2	-	-	-	-
1961	28.4	0.7	-	-	-	-	43.0	0.7	30.1	0.7	23.5	0.9	-	-	-	-
1962	28.8	1.4	-	-	-	-	43.1	0.2	31.1	3.3	23.7	0.9	-	-	-	-
1963	29.1	1.0	-	-	-	-	43.1	0.0	31.3	0.6	24.2	2.1	-	-	-	-
1964	29.4	1.0	-	-	-	-	43.8	1.6	31.4	0.3	24.6	1.7	-	-	-	-
1965	30.0	2.0	-	-	-	-	44.5	1.6	32.6	3.8	25.6	4.1	-	-	-	-
1966	30.7	2.3	-	-	-	-	45.2	1.6	32.8	0.6	27.0	5.5	-	-	-	-
1967	31.3	2.0	-	-	-	-	46.8	3.5	33.2	1.2	29.1	7.8	-	-	-	-
1968	32.4	3.5	-	-	-	-	48.8	4.3	33.6	1.2	30.8	5.8	-	-	-	-
1969	34.3	5.9	-	-	-	-	52.9	8.4	35.4	5.4	32.9	6.8	-	-	-	-
1970	36.2	5.5	-	-	-	-	57.2	8.1	36.8	4.0	34.7	5.5	-	-	-	-
1971	37.6	3.9	-	-	-	-	58.2	1.7	38.9	5.7	36.7	5.8	-	-	-	-
1972	38.7	2.9	-	-	-	-	59.4	2.1	39.7	2.1	37.3	1.6	-	-	-	-
1973	41.1	6.2	-	-	-	-	62.3	4.9	41.9	5.5	39.0	4.6	-	-	-	-
1974	45.1	9.7	-	-	-	-	66.3	6.4	46.5	11.0	42.9	10.0	-	-	-	-
1975	49.1	8.9	-	-	-	-	71.5	7.8	50.4	8.4	47.6	11.0	-	-	-	-
1976	52.3	6.5	61.9	-	43.7	-	75.9	6.2	54.1	7.3	53.2	11.8	64.1	-	57.4	-
1977	55.6	6.3	65.3	5.5	46.9	7.3	79.2	4.3	57.6	6.5	58.0	9.0	70.9	10.6	60.4	5.2
1978	60.5	8.8	72.0	10.3	51.8	10.4	80.2	1.3	61.3	6.4	63.6	9.7	75.4	6.3	64.9	7.5
1979	69.2	14.4	81.1	12.6	61.3	18.3	84.6	5.5	70.9	15.7	69.9	9.9	80.2	6.4	68.9	6.2

[Continued]

622

Milwaukee, WI
Consumer Price Index - Urban Wage Earners
Base 1982-1984 = 100
Annual Averages
[Continued]

For 1935-1997. Columns headed % show percentile change in the index from the previous period for which an index is available.

Year	All Items		Food & Beverage		Housing		Apparel & Upkeep		Trans- portation		Medical Care		Entertain- ment		Other Goods & Services	
	Index	%	Index	%	Index	%	Index	%	Index	%	Index	%	Index	%	Index	%
1980	80.2	15.9	87.8	8.3	74.7	21.9	89.8	6.1	83.3	17.5	79.1	13.2	88.5	10.3	75.1	9.0
1981	89.2	11.2	95.1	8.3	84.7	13.4	95.1	5.9	93.5	12.2	87.6	10.7	94.6	6.9	82.3	9.6
1982	93.8	5.2	98.5	3.6	89.7	5.9	97.8	2.8	98.0	4.8	93.9	7.2	95.7	1.2	92.1	11.9
1983	100.0	6.6	99.7	1.2	100.3	11.8	101.6	3.9	99.1	1.1	100.2	6.7	100.0	4.5	101.0	9.7
1984	106.2	6.2	101.9	2.2	110.0	9.7	100.6	-1.0	102.9	3.8	105.9	5.7	104.3	4.3	106.9	5.8
1985	109.4	3.0	105.6	3.6	113.3	3.0	103.0	2.4	104.5	1.6	110.0	3.9	109.9	5.4	112.9	5.6
1986	109.6	0.2	107.9	2.2	114.1	0.7	105.6	2.5	99.0	-5.3	115.5	5.0	109.7	-0.2	121.1	7.3
1987	113.8	3.8	116.6	8.1	112.5	-1.4	119.1	12.8	107.2	8.3	127.6	10.5	118.1	7.7	126.7	4.6
1988	118.9	4.5	121.7	4.4	116.0	3.1	128.9	8.2	112.3	4.8	134.1	5.1	123.0	4.1	138.1	9.0
1989	124.1	4.4	128.8	5.8	120.0	3.4	126.0	-2.2	117.7	4.8	143.9	7.3	129.2	5.0	148.2	7.3
1990	130.1	4.8	136.4	5.9	124.9	4.1	125.5	-0.4	123.6	5.0	156.1	8.5	139.0	7.6	157.2	6.1
1991	135.6	4.2	140.2	2.8	130.5	4.5	130.9	4.3	125.9	1.9	169.4	8.5	145.9	5.0	172.1	9.5
1992	139.5	2.9	142.1	1.4	132.6	1.6	135.5	3.5	129.1	2.5	181.3	7.0	151.6	3.9	189.7	10.2
1993	142.3	2.0	143.8	1.2	134.7	1.6	135.9	0.3	130.0	0.7	196.0	8.1	155.0	2.2	199.4	5.1
1994	145.9	2.5	149.1	3.7	137.7	2.2	133.5	-1.8	133.4	2.6	214.1	9.2	158.1	2.0	199.5	0.1
1995	149.7	2.6	153.7	3.1	139.7	1.5	127.5	-4.5	139.5	4.6	225.4	5.3	164.1	3.8	207.0	3.8
1996	153.1	2.3	158.1	2.9	142.5	2.0	128.4	0.7	141.4	1.4	232.8	3.3	171.5	4.5	214.0	3.4
1997	159.8	4.4	154.5	-2.3	161.9	13.6	128.0	-0.3	141.9	0.4	230.8	-0.9	140.0	-18.4	225.3	5.3

Source: U.S. Department of Labor, Bureau of Labor Statistics, Division of Consumer Prices and Price Indexes. - indicates no data collected for period.

Milwaukee, WI
Consumer Price Index - All Urban Consumers
Base 1982-1984 = 100
All Items

For 1935-1997. Columns headed % show percentile change in the index from the previous period for which an index is available.

Year	Jan Index	%	Feb Index	%	Mar Index	%	Apr Index	%	May Index	%	Jun Index	%	Jul Index	%	Aug Index	%	Sep Index	%	Oct Index	%	Nov Index	%	Dec Index	%
1935	-		-		13.3	-	-	-	-		-		13.3	0.0	-		-		13.4	0.8	-		-	
1936	13.5	0.7	-		-		13.4	-0.7	-		-		13.6	1.5	-		13.9	2.2	-		-		13.7	-1.4
1937	-		-		14.0	2.2	-		-		14.3	2.1	-		-		14.4	0.7	-		-		14.2	-1.4
1938	-		-		13.9	-2.1	-		-		13.9	0.0	-		-		13.7	-1.4	-		-		13.6	-0.7
1939	-		-		13.4	-1.5	-		-		13.4	0.0	-		-		13.6	1.5	-		-		13.4	-1.5
1940	-		-		13.4	0.0	-		-		13.6	1.5	-		-		13.5	-0.7	-		-		13.6	0.7
1941	-		-		13.6	0.0	-		-		14.2	4.4	-		14.6	2.8	-		-		-		15.0	2.7
1942	-		-		15.4	2.7	-		-		15.8	2.6	-		15.8	0.0	-		-		-		16.2	2.5
1943	-		-		16.5	1.9	-		-		16.8	1.8	-		16.6	-1.2	-		-		-		16.6	0.0
1944	-		-		16.6	0.0	-		-		16.9	1.8	-		17.0	0.6	-		-		-		17.0	0.0
1945	-		-		17.0	0.0	-		-		17.4	2.4	-		17.3	-0.6	-		-		-		17.4	0.6
1946	-		-		17.4	0.0	-		-		17.9	2.9	-		19.6	9.5	-		-		-		20.6	5.1
1947	-		-		21.2	2.9	-		-		21.5	1.4	-		21.8	1.4	-		-		22.5	3.2	-	
1948	-		22.9	1.8	-		-		23.5	2.6	-		-		24.0	2.1	-		-		23.5	-2.1	-	
1949	-		23.2	-1.3	-		-		23.2	0.0	-		-		23.0	-0.9	-		-		23.2	0.9	-	
1950	-		23.1	-0.4	-		-		23.5	1.7	-		-		24.2	3.0	-		-		24.7	2.1	-	
1951	-		25.7	4.0	-		-		26.1	1.6	-		-		26.3	0.8	-		-		26.7	1.5	-	
1952	-		26.7	0.0	-		-		27.1	1.5	-		-		27.3	0.7	-		-		27.2	-0.4	27.1	-0.4
1953	-		26.9	-0.7	-		-		27.1	0.7	-		-		27.3	0.7	-		-		27.1	-0.7	-	
1954	-		27.1	0.0	-		-		27.2	0.4	-		-		27.1	-0.4	-		-		27.1	0.0	-	
1955	-		27.0	-0.4	-		-		27.0	0.0	-		-		27.1	0.4	-		-		27.2	0.4	-	
1956	-		27.1	-0.4	-		-		27.3	0.7	-		-		27.7	1.5	-		-		27.8	0.4	-	
1957	-		28.1	1.1	-		-		28.4	1.1	-		-		28.6	0.7	-		-		28.6	0.0	-	
1958	-		28.8	0.7	-		-		28.9	0.3	-		-		28.9	0.0	-		-		28.8	-0.3	-	
1959	-		28.7	-0.3	-		-		28.7	0.0	-		-		28.9	0.7	-		-		29.0	0.3	-	
1960	-		28.9	-0.3	-		-		29.2	1.0	-		-		29.3	0.3	-		-		29.4	0.3	-	
1961	-		29.4	0.0	-		-		29.3	-0.3	-		-		29.4	0.3	-		-		29.4	0.0	-	
1962	-		29.8	1.4	-		-		29.8	0.0	-		-		29.8	0.0	-		-		29.9	0.3	-	
1963	-		29.9	0.0	-		-		30.0	0.3	-		-		30.1	0.3	-		-		30.2	0.3	-	
1964	-		30.2	0.0	-		-		30.3	0.3	-		-		30.5	0.7	-		-		30.6	0.3	-	
1965	-		30.7	0.3	-		-		31.0	1.0	-		-		31.2	0.6	-		-		31.2	0.0	-	
1966	-		31.4	0.6	-		-		31.6	0.6	-		-		32.0	1.3	-		-		32.0	0.0	-	
1967	-		32.0	0.0	-		-		32.2	0.6	-		-		32.6	1.2	-		-		32.8	0.6	-	
1968	-		33.0	0.6	-		-		33.3	0.9	-		-		33.7	1.2	-		-		34.0	0.9	-	
1969	-		34.6	1.8	-		-		35.2	1.7	-		-		35.5	0.9	-		-		36.4	2.5	-	
1970	-		36.8	1.1	-		-		37.3	1.4	-		-		37.6	0.8	-		-		38.1	1.3	-	
1971	-		38.5	1.0	-		-		38.6	0.3	-		-		39.3	1.8	-		-		39.1	-0.5	-	
1972	-		39.6	1.3	-		-		39.8	0.5	-		-		40.3	1.3	-		-		40.5	0.5	-	
1973	-		41.1	1.5	-		-		42.1	2.4	-		-		43.1	2.4	-		-		43.9	1.9	-	
1974	-		45.0	2.5	-		-		46.0	2.2	-		-		47.2	2.6	-		-		48.6	3.0	-	
1975	-		49.3	1.4	-		-		50.3	2.0	-		-		51.5	2.4	-		-		52.3	1.6	-	
1976	-		52.6	0.6	-		-		53.7	2.1	-		-		54.7	1.9	-		-		55.2	0.9	-	
1977	-		56.2	1.8	-		-		57.6	2.5	-		-		57.9	0.5	-		-		58.8	1.6	-	
1978	59.4	1.0	-		60.3	1.5	-		61.1	1.3	-		62.7	2.6	-		64.2	2.4	-		64.4	0.3	-	
1979	64.9	0.8	-		67.2	3.5	-		70.3	4.6	-		72.1	2.6	-		73.2	1.5	-		74.4	1.6	-	

[Continued]

Milwaukee, WI
Consumer Price Index - All Urban Consumers
Base 1982-1984 = 100
All Items
[Continued]

For 1935-1997. Columns headed % show percentile change in the index from the previous period for which an index is available.

Year	Jan Index	%	Feb Index	%	Mar Index	%	Apr Index	%	May Index	%	Jun Index	%	Jul Index	%	Aug Index	%	Sep Index	%	Oct Index	%	Nov Index	%	Dec Index	%
1980	76.5	2.8	-	-	78.6	2.7	-	-	81.0	3.1	-	-	81.5	0.6	-	-	83.7	2.7	-	-	84.9	1.4	-	-
1981	86.2	1.5	-	-	87.4	1.4	-	-	90.2	3.2	-	-	92.5	2.5	-	-	92.9	0.4	-	-	93.1	0.2	-	-
1982	94.3	1.3	-	-	93.7	-0.6	-	-	94.8	1.2	-	-	96.0	1.3	-	-	97.9	2.0	-	-	98.1	0.2	-	-
1983	98.7	0.6	-	-	98.7	0.0	-	-	100.0	1.3	-	-	100.3	0.3	-	-	101.6	1.3	-	-	101.2	-0.4	-	-
1984	101.7	0.5	-	-	102.6	0.9	-	-	103.8	1.2	-	-	104.0	0.2	-	-	104.9	0.9	-	-	105.0	0.1	-	-
1985	105.1	0.1	-	-	106.1	1.0	-	-	107.1	0.9	-	-	107.2	0.1	-	-	107.6	0.4	-	-	108.1	0.5	-	-
1986	108.1	0.0	-	-	106.6	-1.4	-	-	107.5	0.8	-	-	107.3	-0.2	-	-	107.8	0.5	-	-	107.1	-0.6	107.8	0.7
1987	-	-	-	-	-	-	-	-	-	-	112.8	4.6	-	-	-	-	-	-	-	-	-	-	115.6	2.5
1988	-	-	-	-	-	-	-	-	-	-	117.7	1.8	-	-	-	-	-	-	-	-	-	-	120.9	2.7
1989	-	-	-	-	-	-	-	-	-	-	123.0	1.7	-	-	-	-	-	-	-	-	-	-	126.0	2.4
1990	-	-	-	-	-	-	-	-	-	-	128.9	2.3	-	-	-	-	-	-	-	-	-	-	132.7	2.9
1991	-	-	-	-	-	-	-	-	-	-	135.1	1.8	-	-	-	-	-	-	-	-	-	-	137.6	1.9
1992	-	-	-	-	-	-	-	-	-	-	138.9	0.9	-	-	-	-	-	-	-	-	-	-	141.3	1.7
1993	-	-	-	-	-	-	-	-	-	-	142.6	0.9	-	-	-	-	-	-	-	-	-	-	143.6	0.7
1994	-	-	-	-	-	-	-	-	-	-	145.2	1.1	-	-	-	-	-	-	-	-	-	-	148.5	2.3
1995	-	-	-	-	-	-	-	-	-	-	150.0	1.0	-	-	-	-	-	-	-	-	-	-	151.5	1.0
1996	-	-	-	-	-	-	-	-	-	-	153.2	1.1	-	-	-	-	-	-	-	-	-	-	155.3	1.4
1997	-	-	-	-	-	-	-	-	-	-	156.2	0.6	-	-	-	-	-	-	-	-	-	-	-	-

Source: U.S. Department of Labor, Bureau of Labor Statistics, Division of Consumer Prices and Price Indexes. - indicates no data collected for period.

Milwaukee, WI
Consumer Price Index - Urban Wage Earners
Base 1982-1984 = 100
All Items

For 1935-1997. Columns headed % show percentile change in the index from the previous period for which an index is available.

Year	Jan Index	Jan %	Feb Index	Feb %	Mar Index	Mar %	Apr Index	Apr %	May Index	May %	Jun Index	Jun %	Jul Index	Jul %	Aug Index	Aug %	Sep Index	Sep %	Oct Index	Oct %	Nov Index	Nov %	Dec Index	Dec %
1935	-	-	-	-	12.9	-	-	-	-	-	-	-	12.9	0.0	-	-	-	-	13.0	0.8	-	-	-	-
1936	13.0	0.0	-	-	-	-	13.0	0.0	-	-	-	-	13.2	1.5	-	-	13.4	1.5	-	-	-	-	13.3	-0.7
1937	-	-	-	-	13.5	1.5	-	-	-	-	13.8	2.2	-	-	-	-	13.9	0.7	-	-	-	-	13.7	-1.4
1938	-	-	-	-	13.5	-1.5	-	-	-	-	13.5	0.0	-	-	-	-	13.2	-2.2	-	-	-	-	13.2	0.0
1939	-	-	-	-	13.0	-1.5	-	-	-	-	12.9	-0.8	-	-	-	-	13.1	1.6	-	-	-	-	13.0	-0.8
1940	-	-	-	-	13.0	0.0	-	-	-	-	13.2	1.5	-	-	-	-	13.0	-1.5	-	-	-	-	13.1	0.8
1941	-	-	-	-	13.2	0.8	-	-	-	-	13.7	3.8	-	-	-	-	14.1	2.9	-	-	-	-	14.5	2.8
1942	-	-	-	-	14.9	2.8	-	-	-	-	15.3	2.7	-	-	-	-	15.2	-0.7	-	-	-	-	15.6	2.6
1943	-	-	-	-	16.0	2.6	-	-	-	-	16.2	1.3	-	-	-	-	16.1	-0.6	-	-	-	-	16.1	0.0
1944	-	-	-	-	16.1	0.0	-	-	-	-	16.4	1.9	-	-	-	-	16.4	0.0	-	-	-	-	16.4	0.0
1945	-	-	-	-	16.4	0.0	-	-	-	-	16.8	2.4	-	-	-	-	16.7	-0.6	-	-	-	-	16.8	0.6
1946	-	-	-	-	16.8	0.0	-	-	-	-	17.3	3.0	-	-	-	-	18.9	9.2	-	-	-	-	19.9	5.3
1947	-	-	-	-	20.5	3.0	-	-	-	-	20.7	1.0	-	-	21.1	1.9	-	-	-	-	21.7	2.8	-	-
1948	-	-	22.1	1.8	-	-	-	-	22.7	2.7	-	-	-	-	23.1	1.8	-	-	-	-	22.7	-1.7	-	-
1949	-	-	22.4	-1.3	-	-	-	-	22.5	0.4	-	-	-	-	22.2	-1.3	-	-	-	-	22.4	0.9	-	-
1950	-	-	22.3	-0.4	-	-	-	-	22.7	1.8	-	-	-	-	23.4	3.1	-	-	-	-	23.8	1.7	-	-
1951	-	-	24.8	4.2	-	-	-	-	25.2	1.6	-	-	-	-	25.4	0.8	-	-	-	-	25.8	1.6	-	-
1952	-	-	25.8	0.0	-	-	-	-	26.2	1.6	-	-	-	-	26.3	0.4	-	-	-	-	26.2	-0.4	26.2	0.0
1953	-	-	26.0	-0.8	-	-	-	-	26.2	0.8	-	-	-	-	26.3	0.4	-	-	-	-	26.2	-0.4	-	-
1954	-	-	26.2	0.0	-	-	-	-	26.3	0.4	-	-	-	-	26.2	-0.4	-	-	-	-	26.2	0.0	-	-
1955	-	-	26.1	-0.4	-	-	-	-	26.1	0.0	-	-	-	-	26.2	0.4	-	-	-	-	26.3	0.4	-	-
1956	-	-	26.2	-0.4	-	-	-	-	26.3	0.4	-	-	-	-	26.7	1.5	-	-	-	-	26.9	0.7	-	-
1957	-	-	27.1	0.7	-	-	-	-	27.4	1.1	-	-	-	-	27.7	1.1	-	-	-	-	27.7	0.0	-	-
1958	-	-	27.8	0.4	-	-	-	-	27.9	0.4	-	-	-	-	27.9	0.0	-	-	-	-	27.8	-0.4	-	-
1959	-	-	27.7	-0.4	-	-	-	-	27.7	0.0	-	-	-	-	27.9	0.7	-	-	-	-	28.1	0.7	-	-
1960	-	-	27.9	-0.7	-	-	-	-	28.2	1.1	-	-	-	-	28.3	0.4	-	-	-	-	28.4	0.4	-	-
1961	-	-	28.4	0.0	-	-	-	-	28.3	-0.4	-	-	-	-	28.4	0.4	-	-	-	-	28.4	0.0	-	-
1962	-	-	28.8	1.4	-	-	-	-	28.8	0.0	-	-	-	-	28.7	-0.3	-	-	-	-	28.9	0.7	-	-
1963	-	-	28.9	0.0	-	-	-	-	29.0	0.3	-	-	-	-	29.1	0.3	-	-	-	-	29.2	0.3	-	-
1964	-	-	29.2	0.0	-	-	-	-	29.2	0.0	-	-	-	-	29.5	1.0	-	-	-	-	29.6	0.3	-	-
1965	-	-	29.7	0.3	-	-	-	-	30.0	1.0	-	-	-	-	30.2	0.7	-	-	-	-	30.1	-0.3	-	-
1966	-	-	30.3	0.7	-	-	-	-	30.5	0.7	-	-	-	-	30.9	1.3	-	-	-	-	30.9	0.0	-	-
1967	-	-	30.9	0.0	-	-	-	-	31.1	0.6	-	-	-	-	31.5	1.3	-	-	-	-	31.7	0.6	-	-
1968	-	-	31.9	0.6	-	-	-	-	32.1	0.6	-	-	-	-	32.5	1.2	-	-	-	-	32.9	1.2	-	-
1969	-	-	33.5	1.8	-	-	-	-	34.0	1.5	-	-	-	-	34.3	0.9	-	-	-	-	35.2	2.6	-	-
1970	-	-	35.6	1.1	-	-	-	-	36.0	1.1	-	-	-	-	36.3	0.8	-	-	-	-	36.8	1.4	-	-
1971	-	-	37.2	1.1	-	-	-	-	37.3	0.3	-	-	-	-	38.0	1.9	-	-	-	-	37.8	-0.5	-	-
1972	-	-	38.2	1.1	-	-	-	-	38.4	0.5	-	-	-	-	39.0	1.6	-	-	-	-	39.1	0.3	-	-
1973	-	-	39.7	1.5	-	-	-	-	40.7	2.5	-	-	-	-	41.7	2.5	-	-	-	-	42.4	1.7	-	-
1974	-	-	43.5	2.6	-	-	-	-	44.4	2.1	-	-	-	-	45.6	2.7	-	-	-	-	46.9	2.9	-	-
1975	-	-	47.6	1.5	-	-	-	-	48.6	2.1	-	-	-	-	49.8	2.5	-	-	-	-	50.5	1.4	-	-
1976	-	-	50.8	0.6	-	-	-	-	51.9	2.2	-	-	-	-	52.9	1.9	-	-	-	-	53.3	0.8	-	-
1977	-	-	54.3	1.9	-	-	-	-	55.7	2.6	-	-	-	-	55.9	0.4	-	-	-	-	56.8	1.6	-	-
1978	57.6	1.4	-	-	58.3	1.2	-	-	59.3	1.7	-	-	60.9	2.7	-	-	62.6	2.8	-	-	62.8	0.3	-	-
1979	63.1	0.5	-	-	65.5	3.8	-	-	68.7	4.9	-	-	70.4	2.5	-	-	71.5	1.6	-	-	72.7	1.7	-	-

[Continued]

Milwaukee, WI
Consumer Price Index - Urban Wage Earners
Base 1982-1984 = 100
All Items
[Continued]

For 1935-1997. Columns headed % show percentile change in the index from the previous period for which an index is available.

Year	Jan Index	%	Feb Index	%	Mar Index	%	Apr Index	%	May Index	%	Jun Index	%	Jul Index	%	Aug Index	%	Sep Index	%	Oct Index	%	Nov Index	%	Dec Index	%
1980	75.3	3.6	-	-	77.5	2.9	-	-	79.8	3.0	-	-	80.0	0.3	-	-	82.3	2.9	-	-	83.7	1.7	-	-
1981	85.1	1.7	-	-	85.9	0.9	-	-	88.7	3.3	-	-	91.1	2.7	-	-	91.4	0.3	-	-	91.2	-0.2	-	-
1982	92.4	1.3	-	-	91.5	-1.0	-	-	92.6	1.2	-	-	93.7	1.2	-	-	95.8	2.2	-	-	96.0	0.2	-	-
1983	94.9	-1.1	-	-	97.3	2.5	-	-	98.7	1.4	-	-	101.6	2.9	-	-	102.9	1.3	-	-	102.9	0.0	-	-
1984	102.4	-0.5	-	-	104.9	2.4	-	-	105.8	0.9	-	-	106.9	1.0	-	-	108.8	1.8	-	-	107.2	-1.5	-	-
1985	107.4	0.2	-	-	108.5	1.0	-	-	109.5	0.9	-	-	109.6	0.1	-	-	109.9	0.3	-	-	110.5	0.5	-	-
1986	110.4	-0.1	-	-	108.6	-1.6	-	-	109.7	1.0	-	-	109.5	-0.2	-	-	110.0	0.5	-	-	109.3	-0.6	110.0	0.6
1987	-	-	-	-	-	-	-	-	-	-	112.3	2.1	-	-	-	-	-	-	-	-	-	-	115.3	2.7
1988	-	-	-	-	-	-	-	-	-	-	117.2	1.6	-	-	-	-	-	-	-	-	-	-	120.6	2.9
1989	-	-	-	-	-	-	-	-	-	-	122.6	1.7	-	-	-	-	-	-	-	-	-	-	125.6	2.4
1990	-	-	-	-	-	-	-	-	-	-	128.2	2.1	-	-	-	-	-	-	-	-	-	-	132.0	3.0
1991	-	-	-	-	-	-	-	-	-	-	134.2	1.7	-	-	-	-	-	-	-	-	-	-	136.9	2.0
1992	-	-	-	-	-	-	-	-	-	-	138.3	1.0	-	-	-	-	-	-	-	-	-	-	140.8	1.8
1993	-	-	-	-	-	-	-	-	-	-	141.9	0.8	-	-	-	-	-	-	-	-	-	-	142.7	0.6
1994	-	-	-	-	-	-	-	-	-	-	144.3	1.1	-	-	-	-	-	-	-	-	-	-	147.6	2.3
1995	-	-	-	-	-	-	-	-	-	-	149.0	0.9	-	-	-	-	-	-	-	-	-	-	150.4	0.9
1996	-	-	-	-	-	-	-	-	-	-	152.0	1.1	-	-	-	-	-	-	-	-	-	-	154.2	1.4
1997	-	-	-	-	-	-	-	-	-	-	155.0	0.5	-	-	-	-	-	-	-	-	-	-	-	-

Source: U.S. Department of Labor, Bureau of Labor Statistics, Division of Consumer Prices and Price Indexes. - indicates no data collected for period.

Milwaukee, WI
Consumer Price Index - All Urban Consumers
Base 1982-1984 = 100
Food and Beverages

For 1975-1997. Columns headed % show percentile change in the index from the previous period for which an index is available.

Year	Jan Index	%	Feb Index	%	Mar Index	%	Apr Index	%	May Index	%	Jun Index	%	Jul Index	%	Aug Index	%	Sep Index	%	Oct Index	%	Nov Index	%	Dec Index	%
1975	-	-	-	-	-	-	-	-	-	-	-	-	-	-	-	-	-	-	-	-	62.1	-	-	-
1976	-	-	62.6	0.8	-	-	-	-	63.0	0.6	-	-	-	-	64.1	1.7	-	-	-	-	63.9	-0.3	-	-
1977	-	-	65.6	2.7	-	-	-	-	66.9	2.0	-	-	-	-	67.7	1.2	-	-	-	-	67.3	-0.6	-	-
1978	69.5	3.3	-	-	70.9	2.0	-	-	72.7	2.5	-	-	74.3	2.2	-	-	75.2	1.2	-	-	75.5	0.4	-	-
1979	78.0	3.3	-	-	80.3	2.9	-	-	81.7	1.7	-	-	82.1	0.5	-	-	82.3	0.2	-	-	83.7	1.7	-	-
1980	84.0	0.4	-	-	84.9	1.1	-	-	85.5	0.7	-	-	87.3	2.1	-	-	89.2	2.2	-	-	90.4	1.3	-	-
1981	91.9	1.7	-	-	94.3	2.6	-	-	94.7	0.4	-	-	95.7	1.1	-	-	95.9	0.2	-	-	95.8	-0.1	-	-
1982	96.4	0.6	-	-	97.0	0.6	-	-	98.9	2.0	-	-	99.9	1.0	-	-	99.2	-0.7	-	-	98.6	-0.6	-	-
1983	99.2	0.6	-	-	99.8	0.6	-	-	100.0	0.2	-	-	99.7	-0.3	-	-	99.6	-0.1	-	-	98.9	-0.7	-	-
1984	100.7	1.8	-	-	100.8	0.1	-	-	101.6	0.8	-	-	103.0	1.4	-	-	102.2	-0.8	-	-	102.4	0.2	-	-
1985	104.8	2.3	-	-	105.8	1.0	-	-	106.0	0.2	-	-	106.0	0.0	-	-	105.6	-0.4	-	-	105.8	0.2	-	-
1986	105.6	-0.2	-	-	106.1	0.5	-	-	107.0	0.8	-	-	108.0	0.9	-	-	109.4	1.3	-	-	110.5	1.0	110.1	-0.4
1987	-	-	-	-	-	-	-	-	-	-	115.8	5.2	-	-	-	-	-	-	-	-	-	-	117.8	1.7
1988	-	-	-	-	-	-	-	-	-	-	120.2	2.0	-	-	-	-	-	-	-	-	-	-	123.5	2.7
1989	-	-	-	-	-	-	-	-	-	-	127.6	3.3	-	-	-	-	-	-	-	-	-	-	130.7	2.4
1990	-	-	-	-	-	-	-	-	-	-	135.6	3.7	-	-	-	-	-	-	-	-	-	-	138.2	1.9
1991	-	-	-	-	-	-	-	-	-	-	140.6	1.7	-	-	-	-	-	-	-	-	-	-	140.5	-0.1
1992	-	-	-	-	-	-	-	-	-	-	142.0	1.1	-	-	-	-	-	-	-	-	-	-	142.8	0.6
1993	-	-	-	-	-	-	-	-	-	-	144.0	0.8	-	-	-	-	-	-	-	-	-	-	144.7	0.5
1994	-	-	-	-	-	-	-	-	-	-	149.0	3.0	-	-	-	-	-	-	-	-	-	-	150.3	0.9
1995	-	-	-	-	-	-	-	-	-	-	153.1	1.9	-	-	-	-	-	-	-	-	-	-	155.9	1.8
1996	-	-	-	-	-	-	-	-	-	-	157.3	0.9	-	-	-	-	-	-	-	-	-	-	160.4	2.0
1997	-	-	-	-	-	-	-	-	-	-	160.8	0.2	-	-	-	-	-	-	-	-	-	-	-	-

Source: U.S. Department of Labor, Bureau of Labor Statistics, Division of Consumer Prices and Price Indexes. - indicates no data collected for period.

Milwaukee, WI
Consumer Price Index - Urban Wage Earners
Base 1982-1984 = 100
Food and Beverages

For 1975-1997. Columns headed % show percentile change in the index from the previous period for which an index is available.

Year	Jan Index	%	Feb Index	%	Mar Index	%	Apr Index	%	May Index	%	Jun Index	%	Jul Index	%	Aug Index	%	Sep Index	%	Oct Index	%	Nov Index	%	Dec Index	%
1975	-	-	-	-	-	-	-	-	-	-	-	-	-	-	-	-	-	-	-	-	60.7	-	-	-
1976	-	-	61.1	0.7	-	-	-	-	61.5	0.7	-	-	-	-	62.6	1.8	-	-	-	-	62.4	-0.3	-	-
1977	-	-	64.1	2.7	-	-	-	-	65.3	1.9	-	-	-	-	66.1	1.2	-	-	-	-	65.7	-0.6	-	-
1978	67.9	3.3	-	-	69.3	2.1	-	-	71.5	3.2	-	-	72.6	1.5	-	-	73.9	1.8	-	-	74.6	0.9	-	-
1979	77.1	3.4	-	-	79.9	3.6	-	-	81.6	2.1	-	-	81.9	0.4	-	-	81.8	-0.1	-	-	82.6	1.0	-	-
1980	83.8	1.5	-	-	85.4	1.9	-	-	86.3	1.1	-	-	87.9	1.9	-	-	90.0	2.4	-	-	91.2	1.3	-	-
1981	93.1	2.1	-	-	94.5	1.5	-	-	94.3	-0.2	-	-	95.8	1.6	-	-	96.1	0.3	-	-	95.9	-0.2	-	-
1982	96.5	0.6	-	-	96.8	0.3	-	-	99.0	2.3	-	-	100.1	1.1	-	-	99.3	-0.8	-	-	98.7	-0.6	-	-
1983	99.2	0.5	-	-	99.9	0.7	-	-	100.1	0.2	-	-	99.8	-0.3	-	-	99.7	-0.1	-	-	98.9	-0.8	-	-
1984	100.6	1.7	-	-	100.6	0.0	-	-	101.5	0.9	-	-	102.9	1.4	-	-	102.2	-0.7	-	-	102.2	0.0	-	-
1985	104.7	2.4	-	-	105.8	1.1	-	-	106.0	0.2	-	-	106.0	0.0	-	-	105.5	-0.5	-	-	105.6	0.1	-	-
1986	105.6	0.0	-	-	105.9	0.3	-	-	106.9	0.9	-	-	107.9	0.9	-	-	109.4	1.4	-	-	110.4	0.9	110.1	-0.3
1987	-	-	-	-	-	-	-	-	-	-	115.5	4.9	-	-	-	-	-	-	-	-	-	-	117.7	1.9
1988	-	-	-	-	-	-	-	-	-	-	120.2	2.1	-	-	-	-	-	-	-	-	-	-	123.2	2.5
1989	-	-	-	-	-	-	-	-	-	-	127.3	3.3	-	-	-	-	-	-	-	-	-	-	130.2	2.3
1990	-	-	-	-	-	-	-	-	-	-	135.2	3.8	-	-	-	-	-	-	-	-	-	-	137.7	1.8
1991	-	-	-	-	-	-	-	-	-	-	140.2	1.8	-	-	-	-	-	-	-	-	-	-	140.2	0.0
1992	-	-	-	-	-	-	-	-	-	-	141.7	1.1	-	-	-	-	-	-	-	-	-	-	142.5	0.6
1993	-	-	-	-	-	-	-	-	-	-	143.5	0.7	-	-	-	-	-	-	-	-	-	-	144.2	0.5
1994	-	-	-	-	-	-	-	-	-	-	148.5	3.0	-	-	-	-	-	-	-	-	-	-	149.7	0.8
1995	-	-	-	-	-	-	-	-	-	-	152.3	1.7	-	-	-	-	-	-	-	-	-	-	155.2	1.9
1996	-	-	-	-	-	-	-	-	-	-	156.6	0.9	-	-	-	-	-	-	-	-	-	-	159.6	1.9
1997	-	-	-	-	-	-	-	-	-	-	160.2	0.4	-	-	-	-	-	-	-	-	-	-	-	-

Source: U.S. Department of Labor, Bureau of Labor Statistics, Division of Consumer Prices and Price Indexes. - indicates no data collected for period.

Milwaukee, WI
Consumer Price Index - All Urban Consumers
Base 1982-1984 = 100
Housing

For 1975-1997. Columns headed % show percentile change in the index from the previous period for which an index is available.

Year	Jan Index	%	Feb Index	%	Mar Index	%	Apr Index	%	May Index	%	Jun Index	%	Jul Index	%	Aug Index	%	Sep Index	%	Oct Index	%	Nov Index	%	Dec Index	%
1975	-	-	-	-	-	-	-	-	-	-	-	-	-	-	-	-	-	-	-	-	45.7	-	-	-
1976	-	-	46.0	0.7	-	-	-	-	47.2	2.6	-	-	-	-	47.9	1.5	-	-	-	-	48.5	1.3	-	-
1977	-	-	49.5	2.1	-	-	-	-	50.8	2.6	-	-	-	-	50.8	0.0	-	-	-	-	52.4	3.1	-	-
1978	53.1	1.3	-	-	54.0	1.7	-	-	54.3	0.6	-	-	56.6	4.2	-	-	58.5	3.4	-	-	58.0	-0.9	-	-
1979	57.6	-0.7	-	-	60.6	5.2	-	-	64.9	7.1	-	-	67.0	3.2	-	-	68.1	1.6	-	-	69.2	1.6	-	-
1980	72.5	4.8	-	-	74.5	2.8	-	-	77.9	4.6	-	-	78.3	0.5	-	-	81.0	3.4	-	-	82.3	1.6	-	-
1981	83.0	0.9	-	-	83.0	0.0	-	-	88.1	6.1	-	-	92.2	4.7	-	-	91.3	-1.0	-	-	90.2	-1.2	-	-
1982	92.8	2.9	-	-	91.0	-1.9	-	-	92.4	1.5	-	-	92.8	0.4	-	-	96.9	4.4	-	-	97.5	0.6	-	-
1983	99.2	1.7	-	-	99.4	0.2	-	-	100.6	1.2	-	-	101.7	1.1	-	-	102.1	0.4	-	-	100.8	-1.3	-	-
1984	102.3	1.5	-	-	103.9	1.6	-	-	105.5	1.5	-	-	105.1	-0.4	-	-	106.5	1.3	-	-	106.1	-0.4	-	-
1985	106.5	0.4	-	-	107.2	0.7	-	-	108.8	1.5	-	-	108.7	-0.1	-	-	109.7	0.9	-	-	109.4	-0.3	-	-
1986	110.4	0.9	-	-	109.1	-1.2	-	-	110.2	1.0	-	-	109.8	-0.4	-	-	110.2	0.4	-	-	106.7	-3.2	109.2	2.3
1987	-	-	-	-	-	-	-	-	-	-	112.0	2.6	-	-	-	-	-	-	-	-	-	-	113.2	1.1
1988	-	-	-	-	-	-	-	-	-	-	115.2	1.8	-	-	-	-	-	-	-	-	-	-	117.2	1.7
1989	-	-	-	-	-	-	-	-	-	-	118.4	1.0	-	-	-	-	-	-	-	-	-	-	121.7	2.8
1990	-	-	-	-	-	-	-	-	-	-	123.7	1.6	-	-	-	-	-	-	-	-	-	-	126.8	2.5
1991	-	-	-	-	-	-	-	-	-	-	129.5	2.1	-	-	-	-	-	-	-	-	-	-	132.6	2.4
1992	-	-	-	-	-	-	-	-	-	-	132.3	-0.2	-	-	-	-	-	-	-	-	-	-	134.3	1.5
1993	-	-	-	-	-	-	-	-	-	-	134.5	0.1	-	-	-	-	-	-	-	-	-	-	136.6	1.6
1994	-	-	-	-	-	-	-	-	-	-	137.5	0.7	-	-	-	-	-	-	-	-	-	-	139.3	1.3
1995	-	-	-	-	-	-	-	-	-	-	139.1	-0.1	-	-	-	-	-	-	-	-	-	-	142.2	2.2
1996	-	-	-	-	-	-	-	-	-	-	142.7	0.4	-	-	-	-	-	-	-	-	-	-	144.8	1.5
1997	-	-	-	-	-	-	-	-	-	-	144.8	0.0	-	-	-	-	-	-	-	-	-	-	-	-

Source: U.S. Department of Labor, Bureau of Labor Statistics, Division of Consumer Prices and Price Indexes. - indicates no data collected for period.

Milwaukee, WI
Consumer Price Index - Urban Wage Earners
Base 1982-1984 = 100
Housing

For 1975-1997. Columns headed % show percentile change in the index from the previous period for which an index is available.

Year	Jan Index	%	Feb Index	%	Mar Index	%	Apr Index	%	May Index	%	Jun Index	%	Jul Index	%	Aug Index	%	Sep Index	%	Oct Index	%	Nov Index	%	Dec Index	%
1975	-	-	-	-	-	-	-	-	-	-	-	-	-	-	-	-	-	-	-	-	42.1	-	-	-
1976	-	-	42.5	1.0	-	-	-	-	43.5	2.4	-	-	-	-	44.2	1.6	-	-	-	-	44.7	1.1	-	-
1977	-	-	45.7	2.2	-	-	-	-	46.9	2.6	-	-	-	-	46.9	0.0	-	-	-	-	48.4	3.2	-	-
1978	49.2	1.7	-	-	49.9	1.4	-	-	50.1	0.4	-	-	52.4	4.6	-	-	54.5	4.0	-	-	54.0	-0.9	-	-
1979	53.3	-1.3	-	-	56.5	6.0	-	-	61.1	8.1	-	-	63.1	3.3	-	-	64.1	1.6	-	-	65.5	2.2	-	-
1980	69.2	5.6	-	-	71.2	2.9	-	-	74.2	4.2	-	-	74.5	0.4	-	-	77.4	3.9	-	-	79.2	2.3	-	-
1981	79.3	0.1	-	-	78.9	-0.5	-	-	84.4	7.0	-	-	88.8	5.2	-	-	88.1	-0.8	-	-	86.4	-1.9	-	-
1982	88.9	2.9	-	-	86.6	-2.6	-	-	87.9	1.5	-	-	88.1	0.2	-	-	92.6	5.1	-	-	93.2	0.6	-	-
1983	90.9	-2.5	-	-	96.2	5.8	-	-	97.7	1.6	-	-	104.1	6.6	-	-	105.0	0.9	-	-	104.8	-0.2	-	-
1984	104.0	-0.8	-	-	108.6	4.4	-	-	109.4	0.7	-	-	111.0	1.5	-	-	114.6	3.2	-	-	110.8	-3.3	-	-
1985	111.2	0.4	-	-	112.0	0.7	-	-	113.6	1.4	-	-	113.6	0.0	-	-	114.5	0.8	-	-	114.1	-0.3	-	-
1986	115.2	1.0	-	-	113.7	-1.3	-	-	115.0	1.1	-	-	114.5	-0.4	-	-	114.8	0.3	-	-	111.0	-3.3	113.8	2.5
1987	-	-	-	-	-	-	-	-	-	-	111.8	-1.8	-	-	-	-	-	-	-	-	-	-	113.1	1.2
1988	-	-	-	-	-	-	-	-	-	-	114.9	1.6	-	-	-	-	-	-	-	-	-	-	117.1	1.9
1989	-	-	-	-	-	-	-	-	-	-	118.2	0.9	-	-	-	-	-	-	-	-	-	-	121.7	3.0
1990	-	-	-	-	-	-	-	-	-	-	123.5	1.5	-	-	-	-	-	-	-	-	-	-	126.4	2.3
1991	-	-	-	-	-	-	-	-	-	-	128.8	1.9	-	-	-	-	-	-	-	-	-	-	132.1	2.6
1992	-	-	-	-	-	-	-	-	-	-	131.7	-0.3	-	-	-	-	-	-	-	-	-	-	133.5	1.4
1993	-	-	-	-	-	-	-	-	-	-	133.4	-0.1	-	-	-	-	-	-	-	-	-	-	136.0	1.9
1994	-	-	-	-	-	-	-	-	-	-	136.8	0.6	-	-	-	-	-	-	-	-	-	-	138.7	1.4
1995	-	-	-	-	-	-	-	-	-	-	138.0	-0.5	-	-	-	-	-	-	-	-	-	-	141.3	2.4
1996	-	-	-	-	-	-	-	-	-	-	141.4	0.1	-	-	-	-	-	-	-	-	-	-	143.7	1.6
1997	-	-	-	-	-	-	-	-	-	-	143.6	-0.1	-	-	-	-	-	-	-	-	-	-	-	-

Source: U.S. Department of Labor, Bureau of Labor Statistics, Division of Consumer Prices and Price Indexes. - indicates no data collected for period.

Milwaukee, WI
Consumer Price Index - All Urban Consumers
Base 1982-1984 = 100
Apparel and Upkeep

For 1952-1997. Columns headed % show percentile change in the index from the previous period for which an index is available.

Year	Jan Index	%	Feb Index	%	Mar Index	%	Apr Index	%	May Index	%	Jun Index	%	Jul Index	%	Aug Index	%	Sep Index	%	Oct Index	%	Nov Index	%	Dec Index	%
1952	-	-	-	-	-	-	-	-	-	-	-	-	-	-	-	-	-	-	-	-	39.4	-	-	-
1953	-	-	39.3	-0.3	-	-	-	-	39.5	0.5	-	-	-	-	39.7	0.5	-	-	-	-	39.7	0.0	-	-
1954	-	-	39.9	0.5	-	-	-	-	39.7	-0.5	-	-	-	-	39.4	-0.8	-	-	-	-	39.2	-0.5	-	-
1955	-	-	39.1	-0.3	-	-	-	-	39.2	0.3	-	-	-	-	39.3	0.3	-	-	-	-	39.7	1.0	-	-
1956	-	-	39.9	0.5	-	-	-	-	40.1	0.5	-	-	-	-	40.5	1.0	-	-	-	-	40.6	0.2	-	-
1957	-	-	40.7	0.2	-	-	-	-	40.9	0.5	-	-	-	-	41.1	0.5	-	-	-	-	41.0	-0.2	-	-
1958	-	-	41.1	0.2	-	-	-	-	40.9	-0.5	-	-	-	-	41.0	0.2	-	-	-	-	40.9	-0.2	-	-
1959	-	-	40.7	-0.5	-	-	-	-	41.3	1.5	-	-	-	-	41.4	0.2	-	-	-	-	41.6	0.5	-	-
1960	-	-	41.7	0.2	-	-	-	-	41.9	0.5	-	-	-	-	41.8	-0.2	-	-	-	-	41.8	0.0	-	-
1961	-	-	42.1	0.7	-	-	-	-	42.1	0.0	-	-	-	-	41.7	-1.0	-	-	-	-	42.2	1.2	-	-
1962	-	-	42.1	-0.2	-	-	-	-	42.3	0.5	-	-	-	-	42.2	-0.2	-	-	-	-	42.1	-0.2	-	-
1963	-	-	41.9	-0.5	-	-	-	-	42.0	0.2	-	-	-	-	42.4	1.0	-	-	-	-	42.4	0.0	-	-
1964	-	-	42.3	-0.2	-	-	-	-	42.8	1.2	-	-	-	-	43.1	0.7	-	-	-	-	43.3	0.5	-	-
1965	-	-	43.2	-0.2	-	-	-	-	43.8	1.4	-	-	-	-	43.6	-0.5	-	-	-	-	43.3	-0.7	-	-
1966	-	-	43.6	0.7	-	-	-	-	43.9	0.7	-	-	-	-	44.3	0.9	-	-	-	-	44.8	1.1	-	-
1967	-	-	45.3	1.1	-	-	-	-	46.0	1.5	-	-	-	-	45.7	-0.7	-	-	-	-	46.4	1.5	-	-
1968	-	-	46.5	0.2	-	-	-	-	47.8	2.8	-	-	-	-	48.0	0.4	-	-	-	-	48.7	1.5	-	-
1969	-	-	49.6	1.8	-	-	-	-	51.5	3.8	-	-	-	-	51.5	0.0	-	-	-	-	54.4	5.6	-	-
1970	-	-	54.6	0.4	-	-	-	-	55.5	1.6	-	-	-	-	56.2	1.3	-	-	-	-	57.5	2.3	-	-
1971	-	-	56.7	-1.4	-	-	-	-	56.7	0.0	-	-	-	-	55.8	-1.6	-	-	-	-	58.3	4.5	-	-
1972	-	-	57.2	-1.9	-	-	-	-	58.3	1.9	-	-	-	-	57.2	-1.9	-	-	-	-	59.4	3.8	-	-
1973	-	-	59.8	0.7	-	-	-	-	60.6	1.3	-	-	-	-	60.7	0.2	-	-	-	-	62.7	3.3	-	-
1974	-	-	61.6	-1.8	-	-	-	-	64.2	4.2	-	-	-	-	65.4	1.9	-	-	-	-	68.2	4.3	-	-
1975	-	-	67.7	-0.7	-	-	-	-	69.8	3.1	-	-	-	-	69.6	-0.3	-	-	-	-	72.8	4.6	-	-
1976	-	-	71.7	-1.5	-	-	-	-	74.5	3.9	-	-	-	-	74.8	0.4	-	-	-	-	75.9	1.5	-	-
1977	-	-	75.2	-0.9	-	-	-	-	77.8	3.5	-	-	-	-	77.0	-1.0	-	-	-	-	80.1	4.0	-	-
1978	75.2	-6.1	-	-	77.6	3.2	-	-	80.0	3.1	-	-	76.7	-4.1	-	-	80.1	4.4	-	-	79.6	-0.6	-	-
1979	77.2	-3.0	-	-	81.5	5.6	-	-	80.5	-1.2	-	-	81.4	1.1	-	-	85.4	4.9	-	-	85.7	0.4	-	-
1980	83.5	-2.6	-	-	89.0	6.6	-	-	86.6	-2.7	-	-	83.7	-3.3	-	-	91.3	9.1	-	-	89.3	-2.2	-	-
1981	89.1	-0.2	-	-	91.8	3.0	-	-	89.4	-2.6	-	-	89.2	-0.2	-	-	97.0	8.7	-	-	97.2	0.2	-	-
1982	89.2	-8.2	-	-	94.8	6.3	-	-	96.4	1.7	-	-	96.9	0.5	102.2	5.5	-	-	-	-	100.1	-2.1	-	-
1983	95.6	-4.5	-	-	100.5	5.1	-	-	101.5	1.0	-	-	97.3	-4.1	108.2	11.2	-	-	-	-	107.4	-0.7	-	-
1984	98.8	-8.0	-	-	101.3	2.5	-	-	101.3	0.0	-	-	100.5	-0.8	102.4	1.9	-	-	-	-	103.5	1.1	-	-
1985	98.6	-4.7	-	-	103.6	5.1	-	-	102.5	-1.1	-	-	102.1	-0.4	106.0	3.8	-	-	-	-	106.5	0.5	-	-
1986	102.9	-3.4	-	-	107.3	4.3	-	-	106.3	-0.9	-	-	104.6	-1.6	105.3	0.7	-	-	-	-	105.0	-0.3	103.0	-1.9
1987	-	-	-	-	-	-	-	-	-	-	117.0	13.6	-	-	-	-	-	-	-	-	-	-	122.5	4.7
1988	-	-	-	-	-	-	-	-	-	-	124.6	1.7	-	-	-	-	-	-	-	-	-	-	135.6	8.8
1989	-	-	-	-	-	-	-	-	-	-	130.0	-4.1	-	-	-	-	-	-	-	-	-	-	125.6	-3.4
1990	-	-	-	-	-	-	-	-	-	-	126.9	1.0	-	-	-	-	-	-	-	-	-	-	129.3	1.9
1991	-	-	-	-	-	-	-	-	-	-	133.1	2.9	-	-	-	-	-	-	-	-	-	-	132.6	-0.4
1992	-	-	-	-	-	-	-	-	-	-	137.4	3.6	-	-	-	-	-	-	-	-	-	-	133.1	-3.1
1993	-	-	-	-	-	-	-	-	-	-	137.9	3.6	-	-	-	-	-	-	-	-	-	-	133.9	-2.9
1994	-	-	-	-	-	-	-	-	-	-	134.0	0.1	-	-	-	-	-	-	-	-	-	-	136.6	1.9

[Continued]

Milwaukee, WI
Consumer Price Index - All Urban Consumers
Base 1982-1984 = 100
Apparel and Upkeep
[Continued]

For 1952-1997. Columns headed % show percentile change in the index from the previous period for which an index is available.

Year	Jan Index	%	Feb Index	%	Mar Index	%	Apr Index	%	May Index	%	Jun Index	%	Jul Index	%	Aug Index	%	Sep Index	%	Oct Index	%	Nov Index	%	Dec Index	%
1995	-	-	-	-	-	-	-	-	-	-	135.9	-0.5	-	-	-	-	-	-	-	-	-	-	125.2	-7.9
1996	-	-	-	-	-	-	-	-	-	-	132.7	6.0	-	-	-	-	-	-	-	-	-	-	132.9	0.2
1997	-	-	-	-	-	-	-	-	-	-	135.4	1.9	-	-	-	-	-	-	-	-	-	-	-	-

Source: U.S. Department of Labor, Bureau of Labor Statistics, Division of Consumer Prices and Price Indexes. - indicates no data collected for period.

Milwaukee, WI
Consumer Price Index - Urban Wage Earners
Base 1982-1984 = 100
Apparel and Upkeep

For 1952-1997. Columns headed % show percentile change in the index from the previous period for which an index is available.

Year	Jan Index	%	Feb Index	%	Mar Index	%	Apr Index	%	May Index	%	Jun Index	%	Jul Index	%	Aug Index	%	Sep Index	%	Oct Index	%	Nov Index	%	Dec Index	%
1952	-	-	-	-	-	-	-	-	-	-	-	-	-	-	-	-	-	-	-	-	40.3	-	-	-
1953	-	-	40.2	-0.2	-	-	-	-	40.4	0.5	-	-	-	-	40.6	0.5	-	-	-	-	40.6	0.0	-	-
1954	-	-	40.8	0.5	-	-	-	-	40.6	-0.5	-	-	-	-	40.3	-0.7	-	-	-	-	40.1	-0.5	-	-
1955	-	-	40.0	-0.2	-	-	-	-	40.1	0.2	-	-	-	-	40.1	0.0	-	-	-	-	40.6	1.2	-	-
1956	-	-	40.8	0.5	-	-	-	-	41.0	0.5	-	-	-	-	41.4	1.0	-	-	-	-	41.5	0.2	-	-
1957	-	-	41.6	0.2	-	-	-	-	41.8	0.5	-	-	-	-	42.0	0.5	-	-	-	-	41.9	-0.2	-	-
1958	-	-	42.0	0.2	-	-	-	-	41.8	-0.5	-	-	-	-	41.9	0.2	-	-	-	-	41.8	-0.2	-	-
1959	-	-	41.6	-0.5	-	-	-	-	42.3	1.7	-	-	-	-	42.3	0.0	-	-	-	-	42.5	0.5	-	-
1960	-	-	42.6	0.2	-	-	-	-	42.8	0.5	-	-	-	-	42.7	-0.2	-	-	-	-	42.7	0.0	-	-
1961	-	-	43.0	0.7	-	-	-	-	43.0	0.0	-	-	-	-	42.7	-0.7	-	-	-	-	43.1	0.9	-	-
1962	-	-	43.1	0.0	-	-	-	-	43.2	0.2	-	-	-	-	43.1	-0.2	-	-	-	-	43.0	-0.2	-	-
1963	-	-	42.8	-0.5	-	-	-	-	42.9	0.2	-	-	-	-	43.4	1.2	-	-	-	-	43.4	0.0	-	-
1964	-	-	43.3	-0.2	-	-	-	-	43.8	1.2	-	-	-	-	44.0	0.5	-	-	-	-	44.2	0.5	-	-
1965	-	-	44.2	0.0	-	-	-	-	44.8	1.4	-	-	-	-	44.6	-0.4	-	-	-	-	44.3	-0.7	-	-
1966	-	-	44.6	0.7	-	-	-	-	44.9	0.7	-	-	-	-	45.3	0.9	-	-	-	-	45.8	1.1	-	-
1967	-	-	46.3	1.1	-	-	-	-	47.0	1.5	-	-	-	-	46.7	-0.6	-	-	-	-	47.4	1.5	-	-
1968	-	-	47.5	0.2	-	-	-	-	48.9	2.9	-	-	-	-	49.0	0.2	-	-	-	-	49.8	1.6	-	-
1969	-	-	50.7	1.8	-	-	-	-	52.6	3.7	-	-	-	-	52.7	0.2	-	-	-	-	55.6	5.5	-	-
1970	-	-	55.8	0.4	-	-	-	-	56.7	1.6	-	-	-	-	57.5	1.4	-	-	-	-	58.8	2.3	-	-
1971	-	-	58.0	-1.4	-	-	-	-	58.0	0.0	-	-	-	-	57.1	-1.6	-	-	-	-	59.6	4.4	-	-
1972	-	-	58.5	-1.8	-	-	-	-	59.6	1.9	-	-	-	-	58.5	-1.8	-	-	-	-	60.8	3.9	-	-
1973	-	-	61.1	0.5	-	-	-	-	62.0	1.5	-	-	-	-	62.1	0.2	-	-	-	-	64.1	3.2	-	-
1974	-	-	63.0	-1.7	-	-	-	-	65.6	4.1	-	-	-	-	66.8	1.8	-	-	-	-	69.7	4.3	-	-
1975	-	-	69.2	-0.7	-	-	-	-	71.3	3.0	-	-	-	-	71.2	-0.1	-	-	-	-	74.4	4.5	-	-
1976	-	-	73.4	-1.3	-	-	-	-	76.2	3.8	-	-	-	-	76.5	0.4	-	-	-	-	77.6	1.4	-	-
1977	-	-	76.9	-0.9	-	-	-	-	79.6	3.5	-	-	-	-	78.7	-1.1	-	-	-	-	81.9	4.1	-	-
1978	76.3	-6.8	-	-	78.0	2.2	-	-	80.1	2.7	-	-	78.3	-2.2	-	-	83.6	6.8	-	-	83.7	0.1	-	-
1979	80.2	-4.2	-	-	83.4	4.0	-	-	82.4	-1.2	-	-	82.8	0.5	-	-	88.0	6.3	-	-	89.0	1.1	-	-
1980	87.1	-2.1	-	-	90.2	3.6	-	-	89.6	-0.7	-	-	87.1	-2.8	-	-	93.1	6.9	-	-	90.3	-3.0	-	-
1981	93.4	3.4	-	-	94.9	1.6	-	-	93.4	-1.6	-	-	94.7	1.4	-	-	97.2	2.6	-	-	97.6	0.4	-	-
1982	90.3	-7.5	-	-	96.4	6.8	-	-	97.4	1.0	-	-	97.9	0.5	-	-	102.9	5.1	-	-	100.4	-2.4	-	-
1983	96.3	-4.1	-	-	101.3	5.2	-	-	101.1	-0.2	-	-	96.9	-4.2	-	-	107.2	10.6	-	-	106.4	-0.7	-	-
1984	98.8	-7.1	-	-	101.0	2.2	-	-	101.0	0.0	-	-	99.2	-1.8	-	-	101.4	2.2	-	-	102.2	0.8	-	-
1985	98.8	-3.3	-	-	103.1	4.4	-	-	102.0	-1.1	-	-	101.4	-0.6	-	-	104.8	3.4	-	-	106.7	1.8	-	-
1986	103.2	-3.3	-	-	106.7	3.4	-	-	107.0	0.3	-	-	105.6	-1.3	-	-	105.6	0.0	-	-	105.8	0.2	104.1	-1.6
1987	-	-	-	-	-	-	-	-	-	-	116.6	12.0	-	-	-	-	-	-	-	-	-	-	121.6	4.3
1988	-	-	-	-	-	-	-	-	-	-	122.9	1.1	-	-	-	-	-	-	-	-	-	-	134.9	9.8
1989	-	-	-	-	-	-	-	-	-	-	128.1	-5.0	-	-	-	-	-	-	-	-	-	-	123.8	-3.4
1990	-	-	-	-	-	-	-	-	-	-	124.5	0.6	-	-	-	-	-	-	-	-	-	-	126.5	1.6
1991	-	-	-	-	-	-	-	-	-	-	130.4	3.1	-	-	-	-	-	-	-	-	-	-	131.3	0.7
1992	-	-	-	-	-	-	-	-	-	-	136.9	4.3	-	-	-	-	-	-	-	-	-	-	134.1	-2.0
1993	-	-	-	-	-	-	-	-	-	-	138.4	3.2	-	-	-	-	-	-	-	-	-	-	133.4	-3.6
1994	-	-	-	-	-	-	-	-	-	-	132.3	-0.8	-	-	-	-	-	-	-	-	-	-	134.7	1.8

[Continued]

Milwaukee, WI
Consumer Price Index - Urban Wage Earners
Base 1982-1984 = 100
Apparel and Upkeep

[Continued]

For 1952-1997. Columns headed % show percentile change in the index from the previous period for which an index is available.

Year	Jan Index	%	Feb Index	%	Mar Index	%	Apr Index	%	May Index	%	Jun Index	%	Jul Index	%	Aug Index	%	Sep Index	%	Oct Index	%	Nov Index	%	Dec Index	%
1995	-	-	-	-	-	-	-	-	-	-	133.3	-1.0	-	-	-	-	-	-	-	-	-	-	121.8	-8.6
1996	-	-	-	-	-	-	-	-	-	-	128.1	5.2	-	-	-	-	-	-	-	-	-	-	128.7	0.5
1997	-	-	-	-	-	-	-	-	-	-	131.5	2.2	-	-	-	-	-	-	-	-	-	-	-	-

Source: U.S. Department of Labor, Bureau of Labor Statistics, Division of Consumer Prices and Price Indexes. - indicates no data collected for period.

Milwaukee, WI
Consumer Price Index - All Urban Consumers
Base 1982-1984 = 100
Transportation

For 1946-1997. Columns headed % show percentile change in the index from the previous period for which an index is available.

Year	Jan Index	%	Feb Index	%	Mar Index	%	Apr Index	%	May Index	%	Jun Index	%	Jul Index	%	Aug Index	%	Sep Index	%	Oct Index	%	Nov Index	%	Dec Index	%
1946	-	-	-	-	-	-	-	-	-	-	-	-	-	-	-	-	-	-	-	-	19.9	-	-	-
1947	-	-	-	-	20.0	0.5	-	-	-	-	20.0	0.0	-	-	20.2	1.0	-	-	-	-	20.8	3.0	-	-
1948	-	-	21.2	1.9	-	-	-	-	21.3	0.5	-	-	-	-	22.6	6.1	-	-	-	-	22.7	0.4	-	-
1949	-	-	23.0	1.3	-	-	-	-	23.1	0.4	-	-	-	-	22.9	-0.9	-	-	-	-	22.3	-2.6	-	-
1950	-	-	22.0	-1.3	-	-	-	-	23.2	5.5	-	-	-	-	23.8	2.6	-	-	-	-	23.8	0.0	-	-
1951	-	-	23.9	0.4	-	-	-	-	24.8	3.8	-	-	-	-	24.8	0.0	-	-	-	-	25.6	3.2	-	-
1952	-	-	26.1	2.0	-	-	-	-	26.2	0.4	-	-	-	-	26.2	0.0	-	-	-	-	27.0	3.1	-	-
1953	-	-	27.0	0.0	-	-	-	-	27.0	0.0	-	-	-	-	27.3	1.1	-	-	-	-	27.1	-0.7	-	-
1954	-	-	26.8	-1.1	-	-	-	-	26.8	0.0	-	-	-	-	26.4	-1.5	-	-	-	-	27.2	3.0	-	-
1955	-	-	26.5	-2.6	-	-	-	-	26.4	-0.4	-	-	-	-	26.3	-0.4	-	-	-	-	26.9	2.3	-	-
1956	-	-	26.7	-0.7	-	-	-	-	26.6	-0.4	-	-	-	-	27.3	2.6	-	-	-	-	28.1	2.9	-	-
1957	-	-	28.2	0.4	-	-	-	-	28.2	0.0	-	-	-	-	28.3	0.4	-	-	-	-	28.8	1.8	-	-
1958	-	-	28.5	-1.0	-	-	-	-	28.4	-0.4	-	-	-	-	29.2	2.8	-	-	-	-	29.3	0.3	-	-
1959	-	-	29.4	0.3	-	-	-	-	29.5	0.3	-	-	-	-	29.9	1.4	-	-	-	-	30.5	2.0	-	-
1960	-	-	29.2	-4.3	-	-	-	-	29.5	1.0	-	-	-	-	29.8	1.0	-	-	-	-	29.5	-1.0	-	-
1961	-	-	29.9	1.4	-	-	-	-	29.0	-3.0	-	-	-	-	30.1	3.8	-	-	-	-	29.9	-0.7	-	-
1962	-	-	30.5	2.0	-	-	-	-	31.0	1.6	-	-	-	-	30.3	-2.3	-	-	-	-	31.2	3.0	-	-
1963	-	-	30.5	-2.2	-	-	-	-	31.1	2.0	-	-	-	-	30.8	-1.0	-	-	-	-	31.5	2.3	-	-
1964	-	-	30.9	-1.9	-	-	-	-	30.5	-1.3	-	-	-	-	31.3	2.6	-	-	-	-	31.7	1.3	-	-
1965	-	-	32.1	1.3	-	-	-	-	32.6	1.6	-	-	-	-	32.1	-1.5	-	-	-	-	32.1	0.0	-	-
1966	-	-	32.3	0.6	-	-	-	-	32.0	-0.9	-	-	-	-	32.8	2.5	-	-	-	-	32.7	-0.3	-	-
1967	-	-	32.5	-0.6	-	-	-	-	32.7	0.6	-	-	-	-	32.8	0.3	-	-	-	-	33.7	2.7	-	-
1968	-	-	33.6	-0.3	-	-	-	-	32.8	-2.4	-	-	-	-	32.9	0.3	-	-	-	-	33.6	2.1	-	-
1969	-	-	35.0	4.2	-	-	-	-	34.8	-0.6	-	-	-	-	34.5	-0.9	-	-	-	-	35.8	3.8	-	-
1970	-	-	34.9	-2.5	-	-	-	-	36.6	4.9	-	-	-	-	36.1	-1.4	-	-	-	-	37.8	4.7	-	-
1971	-	-	38.9	2.9	-	-	-	-	37.8	-2.8	-	-	-	-	39.3	4.0	-	-	-	-	38.1	-3.1	-	-
1972	-	-	37.9	-0.5	-	-	-	-	38.6	1.8	-	-	-	-	40.3	4.4	-	-	-	-	40.0	-0.7	-	-
1973	-	-	40.2	0.5	-	-	-	-	41.6	3.5	-	-	-	-	41.5	-0.2	-	-	-	-	42.2	1.7	-	-
1974	-	-	43.4	2.8	-	-	-	-	45.7	5.3	-	-	-	-	47.4	3.7	-	-	-	-	47.8	0.8	-	-
1975	-	-	48.3	1.0	-	-	-	-	49.2	1.9	-	-	-	-	50.9	3.5	-	-	-	-	51.1	0.4	-	-
1976	-	-	51.1	0.0	-	-	-	-	52.4	2.5	-	-	-	-	55.0	5.0	-	-	-	-	55.4	0.7	-	-
1977	-	-	55.7	0.5	-	-	-	-	57.3	2.9	-	-	-	-	57.5	0.3	-	-	-	-	57.7	0.3	-	-
1978	57.9	0.3	-	-	58.2	0.5	-	-	59.1	1.5	-	-	61.1	3.4	-	-	61.7	1.0	-	-	63.5	2.9	-	-
1979	64.4	1.4	-	-	65.5	1.7	-	-	69.1	5.5	-	-	72.5	4.9	-	-	73.3	1.1	-	-	75.0	2.3	-	-
1980	77.4	3.2	-	-	80.7	4.3	-	-	84.5	4.7	-	-	84.0	-0.6	-	-	83.9	-0.1	-	-	86.1	2.6	-	-
1981	88.9	3.3	-	-	90.6	1.9	-	-	92.5	2.1	-	-	93.7	1.3	-	-	95.0	1.4	-	-	98.1	3.3	-	-
1982	98.2	0.1	-	-	97.2	-1.0	-	-	96.8	-0.4	-	-	100.6	3.9	-	-	99.1	-1.5	-	-	98.9	-0.2	-	-
1983	98.1	-0.8	-	-	95.9	-2.2	-	-	98.3	2.5	-	-	99.0	0.7	-	-	100.8	1.8	-	-	101.3	0.5	-	-
1984	100.8	-0.5	-	-	101.3	0.5	-	-	102.8	1.5	-	-	102.7	-0.1	-	-	103.3	0.6	-	-	103.9	0.6	-	-
1985	102.1	-1.7	-	-	103.0	0.9	-	-	104.7	1.7	-	-	104.6	-0.1	-	-	103.4	-1.1	-	-	105.1	1.6	-	-
1986	104.2	-0.9	-	-	97.5	-6.4	-	-	98.8	1.3	-	-	97.7	-1.1	-	-	97.1	-0.6	-	-	98.7	1.6	98.2	-0.5
1987	-	-	-	-	-	-	-	-	-	-	105.0	6.9	-	-	-	-	-	-	-	-	-	-	108.8	3.6
1988	-	-	-	-	-	-	-	-	-	-	110.2	1.3	-	-	-	-	-	-	-	-	-	-	112.8	2.4
1989	-	-	-	-	-	-	-	-	-	-	115.9	2.7	-	-	-	-	-	-	-	-	-	-	118.0	1.8
1990	-	-	-	-	-	-	-	-	-	-	120.1	1.8	-	-	-	-	-	-	-	-	-	-	125.6	4.6

[Continued]

Milwaukee, WI
Consumer Price Index - All Urban Consumers
Base 1982-1984 = 100
Transportation

[Continued]

For 1946-1997. Columns headed % show percentile change in the index from the previous period for which an index is available.

Year	Jan		Feb		Mar		Apr		May		Jun		Jul		Aug		Sep		Oct		Nov		Dec	
	Index	%	Index	%	Index	%	Index	%	Index	%	Index	%	Index	%	Index	%	Index	%	Index	%	Index	%	Index	%
1991	-	-	-	-	-	-	-	-	-	-	124.9	-0.6	-	-	-	-	-	-	-	-	-	-	126.1	1.0
1992	-	-	-	-	-	-	-	-	-	-	127.3	1.0	-	-	-	-	-	-	-	-	-	-	129.7	1.9
1993	-	-	-	-	-	-	-	-	-	-	129.6	-0.1	-	-	-	-	-	-	-	-	-	-	129.7	0.1
1994	-	-	-	-	-	-	-	-	-	-	130.1	0.3	-	-	-	-	-	-	-	-	-	-	135.5	4.2
1995	-	-	-	-	-	-	-	-	-	-	138.7	2.4	-	-	-	-	-	-	-	-	-	-	138.2	-0.4
1996	-	-	-	-	-	-	-	-	-	-	140.1	1.4	-	-	-	-	-	-	-	-	-	-	140.5	0.3
1997	-	-	-	-	-	-	-	-	-	-	142.1	1.1	-	-	-	-	-	-	-	-	-	-	-	-

Source: U.S. Department of Labor, Bureau of Labor Statistics, Division of Consumer Prices and Price Indexes. - indicates no data collected for period.

Milwaukee, WI
Consumer Price Index - Urban Wage Earners
Base 1982-1984 = 100
Transportation

For 1946-1997. Columns headed % show percentile change in the index from the previous period for which an index is available.

Year	Jan Index	%	Feb Index	%	Mar Index	%	Apr Index	%	May Index	%	Jun Index	%	Jul Index	%	Aug Index	%	Sep Index	%	Oct Index	%	Nov Index	%	Dec Index	%
1946	-	-	-	-	-	-	-	-	-	-	-	-	-	-	-	-	-	-	-	-	20.1	-	-	-
1947	-	-	-	-	20.2	0.5	-	-	-	-	20.2	0.0	-	-	20.4	1.0	-	-	-	-	21.1	3.4	-	-
1948	-	-	21.5	1.9	-	-	-	-	21.5	0.0	-	-	-	-	22.8	6.0	-	-	-	-	22.9	0.4	-	-
1949	-	-	23.2	1.3	-	-	-	-	23.3	0.4	-	-	-	-	23.2	-0.4	-	-	-	-	22.6	-2.6	-	-
1950	-	-	22.2	-1.8	-	-	-	-	23.4	5.4	-	-	-	-	24.1	3.0	-	-	-	-	24.1	0.0	-	-
1951	-	-	24.1	0.0	-	-	-	-	25.0	3.7	-	-	-	-	25.1	0.4	-	-	-	-	25.9	3.2	-	-
1952	-	-	26.4	1.9	-	-	-	-	26.5	0.4	-	-	-	-	26.5	0.0	-	-	-	-	27.3	3.0	-	-
1953	-	-	27.3	0.0	-	-	-	-	27.3	0.0	-	-	-	-	27.6	1.1	-	-	-	-	27.4	-0.7	-	-
1954	-	-	27.1	-1.1	-	-	-	-	27.1	0.0	-	-	-	-	26.7	-1.5	-	-	-	-	27.5	3.0	-	-
1955	-	-	26.8	-2.5	-	-	-	-	26.7	-0.4	-	-	-	-	26.6	-0.4	-	-	-	-	27.2	2.3	-	-
1956	-	-	27.0	-0.7	-	-	-	-	26.9	-0.4	-	-	-	-	27.6	2.6	-	-	-	-	28.4	2.9	-	-
1957	-	-	28.6	0.7	-	-	-	-	28.6	0.0	-	-	-	-	28.7	0.3	-	-	-	-	29.1	1.4	-	-
1958	-	-	28.9	-0.7	-	-	-	-	28.7	-0.7	-	-	-	-	29.5	2.8	-	-	-	-	29.6	0.3	-	-
1959	-	-	29.7	0.3	-	-	-	-	29.8	0.3	-	-	-	-	30.3	1.7	-	-	-	-	30.8	1.7	-	-
1960	-	-	29.6	-3.9	-	-	-	-	29.8	0.7	-	-	-	-	30.1	1.0	-	-	-	-	29.9	-0.7	-	-
1961	-	-	30.2	1.0	-	-	-	-	29.4	-2.6	-	-	-	-	30.4	3.4	-	-	-	-	30.2	-0.7	-	-
1962	-	-	30.9	2.3	-	-	-	-	31.4	1.6	-	-	-	-	30.7	-2.2	-	-	-	-	31.6	2.9	-	-
1963	-	-	30.8	-2.5	-	-	-	-	31.4	1.9	-	-	-	-	31.1	-1.0	-	-	-	-	31.8	2.3	-	-
1964	-	-	31.3	-1.6	-	-	-	-	30.8	-1.6	-	-	-	-	31.6	2.6	-	-	-	-	32.0	1.3	-	-
1965	-	-	32.4	1.3	-	-	-	-	32.9	1.5	-	-	-	-	32.5	-1.2	-	-	-	-	32.5	0.0	-	-
1966	-	-	32.6	0.3	-	-	-	-	32.3	-0.9	-	-	-	-	33.1	2.5	-	-	-	-	33.1	0.0	-	-
1967	-	-	32.8	-0.9	-	-	-	-	33.0	0.6	-	-	-	-	33.1	0.3	-	-	-	-	34.0	2.7	-	-
1968	-	-	34.0	0.0	-	-	-	-	33.2	-2.4	-	-	-	-	33.3	0.3	-	-	-	-	33.9	1.8	-	-
1969	-	-	35.4	4.4	-	-	-	-	35.2	-0.6	-	-	-	-	34.9	-0.9	-	-	-	-	36.2	3.7	-	-
1970	-	-	35.2	-2.8	-	-	-	-	37.0	5.1	-	-	-	-	36.5	-1.4	-	-	-	-	38.2	4.7	-	-
1971	-	-	39.3	2.9	-	-	-	-	38.3	-2.5	-	-	-	-	39.8	3.9	-	-	-	-	38.5	-3.3	-	-
1972	-	-	38.4	-0.3	-	-	-	-	39.0	1.6	-	-	-	-	40.7	4.4	-	-	-	-	40.4	-0.7	-	-
1973	-	-	40.7	0.7	-	-	-	-	42.1	3.4	-	-	-	-	42.0	-0.2	-	-	-	-	42.7	1.7	-	-
1974	-	-	43.9	2.8	-	-	-	-	46.2	5.2	-	-	-	-	47.9	3.7	-	-	-	-	48.3	0.8	-	-
1975	-	-	48.8	1.0	-	-	-	-	49.7	1.8	-	-	-	-	51.4	3.4	-	-	-	-	51.7	0.6	-	-
1976	-	-	51.6	-0.2	-	-	-	-	53.0	2.7	-	-	-	-	55.6	4.9	-	-	-	-	56.0	0.7	-	-
1977	-	-	56.3	0.5	-	-	-	-	57.9	2.8	-	-	-	-	58.1	0.3	-	-	-	-	58.3	0.3	-	-
1978	58.6	0.5	-	-	58.9	0.5	-	-	60.2	2.2	-	-	62.1	3.2	-	-	62.7	1.0	-	-	63.7	1.6	-	-
1979	64.6	1.4	-	-	66.2	2.5	-	-	69.1	4.4	-	-	72.4	4.8	-	-	74.1	2.3	-	-	75.6	2.0	-	-
1980	78.1	3.3	-	-	81.1	3.8	-	-	84.3	3.9	-	-	83.6	-0.8	-	-	84.0	0.5	-	-	86.3	2.7	-	-
1981	88.9	3.0	-	-	91.1	2.5	-	-	92.7	1.8	-	-	93.6	1.0	-	-	94.9	1.4	-	-	97.7	3.0	-	-
1982	97.6	-0.1	-	-	96.6	-1.0	-	-	96.2	-0.4	-	-	100.2	4.2	-	-	98.9	-1.3	-	-	98.8	-0.1	-	-
1983	97.9	-0.9	-	-	95.7	-2.2	-	-	98.4	2.8	-	-	99.2	0.8	-	-	101.0	1.8	-	-	101.6	0.6	-	-
1984	101.0	-0.6	-	-	101.6	0.6	-	-	103.2	1.6	-	-	103.0	-0.2	-	-	103.7	0.7	-	-	104.3	0.6	-	-
1985	102.5	-1.7	-	-	103.5	1.0	-	-	105.3	1.7	-	-	105.2	-0.1	-	-	104.0	-1.1	-	-	105.7	1.6	-	-
1986	104.8	-0.9	-	-	97.7	-6.8	-	-	99.2	1.5	-	-	97.9	-1.3	-	-	97.6	-0.3	-	-	98.8	1.2	98.4	-0.4
1987	-	-	-	-	-	-	-	-	-	-	105.0	6.7	-	-	-	-	-	-	-	-	-	-	109.5	4.3
1988	-	-	-	-	-	-	-	-	-	-	111.0	1.4	-	-	-	-	-	-	-	-	-	-	113.6	2.3
1989	-	-	-	-	-	-	-	-	-	-	116.6	2.6	-	-	-	-	-	-	-	-	-	-	118.9	2.0
1990	-	-	-	-	-	-	-	-	-	-	120.8	1.6	-	-	-	-	-	-	-	-	-	-	126.5	4.7

[Continued]

Milwaukee, WI
Consumer Price Index - Urban Wage Earners
Base 1982-1984 = 100
Transportation
[Continued]

For 1946-1997. Columns headed % show percentile change in the index from the previous period for which an index is available.

Year	Jan Index	%	Feb Index	%	Mar Index	%	Apr Index	%	May Index	%	Jun Index	%	Jul Index	%	Aug Index	%	Sep Index	%	Oct Index	%	Nov Index	%	Dec Index	%
1991	-	-	-	-	-	-	-	-	-	-	125.2	-1.0	-	-	-	-	-	-	-	-	-	-	126.6	1.1
1992	-	-	-	-	-	-	-	-	-	-	127.6	0.8	-	-	-	-	-	-	-	-	-	-	130.7	2.4
1993	-	-	-	-	-	-	-	-	-	-	130.0	-0.5	-	-	-	-	-	-	-	-	-	-	130.0	0.0
1994	-	-	-	-	-	-	-	-	-	-	130.5	0.4	-	-	-	-	-	-	-	-	-	-	136.3	4.4
1995	-	-	-	-	-	-	-	-	-	-	139.8	2.6	-	-	-	-	-	-	-	-	-	-	139.3	-0.4
1996	-	-	-	-	-	-	-	-	-	-	141.2	1.4	-	-	-	-	-	-	-	-	-	-	141.7	0.4
1997	-	-	-	-	-	-	-	-	-	-	142.9	0.8	-	-	-	-	-	-	-	-	-	-	-	-

Source: U.S. Department of Labor, Bureau of Labor Statistics, Division of Consumer Prices and Price Indexes. - indicates no data collected for period.

Milwaukee, WI
Consumer Price Index - All Urban Consumers
Base 1982-1984 = 100
Medical Care

For 1946-1997. Columns headed % show percentile change in the index from the previous period for which an index is available.

Year	Jan Index	%	Feb Index	%	Mar Index	%	Apr Index	%	May Index	%	Jun Index	%	Jul Index	%	Aug Index	%	Sep Index	%	Oct Index	%	Nov Index	%	Dec Index	%
1946	-		-		-		-		-		-		-		12.9		-		-		-		12.3	
1947	-		-		12.7	3.3	-		-		12.8	0.8	-		12.9	0.8	-		-		13.0	0.8	-	
1948	-		13.3	2.3	-		-		13.4	0.8	-		-		13.6	1.5	-		-		14.1	3.7	-	
1949	-		14.2	0.7	-		-		14.2	0.0	-		-		14.3	0.7	-		-		14.3	0.0	-	
1950	-		14.4	0.7	-		-		14.5	0.7	-		-		15.1	4.1	-		-		15.6	3.3	-	
1951	-		15.7	0.6	-		-		16.4	4.5	-		-		16.8	2.4	-		-		17.0	1.2	-	
1952	-		17.1	0.6	-		-		17.3	1.2	-		-		17.5	1.2	-		-		17.5	0.0	-	
1953	-		17.7	1.1	-		-		17.8	0.6	-		-		18.1	1.7	-		-		18.2	0.6	-	
1954	-		18.3	0.5	-		-		19.2	4.9	-		-		19.2	0.0	-		-		19.3	0.5	-	
1955	-		19.3	0.0	-		-		19.4	0.5	-		-		19.8	2.1	-		-		19.6	-1.0	-	
1956	-		19.7	0.5	-		-		19.9	1.0	-		-		19.9	0.0	-		-		20.0	0.5	-	
1957	-		20.4	2.0	-		-		21.6	5.9	-		-		21.6	0.0	-		-		21.9	1.4	-	
1958	-		22.0	0.5	-		-		22.1	0.5	-		-		22.1	0.0	-		-		22.1	0.0	-	
1959	-		22.2	0.5	-		-		22.2	0.0	-		-		22.8	2.7	-		-		23.0	0.9	-	
1960	-		23.0	0.0	-		-		23.0	0.0	-		-		23.1	0.4	-		-		23.1	0.0	-	
1961	-		23.1	0.0	-		-		23.2	0.4	-		-		23.3	0.4	-		-		23.3	0.0	-	
1962	-		23.4	0.4	-		-		23.4	0.0	-		-		23.4	0.0	-		-		23.4	0.0	-	
1963	-		23.5	0.4	-		-		24.0	2.1	-		-		24.0	0.0	-		-		24.2	0.8	-	
1964	-		24.2	0.0	-		-		24.3	0.4	-		-		24.4	0.4	-		-		24.5	0.4	-	
1965	-		25.1	2.4	-		-		25.2	0.4	-		-		25.3	0.4	-		-		25.6	1.2	-	
1966	-		25.9	1.2	-		-		26.3	1.5	-		-		26.9	2.3	-		-		27.7	3.0	-	
1967	-		28.1	1.4	-		-		28.3	0.7	-		-		29.0	2.5	-		-		29.8	2.8	-	
1968	-		29.9	0.3	-		-		29.9	0.0	-		-		30.5	2.0	-		-		31.4	3.0	-	
1969	-		32.0	1.9	-		-		32.4	1.3	-		-		32.8	1.2	-		-		33.0	0.6	-	
1970	-		33.9	2.7	-		-		34.2	0.9	-		-		34.6	1.2	-		-		34.6	0.0	-	
1971	-		35.9	3.8	-		-		36.2	0.8	-		-		36.8	1.7	-		-		36.5	-0.8	-	
1972	-		36.6	0.3	-		-		36.7	0.3	-		-		36.9	0.5	-		-		37.2	0.8	-	
1973	-		37.6	1.1	-		-		38.2	1.6	-		-		38.8	1.6	-		-		39.6	2.1	-	
1974	-		40.5	2.3	-		-		41.9	3.5	-		-		43.4	3.6	-		-		44.0	1.4	-	
1975	-		45.3	3.0	-		-		46.4	2.4	-		-		48.0	3.4	-		-		48.7	1.5	-	
1976	-		50.7	4.1	-		-		52.1	2.8	-		-		53.4	2.5	-		-		54.3	1.7	-	
1977	-		55.1	1.5	-		-		57.2	3.8	-		-		58.0	1.4	-		-		58.9	1.6	-	
1978	59.7	1.4	-		60.9	2.0	-		61.4	0.8	-		61.9	0.8	-		63.0	1.8	-		63.2	0.3	-	
1979	66.3	4.9	-		67.2	1.4	-		67.8	0.9	-		69.8	2.9	-		71.0	1.7	-		71.7	1.0	-	
1980	73.6	2.6	-		75.4	2.4	-		75.9	0.7	-		78.0	2.8	-		80.8	3.6	-		81.2	0.5	-	
1981	83.2	2.5	-		86.1	3.5	-		86.3	0.2	-		87.0	0.8	-		87.9	1.0	-		88.1	0.2	-	
1982	90.1	2.3	-		90.4	0.3	-		92.5	2.3	-		93.4	1.0	-		95.4	2.1	-		98.0	2.7	-	
1983	99.2	1.2	-		99.2	0.0	-		99.3	0.1	-		101.0	1.7	-		101.8	0.8	-		102.0	0.2	-	
1984	104.5	2.5	-		104.9	0.4	-		105.2	0.3	-		106.1	0.9	-		106.3	0.2	-		106.5	0.2	-	
1985	107.1	0.6	-		108.3	1.1	-		109.0	0.6	-		109.5	0.5	-		110.1	0.5	-		110.5	0.4	-	
1986	112.1	1.4	-		113.1	0.9	-		113.8	0.6	-		114.9	1.0	-		115.3	0.3	-		117.0	1.5	117.0	0.0
1987	-		-		-		-		-		125.5	7.3	-		-		-		-		-		130.3	3.8
1988	-		-		-		-		-		133.0	2.1	-		-		-		-		-		136.4	2.6
1989	-		-		-		-		-		141.3	3.6	-		-		-		-		-		149.9	6.1
1990	-		-		-		-		-		154.0	2.7	-		-		-		-		-		162.7	5.6

[Continued]

Milwaukee, WI
Consumer Price Index - All Urban Consumers
Base 1982-1984 = 100
Medical Care
[Continued]

For 1946-1997. Columns headed % show percentile change in the index from the previous period for which an index is available.

Year	Jan		Feb		Mar		Apr		May		Jun		Jul		Aug		Sep		Oct		Nov		Dec	
	Index	%	Index	%	Index	%	Index	%	Index	%	Index	%	Index	%	Index	%	Index	%	Index	%	Index	%	Index	%
1991	-	-	-	-	-	-	-	-	-	-	168.9	3.8	-	-	-	-	-	-	-	-	-	-	175.0	3.6
1992	-	-	-	-	-	-	-	-	-	-	180.3	3.0	-	-	-	-	-	-	-	-	-	-	188.5	4.5
1993	-	-	-	-	-	-	-	-	-	-	195.0	3.4	-	-	-	-	-	-	-	-	-	-	202.4	3.8
1994	-	-	-	-	-	-	-	-	-	-	211.8	4.6	-	-	-	-	-	-	-	-	-	-	224.4	5.9
1995	-	-	-	-	-	-	-	-	-	-	229.4	2.2	-	-	-	-	-	-	-	-	-	-	230.6	0.5
1996	-	-	-	-	-	-	-	-	-	-	235.1	2.0	-	-	-	-	-	-	-	-	-	-	239.7	2.0
1997	-	-	-	-	-	-	-	-	-	-	238.0	-0.7	-	-	-	-	-	-	-	-	-	-	-	-

Source: U.S. Department of Labor, Bureau of Labor Statistics, Division of Consumer Prices and Price Indexes. - indicates no data collected for period.

Milwaukee, WI
Consumer Price Index - Urban Wage Earners
Base 1982-1984 = 100
Medical Care

For 1946-1997. Columns headed % show percentile change in the index from the previous period for which an index is available.

Year	Jan Index	%	Feb Index	%	Mar Index	%	Apr Index	%	May Index	%	Jun Index	%	Jul Index	%	Aug Index	%	Sep Index	%	Oct Index	%	Nov Index	%	Dec Index	%
1946	-		-		-		-		-		-		-		-		-		-		-		12.4	-
1947	-		-		12.9	4.0	-		-		12.9	0.0	-		13.0	0.8	-		-		13.1	0.8	-	
1948	-		13.4	2.3	-		-		13.5	0.7	-		-		13.8	2.2	-		-		14.3	3.6	-	
1949	-		14.3	0.0	-		-		14.3	0.0	-		-		14.5	1.4	-		-		14.5	0.0	-	
1950	-		14.5	0.0	-		-		14.7	1.4	-		-		15.3	4.1	-		-		15.7	2.6	-	
1951	-		15.9	1.3					16.6	4.4					17.0	2.4					17.1	0.6	-	
1952	-		17.3	1.2					17.5	1.2					17.7	1.1					17.7	0.0	-	
1953	-		17.9	1.1					18.0	0.6					18.3	1.7					18.4	0.5	-	
1954	-		18.5	0.5					19.4	4.9					19.4	0.0					19.5	0.5	-	
1955	-		19.5	0.0					19.6	0.5					20.0	2.0					19.8	-1.0	-	
1956	-		20.0	1.0					20.1	0.5					20.1	0.0					20.3	1.0	-	
1957	-		20.6	1.5					21.8	5.8					21.9	0.5					22.1	0.9	-	
1958	-		22.3	0.9					22.3	0.0					22.3	0.0					22.4	0.4	-	
1959	-		22.4	0.0					22.5	0.4					23.1	2.7					23.2	0.4	-	
1960	-		23.3	0.4					23.3	0.0					23.4	0.4					23.4	0.0	-	
1961	-		23.4	0.0	-		-		23.5	0.4					23.6	0.4	-		-		23.6	0.0		
1962	-		23.7	0.4	-		-		23.7	0.0					23.7	0.0	-		-		23.7	0.0		
1963	-		23.8	0.4	-		-		24.2	1.7					24.3	0.4	-		-		24.5	0.8		
1964	-		24.5	0.0	-		-		24.6	0.4					24.7	0.4	-		-		24.7	0.0		
1965	-		25.3	2.4	-		-		25.5	0.8					25.6	0.4	-		-		25.9	1.2		
1966	-		26.2	1.2	-		-		26.6	1.5					27.2	2.3	-		-		28.0	2.9		
1967	-		28.4	1.4	-		-		28.6	0.7					29.3	2.4	-		-		30.2	3.1		
1968	-		30.2	0.0	-		-		30.3	0.3					30.9	2.0	-		-		31.8	2.9		
1969	-		32.4	1.9	-		-		32.7	0.9					33.1	1.2	-		-		33.4	0.9		
1970	-		34.3	2.7	-		-		34.6	0.9					35.0	1.2	-		-		35.0	0.0		
1971	-		36.3	3.7	-		-		36.6	0.8					37.2	1.6	-		-		36.9	-0.8	-	
1972	-		37.0	0.3	-		-		37.1	0.3					37.3	0.5	-		-		37.6	0.8	-	
1973	-		38.0	1.1	-		-		38.7	1.8					39.2	1.3	-		-		40.1	2.3	-	
1974	-		40.9	2.0	-		-		42.3	3.4					43.9	3.8	-		-		44.4	1.1	-	
1975	-		45.8	3.2	-		-		46.9	2.4					48.5	3.4	-		-		49.2	1.4	-	
1976	-		51.3	4.3	-		-		52.7	2.7					54.0	2.5	-		-		54.9	1.7	-	
1977	-		55.7	1.5	-		-		57.8	3.8					58.7	1.6	-		-		59.5	1.4	-	
1978	61.4	3.2	-		62.0	1.0	-		63.3	2.1			63.9	0.9	-		64.8	1.4	-		64.9	0.2	-	
1979	67.3	3.7	-		68.0	1.0	-		68.1	0.1			70.5	3.5	-		71.8	1.8	-		72.1	0.4	-	
1980	74.5	3.3	-		77.2	3.6	-		78.1	1.2			79.4	1.7	-		81.3	2.4	-		81.9	0.7	-	
1981	84.0	2.6	-		86.9	3.5	-		87.1	0.2			88.1	1.1	-		88.7	0.7	-		88.9	0.2		
1982	91.0	2.4	-		91.2	0.2	-		92.9	1.9			93.6	0.8	-		95.3	1.8	-		97.3	2.1		
1983	98.5	1.2	-		98.7	0.2	-		98.9	0.2			100.7	1.8	-		101.4	0.7	-		101.6	0.2		
1984	104.4	2.8	-		104.9	0.5	-		105.3	0.4			106.6	1.2	-		106.7	0.1	-		107.0	0.3		
1985	107.8	0.7	-		108.9	1.0	-		109.7	0.7			110.2	0.5	-		110.8	0.5	-		111.3	0.5		
1986	113.0	1.5	-		114.0	0.9	-		114.7	0.6	-		115.6	0.8	-		116.3	0.6	-		117.9	1.4	118.0	0.1
1987	-		-		-		-		-		125.2	6.1	-		-		-		-		-		130.0	3.8
1988	-		-		-		-		-		132.5	1.9	-		-		-		-		-		135.7	2.4
1989	-		-		-		-		-		140.3	3.4	-		-		-		-		-		147.5	5.1
1990	-		-		-		-		-		152.0	3.1	-		-		-		-		-		160.3	5.5

[Continued]

642

Milwaukee, WI
Consumer Price Index - Urban Wage Earners
Base 1982-1984 = 100
Medical Care
[Continued]

For 1946-1997. Columns headed % show percentile change in the index from the previous period for which an index is available.

Year	Jan Index	%	Feb Index	%	Mar Index	%	Apr Index	%	May Index	%	Jun Index	%	Jul Index	%	Aug Index	%	Sep Index	%	Oct Index	%	Nov Index	%	Dec Index	%
1991	-	-	-	-	-	-	-	-	-	-	166.5	3.9	-	-	-	-	-	-	-	-	-	-	172.4	3.5
1992	-	-	-	-	-	-	-	-	-	-	177.1	2.7	-	-	-	-	-	-	-	-	-	-	185.5	4.7
1993	-	-	-	-	-	-	-	-	-	-	192.2	3.6	-	-	-	-	-	-	-	-	-	-	199.7	3.9
1994	-	-	-	-	-	-	-	-	-	-	208.4	4.4	-	-	-	-	-	-	-	-	-	-	219.8	5.5
1995	-	-	-	-	-	-	-	-	-	-	224.8	2.3	-	-	-	-	-	-	-	-	-	-	226.0	0.5
1996	-	-	-	-	-	-	-	-	-	-	230.7	2.1	-	-	-	-	-	-	-	-	-	-	234.8	1.8
1997	-	-	-	-	-	-	-	-	-	-	232.6	-0.9	-	-	-	-	-	-	-	-	-	-	-	-

Source: U.S. Department of Labor, Bureau of Labor Statistics, Division of Consumer Prices and Price Indexes. - indicates no data collected for period.

Milwaukee, WI
Consumer Price Index - All Urban Consumers
Base 1982-1984 = 100
Entertainment

For 1975-1997. Columns headed % show percentile change in the index from the previous period for which an index is available.

Year	Jan Index	%	Feb Index	%	Mar Index	%	Apr Index	%	May Index	%	Jun Index	%	Jul Index	%	Aug Index	%	Sep Index	%	Oct Index	%	Nov Index	%	Dec Index	%
1975	-	-	-	-	-	-	-	-	-	-	-	-	-	-	-	-	-	-	-	-	59.6	-	-	-
1976	-	-	59.8	0.3	-	-	-	-	61.0	2.0	-	-	-	-	62.8	3.0	-	-	-	-	63.3	0.8	-	-
1977	-	-	67.1	6.0	-	-	-	-	68.5	2.1	-	-	-	-	68.7	0.3	-	-	-	-	69.6	1.3	-	-
1978	70.0	0.6	-	-	71.1	1.6	-	-	71.3	0.3	-	-	71.4	0.1	-	-	73.4	2.8	-	-	74.6	1.6	-	-
1979	75.1	0.7	-	-	75.4	0.4	-	-	77.6	2.9	-	-	78.3	0.9	-	-	79.4	1.4	-	-	79.8	0.5	-	-
1980	81.0	1.5	-	-	80.5	-0.6	-	-	84.2	4.6	-	-	84.8	0.7	-	-	86.9	2.5	-	-	86.9	0.0	-	-
1981	88.4	1.7	-	-	92.2	4.3	-	-	92.6	0.4	-	-	91.6	-1.1	-	-	93.2	1.7	-	-	92.6	-0.6	-	-
1982	96.9	4.6	-	-	96.2	-0.7	-	-	95.5	-0.7	-	-	95.4	-0.1	-	-	94.6	-0.8	-	-	96.0	1.5	-	-
1983	97.3	1.4	-	-	98.2	0.9	-	-	100.1	1.9	-	-	100.1	0.0	-	-	102.3	2.2	-	-	103.0	0.7	-	-
1984	101.0	-1.9	-	-	101.7	0.7	-	-	102.5	0.8	-	-	104.8	2.2	-	-	106.1	1.2	-	-	105.8	-0.3	-	-
1985	107.8	1.9	-	-	108.1	0.3	-	-	108.3	0.2	-	-	110.3	1.8	-	-	111.6	1.2	-	-	111.2	-0.4	-	-
1986	109.1	-1.9	-	-	110.9	1.6	-	-	110.8	-0.1	-	-	111.1	0.3	-	-	110.3	-0.7	-	-	109.5	-0.7	109.6	0.1
1987	-	-	-	-	-	-	-	-	-	-	118.3	7.9	-	-	-	-	-	-	-	-	-	-	119.5	1.0
1988	-	-	-	-	-	-	-	-	-	-	121.0	1.3	-	-	-	-	-	-	-	-	-	-	124.5	2.9
1989	-	-	-	-	-	-	-	-	-	-	127.1	2.1	-	-	-	-	-	-	-	-	-	-	130.3	2.5
1990	-	-	-	-	-	-	-	-	-	-	137.7	5.7	-	-	-	-	-	-	-	-	-	-	138.9	0.9
1991	-	-	-	-	-	-	-	-	-	-	141.9	2.2	-	-	-	-	-	-	-	-	-	-	145.7	2.7
1992	-	-	-	-	-	-	-	-	-	-	148.8	2.1	-	-	-	-	-	-	-	-	-	-	149.8	0.7
1993	-	-	-	-	-	-	-	-	-	-	152.2	1.6	-	-	-	-	-	-	-	-	-	-	153.1	0.6
1994	-	-	-	-	-	-	-	-	-	-	152.9	-0.1	-	-	-	-	-	-	-	-	-	-	156.6	2.4
1995	-	-	-	-	-	-	-	-	-	-	158.6	1.3	-	-	-	-	-	-	-	-	-	-	162.5	2.5
1996	-	-	-	-	-	-	-	-	-	-	165.7	2.0	-	-	-	-	-	-	-	-	-	-	168.8	1.9
1997	-	-	-	-	-	-	-	-	-	-	170.6	1.1	-	-	-	-	-	-	-	-	-	-	-	-

Source: U.S. Department of Labor, Bureau of Labor Statistics, Division of Consumer Prices and Price Indexes. - indicates no data collected for period.

Milwaukee, WI
Consumer Price Index - Urban Wage Earners
Base 1982-1984 = 100
Entertainment

For 1975-1997. Columns headed % show percentile change in the index from the previous period for which an index is available.

Year	Jan Index	%	Feb Index	%	Mar Index	%	Apr Index	%	May Index	%	Jun Index	%	Jul Index	%	Aug Index	%	Sep Index	%	Oct Index	%	Nov Index	%	Dec Index	%
1975	-	-	-	-	-	-	-	-	-	-	-	-	-	-	-	-	-	-	-	-	61.8	-	-	-
1976	-	-	62.0	0.3	-	-	-	-	63.3	2.1	-	-	-	-	65.1	2.8	-	-	-	-	65.6	0.8	-	-
1977	-	-	69.5	5.9	-	-	-	-	71.0	2.2	-	-	-	-	71.2	0.3	-	-	-	-	72.1	1.3	-	-
1978	73.3	1.7	-	-	74.4	1.5	-	-	74.6	0.3	-	-	74.7	0.1	-	-	76.3	2.1	-	-	77.6	1.7	-	-
1979	78.2	0.8	-	-	78.0	-0.3	-	-	81.2	4.1	-	-	80.5	-0.9	-	-	81.8	1.6	-	-	80.4	-1.7	-	-
1980	82.9	3.1	-	-	87.5	5.5	-	-	89.3	2.1	-	-	88.5	-0.9	-	-	90.9	2.7	-	-	88.9	-2.2	-	-
1981	94.8	6.6	-	-	98.1	3.5	-	-	96.5	-1.6	-	-	92.7	-3.9	-	-	92.8	0.1	-	-	92.3	-0.5	-	-
1982	96.7	4.8	-	-	96.1	-0.6	-	-	95.8	-0.3	-	-	95.3	-0.5	-	-	94.6	-0.7	-	-	95.7	1.2	-	-
1983	97.0	1.4	-	-	98.0	1.0	-	-	99.8	1.8	-	-	99.9	0.1	-	-	101.9	2.0	-	-	102.6	0.7	-	-
1984	100.8	-1.8	-	-	102.1	1.3	-	-	103.2	1.1	-	-	105.7	2.4	-	-	106.2	0.5	-	-	105.9	-0.3	-	-
1985	107.7	1.7	-	-	108.3	0.6	-	-	108.6	0.3	-	-	110.4	1.7	-	-	112.3	1.7	-	-	112.0	-0.3	-	-
1986	108.4	-3.2	-	-	110.2	1.7	-	-	110.3	0.1	-	-	110.6	0.3	-	-	109.8	-0.7	-	-	109.1	-0.6	109.2	0.1
1987	-	-	-	-	-	-	-	-	-	-	117.1	7.2	-	-	-	-	-	-	-	-	-	-	119.1	1.7
1988	-	-	-	-	-	-	-	-	-	-	121.2	1.8	-	-	-	-	-	-	-	-	-	-	124.7	2.9
1989	-	-	-	-	-	-	-	-	-	-	127.7	2.4	-	-	-	-	-	-	-	-	-	-	130.7	2.3
1990	-	-	-	-	-	-	-	-	-	-	138.1	5.7	-	-	-	-	-	-	-	-	-	-	139.9	1.3
1991	-	-	-	-	-	-	-	-	-	-	143.8	2.8	-	-	-	-	-	-	-	-	-	-	148.0	2.9
1992	-	-	-	-	-	-	-	-	-	-	151.2	2.2	-	-	-	-	-	-	-	-	-	-	152.0	0.5
1993	-	-	-	-	-	-	-	-	-	-	154.3	1.5	-	-	-	-	-	-	-	-	-	-	155.7	0.9
1994	-	-	-	-	-	-	-	-	-	-	156.2	0.3	-	-	-	-	-	-	-	-	-	-	160.1	2.5
1995	-	-	-	-	-	-	-	-	-	-	161.9	1.1	-	-	-	-	-	-	-	-	-	-	166.3	2.7
1996	-	-	-	-	-	-	-	-	-	-	169.8	2.1	-	-	-	-	-	-	-	-	-	-	173.3	2.1
1997	-	-	-	-	-	-	-	-	-	-	175.5	1.3	-	-	-	-	-	-	-	-	-	-	-	-

Source: U.S. Department of Labor, Bureau of Labor Statistics, Division of Consumer Prices and Price Indexes. - indicates no data collected for period.

Milwaukee, WI
Consumer Price Index - All Urban Consumers
Base 1982-1984 = 100
Other Goods and Services

For 1975-1997. Columns headed % show percentile change in the index from the previous period for which an index is available.

Year	Jan Index	%	Feb Index	%	Mar Index	%	Apr Index	%	May Index	%	Jun Index	%	Jul Index	%	Aug Index	%	Sep Index	%	Oct Index	%	Nov Index	%	Dec Index	%
1975	-	-	-	-	-	-	-	-	-	-	-	-	-	-	-	-	-	-	-	-	58.2	-	-	-
1976	-	-	59.3	1.9	-	-	-	-	59.7	0.7	-	-	-	-	59.8	0.2	-	-	-	-	61.1	2.2	-	-
1977	-	-	61.9	1.3	-	-	-	-	62.6	1.1	-	-	-	-	63.1	0.8	-	-	-	-	64.8	2.7	-	-
1978	65.6	1.2	-	-	65.1	-0.8	-	-	65.4	0.5	-	-	65.9	0.8	-	-	67.8	2.9	-	-	68.4	0.9	-	-
1979	68.6	0.3	-	-	69.3	1.0	-	-	69.8	0.7	-	-	69.4	-0.6	-	-	71.9	3.6	-	-	72.6	1.0	-	-
1980	73.9	1.8	-	-	74.0	0.1	-	-	74.7	0.9	-	-	74.8	0.1	-	-	77.3	3.3	-	-	77.7	0.5	-	-
1981	80.2	3.2	-	-	81.2	1.2	-	-	81.9	0.9	-	-	81.9	0.0	-	-	84.9	3.7	-	-	86.9	2.4	-	-
1982	87.6	0.8	-	-	89.2	1.8	-	-	91.3	2.4	-	-	91.9	0.7	-	-	95.1	3.5	-	-	96.3	1.3	-	-
1983	99.7	3.5	-	-	100.1	0.4	-	-	100.0	-0.1	-	-	99.7	-0.3	-	-	101.5	1.8	-	-	102.7	1.2	-	-
1984	103.8	1.1	-	-	104.3	0.5	-	-	104.5	0.2	-	-	105.9	1.3	-	-	110.2	4.1	-	-	110.6	0.4	-	-
1985	110.8	0.2	-	-	111.1	0.3	-	-	111.2	0.1	-	-	111.9	0.6	-	-	114.4	2.2	-	-	117.4	2.6	-	-
1986	118.9	1.3	-	-	119.0	0.1	-	-	119.7	0.6	-	-	120.7	0.8	-	-	124.7	3.3	-	-	125.0	0.2	125.2	0.2
1987	-	-	-	-	-	-	-	-	-	-	122.9	-1.8	-	-	-	-	-	-	-	-	-	-	-	-
1988	-	-	-	-	-	-	-	-	-	-	135.7	10.4	-	-	-	-	-	-	-	-	-	-	-	-
1989	-	-	-	-	-	-	-	-	-	-	146.1	7.7	-	-	-	-	-	-	-	-	-	-	-	-
1990	-	-	-	-	-	-	-	-	-	-	155.6	6.5	-	-	-	-	-	-	-	-	-	-	-	-
1991	-	-	-	-	-	-	-	-	-	-	168.1	8.0	-	-	-	-	-	-	-	-	-	-	-	-
1992	-	-	-	-	-	-	-	-	-	-	182.5	8.6	-	-	-	-	-	-	-	-	-	-	-	-
1993	-	-	-	-	-	-	-	-	-	-	199.6	9.4	-	-	-	-	-	-	-	-	-	-	-	-
1994	-	-	-	-	-	-	-	-	-	-	197.6	-1.0	-	-	-	-	-	-	-	-	-	-	-	-
1995	-	-	-	-	-	-	-	-	-	-	205.7	4.1	-	-	-	-	-	-	-	-	-	-	-	-
1996	-	-	-	-	-	-	-	-	-	-	211.2	2.7	-	-	-	-	-	-	-	-	-	-	-	-
1997	-	-	-	-	-	-	-	-	-	-	221.7	5.0	-	-	-	-	-	-	-	-	-	-	-	-

Source: U.S. Department of Labor, Bureau of Labor Statistics, Division of Consumer Prices and Price Indexes. - indicates no data collected for period.

Milwaukee, WI
Consumer Price Index - Urban Wage Earners
Base 1982-1984 = 100
Other Goods and Services

For 1975-1997. Columns headed % show percentile change in the index from the previous period for which an index is available.

Year	Jan Index	%	Feb Index	%	Mar Index	%	Apr Index	%	May Index	%	Jun Index	%	Jul Index	%	Aug Index	%	Sep Index	%	Oct Index	%	Nov Index	%	Dec Index	%
1975	-	-	-	-	-	-	-	-	-	-	-	-	-	-	-	-	-	-	-	-	55.7	-	-	-
1976	-	-	56.7	1.8	-	-	-	-	57.2	0.9	-	-	-	-	57.2	0.0	-	-	-	-	58.5	2.3	-	-
1977	-	-	59.3	1.4	-	-	-	-	59.9	1.0	-	-	-	-	60.4	0.8	-	-	-	-	62.0	2.6	-	-
1978	63.2	1.9	-	-	63.9	1.1	-	-	64.1	0.3	-	-	64.5	0.6	-	-	66.3	2.8	-	-	66.6	0.5	-	-
1979	66.7	0.2	-	-	67.7	1.5	-	-	67.7	0.0	-	-	68.0	0.4	-	-	70.1	3.1	-	-	71.5	2.0	-	-
1980	73.5	2.8	-	-	73.8	0.4	-	-	74.5	0.9	-	-	74.5	0.0	-	-	76.8	3.1	-	-	76.5	-0.4	-	-
1981	78.6	2.7	-	-	79.7	1.4	-	-	80.9	1.5	-	-	81.3	0.5	-	-	84.5	3.9	-	-	86.6	2.5	-	-
1982	87.0	0.5	-	-	88.6	1.8	-	-	91.1	2.8	-	-	91.7	0.7	-	-	94.8	3.4	-	-	96.1	1.4	-	-
1983	100.0	4.1	-	-	100.3	0.3	-	-	100.2	-0.1	-	-	100.0	-0.2	-	-	101.7	1.7	-	-	102.9	1.2	-	-
1984	104.0	1.1	-	-	104.5	0.5	-	-	104.8	0.3	-	-	106.2	1.3	-	-	110.1	3.7	-	-	110.4	0.3	-	-
1985	110.6	0.2	-	-	111.0	0.4	-	-	111.0	0.0	-	-	111.8	0.7	-	-	113.8	1.8	-	-	116.9	2.7	-	-
1986	118.5	1.4	-	-	118.7	0.2	-	-	119.4	0.6	-	-	120.4	0.8	-	-	123.9	2.9	-	-	124.2	0.2	124.5	0.2
1987	-	-	-	-	-	-	-	-	-	-	122.8	-1.4	-	-	-	-	-	-	-	-	-	-	-	-
1988	-	-	-	-	-	-	-	-	-	-	134.9	9.9	-	-	-	-	-	-	-	-	-	-	-	-
1989	-	-	-	-	-	-	-	-	-	-	145.3	7.7	-	-	-	-	-	-	-	-	-	-	-	-
1990	-	-	-	-	-	-	-	-	-	-	154.3	6.2	-	-	-	-	-	-	-	-	-	-	-	-
1991	-	-	-	-	-	-	-	-	-	-	167.3	8.4	-	-	-	-	-	-	-	-	-	-	-	-
1992	-	-	-	-	-	-	-	-	-	-	183.5	9.7	-	-	-	-	-	-	-	-	-	-	-	-
1993	-	-	-	-	-	-	-	-	-	-	202.1	10.1	-	-	-	-	-	-	-	-	-	-	-	-
1994	-	-	-	-	-	-	-	-	-	-	197.6	-2.2	-	-	-	-	-	-	-	-	-	-	-	-
1995	-	-	-	-	-	-	-	-	-	-	205.4	3.9	-	-	-	-	-	-	-	-	-	-	-	-
1996	-	-	-	-	-	-	-	-	-	-	211.2	2.8	-	-	-	-	-	-	-	-	-	-	-	-
1997	-	-	-	-	-	-	-	-	-	-	222.8	5.5	-	-	-	-	-	-	-	-	-	-	-	-

Source: U.S. Department of Labor, Bureau of Labor Statistics, Division of Consumer Prices and Price Indexes. - indicates no data collected for period.

Minneapolis-St. Paul, MN
Consumer Price Index - All Urban Consumers
Base 1982-1984 = 100
Annual Averages

For 1917-1997. Columns headed % show percentile change in the index from the previous period for which an index is available.

Year	All Items		Food & Beverage		Housing		Apparel & Upkeep		Trans-portation		Medical Care		Entertain-ment		Other Goods & Services	
	Index	%	Index	%	Index	%	Index	%	Index	%	Index	%	Index	%	Index	%
1917	-	-	-	-	-	-	-	-	-	-	-	-	-	-	-	-
1918	14.1	-	-	-	-	-	-	-	-	-	-	-	-	-	-	-
1919	16.0	13.5	-	-	-	-	-	-	-	-	-	-	-	-	-	-
1920	18.6	16.3	-	-	-	-	-	-	-	-	-	-	-	-	-	-
1921	16.7	-10.2	-	-	-	-	-	-	-	-	-	-	-	-	-	-
1922	15.8	-5.4	-	-	-	-	-	-	-	-	-	-	-	-	-	-
1923	15.9	0.6	-	-	-	-	-	-	-	-	-	-	-	-	-	-
1924	15.8	-0.6	-	-	-	-	-	-	-	-	-	-	-	-	-	-
1925	15.9	0.6	-	-	-	-	-	-	-	-	-	-	-	-	-	-
1926	16.1	1.3	-	-	-	-	-	-	-	-	-	-	-	-	-	-
1927	15.7	-2.5	-	-	-	-	-	-	-	-	-	-	-	-	-	-
1928	15.5	-1.3	-	-	-	-	-	-	-	-	-	-	-	-	-	-
1929	15.6	0.6	-	-	-	-	-	-	-	-	-	-	-	-	-	-
1930	15.3	-1.9	-	-	-	-	-	-	-	-	-	-	-	-	-	-
1931	14.2	-7.2	-	-	-	-	-	-	-	-	-	-	-	-	-	-
1932	12.9	-9.2	-	-	-	-	-	-	-	-	-	-	-	-	-	-
1933	12.2	-5.4	-	-	-	-	-	-	-	-	-	-	-	-	-	-
1934	12.6	3.3	-	-	-	-	-	-	-	-	-	-	-	-	-	-
1935	13.0	3.2	-	-	-	-	-	-	-	-	-	-	-	-	-	-
1936	13.2	1.5	-	-	-	-	-	-	-	-	-	-	-	-	-	-
1937	13.8	4.5	-	-	-	-	-	-	-	-	-	-	-	-	-	-
1938	13.6	-1.4	-	-	-	-	-	-	-	-	-	-	-	-	-	-
1939	13.5	-0.7	-	-	-	-	-	-	-	-	-	-	-	-	-	-
1940	13.5	0.0	-	-	-	-	-	-	-	-	-	-	-	-	-	-
1941	14.2	5.2	-	-	-	-	-	-	-	-	-	-	-	-	-	-
1942	15.5	9.2	-	-	-	-	-	-	-	-	-	-	-	-	-	-
1943	16.2	4.5	-	-	-	-	-	-	-	-	-	-	-	-	-	-
1944	16.4	1.2	-	-	-	-	-	-	-	-	-	-	-	-	-	-
1945	16.7	1.8	-	-	-	-	-	-	-	-	-	-	-	-	-	-
1946	18.2	9.0	-	-	-	-	-	-	-	-	-	-	-	-	-	-
1947	21.0	15.4	-	-	-	-	-	-	21.6	-	10.7	-	-	-	-	-
1948	22.9	9.0	-	-	-	-	-	-	24.7	14.4	11.8	10.3	-	-	-	-
1949	22.7	-0.9	-	-	-	-	-	-	26.4	6.9	12.2	3.4	-	-	-	-
1950	22.9	0.9	-	-	-	-	-	-	26.5	0.4	12.6	3.3	-	-	-	-
1951	24.6	7.4	-	-	-	-	-	-	26.9	1.5	13.6	7.9	-	-	-	-
1952	25.4	3.3	-	-	-	-	-	-	28.7	6.7	14.5	6.6	-	-	-	-
1953	25.7	1.2	-	-	-	-	45.9	-	29.5	2.8	15.6	7.6	-	-	-	-
1954	25.9	0.8	-	-	-	-	45.9	0.0	29.2	-1.0	16.4	5.1	-	-	-	-
1955	25.9	0.0	-	-	-	-	45.2	-1.5	28.3	-3.1	17.0	3.7	-	-	-	-
1956	26.0	0.4	-	-	-	-	46.5	2.9	27.9	-1.4	17.3	1.8	-	-	-	-
1957	26.9	3.5	-	-	-	-	47.1	1.3	29.3	5.0	18.7	8.1	-	-	-	-
1958	27.6	2.6	-	-	-	-	47.3	0.4	30.3	3.4	21.2	13.4	-	-	-	-
1959	27.9	1.1	-	-	-	-	47.0	-0.6	31.6	4.3	22.7	7.1	-	-	-	-
1960	28.3	1.4	-	-	-	-	48.0	2.1	32.0	1.3	24.3	7.0	-	-	-	-
1961	28.6	1.1	-	-	-	-	46.9	-2.3	32.2	0.6	25.8	6.2	-	-	-	-

[Continued]

Minneapolis-St. Paul, MN
Consumer Price Index - All Urban Consumers
Base 1982-1984 = 100
Annual Averages
[Continued]

For 1917-1997. Columns headed % show percentile change in the index from the previous period for which an index is available.

Year	All Items		Food & Beverage		Housing		Apparel & Upkeep		Transportation		Medical Care		Entertainment		Other Goods & Services	
	Index	%	Index	%	Index	%	Index	%	Index	%	Index	%	Index	%	Index	%
1962	29.0	1.4	-	-	-	-	47.9	2.1	32.7	1.6	26.7	3.5	-	-	-	-
1963	29.4	1.4	-	-	-	-	48.8	1.9	33.2	1.5	27.0	1.1	-	-	-	-
1964	29.7	1.0	-	-	-	-	48.8	0.0	33.2	0.0	27.5	1.9	-	-	-	-
1965	30.1	1.3	-	-	-	-	49.9	2.3	33.8	1.8	27.6	0.4	-	-	-	-
1966	30.8	2.3	-	-	-	-	51.2	2.6	34.4	1.8	28.9	4.7	-	-	-	-
1967	31.8	3.2	-	-	-	-	53.0	3.5	35.6	3.5	30.4	5.2	-	-	-	-
1968	33.3	4.7	-	-	-	-	55.3	4.3	36.7	3.1	32.0	5.3	-	-	-	-
1969	35.0	5.1	-	-	-	-	58.3	5.4	37.4	1.9	33.6	5.0	-	-	-	-
1970	37.4	6.9	-	-	-	-	61.2	5.0	39.7	6.1	35.8	6.5	-	-	-	-
1971	38.7	3.5	-	-	-	-	62.6	2.3	41.1	3.5	37.7	5.3	-	-	-	-
1972	39.9	3.1	-	-	-	-	63.4	1.3	41.4	0.7	38.4	1.9	-	-	-	-
1973	42.3	6.0	-	-	-	-	66.3	4.6	43.1	4.1	40.3	4.9	-	-	-	-
1974	47.2	11.6	-	-	-	-	72.6	9.5	47.8	10.9	43.9	8.9	-	-	-	-
1975	51.2	8.5	-	-	-	-	74.0	1.9	50.9	6.5	48.6	10.7	-	-	-	-
1976	54.4	6.3	62.5	-	49.0	-	75.0	1.4	55.4	8.8	52.3	7.6	62.2	-	56.8	-
1977	58.2	7.0	65.8	5.3	53.2	8.6	78.1	4.1	59.6	7.6	56.6	8.2	65.5	5.3	60.0	5.6
1978	63.5	9.1	72.3	9.9	59.3	11.5	81.3	4.1	62.5	4.9	61.2	8.1	71.1	8.5	64.9	8.2
1979	70.8	11.5	80.9	11.9	66.3	11.8	85.5	5.2	71.8	14.9	66.2	8.2	75.1	5.6	69.3	6.8
1980	78.9	11.4	87.6	8.3	74.0	11.6	90.8	6.2	83.7	16.6	73.7	11.3	81.3	8.3	75.3	8.7
1981	88.6	12.3	92.7	5.8	85.9	16.1	94.7	4.3	93.6	11.8	80.3	9.0	93.1	14.5	83.2	10.5
1982	97.4	9.9	96.6	4.2	98.7	14.9	99.7	5.3	97.5	4.2	90.0	12.1	97.2	4.4	91.7	10.2
1983	99.5	2.2	99.5	3.0	99.3	0.6	101.5	1.8	99.3	1.8	100.3	11.4	100.2	3.1	100.7	9.8
1984	103.1	3.6	104.0	4.5	102.0	2.7	98.8	-2.7	103.2	3.9	109.7	9.4	102.6	2.4	107.6	6.9
1985	107.0	3.8	106.5	2.4	105.8	3.7	106.2	7.5	106.1	2.8	116.9	6.6	106.6	3.9	114.5	6.4
1986	108.4	1.3	109.4	2.7	107.8	1.9	107.0	0.8	100.5	-5.3	126.8	8.5	111.8	4.9	120.9	5.6
1987	106.5	-1.8	111.8	2.2	97.0	-10.0	113.6	6.2	102.5	2.0	130.4	2.8	118.5	6.0	124.8	3.2
1988	109.5	2.8	116.2	3.9	98.0	1.0	121.1	6.6	104.5	2.0	136.7	4.8	124.5	5.1	131.2	5.1
1989	114.1	4.2	121.7	4.7	100.5	2.6	123.9	2.3	109.2	4.5	148.0	8.3	133.8	7.5	138.5	5.6
1990	120.6	5.7	128.7	5.8	104.8	4.3	132.5	6.9	116.0	6.2	161.2	8.9	134.9	0.8	152.1	9.8
1991	125.1	3.7	131.6	2.3	109.5	4.5	134.8	1.7	119.6	3.1	177.7	10.2	139.6	3.5	157.7	3.7
1992	129.1	3.2	130.8	-0.6	113.2	3.4	135.8	0.7	122.9	2.8	193.6	8.9	146.4	4.9	172.1	9.1
1993	133.4	3.3	132.4	1.2	116.8	3.2	142.1	4.6	128.2	4.3	200.8	3.7	153.2	4.6	180.8	5.1
1994	137.9	3.4	137.5	3.9	120.4	3.1	146.7	3.2	132.9	3.7	204.6	1.9	157.4	2.7	187.6	3.8
1995	139.8	1.4	140.2	2.0	121.1	0.6	138.3	-5.7	137.0	3.1	217.7	6.4	157.3	-0.1	193.4	3.1
1996	142.7	2.1	142.9	1.9	123.9	2.3	137.7	-0.4	140.4	2.5	222.6	2.3	160.4	2.0	197.6	2.2
1997	-	-	-	-	-	-	-	-	-	-	-	-	-	-	-	-

Source: U.S. Department of Labor, Bureau of Labor Statistics, Division of Consumer Prices and Price Indexes. - indicates no data collected for period.

Minneapolis-St. Paul, MN
Consumer Price Index - Urban Wage Earners
Base 1982-1984 = 100
Annual Averages

For 1917-1997. Columns headed % show percentile change in the index from the previous period for which an index is available.

Year	All Items		Food & Beverage		Housing		Apparel & Upkeep		Trans- portation		Medical Care		Entertain- ment		Other Goods & Services	
	Index	%	Index	%	Index	%	Index	%	Index	%	Index	%	Index	%	Index	%
1917	-	-	-	-	-	-	-	-	-	-	-	-	-	-	-	-
1918	14.1	-	-	-	-	-	-	-	-	-	-	-	-	-	-	-
1919	16.1	14.2	-	-	-	-	-	-	-	-	-	-	-	-	-	-
1920	18.6	15.5	-	-	-	-	-	-	-	-	-	-	-	-	-	-
1921	16.8	-9.7	-	-	-	-	-	-	-	-	-	-	-	-	-	-
1922	15.8	-6.0	-	-	-	-	-	-	-	-	-	-	-	-	-	-
1923	15.9	0.6	-	-	-	-	-	-	-	-	-	-	-	-	-	-
1924	15.8	-0.6	-	-	-	-	-	-	-	-	-	-	-	-	-	-
1925	15.9	0.6	-	-	-	-	-	-	-	-	-	-	-	-	-	-
1926	16.1	1.3	-	-	-	-	-	-	-	-	-	-	-	-	-	-
1927	15.7	-2.5	-	-	-	-	-	-	-	-	-	-	-	-	-	-
1928	15.5	-1.3	-	-	-	-	-	-	-	-	-	-	-	-	-	-
1929	15.6	0.6	-	-	-	-	-	-	-	-	-	-	-	-	-	-
1930	15.3	-1.9	-	-	-	-	-	-	-	-	-	-	-	-	-	-
1931	14.2	-7.2	-	-	-	-	-	-	-	-	-	-	-	-	-	-
1932	12.9	-9.2	-	-	-	-	-	-	-	-	-	-	-	-	-	-
1933	12.2	-5.4	-	-	-	-	-	-	-	-	-	-	-	-	-	-
1934	12.6	3.3	-	-	-	-	-	-	-	-	-	-	-	-	-	-
1935	13.0	3.2	-	-	-	-	-	-	-	-	-	-	-	-	-	-
1936	13.2	1.5	-	-	-	-	-	-	-	-	-	-	-	-	-	-
1937	13.8	4.5	-	-	-	-	-	-	-	-	-	-	-	-	-	-
1938	13.6	-1.4	-	-	-	-	-	-	-	-	-	-	-	-	-	-
1939	13.5	-0.7	-	-	-	-	-	-	-	-	-	-	-	-	-	-
1940	13.5	0.0	-	-	-	-	-	-	-	-	-	-	-	-	-	-
1941	14.2	5.2	-	-	-	-	-	-	-	-	-	-	-	-	-	-
1942	15.5	9.2	-	-	-	-	-	-	-	-	-	-	-	-	-	-
1943	16.2	4.5	-	-	-	-	-	-	-	-	-	-	-	-	-	-
1944	16.4	1.2	-	-	-	-	-	-	-	-	-	-	-	-	-	-
1945	16.7	1.8	-	-	-	-	-	-	-	-	-	-	-	-	-	-
1946	18.2	9.0	-	-	-	-	-	-	-	-	-	-	-	-	-	-
1947	21.0	15.4	-	-	-	-	-	-	21.3	-	10.8	-	-	-	-	-
1948	22.9	9.0	-	-	-	-	-	-	24.3	14.1	11.9	10.2	-	-	-	-
1949	22.7	-0.9	-	-	-	-	-	-	26.0	7.0	12.4	4.2	-	-	-	-
1950	22.9	0.9	-	-	-	-	-	-	26.1	0.4	12.8	3.2	-	-	-	-
1951	24.6	7.4	-	-	-	-	-	-	26.5	1.5	13.8	7.8	-	-	-	-
1952	25.4	3.3	-	-	-	-	-	-	28.3	6.8	14.7	6.5	-	-	-	-
1953	25.7	1.2	-	-	-	-	46.9	-	29.0	2.5	15.9	8.2	-	-	-	-
1954	25.9	0.8	-	-	-	-	47.0	0.2	28.8	-0.7	16.6	4.4	-	-	-	-
1955	25.9	0.0	-	-	-	-	46.3	-1.5	27.9	-3.1	17.2	3.6	-	-	-	-
1956	26.0	0.4	-	-	-	-	47.6	2.8	27.5	-1.4	17.5	1.7	-	-	-	-
1957	26.9	3.5	-	-	-	-	48.2	1.3	28.8	4.7	19.0	8.6	-	-	-	-
1958	27.6	2.6	-	-	-	-	48.4	0.4	29.8	3.5	21.5	13.2	-	-	-	-
1959	27.9	1.1	-	-	-	-	48.1	-0.6	31.1	4.4	23.0	7.0	-	-	-	-
1960	28.4	1.8	-	-	-	-	49.1	2.1	31.5	1.3	24.6	7.0	-	-	-	-
1961	28.6	0.7	-	-	-	-	48.0	-2.2	31.7	0.6	26.2	6.5	-	-	-	-

[Continued]

Minneapolis-St. Paul, MN
Consumer Price Index - Urban Wage Earners
Base 1982-1984 = 100
Annual Averages
[Continued]

For 1917-1997. Columns headed % show percentile change in the index from the previous period for which an index is available.

Year	All Items		Food & Beverage		Housing		Apparel & Upkeep		Trans- portation		Medical Care		Entertain- ment		Other Goods & Services	
	Index	%	Index	%	Index	%	Index	%	Index	%	Index	%	Index	%	Index	%
1962	29.0	1.4	-	-	-	-	49.0	2.1	32.2	1.6	27.1	3.4	-	-	-	-
1963	29.4	1.4	-	-	-	-	50.0	2.0	32.7	1.6	27.4	1.1	-	-	-	-
1964	29.7	1.0	-	-	-	-	50.0	0.0	32.7	0.0	27.9	1.8	-	-	-	-
1965	30.1	1.3	-	-	-	-	51.0	2.0	33.3	1.8	28.0	0.4	-	-	-	-
1966	30.8	2.3	-	-	-	-	52.3	2.5	33.9	1.8	29.3	4.6	-	-	-	-
1967	31.9	3.6	-	-	-	-	54.2	3.6	35.0	3.2	30.9	5.5	-	-	-	-
1968	33.3	4.4	-	-	-	-	56.5	4.2	36.2	3.4	32.5	5.2	-	-	-	-
1969	35.0	5.1	-	-	-	-	59.7	5.7	36.8	1.7	34.1	4.9	-	-	-	-
1970	37.4	6.9	-	-	-	-	62.5	4.7	39.1	6.3	36.3	6.5	-	-	-	-
1971	38.8	3.7	-	-	-	-	64.1	2.6	40.5	3.6	38.2	5.2	-	-	-	-
1972	40.0	3.1	-	-	-	-	64.8	1.1	40.8	0.7	38.9	1.8	-	-	-	-
1973	42.4	6.0	-	-	-	-	67.9	4.8	42.4	3.9	40.9	5.1	-	-	-	-
1974	47.3	11.6	-	-	-	-	74.3	9.4	47.1	11.1	44.5	8.8	-	-	-	-
1975	51.3	8.5	-	-	-	-	75.7	1.9	50.1	6.4	49.3	10.8	-	-	-	-
1976	54.5	6.2	63.6	-	48.2	-	76.7	1.3	54.6	9.0	53.1	7.7	63.9	-	58.5	-
1977	58.3	7.0	66.9	5.2	52.4	8.7	79.9	4.2	58.7	7.5	57.4	8.1	67.3	5.3	61.8	5.6
1978	63.7	9.3	73.3	9.6	58.6	11.8	82.9	3.8	61.6	4.9	62.0	8.0	73.1	8.6	66.7	7.9
1979	71.2	11.8	81.6	11.3	65.7	12.1	86.0	3.7	71.5	16.1	66.3	6.9	81.6	11.6	71.1	6.6
1980	79.4	11.5	88.5	8.5	73.2	11.4	91.7	6.6	83.9	17.3	72.9	10.0	88.5	8.5	76.5	7.6
1981	88.9	12.0	92.7	4.7	85.7	17.1	96.3	5.0	93.9	11.9	79.5	9.1	92.6	4.6	83.8	9.5
1982	97.5	9.7	96.5	4.1	98.9	15.4	99.5	3.3	97.7	4.0	89.5	12.6	96.5	4.2	91.8	9.5
1983	99.1	1.6	99.5	3.1	98.2	-0.7	101.4	1.9	99.4	1.7	100.2	12.0	100.6	4.2	101.0	10.0
1984	103.5	4.4	104.1	4.6	102.9	4.8	99.2	-2.2	103.0	3.6	110.4	10.2	102.9	2.3	107.2	6.1
1985	105.7	2.1	106.5	2.3	103.5	0.6	106.6	7.5	105.8	2.7	117.6	6.5	106.7	3.7	114.1	6.4
1986	106.6	0.9	109.5	2.8	105.5	1.9	106.6	0.0	99.5	-6.0	127.4	8.3	112.1	5.1	120.6	5.7
1987	106.4	-0.2	111.7	2.0	96.5	-8.5	112.7	5.7	104.7	5.2	130.9	2.7	120.0	7.0	123.0	2.0
1988	109.7	3.1	116.1	3.9	97.5	1.0	121.1	7.5	107.1	2.3	137.7	5.2	126.3	5.2	130.4	6.0
1989	114.4	4.3	121.7	4.8	100.2	2.8	124.0	2.4	111.9	4.5	149.3	8.4	135.7	7.4	139.1	6.7
1990	120.9	5.7	128.8	5.8	104.5	4.3	132.8	7.1	118.7	6.1	162.3	8.7	136.6	0.7	152.8	9.8
1991	125.3	3.6	131.7	2.3	109.4	4.7	133.9	0.8	122.1	2.9	178.9	10.2	141.2	3.4	157.7	3.2
1992	128.9	2.9	131.0	-0.5	113.3	3.6	134.4	0.4	125.2	2.5	195.3	9.2	148.3	5.0	171.5	8.8
1993	133.0	3.2	132.6	1.2	117.2	3.4	138.9	3.3	129.4	3.4	202.9	3.9	156.2	5.3	179.6	4.7
1994	137.4	3.3	137.7	3.8	120.7	3.0	145.4	4.7	134.0	3.6	206.6	1.8	160.3	2.6	185.1	3.1
1995	139.4	1.5	140.3	1.9	121.2	0.4	137.6	-5.4	138.6	3.4	219.5	6.2	161.3	0.6	190.0	2.6
1996	142.0	1.9	143.1	2.0	123.8	2.1	136.8	-0.6	142.2	2.6	224.6	2.3	164.7	2.1	189.4	-0.3
1997	-	-	-	-	-	-	-	-	-	-	-	-	-	-	-	-

Source: U.S. Department of Labor, Bureau of Labor Statistics, Division of Consumer Prices and Price Indexes. - indicates no data collected for period.

Minneapolis-St. Paul, MN
Consumer Price Index - All Urban Consumers
Base 1982-1984 = 100
All Items

For 1917-1997. Columns headed % show percentile change in the index from the previous period for which an index is available.

Year	Jan Index	%	Feb Index	%	Mar Index	%	Apr Index	%	May Index	%	Jun Index	%	Jul Index	%	Aug Index	%	Sep Index	%	Oct Index	%	Nov Index	%	Dec Index	%
1917	-	-	-	-	-	-	-	-	-	-	-	-	-	-	-	-	-	-	-	-	-	-	13.1	-
1918	-	-	-	-	-	-	-	-	-	-	-	-	-	-	-	-	-	-	-	-	-	-	15.2	16.0
1919	-	-	-	-	-	-	-	-	-	-	15.6	2.6	-	-	-	-	-	-	-	-	-	-	17.5	12.2
1920	-	-	-	-	-	-	-	-	-	-	19.4	10.9	-	-	-	-	-	-	-	-	-	-	18.1	-6.7
1921	-	-	-	-	-	-	-	-	16.6	-8.3	-	-	-	-	-	-	16.5	-0.6	-	-	-	-	16.3	-1.2
1922	-	-	-	-	15.8	-3.1	-	-	-	-	15.9	0.6	-	-	-	-	15.5	-2.5	-	-	-	-	15.8	1.9
1923	-	-	-	-	15.8	0.0	-	-	-	-	15.8	0.0	-	-	-	-	15.9	0.6	-	-	-	-	16.0	0.6
1924	-	-	-	-	15.9	-0.6	-	-	-	-	15.7	-1.3	-	-	-	-	15.5	-1.3	-	-	-	-	15.7	1.3
1925	-	-	-	-	-	-	-	-	-	-	15.8	0.6	-	-	-	-	-	-	-	-	-	-	16.3	3.2
1926	-	-	-	-	-	-	-	-	-	-	16.3	0.0	-	-	-	-	-	-	-	-	-	-	16.0	-1.8
1927	-	-	-	-	-	-	-	-	-	-	16.0	0.0	-	-	-	-	-	-	-	-	-	-	15.6	-2.5
1928	-	-	-	-	-	-	-	-	-	-	15.6	0.0	-	-	-	-	-	-	-	-	-	-	15.5	-0.6
1929	-	-	-	-	-	-	-	-	-	-	15.5	0.0	-	-	-	-	-	-	-	-	-	-	15.7	1.3
1930	-	-	-	-	-	-	-	-	-	-	15.5	-1.3	-	-	-	-	-	-	-	-	-	-	14.9	-3.9
1931	-	-	-	-	-	-	-	-	-	-	14.2	-4.7	-	-	-	-	-	-	-	-	-	-	13.7	-3.5
1932	-	-	-	-	-	-	-	-	-	-	12.9	-5.8	-	-	-	-	-	-	-	-	-	-	12.4	-3.9
1933	-	-	-	-	-	-	-	-	-	-	11.9	-4.0	-	-	-	-	-	-	-	-	-	-	12.4	4.2
1934	-	-	-	-	-	-	-	-	-	-	12.6	1.6	-	-	-	-	-	-	-	-	12.6	0.0	-	-
1935	-	-	-	-	12.9	2.4	-	-	-	-	-	-	12.9	0.0	-	-	-	-	13.0	0.8	-	-	-	-
1936	13.1	0.8	-	-	-	-	13.0	-0.8	-	-	-	-	13.1	0.8	-	-	13.4	2.3	-	-	-	-	13.4	0.0
1937	-	-	-	-	13.6	1.5	-	-	-	-	13.7	0.7	-	-	-	-	13.9	1.5	-	-	-	-	13.8	-0.7
1938	-	-	-	-	13.6	-1.4	-	-	-	-	13.7	0.7	-	-	-	-	13.6	-0.7	-	-	-	-	13.5	-0.7
1939	-	-	-	-	13.4	-0.7	-	-	-	-	13.4	0.0	-	-	-	-	13.6	1.5	-	-	-	-	13.6	0.0
1940	-	-	-	-	13.5	-0.7	-	-	-	-	13.5	0.0	-	-	-	-	13.5	0.0	13.5	0.0	13.6	0.7	13.7	0.7
1941	13.6	-0.7	13.7	0.7	13.7	0.0	13.7	0.0	13.9	1.5	14.2	2.2	14.3	0.7	14.4	0.7	14.6	1.4	14.8	1.4	14.8	0.0	14.8	0.0
1942	15.0	1.4	15.1	0.7	15.3	1.3	15.4	0.7	15.5	0.6	15.5	0.0	15.6	0.6	15.6	0.0	15.7	0.6	15.8	0.6	15.9	0.6	16.0	0.6
1943	15.9	-0.6	16.0	0.6	16.2	1.3	16.2	0.0	16.3	0.6	16.3	0.0	16.2	-0.6	16.2	0.0	16.2	0.0	16.3	0.6	16.3	0.0	16.4	0.6
1944	16.2	-1.2	16.2	0.0	16.3	0.6	16.3	0.0	16.4	0.6	16.4	0.0	16.5	0.6	16.5	0.0	16.5	0.0	16.5	0.0	16.5	0.0	16.5	0.0
1945	16.5	0.0	16.5	0.0	16.5	0.0	16.5	0.0	16.6	0.6	16.7	0.6	16.7	0.0	16.7	0.0	16.8	0.6	16.8	0.0	16.9	0.6	16.9	0.0
1946	16.9	0.0	16.9	0.0	16.9	0.0	17.0	0.6	17.1	0.6	17.3	1.2	18.5	6.9	18.7	1.1	19.1	2.1	19.6	2.6	20.0	2.0	20.1	0.5
1947	19.9	-1.0	20.0	0.5	20.3	1.5	20.3	0.0	20.3	0.0	20.5	1.0	-	-	-	-	21.8	6.3	-	-	-	-	22.3	2.3
1948	-	-	-	-	22.5	0.9	-	-	-	-	23.0	2.2	-	-	-	-	23.3	1.3	-	-	-	-	22.9	-1.7
1949	-	-	-	-	22.8	-0.4	-	-	-	-	22.7	-0.4	-	-	-	-	22.7	0.0	-	-	-	-	22.5	-0.9
1950	-	-	-	-	22.4	-0.4	-	-	-	-	22.7	1.3	-	-	-	-	23.1	1.8	-	-	-	-	23.8	3.0
1951	-	-	-	-	24.5	2.9	-	-	-	-	24.6	0.4	-	-	-	-	24.5	-0.4	-	-	-	-	25.1	2.4
1952	-	-	-	-	25.2	0.4	-	-	-	-	25.5	1.2	-	-	-	-	25.5	0.0	-	-	-	-	25.4	-0.4
1953	25.4	0.0	-	-	-	-	25.5	0.4	-	-	-	-	25.7	0.8	-	-	25.9	0.8	-	-	-	-	-	-
1954	25.9	0.0	-	-	-	-	25.8	-0.4	-	-	-	-	26.0	0.8	-	-	25.9	-0.4	-	-	-	-	-	-
1955	25.9	0.0	-	-	-	-	26.0	0.4	-	-	-	-	26.1	0.4	-	-	25.8	-1.1	-	-	-	-	-	-
1956	25.8	0.0	-	-	-	-	25.7	-0.4	-	-	-	-	26.1	1.6	-	-	26.1	0.0	-	-	-	-	-	-
1957	26.5	1.5	-	-	-	-	26.6	0.4	-	-	-	-	27.0	1.5	-	-	27.1	0.4	-	-	-	-	-	-
1958	27.3	0.7	-	-	-	-	27.5	0.7	-	-	-	-	27.7	0.7	-	-	27.6	-0.4	-	-	-	-	-	-
1959	27.8	0.7	-	-	-	-	27.7	-0.4	-	-	-	-	27.8	0.4	-	-	28.1	1.1	-	-	-	-	-	-
1960	28.0	-0.4	-	-	-	-	28.2	0.7	-	-	-	-	28.3	0.4	-	-	28.5	0.7	-	-	-	-	-	-
1961	28.4	-0.4	-	-	-	-	28.6	0.7	-	-	-	-	28.7	0.3	-	-	28.7	0.0	-	-	-	-	-	-

[Continued]

Minneapolis-St. Paul, MN
Consumer Price Index - All Urban Consumers
Base 1982-1984 = 100
All Items
[Continued]

For 1917-1997. Columns headed % show percentile change in the index from the previous period for which an index is available.

Year	Jan Index	%	Feb Index	%	Mar Index	%	Apr Index	%	May Index	%	Jun Index	%	Jul Index	%	Aug Index	%	Sep Index	%	Oct Index	%	Nov Index	%	Dec Index	%
1962	28.6	-0.3	-	-	-	-	29.0	1.4	-	-	-	-	29.0	0.0	-	-	-	-	29.1	0.3	-	-	-	-
1963	29.1	0.0	-	-	-	-	29.2	0.3	-	-	-	-	29.6	1.4	-	-	-	-	29.5	-0.3	-	-	-	-
1964	29.5	0.0	-	-	-	-	29.5	0.0	-	-	-	-	29.7	0.7	-	-	-	-	29.8	0.3	-	-	-	-
1965	29.8	0.0	-	-	-	-	29.9	0.3	-	-	-	-	30.1	0.7	-	-	-	-	30.2	0.3	-	-	-	-
1966	30.3	0.3	-	-	-	-	30.7	1.3	-	-	-	-	30.7	0.0	-	-	-	-	31.1	1.3	-	-	-	-
1967	31.1	0.0	-	-	-	-	31.3	0.6	-	-	-	-	31.7	1.3	-	-	-	-	32.5	2.5	-	-	-	-
1968	32.7	0.6	-	-	-	-	33.1	1.2	-	-	-	-	33.4	0.9	-	-	-	-	33.5	0.3	-	-	-	-
1969	33.7	0.6	-	-	-	-	34.3	1.8	-	-	-	-	35.1	2.3	-	-	-	-	35.8	2.0	-	-	-	-
1970	36.5	2.0	-	-	-	-	37.1	1.6	-	-	-	-	37.5	1.1	-	-	-	-	37.9	1.1	-	-	-	-
1971	38.2	0.8	-	-	-	-	38.3	0.3	-	-	-	-	38.8	1.3	-	-	-	-	39.3	1.3	-	-	-	-
1972	39.4	0.3	-	-	-	-	39.5	0.3	-	-	-	-	39.9	1.0	-	-	-	-	40.5	1.5	-	-	-	-
1973	40.7	0.5	-	-	-	-	41.6	2.2	-	-	-	-	42.4	1.9	-	-	-	-	43.4	2.4	-	-	-	-
1974	44.6	2.8	-	-	-	-	46.2	3.6	-	-	-	-	47.3	2.4	-	-	-	-	49.0	3.6	-	-	-	-
1975	49.7	1.4	-	-	-	-	49.9	0.4	-	-	-	-	51.5	3.2	-	-	-	-	52.5	1.9	-	-	-	-
1976	53.2	1.3	-	-	-	-	53.7	0.9	-	-	-	-	54.6	1.7	-	-	-	-	55.2	1.1	-	-	-	-
1977	56.0	1.4	-	-	-	-	57.2	2.1	-	-	-	-	58.7	2.6	-	-	-	-	59.5	1.4	-	-	-	-
1978	60.7	2.0	-	-	-	-	62.0	2.1	-	-	63.2	1.9	-	-	64.5	2.1	-	-	65.6	1.7	-	-	66.4	1.2
1979	-	-	67.4	1.5	-	-	68.7	1.9	-	-	70.7	2.9	-	-	72.2	2.1	-	-	73.6	1.9	-	-	74.5	1.2
1980	-	-	75.7	1.6	-	-	77.7	2.6	-	-	78.4	0.9	-	-	79.6	1.5	-	-	81.3	2.1	-	-	82.4	1.4
1981	-	-	82.9	0.6	-	-	84.8	2.3	-	-	87.9	3.7	-	-	91.2	3.8	-	-	92.8	1.8	-	-	95.1	2.5
1982	-	-	97.4	2.4	-	-	96.0	-1.4	-	-	96.8	0.8	-	-	99.9	3.2	-	-	97.9	-2.0	-	-	97.4	-0.5
1983	-	-	97.3	-0.1	-	-	98.5	1.2	-	-	99.5	1.0	-	-	100.6	1.1	-	-	100.8	0.2	-	-	101.0	0.2
1984	-	-	101.7	0.7	-	-	102.5	0.8	-	-	103.1	0.6	-	-	103.4	0.3	-	-	104.4	1.0	-	-	104.3	-0.1
1985	-	-	105.1	0.8	-	-	106.2	1.0	-	-	107.1	0.8	-	-	107.8	0.7	-	-	108.4	0.6	-	-	108.3	-0.1
1986	-	-	108.2	-0.1	-	-	107.7	-0.5	-	-	108.9	1.1	-	-	108.3	-0.6	-	-	108.5	0.2	108.4	-0.1	109.0	0.6
1987	-	-	-	-	-	-	-	-	-	-	105.5	-3.2	-	-	-	-	-	-	-	-	-	-	107.5	1.9
1988	-	-	-	-	-	-	-	-	-	-	108.4	0.8	-	-	-	-	-	-	-	-	-	-	110.7	2.1
1989	-	-	-	-	-	-	-	-	-	-	113.1	2.2	-	-	-	-	-	-	-	-	-	-	115.1	1.8
1990	-	-	-	-	-	-	-	-	-	-	118.6	3.0	-	-	-	-	-	-	-	-	-	-	122.6	3.4
1991	-	-	-	-	-	-	-	-	-	-	124.1	1.2	-	-	-	-	-	-	-	-	-	-	126.2	1.7
1992	-	-	-	-	-	-	-	-	-	-	128.2	1.6	-	-	-	-	-	-	-	-	-	-	130.0	1.4
1993	-	-	-	-	-	-	-	-	-	-	131.8	1.4	-	-	-	-	-	-	-	-	-	-	135.1	2.5
1994	-	-	-	-	-	-	-	-	-	-	137.0	1.4	-	-	-	-	-	-	-	-	-	-	138.7	1.2
1995	-	-	-	-	-	-	-	-	-	-	138.9	0.1	-	-	-	-	-	-	-	-	-	-	140.8	1.4
1996	-	-	-	-	-	-	-	-	-	-	142.3	1.1	-	-	-	-	-	-	-	-	-	-	143.1	0.6
1997	-	-	-	-	-	-	-	-	-	-	144.7	1.1	-	-	-	-	-	-	-	-	-	-	-	-

Source: U.S. Department of Labor, Bureau of Labor Statistics, Division of Consumer Prices and Price Indexes. - indicates no data collected for period.

Minneapolis-St. Paul, MN
Consumer Price Index - Urban Wage Earners
Base 1982-1984 = 100
All Items

For 1917-1997. Columns headed % show percentile change in the index from the previous period for which an index is available.

Year	Jan Index	%	Feb Index	%	Mar Index	%	Apr Index	%	May Index	%	Jun Index	%	Jul Index	%	Aug Index	%	Sep Index	%	Oct Index	%	Nov Index	%	Dec Index	%
1917	-	-	-	-	-	-	-	-	-	-	-	-	-	-	-	-	-	-	-	-	-	-	13.2	-
1918	-	-	-	-	-	-	-	-	-	-	-	-	-	-	-	-	-	-	-	-	-	-	15.2	15.2
1919	-	-	-	-	-	-	-	-	-	-	15.6	2.6	-	-	-	-	-	-	-	-	-	-	17.5	12.2
1920	-	-	-	-	-	-	-	-	-	-	19.4	10.9	-	-	-	-	-	-	-	-	-	-	18.2	-6.2
1921	-	-	-	-	-	-	-	-	16.6	-8.8	-	-	-	-	-	-	16.5	-0.6	-	-	-	-	16.3	-1.2
1922	-	-	-	-	15.8	-3.1	-	-	-	-	15.9	0.6	-	-	-	-	15.5	-2.5	-	-	-	-	15.8	1.9
1923	-	-	-	-	15.9	0.6	-	-	-	-	15.8	-0.6	-	-	-	-	15.9	0.6	-	-	-	-	16.0	0.6
1924	-	-	-	-	15.9	-0.6	-	-	-	-	15.7	-1.3	-	-	-	-	15.5	-1.3	-	-	-	-	15.7	1.3
1925	-	-	-	-	-	-	-	-	-	-	15.8	0.6	-	-	-	-	-	-	-	-	-	-	16.3	3.2
1926	-	-	-	-	-	-	-	-	-	-	16.3	0.0	-	-	-	-	-	-	-	-	-	-	16.0	-1.8
1927	-	-	-	-	-	-	-	-	-	-	16.1	0.6	-	-	-	-	-	-	-	-	-	-	15.6	-3.1
1928	-	-	-	-	-	-	-	-	-	-	15.6	0.0	-	-	-	-	-	-	-	-	-	-	15.5	-0.6
1929	-	-	-	-	-	-	-	-	-	-	15.5	0.0	-	-	-	-	-	-	-	-	-	-	15.7	1.3
1930	-	-	-	-	-	-	-	-	-	-	15.5	-1.3	-	-	-	-	-	-	-	-	-	-	14.9	-3.9
1931	-	-	-	-	-	-	-	-	-	-	14.2	-4.7	-	-	-	-	-	-	-	-	-	-	13.8	-2.8
1932	-	-	-	-	-	-	-	-	-	-	12.9	-6.5	-	-	-	-	-	-	-	-	-	-	12.5	-3.1
1933	-	-	-	-	-	-	-	-	-	-	11.9	-4.8	-	-	-	-	-	-	-	-	-	-	12.5	5.0
1934	-	-	-	-	-	-	-	-	-	-	12.6	0.8	-	-	-	-	-	-	-	-	12.6	0.0	-	-
1935	-	-	-	-	12.9	2.4	-	-	-	-	-	-	12.9	0.0	-	-	-	-	13.0	0.8	-	-	-	-
1936	13.2	1.5	-	-	-	-	13.0	-1.5	-	-	-	-	13.2	1.5	-	-	13.4	1.5	-	-	-	-	13.4	0.0
1937	-	-	-	-	13.6	1.5	-	-	-	-	13.8	1.5	-	-	-	-	14.0	1.4	-	-	-	-	13.9	-0.7
1938	-	-	-	-	13.6	-2.2	-	-	-	-	13.7	0.7	-	-	-	-	13.6	-0.7	-	-	-	-	13.5	-0.7
1939	-	-	-	-	13.4	-0.7	-	-	-	-	13.4	0.0	-	-	-	-	13.6	1.5	-	-	-	-	13.6	0.0
1940	-	-	-	-	13.5	-0.7	-	-	-	-	13.5	0.0	-	-	-	-	13.5	0.0	13.5	0.0	13.6	0.7	13.7	0.7
1941	13.6	-0.7	13.7	0.7	13.7	0.0	13.8	0.7	13.9	0.7	14.2	2.2	14.3	0.7	14.4	0.7	14.6	1.4	14.8	1.4	14.8	0.0	14.8	0.0
1942	15.0	1.4	15.1	0.7	15.3	1.3	15.4	0.7	15.5	0.6	15.5	0.0	15.6	0.6	15.6	0.0	15.7	0.6	15.8	0.6	15.9	0.6	16.0	0.6
1943	16.0	0.0	16.1	0.6	16.2	0.6	16.2	0.0	16.3	0.6	16.3	0.0	16.2	-0.6	16.2	0.0	16.2	0.0	16.3	0.6	16.3	0.0	16.4	0.6
1944	16.2	-1.2	16.2	0.0	16.3	0.6	16.3	0.0	16.4	0.6	16.4	0.0	16.5	0.6	16.5	0.0	16.5	0.0	16.5	0.0	16.5	0.0	16.5	0.0
1945	16.5	0.0	16.5	0.0	16.5	0.0	16.5	0.0	16.6	0.6	16.7	0.6	16.8	0.6	16.8	0.0	16.8	0.0	16.8	0.0	16.9	0.6	16.9	0.0
1946	17.0	0.6	16.9	-0.6	16.9	0.0	17.0	0.6	17.1	0.6	17.4	1.8	18.5	6.3	18.7	1.1	19.1	2.1	19.6	2.6	20.0	2.0	20.1	0.5
1947	19.9	-1.0	20.0	0.5	20.4	2.0	20.3	-0.5	20.4	0.5	20.6	1.0	-	-	-	-	21.8	5.8	-	-	-	-	22.3	2.3
1948	-	-	-	-	22.6	1.3	-	-	-	-	23.0	1.8	-	-	-	-	23.4	1.7	-	-	-	-	23.0	-1.7
1949	-	-	-	-	22.8	-0.9	-	-	-	-	22.7	-0.4	-	-	-	-	22.7	0.0	-	-	-	-	22.6	-0.4
1950	-	-	-	-	22.5	-0.4	-	-	-	-	22.7	0.9	-	-	-	-	23.2	2.2	-	-	-	-	23.8	2.6
1951	-	-	-	-	24.6	3.4	-	-	-	-	24.7	0.4	-	-	-	-	24.6	-0.4	-	-	-	-	25.2	2.4
1952	-	-	-	-	25.2	0.0	-	-	-	-	25.6	1.6	-	-	-	-	25.5	-0.4	-	-	-	-	25.5	0.0
1953	25.4	-0.4	-	-	-	-	25.6	0.8	-	-	-	-	25.7	0.4	-	-	-	-	25.9	0.8	-	-	-	-
1954	25.9	0.0	-	-	-	-	25.8	-0.4	-	-	-	-	26.1	1.2	-	-	-	-	26.0	-0.4	-	-	-	-
1955	25.9	-0.4	-	-	-	-	26.0	0.4	-	-	-	-	26.1	0.4	-	-	-	-	25.9	-0.8	-	-	-	-
1956	25.8	-0.4	-	-	-	-	25.7	-0.4	-	-	-	-	26.2	1.9	-	-	-	-	26.1	-0.4	-	-	-	-
1957	26.5	1.5	-	-	-	-	26.6	0.4	-	-	-	-	27.0	1.5	-	-	-	-	27.1	0.4	-	-	-	-
1958	27.4	1.1	-	-	-	-	27.6	0.7	-	-	-	-	27.8	0.7	-	-	-	-	27.7	-0.4	-	-	-	-
1959	27.8	0.4	-	-	-	-	27.8	0.0	-	-	-	-	27.9	0.4	-	-	-	-	28.1	0.7	-	-	-	-
1960	28.0	-0.4	-	-	-	-	28.2	0.7	-	-	-	-	28.4	0.7	-	-	-	-	28.5	0.4	-	-	-	-
1961	28.4	-0.4	-	-	-	-	28.7	1.1	-	-	-	-	28.7	0.0	-	-	-	-	28.7	0.0	-	-	-	-

[Continued]

Minneapolis-St. Paul, MN
Consumer Price Index - Urban Wage Earners
Base 1982-1984 = 100
All Items
[Continued]

For 1917-1997. Columns headed % show percentile change in the index from the previous period for which an index is available.

Year	Jan Index	%	Feb Index	%	Mar Index	%	Apr Index	%	May Index	%	Jun Index	%	Jul Index	%	Aug Index	%	Sep Index	%	Oct Index	%	Nov Index	%	Dec Index	%
1962	28.7	0.0	-	-	-	-	29.0	1.0	-	-	-	-	29.1	0.3	-	-	-	-	29.1	0.0	-	-	-	-
1963	29.2	0.3	-	-	-	-	29.3	0.3	-	-	-	-	29.6	1.0	-	-	-	-	29.5	-0.3	-	-	-	-
1964	29.6	0.3	-	-	-	-	29.5	-0.3	-	-	-	-	29.7	0.7	-	-	-	-	29.9	0.7	-	-	-	-
1965	29.9	0.0	-	-	-	-	29.9	0.0	-	-	-	-	30.2	1.0	-	-	-	-	30.3	0.3	-	-	-	-
1966	30.4	0.3	-	-	-	-	30.7	1.0	-	-	-	-	30.8	0.3	-	-	-	-	31.2	1.3	-	-	-	-
1967	31.2	0.0	-	-	-	-	31.4	0.6	-	-	-	-	31.8	1.3	-	-	-	-	32.6	2.5	-	-	-	-
1968	32.8	0.6	-	-	-	-	33.1	0.9	-	-	-	-	33.5	1.2	-	-	-	-	33.5	0.0	-	-	-	-
1969	33.8	0.9	-	-	-	-	34.4	1.8	-	-	-	-	35.2	2.3	-	-	-	-	35.8	1.7	-	-	-	-
1970	36.5	2.0	-	-	-	-	37.2	1.9	-	-	-	-	37.6	1.1	-	-	-	-	38.0	1.1	-	-	-	-
1971	38.3	0.8	-	-	-	-	38.3	0.0	-	-	-	-	38.8	1.3	-	-	-	-	39.3	1.3	-	-	-	-
1972	39.4	0.3	-	-	-	-	39.6	0.5	-	-	-	-	40.0	1.0	-	-	-	-	40.5	1.3	-	-	-	-
1973	40.7	0.5	-	-	-	-	41.7	2.5	-	-	-	-	42.4	1.7	-	-	-	-	43.4	2.4	-	-	-	-
1974	44.7	3.0	-	-	-	-	46.2	3.4	-	-	-	-	47.4	2.6	-	-	-	-	49.0	3.4	-	-	-	-
1975	49.8	1.6	-	-	-	-	50.0	0.4	-	-	-	-	51.6	3.2	-	-	-	-	52.6	1.9	-	-	-	-
1976	53.2	1.1	-	-	-	-	53.7	0.9	-	-	-	-	54.7	1.9	-	-	-	-	55.2	0.9	-	-	-	-
1977	56.0	1.4	-	-	-	-	57.2	2.1	-	-	-	-	58.8	2.8	-	-	-	-	59.6	1.4	-	-	-	-
1978	60.8	2.0	-	-	-	-	62.1	2.1	-	-	63.3	1.9	-	-	64.8	2.4	-	-	65.7	1.4	-	-	66.7	1.5
1979	-	-	67.7	1.5	-	-	68.8	1.6	-	-	71.2	3.5	-	-	72.8	2.2	-	-	74.2	1.9	-	-	74.8	0.8
1980	-	-	76.3	2.0	-	-	78.3	2.6	-	-	79.1	1.0	-	-	79.8	0.9	-	-	81.8	2.5	-	-	83.0	1.5
1981	-	-	83.6	0.7	-	-	85.2	1.9	-	-	88.1	3.4	-	-	91.4	3.7	-	-	92.9	1.6	-	-	95.0	2.3
1982	-	-	97.3	2.4	-	-	96.0	-1.3	-	-	96.8	0.8	-	-	99.8	3.1	-	-	98.0	-1.8	-	-	97.5	-0.5
1983	-	-	98.5	1.0	-	-	99.5	1.0	-	-	99.3	-0.2	-	-	98.3	-1.0	-	-	99.6	1.3	-	-	99.6	0.0
1984	-	-	101.5	1.9	-	-	102.3	0.8	-	-	104.8	2.4	-	-	105.9	1.0	-	-	104.2	-1.6	-	-	103.2	-1.0
1985	-	-	103.9	0.7	-	-	104.9	1.0	-	-	105.9	1.0	-	-	106.5	0.6	-	-	107.1	0.6	-	-	107.1	0.0
1986	-	-	106.7	-0.4	-	-	105.9	-0.7	-	-	107.1	1.1	-	-	106.6	-0.5	-	-	106.6	0.0	106.6	0.0	107.0	0.4
1987	-	-	-	-	-	-	-	-	-	-	105.3	-1.6	-	-	-	-	-	-	-	-	-	-	107.4	2.0
1988	-	-	-	-	-	-	-	-	-	-	108.4	0.9	-	-	-	-	-	-	-	-	-	-	111.0	2.4
1989	-	-	-	-	-	-	-	-	-	-	113.4	2.2	-	-	-	-	-	-	-	-	-	-	115.4	1.8
1990	-	-	-	-	-	-	-	-	-	-	118.8	2.9	-	-	-	-	-	-	-	-	-	-	123.0	3.5
1991	-	-	-	-	-	-	-	-	-	-	124.3	1.1	-	-	-	-	-	-	-	-	-	-	126.3	1.6
1992	-	-	-	-	-	-	-	-	-	-	128.0	1.3	-	-	-	-	-	-	-	-	-	-	129.9	1.5
1993	-	-	-	-	-	-	-	-	-	-	131.4	1.2	-	-	-	-	-	-	-	-	-	-	134.6	2.4
1994	-	-	-	-	-	-	-	-	-	-	136.4	1.3	-	-	-	-	-	-	-	-	-	-	138.5	1.5
1995	-	-	-	-	-	-	-	-	-	-	138.5	0.0	-	-	-	-	-	-	-	-	-	-	140.3	1.3
1996	-	-	-	-	-	-	-	-	-	-	141.6	0.9	-	-	-	-	-	-	-	-	-	-	142.5	0.6
1997	-	-	-	-	-	-	-	-	-	-	143.8	0.9	-	-	-	-	-	-	-	-	-	-	-	-

Source: U.S. Department of Labor, Bureau of Labor Statistics, Division of Consumer Prices and Price Indexes. - indicates no data collected for period.

Minneapolis-St. Paul, MN
Consumer Price Index - All Urban Consumers
Base 1982-1984 = 100
Food and Beverages

For 1976-1997. Columns headed % show percentile change in the index from the previous period for which an index is available.

Year	Jan Index	%	Feb Index	%	Mar Index	%	Apr Index	%	May Index	%	Jun Index	%	Jul Index	%	Aug Index	%	Sep Index	%	Oct Index	%	Nov Index	%	Dec Index	%
1976	62.4	-	-	-	-	-	62.0	-0.6	-	-	-	-	62.8	1.3	-	-	-	-	62.7	-0.2	-	-	-	-
1977	63.1	0.6	-	-	-	-	65.0	3.0	-	-	-	-	66.7	2.6	-	-	-	-	66.8	0.1	-	-	-	-
1978	67.9	1.6	-	-	-	-	70.6	4.0	-	-	72.9	3.3	-	-	73.6	1.0	-	-	74.3	1.0	-	-	75.5	1.6
1979	-	-	78.2	3.6	-	-	79.4	1.5	-	-	81.7	2.9	-	-	82.3	0.7	-	-	82.6	0.4	-	-	83.6	1.2
1980	-	-	84.4	1.0	-	-	86.0	1.9	-	-	87.6	1.9	-	-	88.6	1.1	-	-	89.9	1.5	-	-	90.7	0.9
1981	-	-	91.3	0.7	-	-	91.7	0.4	-	-	92.2	0.5	-	-	93.8	1.7	-	-	94.1	0.3	-	-	94.1	0.0
1982	-	-	94.9	0.9	-	-	95.4	0.5	-	-	96.8	1.5	-	-	97.5	0.7	-	-	97.9	0.4	-	-	97.9	0.0
1983	-	-	97.9	0.0	-	-	99.4	1.5	-	-	99.2	-0.2	-	-	99.6	0.4	-	-	100.0	0.4	-	-	101.5	1.5
1984	-	-	103.4	1.9	-	-	103.6	0.2	-	-	103.8	0.2	-	-	104.1	0.3	-	-	104.8	0.7	-	-	105.3	0.5
1985	-	-	106.5	1.1	-	-	106.3	-0.2	-	-	106.2	-0.1	-	-	106.3	0.1	-	-	106.9	0.6	-	-	107.7	0.7
1986	-	-	108.4	0.6	-	-	108.7	0.3	-	-	108.6	-0.1	-	-	109.4	0.7	-	-	110.4	0.9	111.1	0.6	112.2	1.0
1987	-	-	-	-	-	-	-	-	-	-	111.3	-0.8	-	-	-	-	-	-	-	-	-	-	112.3	0.9
1988	-	-	-	-	-	-	-	-	-	-	114.1	1.6	-	-	-	-	-	-	-	-	-	-	118.2	3.6
1989	-	-	-	-	-	-	-	-	-	-	121.4	2.7	-	-	-	-	-	-	-	-	-	-	122.0	0.5
1990	-	-	-	-	-	-	-	-	-	-	127.4	4.4	-	-	-	-	-	-	-	-	-	-	129.9	2.0
1991	-	-	-	-	-	-	-	-	-	-	131.7	1.4	-	-	-	-	-	-	-	-	-	-	131.5	-0.2
1992	-	-	-	-	-	-	-	-	-	-	131.7	0.2	-	-	-	-	-	-	-	-	-	-	129.8	-1.4
1993	-	-	-	-	-	-	-	-	-	-	130.4	0.5	-	-	-	-	-	-	-	-	-	-	134.4	3.1
1994	-	-	-	-	-	-	-	-	-	-	136.7	1.7	-	-	-	-	-	-	-	-	-	-	138.2	1.1
1995	-	-	-	-	-	-	-	-	-	-	140.0	1.3	-	-	-	-	-	-	-	-	-	-	140.4	0.3
1996	-	-	-	-	-	-	-	-	-	-	141.0	0.4	-	-	-	-	-	-	-	-	-	-	144.8	2.7
1997	-	-	-	-	-	-	-	-	-	-	146.7	1.3	-	-	-	-	-	-	-	-	-	-	-	-

Source: U.S. Department of Labor, Bureau of Labor Statistics, Division of Consumer Prices and Price Indexes. - indicates no data collected for period.

Minneapolis-St. Paul, MN
Consumer Price Index - Urban Wage Earners
Base 1982-1984 = 100
Food and Beverages

For 1976-1997. Columns headed % show percentile change in the index from the previous period for which an index is available.

Year	Jan Index	%	Feb Index	%	Mar Index	%	Apr Index	%	May Index	%	Jun Index	%	Jul Index	%	Aug Index	%	Sep Index	%	Oct Index	%	Nov Index	%	Dec Index	%
1976	63.5	-	-	-	-	-	63.1	-0.6	-	-	-	-	63.9	1.3	-	-	-	-	63.8	-0.2	-	-	-	-
1977	64.2	0.6	-	-	-	-	66.1	3.0	-	-	-	-	67.9	2.7	-	-	-	-	68.0	0.1	-	-	-	-
1978	69.0	1.5	-	-	-	-	71.9	4.2	-	-	73.4	2.1	-	-	75.0	2.2	-	-	75.3	0.4	-	-	76.1	1.1
1979	-	-	79.1	3.9	-	-	79.3	0.3	-	-	82.2	3.7	-	-	83.5	1.6	-	-	83.9	0.5	-	-	83.3	-0.7
1980	-	-	85.3	2.4	-	-	86.9	1.9	-	-	88.3	1.6	-	-	89.3	1.1	-	-	91.3	2.2	-	-	91.8	0.5
1981	-	-	91.3	-0.5	-	-	91.7	0.4	-	-	92.1	0.4	-	-	94.1	2.2	-	-	94.0	-0.1	-	-	93.7	-0.3
1982	-	-	94.5	0.9	-	-	95.2	0.7	-	-	96.6	1.5	-	-	97.4	0.8	-	-	98.0	0.6	-	-	98.0	0.0
1983	-	-	97.9	-0.1	-	-	99.4	1.5	-	-	99.1	-0.3	-	-	99.6	0.5	-	-	100.1	0.5	-	-	101.6	1.5
1984	-	-	103.4	1.8	-	-	103.8	0.4	-	-	103.8	0.0	-	-	104.2	0.4	-	-	105.0	0.8	-	-	105.4	0.4
1985	-	-	106.6	1.1	-	-	106.4	-0.2	-	-	106.1	-0.3	-	-	106.2	0.1	-	-	106.8	0.6	-	-	107.6	0.7
1986	-	-	108.5	0.8	-	-	108.6	0.1	-	-	108.6	0.0	-	-	109.6	0.9	-	-	110.4	0.7	111.1	0.6	112.1	0.9
1987	-	-	-	-	-	-	-	-	-	-	111.1	-0.9	-	-	-	-	-	-	-	-	-	-	112.2	1.0
1988	-	-	-	-	-	-	-	-	-	-	113.9	1.5	-	-	-	-	-	-	-	-	-	-	118.2	3.8
1989	-	-	-	-	-	-	-	-	-	-	121.4	2.7	-	-	-	-	-	-	-	-	-	-	122.0	0.5
1990	-	-	-	-	-	-	-	-	-	-	127.6	4.6	-	-	-	-	-	-	-	-	-	-	130.1	2.0
1991	-	-	-	-	-	-	-	-	-	-	131.7	1.2	-	-	-	-	-	-	-	-	-	-	131.7	0.0
1992	-	-	-	-	-	-	-	-	-	-	132.0	0.2	-	-	-	-	-	-	-	-	-	-	130.0	-1.5
1993	-	-	-	-	-	-	-	-	-	-	130.5	0.4	-	-	-	-	-	-	-	-	-	-	134.7	3.2
1994	-	-	-	-	-	-	-	-	-	-	137.1	1.8	-	-	-	-	-	-	-	-	-	-	138.4	0.9
1995	-	-	-	-	-	-	-	-	-	-	140.0	1.2	-	-	-	-	-	-	-	-	-	-	140.5	0.4
1996	-	-	-	-	-	-	-	-	-	-	141.2	0.5	-	-	-	-	-	-	-	-	-	-	145.1	2.8
1997	-	-	-	-	-	-	-	-	-	-	147.0	1.3	-	-	-	-	-	-	-	-	-	-	-	-

Source: U.S. Department of Labor, Bureau of Labor Statistics, Division of Consumer Prices and Price Indexes. - indicates no data collected for period.

Minneapolis-St. Paul, MN
Consumer Price Index - All Urban Consumers
Base 1982-1984 = 100
Housing

For 1976-1997. Columns headed % show percentile change in the index from the previous period for which an index is available.

Year	Jan Index	%	Feb Index	%	Mar Index	%	Apr Index	%	May Index	%	Jun Index	%	Jul Index	%	Aug Index	%	Sep Index	%	Oct Index	%	Nov Index	%	Dec Index	%
1976	47.7	-	-	-	-	-	48.1	0.8	-	-	-	-	49.1	2.1	-	-	-	-	49.8	1.4	-	-	-	-
1977	50.8	2.0	-	-	-	-	51.6	1.6	-	-	-	-	53.7	4.1	-	-	-	-	54.9	2.2	-	-	-	-
1978	56.5	2.9	-	-	-	-	57.5	1.8	-	-	58.7	2.1	-	-	60.3	2.7	-	-	61.6	2.2	-	-	62.2	1.0
1979	-	-	63.0	1.3	-	-	64.1	1.7	-	-	65.8	2.7	-	-	67.2	2.1	-	-	69.6	3.6	-	-	70.0	0.6
1980	-	-	70.7	1.0	-	-	73.0	3.3	-	-	73.4	0.5	-	-	74.4	1.4	-	-	76.7	3.1	-	-	77.8	1.4
1981	-	-	77.5	-0.4	-	-	79.7	2.8	-	-	84.7	6.3	-	-	89.9	6.1	-	-	91.9	2.2	-	-	96.1	4.6
1982	-	-	100.3	4.4	-	-	98.1	-2.2	-	-	97.1	-1.0	-	-	102.2	5.3	-	-	98.2	-3.9	-	-	96.8	-1.4
1983	-	-	97.7	0.9	-	-	98.7	1.0	-	-	99.9	1.2	-	-	100.3	0.4	-	-	100.3	0.0	-	-	99.6	-0.7
1984	-	-	100.0	0.4	-	-	101.5	1.5	-	-	102.3	0.8	-	-	102.5	0.2	-	-	103.3	0.8	-	-	103.0	-0.3
1985	-	-	103.7	0.7	-	-	104.7	1.0	-	-	106.0	1.2	-	-	107.1	1.0	-	-	107.6	0.5	-	-	106.7	-0.8
1986	-	-	106.8	0.1	-	-	107.6	0.7	-	-	109.4	1.7	-	-	109.2	-0.2	-	-	107.2	-1.8	106.4	-0.7	107.5	1.0
1987	-	-	-	-	-	-	-	-	-	-	96.7	-10.0	-	-	-	-	-	-	-	-	-	-	97.2	0.5
1988	-	-	-	-	-	-	-	-	-	-	97.4	0.2	-	-	-	-	-	-	-	-	-	-	98.7	1.3
1989	-	-	-	-	-	-	-	-	-	-	99.8	1.1	-	-	-	-	-	-	-	-	-	-	101.3	1.5
1990	-	-	-	-	-	-	-	-	-	-	103.2	1.9	-	-	-	-	-	-	-	-	-	-	106.4	3.1
1991	-	-	-	-	-	-	-	-	-	-	108.2	1.7	-	-	-	-	-	-	-	-	-	-	110.7	2.3
1992	-	-	-	-	-	-	-	-	-	-	112.1	1.3	-	-	-	-	-	-	-	-	-	-	114.3	2.0
1993	-	-	-	-	-	-	-	-	-	-	115.3	0.9	-	-	-	-	-	-	-	-	-	-	118.3	2.6
1994	-	-	-	-	-	-	-	-	-	-	119.5	1.0	-	-	-	-	-	-	-	-	-	-	121.3	1.5
1995	-	-	-	-	-	-	-	-	-	-	119.9	-1.2	-	-	-	-	-	-	-	-	-	-	122.2	1.9
1996	-	-	-	-	-	-	-	-	-	-	123.2	0.8	-	-	-	-	-	-	-	-	-	-	124.6	1.1
1997	-	-	-	-	-	-	-	-	-	-	125.3	0.6	-	-	-	-	-	-	-	-	-	-	-	-

Source: U.S. Department of Labor, Bureau of Labor Statistics, Division of Consumer Prices and Price Indexes. - indicates no data collected for period.

Minneapolis-St. Paul, MN
Consumer Price Index - Urban Wage Earners
Base 1982-1984 = 100
Housing

For 1976-1997. Columns headed % show percentile change in the index from the previous period for which an index is available.

Year	Jan Index	%	Feb Index	%	Mar Index	%	Apr Index	%	May Index	%	Jun Index	%	Jul Index	%	Aug Index	%	Sep Index	%	Oct Index	%	Nov Index	%	Dec Index	%
1976	47.0	-	-	-	-	-	47.4	0.9	-	-	-	-	48.4	2.1	-	-	-	-	49.1	1.4	-	-	-	-
1977	50.1	2.0	-	-	-	-	50.9	1.6	-	-	-	-	52.9	3.9	-	-	-	-	54.0	2.1	-	-	-	-
1978	55.7	3.1	-	-	-	-	56.6	1.6	-	-	58.1	2.7	-	-	59.9	3.1	-	-	61.0	1.8	-	-	61.7	1.1
1979	-	-	62.5	1.3	-	-	63.5	1.6	-	-	65.4	3.0	-	-	66.8	2.1	-	-	68.8	3.0	-	-	69.3	0.7
1980	-	-	70.1	1.2	-	-	72.0	2.7	-	-	72.5	0.7	-	-	73.5	1.4	-	-	76.0	3.4	-	-	77.4	1.8
1981	-	-	77.3	-0.1	-	-	79.5	2.8	-	-	84.5	6.3	-	-	89.8	6.3	-	-	91.7	2.1	-	-	96.2	4.9
1982	-	-	100.5	4.5	-	-	98.3	-2.2	-	-	97.1	-1.2	-	-	102.5	5.6	-	-	98.3	-4.1	-	-	96.8	-1.5
1983	-	-	99.8	3.1	-	-	100.7	0.9	-	-	99.2	-1.5	-	-	95.2	-4.0	-	-	97.6	2.5	-	-	96.6	-1.0
1984	-	-	99.9	3.4	-	-	101.2	1.3	-	-	105.9	4.6	-	-	107.9	1.9	-	-	103.1	-4.4	-	-	100.7	-2.3
1985	-	-	101.5	0.8	-	-	102.3	0.8	-	-	103.6	1.3	-	-	104.7	1.1	-	-	105.3	0.6	-	-	104.4	-0.9
1986	-	-	104.5	0.1	-	-	105.2	0.7	-	-	107.1	1.8	-	-	106.9	-0.2	-	-	104.7	-2.1	103.9	-0.8	104.9	1.0
1987	-	-	-	-	-	-	-	-	-	-	96.2	-8.3	-	-	-	-	-	-	-	-	-	-	96.8	0.6
1988	-	-	-	-	-	-	-	-	-	-	96.9	0.1	-	-	-	-	-	-	-	-	-	-	98.1	1.2
1989	-	-	-	-	-	-	-	-	-	-	99.2	1.1	-	-	-	-	-	-	-	-	-	-	101.1	1.9
1990	-	-	-	-	-	-	-	-	-	-	102.7	1.6	-	-	-	-	-	-	-	-	-	-	106.3	3.5
1991	-	-	-	-	-	-	-	-	-	-	108.2	1.8	-	-	-	-	-	-	-	-	-	-	110.7	2.3
1992	-	-	-	-	-	-	-	-	-	-	112.0	1.2	-	-	-	-	-	-	-	-	-	-	114.6	2.3
1993	-	-	-	-	-	-	-	-	-	-	115.6	0.9	-	-	-	-	-	-	-	-	-	-	118.8	2.8
1994	-	-	-	-	-	-	-	-	-	-	119.6	0.7	-	-	-	-	-	-	-	-	-	-	121.8	1.8
1995	-	-	-	-	-	-	-	-	-	-	120.0	-1.5	-	-	-	-	-	-	-	-	-	-	122.4	2.0
1996	-	-	-	-	-	-	-	-	-	-	123.0	0.5	-	-	-	-	-	-	-	-	-	-	124.7	1.4
1997	-	-	-	-	-	-	-	-	-	-	125.0	0.2	-	-	-	-	-	-	-	-	-	-	-	-

Source: U.S. Department of Labor, Bureau of Labor Statistics, Division of Consumer Prices and Price Indexes. - indicates no data collected for period.

Minneapolis-St. Paul, MN
Consumer Price Index - All Urban Consumers
Base 1982-1984 = 100
Apparel and Upkeep

For 1952-1997. Columns headed % show percentile change in the index from the previous period for which an index is available.

Year	Jan Index	%	Feb Index	%	Mar Index	%	Apr Index	%	May Index	%	Jun Index	%	Jul Index	%	Aug Index	%	Sep Index	%	Oct Index	%	Nov Index	%	Dec Index	%
1952	-	-	-	-	-	-	-	-	-	-	-	-	-	-	-	-	-	-	-	-	-	-	46.0	-
1953	45.6	-0.9	-	-	-	-	45.9	0.7	-	-	-	-	45.6	-0.7	-	-	-	-	46.4	1.8	-	-	-	-
1954	45.9	-1.1	-	-	-	-	45.9	0.0	-	-	-	-	46.0	0.2	-	-	-	-	46.1	0.2	-	-	-	-
1955	45.2	-2.0	-	-	-	-	45.0	-0.4	-	-	-	-	44.8	-0.4	-	-	-	-	45.7	2.0	-	-	-	-
1956	46.0	0.7	-	-	-	-	46.1	0.2	-	-	-	-	46.5	0.9	-	-	-	-	47.1	1.3	-	-	-	-
1957	46.9	-0.4	-	-	-	-	47.2	0.6	-	-	-	-	46.9	-0.6	-	-	-	-	47.4	1.1	-	-	-	-
1958	47.4	0.0	-	-	-	-	47.3	-0.2	-	-	-	-	47.3	0.0	-	-	-	-	47.5	0.4	-	-	-	-
1959	47.0	-1.1	-	-	-	-	46.9	-0.2	-	-	-	-	46.9	0.0	-	-	-	-	47.1	0.4	-	-	-	-
1960	47.3	0.4	-	-	-	-	47.8	1.1	-	-	-	-	47.9	0.2	-	-	-	-	49.0	2.3	-	-	-	-
1961	46.8	-4.5	-	-	-	-	46.6	-0.4	-	-	-	-	46.6	0.0	-	-	-	-	47.6	2.1	-	-	-	-
1962	47.4	-0.4	-	-	-	-	47.7	0.6	-	-	-	-	47.6	-0.2	-	-	-	-	48.8	2.5	-	-	-	-
1963	48.6	-0.4	-	-	-	-	48.8	0.4	-	-	-	-	49.0	0.4	-	-	-	-	49.3	0.6	-	-	-	-
1964	48.1	-2.4	-	-	-	-	48.6	1.0	-	-	-	-	48.6	0.0	-	-	-	-	49.8	2.5	-	-	-	-
1965	49.2	-1.2	-	-	-	-	49.7	1.0	-	-	-	-	49.4	-0.6	-	-	-	-	50.7	2.6	-	-	-	-
1966	50.3	-0.8	-	-	-	-	50.7	0.8	-	-	-	-	51.2	1.0	-	-	-	-	52.2	2.0	-	-	-	-
1967	51.6	-1.1	-	-	-	-	52.9	2.5	-	-	-	-	52.6	-0.6	-	-	-	-	54.3	3.2	-	-	-	-
1968	53.7	-1.1	-	-	-	-	55.2	2.8	-	-	-	-	55.1	-0.2	-	-	-	-	56.2	2.0	-	-	-	-
1969	56.3	0.2	-	-	-	-	57.8	2.7	-	-	-	-	58.3	0.9	-	-	-	-	60.1	3.1	-	-	-	-
1970	59.3	-1.3	-	-	-	-	60.9	2.7	-	-	-	-	60.1	-1.3	-	-	-	-	63.3	5.3	-	-	-	-
1971	62.1	-1.9	-	-	-	-	62.8	1.1	-	-	-	-	62.2	-1.0	-	-	-	-	63.3	1.8	-	-	-	-
1972	62.4	-1.4	-	-	-	-	63.0	1.0	-	-	-	-	62.2	-1.3	-	-	-	-	65.2	4.8	-	-	-	-
1973	64.5	-1.1	-	-	-	-	65.4	1.4	-	-	-	-	66.1	1.1	-	-	-	-	68.1	3.0	-	-	-	-
1974	68.4	0.4	-	-	-	-	71.0	3.8	-	-	-	-	71.1	0.1	-	-	-	-	77.5	9.0	-	-	-	-
1975	75.8	-2.2	-	-	-	-	73.9	-2.5	-	-	-	-	73.1	-1.1	-	-	-	-	73.8	1.0	-	-	-	-
1976	73.7	-0.1	-	-	-	-	74.5	1.1	-	-	-	-	74.0	-0.7	-	-	-	-	77.0	4.1	-	-	-	-
1977	75.8	-1.6	-	-	-	-	77.2	1.8	-	-	-	-	78.9	2.2	-	-	-	-	79.4	0.6	-	-	-	-
1978	78.8	-0.8	-	-	-	-	81.1	2.9	-	-	80.3	-1.0	-	-	81.8	1.9	-	-	82.4	0.7	-	-	84.2	2.2
1979	-	-	82.8	-1.7	-	-	85.5	3.3	-	-	84.4	-1.3	-	-	86.8	2.8	-	-	86.4	-0.5	-	-	88.1	2.0
1980	-	-	88.5	0.5	-	-	91.2	3.1	-	-	91.5	0.3	-	-	92.1	0.7	-	-	90.9	-1.3	-	-	91.5	0.7
1981	-	-	91.6	0.1	-	-	94.2	2.8	-	-	94.2	0.0	-	-	95.7	1.6	-	-	97.0	1.4	-	-	96.8	-0.2
1982	-	-	97.9	1.1	-	-	99.1	1.2	-	-	97.4	-1.7	-	-	101.2	3.9	-	-	100.9	-0.3	-	-	103.0	2.1
1983	-	-	99.7	-3.2	-	-	104.0	4.3	-	-	101.5	-2.4	-	-	101.6	0.1	-	-	100.8	-0.8	-	-	101.2	0.4
1984	-	-	98.6	-2.6	-	-	99.8	1.2	-	-	98.4	-1.4	-	-	96.7	-1.7	-	-	99.9	3.3	-	-	98.9	-1.0
1985	-	-	103.3	4.4	-	-	107.7	4.3	-	-	108.0	0.3	-	-	104.7	-3.1	-	-	107.2	2.4	-	-	108.7	1.4
1986	-	-	104.5	-3.9	-	-	108.9	4.2	-	-	106.7	-2.0	-	-	105.9	-0.7	-	-	108.7	2.6	107.3	-1.3	107.0	-0.3
1987	-	-	-	-	-	-	-	-	-	-	110.3	3.1	-	-	-	-	-	-	-	-	-	-	116.8	5.9
1988	-	-	-	-	-	-	-	-	-	-	119.9	2.7	-	-	-	-	-	-	-	-	-	-	122.3	2.0
1989	-	-	-	-	-	-	-	-	-	-	123.4	0.9	-	-	-	-	-	-	-	-	-	-	124.5	0.9
1990	-	-	-	-	-	-	-	-	-	-	132.7	6.6	-	-	-	-	-	-	-	-	-	-	132.4	-0.2
1991	-	-	-	-	-	-	-	-	-	-	135.0	2.0	-	-	-	-	-	-	-	-	-	-	134.5	-0.4
1992	-	-	-	-	-	-	-	-	-	-	135.8	1.0	-	-	-	-	-	-	-	-	-	-	135.8	0.0
1993	-	-	-	-	-	-	-	-	-	-	139.2	2.5	-	-	-	-	-	-	-	-	-	-	145.1	4.2
1994	-	-	-	-	-	-	-	-	-	-	149.9	3.3	-	-	-	-	-	-	-	-	-	-	143.4	-4.3

[Continued]

Minneapolis-St. Paul, MN
Consumer Price Index - All Urban Consumers
Base 1982-1984 = 100
Apparel and Upkeep
[Continued]

For 1952-1997. Columns headed % show percentile change in the index from the previous period for which an index is available.

Year	Jan Index	%	Feb Index	%	Mar Index	%	Apr Index	%	May Index	%	Jun Index	%	Jul Index	%	Aug Index	%	Sep Index	%	Oct Index	%	Nov Index	%	Dec Index	%
1995	-	-	-	-	-	-	-	-	-	-	137.6	-4.0	-	-	-	-	-	-	-	-	-	-	139.0	1.0
1996	-	-	-	-	-	-	-	-	-	-	138.6	-0.3	-	-	-	-	-	-	-	-	-	-	136.9	-1.2
1997	-	-	-	-	-	-	-	-	-	-	140.7	2.8	-	-	-	-	-	-	-	-	-	-	-	-

Source: U.S. Department of Labor, Bureau of Labor Statistics, Division of Consumer Prices and Price Indexes. - indicates no data collected for period.

Minneapolis-St. Paul, MN
Consumer Price Index - Urban Wage Earners
Base 1982-1984 = 100
Apparel and Upkeep

For 1952-1997. Columns headed % show percentile change in the index from the previous period for which an index is available.

Year	Jan Index	%	Feb Index	%	Mar Index	%	Apr Index	%	May Index	%	Jun Index	%	Jul Index	%	Aug Index	%	Sep Index	%	Oct Index	%	Nov Index	%	Dec Index	%
1952	-	-	-	-	-	-	-	-	-	-	-	-	-	-	-	-	-	-	-	-	-	-	47.0	-
1953	46.6	-0.9	-	-	-	-	47.0	0.9	-	-	-	-	46.6	-0.9	-	-	-	-	47.5	1.9	-	-	-	-
1954	47.0	-1.1	-	-	-	-	46.9	-0.2	-	-	-	-	47.0	0.2	-	-	-	-	47.1	0.2	-	-	-	-
1955	46.3	-1.7	-	-	-	-	46.0	-0.6	-	-	-	-	45.8	-0.4	-	-	-	-	46.8	2.2	-	-	-	-
1956	47.1	0.6	-	-	-	-	47.2	0.2	-	-	-	-	47.5	0.6	-	-	-	-	48.2	1.5	-	-	-	-
1957	47.9	-0.6	-	-	-	-	48.3	0.8	-	-	-	-	47.9	-0.8	-	-	-	-	48.4	1.0	-	-	-	-
1958	48.5	0.2	-	-	-	-	48.4	-0.2	-	-	-	-	48.3	-0.2	-	-	-	-	48.5	0.4	-	-	-	-
1959	48.1	-0.8	-	-	-	-	47.9	-0.4	-	-	-	-	47.9	0.0	-	-	-	-	48.2	0.6	-	-	-	-
1960	48.4	0.4	-	-	-	-	48.9	1.0	-	-	-	-	49.0	0.2	-	-	-	-	50.1	2.2	-	-	-	-
1961	47.9	-4.4	-	-	-	-	47.7	-0.4	-	-	-	-	47.7	0.0	-	-	-	-	48.7	2.1	-	-	-	-
1962	48.5	-0.4	-	-	-	-	48.8	0.6	-	-	-	-	48.7	-0.2	-	-	-	-	49.9	2.5	-	-	-	-
1963	49.7	-0.4	-	-	-	-	49.9	0.4	-	-	-	-	50.1	0.4	-	-	-	-	50.4	0.6	-	-	-	-
1964	49.2	-2.4	-	-	-	-	49.7	1.0	-	-	-	-	49.7	0.0	-	-	-	-	50.9	2.4	-	-	-	-
1965	50.3	-1.2	-	-	-	-	50.9	1.2	-	-	-	-	50.6	-0.6	-	-	-	-	51.8	2.4	-	-	-	-
1966	51.4	-0.8	-	-	-	-	51.8	0.8	-	-	-	-	52.4	1.2	-	-	-	-	53.4	1.9	-	-	-	-
1967	52.7	-1.3	-	-	-	-	54.1	2.7	-	-	-	-	53.8	-0.6	-	-	-	-	55.5	3.2	-	-	-	-
1968	54.9	-1.1	-	-	-	-	56.5	2.9	-	-	-	-	56.3	-0.4	-	-	-	-	57.4	2.0	-	-	-	-
1969	57.5	0.2	-	-	-	-	59.1	2.8	-	-	-	-	59.7	1.0	-	-	-	-	61.5	3.0	-	-	-	-
1970	60.7	-1.3	-	-	-	-	62.3	2.6	-	-	-	-	61.5	-1.3	-	-	-	-	64.8	5.4	-	-	-	-
1971	63.5	-2.0	-	-	-	-	64.3	1.3	-	-	-	-	63.6	-1.1	-	-	-	-	64.7	1.7	-	-	-	-
1972	63.8	-1.4	-	-	-	-	64.4	0.9	-	-	-	-	63.6	-1.2	-	-	-	-	66.7	4.9	-	-	-	-
1973	66.0	-1.0	-	-	-	-	66.9	1.4	-	-	-	-	67.6	1.0	-	-	-	-	69.6	3.0	-	-	-	-
1974	69.9	0.4	-	-	-	-	72.6	3.9	-	-	-	-	72.7	0.1	-	-	-	-	79.2	8.9	-	-	-	-
1975	77.5	-2.1	-	-	-	-	75.6	-2.5	-	-	-	-	74.8	-1.1	-	-	-	-	75.5	0.9	-	-	-	-
1976	75.4	-0.1	-	-	-	-	76.2	1.1	-	-	-	-	75.7	-0.7	-	-	-	-	78.7	4.0	-	-	-	-
1977	77.6	-1.4	-	-	-	-	79.0	1.8	-	-	-	-	80.7	2.2	-	-	-	-	81.3	0.7	-	-	-	-
1978	80.5	-1.0	-	-	-	-	82.9	3.0	-	-	83.1	0.2	-	-	83.0	-0.1	-	-	83.1	0.1	-	-	85.6	3.0
1979	-	-	83.0	-3.0	-	-	85.8	3.4	-	-	84.3	-1.7	-	-	87.3	3.6	-	-	87.9	0.7	-	-	88.2	0.3
1980	-	-	88.7	0.6	-	-	91.5	3.2	-	-	92.4	1.0	-	-	93.5	1.2	-	-	92.7	-0.9	-	-	92.4	-0.3
1981	-	-	94.1	1.8	-	-	95.8	1.8	-	-	96.7	0.9	-	-	97.8	1.1	-	-	98.1	0.3	-	-	96.7	-1.4
1982	-	-	97.6	0.9	-	-	99.0	1.4	-	-	97.0	-2.0	-	-	101.2	4.3	-	-	100.7	-0.5	-	-	103.3	2.6
1983	-	-	99.8	-3.4	-	-	103.9	4.1	-	-	100.9	-2.9	-	-	101.2	0.3	-	-	100.4	-0.8	-	-	101.6	1.2
1984	-	-	98.9	-2.7	-	-	100.5	1.6	-	-	98.4	-2.1	-	-	97.7	-0.7	-	-	99.8	2.1	-	-	98.8	-1.0
1985	-	-	104.0	5.3	-	-	108.0	3.8	-	-	108.6	0.6	-	-	105.2	-3.1	-	-	107.4	2.1	-	-	109.0	1.5
1986	-	-	104.3	-4.3	-	-	109.4	4.9	-	-	105.4	-3.7	-	-	105.9	0.5	-	-	108.2	2.2	106.9	-1.2	106.0	-0.8
1987	-	-	-	-	-	-	-	-	-	-	109.5	3.3	-	-	-	-	-	-	-	-	-	-	115.9	5.8
1988	-	-	-	-	-	-	-	-	-	-	119.6	3.2	-	-	-	-	-	-	-	-	-	-	122.6	2.5
1989	-	-	-	-	-	-	-	-	-	-	123.8	1.0	-	-	-	-	-	-	-	-	-	-	124.3	0.4
1990	-	-	-	-	-	-	-	-	-	-	133.1	7.1	-	-	-	-	-	-	-	-	-	-	132.4	-0.5
1991	-	-	-	-	-	-	-	-	-	-	134.3	1.4	-	-	-	-	-	-	-	-	-	-	133.5	-0.6
1992	-	-	-	-	-	-	-	-	-	-	134.8	1.0	-	-	-	-	-	-	-	-	-	-	134.1	-0.5
1993	-	-	-	-	-	-	-	-	-	-	135.9	1.3	-	-	-	-	-	-	-	-	-	-	141.9	4.4
1994	-	-	-	-	-	-	-	-	-	-	148.3	4.5	-	-	-	-	-	-	-	-	-	-	142.5	-3.9

[Continued]

Minneapolis-St. Paul, MN
Consumer Price Index - Urban Wage Earners
Base 1982-1984 = 100
Apparel and Upkeep
[Continued]

For 1952-1997. Columns headed % show percentile change in the index from the previous period for which an index is available.

Year	Jan Index	%	Feb Index	%	Mar Index	%	Apr Index	%	May Index	%	Jun Index	%	Jul Index	%	Aug Index	%	Sep Index	%	Oct Index	%	Nov Index	%	Dec Index	%
1995	-	-	-	-	-	-	-	-	-	-	137.3	-3.6	-	-	-	-	-	-	-	-	-	-	138.0	0.5
1996	-	-	-	-	-	-	-	-	-	-	138.0	0.0	-	-	-	-	-	-	-	-	-	-	135.7	-1.7
1997	-	-	-	-	-	-	-	-	-	-	140.0	3.2	-	-	-	-	-	-	-	-	-	-	-	-

Source: U.S. Department of Labor, Bureau of Labor Statistics, Division of Consumer Prices and Price Indexes. - indicates no data collected for period.

Minneapolis-St. Paul, MN
Consumer Price Index - All Urban Consumers
Base 1982-1984 = 100
Transportation

For 1947-1997. Columns headed % show percentile change in the index from the previous period for which an index is available.

Year	Jan Index	%	Feb Index	%	Mar Index	%	Apr Index	%	May Index	%	Jun Index	%	Jul Index	%	Aug Index	%	Sep Index	%	Oct Index	%	Nov Index	%	Dec Index	%
1947	20.9	-	21.0	0.5	21.1	0.5	21.1	0.0	21.3	0.9	21.3	0.0	-	-	-	-	21.9	2.8	-	-	-	-	23.3	6.4
1948	-	-	-	-	23.7	1.7	-	-	-	-	23.7	0.0	-	-	-	-	26.1	10.1	-	-	-	-	25.9	-0.8
1949	-	-	-	-	26.2	1.2	-	-	-	-	26.3	0.4	-	-	-	-	26.6	1.1	-	-	-	-	26.8	0.8
1950	-	-	-	-	26.3	-1.9	-	-	-	-	26.1	-0.8	-	-	-	-	26.7	2.3	-	-	-	-	26.8	0.4
1951	-	-	-	-	27.1	1.1	-	-	-	-	27.1	0.0	-	-	-	-	25.8	-4.8	-	-	-	-	27.8	7.8
1952	-	-	-	-	28.3	1.8	-	-	-	-	28.8	1.8	-	-	-	-	29.2	1.4	-	-	-	-	29.2	0.0
1953	29.3	0.3	-	-	-	-	29.5	0.7	-	-	-	-	29.5	0.0	-	-	-	-	29.4	-0.3	-	-	-	-
1954	29.5	0.3	-	-	-	-	29.3	-0.7	-	-	-	-	29.4	0.3	-	-	-	-	28.7	-2.4	-	-	-	-
1955	29.5	2.8	-	-	-	-	28.5	-3.4	-	-	-	-	28.8	1.1	-	-	-	-	27.1	-5.9	-	-	-	-
1956	27.6	1.8	-	-	-	-	27.0	-2.2	-	-	-	-	28.0	3.7	-	-	-	-	28.6	2.1	-	-	-	-
1957	29.3	2.4	-	-	-	-	29.4	0.3	-	-	-	-	29.4	0.0	-	-	-	-	28.8	-2.0	-	-	-	-
1958	30.1	4.5	-	-	-	-	29.6	-1.7	-	-	-	-	30.3	2.4	-	-	-	-	30.5	0.7	-	-	-	-
1959	31.7	3.9	-	-	-	-	31.5	-0.6	-	-	-	-	30.6	-2.9	-	-	-	-	32.2	5.2	-	-	-	-
1960	32.0	-0.6	-	-	-	-	31.4	-1.9	-	-	-	-	32.1	2.2	-	-	-	-	32.2	0.3	-	-	-	-
1961	32.0	-0.6	-	-	-	-	32.5	1.6	-	-	-	-	32.1	-1.2	-	-	-	-	32.2	0.3	-	-	-	-
1962	32.1	-0.3	-	-	-	-	32.9	2.5	-	-	-	-	32.4	-1.5	-	-	-	-	33.4	3.1	-	-	-	-
1963	32.6	-2.4	-	-	-	-	33.1	1.5	-	-	-	-	33.7	1.8	-	-	-	-	33.2	-1.5	-	-	-	-
1964	33.6	1.2	-	-	-	-	32.5	-3.3	-	-	-	-	33.1	1.8	-	-	-	-	33.5	1.2	-	-	-	-
1965	33.5	0.0	-	-	-	-	33.6	0.3	-	-	-	-	33.8	0.6	-	-	-	-	34.0	0.6	-	-	-	-
1966	34.1	0.3	-	-	-	-	34.2	0.3	-	-	-	-	34.4	0.6	-	-	-	-	34.7	0.9	-	-	-	-
1967	34.7	0.0	-	-	-	-	35.1	1.2	-	-	-	-	35.4	0.9	-	-	-	-	36.5	3.1	-	-	-	-
1968	36.7	0.5	-	-	-	-	36.4	-0.8	-	-	-	-	36.7	0.8	-	-	-	-	37.2	1.4	-	-	-	-
1969	36.6	-1.6	-	-	-	-	37.8	3.3	-	-	-	-	37.0	-2.1	-	-	-	-	37.6	1.6	-	-	-	-
1970	38.2	1.6	-	-	-	-	39.2	2.6	-	-	-	-	39.8	1.5	-	-	-	-	40.5	1.8	-	-	-	-
1971	41.9	3.5	-	-	-	-	40.7	-2.9	-	-	-	-	41.0	0.7	-	-	-	-	40.9	-0.2	-	-	-	-
1972	41.7	2.0	-	-	-	-	40.6	-2.6	-	-	-	-	41.4	2.0	-	-	-	-	41.9	1.2	-	-	-	-
1973	42.2	0.7	-	-	-	-	42.8	1.4	-	-	-	-	43.3	1.2	-	-	-	-	43.2	-0.2	-	-	-	-
1974	44.9	3.9	-	-	-	-	47.0	4.7	-	-	-	-	49.2	4.7	-	-	-	-	48.8	-0.8	-	-	-	-
1975	48.6	-0.4	-	-	-	-	49.2	1.2	-	-	-	-	51.6	4.9	-	-	-	-	52.5	1.7	-	-	-	-
1976	53.0	1.0	-	-	-	-	54.2	2.3	-	-	-	-	56.3	3.9	-	-	-	-	56.7	0.7	-	-	-	-
1977	57.9	2.1	-	-	-	-	59.5	2.8	-	-	-	-	60.3	1.3	-	-	-	-	60.0	-0.5	-	-	-	-
1978	60.4	0.7	-	-	-	-	60.9	0.8	-	-	62.4	2.5	-	-	63.3	1.4	-	-	63.9	0.9	-	-	64.6	1.1
1979	-	-	65.6	1.5	-	-	68.2	4.0	-	-	72.3	6.0	-	-	74.7	3.3	-	-	75.6	1.2	-	-	77.4	2.4
1980	-	-	80.4	3.9	-	-	83.2	3.5	-	-	83.9	0.8	-	-	84.2	0.4	-	-	85.9	2.0	-	-	87.3	1.6
1981	-	-	89.8	2.9	-	-	91.7	2.1	-	-	94.1	2.6	-	-	94.7	0.6	-	-	96.8	2.2	-	-	97.2	0.4
1982	-	-	96.0	-1.2	-	-	93.7	-2.4	-	-	99.2	5.9	-	-	99.3	0.1	-	-	98.7	-0.6	-	-	98.6	-0.1
1983	-	-	96.1	-2.5	-	-	96.9	0.8	-	-	99.1	2.3	-	-	101.1	2.0	-	-	101.4	0.3	-	-	101.9	0.5
1984	-	-	101.9	0.0	-	-	102.3	0.4	-	-	103.5	1.2	-	-	103.6	0.1	-	-	104.2	0.6	-	-	104.4	0.2
1985	-	-	103.4	-1.0	-	-	105.4	1.9	-	-	107.1	1.6	-	-	107.5	0.4	-	-	106.8	-0.7	-	-	107.3	0.5
1986	-	-	104.5	-2.6	-	-	98.8	-5.5	-	-	101.2	2.4	-	-	98.3	-2.9	-	-	98.9	0.6	99.3	0.4	99.0	-0.3
1987	-	-	-	-	-	-	-	-	-	-	101.0	2.0	-	-	-	-	-	-	-	-	-	-	104.0	3.0
1988	-	-	-	-	-	-	-	-	-	-	103.3	-0.7	-	-	-	-	-	-	-	-	-	-	105.7	2.3
1989	-	-	-	-	-	-	-	-	-	-	108.2	2.4	-	-	-	-	-	-	-	-	-	-	110.1	1.8
1990	-	-	-	-	-	-	-	-	-	-	112.7	2.4	-	-	-	-	-	-	-	-	-	-	119.3	5.9
1991	-	-	-	-	-	-	-	-	-	-	118.5	-0.7	-	-	-	-	-	-	-	-	-	-	120.8	1.9

[Continued]

Minneapolis-St. Paul, MN
Consumer Price Index - All Urban Consumers
Base 1982-1984 = 100
Transportation
[Continued]

For 1947-1997. Columns headed % show percentile change in the index from the previous period for which an index is available.

Year	Jan		Feb		Mar		Apr		May		Jun		Jul		Aug		Sep		Oct		Nov		Dec	
	Index	%	Index	%	Index	%	Index	%	Index	%	Index	%	Index	%	Index	%	Index	%	Index	%	Index	%	Index	%
1992	-	-	-	-	-	-	-	-	-	-	122.0	1.0	-	-	-	-	-	-	-	-	-	-	123.8	1.5
1993	-	-	-	-	-	-	-	-	-	-	126.3	2.0	-	-	-	-	-	-	-	-	-	-	130.0	2.9
1994	-	-	-	-	-	-	-	-	-	-	131.2	0.9	-	-	-	-	-	-	-	-	-	-	134.7	2.7
1995	-	-	-	-	-	-	-	-	-	-	136.9	1.6	-	-	-	-	-	-	-	-	-	-	137.0	0.1
1996	-	-	-	-	-	-	-	-	-	-	139.7	2.0	-	-	-	-	-	-	-	-	-	-	141.1	1.0
1997	-	-	-	-	-	-	-	-	-	-	142.4	0.9	-	-	-	-	-	-	-	-	-	-	-	-

Source: U.S. Department of Labor, Bureau of Labor Statistics, Division of Consumer Prices and Price Indexes. - indicates no data collected for period.

Minneapolis-St. Paul, MN
Consumer Price Index - Urban Wage Earners
Base 1982-1984 = 100
Transportation

For 1947-1997. Columns headed % show percentile change in the index from the previous period for which an index is available.

Year	Jan Index	%	Feb Index	%	Mar Index	%	Apr Index	%	May Index	%	Jun Index	%	Jul Index	%	Aug Index	%	Sep Index	%	Oct Index	%	Nov Index	%	Dec Index	%
1947	20.6	-	20.6	0.0	20.7	0.5	20.8	0.5	21.0	1.0	21.0	0.0	-	-	-	-	21.5	2.4	-	-	-	-	22.9	6.5
1948	-	-	-	-	23.3	1.7	-	-	-	-	23.4	0.4	-	-	-	-	25.7	9.8	-	-	-	-	25.5	-0.8
1949	-	-	-	-	25.8	1.2	-	-	-	-	25.9	0.4	-	-	-	-	26.2	1.2	-	-	-	-	26.4	0.8
1950	-	-	-	-	25.9	-1.9	-	-	-	-	25.7	-0.8	-	-	-	-	26.3	2.3	-	-	-	-	26.4	0.4
1951	-	-	-	-	26.7	1.1	-	-	-	-	26.7	0.0	-	-	-	-	25.4	-4.9	-	-	-	-	27.4	7.9
1952	-	-	-	-	27.8	1.5	-	-	-	-	28.3	1.8	-	-	-	-	28.8	1.8	-	-	-	-	28.8	0.0
1953	28.8	0.0	-	-	-	-	29.1	1.0	-	-	-	-	29.1	0.0	-	-	-	-	28.9	-0.7	-	-	-	-
1954	29.1	0.7	-	-	-	-	28.8	-1.0	-	-	-	-	29.0	0.7	-	-	-	-	28.2	-2.8	-	-	-	-
1955	29.0	2.8	-	-	-	-	28.0	-3.4	-	-	-	-	28.3	1.1	-	-	-	-	26.7	-5.7	-	-	-	-
1956	27.2	1.9	-	-	-	-	26.6	-2.2	-	-	-	-	27.5	3.4	-	-	-	-	28.1	2.2	-	-	-	-
1957	28.8	2.5	-	-	-	-	28.9	0.3	-	-	-	-	29.0	0.3	-	-	-	-	28.3	-2.4	-	-	-	-
1958	29.6	4.6	-	-	-	-	29.2	-1.4	-	-	-	-	29.8	2.1	-	-	-	-	30.1	1.0	-	-	-	-
1959	31.3	4.0	-	-	-	-	31.1	-0.6	-	-	-	-	30.2	-2.9	-	-	-	-	31.7	5.0	-	-	-	-
1960	31.5	-0.6	-	-	-	-	30.9	-1.9	-	-	-	-	31.6	2.3	-	-	-	-	31.7	0.3	-	-	-	-
1961	31.5	-0.6	-	-	-	-	32.0	1.6	-	-	-	-	31.6	-1.2	-	-	-	-	31.7	0.3	-	-	-	-
1962	31.6	-0.3	-	-	-	-	32.4	2.5	-	-	-	-	31.9	-1.5	-	-	-	-	32.9	3.1	-	-	-	-
1963	32.1	-2.4	-	-	-	-	32.6	1.6	-	-	-	-	33.2	1.8	-	-	-	-	32.7	-1.5	-	-	-	-
1964	33.1	1.2	-	-	-	-	32.0	-3.3	-	-	-	-	32.6	1.9	-	-	-	-	32.9	0.9	-	-	-	-
1965	32.9	0.0	-	-	-	-	33.1	0.6	-	-	-	-	33.3	0.6	-	-	-	-	33.5	0.6	-	-	-	-
1966	33.5	0.0	-	-	-	-	33.7	0.6	-	-	-	-	33.9	0.6	-	-	-	-	34.2	0.9	-	-	-	-
1967	34.1	-0.3	-	-	-	-	34.5	1.2	-	-	-	-	34.9	1.2	-	-	-	-	36.0	3.2	-	-	-	-
1968	36.2	0.6	-	-	-	-	35.9	-0.8	-	-	-	-	36.1	0.6	-	-	-	-	36.6	1.4	-	-	-	-
1969	36.0	-1.6	-	-	-	-	37.2	3.3	-	-	-	-	36.5	-1.9	-	-	-	-	37.0	1.4	-	-	-	-
1970	37.6	1.6	-	-	-	-	38.6	2.7	-	-	-	-	39.2	1.6	-	-	-	-	39.8	1.5	-	-	-	-
1971	41.2	3.5	-	-	-	-	40.1	-2.7	-	-	-	-	40.3	0.5	-	-	-	-	40.3	0.0	-	-	-	-
1972	41.0	1.7	-	-	-	-	40.0	-2.4	-	-	-	-	40.7	1.7	-	-	-	-	41.2	1.2	-	-	-	-
1973	41.6	1.0	-	-	-	-	42.2	1.4	-	-	-	-	42.6	0.9	-	-	-	-	42.5	-0.2	-	-	-	-
1974	44.2	4.0	-	-	-	-	46.3	4.8	-	-	-	-	48.5	4.8	-	-	-	-	48.1	-0.8	-	-	-	-
1975	47.9	-0.4	-	-	-	-	48.5	1.3	-	-	-	-	50.8	4.7	-	-	-	-	51.7	1.8	-	-	-	-
1976	52.1	0.8	-	-	-	-	53.4	2.5	-	-	-	-	55.5	3.9	-	-	-	-	55.8	0.5	-	-	-	-
1977	57.0	2.2	-	-	-	-	58.6	2.8	-	-	-	-	59.4	1.4	-	-	-	-	59.1	-0.5	-	-	-	-
1978	59.5	0.7	-	-	-	-	60.0	0.8	-	-	61.6	2.7	-	-	62.5	1.5	-	-	63.3	1.3	-	-	64.1	1.3
1979	-	-	65.0	1.4	-	-	67.8	4.3	-	-	72.2	6.5	-	-	74.5	3.2	-	-	75.5	1.3	-	-	77.4	2.5
1980	-	-	80.5	4.0	-	-	83.3	3.5	-	-	84.2	1.1	-	-	84.2	0.0	-	-	85.9	2.0	-	-	87.6	2.0
1981	-	-	90.5	3.3	-	-	92.2	1.9	-	-	94.1	2.1	-	-	95.0	1.0	-	-	96.9	2.0	-	-	97.4	0.5
1982	-	-	96.3	-1.1	-	-	93.7	-2.7	-	-	99.4	6.1	-	-	99.4	0.0	-	-	98.8	-0.6	-	-	98.8	0.0
1983	-	-	96.1	-2.7	-	-	96.9	0.8	-	-	99.4	2.6	-	-	101.3	1.9	-	-	101.4	0.1	-	-	101.8	0.4
1984	-	-	101.7	-0.1	-	-	102.1	0.4	-	-	103.1	1.0	-	-	103.4	0.3	-	-	104.0	0.6	-	-	104.1	0.1
1985	-	-	102.8	-1.2	-	-	105.1	2.2	-	-	106.9	1.7	-	-	107.3	0.4	-	-	106.4	-0.8	-	-	107.1	0.7
1986	-	-	103.9	-3.0	-	-	97.6	-6.1	-	-	100.3	2.8	-	-	97.1	-3.2	-	-	97.7	0.6	98.1	0.4	97.8	-0.3
1987	-	-	-	-	-	-	-	-	-	-	103.0	5.3	-	-	-	-	-	-	-	-	-	-	106.5	3.4
1988	-	-	-	-	-	-	-	-	-	-	105.8	-0.7	-	-	-	-	-	-	-	-	-	-	108.4	2.5
1989	-	-	-	-	-	-	-	-	-	-	111.0	2.4	-	-	-	-	-	-	-	-	-	-	112.8	1.6
1990	-	-	-	-	-	-	-	-	-	-	115.2	2.1	-	-	-	-	-	-	-	-	-	-	122.3	6.2
1991	-	-	-	-	-	-	-	-	-	-	120.8	-1.2	-	-	-	-	-	-	-	-	-	-	123.3	2.1

[Continued]

Minneapolis-St. Paul, MN
Consumer Price Index - Urban Wage Earners
Base 1982-1984 = 100
Transportation
[Continued]

For 1947-1997. Columns headed % show percentile change in the index from the previous period for which an index is available.

Year	Jan Index	%	Feb Index	%	Mar Index	%	Apr Index	%	May Index	%	Jun Index	%	Jul Index	%	Aug Index	%	Sep Index	%	Oct Index	%	Nov Index	%	Dec Index	%
1992	-	-	-	-	-	-	-	-	-	-	124.2	0.7	-	-	-	-	-	-	-	-	-	-	126.2	1.6
1993	-	-	-	-	-	-	-	-	-	-	127.8	1.3	-	-	-	-	-	-	-	-	-	-	131.1	2.6
1994	-	-	-	-	-	-	-	-	-	-	131.8	0.5	-	-	-	-	-	-	-	-	-	-	136.3	3.4
1995	-	-	-	-	-	-	-	-	-	-	138.6	1.7	-	-	-	-	-	-	-	-	-	-	138.6	0.0
1996	-	-	-	-	-	-	-	-	-	-	141.4	2.0	-	-	-	-	-	-	-	-	-	-	143.0	1.1
1997	-	-	-	-	-	-	-	-	-	-	143.7	0.5	-	-	-	-	-	-	-	-	-	-	-	-

Source: U.S. Department of Labor, Bureau of Labor Statistics, Division of Consumer Prices and Price Indexes. - indicates no data collected for period.

Minneapolis-St. Paul, MN
Consumer Price Index - All Urban Consumers
Base 1982-1984 = 100
Medical Care

For 1947-1997. Columns headed % show percentile change in the index from the previous period for which an index is available.

Year	Jan Index	%	Feb Index	%	Mar Index	%	Apr Index	%	May Index	%	Jun Index	%	Jul Index	%	Aug Index	%	Sep Index	%	Oct Index	%	Nov Index	%	Dec Index	%
1947	10.2	-	10.2	0.0	10.2	0.0	10.4	2.0	10.5	1.0	10.6	1.0	-	-	-	-	11.0	3.8	-	-	-	-	11.2	1.8
1948	-	-	-	-	11.4	1.8	-	-	-	-	11.8	3.5	-	-	-	-	11.9	0.8	-	-	-	-	12.1	1.7
1949	-	-	-	-	12.1	0.0	-	-	-	-	12.2	0.8	-	-	-	-	12.3	0.8	-	-	-	-	12.4	0.8
1950	-	-	-	-	12.4	0.0	-	-	-	-	12.4	0.0	-	-	-	-	12.8	3.2	-	-	-	-	12.9	0.8
1951	-	-	-	-	13.6	5.4	-	-	-	-	13.6	0.0	-	-	-	-	13.8	1.5	-	-	-	-	13.9	0.7
1952	-	-	-	-	14.5	4.3	-	-	-	-	14.5	0.0	-	-	-	-	14.6	0.7	-	-	-	-	14.5	-0.7
1953	14.5	0.0	-	-	-	-	15.8	9.0	-	-	-	-	15.9	0.6	-	-	-	-	15.9	0.0	-	-	-	-
1954	16.0	0.6	-	-	-	-	16.4	2.5	-	-	-	-	16.5	0.6	-	-	-	-	16.4	-0.6	-	-	-	-
1955	16.6	1.2	-	-	-	-	17.0	2.4	-	-	-	-	17.1	0.6	-	-	-	-	17.1	0.0	-	-	-	-
1956	17.2	0.6	-	-	-	-	17.2	0.0	-	-	-	-	17.3	0.6	-	-	-	-	17.3	0.0	-	-	-	-
1957	17.4	0.6	-	-	-	-	17.6	1.1	-	-	-	-	19.5	10.8	-	-	-	-	19.6	0.5	-	-	-	-
1958	19.8	1.0	-	-	-	-	20.2	2.0	-	-	-	-	21.9	8.4	-	-	-	-	22.0	0.5	-	-	-	-
1959	22.2	0.9	-	-	-	-	22.2	0.0	-	-	-	-	22.4	0.9	-	-	-	-	23.5	4.9	-	-	-	-
1960	23.5	0.0	-	-	-	-	24.1	2.6	-	-	-	-	24.7	2.5	-	-	-	-	24.4	-1.2	-	-	-	-
1961	24.4	0.0	-	-	-	-	25.4	4.1	-	-	-	-	26.4	3.9	-	-	-	-	26.5	0.4	-	-	-	-
1962	26.5	0.0	-	-	-	-	26.5	0.0	-	-	-	-	26.8	1.1	-	-	-	-	26.9	0.4	-	-	-	-
1963	27.0	0.4	-	-	-	-	27.0	0.0	-	-	-	-	27.0	0.0	-	-	-	-	27.1	0.4	-	-	-	-
1964	27.2	0.4	-	-	-	-	27.6	1.5	-	-	-	-	27.5	-0.4	-	-	-	-	27.5	0.0	-	-	-	-
1965	27.5	0.0	-	-	-	-	27.6	0.4	-	-	-	-	27.6	0.0	-	-	-	-	27.7	0.4	-	-	-	-
1966	27.9	0.7	-	-	-	-	28.6	2.5	-	-	-	-	29.0	1.4	-	-	-	-	29.4	1.4	-	-	-	-
1967	30.0	2.0	-	-	-	-	30.1	0.3	-	-	-	-	30.4	1.0	-	-	-	-	30.8	1.3	-	-	-	-
1968	31.4	1.9	-	-	-	-	31.8	1.3	-	-	-	-	32.0	0.6	-	-	-	-	32.4	1.3	-	-	-	-
1969	32.8	1.2	-	-	-	-	33.3	1.5	-	-	-	-	34.0	2.1	-	-	-	-	33.9	-0.3	-	-	-	-
1970	34.2	0.9	-	-	-	-	35.6	4.1	-	-	-	-	36.3	2.0	-	-	-	-	36.3	0.0	-	-	-	-
1971	36.9	1.7	-	-	-	-	37.5	1.6	-	-	-	-	38.1	1.6	-	-	-	-	37.9	-0.5	-	-	-	-
1972	37.9	0.0	-	-	-	-	38.0	0.3	-	-	-	-	38.3	0.8	-	-	-	-	38.8	1.3	-	-	-	-
1973	39.4	1.5	-	-	-	-	39.8	1.0	-	-	-	-	40.0	0.5	-	-	-	-	41.0	2.5	-	-	-	-
1974	42.0	2.4	-	-	-	-	42.6	1.4	-	-	-	-	43.8	2.8	-	-	-	-	45.3	3.4	-	-	-	-
1975	47.4	4.6	-	-	-	-	47.6	0.4	-	-	-	-	48.9	2.7	-	-	-	-	49.4	1.0	-	-	-	-
1976	50.5	2.2	-	-	-	-	51.4	1.8	-	-	-	-	52.4	1.9	-	-	-	-	53.5	2.1	-	-	-	-
1977	54.9	2.6	-	-	-	-	55.7	1.5	-	-	-	-	56.9	2.2	-	-	-	-	57.5	1.1	-	-	-	-
1978	59.1	2.8	-	-	-	-	60.3	2.0	-	-	60.9	1.0	-	-	62.3	2.3	-	-	62.2	-0.2	-	-	63.2	1.6
1979	-	-	65.1	3.0	-	-	64.0	-1.7	-	-	65.2	1.9	-	-	66.7	2.3	-	-	68.1	2.1	-	-	70.2	3.1
1980	-	-	72.7	3.6	-	-	72.9	0.3	-	-	73.0	0.1	-	-	74.6	2.2	-	-	74.6	0.0	-	-	75.5	1.2
1981	-	-	77.2	2.3	-	-	78.4	1.6	-	-	79.3	1.1	-	-	82.2	3.7	-	-	82.8	0.7	-	-	84.2	1.7
1982	-	-	86.5	2.7	-	-	87.7	1.4	-	-	89.0	1.5	-	-	92.0	3.4	-	-	92.9	1.0	-	-	94.3	1.5
1983	-	-	96.4	2.2	-	-	96.4	0.0	-	-	99.7	3.4	-	-	102.3	2.6	-	-	104.7	2.3	-	-	104.8	0.1
1984	-	-	107.3	2.4	-	-	107.5	0.2	-	-	109.5	1.9	-	-	110.8	1.2	-	-	112.7	1.7	-	-	112.6	-0.1
1985	-	-	114.8	2.0	-	-	115.4	0.5	-	-	116.1	0.6	-	-	117.4	1.1	-	-	119.6	1.9	-	-	120.3	0.6
1986	-	-	123.0	2.2	-	-	124.9	1.5	-	-	125.9	0.8	-	-	127.2	1.0	-	-	130.7	2.8	131.4	0.5	131.6	0.2
1987	-	-	-	-	-	-	-	-	-	-	128.3	-2.5	-	-	-	-	-	-	-	-	-	-	132.6	3.4
1988	-	-	-	-	-	-	-	-	-	-	135.3	2.0	-	-	-	-	-	-	-	-	-	-	138.1	2.1
1989	-	-	-	-	-	-	-	-	-	-	145.4	5.3	-	-	-	-	-	-	-	-	-	-	150.7	3.6
1990	-	-	-	-	-	-	-	-	-	-	156.2	3.6	-	-	-	-	-	-	-	-	-	-	166.1	6.3
1991	-	-	-	-	-	-	-	-	-	-	172.5	3.9	-	-	-	-	-	-	-	-	-	-	182.9	6.0

[Continued]

Minneapolis-St. Paul, MN
Consumer Price Index - All Urban Consumers
Base 1982-1984 = 100
Medical Care
[Continued]

For 1947-1997. Columns headed % show percentile change in the index from the previous period for which an index is available.

Year	Jan		Feb		Mar		Apr		May		Jun		Jul		Aug		Sep		Oct		Nov		Dec	
	Index	%	Index	%	Index	%	Index	%	Index	%	Index	%	Index	%	Index	%	Index	%	Index	%	Index	%	Index	%
1992	-	-	-	-	-	-	-	-	-	-	191.7	4.8	-	-	-	-	-	-	-	-	-	-	195.5	2.0
1993	-	-	-	-	-	-	-	-	-	-	200.4	2.5	-	-	-	-	-	-	-	-	-	-	201.3	0.4
1994	-	-	-	-	-	-	-	-	-	-	202.3	0.5	-	-	-	-	-	-	-	-	-	-	206.9	2.3
1995	-	-	-	-	-	-	-	-	-	-	215.6	4.2	-	-	-	-	-	-	-	-	-	-	219.9	2.0
1996	-	-	-	-	-	-	-	-	-	-	223.9	1.8	-	-	-	-	-	-	-	-	-	-	221.4	-1.1
1997	-	-	-	-	-	-	-	-	-	-	226.8	2.4	-	-	-	-	-	-	-	-	-	-	-	-

Source: U.S. Department of Labor, Bureau of Labor Statistics, Division of Consumer Prices and Price Indexes. - indicates no data collected for period.

Minneapolis-St. Paul, MN
Consumer Price Index - Urban Wage Earners
Base 1982-1984 = 100
Medical Care

For 1947-1997. Columns headed % show percentile change in the index from the previous period for which an index is available.

Year	Jan Index	%	Feb Index	%	Mar Index	%	Apr Index	%	May Index	%	Jun Index	%	Jul Index	%	Aug Index	%	Sep Index	%	Oct Index	%	Nov Index	%	Dec Index	%
1947	10.4	-	10.4	0.0	10.4	0.0	10.5	1.0	10.7	1.9	10.8	0.9	-	-	-	-	11.1	2.8	-	-	-	-	11.4	2.7
1948	-	-	-	-	11.5	0.9	-	-	-	-	12.0	4.3	-	-	-	-	12.1	0.8	-	-	-	-	12.3	1.7
1949	-	-	-	-	12.3	0.0	-	-	-	-	12.4	0.8	-	-	-	-	12.5	0.8	-	-	-	-	12.5	0.0
1950	-	-	-	-	12.6	0.8	-	-	-	-	12.6	0.0	-	-	-	-	12.9	2.4	-	-	-	-	13.1	1.6
1951	-	-	-	-	13.8	5.3	-	-	-	-	13.8	0.0	-	-	-	-	14.0	1.4	-	-	-	-	14.1	0.7
1952	-	-	-	-	14.7	4.3	-	-	-	-	14.7	0.0	-	-	-	-	14.8	0.7	-	-	-	-	14.7	-0.7
1953	14.7	0.0	-	-	-	-	16.0	8.8	-	-	-	-	16.1	0.6	-	-	-	-	16.2	0.6	-	-	-	-
1954	16.3	0.6	-	-	-	-	16.6	1.8	-	-	-	-	16.7	0.6	-	-	-	-	16.6	-0.6	-	-	-	-
1955	16.8	1.2	-	-	-	-	17.2	2.4	-	-	-	-	17.4	1.2	-	-	-	-	17.4	0.0	-	-	-	-
1956	17.4	0.0	-	-	-	-	17.4	0.0	-	-	-	-	17.5	0.6	-	-	-	-	17.5	0.0	-	-	-	-
1957	17.6	0.6	-	-	-	-	17.8	1.1	-	-	-	-	19.8	11.2	-	-	-	-	19.9	0.5	-	-	-	-
1958	20.1	1.0	-	-	-	-	20.4	1.5	-	-	-	-	22.2	8.8	-	-	-	-	22.3	0.5	-	-	-	-
1959	22.5	0.9	-	-	-	-	22.5	0.0	-	-	-	-	22.7	0.9	-	-	-	-	23.8	4.8	-	-	-	-
1960	23.8	0.0	-	-	-	-	24.5	2.9	-	-	-	-	25.0	2.0	-	-	-	-	24.8	-0.8	-	-	-	-
1961	24.7	-0.4	-	-	-	-	25.8	4.5	-	-	-	-	26.8	3.9	-	-	-	-	26.9	0.4	-	-	-	-
1962	26.9	0.0	-	-	-	-	26.9	0.0	-	-	-	-	27.1	0.7	-	-	-	-	27.3	0.7	-	-	-	-
1963	27.4	0.4	-	-	-	-	27.4	0.0	-	-	-	-	27.4	0.0	-	-	-	-	27.5	0.4	-	-	-	-
1964	27.6	0.4	-	-	-	-	27.9	1.1	-	-	-	-	27.9	0.0	-	-	-	-	27.9	0.0	-	-	-	-
1965	27.9	0.0	-	-	-	-	28.0	0.4	-	-	-	-	27.9	-0.4	-	-	-	-	28.1	0.7	-	-	-	-
1966	28.3	0.7	-	-	-	-	29.0	2.5	-	-	-	-	29.4	1.4	-	-	-	-	29.9	1.7	-	-	-	-
1967	30.4	1.7	-	-	-	-	30.6	0.7	-	-	-	-	30.8	0.7	-	-	-	-	31.2	1.3	-	-	-	-
1968	31.8	1.9	-	-	-	-	32.3	1.6	-	-	-	-	32.5	0.6	-	-	-	-	32.9	1.2	-	-	-	-
1969	33.3	1.2	-	-	-	-	33.8	1.5	-	-	-	-	34.5	2.1	-	-	-	-	34.4	-0.3	-	-	-	-
1970	34.7	0.9	-	-	-	-	36.2	4.3	-	-	-	-	36.8	1.7	-	-	-	-	36.9	0.3	-	-	-	-
1971	37.4	1.4	-	-	-	-	38.0	1.6	-	-	-	-	38.7	1.8	-	-	-	-	38.5	-0.5	-	-	-	-
1972	38.4	-0.3	-	-	-	-	38.5	0.3	-	-	-	-	38.9	1.0	-	-	-	-	39.3	1.0	-	-	-	-
1973	39.9	1.5	-	-	-	-	40.4	1.3	-	-	-	-	40.6	0.5	-	-	-	-	41.6	2.5	-	-	-	-
1974	42.6	2.4	-	-	-	-	43.2	1.4	-	-	-	-	44.5	3.0	-	-	-	-	46.0	3.4	-	-	-	-
1975	48.1	4.6	-	-	-	-	48.3	0.4	-	-	-	-	49.6	2.7	-	-	-	-	50.1	1.0	-	-	-	-
1976	51.2	2.2	-	-	-	-	52.2	2.0	-	-	-	-	53.1	1.7	-	-	-	-	54.3	2.3	-	-	-	-
1977	55.7	2.6	-	-	-	-	56.5	1.4	-	-	-	-	57.7	2.1	-	-	-	-	58.3	1.0	-	-	-	-
1978	60.0	2.9	-	-	-	-	61.2	2.0	-	-	61.9	1.1	-	-	62.8	1.5	-	-	63.3	0.8	-	-	63.7	0.6
1979	-	-	64.8	1.7	-	-	64.0	-1.2	-	-	65.1	1.7	-	-	66.1	1.5	-	-	68.6	3.8	-	-	70.7	3.1
1980	-	-	72.4	2.4	-	-	72.1	-0.4	-	-	72.1	0.0	-	-	72.9	1.1	-	-	73.8	1.2	-	-	75.1	1.8
1981	-	-	75.9	1.1	-	-	76.8	1.2	-	-	78.0	1.6	-	-	81.8	4.9	-	-	82.9	1.3	-	-	83.7	1.0
1982	-	-	86.1	2.9	-	-	87.3	1.4	-	-	88.5	1.4	-	-	91.5	3.4	-	-	92.3	0.9	-	-	93.7	1.5
1983	-	-	95.7	2.1	-	-	95.7	0.0	-	-	99.6	4.1	-	-	102.3	2.7	-	-	105.2	2.8	-	-	105.3	0.1
1984	-	-	107.8	2.4	-	-	108.0	0.2	-	-	110.2	2.0	-	-	111.5	1.2	-	-	113.4	1.7	-	-	113.3	-0.1
1985	-	-	115.5	1.9	-	-	116.0	0.4	-	-	116.7	0.6	-	-	118.1	1.2	-	-	120.3	1.9	-	-	121.1	0.7
1986	-	-	123.6	2.1	-	-	125.5	1.5	-	-	126.5	0.8	-	-	127.9	1.1	-	-	131.4	2.7	132.1	0.5	132.4	0.2
1987	-	-	-	-	-	-	-	-	-	-	128.7	-2.8	-	-	-	-	-	-	-	-	-	-	133.1	3.4
1988	-	-	-	-	-	-	-	-	-	-	136.2	2.3	-	-	-	-	-	-	-	-	-	-	139.3	2.3
1989	-	-	-	-	-	-	-	-	-	-	146.6	5.2	-	-	-	-	-	-	-	-	-	-	152.1	3.8
1990	-	-	-	-	-	-	-	-	-	-	157.3	3.4	-	-	-	-	-	-	-	-	-	-	167.3	6.4
1991	-	-	-	-	-	-	-	-	-	-	173.6	3.8	-	-	-	-	-	-	-	-	-	-	184.3	6.2

[Continued]

Minneapolis-St. Paul, MN
Consumer Price Index - Urban Wage Earners
Base 1982-1984 = 100
Medical Care
[Continued]

For 1947-1997. Columns headed % show percentile change in the index from the previous period for which an index is available.

Year	Jan Index	%	Feb Index	%	Mar Index	%	Apr Index	%	May Index	%	Jun Index	%	Jul Index	%	Aug Index	%	Sep Index	%	Oct Index	%	Nov Index	%	Dec Index	%
1992	-		-		-		-		-		193.4	4.9	-		-		-		-		-		197.2	2.0
1993	-		-		-		-		-		202.4	2.6	-		-		-		-		-		203.3	0.4
1994	-		-		-		-		-		204.2	0.4	-		-		-		-		-		208.9	2.3
1995	-		-		-		-		-		217.4	4.1	-		-		-		-		-		221.6	1.9
1996	-		-		-		-		-		225.8	1.9	-		-		-		-		-		223.5	-1.0
1997	-		-		-		-		-		228.6	2.3	-		-		-		-		-		-	-

Source: U.S. Department of Labor, Bureau of Labor Statistics, Division of Consumer Prices and Price Indexes. - indicates no data collected for period.

Minneapolis-St. Paul, MN
Consumer Price Index - All Urban Consumers
Base 1982-1984 = 100
Entertainment

For 1976-1997. Columns headed % show percentile change in the index from the previous period for which an index is available.

Year	Jan Index	%	Feb Index	%	Mar Index	%	Apr Index	%	May Index	%	Jun Index	%	Jul Index	%	Aug Index	%	Sep Index	%	Oct Index	%	Nov Index	%	Dec Index	%
1976	59.5	-	-	-	-	-	62.9	5.7	-	-	-	-	62.7	-0.3	-	-	-	-	62.4	-0.5	-	-	-	-
1977	63.1	1.1	-	-	-	-	64.7	2.5	-	-	-	-	63.7	-1.5	-	-	-	-	68.3	7.2	-	-	-	-
1978	69.4	1.6	-	-	-	-	70.1	1.0	-	-	70.1	0.0	-	-	70.3	0.3	-	-	73.5	4.6	-	-	74.2	1.0
1979	-	-	73.9	-0.4	-	-	74.1	0.3	-	-	76.1	2.7	-	-	78.0	2.5	-	-	74.2	-4.9	-	-	74.4	0.3
1980	-	-	75.9	2.0	-	-	76.9	1.3	-	-	78.1	1.6	-	-	85.7	9.7	-	-	86.3	0.7	-	-	88.4	2.4
1981	-	-	88.9	0.6	-	-	93.2	4.8	-	-	92.6	-0.6	-	-	95.1	2.7	-	-	95.3	0.2	-	-	95.3	0.0
1982	-	-	98.0	2.8	-	-	95.3	-2.8	-	-	98.2	3.0	-	-	99.3	1.1	-	-	96.3	-3.0	-	-	96.4	0.1
1983	-	-	97.0	0.6	-	-	99.4	2.5	-	-	98.8	-0.6	-	-	105.0	6.3	-	-	101.0	-3.8	-	-	101.2	0.2
1984	-	-	101.9	0.7	-	-	102.5	0.6	-	-	102.5	0.0	-	-	102.6	0.1	-	-	103.4	0.8	-	-	103.3	-0.1
1985	-	-	104.6	1.3	-	-	105.3	0.7	-	-	106.4	1.0	-	-	108.3	1.8	-	-	108.6	0.3	-	-	106.9	-1.6
1986	-	-	110.8	3.6	-	-	111.5	0.6	-	-	112.2	0.6	-	-	109.6	-2.3	-	-	114.6	4.6	114.5	-0.1	114.1	-0.3
1987	-	-	-	-	-	-	-	-	-	-	117.3	2.8	-	-	-	-	-	-	-	-	-	-	119.8	2.1
1988	-	-	-	-	-	-	-	-	-	-	123.5	3.1	-	-	-	-	-	-	-	-	-	-	125.6	1.7
1989	-	-	-	-	-	-	-	-	-	-	132.0	5.1	-	-	-	-	-	-	-	-	-	-	135.5	2.7
1990	-	-	-	-	-	-	-	-	-	-	134.0	-1.1	-	-	-	-	-	-	-	-	-	-	135.7	1.3
1991	-	-	-	-	-	-	-	-	-	-	138.6	2.1	-	-	-	-	-	-	-	-	-	-	140.6	1.4
1992	-	-	-	-	-	-	-	-	-	-	144.0	2.4	-	-	-	-	-	-	-	-	-	-	148.9	3.4
1993	-	-	-	-	-	-	-	-	-	-	152.5	2.4	-	-	-	-	-	-	-	-	-	-	153.9	0.9
1994	-	-	-	-	-	-	-	-	-	-	156.5	1.7	-	-	-	-	-	-	-	-	-	-	158.2	1.1
1995	-	-	-	-	-	-	-	-	-	-	153.8	-2.8	-	-	-	-	-	-	-	-	-	-	160.9	4.6
1996	-	-	-	-	-	-	-	-	-	-	161.9	0.6	-	-	-	-	-	-	-	-	-	-	158.9	-1.9
1997	-	-	-	-	-	-	-	-	-	-	161.5	1.6	-	-	-	-	-	-	-	-	-	-	-	-

Source: U.S. Department of Labor, Bureau of Labor Statistics, Division of Consumer Prices and Price Indexes. - indicates no data collected for period.

Minneapolis-St. Paul, MN
Consumer Price Index - Urban Wage Earners
Base 1982-1984 = 100
Entertainment

For 1976-1997. Columns headed % show percentile change in the index from the previous period for which an index is available.

Year	Jan		Feb		Mar		Apr		May		Jun		Jul		Aug		Sep		Oct		Nov		Dec	
	Index	%	Index	%	Index	%	Index	%	Index	%	Index	%	Index	%	Index	%	Index	%	Index	%	Index	%	Index	%
1976	61.1	-	-	-	-	-	64.6	5.7	-	-	-	-	64.4	-0.3	-	-	-	-	64.1	-0.5	-	-	-	-
1977	64.8	1.1	-	-	-	-	66.5	2.6	-	-	-	-	65.4	-1.7	-	-	-	-	70.2	7.3	-	-	-	-
1978	71.3	1.6	-	-	-	-	72.1	1.1	-	-	69.9	-3.1	-	-	72.6	3.9	-	-	74.8	3.0	-	-	79.7	6.6
1979	-	-	78.8	-1.1	-	-	78.2	-0.8	-	-	82.2	5.1	-	-	82.8	0.7	-	-	84.4	1.9	-	-	83.9	-0.6
1980	-	-	84.7	1.0	-	-	86.9	2.6	-	-	91.0	4.7	-	-	90.6	-0.4	-	-	89.2	-1.5	-	-	90.6	1.6
1981	-	-	91.6	1.1	-	-	91.6	0.0	-	-	92.0	0.4	-	-	92.9	1.0	-	-	94.2	1.4	-	-	94.0	-0.2
1982	-	-	97.0	3.2	-	-	95.0	-2.1	-	-	97.0	2.1	-	-	97.8	0.8	-	-	96.2	-1.6	-	-	96.5	0.3
1983	-	-	97.3	0.8	-	-	100.3	3.1	-	-	99.7	-0.6	-	-	104.4	4.7	-	-	101.7	-2.6	-	-	101.7	0.0
1984	-	-	102.4	0.7	-	-	103.1	0.7	-	-	102.8	-0.3	-	-	102.8	0.0	-	-	103.5	0.7	-	-	103.3	-0.2
1985	-	-	104.8	1.5	-	-	105.3	0.5	-	-	106.6	1.2	-	-	108.5	1.8	-	-	108.8	0.3	-	-	107.7	-1.0
1986	-	-	111.1	3.2	-	-	111.6	0.5	-	-	112.4	0.7	-	-	110.3	-1.9	-	-	114.3	3.6	114.9	0.5	114.0	-0.8
1987	-	-	-	-	-	-	-	-	-	-	118.8	4.2	-	-	-	-	-	-	-	-	-	-	121.3	2.1
1988	-	-	-	-	-	-	-	-	-	-	125.2	3.2	-	-	-	-	-	-	-	-	-	-	127.4	1.8
1989	-	-	-	-	-	-	-	-	-	-	133.8	5.0	-	-	-	-	-	-	-	-	-	-	137.6	2.8
1990	-	-	-	-	-	-	-	-	-	-	135.8	-1.3	-	-	-	-	-	-	-	-	-	-	137.5	1.3
1991	-	-	-	-	-	-	-	-	-	-	140.2	2.0	-	-	-	-	-	-	-	-	-	-	142.2	1.4
1992	-	-	-	-	-	-	-	-	-	-	145.3	2.2	-	-	-	-	-	-	-	-	-	-	151.3	4.1
1993	-	-	-	-	-	-	-	-	-	-	155.4	2.7	-	-	-	-	-	-	-	-	-	-	156.9	1.0
1994	-	-	-	-	-	-	-	-	-	-	159.2	1.5	-	-	-	-	-	-	-	-	-	-	161.4	1.4
1995	-	-	-	-	-	-	-	-	-	-	157.4	-2.5	-	-	-	-	-	-	-	-	-	-	165.3	5.0
1996	-	-	-	-	-	-	-	-	-	-	166.2	0.5	-	-	-	-	-	-	-	-	-	-	163.2	-1.8
1997	-	-	-	-	-	-	-	-	-	-	165.9	1.7	-	-	-	-	-	-	-	-	-	-	-	-

Source: U.S. Department of Labor, Bureau of Labor Statistics, Division of Consumer Prices and Price Indexes. - indicates no data collected for period.

Minneapolis-St. Paul, MN
Consumer Price Index - All Urban Consumers
Base 1982-1984 = 100
Other Goods and Services

For 1976-1997. Columns headed % show percentile change in the index from the previous period for which an index is available.

Year	Jan Index	%	Feb Index	%	Mar Index	%	Apr Index	%	May Index	%	Jun Index	%	Jul Index	%	Aug Index	%	Sep Index	%	Oct Index	%	Nov Index	%	Dec Index	%
1976	56.0	-	-	-	-	-	56.5	0.9	-	-	-	-	56.4	-0.2	-	-	-	-	57.5	2.0	-	-	-	-
1977	58.3	1.4	-	-	-	-	59.0	1.2	-	-	-	-	59.7	1.2	-	-	-	-	61.6	3.2	-	-	-	-
1978	62.9	2.1	-	-	-	-	63.9	1.6	-	-	64.1	0.3	-	-	65.4	2.0	-	-	66.9	2.3	-	-	67.3	0.6
1979	-	-	67.8	0.7	-	-	67.8	0.0	-	-	68.4	0.9	-	-	69.4	1.5	-	-	71.7	3.3	-	-	72.2	0.7
1980	-	-	73.5	1.8	-	-	74.0	0.7	-	-	74.4	0.5	-	-	75.4	1.3	-	-	77.6	2.9	-	-	79.0	1.8
1981	-	-	79.6	0.8	-	-	80.7	1.4	-	-	82.6	2.4	-	-	84.0	1.7	-	-	87.2	3.8	-	-	87.4	0.2
1982	-	-	89.1	1.9	-	-	90.1	1.1	-	-	90.1	0.0	-	-	90.7	0.7	-	-	95.8	5.6	-	-	97.0	1.3
1983	-	-	98.6	1.6	-	-	98.5	-0.1	-	-	99.3	0.8	-	-	100.4	1.1	-	-	104.6	4.2	-	-	104.9	0.3
1984	-	-	106.0	1.0	-	-	105.7	-0.3	-	-	106.4	0.7	-	-	107.7	1.2	-	-	110.6	2.7	-	-	110.4	-0.2
1985	-	-	112.0	1.4	-	-	112.2	0.2	-	-	112.7	0.4	-	-	115.2	2.2	-	-	118.6	3.0	-	-	118.1	-0.4
1986	-	-	119.6	1.3	-	-	119.8	0.2	-	-	119.8	0.0	-	-	120.8	0.8	-	-	123.2	2.0	123.4	0.2	123.6	0.2
1987	-	-	-	-	-	-	-	-	-	-	123.2	-0.3	-	-	-	-	-	-	-	-	-	-	-	-
1988	-	-	-	-	-	-	-	-	-	-	129.2	4.9	-	-	-	-	-	-	-	-	-	-	-	-
1989	-	-	-	-	-	-	-	-	-	-	134.6	4.2	-	-	-	-	-	-	-	-	-	-	-	-
1990	-	-	-	-	-	-	-	-	-	-	149.1	10.8	-	-	-	-	-	-	-	-	-	-	-	-
1991	-	-	-	-	-	-	-	-	-	-	156.3	4.8	-	-	-	-	-	-	-	-	-	-	-	-
1992	-	-	-	-	-	-	-	-	-	-	166.5	6.5	-	-	-	-	-	-	-	-	-	-	-	-
1993	-	-	-	-	-	-	-	-	-	-	180.4	8.3	-	-	-	-	-	-	-	-	-	-	-	-
1994	-	-	-	-	-	-	-	-	-	-	185.8	3.0	-	-	-	-	-	-	-	-	-	-	-	-
1995	-	-	-	-	-	-	-	-	-	-	190.8	2.7	-	-	-	-	-	-	-	-	-	-	-	-
1996	-	-	-	-	-	-	-	-	-	-	201.3	5.5	-	-	-	-	-	-	-	-	-	-	-	-
1997	-	-	-	-	-	-	-	-	-	-	195.1	-3.1	-	-	-	-	-	-	-	-	-	-	-	-

Source: U.S. Department of Labor, Bureau of Labor Statistics, Division of Consumer Prices and Price Indexes. - indicates no data collected for period.

Minneapolis-St. Paul, MN
Consumer Price Index - Urban Wage Earners
Base 1982-1984 = 100
Other Goods and Services

For 1976-1997. Columns headed % show percentile change in the index from the previous period for which an index is available.

Year	Jan Index	%	Feb Index	%	Mar Index	%	Apr Index	%	May Index	%	Jun Index	%	Jul Index	%	Aug Index	%	Sep Index	%	Oct Index	%	Nov Index	%	Dec Index	%
1976	57.7	-	-	-	-	-	58.1	0.7	-	-	-	-	58.1	0.0	-	-	-	-	59.2	1.9	-	-	-	-
1977	60.0	1.4	-	-	-	-	60.7	1.2	-	-	-	-	61.5	1.3	-	-	-	-	63.4	3.1	-	-	-	-
1978	64.8	2.2	-	-	-	-	65.8	1.5	-	-	66.3	0.8	-	-	66.9	0.9	-	-	68.2	1.9	-	-	68.8	0.9
1979	-	-	69.5	1.0	-	-	69.6	0.1	-	-	70.3	1.0	-	-	71.8	2.1	-	-	73.2	1.9	-	-	73.4	0.3
1980	-	-	74.5	1.5	-	-	75.5	1.3	-	-	76.0	0.7	-	-	76.7	0.9	-	-	78.3	2.1	-	-	80.0	2.2
1981	-	-	81.2	1.5	-	-	82.0	1.0	-	-	83.2	1.5	-	-	83.9	0.8	-	-	87.2	3.9	-	-	87.1	-0.1
1982	-	-	89.2	2.4	-	-	90.2	1.1	-	-	90.3	0.1	-	-	90.8	0.6	-	-	95.9	5.6	-	-	97.2	1.4
1983	-	-	99.1	2.0	-	-	99.0	-0.1	-	-	99.7	0.7	-	-	101.0	1.3	-	-	104.3	3.3	-	-	104.5	0.2
1984	-	-	105.8	1.2	-	-	105.5	-0.3	-	-	106.2	0.7	-	-	107.8	1.5	-	-	109.7	1.8	-	-	109.7	0.0
1985	-	-	111.6	1.7	-	-	111.7	0.1	-	-	112.3	0.5	-	-	115.4	2.8	-	-	118.2	2.4	-	-	117.7	-0.4
1986	-	-	119.4	1.4	-	-	119.5	0.1	-	-	119.6	0.1	-	-	120.8	1.0	-	-	122.7	1.6	122.9	0.2	123.1	0.2
1987	-	-	-	-	-	-	-	-	-	-	121.3	-1.5	-	-	-	-	-	-	-	-	-	-	-	-
1988	-	-	-	-	-	-	-	-	-	-	127.8	5.4	-	-	-	-	-	-	-	-	-	-	-	-
1989	-	-	-	-	-	-	-	-	-	-	135.1	5.7	-	-	-	-	-	-	-	-	-	-	-	-
1990	-	-	-	-	-	-	-	-	-	-	149.4	10.6	-	-	-	-	-	-	-	-	-	-	-	-
1991	-	-	-	-	-	-	-	-	-	-	156.4	4.7	-	-	-	-	-	-	-	-	-	-	-	-
1992	-	-	-	-	-	-	-	-	-	-	165.7	5.9	-	-	-	-	-	-	-	-	-	-	-	-
1993	-	-	-	-	-	-	-	-	-	-	180.6	9.0	-	-	-	-	-	-	-	-	-	-	-	-
1994	-	-	-	-	-	-	-	-	-	-	183.7	1.7	-	-	-	-	-	-	-	-	-	-	-	-
1995	-	-	-	-	-	-	-	-	-	-	187.4	2.0	-	-	-	-	-	-	-	-	-	-	-	-
1996	-	-	-	-	-	-	-	-	-	-	195.3	4.2	-	-	-	-	-	-	-	-	-	-	-	-
1997	-	-	-	-	-	-	-	-	-	-	184.2	-5.7	-	-	-	-	-	-	-	-	-	-	-	-

Source: U.S. Department of Labor, Bureau of Labor Statistics, Division of Consumer Prices and Price Indexes. - indicates no data collected for period.

New York, NY, NE NJ
Consumer Price Index - All Urban Consumers
Base 1982-1984 = 100
Annual Averages

For 1914-1997. Columns headed % show percentile change in the index from the previous period for which an index is available.

Year	All Items		Food & Beverage		Housing		Apparel & Upkeep		Trans-portation		Medical Care		Entertain-ment		Other Goods & Services	
	Index	%	Index	%	Index	%	Index	%	Index	%	Index	%	Index	%	Index	%
1914	-	-	-	-	-	-	-	-	-	-	-	-	-	-	-	-
1915	9.9	-	-	-	-	-	-	-	-	-	-	-	-	-	-	-
1916	10.6	7.1	-	-	-	-	-	-	-	-	-	-	-	-	-	-
1917	12.8	20.8	-	-	-	-	-	-	-	-	-	-	-	-	-	-
1918	15.1	18.0	-	-	-	-	-	-	-	-	-	-	-	-	-	-
1919	17.7	17.2	-	-	-	-	-	-	-	-	-	-	-	-	-	-
1920	20.2	14.1	-	-	-	-	-	-	-	-	-	-	-	-	-	-
1921	18.1	-10.4	-	-	-	-	-	-	-	-	-	-	-	-	-	-
1922	17.2	-5.0	-	-	-	-	-	-	-	-	-	-	-	-	-	-
1923	17.5	1.7	-	-	-	-	-	-	-	-	-	-	-	-	-	-
1924	17.5	0.0	-	-	-	-	-	-	-	-	-	-	-	-	-	-
1925	17.9	2.3	-	-	-	-	-	-	-	-	-	-	-	-	-	-
1926	18.1	1.1	-	-	-	-	-	-	-	-	-	-	-	-	-	-
1927	17.9	-1.1	-	-	-	-	-	-	-	-	-	-	-	-	-	-
1928	17.8	-0.6	-	-	-	-	-	-	-	-	-	-	-	-	-	-
1929	17.9	0.6	-	-	-	-	-	-	-	-	-	-	-	-	-	-
1930	17.4	-2.8	-	-	-	-	-	-	-	-	-	-	-	-	-	-
1931	16.1	-7.5	-	-	-	-	-	-	-	-	-	-	-	-	-	-
1932	14.7	-8.7	-	-	-	-	-	-	-	-	-	-	-	-	-	-
1933	13.9	-5.4	-	-	-	-	-	-	-	-	-	-	-	-	-	-
1934	14.3	2.9	-	-	-	-	-	-	-	-	-	-	-	-	-	-
1935	14.5	1.4	-	-	-	-	-	-	-	-	-	-	-	-	-	-
1936	14.5	0.0	-	-	-	-	-	-	-	-	-	-	-	-	-	-
1937	14.8	2.1	-	-	-	-	-	-	-	-	-	-	-	-	-	-
1938	14.6	-1.4	-	-	-	-	-	-	-	-	-	-	-	-	-	-
1939	14.5	-0.7	-	-	-	-	-	-	-	-	-	-	-	-	-	-
1940	14.7	1.4	-	-	-	-	-	-	-	-	-	-	-	-	-	-
1941	15.3	4.1	-	-	-	-	-	-	-	-	-	-	-	-	-	-
1942	16.7	9.2	-	-	-	-	-	-	-	-	-	-	-	-	-	-
1943	17.9	7.2	-	-	-	-	-	-	-	-	-	-	-	-	-	-
1944	18.4	2.8	-	-	-	-	-	-	-	-	-	-	-	-	-	-
1945	18.9	2.7	-	-	-	-	-	-	-	-	-	-	-	-	-	-
1946	20.7	9.5	-	-	-	-	-	-	-	-	-	-	-	-	-	-
1947	23.2	12.1	-		-		-	-	16.1	-	14.3	-	-		-	-
1948	24.7	6.5	-		-		-	-	18.8	16.8	15.7	9.8	-		-	-
1949	24.5	-0.8	-		-		-	-	21.5	14.4	16.0	1.9	-		-	-
1950	24.6	0.4	-		-		-	-	22.4	4.2	16.3	1.9	-		-	-
1951	26.5	7.7	-	-	-	-	-	-	23.5	4.9	17.0	4.3	-	-	-	-
1952	26.9	1.5	-	-	-	-	-	-	23.9	1.7	18.1	6.5	-	-	-	-
1953	27.1	0.7	-	-	-	-	44.9	-	24.5	2.5	18.6	2.8	-	-	-	-
1954	27.2	0.4	-	-	-	-	44.5	-0.9	24.9	1.6	19.0	2.2	-	-	-	-
1955	27.1	-0.4	-	-	-	-	43.9	-1.3	24.2	-2.8	19.3	1.6	-	-	-	-
1956	27.5	1.5	-	-	-	-	44.9	2.3	25.0	3.3	19.5	1.0	-	-	-	-
1957	28.4	3.3	-	-	-	-	45.7	1.8	25.9	3.6	19.8	1.5	-	-	-	-
1958	29.2	2.8	-	-	-	-	46.0	0.7	26.3	1.5	20.2	2.0	-	-	-	-

[Continued]

New York, NY, NE NJ
Consumer Price Index - All Urban Consumers
Base 1982-1984 = 100
Annual Averages
[Continued]

For 1914-1997. Columns headed % show percentile change in the index from the previous period for which an index is available.

Year	All Items		Food & Beverage		Housing		Apparel & Upkeep		Trans- portation		Medical Care		Entertain- ment		Other Goods & Services	
	Index	%	Index	%	Index	%	Index	%	Index	%	Index	%	Index	%	Index	%
1959	29.6	1.4	-	-	-	-	46.4	0.9	27.6	4.9	21.5	6.4	-	-	-	-
1960	30.2	2.0	-	-	-	-	47.3	1.9	27.7	0.4	22.2	3.3	-	-	-	-
1961	30.5	1.0	-	-	-	-	47.8	1.1	27.8	0.4	23.0	3.6	-	-	-	-
1962	30.9	1.3	-	-	-	-	48.3	1.0	28.0	0.7	23.5	2.2	-	-	-	-
1963	31.6	2.3	-	-	-	-	49.2	1.9	28.2	0.7	23.9	1.7	-	-	-	-
1964	32.1	1.6	-	-	-	-	50.0	1.6	28.3	0.4	24.4	2.1	-	-	-	-
1965	32.6	1.6	-	-	-	-	50.7	1.4	28.7	1.4	25.3	3.7	-	-	-	-
1966	33.7	3.4	-	-	-	-	51.9	2.4	29.8	3.8	26.6	5.1	-	-	-	-
1967	34.6	2.7	-	-	-	-	54.5	5.0	31.2	4.7	28.4	6.8	-	-	-	-
1968	36.1	4.3	-	-	-	-	57.6	5.7	32.0	2.6	30.3	6.7	-	-	-	-
1969	38.3	6.1	-	-	-	-	61.4	6.6	33.9	5.9	33.1	9.2	-	-	-	-
1970	41.2	7.6	-	-	-	-	64.1	4.4	38.1	12.4	35.6	7.6	-	-	-	-
1971	43.6	5.8	-	-	-	-	65.6	2.3	40.2	5.5	38.6	8.4	-	-	-	-
1972	45.5	4.4	-	-	-	-	67.0	2.1	41.5	3.2	39.8	3.1	-	-	-	-
1973	48.3	6.2	-	-	-	-	68.8	2.7	42.3	1.9	41.2	3.5	-	-	-	-
1974	53.5	10.8	-	-	-	-	74.2	7.8	45.6	7.8	45.6	10.7	-	-	-	-
1975	57.6	7.7	-	-	-	-	76.9	3.6	50.3	10.3	51.4	12.7	-	-	-	-
1976	61.0	5.9	62.7	-	59.9	-	78.9	2.6	57.5	14.3	56.8	10.5	64.5	-	58.6	-
1977	64.2	5.2	65.8	4.9	63.0	5.2	81.3	3.0	60.5	5.2	61.6	8.5	68.5	6.2	62.3	6.3
1978	67.8	5.6	71.4	8.5	66.3	5.2	85.1	4.7	62.6	3.5	65.4	6.2	72.3	5.5	65.1	4.5
1979	73.7	8.7	78.0	9.2	72.1	8.7	86.8	2.0	70.6	12.8	70.5	7.8	75.7	4.7	68.7	5.5
1980	82.1	11.4	85.1	9.1	80.8	12.1	92.7	6.8	82.5	16.9	77.3	9.6	81.5	7.7	74.1	7.9
1981	90.1	9.7	92.7	8.9	89.4	10.6	96.3	3.9	92.4	12.0	84.3	9.1	88.3	8.3	80.9	9.2
1982	95.3	5.8	97.3	5.0	95.0	6.3	97.3	1.0	95.9	3.8	91.8	8.9	95.5	8.2	89.7	10.9
1983	99.8	4.7	99.0	1.7	100.2	5.5	100.6	3.4	99.1	3.3	100.1	9.0	100.4	5.1	101.2	12.8
1984	104.8	5.0	103.7	4.7	104.8	4.6	102.0	1.4	105.0	6.0	108.1	8.0	104.0	3.6	109.0	7.7
1985	108.7	3.7	107.3	3.5	108.7	3.7	104.5	2.5	107.1	2.0	115.9	7.2	108.6	4.4	116.1	6.5
1986	112.3	3.3	112.2	4.6	112.8	3.8	104.2	-0.3	104.8	-2.1	125.6	8.4	115.1	6.0	123.6	6.5
1987	118.0	5.1	118.6	5.7	118.0	4.6	109.9	5.5	108.7	3.7	136.1	8.4	119.2	3.6	130.8	5.8
1988	123.7	4.8	124.8	5.2	125.1	6.0	107.4	-2.3	112.8	3.8	144.8	6.4	122.8	3.0	139.5	6.7
1989	130.6	5.6	132.1	5.8	131.8	5.4	114.0	6.1	116.5	3.3	155.8	7.6	129.5	5.5	151.9	8.9
1990	138.5	6.0	139.6	5.7	139.3	5.7	121.8	6.8	123.1	5.7	172.4	10.7	135.6	4.7	164.0	8.0
1991	144.8	4.5	144.3	3.4	145.7	4.6	124.5	2.2	127.9	3.9	186.6	8.2	140.8	3.8	177.2	8.0
1992	150.0	3.6	146.0	1.2	151.4	3.9	128.5	3.2	131.5	2.8	200.0	7.2	146.4	4.0	191.0	7.8
1993	154.5	3.0	149.0	2.1	155.5	2.7	129.3	0.6	137.7	4.7	209.1	4.6	149.8	2.3	200.1	4.8
1994	158.2	2.4	151.9	1.9	159.9	2.8	126.2	-2.4	141.8	3.0	217.6	4.1	154.0	2.8	204.9	2.4
1995	162.2	2.5	155.9	2.6	163.4	2.2	126.0	-0.2	145.9	2.9	226.8	4.2	158.8	3.1	213.5	4.2
1996	166.9	2.9	159.7	2.4	167.7	2.6	127.7	1.3	152.4	4.5	235.4	3.8	163.5	3.0	221.7	3.8
1997	170.8	2.3	163.0	2.1	171.7	2.4	130.3	2.0	154.1	1.1	244.5	3.9	167.6	2.5	230.1	3.8

Source: U.S. Department of Labor, Bureau of Labor Statistics, Division of Consumer Prices and Price Indexes. - indicates no data collected for period.

New York, NY, NE NJ
Consumer Price Index - Urban Wage Earners
Base 1982-1984 = 100
Annual Averages

For 1914-1997. Columns headed % show percentile change in the index from the previous period for which an index is available.

Year	All Items		Food & Beverage		Housing		Apparel & Upkeep		Trans- portation		Medical Care		Entertain- ment		Other Goods & Services	
	Index	%	Index	%	Index	%	Index	%	Index	%	Index	%	Index	%	Index	%
1914	-	-	-	-	-	-	-	-	-	-	-	-	-	-	-	-
1915	10.0	-	-	-	-	-	-	-	-	-	-	-	-	-	-	-
1916	10.8	8.0	-	-	-	-	-	-	-	-	-	-	-	-	-	-
1917	13.0	20.4	-	-	-	-	-	-	-	-	-	-	-	-	-	-
1918	15.3	17.7	-	-	-	-	-	-	-	-	-	-	-	-	-	-
1919	18.0	17.6	-	-	-	-	-	-	-	-	-	-	-	-	-	-
1920	20.5	13.9	-	-	-	-	-	-	-	-	-	-	-	-	-	-
1921	18.4	-10.2	-	-	-	-	-	-	-	-	-	-	-	-	-	-
1922	17.5	-4.9	-	-	-	-	-	-	-	-	-	-	-	-	-	-
1923	17.7	1.1	-	-	-	-	-	-	-	-	-	-	-	-	-	-
1924	17.7	0.0	-	-	-	-	-	-	-	-	-	-	-	-	-	-
1925	18.2	2.8	-	-	-	-	-	-	-	-	-	-	-	-	-	-
1926	18.4	1.1	-	-	-	-	-	-	-	-	-	-	-	-	-	-
1927	18.2	-1.1	-	-	-	-	-	-	-	-	-	-	-	-	-	-
1928	18.1	-0.5	-	-	-	-	-	-	-	-	-	-	-	-	-	-
1929	18.2	0.6	-	-	-	-	-	-	-	-	-	-	-	-	-	-
1930	17.7	-2.7	-	-	-	-	-	-	-	-	-	-	-	-	-	-
1931	16.4	-7.3	-	-	-	-	-	-	-	-	-	-	-	-	-	-
1932	14.9	-9.1	-	-	-	-	-	-	-	-	-	-	-	-	-	-
1933	14.1	-5.4	-	-	-	-	-	-	-	-	-	-	-	-	-	-
1934	14.5	2.8	-	-	-	-	-	-	-	-	-	-	-	-	-	-
1935	14.7	1.4	-	-	-	-	-	-	-	-	-	-	-	-	-	-
1936	14.7	0.0	-	-	-	-	-	-	-	-	-	-	-	-	-	-
1937	15.1	2.7	-	-	-	-	-	-	-	-	-	-	-	-	-	-
1938	14.8	-2.0	-	-	-	-	-	-	-	-	-	-	-	-	-	-
1939	14.7	-0.7	-	-	-	-	-	-	-	-	-	-	-	-	-	-
1940	14.9	1.4	-	-	-	-	-	-	-	-	-	-	-	-	-	-
1941	15.5	4.0	-	-	-	-	-	-	-	-	-	-	-	-	-	-
1942	17.0	9.7	-	-	-	-	-	-	-	-	-	-	-	-	-	-
1943	18.2	7.1	-	-	-	-	-	-	-	-	-	-	-	-	-	-
1944	18.7	2.7	-	-	-	-	-	-	-	-	-	-	-	-	-	-
1945	19.1	2.1	-	-	-	-	-	-	-	-	-	-	-	-	-	-
1946	21.0	9.9	-	-	-	-	-	-	-	-	-	-	-	-	-	-
1947	23.5	11.9	-	-	-	-	-	-	15.9	-	14.9	-	-	-	-	-
1948	25.1	6.8	-	-	-	-	-	-	18.6	17.0	16.3	9.4	-	-	-	-
1949	24.8	-1.2	-	-	-	-	-	-	21.3	14.5	16.7	2.5	-	-	-	-
1950	25.0	0.8	-	-	-	-	-	-	22.2	4.2	17.0	1.8	-	-	-	-
1951	26.9	7.6	-	-	-	-	-	-	23.3	5.0	17.7	4.1	-	-	-	-
1952	27.3	1.5	-	-	-	-	-	-	23.7	1.7	18.9	6.8	-	-	-	-
1953	27.5	0.7	-	-	-	-	44.8	-	24.2	2.1	19.4	2.6	-	-	-	-
1954	27.6	0.4	-	-	-	-	44.4	-0.9	24.6	1.7	19.8	2.1	-	-	-	-
1955	27.5	-0.4	-	-	-	-	43.8	-1.4	24.0	-2.4	20.1	1.5	-	-	-	-
1956	27.9	1.5	-	-	-	-	44.9	2.5	24.8	3.3	20.3	1.0	-	-	-	-
1957	28.8	3.2	-	-	-	-	45.6	1.6	25.7	3.6	20.6	1.5	-	-	-	-
1958	29.7	3.1	-	-	-	-	46.0	0.9	26.1	1.6	21.1	2.4	-	-	-	-

[Continued]

New York, NY, NE NJ
Consumer Price Index - Urban Wage Earners
Base 1982-1984 = 100
Annual Averages
[Continued]

For 1914-1997. Columns headed % show percentile change in the index from the previous period for which an index is available.

Year	All Items		Food & Beverage		Housing		Apparel & Upkeep		Trans- portation		Medical Care		Entertain- ment		Other Goods & Services	
	Index	%	Index	%	Index	%	Index	%	Index	%	Index	%	Index	%	Index	%
1959	30.1	1.3	-	-	-	-	46.3	0.7	27.3	4.6	22.4	6.2	-	-	-	-
1960	30.7	2.0	-	-	-	-	47.2	1.9	27.5	0.7	23.1	3.1	-	-	-	-
1961	30.9	0.7	-	-	-	-	47.7	1.1	27.5	0.0	24.0	3.9	-	-	-	-
1962	31.4	1.6	-	-	-	-	48.2	1.0	27.7	0.7	24.5	2.1	-	-	-	-
1963	32.1	2.2	-	-	-	-	49.2	2.1	27.9	0.7	25.0	2.0	-	-	-	-
1964	32.6	1.6	-	-	-	-	49.9	1.4	28.0	0.4	25.5	2.0	-	-	-	-
1965	33.1	1.5	-	-	-	-	50.6	1.4	28.4	1.4	26.4	3.5	-	-	-	-
1966	34.2	3.3	-	-	-	-	51.8	2.4	29.5	3.9	27.7	4.9	-	-	-	-
1967	35.1	2.6	-	-	-	-	54.4	5.0	30.9	4.7	29.6	6.9	-	-	-	-
1968	36.6	4.3	-	-	-	-	57.5	5.7	31.7	2.6	31.6	6.8	-	-	-	-
1969	38.9	6.3	-	-	-	-	61.3	6.6	33.6	6.0	34.5	9.2	-	-	-	-
1970	41.8	7.5	-	-	-	-	64.0	4.4	37.8	12.5	37.1	7.5	-	-	-	-
1971	44.2	5.7	-	-	-	-	65.5	2.3	39.8	5.3	40.2	8.4	-	-	-	-
1972	46.1	4.3	-	-	-	-	66.9	2.1	41.1	3.3	41.5	3.2	-	-	-	-
1973	49.1	6.5	-	-	-	-	68.7	2.7	41.9	1.9	43.0	3.6	-	-	-	-
1974	54.4	10.8	-	-	-	-	74.1	7.9	45.1	7.6	47.6	10.7	-	-	-	-
1975	58.5	7.5	-	-	-	-	76.7	3.5	49.8	10.4	53.6	12.6	-	-	-	-
1976	61.9	5.8	63.4	-	61.6	-	78.8	2.7	57.0	14.5	59.2	10.4	66.0	-	59.3	-
1977	65.2	5.3	66.5	4.9	64.8	5.2	81.2	3.0	59.9	5.1	64.3	8.6	70.0	6.1	63.0	6.2
1978	68.6	5.2	72.0	8.3	67.7	4.5	84.1	3.6	62.2	3.8	67.8	5.4	73.2	4.6	66.0	4.8
1979	74.7	8.9	78.7	9.3	73.6	8.7	87.3	3.8	70.3	13.0	72.5	6.9	76.7	4.8	69.6	5.5
1980	83.2	11.4	85.9	9.1	82.5	12.1	93.2	6.8	82.2	16.9	78.7	8.6	82.5	7.6	74.8	7.5
1981	91.3	9.7	92.9	8.1	91.4	10.8	96.0	3.0	92.3	12.3	86.2	9.5	89.4	8.4	80.9	8.2
1982	96.3	5.5	97.3	4.7	97.2	6.3	97.2	1.2	95.8	3.8	91.9	6.6	95.5	6.8	89.7	10.9
1983	100.1	3.9	99.1	1.8	100.9	3.8	100.6	3.5	98.9	3.2	99.9	8.7	100.5	5.2	101.6	13.3
1984	103.6	3.5	103.6	4.5	101.9	1.0	102.1	1.5	105.2	6.4	108.3	8.4	104.1	3.6	108.7	7.0
1985	107.9	4.2	107.0	3.3	107.3	5.3	104.4	2.3	107.2	1.9	116.2	7.3	108.3	4.0	115.4	6.2
1986	111.0	2.9	111.9	4.6	111.2	3.6	104.0	-0.4	104.2	-2.8	125.8	8.3	115.0	6.2	122.7	6.3
1987	116.6	5.0	118.2	5.6	116.0	4.3	110.2	6.0	108.4	4.0	136.8	8.7	120.3	4.6	129.5	5.5
1988	121.8	4.5	124.3	5.2	122.5	5.6	106.3	-3.5	112.4	3.7	145.8	6.6	123.9	3.0	137.9	6.5
1989	128.6	5.6	131.7	6.0	129.0	5.3	112.5	5.8	116.1	3.3	157.0	7.7	130.3	5.2	150.7	9.3
1990	136.3	6.0	139.4	5.8	135.9	5.3	120.1	6.8	123.1	6.0	172.0	9.6	136.2	4.5	163.6	8.6
1991	142.1	4.3	144.0	3.3	141.6	4.2	122.1	1.7	127.8	3.8	186.2	8.3	141.3	3.7	177.5	8.5
1992	146.9	3.4	145.6	1.1	146.7	3.6	125.8	3.0	131.6	3.0	200.3	7.6	146.6	3.8	191.0	7.6
1993	151.1	2.9	148.6	2.1	150.6	2.7	126.2	0.3	137.4	4.4	209.0	4.3	149.5	2.0	200.4	4.9
1994	154.5	2.3	151.5	2.0	154.6	2.7	122.7	-2.8	141.6	3.1	217.9	4.3	153.5	2.7	204.8	2.2
1995	158.3	2.5	155.3	2.5	158.0	2.2	121.8	-0.7	146.0	3.1	227.6	4.5	158.1	3.0	213.1	4.1
1996	163.1	3.0	159.0	2.4	162.2	2.7	123.6	1.5	153.3	5.0	236.0	3.7	162.2	2.6	221.2	3.8
1997	166.8	2.3	162.1	1.9	165.9	2.3	126.2	2.1	154.7	0.9	244.9	3.8	165.3	1.9	231.4	4.6

Source: U.S. Department of Labor, Bureau of Labor Statistics, Division of Consumer Prices and Price Indexes. - indicates no data collected for period.

New York, NY, NE NJ
Consumer Price Index - All Urban Consumers
Base 1982-1984 = 100
All Items

For 1914-1997. Columns headed % show percentile change in the index from the previous period for which an index is available.

Year	Jan Index	%	Feb Index	%	Mar Index	%	Apr Index	%	May Index	%	Jun Index	%	Jul Index	%	Aug Index	%	Sep Index	%	Oct Index	%	Nov Index	%	Dec Index	%
1914	-	-	-	-	-	-	-	-	-	-	-	-	-	-	-	-	-	-	-	-	-	-	9.9	-
1915	-	-	-	-	-	-	-	-	-	-	-	-	-	-	-	-	-	-	-	-	-	-	10.1	2.0
1916	-	-	-	-	-	-	-	-	-	-	-	-	-	-	-	-	-	-	-	-	-	-	11.3	11.9
1917	-	-	-	-	-	-	-	-	-	-	-	-	-	-	-	-	-	-	-	-	-	-	13.8	22.1
1918	-	-	-	-	-	-	-	-	-	-	-	-	-	-	-	-	-	-	-	-	-	-	16.8	21.7
1919	-	-	-	-	-	-	-	-	-	-	17.1	1.8	-	-	-	-	-	-	-	-	-	-	19.3	12.9
1920	-	-	-	-	-	-	-	-	-	-	20.9	8.3	-	-	-	-	-	-	-	-	-	-	19.5	-6.7
1921	-	-	-	-	-	-	-	-	17.9	-8.2	-	-	-	-	-	-	17.8	-0.6	-	-	-	-	17.9	0.6
1922	-	-	-	-	17.1	-4.5	-	-	-	-	17.2	0.6	-	-	-	-	17.1	-0.6	-	-	-	-	17.4	1.8
1923	-	-	-	-	17.3	-0.6	-	-	-	-	17.4	0.6	-	-	-	-	17.6	1.1	-	-	-	-	17.8	1.1
1924	-	-	-	-	17.4	-2.2	-	-	-	-	17.4	0.0	-	-	-	-	17.4	0.0	-	-	-	-	17.7	1.7
1925	-	-	-	-	-	-	-	-	-	-	17.7	0.0	-	-	-	-	-	-	-	-	-	-	18.5	4.5
1926	-	-	-	-	-	-	-	-	-	-	18.1	-2.2	-	-	-	-	-	-	-	-	-	-	18.1	0.0
1927	-	-	-	-	-	-	-	-	-	-	18.0	-0.6	-	-	-	-	-	-	-	-	-	-	18.1	0.6
1928	-	-	-	-	-	-	-	-	-	-	17.7	-2.2	-	-	-	-	-	-	-	-	-	-	17.8	0.6
1929	-	-	-	-	-	-	-	-	-	-	17.8	0.0	-	-	-	-	-	-	-	-	-	-	17.9	0.6
1930	-	-	-	-	-	-	-	-	-	-	17.4	-2.8	-	-	-	-	-	-	-	-	-	-	17.0	-2.3
1931	-	-	-	-	-	-	-	-	-	-	16.0	-5.9	-	-	-	-	-	-	-	-	-	-	15.4	-3.8
1932	-	-	-	-	-	-	-	-	-	-	14.7	-4.5	-	-	-	-	-	-	-	-	-	-	14.2	-3.4
1933	-	-	-	-	-	-	-	-	-	-	13.7	-3.5	-	-	-	-	-	-	-	-	-	-	14.0	2.2
1934	-	-	-	-	-	-	-	-	-	-	14.3	2.1	-	-	-	-	-	-	-	-	14.4	0.7	-	-
1935	-	-	-	-	14.4	0.0	-	-	-	-	-	-	14.3	-0.7	-	-	-	-	14.4	0.7	-	-	-	-
1936	14.6	1.4	-	-	-	-	14.4	-1.4	-	-	-	-	14.5	0.7	-	-	14.7	1.4	-	-	-	-	14.5	-1.4
1937	-	-	-	-	14.8	2.1	-	-	-	-	14.8	0.0	-	-	-	-	15.2	2.7	-	-	-	-	15.0	-1.3
1938	-	-	-	-	14.5	-3.3	-	-	-	-	14.5	0.0	-	-	-	-	14.6	0.7	-	-	-	-	14.6	0.0
1939	-	-	-	-	14.5	-0.7	-	-	-	-	14.3	-1.4	-	-	-	-	14.8	3.5	-	-	-	-	14.6	-1.4
1940	-	-	-	-	14.7	0.7	-	-	-	-	14.8	0.7	-	-	-	-	14.7	-0.7	14.6	-0.7	14.7	0.7	14.7	0.0
1941	14.7	0.0	14.8	0.7	14.8	0.0	14.9	0.7	15.0	0.7	15.2	1.3	15.3	0.7	15.4	0.7	15.6	1.3	15.7	0.6	15.8	0.6	15.8	0.0
1942	16.1	1.9	16.2	0.6	16.3	0.6	16.4	0.6	16.5	0.6	16.7	1.2	16.8	0.6	16.9	0.6	16.9	0.0	17.1	1.2	17.3	1.2	17.4	0.6
1943	17.5	0.6	17.5	0.0	17.8	1.7	17.9	0.6	18.1	1.1	18.1	0.0	18.1	0.0	17.9	-1.1	18.1	1.1	18.2	0.6	18.2	0.0	18.2	0.0
1944	18.2	0.0	18.1	-0.5	18.2	0.6	18.3	0.5	18.4	0.5	18.4	0.0	18.5	0.5	18.5	0.0	18.5	0.0	18.5	0.0	18.6	0.5	18.6	0.0
1945	18.6	0.0	18.6	0.0	18.5	-0.5	18.6	0.5	18.7	0.5	18.9	1.1	19.1	1.1	19.0	-0.5	18.9	-0.5	18.9	0.0	19.0	0.5	19.1	0.5
1946	19.2	0.5	19.2	0.0	19.3	0.5	19.5	1.0	19.6	0.5	19.8	1.0	21.0	6.1	21.3	1.4	21.8	2.3	22.3	2.3	22.5	0.9	22.7	0.9
1947	22.6	-0.4	22.5	-0.4	23.0	2.2	22.9	-0.4	22.7	-0.9	22.9	0.9	23.0	0.4	23.2	0.9	23.6	1.7	23.6	0.0	23.9	1.3	24.1	0.8
1948	24.4	1.2	24.3	-0.4	24.0	-1.2	24.4	1.7	24.5	0.4	24.7	0.8	25.2	2.0	25.3	0.4	25.3	0.0	25.1	-0.8	25.0	-0.4	24.7	-1.2
1949	24.7	0.0	24.4	-1.2	24.5	0.4	24.6	0.4	24.5	-0.4	24.5	0.0	24.5	0.0	24.5	0.0	24.6	0.4	24.3	-1.2	24.3	0.0	24.2	-0.4
1950	24.0	-0.8	24.1	0.4	24.1	0.0	24.2	0.4	24.2	0.0	24.3	0.4	24.7	1.6	24.7	0.0	25.0	1.2	25.1	0.4	25.3	0.8	25.6	1.2
1951	25.9	1.2	26.3	1.5	26.3	0.0	26.3	0.0	26.5	0.8	26.3	-0.8	26.4	0.4	26.4	0.0	26.6	0.8	26.7	0.4	26.8	0.4	26.8	0.0
1952	26.8	0.0	26.7	-0.4	26.6	-0.4	26.7	0.4	26.7	0.0	26.7	0.0	27.1	1.5	27.1	0.0	27.3	0.4	27.3	0.0	27.2	-0.4	27.0	-0.7
1953	26.9	-0.4	26.8	-0.4	26.8	0.0	26.8	0.0	26.8	0.0	27.0	0.7	27.1	0.4	27.2	0.4	27.2	0.0	27.2	0.0	27.2	-0.4	27.3	0.4
1954	27.3	0.0	27.2	-0.4	27.1	-0.4	27.2	0.4	27.2	0.0	27.2	0.0	27.3	0.4	27.3	0.0	27.2	-0.4	27.2	0.0	27.2	0.0	27.1	-0.4
1955	27.1	0.0	27.2	0.4	27.1	-0.4	27.1	0.0	27.0	-0.4	27.0	0.0	27.0	0.0	27.0	0.0	27.2	0.7	27.1	-0.4	27.2	0.4	27.0	-0.7
1956	27.1	0.4	27.1	0.0	27.1	0.0	27.1	0.0	27.3	0.7	27.4	0.4	27.6	0.7	27.6	0.0	27.8	0.7	27.9	0.4	27.9	0.0	27.9	0.0
1957	27.9	0.0	28.0	0.4	28.0	0.0	28.2	0.7	28.3	0.4	28.4	0.4	28.6	0.7	28.6	0.0	28.5	-0.3	28.6	0.4	28.6	0.0	28.6	0.0
1958	29.0	1.4	29.0	0.0	29.2	0.7	29.2	0.0	29.2	0.0	29.2	0.0	29.2	0.0	29.2	0.0	29.3	0.3	29.3	0.0	29.4	0.3	29.3	-0.3

[Continued]

New York, NY, NE NJ
Consumer Price Index - All Urban Consumers
Base 1982-1984 = 100
All Items
[Continued]

For 1914-1997. Columns headed % show percentile change in the index from the previous period for which an index is available.

Year	Jan Index	%	Feb Index	%	Mar Index	%	Apr Index	%	May Index	%	Jun Index	%	Jul Index	%	Aug Index	%	Sep Index	%	Oct Index	%	Nov Index	%	Dec Index	%
1959	29.4	0.3	29.4	0.0	29.4	0.0	29.4	0.0	29.4	0.0	29.6	0.7	29.8	0.7	29.7	-0.3	29.8	0.3	29.9	0.3	30.0	0.3	30.0	0.0
1960	30.0	0.0	30.0	0.0	30.0	0.0	30.1	0.3	30.1	0.0	30.1	0.0	30.1	0.0	30.2	0.3	30.3	0.3	30.4	0.3	30.5	0.3	30.5	0.0
1961	30.4	-0.3	30.4	0.0	30.4	0.0	30.3	-0.3	30.3	0.0	30.3	0.0	30.5	0.7	30.5	0.0	30.6	0.3	30.6	0.0	30.6	0.0	30.6	0.0
1962	30.7	0.3	30.8	0.3	30.8	0.0	30.8	0.0	30.7	-0.3	30.8	0.3	30.9	0.3	31.0	0.3	31.2	0.6	31.2	0.0	31.1	-0.3	31.1	0.0
1963	31.2	0.3	31.3	0.3	31.3	0.0	31.4	0.3	31.3	-0.3	31.6	1.0	31.8	0.6	31.8	0.0	31.8	0.0	31.8	0.0	31.9	0.3	32.0	0.3
1964	31.9	-0.3	32.0	0.3	32.0	0.0	32.0	0.0	32.0	0.0	32.0	0.0	32.1	0.3	32.1	0.0	32.2	0.3	32.2	0.0	32.3	0.3	32.3	0.0
1965	32.2	-0.3	32.3	0.3	32.3	0.0	32.4	0.3	32.5	0.3	32.6	0.3	32.7	0.3	32.7	0.0	32.8	0.3	32.9	0.3	32.9	0.0	33.0	0.3
1966	33.0	0.0	33.2	0.6	33.4	0.6	33.5	0.3	33.5	0.0	33.5	0.0	33.8	0.9	33.9	0.3	34.1	0.6	34.2	0.3	34.2	0.0	34.2	0.0
1967	34.1	-0.3	34.3	0.6	34.3	0.0	34.3	0.0	34.4	0.3	34.5	0.3	34.6	0.3	34.7	0.3	34.8	0.3	34.9	0.3	35.0	0.3	35.1	0.3
1968	35.1	0.0	35.3	0.6	35.5	0.6	35.6	0.3	35.7	0.3	35.9	0.6	36.1	0.6	36.4	0.8	36.6	0.5	36.8	0.5	36.9	0.3	37.0	0.3
1969	37.2	0.5	37.3	0.3	37.7	1.1	37.9	0.5	38.0	0.3	38.3	0.8	38.4	0.3	38.5	0.3	38.8	0.8	39.0	0.5	39.1	0.3	39.5	1.0
1970	39.8	0.8	40.2	1.0	40.4	0.5	40.7	0.7	40.9	0.5	41.2	0.7	41.3	0.2	41.4	0.2	41.7	0.7	41.9	0.5	42.0	0.2	42.3	0.7
1971	42.4	0.2	42.7	0.7	43.0	0.7	43.1	0.2	43.3	0.5	43.6	0.7	43.9	0.7	43.9	0.0	44.0	0.2	44.1	0.2	44.1	0.0	44.3	0.5
1972	44.5	0.5	44.8	0.7	45.0	0.4	45.1	0.2	45.2	0.2	45.3	0.2	45.5	0.4	45.6	0.2	46.0	0.9	46.1	0.2	46.1	0.0	46.2	0.2
1973	46.3	0.2	46.7	0.9	47.2	1.1	47.6	0.8	47.8	0.4	48.1	0.6	48.2	0.2	49.0	1.7	49.2	0.4	49.5	0.6	50.0	1.0	50.5	1.0
1974	50.8	0.6	51.6	1.6	52.2	1.2	52.2	0.0	52.8	1.1	53.2	0.8	53.4	0.4	54.3	1.7	54.9	1.1	55.4	0.9	55.7	0.5	56.0	0.5
1975	56.0	0.0	56.5	0.9	56.5	0.0	56.6	0.2	56.8	0.4	57.1	0.5	57.6	0.9	57.9	0.5	58.6	1.2	58.8	0.3	59.3	0.9	59.6	0.5
1976	59.7	0.2	60.0	0.5	60.2	0.3	60.3	0.2	60.5	0.3	60.9	0.7	61.1	0.3	61.4	0.5	61.8	0.7	61.9	0.2	61.9	0.0	62.2	0.5
1977	62.4	0.3	63.0	1.0	63.3	0.5	63.5	0.3	63.9	0.6	64.4	0.8	64.5	0.2	64.8	0.5	64.8	0.0	64.9	0.2	65.2	0.5	65.3	0.2
1978	65.7	0.6	66.0	0.5	66.5	0.8	66.9	0.6	67.3	0.6	68.0	1.0	68.1	0.1	68.4	0.4	68.8	0.6	69.3	0.7	69.5	0.3	69.7	0.3
1979	70.2	0.7	71.0	1.1	71.4	0.6	72.1	1.0	72.8	1.0	73.5	1.0	74.0	0.7	74.5	0.7	75.4	1.2	76.1	0.9	76.6	0.7	77.1	0.7
1980	78.2	1.4	78.9	0.9	80.0	1.4	80.6	0.7	81.1	0.6	82.1	1.2	82.6	0.6	83.3	0.8	83.6	0.4	84.1	0.6	84.6	0.6	85.5	1.1
1981	86.3	0.9	87.4	1.3	87.8	0.5	88.3	0.6	88.8	0.6	89.5	0.8	90.8	1.5	91.6	0.9	93.0	1.5	92.7	-0.3	92.6	-0.1	92.7	0.1
1982	92.9	0.2	93.1	0.2	92.5	-0.6	92.8	0.3	93.7	1.0	95.7	2.1	95.9	0.2	96.3	0.4	97.1	0.8	98.4	1.3	98.1	-0.3	97.5	-0.6
1983	97.8	0.3	98.0	0.2	98.1	0.1	99.1	1.0	99.4	0.3	99.7	0.3	100.0	0.3	100.1	0.1	101.0	0.9	101.3	0.3	101.7	0.4	101.8	0.1
1984	102.8	1.0	103.4	0.6	103.7	0.3	104.1	0.4	104.1	0.0	104.3	0.2	104.8	0.5	105.5	0.7	106.2	0.7	106.1	-0.1	106.5	0.4	106.5	0.0
1985	106.7	0.2	107.3	0.6	107.5	0.2	107.9	0.4	108.1	0.2	108.3	0.2	108.4	0.1	109.2	0.7	109.6	0.4	109.8	0.2	110.7	0.8	111.0	0.3
1986	111.8	0.7	111.5	-0.3	111.5	0.0	111.2	-0.3	110.9	-0.3	111.7	0.7	112.5	0.7	112.7	0.2	113.0	0.3	113.4	0.4	113.3	-0.1	113.8	0.4
1987	114.7	0.8	115.3	0.5	115.8	0.4	116.6	0.7	117.3	0.6	117.8	0.4	117.9	0.1	118.9	0.8	119.8	0.8	120.2	0.3	120.5	0.2	120.6	0.1
1988	121.3	0.6	121.1	-0.2	121.5	0.3	122.6	0.9	122.7	0.1	123.1	0.3	123.6	0.4	124.2	0.5	126.0	1.4	126.2	0.2	125.9	-0.2	126.0	0.1
1989	127.0	0.8	127.6	0.5	128.9	1.0	129.5	0.5	130.2	0.5	130.5	0.2	130.6	0.1	130.9	0.2	132.2	1.0	132.8	0.5	133.2	0.3	133.3	0.1
1990	135.1	1.4	135.3	0.1	136.6	1.0	137.3	0.5	137.2	-0.1	137.1	-0.1	138.4	0.9	140.0	1.2	140.8	0.6	141.6	0.6	141.5	-0.1	141.6	0.1
1991	143.0	1.0	143.6	0.4	143.4	-0.1	143.7	0.2	144.0	0.2	144.6	0.4	145.2	0.4	145.4	0.1	145.8	0.3	145.7	-0.1	146.6	0.6	146.6	0.0
1992	147.3	0.5	148.0	0.5	149.1	0.7	149.2	0.1	148.9	-0.2	149.5	0.4	149.9	0.3	150.8	0.6	151.4	0.4	152.1	0.5	152.2	0.1	151.9	-0.2
1993	153.0	0.7	153.6	0.4	154.1	0.3	154.0	-0.1	153.8	-0.1	154.2	0.3	154.3	0.1	155.3	0.6	155.3	0.0	155.5	0.1	155.4	-0.1	155.6	0.1
1994	156.0	0.3	157.4	0.9	157.9	0.3	157.7	-0.1	157.3	-0.3	157.8	0.3	158.2	0.3	159.1	0.6	159.0	-0.1	159.5	0.3	159.4	-0.1	158.9	-0.3
1995	159.9	0.6	160.3	0.3	160.9	0.4	161.4	0.3	161.8	0.2	162.2	0.2	162.3	0.1	162.8	0.3	163.2	0.2	163.6	0.2	163.8	0.1	163.7	-0.1
1996	164.8	0.7	165.7	0.5	166.5	0.5	166.0	-0.3	166.4	0.2	166.5	0.1	166.7	0.1	167.2	0.3	168.2	0.6	168.2	0.0	168.4	0.1	168.5	0.1
1997	169.1	0.4	170.1	0.6	170.7	0.4	170.2	-0.3	169.9	-0.2	170.3	0.2	170.8	0.3	170.8	0.0	171.7	0.5	172.3	0.3	172.0	-0.2	171.9	-0.1

Source: U.S. Department of Labor, Bureau of Labor Statistics, Division of Consumer Prices and Price Indexes. - indicates no data collected for period.

New York, NY, NE NJ
Consumer Price Index - Urban Wage Earners
Base 1982-1984 = 100
All Items

For 1914-1997. Columns headed % show percentile change in the index from the previous period for which an index is available.

Year	Jan Index	%	Feb Index	%	Mar Index	%	Apr Index	%	May Index	%	Jun Index	%	Jul Index	%	Aug Index	%	Sep Index	%	Oct Index	%	Nov Index	%	Dec Index	%
1914	-	-	-	-	-	-	-	-	-	-	-	-	-	-	-	-	-	-	-	-	-	-	10.1	-
1915	-	-	-	-	-	-	-	-	-	-	-	-	-	-	-	-	-	-	-	-	-	-	10.3	2.0
1916	-	-	-	-	-	-	-	-	-	-	-	-	-	-	-	-	-	-	-	-	-	-	11.5	11.7
1917	-	-	-	-	-	-	-	-	-	-	-	-	-	-	-	-	-	-	-	-	-	-	14.0	21.7
1918	-	-	-	-	-	-	-	-	-	-	-	-	-	-	-	-	-	-	-	-	-	-	17.1	22.1
1919	-	-	-	-	-	-	-	-	-	-	17.4	1.8	-	-	-	-	-	-	-	-	-	-	19.6	12.6
1920	-	-	-	-	-	-	-	-	-	-	21.2	8.2	-	-	-	-	-	-	-	-	-	-	19.8	-6.6
1921	-	-	-	-	-	-	-	-	18.2	-8.1	-	-	-	-	-	-	18.1	-0.5	-	-	-	-	18.2	0.6
1922	-	-	-	-	17.4	-4.4	-	-	-	-	17.4	0.0	-	-	-	-	17.4	0.0	-	-	-	-	17.7	1.7
1923	-	-	-	-	17.6	-0.6	-	-	-	-	17.7	0.6	-	-	-	-	17.9	1.1	-	-	-	-	18.1	1.1
1924	-	-	-	-	17.7	-2.2	-	-	-	-	17.7	0.0	-	-	-	-	17.7	0.0	-	-	-	-	18.0	1.7
1925	-	-	-	-	-	-	-	-	-	-	18.0	0.0	-	-	-	-	-	-	-	-	-	-	18.8	4.4
1926	-	-	-	-	-	-	-	-	-	-	18.4	-2.1	-	-	-	-	-	-	-	-	-	-	18.4	0.0
1927	-	-	-	-	-	-	-	-	-	-	18.3	-0.5	-	-	-	-	-	-	-	-	-	-	18.4	0.5
1928	-	-	-	-	-	-	-	-	-	-	18.0	-2.2	-	-	-	-	-	-	-	-	-	-	18.1	0.6
1929	-	-	-	-	-	-	-	-	-	-	18.1	0.0	-	-	-	-	-	-	-	-	-	-	18.2	0.6
1930	-	-	-	-	-	-	-	-	-	-	17.7	-2.7	-	-	-	-	-	-	-	-	-	-	17.2	-2.8
1931	-	-	-	-	-	-	-	-	-	-	16.2	-5.8	-	-	-	-	-	-	-	-	-	-	15.7	-3.1
1932	-	-	-	-	-	-	-	-	-	-	15.0	-4.5	-	-	-	-	-	-	-	-	-	-	14.4	-4.0
1933	-	-	-	-	-	-	-	-	-	-	13.9	-3.5	-	-	-	-	-	-	-	-	-	-	14.3	2.9
1934	-	-	-	-	-	-	-	-	-	-	14.5	1.4	-	-	-	-	-	-	-	-	14.6	0.7	-	-
1935	-	-	-	-	14.6	0.0	-	-	-	-	-	-	14.5	-0.7	-	-	-	-	14.6	0.7	-	-	-	-
1936	14.8	1.4	-	-	-	-	14.6	-1.4	-	-	-	-	14.7	0.7	-	-	14.9	1.4	-	-	-	-	14.7	-1.3
1937	-	-	-	-	15.0	2.0	-	-	-	-	15.0	0.0	-	-	-	-	15.4	2.7	-	-	-	-	15.2	-1.3
1938	-	-	-	-	14.8	-2.6	-	-	-	-	14.8	0.0	-	-	-	-	14.9	0.7	-	-	-	-	14.8	-0.7
1939	-	-	-	-	14.7	-0.7	-	-	-	-	14.5	-1.4	-	-	-	-	15.0	3.4	-	-	-	-	14.8	-1.3
1940	-	-	-	-	15.0	1.4	-	-	-	-	15.1	0.7	-	-	-	-	14.9	-1.3	14.8	-0.7	14.9	0.7	14.9	0.0
1941	15.0	0.7	15.0	0.0	15.0	0.0	15.1	0.7	15.2	0.7	15.5	2.0	15.5	0.0	15.6	0.6	15.8	1.3	16.0	1.3	16.1	0.6	16.1	0.0
1942	16.4	1.9	16.4	0.0	16.6	1.2	16.7	0.6	16.8	0.6	16.9	0.6	17.1	1.2	17.2	0.6	17.2	0.0	17.4	1.2	17.6	1.1	17.7	0.6
1943	17.7	0.0	17.8	0.6	18.1	1.7	18.2	0.6	18.4	1.1	18.4	0.0	18.3	-0.5	18.2	-0.5	18.4	1.1	18.4	0.0	18.5	0.5	18.5	0.0
1944	18.5	0.0	18.4	-0.5	18.5	0.5	18.6	0.5	18.6	0.0	18.6	0.0	18.8	1.1	18.8	0.0	18.8	0.0	18.8	0.0	18.9	0.5	18.9	0.0
1945	18.9	0.0	18.9	0.0	18.8	-0.5	18.9	0.5	19.0	0.5	19.2	1.1	19.4	1.0	19.2	-1.0	19.2	0.0	19.1	-0.5	19.3	1.0	19.4	0.5
1946	19.5	0.5	19.5	0.0	19.6	0.5	19.8	1.0	19.9	0.5	20.1	1.0	21.4	6.5	21.6	0.9	22.1	2.3	22.7	2.7	22.9	0.9	23.0	0.4
1947	22.9	-0.4	22.8	-0.4	23.3	2.2	23.3	0.0	23.0	-1.3	23.3	1.3	23.4	0.4	23.5	0.4	24.0	2.1	24.0	0.0	24.2	0.8	24.4	0.8
1948	24.8	1.6	24.7	-0.4	24.4	-1.2	24.8	1.6	24.9	0.4	25.1	0.8	25.6	2.0	25.7	0.4	25.7	0.0	25.5	-0.8	25.4	-0.4	25.1	-1.2
1949	25.1	0.0	24.8	-1.2	24.9	0.4	25.0	0.4	24.8	-0.8	24.8	0.0	24.9	0.4	24.8	-0.4	24.9	0.4	24.7	-0.8	24.7	0.0	24.6	-0.4
1950	24.4	-0.8	24.4	0.0	24.5	0.4	24.6	0.4	24.6	0.0	24.7	0.4	25.1	1.6	25.1	0.0	25.4	1.2	25.5	0.4	25.6	0.4	26.0	1.6
1951	26.3	1.2	26.7	1.5	26.7	0.0	26.7	0.0	26.9	0.7	26.7	-0.7	26.8	0.4	26.8	0.0	27.0	0.7	27.1	0.4	27.3	0.7	27.3	0.0
1952	27.3	0.0	27.1	-0.7	27.0	-0.4	27.1	0.4	27.1	0.0	27.1	0.0	27.5	1.5	27.5	0.0	27.5	0.0	27.5	0.0	27.6	0.4	27.4	-0.7
1953	27.4	0.0	27.2	-0.7	27.3	0.4	27.2	-0.4	27.3	0.4	27.4	0.4	27.5	0.4	27.6	0.4	27.7	0.4	27.7	0.0	27.6	-0.4	27.7	0.4
1954	27.7	0.0	27.6	-0.4	27.5	-0.4	27.6	0.4	27.6	0.0	27.6	0.0	27.7	0.4	27.7	0.0	27.6	-0.4	27.6	0.0	27.6	0.0	27.5	-0.4
1955	27.5	0.0	27.6	0.4	27.5	-0.4	27.5	0.0	27.4	-0.4	27.4	0.0	27.4	0.0	27.4	0.0	27.6	0.7	27.5	-0.4	27.6	0.4	27.4	-0.7
1956	27.5	0.4	27.5	0.0	27.5	0.0	27.5	0.0	27.7	0.7	27.9	0.7	28.1	0.7	28.0	-0.4	28.2	0.7	28.3	0.4	28.3	0.0	28.3	0.0
1957	28.3	0.0	28.4	0.4	28.4	0.0	28.6	0.7	28.7	0.3	28.9	0.7	29.0	0.3	29.1	0.3	29.0	-0.3	29.0	0.0	29.0	0.0	29.1	0.3
1958	29.4	1.0	29.5	0.3	29.7	0.7	29.7	0.0	29.7	0.0	29.6	-0.3	29.7	0.3	29.7	0.0	29.7	0.0	29.7	0.0	29.8	0.3	29.7	-0.3

[Continued]

New York, NY, NE NJ
Consumer Price Index - Urban Wage Earners
Base 1982-1984 = 100
All Items
[Continued]

For 1914-1997. Columns headed % show percentile change in the index from the previous period for which an index is available.

Year	Jan Index	%	Feb Index	%	Mar Index	%	Apr Index	%	May Index	%	Jun Index	%	Jul Index	%	Aug Index	%	Sep Index	%	Oct Index	%	Nov Index	%	Dec Index	%
1959	29.9	0.7	29.8	-0.3	29.8	0.0	29.9	0.3	29.9	0.0	30.0	0.3	30.2	0.7	30.1	-0.3	30.2	0.3	30.3	0.3	30.4	0.3	30.4	0.0
1960	30.4	0.0	30.5	0.3	30.5	0.0	30.6	0.3	30.6	0.0	30.6	0.0	30.6	0.0	30.7	0.3	30.7	0.0	30.9	0.7	31.0	0.3	30.9	-0.3
1961	30.9	0.0	30.9	0.0	30.9	0.0	30.8	-0.3	30.8	0.0	30.8	0.0	31.0	0.6	31.0	0.0	31.0	0.0	31.1	0.3	31.0	-0.3	31.1	0.3
1962	31.2	0.3	31.3	0.3	31.3	0.0	31.3	0.0	31.2	-0.3	31.2	0.0	31.4	0.6	31.5	0.3	31.7	0.6	31.6	-0.3	31.6	0.0	31.5	-0.3
1963	31.7	0.6	31.7	0.0	31.7	0.0	31.9	0.6	31.8	-0.3	32.1	0.9	32.2	0.3	32.2	0.0	32.2	0.0	32.3	0.3	32.4	0.3	32.5	0.3
1964	32.4	-0.3	32.5	0.3	32.5	0.0	32.5	0.0	32.5	0.0	32.5	0.0	32.6	0.3	32.6	0.0	32.7	0.3	32.7	0.0	32.8	0.3	32.8	0.0
1965	32.7	-0.3	32.8	0.3	32.8	0.0	32.9	0.3	33.0	0.3	33.1	0.3	33.2	0.3	33.2	0.0	33.3	0.3	33.4	0.3	33.4	0.0	33.5	0.3
1966	33.5	0.0	33.7	0.6	33.9	0.6	34.0	0.3	34.0	0.0	34.0	0.0	34.3	0.9	34.5	0.6	34.6	0.3	34.8	0.6	34.7	-0.3	34.7	0.0
1967	34.7	0.0	34.8	0.3	34.9	0.3	34.9	0.0	34.9	0.0	35.0	0.3	35.2	0.6	35.2	0.0	35.3	0.3	35.5	0.6	35.5	0.0	35.6	0.3
1968	35.7	0.3	35.9	0.6	36.0	0.3	36.1	0.3	36.3	0.6	36.5	0.6	36.7	0.5	36.9	0.5	37.2	0.8	37.3	0.3	37.4	0.3	37.5	0.3
1969	37.7	0.5	37.9	0.5	38.2	0.8	38.5	0.8	38.6	0.3	38.8	0.5	39.0	0.5	39.1	0.3	39.4	0.8	39.6	0.5	39.7	0.3	40.1	1.0
1970	40.4	0.7	40.8	1.0	41.1	0.7	41.3	0.5	41.5	0.5	41.8	0.7	41.9	0.2	42.1	0.5	42.3	0.5	42.6	0.7	42.7	0.2	43.0	0.7
1971	43.0	0.0	43.4	0.9	43.7	0.7	43.8	0.2	44.0	0.5	44.3	0.7	44.5	0.5	44.6	0.2	44.7	0.2	44.8	0.2	44.8	0.0	45.0	0.4
1972	45.2	0.4	45.5	0.7	45.7	0.4	45.8	0.2	45.9	0.2	46.0	0.2	46.1	0.2	46.3	0.4	46.7	0.9	46.8	0.2	46.8	0.0	47.0	0.4
1973	47.0	0.0	47.4	0.9	47.9	1.1	48.3	0.8	48.5	0.4	48.9	0.8	48.9	0.0	49.8	1.8	50.0	0.4	50.3	0.6	50.7	0.8	51.2	1.0
1974	51.6	0.8	52.4	1.6	53.0	1.1	53.0	0.0	53.6	1.1	54.0	0.7	54.3	0.6	55.1	1.5	55.8	1.3	56.3	0.9	56.5	0.4	56.8	0.5
1975	56.9	0.2	57.3	0.7	57.4	0.2	57.5	0.2	57.7	0.3	58.0	0.5	58.5	0.9	58.8	0.5	59.5	1.2	59.7	0.3	60.2	0.8	60.5	0.5
1976	60.7	0.3	60.9	0.3	61.1	0.3	61.2	0.2	61.4	0.3	61.8	0.7	62.1	0.5	62.4	0.5	62.7	0.5	62.9	0.3	62.9	0.0	63.1	0.3
1977	63.4	0.5	64.0	0.9	64.2	0.3	64.5	0.5	64.8	0.5	65.4	0.9	65.5	0.2	65.7	0.3	65.8	0.2	65.9	0.2	66.2	0.5	66.3	0.2
1978	66.7	0.6	67.0	0.4	67.4	0.6	67.7	0.4	68.0	0.4	68.7	1.0	68.8	0.1	69.1	0.4	69.4	0.4	70.0	0.9	70.2	0.3	70.6	0.6
1979	71.1	0.7	71.9	1.1	72.5	0.8	73.1	0.8	73.9	1.1	74.5	0.8	75.2	0.9	75.6	0.5	76.5	1.2	77.0	0.7	77.5	0.6	78.1	0.8
1980	79.2	1.4	80.0	1.0	81.1	1.4	81.6	0.6	82.2	0.7	83.1	1.1	83.7	0.7	84.5	1.0	84.8	0.4	85.2	0.5	85.8	0.7	86.8	1.2
1981	87.5	0.8	88.8	1.5	89.1	0.3	89.5	0.4	89.9	0.4	90.6	0.8	92.1	1.7	92.7	0.7	94.1	1.5	93.8	-0.3	93.7	-0.1	93.7	0.0
1982	94.0	0.3	94.1	0.1	93.4	-0.7	93.6	0.2	94.6	1.1	96.7	2.2	97.0	0.3	97.3	0.3	98.0	0.7	99.3	1.3	99.0	-0.3	98.4	-0.6
1983	98.6	0.2	98.2	-0.4	98.4	0.2	99.1	0.7	99.7	0.6	100.4	0.7	100.5	0.1	101.3	0.8	101.2	-0.1	101.4	0.2	100.9	-0.5	101.2	0.3
1984	101.9	0.7	102.0	0.1	101.8	-0.2	102.3	0.5	102.4	0.1	102.9	0.5	103.5	0.6	104.3	0.8	105.3	1.0	105.5	0.2	105.8	0.3	105.9	0.1
1985	106.1	0.2	106.6	0.5	106.8	0.2	107.2	0.4	107.4	0.2	107.6	0.2	107.6	0.0	108.4	0.7	108.6	0.2	108.8	0.2	109.8	0.9	110.1	0.3
1986	110.9	0.7	110.5	-0.4	110.5	0.0	110.0	-0.5	109.7	-0.3	110.4	0.6	111.2	0.7	111.4	0.2	111.5	0.1	111.9	0.4	111.9	0.0	112.4	0.4
1987	113.2	0.7	113.8	0.5	114.4	0.5	115.3	0.8	116.0	0.6	116.5	0.4	116.5	0.0	117.4	0.8	118.5	0.9	118.8	0.3	119.1	0.3	119.1	0.0
1988	119.6	0.4	119.3	-0.3	119.7	0.3	120.6	0.8	120.7	0.1	121.2	0.4	121.7	0.4	122.2	0.4	124.1	1.6	124.3	0.2	124.1	-0.2	124.1	0.0
1989	125.1	0.8	125.5	0.3	126.8	1.0	127.5	0.6	128.2	0.5	128.7	0.4	128.7	0.0	128.9	0.2	130.3	1.1	130.8	0.4	131.3	0.4	131.3	0.0
1990	133.0	1.3	133.1	0.1	134.5	1.1	135.0	0.4	134.9	-0.1	135.0	0.1	136.0	0.7	137.4	1.0	138.7	0.9	139.5	0.6	139.5	0.0	139.5	0.0
1991	140.3	0.6	140.6	0.2	140.5	-0.1	141.0	0.4	141.4	0.3	142.1	0.5	142.3	0.1	142.6	0.2	143.2	0.4	143.0	-0.1	144.0	0.7	143.9	-0.1
1992	144.4	0.3	144.8	0.3	145.8	0.7	145.9	0.1	145.8	-0.1	146.5	0.5	146.6	0.1	147.6	0.7	148.3	0.5	149.1	0.5	149.2	0.1	149.1	-0.1
1993	149.9	0.5	150.3	0.3	150.7	0.3	150.7	0.0	150.4	-0.2	150.7	0.2	150.7	0.0	151.7	0.7	151.8	0.1	152.1	0.2	152.0	-0.1	152.1	0.1
1994	152.4	0.2	153.5	0.7	154.0	0.3	153.9	-0.1	153.6	-0.2	154.2	0.4	154.4	0.1	155.3	0.6	155.5	0.1	156.0	0.3	155.9	-0.1	155.4	-0.3
1995	156.3	0.6	156.6	0.2	157.1	0.3	157.5	0.3	158.0	0.3	158.4	0.3	158.3	-0.1	158.9	0.4	159.5	0.4	159.7	0.1	159.9	0.1	159.9	0.0
1996	160.9	0.6	161.7	0.5	162.5	0.5	162.2	-0.2	162.8	0.4	162.8	0.0	162.8	0.0	163.3	0.3	164.4	0.7	164.4	0.0	164.7	0.2	164.7	0.0
1997	165.1	0.2	166.2	0.7	166.6	0.2	166.1	-0.3	166.0	-0.1	166.2	0.1	166.6	0.2	166.7	0.1	167.7	0.6	168.1	0.2	168.0	-0.1	167.7	-0.2

Source: U.S. Department of Labor, Bureau of Labor Statistics, Division of Consumer Prices and Price Indexes. - indicates no data collected for period.

New York, NY, NE NJ
Consumer Price Index - All Urban Consumers
Base 1982-1984 = 100
Food and Beverages

For 1976-1997. Columns headed % show percentile change in the index from the previous period for which an index is available.

Year	Jan Index	%	Feb Index	%	Mar Index	%	Apr Index	%	May Index	%	Jun Index	%	Jul Index	%	Aug Index	%	Sep Index	%	Oct Index	%	Nov Index	%	Dec Index	%
1976	62.5	-	62.3	-0.3	62.0	-0.5	62.1	0.2	62.4	0.5	62.8	0.6	63.2	0.6	63.2	0.0	63.0	-0.3	63.1	0.2	62.8	-0.5	63.2	0.6
1977	63.4	0.3	64.7	2.1	64.8	0.2	65.4	0.9	65.8	0.6	66.3	0.8	66.6	0.5	66.7	0.2	66.1	-0.9	66.2	0.2	66.8	0.9	66.8	0.0
1978	68.0	1.8	68.8	1.2	69.3	0.7	70.4	1.6	71.1	1.0	72.4	1.8	72.5	0.1	72.4	-0.1	72.4	0.0	72.8	0.6	73.3	0.7	73.6	0.4
1979	74.8	1.6	76.1	1.7	76.6	0.7	77.1	0.7	77.7	0.8	78.0	0.4	79.0	1.3	78.3	-0.9	78.9	0.8	79.5	0.8	79.6	0.1	80.3	0.9
1980	81.7	1.7	81.6	-0.1	82.6	1.2	83.3	0.8	83.6	0.4	84.2	0.7	85.1	1.1	86.6	1.8	87.3	0.8	87.6	0.3	88.4	0.9	88.7	0.3
1981	89.5	0.9	90.4	1.0	91.1	0.8	91.9	0.9	92.1	0.2	92.6	0.5	93.7	1.2	94.1	0.4	94.7	0.6	94.1	-0.6	93.8	-0.3	94.0	0.2
1982	96.0	2.1	96.8	0.8	96.9	0.1	97.0	0.1	97.3	0.3	98.6	1.3	98.3	-0.3	97.6	-0.7	97.9	0.3	97.9	0.0	96.8	-1.1	97.1	0.3
1983	97.5	0.4	98.1	0.6	98.5	0.4	98.7	0.2	98.8	0.1	98.9	0.1	98.9	0.0	99.0	0.1	99.9	0.9	99.8	-0.1	99.5	-0.3	100.3	0.8
1984	102.3	2.0	103.0	0.7	103.5	0.5	103.3	-0.2	102.9	-0.4	103.4	0.5	103.7	0.3	104.4	0.7	104.3	-0.1	104.4	0.1	104.1	-0.3	104.8	0.7
1985	105.8	1.0	106.5	0.7	106.8	0.3	107.0	0.2	106.8	-0.2	106.9	0.1	107.0	0.1	107.4	0.4	108.0	0.6	108.1	0.1	108.2	0.1	108.9	0.6
1986	110.1	1.1	109.9	-0.2	110.1	0.2	110.9	0.7	111.2	0.3	110.9	-0.3	112.8	1.7	113.6	0.7	113.5	-0.1	114.2	0.6	114.2	0.0	114.7	0.4
1987	116.3	1.4	116.5	0.2	116.8	0.3	117.2	0.3	117.8	0.5	119.2	1.2	118.9	-0.3	119.2	0.3	119.7	0.4	119.9	0.2	120.1	0.2	121.3	1.0
1988	122.5	1.0	122.7	0.2	122.5	-0.2	124.0	1.2	123.5	-0.4	124.5	0.8	125.5	0.8	126.3	0.6	126.8	0.4	126.2	-0.5	126.8	0.5	126.8	0.0
1989	129.2	1.9	130.2	0.8	130.6	0.3	131.2	0.5	132.2	0.8	132.6	0.3	133.0	0.3	133.3	0.2	133.1	-0.2	132.9	-0.2	133.4	0.4	133.7	0.2
1990	136.9	2.4	138.4	1.1	138.5	0.1	138.7	0.1	138.7	0.0	139.2	0.4	140.4	0.9	140.8	0.3	140.4	-0.3	141.1	0.5	141.1	0.0	141.2	0.1
1991	143.3	1.5	143.8	0.3	144.2	0.3	145.6	1.0	145.2	-0.3	146.1	0.6	144.6	-1.0	143.7	-0.6	143.9	0.1	143.5	-0.3	143.4	-0.1	144.1	0.5
1992	145.2	0.8	145.6	0.3	146.2	0.4	146.2	0.0	145.3	-0.6	145.8	0.3	144.9	-0.6	145.9	0.7	146.0	0.1	146.7	0.5	146.4	-0.2	147.2	0.5
1993	148.7	1.0	148.5	-0.1	148.8	0.2	149.3	0.3	149.3	0.0	147.9	-0.9	147.9	0.0	149.0	0.7	148.9	-0.1	149.1	0.1	149.9	0.5	151.0	0.7
1994	151.8	0.5	150.9	-0.6	150.8	-0.1	150.9	0.1	151.3	0.3	151.2	-0.1	152.3	0.7	152.7	0.3	152.7	0.0	152.8	0.1	152.9	0.1	153.0	0.1
1995	154.6	1.0	154.3	-0.2	154.4	0.1	156.0	1.0	155.5	-0.3	155.7	0.1	155.9	0.1	156.4	0.3	156.8	0.3	157.0	0.1	157.2	0.1	157.0	-0.1
1996	158.1	0.7	158.5	0.3	158.7	0.1	158.5	-0.1	158.8	0.2	159.7	0.6	159.4	-0.2	159.2	-0.1	160.9	1.1	161.0	0.1	161.6	0.4	161.5	-0.1
1997	161.6	0.1	162.3	0.4	162.9	0.4	162.3	-0.4	162.8	0.3	162.9	0.1	162.8	-0.1	163.1	0.2	163.5	0.2	163.5	0.0	164.4	0.6	163.9	-0.3

Source: U.S. Department of Labor, Bureau of Labor Statistics, Division of Consumer Prices and Price Indexes. - indicates no data collected for period.

New York, NY, NE NJ
Consumer Price Index - Urban Wage Earners
Base 1982-1984 = 100
Food and Beverages

For 1976-1997. Columns headed % show percentile change in the index from the previous period for which an index is available.

Year	Jan Index	%	Feb Index	%	Mar Index	%	Apr Index	%	May Index	%	Jun Index	%	Jul Index	%	Aug Index	%	Sep Index	%	Oct Index	%	Nov Index	%	Dec Index	%
1976	63.2	-	63.0	-0.3	62.7	-0.5	62.8	0.2	63.1	0.5	63.5	0.6	63.9	0.6	63.9	0.0	63.7	-0.3	63.8	0.2	63.5	-0.5	63.9	0.6
1977	64.1	0.3	65.4	2.0	65.5	0.2	66.2	1.1	66.5	0.5	67.1	0.9	67.4	0.4	67.4	0.0	66.9	-0.7	66.9	0.0	67.6	1.0	67.5	-0.1
1978	68.5	1.5	69.3	1.2	70.0	1.0	70.7	1.0	71.7	1.4	73.0	1.8	72.9	-0.1	72.9	0.0	73.0	0.1	73.6	0.8	73.9	0.4	74.4	0.7
1979	75.7	1.7	77.2	2.0	77.8	0.8	78.2	0.5	78.5	0.4	78.7	0.3	79.8	1.4	79.0	-1.0	79.4	0.5	79.7	0.4	80.0	0.4	81.0	1.3
1980	82.5	1.9	82.8	0.4	83.3	0.6	84.0	0.8	84.4	0.5	85.2	0.9	85.9	0.8	87.1	1.4	87.9	0.9	88.6	0.8	89.2	0.7	89.6	0.4
1981	90.1	0.6	91.0	1.0	91.5	0.5	92.1	0.7	92.1	0.0	92.7	0.7	93.9	1.3	94.1	0.2	94.6	0.5	94.2	-0.4	94.0	-0.2	94.1	0.1
1982	96.1	2.1	96.8	0.7	96.9	0.1	96.9	0.0	97.3	0.4	98.4	1.1	98.1	-0.3	97.4	-0.7	97.7	0.3	97.5	-0.2	96.8	-0.7	97.2	0.4
1983	97.6	0.4	98.2	0.6	98.6	0.4	98.9	0.3	99.0	0.1	99.0	0.0	98.9	-0.1	99.0	0.1	100.0	1.0	99.9	-0.1	99.6	-0.3	100.5	0.9
1984	102.5	2.0	103.2	0.7	103.6	0.4	103.4	-0.2	102.9	-0.5	103.3	0.4	103.5	0.2	104.2	0.7	104.0	-0.2	104.2	0.2	104.0	-0.2	104.8	0.8
1985	105.8	1.0	106.3	0.5	106.7	0.4	106.7	0.0	106.6	-0.1	106.7	0.1	106.7	0.0	107.0	0.3	107.5	0.5	107.6	0.1	107.9	0.3	108.8	0.8
1986	110.0	1.1	109.7	-0.3	109.9	0.2	110.7	0.7	110.9	0.2	110.7	-0.2	112.5	1.6	113.2	0.6	113.2	0.0	113.9	0.6	113.9	0.0	114.5	0.5
1987	115.9	1.2	116.1	0.2	116.4	0.3	116.8	0.3	117.4	0.5	118.8	1.2	118.5	-0.3	118.8	0.3	119.2	0.3	119.5	0.3	119.6	0.1	120.8	1.0
1988	121.9	0.9	122.1	0.2	121.9	-0.2	123.4	1.2	123.0	-0.3	124.0	0.8	125.1	0.9	125.9	0.6	126.4	0.4	125.7	-0.6	126.2	0.4	126.3	0.1
1989	128.8	2.0	129.8	0.8	130.2	0.3	130.8	0.5	131.7	0.7	132.2	0.4	132.6	0.3	133.0	0.3	132.6	-0.3	132.5	-0.1	133.0	0.4	133.1	0.1
1990	136.6	2.6	138.2	1.2	138.2	0.0	138.4	0.1	138.4	0.0	139.0	0.4	140.2	0.9	140.6	0.3	140.2	-0.3	140.9	0.5	140.9	0.0	141.0	0.1
1991	143.1	1.5	143.6	0.3	143.9	0.2	145.3	1.0	144.9	-0.3	146.0	0.8	144.4	-1.1	143.5	-0.6	143.6	0.1	143.2	-0.3	143.0	-0.1	143.7	0.5
1992	144.8	0.8	145.3	0.3	145.9	0.4	145.9	0.0	144.8	-0.8	145.4	0.4	144.5	-0.6	145.5	0.7	145.6	0.1	146.3	0.5	146.1	-0.1	146.7	0.4
1993	148.3	1.1	147.9	-0.3	148.4	0.3	148.9	0.3	148.9	0.0	147.4	-1.0	147.4	0.0	148.5	0.7	148.5	0.0	148.6	0.1	149.4	0.5	150.4	0.7
1994	151.4	0.7	150.5	-0.6	150.4	-0.1	150.5	0.1	150.9	0.3	151.0	0.1	151.9	0.6	152.4	0.3	152.2	-0.1	152.4	0.1	152.4	0.0	152.5	0.1
1995	154.1	1.0	153.7	-0.3	153.9	0.1	155.5	1.0	154.8	-0.5	155.1	0.2	155.3	0.1	155.7	0.3	156.3	0.4	156.4	0.1	156.5	0.1	156.3	-0.1
1996	157.5	0.8	157.9	0.3	158.0	0.1	157.8	-0.1	158.0	0.1	159.1	0.7	158.7	-0.3	158.4	-0.2	160.3	1.2	160.3	0.0	160.9	0.4	160.7	-0.1
1997	160.8	0.1	161.5	0.4	162.0	0.3	161.4	-0.4	161.9	0.3	162.0	0.1	161.9	-0.1	162.2	0.2	162.6	0.2	162.6	0.0	163.5	0.6	162.7	-0.5

Source: U.S. Department of Labor, Bureau of Labor Statistics, Division of Consumer Prices and Price Indexes. - indicates no data collected for period.

New York, NY, NE NJ
Consumer Price Index - All Urban Consumers
Base 1982-1984 = 100
Housing

For 1976-1997. Columns headed % show percentile change in the index from the previous period for which an index is available.

Year	Jan Index	%	Feb Index	%	Mar Index	%	Apr Index	%	May Index	%	Jun Index	%	Jul Index	%	Aug Index	%	Sep Index	%	Oct Index	%	Nov Index	%	Dec Index	%
1976	58.8	-	59.1	0.5	59.3	0.3	59.4	0.2	59.5	0.2	59.9	0.7	59.9	0.0	60.1	0.3	60.3	0.3	60.6	0.5	60.6	0.0	61.0	0.7
1977	61.6	1.0	61.8	0.3	62.2	0.6	62.4	0.3	62.6	0.3	63.2	1.0	63.2	0.0	63.4	0.3	63.7	0.5	63.8	0.2	63.9	0.2	64.1	0.3
1978	64.4	0.5	64.5	0.2	65.0	0.8	65.2	0.3	65.5	0.5	66.2	1.1	66.4	0.3	66.9	0.8	67.4	0.7	67.9	0.7	67.9	0.0	68.2	0.4
1979	68.7	0.7	69.2	0.7	69.4	0.3	70.1	1.0	70.9	1.1	71.8	1.3	72.2	0.6	73.0	1.1	74.1	1.5	74.7	0.8	75.4	0.9	75.9	0.7
1980	76.9	1.3	77.3	0.5	78.5	1.6	79.0	0.6	79.9	1.1	81.5	2.0	82.0	0.6	82.5	0.6	82.1	-0.5	82.5	0.5	83.1	0.7	84.7	1.9
1981	85.4	0.8	86.4	1.2	86.4	0.0	86.8	0.5	87.5	0.8	88.5	1.1	90.1	1.8	91.3	1.3	93.2	2.1	92.6	-0.6	92.3	-0.3	92.2	-0.1
1982	91.8	-0.4	91.4	-0.4	90.0	-1.5	90.8	0.9	92.7	2.1	95.9	3.5	96.0	0.1	96.7	0.7	97.3	0.6	100.0	2.8	99.7	-0.3	98.1	-1.6
1983	98.4	0.3	98.4	0.0	98.3	-0.1	99.7	1.4	100.0	0.3	100.4	0.4	100.8	0.4	100.4	-0.4	100.9	0.5	101.2	0.3	101.8	0.6	102.0	0.2
1984	102.7	0.7	103.5	0.8	103.3	-0.2	104.0	0.7	103.8	-0.2	104.1	0.3	104.9	0.8	105.5	0.6	106.4	0.9	105.8	-0.6	106.9	1.0	106.6	-0.3
1985	106.5	-0.1	107.1	0.6	106.9	-0.2	107.4	0.5	108.1	0.7	108.4	0.3	108.5	0.1	109.6	1.0	109.6	0.0	109.4	-0.2	111.2	1.6	111.5	0.3
1986	112.0	0.4	111.6	-0.4	112.2	0.5	112.0	-0.2	111.1	-0.8	112.7	1.4	113.7	0.9	113.9	0.2	113.7	-0.2	113.6	-0.1	113.1	-0.4	114.0	0.8
1987	115.2	1.1	115.6	0.3	115.4	-0.2	115.8	0.3	117.1	1.1	118.0	0.8	118.3	0.3	119.5	1.0	119.8	0.3	120.0	0.2	120.3	0.3	121.5	1.0
1988	123.2	1.4	122.8	-0.3	123.0	0.2	123.7	0.6	124.3	0.5	124.9	0.5	125.8	0.7	126.0	0.2	126.9	0.7	126.7	-0.2	126.9	0.2	127.1	0.2
1989	128.2	0.9	128.8	0.5	129.6	0.6	130.2	0.5	131.1	0.7	132.2	0.8	132.7	0.4	132.7	0.0	133.0	0.2	133.7	0.5	134.5	0.6	135.3	0.6
1990	136.3	0.7	135.8	-0.4	137.5	1.3	138.2	0.5	138.3	0.1	138.3	0.0	140.3	1.4	142.1	1.3	141.4	-0.5	141.2	-0.1	140.8	-0.3	141.1	0.2
1991	143.6	1.8	144.8	0.8	144.4	-0.3	144.2	-0.1	144.4	0.1	145.5	0.8	147.4	1.3	147.3	-0.1	146.6	-0.5	145.7	-0.6	147.2	1.0	147.4	0.1
1992	148.3	0.6	149.4	0.7	150.9	1.0	150.8	-0.1	150.2	-0.4	151.6	0.9	152.4	0.5	152.9	0.3	152.6	-0.2	152.6	0.0	152.6	0.0	152.2	-0.3
1993	153.5	0.9	153.8	0.2	154.7	0.6	154.6	-0.1	154.7	0.1	156.5	1.2	156.7	0.1	157.2	0.3	156.4	-0.5	156.2	-0.1	155.6	-0.4	156.3	0.4
1994	157.1	0.5	159.8	1.7	160.3	0.3	159.2	-0.7	158.8	-0.3	159.5	0.4	160.4	0.6	161.8	0.9	160.9	-0.6	160.7	-0.1	160.0	-0.4	159.7	-0.2
1995	160.9	0.8	161.5	0.4	162.0	0.3	162.4	0.2	162.8	0.2	163.9	0.7	165.0	0.7	165.0	0.0	164.1	-0.5	164.2	0.1	164.4	0.1	164.6	0.1
1996	166.6	1.2	166.9	0.2	167.4	0.3	166.4	-0.6	166.7	0.2	167.4	0.4	168.4	0.6	168.9	0.3	168.3	-0.4	168.2	-0.1	168.2	0.0	168.9	0.4
1997	169.8	0.5	170.9	0.6	171.2	0.2	170.5	-0.4	170.2	-0.2	171.3	0.6	172.5	0.7	172.7	0.1	172.5	-0.1	172.6	0.1	172.7	0.1	173.4	0.4

Source: U.S. Department of Labor, Bureau of Labor Statistics, Division of Consumer Prices and Price Indexes. - indicates no data collected for period.

New York, NY, NE NJ
Consumer Price Index - Urban Wage Earners
Base 1982-1984 = 100
Housing

For 1976-1997. Columns headed % show percentile change in the index from the previous period for which an index is available.

Year	Jan Index	%	Feb Index	%	Mar Index	%	Apr Index	%	May Index	%	Jun Index	%	Jul Index	%	Aug Index	%	Sep Index	%	Oct Index	%	Nov Index	%	Dec Index	%
1976	60.6	-	60.9	0.5	61.0	0.2	61.1	0.2	61.2	0.2	61.7	0.8	61.7	0.0	61.8	0.2	62.1	0.5	62.4	0.5	62.4	0.0	62.8	0.6
1977	63.3	0.8	63.6	0.5	64.0	0.6	64.2	0.3	64.4	0.3	65.1	1.1	65.0	-0.2	65.3	0.5	65.5	0.3	65.6	0.2	65.7	0.2	66.0	0.5
1978	66.3	0.5	66.4	0.2	66.7	0.5	66.8	0.1	66.8	0.0	67.5	1.0	67.8	0.4	68.1	0.4	68.5	0.6	69.0	0.7	69.1	0.1	69.5	0.6
1979	70.0	0.7	70.5	0.7	70.8	0.4	71.4	0.8	72.4	1.4	73.3	1.2	73.7	0.5	74.4	0.9	75.6	1.6	76.4	1.1	77.0	0.8	77.5	0.6
1980	78.5	1.3	79.0	0.6	79.9	1.1	80.6	0.9	81.4	1.0	83.2	2.2	83.7	0.6	84.3	0.7	83.6	-0.8	84.0	0.5	84.7	0.8	86.6	2.2
1981	87.2	0.7	88.5	1.5	88.4	-0.1	88.5	0.1	89.2	0.8	90.4	1.3	92.2	2.0	93.3	1.2	95.4	2.3	94.8	-0.6	94.5	-0.3	94.3	-0.2
1982	93.9	-0.4	93.4	-0.5	91.6	-1.9	92.5	1.0	94.6	2.3	98.1	3.7	98.3	0.2	99.0	0.7	99.6	0.6	102.5	2.9	102.3	-0.2	100.5	-1.8
1983	100.6	0.1	99.1	-1.5	99.5	0.4	99.9	0.4	100.7	0.8	102.3	1.6	102.0	-0.3	103.3	1.3	101.5	-1.7	101.6	0.1	100.0	-1.6	100.5	0.5
1984	100.2	-0.3	99.8	-0.4	98.4	-1.4	99.5	1.1	99.6	0.1	100.6	1.0	101.8	1.2	102.8	1.0	104.7	1.8	104.8	0.1	105.4	0.6	105.3	-0.1
1985	105.2	-0.1	105.9	0.7	105.6	-0.3	106.1	0.5	106.7	0.6	107.1	0.4	107.0	-0.1	108.1	1.0	108.0	-0.1	108.0	0.0	109.7	1.6	110.2	0.5
1986	110.6	0.4	110.1	-0.5	110.8	0.6	110.4	-0.4	109.4	-0.9	111.1	1.6	112.0	0.8	112.2	0.2	112.0	-0.2	111.8	-0.2	111.3	-0.4	112.1	0.7
1987	113.1	0.9	113.5	0.4	113.3	-0.2	113.9	0.5	115.2	1.1	116.1	0.8	116.3	0.2	117.4	0.9	117.7	0.3	117.9	0.2	118.2	0.3	119.3	0.9
1988	120.6	1.1	120.2	-0.3	120.4	0.2	120.8	0.3	121.4	0.5	122.5	0.9	123.3	0.7	123.4	0.1	124.2	0.6	123.9	-0.2	124.3	0.3	124.5	0.2
1989	125.5	0.8	125.9	0.3	126.4	0.4	127.4	0.8	128.1	0.5	129.4	1.0	129.9	0.4	129.9	0.0	130.4	0.4	130.9	0.4	131.9	0.8	132.7	0.6
1990	133.3	0.5	132.8	-0.4	134.5	1.3	135.0	0.4	135.1	0.1	135.2	0.1	136.6	1.0	138.0	1.0	137.9	-0.1	137.8	-0.1	137.4	-0.3	137.6	0.1
1991	139.4	1.3	140.2	0.6	139.9	-0.2	140.1	0.1	140.7	0.4	141.7	0.7	143.1	1.0	142.9	-0.1	142.6	-0.2	141.8	-0.6	143.4	1.1	143.5	0.1
1992	144.0	0.3	144.8	0.6	146.0	0.8	146.1	0.1	145.8	-0.2	147.0	0.8	147.5	0.3	147.9	0.3	147.7	-0.1	147.9	0.1	148.1	0.1	148.0	-0.1
1993	149.0	0.7	149.1	0.1	149.8	0.5	149.9	0.1	149.9	0.0	151.6	1.1	151.7	0.1	152.0	0.2	151.4	-0.4	151.1	-0.2	150.6	-0.3	151.4	0.5
1994	151.9	0.3	154.3	1.6	154.9	0.4	154.0	-0.6	153.5	-0.3	154.1	0.4	154.9	0.5	156.2	0.8	156.0	-0.1	155.6	-0.3	155.1	-0.3	154.9	-0.1
1995	155.9	0.6	156.3	0.3	156.7	0.3	157.1	0.3	157.5	0.3	158.4	0.6	159.2	0.5	159.2	0.0	158.8	-0.3	158.7	-0.1	159.1	0.3	159.4	0.2
1996	160.9	0.9	161.1	0.1	161.7	0.4	160.8	-0.6	161.4	0.4	162.0	0.4	162.8	0.5	163.3	0.3	163.1	-0.1	162.9	-0.1	163.0	0.1	163.8	0.5
1997	164.2	0.2	165.2	0.6	165.3	0.1	164.7	-0.4	164.8	0.1	165.7	0.5	166.5	0.5	166.7	0.1	166.8	0.1	166.6	-0.1	166.9	0.2	167.6	0.4

Source: U.S. Department of Labor, Bureau of Labor Statistics, Division of Consumer Prices and Price Indexes. - indicates no data collected for period.

New York, NY, NE NJ
Consumer Price Index - All Urban Consumers
Base 1982-1984 = 100
Apparel and Upkeep

For 1952-1997. Columns headed % show percentile change in the index from the previous period for which an index is available.

Year	Jan Index	%	Feb Index	%	Mar Index	%	Apr Index	%	May Index	%	Jun Index	%	Jul Index	%	Aug Index	%	Sep Index	%	Oct Index	%	Nov Index	%	Dec Index	%
1952	-	-	-	-	-	-	-	-	-	-	-	-	-	-	-	-	-	-	-	-	-	-	45.1	-
1953	45.0	-0.2	44.9	-0.2	45.0	0.2	44.7	-0.7	44.8	0.2	44.7	-0.2	44.6	-0.2	44.5	-0.2	45.1	1.3	45.1	0.0	45.1	0.0	45.0	-0.2
1954	44.8	-0.4	44.7	-0.2	44.6	-0.2	44.4	-0.4	44.4	0.0	44.4	0.0	44.2	-0.5	44.2	0.0	44.6	0.9	44.5	-0.2	44.6	0.2	44.3	-0.7
1955	43.8	-1.1	43.7	-0.2	43.7	0.0	43.5	-0.5	43.6	0.2	43.5	-0.2	43.3	-0.5	43.5	0.5	44.5	2.3	44.5	0.0	44.6	0.2	44.6	0.0
1956	44.2	-0.9	44.5	0.7	44.5	0.0	44.6	0.2	44.5	-0.2	44.7	0.4	44.8	0.2	44.8	0.0	45.6	1.8	45.8	0.4	45.7	-0.2	45.7	0.0
1957	45.5	-0.4	45.2	-0.7	45.7	1.1	45.4	-0.7	45.6	0.4	45.7	0.2	45.6	-0.2	45.7	0.2	46.0	0.7	46.1	0.2	46.2	0.2	46.1	-0.2
1958	46.2	0.2	46.2	0.0	46.2	0.0	45.9	-0.6	45.8	-0.2	45.8	0.0	45.8	0.0	46.0	0.4	46.3	0.7	46.1	-0.4	46.3	0.4	46.2	-0.2
1959	46.0	-0.4	46.0	0.0	46.1	0.2	46.0	-0.2	46.0	0.0	46.1	0.2	46.3	0.4	46.5	0.4	46.6	0.2	46.7	0.2	46.9	0.4	46.9	0.0
1960	46.6	-0.6	46.8	0.4	47.1	0.6	47.2	0.2	47.1	-0.2	47.1	0.0	47.0	-0.2	47.1	0.2	47.7	1.3	48.0	0.6	47.9	-0.2	48.0	0.2
1961	47.6	-0.8	47.6	0.0	47.5	-0.2	47.4	-0.2	47.3	-0.2	47.3	0.0	47.4	0.2	47.7	0.6	48.2	1.0	48.4	0.4	48.4	0.0	48.3	-0.2
1962	47.8	-1.0	47.8	0.0	48.0	0.4	47.9	-0.2	47.7	-0.4	47.9	0.4	48.0	0.2	47.8	-0.4	48.9	2.3	49.1	0.4	49.0	-0.2	48.9	-0.2
1963	48.8	-0.2	48.7	-0.2	48.7	0.0	48.8	0.2	48.5	-0.6	49.0	1.0	49.2	0.4	49.2	0.0	50.0	1.6	50.1	0.2	50.1	0.0	50.2	0.2
1964	49.2	-2.0	49.6	0.8	49.9	0.6	49.8	-0.2	50.0	0.4	49.9	-0.2	49.8	-0.2	49.6	-0.4	50.6	2.0	50.4	-0.4	50.4	0.0	50.6	0.4
1965	49.4	-2.4	50.1	1.4	50.2	0.2	50.2	0.0	50.4	0.4	50.6	0.4	50.0	-1.2	50.6	1.2	51.7	2.2	51.8	0.2	51.6	-0.4	51.4	-0.4
1966	50.3	-2.1	50.8	1.0	51.3	1.0	51.4	0.2	51.7	0.6	51.5	-0.4	51.4	-0.2	51.0	-0.8	53.0	3.9	53.4	0.8	53.3	-0.2	53.4	0.2
1967	52.4	-1.9	53.3	1.7	54.1	1.5	53.9	-0.4	54.3	0.7	54.3	0.0	54.3	0.0	54.1	-0.4	55.5	2.6	55.8	0.5	55.8	0.0	55.8	0.0
1968	54.7	-2.0	55.6	1.6	56.3	1.3	56.5	0.4	57.0	0.9	57.3	0.5	56.9	-0.7	57.5	1.1	59.4	3.3	59.6	0.3	59.9	0.5	60.0	0.2
1969	58.9	-1.8	59.4	0.8	60.8	2.4	60.8	0.0	61.2	0.7	61.3	0.2	61.1	-0.3	60.8	-0.5	62.9	3.5	63.1	0.3	63.2	0.2	63.0	-0.3
1970	61.6	-2.2	63.0	2.3	63.3	0.5	63.1	-0.3	63.5	0.6	63.8	0.5	63.0	-1.3	63.6	1.0	65.9	3.6	65.9	0.0	65.9	0.0	66.0	0.2
1971	64.2	-2.7	65.0	1.2	65.5	0.8	65.0	-0.8	65.7	1.1	65.5	-0.3	64.8	-1.1	64.8	0.0	67.0	3.4	66.9	-0.1	66.7	-0.3	66.7	0.0
1972	65.0	-2.5	66.5	2.3	67.5	1.5	67.3	-0.3	67.3	0.0	66.2	-1.6	65.5	-1.1	65.4	-0.2	68.5	4.7	68.5	0.0	68.4	-0.1	68.3	-0.1
1973	65.1	-4.7	66.3	1.8	68.4	3.2	68.5	0.1	69.0	0.7	68.6	-0.6	67.5	-1.6	68.6	1.6	70.4	2.6	70.7	0.4	71.1	0.6	71.0	-0.1
1974	68.5	-3.5	70.8	3.4	72.9	3.0	72.2	-1.0	73.3	1.5	73.3	0.0	72.3	-1.4	76.1	5.3	77.6	2.0	77.9	0.4	78.2	0.4	76.9	-1.7
1975	75.1	-2.3	77.0	2.5	77.0	0.0	76.2	-1.0	76.6	0.5	75.3	-1.7	75.1	-0.3	77.4	3.1	78.3	1.2	78.3	0.0	78.4	0.1	77.6	-1.0
1976	76.2	-1.8	77.6	1.8	77.7	0.1	77.8	0.1	77.9	0.1	77.4	-0.6	77.4	0.0	80.1	3.5	81.7	2.0	80.9	-1.0	81.3	0.5	81.3	0.0
1977	79.3	-2.5	79.4	0.1	79.5	0.1	79.4	-0.1	79.9	0.6	81.0	1.4	80.8	-0.2	82.7	2.4	83.3	0.7	83.0	-0.4	83.9	1.1	83.6	-0.4
1978	81.8	-2.2	82.2	0.5	83.7	1.8	85.6	2.3	86.2	0.7	86.5	0.3	84.0	-2.9	84.8	1.0	86.2	1.7	87.0	0.9	86.9	-0.1	86.5	-0.5
1979	83.6	-3.4	85.0	1.7	86.7	2.0	86.6	-0.1	87.5	1.0	85.9	-1.8	84.2	-2.0	86.2	2.4	88.4	2.6	88.9	0.6	88.8	-0.1	89.8	1.1
1980	88.5	-1.4	90.3	2.0	92.1	2.0	92.6	0.5	92.4	-0.2	92.3	-0.1	91.2	-1.2	91.9	0.8	94.1	2.4	95.8	1.8	95.8	0.0	95.3	-0.5
1981	93.3	-2.1	95.7	2.6	96.2	0.5	96.6	0.4	96.4	-0.2	95.9	-0.5	95.5	-0.4	96.9	1.5	98.4	1.5	97.1	-1.3	97.1	0.0	96.3	-0.8
1982	94.0	-2.4	96.5	2.7	97.7	1.2	97.5	-0.2	97.0	-0.5	97.2	0.2	97.1	-0.1	97.9	0.8	99.1	1.2	99.0	-0.1	98.2	-0.8	97.3	-0.9
1983	96.7	-0.6	97.9	1.2	99.6	1.7	100.2	0.6	101.9	1.7	100.9	-1.0	100.0	-0.9	100.9	0.9	102.9	2.0	103.2	0.3	102.3	-0.9	100.6	-1.7
1984	99.4	-1.2	99.0	-0.4	101.2	2.2	101.0	-0.2	101.9	0.9	100.3	-1.6	99.4	-0.9	103.9	4.5	104.9	1.0	105.5	0.6	105.0	-0.5	102.9	-2.0
1985	101.2	-1.7	102.8	1.6	104.5	1.7	104.6	0.1	103.6	-1.0	101.9	-1.6	101.6	-0.3	106.7	5.0	107.0	0.3	107.1	0.1	107.4	0.3	105.3	-2.0
1986	103.4	-1.8	102.7	-0.7	103.8	1.1	104.5	0.7	103.9	-0.6	102.4	-1.4	100.9	-1.5	104.3	3.4	107.2	2.8	106.3	-0.8	105.6	-0.7	105.2	-0.4
1987	102.7	-2.4	105.7	2.9	110.4	4.4	112.9	2.3	112.0	-0.8	108.0	-3.6	105.0	-2.8	108.8	3.6	115.2	5.9	115.6	0.3	115.4	-0.2	106.9	-7.4
1988	102.0	-4.6	100.2	-1.8	105.0	4.8	108.9	3.7	106.9	-1.8	103.6	-3.1	100.3	-3.2	102.4	2.1	116.2	13.5	119.9	3.2	112.7	-6.0	111.0	-1.5
1989	107.3	-3.3	108.1	0.7	117.4	8.6	117.0	-0.3	114.5	-2.1	110.7	-3.3	106.7	-3.6	108.7	1.9	120.8	11.1	121.7	0.7	119.8	-1.6	114.7	-4.3
1990	116.9	1.9	116.2	-0.6	122.6	5.5	126.0	2.8	122.1	-3.1	117.7	-3.6	115.1	-2.2	121.2	5.3	126.9	4.7	128.0	0.9	126.1	-1.5	122.9	-2.5
1991	121.0	-1.5	121.9	0.7	123.4	1.2	123.5	0.1	124.0	0.4	122.8	-1.0	120.6	-1.8	123.7	2.6	127.3	2.9	129.5	1.7	130.6	0.8	125.8	-3.7
1992	123.7	-1.7	123.4	-0.2	127.0	2.9	127.1	0.1	127.3	0.2	124.6	-2.1	124.5	-0.1	128.8	3.5	136.1	5.7	135.6	-0.4	134.1	-1.1	129.7	-3.3
1993	126.8	-2.2	133.8	5.5	134.2	0.3	131.7	-1.9	126.8	-3.7	124.6	-1.7	123.4	-1.0	128.5	4.1	132.4	3.0	133.0	0.5	131.4	-1.2	125.3	-4.6
1994	122.2	-2.5	125.9	3.0	129.5	2.9	131.7	1.7	128.4	-2.5	127.7	-0.5	123.4	-3.4	123.4	0.0	126.4	2.4	127.2	0.6	127.2	0.0	121.7	-4.3

[Continued]

New York, NY, NE NJ
Consumer Price Index - All Urban Consumers
Base 1982-1984 = 100
Apparel and Upkeep

[Continued]

For 1952-1997. Columns headed % show percentile change in the index from the previous period for which an index is available.

Year	Jan Index	%	Feb Index	%	Mar Index	%	Apr Index	%	May Index	%	Jun Index	%	Jul Index	%	Aug Index	%	Sep Index	%	Oct Index	%	Nov Index	%	Dec Index	%
1995	122.9	1.0	123.9	0.8	127.9	3.2	127.5	-0.3	127.3	-0.2	123.5	-3.0	119.0	-3.6	123.1	3.4	129.1	4.9	130.5	1.1	130.2	-0.2	126.7	-2.7
1996	123.6	-2.4	128.0	3.6	131.7	2.9	130.4	-1.0	130.1	-0.2	124.9	-4.0	122.0	-2.3	124.7	2.2	132.4	6.2	130.7	-1.3	128.8	-1.5	125.2	-2.8
1997	125.5	0.2	131.1	4.5	134.4	2.5	132.4	-1.5	130.9	-1.1	126.4	-3.4	126.8	0.3	127.0	0.2	132.0	3.9	135.5	2.7	133.1	-1.8	128.9	-3.2

Source: U.S. Department of Labor, Bureau of Labor Statistics, Division of Consumer Prices and Price Indexes. - indicates no data collected for period.

New York, NY, NE NJ
Consumer Price Index - Urban Wage Earners
Base 1982-1984 = 100
Apparel and Upkeep

For 1952-1997. Columns headed % show percentile change in the index from the previous period for which an index is available.

Year	Jan Index	%	Feb Index	%	Mar Index	%	Apr Index	%	May Index	%	Jun Index	%	Jul Index	%	Aug Index	%	Sep Index	%	Oct Index	%	Nov Index	%	Dec Index	%
1952	-	-	-	-	-	-	-	-	-	-	-	-	-	-	-	-	-	-	-	-	-	-	45.0	-
1953	45.0	0.0	44.9	-0.2	44.9	0.0	44.7	-0.4	44.7	0.0	44.7	0.0	44.5	-0.4	44.4	-0.2	45.0	1.4	45.0	0.0	45.0	0.0	44.9	-0.2
1954	44.7	-0.4	44.7	0.0	44.5	-0.4	44.4	-0.2	44.4	0.0	44.3	-0.2	44.2	-0.2	44.1	-0.2	44.5	0.9	44.4	-0.2	44.5	0.2	44.3	-0.4
1955	43.7	-1.4	43.6	-0.2	43.7	0.2	43.5	-0.5	43.5	0.0	43.4	-0.2	43.2	-0.5	43.4	0.5	44.4	2.3	44.4	0.0	44.5	0.2	44.5	0.0
1956	44.1	-0.9	44.4	0.7	44.4	0.0	44.5	0.2	44.4	-0.2	44.6	0.5	44.7	0.2	44.7	0.0	45.5	1.8	45.7	0.4	45.6	-0.2	45.6	0.0
1957	45.5	-0.2	45.1	-0.9	45.6	1.1	45.4	-0.4	45.6	0.4	45.6	0.0	45.6	0.0	45.6	0.0	45.9	0.7	46.0	0.2	46.1	0.2	46.0	-0.2
1958	46.1	0.2	46.2	0.2	46.2	0.0	45.8	-0.9	45.7	-0.2	45.7	0.0	45.7	0.0	45.9	0.4	46.2	0.7	46.1	-0.2	46.2	0.2	46.2	0.0
1959	45.9	-0.6	45.9	0.0	46.0	0.2	46.0	0.0	46.0	0.0	46.1	0.2	46.2	0.2	46.4	0.4	46.5	0.2	46.6	0.2	46.8	0.4	46.8	0.0
1960	46.5	-0.6	46.7	0.4	47.0	0.6	47.1	0.2	47.0	-0.2	47.0	0.0	46.9	-0.2	47.0	0.2	47.6	1.3	47.9	0.6	47.9	0.0	47.9	0.0
1961	47.5	-0.8	47.5	0.0	47.4	-0.2	47.3	-0.2	47.2	-0.2	47.3	0.2	47.4	0.2	47.6	0.4	48.1	1.1	48.3	0.4	48.4	0.2	48.2	-0.4
1962	47.7	-1.0	47.8	0.2	47.9	0.2	47.8	-0.2	47.6	-0.4	47.8	0.4	48.0	0.4	47.8	-0.4	48.8	2.1	49.1	0.6	48.9	-0.4	48.8	-0.2
1963	48.7	-0.2	48.6	-0.2	48.6	0.0	48.7	0.2	48.5	-0.4	48.9	0.8	49.1	0.4	49.2	0.2	49.9	1.4	50.0	0.2	50.0	0.0	50.1	0.2
1964	49.2	-1.8	49.5	0.6	49.8	0.6	49.8	0.0	49.9	0.2	49.8	-0.2	49.8	0.0	49.5	-0.6	50.5	2.0	50.4	-0.2	50.3	-0.2	50.5	0.4
1965	49.3	-2.4	50.0	1.4	50.1	0.2	50.1	0.0	50.4	0.6	50.5	0.2	49.9	-1.2	50.5	1.2	51.6	2.2	51.7	0.2	51.6	-0.2	51.3	-0.6
1966	50.3	-1.9	50.7	0.8	51.2	1.0	51.3	0.2	51.7	0.8	51.4	-0.6	51.3	-0.2	51.0	-0.6	52.9	3.7	53.3	0.8	53.2	-0.2	53.3	0.2
1967	52.3	-1.9	53.2	1.7	54.1	1.7	53.8	-0.6	54.2	0.7	54.2	0.0	54.2	0.0	54.1	-0.2	55.4	2.4	55.7	0.5	55.7	0.0	55.7	0.0
1968	54.6	-2.0	55.5	1.6	56.2	1.3	56.5	0.5	56.9	0.7	57.2	0.5	56.8	-0.7	57.4	1.1	59.3	3.3	59.5	0.3	59.8	0.5	59.9	0.2
1969	58.8	-1.8	59.3	0.9	60.8	2.5	60.8	0.0	61.1	0.5	61.2	0.2	61.0	-0.3	60.8	-0.3	62.8	3.3	63.0	0.3	63.1	0.2	62.9	-0.3
1970	61.5	-2.2	62.9	2.3	63.2	0.5	63.0	-0.3	63.4	0.6	63.7	0.5	62.9	-1.3	63.5	1.0	65.8	3.6	65.8	0.0	65.8	0.0	65.9	0.2
1971	64.1	-2.7	64.9	1.2	65.4	0.8	64.9	-0.8	65.6	1.1	65.4	-0.3	64.7	-1.1	64.7	0.0	66.9	3.4	66.8	-0.1	66.6	-0.3	66.6	0.0
1972	64.9	-2.6	66.4	2.3	67.4	1.5	67.2	-0.3	67.2	0.0	66.1	-1.6	65.4	-1.1	65.3	-0.2	68.4	4.7	68.4	0.0	68.3	-0.1	68.1	-0.3
1973	65.0	-4.6	66.2	1.8	68.3	3.2	68.4	0.1	68.9	0.7	68.5	-0.6	67.4	-1.6	68.5	1.6	70.3	2.6	70.6	0.4	71.0	0.6	70.9	-0.1
1974	68.4	-3.5	70.7	3.4	72.8	3.0	72.1	-1.0	73.2	1.5	73.2	0.0	72.2	-1.4	76.0	5.3	77.5	2.0	77.8	0.4	78.1	0.4	76.7	-1.8
1975	75.0	-2.2	76.9	2.5	76.9	0.0	76.0	-1.2	76.5	0.7	75.2	-1.7	75.0	-0.3	77.2	2.9	78.2	1.3	78.2	0.0	78.3	0.1	77.5	-1.0
1976	76.1	-1.8	77.4	1.7	77.6	0.3	77.7	0.1	77.8	0.1	77.2	-0.8	77.2	0.0	80.0	3.6	81.5	1.9	80.8	-0.9	81.2	0.5	81.1	-0.1
1977	79.1	-2.5	79.3	0.3	79.4	0.1	79.2	-0.3	79.7	0.6	80.9	1.5	80.7	-0.2	82.6	2.4	83.2	0.7	82.8	-0.5	83.8	1.2	83.5	-0.4
1978	81.7	-2.2	82.2	0.6	83.2	1.2	84.7	1.8	84.7	0.0	84.6	-0.1	83.1	-1.8	84.1	1.2	84.6	0.6	85.7	1.3	85.4	-0.4	84.8	-0.7
1979	82.9	-2.2	85.0	2.5	86.9	2.2	87.4	0.6	88.1	0.8	86.2	-2.2	85.4	-0.9	87.2	2.1	89.1	2.2	89.7	0.7	89.7	0.0	90.4	0.8
1980	88.1	-2.5	89.2	1.2	92.7	3.9	92.8	0.1	94.1	1.4	92.5	-1.7	91.6	-1.0	93.9	2.5	95.8	2.0	96.1	0.3	95.8	-0.3	95.6	-0.2
1981	94.7	-0.9	95.3	0.6	95.4	0.1	95.4	0.0	96.1	0.7	95.5	-0.6	95.3	-0.2	97.0	1.8	98.0	1.0	96.8	-1.2	96.3	-0.5	95.9	-0.4
1982	94.0	-2.0	96.4	2.6	97.6	1.2	97.6	0.0	97.0	-0.6	97.1	0.1	96.8	-0.3	97.6	0.8	98.8	1.2	98.9	0.1	97.8	-1.1	97.3	-0.5
1983	96.8	-0.5	98.0	1.2	99.5	1.5	100.3	0.8	102.1	1.8	101.0	-1.1	99.9	-1.1	100.8	0.9	102.8	2.0	103.1	0.3	102.2	-0.9	100.7	-1.5
1984	99.5	-1.2	99.3	-0.2	101.3	2.0	101.1	-0.2	101.8	0.7	100.2	-1.6	99.3	-0.9	104.0	4.7	105.2	1.2	105.6	0.4	105.1	-0.5	103.2	-1.8
1985	101.5	-1.6	102.7	1.2	104.5	1.8	104.6	0.1	103.3	-1.2	101.6	-1.6	101.0	-0.6	106.6	5.5	107.2	0.6	107.1	-0.1	107.4	0.3	105.3	-2.0
1986	103.2	-2.0	102.5	-0.7	103.4	0.9	104.2	0.8	103.4	-0.8	101.7	-1.6	100.6	-1.1	104.3	3.7	107.3	2.9	106.1	-1.1	105.8	-0.3	105.5	-0.3
1987	103.2	-2.2	105.9	2.6	111.3	5.1	114.1	2.5	113.0	-1.0	108.5	-4.0	105.1	-3.1	108.0	2.8	115.3	6.8	115.8	0.4	115.8	0.0	106.7	-7.9
1988	101.3	-5.1	98.8	-2.5	104.3	5.6	108.0	3.5	106.0	-1.9	102.3	-3.5	98.8	-3.4	100.5	1.7	115.1	14.5	118.7	3.1	111.6	-6.0	109.9	-1.5
1989	106.2	-3.4	106.4	0.2	116.2	9.2	115.6	-0.5	112.8	-2.4	109.0	-3.4	104.9	-3.8	106.8	1.8	119.6	12.0	120.3	0.6	118.8	-1.2	113.3	-4.6
1990	115.2	1.7	113.9	-1.1	121.1	6.3	124.4	2.7	120.3	-3.3	116.0	-3.6	113.2	-2.4	119.0	5.1	125.8	.5.7	126.4	0.5	124.6	-1.4	121.1	-2.8
1991	119.0	-1.7	119.2	0.2	121.1	1.6	121.1	0.0	121.4	0.2	120.4	-0.8	117.7	-2.2	121.8	3.5	124.8	2.5	126.8	1.6	127.9	0.9	123.5	-3.4
1992	120.9	-2.1	119.4	-1.2	123.6	3.5	123.3	-0.2	124.3	0.8	121.7	-2.1	121.8	0.1	126.8	4.1	133.8	5.5	134.0	0.1	132.1	-1.4	127.9	-3.2
1993	124.6	-2.6	131.2	5.3	131.5	0.2	128.3	-2.4	123.1	-4.1	121.0	-1.7	119.5	-1.2	124.7	4.4	129.1	3.5	130.1	0.8	128.6	-1.2	122.1	-5.1
1994	119.5	-2.1	123.4	3.3	126.4	2.4	128.1	1.3	124.6	-2.7	124.2	-0.3	119.6	-3.7	119.9	0.3	122.3	2.0	122.9	0.5	123.5	0.5	117.7	-4.7

[Continued]

New York, NY, NE NJ
Consumer Price Index - Urban Wage Earners
Base 1982-1984 = 100
Apparel and Upkeep

[Continued]

For 1952-1997. Columns headed % show percentile change in the index from the previous period for which an index is available.

Year	Jan Index	%	Feb Index	%	Mar Index	%	Apr Index	%	May Index	%	Jun Index	%	Jul Index	%	Aug Index	%	Sep Index	%	Oct Index	%	Nov Index	%	Dec Index	%
1995	119.2	1.3	120.0	0.7	123.6	3.0	123.2	-0.3	123.2	0.0	119.6	-2.9	114.5	-4.3	119.3	4.2	125.5	5.2	126.1	0.5	125.5	-0.5	122.0	-2.8
1996	119.8	-1.8	124.2	3.7	127.6	2.7	126.8	-0.6	126.4	-0.3	121.0	-4.3	118.3	-2.2	120.0	1.4	127.9	6.6	126.4	-1.2	124.4	-1.6	120.6	-3.1
1997	120.8	0.2	127.4	5.5	130.4	2.4	128.0	-1.8	126.9	-0.9	122.5	-3.5	123.6	0.9	123.5	-0.1	127.7	3.4	130.3	2.0	129.3	-0.8	124.5	-3.7

Source: U.S. Department of Labor, Bureau of Labor Statistics, Division of Consumer Prices and Price Indexes. - indicates no data collected for period.

New York, NY, NE NJ
Consumer Price Index - All Urban Consumers
Base 1982-1984 = 100
Transportation

For 1947-1997. Columns headed % show percentile change in the index from the previous period for which an index is available.

Year	Jan Index	%	Feb Index	%	Mar Index	%	Apr Index	%	May Index	%	Jun Index	%	Jul Index	%	Aug Index	%	Sep Index	%	Oct Index	%	Nov Index	%	Dec Index	%
1947	15.8	-	15.8	0.0	15.8	0.0	15.9	0.6	16.0	0.6	16.0	0.0	16.1	0.6	16.1	0.0	16.2	0.6	16.2	0.0	16.3	0.6	16.5	1.2
1948	16.5	0.0	16.5	0.0	16.5	0.0	16.5	0.0	16.5	0.0	16.5	0.0	20.9	26.7	21.1	1.0	21.2	0.5	21.3	0.5	21.3	0.0	21.3	0.0
1949	21.4	0.5	21.4	0.0	21.4	0.0	21.5	0.5	21.5	0.0	21.5	0.0	21.5	0.0	21.5	0.0	21.5	0.0	21.5	0.0	21.5	0.0	21.6	0.5
1950	21.6	0.0	21.6	0.0	21.6	0.0	21.6	0.0	21.6	0.0	21.6	0.0	23.1	6.9	23.2	0.4	23.2	0.0	23.2	0.0	23.3	0.4	23.3	0.0
1951	23.3	0.0	23.3	0.0	23.4	0.4	23.4	0.0	23.4	0.0	23.4	0.0	23.5	0.4	23.5	0.0	23.6	0.4	23.7	0.4	23.8	0.4	23.8	0.0
1952	23.8	0.0	23.9	0.4	23.9	0.0	23.9	0.0	23.9	0.0	23.9	0.0	23.9	0.0	23.9	0.0	24.0	0.4	24.0	0.0	24.0	0.0	24.0	0.0
1953	24.0	0.0	23.9	-0.4	23.9	0.0	23.9	0.0	23.9	0.0	24.0	0.4	24.2	0.8	25.2	4.1	25.2	0.0	25.2	0.0	25.1	-0.4	25.1	0.0
1954	25.5	1.6	25.4	-0.4	25.3	-0.4	25.2	-0.4	25.2	0.0	25.3	0.4	24.3	-4.0	24.2	-0.4	24.3	0.4	24.4	0.4	24.7	1.2	24.6	-0.4
1955	24.4	-0.8	24.4	0.0	24.4	0.0	24.3	-0.4	24.2	-0.4	24.2	0.0	23.9	-1.2	23.8	-0.4	23.8	0.0	24.0	0.8	24.6	2.5	24.3	-1.2
1956	24.5	0.8	24.7	0.8	24.6	-0.4	24.7	0.4	24.7	0.0	24.7	0.0	24.8	0.4	25.1	1.2	25.0	-0.4	25.9	3.6	25.7	-0.8	25.7	0.0
1957	25.7	0.0	25.9	0.8	25.9	0.0	26.0	0.4	26.0	0.0	26.0	0.0	25.8	-0.8	25.8	0.0	25.8	0.0	25.7	-0.4	26.3	2.3	26.2	-0.4
1958	26.2	0.0	26.1	-0.4	26.1	0.0	26.2	0.4	26.2	0.0	26.1	-0.4	26.2	0.4	26.3	0.4	26.3	0.0	26.5	0.8	27.0	1.9	27.2	0.7
1959	27.1	-0.4	27.1	0.0	27.2	0.4	27.4	0.7	27.4	0.0	27.4	0.0	27.6	0.7	27.6	0.0	27.6	0.0	28.0	1.4	28.1	0.4	28.1	0.0
1960	28.1	0.0	28.1	0.0	27.9	-0.7	27.8	-0.4	27.8	0.0	27.7	-0.4	27.6	-0.4	27.6	0.0	27.4	-0.7	27.6	0.7	27.7	0.4	27.7	0.0
1961	27.6	-0.4	27.5	-0.4	27.6	0.4	27.7	0.4	27.8	0.4	27.9	0.4	27.9	0.0	27.9	0.0	27.9	0.0	28.1	0.7	28.0	-0.4	27.8	-0.7
1962	27.9	0.4	27.8	-0.4	27.8	0.0	27.9	0.4	28.1	0.7	28.1	0.0	28.0	-0.4	28.1	0.4	28.0	-0.4	28.1	0.4	28.1	0.0	28.0	-0.4
1963	28.0	0.0	27.9	-0.4	28.0	0.4	28.1	0.4	28.0	-0.4	28.3	1.1	28.3	0.0	28.3	0.0	28.3	0.0	28.4	0.4	28.6	0.7	28.5	-0.3
1964	28.4	-0.4	28.4	0.0	28.3	-0.4	28.3	0.0	28.3	0.0	28.2	-0.4	28.2	0.0	28.2	0.0	28.1	-0.4	28.2	0.4	28.5	1.1	28.6	0.4
1965	28.7	0.3	28.5	-0.7	28.6	0.4	28.6	0.0	28.5	-0.3	28.4	-0.4	28.6	0.7	28.7	0.3	28.7	0.0	28.9	0.7	28.9	0.0	28.9	0.0
1966	29.0	0.3	29.0	0.0	29.1	0.3	29.2	0.3	29.1	-0.3	29.2	0.3	30.5	4.5	30.5	0.0	30.3	-0.7	30.6	1.0	30.7	0.3	30.6	-0.3
1967	30.5	-0.3	30.7	0.7	30.8	0.3	30.9	0.3	31.0	0.3	31.0	0.0	31.2	0.6	31.4	0.6	31.3	-0.3	31.7	1.3	31.6	-0.3	31.7	0.3
1968	31.7	0.0	31.7	0.0	31.7	0.0	31.7	0.0	31.7	0.0	31.9	0.6	32.1	0.6	32.2	0.3	32.1	-0.3	32.4	0.9	32.5	0.3	32.2	-0.9
1969	33.0	2.5	33.3	0.9	33.8	1.5	33.9	0.3	33.7	-0.6	33.9	0.6	33.9	0.0	33.9	0.0	33.6	-0.9	34.2	1.8	34.2	0.0	35.1	2.6
1970	37.4	6.6	37.5	0.3	37.5	0.0	37.8	0.8	38.0	0.5	38.1	0.3	38.2	0.3	38.1	-0.3	38.1	0.0	38.6	1.3	38.9	0.8	39.1	0.5
1971	39.3	0.5	40.0	1.8	40.1	0.2	40.1	0.0	40.2	0.2	40.6	1.0	40.6	0.0	40.5	-0.2	40.1	-1.0	40.3	0.5	40.3	0.0	40.2	-0.2
1972	41.2	2.5	41.2	0.0	41.1	-0.2	41.1	0.0	41.3	0.5	41.4	0.2	41.5	0.2	41.6	0.2	41.7	0.2	41.7	0.0	41.8	0.2	41.8	0.0
1973	41.7	-0.2	41.8	0.2	41.8	0.0	42.0	0.5	42.1	0.2	42.4	0.7	42.4	0.0	42.4	0.0	42.2	-0.5	42.5	0.7	42.7	0.5	43.1	0.9
1974	43.2	0.2	43.4	0.5	43.9	1.2	44.3	0.9	45.0	1.6	45.8	1.8	46.4	1.3	46.5	0.2	46.8	0.6	47.0	0.4	47.1	0.2	47.4	0.6
1975	47.3	-0.2	47.3	0.0	47.8	1.1	48.1	0.6	48.2	0.2	48.8	1.2	49.5	1.4	49.7	0.4	53.3	7.2	53.6	0.6	54.7	2.1	55.3	1.1
1976	55.3	0.0	55.4	0.2	56.4	1.8	56.5	0.2	56.9	0.7	57.5	1.1	57.9	0.7	58.1	0.3	58.7	1.0	59.1	0.7	59.1	0.0	59.0	-0.2
1977	59.4	0.7	59.7	0.5	60.1	0.7	60.4	0.5	60.6	0.3	60.8	0.3	60.8	0.0	60.8	0.0	60.7	-0.2	60.9	0.3	61.0	0.2	61.1	0.2
1978	61.1	0.0	61.3	0.3	61.3	0.0	61.6	0.5	61.8	0.3	62.2	0.6	62.6	0.6	62.8	0.3	63.3	0.8	64.1	1.3	64.4	0.5	64.8	0.6
1979	65.1	0.5	65.7	0.9	66.4	1.1	67.7	2.0	69.0	1.9	70.6	2.3	72.2	2.3	72.9	1.0	73.6	1.0	74.1	0.7	74.7	0.8	75.4	0.9
1980	77.2	2.4	79.1	2.5	80.5	1.8	81.5	1.2	81.8	0.4	82.1	0.4	83.6	1.8	83.9	0.4	84.4	0.6	84.6	0.2	85.3	0.8	86.0	0.8
1981	87.4	1.6	89.3	2.2	90.1	0.9	90.7	0.7	91.0	0.3	91.5	0.5	93.9	2.6	94.0	0.1	94.4	0.4	94.7	0.3	95.4	0.7	95.6	0.2
1982	95.4	-0.2	95.0	-0.4	94.0	-1.1	93.3	-0.7	93.6	0.3	95.6	2.1	96.6	1.0	96.9	0.3	97.4	0.5	97.9	0.5	97.8	-0.1	97.8	0.0
1983	97.5	-0.3	96.9	-0.6	96.1	-0.8	97.8	1.8	98.1	0.3	98.7	0.6	99.2	0.5	99.9	0.7	100.5	0.6	100.9	0.4	101.6	0.7	101.5	-0.1
1984	103.3	1.8	103.5	0.2	104.1	0.6	104.5	0.4	105.0	0.5	105.1	0.1	105.5	0.4	105.5	0.0	105.5	0.0	105.8	0.3	106.1	0.3	106.1	0.0
1985	106.1	0.0	106.1	0.0	106.6	0.5	106.8	0.2	107.1	0.3	107.4	0.3	107.4	0.0	107.1	-0.3	106.8	-0.3	107.6	0.7	108.1	0.5	108.4	0.3
1986	109.5	1.0	108.5	-0.9	106.1	-2.2	103.4	-2.5	103.4	0.0	104.5	1.1	103.9	-0.6	102.9	-1.0	102.4	-0.5	104.0	1.6	104.5	0.5	104.8	0.3
1987	105.4	0.6	105.7	0.3	106.1	0.4	107.4	1.2	108.0	0.6	108.8	0.7	109.4	0.6	110.2	0.7	110.3	0.1	110.7	0.4	111.5	0.7	111.2	-0.3
1988	111.3	0.1	111.3	0.0	110.7	-0.5	111.2	0.5	111.8	0.5	112.6	0.7	113.0	0.4	113.4	0.4	113.7	0.3	114.4	0.6	114.7	0.3	114.9	0.2
1989	115.2	0.3	115.1	-0.1	115.3	0.2	116.3	0.9	117.5	1.0	117.3	-0.2	116.9	-0.3	116.4	-0.4	115.8	-0.5	116.9	0.9	117.3	0.3	117.5	0.2
1990	119.5	1.7	119.8	0.3	119.5	-0.3	119.2	-0.3	119.3	0.1	120.4	0.9	120.8	0.3	122.1	1.1	125.3	2.6	129.0	3.0	130.6	1.2	131.4	0.6
1991	129.1	-1.8	127.8	-1.0	126.6	-0.9	126.2	-0.3	127.3	0.9	127.6	0.2	127.7	0.1	127.6	-0.1	128.1	0.4	128.6	0.4	129.1	0.4	129.1	0.0

[Continued]

New York, NY, NE NJ
Consumer Price Index - All Urban Consumers
Base 1982-1984 = 100
Transportation
[Continued]

For 1947-1997. Columns headed % show percentile change in the index from the previous period for which an index is available.

Year	Jan Index	%	Feb Index	%	Mar Index	%	Apr Index	%	May Index	%	Jun Index	%	Jul Index	%	Aug Index	%	Sep Index	%	Oct Index	%	Nov Index	%	Dec Index	%
1992	129.5	0.3	129.7	0.2	129.9	0.2	129.6	-0.2	129.8	0.2	130.1	0.2	130.9	0.6	130.6	-0.2	130.9	0.2	134.6	2.8	135.5	0.7	136.3	0.6
1993	137.3	0.7	136.9	-0.3	136.2	-0.5	136.4	0.1	137.1	0.5	136.7	-0.3	137.1	0.3	137.2	0.1	137.1	-0.1	139.1	1.5	140.1	0.7	141.0	0.6
1994	140.4	-0.4	140.6	0.1	139.9	-0.5	140.5	0.4	140.3	-0.1	141.2	0.6	141.5	0.2	142.2	0.5	142.3	0.1	143.9	1.1	144.5	0.4	144.6	0.1
1995	144.4	-0.1	144.5	0.1	144.5	0.0	144.1	-0.3	146.0	1.3	147.4	1.0	146.5	-0.6	145.7	-0.5	145.9	0.1	146.8	0.6	146.9	0.1	147.8	0.6
1996	148.6	0.5	149.0	0.3	150.7	1.1	152.5	1.2	153.0	0.3	153.1	0.1	152.8	-0.2	152.3	-0.3	153.3	0.7	153.5	0.1	154.5	0.7	155.8	0.8
1997	154.6	-0.8	154.6	0.0	155.1	0.3	154.1	-0.6	153.6	-0.3	153.9	0.2	153.7	-0.1	152.8	-0.6	154.6	1.2	155.5	0.6	153.4	-1.4	153.3	-0.1

Source: U.S. Department of Labor, Bureau of Labor Statistics, Division of Consumer Prices and Price Indexes. - indicates no data collected for period.

New York, NY, NE NJ
Consumer Price Index - Urban Wage Earners
Base 1982-1984 = 100
Transportation

For 1947-1997. Columns headed % show percentile change in the index from the previous period for which an index is available.

Year	Jan Index	%	Feb Index	%	Mar Index	%	Apr Index	%	May Index	%	Jun Index	%	Jul Index	%	Aug Index	%	Sep Index	%	Oct Index	%	Nov Index	%	Dec Index	%
1947	15.7	-	15.7	0.0	15.7	0.0	15.8	0.6	15.8	0.0	15.9	0.6	15.9	0.0	16.0	0.6	16.1	0.6	16.1	0.0	16.1	0.0	16.3	1.2
1948	16.3	0.0	16.3	0.0	16.3	0.0	16.3	0.0	16.3	0.0	16.3	0.0	20.7	27.0	20.9	1.0	21.0	0.5	21.1	0.5	21.1	0.0	21.1	0.0
1949	21.1	0.0	21.2	0.5	21.2	0.0	21.3	0.5	21.3	0.0	21.3	0.0	21.3	0.0	21.3	0.0	21.3	0.0	21.3	0.0	21.3	0.0	21.4	0.5
1950	21.4	0.0	21.4	0.0	21.4	0.0	21.4	0.0	21.4	0.0	21.4	0.0	22.9	7.0	23.0	0.4	22.9	-0.4	22.9	0.0	23.0	0.4	23.0	0.0
1951	23.0	0.0	23.1	0.4	23.2	0.4	23.2	0.0	23.2	0.0	23.2	0.0	23.3	0.4	23.3	0.0	23.4	0.4	23.5	0.4	23.6	0.4	23.6	0.0
1952	23.6	0.0	23.7	0.4	23.7	0.0	23.7	0.0	23.7	0.0	23.7	0.0	23.7	0.0	23.7	0.0	23.8	0.4	23.8	0.0	23.8	0.0	23.7	-0.4
1953	23.8	0.4	23.7	-0.4	23.7	0.0	23.7	0.0	23.7	0.0	23.7	0.0	23.9	0.8	25.0	4.6	24.9	-0.4	25.0	0.4	24.8	-0.8	24.9	0.4
1954	25.2	1.2	25.1	-0.4	25.0	-0.4	24.9	-0.4	25.0	0.4	25.0	0.0	24.0	-4.0	24.0	0.0	24.1	0.4	24.1	0.0	24.4	1.2	24.3	-0.4
1955	24.2	-0.4	24.2	0.0	24.2	0.0	24.1	-0.4	24.0	-0.4	23.9	-0.4	23.7	-0.8	23.6	-0.4	23.6	0.0	23.8	0.8	24.4	2.5	24.1	-1.2
1956	24.3	0.8	24.4	0.4	24.4	0.0	24.4	0.0	24.5	0.4	24.4	-0.4	24.6	0.8	24.8	0.8	24.8	0.0	25.6	3.2	25.4	-0.8	25.4	0.0
1957	25.5	0.4	25.6	0.4	25.6	0.0	25.7	0.4	25.7	0.0	25.7	0.0	25.6	-0.4	25.6	0.0	25.5	-0.4	25.5	0.0	26.1	2.4	26.0	-0.4
1958	26.0	0.0	25.9	-0.4	25.8	-0.4	25.9	0.4	25.9	0.0	25.9	0.0	25.9	0.0	26.1	0.8	26.1	0.0	26.2	0.4	26.7	1.9	26.9	0.7
1959	26.9	0.0	26.9	0.0	27.0	0.4	27.2	0.7	27.2	0.0	27.2	0.0	27.3	0.4	27.4	0.4	27.3	-0.4	27.7	1.5	27.8	0.4	27.8	0.0
1960	27.8	0.0	27.8	0.0	27.6	-0.7	27.5	-0.4	27.5	0.0	27.4	-0.4	27.3	-0.4	27.3	0.0	27.2	-0.4	27.3	0.4	27.4	0.4	27.5	0.4
1961	27.3	-0.7	27.2	-0.4	27.3	0.4	27.5	0.7	27.5	0.0	27.6	0.4	27.6	0.0	27.6	0.0	27.6	0.0	27.8	0.7	27.8	0.0	27.5	-1.1
1962	27.6	0.4	27.5	-0.4	27.5	0.0	27.7	0.7	27.8	0.4	27.8	0.0	27.8	0.0	27.8	0.0	27.7	-0.4	27.8	0.4	27.9	0.4	27.7	-0.7
1963	27.7	0.0	27.7	0.0	27.7	0.0	27.8	0.4	27.7	-0.4	28.1	1.4	28.1	0.0	28.1	0.0	28.0	-0.4	28.1	0.4	28.3	0.7	28.2	-0.4
1964	28.1	-0.4	28.1	0.0	28.0	-0.4	28.0	0.0	28.0	0.0	27.9	-0.4	28.0	0.4	27.9	-0.4	27.8	-0.4	27.9	0.4	28.2	1.1	28.3	0.4
1965	28.4	0.4	28.2	-0.7	28.3	0.4	28.3	0.0	28.2	-0.4	28.1	-0.4	28.3	0.7	28.4	0.4	28.4	0.0	28.6	0.7	28.6	0.0	28.6	0.0
1966	28.7	0.3	28.7	0.0	28.8	0.3	29.0	0.7	28.9	-0.3	29.0	0.3	30.3	4.5	30.3	0.0	30.0	-1.0	30.3	1.0	30.4	0.3	30.3	-0.3
1967	30.3	0.0	30.4	0.3	30.5	0.3	30.6	0.3	30.7	0.3	30.7	0.0	30.9	0.7	31.1	0.6	31.0	-0.3	31.4	1.3	31.3	-0.3	31.4	0.3
1968	31.4	0.0	31.4	0.0	31.4	0.0	31.4	0.0	31.4	0.0	31.6	0.6	31.8	0.6	31.9	0.3	31.8	-0.3	32.1	0.9	32.2	0.3	31.9	-0.9
1969	32.7	2.5	33.0	0.9	33.5	1.5	33.6	0.3	33.4	-0.6	33.5	0.3	33.6	0.3	33.6	0.0	33.3	-0.9	33.8	1.5	33.8	0.0	34.7	2.7
1970	37.0	6.6	37.1	0.3	37.2	0.3	37.4	0.5	37.6	0.5	37.7	0.3	37.8	0.3	37.7	-0.3	37.7	0.0	38.2	1.3	38.6	1.0	38.7	0.3
1971	38.9	0.5	39.6	1.8	39.8	0.5	39.7	-0.3	39.8	0.3	40.2	1.0	40.3	0.2	40.1	-0.5	39.7	-1.0	39.9	0.5	39.9	0.0	39.8	-0.3
1972	40.8	2.5	40.8	0.0	40.7	-0.2	40.7	0.0	40.9	0.5	41.0	0.2	41.1	0.2	41.1	0.0	41.3	0.5	41.3	0.0	41.4	0.2	41.4	0.0
1973	41.3	-0.2	41.4	0.2	41.4	0.0	41.6	0.5	41.7	0.2	42.0	0.7	42.0	0.0	42.0	0.0	41.8	-0.5	42.1	0.7	42.3	0.5	42.7	0.9
1974	42.8	0.2	43.0	0.5	43.5	1.2	43.9	0.9	44.6	1.6	45.4	1.8	46.0	1.3	46.1	0.2	46.3	0.4	46.5	0.4	46.7	0.4	47.0	0.6
1975	46.9	-0.2	46.9	0.0	47.4	1.1	47.7	0.6	47.8	0.2	48.3	1.0	49.0	1.4	49.3	0.6	52.8	7.1	53.1	0.6	54.2	2.1	54.8	1.1
1976	54.8	0.0	54.9	0.2	55.8	1.6	56.0	0.4	56.4	0.7	57.0	1.1	57.3	0.5	57.5	0.3	58.1	1.0	58.6	0.9	58.6	0.0	58.5	-0.2
1977	58.8	0.5	59.1	0.5	59.5	0.7	59.8	0.5	60.0	0.3	60.2	0.3	60.2	0.0	60.2	0.0	60.1	-0.2	60.3	0.3	60.4	0.2	60.5	0.2
1978	60.5	0.0	60.7	0.3	60.8	0.2	61.1	0.5	61.4	0.5	61.9	0.8	62.3	0.6	62.6	0.5	63.0	0.6	63.6	1.0	64.0	0.6	64.4	0.6
1979	64.7	0.5	65.3	0.9	66.0	1.1	67.4	2.1	68.7	1.9	70.5	2.6	72.0	2.1	72.8	1.1	73.5	1.0	73.7	0.3	74.4	0.9	75.1	0.9
1980	77.0	2.5	78.8	2.3	80.2	1.8	81.1	1.1	81.3	0.2	81.6	0.4	83.3	2.1	83.7	0.5	84.1	0.5	84.4	0.4	85.1	0.8	85.9	0.9
1981	87.2	1.5	89.2	2.3	90.0	0.9	90.7	0.8	90.7	0.0	91.3	0.7	93.9	2.8	94.1	0.2	94.6	0.5	94.9	0.3	95.5	0.6	95.7	0.2
1982	95.5	-0.2	95.0	-0.5	94.0	-1.1	93.0	-1.1	93.4	0.4	95.5	2.2	96.7	1.3	97.0	0.3	97.3	0.3	97.8	0.5	97.5	-0.3	97.6	0.1
1983	97.3	-0.3	96.6	-0.7	95.7	-0.9	97.3	1.7	97.8	0.5	98.5	0.7	99.1	0.6	99.9	0.8	100.6	0.7	101.0	0.4	101.7	0.7	101.7	0.0
1984	103.5	1.8	103.6	0.1	104.2	0.6	104.6	0.4	105.2	0.6	105.5	0.3	105.7	0.2	105.7	0.0	105.8	0.1	106.1	0.3	106.3	0.2	106.3	0.0
1985	106.2	-0.1	106.2	0.0	106.7	0.5	107.0	0.3	107.2	0.2	107.5	0.3	107.5	0.0	107.1	-0.4	106.7	-0.4	107.5	0.7	108.1	0.6	108.3	0.2
1986	109.5	1.1	108.4	-1.0	105.8	-2.4	102.9	-2.7	102.8	-0.1	103.8	1.0	103.1	-0.7	102.1	-1.0	101.5	-0.6	103.1	1.6	103.4	0.3	103.6	0.2
1987	104.4	0.8	105.0	0.6	105.5	0.5	107.0	1.4	107.7	0.7	108.7	0.9	109.3	0.6	110.2	0.8	110.4	0.2	110.7	0.3	111.3	0.5	111.1	-0.2
1988	111.2	0.1	111.1	-0.1	110.5	-0.5	110.8	0.3	111.3	0.5	112.0	0.6	112.5	0.4	113.1	0.5	113.3	0.2	113.9	0.5	114.1	0.2	114.4	0.3
1989	114.5	0.1	114.4	-0.1	114.6	0.2	115.8	1.0	117.4	1.4	117.4	0.0	117.1	-0.3	116.5	-0.5	115.7	-0.7	116.5	0.7	116.9	0.3	116.9	0.0
1990	119.3	2.1	119.4	0.1	119.0	-0.3	118.8	-0.2	118.8	0.0	120.2	1.2	120.9	0.6	122.3	1.2	126.1	3.1	129.7	2.9	131.3	1.2	131.8	0.4
1991	129.1	-2.0	127.3	-1.4	126.0	-1.0	125.9	-0.1	127.2	1.0	127.6	0.3	127.8	0.2	127.7	-0.1	128.4	0.5	128.6	0.2	129.1	0.4	129.0	-0.1

[Continued]

New York, NY, NE NJ
Consumer Price Index - Urban Wage Earners
Base 1982-1984 = 100
Transportation
[Continued]

For 1947-1997. Columns headed % show percentile change in the index from the previous period for which an index is available.

Year	Jan Index	%	Feb Index	%	Mar Index	%	Apr Index	%	May Index	%	Jun Index	%	Jul Index	%	Aug Index	%	Sep Index	%	Oct Index	%	Nov Index	%	Dec Index	%
1992	129.5	0.4	129.4	-0.1	129.6	0.2	129.3	-0.2	129.9	0.5	130.8	0.7	131.4	0.5	131.0	-0.3	131.5	0.4	134.9	2.6	135.7	0.6	136.5	0.6
1993	137.0	0.4	136.5	-0.4	135.9	-0.4	135.8	-0.1	136.7	0.7	136.7	0.0	136.9	0.1	137.0	0.1	136.9	-0.1	139.2	1.7	139.9	0.5	140.6	0.5
1994	139.8	-0.6	139.6	-0.1	139.1	-0.4	139.6	0.4	139.8	0.1	140.9	0.8	141.4	0.4	142.2	0.6	142.7	0.4	144.4	1.2	145.0	0.4	144.9	-0.1
1995	144.5	-0.3	144.5	0.0	144.5	0.0	144.3	-0.1	146.2	1.3	147.5	0.9	147.0	-0.3	146.2	-0.5	146.0	-0.1	146.8	0.5	146.8	0.0	148.1	0.9
1996	149.2	0.7	149.4	0.1	151.5	1.4	153.3	1.2	154.4	0.7	154.3	-0.1	153.7	-0.4	153.4	-0.2	154.1	0.5	154.2	0.1	155.5	0.8	156.6	0.7
1997	155.7	-0.6	155.6	-0.1	155.6	0.0	154.7	-0.6	154.2	-0.3	154.3	0.1	153.8	-0.3	153.6	-0.1	155.3	1.1	155.7	0.3	153.9	-1.2	153.7	-0.1

Source: U.S. Department of Labor, Bureau of Labor Statistics, Division of Consumer Prices and Price Indexes. - indicates no data collected for period.

New York, NY, NE NJ
Consumer Price Index - All Urban Consumers
Base 1982-1984 = 100
Medical Care

For 1947-1997. Columns headed % show percentile change in the index from the previous period for which an index is available.

Year	Jan Index	%	Feb Index	%	Mar Index	%	Apr Index	%	May Index	%	Jun Index	%	Jul Index	%	Aug Index	%	Sep Index	%	Oct Index	%	Nov Index	%	Dec Index	%
1947	14.0	-	14.1	0.7	14.1	0.0	14.1	0.0	14.2	0.7	14.3	0.7	14.3	0.0	14.3	0.0	14.4	0.7	14.5	0.7	14.5	0.0	14.5	0.0
1948	14.8	2.1	14.9	0.7	15.0	0.7	15.6	4.0	15.6	0.0	15.6	0.0	16.0	2.6	16.0	0.0	16.1	0.6	16.1	0.0	16.1	0.0	16.1	0.0
1949	16.2	0.6	16.2	0.0	16.0	-1.2	16.0	0.0	16.0	0.0	16.0	0.0	16.0	0.0	16.0	0.0	16.0	0.0	16.0	0.0	16.0	0.0	16.2	1.3
1950	16.3	0.6	16.3	0.0	16.3	0.0	16.3	0.0	16.3	0.0	16.4	0.6	16.4	0.0	16.4	0.0	16.3	-0.6	16.4	0.6	16.4	0.0	16.4	0.0
1951	16.6	1.2	16.6	0.0	16.9	1.8	17.0	0.6	17.0	0.0	17.0	0.0	17.0	0.0	17.0	0.0	17.2	1.2	17.2	0.0	17.2	0.0	17.4	1.2
1952	17.6	1.1	17.6	0.0	17.6	0.0	17.6	0.0	17.6	0.0	18.3	4.0	18.3	0.0	18.4	0.5	18.6	1.1	18.6	0.0	18.7	0.5	18.6	-0.5
1953	18.6	0.0	18.5	-0.5	18.5	0.0	18.5	0.0	18.5	0.0	18.5	0.0	18.5	0.0	18.6	0.5	18.6	0.0	18.6	0.0	18.9	1.6	18.9	0.0
1954	18.9	0.0	18.9	0.0	18.9	0.0	19.0	0.5	19.0	0.0	19.0	0.0	19.0	0.0	19.0	0.0	19.0	0.0	19.0	0.0	19.1	0.5	19.1	0.0
1955	19.1	0.0	19.2	0.5	19.2	0.0	19.2	0.0	19.3	0.5	19.3	0.0	19.4	0.5	19.4	0.0	19.4	0.0	19.4	0.0	19.4	0.0	19.4	0.0
1956	19.4	0.0	19.4	0.0	19.4	0.0	19.4	0.0	19.4	0.0	19.4	0.0	19.4	0.0	19.6	1.0	19.6	0.0	19.6	0.0	19.6	0.0	19.6	0.0
1957	19.7	0.5	19.7	0.0	19.7	0.0	19.7	0.0	19.8	0.5	19.9	0.5	19.9	0.0	19.8	-0.5	19.8	0.0	19.8	0.0	19.9	0.5	19.9	0.0
1958	19.9	0.0	19.9	0.0	20.0	0.5	20.0	0.0	20.0	0.0	20.0	0.0	20.0	0.0	20.1	0.5	20.7	3.0	20.7	0.0	20.8	0.5	20.8	0.0
1959	20.8	0.0	21.1	1.4	21.1	0.0	21.1	0.0	21.4	1.4	21.5	0.5	21.5	0.0	21.4	-0.5	22.0	2.8	22.0	0.0	22.0	0.0	22.0	0.0
1960	22.0	0.0	22.0	0.0	22.1	0.5	22.1	0.0	22.1	0.0	22.1	0.0	22.1	0.0	22.1	0.0	22.1	0.0	22.1	0.0	22.7	2.7	22.7	0.0
1961	22.7	0.0	22.7	0.0	22.8	0.4	22.8	0.0	23.0	0.9	23.0	0.0	23.0	0.0	23.1	0.4	23.1	0.0	23.1	0.0	23.1	0.0	23.1	0.0
1962	23.1	0.0	23.3	0.9	23.4	0.4	23.4	0.0	23.5	0.4	23.5	0.0	23.5	0.0	23.6	0.4	23.6	0.0	23.5	-0.4	23.6	0.4	23.7	0.4
1963	23.7	0.0	23.9	0.8	23.9	0.0	23.9	0.0	24.0	0.4	23.9	-0.4	23.9	0.0	24.0	0.4	24.0	0.0	24.0	0.0	24.1	0.4	24.1	0.0
1964	24.2	0.4	24.3	0.4	24.3	0.0	24.4	0.4	24.4	0.0	24.4	0.0	24.4	0.0	24.6	0.8	24.4	-0.8	24.5	0.4	24.7	0.8	24.7	0.0
1965	24.9	0.8	25.1	0.8	25.2	0.4	25.2	0.0	25.2	0.0	25.4	0.8	25.4	0.0	25.3	-0.4	25.3	0.0	25.3	0.0	25.4	0.4	25.6	0.8
1966	25.7	0.4	25.8	0.4	26.0	0.8	26.1	0.4	26.3	0.8	26.7	1.5	26.8	0.4	27.0	0.7	27.0	0.0	27.2	0.7	27.3	0.4	27.3	0.0
1967	27.6	1.1	27.8	0.7	27.9	0.4	28.0	0.4	28.1	0.4	28.3	0.7	28.5	0.7	28.7	0.7	28.8	0.3	28.9	0.3	28.9	0.0	29.2	1.0
1968	29.3	0.3	29.4	0.3	29.6	0.7	29.8	0.7	29.8	0.0	30.1	1.0	30.5	1.3	30.5	0.0	30.8	1.0	31.0	0.6	31.1	0.3	31.2	0.3
1969	31.9	2.2	32.0	0.3	32.5	1.6	32.8	0.9	33.0	0.6	33.4	1.2	33.4	0.0	33.6	0.6	33.6	0.0	33.5	-0.3	33.6	0.3	33.8	0.6
1970	34.0	0.6	34.1	0.3	34.6	1.5	34.9	0.9	34.9	0.0	35.6	2.0	35.9	0.8	36.1	0.6	36.4	0.8	36.5	0.3	36.8	0.8	37.3	1.4
1971	37.6	0.8	37.8	0.5	38.2	1.1	38.2	0.0	38.4	0.5	38.5	0.3	38.8	0.8	39.0	0.5	39.0	0.0	38.9	-0.3	39.0	0.3	39.1	0.3
1972	39.4	0.8	39.4	0.0	39.4	0.0	39.5	0.3	39.6	0.3	39.8	0.5	39.8	0.0	39.9	0.3	39.9	0.0	40.1	0.5	40.3	0.5	40.6	0.7
1973	40.7	0.2	40.7	0.0	40.6	-0.2	40.6	0.0	40.9	0.7	41.0	0.2	41.0	0.0	41.1	0.2	41.3	0.5	42.0	1.7	42.1	0.2	42.3	0.5
1974	42.8	1.2	43.2	0.9	43.8	1.4	44.1	0.7	44.7	1.4	45.4	1.6	45.7	0.7	46.9	2.6	47.4	1.1	47.5	0.2	47.8	0.6	48.2	0.8
1975	48.9	1.5	49.6	1.4	50.3	1.4	50.6	0.6	51.0	0.8	51.3	0.6	51.7	0.8	51.9	0.4	52.6	1.3	52.8	0.4	52.6	-0.4	53.4	1.5
1976	54.5	2.1	55.0	0.9	55.5	0.9	55.7	0.4	55.9	0.4	56.5	1.1	57.1	1.1	57.5	0.7	57.9	0.7	57.9	0.0	58.8	1.6	58.9	0.2
1977	59.7	1.4	59.9	0.3	60.7	1.3	61.2	0.8	61.4	0.3	61.7	0.5	62.0	0.5	62.2	0.3	62.3	0.2	62.6	0.5	62.8	0.3	63.3	0.8
1978	64.1	1.3	64.5	0.6	64.6	0.2	64.8	0.3	65.5	1.1	65.5	0.0	65.5	0.0	65.5	0.0	65.7	0.3	65.7	0.0	66.7	1.5	66.3	-0.6
1979	68.1	2.7	69.0	1.3	69.2	0.3	69.7	0.7	69.8	0.1	70.1	0.4	70.2	0.1	70.5	0.4	71.1	0.9	72.2	1.5	73.0	1.1	73.5	0.7
1980	74.5	1.4	75.4	1.2	76.2	1.1	76.9	0.9	76.9	0.0	77.0	0.1	77.2	0.3	77.8	0.8	78.3	0.6	78.7	0.5	79.0	0.4	79.3	0.4
1981	80.2	1.1	80.6	0.5	81.6	1.2	82.5	1.1	82.7	0.2	84.1	1.7	85.0	1.1	85.2	0.2	86.2	1.2	87.2	1.2	87.7	0.6	88.1	0.5
1982	89.1	1.1	89.9	0.9	90.7	0.9	90.9	0.2	91.2	0.3	91.6	0.4	91.5	-0.1	91.9	0.4	92.8	1.0	93.3	0.5	94.1	0.9	94.4	0.3
1983	95.4	1.1	97.3	2.0	98.1	0.8	98.7	0.6	99.4	0.7	99.4	0.0	100.0	0.6	101.2	1.2	101.7	0.5	102.3	0.6	103.2	0.9	103.9	0.7
1984	104.7	0.8	106.1	1.3	106.7	0.6	106.7	0.0	107.3	0.6	107.2	-0.1	107.7	0.5	109.0	1.2	109.8	0.7	110.1	0.3	110.8	0.6	111.4	0.5
1985	112.0	0.5	113.8	1.6	114.3	0.4	114.6	0.3	115.4	0.7	116.2	0.7	116.7	0.4	116.8	0.1	117.2	0.3	117.5	0.3	117.8	0.3	117.7	-0.1
1986	120.0	2.0	122.2	1.8	123.7	1.2	124.2	0.4	124.6	0.3	125.1	0.4	126.0	0.7	126.4	0.3	127.8	1.1	128.7	0.7	128.7	0.0	130.3	1.2
1987	131.1	0.6	132.9	1.4	135.0	1.6	136.1	0.8	136.1	0.0	136.3	0.1	136.8	0.4	137.2	0.3	137.2	0.0	137.5	0.2	137.9	0.3	138.5	0.4
1988	139.7	0.9	141.3	1.1	142.7	1.0	143.2	0.4	144.1	0.6	144.7	0.4	146.1	1.0	145.9	-0.1	146.9	0.7	147.1	0.1	147.6	0.3	147.9	0.2
1989	149.5	1.1	151.1	1.1	152.9	1.2	153.4	0.3	154.3	0.6	155.6	0.8	156.2	0.4	157.1	0.6	157.7	0.4	159.7	1.3	160.5	0.5	161.5	0.6
1990	163.9	1.5	166.7	1.7	169.2	1.5	170.1	0.5	170.5	0.2	171.4	0.5	171.8	0.2	175.1	1.9	175.9	0.5	177.5	0.9	178.0	0.3	178.7	0.4
1991	180.8	1.2	182.8	1.1	183.9	0.6	184.2	0.2	183.9	-0.2	185.3	0.8	187.2	1.0	188.7	0.8	189.3	0.3	189.6	0.2	191.0	0.7	192.0	0.5

[Continued]

New York, NY, NE NJ
Consumer Price Index - All Urban Consumers
Base 1982-1984 = 100
Medical Care
[Continued]

For 1947-1997. Columns headed % show percentile change in the index from the previous period for which an index is available.

Year	Jan Index	%	Feb Index	%	Mar Index	%	Apr Index	%	May Index	%	Jun Index	%	Jul Index	%	Aug Index	%	Sep Index	%	Oct Index	%	Nov Index	%	Dec Index	%
1992	195.1	1.6	196.4	0.7	197.7	0.7	198.4	0.4	199.1	0.4	200.0	0.5	201.2	0.6	200.8	-0.2	201.9	0.5	202.8	0.4	203.1	0.1	203.3	0.1
1993	205.1	0.9	205.5	0.2	206.6	0.5	207.9	0.6	208.9	0.5	208.9	0.0	209.5	0.3	210.7	0.6	211.0	0.1	211.3	0.1	211.4	0.0	212.0	0.3
1994	213.5	0.7	214.2	0.3	215.1	0.4	215.8	0.3	216.5	0.3	217.7	0.6	218.2	0.2	218.7	0.2	218.6	-0.0	220.6	0.9	220.6	0.0	221.7	0.5
1995	223.2	0.7	225.1	0.9	225.3	0.1	225.6	0.1	226.0	0.2	226.0	0.0	226.2	0.1	227.4	0.5	228.0	0.3	229.5	0.7	229.6	0.0	230.0	0.2
1996	231.1	0.5	231.6	0.2	232.6	0.4	232.8	0.1	234.1	0.6	234.0	-0.0	235.0	0.4	237.4	1.0	237.6	0.1	239.2	0.7	239.6	0.2	239.3	-0.1
1997	242.6	1.4	243.1	0.2	243.6	0.2	243.4	-0.1	243.5	0.0	244.1	0.2	244.4	0.1	244.7	0.1	245.4	0.3	246.1	0.3	246.5	0.2	246.9	0.2

Source: U.S. Department of Labor, Bureau of Labor Statistics, Division of Consumer Prices and Price Indexes. - indicates no data collected for period.

New York, NY, NE NJ
Consumer Price Index - Urban Wage Earners
Base 1982-1984 = 100
Medical Care

For 1947-1997. Columns headed % show percentile change in the index from the previous period for which an index is available.

Year	Jan Index	%	Feb Index	%	Mar Index	%	Apr Index	%	May Index	%	Jun Index	%	Jul Index	%	Aug Index	%	Sep Index	%	Oct Index	%	Nov Index	%	Dec Index	%
1947	14.6	-	14.7	0.7	14.7	0.0	14.7	0.0	14.8	0.7	14.9	0.7	14.9	0.0	15.0	0.7	15.0	0.0	15.2	1.3	15.2	0.0	15.2	0.0
1948	15.5	2.0	15.5	0.0	15.6	0.6	16.3	4.5	16.3	0.0	16.3	0.0	16.7	2.5	16.7	0.0	16.8	0.6	16.8	0.0	16.8	0.0	16.8	0.0
1949	16.9	0.6	16.8	-0.6	16.7	-0.6	16.7	0.0	16.7	0.0	16.7	0.0	16.7	0.0	16.6	-0.6	16.6	0.0	16.7	0.6	16.7	0.0	16.9	1.2
1950	17.0	0.6	17.0	0.0	17.0	0.0	17.0	0.0	17.0	0.0	17.1	0.6	17.1	0.0	17.1	0.0	17.0	-0.6	17.1	0.6	17.1	0.0	17.1	0.0
1951	17.3	1.2	17.4	0.6	17.6	1.1	17.7	0.6	17.7	0.0	17.7	0.0	17.7	0.0	17.7	0.0	17.9	1.1	17.9	0.0	17.9	0.0	18.1	1.1
1952	18.3	1.1	18.4	0.5	18.4	0.0	18.4	0.0	18.4	0.0	19.1	3.8	19.1	0.0	19.2	0.5	19.4	1.0	19.4	0.0	19.5	0.5	19.4	-0.5
1953	19.4	0.0	19.3	-0.5	19.3	0.0	19.3	0.0	19.3	0.0	19.3	0.0	19.3	0.0	19.4	0.5	19.4	0.0	19.4	0.0	19.7	1.5	19.7	0.0
1954	19.7	0.0	19.7	0.0	19.7	0.0	19.8	0.5	19.8	0.0	19.8	0.0	19.8	0.0	19.8	0.0	19.8	0.0	19.8	0.0	19.9	0.5	19.9	0.0
1955	20.0	0.5	20.0	0.0	20.0	0.0	20.0	0.0	20.2	1.0	20.2	0.0	20.2	0.0	20.2	0.0	20.2	0.0	20.2	0.0	20.2	0.0	20.2	0.0
1956	20.3	0.5	20.3	0.0	20.3	0.0	20.2	-0.5	20.3	0.5	20.3	0.0	20.3	0.0	20.5	1.0	20.5	0.0	20.5	0.0	20.5	0.0	20.5	0.0
1957	20.5	0.0	20.5	0.0	20.5	0.0	20.5	0.0	20.7	1.0	20.7	0.0	20.7	0.0	20.7	0.0	20.7	0.0	20.7	0.0	20.7	0.0	20.7	0.0
1958	20.8	0.5	20.8	0.0	20.8	0.0	20.8	0.0	20.9	0.5	20.9	0.0	20.9	0.0	21.0	0.5	21.6	2.9	21.6	0.0	21.6	0.0	21.6	0.0
1959	21.7	0.5	22.0	1.4	22.0	0.0	22.0	0.0	22.4	1.8	22.4	0.0	22.4	0.0	22.4	0.0	22.9	2.2	22.9	0.0	22.9	0.0	22.9	0.0
1960	22.9	0.0	23.0	0.4	23.0	0.0	23.0	0.0	23.0	0.0	23.0	0.0	23.0	0.0	23.0	0.0	23.0	0.0	23.0	0.0	23.7	3.0	23.7	0.0
1961	23.7	0.0	23.7	0.0	23.7	0.0	23.8	0.4	24.0	0.8	24.0	0.0	24.0	0.0	24.1	0.4	24.1	0.0	24.1	0.0	24.1	0.0	24.1	0.0
1962	24.1	0.0	24.2	0.4	24.4	0.8	24.4	0.0	24.5	0.4	24.5	0.0	24.5	0.0	24.6	0.4	24.6	0.0	24.5	-0.4	24.6	0.4	24.7	0.4
1963	24.8	0.4	24.9	0.4	25.0	0.4	25.0	0.0	25.0	0.0	24.9	-0.4	24.9	0.0	25.0	0.4	25.0	0.0	25.0	0.0	25.1	0.4	25.1	0.0
1964	25.2	0.4	25.3	0.4	25.4	0.4	25.4	0.0	25.5	0.4	25.4	-0.4	25.4	0.0	25.6	0.8	25.5	-0.4	25.6	0.4	25.7	0.4	25.8	0.4
1965	26.0	0.8	26.1	0.4	26.2	0.4	26.2	0.0	26.3	0.4	26.4	0.4	26.5	0.4	26.4	-0.4	26.4	0.0	26.4	0.0	26.5	0.4	26.7	0.8
1966	26.8	0.4	26.9	0.4	27.1	0.7	27.2	0.4	27.4	0.7	27.8	1.5	28.0	0.7	28.2	0.7	28.2	0.0	28.3	0.4	28.5	0.7	28.5	0.0
1967	28.8	1.1	29.0	0.7	29.1	0.3	29.2	0.3	29.3	0.3	29.5	0.7	29.7	0.7	29.9	0.7	30.0	0.3	30.1	0.3	30.1	0.0	30.4	1.0
1968	30.6	0.7	30.6	0.0	30.9	1.0	31.0	0.3	31.1	0.3	31.4	1.0	31.8	1.3	31.8	0.0	32.1	0.9	32.3	0.6	32.4	0.3	32.5	0.3
1969	33.3	2.5	33.4	0.3	33.9	1.5	34.2	0.9	34.4	0.6	34.8	1.2	34.8	0.0	35.1	0.9	35.1	0.0	35.0	-0.3	35.0	0.0	35.3	0.9
1970	35.4	0.3	35.6	0.6	36.1	1.4	36.4	0.8	36.4	0.0	37.1	1.9	37.4	0.8	37.7	0.8	37.9	0.8	38.1	0.5	38.4	0.8	38.8	1.0
1971	39.2	1.0	39.4	0.5	39.8	1.0	39.8	0.0	40.1	0.8	40.1	0.0	40.5	1.0	40.7	0.5	40.7	0.0	40.5	-0.5	40.7	0.5	40.8	0.2
1972	41.0	0.5	41.0	0.0	41.1	0.2	41.2	0.2	41.2	0.0	41.5	0.7	41.5	0.0	41.6	0.2	41.6	0.0	41.8	0.5	42.0	0.5	42.3	0.7
1973	42.5	0.5	42.4	-0.2	42.3	-0.2	42.4	0.2	42.6	0.5	42.7	0.2	42.8	0.2	42.8	0.0	43.1	0.7	43.8	1.6	43.9	0.2	44.1	0.5
1974	44.6	1.1	45.1	1.1	45.7	1.3	46.0	0.7	46.6	1.3	47.3	1.5	47.7	0.8	48.9	2.5	49.4	1.0	49.5	0.2	49.9	0.8	50.2	0.6
1975	51.0	1.6	51.8	1.6	52.5	1.4	52.8	0.6	53.2	0.8	53.5	0.6	53.9	0.7	54.1	0.4	54.8	1.3	55.0	0.4	54.8	-0.4	55.7	1.6
1976	56.8	2.0	57.4	1.1	57.9	0.9	58.1	0.3	58.3	0.3	59.0	1.2	59.5	0.8	59.9	0.7	60.4	0.8	60.4	0.0	61.3	1.5	61.4	0.2
1977	62.3	1.5	62.4	0.2	63.3	1.4	63.8	0.8	64.0	0.3	64.3	0.5	64.7	0.6	64.8	0.2	65.0	0.3	65.3	0.5	65.5	0.3	66.0	0.8
1978	66.5	0.8	66.9	0.6	67.1	0.3	67.2	0.1	67.8	0.9	67.9	0.1	67.8	-0.1	67.9	0.1	68.0	0.1	68.3	0.4	69.1	1.2	69.5	0.6
1979	70.4	1.3	70.9	0.7	71.3	0.6	71.9	0.8	72.0	0.1	72.3	0.4	72.6	0.4	72.8	0.3	73.2	0.5	73.5	0.4	73.8	0.4	74.4	0.8
1980	75.4	1.3	76.6	1.6	77.5	1.2	78.1	0.8	78.4	0.4	78.3	-0.1	78.6	0.4	79.1	0.6	80.4	1.6	80.4	0.0	80.7	0.4	80.9	0.2
1981	82.3	1.7	82.8	0.6	84.9	2.5	85.9	1.2	86.0	0.1	86.5	0.6	87.2	0.8	87.1	-0.1	87.5	0.5	87.8	0.3	88.1	0.3	88.4	0.3
1982	89.3	1.0	90.2	1.0	91.0	0.9	91.1	0.1	91.5	0.4	91.8	0.3	91.5	-0.3	91.9	0.4	92.8	1.0	93.3	0.5	94.0	0.8	94.2	0.2
1983	95.3	1.2	97.1	1.9	97.8	0.7	98.4	0.6	99.0	0.6	99.2	0.2	99.8	0.6	101.1	1.3	101.6	0.5	102.2	0.6	103.1	0.9	103.8	0.7
1984	104.7	0.9	106.1	1.3	106.7	0.6	106.8	0.1	107.4	0.6	107.4	0.0	107.9	0.5	109.2	1.2	109.9	0.6	110.4	0.5	111.1	0.6	111.6	0.5
1985	112.4	0.7	114.1	1.5	114.6	0.4	115.0	0.3	115.8	0.7	116.5	0.6	117.1	0.5	117.2	0.1	117.6	0.3	117.9	0.3	118.2	0.3	117.8	-0.3
1986	120.3	2.1	122.5	1.8	123.8	1.1	124.4	0.5	124.9	0.4	125.2	0.2	126.2	0.8	126.6	0.3	128.0	1.1	128.8	0.6	128.7	-0.1	130.4	1.3
1987	131.1	0.5	133.1	1.5	135.4	1.7	136.7	1.0	136.7	0.0	137.1	0.3	137.6	0.4	138.1	0.4	138.2	0.1	138.5	0.2	139.3	0.6	140.0	0.5
1988	141.1	0.8	142.5	1.0	143.6	0.8	144.1	0.3	145.0	0.6	145.6	0.4	147.0	1.0	146.9	-0.1	148.1	0.8	148.3	0.1	148.8	0.3	149.1	0.2
1989	150.4	0.9	152.1	1.1	154.1	1.3	154.8	0.5	155.6	0.5	157.0	0.9	157.7	0.4	158.6	0.6	159.2	0.4	160.6	0.9	161.5	0.6	162.5	0.6
1990	164.4	1.2	166.9	1.5	169.3	1.4	170.2	0.5	170.5	0.2	171.4	0.5	172.0	0.4	174.2	1.3	174.9	0.4	176.3	0.8	176.7	0.2	177.3	0.3
1991	180.0	1.5	182.1	1.2	183.3	0.7	183.5	0.1	183.2	-0.2	184.8	0.9	186.9	1.1	188.6	0.9	189.2	0.3	189.7	0.3	191.3	0.8	192.3	0.5

[Continued]

New York, NY, NE NJ
Consumer Price Index - Urban Wage Earners
Base 1982-1984 = 100
Medical Care

[Continued]

For 1947-1997. Columns headed % show percentile change in the index from the previous period for which an index is available.

Year	Jan Index	%	Feb Index	%	Mar Index	%	Apr Index	%	May Index	%	Jun Index	%	Jul Index	%	Aug Index	%	Sep Index	%	Oct Index	%	Nov Index	%	Dec Index	%
1992	195.2	1.5	196.5	0.7	197.7	0.6	198.6	0.5	199.0	0.2	200.0	0.5	201.2	0.6	201.2	0.0	202.5	0.6	203.5	0.5	203.7	0.1	204.0	0.1
1993	205.6	0.8	205.7	0.0	206.8	0.5	208.1	0.6	208.9	0.4	208.9	0.0	209.6	0.3	210.4	0.4	210.7	0.1	211.1	0.2	211.1	0.0	211.6	0.2
1994	213.7	1.0	214.3	0.3	215.3	0.5	216.0	0.3	216.5	0.2	217.9	0.6	218.3	0.2	219.0	0.3	219.0	0.0	221.2	1.0	221.2	0.0	222.3	0.5
1995	224.2	0.9	226.0	0.8	226.2	0.1	226.3	0.0	226.6	0.1	226.7	0.0	226.9	0.1	228.1	0.5	228.7	0.3	230.1	0.6	230.3	0.1	230.6	0.1
1996	231.5	0.4	232.2	0.3	233.1	0.4	233.6	0.2	234.9	0.6	235.0	0.0	235.6	0.3	238.0	1.0	238.2	0.1	239.9	0.7	240.3	0.2	240.1	-0.1
1997	242.7	1.1	243.5	0.3	244.0	0.2	243.7	-0.1	243.8	0.0	244.4	0.2	244.9	0.2	245.1	0.1	245.8	0.3	246.6	0.3	247.0	0.2	247.5	0.2

Source: U.S. Department of Labor, Bureau of Labor Statistics, Division of Consumer Prices and Price Indexes. - indicates no data collected for period.

New York, NY, NE NJ
Consumer Price Index - All Urban Consumers
Base 1982-1984 = 100
Entertainment

For 1976-1997. Columns headed % show percentile change in the index from the previous period for which an index is available.

Year	Jan Index	%	Feb Index	%	Mar Index	%	Apr Index	%	May Index	%	Jun Index	%	Jul Index	%	Aug Index	%	Sep Index	%	Oct Index	%	Nov Index	%	Dec Index	%
1976	62.5	-	62.9	0.6	63.0	0.2	63.3	0.5	63.7	0.6	64.8	1.7	65.0	0.3	65.2	0.3	65.7	0.8	66.1	0.6	65.9	-0.3	66.3	0.6
1977	66.5	0.3	67.1	0.9	66.7	-0.6	66.9	0.3	67.3	0.6	69.1	2.7	69.1	0.0	69.3	0.3	70.4	1.6	70.4	0.0	69.4	-1.4	69.5	0.1
1978	69.9	0.6	71.2	1.9	71.9	1.0	72.5	0.8	72.5	0.0	72.1	-0.6	72.9	1.1	73.2	0.4	73.1	-0.1	72.8	-0.4	72.9	0.1	72.4	-0.7
1979	72.9	0.7	74.5	2.2	75.2	0.9	75.4	0.3	75.3	-0.1	75.7	0.5	75.9	0.3	76.4	0.7	76.6	0.3	76.8	0.3	77.2	0.5	77.1	-0.1
1980	78.0	1.2	79.1	1.4	81.3	2.8	81.5	0.2	81.2	-0.4	81.7	0.6	81.3	-0.5	81.9	0.7	82.4	0.6	83.0	0.7	83.0	0.0	83.4	0.5
1981	84.4	1.2	86.0	1.9	86.9	1.0	87.1	0.2	87.2	0.1	87.8	0.7	87.7	-0.1	89.6	2.2	90.5	1.0	91.3	0.9	90.7	-0.7	90.9	0.2
1982	91.0	0.1	92.3	1.4	94.1	2.0	94.1	0.0	94.2	0.1	95.0	0.8	95.5	0.5	98.0	2.6	97.5	-0.5	98.3	0.8	98.0	-0.3	97.9	-0.1
1983	98.3	0.4	99.0	0.7	100.2	1.2	99.7	-0.5	100.1	0.4	100.3	0.2	100.6	0.3	100.5	-0.1	101.1	0.6	101.8	0.7	102.0	0.2	101.6	-0.4
1984	101.8	0.2	102.2	0.4	102.4	0.2	103.1	0.7	102.9	-0.2	104.4	1.5	104.9	0.5	104.5	-0.4	105.4	0.9	105.6	0.2	105.5	-0.1	106.0	0.5
1985	105.9	-0.1	105.9	0.0	106.9	0.9	107.2	0.3	107.8	0.6	108.2	0.4	108.4	0.2	107.8	-0.6	110.4	2.4	111.2	0.7	111.4	0.2	111.8	0.4
1986	113.8	1.8	114.1	0.3	113.4	-0.6	113.6	0.2	114.1	0.4	115.4	1.1	116.1	0.6	116.3	0.2	115.9	-0.3	115.9	0.0	116.4	0.4	116.1	-0.3
1987	117.3	1.0	116.5	-0.7	117.0	0.4	117.9	0.8	117.8	-0.1	118.5	0.6	120.2	1.4	120.4	0.2	120.7	0.2	121.1	0.3	121.4	0.2	121.6	0.2
1988	122.0	0.3	122.0	0.0	120.4	-1.3	122.1	1.4	120.7	-1.1	122.3	1.3	123.6	1.1	124.1	0.4	123.0	-0.9	124.1	0.9	124.4	0.2	125.3	0.7
1989	127.6	1.8	127.0	-0.5	127.4	0.3	128.8	1.1	128.6	-0.2	127.5	-0.9	129.2	1.3	130.2	0.8	131.8	1.2	131.7	-0.1	132.4	0.5	132.3	-0.1
1990	134.2	1.4	134.5	0.2	133.2	-1.0	134.2	0.8	135.8	1.2	134.5	-1.0	136.8	1.7	134.9	-1.4	136.3	1.0	137.1	0.6	137.8	0.5	137.6	-0.1
1991	140.0	1.7	139.6	-0.3	138.6	-0.7	140.0	1.0	140.4	0.3	138.8	-1.1	140.1	0.9	140.5	0.3	142.3	1.3	142.9	0.4	142.6	-0.2	144.0	1.0
1992	144.0	0.0	145.0	0.7	144.3	-0.5	145.9	1.1	146.3	0.3	147.0	0.5	147.3	0.2	147.3	0.0	146.9	-0.3	146.2	-0.5	148.5	1.6	148.5	0.0
1993	149.4	0.6	149.0	-0.3	149.5	0.3	149.9	0.3	149.1	-0.5	149.1	0.0	148.7	-0.3	150.2	1.0	150.5	0.2	151.4	0.6	151.2	-0.1	149.8	-0.9
1994	151.5	1.1	152.9	0.9	154.1	0.8	152.7	-0.9	153.0	0.2	152.9	-0.1	154.0	0.7	152.4	-1.0	153.2	0.5	156.8	2.3	157.2	0.3	156.9	-0.2
1995	157.7	0.5	157.1	-0.4	157.0	-0.1	158.2	0.8	158.6	0.3	157.7	-0.6	157.8	0.1	158.0	0.1	159.3	0.8	160.5	0.8	162.2	1.1	161.6	-0.4
1996	161.4	-0.1	166.3	3.0	164.0	-1.4	161.2	-1.7	162.8	1.0	162.2	-0.4	162.2	0.0	162.2	0.0	163.6	0.9	164.4	0.5	166.2	1.1	165.9	-0.2
1997	167.1	0.7	166.3	-0.5	167.0	0.4	168.4	0.8	167.9	-0.3	168.7	0.5	168.4	-0.2	167.1	-0.8	167.1	0.0	167.9	0.5	167.9	0.0	167.0	-0.5

Source: U.S. Department of Labor, Bureau of Labor Statistics, Division of Consumer Prices and Price Indexes. - indicates no data collected for period.

New York, NY, NE NJ
Consumer Price Index - Urban Wage Earners
Base 1982-1984 = 100
Entertainment

For 1976-1997. Columns headed % show percentile change in the index from the previous period for which an index is available.

Year	Jan Index	%	Feb Index	%	Mar Index	%	Apr Index	%	May Index	%	Jun Index	%	Jul Index	%	Aug Index	%	Sep Index	%	Oct Index	%	Nov Index	%	Dec Index	%
1976	63.9	-	64.3	0.6	64.5	0.3	64.8	0.5	65.2	0.6	66.3	1.7	66.4	0.2	66.7	0.5	67.2	0.7	67.6	0.6	67.5	-0.1	67.8	0.4
1977	68.0	0.3	68.6	0.9	68.3	-0.4	68.5	0.3	68.8	0.4	70.7	2.8	70.7	0.0	70.9	0.3	72.0	1.6	72.0	0.0	71.0	-1.4	71.1	0.1
1978	71.3	0.3	73.1	2.5	73.5	0.5	73.4	-0.1	72.7	-1.0	72.4	-0.4	72.9	0.7	73.2	0.4	73.6	0.5	73.5	-0.1	73.7	0.3	74.2	0.7
1979	74.5	0.4	74.9	0.5	76.1	1.6	76.1	0.0	76.1	0.0	76.4	0.4	76.6	0.3	77.0	0.5	77.8	1.0	78.4	0.8	79.2	1.0	78.0	-1.5
1980	79.0	1.3	80.1	1.4	82.6	3.1	82.1	-0.6	81.6	-0.6	83.0	1.7	81.7	-1.6	83.1	1.7	84.6	1.8	83.5	-1.3	84.0	0.6	84.6	0.7
1981	85.8	1.4	88.3	2.9	88.8	0.6	88.9	0.1	88.9	0.0	88.9	0.0	89.3	0.4	89.9	0.7	90.4	0.6	91.2	0.9	91.0	-0.2	91.1	0.1
1982	91.3	0.2	92.5	1.3	94.1	1.7	94.1	0.0	94.3	0.2	95.0	0.7	95.9	0.9	97.9	2.1	97.5	-0.4	98.0	0.5	97.6	-0.4	97.4	-0.2
1983	98.0	0.6	99.0	1.0	100.1	1.1	99.9	-0.2	100.2	0.3	100.2	0.0	100.8	0.6	100.7	-0.1	101.1	0.4	101.8	0.7	102.0	0.2	101.5	-0.5
1984	101.9	0.4	102.2	0.3	102.5	0.3	103.2	0.7	103.1	-0.1	104.5	1.4	104.9	0.4	104.7	-0.2	105.4	0.7	105.5	0.1	105.2	-0.3	106.0	0.8
1985	105.8	-0.2	105.8	0.0	106.4	0.6	107.0	0.6	107.7	0.7	108.5	0.7	108.7	0.2	108.0	-0.6	109.8	1.7	110.7	0.8	110.9	0.2	111.0	0.1
1986	113.1	1.9	113.3	0.2	112.7	-0.5	113.1	0.4	113.8	0.6	115.4	1.4	116.1	0.6	116.5	0.3	115.8	-0.6	115.9	0.1	117.0	0.9	116.7	-0.3
1987	118.2	1.3	117.8	-0.3	118.1	0.3	119.1	0.8	118.7	-0.3	119.5	0.7	121.3	1.5	121.4	0.1	121.8	0.3	122.3	0.4	122.8	0.4	123.0	0.2
1988	123.0	0.0	123.1	0.1	121.3	-1.5	123.5	1.8	121.3	-1.8	122.9	1.3	124.4	1.2	124.6	0.2	124.0	-0.5	125.5	1.2	125.9	0.3	126.7	0.6
1989	129.1	1.9	127.9	-0.9	128.4	0.4	129.9	1.2	129.7	-0.2	128.2	-1.2	129.6	1.1	130.3	0.5	132.4	1.6	132.3	-0.1	133.1	0.6	133.0	-0.1
1990	134.7	1.3	134.9	0.1	133.5	-1.0	134.7	0.9	136.6	1.4	135.2	-1.0	137.5	1.7	135.0	-1.8	136.9	1.4	137.8	0.7	138.8	0.7	138.6	-0.1
1991	141.0	1.7	140.4	-0.4	139.4	-0.7	140.8	1.0	140.6	-0.1	138.6	-1.4	140.1	1.1	140.5	0.3	142.7	1.6	143.2	0.4	142.8	-0.3	145.0	1.5
1992	144.6	-0.3	145.4	0.6	144.6	-0.6	146.4	1.2	146.5	0.1	147.1	0.4	147.3	0.1	147.3	0.0	146.5	-0.5	145.4	-0.8	148.8	2.3	148.7	-0.1
1993	149.9	0.8	149.3	-0.4	149.8	0.3	149.5	-0.2	148.9	-0.4	148.7	-0.1	148.0	-0.5	149.9	1.3	150.2	0.2	150.8	0.4	150.5	-0.2	149.0	-1.0
1994	150.8	1.2	151.1	0.2	153.0	1.3	152.5	-0.3	152.7	0.1	152.6	-0.1	153.8	0.8	152.2	-1.0	153.1	0.6	156.4	2.2	157.0	0.4	156.6	-0.3
1995	157.6	0.6	156.7	-0.6	156.6	-0.1	157.5	0.6	158.2	0.4	157.2	-0.6	157.3	0.1	157.3	0.0	158.5	0.8	159.5	0.6	160.9	0.9	160.2	-0.4
1996	160.0	-0.1	165.2	3.2	162.7	-1.5	159.8	-1.8	161.6	1.1	161.1	-0.3	160.9	-0.1	160.9	0.0	162.2	0.8	162.9	0.4	164.9	1.2	164.5	-0.2
1997	165.7	0.7	164.6	-0.7	165.1	0.3	166.3	0.7	165.3	-0.6	166.1	0.5	165.8	-0.2	164.2	-1.0	165.0	0.5	165.6	0.4	165.4	-0.1	164.3	-0.7

Source: U.S. Department of Labor, Bureau of Labor Statistics, Division of Consumer Prices and Price Indexes. - indicates no data collected for period.

New York, NY, NE NJ
Consumer Price Index - All Urban Consumers
Base 1982-1984 = 100
Other Goods and Services

For 1976-1997. Columns headed % show percentile change in the index from the previous period for which an index is available.

Year	Jan Index	%	Feb Index	%	Mar Index	%	Apr Index	%	May Index	%	Jun Index	%	Jul Index	%	Aug Index	%	Sep Index	%	Oct Index	%	Nov Index	%	Dec Index	%
1976	56.5	-	57.3	1.4	57.7	0.7	57.9	0.3	57.9	0.0	58.2	0.5	58.4	0.3	59.0	1.0	59.6	1.0	59.8	0.3	60.1	0.5	60.1	0.0
1977	61.1	1.7	61.5	0.7	61.6	0.2	61.5	-0.2	61.7	0.3	61.9	0.3	62.0	0.2	62.1	0.2	62.7	1.0	62.9	0.3	63.9	1.6	64.0	0.2
1978	64.1	0.2	64.2	0.2	64.4	0.3	64.2	-0.3	64.2	0.0	64.4	0.3	64.9	0.8	65.0	0.2	66.4	2.2	66.4	0.0	66.7	0.5	66.7	0.0
1979	67.0	0.4	67.2	0.3	67.5	0.4	67.6	0.1	67.8	0.3	68.0	0.3	68.0	0.0	68.5	0.7	70.2	2.5	70.5	0.4	70.6	0.1	71.1	0.7
1980	71.7	0.8	72.2	0.7	72.1	-0.1	72.3	0.3	72.8	0.7	73.4	0.8	73.7	0.4	73.9	0.3	76.0	2.8	76.6	0.8	76.8	0.3	77.4	0.8
1981	78.1	0.9	78.2	0.1	78.3	0.1	78.5	0.3	79.1	0.8	79.1	0.0	79.7	0.8	79.9	0.3	84.4	5.6	84.9	0.6	85.1	0.2	85.1	0.0
1982	85.6	0.6	86.1	0.6	86.5	0.5	87.0	0.6	87.3	0.3	87.3	0.0	88.1	0.9	89.0	1.0	93.4	4.9	94.5	1.2	95.4	1.0	96.3	0.9
1983	97.1	0.8	97.3	0.2	97.6	0.3	98.9	1.3	98.7	-0.2	99.2	0.5	100.7	1.5	101.2	0.5	105.0	3.8	105.9	0.9	106.6	0.7	106.6	0.0
1984	107.0	0.4	107.1	0.1	107.0	-0.1	107.1	0.1	107.5	0.4	107.6	0.1	107.9	0.3	108.2	0.3	111.7	3.2	112.0	0.3	112.7	0.6	112.8	0.1
1985	113.6	0.7	113.7	0.1	113.9	0.2	114.3	0.4	114.4	0.1	114.6	0.2	115.2	0.5	115.4	0.2	119.0	3.1	119.4	0.3	119.7	0.3	120.3	0.5
1986	121.4	0.9	121.3	-0.1	122.0	0.6	121.9	-0.1	121.8	-0.1	121.4	-0.3	123.0	1.3	122.7	-0.2	125.9	2.6	126.9	0.8	127.3	0.3	126.9	-0.3
1987	127.9	0.8	127.9	0.0	128.6	0.5	128.8	0.2	128.9	0.1	129.4	0.4	130.1	0.5	130.0	-0.1	133.9	3.0	134.7	0.6	134.8	0.1	135.0	0.1
1988	136.6	1.2	136.9	0.2	137.5	0.4	137.6	0.1	137.4	-0.1	137.5	0.1	138.2	0.5	138.9	0.5	142.9	2.9	143.1	0.1	143.5	0.3	143.6	0.1
1989	146.3	1.9	146.6	0.2	147.0	0.3	146.9	-0.1	149.3	1.6	150.9	1.1	151.2	0.2	153.1	1.3	157.7	3.0	157.3	-0.3	157.7	0.3	158.2	0.3
1990	159.4	0.8	159.8	0.3	160.5	0.4	160.6	0.1	161.3	0.4	162.0	0.4	164.4	1.5	165.2	0.5	168.4	1.9	168.3	-0.1	168.5	0.1	169.2	0.4
1991	171.4	1.3	171.9	0.3	172.0	0.1	173.3	0.8	174.3	0.6	174.7	0.2	175.4	0.4	177.4	1.1	183.2	3.3	183.4	0.1	184.7	0.7	185.1	0.2
1992	187.3	1.2	187.6	0.2	187.6	0.0	187.9	0.2	188.6	0.4	189.0	0.2	189.5	0.3	192.5	1.6	195.4	1.5	195.3	-0.1	195.3	0.0	195.8	0.3
1993	197.4	0.8	198.3	0.5	198.8	0.3	199.3	0.3	199.1	-0.1	200.1	0.5	200.8	0.3	201.7	0.4	202.5	0.4	201.1	-0.7	201.0	-0.0	201.2	0.1
1994	202.0	0.4	202.0	0.0	201.9	-0.0	202.5	0.3	202.8	0.1	204.5	0.8	203.9	-0.3	206.6	1.3	207.5	0.4	208.0	0.2	208.5	0.2	208.4	-0.0
1995	208.8	0.2	210.3	0.7	209.9	-0.2	210.2	0.1	211.0	0.4	211.8	0.4	212.5	0.3	215.6	1.5	217.3	0.8	217.9	0.3	218.2	0.1	218.2	0.0
1996	219.2	0.5	219.7	0.2	219.8	0.0	219.3	-0.2	219.8	0.2	220.2	0.2	220.6	0.2	223.5	1.3	224.7	0.5	224.5	-0.1	225.1	0.3	223.7	-0.6
1997	225.7	0.9	225.8	0.0	226.0	0.1	228.1	0.9	228.3	0.1	229.2	0.4	228.8	-0.2	230.1	0.6	233.3	1.4	235.2	0.8	235.3	0.0	234.8	-0.2

Source: U.S. Department of Labor, Bureau of Labor Statistics, Division of Consumer Prices and Price Indexes. - indicates no data collected for period.

New York, NY, NE NJ
Consumer Price Index - Urban Wage Earners
Base 1982-1984 = 100
Other Goods and Services

For 1976-1997. Columns headed % show percentile change in the index from the previous period for which an index is available.

Year	Jan Index	%	Feb Index	%	Mar Index	%	Apr Index	%	May Index	%	Jun Index	%	Jul Index	%	Aug Index	%	Sep Index	%	Oct Index	%	Nov Index	%	Dec Index	%
1976	57.2	-	58.0	1.4	58.4	0.7	58.6	0.3	58.6	0.0	58.9	0.5	59.1	0.3	59.7	1.0	60.3	1.0	60.5	0.3	60.8	0.5	60.9	0.2
1977	61.8	1.5	62.3	0.8	62.3	0.0	62.2	-0.2	62.4	0.3	62.6	0.3	62.7	0.2	62.9	0.3	63.4	0.8	63.7	0.5	64.7	1.6	64.7	0.0
1978	64.8	0.2	65.1	0.5	65.2	0.2	65.1	-0.2	65.2	0.2	65.7	0.8	66.3	0.9	66.1	-0.3	67.2	1.7	67.1	-0.1	67.5	0.6	67.2	-0.4
1979	67.8	0.9	68.3	0.7	68.6	0.4	68.6	0.0	68.6	0.0	68.7	0.1	69.2	0.7	70.0	1.2	70.9	1.3	71.3	0.6	71.5	0.3	71.9	0.6
1980	72.6	1.0	73.2	0.8	73.0	-0.3	73.3	0.4	73.8	0.7	74.1	0.4	74.4	0.4	74.9	0.7	76.5	2.1	76.9	0.5	76.9	0.0	77.5	0.8
1981	77.6	0.1	78.2	0.8	78.4	0.3	78.9	0.6	79.6	0.9	79.6	0.0	80.3	0.9	80.5	0.2	83.7	4.0	84.2	0.6	84.8	0.7	84.9	0.1
1982	85.4	0.6	86.1	0.8	86.6	0.6	87.1	0.6	87.4	0.3	87.5	0.1	88.5	1.1	89.5	1.1	92.6	3.5	94.1	1.6	95.2	1.2	96.4	1.3
1983	97.4	1.0	97.6	0.2	97.9	0.3	99.6	1.7	99.2	-0.4	99.9	0.7	101.7	1.8	102.4	0.7	104.8	2.3	105.5	0.7	106.4	0.9	106.5	0.1
1984	106.9	0.4	107.1	0.2	106.8	-0.3	107.0	0.2	107.4	0.4	107.6	0.2	108.0	0.4	108.3	0.3	110.8	2.3	111.0	0.2	111.8	0.7	111.9	0.1
1985	112.8	0.8	113.0	0.2	113.2	0.2	113.6	0.4	113.7	0.1	114.0	0.3	114.9	0.8	115.1	0.2	117.9	2.4	118.3	0.3	118.6	0.3	119.4	0.7
1986	120.8	1.2	120.7	-0.1	121.4	0.6	121.4	0.0	121.2	-0.2	120.7	-0.4	122.6	1.6	122.4	-0.2	124.4	1.6	125.4	0.8	126.0	0.5	125.5	-0.4
1987	126.7	1.0	126.8	0.1	127.2	0.3	127.4	0.2	127.5	0.1	127.9	0.3	128.6	0.5	128.7	0.1	132.4	2.9	133.2	0.6	133.4	0.2	133.6	0.1
1988	135.1	1.1	135.3	0.1	135.9	0.4	136.0	0.1	136.0	0.0	136.0	0.0	136.7	0.5	137.4	0.5	141.2	2.8	141.4	0.1	141.8	0.3	141.9	0.1
1989	144.8	2.0	145.2	0.3	145.6	0.3	145.6	0.0	148.4	1.9	150.0	1.1	150.3	0.2	152.0	1.1	156.4	2.9	156.2	-0.1	156.4	0.1	157.1	0.4
1990	158.3	0.8	158.6	0.2	159.3	0.4	159.4	0.1	160.0	0.4	160.9	0.6	164.6	2.3	165.3	0.4	168.8	2.1	168.6	-0.1	169.1	0.3	169.9	0.5
1991	171.6	1.0	171.9	0.2	172.2	0.2	173.5	0.8	174.6	0.6	175.3	0.4	175.8	0.3	178.2	1.4	183.1	2.7	183.7	0.3	184.8	0.6	185.2	0.2
1992	187.3	1.1	187.5	0.1	187.4	-0.1	188.0	0.3	188.7	0.4	189.2	0.3	189.6	0.2	193.1	1.8	195.0	1.0	195.1	0.1	195.2	0.1	195.6	0.2
1993	197.4	0.9	198.3	0.5	198.9	0.3	199.4	0.3	199.3	-0.1	200.6	0.7	201.4	0.4	202.4	0.5	203.4	0.5	201.7	-0.8	201.3	-0.2	200.8	-0.2
1994	201.9	0.5	201.9	0.0	202.0	0.0	202.5	0.2	202.7	0.1	204.7	1.0	203.8	-0.4	206.8	1.5	207.5	0.3	207.9	0.2	208.1	0.1	208.0	-0.0
1995	208.3	0.1	209.8	0.7	209.4	-0.2	209.4	0.0	210.3	0.4	211.4	0.5	211.9	0.2	215.5	1.7	217.3	0.8	217.8	0.2	218.0	0.1	217.7	-0.1
1996	218.7	0.5	219.3	0.3	219.2	-0.0	218.7	-0.2	219.3	0.3	219.5	0.1	219.9	0.2	223.1	1.5	224.3	0.5	224.1	-0.1	224.8	0.3	223.1	-0.8
1997	226.4	1.5	226.4	0.0	226.6	0.1	229.4	1.2	229.4	0.0	230.4	0.4	230.2	-0.1	231.4	0.5	235.5	1.8	237.4	0.8	237.2	-0.1	236.9	-0.1

Source: U.S. Department of Labor, Bureau of Labor Statistics, Division of Consumer Prices and Price Indexes. - indicates no data collected for period.

Philadelphia, PA-NJ
Consumer Price Index - All Urban Consumers
Base 1982-1984 = 100
Annual Averages

For 1914-1997. Columns headed % show percentile change in the index from the previous period for which an index is available.

Year	All Items		Food & Beverage		Housing		Apparel & Upkeep		Trans- portation		Medical Care		Entertain- ment		Other Goods & Services	
	Index	%	Index	%	Index	%	Index	%	Index	%	Index	%	Index	%	Index	%
1914	-	-	-	-	-	-	-	-	-	-	-	-	-	-	-	-
1915	10.1	-	-	-	-	-	-	-	-	-	-	-	-	-	-	-
1916	10.8	6.9	-	-	-	-	-	-	-	-	-	-	-	-	-	-
1917	13.1	21.3	-	-	-	-	-	-	-	-	-	-	-	-	-	-
1918	15.5	18.3	-	-	-	-	-	-	-	-	-	-	-	-	-	-
1919	17.9	15.5	-	-	-	-	-	-	-	-	-	-	-	-	-	-
1920	20.5	14.5	-	-	-	-	-	-	-	-	-	-	-	-	-	-
1921	18.2	-11.2	-	-	-	-	-	-	-	-	-	-	-	-	-	-
1922	17.2	-5.5	-	-	-	-	-	-	-	-	-	-	-	-	-	-
1923	17.6	2.3	-	-	-	-	-	-	-	-	-	-	-	-	-	-
1924	17.7	0.6	-	-	-	-	-	-	-	-	-	-	-	-	-	-
1925	18.4	4.0	-	-	-	-	-	-	-	-	-	-	-	-	-	-
1926	18.7	1.6	-	-	-	-	-	-	-	-	-	-	-	-	-	-
1927	18.3	-2.1	-	-	-	-	-	-	-	-	-	-	-	-	-	-
1928	18.0	-1.6	-	-	-	-	-	-	-	-	-	-	-	-	-	-
1929	17.8	-1.1	-	-	-	-	-	-	-	-	-	-	-	-	-	-
1930	17.4	-2.2	-	-	-	-	-	-	-	-	-	-	-	-	-	-
1931	15.9	-8.6	-	-	-	-	-	-	-	-	-	-	-	-	-	-
1932	14.2	-10.7	-	-	-	-	-	-	-	-	-	-	-	-	-	-
1933	13.5	-4.9	-	-	-	-	-	-	-	-	-	-	-	-	-	-
1934	14.2	5.2	-	-	-	-	-	-	-	-	-	-	-	-	-	-
1935	14.3	0.7	-	-	-	-	-	-	-	-	-	-	-	-	-	-
1936	14.5	1.4	-	-	-	-	-	-	-	-	-	-	-	-	-	-
1937	14.9	2.8	-	-	-	-	-	-	-	-	-	-	-	-	-	-
1938	14.5	-2.7	-	-	-	-	-	-	-	-	-	-	-	-	-	-
1939	14.3	-1.4	-	-	-	-	-	-	-	-	-	-	-	-	-	-
1940	14.3	0.0	-	-	-	-	-	-	-	-	-	-	-	-	-	-
1941	15.0	4.9	-	-	-	-	-	-	-	-	-	-	-	-	-	-
1942	16.7	11.3	-	-	-	-	-	-	-	-	-	-	-	-	-	-
1943	17.8	6.6	-	-	-	-	-	-	-	-	-	-	-	-	-	-
1944	18.0	1.1	-	-	-	-	-	-	-	-	-	-	-	-	-	-
1945	18.5	2.8	-	-	-	-	-	-	-	-	-	-	-	-	-	-
1946	20.1	8.6	-	-	-	-	-	-	-	-	-	-	-	-	-	-
1947	23.0	14.4	-	-	-	-	-	-	16.8	-	12.4	-	-	-	-	-
1948	24.8	7.8	-	-	-	-	-	-	18.4	9.5	13.0	4.8	-	-	-	-
1949	24.5	-1.2	-	-	-	-	-	-	19.5	6.0	13.4	3.1	-	-	-	-
1950	24.7	0.8	-	-	-	-	-	-	19.5	0.0	13.6	1.5	-	-	-	-
1951	27.0	9.3	-	-	-	-	-	-	23.2	19.0	14.2	4.4	-	-	-	-
1952	27.5	1.9	-	-	-	-	-	-	24.1	3.9	15.0	5.6	-	-	-	-
1953	27.6	0.4	-	-	-	-	44.3	-	24.5	1.7	15.6	4.0	-	-	-	-
1954	27.9	1.1	-	-	-	-	44.6	0.7	25.1	2.4	16.4	5.1	-	-	-	-
1955	27.9	0.0	-	-	-	-	44.4	-0.4	24.9	-0.8	17.5	6.7	-	-	-	-
1956	28.2	1.1	-	-	-	-	44.8	0.9	24.9	0.0	17.8	1.7	-	-	-	-
1957	29.1	3.2	-	-	-	-	46.0	2.7	25.8	3.6	18.2	2.2	-	-	-	-
1958	29.7	2.1	-	-	-	-	45.6	-0.9	26.6	3.1	18.9	3.8	-	-	-	-

[Continued]

Philadelphia, PA-NJ
Consumer Price Index - All Urban Consumers
Base 1982-1984 = 100
Annual Averages
[Continued]

For 1914-1997. Columns headed % show percentile change in the index from the previous period for which an index is available.

Year	All Items		Food & Beverage		Housing		Apparel & Upkeep		Trans- portation		Medical Care		Entertain- ment		Other Goods & Services	
	Index	%	Index	%	Index	%	Index	%	Index	%	Index	%	Index	%	Index	%
1959	30.0	1.0	-	-	-	-	46.3	1.5	28.0	5.3	20.0	5.8	-	-	-	-
1960	30.6	2.0	-	-	-	-	48.0	3.7	28.3	1.1	20.8	4.0	-	-	-	-
1961	30.9	1.0	-	-	-	-	49.1	2.3	29.0	2.5	21.7	4.3	-	-	-	-
1962	31.2	1.0	-	-	-	-	49.6	1.0	29.2	0.7	22.6	4.1	-	-	-	-
1963	31.8	1.9	-	-	-	-	50.2	1.2	29.9	2.4	23.1	2.2	-	-	-	-
1964	32.3	1.6	-	-	-	-	50.3	0.2	30.5	2.0	23.4	1.3	-	-	-	-
1965	32.8	1.5	-	-	-	-	51.0	1.4	31.3	2.6	24.0	2.6	-	-	-	-
1966	33.7	2.7	-	-	-	-	52.9	3.7	31.8	1.6	25.1	4.6	-	-	-	-
1967	34.6	2.7	-	-	-	-	55.3	4.5	32.6	2.5	26.7	6.4	-	-	-	-
1968	36.3	4.9	-	-	-	-	58.5	5.8	34.3	5.2	28.9	8.2	-	-	-	-
1969	38.2	5.2	-	-	-	-	61.5	5.1	35.9	4.7	31.4	8.7	-	-	-	-
1970	40.8	6.8	-	-	-	-	64.1	4.2	37.9	5.6	34.0	8.3	-	-	-	-
1971	42.7	4.7	-	-	-	-	65.9	2.8	40.2	6.1	36.7	7.9	-	-	-	-
1972	44.0	3.0	-	-	-	-	66.4	0.8	40.8	1.5	38.0	3.5	-	-	-	-
1973	46.9	6.6	-	-	-	-	69.0	3.9	41.6	2.0	39.8	4.7	-	-	-	-
1974	52.5	11.9	-	-	-	-	73.1	5.9	45.9	10.3	43.4	9.0	-	-	-	-
1975	56.8	8.2	-	-	-	-	75.2	2.9	49.8	8.5	49.3	13.6	-	-	-	-
1976	59.7	5.1	62.2	-	59.1	-	77.1	2.5	54.0	8.4	53.7	8.9	68.8	-	56.0	-
1977	63.5	6.4	66.0	6.1	62.7	6.1	79.1	2.6	59.3	9.8	59.0	9.9	71.6	4.1	59.2	5.7
1978	67.3	6.0	72.4	9.7	65.7	4.8	80.9	2.3	62.5	5.4	63.2	7.1	74.0	3.4	62.4	5.4
1979	73.9	9.8	79.5	9.8	71.9	9.4	86.2	6.6	70.9	13.4	68.4	8.2	81.1	9.6	67.0	7.4
1980	83.6	13.1	86.0	8.2	83.5	16.1	94.4	9.5	83.6	17.9	75.4	10.2	84.0	3.6	73.2	9.3
1981	92.1	10.2	92.5	7.6	93.7	12.2	95.9	1.6	93.2	11.5	83.9	11.3	92.1	9.6	79.5	8.6
1982	96.6	4.9	97.7	5.6	97.6	4.2	98.8	3.0	96.1	3.1	91.7	9.3	96.4	4.7	89.5	12.6
1983	99.4	2.9	100.0	2.4	98.4	0.8	100.3	1.5	99.4	3.4	100.6	9.7	100.5	4.3	101.0	12.8
1984	104.1	4.7	102.4	2.4	104.0	5.7	100.9	0.6	104.5	5.1	107.7	7.1	103.1	2.6	109.5	8.4
1985	108.8	4.5	105.0	2.5	109.1	4.9	101.4	0.5	109.4	4.7	119.1	10.6	105.2	2.0	117.1	6.9
1986	111.5	2.5	107.8	2.7	112.9	3.5	101.3	-0.1	107.1	-2.1	126.6	6.3	109.3	3.9	126.5	8.0
1987	116.8	4.8	112.1	4.0	118.4	4.9	107.7	6.3	111.5	4.1	133.0	5.1	112.2	2.7	135.9	7.4
1988	122.4	4.8	116.0	3.5	124.8	5.4	109.9	2.0	115.6	3.7	142.2	6.9	120.8	7.7	145.1	6.8
1989	128.3	4.8	124.2	7.1	130.8	4.8	99.4	-9.6	121.5	5.1	155.3	9.2	128.6	6.5	155.4	7.1
1990	135.8	5.8	131.2	5.6	138.7	6.0	101.4	2.0	127.7	5.1	167.4	7.8	133.5	3.8	171.9	10.6
1991	142.2	4.7	135.4	3.2	145.6	5.0	103.7	2.3	132.3	3.6	183.5	9.6	138.0	3.4	185.5	7.9
1992	146.6	3.1	137.6	1.6	149.6	2.7	106.5	2.7	136.1	2.9	196.6	7.1	144.4	4.6	195.8	5.6
1993	150.2	2.5	139.7	1.5	151.9	1.5	106.0	-0.5	139.5	2.5	211.6	7.6	147.5	2.1	210.7	7.6
1994	154.6	2.9	142.7	2.1	155.1	2.1	105.8	-0.2	144.0	3.2	223.9	5.8	160.3	8.7	222.2	5.5
1995	158.7	2.7	148.8	4.3	158.4	2.1	102.1	-3.5	148.7	3.3	232.5	3.8	166.7	4.0	227.1	2.2
1996	162.8	2.6	152.2	2.3	162.4	2.5	103.8	1.7	151.5	1.9	242.2	4.2	178.2	6.9	232.9	2.6
1997	166.5	2.3	154.3	1.4	167.3	3.0	104.0	0.2	152.8	0.9	247.8	2.3	181.8	2.0	241.4	3.6

Source: U.S. Department of Labor, Bureau of Labor Statistics, Division of Consumer Prices and Price Indexes. - indicates no data collected for period.

Philadelphia, PA-NJ
Consumer Price Index - Urban Wage Earners
Base 1982-1984 = 100
Annual Averages

For 1914-1997. Columns headed % show percentile change in the index from the previous period for which an index is available.

Year	All Items		Food & Beverage		Housing		Apparel & Upkeep		Trans- portation		Medical Care		Entertain- ment		Other Goods & Services	
	Index	%	Index	%	Index	%	Index	%	Index	%	Index	%	Index	%	Index	%
1914	-	-	-	-	-	-	-	-	-	-	-	-	-	-	-	-
1915	10.0	-	-	-	-	-	-	-	-	-	-	-	-	-	-	-
1916	10.8	8.0	-	-	-	-	-	-	-	-	-	-	-	-	-	-
1917	13.0	20.4	-	-	-	-	-	-	-	-	-	-	-	-	-	-
1918	15.5	19.2	-	-	-	-	-	-	-	-	-	-	-	-	-	-
1919	17.8	14.8	-	-	-	-	-	-	-	-	-	-	-	-	-	-
1920	20.3	14.0	-	-	-	-	-	-	-	-	-	-	-	-	-	-
1921	18.1	-10.8	-	-	-	-	-	-	-	-	-	-	-	-	-	-
1922	17.1	-5.5	-	-	-	-	-	-	-	-	-	-	-	-	-	-
1923	17.5	2.3	-	-	-	-	-	-	-	-	-	-	-	-	-	-
1924	17.6	0.6	-	-	-	-	-	-	-	-	-	-	-	-	-	-
1925	18.3	4.0	-	-	-	-	-	-	-	-	-	-	-	-	-	-
1926	18.6	1.6	-	-	-	-	-	-	-	-	-	-	-	-	-	-
1927	18.2	-2.2	-	-	-	-	-	-	-	-	-	-	-	-	-	-
1928	17.9	-1.6	-	-	-	-	-	-	-	-	-	-	-	-	-	-
1929	17.7	-1.1	-	-	-	-	-	-	-	-	-	-	-	-	-	-
1930	17.3	-2.3	-	-	-	-	-	-	-	-	-	-	-	-	-	-
1931	15.8	-8.7	-	-	-	-	-	-	-	-	-	-	-	-	-	-
1932	14.1	-10.8	-	-	-	-	-	-	-	-	-	-	-	-	-	-
1933	13.4	-5.0	-	-	-	-	-	-	-	-	-	-	-	-	-	-
1934	14.1	5.2	-	-	-	-	-	-	-	-	-	-	-	-	-	-
1935	14.3	1.4	-	-	-	-	-	-	-	-	-	-	-	-	-	-
1936	14.5	1.4	-	-	-	-	-	-	-	-	-	-	-	-	-	-
1937	14.8	2.1	-	-	-	-	-	-	-	-	-	-	-	-	-	-
1938	14.5	-2.0	-	-	-	-	-	-	-	-	-	-	-	-	-	-
1939	14.2	-2.1	-	-	-	-	-	-	-	-	-	-	-	-	-	-
1940	14.3	0.7	-	-	-	-	-	-	-	-	-	-	-	-	-	-
1941	14.9	4.2	-	-	-	-	-	-	-	-	-	-	-	-	-	-
1942	16.6	11.4	-	-	-	-	-	-	-	-	-	-	-	-	-	-
1943	17.7	6.6	-	-	-	-	-	-	-	-	-	-	-	-	-	-
1944	17.9	1.1	-	-	-	-	-	-	-	-	-	-	-	-	-	-
1945	18.4	2.8	-	-	-	-	-	-	-	-	-	-	-	-	-	-
1946	20.0	8.7	-	-	-	-	-	-	-	-	-	-	-	-	-	-
1947	22.9	14.5	-	-	-	-	-	-	16.3	-	11.7	-	-	-	-	-
1948	24.7	7.9	-	-	-	-	-	-	17.9	9.8	12.3	5.1	-	-	-	-
1949	24.4	-1.2	-	-	-	-	-	-	19.0	6.1	12.6	2.4	-	-	-	-
1950	24.5	0.4	-	-	-	-	-	-	19.0	0.0	12.8	1.6	-	-	-	-
1951	26.8	9.4	-	-	-	-	-	-	22.5	18.4	13.4	4.7	-	-	-	-
1952	27.4	2.2	-	-	-	-	-	-	23.4	4.0	14.1	5.2	-	-	-	-
1953	27.5	0.4	-	-	-	-	51.1	-	23.8	1.7	14.7	4.3	-	-	-	-
1954	27.8	1.1	-	-	-	-	51.5	0.8	24.3	2.1	15.5	5.4	-	-	-	-
1955	27.7	-0.4	-	-	-	-	51.2	-0.6	24.1	-0.8	16.5	6.5	-	-	-	-
1956	28.1	1.4	-	-	-	-	51.7	1.0	24.2	0.4	16.8	1.8	-	-	-	-
1957	29.0	3.2	-	-	-	-	53.0	2.5	25.0	3.3	17.1	1.8	-	-	-	-
1958	29.5	1.7	-	-	-	-	52.7	-0.6	25.8	3.2	17.8	4.1	-	-	-	-

[Continued]

706

Philadelphia, PA-NJ
Consumer Price Index - Urban Wage Earners
Base 1982-1984 = 100
Annual Averages
[Continued]

For 1914-1997. Columns headed % show percentile change in the index from the previous period for which an index is available.

Year	All Items		Food & Beverage		Housing		Apparel & Upkeep		Trans-portation		Medical Care		Entertain-ment		Other Goods & Services	
	Index	%	Index	%	Index	%	Index	%	Index	%	Index	%	Index	%	Index	%
1959	29.9	1.4	-	-	-	-	53.4	1.3	27.2	5.4	18.9	6.2	-	-	-	-
1960	30.4	1.7	-	-	-	-	55.4	3.7	27.4	0.7	19.6	3.7	-	-	-	-
1961	30.8	1.3	-	-	-	-	56.7	2.3	28.2	2.9	20.5	4.6	-	-	-	-
1962	31.0	0.6	-	-	-	-	57.2	0.9	28.4	0.7	21.3	3.9	-	-	-	-
1963	31.6	1.9	-	-	-	-	58.0	1.4	29.0	2.1	21.8	2.3	-	-	-	-
1964	32.1	1.6	-	-	-	-	58.1	0.2	29.6	2.1	22.1	1.4	-	-	-	-
1965	32.6	1.6	-	-	-	-	58.9	1.4	30.4	2.7	22.7	2.7	-	-	-	-
1966	33.5	2.8	-	-	-	-	61.0	3.6	30.9	1.6	23.7	4.4	-	-	-	-
1967	34.4	2.7	-	-	-	-	63.8	4.6	31.7	2.6	25.2	6.3	-	-	-	-
1968	36.1	4.9	-	-	-	-	67.5	5.8	33.3	5.0	27.3	8.3	-	-	-	-
1969	38.0	5.3	-	-	-	-	70.9	5.0	34.9	4.8	29.6	8.4	-	-	-	-
1970	40.6	6.8	-	-	-	-	73.9	4.2	36.8	5.4	32.1	8.4	-	-	-	-
1971	42.5	4.7			-	-	76.1	3.0	39.0	6.0	34.7	8.1				
1972	43.7	2.8			-	-	76.6	0.7	39.6	1.5	35.9	3.5	-	-	-	-
1973	46.6	6.6			-	-	79.6	3.9	40.4	2.0	37.6	4.7	-	-	-	-
1974	52.2	12.0	-	-	-	-	84.3	5.9	44.6	10.4	41.0	9.0	-	-	-	-
1975	56.5	8.2	-	-	-	-	86.8	3.0	48.4	8.5	46.5	13.4	-	-	-	-
1976	59.4	5.1	60.5	-	58.9	-	89.0	2.5	52.4	8.3	50.7	9.0	70.9	-	58.2	-
1977	63.2	6.4	64.3	6.3	62.6	6.3	91.3	2.6	57.6	9.9	55.7	9.9	73.8	4.1	61.5	5.7
1978	67.1	6.2	70.8	10.1	65.5	4.6	90.5	-0.9	61.3	6.4	60.2	8.1	77.3	4.7	64.7	5.2
1979	73.9	10.1	79.2	11.9	71.5	9.2	89.4	-1.2	70.1	14.4	66.6	10.6	86.3	11.6	68.4	5.7
1980	83.5	13.0	86.8	9.6	82.4	15.2	94.4	5.6	83.2	18.7	76.0	14.1	86.4	0.1	73.9	8.0
1981	91.9	10.1	93.2	7.4	92.1	11.8	96.3	2.0	93.6	12.5	83.9	10.4	94.1	8.9	80.4	8.8
1982	95.8	4.2	97.7	4.8	95.6	3.8	98.8	2.6	96.2	2.8	91.6	9.2	96.5	2.6	89.4	11.2
1983	99.7	4.1	99.9	2.3	99.3	3.9	100.2	1.4	99.4	3.3	100.6	9.8	100.6	4.2	101.2	13.2
1984	104.5	4.8	102.4	2.5	105.2	5.9	100.9	0.7	104.4	5.0	107.9	7.3	102.9	2.3	109.4	8.1
1985	109.2	4.5	105.1	2.6	110.8	5.3	100.5	-0.4	109.2	4.6	119.0	10.3	104.4	1.5	116.8	6.8
1986	111.5	2.1	107.9	2.7	114.5	3.3	99.7	-0.8	106.0	-2.9	126.3	6.1	108.2	3.6	125.9	7.8
1987	116.7	4.7	112.4	4.2	120.0	4.8	104.4	4.7	110.8	4.5	132.7	5.1	110.6	2.2	134.7	7.0
1988	122.2	4.7	116.5	3.6	126.3	5.2	106.0	1.5	115.1	3.9	141.5	6.6	118.8	7.4	144.3	7.1
1989	128.3	5.0	125.1	7.4	133.0	5.3	94.5	-10.8	121.6	5.6	154.0	8.8	126.1	6.1	153.8	6.6
1990	136.1	6.1	132.3	5.8	140.7	5.8	97.6	3.3	128.4	5.6	165.9	7.7	130.2	3.3	170.7	11.0
1991	142.2	4.5	136.5	3.2	147.5	4.8	99.0	1.4	132.8	3.4	180.9	9.0	134.7	3.5	184.3	8.0
1992	146.4	3.0	138.7	1.6	151.3	2.6	103.3	4.3	136.1	2.5	193.9	7.2	140.2	4.1	194.3	5.4
1993	150.1	2.5	140.9	1.6	153.8	1.7	104.7	1.4	139.2	2.3	208.8	7.7	142.6	1.7	208.5	7.3
1994	154.2	2.7	143.9	2.1	156.9	2.0	101.9	-2.7	144.0	3.4	220.5	5.6	155.7	9.2	218.2	4.7
1995	158.3	2.7	150.0	4.2	160.3	2.2	98.1	-3.7	149.5	3.8	228.5	3.6	162.2	4.2	222.2	1.8
1996	162.2	2.5	153.3	2.2	164.1	2.4	100.1	2.0	152.2	1.8	237.9	4.1	173.5	7.0	227.4	2.3
1997	165.7	2.2	155.3	1.3	168.9	2.9	101.2	1.1	153.5	0.9	243.6	2.4	176.7	1.8	235.4	3.5

Source: U.S. Department of Labor, Bureau of Labor Statistics, Division of Consumer Prices and Price Indexes. - indicates no data collected for period.

Philadelphia, PA-NJ
Consumer Price Index - All Urban Consumers
Base 1982-1984 = 100
All Items

For 1914-1997. Columns headed % show percentile change in the index from the previous period for which an index is available.

Year	Jan Index	%	Feb Index	%	Mar Index	%	Apr Index	%	May Index	%	Jun Index	%	Jul Index	%	Aug Index	%	Sep Index	%	Oct Index	%	Nov Index	%	Dec Index	%
1914	-	-	-	-	-	-	-	-	-	-	-	-	-	-	-	-	-	-	-	-	-	-	10.2	-
1915	-	-	-	-	-	-	-	-	-	-	-	-	-	-	-	-	-	-	-	-	-	-	10.3	1.0
1916	-	-	-	-	-	-	-	-	-	-	-	-	-	-	-	-	-	-	-	-	-	-	11.6	12.6
1917	-	-	-	-	-	-	-	-	-	-	-	-	-	-	-	-	-	-	-	-	-	-	14.1	21.6
1918	-	-	-	-	-	-	-	-	-	-	-	-	-	-	-	-	-	-	-	-	-	-	17.0	20.6
1919	-	-	-	-	-	-	-	-	-	-	17.5	2.9	-	-	-	-	-	-	-	-	-	-	19.2	9.7
1920	-	-	-	-	-	-	-	-	-	-	21.3	10.9	-	-	-	-	-	-	-	-	-	-	19.9	-6.6
1921	-	-	-	-	-	-	-	-	18.1	-9.0	-	-	-	-	-	-	17.9	-1.1	-	-	-	-	17.7	-1.1
1922	-	-	-	-	17.3	-2.3	-	-	-	-	17.3	0.0	-	-	-	-	16.9	-2.3	-	-	-	-	17.3	2.4
1923	-	-	-	-	17.3	0.0	-	-	-	-	17.6	1.7	-	-	-	-	17.8	1.1	-	-	-	-	17.8	0.0
1924	-	-	-	-	17.6	-1.1	-	-	-	-	17.7	0.6	-	-	-	-	17.6	-0.6	-	-	-	-	18.0	2.3
1925	-	-	-	-	-	-	-	-	-	-	18.4	2.2	-	-	-	-	-	-	-	-	-	-	18.9	2.7
1926	-	-	-	-	-	-	-	-	-	-	18.8	-0.5	-	-	-	-	-	-	-	-	-	-	18.7	-0.5
1927	-	-	-	-	-	-	-	-	-	-	18.5	-1.1	-	-	-	-	-	-	-	-	-	-	18.3	-1.1
1928	-	-	-	-	-	-	-	-	-	-	18.1	-1.1	-	-	-	-	-	-	-	-	-	-	17.8	-1.7
1929	-	-	-	-	-	-	-	-	-	-	17.8	0.0	-	-	-	-	-	-	-	-	-	-	17.9	0.6
1930	-	-	-	-	-	-	-	-	-	-	17.5	-2.2	-	-	-	-	-	-	-	-	-	-	16.8	-4.0
1931	-	-	-	-	-	-	-	-	-	-	15.9	-5.4	-	-	-	-	-	-	-	-	-	-	15.3	-3.8
1932	-	-	-	-	-	-	-	-	-	-	14.2	-7.2	-	-	-	-	-	-	-	-	-	-	13.5	-4.9
1933	-	-	-	-	-	-	-	-	-	-	13.2	-2.2	-	-	-	-	-	-	-	-	-	-	13.8	4.5
1934	-	-	-	-	-	-	-	-	-	-	14.2	2.9	-	-	-	-	-	-	-	-	14.1	-0.7	-	-
1935	-	-	-	-	14.2	0.7	-	-	-	-	-	-	14.2	0.0	-	-	-	-	14.4	1.4	-	-	-	-
1936	14.5	0.7	-	-	-	-	14.4	-0.7	-	-	-	-	14.5	0.7	-	-	14.6	0.7	-	-	-	-	14.6	0.0
1937	-	-	-	-	14.8	1.4	-	-	-	-	14.9	0.7	-	-	-	-	15.1	1.3	-	-	-	-	14.7	-2.6
1938	-	-	-	-	14.5	-1.4	-	-	-	-	14.6	0.7	-	-	-	-	14.5	-0.7	-	-	-	-	14.4	-0.7
1939	-	-	-	-	14.2	-1.4	-	-	-	-	14.2	0.0	-	-	-	-	14.5	2.1	-	-	-	-	14.3	-1.4
1940	-	-	-	-	14.3	0.0	-	-	-	-	14.4	0.7	-	-	-	-	14.3	-0.7	14.3	0.0	14.3	0.0	14.4	0.7
1941	14.4	0.0	14.4	0.0	14.5	0.7	14.6	0.7	14.7	0.7	15.0	2.0	15.0	0.0	15.2	1.3	15.5	2.0	15.7	1.3	15.7	0.0	15.8	0.6
1942	16.1	1.9	16.1	0.0	16.3	1.2	16.5	1.2	16.6	0.6	16.7	0.6	16.9	1.2	16.9	0.0	17.0	0.6	17.1	0.6	17.2	0.6	17.4	1.2
1943	17.4	0.0	17.4	0.0	17.6	1.1	18.0	2.3	18.1	0.6	18.0	-0.6	17.8	-1.1	17.8	0.0	17.8	0.0	17.9	0.6	17.9	0.0	17.9	0.0
1944	17.9	0.0	17.9	0.0	17.8	-0.6	17.9	0.6	18.0	0.6	18.1	0.6	18.1	0.0	18.2	0.6	18.2	0.0	18.1	-0.5	18.1	0.0	18.2	0.6
1945	18.3	0.5	18.4	0.5	18.3	-0.5	18.3	0.0	18.5	1.1	18.6	0.5	18.7	0.5	18.7	0.0	18.6	-0.5	18.6	0.0	18.6	0.0	18.7	0.5
1946	18.7	0.0	18.7	0.0	18.8	0.5	18.9	0.5	19.0	0.5	19.2	1.1	20.3	5.7	20.9	3.0	21.2	1.4	21.5	1.4	21.9	1.9	22.2	1.4
1947	22.1	-0.5	22.0	-0.5	22.7	3.2	22.5	-0.9	22.5	0.0	22.8	1.3	23.0	0.9	23.2	0.9	23.7	2.2	23.6	-0.4	23.8	0.8	24.2	1.7
1948	24.4	0.8	24.2	-0.8	24.0	-0.8	24.6	2.5	24.8	0.8	25.0	0.8	25.1	0.4	25.4	1.2	25.4	0.0	25.3	-0.4	25.0	-1.2	24.8	-0.8
1949	24.6	-0.8	24.5	-0.4	24.6	0.4	24.6	0.0	24.7	0.4	24.6	-0.4	24.4	-0.8	24.5	0.4	24.6	0.4	24.6	0.0	24.5	-0.4	24.3	-0.8
1950	24.1	-0.8	24.1	0.0	24.2	0.4	24.2	0.0	24.3	0.4	24.5	0.8	24.7	0.8	24.9	0.8	25.1	0.8	25.2	0.4	25.2	0.0	25.8	2.4
1951	26.3	1.9	26.9	2.3	26.9	0.0	27.0	0.4	27.0	0.0	26.9	-0.4	26.9	0.0	26.9	0.0	27.0	0.4	27.1	0.4	27.4	1.1	27.4	0.0
1952	27.4	0.0	27.1	-1.1	27.2	0.4	27.3	0.4	27.3	0.0	27.4	0.4	27.7	1.1	27.7	0.0	27.7	0.0	27.7	0.0	27.7	0.0	27.7	0.0
1953	27.6	-0.4	27.4	-0.7	27.5	0.4	27.4	-0.4	27.5	0.4	27.7	0.7	27.7	0.0	27.7	0.0	27.8	0.4	27.8	0.0	27.7	-0.4	27.7	0.0
1954	27.8	0.4	27.8	0.0	27.7	-0.4	27.8	0.4	27.8	0.0	28.0	0.7	28.1	0.4	28.0	-0.4	28.0	0.0	28.0	0.0	28.0	0.0	27.9	-0.4
1955	27.9	0.0	27.9	0.0	27.9	0.0	27.9	0.0	27.9	0.0	27.9	0.0	27.9	0.0	27.9	0.0	27.8	-0.4	27.8	0.0	27.7	-0.4	27.7	0.0
1956	27.7	0.0	27.7	0.0	27.9	0.7	28.0	0.4	28.0	0.0	28.2	0.7	28.5	1.1	28.5	0.0	28.6	0.4	28.6	0.0	28.5	-0.3	28.6	0.4
1957	28.7	0.3	28.9	0.7	28.9	0.0	28.9	0.0	28.9	0.0	29.0	0.3	29.2	0.7	29.4	0.7	29.4	0.0	29.4	0.0	29.5	0.3	29.5	0.0
1958	29.5	0.0	29.5	0.0	29.7	0.7	29.7	0.0	29.7	0.0	29.7	0.0	29.8	0.3	29.8	0.0	29.8	0.0	29.8	0.0	29.8	0.0	29.8	0.0

[Continued]

Philadelphia, PA-NJ
Consumer Price Index - All Urban Consumers
Base 1982-1984 = 100
All Items
[Continued]

For 1914-1997. Columns headed % show percentile change in the index from the previous period for which an index is available.

Year	Jan Index	%	Feb Index	%	Mar Index	%	Apr Index	%	May Index	%	Jun Index	%	Jul Index	%	Aug Index	%	Sep Index	%	Oct Index	%	Nov Index	%	Dec Index	%
1959	29.8	0.0	29.8	0.0	29.8	0.0	29.8	0.0	29.7	-0.3	29.9	0.7	30.0	0.3	30.0	0.0	30.4	1.3	30.4	0.0	30.5	0.3	30.5	0.0
1960	30.3	-0.7	30.3	0.0	30.4	0.3	30.5	0.3	30.5	0.0	30.5	0.0	30.6	0.3	30.6	0.0	30.7	0.3	30.8	0.3	30.9	0.3	30.9	0.0
1961	30.8	-0.3	30.9	0.3	30.8	-0.3	30.9	0.3	30.9	0.0	30.8	-0.3	31.0	0.6	30.9	-0.3	31.0	0.3	31.0	0.0	31.1	0.3	31.0	-0.3
1962	31.0	0.0	31.1	0.3	31.1	0.0	31.2	0.3	31.0	-0.6	31.1	0.3	31.2	0.3	31.2	0.0	31.4	0.6	31.4	0.0	31.4	0.0	31.3	-0.3
1963	31.4	0.3	31.5	0.3	31.5	0.0	31.5	0.0	31.5	0.0	31.8	1.0	31.8	0.0	31.8	0.0	31.9	0.3	32.1	0.6	32.1	0.0	32.2	0.3
1964	32.2	0.0	32.2	0.0	32.1	-0.3	32.1	0.0	32.1	0.0	32.2	0.3	32.3	0.3	32.2	-0.3	32.3	0.3	32.4	0.3	32.5	0.3	32.5	0.0
1965	32.5	0.0	32.6	0.3	32.6	0.0	32.5	-0.3	32.6	0.3	32.8	0.6	32.9	0.3	32.8	-0.3	32.8	0.0	32.9	0.3	33.0	0.3	33.1	0.3
1966	33.1	0.0	33.3	0.6	33.4	0.3	33.5	0.3	33.5	0.0	33.6	0.3	33.7	0.3	33.9	0.6	34.0	0.3	34.1	0.3	34.1	0.0	34.2	0.3
1967	34.1	-0.3	34.2	0.3	34.2	0.0	34.3	0.3	34.4	0.3	34.5	0.3	34.6	0.3	34.8	0.6	34.9	0.3	35.1	0.6	35.1	0.0	35.2	0.3
1968	35.4	0.6	35.6	0.6	35.8	0.6	35.9	0.3	36.0	0.3	36.2	0.6	36.3	0.3	36.4	0.3	36.7	0.8	36.9	0.5	37.0	0.3	37.1	0.3
1969	37.1	0.0	37.3	0.5	37.6	0.8	37.8	0.5	37.8	0.0	38.0	0.5	38.3	0.8	38.6	0.8	38.8	0.5	38.9	0.3	39.0	0.3	39.2	0.5
1970	39.4	0.5	39.8	1.0	40.1	0.8	40.2	0.2	40.5	0.7	40.6	0.2	40.7	0.2	40.9	0.5	41.4	1.2	41.7	0.7	41.9	0.5	42.0	0.2
1971	42.0	0.0	42.2	0.5	42.3	0.2	42.4	0.2	42.7	0.7	43.0	0.7	42.8	-0.5	42.8	0.0	43.1	0.7	43.3	0.5	43.2	-0.2	43.3	0.2
1972	43.2	-0.2	43.3	0.2	43.5	0.5	43.6	0.2	43.6	0.0	43.8	0.5	44.0	0.5	44.1	0.2	44.4	0.7	44.5	0.2	44.7	0.4	44.6	-0.2
1973	44.7	0.2	45.2	1.1	45.9	1.5	46.2	0.7	46.4	0.4	46.6	0.4	46.7	0.2	47.5	1.7	47.8	0.6	48.3	1.0	48.6	0.6	48.9	0.6
1974	49.4	1.0	50.2	1.6	50.9	1.4	51.3	0.8	51.7	0.8	52.2	1.0	52.5	0.6	53.1	1.1	53.9	1.5	54.4	0.9	54.9	0.9	55.1	0.4
1975	55.2	0.2	55.5	0.5	55.8	0.5	55.8	0.0	56.1	0.5	56.6	0.9	57.1	0.9	57.3	0.4	57.8	0.9	58.2	0.7	58.3	0.2	58.3	0.0
1976	58.5	0.3	58.7	0.3	58.7	0.0	58.9	0.3	59.2	0.5	59.5	0.5	59.8	0.5	59.9	0.2	60.4	0.8	60.6	0.3	60.8	0.3	60.7	-0.2
1977	61.2	0.8	61.9	1.1	62.4	0.8	63.0	1.0	63.4	0.6	63.6	0.3	64.0	0.6	64.0	0.0	64.6	0.9	64.7	0.2	64.9	0.3	64.7	-0.3
1978	64.9	0.3	65.1	0.3	65.6	0.8	66.0	0.6	66.4	0.6	67.1	1.1	67.9	1.2	68.0	0.1	68.5	0.7	68.7	0.3	69.1	0.6	69.6	0.7
1979	70.0	0.6	70.6	0.9	70.9	0.4	71.9	1.4	72.9	1.4	74.0	1.5	74.8	1.1	75.4	0.8	76.0	0.8	76.2	0.3	77.0	1.0	77.4	0.5
1980	78.6	1.6	80.0	1.8	81.2	1.5	82.2	1.2	82.9	0.9	83.9	1.2	84.5	0.7	85.2	0.8	85.6	0.5	85.8	0.2	86.3	0.6	86.7	0.5
1981	87.6	1.0	88.6	1.1	89.4	0.9	90.3	1.0	90.7	0.4	91.9	1.3	92.7	0.9	93.6	1.0	95.0	1.5	95.1	0.1	94.9	-0.2	95.2	0.3
1982	95.4	0.2	95.4	0.0	95.1	-0.3	95.2	0.1	95.2	0.0	96.8	1.7	97.3	0.5	97.4	0.1	98.0	0.6	97.5	-0.5	97.9	0.4	97.5	-0.4
1983	97.6	0.1	97.6	0.0	98.0	0.4	98.1	0.1	98.4	0.3	99.0	0.6	99.8	0.8	100.3	0.5	100.9	0.6	100.8	-0.1	101.0	0.2	101.0	0.0
1984	101.9	0.9	102.6	0.7	102.7	0.1	103.2	0.5	103.4	0.2	103.8	0.4	104.3	0.5	104.8	0.5	105.2	0.4	105.1	-0.1	105.9	0.8	105.6	-0.3
1985	106.0	0.4	107.0	0.9	107.4	0.4	108.1	0.7	108.8	0.6	108.8	0.0	109.2	0.4	109.3	0.1	109.6	0.3	109.9	0.3	110.4	0.5	110.7	0.3
1986	110.9	0.2	110.8	-0.1	110.5	-0.3	110.0	-0.5	110.4	0.4	111.4	0.9	111.8	0.4	111.8	0.0	112.8	0.9	112.4	-0.4	112.2	-0.2	112.6	0.4
1987	113.4	0.7	113.9	0.4	114.0	0.1	115.5	1.3	116.4	0.8	117.4	0.9	117.4	0.0	118.4	0.9	118.7	0.3	119.1	0.3	118.6	-0.4	118.9	0.3
1988	119.3	0.3	119.3	0.0	119.6	0.3	120.0	0.3	120.9	0.7	121.9	0.8	123.2	1.1	123.9	0.6	125.2	1.0	124.6	-0.5	125.3	0.6	125.6	0.2
1989	125.7	0.1	125.4	-0.2	126.0	0.5	126.7	0.6	127.9	0.9	128.8	0.7	129.3	0.4	129.1	-0.2	130.2	0.9	130.5	0.2	130.1	-0.3	129.9	-0.2
1990	131.2	1.0	132.2	0.8	133.6	1.1	134.3	0.5	134.6	0.2	135.1	0.4	136.3	0.9	137.3	0.7	138.2	0.7	138.8	0.4	139.1	0.2	139.4	0.2
1991	140.4	0.7	140.6	0.1	141.0	0.3	140.8	-0.1	141.3	0.4	141.8	0.4	142.4	0.4	143.3	0.6	143.8	0.3	143.1	-0.5	143.3	0.1	144.4	0.8
1992	144.4	0.0	144.2	-0.1	145.4	0.8	145.4	0.0	145.7	0.2	147.5	1.2	147.3	-0.1	148.0	0.5	148.1	0.1	148.0	-0.1	147.5	-0.3	147.5	0.0
1993	147.5	0.0	148.5	0.7	149.3	0.5	149.6	0.2	149.4	-0.1	150.5	0.7	150.7	0.1	150.6	-0.1	151.1	0.3	152.2	0.7	152.1	-0.1	151.3	-0.5
1994	152.5	0.8	152.9	0.3	153.5	0.4	153.1	-0.3	153.2	0.1	154.6	0.9	155.3	0.5	155.7	0.3	156.2	0.3	156.6	0.3	156.7	0.1	155.4	-0.8
1995	156.6	0.8	157.8	0.8	158.0	0.1	157.8	-0.1	157.8	0.0	158.4	0.4	158.9	0.3	159.6	0.4	160.3	0.4	160.4	0.1	159.6	-0.5	159.1	-0.3
1996	160.3	0.8	161.2	0.6	162.0	0.5	162.1	0.1	161.8	-0.2	162.3	0.3	162.8	0.3	163.6	0.5	164.5	0.6	164.9	0.2	164.3	-0.4	164.3	0.0
1997	165.1	0.5	165.8	0.4	166.1	0.2	166.0	-0.1	166.0	0.0	166.1	0.1	166.4	0.2	166.8	0.2	168.6	1.1	167.7	-0.5	166.4	-0.8	166.4	0.0

Source: U.S. Department of Labor, Bureau of Labor Statistics, Division of Consumer Prices and Price Indexes. - indicates no data collected for period.

Philadelphia, PA-NJ
Consumer Price Index - Urban Wage Earners
Base 1982-1984 = 100
All Items

For 1914-1997. Columns headed % show percentile change in the index from the previous period for which an index is available.

Year	Jan Index	%	Feb Index	%	Mar Index	%	Apr Index	%	May Index	%	Jun Index	%	Jul Index	%	Aug Index	%	Sep Index	%	Oct Index	%	Nov Index	%	Dec Index	%
1914	-	-	-	-	-	-	-	-	-	-	-	-	-	-	-	-	-	-	-	-	-	-	10.1	-
1915	-	-	-	-	-	-	-	-	-	-	-	-	-	-	-	-	-	-	-	-	-	-	10.3	2.0
1916	-	-	-	-	-	-	-	-	-	-	-	-	-	-	-	-	-	-	-	-	-	-	11.5	11.7
1917	-	-	-	-	-	-	-	-	-	-	-	-	-	-	-	-	-	-	-	-	-	-	14.0	21.7
1918	-	-	-	-	-	-	-	-	-	-	-	-	-	-	-	-	-	-	-	-	-	-	16.9	20.7
1919	-	-	-	-	-	-	-	-	-	-	17.4	3.0	-	-	-	-	-	-	-	-	-	-	19.1	9.8
1920	-	-	-	-	-	-	-	-	-	-	21.2	11.0	-	-	-	-	-	-	-	-	-	-	19.8	-6.6
1921	-	-	-	-	-	-	-	-	18.0	-9.1	-	-	-	-	-	-	17.8	-1.1	-	-	-	-	17.6	-1.1
1922	-	-	-	-	17.2	-2.3	-	-	-	-	17.2	0.0	-	-	-	-	16.8	-2.3	-	-	-	-	17.2	2.4
1923	-	-	-	-	17.2	0.0	-	-	-	-	17.5	1.7	-	-	-	-	17.7	1.1	-	-	-	-	17.7	0.0
1924	-	-	-	-	17.5	-1.1	-	-	-	-	17.6	0.6	-	-	-	-	17.5	-0.6	-	-	-	-	17.9	2.3
1925	-	-	-	-	-	-	-	-	-	-	18.3	2.2	-	-	-	-	-	-	-	-	-	-	18.8	2.7
1926	-	-	-	-	-	-	-	-	-	-	18.7	-0.5	-	-	-	-	-	-	-	-	-	-	18.6	-0.5
1927	-	-	-	-	-	-	-	-	-	-	18.4	-1.1	-	-	-	-	-	-	-	-	-	-	18.2	-1.1
1928	-	-	-	-	-	-	-	-	-	-	18.0	-1.1	-	-	-	-	-	-	-	-	-	-	17.7	-1.7
1929	-	-	-	-	-	-	-	-	-	-	17.7	0.0	-	-	-	-	-	-	-	-	-	-	17.8	0.6
1930	-	-	-	-	-	-	-	-	-	-	17.4	-2.2	-	-	-	-	-	-	-	-	-	-	16.7	-4.0
1931	-	-	-	-	-	-	-	-	-	-	15.8	-5.4	-	-	-	-	-	-	-	-	-	-	15.3	-3.2
1932	-	-	-	-	-	-	-	-	-	-	14.1	-7.8	-	-	-	-	-	-	-	-	-	-	13.5	-4.3
1933	-	-	-	-	-	-	-	-	-	-	13.2	-2.2	-	-	-	-	-	-	-	-	-	-	13.8	4.5
1934	-	-	-	-	-	-	-	-	-	-	14.1	2.2	-	-	-	-	-	-	-	-	14.0	-0.7	-	-
1935	-	-	-	-	14.1	0.7	-	-	-	-	-	-	14.1	0.0	-	-	-	-	14.3	1.4	-	-	-	-
1936	14.5	1.4	-	-	-	-	14.3	-1.4	-	-	-	-	14.5	1.4	-	-	14.6	0.7	-	-	-	-	14.5	-0.7
1937	-	-	-	-	14.7	1.4	-	-	-	-	14.8	0.7	-	-	-	-	15.0	1.4	-	-	-	-	14.7	-2.0
1938	-	-	-	-	14.5	-1.4	-	-	-	-	14.5	0.0	-	-	-	-	14.5	0.0	-	-	-	-	14.3	-1.4
1939	-	-	-	-	14.1	-1.4	-	-	-	-	14.1	0.0	-	-	-	-	14.4	2.1	-	-	-	-	14.3	-0.7
1940	-	-	-	-	14.2	-0.7	-	-	-	-	14.3	0.7	-	-	-	-	14.3	0.0	14.3	0.0	14.3	0.0	14.3	0.0
1941	14.3	0.0	14.3	0.0	14.4	0.7	14.5	0.7	14.7	1.4	14.9	1.4	14.9	0.0	15.1	1.3	15.4	2.0	15.6	1.3	15.6	0.0	15.7	0.6
1942	16.0	1.9	16.0	0.0	16.2	1.3	16.4	1.2	16.5	0.6	16.6	0.6	16.8	1.2	16.8	0.0	16.9	0.6	17.0	0.6	17.1	0.6	17.3	1.2
1943	17.3	0.0	17.3	0.0	17.5	1.2	17.9	2.3	18.0	0.6	17.9	-0.6	17.7	-1.1	17.7	0.0	17.7	0.0	17.8	0.6	17.8	0.0	17.8	0.0
1944	17.8	0.0	17.8	0.0	17.7	-0.6	17.8	0.6	17.9	0.6	18.0	0.6	18.0	0.0	18.1	0.6	18.1	0.0	18.0	-0.6	18.0	0.0	18.1	0.6
1945	18.2	0.6	18.3	0.5	18.2	-0.5	18.2	0.0	18.4	1.1	18.5	0.5	18.6	0.5	18.6	0.0	18.5	-0.5	18.5	0.0	18.5	0.0	18.6	0.5
1946	18.6	0.0	18.6	0.0	18.7	0.5	18.8	0.5	18.9	0.5	19.1	1.1	20.2	5.8	20.8	3.0	21.1	1.4	21.3	0.9	21.8	2.3	22.0	0.9
1947	22.0	0.0	21.9	-0.5	22.5	2.7	22.4	-0.4	22.4	0.0	22.7	1.3	22.9	0.9	23.1	0.9	23.6	2.2	23.4	-0.8	23.7	1.3	24.0	1.3
1948	24.3	1.2	24.1	-0.8	23.9	-0.8	24.5	2.5	24.6	0.4	24.9	1.2	25.0	0.4	25.3	1.2	25.3	0.0	25.2	-0.4	24.8	-1.6	24.7	-0.4
1949	24.5	-0.8	24.4	-0.4	24.4	0.0	24.4	0.0	24.5	0.4	24.5	0.0	24.2	-1.2	24.4	0.8	24.5	0.4	24.4	-0.4	24.4	0.0	24.2	-0.8
1950	24.0	-0.8	23.9	-0.4	24.1	0.8	24.1	0.0	24.1	0.0	24.4	1.2	24.6	0.8	24.8	0.8	25.0	0.8	25.1	0.4	25.1	0.0	25.7	2.4
1951	26.1	1.6	26.8	2.7	26.8	0.0	26.8	0.0	26.9	0.4	26.8	-0.4	26.8	0.0	26.8	0.0	26.8	0.0	27.0	0.7	27.3	1.1	27.3	0.0
1952	27.2	-0.4	27.0	-0.7	27.1	0.4	27.2	0.4	27.2	0.0	27.3	0.4	27.6	1.1	27.6	0.0	27.5	-0.4	27.5	0.0	27.5	0.0	27.5	0.0
1953	27.4	-0.4	27.3	-0.4	27.4	0.4	27.3	-0.4	27.3	0.0	27.5	0.7	27.5	0.0	27.6	0.4	27.6	0.0	27.7	0.4	27.5	-0.7	27.6	0.4
1954	27.7	0.4	27.6	-0.4	27.6	0.0	27.6	0.0	27.7	0.4	27.8	0.4	27.9	0.4	27.9	0.0	27.9	0.0	27.9	0.0	27.8	-0.4	27.7	-0.4
1955	27.7	0.0	27.8	0.4	27.8	0.0	27.8	0.0	27.7	-0.4	27.7	0.0	27.8	0.4	27.8	0.0	27.6	-0.7	27.7	0.4	27.6	-0.4	27.6	0.0
1956	27.5	-0.4	27.5	0.0	27.8	1.1	27.9	0.4	27.9	0.0	28.0	0.4	28.3	1.1	28.3	0.0	28.4	0.4	28.5	0.4	28.4	-0.4	28.5	0.4
1957	28.5	0.0	28.7	0.7	28.8	0.3	28.7	-0.3	28.8	0.3	28.8	0.0	29.1	1.0	29.2	0.3	29.3	0.3	29.3	0.0	29.3	0.0	29.3	0.0
1958	29.3	0.0	29.4	0.3	29.5	0.3	29.5	0.0	29.5	0.0	29.5	0.0	29.6	0.3	29.6	0.0	29.6	0.0	29.6	0.0	29.6	0.0	29.6	0.0

[Continued]

Philadelphia, PA-NJ
Consumer Price Index - Urban Wage Earners
Base 1982-1984 = 100
All Items
[Continued]

For 1914-1997. Columns headed % show percentile change in the index from the previous period for which an index is available.

Year	Jan Index	%	Feb Index	%	Mar Index	%	Apr Index	%	May Index	%	Jun Index	%	Jul Index	%	Aug Index	%	Sep Index	%	Oct Index	%	Nov Index	%	Dec Index	%
1959	29.6	0.0	29.6	0.0	29.6	0.0	29.7	0.3	29.6	-0.3	29.8	0.7	29.8	0.0	29.8	0.0	30.2	1.3	30.2	0.0	30.3	0.3	30.4	0.3
1960	30.1	-1.0	30.1	0.0	30.2	0.3	30.3	0.3	30.3	0.0	30.3	0.0	30.4	0.3	30.4	0.0	30.5	0.3	30.6	0.3	30.7	0.3	30.7	0.0
1961	30.7	0.0	30.7	0.0	30.6	-0.3	30.7	0.3	30.7	0.0	30.7	0.0	30.8	0.3	30.7	-0.3	30.8	0.3	30.9	0.3	30.9	0.0	30.9	0.0
1962	30.8	-0.3	31.0	0.6	31.0	0.0	31.0	0.0	30.8	-0.6	30.9	0.3	31.1	0.6	31.0	-0.3	31.3	1.0	31.2	-0.3	31.2	0.0	31.2	0.0
1963	31.2	0.0	31.3	0.3	31.4	0.3	31.4	0.0	31.3	-0.3	31.6	1.0	31.7	0.3	31.7	0.0	31.7	0.0	31.9	0.6	31.9	0.0	32.0	0.3
1964	32.0	0.0	32.1	0.3	31.9	-0.6	31.9	0.0	31.9	0.0	32.0	0.3	32.1	0.3	32.0	-0.3	32.1	0.3	32.2	0.3	32.3	0.3	32.3	0.0
1965	32.3	0.0	32.4	0.3	32.4	0.0	32.3	-0.3	32.5	0.6	32.6	0.3	32.7	0.3	32.6	-0.3	32.7	0.3	32.7	0.0	32.8	0.3	32.9	0.3
1966	32.9	0.0	33.1	0.6	33.2	0.3	33.4	0.6	33.3	-0.3	33.4	0.3	33.5	0.3	33.7	0.6	33.8	0.3	33.9	0.3	33.9	0.0	34.0	0.3
1967	33.9	-0.3	34.0	0.3	34.0	0.0	34.1	0.3	34.2	0.3	34.4	0.6	34.4	0.0	34.6	0.6	34.7	0.3	34.9	0.6	34.9	0.0	35.0	0.3
1968	35.3	0.9	35.4	0.3	35.6	0.6	35.7	0.3	35.8	0.3	36.0	0.6	36.1	0.3	36.3	0.6	36.5	0.6	36.7	0.5	36.8	0.3	36.9	0.3
1969	36.9	0.0	37.1	0.5	37.4	0.8	37.6	0.5	37.6	0.0	37.8	0.5	38.1	0.8	38.4	0.8	38.6	0.5	38.7	0.3	38.8	0.3	39.0	0.5
1970	39.2	0.5	39.6	1.0	39.9	0.8	40.0	0.3	40.2	0.5	40.4	0.5	40.5	0.2	40.7	0.5	41.2	1.2	41.5	0.7	41.7	0.5	41.8	0.2
1971	41.8	0.0	41.9	0.2	42.1	0.5	42.2	0.2	42.5	0.7	42.7	0.5	42.6	-0.2	42.6	0.0	42.9	0.7	43.0	0.2	42.9	-0.2	43.1	0.5
1972	42.9	-0.5	43.1	0.5	43.3	0.5	43.4	0.2	43.4	0.0	43.6	0.5	43.7	0.2	43.9	0.5	44.2	0.7	44.3	0.2	44.4	0.2	44.4	0.0
1973	44.4	0.0	45.0	1.4	45.6	1.3	45.9	0.7	46.2	0.7	46.4	0.4	46.4	0.0	47.2	1.7	47.5	0.6	48.0	1.1	48.4	0.8	48.7	0.6
1974	49.2	1.0	49.9	1.4	50.6	1.4	51.0	0.8	51.4	0.8	52.0	1.2	52.3	0.6	52.8	1.0	53.6	1.5	54.1	0.9	54.6	0.9	54.8	0.4
1975	54.9	0.2	55.2	0.5	55.5	0.5	55.5	0.0	55.8	0.5	56.3	0.9	56.8	0.9	57.0	0.4	57.5	0.9	57.9	0.7	58.0	0.2	58.0	0.0
1976	58.2	0.3	58.4	0.3	58.4	0.0	58.6	0.3	58.9	0.5	59.2	0.5	59.5	0.5	59.6	0.2	60.1	0.8	60.3	0.3	60.5	0.3	60.4	-0.2
1977	60.8	0.7	61.5	1.2	62.1	1.0	62.6	0.8	63.0	0.6	63.3	0.5	63.6	0.5	63.7	0.2	64.2	0.8	64.4	0.3	64.5	0.2	64.3	-0.3
1978	64.5	0.3	65.0	0.8	65.3	0.5	65.9	0.9	66.3	0.6	67.0	1.1	67.4	0.6	68.0	0.9	68.2	0.3	68.5	0.4	69.1	0.9	69.7	0.9
1979	70.2	0.7	70.9	1.0	71.2	0.4	72.0	1.1	72.8	1.1	73.8	1.4	74.7	1.2	75.1	0.5	75.8	0.9	76.2	0.5	77.0	1.0	77.3	0.4
1980	78.5	1.6	79.7	1.5	80.9	1.5	81.9	1.2	82.6	0.9	83.9	1.6	84.5	0.7	85.1	0.7	85.5	0.5	85.9	0.5	86.4	0.6	86.9	0.6
1981	88.0	1.3	88.9	1.0	89.3	0.4	90.0	0.8	90.5	0.6	91.4	1.0	92.4	1.1	93.5	1.2	94.5	1.1	94.7	0.2	94.5	-0.2	94.4	-0.1
1982	94.7	0.3	94.7	0.0	94.4	-0.3	94.5	0.1	94.6	0.1	96.1	1.6	96.7	0.6	96.6	-0.1	97.1	0.5	96.8	-0.3	97.1	0.3	96.7	-0.4
1983	97.3	0.6	97.5	0.2	98.3	0.8	98.7	0.4	98.6	-0.1	99.4	0.8	100.2	0.8	101.0	0.8	101.3	0.3	101.3	0.0	101.5	0.2	101.3	-0.2
1984	102.1	0.8	102.8	0.7	102.9	0.1	102.9	0.0	103.5	0.6	104.2	0.7	104.8	0.6	105.4	0.6	106.2	0.8	106.3	0.1	106.4	0.1	106.0	-0.4
1985	106.5	0.5	107.6	1.0	107.9	0.3	108.5	0.6	109.2	0.6	109.2	0.0	109.7	0.5	109.7	0.0	109.9	0.2	110.3	0.4	110.7	0.4	111.0	0.3
1986	111.2	0.2	111.1	-0.1	110.6	-0.5	110.1	-0.5	110.4	0.3	111.4	0.9	111.8	0.4	111.7	-0.1	112.5	0.7	112.3	-0.2	112.0	-0.3	112.5	0.4
1987	113.3	0.7	113.6	0.3	113.8	0.2	115.3	1.3	116.2	0.8	117.2	0.9	117.3	0.1	118.4	0.9	118.5	0.1	119.0	0.4	118.6	-0.3	119.0	0.3
1988	119.3	0.3	119.0	-0.3	119.5	0.4	119.8	0.3	120.8	0.8	121.8	0.8	123.1	1.1	123.6	0.4	124.9	1.1	124.4	-0.4	125.0	0.5	125.2	0.2
1989	125.5	0.2	125.4	-0.1	125.8	0.3	126.7	0.7	127.9	0.9	128.9	0.8	129.3	0.3	129.3	0.0	130.4	0.9	130.6	0.2	130.1	-0.4	130.0	-0.1
1990	131.0	0.8	132.2	0.9	133.8	1.2	134.4	0.4	134.9	0.4	135.5	0.4	136.6	0.8	137.5	0.7	138.6	0.8	139.1	0.4	139.4	0.2	139.8	0.3
1991	140.4	0.4	140.5	0.1	141.0	0.4	140.8	-0.1	141.2	0.3	141.8	0.4	142.5	0.5	143.2	0.5	143.7	0.3	142.9	-0.6	143.4	0.3	144.4	0.7
1992	144.2	-0.1	143.9	-0.2	145.0	0.8	145.1	0.1	145.5	0.3	147.4	1.3	147.3	-0.1	147.8	0.3	147.9	0.1	147.8	-0.1	147.6	-0.1	147.4	-0.1
1993	147.4	0.0	148.6	0.8	149.0	0.3	149.4	0.3	149.3	-0.1	150.4	0.7	150.6	0.1	150.4	-0.1	150.9	0.3	151.9	0.7	151.9	0.0	151.2	-0.5
1994	152.1	0.6	152.2	0.1	152.8	0.4	152.6	-0.1	152.7	0.1	154.2	1.0	154.9	0.5	155.3	0.3	155.9	0.4	156.1	0.1	156.1	0.0	155.1	-0.6
1995	156.4	0.8	157.5	0.7	157.5	0.0	157.4	-0.1	157.4	0.0	158.1	0.4	158.5	0.3	159.2	0.4	159.8	0.4	159.7	-0.1	159.2	-0.3	158.7	-0.3
1996	159.7	0.6	160.5	0.5	161.3	0.5	161.3	0.0	161.3	0.0	161.7	0.2	162.1	0.2	163.0	0.6	163.7	0.4	164.2	0.3	164.0	-0.1	163.6	-0.2
1997	164.4	0.5	164.9	0.3	165.3	0.2	165.1	-0.1	165.2	0.1	165.3	0.1	165.5	0.1	165.9	0.2	167.9	1.2	166.8	-0.7	165.9	-0.5	165.7	-0.1

Source: U.S. Department of Labor, Bureau of Labor Statistics, Division of Consumer Prices and Price Indexes. - indicates no data collected for period.

Philadelphia, PA-NJ
Consumer Price Index - All Urban Consumers
Base 1982-1984 = 100
Food and Beverages

For 1976-1997. Columns headed % show percentile change in the index from the previous period for which an index is available.

Year	Jan Index	%	Feb Index	%	Mar Index	%	Apr Index	%	May Index	%	Jun Index	%	Jul Index	%	Aug Index	%	Sep Index	%	Oct Index	%	Nov Index	%	Dec Index	%
1976	62.3	-	62.3	0.0	61.7	-1.0	61.8	0.2	62.0	0.3	62.3	0.5	62.4	0.2	62.5	0.2	62.5	0.0	62.4	-0.2	62.3	-0.2	62.2	-0.2
1977	63.1	1.4	64.7	2.5	65.3	0.9	65.8	0.8	65.9	0.2	66.3	0.6	66.7	0.6	66.3	-0.6	66.5	0.3	66.9	0.6	67.4	0.7	67.5	0.1
1978	68.3	1.2	69.3	1.5	70.1	1.2	70.6	0.7	71.6	1.4	73.5	2.7	74.1	0.8	74.0	-0.1	73.9	-0.1	73.8	-0.1	74.7	1.2	75.0	0.4
1979	76.3	1.7	77.4	1.4	78.2	1.0	78.7	0.6	79.2	0.6	79.3	0.1	80.3	1.3	80.1	-0.2	79.8	-0.4	80.9	1.4	81.3	0.5	82.0	0.9
1980	82.3	0.4	82.1	-0.2	83.0	1.1	83.9	1.1	84.8	1.1	86.2	1.7	86.7	0.6	87.5	0.9	87.9	0.5	88.6	0.8	89.3	0.8	89.6	0.3
1981	90.7	1.2	90.8	0.1	90.9	0.1	91.2	0.3	91.6	0.4	91.9	0.3	93.0	1.2	93.4	0.4	94.5	1.2	94.1	-0.4	93.9	-0.2	94.6	0.7
1982	95.5	1.0	96.7	1.3	96.7	0.0	97.7	1.0	97.4	-0.3	98.2	0.8	98.8	0.6	98.5	-0.3	98.7	0.2	98.1	-0.6	98.0	-0.1	97.8	-0.2
1983	98.3	0.5	98.8	0.5	99.1	0.3	99.7	0.6	99.9	0.2	100.7	0.8	100.4	-0.3	100.8	0.4	100.8	0.0	100.6	-0.2	100.1	-0.5	100.2	0.1
1984	101.6	1.4	102.6	1.0	102.7	0.1	102.3	-0.4	102.2	-0.1	102.4	0.2	103.2	0.8	103.6	0.4	102.2	-1.4	102.2	0.0	101.9	-0.3	101.8	-0.1
1985	103.2	1.4	104.5	1.3	104.9	0.4	104.9	0.0	104.9	0.0	104.6	-0.3	105.6	1.0	104.9	-0.7	105.6	0.7	105.8	0.2	105.3	-0.5	106.0	0.7
1986	106.1	0.1	106.0	-0.1	106.9	0.8	106.9	0.0	107.1	0.2	107.1	0.0	107.8	0.7	108.5	0.6	109.4	0.8	109.5	0.1	108.9	-0.5	109.3	0.4
1987	110.8	1.4	110.8	0.0	110.5	-0.3	111.4	0.8	111.9	0.4	112.0	0.1	112.4	0.4	112.7	0.3	112.7	0.0	113.4	0.6	113.1	-0.3	113.0	-0.1
1988	114.2	1.1	113.7	-0.4	112.7	-0.9	114.4	1.5	115.1	0.6	116.1	0.9	117.3	1.0	117.1	-0.2	117.4	0.3	118.5	0.9	117.3	-1.0	118.2	0.8
1989	119.4	1.0	120.1	0.6	121.7	1.3	122.3	0.5	123.1	0.7	125.0	1.5	125.7	0.6	125.4	-0.2	126.0	0.5	127.0	0.8	127.4	0.3	127.7	0.2
1990	128.4	0.5	130.2	1.4	130.6	0.3	130.1	-0.4	130.4	0.2	130.6	0.2	131.6	0.8	132.3	0.5	131.6	-0.5	132.5	0.7	132.5	0.0	133.6	0.8
1991	134.6	0.7	135.2	0.4	135.5	0.2	135.9	0.3	136.0	0.1	136.1	0.1	135.7	-0.3	135.2	-0.4	135.0	-0.1	135.0	0.0	135.1	0.1	135.1	0.0
1992	136.0	0.7	136.4	0.3	137.1	0.5	137.7	0.4	138.0	0.2	137.7	-0.2	138.1	0.3	137.7	-0.3	138.3	0.4	138.1	-0.1	137.6	-0.4	138.4	0.6
1993	138.6	0.1	139.0	0.3	139.4	0.3	140.4	0.7	140.9	0.4	139.5	-1.0	138.6	-0.6	138.6	0.0	140.2	1.2	139.7	-0.4	141.0	0.9	140.3	-0.5
1994	142.0	1.2	140.6	-1.0	141.0	0.3	141.8	0.6	141.1	-0.5	141.7	0.4	142.5	0.6	142.4	-0.1	144.0	1.1	144.9	0.6	144.7	-0.1	146.2	1.0
1995	147.9	1.2	148.4	0.3	147.8	-0.4	148.5	0.5	149.2	0.5	148.2	-0.7	148.7	0.3	149.1	0.3	149.9	0.5	149.7	-0.1	149.6	-0.1	149.0	-0.4
1996	151.1	1.4	150.7	-0.3	150.2	-0.3	151.2	0.7	151.6	0.3	152.2	0.4	152.7	0.3	152.9	0.1	153.1	0.1	152.8	-0.2	153.7	0.6	153.6	-0.1
1997	153.9	0.2	153.7	-0.1	154.0	0.2	153.8	-0.1	155.4	1.0	154.6	-0.5	154.9	0.2	154.9	0.0	155.3	0.3	153.6	-1.1	153.9	0.2	153.8	-0.1

Source: U.S. Department of Labor, Bureau of Labor Statistics, Division of Consumer Prices and Price Indexes. - indicates no data collected for period.

Philadelphia, PA-NJ
Consumer Price Index - Urban Wage Earners
Base 1982-1984 = 100
Food and Beverages

For 1976-1997. Columns headed % show percentile change in the index from the previous period for which an index is available.

Year	Jan Index	%	Feb Index	%	Mar Index	%	Apr Index	%	May Index	%	Jun Index	%	Jul Index	%	Aug Index	%	Sep Index	%	Oct Index	%	Nov Index	%	Dec Index	%
1976	60.6	-	60.6	0.0	60.0	-1.0	60.1	0.2	60.3	0.3	60.6	0.5	60.7	0.2	60.8	0.2	60.8	0.0	60.7	-0.2	60.6	-0.2	60.5	-0.2
1977	61.4	1.5	63.0	2.6	63.5	0.8	64.1	0.9	64.2	0.2	64.5	0.5	64.9	0.6	64.5	-0.6	64.7	0.3	65.1	0.6	65.6	0.8	65.7	0.2
1978	66.3	0.9	68.2	2.9	68.7	0.7	69.3	0.9	70.3	1.4	71.4	1.6	72.0	0.8	72.7	1.0	72.1	-0.8	72.1	0.0	73.1	1.4	73.3	0.3
1979	75.5	3.0	76.9	1.9	78.2	1.7	78.7	0.6	78.9	0.3	78.7	-0.3	79.6	1.1	79.5	-0.1	79.9	0.5	80.9	1.3	81.3	0.5	81.9	0.7
1980	82.1	0.2	82.1	0.0	83.5	1.7	84.7	1.4	85.6	1.1	87.6	2.3	88.1	0.6	88.9	0.9	88.8	-0.1	89.8	1.1	90.3	0.6	90.4	0.1
1981	91.4	1.1	91.6	0.2	92.1	0.5	91.9	-0.2	92.5	0.7	92.9	0.4	93.9	1.1	94.4	0.5	94.7	0.3	94.3	-0.4	93.8	-0.5	94.5	0.7
1982	95.4	1.0	96.7	1.4	96.8	0.1	97.7	0.9	97.4	-0.3	98.3	0.9	98.8	0.5	98.6	-0.2	98.8	0.2	98.0	-0.8	97.8	-0.2	97.7	-0.1
1983	98.3	0.6	98.7	0.4	99.0	0.3	99.6	0.6	99.9	0.3	100.7	0.8	100.5	-0.2	100.9	0.4	100.8	-0.1	100.6	-0.2	100.0	-0.6	100.2	0.2
1984	101.5	1.3	102.6	1.1	102.7	0.1	102.2	-0.5	102.1	-0.1	102.5	0.4	103.2	0.7	103.7	0.5	102.5	-1.2	102.4	-0.1	101.9	-0.5	101.8	-0.1
1985	103.2	1.4	104.5	1.3	105.0	0.5	104.9	-0.1	105.0	0.1	104.6	-0.4	105.7	1.1	105.0	-0.7	105.6	0.6	105.8	0.2	105.3	-0.5	106.1	0.8
1986	106.1	0.0	106.0	-0.1	106.9	0.8	107.0	0.1	107.2	0.2	107.0	-0.2	107.9	0.8	108.6	0.6	109.5	0.8	109.7	0.2	109.0	-0.6	109.4	0.4
1987	111.2	1.6	110.9	-0.3	110.5	-0.4	111.7	1.1	112.2	0.4	112.3	0.1	112.7	0.4	113.2	0.4	113.1	-0.1	113.6	0.4	113.6	0.0	113.3	-0.3
1988	114.7	1.2	114.0	-0.6	113.0	-0.9	114.6	1.4	115.5	0.8	116.6	1.0	117.8	1.0	117.6	-0.2	117.9	0.3	119.1	1.0	117.9	-1.0	118.7	0.7
1989	120.0	1.1	120.8	0.7	122.7	1.6	123.2	0.4	124.0	0.6	125.8	1.5	126.5	0.6	126.1	-0.3	126.9	0.6	128.0	0.9	128.4	0.3	128.6	0.2
1990	129.2	0.5	131.3	1.6	131.6	0.2	131.0	-0.5	131.5	0.4	131.8	0.2	133.0	0.9	133.5	0.4	132.9	-0.4	133.7	0.6	133.8	0.1	134.8	0.7
1991	135.7	0.7	136.4	0.5	136.7	0.2	136.8	0.1	137.1	0.2	137.2	0.1	137.1	-0.1	136.5	-0.4	136.1	-0.3	135.9	-0.1	136.3	0.3	136.2	-0.1
1992	137.0	0.6	137.4	0.3	138.3	0.7	138.8	0.4	139.0	0.1	138.9	-0.1	139.4	0.4	138.9	-0.4	139.5	0.4	139.4	-0.1	138.9	-0.4	139.4	0.4
1993	139.8	0.3	140.0	0.1	140.5	0.4	141.4	0.6	142.0	0.4	140.8	-0.8	140.0	-0.6	139.9	-0.1	141.7	1.3	140.8	-0.6	142.2	1.0	141.5	-0.5
1994	143.2	1.2	141.6	-1.1	142.4	0.6	143.0	0.4	142.3	-0.5	143.1	0.6	143.9	0.6	143.5	-0.3	145.3	1.3	146.2	0.6	145.7	-0.3	147.0	0.9
1995	149.1	1.4	149.3	0.1	148.8	-0.3	149.6	0.5	150.4	0.5	149.4	-0.7	149.7	0.2	150.3	0.4	150.8	0.3	150.9	0.1	150.9	0.0	150.4	-0.3
1996	152.3	1.3	152.1	-0.1	151.6	-0.3	152.2	0.4	152.7	0.3	153.2	0.3	153.7	0.3	154.1	0.3	154.3	0.1	154.0	-0.2	155.2	0.8	154.5	-0.5
1997	155.0	0.3	154.8	-0.1	155.3	0.3	154.8	-0.3	156.5	1.1	155.7	-0.5	156.1	0.3	155.6	-0.3	156.1	0.3	154.3	-1.2	154.9	0.4	154.7	-0.1

Source: U.S. Department of Labor, Bureau of Labor Statistics, Division of Consumer Prices and Price Indexes. - indicates no data collected for period.

Philadelphia, PA-NJ
Consumer Price Index - All Urban Consumers
Base 1982-1984 = 100
Housing

For 1976-1997. Columns headed % show percentile change in the index from the previous period for which an index is available.

Year	Jan Index	%	Feb Index	%	Mar Index	%	Apr Index	%	May Index	%	Jun Index	%	Jul Index	%	Aug Index	%	Sep Index	%	Oct Index	%	Nov Index	%	Dec Index	%
1976	57.8	-	58.1	0.5	58.3	0.3	58.4	0.2	58.7	0.5	58.7	0.0	59.0	0.5	59.0	0.0	59.9	1.5	60.2	0.5	60.5	0.5	60.5	0.0
1977	60.8	0.5	61.0	0.3	61.7	1.1	62.1	0.6	62.6	0.8	62.7	0.2	63.0	0.5	63.4	0.6	64.2	1.3	64.1	-0.2	64.0	-0.2	63.5	-0.8
1978	63.7	0.3	63.8	0.2	64.2	0.6	64.4	0.3	64.5	0.2	64.8	0.5	65.8	1.5	66.3	0.8	67.1	1.2	67.5	0.6	67.8	0.4	68.3	0.7
1979	68.1	-0.3	68.2	0.1	68.1	-0.1	69.3	1.8	70.7	2.0	72.5	2.5	72.8	0.4	73.4	0.8	74.4	1.4	74.5	0.1	75.4	1.2	75.9	0.7
1980	77.6	2.2	79.3	2.2	80.5	1.5	82.1	2.0	82.9	1.0	84.7	2.2	85.3	0.7	85.5	0.2	85.8	0.4	85.7	-0.1	85.9	0.2	86.8	1.0
1981	87.7	1.0	88.8	1.3	90.2	1.6	91.7	1.7	91.8	0.1	94.0	2.4	95.2	1.3	96.5	1.4	97.8	1.3	97.4	-0.4	97.1	-0.3	96.6	-0.5
1982	97.2	0.6	96.9	-0.3	96.4	-0.5	96.0	-0.4	96.2	0.2	98.6	2.5	98.7	0.1	98.5	-0.2	99.2	0.7	97.9	-1.3	98.6	0.7	97.5	-1.1
1983	97.3	-0.2	97.3	0.0	97.4	0.1	97.1	-0.3	97.6	0.5	98.2	0.6	99.4	1.2	99.1	-0.3	99.5	0.4	98.6	-0.9	99.1	0.5	99.7	0.6
1984	100.9	1.2	102.1	1.2	102.2	0.1	102.7	0.5	103.4	0.7	104.3	0.9	104.3	0.0	104.6	0.3	105.4	0.8	105.4	0.0	106.8	1.3	105.8	-0.9
1985	106.0	0.2	107.2	1.1	107.3	0.1	108.2	0.8	109.6	1.3	109.9	0.3	110.2	0.3	110.3	0.1	109.6	-0.6	109.5	-0.1	110.6	1.0	111.5	0.8
1986	111.5	0.0	111.7	0.2	111.2	-0.4	111.5	0.3	111.7	0.2	113.8	1.9	113.7	-0.1	114.1	0.4	114.9	0.7	113.5	-1.2	113.3	-0.2	113.5	0.2
1987	113.5	0.0	114.9	1.2	115.0	0.1	116.2	1.0	118.4	1.9	120.6	1.9	120.1	-0.4	121.4	1.1	120.8	-0.5	120.7	-0.1	119.2	-1.2	120.0	0.7
1988	120.4	0.3	120.5	0.1	120.7	0.2	121.5	0.7	122.3	0.7	125.2	2.4	126.5	1.0	128.0	1.2	129.1	0.9	126.2	-2.2	128.2	1.6	128.6	0.3
1989	127.6	-0.8	127.2	-0.3	128.9	1.3	128.4	-0.4	129.5	0.9	131.3	1.4	132.4	0.8	132.7	0.2	134.2	1.1	132.9	-1.0	131.9	-0.8	132.7	0.6
1990	134.5	1.4	134.6	0.1	136.2	1.2	136.8	0.4	136.9	0.1	138.4	1.1	139.9	1.1	141.4	1.1	141.7	0.2	141.1	-0.4	141.1	0.0	141.3	0.1
1991	143.2	1.3	143.4	0.1	144.5	0.8	143.4	-0.8	144.2	0.6	146.2	1.4	147.8	1.1	148.1	0.2	147.9	-0.1	145.7	-1.5	145.0	-0.5	147.2	1.5
1992	147.9	0.5	148.0	0.1	148.5	0.3	147.3	-0.8	147.4	0.1	151.8	3.0	151.0	-0.5	152.2	0.8	151.8	-0.3	151.0	-0.5	149.1	-1.3	148.9	-0.1
1993	148.9	0.0	151.5	1.7	152.6	0.7	151.7	-0.6	150.3	-0.9	152.8	1.7	152.6	-0.1	153.1	0.3	153.2	0.1	153.1	-0.1	151.6	-1.0	151.6	0.0
1994	152.7	0.7	153.5	0.5	154.2	0.5	152.6	-1.0	153.1	0.3	156.1	2.0	156.6	0.3	157.3	0.4	157.4	0.1	157.0	-0.3	156.4	-0.4	154.0	-1.5
1995	155.5	1.0	156.9	0.9	157.3	0.3	156.8	-0.3	157.0	0.1	158.3	0.8	160.2	1.2	160.1	-0.1	160.3	0.1	160.2	-0.1	158.6	-1.0	159.0	0.3
1996	160.6	1.0	161.3	0.4	162.1	0.5	162.1	0.0	160.3	-1.1	161.3	0.6	163.0	1.1	163.6	0.4	164.6	0.6	164.4	-0.1	162.3	-1.3	162.9	0.4
1997	164.2	0.8	166.7	1.5	166.6	-0.1	166.7	0.1	166.5	-0.1	167.9	0.8	168.8	0.5	169.1	0.2	170.2	0.7	168.6	-0.9	166.0	-1.5	166.6	0.4

Source: U.S. Department of Labor, Bureau of Labor Statistics, Division of Consumer Prices and Price Indexes. - indicates no data collected for period.

Philadelphia, PA-NJ
Consumer Price Index - Urban Wage Earners
Base 1982-1984 = 100
Housing

For 1976-1997. Columns headed % show percentile change in the index from the previous period for which an index is available.

Year	Jan Index	%	Feb Index	%	Mar Index	%	Apr Index	%	May Index	%	Jun Index	%	Jul Index	%	Aug Index	%	Sep Index	%	Oct Index	%	Nov Index	%	Dec Index	%
1976	57.6	-	58.0	0.7	58.1	0.2	58.3	0.3	58.5	0.3	58.5	0.0	58.8	0.5	58.9	0.2	59.8	1.5	60.0	0.3	60.3	0.5	60.4	0.2
1977	60.6	0.3	60.9	0.5	61.5	1.0	62.0	0.8	62.4	0.6	62.6	0.3	62.8	0.3	63.2	0.6	64.0	1.3	63.9	-0.2	63.8	-0.2	63.3	-0.8
1978	63.5	0.3	63.5	0.0	63.9	0.6	64.4	0.8	64.4	0.0	64.7	0.5	65.6	1.4	66.1	0.8	66.8	1.1	67.1	0.4	67.5	0.6	68.1	0.9
1979	67.9	-0.3	68.1	0.3	67.9	-0.3	69.0	1.6	70.1	1.6	71.7	2.3	72.3	0.8	72.9	0.8	73.8	1.2	73.9	0.1	75.0	1.5	75.3	0.4
1980	76.9	2.1	78.1	1.6	79.4	1.7	81.0	2.0	81.5	0.6	83.4	2.3	84.1	0.8	84.5	0.5	84.5	0.0	84.4	-0.1	84.9	0.6	85.7	0.9
1981	86.7	1.2	87.5	0.9	88.3	0.9	89.8	1.7	90.4	0.7	92.1	1.9	93.5	1.5	94.7	1.3	96.0	1.4	95.8	-0.2	95.3	-0.5	94.4	-0.9
1982	95.0	0.6	94.8	-0.2	94.2	-0.6	93.9	-0.3	94.1	0.2	96.6	2.7	96.6	0.0	96.4	-0.2	97.1	0.7	95.9	-1.2	96.7	0.8	95.6	-1.1
1983	96.4	0.8	97.3	0.9	98.4	1.1	98.6	0.2	97.8	-0.8	99.0	1.2	100.4	1.4	100.7	0.3	100.7	0.0	100.2	-0.5	100.9	0.7	100.9	0.0
1984	101.8	0.9	102.7	0.9	102.4	-0.3	102.1	-0.3	103.6	1.5	105.2	1.5	105.4	0.2	106.0	0.6	108.2	2.1	108.7	0.5	108.7	0.0	107.5	-1.1
1985	107.7	0.2	109.0	1.2	109.0	0.0	109.9	0.8	111.3	1.3	111.6	0.3	111.8	0.2	111.9	0.1	111.2	-0.6	111.2	0.0	112.3	1.0	113.2	0.8
1986	113.2	0.0	113.4	0.2	112.9	-0.4	113.3	0.4	113.4	0.1	115.5	1.9	115.3	-0.2	115.7	0.3	116.5	0.7	115.1	-1.2	115.0	-0.1	115.2	0.2
1987	115.2	0.0	116.4	1.0	116.5	0.1	117.5	0.9	119.8	2.0	122.2	2.0	121.7	-0.4	123.0	1.1	122.4	-0.5	122.3	-0.1	120.9	-1.1	121.9	0.8
1988	122.2	0.2	122.0	-0.2	122.2	0.2	122.9	0.6	123.8	0.7	126.8	2.4	128.2	1.1	129.5	1.0	130.7	0.9	127.8	-2.2	129.8	1.6	130.2	0.3
1989	129.6	-0.5	129.1	-0.4	130.8	1.3	130.5	-0.2	131.7	0.9	133.5	1.4	134.7	0.9	135.1	0.3	136.6	1.1	135.0	-1.2	134.1	-0.7	134.9	0.6
1990	136.5	1.2	136.7	0.1	138.3	1.2	138.8	0.4	139.0	0.1	140.7	1.2	141.9	0.9	143.2	0.9	143.8	0.4	143.0	-0.6	143.1	0.1	143.3	0.1
1991	144.7	1.0	145.0	0.2	146.1	0.8	145.2	-0.6	146.2	0.7	148.3	1.4	149.8	1.0	150.1	0.2	150.1	0.0	147.8	-1.5	147.0	-0.5	149.2	1.5
1992	149.6	0.3	149.6	0.0	150.1	0.3	149.1	-0.7	149.3	0.1	153.7	2.9	152.8	-0.6	154.0	0.8	153.6	-0.3	152.3	-0.8	150.9	-0.9	150.9	0.0
1993	150.7	-0.1	153.1	1.6	154.2	0.7	153.7	-0.3	152.3	-0.9	154.8	1.6	154.5	-0.2	155.1	0.4	155.3	0.1	154.8	-0.3	153.7	-0.7	153.7	0.0
1994	154.5	0.5	155.2	0.5	155.8	0.4	154.6	-0.8	155.1	0.3	158.0	1.9	158.4	0.3	159.0	0.4	159.3	0.2	158.6	-0.4	158.0	-0.4	156.3	-1.1
1995	157.4	0.7	158.7	0.8	159.1	0.3	158.6	-0.3	158.9	0.2	160.4	0.9	162.1	1.1	162.0	-0.1	162.2	0.1	161.8	-0.2	160.8	-0.6	161.1	0.2
1996	162.4	0.8	163.0	0.4	163.7	0.4	163.6	-0.1	162.2	-0.9	163.3	0.7	164.8	0.9	165.3	0.3	166.1	0.5	165.7	-0.2	164.3	-0.8	165.0	0.4
1997	165.9	0.5	168.1	1.3	168.0	-0.1	168.1	0.1	167.9	-0.1	169.5	1.0	170.3	0.5	170.6	0.2	171.6	0.6	169.9	-1.0	168.0	-1.1	168.6	0.4

Source: U.S. Department of Labor, Bureau of Labor Statistics, Division of Consumer Prices and Price Indexes. - indicates no data collected for period.

Philadelphia, PA-NJ
Consumer Price Index - All Urban Consumers
Base 1982-1984 = 100
Apparel and Upkeep

For 1952-1997. Columns headed % show percentile change in the index from the previous period for which an index is available.

Year	Jan Index	%	Feb Index	%	Mar Index	%	Apr Index	%	May Index	%	Jun Index	%	Jul Index	%	Aug Index	%	Sep Index	%	Oct Index	%	Nov Index	%	Dec Index	%
1952	-	-	-	-	-	-	-	-	-	-	-	-	-	-	-	-	-	-	-	-	-	-	44.2	-
1953	43.8	-0.9	44.0	0.5	44.1	0.2	43.8	-0.7	44.0	0.5	44.0	0.0	44.0	0.0	44.0	0.0	44.9	2.0	44.9	0.0	45.0	0.2	45.0	0.0
1954	44.7	-0.7	44.6	-0.2	44.5	-0.2	44.5	0.0	44.3	-0.4	44.3	0.0	44.4	0.2	44.5	0.2	44.7	0.4	44.8	0.2	44.9	0.2	44.7	-0.4
1955	44.6	-0.2	44.6	0.0	44.2	-0.9	44.1	-0.2	44.0	-0.2	44.0	0.0	43.8	-0.5	44.0	0.5	44.6	1.4	44.6	0.0	45.0	0.9	44.9	-0.2
1956	43.9	-2.2	44.3	0.9	44.4	0.2	44.4	0.0	44.4	0.0	44.4	0.0	44.5	0.2	44.5	0.0	45.9	3.1	45.6	-0.7	45.8	0.4	45.9	0.2
1957	45.4	-1.1	45.9	1.1	46.1	0.4	45.7	-0.9	45.4	-0.7	45.4	0.0	45.9	1.1	45.9	0.0	46.5	1.3	46.7	0.4	46.6	-0.2	46.2	-0.9
1958	45.2	-2.2	45.2	0.0	45.4	0.4	45.2	-0.4	45.5	0.7	45.4	-0.2	44.9	-1.1	45.1	0.4	46.5	3.1	46.4	-0.2	46.4	0.0	46.4	0.0
1959	45.3	-2.4	45.4	0.2	45.6	0.4	45.6	0.0	45.6	0.0	45.7	0.2	45.9	0.4	46.0	0.2	47.6	3.5	47.7	0.2	47.6	-0.2	47.5	-0.2
1960	46.9	-1.3	47.2	0.6	47.6	0.8	47.6	0.0	47.6	0.0	47.4	-0.4	47.6	0.4	47.6	0.0	48.9	2.7	49.2	0.6	49.2	0.0	49.4	0.4
1961	48.9	-1.0	48.8	-0.2	49.0	0.4	48.8	-0.4	48.6	-0.4	48.6	0.0	48.6	0.0	48.6	0.0	49.7	2.3	50.0	0.6	49.9	-0.2	50.0	0.2
1962	48.8	-2.4	48.9	0.2	49.0	0.2	49.2	0.4	49.2	0.0	49.3	0.2	49.2	-0.2	49.4	0.4	50.4	2.0	50.4	0.0	50.5	0.2	50.3	-0.4
1963	49.9	-0.8	49.9	0.0	50.1	0.4	50.2	0.2	49.8	-0.8	50.0	0.4	50.1	0.2	49.8	-0.6	50.6	1.6	50.8	0.4	50.8	0.0	50.8	0.0
1964	50.1	-1.4	50.2	0.2	50.2	0.0	50.3	0.2	50.1	-0.4	50.0	-0.2	49.7	-0.6	49.8	0.2	50.7	1.8	51.1	0.8	51.2	0.2	51.1	-0.2
1965	50.4	-1.4	50.6	0.4	50.7	0.2	50.6	-0.2	51.1	1.0	51.0	-0.2	50.3	-1.4	50.6	0.6	51.4	1.6	51.7	0.6	51.8	0.2	51.8	0.0
1966	51.0	-1.5	51.6	1.2	52.2	1.2	52.4	0.4	52.5	0.2	52.5	0.0	52.8	0.6	52.4	-0.8	54.1	3.2	54.0	-0.2	54.4	0.7	54.6	0.4
1967	53.5	-2.0	53.9	0.7	54.4	0.9	55.0	1.1	55.3	0.5	55.4	0.2	54.9	-0.9	55.0	0.2	56.3	2.4	56.5	0.4	56.6	0.2	56.6	0.0
1968	56.0	-1.1	56.8	1.4	57.4	1.1	57.9	0.9	58.1	0.3	58.0	-0.2	57.9	-0.2	57.9	0.0	59.8	3.3	60.5	1.2	60.4	-0.2	60.6	0.3
1969	59.6	-1.7	60.3	1.2	61.2	1.5	61.2	0.0	60.9	-0.5	60.6	-0.5	60.1	-0.8	60.6	0.8	62.8	3.6	63.1	0.5	63.3	0.3	63.2	-0.2
1970	62.7	-0.8	63.3	1.0	64.0	1.1	63.1	-1.4	63.3	0.3	63.4	0.2	62.2	-1.9	62.8	1.0	65.5	4.3	66.3	1.2	66.2	-0.2	65.5	-1.1
1971	63.9	-2.4	64.7	1.3	65.4	1.1	66.8	2.1	67.0	0.3	66.9	-0.1	65.0	-2.8	64.6	-0.6	66.9	3.6	67.2	0.4	66.7	-0.7	66.4	-0.4
1972	64.7	-2.6	64.2	-0.8	66.3	3.3	66.7	0.6	66.4	-0.4	66.4	0.0	65.1	-2.0	64.9	-0.3	67.8	4.5	68.1	0.4	67.9	-0.3	67.8	-0.1
1973	66.0	-2.7	67.8	2.7	69.2	2.1	69.4	0.3	69.4	0.0	69.3	-0.1	67.6	-2.5	67.5	-0.1	69.6	3.1	70.6	1.4	70.7	0.1	70.7	0.0
1974	68.6	-3.0	70.7	3.1	72.0	1.8	72.0	0.0	72.1	0.1	73.0	1.2	71.7	-1.8	73.3	2.2	75.2	2.6	75.8	0.8	76.6	1.1	76.0	-0.8
1975	74.2	-2.4	74.5	0.4	74.9	0.5	75.0	0.1	74.7	-0.4	74.3	-0.5	73.4	-1.2	75.2	2.5	76.1	1.2	76.1	0.0	76.8	0.9	76.6	-0.3
1976	74.8	-2.3	75.8	1.3	76.3	0.7	76.4	0.1	76.9	0.7	77.1	0.3	76.2	-1.2	76.8	0.8	78.4	2.1	78.9	0.6	79.2	0.4	78.7	-0.6
1977	77.8	-1.1	77.9	0.1	78.7	1.0	78.8	0.1	78.4	-0.5	78.3	-0.1	78.7	0.5	79.6	1.1	79.9	0.4	80.6	0.9	80.6	0.0	80.2	-0.5
1978	77.9	-2.9	76.1	-2.3	78.0	2.5	79.1	1.4	79.9	1.0	81.4	1.9	83.2	2.2	82.1	-1.3	82.4	0.4	83.6	1.5	83.9	0.4	82.7	-1.4
1979	81.9	-1.0	86.1	5.1	85.3	-0.9	85.5	0.2	85.3	-0.2	85.0	-0.4	83.9	-1.3	87.1	3.8	88.6	1.7	86.6	-2.3	89.0	2.8	89.6	0.7
1980	88.2	-1.6	92.6	5.0	96.7	4.4	96.5	-0.2	95.5	-1.0	93.4	-2.2	93.9	0.5	96.0	2.2	95.2	-0.8	96.9	1.8	95.2	-1.8	93.1	-2.2
1981	92.6	-0.5	92.6	0.0	95.4	3.0	95.4	0.0	95.1	-0.3	95.1	0.0	90.2	-5.2	97.7	8.3	100.4	2.8	100.4	0.0	98.2	-2.2	98.0	-0.2
1982	96.4	-1.6	95.7	-0.7	96.6	0.9	98.6	2.1	97.0	-1.6	98.9	2.0	97.5	-1.4	98.8	1.3	102.8	4.0	102.8	0.0	101.2	-1.6	99.3	-1.9
1983	97.6	-1.7	98.2	0.6	100.6	2.4	100.4	-0.2	98.1	-2.3	99.5	1.4	99.3	-0.2	101.8	2.5	102.7	0.9	103.7	1.0	102.4	-1.3	99.5	-2.8
1984	100.0	0.5	99.2	-0.8	99.2	0.0	100.5	1.3	99.0	-1.5	97.6	-1.4	99.0	1.4	102.4	3.4	103.8	1.4	104.3	0.5	103.1	-1.2	102.4	-0.7
1985	99.6	-2.7	100.3	0.7	101.1	0.8	103.3	2.2	102.4	-0.9	100.2	-2.1	100.0	-0.2	102.7	2.7	101.9	-0.8	101.8	-0.1	103.3	1.5	100.6	-2.6
1986	100.2	-0.4	100.0	-0.2	100.4	0.4	99.7	-0.7	100.0	0.3	97.1	-2.9	100.6	3.6	102.1	1.5	104.8	2.6	104.4	-0.4	103.5	-0.9	102.8	-0.7
1987	104.7	1.8	103.5	-1.1	104.3	0.8	110.6	6.0	106.6	-3.6	103.7	-2.7	102.0	-1.6	110.3	8.1	111.3	0.9	112.4	1.0	113.0	0.5	110.3	-2.4
1988	109.1	-1.1	106.9	-2.0	112.7	5.4	107.9	-4.3	109.2	1.2	104.6	-4.2	108.7	3.9	108.9	0.2	112.7	3.5	113.7	0.9	113.8	0.1	110.3	-3.1
1989	111.3	0.9	108.9	-2.2	101.0	-7.3	102.7	1.7	102.8	0.1	98.4	-4.3	96.4	-2.0	91.8	-4.8	93.4	1.7	97.8	4.7	95.8	-2.0	92.0	-4.0
1990	87.8	-4.6	94.4	7.5	101.4	7.4	107.1	5.6	108.7	1.5	102.8	-5.4	100.4	-2.3	100.7	0.3	105.9	5.2	105.1	-0.8	101.9	-3.0	100.6	-1.3
1991	103.0	2.4	103.1	0.1	106.6	3.4	105.5	-1.0	106.0	0.5	98.9	-6.7	92.8	-6.2	100.3	8.1	107.6	7.3	104.1	-3.3	108.4	4.1	108.6	0.2
1992	104.9	-3.4	100.5	-4.2	107.1	6.6	110.4	3.1	110.9	0.5	105.8	-4.6	103.6	-2.1	107.4	3.7	107.0	-0.4	107.0	0.0	108.8	1.7	104.0	-4.4
1993	103.2	-0.8	107.5	4.2	105.7	-1.7	108.8	2.9	101.0	-7.2	105.6	4.6	106.9	1.2	108.4	1.4	105.3	-2.9	111.8	6.2	108.6	-2.9	99.5	-8.4
1994	103.5	4.0	106.1	2.5	107.1	0.9	107.0	-0.1	107.8	0.7	105.4	-2.2	107.8	2.3	105.3	-2.3	105.2	-0.1	108.0	2.7	106.3	-1.6	99.8	-6.1

[Continued]

Philadelphia, PA-NJ
Consumer Price Index - All Urban Consumers
Base 1982-1984 = 100
Apparel and Upkeep

[Continued]

For 1952-1997. Columns headed % show percentile change in the index from the previous period for which an index is available.

Year	Jan Index	%	Feb Index	%	Mar Index	%	Apr Index	%	May Index	%	Jun Index	%	Jul Index	%	Aug Index	%	Sep Index	%	Oct Index	%	Nov Index	%	Dec Index	%
1995	101.4	1.6	107.7	6.2	107.0	-0.6	103.3	-3.5	99.8	-3.4	98.1	-1.7	95.4	-2.8	102.9	7.9	104.2	1.3	104.4	0.2	104.1	-0.3	96.7	-7.1
1996	97.5	0.8	101.2	3.8	106.9	5.6	105.3	-1.5	104.6	-0.7	101.2	-3.3	98.1	-3.1	102.2	4.2	105.2	2.9	110.8	5.3	108.9	-1.7	103.7	-4.8
1997	101.2	-2.4	101.2	0.0	104.4	3.2	104.8	0.4	102.9	-1.8	100.6	-2.2	99.5	-1.1	102.5	3.0	115.1	12.3	108.1	-6.1	104.9	-3.0	102.7	-2.1

Source: U.S. Department of Labor, Bureau of Labor Statistics, Division of Consumer Prices and Price Indexes. - indicates no data collected for period.

Philadelphia, PA-NJ
Consumer Price Index - Urban Wage Earners
Base 1982-1984 = 100
Apparel and Upkeep

For 1952-1997. Columns headed % show percentile change in the index from the previous period for which an index is available.

Year	Jan Index	%	Feb Index	%	Mar Index	%	Apr Index	%	May Index	%	Jun Index	%	Jul Index	%	Aug Index	%	Sep Index	%	Oct Index	%	Nov Index	%	Dec Index	%
1952	-	-	-	-	-	-	-	-	-	-	-	-	-	-	-	-	-	-	-	-	-	-	51.0	-
1953	50.5	-1.0	50.8	0.6	50.9	0.2	50.5	-0.8	50.8	0.6	50.8	0.0	50.8	0.0	50.8	0.0	51.8	2.0	51.8	0.0	51.9	0.2	51.9	0.0
1954	51.6	-0.6	51.5	-0.2	51.4	-0.2	51.4	0.0	51.1	-0.6	51.1	0.0	51.3	0.4	51.4	0.2	51.6	0.4	51.7	0.2	51.8	0.2	51.6	-0.4
1955	51.5	-0.2	51.5	0.0	51.0	-1.0	50.9	-0.2	50.8	-0.2	50.8	0.0	50.5	-0.6	50.8	0.6	51.5	1.4	51.5	0.0	52.0	1.0	51.8	-0.4
1956	50.7	-2.1	51.1	0.8	51.2	0.2	51.3	0.2	51.2	-0.2	51.2	0.0	51.3	0.2	51.4	0.2	52.9	2.9	52.7	-0.4	52.9	0.4	52.9	0.0
1957	52.3	-1.1	52.9	1.1	53.2	0.6	52.8	-0.8	52.3	-0.9	52.3	0.0	53.0	1.3	52.9	-0.2	53.6	1.3	53.9	0.6	53.8	-0.2	53.4	-0.7
1958	52.2	-2.2	52.2	0.0	52.3	0.2	52.2	-0.2	52.5	0.6	52.3	-0.4	51.8	-1.0	52.0	0.4	53.7	3.3	53.5	-0.4	53.6	0.2	53.5	-0.2
1959	52.3	-2.2	52.4	0.2	52.7	0.6	52.7	0.0	52.7	0.0	52.8	0.2	53.0	0.4	53.0	0.0	55.0	3.8	55.0	0.0	55.0	0.0	54.8	-0.4
1960	54.1	-1.3	54.5	0.7	54.9	0.7	54.9	0.0	54.9	0.0	54.7	-0.4	54.9	0.4	55.0	0.2	56.4	2.5	56.8	0.7	56.8	0.0	57.1	0.5
1961	56.4	-1.2	56.3	-0.2	56.6	0.5	56.3	-0.5	56.1	-0.4	56.1	0.0	56.0	-0.2	56.1	0.2	57.3	2.1	57.7	0.7	57.6	-0.2	57.7	0.2
1962	56.3	-2.4	56.4	0.2	56.6	0.4	56.8	0.4	56.8	0.0	56.9	0.2	56.8	-0.2	57.1	0.5	58.2	1.9	58.2	0.0	58.3	0.2	58.0	-0.5
1963	57.6	-0.7	57.6	0.0	57.8	0.3	57.9	0.2	57.5	-0.7	57.7	0.3	57.8	0.2	57.5	-0.5	58.3	1.4	58.7	0.7	58.6	-0.2	58.6	0.0
1964	57.8	-1.4	58.0	0.3	57.9	-0.2	58.0	0.2	57.8	-0.3	57.7	-0.2	57.4	-0.5	57.5	0.2	58.5	1.7	58.9	0.7	59.0	0.2	59.0	0.0
1965	58.2	-1.4	58.3	0.2	58.5	0.3	58.3	-0.3	58.9	1.0	58.9	0.0	58.0	-1.5	58.3	0.5	59.3	1.7	59.6	0.5	59.8	0.3	59.8	0.0
1966	58.9	-1.5	59.6	1.2	60.2	1.0	60.5	0.5	60.6	0.2	60.6	0.0	61.0	0.7	60.5	-0.8	62.4	3.1	62.4	0.0	62.8	0.6	63.1	0.5
1967	61.8	-2.1	62.2	0.6	62.8	1.0	63.5	1.1	63.8	0.5	64.0	0.3	63.3	-1.1	63.5	0.3	64.9	2.2	65.2	0.5	65.3	0.2	65.3	0.0
1968	64.6	-1.1	65.6	1.5	66.2	0.9	66.8	0.9	67.1	0.4	67.0	-0.1	66.8	-0.3	66.8	0.0	69.1	3.4	69.8	1.0	69.7	-0.1	69.9	0.3
1969	68.8	-1.6	69.6	1.2	70.7	1.6	70.6	-0.1	70.3	-0.4	70.0	-0.4	69.3	-1.0	70.0	1.0	72.5	3.6	72.8	0.4	73.1	0.4	73.0	-0.1
1970	72.3	-1.0	73.1	1.1	73.9	1.1	72.8	-1.5	73.1	0.4	73.2	0.1	71.8	-1.9	72.5	1.0	75.6	4.3	76.5	1.2	76.4	-0.1	75.6	-1.0
1971	73.8	-2.4	74.7	1.2	75.5	1.1	77.1	2.1	77.4	0.4	77.2	-0.3	75.0	-2.8	74.5	-0.7	77.2	3.6	77.5	0.4	76.9	-0.8	76.6	-0.4
1972	74.6	-2.6	74.1	-0.7	76.5	3.2	76.9	0.5	76.7	-0.3	76.6	-0.1	75.1	-2.0	74.9	-0.3	78.2	4.4	78.6	0.5	78.4	-0.3	78.2	-0.3
1973	76.2	-2.6	78.2	2.6	79.9	2.2	80.1	0.3	80.1	0.0	79.9	-0.2	78.0	-2.4	77.9	-0.1	80.4	3.2	81.5	1.4	81.6	0.1	81.6	0.0
1974	79.2	-2.9	81.6	3.0	83.1	1.8	83.1	0.0	83.2	0.1	84.2	1.2	82.8	-1.7	84.6	2.2	86.8	2.6	87.5	0.8	88.4	1.0	87.7	-0.8
1975	85.6	-2.4	86.0	0.5	86.4	0.5	86.6	0.2	86.2	-0.5	85.7	-0.6	84.7	-1.2	86.8	2.5	87.8	1.2	87.8	0.0	88.6	0.9	88.4	-0.2
1976	86.3	-2.4	87.5	1.4	88.1	0.7	88.2	0.1	88.8	0.7	88.9	0.1	87.9	-1.1	88.7	0.9	90.5	2.0	91.1	0.7	91.4	0.3	90.8	-0.7
1977	89.8	-1.1	89.9	0.1	90.8	1.0	91.0	0.2	90.5	-0.5	90.3	-0.2	90.8	0.6	91.9	1.2	92.2	0.3	93.0	0.9	93.1	0.1	92.6	-0.5
1978	89.1	-3.8	87.2	-2.1	87.5	0.3	91.4	4.5	92.2	0.9	92.6	0.4	88.2	-4.8	90.2	2.3	90.7	0.6	91.7	1.1	92.8	1.2	91.7	-1.2
1979	90.7	-1.1	90.8	0.1	89.4	-1.5	88.6	-0.9	88.6	0.0	89.2	0.7	87.2	-2.2	87.9	0.8	89.1	1.4	89.1	0.0	90.3	1.3	91.4	1.2
1980	90.5	-1.0	93.8	3.6	94.4	0.6	94.9	0.5	94.2	-0.7	93.1	-1.2	93.0	-0.1	94.6	1.7	96.6	2.1	96.9	0.3	95.9	-1.0	94.5	-1.5
1981	93.6	-1.0	95.1	1.6	94.3	-0.8	94.7	0.4	94.6	-0.1	95.3	0.7	91.4	-4.1	99.3	8.6	100.7	1.4	99.6	-1.1	99.6	0.0	96.6	-3.0
1982	96.4	-0.2	95.8	-0.6	98.1	2.4	99.5	1.4	98.3	-1.2	99.3	1.0	98.2	-1.1	97.9	-0.3	101.8	4.0	102.1	0.3	100.5	-1.6	98.1	-2.4
1983	96.3	-1.8	97.0	0.7	102.5	5.7	101.3	-1.2	99.3	-2.0	100.2	0.9	99.9	-0.3	101.0	1.1	102.3	1.3	103.0	0.7	101.4	-1.6	98.5	-2.9
1984	99.2	0.7	98.3	-0.9	100.4	2.1	100.9	0.5	98.9	-2.0	97.5	-1.4	99.6	2.2	102.7	3.1	104.4	1.7	104.3	-0.1	103.0	-1.2	101.9	-1.1
1985	99.1	-2.7	100.3	1.2	100.3	0.0	102.3	2.0	101.6	-0.7	99.8	-1.8	99.3	-0.5	100.9	1.6	100.2	-0.7	100.5	0.3	101.8	1.3	99.5	-2.3
1986	98.9	-0.6	99.3	0.4	99.7	0.4	98.7	-1.0	98.4	-0.3	96.1	-2.3	98.4	2.4	100.3	1.9	101.2	0.9	102.6	1.4	101.9	-0.7	101.3	-0.6
1987	101.5	0.2	99.5	-2.0	100.6	1.1	106.9	6.3	103.3	-3.4	100.2	-3.0	99.4	-0.8	106.7	7.3	106.9	0.2	109.8	2.7	110.0	0.2	108.3	-1.5
1988	106.1	-2.0	103.1	-2.8	110.3	7.0	104.8	-5.0	106.8	1.9	101.0	-5.4	103.9	2.9	103.4	-0.5	108.3	4.7	109.2	0.8	109.5	0.3	105.0	-4.1
1989	106.3	1.2	104.2	-2.0	95.2	-8.6	98.0	2.9	97.7	-0.3	93.2	-4.6	90.2	-3.2	87.2	-3.3	88.6	1.6	94.0	6.1	91.7	-2.4	88.0	-4.0
1990	82.6	-6.1	88.7	7.4	98.4	10.9	104.1	5.8	106.3	2.1	99.8	-6.1	96.9	-2.9	95.7	-1.2	101.3	5.9	100.2	-1.1	98.0	-2.2	99.2	1.2
1991	99.8	0.6	99.2	-0.6	102.2	3.0	101.5	-0.7	98.9	-2.6	93.1	-5.9	88.5	-4.9	95.0	7.3	101.1	6.4	98.1	-3.0	105.2	7.2	105.7	0.5
1992	101.5	-4.0	97.5	-3.9	104.1	6.8	107.7	3.5	105.9	-1.7	103.1	-2.6	101.0	-2.0	103.2	2.2	102.6	-0.6	104.0	1.4	107.4	3.3	101.9	-5.1
1993	101.4	-0.5	106.9	5.4	103.4	-3.3	107.5	4.0	99.9	-7.1	103.5	3.6	105.5	1.9	105.9	0.4	103.3	-2.5	110.7	7.2	108.4	-2.1	99.6	-8.1
1994	101.4	1.8	103.1	1.7	103.0	-0.1	103.0	0.0	102.4	-0.6	101.7	-0.7	103.9	2.2	102.3	-1.5	101.7	-0.6	103.4	1.7	101.2	-2.1	95.2	-5.9

[Continued]

Philadelphia, PA-NJ
Consumer Price Index - Urban Wage Earners
Base 1982-1984 = 100
Apparel and Upkeep
[Continued]

For 1952-1997. Columns headed % show percentile change in the index from the previous period for which an index is available.

Year	Jan		Feb		Mar		Apr		May		Jun		Jul		Aug		Sep		Oct		Nov		Dec	
	Index	%	Index	%	Index	%	Index	%	Index	%	Index	%	Index	%	Index	%	Index	%	Index	%	Index	%	Index	%
1995	97.4	2.3	104.4	7.2	103.2	-1.1	99.6	-3.5	95.4	-4.2	94.0	-1.5	91.5	-2.7	98.9	8.1	100.5	1.6	100.0	-0.5	100.1	0.1	92.5	-7.6
1996	93.2	0.8	96.7	3.8	102.8	6.3	100.6	-2.1	100.1	-0.5	96.8	-3.3	94.2	-2.7	99.8	5.9	101.6	1.8	108.9	7.2	106.6	-2.1	100.4	-5.8
1997	97.4	-3.0	98.1	0.7	101.1	3.1	101.2	0.1	99.9	-1.3	97.5	-2.4	96.4	-1.1	99.3	3.0	113.1	13.9	106.8	-5.6	103.2	-3.4	100.0	-3.1

Source: U.S. Department of Labor, Bureau of Labor Statistics, Division of Consumer Prices and Price Indexes. - indicates no data collected for period.

719

Philadelphia, PA-NJ
Consumer Price Index - All Urban Consumers
Base 1982-1984 = 100
Transportation

For 1947-1997. Columns headed % show percentile change in the index from the previous period for which an index is available.

Year	Jan Index	%	Feb Index	%	Mar Index	%	Apr Index	%	May Index	%	Jun Index	%	Jul Index	%	Aug Index	%	Sep Index	%	Oct Index	%	Nov Index	%	Dec Index	%
1947	15.6	-	15.6	0.0	16.8	7.7	16.9	0.6	16.9	0.0	16.9	0.0	16.9	0.0	17.1	1.2	17.2	0.6	17.2	0.0	17.2	0.0	17.3	0.6
1948	17.4	0.6	17.5	0.6	17.5	0.0	18.2	4.0	18.2	0.0	18.4	1.1	18.7	1.6	19.0	1.6	19.0	0.0	19.0	0.0	19.0	0.0	19.1	0.5
1949	19.2	0.5	19.3	0.5	19.3	0.0	19.3	0.0	21.1	9.3	19.4	-8.1	19.5	0.5	19.5	0.0	19.5	0.0	19.5	0.0	19.5	0.0	19.5	0.0
1950	19.5	0.0	19.5	0.0	19.5	0.0	19.4	-0.5	19.4	0.0	19.4	0.0	19.4	0.0	19.5	0.5	19.4	-0.5	19.2	-1.0	19.2	0.0	21.0	9.4
1951	21.2	1.0	23.4	10.4	23.5	0.4	23.5	0.0	23.5	0.0	23.1	-1.7	22.8	-1.3	23.0	0.9	23.0	0.0	22.8	-0.9	23.9	4.8	23.9	0.0
1952	23.9	0.0	23.2	-2.9	24.1	3.9	24.1	0.0	24.1	0.0	24.2	0.4	24.2	0.0	24.2	0.0	24.2	0.0	24.2	0.0	24.2	0.0	24.2	0.0
1953	24.3	0.4	24.2	-0.4	24.2	0.0	24.3	0.4	24.4	0.4	24.4	0.0	24.6	0.8	24.6	0.0	24.7	0.4	24.8	0.4	24.7	-0.4	24.7	0.0
1954	24.8	0.4	25.0	0.8	25.1	0.4	25.1	0.4	25.0	-0.4	25.1	0.4	25.0	-0.4	25.0	0.0	25.1	0.4	25.1	0.0	25.3	0.8	25.2	-0.4
1955	25.1	-0.4	25.2	0.4	25.1	-0.4	25.0	-0.4	25.3	1.2	25.4	0.4	25.3	-0.4	25.3	0.0	23.6	-6.7	24.1	2.1	24.7	2.5	24.5	-0.8
1956	24.8	1.2	24.7	-0.4	24.8	0.4	24.6	-0.8	24.5	-0.4	24.4	-0.4	24.7	1.2	25.0	1.2	25.0	0.0	25.1	0.4	25.6	2.0	25.7	0.4
1957	25.8	0.4	25.8	0.0	25.8	0.0	25.8	0.0	25.8	0.0	25.8	0.0	25.5	-1.2	25.4	-0.4	25.5	0.4	25.5	0.0	26.5	3.9	26.3	-0.8
1958	25.9	-1.5	25.8	-0.4	26.4	2.3	26.5	0.4	26.3	-0.8	26.3	0.0	26.5	0.8	26.7	0.8	26.8	0.4	26.7	-0.4	27.3	2.2	27.4	0.4
1959	27.6	0.7	27.4	-0.7	27.5	0.4	27.6	0.4	27.8	0.7	27.9	0.4	28.1	0.7	28.2	0.4	28.2	0.0	28.4	0.7	28.5	0.4	28.5	0.0
1960	28.5	0.0	28.5	0.0	28.4	-0.4	28.3	-0.4	28.2	-0.4	28.1	-0.4	28.0	-0.4	28.0	0.0	27.9	-0.4	28.4	1.8	28.5	0.4	28.5	0.0
1961	28.4	-0.4	28.5	0.4	28.6	0.4	29.0	1.4	29.1	0.3	29.2	0.3	29.2	0.0	29.2	0.0	29.1	-0.3	29.4	1.0	29.3	-0.3	29.0	-1.0
1962	29.0	0.0	29.0	0.0	29.0	0.0	29.3	1.0	29.1	-0.7	29.1	0.0	29.2	0.3	29.2	0.0	29.4	0.7	29.2	-0.7	29.5	1.0	29.4	-0.3
1963	28.9	-1.7	29.7	2.8	29.8	0.3	29.9	0.3	29.9	0.0	29.9	0.0	29.9	0.0	29.9	0.0	29.9	0.0	30.2	1.0	30.3	0.3	30.3	0.0
1964	30.4	0.3	30.4	0.0	30.4	0.0	30.5	0.3	30.5	0.0	30.2	-1.0	30.5	1.0	30.5	0.0	30.3	-0.7	30.5	0.7	30.8	1.0	31.0	0.6
1965	31.1	0.3	31.4	1.0	31.3	-0.3	31.4	0.3	31.6	0.6	31.4	-0.6	31.4	0.0	31.3	-0.3	31.0	-1.0	31.4	1.3	31.4	0.0	31.4	0.0
1966	31.4	0.0	31.4	0.0	31.5	0.3	31.6	0.3	31.7	0.3	31.8	0.3	31.9	0.3	32.1	0.6	31.8	-0.9	32.1	0.9	32.1	0.0	31.9	-0.6
1967	31.9	0.0	32.0	0.3	32.4	1.3	32.4	0.0	32.4	0.0	32.5	0.3	32.7	0.6	32.8	0.3	32.7	-0.3	33.0	0.9	33.3	0.9	33.3	0.0
1968	33.9	1.8	33.9	0.0	34.0	0.3	33.9	-0.3	34.1	0.6	34.2	0.3	34.4	0.6	34.5	0.3	34.4	-0.3	34.6	0.6	34.9	0.9	34.7	-0.6
1969	34.7	0.0	35.6	2.6	36.0	1.1	36.1	0.3	35.9	-0.6	36.1	0.6	36.1	0.0	35.9	-0.6	35.6	-0.8	36.2	1.7	36.3	0.3	36.3	0.0
1970	36.2	-0.3	37.1	2.5	37.1	0.0	37.6	1.3	37.9	0.8	38.1	0.5	38.1	0.0	38.0	-0.3	37.9	-0.3	38.4	1.3	38.6	0.5	39.1	1.3
1971	39.4	0.8	39.9	1.3	39.8	-0.3	40.1	0.8	40.2	0.2	40.5	0.7	40.6	0.2	40.3	-0.7	40.0	-0.7	40.2	0.5	40.3	0.2	40.4	0.2
1972	40.5	0.2	40.3	-0.5	40.4	0.2	40.4	0.0	40.9	1.2	41.0	0.2	40.9	-0.2	41.0	0.2	41.0	0.0	40.9	-0.2	41.1	0.5	41.2	0.2
1973	41.1	-0.2	41.1	0.0	41.1	0.0	41.4	0.7	41.6	0.5	41.9	0.7	41.9	0.0	41.7	-0.5	41.4	-0.7	41.9	1.2	42.0	0.2	42.5	1.2
1974	42.9	0.9	43.4	1.2	44.3	2.1	44.6	0.7	45.3	1.6	46.1	1.8	46.7	1.3	46.9	0.4	47.2	0.6	47.4	0.4	47.8	0.8	47.9	0.2
1975	47.7	-0.4	47.9	0.4	48.3	0.8	48.6	0.6	48.9	0.6	49.8	1.8	50.4	1.2	50.6	0.4	50.8	0.4	51.3	1.0	51.8	1.0	51.8	0.0
1976	51.7	-0.2	51.7	0.0	52.3	1.2	52.9	1.1	53.5	1.1	54.2	1.3	54.7	0.9	54.9	0.4	55.1	0.4	55.4	0.5	55.6	0.4	55.6	0.0
1977	56.2	1.1	56.8	1.1	57.2	0.7	58.5	2.3	60.0	2.6	60.3	0.5	60.3	0.0	60.1	-0.3	60.6	0.8	60.6	0.0	60.6	0.0	60.5	-0.2
1978	60.7	0.3	60.7	0.0	61.1	0.7	61.4	0.5	61.9	0.8	62.7	1.3	63.1	0.6	63.2	0.2	63.2	0.0	63.0	-0.3	64.2	1.9	64.4	0.3
1979	65.0	0.9	65.4	0.6	66.2	1.2	67.6	2.1	69.3	2.5	71.5	3.2	73.1	2.2	73.7	0.8	74.1	0.5	74.1	0.0	74.7	0.8	75.8	1.5
1980	77.8	2.6	79.9	2.7	81.5	2.0	82.2	0.9	83.4	1.5	83.7	0.4	83.9	0.2	85.2	1.5	85.4	0.2	85.6	0.2	86.9	1.5	87.4	0.6
1981	88.6	1.4	90.6	2.3	91.0	0.4	91.7	0.8	92.3	0.7	92.7	0.4	93.9	1.3	93.8	-0.1	94.4	0.6	95.8	1.5	96.5	0.7	97.2	0.7
1982	96.6	-0.6	95.5	-1.1	94.8	-0.7	93.9	-0.9	94.1	0.2	95.6	1.6	97.1	1.6	96.9	-0.2	96.4	-0.5	97.0	0.6	97.1	0.1	97.5	0.4
1983	98.0	0.5	96.9	-1.1	96.4	-0.5	97.6	1.2	98.4	0.8	98.5	0.1	99.1	0.6	100.7	1.6	101.3	0.6	102.0	0.7	102.4	0.4	102.1	-0.3
1984	102.8	0.7	102.7	-0.1	103.0	0.3	103.8	0.8	104.0	0.2	104.4	0.4	104.8	0.4	105.4	0.6	105.7	0.3	105.3	-0.4	106.0	0.7	106.3	0.3
1985	106.3	0.0	107.1	0.8	107.8	0.7	108.7	0.8	109.2	0.5	109.7	0.5	109.9	0.2	110.0	0.1	110.4	0.4	111.4	0.9	111.5	0.1	111.7	0.2
1986	112.1	0.4	110.9	-1.1	108.4	-2.3	104.7	-3.4	105.8	1.1	107.1	1.2	106.9	-0.2	104.8	-2.0	105.1	0.3	106.1	1.0	106.2	0.1	107.0	0.8
1987	108.5	1.4	108.4	-0.1	108.9	0.5	110.4	1.4	110.7	0.3	111.5	0.7	112.2	0.6	112.0	-0.2	112.6	0.5	113.5	0.8	114.3	0.7	114.6	0.3
1988	114.5	-0.1	114.2	-0.3	114.5	0.3	114.2	-0.3	115.1	0.8	114.8	-0.3	115.3	0.4	115.1	-0.2	115.9	0.7	117.4	1.3	117.7	0.3	117.9	0.2
1989	118.5	0.5	118.0	-0.4	118.0	0.0	120.2	1.9	122.9	2.2	123.3	0.3	123.1	-0.2	122.3	-0.6	122.5	0.2	123.4	0.7	123.0	-0.3	123.1	0.1
1990	124.9	1.5	125.6	0.6	125.2	-0.3	125.2	0.0	125.4	0.2	125.9	0.4	125.3	-0.5	125.9	0.5	128.3	1.9	132.1	3.0	133.8	1.3	134.6	0.6
1991	132.7	-1.4	131.4	-1.0	130.2	-0.9	130.0	-0.2	130.5	0.4	131.0	0.4	132.2	0.9	132.3	0.1	132.5	0.2	134.0	1.1	135.3	1.0	135.7	0.3

[Continued]

Philadelphia, PA-NJ
Consumer Price Index - All Urban Consumers
Base 1982-1984 = 100
Transportation
[Continued]

For 1947-1997. Columns headed % show percentile change in the index from the previous period for which an index is available.

Year	Jan Index	%	Feb Index	%	Mar Index	%	Apr Index	%	May Index	%	Jun Index	%	Jul Index	%	Aug Index	%	Sep Index	%	Oct Index	%	Nov Index	%	Dec Index	%
1992	135.1	-0.4	134.6	-0.4	134.4	-0.1	134.8	0.3	135.0	0.1	136.0	0.7	136.6	0.4	135.9	-0.5	136.1	0.1	137.0	0.7	138.3	0.9	139.4	0.8
1993	139.2	-0.1	138.4	-0.6	138.5	0.1	137.5	-0.7	139.0	1.1	138.4	-0.4	139.4	0.7	137.4	-1.4	139.2	1.3	140.9	1.2	143.2	1.6	143.0	-0.1
1994	142.6	-0.3	142.3	-0.2	142.6	0.2	141.8	-0.6	141.6	-0.1	143.2	1.1	143.5	0.2	144.9	1.0	145.1	0.1	145.7	0.4	147.5	1.2	146.9	-0.4
1995	147.6	0.5	148.0	0.3	148.5	0.3	148.7	0.1	148.5	-0.1	149.5	0.7	148.6	-0.6	148.4	-0.1	148.9	0.3	150.1	0.8	149.1	-0.7	148.6	-0.3
1996	149.2	0.4	150.3	0.7	150.1	-0.1	150.0	-0.1	151.1	0.7	151.9	0.5	151.2	-0.5	151.2	0.0	151.9	0.5	153.2	0.9	154.1	0.6	154.3	0.1
1997	154.5	0.1	153.6	-0.6	153.6	0.0	153.0	-0.4	151.9	-0.7	152.0	0.1	151.8	-0.1	150.8	-0.7	152.2	0.9	153.8	1.1	154.0	0.1	152.9	-0.7

Source: U.S. Department of Labor, Bureau of Labor Statistics, Division of Consumer Prices and Price Indexes. - indicates no data collected for period.

Philadelphia, PA-NJ
Consumer Price Index - Urban Wage Earners
Base 1982-1984 = 100
Transportation

For 1947-1997. Columns headed % show percentile change in the index from the previous period for which an index is available.

Year	Jan Index	%	Feb Index	%	Mar Index	%	Apr Index	%	May Index	%	Jun Index	%	Jul Index	%	Aug Index	%	Sep Index	%	Oct Index	%	Nov Index	%	Dec Index	%
1947	15.1	-	15.1	0.0	16.3	7.9	16.4	0.6	16.4	0.0	16.4	0.0	16.4	0.0	16.6	1.2	16.7	0.6	16.7	0.0	16.7	0.0	16.8	0.6
1948	16.9	0.6	17.0	0.6	17.0	0.0	17.7	4.1	17.7	0.0	17.9	1.1	18.1	1.1	18.4	1.7	18.5	0.5	18.5	0.0	18.4	-0.5	18.5	0.5
1949	18.6	0.5	18.7	0.5	18.7	0.0	18.8	0.5	20.5	9.0	18.9	-7.8	18.9	0.0	18.9	0.0	18.9	0.0	18.9	0.0	19.0	0.5	19.0	0.0
1950	19.0	0.0	19.0	0.0	19.0	0.0	18.8	-1.1	18.9	0.5	18.9	0.0	18.9	0.0	19.0	0.5	18.8	-1.1	18.6	-1.1	18.7	0.5	20.4	9.1
1951	20.6	1.0	22.8	10.7	22.9	0.4	22.9	0.0	22.9	0.0	22.4	-2.2	22.2	-0.9	22.3	0.5	22.4	0.4	22.2	-0.9	23.2	4.5	23.2	0.0
1952	23.2	0.0	22.5	-3.0	23.4	4.0	23.4	0.0	23.4	0.0	23.5	0.4	23.5	0.0	23.5	0.0	23.5	0.0	23.5	0.0	23.5	0.0	23.5	0.0
1953	23.6	0.4	23.5	-0.4	23.5	0.0	23.6	0.4	23.7	0.4	23.7	0.0	23.9	0.8	23.9	0.0	24.0	0.4	24.1	0.4	24.0	-0.4	24.0	0.0
1954	24.1	0.4	24.3	0.8	24.4	0.4	24.3	-0.4	24.3	0.0	24.3	0.0	24.2	-0.4	24.3	0.4	24.3	0.0	24.4	0.4	24.6	0.8	24.4	-0.8
1955	24.4	0.0	24.4	0.0	24.3	-0.4	24.3	0.0	24.6	1.2	24.7	0.4	24.6	-0.4	24.5	-0.4	22.9	-6.5	23.4	2.2	24.0	2.6	23.8	-0.8
1956	24.1	1.3	24.0	-0.4	24.1	0.4	23.9	-0.8	23.8	-0.4	23.7	-0.4	24.0	1.3	24.3	1.2	24.2	-0.4	24.4	0.8	24.9	2.0	25.0	0.4
1957	25.1	0.4	25.1	0.0	25.1	0.0	25.0	-0.4	25.1	0.4	24.8	-1.2	24.7	-0.4	24.7	0.0	24.8	0.4	24.7	-0.4	25.7	4.0	25.6	-0.4
1958	25.2	-1.6	25.1	-0.4	25.6	2.0	25.7	0.4	25.5	-0.8	25.6	0.4	25.8	0.8	26.0	0.8	26.0	0.0	25.9	-0.4	26.6	2.7	26.7	0.4
1959	26.8	0.4	26.6	-0.7	26.7	0.4	26.8	0.4	27.0	0.7	27.1	0.4	27.3	0.7	27.4	0.4	27.4	0.0	27.6	0.7	27.7	0.4	27.7	0.0
1960	27.7	0.0	27.7	0.0	27.6	-0.4	27.5	-0.4	27.4	-0.4	27.3	-0.4	27.2	-0.4	27.2	0.0	27.1	-0.4	27.5	1.5	27.6	0.4	27.7	0.4
1961	27.6	-0.4	27.7	0.4	27.7	0.0	28.2	1.8	28.3	0.4	28.4	0.4	28.4	0.0	28.3	-0.4	28.2	-0.4	28.5	1.1	28.5	0.0	28.1	-1.4
1962	28.2	0.4	28.2	0.0	28.1	-0.4	28.4	1.1	28.3	-0.4	28.3	0.0	28.3	0.0	28.3	0.0	28.5	0.7	28.4	-0.4	28.6	0.7	28.5	-0.3
1963	28.1	-1.4	28.9	2.8	28.9	0.0	29.0	0.3	29.0	0.0	29.0	0.0	29.1	0.3	29.0	-0.3	29.1	0.3	29.3	0.7	29.4	0.3	29.4	0.0
1964	29.5	0.3	29.5	0.0	29.5	0.0	29.6	0.3	29.6	0.0	29.3	-1.0	29.6	1.0	29.7	0.3	29.5	-0.7	29.7	0.7	29.9	0.7	30.1	0.7
1965	30.2	0.3	30.5	1.0	30.4	-0.3	30.5	0.3	30.7	0.7	30.5	-0.7	30.5	0.0	30.4	-0.3	30.1	-1.0	30.5	1.3	30.5	0.0	30.5	0.0
1966	30.5	0.0	30.5	0.0	30.6	0.3	30.7	0.3	30.7	0.0	30.9	0.7	31.0	0.3	31.2	0.6	30.9	-1.0	31.2	1.0	31.2	0.0	31.0	-0.6
1967	31.0	0.0	31.1	0.3	31.5	1.3	31.5	0.0	31.5	0.0	31.6	0.3	31.8	0.6	31.9	0.3	31.8	-0.3	32.1	0.9	32.3	0.6	32.4	0.3
1968	32.9	1.5	32.9	0.0	33.0	0.3	33.0	0.0	33.1	0.3	33.2	0.3	33.4	0.6	33.5	0.3	33.4	-0.3	33.6	0.6	33.9	0.9	33.7	-0.6
1969	33.7	0.0	34.5	2.4	35.0	1.4	35.1	0.3	34.9	-0.6	35.1	0.6	35.0	-0.3	34.9	-0.3	34.6	-0.9	35.1	1.4	35.2	0.3	35.2	0.0
1970	35.2	0.0	36.0	2.3	36.1	0.3	36.5	1.1	36.8	0.8	37.0	0.5	37.0	0.0	37.0	0.0	36.8	-0.5	37.3	1.4	37.5	0.5	38.0	1.3
1971	38.2	0.5	38.8	1.6	38.7	-0.3	38.9	0.5	39.1	0.5	39.4	0.8	39.5	0.3	39.2	-0.8	38.8	-1.0	39.1	0.8	39.2	0.3	39.3	0.3
1972	39.3	0.0	39.2	-0.3	39.3	0.3	39.3	0.0	39.7	1.0	39.8	0.3	39.7	-0.3	39.8	0.3	39.8	0.0	39.7	-0.3	40.0	0.8	40.1	0.2
1973	39.9	-0.5	39.9	0.0	39.9	0.0	40.2	0.8	40.4	0.5	40.7	0.7	40.7	0.0	40.5	-0.5	40.2	-0.7	40.7	1.2	40.8	0.2	41.3	1.2
1974	41.7	1.0	42.1	1.0	43.0	2.1	43.3	0.7	44.0	1.6	44.8	1.8	45.4	1.3	45.6	0.4	45.9	0.7	46.1	0.4	46.5	0.9	46.5	0.0
1975	46.4	-0.2	46.5	0.2	46.9	0.9	47.2	0.6	47.5	0.6	48.4	1.9	48.9	1.0	49.2	0.6	49.3	0.2	49.8	1.0	50.3	1.0	50.3	0.0
1976	50.2	-0.2	50.2	0.0	50.8	1.2	51.3	1.0	52.0	1.4	52.7	1.3	53.1	0.8	53.3	0.4	53.6	0.6	53.8	0.4	54.0	0.4	54.0	0.0
1977	54.5	0.9	55.1	1.1	55.6	0.9	56.8	2.2	58.3	2.6	58.6	0.5	58.6	0.0	58.3	-0.5	58.9	1.0	58.8	-0.2	58.8	0.0	58.8	0.0
1978	58.9	0.2	59.1	0.3	59.6	0.8	59.9	0.5	60.6	1.2	61.4	1.3	61.9	0.8	62.2	0.5	62.1	-0.2	62.4	0.5	63.4	1.6	63.6	0.3
1979	64.0	0.6	64.6	0.9	65.4	1.2	66.9	2.3	68.3	2.1	70.5	3.2	72.3	2.6	72.7	0.6	73.6	1.2	73.4	-0.3	74.3	1.2	75.2	1.2
1980	77.6	3.2	79.8	2.8	81.3	1.9	82.0	0.9	82.9	1.1	83.5	0.7	83.6	0.1	84.6	1.2	84.6	0.0	85.3	0.8	86.4	1.3	87.2	0.9
1981	88.7	1.7	91.0	2.6	91.4	0.4	91.9	0.5	92.7	0.9	93.0	0.3	94.2	1.3	94.3	0.1	94.8	0.5	96.8	2.1	97.0	0.2	97.6	0.6
1982	97.0	-0.6	95.8	-1.2	95.0	-0.8	94.1	-0.9	94.2	0.1	95.8	1.7	97.4	1.7	97.1	-0.3	96.6	-0.5	97.2	0.6	97.2	0.0	97.6	0.4
1983	98.0	0.4	96.8	-1.2	96.2	-0.6	97.5	1.4	98.3	0.8	98.5	0.2	99.2	0.7	100.7	1.5	101.3	0.6	102.0	0.7	102.3	0.3	102.0	-0.3
1984	102.6	0.6	102.6	0.0	102.9	0.3	103.7	0.8	104.0	0.3	104.3	0.3	104.6	0.3	105.2	0.6	105.6	0.4	105.1	-0.5	105.7	0.6	105.9	0.2
1985	106.1	0.2	106.8	0.7	107.5	0.7	108.4	0.8	109.0	0.6	109.5	0.5	109.7	0.2	109.8	0.1	110.1	0.3	111.1	0.9	111.2	0.1	111.3	0.1
1986	111.8	0.4	110.4	-1.3	107.6	-2.5	103.5	-3.8	104.7	1.2	106.0	1.2	105.8	-0.2	103.5	-2.2	103.8	0.3	104.6	0.8	104.7	0.1	105.6	0.9
1987	107.2	1.5	107.3	0.1	107.9	0.6	109.6	1.6	110.1	0.5	110.9	0.7	111.7	0.7	111.8	0.1	112.0	0.2	113.0	0.9	113.7	0.6	113.9	0.2
1988	113.8	-0.1	113.5	-0.3	114.0	0.4	113.8	-0.2	114.7	0.8	114.5	-0.2	115.1	0.5	115.0	-0.1	115.7	0.6	116.9	1.0	117.2	0.3	117.4	0.2
1989	118.0	0.5	117.6	-0.3	117.7	0.1	120.2	2.1	123.2	2.5	123.7	0.4	123.4	-0.2	122.9	-0.4	123.1	0.2	123.9	0.6	123.0	-0.7	123.0	0.0
1990	124.6	1.3	125.8	1.0	125.4	-0.3	125.3	-0.1	125.6	0.2	126.6	0.8	125.8	-0.6	126.8	0.8	129.7	2.3	133.9	3.2	135.2	1.0	135.6	0.3
1991	133.2	-1.8	131.4	-1.4	130.3	-0.8	130.4	0.1	130.9	0.4	131.3	0.3	133.0	1.3	133.0	0.0	133.6	0.5	134.8	0.9	135.6	0.6	135.8	0.1

[Continued]

Philadelphia, PA-NJ
Consumer Price Index - Urban Wage Earners
Base 1982-1984 = 100
Transportation
[Continued]

For 1947-1997. Columns headed % show percentile change in the index from the previous period for which an index is available.

Year	Jan Index	%	Feb Index	%	Mar Index	%	Apr Index	%	May Index	%	Jun Index	%	Jul Index	%	Aug Index	%	Sep Index	%	Oct Index	%	Nov Index	%	Dec Index	%
1992	135.1	-0.5	134.3	-0.6	133.7	-0.4	133.9	0.1	135.0	0.8	136.3	1.0	136.7	0.3	136.4	-0.2	136.4	0.0	137.3	0.7	138.5	0.9	139.1	0.4
1993	138.9	-0.1	138.4	-0.4	138.0	-0.3	137.0	-0.7	138.3	0.9	138.3	0.0	138.9	0.4	137.6	-0.9	138.9	0.9	140.9	1.4	142.8	1.3	142.4	-0.3
1994	141.7	-0.5	141.4	-0.2	141.6	0.1	141.1	-0.4	141.6	0.4	143.2	1.1	143.8	0.4	145.5	1.2	145.6	0.1	146.5	0.6	148.3	1.2	147.9	-0.3
1995	148.4	0.3	149.1	0.5	149.0	-0.1	149.3	0.2	149.6	0.2	150.5	0.6	149.7	-0.5	149.3	-0.3	149.6	0.2	150.5	0.6	149.6	-0.6	149.3	-0.2
1996	149.7	0.3	150.4	0.5	150.6	0.1	150.8	0.1	152.2	0.9	152.7	0.3	151.9	-0.5	152.0	0.1	152.5	0.3	154.1	1.0	154.9	0.5	154.6	-0.2
1997	155.5	0.6	154.2	-0.8	154.1	-0.1	153.6	-0.3	152.5	-0.7	152.7	0.1	152.1	-0.4	151.8	-0.2	153.1	0.9	154.5	0.9	154.6	0.1	153.3	-0.8

Source: U.S. Department of Labor, Bureau of Labor Statistics, Division of Consumer Prices and Price Indexes. - indicates no data collected for period.

Philadelphia, PA-NJ
Consumer Price Index - All Urban Consumers
Base 1982-1984 = 100
Medical Care

For 1947-1997. Columns headed % show percentile change in the index from the previous period for which an index is available.

Year	Jan Index	%	Feb Index	%	Mar Index	%	Apr Index	%	May Index	%	Jun Index	%	Jul Index	%	Aug Index	%	Sep Index	%	Oct Index	%	Nov Index	%	Dec Index	%
1947	12.1	-	12.1	0.0	12.2	0.8	12.4	1.6	12.5	0.8	12.5	0.0	12.5	0.0	12.5	0.0	12.5	0.0	12.6	0.8	12.6	0.0	12.7	0.8
1948	12.8	0.8	12.9	0.8	12.8	-0.8	12.9	0.8	12.9	0.0	12.9	0.0	13.0	0.8	13.0	0.0	13.0	0.0	13.0	0.0	13.2	1.5	13.2	0.0
1949	13.2	0.0	13.3	0.8	13.3	0.0	13.3	0.0	13.3	0.0	13.4	0.8	13.4	0.0	13.4	0.0	13.4	0.0	13.4	0.0	13.4	0.0	13.5	0.7
1950	13.5	0.0	13.5	0.0	13.5	0.0	13.5	0.0	13.6	0.7	13.6	0.0	13.6	0.0	13.6	0.0	13.7	0.7	13.7	0.0	13.7	0.0	13.7	0.0
1951	13.9	1.5	14.0	0.7	14.2	1.4	14.2	0.0	14.2	0.0	14.2	0.0	14.2	0.0	14.2	0.0	14.2	0.0	14.3	0.7	14.3	0.0	14.3	0.0
1952	14.3	0.0	14.3	0.0	14.5	1.4	14.5	0.0	14.5	0.0	15.2	4.8	15.2	0.0	15.2	0.0	15.5	2.0	15.5	0.0	15.5	0.0	15.5	0.0
1953	15.5	0.0	15.5	0.0	15.5	0.0	15.5	0.0	15.5	0.0	15.6	0.6	15.6	0.0	15.6	0.0	15.6	0.0	15.6	0.0	15.6	0.0	15.9	1.9
1954	15.9	0.0	16.0	0.6	16.0	0.0	16.0	0.0	16.0	0.0	16.2	1.3	16.2	0.0	16.2	0.0	17.1	5.6	17.1	0.0	17.1	0.0	17.3	1.2
1955	17.3	0.0	17.3	0.0	17.5	1.2	17.5	0.0	17.5	0.0	17.5	0.0	17.5	0.0	17.5	0.0	17.5	0.0	17.5	0.0	17.5	0.0	17.6	0.6
1956	17.6	0.0	17.6	0.0	17.8	1.1	17.8	0.0	17.8	0.0	17.8	0.0	17.8	0.0	17.8	0.0	17.9	0.6	17.9	0.0	17.9	0.0	17.9	0.0
1957	17.9	0.0	17.9	0.0	18.2	1.7	18.2	0.0	18.2	0.0	18.2	0.0	18.2	0.0	18.2	0.0	18.2	0.0	18.2	0.0	18.2	0.0	18.5	1.6
1958	18.5	0.0	18.5	0.0	18.5	0.0	18.6	0.5	18.6	0.0	18.6	0.0	19.2	3.2	19.2	0.0	19.2	0.0	19.2	0.0	19.2	0.0	19.3	0.5
1959	19.3	0.0	19.3	0.0	19.7	2.1	19.7	0.0	19.7	0.0	19.9	1.0	19.9	0.0	20.5	3.0	20.5	0.0	20.5	0.0	20.5	0.0	20.6	0.5
1960	20.6	0.0	20.6	0.0	20.8	1.0	20.8	0.0	20.8	0.0	20.9	0.5	20.9	0.0	20.9	0.0	20.9	0.0	20.9	0.0	20.9	0.0	21.0	0.5
1961	21.0	0.0	21.0	0.0	21.0	0.0	21.4	1.9	22.0	2.8	22.0	0.0	22.0	0.0	22.0	0.0	22.1	0.5	22.1	0.0	22.1	0.0	22.1	0.0
1962	22.1	0.0	22.1	0.0	22.1	0.0	22.1	0.0	22.1	0.0	22.9	3.6	22.9	0.0	22.9	0.0	22.9	0.0	22.9	0.0	22.9	0.0	22.9	0.0
1963	22.9	0.0	23.0	0.4	23.0	0.0	23.0	0.0	23.0	0.0	23.1	0.4	23.1	0.0	23.1	0.0	23.2	0.4	23.2	0.0	23.2	0.0	23.2	0.0
1964	23.3	0.4	23.3	0.0	23.3	0.0	23.3	0.0	23.3	0.0	23.3	0.0	23.5	0.9	23.4	-0.4	23.5	0.4	23.5	0.0	23.6	0.4	23.6	0.0
1965	23.6	0.0	23.6	0.0	23.8	0.8	23.8	0.0	23.9	0.4	24.1	0.8	24.2	0.4	24.2	0.0	24.3	0.4	24.3	0.0	24.3	0.0	24.4	0.4
1966	24.4	0.0	24.5	0.4	24.7	0.8	24.8	0.4	24.8	0.0	24.9	0.4	25.2	1.2	25.3	0.4	25.3	0.0	25.4	0.4	25.6	0.8	25.9	1.2
1967	26.0	0.4	26.1	0.4	26.1	0.0	26.2	0.4	26.3	0.4	26.6	1.1	26.8	0.8	26.8	0.0	27.3	1.9	27.5	0.7	27.5	0.0	27.7	0.7
1968	27.9	0.7	27.9	0.0	28.0	0.4	28.1	0.4	28.5	1.4	28.7	0.7	29.3	2.1	29.4	0.3	29.5	0.3	29.8	1.0	29.8	0.0	30.0	0.7
1969	30.1	0.3	30.2	0.3	30.6	1.3	30.7	0.3	30.9	0.7	31.1	0.6	32.1	3.2	32.2	0.3	32.4	0.6	32.1	-0.9	32.1	0.0	32.2	0.3
1970	32.5	0.9	32.7	0.6	32.9	0.6	33.1	0.6	33.3	0.6	33.4	0.3	34.6	3.6	34.9	0.9	34.9	0.0	34.8	-0.3	35.6	2.3	35.6	0.0
1971	35.8	0.6	36.0	0.6	36.0	0.0	36.1	0.3	36.2	0.3	36.7	1.4	37.4	1.9	37.4	0.0	37.5	0.3	37.2	-0.8	37.3	0.3	37.3	0.0
1972	37.3	0.0	37.5	0.5	37.5	0.0	37.6	0.3	37.6	0.0	37.7	0.3	38.0	0.8	38.3	0.8	38.3	0.0	38.6	0.8	38.6	0.0	38.7	0.3
1973	38.7	0.0	38.7	0.0	39.2	1.3	39.4	0.5	39.4	0.0	39.4	0.0	39.6	0.5	40.1	1.3	40.2	0.2	41.0	2.0	41.1	0.2	41.1	0.0
1974	41.1	0.0	41.5	1.0	41.7	0.5	41.8	0.2	42.5	1.7	43.6	2.6	44.2	1.4	44.2	0.0	44.4	0.5	45.2	1.8	45.3	0.2	45.7	0.9
1975	46.5	1.8	47.2	1.5	47.7	1.1	47.9	0.4	48.0	0.2	48.7	1.5	50.3	3.3	50.3	0.0	50.9	1.2	51.5	1.2	51.0	-1.0	51.3	0.6
1976	51.7	0.8	52.0	0.6	52.1	0.2	52.4	0.6	52.5	0.2	53.2	1.3	54.5	2.4	54.6	0.2	55.0	0.7	55.3	0.5	55.7	0.7	55.6	-0.2
1977	56.1	0.9	56.8	1.2	57.6	1.4	57.7	0.2	58.1	0.7	58.6	0.9	60.2	2.7	60.4	0.3	60.7	0.5	60.6	-0.2	60.6	0.0	60.5	-0.2
1978	61.7	2.0	62.0	0.5	62.2	0.3	63.0	1.3	61.9	-1.7	61.9	0.0	63.0	1.8	63.6	1.0	64.7	1.7	64.7	0.0	65.1	0.6	65.1	0.0
1979	65.7	0.9	66.4	1.1	66.4	0.0	66.6	0.3	66.9	0.5	67.9	1.5	69.4	2.2	69.9	0.7	69.9	0.0	70.1	0.3	70.3	0.3	71.1	1.1
1980	71.7	0.8	73.6	2.6	73.5	-0.1	73.9	0.5	73.7	-0.3	73.9	0.3	76.3	3.2	77.2	1.2	77.5	0.4	77.7	0.3	78.3	0.8	78.4	0.1
1981	80.1	2.2	81.0	1.1	81.2	0.2	81.7	0.6	81.7	0.0	82.4	0.9	85.2	3.4	86.1	1.1	86.6	0.6	86.5	-0.1	86.7	0.2	87.3	0.7
1982	89.1	2.1	89.2	0.1	89.1	-0.1	89.4	0.3	89.5	0.1	89.9	0.4	93.5	4.0	93.9	0.4	93.3	-0.6	93.6	0.3	95.0	1.5	95.3	0.3
1983	96.1	0.8	97.7	1.7	97.9	0.2	98.3	0.4	98.6	0.3	99.5	0.9	102.4	2.9	103.0	0.6	103.1	0.1	103.7	0.6	103.5	-0.2	103.6	0.1
1984	103.9	0.3	104.8	0.9	104.7	-0.1	105.6	0.9	105.6	0.0	105.9	0.3	107.5	1.5	108.4	0.8	109.0	0.6	109.3	0.3	113.4	3.8	114.0	0.5
1985	115.8	1.6	116.1	0.3	117.1	0.9	117.4	0.3	117.7	0.3	118.5	0.7	119.3	0.7	119.8	0.4	121.0	1.0	121.7	0.6	122.6	0.7	122.2	-0.3
1986	122.5	0.2	123.5	0.8	124.3	0.6	125.5	1.0	125.0	-0.4	125.5	0.4	127.6	1.7	128.3	0.5	129.0	0.5	129.2	0.2	129.2	0.0	130.0	0.6
1987	129.9	-0.1	130.3	0.3	130.7	0.3	130.6	-0.1	131.7	0.8	132.9	0.9	134.0	0.8	134.0	0.0	135.3	1.0	135.3	0.0	135.2	-0.1	136.6	1.0
1988	137.7	0.8	138.7	0.7	138.4	-0.2	139.8	1.0	140.7	0.6	140.7	0.0	143.8	2.2	143.5	-0.2	144.7	0.8	145.5	0.6	146.1	0.4	146.2	0.1
1989	146.9	0.5	147.8	0.6	148.8	0.7	151.1	1.5	152.0	0.6	155.1	2.0	156.0	0.6	155.9	-0.1	159.9	2.6	164.1	2.6	166.1	1.2	159.8	-3.8
1990	160.4	0.4	160.1	-0.2	162.1	1.2	164.2	1.3	165.2	0.6	166.2	0.6	169.2	1.8	170.4	0.7	171.0	0.4	171.5	0.3	174.3	1.6	174.6	0.2
1991	176.0	0.8	178.4	1.4	178.8	0.2	180.5	1.0	181.3	0.4	182.0	0.4	184.7	1.5	186.5	1.0	186.7	0.1	188.4	0.9	188.5	0.1	189.6	0.6

[Continued]

Philadelphia, PA-NJ
Consumer Price Index - All Urban Consumers
Base 1982-1984 = 100
Medical Care
[Continued]

For 1947-1997. Columns headed % show percentile change in the index from the previous period for which an index is available.

Year	Jan Index	%	Feb Index	%	Mar Index	%	Apr Index	%	May Index	%	Jun Index	%	Jul Index	%	Aug Index	%	Sep Index	%	Oct Index	%	Nov Index	%	Dec Index	%
1992	188.0	-0.8	188.7	0.4	192.1	1.8	193.0	0.5	195.6	1.3	196.4	0.4	199.4	1.5	199.5	0.1	200.4	0.5	202.0	0.8	202.0	0.0	202.2	0.1
1993	202.0	-0.1	205.0	1.5	206.3	0.6	207.3	0.5	209.7	1.2	211.2	0.7	214.7	1.7	214.2	-0.2	214.1	-0.0	218.1	1.9	217.8	-0.1	218.3	0.2
1994	219.7	0.6	220.8	0.5	220.3	-0.2	223.2	1.3	223.1	-0.0	222.3	-0.4	224.8	1.1	225.5	0.3	225.5	0.0	226.2	0.3	226.9	0.3	228.1	0.5
1995	228.9	0.4	228.9	0.0	229.1	0.1	229.2	0.0	229.8	0.3	231.7	0.8	234.2	1.1	234.7	0.2	234.9	0.1	235.6	0.3	236.1	0.2	236.6	0.2
1996	236.8	0.1	237.3	0.2	236.8	-0.2	236.8	0.0	240.0	1.4	242.0	0.8	244.4	1.0	247.6	1.3	246.9	-0.3	246.9	0.0	246.3	-0.2	244.8	-0.6
1997	245.7	0.4	246.2	0.2	247.1	0.4	247.0	-0.0	246.8	-0.1	247.5	0.3	249.2	0.7	248.7	-0.2	249.0	0.1	248.7	-0.1	248.9	0.1	249.3	0.2

Source: U.S. Department of Labor, Bureau of Labor Statistics, Division of Consumer Prices and Price Indexes. - indicates no data collected for period.

Philadelphia, PA-NJ
Consumer Price Index - Urban Wage Earners
Base 1982-1984 = 100
Medical Care

For 1947-1997. Columns headed % show percentile change in the index from the previous period for which an index is available.

Year	Jan Index	%	Feb Index	%	Mar Index	%	Apr Index	%	May Index	%	Jun Index	%	Jul Index	%	Aug Index	%	Sep Index	%	Oct Index	%	Nov Index	%	Dec Index	%
1947	11.4	-	11.5	0.9	11.5	0.0	11.7	1.7	11.8	0.9	11.8	0.0	11.8	0.0	11.8	0.0	11.8	0.0	11.9	0.8	11.9	0.0	12.0	0.8
1948	12.1	0.8	12.2	0.8	12.1	-0.8	12.2	0.8	12.2	0.0	12.2	0.0	12.3	0.8	12.3	0.0	12.3	0.0	12.3	0.0	12.5	1.6	12.5	0.0
1949	12.5	0.0	12.5	0.0	12.6	0.8	12.6	0.0	12.6	0.0	12.6	0.0	12.6	0.0	12.6	0.0	12.7	0.8	12.7	0.0	12.7	0.0	12.7	0.0
1950	12.7	0.0	12.7	0.0	12.7	0.0	12.7	0.0	12.8	0.8	12.8	0.0	12.8	0.0	12.8	0.0	12.9	0.8	12.9	0.0	12.9	0.0	13.0	0.8
1951	13.2	1.5	13.2	0.0	13.4	1.5	13.4	0.0	13.4	0.0	13.4	0.0	13.4	0.0	13.4	0.0	13.4	0.0	13.5	0.7	13.5	0.0	13.5	0.0
1952	13.5	0.0	13.5	0.0	13.7	1.5	13.7	0.0	13.7	0.0	14.4	5.1	14.4	0.0	14.4	0.0	14.6	1.4	14.6	0.0	14.6	0.0	14.6	0.0
1953	14.6	0.0	14.6	0.0	14.6	0.0	14.6	0.0	14.6	0.0	14.7	0.7	14.7	0.0	14.7	0.0	14.7	0.0	14.7	0.0	14.7	0.0	15.0	2.0
1954	15.0	0.0	15.1	0.7	15.1	0.0	15.1	0.0	15.1	0.0	15.3	1.3	15.3	0.0	15.3	0.0	16.1	5.2	16.1	0.0	16.2	0.6	16.3	0.6
1955	16.3	0.0	16.3	0.0	16.5	1.2	16.5	0.0	16.5	0.0	16.5	0.0	16.5	0.0	16.5	0.0	16.5	0.0	16.5	0.0	16.5	0.0	16.6	0.6
1956	16.6	0.0	16.6	0.0	16.8	1.2	16.8	0.0	16.8	0.0	16.8	0.0	16.8	0.0	16.8	0.0	16.9	0.6	16.9	0.0	16.9	0.0	16.9	0.0
1957	16.9	0.0	16.9	0.0	17.1	1.2	17.1	0.0	17.1	0.0	17.2	0.6	17.2	0.0	17.2	0.0	17.2	0.0	17.2	0.0	17.2	0.0	17.4	1.2
1958	17.4	0.0	17.4	0.0	17.5	0.6	17.5	0.0	17.5	0.0	17.6	0.6	18.1	2.8	18.1	0.0	18.1	0.0	18.1	0.0	18.1	0.0	18.2	0.6
1959	18.3	0.5	18.3	0.0	18.6	1.6	18.6	0.0	18.6	0.0	18.8	1.1	18.8	0.0	19.3	2.7	19.4	0.5	19.4	0.0	19.4	0.0	19.4	0.0
1960	19.4	0.0	19.4	0.0	19.6	1.0	19.6	0.0	19.6	0.0	19.7	0.5	19.7	0.0	19.7	0.0	19.7	0.0	19.7	0.0	19.7	0.0	19.8	0.5
1961	19.8	0.0	19.8	0.0	19.9	0.5	20.2	1.5	20.8	3.0	20.8	0.0	20.8	0.0	20.8	0.0	20.9	0.5	20.8	-0.5	20.8	0.0	20.8	0.0
1962	20.9	0.5	20.9	0.0	20.9	0.0	20.9	0.0	20.9	0.0	21.6	3.3	21.6	0.0	21.6	0.0	21.7	0.5	21.6	-0.5	21.6	0.0	21.7	0.5
1963	21.7	0.0	21.7	0.0	21.7	0.0	21.7	0.0	21.7	0.0	21.8	0.5	21.8	0.0	21.8	0.0	21.9	0.5	21.9	0.0	21.9	0.0	21.9	0.0
1964	22.0	0.5	22.0	0.0	22.0	0.0	22.0	0.0	22.0	0.0	22.0	0.0	22.2	0.9	22.1	-0.5	22.2	0.5	22.2	0.0	22.3	0.5	22.3	0.0
1965	22.3	0.0	22.3	0.0	22.5	0.9	22.5	0.0	22.6	0.4	22.7	0.4	22.8	0.4	22.8	0.0	22.9	0.4	22.9	0.0	22.9	0.0	23.0	0.4
1966	23.1	0.4	23.1	0.0	23.3	0.9	23.4	0.4	23.4	0.0	23.5	0.4	23.8	1.3	23.9	0.4	23.9	0.0	24.0	0.4	24.2	0.8	24.5	1.2
1967	24.6	0.4	24.6	0.0	24.6	0.0	24.7	0.4	24.9	0.8	25.1	0.8	25.3	0.8	25.3	0.0	25.8	2.0	25.9	0.4	26.0	0.4	26.2	0.8
1968	26.3	0.4	26.4	0.4	26.5	0.4	26.6	0.4	26.9	1.1	27.1	0.7	27.6	1.8	27.7	0.4	27.9	0.7	28.1	0.7	28.2	0.4	28.3	0.4
1969	28.4	0.4	28.5	0.4	28.9	1.4	29.0	0.3	29.2	0.7	29.3	0.3	30.3	3.4	30.4	0.3	30.6	0.7	30.3	-1.0	30.3	0.0	30.4	0.3
1970	30.7	1.0	30.9	0.7	31.0	0.3	31.3	1.0	31.4	0.3	31.6	0.6	32.6	3.2	33.0	1.2	33.0	0.0	32.9	-0.3	33.6	2.1	33.7	0.3
1971	33.8	0.3	34.0	0.6	34.0	0.0	34.1	0.3	34.2	0.3	34.6	1.2	35.3	2.0	35.3	0.0	35.4	0.3	35.2	-0.6	35.2	0.0	35.2	0.0
1972	35.2	0.0	35.4	0.6	35.4	0.0	35.5	0.3	35.5	0.0	35.6	0.3	35.9	0.8	36.2	0.8	36.2	0.0	36.4	0.6	36.5	0.3	36.5	0.0
1973	36.6	0.3	36.6	0.0	37.0	1.1	37.2	0.5	37.2	0.0	37.2	0.0	37.4	0.5	37.8	1.1	38.0	0.5	38.7	1.8	38.8	0.3	38.8	0.0
1974	38.8	0.0	39.2	1.0	39.4	0.5	39.5	0.3	40.1	1.5	41.2	2.7	41.7	1.2	41.7	0.0	41.9	0.5	42.6	1.7	42.7	0.2	43.1	0.9
1975	43.9	1.9	44.6	1.6	45.0	0.9	45.3	0.7	45.4	0.2	46.0	1.3	47.5	3.3	47.5	0.0	48.0	1.1	48.7	1.5	48.2	-1.0	48.4	0.4
1976	48.9	1.0	49.1	0.4	49.2	0.2	49.5	0.6	49.6	0.2	50.3	1.4	51.5	2.4	51.6	0.2	51.9	0.6	52.2	0.6	52.6	0.8	52.5	-0.2
1977	53.0	1.0	53.6	1.1	54.4	1.5	54.5	0.2	54.9	0.7	55.3	0.7	56.9	2.9	57.0	0.2	57.3	0.5	57.2	-0.2	57.3	0.2	57.2	-0.2
1978	58.2	1.7	58.6	0.7	58.6	0.0	58.8	0.3	58.8	0.0	58.8	0.0	59.7	1.5	60.6	1.5	62.2	2.6	62.2	0.0	62.5	0.5	63.3	1.3
1979	63.3	0.0	63.9	0.9	64.0	0.2	64.1	0.2	64.4	0.5	66.8	3.7	67.6	1.2	67.9	0.4	68.3	0.6	69.1	1.2	69.3	0.3	69.8	0.7
1980	70.5	1.0	73.3	4.0	73.2	-0.1	73.8	0.8	74.3	0.7	74.8	0.7	77.3	3.3	78.6	1.7	78.9	0.4	79.2	0.4	79.2	0.0	79.2	0.0
1981	81.0	2.3	80.6	-0.5	80.7	0.1	81.2	0.6	81.2	0.0	81.4	0.2	84.7	4.1	86.2	1.8	87.3	1.3	87.4	0.1	87.7	0.3	87.6	-0.1
1982	89.3	1.9	89.2	-0.1	89.0	-0.2	89.4	0.4	89.6	0.2	89.8	0.2	93.1	3.7	93.7	0.6	93.1	-0.6	93.3	0.2	94.6	1.4	94.8	0.2
1983	95.8	1.1	97.7	2.0	97.8	0.1	98.2	0.4	98.5	0.3	99.7	1.2	102.4	2.7	103.0	0.6	103.1	0.1	103.6	0.5	103.5	-0.1	103.7	0.2
1984	104.0	0.3	105.1	1.1	105.0	-0.1	106.0	1.0	106.0	0.0	106.4	0.4	107.5	1.0	108.5	0.9	109.1	0.6	109.5	0.4	113.3	3.5	113.8	0.4
1985	115.9	1.8	116.2	0.3	117.2	0.9	117.3	0.1	117.7	0.3	118.5	0.7	119.1	0.5	119.6	0.4	120.8	1.0	121.7	0.7	122.6	0.7	122.1	-0.4
1986	122.3	0.2	123.3	0.8	124.1	0.6	125.4	1.0	124.8	-0.5	125.4	0.5	127.0	1.3	127.7	0.6	128.6	0.7	128.8	0.2	128.7	-0.1	129.5	0.6
1987	129.5	0.0	129.9	0.3	130.3	0.3	130.3	0.0	131.5	0.9	132.9	1.1	133.7	0.6	133.6	-0.1	134.5	0.7	134.9	0.3	134.7	-0.1	136.2	1.1
1988	137.3	0.8	138.1	0.6	137.7	-0.3	139.2	1.1	140.2	0.7	140.3	0.1	143.2	2.1	142.8	-0.3	144.1	0.9	144.7	0.4	145.3	0.4	145.3	0.0
1989	146.1	0.6	146.9	0.5	147.9	0.7	150.4	1.7	151.3	0.6	153.8	1.7	154.6	0.5	154.8	0.1	158.2	2.2	161.9	2.3	163.8	1.2	158.4	-3.3
1990	159.1	0.4	158.8	-0.2	160.8	1.3	163.0	1.4	163.9	0.6	164.9	0.6	167.6	1.6	168.7	0.7	169.3	0.4	169.7	0.2	172.3	1.5	172.5	0.1
1991	173.8	0.8	176.2	1.4	176.4	0.1	178.1	1.0	178.8	0.4	179.7	0.5	182.0	1.3	184.0	1.1	184.1	0.1	185.6	0.8	185.7	0.1	186.8	0.6

[Continued]

Philadelphia, PA-NJ
Consumer Price Index - Urban Wage Earners
Base 1982-1984 = 100
Medical Care
[Continued]

For 1947-1997. Columns headed % show percentile change in the index from the previous period for which an index is available.

Year	Jan Index	%	Feb Index	%	Mar Index	%	Apr Index	%	May Index	%	Jun Index	%	Jul Index	%	Aug Index	%	Sep Index	%	Oct Index	%	Nov Index	%	Dec Index	%
1992	185.5	-0.7	186.1	0.3	189.1	1.6	189.9	0.4	192.8	1.5	193.6	0.4	196.7	1.6	196.7	0.0	197.7	0.5	199.2	0.8	199.5	0.2	199.7	0.1
1993	199.4	-0.2	202.7	1.7	203.8	0.5	204.8	0.5	206.8	1.0	208.4	0.8	211.9	1.7	211.4	-0.2	211.2	-0.1	215.2	1.9	214.7	-0.2	215.3	0.3
1994	216.4	0.5	217.6	0.6	217.1	-0.2	219.8	1.2	219.9	0.0	218.9	-0.5	221.4	1.1	221.9	0.2	222.0	0.0	222.8	0.4	223.4	0.3	224.6	0.5
1995	225.1	0.2	225.1	0.0	225.3	0.1	225.3	0.0	225.9	0.3	227.9	0.9	230.0	0.9	230.6	0.3	230.7	0.0	231.3	0.3	231.9	0.3	232.3	0.2
1996	232.4	0.0	232.9	0.2	232.2	-0.3	232.1	-0.0	236.0	1.7	238.3	1.0	240.4	0.9	243.2	1.2	242.6	-0.2	242.5	-0.0	241.9	-0.2	240.6	-0.5
1997	241.5	0.4	241.8	0.1	243.0	0.5	243.0	0.0	242.7	-0.1	243.2	0.2	244.8	0.7	244.4	-0.2	244.7	0.1	244.4	-0.1	244.6	0.1	244.9	0.1

Source: U.S. Department of Labor, Bureau of Labor Statistics, Division of Consumer Prices and Price Indexes. - indicates no data collected for period.

Philadelphia, PA-NJ
Consumer Price Index - All Urban Consumers
Base 1982-1984 = 100
Entertainment

For 1976-1997. Columns headed % show percentile change in the index from the previous period for which an index is available.

Year	Jan Index	%	Feb Index	%	Mar Index	%	Apr Index	%	May Index	%	Jun Index	%	Jul Index	%	Aug Index	%	Sep Index	%	Oct Index	%	Nov Index	%	Dec Index	%
1976	68.7	-	68.1	-0.9	67.8	-0.4	68.4	0.9	68.8	0.6	68.9	0.1	69.2	0.4	69.2	0.0	68.6	-0.9	69.0	0.6	69.2	0.3	69.8	0.9
1977	70.4	0.9	70.4	0.0	70.5	0.1	71.1	0.9	71.2	0.1	72.0	1.1	72.0	0.0	71.7	-0.4	71.9	0.3	72.4	0.7	72.8	0.6	73.2	0.5
1978	73.5	0.4	73.7	0.3	73.5	-0.3	74.2	1.0	74.3	0.1	75.6	1.7	75.1	-0.7	73.3	-2.4	73.3	0.0	73.2	-0.1	71.9	-1.8	76.6	6.5
1979	77.8	1.6	78.1	0.4	78.5	0.5	81.5	3.8	81.2	-0.4	80.3	-1.1	81.8	1.9	82.8	1.2	82.8	0.0	83.6	1.0	84.5	1.1	80.8	-4.4
1980	83.0	2.7	83.1	0.1	83.3	0.2	82.9	-0.5	83.5	0.7	83.5	0.0	83.7	0.2	84.0	0.4	84.8	1.0	85.3	0.6	85.2	-0.1	85.2	0.0
1981	87.2	2.3	88.4	1.4	88.8	0.5	90.5	1.9	91.7	1.3	93.7	2.2	93.9	0.2	92.9	-1.1	93.6	0.8	94.5	1.0	94.3	-0.2	95.9	1.7
1982	94.6	-1.4	94.9	0.3	95.7	0.8	96.3	0.6	96.8	0.5	96.3	-0.5	96.0	-0.3	97.9	2.0	96.2	-1.7	97.4	1.2	97.5	0.1	97.0	-0.5
1983	97.4	0.4	97.7	0.3	100.9	3.3	100.6	-0.3	99.0	-1.6	100.6	1.6	100.9	0.3	100.5	-0.4	100.8	0.3	101.6	0.8	103.1	1.5	102.8	-0.3
1984	101.1	-1.7	102.3	1.2	101.7	-0.6	103.4	1.7	103.2	-0.2	103.7	0.5	104.1	0.4	104.0	-0.1	103.4	-0.6	103.1	-0.3	103.3	0.2	104.2	0.9
1985	103.8	-0.4	103.9	0.1	104.9	1.0	105.1	0.2	105.7	0.6	104.5	-1.1	104.5	0.0	104.5	0.0	104.8	0.3	106.7	1.8	108.0	1.2	106.8	-1.1
1986	107.6	0.7	107.1	-0.5	107.1	0.0	108.9	1.7	108.7	-0.2	109.4	0.6	110.6	1.1	110.5	-0.1	111.2	0.6	109.8	-1.3	110.3	0.5	110.6	0.3
1987	110.9	0.3	109.5	-1.3	109.4	-0.1	111.8	2.2	112.2	0.4	112.4	0.2	112.7	0.3	112.2	-0.4	112.8	0.5	113.8	0.9	113.9	0.1	114.2	0.3
1988	114.8	0.5	116.0	1.0	116.4	0.3	116.9	0.4	119.9	2.6	121.1	1.0	121.8	0.6	122.6	0.7	124.0	1.1	125.1	0.9	124.6	-0.4	126.5	1.5
1989	125.9	-0.5	126.8	0.7	127.3	0.4	129.2	1.5	129.3	0.1	127.9	-1.1	128.3	0.3	128.6	0.2	130.3	1.3	130.3	0.0	129.7	-0.5	130.1	0.3
1990	131.9	1.4	133.4	1.1	133.0	-0.3	132.8	-0.2	133.3	0.4	132.3	-0.8	134.1	1.4	134.2	0.1	134.2	0.0	133.7	-0.4	134.5	0.6	134.1	-0.3
1991	133.2	-0.7	133.1	-0.1	135.0	1.4	139.5	3.3	139.4	-0.1	138.2	-0.9	138.9	0.5	139.3	0.3	140.3	0.7	140.9	0.4	140.0	-0.6	138.5	-1.1
1992	139.2	0.5	139.1	-0.1	142.9	2.7	144.9	1.4	145.2	0.2	146.3	0.8	146.4	0.1	145.9	-0.3	146.6	0.5	145.4	-0.8	145.7	0.2	144.6	-0.8
1993	143.2	-1.0	134.2	-6.3	140.7	4.8	150.6	7.0	149.6	-0.7	149.5	-0.1	149.5	0.0	149.7	0.1	150.3	0.4	151.1	0.5	150.6	-0.3	150.9	0.2
1994	155.7	3.2	157.4	1.1	158.3	0.6	163.8	3.5	161.9	-1.2	160.7	-0.7	161.9	0.7	159.7	-1.4	160.1	0.3	159.3	-0.5	163.0	2.3	161.7	-0.8
1995	163.9	1.4	163.4	-0.3	163.9	0.3	164.1	0.1	165.0	0.5	165.0	0.0	164.7	-0.2	167.4	1.6	170.5	1.9	168.4	-1.2	171.5	1.8	172.7	0.7
1996	172.9	0.1	175.8	1.7	180.0	2.4	178.2	-1.0	178.2	0.0	177.1	-0.6	177.8	0.4	178.9	0.6	179.9	0.6	179.7	-0.1	177.4	-1.3	182.9	3.1
1997	183.8	0.5	182.0	-1.0	183.9	1.0	180.7	-1.7	181.2	0.3	178.9	-1.3	179.0	0.1	178.9	-0.1	183.5	2.6	184.4	0.5	181.3	-1.7	184.1	1.5

Source: U.S. Department of Labor, Bureau of Labor Statistics, Division of Consumer Prices and Price Indexes. - indicates no data collected for period.

Philadelphia, PA-NJ
Consumer Price Index - Urban Wage Earners
Base 1982-1984 = 100
Entertainment

For 1976-1997. Columns headed % show percentile change in the index from the previous period for which an index is available.

Year	Jan Index	%	Feb Index	%	Mar Index	%	Apr Index	%	May Index	%	Jun Index	%	Jul Index	%	Aug Index	%	Sep Index	%	Oct Index	%	Nov Index	%	Dec Index	%
1976	70.8	-	70.2	-0.8	69.9	-0.4	70.5	0.9	70.9	0.6	71.0	0.1	71.3	0.4	71.3	0.0	70.7	-0.8	71.1	0.6	71.4	0.4	72.0	0.8
1977	72.6	0.8	72.5	-0.1	72.7	0.3	73.2	0.7	73.4	0.3	74.2	1.1	74.2	0.0	73.9	-0.4	74.1	0.3	74.7	0.8	75.0	0.4	75.5	0.7
1978	75.5	0.0	75.6	0.1	75.2	-0.5	76.4	1.6	75.7	-0.9	77.7	2.6	77.7	0.0	78.1	0.5	77.9	-0.3	77.8	-0.1	75.8	-2.6	84.4	11.3
1979	85.2	0.9	85.5	0.4	85.7	0.2	86.4	0.8	86.5	0.1	84.3	-2.5	86.5	2.6	87.0	0.6	87.2	0.2	88.7	1.7	90.0	1.5	82.8	-8.0
1980	83.3	0.6	84.1	1.0	85.0	1.1	82.7	-2.7	85.1	2.9	85.3	0.2	85.6	0.4	85.3	-0.4	90.0	5.5	89.3	-0.8	90.8	1.7	90.3	-0.6
1981	92.3	2.2	93.1	0.9	93.1	0.0	93.7	0.6	91.1	-2.8	93.9	3.1	94.1	0.2	94.4	0.3	95.8	1.5	95.9	0.1	95.4	-0.5	95.9	0.5
1982	94.5	-1.5	94.8	0.3	95.4	0.6	95.8	0.4	96.3	0.5	96.1	-0.2	97.4	1.4	97.6	0.2	97.1	-0.5	97.6	0.5	97.7	0.1	97.5	-0.2
1983	97.5	0.0	97.5	0.0	100.4	-3.0	100.9	0.5	100.3	-0.6	100.8	0.5	101.3	0.5	100.7	-0.6	100.6	-0.1	101.5	0.9	103.0	1.5	102.5	-0.5
1984	100.5	-2.0	101.8	1.3	102.1	0.3	102.9	0.8	102.9	0.0	103.7	0.8	104.0	0.3	104.0	0.0	103.3	-0.7	103.1	-0.2	103.3	0.2	103.6	0.3
1985	103.1	-0.5	103.2	0.1	104.0	0.8	104.2	0.2	104.6	0.4	103.3	-1.2	103.8	0.5	103.7	-0.1	104.0	0.3	105.9	1.8	106.8	0.8	105.6	-1.1
1986	106.4	0.8	106.1	-0.3	106.0	-0.1	107.9	1.8	107.7	-0.2	108.5	0.7	109.4	0.8	109.4	0.0	110.1	0.6	108.7	-1.3	109.3	0.6	109.1	-0.2
1987	109.4	0.3	107.2	-2.0	107.1	-0.1	110.4	3.1	110.6	0.2	110.7	0.1	111.5	0.7	110.7	-0.7	111.3	0.5	112.4	1.0	112.5	0.1	112.8	0.3
1988	113.4	0.5	114.3	0.8	114.7	0.3	115.2	0.4	117.8	2.3	118.9	0.9	119.7	0.7	120.6	0.8	121.7	0.9	122.8	0.9	122.0	-0.7	124.1	1.7
1989	123.6	-0.4	124.5	0.7	125.1	0.5	126.4	1.0	126.5	0.1	125.1	-1.1	125.4	0.2	126.0	0.5	127.8	1.4	127.8	0.0	127.4	-0.3	127.7	0.2
1990	129.2	1.2	130.4	0.9	130.3	-0.1	130.0	-0.2	130.3	0.2	129.0	-1.0	130.5	1.2	130.5	0.0	130.7	0.2	130.4	-0.2	131.1	0.5	130.5	-0.5
1991	129.6	-0.7	130.1	0.4	132.1	1.5	135.7	2.7	135.9	0.1	135.1	-0.6	135.8	0.5	136.0	0.1	136.3	0.2	137.2	0.7	136.6	-0.4	135.5	-0.8
1992	136.2	0.5	135.8	-0.3	139.2	2.5	140.4	0.9	140.8	0.3	141.6	0.6	141.6	0.0	141.4	-0.1	142.3	0.6	140.7	-1.1	141.5	0.6	140.4	-0.8
1993	139.3	-0.8	130.6	-6.2	136.7	4.7	145.3	6.3	144.3	-0.7	143.9	-0.3	143.9	0.0	144.2	0.2	145.0	0.6	146.1	0.8	145.4	-0.5	146.1	0.5
1994	151.7	3.8	152.8	0.7	153.9	0.7	158.4	2.9	157.2	-0.8	156.3	-0.6	156.9	0.4	155.6	-0.8	155.1	-0.3	155.0	-0.1	158.4	2.2	156.9	-0.9
1995	159.5	1.7	158.5	-0.6	159.5	0.6	159.7	0.1	160.4	0.4	160.4	0.0	160.4	0.0	163.4	1.9	165.6	1.3	164.1	-0.9	167.0	1.8	168.4	0.8
1996	168.1	-0.2	171.0	1.7	174.8	2.2	173.2	-0.9	173.2	0.0	172.4	-0.5	173.4	0.6	174.3	0.5	175.4	0.6	175.1	-0.2	173.4	-1.0	177.7	2.5
1997	178.7	0.6	177.4	-0.7	178.7	0.7	175.7	-1.7	176.0	0.2	174.5	-0.9	174.7	0.1	174.5	-0.1	177.5	1.7	178.7	0.7	176.1	-1.5	178.1	1.1

Source: U.S. Department of Labor, Bureau of Labor Statistics, Division of Consumer Prices and Price Indexes. - indicates no data collected for period.

Philadelphia, PA-NJ

Consumer Price Index - All Urban Consumers
Base 1982-1984 = 100

Other Goods and Services

For 1976-1997. Columns headed % show percentile change in the index from the previous period for which an index is available.

Year	Jan Index	%	Feb Index	%	Mar Index	%	Apr Index	%	May Index	%	Jun Index	%	Jul Index	%	Aug Index	%	Sep Index	%	Oct Index	%	Nov Index	%	Dec Index	%
1976	54.7	-	55.0	0.5	54.8	-0.4	55.1	0.5	55.2	0.2	55.6	0.7	56.1	0.9	56.1	0.0	56.5	0.7	57.5	1.8	57.6	0.2	57.7	0.2
1977	57.8	0.2	58.0	0.3	58.0	0.0	58.6	1.0	58.5	-0.2	58.7	0.3	58.8	0.2	58.7	-0.2	60.1	2.4	60.7	1.0	60.9	0.3	60.8	-0.2
1978	60.9	0.2	61.1	0.3	61.2	0.2	61.6	0.7	61.4	-0.3	61.8	0.7	62.3	0.8	62.1	-0.3	63.8	2.7	64.0	0.3	63.9	-0.2	64.1	0.3
1979	64.9	1.2	65.4	0.8	65.6	0.3	65.7	0.2	65.7	0.0	65.6	-0.2	66.0	0.6	66.6	0.9	69.1	3.8	69.1	0.0	70.0	1.3	70.0	0.0
1980	71.0	1.4	71.1	0.1	71.1	0.0	71.5	0.6	71.9	0.6	72.2	0.4	72.9	1.0	73.0	0.1	75.7	3.7	75.3	-0.5	76.1	1.1	76.5	0.5
1981	76.6	0.1	76.5	-0.1	76.8	0.4	76.9	0.1	77.9	1.3	78.5	0.8	78.1	-0.5	78.3	0.3	83.3	6.4	83.8	0.6	83.2	-0.7	84.8	1.9
1982	84.7	-0.1	85.2	0.6	85.1	-0.1	86.9	2.1	87.2	0.3	88.2	1.1	87.5	-0.8	88.7	1.4	93.1	5.0	94.9	1.9	95.7	0.8	96.8	1.1
1983	97.8	1.0	97.0	-0.8	98.0	1.0	97.6	-0.4	97.9	0.3	98.1	0.2	99.4	1.3	101.7	2.3	105.1	3.3	106.2	1.0	106.4	0.2	106.5	0.1
1984	107.4	0.8	107.3	-0.1	107.2	-0.1	108.1	0.8	107.7	-0.4	108.2	0.5	109.3	1.0	109.3	0.0	112.3	2.7	112.3	0.0	112.4	0.1	112.5	0.1
1985	113.8	1.2	114.8	0.9	115.0	0.2	116.0	0.9	115.5	-0.4	115.6	0.1	116.5	0.8	116.6	0.1	120.6	3.4	120.5	-0.1	120.4	-0.1	120.2	-0.2
1986	121.6	1.2	123.3	1.4	123.8	0.4	124.5	0.6	125.7	1.0	126.0	0.2	126.6	0.5	126.8	0.2	129.8	2.4	129.8	0.0	129.9	0.1	130.1	0.2
1987	133.2	2.4	133.7	0.4	133.9	0.1	134.1	0.1	134.3	0.1	134.6	0.2	135.2	0.4	135.2	0.0	138.6	2.5	139.3	0.5	139.1	-0.1	139.5	0.3
1988	140.6	0.8	142.7	1.5	142.3	-0.3	143.4	0.8	143.3	-0.1	143.5	0.1	144.1	0.4	144.5	0.3	148.5	2.8	148.8	0.2	148.8	0.0	150.4	1.1
1989	152.0	1.1	152.1	0.1	152.3	0.1	153.8	1.0	153.6	-0.1	153.9	0.2	155.5	1.0	157.7	1.4	158.1	0.3	158.0	-0.1	159.2	0.8	158.4	-0.5
1990	161.9	2.2	162.1	0.1	165.7	2.2	166.1	0.2	166.3	0.1	168.8	1.5	177.4	5.1	179.3	1.1	179.0	-0.2	178.5	-0.3	178.7	0.1	179.0	0.2
1991	182.0	1.7	185.5	1.9	182.0	-1.9	182.7	0.4	182.6	-0.1	182.6	0.0	183.5	0.5	187.5	2.2	188.2	0.4	189.2	0.5	189.7	0.3	190.4	0.4
1992	190.0	-0.2	191.4	0.7	192.5	0.6	192.8	0.2	194.0	0.6	194.9	0.5	195.3	0.2	197.2	1.0	199.5	1.2	200.6	0.6	200.3	-0.1	201.4	0.5
1993	202.6	0.6	202.7	0.0	202.9	0.1	203.1	0.1	211.8	4.3	212.5	0.3	213.3	0.4	212.6	-0.3	212.7	0.0	217.1	2.1	218.1	0.5	218.9	0.4
1994	219.0	0.0	219.1	0.0	220.6	0.7	220.6	0.0	221.2	0.3	221.3	0.0	221.6	0.1	223.0	0.6	225.0	0.9	225.2	0.1	225.1	-0.0	225.1	0.0
1995	224.7	-0.2	224.4	-0.1	224.7	0.1	225.8	0.5	226.2	0.2	227.2	0.4	226.9	-0.1	227.9	0.4	230.0	0.9	229.6	-0.2	228.6	-0.4	229.5	0.4
1996	228.9	-0.3	229.9	0.4	230.9	0.4	231.8	0.4	233.4	0.7	233.4	0.0	232.3	-0.5	233.7	0.6	235.6	0.8	233.6	-0.8	235.8	0.9	234.9	-0.4
1997	239.6	2.0	238.4	-0.5	238.1	-0.1	239.6	0.6	241.5	0.8	239.3	-0.9	238.3	-0.4	242.8	1.9	243.1	0.1	245.2	0.9	245.7	0.2	245.5	-0.1

Source: U.S. Department of Labor, Bureau of Labor Statistics, Division of Consumer Prices and Price Indexes. - indicates no data collected for period.

Philadelphia, PA-NJ
Consumer Price Index - Urban Wage Earners
Base 1982-1984 = 100
Other Goods and Services

For 1976-1997. Columns headed % show percentile change in the index from the previous period for which an index is available.

Year	Jan Index	%	Feb Index	%	Mar Index	%	Apr Index	%	May Index	%	Jun Index	%	Jul Index	%	Aug Index	%	Sep Index	%	Oct Index	%	Nov Index	%	Dec Index	%
1976	56.8	-	57.2	0.7	57.0	-0.3	57.3	0.5	57.3	0.0	57.8	0.9	58.3	0.9	58.3	0.0	58.7	0.7	59.8	1.9	59.9	0.2	59.9	0.0
1977	60.1	0.3	60.3	0.3	60.3	0.0	60.9	1.0	60.8	-0.2	61.0	0.3	61.2	0.3	61.1	-0.2	62.5	2.3	63.1	1.0	63.3	0.3	63.2	-0.2
1978	63.4	0.3	63.6	0.3	63.6	0.0	64.0	0.6	63.8	-0.3	64.3	0.8	65.0	1.1	64.0	-1.5	65.5	2.3	66.2	1.1	66.1	-0.2	66.1	0.0
1979	66.8	1.1	67.3	0.7	67.2	-0.1	67.2	0.0	67.3	0.1	67.0	-0.4	67.5	0.7	68.0	0.7	70.1	3.1	70.0	-0.1	71.3	1.9	71.3	0.0
1980	71.9	0.8	72.0	0.1	72.0	0.0	72.2	0.3	72.8	0.8	73.4	0.8	73.4	0.0	73.8	0.5	75.9	2.8	76.1	0.3	76.6	0.7	77.2	0.8
1981	77.8	0.8	77.7	-0.1	78.1	0.5	78.3	0.3	79.2	1.1	79.0	-0.3	79.2	0.3	79.4	0.3	83.4	5.0	84.0	0.7	84.6	0.7	84.6	0.0
1982	84.5	-0.1	85.1	0.7	85.0	-0.1	86.8	2.1	87.2	0.5	88.2	1.1	87.6	-0.7	88.9	1.5	92.5	4.0	94.6	2.3	95.6	1.1	97.0	1.5
1983	98.0	1.0	97.2	-0.8	98.2	1.0	97.9	-0.3	98.0	0.1	98.3	0.3	99.9	1.6	102.6	2.7	105.3	2.6	106.0	0.7	106.2	0.2	106.3	0.1
1984	107.4	1.0	107.1	-0.3	107.3	0.2	108.2	0.8	107.8	-0.4	108.5	0.6	109.5	0.9	109.6	0.1	111.8	2.0	111.8	0.0	111.9	0.1	112.0	0.1
1985	113.6	1.4	114.5	0.8	114.7	0.2	115.9	1.0	115.5	-0.3	115.6	0.1	116.6	0.9	116.7	0.1	119.8	2.7	119.7	-0.1	119.6	-0.1	119.6	0.0
1986	121.1	1.3	122.8	1.4	123.3	0.4	124.1	0.6	125.5	1.1	125.8	0.2	126.5	0.6	126.5	0.0	128.8	1.8	128.8	0.0	128.9	0.1	129.0	0.1
1987	132.0	2.3	132.4	0.3	132.7	0.2	133.0	0.2	133.1	0.1	133.5	0.3	134.2	0.5	134.1	-0.1	137.3	2.4	138.0	0.5	137.8	-0.1	138.2	0.3
1988	139.4	0.9	141.6	1.6	141.1	-0.4	142.7	1.1	142.7	0.0	143.0	0.2	143.8	0.6	144.1	0.2	147.8	2.6	148.2	0.3	148.1	-0.1	149.5	0.9
1989	150.9	0.9	150.9	0.0	151.0	0.1	152.1	0.7	151.9	-0.1	152.6	0.5	153.9	0.9	156.0	1.4	156.4	0.3	156.3	-0.1	157.5	0.8	156.5	-0.6
1990	160.5	2.6	160.2	-0.2	163.8	2.2	164.2	0.2	164.6	0.2	167.5	1.8	177.0	5.7	178.6	0.9	178.1	-0.3	177.6	-0.3	177.9	0.2	178.2	0.2
1991	181.0	1.6	184.2	1.8	181.5	-1.5	182.2	0.4	182.1	-0.1	182.2	0.1	183.0	0.4	185.5	1.4	186.0	0.3	187.4	0.8	188.1	0.4	188.8	0.4
1992	188.5	-0.2	189.7	0.6	190.7	0.5	190.9	0.1	192.3	0.7	193.9	0.8	194.2	0.2	195.3	0.6	197.7	1.2	199.1	0.7	198.8	-0.2	200.1	0.7
1993	201.4	0.6	201.5	0.0	201.6	0.0	202.0	0.2	210.2	4.1	211.0	0.4	211.8	0.4	210.0	-0.8	209.8	-0.1	213.1	1.6	214.2	0.5	215.2	0.5
1994	215.3	0.0	215.5	0.1	216.8	0.6	216.8	0.0	217.4	0.3	217.5	0.0	217.8	0.1	218.8	0.5	220.5	0.8	220.7	0.1	220.6	-0.0	220.6	0.0
1995	220.1	-0.2	219.8	-0.1	220.1	0.1	221.3	0.5	221.8	0.2	222.6	0.4	221.8	-0.4	222.4	0.3	224.9	1.1	224.2	-0.3	223.4	-0.4	224.2	0.4
1996	223.6	-0.3	224.8	0.5	225.4	0.3	226.4	0.4	228.4	0.9	228.6	0.1	227.3	-0.6	227.8	0.2	229.8	0.9	227.7	-0.9	230.0	1.0	229.2	-0.3
1997	233.5	1.9	232.6	-0.4	231.9	-0.3	233.8	0.8	236.0	0.9	233.5	-1.1	232.1	-0.6	236.2	1.8	236.7	0.2	239.0	1.0	239.3	0.1	239.7	0.2

Source: U.S. Department of Labor, Bureau of Labor Statistics, Division of Consumer Prices and Price Indexes. - indicates no data collected for period.

Pittsburgh, PA
Consumer Price Index - All Urban Consumers
Base 1982-1984 = 100
Annual Averages

For 1917-1997. Columns headed % show percentile change in the index from the previous period for which an index is available.

Year	All Items		Food & Beverage		Housing		Apparel & Upkeep		Trans- portation		Medical Care		Entertain- ment		Other Goods & Services	
	Index	%	Index	%	Index	%	Index	%	Index	%	Index	%	Index	%	Index	%
1917	-	-	-	-	-	-	-	-	-	-	-	-	-	-	-	-
1918	14.8	-	-	-	-	-	-	-	-	-	-	-	-	-	-	-
1919	17.0	14.9	-	-	-	-	-	-	-	-	-	-	-	-	-	-
1920	19.5	14.7	-	-	-	-	-	-	-	-	-	-	-	-	-	-
1921	17.5	-10.3	-	-	-	-	-	-	-	-	-	-	-	-	-	-
1922	16.3	-6.9	-	-	-	-	-	-	-	-	-	-	-	-	-	-
1923	16.6	1.8	-	-	-	-	-	-	-	-	-	-	-	-	-	-
1924	16.8	1.2	-	-	-	-	-	-	-	-	-	-	-	-	-	-
1925	17.4	3.6	-	-	-	-	-	-	-	-	-	-	-	-	-	-
1926	17.5	0.6	-	-	-	-	-	-	-	-	-	-	-	-	-	-
1927	17.2	-1.7	-	-	-	-	-	-	-	-	-	-	-	-	-	-
1928	17.1	-0.6	-	-	-	-	-	-	-	-	-	-	-	-	-	-
1929	17.1	0.0	-	-	-	-	-	-	-	-	-	-	-	-	-	-
1930	16.5	-3.5	-	-	-	-	-	-	-	-	-	-	-	-	-	-
1931	15.0	-9.1	-	-	-	-	-	-	-	-	-	-	-	-	-	-
1932	13.3	-11.3	-	-	-	-	-	-	-	-	-	-	-	-	-	-
1933	12.5	-6.0	-	-	-	-	-	-	-	-	-	-	-	-	-	-
1934	12.9	3.2	-	-	-	-	-	-	-	-	-	-	-	-	-	-
1935	13.3	3.1	-	-	-	-	-	-	-	-	-	-	-	-	-	-
1936	13.5	1.5	-	-	-	-	-	-	-	-	-	-	-	-	-	-
1937	14.0	3.7	-	-	-	-	-	-	-	-	-	-	-	-	-	-
1938	13.7	-2.1	-	-	-	-	-	-	-	-	-	-	-	-	-	-
1939	13.4	-2.2	-	-	-	-	-	-	-	-	-	-	-	-	-	-
1940	13.6	1.5	-	-	-	-	-	-	-	-	-	-	-	-	-	-
1941	14.4	5.9	-	-	-	-	-	-	-	-	-	-	-	-	-	-
1942	15.8	9.7	-	-	-	-	-	-	-	-	-	-	-	-	-	-
1943	16.8	6.3	-	-	-	-	-	-	-	-	-	-	-	-	-	-
1944	17.2	2.4	-	-	-	-	-	-	-	-	-	-	-	-	-	-
1945	17.6	2.3	-	-	-	-	-	-	-	-	-	-	-	-	-	-
1946	19.1	8.5	-	-	-	-	-	-	-	-	-	-	-	-	-	-
1947	22.2	16.2	-	-	-	-	-	-	16.2	-	11.7	-	-	-	-	-
1948	23.8	7.2	-	-	-	-	-	-	17.9	10.5	12.4	6.0	-	-	-	-
1949	23.5	-1.3	-	-	-	-	-	-	18.9	5.6	12.6	1.6	-	-	-	-
1950	23.7	0.9	-	-	-	-	-	-	21.0	11.1	12.9	2.4	-	-	-	-
1951	25.6	8.0	-	-	-	-	-	-	22.8	8.6	13.5	4.7	-	-	-	-
1952	26.1	2.0	-	-	-	-	-	-	24.4	7.0	14.0	3.7	-	-	-	-
1953	26.3	0.8	-	-	-	-	42.9	-	24.7	1.2	14.7	5.0	-	-	-	-
1954	26.5	0.8	-	-	-	-	42.9	0.0	24.3	-1.6	15.4	4.8	-	-	-	-
1955	26.3	-0.8	-	-	-	-	42.2	-1.6	24.2	-0.4	15.8	2.6	-	-	-	-
1956	27.0	2.7	-	-	-	-	43.2	2.4	24.5	1.2	16.8	6.3	-	-	-	-
1957	27.8	3.0	-	-	-	-	44.4	2.8	25.7	4.9	17.7	5.4	-	-	-	-
1958	28.7	3.2	-	-	-	-	44.5	0.2	26.9	4.7	18.5	4.5	-	-	-	-
1959	29.0	1.0	-	-	-	-	44.6	0.2	28.5	5.9	19.7	6.5	-	-	-	-
1960	29.7	2.4	-	-	-	-	45.3	1.6	29.1	2.1	20.7	5.1	-	-	-	-
1961	29.9	0.7	-	-	-	-	45.6	0.7	29.2	0.3	21.4	3.4	-	-	-	-

[Continued]

732

Pittsburgh, PA
Consumer Price Index - All Urban Consumers
Base 1982-1984 = 100
Annual Averages
[Continued]

For 1917-1997. Columns headed % show percentile change in the index from the previous period for which an index is available.

Year	All Items		Food & Beverage		Housing		Apparel & Upkeep		Trans- portation		Medical Care		Entertain- ment		Other Goods & Services	
	Index	%	Index	%	Index	%	Index	%	Index	%	Index	%	Index	%	Index	%
1962	30.2	1.0	-	-	-	-	45.9	0.7	29.9	2.4	22.4	4.7	-	-	-	-
1963	30.5	1.0	-	-	-	-	46.9	2.2	29.9	0.0	23.0	2.7	-	-	-	-
1964	30.9	1.3	-	-	-	-	47.7	1.7	30.3	1.3	23.7	3.0	-	-	-	-
1965	31.4	1.6	-	-	-	-	48.6	1.9	30.8	1.7	24.3	2.5	-	-	-	-
1966	32.2	2.5	-	-	-	-	49.9	2.7	31.1	1.0	25.1	3.3	-	-	-	-
1967	32.8	1.9	-	-	-	-	51.2	2.6	31.6	1.6	26.9	7.2	-	-	-	-
1968	34.3	4.6	-	-	-	-	54.2	5.9	32.7	3.5	28.4	5.6	-	-	-	-
1969	36.2	5.5	-	-	-	-	57.8	6.6	34.1	4.3	30.1	6.0	-	-	-	-
1970	38.1	5.2	-	-	-	-	59.1	2.2	36.0	5.6	31.6	5.0	-	-	-	-
1971	39.8	4.5	-	-	-	-	61.2	3.6	37.9	5.3	32.9	4.1	-	-	-	-
1972	41.1	3.3	-	-	-	-	63.3	3.4	38.3	1.1	34.6	5.2	-	-	-	-
1973	43.6	6.1	-	-	-	-	65.4	3.3	39.3	2.6	36.0	4.0	-	-	-	-
1974	48.3	10.8	-	-	-	-	70.5	7.8	43.4	10.4	39.5	9.7	-	-	-	-
1975	52.4	8.5	-	-	-	-	72.5	2.8	47.0	8.3	43.7	10.6	-	-	-	-
1976	55.2	5.3	62.3	-	50.7	-	73.8	1.8	51.6	9.8	48.2	10.3	65.0	-	57.9	-
1977	58.9	6.7	66.4	6.6	54.4	7.3	75.2	1.9	56.3	9.1	53.3	10.6	68.3	5.1	61.8	6.7
1978	64.1	8.8	72.8	9.6	60.5	11.2	77.6	3.2	59.7	6.0	58.0	8.8	71.3	4.4	65.5	6.0
1979	71.2	11.1	80.0	9.9	67.9	12.2	82.6	6.4	68.5	14.7	64.2	10.7	73.7	3.4	70.3	7.3
1980	81.0	13.8	87.2	9.0	78.9	16.2	87.1	5.4	82.1	19.9	71.2	10.9	82.1	11.4	75.2	7.0
1981	89.3	10.2	93.8	7.6	86.7	9.9	93.7	7.6	93.6	14.0	79.7	11.9	90.3	10.0	82.4	9.6
1982	94.4	5.7	98.0	4.5	92.2	6.3	97.7	4.3	96.6	3.2	89.6	12.4	95.5	5.8	90.8	10.2
1983	101.1	7.1	101.1	3.2	101.7	10.3	101.2	3.6	99.8	3.3	100.9	12.6	100.4	5.1	101.0	11.2
1984	104.5	3.4	100.9	-0.2	106.1	4.3	101.2	0.0	103.6	3.8	109.6	8.6	104.1	3.7	108.2	7.1
1985	106.9	2.3	102.3	1.4	108.5	2.3	102.8	1.6	105.4	1.7	113.4	3.5	109.8	5.5	113.0	4.4
1986	108.2	1.2	105.0	2.6	111.3	2.6	100.4	-2.3	99.5	-5.6	121.2	6.9	118.7	8.1	118.0	4.4
1987	111.4	3.0	109.4	4.2	113.4	1.9	107.0	6.6	100.5	1.0	130.2	7.4	121.4	2.3	122.7	4.0
1988	114.9	3.1	111.9	2.3	115.7	2.0	114.2	6.7	102.3	1.8	138.2	6.1	127.1	4.7	132.7	8.1
1989	120.1	4.5	118.0	5.5	119.2	3.0	121.2	6.1	107.2	4.8	146.8	6.2	133.1	4.7	140.7	6.0
1990	126.2	5.1	124.3	5.3	124.8	4.7	125.0	3.1	112.1	4.6	160.6	9.4	138.8	4.3	150.4	6.9
1991	131.3	4.0	129.2	3.9	131.4	5.3	129.5	3.6	112.9	0.7	175.7	9.4	143.0	3.0	155.0	3.1
1992	136.0	3.6	132.9	2.9	135.8	3.3	133.0	2.7	115.6	2.4	185.9	5.8	145.4	1.7	168.1	8.5
1993	139.9	2.9	137.2	3.2	139.1	2.4	134.5	1.1	118.1	2.2	196.8	5.9	149.8	3.0	177.2	5.4
1994	144.6	3.4	140.6	2.5	145.2	4.4	133.2	-1.0	122.3	3.6	207.0	5.2	153.6	2.5	182.9	3.2
1995	149.2	3.2	143.6	2.1	150.1	3.4	135.3	1.6	127.6	4.3	212.6	2.7	156.4	1.8	192.2	5.1
1996	153.2	2.7	148.9	3.7	153.1	2.0	134.6	-0.5	129.2	1.3	225.4	6.0	163.2	4.3	202.9	5.6
1997	157.0	2.5	151.8	1.9	156.2	2.0	140.9	4.7	132.7	2.7	228.8	1.5	165.7	1.5	214.3	5.6

Source: U.S. Department of Labor, Bureau of Labor Statistics, Division of Consumer Prices and Price Indexes. - indicates no data collected for period.

Pittsburgh, PA
Consumer Price Index - Urban Wage Earners
Base 1982-1984 = 100
Annual Averages

For 1917-1997. Columns headed % show percentile change in the index from the previous period for which an index is available.

Year	All Items		Food & Beverage		Housing		Apparel & Upkeep		Trans-portation		Medical Care		Entertain-ment		Other Goods & Services	
	Index	%	Index	%	Index	%	Index	%	Index	%	Index	%	Index	%	Index	%
1917	-	-	-	-	-	-	-	-	-	-	-	-	-	-	-	-
1918	15.2	-	-	-	-	-	-	-	-	-	-	-	-	-	-	-
1919	17.5	15.1	-	-	-	-	-	-	-	-	-	-	-	-	-	-
1920	20.0	14.3	-	-	-	-	-	-	-	-	-	-	-	-	-	-
1921	17.9	-10.5	-	-	-	-	-	-	-	-	-	-	-	-	-	-
1922	16.7	-6.7	-	-	-	-	-	-	-	-	-	-	-	-	-	-
1923	17.1	2.4	-	-	-	-	-	-	-	-	-	-	-	-	-	-
1924	17.2	0.6	-	-	-	-	-	-	-	-	-	-	-	-	-	-
1925	17.8	3.5	-	-	-	-	-	-	-	-	-	-	-	-	-	-
1926	18.0	1.1	-	-	-	-	-	-	-	-	-	-	-	-	-	-
1927	17.7	-1.7	-	-	-	-	-	-	-	-	-	-	-	-	-	-
1928	17.5	-1.1	-	-	-	-	-	-	-	-	-	-	-	-	-	-
1929	17.5	0.0	-	-	-	-	-	-	-	-	-	-	-	-	-	-
1930	16.9	-3.4	-	-	-	-	-	-	-	-	-	-	-	-	-	-
1931	15.4	-8.9	-	-	-	-	-	-	-	-	-	-	-	-	-	-
1932	13.7	-11.0	-	-	-	-	-	-	-	-	-	-	-	-	-	-
1933	12.8	-6.6	-	-	-	-	-	-	-	-	-	-	-	-	-	-
1934	13.3	3.9	-	-	-	-	-	-	-	-	-	-	-	-	-	-
1935	13.7	3.0	-	-	-	-	-	-	-	-	-	-	-	-	-	-
1936	13.9	1.5	-	-	-	-	-	-	-	-	-	-	-	-	-	-
1937	14.4	3.6	-	-	-	-	-	-	-	-	-	-	-	-	-	-
1938	14.1	-2.1	-	-	-	-	-	-	-	-	-	-	-	-	-	-
1939	13.8	-2.1	-	-	-	-	-	-	-	-	-	-	-	-	-	-
1940	14.0	1.4	-	-	-	-	-	-	-	-	-	-	-	-	-	-
1941	14.7	5.0	-	-	-	-	-	-	-	-	-	-	-	-	-	-
1942	16.2	10.2	-	-	-	-	-	-	-	-	-	-	-	-	-	-
1943	17.3	6.8	-	-	-	-	-	-	-	-	-	-	-	-	-	-
1944	17.6	1.7	-	-	-	-	-	-	-	-	-	-	-	-	-	-
1945	18.1	2.8	-	-	-	-	-	-	-	-	-	-	-	-	-	-
1946	19.6	8.3	-	-	-	-	-	-	-	-	-	-	-	-	-	-
1947	22.8	16.3	-	-	-	-	-	-	16.0	-	11.8	-	-	-	-	-
1948	24.4	7.0	-	-	-	-	-	-	17.7	10.6	12.4	5.1	-	-	-	-
1949	24.1	-1.2	-	-	-	-	-	-	18.7	5.6	12.7	2.4	-	-	-	-
1950	24.3	0.8	-	-	-	-	-	-	20.7	10.7	13.0	2.4	-	-	-	-
1951	26.3	8.2	-	-	-	-	-	-	22.5	8.7	13.6	4.6	-	-	-	-
1952	26.8	1.9	-	-	-	-	-	-	24.1	7.1	14.1	3.7	-	-	-	-
1953	27.0	0.7	-	-	-	-	44.4	-	24.4	1.2	14.8	5.0	-	-	-	-
1954	27.2	0.7	-	-	-	-	44.4	0.0	24.0	-1.6	15.5	4.7	-	-	-	-
1955	27.0	-0.7	-	-	-	-	43.8	-1.4	23.9	-0.4	15.9	2.6	-	-	-	-
1956	27.7	2.6	-	-	-	-	44.8	2.3	24.1	0.8	16.9	6.3	-	-	-	-
1957	28.5	2.9	-	-	-	-	46.0	2.7	25.3	5.0	17.9	5.9	-	-	-	-
1958	29.4	3.2	-	-	-	-	46.1	0.2	26.6	5.1	18.6	3.9	-	-	-	-
1959	29.8	1.4	-	-	-	-	46.3	0.4	28.1	5.6	19.8	6.5	-	-	-	-
1960	30.4	2.0	-	-	-	-	47.0	1.5	28.8	2.5	20.9	5.6	-	-	-	-
1961	30.7	1.0	-	-	-	-	47.3	0.6	28.8	0.0	21.6	3.3	-	-	-	-

[Continued]

734

Pittsburgh, PA
Consumer Price Index - Urban Wage Earners
Base 1982-1984 = 100
Annual Averages
[Continued]

For 1917-1997. Columns headed % show percentile change in the index from the previous period for which an index is available.

Year	All Items		Food & Beverage		Housing		Apparel & Upkeep		Trans-portation		Medical Care		Entertain-ment		Other Goods & Services	
	Index	%	Index	%	Index	%	Index	%	Index	%	Index	%	Index	%	Index	%
1962	31.0	1.0	-	-	-	-	47.6	0.6	29.5	2.4	22.5	4.2	-	-	-	-
1963	31.3	1.0	-	-	-	-	48.7	2.3	29.5	0.0	23.2	3.1	-	-	-	-
1964	31.7	1.3	-	-	-	-	49.4	1.4	29.9	1.4	23.9	3.0	-	-	-	-
1965	32.2	1.6	-	-	-	-	50.4	2.0	30.4	1.7	24.5	2.5	-	-	-	-
1966	33.1	2.8	-	-	-	-	51.8	2.8	30.7	1.0	25.3	3.3	-	-	-	-
1967	33.6	1.5	-	-	-	-	53.1	2.5	31.2	1.6	27.0	6.7	-	-	-	-
1968	35.2	4.8	-	-	-	-	56.2	5.8	32.3	3.5	28.5	5.6	-	-	-	-
1969	37.1	5.4	-	-	-	-	59.9	6.6	33.7	4.3	30.3	6.3	-	-	-	-
1970	39.1	5.4	-	-	-	-	61.3	2.3	35.5	5.3	31.8	5.0	-	-	-	-
1971	40.9	4.6	-	-	-	-	63.5	3.6	37.4	5.4	33.1	4.1	-	-	-	-
1972	42.1	2.9	-	-	-	-	65.6	3.3	37.8	1.1	34.8	5.1	-	-	-	-
1973	44.7	6.2	-	-	-	-	67.8	3.4	38.8	2.6	36.3	4.3	-	-	-	-
1974	49.5	10.7	-	-	-	-	73.1	7.8	42.8	10.3	39.7	9.4	-	-	-	-
1975	53.8	8.7	-	-	-	-	75.2	2.9	46.4	8.4	44.0	10.8	-	-	-	-
1976	56.6	5.2	62.2	-	53.8	-	76.5	1.7	50.9	9.7	48.5	10.2	67.2	-	57.1	-
1977	60.5	6.9	66.2	6.4	57.7	7.2	77.9	1.8	55.6	9.2	53.7	10.7	70.7	5.2	61.0	6.8
1978	65.6	8.4	72.8	10.0	64.1	11.1	78.5	0.8	59.1	6.3	57.9	7.8	73.2	3.5	64.7	6.1
1979	73.1	11.4	80.5	10.6	72.0	12.3	83.8	6.8	67.9	14.9	64.4	11.2	77.2	5.5	69.2	7.0
1980	83.4	14.1	87.4	8.6	83.9	16.5	89.4	6.7	81.4	19.9	73.3	13.8	83.6	8.3	75.2	8.7
1981	92.0	10.3	94.1	7.7	92.5	10.3	93.3	4.4	93.7	15.1	80.6	10.0	90.0	7.7	82.1	9.2
1982	97.0	5.4	98.0	4.1	98.5	6.5	97.7	4.7	96.9	3.4	89.9	11.5	95.4	6.0	89.9	9.5
1983	101.3	4.4	101.1	3.2	102.8	4.4	100.9	3.3	99.4	2.6	100.6	11.9	100.6	5.5	101.1	12.5
1984	101.6	0.3	100.9	-0.2	98.7	-4.0	101.4	0.5	103.7	4.3	109.5	8.8	104.0	3.4	108.9	7.7
1985	103.7	2.1	102.1	1.2	100.4	1.7	102.8	1.4	105.2	1.4	113.6	3.7	109.9	5.7	113.7	4.4
1986	104.2	0.5	104.7	2.5	102.9	2.5	100.0	-2.7	98.2	-6.7	121.7	7.1	118.7	8.0	118.7	4.4
1987	107.1	2.8	109.1	4.2	104.8	1.8	106.1	6.1	99.3	1.1	130.9	7.6	121.4	2.3	123.1	3.7
1988	110.4	3.1	111.9	2.6	106.9	2.0	112.6	6.1	101.7	2.4	139.4	6.5	126.5	4.2	134.3	9.1
1989	115.4	4.5	118.0	5.5	110.3	3.2	118.6	5.3	106.8	5.0	147.5	5.8	131.6	4.0	142.5	.6.1
1990	121.3	5.1	124.5	5.5	115.6	4.8	122.1	3.0	111.5	4.4	161.3	9.4	137.2	4.3	153.4	7.6
1991	125.9	3.8	129.6	4.1	121.6	5.2	124.5	2.0	111.9	0.4	175.4	8.7	140.8	2.6	158.6	3.4
1992	130.1	3.3	133.1	2.7	125.5	3.2	128.0	2.8	114.7	2.5	184.1	5.0	143.0	1.6	172.6	8.8
1993	133.9	2.9	137.4	3.2	128.6	2.5	128.8	0.6	117.5	2.4	194.1	5.4	147.4	3.1	181.6	5.2
1994	138.3	3.3	140.5	2.3	134.1	4.3	128.5	-0.2	121.7	3.6	203.8	5.0	151.5	2.8	186.6	2.8
1995	142.9	3.3	143.4	2.1	138.5	3.3	128.9	0.3	128.5	5.6	208.6	2.4	154.6	2.0	195.2	4.6
1996	146.8	2.7	148.8	3.8	141.3	2.0	129.1	0.2	130.2	1.3	220.0	5.5	161.0	4.1	207.3	6.2
1997	150.5	2.5	151.8	2.0	144.0	1.9	136.8	6.0	133.1	2.2	223.2	1.5	164.5	2.2	219.3	5.8

Source: U.S. Department of Labor, Bureau of Labor Statistics, Division of Consumer Prices and Price Indexes. - indicates no data collected for period.

Pittsburgh, PA
Consumer Price Index - All Urban Consumers
Base 1982-1984 = 100
All Items

For 1917-1997. Columns headed % show percentile change in the index from the previous period for which an index is available.

Year	Jan Index	%	Feb Index	%	Mar Index	%	Apr Index	%	May Index	%	Jun Index	%	Jul Index	%	Aug Index	%	Sep Index	%	Oct Index	%	Nov Index	%	Dec Index	%
1917	-	-	-	-	-	-	-	-	-	-	-	-	-	-	-	-	-	-	-	-	-	-	13.5	-
1918	-	-	-	-	-	-	-	-	-	-	-	-	-	-	-	-	-	-	-	-	-	-	16.2	20.0
1919	-	-	-	-	-	-	-	-	-	-	16.5	1.9	-	-	-	-	-	-	-	-	-	-	18.4	11.5
1920	-	-	-	-	-	-	-	-	-	-	20.4	10.9	-	-	-	-	-	-	-	-	-	-	18.9	-7.4
1921	-	-	-	-	-	-	-	-	17.5	-7.4	-	-	-	-	-	-	17.1	-2.3	-	-	-	-	16.7	-2.3
1922	-	-	-	-	16.2	-3.0	-	-	-	-	16.3	0.6	-	-	-	-	16.2	-0.6	-	-	-	-	16.4	1.2
1923	-	-	-	-	16.4	0.0	-	-	-	-	16.7	1.8	-	-	-	-	16.8	0.6	-	-	-	-	16.7	-0.6
1924	-	-	-	-	16.5	-1.2	-	-	-	-	16.8	1.8	-	-	-	-	16.9	0.6	-	-	-	-	17.0	0.6
1925	-	-	-	-	-	-	-	-	-	-	17.4	2.4	-	-	-	-	-	-	-	-	-	-	17.7	1.7
1926	-	-	-	-	-	-	-	-	-	-	17.6	-0.6	-	-	-	-	-	-	-	-	-	-	17.5	-0.6
1927	-	-	-	-	-	-	-	-	-	-	17.5	0.0	-	-	-	-	-	-	-	-	-	-	17.1	-2.3
1928	-	-	-	-	-	-	-	-	-	-	16.9	-1.2	-	-	-	-	-	-	-	-	-	-	17.1	1.2
1929	-	-	-	-	-	-	-	-	-	-	17.1	0.0	-	-	-	-	-	-	-	-	-	-	17.0	-0.6
1930	-	-	-	-	-	-	-	-	-	-	16.7	-1.8	-	-	-	-	-	-	-	-	-	-	15.9	-4.8
1931	-	-	-	-	-	-	-	-	-	-	14.9	-6.3	-	-	-	-	-	-	-	-	-	-	14.3	-4.0
1932	-	-	-	-	-	-	-	-	-	-	13.2	-7.7	-	-	-	-	-	-	-	-	-	-	12.8	-3.0
1933	-	-	-	-	-	-	-	-	-	-	12.2	-4.7	-	-	-	-	-	-	-	-	-	-	12.7	4.1
1934	-	-	-	-	-	-	-	-	-	-	13.0	2.4	-	-	-	-	-	-	-	-	13.0	0.0	-	-
1935	-	-	-	-	13.2	1.5	-	-	-	-	-	-	13.2	0.0	-	-	-	-	13.4	1.5	-	-	-	-
1936	13.4	0.0	-	-	-	-	13.3	-0.7	-	-	-	-	13.6	2.3	-	-	13.8	1.5	-	-	-	-	13.6	-1.4
1937	-	-	-	-	13.9	2.2	-	-	-	-	14.1	1.4	-	-	-	-	14.3	1.4	-	-	-	-	13.9	-2.8
1938	-	-	-	-	13.7	-1.4	-	-	-	-	13.8	0.7	-	-	-	-	13.8	0.0	-	-	-	-	13.7	-0.7
1939	-	-	-	-	13.3	-2.9	-	-	-	-	13.4	0.8	-	-	-	-	13.6	1.5	-	-	-	-	13.4	-1.5
1940	-	-	-	-	13.5	0.7	-	-	-	-	13.7	1.5	-	-	-	-	13.7	0.0	13.7		13.7	0.0	13.8	0.7
1941	13.8	0.0	13.7	-0.7	13.8	0.7	13.9	0.7	14.1	1.4	14.3	1.4	14.5	1.4	14.5	0.0	14.8	2.1	14.9	0.7	15.0	0.7	15.1	0.7
1942	15.2	0.7	15.4	1.3	15.5	0.6	15.5	0.0	15.8	1.9	15.9	0.6	15.9	0.0	15.9	0.0	16.0	0.6	16.2	1.3	16.2	0.0	16.3	0.6
1943	16.4	0.6	16.5	0.6	16.7	1.2	16.8	0.6	17.0	1.2	17.0	0.0	16.9	-0.6	16.8	-0.6	16.9	0.6	17.0	0.6	17.0	0.0	16.9	-0.6
1944	16.9	0.0	16.9	0.0	16.9	0.0	17.1	1.2	17.1	0.0	17.2	0.6	17.3	0.6	17.4	0.6	17.4	0.0	17.4	0.0	17.3	-0.6	17.4	0.6
1945	17.4	0.0	17.4	0.0	17.4	0.0	17.4	0.0	17.5	0.6	17.8	1.7	17.8	0.0	17.7	-0.6	17.7	0.0	17.7	0.0	17.7	0.0	17.8	0.6
1946	17.9	0.6	17.8	-0.6	17.9	0.6	17.9	0.0	18.0	0.6	18.3	1.7	19.4	6.0	19.8	2.1	20.1	1.5	20.3	1.0	20.9	3.0	21.1	1.0
1947	21.2	0.5	21.3	0.5	21.7	1.9	21.6	-0.5	21.7	0.5	21.9	0.9	22.2	1.4	22.4	0.9	22.9	2.2	22.8	-0.4	22.9	0.4	23.2	1.3
1948	23.5	1.3	23.1	-1.7	23.1	0.0	23.4	1.3	23.6	0.9	23.9	1.3	24.2	1.3	24.3	0.4	24.3	0.0	24.1	-0.8	23.9	-0.8	23.8	-0.4
1949	23.8	0.0	23.4	-1.7	23.5	0.4	23.5	0.0	23.5	0.0	23.6	0.4	23.4	-0.8	23.5	0.4	23.5	0.0	23.3	-0.9	23.3	0.0	23.2	-0.4
1950	23.1	-0.4	23.0	-0.4	23.0	0.0	23.1	0.4	23.3	0.9	23.4	0.4	23.5	0.4	23.9	1.7	24.2	1.3	24.3	0.4	24.3	0.0	24.5	0.8
1951	25.0	2.0	25.2	0.8	25.3	0.4	25.4	0.4	25.6	0.8	25.6	0.0	25.8	0.8	25.7	-0.4	25.9	0.8	26.0	0.4	26.1	0.4	26.1	0.0
1952	26.2	0.4	26.0	-0.8	25.9	-0.4	26.0	0.4	26.0	0.0	26.0	0.0	26.1	0.4	26.2	0.4	26.2	0.0	26.2	0.0	26.2	0.0	26.2	0.0
1953	26.1	-0.4	-	-	-	-	26.1	0.0	-	-	-	-	26.3	0.8	-	-	-	-	26.5	0.8	-	-	-	-
1954	26.5	0.0	-	-	-	-	26.5	0.0	-	-	-	-	26.7	0.8	-	-	-	-	26.4	-1.1	-	-	-	-
1955	26.3	-0.4	-	-	-	-	26.3	0.0	-	-	-	-	26.3	0.0	-	-	-	-	26.3	0.0	-	-	-	-
1956	26.3	0.0	-	-	-	-	26.6	1.1	-	-	-	-	27.1	1.9	-	-	-	-	27.3	0.7	-	-	-	-
1957	27.5	0.7	-	-	-	-	27.5	0.0	-	-	-	-	27.9	1.5	-	-	-	-	28.0	0.4	-	-	-	-
1958	28.3	1.1	-	-	-	-	28.6	1.1	-	-	-	-	28.8	0.7	-	-	-	-	28.8	0.0	-	-	-	-
1959	28.8	0.0	-	-	-	-	28.8	0.0	-	-	-	-	29.1	1.0	-	-	-	-	29.3	0.7	-	-	-	-
1960	29.3	0.0	-	-	-	-	29.6	1.0	-	-	-	-	29.8	0.7	-	-	-	-	29.8	0.0	-	-	-	-
1961	29.9	0.3	-	-	-	-	29.9	0.0	-	-	-	-	30.0	0.3	-	-	-	-	29.9	-0.3	-	-	-	-

[Continued]

Pittsburgh, PA
Consumer Price Index - All Urban Consumers
Base 1982-1984 = 100
All Items
[Continued]

For 1917-1997. Columns headed % show percentile change in the index from the previous period for which an index is available.

Year	Jan Index	%	Feb Index	%	Mar Index	%	Apr Index	%	May Index	%	Jun Index	%	Jul Index	%	Aug Index	%	Sep Index	%	Oct Index	%	Nov Index	%	Dec Index	%
1962	30.0	0.3	-	-	-	-	30.1	0.3	-	-	-	-	30.2	0.3	-	-	-	-	30.3	0.3	-	-	-	-
1963	30.3	0.0	-	-	-	-	30.3	0.0	-	-	-	-	30.7	1.3	-	-	-	-	30.6	-0.3	-	-	-	-
1964	30.7	0.3	-	-	-	-	30.8	0.3	-	-	-	-	31.0	0.6	-	-	-	-	31.0	0.0	-	-	-	-
1965	31.1	0.3	-	-	-	-	31.3	0.6	-	-	-	-	31.6	1.0	-	-	-	-	31.6	0.0	-	-	-	-
1966	31.6	0.0	-	-	-	-	32.2	1.9	-	-	-	-	32.1	-0.3	-	-	-	-	32.5	1.2	-	-	-	-
1967	32.5	0.0	-	-	-	-	32.5	0.0	-	-	-	-	32.8	0.9	-	-	-	-	32.9	0.3	-	-	-	-
1968	33.5	1.8	-	-	-	-	34.0	1.5	-	-	-	-	34.2	0.6	-	-	-	-	34.9	2.0	-	-	-	-
1969	35.3	1.1	-	-	-	-	35.9	1.7	-	-	-	-	36.4	1.4	-	-	-	-	36.6	0.5	-	-	-	-
1970	36.9	0.8	-	-	-	-	37.7	2.2	-	-	-	-	38.3	1.6	-	-	-	-	39.0	1.8	-	-	-	-
1971	39.1	0.3	-	-	-	-	39.6	1.3	-	-	-	-	39.9	0.8	-	-	-	-	40.3	1.0	-	-	-	-
1972	40.4	0.2	-	-	-	-	40.9	1.2	-	-	-	-	41.1	0.5	-	-	-	-	41.5	1.0	-	-	-	-
1973	41.7	0.5	-	-	-	-	43.0	3.1	-	-	-	-	43.5	1.2	-	-	-	-	44.8	3.0	-	-	-	-
1974	45.7	2.0	-	-	-	-	47.2	3.3	-	-	-	-	48.6	3.0	-	-	-	-	49.9	2.7	-	-	-	-
1975	50.6	1.4	-	-	-	-	51.7	2.2	-	-	-	-	53.0	2.5	-	-	-	-	53.4	0.8	-	-	-	-
1976	53.8	0.7	-	-	-	-	54.6	1.5	-	-	-	-	55.2	1.1	-	-	-	-	56.0	1.4	-	-	-	-
1977	56.7	1.3	-	-	-	-	58.4	3.0	-	-	-	-	59.2	1.4	-	-	-	-	60.1	1.5	-	-	-	-
1978	60.6	0.8	-	-	-	-	62.3	2.8	-	-	63.5	1.9	-	-	65.5	3.1	-	-	66.4	1.4	-	-	67.2	1.2
1979	-	-	68.6	2.1	-	-	69.5	1.3	-	-	70.3	1.2	-	-	71.8	2.1	-	-	74.1	3.2	-	-	75.1	1.3
1980	-	-	77.2	2.8	-	-	78.9	2.2	-	-	80.6	2.2	-	-	82.2	2.0	-	-	84.0	2.2	-	-	85.9	2.3
1981	-	-	87.0	1.3	-	-	87.1	0.1	-	-	88.9	2.1	-	-	91.0	2.4	-	-	91.0	0.0	-	-	92.3	1.4
1982	-	-	91.3	-1.1	-	-	90.2	-1.2	-	-	93.4	3.5	-	-	95.5	2.2	-	-	98.5	3.1	-	-	99.0	0.5
1983	-	-	99.9	0.9	-	-	100.0	0.1	-	-	100.1	0.1	-	-	101.7	1.6	-	-	102.8	1.1	-	-	103.0	0.2
1984	-	-	103.4	0.4	-	-	104.4	1.0	-	-	104.8	0.4	-	-	104.6	-0.2	-	-	105.2	0.6	-	-	105.6	0.4
1985	-	-	106.1	0.5	-	-	106.3	0.2	-	-	106.8	0.5	-	-	106.8	0.0	-	-	107.6	0.7	-	-	108.6	0.9
1986	-	-	108.2	-0.4	-	-	107.5	-0.6	-	-	107.7	0.2	-	-	108.2	0.5	-	-	108.7	0.5	-	-	109.1	0.4
1987	-	-	109.8	0.6	-	-	110.8	0.9	-	-	111.1	0.3	-	-	112.0	0.8	-	-	112.8	0.7	-	-	113.0	0.2
1988	-	-	113.3	0.3	-	-	114.5	1.1	-	-	114.3	-0.2	-	-	115.3	0.9	-	-	116.3	0.9	-	-	116.7	0.3
1989	-	-	117.9	1.0	-	-	119.2	1.1	-	-	120.4	1.0	-	-	120.8	0.3	-	-	121.7	0.7	-	-	121.8	0.1
1990	-	-	123.4	1.3	-	-	124.9	1.2	-	-	125.0	0.1	-	-	127.1	1.7	-	-	129.6	2.0	-	-	129.1	-0.4
1991	-	-	129.3	0.2	-	-	130.3	0.8	-	-	130.7	0.3	-	-	131.5	0.6	-	-	133.2	1.3	-	-	134.4	0.9
1992	-	-	134.3	-0.1	-	-	135.1	0.6	-	-	135.2	0.1	-	-	136.9	1.3	-	-	137.7	0.6	-	-	137.3	-0.3
1993	-	-	139.2	1.4	-	-	139.6	0.3	-	-	139.5	-0.1	-	-	140.4	0.6	-	-	140.6	0.1	-	-	141.1	0.4
1994	-	-	142.6	1.1	-	-	143.9	0.9	-	-	144.0	0.1	-	-	145.7	1.2	-	-	146.4	0.5	-	-	146.5	0.1
1995	-	-	147.3	0.5	-	-	148.9	1.1	-	-	149.2	0.2	-	-	150.1	0.6	-	-	150.5	0.3	-	-	150.0	-0.3
1996	-	-	151.1	0.7	-	-	152.8	1.1	-	-	153.2	0.3	-	-	153.6	0.3	-	-	154.5	0.6	-	-	155.4	0.6
1997	-	-	156.2	0.5	-	-	156.6	0.3	-	-	157.4	0.5	-	-	157.5	0.1	-	-	157.9	0.3	-	-	157.1	-0.5

Source: U.S. Department of Labor, Bureau of Labor Statistics, Division of Consumer Prices and Price Indexes. - indicates no data collected for period.

Pittsburgh, PA
Consumer Price Index - Urban Wage Earners
Base 1982-1984 = 100
All Items

For 1917-1997. Columns headed % show percentile change in the index from the previous period for which an index is available.

Year	Jan Index	%	Feb Index	%	Mar Index	%	Apr Index	%	May Index	%	Jun Index	%	Jul Index	%	Aug Index	%	Sep Index	%	Oct Index	%	Nov Index	%	Dec Index	%
1917	-	-	-	-	-	-	-	-	-	-	-	-	-	-	-	-	-	-	-	-	-	-	13.9	-
1918	-	-	-	-	-	-	-	-	-	-	-	-	-	-	-	-	-	-	-	-	-	-	16.6	19.4
1919	-	-	-	-	-	-	-	-	-	-	16.9	1.8	-	-	-	-	-	-	-	-	-	-	18.8	11.2
1920	-	-	-	-	-	-	-	-	-	-	20.9	11.2	-	-	-	-	-	-	-	-	-	-	19.4	-7.2
1921	-	-	-	-	-	-	-	-	17.9	-7.7	-	-	-	-	-	-	17.5	-2.2	-	-	-	-	17.2	-1.7
1922	-	-	-	-	16.6	-3.5	-	-	-	-	16.7	0.6	-	-	-	-	16.6	-0.6	-	-	-	-	16.8	1.2
1923	-	-	-	-	16.8	0.0	-	-	-	-	17.2	2.4	-	-	-	-	17.3	0.6	-	-	-	-	17.2	-0.6
1924	-	-	-	-	17.0	-1.2	-	-	-	-	17.3	1.8	-	-	-	-	17.3	0.0	-	-	-	-	17.5	1.2
1925	-	-	-	-	-	-	-	-	-	-	17.8	1.7	-	-	-	-	-	-	-	-	-	-	18.2	2.2
1926	-	-	-	-	-	-	-	-	-	-	18.0	-1.1	-	-	-	-	-	-	-	-	-	-	18.0	0.0
1927	-	-	-	-	-	-	-	-	-	-	17.9	-0.6	-	-	-	-	-	-	-	-	-	-	17.6	-1.7
1928	-	-	-	-	-	-	-	-	-	-	17.4	-1.1	-	-	-	-	-	-	-	-	-	-	17.6	1.1
1929	-	-	-	-	-	-	-	-	-	-	17.5	-0.6	-	-	-	-	-	-	-	-	-	-	17.5	0.0
1930	-	-	-	-	-	-	-	-	-	-	17.1	-2.3	-	-	-	-	-	-	-	-	-	-	16.3	-4.7
1931	-	-	-	-	-	-	-	-	-	-	15.3	-6.1	-	-	-	-	-	-	-	-	-	-	14.7	-3.9
1932	-	-	-	-	-	-	-	-	-	-	13.6	-7.5	-	-	-	-	-	-	-	-	-	-	13.1	-3.7
1933	-	-	-	-	-	-	-	-	-	-	12.5	-4.6	-	-	-	-	-	-	-	-	-	-	13.0	4.0
1934	-	-	-	-	-	-	-	-	-	-	13.3	2.3	-	-	-	-	-	-	-	-	13.3	0.0	-	-
1935	-	-	-	-	13.6	2.3	-	-	-	-	-	-	13.6	0.0	-	-	13.7	0.7	-	-	-	-	-	-
1936	13.8	0.7	-	-	-	-	13.6	-1.4	-	-	-	-	14.0	2.9	-	-	14.1	0.7	-	-	-	-	14.0	-0.7
1937	-	-	-	-	14.2	1.4	-	-	-	-	14.5	2.1	-	-	-	-	14.7	1.4	-	-	-	-	14.3	-2.7
1938	-	-	-	-	14.1	-1.4	-	-	-	-	14.1	0.0	-	-	-	-	14.1	0.0	-	-	-	-	14.0	-0.7
1939	-	-	-	-	13.7	-2.1	-	-	-	-	13.8	0.7	-	-	-	-	14.0	1.4	-	-	-	-	13.8	-1.4
1940	-	-	-	-	13.8	0.0	-	-	-	-	14.1	2.2	-	-	-	-	14.1	0.0	14.0	-0.7	14.1	0.7	14.1	0.0
1941	14.1	0.0	14.1	0.0	14.2	0.7	14.3	0.7	14.5	1.4	14.7	1.4	14.8	0.7	14.9	0.7	15.2	2.0	15.3	0.7	15.4	0.7	15.5	0.6
1942	15.6	0.6	15.8	1.3	15.9	0.6	15.9	0.0	16.2	1.9	16.3	0.6	16.3	0.0	16.3	0.0	16.4	0.6	16.6	1.2	16.6	0.0	16.7	0.6
1943	16.8	0.6	16.9	0.6	17.1	1.2	17.3	1.2	17.5	1.2	17.5	0.0	17.3	-1.1	17.3	0.0	17.4	0.6	17.5	0.6	17.5	0.0	17.4	-0.6
1944	17.4	0.0	17.3	-0.6	17.3	0.0	17.5	1.2	17.5	0.0	17.7	1.1	17.7	0.0	17.8	0.6	17.8	0.0	17.8	0.0	17.7	-0.6	17.9	1.1
1945	17.9	0.0	17.9	0.0	17.8	-0.6	17.9	0.6	18.0	0.6	18.2	1.1	18.3	0.5	18.2	-0.5	18.1	-0.5	18.2	0.6	18.2	0.0	18.3	0.5
1946	18.3	0.0	18.3	0.0	18.3	0.0	18.4	0.5	18.5	0.5	18.8	1.6	19.9	5.9	20.3	2.0	20.6	1.5	20.8	1.0	21.5	3.4	21.7	0.9
1947	21.8	0.5	21.9	0.5	22.2	1.4	22.2	0.0	22.3	0.5	22.5	0.9	22.7	0.9	23.0	1.3	23.5	2.2	23.4	-0.4	23.5	0.4	23.8	1.3
1948	24.1	1.3	23.7	-1.7	23.7	0.0	24.0	1.3	24.2	0.8	24.5	1.2	24.8	1.2	24.9	0.4	24.9	0.0	24.7	-0.8	24.5	-0.8	24.4	-0.4
1949	24.4	0.0	24.0	-1.6	24.1	0.4	24.1	0.0	24.1	0.0	24.2	0.4	24.0	-0.8	24.1	0.4	24.1	0.0	23.9	-0.8	23.9	0.0	23.8	-0.4
1950	23.7	-0.4	23.6	-0.4	23.6	0.0	23.7	0.4	23.9	0.8	24.0	0.4	24.1	0.4	24.5	1.7	24.8	1.2	25.0	0.8	24.9	-0.4	25.1	0.8
1951	25.6	2.0	25.9	1.2	26.0	0.4	26.1	0.4	26.2	0.4	26.2	0.0	26.4	0.8	26.4	0.0	26.5	0.4	26.7	0.8	26.8	0.4	26.8	0.0
1952	26.8	0.0	26.7	-0.4	26.6	-0.4	26.7	0.4	26.7	0.0	26.6	-0.4	26.8	0.8	26.9	0.4	26.9	0.0	26.9	0.0	26.9	0.0	26.9	0.0
1953	26.7	-0.7	-	-	-	-	26.8	0.4	-	-	-	-	27.0	0.7	-	-	-	-	27.2	0.7	-	-	-	-
1954	27.2	0.0	-	-	-	-	27.2	0.0	-	-	-	-	27.4	0.7	-	-	-	-	27.1	-1.1	-	-	-	-
1955	27.0	-0.4	-	-	-	-	27.0	0.0	-	-	-	-	27.0	0.0	-	-	-	-	27.0	0.0	-	-	-	-
1956	27.0	0.0	-	-	-	-	27.3	1.1	-	-	-	-	27.8	1.8	-	-	-	-	28.0	0.7	-	-	-	-
1957	28.2	0.7	-	-	-	-	28.2	0.0	-	-	-	-	28.6	1.4	-	-	-	-	28.7	0.3	-	-	-	-
1958	29.1	1.4	-	-	-	-	29.4	1.0	-	-	-	-	29.6	0.7	-	-	-	-	29.6	0.0	-	-	-	-
1959	29.5	-0.3	-	-	-	-	29.6	0.3	-	-	-	-	29.8	0.7	-	-	-	-	30.1	1.0	-	-	-	-
1960	30.1	0.0	-	-	-	-	30.4	1.0	-	-	-	-	30.6	0.7	-	-	-	-	30.6	0.0	-	-	-	-
1961	30.7	0.3	-	-	-	-	30.7	0.0	-	-	-	-	30.8	0.3	-	-	-	-	30.7	-0.3	-	-	-	-

[Continued]

Pittsburgh, PA
Consumer Price Index - Urban Wage Earners
Base 1982-1984 = 100
All Items
[Continued]

For 1917-1997. Columns headed % show percentile change in the index from the previous period for which an index is available.

Year	Jan Index	%	Feb Index	%	Mar Index	%	Apr Index	%	May Index	%	Jun Index	%	Jul Index	%	Aug Index	%	Sep Index	%	Oct Index	%	Nov Index	%	Dec Index	%
1962	30.8	0.3	-	-	-	-	30.9	0.3	-	-	-	-	31.0	0.3	-	-	-	-	31.1	0.3	-	-	-	-
1963	31.1	0.0	-	-	-	-	31.1	0.0	-	-	-	-	31.5	1.3	-	-	-	-	31.4	-0.3	-	-	-	-
1964	31.5	0.3	-	-	-	-	31.6	0.3	-	-	-	-	31.8	0.6	-	-	-	-	31.8	0.0	-	-	-	-
1965	31.9	0.3	-	-	-	-	32.1	0.6	-	-	-	-	32.4	0.9	-	-	-	-	32.4	0.0	-	-	-	-
1966	32.4	0.0	-	-	-	-	33.1	2.2	-	-	-	-	33.0	-0.3	-	-	-	-	33.4	1.2	-	-	-	-
1967	33.3	-0.3	-	-	-	-	33.4	0.3	-	-	-	-	33.6	0.6	-	-	-	-	33.8	0.6	-	-	-	-
1968	34.4	1.8	-	-	-	-	34.9	1.5	-	-	-	-	35.1	0.6	-	-	-	-	35.8	2.0	-	-	-	-
1969	36.2	1.1	-	-	-	-	36.9	1.9	-	-	-	-	37.3	1.1	-	-	-	-	37.6	0.8	-	-	-	-
1970	37.8	0.5	-	-	-	-	38.7	2.4	-	-	-	-	39.3	1.6	-	-	-	-	40.0	1.8	-	-	-	-
1971	40.1	0.2	-	-	-	-	40.7	1.5	-	-	-	-	41.0	0.7	-	-	-	-	41.3	0.7	-	-	-	-
1972	41.4	0.2	-	-	-	-	41.9	1.2	-	-	-	-	42.2	0.7	-	-	-	-	42.5	0.7	-	-	-	-
1973	42.8	0.7	-	-	-	-	44.1	3.0	-	-	-	-	44.6	1.1	-	-	-	-	45.9	2.9	-	-	-	-
1974	46.8	2.0	-	-	-	-	48.5	3.6	-	-	-	-	49.9	2.9	-	-	-	-	51.2	2.6	-	-	-	-
1975	51.9	1.4	-	-	-	-	53.0	2.1	-	-	-	-	54.4	2.6	-	-	-	-	54.7	0.6	-	-	-	-
1976	55.2	0.9	-	-	-	-	56.0	1.4	-	-	-	-	56.7	1.3	-	-	-	-	57.5	1.4	-	-	-	-
1977	58.1	1.0	-	-	-	-	59.9	3.1	-	-	-	-	60.7	1.3	-	-	-	-	61.7	1.6	-	-	-	-
1978	62.2	0.8	-	-	-	-	63.9	2.7	-	-	65.1	1.9	-	-	66.9	2.8	-	-	67.8	1.3	-	-	68.7	1.3
1979	-	-	70.1	2.0	-	-	71.4	1.9	-	-	72.3	1.3	-	-	74.0	2.4	-	-	76.0	2.7	-	-	77.2	1.6
1980	-	-	79.3	2.7	-	-	81.4	2.6	-	-	83.0	2.0	-	-	84.5	1.8	-	-	86.6	2.5	-	-	88.4	2.1
1981	-	-	89.6	1.4	-	-	89.9	0.3	-	-	91.8	2.1	-	-	93.5	1.9	-	-	93.6	0.1	-	-	95.0	1.5
1982	-	-	94.1	-0.9	-	-	93.0	-1.2	-	-	96.1	3.3	-	-	98.1	2.1	-	-	101.0	3.0	-	-	101.4	0.4
1983	-	-	99.7	-1.7	-	-	101.1	1.4	-	-	100.7	-0.4	-	-	102.3	1.6	-	-	102.4	0.1	-	-	101.7	-0.7
1984	-	-	100.7	-1.0	-	-	101.4	0.7	-	-	101.3	-0.1	-	-	102.0	0.7	-	-	102.3	0.3	-	-	102.4	0.1
1985	-	-	102.9	0.5	-	-	103.2	0.3	-	-	103.7	0.5	-	-	103.6	-0.1	-	-	104.2	0.6	-	-	105.2	1.0
1986	-	-	104.7	-0.5	-	-	103.5	-1.1	-	-	103.7	0.2	-	-	104.0	0.3	-	-	104.4	0.4	-	-	104.8	0.4
1987	-	-	105.7	0.9	-	-	106.4	0.7	-	-	106.8	0.4	-	-	107.7	0.8	-	-	108.3	0.6	-	-	108.6	0.3
1988	-	-	108.9	0.3	-	-	110.1	1.1	-	-	110.0	-0.1	-	-	110.7	0.6	-	-	111.7	0.9	-	-	112.2	0.4
1989	-	-	113.4	1.1	-	-	114.7	1.1	-	-	115.9	1.0	-	-	116.0	0.1	-	-	116.8	0.7	-	-	117.1	0.3
1990	-	-	118.6	1.3	-	-	120.1	1.3	-	-	120.3	0.2	-	-	122.0	1.4	-	-	124.6	2.1	-	-	124.2	-0.3
1991	-	-	124.1	-0.1	-	-	124.9	0.6	-	-	125.3	0.3	-	-	125.9	0.5	-	-	127.5	1.3	-	-	128.7	0.9
1992	-	-	128.7	0.0	-	-	129.4	0.5	-	-	129.5	0.1	-	-	131.0	1.2	-	-	131.6	0.5	-	-	131.4	-0.2
1993	-	-	133.2	1.4	-	-	133.6	0.3	-	-	133.7	0.1	-	-	134.2	0.4	-	-	134.5	0.2	-	-	135.1	0.4
1994	-	-	136.3	0.9	-	-	137.4	0.8	-	-	137.8	0.3	-	-	139.4	1.2	-	-	140.1	0.5	-	-	140.3	0.1
1995	-	-	141.1	0.6	-	-	142.6	1.1	-	-	143.0	0.3	-	-	143.7	0.5	-	-	144.2	0.3	-	-	143.7	-0.3
1996	-	-	144.7	0.7	-	-	146.5	1.2	-	-	146.9	0.3	-	-	147.2	0.2	-	-	148.0	0.5	-	-	148.8	0.5
1997	-	-	149.6	0.5	-	-	150.1	0.3	-	-	150.8	0.5	-	-	151.0	0.1	-	-	151.3	0.2	-	-	150.6	-0.5

Source: U.S. Department of Labor, Bureau of Labor Statistics, Division of Consumer Prices and Price Indexes. - indicates no data collected for period.

Pittsburgh, PA
Consumer Price Index - All Urban Consumers
Base 1982-1984 = 100
Food and Beverages

For 1976-1997. Columns headed % show percentile change in the index from the previous period for which an index is available.

Year	Jan Index	%	Feb Index	%	Mar Index	%	Apr Index	%	May Index	%	Jun Index	%	Jul Index	%	Aug Index	%	Sep Index	%	Oct Index	%	Nov Index	%	Dec Index	%
1976	62.0	-	-	-	-	-	62.0	0.0	-	-	-	-	62.3	0.5	-	-	-	-	62.7	0.6	-	-	-	-
1977	62.9	0.3	-	-	-	-	66.0	4.9	-	-	-	-	67.1	1.7	-	-	-	-	67.6	0.7	-	-	-	-
1978	68.5	1.3	-	-	-	-	71.4	4.2	-	-	73.6	3.1	-	-	74.4	1.1	-	-	75.1	0.9	-	-	75.3	0.3
1979	-	-	78.5	4.2	-	-	78.8	0.4	-	-	80.0	1.5	-	-	80.4	0.5	-	-	81.7	1.6	-	-	82.6	1.1
1980	-	-	83.5	1.1	-	-	84.5	1.2	-	-	86.7	2.6	-	-	89.0	2.7	-	-	90.1	1.2	-	-	91.5	1.6
1981	-	-	92.5	1.1	-	-	93.2	0.8	-	-	93.4	0.2	-	-	94.8	1.5	-	-	95.1	0.3	-	-	94.9	-0.2
1982	-	-	96.4	1.6	-	-	96.5	0.1	-	-	98.9	2.5	-	-	97.8	-1.1	-	-	99.4	1.6	-	-	99.9	0.5
1983	-	-	100.5	0.6	-	-	101.1	0.6	-	-	101.4	0.3	-	-	101.1	-0.3	-	-	101.2	0.1	-	-	101.7	0.5
1984	-	-	100.4	-1.3	-	-	101.1	0.7	-	-	101.1	0.0	-	-	101.4	0.3	-	-	100.7	-0.7	-	-	100.7	0.0
1985	-	-	102.7	2.0	-	-	102.3	-0.4	-	-	102.5	0.2	-	-	102.3	-0.2	-	-	101.9	-0.4	-	-	102.5	0.6
1986	-	-	104.0	1.5	-	-	103.8	-0.2	-	-	104.0	0.2	-	-	106.7	2.6	-	-	105.6	-1.0	-	-	107.2	1.5
1987	-	-	108.4	1.1	-	-	109.4	0.9	-	-	110.6	1.1	-	-	109.4	-1.1	-	-	109.7	0.3	-	-	109.7	0.0
1988	-	-	110.6	0.8	-	-	112.0	1.3	-	-	111.2	-0.7	-	-	113.1	1.7	-	-	112.3	-0.7	-	-	113.4	1.0
1989	-	-	116.5	2.7	-	-	117.5	0.9	-	-	118.2	0.6	-	-	119.0	0.7	-	-	118.9	-0.1	-	-	119.7	0.7
1990	-	-	122.9	2.7	-	-	123.8	0.7	-	-	124.6	0.6	-	-	125.1	0.4	-	-	125.9	0.6	-	-	124.8	-0.9
1991	-	-	128.7	3.1	-	-	129.3	0.5	-	-	129.5	0.2	-	-	128.9	-0.5	-	-	129.1	0.2	-	-	131.4	1.8
1992	-	-	132.3	0.7	-	-	131.7	-0.5	-	-	133.7	1.5	-	-	133.5	-0.1	-	-	133.3	-0.1	-	-	133.2	-0.1
1993	-	-	135.6	1.8	-	-	137.5	1.4	-	-	137.5	0.0	-	-	137.2	-0.2	-	-	137.9	0.5	-	-	139.1	0.9
1994	-	-	138.4	-0.5	-	-	139.8	1.0	-	-	140.8	0.7	-	-	141.5	0.5	-	-	140.2	-0.9	-	-	143.9	2.6
1995	-	-	140.9	-2.1	-	-	143.9	2.1	-	-	141.9	-1.4	-	-	144.5	1.8	-	-	144.9	0.3	-	-	146.1	0.8
1996	-	-	146.5	0.3	-	-	149.8	2.3	-	-	148.8	-0.7	-	-	149.6	0.5	-	-	149.1	-0.3	-	-	151.1	1.3
1997	-	-	150.8	-0.2	-	-	152.1	0.9	-	-	152.3	0.1	-	-	150.3	-1.3	-	-	153.0	1.8	-	-	152.4	-0.4

Source: U.S. Department of Labor, Bureau of Labor Statistics, Division of Consumer Prices and Price Indexes. - indicates no data collected for period.

Pittsburgh, PA
Consumer Price Index - Urban Wage Earners
Base 1982-1984 = 100
Food and Beverages

For 1976-1997. Columns headed % show percentile change in the index from the previous period for which an index is available.

Year	Jan Index	%	Feb Index	%	Mar Index	%	Apr Index	%	May Index	%	Jun Index	%	Jul Index	%	Aug Index	%	Sep Index	%	Oct Index	%	Nov Index	%	Dec Index	%
1976	61.8	-	-	-	-	-	61.9	0.2	-	-	-	-	62.1	0.3	-	-	-	-	62.6	0.8	-	-	-	-
1977	62.7	0.2	-	-	-	-	65.9	5.1	-	-	-	-	66.9	1.5	-	-	-	-	67.4	0.7	-	-	-	-
1978	68.3	1.3	-	-	-	-	71.2	4.2	-	-	73.3	2.9	-	-	74.9	2.2	-	-	74.8	-0.1	-	-	75.4	0.8
1979	-	-	78.7	4.4	-	-	79.5	1.0	-	-	80.3	1.0	-	-	81.2	1.1	-	-	82.2	1.2	-	-	83.0	1.0
1980	-	-	83.7	0.8	-	-	85.5	2.2	-	-	86.6	1.3	-	-	88.8	2.5	-	-	90.1	1.5	-	-	92.1	2.2
1981	-	-	93.0	1.0	-	-	93.6	0.6	-	-	93.8	0.2	-	-	94.8	1.1	-	-	94.9	0.1	-	-	95.0	0.1
1982	-	-	96.4	1.5	-	-	96.6	0.2	-	-	99.0	2.5	-	-	97.8	-1.2	-	-	99.5	1.7	-	-	99.9	0.4
1983	-	-	100.4	0.5	-	-	101.1	0.7	-	-	101.4	0.3	-	-	101.2	-0.2	-	-	101.3	0.1	-	-	101.7	0.4
1984	-	-	100.3	-1.4	-	-	101.0	0.7	-	-	101.1	0.1	-	-	101.6	0.5	-	-	100.6	-1.0	-	-	100.6	0.0
1985	-	-	102.5	1.9	-	-	102.1	-0.4	-	-	102.4	0.3	-	-	102.1	-0.3	-	-	101.5	-0.6	-	-	102.2	0.7
1986	-	-	103.5	1.3	-	-	103.3	-0.2	-	-	103.6	0.3	-	-	106.5	2.8	-	-	105.3	-1.1	-	-	106.9	1.5
1987	-	-	108.0	1.0	-	-	109.0	0.9	-	-	110.1	1.0	-	-	109.2	-0.8	-	-	109.6	0.4	-	-	109.6	0.0
1988	-	-	110.5	0.8	-	-	111.7	1.1	-	-	111.2	-0.4	-	-	113.0	1.6	-	-	112.5	-0.4	-	-	113.6	1.0
1989	-	-	116.4	2.5	-	-	117.4	0.9	-	-	118.1	0.6	-	-	119.0	0.8	-	-	119.0	0.0	-	-	119.7	0.6
1990	-	-	122.8	2.6	-	-	124.0	1.0	-	-	124.8	0.6	-	-	125.4	0.5	-	-	126.2	0.6	-	-	125.3	-0.7
1991	-	-	129.1	3.0	-	-	129.7	0.5	-	-	129.9	0.2	-	-	129.2	-0.5	-	-	129.6	0.3	-	-	131.8	1.7
1992	-	-	132.6	0.6	-	-	132.1	-0.4	-	-	133.9	1.4	-	-	133.7	-0.1	-	-	133.4	-0.2	-	-	133.4	0.0
1993	-	-	135.7	1.7	-	-	137.7	1.5	-	-	137.7	0.0	-	-	137.6	-0.1	-	-	138.2	0.4	-	-	139.3	0.8
1994	-	-	138.4	-0.6	-	-	139.8	1.0	-	-	140.6	0.6	-	-	141.4	0.6	-	-	140.5	-0.6	-	-	143.6	2.2
1995	-	-	141.0	-1.8	-	-	143.6	1.8	-	-	141.4	-1.5	-	-	144.6	2.3	-	-	144.7	0.1	-	-	145.8	0.8
1996	-	-	146.3	0.3	-	-	149.4	2.1	-	-	148.5	-0.6	-	-	149.5	0.7	-	-	149.2	-0.2	-	-	151.0	1.2
1997	-	-	150.8	-0.1	-	-	152.3	1.0	-	-	152.3	0.0	-	-	150.4	-1.2	-	-	153.0	1.7	-	-	152.5	-0.3

Source: U.S. Department of Labor, Bureau of Labor Statistics, Division of Consumer Prices and Price Indexes. - indicates no data collected for period.

Pittsburgh, PA
Consumer Price Index - All Urban Consumers
Base 1982-1984 = 100
Housing

For 1976-1997. Columns headed % show percentile change in the index from the previous period for which an index is available.

Year	Jan Index	%	Feb Index	%	Mar Index	%	Apr Index	%	May Index	%	Jun Index	%	Jul Index	%	Aug Index	%	Sep Index	%	Oct Index	%	Nov Index	%	Dec Index	%
1976	49.2	-	-	-	-	-	50.6	2.8	-	-	-	-	50.6	0.0	-	-	-	-	51.3	1.4	-	-	-	-
1977	52.6	2.5	-	-	-	-	53.7	2.1	-	-	-	-	54.2	0.9	-	-	-	-	55.7	2.8	-	-	-	-
1978	56.8	2.0	-	-	-	-	58.2	2.5	-	-	59.3	1.9	-	-	61.9	4.4	-	-	63.4	2.4	-	-	64.9	2.4
1979	-	-	65.8	1.4	-	-	66.4	0.9	-	-	66.7	0.5	-	-	67.5	1.2	-	-	71.1	5.3	-	-	72.1	1.4
1980	-	-	74.3	3.1	-	-	76.9	3.5	-	-	78.6	2.2	-	-	79.9	1.7	-	-	82.0	2.6	-	-	84.7	3.3
1981	-	-	84.5	-0.2	-	-	83.3	-1.4	-	-	86.6	4.0	-	-	89.1	2.9	-	-	87.6	-1.7	-	-	90.8	3.7
1982	-	-	87.3	-3.9	-	-	85.4	-2.2	-	-	90.9	6.4	-	-	94.1	3.5	-	-	98.8	5.0	-	-	99.2	0.4
1983	-	-	100.5	1.3	-	-	101.4	0.9	-	-	100.7	-0.7	-	-	102.3	1.6	-	-	103.0	0.7	-	-	103.2	0.2
1984	-	-	104.9	1.6	-	-	106.4	1.4	-	-	106.9	0.5	-	-	105.7	-1.1	-	-	106.4	0.7	-	-	107.4	0.9
1985	-	-	107.8	0.4	-	-	108.1	0.3	-	-	108.7	0.6	-	-	108.6	-0.1	-	-	108.2	-0.4	-	-	110.4	2.0
1986	-	-	109.9	-0.5	-	-	111.8	1.7	-	-	111.0	-0.7	-	-	111.5	0.5	-	-	112.2	0.6	-	-	111.9	-0.3
1987	-	-	113.0	1.0	-	-	112.8	-0.2	-	-	112.8	0.0	-	-	114.1	1.2	-	-	114.0	-0.1	-	-	114.7	0.6
1988	-	-	114.4	-0.3	-	-	115.8	1.2	-	-	116.7	0.8	-	-	115.6	-0.9	-	-	115.6	0.0	-	-	116.6	0.9
1989	-	-	117.8	1.0	-	-	118.0	0.2	-	-	118.8	0.7	-	-	119.7	0.8	-	-	120.8	0.9	-	-	121.2	0.3
1990	-	-	121.3	0.1	-	-	123.6	1.9	-	-	124.0	0.3	-	-	126.7	2.2	-	-	127.6	0.7	-	-	127.0	-0.5
1991	-	-	128.8	1.4	-	-	130.3	1.2	-	-	131.3	0.8	-	-	131.7	0.3	-	-	133.2	1.1	-	-	134.8	1.2
1992	-	-	134.2	-0.4	-	-	135.5	1.0	-	-	134.9	-0.4	-	-	137.7	2.1	-	-	136.6	-0.8	-	-	136.6	0.0
1993	-	-	138.7	1.5	-	-	138.0	-0.5	-	-	138.7	0.5	-	-	139.6	0.6	-	-	139.8	0.1	-	-	141.0	0.9
1994	-	-	144.1	2.2	-	-	144.2	0.1	-	-	144.2	0.0	-	-	146.1	1.3	-	-	147.5	1.0	-	-	146.9	-0.4
1995	-	-	149.0	1.4	-	-	149.6	0.4	-	-	150.2	0.4	-	-	151.0	0.5	-	-	151.0	0.0	-	-	150.4	-0.4
1996	-	-	151.5	0.7	-	-	152.7	0.8	-	-	154.2	1.0	-	-	154.8	0.4	-	-	153.2	-1.0	-	-	153.2	0.0
1997	-	-	155.1	1.2	-	-	155.4	0.2	-	-	157.9	1.6	-	-	157.7	-0.1	-	-	155.9	-1.1	-	-	156.2	0.2

Source: U.S. Department of Labor, Bureau of Labor Statistics, Division of Consumer Prices and Price Indexes. - indicates no data collected for period.

Pittsburgh, PA
Consumer Price Index - Urban Wage Earners
Base 1982-1984 = 100
Housing

For 1976-1997. Columns headed % show percentile change in the index from the previous period for which an index is available.

Year	Jan Index	%	Feb Index	%	Mar Index	%	Apr Index	%	May Index	%	Jun Index	%	Jul Index	%	Aug Index	%	Sep Index	%	Oct Index	%	Nov Index	%	Dec Index	%
1976	52.2	-	-	-	-	-	53.7	2.9	-	-	-	-	53.7	0.0	-	-	-	-	54.4	1.3	-	-	-	-
1977	55.7	2.4	-	-	-	-	57.0	2.3	-	-	-	-	57.4	0.7	-	-	-	-	59.1	3.0	-	-	-	-
1978	60.2	1.9	-	-	-	-	61.7	2.5	-	-	63.1	2.3	-	-	65.3	3.5	-	-	67.1	2.8	-	-	68.5	2.1
1979	-	-	69.5	1.5	-	-	70.3	1.2	-	-	70.6	0.4	-	-	71.6	1.4	-	-	75.4	5.3	-	-	76.6	1.6
1980	-	-	79.0	3.1	-	-	81.9	3.7	-	-	83.7	2.2	-	-	85.0	1.6	-	-	87.2	2.6	-	-	90.1	3.3
1981	-	-	90.1	0.0	-	-	88.8	-1.4	-	-	92.6	4.3	-	-	94.9	2.5	-	-	93.3	-1.7	-	-	96.9	3.9
1982	-	-	93.3	-3.7	-	-	91.3	-2.1	-	-	97.2	6.5	-	-	100.6	3.5	-	-	105.3	4.7	-	-	105.7	0.4
1983	-	-	100.7	-4.7	-	-	104.9	4.2	-	-	103.0	-1.8	-	-	104.3	1.3	-	-	102.5	-1.7	-	-	100.2	-2.2
1984	-	-	98.1	-2.1	-	-	98.7	0.6	-	-	97.9	-0.8	-	-	98.7	0.8	-	-	99.0	0.3	-	-	99.4	0.4
1985	-	-	99.8	0.4	-	-	100.0	0.2	-	-	100.6	0.6	-	-	100.5	-0.1	-	-	100.2	-0.3	-	-	102.2	2.0
1986	-	-	101.9	-0.3	-	-	103.3	1.4	-	-	102.5	-0.8	-	-	103.0	0.5	-	-	103.7	0.7	-	-	103.4	-0.3
1987	-	-	104.4	1.0	-	-	104.1	-0.3	-	-	104.3	0.2	-	-	105.5	1.2	-	-	105.4	-0.1	-	-	106.0	0.6
1988	-	-	105.7	-0.3	-	-	107.0	1.2	-	-	107.8	0.7	-	-	106.8	-0.9	-	-	106.9	0.1	-	-	107.9	0.9
1989	-	-	108.9	0.9	-	-	109.1	0.2	-	-	110.2	1.0	-	-	110.8	0.5	-	-	111.7	0.8	-	-	112.3	0.5
1990	-	-	112.4	0.1	-	-	114.6	2.0	-	-	114.9	0.3	-	-	117.2	2.0	-	-	118.1	0.8	-	-	117.6	-0.4
1991	-	-	119.2	1.4	-	-	120.6	1.2	-	-	121.5	0.7	-	-	121.9	0.3	-	-	123.3	1.1	-	-	124.7	1.1
1992	-	-	124.1	-0.5	-	-	125.2	0.9	-	-	124.6	-0.5	-	-	127.2	2.1	-	-	126.3	-0.7	-	-	126.3	0.0
1993	-	-	128.2	1.5	-	-	127.6	-0.5	-	-	128.3	0.5	-	-	129.0	0.5	-	-	129.1	0.1	-	-	130.3	0.9
1994	-	-	133.0	2.1	-	-	133.1	0.1	-	-	133.2	0.1	-	-	134.9	1.3	-	-	136.1	0.9	-	-	135.5	-0.4
1995	-	-	137.5	1.5	-	-	138.1	0.4	-	-	138.6	0.4	-	-	139.3	0.5	-	-	139.3	0.0	-	-	138.8	-0.4
1996	-	-	139.7	0.6	-	-	141.0	0.9	-	-	142.3	0.9	-	-	142.9	0.4	-	-	141.4	-1.0	-	-	141.5	0.1
1997	-	-	143.0	1.1	-	-	143.3	0.2	-	-	145.5	1.5	-	-	145.2	-0.2	-	-	143.7	-1.0	-	-	144.1	0.3

Source: U.S. Department of Labor, Bureau of Labor Statistics, Division of Consumer Prices and Price Indexes. - indicates no data collected for period.

Pittsburgh, PA
Consumer Price Index - All Urban Consumers
Base 1982-1984 = 100
Apparel and Upkeep

For 1952-1997. Columns headed % show percentile change in the index from the previous period for which an index is available.

Year	Jan Index	%	Feb Index	%	Mar Index	%	Apr Index	%	May Index	%	Jun Index	%	Jul Index	%	Aug Index	%	Sep Index	%	Oct Index	%	Nov Index	%	Dec Index	%
1952	-	-	-	-	-	-	-	-	-	-	-	-	-	-	-	-	-	-	42.4	-	-	-	-	-
1953	42.5	0.2	-	-	-	-	42.9	0.9	-	-	-	-	42.5	-0.9	-	-	-	-	43.1	1.4	-	-	-	-
1954	43.1	0.0	-	-	-	-	42.8	-0.7	-	-	-	-	42.9	0.2	-	-	-	-	42.9	0.0	-	-	-	-
1955	42.3	-1.4	-	-	-	-	42.5	0.5	-	-	-	-	41.9	-1.4	-	-	-	-	42.2	0.7	-	-	-	-
1956	42.7	1.2	-	-	-	-	43.0	0.7	-	-	-	-	43.0	0.0	-	-	-	-	43.5	1.2	-	-	-	-
1957	43.9	0.9	-	-	-	-	44.1	0.5	-	-	-	-	43.9	-0.5	-	-	-	-	45.3	3.2	-	-	-	-
1958	44.9	-0.9	-	-	-	-	44.6	-0.7	-	-	-	-	44.2	-0.9	-	-	-	-	44.5	0.7	-	-	-	-
1959	44.0	-1.1	-	-	-	-	44.5	1.1	-	-	-	-	44.7	0.4	-	-	-	-	45.2	1.1	-	-	-	-
1960	44.6	-1.3	-	-	-	-	45.3	1.6	-	-	-	-	45.3	0.0	-	-	-	-	45.9	1.3	-	-	-	-
1961	45.0	-2.0	-	-	-	-	45.2	0.4	-	-	-	-	45.5	0.7	-	-	-	-	46.3	1.8	-	-	-	-
1962	45.5	-1.7	-	-	-	-	45.7	0.4	-	-	-	-	46.0	0.7	-	-	-	-	46.2	0.4	-	-	-	-
1963	46.5	0.6	-	-	-	-	46.8	0.6	-	-	-	-	46.9	0.2	-	-	-	-	47.3	0.9	-	-	-	-
1964	47.2	-0.2	-	-	-	-	47.6	0.8	-	-	-	-	47.7	0.2	-	-	-	-	48.2	1.0	-	-	-	-
1965	47.6	-1.2	-	-	-	-	49.0	2.9	-	-	-	-	48.4	-1.2	-	-	-	-	49.3	1.9	-	-	-	-
1966	48.2	-2.2	-	-	-	-	49.8	3.3	-	-	-	-	49.7	-0.2	-	-	-	-	51.0	2.6	-	-	-	-
1967	50.8	-0.4	-	-	-	-	51.2	0.8	-	-	-	-	50.8	-0.8	-	-	-	-	51.8	2.0	-	-	-	-
1968	51.4	-0.8	-	-	-	-	54.1	5.3	-	-	-	-	53.7	-0.7	-	-	-	-	56.1	4.5	-	-	-	-
1969	55.9	-0.4	-	-	-	-	57.8	3.4	-	-	-	-	57.4	-0.7	-	-	-	-	59.5	3.7	-	-	-	-
1970	57.2	-3.9	-	-	-	-	58.7	2.6	-	-	-	-	58.3	-0.7	-	-	-	-	61.4	5.3	-	-	-	-
1971	59.1	-3.7	-	-	-	-	60.7	2.7	-	-	-	-	60.0	-1.2	-	-	-	-	64.0	6.7	-	-	-	-
1972	62.4	-2.5	-	-	-	-	63.5	1.8	-	-	-	-	62.4	-1.7	-	-	-	-	64.7	3.7	-	-	-	-
1973	63.0	-2.6	-	-	-	-	64.8	2.9	-	-	-	-	64.3	-0.8	-	-	-	-	68.1	5.9	-	-	-	-
1974	67.3	-1.2	-	-	-	-	70.2	4.3	-	-	-	-	71.4	1.7	-	-	-	-	72.2	1.1	-	-	-	-
1975	69.9	-3.2	-	-	-	-	72.5	3.7	-	-	-	-	71.8	-1.0	-	-	-	-	74.5	3.8	-	-	-	-
1976	73.5	-1.3	-	-	-	-	73.2	-0.4	-	-	-	-	72.9	-0.4	-	-	-	-	75.2	3.2	-	-	-	-
1977	74.5	-0.9	-	-	-	-	74.3	-0.3	-	-	-	-	75.4	1.5	-	-	-	-	76.9	2.0	-	-	-	-
1978	73.3	-4.7	-	-	-	-	75.1	2.5	-	-	75.3	0.3	-	-	80.5	6.9	-	-	81.6	1.4	-	-	81.0	-0.7
1979	-	-	81.3	0.4	-	-	81.5	0.2	-	-	79.7	-2.2	-	-	83.2	4.4	-	-	85.5	2.8	-	-	85.9	0.5
1980	-	-	85.8	-0.1	-	-	86.0	0.2	-	-	84.0	-2.3	-	-	86.9	3.5	-	-	91.1	4.8	-	-	89.6	-1.6
1981	-	-	92.1	2.8	-	-	92.6	0.5	-	-	92.9	0.3	-	-	95.9	3.2	-	-	96.3	0.4	-	-	94.0	-2.4
1982	-	-	95.7	1.8	-	-	96.9	1.3	-	-	95.4	-1.5	-	-	99.0	3.8	-	-	101.3	2.3	-	-	99.0	-2.3
1983	-	-	103.4	4.4	-	-	100.9	-2.4	-	-	98.2	-2.7	-	-	101.1	3.0	-	-	102.8	1.7	-	-	101.4	-1.4
1984	-	-	100.4	-1.0	-	-	103.2	2.8	-	-	99.3	-3.8	-	-	100.3	1.0	-	-	102.7	2.4	-	-	100.9	-1.8
1985	-	-	104.4	3.5	-	-	101.2	-3.1	-	-	99.5	-1.7	-	-	100.0	0.5	-	-	108.8	8.8	-	-	104.0	-4.4
1986	-	-	97.7	-6.1	-	-	98.7	1.0	-	-	96.5	-2.2	-	-	101.9	5.6	-	-	104.8	2.8	-	-	102.4	-2.3
1987	-	-	101.1	-1.3	-	-	107.5	6.3	-	-	104.3	-3.0	-	-	108.3	3.8	-	-	112.4	3.8	-	-	110.5	-1.7
1988	-	-	109.7	-0.7	-	-	114.8	4.6	-	-	107.7	-6.2	-	-	114.7	6.5	-	-	122.7	7.0	-	-	117.3	-4.4
1989	-	-	116.5	-0.7	-	-	119.6	2.7	-	-	119.9	0.3	-	-	123.3	2.8	-	-	127.4	3.3	-	-	121.4	-4.7
1990	-	-	124.3	2.4	-	-	125.7	1.1	-	-	121.0	-3.7	-	-	125.5	3.7	-	-	129.1	2.9	-	-	125.4	-2.9
1991	-	-	125.9	0.4	-	-	131.4	4.4	-	-	125.0	-4.9	-	-	129.4	3.5	-	-	135.5	4.7	-	-	131.7	-2.8
1992	-	-	129.3	-1.8	-	-	133.2	3.0	-	-	127.9	-4.0	-	-	130.8	2.3	-	-	143.2	9.5	-	-	134.8	-5.9
1993	-	-	135.9	0.8	-	-	139.9	2.9	-	-	130.0	-7.1	-	-	140.2	7.8	-	-	131.4	-6.3	-	-	127.7	-2.8
1994	-	-	133.5	4.5	-	-	141.6	6.1	-	-	131.4	-7.2	-	-	133.1	1.3	-	-	133.8	0.5	-	-	125.1	-6.5

[Continued]

Pittsburgh, PA
Consumer Price Index - All Urban Consumers
Base 1982-1984 = 100
Apparel and Upkeep
[Continued]

For 1952-1997. Columns headed % show percentile change in the index from the previous period for which an index is available.

Year	Jan Index	%	Feb Index	%	Mar Index	%	Apr Index	%	May Index	%	Jun Index	%	Jul Index	%	Aug Index	%	Sep Index	%	Oct Index	%	Nov Index	%	Dec Index	%
1995	-	-	133.3	6.6	-	-	140.4	5.3	-	-	134.1	-4.5	-	-	137.3	2.4	-	-	138.2	0.7	-	-	129.5	-6.3
1996	-	-	135.0	4.2	-	-	134.3	-0.5	-	-	129.3	-3.7	-	-	129.4	0.1	-	-	144.0	11.3	-	-	137.5	-4.5
1997	-	-	140.7	2.3	-	-	140.3	-0.3	-	-	136.5	-2.7	-	-	145.7	6.7	-	-	145.4	-0.2	-	-	136.9	-5.8

Source: U.S. Department of Labor, Bureau of Labor Statistics, Division of Consumer Prices and Price Indexes. - indicates no data collected for period.

Pittsburgh, PA
Consumer Price Index - Urban Wage Earners
Base 1982-1984 = 100
Apparel and Upkeep

For 1952-1997. Columns headed % show percentile change in the index from the previous period for which an index is available.

Year	Jan Index	%	Feb Index	%	Mar Index	%	Apr Index	%	May Index	%	Jun Index	%	Jul Index	%	Aug Index	%	Sep Index	%	Oct Index	%	Nov Index	%	Dec Index	%
1952	-	-	-	-	-	-	-	-	-	-	-	-	-	-	-	-	-	-	44.0	-	-	-	-	-
1953	44.1	0.2	-	-	-	-	44.5	0.9	-	-	-	-	44.1	-0.9	-	-	-	-	44.6	1.1	-	-	-	-
1954	44.7	0.2	-	-	-	-	44.4	-0.7	-	-	-	-	44.4	0.0	-	-	-	-	44.4	0.0	-	-	-	-
1955	43.9	-1.1	-	-	-	-	44.1	0.5	-	-	-	-	43.4	-1.6	-	-	-	-	43.7	0.7	-	-	-	-
1956	44.3	1.4	-	-	-	-	44.5	0.5	-	-	-	-	44.5	0.0	-	-	-	-	45.1	1.3	-	-	-	-
1957	45.6	1.1	-	-	-	-	45.8	0.4	-	-	-	-	45.5	-0.7	-	-	-	-	46.9	3.1	-	-	-	-
1958	46.6	-0.6	-	-	-	-	46.2	-0.9	-	-	-	-	45.8	-0.9	-	-	-	-	46.2	0.9	-	-	-	-
1959	45.7	-1.1	-	-	-	-	46.1	0.9	-	-	-	-	46.3	0.4	-	-	-	-	46.9	1.3	-	-	-	-
1960	46.2	-1.5	-	-	-	-	46.9	1.5	-	-	-	-	46.9	0.0	-	-	-	-	47.6	1.5	-	-	-	-
1961	46.7	-1.9	-	-	-	-	46.9	0.4	-	-	-	-	47.2	0.6	-	-	-	-	48.0	1.7	-	-	-	-
1962	47.1	-1.9	-	-	-	-	47.4	0.6	-	-	-	-	47.7	0.6	-	-	-	-	47.9	0.4	-	-	-	-
1963	48.3	0.8	-	-	-	-	48.6	0.6	-	-	-	-	48.7	0.2	-	-	-	-	49.1	0.8	-	-	-	-
1964	48.9	-0.4	-	-	-	-	49.3	0.8	-	-	-	-	49.5	0.4	-	-	-	-	50.0	1.0	-	-	-	-
1965	49.3	-1.4	-	-	-	-	50.8	3.0	-	-	-	-	50.2	-1.2	-	-	-	-	51.1	1.8	-	-	-	-
1966	50.0	-2.2	-	-	-	-	51.7	3.4	-	-	-	-	51.6	-0.2	-	-	-	-	52.9	2.5	-	-	-	-
1967	52.7	-0.4	-	-	-	-	53.1	0.8	-	-	-	-	52.7	-0.8	-	-	-	-	53.7	1.9	-	-	-	-
1968	53.3	-0.7	-	-	-	-	56.1	5.3	-	-	-	-	55.7	-0.7	-	-	-	-	58.1	4.3	-	-	-	-
1969	58.0	-0.2	-	-	-	-	59.9	3.3	-	-	-	-	59.6	-0.5	-	-	-	-	61.7	3.5	-	-	-	-
1970	59.3	-3.9	-	-	-	-	60.8	2.5	-	-	-	-	60.5	-0.5	-	-	-	-	63.7	5.3	-	-	-	-
1971	61.3	-3.8	-	-	-	-	62.9	2.6	-	-	-	-	62.2	-1.1	-	-	-	-	66.4	6.8	-	-	-	-
1972	64.7	-2.6	-	-	-	-	65.8	1.7	-	-	-	-	64.7	-1.7	-	-	-	-	67.1	3.7	-	-	-	-
1973	65.4	-2.5	-	-	-	-	67.2	2.8	-	-	-	-	66.6	-0.9	-	-	-	-	70.7	6.2	-	-	-	-
1974	69.8	-1.3	-	-	-	-	72.8	4.3	-	-	-	-	74.0	1.6	-	-	-	-	74.9	1.2	-	-	-	-
1975	72.5	-3.2	-	-	-	-	75.2	3.7	-	-	-	-	74.4	-1.1	-	-	-	-	77.3	3.9	-	-	-	-
1976	76.2	-1.4	-	-	-	-	75.9	-0.4	-	-	-	-	75.6	-0.4	-	-	-	-	78.0	3.2	-	-	-	-
1977	77.3	-0.9	-	-	-	-	77.0	-0.4	-	-	-	-	78.2	1.6	-	-	-	-	79.7	1.9	-	-	-	-
1978	76.0	-4.6	-	-	-	-	77.8	2.4	-	-	76.5	-1.7	-	-	80.3	5.0	-	-	80.3	0.0	-	-	81.0	0.9
1979	-	-	81.4	0.5	-	-	82.9	1.8	-	-	81.5	-1.7	-	-	84.1	3.2	-	-	87.5	4.0	-	-	87.2	-0.3
1980	-	-	86.6	-0.7	-	-	86.8	0.2	-	-	85.4	-1.6	-	-	91.5	7.1	-	-	96.3	5.2	-	-	90.5	-6.0
1981	-	-	90.4	-0.1	-	-	93.1	3.0	-	-	93.1	0.0	-	-	95.5	2.6	-	-	94.9	-0.6	-	-	93.9	-1.1
1982	-	-	95.9	2.1	-	-	97.3	1.5	-	-	95.3	-2.1	-	-	98.7	3.6	-	-	101.2	2.5	-	-	99.2	-2.0
1983	-	-	102.9	3.7	-	-	100.3	-2.5	-	-	97.2	-3.1	-	-	101.1	4.0	-	-	102.9	1.8	-	-	101.5	-1.4
1984	-	-	101.5	0.0	-	-	103.2	1.7	-	-	99.1	-4.0	-	-	100.8	1.7	-	-	102.6	1.8	-	-	100.9	-1.7
1985	-	-	103.5	2.6	-	-	101.6	-1.8	-	-	100.0	-1.6	-	-	100.3	0.3	-	-	108.6	8.3	-	-	103.6	-4.6
1986	-	-	97.8	-5.6	-	-	98.6	0.8	-	-	96.4	-2.2	-	-	100.9	4.7	-	-	104.1	3.2	-	-	101.5	-2.5
1987	-	-	101.6	0.1	-	-	106.3	4.6	-	-	104.0	-2.2	-	-	107.9	3.8	-	-	110.0	1.9	-	-	108.5	-1.4
1988	-	-	108.5	0.0	-	-	113.1	4.2	-	-	108.2	-4.3	-	-	112.1	3.6	-	-	120.6	7.6	-	-	114.6	-5.0
1989	-	-	113.7	-0.8	-	-	117.8	3.6	-	-	117.7	-0.1	-	-	120.2	2.1	-	-	124.1	3.2	-	-	119.1	-4.0
1990	-	-	121.5	2.0	-	-	124.5	2.5	-	-	119.0	-4.4	-	-	120.1	0.9	-	-	125.7	4.7	-	-	122.6	-2.5
1991	-	-	122.0	-0.5	-	-	126.7	3.9	-	-	121.3	-4.3	-	-	123.2	1.6	-	-	129.3	5.0	-	-	124.9	-3.4
1992	-	-	126.8	1.5	-	-	130.1	2.6	-	-	124.0	-4.7	-	-	123.7	-0.2	-	-	135.7	9.7	-	-	128.5	-5.3
1993	-	-	130.9	1.9	-	-	135.6	3.6	-	-	125.7	-7.3	-	-	132.1	5.1	-	-	125.0	-5.4	-	-	122.3	-2.2
1994	-	-	129.0	5.5	-	-	137.0	6.2	-	-	127.7	-6.8	-	-	128.2	0.4	-	-	128.7	0.4	-	-	119.6	-7.1

[Continued]

Pittsburgh, PA
Consumer Price Index - Urban Wage Earners
Base 1982-1984 = 100
Apparel and Upkeep

[Continued]

For 1952-1997. Columns headed % show percentile change in the index from the previous period for which an index is available.

Year	Jan		Feb		Mar		Apr		May		Jun		Jul		Aug		Sep		Oct		Nov		Dec	
	Index	%	Index	%	Index	%	Index	%	Index	%	Index	%	Index	%	Index	%	Index	%	Index	%	Index	%	Index	%
1995	-	-	127.4	6.5	-	-	134.1	5.3	-	-	128.3	-4.3	-	-	127.9	-0.3	-	-	133.0	4.0	-	-	123.8	-6.9
1996	-	-	130.0	5.0	-	-	129.8	-0.2	-	-	123.6	-4.8	-	-	124.0	0.3	-	-	138.6	11.8	-	-	130.5	-5.8
1997	-	-	135.4	3.8	-	-	136.0	0.4	-	-	132.7	-2.4	-	-	143.2	7.9	-	-	140.9	-1.6	-	-	133.6	-5.2

Source: U.S. Department of Labor, Bureau of Labor Statistics, Division of Consumer Prices and Price Indexes. - indicates no data collected for period.

Pittsburgh, PA
Consumer Price Index - All Urban Consumers
Base 1982-1984 = 100
Transportation

For 1947-1997. Columns headed % show percentile change in the index from the previous period for which an index is available.

Year	Jan Index	%	Feb Index	%	Mar Index	%	Apr Index	%	May Index	%	Jun Index	%	Jul Index	%	Aug Index	%	Sep Index	%	Oct Index	%	Nov Index	%	Dec Index	%
1947	15.9	-	15.8	-0.6	15.9	0.6	16.1	1.3	16.1	0.0	16.1	0.0	16.1	0.0	16.3	1.2	16.5	1.2	16.5	0.0	16.5	0.0	16.5	0.0
1948	17.4	5.5	17.6	1.1	17.6	0.0	17.6	0.0	17.6	0.0	17.6	0.0	18.0	2.3	18.3	1.7	18.3	0.0	18.4	0.5	18.4	0.0	18.4	0.0
1949	18.5	0.5	18.7	1.1	18.6	-0.5	18.7	0.5	18.8	0.5	18.9	0.5	18.9	0.0	18.9	0.0	18.9	0.0	18.9	0.0	18.9	0.0	20.2	6.9
1950	20.3	0.5	20.3	0.0	20.2	-0.5	20.1	-0.5	20.3	1.0	20.3	0.0	20.4	0.5	22.0	7.8	22.1	0.5	22.1	0.0	22.1	0.0	22.1	0.0
1951	22.1	0.0	22.1	0.0	22.3	0.9	22.3	0.0	22.3	0.0	22.3	0.0	22.3	0.0	22.3	0.0	23.3	4.5	23.6	1.3	24.0	1.7	24.0	0.0
1952	24.3	1.2	24.4	0.4	24.4	0.0	24.4	0.0	24.4	0.0	24.4	0.0	24.4	0.0	24.4	0.0	24.4	0.0	24.4	0.0	24.4	0.0	24.6	0.8
1953	24.6	0.0	-	-	-	-	24.6	0.0	-	-	-	-	24.9	1.2	-	-	-	-	24.9	0.0	-	-	-	-
1954	24.6	-1.2	-	-	-	-	24.5	-0.4	-	-	-	-	24.3	-0.8	-	-	-	-	23.7	-2.5	-	-	-	-
1955	24.4	3.0	-	-	-	-	24.3	-0.4	-	-	-	-	24.3	0.0	-	-	-	-	24.0	-1.2	-	-	-	-
1956	23.6	-1.7	-	-	-	-	24.0	1.7	-	-	-	-	24.1	0.4	-	-	-	-	25.4	5.4	-	-	-	-
1957	25.7	1.2	-	-	-	-	25.5	-0.8	-	-	-	-	25.4	-0.4	-	-	-	-	25.7	1.2	-	-	-	-
1958	26.4	2.7	-	-	-	-	26.3	-0.4	-	-	-	-	26.9	2.3	-	-	-	-	27.5	2.2	-	-	-	-
1959	27.8	1.1	-	-	-	-	28.0	0.7	-	-	-	-	28.6	2.1	-	-	-	-	29.1	1.7	-	-	-	-
1960	29.1	0.0	-	-	-	-	29.4	1.0	-	-	-	-	29.1	-1.0	-	-	-	-	29.0	-0.3	-	-	-	-
1961	29.0	0.0	-	-	-	-	29.3	1.0	-	-	-	-	28.9	-1.4	-	-	-	-	29.3	1.4	-	-	-	-
1962	29.7	1.4	-	-	-	-	30.0	1.0	-	-	-	-	29.9	-0.3	-	-	-	-	30.0	0.3	-	-	-	-
1963	29.7	-1.0	-	-	-	-	29.8	0.3	-	-	-	-	30.1	1.0	-	-	-	-	29.7	-1.3	-	-	-	-
1964	30.3	2.0	-	-	-	-	30.2	-0.3	-	-	-	-	30.0	-0.7	-	-	-	-	30.3	1.0	-	-	-	-
1965	30.8	1.7	-	-	-	-	30.8	0.0	-	-	-	-	30.8	0.0	-	-	-	-	30.8	0.0	-	-	-	-
1966	30.7	-0.3	-	-	-	-	30.9	0.7	-	-	-	-	31.2	1.0	-	-	-	-	31.3	0.3	-	-	-	-
1967	31.1	-0.6	-	-	-	-	31.5	1.3	-	-	-	-	31.6	0.3	-	-	-	-	31.9	0.9	-	-	-	-
1968	32.4	1.6	-	-	-	-	32.4	0.0	-	-	-	-	32.6	0.6	-	-	-	-	33.1	1.5	-	-	-	-
1969	33.1	0.0	-	-	-	-	34.3	3.6	-	-	-	-	34.2	-0.3	-	-	-	-	34.3	0.3	-	-	-	-
1970	34.3	0.0	-	-	-	-	35.7	4.1	-	-	-	-	36.3	1.7	-	-	-	-	36.5	0.6	-	-	-	-
1971	37.0	1.4	-	-	-	-	37.8	2.2	-	-	-	-	38.6	2.1	-	-	-	-	38.1	-1.3	-	-	-	-
1972	37.8	-0.8	-	-	-	-	38.1	0.8	-	-	-	-	38.5	1.0	-	-	-	-	38.6	0.3	-	-	-	-
1973	38.5	-0.3	-	-	-	-	39.0	1.3	-	-	-	-	39.5	1.3	-	-	-	-	39.6	0.3	-	-	-	-
1974	40.5	2.3	-	-	-	-	42.2	4.2	-	-	-	-	44.3	5.0	-	-	-	-	45.1	1.8	-	-	-	-
1975	44.9	-0.4	-	-	-	-	45.9	2.2	-	-	-	-	47.7	3.9	-	-	-	-	48.3	1.3	-	-	-	-
1976	48.4	0.2	-	-	-	-	50.3	3.9	-	-	-	-	52.5	4.4	-	-	-	-	53.2	1.3	-	-	-	-
1977	53.9	1.3	-	-	-	-	56.5	4.8	-	-	-	-	57.0	0.9	-	-	-	-	56.8	-0.4	-	-	-	-
1978	56.9	0.2	-	-	-	-	58.4	2.6	-	-	60.0	2.7	-	-	61.0	1.7	-	-	61.1	0.2	-	-	61.9	1.3
1979	-	-	63.0	1.8	-	-	65.3	3.7	-	-	68.0	4.1	-	-	71.3	4.9	-	-	72.4	1.5	-	-	74.0	2.2
1980	-	-	78.0	5.4	-	-	80.0	2.6	-	-	82.4	3.0	-	-	83.2	1.0	-	-	85.0	2.2	-	-	87.3	2.7
1981	-	-	90.7	3.9	-	-	92.1	1.5	-	-	93.4	1.4	-	-	94.9	1.6	-	-	96.1	1.3	-	-	96.5	0.4
1982	-	-	95.7	-0.8	-	-	93.6	-2.2	-	-	95.6	2.1	-	-	97.3	1.8	-	-	98.8	1.5	-	-	99.6	0.8
1983	-	-	97.9	-1.7	-	-	97.1	-0.8	-	-	98.4	1.3	-	-	100.7	2.3	-	-	102.4	1.7	-	-	102.8	0.4
1984	-	-	101.9	-0.9	-	-	102.7	0.8	-	-	104.3	1.6	-	-	104.0	-0.3	-	-	104.6	0.6	-	-	104.7	0.1
1985	-	-	104.0	-0.7	-	-	105.0	1.0	-	-	105.8	0.8	-	-	105.3	-0.5	-	-	106.1	0.8	-	-	107.1	0.9
1986	-	-	105.3	-1.7	-	-	98.1	-6.8	-	-	99.9	1.8	-	-	96.4	-3.5	-	-	97.2	0.8	-	-	97.7	0.5
1987	-	-	98.5	0.8	-	-	99.9	1.4	-	-	100.2	0.3	-	-	101.3	1.1	-	-	101.9	0.6	-	-	102.3	0.4
1988	-	-	100.5	-1.8	-	-	100.3	-0.2	-	-	102.2	1.9	-	-	102.3	0.1	-	-	104.4	2.1	-	-	104.7	0.3
1989	-	-	105.3	0.6	-	-	108.2	2.8	-	-	109.6	1.3	-	-	106.6	-2.7	-	-	107.1	0.5	-	-	107.3	0.2
1990	-	-	109.3	1.9	-	-	108.4	-0.8	-	-	109.2	0.7	-	-	111.4	2.0	-	-	118.8	6.6	-	-	118.7	-0.1
1991	-	-	113.0	-4.8	-	-	110.7	-2.0	-	-	111.9	1.1	-	-	112.1	0.2	-	-	113.7	1.4	-	-	114.8	1.0

[Continued]

Pittsburgh, PA
Consumer Price Index - All Urban Consumers
Base 1982-1984 = 100
Transportation
[Continued]

For 1947-1997. Columns headed % show percentile change in the index from the previous period for which an index is available.

Year	Jan		Feb		Mar		Apr		May		Jun		Jul		Aug		Sep		Oct		Nov		Dec	
	Index	%	Index	%	Index	%	Index	%	Index	%	Index	%	Index	%	Index	%	Index	%	Index	%	Index	%	Index	%
1992	-	-	113.5	-1.1	-	-	114.0	0.4	-	-	115.6	1.4	-	-	116.2	0.5	-	-	117.5	1.1	-	-	117.7	0.2
1993	-	-	117.6	-0.1	-	-	116.9	-0.6	-	-	117.5	0.5	-	-	116.5	-0.9	-	-	120.8	3.7	-	-	119.8	-0.8
1994	-	-	119.5	-0.3	-	-	119.7	0.2	-	-	122.1	2.0	-	-	124.4	1.9	-	-	124.0	-0.3	-	-	125.3	1.0
1995	-	-	126.0	0.6	-	-	126.5	0.4	-	-	130.5	3.2	-	-	127.9	-2.0	-	-	128.2	0.2	-	-	127.3	-0.7
1996	-	-	127.1	-0.2	-	-	128.7	1.3	-	-	129.8	0.9	-	-	127.9	-1.5	-	-	129.7	1.4	-	-	133.5	2.9
1997	-	-	133.1	-0.3	-	-	132.5	-0.5	-	-	132.2	-0.2	-	-	131.2	-0.8	-	-	134.5	2.5	-	-	132.2	-1.7

Source: U.S. Department of Labor, Bureau of Labor Statistics, Division of Consumer Prices and Price Indexes. - indicates no data collected for period.

Pittsburgh, PA
Consumer Price Index - Urban Wage Earners
Base 1982-1984 = 100
Transportation

For 1947-1997. Columns headed % show percentile change in the index from the previous period for which an index is available.

Year	Jan Index	%	Feb Index	%	Mar Index	%	Apr Index	%	May Index	%	Jun Index	%	Jul Index	%	Aug Index	%	Sep Index	%	Oct Index	%	Nov Index	%	Dec Index	%
1947	15.7	-	15.6	-0.6	15.7	0.6	15.9	1.3	15.9	0.0	15.9	0.0	15.9	0.0	16.1	1.3	16.3	1.2	16.3	0.0	16.3	0.0	16.3	0.0
1948	17.2	5.5	17.3	0.6	17.3	0.0	17.3	0.0	17.3	0.0	17.4	0.6	17.8	2.3	18.1	1.7	18.1	0.0	18.2	0.6	18.1	-0.5	18.2	0.6
1949	18.3	0.5	18.4	0.5	18.4	0.0	18.5	0.5	18.6	0.5	18.7	0.5	18.7	0.0	18.7	0.0	18.7	0.0	18.7	0.0	18.7	0.0	20.0	7.0
1950	20.0	0.0	20.0	0.0	20.0	0.0	19.9	-0.5	20.0	0.5	20.1	0.5	20.1	0.0	21.7	8.0	21.8	0.5	21.8	0.0	21.8	0.0	21.8	0.0
1951	21.8	0.0	21.8	0.0	22.0	0.9	22.0	0.0	22.0	0.0	22.0	0.0	22.0	0.0	22.0	0.0	23.0	4.5	23.3	1.3	23.7	1.7	23.7	0.0
1952	24.0	1.3	24.1	0.4	24.1	0.0	24.1	0.0	24.1	0.0	24.1	0.0	24.1	0.0	24.1	0.0	24.1	0.0	24.1	0.0	24.1	0.0	24.3	0.8
1953	24.3	0.0	-	-	-	-	24.3	0.0	-	-	-	-	24.6	1.2	-	-	-	-	24.6	0.0	-	-	-	-
1954	24.3	-1.2	-	-	-	-	24.2	-0.4	-	-	-	-	24.0	-0.8	-	-	-	-	23.4	-2.5	-	-	-	-
1955	24.1	3.0	-	-	-	-	24.0	-0.4	-	-	-	-	24.0	0.0	-	-	-	-	23.7	-1.2	-	-	-	-
1956	23.3	-1.7	-	-	-	-	23.7	1.7	-	-	-	-	23.8	0.4	-	-	-	-	25.1	5.5	-	-	-	-
1957	25.4	1.2	-	-	-	-	25.2	-0.8	-	-	-	-	25.1	-0.4	-	-	-	-	25.4	1.2	-	-	-	-
1958	26.1	2.8	-	-	-	-	26.0	-0.4	-	-	-	-	26.6	2.3	-	-	-	-	27.1	1.9	-	-	-	-
1959	27.5	1.5	-	-	-	-	27.6	0.4	-	-	-	-	28.2	2.2	-	-	-	-	28.8	2.1	-	-	-	-
1960	28.8	0.0	-	-	-	-	29.0	0.7	-	-	-	-	28.8	-0.7	-	-	-	-	28.7	-0.3	-	-	-	-
1961	28.6	-0.3	-	-	-	-	28.9	1.0	-	-	-	-	28.5	-1.4	-	-	-	-	28.9	1.4	-	-	-	-
1962	29.3	1.4	-	-	-	-	29.6	1.0	-	-	-	-	29.5	-0.3	-	-	-	-	29.6	0.3	-	-	-	-
1963	29.3	-1.0	-	-	-	-	29.5	0.7	-	-	-	-	29.7	0.7	-	-	-	-	29.3	-1.3	-	-	-	-
1964	29.9	2.0	-	-	-	-	29.9	0.0	-	-	-	-	29.7	-0.7	-	-	-	-	30.0	1.0	-	-	-	-
1965	30.4	1.3	-	-	-	-	30.4	0.0	-	-	-	-	30.5	0.3	-	-	-	-	30.5	0.0	-	-	-	-
1966	30.3	-0.7	-	-	-	-	30.5	0.7	-	-	-	-	30.8	1.0	-	-	-	-	30.9	0.3	-	-	-	-
1967	30.7	-0.6	-	-	-	-	31.1	1.3	-	-	-	-	31.2	0.3	-	-	-	-	31.5	1.0	-	-	-	-
1968	32.0	1.6	-	-	-	-	32.0	0.0	-	-	-	-	32.2	0.6	-	-	-	-	32.7	1.6	-	-	-	-
1969	32.7	0.0	-	-	-	-	33.9	3.7	-	-	-	-	33.8	-0.3	-	-	-	-	33.9	0.3	-	-	-	-
1970	33.9	0.0	-	-	-	-	35.3	4.1	-	-	-	-	35.9	1.7	-	-	-	-	36.1	0.6	-	-	-	-
1971	36.5	1.1	-	-	-	-	37.3	2.2	-	-	-	-	38.1	2.1	-	-	-	-	37.6	-1.3	-	-	-	-
1972	37.3	-0.8	-	-	-	-	37.6	0.8	-	-	-	-	38.0	1.1	-	-	-	-	38.1	0.3	-	-	-	-
1973	38.0	-0.3	-	-	-	-	38.5	1.3	-	-	-	-	39.0	1.3	-	-	-	-	39.1	0.3	-	-	-	-
1974	40.0	2.3	-	-	-	-	41.7	4.2	-	-	-	-	43.7	4.8	-	-	-	-	44.5	1.8	-	-	-	-
1975	44.4	-0.2	-	-	-	-	45.3	2.0	-	-	-	-	47.1	4.0	-	-	-	-	47.7	1.3	-	-	-	-
1976	47.8	0.2	-	-	-	-	49.7	4.0	-	-	-	-	51.8	4.2	-	-	-	-	52.6	1.5	-	-	-	-
1977	53.3	1.3	-	-	-	-	55.8	4.7	-	-	-	-	56.3	0.9	-	-	-	-	56.1	-0.4	-	-	-	-
1978	56.2	0.2	-	-	-	-	57.7	2.7	-	-	59.3	2.8	-	-	60.3	1.7	-	-	60.8	0.8	-	-	61.3	0.8
1979	-	-	62.5	2.0	-	-	64.6	3.4	-	-	67.5	4.5	-	-	70.9	5.0	-	-	71.8	1.3	-	-	73.2	1.9
1980	-	-	77.4	5.7	-	-	79.4	2.6	-	-	81.8	3.0	-	-	82.0	0.2	-	-	84.7	3.3	-	-	86.9	2.6
1981	-	-	90.5	4.1	-	-	92.1	1.8	-	-	93.5	1.5	-	-	95.0	1.6	-	-	96.5	1.6	-	-	96.9	0.4
1982	-	-	96.0	-0.9	-	-	93.7	-2.4	-	-	95.7	2.1	-	-	97.9	2.3	-	-	99.1	1.2	-	-	99.6	0.5
1983	-	-	97.6	-2.0	-	-	96.6	-1.0	-	-	97.9	1.3	-	-	100.5	2.7	-	-	102.2	1.7	-	-	102.6	0.4
1984	-	-	101.7	-0.9	-	-	102.7	1.0	-	-	104.4	1.7	-	-	104.2	-0.2	-	-	104.7	0.5	-	-	104.8	0.1
1985	-	-	104.1	-0.7	-	-	105.0	0.9	-	-	105.7	0.7	-	-	105.1	-0.6	-	-	105.6	0.5	-	-	106.6	0.9
1986	-	-	104.7	-1.8	-	-	97.0	-7.4	-	-	98.5	1.5	-	-	94.8	-3.8	-	-	95.4	0.6	-	-	95.9	0.5
1987	-	-	97.0	1.1	-	-	98.5	1.5	-	-	99.1	0.6	-	-	100.4	1.3	-	-	101.0	0.6	-	-	101.4	0.4
1988	-	-	99.7	-1.7	-	-	99.7	0.0	-	-	101.5	1.8	-	-	101.7	0.2	-	-	103.9	2.2	-	-	104.1	0.2
1989	-	-	104.8	0.7	-	-	107.9	3.0	-	-	109.3	1.3	-	-	106.3	-2.7	-	-	106.7	0.4	-	-	106.8	0.1
1990	-	-	108.7	1.8	-	-	107.9	-0.7	-	-	108.8	0.8	-	-	110.8	1.8	-	-	117.9	6.4	-	-	117.7	-0.2
1991	-	-	111.8	-5.0	-	-	109.6	-2.0	-	-	111.0	1.3	-	-	111.5	0.5	-	-	113.0	1.3	-	-	113.9	0.8

[Continued]

Pittsburgh, PA
Consumer Price Index - Urban Wage Earners
Base 1982-1984 = 100
Transportation
[Continued]

For 1947-1997. Columns headed % show percentile change in the index from the previous period for which an index is available.

Year	Jan		Feb		Mar		Apr		May		Jun		Jul		Aug		Sep		Oct		Nov		Dec	
	Index	%	Index	%	Index	%	Index	%	Index	%	Index	%	Index	%	Index	%	Index	%	Index	%	Index	%	Index	%
1992	-	-	112.3	-1.4	-	-	112.9	0.5	-	-	114.7	1.6	-	-	115.4	0.6	-	-	116.9	1.3	-	-	116.9	0.0
1993	-	-	116.8	-0.1	-	-	116.2	-0.5	-	-	117.1	0.8	-	-	116.2	-0.8	-	-	120.2	3.4	-	-	119.2	-0.8
1994	-	-	118.4	-0.7	-	-	118.8	0.3	-	-	121.6	2.4	-	-	123.9	1.9	-	-	123.9	0.0	-	-	125.4	1.2
1995	-	-	126.4	0.8	-	-	127.3	0.7	-	-	131.6	3.4	-	-	129.1	-1.9	-	-	129.1	0.0	-	-	128.3	-0.6
1996	-	-	128.2	-0.1	-	-	129.8	1.2	-	-	130.9	0.8	-	-	129.0	-1.5	-	-	130.8	1.4	-	-	134.1	2.5
1997	-	-	133.6	-0.4	-	-	133.1	-0.4	-	-	132.6	-0.4	-	-	131.8	-0.6	-	-	134.8	2.3	-	-	132.5	-1.7

Source: U.S. Department of Labor, Bureau of Labor Statistics, Division of Consumer Prices and Price Indexes. - indicates no data collected for period.

Pittsburgh, PA
Consumer Price Index - All Urban Consumers
Base 1982-1984 = 100
Medical Care

For 1947-1997. Columns headed % show percentile change in the index from the previous period for which an index is available.

Year	Jan Index	%	Feb Index	%	Mar Index	%	Apr Index	%	May Index	%	Jun Index	%	Jul Index	%	Aug Index	%	Sep Index	%	Oct Index	%	Nov Index	%	Dec Index	%
1947	11.5	-	11.5	0.0	11.6	0.9	11.6	0.0	11.6	0.0	11.6	0.0	11.7	0.9	11.6	-0.9	11.7	0.9	11.7	0.0	11.9	1.7	11.9	0.0
1948	12.2	2.5	12.2	0.0	12.2	0.0	12.2	0.0	12.4	1.6	12.4	0.0	12.4	0.0	12.4	0.0	12.4	0.0	12.4	0.0	12.5	0.8	12.6	0.8
1949	12.6	0.0	12.6	0.0	12.6	0.0	12.6	0.0	12.6	0.0	12.6	0.0	12.6	0.0	12.6	0.0	12.6	0.0	12.6	0.0	12.6	0.0	12.7	0.8
1950	12.7	0.0	12.7	0.0	12.9	1.6	12.9	0.0	12.9	0.0	12.9	0.0	12.9	0.0	12.9	0.0	13.0	0.8	12.9	-0.8	13.0	0.8	13.0	0.0
1951	13.1	0.8	13.1	0.0	13.2	0.8	13.3	0.8	13.3	0.0	13.7	3.0	13.7	0.0	13.7	0.0	13.7	0.0	13.7	0.0	13.7	0.0	13.7	0.0
1952	13.8	0.7	13.8	0.0	13.9	0.7	13.9	0.0	13.9	0.0	13.9	0.0	13.9	0.0	13.9	0.0	14.1	1.4	14.1	0.0	14.1	0.0	14.3	1.4
1953	14.3	0.0	-	-	-	-	14.8	3.5	-	-	-	-	14.8	0.0	-	-	-	-	14.7	-0.7	-	-	-	-
1954	14.8	0.7	-	-	-	-	15.6	5.4	-	-	-	-	15.6	0.0	-	-	-	-	15.4	-1.3	-	-	-	-
1955	15.4	0.0	-	-	-	-	15.5	0.6	-	-	-	-	16.1	3.9	-	-	-	-	16.1	0.0	-	-	-	-
1956	16.1	0.0	-	-	-	-	16.5	2.5	-	-	-	-	16.5	0.0	-	-	-	-	17.5	6.1	-	-	-	-
1957	17.6	0.6	-	-	-	-	17.7	0.6	-	-	-	-	17.7	0.0	-	-	-	-	17.9	1.1	-	-	-	-
1958	18.0	0.6	-	-	-	-	18.0	0.0	-	-	-	-	18.8	4.4	-	-	-	-	18.9	0.5	-	-	-	-
1959	19.1	1.1	-	-	-	-	19.3	1.0	-	-	-	-	19.3	0.0	-	-	-	-	20.5	6.2	-	-	-	-
1960	20.6	0.5	-	-	-	-	20.7	0.5	-	-	-	-	20.7	0.0	-	-	-	-	20.8	0.5	-	-	-	-
1961	20.9	0.5	-	-	-	-	21.5	2.9	-	-	-	-	21.5	0.0	-	-	-	-	21.6	0.5	-	-	-	-
1962	21.7	0.5	-	-	-	-	21.7	0.0	-	-	-	-	22.8	5.1	-	-	-	-	23.0	0.9	-	-	-	-
1963	23.0	0.0	-	-	-	-	23.0	0.0	-	-	-	-	23.0	0.0	-	-	-	-	23.1	0.4	-	-	-	-
1964	23.2	0.4	-	-	-	-	23.6	1.7	-	-	-	-	23.9	1.3	-	-	-	-	23.9	0.0	-	-	-	-
1965	24.0	0.4	-	-	-	-	24.2	0.8	-	-	-	-	24.4	0.8	-	-	-	-	24.5	0.4	-	-	-	-
1966	24.6	0.4	-	-	-	-	24.8	0.8	-	-	-	-	25.1	1.2	-	-	-	-	25.3	0.8	-	-	-	-
1967	26.5	4.7	-	-	-	-	26.7	0.8	-	-	-	-	26.8	0.4	-	-	-	-	27.1	1.1	-	-	-	-
1968	27.5	1.5	-	-	-	-	27.7	0.7	-	-	-	-	28.5	2.9	-	-	-	-	29.1	2.1	-	-	-	-
1969	29.4	1.0	-	-	-	-	29.9	1.7	-	-	-	-	30.2	1.0	-	-	-	-	30.4	0.7	-	-	-	-
1970	30.6	0.7	-	-	-	-	31.3	2.3	-	-	-	-	31.8	1.6	-	-	-	-	32.1	0.9	-	-	-	-
1971	32.5	1.2	-	-	-	-	32.8	0.9	-	-	-	-	32.9	0.3	-	-	-	-	33.2	0.9	-	-	-	-
1972	33.6	1.2	-	-	-	-	34.2	1.8	-	-	-	-	34.9	2.0	-	-	-	-	35.0	0.3	-	-	-	-
1973	35.4	1.1	-	-	-	-	35.6	0.6	-	-	-	-	35.9	0.8	-	-	-	-	36.7	2.2	-	-	-	-
1974	37.3	1.6	-	-	-	-	38.0	1.9	-	-	-	-	40.1	5.5	-	-	-	-	40.9	2.0	-	-	-	-
1975	41.6	1.7	-	-	-	-	42.5	2.2	-	-	-	-	44.2	4.0	-	-	-	-	45.3	2.5	-	-	-	-
1976	45.8	1.1	-	-	-	-	46.4	1.3	-	-	-	-	49.1	5.8	-	-	-	-	49.9	1.6	-	-	-	-
1977	50.7	1.6	-	-	-	-	51.7	2.0	-	-	-	-	54.1	4.6	-	-	-	-	55.1	1.8	-	-	-	-
1978	55.5	0.7	-	-	-	-	56.7	2.2	-	-	57.0	0.5	-	-	59.5	4.4	-	-	59.7	0.3	-	-	60.3	1.0
1979	-	-	61.3	1.7	-	-	62.4	1.8	-	-	63.7	2.1	-	-	65.7	3.1	-	-	66.7	1.5	-	-	66.9	0.3
1980	-	-	67.9	1.5	-	-	69.1	1.8	-	-	70.8	2.5	-	-	73.4	3.7	-	-	73.4	0.0	-	-	74.2	1.1
1981	-	-	75.8	2.2	-	-	77.6	2.4	-	-	78.1	0.6	-	-	81.7	4.6	-	-	83.5	2.2	-	-	84.2	0.8
1982	-	-	85.7	1.8	-	-	86.8	1.3	-	-	87.8	1.2	-	-	92.3	5.1	-	-	93.0	0.8	-	-	94.3	1.4
1983	-	-	97.8	3.7	-	-	97.7	-0.1	-	-	99.4	1.7	-	-	102.1	2.7	-	-	105.6	3.4	-	-	105.6	0.0
1984	-	-	108.5	2.7	-	-	109.0	0.5	-	-	109.4	0.4	-	-	110.1	0.6	-	-	110.8	0.6	-	-	110.9	0.1
1985	-	-	111.4	0.5	-	-	112.1	0.6	-	-	112.3	0.2	-	-	114.0	1.5	-	-	115.0	0.9	-	-	117.0	1.7
1986	-	-	118.6	1.4	-	-	119.2	0.5	-	-	120.9	1.4	-	-	122.0	0.9	-	-	123.9	1.6	-	-	124.5	0.5
1987	-	-	125.5	0.8	-	-	127.8	1.8	-	-	130.7	2.3	-	-	132.4	1.3	-	-	133.2	0.6	-	-	134.1	0.7
1988	-	-	135.5	1.0	-	-	136.0	0.4	-	-	137.8	1.3	-	-	139.2	1.0	-	-	140.8	1.1	-	-	142.2	1.0
1989	-	-	142.3	0.1	-	-	144.0	1.2	-	-	146.3	1.6	-	-	149.2	2.0	-	-	149.9	0.5	-	-	151.3	0.9
1990	-	-	154.4	2.0	-	-	159.1	3.0	-	-	159.6	0.3	-	-	162.4	1.8	-	-	165.1	1.7	-	-	166.7	1.0
1991	-	-	168.9	1.3	-	-	171.2	1.4	-	-	175.3	2.4	-	-	179.6	2.5	-	-	181.3	0.9	-	-	182.1	0.4

[Continued]

Pittsburgh, PA
Consumer Price Index - All Urban Consumers
Base 1982-1984 = 100
Medical Care
[Continued]

For 1947-1997. Columns headed % show percentile change in the index from the previous period for which an index is available.

Year	Jan		Feb		Mar		Apr		May		Jun		Jul		Aug		Sep		Oct		Nov		Dec	
	Index	%	Index	%	Index	%	Index	%	Index	%	Index	%	Index	%	Index	%	Index	%	Index	%	Index	%	Index	%
1992	-	-	184.6	1.4	-	-	184.5	-0.1	-	-	182.8	-0.9	-	-	186.6	2.1	-	-	189.1	1.3	-	-	190.2	0.6
1993	-	-	194.1	2.1	-	-	194.7	0.3	-	-	197.7	1.5	-	-	198.4	0.4	-	-	199.1	0.4	-	-	199.3	0.1
1994	-	-	202.4	1.6	-	-	204.8	1.2	-	-	207.0	1.1	-	-	208.5	0.7	-	-	211.0	1.2	-	-	211.6	0.3
1995	-	-	208.2	-1.6	-	-	210.2	1.0	-	-	210.9	0.3	-	-	215.3	2.1	-	-	214.3	-0.5	-	-	218.5	2.0
1996	-	-	223.4	2.2	-	-	224.7	0.6	-	-	226.0	0.6	-	-	226.9	0.4	-	-	226.8	-0.0	-	-	226.7	-0.0
1997	-	-	226.8	0.0	-	-	229.0	1.0	-	-	231.0	0.9	-	-	229.4	-0.7	-	-	227.9	-0.7	-	-	229.5	0.7

Source: U.S. Department of Labor, Bureau of Labor Statistics, Division of Consumer Prices and Price Indexes. - indicates no data collected for period.

Pittsburgh, PA
Consumer Price Index - Urban Wage Earners
Base 1982-1984 = 100
Medical Care

For 1947-1997. Columns headed % show percentile change in the index from the previous period for which an index is available.

Year	Jan Index	%	Feb Index	%	Mar Index	%	Apr Index	%	May Index	%	Jun Index	%	Jul Index	%	Aug Index	%	Sep Index	%	Oct Index	%	Nov Index	%	Dec Index	%
1947	11.6	-	11.6	0.0	11.6	0.0	11.7	0.9	11.7	0.0	11.7	0.0	11.8	0.9	11.7	-0.8	11.7	0.0	11.8	0.9	11.9	0.8	11.9	0.0
1948	12.2	2.5	12.3	0.8	12.3	0.0	12.3	0.0	12.5	1.6	12.5	0.0	12.5	0.0	12.4	-0.8	12.4	0.0	12.4	0.0	12.6	1.6	12.7	0.8
1949	12.7	0.0	12.7	0.0	12.7	0.0	12.7	0.0	12.7	0.0	12.7	0.0	12.7	0.0	12.7	0.0	12.7	0.0	12.7	0.0	12.7	0.0	12.8	0.8
1950	12.8	0.0	12.8	0.0	12.9	0.8	12.9	0.0	12.9	0.0	13.0	0.8	13.0	0.0	13.0	0.0	13.1	0.8	13.0	-0.8	13.1	0.8	13.1	0.0
1951	13.2	0.8	13.2	0.0	13.3	0.8	13.4	0.8	13.4	0.0	13.8	3.0	13.8	0.0	13.8	0.0	13.8	0.0	13.8	0.0	13.8	0.0	13.8	0.0
1952	13.9	0.7	13.9	0.0	14.0	0.7	14.0	0.0	14.0	0.0	14.0	0.0	14.0	0.0	14.0	0.0	14.2	1.4	14.2	0.0	14.2	0.0	14.4	1.4
1953	14.4	0.0	-	-	-	-	14.9	3.5	-	-	-	-	14.9	0.0	-	-	-	-	14.8	-0.7	-	-	-	-
1954	14.9	0.7	-	-	-	-	15.7	5.4	-	-	-	-	15.7	0.0	-	-	-	-	15.5	-1.3	-	-	-	-
1955	15.5	0.0	-	-	-	-	15.6	0.6	-	-	-	-	16.2	3.8	-	-	-	-	16.2	0.0	-	-	-	-
1956	16.2	0.0	-	-	-	-	16.6	2.5	-	-	-	-	16.6	0.0	-	-	-	-	17.6	6.0	-	-	-	-
1957	17.7	0.6	-	-	-	-	17.8	0.6	-	-	-	-	17.8	0.0	-	-	-	-	18.0	1.1	-	-	-	-
1958	18.1	0.6	-	-	-	-	18.1	0.0	-	-	-	-	18.9	4.4	-	-	-	-	19.0	0.5	-	-	-	-
1959	19.2	1.1	-	-	-	-	19.4	1.0	-	-	-	-	19.4	0.0	-	-	-	-	20.7	6.7	-	-	-	-
1960	20.7	0.0	-	-	-	-	20.8	0.5	-	-	-	-	20.9	0.5	-	-	-	-	20.9	0.0	-	-	-	-
1961	21.1	1.0	-	-	-	-	21.6	2.4	-	-	-	-	21.7	0.5	-	-	-	-	21.7	0.0	-	-	-	-
1962	21.8	0.5	-	-	-	-	21.8	0.0	-	-	-	-	22.9	5.0	-	-	-	-	23.1	0.9	-	-	-	-
1963	23.1	0.0	-	-	-	-	23.1	0.0	-	-	-	-	23.2	0.4	-	-	-	-	23.2	0.0	-	-	-	-
1964	23.4	0.9	-	-	-	-	23.8	1.7	-	-	-	-	24.1	1.3	-	-	-	-	24.1	0.0	-	-	-	-
1965	24.2	0.4	-	-	-	-	24.4	0.8	-	-	-	-	24.5	0.4	-	-	-	-	24.7	0.8	-	-	-	-
1966	24.7	0.0	-	-	-	-	24.9	0.8	-	-	-	-	25.2	1.2	-	-	-	-	25.5	1.2	-	-	-	-
1967	26.7	4.7	-	-	-	-	26.9	0.7	-	-	-	-	27.0	0.4	-	-	-	-	27.2	0.7	-	-	-	-
1968	27.7	1.8	-	-	-	-	27.9	0.7	-	-	-	-	28.7	2.9	-	-	-	-	29.3	2.1	-	-	-	-
1969	29.6	1.0	-	-	-	-	30.1	1.7	-	-	-	-	30.4	1.0	-	-	-	-	30.6	0.7	-	-	-	-
1970	30.8	0.7	-	-	-	-	31.5	2.3	-	-	-	-	32.0	1.6	-	-	-	-	32.4	1.3	-	-	-	-
1971	32.7	0.9	-	-	-	-	33.0	0.9	-	-	-	-	33.1	0.3	-	-	-	-	33.4	0.9	-	-	-	-
1972	33.8	1.2	-	-	-	-	34.4	1.8	-	-	-	-	35.1	2.0	-	-	-	-	35.2	0.3	-	-	-	-
1973	35.6	1.1	-	-	-	-	35.8	0.6	-	-	-	-	36.2	1.1	-	-	-	-	36.9	1.9	-	-	-	-
1974	37.5	1.6	-	-	-	-	38.3	2.1	-	-	-	-	40.4	5.5	-	-	-	-	41.2	2.0	-	-	-	-
1975	41.9	1.7	-	-	-	-	42.8	2.1	-	-	-	-	44.5	4.0	-	-	-	-	45.6	2.5	-	-	-	-
1976	46.1	1.1	-	-	-	-	46.7	1.3	-	-	-	-	49.4	5.8	-	-	-	-	50.3	1.8	-	-	-	-
1977	51.0	1.4	-	-	-	-	52.1	2.2	-	-	-	-	54.5	4.6	-	-	-	-	55.4	1.7	-	-	-	-
1978	55.9	0.9	-	-	-	-	57.1	2.1	-	-	56.8	-0.5	-	-	58.6	3.2	-	-	59.1	0.9	-	-	60.5	2.4
1979	-	-	62.0	2.5	-	-	62.7	1.1	-	-	63.4	1.1	-	-	65.5	3.3	-	-	66.6	1.7	-	-	68.4	2.7
1980	-	-	68.8	0.6	-	-	70.7	2.8	-	-	73.4	3.8	-	-	76.2	3.8	-	-	76.2	0.0	-	-	76.4	0.3
1981	-	-	77.3	1.2	-	-	78.2	1.2	-	-	78.4	0.3	-	-	82.9	5.7	-	-	84.3	1.7	-	-	84.8	0.6
1982	-	-	86.3	1.8	-	-	87.5	1.4	-	-	88.4	1.0	-	-	92.4	4.5	-	-	93.1	0.8	-	-	94.3	1.3
1983	-	-	97.6	3.5	-	-	97.5	-0.1	-	-	99.2	1.7	-	-	101.7	2.5	-	-	105.0	3.2	-	-	105.1	0.1
1984	-	-	108.4	3.1	-	-	108.9	0.5	-	-	109.4	0.5	-	-	110.0	0.5	-	-	110.8	0.7	-	-	110.9	0.1
1985	-	-	111.4	0.5	-	-	112.2	0.7	-	-	112.5	0.3	-	-	114.2	1.5	-	-	115.3	1.0	-	-	117.5	1.9
1986	-	-	119.1	1.4	-	-	119.8	0.6	-	-	121.4	1.3	-	-	122.5	0.9	-	-	124.4	1.6	-	-	125.2	0.6
1987	-	-	126.0	0.6	-	-	128.6	2.1	-	-	131.6	2.3	-	-	133.0	1.1	-	-	133.8	0.6	-	-	135.0	0.9
1988	-	-	136.6	1.2	-	-	137.3	0.5	-	-	139.1	1.3	-	-	140.3	0.9	-	-	141.7	1.0	-	-	143.3	1.1
1989	-	-	143.2	-0.1	-	-	145.0	1.3	-	-	147.2	1.5	-	-	149.7	1.7	-	-	150.1	0.3	-	-	152.0	1.3
1990	-	-	155.4	2.2	-	-	160.0	3.0	-	-	160.5	0.3	-	-	163.0	1.6	-	-	165.8	1.7	-	-	167.2	0.8
1991	-	-	169.4	1.3	-	-	171.9	1.5	-	-	174.9	1.7	-	-	178.4	2.0	-	-	180.2	1.0	-	-	181.0	0.4

[Continued]

Pittsburgh, PA
Consumer Price Index - Urban Wage Earners
Base 1982-1984 = 100
Medical Care
[Continued]

For 1947-1997. Columns headed % show percentile change in the index from the previous period for which an index is available.

Year	Jan Index	%	Feb Index	%	Mar Index	%	Apr Index	%	May Index	%	Jun Index	%	Jul Index	%	Aug Index	%	Sep Index	%	Oct Index	%	Nov Index	%	Dec Index	%
1992	-	-	183.3	1.3	-	-	183.1	-0.1	-	-	181.1	-1.1	-	-	184.2	1.7	-	-	186.9	1.5	-	-	187.8	0.5
1993	-	-	191.9	2.2	-	-	192.0	0.1	-	-	195.0	1.6	-	-	195.7	0.4	-	-	196.1	0.2	-	-	196.1	0.0
1994	-	-	199.3	1.6	-	-	201.6	1.2	-	-	204.0	1.2	-	-	204.9	0.4	-	-	207.7	1.4	-	-	208.3	0.3
1995	-	-	204.2	-2.0	-	-	206.5	1.1	-	-	207.2	0.3	-	-	211.2	1.9	-	-	209.9	-0.6	-	-	214.5	2.2
1996	-	-	218.3	1.8	-	-	219.4	0.5	-	-	220.9	0.7	-	-	221.4	0.2	-	-	221.0	-0.2	-	-	220.9	-0.0
1997	-	-	221.1	0.1	-	-	223.5	1.1	-	-	225.6	0.9	-	-	223.8	-0.8	-	-	222.1	-0.8	-	-	223.9	0.8

Source: U.S. Department of Labor, Bureau of Labor Statistics, Division of Consumer Prices and Price Indexes. - indicates no data collected for period.

Pittsburgh, PA
Consumer Price Index - All Urban Consumers
Base 1982-1984 = 100
Entertainment

For 1976-1997. Columns headed % show percentile change in the index from the previous period for which an index is available.

Year	Jan Index	%	Feb Index	%	Mar Index	%	Apr Index	%	May Index	%	Jun Index	%	Jul Index	%	Aug Index	%	Sep Index	%	Oct Index	%	Nov Index	%	Dec Index	%
1976	64.0	-	-	-	-	-	64.4	0.6	-	-	-	-	64.9	0.8	-	-	-	-	65.7	1.2	-	-	-	-
1977	66.7	1.5	-	-	-	-	67.5	1.2	-	-	-	-	68.6	1.6	-	-	-	-	69.4	1.2	-	-	-	-
1978	70.4	1.4	-	-	-	-	71.1	1.0	-	-	71.4	0.4	-	-	72.3	1.3	-	-	71.3	-1.4	-	-	70.9	-0.6
1979	-	-	71.6	1.0	-	-	72.9	1.8	-	-	72.9	0.0	-	-	74.6	2.3	-	-	74.4	-0.3	-	-	77.7	4.4
1980	-	-	80.0	3.0	-	-	80.4	0.5	-	-	82.0	2.0	-	-	82.7	0.9	-	-	84.9	2.7	-	-	84.5	-0.5
1981	-	-	88.9	5.2	-	-	89.5	0.7	-	-	90.8	1.5	-	-	90.0	-0.9	-	-	92.5	2.8	-	-	91.5	-1.1
1982	-	-	94.5	3.3	-	-	94.5	0.0	-	-	94.5	0.0	-	-	95.1	0.6	-	-	98.5	3.6	-	-	97.8	-0.7
1983	-	-	98.9	1.1	-	-	99.1	0.2	-	-	100.8	1.7	-	-	101.1	0.3	-	-	101.3	0.2	-	-	102.1	0.8
1984	-	-	102.5	0.4	-	-	101.8	-0.7	-	-	102.7	0.9	-	-	105.2	2.4	-	-	106.3	1.0	-	-	107.6	1.2
1985	-	-	105.4	-2.0	-	-	107.3	1.8	-	-	110.5	3.0	-	-	109.6	-0.8	-	-	113.4	3.5	-	-	114.4	0.9
1986	-	-	115.5	1.0	-	-	117.4	1.6	-	-	120.1	2.3	-	-	120.4	0.2	-	-	118.8	-1.3	-	-	122.1	2.8
1987	-	-	119.5	-2.1	-	-	120.1	0.5	-	-	119.9	-0.2	-	-	119.1	-0.7	-	-	125.5	5.4	-	-	124.9	-0.5
1988	-	-	126.6	1.4	-	-	128.0	1.1	-	-	127.8	-0.2	-	-	127.6	-0.2	-	-	125.5	-1.6	-	-	127.9	1.9
1989	-	-	127.5	-0.3	-	-	129.4	1.5	-	-	135.9	5.0	-	-	136.2	0.2	-	-	135.7	-0.4	-	-	135.8	0.1
1990	-	-	136.7	0.7	-	-	138.2	1.1	-	-	139.9	1.2	-	-	139.8	-0.1	-	-	139.1	-0.5	-	-	140.6	1.1
1991	-	-	139.5	-0.8	-	-	143.2	2.7	-	-	143.1	-0.1	-	-	144.6	1.0	-	-	144.0	-0.4	-	-	144.9	0.6
1992	-	-	146.0	0.8	-	-	145.2	-0.5	-	-	144.6	-0.4	-	-	144.9	0.2	-	-	145.6	0.5	-	-	146.9	0.9
1993	-	-	147.4	0.3	-	-	148.4	0.7	-	-	151.0	1.8	-	-	152.0	0.7	-	-	150.7	-0.9	-	-	150.3	-0.3
1994	-	-	150.7	0.3	-	-	152.2	1.0	-	-	155.2	2.0	-	-	155.1	-0.1	-	-	154.9	-0.1	-	-	154.6	-0.2
1995	-	-	154.0	-0.4	-	-	155.6	1.0	-	-	157.0	0.9	-	-	155.9	-0.7	-	-	157.0	0.7	-	-	160.2	2.0
1996	-	-	161.1	0.6	-	-	162.1	0.6	-	-	162.4	0.2	-	-	163.3	0.6	-	-	165.8	1.5	-	-	165.9	0.1
1997	-	-	164.2	-1.0	-	-	164.6	0.2	-	-	165.0	0.2	-	-	166.3	0.8	-	-	166.5	0.1	-	-	168.2	1.0

Source: U.S. Department of Labor, Bureau of Labor Statistics, Division of Consumer Prices and Price Indexes. - indicates no data collected for period.

Pittsburgh, PA
Consumer Price Index - Urban Wage Earners
Base 1982-1984 = 100
Entertainment

For 1976-1997. Columns headed % show percentile change in the index from the previous period for which an index is available.

Year	Jan Index	%	Feb Index	%	Mar Index	%	Apr Index	%	May Index	%	Jun Index	%	Jul Index	%	Aug Index	%	Sep Index	%	Oct Index	%	Nov Index	%	Dec Index	%
1976	66.2	-	-	-	-	-	66.7	0.8	-	-	-	-	67.2	0.7	-	-	-	-	68.0	1.2	-	-	-	-
1977	69.0	1.5	-	-	-	-	69.9	1.3	-	-	-	-	71.0	1.6	-	-	-	-	71.8	1.1	-	-	-	-
1978	72.8	1.4	-	-	-	-	73.6	1.1	-	-	72.7	-1.2	-	-	73.5	1.1	-	-	73.6	0.1	-	-	72.8	-1.1
1979	-	-	75.2	3.3	-	-	77.5	3.1	-	-	77.7	0.3	-	-	77.8	0.1	-	-	76.2	-2.1	-	-	80.7	5.9
1980	-	-	81.7	1.2	-	-	82.8	1.3	-	-	83.6	1.0	-	-	83.2	-0.5	-	-	85.5	2.8	-	-	86.3	0.9
1981	-	-	87.9	1.9	-	-	89.3	1.6	-	-	91.8	2.8	-	-	89.4	-2.6	-	-	91.4	2.2	-	-	91.5	0.1
1982	-	-	94.3	3.1	-	-	94.1	-0.2	-	-	94.3	0.2	-	-	95.1	0.8	-	-	98.3	3.4	-	-	98.0	-0.3
1983	-	-	99.2	1.2	-	-	99.4	0.2	-	-	101.1	1.7	-	-	101.3	0.2	-	-	101.5	0.2	-	-	102.4	0.9
1984	-	-	102.4	0.0	-	-	100.9	-1.5	-	-	102.6	1.7	-	-	105.3	2.6	-	-	106.2	0.9	-	-	107.6	1.3
1985	-	-	105.2	-2.2	-	-	107.4	2.1	-	-	110.8	3.2	-	-	109.9	-0.8	-	-	113.6	3.4	-	-	114.5	0.8
1986	-	-	115.6	1.0	-	-	117.4	1.6	-	-	120.2	2.4	-	-	120.5	0.2	-	-	118.7	-1.5	-	-	121.9	2.7
1987	-	-	119.9	-1.6	-	-	120.6	0.6	-	-	119.8	-0.7	-	-	119.2	-0.5	-	-	125.1	4.9	-	-	124.6	-0.4
1988	-	-	126.3	1.4	-	-	127.3	0.8	-	-	126.8	-0.4	-	-	126.6	-0.2	-	-	125.2	-1.1	-	-	127.4	1.8
1989	-	-	126.8	-0.5	-	-	128.1	1.0	-	-	134.1	4.7	-	-	134.3	0.1	-	-	134.1	-0.1	-	-	134.0	-0.1
1990	-	-	135.3	1.0	-	-	136.4	0.8	-	-	138.2	1.3	-	-	138.1	-0.1	-	-	137.5	-0.4	-	-	138.8	0.9
1991	-	-	137.5	-0.9	-	-	141.0	2.5	-	-	140.9	-0.1	-	-	142.4	1.1	-	-	141.4	-0.7	-	-	142.4	0.7
1992	-	-	143.5	0.8	-	-	142.8	-0.5	-	-	142.2	-0.4	-	-	142.4	0.1	-	-	143.0	0.4	-	-	144.4	1.0
1993	-	-	144.9	0.3	-	-	146.0	0.8	-	-	148.6	1.8	-	-	149.5	0.6	-	-	148.3	-0.8	-	-	148.1	-0.1
1994	-	-	148.4	0.2	-	-	150.1	1.1	-	-	152.9	1.9	-	-	152.5	-0.3	-	-	153.4	0.6	-	-	153.1	-0.2
1995	-	-	152.4	-0.5	-	-	154.1	1.1	-	-	155.1	0.6	-	-	154.2	-0.6	-	-	155.0	0.5	-	-	157.8	1.8
1996	-	-	159.0	0.8	-	-	160.0	0.6	-	-	160.3	0.2	-	-	161.2	0.6	-	-	163.6	1.5	-	-	163.6	0.0
1997	-	-	161.7	-1.2	-	-	163.7	1.2	-	-	164.1	0.2	-	-	165.4	0.8	-	-	165.5	0.1	-	-	167.3	1.1

Source: U.S. Department of Labor, Bureau of Labor Statistics, Division of Consumer Prices and Price Indexes. - indicates no data collected for period.

Pittsburgh, PA
Consumer Price Index - All Urban Consumers
Base 1982-1984 = 100
Other Goods and Services

For 1976-1997. Columns headed % show percentile change in the index from the previous period for which an index is available.

Year	Jan Index	%	Feb Index	%	Mar Index	%	Apr Index	%	May Index	%	Jun Index	%	Jul Index	%	Aug Index	%	Sep Index	%	Oct Index	%	Nov Index	%	Dec Index	%
1976	56.7	-	-	-	-	-	57.2	0.9	-	-	-	-	57.8	1.0	-	-	-	-	58.7	1.6	-	-	-	-
1977	59.9	2.0	-	-	-	-	60.7	1.3	-	-	-	-	61.6	1.5	-	-	-	-	63.5	3.1	-	-	-	-
1978	64.0	0.8	-	-	-	-	64.6	0.9	-	-	64.5	-0.2	-	-	65.8	2.0	-	-	67.4	2.4	-	-	67.6	0.3
1979	-	-	68.5	1.3	-	-	68.9	0.6	-	-	69.1	0.3	-	-	70.9	2.6	-	-	72.5	2.3	-	-	72.9	0.6
1980	-	-	73.5	0.8	-	-	73.9	0.5	-	-	74.5	0.8	-	-	75.2	0.9	-	-	77.2	2.7	-	-	78.3	1.4
1981	-	-	78.9	0.8	-	-	79.5	0.8	-	-	81.0	1.9	-	-	83.1	2.6	-	-	87.0	4.7	-	-	87.3	0.3
1982	-	-	88.2	1.0	-	-	88.5	0.3	-	-	88.9	0.5	-	-	90.4	1.7	-	-	94.3	4.3	-	-	96.8	2.7
1983	-	-	98.7	2.0	-	-	98.7	0.0	-	-	98.0	-0.7	-	-	101.9	4.0	-	-	105.2	3.2	-	-	105.3	0.1
1984	-	-	107.3	1.9	-	-	106.7	-0.6	-	-	106.7	0.0	-	-	107.7	0.9	-	-	111.4	3.4	-	-	111.3	-0.1
1985	-	-	111.1	-0.2	-	-	111.3	0.2	-	-	112.1	0.7	-	-	112.9	0.7	-	-	115.7	2.5	-	-	116.2	0.4
1986	-	-	116.4	0.2	-	-	117.1	0.6	-	-	116.7	-0.3	-	-	117.7	0.9	-	-	120.4	2.3	-	-	120.7	0.2
1987	-	-	121.3	0.5	-	-	121.5	0.2	-	-	122.1	0.5	-	-	123.3	1.0	-	-	124.5	1.0	-	-	124.1	-0.3
1988	-	-	132.4	6.7	-	-	132.9	0.4	-	-	126.9	-4.5	-	-	134.0	5.6	-	-	136.4	1.8	-	-	136.6	0.1
1989	-	-	138.7	1.5	-	-	139.4	0.5	-	-	139.7	0.2	-	-	140.8	0.8	-	-	143.1	1.6	-	-	144.9	1.3
1990	-	-	147.1	1.5	-	-	149.7	1.8	-	-	148.4	-0.9	-	-	150.5	1.4	-	-	153.8	2.2	-	-	155.3	1.0
1991	-	-	151.2	-2.6	-	-	152.4	0.8	-	-	152.5	0.1	-	-	154.4	1.2	-	-	159.5	3.3	-	-	161.9	1.5
1992	-	-	165.4	2.2	-	-	166.3	0.5	-	-	167.7	0.8	-	-	170.6	1.7	-	-	169.7	-0.5	-	-	171.5	1.1
1993	-	-	176.5	2.9	-	-	177.4	0.5	-	-	178.7	0.7	-	-	178.0	-0.4	-	-	175.1	-1.6	-	-	179.3	2.4
1994	-	-	178.2	-0.6	-	-	179.7	0.8	-	-	180.3	0.3	-	-	183.7	1.9	-	-	188.9	2.8	-	-	188.7	-0.1
1995	-	-	189.6	0.5	-	-	189.4	-0.1	-	-	190.8	0.7	-	-	193.1	1.2	-	-	196.4	1.7	-	-	195.9	-0.3
1996	-	-	196.1	0.1	-	-	199.6	1.8	-	-	202.2	1.3	-	-	205.6	1.7	-	-	206.9	0.6	-	-	211.1	2.0
1997	-	-	212.1	0.5	-	-	212.9	0.4	-	-	213.7	0.4	-	-	216.4	1.3	-	-	215.5	-0.4	-	-	216.9	0.6

Source: U.S. Department of Labor, Bureau of Labor Statistics, Division of Consumer Prices and Price Indexes. - indicates no data collected for period.

Pittsburgh, PA
Consumer Price Index - Urban Wage Earners
Base 1982-1984 = 100
Other Goods and Services

For 1976-1997. Columns headed % show percentile change in the index from the previous period for which an index is available.

Year	Jan Index	%	Feb Index	%	Mar Index	%	Apr Index	%	May Index	%	Jun Index	%	Jul Index	%	Aug Index	%	Sep Index	%	Oct Index	%	Nov Index	%	Dec Index	%
1976	56.0	-	-	-	-	-	56.5	0.9	-	-	-	-	57.1	1.1	-	-	-	-	58.0	1.6	-	-	-	-
1977	59.2	2.1	-	-	-	-	59.9	1.2	-	-	-	-	60.8	1.5	-	-	-	-	62.7	3.1	-	-	-	-
1978	63.2	0.8	-	-	-	-	63.8	0.9	-	-	63.7	-0.2	-	-	65.2	2.4	-	-	66.4	1.8	-	-	66.4	0.0
1979	-	-	67.2	1.2	-	-	67.7	0.7	-	-	68.5	1.2	-	-	69.7	1.8	-	-	71.2	2.2	-	-	72.3	1.5
1980	-	-	73.4	1.5	-	-	73.8	0.5	-	-	74.6	1.1	-	-	75.3	0.9	-	-	77.1	2.4	-	-	78.6	1.9
1981	-	-	79.1	0.6	-	-	79.9	1.0	-	-	81.2	1.6	-	-	82.2	1.2	-	-	85.8	4.4	-	-	86.3	0.6
1982	-	-	87.3	1.2	-	-	87.7	0.5	-	-	88.1	0.5	-	-	89.4	1.5	-	-	93.3	4.4	-	-	96.5	3.4
1983	-	-	98.5	2.1	-	-	98.6	0.1	-	-	98.0	-0.6	-	-	102.7	4.8	-	-	105.6	2.8	-	-	105.7	0.1
1984	-	-	108.2	2.4	-	-	107.6	-0.6	-	-	107.6	0.0	-	-	108.6	0.9	-	-	111.7	2.9	-	-	111.5	-0.2
1985	-	-	112.0	0.4	-	-	112.1	0.1	-	-	112.8	0.6	-	-	113.9	1.0	-	-	116.2	2.0	-	-	116.7	0.4
1986	-	-	117.0	0.3	-	-	117.8	0.7	-	-	117.5	-0.3	-	-	118.9	1.2	-	-	120.9	1.7	-	-	121.3	0.3
1987	-	-	121.8	0.4	-	-	121.9	0.1	-	-	122.5	0.5	-	-	123.4	0.7	-	-	125.3	1.5	-	-	125.0	-0.2
1988	-	-	134.1	7.3	-	-	134.4	0.2	-	-	127.9	-4.8	-	-	135.6	6.0	-	-	138.5	2.1	-	-	138.7	0.1
1989	-	-	140.6	1.4	-	-	141.1	0.4	-	-	141.4	0.2	-	-	142.2	0.6	-	-	144.9	1.9	-	-	147.2	1.6
1990	-	-	149.6	1.6	-	-	152.3	1.8	-	-	151.5	-0.5	-	-	153.7	1.5	-	-	157.4	2.4	-	-	159.0	1.0
1991	-	-	154.8	-2.6	-	-	155.7	0.6	-	-	155.9	0.1	-	-	157.8	1.2	-	-	163.3	3.5	-	-	165.9	1.6
1992	-	-	169.3	2.0	-	-	170.2	0.5	-	-	171.9	1.0	-	-	175.7	2.2	-	-	174.5	-0.7	-	-	176.5	1.1
1993	-	-	181.3	2.7	-	-	182.3	0.6	-	-	183.5	0.7	-	-	182.3	-0.7	-	-	179.0	-1.8	-	-	182.6	2.0
1994	-	-	181.8	-0.4	-	-	183.8	1.1	-	-	184.4	0.3	-	-	188.4	2.2	-	-	191.7	1.8	-	-	191.6	-0.1
1995	-	-	192.3	0.4	-	-	192.2	-0.1	-	-	193.5	0.7	-	-	196.4	1.5	-	-	199.6	1.6	-	-	199.2	-0.2
1996	-	-	199.5	0.2	-	-	204.3	2.4	-	-	206.6	1.1	-	-	210.2	1.7	-	-	211.8	0.8	-	-	215.6	1.8
1997	-	-	216.6	0.5	-	-	217.7	0.5	-	-	218.5	0.4	-	-	221.4	1.3	-	-	220.8	-0.3	-	-	222.5	0.8

Source: U.S. Department of Labor, Bureau of Labor Statistics, Division of Consumer Prices and Price Indexes. - indicates no data collected for period.

Portland, OR-WA

Consumer Price Index - All Urban Consumers
Base 1982-1984 = 100
Annual Averages

For 1914-1997. Columns headed % show percentile change in the index from the previous period for which an index is available.

Year	All Items		Food & Beverage		Housing		Apparel & Upkeep		Trans- portation		Medical Care		Entertain- ment		Other Goods & Services	
	Index	%	Index	%	Index	%	Index	%	Index	%	Index	%	Index	%	Index	%
1914	10.5	-	-	-	-	-	16.5	-	-	-	-	-	-	-	-	-
1915	10.2	-2.9	-	-	-	-	16.8	1.8	-	-	-	-	-	-	-	-
1916	10.5	2.9	-	-	-	-	18.2	8.3	-	-	-	-	-	-	-	-
1917	12.3	17.1	-	-	-	-	21.7	19.2	-	-	-	-	-	-	-	-
1918	15.1	22.8	-	-	-	-	28.6	31.8	-	-	-	-	-	-	-	-
1919	17.7	17.2	-	-	-	-	36.3	26.9	-	-	-	-	-	-	-	-
1920	20.0	13.0	-	-	-	-	40.5	11.6	-	-	-	-	-	-	-	-
1921	17.3	-13.5	-	-	-	-	30.8	-24.0	-	-	-	-	-	-	-	-
1922	16.4	-5.2	-	-	-	-	25.7	-16.6	-	-	-	-	-	-	-	-
1923	16.6	1.2	-	-	-	-	26.6	3.5	-	-	-	-	-	-	-	-
1924	16.5	-0.6	-	-	-	-	26.6	0.0	-	-	-	-	-	-	-	-
1925	16.6	0.6	-	-	-	-	26.1	-1.9	-	-	-	-	-	-	-	-
1926	16.4	-1.2	-	-	-	-	25.9	-0.8	-	-	-	-	-	-	-	-
1927	16.2	-1.2	-	-	-	-	25.2	-2.7	-	-	-	-	-	-	-	-
1928	16.0	-1.2	-	-	-	-	24.9	-1.2	-	-	-	-	-	-	-	-
1929	15.8	-1.2	-	-	-	-	24.5	-1.6	-	-	-	-	-	-	-	-
1930	15.5	-1.9	-	-	-	-	23.8	-2.9	-	-	-	-	-	-	-	-
1931	14.0	-9.7	-	-	-	-	21.7	-8.8	-	-	-	-	-	-	-	-
1932	12.7	-9.3	-	-	-	-	19.2	-11.5	-	-	-	-	-	-	-	-
1933	12.1	-4.7	-	-	-	-	18.8	-2.1	-	-	-	-	-	-	-	-
1934	12.5	3.3	-	-	-	-	20.5	9.0	-	-	-	-	-	-	-	-
1935	12.9	3.2	-	-	-	-	20.5	0.0	-	-	-	-	-	-	-	-
1936	13.2	2.3	-	-	-	-	20.6	0.5	-	-	-	-	-	-	-	-
1937	13.9	5.3	-	-	-	-	21.5	4.4	-	-	-	-	-	-	-	-
1938	13.7	-1.4	-	-	-	-	21.4	-0.5	-	-	-	-	-	-	-	-
1939	13.6	-0.7	-	-	-	-	21.3	-0.5	-	-	-	-	-	-	-	-
1940	13.6	0.0	-	-	-	-	21.7	1.9	-	-	-	-	-	-	-	-
1941	14.4	5.9	-	-	-	-	22.5	3.7	-	-	-	-	-	-	-	-
1942	16.5	14.6	-	-	-	-	26.0	15.6	-	-	-	-	-	-	-	-
1943	17.5	6.1	-	-	-	-	27.6	6.2	-	-	-	-	-	-	-	-
1944	17.7	1.1	-	-	-	-	29.4	6.5	-	-	-	-	-	-	-	-
1945	18.2	2.8	-	-	-	-	30.0	2.0	-	-	-	-	-	-	-	-
1946	19.5	7.1	-	-	-	-	32.1	7.0	-	-	-	-	-	-	-	-
1947	22.1	13.3	-	-	-	-	37.9	18.1	19.8	-	14.2	-	-	-	-	-
1948	24.1	9.0	-	-	-	-	41.2	8.7	21.9	10.6	14.7	3.5	-	-	-	-
1949	23.8	-1.2	-	-	-	-	39.8	-3.4	23.6	7.8	15.0	2.0	-	-	-	-
1950	24.3	2.1	-	-	-	-	39.5	-0.8	24.0	1.7	15.4	2.7	-	-	-	-
1951	26.2	7.8	-	-	-	-	42.3	7.1	25.1	4.6	16.3	5.8	-	-	-	-
1952	26.8	2.3	-	-	-	-	41.9	-0.9	26.8	6.8	17.1	4.9	-	-	-	-
1953	26.9	0.4	-	-	-	-	41.6	-0.7	27.6	3.0	17.5	2.3	-	-	-	-
1954	26.9	0.0	-	-	-	-	41.9	0.7	26.8	-2.9	17.9	2.3	-	-	-	-
1955	26.8	-0.4	-	-	-	-	42.2	0.7	26.9	0.4	18.6	3.9	-	-	-	-
1956	27.5	2.6	-	-	-	-	43.2	2.4	26.9	0.0	19.2	3.2	-	-	-	-
1957	28.4	3.3	-	-	-	-	44.1	2.1	28.2	4.8	20.3	5.7	-	-	-	-
1958	29.0	2.1	-	-	-	-	44.2	0.2	29.8	5.7	20.6	1.5	-	-	-	-

[Continued]

Portland, OR-WA
Consumer Price Index - All Urban Consumers
Base 1982-1984 = 100
Annual Averages
[Continued]

For 1914-1997. Columns headed % show percentile change in the index from the previous period for which an index is available.

Year	All Items		Food & Beverage		Housing		Apparel & Upkeep		Trans- portation		Medical Care		Entertain- ment		Other Goods & Services	
	Index	%	Index	%	Index	%	Index	%	Index	%	Index	%	Index	%	Index	%
1959	29.3	1.0	-	-	-	-	44.5	0.7	31.1	4.4	20.8	1.0	-	-	-	-
1960	29.8	1.7	-	-	-	-	45.5	2.2	30.8	-1.0	21.8	4.8	-	-	-	-
1961	30.1	1.0	-	-	-	-	45.8	0.7	30.9	0.3	22.4	2.8	-	-	-	-
1962	30.2	0.3	-	-	-	-	45.5	-0.7	31.2	1.0	22.5	0.4	-	-	-	-
1963	30.8	2.0	-	-	-	-	46.3	1.8	31.5	1.0	23.0	2.2	-	-	-	-
1964	31.5	2.3	-	-	-	-	46.8	1.1	32.0	1.6	24.4	6.1	-	-	-	-
1965	32.3	2.5	-	-	-	-	48.2	3.0	32.4	1.3	25.2	3.3	-	-	-	-
1966	33.3	3.1	-	-	-	-	49.8	3.3	32.7	0.9	26.0	3.2	-	-	-	-
1967	34.2	2.7	-	-	-	-	51.0	2.4	34.1	4.3	27.7	6.5	-	-	-	-
1968	35.4	3.5	-	-	-	-	53.2	4.3	34.9	2.3	29.2	5.4	-	-	-	-
1969	37.1	4.8	-	-	-	-	56.2	5.6	36.1	3.4	30.9	5.8	-	-	-	-
1970	38.7	4.3	-	-	-	-	58.8	4.6	37.1	2.8	32.9	6.5	-	-	-	-
1971	39.7	2.6	-	-	-	-	59.5	1.2	37.3	0.5	34.2	4.0	-	-	-	-
1972	40.8	2.8	-	-	-	-	61.1	2.7	37.6	0.8	35.3	3.2	-	-	-	-
1973	43.5	6.6	-	-	-	-	65.0	6.4	38.6	2.7	37.6	6.5	-	-	-	-
1974	48.8	12.2	-	-	-	-	68.9	6.0	42.4	9.8	41.4	10.1	-	-	-	-
1975	53.5	9.6	-	-	-	-	72.9	5.8	46.8	10.4	46.0	11.1	-	-	-	-
1976	57.0	6.5	60.8	-	56.3	-	76.7	5.2	51.3	9.6	50.1	8.9	68.8	-	52.2	-
1977	61.6	8.1	64.6	6.3	61.2	8.7	82.1	7.0	56.2	9.6	55.2	10.2	71.4	3.8	56.3	7.9
1978	67.8	10.1	71.1	10.1	69.1	12.9	84.5	2.9	60.4	7.5	60.2	9.1	75.9	6.3	60.3	7.1
1979	77.0	13.6	79.8	12.2	79.7	15.3	85.7	1.4	70.6	16.9	65.9	9.5	80.7	6.3	65.5	8.6
1980	87.2	13.2	85.5	7.1	92.4	15.9	87.8	2.5	81.7	15.7	74.3	12.7	86.9	7.7	73.6	12.4
1981	95.0	8.9	92.3	8.0	100.0	8.2	92.6	5.5	91.8	12.4	83.3	12.1	90.4	4.0	82.1	11.5
1982	98.0	3.2	97.2	5.3	100.1	0.1	95.5	3.1	97.8	6.5	93.6	12.4	94.8	4.9	92.5	12.7
1983	99.1	1.1	99.7	2.6	98.6	-1.5	99.6	4.3	98.5	0.7	100.6	7.5	101.4	7.0	101.5	9.7
1984	102.8	3.7	103.2	3.5	101.2	2.6	104.9	5.3	103.6	5.2	105.8	5.2	103.8	2.4	106.0	4.4
1985	106.7	3.8	105.6	2.3	104.8	3.6	107.5	2.5	108.3	4.5	111.2	5.1	109.6	5.6	111.6	5.3
1986	108.2	1.4	108.2	2.5	106.2	1.3	100.5	-6.5	107.4	-0.8	119.1	7.1	111.2	1.5	121.0	8.4
1987	115.4	6.7	113.7	5.1	121.5	14.4	104.6	4.1	102.4	-4.7	128.7	8.1	121.6	9.4	130.9	8.2
1988	120.5	4.4	120.4	5.9	126.9	4.4	102.4	-2.1	105.3	2.8	136.9	6.4	129.1	6.2	140.1	7.0
1989	126.4	4.9	128.2	6.5	132.4	4.3	104.2	1.8	109.6	4.1	147.9	8.0	133.1	3.1	152.2	8.6
1990	132.1	4.5	134.7	5.1	137.3	3.7	107.5	3.2	114.7	4.7	160.5	8.5	140.7	5.7	161.0	5.8
1991	137.9	4.4	140.3	4.2	142.7	3.9	113.1	5.2	117.1	2.1	172.9	7.7	152.4	8.3	174.5	8.4
1992	142.5	3.3	143.3	2.1	146.2	2.5	117.8	4.2	119.8	2.3	187.0	8.2	156.5	2.7	195.9	12.3
1993	146.3	2.7	146.2	2.0	149.2	2.1	118.2	0.3	123.7	3.3	199.1	6.5	162.3	3.7	207.0	5.7
1994	148.7	1.6	148.9	1.8	151.5	1.5	115.5	-2.3	125.7	1.6	204.3	2.6	164.5	1.4	213.2	3.0
1995	151.6	2.0	151.6	1.8	154.5	2.0	114.0	-1.3	129.0	2.6	209.0	2.3	166.2	1.0	220.6	3.5
1996	155.1	2.3	155.3	2.4	157.4	1.9	116.9	2.5	133.5	3.5	214.5	2.6	166.8	0.4	227.8	3.3
1997	-	-	-	-	-	-	-	-	-	-	-	-	-	-	-	-

Source: U.S. Department of Labor, Bureau of Labor Statistics, Division of Consumer Prices and Price Indexes. - indicates no data collected for period.

Portland, OR-WA
Consumer Price Index - Urban Wage Earners
Base 1982-1984 = 100
Annual Averages

For 1914-1997. Columns headed % show percentile change in the index from the previous period for which an index is available.

Year	All Items		Food & Beverage		Housing		Apparel & Upkeep		Trans-portation		Medical Care		Entertain-ment		Other Goods & Services	
	Index	%	Index	%	Index	%	Index	%	Index	%	Index	%	Index	%	Index	%
1914	10.6	-	-	-	-	-	16.6	-	-	-	-	-	-	-	-	-
1915	10.4	-1.9	-	-	-	-	16.9	1.8	-	-	-	-	-	-	-	-
1916	10.7	2.9	-	-	-	-	18.3	8.3	-	-	-	-	-	-	-	-
1917	12.5	16.8	-	-	-	-	21.9	19.7	-	-	-	-	-	-	-	-
1918	15.3	22.4	-	-	-	-	28.8	31.5	-	-	-	-	-	-	-	-
1919	17.9	17.0	-	-	-	-	36.5	26.7	-	-	-	-	-	-	-	-
1920	20.3	13.4	-	-	-	-	40.7	11.5	-	-	-	-	-	-	-	-
1921	17.6	-13.3	-	-	-	-	31.0	-23.8	-	-	-	-	-	-	-	-
1922	16.7	-5.1	-	-	-	-	25.9	-16.5	-	-	-	-	-	-	-	-
1923	16.8	0.6	-	-	-	-	26.8	3.5	-	-	-	-	-	-	-	-
1924	16.8	0.0	-	-	-	-	26.7	-0.4	-	-	-	-	-	-	-	-
1925	16.8	0.0	-	-	-	-	26.3	-1.5	-	-	-	-	-	-	-	-
1926	16.7	-0.6	-	-	-	-	26.0	-1.1	-	-	-	-	-	-	-	-
1927	16.5	-1.2	-	-	-	-	25.4	-2.3	-	-	-	-	-	-	-	-
1928	16.2	-1.8	-	-	-	-	25.0	-1.6	-	-	-	-	-	-	-	-
1929	16.1	-0.6	-	-	-	-	24.7	-1.2	-	-	-	-	-	-	-	-
1930	15.7	-2.5	-	-	-	-	23.9	-3.2	-	-	-	-	-	-	-	-
1931	14.2	-9.6	-	-	-	-	21.9	-8.4	-	-	-	-	-	-	-	-
1932	12.9	-9.2	-	-	-	-	19.3	-11.9	-	-	-	-	-	-	-	-
1933	12.3	-4.7	-	-	-	-	18.9	-2.1	-	-	-	-	-	-	-	-
1934	12.7	3.3	-	-	-	-	20.6	9.0	-	-	-	-	-	-	-	-
1935	13.2	3.9	-	-	-	-	20.6	0.0	-	-	-	-	-	-	-	-
1936	13.4	1.5	-	-	-	-	20.7	0.5	-	-	-	-	-	-	-	-
1937	14.1	5.2	-	-	-	-	21.6	4.3	-	-	-	-	-	-	-	-
1938	13.9	-1.4	-	-	-	-	21.6	0.0	-	-	-	-	-	-	-	-
1939	13.8	-0.7	-	-	-	-	21.4	-0.9	-	-	-	-	-	-	-	-
1940	13.8	0.0	-	-	-	-	21.8	1.9	-	-	-	-	-	-	-	-
1941	14.7	6.5	-	-	-	-	22.6	3.7	-	-	-	-	-	-	-	-
1942	16.7	13.6	-	-	-	-	26.2	15.9	-	-	-	-	-	-	-	-
1943	17.8	6.6	-	-	-	-	27.8	6.1	-	-	-	-	-	-	-	-
1944	18.0	1.1	-	-	-	-	29.6	6.5	-	-	-	-	-	-	-	-
1945	18.5	2.8	-	-	-	-	30.2	2.0	-	-	-	-	-	-	-	-
1946	19.8	7.0	-	-	-	-	32.3	7.0	-	-	-	-	-	-	-	-
1947	22.4	13.1	-	-	-	-	38.2	18.3	19.7	-	15.8	-	-	-	-	-
1948	24.5	9.4	-	-	-	-	41.5	8.6	21.9	11.2	16.4	3.8	-	-	-	-
1949	24.2	-1.2	-	-	-	-	40.1	-3.4	23.6	7.8	16.7	1.8	-	-	-	-
1950	24.6	1.7	-	-	-	-	39.8	-0.7	24.0	1.7	17.2	3.0	-	-	-	-
1951	26.6	8.1	-	-	-	-	42.6	7.0	25.1	4.6	18.2	5.8	-	-	-	-
1952	27.2	2.3	-	-	-	-	42.2	-0.9	26.8	6.8	19.0	4.4	-	-	-	-
1953	27.3	0.4	-	-	-	-	41.8	-0.9	27.6	3.0	19.5	2.6	-	-	-	-
1954	27.3	0.0	-	-	-	-	42.1	0.7	26.8	-2.9	19.9	2.1	-	-	-	-
1955	27.3	0.0	-	-	-	-	42.5	1.0	26.9	0.4	20.7	4.0	-	-	-	-
1956	27.9	2.2	-	-	-	-	43.5	2.4	26.9	0.0	21.4	3.4	-	-	-	-
1957	28.8	3.2	-	-	-	-	44.3	1.8	28.2	4.8	22.6	5.6	-	-	-	-
1958	29.5	2.4	-	-	-	-	44.4	0.2	29.8	5.7	22.9	1.3	-	-	-	-

[Continued]

Portland, OR-WA
Consumer Price Index - Urban Wage Earners
Base 1982-1984 = 100
Annual Averages
[Continued]

For 1914-1997. Columns headed % show percentile change in the index from the previous period for which an index is available.

Year	All Items Index	%	Food & Beverage Index	%	Housing Index	%	Apparel & Upkeep Index	%	Trans-portation Index	%	Medical Care Index	%	Entertain-ment Index	%	Other Goods & Services Index	%
1959	29.8	1.0	-	-	-	-	44.7	0.7	31.0	4.0	23.2	1.3	-	-	-	-
1960	30.2	1.3	-	-	-	-	45.8	2.5	30.8	-0.6	24.3	4.7	-	-	-	-
1961	30.6	1.3	-	-	-	-	46.1	0.7	30.9	0.3	25.0	2.9	-	-	-	-
1962	30.7	0.3	-	-	-	-	45.8	-0.7	31.1	0.6	25.1	0.4	-	-	-	-
1963	31.3	2.0	-	-	-	-	46.6	1.7	31.5	1.3	25.7	2.4	-	-	-	-
1964	32.0	2.2	-	-	-	-	47.1	1.1	31.9	1.3	27.2	5.8	-	-	-	-
1965	32.8	2.5	-	-	-	-	48.5	3.0	32.4	1.6	28.1	3.3	-	-	-	-
1966	33.8	3.0	-	-	-	-	50.1	3.3	32.7	0.9	29.0	3.2	-	-	-	-
1967	34.7	2.7	-	-	-	-	51.3	2.4	34.1	4.3	30.9	6.6	-	-	-	-
1968	35.9	3.5	-	-	-	-	53.6	4.5	34.9	2.3	32.5	5.2	-	-	-	-
1969	37.7	5.0	-	-	-	-	56.6	5.6	36.0	3.2	34.4	5.8	-	-	-	-
1970	39.3	4.2	-	-	-	-	59.2	4.6	37.0	2.8	36.6	6.4	-	-	-	-
1971	40.3	2.5			-	-	59.9	1.2	37.3	0.8	38.1	4.1	-	-	-	-
1972	41.5	3.0			-	-	61.5	2.7	37.6	0.8	39.4	3.4	-	-	-	-
1973	44.2	6.5	-	-	-	-	65.4	6.3	38.5	2.4	41.9	6.3	-	-	-	-
1974	49.5	12.0	-	-	-	-	69.4	6.1	42.3	9.9	46.1	10.0	-	-	-	-
1975	54.3	9.7	-	-	-	-	73.4	5.8	46.8	10.6	51.2	11.1	-	-	-	-
1976	57.9	6.6	60.6	-	57.1	-	77.2	5.2	51.2	9.4	55.8	9.0	75.7	-	55.7	-
1977	62.5	7.9	64.4	6.3	62.1	8.8	82.6	7.0	56.2	9.8	61.5	10.2	78.5	3.7	60.0	7.7
1978	69.0	10.4	71.8	11.5	70.1	12.9	85.3	3.3	61.3	9.1	66.1	7.5	82.5	5.1	63.4	5.7
1979	78.3	13.5	81.0	12.8	81.1	15.7	86.9	1.9	70.7	15.3	71.8	8.6	86.9	5.3	67.6	6.6
1980	88.2	12.6	86.3	6.5	94.2	16.2	88.8	2.2	80.6	14.0	77.6	8.1	94.6	8.9	74.0	9.5
1981	95.8	8.6	92.5	7.2	102.2	8.5	93.2	5.0	91.3	13.3	83.8	8.0	91.8	-3.0	81.3	9.9
1982	98.8	3.1	97.1	5.0	101.9	-0.3	95.3	2.3	97.0	6.2	93.8	11.9	95.1	3.6	92.2	13.4
1983	99.2	0.4	99.7	2.7	98.7	-3.1	98.9	3.8	98.5	1.5	100.8	7.5	101.2	6.4	102.1	10.7
1984	102.1	2.9	103.2	3.5	99.4	0.7	105.8	7.0	104.4	6.0	105.4	4.6	103.7	2.5	105.8	3.6
1985	105.1	2.9	105.6	2.3	101.3	1.9	108.8	2.8	109.0	4.4	111.1	5.4	109.2	5.3	111.2	5.1
1986	106.0	0.9	108.0	2.3	102.6	1.3	100.4	-7.7	107.5	-1.4	118.7	6.8	110.3	1.0	120.2	8.1
1987	114.3	7.8	113.8	5.4	119.4	16.4	105.4	5.0	103.7	-3.5	130.0	9.5	117.3	6.3	130.4	8.5
1988	119.4	4.5	120.4	5.8	124.6	4.4	104.4	-0.9	107.1	3.3	138.1	6.2	124.0	5.7	140.1	7.4
1989	125.5	5.1	128.3	6.6	129.7	4.1	107.0	2.5	111.8	4.4	149.0	7.9	130.1	4.9	154.6	10.3
1990	131.1	4.5	134.7	5.0	134.6	3.8	110.6	3.4	116.7	4.4	160.8	7.9	136.3	4.8	164.5	6.4
1991	136.3	4.0	140.4	4.2	139.7	3.8	116.2	5.1	118.6	1.6	172.1	7.0	143.5	5.3	177.8	8.1
1992	140.6	3.2	143.3	2.1	143.1	2.4	121.5	4.6	121.9	2.8	186.4	8.3	147.5	2.8	195.8	10.1
1993	144.3	2.6	146.4	2.2	146.1	2.1	122.7	1.0	125.7	3.1	197.9	6.2	151.6	2.8	204.8	4.6
1994	146.3	1.4	149.2	1.9	148.3	1.5	120.6	-1.7	127.9	1.8	202.4	2.3	152.9	0.9	208.8	2.0
1995	149.3	2.1	151.8	1.7	151.1	1.9	120.0	-0.5	132.1	3.3	206.8	2.2	154.8	1.2	215.1	3.0
1996	152.6	2.2	155.6	2.5	153.8	1.8	122.7	2.2	136.4	3.3	212.2	2.6	156.2	0.9	220.5	2.5
1997	-	-	-	-	-	-	-	-	-	-	-	-	-	-	-	-

Source: U.S. Department of Labor, Bureau of Labor Statistics, Division of Consumer Prices and Price Indexes. - indicates no data collected for period.

Portland, OR-WA
Consumer Price Index - All Urban Consumers
Base 1982-1984 = 100
All Items

For 1914-1997. Columns headed % show percentile change in the index from the previous period for which an index is available.

Year	Jan Index	Jan %	Feb Index	Feb %	Mar Index	Mar %	Apr Index	Apr %	May Index	May %	Jun Index	Jun %	Jul Index	Jul %	Aug Index	Aug %	Sep Index	Sep %	Oct Index	Oct %	Nov Index	Nov %	Dec Index	Dec %
1914	-	-	-	-	-	-	-	-	-	-	-	-	-	-	-	-	-	-	-	-	-	-	10.5	-
1915	-	-	-	-	-	-	-	-	-	-	-	-	-	-	-	-	-	-	-	-	-	-	10.1	-3.8
1916	-	-	-	-	-	-	-	-	-	-	-	-	-	-	-	-	-	-	-	-	-	-	10.9	7.9
1917	-	-	-	-	-	-	-	-	-	-	-	-	-	-	-	-	-	-	-	-	-	-	13.2	21.1
1918	-	-	-	-	-	-	-	-	-	-	-	-	-	-	-	-	-	-	-	-	-	-	16.6	25.8
1919	-	-	-	-	-	-	-	-	-	-	17.3	4.2	-	-	-	-	-	-	-	-	-	-	19.0	9.8
1920	-	-	-	-	-	-	-	-	-	-	21.1	11.1	-	-	-	-	-	-	-	-	-	-	18.8	-10.9
1921	-	-	-	-	17.1	-9.0	-	-	-	-	-	-	-	-	-	-	17.0	-0.6	-	-	-	-	16.8	-1.2
1922	-	-	-	-	16.3	-3.0	-	-	-	-	16.2	-0.6	-	-	-	-	16.4	1.2	-	-	-	-	16.5	0.6
1923	-	-	-	-	16.4	-0.6	-	-	-	-	16.5	0.6	-	-	-	-	16.6	0.6	-	-	-	-	16.7	0.6
1924	-	-	-	-	16.6	-0.6	-	-	-	-	16.4	-1.2	-	-	-	-	16.5	0.6	-	-	-	-	16.5	0.0
1925	-	-	-	-	-	-	-	-	-	-	16.6	0.6	-	-	-	-	-	-	-	-	-	-	16.7	0.6
1926	-	-	-	-	-	-	-	-	-	-	16.5	-1.2	-	-	-	-	-	-	-	-	-	-	16.4	-0.6
1927	-	-	-	-	-	-	-	-	-	-	16.4	0.0	-	-	-	-	-	-	-	-	-	-	16.1	-1.8
1928	-	-	-	-	-	-	-	-	-	-	15.8	-1.9	-	-	-	-	-	-	-	-	-	-	15.9	0.6
1929	-	-	-	-	-	-	-	-	-	-	15.7	-1.3	-	-	-	-	-	-	-	-	-	-	15.8	0.6
1930	-	-	-	-	-	-	-	-	-	-	15.7	-0.6	-	-	-	-	-	-	-	-	-	-	14.8	-5.7
1931	-	-	-	-	-	-	-	-	-	-	14.1	-4.7	-	-	-	-	-	-	-	-	-	-	13.6	-3.5
1932	-	-	-	-	-	-	-	-	-	-	12.7	-6.6	-	-	-	-	-	-	-	-	-	-	12.4	-2.4
1933	-	-	-	-	-	-	-	-	-	-	11.9	-4.0	-	-	-	-	-	-	-	-	-	-	12.2	2.5
1934	-	-	-	-	-	-	-	-	-	-	12.4	1.6	-	-	-	-	-	-	-	-	12.7	2.4	-	-
1935	-	-	-	-	13.0	2.4	-	-	-	-	-	-	12.8	-1.5	-	-	-	-	12.9	0.8	-	-	-	-
1936	13.0	0.8	-	-	-	-	12.9	-0.8	-	-	-	-	13.2	2.3	-	-	13.4	1.5	-	-	-	-	13.4	0.0
1937	-	-	-	-	13.7	2.2	-	-	-	-	13.9	1.5	-	-	-	-	14.1	1.4	-	-	-	-	13.9	-1.4
1938	-	-	-	-	13.8	-0.7	-	-	-	-	13.7	-0.7	-	-	-	-	13.7	0.0	-	-	-	-	13.7	0.0
1939	-	-	-	-	13.6	-0.7	-	-	-	-	13.5	-0.7	-	-	-	-	13.7	1.5	-	-	-	-	13.6	-0.7
1940	-	-	-	-	13.4	-1.5	-	-	-	-	13.6	1.5	-	-	-	-	13.7	0.7	-	-	-	-	13.7	0.0
1941	-	-	-	-	13.8	0.7	-	-	-	-	14.3	3.6	-	-	-	-	14.9	4.2	-	-	-	-	15.3	2.7
1942	-	-	-	-	16.1	5.2	-	-	-	-	16.5	2.5	-	-	-	-	16.8	1.8	-	-	-	-	17.1	1.8
1943	-	-	-	-	17.4	1.8	-	-	-	-	17.7	1.7	-	-	-	-	17.5	-1.1	-	-	-	-	17.5	0.0
1944	-	-	-	-	17.5	0.0	-	-	-	-	17.5	0.0	-	-	-	-	17.8	1.7	-	-	-	-	18.0	1.1
1945	-	-	-	-	18.0	0.0	-	-	-	-	18.3	1.7	-	-	-	-	18.3	0.0	-	-	-	-	18.5	1.1
1946	-	-	-	-	18.4	-0.5	-	-	-	-	19.0	3.3	-	-	-	-	20.4	7.4	-	-	-	-	21.3	4.4
1947	-	-	-	-	21.7	1.9	-	-	-	-	21.8	0.5	21.9	0.5	-	-	-	-	22.5	2.7	-	-	-	-
1948	23.6	4.9	-	-	-	-	23.8	0.8	-	-	-	-	24.4	2.5	-	-	-	-	24.4	0.0	-	-	-	-
1949	24.1	-1.2	-	-	-	-	24.0	-0.4	-	-	-	-	23.7	-1.2	-	-	-	-	23.5	-0.8	-	-	-	-
1950	23.6	0.4	-	-	-	-	23.7	0.4	-	-	-	-	24.1	1.7	-	-	-	-	24.8	2.9	-	-	-	-
1951	25.6	3.2	-	-	-	-	26.2	2.3	-	-	-	-	26.4	0.8	-	-	-	-	26.4	0.0	-	-	-	-
1952	26.8	1.5	-	-	-	-	26.7	-0.4	-	-	-	-	26.7	0.0	-	-	-	-	26.8	0.4	-	-	26.7	-0.4
1953	26.7	0.0	-	-	-	-	26.9	0.7	-	-	-	-	26.9	0.0	-	-	-	-	27.1	0.7	-	-	-	-
1954	26.9	-0.7	-	-	-	-	26.8	-0.4	-	-	-	-	26.9	0.4	-	-	-	-	26.9	0.0	-	-	-	-
1955	26.7	-0.7	-	-	-	-	26.6	-0.4	-	-	-	-	26.7	0.4	-	-	-	-	27.1	1.5	-	-	-	-
1956	27.1	0.0	-	-	-	-	27.1	0.0	-	-	-	-	27.7	2.2	-	-	-	-	27.9	0.7	-	-	-	-
1957	28.0	0.4	-	-	-	-	28.4	1.4	-	-	-	-	28.5	0.4	-	-	-	-	28.4	-0.4	-	-	-	-
1958	28.8	1.4	-	-	-	-	29.2	1.4	-	-	-	-	29.1	-0.3	-	-	-	-	29.0	-0.3	-	-	-	-

[Continued]

Portland, OR-WA
Consumer Price Index - All Urban Consumers
Base 1982-1984 = 100
All Items
[Continued]

For 1914-1997. Columns headed % show percentile change in the index from the previous period for which an index is available.

Year	Jan Index	%	Feb Index	%	Mar Index	%	Apr Index	%	May Index	%	Jun Index	%	Jul Index	%	Aug Index	%	Sep Index	%	Oct Index	%	Nov Index	%	Dec Index	%
1959	29.0	0.0	-	-	-	-	29.2	0.7	-	-	-	-	29.4	0.7	-	-	-	-	29.4	0.0	-	-	-	-
1960	29.7	1.0	-	-	-	-	29.8	0.3	-	-	-	-	29.8	0.0	-	-	-	-	29.7	-0.3	-	-	-	-
1961	30.1	1.3	-	-	-	-	29.9	-0.7	-	-	-	-	30.2	1.0	-	-	-	-	30.2	0.0	-	-	-	-
1962	30.0	-0.7	-	-	-	-	30.0	0.0	-	-	-	-	30.3	1.0	-	-	-	-	30.4	0.3	-	-	-	-
1963	30.5	0.3	-	-	-	-	30.7	0.7	-	-	-	-	30.9	0.7	-	-	-	-	30.9	0.0	-	-	-	-
1964	31.1	0.6	-	-	-	-	31.4	1.0	-	-	-	-	31.6	0.6	-	-	-	-	31.7	0.3	-	-	-	-
1965	31.8	0.3	-	-	-	-	32.1	0.9	-	-	-	-	32.5	1.2	-	-	-	-	32.6	0.3	-	-	-	-
1966	32.6	0.0	-	-	-	-	33.1	1.5	-	-	-	-	33.4	0.9	-	-	-	-	33.7	0.9	-	-	-	-
1967	33.9	0.6	-	-	-	-	33.9	0.0	-	-	-	-	34.2	0.9	-	-	-	-	34.5	0.9	-	-	-	-
1968	34.6	0.3	-	-	-	-	35.0	1.2	-	-	-	-	35.4	1.1	-	-	-	-	35.8	1.1	-	-	-	-
1969	36.2	1.1	-	-	-	-	37.0	2.2	-	-	-	-	37.1	0.3	-	-	-	-	37.6	1.3	-	-	-	-
1970	37.8	0.5	-	-	-	-	38.6	2.1	-	-	-	-	38.8	0.5	-	-	-	-	39.1	0.8	-	-	-	-
1971	39.2	0.3	-	-	-	-	39.2	0.0	-	-	-	-	39.7	1.3	-	-	-	-	40.1	1.0	-	-	-	-
1972	40.3	0.5	-	-	-	-	40.4	0.2	-	-	-	-	40.9	1.2	-	-	-	-	41.2	0.7	-	-	-	-
1973	41.6	1.0	-	-	-	-	42.8	2.9	-	-	-	-	43.4	1.4	-	-	-	-	44.7	3.0	-	-	-	-
1974	45.7	2.2	-	-	-	-	47.5	3.9	-	-	-	-	49.1	3.4	-	-	-	-	50.6	3.1	-	-	-	-
1975	52.1	3.0	-	-	-	-	52.7	1.2	-	-	-	-	53.7	1.9	-	-	-	-	54.4	1.3	-	-	-	-
1976	55.4	1.8	-	-	-	-	56.2	1.4	-	-	-	-	57.4	2.1	-	-	-	-	58.0	1.0	-	-	-	-
1977	58.9	1.6	-	-	-	-	60.7	3.1	-	-	-	-	62.0	2.1	-	-	-	-	62.8	1.3	-	-	-	-
1978	64.2	2.2	-	-	65.5	2.0	-	-	66.7	1.8	-	-	68.0	1.9	-	-	69.4	2.1	-	-	70.7	1.9	-	-
1979	72.3	2.3	-	-	73.6	1.8	-	-	75.4	2.4	-	-	77.7	3.1	-	-	79.3	2.1	-	-	80.8	1.9	-	-
1980	83.6	3.5	-	-	86.6	3.6	-	-	87.9	1.5	-	-	86.3	-1.8	-	-	87.8	1.7	-	-	89.5	1.9	-	-
1981	91.0	1.7	-	-	91.6	0.7	-	-	95.1	3.8	-	-	95.9	0.8	-	-	99.4	3.6	-	-	95.2	-4.2	-	-
1982	98.5	3.5	-	-	97.9	-0.6	-	-	96.4	-1.5	-	-	99.9	3.6	-	-	98.4	-1.5	-	-	97.6	-0.8	-	-
1983	97.9	0.3	-	-	97.2	-0.7	-	-	98.5	1.3	-	-	99.6	1.1	-	-	100.2	0.6	-	-	100.4	0.2	-	-
1984	100.8	0.4	-	-	101.8	1.0	-	-	103.1	1.3	-	-	102.8	-0.3	-	-	103.3	0.5	-	-	104.1	0.8	-	-
1985	104.8	0.7	-	-	105.5	0.7	-	-	106.0	0.5	-	-	106.9	0.8	-	-	107.6	0.7	-	-	108.3	0.7	-	-
1986	109.7	1.3	-	-	107.6	-1.9	-	-	107.5	-0.1	-	-	107.5	0.0	-	-	108.6	1.0	-	-	108.6	0.0	-	-
1987	-	-	-	-	-	-	-	-	-	-	114.1	5.1	-	-	-	-	-	-	-	-	-	-	116.7	2.3
1988	-	-	-	-	-	-	-	-	-	-	119.0	2.0	-	-	-	-	-	-	-	-	-	-	122.0	2.5
1989	-	-	-	-	-	-	-	-	-	-	125.3	2.7	-	-	-	-	-	-	-	-	-	-	127.4	1.7
1990	-	-	-	-	-	-	-	-	-	-	130.1	2.1	-	-	-	-	-	-	-	-	-	-	134.0	3.0
1991	-	-	-	-	-	-	-	-	-	-	136.5	1.9	-	-	-	-	-	-	-	-	-	-	139.4	2.1
1992	-	-	-	-	-	-	-	-	-	-	141.4	1.4	-	-	-	-	-	-	-	-	-	-	143.6	1.6
1993	-	-	-	-	-	-	-	-	-	-	146.0	1.7	-	-	-	-	-	-	-	-	-	-	146.7	0.5
1994	-	-	-	-	-	-	-	-	-	-	147.9	0.8	-	-	-	-	-	-	-	-	-	-	149.4	1.0
1995	-	-	-	-	-	-	-	-	-	-	151.1	1.1	-	-	-	-	-	-	-	-	-	-	152.1	0.7
1996	-	-	-	-	-	-	-	-	-	-	153.9	1.2	-	-	-	-	-	-	-	-	-	-	156.3	1.6
1997	-	-	-	-	-	-	-	-	-	-	158.9	1.7	-	-	-	-	-	-	-	-	-	-	-	-

Source: U.S. Department of Labor, Bureau of Labor Statistics, Division of Consumer Prices and Price Indexes. - indicates no data collected for period.

Portland, OR-WA
Consumer Price Index - Urban Wage Earners
Base 1982-1984 = 100
All Items

For 1914-1997. Columns headed % show percentile change in the index from the previous period for which an index is available.

Year	Jan Index	%	Feb Index	%	Mar Index	%	Apr Index	%	May Index	%	Jun Index	%	Jul Index	%	Aug Index	%	Sep Index	%	Oct Index	%	Nov Index	%	Dec Index	%
1914	-	-	-	-	-	-	-	-	-	-	-	-	-	-	-	-	-	-	-	-	-	-	10.6	-
1915	-	-	-	-	-	-	-	-	-	-	-	-	-	-	-	-	-	-	-	-	-	-	10.2	-3.8
1916	-	-	-	-	-	-	-	-	-	-	-	-	-	-	-	-	-	-	-	-	-	-	11.0	7.8
1917	-	-	-	-	-	-	-	-	-	-	-	-	-	-	-	-	-	-	-	-	-	-	13.4	21.8
1918	-	-	-	-	-	-	-	-	-	-	-	-	-	-	-	-	-	-	-	-	-	-	16.9	26.1
1919	-	-	-	-	-	-	-	-	-	-	17.6	4.1	-	-	-	-	-	-	-	-	-	-	19.3	9.7
1920	-	-	-	-	-	-	-	-	-	-	21.4	10.9	-	-	-	-	-	-	-	-	-	-	19.1	-10.7
1921	-	-	-	-	17.4	-8.9	-	-	-	-	-	-	-	-	-	-	17.3	-0.6	-	-	-	-	17.1	-1.2
1922	-	-	-	-	16.5	-3.5	-	-	-	-	16.5	0.0	-	-	-	-	16.7	1.2	-	-	-	-	16.8	0.6
1923	-	-	-	-	16.7	-0.6	-	-	-	-	16.7	0.0	-	-	-	-	16.9	1.2	-	-	-	-	17.0	0.6
1924	-	-	-	-	16.8	-1.2	-	-	-	-	16.6	-1.2	-	-	-	-	16.7	0.6	-	-	-	-	16.8	0.6
1925	-	-	-	-	-	-	-	-	-	-	16.9	0.6	-	-	-	-	-	-	-	-	-	-	16.9	0.0
1926	-	-	-	-	-	-	-	-	-	-	16.7	-1.2	-	-	-	-	-	-	-	-	-	-	16.7	0.0
1927	-	-	-	-	-	-	-	-	-	-	16.7	0.0	-	-	-	-	-	-	-	-	-	-	16.4	-1.8
1928	-	-	-	-	-	-	-	-	-	-	16.1	-1.8	-	-	-	-	-	-	-	-	-	-	16.2	0.6
1929	-	-	-	-	-	-	-	-	-	-	16.0	-1.2	-	-	-	-	-	-	-	-	-	-	16.1	0.6
1930	-	-	-	-	-	-	-	-	-	-	16.0	-0.6	-	-	-	-	-	-	-	-	-	-	15.0	-6.3
1931	-	-	-	-	-	-	-	-	-	-	14.3	-4.7	-	-	-	-	-	-	-	-	-	-	13.8	-3.5
1932	-	-	-	-	-	-	-	-	-	-	12.9	-6.5	-	-	-	-	-	-	-	-	-	-	12.6	-2.3
1933	-	-	-	-	-	-	-	-	-	-	12.1	-4.0	-	-	-	-	-	-	-	-	-	-	12.4	2.5
1934	-	-	-	-	-	-	-	-	-	-	12.6	1.6	-	-	-	-	-	-	-	-	12.9	2.4	-	-
1935	-	-	-	-	13.2	2.3	-	-	-	-	-	-	13.0	-1.5	-	-	-	-	13.1	0.8	-	-	-	-
1936	13.3	1.5	-	-	-	-	13.2	-0.8	-	-	-	-	13.4	1.5	-	-	13.6	1.5	-	-	-	-	13.6	0.0
1937	-	-	-	-	13.9	2.2	-	-	-	-	14.1	1.4	-	-	-	-	14.3	1.4	-	-	-	-	14.1	-1.4
1938	-	-	-	-	14.1	0.0	-	-	-	-	13.9	-1.4	-	-	-	-	13.9	0.0	-	-	-	-	13.9	0.0
1939	-	-	-	-	13.8	-0.7	-	-	-	-	13.7	-0.7	-	-	-	-	13.9	1.5	-	-	-	-	13.8	-0.7
1940	-	-	-	-	13.6	-1.4	-	-	-	-	13.8	1.5	-	-	-	-	13.9	0.7	-	-	-	-	13.9	0.0
1941	-	-	-	-	14.1	1.4	-	-	-	-	14.5	2.8	-	-	-	-	15.2	4.8	-	-	-	-	15.5	2.0
1942	-	-	-	-	16.3	5.2	-	-	-	-	16.7	2.5	-	-	-	-	17.1	2.4	-	-	-	-	17.4	1.8
1943	-	-	-	-	17.6	1.1	-	-	-	-	17.9	1.7	-	-	-	-	17.7	-1.1	-	-	-	-	17.8	0.6
1944	-	-	-	-	17.8	0.0	-	-	-	-	17.8	0.0	-	-	-	-	18.1	1.7	-	-	-	-	18.3	1.1
1945	-	-	-	-	18.3	0.0	-	-	-	-	18.6	1.6	-	-	-	-	18.6	0.0	-	-	-	-	18.8	1.1
1946	-	-	-	-	18.7	-0.5	-	-	-	-	19.3	3.2	-	-	-	-	20.7	7.3	-	-	-	-	21.7	4.8
1947	-	-	-	-	22.0	1.4	-	-	-	-	22.2	0.9	22.2	0.0	-	-	-	-	22.9	3.2	-	-	-	-
1948	24.0	4.8	-	-	-	-	24.1	0.4	-	-	-	-	24.8	2.9	-	-	-	-	24.7	-0.4	-	-	-	-
1949	24.5	-0.8	-	-	-	-	24.4	-0.4	-	-	-	-	24.1	-1.2	-	-	-	-	23.9	-0.8	-	-	-	-
1950	23.9	0.0	-	-	-	-	24.0	0.4	-	-	-	-	24.5	2.1	-	-	-	-	25.2	2.9	-	-	-	-
1951	26.0	3.2	-	-	-	-	26.6	2.3	-	-	-	-	26.8	0.8	-	-	-	-	26.8	0.0	-	-	-	-
1952	27.2	1.5	-	-	-	-	27.2	0.0	-	-	-	-	27.2	0.0	-	-	-	-	27.2	0.0	-	-	27.2	0.0
1953	27.2	0.0	-	-	-	-	27.3	0.4	-	-	-	-	27.3	0.0	-	-	-	-	27.5	0.7	-	-	-	-
1954	27.3	-0.7	-	-	-	-	27.2	-0.4	-	-	-	-	27.3	0.4	-	-	-	-	27.3	0.0	-	-	-	-
1955	27.2	-0.4	-	-	-	-	27.1	-0.4	-	-	-	-	27.2	0.4	-	-	-	-	27.6	1.5	-	-	-	-
1956	27.6	0.0	-	-	-	-	27.6	0.0	-	-	-	-	28.1	1.8	-	-	-	-	28.3	0.7	-	-	-	-
1957	28.5	0.7	-	-	-	-	28.8	1.1	-	-	-	-	28.9	0.3	-	-	-	-	28.9	0.0	-	-	-	-
1958	29.2	1.0	-	-	-	-	29.6	1.4	-	-	-	-	29.5	-0.3	-	-	-	-	29.5	0.0	-	-	-	-

[Continued]

Portland, OR-WA
Consumer Price Index - Urban Wage Earners
Base 1982-1984 = 100
All Items
[Continued]

For 1914-1997. Columns headed % show percentile change in the index from the previous period for which an index is available.

Year	Jan Index	%	Feb Index	%	Mar Index	%	Apr Index	%	May Index	%	Jun Index	%	Jul Index	%	Aug Index	%	Sep Index	%	Oct Index	%	Nov Index	%	Dec Index	%
1959	29.4	-0.3	-	-	-	-	29.7	1.0	-	-	-	-	29.9	0.7	-	-	-	-	29.9	0.0	-	-	-	-
1960	30.2	1.0	-	-	-	-	30.2	0.0	-	-	-	-	30.2	0.0	-	-	-	-	30.2	0.0	-	-	-	-
1961	30.5	1.0	-	-	-	-	30.4	-0.3	-	-	-	-	30.6	0.7	-	-	-	-	30.7	0.3	-	-	-	-
1962	30.5	-0.7	-	-	-	-	30.5	0.0	-	-	-	-	30.8	1.0	-	-	-	-	30.9	0.3	-	-	-	-
1963	31.0	0.3	-	-	-	-	31.2	0.6	-	-	-	-	31.4	0.6	-	-	-	-	31.4	0.0	-	-	-	-
1964	31.6	0.6	-	-	-	-	31.9	0.9	-	-	-	-	32.1	0.6	-	-	-	-	32.2	0.3	-	-	-	-
1965	32.3	0.3	-	-	-	-	32.6	0.9	-	-	-	-	33.0	1.2	-	-	-	-	33.1	0.3	-	-	-	-
1966	33.1	0.0	-	-	-	-	33.7	1.8	-	-	-	-	33.9	0.6	-	-	-	-	34.2	0.9	-	-	-	-
1967	34.4	0.6	-	-	-	-	34.5	0.3	-	-	-	-	34.7	0.6	-	-	-	-	35.0	0.9	-	-	-	-
1968	35.2	0.6	-	-	-	-	35.6	1.1	-	-	-	-	35.9	0.8	-	-	-	-	36.4	1.4	-	-	-	-
1969	36.8	1.1	-	-	-	-	37.5	1.9	-	-	-	-	37.7	0.5	-	-	-	-	38.2	1.3	-	-	-	-
1970	38.4	0.5	-	-	-	-	39.2	2.1	-	-	-	-	39.4	0.5	-	-	-	-	39.7	0.8	-	-	-	-
1971	39.9	0.5	-	-	-	-	39.8	-0.3	-	-	-	-	40.3	1.3	-	-	-	-	40.7	1.0	-	-	-	-
1972	41.0	0.7	-	-	-	-	41.1	0.2	-	-	-	-	41.5	1.0	-	-	-	-	41.8	0.7	-	-	-	-
1973	42.3	1.2	-	-	-	-	43.5	2.8	-	-	-	-	44.1	1.4	-	-	-	-	45.4	2.9	-	-	-	-
1974	46.5	2.4	-	-	-	-	48.3	3.9	-	-	-	-	49.9	3.3	-	-	-	-	51.4	3.0	-	-	-	-
1975	52.9	2.9	-	-	-	-	53.5	1.1	-	-	-	-	54.5	1.9	-	-	-	-	55.2	1.3	-	-	-	-
1976	56.2	1.8	-	-	-	-	57.0	1.4	-	-	-	-	58.3	2.3	-	-	-	-	58.9	1.0	-	-	-	-
1977	59.8	1.5	-	-	-	-	61.7	3.2	-	-	-	-	63.0	2.1	-	-	-	-	63.8	1.3	-	-	-	-
1978	65.2	2.2	-	-	66.6	2.1	-	-	68.0	2.1	-	-	69.4	2.1	-	-	70.9	2.2	-	-	72.1	1.7	-	-
1979	73.6	2.1	-	-	74.9	1.8	-	-	77.0	2.8	-	-	79.1	2.7	-	-	80.7	2.0	-	-	82.1	1.7	-	-
1980	84.5	2.9	-	-	87.3	3.3	-	-	88.8	1.7	-	-	87.5	-1.5	-	-	88.6	1.3	-	-	90.5	2.1	-	-
1981	91.9	1.5	-	-	92.6	0.8	-	-	95.8	3.5	-	-	96.9	1.1	-	-	100.2	3.4	-	-	95.9	-4.3	-	-
1982	99.1	3.3	-	-	98.5	-0.6	-	-	97.0	-1.5	-	-	100.8	3.9	-	-	99.2	-1.6	-	-	98.4	-0.8	-	-
1983	97.7	-0.7	-	-	98.2	0.5	-	-	98.5	0.3	-	-	99.4	0.9	-	-	100.0	0.6	-	-	100.5	0.5	-	-
1984	100.5	0.0	-	-	101.4	0.9	-	-	103.2	1.8	-	-	102.2	-1.0	-	-	101.9	-0.3	-	-	102.6	0.7	-	-
1985	103.2	0.6	-	-	104.0	0.8	-	-	104.5	0.5	-	-	105.2	0.7	-	-	106.0	0.8	-	-	106.6	0.6	-	-
1986	107.9	1.2	-	-	105.6	-2.1	-	-	105.2	-0.4	-	-	105.3	0.1	-	-	106.3	0.9	-	-	106.2	-0.1	-	-
1987	-	-	-	-	-	-	-	-	-	-	113.1	6.5	-	-	-	-	-	-	-	-	-	-	115.6	2.2
1988	-	-	-	-	-	-	-	-	-	-	118.0	2.1	-	-	-	-	-	-	-	-	-	-	120.9	2.5
1989	-	-	-	-	-	-	-	-	-	-	124.4	2.9	-	-	-	-	-	-	-	-	-	-	126.5	1.7
1990	-	-	-	-	-	-	-	-	-	-	129.2	2.1	-	-	-	-	-	-	-	-	-	-	132.9	2.9
1991	-	-	-	-	-	-	-	-	-	-	134.9	1.5	-	-	-	-	-	-	-	-	-	-	137.6	2.0
1992	-	-	-	-	-	-	-	-	-	-	139.6	1.5	-	-	-	-	-	-	-	-	-	-	141.7	1.5
1993	-	-	-	-	-	-	-	-	-	-	144.0	1.6	-	-	-	-	-	-	-	-	-	-	144.5	0.3
1994	-	-	-	-	-	-	-	-	-	-	145.6	0.8	-	-	-	-	-	-	-	-	-	-	147.1	1.0
1995	-	-	-	-	-	-	-	-	-	-	148.9	1.2	-	-	-	-	-	-	-	-	-	-	149.7	0.5
1996	-	-	-	-	-	-	-	-	-	-	151.6	1.3	-	-	-	-	-	-	-	-	-	-	153.6	1.3
1997	-	-	-	-	-	-	-	-	-	-	156.0	1.6	-	-	-	-	-	-	-	-	-	-	-	-

Source: U.S. Department of Labor, Bureau of Labor Statistics, Division of Consumer Prices and Price Indexes. - indicates no data collected for period.

Portland, OR-WA
Consumer Price Index - All Urban Consumers
Base 1982-1984 = 100
Food and Beverages

For 1976-1997. Columns headed % show percentile change in the index from the previous period for which an index is available.

Year	Jan Index	%	Feb Index	%	Mar Index	%	Apr Index	%	May Index	%	Jun Index	%	Jul Index	%	Aug Index	%	Sep Index	%	Oct Index	%	Nov Index	%	Dec Index	%
1976	60.1	-	-	-	-	-	60.2	0.2	-	-	-	-	61.3	1.8	-	-	-	-	61.0	-0.5	-	-	-	-
1977	61.6	1.0	-	-	-	-	64.1	4.1	-	-	-	-	65.4	2.0	-	-	-	-	65.4	0.0	-	-	-	-
1978	66.7	2.0	-	-	68.3	2.4	-	-	70.6	3.4	-	-	72.5	2.7	-	-	73.0	0.7	-	-	73.3	0.4	-	-
1979	76.1	3.8	-	-	78.2	2.8	-	-	79.6	1.8	-	-	80.4	1.0	-	-	80.7	0.4	-	-	81.8	1.4	-	-
1980	82.7	1.1	-	-	84.0	1.6	-	-	84.7	0.8	-	-	85.8	1.3	-	-	86.4	0.7	-	-	87.9	1.7	-	-
1981	89.4	1.7	-	-	91.0	1.8	-	-	91.9	1.0	-	-	93.1	1.3	-	-	93.6	0.5	-	-	93.4	-0.2	-	-
1982	94.7	1.4	-	-	95.1	0.4	-	-	95.5	0.4	-	-	99.6	4.3	-	-	98.7	-0.9	-	-	98.4	-0.3	-	-
1983	98.7	0.3	-	-	99.0	0.3	-	-	99.6	0.6	-	-	100.0	0.4	-	-	100.0	0.0	-	-	100.2	0.2	-	-
1984	101.2	1.0	-	-	102.6	1.4	-	-	103.3	0.7	-	-	103.6	0.3	-	-	103.4	-0.2	-	-	104.1	0.7	-	-
1985	104.1	0.0	-	-	105.1	1.0	-	-	105.1	0.0	-	-	105.7	0.6	-	-	106.4	0.7	-	-	106.3	-0.1	-	-
1986	108.1	1.7	-	-	107.7	-0.4	-	-	107.2	-0.5	-	-	106.8	-0.4	-	-	108.9	2.0	-	-	109.6	0.6	-	-
1987	-	-	-	-	-	-	-	-	-	-	113.0	3.1	-	-	-	-	-	-	-	-	-	-	114.4	1.2
1988	-	-	-	-	-	-	-	-	-	-	118.3	3.9	-	-	-	-	-	-	-	-	-	-	122.6	3.6
1989	-	-	-	-	-	-	-	-	-	-	127.1	3.7	-	-	-	-	-	-	-	-	-	-	129.4	1.8
1990	-	-	-	-	-	-	-	-	-	-	133.2	2.9	-	-	-	-	-	-	-	-	-	-	136.1	2.2
1991	-	-	-	-	-	-	-	-	-	-	139.9	2.8	-	-	-	-	-	-	-	-	-	-	140.7	0.6
1992	-	-	-	-	-	-	-	-	-	-	142.8	1.5	-	-	-	-	-	-	-	-	-	-	143.9	0.8
1993	-	-	-	-	-	-	-	-	-	-	146.5	1.8	-	-	-	-	-	-	-	-	-	-	146.0	-0.3
1994	-	-	-	-	-	-	-	-	-	-	148.4	1.6	-	-	-	-	-	-	-	-	-	-	149.4	0.7
1995	-	-	-	-	-	-	-	-	-	-	152.1	1.8	-	-	-	-	-	-	-	-	-	-	151.1	-0.7
1996	-	-	-	-	-	-	-	-	-	-	154.0	1.9	-	-	-	-	-	-	-	-	-	-	156.6	1.7
1997	-	-	-	-	-	-	-	-	-	-	159.1	1.6	-	-	-	-	-	-	-	-	-	-	-	-

Source: U.S. Department of Labor, Bureau of Labor Statistics, Division of Consumer Prices and Price Indexes. - indicates no data collected for period.

Portland, OR-WA
Consumer Price Index - Urban Wage Earners
Base 1982-1984 = 100
Food and Beverages

For 1976-1997. Columns headed % show percentile change in the index from the previous period for which an index is available.

Year	Jan Index	%	Feb Index	%	Mar Index	%	Apr Index	%	May Index	%	Jun Index	%	Jul Index	%	Aug Index	%	Sep Index	%	Oct Index	%	Nov Index	%	Dec Index	%
1976	59.9	-	-	-	-	-	60.1	0.3	-	-	-	-	61.1	1.7	-	-	-	-	60.8	-0.5	-	-	-	-
1977	61.5	1.2	-	-	-	-	63.9	3.9	-	-	-	-	65.2	2.0	-	-	-	-	65.2	0.0	-	-	-	-
1978	66.5	2.0	-	-	69.4	4.4	-	-	71.4	2.9	-	-	73.3	2.7	-	-	73.5	0.3	-	-	74.4	1.2	-	-
1979	77.3	3.9	-	-	79.2	2.5	-	-	81.3	2.7	-	-	81.8	0.6	-	-	82.3	0.6	-	-	82.5	0.2	-	-
1980	83.8	1.6	-	-	84.7	1.1	-	-	85.7	1.2	-	-	86.8	1.3	-	-	86.6	-0.2	-	-	88.3	2.0	-	-
1981	90.4	2.4	-	-	91.2	0.9	-	-	92.2	1.1	-	-	93.2	1.1	-	-	93.3	0.1	-	-	93.6	0.3	-	-
1982	94.8	1.3	-	-	95.0	0.2	-	-	95.7	0.7	-	-	99.4	3.9	-	-	98.5	-0.9	-	-	98.3	-0.2	-	-
1983	98.8	0.5	-	-	99.0	0.2	-	-	99.6	0.6	-	-	100.1	0.5	-	-	99.9	-0.2	-	-	100.3	0.4	-	-
1984	101.2	0.9	-	-	102.5	1.3	-	-	103.3	0.8	-	-	103.7	0.4	-	-	103.4	-0.3	-	-	104.2	0.8	-	-
1985	104.2	0.0	-	-	105.1	0.9	-	-	105.2	0.1	-	-	105.6	0.4	-	-	106.5	0.9	-	-	106.3	-0.2	-	-
1986	108.2	1.8	-	-	107.6	-0.6	-	-	107.1	-0.5	-	-	106.4	-0.7	-	-	108.6	2.1	-	-	109.4	0.7	-	-
1987	-	-	-	-	-	-	-	-	-	-	113.1	3.4	-	-	-	-	-	-	-	-	-	-	114.4	1.1
1988	-	-	-	-	-	-	-	-	-	-	118.3	3.4	-	-	-	-	-	-	-	-	-	-	122.6	3.6
1989	-	-	-	-	-	-	-	-	-	-	127.2	3.8	-	-	-	-	-	-	-	-	-	-	129.5	1.8
1990	-	-	-	-	-	-	-	-	-	-	133.3	2.9	-	-	-	-	-	-	-	-	-	-	136.2	2.2
1991	-	-	-	-	-	-	-	-	-	-	140.0	2.8	-	-	-	-	-	-	-	-	-	-	140.7	0.5
1992	-	-	-	-	-	-	-	-	-	-	142.8	1.5	-	-	-	-	-	-	-	-	-	-	143.9	0.8
1993	-	-	-	-	-	-	-	-	-	-	146.6	1.9	-	-	-	-	-	-	-	-	-	-	146.2	-0.3
1994	-	-	-	-	-	-	-	-	-	-	148.7	1.7	-	-	-	-	-	-	-	-	-	-	149.7	0.7
1995	-	-	-	-	-	-	-	-	-	-	152.1	1.6	-	-	-	-	-	-	-	-	-	-	151.4	-0.5
1996	-	-	-	-	-	-	-	-	-	-	154.3	1.9	-	-	-	-	-	-	-	-	-	-	157.0	1.7
1997	-	-	-	-	-	-	-	-	-	-	159.4	1.5	-	-	-	-	-	-	-	-	-	-	-	-

Source: U.S. Department of Labor, Bureau of Labor Statistics, Division of Consumer Prices and Price Indexes. - indicates no data collected for period.

Portland, OR-WA
Consumer Price Index - All Urban Consumers
Base 1982-1984 = 100
Housing

For 1976-1997. Columns headed % show percentile change in the index from the previous period for which an index is available.

Year	Jan Index	%	Feb Index	%	Mar Index	%	Apr Index	%	May Index	%	Jun Index	%	Jul Index	%	Aug Index	%	Sep Index	%	Oct Index	%	Nov Index	%	Dec Index	%
1976	54.3	-	-	-	-	-	55.5	2.2	-	-	-	-	56.6	2.0	-	-	-	-	57.4	1.4	-	-	-	-
1977	58.2	1.4	-	-	-	-	60.0	3.1	-	-	-	-	61.7	2.8	-	-	-	-	62.9	1.9	-	-	-	-
1978	64.7	2.9	-	-	66.6	2.9	-	-	67.5	1.4	-	-	69.1	2.4	-	-	70.8	2.5	-	-	73.0	3.1	-	-
1979	74.8	2.5	-	-	75.3	0.7	-	-	77.2	2.5	-	-	80.3	4.0	-	-	82.5	2.7	-	-	84.9	2.9	-	-
1980	88.4	4.1	-	-	92.5	4.6	-	-	94.3	1.9	-	-	90.6	-3.9	-	-	92.2	1.8	-	-	94.4	2.4	-	-
1981	96.0	1.7	-	-	95.1	-0.9	-	-	101.2	6.4	-	-	101.6	0.4	-	-	107.2	5.5	-	-	97.6	-9.0	-	-
1982	102.8	5.3	-	-	101.7	-1.1	-	-	97.9	-3.7	-	-	102.5	4.7	-	-	99.4	-3.0	-	-	97.8	-1.6	-	-
1983	98.2	0.4	-	-	97.3	-0.9	-	-	98.4	1.1	-	-	98.9	0.5	-	-	99.2	0.3	-	-	99.3	0.1	-	-
1984	99.9	0.6	-	-	100.5	0.6	-	-	101.3	0.8	-	-	101.0	-0.3	-	-	101.7	0.7	-	-	102.2	0.5	-	-
1985	103.5	1.3	-	-	103.7	0.2	-	-	103.8	0.1	-	-	105.6	1.7	-	-	105.2	-0.4	-	-	105.8	0.6	-	-
1986	108.1	2.2	-	-	106.0	-1.9	-	-	105.6	-0.4	-	-	104.7	-0.9	-	-	106.5	1.7	-	-	106.7	0.2	-	-
1987	-	-	-	-	-	-	-	-	-	-	120.0	12.5	-	-	-	-	-	-	-	-	-	-	123.0	2.5
1988	-	-	-	-	-	-	-	-	-	-	125.0	1.6	-	-	-	-	-	-	-	-	-	-	128.8	3.0
1989	-	-	-	-	-	-	-	-	-	-	131.1	1.8	-	-	-	-	-	-	-	-	-	-	133.6	1.9
1990	-	-	-	-	-	-	-	-	-	-	135.8	1.6	-	-	-	-	-	-	-	-	-	-	138.7	2.1
1991	-	-	-	-	-	-	-	-	-	-	141.2	1.8	-	-	-	-	-	-	-	-	-	-	144.2	2.1
1992	-	-	-	-	-	-	-	-	-	-	145.5	0.9	-	-	-	-	-	-	-	-	-	-	147.0	1.0
1993	-	-	-	-	-	-	-	-	-	-	148.6	1.1	-	-	-	-	-	-	-	-	-	-	149.8	0.8
1994	-	-	-	-	-	-	-	-	-	-	150.8	0.7	-	-	-	-	-	-	-	-	-	-	152.3	1.0
1995	-	-	-	-	-	-	-	-	-	-	153.7	0.9	-	-	-	-	-	-	-	-	-	-	155.3	1.0
1996	-	-	-	-	-	-	-	-	-	-	155.4	0.1	-	-	-	-	-	-	-	-	-	-	159.4	2.6
1997	-	-	-	-	-	-	-	-	-	-	163.1	2.3	-	-	-	-	-	-	-	-	-	-	-	-

Source: U.S. Department of Labor, Bureau of Labor Statistics, Division of Consumer Prices and Price Indexes. - indicates no data collected for period.

Portland, OR-WA
Consumer Price Index - Urban Wage Earners
Base 1982-1984 = 100
Housing

For 1976-1997. Columns headed % show percentile change in the index from the previous period for which an index is available.

Year	Jan Index	%	Feb Index	%	Mar Index	%	Apr Index	%	May Index	%	Jun Index	%	Jul Index	%	Aug Index	%	Sep Index	%	Oct Index	%	Nov Index	%	Dec Index	%
1976	55.1	-	-	-	-	-	56.3	2.2	-	-	-	-	57.4	2.0	-	-	-	-	58.2	1.4	-	-	-	-
1977	59.0	1.4	-	-	-	-	60.9	3.2	-	-	-	-	62.6	2.8	-	-	-	-	63.8	1.9	-	-	-	-
1978	65.7	3.0	-	-	67.5	2.7	-	-	68.5	1.5	-	-	70.0	2.2	-	-	72.0	2.9	-	-	74.1	2.9	-	-
1979	76.0	2.6	-	-	76.6	0.8	-	-	78.6	2.6	-	-	81.6	3.8	-	-	84.0	2.9	-	-	86.6	3.1	-	-
1980	90.4	4.4	-	-	94.4	4.4	-	-	96.4	2.1	-	-	92.2	-4.4	-	-	93.7	1.6	-	-	96.2	2.7	-	-
1981	97.8	1.7	-	-	97.3	-0.5	-	-	103.0	5.9	-	-	104.0	1.0	-	-	110.2	6.0	-	-	99.2	-10.0	-	-
1982	104.6	5.4	-	-	103.7	-0.9	-	-	99.5	-4.1	-	-	104.7	5.2	-	-	101.0	-3.5	-	-	99.4	-1.6	-	-
1983	97.8	-1.6	-	-	99.6	1.8	-	-	98.2	-1.4	-	-	98.3	0.1	-	-	98.8	0.5	-	-	99.4	0.6	-	-
1984	98.9	-0.5	-	-	99.4	0.5	-	-	101.2	1.8	-	-	99.5	-1.7	-	-	98.4	-1.1	-	-	98.8	0.4	-	-
1985	100.0	1.2	-	-	100.2	0.2	-	-	100.3	0.1	-	-	102.2	1.9	-	-	101.8	-0.4	-	-	102.2	0.4	-	-
1986	104.3	2.1	-	-	102.4	-1.8	-	-	102.0	-0.4	-	-	101.3	-0.7	-	-	103.0	1.7	-	-	103.1	0.1	-	-
1987	-	-	-	-	-	-	-	-	-	-	118.0	14.5	-	-	-	-	-	-	-	-	-	-	120.7	2.3
1988	-	-	-	-	-	-	-	-	-	-	122.9	1.8	-	-	-	-	-	-	-	-	-	-	126.3	2.8
1989	-	-	-	-	-	-	-	-	-	-	128.4	1.7	-	-	-	-	-	-	-	-	-	-	130.9	1.9
1990	-	-	-	-	-	-	-	-	-	-	133.3	1.8	-	-	-	-	-	-	-	-	-	-	136.0	2.0
1991	-	-	-	-	-	-	-	-	-	-	138.2	1.6	-	-	-	-	-	-	-	-	-	-	141.2	2.2
1992	-	-	-	-	-	-	-	-	-	-	142.4	0.8	-	-	-	-	-	-	-	-	-	-	143.9	1.1
1993	-	-	-	-	-	-	-	-	-	-	145.6	1.2	-	-	-	-	-	-	-	-	-	-	146.7	0.8
1994	-	-	-	-	-	-	-	-	-	-	147.6	0.6	-	-	-	-	-	-	-	-	-	-	149.0	0.9
1995	-	-	-	-	-	-	-	-	-	-	150.4	0.9	-	-	-	-	-	-	-	-	-	-	151.9	1.0
1996	-	-	-	-	-	-	-	-	-	-	151.9	0.0	-	-	-	-	-	-	-	-	-	-	155.6	2.4
1997	-	-	-	-	-	-	-	-	-	-	159.2	2.3	-	-	-	-	-	-	-	-	-	-	-	-

Source: U.S. Department of Labor, Bureau of Labor Statistics, Division of Consumer Prices and Price Indexes. - indicates no data collected for period.

Portland, OR-WA
Consumer Price Index - All Urban Consumers
Base 1982-1984 = 100
Apparel and Upkeep

For 1914-1997. Columns headed % show percentile change in the index from the previous period for which an index is available.

Year	Jan Index	%	Feb Index	%	Mar Index	%	Apr Index	%	May Index	%	Jun Index	%	Jul Index	%	Aug Index	%	Sep Index	%	Oct Index	%	Nov Index	%	Dec Index	%
1914	-	-	-	-	-	-	-	-	-	-	-	-	-	-	-	-	-	-	-	-	-	-	16.5	-
1915	-	-	-	-	-	-	-	-	-	-	-	-	-	-	-	-	-	-	-	-	-	-	17.1	3.6
1916	-	-	-	-	-	-	-	-	-	-	-	-	-	-	-	-	-	-	-	-	-	-	19.2	12.3
1917	-	-	-	-	-	-	-	-	-	-	-	-	-	-	-	-	-	-	-	-	-	-	23.9	24.5
1918	-	-	-	-	-	-	-	-	-	-	-	-	-	-	-	-	-	-	-	-	-	-	32.5	36.0
1919	-	-	-	-	-	-	-	-	-	-	35.6	9.5	-	-	-	-	-	-	-	-	-	-	40.1	12.6
1920	-	-	-	-	-	-	-	-	-	-	42.8	6.7	-	-	-	-	-	-	-	-	-	-	36.8	-14.0
1921	-	-	-	-	31.7	-13.9	-	-	-	-	-	-	-	-	-	-	28.2	-11.0	-	-	-	-	27.4	-2.8
1922	-	-	-	-	25.8	-5.8	-	-	-	-	25.4	-1.6	-	-	-	-	25.4	0.0	-	-	-	-	25.6	0.8
1923	-	-	-	-	26.5	3.5	-	-	-	-	26.7	0.8	-	-	-	-	26.8	0.4	-	-	-	-	26.8	0.0
1924	-	-	-	-	26.8	0.0	-	-	-	-	26.7	-0.4	-	-	-	-	26.3	-1.5	-	-	-	-	26.4	0.4
1925	-	-	-	-	-	-	-	-	-	-	26.1	-1.1	-	-	-	-	-	-	-	-	-	-	26.0	-0.4
1926	-	-	-	-	-	-	-	-	-	-	25.9	-0.4	-	-	-	-	-	-	-	-	-	-	25.5	-1.5
1927	-	-	-	-	-	-	-	-	-	-	25.4	-0.4	-	-	-	-	-	-	-	-	-	-	25.0	-1.6
1928	-	-	-	-	-	-	-	-	-	-	25.0	0.0	-	-	-	-	-	-	-	-	-	-	24.8	-0.8
1929	-	-	-	-	-	-	-	-	-	-	24.5	-1.2	-	-	-	-	-	-	-	-	-	-	24.5	0.0
1930	-	-	-	-	-	-	-	-	-	-	24.0	-2.0	-	-	-	-	-	-	-	-	-	-	22.8	-5.0
1931	-	-	-	-	-	-	-	-	-	-	22.0	-3.5	-	-	-	-	-	-	-	-	-	-	20.4	-7.3
1932	-	-	-	-	-	-	-	-	-	-	19.2	-5.9	-	-	-	-	-	-	-	-	-	-	18.2	-5.2
1933	-	-	-	-	-	-	-	-	-	-	18.3	0.5	-	-	-	-	-	-	-	-	-	-	20.1	9.8
1934	-	-	-	-	-	-	-	-	-	-	20.6	2.5	-	-	-	-	-	-	-	-	20.5	-0.5	-	-
1935	-	-	-	-	20.5	0.0	-	-	-	-	-	-	20.5	0.0	-	-	-	-	20.5	0.0	-	-	-	-
1936	20.6	0.5	-	-	-	-	20.7	0.5	-	-	-	-	20.6	-0.5	-	-	20.6	0.0	-	-	-	-	20.8	1.0
1937	-	-	-	-	21.3	2.4	-	-	-	-	21.5	0.9	-	-	-	-	21.8	1.4	-	-	-	-	21.7	-0.5
1938	-	-	-	-	21.5	-0.9	-	-	-	-	21.4	-0.5	-	-	-	-	21.4	0.0	-	-	-	-	21.3	-0.5
1939	-	-	-	-	21.2	-0.5	-	-	-	-	21.2	0.0	-	-	-	-	21.3	0.5	-	-	-	-	21.4	0.5
1940	-	-	-	-	21.7	1.4	-	-	-	-	21.7	0.0	-	-	-	-	21.7	0.0	-	-	-	-	21.7	0.0
1941	-	-	-	-	21.7	0.0	-	-	-	-	21.8	0.5	-	-	-	-	23.2	6.4	-	-	-	-	23.8	2.6
1942	-	-	-	-	25.8	8.4	-	-	-	-	26.2	1.6	-	-	-	-	26.5	1.1	-	-	-	-	26.5	0.0
1943	-	-	-	-	27.1	2.3	-	-	-	-	27.2	0.4	-	-	-	-	28.2	3.7	-	-	-	-	28.5	1.1
1944	-	-	-	-	29.1	2.1	-	-	-	-	29.5	1.4	-	-	-	-	29.8	1.0	-	-	-	-	29.8	0.0
1945	-	-	-	-	29.9	0.3	-	-	-	-	30.0	0.3	-	-	-	-	30.2	0.7	-	-	-	-	30.0	-0.7
1946	-	-	-	-	30.2	0.7	-	-	-	-	31.5	4.3	-	-	-	-	32.9	4.4	-	-	-	-	35.2	7.0
1947	-	-	-	-	37.5	6.5	-	-	-	-	37.9	1.1	37.5	-1.1	-	-	-	-	38.9	3.7	-	-	-	-
1948	40.0	2.8	-	-	-	-	41.3	3.2	-	-	-	-	41.0	-0.7	-	-	-	-	42.3	3.2	-	-	-	-
1949	41.1	-2.8	-	-	-	-	40.2	-2.2	-	-	-	-	39.7	-1.2	-	-	-	-	39.2	-1.3	-	-	-	-
1950	38.7	-1.3	-	-	-	-	39.0	0.8	-	-	-	-	38.8	-0.5	-	-	-	-	40.7	4.9	-	-	-	-
1951	41.4	1.7	-	-	-	-	42.0	1.4	-	-	-	-	42.5	1.2	-	-	-	-	42.9	0.9	-	-	-	-
1952	42.8	-0.2	-	-	-	-	41.8	-2.3	-	-	-	-	41.6	-0.5	-	-	-	-	42.1	1.2	-	-	-	-
1953	41.4	-1.7	-	-	-	-	41.3	-0.2	-	-	-	-	41.2	-0.2	-	-	-	-	42.4	2.9	-	-	-	-
1954	41.8	-1.4	-	-	-	-	41.5	-0.7	-	-	-	-	41.5	0.0	-	-	-	-	42.6	2.7	-	-	-	-
1955	42.1	-1.2	-	-	-	-	42.1	0.0	-	-	-	-	41.7	-1.0	-	-	-	-	42.8	2.6	-	-	-	-
1956	43.1	0.7	-	-	-	-	43.0	-0.2	-	-	-	-	42.9	-0.2	-	-	-	-	43.7	1.9	-	-	-	-
1957	43.5	-0.5	-	-	-	-	44.0	1.1	-	-	-	-	44.1	0.2	-	-	-	-	44.4	0.7	-	-	-	-
1958	44.2	-0.5	-	-	-	-	44.3	0.2	-	-	-	-	44.2	-0.2	-	-	-	-	44.1	-0.2	-	-	-	-

[Continued]

Portland, OR-WA
Consumer Price Index - All Urban Consumers
Base 1982-1984 = 100
Apparel and Upkeep
[Continued]

For 1914-1997. Columns headed % show percentile change in the index from the previous period for which an index is available.

Year	Jan Index	%	Feb Index	%	Mar Index	%	Apr Index	%	May Index	%	Jun Index	%	Jul Index	%	Aug Index	%	Sep Index	%	Oct Index	%	Nov Index	%	Dec Index	%
1959	44.0	-0.2	-	-	-	-	44.0	0.0	-	-	-	-	44.4	0.9	-	-	-	-	45.2	1.8	-	-	-	-
1960	45.2	0.0	-	-	-	-	45.5	0.7	-	-	-	-	45.5	0.0	-	-	-	-	45.7	0.4	-	-	-	-
1961	45.8	0.2	-	-	-	-	45.8	0.0	-	-	-	-	45.8	0.0	-	-	-	-	45.9	0.2	-	-	-	-
1962	45.3	-1.3	-	-	-	-	45.2	-0.2	-	-	-	-	45.1	-0.2	-	-	-	-	46.2	2.4	-	-	-	-
1963	46.2	0.0	-	-	-	-	46.4	0.4	-	-	-	-	46.2	-0.4	-	-	-	-	46.6	0.9	-	-	-	-
1964	45.9	-1.5	-	-	-	-	46.8	2.0	-	-	-	-	46.5	-0.6	-	-	-	-	47.6	2.4	-	-	-	-
1965	46.7	-1.9	-	-	-	-	47.5	1.7	-	-	-	-	47.9	0.8	-	-	-	-	50.0	4.4	-	-	-	-
1966	49.2	-1.6	-	-	-	-	49.7	1.0	-	-	-	-	49.8	0.2	-	-	-	-	50.3	1.0	-	-	-	-
1967	50.3	0.0	-	-	-	-	50.8	1.0	-	-	-	-	50.8	0.0	-	-	-	-	51.8	2.0	-	-	-	-
1968	51.1	-1.4	-	-	-	-	53.0	3.7	-	-	-	-	53.2	0.4	-	-	-	-	54.5	2.4	-	-	-	-
1969	54.2	-0.6	-	-	-	-	55.7	2.8	-	-	-	-	55.7	0.0	-	-	-	-	58.4	4.8	-	-	-	-
1970	57.2	-2.1	-	-	-	-	58.6	2.4	-	-	-	-	59.1	0.9	-	-	-	-	60.0	1.5	-	-	-	-
1971	58.2	-3.0	-	-	-	-	58.5	0.5	-	-	-	-	58.9	0.7	-	-	-	-	61.7	4.8	-	-	-	-
1972	60.3	-2.3	-	-	-	-	60.4	0.2	-	-	-	-	61.0	1.0	-	-	-	-	62.3	2.1	-	-	-	-
1973	61.9	-0.6	-	-	-	-	64.3	3.9	-	-	-	-	65.0	1.1	-	-	-	-	67.4	3.7	-	-	-	-
1974	66.3	-1.6	-	-	-	-	67.3	1.5	-	-	-	-	69.0	2.5	-	-	-	-	71.4	3.5	-	-	-	-
1975	71.3	-0.1	-	-	-	-	72.7	2.0	-	-	-	-	72.5	-0.3	-	-	-	-	74.6	2.9	-	-	-	-
1976	73.3	-1.7	-	-	-	-	75.5	3.0	-	-	-	-	76.9	1.9	-	-	-	-	79.2	3.0	-	-	-	-
1977	79.2	0.0	-	-	-	-	80.7	1.9	-	-	-	-	81.9	1.5	-	-	-	-	84.8	3.5	-	-	-	-
1978	84.0	-0.9	-	-	84.4	0.5	-	-	84.8	0.5	-	-	81.9	-3.4	-	-	86.0	5.0	-	-	85.6	-0.5	-	-
1979	83.9	-2.0	-	-	86.5	3.1	-	-	85.8	-0.8	-	-	84.5	-1.5	-	-	87.6	3.7	-	-	86.0	-1.8	-	-
1980	84.4	-1.9	-	-	88.3	4.6	-	-	87.3	-1.1	-	-	87.5	0.2	-	-	88.6	1.3	-	-	89.3	0.8	-	-
1981	89.6	0.3	-	-	93.1	3.9	-	-	92.2	-1.0	-	-	90.8	-1.5	-	-	94.6	4.2	-	-	94.4	-0.2	-	-
1982	92.8	-1.7	-	-	95.1	2.5	-	-	95.8	0.7	-	-	93.4	-2.5	-	-	96.6	3.4	-	-	98.2	1.7	-	-
1983	96.6	-1.6	-	-	98.2	1.7	-	-	98.8	0.6	-	-	98.8	0.0	-	-	103.4	4.7	-	-	101.4	-1.9	-	-
1984	100.0	-1.4	-	-	107.7	7.7	-	-	107.0	-0.6	-	-	101.4	-5.2	-	-	107.0	5.5	-	-	106.1	-0.8	-	-
1985	100.5	-5.3	-	-	110.6	10.0	-	-	113.6	2.7	-	-	103.3	-9.1	-	-	108.7	5.2	-	-	108.2	-0.5	-	-
1986	102.3	-5.5	-	-	100.7	-1.6	-	-	100.1	-0.6	-	-	96.1	-4.0	-	-	102.8	7.0	-	-	102.3	-0.5	-	-
1987	-	-	-	-	-	-	-	-	-	-	103.5	1.2	-	-	-	-	-	-	-	-	-	-	105.6	2.0
1988	-	-	-	-	-	-	-	-	-	-	105.0	-0.6	-	-	-	-	-	-	-	-	-	-	99.7	-5.0
1989	-	-	-	-	-	-	-	-	-	-	103.7	4.0	-	-	-	-	-	-	-	-	-	-	104.7	1.0
1990	-	-	-	-	-	-	-	-	-	-	105.5	0.8	-	-	-	-	-	-	-	-	-	-	109.5	3.8
1991	-	-	-	-	-	-	-	-	-	-	111.6	1.9	-	-	-	-	-	-	-	-	-	-	114.6	2.7
1992	-	-	-	-	-	-	-	-	-	-	118.8	3.7	-	-	-	-	-	-	-	-	-	-	116.7	-1.8
1993	-	-	-	-	-	-	-	-	-	-	119.5	2.4	-	-	-	-	-	-	-	-	-	-	116.9	-2.2
1994	-	-	-	-	-	-	-	-	-	-	115.5	-1.2	-	-	-	-	-	-	-	-	-	-	115.5	0.0
1995	-	-	-	-	-	-	-	-	-	-	115.2	-0.3	-	-	-	-	-	-	-	-	-	-	112.7	-2.2
1996	-	-	-	-	-	-	-	-	-	-	118.9	5.5	-	-	-	-	-	-	-	-	-	-	115.0	-3.3
1997	-	-	-	-	-	-	-	-	-	-	115.6	0.5	-	-	-	-	-	-	-	-	-	-	-	-

Source: U.S. Department of Labor, Bureau of Labor Statistics, Division of Consumer Prices and Price Indexes. - indicates no data collected for period.

Portland, OR-WA
Consumer Price Index - Urban Wage Earners
Base 1982-1984 = 100
Apparel and Upkeep

For 1914-1997. Columns headed % show percentile change in the index from the previous period for which an index is available.

Year	Jan Index	%	Feb Index	%	Mar Index	%	Apr Index	%	May Index	%	Jun Index	%	Jul Index	%	Aug Index	%	Sep Index	%	Oct Index	%	Nov Index	%	Dec Index	%
1914	-	-	-	-	-	-	-	-	-	-	-	-	-	-	-	-	-	-	-	-	-	-	16.6	-
1915	-	-	-	-	-	-	-	-	-	-	-	-	-	-	-	-	-	-	-	-	-	-	17.2	3.6
1916	-	-	-	-	-	-	-	-	-	-	-	-	-	-	-	-	-	-	-	-	-	-	19.3	12.2
1917	-	-	-	-	-	-	-	-	-	-	-	-	-	-	-	-	-	-	-	-	-	-	24.0	24.4
1918	-	-	-	-	-	-	-	-	-	-	-	-	-	-	-	-	-	-	-	-	-	-	32.7	36.3
1919	-	-	-	-	-	-	-	-	-	-	35.9	9.8	-	-	-	-	-	-	-	-	-	-	40.4	12.5
1920	-	-	-	-	-	-	-	-	-	-	43.1	6.7	-	-	-	-	-	-	-	-	-	-	37.0	-14.2
1921	-	-	-	-	31.9	-13.8	-	-	-	-	-	-	-	-	-	-	28.4	-11.0	-	-	-	-	27.6	-2.8
1922	-	-	-	-	25.9	-6.2	-	-	-	-	25.6	-1.2	-	-	-	-	25.6	0.0	-	-	-	-	25.8	0.8
1923	-	-	-	-	26.7	3.5	-	-	-	-	26.9	0.7	-	-	-	-	26.9	0.0	-	-	-	-	26.9	0.0
1924	-	-	-	-	27.0	0.4	-	-	-	-	26.9	-0.4	-	-	-	-	26.4	-1.9	-	-	-	-	26.5	0.4
1925	-	-	-	-	-	-	-	-	-	-	26.3	-0.8	-	-	-	-	-	-	-	-	-	-	26.1	-0.8
1926	-	-	-	-	-	-	-	-	-	-	26.1	0.0	-	-	-	-	-	-	-	-	-	-	25.7	-1.5
1927	-	-	-	-	-	-	-	-	-	-	25.6	-0.4	-	-	-	-	-	-	-	-	-	-	25.2	-1.6
1928	-	-	-	-	-	-	-	-	-	-	25.1	-0.4	-	-	-	-	-	-	-	-	-	-	24.9	-0.8
1929	-	-	-	-	-	-	-	-	-	-	24.7	-0.8	-	-	-	-	-	-	-	-	-	-	24.6	-0.4
1930	-	-	-	-	-	-	-	-	-	-	24.2	-1.6	-	-	-	-	-	-	-	-	-	-	23.0	-5.0
1931	-	-	-	-	-	-	-	-	-	-	22.2	-3.5	-	-	-	-	-	-	-	-	-	-	20.5	-7.7
1932	-	-	-	-	-	-	-	-	-	-	19.3	-5.9	-	-	-	-	-	-	-	-	-	-	18.3	-5.2
1933	-	-	-	-	-	-	-	-	-	-	18.4	0.5	-	-	-	-	-	-	-	-	-	-	20.3	10.3
1934	-	-	-	-	-	-	-	-	-	-	20.7	2.0	-	-	-	-	-	-	-	-	20.6	-0.5	-	-
1935	-	-	-	-	20.6	0.0	-	-	-	-	-	-	20.6	0.0	-	-	-	-	20.6	0.0	-	-	-	-
1936	20.7	0.5	-	-	-	-	20.8	0.5	-	-	-	-	20.7	-0.5	-	-	20.7	0.0	-	-	-	-	20.9	1.0
1937	-	-	-	-	21.4	2.4	-	-	-	-	21.6	0.9	-	-	-	-	21.9	1.4	-	-	-	-	21.9	0.0
1938	-	-	-	-	21.6	-1.4	-	-	-	-	21.5	-0.5	-	-	-	-	21.5	0.0	-	-	-	-	21.5	0.0
1939	-	-	-	-	21.3	-0.9	-	-	-	-	21.3	0.0	-	-	-	-	21.4	0.5	-	-	-	-	21.5	0.5
1940	-	-	-	-	21.9	1.9	-	-	-	-	21.9	0.0	-	-	-	-	21.8	-0.5	-	-	-	-	21.8	0.0
1941	-	-	-	-	21.8	0.0	-	-	-	-	22.0	0.9	-	-	-	-	23.3	5.9	-	-	-	-	24.0	3.0
1942	-	-	-	-	26.0	8.3	-	-	-	-	26.4	1.5	-	-	-	-	26.7	1.1	-	-	-	-	26.7	0.0
1943	-	-	-	-	27.3	2.2	-	-	-	-	27.4	0.4	-	-	-	-	28.4	3.6	-	-	-	-	28.6	0.7
1944	-	-	-	-	29.3	2.4	-	-	-	-	29.7	1.4	-	-	-	-	30.0	1.0	-	-	-	-	30.0	0.0
1945	-	-	-	-	30.1	0.3	-	-	-	-	30.2	0.3	-	-	-	-	30.4	0.7	-	-	-	-	30.2	-0.7
1946	-	-	-	-	30.4	0.7	-	-	-	-	31.7	4.3	-	-	-	-	33.1	4.4	-	-	-	-	35.5	7.3
1947	-	-	-	-	37.8	6.5	-	-	-	-	38.1	0.8	37.8	-0.8	-	-	-	-	39.2	3.7	-	-	-	-
1948	40.2	2.6	-	-	-	-	41.5	3.2	-	-	-	-	41.3	-0.5	-	-	-	-	42.5	2.9	-	-	-	-
1949	41.3	-2.8	-	-	-	-	40.4	-2.2	-	-	-	-	39.9	-1.2	-	-	-	-	39.4	-1.3	-	-	-	-
1950	38.9	-1.3	-	-	-	-	39.2	0.8	-	-	-	-	39.0	-0.5	-	-	-	-	41.0	5.1	-	-	-	-
1951	41.6	1.5	-	-	-	-	42.3	1.7	-	-	-	-	42.8	1.2	-	-	-	-	43.2	0.9	-	-	-	-
1952	43.1	-0.2	-	-	-	-	42.1	-2.3	-	-	-	-	41.8	-0.7	-	-	-	-	42.4	1.4	-	-	-	-
1953	41.6	-1.9	-	-	-	-	41.5	-0.2	-	-	-	-	41.5	0.0	-	-	-	-	42.6	2.7	-	-	-	-
1954	42.1	-1.2	-	-	-	-	41.8	-0.7	-	-	-	-	41.8	0.0	-	-	-	-	42.9	2.6	-	-	-	-
1955	42.3	-1.4	-	-	-	-	42.3	0.0	-	-	-	-	42.0	-0.7	-	-	-	-	43.1	2.6	-	-	-	-
1956	43.4	0.7	-	-	-	-	43.3	-0.2	-	-	-	-	43.2	-0.2	-	-	-	-	43.9	1.6	-	-	-	-
1957	43.8	-0.2	-	-	-	-	44.2	0.9	-	-	-	-	44.3	0.2	-	-	-	-	44.7	0.9	-	-	-	-
1958	44.4	-0.7	-	-	-	-	44.6	0.5	-	-	-	-	44.4	-0.4	-	-	-	-	44.4	0.0	-	-	-	-

[Continued]

Portland, OR-WA
Consumer Price Index - Urban Wage Earners
Base 1982-1984 = 100
Apparel and Upkeep
[Continued]

For 1914-1997. Columns headed % show percentile change in the index from the previous period for which an index is available.

Year	Jan Index	%	Feb Index	%	Mar Index	%	Apr Index	%	May Index	%	Jun Index	%	Jul Index	%	Aug Index	%	Sep Index	%	Oct Index	%	Nov Index	%	Dec Index	%
1959	44.2	-0.5	-	-	-	-	44.2	0.0	-	-	-	-	44.7	1.1	-	-	-	-	45.5	1.8	-	-	-	-
1960	45.5	0.0	-	-	-	-	45.8	0.7	-	-	-	-	45.8	0.0	-	-	-	-	46.0	0.4	-	-	-	-
1961	46.1	0.2	-	-	-	-	46.1	0.0	-	-	-	-	46.1	0.0	-	-	-	-	46.2	0.2	-	-	-	-
1962	45.6	-1.3	-	-	-	-	45.5	-0.2	-	-	-	-	45.4	-0.2	-	-	-	-	46.4	2.2	-	-	-	-
1963	46.4	0.0	-	-	-	-	46.7	0.6	-	-	-	-	46.4	-0.6	-	-	-	-	46.9	1.1	-	-	-	-
1964	46.2	-1.5	-	-	-	-	47.1	1.9	-	-	-	-	46.8	-0.6	-	-	-	-	47.9	2.4	-	-	-	-
1965	47.0	-1.9	-	-	-	-	47.8	1.7	-	-	-	-	48.2	0.8	-	-	-	-	50.3	4.4	-	-	-	-
1966	49.5	-1.6	-	-	-	-	50.0	1.0	-	-	-	-	50.1	0.2	-	-	-	-	50.6	1.0	-	-	-	-
1967	50.6	0.0	-	-	-	-	51.2	1.2	-	-	-	-	51.1	-0.2	-	-	-	-	52.1	2.0	-	-	-	-
1968	51.5	-1.2	-	-	-	-	53.4	3.7	-	-	-	-	53.5	0.2	-	-	-	-	54.9	2.6	-	-	-	-
1969	54.5	-0.7	-	-	-	-	56.1	2.9	-	-	-	-	56.1	0.0	-	-	-	-	58.8	4.8	-	-	-	-
1970	57.5	-2.2	-	-	-	-	59.0	2.6	-	-	-	-	59.5	0.8	-	-	-	-	60.3	1.3	-	-	-	-
1971	58.6	-2.8	-	-	-	-	58.9	0.5	-	-	-	-	59.3	0.7	-	-	-	-	62.1	4.7	-	-	-	-
1972	60.7	-2.3	-	-	-	-	60.8	0.2	-	-	-	-	61.4	1.0	-	-	-	-	62.7	2.1	-	-	-	-
1973	62.2	-0.8	-	-	-	-	64.7	4.0	-	-	-	-	65.4	1.1	-	-	-	-	67.8	3.7	-	-	-	-
1974	66.8	-1.5	-	-	-	-	67.7	1.3	-	-	-	-	69.5	2.7	-	-	-	-	71.9	3.5	-	-	-	-
1975	71.7	-0.3	-	-	-	-	73.1	2.0	-	-	-	-	72.9	-0.3	-	-	-	-	75.0	2.9	-	-	-	-
1976	73.7	-1.7	-	-	-	-	76.0	3.1	-	-	-	-	77.3	1.7	-	-	-	-	79.7	3.1	-	-	-	-
1977	79.7	0.0	-	-	-	-	81.2	1.9	-	-	-	-	82.4	1.5	-	-	-	-	85.3	3.5	-	-	-	-
1978	84.5	-0.9	-	-	84.4	-0.1	-	-	85.9	1.8	-	-	82.8	-3.6	-	-	87.7	5.9	-	-	86.7	-1.1	-	-
1979	85.4	-1.5	-	-	84.8	-0.7	-	-	85.4	0.7	-	-	85.4	0.0	-	-	90.3	5.7	-	-	90.3	0.0	-	-
1980	85.0	-5.9	-	-	87.6	3.1	-	-	86.5	-1.3	-	-	89.0	2.9	-	-	91.1	2.4	-	-	92.1	1.1	-	-
1981	92.0	-0.1	-	-	93.5	1.6	-	-	93.8	0.3	-	-	91.0	-3.0	-	-	94.5	3.8	-	-	94.4	-0.1	-	-
1982	92.5	-2.0	-	-	95.1	2.8	-	-	96.2	1.2	-	-	93.8	-2.5	-	-	96.1	2.5	-	-	97.2	1.1	-	-
1983	95.4	-1.9	-	-	98.1	2.8	-	-	99.0	0.9	-	-	98.0	-1.0	-	-	102.3	4.4	-	-	99.8	-2.4	-	-
1984	99.7	-0.1	-	-	110.1	10.4	-	-	108.8	-1.2	-	-	102.4	-5.9	-	-	107.5	5.0	-	-	106.3	-1.1	-	-
1985	99.6	-6.3	-	-	112.8	13.3	-	-	116.3	3.1	-	-	102.8	-11.6	-	-	110.6	7.6	-	-	110.0	-0.5	-	-
1986	103.6	-5.8	-	-	100.7	-2.8	-	-	99.9	-0.8	-	-	95.6	-4.3	-	-	102.5	7.2	-	-	102.0	-0.5	-	-
1987	-	-	-	-	-	-	-	-	-	-	103.9	1.9	-	-	-	-	-	-	-	-	-	-	106.8	2.8
1988	-	-	-	-	-	-	-	-	-	-	106.8	0.0	-	-	-	-	-	-	-	-	-	-	102.0	-4.5
1989	-	-	-	-	-	-	-	-	-	-	106.5	4.4	-	-	-	-	-	-	-	-	-	-	107.6	1.0
1990	-	-	-	-	-	-	-	-	-	-	108.6	0.9	-	-	-	-	-	-	-	-	-	-	112.7	3.8
1991	-	-	-	-	-	-	-	-	-	-	114.5	1.6	-	-	-	-	-	-	-	-	-	-	117.9	3.0
1992	-	-	-	-	-	-	-	-	-	-	122.1	3.6	-	-	-	-	-	-	-	-	-	-	120.8	-1.1
1993	-	-	-	-	-	-	-	-	-	-	123.5	2.2	-	-	-	-	-	-	-	-	-	-	121.9	-1.3
1994	-	-	-	-	-	-	-	-	-	-	120.6	-1.1	-	-	-	-	-	-	-	-	-	-	120.5	-0.1
1995	-	-	-	-	-	-	-	-	-	-	121.8	1.1	-	-	-	-	-	-	-	-	-	-	118.2	-3.0
1996	-	-	-	-	-	-	-	-	-	-	125.0	5.8	-	-	-	-	-	-	-	-	-	-	120.5	-3.6
1997	-	-	-	-	-	-	-	-	-	-	121.0	0.4	-	-	-	-	-	-	-	-	-	-	-	-

Source: U.S. Department of Labor, Bureau of Labor Statistics, Division of Consumer Prices and Price Indexes. - indicates no data collected for period.

Portland, OR-WA
Consumer Price Index - All Urban Consumers
Base 1982-1984 = 100
Transportation

For 1947-1997. Columns headed % show percentile change in the index from the previous period for which an index is available.

Year	Jan Index	%	Feb Index	%	Mar Index	%	Apr Index	%	May Index	%	Jun Index	%	Jul Index	%	Aug Index	%	Sep Index	%	Oct Index	%	Nov Index	%	Dec Index	%
1947	-	-	-	-	19.5		-	-	-	-	19.6	0.5	19.6	0.0	-	-	-	-	20.0	2.0	-	-	-	-
1948	20.9	4.5	-	-	-	-	21.0	0.5	-	-	-	-	22.2	5.7	-	-	-	-	22.6	1.8	-	-	-	-
1949	22.9	1.3	-	-	-	-	23.2	1.3	-	-	-	-	24.0	3.4	-	-	-	-	24.0	0.0	-	-	-	-
1950	24.2	0.8	-	-	-	-	23.7	-2.1	-	-	-	-	23.8	0.4	-	-	-	-	24.2	1.7	-	-	-	-
1951	24.4	0.8	-	-	-	-	24.8	1.6	-	-	-	-	25.0	0.8	-	-	-	-	25.5	2.0	-	-	-	-
1952	26.0	2.0	-	-	-	-	26.7	2.7	-	-	-	-	26.7	0.0	-	-	-	-	27.3	2.2	-	-	-	-
1953	27.5	0.7	-	-	-	-	27.7	0.7	-	-	-	-	27.5	-0.7	-	-	-	-	27.5	0.0	-	-	-	-
1954	27.4	-0.4	-	-	-	-	27.1	-1.1	-	-	-	-	26.6	-1.8	-	-	-	-	26.4	-0.8	-	-	-	-
1955	26.9	1.9	-	-	-	-	26.7	-0.7	-	-	-	-	26.6	-0.4	-	-	-	-	27.4	3.0	-	-	-	-
1956	27.1	-1.1	-	-	-	-	26.1	-3.7	-	-	-	-	26.7	2.3	-	-	-	-	27.6	3.4	-	-	-	-
1957	27.6	0.0	-	-	-	-	28.1	1.8	-	-	-	-	28.6	1.8	-	-	-	-	28.1	-1.7	-	-	-	-
1958	29.0	3.2	-	-	-	-	29.8	2.8	-	-	-	-	30.0	0.7	-	-	-	-	30.3	1.0	-	-	-	-
1959	29.6	-2.3	-	-	-	-	31.4	6.1	-	-	-	-	30.6	-2.5	-	-	-	-	31.8	3.9	-	-	-	-
1960	31.6	-0.6	-	-	-	-	31.1	-1.6	-	-	-	-	30.6	-1.6	-	-	-	-	30.1	-1.6	-	-	-	-
1961	31.1	3.3	-	-	-	-	29.2	-6.1	-	-	-	-	31.5	7.9	-	-	-	-	31.8	1.0	-	-	-	-
1962	31.4	-1.3	-	-	-	-	30.7	-2.2	-	-	-	-	31.5	2.6	-	-	-	-	31.1	-1.3	-	-	-	-
1963	31.0	-0.3	-	-	-	-	31.6	1.9	-	-	-	-	31.5	-0.3	-	-	-	-	31.7	0.6	-	-	-	-
1964	32.0	0.9	-	-	-	-	32.1	0.3	-	-	-	-	32.2	0.3	-	-	-	-	31.5	-2.2	-	-	-	-
1965	32.4	2.9	-	-	-	-	32.5	0.3	-	-	-	-	32.7	0.6	-	-	-	-	32.2	-1.5	-	-	-	-
1966	32.1	-0.3	-	-	-	-	32.6	1.6	-	-	-	-	32.7	0.3	-	-	-	-	33.3	1.8	-	-	-	-
1967	33.1	-0.6	-	-	-	-	33.9	2.4	-	-	-	-	34.4	1.5	-	-	-	-	34.6	0.6	-	-	-	-
1968	34.7	0.3	-	-	-	-	34.7	0.0	-	-	-	-	35.0	0.9	-	-	-	-	35.0	0.0	-	-	-	-
1969	35.6	1.7	-	-	-	-	36.1	1.4	-	-	-	-	35.9	-0.6	-	-	-	-	36.3	1.1	-	-	-	-
1970	36.7	1.1	-	-	-	-	36.9	0.5	-	-	-	-	37.2	0.8	-	-	-	-	37.1	-0.3	-	-	-	-
1971	38.1	2.7	-	-	-	-	36.9	-3.1	-	-	-	-	37.3	1.1	-	-	-	-	37.3	0.0	-	-	-	-
1972	37.5	0.5	-	-	-	-	37.1	-1.1	-	-	-	-	37.4	0.8	-	-	-	-	38.1	1.9	-	-	-	-
1973	37.9	-0.5	-	-	-	-	38.2	0.8	-	-	-	-	38.7	1.3	-	-	-	-	38.8	0.3	-	-	-	-
1974	39.8	2.6	-	-	-	-	41.1	3.3	-	-	-	-	43.2	5.1	-	-	-	-	43.6	0.9	-	-	-	-
1975	45.0	3.2	-	-	-	-	45.3	0.7	-	-	-	-	47.7	5.3	-	-	-	-	48.0	0.6	-	-	-	-
1976	49.0	2.1	-	-	-	-	49.4	0.8	-	-	-	-	52.3	5.9	-	-	-	-	53.0	1.3	-	-	-	-
1977	53.6	1.1	-	-	-	-	56.4	5.2	-	-	-	-	56.6	0.4	-	-	-	-	56.7	0.2	-	-	-	-
1978	58.3	2.8	-	-	57.9	-0.7	-	-	59.5	2.8	-	-	60.9	2.4	-	-	61.9	1.6	-	-	62.8	1.5	-	-
1979	63.3	0.8	-	-	65.9	4.1	-	-	69.2	5.0	-	-	73.0	5.5	-	-	74.1	1.5	-	-	74.5	0.5	-	-
1980	77.6	4.2	-	-	79.9	3.0	-	-	80.8	1.1	-	-	81.6	1.0	-	-	83.1	1.8	-	-	85.0	2.3	-	-
1981	85.9	1.1	-	-	88.7	3.3	-	-	90.5	2.0	-	-	92.3	2.0	-	-	94.1	2.0	-	-	96.2	2.2	-	-
1982	97.9	1.8	-	-	96.1	-1.8	-	-	96.1	0.0	-	-	99.3	3.3	-	-	99.3	0.0	-	-	98.6	-0.7	-	-
1983	97.2	-1.4	-	-	94.4	-2.9	-	-	96.9	2.6	-	-	99.9	3.1	-	-	100.7	0.8	-	-	101.2	0.5	-	-
1984	100.8	-0.4	-	-	100.8	0.0	-	-	104.6	3.8	-	-	104.4	-0.2	-	-	104.2	-0.2	-	-	105.7	1.4	-	-
1985	106.6	0.9	-	-	106.2	-0.4	-	-	107.4	1.1	-	-	108.3	0.8	-	-	109.3	0.9	-	-	110.9	1.5	-	-
1986	112.5	1.4	-	-	107.3	-4.6	-	-	106.0	-1.2	-	-	108.1	2.0	-	-	106.8	-1.2	-	-	105.1	-1.6	-	-
1987	-	-	-	-	-	-	-	-	-	-	101.2	-3.7	-	-	-	-	-	-	-	-	-	-	103.6	2.4
1988	-	-	-	-	-	-	-	-	-	-	104.1	0.5	-	-	-	-	-	-	-	-	-	-	106.4	2.2
1989	-	-	-	-	-	-	-	-	-	-	109.4	2.8	-	-	-	-	-	-	-	-	-	-	109.8	0.4
1990	-	-	-	-	-	-	-	-	-	-	111.7	1.7	-	-	-	-	-	-	-	-	-	-	117.7	5.4
1991	-	-	-	-	-	-	-	-	-	-	116.5	-1.0	-	-	-	-	-	-	-	-	-	-	117.7	1.0

[Continued]

Portland, OR-WA
Consumer Price Index - All Urban Consumers
Base 1982-1984 = 100
Transportation
[Continued]

For 1947-1997. Columns headed % show percentile change in the index from the previous period for which an index is available.

Year	Jan		Feb		Mar		Apr		May		Jun		Jul		Aug		Sep		Oct		Nov		Dec	
	Index	%	Index	%	Index	%	Index	%	Index	%	Index	%	Index	%	Index	%	Index	%	Index	%	Index	%	Index	%
1992	-	-	-	-	-	-	-	-	-	-	117.7	0.0	-	-	-	-	-	-	-	-	-	-	122.0	3.7
1993	-	-	-	-	-	-	-	-	-	-	123.8	1.5	-	-	-	-	-	-	-	-	-	-	123.6	-0.2
1994	-	-	-	-	-	-	-	-	-	-	124.7	0.9	-	-	-	-	-	-	-	-	-	-	126.7	1.6
1995	-	-	-	-	-	-	-	-	-	-	128.1	1.1	-	-	-	-	-	-	-	-	-	-	130.0	1.5
1996	-	-	-	-	-	-	-	-	-	-	133.4	2.6	-	-	-	-	-	-	-	-	-	-	133.6	0.1
1997	-	-	-	-	-	-	-	-	-	-	133.9	0.2	-	-	-	-	-	-	-	-	-	-	-	-

Source: U.S. Department of Labor, Bureau of Labor Statistics, Division of Consumer Prices and Price Indexes. - indicates no data collected for period.

Portland, OR-WA
Consumer Price Index - Urban Wage Earners
Base 1982-1984 = 100
Transportation

For 1947-1997. Columns headed % show percentile change in the index from the previous period for which an index is available.

Year	Jan Index	%	Feb Index	%	Mar Index	%	Apr Index	%	May Index	%	Jun Index	%	Jul Index	%	Aug Index	%	Sep Index	%	Oct Index	%	Nov Index	%	Dec Index	%
1947	-	-	-	-	19.5	-	-	-	-	-	19.6	0.5	19.6	0.0	-	-	-	-	20.0	2.0	-	-	-	-
1948	20.9	4.5	-	-	-	-	21.0	0.5	-	-	-	-	22.2	5.7	-	-	-	-	22.6	1.8	-	-	-	-
1949	22.9	1.3	-	-	-	-	23.2	1.3	-	-	-	-	23.9	3.0	-	-	-	-	24.0	0.4	-	-	-	-
1950	24.1	0.4	-	-	-	-	23.7	-1.7	-	-	-	-	23.8	0.4	-	-	-	-	24.2	1.7	-	-	-	-
1951	24.4	0.8	-	-	-	-	24.8	1.6	-	-	-	-	25.0	0.8	-	-	-	-	25.5	2.0	-	-	-	-
1952	26.0	2.0	-	-	-	-	26.6	2.3	-	-	-	-	26.7	0.4	-	-	-	-	27.3	2.2	-	-	-	-
1953	27.4	0.4	-	-	-	-	27.7	1.1	-	-	-	-	27.5	-0.7	-	-	-	-	27.5	0.0	-	-	-	-
1954	27.3	-0.7	-	-	-	-	27.1	-0.7	-	-	-	-	26.6	-1.8	-	-	-	-	26.4	-0.8	-	-	-	-
1955	26.9	1.9	-	-	-	-	26.7	-0.7	-	-	-	-	26.6	-0.4	-	-	-	-	27.3	2.6	-	-	-	-
1956	27.1	-0.7	-	-	-	-	26.0	-4.1	-	-	-	-	26.7	2.7	-	-	-	-	27.6	3.4	-	-	-	-
1957	27.6	0.0	-	-	-	-	28.1	1.8	-	-	-	-	28.5	1.4	-	-	-	-	28.1	-1.4	-	-	-	-
1958	29.0	3.2	-	-	-	-	29.7	2.4	-	-	-	-	30.0	1.0	-	-	-	-	30.3	1.0	-	-	-	-
1959	29.6	-2.3	-	-	-	-	31.3	5.7	-	-	-	-	30.6	-2.2	-	-	-	-	31.8	3.9	-	-	-	-
1960	31.5	-0.9	-	-	-	-	31.1	-1.3	-	-	-	-	30.6	-1.6	-	-	-	-	30.0	-2.0	-	-	-	-
1961	31.1	3.7	-	-	-	-	29.2	-6.1	-	-	-	-	31.4	7.5	-	-	-	-	31.7	1.0	-	-	-	-
1962	31.4	-0.9	-	-	-	-	30.7	-2.2	-	-	-	-	31.4	2.3	-	-	-	-	31.1	-1.0	-	-	-	-
1963	31.0	-0.3	-	-	-	-	31.6	1.9	-	-	-	-	31.4	-0.6	-	-	-	-	31.6	0.6	-	-	-	-
1964	32.0	1.3	-	-	-	-	32.1	0.3	-	-	-	-	32.2	0.3	-	-	-	-	31.5	-2.2	-	-	-	-
1965	32.4	2.9	-	-	-	-	32.4	0.0	-	-	-	-	32.7	0.9	-	-	-	-	32.2	-1.5	-	-	-	-
1966	32.1	-0.3	-	-	-	-	32.6	1.6	-	-	-	-	32.7	0.3	-	-	-	-	33.2	1.5	-	-	-	-
1967	33.1	-0.3	-	-	-	-	33.8	2.1	-	-	-	-	34.3	1.5	-	-	-	-	34.6	0.9	-	-	-	-
1968	34.7	0.3	-	-	-	-	34.7	0.0	-	-	-	-	35.0	0.9	-	-	-	-	35.0	0.0	-	-	-	-
1969	35.6	1.7	-	-	-	-	36.1	1.4	-	-	-	-	35.8	-0.8	-	-	-	-	36.3	1.4	-	-	-	-
1970	36.7	1.1	-	-	-	-	36.8	0.3	-	-	-	-	37.1	0.8	-	-	-	-	37.1	0.0	-	-	-	-
1971	38.1	2.7	-	-	-	-	36.9	-3.1	-	-	-	-	37.2	0.8	-	-	-	-	37.3	0.3	-	-	-	-
1972	37.5	0.5	-	-	-	-	37.1	-1.1	-	-	-	-	37.4	0.8	-	-	-	-	38.1	1.9	-	-	-	-
1973	37.9	-0.5	-	-	-	-	38.2	0.8	-	-	-	-	38.7	1.3	-	-	-	-	38.7	0.0	-	-	-	-
1974	39.8	2.8	-	-	-	-	41.1	3.3	-	-	-	-	43.2	5.1	-	-	-	-	43.6	0.9	-	-	-	-
1975	45.0	3.2	-	-	-	-	45.2	0.4	-	-	-	-	47.6	5.3	-	-	-	-	48.0	0.8	-	-	-	-
1976	49.0	2.1	-	-	-	-	49.4	0.8	-	-	-	-	52.2	5.7	-	-	-	-	52.9	1.3	-	-	-	-
1977	53.6	1.3	-	-	-	-	56.4	5.2	-	-	-	-	56.6	0.4	-	-	-	-	56.6	0.0	-	-	-	-
1978	58.2	2.8	-	-	58.0	-0.3	-	-	60.7	4.7	-	-	62.3	2.6	-	-	63.3	1.6	-	-	63.8	0.8	-	-
1979	64.2	0.6	-	-	66.8	4.0	-	-	69.8	4.5	-	-	72.8	4.3	-	-	73.5	1.0	-	-	74.2	1.0	-	-
1980	76.3	2.8	-	-	78.5	2.9	-	-	79.8	1.7	-	-	80.8	1.3	-	-	82.1	1.6	-	-	83.9	2.2	-	-
1981	85.8	2.3	-	-	88.5	3.1	-	-	90.3	2.0	-	-	92.1	2.0	-	-	93.6	1.6	-	-	95.2	1.7	-	-
1982	96.8	1.7	-	-	95.1	-1.8	-	-	95.2	0.1	-	-	98.5	3.5	-	-	98.5	0.0	-	-	98.1	-0.4	-	-
1983	96.7	-1.4	-	-	94.0	-2.8	-	-	96.7	2.9	-	-	99.9	3.3	-	-	100.9	1.0	-	-	101.7	0.8	-	-
1984	101.4	-0.3	-	-	101.5	0.1	-	-	105.5	3.9	-	-	105.3	-0.2	-	-	105.1	-0.2	-	-	106.5	1.3	-	-
1985	107.4	0.8	-	-	107.0	-0.4	-	-	108.2	1.1	-	-	108.9	0.6	-	-	109.9	0.9	-	-	111.3	1.3	-	-
1986	112.7	1.3	-	-	107.6	-4.5	-	-	106.1	-1.4	-	-	108.0	1.8	-	-	106.8	-1.1	-	-	105.2	-1.5	-	-
1987	-	-	-	-	-	-	-	-	-	-	102.2	-2.9	-	-	-	-	-	-	-	-	-	-	105.2	2.9
1988	-	-	-	-	-	-	-	-	-	-	106.0	0.8	-	-	-	-	-	-	-	-	-	-	108.1	2.0
1989	-	-	-	-	-	-	-	-	-	-	111.6	3.2	-	-	-	-	-	-	-	-	-	-	112.1	0.4
1990	-	-	-	-	-	-	-	-	-	-	113.4	1.2	-	-	-	-	-	-	-	-	-	-	120.0	5.8
1991	-	-	-	-	-	-	-	-	-	-	117.7	-1.9	-	-	-	-	-	-	-	-	-	-	119.4	1.4

[Continued]

Portland, OR-WA
Consumer Price Index - Urban Wage Earners
Base 1982-1984 = 100
Transportation
[Continued]

For 1947-1997. Columns headed % show percentile change in the index from the previous period for which an index is available.

Year	Jan		Feb		Mar		Apr		May		Jun		Jul		Aug		Sep		Oct		Nov		Dec	
	Index	%	Index	%	Index	%	Index	%	Index	%	Index	%	Index	%	Index	%	Index	%	Index	%	Index	%	Index	%
1992	-	-	-	-	-	-	-	-	-	-	119.6	0.2	-	-	-	-	-	-	-	-	-	-	124.2	3.8
1993	-	-	-	-	-	-	-	-	-	-	125.5	1.0	-	-	-	-	-	-	-	-	-	-	125.9	0.3
1994	-	-	-	-	-	-	-	-	-	-	126.0	0.1	-	-	-	-	-	-	-	-	-	-	129.7	2.9
1995	-	-	-	-	-	-	-	-	-	-	131.3	1.2	-	-	-	-	-	-	-	-	-	-	133.0	1.3
1996	-	-	-	-	-	-	-	-	-	-	136.6	2.7	-	-	-	-	-	-	-	-	-	-	136.2	-0.3
1997	-	-	-	-	-	-	-	-	-	-	136.3	0.1	-	-	-	-	-	-	-	-	-	-	-	-

Source: U.S. Department of Labor, Bureau of Labor Statistics, Division of Consumer Prices and Price Indexes. - indicates no data collected for period.

Portland, OR-WA
Consumer Price Index - All Urban Consumers
Base 1982-1984 = 100
Medical Care

For 1947-1997. Columns headed % show percentile change in the index from the previous period for which an index is available.

Year	Jan Index	%	Feb Index	%	Mar Index	%	Apr Index	%	May Index	%	Jun Index	%	Jul Index	%	Aug Index	%	Sep Index	%	Oct Index	%	Nov Index	%	Dec Index	%
1947	-	-	-	-	14.1	-	-	-	-	-	14.1	0.0	14.1	0.0	-	-	-	-	14.5	2.8	-	-	-	-
1948	14.6	0.7	-	-	-	-	14.6	0.0	-	-	-	-	14.8	1.4	-	-	-	-	14.8	0.0	-	-	-	-
1949	14.9	0.7	-	-	-	-	15.0	0.7	-	-	-	-	15.0	0.0	-	-	-	-	15.1	0.7	-	-	-	-
1950	15.1	0.0	-	-	-	-	15.1	0.0	-	-	-	-	15.6	3.3	-	-	-	-	15.8	1.3	-	-	-	-
1951	15.8	0.0	-	-	-	-	16.2	2.5	-	-	-	-	16.2	0.0	-	-	-	-	16.7	3.1	-	-	-	-
1952	16.8	0.6	-	-	-	-	17.0	1.2	-	-	-	-	17.2	1.2	-	-	-	-	17.2	0.0	-	-	-	-
1953	17.2	0.0	-	-	-	-	17.3	0.6	-	-	-	-	17.5	1.2	-	-	-	-	17.7	1.1	-	-	-	-
1954	17.7	0.0	-	-	-	-	17.8	0.6	-	-	-	-	17.9	0.6	-	-	-	-	18.0	0.6	-	-	-	-
1955	18.4	2.2	-	-	-	-	18.5	0.5	-	-	-	-	18.4	-0.5	-	-	-	-	18.9	2.7	-	-	-	-
1956	18.9	0.0	-	-	-	-	19.0	0.5	-	-	-	-	19.2	1.1	-	-	-	-	19.5	1.6	-	-	-	-
1957	20.0	2.6	-	-	-	-	20.2	1.0	-	-	-	-	20.3	0.5	-	-	-	-	20.4	0.5	-	-	-	-
1958	20.5	0.5	-	-	-	-	20.6	0.5	-	-	-	-	20.6	0.0	-	-	-	-	20.7	0.5	-	-	-	-
1959	20.7	0.0	-	-	-	-	20.7	0.0	-	-	-	-	20.8	0.5	-	-	-	-	20.8	0.0	-	-	-	-
1960	20.8	0.0	-	-	-	-	21.8	4.8	-	-	-	-	21.9	0.5	-	-	-	-	22.2	1.4	-	-	-	-
1961	22.2	0.0	-	-	-	-	22.4	0.9	-	-	-	-	22.6	0.9	-	-	-	-	22.5	-0.4	-	-	-	-
1962	22.3	-0.9	-	-	-	-	22.4	0.4	-	-	-	-	22.5	0.4	-	-	-	-	22.6	0.4	-	-	-	-
1963	22.8	0.9	-	-	-	-	22.8	0.0	-	-	-	-	23.0	0.9	-	-	-	-	23.4	1.7	-	-	-	-
1964	23.4	0.0	-	-	-	-	24.1	3.0	-	-	-	-	24.7	2.5	-	-	-	-	24.8	0.4	-	-	-	-
1965	24.9	0.4	-	-	-	-	25.0	0.4	-	-	-	-	25.3	1.2	-	-	-	-	25.3	0.0	-	-	-	-
1966	25.6	1.2	-	-	-	-	25.7	0.4	-	-	-	-	25.9	0.8	-	-	-	-	26.4	1.9	-	-	-	-
1967	27.1	2.7	-	-	-	-	27.2	0.4	-	-	-	-	27.7	1.8	-	-	-	-	28.2	1.8	-	-	-	-
1968	28.8	2.1	-	-	-	-	28.8	0.0	-	-	-	-	29.0	0.7	-	-	-	-	29.6	2.1	-	-	-	-
1969	30.0	1.4	-	-	-	-	30.5	1.7	-	-	-	-	31.0	1.6	-	-	-	-	31.2	0.6	-	-	-	-
1970	32.1	2.9	-	-	-	-	32.6	1.6	-	-	-	-	33.1	1.5	-	-	-	-	33.2	0.3	-	-	-	-
1971	34.1	2.7	-	-	-	-	34.2	0.3	-	-	-	-	34.2	0.0	-	-	-	-	34.1	-0.3	-	-	-	-
1972	34.6	1.5	-	-	-	-	34.9	0.9	-	-	-	-	35.3	1.1	-	-	-	-	36.0	2.0	-	-	-	-
1973	36.3	0.8	-	-	-	-	37.3	2.8	-	-	-	-	37.3	0.0	-	-	-	-	38.6	3.5	-	-	-	-
1974	39.3	1.8	-	-	-	-	40.1	2.0	-	-	-	-	42.1	5.0	-	-	-	-	42.6	1.2	-	-	-	-
1975	44.1	3.5	-	-	-	-	45.0	2.0	-	-	-	-	46.6	3.6	-	-	-	-	46.9	0.6	-	-	-	-
1976	48.7	3.8	-	-	-	-	49.0	0.6	-	-	-	-	50.3	2.7	-	-	-	-	50.9	1.2	-	-	-	-
1977	53.3	4.7	-	-	-	-	54.4	2.1	-	-	-	-	55.7	2.4	-	-	-	-	56.1	0.7	-	-	-	-
1978	57.6	2.7	-	-	59.2	2.8	-	-	59.7	0.8	-	-	60.6	1.5	-	-	61.0	0.7	-	-	61.8	1.3	-	-
1979	63.5	2.8	-	-	64.0	0.8	-	-	64.5	0.8	-	-	65.6	1.7	-	-	67.2	2.4	-	-	68.8	2.4	-	-
1980	70.6	2.6	-	-	73.0	3.4	-	-	73.7	1.0	-	-	74.0	0.4	-	-	76.1	2.8	-	-	76.6	0.7	-	-
1981	78.6	2.6	-	-	79.3	0.9	-	-	81.2	2.4	-	-	84.5	4.1	-	-	85.3	0.9	-	-	88.0	3.2	-	-
1982	89.4	1.6	-	-	91.0	1.8	-	-	92.3	1.4	-	-	94.3	2.2	-	-	95.4	1.2	-	-	96.7	1.4	-	-
1983	99.0	2.4	-	-	99.8	0.8	-	-	100.3	0.5	-	-	100.7	0.4	-	-	100.4	-0.3	-	-	102.1	1.7	-	-
1984	104.7	2.5	-	-	105.0	0.3	-	-	104.8	-0.2	-	-	105.9	1.0	-	-	106.4	0.5	-	-	107.1	0.7	-	-
1985	108.7	1.5	-	-	109.0	0.3	-	-	109.6	0.6	-	-	112.0	2.2	-	-	112.3	0.3	-	-	114.0	1.5	-	-
1986	116.0	1.8	-	-	116.9	0.8	-	-	119.4	2.1	-	-	120.1	0.6	-	-	119.7	-0.3	-	-	121.1	1.2	-	-
1987	-	-	-	-	-	-	-	-	-	-	126.1	4.1	-	-	-	-	-	-	-	-	-	-	131.4	4.2
1988	-	-	-	-	-	-	-	-	-	-	134.2	2.1	-	-	-	-	-	-	-	-	-	-	139.5	3.9
1989	-	-	-	-	-	-	-	-	-	-	145.1	4.0	-	-	-	-	-	-	-	-	-	-	150.6	3.8
1990	-	-	-	-	-	-	-	-	-	-	157.5	4.6	-	-	-	-	-	-	-	-	-	-	163.5	3.8
1991	-	-	-	-	-	-	-	-	-	-	168.4	3.0	-	-	-	-	-	-	-	-	-	-	177.4	5.3

[Continued]

Portland, OR-WA
Consumer Price Index - All Urban Consumers
Base 1982-1984 = 100
Medical Care
[Continued]

For 1947-1997. Columns headed % show percentile change in the index from the previous period for which an index is available.

Year	Jan		Feb		Mar		Apr		May		Jun		Jul		Aug		Sep		Oct		Nov		Dec	
	Index	%	Index	%	Index	%	Index	%	Index	%	Index	%	Index	%	Index	%	Index	%	Index	%	Index	%	Index	%
1992	-	-	-	-	-	-	-	-	-	-	183.8	3.6	-	-	-	-	-	-	-	-	-	-	190.2	3.5
1993	-	-	-	-	-	-	-	-	-	-	196.3	3.2	-	-	-	-	-	-	-	-	-	-	201.8	2.8
1994	-	-	-	-	-	-	-	-	-	-	203.2	0.7	-	-	-	-	-	-	-	-	-	-	205.5	1.1
1995	-	-	-	-	-	-	-	-	-	-	208.2	1.3	-	-	-	-	-	-	-	-	-	-	209.8	0.8
1996	-	-	-	-	-	-	-	-	-	-	213.1	1.6	-	-	-	-	-	-	-	-	-	-	215.9	1.3
1997	-	-	-	-	-	-	-	-	-	-	220.2	2.0	-	-	-	-	-	-	-	-	-	-	-	-

Source: U.S. Department of Labor, Bureau of Labor Statistics, Division of Consumer Prices and Price Indexes. - indicates no data collected for period.

Portland, OR-WA
Consumer Price Index - Urban Wage Earners
Base 1982-1984 = 100
Medical Care

For 1947-1997. Columns headed % show percentile change in the index from the previous period for which an index is available.

Year	Jan Index	%	Feb Index	%	Mar Index	%	Apr Index	%	May Index	%	Jun Index	%	Jul Index	%	Aug Index	%	Sep Index	%	Oct Index	%	Nov Index	%	Dec Index	%
1947	-	-	-	-	15.7	-	-	-	-	-	15.7	0.0	15.7	0.0	-	-	-	-	16.2	3.2	-	-	-	-
1948	16.2	0.0	-	-	-	-	16.3	0.6	-	-	-	-	16.5	1.2	-	-	-	-	16.5	0.0	-	-	-	-
1949	16.6	0.6	-	-	-	-	16.7	0.6	-	-	-	-	16.7	0.0	-	-	-	-	16.8	0.6	-	-	-	-
1950	16.8	0.0	-	-	-	-	16.8	0.0	-	-	-	-	17.3	3.0	-	-	-	-	17.6	1.7	-	-	-	-
1951	17.6	0.0	-	-	-	-	18.1	2.8	-	-	-	-	18.1	0.0	-	-	-	-	18.6	2.8	-	-	-	-
1952	18.7	0.5	-	-	-	-	18.9	1.1	-	-	-	-	19.1	1.1	-	-	-	-	19.1	0.0	-	-	-	-
1953	19.2	0.5	-	-	-	-	19.2	0.0	-	-	-	-	19.5	1.6	-	-	-	-	19.7	1.0	-	-	-	-
1954	19.7	0.0	-	-	-	-	19.8	0.5	-	-	-	-	19.9	0.5	-	-	-	-	20.0	0.5	-	-	-	-
1955	20.4	2.0	-	-	-	-	20.6	1.0	-	-	-	-	20.5	-0.5	-	-	-	-	21.0	2.4	-	-	-	-
1956	21.0	0.0	-	-	-	-	21.2	1.0	-	-	-	-	21.4	0.9	-	-	-	-	21.7	1.4	-	-	-	-
1957	22.3	2.8	-	-	-	-	22.5	0.9	-	-	-	-	22.7	0.9	-	-	-	-	22.7	0.0	-	-	-	-
1958	22.8	0.4	-	-	-	-	22.9	0.4	-	-	-	-	22.9	0.0	-	-	-	-	23.0	0.4	-	-	-	-
1959	23.0	0.0	-	-	-	-	23.0	0.0	-	-	-	-	23.2	0.9	-	-	-	-	23.2	0.0	-	-	-	-
1960	23.2	0.0	-	-	-	-	24.3	4.7	-	-	-	-	24.4	0.4	-	-	-	-	24.7	1.2	-	-	-	-
1961	24.7	0.0	-	-	-	-	25.0	1.2	-	-	-	-	25.2	0.8	-	-	-	-	25.1	-0.4	-	-	-	-
1962	24.8	-1.2	-	-	-	-	24.9	0.4	-	-	-	-	25.1	0.8	-	-	-	-	25.2	0.4	-	-	-	-
1963	25.4	0.8	-	-	-	-	25.4	0.0	-	-	-	-	25.6	0.8	-	-	-	-	26.0	1.6	-	-	-	-
1964	26.1	0.4	-	-	-	-	26.8	2.7	-	-	-	-	27.5	2.6	-	-	-	-	27.6	0.4	-	-	-	-
1965	27.7	0.4	-	-	-	-	27.8	0.4	-	-	-	-	28.2	1.4	-	-	-	-	28.2	0.0	-	-	-	-
1966	28.5	1.1	-	-	-	-	28.6	0.4	-	-	-	-	28.8	0.7	-	-	-	-	29.4	2.1	-	-	-	-
1967	30.2	2.7	-	-	-	-	30.3	0.3	-	-	-	-	30.9	2.0	-	-	-	-	31.4	1.6	-	-	-	-
1968	32.1	2.2	-	-	-	-	32.1	0.0	-	-	-	-	32.3	0.6	-	-	-	-	33.0	2.2	-	-	-	-
1969	33.4	1.2	-	-	-	-	34.0	1.8	-	-	-	-	34.5	1.5	-	-	-	-	34.8	0.9	-	-	-	-
1970	35.7	2.6	-	-	-	-	36.3	1.7	-	-	-	-	36.9	1.7	-	-	-	-	36.9	0.0	-	-	-	-
1971	37.9	2.7	-	-	-	-	38.1	0.5	-	-	-	-	38.1	0.0	-	-	-	-	37.9	-0.5	-	-	-	-
1972	38.6	1.8	-	-	-	-	38.8	0.5	-	-	-	-	39.4	1.5	-	-	-	-	40.0	1.5	-	-	-	-
1973	40.4	1.0	-	-	-	-	41.5	2.7	-	-	-	-	41.5	0.0	-	-	-	-	42.9	3.4	-	-	-	-
1974	43.8	2.1	-	-	-	-	44.6	1.8	-	-	-	-	46.8	4.9	-	-	-	-	47.4	1.3	-	-	-	-
1975	49.1	3.6	-	-	-	-	50.1	2.0	-	-	-	-	51.9	3.6	-	-	-	-	52.2	0.6	-	-	-	-
1976	54.2	3.8	-	-	-	-	54.5	0.6	-	-	-	-	56.0	2.8	-	-	-	-	56.6	1.1	-	-	-	-
1977	59.4	4.9	-	-	-	-	60.5	1.9	-	-	-	-	62.0	2.5	-	-	-	-	62.4	0.6	-	-	-	-
1978	64.1	2.7	-	-	65.1	1.6	-	-	65.3	0.3	-	-	66.2	1.4	-	-	66.9	1.1	-	-	68.0	1.6	-	-
1979	68.8	1.2	-	-	70.2	2.0	-	-	71.4	1.7	-	-	72.6	1.7	-	-	72.7	0.1	-	-	73.8	1.5	-	-
1980	74.8	1.4	-	-	76.0	1.6	-	-	77.7	2.2	-	-	78.2	0.6	-	-	78.7	0.6	-	-	79.2	0.6	-	-
1981	79.7	0.6	-	-	80.5	1.0	-	-	82.4	2.4	-	-	85.3	3.5	-	-	84.8	-0.6	-	-	87.9	3.7	-	-
1982	89.5	1.8	-	-	91.0	1.7	-	-	92.4	1.5	-	-	94.6	2.4	-	-	95.7	1.2	-	-	97.0	1.4	-	-
1983	99.5	2.6	-	-	100.2	0.7	-	-	100.7	0.5	-	-	100.9	0.2	-	-	100.6	-0.3	-	-	102.0	1.4	-	-
1984	104.4	2.4	-	-	104.6	0.2	-	-	104.3	-0.3	-	-	105.4	1.1	-	-	106.1	0.7	-	-	106.6	0.5	-	-
1985	108.3	1.6	-	-	108.7	0.4	-	-	109.2	0.5	-	-	111.9	2.5	-	-	112.4	0.4	-	-	114.1	1.5	-	-
1986	115.8	1.5	-	-	116.8	0.9	-	-	119.0	1.9	-	-	119.6	0.5	-	-	119.0	-0.5	-	-	120.6	1.3	-	-
1987	-	-	-	-	-	-	-	-	-	-	127.2	5.5	-	-	-	-	-	-	-	-	-	-	132.7	4.3
1988	-	-	-	-	-	-	-	-	-	-	135.5	2.1	-	-	-	-	-	-	-	-	-	-	140.7	3.8
1989	-	-	-	-	-	-	-	-	-	-	146.4	4.1	-	-	-	-	-	-	-	-	-	-	151.6	3.6
1990	-	-	-	-	-	-	-	-	-	-	158.0	4.2	-	-	-	-	-	-	-	-	-	-	163.5	3.5
1991	-	-	-	-	-	-	-	-	-	-	167.9	2.7	-	-	-	-	-	-	-	-	-	-	176.3	5.0

[Continued]

Portland, OR-WA
Consumer Price Index - Urban Wage Earners
Base 1982-1984 = 100
Medical Care
[Continued]

For 1947-1997. Columns headed % show percentile change in the index from the previous period for which an index is available.

Year	Jan		Feb		Mar		Apr		May		Jun		Jul		Aug		Sep		Oct		Nov		Dec	
	Index	%	Index	%	Index	%	Index	%	Index	%	Index	%	Index	%	Index	%	Index	%	Index	%	Index	%	Index	%
1992	-	-	-	-	-	-	-	-	-	-	183.0	3.8	-	-	-	-	-	-	-	-	-	-	189.7	3.7
1993	-	-	-	-	-	-	-	-	-	-	195.4	3.0	-	-	-	-	-	-	-	-	-	-	200.4	2.6
1994	-	-	-	-	-	-	-	-	-	-	201.4	0.5	-	-	-	-	-	-	-	-	-	-	203.4	1.0
1995	-	-	-	-	-	-	-	-	-	-	206.1	1.3	-	-	-	-	-	-	-	-	-	-	207.6	0.7
1996	-	-	-	-	-	-	-	-	-	-	211.0	1.6	-	-	-	-	-	-	-	-	-	-	213.5	1.2
1997	-	-	-	-	-	-	-	-	-	-	217.8	2.0	-	-	-	-	-	-	-	-	-	-	-	-

Source: U.S. Department of Labor, Bureau of Labor Statistics, Division of Consumer Prices and Price Indexes. - indicates no data collected for period.

Portland, OR-WA
Consumer Price Index - All Urban Consumers
Base 1982-1984 = 100
Entertainment

For 1976-1997. Columns headed % show percentile change in the index from the previous period for which an index is available.

Year	Jan Index	%	Feb Index	%	Mar Index	%	Apr Index	%	May Index	%	Jun Index	%	Jul Index	%	Aug Index	%	Sep Index	%	Oct Index	%	Nov Index	%	Dec Index	%
1976	68.4	-	-	-	-	-	68.4	0.0	-	-	-	-	68.3	-0.1	-	-	-	-	69.4	1.6	-	-	-	-
1977	70.8	2.0	-	-	-	-	71.2	0.6	-	-	-	-	70.4	-1.1	-	-	-	-	72.3	2.7	-	-	-	-
1978	72.9	0.8	-	-	74.5	2.2	-	-	75.7	1.6	-	-	76.8	1.5	-	-	76.9	0.1	-	-	77.1	0.3	-	-
1979	78.2	1.4	-	-	80.6	3.1	-	-	81.6	1.2	-	-	81.0	-0.7	-	-	80.7	-0.4	-	-	80.7	0.0	-	-
1980	83.7	3.7	-	-	87.6	4.7	-	-	87.9	0.3	-	-	87.0	-1.0	-	-	87.5	0.6	-	-	86.3	-1.4	-	-
1981	91.2	5.7	-	-	92.3	1.2	-	-	90.1	-2.4	-	-	88.9	-1.3	-	-	89.5	0.7	-	-	90.2	0.8	-	-
1982	92.9	3.0	-	-	93.6	0.8	-	-	96.4	3.0	-	-	96.6	0.2	-	-	94.7	-2.0	-	-	93.5	-1.3	-	-
1983	98.1	4.9	-	-	100.2	2.1	-	-	102.5	2.3	-	-	102.1	-0.4	-	-	102.8	0.7	-	-	101.6	-1.2	-	-
1984	102.3	0.7	-	-	103.0	0.7	-	-	104.0	1.0	-	-	103.3	-0.7	-	-	103.1	-0.2	-	-	105.9	2.7	-	-
1985	107.7	1.7	-	-	109.2	1.4	-	-	108.5	-0.6	-	-	111.3	2.6	-	-	110.8	-0.4	-	-	109.7	-1.0	-	-
1986	109.0	-0.6	-	-	107.1	-1.7	-	-	110.7	3.4	-	-	112.4	1.5	-	-	112.2	-0.2	-	-	114.3	1.9	-	-
1987	-	-	-	-	-	-	-	-	-	-	121.0	5.9	-	-	-	-	-	-	-	-	-	-	122.3	1.1
1988	-	-	-	-	-	-	-	-	-	-	127.9	4.6	-	-	-	-	-	-	-	-	-	-	130.3	1.9
1989	-	-	-	-	-	-	-	-	-	-	133.8	2.7	-	-	-	-	-	-	-	-	-	-	132.5	-1.0
1990	-	-	-	-	-	-	-	-	-	-	136.7	3.2	-	-	-	-	-	-	-	-	-	-	144.7	5.9
1991	-	-	-	-	-	-	-	-	-	-	149.8	3.5	-	-	-	-	-	-	-	-	-	-	154.9	3.4
1992	-	-	-	-	-	-	-	-	-	-	156.6	1.1	-	-	-	-	-	-	-	-	-	-	156.5	-0.1
1993	-	-	-	-	-	-	-	-	-	-	161.0	2.9	-	-	-	-	-	-	-	-	-	-	163.6	1.6
1994	-	-	-	-	-	-	-	-	-	-	165.0	0.9	-	-	-	-	-	-	-	-	-	-	164.1	-0.5
1995	-	-	-	-	-	-	-	-	-	-	166.2	1.3	-	-	-	-	-	-	-	-	-	-	166.3	0.1
1996	-	-	-	-	-	-	-	-	-	-	166.9	0.4	-	-	-	-	-	-	-	-	-	-	166.7	-0.1
1997	-	-	-	-	-	-	-	-	-	-	167.8	0.7	-	-	-	-	-	-	-	-	-	-	-	-

Source: U.S. Department of Labor, Bureau of Labor Statistics, Division of Consumer Prices and Price Indexes. - indicates no data collected for period.

Portland, OR-WA
Consumer Price Index - Urban Wage Earners
Base 1982-1984 = 100
Entertainment

For 1976-1997. Columns headed % show percentile change in the index from the previous period for which an index is available.

Year	Jan Index	%	Feb Index	%	Mar Index	%	Apr Index	%	May Index	%	Jun Index	%	Jul Index	%	Aug Index	%	Sep Index	%	Oct Index	%	Nov Index	%	Dec Index	%
1976	75.2	-	-	-	-	-	75.3	0.1	-	-	-	-	75.2	-0.1	-	-	-	-	76.3	1.5	-	-	-	-
1977	77.9	2.1	-	-	-	-	78.4	0.6	-	-	-	-	77.4	-1.3	-	-	-	-	79.5	2.7	-	-	-	-
1978	80.2	0.9	-	-	81.1	1.1	-	-	81.1	0.0	-	-	83.0	2.3	-	-	83.9	1.1	-	-	84.6	0.8	-	-
1979	84.9	0.4	-	-	85.4	0.6	-	-	88.2	3.3	-	-	86.7	-1.7	-	-	87.4	0.8	-	-	87.6	0.2	-	-
1980	88.2	0.7	-	-	94.8	7.5	-	-	96.1	1.4	-	-	96.2	0.1	-	-	96.2	0.0	-	-	94.8	-1.5	-	-
1981	93.5	-1.4	-	-	94.2	0.7	-	-	90.1	-4.4	-	-	90.5	0.4	-	-	92.0	1.7	-	-	90.8	-1.3	-	-
1982	93.4	2.9	-	-	94.1	0.7	-	-	97.6	3.7	-	-	97.4	-0.2	-	-	95.1	-2.4	-	-	92.4	-2.8	-	-
1983	97.2	5.2	-	-	99.7	2.6	-	-	102.2	2.5	-	-	102.1	-0.1	-	-	103.0	0.9	-	-	101.4	-1.6	-	-
1984	102.8	1.4	-	-	102.9	0.1	-	-	104.1	1.2	-	-	103.2	-0.9	-	-	103.0	-0.2	-	-	105.2	2.1	-	-
1985	107.0	1.7	-	-	108.4	1.3	-	-	107.8	-0.6	-	-	111.6	3.5	-	-	110.9	-0.6	-	-	109.4	-1.4	-	-
1986	108.7	-0.6	-	-	106.5	-2.0	-	-	109.6	2.9	-	-	111.6	1.8	-	-	111.2	-0.4	-	-	113.3	1.9	-	-
1987	-	-	-	-	-	-	-	-	-	-	116.9	3.2	-	-	-	-	-	-	-	-	-	-	117.8	0.8
1988	-	-	-	-	-	-	-	-	-	-	122.8	4.2	-	-	-	-	-	-	-	-	-	-	125.2	2.0
1989	-	-	-	-	-	-	-	-	-	-	129.8	3.7	-	-	-	-	-	-	-	-	-	-	130.3	0.4
1990	-	-	-	-	-	-	-	-	-	-	134.6	3.3	-	-	-	-	-	-	-	-	-	-	138.0	2.5
1991	-	-	-	-	-	-	-	-	-	-	141.6	2.6	-	-	-	-	-	-	-	-	-	-	145.3	2.6
1992	-	-	-	-	-	-	-	-	-	-	147.6	1.6	-	-	-	-	-	-	-	-	-	-	147.3	-0.2
1993	-	-	-	-	-	-	-	-	-	-	150.5	2.2	-	-	-	-	-	-	-	-	-	-	152.7	1.5
1994	-	-	-	-	-	-	-	-	-	-	153.5	0.5	-	-	-	-	-	-	-	-	-	-	152.3	-0.8
1995	-	-	-	-	-	-	-	-	-	-	154.8	1.6	-	-	-	-	-	-	-	-	-	-	154.9	0.1
1996	-	-	-	-	-	-	-	-	-	-	156.5	1.0	-	-	-	-	-	-	-	-	-	-	155.9	-0.4
1997	-	-	-	-	-	-	-	-	-	-	156.2	0.2	-	-	-	-	-	-	-	-	-	-	-	-

Source: U.S. Department of Labor, Bureau of Labor Statistics, Division of Consumer Prices and Price Indexes. - indicates no data collected for period.

Portland, OR-WA

Consumer Price Index - All Urban Consumers
Base 1982-1984 = 100
Other Goods and Services

For 1976-1997. Columns headed % show percentile change in the index from the previous period for which an index is available.

Year	Jan Index	%	Feb Index	%	Mar Index	%	Apr Index	%	May Index	%	Jun Index	%	Jul Index	%	Aug Index	%	Sep Index	%	Oct Index	%	Nov Index	%	Dec Index	%
1976	50.4	-	-	-	-	-	51.2	1.6	-	-	-	-	52.7	2.9	-	-	-	-	53.1	0.8	-	-	-	-
1977	54.8	3.2	-	-	-	-	55.3	0.9	-	-	-	-	56.2	1.6	-	-	-	-	57.6	2.5	-	-	-	-
1978	58.3	1.2	-	-	58.5	0.3	-	-	59.3	1.4	-	-	60.2	1.5	-	-	62.1	3.2	-	-	62.2	0.2	-	-
1979	63.5	2.1	-	-	64.3	1.3	-	-	64.4	0.2	-	-	64.0	-0.6	-	-	67.0	4.7	-	-	68.1	1.6	-	-
1980	71.0	4.3	-	-	71.3	0.4	-	-	72.7	2.0	-	-	73.4	1.0	-	-	75.4	2.7	-	-	76.1	0.9	-	-
1981	78.5	3.2	-	-	79.7	1.5	-	-	80.5	1.0	-	-	81.5	1.2	-	-	84.2	3.3	-	-	85.9	2.0	-	-
1982	88.6	3.1	-	-	89.8	1.4	-	-	90.8	1.1	-	-	92.5	1.9	-	-	95.0	2.7	-	-	95.8	0.8	-	-
1983	99.3	3.7	-	-	99.0	-0.3	-	-	100.3	1.3	-	-	101.4	1.1	-	-	103.0	1.6	-	-	105.0	1.9	-	-
1984	103.8	-1.1	-	-	105.5	1.6	-	-	105.2	-0.3	-	-	105.7	0.5	-	-	107.4	1.6	-	-	106.9	-0.5	-	-
1985	108.5	1.5	-	-	109.1	0.6	-	-	108.5	-0.5	-	-	110.0	1.4	-	-	113.9	3.5	-	-	116.9	2.6	-	-
1986	118.8	1.6	-	-	119.0	0.2	-	-	120.7	1.4	-	-	121.1	0.3	-	-	121.9	0.7	-	-	122.4	0.4	-	-
1987	-	-	-	-	-	-	-	-	-	-	128.6	5.1	-	-	-	-	-	-	-	-	-	-	-	-
1988	-	-	-	-	-	-	-	-	-	-	137.9	7.2	-	-	-	-	-	-	-	-	-	-	-	-
1989	-	-	-	-	-	-	-	-	-	-	149.2	8.2	-	-	-	-	-	-	-	-	-	-	-	-
1990	-	-	-	-	-	-	-	-	-	-	159.3	6.8	-	-	-	-	-	-	-	-	-	-	-	-
1991	-	-	-	-	-	-	-	-	-	-	169.8	6.6	-	-	-	-	-	-	-	-	-	-	-	-
1992	-	-	-	-	-	-	-	-	-	-	191.6	12.8	-	-	-	-	-	-	-	-	-	-	-	-
1993	-	-	-	-	-	-	-	-	-	-	206.6	7.8	-	-	-	-	-	-	-	-	-	-	-	-
1994	-	-	-	-	-	-	-	-	-	-	211.1	2.2	-	-	-	-	-	-	-	-	-	-	-	-
1995	-	-	-	-	-	-	-	-	-	-	218.3	3.4	-	-	-	-	-	-	-	-	-	-	-	-
1996	-	-	-	-	-	-	-	-	-	-	225.5	3.3	-	-	-	-	-	-	-	-	-	-	-	-
1997	-	-	-	-	-	-	-	-	-	-	235.2	4.3	-	-	-	-	-	-	-	-	-	-	-	-

Source: U.S. Department of Labor, Bureau of Labor Statistics, Division of Consumer Prices and Price Indexes. - indicates no data collected for period.

Portland, OR-WA
Consumer Price Index - Urban Wage Earners
Base 1982-1984 = 100
Other Goods and Services

For 1976-1997. Columns headed % show percentile change in the index from the previous period for which an index is available.

Year	Jan Index	%	Feb Index	%	Mar Index	%	Apr Index	%	May Index	%	Jun Index	%	Jul Index	%	Aug Index	%	Sep Index	%	Oct Index	%	Nov Index	%	Dec Index	%
1976	53.8	-	-	-	-	-	54.6	1.5	-	-	-	-	56.2	2.9	-	-	-	-	56.6	0.7	-	-	-	-
1977	58.5	3.4	-	-	-	-	58.9	0.7	-	-	-	-	60.0	1.9	-	-	-	-	61.4	2.3	-	-	-	-
1978	62.1	1.1	-	-	62.2	0.2	-	-	62.7	0.8	-	-	63.3	1.0	-	-	64.4	1.7	-	-	64.7	0.5	-	-
1979	65.6	1.4	-	-	66.6	1.5	-	-	66.5	-0.2	-	-	66.6	0.2	-	-	68.7	3.2	-	-	69.9	1.7	-	-
1980	72.2	3.3	-	-	72.3	0.1	-	-	72.9	0.8	-	-	73.9	1.4	-	-	75.4	2.0	-	-	76.1	0.9	-	-
1981	78.0	2.5	-	-	78.7	0.9	-	-	80.3	2.0	-	-	80.9	0.7	-	-	82.7	2.2	-	-	84.7	2.4	-	-
1982	87.7	3.5	-	-	89.2	1.7	-	-	90.2	1.1	-	-	92.1	2.1	-	-	94.8	2.9	-	-	95.9	1.2	-	-
1983	100.0	4.3	-	-	99.3	-0.7	-	-	100.9	1.6	-	-	102.3	1.4	-	-	103.5	1.2	-	-	105.5	1.9	-	-
1984	104.0	-1.4	-	-	105.3	1.3	-	-	105.2	-0.1	-	-	105.8	0.6	-	-	107.1	1.2	-	-	106.1	-0.9	-	-
1985	108.1	1.9	-	-	108.8	0.6	-	-	108.1	-0.6	-	-	110.0	1.8	-	-	113.0	2.7	-	-	116.8	3.4	-	-
1986	118.6	1.5	-	-	118.1	-0.4	-	-	119.9	1.5	-	-	120.4	0.4	-	-	120.9	0.4	-	-	121.1	0.2	-	-
1987	-	-	-	-	-	-	-	-	-	-	128.1	5.8	-	-	-	-	-	-	-	-	-	-	-	-
1988	-	-	-	-	-	-	-	-	-	-	137.6	7.4	-	-	-	-	-	-	-	-	-	-	-	-
1989	-	-	-	-	-	-	-	-	-	-	151.2	9.9	-	-	-	-	-	-	-	-	-	-	-	-
1990	-	-	-	-	-	-	-	-	-	-	162.6	7.5	-	-	-	-	-	-	-	-	-	-	-	-
1991	-	-	-	-	-	-	-	-	-	-	173.7	6.8	-	-	-	-	-	-	-	-	-	-	-	-
1992	-	-	-	-	-	-	-	-	-	-	192.2	10.7	-	-	-	-	-	-	-	-	-	-	-	-
1993	-	-	-	-	-	-	-	-	-	-	205.9	7.1	-	-	-	-	-	-	-	-	-	-	-	-
1994	-	-	-	-	-	-	-	-	-	-	207.2	0.6	-	-	-	-	-	-	-	-	-	-	-	-
1995	-	-	-	-	-	-	-	-	-	-	213.2	2.9	-	-	-	-	-	-	-	-	-	-	-	-
1996	-	-	-	-	-	-	-	-	-	-	218.2	2.3	-	-	-	-	-	-	-	-	-	-	-	-
1997	-	-	-	-	-	-	-	-	-	-	226.8	3.9	-	-	-	-	-	-	-	-	-	-	-	-

Source: U.S. Department of Labor, Bureau of Labor Statistics, Division of Consumer Prices and Price Indexes. - indicates no data collected for period.

San Diego, CA
Consumer Price Index - All Urban Consumers
Base 1982-1984 = 100
Annual Averages

For 1965-1997. Columns headed % show percentile change in the index from the previous period for which an index is available.

Year	All Items		Food & Beverage		Housing		Apparel & Upkeep		Trans- portation		Medical Care		Entertain- ment		Other Goods & Services	
	Index	%	Index	%	Index	%	Index	%	Index	%	Index	%	Index	%	Index	%
1965	28.2	-	-	-	-	-	48.1	-	32.1	-	26.6	-	-	-	-	-
1966	28.7	1.8	-	-	-	-	48.7	1.2	32.1	0.0	28.0	5.3	-	-	-	-
1967	29.6	3.1	-	-	-	-	49.5	1.6	33.3	3.7	30.0	7.1	-	-	-	-
1968	30.8	4.1	-	-	-	-	52.4	5.9	34.1	2.4	30.8	2.7	-		-	-
1969	32.4	5.2	-	-	-	-	54.7	4.4	34.9	2.3	32.4	5.2	-	-	-	-
1970	34.1	5.2	-	-	-	-	56.8	3.8	35.9	2.9	34.5	6.5	-	-	-	-
1971	35.4	3.8	-	-	-	-	58.3	2.6	37.9	5.6	36.3	5.2	-	-	-	-
1972	36.8	4.0	-	-	-	-	60.4	3.6	39.0	2.9	37.2	2.5	-	-	-	-
1973	39.2	6.5	-	-	-	-	62.7	3.8	40.7	4.4	39.0	4.8	-	-	-	-
1974	43.5	11.0	-	-	-	-	67.9	8.3	46.1	13.3	43.2	10.8	-	-	-	-
1975	47.6	9.4	-	-	-	-	69.5	2.4	51.0	10.6	48.5	12.3	-	-	-	-
1976	50.5	6.1	59.3	-	44.3	-	71.4	2.7	54.6	7.1	53.6	10.5	62.6	-	58.0	-
1977	53.8	6.5	62.9	6.1	47.9	8.1	72.8	2.0	58.1	6.4	58.6	9.3	65.1	4.0	61.1	5.3
1978	59.2	10.0	69.7	10.8	53.8	12.3	76.9	5.6	61.2	5.3	63.6	8.5	69.3	6.5	66.2	8.3
1979	68.9	16.4	77.3	10.9	65.2	21.2	81.5	6.0	69.9	14.2	69.5	9.3	75.0	8.2	71.3	7.7
1980	79.4	15.2	84.4	9.2	76.8	17.8	87.4	7.2	82.2	17.6	76.2	9.6	83.1	10.8	77.2	8.3
1981	90.1	13.5	90.5	7.2	89.6	16.7	92.2	5.5	91.4	11.2	83.0	8.9	89.9	8.2	85.1	10.2
1982	96.2	6.8	94.8	4.8	96.3	7.5	96.5	4.7	95.7	4.7	93.1	12.2	96.1	6.9	91.5	7.5
1983	99.0	2.9	100.4	5.9	98.6	2.4	99.7	3.3	98.8	3.2	100.7	8.2	100.8	4.9	100.2	9.5
1984	104.8	5.9	104.8	4.4	104.9	6.4	103.8	4.1	105.5	6.8	106.2	5.5	103.1	2.3	108.4	8.2
1985	110.4	5.3	107.2	2.3	113.7	8.4	105.9	2.0	109.4	3.7	110.1	3.7	107.4	4.2	115.7	6.7
1986	113.5	2.8	111.2	3.7	119.2	4.8	107.3	1.3	105.6	-3.5	118.2	7.4	111.9	4.2	120.0	3.7
1987	109.2	-3.8	111.9	0.6	108.1	-9.3	109.4	2.0	102.3	-3.1	124.6	5.4	110.9	-0.9	122.5	2.1
1988	112.8	3.3	114.9	2.7	111.9	3.5	115.6	5.7	103.5	1.2	132.9	6.7	115.5	4.1	127.4	4.0
1989	118.1	4.7	123.1	7.1	116.3	3.9	107.4	-7.1	109.2	5.5	141.6	6.5	126.0	9.1	135.4	6.3
1990	126.8	7.4	133.0	8.0	125.4	7.8	112.0	4.3	116.1	6.3	154.6	9.2	129.9	3.1	146.8	8.4
1991	134.1	5.8	140.6	5.7	134.0	6.9	113.4	1.3	119.9	3.3	169.4	9.6	135.9	4.6	156.5	6.6
1992	139.0	3.7	141.1	0.4	139.3	4.0	118.7	4.7	123.9	3.3	184.2	8.7	140.1	3.1	169.1	8.1
1993	142.9	2.8	142.4	0.9	143.5	3.0	115.5	-2.7	128.4	3.6	193.1	4.8	144.2	2.9	179.5	6.2
1994	147.8	3.4	146.9	3.2	147.9	3.1	120.9	4.7	135.0	5.1	199.8	3.5	146.7	1.7	184.9	3.0
1995	152.3	3.0	152.0	3.5	151.5	2.4	121.2	0.2	139.5	3.3	209.4	4.8	147.6	0.6	198.0	7.1
1996	157.5	3.4	155.5	2.3	156.9	3.6	125.7	3.7	144.0	3.2	217.4	3.8	149.8	1.5	210.7	6.4
1997	-		-		-		-		-		-		-		-	

Source: U.S. Department of Labor, Bureau of Labor Statistics, Division of Consumer Prices and Price Indexes. - indicates no data collected for period.

San Diego, CA
Consumer Price Index - Urban Wage Earners
Base 1982-1984 = 100
Annual Averages

For 1965-1997. Columns headed % show percentile change in the index from the previous period for which an index is available.

Year	All Items		Food & Beverage		Housing		Apparel & Upkeep		Trans-portation		Medical Care		Entertain-ment		Other Goods & Services	
	Index	%	Index	%	Index	%	Index	%	Index	%	Index	%	Index	%	Index	%
1965	29.5	-	-	-	-	-	50.2	-	31.9	-	26.0	-	-	-	-	-
1966	30.1	2.0	-	-	-	-	50.8	1.2	31.9	0.0	27.4	5.4	-	-	-	-
1967	31.0	3.0	-	-	-	-	51.6	1.6	33.1	3.8	29.4	7.3	-	-	-	-
1968	32.3	4.2	-	-	-	-	54.7	6.0	33.9	2.4	30.1	2.4	-	-	-	-
1969	34.0	5.3	-	-	-	-	57.1	4.4	34.7	2.4	31.7	5.3	-	-	-	-
1970	35.8	5.3	-	-	-	-	59.3	3.9	35.7	2.9	33.7	6.3	-	-	-	-
1971	37.1	3.6	-	-	-	-	60.8	2.5	37.7	5.6	35.5	5.3	-	-	-	-
1972	38.6	4.0	-	-	-	-	63.1	3.8	38.8	2.9	36.4	2.5	-	-	-	-
1973	41.1	6.5	-	-	-	-	65.5	3.8	40.5	4.4	38.2	4.9	-	-	-	-
1974	45.6	10.9	-	-	-	-	70.9	8.2	45.8	13.1	42.3	10.7	-	-	-	-
1975	49.9	9.4	-	-	-	-	72.6	2.4	50.6	10.5	47.4	12.1	-	-	-	-
1976	52.9	6.0	57.9	-	48.1	-	74.6	2.8	54.2	7.1	52.4	10.5	60.8	-	59.3	-
1977	56.4	6.6	61.4	6.0	52.0	8.1	76.0	1.9	57.7	6.5	57.3	9.4	63.2	3.9	62.5	5.4
1978	61.9	9.8	67.9	10.6	58.4	12.3	77.9	2.5	61.0	5.7	62.0	8.2	67.5	6.8	67.6	8.2
1979	71.4	15.3	75.9	11.8	69.9	19.7	81.0	4.0	69.6	14.1	69.4	11.9	73.4	8.7	72.5	7.2
1980	82.1	15.0	82.9	9.2	82.4	17.9	88.5	9.3	81.2	16.7	76.2	9.8	81.8	11.4	78.5	8.3
1981	92.8	13.0	89.9	8.4	96.2	16.7	92.5	4.5	90.2	11.1	83.5	9.6	88.7	8.4	85.0	8.3
1982	99.4	7.1	94.6	5.2	103.7	7.8	96.5	4.3	95.4	5.8	93.1	11.5	96.1	8.3	91.4	7.5
1983	99.0	-0.4	100.5	6.2	98.2	-5.3	99.8	3.4	98.8	3.6	100.6	8.1	100.9	5.0	100.3	9.7
1984	101.7	2.7	104.9	4.4	98.1	-0.1	103.8	4.0	105.9	7.2	106.3	5.7	103.0	2.1	108.3	8.0
1985	104.5	2.8	107.4	2.4	100.8	2.8	106.3	2.4	109.6	3.5	110.6	4.0	107.7	4.6	115.0	6.2
1986	107.2	2.6	111.2	3.5	105.6	4.8	107.5	1.1	106.2	-3.1	118.9	7.5	113.1	5.0	118.9	3.4
1987	107.4	0.2	111.6	0.4	104.5	-1.0	108.3	0.7	102.7	-3.3	126.2	6.1	109.6	-3.1	123.0	3.4
1988	110.9	3.3	114.6	2.7	108.0	3.3	114.1	5.4	104.6	1.9	134.7	6.7	113.4	3.5	128.0	4.1
1989	116.1	4.7	122.7	7.1	111.9	3.6	105.7	-7.4	110.2	5.4	143.4	6.5	124.2	9.5	136.3	6.5
1990	124.4	7.1	132.7	8.1	120.5	7.7	111.0	5.0	116.7	5.9	156.0	8.8	127.8	2.9	147.7	8.4
1991	131.3	5.5	140.2	5.7	128.4	6.6	112.2	1.1	120.6	3.3	170.0	9.0	132.9	4.0	157.4	6.6
1992	136.0	3.6	140.8	0.4	133.0	3.6	117.7	4.9	125.0	3.6	184.9	8.8	136.4	2.6	170.4	8.3
1993	140.0	2.9	142.5	1.2	137.0	3.0	115.0	-2.3	130.1	4.1	193.9	4.9	140.2	2.8	181.6	6.6
1994	145.1	3.6	146.6	2.9	141.4	3.2	120.5	4.8	137.8	5.9	200.2	3.2	143.0	2.0	186.7	2.8
1995	149.3	2.9	151.0	3.0	144.5	2.2	120.4	-0.1	143.1	3.8	209.1	4.4	142.4	-0.4	200.3	7.3
1996	154.3	3.3	154.5	2.3	149.3	3.3	124.1	3.1	147.5	3.1	217.8	4.2	144.6	1.5	214.8	7.2
1997	-	-	-	-	-	-	-	-	-	-	-	-	-	-	-	-

Source: U.S. Department of Labor, Bureau of Labor Statistics, Division of Consumer Prices and Price Indexes. - indicates no data collected for period.

San Diego, CA
Consumer Price Index - All Urban Consumers
Base 1982-1984 = 100
All Items

For 1965-1997. Columns headed % show percentile change in the index from the previous period for which an index is available.

Year	Jan Index	%	Feb Index	%	Mar Index	%	Apr Index	%	May Index	%	Jun Index	%	Jul Index	%	Aug Index	%	Sep Index	%	Oct Index	%	Nov Index	%	Dec Index	%
1965	-	-	28.1	-	-	-	-	-	28.3	0.7	-	-	-	-	28.0	-1.1	-	-	-	-	28.2	0.7	-	-
1966	-	-	28.5	1.1	-	-	-	-	28.6	0.4	-	-	-	-	28.7	0.3	-	-	-	-	29.1	1.4	-	-
1967	-	-	29.2	0.3	-	-	-	-	29.3	0.3	-	-	-	-	29.8	1.7	-	-	-	-	30.0	0.7	-	-
1968	-	-	30.3	1.0	-	-	-	-	30.6	1.0	-	-	-	-	31.0	1.3	-	-	-	-	31.3	1.0	-	-
1969	-	-	31.7	1.3	-	-	-	-	32.2	1.6	-	-	-	-	32.7	1.6	-	-	-	-	32.9	0.6	-	-
1970	-	-	33.4	1.5	-	-	-	-	34.0	1.8	-	-	-	-	34.3	0.9	-	-	-	-	34.8	1.5	-	-
1971	-	-	35.0	0.6	-	-	-	-	35.3	0.9	-	-	-	-	35.6	0.8	-	-	-	-	35.7	0.3	-	-
1972	-	-	36.1	1.1	-	-	-	-	36.6	1.4	-	-	-	-	37.0	1.1	-	-	-	-	37.5	1.4	-	-
1973	-	-	37.9	1.1	-	-	-	-	38.7	2.1	-	-	-	-	39.7	2.6	-	-	-	-	40.4	1.8	-	-
1974	-	-	41.5	2.7	-	-	-	-	42.9	3.4	-	-	-	-	44.3	3.3	-	-	-	-	45.4	2.5	-	-
1975	-	-	46.5	2.4	-	-	-	-	47.0	1.1	-	-	-	-	48.1	2.3	-	-	-	-	48.8	1.5	-	-
1976	-	-	49.5	1.4	-	-	-	-	50.1	1.2	-	-	-	-	50.9	1.6	-	-	-	-	51.4	1.0	-	-
1977	-	-	52.2	1.6	-	-	-	-	53.4	2.3	-	-	-	-	54.4	1.9	-	-	-	-	55.2	1.5	-	-
1978	55.9	1.3	-	-	56.6	1.3	-	-	57.8	2.1	-	-	59.7	3.3	-	-	61.1	2.3	-	-	62.0	1.5	-	-
1979	63.5	2.4	-	-	65.5	3.1	-	-	67.5	3.1	-	-	69.8	3.4	-	-	71.1	1.9	-	-	73.3	3.1	-	-
1980	75.1	2.5	-	-	76.4	1.7	-	-	79.8	4.5	-	-	79.8	0.0	-	-	80.4	0.8	-	-	82.5	2.6	-	-
1981	85.1	3.2	-	-	86.7	1.9	-	-	88.0	1.5	-	-	90.3	2.6	-	-	92.8	2.8	-	-	95.0	2.4	-	-
1982	95.6	0.6	-	-	94.3	-1.4	-	-	97.4	3.3	-	-	99.0	1.6	-	-	96.3	-2.7	-	-	95.1	-1.2	-	-
1983	96.1	1.1	-	-	96.9	0.8	-	-	98.2	1.3	-	-	99.1	0.9	-	-	100.7	1.6	-	-	101.2	0.5	-	-
1984	102.4	1.2	-	-	103.3	0.9	-	-	104.4	1.1	-	-	103.9	-0.5	-	-	105.6	1.6	-	-	107.6	1.9	-	-
1985	107.7	0.1	-	-	109.2	1.4	-	-	110.0	0.7	-	-	110.3	0.3	-	-	111.6	1.2	-	-	112.1	0.4	-	-
1986	112.9	0.7	-	-	112.1	-0.7	-	-	113.2	1.0	-	-	113.3	0.1	-	-	114.1	0.7	-	-	114.6	0.4	-	-
1987	-	-	-	-	-	-	-	-	-	-	108.2	-5.6	-	-	-	-	-	-	-	-	-	-	110.3	1.9
1988	-	-	-	-	-	-	-	-	-	-	111.9	1.5	-	-	-	-	-	-	-	-	-	-	113.8	1.7
1989	-	-	-	-	-	-	-	-	-	-	116.7	2.5	-	-	-	-	-	-	-	-	-	-	119.6	2.5
1990	-	-	-	-	-	-	-	-	-	-	124.2	3.8	-	-	-	-	-	-	-	-	-	-	129.4	4.2
1991	-	-	-	-	-	-	-	-	-	-	133.0	2.8	-	-	-	-	-	-	-	-	-	-	135.2	1.7
1992	-	-	-	-	-	-	-	-	-	-	137.8	1.9	-	-	-	-	-	-	-	-	-	-	140.2	1.7
1993	-	-	-	-	-	-	-	-	-	-	141.9	1.2	-	-	-	-	-	-	-	-	-	-	143.9	1.4
1994	-	-	-	-	-	-	-	-	-	-	146.4	1.7	-	-	-	-	-	-	-	-	-	-	149.2	1.9
1995	-	-	-	-	-	-	-	-	-	-	151.2	1.3	-	-	-	-	-	-	-	-	-	-	153.3	1.4
1996	-	-	-	-	-	-	-	-	-	-	155.6	1.5	-	-	-	-	-	-	-	-	-	-	159.4	2.4
1997	-	-	-	-	-	-	-	-	-	-	161.9	1.6	-	-	-	-	-	-	-	-	-	-	-	-

Source: U.S. Department of Labor, Bureau of Labor Statistics, Division of Consumer Prices and Price Indexes. - indicates no data collected for period.

San Diego, CA
Consumer Price Index - Urban Wage Earners
Base 1982-1984 = 100
All Items

For 1965-1997. Columns headed % show percentile change in the index from the previous period for which an index is available.

Year	Jan Index	Jan %	Feb Index	Feb %	Mar Index	Mar %	Apr Index	Apr %	May Index	May %	Jun Index	Jun %	Jul Index	Jul %	Aug Index	Aug %	Sep Index	Sep %	Oct Index	Oct %	Nov Index	Nov %	Dec Index	Dec %
1965	-	-	29.5	-	-	-	-	-	29.6	0.3	-	-	-	-	29.4	-0.7	-	-	-	-	29.6	0.7	-	-
1966	-	-	29.9	1.0	-	-	-	-	30.0	0.3	-	-	-	-	30.1	0.3	-	-	-	-	30.5	1.3	-	-
1967	-	-	30.6	0.3	-	-	-	-	30.7	0.3	-	-	-	-	31.3	2.0	-	-	-	-	31.4	0.3	-	-
1968	-	-	31.8	1.3	-	-	-	-	32.1	0.9	-	-	-	-	32.5	1.2	-	-	-	-	32.8	0.9	-	-
1969	-	-	33.3	1.5	-	-	-	-	33.7	1.2	-	-	-	-	34.2	1.5	-	-	-	-	34.5	0.9	-	-
1970	-	-	35.0	1.4	-	-	-	-	35.7	2.0	-	-	-	-	35.9	0.6	-	-	-	-	36.5	1.7	-	-
1971	-	-	36.7	0.5	-	-	-	-	37.1	1.1	-	-	-	-	37.4	0.8	-	-	-	-	37.5	0.3	-	-
1972	-	-	37.9	1.1	-	-	-	-	38.3	1.1	-	-	-	-	38.8	1.3	-	-	-	-	39.3	1.3	-	-
1973	-	-	39.8	1.3	-	-	-	-	40.5	1.8	-	-	-	-	41.7	3.0	-	-	-	-	42.3	1.4	-	-
1974	-	-	43.5	2.8	-	-	-	-	45.0	3.4	-	-	-	-	46.5	3.3	-	-	-	-	47.6	2.4	-	-
1975	-	-	48.7	2.3	-	-	-	-	49.2	1.0	-	-	-	-	50.4	2.4	-	-	-	-	51.1	1.4	-	-
1976	-	-	51.9	1.6	-	-	-	-	52.5	1.2	-	-	-	-	53.4	1.7	-	-	-	-	53.9	0.9	-	-
1977	-	-	54.8	1.7	-	-	-	-	56.0	2.2	-	-	-	-	57.1	2.0	-	-	-	-	57.9	1.4	-	-
1978	58.6	1.2	-	-	59.3	1.2	-	-	60.6	2.2	-	-	62.5	3.1	-	-	63.7	1.9	-	-	64.7	1.6	-	-
1979	65.9	1.9	-	-	67.8	2.9	-	-	70.1	3.4	-	-	72.3	3.1	-	-	73.7	1.9	-	-	75.9	3.0	-	-
1980	77.8	2.5	-	-	79.3	1.9	-	-	82.1	3.5	-	-	82.4	0.4	-	-	83.0	0.7	-	-	85.3	2.8	-	-
1981	87.7	2.8	-	-	89.3	1.8	-	-	90.7	1.6	-	-	93.2	2.8	-	-	95.5	2.5	-	-	97.7	2.3	-	-
1982	98.4	0.7	-	-	97.3	-1.1	-	-	100.3	3.1	-	-	102.1	1.8	-	-	99.6	-2.4	-	-	98.7	-0.9	-	-
1983	97.2	-1.5	-	-	97.8	0.6	-	-	97.6	-0.2	-	-	99.2	1.6	-	-	100.4	1.2	-	-	100.4	0.0	-	-
1984	102.1	1.7	-	-	101.2	-0.9	-	-	101.6	0.4	-	-	100.7	-0.9	-	-	102.5	1.8	-	-	102.0	-0.5	-	-
1985	102.1	0.1	-	-	103.5	1.4	-	-	104.3	0.8	-	-	104.5	0.2	-	-	105.5	1.0	-	-	106.0	0.5	-	-
1986	106.9	0.8	-	-	106.0	-0.8	-	-	107.0	0.9	-	-	107.0	0.0	-	-	107.7	0.7	-	-	108.2	0.5	-	-
1987	-	-	-	-	-	-	-	-	-	-	106.4	-1.7	-	-	-	-	-	-	-	-	-	-	108.4	1.9
1988	-	-	-	-	-	-	-	-	-	-	109.9	1.4	-	-	-	-	-	-	-	-	-	-	112.0	1.9
1989	-	-	-	-	-	-	-	-	-	-	114.7	2.4	-	-	-	-	-	-	-	-	-	-	117.6	2.5
1990	-	-	-	-	-	-	-	-	-	-	122.0	3.7	-	-	-	-	-	-	-	-	-	-	126.9	4.0
1991	-	-	-	-	-	-	-	-	-	-	130.2	2.6	-	-	-	-	-	-	-	-	-	-	132.4	1.7
1992	-	-	-	-	-	-	-	-	-	-	134.8	1.8	-	-	-	-	-	-	-	-	-	-	137.2	1.8
1993	-	-	-	-	-	-	-	-	-	-	138.9	1.2	-	-	-	-	-	-	-	-	-	-	141.1	1.6
1994	-	-	-	-	-	-	-	-	-	-	143.7	1.8	-	-	-	-	-	-	-	-	-	-	146.5	1.9
1995	-	-	-	-	-	-	-	-	-	-	148.3	1.2	-	-	-	-	-	-	-	-	-	-	150.4	1.4
1996	-	-	-	-	-	-	-	-	-	-	152.6	1.5	-	-	-	-	-	-	-	-	-	-	155.9	2.2
1997	-	-	-	-	-	-	-	-	-	-	158.2	1.5	-	-	-	-	-	-	-	-	-	-	-	-

Source: U.S. Department of Labor, Bureau of Labor Statistics, Division of Consumer Prices and Price Indexes. - indicates no data collected for period.

San Diego, CA
Consumer Price Index - All Urban Consumers
Base 1982-1984 = 100
Food and Beverages

For 1975-1997. Columns headed % show percentile change in the index from the previous period for which an index is available.

Year	Jan Index	%	Feb Index	%	Mar Index	%	Apr Index	%	May Index	%	Jun Index	%	Jul Index	%	Aug Index	%	Sep Index	%	Oct Index	%	Nov Index	%	Dec Index	%
1975	-	-	-	-	-	-	-	-	-	-	-	-	-	-	-	-	-	-	-	-	58.9	-	-	-
1976	-	-	58.9	0.0	-	-	-	-	59.2	0.5	-	-	-	-	59.7	0.8	-	-	-	-	59.6	-0.2	-	-
1977	-	-	61.0	2.3	-	-	-	-	62.8	3.0	-	-	-	-	63.6	1.3	-	-	-	-	64.3	1.1	-	-
1978	65.8	2.3	-	-	67.3	2.3	-	-	69.8	3.7	-	-	71.0	1.7	-	-	71.3	0.4	-	-	71.0	-0.4	-	-
1979	73.6	3.7	-	-	75.6	2.7	-	-	77.4	2.4	-	-	77.5	0.1	-	-	78.4	1.2	-	-	79.4	1.3	-	-
1980	81.0	2.0	-	-	82.2	1.5	-	-	83.5	1.6	-	-	84.1	0.7	-	-	86.2	2.5	-	-	87.5	1.5	-	-
1981	88.7	1.4	-	-	89.6	1.0	-	-	89.7	0.1	-	-	90.9	1.3	-	-	91.8	1.0	-	-	91.2	-0.7	-	-
1982	93.2	2.2	-	-	93.7	0.5	-	-	94.2	0.5	-	-	95.5	1.4	-	-	95.0	-0.5	-	-	96.7	1.8	-	-
1983	96.1	-0.6	-	-	100.3	4.4	-	-	100.5	0.2	-	-	100.2	-0.3	-	-	101.0	0.8	-	-	102.1	1.1	-	-
1984	104.7	2.5	-	-	105.3	0.6	-	-	103.6	-1.6	-	-	103.9	0.3	-	-	105.1	1.2	-	-	105.6	0.5	-	-
1985	107.4	1.7	-	-	106.9	-0.5	-	-	106.9	0.0	-	-	105.9	-0.9	-	-	106.8	0.8	-	-	108.0	1.1	-	-
1986	111.2	3.0	-	-	108.9	-2.1	-	-	111.0	1.9	-	-	110.1	-0.8	-	-	111.0	0.8	-	-	113.7	2.4	-	-
1987	-	-	-	-	-	-	-	-	-	-	111.7	-1.8	-	-	-	-	-	-	-	-	-	-	112.2	0.4
1988	-	-	-	-	-	-	-	-	-	-	114.0	1.6	-	-	-	-	-	-	-	-	-	-	115.8	1.6
1989	-	-	-	-	-	-	-	-	-	-	121.7	5.1	-	-	-	-	-	-	-	-	-	-	124.4	2.2
1990	-	-	-	-	-	-	-	-	-	-	131.8	5.9	-	-	-	-	-	-	-	-	-	-	134.2	1.8
1991	-	-	-	-	-	-	-	-	-	-	141.1	5.1	-	-	-	-	-	-	-	-	-	-	140.2	-0.6
1992	-	-	-	-	-	-	-	-	-	-	141.1	0.6	-	-	-	-	-	-	-	-	-	-	141.1	0.0
1993	-	-	-	-	-	-	-	-	-	-	142.8	1.2	-	-	-	-	-	-	-	-	-	-	142.1	-0.5
1994	-	-	-	-	-	-	-	-	-	-	145.3	2.3	-	-	-	-	-	-	-	-	-	-	148.5	2.2
1995	-	-	-	-	-	-	-	-	-	-	151.9	2.3	-	-	-	-	-	-	-	-	-	-	152.1	0.1
1996	-	-	-	-	-	-	-	-	-	-	153.5	0.9	-	-	-	-	-	-	-	-	-	-	157.5	2.6
1997	-	-	-	-	-	-	-	-	-	-	159.0	1.0	-	-	-	-	-	-	-	-	-	-	-	-

Source: U.S. Department of Labor, Bureau of Labor Statistics, Division of Consumer Prices and Price Indexes. - indicates no data collected for period.

San Diego, CA
Consumer Price Index - Urban Wage Earners
Base 1982-1984 = 100
Food and Beverages

For 1975-1997. Columns headed % show percentile change in the index from the previous period for which an index is available.

Year	Jan Index	%	Feb Index	%	Mar Index	%	Apr Index	%	May Index	%	Jun Index	%	Jul Index	%	Aug Index	%	Sep Index	%	Oct Index	%	Nov Index	%	Dec Index	%
1975	-	-	-	-	-	-	-	-	-	-	-	-	-	-	-	-	-	-	-	-	57.4	-	-	-
1976	-	-	57.5	0.2	-	-	-	-	57.7	0.3	-	-	-	-	58.2	0.9	-	-	-	-	58.1	-0.2	-	-
1977	-	-	59.6	2.6	-	-	-	-	61.3	2.9	-	-	-	-	62.1	1.3	-	-	-	-	62.7	1.0	-	-
1978	63.9	1.9	-	-	65.4	2.3	-	-	67.9	3.8	-	-	69.3	2.1	-	-	69.7	0.6	-	-	69.4	-0.4	-	-
1979	72.0	3.7	-	-	74.2	3.1	-	-	76.0	2.4	-	-	76.5	0.7	-	-	77.1	0.8	-	-	77.9	1.0	-	-
1980	79.5	2.1	-	-	80.9	1.8	-	-	81.5	0.7	-	-	82.1	0.7	-	-	84.6	3.0	-	-	86.8	2.6	-	-
1981	87.6	0.9	-	-	88.8	1.4	-	-	89.1	0.3	-	-	90.2	1.2	-	-	91.3	1.2	-	-	90.8	-0.5	-	-
1982	92.6	2.0	-	-	93.3	0.8	-	-	93.9	0.6	-	-	95.4	1.6	-	-	94.9	-0.5	-	-	96.7	1.9	-	-
1983	96.0	-0.7	-	-	100.5	4.7	-	-	100.6	0.1	-	-	100.2	-0.4	-	-	101.0	0.8	-	-	102.3	1.3	-	-
1984	104.8	2.4	-	-	105.2	0.4	-	-	103.8	-1.3	-	-	104.0	0.2	-	-	105.4	1.3	-	-	105.8	0.4	-	-
1985	107.5	1.6	-	-	107.1	-0.4	-	-	107.2	0.1	-	-	106.2	-0.9	-	-	107.0	0.8	-	-	108.4	1.3	-	-
1986	111.4	2.8	-	-	108.9	-2.2	-	-	110.9	1.8	-	-	110.2	-0.6	-	-	111.0	0.7	-	-	114.0	2.7	-	-
1987	-	-	-	-	-	-	-	-	-	-	111.3	-2.4	-	-	-	-	-	-	-	-	-	-	111.8	0.4
1988	-	-	-	-	-	-	-	-	-	-	113.6	1.6	-	-	-	-	-	-	-	-	-	-	115.6	1.8
1989	-	-	-	-	-	-	-	-	-	-	121.3	4.9	-	-	-	-	-	-	-	-	-	-	124.1	2.3
1990	-	-	-	-	-	-	-	-	-	-	131.5	6.0	-	-	-	-	-	-	-	-	-	-	134.0	1.9
1991	-	-	-	-	-	-	-	-	-	-	140.5	4.9	-	-	-	-	-	-	-	-	-	-	140.0	-0.4
1992	-	-	-	-	-	-	-	-	-	-	140.5	0.4	-	-	-	-	-	-	-	-	-	-	141.0	0.4
1993	-	-	-	-	-	-	-	-	-	-	142.4	1.0	-	-	-	-	-	-	-	-	-	-	142.5	0.1
1994	-	-	-	-	-	-	-	-	-	-	145.2	1.9	-	-	-	-	-	-	-	-	-	-	147.9	1.9
1995	-	-	-	-	-	-	-	-	-	-	150.8	2.0	-	-	-	-	-	-	-	-	-	-	151.3	0.3
1996	-	-	-	-	-	-	-	-	-	-	152.7	0.9	-	-	-	-	-	-	-	-	-	-	156.4	2.4
1997	-	-	-	-	-	-	-	-	-	-	158.0	1.0	-	-	-	-	-	-	-	-	-	-	-	-

Source: U.S. Department of Labor, Bureau of Labor Statistics, Division of Consumer Prices and Price Indexes. - indicates no data collected for period.

San Diego, CA
Consumer Price Index - All Urban Consumers
Base 1982-1984 = 100
Housing

For 1975-1997. Columns headed % show percentile change in the index from the previous period for which an index is available.

Year	Jan Index	%	Feb Index	%	Mar Index	%	Apr Index	%	May Index	%	Jun Index	%	Jul Index	%	Aug Index	%	Sep Index	%	Oct Index	%	Nov Index	%	Dec Index	%
1975	-		-		-			-	-				-		-		-			-	42.4		-	-
1976	-		43.5	2.6	-			-	43.8	0.7	-			-	44.6	1.8	-			-	45.4	1.8	-	-
1977	-		46.2	1.8	-			-	47.0	1.7	-			-	48.7	3.6	-			-	49.6	1.8	-	-
1978	50.3	1.4	-		51.0	1.4		-	51.9	1.8	-		54.1	4.2	-		56.1	3.7		-	57.3	2.1	-	-
1979	58.9	2.8	-		61.3	4.1		-	63.2	3.1	-		66.4	5.1	-		67.5	1.7		-	70.5	4.4	-	-
1980	72.5	2.8	-		72.8	0.4		-	77.7	6.7	-		77.3	-0.5	-		77.3	0.0		-	80.2	3.8	-	-
1981	83.7	4.4	-		85.3	1.9		-	86.8	1.8	-		89.5	3.1	-		92.9	3.8		-	96.2	3.6	-	-
1982	96.7	0.5	-		94.6	-2.2		-	99.3	5.0	-		100.4	1.1	-		95.5	-4.9		-	93.2	-2.4	-	-
1983	95.5	2.5	-		96.5	1.0		-	97.1	0.6	-		98.3	1.2	-		101.1	2.8		-	101.2	0.1	-	-
1984	101.3	0.1	-		103.1	1.8		-	104.1	1.0	-		103.8	-0.3	-		106.1	2.2		-	109.1	2.8	-	-
1985	108.9	-0.2	-		111.8	2.7		-	112.1	0.3	-		113.6	1.3	-		116.7	2.7		-	116.9	0.2	-	-
1986	117.1	0.2	-		117.2	0.1		-	118.3	0.9	-		119.8	1.3	-		120.8	0.8		-	121.1	0.2	-	-
1987	-		-		-			-	-		107.2	-11.5	-		-		-			-	-		109.1	1.8
1988	-		-		-			-	-		111.0	1.7	-		-		-			-	-		112.9	1.7
1989	-		-		-			-	-		114.6	1.5	-		-		-			-	-		118.1	3.1
1990	-		-		-			-	-		122.0	3.3	-		-		-			-	-		128.9	5.7
1991	-		-		-			-	-		132.3	2.6	-		-		-			-	-		135.8	2.6
1992	-		-		-			-	-		138.3	1.8	-		-		-			-	-		140.2	1.4
1993	-		-		-			-	-		142.0	1.3	-		-		-			-	-		144.9	2.0
1994	-		-		-			-	-		147.0	1.4	-		-		-			-	-		148.9	1.3
1995	-		-		-			-	-		150.5	1.1	-		-		-			-	-		152.5	1.3
1996	-		-		-			-	-		154.6	1.4	-		-		-			-	-		159.2	3.0
1997	-		-		-		-		-		163.1	2.4	-		-		-		-		-		-	-

Source: U.S. Department of Labor, Bureau of Labor Statistics, Division of Consumer Prices and Price Indexes. - indicates no data collected for period.

San Diego, CA
Consumer Price Index - Urban Wage Earners
Base 1982-1984 = 100
Housing

For 1975-1997. Columns headed % show percentile change in the index from the previous period for which an index is available.

Year	Jan Index	%	Feb Index	%	Mar Index	%	Apr Index	%	May Index	%	Jun Index	%	Jul Index	%	Aug Index	%	Sep Index	%	Oct Index	%	Nov Index	%	Dec Index	%
1975	-	-	-	-	-	-	-	-	-	-	-	-	-	-	-	-	-	-	-	-	46.0	-	-	-
1976	-	-	47.2	2.6	-	-	-	-	47.6	0.8	-	-	-	-	48.4	1.7	-	-	-	-	49.3	1.9	-	-
1977	-	-	50.2	1.8	-	-	-	-	51.1	1.8	-	-	-	-	52.8	3.3	-	-	-	-	53.9	2.1	-	-
1978	54.7	1.5	-	-	55.3	1.1	-	-	56.4	2.0	-	-	58.8	4.3	-	-	60.8	3.4	-	-	62.1	2.1	-	-
1979	63.3	1.9	-	-	65.8	3.9	-	-	67.8	3.0	-	-	70.9	4.6	-	-	72.3	2.0	-	-	75.8	4.8	-	-
1980	77.9	2.8	-	-	78.2	0.4	-	-	83.1	6.3	-	-	82.9	-0.2	-	-	82.9	0.0	-	-	86.0	3.7	-	-
1981	90.0	4.7	-	-	91.5	1.7	-	-	93.0	1.6	-	-	96.2	3.4	-	-	99.6	3.5	-	-	103.3	3.7	-	-
1982	104.1	0.8	-	-	101.8	-2.2	-	-	107.0	5.1	-	-	108.1	1.0	-	-	102.7	-5.0	-	-	100.4	-2.2	-	-
1983	97.7	-2.7	-	-	97.9	0.2	-	-	95.8	-2.1	-	-	98.3	2.6	-	-	99.9	1.6	-	-	98.8	-1.1	-	-
1984	100.4	1.6	-	-	98.2	-2.2	-	-	98.1	-0.1	-	-	96.6	-1.5	-	-	99.2	2.7	-	-	96.9	-2.3	-	-
1985	96.5	-0.4	-	-	99.1	2.7	-	-	99.5	0.4	-	-	100.9	1.4	-	-	103.5	2.6	-	-	103.6	0.1	-	-
1986	103.7	0.1	-	-	103.8	0.1	-	-	104.8	1.0	-	-	106.1	1.2	-	-	107.1	0.9	-	-	107.3	0.2	-	-
1987	-	-	-	-	-	-	-	-	-	-	103.7	-3.4	-	-	-	-	-	-	-	-	-	-	105.2	1.4
1988	-	-	-	-	-	-	-	-	-	-	107.1	1.8	-	-	-	-	-	-	-	-	-	-	108.9	1.7
1989	-	-	-	-	-	-	-	-	-	-	110.3	1.3	-	-	-	-	-	-	-	-	-	-	113.5	2.9
1990	-	-	-	-	-	-	-	-	-	-	117.4	3.4	-	-	-	-	-	-	-	-	-	-	123.6	5.3
1991	-	-	-	-	-	-	-	-	-	-	126.7	2.5	-	-	-	-	-	-	-	-	-	-	130.1	2.7
1992	-	-	-	-	-	-	-	-	-	-	132.2	1.6	-	-	-	-	-	-	-	-	-	-	133.8	1.2
1993	-	-	-	-	-	-	-	-	-	-	135.7	1.4	-	-	-	-	-	-	-	-	-	-	138.4	2.0
1994	-	-	-	-	-	-	-	-	-	-	140.5	1.5	-	-	-	-	-	-	-	-	-	-	142.3	1.3
1995	-	-	-	-	-	-	-	-	-	-	143.6	0.9	-	-	-	-	-	-	-	-	-	-	145.5	1.3
1996	-	-	-	-	-	-	-	-	-	-	147.5	1.4	-	-	-	-	-	-	-	-	-	-	151.2	2.5
1997	-	-	-	-	-	-	-	-	-	-	154.6	2.2	-	-	-	-	-	-	-	-	-	-	-	-

Source: U.S. Department of Labor, Bureau of Labor Statistics, Division of Consumer Prices and Price Indexes. - indicates no data collected for period.

San Diego, CA
Consumer Price Index - All Urban Consumers
Base 1982-1984 = 100
Apparel and Upkeep

For 1965-1997. Columns headed % show percentile change in the index from the previous period for which an index is available.

Year	Jan Index	%	Feb Index	%	Mar Index	%	Apr Index	%	May Index	%	Jun Index	%	Jul Index	%	Aug Index	%	Sep Index	%	Oct Index	%	Nov Index	%	Dec Index	%
1965	-		48.5	-	-	-	-	-	48.4	-0.2	-	-	-	-	47.7	-1.4	-	-	-	-	47.8	0.2	-	-
1966	-		48.0	0.4	-	-	-	-	48.8	1.7	-	-	-	-	48.9	0.2	-	-	-	-	49.2	0.6	-	-
1967	-		48.8	-0.8	-	-	-	-	49.3	1.0	-	-	-	-	49.2	-0.2	-	-	-	-	50.5	2.6	-	-
1968	-		50.9	0.8	-	-	-	-	51.9	2.0	-	-	-	-	52.8	1.7	-	-	-	-	54.2	2.7	-	-
1969	-		53.9	-0.6	-	-	-	-	54.4	0.9	-	-	-	-	55.0	1.1	-	-	-	-	55.2	0.4	-	-
1970	-		55.8	1.1	-	-	-	-	57.2	2.5	-	-	-	-	56.8	-0.7	-	-	-	-	57.5	1.2	-	-
1971	-		57.5	0.0	-	-	-	-	58.4	1.6	-	-	-	-	58.5	0.2	-	-	-	-	58.7	0.3	-	-
1972	-		59.8	1.9	-	-	-	-	60.7	1.5	-	-	-	-	59.8	-1.5	-	-	-	-	61.4	2.7	-	-
1973	-		60.9	-0.8	-	-	-	-	61.7	1.3	-	-	-	-	63.3	2.6	-	-	-	-	64.7	2.2	-	-
1974	-		66.2	2.3	-	-	-	-	68.6	3.6	-	-	-	-	67.9	-1.0	-	-	-	-	69.1	1.8	-	-
1975	-		68.6	-0.7	-	-	-	-	70.3	2.5	-	-	-	-	69.2	-1.6	-	-	-	-	70.0	1.2	-	-
1976	-		71.0	1.4	-	-	-	-	71.5	0.7	-	-	-	-	71.9	0.6	-	-	-	-	71.5	-0.6	-	-
1977	-		71.1	-0.6	-	-	-	-	73.0	2.7	-	-	-	-	73.0	0.0	-	-	-	-	73.8	1.1	-	-
1978	74.0	0.3	-	-	73.8	-0.3	-	-	76.9	4.2	-	-	77.3	0.5	-	-	78.5	1.6	-	-	79.5	1.3	-	-
1979	79.2	-0.4	-	-	79.7	0.6	-	-	81.8	2.6	-	-	81.2	-0.7	-	-	82.9	2.1	-	-	82.9	0.0	-	-
1980	83.4	0.6	-	-	88.6	6.2	-	-	87.5	-1.2	-	-	86.7	-0.9	-	-	87.8	1.3	-	-	89.5	1.9	-	-
1981	87.9	-1.8	-	-	90.8	3.3	-	-	90.3	-0.6	-	-	93.5	3.5	-	-	95.0	1.6	-	-	95.0	0.0	-	-
1982	92.2	-2.9	-	-	95.1	3.1	-	-	96.4	1.4	-	-	95.9	-0.5	-	-	99.4	3.6	-	-	98.7	-0.7	-	-
1983	97.8	-0.9	-	-	97.3	-0.5	-	-	98.4	1.1	-	-	101.3	2.9	-	-	101.6	0.3	-	-	100.5	-1.1	-	-
1984	101.8	1.3	-	-	101.6	-0.2	-	-	103.8	2.2	-	-	100.6	-3.1	-	-	106.4	5.8	-	-	108.0	1.5	-	-
1985	105.1	-2.7	-	-	105.5	0.4	-	-	107.5	1.9	-	-	105.1	-2.2	-	-	106.1	1.0	-	-	106.3	0.2	-	-
1986	105.1	-1.1	-	-	108.3	3.0	-	-	108.1	-0.2	-	-	104.5	-3.3	-	-	109.0	4.3	-	-	108.2	-0.7	-	-
1987	-	-	-	-	-	-	-	-	-	-	107.0	-1.1	-	-	-	-	-	-	-	-	-	-	111.9	4.6
1988	-	-	-	-	-	-	-	-	-	-	115.7	3.4	-	-	-	-	-	-	-	-	-	-	115.6	-0.1
1989	-	-	-	-	-	-	-	-	-	-	110.4	-4.5	-	-	-	-	-	-	-	-	-	-	104.4	-5.4
1990	-	-	-	-	-	-	-	-	-	-	110.4	5.7	-	-	-	-	-	-	-	-	-	-	113.6	2.9
1991	-	-	-	-	-	-	-	-	-	-	112.3	-1.1	-	-	-	-	-	-	-	-	-	-	114.4	1.9
1992	-	-	-	-	-	-	-	-	-	-	118.5	3.6	-	-	-	-	-	-	-	-	-	-	118.9	0.3
1993	-	-	-	-	-	-	-	-	-	-	115.5	-2.9	-	-	-	-	-	-	-	-	-	-	115.5	0.0
1994	-	-	-	-	-	-	-	-	-	-	122.5	6.1	-	-	-	-	-	-	-	-	-	-	119.3	-2.6
1995	-	-	-	-	-	-	-	-	-	-	120.3	0.8	-	-	-	-	-	-	-	-	-	-	122.2	1.6
1996	-	-	-	-	-	-	-	-	-	-	125.2	2.5	-	-	-	-	-	-	-	-	-	-	126.3	0.9
1997	-	-	-	-	-	-	-	-	-	-	126.5	0.2	-	-	-	-	-	-	-	-	-	-	-	-

Source: U.S. Department of Labor, Bureau of Labor Statistics, Division of Consumer Prices and Price Indexes. - indicates no data collected for period.

San Diego, CA
Consumer Price Index - Urban Wage Earners
Base 1982-1984 = 100
Apparel and Upkeep

For 1965-1997. Columns headed % show percentile change in the index from the previous period for which an index is available.

Year	Jan Index	%	Feb Index	%	Mar Index	%	Apr Index	%	May Index	%	Jun Index	%	Jul Index	%	Aug Index	%	Sep Index	%	Oct Index	%	Nov Index	%	Dec Index	%
1965	-	-	50.6	-	-	-	-	-	50.6	0.0	-	-	-	-	49.8	-1.6	-	-	-	-	49.9	0.2	-	-
1966	-	-	50.1	0.4	-	-	-	-	50.9	1.6	-	-	-	-	51.0	0.2	-	-	-	-	51.3	0.6	-	-
1967	-	-	51.0	-0.6	-	-	-	-	51.5	1.0	-	-	-	-	51.4	-0.2	-	-	-	-	52.7	2.5	-	-
1968	-	-	53.2	0.9	-	-	-	-	54.2	1.9	-	-	-	-	55.1	1.7	-	-	-	-	56.5	2.5	-	-
1969	-	-	56.2	-0.5	-	-	-	-	56.8	1.1	-	-	-	-	57.5	1.2	-	-	-	-	57.7	0.3	-	-
1970	-	-	58.3	1.0	-	-	-	-	59.7	2.4	-	-	-	-	59.3	-0.7	-	-	-	-	60.0	1.2	-	-
1971	-	-	60.0	0.0	-	-	-	-	60.9	1.5	-	-	-	-	61.0	0.2	-	-	-	-	61.2	0.3	-	-
1972	-	-	62.4	2.0	-	-	-	-	63.4	1.6	-	-	-	-	62.5	-1.4	-	-	-	-	64.1	2.6	-	-
1973	-	-	63.6	-0.8	-	-	-	-	64.4	1.3	-	-	-	-	66.0	2.5	-	-	-	-	67.5	2.3	-	-
1974	-	-	69.1	2.4	-	-	-	-	71.6	3.6	-	-	-	-	70.8	-1.1	-	-	-	-	72.2	2.0	-	-
1975	-	-	71.6	-0.8	-	-	-	-	73.4	2.5	-	-	-	-	72.2	-1.6	-	-	-	-	73.1	1.2	-	-
1976	-	-	74.1	1.4	-	-	-	-	74.6	0.7	-	-	-	-	75.0	0.5	-	-	-	-	74.7	-0.4	-	-
1977	-	-	74.2	-0.7	-	-	-	-	76.3	2.8	-	-	-	-	76.2	-0.1	-	-	-	-	77.0	1.0	-	-
1978	75.9	-1.4	-	-	76.7	1.1	-	-	77.8	1.4	-	-	78.2	0.5	-	-	79.0	1.0	-	-	79.6	0.8	-	-
1979	77.5	-2.6	-	-	77.0	-0.6	-	-	80.3	4.3	-	-	81.4	1.4	-	-	83.4	2.5	-	-	84.6	1.4	-	-
1980	84.5	-0.1	-	-	90.0	6.5	-	-	90.1	0.1	-	-	87.6	-2.8	-	-	87.9	0.3	-	-	89.6	1.9	-	-
1981	88.8	-0.9	-	-	91.1	2.6	-	-	92.5	1.5	-	-	93.2	0.8	-	-	93.9	0.8	-	-	94.6	0.7	-	-
1982	92.3	-2.4	-	-	95.0	2.9	-	-	95.9	0.9	-	-	95.8	-0.1	-	-	99.2	3.5	-	-	98.9	-0.3	-	-
1983	98.5	-0.4	-	-	97.9	-0.6	-	-	98.6	0.7	-	-	101.0	2.4	-	-	101.7	0.7	-	-	100.4	-1.3	-	-
1984	101.5	1.1	-	-	101.7	0.2	-	-	103.7	2.0	-	-	100.8	-2.8	-	-	106.2	5.4	-	-	107.8	1.5	-	-
1985	105.0	-2.6	-	-	105.8	0.8	-	-	107.8	1.9	-	-	105.5	-2.1	-	-	106.4	0.9	-	-	106.8	0.4	-	-
1986	106.4	-0.4	-	-	108.8	2.3	-	-	109.0	0.2	-	-	104.3	-4.3	-	-	107.9	3.5	-	-	108.0	0.1	-	-
1987	-	-	-	-	-	-	-	-	-	-	105.3	-2.5	-	-	-	-	-	-	-	-	-	-	111.3	5.7
1988	-	-	-	-	-	-	-	-	-	-	114.2	2.6	-	-	-	-	-	-	-	-	-	-	114.0	-0.2
1989	-	-	-	-	-	-	-	-	-	-	108.5	-4.8	-	-	-	-	-	-	-	-	-	-	103.0	-5.1
1990	-	-	-	-	-	-	-	-	-	-	109.1	5.9	-	-	-	-	-	-	-	-	-	-	112.8	3.4
1991	-	-	-	-	-	-	-	-	-	-	111.1	-1.5	-	-	-	-	-	-	-	-	-	-	113.2	1.9
1992	-	-	-	-	-	-	-	-	-	-	117.0	3.4	-	-	-	-	-	-	-	-	-	-	118.4	1.2
1993	-	-	-	-	-	-	-	-	-	-	114.3	-3.5	-	-	-	-	-	-	-	-	-	-	115.7	1.2
1994	-	-	-	-	-	-	-	-	-	-	122.2	5.6	-	-	-	-	-	-	-	-	-	-	118.8	-2.8
1995	-	-	-	-	-	-	-	-	-	-	119.6	0.7	-	-	-	-	-	-	-	-	-	-	121.2	1.3
1996	-	-	-	-	-	-	-	-	-	-	123.4	1.8	-	-	-	-	-	-	-	-	-	-	124.8	1.1
1997	-	-	-	-	-	-	-	-	-	-	126.1	1.0	-	-	-	-	-	-	-	-	-	-	-	-

Source: U.S. Department of Labor, Bureau of Labor Statistics, Division of Consumer Prices and Price Indexes. - indicates no data collected for period.

San Diego, CA
Consumer Price Index - All Urban Consumers
Base 1982-1984 = 100
Transportation

For 1965-1997. Columns headed % show percentile change in the index from the previous period for which an index is available.

Year	Jan Index	%	Feb Index	%	Mar Index	%	Apr Index	%	May Index	%	Jun Index	%	Jul Index	%	Aug Index	%	Sep Index	%	Oct Index	%	Nov Index	%	Dec Index	%
1965	-	-	32.0	-	-	-	-	-	32.7	2.2	-	-	-	-	32.4	-0.9	-	-	-	-	31.4	-3.1	-	-
1966	-	-	31.7	1.0	-	-	-	-	31.8	0.3	-	-	-	-	31.9	0.3	-	-	-	-	33.2	4.1	-	-
1967	-	-	33.0	-0.6	-	-	-	-	33.0	0.0	-	-	-	-	33.7	2.1	-	-	-	-	33.5	-0.6	-	-
1968	-	-	33.8	0.9	-	-	-	-	34.0	0.6	-	-	-	-	34.2	0.6	-	-	-	-	34.4	0.6	-	-
1969	-	-	34.5	0.3	-	-	-	-	35.0	1.4	-	-	-	-	35.1	0.3	-	-	-	-	35.0	-0.3	-	-
1970	-	-	34.8	-0.6	-	-	-	-	35.6	2.3	-	-	-	-	35.7	0.3	-	-	-	-	37.5	5.0	-	-
1971	-	-	36.9	-1.6	-	-	-	-	38.0	3.0	-	-	-	-	38.6	1.6	-	-	-	-	38.2	-1.0	-	-
1972	-	-	37.5	-1.8	-	-	-	-	38.8	3.5	-	-	-	-	39.7	2.3	-	-	-	-	40.2	1.3	-	-
1973	-	-	39.5	-1.7	-	-	-	-	40.6	2.8	-	-	-	-	41.2	1.5	-	-	-	-	41.3	0.2	-	-
1974	-	-	43.4	5.1	-	-	-	-	45.8	5.5	-	-	-	-	47.4	3.5	-	-	-	-	48.1	1.5	-	-
1975	-	-	48.8	1.5	-	-	-	-	50.1	2.7	-	-	-	-	52.5	4.8	-	-	-	-	52.6	0.2	-	-
1976	-	-	52.5	-0.2	-	-	-	-	53.8	2.5	-	-	-	-	55.5	3.2	-	-	-	-	56.4	1.6	-	-
1977	-	-	56.8	0.7	-	-	-	-	58.1	2.3	-	-	-	-	58.6	0.9	-	-	-	-	58.9	0.5	-	-
1978	58.8	-0.2	-	-	58.8	0.0	-	-	60.1	2.2	-	-	62.2	3.5	-	-	62.4	0.3	-	-	63.4	1.6	-	-
1979	64.1	1.1	-	-	65.2	1.7	-	-	68.9	5.7	-	-	71.2	3.3	-	-	72.9	2.4	-	-	74.2	1.8	-	-
1980	77.0	3.8	-	-	80.7	4.8	-	-	82.0	1.6	-	-	82.9	1.1	-	-	84.0	1.3	-	-	84.6	0.7	-	-
1981	86.0	1.7	-	-	88.6	3.0	-	-	90.7	2.4	-	-	92.8	2.3	-	-	93.7	1.0	-	-	94.7	1.1	-	-
1982	94.6	-0.1	-	-	93.2	-1.5	-	-	93.4	0.2	-	-	98.2	5.1	-	-	97.8	-0.4	-	-	96.6	-1.2	-	-
1983	96.2	-0.4	-	-	94.4	-1.9	-	-	98.5	4.3	-	-	100.3	1.8	-	-	100.6	0.3	-	-	101.3	0.7	-	-
1984	103.1	1.8	-	-	103.3	0.2	-	-	106.9	3.5	-	-	105.2	-1.6	-	-	105.9	0.7	-	-	107.6	1.6	-	-
1985	107.5	-0.1	-	-	108.6	1.0	-	-	111.1	2.3	-	-	110.1	-0.9	-	-	108.9	-1.1	-	-	109.3	0.4	-	-
1986	110.0	0.6	-	-	106.3	-3.4	-	-	106.6	0.3	-	-	105.3	-1.2	-	-	104.1	-1.1	-	-	102.9	-1.2	-	-
1987	-	-	-	-	-	-	-	-	-	-	100.9	-1.9	-	-	-	-	-	-	-	-	-	-	103.8	2.9
1988	-	-	-	-	-	-	-	-	-	-	102.5	-1.3	-	-	-	-	-	-	-	-	-	-	104.6	2.0
1989	-	-	-	-	-	-	-	-	-	-	107.5	2.8	-	-	-	-	-	-	-	-	-	-	110.8	3.1
1990	-	-	-	-	-	-	-	-	-	-	113.4	2.3	-	-	-	-	-	-	-	-	-	-	118.9	4.9
1991	-	-	-	-	-	-	-	-	-	-	119.3	0.3	-	-	-	-	-	-	-	-	-	-	120.6	1.1
1992	-	-	-	-	-	-	-	-	-	-	121.8	1.0	-	-	-	-	-	-	-	-	-	-	126.0	3.4
1993	-	-	-	-	-	-	-	-	-	-	126.6	0.5	-	-	-	-	-	-	-	-	-	-	130.1	2.8
1994	-	-	-	-	-	-	-	-	-	-	133.0	2.2	-	-	-	-	-	-	-	-	-	-	137.0	3.0
1995	-	-	-	-	-	-	-	-	-	-	138.2	0.9	-	-	-	-	-	-	-	-	-	-	140.8	1.9
1996	-	-	-	-	-	-	-	-	-	-	142.5	1.2	-	-	-	-	-	-	-	-	-	-	145.5	2.1
1997	-	-	-	-	-	-	-	-	-	-	145.4	-0.1	-	-	-	-	-	-	-	-	-	-	-	-

Source: U.S. Department of Labor, Bureau of Labor Statistics, Division of Consumer Prices and Price Indexes. - indicates no data collected for period.

San Diego, CA
Consumer Price Index - Urban Wage Earners
Base 1982-1984 = 100
Transportation

For 1965-1997. Columns headed % show percentile change in the index from the previous period for which an index is available.

Year	Jan Index	%	Feb Index	%	Mar Index	%	Apr Index	%	May Index	%	Jun Index	%	Jul Index	%	Aug Index	%	Sep Index	%	Oct Index	%	Nov Index	%	Dec Index	%
1965	-	-	31.8	-	-	-	-	-	32.5	2.2	-	-	-	-	32.1	-1.2	-	-	-	-	31.2	-2.8	-	-
1966	-	-	31.5	1.0	-	-	-	-	31.5	0.0	-	-	-	-	31.6	0.3	-	-	-	-	33.0	4.4	-	-
1967	-	-	32.8	-0.6	-	-	-	-	32.8	0.0	-	-	-	-	33.5	2.1	-	-	-	-	33.3	-0.6	-	-
1968	-	-	33.6	0.9	-	-	-	-	33.8	0.6	-	-	-	-	33.9	0.3	-	-	-	-	34.2	0.9	-	-
1969	-	-	34.3	0.3	-	-	-	-	34.8	1.5	-	-	-	-	34.9	0.3	-	-	-	-	34.7	-0.6	-	-
1970	-	-	34.6	-0.3	-	-	-	-	35.4	2.3	-	-	-	-	35.5	0.3	-	-	-	-	37.2	4.8	-	-
1971	-	-	36.6	-1.6	-	-	-	-	37.8	3.3	-	-	-	-	38.3	1.3	-	-	-	-	38.0	-0.8	-	-
1972	-	-	37.2	-2.1	-	-	-	-	38.6	3.8	-	-	-	-	39.4	2.1	-	-	-	-	39.9	1.3	-	-
1973	-	-	39.2	-1.8	-	-	-	-	40.3	2.8	-	-	-	-	40.9	1.5	-	-	-	-	41.0	0.2	-	-
1974	-	-	43.1	5.1	-	-	-	-	45.5	5.6	-	-	-	-	47.1	3.5	-	-	-	-	47.8	1.5	-	-
1975	-	-	48.4	1.3	-	-	-	-	49.8	2.9	-	-	-	-	52.1	4.6	-	-	-	-	52.2	0.2	-	-
1976	-	-	52.2	0.0	-	-	-	-	53.4	2.3	-	-	-	-	55.1	3.2	-	-	-	-	56.0	1.6	-	-
1977	-	-	56.4	0.7	-	-	-	-	57.7	2.3	-	-	-	-	58.2	0.9	-	-	-	-	58.5	0.5	-	-
1978	58.7	0.3	-	-	58.8	0.2	-	-	60.0	2.0	-	-	61.9	3.2	-	-	62.0	0.2	-	-	63.3	2.1	-	-
1979	64.0	1.1	-	-	65.1	1.7	-	-	68.8	5.7	-	-	70.9	3.1	-	-	72.6	2.4	-	-	73.5	1.2	-	-
1980	76.3	3.8	-	-	79.9	4.7	-	-	80.9	1.3	-	-	81.8	1.1	-	-	82.5	0.9	-	-	83.5	1.2	-	-
1981	84.7	1.4	-	-	87.1	2.8	-	-	89.3	2.5	-	-	91.5	2.5	-	-	92.4	1.0	-	-	93.8	1.5	-	-
1982	93.9	0.1	-	-	92.7	-1.3	-	-	93.0	0.3	-	-	98.0	5.4	-	-	97.6	-0.4	-	-	96.4	-1.2	-	-
1983	95.9	-0.5	-	-	94.4	-1.6	-	-	98.4	4.2	-	-	100.2	1.8	-	-	100.6	0.4	-	-	101.4	0.8	-	-
1984	103.3	1.9	-	-	103.6	0.3	-	-	107.1	3.4	-	-	105.8	-1.2	-	-	106.2	0.4	-	-	107.9	1.6	-	-
1985	107.9	0.0	-	-	108.8	0.8	-	-	111.3	2.3	-	-	110.4	-0.8	-	-	109.1	-1.2	-	-	109.5	0.4	-	-
1986	110.1	0.5	-	-	106.9	-2.9	-	-	107.2	0.3	-	-	105.8	-1.3	-	-	104.7	-1.0	-	-	103.5	-1.1	-	-
1987	-	-	-	-	-	-	-	-	-	-	101.1	-2.3	-	-	-	-	-	-	-	-	-	-	104.2	3.1
1988	-	-	-	-	-	-	-	-	-	-	103.6	-0.6	-	-	-	-	-	-	-	-	-	-	105.7	2.0
1989	-	-	-	-	-	-	-	-	-	-	108.6	2.7	-	-	-	-	-	-	-	-	-	-	111.9	3.0
1990	-	-	-	-	-	-	-	-	-	-	113.8	1.7	-	-	-	-	-	-	-	-	-	-	119.5	5.0
1991	-	-	-	-	-	-	-	-	-	-	119.7	0.2	-	-	-	-	-	-	-	-	-	-	121.5	1.5
1992	-	-	-	-	-	-	-	-	-	-	122.8	1.1	-	-	-	-	-	-	-	-	-	-	127.2	3.6
1993	-	-	-	-	-	-	-	-	-	-	127.9	0.6	-	-	-	-	-	-	-	-	-	-	132.3	3.4
1994	-	-	-	-	-	-	-	-	-	-	135.4	2.3	-	-	-	-	-	-	-	-	-	-	140.2	3.5
1995	-	-	-	-	-	-	-	-	-	-	141.9	1.2	-	-	-	-	-	-	-	-	-	-	144.3	1.7
1996	-	-	-	-	-	-	-	-	-	-	146.2	1.3	-	-	-	-	-	-	-	-	-	-	148.8	1.8
1997	-	-	-	-	-	-	-	-	-	-	148.4	-0.3	-	-	-	-	-	-	-	-	-	-	-	-

Source: U.S. Department of Labor, Bureau of Labor Statistics, Division of Consumer Prices and Price Indexes. - indicates no data collected for period.

San Diego, CA
Consumer Price Index - All Urban Consumers
Base 1982-1984 = 100
Medical Care

For 1965-1997. Columns headed % show percentile change in the index from the previous period for which an index is available.

Year	Jan Index	%	Feb Index	%	Mar Index	%	Apr Index	%	May Index	%	Jun Index	%	Jul Index	%	Aug Index	%	Sep Index	%	Oct Index	%	Nov Index	%	Dec Index	%
1965	-	-	26.4	-	-	-	-	-	26.5	0.4	-	-	-	-	26.6	0.4	-	-	-	-	26.8	0.8	-	-
1966	-	-	27.2	1.5	-	-	-	-	27.7	1.8	-	-	-	-	27.9	0.7	-	-	-	-	29.2	4.7	-	-
1967	-	-	29.4	0.7	-	-	-	-	29.9	1.7	-	-	-	-	30.2	1.0	-	-	-	-	30.5	1.0	-	-
1968	-	-	30.5	0.0	-	-	-	-	30.5	0.0	-	-	-	-	30.9	1.3	-	-	-	-	31.2	1.0	-	-
1969	-	-	31.9	2.2	-	-	-	-	32.3	1.3	-	-	-	-	32.7	1.2	-	-	-	-	32.7	0.0	-	-
1970	-	-	33.4	2.1	-	-	-	-	34.3	2.7	-	-	-	-	34.9	1.7	-	-	-	-	35.2	0.9	-	-
1971	-	-	35.6	1.1	-	-	-	-	36.3	2.0	-	-	-	-	36.8	1.4	-	-	-	-	36.6	-0.5	-	-
1972	-	-	36.7	0.3	-	-	-	-	36.8	0.3	-	-	-	-	37.2	1.1	-	-	-	-	38.0	2.2	-	-
1973	-	-	38.1	0.3	-	-	-	-	38.5	1.0	-	-	-	-	39.3	2.1	-	-	-	-	40.2	2.3	-	-
1974	-	-	41.1	2.2	-	-	-	-	42.2	2.7	-	-	-	-	44.4	5.2	-	-	-	-	45.0	1.4	-	-
1975	-	-	47.1	4.7	-	-	-	-	47.8	1.5	-	-	-	-	49.0	2.5	-	-	-	-	50.1	2.2	-	-
1976	-	-	52.0	3.8	-	-	-	-	52.8	1.5	-	-	-	-	54.3	2.8	-	-	-	-	55.3	1.8	-	-
1977	-	-	56.7	2.5	-	-	-	-	58.3	2.8	-	-	-	-	59.3	1.7	-	-	-	-	60.0	1.2	-	-
1978	61.2	2.0	-	-	62.5	2.1	-	-	62.7	0.3	-	-	63.8	1.8	-	-	64.0	0.3	-	-	65.7	2.7	-	-
1979	67.2	2.3	-	-	67.6	0.6	-	-	68.4	1.2	-	-	69.2	1.2	-	-	71.1	2.7	-	-	72.3	1.7	-	-
1980	72.7	0.6	-	-	73.8	1.5	-	-	76.2	3.3	-	-	76.5	0.4	-	-	77.1	0.8	-	-	79.1	2.6	-	-
1981	79.4	0.4	-	-	79.5	0.1	-	-	80.4	1.1	-	-	84.1	4.6	-	-	84.9	1.0	-	-	87.4	2.9	-	-
1982	88.7	1.5	-	-	89.2	0.6	-	-	90.1	1.0	-	-	93.7	4.0	-	-	95.4	1.8	-	-	98.8	3.6	-	-
1983	99.9	1.1	-	-	99.9	0.0	-	-	99.9	0.0	-	-	99.7	-0.2	-	-	101.1	1.4	-	-	102.8	1.7	-	-
1984	104.3	1.5	-	-	105.2	0.9	-	-	105.5	0.3	-	-	107.5	1.9	-	-	106.9	-0.6	-	-	107.2	0.3	-	-
1985	106.9	-0.3	-	-	108.8	1.8	-	-	109.9	1.0	-	-	110.6	0.6	-	-	110.9	0.3	-	-	112.1	1.1	-	-
1986	112.8	0.6	-	-	115.0	2.0	-	-	116.4	1.2	-	-	117.8	1.2	-	-	121.4	3.1	-	-	123.0	1.3	-	-
1987	-	-	-	-	-	-	-	-	-	-	122.6	-0.3	-	-	-	-	-	-	-	-	-	-	126.6	3.3
1988	-	-	-	-	-	-	-	-	-	-	131.2	3.6	-	-	-	-	-	-	-	-	-	-	134.6	2.6
1989	-	-	-	-	-	-	-	-	-	-	140.6	4.5	-	-	-	-	-	-	-	-	-	-	142.6	1.4
1990	-	-	-	-	-	-	-	-	-	-	152.6	7.0	-	-	-	-	-	-	-	-	-	-	156.6	2.6
1991	-	-	-	-	-	-	-	-	-	-	166.2	6.1	-	-	-	-	-	-	-	-	-	-	172.6	3.9
1992	-	-	-	-	-	-	-	-	-	-	181.2	5.0	-	-	-	-	-	-	-	-	-	-	187.1	3.3
1993	-	-	-	-	-	-	-	-	-	-	192.4	2.8	-	-	-	-	-	-	-	-	-	-	193.8	0.7
1994	-	-	-	-	-	-	-	-	-	-	197.3	1.8	-	-	-	-	-	-	-	-	-	-	202.4	2.6
1995	-	-	-	-	-	-	-	-	-	-	207.5	2.5	-	-	-	-	-	-	-	-	-	-	211.3	1.8
1996	-	-	-	-	-	-	-	-	-	-	216.9	2.7	-	-	-	-	-	-	-	-	-	-	217.9	0.5
1997	-	-	-	-	-	-	-	-	-	-	222.5	2.1	-	-	-	-	-	-	-	-	-	-	-	-

Source: U.S. Department of Labor, Bureau of Labor Statistics, Division of Consumer Prices and Price Indexes. - indicates no data collected for period.

San Diego, CA
Consumer Price Index - Urban Wage Earners
Base 1982-1984 = 100
Medical Care

For 1965-1997. Columns headed % show percentile change in the index from the previous period for which an index is available.

Year	Jan Index	%	Feb Index	%	Mar Index	%	Apr Index	%	May Index	%	Jun Index	%	Jul Index	%	Aug Index	%	Sep Index	%	Oct Index	%	Nov Index	%	Dec Index	%
1965	-	-	25.8	-	-	-	-	-	26.0	0.8	-	-	-	-	26.1	0.4	-	-	-	-	26.2	0.4	-	-
1966	-	-	26.6	1.5	-	-	-	-	27.1	1.9	-	-	-	-	27.3	0.7	-	-	-	-	28.6	4.8	-	-
1967	-	-	28.8	0.7	-	-	-	-	29.2	1.4	-	-	-	-	29.6	1.4	-	-	-	-	29.9	1.0	-	-
1968	-	-	29.9	0.0	-	-	-	-	29.9	0.0	-	-	-	-	30.2	1.0	-	-	-	-	30.5	1.0	-	-
1969	-	-	31.2	2.3	-	-	-	-	31.6	1.3	-	-	-	-	32.0	1.3	-	-	-	-	32.0	0.0	-	-
1970	-	-	32.7	2.2	-	-	-	-	33.5	2.4	-	-	-	-	34.1	1.8	-	-	-	-	34.4	0.9	-	-
1971	-	-	34.9	1.5	-	-	-	-	35.5	1.7	-	-	-	-	36.0	1.4	-	-	-	-	35.8	-0.6	-	-
1972	-	-	35.9	0.3	-	-	-	-	36.0	0.3	-	-	-	-	36.4	1.1	-	-	-	-	37.1	1.9	-	-
1973	-	-	37.3	0.5	-	-	-	-	37.7	1.1	-	-	-	-	38.4	1.9	-	-	-	-	39.3	2.3	-	-
1974	-	-	40.2	2.3	-	-	-	-	41.3	2.7	-	-	-	-	43.4	5.1	-	-	-	-	44.0	1.4	-	-
1975	-	-	46.0	4.5	-	-	-	-	46.8	1.7	-	-	-	-	47.9	2.4	-	-	-	-	49.0	2.3	-	-
1976	-	-	50.9	3.9	-	-	-	-	51.6	1.4	-	-	-	-	53.1	2.9	-	-	-	-	54.1	1.9	-	-
1977	-	-	55.5	2.6	-	-	-	-	57.1	2.9	-	-	-	-	58.0	1.6	-	-	-	-	58.8	1.4	-	-
1978	60.3	2.6	-	-	60.8	0.8	-	-	61.1	0.5	-	-	62.5	2.3	-	-	62.8	0.5	-	-	63.7	1.4	-	-
1979	65.2	2.4	-	-	66.2	1.5	-	-	68.7	3.8	-	-	69.4	1.0	-	-	72.0	3.7	-	-	73.0	1.4	-	-
1980	73.8	1.1	-	-	74.4	0.8	-	-	75.1	0.9	-	-	77.0	2.5	-	-	77.6	0.8	-	-	77.9	0.4	-	-
1981	79.5	2.1	-	-	79.4	-0.1	-	-	80.1	0.9	-	-	85.4	6.6	-	-	86.5	1.3	-	-	87.9	1.6	-	-
1982	89.1	1.4	-	-	89.5	0.4	-	-	90.3	0.9	-	-	93.5	3.5	-	-	95.0	1.6	-	-	98.6	3.8	-	-
1983	99.5	0.9	-	-	99.6	0.1	-	-	99.6	0.0	-	-	99.4	-0.2	-	-	101.2	1.8	-	-	102.9	1.7	-	-
1984	104.4	1.5	-	-	105.3	0.9	-	-	105.6	0.3	-	-	107.5	1.8	-	-	107.1	-0.4	-	-	107.4	0.3	-	-
1985	107.3	-0.1	-	-	109.3	1.9	-	-	110.5	1.1	-	-	111.1	0.5	-	-	111.5	0.4	-	-	112.6	1.0	-	-
1986	113.3	0.6	-	-	115.6	2.0	-	-	117.1	1.3	-	-	118.5	1.2	-	-	122.4	3.3	-	-	123.8	1.1	-	-
1987	-	-	-	-	-	-	-	-	-	-	124.3	0.4	-	-	-	-	-	-	-	-	-	-	128.2	3.1
1988	-	-	-	-	-	-	-	-	-	-	133.0	3.7	-	-	-	-	-	-	-	-	-	-	136.5	2.6
1989	-	-	-	-	-	-	-	-	-	-	142.5	4.4	-	-	-	-	-	-	-	-	-	-	144.3	1.3
1990	-	-	-	-	-	-	-	-	-	-	154.0	6.7	-	-	-	-	-	-	-	-	-	-	157.9	2.5
1991	-	-	-	-	-	-	-	-	-	-	166.9	5.7	-	-	-	-	-	-	-	-	-	-	173.1	3.7
1992	-	-	-	-	-	-	-	-	-	-	181.9	5.1	-	-	-	-	-	-	-	-	-	-	188.0	3.4
1993	-	-	-	-	-	-	-	-	-	-	193.2	2.8	-	-	-	-	-	-	-	-	-	-	194.5	0.7
1994	-	-	-	-	-	-	-	-	-	-	197.7	1.6	-	-	-	-	-	-	-	-	-	-	202.7	2.5
1995	-	-	-	-	-	-	-	-	-	-	207.4	2.3	-	-	-	-	-	-	-	-	-	-	210.8	1.6
1996	-	-	-	-	-	-	-	-	-	-	217.3	3.1	-	-	-	-	-	-	-	-	-	-	218.3	0.5
1997	-	-	-	-	-	-	-	-	-	-	222.9	2.1	-	-	-	-	-	-	-	-	-	-	-	-

Source: U.S. Department of Labor, Bureau of Labor Statistics, Division of Consumer Prices and Price Indexes. - indicates no data collected for period.

San Diego, CA
Consumer Price Index - All Urban Consumers
Base 1982-1984 = 100
Entertainment

For 1975-1997. Columns headed % show percentile change in the index from the previous period for which an index is available.

Year	Jan Index	%	Feb Index	%	Mar Index	%	Apr Index	%	May Index	%	Jun Index	%	Jul Index	%	Aug Index	%	Sep Index	%	Oct Index	%	Nov Index	%	Dec Index	%
1975	-	-	-	-	-	-	-	-	-	-	-	-	-	-	-	-	-	-	-	-	60.3	-	-	-
1976	-	-	61.6	2.2	-	-	-	-	62.6	1.6	-	-	-	-	63.1	0.8	-	-	-	-	63.1	0.0	-	-
1977	-	-	63.4	0.5	-	-	-	-	64.9	2.4	-	-	-	-	65.9	1.5	-	-	-	-	66.1	0.3	-	-
1978	67.1	1.5	-	-	67.8	1.0	-	-	68.7	1.3	-	-	69.5	1.2	-	-	70.7	1.7	-	-	70.7	0.0	-	-
1979	72.6	2.7	-	-	73.3	1.0	-	-	74.3	1.4	-	-	75.5	1.6	-	-	76.0	0.7	-	-	76.5	0.7	-	-
1980	77.8	1.7	-	-	81.5	4.8	-	-	83.4	2.3	-	-	84.4	1.2	-	-	84.3	-0.1	-	-	85.1	0.9	-	-
1981	86.5	1.6	-	-	87.6	1.3	-	-	89.3	1.9	-	-	90.2	1.0	-	-	91.9	1.9	-	-	92.2	0.3	-	-
1982	93.3	1.2	-	-	94.6	1.4	-	-	95.4	0.8	-	-	96.5	1.2	-	-	96.7	0.2	-	-	98.4	1.8	-	-
1983	99.7	1.3	-	-	99.5	-0.2	-	-	101.5	2.0	-	-	101.0	-0.5	-	-	101.2	0.2	-	-	101.4	0.2	-	-
1984	101.9	0.5	-	-	102.4	0.5	-	-	102.7	0.3	-	-	102.4	-0.3	-	-	103.2	0.8	-	-	105.3	2.0	-	-
1985	105.4	0.1	-	-	106.5	1.0	-	-	107.3	0.8	-	-	108.4	1.0	-	-	108.2	-0.2	-	-	108.1	-0.1	-	-
1986	108.7	0.6	-	-	110.5	1.7	-	-	112.0	1.4	-	-	113.2	1.1	-	-	112.9	-0.3	-	-	112.7	-0.2	-	-
1987	-	-	-	-	-	-	-	-	-	-	110.0	-2.4	-	-	-	-	-	-	-	-	-	-	111.8	1.6
1988	-	-	-	-	-	-	-	-	-	-	113.9	1.9	-	-	-	-	-	-	-	-	-	-	117.1	2.8
1989	-	-	-	-	-	-	-	-	-	-	124.1	6.0	-	-	-	-	-	-	-	-	-	-	127.9	3.1
1990	-	-	-	-	-	-	-	-	-	-	129.1	0.9	-	-	-	-	-	-	-	-	-	-	130.8	1.3
1991	-	-	-	-	-	-	-	-	-	-	135.3	3.4	-	-	-	-	-	-	-	-	-	-	136.5	0.9
1992	-	-	-	-	-	-	-	-	-	-	138.0	1.1	-	-	-	-	-	-	-	-	-	-	142.3	3.1
1993	-	-	-	-	-	-	-	-	-	-	143.8	1.1	-	-	-	-	-	-	-	-	-	-	144.7	0.6
1994	-	-	-	-	-	-	-	-	-	-	145.4	0.5	-	-	-	-	-	-	-	-	-	-	148.0	1.8
1995	-	-	-	-	-	-	-	-	-	-	148.2	0.1	-	-	-	-	-	-	-	-	-	-	146.9	-0.9
1996	-	-	-	-	-	-	-	-	-	-	148.1	0.8	-	-	-	-	-	-	-	-	-	-	151.5	2.3
1997	-	-	-	-	-	-	-	-	-	-	151.7	0.1	-	-	-	-	-	-	-	-	-	-	-	-

Source: U.S. Department of Labor, Bureau of Labor Statistics, Division of Consumer Prices and Price Indexes. - indicates no data collected for period.

San Diego, CA
Consumer Price Index - Urban Wage Earners
Base 1982-1984 = 100
Entertainment

For 1975-1997. Columns headed % show percentile change in the index from the previous period for which an index is available.

Year	Jan Index	%	Feb Index	%	Mar Index	%	Apr Index	%	May Index	%	Jun Index	%	Jul Index	%	Aug Index	%	Sep Index	%	Oct Index	%	Nov Index	%	Dec Index	%
1975	-	-	-	-	-	-	-	-	-	-	-	-	-	-	-	-	-	-	-	-	58.6	-	-	-
1976	-	-	59.9	2.2	-	-	-	-	60.8	1.5	-	-	-	-	61.3	0.8	-	-	-	-	61.3	0.0	-	-
1977	-	-	61.6	0.5	-	-	-	-	63.0	2.3	-	-	-	-	64.0	1.6	-	-	-	-	64.3	0.5	-	-
1978	64.8	0.8	-	-	65.4	0.9	-	-	66.2	1.2	-	-	68.2	3.0	-	-	69.3	1.6	-	-	69.5	0.3	-	-
1979	70.6	1.6	-	-	71.2	0.8	-	-	73.1	2.7	-	-	73.5	0.5	-	-	74.6	1.5	-	-	76.0	1.9	-	-
1980	76.2	0.3	-	-	79.8	4.7	-	-	80.7	1.1	-	-	83.2	3.1	-	-	84.7	1.8	-	-	84.6	-0.1	-	-
1981	84.2	-0.5	-	-	86.7	3.0	-	-	86.9	0.2	-	-	88.9	2.3	-	-	91.4	2.8	-	-	91.8	0.4	-	-
1982	93.2	1.5	-	-	94.4	1.3	-	-	95.4	1.1	-	-	96.8	1.5	-	-	96.6	-0.2	-	-	98.2	1.7	-	-
1983	99.8	1.6	-	-	99.2	-0.6	-	-	101.7	2.5	-	-	101.3	-0.4	-	-	101.4	0.1	-	-	101.6	0.2	-	-
1984	101.9	0.3	-	-	102.4	0.5	-	-	102.6	0.2	-	-	102.2	-0.4	-	-	103.0	0.8	-	-	105.2	2.1	-	-
1985	105.3	0.1	-	-	106.4	1.0	-	-	107.3	0.8	-	-	108.7	1.3	-	-	108.6	-0.1	-	-	108.8	0.2	-	-
1986	109.6	0.7	-	-	111.5	1.7	-	-	113.0	1.3	-	-	114.3	1.2	-	-	114.3	0.0	-	-	114.2	-0.1	-	-
1987	-	-	-	-	-	-	-	-	-	-	109.0	-4.6	-	-	-	-	-	-	-	-	110.2	1.1		
1988	-	-	-	-	-	-	-	-	-	-	111.2	0.9	-	-	-	-	-	-	-	-	115.5	3.9		
1989	-	-	-	-	-	-	-	-	-	-	122.1	5.7	-	-	-	-	-	-	-	-	126.3	3.4		
1990	-	-	-	-	-	-	-	-	-	-	127.2	0.7	-	-	-	-	-	-	-	-	128.4	0.9		
1991	-	-	-	-	-	-	-	-	-	-	133.1	3.7	-	-	-	-	-	-	-	-	132.8	-0.2		
1992	-	-	-	-	-	-	-	-	-	-	135.1	1.7	-	-	-	-	-	-	-	-	137.7	1.9		
1993	-	-	-	-	-	-	-	-	-	-	139.3	1.2	-	-	-	-	-	-	-	-	141.1	1.3		
1994	-	-	-	-	-	-	-	-	-	-	141.9	0.6	-	-	-	-	-	-	-	-	144.2	1.6		
1995	-	-	-	-	-	-	-	-	-	-	143.2	-0.7	-	-	-	-	-	-	-	-	141.6	-1.1		
1996	-	-	-	-	-	-	-	-	-	-	143.3	1.2	-	-	-	-	-	-	-	-	145.9	1.8		
1997	-	-	-	-	-	-	-	-	-	-	146.4	0.3	-	-	-	-	-	-	-	-	-	-	-	-

Source: U.S. Department of Labor, Bureau of Labor Statistics, Division of Consumer Prices and Price Indexes. - indicates no data collected for period.

San Diego, CA
Consumer Price Index - All Urban Consumers
Base 1982-1984 = 100
Other Goods and Services

For 1975-1997. Columns headed % show percentile change in the index from the previous period for which an index is available.

Year	Jan Index	%	Feb Index	%	Mar Index	%	Apr Index	%	May Index	%	Jun Index	%	Jul Index	%	Aug Index	%	Sep Index	%	Oct Index	%	Nov Index	%	Dec Index	%
1975	-	-	-	-	-	-	-	-	57.8	-	-	-	-	-	-	-	-	-	-	-	55.4	-	-	-
1976	-	-	56.6	2.2	-	-	-	-	57.8	2.1	-	-	-	-	58.3	0.9	-	-	-	-	59.5	2.1	-	-
1977	-	-	59.7	0.3	-	-	-	-	60.5	1.3	-	-	-	-	61.5	1.7	-	-	-	-	62.7	2.0	-	-
1978	63.8	1.8	-	-	64.7	1.4	-	-	65.1	0.6	-	-	65.7	0.9	-	-	67.8	3.2	-	-	68.8	1.5	-	-
1979	69.4	0.9	-	-	70.0	0.9	-	-	70.2	0.3	-	-	70.7	0.7	-	-	72.8	3.0	-	-	73.4	0.8	-	-
1980	73.9	0.7	-	-	75.1	1.6	-	-	75.2	0.1	-	-	76.7	2.0	-	-	79.3	3.4	-	-	80.7	1.8	-	-
1981	83.0	2.9	-	-	83.1	0.1	-	-	84.4	1.6	-	-	84.3	-0.1	-	-	86.7	2.8	-	-	87.6	1.0	-	-
1982	88.9	1.5	-	-	89.6	0.8	-	-	90.2	0.7	-	-	88.6	-1.8	-	-	94.2	6.3	-	-	95.4	1.3	-	-
1983	98.0	2.7	-	-	97.1	-0.9	-	-	98.8	1.8	-	-	99.2	0.4	-	-	101.7	2.5	-	-	104.5	2.8	-	-
1984	104.9	0.4	-	-	105.0	0.1	-	-	107.6	2.5	-	-	107.1	-0.5	-	-	110.5	3.2	-	-	112.6	1.9	-	-
1985	114.2	1.4	-	-	115.1	0.8	-	-	114.6	-0.4	-	-	114.5	-0.1	-	-	117.6	2.7	-	-	117.2	-0.3	-	-
1986	118.6	1.2	-	-	119.4	0.7	-	-	119.6	0.2	-	-	118.4	-1.0	-	-	120.9	2.1	-	-	121.7	0.7	-	-
1987	-	-	-	-	-	-	-	-	-	-	121.0	-0.6	-	-	-	-	-	-	-	-	-	-	-	-
1988	-	-	-	-	-	-	-	-	-	-	126.5	4.5	-	-	-	-	-	-	-	-	-	-	-	-
1989	-	-	-	-	-	-	-	-	-	-	132.9	5.1	-	-	-	-	-	-	-	-	-	-	-	-
1990	-	-	-	-	-	-	-	-	-	-	144.2	8.5	-	-	-	-	-	-	-	-	-	-	-	-
1991	-	-	-	-	-	-	-	-	-	-	154.1	6.9	-	-	-	-	-	-	-	-	-	-	-	-
1992	-	-	-	-	-	-	-	-	-	-	166.0	7.7	-	-	-	-	-	-	-	-	-	-	-	-
1993	-	-	-	-	-	-	-	-	-	-	178.6	7.6	-	-	-	-	-	-	-	-	-	-	-	-
1994	-	-	-	-	-	-	-	-	-	-	181.4	1.6	-	-	-	-	-	-	-	-	-	-	-	-
1995	-	-	-	-	-	-	-	-	-	-	193.3	6.6	-	-	-	-	-	-	-	-	-	-	-	-
1996	-	-	-	-	-	-	-	-	-	-	208.5	7.9	-	-	-	-	-	-	-	-	-	-	-	-
1997	-	-	-	-	-	-	-	-	-	-	219.6	5.3	-	-	-	-	-	-	-	-	-	-	-	-

Source: U.S. Department of Labor, Bureau of Labor Statistics, Division of Consumer Prices and Price Indexes. - indicates no data collected for period.

San Diego, CA
Consumer Price Index - Urban Wage Earners
Base 1982-1984 = 100
Other Goods and Services

For 1975-1997. Columns headed % show percentile change in the index from the previous period for which an index is available.

Year	Jan Index	%	Feb Index	%	Mar Index	%	Apr Index	%	May Index	%	Jun Index	%	Jul Index	%	Aug Index	%	Sep Index	%	Oct Index	%	Nov Index	%	Dec Index	%
1975	-	-	-	-	-	-	-	-	-	-	-	-	-	-	-	-	-	-	-	-	56.6	-	-	-
1976	-	-	57.8	2.1	-	-	-	-	59.1	2.2	-	-	-	-	59.5	0.7	-	-	-	-	60.8	2.2	-	-
1977	-	-	61.0	0.3	-	-	-	-	61.9	1.5	-	-	-	-	62.9	1.6	-	-	-	-	64.1	1.9	-	-
1978	64.7	0.9	-	-	66.9	3.4	-	-	67.1	0.3	-	-	67.1	0.0	-	-	68.6	2.2	-	-	69.5	1.3	-	-
1979	70.4	1.3	-	-	71.0	0.9	-	-	71.0	0.0	-	-	71.9	1.3	-	-	74.5	3.6	-	-	74.8	0.4	-	-
1980	76.1	1.7	-	-	77.1	1.3	-	-	76.9	-0.3	-	-	78.3	1.8	-	-	80.0	2.2	-	-	81.2	1.5	-	-
1981	82.8	2.0	-	-	82.6	-0.2	-	-	84.6	2.4	-	-	83.8	-0.9	-	-	87.0	3.8	-	-	87.6	0.7	-	-
1982	88.8	1.4	-	-	89.7	1.0	-	-	90.2	0.6	-	-	88.9	-1.4	-	-	93.4	5.1	-	-	94.9	1.6	-	-
1983	98.4	3.7	-	-	97.3	-1.1	-	-	98.9	1.6	-	-	99.6	0.7	-	-	101.5	1.9	-	-	104.5	3.0	-	-
1984	105.3	0.8	-	-	105.5	0.2	-	-	107.7	2.1	-	-	107.9	0.2	-	-	109.7	1.7	-	-	111.8	1.9	-	-
1985	113.5	1.5	-	-	114.5	0.9	-	-	114.3	-0.2	-	-	114.3	0.0	-	-	116.6	2.0	-	-	116.0	-0.5	-	-
1986	117.7	1.5	-	-	118.7	0.8	-	-	118.9	0.2	-	-	117.8	-0.9	-	-	119.0	1.0	-	-	119.9	0.8	-	-
1987	-	-	-	-	-	-	-	-	-	-	121.6	1.4	-	-	-	-	-	-	-	-	-	-	-	-
1988	-	-	-	-	-	-	-	-	-	-	126.8	4.3	-	-	-	-	-	-	-	-	-	-	-	-
1989	-	-	-	-	-	-	-	-	-	-	134.0	5.7	-	-	-	-	-	-	-	-	-	-	-	-
1990	-	-	-	-	-	-	-	-	-	-	145.6	8.7	-	-	-	-	-	-	-	-	-	-	-	-
1991	-	-	-	-	-	-	-	-	-	-	154.9	6.4	-	-	-	-	-	-	-	-	-	-	-	-
1992	-	-	-	-	-	-	-	-	-	-	167.2	7.9	-	-	-	-	-	-	-	-	-	-	-	-
1993	-	-	-	-	-	-	-	-	-	-	181.6	8.6	-	-	-	-	-	-	-	-	-	-	-	-
1994	-	-	-	-	-	-	-	-	-	-	182.4	0.4	-	-	-	-	-	-	-	-	-	-	-	-
1995	-	-	-	-	-	-	-	-	-	-	194.6	6.7	-	-	-	-	-	-	-	-	-	-	-	-
1996	-	-	-	-	-	-	-	-	-	-	212.7	9.3	-	-	-	-	-	-	-	-	-	-	-	-
1997	-	-	-	-	-	-	-	-	-	-	223.2	4.9	-	-	-	-	-	-	-	-	-	-	-	-

Source: U.S. Department of Labor, Bureau of Labor Statistics, Division of Consumer Prices and Price Indexes. - indicates no data collected for period.

San Francisco-Oakland, CA
Consumer Price Index - All Urban Consumers
Base 1982-1984 = 100
Annual Averages

For 1914-1997. Columns headed % show percentile change in the index from the previous period for which an index is available.

Year	All Items		Food & Beverage		Housing		Apparel & Upkeep		Trans-portation		Medical Care		Entertain-ment		Other Goods & Services	
	Index	%	Index	%	Index	%	Index	%	Index	%	Index	%	Index	%	Index	%
1914	-	-	-	-	-	-	-	-	-	-	-	-	-	-	-	-
1915	9.2	-	-	-	-	-	-	-	-	-	-	-	-	-	-	-
1916	9.5	3.3	-	-	-	-	-	-	-	-	-	-	-	-	-	-
1917	10.9	14.7	-	-	-	-	-	-	-	-	-	-	-	-	-	-
1918	12.9	18.3	-	-	-	-	-	-	-	-	-	-	-	-	-	-
1919	15.0	16.3	-	-	-	-	-	-	-	-	-	-	-	-	-	-
1920	17.0	13.3	-	-	-	-	-	-	-	-	-	-	-	-	-	-
1921	15.3	-10.0	-	-	-	-	-	-	-	-	-	-	-	-	-	-
1922	14.6	-4.6	-	-	-	-	-	-	-	-	-	-	-	-	-	-
1923	14.7	0.7	-	-	-	-	-	-	-	-	-	-	-	-	-	-
1924	14.7	0.0	-	-	-	-	-	-	-	-	-	-	-	-	-	-
1925	15.1	2.7	-	-	-	-	-	-	-	-	-	-	-	-	-	-
1926	15.0	-0.7	-	-	-	-	-	-	-	-	-	-	-	-	-	-
1927	14.9	-0.7	-	-	-	-	-	-	-	-	-	-	-	-	-	-
1928	14.8	-0.7	-	-	-	-	-	-	-	-	-	-	-	-	-	-
1929	14.9	0.7	-	-	-	-	-	-	-	-	-	-	-	-	-	-
1930	14.5	-2.7	-	-	-	-	-	-	-	-	-	-	-	-	-	-
1931	13.3	-8.3	-	-	-	-	-	-	-	-	-	-	-	-	-	-
1932	12.3	-7.5	-	-	-	-	-	-	-	-	-	-	-	-	-	-
1933	11.8	-4.1	-	-	-	-	-	-	-	-	-	-	-	-	-	-
1934	12.1	2.5	-	-	-	-	-	-	-	-	-	-	-	-	-	-
1935	12.4	2.5	-	-	-	-	-	-	-	-	-	-	-	-	-	-
1936	12.4	0.0	-	-	-	-	-	-	-	-	-	-	-	-	-	-
1937	12.8	3.2	-	-	-	-	-	-	-	-	-	-	-	-	-	-
1938	12.8	0.0	-	-	-	-	-	-	-	-	-	-	-	-	-	-
1939	12.6	-1.6	-	-	-	-	-	-	-	-	-	-	-	-	-	-
1940	12.7	0.8	-	-	-	-	-	-	-	-	-	-	-	-	-	-
1941	13.4	5.5	-	-	-	-	-	-	-	-	-	-	-	-	-	-
1942	15.0	11.9	-	-	-	-	-	-	-	-	-	-	-	-	-	-
1943	16.0	6.7	-	-	-	-	-	-	-	-	-	-	-	-	-	-
1944	16.4	2.5	-	-	-	-	-	-	-	-	-	-	-	-	-	-
1945	16.8	2.4	-	-	-	-	-	-	-	-	-	-	-	-	-	-
1946	18.2	8.3	-	-	-	-	-	-	-	-	-	-	-	-	-	-
1947	20.6	13.2	-	-	-	-	-	-	16.4	-	13.6	-	-	-	-	-
1948	22.0	6.8	-	-	-	-	-	-	18.0	9.8	14.3	5.1	-	-	-	-
1949	22.0	0.0	-	-	-	-	-	-	19.4	7.8	14.7	2.8	-	-	-	-
1950	22.0	0.0	-	-	-	-	-	-	19.5	0.5	15.1	2.7	-	-	-	-
1951	23.8	8.2	-	-	-	-	-	-	20.8	6.7	15.8	4.6	-	-	-	-
1952	24.6	3.4	-	-	-	-	-	-	23.7	13.9	16.8	6.3	-	-	-	-
1953	25.0	1.6	-	-	-	-	39.3	-	25.7	8.4	17.2	2.4	-	-	-	-
1954	25.1	0.4	-	-	-	-	38.8	-1.3	25.5	-0.8	17.5	1.7	-	-	-	-
1955	24.9	-0.8	-	-	-	-	39.0	0.5	25.1	-1.6	17.6	0.6	-	-	-	-
1956	25.5	2.4	-	-	-	-	39.8	2.1	25.4	1.2	18.6	5.7	-	-	-	-
1957	26.5	3.9	-	-	-	-	40.7	2.3	27.1	6.7	19.6	5.4	-	-	-	-
1958	27.5	3.8	-	-	-	-	41.0	0.7	28.3	4.4	21.0	7.1	-	-	-	-

[Continued]

San Francisco-Oakland, CA
Consumer Price Index - All Urban Consumers
Base 1982-1984 = 100
Annual Averages
[Continued]

For 1914-1997. Columns headed % show percentile change in the index from the previous period for which an index is available.

Year	All Items		Food & Beverage		Housing		Apparel & Upkeep		Trans- portation		Medical Care		Entertain- ment		Other Goods & Services	
	Index	%	Index	%	Index	%	Index	%	Index	%	Index	%	Index	%	Index	%
1959	28.0	1.8	-	-	-	-	41.4	1.0	29.8	5.3	21.9	4.3	-	-	-	-
1960	28.6	2.1	-	-	-	-	42.5	2.7	29.6	-0.7	22.5	2.7	-	-	-	-
1961	28.9	1.0	-	-	-	-	43.2	1.6	29.8	0.7	23.0	2.2	-	-	-	-
1962	29.4	1.7	-	-	-	-	43.8	1.4	30.4	2.0	24.1	4.8	-	-	-	-
1963	29.8	1.4	-	-	-	-	44.2	0.9	30.7	1.0	24.7	2.5	-	-	-	-
1964	30.2	1.3	-	-	-	-	44.7	1.1	31.5	2.6	25.3	2.4	-	-	-	-
1965	30.8	2.0	-	-	-	-	45.4	1.6	31.7	0.6	25.9	2.4	-	-	-	-
1966	31.6	2.6	-	-	-	-	46.5	2.4	32.0	0.9	27.3	5.4	-	-	-	-
1967	32.5	2.8	-	-	-	-	48.5	4.3	32.9	2.8	28.9	5.9	-	-	-	-
1968	34.0	4.6	-	-	-	-	51.2	5.6	33.8	2.7	30.4	5.2	-	-	-	-
1969	35.8	5.3	-	-	-	-	53.7	4.9	35.3	4.4	31.9	4.9	-	-	-	-
1970	37.7	5.3	-	-	-	-	55.3	3.0	36.7	4.0	33.6	5.3	-	-	-	-
1971	39.1	3.7	-	-	-	-	57.7	4.3	38.8	5.7	35.6	6.0	-	-	-	-
1972	40.4	3.3	-	-	-	-	59.0	2.3	39.6	2.1	36.8	3.4	-	-	-	-
1973	42.8	5.9	-	-	-	-	61.4	4.1	40.5	2.3	38.2	3.8	-	-	-	-
1974	47.0	9.8	-	-	-	-	65.9	7.3	44.8	10.6	41.5	8.6	-	-	-	-
1975	51.8	10.2	-	-	-	-	68.7	4.2	49.9	11.4	47.7	14.9	-	-	-	-
1976	54.6	5.4	59.5	-	50.5	-	70.5	2.6	54.2	8.6	52.5	10.1	64.8	-	54.3	-
1977	58.8	7.7	64.0	7.6	55.0	8.9	73.1	3.7	58.0	7.0	57.8	10.1	67.6	4.3	58.2	7.2
1978	64.3	9.4	70.7	10.5	61.6	12.0	77.2	5.6	61.4	5.9	63.3	9.5	71.8	6.2	63.4	8.9
1979	69.8	8.6	79.3	12.2	65.1	5.7	82.0	6.2	70.4	14.7	69.1	9.2	75.5	5.2	67.6	6.6
1980	80.4	15.2	85.2	7.4	77.2	18.6	88.6	8.0	83.7	18.9	76.6	10.9	84.8	12.3	72.7	7.5
1981	90.8	12.9	91.2	7.0	90.5	17.2	92.6	4.5	92.0	9.9	84.6	10.4	92.4	9.0	79.8	9.8
1982	97.6	7.5	97.1	6.5	97.8	8.1	97.6	5.4	97.2	5.7	94.2	11.3	98.4	6.5	90.7	13.7
1983	98.4	0.8	99.3	2.3	97.7	-0.1	97.8	0.2	99.1	2.0	100.7	6.9	98.7	0.3	101.2	11.6
1984	104.0	5.7	103.7	4.4	104.5	7.0	104.6	7.0	103.7	4.6	105.1	4.4	102.8	4.2	108.2	6.9
1985	108.4	4.2	105.9	2.1	111.2	6.4	103.5	-1.1	105.5	1.7	111.1	5.7	108.6	5.6	116.3	7.5
1986	111.6	3.0	109.5	3.4	117.5	5.7	101.7	-1.7	101.2	-4.1	119.7	7.7	117.4	8.1	123.2	5.9
1987	115.4	3.4	113.7	3.8	121.5	3.4	104.6	2.9	102.4	1.2	128.7	7.5	121.6	3.6	130.9	6.3
1988	120.5	4.4	120.4	5.9	126.9	4.4	102.4	-2.1	105.3	2.8	136.9	6.4	129.1	6.2	140.1	7.0
1989	126.4	4.9	128.2	6.5	132.4	4.3	104.2	1.8	109.6	4.1	147.9	8.0	133.1	3.1	152.2	8.6
1990	132.1	4.5	134.7	5.1	137.3	3.7	107.5	3.2	114.7	4.7	160.5	8.5	140.7	5.7	161.0	5.8
1991	137.9	4.4	140.3	4.2	142.7	3.9	113.1	5.2	117.1	2.1	172.9	7.7	152.4	8.3	174.5	8.4
1992	142.5	3.3	143.3	2.1	146.2	2.5	117.8	4.2	119.8	2.3	187.0	8.2	156.5	2.7	195.9	12.3
1993	146.3	2.7	146.2	2.0	149.2	2.1	118.2	0.3	123.7	3.3	199.1	6.5	162.3	3.7	207.0	5.7
1994	148.7	1.6	148.9	1.8	151.5	1.5	115.5	-2.3	125.7	1.6	204.3	2.6	164.5	1.4	213.2	3.0
1995	151.6	2.0	151.6	1.8	154.5	2.0	114.0	-1.3	129.0	2.6	209.0	2.3	166.2	1.0	220.6	3.5
1996	155.1	2.3	155.3	2.4	157.4	1.9	116.9	2.5	133.5	3.5	214.5	2.6	166.8	0.4	227.8	3.3
1997	160.4	3.4	160.1	3.1	165.6	5.2	116.1	-0.7	133.6	0.1	221.8	3.4	165.7	-0.7	239.9	5.3

Source: U.S. Department of Labor, Bureau of Labor Statistics, Division of Consumer Prices and Price Indexes. - indicates no data collected for period.

San Francisco-Oakland, CA
Consumer Price Index - Urban Wage Earners
Base 1982-1984 = 100
Annual Averages

For 1914-1997. Columns headed % show percentile change in the index from the previous period for which an index is available.

Year	All Items		Food & Beverage		Housing		Apparel & Upkeep		Trans- portation		Medical Care		Entertain- ment		Other Goods & Services	
	Index	%	Index	%	Index	%	Index	%	Index	%	Index	%	Index	%	Index	%
1914	-	-	-	-	-	-	-	-	-	-	-	-	-	-	-	-
1915	9.3	-	-	-	-	-	-	-	-	-	-	-	-	-	-	-
1916	9.6	3.2	-	-	-	-	-	-	-	-	-	-	-	-	-	-
1917	11.0	14.6	-	-	-	-	-	-	-	-	-	-	-	-	-	-
1918	13.0	18.2	-	-	-	-	-	-	-	-	-	-	-	-	-	-
1919	15.2	16.9	-	-	-	-	-	-	-	-	-	-	-	-	-	-
1920	17.1	12.5	-	-	-	-	-	-	-	-	-	-	-	-	-	-
1921	15.5	-9.4	-	-	-	-	-	-	-	-	-	-	-	-	-	-
1922	14.8	-4.5	-	-	-	-	-	-	-	-	-	-	-	-	-	-
1923	14.8	0.0	-	-	-	-	-	-	-	-	-	-	-	-	-	-
1924	14.8	0.0	-	-	-	-	-	-	-	-	-	-	-	-	-	-
1925	15.2	2.7	-	-	-	-	-	-	-	-	-	-	-	-	-	-
1926	15.2	0.0	-	-	-	-	-	-	-	-	-	-	-	-	-	-
1927	15.0	-1.3	-	-	-	-	-	-	-	-	-	-	-	-	-	-
1928	15.0	0.0	-	-	-	-	-	-	-	-	-	-	-	-	-	-
1929	15.0	0.0	-	-	-	-	-	-	-	-	-	-	-	-	-	-
1930	14.7	-2.0	-	-	-	-	-	-	-	-	-	-	-	-	-	-
1931	13.4	-8.8	-	-	-	-	-	-	-	-	-	-	-	-	-	-
1932	12.4	-7.5	-	-	-	-	-	-	-	-	-	-	-	-	-	-
1933	11.9	-4.0	-	-	-	-	-	-	-	-	-	-	-	-	-	-
1934	12.2	2.5	-	-	-	-	-	-	-	-	-	-	-	-	-	-
1935	12.5	2.5	-	-	-	-	-	-	-	-	-	-	-	-	-	-
1936	12.5	0.0	-	-	-	-	-	-	-	-	-	-	-	-	-	-
1937	13.0	4.0	-	-	-	-	-	-	-	-	-	-	-	-	-	-
1938	12.9	-0.8	-	-	-	-	-	-	-	-	-	-	-	-	-	-
1939	12.7	-1.6	-	-	-	-	-	-	-	-	-	-	-	-	-	-
1940	12.8	0.8	-	-	-	-	-	-	-	-	-	-	-	-	-	-
1941	13.5	5.5	-	-	-	-	-	-	-	-	-	-	-	-	-	-
1942	15.1	11.9	-	-	-	-	-	-	-	-	-	-	-	-	-	-
1943	16.1	6.6	-	-	-	-	-	-	-	-	-	-	-	-	-	-
1944	16.5	2.5	-	-	-	-	-	-	-	-	-	-	-	-	-	-
1945	17.0	3.0	-	-	-	-	-	-	-	-	-	-	-	-	-	-
1946	18.3	7.6	-	-	-	-	-	-	-	-	-	-	-	-	-	-
1947	20.8	13.7	-	-	-	-	-	-	16.0	-	13.7	-	-	-	-	-
1948	22.2	6.7	-	-	-	-	-	-	17.6	10.0	14.4	5.1	-	-	-	-
1949	22.2	0.0	-	-	-	-	-	-	19.0	8.0	14.8	2.8	-	-	-	-
1950	22.2	0.0	-	-	-	-	-	-	19.0	0.0	15.2	2.7	-	-	-	-
1951	24.0	8.1	-	-	-	-	-	-	20.3	6.8	15.9	4.6	-	-	-	-
1952	24.9	3.8	-	-	-	-	-	-	23.2	14.3	16.9	6.3	-	-	-	-
1953	25.3	1.6	-	-	-	-	40.8	-	25.1	8.2	17.4	3.0	-	-	-	-
1954	25.3	0.0	-	-	-	-	40.3	-1.2	24.9	-0.8	17.6	1.1	-	-	-	-
1955	25.2	-0.4	-	-	-	-	40.4	0.2	24.5	-1.6	17.8	1.1	-	-	-	-
1956	25.7	2.0	-	-	-	-	41.3	2.2	24.8	1.2	18.7	5.1	-	-	-	-
1957	26.8	4.3	-	-	-	-	42.2	2.2	26.4	6.5	19.7	5.3	-	-	-	-
1958	27.7	3.4	-	-	-	-	42.5	0.7	27.6	4.5	21.2	7.6	-	-	-	-

[Continued]

San Francisco-Oakland, CA
Consumer Price Index - Urban Wage Earners
Base 1982-1984 = 100
Annual Averages
[Continued]

For 1914-1997. Columns headed % show percentile change in the index from the previous period for which an index is available.

Year	All Items		Food & Beverage		Housing		Apparel & Upkeep		Trans- portation		Medical Care		Entertain- ment		Other Goods & Services	
	Index	%	Index	%	Index	%	Index	%	Index	%	Index	%	Index	%	Index	%
1959	28.3	2.2	-	-	-	-	43.0	1.2	29.1	5.4	22.0	3.8	-	-	-	-
1960	28.8	1.8	-	-	-	-	44.2	2.8	28.9	-0.7	22.7	3.2	-	-	-	-
1961	29.2	1.4	-	-	-	-	44.8	1.4	29.1	0.7	23.2	2.2	-	-	-	-
1962	29.7	1.7	-	-	-	-	45.4	1.3	29.7	2.1	24.2	4.3	-	-	-	-
1963	30.0	1.0	-	-	-	-	45.9	1.1	30.0	1.0	24.8	2.5	-	-	-	-
1964	30.5	1.7	-	-	-	-	46.4	1.1	30.8	2.7	25.4	2.4	-	-	-	-
1965	31.1	2.0	-	-	-	-	47.1	1.5	31.0	0.6	26.1	2.8	-	-	-	-
1966	31.9	2.6	-	-	-	-	48.3	2.5	31.2	0.6	27.5	5.4	-	-	-	-
1967	32.8	2.8	-	-	-	-	50.3	4.1	32.1	2.9	29.1	5.8	-	-	-	-
1968	34.3	4.6	-	-	-	-	53.2	5.8	33.0	2.8	30.6	5.2	-	-	-	-
1969	36.2	5.5	-	-	-	-	55.7	4.7	34.5	4.5	32.1	4.9	-	-	-	-
1970	38.0	5.0	-	-	-	-	57.4	3.1	35.9	4.1	33.8	5.3	-	-	-	-
1971	39.4	3.7					59.8	4.2	37.9	5.6	35.9	6.2				
1972	40.8	3.6					61.2	2.3	38.6	1.8	37.0	3.1				
1973	43.2	5.9					63.7	4.1	39.5	2.3	38.5	4.1				
1974	47.4	9.7					68.4	7.4	43.8	10.9	41.8	8.6				
1975	52.2	10.1	-	-	51.8	-	71.3	4.2	48.7	11.2	48.0	14.8	-	-	-	-
1976	55.2	5.7	59.1	-	51.8	-	73.1	2.5	52.9	8.6	52.9	10.2	72.6	-	54.0	-
1977	59.4	7.6	63.6	7.6	56.4	8.9	75.8	3.7	56.6	7.0	58.2	10.0	75.7	4.3	57.9	7.2
1978	64.8	9.1	70.3	10.5	63.0	11.7	78.4	3.4	60.3	6.5	63.5	9.1	81.2	7.3	61.7	6.6
1979	70.5	8.8	78.4	11.5	66.5	5.6	82.9	5.7	69.5	15.3	69.2	9.0	83.8	3.2	66.7	8.1
1980	81.2	15.2	84.9	8.3	78.9	18.6	88.8	7.1	82.3	18.4	76.9	11.1	91.7	9.4	73.1	9.6
1981	91.6	12.8	91.8	8.1	92.3	17.0	95.1	7.1	91.1	10.7	85.1	10.7	98.8	7.7	80.2	9.7
1982	98.2	7.2	97.0	5.7	100.0	8.3	98.1	3.2	96.8	6.3	94.1	10.6	100.0	1.2	91.0	13.5
1983	98.2	0.0	99.3	2.4	96.9	-3.1	97.7	-0.4	99.2	2.5	100.6	6.9	97.7	-2.3	101.1	11.1
1984	103.7	5.6	103.7	4.4	103.2	6.5	104.2	6.7	104.0	4.8	105.4	4.8	102.3	4.7	107.9	6.7
1985	107.8	4.0	105.9	2.1	109.6	6.2	103.9	-0.3	105.7	1.6	111.8	6.1	107.2	4.8	115.9	7.4
1986	110.7	2.7	109.5	3.4	115.9	5.7	102.3	-1.5	101.5	-4.0	120.5	7.8	114.1	6.4	122.5	5.7
1987	114.3	3.3	113.8	3.9	119.4	3.0	105.4	3.0	103.7	2.2	130.0	7.9	117.3	2.8	130.4	6.4
1988	119.4	4.5	120.4	5.8	124.6	4.4	104.4	-0.9	107.1	3.3	138.1	6.2	124.0	5.7	140.1	7.4
1989	125.5	5.1	128.3	6.6	129.7	4.1	107.0	2.5	111.8	4.4	149.0	7.9	130.1	4.9	154.6	10.3
1990	131.1	4.5	134.7	5.0	134.6	3.8	110.6	3.4	116.7	4.4	160.8	7.9	136.3	4.8	164.5	6.4
1991	136.3	4.0	140.4	4.2	139.7	3.8	116.2	5.1	118.6	1.6	172.1	7.0	143.5	5.3	177.8	8.1
1992	140.6	3.2	143.3	2.1	143.1	2.4	121.5	4.6	121.9	2.8	186.4	8.3	147.5	2.8	195.8	10.1
1993	144.3	2.6	146.4	2.2	146.1	2.1	122.7	1.0	125.7	3.1	197.9	6.2	151.6	2.8	204.8	4.6
1994	146.3	1.4	149.2	1.9	148.3	1.5	120.6	-1.7	127.9	1.8	202.4	2.3	152.9	0.9	208.8	2.0
1995	149.3	2.1	151.8	1.7	151.1	1.9	120.0	-0.5	132.1	3.3	206.8	2.2	154.8	1.2	215.1	3.0
1996	152.6	2.2	155.6	2.5	153.8	1.8	122.7	2.2	136.4	3.3	212.2	2.6	156.2	0.9	220.5	2.5
1997	157.4	3.1	160.4	3.1	161.8	5.2	121.5	-1.0	135.8	-0.4	219.4	3.4	155.0	-0.8	230.8	4.7

Source: U.S. Department of Labor, Bureau of Labor Statistics, Division of Consumer Prices and Price Indexes. - indicates no data collected for period.

San Francisco-Oakland, CA
Consumer Price Index - All Urban Consumers
Base 1982-1984 = 100
All Items

For 1914-1997. Columns headed % show percentile change in the index from the previous period for which an index is available.

Year	Jan Index	Jan %	Feb Index	Feb %	Mar Index	Mar %	Apr Index	Apr %	May Index	May %	Jun Index	Jun %	Jul Index	Jul %	Aug Index	Aug %	Sep Index	Sep %	Oct Index	Oct %	Nov Index	Nov %	Dec Index	Dec %
1914	-	-	-	-	-	-	-	-	-	-	-	-	-	-	-	-	-	-	-	-	-	-	9.2	-
1915	-	-	-	-	-	-	-	-	-	-	-	-	-	-	-	-	-	-	-	-	-	-	9.2	0.0
1916	-	-	-	-	-	-	-	-	-	-	-	-	-	-	-	-	-	-	-	-	-	-	10.0	8.7
1917	-	-	-	-	-	-	-	-	-	-	-	-	-	-	-	-	-	-	-	-	-	-	11.6	16.0
1918	-	-	-	-	-	-	-	-	-	-	-	-	-	-	-	-	-	-	-	-	-	-	14.1	21.6
1919	-	-	-	-	-	-	-	-	-	-	14.7	4.3	-	-	-	-	-	-	-	-	-	-	16.3	10.9
1920	-	-	-	-	-	-	-	-	-	-	17.5	7.4	-	-	-	-	-	-	-	-	-	-	16.5	-5.7
1921	-	-	-	-	-	-	-	-	15.2	-7.9	-	-	-	-	-	-	15.0	-1.3	-	-	-	-	15.0	0.0
1922	-	-	-	-	14.7	-2.0	-	-	-	-	14.6	-0.7	-	-	-	-	14.5	-0.7	-	-	-	-	14.6	0.7
1923	-	-	-	-	14.4	-1.4	-	-	-	-	14.6	1.4	-	-	-	-	14.8	1.4	-	-	-	-	15.0	1.4
1924	-	-	-	-	14.6	-2.7	-	-	-	-	14.6	0.0	-	-	-	-	14.7	0.7	-	-	-	-	14.8	0.7
1925	-	-	-	-	-	-	-	-	-	-	15.1	2.0	-	-	-	-	-	-	-	-	-	-	15.3	1.3
1926	-	-	-	-	-	-	-	-	-	-	15.0	-2.0	-	-	-	-	-	-	-	-	-	-	15.0	0.0
1927	-	-	-	-	-	-	-	-	-	-	15.0	0.0	-	-	-	-	-	-	-	-	-	-	14.9	-0.7
1928	-	-	-	-	-	-	-	-	-	-	14.8	-0.7	-	-	-	-	-	-	-	-	-	-	15.0	1.4
1929	-	-	-	-	-	-	-	-	-	-	14.8	-1.3	-	-	-	-	-	-	-	-	-	-	14.9	0.7
1930	-	-	-	-	-	-	-	-	-	-	14.6	-2.0	-	-	-	-	-	-	-	-	-	-	14.1	-3.4
1931	-	-	-	-	-	-	-	-	-	-	13.3	-5.7	-	-	-	-	-	-	-	-	-	-	12.9	-3.0
1932	-	-	-	-	-	-	-	-	-	-	12.2	-5.4	-	-	-	-	-	-	-	-	-	-	12.0	-1.6
1933	-	-	-	-	-	-	-	-	-	-	11.7	-2.5	-	-	-	-	-	-	-	-	-	-	12.1	3.4
1934	-	-	-	-	-	-	-	-	-	-	12.2	0.8	-	-	-	-	-	-	-	-	12.5	2.5	-	-
1935	-	-	-	-	12.6	0.8	-	-	-	-	-	-	12.3	-2.4	-	-	-	-	12.3	0.0	-	-	-	-
1936	12.4	0.8	-	-	-	-	12.2	-1.6	-	-	-	-	12.4	1.6	-	-	12.4	0.0	-	-	-	-	12.4	0.0
1937	-	-	-	-	12.8	3.2	-	-	-	-	12.8	0.0	-	-	-	-	12.9	0.8	-	-	-	-	13.0	0.8
1938	-	-	-	-	12.8	-1.5	-	-	-	-	12.8	0.0	-	-	-	-	12.8	0.0	-	-	-	-	12.8	0.0
1939	-	-	-	-	12.7	-0.8	-	-	-	-	12.5	-1.6	-	-	-	-	12.8	2.4	-	-	-	-	12.6	-1.6
1940	-	-	-	-	12.6	0.0	-	-	-	-	12.6	0.0	-	-	-	-	12.7	0.8	12.8	0.8	12.8	0.0	12.8	0.0
1941	12.8	0.0	12.9	0.8	12.9	0.0	13.1	1.6	13.1	0.0	13.3	1.5	13.3	0.0	13.4	0.8	13.6	1.5	13.8	1.5	14.0	1.4	14.0	0.0
1942	14.3	2.1	14.4	0.7	14.6	1.4	14.8	1.4	14.8	0.0	14.9	0.7	14.9	0.0	15.1	1.3	15.2	0.7	15.3	0.7	15.6	2.0	15.6	0.0
1943	15.7	0.6	15.7	0.0	15.9	1.3	16.2	1.9	16.2	0.0	16.2	0.0	15.8	-2.5	15.7	-0.6	15.8	0.6	16.0	1.3	16.1	0.6	16.1	0.0
1944	16.1	0.0	16.0	-0.6	16.1	0.6	16.2	0.6	16.4	1.2	16.3	-0.6	16.4	0.6	16.4	0.0	16.4	0.0	16.6	1.2	16.6	0.0	16.8	1.2
1945	16.7	-0.6	16.6	-0.6	16.7	0.6	16.8	0.6	16.7	-0.6	16.8	0.6	16.9	0.6	16.8	-0.6	16.8	0.0	16.8	0.0	17.0	1.2	17.2	1.2
1946	17.0	-1.2	16.8	-1.2	16.9	0.6	16.9	0.0	17.0	0.6	17.4	2.4	18.2	4.6	18.7	2.7	19.1	2.1	19.4	1.6	20.1	3.6	20.3	1.0
1947	20.1	-1.0	20.0	-0.5	20.3	1.5	20.4	0.5	20.3	-0.5	20.1	-1.0	-	-	-	-	21.0	4.5	-	-	-	-	21.4	1.9
1948	-	-	-	-	21.7	1.4	-	-	-	-	22.0	1.4	-	-	-	-	22.4	1.8	-	-	-	-	22.4	0.0
1949	-	-	-	-	22.1	-1.3	-	-	-	-	22.0	-0.5	-	-	-	-	21.9	-0.5	-	-	-	-	21.7	-0.9
1950	-	-	-	-	21.8	0.5	-	-	-	-	21.7	-0.5	-	-	-	-	22.1	1.8	-	-	-	-	22.9	3.6
1951	-	-	-	-	23.8	3.9	-	-	-	-	23.7	-0.4	-	-	-	-	23.7	0.0	-	-	-	-	24.3	2.5
1952	-	-	-	-	24.3	0.0	-	-	-	-	24.8	2.1	-	-	-	-	24.7	-0.4	-	-	-	-	24.9	0.8
1953	-	-	-	-	24.9	0.0	-	-	-	-	25.0	0.4	-	-	-	-	25.2	0.8	-	-	-	-	25.2	0.0
1954	-	-	-	-	25.1	-0.4	-	-	-	-	25.1	0.0	-	-	-	-	25.0	-0.4	-	-	-	-	24.9	-0.4
1955	-	-	-	-	24.9	0.0	-	-	-	-	24.9	0.0	-	-	-	-	24.9	0.0	-	-	-	-	24.9	0.0
1956	-	-	-	-	25.1	0.8	-	-	-	-	25.4	1.2	-	-	-	-	25.6	0.8	-	-	-	-	26.2	2.3
1957	-	-	-	-	26.3	0.4	-	-	-	-	26.4	0.4	-	-	-	-	26.6	0.8	-	-	-	-	26.9	1.1
1958	-	-	-	-	27.3	1.5	-	-	-	-	27.6	1.1	-	-	-	-	27.6	0.0	-	-	-	-	27.6	0.0

[Continued]

San Francisco-Oakland, CA
Consumer Price Index - All Urban Consumers
Base 1982-1984 = 100
All Items
[Continued]

For 1914-1997. Columns headed % show percentile change in the index from the previous period for which an index is available.

Year	Jan Index	%	Feb Index	%	Mar Index	%	Apr Index	%	May Index	%	Jun Index	%	Jul Index	%	Aug Index	%	Sep Index	%	Oct Index	%	Nov Index	%	Dec Index	%
1959	-	-	-	-	27.8	0.7	-	-	-	-	27.9	0.4	-	-	-	-	28.2	1.1	-	-	-	-	28.4	0.7
1960	-	-	-	-	28.3	-0.4	-	-	-	-	28.5	0.7	-	-	-	-	28.7	0.7	-	-	-	-	28.9	0.7
1961	-	-	-	-	28.8	-0.3	-	-	-	-	28.8	0.0	-	-	-	-	29.0	0.7	-	-	-	-	29.1	0.3
1962	-	-	-	-	29.3	0.7	-	-	-	-	29.4	0.3	-	-	-	-	29.4	0.0	-	-	-	-	29.5	0.3
1963	-	-	-	-	29.6	0.3	-	-	-	-	29.8	0.7	-	-	-	-	29.9	0.3	-	-	-	-	30.1	0.7
1964	-	-	-	-	30.1	0.0	-	-	-	-	30.2	0.3	-	-	-	-	30.3	0.3	-	-	-	-	30.5	0.7
1965	-	-	-	-	30.7	0.7	-	-	-	-	30.9	0.7	-	-	-	-	30.8	-0.3	-	-	-	-	31.1	1.0
1966	-	-	-	-	31.4	1.0	-	-	-	-	31.5	0.3	-	-	-	-	31.8	1.0	-	-	-	-	32.0	0.6
1967	-	-	-	-	32.0	0.0	-	-	-	-	32.4	1.3	-	-	-	-	32.9	1.5	-	-	-	-	33.1	0.6
1968	-	-	-	-	33.5	1.2	-	-	-	-	34.0	1.5	-	-	-	-	34.3	0.9	-	-	-	-	34.6	0.9
1969	-	-	-	-	35.2	1.7	-	-	-	-	35.7	1.4	-	-	-	-	36.3	1.7	-	-	-	-	36.8	1.4
1970	-	-	-	-	37.2	1.1	-	-	-	-	37.6	1.1	-	-	-	-	38.0	1.1	-	-	-	-	38.5	1.3
1971	-	-	-	-	38.7	0.5	-	-	-	-	39.0	0.8	-	-	-	-	39.3	0.8	-	-	-	-	39.6	0.8
1972	-	-	-	-	39.9	0.8	-	-	-	-	40.4	1.3	-	-	-	-	40.9	1.2	-	-	-	-	41.1	0.5
1973	-	-	-	-	41.9	1.9	-	-	-	-	42.5	1.4	-	-	-	-	43.8	3.1	-	-	-	-	44.0	0.5
1974	-	-	-	-	45.3	3.0	-	-	-	-	46.8	3.3	-	-	-	-	48.2	3.0	-	-	-	-	49.5	2.7
1975	-	-	-	-	50.7	2.4	-	-	-	-	51.6	1.8	-	-	-	-	52.5	1.7	-	-	-	-	53.4	1.7
1976	-	-	-	-	53.8	0.7	-	-	-	-	54.3	0.9	-	-	-	-	55.3	1.8	-	-	-	-	56.0	1.3
1977	-	-	-	-	57.2	2.1	-	-	-	-	58.8	2.8	-	-	-	-	59.9	1.9	-	-	-	-	60.9	1.7
1978	-	-	61.5	1.0	-	-	62.7	2.0	-	-	64.8	3.3	-	-	66.6	2.8	-	-	66.1	-0.8	-	-	65.3	-1.2
1979	-	-	66.3	1.5	-	-	67.9	2.4	-	-	69.1	1.8	-	-	71.0	2.7	-	-	72.0	1.4	-	-	74.9	4.0
1980	-	-	78.3	4.5	-	-	79.2	1.1	-	-	80.7	1.9	-	-	81.6	1.1	-	-	81.9	0.4	-	-	82.9	1.2
1981	-	-	84.7	2.2	-	-	87.9	3.8	-	-	89.1	1.4	-	-	93.6	5.1	-	-	96.6	3.2	-	-	95.6	-1.0
1982	-	-	96.2	0.6	-	-	97.2	1.0	-	-	99.1	2.0	-	-	99.0	-0.1	-	-	98.4	-0.6	-	-	95.6	-2.8
1983	-	-	96.7	1.2	-	-	97.4	0.7	-	-	98.6	1.2	-	-	99.5	0.9	-	-	99.4	-0.1	-	-	100.0	0.6
1984	-	-	101.4	1.4	-	-	102.9	1.5	-	-	103.7	0.8	-	-	105.2	1.4	-	-	106.5	1.2	-	-	106.0	-0.5
1985	-	-	106.9	0.8	-	-	107.5	0.6	-	-	108.4	0.8	-	-	109.2	0.7	-	-	109.5	0.3	-	-	109.4	-0.1
1986	-	-	111.0	1.5	-	-	110.4	-0.5	-	-	111.9	1.4	-	-	112.4	0.4	-	-	113.1	0.6	-	-	111.8	-1.1
1987	112.5	0.6	113.4	0.8	113.7	0.3	114.8	1.0	115.0	0.2	115.0	0.0	115.8	0.7	116.1	0.3	116.6	0.4	117.1	0.4	117.3	0.2	117.4	0.1
1988	118.4	0.9	117.9	-0.4	119.1	1.0	118.7	-0.3	119.7	0.8	120.1	0.3	120.9	0.7	122.0	0.9	122.1	0.1	122.3	0.2	122.2	-0.1	122.6	0.3
1989	124.0	1.1	124.0	0.0	125.9	1.5	125.4	-0.4	126.3	0.7	126.2	-0.1	127.4	1.0	128.1	0.5	126.8	-1.0	127.5	0.6	127.2	-0.2	127.4	0.2
1990	128.5	0.9	129.2	0.5	130.0	0.6	130.7	0.5	130.8	0.1	131.6	0.6	132.3	0.5	133.1	0.6	134.0	0.7	134.6	0.4	134.7	0.1	135.1	0.3
1991	136.7	1.2	136.1	-0.4	136.3	0.1	135.8	-0.4	136.2	0.3	137.6	1.0	138.2	0.4	139.1	0.7	139.7	0.4	139.6	-0.1	139.8	0.1	139.8	0.0
1992	140.3	0.4	141.0	0.5	141.9	0.6	141.6	-0.2	141.9	0.2	141.9	0.0	142.2	0.2	142.7	0.4	143.7	0.7	144.3	0.4	144.2	-0.1	144.3	0.1
1993	145.1	0.6	145.5	0.3	145.7	0.1	146.8	0.8	146.9	0.1	146.1	-0.5	146.1	0.0	146.2	0.1	146.5	0.2	147.0	0.3	147.2	0.1	147.0	-0.1
1994	147.5	0.3	147.4	-0.1	148.2	0.5	148.0	-0.1	148.3	0.2	148.1	-0.1	148.9	0.5	149.4	0.3	149.4	0.0	149.4	0.0	149.8	0.3	149.4	-0.3
1995	150.3	0.6	150.5	0.1	151.1	0.4	151.5	0.3	151.3	-0.1	151.7	0.3	151.5	-0.1	151.5	0.0	152.3	0.5	152.6	0.2	152.4	-0.1	152.1	-0.2
1996	152.9	0.5	153.2	0.2	152.9	-0.2	153.9	0.7	155.1	0.8	155.2	0.1	155.9	0.5	155.6	-0.2	156.3	0.4	156.9	0.4	156.9	0.0	156.0	-0.6
1997	157.0	0.6	157.9	0.6	159.2	0.8	159.6	0.3	159.8	0.1	160.0	0.1	160.6	0.4	161.2	0.4	161.6	0.2	162.5	0.6	162.6	0.1	162.6	0.0

Source: U.S. Department of Labor, Bureau of Labor Statistics, Division of Consumer Prices and Price Indexes. - indicates no data collected for period.

San Francisco-Oakland, CA
Consumer Price Index - Urban Wage Earners
Base 1982-1984 = 100
All Items

For 1914-1997. Columns headed % show percentile change in the index from the previous period for which an index is available.

Year	Jan Index	%	Feb Index	%	Mar Index	%	Apr Index	%	May Index	%	Jun Index	%	Jul Index	%	Aug Index	%	Sep Index	%	Oct Index	%	Nov Index	%	Dec Index	%
1914	-	-	-	-	-	-	-	-	-	-	-	-	-	-	-	-	-	-	-	-	-	-	9.3	-
1915	-	-	-	-	-	-	-	-	-	-	-	-	-	-	-	-	-	-	-	-	-	-	9.3	0.0
1916	-	-	-	-	-	-	-	-	-	-	-	-	-	-	-	-	-	-	-	-	-	-	10.0	7.5
1917	-	-	-	-	-	-	-	-	-	-	-	-	-	-	-	-	-	-	-	-	-	-	11.7	17.0
1918	-	-	-	-	-	-	-	-	-	-	-	-	-	-	-	-	-	-	-	-	-	-	14.3	22.2
1919	-	-	-	-	-	-	-	-	-	-	14.8	3.5	-	-	-	-	-	-	-	-	-	-	16.4	10.8
1920	-	-	-	-	-	-	-	-	-	-	17.7	7.9	-	-	-	-	-	-	-	-	-	-	16.7	-5.6
1921	-	-	-	-	-	-	-	-	15.3	-8.4	-	-	-	-	-	-	15.2	-0.7	-	-	-	-	15.1	-0.7
1922	-	-	-	-	14.8	-2.0	-	-	-	-	14.7	-0.7	-	-	-	-	14.6	-0.7	-	-	-	-	14.8	1.4
1923	-	-	-	-	14.6	-1.4	-	-	-	-	14.7	0.7	-	-	-	-	14.9	1.4	-	-	-	-	15.1	1.3
1924	-	-	-	-	14.7	-2.6	-	-	-	-	14.7	0.0	-	-	-	-	14.8	0.7	-	-	-	-	14.9	0.7
1925	-	-	-	-	-	-	-	-	-	-	15.3	2.7	-	-	-	-	-	-	-	-	-	-	15.4	0.7
1926	-	-	-	-	-	-	-	-	-	-	15.1	-1.9	-	-	-	-	-	-	-	-	-	-	15.1	0.0
1927	-	-	-	-	-	-	-	-	-	-	15.2	0.7	-	-	-	-	-	-	-	-	-	-	15.0	-1.3
1928	-	-	-	-	-	-	-	-	-	-	14.9	-0.7	-	-	-	-	-	-	-	-	-	-	15.1	1.3
1929	-	-	-	-	-	-	-	-	-	-	15.0	-0.7	-	-	-	-	-	-	-	-	-	-	15.0	0.0
1930	-	-	-	-	-	-	-	-	-	-	14.7	-2.0	-	-	-	-	-	-	-	-	-	-	14.2	-3.4
1931	-	-	-	-	-	-	-	-	-	-	13.4	-5.6	-	-	-	-	-	-	-	-	-	-	13.0	-3.0
1932	-	-	-	-	-	-	-	-	-	-	12.3	-5.4	-	-	-	-	-	-	-	-	-	-	12.1	-1.6
1933	-	-	-	-	-	-	-	-	-	-	11.8	-2.5	-	-	-	-	-	-	-	-	-	-	12.2	3.4
1934	-	-	-	-	-	-	-	-	-	-	12.3	0.8	-	-	-	-	-	-	-	-	12.6	2.4	-	-
1935	-	-	-	-	12.7	0.8	-	-	-	-	-	-	12.4	-2.4	-	-	-	-	12.4	0.0	-	-	-	-
1936	12.5	0.8	-	-	-	-	12.3	-1.6	-	-	-	-	12.5	1.6	-	-	12.5	0.0	-	-	-	-	12.5	0.0
1937	-	-	-	-	12.9	3.2	-	-	-	-	12.9	0.0	-	-	-	-	13.1	1.6	-	-	-	-	13.1	0.0
1938	-	-	-	-	12.9	-1.5	-	-	-	-	12.9	0.0	-	-	-	-	12.9	0.0	-	-	-	-	12.9	0.0
1939	-	-	-	-	12.8	-0.8	-	-	-	-	12.6	-1.6	-	-	-	-	12.9	2.4	-	-	-	-	12.7	-1.6
1940	-	-	-	-	12.7	0.0	-	-	-	-	12.7	0.0	-	-	-	-	12.8	0.8	12.9	0.8	12.9	0.0	12.9	0.0
1941	13.0	0.8	13.0	0.0	13.0	0.0	13.2	1.5	13.3	0.8	13.4	0.8	13.4	0.0	13.5	0.7	13.7	1.5	13.9	1.5	14.1	1.4	14.2	0.7
1942	14.5	2.1	14.5	0.0	14.7	1.4	14.9	1.4	14.9	0.0	15.0	0.7	15.0	0.0	15.2	1.3	15.4	1.3	15.5	0.6	15.7	1.3	15.8	0.6
1943	15.8	0.0	15.8	0.0	16.1	1.9	16.4	1.9	16.3	-0.6	16.4	0.6	16.0	-2.4	15.8	-1.2	16.0	1.3	16.2	1.3	16.3	0.6	16.3	0.0
1944	16.3	0.0	16.2	-0.6	16.3	0.6	16.4	0.6	16.5	0.6	16.5	0.0	16.5	0.0	16.5	0.0	16.6	0.6	16.7	0.6	16.8	0.6	16.9	0.6
1945	16.8	-0.6	16.7	-0.6	16.8	0.6	16.9	0.6	16.8	-0.6	16.9	0.6	17.0	0.6	16.9	-0.6	16.9	0.0	17.0	0.6	17.2	1.2	17.3	0.6
1946	17.1	-1.2	17.0	-0.6	17.0	0.0	17.1	0.6	17.2	0.6	17.6	2.3	18.4	4.5	18.9	2.7	19.3	2.1	19.6	1.6	20.3	3.6	20.5	1.0
1947	20.3	-1.0	20.2	-0.5	20.5	1.5	20.6	0.5	20.5	-0.5	20.3	-1.0	-	-	-	-	21.2	4.4	-	-	-	-	21.6	1.9
1948	-	-	-	-	21.9	1.4	-	-	-	-	22.2	1.4	-	-	-	-	22.6	1.8	-	-	-	-	22.6	0.0
1949	-	-	-	-	22.3	-1.3	-	-	-	-	22.2	-0.4	-	-	-	-	22.1	-0.5	-	-	-	-	21.9	-0.9
1950	-	-	-	-	22.0	0.5	-	-	-	-	21.9	-0.5	-	-	-	-	22.3	1.8	-	-	-	-	23.1	3.6
1951	-	-	-	-	24.0	3.9	-	-	-	-	23.9	-0.4	-	-	-	-	23.9	0.0	-	-	-	-	24.6	2.9
1952	-	-	-	-	24.6	0.0	-	-	-	-	25.0	1.6	-	-	-	-	24.9	-0.4	-	-	-	-	25.2	1.2
1953	-	-	-	-	25.1	-0.4	-	-	-	-	25.3	0.8	-	-	-	-	25.4	0.4	-	-	-	-	25.4	0.0
1954	-	-	-	-	25.3	-0.4	-	-	-	-	25.4	0.4	-	-	-	-	25.3	-0.4	-	-	-	-	25.2	-0.4
1955	-	-	-	-	25.2	0.0	-	-	-	-	25.1	-0.4	-	-	-	-	25.2	0.4	-	-	-	-	25.2	0.0
1956	-	-	-	-	25.4	0.8	-	-	-	-	25.6	0.8	-	-	-	-	25.9	1.2	-	-	-	-	26.4	1.9
1957	-	-	-	-	26.6	0.8	-	-	-	-	26.7	0.4	-	-	-	-	26.9	0.7	-	-	-	-	27.1	0.7
1958	-	-	-	-	27.6	1.8	-	-	-	-	27.8	0.7	-	-	-	-	27.9	0.4	-	-	-	-	27.8	-0.4

[Continued]

San Francisco-Oakland, CA
Consumer Price Index - Urban Wage Earners
Base 1982-1984 = 100
All Items
[Continued]

For 1914-1997. Columns headed % show percentile change in the index from the previous period for which an index is available.

Year	Jan Index	%	Feb Index	%	Mar Index	%	Apr Index	%	May Index	%	Jun Index	%	Jul Index	%	Aug Index	%	Sep Index	%	Oct Index	%	Nov Index	%	Dec Index	%
1959	-	-	-	-	28.1	1.1	-	-	-	-	28.2	0.4	-	-	-	-	28.4	0.7	-	-	-	-	28.7	1.1
1960	-	-	-	-	28.6	-0.3	-	-	-	-	28.8	0.7	-	-	-	-	28.9	0.3	-	-	-	-	29.1	0.7
1961	-	-	-	-	29.1	0.0	-	-	-	-	29.1	0.0	-	-	-	-	29.3	0.7	-	-	-	-	29.4	0.3
1962	-	-	-	-	29.6	0.7	-	-	-	-	29.7	0.3	-	-	-	-	29.7	0.0	-	-	-	-	29.8	0.3
1963	-	-	-	-	29.9	0.3	-	-	-	-	30.0	0.3	-	-	-	-	30.1	0.3	-	-	-	-	30.3	0.7
1964	-	-	-	-	30.3	0.0	-	-	-	-	30.5	0.7	-	-	-	-	30.6	0.3	-	-	-	-	30.8	0.7
1965	-	-	-	-	31.0	0.6	-	-	-	-	31.2	0.6	-	-	-	-	31.1	-0.3	-	-	-	-	31.4	1.0
1966	-	-	-	-	31.7	1.0	-	-	-	-	31.8	0.3	-	-	-	-	32.1	0.9	-	-	-	-	32.3	0.6
1967	-	-	-	-	32.3	0.0	-	-	-	-	32.7	1.2	-	-	-	-	33.2	1.5	-	-	-	-	33.5	0.9
1968	-	-	-	-	33.9	1.2	-	-	-	-	34.3	1.2	-	-	-	-	34.6	0.9	-	-	-	-	35.0	1.2
1969	-	-	-	-	35.6	1.7	-	-	-	-	36.1	1.4	-	-	-	-	36.6	1.4	-	-	-	-	37.1	1.4
1970	-	-	-	-	37.6	1.3	-	-	-	-	37.9	0.8	-	-	-	-	38.3	1.1	-	-	-	-	38.9	1.6
1971	-	-	-	-	39.1	0.5	-	-	-	-	39.4	0.8	-	-	-	-	39.6	0.5	-	-	-	-	39.9	0.8
1972	-	-	-	-	40.3	1.0	-	-	-	-	40.8	1.2	-	-	-	-	41.2	1.0	-	-	-	-	41.5	0.7
1973	-	-	-	-	42.3	1.9	-	-	-	-	42.9	1.4	-	-	-	-	44.2	3.0	-	-	-	-	44.4	0.5
1974	-	-	-	-	45.7	2.9	-	-	-	-	47.2	3.3	-	-	-	-	48.6	3.0	-	-	-	-	49.9	2.7
1975	-	-	-	-	51.2	2.6	-	-	-	-	52.1	1.8	-	-	-	-	53.0	1.7	-	-	-	-	53.9	1.7
1976	-	-	-	-	54.3	0.7	-	-	-	-	54.8	0.9	-	-	-	-	55.8	1.8	-	-	-	-	56.6	1.4
1977	-	-	-	-	57.8	2.1	-	-	-	-	59.3	2.6	-	-	-	-	60.4	1.9	-	-	-	-	61.5	1.8
1978	-	-	62.2	1.1	-	-	63.2	1.6	-	-	65.3	3.3	-	-	67.0	2.6	-	-	66.5	-0.7	-	-	65.8	-1.1
1979	-	-	67.1	2.0	-	-	68.7	2.4	-	-	70.2	2.2	-	-	71.8	2.3	-	-	72.5	1.0	-	-	75.2	3.7
1980	-	-	78.8	4.8	-	-	79.7	1.1	-	-	81.3	2.0	-	-	82.6	1.6	-	-	83.0	0.5	-	-	84.0	1.2
1981	-	-	85.9	2.3	-	-	89.0	3.6	-	-	90.1	1.2	-	-	94.3	4.7	-	-	97.1	3.0	-	-	96.1	-1.0
1982	-	-	96.8	0.7	-	-	97.8	1.0	-	-	99.6	1.8	-	-	99.4	-0.2	-	-	98.9	-0.5	-	-	96.4	-2.5
1983	-	-	96.5	0.1	-	-	96.8	0.3	-	-	98.1	1.3	-	-	99.0	0.9	-	-	99.0	0.0	-	-	100.5	1.5
1984	-	-	101.4	0.9	-	-	102.2	0.8	-	-	103.5	1.3	-	-	106.0	2.4	-	-	104.9	-1.0	-	-	105.6	0.7
1985	-	-	106.5	0.9	-	-	107.1	0.6	-	-	107.9	0.7	-	-	108.6	0.6	-	-	108.7	0.1	-	-	108.8	0.1
1986	-	-	110.3	1.4	-	-	109.4	-0.8	-	-	111.0	1.5	-	-	111.3	0.3	-	-	112.0	0.6	-	-	110.7	-1.2
1987	111.3	0.5	112.4	1.0	112.8	0.4	113.9	1.0	113.9	0.0	114.0	0.1	114.7	0.6	114.9	0.2	115.4	0.4	116.0	0.5	116.2	0.2	116.4	0.2
1988	117.5	0.9	117.0	-0.4	117.9	0.8	117.8	-0.1	118.7	0.8	119.0	0.3	119.7	0.6	120.5	0.7	121.1	0.5	121.3	0.2	121.1	-0.2	121.5	0.3
1989	122.8	1.1	122.9	0.1	124.6	1.4	124.8	0.2	125.7	0.7	125.6	-0.1	126.4	0.6	127.0	0.5	126.1	-0.7	126.7	0.5	126.4	-0.2	126.6	0.2
1990	127.6	0.8	128.2	0.5	129.0	0.6	129.8	0.6	129.9	0.1	130.7	0.6	131.3	0.5	132.0	0.5	132.9	0.7	133.6	0.5	133.7	0.1	133.9	0.1
1991	135.3	1.0	134.5	-0.6	134.7	0.1	134.2	-0.4	134.8	0.4	136.0	0.9	136.4	0.3	137.2	0.6	137.9	0.5	137.8	-0.1	138.1	0.2	138.2	0.1
1992	138.5	0.2	139.1	0.4	139.9	0.6	139.6	-0.2	140.1	0.4	140.3	0.1	140.4	0.1	141.0	0.4	141.8	0.6	142.3	0.4	142.3	0.0	142.3	0.0
1993	143.0	0.5	143.5	0.3	143.8	0.2	144.8	0.7	144.8	0.0	144.0	-0.6	144.1	0.1	144.0	-0.1	144.4	0.3	145.0	0.4	145.0	0.0	144.7	-0.2
1994	145.3	0.4	145.0	-0.2	145.6	0.4	145.6	0.0	146.1	0.3	145.7	-0.3	146.6	0.6	147.1	0.3	147.1	0.0	147.0	-0.1	147.6	0.4	147.4	-0.1
1995	148.2	0.5	148.3	0.1	148.9	0.4	149.4	0.3	149.0	-0.3	149.6	0.4	149.3	-0.2	149.3	0.0	150.0	0.5	150.2	0.1	149.9	-0.2	149.6	-0.2
1996	150.5	0.6	150.5	0.0	150.7	0.1	151.9	0.8	153.0	0.7	152.9	-0.1	153.4	0.3	153.0	-0.3	153.8	0.5	154.3	0.3	154.2	-0.1	153.1	-0.7
1997	154.1	0.7	155.0	0.6	156.2	0.8	156.7	0.3	156.8	0.1	157.0	0.1	157.5	0.3	158.1	0.4	158.6	0.3	159.5	0.6	159.5	0.0	159.4	-0.1

Source: U.S. Department of Labor, Bureau of Labor Statistics, Division of Consumer Prices and Price Indexes. - indicates no data collected for period.

813

San Francisco-Oakland, CA
Consumer Price Index - All Urban Consumers
Base 1982-1984 = 100
Food and Beverages

For 1975-1997. Columns headed % show percentile change in the index from the previous period for which an index is available.

Year	Jan Index	%	Feb Index	%	Mar Index	%	Apr Index	%	May Index	%	Jun Index	%	Jul Index	%	Aug Index	%	Sep Index	%	Oct Index	%	Nov Index	%	Dec Index	%
1975	-	-	-	-	-	-	-	-	-	-	-	-	-	-	-	-	-	-	-	-	-	-	60.2	-
1976	-	-	-	-	59.1	-1.8	-	-	-	-	59.3	0.3	-	-	-	-	59.7	0.7	-	-	-	-	60.0	0.5
1977	-	-	-	-	62.5	4.2	-	-	-	-	64.6	3.4	-	-	-	-	65.0	0.6	-	-	-	-	65.9	1.4
1978	-	-	67.3	2.1	-	-	69.1	2.7	-	-	71.4	3.3	-	-	72.3	1.3	-	-	72.9	0.8	-	-	73.0	0.1
1979	-	-	76.5	4.8	-	-	78.8	3.0	-	-	79.6	1.0	-	-	79.8	0.3	-	-	81.3	1.9	-	-	81.9	0.7
1980	-	-	82.5	0.7	-	-	83.7	1.5	-	-	84.2	0.6	-	-	85.9	2.0	-	-	87.7	2.1	-	-	89.3	1.8
1981	-	-	90.1	0.9	-	-	91.0	1.0	-	-	90.1	-1.0	-	-	92.7	2.9	-	-	91.9	-0.9	-	-	92.3	0.4
1982	-	-	95.8	3.8	-	-	96.2	0.4	-	-	97.5	1.4	-	-	97.8	0.3	-	-	99.0	1.2	-	-	97.7	-1.3
1983	-	-	98.3	0.6	-	-	100.1	1.8	-	-	98.9	-1.2	-	-	98.9	0.0	-	-	99.4	0.5	-	-	100.7	1.3
1984	-	-	102.7	2.0	-	-	103.2	0.5	-	-	103.4	0.2	-	-	103.9	0.5	-	-	104.6	0.7	-	-	105.3	0.7
1985	-	-	106.1	0.8	-	-	105.8	-0.3	-	-	105.3	-0.5	-	-	106.0	0.7	-	-	105.3	-0.7	-	-	107.2	1.8
1986	-	-	107.9	0.7	-	-	108.8	0.8	-	-	109.1	0.3	-	-	110.5	1.3	-	-	111.0	0.5	-	-	110.7	-0.3
1987	112.5	1.6	111.9	-0.5	112.5	0.5	113.5	0.9	113.5	0.0	114.0	0.4	114.1	0.1	114.2	0.1	114.0	-0.2	114.0	0.0	114.1	0.1	115.8	1.5
1988	117.3	1.3	116.6	-0.6	117.8	1.0	118.5	0.6	119.4	0.8	119.9	0.4	121.2	1.1	121.6	0.3	122.8	1.0	122.8	0.0	122.6	-0.2	124.3	1.4
1989	126.1	1.4	126.8	0.6	126.9	0.1	127.0	0.1	128.2	0.9	127.8	-0.3	127.4	-0.3	128.2	0.6	129.0	0.6	130.0	0.8	130.5	0.4	131.0	0.4
1990	132.8	1.4	133.2	0.3	133.0	-0.2	133.6	0.5	133.0	-0.4	133.7	0.5	135.1	1.0	134.9	-0.1	135.7	0.6	136.5	0.6	137.2	0.5	137.1	-0.1
1991	140.0	2.1	139.1	-0.6	140.0	0.6	140.1	0.1	139.8	-0.2	140.2	0.3	139.3	-0.6	139.1	-0.1	139.8	0.5	140.1	0.2	142.4	1.6	143.6	0.8
1992	142.2	-1.0	142.9	0.5	143.1	0.1	142.8	-0.2	142.8	0.0	142.9	0.1	142.3	-0.4	144.0	1.2	143.9	-0.1	143.9	0.0	144.0	0.1	145.1	0.8
1993	146.6	1.0	146.6	0.0	146.6	0.0	146.9	0.2	146.5	-0.3	145.5	-0.7	145.8	0.2	145.1	-0.5	145.1	0.0	146.6	1.0	146.3	-0.2	147.3	0.7
1994	148.9	1.1	148.2	-0.5	148.4	0.1	149.2	0.5	148.0	-0.8	147.6	-0.3	148.7	0.7	148.2	-0.3	148.2	0.0	148.9	0.5	150.4	1.0	152.2	1.2
1995	152.9	0.5	151.7	-0.8	152.2	0.3	153.1	0.6	151.5	-1.0	150.9	-0.4	151.3	0.3	149.9	-0.9	151.5	1.1	151.8	0.2	150.7	-0.7	151.6	0.6
1996	152.7	0.7	152.2	-0.3	154.8	1.7	155.4	0.4	154.0	-0.9	154.8	0.5	155.1	0.2	155.9	0.5	156.3	0.3	157.7	0.9	157.5	-0.1	157.2	-0.2
1997	157.9	0.4	159.5	1.0	159.9	0.3	159.8	-0.1	158.8	-0.6	158.4	-0.3	158.8	0.3	160.7	1.2	160.6	-0.1	162.0	0.9	162.0	0.0	163.1	0.7

Source: U.S. Department of Labor, Bureau of Labor Statistics, Division of Consumer Prices and Price Indexes. - indicates no data collected for period.

San Francisco-Oakland, CA
Consumer Price Index - Urban Wage Earners
Base 1982-1984 = 100
Food and Beverages

For 1975-1997. Columns headed % show percentile change in the index from the previous period for which an index is available.

Year	Jan Index	%	Feb Index	%	Mar Index	%	Apr Index	%	May Index	%	Jun Index	%	Jul Index	%	Aug Index	%	Sep Index	%	Oct Index	%	Nov Index	%	Dec Index	%
1975	-	-	-	-	-	-	-	-	-	-	-	-	-	-	-	-	-	-	-	-	-	-	59.8	-
1976	-	-	-	-	58.7	-1.8	-	-	-	-	58.8	0.2	-	-	-	-	59.3	0.9	-	-	-	-	59.6	0.5
1977	-	-	-	-	62.1	4.2	-	-	-	-	64.1	3.2	-	-	-	-	64.6	0.8	-	-	-	-	65.4	1.2
1978	-	-	67.0	2.4	-	-	68.7	2.5	-	-	70.9	3.2	-	-	71.9	1.4	-	-	72.3	0.6	-	-	72.7	0.6
1979	-	-	76.2	4.8	-	-	78.1	2.5	-	-	79.0	1.2	-	-	78.9	-0.1	-	-	79.9	1.3	-	-	80.5	0.8
1980	-	-	82.5	2.5	-	-	83.1	0.7	-	-	83.9	1.0	-	-	85.5	1.9	-	-	87.3	2.1	-	-	89.1	2.1
1981	-	-	90.6	1.7	-	-	92.1	1.7	-	-	91.2	-1.0	-	-	93.0	2.0	-	-	92.4	-0.6	-	-	92.4	0.0
1982	-	-	95.8	3.7	-	-	96.3	0.5	-	-	97.5	1.2	-	-	97.6	0.1	-	-	98.7	1.1	-	-	97.6	-1.1
1983	-	-	98.3	0.7	-	-	100.0	1.7	-	-	98.9	-1.1	-	-	99.0	0.1	-	-	99.5	0.5	-	-	100.9	1.4
1984	-	-	102.8	1.9	-	-	103.4	0.6	-	-	103.4	0.0	-	-	103.9	0.5	-	-	104.5	0.6	-	-	105.2	0.7
1985	-	-	106.1	0.9	-	-	105.9	-0.2	-	-	105.2	-0.7	-	-	106.0	0.8	-	-	105.3	-0.7	-	-	107.2	1.8
1986	-	-	108.0	0.7	-	-	108.8	0.7	-	-	109.0	0.2	-	-	110.5	1.4	-	-	110.8	0.3	-	-	110.7	-0.1
1987	112.6	1.7	111.9	-0.6	112.6	0.6	113.7	1.0	113.7	0.0	114.2	0.4	114.3	0.1	114.4	0.1	114.1	-0.3	114.0	-0.1	114.1	0.1	115.7	1.4
1988	117.2	1.3	116.6	-0.5	117.7	0.9	118.6	0.8	119.5	0.8	120.0	0.4	121.3	1.1	121.7	0.3	122.9	1.0	122.8	-0.1	122.6	-0.2	124.3	1.4
1989	125.9	1.3	126.9	0.8	127.0	0.1	127.2	0.2	128.4	0.9	128.0	-0.3	127.5	-0.4	128.3	0.6	129.1	0.6	130.1	0.8	130.6	0.4	131.1	0.4
1990	132.8	1.3	133.4	0.5	133.1	-0.2	133.7	0.5	133.1	-0.4	133.8	0.5	135.2	1.0	135.0	-0.1	135.8	0.6	136.6	0.6	137.2	0.4	137.2	0.0
1991	140.1	2.1	139.3	-0.6	140.2	0.6	140.3	0.1	139.9	-0.3	140.4	0.4	139.4	-0.7	139.1	-0.2	139.8	0.5	140.0	0.1	142.3	1.6	143.5	0.8
1992	142.2	-0.9	143.0	0.6	143.2	0.1	142.8	-0.3	142.7	-0.1	142.9	0.1	142.4	-0.3	144.0	1.1	143.8	-0.1	143.9	0.1	144.0	0.1	145.2	0.8
1993	146.6	1.0	146.8	0.1	146.8	0.0	147.1	0.2	146.7	-0.3	145.7	-0.7	146.0	0.2	145.3	-0.5	145.4	0.1	146.8	1.0	146.5	-0.2	147.4	0.6
1994	149.1	1.2	148.4	-0.5	148.7	0.2	149.6	0.6	148.4	-0.8	148.0	-0.3	149.1	0.7	148.5	-0.4	148.5	0.0	149.1	0.4	150.5	0.9	152.3	1.2
1995	152.9	0.4	151.8	-0.7	152.3	0.3	153.1	0.5	151.6	-1.0	151.1	-0.3	151.6	0.3	150.2	-0.9	151.9	1.1	152.1	0.1	150.9	-0.8	151.9	0.7
1996	152.9	0.7	152.4	-0.3	155.1	1.8	155.8	0.5	154.3	-1.0	155.1	0.5	155.4	0.2	156.3	0.6	156.7	0.3	158.0	0.8	157.8	-0.1	157.5	-0.2
1997	158.3	0.5	159.8	0.9	160.2	0.3	160.2	0.0	159.1	-0.7	158.8	-0.2	159.1	0.2	161.1	1.3	160.8	-0.2	162.2	0.9	162.1	-0.1	163.2	0.7

Source: U.S. Department of Labor, Bureau of Labor Statistics, Division of Consumer Prices and Price Indexes. - indicates no data collected for period.

San Francisco-Oakland, CA
Consumer Price Index - All Urban Consumers
Base 1982-1984 = 100
Housing

For 1975-1997. Columns headed % show percentile change in the index from the previous period for which an index is available.

Year	Jan Index	%	Feb Index	%	Mar Index	%	Apr Index	%	May Index	%	Jun Index	%	Jul Index	%	Aug Index	%	Sep Index	%	Oct Index	%	Nov Index	%	Dec Index	%
1975	-	-	-	-	-	-	-	-	-	-	-	-	-	-	-	-	-	-	-	-	-	-	49.3	-
1976	-	-	-	-	50.0	1.4	-	-	-	-	50.4	0.8	-	-	-	-	51.4	2.0	-	-	-	-	50.9	-1.0
1977	-	-	-	-	53.1	4.3	-	-	-	-	54.8	3.2	-	-	-	-	56.5	3.1	-	-	-	-	58.2	3.0
1978	-	-	58.9	1.2	-	-	59.7	1.4	-	-	62.5	4.7	-	-	64.9	3.8	-	-	63.1	-2.8	-	-	61.0	-3.3
1979	-	-	61.7	1.1	-	-	63.0	2.1	-	-	63.9	1.4	-	-	66.4	3.9	-	-	67.0	0.9	-	-	71.4	6.6
1980	-	-	75.8	6.2	-	-	75.2	-0.8	-	-	78.1	3.9	-	-	78.6	0.6	-	-	78.2	-0.5	-	-	79.1	1.2
1981	-	-	81.1	2.5	-	-	86.2	6.3	-	-	87.7	1.7	-	-	95.2	8.6	-	-	100.1	5.1	-	-	97.3	-2.8
1982	-	-	97.4	0.1	-	-	98.5	1.1	-	-	100.2	1.7	-	-	99.5	-0.7	-	-	97.3	-2.2	-	-	92.9	-4.5
1983	-	-	95.7	3.0	-	-	96.2	0.5	-	-	97.4	1.2	-	-	99.3	2.0	-	-	99.6	0.3	-	-	99.4	-0.2
1984	-	-	100.9	1.5	-	-	102.7	1.8	-	-	103.7	1.0	-	-	106.9	3.1	-	-	108.0	1.0	-	-	106.7	-1.2
1985	-	-	108.2	1.4	-	-	109.3	1.0	-	-	111.0	1.6	-	-	113.4	2.2	-	-	114.2	0.7	-	-	112.8	-1.2
1986	-	-	115.7	2.6	-	-	115.5	-0.2	-	-	117.9	2.1	-	-	119.4	1.3	-	-	120.1	0.6	-	-	117.8	-1.9
1987	118.5	0.6	119.5	0.8	119.1	-0.3	120.4	1.1	121.2	0.7	121.2	0.0	122.7	1.2	122.9	0.2	123.3	0.3	123.7	0.3	122.6	-0.9	122.6	0.0
1988	123.7	0.9	123.8	0.1	125.6	1.5	124.2	-1.1	126.1	1.5	126.7	0.5	127.9	0.9	130.0	1.6	128.5	-1.2	128.9	0.3	128.5	-0.3	128.9	0.3
1989	130.4	1.2	130.0	-0.3	133.0	2.3	130.1	-2.2	131.3	0.9	131.6	0.2	134.4	2.1	135.0	0.4	133.0	-1.5	133.4	0.3	132.7	-0.5	133.3	0.5
1990	134.2	0.7	135.1	0.7	135.7	0.4	135.9	0.1	136.5	0.4	137.5	0.7	138.1	0.4	138.5	0.3	138.8	0.2	138.6	-0.1	139.1	0.4	139.2	0.1
1991	141.2	1.4	140.9	-0.2	141.2	0.2	140.2	-0.7	140.8	0.4	142.8	1.4	143.8	0.7	144.5	0.5	145.0	0.3	144.1	-0.6	144.1	0.0	143.7	-0.3
1992	144.7	0.7	145.3	0.4	146.6	0.9	145.5	-0.8	145.6	0.1	145.3	-0.2	146.0	0.5	145.9	-0.1	147.5	1.1	147.9	0.3	147.1	-0.5	147.3	0.1
1993	147.5	0.1	147.6	0.1	147.8	0.1	149.5	1.2	150.0	0.3	149.4	-0.4	149.1	-0.2	149.4	0.2	149.7	0.2	149.8	0.1	150.3	0.3	150.4	0.1
1994	150.4	0.0	150.4	0.0	150.8	0.3	150.2	-0.4	151.2	0.7	151.7	0.3	152.5	0.5	153.0	0.3	152.7	-0.2	152.2	-0.3	151.7	-0.3	151.6	-0.1
1995	152.6	0.7	153.2	0.4	153.5	0.2	153.9	0.3	154.4	0.3	154.8	0.3	154.8	0.0	155.0	0.1	155.7	0.5	155.6	-0.1	155.5	-0.1	155.2	-0.2
1996	155.6	0.3	155.9	0.2	153.1	-1.8	153.7	0.4	156.8	2.0	157.3	0.3	158.7	0.9	158.9	0.1	159.2	0.2	159.9	0.4	160.0	0.1	159.8	-0.1
1997	161.2	0.9	161.7	0.3	162.7	0.6	163.2	0.3	164.5	0.8	165.1	0.4	165.8	0.4	167.0	0.7	167.6	0.4	169.0	0.8	169.3	0.2	169.7	0.2

Source: U.S. Department of Labor, Bureau of Labor Statistics, Division of Consumer Prices and Price Indexes. - indicates no data collected for period.

San Francisco-Oakland, CA
Consumer Price Index - Urban Wage Earners
Base 1982-1984 = 100
Housing

For 1975-1997. Columns headed % show percentile change in the index from the previous period for which an index is available.

Year	Jan Index	%	Feb Index	%	Mar Index	%	Apr Index	%	May Index	%	Jun Index	%	Jul Index	%	Aug Index	%	Sep Index	%	Oct Index	%	Nov Index	%	Dec Index	%
1975	-	-	-	-	-	-	-	-	-	-	-	-	-	-	-	-	-	-	-	-	-	-	50.6	-
1976	-	-	-	-	51.2	1.2	-	-	-	-	51.7	1.0	-	-	-	-	52.7	1.9	-	-	-	-	52.1	-1.1
1977	-	-	-	-	54.4	4.4	-	-	-	-	56.2	3.3	-	-	-	-	57.9	3.0	-	-	-	-	59.7	3.1
1978	-	-	60.3	1.0	-	-	61.1	1.3	-	-	63.8	4.4	-	-	66.3	3.9	-	-	64.5	-2.7	-	-	62.4	-3.3
1979	-	-	63.2	1.3	-	-	64.4	1.9	-	-	65.4	1.6	-	-	67.7	3.5	-	-	68.3	0.9	-	-	72.8	6.6
1980	-	-	77.4	6.3	-	-	76.9	-0.6	-	-	80.1	4.2	-	-	80.6	0.6	-	-	79.8	-1.0	-	-	81.0	1.5
1981	-	-	83.0	2.5	-	-	87.8	5.8	-	-	89.4	1.8	-	-	96.9	8.4	-	-	101.9	5.2	-	-	99.3	-2.6
1982	-	-	99.6	0.3	-	-	100.7	1.1	-	-	102.4	1.7	-	-	101.5	-0.9	-	-	99.4	-2.1	-	-	95.0	-4.4
1983	-	-	95.5	0.5	-	-	95.2	-0.3	-	-	96.2	1.1	-	-	97.8	1.7	-	-	98.0	0.2	-	-	100.0	2.0
1984	-	-	100.5	0.5	-	-	100.5	0.0	-	-	102.8	2.3	-	-	107.7	4.8	-	-	103.6	-3.8	-	-	105.2	1.5
1985	-	-	106.7	1.4	-	-	107.8	1.0	-	-	109.5	1.6	-	-	111.6	1.9	-	-	112.2	0.5	-	-	111.1	-1.0
1986	-	-	114.1	2.7	-	-	113.9	-0.2	-	-	116.3	2.1	-	-	117.7	1.2	-	-	118.5	0.7	-	-	116.0	-2.1
1987	116.7	0.6	117.7	0.9	117.2	-0.4	118.5	1.1	119.0	0.4	119.0	0.0	120.4	1.2	120.5	0.1	120.9	0.3	121.4	0.4	120.5	-0.7	120.5	0.0
1988	121.7	1.0	121.9	0.2	123.1	1.0	122.2	-0.7	123.9	1.4	124.5	0.5	125.4	0.7	127.0	1.3	126.2	-0.6	126.6	0.3	126.0	-0.5	126.4	0.3
1989	127.6	0.9	127.3	-0.2	129.8	2.0	127.8	-1.5	128.9	0.9	129.1	0.2	131.2	1.6	131.9	0.5	130.4	-1.1	131.0	0.5	130.3	-0.5	130.8	0.4
1990	131.7	0.7	132.6	0.7	133.0	0.3	133.4	0.3	134.1	0.5	135.0	0.7	135.4	0.3	135.8	0.3	136.0	0.1	136.0	0.0	136.4	0.3	136.3	-0.1
1991	138.2	1.4	137.9	-0.2	138.1	0.1	137.1	-0.7	138.1	0.7	140.0	1.4	140.8	0.6	141.3	0.4	141.9	0.4	141.0	-0.6	141.2	0.1	140.7	-0.4
1992	141.6	0.6	142.1	0.4	143.2	0.8	142.2	-0.7	142.5	0.2	142.5	0.0	143.0	0.4	142.8	-0.1	144.3	1.1	144.8	0.3	144.1	-0.5	144.1	0.0
1993	144.3	0.1	144.5	0.1	144.8	0.2	146.6	1.2	146.9	0.2	146.2	-0.5	146.0	-0.1	146.3	0.2	146.5	0.1	146.8	0.2	147.3	0.3	147.2	-0.1
1994	147.2	0.0	147.2	0.0	147.6	0.3	147.1	-0.3	148.0	0.6	148.6	0.4	149.3	0.5	149.6	0.2	149.4	-0.1	148.9	-0.3	148.5	-0.3	148.4	-0.1
1995	149.4	0.7	149.9	0.3	150.1	0.1	150.5	0.3	151.0	0.3	151.4	0.3	151.4	0.0	151.5	0.1	152.2	0.5	152.2	0.0	152.1	-0.1	151.8	-0.2
1996	152.1	0.2	152.4	0.2	149.5	-1.9	150.2	0.5	153.3	2.1	153.7	0.3	154.9	0.8	155.1	0.1	155.4	0.2	156.1	0.5	156.2	0.1	156.1	-0.1
1997	157.3	0.8	157.9	0.4	158.8	0.6	159.3	0.3	160.7	0.9	161.3	0.4	162.0	0.4	163.1	0.7	163.9	0.5	165.2	0.8	165.5	0.2	166.1	0.4

Source: U.S. Department of Labor, Bureau of Labor Statistics, Division of Consumer Prices and Price Indexes. - indicates no data collected for period.

San Francisco-Oakland, CA
Consumer Price Index - All Urban Consumers
Base 1982-1984 = 100
Apparel and Upkeep

For 1952-1997. Columns headed % show percentile change in the index from the previous period for which an index is available.

Year	Jan Index	%	Feb Index	%	Mar Index	%	Apr Index	%	May Index	%	Jun Index	%	Jul Index	%	Aug Index	%	Sep Index	%	Oct Index	%	Nov Index	%	Dec Index	%
1952	-	-	-	-	-	-	-	-	-	-	-	-	-	-	-	-	-	-	-	-	-	-	39.3	-
1953	-	-	-	-	39.4	0.3	-	-	-	-	38.9	-1.3	-	-	-	-	39.4	1.3	-	-	-	-	39.4	0.0
1954	-	-	-	-	38.9	-1.3	-	-	-	-	38.8	-0.3	-	-	-	-	38.8	0.0	-	-	-	-	38.4	-1.0
1955	-	-	-	-	38.8	1.0	-	-	-	-	38.8	0.0	-	-	-	-	39.3	1.3	-	-	-	-	39.3	0.0
1956	-	-	-	-	39.6	0.8	-	-	-	-	39.7	0.3	-	-	-	-	39.8	0.3	-	-	-	-	40.5	1.8
1957	-	-	-	-	40.7	0.5	-	-	-	-	40.6	-0.2	-	-	-	-	40.8	0.5	-	-	-	-	41.0	0.5
1958	-	-	-	-	41.0	0.0	-	-	-	-	40.9	-0.2	-	-	-	-	40.9	0.0	-	-	-	-	41.0	0.2
1959	-	-	-	-	41.0	0.0	-	-	-	-	41.2	0.5	-	-	-	-	41.9	1.7	-	-	-	-	42.1	0.5
1960	-	-	-	-	42.1	0.0	-	-	-	-	42.4	0.7	-	-	-	-	42.9	1.2	-	-	-	-	43.0	0.2
1961	-	-	-	-	43.0	0.0	-	-	-	-	43.2	0.5	-	-	-	-	43.2	0.0	-	-	-	-	43.4	0.5
1962	-	-	-	-	43.7	0.7	-	-	-	-	43.9	0.5	-	-	-	-	43.8	-0.2	-	-	-	-	44.0	0.5
1963	-	-	-	-	44.0	0.0	-	-	-	-	44.1	0.2	-	-	-	-	44.3	0.5	-	-	-	-	44.5	0.5
1964	-	-	-	-	44.6	0.2	-	-	-	-	44.6	0.0	-	-	-	-	44.6	0.0	-	-	-	-	44.9	0.7
1965	-	-	-	-	45.2	0.7	-	-	-	-	45.5	0.7	-	-	-	-	45.2	-0.7	-	-	-	-	45.6	0.9
1966	-	-	-	-	46.3	1.5	-	-	-	-	46.5	0.4	-	-	-	-	46.8	0.6	-	-	-	-	47.1	0.6
1967	-	-	-	-	47.7	1.3	-	-	-	-	47.8	0.2	-	-	-	-	49.5	3.6	-	-	-	-	49.7	0.4
1968	-	-	-	-	50.5	1.6	-	-	-	-	51.0	1.0	-	-	-	-	51.9	1.8	-	-	-	-	52.3	0.8
1969	-	-	-	-	53.1	1.5	-	-	-	-	53.3	0.4	-	-	-	-	54.5	2.3	-	-	-	-	54.7	0.4
1970	-	-	-	-	54.6	-0.2	-	-	-	-	54.5	-0.2	-	-	-	-	56.1	2.9	-	-	-	-	56.5	0.7
1971	-	-	-	-	57.2	1.2	-	-	-	-	57.5	0.5	-	-	-	-	58.5	1.7	-	-	-	-	58.0	-0.9
1972	-	-	-	-	58.2	0.3	-	-	-	-	58.0	-0.3	-	-	-	-	60.1	3.6	-	-	-	-	60.1	0.0
1973	-	-	-	-	60.4	0.5	-	-	-	-	61.0	1.0	-	-	-	-	62.4	2.3	-	-	-	-	62.7	0.5
1974	-	-	-	-	64.1	2.2	-	-	-	-	65.9	2.8	-	-	-	-	67.4	2.3	-	-	-	-	68.4	1.5
1975	-	-	-	-	68.4	0.0	-	-	-	-	68.1	-0.4	-	-	-	-	68.8	1.0	-	-	-	-	69.8	1.5
1976	-	-	-	-	70.5	1.0	-	-	-	-	69.8	-1.0	-	-	-	-	70.6	1.1	-	-	-	-	71.4	1.1
1977	-	-	-	-	72.6	1.7	-	-	-	-	72.7	0.1	-	-	-	-	73.7	1.4	-	-	-	-	74.1	0.5
1978	-	-	73.6	-0.7	-	-	78.3	6.4	-	-	76.5	-2.3	-	-	77.2	0.9	-	-	79.6	3.1	-	-	79.3	-0.4
1979	-	-	80.1	1.0	-	-	80.1	0.0	-	-	81.3	1.5	-	-	81.4	0.1	-	-	84.3	3.6	-	-	86.7	2.8
1980	-	-	86.9	0.2	-	-	88.3	1.6	-	-	85.4	-3.3	-	-	90.7	6.2	-	-	91.0	0.3	-	-	90.5	-0.5
1981	-	-	89.6	-1.0	-	-	91.0	1.6	-	-	92.2	1.3	-	-	94.3	2.3	-	-	93.8	-0.5	-	-	96.4	2.8
1982	-	-	97.3	0.9	-	-	97.3	0.0	-	-	97.1	-0.2	-	-	98.9	1.9	-	-	98.6	-0.3	-	-	96.4	-2.2
1983	-	-	98.8	2.5	-	-	99.1	0.3	-	-	97.8	-1.3	-	-	98.2	0.4	-	-	95.5	-2.7	-	-	98.0	2.6
1984	-	-	102.1	4.2	-	-	104.4	2.3	-	-	100.6	-3.6	-	-	107.1	6.5	-	-	109.5	2.2	-	-	105.7	-3.5
1985	-	-	108.1	2.3	-	-	105.0	-2.9	-	-	104.7	-0.3	-	-	100.6	-3.9	-	-	102.2	1.6	-	-	99.1	-3.0
1986	-	-	98.1	-1.0	-	-	103.9	5.9	-	-	100.0	-3.8	-	-	102.6	2.6	-	-	105.9	3.2	-	-	99.6	-5.9
1987	96.8	-2.8	103.1	6.5	106.6	3.4	108.6	1.9	103.7	-4.5	102.2	-1.4	100.4	-1.8	100.2	-0.2	105.1	4.9	107.4	2.2	112.2	4.5	108.4	-3.4
1988	108.9	0.5	106.3	-2.4	106.2	-0.1	105.4	-0.8	103.6	-1.7	99.7	-3.8	97.3	-2.4	95.2	-2.2	101.9	7.0	101.7	-0.2	102.7	1.0	99.5	-3.1
1989	100.6	1.1	100.2	-0.4	104.7	4.5	107.5	2.7	105.6	-1.8	103.5	-2.0	101.3	-2.1	103.1	1.8	106.9	3.7	108.2	1.2	105.5	-2.5	103.0	-2.4
1990	99.6	-3.3	104.5	4.9	107.3	2.7	108.4	1.0	106.5	-1.8	106.5	0.0	105.7	-0.8	107.6	1.8	112.2	4.3	113.2	0.9	109.2	-3.5	109.1	-0.1
1991	112.1	2.7	110.9	-1.1	112.0	1.0	114.0	1.8	111.3	-2.4	109.1	-2.0	109.2	0.1	115.6	5.9	115.8	0.2	116.6	0.7	115.8	-0.7	114.8	-0.9
1992	114.2	-0.5	117.7	3.1	121.6	3.3	119.5	-1.7	121.3	1.5	118.4	-2.4	115.4	-2.5	118.0	2.3	117.6	-0.3	117.0	-0.5	117.9	0.8	114.4	-3.0
1993	114.7	0.3	117.2	2.2	121.9	4.0	124.3	2.0	121.6	-2.2	117.1	-3.7	116.2	-0.8	115.2	-0.9	120.0	4.2	119.0	-0.8	117.3	-1.4	113.5	-3.2
1994	115.1	1.4	114.7	-0.3	116.3	1.4	116.1	-0.2	119.0	2.5	111.9	-6.0	114.5	2.3	116.4	1.7	117.8	1.2	113.7	-3.5	118.3	4.0	112.5	-4.9

[Continued]

San Francisco-Oakland, CA
Consumer Price Index - All Urban Consumers
Base 1982-1984 = 100
Apparel and Upkeep

[Continued]

For 1952-1997. Columns headed % show percentile change in the index from the previous period for which an index is available.

Year	Jan Index	%	Feb Index	%	Mar Index	%	Apr Index	%	May Index	%	Jun Index	%	Jul Index	%	Aug Index	%	Sep Index	%	Oct Index	%	Nov Index	%	Dec Index	%
1995	113.4	0.8	115.0	1.4	117.8	2.4	118.3	0.4	111.9	-5.4	115.0	2.8	110.5	-3.9	114.7	3.8	113.4	-1.1	114.6	1.1	114.1	-0.4	108.7	-4.7
1996	114.8	5.6	113.3	-1.3	122.2	7.9	122.8	0.5	121.5	-1.1	118.5	-2.5	116.7	-1.5	112.7	-3.4	117.9	4.6	116.6	-1.1	117.3	0.6	108.8	-7.2
1997	112.2	3.1	113.4	1.1	117.3	3.4	117.9	0.5	115.7	-1.9	117.3	1.4	121.7	3.8	119.2	-2.1	117.6	-1.3	115.9	-1.4	116.3	0.3	109.0	-6.3

Source: U.S. Department of Labor, Bureau of Labor Statistics, Division of Consumer Prices and Price Indexes. - indicates no data collected for period.

San Francisco-Oakland, CA
Consumer Price Index - Urban Wage Earners
Base 1982-1984 = 100
Apparel and Upkeep

For 1952-1997. Columns headed % show percentile change in the index from the previous period for which an index is available.

Year	Jan Index	Jan %	Feb Index	Feb %	Mar Index	Mar %	Apr Index	Apr %	May Index	May %	Jun Index	Jun %	Jul Index	Jul %	Aug Index	Aug %	Sep Index	Sep %	Oct Index	Oct %	Nov Index	Nov %	Dec Index	Dec %
1952	-	-	-	-	-	-	-	-	-	-	-	-	-	-	-	-	-	-	-	-	-	-	40.8	-
1953	-	-	-	-	40.9	0.2	-	-	-	-	40.4	-1.2	-	-	-	-	40.9	1.2	-	-	-	-	40.9	0.0
1954	-	-	-	-	40.4	-1.2	-	-	-	-	40.3	-0.2	-	-	-	-	40.2	-0.2	-	-	-	-	39.8	-1.0
1955	-	-	-	-	40.3	1.3	-	-	-	-	40.3	0.0	-	-	-	-	40.8	1.2	-	-	-	-	40.8	0.0
1956	-	-	-	-	41.1	0.7	-	-	-	-	41.2	0.2	-	-	-	-	41.3	0.2	-	-	-	-	42.0	1.7
1957	-	-	-	-	42.2	0.5	-	-	-	-	42.1	-0.2	-	-	-	-	42.3	0.5	-	-	-	-	42.5	0.5
1958	-	-	-	-	42.5	0.0	-	-	-	-	42.5	0.0	-	-	-	-	42.5	0.0	-	-	-	-	42.5	0.0
1959	-	-	-	-	42.6	0.2	-	-	-	-	42.7	0.2	-	-	-	-	43.5	1.9	-	-	-	-	43.7	0.5
1960	-	-	-	-	43.7	0.0	-	-	-	-	44.0	0.7	-	-	-	-	44.6	1.4	-	-	-	-	44.7	0.2
1961	-	-	-	-	44.6	-0.2	-	-	-	-	44.9	0.7	-	-	-	-	44.9	0.0	-	-	-	-	45.0	0.2
1962	-	-	-	-	45.3	0.7	-	-	-	-	45.5	0.4	-	-	-	-	45.5	0.0	-	-	-	-	45.7	0.4
1963	-	-	-	-	45.7	0.0	-	-	-	-	45.8	0.2	-	-	-	-	46.0	0.4	-	-	-	-	46.2	0.4
1964	-	-	-	-	46.3	0.2	-	-	-	-	46.3	0.0	-	-	-	-	46.3	0.0	-	-	-	-	46.6	0.6
1965	-	-	-	-	46.9	0.6	-	-	-	-	47.2	0.6	-	-	-	-	46.9	-0.6	-	-	-	-	47.4	1.1
1966	-	-	-	-	48.0	1.3	-	-	-	-	48.2	0.4	-	-	-	-	48.5	0.6	-	-	-	-	48.9	0.8
1967	-	-	-	-	49.5	1.2	-	-	-	-	49.6	0.2	-	-	-	-	51.4	3.6	-	-	-	-	51.5	0.2
1968	-	-	-	-	52.4	1.7	-	-	-	-	52.9	1.0	-	-	-	-	53.9	1.9	-	-	-	-	54.3	0.7
1969	-	-	-	-	55.1	1.5	-	-	-	-	55.3	0.4	-	-	-	-	56.6	2.4	-	-	-	-	56.7	0.2
1970	-	-	-	-	56.7	0.0	-	-	-	-	56.5	-0.4	-	-	-	-	58.2	3.0	-	-	-	-	58.7	0.9
1971	-	-	-	-	59.4	1.2	-	-	-	-	59.6	0.3	-	-	-	-	60.8	2.0	-	-	-	-	60.1	-1.2
1972	-	-	-	-	60.4	0.5	-	-	-	-	60.2	-0.3	-	-	-	-	62.4	3.7	-	-	-	-	62.4	0.0
1973	-	-	-	-	62.7	0.5	-	-	-	-	63.3	1.0	-	-	-	-	64.8	2.4	-	-	-	-	65.0	0.3
1974	-	-	-	-	66.5	2.3	-	-	-	-	68.4	2.9	-	-	-	-	69.9	2.2	-	-	-	-	71.0	1.6
1975	-	-	-	-	71.0	0.0	-	-	-	-	70.7	-0.4	-	-	-	-	71.4	1.0	-	-	-	-	72.4	1.4
1976	-	-	-	-	73.2	1.1	-	-	-	-	72.4	-1.1	-	-	-	-	73.3	1.2	-	-	-	-	74.1	1.1
1977	-	-	-	-	75.3	1.6	-	-	-	-	75.4	0.1	-	-	-	-	76.5	1.5	-	-	-	-	76.9	0.5
1978	-	-	75.1	-2.3	-	-	79.0	5.2	-	-	78.1	-1.1	-	-	78.8	0.9	-	-	80.4	2.0	-	-	79.9	-0.6
1979	-	-	81.3	1.8	-	-	81.8	0.6	-	-	83.9	2.6	-	-	82.6	-1.5	-	-	83.6	1.2	-	-	85.9	2.8
1980	-	-	86.2	0.3	-	-	87.2	1.2	-	-	85.9	-1.5	-	-	90.8	5.7	-	-	92.3	1.7	-	-	91.7	-0.7
1981	-	-	92.7	1.1	-	-	94.5	1.9	-	-	95.1	0.6	-	-	96.1	1.1	-	-	97.0	0.9	-	-	96.6	-0.4
1982	-	-	97.7	1.1	-	-	97.8	0.1	-	-	98.3	0.5	-	-	99.1	0.8	-	-	98.9	-0.2	-	-	97.1	-1.8
1983	-	-	98.5	1.4	-	-	98.5	0.0	-	-	97.6	-0.9	-	-	98.2	0.6	-	-	95.8	-2.4	-	-	98.0	2.3
1984	-	-	102.0	4.1	-	-	103.6	1.6	-	-	100.0	-3.5	-	-	106.6	6.6	-	-	109.0	2.3	-	-	105.9	-2.8
1985	-	-	107.7	1.7	-	-	105.3	-2.2	-	-	104.7	-0.6	-	-	101.7	-2.9	-	-	102.7	1.0	-	-	100.2	-2.4
1986	-	-	99.5	-0.7	-	-	104.5	5.0	-	-	100.5	-3.8	-	-	103.0	2.5	-	-	106.1	3.0	-	-	100.4	-5.4
1987	97.5	-2.9	103.1	5.7	106.7	3.5	109.2	2.3	104.0	-4.8	103.0	-1.0	101.2	-1.7	100.8	-0.4	105.6	4.8	109.3	3.5	113.8	4.1	110.0	-3.3
1988	110.8	0.7	108.0	-2.5	108.1	0.1	107.2	-0.8	105.2	-1.9	101.4	-3.6	99.4	-2.0	97.0	-2.4	104.4	7.6	104.1	-0.3	105.2	1.1	101.9	-3.1
1989	103.7	1.8	103.2	-0.5	107.0	3.7	110.1	2.9	108.0	-1.9	106.9	-1.0	104.8	-2.0	106.4	1.5	109.5	2.9	111.3	1.6	108.1	-2.9	105.5	-2.4
1990	103.7	-1.7	106.9	3.1	110.1	3.0	111.3	1.1	109.6	-1.5	109.7	0.1	108.9	-0.7	110.2	1.2	115.4	4.7	116.7	1.1	112.2	-3.9	112.8	0.5
1991	115.8	2.7	113.5	-2.0	114.8	1.1	117.0	1.9	114.2	-2.4	111.7	-2.2	112.1	0.4	118.6	5.8	118.9	0.3	120.2	1.1	119.3	-0.7	118.4	-0.8
1992	117.6	-0.7	120.7	2.6	124.9	3.5	122.7	-1.8	124.8	1.7	122.0	-2.2	119.2	-2.3	121.9	2.3	121.4	-0.4	120.8	-0.5	122.4	1.3	119.1	-2.7
1993	118.8	-0.3	121.4	2.2	125.2	3.1	128.7	2.8	126.0	-2.1	121.1	-3.9	120.7	-0.3	119.2	-1.2	125.6	5.4	124.9	-0.6	122.7	-1.8	118.5	-3.4
1994	120.8	1.9	119.5	-1.1	120.9	1.2	120.9	0.0	125.4	3.7	116.3	-7.3	119.4	2.7	122.0	2.2	122.8	0.7	117.8	-4.1	123.7	5.0	117.4	-5.1

[Continued]

San Francisco-Oakland, CA
Consumer Price Index - Urban Wage Earners
Base 1982-1984 = 100
Apparel and Upkeep

[Continued]

For 1952-1997. Columns headed % show percentile change in the index from the previous period for which an index is available.

Year	Jan		Feb		Mar		Apr		May		Jun		Jul		Aug		Sep		Oct		Nov		Dec	
	Index	%	Index	%	Index	%	Index	%	Index	%	Index	%	Index	%	Index	%	Index	%	Index	%	Index	%	Index	%
1995	119.8	2.0	121.1	1.1	124.4	2.7	125.2	0.6	116.8	-6.7	123.2	5.5	115.9	-5.9	122.3	5.5	120.0	-1.9	119.4	-0.5	119.1	-0.3	112.7	-5.4
1996	120.8	7.2	117.2	-3.0	128.9	10.0	129.2	0.2	128.4	-0.6	125.2	-2.5	122.2	-2.4	116.6	-4.6	124.3	6.6	122.8	-1.2	124.4	1.3	112.8	-9.3
1997	117.9	4.5	118.3	0.3	122.9	3.9	123.3	0.3	120.4	-2.4	123.1	2.2	128.1	4.1	125.1	-2.3	122.6	-2.0	121.7	-0.7	122.0	0.2	112.2	-8.0

Source: U.S. Department of Labor, Bureau of Labor Statistics, Division of Consumer Prices and Price Indexes. - indicates no data collected for period.

San Francisco-Oakland, CA
Consumer Price Index - All Urban Consumers
Base 1982-1984 = 100
Transportation

For 1947-1997. Columns headed % show percentile change in the index from the previous period for which an index is available.

Year	Jan Index	%	Feb Index	%	Mar Index	%	Apr Index	%	May Index	%	Jun Index	%	Jul Index	%	Aug Index	%	Sep Index	%	Oct Index	%	Nov Index	%	Dec Index	%
1947	16.0	-	16.1	0.6	16.1	0.0	16.3	1.2	16.2	-0.6	16.2	0.0	-	-	-	-	16.7	3.1	-	-	-	-	17.0	1.8
1948	-	-	-	-	17.4	2.4	-	-	-	-	18.0	3.4	-	-	-	-	18.6	3.3	-	-	-	-	18.7	0.5
1949	-	-	-	-	19.3	3.2	-	-	-	-	19.5	1.0	-	-	-	-	19.5	0.0	-	-	-	-	19.6	0.5
1950	-	-	-	-	19.6	0.0	-	-	-	-	19.2	-2.0	-	-	-	-	19.4	1.0	-	-	-	-	19.5	0.5
1951	-	-	-	-	20.6	5.6	-	-	-	-	20.8	1.0	-	-	-	-	21.3	2.4	-	-	-	-	21.4	0.5
1952	-	-	-	-	21.6	0.9	-	-	-	-	24.1	11.6	-	-	-	-	25.2	4.6	-	-	-	-	25.2	0.0
1953	-	-	-	-	25.7	2.0	-	-	-	-	25.5	-0.8	-	-	-	-	25.8	1.2	-	-	-	-	25.9	0.4
1954	-	-	-	-	25.8	-0.4	-	-	-	-	25.7	-0.4	-	-	-	-	25.2	-1.9	-	-	-	-	25.4	0.8
1955	-	-	-	-	25.3	-0.4	-	-	-	-	24.8	-2.0	-	-	-	-	24.8	0.0	-	-	-	-	25.3	2.0
1956	-	-	-	-	25.0	-1.2	-	-	-	-	25.1	0.4	-	-	-	-	25.3	0.8	-	-	-	-	26.7	5.5
1957	-	-	-	-	27.1	1.5	-	-	-	-	26.9	-0.7	-	-	-	-	27.1	0.7	-	-	-	-	27.4	1.1
1958	-	-	-	-	28.0	2.2	-	-	-	-	28.4	1.4	-	-	-	-	28.8	1.4	-	-	-	-	28.4	-1.4
1959	-	-	-	-	29.7	4.6	-	-	-	-	29.6	-0.3	-	-	-	-	30.0	1.4	-	-	-	-	30.5	1.7
1960	-	-	-	-	29.6	-3.0	-	-	-	-	29.5	-0.3	-	-	-	-	29.3	-0.7	-	-	-	-	29.9	2.0
1961	-	-	-	-	29.6	-1.0	-	-	-	-	29.3	-1.0	-	-	-	-	30.1	2.7	-	-	-	-	30.5	1.3
1962	-	-	-	-	30.2	-1.0	-	-	-	-	30.5	1.0	-	-	-	-	30.5	0.0	-	-	-	-	30.4	-0.3
1963	-	-	-	-	30.5	0.3	-	-	-	-	30.6	0.3	-	-	-	-	30.8	0.7	-	-	-	-	31.4	1.9
1964	-	-	-	-	31.4	0.0	-	-	-	-	31.6	0.6	-	-	-	-	31.4	-0.6	-	-	-	-	31.9	1.6
1965	-	-	-	-	31.7	-0.6	-	-	-	-	31.7	0.0	-	-	-	-	31.6	-0.3	-	-	-	-	31.9	0.9
1966	-	-	-	-	31.9	0.0	-	-	-	-	31.6	-0.9	-	-	-	-	32.2	1.9	-	-	-	-	32.4	0.6
1967	-	-	-	-	32.4	0.0	-	-	-	-	32.9	1.5	-	-	-	-	33.2	0.9	-	-	-	-	33.4	0.6
1968	-	-	-	-	33.6	0.6	-	-	-	-	33.8	0.6	-	-	-	-	33.8	0.0	-	-	-	-	34.1	0.9
1969	-	-	-	-	35.0	2.6	-	-	-	-	35.3	0.9	-	-	-	-	35.4	0.3	-	-	-	-	36.1	2.0
1970	-	-	-	-	35.6	-1.4	-	-	-	-	36.5	2.5	-	-	-	-	37.0	1.4	-	-	-	-	38.6	4.3
1971	-	-	-	-	38.8	0.5	-	-	-	-	38.9	0.3	-	-	-	-	38.7	-0.5	-	-	-	-	38.6	-0.3
1972	-	-	-	-	39.0	1.0	-	-	-	-	39.5	1.3	-	-	-	-	40.1	1.5	-	-	-	-	40.2	0.2
1973	-	-	-	-	39.8	-1.0	-	-	-	-	40.7	2.3	-	-	-	-	40.6	-0.2	-	-	-	-	41.1	1.2
1974	-	-	-	-	42.6	3.6	-	-	-	-	45.0	5.6	-	-	-	-	46.5	3.3	-	-	-	-	47.3	1.7
1975	-	-	-	-	48.3	2.1	-	-	-	-	50.0	3.5	-	-	-	-	51.0	2.0	-	-	-	-	51.6	1.2
1976	-	-	-	-	52.5	1.7	-	-	-	-	53.9	2.7	-	-	-	-	55.7	3.3	-	-	-	-	56.3	1.1
1977	-	-	-	-	56.9	1.1	-	-	-	-	58.5	2.8	-	-	-	-	58.4	-0.2	-	-	-	-	59.1	1.2
1978	-	-	59.5	0.7	-	-	59.7	0.3	-	-	61.5	3.0	-	-	62.2	1.1	-	-	62.9	1.1	-	-	64.0	1.7
1979	-	-	64.7	1.1	-	-	67.4	4.2	-	-	70.5	4.6	-	-	72.9	3.4	-	-	74.3	1.9	-	-	76.0	2.3
1980	-	-	80.7	6.2	-	-	83.7	3.7	-	-	83.7	0.0	-	-	84.9	1.4	-	-	85.6	0.8	-	-	86.5	1.1
1981	-	-	88.6	2.4	-	-	90.6	2.3	-	-	92.8	2.4	-	-	93.0	0.2	-	-	94.1	1.2	-	-	94.9	0.9
1982	-	-	94.0	-0.9	-	-	94.5	0.5	-	-	98.1	3.8	-	-	99.6	1.5	-	-	99.8	0.2	-	-	98.2	-1.6
1983	-	-	96.2	-2.0	-	-	96.5	0.3	-	-	100.4	4.0	-	-	101.2	0.8	-	-	100.0	-1.2	-	-	100.8	0.8
1984	-	-	100.6	-0.2	-	-	103.2	2.6	-	-	104.9	1.6	-	-	103.8	-1.0	-	-	105.9	2.0	-	-	105.1	-0.8
1985	-	-	104.6	-0.5	-	-	105.9	1.2	-	-	106.7	0.8	-	-	105.3	-1.3	-	-	105.0	-0.3	-	-	105.5	0.5
1986	-	-	105.3	-0.2	-	-	99.8	-5.2	-	-	102.8	3.0	-	-	99.4	-3.3	-	-	99.7	0.3	-	-	98.5	-1.2
1987	99.4	0.9	100.2	0.8	101.4	1.2	101.8	0.4	102.0	0.2	102.1	0.1	102.6	0.5	103.2	0.6	103.3	0.1	103.5	0.2	104.6	1.1	104.5	-0.1
1988	104.4	-0.1	103.5	-0.9	103.4	-0.1	103.7	0.3	104.4	0.7	105.3	0.9	105.7	0.4	106.5	0.8	106.7	0.2	107.0	0.3	106.1	-0.8	106.4	0.3
1989	106.8	0.4	107.2	0.4	107.6	0.4	110.9	3.1	112.1	1.1	111.6	-0.4	111.5	-0.1	110.7	-0.7	108.7	-1.8	109.0	0.3	109.5	0.5	109.1	-0.4
1990	110.4	1.2	110.4	0.0	111.5	1.0	112.0	0.4	112.7	0.6	113.4	0.6	113.8	0.4	115.4	1.4	116.8	1.2	119.1	2.0	119.6	0.4	121.2	1.3
1991	119.5	-1.4	117.0	-2.1	115.2	-1.5	113.7	-1.3	115.9	1.9	117.6	1.5	117.7	0.1	118.4	0.6	117.5	-0.8	117.9	0.3	117.4	-0.4	117.0	-0.3

[Continued]

San Francisco-Oakland, CA
Consumer Price Index - All Urban Consumers
Base 1982-1984 = 100
Transportation
[Continued]

For 1947-1997. Columns headed % show percentile change in the index from the previous period for which an index is available.

Year	Jan Index	%	Feb Index	%	Mar Index	%	Apr Index	%	May Index	%	Jun Index	%	Jul Index	%	Aug Index	%	Sep Index	%	Oct Index	%	Nov Index	%	Dec Index	%
1992	116.6	-0.3	116.2	-0.3	116.7	0.4	117.6	0.8	119.1	1.3	120.1	0.8	121.4	1.1	121.5	0.1	120.7	-0.7	122.1	1.2	122.7	0.5	123.3	0.5
1993	125.1	1.5	124.3	-0.6	123.5	-0.6	123.1	-0.3	123.4	0.2	123.1	-0.2	123.0	-0.1	123.6	0.5	122.2	-1.1	124.4	1.8	124.7	0.2	123.5	-1.0
1994	123.9	0.3	123.4	-0.4	124.9	1.2	125.3	0.3	125.1	-0.2	125.6	0.4	126.1	0.4	127.2	0.9	126.3	-0.7	127.3	0.8	127.2	-0.1	126.2	-0.8
1995	126.7	0.4	126.6	-0.1	127.4	0.6	128.2	0.6	129.1	0.7	130.4	1.0	130.3	-0.1	129.5	-0.6	129.8	0.2	130.4	0.5	130.0	-0.3	129.9	-0.1
1996	129.9	0.0	131.7	1.4	131.9	0.2	134.9	2.3	135.8	0.7	135.9	0.1	135.2	-0.5	134.2	-0.7	134.1	-0.1	134.2	0.1	132.8	-1.0	131.3	-1.1
1997	131.2	-0.1	133.1	1.4	134.7	1.2	135.3	0.4	134.7	-0.4	134.1	-0.4	134.0	-0.1	133.0	-0.7	133.4	0.3	133.5	0.1	133.0	-0.4	132.6	-0.3

Source: U.S. Department of Labor, Bureau of Labor Statistics, Division of Consumer Prices and Price Indexes. - indicates no data collected for period.

San Francisco-Oakland, CA
Consumer Price Index - Urban Wage Earners
Base 1982-1984 = 100
Transportation

For 1947-1997. Columns headed % show percentile change in the index from the previous period for which an index is available.

Year	Jan Index	%	Feb Index	%	Mar Index	%	Apr Index	%	May Index	%	Jun Index	%	Jul Index	%	Aug Index	%	Sep Index	%	Oct Index	%	Nov Index	%	Dec Index	%
1947	15.7	-	15.7	0.0	15.8	0.6	15.9	0.6	15.8	-0.6	15.8	0.0	-	-	-	-	16.3	3.2	-	-	-	-	16.6	1.8
1948	-	-	-	-	17.0	2.4	-	-	-	-	17.5	2.9	-	-	-	-	18.2	4.0	-	-	-	-	18.3	0.5
1949	-	-	-	-	18.9	3.3	-	-	-	-	19.0	0.5	-	-	-	-	19.1	0.5	-	-	-	-	19.2	0.5
1950	-	-	-	-	19.2	0.0	-	-	-	-	18.8	-2.1	-	-	-	-	19.0	1.1	-	-	-	-	19.0	0.0
1951	-	-	-	-	20.1	5.8	-	-	-	-	20.3	1.0	-	-	-	-	20.8	2.5	-	-	-	-	20.9	0.5
1952	-	-	-	-	21.1	1.0	-	-	-	-	23.6	11.8	-	-	-	-	24.6	4.2	-	-	-	-	24.6	0.0
1953	-	-	-	-	25.1	2.0	-	-	-	-	24.9	-0.8	-	-	-	-	25.2	1.2	-	-	-	-	25.3	0.4
1954	-	-	-	-	25.2	-0.4	-	-	-	-	25.1	-0.4	-	-	-	-	24.6	-2.0	-	-	-	-	24.8	0.8
1955	-	-	-	-	24.7	-0.4	-	-	-	-	24.2	-2.0	-	-	-	-	24.3	0.4	-	-	-	-	24.7	1.6
1956	-	-	-	-	24.4	-1.2	-	-	-	-	24.5	0.4	-	-	-	-	24.7	0.8	-	-	-	-	26.1	5.7
1957	-	-	-	-	26.5	1.5	-	-	-	-	26.3	-0.8	-	-	-	-	26.4	0.4	-	-	-	-	26.7	1.1
1958	-	-	-	-	27.3	2.2	-	-	-	-	27.7	1.5	-	-	-	-	28.2	1.8	-	-	-	-	27.7	-1.8
1959	-	-	-	-	29.0	4.7	-	-	-	-	28.9	-0.3	-	-	-	-	29.3	1.4	-	-	-	-	29.7	1.4
1960	-	-	-	-	28.9	-2.7	-	-	-	-	28.8	-0.3	-	-	-	-	28.6	-0.7	-	-	-	-	29.2	2.1
1961	-	-	-	-	28.9	-1.0	-	-	-	-	28.6	-1.0	-	-	-	-	29.4	2.8	-	-	-	-	29.8	1.4
1962	-	-	-	-	29.4	-1.3	-	-	-	-	29.7	1.0	-	-	-	-	29.8	0.3	-	-	-	-	29.7	-0.3
1963	-	-	-	-	29.7	0.0	-	-	-	-	29.9	0.7	-	-	-	-	30.0	0.3	-	-	-	-	30.6	2.0
1964	-	-	-	-	30.6	0.0	-	-	-	-	30.9	1.0	-	-	-	-	30.7	-0.6	-	-	-	-	31.1	1.3
1965	-	-	-	-	31.0	-0.3	-	-	-	-	31.0	0.0	-	-	-	-	30.8	-0.6	-	-	-	-	31.2	1.3
1966	-	-	-	-	31.2	0.0	-	-	-	-	30.9	-1.0	-	-	-	-	31.5	1.9	-	-	-	-	31.6	0.3
1967	-	-	-	-	31.6	0.0	-	-	-	-	32.1	1.6	-	-	-	-	32.4	0.9	-	-	-	-	32.6	0.6
1968	-	-	-	-	32.8	0.6	-	-	-	-	33.0	0.6	-	-	-	-	33.0	0.0	-	-	-	-	33.3	0.9
1969	-	-	-	-	34.2	2.7	-	-	-	-	34.4	0.6	-	-	-	-	34.6	0.6	-	-	-	-	35.2	1.7
1970	-	-	-	-	34.8	-1.1	-	-	-	-	35.7	2.6	-	-	-	-	36.2	1.4	-	-	-	-	37.7	4.1
1971	-	-	-	-	37.9	0.5	-	-	-	-	38.0	0.3	-	-	-	-	37.8	-0.5	-	-	-	-	37.7	-0.3
1972	-	-	-	-	38.1	1.1	-	-	-	-	38.5	1.0	-	-	-	-	39.2	1.8	-	-	-	-	39.2	0.0
1973	-	-	-	-	38.8	-1.0	-	-	-	-	39.8	2.6	-	-	-	-	39.7	-0.3	-	-	-	-	40.1	1.0
1974	-	-	-	-	41.6	3.7	-	-	-	-	44.0	5.8	-	-	-	-	45.4	3.2	-	-	-	-	46.2	1.8
1975	-	-	-	-	47.2	2.2	-	-	-	-	48.8	3.4	-	-	-	-	49.8	2.0	-	-	-	-	50.4	1.2
1976	-	-	-	-	51.2	1.6	-	-	-	-	52.6	2.7	-	-	-	-	54.4	3.4	-	-	-	-	55.0	1.1
1977	-	-	-	-	55.6	1.1	-	-	-	-	57.1	2.7	-	-	-	-	57.0	-0.2	-	-	-	-	57.7	1.2
1978	-	-	58.1	0.7	-	-	58.4	0.5	-	-	60.3	3.3	-	-	61.2	1.5	-	-	61.9	1.1	-	-	63.0	1.8
1979	-	-	63.6	1.0	-	-	66.6	4.7	-	-	69.8	4.8	-	-	72.1	3.3	-	-	73.2	1.5	-	-	75.0	2.5
1980	-	-	79.4	5.9	-	-	81.9	3.1	-	-	81.9	0.0	-	-	83.5	2.0	-	-	84.4	1.1	-	-	85.2	0.9
1981	-	-	87.8	3.1	-	-	89.8	2.3	-	-	91.5	1.9	-	-	92.3	0.9	-	-	93.5	1.3	-	-	94.3	0.9
1982	-	-	93.4	-1.0	-	-	94.2	0.9	-	-	97.6	3.6	-	-	99.2	1.6	-	-	99.4	0.2	-	-	98.0	-1.4
1983	-	-	96.0	-2.0	-	-	96.4	0.4	-	-	100.5	4.3	-	-	101.3	0.8	-	-	100.4	-0.9	-	-	101.3	0.9
1984	-	-	101.1	-0.2	-	-	103.6	2.5	-	-	105.1	1.4	-	-	103.9	-1.1	-	-	106.0	2.0	-	-	105.3	-0.7
1985	-	-	104.8	-0.5	-	-	106.1	1.2	-	-	107.0	0.8	-	-	105.6	-1.3	-	-	105.2	-0.4	-	-	105.7	0.5
1986	-	-	105.6	-0.1	-	-	100.0	-5.3	-	-	102.9	2.9	-	-	99.7	-3.1	-	-	100.0	0.3	-	-	98.8	-1.2
1987	99.3	0.5	100.8	1.5	102.3	1.5	103.2	0.9	103.5	0.3	103.8	0.3	104.1	0.3	104.8	0.7	104.8	0.0	105.3	0.5	105.9	0.6	106.1	0.2
1988	106.1	0.0	105.5	-0.6	105.4	-0.1	105.5	0.1	106.2	0.7	107.1	0.8	107.6	0.5	108.1	0.5	108.3	0.2	108.8	0.5	108.0	-0.7	108.0	0.0
1989	108.5	0.5	108.9	0.4	109.6	0.6	113.4	3.5	114.9	1.3	114.4	-0.4	114.1	-0.3	113.3	-0.7	111.3	-1.8	111.1	-0.2	111.5	0.4	111.1	-0.4
1990	111.7	0.5	112.1	0.4	113.2	1.0	113.7	0.4	114.4	0.6	115.4	0.9	115.7	0.3	117.6	1.6	119.2	1.4	122.0	2.3	122.3	0.2	123.2	0.7
1991	121.0	-1.8	118.1	-2.4	116.2	-1.6	114.8	-1.2	117.2	2.1	118.9	1.5	119.2	0.3	119.8	0.5	119.5	-0.3	120.0	0.4	119.1	-0.8	118.9	-0.2

[Continued]

San Francisco-Oakland, CA
Consumer Price Index - Urban Wage Earners
Base 1982-1984 = 100
Transportation
[Continued]

For 1947-1997. Columns headed % show percentile change in the index from the previous period for which an index is available.

Year	Jan		Feb		Mar		Apr		May		Jun		Jul		Aug		Sep		Oct		Nov		Dec	
	Index	%	Index	%	Index	%	Index	%	Index	%	Index	%	Index	%	Index	%	Index	%	Index	%	Index	%	Index	%
1992	118.3	-0.5	118.0	-0.3	118.3	0.3	119.2	0.8	121.1	1.6	122.5	1.2	123.5	0.8	123.8	0.2	123.4	-0.3	124.3	0.7	125.0	0.6	125.3	0.2
1993	126.4	0.9	125.8	-0.5	125.2	-0.5	125.0	-0.2	125.3	0.2	125.3	0.0	125.3	0.0	125.7	0.3	125.1	-0.5	127.0	1.5	126.9	-0.1	125.6	-1.0
1994	125.5	-0.1	124.7	-0.6	125.6	0.7	126.3	0.6	126.5	0.2	127.4	0.7	128.3	0.7	129.6	1.0	129.3	-0.2	130.5	0.9	130.5	0.0	130.1	-0.3
1995	129.8	-0.2	129.7	-0.1	130.6	0.7	131.6	0.8	132.4	0.6	133.4	0.8	133.2	-0.1	132.6	-0.5	132.4	-0.2	133.5	0.8	133.2	-0.2	133.1	-0.1
1996	133.3	0.2	134.3	0.8	134.7	0.3	138.5	2.8	139.7	0.9	139.0	-0.5	138.3	-0.5	137.1	-0.9	136.7	-0.3	136.5	-0.1	135.1	-1.0	133.2	-1.4
1997	133.7	0.4	135.7	1.5	136.7	0.7	138.1	1.0	137.2	-0.7	136.2	-0.7	135.4	-0.6	134.9	-0.4	135.9	0.7	135.8	-0.1	135.2	-0.4	135.0	-0.1

Source: U.S. Department of Labor, Bureau of Labor Statistics, Division of Consumer Prices and Price Indexes. - indicates no data collected for period.

San Francisco-Oakland, CA
Consumer Price Index - All Urban Consumers
Base 1982-1984 = 100
Medical Care

For 1947-1997. Columns headed % show percentile change in the index from the previous period for which an index is available.

Year	Jan Index	%	Feb Index	%	Mar Index	%	Apr Index	%	May Index	%	Jun Index	%	Jul Index	%	Aug Index	%	Sep Index	%	Oct Index	%	Nov Index	%	Dec Index	%
1947	13.3	-	13.4	0.8	13.4	0.0	13.4	0.0	13.4	0.0	13.4	0.0	-	-	-	-	13.8	3.0	-	-	-	-	13.9	0.7
1948	-	-	-	-	14.0	0.7	-	-	-	-	14.2	1.4	-	-	-	-	14.4	1.4	-	-	-	-	14.6	1.4
1949	-	-	-	-	14.7	0.7	-	-	-	-	14.7	0.0	-	-	-	-	14.8	0.7	-	-	-	-	14.8	0.0
1950	-	-	-	-	14.8	0.0	-	-	-	-	14.8	0.0	-	-	-	-	15.5	4.7	-	-	-	-	15.7	1.3
1951	-	-	-	-	15.7	0.0	-	-	-	-	15.8	0.6	-	-	-	-	15.8	0.0	-	-	-	-	16.0	1.3
1952	-	-	-	-	16.8	5.0	-	-	-	-	16.9	0.6	-	-	-	-	16.9	0.0	-	-	-	-	17.0	0.6
1953	-	-	-	-	17.0	0.0	-	-	-	-	17.2	1.2	-	-	-	-	17.4	1.2	-	-	-	-	17.4	0.0
1954	-	-	-	-	17.5	0.6	-	-	-	-	17.5	0.0	-	-	-	-	17.5	0.0	-	-	-	-	17.5	0.0
1955	-	-	-	-	17.5	0.0	-	-	-	-	17.6	0.6	-	-	-	-	17.8	1.1	-	-	-	-	17.9	0.6
1956	-	-	-	-	18.2	1.7	-	-	-	-	18.2	0.0	-	-	-	-	19.2	5.5	-	-	-	-	19.3	0.5
1957	-	-	-	-	19.3	0.0	-	-	-	-	19.5	1.0	-	-	-	-	19.6	0.5	-	-	-	-	20.0	2.0
1958	-	-	-	-	20.3	1.5	-	-	-	-	21.4	5.4	-	-	-	-	21.5	0.5	-	-	-	-	21.6	0.5
1959	-	-	-	-	21.7	0.5	-	-	-	-	22.0	1.4	-	-	-	-	22.0	0.0	-	-	-	-	22.0	0.0
1960	-	-	-	-	22.4	1.8	-	-	-	-	22.5	0.4	-	-	-	-	22.7	0.9	-	-	-	-	22.8	0.4
1961	-	-	-	-	22.9	0.4	-	-	-	-	23.0	0.4	-	-	-	-	23.1	0.4	-	-	-	-	23.2	0.4
1962	-	-	-	-	24.0	3.4	-	-	-	-	24.1	0.4	-	-	-	-	24.2	0.4	-	-	-	-	24.4	0.8
1963	-	-	-	-	24.5	0.4	-	-	-	-	24.6	0.4	-	-	-	-	24.7	0.4	-	-	-	-	24.8	0.4
1964	-	-	-	-	25.1	1.2	-	-	-	-	25.3	0.8	-	-	-	-	25.5	0.8	-	-	-	-	25.5	0.0
1965	-	-	-	-	25.8	1.2	-	-	-	-	25.9	0.4	-	-	-	-	25.9	0.0	-	-	-	-	26.3	1.5
1966	-	-	-	-	26.6	1.1	-	-	-	-	27.1	1.9	-	-	-	-	27.8	2.6	-	-	-	-	28.2	1.4
1967	-	-	-	-	28.7	1.8	-	-	-	-	28.9	0.7	-	-	-	-	29.1	0.7	-	-	-	-	29.4	1.0
1968	-	-	-	-	30.1	2.4	-	-	-	-	30.3	0.7	-	-	-	-	30.5	0.7	-	-	-	-	30.9	1.3
1969	-	-	-	-	31.4	1.6	-	-	-	-	31.7	1.0	-	-	-	-	32.2	1.6	-	-	-	-	32.5	0.9
1970	-	-	-	-	33.2	2.2	-	-	-	-	33.5	0.9	-	-	-	-	34.1	1.8	-	-	-	-	34.2	0.3
1971	-	-	-	-	35.3	3.2	-	-	-	-	35.7	1.1	-	-	-	-	36.2	1.4	-	-	-	-	35.9	-0.8
1972	-	-	-	-	36.4	1.4	-	-	-	-	36.7	0.8	-	-	-	-	37.1	1.1	-	-	-	-	37.4	0.8
1973	-	-	-	-	37.9	1.3	-	-	-	-	38.0	0.3	-	-	-	-	38.4	1.1	-	-	-	-	39.0	1.6
1974	-	-	-	-	40.1	2.8	-	-	-	-	41.2	2.7	-	-	-	-	42.7	3.6	-	-	-	-	43.5	1.9
1975	-	-	-	-	45.7	5.1	-	-	-	-	48.3	5.7	-	-	-	-	49.1	1.7	-	-	-	-	49.8	1.4
1976	-	-	-	-	51.7	3.8	-	-	-	-	52.3	1.2	-	-	-	-	53.2	1.7	-	-	-	-	54.6	2.6
1977	-	-	-	-	56.4	3.3	-	-	-	-	57.4	1.8	-	-	-	-	59.3	3.3	-	-	-	-	59.7	0.7
1978	-	-	61.0	2.2	-	-	62.6	2.6	-	-	62.6	0.0	-	-	63.7	1.8	-	-	65.5	2.8	-	-	65.9	0.6
1979	-	-	67.0	1.7	-	-	67.3	0.4	-	-	67.8	0.7	-	-	69.3	2.2	-	-	72.1	4.0	-	-	73.2	1.5
1980	-	-	74.4	1.6	-	-	76.0	2.2	-	-	76.4	0.5	-	-	76.8	0.5	-	-	78.4	2.1	-	-	78.6	0.3
1981	-	-	81.1	3.2	-	-	82.9	2.2	-	-	84.0	1.3	-	-	85.7	2.0	-	-	87.2	1.8	-	-	89.1	2.2
1982	-	-	90.8	1.9	-	-	93.1	2.5	-	-	94.3	1.3	-	-	95.2	1.0	-	-	96.3	1.2	-	-	97.6	1.3
1983	-	-	99.5	1.9	-	-	99.7	0.2	-	-	101.2	1.5	-	-	101.9	0.7	-	-	101.6	-0.3	-	-	101.7	0.1
1984	-	-	103.8	2.1	-	-	104.4	0.6	-	-	104.6	0.2	-	-	105.4	0.8	-	-	106.4	0.9	-	-	107.0	0.6
1985	-	-	107.8	0.7	-	-	108.5	0.6	-	-	110.3	1.7	-	-	113.2	2.6	-	-	113.9	0.6	-	-	115.1	1.1
1986	-	-	115.9	0.7	-	-	117.4	1.3	-	-	118.9	1.3	-	-	121.9	2.5	-	-	122.4	0.4	-	-	124.0	1.3
1987	125.1	0.9	125.2	0.1	125.8	0.5	126.6	0.6	126.4	-0.2	127.3	0.7	130.1	2.2	131.3	0.9	131.1	-0.2	131.4	0.2	132.0	0.5	132.2	0.2
1988	133.2	0.8	133.1	-0.1	133.7	0.5	134.3	0.4	134.7	0.3	136.1	1.0	137.9	1.3	138.1	0.1	139.1	0.7	140.1	0.7	140.5	0.3	141.4	0.6
1989	143.0	1.1	144.6	1.1	145.0	0.3	145.7	0.5	145.8	0.1	146.6	0.5	147.8	0.8	148.4	0.4	149.9	1.0	150.4	0.3	154.1	2.5	152.9	-0.8
1990	155.2	1.5	156.1	0.6	158.3	1.4	158.3	0.0	158.3	0.0	158.7	0.3	161.3	1.6	162.7	0.9	163.1	0.2	164.2	0.7	164.8	0.4	164.9	0.1
1991	166.6	1.0	167.8	0.7	168.7	0.5	168.7	0.0	169.0	0.2	169.7	0.4	173.2	2.1	176.6	2.0	177.9	0.7	178.2	0.2	178.9	0.4	179.4	0.3

[Continued]

San Francisco-Oakland, CA
Consumer Price Index - All Urban Consumers
Base 1982-1984 = 100
Medical Care
[Continued]

For 1947-1997. Columns headed % show percentile change in the index from the previous period for which an index is available.

Year	Jan Index	%	Feb Index	%	Mar Index	%	Apr Index	%	May Index	%	Jun Index	%	Jul Index	%	Aug Index	%	Sep Index	%	Oct Index	%	Nov Index	%	Dec Index	%
1992	180.1	0.4	182.2	1.2	183.1	0.5	185.3	1.2	185.2	-0.1	186.7	0.8	188.5	1.0	188.7	0.1	190.3	0.8	190.9	0.3	191.2	0.2	191.4	0.1
1993	193.1	0.9	194.9	0.9	194.7	-0.1	197.8	1.6	197.8	0.0	199.5	0.9	201.4	1.0	201.6	0.1	201.2	-0.2	202.2	0.5	202.0	-0.1	202.4	0.2
1994	202.4	0.0	202.5	0.0	203.1	0.3	203.9	0.4	203.5	-0.2	203.9	0.2	203.3	-0.3	204.9	0.8	205.7	0.4	205.8	0.0	206.3	0.2	206.8	0.2
1995	209.0	1.1	208.6	-0.2	209.2	0.3	207.7	-0.7	207.7	0.0	207.1	-0.3	208.8	0.8	208.8	0.0	209.9	0.5	210.1	0.1	210.6	0.2	210.6	0.0
1996	212.4	0.9	212.2	-0.1	213.3	0.5	214.1	0.4	213.2	-0.4	213.3	0.0	214.2	0.4	214.6	0.2	214.3	-0.1	217.3	1.4	217.2	-0.0	217.9	0.3
1997	218.3	0.2	218.6	0.1	219.3	0.3	220.6	0.6	222.2	0.7	222.3	0.0	222.3	0.0	222.7	0.2	221.8	-0.4	223.3	0.7	224.6	0.6	225.9	0.6

Source: U.S. Department of Labor, Bureau of Labor Statistics, Division of Consumer Prices and Price Indexes. - indicates no data collected for period.

San Francisco-Oakland, CA
Consumer Price Index - Urban Wage Earners
Base 1982-1984 = 100
Medical Care

For 1947-1997. Columns headed % show percentile change in the index from the previous period for which an index is available.

Year	Jan Index	%	Feb Index	%	Mar Index	%	Apr Index	%	May Index	%	Jun Index	%	Jul Index	%	Aug Index	%	Sep Index	%	Oct Index	%	Nov Index	%	Dec Index	%
1947	13.4	-	13.5	0.7	13.5	0.0	13.5	0.0	13.5	0.0	13.5	0.0	-	-	-	-	13.9	3.0	-	-	-	-	14.0	0.7
1948	-	-	-	-	14.1	0.7	-	-	-	-	14.3	1.4	-	-	-	-	14.5	1.4	-	-	-	-	14.7	1.4
1949	-	-	-	-	14.8	0.7	-	-	-	-	14.8	0.0	-	-	-	-	14.9	0.7	-	-	-	-	14.9	0.0
1950	-	-	-	-	14.9	0.0	-	-	-	-	14.9	0.0	-	-	-	-	15.6	4.7	-	-	-	-	15.8	1.3
1951	-	-	-	-	15.8	0.0	-	-	-	-	15.9	0.6	-	-	-	-	15.9	0.0	-	-	-	-	16.1	1.3
1952	-	-	-	-	16.9	5.0	-	-	-	-	17.0	0.6	-	-	-	-	17.0	0.0	-	-	-	-	17.1	0.6
1953	-	-	-	-	17.1	0.0	-	-	-	-	17.3	1.2	-	-	-	-	17.5	1.2	-	-	-	-	17.6	0.6
1954	-	-	-	-	17.6	0.0	-	-	-	-	17.6	0.0	-	-	-	-	17.6	0.0	-	-	-	-	17.7	0.6
1955	-	-	-	-	17.7	0.0	-	-	-	-	17.7	0.0	-	-	-	-	17.9	1.1	-	-	-	-	18.0	0.6
1956	-	-	-	-	18.3	1.7	-	-	-	-	18.3	0.0	-	-	-	-	19.4	6.0	-	-	-	-	19.4	0.0
1957	-	-	-	-	19.5	0.5	-	-	-	-	19.6	0.5	-	-	-	-	19.7	0.5	-	-	-	-	20.1	2.0
1958	-	-	-	-	20.4	1.5	-	-	-	-	21.6	5.9	-	-	-	-	21.6	0.0	-	-	-	-	21.7	0.5
1959	-	-	-	-	21.8	0.5	-	-	-	-	22.1	1.4	-	-	-	-	22.1	0.0	-	-	-	-	22.2	0.5
1960	-	-	-	-	22.5	1.4	-	-	-	-	22.7	0.9	-	-	-	-	22.8	0.4	-	-	-	-	22.9	0.4
1961	-	-	-	-	23.0	0.4	-	-	-	-	23.1	0.4	-	-	-	-	23.3	0.9	-	-	-	-	23.4	0.4
1962	-	-	-	-	24.2	3.4	-	-	-	-	24.3	0.4	-	-	-	-	24.4	0.4	-	-	-	-	24.5	0.4
1963	-	-	-	-	24.7	0.8	-	-	-	-	24.8	0.4	-	-	-	-	24.9	0.4	-	-	-	-	25.0	0.4
1964	-	-	-	-	25.2	0.8	-	-	-	-	25.4	0.8	-	-	-	-	25.7	1.2	-	-	-	-	25.7	0.0
1965	-	-	-	-	26.0	1.2	-	-	-	-	26.0	0.0	-	-	-	-	26.1	0.4	-	-	-	-	26.5	1.5
1966	-	-	-	-	26.8	1.1	-	-	-	-	27.3	1.9	-	-	-	-	28.0	2.6	-	-	-	-	28.4	1.4
1967	-	-	-	-	28.9	1.8	-	-	-	-	29.1	0.7	-	-	-	-	29.3	0.7	-	-	-	-	29.6	1.0
1968	-	-	-	-	30.3	2.4	-	-	-	-	30.5	0.7	-	-	-	-	30.7	0.7	-	-	-	-	31.1	1.3
1969	-	-	-	-	31.6	1.6	-	-	-	-	32.0	1.3	-	-	-	-	32.4	1.3	-	-	-	-	32.7	0.9
1970	-	-	-	-	33.4	2.1	-	-	-	-	33.7	0.9	-	-	-	-	34.3	1.8	-	-	-	-	34.5	0.6
1971	-	-	-	-	35.5	2.9	-	-	-	-	35.9	1.1	-	-	-	-	36.4	1.4	-	-	-	-	36.2	-0.5
1972	-	-	-	-	36.6	1.1	-	-	-	-	36.9	0.8	-	-	-	-	37.3	1.1	-	-	-	-	37.7	1.1
1973	-	-	-	-	38.2	1.3	-	-	-	-	38.3	0.3	-	-	-	-	38.6	0.8	-	-	-	-	39.3	1.8
1974	-	-	-	-	40.4	2.8	-	-	-	-	41.5	2.7	-	-	-	-	43.0	3.6	-	-	-	-	43.8	1.9
1975	-	-	-	-	46.0	5.0	-	-	-	-	48.6	5.7	-	-	-	-	49.5	1.9	-	-	-	-	50.1	1.2
1976	-	-	-	-	52.1	4.0	-	-	-	-	52.6	1.0	-	-	-	-	53.6	1.9	-	-	-	-	54.9	2.4
1977	-	-	-	-	56.8	3.5	-	-	-	-	57.8	1.8	-	-	-	-	59.7	3.3	-	-	-	-	60.1	0.7
1978	-	-	62.3	3.7	-	-	62.7	0.6	-	-	62.3	-0.6	-	-	64.4	3.4	-	-	65.0	0.9	-	-	65.8	1.2
1979	-	-	66.4	0.9	-	-	66.9	0.8	-	-	68.2	1.9	-	-	69.9	2.5	-	-	72.2	3.3	-	-	73.4	1.7
1980	-	-	74.7	1.8	-	-	75.8	1.5	-	-	76.0	0.3	-	-	77.4	1.8	-	-	79.1	2.2	-	-	80.0	1.1
1981	-	-	82.2	2.8	-	-	83.2	1.2	-	-	83.8	0.7	-	-	87.0	3.8	-	-	87.5	0.6	-	-	89.2	1.9
1982	-	-	90.9	1.9	-	-	93.1	2.4	-	-	94.3	1.3	-	-	95.0	0.7	-	-	96.0	1.1	-	-	97.1	1.1
1983	-	-	99.1	2.1	-	-	99.5	0.4	-	-	101.0	1.5	-	-	101.7	0.7	-	-	101.5	-0.2	-	-	101.7	0.2
1984	-	-	103.8	2.1	-	-	104.6	0.8	-	-	104.9	0.3	-	-	105.8	0.9	-	-	106.9	1.0	-	-	107.6	0.7
1985	-	-	108.5	0.8	-	-	109.1	0.6	-	-	110.8	1.6	-	-	113.8	2.7	-	-	114.5	0.6	-	-	115.8	1.1
1986	-	-	116.6	0.7	-	-	118.0	1.2	-	-	119.8	1.5	-	-	122.7	2.4	-	-	123.1	0.3	-	-	124.7	1.3
1987	126.0	1.0	126.3	0.2	126.9	0.5	127.7	0.6	127.7	0.0	128.7	0.8	131.5	2.2	132.6	0.8	132.4	-0.2	132.8	0.3	133.4	0.5	133.6	0.1
1988	134.4	0.6	134.4	0.0	135.0	0.4	135.6	0.4	136.0	0.3	137.3	1.0	138.9	1.2	139.3	0.3	140.0	0.5	141.5	1.1	142.0	0.4	142.5	0.4
1989	144.3	1.3	146.0	1.2	145.9	-0.1	147.0	0.8	147.1	0.1	147.9	0.5	149.1	0.8	149.4	0.2	151.0	1.1	151.5	0.3	155.1	2.4	153.6	-1.0
1990	156.1	1.6	156.8	0.4	158.9	1.3	158.8	-0.1	158.5	-0.2	158.9	0.3	161.3	1.5	163.1	1.1	163.4	0.2	164.3	0.6	164.9	0.4	164.1	-0.5
1991	166.3	1.3	167.1	0.5	168.0	0.5	168.3	0.2	168.6	0.2	169.3	0.4	172.3	1.8	175.8	2.0	177.1	0.7	176.6	-0.3	177.6	0.6	178.3	0.4

[Continued]

San Francisco-Oakland, CA
Consumer Price Index - Urban Wage Earners
Base 1982-1984 = 100
Medical Care
[Continued]

For 1947-1997. Columns headed % show percentile change in the index from the previous period for which an index is available.

Year	Jan Index	%	Feb Index	%	Mar Index	%	Apr Index	%	May Index	%	Jun Index	%	Jul Index	%	Aug Index	%	Sep Index	%	Oct Index	%	Nov Index	%	Dec Index	%
1992	178.6	0.2	181.4	1.6	182.2	0.4	184.7	1.4	184.4	-0.2	186.8	1.3	188.5	0.9	188.7	0.1	190.0	0.7	190.2	0.1	190.3	0.1	190.6	0.2
1993	192.2	0.8	194.2	1.0	194.0	-0.1	196.8	1.4	196.8	0.0	198.3	0.8	200.1	0.9	200.5	0.2	199.4	-0.5	201.0	0.8	200.6	-0.2	201.0	0.2
1994	200.9	-0.0	200.3	-0.3	201.4	0.5	202.2	0.4	201.5	-0.3	201.9	0.2	201.4	-0.2	203.0	0.8	203.6	0.3	203.6	0.0	204.1	0.2	204.7	0.3
1995	206.7	1.0	206.4	-0.1	207.1	0.3	205.6	-0.7	205.6	0.0	204.9	-0.3	206.6	0.8	206.6	0.0	207.6	0.5	207.8	0.1	208.3	0.2	208.4	0.0
1996	210.1	0.8	209.9	-0.1	211.2	0.6	211.9	0.3	211.3	-0.3	211.3	0.0	212.2	0.4	212.6	0.2	212.0	-0.3	214.6	1.2	214.1	-0.2	215.2	0.5
1997	215.8	0.3	216.1	0.1	216.9	0.4	218.0	0.5	219.7	0.8	220.0	0.1	220.0	0.0	220.5	0.2	219.6	-0.4	220.9	0.6	222.3	0.6	223.2	0.4

Source: U.S. Department of Labor, Bureau of Labor Statistics, Division of Consumer Prices and Price Indexes. - indicates no data collected for period.

San Francisco-Oakland, CA
Consumer Price Index - All Urban Consumers
Base 1982-1984 = 100
Entertainment

For 1975-1997. Columns headed % show percentile change in the index from the previous period for which an index is available.

Year	Jan Index	%	Feb Index	%	Mar Index	%	Apr Index	%	May Index	%	Jun Index	%	Jul Index	%	Aug Index	%	Sep Index	%	Oct Index	%	Nov Index	%	Dec Index	%
1975	-	-	-	-	-	-	-	-	-	-	-	-	-	-	-	-	-	-	-	-	-	-	62.9	-
1976	-	-	-	-	63.8	1.4	-	-	-	-	64.5	1.1	-	-	-	-	65.6	1.7	-	-	-	-	66.2	0.9
1977	-	-	-	-	66.7	0.8	-	-	-	-	67.4	1.0	-	-	-	-	68.2	1.2	-	-	-	-	68.8	0.9
1978	-	-	66.6	-3.2	-	-	70.2	5.4	-	-	71.2	1.4	-	-	73.9	3.8	-	-	75.2	1.8	-	-	75.5	0.4
1979	-	-	73.6	-2.5	-	-	76.2	3.5	-	-	76.1	-0.1	-	-	76.9	1.1	-	-	74.5	-3.1	-	-	75.7	1.6
1980	-	-	77.9	2.9	-	-	86.7	11.3	-	-	87.7	1.2	-	-	85.9	-2.1	-	-	85.8	-0.1	-	-	87.7	2.2
1981	-	-	91.5	4.3	-	-	89.6	-2.1	-	-	89.7	0.1	-	-	90.8	1.2	-	-	97.3	7.2	-	-	97.7	0.4
1982	-	-	97.0	-0.7	-	-	98.8	1.9	-	-	101.7	2.9	-	-	97.2	-4.4	-	-	98.1	0.9	-	-	98.0	-0.1
1983	-	-	97.5	-0.5	-	-	97.9	0.4	-	-	99.1	1.2	-	-	99.3	0.2	-	-	99.3	0.0	-	-	99.8	0.5
1984	-	-	101.5	1.7	-	-	101.5	0.0	-	-	102.6	1.1	-	-	103.3	0.7	-	-	103.7	0.4	-	-	106.1	2.3
1985	-	-	106.5	0.4	-	-	107.1	0.6	-	-	108.1	0.9	-	-	109.3	1.1	-	-	110.6	1.2	-	-	110.7	0.1
1986	-	-	114.9	3.8	-	-	117.1	1.9	-	-	116.7	-0.3	-	-	118.9	1.9	-	-	119.3	0.3	-	-	119.5	0.2
1987	120.1	0.5	121.2	0.9	119.3	-1.6	120.7	1.2	122.6	1.6	121.9	-0.6	120.7	-1.0	120.9	0.2	119.6	-1.1	121.8	1.8	124.8	2.5	126.0	1.0
1988	127.3	1.0	124.1	-2.5	128.9	3.9	129.1	0.2	128.6	-0.4	129.3	0.5	130.0	0.5	129.3	-0.5	131.2	1.5	128.7	-1.9	130.9	1.7	131.7	0.6
1989	133.8	1.6	133.3	-0.4	132.9	-0.3	134.4	1.1	134.3	-0.1	134.2	-0.1	135.0	0.6	137.4	1.8	130.0	-5.4	131.6	1.2	129.2	-1.8	131.5	1.8
1990	133.5	1.5	130.6	-2.2	134.8	3.2	139.8	3.7	139.9	0.1	141.3	1.0	142.6	0.9	145.4	2.0	146.0	0.4	144.6	-1.0	143.7	-0.6	145.7	1.4
1991	147.9	1.5	148.0	0.1	150.1	1.4	151.1	0.7	149.1	-1.3	152.7	2.4	154.4	1.1	154.3	-0.1	155.1	0.5	155.8	0.5	153.8	-1.3	156.0	1.4
1992	156.6	0.4	156.7	0.1	156.0	-0.4	157.5	1.0	155.4	-1.3	157.1	1.1	154.8	-1.5	155.5	0.5	155.2	-0.2	156.4	0.8	158.7	1.5	158.1	-0.4
1993	155.5	-1.6	160.9	3.5	161.3	0.2	161.7	0.2	163.5	1.1	163.1	-0.2	162.8	-0.2	163.1	0.2	162.9	-0.1	163.6	0.4	164.3	0.4	164.6	0.2
1994	164.0	-0.4	164.9	0.5	166.6	1.0	165.5	-0.7	164.4	-0.7	164.3	-0.1	163.8	-0.3	163.0	-0.5	162.7	-0.2	164.4	1.0	165.7	0.8	164.9	-0.5
1995	165.8	0.5	166.9	0.7	166.6	-0.2	165.9	-0.4	166.4	0.3	165.4	-0.6	164.7	-0.4	163.7	-0.6	166.6	1.8	166.4	-0.1	167.5	0.7	168.6	0.7
1996	167.7	-0.5	167.8	0.1	165.9	-1.1	166.8	0.5	167.2	0.2	166.2	-0.6	166.9	0.4	164.3	-1.6	166.3	1.2	165.8	-0.3	168.2	1.4	168.7	0.3
1997	168.2	-0.3	168.2	0.0	167.6	-0.4	167.2	-0.2	168.0	0.5	167.8	-0.1	165.9	-1.1	161.7	-2.5	163.3	1.0	163.9	0.4	163.7	-0.1	163.3	-0.2

Source: U.S. Department of Labor, Bureau of Labor Statistics, Division of Consumer Prices and Price Indexes. - indicates no data collected for period.

San Francisco-Oakland, CA
Consumer Price Index - Urban Wage Earners
Base 1982-1984 = 100
Entertainment

For 1975-1997. Columns headed % show percentile change in the index from the previous period for which an index is available.

Year	Jan Index	%	Feb Index	%	Mar Index	%	Apr Index	%	May Index	%	Jun Index	%	Jul Index	%	Aug Index	%	Sep Index	%	Oct Index	%	Nov Index	%	Dec Index	%
1975	-	-	-	-	-	-	-	-	-	-	-	-	-	-	-	-	-	-	-	-	-	-	70.5	-
1976	-	-	-	-	71.5	1.4	-	-	-	-	72.3	1.1	-	-	-	-	73.6	1.8	-	-	-	-	74.2	0.8
1977	-	-	-	-	74.8	0.8	-	-	-	-	75.6	1.1	-	-	-	-	76.4	1.1	-	-	-	-	77.1	0.9
1978	-	-	78.7	2.1	-	-	79.7	1.3	-	-	80.7	1.3	-	-	83.2	3.1	-	-	83.2	0.0	-	-	83.0	-0.2
1979	-	-	82.9	-0.1	-	-	86.1	3.9	-	-	85.6	-0.6	-	-	86.7	1.3	-	-	80.3	-7.4	-	-	80.4	0.1
1980	-	-	81.7	1.6	-	-	92.6	13.3	-	-	92.9	0.3	-	-	94.8	2.0	-	-	96.9	2.2	-	-	95.1	-1.9
1981	-	-	97.0	2.0	-	-	95.9	-1.1	-	-	98.1	2.3	-	-	99.6	1.5	-	-	102.4	2.8	-	-	101.4	-1.0
1982	-	-	101.4	0.0	-	-	102.6	1.2	-	-	105.0	2.3	-	-	96.0	-8.6	-	-	97.0	1.0	-	-	96.9	-0.1
1983	-	-	96.3	-0.6	-	-	96.5	0.2	-	-	97.9	1.5	-	-	98.5	0.6	-	-	98.6	0.1	-	-	99.2	0.6
1984	-	-	101.1	1.9	-	-	100.8	-0.3	-	-	102.1	1.3	-	-	103.1	1.0	-	-	102.8	-0.3	-	-	105.3	2.4
1985	-	-	105.8	0.5	-	-	106.4	0.6	-	-	107.5	1.0	-	-	107.8	0.3	-	-	108.1	0.3	-	-	108.3	0.2
1986	-	-	112.6	4.0	-	-	113.9	1.2	-	-	113.5	-0.4	-	-	115.3	1.6	-	-	115.6	0.3	-	-	115.8	0.2
1987	115.8	0.0	117.4	1.4	115.6	-1.5	116.4	0.7	118.6	1.9	117.8	-0.7	116.6	-1.0	116.9	0.3	115.5	-1.2	116.7	1.0	120.0	2.8	120.8	0.7
1988	122.0	1.0	119.2	-2.3	123.4	3.5	123.8	0.3	123.6	-0.2	124.5	0.7	124.9	0.3	124.1	-0.6	125.7	1.3	123.7	-1.6	125.9	1.8	126.6	0.6
1989	128.4	1.4	128.4	0.0	129.6	0.9	130.9	1.0	130.5	-0.3	131.2	0.5	131.9	0.5	133.3	1.1	128.2	-3.8	130.1	1.5	127.5	-2.0	130.6	2.4
1990	131.9	1.0	127.7	-3.2	133.1	4.2	138.1	3.8	138.3	0.1	138.4	0.1	138.7	0.2	140.1	1.0	138.4	-1.2	136.9	-1.1	135.8	-0.8	137.9	1.5
1991	139.7	1.3	140.2	0.4	142.0	1.3	143.0	0.7	141.0	-1.4	143.9	2.1	145.1	0.8	144.5	-0.4	145.5	0.7	145.7	0.1	143.5	-1.5	147.4	2.7
1992	148.2	0.5	147.7	-0.3	146.7	-0.7	148.6	1.3	146.4	-1.5	148.1	1.2	146.1	-1.4	146.5	0.3	146.2	-0.2	147.3	0.8	149.1	1.2	148.6	-0.3
1993	146.2	-1.6	150.4	2.9	150.9	0.3	150.8	-0.1	152.5	1.1	152.0	-0.3	152.0	0.0	152.3	0.2	152.1	-0.1	152.7	0.4	152.9	0.1	154.4	1.0
1994	152.8	-1.0	153.6	0.5	155.0	0.9	153.8	-0.8	153.1	-0.5	152.9	-0.1	152.4	-0.3	151.8	-0.4	151.5	-0.2	151.6	0.1	152.8	0.8	153.6	0.5
1995	154.5	0.6	155.6	0.7	155.1	-0.3	154.5	-0.4	155.0	0.3	154.2	-0.5	154.0	-0.1	152.7	-0.8	155.2	1.6	154.4	-0.5	155.8	0.9	157.0	0.8
1996	156.5	-0.3	157.0	0.3	155.6	-0.9	156.5	0.6	157.0	0.3	156.3	-0.4	155.7	-0.4	154.5	-0.8	156.0	1.0	155.4	-0.4	156.6	0.8	157.0	0.3
1997	156.6	-0.3	156.3	-0.2	155.8	-0.3	155.4	-0.3	156.7	0.8	156.4	-0.2	154.6	-1.2	152.5	-1.4	153.7	0.8	154.2	0.3	154.4	0.1	153.9	-0.3

Source: U.S. Department of Labor, Bureau of Labor Statistics, Division of Consumer Prices and Price Indexes. - indicates no data collected for period.

San Francisco-Oakland, CA
Consumer Price Index - All Urban Consumers
Base 1982-1984 = 100
Other Goods and Services

For 1975-1997. Columns headed % show percentile change in the index from the previous period for which an index is available.

Year	Jan Index	%	Feb Index	%	Mar Index	%	Apr Index	%	May Index	%	Jun Index	%	Jul Index	%	Aug Index	%	Sep Index	%	Oct Index	%	Nov Index	%	Dec Index	%
1975	-	-	-	-	-	-	-	-	-	-	-	-	-	-	-	-	-	-	-	-	-	-	53.0	-
1976	-	-	-	-	53.4	0.8	-	-	-	-	53.9	0.9	-	-	-	-	54.9	1.9	-	-	-	-	56.0	2.0
1977	-	-	-	-	56.8	1.4	-	-	-	-	57.8	1.8	-	-	-	-	59.6	3.1	-	-	-	-	59.9	0.5
1978	-	-	60.4	0.8	-	-	61.6	2.0	-	-	63.4	2.9	-	-	64.7	2.1	-	-	66.0	2.0	-	-	66.2	0.3
1979	-	-	66.5	0.5	-	-	66.9	0.6	-	-	66.8	-0.1	-	-	67.4	0.9	-	-	69.3	2.8	-	-	69.6	0.4
1980	-	-	70.6	1.4	-	-	71.9	1.8	-	-	71.3	-0.8	-	-	73.2	2.7	-	-	74.8	2.2	-	-	76.1	1.7
1981	-	-	77.1	1.3	-	-	77.8	0.9	-	-	79.7	2.4	-	-	79.9	0.3	-	-	82.8	3.6	-	-	83.8	1.2
1982	-	-	86.5	3.2	-	-	88.6	2.4	-	-	88.7	0.1	-	-	89.9	1.4	-	-	96.2	7.0	-	-	97.7	1.6
1983	-	-	100.0	2.4	-	-	100.2	0.2	-	-	101.3	1.1	-	-	100.5	-0.8	-	-	102.7	2.2	-	-	103.9	1.2
1984	-	-	105.6	1.6	-	-	105.9	0.3	-	-	107.6	1.6	-	-	108.0	0.4	-	-	111.6	3.3	-	-	112.4	0.7
1985	-	-	115.0	2.3	-	-	115.5	0.4	-	-	115.7	0.2	-	-	117.0	1.1	-	-	117.4	0.3	-	-	119.0	1.4
1986	-	-	122.2	2.7	-	-	122.3	0.1	-	-	123.2	0.7	-	-	122.6	-0.5	-	-	124.2	1.3	-	-	126.2	1.6
1987	127.5	1.0	128.5	0.8	128.7	0.2	129.0	0.2	128.8	-0.2	129.1	0.2	130.3	0.9	131.5	0.9	133.7	1.7	134.1	0.3	134.6	0.4	134.4	-0.1
1988	137.2	2.1	137.2	0.0	137.2	0.0	138.3	0.8	138.7	0.3	138.5	-0.1	139.1	0.4	140.6	1.1	142.1	1.1	142.6	0.4	144.3	1.2	144.9	0.4
1989	148.0	2.1	146.4	-1.1	149.5	2.1	149.6	0.1	150.4	0.5	151.5	0.7	153.3	1.2	156.2	1.9	155.0	-0.8	155.0	0.0	155.1	0.1	156.0	0.6
1990	159.2	2.1	158.6	-0.4	158.3	-0.2	160.2	1.2	159.3	-0.6	160.3	0.6	160.3	0.0	161.4	0.7	162.8	0.9	163.8	0.6	164.1	0.2	164.2	0.1
1991	165.5	0.8	170.0	2.7	169.3	-0.4	170.2	0.5	171.4	0.7	172.2	0.5	173.2	0.6	175.0	1.0	180.8	3.3	181.6	0.4	182.4	0.4	182.4	0.0
1992	190.4	4.4	191.2	0.4	191.4	0.1	192.5	0.6	192.0	-0.3	192.0	0.0	192.7	0.4	193.7	0.5	202.8	4.7	204.1	0.6	203.9	-0.1	203.7	-0.1
1993	205.9	1.1	207.3	0.7	207.1	-0.1	206.5	-0.3	207.0	0.2	205.7	-0.6	206.8	0.5	206.7	-0.0	209.6	1.4	207.1	-1.2	207.1	0.0	207.2	0.0
1994	210.1	1.4	210.7	0.3	212.3	0.8	211.5	-0.4	211.1	-0.2	210.6	-0.2	211.1	0.2	211.6	0.2	216.9	2.5	217.5	0.3	218.2	0.3	216.9	-0.6
1995	217.2	0.1	217.2	0.0	218.1	0.4	218.5	0.2	219.2	0.3	219.7	0.2	219.7	0.0	220.7	0.5	223.2	1.1	223.9	0.3	224.7	0.4	224.7	0.0
1996	225.6	0.4	225.8	0.1	225.9	0.0	226.1	0.1	225.0	-0.5	224.7	-0.1	227.8	1.4	227.9	0.0	230.1	1.0	230.9	0.3	232.0	0.5	231.9	-0.0
1997	231.8	-0.0	231.4	-0.2	236.9	2.4	237.4	0.2	235.9	-0.6	237.6	0.7	238.1	0.2	243.0	2.1	246.1	1.3	246.4	0.1	246.5	0.0	247.8	0.5

Source: U.S. Department of Labor, Bureau of Labor Statistics, Division of Consumer Prices and Price Indexes. - indicates no data collected for period.

San Francisco-Oakland, CA
Consumer Price Index - Urban Wage Earners
Base 1982-1984 = 100
Other Goods and Services

For 1975-1997. Columns headed % show percentile change in the index from the previous period for which an index is available.

Year	Jan Index	%	Feb Index	%	Mar Index	%	Apr Index	%	May Index	%	Jun Index	%	Jul Index	%	Aug Index	%	Sep Index	%	Oct Index	%	Nov Index	%	Dec Index	%
1975	-	-	-	-	-	-	-	-	-	-	-	-	-	-	-	-	-	-	-	-	-	-	52.7	-
1976	-	-	-	-	53.1	0.8	-	-	-	-	53.6	0.9	-	-	-	-	54.5	1.7	-	-	-	-	55.7	2.2
1977	-	-	-	-	56.5	1.4	-	-	-	-	57.5	1.8	-	-	-	-	59.2	3.0	-	-	-	-	59.5	0.5
1978	-	-	59.5	0.0	-	-	60.4	1.5	-	-	61.3	1.5	-	-	62.5	2.0	-	-	63.9	2.2	-	-	63.4	-0.8
1979	-	-	64.9	2.4	-	-	65.1	0.3	-	-	66.5	2.2	-	-	67.1	0.9	-	-	68.7	2.4	-	-	69.3	0.9
1980	-	-	70.3	1.4	-	-	72.0	2.4	-	-	72.9	1.3	-	-	73.5	0.8	-	-	75.2	2.3	-	-	76.7	2.0
1981	-	-	77.3	0.8	-	-	78.1	1.0	-	-	79.8	2.2	-	-	80.3	0.6	-	-	83.3	3.7	-	-	84.5	1.4
1982	-	-	87.0	3.0	-	-	88.9	2.2	-	-	89.0	0.1	-	-	90.3	1.5	-	-	96.2	6.5	-	-	97.9	1.8
1983	-	-	99.9	2.0	-	-	100.0	0.1	-	-	101.1	1.1	-	-	100.7	-0.4	-	-	102.7	2.0	-	-	103.7	1.0
1984	-	-	105.5	1.7	-	-	105.8	0.3	-	-	107.2	1.3	-	-	107.6	0.4	-	-	111.4	3.5	-	-	112.2	0.7
1985	-	-	114.7	2.2	-	-	115.3	0.5	-	-	115.2	-0.1	-	-	116.7	1.3	-	-	116.8	0.1	-	-	118.3	1.3
1986	-	-	121.5	2.7	-	-	121.5	0.0	-	-	122.5	0.8	-	-	122.1	-0.3	-	-	123.6	1.2	-	-	125.7	1.7
1987	126.7	0.8	128.0	1.0	128.4	0.3	128.6	0.2	128.2	-0.3	128.7	0.4	130.1	1.1	131.1	0.8	133.5	1.8	133.7	0.1	134.0	0.2	133.7	-0.2
1988	137.0	2.5	137.0	0.0	137.0	0.0	138.0	0.7	138.3	0.2	138.1	-0.1	138.9	0.6	140.9	1.4	142.3	1.0	142.8	0.4	144.9	1.5	145.8	0.6
1989	149.8	2.7	147.4	-1.6	151.9	3.1	151.9	0.0	152.2	0.2	153.8	1.1	156.4	1.7	159.1	1.7	157.6	-0.9	157.6	0.0	157.8	0.1	159.1	0.8
1990	162.3	2.0	161.4	-0.6	161.4	0.0	163.6	1.4	162.8	-0.5	164.2	0.9	164.2	0.0	165.2	0.6	165.8	0.4	167.4	1.0	167.8	0.2	168.0	0.1
1991	169.3	0.8	173.7	2.6	173.3	-0.2	174.3	0.6	175.4	0.6	176.0	0.3	177.1	0.6	178.6	0.8	182.4	2.1	183.6	0.7	184.7	0.6	184.7	0.0
1992	191.6	3.7	191.8	0.1	192.0	0.1	193.1	0.6	192.4	-0.4	192.4	0.0	193.5	0.6	194.4	0.5	201.2	3.5	202.6	0.7	202.4	-0.1	202.2	-0.1
1993	205.1	1.4	207.0	0.9	206.7	-0.1	205.8	-0.4	206.3	0.2	204.5	-0.9	206.1	0.8	204.9	-0.6	205.4	0.2	201.8	-1.8	201.9	0.0	202.0	0.0
1994	206.4	2.2	207.0	0.3	208.6	0.8	207.7	-0.4	207.1	-0.3	206.4	-0.3	207.1	0.3	207.5	0.2	211.4	1.9	212.1	0.3	213.0	0.4	211.1	-0.9
1995	211.6	0.2	211.7	0.0	212.9	0.6	213.3	0.2	214.4	0.5	215.0	0.3	214.4	-0.3	215.0	0.3	217.2	1.0	218.3	0.5	218.9	0.3	218.5	-0.2
1996	218.5	0.0	218.7	0.1	218.8	0.0	218.9	0.0	217.5	-0.6	217.0	-0.2	221.3	2.0	220.7	-0.3	222.5	0.8	223.5	0.4	224.6	0.5	224.5	-0.0
1997	224.3	-0.1	223.3	-0.4	228.1	2.1	229.6	0.7	226.5	-1.4	228.8	1.0	229.6	0.3	232.4	1.2	236.0	1.5	236.5	0.2	236.6	0.0	238.4	0.8

Source: U.S. Department of Labor, Bureau of Labor Statistics, Division of Consumer Prices and Price Indexes. - indicates no data collected for period.

Seattle-Everett, WA
Consumer Price Index - All Urban Consumers
Base 1982-1984 = 100
Annual Averages

For 1914-1997. Columns headed % show percentile change in the index from the previous period for which an index is available.

Year	All Items Index	%	Food & Beverage Index	%	Housing Index	%	Apparel & Upkeep Index	%	Trans-portation Index	%	Medical Care Index	%	Entertain-ment Index	%	Other Goods & Services Index	%
1914	-	-	-	-	-	-	-	-	-	-	-	-	-	-	-	-
1915	9.0	-	-	-	-	-	-	-	-	-	-	-	-	-	-	-
1916	9.4	4.4	-	-	-	-	-	-	-	-	-	-	-	-	-	-
1917	11.0	17.0	-	-	-	-	-	-	-	-	-	-	-	-	-	-
1918	13.7	24.5	-	-	-	-	-	-	-	-	-	-	-	-	-	-
1919	16.5	20.4	-	-	-	-	-	-	-	-	-	-	-	-	-	-
1920	18.8	13.9	-	-	-	-	-	-	-	-	-	-	-	-	-	-
1921	16.7	-11.2	-	-	-	-	-	-	-	-	-	-	-	-	-	-
1922	15.6	-6.6	-	-	-	-	-	-	-	-	-	-	-	-	-	-
1923	15.5	-0.6	-	-	-	-	-	-	-	-	-	-	-	-	-	-
1924	15.5	0.0	-	-	-	-	-	-	-	-	-	-	-	-	-	-
1925	15.8	1.9	-	-	-	-	-	-	-	-	-	-	-	-	-	-
1926	15.8	0.0	-	-	-	-	-	-	-	-	-	-	-	-	-	-
1927	15.5	-1.9	-	-	-	-	-	-	-	-	-	-	-	-	-	-
1928	15.4	-0.6	-	-	-	-	-	-	-	-	-	-	-	-	-	-
1929	15.5	0.6	-	-	-	-	-	-	-	-	-	-	-	-	-	-
1930	15.2	-1.9	-	-	-	-	-	-	-	-	-	-	-	-	-	-
1931	13.8	-9.2	-	-	-	-	-	-	-	-	-	-	-	-	-	-
1932	12.6	-8.7	-	-	-	-	-	-	-	-	-	-	-	-	-	-
1933	12.0	-4.8	-	-	-	-	-	-	-	-	-	-	-	-	-	-
1934	12.3	2.5	-	-	-	-	-	-	-	-	-	-	-	-	-	-
1935	12.6	2.4	-	-	-	-	-	-	-	-	-	-	-	-	-	-
1936	12.7	0.8	-	-	-	-	-	-	-	-	-	-	-	-	-	-
1937	13.4	5.5	-	-	-	-	-	-	-	-	-	-	-	-	-	-
1938	13.2	-1.5	-	-	-	-	-	-	-	-	-	-	-	-	-	-
1939	13.2	0.0	-	-	-	-	-	-	-	-	-	-	-	-	-	-
1940	13.2	0.0	-	-	-	-	-	-	-	-	-	-	-	-	-	-
1941	14.0	6.1	-	-	-	-	-	-	-	-	-	-	-	-	-	-
1942	15.8	12.9	-	-	-	-	-	-	-	-	-	-	-	-	-	-
1943	16.7	5.7	-	-	-	-	-	-	-	-	-	-	-	-	-	-
1944	16.9	1.2	-	-	-	-	-	-	-	-	-	-	-	-	-	-
1945	17.3	2.4	-	-	-	-	-	-	-	-	-	-	-	-	-	-
1946	18.6	7.5	-	-	-	-	-	-	-	-	-	-	-	-	-	-
1947	21.1	13.4	-	-	-	-	-	-	19.1	-	14.4	-	-	-	-	-
1948	22.8	8.1	-	-	-	-	-	-	20.8	8.9	15.1	4.9	-	-	-	-
1949	22.7	-0.4	-	-	-	-	-	-	22.2	6.7	15.8	4.6	-	-	-	-
1950	23.1	1.8	-	-	-	-	-	-	22.9	3.2	16.1	1.9	-	-	-	-
1951	24.8	7.4	-	-	-	-	-	-	24.2	5.7	17.1	6.2	-	-	-	-
1952	25.5	2.8	-	-	-	-	-	-	25.6	5.8	18.4	7.6	-	-	-	-
1953	25.8	1.2	-	-	-	-	43.9	-	27.4	7.0	19.0	3.3	-	-	-	-
1954	25.8	0.0	-	-	-	-	43.6	-0.7	26.9	-1.8	19.7	3.7	-	-	-	-
1955	25.9	0.4	-	-	-	-	43.8	0.5	26.4	-1.9	20.1	2.0	-	-	-	-
1956	26.2	1.2	-	-	-	-	44.2	0.9	26.6	0.8	20.6	2.5	-	-	-	-
1957	27.3	4.2	-	-	-	-	45.1	2.0	28.6	7.5	21.3	3.4	-	-	-	-
1958	27.9	2.2	-	-	-	-	44.9	-0.4	29.7	3.8	22.3	4.7	-	-	-	-

[Continued]

834

Seattle-Everett, WA
Consumer Price Index - All Urban Consumers
Base 1982-1984 = 100
Annual Averages
[Continued]

For 1914-1997. Columns headed % show percentile change in the index from the previous period for which an index is available.

Year	All Items		Food & Beverage		Housing		Apparel & Upkeep		Trans- portation		Medical Care		Entertain- ment		Other Goods & Services	
	Index	%	Index	%	Index	%	Index	%	Index	%	Index	%	Index	%	Index	%
1959	28.5	2.2	-	-	-	-	45.4	1.1	31.1	4.7	22.8	2.2	-	-	-	-
1960	28.8	1.1	-	-	-	-	46.0	1.3	30.8	-1.0	23.9	4.8	-	-	-	-
1961	29.3	1.7	-	-	-	-	46.7	1.5	31.7	2.9	24.0	0.4	-	-	-	-
1962	29.7	1.4	-	-	-	-	47.5	1.7	32.6	2.8	24.3	1.2	-	-	-	-
1963	30.2	1.7	-	-	-	-	48.2	1.5	32.5	-0.3	24.5	0.8	-	-	-	-
1964	30.6	1.3	-	-	-	-	48.7	1.0	32.6	0.3	25.0	2.0	-	-	-	-
1965	31.0	1.3	-	-	-	-	49.0	0.6	33.5	2.8	26.0	4.0	-	-	-	-
1966	31.9	2.9	-	-	-	-	50.4	2.9	34.0	1.5	27.6	6.2	-	-	-	-
1967	32.8	2.8	-	-	-	-	52.2	3.6	35.3	3.8	29.1	5.4	-	-	-	-
1968	34.1	4.0	-	-	-	-	53.7	2.9	35.9	1.7	30.8	5.8	-	-	-	-
1969	35.8	5.0	-	-	-	-	55.8	3.9	36.2	0.8	32.9	6.8	-	-	-	-
1970	37.4	4.5	-	-	-	-	58.3	4.5	37.1	2.5	34.5	4.9	-	-	-	-
1971	38.2	2.1	-	-	-	-	60.6	3.9	37.8	1.9	35.8	3.8	-	-	-	-
1972	39.3	2.9	-	-	-	-	61.4	1.3	38.6	2.1	36.5	2.0	-	-	-	-
1973	41.8	6.4	-	-	-	-	64.2	4.6	39.6	2.6	37.8	3.6	-	-	-	-
1974	46.4	11.0	-	-	-	-	68.2	6.2	44.0	11.1	41.2	9.0	-	-	-	-
1975	51.1	10.1	-	-	-	-	72.7	6.6	48.1	9.3	46.1	11.9	-	-	-	-
1976	54.0	5.7	61.3	-	50.3	-	76.9	5.8	51.8	7.7	50.9	10.4	62.2	-	50.8	-
1977	58.3	8.0	65.6	7.0	54.8	8.9	80.4	4.6	56.9	9.8	56.0	10.0	65.4	5.1	54.2	6.7
1978	63.9	9.6	71.0	8.2	61.7	12.6	82.6	2.7	61.2	7.6	62.2	11.1	68.5	4.7	57.8	6.6
1979	71.0	11.1	78.3	10.3	68.1	10.4	87.9	6.4	71.1	16.2	67.4	8.4	73.3	7.0	64.2	11.1
1980	82.7	16.5	84.5	7.9	82.7	21.4	95.0	8.1	83.1	16.9	75.8	12.5	82.0	11.9	71.5	11.4
1981	91.8	11.0	91.6	8.4	92.2	11.5	99.0	4.2	94.2	13.4	84.9	12.0	88.2	7.6	80.0	11.9
1982	97.7	6.4	98.3	7.3	98.4	6.7	99.6	0.6	98.0	4.0	93.5	10.1	93.8	6.3	91.7	14.6
1983	99.3	1.6	100.1	1.8	98.7	0.3	101.2	1.6	98.9	0.9	100.9	7.9	100.0	6.6	101.1	10.3
1984	103.0	3.7	101.6	1.5	102.8	4.2	99.2	-2.0	103.1	4.2	105.6	4.7	106.2	6.2	107.3	6.1
1985	105.6	2.5	103.2	1.6	105.5	2.6	102.5	3.3	105.0	1.8	112.2	6.3	108.5	2.2	111.9	4.3
1986	106.7	1.0	106.8	3.5	106.8	1.2	104.7	2.1	101.7	-3.1	117.6	4.8	108.6	0.1	117.1	4.6
1987	110.9	3.9	111.3	4.2	108.1	1.2	102.1	-2.5	109.2	7.4	126.8	7.8	116.6	7.4	128.7	9.9
1988	114.7	3.4	112.0	0.6	111.8	3.4	111.9	9.6	110.6	1.3	138.8	9.5	120.9	3.7	136.0	5.7
1989	120.4	5.0	118.7	6.0	116.5	4.2	114.4	2.2	118.3	7.0	145.2	4.6	124.4	2.9	145.1	6.7
1990	127.4	5.8	126.1	6.2	122.6	5.2	120.7	5.5	125.5	6.1	154.4	6.3	128.6	3.4	157.9	8.8
1991	133.9	5.1	130.7	3.6	130.4	6.4	122.3	1.3	130.1	3.7	166.0	7.5	132.6	3.1	172.2	9.1
1992	139.8	4.4	131.7	0.8	138.2	6.0	124.8	2.0	134.0	3.0	176.3	6.2	139.9	5.5	183.6	6.6
1993	144.7	3.5	134.0	1.7	143.7	4.0	122.2	-2.1	136.2	1.6	186.6	5.8	148.7	6.3	201.2	9.6
1994	148.9	2.9	135.9	1.4	149.5	4.0	123.7	1.2	138.6	1.8	192.8	3.3	157.7	6.1	203.1	0.9
1995	153.2	2.9	137.1	0.9	154.6	3.4	123.4	-0.2	141.9	2.4	198.1	2.7	165.2	4.8	217.2	6.9
1996	158.6	3.5	143.1	4.4	158.3	2.4	124.5	0.9	147.0	3.6	211.8	6.9	168.8	2.2	235.6	8.5
1997	-	-	-	-	-	-	-	-	-	-	-	-	-	-	-	-

Source: U.S. Department of Labor, Bureau of Labor Statistics, Division of Consumer Prices and Price Indexes. - indicates no data collected for period.

Seattle-Everett, WA
Consumer Price Index - Urban Wage Earners
Base 1982-1984 = 100
Annual Averages

For 1914-1997. Columns headed % show percentile change in the index from the previous period for which an index is available.

Year	All Items		Food & Beverage		Housing		Apparel & Upkeep		Trans- portation		Medical Care		Entertain- ment		Other Goods & Services	
	Index	%	Index	%	Index	%	Index	%	Index	%	Index	%	Index	%	Index	%
1914	-	-	-	-	-	-	-	-	-	-	-	-	-	-	-	-
1915	9.3	-	-	-	-	-	-	-	-	-	-	-	-	-	-	-
1916	9.6	3.2	-	-	-	-	-	-	-	-	-	-	-	-	-	-
1917	11.3	17.7	-	-	-	-	-	-	-	-	-	-	-	-	-	-
1918	14.1	24.8	-	-	-	-	-	-	-	-	-	-	-	-	-	-
1919	17.0	20.6	-	-	-	-	-	-	-	-	-	-	-	-	-	-
1920	19.4	14.1	-	-	-	-	-	-	-	-	-	-	-	-	-	-
1921	17.1	-11.9	-	-	-	-	-	-	-	-	-	-	-	-	-	-
1922	16.0	-6.4	-	-	-	-	-	-	-	-	-	-	-	-	-	-
1923	15.9	-0.6	-	-	-	-	-	-	-	-	-	-	-	-	-	-
1924	15.9	0.0	-	-	-	-	-	-	-	-	-	-	-	-	-	-
1925	16.3	2.5	-	-	-	-	-	-	-	-	-	-	-	-	-	-
1926	16.3	0.0	-	-	-	-	-	-	-	-	-	-	-	-	-	-
1927	15.9	-2.5	-	-	-	-	-	-	-	-	-	-	-	-	-	-
1928	15.8	-0.6	-	-	-	-	-	-	-	-	-	-	-	-	-	-
1929	15.9	0.6	-	-	-	-	-	-	-	-	-	-	-	-	-	-
1930	15.6	-1.9	-	-	-	-	-	-	-	-	-	-	-	-	-	-
1931	14.2	-9.0	-	-	-	-	-	-	-	-	-	-	-	-	-	-
1932	12.9	-9.2	-	-	-	-	-	-	-	-	-	-	-	-	-	-
1933	12.3	-4.7	-	-	-	-	-	-	-	-	-	-	-	-	-	-
1934	12.6	2.4	-	-	-	-	-	-	-	-	-	-	-	-	-	-
1935	12.9	2.4	-	-	-	-	-	-	-	-	-	-	-	-	-	-
1936	13.1	1.6	-	-	-	-	-	-	-	-	-	-	-	-	-	-
1937	13.7	4.6	-	-	-	-	-	-	-	-	-	-	-	-	-	-
1938	13.6	-0.7	-	-	-	-	-	-	-	-	-	-	-	-	-	-
1939	13.5	-0.7	-	-	-	-	-	-	-	-	-	-	-	-	-	-
1940	13.6	0.7	-	-	-	-	-	-	-	-	-	-	-	-	-	-
1941	14.4	5.9	-	-	-	-	-	-	-	-	-	-	-	-	-	-
1942	16.2	12.5	-	-	-	-	-	-	-	-	-	-	-	-	-	-
1943	17.1	5.6	-	-	-	-	-	-	-	-	-	-	-	-	-	-
1944	17.4	1.8	-	-	-	-	-	-	-	-	-	-	-	-	-	-
1945	17.8	2.3	-	-	-	-	-	-	-	-	-	-	-	-	-	-
1946	19.2	7.9	-	-	-	-	-	-	-	-	-	-	-	-	-	-
1947	21.7	13.0	-	-	-	-	-	-	19.5	-	14.3	-	-	-	-	-
1948	23.5	8.3	-	-	-	-	-	-	21.2	8.7	15.0	4.9	-	-	-	-
1949	23.4	-0.4	-	-	-	-	-	-	22.7	7.1	15.7	4.7	-	-	-	-
1950	23.7	1.3	-	-	-	-	-	-	23.3	2.6	15.9	1.3	-	-	-	-
1951	25.5	7.6	-	-	-	-	-	-	24.7	6.0	16.9	6.3	-	-	-	-
1952	26.2	2.7	-	-	-	-	-	-	26.1	5.7	18.2	7.7	-	-	-	-
1953	26.5	1.1	-	-	-	-	44.4	-	27.9	6.9	18.9	3.8	-	-	-	-
1954	26.5	0.0	-	-	-	-	44.1	-0.7	27.4	-1.8	19.5	3.2	-	-	-	-
1955	26.6	0.4	-	-	-	-	44.3	0.5	27.0	-1.5	19.9	2.1	-	-	-	-
1956	27.0	1.5	-	-	-	-	44.7	0.9	27.1	0.4	20.4	2.5	-	-	-	-
1957	28.1	4.1	-	-	-	-	45.6	2.0	29.2	7.7	21.1	3.4	-	-	-	-
1958	28.7	2.1	-	-	-	-	45.4	-0.4	30.3	3.8	22.1	4.7	-	-	-	-

[Continued]

Seattle-Everett, WA
Consumer Price Index - Urban Wage Earners
Base 1982-1984 = 100
Annual Averages
[Continued]

For 1914-1997. Columns headed % show percentile change in the index from the previous period for which an index is available.

Year	All Items		Food & Beverage		Housing		Apparel & Upkeep		Transportation		Medical Care		Entertainment		Other Goods & Services	
	Index	%	Index	%	Index	%	Index	%	Index	%	Index	%	Index	%	Index	%
1959	29.3	2.1	-	-	-	-	45.9	1.1	31.7	4.6	22.6	2.3	-	-	-	-
1960	29.6	1.0	-	-	-	-	46.5	1.3	31.4	-0.9	23.7	4.9	-	-	-	-
1961	30.1	1.7	-	-	-	-	47.2	1.5	32.3	2.9	23.8	0.4	-	-	-	-
1962	30.5	1.3	-	-	-	-	48.0	1.7	33.3	3.1	24.1	1.3	-	-	-	-
1963	31.1	2.0	-	-	-	-	48.8	1.7	33.2	-0.3	24.3	0.8	-	-	-	-
1964	31.5	1.3	-	-	-	-	49.3	1.0	33.3	0.3	24.7	1.6	-	-	-	-
1965	31.9	1.3	-	-	-	-	49.6	0.6	34.2	2.7	25.7	4.0	-	-	-	-
1966	32.7	2.5	-	-	-	-	51.0	2.8	34.7	1.5	27.4	6.6	-	-	-	-
1967	33.7	3.1	-	-	-	-	52.8	3.5	36.0	3.7	28.8	5.1	-	-	-	-
1968	35.1	4.2	-	-	-	-	54.3	2.8	36.6	1.7	30.5	5.9	-	-	-	-
1969	36.8	4.8	-	-	-	-	56.5	4.1	36.9	0.8	32.6	6.9	-	-	-	-
1970	38.4	4.3	-	-	-	-	59.0	4.4	37.9	2.7	34.1	4.6	-	-	-	-
1971	39.2	2.1	-	-	-	-	61.3	3.9	38.6	1.8	35.4	3.8	-	-	-	-
1972	40.4	3.1	-	-	-	-	62.1	1.3	39.4	2.1	36.2	2.3	-	-	-	-
1973	43.0	6.4	-	-	-	-	65.0	4.7	40.4	2.5	37.4	3.3	-	-	-	-
1974	47.7	10.9	-	-	-	-	69.1	6.3	44.9	11.1	40.8	9.1	-	-	-	-
1975	52.5	10.1	-	-	-	-	73.5	6.4	49.1	9.4	45.7	12.0	-	-	-	-
1976	55.5	5.7	61.6	-	52.5	-	77.8	5.9	52.8	7.5	50.4	10.3	60.0	-	52.6	-
1977	59.9	7.9	65.9	7.0	57.2	9.0	81.3	4.5	58.1	10.0	55.4	9.9	63.1	5.2	56.1	6.7
1978	65.3	9.0	71.2	8.0	64.4	12.6	83.5	2.7	61.4	5.7	61.1	10.3	66.5	5.4	60.0	7.0
1979	72.4	10.9	78.3	10.0	70.9	10.1	87.9	5.3	70.8	15.3	67.4	10.3	71.4	7.4	65.2	8.7
1980	84.0	16.0	84.8	8.3	85.9	21.2	93.9	6.8	82.3	16.2	75.1	11.4	80.3	12.5	71.6	9.8
1981	93.1	10.8	92.1	8.6	95.5	11.2	97.9	4.3	93.4	13.5	84.1	12.0	87.1	8.5	79.9	11.6
1982	99.1	6.4	98.3	6.7	101.7	6.5	99.7	1.8	97.8	4.7	93.4	11.1	94.2	8.2	91.2	14.1
1983	98.9	-0.2	100.1	1.8	97.6	-4.0	100.9	1.2	98.9	1.1	100.8	7.9	100.1	6.3	101.5	11.3
1984	102.1	3.2	101.6	1.5	100.8	3.3	99.4	-1.5	103.3	4.4	105.8	5.0	105.7	5.6	107.3	5.7
1985	104.2	2.1	103.3	1.7	102.2	1.4	102.5	3.1	105.4	2.0	112.6	6.4	108.0	2.2	111.9	4.3
1986	105.0	0.8	106.6	3.2	103.3	1.1	103.7	1.2	101.8	-3.4	118.4	5.2	107.9	-0.1	117.2	4.7
1987	108.5	3.3	111.1	4.2	104.4	1.1	101.8	-1.8	109.3	7.4	126.4	6.8	115.5	7.0	127.7	9.0
1988	112.0	3.2	111.9	0.7	107.8	3.3	112.0	10.0	110.7	1.3	138.3	9.4	119.6	3.5	135.7	6.3
1989	117.6	5.0	118.6	6.0	112.3	4.2	114.4	2.1	117.9	6.5	144.7	4.6	123.0	2.8	145.6	7.3
1990	124.2	5.6	125.9	6.2	118.1	5.2	120.9	5.7	124.2	5.3	153.2	5.9	127.0	3.3	158.4	8.8
1991	130.8	5.3	130.5	3.7	125.9	6.6	123.6	2.2	129.1	3.9	164.3	7.2	131.1	3.2	171.9	8.5
1992	136.6	4.4	131.7	0.9	133.7	6.2	125.1	1.2	133.1	3.1	174.9	6.5	139.2	6.2	183.0	6.5
1993	141.5	3.6	133.9	1.7	139.1	4.0	123.0	-1.7	136.0	2.2	185.0	5.8	148.8	6.9	200.1	9.3
1994	145.6	2.9	135.5	1.2	144.8	4.1	123.8	0.7	138.8	2.1	191.1	3.3	158.1	6.3	203.1	1.5
1995	149.9	3.0	136.4	0.7	149.4	3.2	124.3	0.4	143.0	3.0	197.0	3.1	166.7	5.4	216.9	6.8
1996	155.2	3.5	142.2	4.3	152.9	2.3	125.4	0.9	148.2	3.6	210.6	6.9	171.7	3.0	235.0	8.3
1997	-	-	-	-	-	-	-	-	-	-	-	-	-	-	-	-

Source: U.S. Department of Labor, Bureau of Labor Statistics, Division of Consumer Prices and Price Indexes. - indicates no data collected for period.

Seattle-Everett, WA
Consumer Price Index - All Urban Consumers
Base 1982-1984 = 100
All Items

For 1914-1997. Columns headed % show percentile change in the index from the previous period for which an index is available.

Year	Jan Index	%	Feb Index	%	Mar Index	%	Apr Index	%	May Index	%	Jun Index	%	Jul Index	%	Aug Index	%	Sep Index	%	Oct Index	%	Nov Index	%	Dec Index	%
1914	-	-	-	-	-	-	-	-	-	-	-	-	-	-	-	-	-	-	-	-	-	-	9.2	-
1915	-	-	-	-	-	-	-	-	-	-	-	-	-	-	-	-	-	-	-	-	-	-	9.1	-1.1
1916	-	-	-	-	-	-	-	-	-	-	-	-	-	-	-	-	-	-	-	-	-	-	9.7	6.6
1917	-	-	-	-	-	-	-	-	-	-	-	-	-	-	-	-	-	-	-	-	-	-	11.8	21.6
1918	-	-	-	-	-	-	-	-	-	-	-	-	-	-	-	-	-	-	-	-	-	-	15.4	30.5
1919	-	-	-	-	-	-	-	-	-	-	16.0	3.9	-	-	-	-	-	-	-	-	-	-	18.2	13.8
1920	-	-	-	-	-	-	-	-	-	-	19.6	7.7	-	-	-	-	-	-	-	-	-	-	17.9	-8.7
1921	-	-	-	-	-	-	-	-	16.8	-6.1	-	-	-	-	-	-	16.3	-3.0	-	-	-	-	16.0	-1.8
1922	-	-	-	-	15.7	-1.9	-	-	-	-	15.6	-0.6	-	-	-	-	15.5	-0.6	-	-	-	-	15.5	0.0
1923	-	-	-	-	15.1	-2.6	-	-	-	-	15.5	2.6	-	-	-	-	15.6	0.6	-	-	-	-	15.6	0.0
1924	-	-	-	-	15.5	-0.6	-	-	-	-	15.6	0.6	-	-	-	-	15.5	-0.6	-	-	-	-	15.6	0.6
1925	-	-	-	-	-	-	-	-	-	-	16.0	2.6	-	-	-	-	-	-	-	-	-	-	16.0	0.0
1926	-	-	-	-	-	-	-	-	-	-	15.8	-1.2	-	-	-	-	-	-	-	-	-	-	15.7	-0.6
1927	-	-	-	-	-	-	-	-	-	-	15.8	0.6	-	-	-	-	-	-	-	-	-	-	15.4	-2.5
1928	-	-	-	-	-	-	-	-	-	-	15.3	-0.6	-	-	-	-	-	-	-	-	-	-	15.4	0.7
1929	-	-	-	-	-	-	-	-	-	-	15.5	0.6	-	-	-	-	-	-	-	-	-	-	15.5	0.0
1930	-	-	-	-	-	-	-	-	-	-	15.5	0.0	-	-	-	-	-	-	-	-	-	-	14.4	-7.1
1931	-	-	-	-	-	-	-	-	-	-	13.9	-3.5	-	-	-	-	-	-	-	-	-	-	13.4	-3.6
1932	-	-	-	-	-	-	-	-	-	-	12.6	-6.0	-	-	-	-	-	-	-	-	-	-	12.1	-4.0
1933	-	-	-	-	-	-	-	-	-	-	12.0	-0.8	-	-	-	-	-	-	-	-	-	-	12.1	0.8
1934	-	-	-	-	-	-	-	-	-	-	12.2	0.8	-	-	-	-	-	-	-	-	12.4	1.6	-	-
1935	-	-	-	-	12.7	2.4	-	-	-	-	-	-	12.5	-1.6	-	-	-	-	12.5	0.0	-	-	-	-
1936	12.7	1.6	-	-	-	-	12.5	-1.6	-	-	-	-	12.7	1.6	-	-	12.9	1.6	-	-	-	-	12.9	0.0
1937	-	-	-	-	13.3	3.1	-	-	-	-	13.3	0.0	-	-	-	-	13.5	1.5	-	-	-	-	13.4	-0.7
1938	-	-	-	-	13.3	-0.7	-	-	-	-	13.2	-0.8	-	-	-	-	13.2	0.0	-	-	-	-	13.2	0.0
1939	-	-	-	-	13.1	-0.8	-	-	-	-	13.1	0.0	-	-	-	-	13.3	1.5	-	-	-	-	13.1	-1.5
1940	-	-	-	-	13.2	0.8	-	-	-	-	13.2	0.0	-	-	-	-	13.2	0.0	13.2	0.0	13.2	0.0	13.3	0.8
1941	13.3	0.0	13.3	0.0	13.4	0.8	13.5	0.7	13.8	2.2	13.9	0.7	14.0	0.7	14.1	0.7	14.5	2.8	14.7	1.4	14.7	0.0	14.9	1.4
1942	15.2	2.0	15.3	0.7	15.5	1.3	15.6	0.6	15.8	1.3	15.5	-1.9	15.6	0.6	15.8	1.3	16.0	1.3	16.1	0.6	16.2	0.6	16.4	1.2
1943	16.4	0.0	16.4	0.0	16.6	1.2	16.7	0.6	16.9	1.2	16.8	-0.6	16.5	-1.8	16.4	-0.6	16.7	1.8	16.8	0.6	16.8	0.0	16.8	0.0
1944	16.8	0.0	16.7	-0.6	16.8	0.6	16.8	0.0	16.9	0.6	16.9	0.0	17.0	0.6	17.0	0.0	17.0	0.0	17.1	0.6	17.1	0.0	17.2	0.6
1945	17.2	0.0	17.1	-0.6	17.2	0.6	17.2	0.0	17.3	0.6	17.3	0.0	17.4	0.6	17.4	0.0	17.4	0.0	17.3	-0.6	17.4	0.6	17.6	1.1
1946	17.5	-0.6	17.5	0.0	17.6	0.6	17.6	0.0	17.7	0.6	17.9	1.1	18.7	4.5	19.0	1.6	19.4	2.1	19.9	2.6	20.3	2.0	20.6	1.5
1947	20.4	-1.0	20.3	-0.5	20.7	2.0	20.8	0.5	20.8	0.0	20.7	-0.5	-	-	21.2	2.4	-	-	-	-	21.8	2.8	-	-
1948	-	-	22.4	2.8	-	-	-	-	22.9	2.2	-	-	-	-	23.2	1.3	-	-	-	-	22.9	-1.3	-	-
1949	-	-	23.0	0.4	-	-	-	-	22.8	-0.9	-	-	-	-	22.5	-1.3	-	-	-	-	22.7	0.9	-	-
1950	-	-	22.6	-0.4	-	-	-	-	22.6	0.0	-	-	-	-	23.0	1.8	-	-	-	-	23.8	3.5	-	-
1951	-	-	24.5	2.9	-	-	-	-	24.9	1.6	-	-	-	-	24.8	-0.4	-	-	-	-	25.3	2.0	-	-
1952	-	-	25.4	0.4	-	-	-	-	25.5	0.4	-	-	-	-	25.5	0.0	-	-	-	-	25.7	0.8	-	-
1953	-	-	25.5	-0.8	-	-	-	-	25.8	1.2	-	-	-	-	25.9	0.4	-	-	-	-	25.8	-0.4	-	-
1954	-	-	25.8	0.0	-	-	-	-	25.8	0.0	-	-	-	-	25.8	0.0	-	-	-	-	25.7	-0.4	-	-
1955	-	-	25.8	0.4	-	-	-	-	25.9	0.4	-	-	-	-	25.9	0.0	-	-	-	-	26.1	0.8	-	-
1956	-	-	25.8	-1.1	-	-	-	-	26.0	0.8	-	-	-	-	26.4	1.5	-	-	-	-	26.7	1.1	-	-
1957	-	-	27.1	1.5	-	-	-	-	27.3	0.7	-	-	-	-	27.5	0.7	-	-	-	-	27.5	0.0	-	-
1958	-	-	27.8	1.1	-	-	-	-	28.0	0.7	-	-	-	-	28.0	0.0	-	-	-	-	28.0	0.0	-	-

[Continued]

Seattle-Everett, WA
Consumer Price Index - All Urban Consumers
Base 1982-1984 = 100
All Items
[Continued]

For 1914-1997. Columns headed % show percentile change in the index from the previous period for which an index is available.

Year	Jan Index	%	Feb Index	%	Mar Index	%	Apr Index	%	May Index	%	Jun Index	%	Jul Index	%	Aug Index	%	Sep Index	%	Oct Index	%	Nov Index	%	Dec Index	%
1959	-	-	28.2	0.7	-	-	-	-	28.4	0.7	-	-	-	-	28.6	0.7	-	-	-	-	28.7	0.3	-	-
1960	-	-	28.6	-0.3	-	-	-	-	28.8	0.7	-	-	-	-	28.8	0.0	-	-	-	-	29.0	0.7	-	-
1961	-	-	29.1	0.3	-	-	-	-	29.3	0.7	-	-	-	-	29.3	0.0	-	-	-	-	29.5	0.7	-	-
1962	-	-	29.6	0.3	-	-	-	-	29.7	0.3	-	-	-	-	29.8	0.3	-	-	-	-	29.9	0.3	-	-
1963	-	-	29.9	0.0	-	-	-	-	30.0	0.3	-	-	-	-	30.5	1.7	-	-	-	-	30.5	0.0	-	-
1964	-	-	30.5	0.0	-	-	-	-	30.5	0.0	-	-	-	-	30.8	1.0	-	-	-	-	30.7	-0.3	-	-
1965	-	-	30.6	-0.3	-	-	-	-	30.9	1.0	-	-	-	-	31.1	0.6	-	-	-	-	31.2	0.3	-	-
1966	-	-	31.4	0.6	-	-	-	-	31.8	1.3	-	-	-	-	32.0	0.6	-	-	-	-	32.3	0.9	-	-
1967	-	-	32.3	0.0	-	-	-	-	32.6	0.9	-	-	-	-	33.0	1.2	-	-	-	-	33.3	0.9	-	-
1968	-	-	33.6	0.9	-	-	-	-	33.8	0.6	-	-	-	-	34.4	1.8	-	-	-	-	34.8	1.2	-	-
1969	-	-	35.1	0.9	-	-	-	-	35.6	1.4	-	-	-	-	36.2	1.7	-	-	-	-	36.3	0.3	-	-
1970	-	-	36.9	1.7	-	-	-	-	37.4	1.4	-	-	-	-	37.6	0.5	-	-	-	-	37.7	0.3	-	-
1971	-	-	37.6	-0.3	-	-	-	-	37.9	0.8	-	-	-	-	38.6	1.8	-	-	-	-	38.6	0.0	-	-
1972	-	-	39.0	1.0	-	-	-	-	39.0	0.0	-	-	-	-	39.3	0.8	-	-	-	-	39.8	1.3	-	-
1973	-	-	40.4	1.5	-	-	-	-	41.4	2.5	-	-	-	-	42.3	2.2	-	-	-	-	43.1	1.9	-	-
1974	-	-	44.5	3.2	-	-	-	-	45.7	2.7	-	-	-	-	46.9	2.6	-	-	-	-	48.5	3.4	-	-
1975	-	-	49.8	2.7	-	-	-	-	50.7	1.8	-	-	-	-	51.6	1.8	-	-	-	-	52.4	1.6	-	-
1976	-	-	53.0	1.1	-	-	-	-	53.3	0.6	-	-	-	-	54.4	2.1	-	-	-	-	55.1	1.3	-	-
1977	-	-	56.2	2.0	-	-	-	-	57.8	2.8	-	-	-	-	59.1	2.2	-	-	-	-	59.9	1.4	-	-
1978	60.4	0.8	-	-	61.4	1.7	-	-	63.5	3.4	-	-	63.9	0.6	-	-	65.9	3.1	-	-	66.8	1.4	-	-
1979	66.3	-0.7	-	-	67.9	2.4	-	-	69.7	2.7	-	-	71.3	2.3	-	-	73.0	2.4	-	-	74.7	2.3	-	-
1980	77.4	3.6	-	-	80.0	3.4	-	-	81.9	2.4	-	-	83.7	2.2	-	-	84.7	1.2	-	-	86.1	1.7	-	-
1981	86.9	0.9	-	-	88.9	2.3	-	-	90.1	1.3	-	-	92.6	2.8	-	-	94.7	2.3	-	-	94.9	0.2	-	-
1982	97.1	2.3	-	-	96.2	-0.9	-	-	98.8	2.7	-	-	97.3	-1.5	-	-	99.1	1.8	-	-	97.6	-1.5	-	-
1983	97.6	0.0	-	-	97.7	0.1	-	-	98.7	1.0	-	-	99.7	1.0	-	-	100.5	0.8	-	-	100.7	0.2	-	-
1984	101.3	0.6	-	-	101.8	0.5	-	-	102.7	0.9	-	-	103.1	0.4	-	-	103.8	0.7	-	-	104.4	0.6	-	-
1985	104.8	0.4	-	-	105.4	0.6	-	-	105.3	-0.1	-	-	105.6	0.3	-	-	105.6	0.0	-	-	106.3	0.7	-	-
1986	107.3	0.9	-	-	106.6	-0.7	-	-	106.1	-0.5	-	-	106.2	0.1	-	-	107.0	0.8	-	-	106.9	-0.1	106.8	-0.1
1987	-	-	-	-	-	-	-	-	-	-	109.9	2.9	-	-	-	-	-	-	-	-	-	-	111.9	1.8
1988	-	-	-	-	-	-	-	-	-	-	113.6	1.5	-	-	-	-	-	-	-	-	-	-	115.9	2.0
1989	-	-	-	-	-	-	-	-	-	-	119.3	2.9	-	-	-	-	-	-	-	-	-	-	121.6	1.9
1990	-	-	-	-	-	-	-	-	-	-	124.9	2.7	-	-	-	-	-	-	-	-	-	-	129.8	3.9
1991	-	-	-	-	-	-	-	-	-	-	132.8	2.3	-	-	-	-	-	-	-	-	-	-	135.1	1.7
1992	-	-	-	-	-	-	-	-	-	-	138.8	2.7	-	-	-	-	-	-	-	-	-	-	140.9	1.5
1993	-	-	-	-	-	-	-	-	-	-	143.6	1.9	-	-	-	-	-	-	-	-	-	-	145.8	1.5
1994	-	-	-	-	-	-	-	-	-	-	147.7	1.3	-	-	-	-	-	-	-	-	-	-	150.1	1.6
1995	-	-	-	-	-	-	-	-	-	-	152.5	1.6	-	-	-	-	-	-	-	-	-	-	153.9	0.9
1996	-	-	-	-	-	-	-	-	-	-	157.2	2.1	-	-	-	-	-	-	-	-	-	-	160.0	1.8
1997	-	-	-	-	-	-	-	-	-	-	162.6	1.6	-	-	-	-	-	-	-	-	-	-	-	-

Source: U.S. Department of Labor, Bureau of Labor Statistics, Division of Consumer Prices and Price Indexes. - indicates no data collected for period.

Seattle-Everett, WA
Consumer Price Index - Urban Wage Earners
Base 1982-1984 = 100
All Items

For 1914-1997. Columns headed % show percentile change in the index from the previous period for which an index is available.

Year	Jan Index	%	Feb Index	%	Mar Index	%	Apr Index	%	May Index	%	Jun Index	%	Jul Index	%	Aug Index	%	Sep Index	%	Oct Index	%	Nov Index	%	Dec Index	%
1914	-	-	-	-	-	-	-	-	-	-	-	-	-	-	-	-	-	-	-	-	-	-	9.4	-
1915	-	-	-	-	-	-	-	-	-	-	-	-	-	-	-	-	-	-	-	-	-	-	9.3	-1.1
1916	-	-	-	-	-	-	-	-	-	-	-	-	-	-	-	-	-	-	-	-	-	-	10.0	7.5
1917	-	-	-	-	-	-	-	-	-	-	-	-	-	-	-	-	-	-	-	-	-	-	12.1	21.0
1918	-	-	-	-	-	-	-	-	-	-	-	-	-	-	-	-	-	-	-	-	-	-	15.8	30.6
1919	-	-	-	-	-	-	-	-	-	-	16.5	4.4	-	-	-	-	-	-	-	-	-	-	18.7	13.3
1920	-	-	-	-	-	-	-	-	-	-	20.2	8.0	-	-	-	-	-	-	-	-	-	-	18.4	-8.9
1921	-	-	-	-	-	-	-	-	17.2	-6.5	-	-	-	-	-	-	16.7	-2.9	-	-	-	-	16.4	-1.8
1922	-	-	-	-	16.1	-1.8	-	-	-	-	16.0	-0.6	-	-	-	-	15.9	-0.6	-	-	-	-	15.9	0.0
1923	-	-	-	-	15.5	-2.5	-	-	-	-	15.9	2.6	-	-	-	-	16.1	1.3	-	-	-	-	16.0	-0.6
1924	-	-	-	-	15.9	-0.6	-	-	-	-	16.0	0.6	-	-	-	-	15.9	-0.6	-	-	-	-	16.0	0.6
1925	-	-	-	-	-	-	-	-	-	-	16.4	2.5	-	-	-	-	-	-	-	-	-	-	16.5	0.6
1926	-	-	-	-	-	-	-	-	-	-	16.3	-1.2	-	-	-	-	-	-	-	-	-	-	16.1	-1.2
1927	-	-	-	-	-	-	-	-	-	-	16.3	1.2	-	-	-	-	-	-	-	-	-	-	15.8	-3.1
1928	-	-	-	-	-	-	-	-	-	-	15.7	-0.6	-	-	-	-	-	-	-	-	-	-	15.8	0.6
1929	-	-	-	-	-	-	-	-	-	-	15.9	0.6	-	-	-	-	-	-	-	-	-	-	16.0	0.6
1930	-	-	-	-	-	-	-	-	-	-	15.9	-0.6	-	-	-	-	-	-	-	-	-	-	14.8	-6.9
1931	-	-	-	-	-	-	-	-	-	-	14.3	-3.4	-	-	-	-	-	-	-	-	-	-	13.8	-3.5
1932	-	-	-	-	-	-	-	-	-	-	13.0	-5.8	-	-	-	-	-	-	-	-	-	-	12.4	-4.6
1933	-	-	-	-	-	-	-	-	-	-	12.3	-0.8	-	-	-	-	-	-	-	-	-	-	12.4	0.8
1934	-	-	-	-	-	-	-	-	-	-	12.5	0.8	-	-	-	-	-	-	-	-	12.8	2.4	-	-
1935	-	-	-	-	13.0	1.6	-	-	-	-	-	-	12.8	-1.5	-	-	-	-	12.8	0.0	-	-	-	-
1936	13.0	1.6	-	-	-	-	12.9	-0.8	-	-	-	-	13.0	0.8	-	-	13.2	1.5	-	-	-	-	13.3	0.8
1937	-	-	-	-	13.6	2.3	-	-	-	-	13.7	0.7	-	-	-	-	13.9	1.5	-	-	-	-	13.8	-0.7
1938	-	-	-	-	13.7	-0.7	-	-	-	-	13.5	-1.5	-	-	-	-	13.5	0.0	-	-	-	-	13.5	0.0
1939	-	-	-	-	13.5	0.0	-	-	-	-	13.5	0.0	-	-	-	-	13.7	1.5	-	-	-	-	13.5	-1.5
1940	-	-	-	-	13.6	0.7	-	-	-	-	13.6	0.0	-	-	-	-	13.6	0.0	13.6	0.0	13.6	0.0	13.6	0.0
1941	13.7	0.7	13.7	0.0	13.8	0.7	13.9	0.7	14.2	2.2	14.3	0.7	14.4	0.7	14.5	0.7	14.9	2.8	15.1	1.3	15.1	0.0	15.3	1.3
1942	15.6	2.0	15.7	0.6	16.0	1.9	16.1	0.6	16.2	0.6	15.9	-1.9	16.0	0.6	16.3	1.9	16.5	1.2	16.6	0.6	16.7	0.6	16.8	0.6
1943	16.9	0.6	16.9	0.0	17.0	0.6	17.2	1.2	17.4	1.2	17.2	-1.1	17.0	-1.2	16.9	-0.6	17.2	1.8	17.2	0.0	17.3	0.6	17.3	0.0
1944	17.3	0.0	17.2	-0.6	17.2	0.0	17.2	0.0	17.4	1.2	17.3	-0.6	17.4	0.6	17.4	0.0	17.5	0.6	17.6	0.6	17.5	-0.6	17.6	0.6
1945	17.6	0.0	17.6	0.0	17.7	0.6	17.7	0.0	17.8	0.6	17.8	0.0	17.8	0.0	17.9	0.6	17.8	-0.6	17.8	0.0	17.9	0.6	18.1	1.1
1946	18.0	-0.6	18.0	0.0	18.0	0.0	18.1	0.6	18.2	0.6	18.4	1.1	19.3	4.9	19.5	1.0	19.9	2.1	20.4	2.5	20.9	2.5	21.1	1.0
1947	20.9	-0.9	20.9	0.0	21.3	1.9	21.4	0.5	21.3	-0.5	21.3	0.0	-	-	21.8	2.3	-	-	-	-	22.4	2.8	-	-
1948	-	-	23.0	2.7	-	-	-	-	23.5	2.2	-	-	-	-	23.8	1.3	-	-	-	-	23.6	-0.8	-	-
1949	-	-	23.6	0.0	-	-	-	-	23.4	-0.8	-	-	-	-	23.2	-0.9	-	-	-	-	23.3	0.4	-	-
1950	-	-	23.3	0.0	-	-	-	-	23.3	0.0	-	-	-	-	23.7	1.7	-	-	-	-	24.4	3.0	-	-
1951	-	-	25.2	3.3	-	-	-	-	25.6	1.6	-	-	-	-	25.5	-0.4	-	-	-	-	26.0	2.0	-	-
1952	-	-	26.1	0.4	-	-	-	-	26.2	0.4	-	-	-	-	26.2	0.0	-	-	-	-	26.4	0.8	-	-
1953	-	-	26.2	-0.8	-	-	-	-	26.5	1.1	-	-	-	-	26.7	0.8	-	-	-	-	26.6	-0.4	-	-
1954	-	-	26.5	-0.4	-	-	-	-	26.5	0.0	-	-	-	-	26.5	0.0	-	-	-	-	26.4	-0.4	-	-
1955	-	-	26.5	0.4	-	-	-	-	26.7	0.8	-	-	-	-	26.6	-0.4	-	-	-	-	26.8	0.8	-	-
1956	-	-	26.5	-1.1	-	-	-	-	26.7	0.8	-	-	-	-	27.1	1.5	-	-	-	-	27.4	1.1	-	-
1957	-	-	27.9	1.8	-	-	-	-	28.0	0.4	-	-	-	-	28.2	0.7	-	-	-	-	28.3	0.4	-	-
1958	-	-	28.5	0.7	-	-	-	-	28.8	1.1	-	-	-	-	28.8	0.0	-	-	-	-	28.8	0.0	-	-

[Continued]

Seattle-Everett, WA
Consumer Price Index - Urban Wage Earners
Base 1982-1984 = 100
All Items
[Continued]

For 1914-1997. Columns headed % show percentile change in the index from the previous period for which an index is available.

Year	Jan Index	%	Feb Index	%	Mar Index	%	Apr Index	%	May Index	%	Jun Index	%	Jul Index	%	Aug Index	%	Sep Index	%	Oct Index	%	Nov Index	%	Dec Index	%
1959	-	-	29.0	0.7	-	-	-	-	29.2	0.7	-	-	-	-	29.4	0.7	-	-	-	-	29.5	0.3	-	-
1960	-	-	29.4	-0.3	-	-	-	-	29.6	0.7	-	-	-	-	29.6	0.0	-	-	-	-	29.8	0.7	-	-
1961	-	-	29.9	0.3	-	-	-	-	30.1	0.7	-	-	-	-	30.1	0.0	-	-	-	-	30.3	0.7	-	-
1962	-	-	30.4	0.3	-	-	-	-	30.5	0.3	-	-	-	-	30.6	0.3	-	-	-	-	30.7	0.3	-	-
1963	-	-	30.7	0.0	-	-	-	-	30.8	0.3	-	-	-	-	31.3	1.6	-	-	-	-	31.4	0.3	-	-
1964	-	-	31.4	0.0	-	-	-	-	31.3	-0.3	-	-	-	-	31.7	1.3	-	-	-	-	31.6	-0.3	-	-
1965	-	-	31.5	-0.3	-	-	-	-	31.8	1.0	-	-	-	-	32.0	0.6	-	-	-	-	32.1	0.3	-	-
1966	-	-	32.3	0.6	-	-	-	-	32.6	0.9	-	-	-	-	32.8	0.6	-	-	-	-	33.2	1.2	-	-
1967	-	-	33.2	0.0	-	-	-	-	33.5	0.9	-	-	-	-	33.9	1.2	-	-	-	-	34.2	0.9	-	-
1968	-	-	34.5	0.9	-	-	-	-	34.8	0.9	-	-	-	-	35.4	1.7	-	-	-	-	35.7	0.8	-	-
1969	-	-	36.1	1.1	-	-	-	-	36.6	1.4	-	-	-	-	37.2	1.6	-	-	-	-	37.3	0.3	-	-
1970	-	-	37.9	1.6	-	-	-	-	38.4	1.3	-	-	-	-	38.6	0.5	-	-	-	-	38.7	0.3	-	-
1971	-	-	38.6	-0.3	-	-	-	-	38.9	0.8	-	-	-	-	39.6	1.8	-	-	-	-	39.6	0.0	-	-
1972	-	-	40.1	1.3	-	-	-	-	40.1	0.0	-	-	-	-	40.4	0.7	-	-	-	-	40.9	1.2	-	-
1973	-	-	41.5	1.5	-	-	-	-	42.6	2.7	-	-	-	-	43.4	1.9	-	-	-	-	44.3	2.1	-	-
1974	-	-	45.8	3.4	-	-	-	-	47.0	2.6	-	-	-	-	48.2	2.6	-	-	-	-	49.9	3.5	-	-
1975	-	-	51.2	2.6	-	-	-	-	52.1	1.8	-	-	-	-	53.0	1.7	-	-	-	-	53.8	1.5	-	-
1976	-	-	54.5	1.3	-	-	-	-	54.8	0.6	-	-	-	-	55.9	2.0	-	-	-	-	56.6	1.3	-	-
1977	-	-	57.8	2.1	-	-	-	-	59.4	2.8	-	-	-	-	60.8	2.4	-	-	-	-	61.5	1.2	-	-
1978	62.0	0.8	-	-	63.0	1.6	-	-	64.9	3.0	-	-	65.4	0.8	-	-	67.3	2.9	-	-	68.1	1.2	-	-
1979	67.6	-0.7	-	-	69.4	2.7	-	-	71.1	2.4	-	-	72.8	2.4	-	-	74.5	2.3	-	-	76.0	2.0	-	-
1980	78.8	3.7	-	-	81.4	3.3	-	-	83.2	2.2	-	-	84.8	1.9	-	-	85.8	1.2	-	-	87.5	2.0	-	-
1981	88.4	1.0	-	-	90.3	2.1	-	-	91.5	1.3	-	-	93.7	2.4	-	-	95.9	2.3	-	-	96.3	0.4	-	-
1982	98.4	2.2	-	-	97.6	-0.8	-	-	100.2	2.7	-	-	98.8	-1.4	-	-	100.6	1.8	-	-	99.2	-1.4	-	-
1983	98.2	-1.0	-	-	98.0	-0.2	-	-	97.9	-0.1	-	-	98.5	0.6	-	-	99.7	1.2	-	-	100.1	0.4	-	-
1984	100.2	0.1	-	-	101.1	0.9	-	-	102.1	1.0	-	-	102.2	0.1	-	-	102.9	0.7	-	-	103.0	0.1	-	-
1985	103.4	0.4	-	-	104.2	0.8	-	-	104.0	-0.2	-	-	104.2	0.2	-	-	104.1	-0.1	-	-	104.8	0.7	-	-
1986	105.7	0.9	-	-	105.0	-0.7	-	-	104.3	-0.7	-	-	104.6	0.3	-	-	105.3	0.7	-	-	105.1	-0.2	105.1	0.0
1987	-	-	-	-	-	-	-	-	-	-	107.5	2.3	-	-	-	-	-	-	-	-	-	-	109.5	1.9
1988	-	-	-	-	-	-	-	-	-	-	110.9	1.3	-	-	-	-	-	-	-	-	-	-	113.0	1.9
1989	-	-	-	-	-	-	-	-	-	-	116.4	3.0	-	-	-	-	-	-	-	-	-	-	118.7	2.0
1990	-	-	-	-	-	-	-	-	-	-	121.8	2.6	-	-	-	-	-	-	-	-	-	-	126.6	3.9
1991	-	-	-	-	-	-	-	-	-	-	129.6	2.4	-	-	-	-	-	-	-	-	-	-	132.1	1.9
1992	-	-	-	-	-	-	-	-	-	-	135.5	2.6	-	-	-	-	-	-	-	-	-	-	137.7	1.6
1993	-	-	-	-	-	-	-	-	-	-	140.3	1.9	-	-	-	-	-	-	-	-	-	-	142.6	1.6
1994	-	-	-	-	-	-	-	-	-	-	144.3	1.2	-	-	-	-	-	-	-	-	-	-	146.8	1.7
1995	-	-	-	-	-	-	-	-	-	-	149.1	1.6	-	-	-	-	-	-	-	-	-	-	150.7	1.1
1996	-	-	-	-	-	-	-	-	-	-	153.9	2.1	-	-	-	-	-	-	-	-	-	-	156.5	1.7
1997	-	-	-	-	-	-	-	-	-	-	159.0	1.6	-	-	-	-	-	-	-	-	-	-	-	-

Source: U.S. Department of Labor, Bureau of Labor Statistics, Division of Consumer Prices and Price Indexes. - indicates no data collected for period.

Seattle-Everett, WA
Consumer Price Index - All Urban Consumers
Base 1982-1984 = 100
Food and Beverages

For 1975-1997. Columns headed % show percentile change in the index from the previous period for which an index is available.

Year	Jan Index	%	Feb Index	%	Mar Index	%	Apr Index	%	May Index	%	Jun Index	%	Jul Index	%	Aug Index	%	Sep Index	%	Oct Index	%	Nov Index	%	Dec Index	%
1975	-	-	-	-	-	-	-	-	-	-	-	-	-	-	-	-	-	-	-	-	60.8	-	-	-
1976	-	-	60.6	-0.3	-	-	-	-	60.8	0.3	-	-	-	-	61.8	1.6	-	-	-	-	61.8	0.0	-	-
1977	-	-	63.5	2.8	-	-	-	-	65.2	2.7	-	-	-	-	66.8	2.5	-	-	-	-	66.8	0.0	-	-
1978	67.1	0.4	-	-	69.2	3.1	-	-	72.5	4.8	-	-	70.9	-2.2	-	-	71.9	1.4	-	-	72.5	0.8	-	-
1979	74.1	2.2	-	-	77.5	4.6	-	-	78.8	1.7	-	-	78.8	0.0	-	-	78.5	-0.4	-	-	80.1	2.0	-	-
1980	81.4	1.6	-	-	82.5	1.4	-	-	83.6	1.3	-	-	84.4	1.0	-	-	86.4	2.4	-	-	87.2	0.9	-	-
1981	88.7	1.7	-	-	90.4	1.9	-	-	90.7	0.3	-	-	92.0	1.4	-	-	93.1	1.2	-	-	93.1	0.0	-	-
1982	95.1	2.1	-	-	94.6	-0.5	-	-	99.6	5.3	-	-	100.0	0.4	-	-	99.8	-0.2	-	-	99.5	-0.3	-	-
1983	100.0	0.5	-	-	101.5	1.5	-	-	102.4	0.9	-	-	98.9	-3.4	-	-	98.7	-0.2	-	-	99.0	0.3	-	-
1984	100.8	1.8	-	-	101.3	0.5	-	-	101.4	0.1	-	-	101.7	0.3	-	-	102.1	0.4	-	-	102.1	0.0	-	-
1985	101.7	-0.4	-	-	103.3	1.6	-	-	103.3	0.0	-	-	103.6	0.3	-	-	103.5	-0.1	-	-	103.3	0.2	-	-
1986	104.9	1.5	-	-	105.9	1.0	-	-	107.1	1.1	-	-	106.7	-0.4	-	-	107.5	0.7	-	-	107.9	0.4	108.1	0.2
1987	-	-	-	-	-	-	-	-	111.7	3.3	-	-	-	-	-	-	-	-	-	-	-	-	110.9	-0.7
1988	-	-	-	-	-	-	-	-	111.0	0.1	-	-	-	-	-	-	-	-	-	-	-	-	113.0	1.8
1989	-	-	-	-	-	-	-	-	118.0	4.4	-	-	-	-	-	-	-	-	-	-	-	-	119.5	1.3
1990	-	-	-	-	-	-	-	-	124.9	4.5	-	-	-	-	-	-	-	-	-	-	-	-	127.4	2.0
1991	-	-	-	-	-	-	-	-	131.4	3.1	-	-	-	-	-	-	-	-	-	-	-	-	129.9	-1.1
1992	-	-	-	-	-	-	-	-	132.1	1.7	-	-	-	-	-	-	-	-	-	-	-	-	131.3	-0.6
1993	-	-	-	-	-	-	-	-	133.8	1.9	-	-	-	-	-	-	-	-	-	-	-	-	134.3	0.4
1994	-	-	-	-	-	-	-	-	135.5	0.9	-	-	-	-	-	-	-	-	-	-	-	-	136.2	0.5
1995	-	-	-	-	-	-	-	-	137.3	0.8	-	-	-	-	-	-	-	-	-	-	-	-	136.8	-0.4
1996	-	-	-	-	-	-	-	-	141.6	3.5	-	-	-	-	-	-	-	-	-	-	-	-	144.7	2.2
1997	-	-	-	-	-	-	-	-	147.0	1.6	-	-	-	-	-	-	-	-	-	-	-	-	-	-

Source: U.S. Department of Labor, Bureau of Labor Statistics, Division of Consumer Prices and Price Indexes. - indicates no data collected for period.

Seattle-Everett, WA
Consumer Price Index - Urban Wage Earners
Base 1982-1984 = 100
Food and Beverages

For 1975-1997. Columns headed % show percentile change in the index from the previous period for which an index is available.

Year	Jan Index	%	Feb Index	%	Mar Index	%	Apr Index	%	May Index	%	Jun Index	%	Jul Index	%	Aug Index	%	Sep Index	%	Oct Index	%	Nov Index	%	Dec Index	%
1975	-	-	-	-	-	-	-	-	-	-	-	-	-	-	-	-	-	-	-	-	61.1	-	-	-
1976	-	-	60.9	-0.3	-	-	-	-	61.1	0.3	-	-	-	-	62.1	1.6	-	-	-	-	62.1	0.0	-	-
1977	-	-	63.8	2.7	-	-	-	-	65.5	2.7	-	-	-	-	67.1	2.4	-	-	-	-	67.1	0.0	-	-
1978	67.7	0.9	-	-	69.8	3.1	-	-	72.1	3.3	-	-	71.0	-1.5	-	-	72.3	1.8	-	-	72.7	0.6	-	-
1979	74.4	2.3	-	-	77.8	4.6	-	-	78.8	1.3	-	-	78.7	-0.1	-	-	79.0	0.4	-	-	79.3	0.4	-	-
1980	81.4	2.6	-	-	82.6	1.5	-	-	83.7	1.3	-	-	84.7	1.2	-	-	86.6	2.2	-	-	87.6	1.2	-	-
1981	89.6	2.3	-	-	91.2	1.8	-	-	91.5	0.3	-	-	92.5	1.1	-	-	93.5	1.1	-	-	93.1	-0.4	-	-
1982	95.1	2.1	-	-	94.7	-0.4	-	-	99.5	5.1	-	-	99.9	0.4	-	-	99.7	-0.2	-	-	99.5	-0.2	-	-
1983	100.0	0.5	-	-	101.6	1.6	-	-	102.5	0.9	-	-	98.9	-3.5	-	-	98.6	-0.3	-	-	99.0	0.4	-	-
1984	100.7	1.7	-	-	101.3	0.6	-	-	101.4	0.1	-	-	101.6	0.2	-	-	102.2	0.6	-	-	102.2	0.0	-	-
1985	101.7	-0.5	-	-	103.4	1.7	-	-	103.3	-0.1	-	-	103.6	0.3	-	-	103.7	0.1	-	-	103.3	-0.4	-	-
1986	104.9	1.5	-	-	105.8	0.9	-	-	106.9	1.0	-	-	106.6	-0.3	-	-	107.2	0.6	-	-	107.6	0.4	107.9	0.3
1987	-	-	-	-	-	-	-	-	-	-	111.4	3.2	-	-	-	-	-	-	-	-	-	-	110.8	-0.5
1988	-	-	-	-	-	-	-	-	-	-	110.8	0.0	-	-	-	-	-	-	-	-	-	-	112.9	1.9
1989	-	-	-	-	-	-	-	-	-	-	117.8	4.3	-	-	-	-	-	-	-	-	-	-	119.4	1.4
1990	-	-	-	-	-	-	-	-	-	-	124.6	4.4	-	-	-	-	-	-	-	-	-	-	127.2	2.1
1991	-	-	-	-	-	-	-	-	-	-	131.1	3.1	-	-	-	-	-	-	-	-	-	-	130.0	-0.8
1992	-	-	-	-	-	-	-	-	-	-	132.1	1.6	-	-	-	-	-	-	-	-	-	-	131.4	-0.5
1993	-	-	-	-	-	-	-	-	-	-	133.8	1.8	-	-	-	-	-	-	-	-	-	-	134.1	0.2
1994	-	-	-	-	-	-	-	-	-	-	135.1	0.7	-	-	-	-	-	-	-	-	-	-	135.8	0.5
1995	-	-	-	-	-	-	-	-	-	-	136.6	0.6	-	-	-	-	-	-	-	-	-	-	136.1	-0.4
1996	-	-	-	-	-	-	-	-	-	-	140.6	3.3	-	-	-	-	-	-	-	-	-	-	143.7	2.2
1997	-	-	-	-	-	-	-	-	-	-	146.1	1.7	-	-	-	-	-	-	-	-	-	-	-	-

Source: U.S. Department of Labor, Bureau of Labor Statistics, Division of Consumer Prices and Price Indexes. - indicates no data collected for period.

Seattle-Everett, WA
Consumer Price Index - All Urban Consumers
Base 1982-1984 = 100
Housing

For 1975-1997. Columns headed % show percentile change in the index from the previous period for which an index is available.

Year	Jan Index	%	Feb Index	%	Mar Index	%	Apr Index	%	May Index	%	Jun Index	%	Jul Index	%	Aug Index	%	Sep Index	%	Oct Index	%	Nov Index	%	Dec Index	%
1975	-	-	-	-	-	-	-	-	-	-	-	-	-	-	-	-	-	-	-	-	48.9	-	-	-
1976	-	-	49.8	1.8	-	-	-	-	49.2	-1.2	-	-	-	-	50.7	3.0	-	-	-	-	51.5	1.6	-	-
1977	-	-	52.2	1.4	-	-	-	-	54.2	3.8	-	-	-	-	55.8	3.0	-	-	-	-	57.0	2.2	-	-
1978	57.5	0.9	-	-	58.7	2.1	-	-	60.9	3.7	-	-	61.6	1.1	-	-	64.5	4.7	-	-	65.5	1.6	-	-
1979	63.6	-2.9	-	-	64.8	1.9	-	-	66.3	2.3	-	-	68.4	3.2	-	-	70.3	2.8	-	-	72.1	2.6	-	-
1980	76.3	5.8	-	-	79.2	3.8	-	-	82.0	3.5	-	-	84.5	3.0	-	-	84.8	0.4	-	-	86.7	2.2	-	-
1981	87.2	0.6	-	-	88.8	1.8	-	-	89.8	1.1	-	-	93.1	3.7	-	-	95.9	3.0	-	-	95.7	-0.2	-	-
1982	99.0	3.4	-	-	97.7	-1.3	-	-	101.1	3.5	-	-	96.6	-4.5	-	-	99.8	3.3	-	-	97.1	-2.7	-	-
1983	97.2	0.1	-	-	97.0	-0.2	-	-	97.7	0.7	-	-	99.2	1.5	-	-	100.0	0.8	-	-	100.2	0.2	-	-
1984	100.9	0.7	-	-	101.9	1.0	-	-	102.1	0.2	-	-	102.6	0.5	-	-	103.8	1.2	-	-	104.6	0.8	-	-
1985	105.2	0.6	-	-	105.4	0.2	-	-	105.3	-0.1	-	-	105.0	-0.3	-	-	104.8	-0.2	-	-	106.5	1.6	-	-
1986	107.7	1.1	-	-	107.0	-0.6	-	-	106.2	-0.7	-	-	105.9	-0.3	-	-	107.3	1.3	-	-	107.1	-0.2	106.6	-0.5
1987	-	-	-	-	-	-	-	-	-	-	107.1	0.5	-	-	-	-	-	-	-	-	-	-	109.2	2.0
1988	-	-	-	-	-	-	-	-	-	-	111.0	1.6	-	-	-	-	-	-	-	-	-	-	112.7	1.5
1989	-	-	-	-	-	-	-	-	-	-	115.1	2.1	-	-	-	-	-	-	-	-	-	-	118.0	2.5
1990	-	-	-	-	-	-	-	-	-	-	120.7	2.3	-	-	-	-	-	-	-	-	-	-	124.6	3.2
1991	-	-	-	-	-	-	-	-	-	-	128.0	2.7	-	-	-	-	-	-	-	-	-	-	132.7	3.7
1992	-	-	-	-	-	-	-	-	-	-	137.4	3.5	-	-	-	-	-	-	-	-	-	-	139.0	1.2
1993	-	-	-	-	-	-	-	-	-	-	141.6	1.9	-	-	-	-	-	-	-	-	-	-	145.8	3.0
1994	-	-	-	-	-	-	-	-	-	-	148.3	1.7	-	-	-	-	-	-	-	-	-	-	150.8	1.7
1995	-	-	-	-	-	-	-	-	-	-	153.8	2.0	-	-	-	-	-	-	-	-	-	-	155.4	1.0
1996	-	-	-	-	-	-	-	-	-	-	157.0	1.0	-	-	-	-	-	-	-	-	-	-	159.6	1.7
1997	-	-	-	-	-	-	-	-	-	-	161.2	1.0	-	-	-	-	-	-	-	-	-	-	-	-

Source: U.S. Department of Labor, Bureau of Labor Statistics, Division of Consumer Prices and Price Indexes. - indicates no data collected for period.

Seattle-Everett, WA
Consumer Price Index - Urban Wage Earners
Base 1982-1984 = 100
Housing

For 1975-1997. Columns headed % show percentile change in the index from the previous period for which an index is available.

Year	Jan Index	%	Feb Index	%	Mar Index	%	Apr Index	%	May Index	%	Jun Index	%	Jul Index	%	Aug Index	%	Sep Index	%	Oct Index	%	Nov Index	%	Dec Index	%
1975	-	-			-	-	-	-			-				-	-			-	-	51.0	-	-	-
1976	-	-	51.9	1.8	-	-	-	-	51.4	-1.0	-	-	-	-	52.9	2.9	-	-	-	-	53.7	1.5	-	-
1977	-	-	54.5	1.5	-	-	-	-	56.6	3.9	-	-	-	-	58.3	3.0	-	-	-	-	59.5	2.1	-	-
1978	60.1	1.0	-	-	61.3	2.0	-	-	63.5	3.6	-	-	64.2	1.1	-	-	67.3	4.8	-	-	68.2	1.3	-	-
1979	66.1	-3.1	-	-	67.6	2.3	-	-	69.1	2.2	-	-	71.1	2.9	-	-	73.1	2.8	-	-	75.1	2.7	-	-
1980	79.5	5.9	-	-	82.3	3.5	-	-	85.4	3.8	-	-	87.8	2.8	-	-	88.0	0.2	-	-	90.0	2.3	-	-
1981	90.4	0.4	-	-	92.4	2.2	-	-	93.2	0.9	-	-	96.0	3.0	-	-	99.1	3.2	-	-	99.0	-0.1	-	-
1982	102.3	3.3	-	-	100.9	-1.4	-	-	104.5	3.6	-	-	99.7	-4.6	-	-	103.1	3.4	-	-	100.5	-2.5	-	-
1983	98.7	-1.8	-	-	97.9	-0.8	-	-	96.1	-1.8	-	-	96.4	0.3	-	-	97.9	1.6	-	-	98.7	0.8	-	-
1984	98.7	0.0	-	-	100.3	1.6	-	-	100.7	0.4	-	-	100.6	-0.1	-	-	101.8	1.2	-	-	101.4	-0.4	-	-
1985	102.1	0.7	-	-	102.4	0.3	-	-	102.0	-0.4	-	-	101.5	-0.5	-	-	101.4	-0.1	-	-	103.0	1.6	-	-
1986	104.1	1.1	-	-	103.5	-0.6	-	-	102.6	-0.9	-	-	102.5	-0.1	-	-	103.9	1.4	-	-	103.6	-0.3	103.2	-0.4
1987	-	-	-	-	-	-	-	-	-	-	103.3	0.1	-	-	-	-	-	-	-	-	-	-	105.3	1.9
1988	-	-	-	-	-	-	-	-	-	-	107.0	1.6	-	-	-	-	-	-	-	-	-	-	108.6	1.5
1989	-	-	-	-	-	-	-	-	-	-	110.9	2.1	-	-	-	-	-	-	-	-	-	-	113.7	2.5
1990	-	-	-	-	-	-	-	-	-	-	116.2	2.2	-	-	-	-	-	-	-	-	-	-	120.0	3.3
1991	-	-	-	-	-	-	-	-	-	-	123.5	2.9	-	-	-	-	-	-	-	-	-	-	128.2	3.8
1992	-	-	-	-	-	-	-	-	-	-	132.9	3.7	-	-	-	-	-	-	-	-	-	-	134.6	1.3
1993	-	-	-	-	-	-	-	-	-	-	137.1	1.9	-	-	-	-	-	-	-	-	-	-	141.1	2.9
1994	-	-	-	-	-	-	-	-	-	-	143.6	1.8	-	-	-	-	-	-	-	-	-	-	146.1	1.7
1995	-	-	-	-	-	-	-	-	-	-	148.7	1.8	-	-	-	-	-	-	-	-	-	-	150.2	1.0
1996	-	-	-	-	-	-	-	-	-	-	151.7	1.0	-	-	-	-	-	-	-	-	-	-	154.2	1.6
1997	-	-	-	-	-	-	-	-	-	-	155.7	1.0	-	-	-	-	-	-	-	-	-	-	-	-

Source: U.S. Department of Labor, Bureau of Labor Statistics, Division of Consumer Prices and Price Indexes. - indicates no data collected for period.

Seattle-Everett, WA
Consumer Price Index - All Urban Consumers
Base 1982-1984 = 100
Apparel and Upkeep

For 1952-1997. Columns headed % show percentile change in the index from the previous period for which an index is available.

Year	Jan Index	%	Feb Index	%	Mar Index	%	Apr Index	%	May Index	%	Jun Index	%	Jul Index	%	Aug Index	%	Sep Index	%	Oct Index	%	Nov Index	%	Dec Index	%
1952	-		-		-		-		-						-		-		-		43.9	-	-	-
1953	-		43.9	0.0	-		-		43.8	-0.2					44.1	0.7	-		-		44.0	-0.2		
1954	-		43.5	-1.1	-		-		43.7	0.5					43.6	-0.2	-		-		43.5	-0.2		
1955	-		43.7	0.5	-		-		43.4	-0.7					43.9	1.2	-		-		44.1	0.5		
1956	-		43.8	-0.7	-		-		44.0	0.5					44.1	0.2	-		-		45.0	2.0		
1957	-		44.8	-0.4	-		-		45.0	0.4					45.3	0.7	-		-		45.2	-0.2		
1958	-		45.1	-0.2	-		-		45.1	0.0					44.8	-0.7	-		-		44.7	-0.2		
1959	-		44.7	0.0	-		-		45.1	0.9					45.5	0.9	-		-		46.1	1.3		
1960	-		46.0	-0.2	-		-		45.4	-1.3					45.8	0.9	-		-		46.6	1.7		
1961	-		46.5	-0.2	-		-		46.7	0.4					46.2	-1.1	-		-		47.4	2.6		
1962	-		47.2	-0.4	-		-		47.4	0.4					47.5	0.2	-		-		47.8	0.6		
1963	-		48.2	0.8	-		-		47.7	-1.0					48.1	0.8	-		-		48.8	1.5		
1964	-		48.9	0.2	-		-		49.1	0.4					48.1	-2.0	-		-		48.9	1.7		
1965	-		48.8	-0.2	-		-		49.0	0.4					48.7	-0.6	-		-		49.7	2.1		
1966	-		50.1	0.8	-		-		50.6	1.0					50.2	-0.8	-		-		51.0	1.6		
1967	-		51.4	0.8	-		-		52.2	1.6					52.3	0.2	-		-		53.1	1.5		
1968	-		52.9	-0.4	-		-		53.5	1.1					53.6	0.2	-		-		54.6	1.9		
1969	-		54.7	0.2	-		-		55.7	1.8					55.7	0.0	-		-		57.2	2.7		
1970	-		57.1	-0.2	-		-		58.1	1.8					58.0	-0.2	-		-		60.0	3.4		
1971	-		59.5	-0.8	-		-		61.1	2.7					60.3	-1.3	-		-		61.4	1.8		
1972	-		61.0	-0.7	-		-		61.0	0.0					60.8	-0.3	-		-		62.6	3.0		
1973	-		62.9	0.5	-		-		64.3	2.2					64.1	-0.3	-		-		65.5	2.2		
1974	-		65.8	0.5	-		-		67.5	2.6					68.6	1.6	-		-		71.1	3.6		
1975	-		71.8	1.0	-		-		72.9	1.5					72.5	-0.5	-		-		73.4	1.2		
1976	-		75.4	2.7	-		-		77.4	2.7					76.9	-0.6	-		-		77.9	1.3		
1977	-		78.5	0.8	-		-		79.9	1.8					80.6	0.9	-		-		82.4	2.2		
1978	81.6	-1.0	-		81.4	-0.2	-		82.8	1.7			81.5	-1.6	-		84.2	3.3	-		84.0	-0.2		
1979	82.8	-1.4	-		86.1	4.0	-		87.6	1.7			86.9	-0.8	-		89.4	2.9	-		92.7	3.7		
1980	90.6	-2.3	-		93.7	3.4	-		92.3	-1.5			94.5	2.4	-		98.8	4.6	-		98.5	-0.3		
1981	96.8	-1.7	-		98.0	1.2	-		98.8	0.8			99.4	0.6	-		100.4	1.0	-		100.6	0.2		
1982	97.7	-2.9	-		99.9	2.3	-		99.3	-0.6			97.5	-1.8	-		102.9	5.5	-		100.5	-2.3		
1983	96.9	-3.6	-		101.6	4.9	-		103.1	1.5			101.6	-1.5	-		103.6	2.0	-		100.3	-3.2		
1984	97.3	-3.0	-		100.2	3.0	-		98.2	-2.0			97.8	-0.4	-		101.6	3.9	-		100.4	-1.2		
1985	96.9	-3.5	-		104.6	7.9	-		100.6	-3.8			100.8	0.2	-		107.8	6.9	-		103.7	-3.8		
1986	99.2	-4.3	-		104.0	4.8	-		103.9	-0.1			103.9	0.0	-		108.3	4.2	-		108.6	0.3	105.1	-3.2
1987	-		-		-		-		-		98.5	-6.3	-		-		-		-		-		105.7	7.3
1988	-		-		-		-		-		109.4	3.5	-		-		-		-		-		114.5	4.7
1989	-		-		-		-		-		114.5	0.0	-		-		-		-		-		114.3	-0.2
1990	-		-		-		-		-		118.4	3.6	-		-		-		-		-		123.0	3.9
1991	-		-		-		-		-		123.2	0.2	-		-		-		-		-		121.4	-1.5
1992	-		-		-		-		-		124.3	2.4	-		-		-		-		-		125.3	0.8
1993	-		-		-		-		-		124.8	-0.4	-		-		-		-		-		119.6	-4.2
1994	-		-		-		-		-		124.7	4.3	-		-		-		-		-		122.8	-1.5

[Continued]

Seattle-Everett, WA
Consumer Price Index - All Urban Consumers
Base 1982-1984 = 100
Apparel and Upkeep

[Continued]

For 1952-1997. Columns headed % show percentile change in the index from the previous period for which an index is available.

Year	Jan		Feb		Mar		Apr		May		Jun		Jul		Aug		Sep		Oct		Nov		Dec	
	Index	%	Index	%	Index	%	Index	%	Index	%	Index	%	Index	%	Index	%	Index	%	Index	%	Index	%	Index	%
1995	-	-	-	-	-	-	-	-	-	-	127.8	4.1	-	-	-	-	-	-	-	-	-	-	119.1	-6.8
1996	-	-	-	-	-	-	-	-	-	-	122.4	2.8	-	-	-	-	-	-	-	-	-	-	126.6	3.4
1997	-	-	-	-	-	-	-	-	-	-	128.7	1.7	-	-	-	-	-	-	-	-	-	-	-	-

Source: U.S. Department of Labor, Bureau of Labor Statistics, Division of Consumer Prices and Price Indexes. - indicates no data collected for period.

Seattle-Everett, WA
Consumer Price Index - Urban Wage Earners
Base 1982-1984 = 100
Apparel and Upkeep

For 1952-1997. Columns headed % show percentile change in the index from the previous period for which an index is available.

Year	Jan Index	%	Feb Index	%	Mar Index	%	Apr Index	%	May Index	%	Jun Index	%	Jul Index	%	Aug Index	%	Sep Index	%	Oct Index	%	Nov Index	%	Dec Index	%
1952	-	-	-	-	-	-	-	-	-	-	-	-	-	-	-	-	-	-	-	-	44.4	-	-	-
1953	-	-	44.4	0.0	-	-	-	-	44.3	-0.2	-	-	-	-	44.6	0.7	-	-	-	-	44.5	-0.2	-	-
1954	-	-	44.1	-0.9	-	-	-	-	44.2	0.2	-	-	-	-	44.1	-0.2	-	-	-	-	44.0	-0.2	-	-
1955	-	-	44.2	0.5	-	-	-	-	43.9	-0.7	-	-	-	-	44.4	1.1	-	-	-	-	44.6	0.5	-	-
1956	-	-	44.3	-0.7	-	-	-	-	44.5	0.5	-	-	-	-	44.6	0.2	-	-	-	-	45.5	2.0	-	-
1957	-	-	45.3	-0.4	-	-	-	-	45.5	0.4	-	-	-	-	45.8	0.7	-	-	-	-	45.7	-0.2	-	-
1958	-	-	45.6	-0.2	-	-	-	-	45.6	0.0	-	-	-	-	45.3	-0.7	-	-	-	-	45.2	-0.2	-	-
1959	-	-	45.3	0.2	-	-	-	-	45.6	0.7	-	-	-	-	46.1	1.1	-	-	-	-	46.6	1.1	-	-
1960	-	-	46.5	-0.2	-	-	-	-	46.0	-1.1	-	-	-	-	46.4	0.9	-	-	-	-	47.1	1.5	-	-
1961	-	-	47.0	-0.2	-	-	-	-	47.2	0.4	-	-	-	-	46.7	-1.1	-	-	-	-	47.9	2.6	-	-
1962	-	-	47.8	-0.2	-	-	-	-	48.0	0.4	-	-	-	-	48.0	0.0	-	-	-	-	48.4	0.8	-	-
1963	-	-	48.8	0.8	-	-	-	-	48.3	-1.0	-	-	-	-	48.7	0.8	-	-	-	-	49.4	1.4	-	-
1964	-	-	49.5	0.2	-	-	-	-	49.7	0.4	-	-	-	-	48.7	-2.0	-	-	-	-	49.5	1.6	-	-
1965	-	-	49.4	-0.2	-	-	-	-	49.6	0.4	-	-	-	-	49.2	-0.8	-	-	-	-	50.2	2.0	-	-
1966	-	-	50.7	1.0	-	-	-	-	51.2	1.0	-	-	-	-	50.8	-0.8	-	-	-	-	51.6	1.6	-	-
1967	-	-	52.0	0.8	-	-	-	-	52.8	1.5	-	-	-	-	52.9	0.2	-	-	-	-	53.7	1.5	-	-
1968	-	-	53.5	-0.4	-	-	-	-	54.2	1.3	-	-	-	-	54.3	0.2	-	-	-	-	55.3	1.8	-	-
1969	-	-	55.4	0.2	-	-	-	-	56.4	1.8	-	-	-	-	56.4	0.0	-	-	-	-	57.9	2.7	-	-
1970	-	-	57.8	-0.2	-	-	-	-	58.8	1.7	-	-	-	-	58.7	-0.2	-	-	-	-	60.8	3.6	-	-
1971	-	-	60.2	-1.0	-	-	-	-	61.9	2.8	-	-	-	-	61.0	-1.5	-	-	-	-	62.1	1.8	-	-
1972	-	-	61.8	-0.5	-	-	-	-	61.7	-0.2	-	-	-	-	61.5	-0.3	-	-	-	-	63.3	2.9	-	-
1973	-	-	63.7	0.6	-	-	-	-	65.1	2.2	-	-	-	-	64.9	-0.3	-	-	-	-	66.3	2.2	-	-
1974	-	-	66.6	0.5	-	-	-	-	68.3	2.6	-	-	-	-	69.4	1.6	-	-	-	-	72.0	3.7	-	-
1975	-	-	72.6	0.8	-	-	-	-	73.8	1.7	-	-	-	-	73.4	-0.5	-	-	-	-	74.3	1.2	-	-
1976	-	-	76.3	2.7	-	-	-	-	78.3	2.6	-	-	-	-	77.8	-0.6	-	-	-	-	78.8	1.3	-	-
1977	-	-	79.5	0.9	-	-	-	-	80.9	1.8	-	-	-	-	81.5	0.7	-	-	-	-	83.4	2.3	-	-
1978	82.2	-1.4	-	-	82.7	0.6	-	-	84.3	1.9	-	-	81.9	-2.8	-	-	85.5	4.4	-	-	84.7	-0.9	-	-
1979	82.1	-3.1	-	-	85.6	4.3	-	-	87.6	2.3	-	-	88.1	0.6	-	-	90.1	2.3	-	-	92.0	2.1	-	-
1980	89.8	-2.4	-	-	92.8	3.3	-	-	91.8	-1.1	-	-	94.6	3.1	-	-	96.1	1.6	-	-	97.3	1.2	-	-
1981	95.4	-2.0	-	-	98.4	3.1	-	-	97.3	-1.1	-	-	97.0	-0.3	-	-	99.3	2.4	-	-	99.7	0.4	-	-
1982	97.3	-2.4	-	-	100.1	2.9	-	-	100.1	0.0	-	-	98.1	-2.0	-	-	102.6	4.6	-	-	100.4	-2.1	-	-
1983	96.3	-4.1	-	-	101.0	4.9	-	-	102.5	1.5	-	-	101.9	-0.6	-	-	103.4	1.5	-	-	100.3	-3.0	-	-
1984	97.2	-3.1	-	-	100.5	3.4	-	-	98.2	-2.3	-	-	98.0	-0.2	-	-	101.6	3.7	-	-	100.8	-0.8	-	-
1985	96.6	-4.2	-	-	104.7	8.4	-	-	101.0	-3.5	-	-	101.5	0.5	-	-	107.9	6.3	-	-	103.1	-4.4	-	-
1986	99.0	-4.0	-	-	103.0	4.0	-	-	103.4	0.4	-	-	102.9	-0.5	-	-	106.7	3.7	-	-	107.0	0.3	103.9	-2.9
1987	-	-	-	-	-	-	-	-	-	-	98.5	-5.2	-	-	-	-	-	-	-	-	-	-	105.2	6.8
1988	-	-	-	-	-	-	-	-	-	-	109.3	3.9	-	-	-	-	-	-	-	-	-	-	114.8	5.0
1989	-	-	-	-	-	-	-	-	-	-	114.7	-0.1	-	-	-	-	-	-	-	-	-	-	114.1	-0.5
1990	-	-	-	-	-	-	-	-	-	-	118.7	4.0	-	-	-	-	-	-	-	-	-	-	123.2	3.8
1991	-	-	-	-	-	-	-	-	-	-	124.6	1.1	-	-	-	-	-	-	-	-	-	-	122.6	-1.6
1992	-	-	-	-	-	-	-	-	-	-	124.6	1.6	-	-	-	-	-	-	-	-	-	-	125.6	0.8
1993	-	-	-	-	-	-	-	-	-	-	125.4	-0.2	-	-	-	-	-	-	-	-	-	-	120.6	-3.8
1994	-	-	-	-	-	-	-	-	-	-	124.6	3.3	-	-	-	-	-	-	-	-	-	-	123.1	-1.2

[Continued]

Seattle-Everett, WA
Consumer Price Index - Urban Wage Earners
Base 1982-1984 = 100
Apparel and Upkeep
[Continued]

For 1952-1997. Columns headed % show percentile change in the index from the previous period for which an index is available.

Year	Jan		Feb		Mar		Apr		May		Jun		Jul		Aug		Sep		Oct		Nov		Dec	
	Index	%	Index	%	Index	%	Index	%	Index	%	Index	%	Index	%	Index	%	Index	%	Index	%	Index	%	Index	%
1995	-	-	-	-	-	-	-	-	-	-	128.0	4.0	-	-	-	-	-	-	-	-	-	-	120.5	-5.9
1996	-	-	-	-	-	-	-	-	-	-	123.6	2.6	-	-	-	-	-	-	-	-	-	-	127.2	2.9
1997	-	-	-	-	-	-	-	-	-	-	129.1	1.5	-	-	-	-	-	-	-	-	-	-	-	-

Source: U.S. Department of Labor, Bureau of Labor Statistics, Division of Consumer Prices and Price Indexes. - indicates no data collected for period.

Seattle-Everett, WA
Consumer Price Index - All Urban Consumers
Base 1982-1984 = 100
Transportation

For 1947-1997. Columns headed % show percentile change in the index from the previous period for which an index is available.

Year	Jan Index	%	Feb Index	%	Mar Index	%	Apr Index	%	May Index	%	Jun Index	%	Jul Index	%	Aug Index	%	Sep Index	%	Oct Index	%	Nov Index	%	Dec Index	%
1947	18.7	-	18.7	0.0	18.8	0.5	18.9	0.5	18.9	0.0	18.9	0.0	-	-	19.1	1.1	-	-	-	-	19.5	2.1	-	-
1948	-	-	20.4	4.6	-	-	-	-	20.4	0.0	-	-	-	-	21.1	3.4	-	-	-	-	21.4	1.4	-	-
1949	-	-	21.6	0.9	-	-	-	-	22.0	1.9	-	-	-	-	22.6	2.7	-	-	-	-	22.6	0.0	-	-
1950	-	-	22.8	0.9	-	-	-	-	22.3	-2.2	-	-	-	-	22.6	1.3	-	-	-	-	23.7	4.9	-	-
1951	-	-	23.8	0.4	-	-	-	-	24.0	0.8	-	-	-	-	24.2	0.8	-	-	-	-	24.8	2.5	-	-
1952	-	-	25.0	0.8	-	-	-	-	25.2	0.8	-	-	-	-	25.2	0.0	-	-	-	-	26.8	6.3	-	-
1953	-	-	26.9	0.4	-	-	-	-	27.6	2.6	-	-	-	-	27.6	0.0	-	-	-	-	27.4	-0.7	-	-
1954	-	-	27.5	0.4	-	-	-	-	26.9	-2.2	-	-	-	-	26.6	-1.1	-	-	-	-	26.7	0.4	-	-
1955	-	-	26.6	-0.4	-	-	-	-	26.2	-1.5	-	-	-	-	26.1	-0.4	-	-	-	-	26.9	3.1	-	-
1956	-	-	25.8	-4.1	-	-	-	-	25.9	0.4	-	-	-	-	26.7	3.1	-	-	-	-	27.6	3.4	-	-
1957	-	-	28.4	2.9	-	-	-	-	28.6	0.7	-	-	-	-	28.1	-1.7	-	-	-	-	29.2	3.9	-	-
1958	-	-	29.1	-0.3	-	-	-	-	29.4	1.0	-	-	-	-	30.1	2.4	-	-	-	-	29.9	-0.7	-	-
1959	-	-	30.7	2.7	-	-	-	-	30.8	0.3	-	-	-	-	32.0	3.9	-	-	-	-	31.0	-3.1	-	-
1960	-	-	30.3	-2.3	-	-	-	-	31.0	2.3	-	-	-	-	30.7	-1.0	-	-	-	-	31.0	1.0	-	-
1961	-	-	30.9	-0.3	-	-	-	-	31.4	1.6	-	-	-	-	31.8	1.3	-	-	-	-	32.6	2.5	-	-
1962	-	-	32.3	-0.9	-	-	-	-	32.5	0.6	-	-	-	-	32.6	0.3	-	-	-	-	33.0	1.2	-	-
1963	-	-	32.3	-2.1	-	-	-	-	32.2	-0.3	-	-	-	-	32.9	2.2	-	-	-	-	32.4	-1.5	-	-
1964	-	-	32.4	0.0	-	-	-	-	31.8	-1.9	-	-	-	-	33.5	5.3	-	-	-	-	32.8	-2.1	-	-
1965	-	-	32.4	-1.2	-	-	-	-	33.9	4.6	-	-	-	-	33.8	-0.3	-	-	-	-	33.8	0.0	-	-
1966	-	-	33.7	-0.3	-	-	-	-	33.4	-0.9	-	-	-	-	34.1	2.1	-	-	-	-	34.8	2.1	-	-
1967	-	-	34.6	-0.6	-	-	-	-	35.3	2.0	-	-	-	-	35.6	0.8	-	-	-	-	35.7	0.3	-	-
1968	-	-	35.7	0.0	-	-	-	-	35.6	-0.3	-	-	-	-	36.2	1.7	-	-	-	-	36.2	0.0	-	-
1969	-	-	36.3	0.3	-	-	-	-	36.0	-0.8	-	-	-	-	36.5	1.4	-	-	-	-	35.9	-1.6	-	-
1970	-	-	36.9	2.8	-	-	-	-	37.1	0.5	-	-	-	-	37.5	1.1	-	-	-	-	37.1	-1.1	-	-
1971	-	-	37.4	0.8	-	-	-	-	37.6	0.5	-	-	-	-	38.5	2.4	-	-	-	-	37.7	-2.1	-	-
1972	-	-	38.2	1.3	-	-	-	-	38.3	0.3	-	-	-	-	38.7	1.0	-	-	-	-	39.4	1.8	-	-
1973	-	-	39.0	-1.0	-	-	-	-	39.4	1.0	-	-	-	-	39.7	0.8	-	-	-	-	40.0	0.8	-	-
1974	-	-	41.3	3.2	-	-	-	-	43.6	5.6	-	-	-	-	45.4	4.1	-	-	-	-	45.8	0.9	-	-
1975	-	-	46.1	0.7	-	-	-	-	47.5	3.0	-	-	-	-	49.0	3.2	-	-	-	-	49.7	1.4	-	-
1976	-	-	49.7	0.0	-	-	-	-	51.1	2.8	-	-	-	-	52.8	3.3	-	-	-	-	53.3	0.9	-	-
1977	-	-	55.2	3.6	-	-	-	-	56.5	2.4	-	-	-	-	58.3	3.2	-	-	-	-	57.8	-0.9	-	-
1978	58.3	0.9	-	-	58.5	0.3	-	-	60.2	2.9	-	-	61.8	2.7	-	-	63.1	2.1	-	-	63.8	1.1	-	-
1979	64.5	1.1	-	-	66.0	2.3	-	-	69.6	5.5	-	-	72.5	4.2	-	-	74.7	3.0	-	-	76.1	1.9	-	-
1980	78.0	2.5	-	-	81.3	4.2	-	-	82.5	1.5	-	-	83.7	1.5	-	-	84.7	1.2	-	-	85.9	1.4	-	-
1981	86.8	1.0	-	-	91.0	4.8	-	-	93.6	2.9	-	-	96.2	2.8	-	-	97.1	0.9	-	-	97.7	0.6	-	-
1982	98.2	0.5	-	-	97.0	-1.2	-	-	96.6	-0.4	-	-	99.7	3.2	-	-	99.1	-0.6	-	-	97.8	-1.3	-	-
1983	96.4	-1.4	-	-	94.0	-2.5	-	-	96.8	3.0	-	-	100.9	4.2	-	-	102.0	1.1	Oct	-	102.2	0.2	-	-
1984	101.0	-1.2	-	-	99.9	-1.1	-	-	103.8	3.9	-	-	104.5	0.7	-	-	104.0	-0.5	-	-	104.4	0.4	-	-
1985	105.1	0.7	-	-	104.4	-0.7	-	-	105.0	0.6	-	-	105.5	0.5	-	-	104.5	-0.9	-	-	105.1	0.6	-	-
1986	106.5	1.3	-	-	102.9	-3.4	-	-	100.9	-1.9	-	-	100.9	0.0	-	-	100.4	-0.5	-	-	99.7	-0.7	100.4	0.7
1987	-	-	-	-	-	-	-	-	-	-	108.1	7.7	-	-	-	-	-	-	-	-	-	-	110.2	1.9
1988	-	-	-	-	-	-	-	-	-	-	109.7	-0.5	-	-	-	-	-	-	-	-	-	-	111.5	1.6
1989	-	-	-	-	-	-	-	-	-	-	117.8	5.7	-	-	-	-	-	-	-	-	-	-	118.8	0.8
1990	-	-	-	-	-	-	-	-	-	-	120.1	1.1	-	-	-	-	-	-	-	-	-	-	130.8	8.9
1991	-	-	-	-	-	-	-	-	-	-	130.0	-0.6	-	-	-	-	-	-	-	-	-	-	130.1	0.1

[Continued]

Seattle-Everett, WA
Consumer Price Index - All Urban Consumers
Base 1982-1984 = 100
Transportation
[Continued]

For 1947-1997. Columns headed % show percentile change in the index from the previous period for which an index is available.

Year	Jan		Feb		Mar		Apr		May		Jun		Jul		Aug		Sep		Oct		Nov		Dec	
	Index	%	Index	%	Index	%	Index	%	Index	%	Index	%	Index	%	Index	%	Index	%	Index	%	Index	%	Index	%
1992	-	-	-	-	-	-	-	-	-	-	131.7	1.2	-	-	-	-	-	-	-	-	-	-	136.4	3.6
1993	-	-	-	-	-	-	-	-	-	-	135.5	-0.7	-	-	-	-	-	-	-	-	-	-	136.9	1.0
1994	-	-	-	-	-	-	-	-	-	-	136.6	-0.2	-	-	-	-	-	-	-	-	-	-	140.6	2.9
1995	-	-	-	-	-	-	-	-	-	-	141.6	0.7	-	-	-	-	-	-	-	-	-	-	142.2	0.4
1996	-	-	-	-	-	-	-	-	-	-	145.1	2.0	-	-	-	-	-	-	-	-	-	-	148.9	2.6
1997	-	-	-	-	-	-	-	-	-	-	150.8	1.3	-	-	-	-	-	-	-	-	-	-	-	-

Source: U.S. Department of Labor, Bureau of Labor Statistics, Division of Consumer Prices and Price Indexes. - indicates no data collected for period.

Seattle-Everett, WA
Consumer Price Index - Urban Wage Earners
Base 1982-1984 = 100
Transportation

For 1947-1997. Columns headed % show percentile change in the index from the previous period for which an index is available.

Year	Jan Index	%	Feb Index	%	Mar Index	%	Apr Index	%	May Index	%	Jun Index	%	Jul Index	%	Aug Index	%	Sep Index	%	Oct Index	%	Nov Index	%	Dec Index	%
1947	19.1	-	19.1	0.0	19.2	0.5	19.2	0.0	19.3	0.5	19.3	0.0	-	-	19.5	1.0	-	-	-	-	19.9	2.1	-	-
1948	-	-	20.8	4.5	-	-	-	-	20.8	0.0	-	-	-	-	21.5	3.4	-	-	-	-	21.8	1.4	-	-
1949	-	-	22.0	0.9	-	-	-	-	22.5	2.3	-	-	-	-	23.0	2.2	-	-	-	-	23.1	0.4	-	-
1950	-	-	23.3	0.9	-	-	-	-	22.8	-2.1	-	-	-	-	23.1	1.3	-	-	-	-	24.1	4.3	-	-
1951	-	-	24.3	0.8	-	-	-	-	24.5	0.8	-	-	-	-	24.6	0.4	-	-	-	-	25.3	2.8	-	-
1952	-	-	25.5	0.8	-	-	-	-	25.8	1.2	-	-	-	-	25.8	0.0	-	-	-	-	27.4	6.2	-	-
1953	-	-	27.4	0.0	-	-	-	-	28.2	2.9	-	-	-	-	28.1	-0.4	-	-	-	-	28.0	-0.4	-	-
1954	-	-	28.1	0.4	-	-	-	-	27.4	-2.5	-	-	-	-	27.1	-1.1	-	-	-	-	27.2	0.4	-	-
1955	-	-	27.1	-0.4	-	-	-	-	26.8	-1.1	-	-	-	-	26.6	-0.7	-	-	-	-	27.4	3.0	-	-
1956	-	-	26.3	-4.0	-	-	-	-	26.4	0.4	-	-	-	-	27.2	3.0	-	-	-	-	28.2	3.7	-	-
1957	-	-	29.0	2.8	-	-	-	-	29.2	0.7	-	-	-	-	28.7	-1.7	-	-	-	-	29.8	3.8	-	-
1958	-	-	29.7	-0.3	-	-	-	-	30.0	1.0	-	-	-	-	30.7	2.3	-	-	-	-	30.5	-0.7	-	-
1959	-	-	31.3	2.6	-	-	-	-	31.4	0.3	-	-	-	-	32.7	4.1	-	-	-	-	31.6	-3.4	-	-
1960	-	-	30.9	-2.2	-	-	-	-	31.6	2.3	-	-	-	-	31.3	-0.9	-	-	-	-	31.6	1.0	-	-
1961	-	-	31.5	-0.3	-	-	-	-	32.1	1.9	-	-	-	-	32.4	0.9	-	-	-	-	33.3	2.8	-	-
1962	-	-	33.0	-0.9	-	-	-	-	33.2	0.6	-	-	-	-	33.3	0.3	-	-	-	-	33.7	1.2	-	-
1963	-	-	33.0	-2.1	-	-	-	-	32.8	-0.6	-	-	-	-	33.6	2.4	-	-	-	-	33.0	-1.8	-	-
1964	-	-	33.1	0.3	-	-	-	-	32.5	-1.8	-	-	-	-	34.2	5.2	-	-	-	-	33.5	-2.0	-	-
1965	-	-	33.1	-1.2	-	-	-	-	34.6	4.5	-	-	-	-	34.5	-0.3	-	-	-	-	34.5	0.0	-	-
1966	-	-	34.4	-0.3	-	-	-	-	34.1	-0.9	-	-	-	-	34.8	2.1	-	-	-	-	35.6	2.3	-	-
1967	-	-	35.3	-0.8	-	-	-	-	36.1	2.3	-	-	-	-	36.3	0.6	-	-	-	-	36.4	0.3	-	-
1968	-	-	36.5	0.3	-	-	-	-	36.3	-0.5	-	-	-	-	36.9	1.7	-	-	-	-	37.0	0.3	-	-
1969	-	-	37.0	0.0	-	-	-	-	36.8	-0.5	-	-	-	-	37.3	1.4	-	-	-	-	36.6	-1.9	-	-
1970	-	-	37.7	3.0	-	-	-	-	37.9	0.5	-	-	-	-	38.3	1.1	-	-	-	-	37.8	-1.3	-	-
1971	-	-	38.2	1.1	-	-	-	-	38.3	0.3	-	-	-	-	39.3	2.6	-	-	-	-	38.4	-2.3	-	-
1972	-	-	39.0	1.6	-	-	-	-	39.1	0.3	-	-	-	-	39.5	1.0	-	-	-	-	40.2	1.8	-	-
1973	-	-	39.9	-0.7	-	-	-	-	40.2	0.8	-	-	-	-	40.5	0.7	-	-	-	-	40.9	1.0	-	-
1974	-	-	42.2	3.2	-	-	-	-	44.5	5.5	-	-	-	-	46.3	4.0	-	-	-	-	46.7	0.9	-	-
1975	-	-	47.1	0.9	-	-	-	-	48.5	3.0	-	-	-	-	50.1	3.3	-	-	-	-	50.7	1.2	-	-
1976	-	-	50.7	0.0	-	-	-	-	52.1	2.8	-	-	-	-	53.9	3.5	-	-	-	-	54.4	0.9	-	-
1977	-	-	56.4	3.7	-	-	-	-	57.7	2.3	-	-	-	-	59.5	3.1	-	-	-	-	59.0	-0.8	-	-
1978	59.0	0.0	-	-	59.2	0.3	-	-	60.6	2.4	-	-	62.2	2.6	-	-	62.8	1.0	-	-	63.5	1.1	-	-
1979	64.2	1.1	-	-	65.9	2.6	-	-	69.4	5.3	-	-	72.2	4.0	-	-	74.3	2.9	-	-	75.7	1.9	-	-
1980	77.2	2.0	-	-	80.9	4.8	-	-	81.9	1.2	-	-	82.7	1.0	-	-	83.8	1.3	-	-	85.3	1.8	-	-
1981	86.4	1.3	-	-	89.8	3.9	-	-	92.6	3.1	-	-	95.2	2.8	-	-	95.8	0.6	-	-	97.6	1.9	-	-
1982	98.1	0.5	-	-	96.8	-1.3	-	-	96.4	-0.4	-	-	99.5	3.2	-	-	98.8	-0.7	-	-	97.7	-1.1	-	-
1983	96.2	-1.5	-	-	93.9	-2.4	-	-	96.8	3.1	-	-	101.0	4.3	-	-	102.2	1.2	-	-	102.3	0.1	-	-
1984	101.2	-1.1	-	-	100.2	-1.0	-	-	103.9	3.7	-	-	104.5	0.6	-	-	104.1	-0.4	-	-	104.7	0.6	-	-
1985	105.4	0.7	-	-	104.7	-0.7	-	-	105.5	0.8	-	-	105.9	0.4	-	-	105.0	-0.8	-	-	105.6	0.6	-	-
1986	106.7	1.0	-	-	103.1	-3.4	-	-	101.0	-2.0	-	-	101.0	0.0	-	-	100.5	-0.5	-	-	99.8	-0.7	100.2	0.4
1987	-	-	-	-	-	-	-	-	-	-	108.3	8.1	-	-	-	-	-	-	-	-	-	-	110.2	1.8
1988	-	-	-	-	-	-	-	-	-	-	109.9	-0.3	-	-	-	-	-	-	-	-	-	-	111.5	1.5
1989	-	-	-	-	-	-	-	-	-	-	117.4	5.3	-	-	-	-	-	-	-	-	-	-	118.3	0.8
1990	-	-	-	-	-	-	-	-	-	-	119.3	0.8	-	-	-	-	-	-	-	-	-	-	129.1	8.2
1991	-	-	-	-	-	-	-	-	-	-	128.9	-0.2	-	-	-	-	-	-	-	-	-	-	129.3	0.3

[Continued]

Seattle-Everett, WA
Consumer Price Index - Urban Wage Earners
Base 1982-1984 = 100
Transportation
[Continued]

For 1947-1997. Columns headed % show percentile change in the index from the previous period for which an index is available.

Year	Jan		Feb		Mar		Apr		May		Jun		Jul		Aug		Sep		Oct		Nov		Dec	
	Index	%	Index	%	Index	%	Index	%	Index	%	Index	%	Index	%	Index	%	Index	%	Index	%	Index	%	Index	%
1992	-	-	-	-	-	-	-	-	-	-	130.8	1.2	-	-	-	-	-	-	-	-	-	-	135.4	3.5
1993	-	-	-	-	-	-	-	-	-	-	135.1	-0.2	-	-	-	-	-	-	-	-	-	-	137.0	1.4
1994	-	-	-	-	-	-	-	-	-	-	136.7	-0.2	-	-	-	-	-	-	-	-	-	-	141.0	3.1
1995	-	-	-	-	-	-	-	-	-	-	142.5	1.1	-	-	-	-	-	-	-	-	-	-	143.5	0.7
1996	-	-	-	-	-	-	-	-	-	-	146.5	2.1	-	-	-	-	-	-	-	-	-	-	149.9	2.3
1997	-	-	-	-	-	-	-	-	-	-	151.9	1.3	-	-	-	-	-	-	-	-	-	-	-	-

Source: U.S. Department of Labor, Bureau of Labor Statistics, Division of Consumer Prices and Price Indexes. - indicates no data collected for period.

Seattle-Everett, WA
Consumer Price Index - All Urban Consumers
Base 1982-1984 = 100
Medical Care

For 1947-1997. Columns headed % show percentile change in the index from the previous period for which an index is available.

Year	Jan Index	%	Feb Index	%	Mar Index	%	Apr Index	%	May Index	%	Jun Index	%	Jul Index	%	Aug Index	%	Sep Index	%	Oct Index	%	Nov Index	%	Dec Index	%
1947	14.1	-	14.3	1.4	14.3	0.0	14.4	0.7	14.4	0.0	14.4	0.0	-	-	14.4	0.0	-	-	-	-	14.6	1.4	-	-
1948	-	-	14.7	0.7	-	-	-	-	15.0	2.0	-	-	-	-	15.3	2.0	-	-	-	-	15.6	2.0	-	-
1949	-	-	15.6	0.0	-	-	-	-	15.9	1.9	-	-	-	-	15.9	0.0	-	-	-	-	16.0	0.6	-	-
1950	-	-	16.0	0.0	-	-	-	-	16.0	0.0	-	-	-	-	16.0	0.0	-	-	-	-	16.1	0.6	-	-
1951	-	-	16.6	3.1	-	-	-	-	17.1	3.0	-	-	-	-	17.2	0.6	-	-	-	-	17.4	1.2	-	-
1952	-	-	17.8	2.3	-	-	-	-	18.3	2.8	-	-	-	-	18.7	2.2	-	-	-	-	18.7	0.0	-	-
1953	-	-	18.7	0.0	-	-	-	-	18.9	1.1	-	-	-	-	19.0	0.5	-	-	-	-	19.6	3.2	-	-
1954	-	-	19.6	0.0	-	-	-	-	19.8	1.0	-	-	-	-	19.6	-1.0	-	-	-	-	19.7	0.5	-	-
1955	-	-	19.8	0.5	-	-	-	-	19.8	0.0	-	-	-	-	19.9	0.5	-	-	-	-	21.1	6.0	-	-
1956	-	-	20.4	-3.3	-	-	-	-	20.5	0.5	-	-	-	-	20.8	1.5	-	-	-	-	20.7	-0.5	-	-
1957	-	-	20.9	1.0	-	-	-	-	21.0	0.5	-	-	-	-	21.6	2.9	-	-	-	-	21.7	0.5	-	-
1958	-	-	22.1	1.8	-	-	-	-	22.2	0.5	-	-	-	-	22.4	0.9	-	-	-	-	22.5	0.4	-	-
1959	-	-	22.6	0.4	-	-	-	-	22.6	0.0	-	-	-	-	22.9	1.3	-	-	-	-	23.3	1.7	-	-
1960	-	-	23.9	2.6	-	-	-	-	23.9	0.0	-	-	-	-	24.1	0.8	-	-	-	-	23.9	-0.8	-	-
1961	-	-	23.9	0.0	-	-	-	-	24.0	0.4	-	-	-	-	24.0	0.0	-	-	-	-	24.1	0.4	-	-
1962	-	-	24.2	0.4	-	-	-	-	24.3	0.4	-	-	-	-	24.4	0.4	-	-	-	-	24.4	0.0	-	-
1963	-	-	24.4	0.0	-	-	-	-	24.5	0.4	-	-	-	-	24.6	0.4	-	-	-	-	24.6	0.0	-	-
1964	-	-	24.6	0.0	-	-	-	-	24.9	1.2	-	-	-	-	25.1	0.8	-	-	-	-	25.2	0.4	-	-
1965	-	-	25.4	0.8	-	-	-	-	25.9	2.0	-	-	-	-	26.1	0.8	-	-	-	-	26.6	1.9	-	-
1966	-	-	26.8	0.8	-	-	-	-	27.3	1.9	-	-	-	-	27.8	1.8	-	-	-	-	28.5	2.5	-	-
1967	-	-	28.5	0.0	-	-	-	-	28.8	1.1	-	-	-	-	29.3	1.7	-	-	-	-	29.8	1.7	-	-
1968	-	-	30.1	1.0	-	-	-	-	30.6	1.7	-	-	-	-	31.1	1.6	-	-	-	-	31.5	1.3	-	-
1969	-	-	32.1	1.9	-	-	-	-	32.7	1.9	-	-	-	-	33.3	1.8	-	-	-	-	33.5	0.6	-	-
1970	-	-	34.0	1.5	-	-	-	-	34.3	0.9	-	-	-	-	34.7	1.2	-	-	-	-	34.8	0.3	-	-
1971	-	-	35.4	1.7	-	-	-	-	35.6	0.6	-	-	-	-	36.1	1.4	-	-	-	-	36.0	-0.3	-	-
1972	-	-	36.2	0.6	-	-	-	-	36.4	0.6	-	-	-	-	36.7	0.8	-	-	-	-	36.7	0.0	-	-
1973	-	-	37.2	1.4	-	-	-	-	37.4	0.5	-	-	-	-	37.9	1.3	-	-	-	-	38.6	1.8	-	-
1974	-	-	39.4	2.1	-	-	-	-	40.7	3.3	-	-	-	-	41.7	2.5	-	-	-	-	42.8	2.6	-	-
1975	-	-	44.8	4.7	-	-	-	-	45.7	2.0	-	-	-	-	46.7	2.2	-	-	-	-	47.4	1.5	-	-
1976	-	-	49.4	4.2	-	-	-	-	50.5	2.2	-	-	-	-	51.1	1.2	-	-	-	-	52.8	3.3	-	-
1977	-	-	54.6	3.4	-	-	-	-	55.5	1.6	-	-	-	-	56.4	1.6	-	-	-	-	57.3	1.6	-	-
1978	60.6	5.8	-	-	60.7	0.2	-	-	61.3	1.0	-	-	62.4	1.8	-	-	62.8	0.6	-	-	64.0	1.9	-	-
1979	64.7	1.1	-	-	66.1	2.2	-	-	66.3	0.3	-	-	67.4	1.7	-	-	68.1	1.0	-	-	69.8	2.5	-	-
1980	72.6	4.0	-	-	73.9	1.8	-	-	75.1	1.6	-	-	76.4	1.7	-	-	76.4	0.0	-	-	78.4	2.6	-	-
1981	81.2	3.6	-	-	83.2	2.5	-	-	83.8	0.7	-	-	85.3	1.8	-	-	86.1	0.9	-	-	87.5	1.6	-	-
1982	89.7	2.5	-	-	91.7	2.2	-	-	92.4	0.8	-	-	93.8	1.5	-	-	94.8	1.1	-	-	96.1	1.4	-	-
1983	99.5	3.5	-	-	101.1	1.6	-	-	100.6	-0.5	-	-	101.3	0.7	-	-	101.3	0.0	-	-	100.7	-0.6	-	-
1984	103.2	2.5	-	-	104.6	1.4	-	-	104.7	0.1	-	-	105.7	1.0	-	-	106.5	0.8	-	-	107.4	0.8	-	-
1985	109.7	2.1	-	-	111.9	2.0	-	-	112.3	0.4	-	-	113.1	0.7	-	-	113.2	0.1	-	-	112.1	-1.0	-	-
1986	113.2	1.0	-	-	116.0	2.5	-	-	116.0	0.0	-	-	118.9	2.5	-	-	119.9	0.8	-	-	119.6	-0.3	120.5	0.8
1987	-	-	-	-	-	-	-	-	-	-	123.7	2.7	-	-	-	-	-	-	-	-	-	-	129.8	4.9
1988	-	-	-	-	-	-	-	-	-	-	136.2	4.9	-	-	-	-	-	-	-	-	-	-	141.3	3.7
1989	-	-	-	-	-	-	-	-	-	-	143.9	1.8	-	-	-	-	-	-	-	-	-	-	146.5	1.8
1990	-	-	-	-	-	-	-	-	-	-	152.0	3.8	-	-	-	-	-	-	-	-	-	-	156.7	3.1
1991	-	-	-	-	-	-	-	-	-	-	163.5	4.3	-	-	-	-	-	-	-	-	-	-	168.4	3.0

[Continued]

Seattle-Everett, WA
Consumer Price Index - All Urban Consumers
Base 1982-1984 = 100
Medical Care
[Continued]

For 1947-1997. Columns headed % show percentile change in the index from the previous period for which an index is available.

Year	Jan Index	%	Feb Index	%	Mar Index	%	Apr Index	%	May Index	%	Jun Index	%	Jul Index	%	Aug Index	%	Sep Index	%	Oct Index	%	Nov Index	%	Dec Index	%
1992	-	-	-	-	-	-	-	-	-	-	174.5	3.6	-	-	-	-	-	-	-	-	-	-	178.2	2.1
1993	-	-	-	-	-	-	-	-	-	-	184.8	3.7	-	-	-	-	-	-	-	-	-	-	188.4	1.9
1994	-	-	-	-	-	-	-	-	-	-	190.8	1.3	-	-	-	-	-	-	-	-	-	-	194.7	2.0
1995	-	-	-	-	-	-	-	-	-	-	195.9	0.6	-	-	-	-	-	-	-	-	-	-	200.2	2.2
1996	-	-	-	-	-	-	-	-	-	-	210.2	5.0	-	-	-	-	-	-	-	-	-	-	213.5	1.6
1997	-	-	-	-	-	-	-	-	-	-	216.6	1.5	-	-	-	-	-	-	-	-	-	-	-	-

Source: U.S. Department of Labor, Bureau of Labor Statistics, Division of Consumer Prices and Price Indexes. - indicates no data collected for period.

Seattle-Everett, WA
Consumer Price Index - Urban Wage Earners
Base 1982-1984 = 100
Medical Care

For 1947-1997. Columns headed % show percentile change in the index from the previous period for which an index is available.

Year	Jan Index	%	Feb Index	%	Mar Index	%	Apr Index	%	May Index	%	Jun Index	%	Jul Index	%	Aug Index	%	Sep Index	%	Oct Index	%	Nov Index	%	Dec Index	%
1947	14.0	-	14.2	1.4	14.2	0.0	14.2	0.0	14.2	0.0	14.3	0.7	-	-	14.3	0.0	-	-	-	-	14.5	1.4	-	-
1948	-	-	14.6	0.7	-	-	-	-	14.8	1.4	-	-	-	-	15.2	2.7	-	-	-	-	15.4	1.3	-	-
1949	-	-	15.4	0.0	-	-	-	-	15.7	1.9	-	-	-	-	15.7	0.0	-	-	-	-	15.9	1.3	-	-
1950	-	-	15.9	0.0	-	-	-	-	15.9	0.0	-	-	-	-	15.9	0.0	-	-	-	-	16.0	0.6	-	-
1951	-	-	16.4	2.5	-	-	-	-	17.0	3.7	-	-	-	-	17.0	0.0	-	-	-	-	17.2	1.2	-	-
1952	-	-	17.7	2.9	-	-	-	-	18.1	2.3	-	-	-	-	18.5	2.2	-	-	-	-	18.5	0.0	-	-
1953	-	-	18.5	0.0	-	-	-	-	18.7	1.1	-	-	-	-	18.8	0.5	-	-	-	-	19.4	3.2	-	-
1954	-	-	19.4	0.0	-	-	-	-	19.6	1.0	-	-	-	-	19.4	-1.0	-	-	-	-	19.5	0.5	-	-
1955	-	-	19.6	0.5	-	-	-	-	19.6	0.0	-	-	-	-	19.7	0.5	-	-	-	-	20.9	6.1	-	-
1956	-	-	20.2	-3.3	-	-	-	-	20.3	0.5	-	-	-	-	20.6	1.5	-	-	-	-	20.5	-0.5	-	-
1957	-	-	20.7	1.0	-	-	-	-	20.8	0.5	-	-	-	-	21.4	2.9	-	-	-	-	21.5	0.5	-	-
1958	-	-	21.9	1.9	-	-	-	-	22.0	0.5	-	-	-	-	22.2	0.9	-	-	-	-	22.3	0.5	-	-
1959	-	-	22.4	0.4	-	-	-	-	22.4	0.0	-	-	-	-	22.7	1.3	-	-	-	-	23.1	1.8	-	-
1960	-	-	23.7	2.6	-	-	-	-	23.7	0.0	-	-	-	-	23.9	0.8	-	-	-	-	23.7	-0.8	-	-
1961	-	-	23.7	0.0	-	-	-	-	23.8	0.4	-	-	-	-	23.8	0.0	-	-	-	-	23.9	0.4	-	-
1962	-	-	24.0	0.4	-	-	-	-	24.1	0.4	-	-	-	-	24.1	0.0	-	-	-	-	24.2	0.4	-	-
1963	-	-	24.2	0.0	-	-	-	-	24.3	0.4	-	-	-	-	24.4	0.4	-	-	-	-	24.4	0.0	-	-
1964	-	-	24.4	0.0	-	-	-	-	24.6	0.8	-	-	-	-	24.8	0.8	-	-	-	-	25.0	0.8	-	-
1965	-	-	25.2	0.8	-	-	-	-	25.6	1.6	-	-	-	-	25.8	0.8	-	-	-	-	26.4	2.3	-	-
1966	-	-	26.6	0.8	-	-	-	-	27.0	1.5	-	-	-	-	27.5	1.9	-	-	-	-	28.3	2.9	-	-
1967	-	-	28.2	-0.4	-	-	-	-	28.5	1.1	-	-	-	-	29.1	2.1	-	-	-	-	29.5	1.4	-	-
1968	-	-	29.9	1.4	-	-	-	-	30.3	1.3	-	-	-	-	30.8	1.7	-	-	-	-	31.2	1.3	-	-
1969	-	-	31.8	1.9	-	-	-	-	32.4	1.9	-	-	-	-	33.0	1.9	-	-	-	-	33.2	0.6	-	-
1970	-	-	33.6	1.2	-	-	-	-	34.0	1.2	-	-	-	-	34.4	1.2	-	-	-	-	34.5	0.3	-	-
1971	-	-	35.0	1.4	-	-	-	-	35.3	0.9	-	-	-	-	35.8	1.4	-	-	-	-	35.7	-0.3	-	-
1972	-	-	35.9	0.6	-	-	-	-	36.1	0.6	-	-	-	-	36.4	0.8	-	-	-	-	36.3	-0.3	-	-
1973	-	-	36.9	1.7	-	-	-	-	37.1	0.5	-	-	-	-	37.6	1.3	-	-	-	-	38.3	1.9	-	-
1974	-	-	39.1	2.1	-	-	-	-	40.3	3.1	-	-	-	-	41.3	2.5	-	-	-	-	42.4	2.7	-	-
1975	-	-	44.3	4.5	-	-	-	-	45.2	2.0	-	-	-	-	46.3	2.4	-	-	-	-	47.0	1.5	-	-
1976	-	-	48.9	4.0	-	-	-	-	50.0	2.2	-	-	-	-	50.6	1.2	-	-	-	-	52.3	3.4	-	-
1977	-	-	54.0	3.3	-	-	-	-	55.0	1.9	-	-	-	-	55.8	1.5	-	-	-	-	56.8	1.8	-	-
1978	59.0	3.9	-	-	59.2	0.3	-	-	60.1	1.5	-	-	61.2	1.8	-	-	61.5	0.5	-	-	63.9	3.9	-	-
1979	64.6	1.1	-	-	65.5	1.4	-	-	66.2	1.1	-	-	67.8	2.4	-	-	68.2	0.6	-	-	69.9	2.5	-	-
1980	72.4	3.6	-	-	73.2	1.1	-	-	74.6	1.9	-	-	74.4	-0.3	-	-	76.0	2.2	-	-	78.0	2.6	-	-
1981	79.9	2.4	-	-	81.4	1.9	-	-	82.9	1.8	-	-	84.1	1.4	-	-	86.2	2.5	-	-	87.9	2.0	-	-
1982	89.8	2.2	-	-	91.7	2.1	-	-	92.4	0.8	-	-	93.8	1.5	-	-	94.5	0.7	-	-	95.9	1.5	-	-
1983	99.2	3.4	-	-	100.7	1.5	-	-	100.5	-0.2	-	-	101.3	0.8	-	-	101.2	-0.1	-	-	100.9	-0.3	-	-
1984	103.2	2.3	-	-	104.7	1.5	-	-	104.9	0.2	-	-	106.0	1.0	-	-	106.9	0.8	-	-	107.5	0.6	-	-
1985	109.9	2.2	-	-	112.2	2.1	-	-	112.5	0.3	-	-	113.3	0.7	-	-	113.6	0.3	-	-	112.8	-0.7	-	-
1986	114.0	1.1	-	-	116.9	2.5	-	-	116.8	-0.1	-	-	119.8	2.6	-	-	120.7	0.8	-	-	120.4	-0.2	121.5	0.9
1987	-	-	-	-	-	-	-	-	-	-	123.3	1.5	-	-	-	-	-	-	-	-	-	-	129.5	5.0
1988	-	-	-	-	-	-	-	-	-	-	135.7	4.8	-	-	-	-	-	-	-	-	-	-	140.9	3.8
1989	-	-	-	-	-	-	-	-	-	-	143.6	1.9	-	-	-	-	-	-	-	-	-	-	145.9	1.6
1990	-	-	-	-	-	-	-	-	-	-	151.0	3.5	-	-	-	-	-	-	-	-	-	-	155.3	2.8
1991	-	-	-	-	-	-	-	-	-	-	161.8	4.2	-	-	-	-	-	-	-	-	-	-	166.8	3.1

[Continued]

Seattle-Everett, WA
Consumer Price Index - Urban Wage Earners
Base 1982-1984 = 100
Medical Care
[Continued]

For 1947-1997. Columns headed % show percentile change in the index from the previous period for which an index is available.

Year	Jan		Feb		Mar		Apr		May		Jun		Jul		Aug		Sep		Oct		Nov		Dec	
	Index	%	Index	%	Index	%	Index	%	Index	%	Index	%	Index	%	Index	%	Index	%	Index	%	Index	%	Index	%
1992	-	-	-	-	-	-	-	-	-	-	173.0	3.7	-	-	-	-	-	-	-	-	-	-	176.8	2.2
1993	-	-	-	-	-	-	-	-	-	-	183.1	3.6	-	-	-	-	-	-	-	-	-	-	186.8	2.0
1994	-	-	-	-	-	-	-	-	-	-	189.0	1.2	-	-	-	-	-	-	-	-	-	-	193.3	2.3
1995	-	-	-	-	-	-	-	-	-	-	194.7	0.7	-	-	-	-	-	-	-	-	-	-	199.3	2.4
1996	-	-	-	-	-	-	-	-	-	-	208.9	4.8	-	-	-	-	-	-	-	-	-	-	212.3	1.6
1997	-	-	-	-	-	-	-	-	-	-	215.5	1.5	-	-	-	-	-	-	-	-	-	-	-	-

Source: U.S. Department of Labor, Bureau of Labor Statistics, Division of Consumer Prices and Price Indexes. - indicates no data collected for period.

Seattle-Everett, WA
Consumer Price Index - All Urban Consumers
Base 1982-1984 = 100
Entertainment

For 1975-1997. Columns headed % show percentile change in the index from the previous period for which an index is available.

Year	Jan Index	%	Feb Index	%	Mar Index	%	Apr Index	%	May Index	%	Jun Index	%	Jul Index	%	Aug Index	%	Sep Index	%	Oct Index	%	Nov Index	%	Dec Index	%
1975	-	-	-	-	-	-	-	-	-	-	-	-	-	-	-	-	-	-	-	-	61.1	-	-	-
1976	-	-	61.2	0.2	-	-	-	-	61.7	0.8	-	-	-	-	62.1	0.6	-	-	-	-	63.4	2.1	-	-
1977	-	-	65.2	2.8	-	-	-	-	65.1	-0.2	-	-	-	-	65.2	0.2	-	-	-	-	66.5	2.0	-	-
1978	66.6	0.2	-	-	67.2	0.9	-	-	68.4	1.8	-	-	68.9	0.7	-	-	69.0	0.1	-	-	69.9	1.3	-	-
1979	70.1	0.3	-	-	70.3	0.3	-	-	72.8	3.6	-	-	73.3	0.7	-	-	75.5	3.0	-	-	76.2	0.9	-	-
1980	77.3	1.4	-	-	79.1	2.3	-	-	80.2	1.4	-	-	81.9	2.1	-	-	84.6	3.3	-	-	86.4	2.1	-	-
1981	87.0	0.7	-	-	86.6	-0.5	-	-	87.8	1.4	-	-	87.4	-0.5	-	-	89.4	2.3	-	-	89.6	0.2	-	-
1982	91.5	2.1	-	-	90.9	-0.7	-	-	93.3	2.6	-	-	94.0	0.8	-	-	96.1	2.2	-	-	95.9	-0.2	-	-
1983	96.9	1.0	-	-	99.4	2.6	-	-	97.6	-1.8	-	-	99.7	2.2	-	-	101.6	1.9	-	-	102.5	0.9	-	-
1984	105.1	2.5	-	-	105.9	0.8	-	-	106.4	0.5	-	-	106.3	-0.1	-	-	105.2	-1.0	-	-	107.6	2.3	-	-
1985	108.0	0.4	-	-	108.1	0.1	-	-	107.6	-0.5	-	-	109.6	1.9	-	-	107.6	-1.8	-	-	109.4	1.7	-	-
1986	110.3	0.8	-	-	109.0	-1.2	-	-	107.4	-1.5	-	-	109.2	1.7	-	-	107.6	-1.5	-	-	108.6	0.9	108.6	0.0
1987	-	-	-	-	-	-	-	-	-	-	115.5	6.4	-	-	-	-	-	-	-	-	-	-	117.7	1.9
1988	-	-	-	-	-	-	-	-	-	-	119.4	1.4	-	-	-	-	-	-	-	-	-	-	122.5	2.6
1989	-	-	-	-	-	-	-	-	-	-	122.8	0.2	-	-	-	-	-	-	-	-	-	-	126.1	2.7
1990	-	-	-	-	-	-	-	-	-	-	127.5	1.1	-	-	-	-	-	-	-	-	-	-	129.8	1.8
1991	-	-	-	-	-	-	-	-	-	-	131.5	1.3	-	-	-	-	-	-	-	-	-	-	133.6	1.6
1992	-	-	-	-	-	-	-	-	-	-	138.5	3.7	-	-	-	-	-	-	-	-	-	-	141.4	2.1
1993	-	-	-	-	-	-	-	-	-	-	146.6	3.7	-	-	-	-	-	-	-	-	-	-	150.8	2.9
1994	-	-	-	-	-	-	-	-	-	-	154.9	2.7	-	-	-	-	-	-	-	-	-	-	160.5	3.6
1995	-	-	-	-	-	-	-	-	-	-	162.9	1.5	-	-	-	-	-	-	-	-	-	-	167.4	2.8
1996	-	-	-	-	-	-	-	-	-	-	169.3	1.1	-	-	-	-	-	-	-	-	-	-	168.3	-0.6
1997	-	-	-	-	-	-	-	-	-	-	170.4	1.2	-	-	-	-	-	-	-	-	-	-	-	-

Source: U.S. Department of Labor, Bureau of Labor Statistics, Division of Consumer Prices and Price Indexes. - indicates no data collected for period.

Seattle-Everett, WA
Consumer Price Index - Urban Wage Earners
Base 1982-1984 = 100
Entertainment

For 1975-1997. Columns headed % show percentile change in the index from the previous period for which an index is available.

Year	Jan Index	%	Feb Index	%	Mar Index	%	Apr Index	%	May Index	%	Jun Index	%	Jul Index	%	Aug Index	%	Sep Index	%	Oct Index	%	Nov Index	%	Dec Index	%
1975	-	-	-	-	-	-	-	-	-	-	-	-	-	-	-	-	-	-	-	-	58.9	-	-	-
1976	-	-	59.1	0.3	-	-	-	-	59.5	0.7	-	-	-	-	60.0	0.8	-	-	-	-	61.2	2.0	-	-
1977	-	-	62.9	2.8	-	-	-	-	62.8	-0.2	-	-	-	-	62.9	0.2	-	-	-	-	64.2	2.1	-	-
1978	64.4	0.3	-	-	64.5	0.2	-	-	66.7	3.4	-	-	67.3	0.9	-	-	66.6	-1.0	-	-	68.3	2.6	-	-
1979	68.9	0.9	-	-	68.8	-0.1	-	-	69.9	1.6	-	-	70.5	0.9	-	-	73.5	4.3	-	-	74.9	1.9	-	-
1980	76.1	1.6	-	-	77.9	2.4	-	-	78.0	0.1	-	-	79.9	2.4	-	-	82.8	3.6	-	-	84.2	1.7	-	-
1981	87.3	3.7	-	-	83.4	-4.5	-	-	86.0	3.1	-	-	86.4	0.5	-	-	88.6	2.5	-	-	89.4	0.9	-	-
1982	91.1	1.9	-	-	91.3	0.2	-	-	93.6	2.5	-	-	94.3	0.7	-	-	97.1	3.0	-	-	96.6	-0.5	-	-
1983	96.8	0.2	-	-	100.0	3.3	-	-	96.5	-3.5	-	-	99.7	3.3	-	-	102.5	2.8	-	-	103.2	0.7	-	-
1984	104.4	1.2	-	-	105.6	1.1	-	-	106.0	0.4	-	-	105.9	-0.1	-	-	104.7	-1.1	-	-	106.7	1.9	-	-
1985	107.4	0.7	-	-	108.2	0.7	-	-	107.0	-1.1	-	-	109.5	2.3	-	-	106.5	-2.7	-	-	109.2	2.5	-	-
1986	109.7	0.5	-	-	108.7	-0.9	-	-	105.3	-3.1	-	-	108.7	3.2	-	-	107.5	-1.1	-	-	108.0	0.5	108.1	0.1
1987	-	-	-	-	-	-	-	-	-	-	114.5	5.9	-	-	-	-	-	-	-	-	-	-	116.6	1.8
1988	-	-	-	-	-	-	-	-	-	-	118.2	1.4	-	-	-	-	-	-	-	-	-	-	121.1	2.5
1989	-	-	-	-	-	-	-	-	-	-	121.2	0.1	-	-	-	-	-	-	-	-	-	-	124.8	3.0
1990	-	-	-	-	-	-	-	-	-	-	126.1	1.0	-	-	-	-	-	-	-	-	-	-	128.0	1.5
1991	-	-	-	-	-	-	-	-	-	-	129.8	1.4	-	-	-	-	-	-	-	-	-	-	132.4	2.0
1992	-	-	-	-	-	-	-	-	-	-	137.7	4.0	-	-	-	-	-	-	-	-	-	-	140.7	2.2
1993	-	-	-	-	-	-	-	-	-	-	146.8	4.3	-	-	-	-	-	-	-	-	-	-	150.9	2.8
1994	-	-	-	-	-	-	-	-	-	-	155.0	2.7	-	-	-	-	-	-	-	-	-	-	161.2	4.0
1995	-	-	-	-	-	-	-	-	-	-	163.7	1.6	-	-	-	-	-	-	-	-	-	-	169.7	3.7
1996	-	-	-	-	-	-	-	-	-	-	172.2	1.5	-	-	-	-	-	-	-	-	-	-	171.3	-0.5
1997	-	-	-	-	-	-	-	-	-	-	172.9	0.9	-	-	-	-	-	-	-	-	-	-	-	-

Source: U.S. Department of Labor, Bureau of Labor Statistics, Division of Consumer Prices and Price Indexes. - indicates no data collected for period.

Seattle-Everett, WA
Consumer Price Index - All Urban Consumers
Base 1982-1984 = 100
Other Goods and Services

For 1975-1997. Columns headed % show percentile change in the index from the previous period for which an index is available.

Year	Jan Index	%	Feb Index	%	Mar Index	%	Apr Index	%	May Index	%	Jun Index	%	Jul Index	%	Aug Index	%	Sep Index	%	Oct Index	%	Nov Index	%	Dec Index	%
1975	-	-	-	-	-	-	-	-	-	-	-	-	-	-	-	-	-	-	-	-	48.2	-	-	-
1976	-	-	49.2	2.1	-	-	-	-	50.6	2.8	-	-	-	-	50.9	0.6	-	-	-	-	52.3	2.8	-	-
1977	-	-	53.3	1.9	-	-	-	-	53.6	0.6	-	-	-	-	54.2	1.1	-	-	-	-	55.6	2.6	-	-
1978	55.8	0.4	-	-	55.9	0.2	-	-	56.6	1.3	-	-	57.3	1.2	-	-	58.9	2.8	-	-	60.9	3.4	-	-
1979	60.8	-0.2	-	-	62.5	2.8	-	-	62.4	-0.2	-	-	63.6	1.9	-	-	66.7	4.9	-	-	67.3	0.9	-	-
1980	67.9	0.9	-	-	69.9	2.9	-	-	70.9	1.4	-	-	71.2	0.4	-	-	73.6	3.4	-	-	73.9	0.4	-	-
1981	74.7	1.1	-	-	75.2	0.7	-	-	76.7	2.0	-	-	79.4	3.5	-	-	84.3	6.2	-	-	86.7	2.8	-	-
1982	88.1	1.6	-	-	89.2	1.2	-	-	90.3	1.2	-	-	91.1	0.9	-	-	92.9	2.0	-	-	96.0	3.3	-	-
1983	98.1	2.2	-	-	99.1	1.0	-	-	99.4	0.3	-	-	99.6	0.2	-	-	102.5	2.9	-	-	105.6	3.0	-	-
1984	106.4	0.8	-	-	106.5	0.1	-	-	105.9	-0.6	-	-	106.6	0.7	-	-	108.2	1.5	-	-	108.8	0.6	-	-
1985	110.6	1.7	-	-	110.5	-0.1	-	-	109.8	-0.6	-	-	111.9	1.9	-	-	112.7	0.7	-	-	114.9	2.0	-	-
1986	115.0	0.1	-	-	114.3	-0.6	-	-	117.0	2.4	-	-	117.7	0.6	-	-	118.5	0.7	-	-	118.6	0.1	119.8	1.0
1987	-	-	-	-	-	-	-	-	-	-	127.3	6.3	-	-	-	-	-	-	-	-	-	-	-	-
1988	-	-	-	-	-	-	-	-	-	-	134.7	5.8	-	-	-	-	-	-	-	-	-	-	-	-
1989	-	-	-	-	-	-	-	-	-	-	141.6	5.1	-	-	-	-	-	-	-	-	-	-	-	-
1990	-	-	-	-	-	-	-	-	-	-	155.0	9.5	-	-	-	-	-	-	-	-	-	-	-	-
1991	-	-	-	-	-	-	-	-	-	-	169.0	9.0	-	-	-	-	-	-	-	-	-	-	-	-
1992	-	-	-	-	-	-	-	-	-	-	179.8	6.4	-	-	-	-	-	-	-	-	-	-	-	-
1993	-	-	-	-	-	-	-	-	-	-	201.1	11.8	-	-	-	-	-	-	-	-	-	-	-	-
1994	-	-	-	-	-	-	-	-	-	-	202.1	0.5	-	-	-	-	-	-	-	-	-	-	-	-
1995	-	-	-	-	-	-	-	-	-	-	209.1	3.5	-	-	-	-	-	-	-	-	-	-	-	-
1996	-	-	-	-	-	-	-	-	-	-	235.0	12.4	-	-	-	-	-	-	-	-	-	-	-	-
1997	-	-	-	-	-	-	-	-	-	-	249.1	6.0	-	-	-	-	-	-	-	-	-	-	-	-

Source: U.S. Department of Labor, Bureau of Labor Statistics, Division of Consumer Prices and Price Indexes. - indicates no data collected for period.

Seattle-Everett, WA
Consumer Price Index - Urban Wage Earners
Base 1982-1984 = 100
Other Goods and Services

For 1975-1997. Columns headed % show percentile change in the index from the previous period for which an index is available.

Year	Jan Index	%	Feb Index	%	Mar Index	%	Apr Index	%	May Index	%	Jun Index	%	Jul Index	%	Aug Index	%	Sep Index	%	Oct Index	%	Nov Index	%	Dec Index	%
1975	-	-	-		-	-	-	-	-	-	-	-	-	-	-	-	-	-	-	-	49.9	-	-	-
1976	-	-	50.9	2.0	-	-	-	-	52.4	2.9	-	-	-	-	52.7	0.6	-	-	-	-	54.2	2.8	-	-
1977	-	-	55.1	1.7	-	-	-	-	55.5	0.7	-	-	-	-	56.2	1.3	-	-	-	-	57.6	2.5	-	-
1978	58.1	0.9	-	-	58.4	0.5	-	-	59.0	1.0	-	-	59.9	1.5	-	-	61.4	2.5	-	-	62.0	1.0	-	-
1979	62.5	0.8	-	-	64.1	2.6	-	-	63.7	-0.6	-	-	64.6	1.4	-	-	67.0	3.7	-	-	67.9	1.3	-	-
1980	68.6	1.0	-	-	70.1	2.2	-	-	70.5	0.6	-	-	71.1	0.9	-	-	73.4	3.2	-	-	73.9	0.7	-	-
1981	75.5	2.2	-	-	75.8	0.4	-	-	77.5	2.2	-	-	79.0	1.9	-	-	83.5	5.7	-	-	85.4	2.3	-	-
1982	87.3	2.2	-	-	88.7	1.6	-	-	89.6	1.0	-	-	90.6	1.1	-	-	92.5	2.1	-	-	96.0	3.8	-	-
1983	98.6	2.7	-	-	99.6	1.0	-	-	99.8	0.2	-	-	100.2	0.4	-	-	103.1	2.9	-	-	105.5	2.3	-	-
1984	106.5	0.9	-	-	106.5	0.0	-	-	106.1	-0.4	-	-	107.0	0.8	-	-	108.0	0.9	-	-	108.6	0.6	-	-
1985	110.6	1.8	-	-	110.6	0.0	-	-	109.8	-0.7	-	-	112.1	2.1	-	-	112.6	0.4	-	-	114.6	1.8	-	-
1986	114.7	0.1	-	-	113.9	-0.7	-	-	117.3	3.0	-	-	118.2	0.8	-	-	118.9	0.6	-	-	118.5	-0.3	119.9	1.2
1987	-	-	-	-	-	-	-	-	-	-	125.9	5.0	-	-	-	-	-	-	-	-	-	-	-	-
1988	-	-	-	-	-	-	-	-	-	-	134.2	6.6	-	-	-	-	-	-	-	-	-	-	-	-
1989	-	-	-	-	-	-	-	-	-	-	141.9	5.7	-	-	-	-	-	-	-	-	-	-	-	-
1990	-	-	-	-	-	-	-	-	-	-	155.5	9.6	-	-	-	-	-	-	-	-	-	-	-	-
1991	-	-	-	-	-	-	-	-	-	-	168.4	8.3	-	-	-	-	-	-	-	-	-	-	-	-
1992	-	-	-	-	-	-	-	-	-	-	179.6	6.7	-	-	-	-	-	-	-	-	-	-	-	-
1993	-	-	-	-	-	-	-	-	-	-	199.8	11.2	-	-	-	-	-	-	-	-	-	-	-	-
1994	-	-	-	-	-	-	-	-	-	-	202.1	1.2	-	-	-	-	-	-	-	-	-	-	-	-
1995	-	-	-	-	-	-	-	-	-	-	208.8	3.3	-	-	-	-	-	-	-	-	-	-	-	-
1996	-	-	-	-	-	-	-	-	-	-	234.2	12.2	-	-	-	-	-	-	-	-	-	-	-	-
1997	-	-	-	-	-	-	-	-	-	-	249.0	6.3	-	-	-	-	-	-	-	-	-	-	-	-

Source: U.S. Department of Labor, Bureau of Labor Statistics, Division of Consumer Prices and Price Indexes. - indicates no data collected for period.

St. Louis, MO-IL
Consumer Price Index - All Urban Consumers
Base 1982-1984 = 100
Annual Averages

For 1917-1997. Columns headed % show percentile change in the index from the previous period for which an index is available.

Year	All Items		Food & Beverage		Housing		Apparel & Upkeep		Trans- portation		Medical Care		Entertain- ment		Other Goods & Services	
	Index	%	Index	%	Index	%	Index	%	Index	%	Index	%	Index	%	Index	%
1917	-	-	-	-	-	-	-	-	-	-	-	-	-	-	-	-
1918	14.8	-	-	-	-	-	-	-	-	-	-	-	-	-	-	-
1919	16.8	13.5	-	-	-	-	-	-	-	-	-	-	-	-	-	-
1920	19.9	18.5	-	-	-	-	-	-	-	-	-	-	-	-	-	-
1921	17.4	-12.6	-	-	-	-	-	-	-	-	-	-	-	-	-	-
1922	16.3	-6.3	-	-	-	-	-	-	-	-	-	-	-	-	-	-
1923	16.7	2.5	-	-	-	-	-	-	-	-	-	-	-	-	-	-
1924	16.8	0.6	-	-	-	-	-	-	-	-	-	-	-	-	-	-
1925	17.3	3.0	-	-	-	-	-	-	-	-	-	-	-	-	-	-
1926	17.6	1.7	-	-	-	-	-	-	-	-	-	-	-	-	-	-
1927	17.3	-1.7	-	-	-	-	-	-	-	-	-	-	-	-	-	-
1928	16.9	-2.3	-	-	-	-	-	-	-	-	-	-	-	-	-	-
1929	17.1	1.2	-	-	-	-	-	-	-	-	-	-	-	-	-	-
1930	16.7	-2.3	-	-	-	-	-	-	-	-	-	-	-	-	-	-
1931	15.0	-10.2	-	-	-	-	-	-	-	-	-	-	-	-	-	-
1932	13.4	-10.7	-	-	-	-	-	-	-	-	-	-	-	-	-	-
1933	12.8	-4.5	-	-	-	-	-	-	-	-	-	-	-	-	-	-
1934	13.3	3.9	-	-	-	-	-	-	-	-	-	-	-	-	-	-
1935	13.7	3.0	-	-	-	-	-	-	-	-	-	-	-	-	-	-
1936	13.8	0.7	-	-	-	-	-	-	-	-	-	-	-	-	-	-
1937	14.3	3.6	-	-	-	-	-	-	-	-	-	-	-	-	-	-
1938	13.9	-2.8	-	-	-	-	-	-	-	-	-	-	-	-	-	-
1939	13.8	-0.7	-	-	-	-	-	-	-	-	-	-	-	-	-	-
1940	13.9	0.7	-	-	-	-	-	-	-	-	-	-	-	-	-	-
1941	14.6	5.0	-	-	-	-	-	-	-	-	-	-	-	-	-	-
1942	16.2	11.0	-	-	-	-	-	-	-	-	-	-	-	-	-	-
1943	17.0	4.9	-	-	-	-	-	-	-	-	-	-	-	-	-	-
1944	17.3	1.8	-	-	-	-	-	-	-	-	-	-	-	-	-	-
1945	17.6	1.7	-	-	-	-	-	-	-	-	-	-	-	-	-	-
1946	19.1	8.5	-	-	-	-	-	-	-	-	-	-	-	-	-	-
1947	22.2	16.2	-	-	-	-	-	-	18.2	-	13.2	-	-	-	-	-
1948	23.9	7.7	-	-	-	-	-	-	19.8	8.8	14.0	6.1	-	-	-	-
1949	23.6	-1.3	-	-	-	-	-	-	20.8	5.1	14.4	2.9	-	-	-	-
1950	23.9	1.3	-	-	-	-	-	-	21.3	2.4	14.5	0.7	-	-	-	-
1951	25.9	8.4	-	-	-	-	-	-	23.5	10.3	15.5	6.9	-	-	-	-
1952	26.7	3.1	-	-	-	-	-	-	25.8	9.8	18.0	16.1	-	-	-	-
1953	27.0	1.1	-	-	-	-	44.1	-	26.8	3.9	18.5	2.8	-	-	-	-
1954	27.1	0.4	-	-	-	-	44.0	-0.2	26.0	-3.0	18.9	2.2	-	-	-	-
1955	27.0	-0.4	-	-	-	-	44.0	0.0	26.1	0.4	19.5	3.2	-	-	-	-
1956	27.2	0.7	-	-	-	-	44.4	0.9	26.3	0.8	19.9	2.1	-	-	-	-
1957	28.1	3.3	-	-	-	-	45.0	1.4	28.0	6.5	21.5	8.0	-	-	-	-
1958	29.0	3.2	-	-	-	-	45.8	1.8	29.6	5.7	22.2	3.3	-	-	-	-
1959	29.4	1.4	-	-	-	-	46.2	0.9	31.6	6.8	23.3	5.0	-	-	-	-
1960	29.5	0.3	-	-	-	-	47.1	1.9	31.4	-0.6	23.7	1.7	-	-	-	-
1961	30.0	1.7	-	-	-	-	47.6	1.1	32.0	1.9	24.2	2.1	-	-	-	-

[Continued]

862

St. Louis, MO-IL
Consumer Price Index - All Urban Consumers
Base 1982-1984 = 100
Annual Averages
[Continued]

For 1917-1997. Columns headed % show percentile change in the index from the previous period for which an index is available.

Year	All Items		Food & Beverage		Housing		Apparel & Upkeep		Trans- portation		Medical Care		Entertain- ment		Other Goods & Services	
	Index	%	Index	%	Index	%	Index	%	Index	%	Index	%	Index	%	Index	%
1962	30.3	1.0	-	-	-	-	47.6	0.0	32.4	1.3	25.5	5.4	-	-	-	-
1963	30.6	1.0	-	-	-	-	48.0	0.8	32.3	-0.3	25.7	0.8	-	-	-	-
1964	31.2	2.0	-	-	-	-	48.7	1.5	32.7	1.2	25.9	0.8	-	-	-	-
1965	31.7	1.6	-	-	-	-	49.2	1.0	33.0	0.9	26.8	3.5	-	-	-	-
1966	32.7	3.2	-	-	-	-	50.7	3.0	34.0	3.0	28.2	5.2	-	-	-	-
1967	33.7	3.1	-	-	-	-	52.4	3.4	35.3	3.8	29.7	5.3	-	-	-	-
1968	35.0	3.9	-	-	-	-	55.4	5.7	36.0	2.0	31.1	4.7	-	-	-	-
1969	36.8	5.1	-	-	-	-	58.2	5.1	37.2	3.3	33.0	6.1	-	-	-	-
1970	38.8	5.4	-	-	-	-	60.4	3.8	39.4	5.9	35.2	6.7	-	-	-	-
1971	40.3	3.9	-	-	-	-	62.4	3.3	42.1	6.9	36.7	4.3	-	-	-	-
1972	41.2	2.2	-	-	-	-	63.0	1.0	42.4	0.7	37.4	1.9	-	-	-	-
1973	43.5	5.6	-	-	-	-	64.5	2.4	43.8	3.3	38.6	3.2	-	-	-	-
1974	47.9	10.1	-	-	-	-	68.0	5.4	47.4	8.2	41.8	8.3	-	-	-	-
1975	52.6	9.8	-	-	-	-	70.8	4.1	51.5	8.6	46.3	10.8	-	-	-	-
1976	55.6	5.7	62.5	-	50.5	-	74.3	4.9	56.1	8.9	50.2	8.4	66.4	-	57.2	-
1977	59.5	7.0	66.8	6.9	54.0	6.9	79.2	6.6	59.5	6.1	55.4	10.4	70.2	5.7	60.5	5.8
1978	64.5	8.4	72.7	8.8	59.4	10.0	80.2	1.3	63.5	6.7	59.6	7.6	77.5	10.4	64.6	6.8
1979	72.7	12.7	81.0	11.4	67.9	14.3	85.2	6.2	73.8	16.2	64.8	8.7	81.5	5.2	68.7	6.3
1980	82.5	13.5	87.1	7.5	79.8	17.5	91.7	7.6	85.1	15.3	72.9	12.5	88.2	8.2	74.7	8.7
1981	90.1	9.2	93.5	7.3	87.6	9.8	95.3	3.9	94.4	10.9	81.8	12.2	93.9	6.5	82.0	9.8
1982	96.6	7.2	97.1	3.9	96.6	10.3	97.6	2.4	97.8	3.6	93.4	14.2	96.3	2.6	90.6	10.5
1983	100.1	3.6	99.7	2.7	100.4	3.9	100.8	3.3	99.2	1.4	100.9	8.0	101.3	5.2	101.0	11.5
1984	103.3	3.2	103.2	3.5	102.9	2.5	101.6	0.8	102.9	3.7	105.8	4.9	102.4	1.1	108.5	7.4
1985	107.1	3.7	105.7	2.4	107.8	4.8	104.4	2.8	105.3	2.3	111.0	4.9	106.0	3.5	115.4	6.4
1986	108.6	1.4	109.7	3.8	110.4	2.4	102.7	-1.6	100.3	-4.7	120.3	8.4	110.2	4.0	122.1	5.8
1987	112.2	3.3	114.0	3.9	112.1	1.5	107.6	4.8	103.9	3.6	127.9	6.3	113.9	3.4	128.1	4.9
1988	115.7	3.1	117.7	3.2	114.9	2.5	112.5	4.6	106.0	2.0	135.6	6.0	117.9	3.5	136.8	6.8
1989	121.8	5.3	125.8	6.9	120.3	4.7	118.4	5.2	110.5	4.2	145.6	7.4	122.3	3.7	145.4	6.3
1990	128.1	5.2	134.9	7.2	124.9	3.8	120.9	2.1	117.4	6.2	159.0	9.2	124.4	1.7	153.6	5.6
1991	132.1	3.1	139.6	3.5	127.7	2.2	122.5	1.3	118.5	0.9	171.7	8.0	134.5	8.1	163.4	6.4
1992	134.7	2.0	140.1	0.4	129.7	1.6	121.7	-0.7	121.9	2.9	181.0	5.4	137.8	2.5	172.3	5.4
1993	137.5	2.1	140.1	0.0	133.0	2.5	122.8	0.9	125.1	2.6	191.5	5.8	137.3	-0.4	175.9	2.1
1994	141.3	2.8	144.0	2.8	136.7	2.8	125.1	1.9	129.2	3.3	201.7	5.3	142.6	3.9	174.0	-1.1
1995	145.2	2.8	146.9	2.0	139.5	2.0	119.2	-4.7	136.0	5.3	210.0	4.1	155.4	9.0	180.4	3.7
1996	149.6	3.0	151.2	2.9	142.6	2.2	122.2	2.5	141.8	4.3	218.4	4.0	160.8	3.5	186.3	3.3
1997	-	-	-	-	-	-	-	-	-	-	-	-	-	-	-	-

Source: U.S. Department of Labor, Bureau of Labor Statistics, Division of Consumer Prices and Price Indexes. - indicates no data collected for period.

St. Louis, MO-IL
Consumer Price Index - Urban Wage Earners
Base 1982-1984 = 100
Annual Averages

For 1917-1997. Columns headed % show percentile change in the index from the previous period for which an index is available.

Year	All Items		Food & Beverage		Housing		Apparel & Upkeep		Trans- portation		Medical Care		Entertain- ment		Other Goods & Services	
	Index	%	Index	%	Index	%	Index	%	Index	%	Index	%	Index	%	Index	%
1917	-	-	-	-	-	-	-	-	-	-	-	-	-	-	-	-
1918	15.0	-	-	-	-	-	-	-	-	-	-	-	-	-	-	-
1919	17.0	13.3	-	-	-	-	-	-	-	-	-	-	-	-	-	-
1920	20.1	18.2	-	-	-	-	-	-	-	-	-	-	-	-	-	-
1921	17.6	-12.4	-	-	-	-	-	-	-	-	-	-	-	-	-	-
1922	16.5	-6.3	-	-	-	-	-	-	-	-	-	-	-	-	-	-
1923	16.8	1.8	-	-	-	-	-	-	-	-	-	-	-	-	-	-
1924	17.0	1.2	-	-	-	-	-	-	-	-	-	-	-	-	-	-
1925	17.5	2.9	-	-	-	-	-	-	-	-	-	-	-	-	-	-
1926	17.7	1.1	-	-	-	-	-	-	-	-	-	-	-	-	-	-
1927	17.5	-1.1	-	-	-	-	-	-	-	-	-	-	-	-	-	-
1928	17.1	-2.3	-	-	-	-	-	-	-	-	-	-	-	-	-	-
1929	17.2	0.6	-	-	-	-	-	-	-	-	-	-	-	-	-	-
1930	16.9	-1.7	-	-	-	-	-	-	-	-	-	-	-	-	-	-
1931	15.1	-10.7	-	-	-	-	-	-	-	-	-	-	-	-	-	-
1932	13.6	-9.9	-	-	-	-	-	-	-	-	-	-	-	-	-	-
1933	12.9	-5.1	-	-	-	-	-	-	-	-	-	-	-	-	-	-
1934	13.4	3.9	-	-	-	-	-	-	-	-	-	-	-	-	-	-
1935	13.8	3.0	-	-	-	-	-	-	-	-	-	-	-	-	-	-
1936	14.0	1.4	-	-	-	-	-	-	-	-	-	-	-	-	-	-
1937	14.4	2.9	-	-	-	-	-	-	-	-	-	-	-	-	-	-
1938	14.1	-2.1	-	-	-	-	-	-	-	-	-	-	-	-	-	-
1939	13.9	-1.4	-	-	-	-	-	-	-	-	-	-	-	-	-	-
1940	14.0	0.7	-	-	-	-	-	-	-	-	-	-	-	-	-	-
1941	14.7	5.0	-	-	-	-	-	-	-	-	-	-	-	-	-	-
1942	16.3	10.9	-	-	-	-	-	-	-	-	-	-	-	-	-	-
1943	17.2	5.5	-	-	-	-	-	-	-	-	-	-	-	-	-	-
1944	17.5	1.7	-	-	-	-	-	-	-	-	-	-	-	-	-	-
1945	17.8	1.7	-	-	-	-	-	-	-	-	-	-	-	-	-	-
1946	19.3	8.4	-	-	-	-	-	-	-	-	-	-	-	-	-	-
1947	22.4	16.1	-	-	-	-	-	-	18.5	-	13.1	-	-	-	-	-
1948	24.1	7.6	-	-	-	-	-	-	20.1	8.6	13.9	6.1	-	-	-	-
1949	23.8	-1.2	-	-	-	-	-	-	21.2	5.5	14.3	2.9	-	-	-	-
1950	24.1	1.3	-	-	-	-	-	-	21.7	2.4	14.4	0.7	-	-	-	-
1951	26.1	8.3	-	-	-	-	-	-	23.9	10.1	15.3	6.3	-	-	-	-
1952	27.0	3.4	-	-	-	-	-	-	26.2	9.6	17.9	17.0	-	-	-	-
1953	27.2	0.7	-	-	-	-	45.0	-	27.2	3.8	18.3	2.2	-	-	-	-
1954	27.3	0.4	-	-	-	-	44.9	-0.2	26.4	-2.9	18.7	2.2	-	-	-	-
1955	27.2	-0.4	-	-	-	-	44.8	-0.2	26.5	0.4	19.3	3.2	-	-	-	-
1956	27.5	1.1	-	-	-	-	45.3	1.1	26.7	0.8	19.7	2.1	-	-	-	-
1957	28.4	3.3	-	-	-	-	45.9	1.3	28.5	6.7	21.3	8.1	-	-	-	-
1958	29.2	2.8	-	-	-	-	46.7	1.7	30.1	5.6	22.0	3.3	-	-	-	-
1959	29.6	1.4	-	-	-	-	47.1	0.9	32.1	6.6	23.1	5.0	-	-	-	-
1960	29.8	0.7	-	-	-	-	48.0	1.9	31.9	-0.6	23.5	1.7	-	-	-	-
1961	30.3	1.7	-	-	-	-	48.5	1.0	32.5	1.9	24.0	2.1	-	-	-	-

[Continued]

St. Louis, MO-IL
Consumer Price Index - Urban Wage Earners
Base 1982-1984 = 100
Annual Averages

[Continued]

For 1917-1997. Columns headed % show percentile change in the index from the previous period for which an index is available.

Year	All Items		Food & Beverage		Housing		Apparel & Upkeep		Trans- portation		Medical Care		Entertain- ment		Other Goods & Services	
	Index	%	Index	%	Index	%	Index	%	Index	%	Index	%	Index	%	Index	%
1962	30.6	1.0	-	-	-	-	48.5	0.0	32.9	1.2	25.3	5.4	-	-	-	-
1963	30.9	1.0	-	-	-	-	48.9	0.8	32.8	-0.3	25.5	0.8	-	-	-	-
1964	31.5	1.9	-	-	-	-	49.6	1.4	33.2	1.2	25.6	0.4	-	-	-	-
1965	32.0	1.6	-	-	-	-	50.1	1.0	33.6	1.2	26.5	3.5	-	-	-	-
1966	33.0	3.1	-	-	-	-	51.6	3.0	34.6	3.0	28.0	5.7	-	-	-	-
1967	34.0	3.0	-	-	-	-	53.4	3.5	35.8	3.5	29.4	5.0	-	-	-	-
1968	35.3	3.8	-	-	-	-	56.5	5.8	36.6	2.2	30.8	4.8	-	-	-	-
1969	37.1	5.1	-	-	-	-	59.3	5.0	37.8	3.3	32.7	6.2	-	-	-	-
1970	39.2	5.7	-	-	-	-	61.6	3.9	40.1	6.1	34.8	6.4	-	-	-	-
1971	40.7	3.8	-	-	-	-	63.6	3.2	42.8	6.7	36.3	4.3	-	-	-	-
1972	41.6	2.2	-	-	-	-	64.2	0.9	43.1	0.7	37.0	1.9	-	-	-	-
1973	43.9	5.5	-	-	-	-	65.7	2.3	44.5	3.2	38.2	3.2	-	-	-	-
1974	48.3	10.0	-	-	-	-	69.3	5.5	48.2	8.3	41.4	8.4	-	-	-	-
1975	53.1	9.9	-	-	-	-	72.2	4.2	52.3	8.5	45.9	10.9	-	-	-	-
1976	56.1	5.6	62.5	-	51.0	-	75.7	4.8	57.0	9.0	49.7	8.3	72.4	-	56.8	-
1977	60.0	7.0	66.8	6.9	54.5	6.9	80.8	6.7	60.5	6.1	55.0	10.7	76.6	5.8	60.0	5.6
1978	64.7	7.8	72.5	8.5	59.9	9.9	80.9	0.1	63.1	4.3	59.5	8.2	82.3	7.4	64.2	7.0
1979	73.2	13.1	81.5	12.4	68.9	15.0	84.4	4.3	73.3	16.2	65.1	9.4	86.2	4.7	68.7	7.0
1980	83.4	13.9	87.4	7.2	81.0	17.6	90.5	7.2	85.6	16.8	73.5	12.9	93.6	8.6	75.5	9.9
1981	90.9	9.0	93.6	7.1	88.7	9.5	95.3	5.3	94.5	10.4	82.2	11.8	96.3	2.9	82.6	9.4
1982	97.1	6.8	97.1	3.7	97.8	10.3	97.5	2.3	97.8	3.5	93.4	13.6	96.5	0.2	90.6	9.7
1983	100.3	3.3	99.8	2.8	100.8	3.1	101.0	3.6	99.1	1.3	100.7	7.8	101.4	5.1	101.4	11.9
1984	102.6	2.3	103.2	3.4	101.3	0.5	101.5	0.5	103.2	4.1	105.9	5.2	102.1	0.7	108.0	6.5
1985	107.1	4.4	105.6	2.3	109.1	7.7	104.1	2.6	105.3	2.0	111.0	4.8	105.1	2.9	114.6	6.1
1986	108.2	1.0	109.8	4.0	111.9	2.6	102.4	-1.6	99.2	-5.8	119.8	7.9	109.2	3.9	121.1	5.7
1987	111.8	3.3	114.0	3.8	113.9	1.8	107.7	5.2	103.2	4.0	127.5	6.4	112.9	3.4	126.8	4.7
1988	115.4	3.2	117.8	3.3	116.6	2.4	112.6	4.5	105.8	2.5	135.2	6.0	117.1	3.7	135.7	7.0
1989	121.5	5.3	125.8	6.8	122.0	4.6	118.5	5.2	110.1	4.1	145.6	7.7	121.3	3.6	144.7	6.6
1990	127.5	4.9	134.8	7.2	126.7	3.9	121.2	2.3	115.5	4.9	158.3	8.7	123.3	1.6	153.7	6.2
1991	131.5	3.1	139.6	3.6	129.5	2.2	122.8	1.3	117.2	1.5	170.6	7.8	132.9	7.8	165.4	7.6
1992	134.3	2.1	140.2	0.4	131.9	1.9	122.1	-0.6	121.0	3.2	180.0	5.5	135.7	2.1	175.4	6.0
1993	136.9	1.9	140.3	0.1	135.2	2.5	123.0	0.7	124.6	3.0	190.5	5.8	135.3	-0.3	175.9	0.3
1994	140.7	2.8	144.3	2.9	138.9	2.7	125.9	2.4	129.2	3.7	200.1	5.0	140.7	4.0	170.4	-3.1
1995	144.7	2.8	147.0	1.9	141.6	1.9	119.7	-4.9	138.0	6.8	208.2	4.0	151.0	7.3	175.4	2.9
1996	148.7	2.8	151.1	2.8	144.8	2.3	122.5	2.3	143.0	3.6	216.6	4.0	154.3	2.2	180.2	2.7
1997	-	-	-	-	-	-	-	-	-	-	-	-	-	-	-	-

Source: U.S. Department of Labor, Bureau of Labor Statistics, Division of Consumer Prices and Price Indexes. - indicates no data collected for period.

St. Louis, MO-IL
Consumer Price Index - All Urban Consumers
Base 1982-1984 = 100
All Items

For 1917-1997. Columns headed % show percentile change in the index from the previous period for which an index is available.

Year	Jan Index	%	Feb Index	%	Mar Index	%	Apr Index	%	May Index	%	Jun Index	%	Jul Index	%	Aug Index	%	Sep Index	%	Oct Index	%	Nov Index	%	Dec Index	%
1917	-	-	-	-	-	-	-	-	-	-	-	-	-	-	-	-	-	-	-	-	-	-	13.7	-
1918	-	-	-	-	-	-	-	-	-	-	-	-	-	-	-	-	-	-	-	-	-	-	16.0	16.8
1919	-	-	-	-	-	-	-	-	-	-	16.2	1.3	-	-	-	-	-	-	-	-	-	-	18.4	13.6
1920	-	-	-	-	-	-	-	-	-	-	21.1	14.7	-	-	-	-	-	-	-	-	-	-	18.8	-10.9
1921	-	-	-	-	-	-	-	-	17.2	-8.5	-	-	-	-	-	-	17.2	0.0	-	-	-	-	16.7	-2.9
1922	-	-	-	-	16.3	-2.4	-	-	-	-	16.5	1.2	-	-	-	-	16.2	-1.8	-	-	-	-	16.4	1.2
1923	-	-	-	-	16.5	0.6	-	-	-	-	16.6	0.6	-	-	-	-	16.9	1.8	-	-	-	-	16.8	-0.6
1924	-	-	-	-	16.7	-0.6	-	-	-	-	16.7	0.0	-	-	-	-	16.7	0.0	-	-	-	-	16.9	1.2
1925	-	-	-	-	-	-	-	-	-	-	17.3	2.4	-	-	-	-	-	-	-	-	-	-	17.7	2.3
1926	-	-	-	-	-	-	-	-	-	-	17.6	-0.6	-	-	-	-	-	-	-	-	-	-	17.6	0.0
1927	-	-	-	-	-	-	-	-	-	-	17.6	0.0	-	-	-	-	-	-	-	-	-	-	17.1	-2.8
1928	-	-	-	-	-	-	-	-	-	-	16.9	-1.2	-	-	-	-	-	-	-	-	-	-	16.9	0.0
1929	-	-	-	-	-	-	-	-	-	-	17.1	1.2	-	-	-	-	-	-	-	-	-	-	17.2	0.6
1930	-	-	-	-	-	-	-	-	-	-	16.8	-2.3	-	-	-	-	-	-	-	-	-	-	16.0	-4.8
1931	-	-	-	-	-	-	-	-	-	-	14.9	-6.9	-	-	-	-	-	-	-	-	-	-	14.2	-4.7
1932	-	-	-	-	-	-	-	-	-	-	13.4	-5.6	-	-	-	-	-	-	-	-	-	-	12.9	-3.7
1933	-	-	-	-	-	-	-	-	-	-	12.6	-2.3	-	-	-	-	-	-	-	-	-	-	12.9	2.4
1934	-	-	-	-	-	-	-	-	-	-	13.2	2.3	-	-	-	-	-	-	-	-	13.3	0.8	-	-
1935	-	-	-	-	13.6	2.3	-	-	-	-	-	-	13.7	0.7	-	-	-	-	13.7	0.0	-	-	-	-
1936	13.8	0.7	-	-	-	-	13.7	-0.7	-	-	-	-	13.9	1.5	-	-	14.1	1.4	-	-	-	-	13.9	-1.4
1937	-	-	-	-	14.2	2.2	-	-	-	-	14.3	0.7	-	-	-	-	14.5	1.4	-	-	-	-	14.3	-1.4
1938	-	-	-	-	14.0	-2.1	-	-	-	-	14.0	0.0	-	-	-	-	14.0	0.0	-	-	-	-	13.8	-1.4
1939	-	-	-	-	13.8	0.0	-	-	-	-	13.6	-1.4	-	-	-	-	14.0	2.9	-	-	-	-	13.8	-1.4
1940	-	-	-	-	13.8	0.0	-	-	-	-	13.8	0.0	-	-	-	-	13.9	0.7	13.9	0.0	13.9	0.0	14.1	1.4
1941	14.1	0.0	14.0	-0.7	14.1	0.7	14.2	0.7	14.2	0.0	14.5	2.1	14.5	0.0	14.6	0.7	15.0	2.7	15.1	0.7	15.3	1.3	15.4	0.7
1942	15.6	1.3	15.7	0.6	16.0	1.9	16.1	0.6	16.1	0.0	16.2	0.6	16.2	0.0	16.3	0.6	16.2	-0.6	16.4	1.2	16.5	0.6	16.7	1.2
1943	16.6	-0.6	16.7	0.6	16.9	1.2	17.1	1.2	17.3	1.2	17.2	-0.6	17.1	-0.6	17.1	0.0	17.1	0.0	17.1	0.0	17.1	0.0	17.1	0.0
1944	17.1	0.0	17.0	-0.6	17.1	0.6	17.2	0.6	17.3	0.6	17.3	0.0	17.5	1.2	17.4	-0.6	17.4	0.0	17.3	-0.6	17.4	0.6	17.4	0.0
1945	17.5	0.6	17.4	-0.6	17.4	0.0	17.4	0.0	17.6	1.1	17.7	0.6	17.7	0.0	17.7	0.0	17.6	-0.6	17.7	0.6	17.6	-0.6	17.9	1.7
1946	17.9	0.0	17.8	-0.6	17.9	0.6	18.0	0.6	18.0	0.0	18.3	1.7	19.5	6.6	19.9	2.1	19.9	0.0	20.4	2.5	21.0	2.9	21.1	0.5
1947	21.1	0.0	21.1	0.0	21.7	2.8	21.6	-0.5	21.5	-0.5	21.7	0.9	-	-	-	-	23.1	6.5	-	-	-	-	23.4	1.3
1948	-	-	-	-	23.4	0.0	-	-	-	-	24.0	2.6	-	-	-	-	24.4	1.7	-	-	-	-	23.9	-2.0
1949	-	-	-	-	23.6	-1.3	-	-	-	-	23.7	0.4	-	-	-	-	23.6	-0.4	-	-	-	-	23.4	-0.8
1950	-	-	-	-	23.4	0.0	-	-	-	-	23.5	0.4	-	-	-	-	24.2	3.0	-	-	-	-	24.9	2.9
1951	-	-	-	-	25.8	3.6	-	-	-	-	25.8	0.0	-	-	-	-	25.9	0.4	-	-	-	-	26.5	2.3
1952	-	-	-	-	26.5	0.0	-	-	-	-	26.8	1.1	-	-	-	-	26.8	0.0	-	-	-	-	26.7	-0.4
1953	-	-	-	-	26.6	-0.4	-	-	-	-	26.9	1.1	-	-	-	-	27.2	1.1	-	-	-	-	27.2	0.0
1954	-	-	-	-	27.2	0.0	-	-	-	-	27.3	0.4	-	-	-	-	26.9	-1.5	-	-	-	-	26.8	-0.4
1955	-	-	-	-	26.9	0.4	-	-	-	-	26.9	0.0	-	-	-	-	27.1	0.7	-	-	-	-	27.0	-0.4
1956	-	-	-	-	26.9	-0.4	-	-	-	-	27.2	1.1	-	-	-	-	27.4	0.7	-	-	-	-	27.7	1.1
1957	-	-	-	-	27.9	0.7	-	-	-	-	28.1	0.7	-	-	-	-	28.3	0.7	-	-	-	-	28.4	0.4
1958	-	-	-	-	28.9	1.8	-	-	-	-	28.9	0.0	-	-	-	-	29.1	0.7	-	-	-	-	29.2	0.3
1959	-	-	-	-	29.3	0.3	-	-	-	-	29.4	0.3	-	-	-	-	29.4	0.0	-	-	-	-	29.4	0.0
1960	-	-	-	-	29.4	0.0	-	-	-	-	29.6	0.7	-	-	-	-	29.6	0.0	-	-	-	-	29.7	0.3
1961	-	-	-	-	30.0	1.0	-	-	-	-	30.0	0.0	-	-	-	-	30.0	0.0	-	-	-	-	30.1	0.3

[Continued]

866

St. Louis, MO-IL
Consumer Price Index - All Urban Consumers
Base 1982-1984 = 100
All Items
[Continued]

For 1917-1997. Columns headed % show percentile change in the index from the previous period for which an index is available.

Year	Jan Index	%	Feb Index	%	Mar Index	%	Apr Index	%	May Index	%	Jun Index	%	Jul Index	%	Aug Index	%	Sep Index	%	Oct Index	%	Nov Index	%	Dec Index	%
1962	-	-	-	-	30.2	0.3	-	-	-	-	30.1	-0.3	-	-	-	-	30.4	1.0	-	-	-	-	30.6	0.7
1963	-	-	-	-	30.5	-0.3	-	-	-	-	30.4	-0.3	-	-	-	-	30.7	1.0	-	-	-	-	30.9	0.7
1964	-	-	-	-	31.0	0.3	-	-	-	-	31.0	0.0	-	-	-	-	31.3	1.0	-	-	-	-	31.4	0.3
1965	-	-	-	-	31.4	0.0	-	-	-	-	31.7	1.0	-	-	-	-	31.7	0.0	-	-	-	-	32.2	1.6
1966	-	-	-	-	32.3	0.3	-	-	-	-	32.8	1.5	-	-	-	-	33.1	0.9	-	-	-	-	33.1	0.0
1967	-	-	-	-	33.3	0.6	-	-	-	-	33.6	0.9	-	-	-	-	33.9	0.9	-	-	-	-	34.3	1.2
1968	-	-	-	-	34.6	0.9	-	-	-	-	35.0	1.2	-	-	-	-	35.4	1.1	-	-	-	-	35.6	0.6
1969	-	-	-	-	36.2	1.7	-	-	-	-	36.6	1.1	-	-	-	-	37.2	1.6	-	-	-	-	37.7	1.3
1970	-	-	-	-	38.2	1.3	-	-	-	-	38.7	1.3	-	-	-	-	39.3	1.6	-	-	-	-	39.6	0.8
1971	-	-	-	-	39.8	0.5	-	-	-	-	40.4	1.5	-	-	-	-	40.6	0.5	-	-	-	-	40.7	0.2
1972	-	-	-	-	40.7	0.0	-	-	-	-	41.0	0.7	-	-	-	-	41.6	1.5	-	-	-	-	41.6	0.0
1973	-	-	-	-	42.5	2.2	-	-	-	-	43.1	1.4	-	-	-	-	44.5	3.2	-	-	-	-	45.0	1.1
1974	-	-	-	-	46.5	3.3	-	-	-	-	47.5	2.2	-	-	-	-	49.1	3.4	-	-	-	-	50.0	1.8
1975	-	-	-	-	51.3	2.6	-	-	-	-	52.8	2.9	-	-	-	-	53.5	1.3	-	-	-	-	54.0	0.9
1976	-	-	-	-	54.8	1.5	-	-	-	-	55.6	1.5	-	-	-	-	56.3	1.3	-	-	-	-	56.6	0.5
1977	-	-	-	-	58.3	3.0	-	-	-	-	59.7	2.4	-	-	-	-	60.4	1.2	-	-	-	-	60.8	0.7
1978	-	-	-	-	61.9	1.8	-	-	63.8	3.1	-	-	65.0	1.9	-	-	66.0	1.5	-	-	67.1	1.7	-	-
1979	68.5	2.1	-	-	70.2	2.5	-	-	71.1	1.3	-	-	73.0	2.7	-	-	74.8	2.5	-	-	76.0	1.6	-	-
1980	78.3	3.0	-	-	80.2	2.4	-	-	81.4	1.5	-	-	82.5	1.4	-	-	85.0	3.0	-	-	85.4	0.5	-	-
1981	86.1	0.8	-	-	87.3	1.4	-	-	90.2	3.3	-	-	90.7	0.6	-	-	92.0	1.4	-	-	92.2	0.2	-	-
1982	93.7	1.6	-	-	94.5	0.9	-	-	96.2	1.8	-	-	97.7	1.6	-	-	99.0	1.3	-	-	97.6	-1.4	-	-
1983	98.0	0.4	-	-	98.7	0.7	-	-	99.5	0.8	-	-	100.8	1.3	-	-	101.7	0.9	-	-	100.9	-0.8	-	-
1984	101.3	0.4	-	-	101.9	0.6	-	-	102.8	0.9	-	-	103.9	1.1	-	-	104.8	0.9	-	-	104.1	-0.7	-	-
1985	105.5	1.3	-	-	105.8	0.3	-	-	106.4	0.6	-	-	107.7	1.2	-	-	108.3	0.6	-	-	108.3	0.0	-	-
1986	108.5	0.2	-	-	107.5	-0.9	-	-	107.3	-0.2	-	-	109.6	2.1	-	-	109.7	0.1	-	-	109.0	-0.6	-	-
1987	110.0	0.9	-	-	110.7	0.6	-	-	111.3	0.5	-	-	112.7	1.3	-	-	114.3	1.4	-	-	113.1	-1.0	-	-
1988	113.4	0.3	-	-	114.2	0.7	-	-	114.1	-0.1	-	-	116.0	1.7	-	-	117.3	1.1	-	-	118.3	0.9	-	-
1989	118.4	0.1	-	-	119.4	0.8	-	-	121.5	1.8	-	-	123.1	1.3	-	-	123.9	0.6	-	-	123.1	-0.6	-	-
1990	125.1	1.6	-	-	127.2	1.7	-	-	126.7	-0.4	-	-	128.0	1.0	-	-	129.9	1.5	-	-	130.4	0.4	-	-
1991	131.0	0.5	-	-	130.7	-0.2	-	-	131.3	0.5	-	-	132.7	1.1	-	-	133.5	0.6	-	-	133.2	-0.2	-	-
1992	132.5	-0.5	-	-	132.6	0.1	-	-	134.0	1.1	-	-	135.7	1.3	-	-	136.6	0.7	-	-	136.0	-0.4	-	-
1993	135.9	-0.1	-	-	136.1	0.1	-	-	136.8	0.5	-	-	138.8	1.5	-	-	138.4	-0.3	-	-	138.1	-0.2	-	-
1994	138.6	0.4	-	-	139.7	0.8	-	-	140.0	0.2	-	-	141.9	1.4	-	-	143.4	1.1	-	-	143.3	-0.1	-	-
1995	142.9	-0.3	-	-	144.5	1.1	-	-	144.6	0.1	-	-	145.6	0.7	-	-	147.1	1.0	-	-	145.7	-1.0	-	-
1996	147.2	1.0	-	-	148.9	1.2	-	-	148.1	-0.5	-	-	149.9	1.2	-	-	151.0	0.7	-	-	151.4	0.3	-	-
1997	151.5	0.1	-	-	152.2	0.5	-	-	152.1	-0.1	152.1	0.0	153.3	0.8	-	-	155.1	1.2	-	-	152.9	-1.4	-	-

Source: U.S. Department of Labor, Bureau of Labor Statistics, Division of Consumer Prices and Price Indexes. - indicates no data collected for period.

St. Louis, MO-IL
Consumer Price Index - Urban Wage Earners
Base 1982-1984 = 100
All Items

For 1917-1997. Columns headed % show percentile change in the index from the previous period for which an index is available.

Year	Jan Index	%	Feb Index	%	Mar Index	%	Apr Index	%	May Index	%	Jun Index	%	Jul Index	%	Aug Index	%	Sep Index	%	Oct Index	%	Nov Index	%	Dec Index	%
1917	-	-	-	-	-	-	-	-	-	-	-	-	-	-	-	-	-	-	-	-	-	-	13.9	-
1918	-	-	-	-	-	-	-	-	-	-	-	-	-	-	-	-	-	-	-	-	-	-	16.2	16.5
1919	-	-	-	-	-	-	-	-	-	-	16.4	1.2	-	-	-	-	-	-	-	-	-	-	18.6	13.4
1920	-	-	-	-	-	-	-	-	-	-	21.3	14.5	-	-	-	-	-	-	-	-	-	-	18.9	-11.3
1921	-	-	-	-	-	-	-	-	17.4	-7.9	-	-	-	-	-	-	17.4	0.0	-	-	-	-	16.9	-2.9
1922	-	-	-	-	16.5	-2.4	-	-	-	-	16.6	0.6	-	-	-	-	16.3	-1.8	-	-	-	-	16.5	1.2
1923	-	-	-	-	16.6	0.6	-	-	-	-	16.7	0.6	-	-	-	-	17.1	2.4	-	-	-	-	17.0	-0.6
1924	-	-	-	-	16.9	-0.6	-	-	-	-	16.9	0.0	-	-	-	-	16.9	0.0	-	-	-	-	17.1	1.2
1925	-	-	-	-	-	-	-	-	-	-	17.5	2.3	-	-	-	-	-	-	-	-	-	-	17.9	2.3
1926	-	-	-	-	-	-	-	-	-	-	17.8	-0.6	-	-	-	-	-	-	-	-	-	-	17.7	-0.6
1927	-	-	-	-	-	-	-	-	-	-	17.8	0.6	-	-	-	-	-	-	-	-	-	-	17.2	-3.4
1928	-	-	-	-	-	-	-	-	-	-	17.1	-0.6	-	-	-	-	-	-	-	-	-	-	17.1	0.0
1929	-	-	-	-	-	-	-	-	-	-	17.2	0.6	-	-	-	-	-	-	-	-	-	-	17.4	1.2
1930	-	-	-	-	-	-	-	-	-	-	17.0	-2.3	-	-	-	-	-	-	-	-	-	-	16.1	-5.3
1931	-	-	-	-	-	-	-	-	-	-	15.1	-6.2	-	-	-	-	-	-	-	-	-	-	14.3	-5.3
1932	-	-	-	-	-	-	-	-	-	-	13.5	-5.6	-	-	-	-	-	-	-	-	-	-	13.0	-3.7
1933	-	-	-	-	-	-	-	-	-	-	12.7	-2.3	-	-	-	-	-	-	-	-	-	-	13.1	3.1
1934	-	-	-	-	-	-	-	-	-	-	13.4	2.3	-	-	-	-	-	-	-	-	13.5	0.7	-	-
1935	-	-	-	-	13.8	2.2	-	-	-	-	-	-	13.8	0.0	-	-	-	-	13.8	0.0	-	-	-	-
1936	14.0	1.4	-	-	-	-	13.8	-1.4	-	-	-	-	14.0	1.4	-	-	14.2	1.4	-	-	-	-	14.0	-1.4
1937	-	-	-	-	14.3	2.1	-	-	-	-	14.5	1.4	-	-	-	-	14.6	0.7	-	-	-	-	14.4	-1.4
1938	-	-	-	-	14.1	-2.1	-	-	-	-	14.1	0.0	-	-	-	-	14.1	0.0	-	-	-	-	14.0	-0.7
1939	-	-	-	-	13.9	-0.7	-	-	-	-	13.7	-1.4	-	-	-	-	14.1	2.9	-	-	-	-	13.9	-1.4
1940	-	-	-	-	13.9	0.0	-	-	-	-	14.0	0.7	-	-	-	-	14.0	0.0	14.1	0.7	14.0	-0.7	14.2	1.4
1941	14.2	0.0	14.2	0.0	14.2	0.0	14.3	0.7	14.3	0.0	14.6	2.1	14.7	0.7	14.8	0.7	15.2	2.7	15.3	0.7	15.4	0.7	15.5	0.6
1942	15.7	1.3	15.9	1.3	16.1	1.3	16.2	0.6	16.2	0.0	16.4	1.2	16.3	-0.6	16.5	1.2	16.4	-0.6	16.6	1.2	16.6	0.0	16.9	1.8
1943	16.8	-0.6	16.9	0.6	17.1	1.2	17.3	1.2	17.4	0.6	17.4	0.0	17.3	-0.6	17.3	0.0	17.2	-0.6	17.3	0.6	17.3	0.0	17.3	0.0
1944	17.3	0.0	17.2	-0.6	17.2	0.0	17.4	1.2	17.4	0.0	17.5	0.6	17.7	1.1	17.6	-0.6	17.6	0.0	17.5	-0.6	17.6	0.6	17.6	0.0
1945	17.7	0.6	17.6	-0.6	17.6	0.0	17.6	0.0	17.8	1.1	17.9	0.6	17.9	0.0	17.9	0.0	17.8	-0.6	17.8	0.0	17.8	0.0	18.0	1.1
1946	18.1	0.6	18.0	-0.6	18.0	0.0	18.2	1.1	18.2	0.0	18.5	1.6	19.6	5.9	20.1	2.6	20.1	0.0	20.6	2.5	21.2	2.9	21.3	0.5
1947	21.3	0.0	21.3	0.0	21.9	2.8	21.8	-0.5	21.8	0.0	21.9	0.5	-	-	-	-	23.3	6.4	-	-	-	-	23.6	1.3
1948	-	-	-	-	23.6	0.0	-	-	-	-	24.2	2.5	-	-	-	-	24.6	1.7	-	-	-	-	24.1	-2.0
1949	-	-	-	-	23.8	-1.2	-	-	-	-	23.9	0.4	-	-	-	-	23.8	-0.4	-	-	-	-	23.6	-0.8
1950	-	-	-	-	23.6	0.0	-	-	-	-	23.7	0.4	-	-	-	-	24.4	3.0	-	-	-	-	25.1	2.9
1951	-	-	-	-	26.0	3.6	-	-	-	-	26.0	0.0	-	-	-	-	26.2	0.8	-	-	-	-	26.8	2.3
1952	-	-	-	-	26.8	0.0	-	-	-	-	27.1	1.1	-	-	-	-	27.1	0.0	-	-	-	-	27.0	-0.4
1953	-	-	-	-	26.9	-0.4	-	-	-	-	27.2	1.1	-	-	-	-	27.5	1.1	-	-	-	-	27.4	-0.4
1954	-	-	-	-	27.4	0.0	-	-	-	-	27.5	0.4	-	-	-	-	27.1	-1.5	-	-	-	-	27.1	0.0
1955	-	-	-	-	27.1	0.0	-	-	-	-	27.2	0.4	-	-	-	-	27.3	0.4	-	-	-	-	27.2	-0.4
1956	-	-	-	-	27.1	-0.4	-	-	-	-	27.4	1.1	-	-	-	-	27.7	1.1	-	-	-	-	27.9	0.7
1957	-	-	-	-	28.2	1.1	-	-	-	-	28.4	0.7	-	-	-	-	28.6	0.7	-	-	-	-	28.7	0.3
1958	-	-	-	-	29.2	1.7	-	-	-	-	29.2	0.0	-	-	-	-	29.4	0.7	-	-	-	-	29.5	0.3
1959	-	-	-	-	29.5	0.0	-	-	-	-	29.6	0.3	-	-	-	-	29.6	0.0	-	-	-	-	29.7	0.3
1960	-	-	-	-	29.6	-0.3	-	-	-	-	29.8	0.7	-	-	-	-	29.9	0.3	-	-	-	-	30.0	0.3
1961	-	-	-	-	30.3	1.0	-	-	-	-	30.3	0.0	-	-	-	-	30.3	0.0	-	-	-	-	30.4	0.3

[Continued]

St. Louis, MO-IL
Consumer Price Index - Urban Wage Earners
Base 1982-1984 = 100
All Items
[Continued]

For 1917-1997. Columns headed % show percentile change in the index from the previous period for which an index is available.

Year	Jan Index	%	Feb Index	%	Mar Index	%	Apr Index	%	May Index	%	Jun Index	%	Jul Index	%	Aug Index	%	Sep Index	%	Oct Index	%	Nov Index	%	Dec Index	%
1962	-	-	-	-	30.5	0.3	-	-	-	-	30.4	-0.3	-	-	-	-	30.7	1.0	-	-	-	-	30.9	0.7
1963	-	-	-	-	30.8	-0.3	-	-	-	-	30.7	-0.3	-	-	-	-	31.0	1.0	-	-	-	-	31.2	0.6
1964	-	-	-	-	31.3	0.3	-	-	-	-	31.3	0.0	-	-	-	-	31.6	1.0	-	-	-	-	31.7	0.3
1965	-	-	-	-	31.7	0.0	-	-	-	-	32.1	1.3	-	-	-	-	32.0	-0.3	-	-	-	-	32.5	1.6
1966	-	-	-	-	32.6	0.3	-	-	-	-	33.1	1.5	-	-	-	-	33.4	0.9	-	-	-	-	33.4	0.0
1967	-	-	-	-	33.6	0.6	-	-	-	-	33.9	0.9	-	-	-	-	34.3	1.2	-	-	-	-	34.6	0.9
1968	-	-	-	-	35.0	1.2	-	-	-	-	35.3	0.9	-	-	-	-	35.7	1.1	-	-	-	-	35.9	0.6
1969	-	-	-	-	36.5	1.7	-	-	-	-	36.9	1.1	-	-	-	-	37.6	1.9	-	-	-	-	38.0	1.1
1970	-	-	-	-	38.5	1.3	-	-	-	-	39.0	1.3	-	-	-	-	39.6	1.5	-	-	-	-	40.0	1.0
1971	-	-	-	-	40.2	0.5	-	-	-	-	40.8	1.5	-	-	-	-	41.0	0.5	-	-	-	-	41.1	0.2
1972	-	-	-	-	41.1	0.0	-	-	-	-	41.4	0.7	-	-	-	-	42.0	1.4	-	-	-	-	42.0	0.0
1973	-	-	-	-	42.9	2.1	-	-	-	-	43.5	1.4	-	-	-	-	45.0	3.4	-	-	-	-	45.5	1.1
1974	-	-	-	-	47.0	3.3	-	-	-	-	48.0	2.1	-	-	-	-	49.6	3.3	-	-	-	-	50.5	1.8
1975	-	-	-	-	51.8	2.6	-	-	-	-	53.3	2.9	-	-	-	-	54.0	1.3	-	-	-	-	54.5	0.9
1976	-	-	-	-	55.3	1.5	-	-	-	-	56.2	1.6	-	-	-	-	56.8	1.1	-	-	-	-	57.2	0.7
1977	-	-	-	-	58.9	3.0	-	-	-	-	60.3	2.4	-	-	-	-	60.9	1.0	-	-	-	-	61.4	0.8
1978	-	-	-	-	62.5	1.8	-	-	63.9	2.2	-	-	64.9	1.6	-	-	66.2	2.0	-	-	67.2	1.5	-	-
1979	68.5	1.9	-	-	70.4	2.8	-	-	71.5	1.6	-	-	73.9	3.4	-	-	75.6	2.3	-	-	76.9	1.7	-	-
1980	79.4	3.3	-	-	81.1	2.1	-	-	82.5	1.7	-	-	83.6	1.3	-	-	85.9	2.8	-	-	86.4	0.6	-	-
1981	87.0	0.7	-	-	88.2	1.4	-	-	91.2	3.4	-	-	91.5	0.3	-	-	92.8	1.4	-	-	92.8	0.0	-	-
1982	94.2	1.5	-	-	94.9	0.7	-	-	96.7	1.9	-	-	98.3	1.7	-	-	99.6	1.3	-	-	98.2	-1.4	-	-
1983	97.0	-1.2	-	-	99.7	2.8	-	-	99.9	0.2	-	-	100.8	0.9	-	-	101.7	0.9	-	-	101.7	0.0	-	-
1984	100.9	-0.8	-	-	101.1	0.2	-	-	101.1	0.0	-	-	102.4	1.3	-	-	104.7	2.2	-	-	104.4	-0.3	-	-
1985	105.5	1.1	-	-	105.7	0.2	-	-	106.4	0.7	-	-	107.6	1.1	-	-	108.3	0.7	-	-	108.3	0.0	-	-
1986	108.5	0.2	-	-	107.1	-1.3	-	-	106.8	-0.3	-	-	109.0	2.1	-	-	109.0	0.0	-	-	108.4	-0.6	-	-
1987	109.4	0.9	-	-	110.2	0.7	-	-	110.9	0.6	-	-	112.5	1.4	-	-	114.1	1.4	-	-	112.7	-1.2	-	-
1988	113.0	0.3	-	-	113.8	0.7	-	-	113.7	-0.1	-	-	115.7	1.8	-	-	117.1	1.2	-	-	117.8	0.6	-	-
1989	118.0	0.2	-	-	119.1	0.9	-	-	121.2	1.8	-	-	122.8	1.3	-	-	123.5	0.6	-	-	122.6	-0.7	-	-
1990	124.6	1.6	-	-	126.5	1.5	-	-	126.0	-0.4	-	-	127.3	1.0	-	-	129.3	1.6	-	-	129.9	0.5	-	-
1991	130.3	0.3	-	-	130.1	-0.2	-	-	130.6	0.4	-	-	132.0	1.1	-	-	133.0	0.8	-	-	132.7	-0.2	-	-
1992	132.0	-0.5	-	-	132.0	0.0	-	-	133.6	1.2	-	-	135.4	1.3	-	-	136.5	0.8	-	-	135.6	-0.7	-	-
1993	135.4	-0.1	-	-	135.5	0.1	-	-	136.4	0.7	-	-	138.3	1.4	-	-	137.6	-0.5	-	-	137.5	-0.1	-	-
1994	137.7	0.1	-	-	138.7	0.7	-	-	139.2	0.4	-	-	141.4	1.6	-	-	143.0	1.1	-	-	142.9	-0.1	-	-
1995	142.3	-0.4	-	-	143.9	1.1	-	-	144.2	0.2	-	-	145.2	0.7	-	-	146.5	0.9	-	-	145.0	-1.0	-	-
1996	146.5	1.0	-	-	148.0	1.0	-	-	147.4	-0.4	-	-	149.0	1.1	-	-	150.1	0.7	-	-	150.5	0.3	-	-
1997	150.6	0.1	-	-	151.1	0.3	-	-	151.2	0.1	151.1	-0.1	152.5	0.9	-	-	154.0	1.0	-	-	151.9	-1.4	-	-

Source: U.S. Department of Labor, Bureau of Labor Statistics, Division of Consumer Prices and Price Indexes. - indicates no data collected for period.

St. Louis, MO-IL
Consumer Price Index - All Urban Consumers
Base 1982-1984 = 100
Food and Beverages

For 1975-1997. Columns headed % show percentile change in the index from the previous period for which an index is available.

Year	Jan Index	%	Feb Index	%	Mar Index	%	Apr Index	%	May Index	%	Jun Index	%	Jul Index	%	Aug Index	%	Sep Index	%	Oct Index	%	Nov Index	%	Dec Index	%
1975	-	-	-	-	-	-	-	-	-	-	-	-	-	-	-	-	-	-	-	-	-	-	62.0	-
1976	-	-	-	-	61.8	-0.3	-	-	-	-	62.6	1.3	-	-	-	-	62.9	0.5	-	-	-	-	62.8	-0.2
1977	-	-	-	-	65.4	4.1	-	-	-	-	67.9	3.8	-	-	-	-	67.9	0.0	-	-	-	-	67.8	-0.1
1978	-	-	-	-	70.1	3.4	-	-	72.6	3.6	-	-	74.2	2.2	-	-	74.2	0.0	-	-	74.6	0.5	-	-
1979	77.6	4.0	-	-	79.5	2.4	-	-	81.3	2.3	-	-	82.4	1.4	-	-	82.1	-0.4	-	-	81.7	-0.5	-	-
1980	83.7	2.4	-	-	84.1	0.5	-	-	85.3	1.4	-	-	86.9	1.9	-	-	89.9	3.5	-	-	90.8	1.0	-	-
1981	91.2	0.4	-	-	92.3	1.2	-	-	92.7	0.4	-	-	94.2	1.6	-	-	94.6	0.4	-	-	94.8	0.2		
1982	95.5	0.7	-	-	95.7	0.2	-	-	96.7	1.0	-	-	98.0	1.3	-	-	98.1	0.1	-	-	98.1	0.0		
1983	98.2	0.1	-	-	99.5	1.3	-	-	99.8	0.3	-	-	99.7	-0.1	-	-	100.2	0.5	-	-	100.0	-0.2		
1984	101.3	1.3	-	-	102.3	1.0	-	-	102.2	-0.1	-	-	103.8	1.6	-	-	104.3	0.5	-	-	104.3	0.0		
1985	105.0	0.7	-	-	106.1	1.0	-	-	105.0	-1.0	-	-	105.4	0.4	-	-	106.7	1.2	-	-	105.7	-0.9		
1986	107.3	1.5	-	-	107.6	0.3	-	-	108.1	0.5	-	-	110.0	1.8	-	-	111.9	1.7	-	-	112.1	0.2		
1987	113.4	1.2	-	-	113.7	0.3	-	-	114.1	0.4	-	-	114.2	0.1	-	-	115.0	0.7	-	-	113.3	-1.5		
1988	113.9	0.5	-	-	114.3	0.4	-	-	115.8	1.3	-	-	118.3	2.2	-	-	120.5	1.9	-	-	121.8	1.1		
1989	121.3	-0.4	-	-	124.4	2.6	-	-	125.4	0.8	-	-	125.3	-0.1	-	-	127.2	1.5	-	-	128.4	0.9		
1990	132.8	3.4	-	-	133.6	0.6	-	-	134.0	0.3	-	-	134.2	0.1	-	-	135.3	0.8	-	-	137.6	1.7		
1991	139.8	1.6	-	-	139.1	-0.5	-	-	139.4	0.2	-	-	139.5	0.1	-	-	139.6	0.1	-	-	140.4	0.6		
1992	140.5	0.1	-	-	139.2	-0.9	-	-	140.6	1.0	-	-	139.7	-0.6	-	-	139.9	0.1	-	-	140.8	0.6		
1993	139.8	-0.7	-	-	138.9	-0.6	-	-	138.8	-0.1	-	-	140.0	0.9	-	-	140.9	0.6	-	-	141.1	0.1		
1994	143.9	2.0	-	-	143.6	-0.2	-	-	143.6	0.0	-	-	143.6	0.0	-	-	143.8	0.1	-	-	145.2	1.0		
1995	145.7	0.3	-	-	145.7	0.0	-	-	147.5	1.2	-	-	146.3	-0.8	-	-	147.2	0.6	-	-	148.3	0.7		
1996	149.8	1.0	-	-	150.2	0.3	-	-	150.3	0.1	-	-	151.4	0.7	-	-	151.3	-0.1	-	-	153.6	1.5		
1997	153.6	0.0	-	-	153.9	0.2	-	-	154.3	0.3	154.1	-0.1	155.8	1.1	-	-	156.7	0.6	-	-	154.7	-1.3		

Source: U.S. Department of Labor, Bureau of Labor Statistics, Division of Consumer Prices and Price Indexes. - indicates no data collected for period.

St. Louis, MO-IL
Consumer Price Index - Urban Wage Earners
Base 1982-1984 = 100
Food and Beverages

For 1975-1997. Columns headed % show percentile change in the index from the previous period for which an index is available.

Year	Jan Index	%	Feb Index	%	Mar Index	%	Apr Index	%	May Index	%	Jun Index	%	Jul Index	%	Aug Index	%	Sep Index	%	Oct Index	%	Nov Index	%	Dec Index	%
1975	-	-	-	-	-	-	-	-	-	-	-	-	-	-	-	-	-	-	-	-	-	-	62.0	-
1976	-	-	-	-	61.8	-0.3	-	-	-	-	62.6	1.3	-	-	-	-	62.9	0.5	-	-	-	-	62.8	-0.2
1977	-	-	-	-	65.4	4.1	-	-	-	-	67.9	3.8	-	-	-	-	67.9	0.0	-	-	-	-	67.8	-0.1
1978	-	-	-	-	70.1	3.4	-	-	72.3	3.1	-	-	73.1	1.1	-	-	74.2	1.5	-	-	74.5	0.4	-	-
1979	77.3	3.8	-	-	79.7	3.1	-	-	80.8	1.4	-	-	83.0	2.7	-	-	83.3	0.4	-	-	83.1	-0.2	-	-
1980	84.7	1.9	-	-	84.5	-0.2	-	-	85.0	0.6	-	-	87.2	2.6	-	-	90.5	3.8	-	-	91.1	0.7	-	-
1981	91.6	0.5	-	-	92.3	0.8	-	-	93.0	0.8	-	-	94.2	1.3	-	-	95.0	0.8	-	-	94.9	-0.1	-	-
1982	95.3	0.4	-	-	95.7	0.4	-	-	96.6	0.9	-	-	97.9	1.3	-	-	98.1	0.2	-	-	98.1	0.0	-	-
1983	98.3	0.2	-	-	99.6	1.3	-	-	99.9	0.3	-	-	99.8	-0.1	-	-	100.4	0.6	-	-	100.1	-0.3	-	-
1984	101.2	1.1	-	-	102.3	1.1	-	-	102.2	-0.1	-	-	103.8	1.6	-	-	104.2	0.4	-	-	104.3	0.1	-	-
1985	104.9	0.6	-	-	105.9	1.0	-	-	104.9	-0.9	-	-	105.3	0.4	-	-	106.5	1.1	-	-	105.6	-0.8	-	-
1986	107.1	1.4	-	-	107.6	0.5	-	-	108.1	0.5	-	-	109.9	1.7	-	-	112.0	1.9	-	-	112.2	0.2	-	-
1987	113.6	1.2	-	-	113.8	0.2	-	-	114.0	0.2	-	-	114.2	0.2	-	-	115.1	0.8	-	-	113.5	-1.4	-	-
1988	114.0	0.4	-	-	114.5	0.4	-	-	115.7	1.0	-	-	118.3	2.2	-	-	120.5	1.9	-	-	121.9	1.2	-	-
1989	121.2	-0.6	-	-	124.3	2.6	-	-	125.3	0.8	-	-	125.3	0.0	-	-	127.3	1.6	-	-	128.6	1.0	-	-
1990	132.6	3.1	-	-	133.6	0.8	-	-	134.1	0.4	-	-	134.3	0.1	-	-	135.3	0.7	-	-	137.4	1.6	-	-
1991	139.6	1.6	-	-	139.1	-0.4	-	-	139.3	0.1	-	-	139.5	0.1	-	-	139.8	0.2	-	-	140.3	0.4	-	-
1992	140.5	0.1	-	-	139.3	-0.9	-	-	140.6	0.9	-	-	140.0	-0.4	-	-	140.1	0.1	-	-	140.8	0.5	-	-
1993	140.0	-0.6	-	-	139.1	-0.6	-	-	139.1	0.0	-	-	140.3	0.9	-	-	141.1	0.6	-	-	141.3	0.1	-	-
1994	143.9	1.8	-	-	143.9	0.0	-	-	144.1	0.1	-	-	144.1	0.0	-	-	144.2	0.1	-	-	145.4	0.8	-	-
1995	145.7	0.2	-	-	145.9	0.1	-	-	147.7	1.2	-	-	146.4	-0.9	-	-	147.2	0.5	-	-	148.1	0.6	-	-
1996	149.6	1.0	-	-	149.9	0.2	-	-	150.3	0.3	-	-	151.2	0.6	-	-	151.2	0.0	-	-	153.4	1.5	-	-
1997	153.7	0.2	-	-	154.1	0.3	-	-	154.5	0.3	154.3	-0.1	156.1	1.2	-	-	156.7	0.4	-	-	155.0	-1.1	-	-

Source: U.S. Department of Labor, Bureau of Labor Statistics, Division of Consumer Prices and Price Indexes. - indicates no data collected for period.

St. Louis, MO-IL
Consumer Price Index - All Urban Consumers
Base 1982-1984 = 100
Housing

For 1975-1997. Columns headed % show percentile change in the index from the previous period for which an index is available.

Year	Jan Index	%	Feb Index	%	Mar Index	%	Apr Index	%	May Index	%	Jun Index	%	Jul Index	%	Aug Index	%	Sep Index	%	Oct Index	%	Nov Index	%	Dec Index	%
1975	-	-	-	-	-	-	-	-	-	-	-	-	-	-	-	-	-	-	-	-	-	-	48.7	-
1976	-	-	-	-	50.1	2.9	-	-	-	-	50.5	0.8	-	-	-	-	51.1	1.2	-	-	-	-	51.3	0.4
1977	-	-	-	-	52.8	2.9	-	-	-	-	53.9	2.1	-	-	-	-	55.1	2.2	-	-	-	-	55.7	1.1
1978	-	-	-	-	56.9	2.2	-	-	58.5	2.8	-	-	59.6	1.9	-	-	61.0	2.3	-	-	62.3	2.1	-	-
1979	63.7	2.2	-	-	65.4	2.7	-	-	65.3	-0.2	-	-	67.4	3.2	-	-	70.6	4.7	-	-	72.2	2.3	-	-
1980	75.4	4.4	-	-	77.2	2.4	-	-	78.4	1.6	-	-	79.7	1.7	-	-	83.1	4.3	-	-	82.9	-0.2	-	-
1981	82.6	-0.4	-	-	83.1	0.6	-	-	88.7	6.7	-	-	88.7	0.0	-	-	90.5	2.0	-	-	89.4	-1.2	-	-
1982	92.4	3.4	-	-	94.3	2.1	-	-	96.9	2.8	-	-	98.0	1.1	-	-	100.5	2.6	-	-	97.1	-3.4	-	-
1983	97.8	0.7	-	-	98.9	1.1	-	-	99.3	0.4	-	-	102.0	2.7	-	-	103.0	1.0	-	-	100.6	-2.3	-	-
1984	101.3	0.7	-	-	100.9	-0.4	-	-	102.7	1.8	-	-	104.4	1.7	-	-	104.8	0.4	-	-	101.9	-2.8	-	-
1985	106.2	4.2	-	-	105.2	-0.9	-	-	105.9	0.7	-	-	109.5	3.4	-	-	110.0	0.5	-	-	109.4	-0.5	-	-
1986	109.3	-0.1	-	-	108.5	-0.7	-	-	108.2	-0.3	-	-	114.2	5.5	-	-	112.9	-1.1	-	-	108.8	-3.6	-	-
1987	109.9	1.0	-	-	110.3	0.4	-	-	110.8	0.5	-	-	114.1	3.0	-	-	114.5	0.4	-	-	112.3	-1.9	-	-
1988	112.8	0.4	-	-	113.7	0.8	-	-	112.8	-0.8	-	-	115.8	2.7	-	-	116.1	0.3	-	-	117.1	0.9	-	-
1989	117.8	0.6	-	-	117.2	-0.5	-	-	118.4	1.0	-	-	122.5	3.5	-	-	124.3	1.5	-	-	120.6	-3.0	-	-
1990	121.6	0.8	-	-	124.5	2.4	-	-	123.9	-0.5	-	-	126.4	2.0	-	-	126.4	0.0	-	-	125.6	-0.6	-	-
1991	125.6	0.0	-	-	126.4	0.6	-	-	127.1	0.6	-	-	129.8	2.1	-	-	129.5	-0.2	-	-	127.4	-1.6	-	-
1992	126.5	-0.7	-	-	126.8	0.2	-	-	128.0	0.9	-	-	132.1	3.2	-	-	133.1	0.8	-	-	130.4	-2.0	-	-
1993	131.0	0.5	-	-	131.3	0.2	-	-	131.1	-0.2	-	-	135.4	3.3	-	-	135.6	0.1	-	-	132.7	-2.1	-	-
1994	133.8	0.8	-	-	135.7	1.4	-	-	135.2	-0.4	-	-	138.8	2.7	-	-	139.0	0.1	-	-	137.0	-1.4	-	-
1995	137.0	0.0	-	-	138.9	1.4	-	-	137.3	-1.2	-	-	141.1	2.8	-	-	142.1	0.7	-	-	139.7	-1.7	-	-
1996	140.2	0.4	-	-	141.8	1.1	-	-	140.1	-1.2	-	-	144.4	3.1	-	-	144.9	0.3	-	-	143.1	-1.2	-	-
1997	145.1	1.4	-	-	144.6	-0.3	-	-	143.6	-0.7	144.6	0.7	147.0	1.7	-	-	148.2	0.8	-	-	144.4	-2.6	-	-

Source: U.S. Department of Labor, Bureau of Labor Statistics, Division of Consumer Prices and Price Indexes. - indicates no data collected for period.

St. Louis, MO-IL
Consumer Price Index - Urban Wage Earners
Base 1982-1984 = 100
Housing

For 1975-1997. Columns headed % show percentile change in the index from the previous period for which an index is available.

Year	Jan Index	%	Feb Index	%	Mar Index	%	Apr Index	%	May Index	%	Jun Index	%	Jul Index	%	Aug Index	%	Sep Index	%	Oct Index	%	Nov Index	%	Dec Index	%
1975	-	-	-	-	-	-			-	-			-	-	-	-	-	-	-	-	-	-	49.1	-
1976	-	-	-	-	50.5	2.9	-	-	-	-	51.0	1.0	-	-	-	-	51.6	1.2	-	-	-	-	51.8	0.4
1977	-	-	-	-	53.3	2.9	-	-	-	-	54.3	1.9	-	-	-	-	55.6	2.4	-	-	-	-	56.2	1.1
1978	-	-	-	-	57.4	2.1	-	-	58.8	2.4	-	-	60.0	2.0	-	-	61.7	2.8	-	-	63.1	2.3	-	-
1979	64.2	1.7	-	-	66.2	3.1	-	-	66.4	0.3	-	-	68.6	3.3	-	-	71.5	4.2	-	-	73.3	2.5	-	-
1980	76.5	4.4	-	-	78.4	2.5	-	-	80.0	2.0	-	-	81.2	1.5	-	-	84.1	3.6	-	-	84.1	0.0	-	-
1981	83.5	-0.7	-	-	84.0	0.6	-	-	90.1	7.3	-	-	89.8	-0.3	-	-	91.8	2.2	-	-	90.4	-1.5	-	-
1982	93.5	3.4	-	-	95.4	2.0	-	-	98.1	2.8	-	-	99.2	1.1	-	-	101.9	2.7	-	-	98.3	-3.5	-	-
1983	95.6	-2.7	-	-	101.4	6.1	-	-	100.4	-1.0	-	-	101.6	1.2	-	-	102.3	0.7	-	-	102.6	0.3	-	-
1984	100.4	-2.1	-	-	99.4	-1.0	-	-	98.5	-0.9	-	-	100.6	2.1	-	-	104.4	3.8	-	-	103.2	-1.1	-	-
1985	107.4	4.1	-	-	106.3	-1.0	-	-	107.0	0.7	-	-	110.6	3.4	-	-	111.4	0.7	-	-	110.8	-0.5	-	-
1986	110.8	0.0	-	-	110.0	-0.7	-	-	109.7	-0.3	-	-	115.6	5.4	-	-	114.4	-1.0	-	-	110.4	-3.5	-	-
1987	111.7	1.2	-	-	112.1	0.4	-	-	112.5	0.4	-	-	116.2	3.3	-	-	116.4	0.2	-	-	113.8	-2.2	-	-
1988	114.4	0.5	-	-	115.3	0.8	-	-	114.3	-0.9	-	-	117.6	2.9	-	-	117.9	0.3	-	-	118.7	0.7	-	-
1989	119.4	0.6	-	-	118.9	-0.4	-	-	120.1	1.0	-	-	124.4	3.6	-	-	126.2	1.4	-	-	122.1	-3.2	-	-
1990	123.3	1.0	-	-	126.3	2.4	-	-	125.5	-0.6	-	-	128.4	2.3	-	-	128.5	0.1	-	-	127.5	-0.8	-	-
1991	127.4	-0.1	-	-	128.1	0.5	-	-	128.8	0.5	-	-	131.7	2.3	-	-	131.6	-0.1	-	-	129.3	-1.7	-	-
1992	128.5	-0.6	-	-	128.9	0.3	-	-	130.1	0.9	-	-	134.6	3.5	-	-	135.5	0.7	-	-	132.6	-2.1	-	-
1993	133.2	0.5	-	-	133.4	0.2	-	-	133.2	-0.1	-	-	137.9	3.5	-	-	137.9	0.0	-	-	134.8	-2.2	-	-
1994	136.0	0.9	-	-	137.8	1.3	-	-	137.4	-0.3	-	-	141.2	2.8	-	-	141.4	0.1	-	-	139.1	-1.6	-	-
1995	139.1	0.0	-	-	141.0	1.4	-	-	139.3	-1.2	-	-	143.4	2.9	-	-	144.2	0.6	-	-	141.6	-1.8	-	-
1996	142.4	0.6	-	-	143.7	0.9	-	-	142.1	-1.1	-	-	146.7	3.2	-	-	147.4	0.5	-	-	145.2	-1.5	-	-
1997	147.3	1.4	-	-	146.9	-0.3	-	-	145.9	-0.7	146.9	0.7	149.6	1.8	-	-	150.8	0.8	-	-	146.6	-2.8	-	-

Source: U.S. Department of Labor, Bureau of Labor Statistics, Division of Consumer Prices and Price Indexes. - indicates no data collected for period.

St. Louis, MO-IL
Consumer Price Index - All Urban Consumers
Base 1982-1984 = 100
Apparel and Upkeep

For 1952-1997. Columns headed % show percentile change in the index from the previous period for which an index is available.

Year	Jan Index	%	Feb Index	%	Mar Index	%	Apr Index	%	May Index	%	Jun Index	%	Jul Index	%	Aug Index	%	Sep Index	%	Oct Index	%	Nov Index	%	Dec Index	%
1952	-	-	-	-	-	-	-	-	-	-	-	-	-	-	-	-	-	-	-	-	-	-	43.8	-
1953	-	-	-	-	43.9	0.2	-	-	-	-	44.0	0.2	-	-	-	-	44.5	1.1	-	-	-	-	44.3	-0.4
1954	-	-	-	-	44.0	-0.7	-	-	-	-	44.1	0.2	-	-	-	-	43.9	-0.5	-	-	-	-	43.8	-0.2
1955	-	-	-	-	44.0	0.5	-	-	-	-	43.8	-0.5	-	-	-	-	43.9	0.2	-	-	-	-	44.1	0.5
1956	-	-	-	-	44.2	0.2	-	-	-	-	44.4	0.5	-	-	-	-	44.6	0.5	-	-	-	-	44.8	0.4
1957	-	-	-	-	45.0	0.4	-	-	-	-	44.8	-0.4	-	-	-	-	45.1	0.7	-	-	-	-	45.4	0.7
1958	-	-	-	-	45.9	1.1	-	-	-	-	45.7	-0.4	-	-	-	-	46.0	0.7	-	-	-	-	45.9	-0.2
1959	-	-	-	-	45.9	0.0	-	-	-	-	45.9	0.0	-	-	-	-	46.5	1.3	-	-	-	-	46.6	0.2
1960	-	-	-	-	46.8	0.4	-	-	-	-	46.9	0.2	-	-	-	-	47.5	1.3	-	-	-	-	47.5	0.0
1961	-	-	-	-	47.7	0.4	-	-	-	-	47.6	-0.2	-	-	-	-	47.6	0.0	-	-	-	-	47.4	-0.4
1962	-	-	-	-	47.5	0.2	-	-	-	-	47.6	0.2	-	-	-	-	47.8	0.4	-	-	-	-	47.5	-0.6
1963	-	-	-	-	47.6	0.2	-	-	-	-	48.0	0.8	-	-	-	-	48.3	0.6	-	-	-	-	48.7	0.8
1964	-	-	-	-	48.5	-0.4	-	-	-	-	48.5	0.0	-	-	-	-	48.8	0.6	-	-	-	-	48.9	0.2
1965	-	-	-	-	48.8	-0.2	-	-	-	-	48.9	0.2	-	-	-	-	49.6	1.4	-	-	-	-	49.7	0.2
1966	-	-	-	-	49.9	0.4	-	-	-	-	50.7	1.6	-	-	-	-	51.2	1.0	-	-	-	-	51.4	0.4
1967	-	-	-	-	52.1	1.4	-	-	-	-	52.2	0.2	-	-	-	-	52.6	0.8	-	-	-	-	53.4	1.5
1968	-	-	-	-	54.7	2.4	-	-	-	-	54.8	0.2	-	-	-	-	56.5	3.1	-	-	-	-	56.8	0.5
1969	-	-	-	-	57.5	1.2	-	-	-	-	57.9	0.7	-	-	-	-	58.8	1.6	-	-	-	-	59.1	0.5
1970	-	-	-	-	59.3	0.3	-	-	-	-	60.1	1.3	-	-	-	-	61.6	2.5	-	-	-	-	61.3	-0.5
1971	-	-	-	-	61.8	0.8	-	-	-	-	61.9	0.2	-	-	-	-	63.4	2.4	-	-	-	-	63.3	-0.2
1972	-	-	-	-	63.0	-0.5	-	-	-	-	62.6	-0.6	-	-	-	-	63.4	1.3	-	-	-	-	63.1	-0.5
1973	-	-	-	-	63.2	0.2	-	-	-	-	63.3	0.2	-	-	-	-	66.5	5.1	-	-	-	-	66.0	-0.8
1974	-	-	-	-	66.1	0.2	-	-	-	-	67.5	2.1	-	-	-	-	69.8	3.4	-	-	-	-	70.0	0.3
1975	-	-	-	-	70.2	0.3	-	-	-	-	70.6	0.6	-	-	-	-	71.3	1.0	-	-	-	-	72.0	1.0
1976	-	-	-	-	73.5	2.1	-	-	-	-	73.8	0.4	-	-	-	-	75.4	2.2	-	-	-	-	75.7	0.4
1977	-	-	-	-	78.8	4.1	-	-	-	-	79.0	0.3	-	-	-	-	80.0	1.3	-	-	-	-	80.9	1.1
1978	-	-	-	-	79.6	-1.6	-	-	78.0	-2.0	-	-	77.9	-0.1	-	-	80.6	3.5	-	-	84.1	4.3	-	-
1979	81.8	-2.7	-	-	87.3	6.7	-	-	85.4	-2.2	-	-	81.4	-4.7	-	-	86.9	6.8	-	-	87.5	0.7	-	-
1980	85.4	-2.4	-	-	92.0	7.7	-	-	92.9	1.0	-	-	91.0	-2.0	-	-	94.4	3.7	-	-	93.2	-1.3	-	-
1981	91.6	-1.7	-	-	96.2	5.0	-	-	94.1	-2.2	-	-	95.4	1.4	-	-	97.7	2.4	-	-	95.9	-1.8	-	-
1982	94.1	-1.9	-	-	99.2	5.4	-	-	97.5	-1.7	-	-	97.6	0.1	-	-	99.4	1.8	-	-	97.1	-2.3	-	-
1983	97.4	0.3	-	-	103.3	6.1	-	-	100.9	-2.3	-	-	100.5	-0.4	-	-	102.0	1.5	-	-	100.5	-1.5	-	-
1984	98.0	-2.5	-	-	102.5	4.6	-	-	100.0	-2.4	-	-	99.8	-0.2	-	-	105.3	5.5	-	-	103.8	-1.4	-	-
1985	99.6	-4.0	-	-	106.9	7.3	-	-	107.4	0.5	-	-	104.3	-2.9	-	-	105.2	0.9	-	-	103.9	-1.2	-	-
1986	98.0	-5.7	-	-	103.5	5.6	-	-	103.2	-0.3	-	-	99.2	-3.9	-	-	104.7	5.5	-	-	106.1	1.3	-	-
1987	102.0	-3.9	-	-	107.1	5.0	-	-	107.1	0.0	-	-	100.2	-6.4	-	-	114.6	14.4	-	-	113.1	-1.3	-	-
1988	109.1	-3.5	-	-	115.1	5.5	-	-	110.6	-3.9	-	-	107.4	-2.9	-	-	116.1	8.1	-	-	116.2	0.1	-	-
1989	111.5	-4.0	-	-	119.6	7.3	-	-	121.0	1.2	-	-	118.5	-2.1	-	-	119.3	0.7	-	-	119.0	-0.3	-	-
1990	118.7	-0.3	-	-	128.6	8.3	-	-	119.2	-7.3	-	-	116.7	-2.1	-	-	121.2	3.9	-	-	121.0	-0.2	-	-
1991	119.1	-1.6	-	-	124.6	4.6	-	-	121.4	-2.6	-	-	119.1	-1.9	-	-	125.8	5.6	-	-	124.6	-1.0	-	-
1992	121.4	-2.6	-	-	122.6	1.0	-	-	119.7	-2.4	-	-	118.0	-1.4	-	-	124.5	5.5	-	-	123.9	-0.5	-	-
1993	120.9	-2.4	-	-	122.8	1.6	-	-	126.0	2.6	-	-	122.6	-2.7	-	-	121.2	-1.1	-	-	123.5	1.9	-	-
1994	120.8	-2.2	-	-	123.1	1.9	-	-	123.7	0.5	-	-	121.4	-1.9	-	-	131.3	8.2	-	-	130.7	-0.5	-	-

[Continued]

St. Louis, MO-IL
Consumer Price Index - All Urban Consumers
Base 1982-1984 = 100
Apparel and Upkeep

[Continued]

For 1952-1997. Columns headed % show percentile change in the index from the previous period for which an index is available.

Year	Jan		Feb		Mar		Apr		May		Jun		Jul		Aug		Sep		Oct		Nov		Dec	
	Index	%	Index	%	Index	%	Index	%	Index	%	Index	%	Index	%	Index	%	Index	%	Index	%	Index	%	Index	%
1995	120.5	-7.8	-	-	120.7	0.2	-	-	117.9	-2.3	-	-	117.5	-0.3	-	-	123.0	4.7	-	-	116.4	-5.4	-	-
1996	117.8	1.2	-	-	124.1	5.3	-	-	120.7	-2.7	-	-	119.7	-0.8	-	-	127.6	6.6	-	-	123.6	-3.1	-	-
1997	117.6	-4.9	-	-	125.6	6.8	-	-	128.7	2.5	123.9	-3.7	117.5	-5.2	-	-	127.1	8.2	-	-	126.2	-0.7	-	-

Source: U.S. Department of Labor, Bureau of Labor Statistics, Division of Consumer Prices and Price Indexes. - indicates no data collected for period.

St. Louis, MO-IL
Consumer Price Index - Urban Wage Earners
Base 1982-1984 = 100
Apparel and Upkeep

For 1952-1997. Columns headed % show percentile change in the index from the previous period for which an index is available.

Year	Jan Index	%	Feb Index	%	Mar Index	%	Apr Index	%	May Index	%	Jun Index	%	Jul Index	%	Aug Index	%	Sep Index	%	Oct Index	%	Nov Index	%	Dec Index	%
1952	-	-	-	-	-	-	-	-	-	-	-	-	-	-	-	-	-	-	-	-	-	-	44.6	-
1953	-	-	-	-	44.8	0.4	-	-	-	-	44.9	0.2	-	-	-	-	45.4	1.1	-	-	-	-	45.2	-0.4
1954	-	-	-	-	44.9	-0.7	-	-	-	-	44.9	0.0	-	-	-	-	44.7	-0.4	-	-	-	-	44.6	-0.2
1955	-	-	-	-	44.9	0.7	-	-	-	-	44.6	-0.7	-	-	-	-	44.8	0.4	-	-	-	-	44.9	0.2
1956	-	-	-	-	45.1	0.4	-	-	-	-	45.2	0.2	-	-	-	-	45.5	0.7	-	-	-	-	45.6	0.2
1957	-	-	-	-	45.8	0.4	-	-	-	-	45.6	-0.4	-	-	-	-	46.0	0.9	-	-	-	-	46.3	0.7
1958	-	-	-	-	46.8	1.1	-	-	-	-	46.6	-0.4	-	-	-	-	46.8	0.4	-	-	-	-	46.7	-0.2
1959	-	-	-	-	46.8	0.2	-	-	-	-	46.7	-0.2	-	-	-	-	47.4	1.5	-	-	-	-	47.5	0.2
1960	-	-	-	-	47.7	0.4	-	-	-	-	47.8	0.2	-	-	-	-	48.4	1.3	-	-	-	-	48.4	0.0
1961	-	-	-	-	48.6	0.4	-	-	-	-	48.5	-0.2	-	-	-	-	48.5	0.0	-	-	-	-	48.3	-0.4
1962	-	-	-	-	48.4	0.2	-	-	-	-	48.5	0.2	-	-	-	-	48.7	0.4	-	-	-	-	48.4	-0.6
1963	-	-	-	-	48.5	0.2	-	-	-	-	48.9	0.8	-	-	-	-	49.2	0.6	-	-	-	-	49.6	0.8
1964	-	-	-	-	49.4	-0.4	-	-	-	-	49.5	0.2	-	-	-	-	49.8	0.6	-	-	-	-	49.8	0.0
1965	-	-	-	-	49.7	-0.2	-	-	-	-	49.8	0.2	-	-	-	-	50.6	1.6	-	-	-	-	50.7	0.2
1966	-	-	-	-	50.9	0.4	-	-	-	-	51.6	1.4	-	-	-	-	52.2	1.2	-	-	-	-	52.4	0.4
1967	-	-	-	-	53.1	1.3	-	-	-	-	53.2	0.2	-	-	-	-	53.6	0.8	-	-	-	-	54.5	1.7
1968	-	-	-	-	55.7	2.2	-	-	-	-	55.8	0.2	-	-	-	-	57.6	3.2	-	-	-	-	57.8	0.3
1969	-	-	-	-	58.6	1.4	-	-	-	-	59.0	0.7	-	-	-	-	59.9	1.5	-	-	-	-	60.2	0.5
1970	-	-	-	-	60.5	0.5	-	-	-	-	61.2	1.2	-	-	-	-	62.8	2.6	-	-	-	-	62.4	-0.6
1971	-	-	-	-	63.0	1.0	-	-	-	-	63.1	0.2	-	-	-	-	64.6	2.4	-	-	-	-	64.5	-0.2
1972	-	-	-	-	64.2	-0.5	-	-	-	-	63.8	-0.6	-	-	-	-	64.6	1.3	-	-	-	-	64.4	-0.3
1973	-	-	-	-	64.4	0.0	-	-	-	-	64.5	0.2	-	-	-	-	67.8	5.1	-	-	-	-	67.3	-0.7
1974	-	-	-	-	67.3	0.0	-	-	-	-	68.8	2.2	-	-	-	-	71.1	3.3	-	-	-	-	71.4	0.4
1975	-	-	-	-	71.5	0.1	-	-	-	-	71.9	0.6	-	-	-	-	72.7	1.1	-	-	-	-	73.4	1.0
1976	-	-	-	-	74.9	2.0	-	-	-	-	75.2	0.4	-	-	-	-	76.8	2.1	-	-	-	-	77.2	0.5
1977	-	-	-	-	80.3	4.0	-	-	-	-	80.5	0.2	-	-	-	-	81.5	1.2	-	-	-	-	82.4	1.1
1978	-	-	-	-	81.1	-1.6	-	-	79.3	-2.2	-	-	79.4	0.1	-	-	82.1	3.4	-	-	82.0	-0.1	-	-
1979	80.3	-2.1	-	-	85.3	6.2	-	-	84.7	-0.7	-	-	81.2	-4.1	-	-	86.6	6.7	-	-	87.1	0.6	-	-
1980	85.6	-1.7	-	-	90.3	5.5	-	-	90.7	0.4	-	-	89.3	-1.5	-	-	93.1	4.3	-	-	92.3	-0.9	-	-
1981	92.1	-0.2	-	-	97.0	5.3	-	-	95.2	-1.9	-	-	95.2	0.0	-	-	96.7	1.6	-	-	95.3	-1.4	-	-
1982	93.1	-2.3	-	-	98.9	6.2	-	-	96.9	-2.0	-	-	97.5	0.6	-	-	99.4	1.9	-	-	98.0	-1.4	-	-
1983	97.5	-0.5	-	-	102.8	5.4	-	-	101.4	-1.4	-	-	101.3	-0.1	-	-	102.5	1.2	-	-	100.6	-1.9	-	-
1984	97.4	-3.2	-	-	101.1	3.8	-	-	98.6	-2.5	-	-	100.5	1.9	-	-	106.0	5.5	-	-	104.9	-1.0	-	-
1985	99.9	-4.8	-	-	106.0	6.1	-	-	106.9	0.8	-	-	103.3	-3.4	-	-	105.2	1.8	-	-	104.1	-1.0	-	-
1986	99.0	-4.9	-	-	102.6	3.6	-	-	102.1	-0.5	-	-	99.0	-3.0	-	-	105.1	6.2	-	-	105.9	0.8	-	-
1987	101.9	-3.8	-	-	107.2	5.2	-	-	107.4	0.2	-	-	100.7	-6.2	-	-	114.5	13.7	-	-	112.9	-1.4	-	-
1988	109.6	-2.9	-	-	115.3	5.2	-	-	110.8	-3.9	-	-	107.1	-3.3	-	-	116.4	8.7	-	-	116.1	-0.3	-	-
1989	111.8	-3.7	-	-	119.4	6.8	-	-	120.7	1.1	-	-	119.0	-1.4	-	-	119.2	0.2	-	-	119.4	0.2	-	-
1990	119.1	-0.3	-	-	129.6	8.8	-	-	119.2	-8.0	-	-	116.8	-2.0	-	-	121.4	3.9	-	-	121.0	-0.3	-	-
1991	119.6	-1.2	-	-	125.0	4.5	-	-	121.4	-2.9	-	-	119.0	-2.0	-	-	126.3	6.1	-	-	125.2	-0.9	-	-
1992	121.8	-2.7	-	-	123.1	1.1	-	-	119.9	-2.6	-	-	118.2	-1.4	-	-	125.3	6.0	-	-	124.7	-0.5	-	-
1993	121.0	-3.0	-	-	123.4	2.0	-	-	126.3	2.4	-	-	122.5	-3.0	-	-	120.9	-1.3	-	-	124.3	2.8	-	-
1994	120.6	-3.0	-	-	123.1	2.1	-	-	123.7	0.5	-	-	122.4	-1.1	-	-	133.0	8.7	-	-	132.7	-0.2	-	-

[Continued]

St. Louis, MO-IL
Consumer Price Index - Urban Wage Earners
Base 1982-1984 = 100
Apparel and Upkeep

[Continued]

For 1952-1997. Columns headed % show percentile change in the index from the previous period for which an index is available.

Year	Jan Index	%	Feb Index	%	Mar Index	%	Apr Index	%	May Index	%	Jun Index	%	Jul Index	%	Aug Index	%	Sep Index	%	Oct Index	%	Nov Index	%	Dec Index	%
1995	120.7	-9.0	-	-	120.9	0.2	-	-	117.7	-2.6	-	-	118.3	0.5	-	-	124.0	4.8	-	-	117.1	-5.6	-	-
1996	118.2	0.9	-	-	124.9	5.7	-	-	121.5	-2.7	-	-	119.9	-1.3	-	-	127.7	6.5	-	-	123.4	-3.4	-	-
1997	116.8	-5.3	-	-	125.6	7.5	-	-	129.0	2.7	123.9	-4.0	117.8	-4.9	-	-	127.3	8.1	-	-	126.2	-0.9	-	-

Source: U.S. Department of Labor, Bureau of Labor Statistics, Division of Consumer Prices and Price Indexes. - indicates no data collected for period.

St. Louis, MO-IL
Consumer Price Index - All Urban Consumers
Base 1982-1984 = 100
Transportation

For 1947-1997. Columns headed % show percentile change in the index from the previous period for which an index is available.

Year	Jan Index	Jan %	Feb Index	Feb %	Mar Index	Mar %	Apr Index	Apr %	May Index	May %	Jun Index	Jun %	Jul Index	Jul %	Aug Index	Aug %	Sep Index	Sep %	Oct Index	Oct %	Nov Index	Nov %	Dec Index	Dec %
1947	17.7	-	17.7	0.0	17.9	1.1	18.0	0.6	18.0	0.0	18.0	0.0	-	-	-	-	18.4	2.2	-	-	-	-	18.9	2.7
1948	-	-	-	-	19.2	1.6	-	-	-	-	19.6	2.1	-	-	-	-	20.4	4.1	-	-	-	-	20.4	0.0
1949	-	-	-	-	20.7	1.5	-	-	-	-	20.7	0.0	-	-	-	-	20.7	0.0	-	-	-	-	21.5	3.9
1950	-	-	-	-	21.3	-0.9	-	-	-	-	21.1	-0.9	-	-	-	-	21.4	1.4	-	-	-	-	21.6	0.9
1951	-	-	-	-	23.5	8.8	-	-	-	-	23.4	-0.4	-	-	-	-	23.7	1.3	-	-	-	-	24.3	2.5
1952	-	-	-	-	25.6	5.3	-	-	-	-	25.6	0.0	-	-	-	-	26.3	2.7	-	-	-	-	26.1	-0.8
1953	-	-	-	-	26.9	3.1	-	-	-	-	26.8	-0.4	-	-	-	-	26.8	0.0	-	-	-	-	26.7	-0.4
1954	-	-	-	-	26.7	0.0	-	-	-	-	26.7	0.0	-	-	-	-	24.5	-8.2	-	-	-	-	25.6	4.5
1955	-	-	-	-	26.4	3.1	-	-	-	-	26.4	0.0	-	-	-	-	25.7	-2.7	-	-	-	-	26.2	1.9
1956	-	-	-	-	25.9	-1.1	-	-	-	-	26.2	1.2	-	-	-	-	26.3	0.4	-	-	-	-	27.3	3.8
1957	-	-	-	-	27.6	1.1	-	-	-	-	28.0	1.4	-	-	-	-	28.3	1.1	-	-	-	-	28.6	1.1
1958	-	-	-	-	28.9	1.0	-	-	-	-	29.1	0.7	-	-	-	-	30.1	3.4	-	-	-	-	31.3	4.0
1959	-	-	-	-	31.7	1.3	-	-	-	-	31.7	0.0	-	-	-	-	31.3	-1.3	-	-	-	-	32.0	2.2
1960	-	-	-	-	31.6	-1.2	-	-	-	-	31.6	0.0	-	-	-	-	31.2	-1.3	-	-	-	-	30.6	-1.9
1961	-	-	-	-	32.0	4.6	-	-	-	-	32.2	0.6	-	-	-	-	32.0	-0.6	-	-	-	-	32.5	1.6
1962	-	-	-	-	32.1	-1.2	-	-	-	-	31.8	-0.9	-	-	-	-	32.8	3.1	-	-	-	-	33.2	1.2
1963	-	-	-	-	32.7	-1.5	-	-	-	-	31.3	-4.3	-	-	-	-	32.2	2.9	-	-	-	-	32.8	1.9
1964	-	-	-	-	32.7	-0.3	-	-	-	-	32.1	-1.8	-	-	-	-	32.9	2.5	-	-	-	-	33.3	1.2
1965	-	-	-	-	33.0	-0.9	-	-	-	-	32.9	-0.3	-	-	-	-	32.7	-0.6	-	-	-	-	33.5	2.4
1966	-	-	-	-	33.5	0.0	-	-	-	-	34.4	2.7	-	-	-	-	34.4	0.0	-	-	-	-	34.4	0.0
1967	-	-	-	-	34.8	1.2	-	-	-	-	35.2	1.1	-	-	-	-	35.7	1.4	-	-	-	-	36.0	0.8
1968	-	-	-	-	36.0	0.0	-	-	-	-	36.1	0.3	-	-	-	-	36.1	0.0	-	-	-	-	35.9	-0.6
1969	-	-	-	-	36.9	2.8	-	-	-	-	37.3	1.1	-	-	-	-	37.4	0.3	-	-	-	-	37.7	0.8
1970	-	-	-	-	37.4	-0.8	-	-	-	-	39.4	5.3	-	-	-	-	40.3	2.3	-	-	-	-	42.2	4.7
1971	-	-	-	-	41.2	-2.4	-	-	-	-	42.7	3.6	-	-	-	-	42.0	-1.6	-	-	-	-	42.6	1.4
1972	-	-	-	-	41.2	-3.3	-	-	-	-	42.3	2.7	-	-	-	-	42.9	1.4	-	-	-	-	43.3	0.9
1973	-	-	-	-	43.5	0.5	-	-	-	-	44.3	1.8	-	-	-	-	43.9	-0.9	-	-	-	-	43.6	-0.7
1974	-	-	-	-	45.5	4.4	-	-	-	-	47.9	5.3	-	-	-	-	49.0	2.3	-	-	-	-	49.2	0.4
1975	-	-	-	-	49.5	0.6	-	-	-	-	51.3	3.6	-	-	-	-	53.1	3.5	-	-	-	-	53.5	0.8
1976	-	-	-	-	54.0	0.9	-	-	-	-	56.5	4.6	-	-	-	-	57.4	1.6	-	-	-	-	58.3	1.6
1977	-	-	-	-	58.7	0.7	-	-	-	-	60.3	2.7	-	-	-	-	59.8	-0.8	-	-	-	-	60.0	0.3
1978	-	-	-	-	59.9	-0.2	-	-	63.4	5.8	-	-	64.4	1.6	-	-	65.2	1.2	-	-	66.5	2.0	-	-
1979	67.4	1.4	-	-	68.9	2.2	-	-	72.0	4.5	-	-	76.3	6.0	-	-	76.7	0.5	-	-	78.4	2.2	-	-
1980	80.9	3.2	-	-	83.3	3.0	-	-	84.8	1.8	-	-	85.5	0.8	-	-	86.0	0.6	-	-	88.1	2.4	-	-
1981	90.3	2.5	-	-	92.5	2.4	-	-	94.1	1.7	-	-	94.8	0.7	-	-	95.4	0.6	-	-	97.6	2.3	-	-
1982	96.9	-0.7	-	-	94.6	-2.4	-	-	97.1	2.6	-	-	100.0	3.0	-	-	99.2	-0.8	-	-	99.0	-0.2	-	-
1983	97.6	-1.4	-	-	95.8	-1.8	-	-	99.0	3.3	-	-	100.3	1.3	-	-	100.9	0.6	-	-	101.2	0.3	-	-
1984	100.5	-0.7	-	-	101.3	0.8	-	-	103.0	1.7	-	-	103.4	0.4	-	-	103.9	0.5	-	-	104.6	0.7	-	-
1985	103.9	-0.7	-	-	103.8	-0.1	-	-	106.0	2.1	-	-	105.8	-0.2	-	-	105.4	-0.4	-	-	106.5	1.0	-	-
1986	106.1	-0.4	-	-	100.7	-5.1	-	-	99.7	-1.0	-	-	99.3	-0.4	-	-	97.7	-1.6	-	-	99.8	2.1	-	-
1987	101.4	1.6	-	-	102.1	0.7	-	-	103.2	1.1	-	-	104.7	1.5	-	-	105.7	1.0	-	-	105.7	0.0	-	-
1988	105.2	-0.5	-	-	104.0	-1.1	-	-	105.8	1.7	-	-	106.5	0.7	-	-	106.7	0.2	-	-	107.1	0.4	-	-
1989	107.2	0.1	-	-	107.4	0.2	-	-	113.3	5.5	-	-	112.0	-1.1	-	-	109.2	-2.5	-	-	111.6	2.2	-	-
1990	115.4	3.4	-	-	114.0	-1.2	-	-	115.1	1.0	-	-	114.8	-0.3	-	-	120.9	5.3	-	-	122.6	1.4	-	-
1991	121.6	-0.8	-	-	115.8	-4.8	-	-	118.2	2.1	-	-	117.2	-0.8	-	-	118.9	1.5	-	-	120.3	1.2	-	-

[Continued]

St. Louis, MO-IL
Consumer Price Index - All Urban Consumers
Base 1982-1984 = 100
Transportation
[Continued]

For 1947-1997. Columns headed % show percentile change in the index from the previous period for which an index is available.

Year	Jan Index	%	Feb Index	%	Mar Index	%	Apr Index	%	May Index	%	Jun Index	%	Jul Index	%	Aug Index	%	Sep Index	%	Oct Index	%	Nov Index	%	Dec Index	%
1992	118.8	-1.2	-	-	119.0	0.2	-	-	122.7	3.1	-	-	122.6	-0.1	-	-	122.7	0.1	-	-	124.8	1.7	-	-
1993	122.8	-1.6	-	-	123.5	0.6	-	-	126.0	2.0	-	-	125.8	-0.2	-	-	125.1	-0.6	-	-	127.1	1.6	-	-
1994	124.7	-1.9	-	-	125.8	0.9	-	-	127.0	1.0	-	-	130.8	3.0	-	-	132.3	1.1	-	-	132.9	0.5	-	-
1995	131.4	-1.1	-	-	135.3	3.0	-	-	137.8	1.8	-	-	136.6	-0.9	-	-	136.9	0.2	-	-	136.1	-0.6	-	-
1996	138.7	1.9	-	-	141.5	2.0	-	-	142.6	0.8	-	-	141.0	-1.1	-	-	141.0	0.0	-	-	144.9	2.8	-	-
1997	143.4	-1.0	-	-	144.6	0.8	-	-	144.5	-0.1	144.3	-0.1	144.7	0.3	-	-	143.8	-0.6	-	-	142.8	-0.7	-	-

Source: U.S. Department of Labor, Bureau of Labor Statistics, Division of Consumer Prices and Price Indexes. - indicates no data collected for period.

St. Louis, MO-IL
Consumer Price Index - Urban Wage Earners
Base 1982-1984 = 100
Transportation

For 1947-1997. Columns headed % show percentile change in the index from the previous period for which an index is available.

Year	Jan Index	%	Feb Index	%	Mar Index	%	Apr Index	%	May Index	%	Jun Index	%	Jul Index	%	Aug Index	%	Sep Index	%	Oct Index	%	Nov Index	%	Dec Index	%
1947	18.0	-	18.0	0.0	18.2	1.1	18.3	0.5	18.3	0.0	18.2	-0.5	-	-	-	-	18.7	2.7	-	-	-	-	19.2	2.7
1948	-	-	-	-	19.5	1.6	-	-	-	-	19.9	2.1	-	-	-	-	20.7	4.0	-	-	-	-	20.7	0.0
1949	-	-	-	-	21.1	1.9	-	-	-	-	21.1	0.0	-	-	-	-	21.0	-0.5	-	-	-	-	21.9	4.3
1950	-	-	-	-	21.7	-0.9	-	-	-	-	21.4	-1.4	-	-	-	-	21.8	1.9	-	-	-	-	22.0	0.9
1951	-	-	-	-	23.8	8.2	-	-	-	-	23.8	0.0	-	-	-	-	24.1	1.3	-	-	-	-	24.7	2.5
1952	-	-	-	-	26.0	5.3	-	-	-	-	26.1	0.4	-	-	-	-	26.7	2.3	-	-	-	-	26.5	-0.7
1953	-	-	-	-	27.3	3.0	-	-	-	-	27.3	0.0	-	-	-	-	27.3	0.0	-	-	-	-	27.2	-0.4
1954	-	-	-	-	27.1	-0.4	-	-	-	-	27.1	0.0	-	-	-	-	24.9	-8.1	-	-	-	-	26.0	4.4
1955	-	-	-	-	26.9	3.5	-	-	-	-	26.9	0.0	-	-	-	-	26.1	-3.0	-	-	-	-	26.6	1.9
1956	-	-	-	-	26.3	-1.1	-	-	-	-	26.6	1.1	-	-	-	-	26.7	0.4	-	-	-	-	27.7	3.7
1957	-	-	-	-	28.0	1.1	-	-	-	-	28.5	1.8	-	-	-	-	28.8	1.1	-	-	-	-	29.1	1.0
1958	-	-	-	-	29.4	1.0	-	-	-	-	29.5	0.3	-	-	-	-	30.5	3.4	-	-	-	-	31.8	4.3
1959	-	-	-	-	32.3	1.6	-	-	-	-	32.2	-0.3	-	-	-	-	31.8	-1.2	-	-	-	-	32.5	2.2
1960	-	-	-	-	32.1	-1.2	-	-	-	-	32.1	0.0	-	-	-	-	31.7	-1.2	-	-	-	-	31.1	-1.9
1961	-	-	-	-	32.5	4.5	-	-	-	-	32.7	0.6	-	-	-	-	32.5	-0.6	-	-	-	-	33.0	1.5
1962	-	-	-	-	32.6	-1.2	-	-	-	-	32.3	-0.9	-	-	-	-	33.4	3.4	-	-	-	-	33.7	0.9
1963	-	-	-	-	33.2	-1.5	-	-	-	-	31.8	-4.2	-	-	-	-	32.7	2.8	-	-	-	-	33.3	1.8
1964	-	-	-	-	33.2	-0.3	-	-	-	-	32.6	-1.8	-	-	-	-	33.5	2.8	-	-	-	-	33.9	1.2
1965	-	-	-	-	33.5	-1.2	-	-	-	-	33.4	-0.3	-	-	-	-	33.2	-0.6	-	-	-	-	34.1	2.7
1966	-	-	-	-	34.0	-0.3	-	-	-	-	34.9	2.6	-	-	-	-	35.0	0.3	-	-	-	-	35.0	0.0
1967	-	-	-	-	35.3	0.9	-	-	-	-	35.8	1.4	-	-	-	-	36.2	1.1	-	-	-	-	36.6	1.1
1968	-	-	-	-	36.6	0.0	-	-	-	-	36.6	0.0	-	-	-	-	36.7	0.3	-	-	-	-	36.5	-0.5
1969	-	-	-	-	37.5	2.7	-	-	-	-	37.9	1.1	-	-	-	-	38.0	0.3	-	-	-	-	38.3	0.8
1970	-	-	-	-	38.0	-0.8	-	-	-	-	40.0	5.3	-	-	-	-	40.9	2.3	-	-	-	-	42.9	4.9
1971	-	-	-	-	41.8	-2.6	-	-	-	-	43.4	3.8	-	-	-	-	42.7	-1.6	-	-	-	-	43.3	1.4
1972	-	-	-	-	41.9	-3.2	-	-	-	-	43.0	2.6	-	-	-	-	43.6	1.4	-	-	-	-	44.0	0.9
1973	-	-	-	-	44.2	0.5	-	-	-	-	45.0	1.8	-	-	-	-	44.6	-0.9	-	-	-	-	44.3	-0.7
1974	-	-	-	-	46.3	4.5	-	-	-	-	48.7	5.2	-	-	-	-	49.8	2.3	-	-	-	-	50.0	0.4
1975	-	-	-	-	50.3	0.6	-	-	-	-	52.1	3.6	-	-	-	-	54.0	3.6	-	-	-	-	54.4	0.7
1976	-	-	-	-	54.9	0.9	-	-	-	-	57.4	4.6	-	-	-	-	58.3	1.6	-	-	-	-	59.3	1.7
1977	-	-	-	-	59.6	0.5	-	-	-	-	61.2	2.7	-	-	-	-	60.8	-0.7	-	-	-	-	61.0	0.3
1978	-	-	-	-	60.9	-0.2	-	-	62.2	2.1	-	-	63.4	1.9	-	-	64.3	1.4	-	-	65.3	1.6	-	-
1979	66.4	1.7	-	-	67.8	2.1	-	-	71.3	5.2	-	-	76.3	7.0	-	-	76.5	0.3	-	-	78.1	2.1	-	-
1980	81.2	4.0	-	-	83.5	2.8	-	-	85.4	2.3	-	-	86.3	1.1	-	-	86.6	0.3	-	-	88.4	2.1	-	-
1981	90.6	2.5	-	-	92.8	2.4	-	-	94.3	1.6	-	-	94.9	0.6	-	-	95.5	0.6	-	-	97.7	2.3	-	-
1982	96.9	-0.8	-	-	94.3	-2.7	-	-	96.9	2.8	-	-	100.1	3.3	-	-	99.2	-0.9	-	-	99.0	-0.2	-	-
1983	97.3	-1.7	-	-	95.3	-2.1	-	-	98.7	3.6	-	-	100.2	1.5	-	-	101.0	0.8	-	-	101.3	0.3	-	-
1984	100.5	-0.8	-	-	101.5	1.0	-	-	103.4	1.9	-	-	103.8	0.4	-	-	104.2	0.4	-	-	104.9	0.7	-	-
1985	103.8	-1.0	-	-	103.7	-0.1	-	-	106.1	2.3	-	-	105.9	-0.2	-	-	105.3	-0.6	-	-	106.3	0.9	-	-
1986	105.8	-0.5	-	-	99.9	-5.6	-	-	98.6	-1.3	-	-	98.2	-0.4	-	-	96.4	-1.8	-	-	98.3	2.0	-	-
1987	99.6	1.3	-	-	100.7	1.1	-	-	102.3	1.6	-	-	104.4	2.1	-	-	105.5	1.1	-	-	105.4	-0.1	-	-
1988	105.0	-0.4	-	-	103.9	-1.0	-	-	105.6	1.6	-	-	106.2	0.6	-	-	106.6	0.4	-	-	106.8	0.2	-	-
1989	106.9	0.1	-	-	107.4	0.5	-	-	112.9	5.1	-	-	111.7	-1.1	-	-	109.2	-2.2	-	-	111.0	1.6	-	-
1990	114.0	2.7	-	-	112.0	-1.8	-	-	113.1	1.0	-	-	113.1	0.0	-	-	118.9	5.1	-	-	120.7	1.5	-	-
1991	119.4	-1.1	-	-	114.4	-4.2	-	-	116.8	2.1	-	-	116.1	-0.6	-	-	117.9	1.6	-	-	119.2	1.1	-	-

[Continued]

St. Louis, MO-IL
Consumer Price Index - Urban Wage Earners
Base 1982-1984 = 100
Transportation
[Continued]

For 1947-1997. Columns headed % show percentile change in the index from the previous period for which an index is available.

Year	Jan Index	%	Feb Index	%	Mar Index	%	Apr Index	%	May Index	%	Jun Index	%	Jul Index	%	Aug Index	%	Sep Index	%	Oct Index	%	Nov Index	%	Dec Index	%
1992	117.5	-1.4	-	-	117.2	-0.3	-	-	121.3	3.5	-	-	122.1	0.7	-	-	122.4	0.2	-	-	124.2	1.5	-	-
1993	122.2	-1.6	-	-	122.3	0.1	-	-	125.2	2.4	-	-	125.5	0.2	-	-	125.0	-0.4	-	-	126.9	1.5	-	-
1994	124.3	-2.0	-	-	124.7	0.3	-	-	126.6	1.5	-	-	130.9	3.4	-	-	132.8	1.5	-	-	134.0	0.9	-	-
1995	133.1	-0.7	-	-	136.5	2.6	-	-	139.9	2.5	-	-	139.1	-0.6	-	-	138.9	-0.1	-	-	138.4	-0.4	-	-
1996	140.6	1.6	-	-	142.4	1.3	-	-	144.0	1.1	-	-	142.3	-1.2	-	-	142.1	-0.1	-	-	145.8	2.6	-	-
1997	144.6	-0.8	-	-	144.3	-0.2	-	-	144.7	0.3	144.5	-0.1	144.7	0.1	-	-	143.9	-0.6	-	-	143.1	-0.6	-	-

Source: U.S. Department of Labor, Bureau of Labor Statistics, Division of Consumer Prices and Price Indexes. - indicates no data collected for period.

St. Louis, MO-IL
Consumer Price Index - All Urban Consumers
Base 1982-1984 = 100
Medical Care

For 1947-1997. Columns headed % show percentile change in the index from the previous period for which an index is available.

Year	Jan Index	%	Feb Index	%	Mar Index	%	Apr Index	%	May Index	%	Jun Index	%	Jul Index	%	Aug Index	%	Sep Index	%	Oct Index	%	Nov Index	%	Dec Index	%
1947	12.9	-	12.9	0.0	13.0	0.8	13.0	0.0	13.0	0.0	13.0	0.0	-	-	-	-	13.4	3.1	-	-	-	-	13.7	2.2
1948	-	-	-	-	13.8	0.7	-	-	-	-	13.8	0.0	-	-	-	-	14.3	3.6	-	-	-	-	14.4	0.7
1949	-	-	-	-	14.5	0.7	-	-	-	-	14.4	-0.7	-	-	-	-	14.4	0.0	-	-	-	-	14.5	0.7
1950	-	-	-	-	14.5	0.0	-	-	-	-	14.5	0.0	-	-	-	-	14.6	0.7	-	-	-	-	14.7	0.7
1951	-	-	-	-	15.0	2.0	-	-	-	-	15.0	0.0	-	-	-	-	15.1	0.7	-	-	-	-	17.7	17.2
1952	-	-	-	-	17.8	0.6	-	-	-	-	18.1	1.7	-	-	-	-	18.1	0.0	-	-	-	-	18.3	1.1
1953	-	-	-	-	18.4	0.5	-	-	-	-	18.5	0.5	-	-	-	-	18.5	0.0	-	-	-	-	18.6	0.5
1954	-	-	-	-	18.7	0.5	-	-	-	-	18.7	0.0	-	-	-	-	18.9	1.1	-	-	-	-	19.4	2.6
1955	-	-	-	-	19.5	0.5	-	-	-	-	19.5	0.0	-	-	-	-	19.5	0.0	-	-	-	-	19.5	0.0
1956	-	-	-	-	19.5	0.0	-	-	-	-	19.5	0.0	-	-	-	-	19.9	2.1	-	-	-	-	21.2	6.5
1957	-	-	-	-	21.4	0.9	-	-	-	-	21.4	0.0	-	-	-	-	21.5	0.5	-	-	-	-	21.7	0.9
1958	-	-	-	-	22.0	1.4	-	-	-	-	22.0	0.0	-	-	-	-	22.1	0.5	-	-	-	-	23.1	4.5
1959	-	-	-	-	23.2	0.4	-	-	-	-	23.3	0.4	-	-	-	-	23.5	0.9	-	-	-	-	23.7	0.9
1960	-	-	-	-	23.7	0.0	-	-	-	-	23.6	-0.4	-	-	-	-	23.6	0.0	-	-	-	-	23.8	0.8
1961	-	-	-	-	24.0	0.8	-	-	-	-	24.0	0.0	-	-	-	-	24.2	0.8	-	-	-	-	25.3	4.5
1962	-	-	-	-	25.4	0.4	-	-	-	-	25.5	0.4	-	-	-	-	25.6	0.4	-	-	-	-	25.6	0.0
1963	-	-	-	-	25.7	0.4	-	-	-	-	25.7	0.0	-	-	-	-	25.8	0.4	-	-	-	-	25.8	0.0
1964	-	-	-	-	25.8	0.0	-	-	-	-	25.7	-0.4	-	-	-	-	25.9	0.8	-	-	-	-	26.0	0.4
1965	-	-	-	-	26.5	1.9	-	-	-	-	26.9	1.5	-	-	-	-	27.0	0.4	-	-	-	-	27.1	0.4
1966	-	-	-	-	27.6	1.8	-	-	-	-	28.2	2.2	-	-	-	-	28.7	1.8	-	-	-	-	29.1	1.4
1967	-	-	-	-	29.5	1.4	-	-	-	-	29.5	0.0	-	-	-	-	30.0	1.7	-	-	-	-	30.3	1.0
1968	-	-	-	-	30.9	2.0	-	-	-	-	30.9	0.0	-	-	-	-	31.4	1.6	-	-	-	-	31.7	1.0
1969	-	-	-	-	32.6	2.8	-	-	-	-	33.1	1.5	-	-	-	-	33.4	0.9	-	-	-	-	33.5	0.3
1970	-	-	-	-	34.7	3.6	-	-	-	-	35.3	1.7	-	-	-	-	35.6	0.8	-	-	-	-	35.7	0.3
1971	-	-	-	-	36.4	2.0	-	-	-	-	36.8	1.1	-	-	-	-	37.1	0.8	-	-	-	-	36.8	-0.8
1972	-	-	-	-	37.2	1.1	-	-	-	-	37.4	0.5	-	-	-	-	37.5	0.3	-	-	-	-	37.6	0.3
1973	-	-	-	-	38.2	1.6	-	-	-	-	38.3	0.3	-	-	-	-	38.8	1.3	-	-	-	-	39.7	2.3
1974	-	-	-	-	40.7	2.5	-	-	-	-	41.2	1.2	-	-	-	-	42.7	3.6	-	-	-	-	44.1	3.3
1975	-	-	-	-	45.2	2.5	-	-	-	-	46.2	2.2	-	-	-	-	47.4	2.6	-	-	-	-	47.5	0.2
1976	-	-	-	-	49.1	3.4	-	-	-	-	50.1	2.0	-	-	-	-	50.7	1.2	-	-	-	-	52.4	3.4
1977	-	-	-	-	54.4	3.8	-	-	-	-	55.2	1.5	-	-	-	-	56.5	2.4	-	-	-	-	57.2	1.2
1978	-	-	-	-	58.9	3.0	-	-	59.1	0.3	-	-	60.1	1.7	-	-	60.3	0.3	-	-	60.5	0.3	-	-
1979	62.4	3.1	-	-	62.5	0.2	-	-	63.5	1.6	-	-	65.6	3.3	-	-	65.7	0.2	-	-	66.8	1.7	-	-
1980	70.7	5.8	-	-	71.2	0.7	-	-	72.1	1.3	-	-	73.4	1.8	-	-	73.4	0.0	-	-	75.1	2.3	-	-
1981	77.7	3.5	-	-	79.6	2.4	-	-	81.2	2.0	-	-	81.6	0.5	-	-	83.0	1.7	-	-	84.6	1.9		
1982	90.2	6.6	-	-	91.5	1.4	-	-	92.1	0.7	-	-	93.7	1.7	-	-	94.5	0.9	-	-	95.9	1.5		
1983	99.9	4.2	-	-	100.0	0.1	-	-	100.0	0.0	-	-	101.2	1.2	-	-	101.1	-0.1	Oct	-	101.7	0.6		
1984	104.6	2.9	-	-	105.1	0.5	-	-	105.3	0.2	-	-	105.6	0.3	-	-	106.2	0.6	-	-	106.8	0.6		
1985	108.6	1.7	-	-	109.5	0.8	-	-	110.3	0.7	-	-	111.3	0.9	-	-	111.5	0.2	-	-	112.6	1.0		
1986	117.4	4.3	-	-	118.4	0.9	-	-	119.2	0.7	-	-	121.4	1.8	-	-	121.3	-0.1	-	-	122.1	0.7		
1987	124.5	2.0	-	-	126.5	1.6	-	-	127.0	0.4	-	-	128.6	1.3	-	-	129.3	0.5	-	-	129.8	0.4		
1988	132.4	2.0	-	-	133.4	0.8	-	-	134.0	0.4	-	-	136.5	1.9	-	-	136.6	0.1	-	-	138.8	1.6		
1989	140.5	1.2	-	-	142.3	1.3	-	-	143.7	1.0	-	-	146.9	2.2	-	-	148.4	1.0	-	-	148.9	0.3		
1990	152.4	2.4	-	-	156.5	2.7	-	-	158.7	1.4	-	-	159.6	0.6	-	-	160.5	0.6	-	-	162.3	1.1		
1991	168.0	3.5	-	-	169.5	0.9	-	-	170.0	0.3	-	-	172.9	1.7	-	-	173.6	0.4	-	-	174.1	0.3		

[Continued]

St. Louis, MO-IL
Consumer Price Index - All Urban Consumers
Base 1982-1984 = 100
Medical Care
[Continued]

For 1947-1997. Columns headed % show percentile change in the index from the previous period for which an index is available.

Year	Jan Index	%	Feb Index	%	Mar Index	%	Apr Index	%	May Index	%	Jun Index	%	Jul Index	%	Aug Index	%	Sep Index	%	Oct Index	%	Nov Index	%	Dec Index	%
1992	177.1	1.7	-	-	178.8	1.0	-	-	179.4	0.3	-	-	182.4	1.7	-	-	183.1	0.4	-	-	182.9	-0.1	-	-
1993	186.3	1.9	-	-	188.7	1.3	-	-	190.2	0.8	-	-	192.0	0.9	-	-	194.3	1.2	-	-	195.0	0.4	-	-
1994	197.5	1.3	-	-	199.2	0.9	-	-	199.9	0.4	-	-	202.5	1.3	-	-	204.2	0.8	-	-	204.6	0.2	-	-
1995	207.0	1.2	-	-	208.3	0.6	-	-	210.6	1.1	-	-	210.0	-0.3	-	-	210.6	0.3	-	-	211.1	0.2	-	-
1996	215.9	2.3	-	-	216.1	0.1	-	-	216.8	0.3	-	-	219.0	1.0	-	-	218.7	-0.1	-	-	222.6	1.8	-	-
1997	222.1	-0.2	-	-	224.6	1.1	-	-	226.3	0.8	224.7	-0.7	226.9	1.0	-	-	227.8	0.4	-	-	229.0	0.5	-	-

Source: U.S. Department of Labor, Bureau of Labor Statistics, Division of Consumer Prices and Price Indexes. - indicates no data collected for period.

St. Louis, MO-IL
Consumer Price Index - Urban Wage Earners
Base 1982-1984 = 100
Medical Care

For 1947-1997. Columns headed % show percentile change in the index from the previous period for which an index is available.

Year	Jan Index	%	Feb Index	%	Mar Index	%	Apr Index	%	May Index	%	Jun Index	%	Jul Index	%	Aug Index	%	Sep Index	%	Oct Index	%	Nov Index	%	Dec Index	%
1947	12.8	-	12.8	0.0	12.9	0.8	12.9	0.0	12.9	0.0	12.9	0.0	-	-	-	-	13.2	2.3	-	-	-	-	13.6	3.0
1948	-	-	-	-	13.7	0.7	-	-	-	-	13.7	0.0	-	-	-	-	14.2	3.6	-	-	-	-	14.2	0.0
1949	-	-	-	-	14.3	0.7	-	-	-	-	14.3	0.0	-	-	-	-	14.3	0.0	-	-	-	-	14.3	0.0
1950	-	-	-	-	14.4	0.7	-	-	-	-	14.4	0.0	-	-	-	-	14.4	0.0	-	-	-	-	14.5	0.7
1951	-	-	-	-	14.9	2.8	-	-	-	-	14.9	0.0	-	-	-	-	14.9	0.0	-	-	-	-	17.6	18.1
1952	-	-	-	-	17.7	0.6	-	-	-	-	17.9	1.1	-	-	-	-	17.9	0.0	-	-	-	-	18.2	1.7
1953	-	-	-	-	18.2	0.0	-	-	-	-	18.3	0.5	-	-	-	-	18.3	0.0	-	-	-	-	18.4	0.5
1954	-	-	-	-	18.5	0.5	-	-	-	-	18.6	0.5	-	-	-	-	18.7	0.5	-	-	-	-	19.2	2.7
1955	-	-	-	-	19.3	0.5	-	-	-	-	19.3	0.0	-	-	-	-	19.3	0.0	-	-	-	-	19.3	0.0
1956	-	-	-	-	19.3	0.0	-	-	-	-	19.4	0.5	-	-	-	-	19.7	1.5	-	-	-	-	21.0	6.6
1957	-	-	-	-	21.3	1.4	-	-	-	-	21.3	0.0	-	-	-	-	21.3	0.0	-	-	-	-	21.5	0.9
1958	-	-	-	-	21.8	1.4	-	-	-	-	21.8	0.0	-	-	-	-	21.9	0.5	-	-	-	-	22.9	4.6
1959	-	-	-	-	23.0	0.4	-	-	-	-	23.0	0.0	-	-	-	-	23.3	1.3	-	-	-	-	23.5	0.9
1960	-	-	-	-	23.5	0.0	-	-	-	-	23.4	-0.4	-	-	-	-	23.4	0.0	-	-	-	-	23.6	0.9
1961	-	-	-	-	23.8	0.8	-	-	-	-	23.8	0.0	-	-	-	-	24.0	0.8	-	-	-	-	25.1	4.6
1962	-	-	-	-	25.1	0.0	-	-	-	-	25.3	0.8	-	-	-	-	25.3	0.0	-	-	-	-	25.3	0.0
1963	-	-	-	-	25.5	0.8	-	-	-	-	25.5	0.0	-	-	-	-	25.5	0.0	-	-	-	-	25.6	0.4
1964	-	-	-	-	25.6	0.0	-	-	-	-	25.5	-0.4	-	-	-	-	25.7	0.8	-	-	-	-	25.8	0.4
1965	-	-	-	-	26.3	1.9	-	-	-	-	26.7	1.5	-	-	-	-	26.7	0.0	-	-	-	-	26.9	0.7
1966	-	-	-	-	27.3	1.5	-	-	-	-	28.0	2.6	-	-	-	-	28.4	1.4	-	-	-	-	28.8	1.4
1967	-	-	-	-	29.2	1.4	-	-	-	-	29.2	0.0	-	-	-	-	29.7	1.7	-	-	-	-	30.0	1.0
1968	-	-	-	-	30.6	2.0	-	-	-	-	30.7	0.3	-	-	-	-	31.1	1.3	-	-	-	-	31.5	1.3
1969	-	-	-	-	32.3	2.5	-	-	-	-	32.8	1.5	-	-	-	-	33.1	0.9	-	-	-	-	33.2	0.3
1970	-	-	-	-	34.4	3.6	-	-	-	-	34.9	1.5	-	-	-	-	35.3	1.1	-	-	-	-	35.4	0.3
1971	-	-	-	-	36.0	1.7	-	-	-	-	36.4	1.1	-	-	-	-	36.8	1.1	-	-	-	-	36.5	-0.8
1972	-	-	-	-	36.8	0.8	-	-	-	-	37.1	0.8	-	-	-	-	37.1	0.0	-	-	-	-	37.3	0.5
1973	-	-	-	-	37.9	1.6	-	-	-	-	38.0	0.3	-	-	-	-	38.4	1.1	-	-	-	-	39.3	2.3
1974	-	-	-	-	40.4	2.8	-	-	-	-	40.8	1.0	-	-	-	-	42.3	3.7	-	-	-	-	43.7	3.3
1975	-	-	-	-	44.8	2.5	-	-	-	-	45.8	2.2	-	-	-	-	47.0	2.6	-	-	-	-	47.1	0.2
1976	-	-	-	-	48.6	3.2	-	-	-	-	49.6	2.1	-	-	-	-	50.2	1.2	-	-	-	-	51.9	3.4
1977	-	-	-	-	53.9	3.9	-	-	-	-	54.7	1.5	-	-	-	-	56.0	2.4	-	-	-	-	56.7	1.3
1978	-	-	-	-	58.4	3.0	-	-	59.0	1.0	-	-	59.6	1.0	-	-	60.2	1.0	-	-	61.3	1.8	-	-
1979	62.8	2.4	-	-	63.2	0.6	-	-	63.7	0.8	-	-	65.2	2.4	-	-	65.9	1.1	-	-	67.8	2.9	-	-
1980	70.9	4.6	-	-	72.3	2.0	-	-	72.6	0.4	-	-	73.7	1.5	-	-	74.0	0.4	-	-	75.8	2.4	-	-
1981	78.1	3.0	-	-	80.7	3.3	-	-	81.4	0.9	-	-	81.8	0.5	-	-	83.3	1.8	-	-	85.0	2.0	-	-
1982	90.4	6.4	-	-	91.6	1.3	-	-	92.1	0.5	-	-	93.7	1.7	-	-	94.4	0.7	-	-	95.8	1.5	-	-
1983	99.5	3.9	-	-	99.7	0.2	-	-	99.8	0.1	-	-	101.2	1.4	-	-	101.2	0.0	-	-	101.8	0.6	-	-
1984	104.6	2.8	-	-	105.1	0.5	-	-	105.3	0.2	-	-	105.7	0.4	-	-	106.4	0.7	-	-	107.0	0.6	-	-
1985	108.8	1.7	-	-	109.6	0.7	-	-	110.3	0.6	-	-	111.3	0.9	-	-	111.5	0.2	-	-	112.5	0.9	-	-
1986	117.2	4.2	-	-	118.1	0.8	-	-	118.9	0.7	-	-	121.0	1.8	-	-	120.7	-0.2	-	-	121.5	0.7	-	-
1987	123.9	2.0	-	-	126.0	1.7	-	-	126.7	0.6	-	-	128.3	1.3	-	-	129.1	0.6	-	-	129.3	0.2	-	-
1988	131.9	2.0	-	-	132.9	0.8	-	-	133.6	0.5	-	-	136.1	1.9	-	-	136.3	0.1	-	-	138.5	1.6	-	-
1989	140.4	1.4	-	-	142.2	1.3	-	-	143.6	1.0	-	-	147.1	2.4	-	-	148.6	1.0	-	-	148.8	0.1	-	-
1990	152.4	2.4	-	-	156.0	2.4	-	-	158.1	1.3	-	-	158.9	0.5	-	-	159.7	0.5	-	-	161.3	1.0	-	-
1991	167.0	3.5	-	-	168.4	0.8	-	-	169.0	0.4	-	-	171.8	1.7	-	-	172.4	0.3	-	-	172.9	0.3	-	-

[Continued]

St. Louis, MO-IL
Consumer Price Index - Urban Wage Earners
Base 1982-1984 = 100
Medical Care
[Continued]

For 1947-1997. Columns headed % show percentile change in the index from the previous period for which an index is available.

Year	Jan Index	%	Feb Index	%	Mar Index	%	Apr Index	%	May Index	%	Jun Index	%	Jul Index	%	Aug Index	%	Sep Index	%	Oct Index	%	Nov Index	%	Dec Index	%
1992	175.9	1.7	-	-	177.8	1.1	-	-	178.4	0.3	-	-	181.6	1.8	-	-	182.2	0.3	-	-	182.0	-0.1	-	-
1993	185.3	1.8	-	-	187.9	1.4	-	-	189.2	0.7	-	-	190.8	0.8	-	-	193.2	1.3	-	-	193.8	0.3	-	-
1994	196.2	1.2	-	-	197.7	0.8	-	-	198.3	0.3	-	-	200.8	1.3	-	-	202.5	0.8	-	-	202.9	0.2	-	-
1995	205.2	1.1	-	-	206.5	0.6	-	-	208.9	1.2	-	-	208.3	-0.3	-	-	208.8	0.2	-	-	209.5	0.3	-	-
1996	214.2	2.2	-	-	214.4	0.1	-	-	214.9	0.2	-	-	217.2	1.1	-	-	216.9	-0.1	-	-	220.7	1.8	-	-
1997	220.5	-0.1	-	-	223.0	1.1	-	-	225.0	0.9	223.2	-0.8	225.5	1.0	-	-	226.3	0.4	-	-	227.4	0.5	-	-

Source: U.S. Department of Labor, Bureau of Labor Statistics, Division of Consumer Prices and Price Indexes. - indicates no data collected for period.

St. Louis, MO-IL
Consumer Price Index - All Urban Consumers
Base 1982-1984 = 100
Entertainment

For 1975-1997. Columns headed % show percentile change in the index from the previous period for which an index is available.

Year	Jan Index	%	Feb Index	%	Mar Index	%	Apr Index	%	May Index	%	Jun Index	%	Jul Index	%	Aug Index	%	Sep Index	%	Oct Index	%	Nov Index	%	Dec Index	%
1975	-	-	-	-	-	-	-	-	-	-	-	-	-	-	-	-	-	-	-	-	-	-	65.1	-
1976	-	-	-	-	65.4	0.5	-	-	-	-	66.5	1.7	-	-	-	-	66.8	0.5	-	-	-	-	67.5	1.0
1977	-	-	-	-	68.6	1.6	-	-	-	-	70.3	2.5	-	-	-	-	71.0	1.0	-	-	-	-	72.7	2.4
1978	-	-	-	-	75.1	3.3	-	-	76.2	1.5	-	-	78.6	3.1	-	-	79.9	1.7	-	-	80.0	0.1	-	-
1979	80.8	1.0	-	-	80.4	-0.5	-	-	80.6	0.2	-	-	80.5	-0.1	-	-	81.4	1.1	-	-	84.5	3.8	-	-
1980	83.8	-0.8	-	-	86.4	3.1	-	-	87.4	1.2	-	-	89.2	2.1	-	-	89.8	0.7	-	-	89.9	0.1	-	-
1981	93.9	4.4	-	-	94.0	0.1	-	-	94.2	0.2	-	-	91.7	-2.7	-	-	94.7	3.3	-	-	94.7	0.0	-	-
1982	95.6	1.0	-	-	96.4	0.8	-	-	93.9	-2.6	-	-	95.6	1.8	-	-	97.3	1.8	-	-	97.9	0.6	-	-
1983	99.9	2.0	-	-	101.4	1.5	-	-	101.0	-0.4	-	-	101.3	0.3	-	-	102.7	1.4	-	-	101.4	-1.3	-	-
1984	100.4	-1.0	-	-	100.8	0.4	-	-	101.9	1.1	-	-	102.0	0.1	-	-	103.0	1.0	-	-	105.1	2.0	-	-
1985	105.3	0.2	-	-	104.8	-0.5	-	-	104.5	-0.3	-	-	105.6	1.1	-	-	106.4	0.8	-	-	108.6	2.1	-	-
1986	108.4	-0.2	-	-	109.8	1.3	-	-	110.4	0.5	-	-	109.2	-1.1	-	-	110.3	1.0	-	-	111.9	1.5	-	-
1987	112.4	0.4	-	-	111.7	-0.6	-	-	112.7	0.9	-	-	114.3	1.4	-	-	115.5	1.0	-	-	116.0	0.4	-	-
1988	115.8	-0.2	-	-	117.8	1.7	-	-	116.8	-0.8	-	-	117.0	0.2	-	-	118.8	1.5	-	-	119.8	0.8	-	-
1989	120.6	0.7	-	-	121.0	0.3	-	-	122.8	1.5	-	-	123.0	0.2	-	-	123.6	0.5	-	-	123.0	-0.5	-	-
1990	120.3	-2.2	-	-	122.1	1.5	-	-	121.9	-0.2	-	-	124.3	2.0	-	-	128.4	3.3	-	-	127.7	-0.5	-	-
1991	127.5	-0.2	-	-	132.6	4.0	-	-	133.9	1.0	-	-	136.4	1.9	-	-	137.4	0.7	-	-	136.9	-0.4	-	-
1992	137.3	0.3	-	-	137.8	0.4	-	-	139.5	1.2	-	-	139.5	0.0	-	-	136.6	-2.1	-	-	135.9	-0.5	-	-
1993	137.3	1.0	-	-	137.3	0.0	-	-	135.4	-1.4	-	-	137.7	1.7	-	-	136.4	-0.9	-	-	139.5	2.3	-	-
1994	138.1	-1.0	-	-	137.6	-0.4	-	-	144.7	5.2	-	-	140.5	-2.9	-	-	142.0	1.1	-	-	148.9	4.9	-	-
1995	153.2	2.9	-	-	154.3	0.7	-	-	154.5	0.1	-	-	152.4	-1.4	-	-	159.0	4.3	-	-	157.7	-0.8	-	-
1996	159.8	1.3	-	-	162.7	1.8	-	-	158.4	-2.6	-	-	158.6	0.1	-	-	162.3	2.3	-	-	162.3	0.0	-	-
1997	163.1	0.5	-	-	163.6	0.3	-	-	162.2	-0.9	162.9	0.4	162.1	-0.5	-	-	167.5	3.3	-	-	166.3	-0.7	-	-

Source: U.S. Department of Labor, Bureau of Labor Statistics, Division of Consumer Prices and Price Indexes. - indicates no data collected for period.

St. Louis, MO-IL
Consumer Price Index - Urban Wage Earners
Base 1982-1984 = 100
Entertainment

For 1975-1997. Columns headed % show percentile change in the index from the previous period for which an index is available.

Year	Jan Index	%	Feb Index	%	Mar Index	%	Apr Index	%	May Index	%	Jun Index	%	Jul Index	%	Aug Index	%	Sep Index	%	Oct Index	%	Nov Index	%	Dec Index	%
1975	-	-	-	-	-	-	-	-	-	-	-	-	-	-	-	-	-	-	-	-	-	-	71.0	-
1976	-	-	-	-	71.4	0.6	-	-	-	-	72.5	1.5	-	-	-	-	72.9	0.6	-	-	-	-	73.7	1.1
1977	-	-	-	-	74.8	1.5	-	-	-	-	76.7	2.5	-	-	-	-	77.5	1.0	-	-	-	-	79.3	2.3
1978	-	-	-	-	81.9	3.3	-	-	82.3	0.5	-	-	81.7	-0.7	-	-	83.1	1.7	-	-	83.4	0.4	-	-
1979	83.3	-0.1	-	-	83.2	-0.1	-	-	85.8	3.1	-	-	86.0	0.2	-	-	87.0	1.2	-	-	90.5	4.0	-	-
1980	88.6	-2.1	-	-	92.1	4.0	-	-	94.9	3.0	-	-	94.7	-0.2	-	-	95.7	1.1	-	-	93.3	-2.5	-	-
1981	98.0	5.0	-	-	97.5	-0.5	-	-	96.2	-1.3	-	-	94.5	-1.8	-	-	97.0	2.6	-	-	95.5	-1.5	-	-
1982	96.2	0.7	-	-	96.6	0.4	-	-	93.8	-2.9	-	-	95.8	2.1	-	-	97.6	1.9	-	-	98.0	0.4	-	-
1983	100.1	2.1	-	-	101.6	1.5	-	-	101.0	-0.6	-	-	101.5	0.5	-	-	102.9	1.4	-	-	101.3	-1.6	-	-
1984	100.4	-0.9	-	-	100.7	0.3	-	-	101.7	1.0	-	-	101.5	-0.2	-	-	102.3	0.8	-	-	105.0	2.6	-	-
1985	105.1	0.1	-	-	103.8	-1.2	-	-	103.7	-0.1	-	-	104.6	0.9	-	-	105.2	0.6	-	-	107.4	2.1	-	-
1986	107.3	-0.1	-	-	108.6	1.2	-	-	109.2	0.6	-	-	108.4	-0.7	-	-	109.8	1.3	-	-	111.0	1.1	-	-
1987	111.4	0.4	-	-	110.8	-0.5	-	-	111.8	0.9	-	-	113.3	1.3	-	-	114.5	1.1	-	-	114.9	0.3	-	-
1988	115.1	0.2	-	-	117.3	1.9	-	-	115.7	-1.4	-	-	116.4	0.6	-	-	117.9	1.3	-	-	118.8	0.8	-	-
1989	119.9	0.9	-	-	120.0	0.1	-	-	122.2	1.8	-	-	122.0	-0.2	-	-	122.6	0.5	-	-	121.6	-0.8	-	-
1990	118.9	-2.2	-	-	120.7	1.5	-	-	120.8	0.1	-	-	123.0	1.8	-	-	127.5	3.7	-	-	126.9	-0.5	-	-
1991	126.7	-0.2	-	-	131.5	3.8	-	-	132.2	0.5	-	-	134.5	1.7	-	-	135.7	0.9	-	-	134.9	-0.6	-	-
1992	135.1	0.1	-	-	135.8	0.5	-	-	137.4	1.2	-	-	137.4	0.0	-	-	134.8	-1.9	-	-	134.0	-0.6	-	-
1993	135.0	0.7	-	-	134.8	-0.1	-	-	133.4	-1.0	-	-	135.7	1.7	-	-	134.7	-0.7	-	-	137.9	2.4	-	-
1994	136.6	-0.9	-	-	137.3	0.5	-	-	142.4	3.7	-	-	138.9	-2.5	-	-	139.9	0.7	-	-	146.1	4.4	-	-
1995	149.8	2.5	-	-	150.6	0.5	-	-	150.2	-0.3	-	-	148.3	-1.3	-	-	154.1	3.9	-	-	152.2	-1.2	-	-
1996	153.9	1.1	-	-	156.0	1.4	-	-	152.2	-2.4	-	-	152.3	0.1	-	-	155.5	2.1	-	-	155.4	-0.1	-	-
1997	156.1	0.5	-	-	156.5	0.3	-	-	155.9	-0.4	156.2	0.2	156.4	0.1	-	-	160.7	2.7	-	-	159.3	-0.9	-	-

Source: U.S. Department of Labor, Bureau of Labor Statistics, Division of Consumer Prices and Price Indexes. - indicates no data collected for period.

St. Louis, MO-IL
Consumer Price Index - All Urban Consumers
Base 1982-1984 = 100
Other Goods and Services

For 1975-1997. Columns headed % show percentile change in the index from the previous period for which an index is available.

Year	Jan Index	%	Feb Index	%	Mar Index	%	Apr Index	%	May Index	%	Jun Index	%	Jul Index	%	Aug Index	%	Sep Index	%	Oct Index	%	Nov Index	%	Dec Index	%
1975	-	-	-	-	-	-	-	-	-	-	-	-	-	-	-	-	-	-	-	-	-	-	55.7	-
1976	-	-	-	-	56.1	0.7	-	-	-	-	57.0	1.6	-	-	-	-	58.0	1.8	-	-	-	-	58.8	1.4
1977	-	-	-	-	59.2	0.7	-	-	-	-	60.1	1.5	-	-	-	-	61.4	2.2	-	-	-	-	62.6	2.0
1978	-	-	-	-	63.2	1.0	-	-	63.4	0.3	-	-	64.8	2.2	-	-	66.1	2.0	-	-	66.5	0.6	-	-
1979	66.8	0.5	-	-	67.0	0.3	-	-	67.8	1.2	-	-	68.6	1.2	-	-	70.3	2.5	-	-	70.4	0.1	-	-
1980	71.1	1.0	-	-	72.5	2.0	-	-	73.5	1.4	-	-	74.2	1.0	-	-	78.0	5.1	-	-	77.3	-0.9	-	-
1981	77.9	0.8	-	-	78.7	1.0	-	-	81.2	3.2	-	-	81.8	0.7	-	-	84.0	2.7	-	-	86.3	2.7	-	-
1982	86.7	0.5	-	-	88.3	1.8	-	-	87.6	-0.8	-	-	88.5	1.0	-	-	92.8	4.9	-	-	96.6	4.1	-	-
1983	98.3	1.8	-	-	99.7	1.4	-	-	98.8	-0.9	-	-	99.8	1.0	-	-	102.9	3.1	-	-	104.6	1.7	-	-
1984	105.8	1.1	-	-	106.2	0.4	-	-	106.5	0.3	-	-	107.5	0.9	-	-	111.5	3.7	-	-	111.6	0.1	-	-
1985	112.7	1.0	-	-	113.7	0.9	-	-	113.0	-0.6	-	-	114.6	1.4	-	-	117.0	2.1	-	-	119.5	2.1	-	-
1986	120.2	0.6	-	-	120.3	0.1	-	-	120.3	0.0	-	-	121.1	0.7	-	-	123.6	2.1	-	-	125.4	1.5	-	-
1987	126.6	1.0	-	-	125.9	-0.6	-	-	126.7	0.6	-	-	126.9	0.2	-	-	129.9	2.4	-	-	131.0	0.8	-	-
1988	133.7	2.1	-	-	135.1	1.0	-	-	134.7	-0.3	-	-	136.2	1.1	-	-	138.8	1.9	-	-	140.5	1.2	-	-
1989	141.8	0.9	-	-	143.1	0.9	-	-	143.7	0.4	-	-	145.9	1.5	-	-	146.7	0.5	-	-	149.2	1.7	-	-
1990	150.2	0.7	-	-	150.9	0.5	-	-	151.1	0.1	-	-	154.1	2.0	-	-	155.6	1.0	-	-	157.1	1.0	-	-
1991	159.7	1.7	-	-	160.6	0.6	-	-	158.1	-1.6	-	-	163.7	3.5	-	-	166.3	1.6	-	-	169.7	2.0	-	-
1992	169.9	0.1	-	-	169.9	0.0	-	-	170.9	0.6	-	-	171.6	0.4	-	-	175.0	2.0	-	-	174.8	-0.1	-	-
1993	177.4	1.5	-	-	176.6	-0.5	-	-	179.6	1.7	-	-	178.8	-0.4	-	-	170.3	-4.8	-	-	173.7	2.0	-	-
1994	174.1	0.2	-	-	172.8	-0.7	-	-	171.5	-0.8	-	-	168.8	-1.6	-	-	177.0	4.9	-	-	178.6	0.9	-	-
1995	179.0	0.2	-	-	178.6	-0.2	-	-	179.6	0.6	-	-	178.9	-0.4	-	-	183.0	2.3	-	-	182.4	-0.3	-	-
1996	183.9	0.8	-	-	183.4	-0.3	-	-	183.9	0.3	-	-	184.9	0.5	-	-	189.2	2.3	-	-	191.3	1.1	-	-
1997	188.7	-1.4	-	-	188.2	-0.3	-	-	189.2	0.5	189.0	-0.1	192.2	1.7	-	-	198.7	3.4	-	-	199.6	0.5	-	-

Source: U.S. Department of Labor, Bureau of Labor Statistics, Division of Consumer Prices and Price Indexes. - indicates no data collected for period.

St. Louis, MO-IL
Consumer Price Index - Urban Wage Earners
Base 1982-1984 = 100
Other Goods and Services

For 1975-1997. Columns headed % show percentile change in the index from the previous period for which an index is available.

Year	Jan Index	%	Feb Index	%	Mar Index	%	Apr Index	%	May Index	%	Jun Index	%	Jul Index	%	Aug Index	%	Sep Index	%	Oct Index	%	Nov Index	%	Dec Index	%
1975	-	-	-	-	-	-	-	-	-	-			-	-	-	-	-	-	-	-	-	-	55.3	-
1976	-	-	-	-	55.7	0.7	-	-	-	-	56.6	1.6	-	-	-	-	57.6	1.8	-	-	-	-	58.3	1.2
1977	-	-	-	-	58.8	0.9	-	-	-	-	59.7	1.5	-	-	-	-	60.9	2.0	-	-	-	-	62.1	2.0
1978	-	-	-	-	62.7	1.0	-	-	63.3	1.0	-	-	64.8	2.4	-	-	64.9	0.2	-	-	65.7	1.2	-	-
1979	67.7	3.0	-	-	67.3	-0.6	-	-	68.2	1.3	-	-	68.3	0.1	-	-	69.8	2.2	-	-	69.9	0.1	-	-
1980	71.8	2.7	-	-	73.0	1.7	-	-	74.3	1.8	-	-	74.7	0.5	-	-	78.3	4.8	-	-	78.9	0.8	-	-
1981	79.5	0.8	-	-	80.0	0.6	-	-	82.2	2.8	-	-	82.8	0.7	-	-	83.0	0.2	-	-	86.2	3.9	-	-
1982	86.4	0.2	-	-	88.5	2.4	-	-	87.8	-0.8	-	-	88.7	1.0	-	-	92.8	4.6	-	-	96.5	4.0	-	-
1983	98.6	2.2	-	-	100.5	1.9	-	-	99.3	-1.2	-	-	100.6	1.3	-	-	103.1	2.5	-	-	104.3	1.2	-	-
1984	105.8	1.4	-	-	106.0	0.2	-	-	106.2	0.2	-	-	107.5	1.2	-	-	110.5	2.8	-	-	110.5	0.0	-	-
1985	111.9	1.3	-	-	112.9	0.9	-	-	112.1	-0.7	-	-	114.2	1.9	-	-	116.4	1.9	-	-	118.5	1.8	-	-
1986	119.4	0.8	-	-	119.5	0.1	-	-	119.5	0.0	-	-	120.7	1.0	-	-	121.9	1.0	-	-	123.8	1.6	-	-
1987	125.2	1.1	-	-	124.5	-0.6	-	-	125.4	0.7	-	-	125.8	0.3	-	-	128.6	2.2	-	-	129.5	0.7	-	-
1988	132.1	2.0	-	-	133.7	1.2	-	-	133.6	-0.1	-	-	135.5	1.4	-	-	138.1	1.9	-	-	139.1	0.7	-	-
1989	141.3	1.6	-	-	142.2	0.6	-	-	143.0	0.6	-	-	145.3	1.6	-	-	145.9	0.4	-	-	148.5	1.8	-	-
1990	149.7	0.8	-	-	150.4	0.5	-	-	150.8	0.3	-	-	154.8	2.7	-	-	155.6	0.5	-	-	157.9	1.5	-	-
1991	161.4	2.2	-	-	162.8	0.9	-	-	160.1	-1.7	-	-	165.3	3.2	-	-	168.0	1.6	-	-	172.3	2.6	-	-
1992	172.5	0.1	-	-	172.5	0.0	-	-	174.6	1.2	-	-	174.7	0.1	-	-	179.0	2.5	-	-	177.0	-1.1	-	-
1993	181.1	2.3	-	-	178.7	-1.3	-	-	182.4	2.1	-	-	180.3	-1.2	-	-	165.6	-8.2	-	-	170.2	2.8	-	-
1994	170.4	0.1	-	-	169.5	-0.5	-	-	168.5	-0.6	-	-	166.7	-1.1	-	-	172.6	3.5	-	-	173.9	0.8	-	-
1995	174.2	0.2	-	-	173.9	-0.2	-	-	174.9	0.6	-	-	174.2	-0.4	-	-	177.6	2.0	-	-	177.0	-0.3	-	-
1996	177.8	0.5	-	-	177.4	-0.2	-	-	178.0	0.3	-	-	179.0	0.6	-	-	182.1	1.7	-	-	185.8	2.0	-	-
1997	182.1	-2.0	-	-	181.3	-0.4	-	-	182.8	0.8	182.5	-0.2	187.2	2.6	-	-	193.7	3.5	-	-	194.7	0.5	-	-

Source: U.S. Department of Labor, Bureau of Labor Statistics, Division of Consumer Prices and Price Indexes. - indicates no data collected for period.

Washington, DC-MD-VA
Consumer Price Index - All Urban Consumers
Base 1982-1984 = 100
Annual Averages

For 1914-1997. Columns headed % show percentile change in the index from the previous period for which an index is available.

Year	All Items		Food & Beverage		Housing		Apparel & Upkeep		Trans- portation		Medical Care		Entertain- ment		Other Goods & Services	
	Index	%	Index	%	Index	%	Index	%	Index	%	Index	%	Index	%	Index	%
1914	-	-	-	-	-	-	-	-	-	-	-	-	-	-	-	-
1915	10.6	-	-	-	-	-	-	-	-	-	-	-	-	-	-	-
1916	11.4	7.5	-	-	-	-	-	-	-	-	-	-	-	-	-	-
1917	13.8	21.1	-	-	-	-	-	-	-	-	-	-	-	-	-	-
1918	16.3	18.1	-	-	-	-	-	-	-	-	-	-	-	-	-	-
1919	17.8	9.2	-	-	-	-	-	-	-	-	-	-	-	-	-	-
1920	20.0	12.4	-	-	-	-	-	-	-	-	-	-	-	-	-	-
1921	17.6	-12.0	-	-	-	-	-	-	-	-	-	-	-	-	-	-
1922	16.7	-5.1	-	-	-	-	-	-	-	-	-	-	-	-	-	-
1923	16.9	1.2	-	-	-	-	-	-	-	-	-	-	-	-	-	-
1924	16.9	0.0	-	-	-	-	-	-	-	-	-	-	-	-	-	-
1925	17.3	2.4	-	-	-	-	-	-	-	-	-	-	-	-	-	-
1926	17.5	1.2	-	-	-	-	-	-	-	-	-	-	-	-	-	-
1927	17.0	-2.9	-	-	-	-	-	-	-	-	-	-	-	-	-	-
1928	16.9	-0.6	-	-	-	-	-	-	-	-	-	-	-	-	-	-
1929	16.8	-0.6	-	-	-	-	-	-	-	-	-	-	-	-	-	-
1930	16.5	-1.8	-	-	-	-	-	-	-	-	-	-	-	-	-	-
1931	15.5	-6.1	-	-	-	-	-	-	-	-	-	-	-	-	-	-
1932	14.3	-7.7	-	-	-	-	-	-	-	-	-	-	-	-	-	-
1933	13.9	-2.8	-	-	-	-	-	-	-	-	-	-	-	-	-	-
1934	14.3	2.9	-	-	-	-	-	-	-	-	-	-	-	-	-	-
1935	14.6	2.1	-	-	-	-	-	-	-	-	-	-	-	-	-	-
1936	14.7	0.7	-	-	-	-	-	-	-	-	-	-	-	-	-	-
1937	15.0	2.0	-	-	-	-	-	-	-	-	-	-	-	-	-	-
1938	14.7	-2.0	-	-	-	-	-	-	-	-	-	-	-	-	-	-
1939	14.6	-0.7	-	-	-	-	-	-	-	-	-	-	-	-	-	-
1940	14.7	0.7	-	-	-	-	-	-	-	-	-	-	-	-	-	-
1941	15.3	4.1	-	-	-	-	-	-	-	-	-	-	-	-	-	-
1942	17.0	11.1	-	-	-	-	-	-	-	-	-	-	-	-	-	-
1943	18.1	6.5	-	-	-	-	-	-	-	-	-	-	-	-	-	-
1944	18.4	1.7	-	-	-	-	-	-	-	-	-	-	-	-	-	-
1945	18.9	2.7	-	-	-	-	-	-	-	-	-	-	-	-	-	-
1946	20.6	9.0	-	-	-	-	-	-	-	-	-	-	-	-	-	-
1947	23.2	12.6	-	-	-	-	-	-	19.1	-	12.4	-	-	-	-	-
1948	24.6	6.0	-	-	-	-	-	-	21.2	11.0	12.8	3.2	-	-	-	-
1949	24.6	0.0	-	-	-	-	-	-	22.8	7.5	13.1	2.3	-	-	-	-
1950	24.9	1.2	-	-	-	-	-	-	23.3	2.2	13.2	0.8	-	-	-	-
1951	26.6	6.8	-	-	-	-	-	-	24.2	3.9	14.0	6.1	-	-	-	-
1952	27.3	2.6	-	-	-	-	-	-	25.8	6.6	14.8	5.7	-	-	-	-
1953	27.5	0.7	-	-	-	-	40.5	-	26.9	4.3	15.0	1.4	-	-	-	-
1954	27.5	0.0	-	-	-	-	40.3	-0.5	26.8	-0.4	15.0	0.0	-	-	-	-
1955	27.4	-0.4	-	-	-	-	40.0	-0.7	27.2	1.5	15.3	2.0	-	-	-	-
1956	27.7	1.1	-	-	-	-	41.1	2.8	27.5	1.1	16.0	4.6	-	-	-	-
1957	28.6	3.2	-	-	-	-	41.3	0.5	28.9	5.1	16.8	5.0	-	-	-	-
1958	29.3	2.4	-	-	-	-	41.1	-0.5	29.5	2.1	17.9	6.5	-	-	-	-

[Continued]

Washington, DC-MD-VA
Consumer Price Index - All Urban Consumers
Base 1982-1984 = 100
Annual Averages
[Continued]

For 1914-1997. Columns headed % show percentile change in the index from the previous period for which an index is available.

Year	All Items		Food & Beverage		Housing		Apparel & Upkeep		Trans- portation		Medical Care		Entertain- ment		Other Goods & Services	
	Index	%	Index	%	Index	%	Index	%	Index	%	Index	%	Index	%	Index	%
1959	29.4	0.3	-	-	-	-	41.7	1.5	30.4	3.1	19.1	6.7	-	-	-	-
1960	29.7	1.0	-	-	-	-	42.1	1.0	30.7	1.0	19.7	3.1	-	-	-	-
1961	30.1	1.3	-	-	-	-	42.8	1.7	31.0	1.0	20.4	3.6	-	-	-	-
1962	30.4	1.0	-	-	-	-	44.1	3.0	31.3	1.0	21.5	5.4	-	-	-	-
1963	30.9	1.6	-	-	-	-	44.3	0.5	31.6	1.0	22.4	4.2	-	-	-	-
1964	31.4	1.6	-	-	-	-	44.6	0.7	32.4	2.5	23.0	2.7	-	-	-	-
1965	31.9	1.6	-	-	-	-	44.9	0.7	32.7	0.9	23.7	3.0	-	-	-	-
1966	33.0	3.4	-	-	-	-	46.4	3.3	32.9	0.6	24.9	5.1	-	-	-	-
1967	33.9	2.7	-	-	-	-	48.7	5.0	34.1	3.6	27.0	8.4	-	-	-	-
1968	35.5	4.7	-	-	-	-	52.3	7.4	35.4	3.8	29.6	9.6	-	-	-	-
1969	37.7	6.2	-	-	-	-	55.7	6.5	37.1	4.8	31.9	7.8	-	-	-	-
1970	39.8	5.6	-	-	-	-	58.2	4.5	39.7	7.0	34.3	7.5	-	-	-	-
1971	41.6	4.5	-	-	-	-	59.9	2.9	42.1	6.0	36.9	7.6	-	-	-	-
1972	43.0	3.4	-	-	-	-	60.8	1.5	42.2	0.2	37.8	2.4	-	-	-	-
1973	45.7	6.3	-	-	-	-	63.7	4.8	43.0	1.9	39.0	3.2	-	-	-	-
1974	50.8	11.2	-	-	-	-	68.5	7.5	47.6	10.7	43.5	11.5	-	-	-	-
1975	54.7	7.7	-	-	-	-	70.5	2.9	51.8	8.8	48.5	11.5	-	-	-	-
1976	58.0	6.0	62.5	-	55.2	-	72.7	3.1	55.6	7.3	53.4	10.1	68.6	-	58.4	-
1977	62.0	6.9	66.8	6.9	59.4	7.6	74.3	2.2	59.8	7.6	58.3	9.2	73.8	7.6	62.1	6.3
1978	66.7	7.6	73.4	9.9	64.6	8.8	78.0	5.0	63.4	6.0	62.2	6.7	74.9	1.5	65.6	5.6
1979	74.0	10.9	81.8	11.4	71.9	11.3	83.5	7.1	71.8	13.2	68.3	9.8	78.6	4.9	70.0	6.7
1980	82.9	12.0	88.0	7.6	81.0	12.7	90.2	8.0	84.8	18.1	74.2	8.6	84.7	7.8	75.8	8.3
1981	90.5	9.2	92.6	5.2	90.1	11.2	90.5	0.3	94.4	11.3	80.1	8.0	88.9	5.0	83.4	10.0
1982	95.5	5.5	97.2	5.0	95.4	5.9	94.7	4.6	97.0	2.8	90.6	13.1	94.1	5.8	91.3	9.5
1983	99.8	4.5	99.8	2.7	99.7	4.5	100.6	6.2	99.3	2.4	101.5	12.0	99.1	5.3	101.0	10.6
1984	104.6	4.8	103.0	3.2	104.9	5.2	104.7	4.1	103.7	4.4	107.9	6.3	106.7	7.7	107.7	6.6
1985	109.0	4.2	106.1	3.0	110.1	5.0	109.9	5.0	105.6	1.8	114.7	6.3	113.7	6.6	114.5	6.3
1986	112.2	2.9	110.1	3.8	114.8	4.3	108.7	-1.1	103.8	-1.7	122.6	6.9	116.5	2.5	121.9	6.5
1987	116.2	3.6	113.6	3.2	118.9	3.6	116.3	7.0	105.9	2.0	129.1	5.3	121.5	4.3	129.4	6.2
1988	121.0	4.1	119.2	4.9	123.4	3.8	123.1	5.8	108.1	2.1	137.8	6.7	124.8	2.7	138.4	7.0
1989	128.0	5.8	126.1	5.8	129.3	4.8	134.9	9.6	114.4	5.8	146.4	6.2	127.5	2.2	152.2	10.0
1990	135.6	5.9	133.4	5.8	136.6	5.6	139.4	3.3	120.7	5.5	162.4	10.9	135.6	6.4	165.4	8.7
1991	141.2	4.1	137.7	3.2	140.8	3.1	142.4	2.2	126.2	4.6	176.4	8.6	142.7	5.2	178.6	8.0
1992	144.7	2.5	140.9	2.3	143.9	2.2	139.6	-2.0	129.9	2.9	186.3	5.6	147.6	3.4	186.9	4.6
1993	149.3	3.2	142.8	1.3	148.0	2.8	144.4	3.4	134.9	3.8	195.3	4.8	151.0	2.3	199.4	6.7
1994	152.2	1.9	144.2	1.0	150.9	2.0	141.5	-2.0	137.0	1.6	203.5	4.2	155.9	3.2	208.8	4.7
1995	155.3	2.0	147.2	2.1	153.1	1.5	141.0	-0.4	140.2	2.3	212.1	4.2	163.1	4.6	214.9	2.9
1996	159.6	2.8	152.5	3.6	156.0	1.9	140.4	-0.4	144.5	3.1	220.9	4.1	169.1	3.7	227.8	6.0
1997	-	-	-	-	-	-	-	-	-	-	-	-	-	-	-	-

Source: U.S. Department of Labor, Bureau of Labor Statistics, Division of Consumer Prices and Price Indexes. - indicates no data collected for period.

Washington, DC-MD-VA
Consumer Price Index - Urban Wage Earners
Base 1982-1984 = 100
Annual Averages

For 1914-1997. Columns headed % show percentile change in the index from the previous period for which an index is available.

Year	All Items		Food & Beverage		Housing		Apparel & Upkeep		Trans-portation		Medical Care		Entertain-ment		Other Goods & Services	
	Index	%	Index	%	Index	%	Index	%	Index	%	Index	%	Index	%	Index	%
1914	-	-	-	-	-	-	-	-	-	-	-	-	-	-	-	-
1915	10.5	-	-	-	-	-	-	-	-	-	-	-	-	-	-	-
1916	11.2	6.7	-	-	-	-	-	-	-	-	-	-	-	-	-	-
1917	13.6	21.4	-	-	-	-	-	-	-	-	-	-	-	-	-	-
1918	16.1	18.4	-	-	-	-	-	-	-	-	-	-	-	-	-	-
1919	17.6	9.3	-	-	-	-	-	-	-	-	-	-	-	-	-	-
1920	19.7	11.9	-	-	-	-	-	-	-	-	-	-	-	-	-	-
1921	17.4	-11.7	-	-	-	-	-	-	-	-	-	-	-	-	-	-
1922	16.4	-5.7	-	-	-	-	-	-	-	-	-	-	-	-	-	-
1923	16.7	1.8	-	-	-	-	-	-	-	-	-	-	-	-	-	-
1924	16.7	0.0	-	-	-	-	-	-	-	-	-	-	-	-	-	-
1925	17.1	2.4	-	-	-	-	-	-	-	-	-	-	-	-	-	-
1926	17.3	1.2	-	-	-	-	-	-	-	-	-	-	-	-	-	-
1927	16.8	-2.9	-	-	-	-	-	-	-	-	-	-	-	-	-	-
1928	16.7	-0.6	-	-	-	-	-	-	-	-	-	-	-	-	-	-
1929	16.6	-0.6	-	-	-	-	-	-	-	-	-	-	-	-	-	-
1930	16.3	-1.8	-	-	-	-	-	-	-	-	-	-	-	-	-	-
1931	15.3	-6.1	-	-	-	-	-	-	-	-	-	-	-	-	-	-
1932	14.1	-7.8	-	-	-	-	-	-	-	-	-	-	-	-	-	-
1933	13.7	-2.8	-	-	-	-	-	-	-	-	-	-	-	-	-	-
1934	14.1	2.9	-	-	-	-	-	-	-	-	-	-	-	-	-	-
1935	14.4	2.1	-	-	-	-	-	-	-	-	-	-	-	-	-	-
1936	14.5	0.7	-	-	-	-	-	-	-	-	-	-	-	-	-	-
1937	14.8	2.1	-	-	-	-	-	-	-	-	-	-	-	-	-	-
1938	14.5	-2.0	-	-	-	-	-	-	-	-	-	-	-	-	-	-
1939	14.4	-0.7	-	-	-	-	-	-	-	-	-	-	-	-	-	-
1940	14.5	0.7	-	-	-	-	-	-	-	-	-	-	-	-	-	-
1941	15.1	4.1	-	-	-	-	-	-	-	-	-	-	-	-	-	-
1942	16.8	11.3	-	-	-	-	-	-	-	-	-	-	-	-	-	-
1943	17.8	6.0	-	-	-	-	-	-	-	-	-	-	-	-	-	-
1944	18.1	1.7	-	-	-	-	-	-	-	-	-	-	-	-	-	-
1945	18.6	2.8	-	-	-	-	-	-	-	-	-	-	-	-	-	-
1946	20.3	9.1	-	-	-	-	-	-	-	-	-	-	-	-	-	-
1947	22.9	12.8	-	-	-	-	-	-	19.1	-	11.9	-	-	-	-	-
1948	24.3	6.1	-	-	-	-	-	-	21.1	10.5	12.3	3.4	-	-	-	-
1949	24.2	-0.4	-	-	-	-	-	-	22.7	7.6	12.5	1.6	-	-	-	-
1950	24.6	1.7	-	-	-	-	-	-	23.3	2.6	12.6	0.8	-	-	-	-
1951	26.2	6.5	-	-	-	-	-	-	24.1	3.4	13.4	6.3	-	-	-	-
1952	26.9	2.7	-	-	-	-	-	-	25.7	6.6	14.1	5.2	-	-	-	-
1953	27.1	0.7	-	-	-	-	36.4	-	26.8	4.3	14.3	1.4	-	-	-	-
1954	27.1	0.0	-	-	-	-	36.2	-0.5	26.7	-0.4	14.4	0.7	-	-	-	-
1955	27.0	-0.4	-	-	-	-	36.0	-0.6	27.1	1.5	14.6	1.4	-	-	-	-
1956	27.3	1.1	-	-	-	-	37.0	2.8	27.5	1.5	15.4	5.5	-	-	-	-
1957	28.2	3.3	-	-	-	-	37.2	0.5	28.9	5.1	16.1	4.5	-	-	-	-
1958	28.8	2.1	-	-	-	-	37.0	-0.5	29.4	1.7	17.1	6.2	-	-	-	-

[Continued]

Washington, DC-MD-VA
Consumer Price Index - Urban Wage Earners
Base 1982-1984 = 100
Annual Averages
[Continued]

For 1914-1997. Columns headed % show percentile change in the index from the previous period for which an index is available.

Year	All Items		Food & Beverage		Housing		Apparel & Upkeep		Trans- portation		Medical Care		Entertain- ment		Other Goods & Services	
	Index	%	Index	%	Index	%	Index	%	Index	%	Index	%	Index	%	Index	%
1959	29.0	0.7	-	-	-	-	37.5	1.4	30.4	3.4	18.2	6.4	-	-	-	-
1960	29.3	1.0	-	-	-	-	37.9	1.1	30.6	0.7	18.9	3.8	-	-	-	-
1961	29.7	1.4	-	-	-	-	38.5	1.6	30.9	1.0	19.5	3.2	-	-	-	-
1962	30.0	1.0	-	-	-	-	39.7	3.1	31.3	1.3	20.6	5.6	-	-	-	-
1963	30.5	1.7	-	-	-	-	39.8	0.3	31.5	0.6	21.4	3.9	-	-	-	-
1964	31.0	1.6	-	-	-	-	40.1	0.8	32.3	2.5	22.0	2.8	-	-	-	-
1965	31.4	1.3	-	-	-	-	40.4	0.7	32.6	0.9	22.7	3.2	-	-	-	-
1966	32.5	3.5	-	-	-	-	41.8	3.5	32.9	0.9	23.8	4.8	-	-	-	-
1967	33.4	2.8	-	-	-	-	43.8	4.8	34.0	3.3	25.8	8.4	-	-	-	-
1968	35.0	4.8	-	-	-	-	47.0	7.3	35.3	3.8	28.3	9.7	-	-	-	-
1969	37.1	6.0	-	-	-	-	50.1	6.6	37.0	4.8	30.5	7.8	-	-	-	-
1970	39.3	5.9	-	-	-	-	52.4	4.6	39.6	7.0	32.8	7.5	-	-	-	-
1971	41.0	4.3	-	-	-	-	53.8	2.7	42.0	6.1	35.3	7.6	-	-	-	-
1972	42.4	3.4	-	-	-	-	54.7	1.7	42.1	0.2	36.2	2.5	-	-	-	-
1973	45.1	6.4	-	-	-	-	57.3	4.8	42.9	1.9	37.3	3.0	-	-	-	-
1974	50.1	11.1	-	-	-	-	61.6	7.5	47.5	10.7	41.6	11.5	-	-	-	-
1975	54.0	7.8	-	-	-	-	63.4	2.9	51.7	8.8	46.4	11.5	-	-	-	-
1976	57.1	5.7	61.6	-	55.7	-	65.4	3.2	55.5	7.4	51.1	10.1	58.3	-	56.3	-
1977	61.1	7.0	65.8	6.8	59.8	7.4	66.8	2.1	59.6	7.4	55.8	9.2	62.6	7.4	59.8	6.2
1978	66.2	8.3	72.4	10.0	65.8	10.0	68.3	2.2	62.8	5.4	61.1	9.5	68.4	9.3	65.4	9.4
1979	73.4	10.9	79.7	10.1	73.1	11.1	72.2	5.7	70.9	12.9	68.5	12.1	75.8	10.8	70.0	7.0
1980	82.2	12.0	85.6	7.4	81.9	12.0	80.8	11.9	83.0	17.1	74.7	9.1	82.7	9.1	76.6	9.4
1981	90.3	9.9	91.8	7.2	90.5	10.5	89.2	10.4	92.9	11.9	79.8	6.8	88.0	6.4	84.3	10.1
1982	95.8	6.1	97.3	6.0	96.2	6.3	94.1	5.5	96.6	4.0	90.3	13.2	94.5	7.4	91.3	8.3
1983	99.8	4.2	99.7	2.5	99.5	3.4	102.8	9.2	99.3	2.8	101.4	12.3	99.2	5.0	101.3	11.0
1984	104.4	4.6	103.0	3.3	104.3	4.8	103.2	0.4	104.2	4.9	108.4	6.9	106.3	7.2	107.5	6.1
1985	108.6	4.0	106.0	2.9	109.6	5.1	108.7	5.3	106.1	1.8	115.6	6.6	111.9	5.3	112.7	4.8
1986	111.0	2.2	109.9	3.7	114.3	4.3	104.0	-4.3	104.3	-1.7	123.6	6.9	112.7	0.7	119.1	5.7
1987	115.4	4.0	113.9	3.6	118.2	3.4	114.6	10.2	108.0	3.5	130.5	5.6	118.0	4.7	125.7	5.5
1988	120.3	4.2	119.3	4.7	122.6	3.7	120.8	5.4	111.2	3.0	139.5	6.9	121.8	3.2	134.6	7.1
1989	127.3	5.8	126.5	6.0	128.4	4.7	133.4	10.4	117.9	6.0	148.2	6.2	124.6	2.3	148.5	10.3
1990	134.5	5.7	133.8	5.8	135.0	5.1	137.0	2.7	124.6	5.7	163.5	10.3	132.0	5.9	160.6	8.1
1991	139.7	3.9	137.8	3.0	139.0	3.0	141.2	3.1	129.8	4.2	176.8	8.1	138.7	5.1	172.5	7.4
1992	143.0	2.4	141.0	2.3	141.7	1.9	140.0	-0.8	133.3	2.7	186.8	5.7	143.7	3.6	180.5	4.6
1993	147.1	2.9	142.8	1.3	145.3	2.5	143.7	2.6	137.8	3.4	195.9	4.9	146.6	2.0	192.5	6.6
1994	149.8	1.8	144.4	1.1	148.1	1.9	141.1	-1.8	140.4	1.9	204.1	4.2	151.0	3.0	199.5	3.6
1995	152.7	1.9	147.4	2.1	150.4	1.6	140.7	-0.3	144.0	2.6	212.0	3.9	156.7	3.8	203.4	2.0
1996	156.9	2.8	152.6	3.5	153.0	1.7	141.8	0.8	149.0	3.5	220.9	4.2	162.8	3.9	215.4	5.9
1997	-	-	-	-	-	-	-	-	-	-	-	-	-	-	-	-

Source: U.S. Department of Labor, Bureau of Labor Statistics, Division of Consumer Prices and Price Indexes. - indicates no data collected for period.

Washington, DC-MD-VA
Consumer Price Index - All Urban Consumers
Base 1982-1984 = 100
All Items

For 1914-1997. Columns headed % show percentile change in the index from the previous period for which an index is available.

Year	Jan Index	%	Feb Index	%	Mar Index	%	Apr Index	%	May Index	%	Jun Index	%	Jul Index	%	Aug Index	%	Sep Index	%	Oct Index	%	Nov Index	%	Dec Index	%
1914	-	-	-	-	-	-	-	-	-	-	-	-	-	-	-	-	-	-	-	-	-	-	10.7	-
1915	-	-	-	-	-	-	-	-	-	-	-	-	-	-	-	-	-	-	-	-	-	-	10.8	0.9
1916	-	-	-	-	-	-	-	-	-	-	-	-	-	-	-	-	-	-	-	-	-	-	12.0	11.1
1917	-	-	-	-	-	-	-	-	-	-	-	-	-	-	-	-	-	-	-	-	-	-	15.1	25.8
1918	-	-	-	-	-	-	-	-	-	-	-	-	-	-	-	-	-	-	-	-	-	-	17.6	16.6
1919	-	-	-	-	-	-	-	-	-	-	17.3	-1.7	-	-	-	-	-	-	-	-	-	-	18.8	8.7
1920	-	-	-	-	-	-	-	-	-	-	20.9	11.2	-	-	-	-	-	-	-	-	-	-	19.1	-8.6
1921	-	-	-	-	-	-	-	-	17.4	-8.9	-	-	-	-	-	-	17.5	0.6	-	-	-	-	17.1	-2.3
1922	-	-	-	-	16.6	-2.9	-	-	-	-	16.7	0.6	-	-	-	-	16.5	-1.2	-	-	-	-	16.7	1.2
1923	-	-	-	-	16.6	-0.6	-	-	-	-	17.0	2.4	-	-	-	-	17.2	1.2	-	-	-	-	17.0	-1.2
1924	-	-	-	-	16.8	-1.2	-	-	-	-	16.8	0.0	-	-	-	-	16.8	0.0	-	-	-	-	17.0	1.2
1925	-	-	-	-	-	-	-	-	-	-	17.3	1.8	-	-	-	-	-	-	-	-	-	-	17.6	1.7
1926	-	-	-	-	-	-	-	-	-	-	17.5	-0.6	-	-	-	-	-	-	-	-	-	-	17.4	-0.6
1927	-	-	-	-	-	-	-	-	-	-	17.1	-1.7	-	-	-	-	-	-	-	-	-	-	16.9	-1.2
1928	-	-	-	-	-	-	-	-	-	-	16.9	0.0	-	-	-	-	-	-	-	-	-	-	16.8	-0.6
1929	-	-	-	-	-	-	-	-	-	-	16.9	0.6	-	-	-	-	-	-	-	-	-	-	16.8	-0.6
1930	-	-	-	-	-	-	-	-	-	-	16.6	-1.2	-	-	-	-	-	-	-	-	-	-	16.2	-2.4
1931	-	-	-	-	-	-	-	-	-	-	15.4	-4.9	-	-	-	-	-	-	-	-	-	-	15.1	-1.9
1932	-	-	-	-	-	-	-	-	-	-	14.3	-5.3	-	-	-	-	-	-	-	-	-	-	13.9	-2.8
1933	-	-	-	-	-	-	-	-	-	-	13.7	-1.4	-	-	-	-	-	-	-	-	-	-	14.2	3.6
1934	-	-	-	-	-	-	-	-	-	-	14.3	0.7	-	-	-	-	-	-	-	-	14.5	1.4	-	-
1935	-	-	-	-	14.5	0.0	-	-	-	-	-	-	14.5	0.0	-	-	-	-	14.6	0.7	-	-	-	-
1936	14.7	0.7	-	-	-	-	14.5	-1.4	-	-	-	-	14.7	1.4	-	-	14.8	0.7	-	-	-	-	14.7	-0.7
1937	-	-	-	-	15.0	2.0	-	-	-	-	15.1	0.7	-	-	-	-	15.2	0.7	-	-	-	-	15.0	-1.3
1938	-	-	-	-	14.7	-2.0	-	-	-	-	14.7	0.0	-	-	-	-	14.7	0.0	-	-	-	-	14.7	0.0
1939	-	-	-	-	14.5	-1.4	-	-	-	-	14.5	0.0	-	-	-	-	14.7	1.4	-	-	-	-	14.5	-1.4
1940	-	-	-	-	14.7	1.4	-	-	-	-	14.7	0.0	-	-	-	-	14.7	0.0	-	-	-	-	14.7	0.0
1941	-	-	-	-	14.8	0.7	-	-	-	-	15.2	2.7	-	-	-	-	15.7	3.3	16.0	1.9	16.0	0.0	16.2	1.3
1942	16.3	0.6	16.5	1.2	16.7	1.2	16.7	0.0	16.9	1.2	17.0	0.6	17.1	0.6	17.2	0.6	17.3	0.6	17.3	0.0	17.4	0.6	17.5	0.6
1943	17.6	0.6	17.6	0.0	17.9	1.7	18.1	1.1	18.3	1.1	18.3	0.0	18.2	-0.5	18.2	0.0	18.2	0.0	18.3	0.5	18.2	-0.5	18.2	0.0
1944	18.3	0.5	18.2	-0.5	18.1	-0.5	18.2	0.6	18.3	0.5	18.4	0.5	18.4	0.0	18.5	0.5	18.5	0.0	18.5	0.0	18.6	0.5	18.6	0.0
1945	18.6	0.0	18.6	0.0	18.6	0.0	18.7	0.5	18.9	1.1	19.0	0.5	19.0	0.0	19.0	0.0	19.1	0.5	19.0	-0.5	19.1	0.5	19.2	0.5
1946	19.3	0.5	19.2	-0.5	19.4	1.0	19.4	0.0	19.4	0.0	19.8	2.1	20.8	5.1	21.1	1.4	21.4	1.4	21.8	1.9	22.2	1.8	22.5	1.4
1947	22.5	0.0	22.4	-0.4	22.9	2.2	22.9	0.0	22.9	0.0	22.9	0.0	23.1	0.9	23.5	1.7	-	-	-	-	23.9	1.7	-	-
1948	-	-	24.1	0.8	-	-	-	-	24.7	2.5	-	-	-	-	25.0	1.2	-	-	-	-	24.7	-1.2	-	-
1949	-	-	24.4	-1.2	-	-	-	-	24.6	0.8	-	-	-	-	24.7	0.4	-	-	-	-	24.8	0.4	-	-
1950	-	-	24.4	-1.6	-	-	-	-	24.5	0.4	-	-	-	-	25.1	2.4	-	-	-	-	25.5	1.6	-	-
1951	-	-	26.4	3.5	-	-	-	-	26.5	0.4	-	-	-	-	26.6	0.4	-	-	-	-	27.2	2.3	-	-
1952	-	-	27.0	-0.7	-	-	-	-	27.2	0.7	-	-	-	-	27.6	1.5	-	-	-	-	27.5	-0.4	-	-
1953	-	-	27.3	-0.7	-	-	-	-	27.4	0.4	-	-	-	-	27.6	0.7	-	-	-	-	27.6	0.0	-	-
1954	-	-	27.6	0.0	-	-	-	-	27.4	-0.7	-	-	-	-	27.6	0.7	-	-	-	-	27.4	-0.7	-	-
1955	-	-	27.3	-0.4	-	-	-	-	27.4	0.4	-	-	-	-	27.5	0.4	-	-	-	-	27.4	-0.4	-	-
1956	-	-	27.4	0.0	-	-	-	-	27.6	0.7	-	-	-	-	27.9	1.1	-	-	-	-	28.0	0.4	-	-
1957	-	-	28.4	1.4	-	-	-	-	28.3	-0.4	-	-	-	-	28.8	1.8	-	-	-	-	28.9	0.3	-	-
1958	-	-	29.1	0.7	-	-	-	-	29.3	0.7	-	-	-	-	29.3	0.0	-	-	-	-	29.3	0.0	-	-

[Continued]

Washington, DC-MD-VA
Consumer Price Index - All Urban Consumers
Base 1982-1984 = 100
All Items
[Continued]

For 1914-1997. Columns headed % show percentile change in the index from the previous period for which an index is available.

Year	Jan Index	%	Feb Index	%	Mar Index	%	Apr Index	%	May Index	%	Jun Index	%	Jul Index	%	Aug Index	%	Sep Index	%	Oct Index	%	Nov Index	%	Dec Index	%
1959	-	-	29.3	0.0	-	-	-	-	29.4	0.3	-	-	-	-	29.5	0.3	-	-	-	-	29.4	-0.3	-	-
1960	-	-	29.4	0.0	-	-	-	-	29.7	1.0	-	-	-	-	29.7	0.0	-	-	-	-	29.9	0.7	-	-
1961	-	-	30.1	0.7	-	-	-	-	30.0	-0.3	-	-	-	-	30.2	0.7	-	-	-	-	30.3	0.3	-	-
1962	-	-	30.2	-0.3	-	-	-	-	30.3	0.3	-	-	-	-	30.5	0.7	-	-	-	-	30.6	0.3	-	-
1963	-	-	30.7	0.3	-	-	-	-	30.9	0.7	-	-	-	-	31.1	0.6	-	-	-	-	31.1	0.0	-	-
1964	-	-	31.2	0.3	-	-	-	-	31.3	0.3	-	-	-	-	31.6	1.0	-	-	-	-	31.7	0.3	-	-
1965	-	-	31.6	-0.3	-	-	-	-	31.8	0.6	-	-	-	-	31.9	0.3	-	-	-	-	32.1	0.6	-	-
1966	-	-	32.6	1.6	-	-	-	-	32.8	0.6	-	-	-	-	33.2	1.2	-	-	-	-	33.3	0.3	-	-
1967	-	-	33.5	0.6	-	-	-	-	33.6	0.3	-	-	-	-	34.1	1.5	-	-	-	-	34.2	0.3	-	-
1968	-	-	34.6	1.2	-	-	-	-	35.2	1.7	-	-	-	-	35.8	1.7	-	-	-	-	36.3	1.4	-	-
1969	-	-	36.7	1.1	-	-	-	-	37.5	2.2	-	-	-	-	38.0	1.3	-	-	-	-	38.4	1.1	-	-
1970	-	-	39.1	1.8	-	-	-	-	39.7	1.5	-	-	-	-	40.1	1.0	-	-	-	-	40.4	0.7	-	-
1971	-	-	41.0	1.5	-	-	-	-	41.4	1.0	-	-	-	-	41.8	1.0	-	-	-	-	42.1	0.7	-	-
1972	-	-	42.2	0.2	-	-	-	-	42.5	0.7	-	-	-	-	43.3	1.9	-	-	-	-	43.9	1.4	-	-
1973	-	-	44.3	0.9	-	-	-	-	45.2	2.0	-	-	-	-	46.2	2.2	-	-	-	-	47.2	2.2	-	-
1974	-	-	48.8	3.4	-	-	-	-	50.0	2.5	-	-	-	-	51.7	3.4	-	-	-	-	52.9	2.3	-	-
1975	-	-	53.5	1.1	-	-	-	-	54.2	1.3	-	-	-	-	55.3	2.0	-	-	-	-	56.0	1.3	-	-
1976	-	-	56.6	1.1	-	-	-	-	57.6	1.8	-	-	-	-	58.6	1.7	-	-	-	-	59.0	0.7	-	-
1977	-	-	60.3	2.2	-	-	-	-	61.5	2.0	-	-	-	-	62.6	1.8	-	-	-	-	63.5	1.4	-	-
1978	64.3	1.3	-	-	64.7	0.6	-	-	65.8	1.7	-	-	67.0	1.8	-	-	68.0	1.5	-	-	69.1	1.6	-	-
1979	70.7	2.3	-	-	72.0	1.8	-	-	73.2	1.7	-	-	74.7	2.0	-	-	75.5	1.1	-	-	76.3	1.1	-	-
1980	78.5	2.9	-	-	80.9	3.1	-	-	81.7	1.0	-	-	83.7	2.4	-	-	84.4	0.8	-	-	85.9	1.8	-	-
1981	87.1	1.4	-	-	88.8	2.0	-	-	89.7	1.0	-	-	90.5	0.9	-	-	92.1	1.8	-	-	93.3	1.3	-	-
1982	94.2	1.0	-	-	94.4	0.2	-	-	94.3	-0.1	-	-	95.3	1.1	-	-	97.0	1.8	-	-	97.0	0.0	-	-
1983	98.0	1.0	-	-	98.0	0.0	-	-	99.2	1.2	-	-	100.6	1.4	-	-	100.7	0.1	-	-	101.2	0.5	-	-
1984	102.9	1.7	-	-	103.3	0.4	-	-	103.5	0.2	-	-	104.4	0.9	-	-	106.0	1.5	-	-	106.7	0.7	-	-
1985	106.6	-0.1	-	-	108.1	1.4	-	-	108.3	0.2	-	-	109.5	1.1	-	-	109.6	0.1	-	-	110.7	1.0	-	-
1986	112.2	1.4	-	-	111.5	-0.6	-	-	111.6	0.1	-	-	111.5	-0.1	-	-	112.6	1.0	-	-	113.1	0.4	-	-
1987	113.7	0.5	-	-	114.5	0.7	-	-	115.3	0.7	-	-	116.2	0.8	-	-	117.8	1.4	-	-	118.5	0.6	-	-
1988	118.3	-0.2	-	-	119.2	0.8	-	-	120.1	0.8	-	-	120.7	0.5	-	-	122.8	1.7	-	-	123.2	0.3	-	-
1989	124.3	0.9	-	-	126.1	1.4	-	-	127.1	0.8	-	-	127.8	0.6	-	-	130.1	1.8	-	-	130.5	0.3	-	-
1990	132.0	1.1	-	-	133.8	1.4	-	-	134.0	0.1	-	-	135.7	1.3	-	-	138.0	1.7	-	-	138.4	0.3	-	-
1991	139.1	0.5	-	-	139.3	0.1	-	-	140.9	1.1	-	-	140.9	0.0	-	-	143.3	1.7	-	-	142.6	-0.5	-	-
1992	142.9	0.2	-	-	143.0	0.1	-	-	143.2	0.1	-	-	144.8	1.1	-	-	146.0	0.8	-	-	146.9	0.6	-	-
1993	147.8	0.6	-	-	148.5	0.5	-	-	149.2	0.5	-	-	149.2	0.0	-	-	149.7	0.3	-	-	150.9	0.8	-	-
1994	150.9	0.0	-	-	151.5	0.4	-	-	151.4	-0.1	-	-	151.8	0.3	-	-	153.7	1.3	-	-	153.0	-0.5	-	-
1995	153.8	0.5	-	-	155.1	0.8	-	-	154.7	-0.3	-	-	156.1	0.9	-	-	156.2	0.1	-	-	155.2	-0.6	-	-
1996	156.8	1.0	-	-	158.4	1.0	-	-	159.0	0.4	-	-	160.1	0.7	-	-	160.8	0.4	-	-	161.2	0.2	-	-
1997	161.6	0.2	-	-	161.9	0.2	-	-	162.1	0.1	162.0	-0.1	162.9	0.6	-	-	163.6	0.4	-	-	161.8	-1.1	-	-

Source: U.S. Department of Labor, Bureau of Labor Statistics, Division of Consumer Prices and Price Indexes. - indicates no data collected for period.

Washington, DC-MD-VA
Consumer Price Index - Urban Wage Earners
Base 1982-1984 = 100
All Items

For 1914-1997. Columns headed % show percentile change in the index from the previous period for which an index is available.

Year	Jan Index	%	Feb Index	%	Mar Index	%	Apr Index	%	May Index	%	Jun Index	%	Jul Index	%	Aug Index	%	Sep Index	%	Oct Index	%	Nov Index	%	Dec Index	%
1914	-	-	-	-	-	-	-	-	-	-	-	-	-	-	-	-	-	-	-	-	-	-	10.5	-
1915	-	-	-	-	-	-	-	-	-	-	-	-	-	-	-	-	-	-	-	-	-	-	10.6	1.0
1916	-	-	-	-	-	-	-	-	-	-	-	-	-	-	-	-	-	-	-	-	-	-	11.8	11.3
1917	-	-	-	-	-	-	-	-	-	-	-	-	-	-	-	-	-	-	-	-	-	-	14.9	26.3
1918	-	-	-	-	-	-	-	-	-	-	-	-	-	-	-	-	-	-	-	-	-	-	17.3	16.1
1919	-	-	-	-	-	-	-	-	-	-	17.1	-1.2	-	-	-	-	-	-	-	-	-	-	18.5	8.2
1920	-	-	-	-	-	-	-	-	-	-	20.6	11.4	-	-	-	-	-	-	-	-	-	-	18.9	-8.3
1921	-	-	-	-	-	-	-	-	17.1	-9.5	-	-	-	-	-	-	17.3	1.2	-	-	-	-	16.9	-2.3
1922	-	-	-	-	16.4	-3.0	-	-	-	-	16.5	0.6	-	-	-	-	16.3	-1.2	-	-	-	-	16.5	1.2
1923	-	-	-	-	16.4	-0.6	-	-	-	-	16.8	2.4	-	-	-	-	16.9	0.6	-	-	-	-	16.8	-0.6
1924	-	-	-	-	16.6	-1.2	-	-	-	-	16.6	0.0	-	-	-	-	16.6	0.0	-	-	-	-	16.8	1.2
1925	-	-	-	-	-	-	-	-	-	-	17.0	1.2	-	-	-	-	-	-	-	-	-	-	17.4	2.4
1926	-	-	-	-	-	-	-	-	-	-	17.3	-0.6	-	-	-	-	-	-	-	-	-	-	17.2	-0.6
1927	-	-	-	-	-	-	-	-	-	-	16.9	-1.7	-	-	-	-	-	-	-	-	-	-	16.7	-1.2
1928	-	-	-	-	-	-	-	-	-	-	16.7	0.0	-	-	-	-	-	-	-	-	-	-	16.5	-1.2
1929	-	-	-	-	-	-	-	-	-	-	16.6	0.6	-	-	-	-	-	-	-	-	-	-	16.6	0.0
1930	-	-	-	-	-	-	-	-	-	-	16.4	-1.2	-	-	-	-	-	-	-	-	-	-	16.0	-2.4
1931	-	-	-	-	-	-	-	-	-	-	15.2	-5.0	-	-	-	-	-	-	-	-	-	-	14.9	-2.0
1932	-	-	-	-	-	-	-	-	-	-	14.1	-5.4	-	-	-	-	-	-	-	-	-	-	13.7	-2.8
1933	-	-	-	-	-	-	-	-	-	-	13.5	-1.5	-	-	-	-	-	-	-	-	-	-	14.0	3.7
1934	-	-	-	-	-	-	-	-	-	-	14.1	0.7	-	-	-	-	-	-	-	-	14.3	1.4	-	-
1935	-	-	-	-	14.3	0.0	-	-	-	-	-	-	14.3	0.0	-	-	-	-	14.4	0.7	-	-	-	-
1936	14.5	0.7	-	-	-	-	14.3	-1.4	-	-	-	-	14.5	1.4	-	-	14.6	0.7	-	-	-	-	14.5	-0.7
1937	-	-	-	-	14.8	2.1	-	-	-	-	14.9	0.7	-	-	-	-	15.0	0.7	-	-	-	-	14.8	-1.3
1938	-	-	-	-	14.5	-2.0	-	-	-	-	14.5	0.0	-	-	-	-	14.5	0.0	-	-	-	-	14.5	0.0
1939	-	-	-	-	14.3	-1.4	-	-	-	-	14.3	0.0	-	-	-	-	14.5	1.4	-	-	-	-	14.3	-1.4
1940	-	-	-	-	14.5	1.4	-	-	-	-	14.5	0.0	-	-	-	-	14.5	0.0	-	-	-	-	14.5	0.0
1941	-	-	-	-	14.6	0.7	-	-	-	-	15.0	2.7	-	-	-	-	15.5	3.3	15.7	1.3	15.8	0.6	15.9	0.6
1942	16.1	1.3	16.2	0.6	16.5	1.9	16.5	0.0	16.7	1.2	16.8	0.6	16.9	0.6	17.0	0.6	17.0	0.0	17.1	0.6	17.2	0.6	17.3	0.6
1943	17.4	0.6	17.3	-0.6	17.6	1.7	17.8	1.1	18.0	1.1	18.0	0.0	17.9	-0.6	17.9	0.0	18.0	0.6	18.1	0.6	18.0	-0.6	18.0	0.0
1944	18.0	0.0	17.9	-0.6	17.8	-0.6	17.9	0.6	18.1	1.1	18.1	0.0	18.1	0.0	18.2	0.6	18.2	0.0	18.2	0.0	18.3	0.5	18.3	0.0
1945	18.4	0.5	18.4	0.0	18.3	-0.5	18.4	0.5	18.6	1.1	18.7	0.5	18.8	0.5	18.8	0.0	18.8	0.0	18.8	0.0	18.9	0.5	18.9	0.0
1946	19.1	1.1	19.0	-0.5	19.1	0.5	19.2	0.5	19.2	0.0	19.5	1.6	20.5	5.1	20.8	1.5	21.1	1.4	21.5	1.9	21.9	1.9	22.2	1.4
1947	22.2	0.0	22.1	-0.5	22.6	2.3	22.6	0.0	22.5	-0.4	22.7	0.9	-	-	23.2	2.2	-	-	-	-	23.6	1.7	-	-
1948	-	-	23.8	0.8	-	-	-	-	24.3	2.1	-	-	-	-	24.7	1.6	-	-	-	-	24.4	-1.2	-	-
1949	-	-	24.0	-1.6	-	-	-	-	24.2	0.8	-	-	-	-	24.4	0.8	-	-	-	-	24.4	0.0	-	-
1950	-	-	24.1	-1.2	-	-	-	-	24.2	0.4	-	-	-	-	24.8	2.5	-	-	-	-	25.2	1.6	-	-
1951	-	-	26.0	3.2	-	-	-	-	26.1	0.4	-	-	-	-	26.2	0.4	-	-	-	-	26.8	2.3	-	-
1952	-	-	26.6	-0.7	-	-	-	-	26.8	0.8	-	-	-	-	27.2	1.5	-	-	-	-	27.1	-0.4	-	-
1953	-	-	26.9	-0.7	-	-	-	-	27.0	0.4	-	-	-	-	27.2	0.7	-	-	-	-	27.2	0.0	-	-
1954	-	-	27.2	0.0	-	-	-	-	27.0	-0.7	-	-	-	-	27.2	0.7	-	-	-	-	27.0	-0.7	-	-
1955	-	-	26.9	-0.4	-	-	-	-	27.0	0.4	-	-	-	-	27.1	0.4	-	-	-	-	27.0	-0.4	-	-
1956	-	-	27.0	0.0	-	-	-	-	27.2	0.7	-	-	-	-	27.5	1.1	-	-	-	-	27.6	0.4	-	-
1957	-	-	28.0	1.4	-	-	-	-	27.9	-0.4	-	-	-	-	28.3	1.4	-	-	-	-	28.4	0.4	-	-
1958	-	-	28.6	0.7	-	-	-	-	28.8	0.7	-	-	-	-	28.8	0.0	-	-	-	-	28.9	0.3	-	-

[Continued]

Washington, DC-MD-VA
Consumer Price Index - Urban Wage Earners
Base 1982-1984 = 100
All Items
[Continued]

For 1914-1997. Columns headed % show percentile change in the index from the previous period for which an index is available.

Year	Jan Index	%	Feb Index	%	Mar Index	%	Apr Index	%	May Index	%	Jun Index	%	Jul Index	%	Aug Index	%	Sep Index	%	Oct Index	%	Nov Index	%	Dec Index	%
1959	-	-	28.8	-0.3	-	-	-	-	29.0	0.7	-	-	-	-	29.0	0.0	-	-	-	-	29.0	0.0	-	-
1960	-	-	29.0	0.0	-	-	-	-	29.3	1.0	-	-	-	-	29.3	0.0	-	-	-	-	29.5	0.7	-	-
1961	-	-	29.7	0.7	-	-	-	-	29.6	-0.3	-	-	-	-	29.8	0.7	-	-	-	-	29.9	0.3	-	-
1962	-	-	29.8	-0.3	-	-	-	-	29.9	0.3	-	-	-	-	30.1	0.7	-	-	-	-	30.2	0.3	-	-
1963	-	-	30.3	0.3	-	-	-	-	30.4	0.3	-	-	-	-	30.6	0.7	-	-	-	-	30.7	0.3	-	-
1964	-	-	30.8	0.3	-	-	-	-	30.8	0.0	-	-	-	-	31.2	1.3	-	-	-	-	31.2	0.0	-	-
1965	-	-	31.2	0.0	-	-	-	-	31.4	0.6	-	-	-	-	31.4	0.0	-	-	-	-	31.7	1.0	-	-
1966	-	-	32.1	1.3	-	-	-	-	32.3	0.6	-	-	-	-	32.7	1.2	-	-	-	-	32.9	0.6	-	-
1967	-	-	33.0	0.3	-	-	-	-	33.2	0.6	-	-	-	-	33.6	1.2	-	-	-	-	33.8	0.6	-	-
1968	-	-	34.1	0.9	-	-	-	-	34.7	1.8	-	-	-	-	35.3	1.7	-	-	-	-	35.8	1.4	-	-
1969	-	-	36.2	1.1	-	-	-	-	36.9	1.9	-	-	-	-	37.5	1.6	-	-	-	-	37.8	0.8	-	-
1970	-	-	38.6	2.1	-	-	-	-	39.2	1.6	-	-	-	-	39.5	0.8	-	-	-	-	39.8	0.8	-	-
1971	-	-	40.4	1.5	-	-	-	-	40.8	1.0	-	-	-	-	41.2	1.0	-	-	-	-	41.5	0.7	-	-
1972	-	-	41.6	0.2	-	-	-	-	41.9	0.7	-	-	-	-	42.6	1.7	-	-	-	-	43.3	1.6	-	-
1973	-	-	43.6	0.7	-	-	-	-	44.5	2.1	-	-	-	-	45.5	2.2	-	-	-	-	46.5	2.2	-	-
1974	-	-	48.1	3.4	-	-	-	-	49.3	2.5	-	-	-	-	51.0	3.4	-	-	-	-	52.1	2.2	-	-
1975	-	-	52.7	1.2	-	-	-	-	53.4	1.3	-	-	-	-	54.6	2.2	-	-	-	-	55.2	1.1	-	-
1976	-	-	55.8	1.1	-	-	-	-	56.8	1.8	-	-	-	-	57.8	1.8	-	-	-	-	58.2	0.7	-	-
1977	-	-	59.4	2.1	-	-	-	-	60.7	2.2	-	-	-	-	61.7	1.6	-	-	-	-	62.6	1.5	-	-
1978	63.1	0.8	-	-	63.7	1.0	-	-	65.5	2.8	-	-	67.0	2.3	-	-	67.7	1.0	-	-	68.6	1.3	-	-
1979	69.9	1.9	-	-	71.3	2.0	-	-	72.7	2.0	-	-	74.1	1.9	-	-	74.9	1.1	-	-	75.7	1.1	-	-
1980	77.8	2.8	-	-	79.9	2.7	-	-	80.8	1.1	-	-	83.0	2.7	-	-	84.1	1.3	-	-	85.4	1.5	-	-
1981	86.6	1.4	-	-	88.2	1.8	-	-	89.4	1.4	-	-	90.6	1.3	-	-	92.1	1.7	-	-	93.3	1.3	-	-
1982	94.1	0.9	-	-	94.8	0.7	-	-	94.6	-0.2	-	-	95.6	1.1	-	-	97.5	2.0	-	-	97.4	-0.1	-	-
1983	97.9	0.5	-	-	98.4	0.5	-	-	99.4	1.0	-	-	100.3	0.9	-	-	100.6	0.3	-	-	101.2	0.6	-	-
1984	102.9	1.7	-	-	102.9	0.0	-	-	103.1	0.2	-	-	103.8	0.7	-	-	106.1	2.2	-	-	106.6	0.5	-	-
1985	106.1	-0.5	-	-	107.6	1.4	-	-	107.9	0.3	-	-	108.8	0.8	-	-	109.3	0.5	-	-	110.4	1.0	-	-
1986	111.1	0.6	-	-	110.4	-0.6	-	-	110.3	-0.1	-	-	110.3	0.0	-	-	111.7	1.3	-	-	112.2	0.4	-	-
1987	112.7	0.4	-	-	113.6	0.8	-	-	114.6	0.9	-	-	115.3	0.6	-	-	117.1	1.6	-	-	117.9	0.7	-	-
1988	117.6	-0.3	-	-	118.5	0.8	-	-	119.3	0.7	-	-	119.9	0.5	-	-	122.3	2.0	-	-	122.6	0.2	-	-
1989	123.7	0.9	-	-	125.6	1.5	-	-	126.6	0.8	-	-	127.3	0.6	-	-	129.5	1.7	-	-	129.6	0.1	-	-
1990	131.1	1.2	-	-	132.9	1.4	-	-	132.8	-0.1	-	-	134.6	1.4	-	-	136.9	1.7	-	-	137.2	0.2	-	-
1991	137.7	0.4	-	-	137.9	0.1	-	-	139.6	1.2	-	-	139.2	-0.3	-	-	141.8	1.9	-	-	141.1	-0.5	-	-
1992	141.3	0.1	-	-	141.3	0.0	-	-	141.6	0.2	-	-	143.3	1.2	-	-	144.2	0.6	-	-	145.1	0.6	-	-
1993	145.6	0.3	-	-	146.2	0.4	-	-	147.0	0.5	-	-	147.0	0.0	-	-	147.5	0.3	-	-	148.5	0.7	-	-
1994	148.3	-0.1	-	-	148.9	0.4	-	-	149.2	0.2	-	-	149.4	0.1	-	-	151.5	1.4	-	-	150.6	-0.6	-	-
1995	151.2	0.4	-	-	152.4	0.8	-	-	152.3	-0.1	-	-	153.5	0.8	-	-	153.5	0.0	-	-	152.5	-0.7	-	-
1996	153.9	0.9	-	-	155.4	1.0	-	-	156.7	0.8	-	-	157.6	0.6	-	-	158.2	0.4	-	-	158.7	0.3	-	-
1997	158.9	0.1	-	-	159.1	0.1	-	-	159.7	0.4	159.3	-0.3	160.2	0.6	-	-	161.1	0.6	-	-	159.1	-1.2	-	-

Source: U.S. Department of Labor, Bureau of Labor Statistics, Division of Consumer Prices and Price Indexes. - indicates no data collected for period.

Washington, DC-MD-VA
Consumer Price Index - All Urban Consumers
Base 1982-1984 = 100
Food and Beverages

For 1975-1997. Columns headed % show percentile change in the index from the previous period for which an index is available.

Year	Jan Index	%	Feb Index	%	Mar Index	%	Apr Index	%	May Index	%	Jun Index	%	Jul Index	%	Aug Index	%	Sep Index	%	Oct Index	%	Nov Index	%	Dec Index	%
1975	-	-	-	-	-	-	-	-	-	-	-	-	-	-	-	-	-	-	-	-	61.5	-	-	-
1976	-	-	61.5	0.0	-	-	-	-	61.7	0.3	-	-	-	-	63.5	2.9	-	-	-	-	63.0	-0.8	-	-
1977	-	-	65.1	3.3	-	-	-	-	66.4	2.0	-	-	-	-	67.5	1.7	-	-	-	-	68.3	1.2	-	-
1978	69.3	1.5	-	-	70.7	2.0	-	-	72.9	3.1	-	-	74.9	2.7	-	-	74.8	-0.1	-	-	75.4	0.8	-	-
1979	78.2	3.7	-	-	80.4	2.8	-	-	82.0	2.0	-	-	82.4	0.5	-	-	83.3	1.1	-	-	83.1	-0.2	-	-
1980	84.1	1.2	-	-	85.3	1.4	-	-	85.7	0.5	-	-	88.5	3.3	-	-	90.3	2.0	-	-	91.9	1.8	-	-
1981	93.0	1.2	-	-	93.6	0.6	-	-	90.7	-3.1	-	-	91.1	0.4	-	-	93.1	2.2	-	-	93.5	0.4	-	-
1982	95.0	1.6	-	-	96.2	1.3	-	-	97.0	0.8	-	-	97.9	0.9	-	-	98.5	0.6	-	-	97.6	-0.9	-	-
1983	98.4	0.8	-	-	99.7	1.3	-	-	100.9	1.2	-	-	100.3	-0.6	-	-	99.5	-0.8	-	-	99.2	-0.3	-	-
1984	101.8	2.6	-	-	103.4	1.6	-	-	102.5	-0.9	-	-	102.9	0.4	-	-	103.5	0.6	-	-	103.5	0.0	-	-
1985	104.2	0.7	-	-	105.7	1.4	-	-	105.9	0.2	-	-	106.0	0.1	-	-	106.4	0.4	-	-	107.3	0.8	-	-
1986	109.4	2.0	-	-	109.2	-0.2	-	-	110.9	1.6	-	-	110.5	-0.4	-	-	110.7	0.2	-	-	109.4	-1.2	-	-
1987	111.6	2.0	-	-	111.9	0.3	-	-	113.6	1.5	-	-	114.2	0.5	-	-	114.5	0.3	-	-	114.8	0.3	-	-
1988	116.0	1.0	-	-	116.7	0.6	-	-	117.9	1.0	-	-	120.5	2.2	-	-	121.3	0.7	-	-	121.1	-0.2	-	-
1989	122.7	1.3	-	-	124.4	1.4	-	-	126.5	1.7	-	-	126.4	-0.1	-	-	126.8	0.3	-	-	127.8	0.8	-	-
1990	131.7	3.1	-	-	133.3	1.2	-	-	132.8	-0.4	-	-	133.9	0.8	-	-	133.9	0.0	-	-	133.8	-0.1	-	-
1991	135.9	1.6	-	-	137.3	1.0	-	-	137.1	-0.1	-	-	137.7	0.4	-	-	138.1	0.3	-	-	139.0	0.7	-	-
1992	140.5	1.1	-	-	142.3	1.3	-	-	141.3	-0.7	-	-	140.2	-0.8	-	-	140.1	-0.1	-	-	140.9	0.6	-	-
1993	141.8	0.6	-	-	142.2	0.3	-	-	144.0	1.3	-	-	142.4	-1.1	-	-	141.9	-0.4	-	-	144.1	1.6	-	-
1994	143.8	-0.2	-	-	144.6	0.6	-	-	144.3	-0.2	-	-	143.0	-0.9	-	-	144.7	1.2	-	-	144.6	-0.1	-	-
1995	146.1	1.0	-	-	146.7	0.4	-	-	147.6	0.6	-	-	147.9	0.2	-	-	146.9	-0.7	-	-	147.4	0.3	-	-
1996	149.3	1.3	-	-	151.1	1.2	-	-	152.5	0.9	-	-	152.0	-0.3	-	-	154.0	1.3	-	-	154.8	0.5	-	-
1997	154.4	-0.3	-	-	154.5	0.1	-	-	154.9	0.3	154.7	-0.1	155.4	0.5	-	-	155.4	0.0	-	-	156.2	0.5	-	-

Source: U.S. Department of Labor, Bureau of Labor Statistics, Division of Consumer Prices and Price Indexes. - indicates no data collected for period.

Washington, DC-MD-VA
Consumer Price Index - Urban Wage Earners
Base 1982-1984 = 100
Food and Beverages

For 1975-1997. Columns headed % show percentile change in the index from the previous period for which an index is available.

Year	Jan Index	Jan %	Feb Index	Feb %	Mar Index	Mar %	Apr Index	Apr %	May Index	May %	Jun Index	Jun %	Jul Index	Jul %	Aug Index	Aug %	Sep Index	Sep %	Oct Index	Oct %	Nov Index	Nov %	Dec Index	Dec %
1975	-	-	-	-	-	-	-	-	-	-	-	-	-	-	-	-	-	-	-	-	60.6	-	-	-
1976	-	-	60.6	0.0	-	-	-	-	60.8	0.3	-	-	-	-	62.6	3.0	-	-	-	-	62.0	-1.0	-	-
1977	-	-	64.1	3.4	-	-	-	-	65.4	2.0	-	-	-	-	66.5	1.7	-	-	-	-	67.3	1.2	-	-
1978	68.2	1.3	-	-	69.4	1.8	-	-	72.8	4.9	-	-	74.3	2.1	-	-	73.8	-0.7	-	-	73.9	0.1	-	-
1979	76.4	3.4	-	-	78.2	2.4	-	-	80.2	2.6	-	-	80.4	0.2	-	-	81.2	1.0	-	-	80.6	-0.7	-	-
1980	81.6	1.2	-	-	82.6	1.2	-	-	82.5	-0.1	-	-	85.7	3.9	-	-	88.0	2.7	-	-	90.8	3.2	-	-
1981	91.7	1.0	-	-	92.1	0.4	-	-	89.6	-2.7	-	-	90.5	1.0	-	-	92.7	2.4	-	-	93.3	0.6	-	-
1982	95.0	1.8	-	-	96.3	1.4	-	-	97.0	0.7	-	-	98.1	1.1	-	-	98.8	0.7	-	-	97.9	-0.9	-	-
1983	98.5	0.6	-	-	99.7	1.2	-	-	100.6	0.9	-	-	100.2	-0.4	-	-	99.2	-1.0	-	-	99.0	-0.2	-	-
1984	101.9	2.9	-	-	103.3	1.4	-	-	102.5	-0.8	-	-	102.8	0.3	-	-	103.5	0.7	-	-	103.5	0.0	-	-
1985	104.0	0.5	-	-	105.7	1.6	-	-	105.9	0.2	-	-	105.9	0.0	-	-	106.3	0.4	-	-	107.2	0.8	-	-
1986	108.9	1.6	-	-	108.8	-0.1	-	-	110.5	1.6	-	-	110.2	-0.3	-	-	110.7	0.5	-	-	109.6	-1.0	-	-
1987	112.0	2.2	-	-	112.2	0.2	-	-	114.0	1.6	-	-	114.6	0.5	-	-	114.7	0.1	-	-	114.9	0.2	-	-
1988	116.2	1.1	-	-	116.9	0.6	-	-	118.1	1.0	-	-	120.6	2.1	-	-	121.4	0.7	-	-	121.2	-0.2	-	-
1989	123.0	1.5	-	-	124.7	1.4	-	-	126.7	1.6	-	-	126.6	-0.1	-	-	127.3	0.6	-	-	128.2	0.7	-	-
1990	132.2	3.1	-	-	134.3	1.6	-	-	133.1	-0.9	-	-	134.2	0.8	-	-	134.2	0.0	-	-	134.0	-0.1	-	-
1991	136.1	1.6	-	-	137.5	1.0	-	-	137.2	-0.2	-	-	137.9	0.5	-	-	138.3	0.3	-	-	138.9	0.4	-	-
1992	140.5	1.2	-	-	142.4	1.4	-	-	141.2	-0.8	-	-	140.3	-0.6	-	-	140.1	-0.1	-	-	141.0	0.6	-	-
1993	141.8	0.6	-	-	142.3	0.4	-	-	144.2	1.3	-	-	142.3	-1.3	-	-	141.9	-0.3	-	-	143.8	1.3	-	-
1994	143.8	0.0	-	-	144.7	0.6	-	-	144.2	-0.3	-	-	143.2	-0.7	-	-	145.0	1.3	-	-	144.7	-0.2	-	-
1995	146.3	1.1	-	-	146.6	0.2	-	-	147.8	0.8	-	-	148.2	0.3	-	-	147.0	-0.8	-	-	147.6	0.4	-	-
1996	149.4	1.2	-	-	151.1	1.1	-	-	152.8	1.1	-	-	152.0	-0.5	-	-	154.0	1.3	-	-	155.1	0.7	-	-
1997	154.7	-0.3	-	-	154.8	0.1	-	-	155.2	0.3	155.0	-0.1	155.5	0.3	-	-	155.4	-0.1	-	-	156.3	0.6	-	-

Source: U.S. Department of Labor, Bureau of Labor Statistics, Division of Consumer Prices and Price Indexes. - indicates no data collected for period.

Washington, DC-MD-VA
Consumer Price Index - All Urban Consumers
Base 1982-1984 = 100
Housing

For 1975-1997. Columns headed % show percentile change in the index from the previous period for which an index is available.

Year	Jan Index	%	Feb Index	%	Mar Index	%	Apr Index	%	May Index	%	Jun Index	%	Jul Index	%	Aug Index	%	Sep Index	%	Oct Index	%	Nov Index	%	Dec Index	%
1975	-	-	-	-	-	-	-	-	-	-	-	-	-	-	-	-	-	-	-	-	53.0	-	-	-
1976	-	-	53.8	1.5	-	-	-	-	54.9	2.0	-	-	-	-	55.7	1.5	-	-	-	-	56.4	1.3	-	-
1977	-	-	57.6	2.1	-	-	-	-	58.7	1.9	-	-	-	-	60.0	2.2	-	-	-	-	61.2	2.0	-	-
1978	62.2	1.6	-	-	62.4	0.3	-	-	63.4	1.6	-	-	64.6	1.9	-	-	66.0	2.2	-	-	67.0	1.5	-	-
1979	69.5	3.7	-	-	70.2	1.0	-	-	70.8	0.9	-	-	72.9	3.0	-	-	72.7	-0.3	-	-	73.6	1.2	-	-
1980	76.5	3.9	-	-	79.0	3.3	-	-	80.2	1.5	-	-	82.5	2.9	-	-	81.8	-0.8	-	-	83.9	2.6	-	-
1981	85.3	1.7	-	-	87.5	2.6	-	-	89.3	2.1	-	-	90.6	1.5	-	-	91.8	1.3	-	-	93.8	2.2	-	-
1982	94.7	1.0	-	-	94.6	-0.1	-	-	94.1	-0.5	-	-	94.7	0.6	-	-	97.0	2.4	-	-	96.6	-0.4	-	-
1983	98.2	1.7	-	-	97.8	-0.4	-	-	98.6	0.8	-	-	101.2	2.6	-	-	100.3	-0.9	-	-	101.1	0.8	-	-
1984	103.3	2.2	-	-	103.5	0.2	-	-	103.2	-0.3	-	-	104.2	1.0	-	-	106.5	2.2	-	-	107.4	0.8	-	-
1985	107.4	0.0	-	-	109.1	1.6	-	-	108.9	-0.2	-	-	111.6	2.5	-	-	110.4	-1.1	-	-	111.4	0.9	-	-
1986	114.4	2.7	-	-	114.0	-0.3	-	-	114.5	0.4	-	-	113.9	-0.5	-	-	114.7	0.7	-	-	116.3	1.4	-	-
1987	117.1	0.7	-	-	116.7	-0.3	-	-	117.7	0.9	-	-	118.8	0.9	-	-	121.0	1.9	-	-	121.0	0.0	-	-
1988	121.1	0.1	-	-	121.2	0.1	-	-	122.3	0.9	-	-	124.7	2.0	-	-	125.3	0.5	-	-	124.4	-0.7	-	-
1989	125.9	1.2	-	-	127.6	1.4	-	-	128.1	0.4	-	-	129.5	1.1	-	-	131.7	1.7	-	-	131.2	-0.4	-	-
1990	134.1	2.2	-	-	134.8	0.5	-	-	134.6	-0.1	-	-	138.4	2.8	-	-	138.8	0.3	-	-	137.7	-0.8	-	-
1991	138.2	0.4	-	-	138.9	0.5	-	-	142.0	2.2	-	-	141.8	-0.1	-	-	142.9	0.8	-	-	140.2	-1.9	-	-
1992	142.1	1.4	-	-	142.2	0.1	-	-	142.4	0.1	-	-	144.9	1.8	-	-	146.0	0.8	-	-	145.2	-0.5	-	-
1993	145.2	0.0	-	-	145.9	0.5	-	-	147.3	1.0	-	-	149.2	1.3	-	-	149.4	0.1	-	-	149.6	0.1	-	-
1994	150.5	0.6	-	-	150.4	-0.1	-	-	150.1	-0.2	-	-	151.5	0.9	-	-	152.6	0.7	-	-	150.0	-1.7	-	-
1995	151.3	0.9	-	-	152.5	0.8	-	-	152.0	-0.3	-	-	154.7	1.8	-	-	154.7	0.0	-	-	152.8	-1.2	-	-
1996	154.7	1.2	-	-	155.6	0.6	-	-	154.4	-0.8	-	-	157.5	2.0	-	-	157.4	-0.1	-	-	156.2	-0.8	-	-
1997	156.4	0.1	-	-	156.4	0.0	-	-	156.7	0.2	156.7	0.0	159.2	1.6	-	-	158.6	-0.4	-	-	155.2	-2.1	-	-

Source: U.S. Department of Labor, Bureau of Labor Statistics, Division of Consumer Prices and Price Indexes. - indicates no data collected for period.

Washington, DC-MD-VA
Consumer Price Index - Urban Wage Earners
Base 1982-1984 = 100
Housing

For 1975-1997. Columns headed % show percentile change in the index from the previous period for which an index is available.

Year	Jan Index	%	Feb Index	%	Mar Index	%	Apr Index	%	May Index	%	Jun Index	%	Jul Index	%	Aug Index	%	Sep Index	%	Oct Index	%	Nov Index	%	Dec Index	%
1975	-	-	-	-	-	-	-	-	-	-	-	-	-	-	-	-	-	-	-	-	53.4	-	-	-
1976	-	-	54.3	1.7	-	-	-	-	55.4	2.0	-	-	-	-	56.2	1.4	-	-	-	-	56.8	1.1	-	-
1977	-	-	58.1	2.3	-	-	-	-	59.1	1.7	-	-	-	-	60.5	2.4	-	-	-	-	61.7	2.0	-	-
1978	62.6	1.5	-	-	62.9	0.5	-	-	64.6	2.7	-	-	66.4	2.8	-	-	67.8	2.1	-	-	68.3	0.7	-	-
1979	70.5	3.2	-	-	71.5	1.4	-	-	72.2	1.0	-	-	73.9	2.4	-	-	74.0	0.1	-	-	74.8	1.1	-	-
1980	77.5	3.6	-	-	79.7	2.8	-	-	81.2	1.9	-	-	83.4	2.7	-	-	83.0	-0.5	-	-	84.5	1.8	-	-
1981	86.1	1.9	-	-	87.8	2.0	-	-	89.6	2.1	-	-	91.0	1.6	-	-	92.3	1.4	-	-	94.2	2.1	-	-
1982	95.1	1.0	-	-	95.1	0.0	-	-	95.1	0.0	-	-	95.7	0.6	-	-	98.1	2.5	-	-	97.7	-0.4	-	-
1983	98.0	0.3	-	-	98.6	0.6	-	-	98.9	0.3	-	-	100.0	1.1	-	-	99.5	-0.5	-	-	100.6	1.1	-	-
1984	103.2	2.6	-	-	102.5	-0.7	-	-	102.6	0.1	-	-	103.1	0.5	-	-	106.4	3.2	-	-	106.9	0.5	-	-
1985	106.6	-0.3	-	-	108.3	1.6	-	-	108.5	0.2	-	-	111.1	2.4	-	-	110.1	-0.9	-	-	111.2	1.0	-	-
1986	113.8	2.3	-	-	113.5	-0.3	-	-	114.1	0.5	-	-	113.4	-0.6	-	-	114.2	0.7	-	-	115.9	1.5	-	-
1987	116.7	0.7	-	-	116.1	-0.5	-	-	117.0	0.8	-	-	118.0	0.9	-	-	120.1	1.8	-	-	120.3	0.2	-	-
1988	120.4	0.1	-	-	120.5	0.1	-	-	121.5	0.8	-	-	123.9	2.0	-	-	124.7	0.6	-	-	123.5	-1.0	-	-
1989	125.2	1.4	-	-	126.9	1.4	-	-	127.2	0.2	-	-	128.7	1.2	-	-	130.9	1.7	-	-	129.8	-0.8	-	-
1990	133.0	2.5	-	-	133.2	0.2	-	-	132.8	-0.3	-	-	136.9	3.1	-	-	137.3	0.3	-	-	135.8	-1.1	-	-
1991	136.4	0.4	-	-	137.2	0.6	-	-	140.5	2.4	-	-	139.6	-0.6	-	-	141.1	1.1	-	-	138.5	-1.8	-	-
1992	140.1	1.2	-	-	140.0	-0.1	-	-	140.3	0.2	-	-	142.8	1.8	-	-	143.4	0.4	-	-	142.9	-0.3	-	-
1993	142.4	-0.3	-	-	143.1	0.5	-	-	144.6	1.0	-	-	146.7	1.5	-	-	146.9	0.1	-	-	146.9	0.0	-	-
1994	147.3	0.3	-	-	147.2	-0.1	-	-	147.5	0.2	-	-	148.7	0.8	-	-	150.4	1.1	-	-	147.5	-1.9	-	-
1995	148.5	0.7	-	-	149.5	0.7	-	-	149.5	0.0	-	-	151.8	1.5	-	-	152.1	0.2	-	-	150.3	-1.2	-	-
1996	151.4	0.7	-	-	152.2	0.5	-	-	151.6	-0.4	-	-	154.6	2.0	-	-	154.5	-0.1	-	-	153.2	-0.8	-	-
1997	153.2	0.0	-	-	152.8	-0.3	-	-	153.6	0.5	153.4	-0.1	155.8	1.6	-	-	155.6	-0.1	-	-	151.9	-2.4	-	-

Source: U.S. Department of Labor, Bureau of Labor Statistics, Division of Consumer Prices and Price Indexes. - indicates no data collected for period.

Washington, DC-MD-VA
Consumer Price Index - All Urban Consumers
Base 1982-1984 = 100
Apparel and Upkeep

For 1952-1997. Columns headed % show percentile change in the index from the previous period for which an index is available.

Year	Jan Index	%	Feb Index	%	Mar Index	%	Apr Index	%	May Index	%	Jun Index	%	Jul Index	%	Aug Index	%	Sep Index	%	Oct Index	%	Nov Index	%	Dec Index	%
1952	-	-	-	-	-	-	-	-	-	-	-	-	-	-	-	-	-	-	-	-	40.1	-	-	-
1953	-	-	40.3	0.5	-	-	-	-	40.5	0.5	-	-	-	-	40.5	0.0	-	-	-	-	40.6	0.2	-	-
1954	-	-	40.5	-0.2	-	-	-	-	40.3	-0.5	-	-	-	-	40.0	-0.7	-	-	-	-	40.2	0.5	-	-
1955	-	-	39.8	-1.0	-	-	-	-	39.8	0.0	-	-	-	-	40.0	0.5	-	-	-	-	40.4	1.0	-	-
1956	-	-	40.7	0.7	-	-	-	-	41.1	1.0	-	-	-	-	41.2	0.2	-	-	-	-	41.2	0.0	-	-
1957	-	-	41.3	0.2	-	-	-	-	41.3	0.0	-	-	-	-	41.4	0.2	-	-	-	-	41.2	-0.5	-	-
1958	-	-	41.1	-0.2	-	-	-	-	41.1	0.0	-	-	-	-	41.2	0.2	-	-	-	-	41.2	0.0	-	-
1959	-	-	41.3	0.2	-	-	-	-	41.6	0.7	-	-	-	-	42.0	1.0	-	-	-	-	42.0	0.0	-	-
1960	-	-	41.7	-0.7	-	-	-	-	42.0	0.7	-	-	-	-	42.2	0.5	-	-	-	-	42.3	0.2	-	-
1961	-	-	42.4	0.2	-	-	-	-	42.6	0.5	-	-	-	-	42.6	0.0	-	-	-	-	43.7	2.6	-	-
1962	-	-	43.9	0.5	-	-	-	-	43.9	0.0	-	-	-	-	44.0	0.2	-	-	-	-	44.7	1.6	-	-
1963	-	-	44.2	-1.1	-	-	-	-	44.3	0.2	-	-	-	-	43.9	-0.9	-	-	-	-	44.5	1.4	-	-
1964	-	-	44.4	-0.2	-	-	-	-	44.7	0.7	-	-	-	-	44.6	-0.2	-	-	-	-	44.7	0.2	-	-
1965	-	-	44.3	-0.9	-	-	-	-	45.2	2.0	-	-	-	-	44.5	-1.5	-	-	-	-	45.3	1.8	-	-
1966	-	-	45.5	0.4	-	-	-	-	46.5	2.2	-	-	-	-	46.3	-0.4	-	-	-	-	47.5	2.6	-	-
1967	-	-	47.7	0.4	-	-	-	-	48.6	1.9	-	-	-	-	48.5	-0.2	-	-	-	-	49.7	2.5	-	-
1968	-	-	50.2	1.0	-	-	-	-	52.3	4.2	-	-	-	-	52.6	0.6	-	-	-	-	54.1	2.9	-	-
1969	-	-	54.3	0.4	-	-	-	-	55.9	2.9	-	-	-	-	55.7	-0.4	-	-	-	-	57.0	2.3	-	-
1970	-	-	57.0	0.0	-	-	-	-	58.5	2.6	-	-	-	-	58.0	-0.9	-	-	-	-	59.5	2.6	-	-
1971	-	-	58.8	-1.2	-	-	-	-	60.0	2.0	-	-	-	-	59.7	-0.5	-	-	-	-	61.1	2.3	-	-
1972	-	-	60.0	-1.8	-	-	-	-	61.0	1.7	-	-	-	-	60.3	-1.1	-	-	-	-	61.9	2.7	-	-
1973	-	-	62.2	0.5	-	-	-	-	64.1	3.1	-	-	-	-	63.7	-0.6	-	-	-	-	64.8	1.7	-	-
1974	-	-	66.3	2.3	-	-	-	-	68.2	2.9	-	-	-	-	69.2	1.5	-	-	-	-	70.5	1.9	-	-
1975	-	-	70.1	-0.6	-	-	-	-	70.5	0.6	-	-	-	-	69.9	-0.9	-	-	-	-	71.4	2.1	-	-
1976	-	-	70.6	-1.1	-	-	-	-	73.3	3.8	-	-	-	-	73.1	-0.3	-	-	-	-	73.8	1.0	-	-
1977	-	-	72.4	-1.9	-	-	-	-	74.1	2.3	-	-	-	-	74.6	0.7	-	-	-	-	75.8	1.6	-	-
1978	75.6	-0.3	-	-	76.8	1.6	-	-	78.2	1.8	-	-	76.5	-2.2	-	-	79.8	4.3	-	-	80.6	1.0	-	-
1979	77.3	-4.1	-	-	81.6	5.6	-	-	83.3	2.1	-	-	81.4	-2.3	-	-	87.2	7.1	-	-	87.7	0.6	-	-
1980	86.7	-1.1	-	-	91.5	5.5	-	-	89.9	-1.7	-	-	87.9	-2.2	-	-	91.8	4.4	-	-	93.0	1.3	-	-
1981	89.7	-3.5	-	-	89.7	0.0	-	-	90.8	1.2	-	-	87.6	-3.5	-	-	93.4	6.6	-	-	91.8	-1.7	-	-
1982	90.7	-1.2	-	-	95.5	5.3	-	-	93.7	-1.9	-	-	92.2	-1.6	-	-	96.6	4.8	-	-	97.8	1.2	-	-
1983	97.0	-0.8	-	-	100.4	3.5	-	-	102.6	2.2	-	-	103.0	0.4	-	-	100.9	-2.0	-	-	99.0	-1.9	-	-
1984	99.9	0.9	-	-	101.1	1.2	-	-	104.4	3.3	-	-	103.4	-1.0	-	-	109.8	6.2	-	-	108.6	-1.1	-	-
1985	104.8	-3.5	-	-	110.4	5.3	-	-	109.4	-0.9	-	-	106.7	-2.5	-	-	113.8	6.7	-	-	114.3	0.4	-	-
1986	106.2	-7.1	-	-	105.3	-0.8	-	-	104.4	-0.9	-	-	104.5	0.1	-	-	115.6	10.6	-	-	115.4	-0.2	-	-
1987	110.7	-4.1	-	-	113.0	2.1	-	-	115.0	1.8	-	-	112.1	-2.5	-	-	122.0	8.8	-	-	123.5	1.2	-	-
1988	116.4	-5.7	-	-	124.9	7.3	-	-	122.3	-2.1	-	-	111.6	-8.7	-	-	130.8	17.2	-	-	131.0	0.2	-	-
1989	125.0	-4.6	-	-	135.6	8.5	-	-	135.7	0.1	-	-	130.8	-3.6	-	-	142.1	8.6	-	-	139.7	-1.7	-	-
1990	128.2	-8.2	-	-	141.9	10.7	-	-	140.4	-1.1	-	-	135.0	-3.8	-	-	147.0	8.9	-	-	141.1	-4.0	-	-
1991	138.9	-1.6	-	-	138.8	-0.1	-	-	139.3	0.4	-	-	135.2	-2.9	-	-	153.3	13.4	-	-	149.9	-2.2	-	-
1992	136.5	-8.9	-	-	138.4	1.4	-	-	134.5	-2.8	-	-	136.2	1.3	-	-	145.3	6.7	-	-	144.8	-0.3	-	-
1993	145.7	0.6	-	-	150.6	3.4	-	-	146.4	-2.8	-	-	136.4	-6.8	-	-	144.3	5.8	-	-	145.2	0.6	-	-
1994	137.5	-5.3	-	-	143.7	4.5	-	-	144.9	0.8	-	-	137.0	-5.5	-	-	144.9	5.8	-	-	141.4	-2.4	-	-

[Continued]

Washington, DC-MD-VA
Consumer Price Index - All Urban Consumers
Base 1982-1984 = 100
Apparel and Upkeep

[Continued]

For 1952-1997. Columns headed % show percentile change in the index from the previous period for which an index is available.

Year	Jan Index	%	Feb Index	%	Mar Index	%	Apr Index	%	May Index	%	Jun Index	%	Jul Index	%	Aug Index	%	Sep Index	%	Oct Index	%	Nov Index	%	Dec Index	%
1995	135.8	-4.0	-	-	149.1	9.8	-	-	143.6	-3.7	-	-	140.9	-1.9	-	-	142.5	1.1	-	-	133.5	-6.3	-	-
1996	138.2	3.5	-	-	142.8	3.3	-	-	139.5	-2.3	-	-	134.9	-3.3	-	-	139.6	3.5	-	-	145.9	4.5	-	-
1997	145.0	-0.6	-	-	145.0	0.0	-	-	147.1	1.4	145.3	-1.2	140.3	-3.4	-	-	145.5	3.7	-	-	138.2	-5.0	-	-

Source: U.S. Department of Labor, Bureau of Labor Statistics, Division of Consumer Prices and Price Indexes. - indicates no data collected for period.

Washington, DC-MD-VA
Consumer Price Index - Urban Wage Earners
Base 1982-1984 = 100
Apparel and Upkeep

For 1952-1997. Columns headed % show percentile change in the index from the previous period for which an index is available.

Year	Jan Index	%	Feb Index	%	Mar Index	%	Apr Index	%	May Index	%	Jun Index	%	Jul Index	%	Aug Index	%	Sep Index	%	Oct Index	%	Nov Index	%	Dec Index	%
1952	-	-	-	-	-	-	-	-	-	-	-	-	-	-	-	-	-	-	-	-	36.0	-	-	-
1953	-	-	36.3	0.8	-	-	-	-	36.4	0.3	-	-	-	-	36.5	0.3	-	-	-	-	36.6	0.3	-	-
1954	-	-	36.4	-0.5	-	-	-	-	36.2	-0.5	-	-	-	-	35.9	-0.8	-	-	-	-	36.2	0.8	-	-
1955	-	-	35.8	-1.1	-	-	-	-	35.8	0.0	-	-	-	-	36.0	0.6	-	-	-	-	36.3	0.8	-	-
1956	-	-	36.6	0.8	-	-	-	-	37.0	1.1	-	-	-	-	37.1	0.3	-	-	-	-	37.0	-0.3	-	-
1957	-	-	37.2	0.5	-	-	-	-	37.1	-0.3	-	-	-	-	37.3	0.5	-	-	-	-	37.1	-0.5	-	-
1958	-	-	37.0	-0.3	-	-	-	-	37.0	0.0	-	-	-	-	37.0	0.0	-	-	-	-	37.1	0.3	-	-
1959	-	-	37.1	0.0	-	-	-	-	37.4	0.8	-	-	-	-	37.8	1.1	-	-	-	-	37.7	-0.3	-	-
1960	-	-	37.5	-0.5	-	-	-	-	37.8	0.8	-	-	-	-	38.0	0.5	-	-	-	-	38.1	0.3	-	-
1961	-	-	38.1	0.0	-	-	-	-	38.3	0.5	-	-	-	-	38.4	0.3	-	-	-	-	39.3	2.3	-	-
1962	-	-	39.4	0.3	-	-	-	-	39.5	0.3	-	-	-	-	39.6	0.3	-	-	-	-	40.2	1.5	-	-
1963	-	-	39.8	-1.0	-	-	-	-	39.9	0.3	-	-	-	-	39.5	-1.0	-	-	-	-	40.1	1.5	-	-
1964	-	-	39.9	-0.5	-	-	-	-	40.2	0.8	-	-	-	-	40.1	-0.2	-	-	-	-	40.2	0.2	-	-
1965	-	-	39.9	-0.7	-	-	-	-	40.7	2.0	-	-	-	-	40.1	-1.5	-	-	-	-	40.7	1.5	-	-
1966	-	-	40.9	0.5	-	-	-	-	41.8	2.2	-	-	-	-	41.7	-0.2	-	-	-	-	42.7	2.4	-	-
1967	-	-	42.9	0.5	-	-	-	-	43.7	1.9	-	-	-	-	43.6	-0.2	-	-	-	-	44.7	2.5	-	-
1968	-	-	45.1	0.9	-	-	-	-	47.0	4.2	-	-	-	-	47.3	0.6	-	-	-	-	48.6	2.7	-	-
1969	-	-	48.9	0.6	-	-	-	-	50.3	2.9	-	-	-	-	50.1	-0.4	-	-	-	-	51.3	2.4	-	-
1970	-	-	51.3	0.0	-	-	-	-	52.6	2.5	-	-	-	-	52.1	-1.0	-	-	-	-	53.5	2.7	-	-
1971	-	-	52.9	-1.1	-	-	-	-	54.0	2.1	-	-	-	-	53.7	-0.6	-	-	-	-	55.0	2.4	-	-
1972	-	-	53.9	-2.0	-	-	-	-	54.9	1.9	-	-	-	-	54.2	-1.3	-	-	-	-	55.7	2.8	-	-
1973	-	-	55.9	0.4	-	-	-	-	57.7	3.2	-	-	-	-	57.3	-0.7	-	-	-	-	58.3	1.7	-	-
1974	-	-	59.7	2.4	-	-	-	-	61.4	2.8	-	-	-	-	62.2	1.3	-	-	-	-	63.4	1.9	-	-
1975	-	-	63.0	-0.6	-	-	-	-	63.4	0.6	-	-	-	-	62.9	-0.8	-	-	-	-	64.3	2.2	-	-
1976	-	-	63.5	-1.2	-	-	-	-	65.9	3.8	-	-	-	-	65.7	-0.3	-	-	-	-	66.4	1.1	-	-
1977	-	-	65.1	-2.0	-	-	-	-	66.6	2.3	-	-	-	-	67.1	0.8	-	-	-	-	68.2	1.6	-	-
1978	65.9	-3.4	-	-	66.6	1.1	-	-	68.2	2.4	-	-	67.9	-0.4	-	-	70.2	3.4	-	-	70.9	1.0	-	-
1979	67.6	-4.7	-	-	70.4	4.1	-	-	71.4	1.4	-	-	71.4	0.0	-	-	75.3	5.5	-	-	75.5	0.3	-	-
1980	75.7	0.3	-	-	78.4	3.6	-	-	78.7	0.4	-	-	78.3	-0.5	-	-	86.5	10.5	-	-	85.3	-1.4	-	-
1981	84.1	-1.4	-	-	87.1	3.6	-	-	90.1	3.4	-	-	90.0	-0.1	-	-	93.0	3.3	-	-	90.1	-3.1	-	-
1982	88.3	-2.0	-	-	98.0	11.0	-	-	90.8	-7.3	-	-	89.0	-2.0	-	-	97.1	9.1	-	-	99.0	2.0	-	-
1983	97.7	-1.3	-	-	102.8	5.2	-	-	105.6	2.7	-	-	105.9	0.3	-	-	104.2	-1.6	-	-	99.6	-4.4	-	-
1984	100.4	0.8	-	-	99.4	-1.0	-	-	99.1	-0.3	-	-	97.5	-1.6	-	-	111.9	14.8	-	-	110.1	-1.6	-	-
1985	103.5	-6.0	-	-	109.2	5.5	-	-	106.0	-2.9	-	-	103.3	-2.5	-	-	116.1	12.4	-	-	114.7	-1.2	-	-
1986	100.8	-12.1	-	-	98.5	-2.3	-	-	96.3	-2.2	-	-	97.2	0.9	-	-	116.1	19.4	-	-	113.8	-2.0	-	-
1987	108.3	-4.8	-	-	111.1	2.6	-	-	114.0	2.6	-	-	109.1	-4.3	-	-	120.6	10.5	-	-	123.1	2.1	-	-
1988	113.8	-7.6	-	-	123.5	8.5	-	-	119.9	-2.9	-	-	107.5	-10.3	-	-	127.8	18.9	-	-	130.5	2.1	-	-
1989	123.2	-5.6	-	-	134.1	8.8	-	-	133.7	-0.3	-	-	129.5	-3.1	-	-	141.5	9.3	-	-	138.3	-2.3	-	-
1990	124.8	-9.8	-	-	139.5	11.8	-	-	138.7	-0.6	-	-	130.8	-5.7	-	-	145.1	10.9	-	-	140.7	-3.0	-	-
1991	136.2	-3.2	-	-	137.6	1.0	-	-	138.0	0.3	-	-	133.0	-3.6	-	-	152.0	14.3	-	-	150.1	-1.2	-	-
1992	137.1	-8.7	-	-	139.6	1.8	-	-	134.8	-3.4	-	-	136.9	1.6	-	-	145.4	6.2	-	-	144.9	-0.3	-	-
1993	143.7	-0.8	-	-	149.2	3.8	-	-	145.2	-2.7	-	-	135.8	-6.5	-	-	144.7	6.6	-	-	145.0	0.2	-	-
1994	137.8	-5.0	-	-	143.7	4.3	-	-	144.7	0.7	-	-	135.2	-6.6	-	-	144.7	7.0	-	-	140.7	-2.8	-	-

[Continued]

Washington, DC-MD-VA
Consumer Price Index - Urban Wage Earners
Base 1982-1984 = 100
Apparel and Upkeep

[Continued]

For 1952-1997. Columns headed % show percentile change in the index from the previous period for which an index is available.

Year	Jan Index	%	Feb Index	%	Mar Index	%	Apr Index	%	May Index	%	Jun Index	%	Jul Index	%	Aug Index	%	Sep Index	%	Oct Index	%	Nov Index	%	Dec Index	%
1995	136.1	-3.3	-	-	150.0	10.2	-	-	143.2	-4.5	-	-	140.7	-1.7	-	-	142.2	1.1	-	-	131.9	-7.2	-	-
1996	137.7	4.4	-	-	143.0	3.8	-	-	141.5	-1.0	-	-	136.5	-3.5	-	-	140.3	2.8	-	-	149.3	6.4	-	-
1997	147.1	-1.5	-	-	149.2	1.4	-	-	152.8	2.4	149.4	-2.2	144.1	-3.5	-	-	149.7	3.9	-	-	143.3	-4.3	-	-

Source: U.S. Department of Labor, Bureau of Labor Statistics, Division of Consumer Prices and Price Indexes. - indicates no data collected for period.

Washington, DC-MD-VA
Consumer Price Index - All Urban Consumers
Base 1982-1984 = 100
Transportation

For 1947-1997. Columns headed % show percentile change in the index from the previous period for which an index is available.

Year	Jan Index	%	Feb Index	%	Mar Index	%	Apr Index	%	May Index	%	Jun Index	%	Jul Index	%	Aug Index	%	Sep Index	%	Oct Index	%	Nov Index	%	Dec Index	%
1947	18.0	-	18.0	0.0	18.1	0.6	18.3	1.1	19.1	4.4	19.3	1.0	-	-	19.6	1.6	-	-	-	-	19.8	1.0	-	-
1948	-	-	20.2	2.0	-	-	-	-	20.4	1.0	-	-	-	-	21.5	5.4	-	-	-	-	22.6	5.1	-	-
1949	-	-	22.7	0.4	-	-	-	-	22.8	0.4	-	-	-	-	22.8	0.0	-	-	-	-	22.9	0.4	-	-
1950	-	-	22.9	0.0	-	-	-	-	22.9	0.0	-	-	-	-	23.7	3.5	-	-	-	-	23.8	0.4	-	-
1951	-	-	23.8	0.0	-	-	-	-	24.0	0.8	-	-	-	-	24.1	0.4	-	-	-	-	24.7	2.5	-	-
1952	-	-	25.3	2.4	-	-	-	-	25.3	0.0	-	-	-	-	25.9	2.4	-	-	-	-	26.8	3.5	-	-
1953	-	-	26.7	-0.4	-	-	-	-	26.8	0.4	-	-	-	-	27.1	1.1	-	-	-	-	27.0	-0.4	-	-
1954	-	-	26.9	-0.4	-	-	-	-	26.7	-0.7	-	-	-	-	26.3	-1.5	-	-	-	-	27.2	3.4	-	-
1955	-	-	27.1	-0.4	-	-	-	-	27.0	-0.4	-	-	-	-	27.1	0.4	-	-	-	-	27.6	1.8	-	-
1956	-	-	27.4	-0.7	-	-	-	-	27.1	-1.1	-	-	-	-	27.4	1.1	-	-	-	-	28.4	3.6	-	-
1957	-	-	28.4	0.0	-	-	-	-	28.6	0.7	-	-	-	-	29.0	1.4	-	-	-	-	29.8	2.8	-	-
1958	-	-	29.0	-2.7	-	-	-	-	29.0	0.0	-	-	-	-	29.4	1.4	-	-	-	-	30.6	4.1	-	-
1959	-	-	30.2	-1.3	-	-	-	-	30.2	0.0	-	-	-	-	30.6	1.3	-	-	-	-	30.8	0.7	-	-
1960	-	-	30.7	-0.3	-	-	-	-	30.7	0.0	-	-	-	-	30.8	0.3	-	-	-	-	30.7	-0.3	-	-
1961	-	-	30.4	-1.0	-	-	-	-	30.8	1.3	-	-	-	-	31.3	1.6	-	-	-	-	31.4	0.3	-	-
1962	-	-	31.1	-1.0	-	-	-	-	31.3	0.6	-	-	-	-	31.4	0.3	-	-	-	-	31.5	0.3	-	-
1963	-	-	31.0	-1.6	-	-	-	-	31.5	1.6	-	-	-	-	31.7	0.6	-	-	-	-	32.2	1.6	-	-
1964	-	-	32.2	0.0	-	-	-	-	32.2	0.0	-	-	-	-	32.3	0.3	-	-	-	-	32.7	1.2	-	-
1965	-	-	32.7	0.0	-	-	-	-	32.7	0.0	-	-	-	-	32.5	-0.6	-	-	-	-	32.7	0.6	-	-
1966	-	-	32.6	-0.3	-	-	-	-	32.9	0.9	-	-	-	-	32.9	0.0	-	-	-	-	33.3	1.2	-	-
1967	-	-	33.3	0.0	-	-	-	-	34.1	2.4	-	-	-	-	34.3	0.6	-	-	-	-	34.7	1.2	-	-
1968	-	-	35.0	0.9	-	-	-	-	35.2	0.6	-	-	-	-	35.5	0.9	-	-	-	-	36.0	1.4	-	-
1969	-	-	36.4	1.1	-	-	-	-	36.9	1.4	-	-	-	-	37.3	1.1	-	-	-	-	38.0	1.9	-	-
1970	-	-	38.3	0.8	-	-	-	-	39.4	2.9	-	-	-	-	40.4	2.5	-	-	-	-	40.7	0.7	-	-
1971	-	-	41.8	2.7	-	-	-	-	42.5	1.7	-	-	-	-	42.3	-0.5	-	-	-	-	42.1	-0.5	-	-
1972	-	-	41.8	-0.7	-	-	-	-	42.0	0.5	-	-	-	-	42.4	1.0	-	-	-	-	42.6	0.5	-	-
1973	-	-	42.6	0.0	-	-	-	-	42.9	0.7	-	-	-	-	43.0	0.2	-	-	-	-	43.6	1.4	-	-
1974	-	-	45.1	3.4	-	-	-	-	47.1	4.4	-	-	-	-	48.8	3.6	-	-	-	-	49.4	1.2	-	-
1975	-	-	49.9	1.0	-	-	-	-	51.2	2.6	-	-	-	-	52.8	3.1	-	-	-	-	53.5	1.3	-	-
1976	-	-	53.7	0.4	-	-	-	-	55.3	3.0	-	-	-	-	56.6	2.4	-	-	-	-	56.8	0.4	-	-
1977	-	-	58.1	2.3	-	-	-	-	59.9	3.1	-	-	-	-	60.6	1.2	-	-	-	-	60.7	0.2	-	-
1978	61.0	0.5	-	-	61.3	0.5	-	-	62.3	1.6	-	-	64.0	2.7	-	-	64.5	0.8	-	-	65.9	2.2	-	-
1979	66.3	0.6	-	-	67.5	1.8	-	-	70.1	3.9	-	-	72.9	4.0	-	-	74.5	2.2	-	-	76.3	2.4	-	-
1980	79.1	3.7	-	-	82.5	4.3	-	-	83.5	1.2	-	-	85.4	2.3	-	-	87.2	2.1	-	-	88.3	1.3	-	-
1981	90.4	2.4	-	-	92.8	2.7	-	-	94.2	1.5	-	-	95.0	0.8	-	-	95.7	0.7	-	-	96.5	0.8	-	-
1982	97.1	0.6	-	-	95.2	-2.0	-	-	95.2	0.0	-	-	98.2	3.2	-	-	98.0	-0.2	-	-	98.0	0.0	-	-
1983	97.5	-0.5	-	-	96.0	-1.5	-	-	98.6	2.7	-	-	99.9	1.3	-	-	100.8	0.9	-	-	102.1	1.3	-	-
1984	102.3	0.2	-	-	102.2	-0.1	-	-	103.7	1.5	-	-	104.5	0.8	-	-	104.5	0.0	-	-	104.6	0.1	-	-
1985	104.1	-0.5	-	-	104.6	0.5	-	-	105.8	1.1	-	-	106.0	0.2	-	-	105.7	-0.3	-	-	107.0	1.2	-	-
1986	107.3	0.3	-	-	104.8	-2.3	-	-	103.2	-1.5	-	-	103.4	0.2	-	-	102.4	-1.0	-	-	102.6	0.2	-	-
1987	103.8	1.2	-	-	105.4	1.5	-	-	104.9	-0.5	-	-	107.2	2.2	-	-	106.4	-0.7	-	-	107.1	0.7	-	-
1988	106.0	-1.0	-	-	106.2	0.2	-	-	107.5	1.2	-	-	107.9	0.4	-	-	108.4	0.5	-	-	111.2	2.6	-	-
1989	112.5	1.2	-	-	112.3	-0.2	-	-	113.8	1.3	-	-	114.8	0.9	-	-	114.4	-0.3	-	-	117.0	2.3	-	-
1990	118.1	0.9	-	-	117.8	-0.3	-	-	117.9	0.1	-	-	118.7	0.7	-	-	122.3	3.0	-	-	127.1	3.9	-	-
1991	127.4	0.2	-	-	123.9	-2.7	-	-	124.8	0.7	-	-	124.7	-0.1	-	-	127.1	1.9	-	-	128.7	1.3	-	-

[Continued]

Washington, DC-MD-VA
Consumer Price Index - All Urban Consumers
Base 1982-1984 = 100
Transportation
[Continued]

For 1947-1997. Columns headed % show percentile change in the index from the previous period for which an index is available.

Year	Jan Index	%	Feb Index	%	Mar Index	%	Apr Index	%	May Index	%	Jun Index	%	Jul Index	%	Aug Index	%	Sep Index	%	Oct Index	%	Nov Index	%	Dec Index	%
1992	129.6	0.7	-	-	127.5	-1.6	-	-	129.0	1.2	-	-	130.9	1.5	-	-	127.8	-2.4	-	-	133.1	4.1	-	-
1993	135.5	1.8	-	-	134.8	-0.5	-	-	135.2	0.3	-	-	135.2	0.0	-	-	132.4	-2.1	-	-	136.3	2.9	-	-
1994	135.7	-0.4	-	-	136.0	0.2	-	-	135.6	-0.3	-	-	136.9	1.0	-	-	136.9	0.0	-	-	139.9	2.2	-	-
1995	140.6	0.5	-	-	139.7	-0.6	-	-	140.5	0.6	-	-	141.2	0.5	-	-	139.6	-1.1	-	-	140.1	0.4	-	-
1996	139.8	-0.2	-	-	142.0	1.6	-	-	145.8	2.7	-	-	146.3	0.3	-	-	145.6	-0.5	-	-	146.0	0.3	-	-
1997	146.0	0.0	-	-	146.5	0.3	-	-	145.6	-0.6	146.0	0.3	145.3	-0.5	-	-	147.1	1.2	-	-	146.6	-0.3	-	-

Source: U.S. Department of Labor, Bureau of Labor Statistics, Division of Consumer Prices and Price Indexes. - indicates no data collected for period.

Washington, DC-MD-VA
Consumer Price Index - Urban Wage Earners
Base 1982-1984 = 100
Transportation

For 1947-1997. Columns headed % show percentile change in the index from the previous period for which an index is available.

Year	Jan Index	%	Feb Index	%	Mar Index	%	Apr Index	%	May Index	%	Jun Index	%	Jul Index	%	Aug Index	%	Sep Index	%	Oct Index	%	Nov Index	%	Dec Index	%
1947	18.0	-	18.0	0.0	18.0	0.0	18.3	1.7	19.1	4.4	19.2	0.5	-	-	19.6	2.1	-	-	-	-	19.8	1.0	-	-
1948	-	-	20.2	2.0	-	-	-	-	20.4	1.0	-	-	-	-	21.4	4.9	-	-	-	-	22.5	5.1	-	-
1949	-	-	22.6	0.4	-	-	-	-	22.8	0.9	-	-	-	-	22.7	-0.4	-	-	-	-	22.8	0.4	-	-
1950	-	-	22.9	0.4	-	-	-	-	22.9	0.0	-	-	-	-	23.6	3.1	-	-	-	-	23.7	0.4	-	-
1951	-	-	23.8	0.4	-	-	-	-	24.0	0.8	-	-	-	-	24.0	0.0	-	-	-	-	24.7	2.9	-	-
1952	-	-	25.2	2.0	-	-	-	-	25.2	0.0	-	-	-	-	25.9	2.8	-	-	-	-	26.7	3.1	-	-
1953	-	-	26.6	-0.4	-	-	-	-	26.7	0.4	-	-	-	-	27.0	1.1	-	-	-	-	26.9	-0.4	-	-
1954	-	-	26.9	0.0	-	-	-	-	26.6	-1.1	-	-	-	-	26.2	-1.5	-	-	-	-	27.1	3.4	-	-
1955	-	-	27.0	-0.4	-	-	-	-	27.0	0.0	-	-	-	-	27.1	0.4	-	-	-	-	27.5	1.5	-	-
1956	-	-	27.3	-0.7	-	-	-	-	27.0	-1.1	-	-	-	-	27.3	1.1	-	-	-	-	28.3	3.7	-	-
1957	-	-	28.4	0.4	-	-	-	-	28.6	0.7	-	-	-	-	28.9	1.0	-	-	-	-	29.7	2.8	-	-
1958	-	-	28.9	-2.7	-	-	-	-	28.9	0.0	-	-	-	-	29.3	1.4	-	-	-	-	30.5	4.1	-	-
1959	-	-	30.2	-1.0	-	-	-	-	30.1	-0.3	-	-	-	-	30.5	1.3	-	-	-	-	30.7	0.7	-	-
1960	-	-	30.6	-0.3	-	-	-	-	30.6	0.0	-	-	-	-	30.7	0.3	-	-	-	-	30.6	-0.3	-	-
1961	-	-	30.3	-1.0	-	-	-	-	30.7	1.3	-	-	-	-	31.3	2.0	-	-	-	-	31.3	0.0	-	-
1962	-	-	31.0	-1.0	-	-	-	-	31.2	0.6	-	-	-	-	31.3	0.3	-	-	-	-	31.5	0.6	-	-
1963	-	-	30.9	-1.9	-	-	-	-	31.4	1.6	-	-	-	-	31.6	0.6	-	-	-	-	32.1	1.6	-	-
1964	-	-	32.1	0.0	-	-	-	-	32.1	0.0	-	-	-	-	32.2	0.3	-	-	-	-	32.6	1.2	-	-
1965	-	-	32.6	0.0	-	-	-	-	32.6	0.0	-	-	-	-	32.4	-0.6	-	-	-	-	32.6	0.6	-	-
1966	-	-	32.5	-0.3	-	-	-	-	32.8	0.9	-	-	-	-	32.9	0.3	-	-	-	-	33.3	1.2	-	-
1967	-	-	33.3	0.0	-	-	-	-	34.0	2.1	-	-	-	-	34.2	0.6	-	-	-	-	34.6	1.2	-	-
1968	-	-	34.9	0.9	-	-	-	-	35.1	0.6	-	-	-	-	35.4	0.9	-	-	-	-	35.9	1.4	-	-
1969	-	-	36.3	1.1	-	-	-	-	36.8	1.4	-	-	-	-	37.2	1.1	-	-	-	-	37.9	1.9	-	-
1970	-	-	38.2	0.8	-	-	-	-	39.3	2.9	-	-	-	-	40.3	2.5	-	-	-	-	40.6	0.7	-	-
1971	-	-	41.7	2.7	-	-	-	-	42.4	1.7	-	-	-	-	42.2	-0.5	-	-	-	-	42.0	-0.5	-	-
1972	-	-	41.7	-0.7	-	-	-	-	41.8	0.2	-	-	-	-	42.3	1.2	-	-	-	-	42.5	0.5	-	-
1973	-	-	42.5	0.0	-	-	-	-	42.8	0.7	-	-	-	-	42.9	0.2	-	-	-	-	43.4	1.2	-	-
1974	-	-	45.0	3.7	-	-	-	-	47.0	4.4	-	-	-	-	48.7	3.6	-	-	-	-	49.3	1.2	-	-
1975	-	-	49.8	1.0	-	-	-	-	51.1	2.6	-	-	-	-	52.7	3.1	-	-	-	-	53.4	1.3	-	-
1976	-	-	53.5	0.2	-	-	-	-	55.1	3.0	-	-	-	-	56.4	2.4	-	-	-	-	56.7	0.5	-	-
1977	-	-	58.0	2.3	-	-	-	-	59.7	2.9	-	-	-	-	60.4	1.2	-	-	-	-	60.5	0.2	-	-
1978	60.6	0.2	-	-	60.8	0.3	-	-	62.0	2.0	-	-	63.3	2.1	-	-	63.6	0.5	-	-	65.5	3.0	-	-
1979	65.9	0.6	-	-	67.0	1.7	-	-	69.7	4.0	-	-	71.8	3.0	-	-	73.1	1.8	-	-	74.8	2.3	-	-
1980	77.8	4.0	-	-	80.9	4.0	-	-	81.5	0.7	-	-	84.2	3.3	-	-	85.3	1.3	-	-	86.0	0.8	-	-
1981	87.9	2.2	-	-	90.4	2.8	-	-	92.5	2.3	-	-	94.0	1.6	-	-	94.5	0.5	-	-	95.9	1.5	-	-
1982	96.4	0.5	-	-	94.8	-1.7	-	-	95.0	0.2	-	-	97.7	2.8	-	-	97.6	-0.1	-	-	97.5	-0.1	-	-
1983	97.3	-0.2	-	-	95.9	-1.4	-	-	98.4	2.6	-	-	99.7	1.3	-	-	100.8	1.1	-	-	102.3	1.5	-	-
1984	102.5	0.2	-	-	102.5	0.0	-	-	104.2	1.7	-	-	105.0	0.8	-	-	105.0	0.0	-	-	105.3	0.3	-	-
1985	104.8	-0.5	-	-	105.2	0.4	-	-	106.2	1.0	-	-	106.2	0.0	-	-	105.9	-0.3	-	-	107.3	1.3	-	-
1986	107.6	0.3	-	-	105.5	-2.0	-	-	103.5	-1.9	-	-	103.8	0.3	-	-	103.0	-0.8	-	-	103.3	0.3	-	-
1987	104.4	1.1	-	-	106.4	1.9	-	-	106.9	0.5	-	-	109.4	2.3	-	-	109.6	0.2	-	-	110.2	0.5	-	-
1988	108.9	-1.2	-	-	109.0	0.1	-	-	110.5	1.4	-	-	111.0	0.5	-	-	112.0	0.9	-	-	114.3	2.1	-	-
1989	115.6	1.1	-	-	115.6	0.0	-	-	117.5	1.6	-	-	118.5	0.9	-	-	117.9	-0.5	-	-	120.5	2.2	-	-
1990	121.9	1.2	-	-	121.3	-0.5	-	-	121.5	0.2	-	-	122.5	0.8	-	-	126.6	3.3	-	-	131.6	3.9	-	-
1991	131.4	-0.2	-	-	127.3	-3.1	-	-	128.5	0.9	-	-	128.5	0.0	-	-	130.7	1.7	-	-	132.4	1.3	-	-

[Continued]

Washington, DC-MD-VA
Consumer Price Index - Urban Wage Earners
Base 1982-1984 = 100
Transportation
[Continued]

For 1947-1997. Columns headed % show percentile change in the index from the previous period for which an index is available.

Year	Jan		Feb		Mar		Apr		May		Jun		Jul		Aug		Sep		Oct		Nov		Dec	
	Index	%	Index	%	Index	%	Index	%	Index	%	Index	%	Index	%	Index	%	Index	%	Index	%	Index	%	Index	%
1992	132.7	0.2	-	-	130.5	-1.7	-	-	132.4	1.5	-	-	134.5	1.6	-	-	131.9	-1.9	-	-	136.3	3.3	-	-
1993	138.6	1.7	-	-	137.5	-0.8	-	-	138.0	0.4	-	-	137.9	-0.1	-	-	135.6	-1.7	-	-	139.2	2.7	-	-
1994	138.2	-0.7	-	-	138.4	0.1	-	-	139.1	0.5	-	-	140.5	1.0	-	-	140.8	0.2	-	-	143.8	2.1	-	-
1995	144.3	0.3	-	-	143.3	-0.7	-	-	144.6	0.9	-	-	144.9	0.2	-	-	143.3	-1.1	-	-	143.9	0.4	-	-
1996	144.0	0.1	-	-	146.1	1.5	-	-	150.6	3.1	-	-	151.0	0.3	-	-	150.1	-0.6	-	-	150.7	0.4	-	-
1997	150.9	0.1	-	-	151.0	0.1	-	-	150.4	-0.4	150.7	0.2	150.2	-0.3	-	-	152.0	1.2	-	-	151.5	-0.3	-	-

Source: U.S. Department of Labor, Bureau of Labor Statistics, Division of Consumer Prices and Price Indexes. - indicates no data collected for period.

Washington, DC-MD-VA
Consumer Price Index - All Urban Consumers
Base 1982-1984 = 100
Medical Care

For 1947-1997. Columns headed % show percentile change in the index from the previous period for which an index is available.

Year	Jan Index	%	Feb Index	%	Mar Index	%	Apr Index	%	May Index	%	Jun Index	%	Jul Index	%	Aug Index	%	Sep Index	%	Oct Index	%	Nov Index	%	Dec Index	%
1947	12.3	-	12.4	0.8	12.4	0.0	12.4	0.0	12.3	-0.8	12.3	0.0	-	-	12.5	1.6	-	-	-	-	12.5	0.0	-	-
1948	-	-	12.6	0.8	-	-	-	-	12.8	1.6	-	-	-	-	12.8	0.0	-	-	-	-	13.0	1.6	-	-
1949	-	-	13.1	0.8	-	-	-	-	13.1	0.0	-	-	-	-	13.1	0.0	-	-	-	-	13.1	0.0	-	-
1950	-	-	13.1	0.0	-	-	-	-	13.0	-0.8	-	-	-	-	13.2	1.5	-	-	-	-	13.3	0.8	-	-
1951	-	-	13.7	3.0	-	-	-	-	13.9	1.5	-	-	-	-	14.2	2.2	-	-	-	-	14.4	1.4	-	-
1952	-	-	14.5	0.7	-	-	-	-	14.9	2.8	-	-	-	-	14.9	0.0	-	-	-	-	14.9	0.0	-	-
1953	-	-	14.9	0.0	-	-	-	-	15.0	0.7	-	-	-	-	15.0	0.0	-	-	-	-	15.0	0.0	-	-
1954	-	-	15.0	0.0	-	-	-	-	15.0	0.0	-	-	-	-	15.1	0.7	-	-	-	-	15.2	0.7	-	-
1955	-	-	15.1	-0.7	-	-	-	-	15.1	0.0	-	-	-	-	15.1	0.0	-	-	-	-	15.7	4.0	-	-
1956	-	-	15.7	0.0	-	-	-	-	15.8	0.6	-	-	-	-	16.3	3.2	-	-	-	-	16.4	0.6	-	-
1957	-	-	16.5	0.6	-	-	-	-	16.8	1.8	-	-	-	-	16.8	0.0	-	-	-	-	17.0	1.2	-	-
1958	-	-	17.5	2.9	-	-	-	-	17.5	0.0	-	-	-	-	17.9	2.3	-	-	-	-	18.8	5.0	-	-
1959	-	-	18.9	0.5	-	-	-	-	19.2	1.6	-	-	-	-	19.0	-1.0	-	-	-	-	19.2	1.1	-	-
1960	-	-	19.6	2.1	-	-	-	-	19.7	0.5	-	-	-	-	19.7	0.0	-	-	-	-	19.9	1.0	-	-
1961	-	-	20.2	1.5	-	-	-	-	20.3	0.5	-	-	-	-	20.5	1.0	-	-	-	-	20.6	0.5	-	-
1962	-	-	21.0	1.9	-	-	-	-	21.1	0.5	-	-	-	-	21.9	3.8	-	-	-	-	22.0	0.5	-	-
1963	-	-	22.2	0.9	-	-	-	-	22.4	0.9	-	-	-	-	22.4	0.0	-	-	-	-	22.6	0.9	-	-
1964	-	-	22.8	0.9	-	-	-	-	23.0	0.9	-	-	-	-	23.0	0.0	-	-	-	-	23.2	0.9	-	-
1965	-	-	23.4	0.9	-	-	-	-	23.5	0.4	-	-	-	-	23.8	1.3	-	-	-	-	24.0	0.8	-	-
1966	-	-	24.3	1.2	-	-	-	-	24.8	2.1	-	-	-	-	25.1	1.2	-	-	-	-	25.4	1.2	-	-
1967	-	-	26.3	3.5	-	-	-	-	26.8	1.9	-	-	-	-	27.0	0.7	-	-	-	-	28.0	3.7	-	-
1968	-	-	28.8	2.9	-	-	-	-	29.4	2.1	-	-	-	-	29.7	1.0	-	-	-	-	30.3	2.0	-	-
1969	-	-	31.3	3.3	-	-	-	-	31.6	1.0	-	-	-	-	32.2	1.9	-	-	-	-	32.3	0.3	-	-
1970	-	-	33.7	4.3	-	-	-	-	34.0	0.9	-	-	-	-	34.6	1.8	-	-	-	-	35.0	1.2	-	-
1971	-	-	36.4	4.0	-	-	-	-	36.8	1.1	-	-	-	-	37.4	1.6	-	-	-	-	37.0	-1.1	-	-
1972	-	-	37.3	0.8	-	-	-	-	37.8	1.3	-	-	-	-	38.0	0.5	-	-	-	-	38.2	0.5	-	-
1973	-	-	38.4	0.5	-	-	-	-	38.6	0.5	-	-	-	-	39.1	1.3	-	-	-	-	39.9	2.0	-	-
1974	-	-	41.1	3.0	-	-	-	-	42.6	3.6	-	-	-	-	44.8	5.2	-	-	-	-	45.6	1.8	-	-
1975	-	-	47.3	3.7	-	-	-	-	48.1	1.7	-	-	-	-	48.9	1.7	-	-	-	-	49.6	1.4	-	-
1976	-	-	51.7	4.2	-	-	-	-	52.6	1.7	-	-	-	-	53.9	2.5	-	-	-	-	55.4	2.8	-	-
1977	-	-	56.7	2.3	-	-	-	-	57.9	2.1	-	-	-	-	59.1	2.1	-	-	-	-	59.6	0.8	-	-
1978	61.0	2.3	-	-	61.2	0.3	-	-	60.9	-0.5	-	-	62.3	2.3	-	-	62.6	0.5	-	-	64.2	2.6	-	-
1979	65.2	1.6	-	-	66.8	2.5	-	-	67.1	0.4	-	-	68.1	1.5	-	-	70.2	3.1	-	-	70.7	0.7	-	-
1980	71.4	1.0	-	-	72.4	1.4	-	-	74.2	2.5	-	-	74.9	0.9	-	-	75.6	0.9	-	-	75.5	-0.1	-	-
1981	77.2	2.3	-	-	78.4	1.6	-	-	78.0	-0.5	-	-	80.7	3.5	-	-	81.8	1.4	-	-	82.9	1.3	-	-
1982	84.3	1.7	-	-	87.9	4.3	-	-	88.8	1.0	-	-	90.2	1.6	-	-	93.9	4.1	-	-	94.9	1.1	-	-
1983	98.9	4.2	-	-	99.5	0.6	-	-	100.1	0.6	-	-	99.7	-0.4	-	-	103.4	3.7	-	-	105.6	2.1	-	-
1984	107.0	1.3	-	-	106.3	-0.7	-	-	107.1	0.8	-	-	107.2	0.1	-	-	108.5	1.2	-	-	110.5	1.8	-	-
1985	110.1	-0.4	-	-	112.5	2.2	-	-	113.4	0.8	-	-	115.8	2.1	-	-	116.1	0.3	-	-	117.9	1.6	-	-
1986	119.4	1.3	-	-	121.1	1.4	-	-	122.7	1.3	-	-	123.0	0.2	-	-	123.6	0.5	-	-	124.5	0.7	-	-
1987	126.0	1.2	-	-	127.5	1.2	-	-	128.6	0.9	-	-	128.3	-0.2	-	-	129.4	0.9	-	-	132.4	2.3	-	-
1988	135.1	2.0	-	-	136.4	1.0	-	-	137.3	0.7	-	-	137.9	0.4	-	-	138.0	0.1	-	-	140.2	1.6	-	-
1989	142.6	1.7	-	-	144.1	1.1	-	-	145.4	0.9	-	-	146.4	0.7	-	-	147.2	0.5	-	-	149.6	1.6	-	-
1990	155.3	3.8	-	-	157.9	1.7	-	-	160.1	1.4	-	-	162.4	1.4	-	-	164.3	1.2	-	-	170.2	3.6	-	-
1991	173.0	1.6	-	-	175.3	1.3	-	-	175.9	0.3	-	-	176.6	0.4	-	-	176.3	-0.2	-	-	178.7	1.4	-	-

[Continued]

Washington, DC-MD-VA
Consumer Price Index - All Urban Consumers
Base 1982-1984 = 100
Medical Care

[Continued]

For 1947-1997. Columns headed % show percentile change in the index from the previous period for which an index is available.

Year	Jan Index	%	Feb Index	%	Mar Index	%	Apr Index	%	May Index	%	Jun Index	%	Jul Index	%	Aug Index	%	Sep Index	%	Oct Index	%	Nov Index	%	Dec Index	%
1992	184.1	3.0	-	-	181.9	-1.2	-	-	182.0	0.1	-	-	187.1	2.8	-	-	189.6	1.3	-	-	191.1	0.8	-	-
1993	192.6	0.8	-	-	193.6	0.5	-	-	194.3	0.4	-	-	196.1	0.9	-	-	197.0	0.5	-	-	196.8	-0.1	-	-
1994	198.5	0.9	-	-	199.9	0.7	-	-	202.1	1.1	-	-	204.5	1.2	-	-	205.6	0.5	-	-	207.7	1.0	-	-
1995	208.5	0.4	-	-	209.0	0.2	-	-	209.3	0.1	-	-	213.8	2.2	-	-	213.6	-0.1	-	-	216.0	1.1	-	-
1996	217.8	0.8	-	-	219.1	0.6	-	-	220.9	0.8	-	-	220.8	-0.0	-	-	220.4	-0.2	-	-	222.8	1.1	-	-
1997	231.4	3.9	-	-	231.9	0.2	-	-	230.4	-0.6	231.1	0.3	229.9	-0.5	-	-	231.7	0.8	-	-	233.1	0.6	-	-

Source: U.S. Department of Labor, Bureau of Labor Statistics, Division of Consumer Prices and Price Indexes. - indicates no data collected for period.

Washington, DC-MD-VA
Consumer Price Index - Urban Wage Earners
Base 1982-1984 = 100
Medical Care

For 1947-1997. Columns headed % show percentile change in the index from the previous period for which an index is available.

Year	Jan Index	%	Feb Index	%	Mar Index	%	Apr Index	%	May Index	%	Jun Index	%	Jul Index	%	Aug Index	%	Sep Index	%	Oct Index	%	Nov Index	%	Dec Index	%
1947	11.8	-	11.9	0.8	11.9	0.0	11.8	-0.8	11.8	0.0	11.8	0.0	-	-	11.9	0.8	-	-	-	-	11.9	0.0	-	-
1948	-	-	12.1	1.7	-	-	-	-	12.3	1.7	-	-	-	-	12.3	0.0	-	-	-	-	12.5	1.6	-	-
1949	-	-	12.5	0.0	-	-	-	-	12.5	0.0	-	-	-	-	12.6	0.8	-	-	-	-	12.6	0.0	-	-
1950	-	-	12.6	0.0	-	-	-	-	12.4	-1.6	-	-	-	-	12.6	1.6	-	-	-	-	12.7	0.8	-	-
1951	-	-	13.1	3.1	-	-	-	-	13.3	1.5	-	-	-	-	13.6	2.3	-	-	-	-	13.8	1.5	-	-
1952	-	-	13.9	0.7	-	-	-	-	14.2	2.2	-	-	-	-	14.3	0.7	-	-	-	-	14.2	-0.7	-	-
1953	-	-	14.2	0.0	-	-	-	-	14.3	0.7	-	-	-	-	14.4	0.7	-	-	-	-	14.4	0.0	-	-
1954	-	-	14.3	-0.7	-	-	-	-	14.3	0.0	-	-	-	-	14.4	0.7	-	-	-	-	14.5	0.7	-	-
1955	-	-	14.4	-0.7	-	-	-	-	14.5	0.7	-	-	-	-	14.5	0.0	-	-	-	-	15.0	3.4	-	-
1956	-	-	15.0	0.0	-	-	-	-	15.1	0.7	-	-	-	-	15.6	3.3	-	-	-	-	15.7	0.6	-	-
1957	-	-	15.8	0.6	-	-	-	-	16.1	1.9	-	-	-	-	16.1	0.0	-	-	-	-	16.3	1.2	-	-
1958	-	-	16.7	2.5	-	-	-	-	16.7	0.0	-	-	-	-	17.1	2.4	-	-	-	-	18.0	5.3	-	-
1959	-	-	18.1	0.6	-	-	-	-	18.3	1.1	-	-	-	-	18.1	-1.1	-	-	-	-	18.4	1.7	-	-
1960	-	-	18.8	2.2	-	-	-	-	18.8	0.0	-	-	-	-	18.9	0.5	-	-	-	-	19.0	0.5	-	-
1961	-	-	19.3	1.6	-	-	-	-	19.5	1.0	-	-	-	-	19.6	0.5	-	-	-	-	19.7	0.5	-	-
1962	-	-	20.1	2.0	-	-	-	-	20.2	0.5	-	-	-	-	21.0	4.0	-	-	-	-	21.1	0.5	-	-
1963	-	-	21.2	0.5	-	-	-	-	21.5	1.4	-	-	-	-	21.5	0.0	-	-	-	-	21.6	0.5	-	-
1964	-	-	21.8	0.9	-	-	-	-	22.0	0.9	-	-	-	-	22.0	0.0	-	-	-	-	22.2	0.9	-	-
1965	-	-	22.4	0.9	-	-	-	-	22.5	0.4	-	-	-	-	22.8	1.3	-	-	-	-	22.9	0.4	-	-
1966	-	-	23.3	1.7	-	-	-	-	23.7	1.7	-	-	-	-	24.0	1.3	-	-	-	-	24.3	1.2	-	-
1967	-	-	25.1	3.3	-	-	-	-	25.6	2.0	-	-	-	-	25.9	1.2	-	-	-	-	26.8	3.5	-	-
1968	-	-	27.6	3.0	-	-	-	-	28.1	1.8	-	-	-	-	28.4	1.1	-	-	-	-	29.0	2.1	-	-
1969	-	-	29.9	3.1	-	-	-	-	30.2	1.0	-	-	-	-	30.8	2.0	-	-	-	-	30.9	0.3	-	-
1970	-	-	32.3	4.5	-	-	-	-	32.5	0.6	-	-	-	-	33.1	1.8	-	-	-	-	33.5	1.2	-	-
1971	-	-	34.8	3.9	-	-	-	-	35.2	1.1	-	-	-	-	35.8	1.7	-	-	-	-	35.4	-1.1	-	-
1972	-	-	35.7	0.8	-	-	-	-	36.1	1.1	-	-	-	-	36.3	0.6	-	-	-	-	36.5	0.6	-	-
1973	-	-	36.7	0.5	-	-	-	-	37.0	0.8	-	-	-	-	37.4	1.1	-	-	-	-	38.1	1.9	-	-
1974	-	-	39.3	3.1	-	-	-	-	40.7	3.6	-	-	-	-	42.8	5.2	-	-	-	-	43.6	1.9	-	-
1975	-	-	45.3	3.9	-	-	-	-	46.0	1.5	-	-	-	-	46.8	1.7	-	-	-	-	47.5	1.5	-	-
1976	-	-	49.5	4.2	-	-	-	-	50.3	1.6	-	-	-	-	51.5	2.4	-	-	-	-	53.0	2.9	-	-
1977	-	-	54.2	2.3	-	-	-	-	55.4	2.2	-	-	-	-	56.6	2.2	-	-	-	-	57.0	0.7	-	-
1978	58.3	2.3	-	-	59.6	2.2	-	-	60.1	0.8	-	-	61.5	2.3	-	-	62.8	2.1	-	-	63.0	0.3	-	-
1979	63.9	1.4	-	-	67.1	5.0	-	-	67.9	1.2	-	-	68.4	0.7	-	-	70.3	2.8	-	-	71.2	1.3	-	-
1980	72.2	1.4	-	-	73.1	1.2	-	-	73.6	0.7	-	-	75.5	2.6	-	-	75.8	0.4	-	-	76.7	1.2	-	-
1981	77.4	0.9	-	-	78.0	0.8	-	-	77.9	-0.1	-	-	79.9	2.6	-	-	80.7	1.0	-	-	83.1	3.0	-	-
1982	84.5	1.7	-	-	88.0	4.1	-	-	88.5	0.6	-	-	89.7	1.4	-	-	93.3	4.0	-	-	94.2	1.0	-	-
1983	98.2	4.2	-	-	99.0	0.8	-	-	99.8	0.8	-	-	99.6	-0.2	-	-	103.6	4.0	-	-	105.9	2.2	-	-
1984	107.2	1.2	-	-	106.8	-0.4	-	-	107.5	0.7	-	-	107.8	0.3	-	-	109.0	1.1	-	-	111.0	1.8	-	-
1985	110.8	-0.2	-	-	113.4	2.3	-	-	114.3	0.8	-	-	116.7	2.1	-	-	116.9	0.2	-	-	118.8	1.6	-	-
1986	120.2	1.2	-	-	122.1	1.6	-	-	123.8	1.4	-	-	124.0	0.2	-	-	124.4	0.3	-	-	125.5	0.9	-	-
1987	127.2	1.4	-	-	128.7	1.2	-	-	129.9	0.9	-	-	129.7	-0.2	-	-	131.0	1.0	-	-	134.0	2.3	-	-
1988	136.9	2.2	-	-	137.9	0.7	-	-	138.9	0.7	-	-	139.5	0.4	-	-	139.8	0.2	-	-	142.2	1.7	-	-
1989	144.5	1.6	-	-	146.1	1.1	-	-	147.4	0.9	-	-	148.3	0.6	-	-	148.9	0.4	-	-	151.2	1.5	-	-
1990	156.9	3.8	-	-	159.4	1.6	-	-	161.3	1.2	-	-	163.4	1.3	-	-	165.2	1.1	-	-	170.7	3.3	-	-
1991	173.4	1.6	-	-	175.7	1.3	-	-	176.4	0.4	-	-	177.1	0.4	-	-	176.8	-0.2	-	-	179.0	1.2	-	-

[Continued]

Washington, DC-MD-VA
Consumer Price Index - Urban Wage Earners
Base 1982-1984 = 100
Medical Care
[Continued]

For 1947-1997. Columns headed % show percentile change in the index from the previous period for which an index is available.

Year	Jan Index	%	Feb Index	%	Mar Index	%	Apr Index	%	May Index	%	Jun Index	%	Jul Index	%	Aug Index	%	Sep Index	%	Oct Index	%	Nov Index	%	Dec Index	%
1992	184.5	3.1	-	-	182.1	-1.3	-	-	182.3	0.1	-	-	187.5	2.9	-	-	190.3	1.5	-	-	191.7	0.7	-	-
1993	193.3	0.8	-	-	194.0	0.4	-	-	194.8	0.4	-	-	196.9	1.1	-	-	197.7	0.4	-	-	197.5	-0.1	-	-
1994	199.1	0.8	-	-	200.4	0.7	-	-	202.9	1.2	-	-	205.2	1.1	-	-	206.2	0.5	-	-	208.2	1.0	-	-
1995	208.9	0.3	-	-	208.8	-0.0	-	-	208.9	0.0	-	-	213.7	2.3	-	-	213.6	-0.0	-	-	216.0	1.1	-	-
1996	217.6	0.7	-	-	219.1	0.7	-	-	220.9	0.8	-	-	220.9	0.0	-	-	220.6	-0.1	-	-	222.9	1.0	-	-
1997	231.9	4.0	-	-	232.3	0.2	-	-	231.0	-0.6	231.6	0.3	230.4	-0.5	-	-	232.3	0.8	-	-	233.6	0.6	-	-

Source: U.S. Department of Labor, Bureau of Labor Statistics, Division of Consumer Prices and Price Indexes. - indicates no data collected for period.

Washington, DC-MD-VA
Consumer Price Index - All Urban Consumers
Base 1982-1984 = 100
Entertainment

For 1975-1997. Columns headed % show percentile change in the index from the previous period for which an index is available.

Year	Jan Index	Jan %	Feb Index	Feb %	Mar Index	Mar %	Apr Index	Apr %	May Index	May %	Jun Index	Jun %	Jul Index	Jul %	Aug Index	Aug %	Sep Index	Sep %	Oct Index	Oct %	Nov Index	Nov %	Dec Index	Dec %
1975	-		-		-		-		-		-		-		-		-		-		66.3	-	-	
1976	-		67.3	1.5	-		-		68.3	1.5	-		-		68.7	0.6	-		-		70.0	1.9	-	
1977	-		72.0	2.9	-		-		73.2	1.7	-		-		74.7	2.0	-		-		75.2	0.7	-	
1978	74.8	-0.5	-		74.9	0.1	-		74.2	-0.9	-		74.4	0.3	-		74.4	0.0	-		76.4	2.7	-	
1979	76.5	0.1	-		77.9	1.8	-		78.0	0.1	-		78.4	0.5	-		79.5	1.4	-		79.6	0.1	-	
1980	83.8	5.3	-		83.0	-1.0	-		82.2	-1.0	-		86.0	4.6	-		86.8	0.9	-		85.7	-1.3	-	
1981	87.0	1.5	-		86.1	-1.0	-		89.1	3.5	-		89.0	-0.1	-		90.2	1.3	-		90.9	0.8	-	
1982	92.3	1.5	-		93.7	1.5	-		94.1	0.4	-		93.9	-0.2	-		94.6	0.7	-		95.3	0.7	-	
1983	96.0	0.7	-		96.2	0.2	-		96.5	0.3	-		98.1	1.7	-		103.7	5.7	-		102.8	-0.9	-	
1984	102.1	-0.7	-		104.3	2.2	-		102.9	-1.3	-		108.0	5.0	-		108.3	0.3	-		112.2	3.6	-	
1985	112.8	0.5	-		112.4	-0.4	-		112.1	-0.3	-		113.6	1.3	-		114.2	0.5	-		116.0	1.6	-	
1986	116.8	0.7	-		116.5	-0.3	-		115.2	-1.1	-		116.6	1.2	-		117.8	1.0	-		117.0	-0.7	-	
1987	115.2	-1.5	-		121.8	5.7	-		122.1	0.2	-		123.6	1.2	-		121.3	-1.9	-		122.7	1.2	-	
1988	125.4	2.2	-		126.5	0.9	-		127.5	0.8	-		122.1	-4.2	-		124.2	1.7	-		123.4	-0.6	-	
1989	125.4	1.6	-		125.9	0.4	-		126.2	0.2	-		127.9	1.3	-		130.5	2.0	-		128.8	-1.3	-	
1990	127.8	-0.8	-		131.1	2.6	-		136.9	4.4	-		137.0	0.1	-		139.6	1.9	-		139.0	-0.4	-	
1991	137.2	-1.3	-		140.7	2.6	-		141.4	0.5	-		143.4	1.4	-		145.4	1.4	-		146.4	0.7	-	
1992	143.4	-2.0	-		146.4	2.1	-		147.7	0.9	-		147.4	-0.2	-		149.3	1.3	-		149.8	0.3	-	
1993	150.6	0.5	-		150.1	-0.3	-		148.3	-1.2	-		149.7	0.9	-		153.9	2.8	-		152.5	-0.9	-	
1994	154.0	1.0	-		152.8	-0.8	-		151.6	-0.8	-		155.2	2.4	-		159.9	3.0	-		159.3	-0.4	-	
1995	164.3	3.1	-		163.2	-0.7	-		161.2	-1.2	-		162.1	0.6	-		163.3	0.7	-		164.4	0.7	-	
1996	164.9	0.3	-		165.8	0.5	-		168.9	1.9	-		170.2	0.8	-		171.5	0.8	-		171.8	0.2	-	
1997	172.1	0.2	-		173.1	0.6	-		173.3	0.1	173.2	-0.1	176.2	1.7	-		176.2	0.0	-		175.9	-0.2	-	

Source: U.S. Department of Labor, Bureau of Labor Statistics, Division of Consumer Prices and Price Indexes. - indicates no data collected for period.

Washington, DC-MD-VA
Consumer Price Index - Urban Wage Earners
Base 1982-1984 = 100
Entertainment

For 1975-1997. Columns headed % show percentile change in the index from the previous period for which an index is available.

Year	Jan Index	%	Feb Index	%	Mar Index	%	Apr Index	%	May Index	%	Jun Index	%	Jul Index	%	Aug Index	%	Sep Index	%	Oct Index	%	Nov Index	%	Dec Index	%
1975	-	-	-	-	-	-	-	-	-	-	-	-	-	-	-	-	-	-	-	-	56.3	-	-	-
1976	-	-	57.1	1.4	-	-	-	-	58.0	1.6	-	-	-	-	58.3	0.5	-	-	-	-	59.4	1.9	-	-
1977	-	-	61.1	2.9	-	-	-	-	62.1	1.6	-	-	-	-	63.4	2.1	-	-	-	-	63.8	0.6	-	-
1978	64.2	0.6	-	-	67.3	4.8	-	-	66.9	-0.6	-	-	69.0	3.1	-	-	69.2	0.3	-	-	71.7	3.6	-	-
1979	72.4	1.0	-	-	73.5	1.5	-	-	75.3	2.4	-	-	76.6	1.7	-	-	77.6	1.3	-	-	78.0	0.5	-	-
1980	79.3	1.7	-	-	80.3	1.3	-	-	83.3	3.7	-	-	84.2	1.1	-	-	83.6	-0.7	-	-	84.4	1.0	-	-
1981	84.2	-0.2	-	-	83.5	-0.8	-	-	86.6	3.7	-	-	89.5	3.3	-	-	90.7	1.3	-	-	91.1	0.4	-	-
1982	92.7	1.8	-	-	94.0	1.4	-	-	94.8	0.9	-	-	94.4	-0.4	-	-	95.2	0.8	-	-	95.2	0.0	-	-
1983	96.1	0.9	-	-	95.9	-0.2	-	-	96.8	0.9	-	-	98.0	1.2	-	-	103.6	5.7	-	-	103.3	-0.3	-	-
1984	102.7	-0.6	-	-	104.8	2.0	-	-	102.2	-2.5	-	-	107.4	5.1	-	-	107.6	0.2	-	-	110.6	2.8	-	-
1985	111.5	0.8	-	-	110.6	-0.8	-	-	110.2	-0.4	-	-	111.7	1.4	-	-	112.5	0.7	-	-	113.9	1.2	-	-
1986	114.8	0.8	-	-	113.9	-0.8	-	-	110.5	-3.0	-	-	111.6	1.0	-	-	114.4	2.5	-	-	113.1	-1.1	-	-
1987	110.8	-2.0	-	-	118.8	7.2	-	-	118.7	-0.1	-	-	120.0	1.1	-	-	117.3	-2.3	-	-	119.8	2.1	-	-
1988	122.0	1.8	-	-	123.1	0.9	-	-	124.0	0.7	-	-	119.1	-4.0	-	-	121.6	2.1	-	-	120.8	-0.7	-	-
1989	122.9	1.7	-	-	123.3	0.3	-	-	123.5	0.2	-	-	124.5	0.8	-	-	127.0	2.0	-	-	125.7	-1.0	-	-
1990	124.8	-0.7	-	-	127.7	2.3	-	-	133.2	4.3	-	-	133.2	0.0	-	-	135.9	2.0	-	-	135.1	-0.6	-	-
1991	133.5	-1.2	-	-	137.1	2.7	-	-	137.3	0.1	-	-	139.2	1.4	-	-	141.1	1.4	-	-	142.4	0.9	-	-
1992	139.6	-2.0	-	-	142.4	2.0	-	-	143.8	1.0	-	-	143.6	-0.1	-	-	145.5	1.3	-	-	145.8	0.2	-	-
1993	146.2	0.3	-	-	146.1	-0.1	-	-	144.6	-1.0	-	-	145.4	0.6	-	-	149.4	2.8	-	-	147.4	-1.3	-	-
1994	148.9	1.0	-	-	147.7	-0.8	-	-	146.7	-0.7	-	-	150.5	2.6	-	-	155.1	3.1	-	-	154.5	-0.4	-	-
1995	158.2	2.4	-	-	157.1	-0.7	-	-	155.1	-1.3	-	-	156.0	0.6	-	-	156.2	0.1	-	-	157.6	0.9	-	-
1996	158.4	0.5	-	-	158.7	0.2	-	-	162.9	2.6	-	-	164.2	0.8	-	-	165.4	0.7	-	-	165.5	0.1	-	-
1997	165.7	0.1	-	-	166.1	0.2	-	-	166.3	0.1	166.3	0.0	168.8	1.5	-	-	169.0	0.1	-	-	169.5	0.3	-	-

Source: U.S. Department of Labor, Bureau of Labor Statistics, Division of Consumer Prices and Price Indexes. - indicates no data collected for period.

Washington, DC-MD-VA
Consumer Price Index - All Urban Consumers
Base 1982-1984 = 100
Other Goods and Services

For 1975-1997. Columns headed % show percentile change in the index from the previous period for which an index is available.

Year	Jan Index	%	Feb Index	%	Mar Index	%	Apr Index	%	May Index	%	Jun Index	%	Jul Index	%	Aug Index	%	Sep Index	%	Oct Index	%	Nov Index	%	Dec Index	%
1975	-	-	-	-	-	-	-	-	-	-	-	-	-	-	-	-	-	-	-	-	54.9	-	-	-
1976	-	-	57.3	4.4	-	-	-	-	57.7	0.7	-	-	-	-	58.6	1.6	-	-	-	-	59.9	2.2	-	-
1977	-	-	60.6	1.2	-	-	-	-	61.4	1.3	-	-	-	-	61.9	0.8	-	-	-	-	64.4	4.0	-	-
1978	63.9	-0.8	-	-	64.4	0.8	-	-	64.6	0.3	-	-	65.2	0.9	-	-	67.1	2.9	-	-	67.3	0.3	-	-
1979	68.4	1.6	-	-	69.0	0.9	-	-	69.4	0.6	-	-	69.3	-0.1	-	-	71.3	2.9	-	-	71.5	0.3	-	-
1980	73.1	2.2	-	-	73.2	0.1	-	-	74.3	1.5	-	-	75.7	1.9	-	-	78.4	3.6	-	-	78.6	0.3	-	-
1981	79.2	0.8	-	-	81.1	2.4	-	-	81.7	0.7	-	-	82.1	0.5	-	-	86.5	5.4	-	-	87.6	1.3	-	-
1982	87.7	0.1	-	-	89.1	1.6	-	-	89.3	0.2	-	-	89.5	0.2	-	-	93.3	4.2	-	-	96.1	3.0	-	-
1983	98.9	2.9	-	-	99.1	0.2	-	-	98.9	-0.2	-	-	100.8	1.9	-	-	103.0	2.2	-	-	103.6	0.6	-	-
1984	105.4	1.7	-	-	105.4	0.0	-	-	106.1	0.7	-	-	106.9	0.8	-	-	109.4	2.3	-	-	111.5	1.9	-	-
1985	112.0	0.4	-	-	112.9	0.8	-	-	113.0	0.1	-	-	113.5	0.4	-	-	116.2	2.4	-	-	117.7	1.3	-	-
1986	119.0	1.1	-	-	119.2	0.2	-	-	119.6	0.3	-	-	121.4	1.5	-	-	124.1	2.2	-	-	126.2	1.7	-	-
1987	126.9	0.6	-	-	127.4	0.4	-	-	127.7	0.2	-	-	128.2	0.4	-	-	130.8	2.0	-	-	133.4	2.0	-	-
1988	135.1	1.3	-	-	134.9	-0.1	-	-	135.4	0.4	-	-	138.8	2.5	-	-	140.3	1.1	-	-	142.9	1.9	-	-
1989	146.2	2.3	-	-	147.1	0.6	-	-	148.4	0.9	-	-	150.5	1.4	-	-	157.7	4.8	-	-	160.0	1.5	-	-
1990	160.7	0.4	-	-	162.4	1.1	-	-	162.3	-0.1	-	-	164.4	1.3	-	-	168.3	2.4	-	-	170.7	1.4	-	-
1991	174.6	2.3	-	-	175.8	0.7	-	-	177.0	0.7	-	-	180.0	1.7	-	-	181.1	0.6	-	-	181.2	0.1	-	-
1992	181.2	0.0	-	-	181.5	0.2	-	-	183.9	1.3	-	-	184.7	0.4	-	-	193.2	4.6	-	-	193.3	0.1	-	-
1993	195.1	0.9	-	-	196.2	0.6	-	-	197.7	0.8	-	-	199.5	0.9	-	-	202.6	1.6	-	-	202.7	0.0	-	-
1994	206.0	1.6	-	-	206.3	0.1	-	-	207.2	0.4	-	-	207.3	0.0	-	-	212.2	2.4	-	-	212.2	0.0	-	-
1995	212.0	-0.1	-	-	211.5	-0.2	-	-	211.6	0.0	-	-	212.6	0.5	-	-	218.9	3.0	-	-	220.3	0.6	-	-
1996	222.7	1.1	-	-	224.5	0.8	-	-	226.9	1.1	-	-	227.0	0.0	-	-	231.0	1.8	-	-	232.2	0.5	-	-
1997	232.6	0.2	-	-	234.7	0.9	-	-	235.9	0.5	234.8	-0.5	238.0	1.4	-	-	241.0	1.3	-	-	240.6	-0.2	-	-

Source: U.S. Department of Labor, Bureau of Labor Statistics, Division of Consumer Prices and Price Indexes. - indicates no data collected for period.

Washington, DC-MD-VA
Consumer Price Index - Urban Wage Earners
Base 1982-1984 = 100
Other Goods and Services

For 1975-1997. Columns headed % show percentile change in the index from the previous period for which an index is available.

Year	Jan Index	%	Feb Index	%	Mar Index	%	Apr Index	%	May Index	%	Jun Index	%	Jul Index	%	Aug Index	%	Sep Index	%	Oct Index	%	Nov Index	%	Dec Index	%
1975	-	-			-	-	-	-	-	-	-	-	-	-	-	-	-	-	-	-	52.9	-	-	-
1976	-	-	55.3	4.5	-	-	-	-	55.7	0.7	-	-	-	-	56.5	1.4	-	-	-	-	57.8	2.3	-	-
1977	-	-	58.4	1.0	-	-	-	-	59.2	1.4	-	-	-	-	59.7	0.8	-	-	-	-	62.1	4.0	-	-
1978	62.2	0.2	-	-	63.0	1.3	-	-	64.8	2.9	-	-	66.9	3.2	-	-	66.8	-0.1	-	-	67.2	0.6	-	-
1979	67.8	0.9	-	-	68.5	1.0	-	-	68.7	0.3	-	-	70.2	2.2	-	-	71.3	1.6	-	-	72.1	1.1	-	-
1980	73.7	2.2	-	-	74.4	0.9	-	-	75.5	1.5	-	-	76.9	1.9	-	-	78.1	1.6	-	-	79.3	1.5	-	-
1981	80.0	0.9	-	-	82.2	2.8	-	-	83.8	1.9	-	-	83.7	-0.1	-	-	86.6	3.5	-	-	87.6	1.2	-	-
1982	87.8	0.2	-	-	89.4	1.8	-	-	89.7	0.3	-	-	90.1	0.4	-	-	92.6	2.8	-	-	95.3	2.9	-	-
1983	98.9	3.8	-	-	99.6	0.7	-	-	99.4	-0.2	-	-	101.9	2.5	-	-	103.1	1.2	-	-	103.1	0.0	-	-
1984	105.6	2.4	-	-	105.4	-0.2	-	-	106.2	0.8	-	-	107.4	1.1	-	-	109.2	1.7	-	-	109.8	0.5	-	-
1985	110.4	0.5	-	-	111.6	1.1	-	-	111.6	0.0	-	-	112.3	0.6	-	-	114.3	1.8	-	-	114.7	0.3	-	-
1986	116.3	1.4	-	-	116.7	0.3	-	-	117.1	0.3	-	-	119.4	2.0	-	-	120.9	1.3	-	-	122.4	1.2	-	-
1987	123.4	0.8	-	-	124.1	0.6	-	-	124.5	0.3	-	-	125.0	0.4	-	-	126.9	1.5	-	-	128.5	1.3	-	-
1988	130.7	1.7	-	-	130.6	-0.1	-	-	131.3	0.5	-	-	135.4	3.1	-	-	137.3	1.4	-	-	139.6	1.7	-	-
1989	142.7	2.2	-	-	144.0	0.9	-	-	145.5	1.0	-	-	147.6	1.4	-	-	153.4	3.9	-	-	154.7	0.8	-	-
1990	155.7	0.6	-	-	157.9	1.4	-	-	157.6	-0.2	-	-	160.2	1.6	-	-	163.4	2.0	-	-	165.3	1.2	-	-
1991	169.6	2.6	-	-	170.5	0.5	-	-	171.6	0.6	-	-	174.3	1.6	-	-	174.0	-0.2	-	-	174.2	0.1	-	-
1992	174.2	0.0	-	-	174.4	0.1	-	-	178.1	2.1	-	-	178.8	0.4	-	-	186.8	4.5	-	-	187.0	0.1	-	-
1993	189.1	1.1	-	-	190.8	0.9	-	-	191.8	0.5	-	-	192.8	0.5	-	-	194.1	0.7	-	-	194.3	0.1	-	-
1994	197.6	1.7	-	-	198.1	0.3	-	-	198.8	0.4	-	-	198.1	-0.4	-	-	201.9	1.9	-	-	201.9	0.0	-	-
1995	200.5	-0.7	-	-	200.2	-0.1	-	-	200.7	0.2	-	-	201.1	0.2	-	-	206.6	2.7	-	-	208.6	1.0	-	-
1996	211.4	1.3	-	-	211.7	0.1	-	-	215.0	1.6	-	-	214.7	-0.1	-	-	218.4	1.7	-	-	219.2	0.4	-	-
1997	219.3	0.0	-	-	222.3	1.4	-	-	223.8	0.7	222.3	-0.7	225.6	1.5	-	-	228.0	1.1	-	-	226.1	-0.8	-	-

Source: U.S. Department of Labor, Bureau of Labor Statistics, Division of Consumer Prices and Price Indexes. - indicates no data collected for period.

CHAPTER 7

PRODUCER PRICE INDEX

PRODUCER PRICE INDEX

The Producer Price Index (PPI) is a program of the Bureau of Labor Statistics (BLS), U.S. Department of Labor. In one of its publications, BLS describes the Producer Price Index (PPI) as follows:

> The Producer Price Index . . . measures average changes in selling prices received by domestic producers for their output. Most of the information used in calculating the Producer Price Index is obtained through the systematic sampling of virtually every industry in the mining and manufacturing sectors of the economy. The PPI program (also known as the industrial price program) includes some data from other sectors as well—agriculture, fishing, forestry, services, and gas and electricity. Thus the title "Producer Price Index" refers to an entire "family" or system of indexes. (Reference 1, p. 125.)

Description of the PPI

The PPI covers nearly 500 mining and manufacturing industries and about 8,000 specific products and product categories. More than 3,000 commodity prices are included, organized by type of product and end use. Data are reported by product groupings and sub-groups as well as in large aggregates.

Important aspects of the PPI include the definition of *price*, the selection of a *sample universe*, *data collection*, and the analytical management of the collected data, including the use of *weights*. Data are expressed as an index; the base year at present (1996) is 1982, meaning that prices for 1982 are indexed at 100.

Price. Price is defined as "the net revenue accruing to a specified producing establishment from a specified kind of buyer for a specified product shipped under specified transaction terms on a specified day of the month." (Reference 1). Under this definition, companies voluntarily providing pricing information to the BLS thus report on *actual* shipments in a given month rather than average price levels. Prices exclude taxes paid but reflect discounts, low-interest financing, and other forms of incentives, rebates, and the like.

Sampling. Samples are chosen from each industry surveyed using Unemployment Insurance System data for identifying establishments—because virtually all employers are required to report to the system. Establishments are stratified, meaning that they are assigned to groups with like characteristics within an industry. Within strata, units are ordered by size. The number of units required for the sample is selected within each stratum based on employment. Selection of each establishment is then accomplished systematically with a probability of selection proportionate to its size.

Data Collection. Data are collected by companies in the sample on a voluntary basis. Within each establishment, a portion of the transactions is selected by the BLS field representative; these transactions are then priced every month. The selection of the transactions is also made systematically so that the probability of a product or commodity being selected is proportional to its relative importance to the reporting unit.

Weights. In order to create price indexes for aggregations of products, price indexes for individual products/commodities must be combined to form a composite index. This is accomplished by giving each component a weight appropriate to its importance in the aggregate as a whole. Industrial products are weighted by their proportion of total industry shipments as measured by the Standard Industrial Classification (SIC) system and reported by the *Census of Manufactures*. Commodities are weighted based on gross value of shipments data.

Base of Index. The index shows prices relative to 1982, which is defined as 100. Changes in the index are usually expressed as increases or decreases in percent, derived by the following formula:

((Current Index / Previous Index) - 1) x 100.

If the current index is 220.5 and the last index is 219.7, the formula produces a 0.36% change. This is the actual price increase from the last measured index to the current index.

This brief description hides much of the complexity of the PPI. For more details, the reader is referred to Reference 1. In summary, the methodology used is designed to present an accurate picture of price movements. The accuracy of the index is dependent on voluntary reporting; however, price definitions, sampling, and analytical factors are designed to take into account producers of all sizes operating in all kinds of markets and geographies; prices are actual, excluding taxes but including sales incentives; industrial establishments as well as products and commodities are selected to reflect, in the index, in proportion to their relative importance overall.

History of the PPI

The PPI (then called the Wholesale Price Index or WPI), was first published in 1902 and covered the 1890-1901 period. The WPI was initially an average of prices. Weighting of components was first incorporated in 1914. Major sample expansions and reclassifications took place in 1952 and 1967. In 1978, the index was renamed Producer Price Index in recognition of the fact that the meaning of the word "wholesale"—which had been understood earlier to mean goods sold in large quantities—had come to mean prices charged by wholesalers, jobbers, and distributors. The PPI is based on prices received by producers from the party that makes the first purchase, be that a distributor, a retailer, or the final consumer. The last comprehensive revision of the PPI, begun in 1978, culminated in January 1986 with the introduction of the current methods of price definition, sampling, data collection, and analysis.

Uses of the PPI

The PPI is widely used by government, industry, labor organization, and in the academic sector. It is an early measure of inflation—because producer sales predate retail sales; the latter form the backbone of the Consumer Price Index (CPI). The CPI, however, does not mirror the movements of the PPI at some lag in time. The PPI excludes imported goods, the CPI does not; the CPI includes services, the PPI largely does not. The CPI does not directly include the prices of capital equipment (industrial tooling and the like);the PPI does. Sharp swings in the prices of goods and other items may not reflect in consumer prices in the same way—because distributors and retailers absorb price rises/drops rather than cause wide price swings at the consumer level. The PPI is used in the construction of the implicit GNP deflator. In addition to the use of the index for analytical purposes in industry, it is used in contracts in price escalation clauses and in inventory valuation.

Presentation of Data

Six summary tables of the Producer Price Index are presented in Chapter 4, Other Cyclic Indicators, in the section on Prices and Productivity. In this chapter, 120 detailed PPI tables are shown. The first four tables show annual averages for 15 major product and commodity groupings and 100 subdivisions from 1926 to

1995. Thereafter, monthly data, from 1913 or a later date to 1995 are shown, first by the major group ("Farm Products") and then followed by the next level of detail provided by the PPI ("Fruits & Melons, Fresh/Dry Vegetables & Nuts," "Grains," "Livestock," etc.). All tables show a 1982 base (1982 = 100). Percent changes in the index from month to month are precalculated.

Bibliography

1. U.S. Department of Labor, Bureau of Labor Statistics. *BLS Handbook of Methods*, Bulletin 2285, 1987. Washington, D.C.

Producer Price Index
Annual Averages, 1926-1934
Base 1982 = 100

Columns headed % show percentile change in the index from the previous period for which an index is available.

	1926 Index	%	1927 Index	%	1928 Index	%	1929 Index	%	1930 Index	%	1931 Index	%	1932 Index	%	1933 Index	%	1934 Index	%
Farm Products	25.3	-	25.1	-0.8	26.7	6.4	26.4	-1.1	22.4	-15.2	16.4	-26.8	12.2	-25.6	13.0	6.6	16.5	26.9
Fruits & Melons, Fresh/Dry Vegetables & Nuts	27.0	-	25.8	-4.4	25.6	-0.8	25.7	0.4	25.8	0.4	18.5	-28.3	14.3	-22.7	15.5	8.4	16.9	9.0
Grains	33.7	-	34.0	0.9	36.0	5.9	32.8	-8.9	26.4	-19.5	17.9	-32.2	13.3	-25.7	17.9	34.6	25.1	40.2
Slaughter Livestock	18.8	-	18.8	0.0	20.0	6.4	20.0	0.0	16.8	-16.0	11.9	-29.2	8.9	-25.2	8.2	-7.9	9.8	19.5
Slaughter Poultry	102.5	-	91.9	-10.3	98.5	7.2	109.0	10.7	88.4	-18.9	75.4	-14.7	60.0	-20.4	47.4	-21.0	53.3	12.4
Plant and Animal Fibers	45.0	-	44.0	-2.2	48.0	9.1	45.6	-5.0	32.3	-29.2	21.2	-34.4	15.4	-27.4	19.8	28.6	26.3	32.8
Fluid Milk	19.5	-	19.9	2.1	20.3	2.0	21.2	4.4	20.6	-2.8	18.5	-10.2	13.6	-26.5	13.2	-2.9	16.2	22.7
Chicken Eggs	67.4	-	60.5	-10.2	63.7	5.3	70.3	10.4	54.1	-23.0	41.7	-22.9	37.5	-10.1	32.9	-12.3	39.1	18.8
Hay, Hayseeds and Oilseeds	29.5	-	26.2	-11.2	28.9	10.3	30.4	5.2	27.7	-8.9	21.1	-23.8	15.4	-27.0	16.0	3.9	23.3	45.6
Other Farm Products	13.2	-	13.1	-0.8	14.8	13.0	14.4	-2.7	9.7	-32.6	6.8	-29.9	6.0	-11.8	6.6	10.0	8.2	24.2
Processed Foods and Feeds	-	-	-		-		-		-		-		-		-		-	
Cereal and Bakery Products	18.8	-	17.8	-5.3	17.6	-1.1	16.5	-6.3	15.3	-7.3	13.8	-9.8	12.5	-9.4	14.1	12.8	16.7	18.4
Meats, Poultry, and Fish	17.5	-	16.2	-7.4	18.7	15.4	19.1	2.1	17.2	-9.9	13.2	-23.3	10.2	-22.7	8.8	-13.7	11.0	25.0
Dairy Products	17.5	-	18.1	3.4	18.4	1.7	18.4	0.0	16.7	-9.2	14.3	-14.4	10.7	-25.2	10.6	-0.9	12.7	19.8
Processed Fruits and Vegetables	20.3	-	20.1	-1.0	21.5	7.0	22.4	4.2	21.0	-6.3	17.6	-16.2	15.7	-10.8	15.9	1.3	17.9	12.6
Sugar and Confectionery	19.3	-	20.7	7.3	19.5	-5.8	17.5	-10.3	16.1	-8.0	15.5	-3.7	13.8	-11.0	14.9	8.0	14.9	0.0
Beverages and Beverage Materials	-	-	-		-		-		-		-		-		-		-	
Fats and Oils	-	-	-		-		-		-		-		-		-		-	
Miscellaneous Processed Foods	-	-	-		-		-		-		-		-		-		-	
Prepared Animal Feeds	-	-	-		-		-		-		-		-		-		-	
Textile Products and Apparel	-	-	-		-		-		-		-		-		-		-	
Synthetic Fibers	-	-	-		-		-		-		-		-		-		-	
Processed Yarns and Threads	-	-	-		-		-		-		-		-		-		-	
Gray Fabrics	-	-	-		-		-		-		-		-		-		-	
Finished Fabrics	-	-	-		-		-		-		-		-		-		-	
Apparel	-	-	-		-		-		-		-		-		-		-	
Textile Housefurnishings	-	-	-		-		-		-		-		-		-		-	
Miscellaneous Textile Products	-	-	-		-		-		-		-		-		-		-	
Apparel & Other Fabricated Textile Products	-	-	-		-		-		-		-		-		-		-	
Miscellaneous Textile Products/Services	-	-	-		-		-		-		-		-		-		-	
Hides, Skins, Leather, and Related Products	17.1	-	18.4	7.6	20.7	12.5	18.6	-10.1	17.1	-8.1	14.7	-14.0	12.5	-15.0	13.8	10.4	14.8	7.2
Hides and Skins	20.5	-	24.6	20.0	30.4	23.6	23.0	-24.3	18.7	-18.7	12.3	-34.2	8.6	-30.1	13.6	58.1	14.0	2.9

Source: U.S. Department of Labor, Bureau of Labor Statistics, Division of Industry Prices and Price Indexes. n.e.c. stands for not elsewhere classified. - indicates no data collected for period or unavailable.

Producer Price Index
Annual Averages, 1935-1943
Base 1982 = 100

Columns headed % show percentile change in the index from the previous period for which an index is available.

	1935		1936		1937		1938		1939		1940		1941		1942		1943	
	Index	%	Index	%	Index	%	Index	%	Index	%	Index	%	Index	%	Index	%	Index	%
Farm Products	19.8	20.0	20.4	3.0	21.8	6.9	17.3	-20.6	16.5	-4.6	17.1	3.6	20.8	21.6	26.7	28.4	30.9	15.7
Fruits & Melons, Fresh/Dry Vegetables & Nuts	15.6	-7.7	18.4	17.9	18.9	2.7	14.2	-24.9	15.7	10.6	16.0	1.9	16.8	5.0	24.8	47.6	33.5	35.1
Grains	27.8	10.8	29.7	6.8	33.2	11.8	20.5	-38.3	19.8	-3.4	22.9	15.7	25.7	12.2	31.2	21.4	39.1	25.3
Slaughter Livestock	16.8	71.4	16.8	0.0	19.2	14.3	15.5	-19.3	13.7	-11.6	13.3	-2.9	18.0	35.3	23.7	31.7	25.4	7.2
Slaughter Poultry	71.1	33.4	70.9	-0.3	72.4	2.1	70.2	-3.0	58.5	-16.7	58.2	-0.5	74.9	28.7	86.1	15.0	97.8	13.6
Plant and Animal Fibers	25.7	-2.3	27.1	5.4	26.6	-1.8	20.4	-23.3	23.5	15.2	23.3	-0.9	29.9	28.3	38.7	29.4	40.3	4.1
Fluid Milk	17.0	4.9	17.0	0.0	16.4	-3.5	15.0	-8.5	14.2	-5.3	15.8	11.3	17.1	8.2	19.3	12.9	21.8	13.0
Chicken Eggs	50.7	29.7	48.6	-4.1	44.9	-7.6	44.1	-1.8	35.8	-18.8	38.1	6.4	50.4	32.3	64.5	28.0	76.8	19.1
Hay, Hayseeds and Oilseeds	23.0	-1.3	22.5	-2.2	26.8	19.1	22.4	-16.4	20.8	-7.1	20.5	-1.4	21.7	5.9	30.0	38.2	36.6	22.0
Other Farm Products	9.3	13.4	8.9	-4.3	10.7	20.2	8.9	-16.8	8.5	-4.5	7.7	-9.4	10.1	31.2	14.7	45.5	16.7	13.6
Processed Foods and Feeds	-	-	-	-	-	-	-	-	-	-	-	-	-	-	-	-	-	-
Cereal and Bakery Products	17.7	6.0	16.2	-8.5	16.5	1.9	14.8	-10.3	14.1	-4.7	14.7	4.3	15.2	3.4	16.8	10.5	17.6	4.8
Meats, Poultry, and Fish	16.5	50.0	15.3	-7.3	17.3	13.1	14.6	-15.6	13.5	-7.5	12.8	-5.2	15.8	23.4	19.6	24.1	19.3	-1.5
Dairy Products	13.9	9.4	14.6	5.0	14.5	-0.7	12.7	-12.4	12.0	-5.5	13.5	12.5	15.2	12.6	17.4	14.5	19.4	11.5
Processed Fruits and Vegetables	17.8	-0.6	17.5	-1.7	18.2	4.0	16.3	-10.4	15.7	-3.7	15.9	1.3	18.4	15.7	21.8	18.5	22.5	3.2
Sugar and Confectionery	16.3	9.4	16.8	3.1	16.4	-2.4	14.9	-9.1	15.2	2.0	14.4	-5.3	16.7	16.0	18.5	10.8	18.6	0.5
Beverages and Beverage Materials	-	-	-	-	-	-	-	-	-	-	-	-	-	-	-	-	-	-
Fats and Oils	-	-	-	-	-	-	-	-	-	-	-	-	-	-	-	-	-	-
Miscellaneous Processed Foods	-	-	-	-	-	-	-	-	-	-	-	-	-	-	-	-	-	-
Prepared Animal Feeds	-	-	-	-	-	-	-	-	-	-	-	-	-	-	-	-	-	-
Textile Products and Apparel	-	-	-	-	-	-	-	-	-	-	-	-	-	-	-	-	-	-
Synthetic Fibers	-	-	-	-	-	-	-	-	-	-	-	-	-	-	-	-	-	-
Processed Yarns and Threads	-	-	-	-	-	-	-	-	-	-	-	-	-	-	-	-	-	-
Gray Fabrics	-	-	-	-	-	-	-	-	-	-	-	-	-	-	-	-	-	-
Finished Fabrics	-	-	-	-	-	-	-	-	-	-	-	-	-	-	-	-	-	-
Apparel	-	-	-	-	-	-	-	-	-	-	-	-	-	-	-	-	-	-
Textile Housefurnishings	-	-	-	-	-	-	-	-	-	-	-	-	-	-	-	-	-	-
Miscellaneous Textile Products	-	-	-	-	-	-	-	-	-	-	-	-	-	-	-	-	-	-
Apparel & Other Fabricated Textile Products	-	-	-	-	-	-	-	-	-	-	-	-	-	-	-	-	-	-
Miscellaneous Textile Products/Services	-	-	-	-	-	-	-	-	-	-	-	-	-	-	-	-	-	-
Hides, Skins, Leather, and Related Products	15.3	3.4	16.3	6.5	17.9	9.8	15.8	-11.7	16.3	3.2	17.2	5.5	18.4	7.0	20.1	9.2	20.1	0.0
Hides and Skins	16.4	17.1	19.3	17.7	23.2	20.2	15.1	-34.9	17.3	14.6	18.8	8.7	22.2	18.1	24.1	8.6	23.5	-2.5

Source: U.S. Department of Labor, Bureau of Labor Statistics, Division of Industry Prices and Price Indexes. n.e.c. stands for not elsewhere classified. - indicates no data collected for period or unavailable.

Producer Price Index
Annual Averages, 1944-1952
Base 1982 = 100

Columns headed % show percentile change in the index from the previous period for which an index is available.

	1944		1945		1946		1947		1948		1949		1950		1951		1952	
	Index	%	Index	%	Index	%	Index	%	Index	%	Index	%	Index	%	Index	%	Index	%
Farm Products	31.2	1.0	32.4	3.8	37.5	15.7	45.1	20.3	48.5	7.5	41.9	-13.6	44.0	5.0	51.2	16.4	48.4	-5.5
Fruits & Melons, Fresh/Dry Vegetables & Nuts	33.4	-0.3	33.7	0.9	35.7	5.9	36.0	0.8	37.4	3.9	36.3	-2.9	33.4	-8.0	35.6	6.6	44.0	23.6
Grains	42.7	9.2	43.7	2.3	52.3	19.7	71.0	35.8	67.2	-5.4	54.0	-19.6	57.5	6.5	63.6	10.6	62.9	-1.1
Slaughter Livestock	24.8	-2.4	25.8	4.0	30.4	17.8	41.4	36.2	46.7	12.8	39.1	-16.3	42.7	9.2	50.8	19.0	44.1	-13.2
Slaughter Poultry	95.3	-2.6	100.7	5.7	108.9	8.1	111.8	2.7	128.7	15.1	105.6	-17.9	96.8	-8.3	106.4	9.9	101.4	-4.7
Plant and Animal Fibers	41.0	1.7	42.9	4.6	56.9	32.6	65.7	15.5	69.7	6.1	67.1	-3.7	78.4	16.8	97.1	23.9	77.7	-20.0
Fluid Milk	22.5	3.2	22.5	0.0	27.2	20.9	30.0	10.3	34.1	13.7	27.6	-19.1	27.1	-1.8	32.1	18.5	33.5	4.4
Chicken Eggs	67.8	-11.7	73.1	7.8	70.5	-3.6	85.1	20.7	92.2	8.3	88.7	-3.8	75.3	-15.1	95.7	27.1	84.9	-11.3
Hay, Hayseeds and Oilseeds	40.5	10.7	40.3	-0.5	43.5	7.9	55.5	27.6	56.9	2.5	43.2	-24.1	46.6	7.9	53.2	14.2	51.0	-4.1
Other Farm Products	17.5	4.8	17.2	-1.7	19.7	14.5	25.3	28.4	26.3	4.0	27.3	3.8	33.6	23.1	36.4	8.3	35.9	-1.4
Processed Foods and Feeds	-		-		-		33.0	-	35.3	7.0	32.1	-9.1	33.2	3.4	36.9	11.1	36.4	-1.4
Cereal and Bakery Products	17.9	1.7	17.9	0.0	21.5	20.1	28.7	33.5	29.2	1.7	27.7	-5.1	28.2	1.8	30.5	8.2	30.5	0.0
Meats, Poultry, and Fish	18.5	-4.1	18.8	1.6	25.3	34.6	35.3	39.5	41.0	16.1	35.8	-12.7	37.9	5.9	43.6	15.0	40.5	-7.1
Dairy Products	19.3	-0.5	19.4	0.5	25.4	30.9	28.0	10.2	31.3	11.8	28.2	-9.9	27.7	-1.8	31.5	13.7	33.1	5.1
Processed Fruits and Vegetables	22.8	1.3	23.0	0.9	24.4	6.1	31.7	29.9	31.6	-0.3	31.4	-0.6	31.6	0.6	33.3	5.4	33.2	-0.3
Sugar and Confectionery	18.6	0.0	18.5	-0.5	22.0	18.9	28.9	31.4	29.6	2.4	27.4	-7.4	27.9	1.8	30.3	8.6	31.1	2.6
Beverages and Beverage Materials	-		-		-		26.6	-	27.8	4.5	28.3	1.8	30.5	7.8	32.5	6.6	33.2	2.2
Fats and Oils	-		-		-		-		-		-		-		-		-	
Miscellaneous Processed Foods	-		-		-		34.8	-	36.5	4.9	40.0	9.6	43.9	9.7	45.6	3.9	44.2	-3.1
Prepared Animal Feeds	-		-		-		55.3	-	56.0	1.3	49.0	-12.5	48.8	-0.4	53.7	10.0	57.7	7.4
Textile Products and Apparel	-		-		-		50.6	-	52.8	4.3	48.3	-8.5	50.2	3.9	56.0	11.6	50.5	-9.8
Synthetic Fibers	-		-		-		-		-		-		-		-		-	
Processed Yarns and Threads	-		-		-		-		-		-		-		-		-	
Gray Fabrics	-		-		-		-		-		-		-		-		-	
Finished Fabrics	-		-		-		-		-		-		-		-		-	
Apparel	-		-		-		95.1	-	97.0	2.0	89.9	-7.3	90.5	0.7	97.6	7.8	94.0	-3.7
Textile Housefurnishings	-		-		-		97.2	-	103.1	6.1	95.7	-7.2	99.9	4.4	111.5	11.6	100.8	-9.6
Miscellaneous Textile Products	-		-		-		-		-		-		-		-		-	
Apparel & Other Fabricated Textile Products	-		-		-		-		-		-		-		-		-	
Miscellaneous Textile Products/Services	-		-		-		-		-		-		-		-		-	
Hides, Skins, Leather, and Related Products	19.9	-1.0	20.1	1.0	23.3	15.9	31.7	36.1	32.1	1.3	30.4	-5.3	32.9	8.2	37.7	14.6	30.5	-19.1
Hides and Skins	22.4	-4.7	23.9	6.7	30.3	26.8	47.6	57.1	44.5	-6.5	38.8	-12.8	45.0	16.0	51.9	15.3	27.5	-47.0

Source: U.S. Department of Labor, Bureau of Labor Statistics, Division of Industry Prices and Price Indexes. n.e.c. stands for not elsewhere classified. - indicates no data collected for period or unavailable.

Producer Price Index
Annual Averages, 1953-1961
Base 1982 = 100

Columns headed % show percentile change in the index from the previous period for which an index is available.

	1953		1954		1955		1956		1957		1958		1959		1960		1961	
	Index	%	Index	%	Index	%	Index	%	Index	%	Index	%	Index	%	Index	%	Index	%
Farm Products	43.8	-9.5	43.2	-1.4	40.5	-6.3	40.0	-1.2	41.1	2.8	42.9	4.4	40.2	-6.3	40.1	-0.2	39.7	-1.0
Fruits & Melons, Fresh/Dry Vegetables & Nuts	36.7	-16.6	36.3	-1.1	38.1	5.0	38.1	0.0	37.9	-0.5	41.0	8.2	37.6	-8.3	39.0	3.7	36.3	-6.9
Grains	57.8	-8.1	58.6	1.4	55.8	-4.8	55.8	0.0	53.9	-3.4	50.9	-5.6	49.5	-2.8	48.5	-2.0	49.2	1.4
Slaughter Livestock	37.5	-15.0	37.0	-1.3	31.8	-14.1	30.6	-3.8	35.3	15.4	41.6	17.8	38.2	-8.2	36.6	-4.2	36.0	-1.6
Slaughter Poultry	100.5	-0.9	81.8	-18.6	87.0	6.4	71.4	-17.9	66.4	-7.0	65.1	-2.0	59.4	-8.8	63.4	6.7	52.7	-16.9
Plant and Animal Fibers	69.8	-10.2	71.7	2.7	69.2	-3.5	69.4	0.3	70.2	1.2	68.6	-2.3	66.3	-3.4	63.6	-4.1	64.8	1.9
Fluid Milk	30.2	-9.9	27.9	-7.6	28.0	0.4	28.9	3.2	29.3	1.4	28.9	-1.4	28.9	0.0	30.0	3.8	30.2	0.7
Chicken Eggs	93.7	10.4	70.8	-24.4	76.0	7.3	72.6	-4.5	68.5	-5.6	72.5	5.8	58.1	-19.9	68.5	17.9	65.7	-4.1
Hay, Hayseeds and Oilseeds	46.8	-8.2	48.3	3.2	44.0	-8.9	42.9	-2.5	42.6	-0.7	39.9	-6.3	39.8	-0.3	38.8	-2.5	43.7	12.6
Other Farm Products	37.1	3.3	45.0	21.3	37.5	-16.7	38.6	2.9	38.0	-1.6	36.9	-2.9	34.9	-5.4	33.8	-3.2	34.1	0.9
Processed Foods and Feeds	34.8	-4.4	35.4	1.7	33.8	-4.5	33.8	0.0	34.8	3.0	36.5	4.9	35.6	-2.5	35.6	0.0	36.2	1.7
Cereal and Bakery Products	31.2	2.3	32.5	4.2	33.1	1.8	32.8	-0.9	33.3	1.5	33.6	0.9	34.0	1.2	34.7	2.1	35.4	2.0
Meats, Poultry, and Fish	34.7	-14.3	34.4	-0.9	31.7	-7.8	30.5	-3.8	34.4	12.8	39.9	16.0	36.7	-8.0	36.1	-1.6	35.3	-2.2
Dairy Products	32.3	-2.4	31.0	-4.0	31.0	0.0	31.7	2.3	32.6	2.8	32.9	0.9	33.4	1.5	34.6	3.6	35.4	2.3
Processed Fruits and Vegetables	33.1	-0.3	33.0	-0.3	33.3	0.9	34.1	2.4	32.8	-3.8	34.7	5.8	34.5	-0.6	33.8	-2.0	34.6	2.4
Sugar and Confectionery	31.3	0.6	32.2	2.9	31.6	-1.9	31.4	-0.6	32.4	3.2	33.1	2.2	32.9	-0.6	33.4	1.5	33.2	-0.6
Beverages and Beverage Materials	33.8	1.8	37.6	11.2	36.2	-3.7	37.1	2.5	37.1	0.0	36.3	-2.2	36.2	-0.3	36.1	-0.3	36.1	0.0
Fats and Oils	-		-		-		-		-		-		-		-		-	
Miscellaneous Processed Foods	43.4	-1.8	38.3	-11.8	36.9	-3.7	35.9	-2.7	35.4	-1.4	35.8	1.1	35.9	0.3	37.9	5.6	37.8	-0.3
Prepared Animal Feeds	46.9	-18.7	51.3	9.4	40.5	-21.1	38.5	-4.9	36.0	-6.5	39.8	10.6	40.2	1.0	37.2	-7.5	40.4	8.6
Textile Products and Apparel	49.3	-2.4	48.2	-2.2	48.2	0.0	48.2	0.0	48.3	0.2	47.4	-1.9	48.1	1.5	48.6	1.0	47.8	-1.6
Synthetic Fibers	-		-		-		-		-		-		-		-		-	
Processed Yarns and Threads	-		-		-		-		-		-		-		-		-	
Gray Fabrics	-		-		-		-		-		-		-		-		-	
Finished Fabrics	-		-		-		-		-		-		-		-		-	
Apparel	93.4	-0.6	92.6	-0.9	92.6	0.0	93.6	1.1	93.6	0.0	93.4	-0.2	94.0	0.6	94.9	1.0	94.6	-0.3
Textile Housefurnishings	96.6	-4.2	94.3	-2.4	94.9	0.6	95.8	0.9	96.5	0.7	92.7	-3.9	93.8	1.2	96.1	2.5	96.6	0.5
Miscellaneous Textile Products	-		-		-		-		-		-		-		-		-	
Apparel & Other Fabricated Textile Products	-		-		-		-		-		-		-		-		-	
Miscellaneous Textile Products/Services	-		-		-		-		-		-		-		-		-	
Hides, Skins, Leather, and Related Products	31.0	1.6	29.5	-4.8	29.4	-0.3	31.2	6.1	31.2	0.0	31.6	1.3	35.9	13.6	34.6	-3.6	34.9	0.9
Hides and Skins	29.8	8.4	24.1	-19.1	24.7	2.5	25.8	4.5	24.1	-6.6	25.1	4.1	39.6	57.8	29.7	-25.0	31.9	7.4

Source: U.S. Department of Labor, Bureau of Labor Statistics, Division of Industry Prices and Price Indexes. n.e.c. stands for not elsewhere classified. - indicates no data collected for period or unavailable.

Producer Price Index
Annual Averages, 1962-1970
Base 1982 = 100

Columns headed % show percentile change in the index from the previous period for which an index is available.

	1962		1963		1964		1965		1966		1967		1968		1969		1970	
	Index	%	Index	%	Index	%	Index	%	Index	%	Index	%	Index	%	Index	%	Index	%
Farm Products	40.4	1.8	39.6	-2.0	39.0	-1.5	40.7	4.4	43.7	7.4	41.3	-5.5	42.3	2.4	45.0	6.4	45.8	1.8
Fruits & Melons, Fresh/Dry Vegetables & Nuts	37.9	4.4	37.3	-1.6	40.1	7.5	39.5	-1.5	39.8	0.8	39.4	-1.0	42.0	6.6	43.4	3.3	44.0	1.4
Grains	50.8	3.3	52.4	3.1	48.4	-7.6	46.1	-4.8	50.0	8.5	47.4	-5.2	42.1	-11.2	42.8	1.7	46.8	9.3
Slaughter Livestock	37.4	3.9	34.2	-8.6	32.6	-4.7	38.6	18.4	42.2	9.3	38.8	-8.1	40.2	3.6	45.4	12.9	45.3	-0.2
Slaughter Poultry	54.3	3.0	53.9	-0.7	52.2	-3.2	55.0	5.4	58.2	5.8	52.1	-10.5	54.0	3.6	58.8	8.9	51.9	-11.7
Plant and Animal Fibers	67.3	3.9	68.7	2.1	67.2	-2.2	62.3	-7.3	56.2	-9.8	49.3	-12.3	51.5	4.5	45.9	-10.9	44.5	-3.1
Fluid Milk	29.4	-2.6	29.2	-0.7	29.6	1.4	30.1	1.7	34.2	13.6	35.4	3.5	37.5	5.9	39.2	4.5	40.8	4.1
Chicken Eggs	63.2	-3.8	62.4	-1.3	60.3	-3.4	62.1	3.0	71.6	15.3	56.0	-21.8	62.3	11.2	74.9	20.2	71.0	-5.2
Hay, Hayseeds and Oilseeds	42.9	-1.8	46.0	7.2	44.8	-2.6	46.0	2.7	50.0	8.7	47.0	-6.0	45.4	-3.4	44.5	-2.0	46.7	4.9
Other Farm Products	33.6	-1.5	32.7	-2.7	36.1	10.4	35.7	-1.1	37.1	3.9	36.4	-1.9	37.7	3.6	39.9	5.8	42.7	7.0
Processed Foods and Feeds	36.5	0.8	36.8	0.8	36.7	-0.3	38.0	3.5	40.2	5.8	39.8	-1.0	40.6	2.0	42.7	5.2	44.6	4.4
Cereal and Bakery Products	36.2	2.3	36.1	-0.3	36.3	0.6	36.7	1.1	38.8	5.7	39.4	1.5	39.8	1.0	40.5	1.8	42.4	4.7
Meats, Poultry, and Fish	36.6	3.7	34.5	-5.7	33.6	-2.6	37.3	11.0	40.8	9.4	38.8	-4.9	40.0	3.1	44.2	10.5	45.0	1.8
Dairy Products	35.2	-0.6	35.4	0.6	35.5	0.3	35.8	0.8	39.1	9.2	40.2	2.8	42.1	4.7	43.5	3.3	44.7	2.8
Processed Fruits and Vegetables	33.3	-3.8	35.3	6.0	35.6	0.8	34.7	-2.5	35.6	2.6	36.4	2.2	38.8	6.6	39.4	1.5	40.3	2.3
Sugar and Confectionery	33.5	0.9	38.9	16.1	36.7	-5.7	35.8	-2.5	36.3	1.4	37.1	2.2	38.1	2.7	40.8	7.1	42.9	5.1
Beverages and Beverage Materials	36.2	0.3	36.9	1.9	38.8	5.1	38.6	-0.5	38.7	0.3	38.9	0.5	40.0	2.8	41.3	3.2	44.0	6.5
Fats and Oils	-	-	-	-	-	-	-	-	-	-	46.5	-	44.8	-3.7	46.9	4.7	55.1	17.5
Miscellaneous Processed Foods	36.4	-3.7	37.3	2.5	38.9	4.3	40.6	4.4	40.7	0.2	40.2	-1.2	41.3	2.7	43.4	5.1	45.5	4.8
Prepared Animal Feeds	42.7	5.7	45.0	5.4	44.0	-2.2	44.9	2.0	48.9	8.9	47.3	-3.3	45.8	-3.2	45.7	-0.2	49.1	7.4
Textile Products and Apparel	48.2	0.8	48.2	0.0	48.5	0.6	48.8	0.6	48.9	0.2	48.9	0.0	50.7	3.7	51.8	2.2	52.4	1.2
Synthetic Fibers	-	-	-	-	-	-	-	-	-	-	-	-	-	-	-	-	-	-
Processed Yarns and Threads	-	-	-	-	-	-	-	-	-	-	-	-	-	-	-	-	-	-
Gray Fabrics	-	-	-	-	-	-	-	-	-	-	-	-	-	-	-	-	-	-
Finished Fabrics	-	-	-	-	-	-	-	-	-	-	-	-	-	-	-	-	-	-
Apparel	95.0	0.4	95.4	0.4	96.3	0.9	97.1	0.8	98.3	1.2	100.0	1.7	103.6	3.6	107.4	3.7	110.8	3.2
Textile Housefurnishings	98.3	1.8	97.1	-1.2	97.6	0.5	97.3	-0.3	98.5	1.2	100.0	1.5	104.2	4.2	100.8	-3.3	103.5	2.7
Miscellaneous Textile Products	-	-	-	-	-	-	-	-	-	-	-	-	-	-	-	-	-	-
Apparel & Other Fabricated Textile Products	-	-	-	-	-	-	-	-	-	-	-	-	-	-	-	-	-	-
Miscellaneous Textile Products/Services	-	-	-	-	-	-	-	-	-	-	-	-	-	-	-	-	-	-
Hides, Skins, Leather, and Related Products	35.3	1.1	34.3	-2.8	34.4	0.3	35.9	4.4	39.4	9.7	38.1	-3.3	39.3	3.1	41.5	5.6	42.0	1.2
Hides and Skins	31.4	-1.6	24.9	-20.7	25.9	4.0	32.9	27.0	41.7	26.7	27.9	-33.1	29.6	6.1	34.6	16.9	29.0	-16.2

Source: U.S. Department of Labor, Bureau of Labor Statistics, Division of Industry Prices and Price Indexes. n.e.c. stands for not elsewhere classified. - indicates no data collected for period or unavailable.

Producer Price Index
Annual Averages, 1971-1979
Base 1982 = 100

Columns headed % show percentile change in the index from the previous period for which an index is available.

	1971		1972		1973		1974		1975		1976		1977		1978		1979	
	Index	%	Index	%	Index	%	Index	%	Index	%	Index	%	Index	%	Index	%	Index	%
Farm Products	46.6	1.7	51.6	10.7	72.7	40.9	77.4	6.5	77.0	-0.5	78.8	2.3	79.4	0.8	87.7	10.5	99.6	13.6
Fruits & Melons, Fresh/Dry Vegetables & Nuts	47.3	7.5	50.3	6.3	66.3	31.8	75.8	14.3	72.4	-4.5	70.3	-2.9	75.8	7.8	85.3	12.5	90.3	5.9
Grains	47.8	2.1	48.8	2.1	87.1	78.5	122.3	40.4	106.2	-13.2	97.6	-8.1	78.2	-19.9	86.5	10.6	101.8	17.7
Slaughter Livestock	45.9	1.3	55.3	20.5	73.8	33.5	66.2	-10.3	72.9	10.1	67.2	-7.8	67.1	-0.1	85.4	27.3	100.9	18.1
Slaughter Poultry	52.2	0.6	54.2	3.8	93.5	72.5	82.0	-12.3	98.9	20.6	87.0	-12.0	91.4	5.1	104.1	13.9	101.2	-2.8
Plant and Animal Fibers	45.7	2.7	57.9	26.7	97.5	68.4	95.6	-1.9	75.5	-21.0	110.3	46.1	99.7	-9.6	95.3	-4.4	103.4	8.5
Fluid Milk	42.0	2.9	43.3	3.1	51.3	18.5	61.2	19.3	63.8	4.2	71.2	11.6	71.8	0.8	77.8	8.4	88.5	13.8
Chicken Eggs	56.4	-20.6	58.0	2.8	92.7	59.8	89.9	-3.0	89.4	-0.6	100.2	12.1	90.6	-9.6	88.7	-2.1	98.8	11.4
Hay, Hayseeds and Oilseeds	51.3	9.9	55.5	8.2	103.4	86.3	107.4	3.9	94.1	-12.4	98.9	5.1	110.1	11.3	101.4	-7.9	114.8	13.2
Other Farm Products	42.1	-1.4	45.5	8.1	53.7	18.0	59.9	11.5	61.8	3.2	81.4	31.7	118.7	45.8	100.2	-15.6	105.3	5.1
Processed Foods and Feeds	45.5	2.0	48.0	5.5	58.9	22.7	68.0	15.4	72.6	6.8	70.8	-2.5	74.0	4.5	80.6	8.9	88.5	9.8
Cereal and Bakery Products	44.0	3.8	45.2	2.7	53.0	17.3	67.5	27.4	70.1	3.9	67.8	-3.3	68.3	0.7	75.0	9.8	82.9	10.5
Meats, Poultry, and Fish	45.0	0.0	50.5	12.2	65.0	28.7	63.5	-2.3	74.2	16.9	70.5	-5.0	70.7	0.3	84.3	19.2	93.9	11.4
Dairy Products	46.5	4.0	47.7	2.6	52.7	10.5	58.8	11.6	62.6	6.5	67.7	8.1	69.7	3.0	75.7	8.6	84.9	12.2
Processed Fruits and Vegetables	41.7	3.5	43.6	4.6	47.2	8.3	56.3	19.3	61.9	9.9	62.0	0.2	68.3	10.2	73.8	8.1	80.9	9.6
Sugar and Confectionery	44.3	3.3	45.1	1.8	49.1	8.9	96.0	95.5	94.3	-1.8	70.8	-24.9	65.8	-7.1	73.3	11.4	79.6	8.6
Beverages and Beverage Materials	45.2	2.7	45.9	1.5	47.4	3.3	54.8	15.6	63.2	15.3	67.5	6.8	78.3	16.0	77.9	-0.5	82.0	5.3
Fats and Oils	58.6	6.4	54.6	-6.8	75.6	38.5	120.5	59.4	104.7	-13.1	82.8	-20.9	96.5	16.5	104.7	8.5	113.1	8.0
Miscellaneous Processed Foods	45.6	0.2	46.2	1.3	49.6	7.4	63.8	28.6	71.8	12.5	70.3	-2.1	76.5	8.8	80.1	4.7	87.1	8.7
Prepared Animal Feeds	49.4	0.6	54.9	11.1	94.0	71.2	87.1	-7.3	81.5	-6.4	92.0	12.9	96.8	5.2	93.4	-3.5	103.8	11.1
Textile Products and Apparel	53.3	1.7	55.5	4.1	60.5	9.0	68.0	12.4	67.4	-0.9	72.4	7.4	75.3	4.0	78.1	3.7	82.5	5.6
Synthetic Fibers	-		-		-		-		-		63.2	-	66.2	4.7	67.6	2.1	73.4	8.6
Processed Yarns and Threads	-		-		-		-		-		71.9	-	73.0	1.5	74.0	1.4	78.9	6.6
Gray Fabrics	-		-		-		-		-		73.0	-	72.1	-1.2	81.6	13.2	87.5	7.2
Finished Fabrics	-		-		-		-		-		81.2	-	83.3	2.6	83.3	0.0	86.2	3.5
Apparel	113.6	2.5	114.8	1.1	119.0	3.7	129.5	8.8	133.4	3.0	139.9	4.9	-		-		-	
Textile Housefurnishings	104.9	1.4	109.2	4.1	113.3	3.8	143.1	26.3	151.9	6.1	159.3	4.9	-		-		-	
Miscellaneous Textile Products	-		-		-		-		-		-		-		-		-	
Apparel & Other Fabricated Textile Products	-		-		-		-		-		-		-		77.9	-	82.1	5.4
Miscellaneous Textile Products/Services	-		-		-		-		-		-		-		-		-	
Hides, Skins, Leather, and Related Products	43.4	3.3	50.0	15.2	54.5	9.0	55.2	1.3	56.5	2.4	63.9	13.1	68.3	6.9	76.1	11.4	96.1	26.3
Hides and Skins	32.1	10.7	59.6	85.7	70.8	18.8	54.6	-22.9	48.6	-11.0	72.0	48.1	79.9	11.0	100.5	25.8	149.2	48.5

Source: U.S. Department of Labor, Bureau of Labor Statistics, Division of Industry Prices and Price Indexes. n.e.c. stands for not elsewhere classified. - indicates no data collected for period or unavailable.

Producer Price Index
Annual Averages, 1980-1988
Base 1982 = 100

Columns headed % show percentile change in the index from the previous period for which an index is available.

	1980		1981		1982		1983		1984		1985		1986		1987		1988	
	Index	%	Index	%	Index	%	Index	%	Index	%	Index	%	Index	%	Index	%	Index	%
Farm Products	102.9	3.3	105.2	2.2	100.0	-4.9	102.4	2.4	105.5	3.0	95.1	-9.9	92.9	-2.3	95.5	2.8	104.9	9.8
Fruits & Melons, Fresh/Dry Vegetables & Nuts	94.1	4.2	105.4	12.0	100.0	-5.1	103.3	3.3	109.6	6.1	102.7	-6.3	103.9	1.2	106.8	2.8	108.5	1.6
Grains	113.3	11.3	117.8	4.0	100.0	-15.1	114.0	14.0	113.7	-0.3	96.1	-15.5	79.3	-17.5	71.1	-10.3	97.9	37.7
Slaughter Livestock	98.0	-2.9	96.2	-1.8	100.0	4.0	94.3	-5.7	97.7	3.6	89.2	-8.7	91.8	2.9	102.0	11.1	103.3	1.3
Slaughter Poultry	105.3	4.1	104.8	-0.5	100.0	-4.6	107.6	7.6	125.4	16.5	117.9	-6.0	129.7	10.0	101.2	-22.0	121.5	20.1
Plant and Animal Fibers	133.6	29.2	119.2	-10.8	100.0	-16.1	111.9	11.9	112.6	0.6	97.5	-13.4	88.4	-9.3	106.5	20.5	98.4	-7.6
Fluid Milk	96.0	8.5	101.7	5.9	100.0	-1.7	99.8	-0.2	98.5	-1.3	93.7	-4.9	91.0	-2.9	91.9	1.0	89.4	-2.7
Chicken Eggs	95.7	-3.1	104.7	9.4	100.0	-4.5	-	-	117.9	17.9	95.7	-18.8	99.6	4.1	87.6	-12.0	88.6	1.1
Hay, Hayseeds and Oilseeds	116.1	1.1	128.8	10.9	100.0	-22.4	116.0	16.0	120.5	3.9	96.8	-19.7	92.9	-4.0	101.4	9.1	138.4	36.5
Other Farm Products	108.9	3.4	99.7	-8.4	100.0	0.3	102.8	2.8	104.1	1.3	103.1	-1.0	96.3	-6.6	94.4	-2.0	95.4	1.1
Processed Foods and Feeds	95.9	8.4	98.9	3.1	100.0	1.1	101.8	1.8	105.4	3.5	103.5	-1.8	105.4	1.8	107.9	2.4	112.7	4.4
Cereal and Bakery Products	93.0	12.2	100.7	8.3	100.0	-0.7	102.8	2.8	106.6	3.7	110.3	3.5	111.0	0.6	112.6	1.4	123.0	9.2
Meats, Poultry, and Fish	94.4	0.5	95.6	1.3	100.0	4.6	96.7	-3.3	98.8	2.2	95.9	-2.9	100.2	4.5	104.9	4.7	106.6	1.6
Dairy Products	92.7	9.2	98.7	6.5	100.0	1.3	100.7	0.7	101.1	0.4	100.2	-0.9	99.9	-0.3	101.6	1.7	102.2	0.6
Processed Fruits and Vegetables	83.3	3.0	95.2	14.3	100.0	5.0	101.1	1.1	107.3	6.1	108.0	0.7	104.9	-2.9	108.6	3.5	113.8	4.8
Sugar and Confectionery	119.6	50.3	102.3	-14.5	100.0	-2.2	108.6	8.6	111.7	2.9	107.9	-3.4	109.7	1.7	112.7	2.7	114.7	1.8
Beverages and Beverage Materials	90.7	10.6	96.5	6.4	100.0	3.6	102.6	2.6	106.3	3.6	107.7	1.3	114.6	6.4	112.5	-1.8	114.3	1.6
Fats and Oils	105.4	-6.8	105.7	0.3	100.0	-5.4	111.0	11.0	140.1	26.2	125.5	-10.4	96.5	-23.1	97.9	1.5	117.2	19.7
Miscellaneous Processed Foods	91.4	4.9	100.6	10.1	100.0	-0.6	102.5	2.5	111.8	9.1	114.1	2.1	116.2	1.8	119.8	3.1	122.5	2.3
Prepared Animal Feeds	107.3	3.4	109.0	1.6	100.0	-8.3	108.3	8.3	104.4	-3.6	90.1	-13.7	94.6	5.0	98.5	4.1	116.0	17.8
Textile Products and Apparel	89.7	8.7	97.6	8.8	100.0	2.5	100.3	0.3	102.7	2.4	102.9	0.2	103.2	0.3	105.1	1.8	109.2	3.9
Synthetic Fibers	83.1	13.2	96.5	16.1	100.0	3.6	96.7	-3.3	98.5	1.9	95.5	-3.0	92.5	-3.1	91.8	-0.8	97.3	6.0
Processed Yarns and Threads	88.6	12.3	99.8	12.6	100.0	0.2	100.1	0.1	103.2	3.1	102.1	-1.1	101.7	-0.4	103.8	2.1	108.0	4.0
Gray Fabrics	95.0	8.6	101.0	6.3	100.0	-1.0	101.2	1.2	105.8	4.5	104.4	-1.3	103.7	-0.7	107.2	3.4	114.0	6.3
Finished Fabrics	92.9	7.8	100.5	8.2	100.0	-0.5	98.9	-1.1	101.7	2.8	101.4	-0.3	101.4	0.0	104.2	2.8	109.4	5.0
Apparel	-		-		-		-		-		-		-		-		-	
Textile Housefurnishings	-		-		-		-		-		-		-		-		-	
Miscellaneous Textile Products	-		-		-		-		-		-		-		-		-	
Apparel & Other Fabricated Textile Products	88.7	8.0	95.8	8.0	100.0	4.4	101.0	1.0	102.8	1.8	104.2	1.4	105.5	1.2	107.3	1.7	110.4	2.9
Miscellaneous Textile Products/Services	-		-		-		-		-		-		96.4	-	98.7	2.4	105.3	6.7
Hides, Skins, Leather, and Related Products	94.7	-1.5	99.3	4.9	100.0	0.7	103.2	3.2	109.0	5.6	108.9	-0.1	113.0	3.8	120.4	6.5	131.4	9.1
Hides and Skins	103.4	-30.7	104.7	1.3	100.0	-4.5	109.8	9.8	143.8	31.0	126.1	-12.3	147.7	17.1	179.9	21.8	-	-

Source: U.S. Department of Labor, Bureau of Labor Statistics, Division of Industry Prices and Price Indexes. n.e.c. stands for not elsewhere classified. - indicates no data collected for period or unavailable.

Producer Price Index
Annual Averages, 1989-1997
Base 1982 = 100

Columns headed % show percentile change in the index from the previous period for which an index is available.

	1989		1990		1991		1992		1993		1994		1995		1996		1997	
	Index	%	Index	%	Index	%	Index	%	Index	%	Index	%	Index	%	Index	%	Index	%
Farm Products	110.9	5.7	112.2	1.2	105.7	-5.8	103.6	-2.0	107.1	3.4	106.3	-0.7	107.4	1.0	122.4	14.0	112.8	-7.8
Fruits & Melons, Fresh/Dry Vegetables & Nuts	114.6	5.6	117.5	2.5	114.7	-2.4	96.9	-15.5	106.9	10.3	104.6	-2.2	108.5	3.7	122.5	12.9	115.1	-6.0
Grains	106.4	8.7	97.4	-8.5	92.0	-5.5	97.3	5.8	94.5	-2.9	102.7	8.7	112.6	9.6	151.1	34.2	111.2	-26.4
Slaughter Livestock	106.1	2.7	115.6	9.0	107.9	-6.7	104.7	-3.0	107.0	2.2	96.4	-9.9	92.8	-3.7	95.2	2.6	96.3	1.2
Slaughter Poultry	128.8	6.0	118.8	-7.8	111.2	-6.4	112.6	1.3	122.0	8.3	124.4	2.0	125.6	1.0	140.5	11.9	131.0	-6.8
Plant and Animal Fibers	107.8	9.6	117.8	9.3	115.1	-2.3	89.8	-22.0	91.3	1.7	120.7	32.2	155.3	28.7	129.3	-16.7	117.0	-9.5
Fluid Milk	98.8	10.5	100.8	2.0	89.5	-11.2	96.1	7.4	94.1	-2.1	95.7	1.7	93.6	-2.2	107.9	15.3	96.9	-10.2
Chicken Eggs	119.6	35.0	117.6	-1.7	110.7	-5.9	94.1	-15.0	105.9	12.5	97.8	-7.6	104.1	6.4	130.7	25.6	119.0	-9.0
Hay, Hayseeds and Oilseeds	137.0	-1.0	122.1	-10.9	112.1	-8.2	111.2	-0.8	126.2	13.5	132.4	4.9	122.9	-7.2	146.3	19.0	153.2	4.7
Other Farm Products	103.3	8.3	125.3	21.3	151.6	21.0	150.6	-0.7	149.6	-0.7	149.5	-0.1	152.9	2.3	156.8	2.6	-	-
Processed Foods and Feeds	117.8	4.5	121.9	3.5	121.9	0.0	122.1	0.2	124.0	1.6	125.5	1.2	127.0	1.2	133.3	5.0	134.0	0.5
Cereal and Bakery Products	131.1	6.6	134.2	2.4	137.9	2.8	144.2	4.6	147.6	2.4	151.1	2.4	154.7	2.4	159.9	3.4	158.1	-1.1
Meats, Poultry, and Fish	111.0	4.1	119.6	7.7	116.6	-2.5	112.2	-3.8	115.5	2.9	112.2	-2.9	111.8	-0.4	116.5	4.2	118.6	1.8
Dairy Products	110.6	8.2	117.2	6.0	114.6	-2.2	117.9	2.9	118.1	0.2	119.4	1.1	119.7	0.3	130.4	8.9	128.1	-1.8
Processed Fruits and Vegetables	119.9	5.4	124.7	4.0	119.6	-4.1	120.8	1.0	118.2	-2.2	121.1	2.5	122.4	1.1	127.6	4.2	126.4	-0.9
Sugar and Confectionery	120.1	4.7	123.1	2.5	128.4	4.3	127.7	-0.5	127.9	0.2	132.5	3.6	134.0	1.1	137.5	2.6	137.4	-0.1
Beverages and Beverage Materials	118.4	3.6	120.8	2.0	124.1	2.7	124.4	0.2	124.8	0.3	127.7	2.3	133.8	4.8	134.6	0.6	137.7	2.3
Fats and Oils	112.1	-4.4	119.4	6.5	112.0	-6.2	108.8	-2.9	116.9	7.4	135.8	16.2	138.5	2.0	130.7	-5.6	130.8	0.1
Miscellaneous Processed Foods	129.4	5.6	134.2	3.7	138.3	3.1	139.2	0.7	142.3	2.2	144.3	1.4	146.2	1.3	149.9	2.5	152.9	2.0
Prepared Animal Feeds	116.6	0.5	107.4	-7.9	106.8	-0.6	108.3	1.4	111.0	2.5	111.3	0.3	109.1	-2.0	135.3	24.0	132.9	-1.8
Textile Products and Apparel	112.3	2.8	115.0	2.4	116.3	1.1	117.8	1.3	118.0	0.2	118.3	0.3	120.8	2.1	122.4	1.3	122.6	0.2
Synthetic Fibers	104.8	7.7	106.7	1.8	105.3	-1.3	103.4	-1.8	103.6	0.2	104.1	0.5	109.4	5.1	111.3	1.7	111.1	-0.2
Processed Yarns and Threads	110.4	2.2	112.6	2.0	112.6	0.0	110.8	-1.6	107.8	-2.7	108.4	0.6	112.8	4.1	114.7	1.7	113.8	-0.8
Gray Fabrics	115.2	1.1	117.2	1.7	117.4	0.2	120.6	2.7	118.6	-1.7	116.8	-1.5	121.2	3.8	121.4	0.2	121.8	0.3
Finished Fabrics	113.6	3.8	116.0	2.1	117.5	1.3	118.8	1.1	119.5	0.6	119.2	-0.3	121.7	2.1	123.6	1.6	123.9	0.2
Apparel	-	-	-	-	-	-	-	-	-	-	-	-	-	-	-	-	-	-
Textile Housefurnishings	-	-	-	-	-	-	-	-	-	-	-	-	-	-	-	-	-	-
Miscellaneous Textile Products	-	-	-	-	-	-	-	-	-	-	-	-	-	-	-	-	-	-
Apparel & Other Fabricated Textile Products	113.0	2.4	116.0	2.7	118.1	1.8	120.4	1.9	121.6	1.0	122.1	0.4	123.2	0.9	125.0	1.5	125.6	0.5
Miscellaneous Textile Products/Services	111.8	6.2	114.0	2.0	113.5	-0.4	114.9	1.2	115.9	0.9	118.1	1.9	123.6	4.7	123.5	-0.1	120.1	-2.8
Hides, Skins, Leather, and Related Products	136.3	3.7	141.7	4.0	138.9	-2.0	140.4	1.1	143.7	2.4	148.5	3.3	153.7	3.5	150.5	-2.1	154.3	2.5
Hides and Skins	212.9	-	217.9	2.3	174.2	-20.1	174.0	-0.1	184.2	5.9	206.3	12.0	215.5	4.5	191.8	-11.0	202.0	5.3

Source: U.S. Department of Labor, Bureau of Labor Statistics, Division of Industry Prices and Price Indexes. n.e.c. stands for not elsewhere classified. - indicates no data collected for period or unavailable.

Producer Price Index
Annual Averages, 1926-1934
Base 1982 = 100

Columns headed % show percentile change in the index from the previous period for which an index is available.

	1926		1927		1928		1929		1930		1931		1932		1933		1934	
	Index	%	Index	%	Index	%	Index	%	Index	%	Index	%	Index	%	Index	%	Index	%
Leather	16.2	-	17.7	9.3	20.4	15.3	18.3	-10.3	16.4	-10.4	13.9	-15.2	10.5	-24.5	11.5	9.5	12.1	5.2
Footwear	14.6	-	14.9	2.1	16.0	7.4	15.5	-3.1	14.9	-3.9	13.7	-8.1	12.6	-8.0	13.1	4.0	14.3	9.2
Other Leather and Related Products	-	-	-	-	-	-	-	-	-	-	-	-	-	-	-	-	-	-
Fuels and Related Products and Power	10.3	-	9.1	-11.7	8.7	-4.4	8.6	-1.1	8.1	-5.8	7.0	-13.6	7.3	4.3	6.9	-5.5	7.6	10.1
Coal	8.5	-	8.4	-1.2	7.9	-6.0	7.7	-2.5	7.6	-1.3	7.3	-3.9	7.1	-2.7	7.0	-1.4	7.7	10.0
Coke Oven Products	6.0	-	5.6	-6.7	5.0	-10.7	5.0	0.0	5.0	0.0	4.9	-2.0	4.6	-6.1	4.6	0.0	5.0	8.7
Gas Fuels	-	-	-	-	-	-	-	-	-	-	-	-	-	-	-	-	-	-
Electric Power	-	-	-	-	-	-	-	-	-	-	-	-	-	-	-	-	-	-
Utility Natural Gas	-	-	-	-	-	-	-	-	-	-	-	-	-	-	-	-	-	-
Crude Petroleum (domestic production)	-	-	-	-	-	-	-	-	-	-	-	-	-	-	-	-	-	-
Petroleum Products, Refined	-	-	-	-	-	-	-	-	-	-	-	-	-	-	-	-	-	-
Petroleum and Coal Products, n.e.c.	-	-	-	-	-	-	-	-	-	-	-	-	-	-	-	-	-	-
Chemicals and Allied Products	-	-	-	-	-	-	-	-	-	-	-	-	-	-	16.2	-	17.0	4.9
Industrial Chemicals	19.9	-	19.8	-0.5	19.6	-1.0	19.8	1.0	19.3	-2.5	17.9	-7.3	17.7	-1.1	17.3	-2.3	17.3	0.0
Paints and Allied Products	-	-	-	-	-	-	-	-	-	-	-	-	-	-	-	-	-	-
Drugs and Pharmaceuticals	-	-	-	-	-	-	-	-	-	-	-	-	-	-	-	-	-	-
Fats and Oils, Inedible	52.9	-	49.0	-7.4	50.5	3.1	47.1	-6.7	37.6	-20.2	25.9	-31.1	21.2	-18.1	20.9	-1.4	21.5	2.9
Agricultural Chemicals and Chemical Products	-	-	-	-	-	-	-	-	-	-	-	-	-	-	-	-	-	-
Plastic Resins and Materials	-	-	-	-	-	-	-	-	-	-	-	-	-	-	-	-	-	-
Other Chemicals and Allied Products	-	-	-	-	-	-	-	-	-	-	-	-	-	-	-	-	-	-
Rubber and Plastic Products	47.1	-	35.7	-24.2	28.3	-20.7	24.6	-13.1	21.5	-12.6	18.3	-14.9	15.9	-13.1	16.7	5.0	19.5	16.8
Rubber and Rubber Products	-	-	-	-	-	-	-	-	-	-	-	-	-	-	-	-	-	-
Plastic Products	-	-	-	-	-	-	-	-	-	-	-	-	-	-	-	-	-	-
Lumber and Wood Products	9.3	-	8.8	-5.4	8.5	-3.4	8.8	3.5	8.0	-9.1	6.5	-18.8	5.6	-13.8	6.7	19.6	7.8	16.4
Lumber	8.1	-	7.6	-6.2	7.3	-3.9	7.6	4.1	6.9	-9.2	5.6	-18.8	4.8	-14.3	5.7	18.7	6.8	19.3
Millwork	10.7	-	10.7	0.0	10.7	0.0	10.8	0.9	10.2	-5.6	8.5	-16.7	8.4	-1.2	8.8	4.8	9.2	4.5
Plywood	-	-	-	-	-	-	-	-	-	-	-	-	-	-	-	-	-	-
Other Wood Products	-	-	-	-	-	-	-	-	-	-	-	-	-	-	-	-	-	-
Logs, Bolts, Timber and Pulpwood	-	-	-	-	-	-	-	-	-	-	-	-	-	-	-	-	-	-
Prefabricated Wood Buildings & Components	-	-	-	-	-	-	-	-	-	-	-	-	-	-	-	-	-	-
Treated Wood and Contract Wood Preserving	-	-	-	-	-	-	-	-	-	-	-	-	-	-	-	-	-	-

Source: U.S. Department of Labor, Bureau of Labor Statistics, Division of Industry Prices and Price Indexes. n.e.c. stands for not elsewhere classified. - indicates no data collected for period or unavailable.

Producer Price Index
Annual Averages, 1935-1943
Base 1982 = 100

Columns headed % show percentile change in the index from the previous period for which an index is available.

	1935		1936		1937		1938		1939		1940		1941		1942		1943	
	Index	%	Index	%	Index	%	Index	%	Index	%	Index	%	Index	%	Index	%	Index	%
Leather	13.0	7.4	13.8	6.2	15.7	13.8	13.6	-13.4	14.2	4.4	15.0	5.6	15.8	5.3	16.4	3.8	16.4	0.0
Footwear	14.3	0.0	14.6	2.1	15.3	4.8	14.9	-2.6	15.0	0.7	15.7	4.7	16.5	5.1	18.3	10.9	18.4	0.5
Other Leather and Related Products	-	-	-	-	-	-	-	-	-	-	-	-	-	-	-	-	-	-
Fuels and Related Products and Power	7.6	0.0	7.9	3.9	8.0	1.3	7.9	-1.2	7.5	-5.1	7.4	-1.3	7.9	6.8	8.1	2.5	8.3	2.5
Coal	7.8	1.3	7.9	1.3	7.9	0.0	7.9	0.0	7.8	-1.3	7.8	0.0	8.3	6.4	8.7	4.8	9.2	5.7
Coke Oven Products	5.3	6.0	5.6	5.7	6.1	8.9	6.2	1.6	6.3	1.6	6.6	4.8	7.1	7.6	7.3	2.8	7.3	0.0
Gas Fuels	-	-	-	-	-	-	-	-	-	-	-	-	-	-	-	-	-	-
Electric Power	-	-	-	-	-	-	-	-	-	-	-	-	-	-	-	-	-	-
Utility Natural Gas	-	-	-	-	-	-	-	-	-	-	-	-	-	-	-	-	-	-
Crude Petroleum (domestic production)	-	-	-	-	-	-	-	-	-	-	-	-	-	-	-	-	-	-
Petroleum Products, Refined	-	-	-	-	-	-	-	-	-	-	-	-	-	-	-	-	-	-
Petroleum and Coal Products, n.e.c.	-	-	-	-	-	-	-	-	-	-	-	-	-	-	-	-	-	-
Chemicals and Allied Products	17.7	4.1	17.8	0.6	18.6	4.5	17.7	-4.8	17.6	-0.6	17.9	1.7	19.5	8.9	21.7	11.3	21.9	0.9
Industrial Chemicals	17.6	1.7	17.5	-0.6	17.5	0.0	17.2	-1.7	16.8	-2.3	16.9	0.6	17.4	3.0	19.2	10.3	19.2	0.0
Paints and Allied Products	-	-	-	-	-	-	-	-	-	-	-	-	-	-	-	-	-	-
Drugs and Pharmaceuticals	-	-	-	-	-	-	-	-	-	-	-	-	-	-	-	-	-	-
Fats and Oils, Inedible	32.7	52.1	33.5	2.4	40.7	21.5	26.2	-35.6	25.7	-1.9	23.6	-8.2	41.0	73.7	55.7	35.9	53.9	-3.2
Agricultural Chemicals and Chemical Products	-	-	-	-	-	-	-	-	-	-	-	-	-	-	-	-	-	-
Plastic Resins and Materials	-	-	-	-	-	-	-	-	-	-	-	-	-	-	-	-	-	-
Other Chemicals and Allied Products	-	-	-	-	-	-	-	-	-	-	-	-	-	-	-	-	-	-
Rubber and Plastic Products	19.6	0.5	21.1	7.7	24.9	18.0	24.4	-2.0	25.4	4.1	23.7	-6.7	25.5	7.6	29.7	16.5	30.5	2.7
Rubber and Rubber Products	-	-	-	-	-	-	-	-	-	-	-	-	-	-	-	-	-	-
Plastic Products	-	-	-	-	-	-	-	-	-	-	-	-	-	-	-	-	-	-
Lumber and Wood Products	7.5	-3.8	7.9	5.3	9.3	17.7	8.5	-8.6	8.7	2.4	9.6	10.3	11.5	19.8	12.5	8.7	13.2	5.6
Lumber	6.6	-2.9	7.0	6.1	8.1	15.7	7.1	-12.3	7.5	5.6	8.3	10.7	9.9	19.3	10.7	8.1	11.4	6.5
Millwork	9.1	-1.1	9.7	6.6	11.7	20.6	10.5	-10.3	10.3	-1.9	11.2	8.7	12.8	14.3	14.0	9.4	14.1	0.7
Plywood	-	-	-	-	-	-	-	-	-	-	-	-	-	-	-	-	-	-
Other Wood Products	-	-	-	-	-	-	-	-	-	-	-	-	-	-	-	-	-	-
Logs, Bolts, Timber and Pulpwood	-	-	-	-	-	-	-	-	-	-	-	-	-	-	-	-	-	-
Prefabricated Wood Buildings & Components	-	-	-	-	-	-	-	-	-	-	-	-	-	-	-	-	-	-
Treated Wood and Contract Wood Preserving	-	-	-	-	-	-	-	-	-	-	-	-	-	-	-	-	-	-

Source: U.S. Department of Labor, Bureau of Labor Statistics, Division of Industry Prices and Price Indexes. n.e.c. stands for not elsewhere classified. - indicates no data collected for period or unavailable.

Producer Price Index
Annual Averages, 1944-1952
Base 1982 = 100

Columns headed % show percentile change in the index from the previous period for which an index is available.

	1944		1945		1946		1947		1948		1949		1950		1951		1952	
	Index	%	Index	%	Index	%	Index	%	Index	%	Index	%	Index	%	Index	%	Index	%
Leather	16.4	0.0	16.5	0.6	20.7	25.5	31.4	51.7	29.9	-4.8	27.7	-7.4	31.8	14.8	37.0	16.4	26.6	-28.1
Footwear	18.4	0.0	18.4	0.0	20.4	10.9	25.8	26.5	27.6	7.0	27.2	-1.4	28.7	5.5	32.7	13.9	30.2	-7.6
Other Leather and Related Products	-	-	-	-	-	-	35.1	-	36.0	2.6	34.3	-4.7	34.5	0.6	39.5	14.5	35.4	-10.4
Fuels and Related Products and Power	8.6	3.6	8.7	1.2	9.3	6.9	11.1	19.4	13.1	18.0	12.4	-5.3	12.6	1.6	13.0	3.2	13.0	0.0
Coal	9.6	4.3	9.9	3.1	10.6	7.1	12.9	21.7	15.6	20.9	15.5	-0.6	15.6	0.6	15.9	1.9	16.0	0.6
Coke Oven Products	7.7	5.5	7.9	2.6	8.4	6.3	9.9	17.9	12.3	24.2	13.1	6.5	13.6	3.8	14.6	7.4	14.7	0.7
Gas Fuels	-	-	-	-	-	-	-	-	-	-	-	-	-	-	-	-	-	-
Electric Power	-	-	-	-	-	-	-	-	-	-	-	-	-	-	-	-	-	-
Utility Natural Gas	-	-	-	-	-	-	-	-	-	-	-	-	-	-	-	-	-	-
Crude Petroleum (domestic production)	-	-	-	-	-	-	-	-	-	-	-	-	-	-	-	-	-	-
Petroleum Products, Refined	-	-	-	-	-	-	9.7	-	12.2	25.8	10.7	-12.3	11.2	4.7	12.1	8.0	11.9	-1.7
Petroleum and Coal Products, n.e.c.	-	-	-	-	-	-	-	-	-	-	-	-	-	-	-	-	-	-
Chemicals and Allied Products	22.2	1.4	22.3	0.5	24.1	8.1	32.1	33.2	32.8	2.2	30.0	-8.5	30.4	1.3	34.8	14.5	33.0	-5.2
Industrial Chemicals	19.1	-0.5	19.1	0.0	19.8	3.7	23.3	17.7	24.7	6.0	22.7	-8.1	23.8	4.8	28.4	19.3	27.1	-4.6
Paints and Allied Products	-	-	-	-	-	-	-	-	-	-	-	-	-	-	-	-	-	-
Drugs and Pharmaceuticals	-	-	-	-	-	-	57.0	-	54.7	-4.0	50.7	-7.3	50.1	-1.2	51.8	3.4	50.1	-3.3
Fats and Oils, Inedible	54.0	0.2	54.0	0.0	63.4	17.4	97.6	53.9	88.7	-9.1	43.2	-51.3	52.5	21.5	67.9	29.3	38.3	-43.6
Agricultural Chemicals and Chemical Products	-	-	-	-	-	-	29.0	-	30.4	4.8	31.4	3.3	30.6	-2.5	32.5	6.2	33.1	1.8
Plastic Resins and Materials	-	-	-	-	-	-	37.4	-	37.2	-0.5	37.7	1.3	37.9	0.5	47.4	25.1	47.1	-0.6
Other Chemicals and Allied Products	-	-	-	-	-	-	31.7	-	32.5	2.5	28.6	-12.0	28.5	-0.3	31.8	11.6	29.7	-6.6
Rubber and Plastic Products	30.1	-1.3	29.2	-3.0	29.3	0.3	29.2	-0.3	30.2	3.4	29.2	-3.3	35.6	21.9	43.7	22.8	39.6	-9.4
Rubber and Rubber Products	-	-	-	-	-	-	-	-	-	-	-	-	-	-	-	-	-	-
Plastic Products	-	-	-	-	-	-	-	-	-	-	-	-	-	-	-	-	-	-
Lumber and Wood Products	14.3	8.3	14.5	1.4	16.6	14.5	25.8	55.4	29.5	14.3	27.3	-7.5	31.4	15.0	34.1	8.6	33.2	-2.6
Lumber	12.4	8.8	12.5	0.8	14.4	15.2	23.0	59.7	26.1	13.5	23.9	-8.4	27.9	16.7	30.2	8.2	29.4	-2.6
Millwork	14.6	3.5	14.7	0.7	16.6	12.9	21.3	28.3	25.7	20.7	26.3	2.3	28.0	6.5	31.7	13.2	31.0	-2.2
Plywood	-	-	-	-	-	-	47.1	-	53.5	13.6	46.8	-12.5	52.3	11.8	56.6	8.2	51.6	-8.8
Other Wood Products	-	-	-	-	-	-	-	-	-	-	-	-	-	-	-	-	-	-
Logs, Bolts, Timber and Pulpwood	-	-	-	-	-	-	-	-	-	-	-	-	-	-	-	-	-	-
Prefabricated Wood Buildings & Components	-	-	-	-	-	-	-	-	-	-	-	-	-	-	-	-	-	-
Treated Wood and Contract Wood Preserving	-	-	-	-	-	-	-	-	-	-	-	-	-	-	-	-	-	-

Source: U.S. Department of Labor, Bureau of Labor Statistics, Division of Industry Prices and Price Indexes. n.e.c. stands for not elsewhere classified. - indicates no data collected for period or unavailable.

Producer Price Index
Annual Averages, 1953-1961
Base 1982 = 100

Columns headed % show percentile change in the index from the previous period for which an index is available.

	1953		1954		1955		1956		1957		1958		1959		1960		1961	
	Index	%	Index	%	Index	%	Index	%	Index	%	Index	%	Index	%	Index	%	Index	%
Leather	27.7	4.1	25.3	-8.7	25.1	-0.8	27.1	8.0	26.8	-1.1	27.4	2.2	33.2	21.2	30.1	-9.3	30.9	2.7
Footwear	30.1	-0.3	30.1	0.0	30.2	0.3	32.1	6.3	32.6	1.6	32.9	0.9	34.9	6.1	35.8	2.6	35.9	0.3
Other Leather and Related Products	34.9	-1.4	34.1	-2.3	33.7	-1.2	34.6	2.7	34.4	-0.6	34.2	-0.6	38.3	12.0	37.2	-2.9	36.8	-1.1
Fuels and Related Products and Power	13.4	3.1	13.2	-1.5	13.2	0.0	13.6	3.0	14.3	5.1	13.7	-4.2	13.7	0.0	13.9	1.5	14.0	0.7
Coal	16.6	3.8	15.6	-6.0	15.4	-1.3	16.8	9.1	18.3	8.9	18.0	-1.6	18.0	0.0	17.9	-0.6	17.7	-1.1
Coke Oven Products	15.5	5.4	15.6	0.6	15.9	1.9	17.6	10.7	19.0	8.0	19.0	0.0	19.9	4.7	20.0	0.5	20.0	0.0
Gas Fuels	-	-	-	-	-	-	-	-	-	-	7.2	-	7.8	8.3	8.2	5.1	8.4	2.4
Electric Power	-	-	-	-	-	-	-	-	-	-	24.5	-	24.6	0.4	24.9	1.2	25.0	0.4
Utility Natural Gas	-	-	-	-	-	-	-	-	-	-	-	-	-	-	-	-	-	-
Crude Petroleum (domestic production)	-	-	-	-	-	-	-	-	-	-	-	-	-	-	-	-	-	-
Petroleum Products, Refined	12.2	2.5	11.8	-3.3	12.1	2.5	12.8	5.8	13.7	7.0	12.5	-8.8	12.4	-0.8	12.5	0.8	12.8	2.4
Petroleum and Coal Products, n.e.c.	-	-	-	-	-	-	-	-	-	-	-	-	-	-	-	-	-	-
Chemicals and Allied Products	33.4	1.2	33.8	1.2	33.7	-0.3	33.9	0.6	34.6	2.1	34.9	0.9	34.8	-0.3	34.8	0.0	34.5	-0.9
Industrial Chemicals	27.7	2.2	27.7	0.0	27.9	0.7	28.6	2.5	29.1	1.7	29.1	0.0	29.2	0.3	29.3	0.3	28.6	-2.4
Paints and Allied Products	-	-	-	-	-	-	-	-	-	-	-	-	-	-	-	-	-	-
Drugs and Pharmaceuticals	50.3	0.4	50.8	1.0	50.3	-1.0	49.9	-0.8	50.6	1.4	50.9	0.6	50.5	-0.8	50.7	0.4	49.8	-1.8
Fats and Oils, Inedible	40.3	5.2	44.2	9.7	43.3	-2.0	43.0	-0.7	46.9	9.1	47.9	2.1	43.3	-9.6	37.5	-13.4	40.3	7.5
Agricultural Chemicals and Chemical Products	33.0	-0.3	33.2	0.6	33.0	-0.6	32.5	-1.5	32.6	0.3	33.2	1.8	33.3	0.3	33.7	1.2	33.8	0.3
Plastic Resins and Materials	47.1	0.0	46.8	-0.6	44.6	-4.7	40.5	-9.2	40.6	0.2	40.0	-1.5	38.3	-4.3	38.2	-0.3	36.5	-4.5
Other Chemicals and Allied Products	29.7	0.0	31.2	5.1	31.5	1.0	32.4	2.9	33.6	3.7	34.3	2.1	34.6	0.9	34.7	0.3	35.0	0.9
Rubber and Plastic Products	36.9	-6.8	37.5	1.6	42.4	13.1	43.0	1.4	42.8	-0.5	42.8	0.0	42.6	-0.5	42.7	0.2	41.1	-3.7
Rubber and Rubber Products	-	-	-	-	-	-	-	-	-	-	-	-	-	-	-	-	-	-
Plastic Products	-	-	-	-	-	-	-	-	-	-	-	-	-	-	-	-	-	-
Lumber and Wood Products	33.1	-0.3	32.5	-1.8	34.1	4.9	34.6	1.5	32.8	-5.2	32.5	-0.9	34.7	6.8	33.5	-3.5	32.0	-4.5
Lumber	29.1	-1.0	28.6	-1.7	30.4	6.3	31.1	2.3	29.2	-6.1	28.8	-1.4	31.0	7.6	29.6	-4.5	28.1	-5.1
Millwork	32.1	3.5	31.8	-0.9	31.4	-1.3	31.5	0.3	31.3	-0.6	31.2	-0.3	33.1	6.1	33.3	0.6	32.5	-2.4
Plywood	53.8	4.3	50.7	-5.8	51.9	2.4	50.0	-3.7	47.4	-5.2	47.8	0.8	49.8	4.2	47.2	-5.2	46.2	-2.1
Other Wood Products	-	-	-	-	-	-	-	-	-	-	-	-	-	-	-	-	-	-
Logs, Bolts, Timber and Pulpwood	-	-	-	-	-	-	-	-	-	-	-	-	-	-	-	-	-	-
Prefabricated Wood Buildings & Components	-	-	-	-	-	-	-	-	-	-	-	-	-	-	-	-	-	-
Treated Wood and Contract Wood Preserving	-	-	-	-	-	-	-	-	-	-	-	-	-	-	-	-	-	-

Source: U.S. Department of Labor, Bureau of Labor Statistics, Division of Industry Prices and Price Indexes. n.e.c. stands for not elsewhere classified. - indicates no data collected for period or unavailable.

Producer Price Index
Annual Averages, 1962-1970
Base 1982 = 100

Columns headed % show percentile change in the index from the previous period for which an index is available.

	1962 Index	%	1963 Index	%	1964 Index	%	1965 Index	%	1966 Index	%	1967 Index	%	1968 Index	%	1969 Index	%	1970 Index	%
Leather	31.6	2.3	29.7	-6.0	30.0	1.0	31.5	5.0	35.3	12.1	32.1	-9.1	32.8	2.2	34.9	6.4	34.6	-0.9
Footwear	36.3	1.1	36.2	-0.3	36.3	0.3	37.0	1.9	39.5	6.8	40.8	3.3	42.8	4.9	44.7	4.4	46.2	3.4
Other Leather and Related Products	37.2	1.1	37.1	-0.3	36.8	-0.8	37.8	2.7	40.8	7.9	40.4	-1.0	40.2	-0.5	41.8	4.0	43.0	2.9
Fuels and Related Products and Power	14.0	0.0	13.9	-0.7	13.5	-2.9	13.8	2.2	14.1	2.2	14.4	2.1	14.3	-0.7	14.6	2.1	15.3	4.8
Coal	17.5	-1.1	17.5	0.0	17.5	0.0	17.5	0.0	17.9	2.3	18.7	4.5	19.4	3.7	21.1	8.8	28.1	33.2
Coke Oven Products	20.0	0.0	20.0	0.0	20.6	3.0	20.8	1.0	21.2	1.9	21.7	2.4	22.4	3.2	23.6	5.4	27.6	16.9
Gas Fuels	8.4	0.0	8.7	3.6	8.5	-2.3	8.7	2.4	9.1	4.6	9.4	3.3	8.7	-7.4	8.8	1.1	9.8	11.4
Electric Power	25.1	0.4	24.9	-0.8	24.7	-0.8	24.6	-0.4	24.5	-0.4	24.6	0.4	24.8	0.8	25.0	0.8	26.1	4.4
Utility Natural Gas	-	-	-	-	-	-	-	-	-	-	-	-	-	-	-	-	-	-
Crude Petroleum (domestic production)	-	-	-	-	-	-	-	-	-	-	-	-	-	-	-	-	-	-
Petroleum Products, Refined	12.6	-1.6	12.5	-0.8	11.9	-4.8	12.3	3.4	12.8	4.1	13.1	2.3	12.9	-1.5	13.1	1.6	13.3	1.5
Petroleum and Coal Products, n.e.c.	-	-	-	-	-	-	-	-	-	-	-	-	-	-	-	-	-	-
Chemicals and Allied Products	33.9	-1.7	33.5	-1.2	33.6	0.3	33.9	0.9	34.0	0.3	34.2	0.6	34.1	-0.3	34.2	0.3	35.0	2.3
Industrial Chemicals	28.1	-1.7	27.6	-1.8	27.4	-0.7	27.7	1.1	27.9	0.7	28.4	1.8	28.6	0.7	28.4	-0.7	28.6	0.7
Paints and Allied Products	-	-	-	-	-	-	-	-	-	-	-	-	-	-	-	-	-	-
Drugs and Pharmaceuticals	48.6	-2.4	48.2	-0.8	48.1	-0.2	47.8	-0.6	47.8	0.0	47.6	-0.4	47.3	-0.6	47.6	0.6	48.2	1.3
Fats and Oils, Inedible	35.1	-12.9	37.0	5.4	44.6	20.5	51.9	16.4	47.3	-8.9	37.4	-20.9	34.0	-9.1	40.9	20.3	49.7	21.5
Agricultural Chemicals and Chemical Products	33.6	-0.6	33.1	-1.5	32.9	-0.6	33.6	2.1	33.9	0.9	34.2	0.9	32.9	-3.8	29.6	-10.0	30.3	2.4
Plastic Resins and Materials	36.3	-0.5	35.6	-1.9	35.3	-0.8	35.0	-0.8	35.3	0.9	35.3	0.0	32.4	-8.2	31.9	-1.5	32.0	0.3
Other Chemicals and Allied Products	34.9	-0.3	35.3	1.1	35.6	0.8	36.0	1.1	36.4	1.1	37.0	1.6	37.6	1.6	38.6	2.7	40.2	4.1
Rubber and Plastic Products	39.9	-2.9	40.1	0.5	39.6	-1.2	39.7	0.3	40.5	2.0	41.4	2.2	42.8	3.4	43.6	1.9	44.9	3.0
Rubber and Rubber Products	-	-	-	-	-	-	-	-	-	-	37.3	-	38.6	3.5	39.3	1.8	41.1	4.6
Plastic Products	-	-	-	-	-	-	-	-	-	-	-	-	-	-	-	-	-	-
Lumber and Wood Products	32.2	0.6	32.8	1.9	33.5	2.1	33.7	0.6	35.2	4.5	35.1	-0.3	39.8	13.4	44.0	10.6	39.9	-9.3
Lumber	28.6	1.8	29.3	2.4	29.9	2.0	30.2	1.0	32.2	6.6	32.2	0.0	37.8	17.4	42.3	11.9	36.6	-13.5
Millwork	32.5	0.0	33.2	2.2	34.6	4.2	34.4	-0.6	35.1	2.0	35.8	2.0	37.9	5.9	42.2	11.3	41.5	-1.7
Plywood	44.6	-3.5	45.1	1.1	44.6	-1.1	44.6	0.0	44.8	0.4	43.1	-3.8	49.8	15.5	52.8	6.0	46.7	-11.6
Other Wood Products	-	-	-	-	-	-	-	-	41.6	-	42.3	1.7	44.4	5.0	47.7	7.4	49.7	4.2
Logs, Bolts, Timber and Pulpwood	-	-	-	-	-	-	-	-	-	-	-	-	-	-	-	-	-	-
Prefabricated Wood Buildings & Components	-	-	-	-	-	-	-	-	-	-	-	-	-	-	-	-	-	-
Treated Wood and Contract Wood Preserving	-	-	-	-	-	-	-	-	-	-	-	-	-	-	-	-	-	-

Source: U.S. Department of Labor, Bureau of Labor Statistics, Division of Industry Prices and Price Indexes. n.e.c. stands for not elsewhere classified. - indicates no data collected for period or unavailable.

Producer Price Index
Annual Averages, 1971-1979
Base 1982 = 100

Columns headed % show percentile change in the index from the previous period for which an index is available.

	1971		1972		1973		1974		1975		1976		1977		1978		1979	
	Index	%	Index	%	Index	%	Index	%	Index	%	Index	%	Index	%	Index	%	Index	%
Leather	36.2	4.6	45.1	24.6	51.4	14.0	49.6	-3.5	48.7	-1.8	60.4	24.0	64.6	7.0	76.6	18.6	114.6	49.6
Footwear	47.7	3.2	50.8	6.5	53.3	4.9	57.1	7.1	60.3	5.6	64.8	7.5	68.8	6.2	74.7	8.6	89.0	19.1
Other Leather and Related Products	43.8	1.9	47.6	8.7	52.5	10.3	55.2	5.1	57.0	3.3	61.8	8.4	66.0	6.8	71.5	8.3	82.9	15.9
Fuels and Related Products and Power	16.6	8.5	17.1	3.0	19.4	13.5	30.1	55.2	35.4	17.6	38.3	8.2	43.6	13.8	46.5	6.7	58.9	26.7
Coal	34.0	21.0	36.2	6.5	40.8	12.7	62.2	52.5	72.2	16.1	68.9	-4.6	72.8	5.7	80.4	10.4	84.3	4.9
Coke Oven Products	32.2	16.7	33.7	4.7	36.1	7.1	53.7	48.8	71.7	33.5	75.1	4.7	82.2	9.5	89.2	8.5	93.0	4.3
Gas Fuels	10.2	4.1	10.8	5.9	11.9	10.2	15.3	28.6	20.4	33.3	27.0	32.4	36.6	35.6	40.4	10.4	51.3	27.0
Electric Power	28.6	9.6	29.9	4.5	31.8	6.4	40.1	26.1	47.6	18.7	51.1	7.4	57.3	12.1	61.6	7.5	66.5	8.0
Utility Natural Gas	-	-	-	-	-	-	-	-	-	-	-	-	-	-	-	-	-	-
Crude Petroleum (domestic production)	-	-	-	-	-	-	-	-	-	-	-	-	-	-	-	-	-	-
Petroleum Products, Refined	14.1	6.0	14.3	1.4	16.9	18.2	29.3	73.4	33.8	15.4	36.3	7.4	40.5	11.6	42.2	4.2	58.4	38.4
Petroleum and Coal Products, n.e.c.	-	-	-	-	-	-	-	-	-	-	-	-	-	-	-	-	-	-
Chemicals and Allied Products	35.6	1.7	35.6	0.0	37.6	5.6	50.2	33.5	62.0	23.5	64.0	3.2	65.9	3.0	68.0	3.2	76.0	11.8
Industrial Chemicals	28.9	1.0	28.7	-0.7	29.3	2.1	43.0	46.8	58.7	36.5	62.2	6.0	63.5	2.1	64.0	0.8	74.9	17.0
Paints and Allied Products	39.5	.	-	-	-	-	-	-	60.5	53.2	64.3	6.3	68.5	6.5	71.4	4.2	78.5	9.9
Drugs and Pharmaceuticals	48.8	1.2	49.0	0.4	49.6	1.2	53.6	8.1	60.3	12.5	63.8	5.8	66.9	4.9	70.5	5.4	75.9	7.7
Fats and Oils, Inedible	50.0	0.6	43.4	-13.2	85.5	97.0	126.6	48.1	95.5	-24.6	93.6	-2.0	104.5	11.6	118.3	13.2	141.0	19.2
Agricultural Chemicals and Chemical Products	31.5	4.0	31.4	-0.3	33.0	5.1	47.1	42.7	69.6	47.8	64.4	-7.5	64.2	-0.3	67.8	5.6	73.3	8.1
Plastic Resins and Materials	31.3	-2.2	31.3	0.0	32.5	3.8	50.7	56.0	63.8	25.8	68.4	7.2	69.7	1.9	70.5	1.1	83.2	18.0
Other Chemicals and Allied Products	41.5	3.2	42.0	1.2	43.7	4.0	54.6	24.9	62.4	14.3	63.2	1.3	65.1	3.0	67.3	3.4	71.0	5.5
Rubber and Plastic Products	45.2	0.7	45.3	0.2	46.6	2.9	56.4	21.0	62.2	10.3	66.0	6.1	69.4	5.2	72.4	4.3	80.5	11.2
Rubber and Rubber Products	41.9	1.9	42.5	1.4	44.1	3.8	51.5	16.8	56.7	10.1	60.9	7.4	64.9	6.6	69.2	6.6	78.1	12.9
Plastic Products	48.5	-	-	-	-	-	-	-	68.7	41.6	71.5	4.1	74.5	4.2	-	-	83.1	11.5
Lumber and Wood Products	44.7	12.0	50.7	13.4	62.2	22.7	64.5	3.7	62.1	-3.7	72.2	16.3	83.0	15.0	96.9	16.7	105.5	8.9
Lumber	43.8	19.7	51.3	17.1	66.0	28.7	66.6	0.9	61.9	-7.1	75.0	21.2	89.0	18.7	103.7	16.5	114.0	9.9
Millwork	43.2	4.1	46.0	6.5	51.6	12.2	56.2	8.9	57.4	2.1	63.3	10.3	69.3	9.5	84.3	21.6	91.0	7.9
Plywood	49.4	5.8	56.3	14.0	66.9	18.8	69.4	3.7	69.4	0.0	80.6	16.1	91.4	13.4	101.5	11.1	107.9	6.3
Other Wood Products	50.3	1.2	52.8	5.0	63.4	20.1	70.5	11.2	68.5	-2.8	70.4	2.8	78.0	10.8	89.7	15.0	99.7	11.1
Logs, Bolts, Timber and Pulpwood	-	-	-	-	-	-	-	-	-	-	-	-	-	-	-	-	-	-
Prefabricated Wood Buildings & Components	-	-	-	-	-	-	-	-	-	-	-	-	-	-	-	-	-	-
Treated Wood and Contract Wood Preserving	-	-	-	-	-	-	-	-	-	-	-	-	-	-	-	-	-	-

Source: U.S. Department of Labor, Bureau of Labor Statistics, Division of Industry Prices and Price Indexes. n.e.c. stands for not elsewhere classified. - indicates no data collected for period or unavailable.

Producer Price Index
Annual Averages, 1980-1988
Base 1982 = 100

Columns headed % show percentile change in the index from the previous period for which an index is available.

	1980 Index	%	1981 Index	%	1982 Index	%	1983 Index	%	1984 Index	%	1985 Index	%	1986 Index	%	1987 Index	%	1988 Index	%
Leather	99.8	-12.9	102.7	2.9	100.0	-2.6	106.2	6.2	119.6	12.6	113.4	-5.2	122.9	8.4	140.9	14.6	167.5	18.9
Footwear	95.2	7.0	98.3	3.3	100.0	1.7	102.1	2.1	102.7	0.6	104.8	2.0	106.9	2.0	109.4	2.3	115.1	5.2
Other Leather and Related Products	88.3	6.5	97.7	10.6	100.0	2.4	102.2	2.2	106.6	4.3	110.3	3.5	110.3	0.0	113.0	2.4	119.1	5.4
Fuels and Related Products and Power	82.8	40.6	100.2	21.0	100.0	-0.2	95.9	-4.1	94.8	-1.1	91.4	-3.6	69.8	-23.6	70.2	0.6	66.7	-5.0
Coal	87.4	3.7	93.0	6.4	100.0	7.5	100.5	0.5	102.2	1.7	102.2	0.0	100.8	-1.4	97.1	-3.7	95.4	-1.8
Coke Oven Products	93.3	0.3	98.8	5.9	100.0	1.2	96.3	-3.7	94.5	-1.9	93.2	-1.4	88.0	-5.6	82.8	-5.9	84.9	2.5
Gas Fuels	71.7	39.8	88.6	23.6	100.0	12.9	108.1	8.1	104.5	-3.3	98.7	-5.6	83.2	-15.7	74.1	-10.9	71.4	-3.6
Electric Power	79.1	18.9	90.3	14.2	100.0	10.7	102.8	2.8	108.2	5.3	111.6	3.1	112.6	0.9	110.6	-1.8	111.2	0.5
Utility Natural Gas	-	-	-	-	-	-	-	-	-	-	-	-	-	-	-	-	-	-
Crude Petroleum (domestic production)	-	-	-	-	-	-	-	-	-	-	-	-	-	-	-	-	-	-
Petroleum Products, Refined	88.6	51.7	105.9	19.5	100.0	-5.6	89.9	-10.1	87.4	-2.8	83.2	-4.8	53.2	-36.1	56.8	6.8	53.9	-5.1
Petroleum and Coal Products, n.e.c.	-	-	-	-	-	-	-	-	-	-	100.5	-	77.1	-23.3	63.7	-17.4	66.4	4.2
Chemicals and Allied Products	89.0	17.1	98.4	10.6	100.0	1.6	100.3	0.3	102.9	2.6	103.7	0.8	102.6	-1.1	106.4	3.7	116.3	9.3
Industrial Chemicals	91.9	22.7	103.1	12.2	100.0	-3.0	97.3	-2.7	96.8	-0.5	96.0	-0.8	91.5	-4.7	95.5	4.4	106.8	11.8
Paints and Allied Products	89.7	14.3	-	-	100.0	11.5	100.5	0.5	105.1	4.6	106.7	1.5	105.7	-0.9	107.4	1.6	113.1	5.3
Drugs and Pharmaceuticals	83.0	9.4	92.1	11.0	100.0	8.6	107.6	7.6	114.2	6.1	122.0	6.8	130.1	6.6	139.1	6.9	148.4	6.7
Fats and Oils, Inedible	111.6	-20.9	110.7	-0.8	100.0	-9.7	106.9	6.9	139.1	30.1	110.6	-20.5	80.1	-27.6	92.7	15.7	110.9	19.6
Agricultural Chemicals and Chemical Products	87.9	19.9	97.4	10.8	100.0	2.7	95.9	-4.1	97.4	1.6	96.2	-1.2	94.2	-2.1	96.4	2.3	104.5	8.4
Plastic Resins and Materials	98.5	18.4	102.0	3.6	100.0	-2.0	102.8	2.8	108.9	5.9	107.5	-1.3	104.4	-2.9	110.3	5.7	132.4	20.0
Other Chemicals and Allied Products	83.1	17.0	94.1	13.2	100.0	6.3	101.3	1.3	102.7	1.4	105.2	2.4	105.8	0.6	107.0	1.1	111.9	4.6
Rubber and Plastic Products	90.1	11.9	96.4	7.0	100.0	3.7	100.8	0.8	102.3	1.5	101.9	-0.4	101.9	0.0	103.0	1.1	109.3	6.1
Rubber and Rubber Products	88.7	13.6	95.7	7.9	100.0	4.5	99.3	-0.7	99.4	0.1	98.7	-0.7	98.1	-0.6	99.4	1.3	103.6	4.2
Plastic Products	91.5	10.1	97.1	6.1	100.0	3.0	102.3	2.3	105.5	3.1	105.4	-0.1	106.1	0.7	107.3	1.1	115.0	7.2
Lumber and Wood Products	101.5	-3.8	102.8	1.3	100.0	-2.7	107.9	7.9	108.0	0.1	106.6	-1.3	107.2	0.6	112.8	5.2	118.9	5.4
Lumber	104.9	-8.0	104.6	-0.3	100.0	-4.4	113.5	13.5	112.5	-0.9	109.6	-2.6	110.5	0.8	118.2	7.0	122.1	3.3
Millwork	93.2	2.4	97.8	4.9	100.0	2.2	108.2	8.2	110.2	1.8	111.7	1.4	113.7	1.8	117.7	3.5	121.9	3.6
Plywood	106.2	-1.6	105.9	-0.3	100.0	-5.6	105.2	5.2	104.1	-1.0	99.6	-4.3	101.4	1.8	102.6	1.2	103.4	0.8
Other Wood Products	101.2	1.5	101.2	0.0	100.0	-1.2	97.6	-2.4	99.3	1.7	100.1	0.8	100.9	0.8	103.7	2.8	107.2	3.4
Logs, Bolts, Timber and Pulpwood	-	-	-	-	100.0	-	96.6	-3.4	97.0	0.4	96.0	-1.0	92.3	-3.9	101.8	10.3	117.7	15.6
Prefabricated Wood Buildings & Components	-	-	-	-	-	-	-	-	-	-	101.4	-	104.1	2.7	105.5	1.3	108.2	2.6
Treated Wood and Contract Wood Preserving	-	-	-	-	-	-	-	-	-	-	-	-	98.0	-	98.8	0.8	102.2	3.4

Source: U.S. Department of Labor, Bureau of Labor Statistics, Division of Industry Prices and Price Indexes. n.e.c. stands for not elsewhere classified. - indicates no data collected for period or unavailable.

Producer Price Index
Annual Averages, 1989-1997
Base 1982 = 100

Columns headed % show percentile change in the index from the previous period for which an index is available.

	1989		1990		1991		1992		1993		1994		1995		1996		1997	
	Index	%	Index	%	Index	%	Index	%	Index	%	Index	%	Index	%	Index	%	Index	%
Leather	170.4	1.7	177.5	4.2	168.4	-5.1	163.7	-2.8	168.6	3.0	179.6	6.5	191.4	6.6	177.9	-7.1	182.7	2.7
Footwear	120.8	5.0	125.6	4.0	128.6	2.4	132.0	2.6	134.4	1.8	135.5	0.8	139.2	2.7	141.6	1.7	143.8	1.6
Other Leather and Related Products	123.1	3.4	128.9	4.7	132.6	2.9	134.9	1.7	136.3	1.0	136.8	0.4	138.9	1.5	141.0	1.5	143.5	1.8
Fuels and Related Products and Power	72.9	9.3	82.3	12.9	81.2	-1.3	80.4	-1.0	80.0	-0.5	77.8	-2.7	78.0	0.3	85.8	10.0	85.9	0.1
Coal	95.5	0.1	97.5	2.1	97.2	-0.3	95.0	-2.3	96.1	1.2	96.7	0.6	95.0	-1.8	94.5	-0.5	96.0	1.6
Coke Oven Products	89.9	5.9	91.4	1.7	93.9	2.7	91.3	-2.8	89.2	-2.3	88.6	-0.7	92.0	3.8	95.8	4.1	95.1	-0.7
Gas Fuels	75.3	5.5	78.4	4.1	77.0	-1.8	75.9	-1.4	78.5	3.4	72.8	-7.3	65.2	-10.4	88.3	35.4	95.1	7.7
Electric Power	114.8	3.2	117.6	2.4	124.3	5.7	126.3	1.6	128.6	1.8	128.7	0.1	130.9	1.7	131.6	0.5	131.5	-0.1
Utility Natural Gas	-	-	-	-	97.2	-	98.6	1.4	104.1	5.6	104.4	0.3	98.8	-5.4	105.2	6.5	112.0	6.5
Crude Petroleum (domestic production)	-	-	-	-	-	-	58.0	-	51.4	-11.4	47.1	-8.4	51.1	8.5	62.6	22.5	57.5	-8.1
Petroleum Products, Refined	61.2	13.5	74.8	22.2	67.2	-10.2	64.7	-3.7	62.0	-4.2	59.1	-4.7	60.8	2.9	70.1	15.3	67.9	-3.1
Petroleum and Coal Products, n.e.c.	65.0	-2.1	67.3	3.5	63.6	-5.5	58.8	-7.5	66.4	12.9	65.8	-0.9	69.8	6.1	70.2	0.6	72.5	3.3
Chemicals and Allied Products	123.0	5.8	123.6	0.5	125.6	1.6	125.9	0.2	128.2	1.8	132.1	3.0	142.5	7.9	142.1	-0.3	143.7	1.1
Industrial Chemicals	114.8	7.5	113.2	-1.4	111.8	-1.2	109.3	-2.2	110.4	1.0	114.3	3.5	128.4	12.3	126.7	-1.3	126.7	0.0
Paints and Allied Products	122.6	8.4	128.5	4.8	131.6	2.4	131.0	-0.5	132.2	0.9	133.9	1.3	141.0	5.3	144.8	2.7	148.1	2.3
Drugs and Pharmaceuticals	160.0	7.8	170.8	6.8	182.6	6.9	192.2	5.3	200.9	4.5	206.0	2.5	210.9	2.4	214.7	1.8	219.0	2.0
Fats and Oils, Inedible	95.5	-13.9	88.1	-7.7	86.8	-1.5	93.0	7.1	95.6	2.8	110.6	15.7	126.9	14.7	133.3	5.0	132.3	-0.8
Agricultural Chemicals and Chemical Products	108.7	4.0	107.4	-1.2	111.7	4.0	110.3	-1.3	109.9	-0.4	119.9	9.1	130.1	8.5	133.7	2.8	132.9	-0.6
Plastic Resins and Materials	133.4	0.8	124.1	-7.0	120.0	-3.3	116.4	-3.0	117.1	0.6	122.4	4.5	143.5	17.2	133.1	-7.2	137.3	3.2
Other Chemicals and Allied Products	117.3	4.8	118.9	1.4	121.5	2.2	123.3	1.5	125.5	1.8	127.1	1.3	130.6	2.8	132.4	1.4	133.3	0.7
Rubber and Plastic Products	112.6	3.0	113.6	0.9	115.1	1.3	115.1	0.0	116.0	0.8	117.6	1.4	124.3	5.7	123.8	-0.4	123.2	-0.5
Rubber and Rubber Products	107.0	3.3	108.6	1.5	109.6	0.9	109.8	0.2	110.8	0.9	111.9	1.0	117.1	4.6	116.4	-0.6	115.8	-0.5
Plastic Products	118.3	2.9	119.0	0.6	120.8	1.5	120.7	-0.1	121.6	0.7	123.5	1.6	131.1	6.2	130.5	-0.5	129.9	-0.5
Lumber and Wood Products	126.7	6.6	129.7	2.4	132.1	1.9	146.6	11.0	174.0	18.7	180.0	3.4	178.1	-1.1	176.1	-1.1	183.8	4.4
Lumber	125.7	2.9	124.6	-0.9	124.9	0.2	144.7	15.9	183.4	26.7	188.4	2.7	173.4	-8.0	179.8	3.7	194.6	8.2
Millwork	127.3	4.4	130.4	2.4	135.5	3.9	143.3	5.8	156.6	9.3	162.4	3.7	163.8	0.9	166.6	1.7	170.9	2.6
Plywood	115.9	12.1	114.2	-1.5	114.3	0.1	133.3	16.6	152.8	14.6	158.6	3.8	165.3	4.2	156.4	-5.4	159.3	1.9
Other Wood Products	113.1	5.5	114.7	1.4	118.6	3.4	124.5	5.0	135.3	8.7	137.7	1.8	143.7	4.4	127.5	-11.3	128.3	0.6
Logs, Bolts, Timber and Pulpwood	131.9	12.1	142.8	8.3	144.1	0.9	164.8	14.4	212.3	28.8	219.1	3.2	220.4	0.6	206.8	-6.2	214.5	3.7
Prefabricated Wood Buildings & Components	110.7	2.3	113.1	2.2	118.2	4.5	122.8	3.9	132.5	7.9	141.6	6.9	147.8	4.4	150.7	2.0	156.4	3.8
Treated Wood and Contract Wood Preserving	109.7	7.3	112.6	2.6	115.6	2.7	123.5	6.8	138.1	11.8	149.0	7.9	149.2	0.1	154.9	3.8	164.1	5.9

Source: U.S. Department of Labor, Bureau of Labor Statistics, Division of Industry Prices and Price Indexes. n.e.c. stands for not elsewhere classified. - indicates no data collected for period or unavailable.

Producer Price Index
Annual Averages, 1926-1934
Base 1982 = 100

Columns headed % show percentile change in the index from the previous period for which an index is available.

	1926		1927		1928		1929		1930		1931		1932		1933		1934	
	Index	%	Index	%	Index	%	Index	%	Index	%	Index	%	Index	%	Index	%	Index	%
Pulp, Paper, and Allied Products	-	-	-	-	-	-	-	-	-	-	-	-	-	-	-	-	-	-
Pulp, Paper, and Products, ex. Building Paper	-	-	-	-	-	-	-	-	-	-	-	-	-	-	-	-	-	-
Building Paper & Building Board Mill Products	-	-	-	-	-	-	-	-	-	-	-	-	-	-	-	-	-	-
Publications, Printed Matter & Printing Materials	-	-	-	-	-	-	-	-	-	-	-	-	-	-	-	-	-	-
Metals and Metal Products	13.7	-	12.9	-5.8	12.9	0.0	13.3	3.1	12.0	-9.8	10.8	-10.0	9.9	-8.3	10.2	3.0	11.2	9.8
Iron and Steel	11.3	-	10.6	-6.2	10.6	0.0	10.7	0.9	10.1	-5.6	9.4	-6.9	9.0	-4.3	8.9	-1.1	9.8	10.1
Nonferrous Metals	16.5	-	15.3	-7.3	15.5	1.3	17.5	12.9	13.6	-22.3	10.2	-25.0	8.2	-19.6	9.8	19.5	11.2	14.3
Metal Containers	15.2	-	15.2	0.0	14.7	-3.3	14.9	1.4	14.7	-1.3	14.1	-4.1	13.5	-4.3	12.6	-6.7	14.5	15.1
Hardware	-	-	-	-	-	-	-	-	-	-	-	-	-	-	-	-	-	-
Plumbing Fixtures and Brass Fittings	26.2	-	23.4	-10.7	23.8	1.7	22.5	-5.5	21.3	-5.3	20.1	-5.6	16.4	-18.4	16.1	-1.8	16.8	4.3
Heating Equipment	-	-	-	-	-	-	-	-	-	-	-	-	-	-	-	-	-	-
Fabricated Structural Metal Products	-	-	-	-	-	-	-	-	-	-	-	-	-	-	-	-	-	-
Miscellaneous Metal Products	-	-	-	-	-	-	-	-	-	-	-	-	-	-	-	-	-	-
Metal Treatment Services	-	-	-	-	-	-	-	-	-	-	-	-	-	-	-	-	-	-
Machinery and Equipment	-	-	-	-	-	-	-	-	-	-	-	-	-	-	-	-	-	-
Agricultural Machinery and Equipment	14.1	-	14.1	0.0	14.0	-0.7	13.9	-0.7	13.4	-3.6	13.0	-3.0	12.0	-7.7	11.8	-1.7	12.7	7.6
Construction Machinery and Equipment	-	-	-	-	-	-	-	-	-	-	-	-	-	-	-	-	-	-
Metalworking Machinery and Equipment	-	-	-	-	-	-	-	-	-	-	-	-	-	-	-	-	-	-
General Purpose Machinery and Equipment	-	-	-	-	-	-	-	-	-	-	-	-	-	-	-	-	-	-
Electronic Computers and Computer Equipment	-	-	-	-	-	-	-	-	-	-	-	-	-	-	-	-	-	-
Special Industry Machinery and Equipment	-	-	-	-	-	-	-	-	-	-	-	-	-	-	-	-	-	-
Electrical Machinery and Equipment	-	-	-	-	-	-	-	-	-	-	-	-	-	-	-	-	-	-
Miscellaneous Instruments	-	-	-	-	-	-	-	-	-	-	-	-	-	-	-	-	-	-
Miscellaneous Machinery	-	-	-	-	-	-	-	-	-	-	-	-	-	-	-	-	-	-
Furniture and Household Durables	28.6	-	27.9	-2.4	27.2	-2.5	27.0	-0.7	26.5	-1.9	24.4	-7.9	21.5	-11.9	21.6	0.5	23.4	8.3
Household Furniture	22.9	-	22.3	-2.6	22.1	-0.9	21.7	-1.8	21.5	-0.9	20.1	-6.5	17.1	-14.9	17.2	0.6	18.1	5.2
Commercial Furniture	-	-	-	-	-	-	-	-	-	-	-	-	-	-	-	-	-	-

Source: U.S. Department of Labor, Bureau of Labor Statistics, Division of Industry Prices and Price Indexes. n.e.c. stands for not elsewhere classified. - indicates no data collected for period or unavailable.

Producer Price Index
Annual Averages, 1935-1943
Base 1982 = 100

Columns headed % show percentile change in the index from the previous period for which an index is available.

	1935		1936		1937		1938		1939		1940		1941		1942		1943	
	Index	%	Index	%	Index	%	Index	%	Index	%	Index	%	Index	%	Index	%	Index	%
Pulp, Paper, and Allied Products	-	-	-	-	-	-	-	-	-	-	-	-	-	-	-	-	-	-
Pulp, Paper, and Products, ex. Building Paper	-	-	-	-	-	-	-	-	-	-	-	-	-	-	-	-	-	-
Building Paper & Building Board Mill Products	-	-	-	-	-	-	-	-	-	-	-	-	-	-	-	-	-	-
Publications, Printed Matter & Printing Materials	-	-	-	-	-	-	-	-	-	-	-	-	-	-	-	-	-	-
Metals and Metal Products	11.2	0.0	11.4	1.8	13.1	14.9	12.6	-3.8	12.5	-0.8	12.5	0.0	12.8	2.4	13.0	1.6	12.9	-0.8
Iron and Steel	9.8	0.0	9.9	1.0	11.1	12.1	11.1	0.0	10.8	-2.7	10.7	-0.9	10.9	1.9	11.0	0.9	11.0	0.0
Nonferrous Metals	11.3	0.9	11.8	4.4	14.8	25.4	12.0	-18.9	12.9	7.5	13.4	3.9	13.9	3.7	14.1	1.4	14.2	0.7
Metal Containers	14.4	-0.7	14.5	0.7	13.5	-6.9	14.4	6.7	13.8	-4.2	13.5	-2.2	13.6	0.7	13.8	1.5	13.8	0.0
Hardware	-	-	-	-	-	-	-	-	-	-	-	-	-	-	-	-	-	-
Plumbing Fixtures and Brass Fittings	14.7	-12.5	16.8	14.3	17.1	1.8	16.9	-1.2	16.9	0.0	17.9	5.9	18.3	2.2	20.3	10.9	19.7	-3.0
Heating Equipment	-	-	-	-	-	-	-	-	-	-	-	-	-	-	-	-	-	-
Fabricated Structural Metal Products	-	-	-	-	-	-	-	-	-	-	-	-	-	-	-	-	-	-
Miscellaneous Metal Products	-	-	-	-	-	-	-	-	-	-	-	-	-	-	-	-	-	-
Metal Treatment Services	-	-	-	-	-	-	-	-	-	-	-	-	-	-	-	-	-	-
Machinery and Equipment	-	-	-	-	-	-	-	-	14.8	-	14.9	0.7	15.1	1.3	15.4	2.0	15.2	-1.3
Agricultural Machinery and Equipment	13.2	3.9	13.3	0.8	13.3	0.0	13.5	1.5	13.2	-2.2	13.1	-0.8	13.2	0.8	13.7	3.8	13.7	0.0
Construction Machinery and Equipment	-	-	-	-	-	-	-	-	9.3	-	9.5	2.2	10.0	5.3	10.3	3.0	10.3	0.0
Metalworking Machinery and Equipment	-	-	-	-	-	-	-	-	-	-	-	-	-	-	-	-	-	-
General Purpose Machinery and Equipment	-	-	-	-	-	-	-	-	13.3	-	13.3	0.0	13.6	2.3	13.7	0.7	13.4	-2.2
Electronic Computers and Computer Equipment	-	-	-	-	-	-	-	-	-	-	-	-	-	-	-	-	-	-
Special Industry Machinery and Equipment	-	-	-	-	-	-	-	-	-	-	-	-	-	-	-	-	-	-
Electrical Machinery and Equipment	-	-	-	-	-	-	-	-	19.6	-	19.5	-0.5	19.6	0.5	19.6	0.0	19.5	-0.5
Miscellaneous Instruments	-	-	-	-	-	-	-	-	-	-	-	-	-	-	-	-	-	-
Miscellaneous Machinery	-	-	-	-	-	-	-	-	-	-	-	-	-	-	-	-	-	-
Furniture and Household Durables	23.2	-0.9	23.6	1.7	26.1	10.6	25.5	-2.3	25.4	-0.4	26.0	2.4	27.6	6.2	29.9	8.3	29.7	-0.7
Household Furniture	17.7	-2.2	17.8	0.6	19.7	10.7	19.0	-3.6	18.6	-2.1	18.7	0.5	20.2	8.0	22.3	10.4	22.4	0.4
Commercial Furniture	-	-	-	-	-	-	-	-	-	-	-	-	-	-	-	-	-	-

Source: U.S. Department of Labor, Bureau of Labor Statistics, Division of Industry Prices and Price Indexes. n.e.c. stands for not elsewhere classified. - indicates no data collected for period or unavailable.

Producer Price Index
Annual Averages, 1944-1952
Base 1982 = 100

Columns headed % show percentile change in the index from the previous period for which an index is available.

	1944		1945		1946		1947		1948		1949		1950		1951		1952	
	Index	%	Index	%	Index	%	Index	%	Index	%	Index	%	Index	%	Index	%	Index	%
Pulp, Paper, and Allied Products	-	-	-	-	-	-	25.1	-	26.2	4.4	25.1	-4.2	25.7	2.4	30.5	18.7	29.7	-2.6
Pulp, Paper, and Products, ex. Building Paper	-	-	-	-	-	-	26.6	-	27.7	4.1	26.5	-4.3	27.1	2.3	32.2	18.8	31.4	-2.5
Building Paper & Building Board Mill Products	-	-	-	-	-	-	29.4	-	32.5	10.5	32.9	1.2	34.0	3.3	35.9	5.6	36.5	1.7
Publications, Printed Matter & Printing Materials	-	-	-	-	-	-	-	-	-	-	-	-	-	-	-	-	-	-
Metals and Metal Products	12.9	0.0	13.1	1.6	14.7	12.2	18.2	23.8	20.7	13.7	20.9	1.0	22.0	5.3	24.5	11.4	24.5	0.0
Iron and Steel	11.0	0.0	11.2	1.8	12.4	10.7	15.1	21.8	17.6	16.6	17.8	1.1	19.1	7.3	20.8	8.9	21.0	1.0
Nonferrous Metals	14.1	-0.7	14.1	0.0	16.3	15.6	22.4	37.4	24.8	10.7	23.1	-6.9	24.4	5.6	29.1	19.3	28.9	-0.7
Metal Containers	13.8	0.0	13.8	0.0	14.2	2.9	16.0	12.7	17.8	11.2	19.3	8.4	19.4	0.5	21.5	10.8	21.6	0.5
Hardware	-	-	-	-	-	-	17.2	-	18.7	8.7	19.6	4.8	21.1	7.7	23.3	10.4	23.2	-0.4
Plumbing Fixtures and Brass Fittings	19.0	-3.6	18.8	-1.1	20.1	6.9	24.0	19.4	26.1	8.7	26.1	0.0	27.4	5.0	31.1	13.5	29.8	-4.2
Heating Equipment	-	-	-	-	-	-	35.8	-	38.0	6.1	38.9	2.4	39.4	1.3	43.0	9.1	42.7	-0.7
Fabricated Structural Metal Products	-	-	-	-	-	-	22.6	-	23.9	5.8	23.5	-1.7	24.3	3.4	27.4	12.8	26.8	-2.2
Miscellaneous Metal Products	-	-	-	-	-	-	18.0	-	22.2	23.3	23.9	7.7	24.7	3.3	26.8	8.5	26.7	-0.4
Metal Treatment Services	-	-	-	-	-	-	-	-	-	-	-	-	-	-	-	-	-	-
Machinery and Equipment	15.1	-0.7	15.1	0.0	16.6	9.9	19.3	16.3	20.9	8.3	21.9	4.8	22.6	3.2	25.3	11.9	25.3	0.0
Agricultural Machinery and Equipment	13.7	0.0	13.8	0.7	14.8	7.2	17.1	15.5	19.2	12.3	20.5	6.8	21.0	2.4	22.8	8.6	23.0	0.9
Construction Machinery and Equipment	10.3	0.0	10.4	1.0	11.3	8.7	12.8	13.3	14.5	13.3	15.4	6.2	15.8	2.6	17.6	11.4	17.9	1.7
Metalworking Machinery and Equipment	-	-	-	-	-	-	14.3	-	15.4	7.7	16.2	5.2	17.2	6.2	19.2	11.6	19.5	1.6
General Purpose Machinery and Equipment	13.4	0.0	13.4	0.0	14.4	7.5	16.7	16.0	18.2	9.0	19.2	5.5	19.9	3.6	22.2	11.6	22.0	-0.9
Electronic Computers and Computer Equipment	-	-	-	-	-	-	-	-	-	-	-	-	-	-	-	-	-	-
Special Industry Machinery and Equipment	-	-	-	-	-	-	-	-	-	-	-	-	-	-	-	-	-	-
Electrical Machinery and Equipment	19.2	-1.5	19.3	0.5	22.0	14.0	26.9	22.3	28.1	4.5	28.8	2.5	29.8	3.5	34.1	14.4	33.6	-1.5
Miscellaneous Instruments	-	-	-	-	-	-	-	-	-	-	-	-	-	-	-	-	-	-
Miscellaneous Machinery	-	-	-	-	-	-	21.7	-	23.4	7.8	24.3	3.8	24.8	2.1	27.6	11.3	27.6	0.0
Furniture and Household Durables	30.5	2.7	30.5	0.0	32.4	6.2	37.2	14.8	39.4	5.9	40.1	1.8	40.9	2.0	44.4	8.6	43.5	-2.0
Household Furniture	23.1	3.1	23.4	1.3	25.0	6.8	29.9	19.6	32.2	7.7	31.8	-1.2	32.9	3.5	36.4	10.6	35.3	-3.0
Commercial Furniture	-	-	-	-	-	-	20.1	-	21.5	7.0	22.2	3.3	23.4	5.4	26.5	13.2	26.2	-1.1

Source: U.S. Department of Labor, Bureau of Labor Statistics, Division of Industry Prices and Price Indexes. n.e.c. stands for not elsewhere classified. - indicates no data collected for period or unavailable.

Producer Price Index
Annual Averages, 1953-1961
Base 1982 = 100

Columns headed % show percentile change in the index from the previous period for which an index is available.

	1953		1954		1955		1956		1957		1958		1959		1960		1961	
	Index	%	Index	%	Index	%	Index	%	Index	%	Index	%	Index	%	Index	%	Index	%
Pulp, Paper, and Allied Products	29.6	-0.3	29.6	0.0	30.4	2.7	32.4	6.6	33.0	1.9	33.4	1.2	33.7	0.9	34.0	0.9	33.0	-2.9
Pulp, Paper, and Products, ex. Building Paper	31.2	-0.6	31.2	0.0	32.0	2.6	34.1	6.6	34.8	2.1	35.2	1.1	35.4	0.6	35.8	1.1	34.7	-3.1
Building Paper & Building Board Mill Products	38.4	5.2	40.4	5.2	41.4	2.5	43.3	4.6	44.8	3.5	45.3	1.1	46.3	2.2	46.1	-0.4	45.8	-0.7
Publications, Printed Matter & Printing Materials	-	-	-	-	-	-	-	-	-	-	-	-	-	-	-	-	-	-
Metals and Metal Products	25.3	3.3	25.5	0.8	27.2	6.7	29.6	8.8	30.2	2.0	30.0	-0.7	30.6	2.0	30.6	0.0	30.5	-0.3
Iron and Steel	22.1	5.2	22.4	1.4	23.7	5.8	26.1	10.1	28.0	7.3	28.4	1.4	29.0	2.1	28.6	-1.4	28.7	0.3
Nonferrous Metals	29.3	1.4	29.1	-0.7	33.5	15.1	36.6	9.3	32.2	-12.0	30.0	-6.8	31.9	6.3	32.6	2.2	31.5	-3.4
Metal Containers	22.6	4.6	23.2	2.7	23.6	1.7	25.1	6.4	26.8	6.8	27.6	3.0	27.2	-1.4	27.3	0.4	27.8	1.8
Hardware	24.5	5.6	25.7	4.9	27.1	5.4	28.8	6.3	30.5	5.9	31.6	3.6	32.0	1.3	32.2	0.6	32.5	0.9
Plumbing Fixtures and Brass Fittings	29.4	-1.3	30.0	2.0	31.8	6.0	34.0	6.9	33.0	-2.9	31.4	-4.8	33.0	5.1	33.5	1.5	33.5	0.0
Heating Equipment	43.1	0.9	42.9	-0.5	43.2	0.7	44.6	3.2	45.7	2.5	45.3	-0.9	45.5	0.4	44.6	-2.0	42.9	-3.8
Fabricated Structural Metal Products	27.0	0.7	27.3	1.1	28.5	4.4	30.9	8.4	31.2	1.0	31.2	0.0	31.1	-0.3	31.4	1.0	30.8	-1.9
Miscellaneous Metal Products	26.8	0.4	26.9	0.4	27.4	1.9	28.9	5.5	31.0	7.3	31.2	0.6	31.2	0.0	31.3	0.3	32.1	2.6
Metal Treatment Services	-	-	-	-	-	-	-	-	-	-	-	-	-	-	-	-	-	-
Machinery and Equipment	25.9	2.4	26.3	1.5	27.2	3.4	29.3	7.7	31.4	7.2	32.1	2.2	32.8	2.2	33.0	0.6	33.0	0.0
Agricultural Machinery and Equipment	23.2	0.9	23.1	-0.4	23.3	0.9	24.2	3.9	25.3	4.5	26.3	4.0	27.2	3.4	27.7	1.8	28.2	1.8
Construction Machinery and Equipment	18.4	2.8	18.7	1.6	19.5	4.3	21.1	8.2	22.7	7.6	23.6	4.0	24.5	3.8	25.0	2.0	25.4	1.6
Metalworking Machinery and Equipment	19.8	1.5	20.1	1.5	21.2	5.5	23.2	9.4	24.6	6.0	25.2	2.4	25.8	2.4	26.5	2.7	26.8	1.1
General Purpose Machinery and Equipment	22.6	2.7	23.1	2.2	24.1	4.3	26.5	10.0	28.4	7.2	28.8	1.4	29.7	3.1	30.0	1.0	29.8	-0.7
Electronic Computers and Computer Equipment	-	-	-	-	-	-	-	-	-	-	-	-	-	-	-	-	-	-
Special Industry Machinery and Equipment	-	-	-	-	-	-	-	-	-	-	-	-	-	-	-	-	26.5	-
Electrical Machinery and Equipment	34.5	2.7	35.2	2.0	35.8	1.7	38.7	8.1	41.6	7.5	42.5	2.2	43.1	1.4	43.0	-0.2	42.4	-1.4
Miscellaneous Instruments	-	-	-	-	-	-	-	-	-	-	-	-	-	-	-	-	-	-
Miscellaneous Machinery	28.3	2.5	29.0	2.5	29.8	2.8	31.6	6.0	33.5	6.0	34.2	2.1	34.5	0.9	34.7	0.6	35.1	1.2
Furniture and Household Durables	44.4	2.1	44.9	1.1	45.1	0.4	46.3	2.7	47.5	2.6	47.9	0.8	48.0	0.2	47.8	-0.4	47.5	-0.6
Household Furniture	35.6	0.8	35.5	-0.3	35.6	0.3	37.2	4.5	38.3	3.0	38.5	0.5	38.8	0.8	39.2	1.0	39.6	1.0
Commercial Furniture	26.6	1.5	27.0	1.5	28.1	4.1	30.2	7.5	32.1	6.3	32.9	2.5	33.1	0.6	33.4	0.9	33.2	-0.6

Source: U.S. Department of Labor, Bureau of Labor Statistics, Division of Industry Prices and Price Indexes. n.e.c. stands for not elsewhere classified. - indicates no data collected for period or unavailable.

Producer Price Index
Annual Averages, 1962-1970
Base 1982 = 100

Columns headed % show percentile change in the index from the previous period for which an index is available.

	1962		1963		1964		1965		1966		1967		1968		1969		1970	
	Index	%	Index	%	Index	%	Index	%	Index	%	Index	%	Index	%	Index	%	Index	%
Pulp, Paper, and Allied Products	33.4	1.2	33.1	-0.9	33.0	-0.3	33.3	0.9	34.2	2.7	34.6	1.2	35.0	1.2	36.0	2.9	37.5	4.2
Pulp, Paper, and Products, ex. Building Paper	35.2	1.4	34.9	-0.9	34.9	0.0	35.2	0.9	36.2	2.8	36.6	1.1	37.0	1.1	38.1	3.0	39.7	4.2
Building Paper & Building Board Mill Products	44.2	-3.5	43.6	-1.4	42.7	-2.1	42.1	-1.4	42.1	0.0	41.8	-0.7	42.1	0.7	44.1	4.8	42.2	-4.3
Publications, Printed Matter & Printing Materials	-		-		-		-		-		-		-		-		-	
Metals and Metal Products	30.2	-1.0	30.3	0.3	31.1	2.6	32.0	2.9	32.8	2.5	33.2	1.2	34.0	2.4	36.0	5.9	38.7	7.5
Iron and Steel	28.3	-1.4	28.2	-0.4	28.6	1.4	28.9	1.0	29.1	0.7	29.5	1.4	30.1	2.0	31.6	5.0	34.0	7.6
Nonferrous Metals	31.1	-1.3	31.1	0.0	33.2	6.8	36.2	9.0	37.9	4.7	37.9	0.0	39.3	3.7	43.1	9.7	47.3	9.7
Metal Containers	28.2	1.4	28.5	1.1	28.7	0.7	29.3	2.1	29.9	2.0	30.4	1.7	31.6	3.9	32.5	2.8	34.3	5.5
Hardware	32.6	0.3	32.6	0.0	32.9	0.9	33.2	0.9	34.4	3.6	35.7	3.8	36.6	2.5	37.9	3.6	39.8	5.0
Plumbing Fixtures and Brass Fittings	32.5	-3.0	32.5	0.0	32.8	0.9	33.5	2.1	35.2	5.1	35.9	2.0	37.1	3.3	38.5	3.8	39.9	3.6
Heating Equipment	42.4	-1.2	42.2	-0.5	41.8	-0.9	41.7	-0.2	42.1	1.0	42.2	0.2	43.3	2.6	44.4	2.5	46.6	5.0
Fabricated Structural Metal Products	30.6	-0.6	30.6	0.0	30.9	1.0	31.5	1.9	32.4	2.9	32.8	1.2	33.5	2.1	34.7	3.6	36.7	5.8
Miscellaneous Metal Products	32.3	0.6	32.7	1.2	33.8	3.4	34.0	0.6	34.7	2.1	35.4	2.0	36.1	2.0	38.0	5.3	40.5	6.6
Metal Treatment Services	-		-		-		-		-		-		-		-		-	
Machinery and Equipment	33.0	0.0	33.1	0.3	33.3	0.6	33.7	1.2	34.7	3.0	35.9	3.5	37.0	3.1	38.2	3.2	40.0	4.7
Agricultural Machinery and Equipment	28.8	2.1	29.2	1.4	29.6	1.4	30.2	2.0	31.1	3.0	32.1	3.2	33.4	4.0	34.9	4.5	36.4	4.3
Construction Machinery and Equipment	25.4	0.0	25.9	2.0	26.5	2.3	27.2	2.6	28.1	3.3	29.1	3.6	30.7	5.5	32.1	4.6	33.7	5.0
Metalworking Machinery and Equipment	27.2	1.5	27.3	0.4	27.8	1.8	28.6	2.9	29.9	4.5	31.2	4.3	32.4	3.8	33.7	4.0	35.6	5.6
General Purpose Machinery and Equipment	29.9	0.3	30.1	0.7	30.2	0.3	30.4	0.7	31.8	4.6	32.9	3.5	34.0	3.3	35.2	3.5	37.4	6.3
Electronic Computers and Computer Equipment	-		-		-				-		-		-		-		-	
Special Industry Machinery and Equipment	26.9	1.5	27.4	1.9	27.9	1.8	28.4	1.8	29.5	3.9	30.8	4.4	32.4	5.2	33.8	4.3	35.6	5.3
Electrical Machinery and Equipment	41.8	-1.4	41.3	-1.2	41.1	-0.5	41.1	0.0	42.0	2.2	43.2	2.9	43.7	1.2	44.4	1.6	45.9	3.4
Miscellaneous Instruments	-		-		-		-		-		-		-		-		-	
Miscellaneous Machinery	35.2	0.3	35.3	0.3	35.6	0.8	35.8	0.6	36.3	1.4	37.3	2.8	38.9	4.3	40.3	3.6	42.0	4.2
Furniture and Household Durables	47.2	-0.6	46.9	-0.6	47.1	0.4	46.8	-0.6	47.4	1.3	48.3	1.9	49.7	2.9	50.7	2.0	51.9	2.4
Household Furniture	40.0	1.0	40.3	0.7	40.6	0.7	40.9	0.7	42.0	2.7	43.5	3.6	45.2	3.9	47.2	4.4	48.6	3.0
Commercial Furniture	33.4	0.6	33.5	0.3	33.7	0.6	33.9	0.6	34.5	1.8	36.3	5.2	37.7	3.9	39.2	4.0	41.6	6.1

Source: U.S. Department of Labor, Bureau of Labor Statistics, Division of Industry Prices and Price Indexes. n.e.c. stands for not elsewhere classified. - indicates no data collected for period or unavailable.

Producer Price Index
Annual Averages, 1971-1979
Base 1982 = 100

Columns headed % show percentile change in the index from the previous period for which an index is available.

	1971		1972		1973		1974		1975		1976		1977		1978		1979	
	Index	%	Index	%	Index	%	Index	%	Index	%	Index	%	Index	%	Index	%	Index	%
Pulp, Paper, and Allied Products	38.1	1.6	39.3	3.1	42.3	7.6	52.5	24.1	59.0	12.4	62.1	5.3	64.6	4.0	67.7	4.8	75.9	12.1
Pulp, Paper, and Products, ex. Building Paper	40.4	1.8	41.6	3.0	44.8	7.7	55.9	24.8	62.9	12.5	66.2	5.2	68.6	3.6	71.6	4.4	80.6	12.6
Building Paper & Building Board Mill Products	42.9	1.7	44.4	3.5	47.1	6.1	51.6	9.6	53.1	2.9	57.9	9.0	65.6	13.3	78.2	19.2	76.2	-2.6
Publications, Printed Matter & Printing Materials	-	-	-	-	-	-	-	-	-	-	-	-	-	-	-	-	-	-
Metals and Metal Products	39.4	1.8	40.9	3.8	44.0	7.6	57.0	29.5	61.5	7.9	65.0	5.7	69.3	6.6	75.3	8.7	86.0	14.2
Iron and Steel	35.9	5.6	37.9	5.6	40.2	6.1	52.7	31.1	59.3	12.5	63.7	7.4	68.0	6.8	74.8	10.0	83.6	11.8
Nonferrous Metals	43.5	-8.0	44.3	1.8	51.2	15.6	71.0	38.7	65.1	-8.3	68.9	5.8	74.1	7.5	78.8	6.3	99.3	26.0
Metal Containers	37.1	8.2	39.2	5.7	41.0	4.6	50.1	22.2	58.5	16.8	61.5	5.1	66.4	8.0	74.1	11.6	81.9	10.5
Hardware	41.7	4.8	42.9	2.9	44.5	3.7	50.2	12.8	58.2	15.9	61.8	6.2	66.2	7.1	71.5	8.0	78.0	9.1
Plumbing Fixtures and Brass Fittings	41.8	4.8	43.0	2.9	45.1	4.9	53.5	18.6	58.2	8.8	62.5	7.4	67.0	7.2	71.4	6.6	77.9	9.1
Heating Equipment	48.6	4.3	49.8	2.5	50.8	2.0	56.9	12.0	63.5	11.6	66.6	4.9	69.8	4.8	73.5	5.3	78.9	7.3
Fabricated Structural Metal Products	38.8	5.7	40.2	3.6	41.8	4.0	52.9	26.6	62.0	17.2	63.6	2.6	67.8	6.6	74.3	9.6	81.6	9.8
Miscellaneous Metal Products	42.1	4.0	44.0	4.5	45.9	4.3	55.7	21.4	64.1	15.1	66.2	3.3	69.5	5.0	75.1	8.1	81.9	9.1
Metal Treatment Services	-	-	-	-	-	-	-	-	-	-	-	-	-	-	-	-	-	-
Machinery and Equipment	41.4	3.5	42.3	2.2	43.7	3.3	50.0	14.4	57.9	15.8	61.3	5.9	65.2	6.4	70.3	7.8	76.7	9.1
Agricultural Machinery and Equipment	37.8	3.8	39.3	4.0	40.5	3.1	46.2	14.1	54.2	17.3	58.8	8.5	63.6	8.2	68.5	7.7	74.6	8.9
Construction Machinery and Equipment	35.4	5.0	36.6	3.4	38.0	3.8	44.3	16.6	53.8	21.4	57.8	7.4	62.1	7.4	67.7	9.0	74.5	10.0
Metalworking Machinery and Equipment	36.7	3.1	37.5	2.2	39.1	4.3	45.8	17.1	53.5	16.8	56.9	6.4	61.9	8.8	67.6	9.2	75.2	11.2
General Purpose Machinery and Equipment	39.2	4.8	40.3	2.8	41.8	3.7	49.7	18.9	58.7	18.1	62.4	6.3	66.4	6.4	71.2	7.2	77.8	9.3
Electronic Computers and Computer Equipment	-	-	-	-	-	-	-	-	-	-	-	-	-	-	-	-	-	-
Special Industry Machinery and Equipment	37.2	4.5	38.0	2.2	40.0	5.3	46.4	16.0	53.8	15.9	58.0	7.8	62.3	7.4	68.6	10.1	76.0	10.8
Electrical Machinery and Equipment	47.1	2.6	47.7	1.3	48.5	1.7	54.0	11.3	60.7	12.4	63.4	4.4	66.6	5.0	71.2	6.9	77.2	8.4
Miscellaneous Instruments	-	-	-	-	-	-	-	-	-	-	-	-	-	-	-	-	-	-
Miscellaneous Machinery	43.7	4.0	44.8	2.5	46.2	3.1	52.0	12.6	60.5	16.3	64.1	6.0	67.3	5.0	72.5	7.7	77.8	7.3
Furniture and Household Durables	53.1	2.3	53.8	1.3	55.7	3.5	61.8	11.0	67.5	9.2	70.3	4.1	73.2	4.1	77.5	5.9	82.8	6.8
Household Furniture	50.0	2.9	51.0	2.0	53.5	4.9	59.4	11.0	63.6	7.1	66.8	5.0	70.6	5.7	75.5	6.9	81.0	7.3
Commercial Furniture	42.9	3.1	43.6	1.6	47.0	7.8	55.3	17.7	60.5	9.4	63.0	4.1	67.5	7.1	73.1	8.3	80.5	10.1

Source: U.S. Department of Labor, Bureau of Labor Statistics, Division of Industry Prices and Price Indexes. n.e.c. stands for not elsewhere classified. - indicates no data collected for period or unavailable.

Producer Price Index
Annual Averages, 1980-1988
Base 1982 = 100

Columns headed % show percentile change in the index from the previous period for which an index is available.

	1980		1981		1982		1983		1984		1985		1986		1987		1988	
	Index	%	Index	%	Index	%	Index	%	Index	%	Index	%	Index	%	Index	%	Index	%
Pulp, Paper, and Allied Products	86.3	13.7	94.8	9.8	100.0	5.5	103.3	3.3	110.3	6.8	113.3	2.7	116.1	2.5	121.8	4.9	130.4	7.1
Pulp, Paper, and Products, ex. Building Paper	91.7	13.8	99.1	8.1	100.0	0.9	99.3	-0.7	107.3	8.1	106.9	-0.4	107.6	0.7	114.3	6.2	124.9	9.3
Building Paper & Building Board Mill Products	86.1	13.0	96.7	12.3	100.0	3.4	104.4	4.4	108.2	3.6	107.4	-0.7	108.8	1.3	111.2	2.2	113.3	1.9
Publications, Printed Matter & Printing Materials	-	-	91.4	-	100.0	9.4	106.3	6.3	112.7	6.0	118.7	5.3	123.3	3.9	128.1	3.9	134.7	5.2
Metals and Metal Products	95.0	10.5	99.6	4.8	100.0	0.4	101.8	1.8	104.8	2.9	104.4	-0.4	103.2	-1.1	107.1	3.8	118.7	10.8
Iron and Steel	90.0	7.7	98.5	9.4	100.0	1.5	101.3	1.3	105.3	3.9	104.8	-0.5	101.1	-3.5	104.6	3.5	115.7	10.6
Nonferrous Metals	115.7	16.5	108.4	-6.3	100.0	-7.7	104.7	4.7	105.1	0.4	99.6	-5.2	98.5	-1.1	108.8	10.5	133.2	22.4
Metal Containers	90.9	11.0	96.1	5.7	100.0	4.1	102.1	2.1	106.5	4.3	109.0	2.3	110.2	1.1	109.5	-0.6	110.2	0.6
Hardware	85.8	10.0	93.9	9.4	100.0	6.5	103.7	3.7	105.9	2.1	109.1	3.0	109.5	0.4	109.6	0.1	113.7	3.7
Plumbing Fixtures and Brass Fittings	88.5	13.6	96.0	8.5	100.0	4.2	103.8	3.8	108.6	4.6	111.9	3.0	115.5	3.2	119.7	3.6	128.7	7.5
Heating Equipment	87.0	10.3	94.5	8.6	100.0	5.8	102.7	2.7	106.6	3.8	109.5	2.7	113.0	3.2	115.5	2.2	119.2	3.2
Fabricated Structural Metal Products	88.8	8.8	96.9	9.1	100.0	3.2	99.6	-0.4	101.9	2.3	103.2	1.3	103.6	0.4	105.4	1.7	114.3	8.4
Miscellaneous Metal Products	88.5	8.1	95.8	8.2	100.0	4.4	100.5	0.5	104.6	4.1	107.1	2.4	107.0	-0.1	107.8	0.7	112.1	4.0
Metal Treatment Services	-	-	-	-	-	-	-	-	-	-	102.4	-	104.7	2.2	106.2	1.4	109.8	3.4
Machinery and Equipment	86.0	12.1	94.4	9.8	100.0	5.9	102.7	2.7	105.1	2.3	107.2	2.0	108.8	1.5	110.4	1.5	113.2	2.5
Agricultural Machinery and Equipment	83.3	11.7	92.7	11.3	100.0	7.9	104.9	4.9	108.0	3.0	108.7	0.6	109.2	0.5	109.6	0.4	112.7	2.8
Construction Machinery and Equipment	84.2	13.0	93.3	10.8	100.0	7.2	102.3	2.3	103.8	1.5	105.4	1.5	106.7	1.2	108.9	2.1	111.8	2.7
Metalworking Machinery and Equipment	85.5	13.7	93.9	9.8	100.0	6.5	101.7	1.7	104.1	2.4	106.6	2.4	108.4	1.7	110.1	1.6	113.5	3.1
General Purpose Machinery and Equipment	87.0	11.8	95.0	9.2	100.0	5.3	101.4	1.4	103.3	1.9	105.7	2.3	107.2	1.4	108.3	1.0	112.8	4.2
Electronic Computers and Computer Equipment	-	-	-	-	-	-	-	-	-	-	-	-	-	-	-	-	-	-
Special Industry Machinery and Equipment	84.8	11.6	94.7	11.7	100.0	5.6	103.7	3.7	107.3	3.5	110.8	3.3	114.2	3.1	117.3	2.7	121.7	3.8
Electrical Machinery and Equipment	87.1	12.8	95.1	9.2	100.0	5.2	103.7	3.7	107.4	3.6	109.6	2.0	111.2	1.5	112.6	1.3	114.5	1.7
Miscellaneous Instruments	-	-	91.9	-	100.0	8.8	105.3	5.3	106.6	1.2	109.8	3.0	112.7	2.6	115.7	2.7	118.9	2.8
Miscellaneous Machinery	85.7	10.2	94.1	9.8	100.0	6.3	102.1	2.1	102.2	0.1	103.3	1.1	104.2	0.9	105.7	1.4	108.6	2.7
Furniture and Household Durables	90.7	9.5	95.9	5.7	100.0	4.3	103.4	3.4	105.7	2.2	107.1	1.3	108.2	1.0	109.9	1.6	113.1	2.9
Household Furniture	89.1	10.0	95.4	7.1	100.0	4.8	102.1	2.1	105.3	3.1	108.5	3.0	110.3	1.7	113.0	2.4	117.6	4.1
Commercial Furniture	85.7	6.5	93.5	9.1	100.0	7.0	103.9	3.9	107.8	3.8	111.9	3.8	115.3	3.0	118.6	2.9	124.2	4.7

Source: U.S. Department of Labor, Bureau of Labor Statistics, Division of Industry Prices and Price Indexes. n.e.c. stands for not elsewhere classified. - indicates no data collected for period or unavailable.

Producer Price Index
Annual Averages, 1989-1997
Base 1982 = 100

Columns headed % show percentile change in the index from the previous period for which an index is available.

	1989		1990		1991		1992		1993		1994		1995		1996		1997	
	Index	%	Index	%	Index	%	Index	%	Index	%	Index	%	Index	%	Index	%	Index	%
Pulp, Paper, and Allied Products	137.8	5.7	141.2	2.5	142.9	1.2	145.2	1.6	147.3	1.4	152.5	3.5	172.2	12.9	168.7	-2.0	167.9	-0.5
Pulp, Paper, and Products, ex. Building Paper	132.4	6.0	132.9	0.4	129.8	-2.3	129.2	-0.5	127.6	-1.2	133.1	4.3	163.4	22.8	149.7	-8.4	144.7	-3.3
Building Paper & Building Board Mill Products	115.6	2.0	112.2	-2.9	111.8	-0.4	119.6	7.0	132.7	11.0	144.1	8.6	144.9	0.6	137.2	-5.3	130.0	-5.2
Publications, Printed Matter & Printing Materials	142.1	5.5	148.4	4.4	154.8	4.3	159.6	3.1	164.9	3.3	169.6	2.9	179.9	6.1	186.9	3.9	190.5	1.9
Metals and Metal Products	124.1	4.5	122.9	-1.0	120.2	-2.2	119.2	-0.8	119.2	0.0	124.8	4.7	134.5	7.8	131.0	-2.6	131.8	0.6
Iron and Steel	119.1	2.9	117.2	-1.6	114.1	-2.6	111.5	-2.3	116.0	4.0	122.0	5.2	128.8	5.6	125.8	-2.3	126.5	0.6
Nonferrous Metals	141.5	6.2	133.8	-5.4	123.4	-7.8	120.9	-2.0	114.4	-5.4	126.6	10.7	149.6	18.2	136.5	-8.8	136.6	0.1
Metal Containers	111.5	1.2	114.0	2.2	115.5	1.3	113.9	-1.4	109.7	-3.7	108.1	-1.5	117.2	8.4	110.0	-6.1	107.9	-1.9
Hardware	120.4	5.9	125.9	4.6	130.2	3.4	132.7	1.9	135.2	1.9	137.5	1.7	141.1	2.6	143.8	1.9	145.6	1.3
Plumbing Fixtures and Brass Fittings	137.7	7.0	144.3	4.8	149.7	3.7	153.1	2.3	155.9	1.8	159.6	2.4	166.0	4.0	171.1	3.1	174.6	2.0
Heating Equipment	125.1	4.9	131.6	5.2	134.1	1.9	137.3	2.4	140.4	2.3	142.5	1.5	147.5	3.5	151.2	2.5	152.6	0.9
Fabricated Structural Metal Products	120.3	5.2	121.8	1.2	122.4	0.5	122.1	-0.2	123.2	0.9	127.3	3.3	135.1	6.1	137.8	2.0	140.3	1.8
Miscellaneous Metal Products	117.0	4.4	119.4	2.1	120.4	0.8	121.4	0.8	122.3	0.7	123.6	1.1	125.9	1.9	126.9	0.8	127.6	0.6
Metal Treatment Services	114.5	4.3	116.3	1.6	117.4	0.9	118.2	0.7	119.8	1.4	121.4	1.3	123.5	1.7	124.8	1.1	126.0	1.0
Machinery and Equipment	117.4	3.7	120.7	2.8	123.0	1.9	123.4	0.3	124.0	0.5	125.1	0.9	126.6	1.2	126.5	-0.1	125.9	-0.5
Agricultural Machinery and Equipment	117.7	4.4	121.7	3.4	125.7	3.3	129.5	3.0	133.6	3.2	137.0	2.5	142.9	4.3	146.8	2.7	148.6	1.2
Construction Machinery and Equipment	117.2	4.8	121.6	3.8	125.2	3.0	128.7	2.8	132.0	2.6	133.7	1.3	136.7	2.2	139.8	2.3	142.2	1.7
Metalworking Machinery and Equipment	118.2	4.1	123.0	4.1	127.6	3.7	130.9	2.6	133.5	2.0	136.5	2.2	139.8	2.4	143.1	2.4	145.4	1.6
General Purpose Machinery and Equipment	119.0	5.5	123.7	3.9	127.8	3.3	129.9	1.6	132.2	1.8	134.8	2.0	139.1	3.2	142.5	2.4	145.0	1.8
Electronic Computers and Computer Equipment	-	-	-	-	88.9	-	73.2	-17.7	62.2	-15.0	57.0	-8.4	52.2	-8.4	45.5	-12.8	39.2	-13.8
Special Industry Machinery and Equipment	127.0	4.4	131.5	3.5	135.9	3.3	139.5	2.6	143.7	3.0	146.2	1.7	149.8	2.5	153.3	2.3	156.7	2.2
Electrical Machinery and Equipment	117.5	2.6	119.3	1.5	120.8	1.3	121.3	0.4	122.5	1.0	123.4	0.7	124.2	0.6	123.4	-0.6	122.4	-0.8
Miscellaneous Instruments	122.5	3.0	126.7	3.4	130.3	2.8	133.7	2.6	137.8	3.1	139.6	1.3	141.0	1.0	143.3	1.6	146.0	1.9
Miscellaneous Machinery	112.7	3.8	116.7	3.5	120.3	3.1	121.7	1.2	122.7	0.8	124.7	1.6	127.0	1.8	129.2	1.7	130.9	1.3
Furniture and Household Durables	116.9	3.4	119.2	2.0	121.2	1.7	122.2	0.8	123.7	1.2	126.1	1.9	128.2	1.7	130.4	1.7	130.8	0.3
Household Furniture	121.8	3.6	125.1	2.7	128.0	2.3	130.0	1.6	133.4	2.6	138.0	3.4	141.8	2.8	144.5	1.9	146.2	1.2
Commercial Furniture	129.0	3.9	133.4	3.4	136.2	2.1	138.1	1.4	140.5	1.7	144.7	3.0	148.2	2.4	151.7	2.4	154.2	1.6

Source: U.S. Department of Labor, Bureau of Labor Statistics, Division of Industry Prices and Price Indexes. n.e.c. stands for not elsewhere classified. - indicates no data collected for period or unavailable.

Producer Price Index
Annual Averages, 1926-1934
Base 1982 = 100

Columns headed % show percentile change in the index from the previous period for which an index is available.

	1926		1927		1928		1929		1930		1931		1932		1933		1934	
	Index	%	Index	%	Index	%	Index	%	Index	%	Index	%	Index	%	Index	%	Index	%
Floor Coverings	31.7	-	30.3	-4.4	29.7	-2.0	29.7	0.0	30.0	1.0	25.4	-15.3	22.7	-10.6	23.6	4.0	25.8	9.3
Household Appliances	-	-	-	-	-	-	-	-	-	-	-	-	-	-	-	-	-	-
Home Electronic Equipment	-	-	-	-	-	-	-	-	-	-	-	-	-	-	-	-	-	-
Other Household Durable Goods	-	-	-	-	-	-	-	-	-	-	-	-	-	-	-	-	-	-
Nonmetallic Mineral Products	16.4	-	15.7	-4.3	16.2	3.2	16.0	-1.2	15.9	-0.6	14.9	-6.3	13.9	-6.7	14.7	5.8	15.7	6.8
Glass	-	-	-	-	-	-	-	-	-	-	-	-	-	-	-	-	-	-
Concrete Ingredients and Related Products	14.9	-	14.5	-2.7	16.4	13.1	16.5	0.6	16.6	0.6	15.1	-9.0	14.4	-4.6	15.6	8.3	16.6	6.4
Concrete Products	23.7	-	23.7	0.0	23.7	0.0	23.3	-1.7	23.6	1.3	22.3	-5.5	20.5	-8.1	20.9	2.0	20.9	0.0
Clay Construction Products ex. Refractories	-	-	-	-	-	-	-	-	-	-	-	-	-	-	-	-	-	-
Refractories	-	-	-	-	-	-	-	-	-	-	-	-	-	-	-	-	-	-
Asphalt Felts and Coatings	21.2	-	20.0	-5.7	17.9	-10.5	15.8	-11.7	16.1	1.9	16.7	3.7	15.3	-8.4	15.7	2.6	16.9	7.6
Gypsum Products	-	-	-	-	-	-	-	-	-	-	-	-	-	-	-	-	-	-
Glass Containers	-	-	-	-	-	-	-	-	-	-	-	-	-	-	-	-	-	-
Other Nonmetallic Minerals	-	-	-	-	-	-	-	-	-	-	-	-	-	-	-	-	-	-
Transportation Equipment	-	-	-	-	-	-	-	-	-	-	-	-	-	-	-	-	-	-
Motor Vehicles and Equipment	16.7	-	16.0	-4.2	16.2	1.3	16.7	3.1	15.7	-6.0	14.9	-5.1	14.5	-2.7	13.9	-4.1	14.6	5.0
Aircraft and Aircraft Equipment	-	-	-	-	-	-	-	-	-	-	-	-	-	-	-	-	-	-
Ships and Boats	-	-	-	-	-	-	-	-	-	-	-	-	-	-	-	-	-	-
Railroad Equipment	-	-	-	-	-	-	-	-	-	-	-	-	-	-	-	-	-	-
Transportation Equipment, n.e.c.	-	-	-	-	-	-	-	-	-	-	-	-	-	-	-	-	-	-
Miscellaneous Products	-	-	-	-	-	-	-	-	-	-	-	-	-	-	-	-	-	-
Toys, Sporting Goods, Small Arms, etc.	-	-	-	-	-	-	-	-	-	-	-	-	-	-	-	-	-	-
Tobacco Products, incl. Stemmed & Redried	-	-	-	-	-	-	-	-	-	-	-	-	-	-	-	-	-	-
Notions	-	-	-	-	-	-	-	-	-	-	-	-	-	-	-	-	-	-
Photographic Equipment and Supplies	-	-	-	-	-	-	-	-	-	-	-	-	-	-	-	-	-	-
Mobile Homes	-	-	-	-	-	-	-	-	-	-	-	-	-	-	-	-	-	-
Medical, Surgical & Personal Aid Devices	-	-	-	-	-	-	-	-	-	-	-	-	-	-	-	-	-	-
Industrial Safety Equipment	-	-	-	-	-	-	-	-	-	-	-	-	-	-	-	-	-	-
Mining Services	-	-	-	-	-	-	-	-	-	-	-	-	-	-	-	-	-	-
Other Miscellaneous Products	-	-	-	-	-	-	-	-	-	-	-	-	-	-	-	-	-	-

Source: U.S. Department of Labor, Bureau of Labor Statistics, Division of Industry Prices and Price Indexes. n.e.c. stands for not elsewhere classified. - indicates no data collected for period or unavailable.

Producer Price Index
Annual Averages, 1935-1943
Base 1982 = 100

Columns headed % show percentile change in the index from the previous period for which an index is available.

	1935		1936		1937		1938		1939		1940		1941		1942		1943	
	Index	%	Index	%	Index	%	Index	%	Index	%	Index	%	Index	%	Index	%	Index	%
Floor Coverings	26.2	1.6	26.3	0.4	29.5	12.2	28.2	-4.4	28.9	2.5	31.2	8.0	32.1	2.9	33.2	3.4	33.2	0.0
Household Appliances	-	-	-	-	-	-	-	-	-	-	-	-	-	-	-	-	-	-
Home Electronic Equipment	-	-	-	-	-	-	-	-	-	-	-	-	-	-	-	-	-	-
Other Household Durable Goods	-	-	-	-	-	-	-	-	-	-	-	-	-	-	-	-	-	-
Nonmetallic Mineral Products	15.7	0.0	15.8	0.6	16.1	1.9	15.6	-3.1	15.3	-1.9	15.3	0.0	15.7	2.6	16.3	3.8	16.4	0.6
Glass	-	-	-	-	-	-	-	-	-	-	-	-	-	-	-	-	-	-
Concrete Ingredients and Related Products	16.6	0.0	16.7	0.6	16.6	-0.6	16.7	0.6	16.7	0.0	16.6	-0.6	16.8	1.2	17.3	3.0	17.3	0.0
Concrete Products	19.0	-9.1	20.2	6.3	20.3	0.5	18.7	-7.9	18.6	-0.5	16.6	-10.8	19.2	15.7	19.9	3.6	19.9	0.0
Clay Construction Products ex. Refractories	-	-	-	-	-	-	-	-	-	-	-	-	-	-	-	-	-	-
Refractories	-	-	-	-	-	-	-	-	-	-	-	-	-	-	-	-	-	-
Asphalt Felts and Coatings	17.7	4.7	17.4	-1.7	19.1	9.8	15.4	-19.4	15.9	3.2	17.4	9.4	17.9	2.9	17.5	-2.2	17.5	0.0
Gypsum Products	-	-	-	-	-	-	-	-	-	-	-	-	-	-	-	-	-	-
Glass Containers	-	-	-	-	-	-	-	-	-	-	-	-	-	-	-	-	-	-
Other Nonmetallic Minerals	-	-	-	-	-	-	-	-	-	-	-	-	-	-	-	-	-	-
Transportation Equipment	-	-	-	-	-	-	-	-	-	-	-	-	-	-	-	-	-	-
Motor Vehicles and Equipment	14.0	-4.1	13.9	-0.7	14.9	7.2	15.9	6.7	15.6	-1.9	16.1	3.2	17.2	6.8	18.8	9.3	18.8	0.0
Aircraft and Aircraft Equipment	-	-	-	-	-	-	-	-	-	-	-	-	-	-	-	-	-	-
Ships and Boats	-	-	-	-	-	-	-	-	-	-	-	-	-	-	-	-	-	-
Railroad Equipment	-	-	-	-	-	-	-	-	-	-	-	-	-	-	-	-	-	-
Transportation Equipment, n.e.c.	-	-	-	-	-	-	-	-	-	-	-	-	-	-	-	-	-	-
Miscellaneous Products	-	-	-	-	-	-	-	-	-	-	-	-	-	-	-	-	-	-
Toys, Sporting Goods, Small Arms, etc.	-	-	-	-	-	-	-	-	-	-	-	-	-	-	-	-	-	-
Tobacco Products, incl. Stemmed & Redried	-	-	-	-	-	-	-	-	-	-	-	-	-	-	-	-	-	-
Notions	-	-	-	-	-	-	-	-	-	-	-	-	-	-	-	-	-	-
Photographic Equipment and Supplies	-	-	-	-	-	-	-	-	-	-	-	-	-	-	-	-	-	-
Mobile Homes	-	-	-	-	-	-	-	-	-	-	-	-	-	-	-	-	-	-
Medical, Surgical & Personal Aid Devices	-	-	-	-	-	-	-	-	-	-	-	-	-	-	-	-	-	-
Industrial Safety Equipment	-	-	-	-	-	-	-	-	-	-	-	-	-	-	-	-	-	-
Mining Services	-	-	-	-	-	-	-	-	-	-	-	-	-	-	-	-	-	-
Other Miscellaneous Products	-	-	-	-	-	-	-	-	-	-	-	-	-	-	-	-	-	-

Source: U.S. Department of Labor, Bureau of Labor Statistics, Division of Industry Prices and Price Indexes. n.e.c. stands for not elsewhere classified. - indicates no data collected for period or unavailable.

Producer Price Index
Annual Averages, 1944-1952
Base 1982 = 100

Columns headed % show percentile change in the index from the previous period for which an index is available.

	1944 Index	%	1945 Index	%	1946 Index	%	1947 Index	%	1948 Index	%	1949 Index	%	1950 Index	%	1951 Index	%	1952 Index	%
Floor Coverings	33.2	0.0	33.1	-0.3	36.8	11.2	43.6	18.5	46.4	6.4	46.6	0.4	52.3	12.2	62.7	19.9	55.9	-10.8
Household Appliances	-	-	-	-	-	-	51.5	-	54.0	4.9	53.7	-0.6	54.0	0.6	57.3	6.1	57.0	-0.5
Home Electronic Equipment	-	-	-	-	-	-	141.0	-	146.7	4.0	151.8	3.5	141.8	-6.6	136.2	-3.9	135.9	-0.2
Other Household Durable Goods	-	-	-	-	-	-	19.5	-	20.0	2.6	20.9	4.5	21.5	2.9	23.1	7.4	23.3	0.9
Nonmetallic Mineral Products	16.7	1.8	17.4	4.2	18.5	6.3	20.7	11.9	22.4	8.2	23.0	2.7	23.5	2.2	25.0	6.4	25.0	0.0
Glass	-	-	-	-	-	-	30.2	-	31.8	5.3	33.4	5.0	34.1	2.1	36.3	6.5	36.3	0.0
Concrete Ingredients and Related Products	17.5	1.2	18.0	2.9	18.7	3.9	20.5	9.6	22.4	9.3	23.2	3.6	23.5	1.3	24.9	6.0	24.9	0.0
Concrete Products	19.9	0.0	19.9	0.0	21.1	6.0	23.9	13.3	25.1	5.0	25.7	2.4	26.3	2.3	28.0	6.5	28.0	0.0
Clay Construction Products ex. Refractories	-	-	-	-	-	-	23.9	-	25.7	7.5	26.5	3.1	27.6	4.2	29.9	8.3	29.8	-0.3
Refractories	-	-	-	-	-	-	14.3	-	15.8	10.5	16.5	4.4	18.2	10.3	19.6	7.7	19.8	1.0
Asphalt Felts and Coatings	17.6	0.6	18.0	2.3	18.8	4.4	21.4	13.8	23.5	9.8	23.4	-0.4	23.1	-1.3	23.9	3.5	23.4	-2.1
Gypsum Products	-	-	-	-	-	-	27.5	-	30.0	9.1	29.7	-1.0	30.4	2.4	34.1	12.2	34.2	0.3
Glass Containers	-	-	-	-	-	-	14.7	-	16.9	15.0	19.0	12.4	19.1	0.5	20.6	7.9	21.1	2.4
Other Nonmetallic Minerals	-	-	-	-	-	-	14.9	-	16.3	9.4	16.5	1.2	17.0	3.0	17.7	4.1	17.9	1.1
Transportation Equipment	-	-	-	-	-	-	-	-	-	-	-	-	-	-	-	-	-	-
Motor Vehicles and Equipment	18.9	0.5	19.2	1.6	22.3	16.1	25.5	14.3	28.2	10.6	30.1	6.7	30.0	-0.3	31.6	5.3	33.4	5.7
Aircraft and Aircraft Equipment	-	-	-	-	-	-	-	-	-	-	-	-	-	-	-	-	-	-
Ships and Boats	-	-	-	-	-	-	-	-	-	-	-	-	-	-	-	-	-	-
Railroad Equipment	-	-	-	-	-	-	-	-	-	-	-	-	-	-	-	-	-	-
Transportation Equipment, n.e.c.	-	-	-	-	-	-	-	-	-	-	-	-	-	-	-	-	-	-
Miscellaneous Products	-	-	-	-	-	-	26.6	-	27.7	4.1	28.2	1.8	28.6	1.4	30.3	5.9	30.2	-0.3
Toys, Sporting Goods, Small Arms, etc.	-	-	-	-	-	-	35.1	-	36.7	4.6	36.7	0.0	38.7	5.4	42.0	8.5	41.0	-2.4
Tobacco Products, incl. Stemmed & Redried	-	-	-	-	-	-	20.5	-	21.3	3.9	22.3	4.7	22.8	2.2	23.5	3.1	23.6	0.4
Notions	-	-	-	-	-	-	37.8	-	37.9	0.3	34.2	-9.8	33.7	-1.5	37.0	9.8	34.4	-7.0
Photographic Equipment and Supplies	-	-	-	-	-	-	32.2	-	35.3	9.6	36.6	3.7	36.3	-0.8	37.5	3.3	38.0	1.3
Mobile Homes	-	-	-	-	-	-	-	-	-	-	-	-	-	-	-	-	-	-
Medical, Surgical & Personal Aid Devices	-	-	-	-	-	-	-	-	-	-	-	-	-	-	-	-	-	-
Industrial Safety Equipment	-	-	-	-	-	-	-	-	-	-	-	-	-	-	-	-	-	-
Mining Services	-	-	-	-	-	-	-	-	-	-	-	-	-	-	-	-	-	-
Other Miscellaneous Products	-	-	-	-	-	-	23.2	-	23.8	2.6	23.9	0.4	24.1	0.8	25.7	6.6	25.7	0.0

Source: U.S. Department of Labor, Bureau of Labor Statistics, Division of Industry Prices and Price Indexes. n.e.c. stands for not elsewhere classified. - indicates no data collected for period or unavailable.

Producer Price Index
Annual Averages, 1953-1961
Base 1982 = 100

Columns headed % show percentile change in the index from the previous period for which an index is available.

	1953		1954		1955		1956		1957		1958		1959		1960		1961	
	Index	%	Index	%	Index	%	Index	%	Index	%	Index	%	Index	%	Index	%	Index	%
Floor Coverings	56.8	1.6	56.0	-1.4	57.6	2.9	59.7	3.6	60.7	1.7	58.1	-4.3	58.3	0.3	59.3	1.7	58.6	-1.2
Household Appliances	57.5	0.9	58.1	1.0	56.7	-2.4	56.0	-1.2	56.0	0.0	55.6	-0.7	55.5	-0.2	54.0	-2.7	53.0	-1.9
Home Electronic Equipment	-	-	-	-	136.3	0.3	136.4	0.1	138.3	1.4	138.2	-0.1	135.9	-1.7	133.8	-1.5	131.0	-2.1
Other Household Durable Goods	24.2	3.9	25.0	3.3	25.9	3.6	27.3	5.4	28.7	5.1	29.8	3.8	30.2	1.3	30.8	2.0	30.8	0.0
Nonmetallic Mineral Products	26.0	4.0	26.6	2.3	27.3	2.6	28.5	4.4	29.6	3.9	29.9	1.0	30.3	1.3	30.4	0.3	30.5	0.3
Glass	38.4	5.8	39.6	3.1	40.7	2.8	42.4	4.2	43.1	1.7	43.0	-0.2	43.0	0.0	42.1	-2.1	41.7	-1.0
Concrete Ingredients and Related Products	25.8	3.6	26.6	3.1	27.5	3.4	28.7	4.4	29.9	4.2	30.6	2.3	30.9	1.0	31.3	1.3	31.3	0.0
Concrete Products	28.7	2.5	29.2	1.7	29.5	1.0	30.6	3.7	31.4	2.6	31.9	1.6	32.3	1.3	32.6	0.9	32.6	0.0
Clay Construction Products ex. Refractories	30.4	2.0	30.9	1.6	32.1	3.9	33.8	5.3	34.3	1.5	34.5	0.6	35.4	2.6	35.9	1.4	36.1	0.6
Refractories	21.6	9.1	22.9	6.0	24.4	6.6	25.8	5.7	27.6	7.0	28.2	2.2	29.0	2.8	29.0	0.0	28.8	-0.7
Asphalt Felts and Coatings	24.4	4.3	23.7	-2.9	24.2	2.1	25.5	5.4	27.9	9.4	25.7	-7.9	26.5	3.1	24.4	-7.9	26.3	7.8
Gypsum Products	35.2	2.9	35.5	0.9	35.5	0.0	36.9	3.9	36.9	0.0	38.4	4.1	38.7	0.8	38.7	0.0	39.4	1.8
Glass Containers	22.7	7.6	23.8	4.8	24.1	1.3	25.4	5.4	26.8	5.5	28.3	5.6	28.3	0.0	27.6	-2.5	27.4	-0.7
Other Nonmetallic Minerals	18.6	3.9	19.1	2.7	19.3	1.0	19.6	1.6	20.4	4.1	20.9	2.5	21.1	1.0	21.4	1.4	21.2	-0.9
Transportation Equipment	-	-	-	-	-	-	-	-	-	-	-	-	-	-	-	-	-	-
Motor Vehicles and Equipment	33.3	-0.3	33.4	0.3	34.3	2.7	36.3	5.8	37.9	4.4	39.0	2.9	39.9	2.3	39.3	-1.5	39.2	-0.3
Aircraft and Aircraft Equipment	-	-	-	-	-	-	-	-	-	-	-	-	-	-	-	-	-	-
Ships and Boats	-	-	-	-	-	-	-	-	-	-	-	-	-	-	-	-	-	-
Railroad Equipment	-	-	-	-	-	-	-	-	-	-	-	-	-	-	-	-	27.9	-
Transportation Equipment, n.e.c.	-	-	-	-	-	-	-	-	-	-	-	-	-	-	-	-	-	-
Miscellaneous Products	31.0	2.6	31.3	1.0	31.3	0.0	31.7	1.3	32.6	2.8	33.3	2.1	33.4	0.3	33.6	0.6	33.7	0.3
Toys, Sporting Goods, Small Arms, etc.	41.1	0.2	40.9	-0.5	41.0	0.2	42.0	2.4	42.5	1.2	43.0	1.2	42.4	-1.4	42.8	0.9	43.1	0.7
Tobacco Products, incl. Stemmed & Redried	25.3	7.2	25.6	1.2	25.6	0.0	25.6	0.0	26.7	4.3	27.7	3.7	27.9	0.7	27.9	0.0	27.9	0.0
Notions	34.2	-0.6	34.8	1.8	33.7	-3.2	34.9	3.6	35.6	2.0	35.7	0.3	35.6	-0.3	35.5	-0.3	35.2	-0.8
Photographic Equipment and Supplies	38.3	0.8	38.7	1.0	39.1	1.0	39.8	1.8	41.5	4.3	42.6	2.7	44.0	3.3	44.4	0.9	45.0	1.4
Mobile Homes	-	-	-	-	-	-	-	-	-	-	-	-	-	-	-	-	-	-
Medical, Surgical & Personal Aid Devices	-	-	-	-	-	-	-	-	-	-	-	-	-	-	-	-	-	-
Industrial Safety Equipment	-	-	-	-	-	-	-	-	-	-	-	-	-	-	-	-	-	-
Mining Services	-	-	-	-	-	-	-	-	-	-	-	-	-	-	-	-	-	-
Other Miscellaneous Products	25.7	0.0	26.0	1.2	26.1	0.4	26.5	1.5	27.2	2.6	27.4	0.7	27.5	0.4	27.9	1.5	28.0	0.4

Source: U.S. Department of Labor, Bureau of Labor Statistics, Division of Industry Prices and Price Indexes. n.e.c. stands for not elsewhere classified. - indicates no data collected for period or unavailable.

Producer Price Index
Annual Averages, 1962-1970
Base 1982 = 100

Columns headed % show percentile change in the index from the previous period for which an index is available.

	1962		1963		1964		1965		1966		1967		1968		1969		1970	
	Index	%	Index	%	Index	%	Index	%	Index	%	Index	%	Index	%	Index	%	Index	%
Floor Coverings	57.2	-2.4	57.0	-0.3	58.7	3.0	57.7	-1.7	57.2	-0.9	55.2	-3.5	55.9	1.3	55.4	-0.9	54.9	-0.9
Household Appliances	52.3	-1.3	51.1	-2.3	50.8	-0.6	49.7	-2.2	49.6	-0.2	50.2	1.2	51.1	1.8	51.7	1.2	52.9	2.3
Home Electronic Equipment	125.3	-4.4	121.8	-2.8	119.9	-1.6	117.1	-2.3	114.9	-1.9	113.6	-1.1	111.4	-1.9	107.4	-3.6	106.0	-1.3
Other Household Durable Goods	31.3	1.6	31.4	0.3	31.8	1.3	32.2	1.3	33.0	2.5	34.6	4.8	36.9	6.6	38.6	4.6	40.1	3.9
Nonmetallic Mineral Products	30.5	0.0	30.3	-0.7	30.4	0.3	30.4	0.0	30.7	1.0	31.2	1.6	32.4	3.8	33.6	3.7	35.3	5.1
Glass	41.8	0.2	42.3	1.2	44.1	4.3	43.4	-1.6	43.3	-0.2	-	-	-	-	-	-	-	-
Concrete Ingredients and Related Products	31.5	0.6	31.4	-0.3	31.3	-0.3	31.5	0.6	31.6	0.3	32.3	2.2	33.3	3.1	34.4	3.3	36.3	5.5
Concrete Products	32.7	0.3	32.4	-0.9	32.1	-0.9	32.3	0.6	32.8	1.5	33.6	2.4	34.5	2.7	35.8	3.8	37.7	5.3
Clay Construction Products ex. Refractories	36.4	0.8	36.6	0.5	36.7	0.3	37.0	0.8	37.7	1.9	38.3	1.6	39.3	2.6	40.7	3.6	42.1	3.4
Refractories	28.7	-0.3	28.6	-0.3	28.8	0.7	29.1	1.0	29.3	0.7	29.7	1.4	31.7	6.7	32.5	2.5	35.9	10.5
Asphalt Felts and Coatings	25.3	-3.8	24.0	-5.1	23.7	-1.2	24.8	4.6	25.6	3.2	25.1	-2.0	25.9	3.2	25.8	-0.4	25.8	0.0
Gypsum Products	39.9	1.3	40.0	0.3	41.1	2.8	39.5	-3.9	38.9	-1.5	39.1	0.5	40.5	3.6	40.5	0.0	38.9	-4.0
Glass Containers	26.9	-1.8	26.9	0.0	27.0	0.4	27.3	1.1	27.8	1.8	28.1	1.1	30.2	7.5	32.3	7.0	33.9	5.0
Other Nonmetallic Minerals	21.2	0.0	21.1	-0.5	21.1	0.0	21.0	-0.5	21.1	0.5	21.2	0.5	21.9	3.3	22.7	3.7	23.8	4.8
Transportation Equipment	-	-	-	-	-	-	-	-	-	-	-	-	-	-	40.4	-	41.9	3.7
Motor Vehicles and Equipment	39.2	0.0	38.9	-0.8	39.1	0.5	39.2	0.3	39.2	0.0	39.8	1.5	40.9	2.8	41.7	2.0	43.3	3.8
Aircraft and Aircraft Equipment	-	-	-	-	-	-	-	-	-	-	-	-	-	-	-	-	-	-
Ships and Boats	-	-	-	-	-	-	-	-	-	-	-	-	-	-	-	-	-	-
Railroad Equipment	28.0	0.4	28.0	0.0	28.0	0.0	28.1	0.4	28.2	0.4	28.9	2.5	29.8	3.1	31.4	5.4	33.2	5.7
Transportation Equipment, n.e.c.																		
Miscellaneous Products	33.9	0.6	34.2	0.9	34.4	0.6	34.7	0.9	35.3	1.7	36.2	2.5	37.0	2.2	38.1	3.0	39.8	4.5
Toys, Sporting Goods, Small Arms, etc.	43.0	-0.2	43.1	0.2	43.1	0.0	43.8	1.6	44.4	1.4	45.2	1.8	46.2	2.2	47.6	3.0	49.5	4.0
Tobacco Products, incl. Stemmed & Redried	28.0	0.4	28.7	2.5	29.1	1.4	29.1	0.0	30.1	3.4	31.0	3.0	31.6	1.9	33.1	4.7	35.2	6.3
Notions	35.2	0.0	35.2	0.0	35.3	0.3	35.3	0.0	35.8	1.4	36.1	0.8	36.1	0.0	37.2	3.0	39.1	5.1
Photographic Equipment and Supplies	46.1	2.4	46.0	-0.2	46.3	0.7	46.7	0.9	46.5	-0.4	47.5	2.2	48.6	2.3	48.7	0.2	49.9	2.5
Mobile Homes	-	-	-	-	-	-	-	-	-	-	-	-	-	-	-	-	-	-
Medical, Surgical & Personal Aid Devices	-	-	-	-	-	-	-	-	-	-	-	-	-	-	-	-	-	-
Industrial Safety Equipment	-	-	-	-	-	-	-	-	-	-	-	-	-	-	-	-	-	-
Mining Services	-	-	-	-	-	-	-	-	-	-	-	-	-	-	-	-	-	-
Other Miscellaneous Products	28.1	0.4	28.0	-0.4	28.1	0.4	28.4	1.1	28.8	1.4	29.6	2.8	30.3	2.4	30.9	2.0	32.1	3.9

Source: U.S. Department of Labor, Bureau of Labor Statistics, Division of Industry Prices and Price Indexes. n.e.c. stands for not elsewhere classified. - indicates no data collected for period or unavailable.

Producer Price Index
Annual Averages, 1971-1979
Base 1982 = 100

Columns headed % show percentile change in the index from the previous period for which an index is available.

	1971		1972		1973		1974		1975		1976		1977		1978		1979	
	Index	%	Index	%	Index	%	Index	%	Index	%	Index	%	Index	%	Index	%	Index	%
Floor Coverings	54.6	-0.5	54.4	-0.4	56.4	3.7	63.7	12.9	69.0	8.3	72.5	5.1	75.3	3.9	78.2	3.9	81.7	4.5
Household Appliances	54.0	2.1	54.0	0.0	54.5	0.9	59.2	8.6	66.5	12.3	69.9	5.1	72.9	4.3	76.8	5.3	80.8	5.2
Home Electronic Equipment	106.1	0.1	105.3	-0.8	104.4	-0.9	105.7	1.2	106.2	0.5	103.7	-2.4	99.6	-4.0	102.4	2.8	103.7	1.3
Other Household Durable Goods	41.8	4.2	43.4	3.8	45.1	3.9	51.4	14.0	58.3	13.4	61.9	6.2	65.7	6.1	70.2	6.8	78.9	12.4
Nonmetallic Mineral Products	38.2	8.2	39.4	3.1	40.7	3.3	47.8	17.4	54.4	13.8	58.2	7.0	62.6	7.6	69.6	11.2	77.6	11.5
Glass	55.6	-	-	-	-	-	-	-	62.8	12.9	67.7	7.8	72.6	7.2	78.0	7.4	83.0	6.4
Concrete Ingredients and Related Products	39.3	8.3	40.9	4.1	42.3	3.4	48.0	13.5	55.6	15.8	60.2	8.3	64.2	6.6	70.2	9.3	78.7	12.1
Concrete Products	40.5	7.4	42.2	4.2	44.2	4.7	50.9	15.2	57.3	12.6	60.5	5.6	64.4	6.4	71.9	11.6	82.0	14.0
Clay Construction Products ex. Refractories	43.9	4.3	45.0	2.5	47.3	5.1	51.8	9.5	58.0	12.0	62.7	8.1	69.0	10.0	75.6	9.6	83.6	10.6
Refractories	37.6	4.7	38.3	1.9	40.4	5.5	42.6	5.4	49.2	15.5	54.6	11.0	59.2	8.4	64.2	8.4	70.2	9.3
Asphalt Felts and Coatings	31.5	22.1	32.9	4.4	34.0	3.3	49.2	44.7	56.7	15.2	59.8	5.5	63.5	6.2	73.3	15.4	81.7	11.5
Gypsum Products	42.7	9.8	44.8	4.9	47.2	5.4	53.7	13.8	56.2	4.7	60.3	7.3	71.7	18.9	89.5	24.8	98.5	10.1
Glass Containers	37.0	9.1	38.0	2.7	39.1	2.9	43.7	11.8	50.5	15.6	55.0	8.9	60.2	9.5	68.7	14.1	73.4	6.8
Other Nonmetallic Minerals	26.3	10.5	26.9	2.3	27.2	1.1	40.0	47.1	46.7	16.7	49.3	5.6	53.1	7.7	58.4	10.0	66.5	13.9
Transportation Equipment	44.2	5.5	45.5	2.9	46.1	1.3	50.3	9.1	56.7	12.7	60.5	6.7	64.6	6.8	69.5	7.6	75.3	8.3
Motor Vehicles and Equipment	45.7	5.5	47.0	2.8	47.4	0.9	51.4	8.4	57.6	12.1	61.2	6.3	65.2	6.5	70.0	7.4	75.8	8.3
Aircraft and Aircraft Equipment	36.6	-	-	-	-	-	-	-	48.5	32.5	54.5	12.4	59.3	8.8	64.1	8.1	69.9	9.0
Ships and Boats	-	-	-	-	-	-	-	-	-	-	-	-	-	-	-	-	-	-
Railroad Equipment	34.9	5.1	37.1	6.3	38.9	4.9	47.3	21.6	58.1	22.8	62.5	7.6	67.4	7.8	73.0	8.3	80.0	9.6
Transportation Equipment, n.e.c.																		
Miscellaneous Products	40.8	2.5	41.5	1.7	43.3	4.3	48.1	11.1	53.4	11.0	55.6	4.1	59.4	6.8	66.7	12.3	75.5	13.2
Toys, Sporting Goods, Small Arms, etc.	50.9	2.8	51.7	1.6	53.2	2.9	59.7	12.2	65.9	10.4	67.7	2.7	70.1	3.5	73.7	5.1	79.6	8.0
Tobacco Products, incl. Stemmed & Redried	36.1	2.6	36.4	0.8	37.7	3.6	41.1	9.0	46.3	12.7	50.5	9.1	55.6	10.1	61.4	10.4	67.4	9.8
Notions	40.4	3.3	40.5	0.2	41.3	2.0	49.6	20.1	54.5	9.9	58.6	7.5	62.2	6.1	65.7	5.6	69.3	5.5
Photographic Equipment and Supplies	50.5	1.2	50.7	0.4	51.5	1.6	55.5	7.8	62.1	11.9	64.7	4.2	66.5	2.8	69.3	4.2	73.0	5.3
Mobile Homes	-	-	-	-	-	-	-	-	-	-	-	-	-	-	-	-	-	-
Medical, Surgical & Personal Aid Devices	-	-	-	-	-	-	-	-	-	-	-	-	-	-	-	-	89.5	-
Industrial Safety Equipment	-	-	-	-	-	-	-	-	-	-	-	-	-	-	-	-	83.3	-
Mining Services	-	-	-	-	-	-	-	-	-	-	-	-	-	-	-	-	-	-
Other Miscellaneous Products	33.3	3.7	34.3	3.0	37.1	8.2	42.0	13.2	46.0	9.5	45.2	-1.7	49.5	9.5	62.2	25.7	77.9	25.2

Source: U.S. Department of Labor, Bureau of Labor Statistics, Division of Industry Prices and Price Indexes. n.e.c. stands for not elsewhere classified. - indicates no data collected for period or unavailable.

Producer Price Index
Annual Averages, 1980-1988
Base 1982 = 100

Columns headed % show percentile change in the index from the previous period for which an index is available.

	1980		1981		1982		1983		1984		1985		1986		1987		1988	
	Index	%	Index	%	Index	%	Index	%	Index	%	Index	%	Index	%	Index	%	Index	%
Floor Coverings	90.0	10.2	98.7	9.7	100.0	1.3	102.4	2.4	105.6	3.1	105.6	0.0	108.3	2.6	110.7	2.2	114.7	3.6
Household Appliances	87.5	8.3	94.1	7.5	100.0	6.3	103.9	3.9	106.0	2.0	106.7	0.7	105.7	-0.9	105.6	-0.1	106.0	0.4
Home Electronic Equipment	103.8	0.1	101.3	-2.4	100.0	-1.3	97.8	-2.2	95.2	-2.7	90.8	-4.6	89.9	-1.0	88.8	-1.2	87.2	-1.8
Other Household Durable Goods	96.3	22.1	97.1	0.8	100.0	3.0	108.2	8.2	110.1	1.8	111.7	1.5	112.9	1.1	115.4	2.2	119.8	3.8
Nonmetallic Mineral Products	88.4	13.9	96.7	9.4	100.0	3.4	101.6	1.6	105.4	3.7	108.6	3.0	110.0	1.3	110.0	0.0	111.2	1.1
Glass	88.7	6.9	96.0	8.2	100.0	4.2	104.0	4.0	105.6	1.5	104.7	-0.9	107.4	2.6	109.4	1.9	112.3	2.7
Concrete Ingredients and Related Products	88.4	12.3	95.6	8.1	100.0	4.6	101.1	1.1	105.1	4.0	108.5	3.2	109.4	0.8	110.4	0.9	112.0	1.4
Concrete Products	92.0	12.2	97.8	6.3	100.0	2.2	101.4	1.4	103.9	2.5	107.5	3.5	109.2	1.6	109.4	0.2	110.0	0.5
Clay Construction Products ex. Refractories	88.8	6.2	95.8	7.9	100.0	4.4	106.5	6.5	110.0	3.3	113.5	3.2	118.0	4.0	121.4	2.9	124.9	2.9
Refractories	78.5	11.8	89.7	14.3	100.0	11.5	101.2	1.2	107.1	5.8	109.7	2.4	110.2	0.5	110.5	0.3	113.8	3.0
Asphalt Felts and Coatings	99.6	21.9	102.3	2.7	100.0	-2.2	96.4	-3.6	100.3	4.0	102.6	2.3	97.9	-4.6	92.4	-5.6	94.7	2.5
Gypsum Products	100.1	1.6	100.1	0.0	100.0	-0.1	111.7	11.7	135.4	21.2	132.3	-2.3	137.0	3.6	125.2	-8.6	112.9	-9.8
Glass Containers	82.3	12.1	92.5	12.4	100.0	8.1	99.1	-0.9	101.4	2.3	106.8	5.3	111.9	4.8	113.0	1.0	112.3	-0.6
Other Nonmetallic Minerals	83.6	25.7	98.3	17.6	100.0	1.7	101.8	1.8	106.0	4.1	110.5	4.2	110.2	-0.3	110.3	0.1	112.9	2.4
Transportation Equipment	82.9	10.1	94.3	13.8	100.0	6.0	102.8	2.8	105.2	2.3	107.9	2.6	110.5	2.4	112.5	1.8	114.3	1.6
Motor Vehicles and Equipment	83.1	9.6	94.6	13.8	100.0	5.7	102.2	2.2	104.1	1.9	106.4	2.2	109.1	2.5	111.7	2.4	113.1	1.3
Aircraft and Aircraft Equipment	78.8	12.7	91.3	15.9	100.0	9.5	108.3	8.3	115.0	6.2	-	-	123.8	7.7	123.3	-0.4	126.0	2.2
Ships and Boats	-	-	-	-	100.0	-	103.0	3.0	107.3	4.2	110.3	2.8	113.4	2.8	114.1	0.6	115.1	0.9
Railroad Equipment	90.4	13.0	97.0	7.3	100.0	3.1	101.1	1.1	102.6	1.5	104.9	2.2	105.4	0.5	104.7	-0.7	107.5	2.7
Transportation Equipment, n.e.c.	-	-	-	-	-	-	-	-	-	-	-	-	100.2	-	102.0	1.8	106.1	4.0
Miscellaneous Products	93.6	24.0	96.1	2.7	100.0	4.1	104.8	4.8	107.0	2.1	109.4	2.2	111.6	2.0	114.9	3.0	120.2	4.6
Toys, Sporting Goods, Small Arms, etc.	89.7	12.7	95.7	6.7	100.0	4.5	101.7	1.7	102.6	0.9	104.5	1.9	106.6	2.0	107.8	1.1	111.8	3.7
Tobacco Products, incl. Stemmed & Redried	76.0	12.8	83.1	9.3	100.0	20.3	113.1	13.1	123.3	9.0	132.5	7.5	142.5	7.5	154.7	8.6	171.9	11.1
Notions	78.4	13.1	93.8	19.6	100.0	6.6	101.1	1.1	102.3	1.2	102.9	0.6	103.7	0.8	105.2	1.4	107.9	2.6
Photographic Equipment and Supplies	96.4	32.1	99.8	3.5	100.0	0.2	102.5	2.5	102.0	-0.5	102.6	0.6	104.0	1.4	105.4	1.3	107.2	1.7
Mobile Homes	-	-	96.9	-	100.0	3.2	100.9	0.9	100.9	0.0	101.7	0.8	102.8	1.1	104.3	1.5	109.3	4.8
Medical, Surgical & Personal Aid Devices	93.3	4.2	97.2	4.2	-	-	103.8	6.8	108.3	4.3	109.0	0.6	111.8	2.6	117.0	4.7	118.9	1.6
Industrial Safety Equipment	89.6	7.6	95.3	6.4	100.0	4.9	103.0	3.0	106.9	3.8	111.3	4.1	121.0	8.7	129.1	6.7	136.7	5.9
Mining Services	-	-	-	-	-	-	-	-	-	-	-	-	91.3	-	87.3	-4.4	90.6	3.8
Other Miscellaneous Products	107.4	37.9	102.7	-4.4	100.0	-2.6	104.0	4.0	103.6	-0.4	103.4	-0.2	104.8	1.4	108.0	3.1	111.0	2.8

Source: U.S. Department of Labor, Bureau of Labor Statistics, Division of Industry Prices and Price Indexes. n.e.c. stands for not elsewhere classified. - indicates no data collected for period or unavailable.

Producer Price Index
Annual Averages, 1989-1997
Base 1982 = 100

Columns headed % show percentile change in the index from the previous period for which an index is available.

	1989 Index	%	1990 Index	%	1991 Index	%	1992 Index	%	1993 Index	%	1994 Index	%	1995 Index	%	1996 Index	%	1997 Index	%
Floor Coverings	117.6	2.5	119.0	1.2	120.4	1.2	120.3	-0.1	120.2	-0.1	121.5	1.1	123.7	1.8	126.6	2.3	127.7	0.9
Household Appliances	108.7	2.5	110.8	1.9	111.3	0.5	111.4	0.1	112.9	1.3	112.8	-0.1	112.4	-0.4	112.7	0.3	110.2	-2.2
Home Electronic Equipment	86.9	-0.3	82.7	-4.8	83.2	0.6	82.0	-1.4	80.2	-2.2	80.3	0.1	78.9	-1.7	79.0	0.1	77.5	-1.9
Other Household Durable Goods	127.2	6.2	130.7	2.8	134.2	2.7	136.6	1.8	138.0	1.0	140.8	2.0	144.8	2.8	148.1	2.3	149.7	1.1
Nonmetallic Mineral Products	112.6	1.3	114.7	1.9	117.2	2.2	117.3	0.1	120.0	2.3	124.2	3.5	129.0	3.9	131.0	1.6	133.2	1.7
Glass	113.2	0.8	113.8	0.5	114.4	0.5	115.7	1.1	116.9	1.0	120.1	2.7	122.9	2.3	120.9	-1.6	120.3	-0.5
Concrete Ingredients and Related Products	113.2	1.1	115.3	1.9	118.4	2.7	119.4	0.8	123.4	3.4	128.7	4.3	134.7	4.7	138.8	3.0	142.5	2.7
Concrete Products	111.2	1.1	113.5	2.1	116.6	2.7	117.2	0.5	120.2	2.6	124.6	3.7	129.4	3.9	133.2	2.9	136.0	2.1
Clay Construction Products ex. Refractories	127.0	1.7	129.9	2.3	130.2	0.2	132.0	1.4	135.1	2.3	138.3	2.4	141.3	2.2	142.3	0.7	143.4	0.8
Refractories	119.4	4.9	122.3	2.4	125.4	2.5	126.4	0.8	127.1	0.6	128.2	0.9	132.1	3.0	136.8	3.6	138.7	1.4
Asphalt Felts and Coatings	95.8	1.2	97.1	1.4	98.2	1.1	96.2	-2.0	96.8	0.6	95.3	-1.5	100.0	4.9	100.0	0.0	99.9	-0.1
Gypsum Products	110.0	-2.6	105.2	-4.4	99.3	-5.6	99.9	0.6	108.3	8.4	136.1	25.7	154.5	13.5	154.0	-0.3	170.7	10.8
Glass Containers	115.2	2.6	120.4	4.5	125.4	4.2	125.1	-0.2	125.8	0.6	127.5	1.4	130.5	2.4	129.1	-1.1	125.7	-2.6
Other Nonmetallic Minerals	114.2	1.2	116.0	1.6	118.4	2.1	116.4	-1.7	119.2	2.4	121.6	2.0	125.4	3.1	127.7	1.8	130.2	2.0
Transportation Equipment	117.7	3.0	121.5	3.2	126.4	4.0	130.4	3.2	133.7	2.5	137.2	2.6	139.7	1.8	141.7	1.4	141.6	-0.1
Motor Vehicles and Equipment	116.2	2.7	118.2	1.7	122.1	3.3	124.9	2.3	128.0	2.5	131.4	2.7	133.0	1.2	134.1	0.8	132.8	-1.0
Aircraft and Aircraft Equipment	129.9	3.1	136.8	5.3	144.3	5.5	151.3	4.9	154.9	2.4	159.2	2.8	163.7	2.8	167.8	2.5	169.8	1.2
Ships and Boats	120.1	4.3	125.4	4.4	130.3	3.9	137.4	5.4	143.3	4.3	145.4	1.5	147.8	1.7	154.1	4.3	159.4	3.4
Railroad Equipment	114.0	6.0	118.6	4.0	122.2	3.0	123.7	1.2	125.2	1.2	129.2	3.2	134.8	4.3	137.2	1.8	134.8	-1.7
Transportation Equipment, n.e.c.	109.8	3.5	111.6	1.6	113.6	1.8	114.7	1.0	115.7	0.9	117.5	1.6	121.5	3.4	124.9	2.8	127.0	1.7
Miscellaneous Products	126.5	5.2	134.2	6.1	140.8	4.9	145.3	3.2	145.4	0.1	141.9	-2.4	145.4	2.5	147.7	1.6	150.9	2.2
Toys, Sporting Goods, Small Arms, etc.	116.7	4.4	119.6	2.5	122.6	2.5	124.6	1.6	125.5	0.7	127.0	1.2	129.1	1.7	130.4	1.0	131.5	0.8
Tobacco Products, incl. Stemmed & Redried	194.8	13.3	221.4	13.7	249.7	12.8	275.3	10.3	260.3	-5.4	224.7	-13.7	231.3	2.9	237.4	2.6	248.8	4.8
Notions	112.4	4.2	115.8	3.0	117.9	1.8	119.3	1.2	120.5	1.0	121.8	1.1	123.9	1.7	125.7	1.5	125.8	0.1
Photographic Equipment and Supplies	114.3	6.6	118.4	3.6	118.1	-0.3	118.6	0.4	117.9	-0.6	116.9	-0.8	118.4	1.3	119.9	1.3	118.7	-1.0
Mobile Homes	114.0	4.3	117.5	3.1	120.4	2.5	121.7	1.1	127.8	5.0	137.0	7.2	145.6	6.3	149.8	2.9	152.2	1.6
Medical, Surgical & Personal Aid Devices	123.0	3.4	127.3	3.5	130.3	2.4	133.9	2.8	137.8	2.9	140.4	1.9	141.3	0.6	143.1	1.3	143.0	-0.1
Industrial Safety Equipment	144.2	5.5	149.7	3.8	157.7	5.3	163.6	3.7	166.5	1.8	172.6	3.7	178.5	3.4	182.7	2.4	186.1	1.9
Mining Services	90.9	0.3	95.5	5.1	98.6	3.2	95.1	-3.5	100.0	5.2	102.9	2.9	106.1	3.1	107.6	1.4	118.9	10.5
Other Miscellaneous Products	114.0	2.7	117.7	3.2	120.5	2.4	122.4	1.6	125.3	2.4	127.5	1.8	131.9	3.5	132.8	0.7	133.5	0.5

Source: U.S. Department of Labor, Bureau of Labor Statistics, Division of Industry Prices and Price Indexes. n.e.c. stands for not elsewhere classified. - indicates no data collected for period or unavailable.

FARM PRODUCTS
Producer Price Index
Base 1982 = 100

For 1913-1997. Columns headed % show percentile change in the index from the previous period for which an index is available.

Year	Jan Index	%	Feb Index	%	Mar Index	%	Apr Index	%	May Index	%	Jun Index	%	Jul Index	%	Aug Index	%	Sep Index	%	Oct Index	%	Nov Index	%	Dec Index	%
1913	17.6	-	17.5	-0.6	17.6	0.6	17.5	-0.6	17.4	-0.6	17.6	1.1	18.1	2.8	18.2	0.6	18.8	3.3	18.8	0.0	18.9	0.5	18.5	-2.1
1914	18.4	-0.5	18.3	-0.5	18.2	-0.5	18.0	-1.1	18.0	0.0	18.1	0.6	18.0	-0.6	18.3	1.7	17.9	-2.2	17.2	-3.9	17.6	2.3	17.4	-1.1
1915	18.1	4.0	18.4	1.7	17.9	-2.7	18.2	1.7	18.2	0.0	17.7	-2.7	18.1	2.3	17.9	-1.1	17.5	-2.2	18.1	3.4	18.0	-0.6	18.4	2.2
1916	19.4	5.4	19.4	0.0	19.4	0.0	19.6	1.0	19.8	1.0	19.7	-0.5	20.3	3.0	21.7	6.9	22.6	4.1	23.7	4.9	25.3	6.8	25.0	-1.2
1917	26.2	4.8	27.2	3.8	28.6	5.1	31.6	10.5	33.6	6.3	33.8	0.6	34.0	0.6	34.6	1.8	34.3	-0.9	35.2	2.6	36.0	2.3	35.6	-1.1
1918	37.0	3.9	37.1	0.3	37.3	0.5	36.6	-1.9	35.4	-3.3	35.4	0.0	37.0	4.5	38.6	4.3	39.6	2.6	38.2	-3.5	38.0	-0.5	38.1	0.3
1919	38.9	2.1	37.5	-3.6	38.5	2.7	40.0	3.9	40.9	2.3	39.6	-3.2	41.5	4.8	41.3	-0.5	38.7	-6.3	38.5	-0.5	40.3	4.7	41.8	3.7
1920	43.0	2.9	41.2	-4.2	41.5	0.7	42.5	2.4	42.8	0.7	42.3	-1.2	40.5	-4.3	37.8	-6.7	36.4	-3.7	32.2	-11.5	30.0	-6.8	26.4	-12.0
1921	25.6	-3.0	23.4	-8.6	22.7	-3.0	20.9	-7.9	21.0	0.5	20.3	-3.3	21.8	7.4	22.5	3.2	22.7	0.9	22.7	0.0	22.1	-2.6	22.2	0.5
1922	22.2	0.0	24.0	8.1	23.6	-1.7	23.4	-0.8	23.8	1.7	23.4	-1.7	24.1	3.0	23.0	-4.6	23.3	1.3	23.8	2.1	24.7	3.8	25.0	1.2
1923	25.1	0.4	25.3	0.8	25.3	0.0	24.8	-2.0	24.4	-1.6	24.2	-0.8	23.7	-2.1	24.2	2.1	25.3	4.5	25.4	0.4	25.7	1.2	25.5	-0.8
1924	25.6	0.4	25.0	-2.3	24.2	-3.2	24.6	1.7	24.0	-2.4	23.8	-0.8	24.9	4.6	25.7	3.2	25.3	-1.6	26.0	2.8	26.2	0.8	27.3	4.2
1925	28.7	5.1	28.4	-1.0	28.5	0.4	27.1	-4.9	27.1	0.0	27.6	1.8	28.3	2.5	28.1	-0.7	27.7	-1.4	27.0	-2.5	27.3	1.1	26.6	-2.6
1926	27.1	1.9	26.5	-2.2	25.7	-3.0	26.0	1.2	25.8	-0.8	25.5	-1.2	24.9	-2.4	24.6	-1.2	25.1	2.0	24.7	-1.6	23.9	-3.2	24.0	0.4
1927	24.3	1.2	24.1	-0.8	23.8	-1.2	23.8	0.0	24.3	2.1	24.3	0.0	24.6	1.2	25.8	4.9	26.7	3.5	26.5	-0.7	26.3	-0.8	26.3	0.0
1928	26.8	1.9	26.4	-1.5	26.1	-1.1	27.1	3.8	27.7	2.2	26.9	-2.9	27.4	1.9	27.0	-1.5	27.5	1.9	26.1	-5.1	25.7	-1.5	26.2	1.9
1929	26.7	1.9	26.6	-0.4	27.1	1.9	26.5	-2.2	25.8	-2.6	26.1	1.2	27.1	3.8	27.1	0.0	26.9	-0.7	26.2	-2.6	25.5	-2.7	25.7	0.8
1930	25.5	-0.8	24.7	-3.1	23.9	-3.2	24.2	1.3	23.5	-2.9	22.5	-4.3	21.0	-6.7	21.4	1.9	21.5	0.5	20.8	-3.3	20.0	-3.8	19.0	-5.0
1931	18.4	-3.2	17.7	-3.8	17.8	0.6	17.7	-0.6	16.9	-4.5	16.5	-2.4	16.4	-0.6	16.1	-1.8	15.3	-5.0	14.8	-3.3	14.8	0.0	14.1	-4.7
1932	13.3	-5.7	12.8	-3.8	12.7	-0.8	12.4	-2.4	11.8	-4.8	11.6	-1.7	12.1	4.3	12.4	2.5	12.4	0.0	11.8	-4.8	11.8	0.0	11.1	-5.9
1933	10.8	-2.7	10.3	-4.6	10.8	4.9	11.2	3.7	12.7	13.4	13.4	5.5	15.2	13.4	14.6	-3.9	14.4	-1.4	14.1	-2.1	14.3	1.4	14.0	-2.1
1934	14.8	5.7	15.5	4.7	15.5	0.0	15.1	-2.6	15.1	0.0	16.0	6.0	16.3	1.9	17.6	8.0	18.5	5.1	17.8	-3.8	17.8	0.0	18.2	2.2
1935	19.6	7.7	20.0	2.0	19.7	-1.5	20.3	3.0	20.3	0.0	19.8	-2.5	19.5	-1.5	20.0	2.6	20.1	0.5	19.7	-2.0	19.6	-0.5	19.8	1.0
1936	19.7	-0.5	20.1	2.0	19.3	-4.0	19.4	0.5	19.0	-2.1	19.7	3.7	20.5	4.1	21.2	3.4	21.2	0.0	21.2	0.0	21.5	1.4	22.4	4.2
1937	23.1	3.1	23.1	0.0	23.8	3.0	23.3	-2.1	22.7	-2.6	22.3	-1.8	22.6	1.3	21.8	-3.5	21.7	-0.5	20.3	-6.5	19.1	-5.9	18.4	-3.7
1938	18.1	-1.6	17.6	-2.8	17.7	0.6	17.2	-2.8	17.0	-1.2	17.3	1.8	17.5	1.2	17.0	-2.9	17.2	1.2	16.8	-2.3	17.1	1.8	17.0	-0.6
1939	17.0	0.0	16.9	-0.6	16.6	-1.8	16.1	-3.0	16.1	0.0	15.7	-2.5	15.8	0.6	15.4	-2.5	17.3	12.3	16.9	-2.3	17.0	0.6	17.1	0.6
1940	17.4	1.8	17.3	-0.6	17.1	-1.2	17.5	2.3	17.1	-2.3	16.7	-2.3	16.8	0.6	16.5	-1.8	16.7	1.2	16.8	0.6	17.2	2.4	17.6	2.3
1941	18.1	2.8	17.7	-2.2	18.1	2.3	18.8	3.9	19.3	2.7	20.7	7.3	21.7	4.8	22.1	1.8	23.0	4.1	22.7	-1.3	22.9	0.9	23.9	4.4
1942	25.5	6.7	25.6	0.4	26.0	1.6	26.4	1.5	26.3	-0.4	26.3	0.0	26.6	1.1	26.8	0.8	27.2	1.5	27.5	1.1	27.9	1.5	28.7	2.9
1943	29.5	2.8	30.0	1.7	31.0	3.3	31.2	0.6	31.7	1.6	31.9	0.6	31.5	-1.3	31.2	-1.0	31.0	-0.6	30.9	-0.3	30.6	-1.0	30.7	0.3
1944	30.7	0.0	30.9	0.7	31.2	1.0	31.1	-0.3	31.0	-0.3	31.5	1.6	31.3	-0.6	30.9	-1.3	31.0	0.3	31.2	0.6	31.4	0.6	31.6	0.6
1945	31.9	0.9	32.1	0.6	32.1	0.0	32.5	1.2	32.8	0.9	32.9	0.3	32.5	-1.2	32.0	-1.5	31.4	-1.9	32.1	2.2	33.1	3.1	33.2	0.3
1946	32.7	-1.5	33.0	0.9	33.6	1.8	34.1	1.5	34.7	1.8	35.4	2.0	39.6	11.9	40.6	2.5	39.0	-3.9	41.7	6.9	42.8	2.6	42.4	-0.9
1947	41.6	-1.9	42.6	2.4	45.5	6.8	44.0	-3.3	43.6	-0.9	43.8	0.5	44.3	1.1	44.8	1.1	46.6	4.0	47.4	1.7	47.7	0.6	50.1	5.0
1948	51.2	2.2	47.7	-6.8	47.6	-0.2	48.3	1.5	49.4	2.3	50.4	2.0	50.2	-0.4	49.6	-1.2	48.8	-1.6	46.9	-3.9	46.3	-1.3	45.2	-2.4
1949	43.8	-3.1	42.0	-4.1	42.7	1.7	42.7	0.0	42.7	0.0	41.8	-2.1	41.7	-0.2	41.7	0.0	41.8	0.2	41.0	-1.9	40.9	-0.2	40.3	-1.5
1950	40.1	-0.5	41.0	2.2	41.7	1.7	41.5	-0.5	42.6	2.7	42.7	0.2	45.3	6.1	45.8	1.1	46.5	1.5	45.6	-1.9	47.1	3.3	48.8	3.6
1951	50.8	4.1	52.9	4.1	53.1	0.4	53.1	0.0	52.3	-1.5	51.5	-1.5	50.2	-2.5	49.9	-0.6	49.7	-0.4	50.4	1.4	50.6	0.4	50.3	-0.6
1952	49.7	-1.2	48.7	-2.0	48.9	0.4	49.1	0.4	48.8	-0.6	48.4	-0.8	49.8	2.9	49.7	-0.2	48.2	-3.0	47.4	-1.7	46.8	-1.3	44.8	-4.3
1953	45.0	0.4	44.2	-1.8	45.1	2.0	43.9	-2.7	44.2	0.7	43.1	-2.5	44.2	2.6	43.5	-1.6	44.3	1.8	43.0	-2.9	42.3	-1.6	42.7	0.9
1954	44.2	3.5	44.1	-0.2	44.4	0.7	44.9	1.1	44.2	-1.6	42.8	-3.2	43.4	1.4	43.3	-0.2	42.3	-2.3	42.0	-0.7	42.1	0.2	40.6	-3.6
1955	41.8	3.0	42.0	0.5	41.6	-1.0	42.5	2.2	41.2	-3.1	41.5	0.7	40.4	-2.7	39.8	-1.5	40.4	1.5	39.2	-3.0	38.0	-3.1	37.5	-1.3
1956	38.0	1.3	38.9	2.4	39.1	0.5	39.8	1.8	41.1	3.3	41.2	0.2	40.7	-1.2	40.3	-1.0	40.7	1.0	39.9	-2.0	39.7	-0.5	40.1	1.0
1957	40.4	0.7	40.1	-0.7	40.1	0.0	40.9	2.0	40.4	-1.2	41.1	1.7	41.9	1.9	42.0	0.2	41.1	-2.1	41.3	0.5	41.5	0.5	41.8	0.7

[Continued]

FARM PRODUCTS
Producer Price Index
Base 1982 = 100
[Continued]

For 1913-1997. Columns headed % show percentile change in the index from the previous period for which an index is available.

Year	Jan Index	%	Feb Index	%	Mar Index	%	Apr Index	%	May Index	%	Jun Index	%	Jul Index	%	Aug Index	%	Sep Index	%	Oct Index	%	Nov Index	%	Dec Index	%
1958	42.3	1.2	43.4	2.6	45.4	4.6	44.1	-2.9	44.5	0.9	43.2	-2.9	42.9	-0.7	42.1	-1.9	42.0	-0.2	41.7	-0.7	41.6	-0.2	40.9	-1.7
1959	41.3	1.0	41.2	-0.2	41.0	-0.5	41.8	2.0	41.0	-1.9	40.6	-1.0	39.9	-1.7	39.4	-1.3	40.1	1.8	39.1	-2.5	38.6	-1.3	38.8	0.5
1960	39.1	0.8	39.3	0.5	40.8	3.8	41.2	1.0	40.8	-1.0	40.2	-1.5	40.1	-0.2	39.1	-2.5	39.6	1.3	40.4	2.0	40.6	0.5	40.1	-1.2
1961	40.5	1.0	40.7	0.5	40.6	-0.2	40.0	-1.5	39.2	-2.0	38.5	-1.8	39.4	2.3	40.0	1.5	39.4	-1.5	39.4	0.0	39.6	0.5	39.7	0.3
1962	40.5	2.0	40.6	0.2	40.7	0.2	40.1	-1.5	39.8	-0.7	39.4	-1.0	39.9	1.3	40.4	1.3	41.6	3.0	40.8	-1.9	41.1	0.7	40.3	-1.9
1963	40.8	1.2	39.9	-2.2	39.5	-1.0	39.5	0.0	39.1	-1.0	39.3	0.5	40.1	2.0	39.9	-0.5	39.5	-1.0	39.4	-0.3	39.8	1.0	38.6	-3.0
1964	39.9	3.4	39.1	-2.0	39.4	0.8	39.1	-0.8	38.8	-0.8	38.6	-0.5	39.0	1.0	38.7	-0.8	39.6	2.3	38.8	-2.0	38.9	0.3	38.4	-1.3
1965	38.5	0.3	39.1	1.6	39.5	1.0	40.4	2.3	40.7	0.7	41.5	2.0	41.4	-0.2	41.0	-1.0	41.2	0.5	41.1	-0.2	41.5	1.0	42.6	2.7
1966	43.2	1.4	44.4	2.8	44.2	-0.5	44.0	-0.5	43.2	-1.8	43.1	-0.2	44.6	3.5	44.7	0.2	45.0	0.7	43.2	-4.0	42.4	-1.9	42.1	-0.7
1967	42.5	1.0	41.8	-1.6	41.3	-1.2	40.4	-2.2	41.7	3.2	42.4	1.7	42.5	0.2	41.1	-3.3	40.7	-1.0	40.2	-1.2	39.9	-0.7	41.0	2.8
1968	41.0	0.0	41.9	2.2	42.3	1.0	42.3	0.0	42.9	1.4	42.4	-1.2	43.0	1.4	42.0	-2.3	42.5	1.2	41.9	-1.4	42.7	1.9	42.8	0.2
1969	43.4	1.4	43.5	0.2	44.1	1.4	43.9	-0.5	45.9	4.6	46.2	0.7	46.0	-0.4	45.1	-2.0	44.9	-0.4	44.6	-0.7	46.0	3.1	46.4	0.9
1970	46.6	0.4	47.0	0.9	47.3	0.6	46.0	-2.7	45.9	-0.2	46.0	0.2	46.8	1.7	44.8	-4.3	46.3	3.3	44.5	-3.9	44.1	-0.9	44.2	0.2
1971	44.9	1.6	47.0	4.7	46.6	-0.9	46.6	0.0	47.0	0.9	47.9	1.9	46.8	-2.3	46.7	-0.2	45.6	-2.4	45.9	0.7	46.3	0.9	47.8	3.2
1972	48.6	1.7	49.8	2.5	49.4	-0.8	49.1	-0.6	50.4	2.6	51.1	1.4	52.8	3.3	52.9	0.2	53.1	0.4	51.8	-2.4	53.1	2.5	56.7	6.8
1973	59.5	4.9	62.3	4.7	66.4	6.6	66.3	-0.2	70.3	6.0	75.2	7.0	71.5	-4.9	88.0	23.1	82.7	-6.0	77.7	-6.0	75.9	-2.3	77.3	1.8
1974	83.6	8.2	84.8	1.4	81.3	-4.1	76.8	-5.5	74.6	-2.9	69.6	-6.7	74.6	7.2	78.1	4.7	75.4	-3.5	77.4	2.7	77.5	0.1	75.8	-2.2
1975	74.1	-2.2	72.1	-2.7	70.6	-2.1	73.3	3.8	76.1	3.8	76.8	0.9	79.9	4.0	79.7	-0.3	81.3	2.0	81.4	0.1	79.1	-2.8	80.0	1.1
1976	79.5	-0.6	78.7	-1.0	77.0	-2.2	79.6	3.4	79.5	-0.1	81.1	2.0	81.2	0.1	78.3	-3.6	79.2	1.1	77.0	-2.8	75.7	-1.7	79.1	4.5
1977	79.8	0.9	82.1	2.9	83.5	1.7	85.9	2.9	84.3	-1.9	79.5	-5.7	78.5	-1.3	75.0	-4.5	75.1	0.1	75.1	0.0	76.6	2.0	77.7	1.4
1978	79.3	2.1	82.1	3.5	84.2	2.6	88.2	4.8	89.0	0.9	90.6	1.8	90.7	0.1	86.8	-4.3	88.8	2.3	90.5	1.9	90.0	-0.6	91.9	2.1
1979	95.0	3.4	99.4	4.6	100.2	0.8	101.5	1.3	101.2	-0.3	100.2	-1.0	101.8	1.6	98.4	-3.3	99.5	1.1	98.9	-0.6	99.1	0.2	100.1	1.0
1980	97.6	-2.5	100.0	2.5	98.7	-1.3	94.5	-4.3	96.3	1.9	96.3	0.0	104.9	8.9	108.9	3.8	110.2	1.2	108.8	-1.3	109.3	0.5	109.5	0.2
1981	109.1	-0.4	108.3	-0.7	107.6	-0.6	108.7	1.0	107.1	-1.5	107.6	0.5	108.7	1.0	106.4	-2.1	103.6	-2.6	100.3	-3.2	97.9	-2.4	96.8	-1.1
1982	99.9	3.2	102.0	2.1	101.0	-1.0	103.4	2.4	105.8	2.3	104.3	-1.4	101.8	-2.4	99.4	-2.4	96.8	-2.6	94.6	-2.3	95.2	0.6	96.0	0.8
1983	96.2	0.2	99.3	3.2	99.6	0.3	103.4	3.8	103.3	-0.1	102.1	-1.2	100.8	-1.3	104.6	3.8	105.8	1.1	105.3	-0.5	103.6	-1.6	104.8	1.2
1984	108.7	3.7	107.9	-0.7	110.3	2.2	109.5	-0.7	107.6	-1.7	106.1	-1.4	106.7	0.6	104.5	-2.1	103.1	-1.3	99.1	-3.9	101.4	2.3	101.4	0.0
1985	100.4	-1.0	101.2	0.8	98.5	-2.7	97.7	-0.8	95.1	-2.7	94.7	-0.4	94.6	-0.1	90.0	-4.9	87.8	-2.4	90.7	3.3	95.1	4.9	95.8	0.7
1986	93.8	-2.1	91.5	-2.5	90.9	-0.7	90.2	-0.8	93.7	3.9	91.8	-2.0	94.3	2.7	93.7	-0.6	92.5	-1.3	93.8	1.4	95.0	1.3	93.8	-1.3
1987	91.1	-2.9	92.0	1.0	92.2	0.2	95.7	3.8	99.9	4.4	98.8	-1.1	97.9	-0.9	95.7	-2.2	96.1	0.4	94.9	-1.2	96.3	1.5	95.7	-0.6
1988	97.3	1.7	97.9	0.6	98.2	0.3	99.2	1.0	102.2	3.0	106.8	4.5	109.1	2.2	109.3	0.2	111.6	2.1	110.9	-0.6	107.9	-2.7	108.9	0.9
1989	112.0	2.8	110.8	-1.1	113.8	2.7	111.0	-2.5	115.1	3.7	111.8	-2.9	110.5	-1.2	109.3	-1.1	108.0	-1.2	107.8	-0.2	109.0	1.1	111.5	2.3
1990	114.9	3.0	115.7	0.7	115.3	-0.3	113.3	-1.7	113.7	0.4	113.6	-0.1	113.8	0.2	111.4	-2.1	109.2	-2.0	109.5	0.3	108.5	-0.9	107.2	-1.2
1991	106.9	-0.3	106.9	0.0	109.7	2.6	109.6	-0.1	110.4	0.7	109.1	-1.2	105.6	-3.2	102.9	-2.6	103.1	0.2	101.5	-1.6	101.6	0.1	100.6	-1.0
1992	102.8	2.2	105.5	2.6	106.4	0.9	103.2	-3.0	105.8	2.5	104.7	-1.0	102.5	-2.1	102.2	-0.3	101.6	-0.6	102.7	1.1	101.8	-0.9	103.7	1.9
1993	104.3	0.6	104.4	0.1	106.4	1.9	109.7	3.1	111.0	1.2	104.3	-6.0	105.4	1.1	106.6	1.1	106.3	-0.3	104.2	-2.0	110.1	5.7	113.0	2.6
1994	112.0	-0.9	112.3	0.3	112.8	0.4	111.5	-1.2	108.7	-2.5	107.2	-1.4	102.8	-4.1	101.0	-1.8	101.3	0.3	98.8	-2.5	101.4	2.6	105.5	4.0
1995	103.6	-1.8	104.9	1.3	105.1	0.2	104.8	-0.3	102.6	-2.1	104.2	1.6	106.2	1.9	105.1	-1.0	110.7	5.3	110.2	-0.5	115.4	4.7	116.5	1.0
1996	116.4	-0.1	116.6	0.2	119.5	2.5	121.7	1.8	128.1	5.3	129.6	1.2	129.9	0.2	128.6	-1.0	125.1	-2.7	120.2	-3.9	117.9	-1.9	114.8	-2.6
1997	113.0	-1.6	113.0	0.0	116.2	2.8	116.7	0.4	117.4	0.6	111.6	-4.9	111.6	0.0	111.4	-0.2	111.2	-0.2	110.4	-0.7	110.6	0.2	110.1	-0.5

Source: U.S. Department of Labor, Bureau of Labor Statistics, Division of Industry Prices and Price Indexes. n.e.c. stands for not elsewhere classified. - indicates no data collected for period or unavailable.

Fruits & Melons, Fresh/Dry Vegetables & Nuts
Producer Price Index
Base 1982 = 100

For 1926-1997. Columns headed % show percentile change in the index from the previous period for which an index is available.

Year	Jan		Feb		Mar		Apr		May		Jun		Jul		Aug		Sep		Oct		Nov		Dec	
	Index	%	Index	%	Index	%	Index	%	Index	%	Index	%	Index	%	Index	%	Index	%	Index	%	Index	%	Index	%
1926	29.4	-	28.9	-1.7	28.8	-0.3	32.4	12.5	29.7	-8.3	28.0	-5.7	24.1	-13.9	22.7	-5.8	24.4	7.5	26.1	7.0	25.1	-3.8	24.2	-3.6
1927	25.4	5.0	25.0	-1.6	23.6	-5.6	24.3	3.0	28.4	16.9	28.6	0.7	25.6	-10.5	26.3	2.7	24.7	-6.1	25.0	1.2	26.8	7.2	25.7	-4.1
1928	26.4	2.7	27.5	4.2	28.6	4.0	28.6	0.0	28.3	-1.0	26.7	-5.7	25.4	-4.9	25.0	-1.6	24.6	-1.6	22.6	-8.1	22.0	-2.7	21.8	-0.9
1929	22.5	3.2	21.5	-4.4	20.9	-2.8	21.3	1.9	22.6	6.1	25.3	11.9	28.1	11.1	29.6	5.3	29.6	0.0	29.3	-1.0	28.5	-2.7	28.9	1.4
1930	27.6	-4.5	27.4	-0.7	27.1	-1.1	29.8	10.0	30.3	1.7	30.2	-0.3	25.5	-15.6	23.1	-9.4	23.8	3.0	23.8	0.0	21.4	-10.1	19.0	-11.2
1931	19.6	3.2	18.6	-5.1	18.8	1.1	19.6	4.3	19.8	1.0	20.0	1.0	19.2	-4.0	19.0	-1.0	18.3	-3.7	17.3	-5.5	16.5	-4.6	15.9	-3.6
1932	15.5	-2.5	15.4	-0.6	15.5	0.6	15.5	0.0	15.2	-1.9	15.6	2.6	14.9	-4.5	13.6	-8.7	12.7	-6.6	12.5	-1.6	12.6	0.8	12.7	0.8
1933	12.9	1.6	12.7	-1.6	13.4	5.5	14.5	8.2	14.8	2.1	16.2	9.5	20.1	24.1	18.4	-8.5	16.8	-8.7	15.4	-8.3	15.1	-1.9	15.6	3.3
1934	17.2	10.3	18.4	7.0	18.3	-0.5	17.0	-7.1	17.1	0.6	17.7	3.5	17.0	-4.0	16.3	-4.1	16.2	-0.6	16.6	2.5	15.9	-4.2	14.9	-6.3
1935	15.0	0.7	15.3	2.0	15.1	-1.3	16.5	9.3	16.2	-1.8	17.1	5.6	16.0	-6.4	14.7	-8.1	14.6	-0.7	14.3	-2.1	15.7	9.8	15.9	1.3
1936	15.5	-2.5	15.5	0.0	16.3	5.2	17.2	5.5	18.6	8.1	22.0	18.3	21.1	-4.1	19.6	-7.1	18.1	-7.7	18.8	3.9	19.1	1.6	19.3	1.0
1937	21.5	11.4	23.4	8.8	23.0	-1.7	22.0	-4.3	22.2	0.9	22.2	0.0	17.9	-19.4	16.1	-10.1	15.7	-2.5	15.1	-3.8	14.8	-2.0	13.6	-8.1
1938	13.6	0.0	13.4	-1.5	13.2	-1.5	13.5	2.3	14.1	4.4	15.3	8.5	13.8	-9.8	13.6	-1.4	14.1	3.7	13.9	-1.4	16.0	15.1	15.5	-3.1
1939	15.5	0.0	15.9	2.6	16.2	1.9	16.5	1.9	16.3	-1.2	15.8	-3.1	15.7	-0.6	14.5	-7.6	15.8	9.0	14.9	-5.7	15.2	2.0	15.8	3.9
1940	15.0	-5.1	14.4	-4.0	14.5	0.7	16.9	16.6	18.1	7.1	19.6	8.3	17.9	-8.7	16.0	-10.6	15.3	-4.4	14.6	-4.6	15.1	3.4	15.4	2.0
1941	14.9	-3.2	14.7	-1.3	15.0	2.0	15.9	6.0	15.9	0.0	18.7	17.6	17.1	-8.6	17.1	0.0	17.3	1.2	18.8	8.7	18.2	-3.2	17.9	-1.6
1942	19.0	6.1	20.9	10.0	21.7	3.8	25.0	15.2	25.3	1.2	27.9	10.3	26.3	-5.7	26.0	-1.1	25.6	-1.5	25.7	0.4	26.9	4.7	27.7	3.0
1943	27.0	-2.5	29.0	7.4	31.4	8.3	33.9	8.0	38.7	14.2	40.6	4.9	38.7	-4.7	34.7	-10.3	31.7	-8.6	31.2	-1.6	32.3	3.5	32.6	0.9
1944	32.2	-1.2	33.0	2.5	33.9	2.7	34.9	2.9	35.0	0.3	38.6	10.3	36.0	-6.7	33.6	-6.7	31.3	-6.8	30.2	-3.5	30.6	1.3	31.4	2.6
1945	30.8	-1.9	32.0	3.9	31.3	-2.2	33.8	8.0	36.4	7.7	37.5	3.0	36.0	-4.0	34.1	-5.3	31.8	-6.7	31.4	-1.3	33.9	8.0	35.6	5.0
1946	34.5	-3.1	35.2	2.0	37.0	5.1	38.6	4.3	39.3	1.8	37.8	-3.8	35.8	-5.3	32.6	-8.9	30.9	-5.2	33.3	7.8	37.1	11.4	35.4	-4.6
1947	33.7	-4.8	35.4	5.0	38.2	7.9	38.2	0.0	39.3	2.9	37.1	-5.6	33.9	-8.6	34.5	1.8	34.0	-1.4	33.5	-1.5	37.1	10.7	37.2	0.3
1948	38.7	4.0	39.6	2.3	39.5	-0.3	42.1	6.6	43.5	3.3	38.2	-12.2	36.1	-5.5	35.4	-1.9	33.8	-4.5	33.9	0.3	34.7	2.4	33.9	-2.3
1949	37.6	10.9	38.2	1.6	37.8	-1.0	40.8	7.9	42.4	3.9	36.7	-13.4	36.0	-1.9	34.1	-5.3	33.0	-3.2	31.4	-4.8	33.8	7.6	33.4	-1.2
1950	33.0	-1.2	32.5	-1.5	33.3	2.5	35.4	6.3	35.2	-0.6	32.8	-6.8	34.9	6.4	32.9	-5.7	31.5	-4.3	30.6	-2.9	34.1	11.4	35.0	2.6
1951	33.2	-5.1	35.8	7.8	32.4	-9.5	36.0	11.1	38.0	5.6	34.5	-9.2	33.2	-3.8	32.7	-1.5	33.9	3.7	35.2	3.8	39.1	11.1	43.0	10.0
1952	44.4	3.3	41.2	-7.2	45.3	10.0	46.6	2.9	47.1	1.1	45.5	-3.4	46.9	3.1	45.5	-3.0	42.3	-7.0	40.8	-3.5	41.4	1.5	41.0	-1.0
1953	39.2	-4.4	37.4	-4.6	38.7	3.5	39.1	1.0	38.5	-1.5	40.2	4.4	34.7	-13.7	35.8	3.2	35.1	-2.0	34.5	-1.7	34.5	0.0	32.8	-4.9
1954	33.3	1.5	32.8	-1.5	32.8	0.0	35.6	8.5	38.2	7.3	35.4	-7.3	40.6	14.7	39.6	-2.5	36.5	-7.8	37.3	2.2	37.8	1.3	35.4	-6.3
1955	38.5	8.8	38.0	-1.3	38.2	0.5	44.2	15.7	43.4	-1.8	38.3	-11.8	36.1	-5.7	36.4	0.8	37.3	2.5	34.0	-8.8	37.5	10.3	35.0	-6.7
1956	38.4	9.7	35.9	-6.5	38.9	8.4	37.3	-4.1	40.9	9.7	44.0	7.6	40.9	-7.0	34.7	-15.2	34.8	0.3	35.7	2.6	38.2	7.0	37.5	-1.8
1957	36.8	-1.9	35.2	-4.3	34.4	-2.3	37.7	9.6	39.9	5.8	38.5	-3.5	39.5	2.6	38.9	-1.5	36.1	-7.2	39.4	9.1	38.9	-1.3	39.6	1.8
1958	44.2	11.6	46.4	5.0	52.1	12.3	47.3	-9.2	44.6	-5.7	37.3	-16.4	38.9	4.3	35.6	-8.5	35.8	0.6	37.1	3.6	35.9	-3.2	36.3	1.1
1959	37.5	3.3	38.7	3.2	34.2	-11.6	41.7	21.9	39.1	-6.2	36.9	-5.6	36.0	-2.4	33.9	-5.8	37.7	11.2	37.4	-0.8	37.8	1.1	39.5	4.5
1960	38.4	-2.8	36.7	-4.4	38.2	4.1	40.8	6.8	42.8	4.9	40.1	-6.3	41.3	3.0	36.1	-12.6	38.3	6.1	39.9	4.2	39.3	-1.5	36.4	-7.4
1961	37.9	4.1	36.5	-3.7	38.7	6.0	36.6	-5.4	37.1	1.4	37.8	1.9	38.2	1.1	35.6	-6.8	34.7	-2.5	34.6	-0.3	34.9	0.9	33.8	-3.2
1962	37.6	11.2	40.5	7.7	41.1	1.5	38.4	-6.6	41.5	8.1	38.3	-7.7	35.8	-6.5	35.3	-1.4	36.8	4.2	37.8	2.7	37.4	-1.1	34.3	-8.3
1963	40.4	17.8	37.4	-7.4	38.4	2.7	38.6	0.5	38.7	0.3	37.7	-2.6	37.6	-0.3	35.9	-4.5	34.1	-5.0	34.6	1.5	37.3	7.8	36.8	-1.3
1964	37.2	1.1	38.0	2.2	40.7	7.1	41.1	1.0	41.7	1.5	43.9	5.3	42.3	-3.6	38.0	-10.2	39.4	3.7	38.1	-3.3	41.9	10.0	38.4	-8.4
1965	38.2	-0.5	39.8	4.2	41.8	5.0	45.6	9.1	46.0	0.9	42.3	-8.0	40.3	-4.7	33.2	-17.6	37.3	12.3	37.1	-0.5	40.4	-1.6	39.3	-1.9
1966	37.8	5.6	38.0	0.5	39.5	3.9	43.1	9.1	40.1	-7.0	38.7	-3.5	41.5	7.2	37.9	-8.7	42.8	12.9	38.0	-11.2	40.4	6.3	40.7	-2.7
1967	39.5	0.5	40.6	2.8	38.3	-5.7	38.7	1.0	40.6	4.9	44.3	9.1	41.9	-5.4	37.5	-10.5	35.8	-4.5	35.6	-0.6	39.8	11.8	40.7	2.3
1968	41.9	2.9	43.5	3.8	44.3	1.8	43.4	-2.0	47.9	10.4	41.3	-13.8	42.0	1.7	37.8	-10.0	37.9	0.3	38.7	2.1	42.7	10.3	42.8	0.2
1969	43.8	2.3	42.8	-2.3	44.1	3.0	41.9	-5.0	49.7	18.6	44.2	-11.1	40.6	-8.1	41.5	2.2	40.2	-3.1	39.3	-2.2	48.6	23.7	43.6	-10.3
1970	45.3	3.9	45.6	0.7	45.9	0.7	43.7	-4.8	48.0	9.8	47.4	-1.2	43.6	-8.0	38.6	-11.5	44.0	14.0	39.7	-9.8	42.3	6.5	43.8	3.5

[Continued]

958

Fruits & Melons, Fresh/Dry Vegetables & Nuts
Producer Price Index
Base 1982 = 100
[Continued]

For 1926-1997. Columns headed % show percentile change in the index from the previous period for which an index is available.

Year	Jan Index	%	Feb Index	%	Mar Index	%	Apr Index	%	May Index	%	Jun Index	%	Jul Index	%	Aug Index	%	Sep Index	%	Oct Index	%	Nov Index	%	Dec Index	%
1971	45.6	4.1	46.6	2.2	49.3	5.8	47.6	-3.4	50.2	5.5	53.7	7.0	43.1	-19.7	45.7	6.0	40.9	-10.5	45.6	11.5	50.1	9.9	49.8	-0.6
1972	49.2	-1.2	50.3	2.2	44.5	-11.5	46.3	4.0	47.5	2.6	48.0	1.1	51.2	6.7	54.7	6.8	54.4	-0.5	48.4	-11.0	55.9	15.5	53.1	-5.0
1973	59.6	12.2	57.9	-2.9	62.5	7.9	69.4	11.0	73.3	5.6	77.9	6.3	74.0	-5.0	63.9	-13.6	58.7	-8.1	63.9	8.9	66.3	3.8	67.6	2.0
1974	72.7	7.5	84.6	16.4	83.0	-1.9	89.5	7.8	93.3	4.2	80.6	-13.6	73.7	-8.6	64.1	-13.0	64.3	0.3	65.5	1.9	73.7	12.5	64.5	-12.5
1975	69.0	7.0	66.6	-3.5	64.6	-3.0	72.3	11.9	72.2	-0.1	81.5	12.9	82.2	0.9	70.8	-13.9	72.0	1.7	72.2	0.3	70.5	-2.4	75.0	6.4
1976	76.8	2.4	74.6	-2.9	72.7	-2.5	76.9	5.8	70.6	-8.2	63.3	-10.3	64.9	2.5	62.8	-3.2	71.0	13.1	75.9	6.9	65.7	-13.4	68.8	4.7
1977	78.3	13.8	83.9	7.2	86.4	3.0	81.1	-6.1	79.6	-1.8	69.5	-12.7	71.8	3.3	69.6	-3.1	72.1	3.6	74.1	2.8	76.3	3.0	66.8	-12.5
1978	77.5	16.0	80.5	3.9	79.3	-1.5	89.6	13.0	86.8	-3.1	90.8	4.6	99.5	9.6	84.9	-14.7	82.0	-3.4	84.4	2.9	81.6	-3.3	87.3	7.0
1979	92.1	5.5	103.7	12.6	92.9	-10.4	94.2	1.4	90.0	-4.5	89.2	-0.9	89.4	0.2	95.3	6.6	82.1	-13.9	85.9	4.6	85.3	-0.7	83.1	-2.6
1980	86.3	3.9	87.0	0.8	86.1	-1.0	88.0	2.2	96.2	9.3	92.1	-4.3	99.4	7.9	100.1	0.7	104.9	4.8	95.0	-9.4	97.2	2.3	96.6	-0.6
1981	102.0	5.6	107.0	4.9	115.4	7.9	112.8	-2.3	108.5	-3.8	103.8	-4.3	104.7	0.9	101.7	-2.9	99.7	-2.0	98.1	-1.6	100.1	2.0	110.6	10.5
1982	114.0	3.1	114.4	0.4	101.4	-11.4	105.5	4.0	107.0	1.4	104.3	-2.5	94.3	-9.6	94.1	-0.2	87.1	-7.4	87.9	0.9	92.0	4.7	98.1	6.6
1983	89.7	-8.6	89.8	0.1	92.6	3.1	105.1	13.5	102.5	-2.5	104.2	1.7	101.8	-2.3	106.6	4.7	108.8	2.1	121.5	11.7	108.5	-10.7	108.9	0.4
1984	114.8	5.4	123.1	7.2	121.4	-1.4	104.0	-14.3	99.3	-4.5	107.9	8.7	111.1	3.0	115.8	4.2	114.4	-1.2	105.4	-7.9	99.0	-6.1	99.3	0.3
1985	102.1	2.8	114.1	11.8	109.6	-3.9	109.6	0.0	99.0	-9.7	100.2	1.2	108.7	8.5	103.0	-5.2	93.9	-8.8	92.2	-1.8	94.6	2.6	105.3	11.3
1986	101.1	-4.0	92.5	-8.5	93.5	1.1	103.8	11.0	108.1	4.1	102.8	-4.9	105.2	2.3	104.5	-0.7	105.7	1.1	113.4	7.3	109.7	-3.3	107.3	-2.2
1987	98.4	-8.3	101.9	3.6	108.3	6.3	105.1	-3.0	104.5	-0.6	110.3	5.6	112.2	1.7	99.5	-11.3	102.5	3.0	101.5	-1.0	124.1	22.3	113.8	-8.3
1988	118.2	3.9	100.5	-15.0	101.5	1.0	101.0	-0.5	101.2	0.2	100.8	-0.4	109.9	9.0	105.9	-3.6	117.4	10.9	111.3	-5.2	119.0	6.9	114.7	-3.6
1989	109.4	-4.6	123.8	13.2	118.7	-4.1	115.3	-2.9	128.9	11.8	122.3	-5.1	120.8	-1.2	109.7	-9.2	101.8	-7.2	114.3	12.3	102.9	-10.0	106.7	3.7
1990	139.1	30.4	156.9	12.8	133.3	-15.0	106.9	-19.8	103.6	-3.1	106.9	3.2	117.3	9.7	107.4	-8.4	104.0	-3.2	109.0	4.8	119.3	9.4	106.7	-10.6
1991	109.8	2.9	111.4	1.5	113.3	1.7	124.4	9.8	141.9	14.1	137.0	-3.5	124.8	-8.9	110.9	-11.1	108.1	-2.5	98.1	-9.3	108.5	10.6	88.7	-18.2
1992	99.6	12.3	106.9	7.3	104.6	-2.2	92.7	-11.4	91.3	-1.5	83.3	-8.8	85.2	2.3	95.9	12.6	89.3	-6.9	105.2	17.8	102.0	-3.0	106.3	4.2
1993	103.7	-2.4	105.2	1.4	101.6	-3.4	118.3	16.4	120.8	2.1	93.9	-22.3	97.5	3.8	99.7	2.3	102.3	2.6	94.6	-7.5	118.4	25.2	126.4	6.8
1994	113.3	-10.4	99.4	-12.3	100.0	0.6	96.6	-3.4	101.4	5.0	99.2	-2.2	100.3	1.1	95.3	-5.0	97.2	2.0	99.9	2.8	115.7	15.8	137.1	18.5
1995	110.9	-19.1	105.9	-4.5	107.7	1.7	118.9	10.4	117.0	-1.6	101.3	-13.4	101.5	0.2	96.9	-4.5	113.5	17.1	98.6	-13.1	113.6	15.2	115.5	1.7
1996	117.3	1.6	115.7	-1.4	138.3	19.5	125.0	-9.6	117.1	-6.3	129.5	10.6	118.8	-8.3	112.1	-5.6	122.4	9.2	130.3	6.5	123.8	-5.0	119.6	-3.4
1997	117.0	-2.2	122.8	5.0	127.2	3.6	112.5	-11.6	117.5	4.4	105.8	-10.0	101.8	-3.8	109.0	7.1	112.8	3.5	122.7	8.8	111.8	-8.9	121.4	8.6

Source: U.S. Department of Labor, Bureau of Labor Statistics, Division of Industry Prices and Price Indexes. n.e.c. stands for not elsewhere classified. - indicates no data collected for period or unavailable.

Grains

Producer Price Index
Base 1982 = 100

For 1926-1997. Columns headed % show percentile change in the index from the previous period for which an index is available.

Year	Jan Index	%	Feb Index	%	Mar Index	%	Apr Index	%	May Index	%	Jun Index	%	Jul Index	%	Aug Index	%	Sep Index	%	Oct Index	%	Nov Index	%	Dec Index	%
1926	37.9	-	36.5	-3.7	34.2	-6.3	34.7	1.5	33.7	-2.9	32.9	-2.4	33.9	3.0	32.2	-5.0	32.1	-0.3	32.8	2.2	31.5	-4.0	32.6	3.5
1927	32.3	-0.9	32.1	-0.6	31.3	-2.5	31.4	0.3	35.1	11.8	36.9	5.1	36.0	-2.4	36.5	1.4	34.7	-4.9	33.4	-3.7	33.6	0.6	34.4	2.4
1928	35.2	2.3	36.5	3.7	38.3	4.9	40.9	6.8	42.8	4.6	40.4	-5.6	37.5	-7.2	32.1	-14.4	32.8	2.2	32.6	-0.6	31.8	-2.5	31.8	0.0
1929	33.1	4.1	34.4	3.9	33.2	-3.5	31.8	-4.2	29.7	-6.6	30.6	3.0	34.4	12.4	33.4	-2.9	34.2	2.4	33.4	-2.3	32.0	-4.2	32.9	2.8
1930	31.6	-4.0	30.0	-5.1	28.1	-6.3	28.4	1.1	27.7	-2.5	26.4	-4.7	24.9	-5.7	27.1	8.8	25.9	-4.4	24.3	-6.2	21.5	-11.5	21.5	0.0
1931	21.1	-1.9	20.4	-3.3	20.0	-2.0	20.1	0.5	20.1	0.0	18.9	-6.0	16.5	-12.7	15.1	-8.5	14.8	-2.0	14.9	0.7	17.3	16.1	15.8	-8.7
1932	15.7	-0.6	15.5	-1.3	14.7	-5.2	15.0	2.0	14.4	-4.0	12.7	-11.8	12.3	-3.1	12.9	4.9	12.6	-2.3	11.6	-7.9	11.1	-4.3	10.7	-3.6
1933	11.0	2.8	11.0	0.0	12.1	10.0	15.1	24.8	17.7	17.2	19.3	9.0	24.8	28.5	21.8	-12.1	21.5	-1.4	19.6	-8.8	20.6	5.1	20.4	-1.0
1934	21.4	4.9	21.3	-0.5	20.9	-1.9	19.8	-5.3	21.5	8.6	24.4	13.5	25.1	2.9	29.0	15.5	29.7	2.4	28.6	-3.7	29.3	2.4	30.8	5.1
1935	29.9	-2.9	29.4	-1.7	27.9	-5.1	29.6	6.1	28.1	-5.1	25.9	-7.8	26.4	1.9	26.7	1.1	28.1	5.2	29.1	3.6	26.2	-10.0	25.8	-1.5
1936	26.6	3.1	26.3	-1.1	25.4	-3.4	24.9	-2.0	23.8	-4.4	24.6	3.4	29.9	21.5	34.5	15.4	34.4	-0.3	34.4	0.0	34.7	0.9	36.7	5.8
1937	38.1	3.8	37.6	-1.3	38.1	1.3	40.1	5.2	38.3	-4.5	35.5	-7.3	35.4	-0.3	31.0	-12.4	31.0	0.0	25.9	-16.5	23.3	-10.0	24.1	3.4
1938	25.3	5.0	24.6	-2.8	23.2	-5.7	22.2	-4.3	21.1	-5.0	21.1	0.0	19.6	-7.1	18.0	-8.2	17.9	-0.6	17.1	-4.5	17.1	0.0	18.3	7.0
1939	19.0	3.8	18.4	-3.2	18.3	-0.5	18.6	1.6	20.1	8.1	19.6	-2.5	17.6	-10.2	17.4	-1.1	21.9	25.9	20.8	-5.0	21.6	3.8	24.2	12.0
1940	24.8	2.5	24.5	-1.2	24.8	1.2	26.0	4.8	23.9	-8.1	21.7	-9.2	20.5	-5.5	20.0	-2.4	20.8	4.0	22.0	5.8	22.8	3.6	22.5	-1.3
1941	22.8	1.3	21.7	-4.8	22.8	5.1	23.9	4.8	25.1	5.0	25.6	2.0	25.7	0.4	26.8	4.3	28.7	7.1	27.4	-4.5	28.4	3.6	30.6	7.7
1942	32.3	5.6	32.1	-0.6	31.6	-1.6	30.8	-2.5	31.1	1.0	29.9	-3.9	30.0	0.3	30.3	1.0	31.5	4.0	30.8	-2.2	31.2	1.3	33.9	8.7
1943	36.1	6.5	36.6	1.4	37.8	3.3	37.8	0.0	38.1	0.8	38.3	0.5	39.1	2.1	39.4	0.8	40.3	2.3	41.3	2.5	41.5	0.5	43.2	4.1
1944	43.6	0.9	43.6	0.0	43.6	0.0	43.6	0.0	43.7	0.2	42.8	-2.1	42.2	-1.4	41.3	-2.1	41.0	-0.7	42.2	2.9	42.0	-0.5	43.0	2.4
1945	43.6	1.4	43.7	0.2	43.7	0.0	43.9	0.5	43.5	-0.9	43.8	0.7	43.3	-1.1	42.5	-1.8	42.7	0.5	43.8	2.6	44.8	2.3	44.9	0.2
1946	45.0	0.2	45.1	0.2	46.0	2.0	46.1	0.2	49.9	8.2	51.1	2.4	61.0	19.4	56.9	-6.7	57.4	0.9	58.7	2.3	55.7	-5.1	54.9	-1.4
1947	54.8	-0.2	57.7	5.3	68.9	19.4	67.9	-1.5	69.1	1.8	69.1	0.0	67.5	-2.3	70.0	3.7	77.2	10.3	81.4	5.4	83.2	2.2	85.5	2.8
1948	86.9	1.6	74.3	-14.5	73.5	-1.1	73.5	0.0	72.1	-1.9	69.9	-3.1	63.6	-9.0	60.1	-5.5	59.3	-1.3	57.5	-3.0	57.9	0.7	57.9	0.0
1949	56.8	-1.9	53.6	-5.6	55.5	3.5	55.9	0.7	54.6	-2.3	52.4	-4.0	52.0	-0.8	51.3	-1.3	53.5	4.3	53.4	-0.2	53.7	0.6	55.0	2.4
1950	54.8	-0.4	55.2	0.7	56.7	2.7	57.9	2.1	58.9	1.7	57.4	-2.5	58.8	2.4	56.9	-3.2	56.6	-0.5	56.6	0.0	58.5	3.4	61.5	5.1
1951	63.7	3.6	65.5	2.8	64.2	-2.0	64.2	0.0	63.0	-1.9	60.7	-3.7	60.4	-0.5	61.4	1.7	61.9	0.8	64.8	4.7	66.5	2.6	67.3	1.2
1952	66.3	-1.5	65.2	-1.7	65.3	0.2	64.6	-1.1	63.3	-2.0	61.1	-3.5	60.8	-0.5	62.1	2.1	62.1	0.0	60.8	-2.1	61.8	1.6	61.5	-0.5
1953	60.6	-1.5	59.7	-1.5	60.7	1.7	60.1	-1.0	59.8	-0.5	54.0	-9.7	54.7	1.3	55.4	1.3	56.6	2.2	56.3	-0.5	57.2	1.6	58.0	1.4
1954	58.5	0.9	58.7	0.3	59.6	1.5	59.5	-0.2	58.4	-1.8	55.4	-5.1	56.4	1.8	58.4	3.5	60.0	2.7	59.5	-0.8	59.9	0.7	59.2	-1.2
1955	59.9	1.2	59.7	-0.3	59.0	-1.2	58.3	-1.2	59.2	1.5	57.9	-2.2	55.5	-4.1	50.4	-9.2	52.2	3.6	52.8	1.1	51.1	-3.2	53.0	3.7
1956	52.2	-1.5	53.1	1.7	54.1	1.9	57.3	5.9	57.9	1.0	55.7	-3.8	56.6	1.6	56.9	0.5	58.1	2.1	53.8	-7.4	56.3	4.6	56.9	1.1
1957	57.3	0.7	55.8	-2.6	56.0	0.4	55.9	-0.2	54.7	-2.1	53.7	-1.8	53.0	-1.3	52.8	-0.4	52.0	-1.5	51.6	-0.8	51.8	0.4	51.6	-0.4
1958	50.6	-1.9	51.2	1.2	52.7	2.9	54.9	4.2	54.0	-1.6	52.1	-3.5	51.1	-1.9	49.5	-3.1	48.7	-1.6	49.2	1.0	48.2	-2.0	48.7	1.0
1959	48.7	0.0	49.3	1.2	49.8	1.0	51.1	2.6	50.4	-1.4	50.1	-0.6	50.1	0.0	49.8	-0.6	48.8	-2.0	48.5	-0.6	49.0	1.0	48.7	-0.6
1960	49.5	1.6	49.1	-0.8	50.1	2.0	50.9	1.6	49.8	-2.2	49.6	-0.4	48.4	-2.4	47.6	-1.7	48.0	0.8	47.0	-2.1	45.0	-4.3	46.6	3.6
1961	48.2	3.4	48.7	1.0	49.0	0.6	47.3	-3.5	47.9	1.3	47.5	-0.8	49.8	4.8	50.0	0.4	50.0	0.0	49.9	-0.2	50.8	1.8	50.6	-0.4
1962	50.0	-1.2	49.7	-0.6	50.1	0.8	50.6	1.0	51.9	2.6	51.4	-1.0	51.0	-0.8	50.5	-1.0	50.7	0.4	50.6	-0.2	51.2	1.2	52.0	1.6
1963	52.4	0.8	53.0	1.1	53.3	0.6	54.1	1.5	52.9	-2.2	52.2	-1.3	51.2	-1.9	50.6	-1.2	52.9	4.5	52.3	-1.1	51.6	-1.3	52.3	1.4
1964	53.4	2.1	52.4	-1.9	51.0	-2.7	53.1	4.1	53.1	0.0	46.2	-13.0	44.1	-4.5	44.1	0.0	45.9	1.1	45.6	-0.7	45.0	-1.3	46.3	2.9
1965	46.5	0.4	46.6	0.2	46.6	0.0	46.9	0.6	46.8	-0.2	46.1	-1.5	45.5	-1.3	45.4	-0.2	45.9	1.1	45.6	-0.7	45.0	-1.0	52.2	3.6
1966	47.5	2.6	47.8	0.6	46.7	-2.3	46.9	0.4	48.1	2.6	48.8	1.5	53.0	8.6	54.3	2.5	53.8	-0.9	50.9	-5.4	50.4	-1.0	52.2	3.6
1967	51.8	-0.8	49.3	-4.8	51.4	4.3	50.5	-1.8	50.4	-0.2	49.4	-2.0	47.6	-3.6	44.3	-6.9	44.0	-0.7	44.5	1.1	41.8	-6.1	43.9	5.0
1968	43.7	-0.5	44.4	1.6	43.8	-1.4	43.6	-0.5	44.4	1.8	42.2	-5.0	41.2	-2.4	38.6	-6.3	39.4	2.1	40.5	2.8	42.2	4.2	41.3	-2.1
1969	42.4	2.7	42.2	-0.5	42.0	-0.5	42.7	1.7	44.6	4.4	44.0	-1.3	43.1	-2.0	42.1	-2.3	42.9	1.9	43.6	1.6	42.0	-3.7	42.6	1.4
1970	44.2	3.8	44.2	0.0	44.0	-0.5	45.1	2.5	45.5	0.9	45.9	0.9	45.9	0.0	45.9	0.0	51.7	12.6	49.4	-4.4	49.4	0.0	51.2	3.6

[Continued]

Grains
Producer Price Index
Base 1982 = 100
[Continued]

For 1926-1997. Columns headed % show percentile change in the index from the previous period for which an index is available.

Year	Jan Index	%	Feb Index	%	Mar Index	%	Apr Index	%	May Index	%	Jun Index	%	Jul Index	%	Aug Index	%	Sep Index	%	Oct Index	%	Nov Index	%	Dec Index	%
1971	52.6	2.7	53.0	0.8	51.4	-3.0	50.7	-1.4	50.8	0.2	51.9	2.2	48.6	-6.4	44.0	-9.5	42.2	-4.1	41.9	-0.7	41.6	-0.7	45.3	8.9
1972	44.6	-1.5	44.1	-1.1	44.5	0.9	45.5	2.2	46.2	1.5	44.8	-3.0	45.7	2.0	47.3	3.5	51.9	9.7	51.8	-0.2	53.9	4.1	65.3	21.2
1973	64.3	-1.5	60.8	-5.4	59.8	-1.6	62.1	3.8	71.1	14.5	84.7	19.1	74.6	-11.9	126.3	69.3	109.8	-13.1	108.6	-1.1	104.7	-3.6	117.9	12.6
1974	128.4	8.9	131.9	2.7	124.7	-5.5	101.0	-19.0	99.8	-1.2	106.3	6.5	117.2	10.3	131.7	12.4	123.0	-6.6	138.1	12.3	134.4	-2.7	130.9	-2.6
1975	121.1	-7.5	115.2	-4.9	106.0	-8.0	103.6	-2.3	101.0	-2.5	96.4	-4.6	104.0	7.9	112.7	8.4	110.4	-2.0	107.8	-2.4	98.6	-8.5	97.5	-1.1
1976	99.8	2.4	101.6	1.8	103.3	1.7	99.1	-4.1	101.2	2.1	106.7	5.4	106.4	-0.3	98.5	-7.4	97.5	-1.0	88.5	-9.2	83.2	-6.0	85.7	3.0
1977	87.7	2.3	88.1	0.5	87.0	-1.2	87.4	0.5	81.2	-7.1	74.8	-7.9	71.7	-4.1	66.6	-7.1	68.4	2.7	68.6	0.3	78.0	13.7	79.3	1.7
1978	80.2	1.1	81.0	1.0	84.8	4.7	94.2	11.1	89.7	-4.8	89.2	-0.6	87.1	-2.4	84.8	-2.6	83.9	-1.1	86.3	2.9	89.6	3.8	87.6	-2.2
1979	87.4	-0.2	89.7	2.6	91.0	1.4	94.0	3.3	99.7	6.1	103.7	4.0	117.3	13.1	108.6	-7.4	106.4	-2.0	108.6	2.1	107.5	-1.0	108.1	0.6
1980	101.8	-5.8	105.9	4.0	103.3	-2.5	99.9	-3.3	103.8	3.9	102.1	-1.6	116.1	13.7	121.6	4.7	123.6	1.6	127.7	3.3	128.5	0.6	125.7	-2.2
1981	131.7	4.8	126.8	-3.7	124.1	-2.1	125.5	1.1	122.2	-2.6	121.9	-0.2	122.0	0.1	115.1	-5.7	107.7	-6.4	107.9	0.2	107.4	-0.5	101.3	-5.7
1982	106.8	5.4	105.8	-0.9	104.7	-1.0	107.1	2.3	108.2	1.0	107.0	-1.1	100.9	-5.7	93.5	-7.3	88.8	-5.0	86.9	-2.1	94.2	8.4	95.9	1.8
1983	97.8	2.0	105.4	7.8	107.8	2.3	115.6	7.2	114.8	-0.7	114.5	-0.3	112.2	-2.0	119.4	6.4	122.3	2.4	120.3	-1.6	122.1	1.5	115.5	-5.4
1984	116.4	0.8	111.6	-4.1	119.0	6.6	124.3	4.5	121.5	-2.3	122.3	0.7	118.0	-3.5	112.3	-4.8	109.7	-2.3	103.9	-5.3	104.2	0.3	100.8	-3.3
1985	103.1	2.3	103.0	-0.1	102.5	-0.5	104.6	2.0	101.5	-3.0	100.9	-0.6	97.2	-3.7	87.8	-9.7	85.9	-2.2	83.6	-2.7	91.0	8.9	92.8	2.0
1986	91.7	-1.2	91.8	0.1	90.8	-1.1	90.7	-0.1	94.6	4.3	86.4	-8.7	72.2	-16.4	65.9	-8.7	62.9	-4.6	63.9	1.6	69.4	8.6	71.0	2.3
1987	66.8	-5.9	66.7	-0.1	67.5	1.2	71.0	5.2	79.0	11.3	74.0	-6.3	68.8	-7.0	63.4	-7.8	69.5	9.6	72.8	4.7	74.9	2.9	78.9	5.3
1988	77.5	-1.8	83.5	7.7	80.6	-3.5	82.3	2.1	82.9	0.7	103.4	24.7	111.5	7.8	109.9	-1.4	112.9	2.7	114.2	1.2	107.4	-6.0	108.9	1.4
1989	115.2	5.8	111.3	-3.4	115.1	3.4	109.8	-4.6	114.1	3.9	105.8	-7.3	105.1	-0.7	100.3	-4.6	100.1	-0.2	98.2	-1.9	101.1	3.0	101.0	-0.1
1990	100.8	-0.2	100.4	-0.4	100.2	-0.2	107.2	7.0	108.6	1.3	110.4	1.7	103.1	-6.6	92.1	-10.7	88.3	-4.1	85.8	-2.8	85.1	-0.8	87.0	2.2
1991	85.9	-1.3	88.0	2.4	94.0	6.8	94.1	0.1	92.7	-1.5	90.2	-2.7	84.3	-6.5	93.2	10.6	92.4	-0.9	94.8	2.6	96.4	1.7	97.7	1.3
1992	103.1	5.5	106.2	3.0	108.5	2.2	102.7	-5.3	103.5	0.8	105.7	2.1	95.0	-10.1	88.5	-6.8	90.6	2.4	87.8	-3.1	86.6	-1.4	89.2	3.0
1993	89.9	0.8	88.1	-2.0	89.3	1.4	93.7	4.9	91.1	-2.8	85.3	-6.4	91.2	6.9	93.9	3.0	92.2	-1.8	96.4	4.6	106.1	10.1	116.4	9.7
1994	118.0	1.4	116.8	-1.0	112.5	-3.7	109.3	-2.8	106.8	-2.3	110.1	3.1	96.4	-12.4	90.2	-6.4	94.2	4.4	91.1	-3.3	91.2	0.1	95.3	4.5
1995	95.5	0.2	96.9	1.5	98.2	1.3	101.1	3.0	104.2	3.1	110.5	6.0	116.2	5.2	114.0	-1.9	119.3	4.6	126.2	5.8	131.1	3.9	137.6	5.0
1996	141.4	2.8	146.5	3.6	151.5	3.4	166.9	10.2	190.5	14.1	181.9	-4.5	184.9	1.6	170.6	-7.7	138.7	-18.7	118.8	-14.3	112.2	-5.6	109.6	-2.3
1997	111.1	1.4	111.0	-0.1	119.3	7.5	121.2	1.6	116.6	-3.8	112.4	-3.6	105.9	-5.8	106.3	0.4	107.2	0.8	109.1	1.8	107.1	-1.8	107.4	0.3

Source: U.S. Department of Labor, Bureau of Labor Statistics, Division of Industry Prices and Price Indexes. n.e.c. stands for not elsewhere classified. - indicates no data collected for period or unavailable.

Slaughter Livestock
Producer Price Index
Base 1982 = 100

For 1926-1997. Columns headed % show percentile change in the index from the previous period for which an index is available.

Year	Jan Index	%	Feb Index	%	Mar Index	%	Apr Index	%	May Index	%	Jun Index	%	Jul Index	%	Aug Index	%	Sep Index	%	Oct Index	%	Nov Index	%	Dec Index	%
1926	-	-	-	-	-	-	-	-	-	-	-	-	-	-	-	-	-	-	-	-	-	-	-	-
1927	-	-	-	-	-	-	-	-	-	-	-	-	-	-	-	-	-	-	-	-	-	-	-	-
1928	-	-	-	-	-	-	-	-	-	-	-	-	-	-	-	-	-	-	-	-	-	-	-	-
1929	-	-	-	-	-	-	-	-	-	-	-	-	-	-	-	-	-	-	-	-	-	-	-	-
1930	-	-	-	-	-	-	-	-	-	-	-	-	-	-	-	-	-	-	-	-	-	-	-	-
1931	-	-	-	-	-	-	-	-	-	-	-	-	-	-	-	-	-	-	-	-	-	-	-	-
1932	-	-	-	-	-	-	-	-	-	-	-	-	-	-	-	-	-	-	-	-	-	-	-	-
1933	-	-	-	-	-	-	-	-	-	-	-	-	-	-	-	-	-	-	-	-	-	-	-	-
1934	-	-	-	-	-	-	-	-	-	-	-	-	-	-	-	-	-	-	-	-	-	-	-	-
1935	-	-	-	-	-	-	-	-	-	-	-	-	-	-	-	-	-	-	-	-	-	-	-	-
1936	-	-	-	-	-	-	-	-	-	-	-	-	-	-	-	-	-	-	-	-	-	-	-	-
1937	-	-	-	-	-	-	-	-	-	-	-	-	-	-	-	-	-	-	-	-	-	-	-	-
1938	-	-	-	-	-	-	-	-	-	-	-	-	-	-	-	-	-	-	-	-	-	-	-	-
1939	-	-	-	-	15.0	-	-	-	-	-	13.6	-9.3	-	-	12.8	-5.9	14.7	14.8	-	-	-	-	12.3	-16.3
1940	-	-	-	-	12.6	2.4	-	-	-	-	12.6	0.0	-	-	-	-	14.0	11.1	-	-	-	-	14.1	0.7
1941	-	-	-	-	15.7	11.3	-	-	-	-	17.9	14.0	-	-	-	-	19.4	8.4	-	-	-	-	19.0	-2.1
1942	-	-	-	-	22.2	16.8	-	-	-	-	23.7	6.8	-	-	-	-	24.3	2.5	-	-	-	-	24.4	0.4
1943	-	-	-	-	27.3	11.9	-	-	-	-	25.3	-7.3	-	-	-	-	25.3	0.0	-	-	-	-	23.4	-7.5
1944	-	-	-	-	24.8	6.0	-	-	-	-	24.6	-0.8	-	-	-	-	25.0	1.6	-	-	-	-	24.8	-0.8
1945	-	-	-	-	26.1	5.2	-	-	-	-	26.1	0.0	-	-	-	-	25.1	-3.8	-	-	-	-	25.8	2.8
1946	26.2	1.6	26.1	-0.4	26.5	1.5	26.6	0.4	26.6	0.0	27.0	1.5	31.8	17.8	34.2	7.5	28.8	-15.8	33.7	17.0	38.7	14.8	38.5	-0.5
1947	37.2	-3.4	39.6	6.5	41.6	5.1	38.6	-7.2	39.5	2.3	40.4	2.3	42.0	4.0	42.0	0.0	44.1	5.0	44.4	0.7	42.3	-4.7	45.1	6.6
1948	47.5	5.3	43.0	-9.5	42.9	-0.2	42.4	-1.2	45.7	7.8	49.7	8.8	51.9	4.4	51.8	-0.2	50.9	-1.7	47.0	-7.7	44.9	-4.5	42.7	-4.9
1949	40.4	-5.4	38.4	-5.0	40.1	4.4	39.1	-2.5	40.1	2.6	40.8	1.7	40.0	-2.0	39.3	-1.7	39.6	0.8	38.2	-3.5	36.8	-3.7	36.7	-0.3
1950	37.7	2.7	39.2	4.0	39.1	-0.3	38.8	-0.8	42.6	9.8	43.3	1.6	46.7	7.9	46.8	0.2	45.9	-1.9	43.4	-5.4	43.8	0.9	45.5	3.9
1951	49.1	7.9	52.4	6.7	53.1	1.3	53.2	0.2	51.9	-2.4	52.0	0.2	51.5	-1.0	51.4	-0.2	50.7	-1.4	50.3	-0.8	47.5	-5.6	46.8	-1.5
1952	46.0	-1.7	45.6	-0.9	45.4	-0.4	46.3	2.0	47.7	3.0	46.8	-1.9	46.9	0.2	45.9	-2.1	42.5	-7.4	40.6	-4.5	39.2	-3.4	36.9	-5.9
1953	39.4	6.8	38.7	-1.8	38.8	0.3	36.6	-5.7	38.9	6.3	37.0	-4.9	40.8	10.3	37.3	-8.6	38.6	3.5	34.9	-9.6	33.2	-4.9	36.2	9.0
1954	39.6	9.4	39.5	-0.3	39.8	0.8	41.1	3.3	40.5	-1.5	37.9	-6.4	35.8	-5.5	35.9	0.3	34.9	-2.8	33.5	-4.0	33.2	-0.9	32.2	-3.0
1955	34.0	5.6	34.2	0.6	33.0	-3.5	35.2	6.7	32.8	-6.8	35.0	6.7	33.4	-4.6	31.3	-6.3	31.5	0.6	30.3	-3.8	25.8	-14.9	24.6	-4.7
1956	26.3	6.9	28.4	8.0	28.0	-1.4	30.0	7.1	31.7	5.7	32.3	1.9	31.1	-3.7	33.0	6.1	33.2	0.6	32.0	-3.6	29.7	-7.2	31.2	5.1
1957	32.3	3.5	32.6	0.9	33.3	2.1	34.7	4.2	34.5	-0.6	36.7	6.4	38.0	3.5	38.2	0.5	36.1	-5.5	34.8	-3.6	35.1	0.9	36.9	5.1
1958	38.0	3.0	40.4	6.3	42.4	5.0	42.4	0.0	44.6	5.2	44.0	-1.3	43.4	-1.4	42.3	-2.5	41.4	-2.1	40.1	-3.1	40.7	1.5	39.7	-2.5
1959	40.5	2.0	39.5	-2.5	40.9	3.5	41.7	2.0	40.9	-1.9	40.4	-1.2	38.1	-5.7	37.5	-1.6	37.0	-1.3	35.3	-4.6	33.5	-5.1	33.0	-1.5
1960	34.5	4.5	35.5	2.9	38.1	7.3	37.9	-0.5	38.1	0.5	37.8	-0.8	37.4	-1.1	35.9	-4.0	35.1	-2.2	36.0	2.6	36.5	1.4	36.9	1.1
1961	37.6	1.9	37.6	0.0	36.8	-2.1	36.7	-0.3	34.9	-4.9	34.4	-1.4	34.4	0.0	36.8	7.0	35.9	-2.4	35.4	-1.4	35.3	-0.3	35.9	1.7
1962	37.0	3.1	36.5	-1.4	37.0	1.4	36.7	-0.8	35.6	-3.0	35.8	0.6	37.3	4.2	38.5	3.2	40.7	5.7	38.5	-5.4	38.4	-0.3	37.3	-2.9
1963	36.5	-2.1	34.2	-6.3	32.6	-4.7	33.7	3.4	33.4	-0.9	34.4	3.0	36.7	6.7	36.5	-0.5	34.3	-6.0	34.0	-0.9	33.7	-0.9	30.8	-8.6
1964	32.4	5.2	31.7	-2.2	32.2	1.6	31.6	-1.9	31.3	-0.9	31.6	1.0	33.8	7.0	34.2	1.2	35.3	3.2	33.2	-5.9	32.0	-3.6	32.0	0.0
1965	32.9	2.8	34.0	3.3	34.4	1.2	35.3	2.6	37.5	6.2	41.0	9.3	41.1	0.2	41.8	1.7	40.2	-3.8	40.5	0.7	40.8	0.7	42.9	5.1
1966	44.2	3.0	45.8	3.6	44.4	-3.1	44.0	-0.9	42.8	-2.7	42.2	-1.4	41.7	-1.2	43.0	3.1	41.9	-2.6	40.8	-2.6	37.7	-7.6	37.5	-0.5
1967	38.9	3.7	38.2	-1.8	37.3	-2.4	36.1	-3.2	39.4	9.1	40.3	2.3	41.2	2.2	40.8	-1.0	39.7	-2.7	39.1	-1.5	37.0	-5.4	37.5	1.4
1968	37.9	1.1	39.4	4.0	40.5	2.8	40.4	-0.2	40.5	0.2	40.7	0.5	42.0	3.2	40.7	-3.1	40.6	-0.2	39.9	-1.7	39.9	0.0	40.0	0.3
1969	40.7	1.7	41.9	2.9	43.2	3.1	43.7	1.2	47.2	8.0	50.0	5.9	48.6	-2.8	47.4	-2.5	45.7	-3.6	45.5	-0.4	44.7	-1.8	46.1	3.1
1970	45.0	-2.4	47.9	6.4	49.7	3.8	47.9	-3.6	46.9	-2.1	47.2	0.6	48.4	2.5	45.5	-6.0	44.1	-3.1	42.9	-2.7	39.2	-8.6	38.6	-1.5

[Continued]

Slaughter Livestock
Producer Price Index
Base 1982 = 100
[Continued]

For 1926-1997. Columns headed % show percentile change in the index from the previous period for which an index is available.

Year	Jan Index	%	Feb Index	%	Mar Index	%	Apr Index	%	May Index	%	Jun Index	%	Jul Index	%	Aug Index	%	Sep Index	%	Oct Index	%	Nov Index	%	Dec Index	%
1971	39.7	2.8	46.1	16.1	44.5	-3.5	45.3	1.8	46.1	1.8	46.1	0.0	47.0	2.0	47.0	0.0	46.2	-1.7	46.9	1.5	46.9	0.0	48.4	3.2
1972	51.3	6.0	54.1	5.5	53.0	-2.0	51.9	-2.1	54.2	4.4	56.8	4.8	59.1	4.0	57.4	-2.9	56.2	-2.1	55.9	-0.5	54.1	-3.2	59.2	9.4
1973	61.8	4.4	69.0	11.7	75.4	9.3	71.4	-5.3	73.2	2.5	75.2	2.7	77.3	2.8	94.4	22.1	80.4	-14.8	72.0	-10.4	69.8	-3.1	66.3	-5.0
1974	76.5	15.4	75.6	-1.2	70.2	-7.1	65.5	-6.7	61.7	-5.8	53.5	-13.3	67.3	25.8	71.6	6.4	65.4	-8.7	64.0	-2.1	60.7	-5.2	61.9	2.0
1975	60.5	-2.3	59.0	-2.5	60.3	2.2	67.3	11.6	76.8	14.1	78.5	2.2	81.9	4.3	78.7	-3.9	81.4	3.4	80.6	-1.0	75.0	-6.9	74.3	-0.9
1976	71.6	-3.6	69.6	-2.8	66.3	-4.7	74.6	12.5	72.5	-2.8	71.8	-1.0	68.2	-5.0	64.4	-5.6	62.7	-2.6	60.5	-3.5	59.9	-1.0	64.4	7.5
1977	64.4	0.0	64.5	0.2	63.4	-1.7	65.1	2.7	69.9	7.4	66.8	-4.4	70.0	4.8	68.0	-2.9	67.0	-1.5	68.8	2.7	66.5	-3.3	70.8	6.5
1978	73.0	3.1	78.4	7.4	80.8	3.1	84.6	4.7	89.3	5.6	91.6	2.6	87.9	-4.0	84.0	-4.4	88.0	4.8	91.2	3.6	86.3	-5.4	89.3	3.5
1979	95.9	7.4	103.4	7.8	107.0	3.5	110.2	3.0	108.8	-1.3	102.4	-5.9	99.3	-3.0	93.1	-6.2	99.4	6.8	97.6	-1.8	96.3	-1.3	97.9	1.7
1980	96.1	-1.8	99.7	3.7	97.7	-2.0	89.4	-8.5	90.5	1.2	93.1	2.9	101.0	8.5	106.9	5.8	103.5	-3.2	102.0	-1.4	98.8	-3.1	97.5	-1.3
1981	94.7	-2.9	94.9	0.2	92.8	-2.2	95.7	3.1	97.6	2.0	102.0	4.5	103.4	1.4	101.6	-1.7	99.8	-1.8	94.8	-5.0	89.6	-5.5	87.3	-2.6
1982	91.8	5.2	97.4	6.1	99.1	1.7	103.8	4.7	109.7	5.7	107.6	-1.9	104.8	-2.6	104.1	-0.7	100.4	-3.6	96.4	-4.0	92.7	-3.8	92.0	-0.8
1983	94.0	2.2	97.4	3.6	97.5	0.1	101.1	3.7	100.0	-1.1	97.6	-2.4	93.3	-4.4	93.9	0.6	89.8	-4.4	89.0	-0.9	85.5	-3.9	92.4	8.1
1984	97.2	5.2	97.7	0.5	101.2	3.6	101.1	-0.1	98.8	-2.3	97.0	-1.8	100.9	4.0	98.4	-2.5	95.0	-3.5	90.7	-4.5	96.1	6.0	97.8	1.8
1985	96.0	-1.8	96.8	0.8	91.8	-5.2	89.7	-2.3	88.3	-1.6	87.9	-0.5	86.9	-1.1	82.1	-5.5	77.0	-6.2	88.2	14.5	92.8	5.2	92.8	0.0
1986	90.2	-2.8	87.7	-2.8	85.4	-2.6	82.9	-2.9	88.9	7.2	87.3	-1.8	95.1	8.9	98.1	3.2	98.2	0.1	95.9	-2.3	96.6	0.7	95.6	-1.0
1987	93.1	-2.6	95.9	3.0	96.0	0.1	104.3	8.6	109.6	5.1	109.8	0.2	107.3	-2.3	106.5	-0.7	104.1	-2.3	102.6	-1.4	96.8	-5.7	98.1	1.3
1988	99.3	1.2	105.7	6.4	106.3	0.6	107.7	1.3	111.8	3.8	106.1	-5.1	99.7	-6.0	100.6	0.9	100.7	0.1	101.8	1.1	98.3	-3.4	101.0	2.7
1989	104.5	3.5	104.6	0.1	106.8	2.1	106.4	-0.4	107.4	0.9	106.0	-1.3	104.8	-1.1	108.8	3.8	103.7	-4.7	104.6	0.9	105.6	1.0	110.5	4.6
1990	110.7	0.2	113.2	2.3	117.0	3.4	117.9	0.8	120.5	2.2	117.8	-2.2	114.7	-2.6	117.8	2.7	113.3	-3.8	116.5	2.8	113.9	-2.2	114.3	0.4
1991	112.8	-1.3	113.9	1.0	117.1	2.8	115.8	-1.1	115.2	-0.5	112.8	-2.1	110.2	-2.3	100.7	-8.6	101.1	0.4	100.9	-0.2	96.6	-4.3	97.7	1.1
1992	100.0	2.4	106.0	6.0	107.0	0.9	106.7	-0.3	108.0	1.2	105.3	-2.5	103.7	-1.5	104.2	0.5	103.4	-0.8	104.2	0.8	101.8	-2.3	106.3	4.4
1993	108.3	1.9	110.0	1.6	112.6	2.4	113.0	0.4	112.8	-0.2	109.8	-2.7	105.0	-4.4	107.1	2.0	105.7	-1.3	100.0	-5.4	100.5	0.5	99.2	-1.3
1994	100.7	1.5	103.6	2.9	104.7	1.1	104.9	0.2	98.5	-6.1	92.4	-6.2	94.3	2.1	96.8	2.7	91.3	-5.7	88.1	-3.5	89.6	1.7	91.6	2.2
1995	96.4	5.2	100.5	4.3	96.9	-3.6	92.3	-4.7	87.4	-5.3	90.7	3.8	90.7	0.0	90.8	0.1	92.0	1.3	91.4	-0.7	91.9	0.5	92.3	0.4
1996	89.6	-2.9	90.5	1.0	89.9	-0.7	89.6	-0.3	93.5	4.4	95.0	1.6	97.4	2.5	99.6	2.3	100.5	0.9	100.5	0.0	100.7	0.2	95.8	-4.9
1997	95.4	-0.4	93.8	-1.7	96.3	2.7	101.6	5.5	102.6	1.0	96.2	-6.2	98.8	2.7	97.9	-0.9	95.8	-2.1	93.0	-2.9	93.1	0.1	91.4	-1.8

Source: U.S. Department of Labor, Bureau of Labor Statistics, Division of Industry Prices and Price Indexes. n.e.c. stands for not elsewhere classified. - indicates no data collected for period or unavailable.

Slaughter Poultry
Producer Price Index
Base 1982 = 100

For 1926-1997. Columns headed % show percentile change in the index from the previous period for which an index is available.

Year	Jan Index	%	Feb Index	%	Mar Index	%	Apr Index	%	May Index	%	Jun Index	%	Jul Index	%	Aug Index	%	Sep Index	%	Oct Index	%	Nov Index	%	Dec Index	%
1926	-	-	-	-	-	-	-	-	-	-	-	-	-	-	-	-	-	-	-	-	-	-	-	-
1927	-	-	-	-	-	-	-	-	-	-	-	-	-	-	-	-	-	-	-	-	-	-	-	-
1928	-	-	-	-	-	-	-	-	-	-	-	-	-	-	-	-	-	-	-	-	-	-	-	-
1929	-	-	-	-	-	-	-	-	-	-	-	-	-	-	-	-	-	-	-	-	-	-	-	-
1930	-	-	-	-	-	-	-	-	-	-	-	-	-	-	-	-	-	-	-	-	-	-	-	-
1931	-	-	-	-	-	-	-	-	-	-	-	-	-	-	-	-	-	-	-	-	-	-	-	-
1932	-	-	-	-	-	-	-	-	-	-	-	-	-	-	-	-	-	-	-	-	-	-	-	-
1933	-	-	-	-	-	-	-	-	-	-	-	-	-	-	-	-	-	-	-	-	-	-	-	-
1934	-	-	-	-	-	-	-	-	-	-	-	-	-	-	-	-	-	-	-	-	-	-	-	-
1935	-	-	-	-	-	-	-	-	-	-	-	-	-	-	-	-	-	-	-	-	-	-	-	-
1936	-	-	-	-	-	-	-	-	-	-	-	-	-	-	-	-	-	-	-	-	-	-	-	-
1937	-	-	-	-	-	-	-	-	-	-	-	-	-	-	-	-	-	-	-	-	-	-	-	-
1938	-	-	-	-	-	-	-	-	-	-	-	-	-	-	-	-	-	-	-	-	-	-	-	-
1939	-	-	-	-	67.7		-	-	-	-	55.3	-18.3	-	-	56.3	1.8	60.8	8.0	-	-	-	-	52.5	-13.7
1940	-	-	-	-	60.0	14.3	-	-	-	-	54.9	-8.5	-	-	-	-	59.6	8.6	-	-	-	-	58.2	-2.3
1941	-	-	-	-	72.2	24.1	-	-	-	-	77.2	6.9	-	-	-	-	76.8	-0.5	-	-	-	-	73.8	-3.9
1942	-	-	-	-	89.3	21.0	-	-	-	-	77.6	-13.1	-	-	-	-	87.0	12.1	-	-	-	-	90.9	4.5
1943	-	-	-	-	98.8	8.7	-	-	-	-	99.8	1.0	-	-	-	-	96.5	-3.3	-	-	-	-	96.2	-0.3
1944	-	-	-	-	98.8	2.7	-	-	-	-	89.2	-9.7	-	-	-	-	94.8	6.3	-	-	-	-	98.2	3.6
1945	-	-	-	-	104.0	5.9	-	-	-	-	103.0	-1.0	-	-	-	-	97.3	-5.5	-	-	-	-	98.4	1.1
1946	102.6	4.3	104.3	1.7	103.2	-1.1	108.9	5.5	108.9	0.0	108.0	-0.8	110.6	2.4	103.9	-6.1	125.7	21.0	121.0	-3.7	101.9	-15.8	107.9	5.9
1947	103.7	-3.9	103.7	0.0	115.2	11.1	115.4	0.2	116.9	1.3	111.9	-4.3	110.6	-1.2	111.9	1.2	119.5	6.8	108.2	-9.5	107.4	-0.7	117.5	9.4
1948	128.5	9.4	119.1	-7.3	131.4	10.3	135.1	2.8	131.7	-2.5	133.2	1.1	129.2	-3.0	131.0	1.4	130.3	-0.5	119.4	-8.4	123.9	3.8	131.5	6.1
1949	123.9	-5.8	116.4	-6.1	122.8	5.5	120.5	-1.9	108.3	-10.1	97.8	-9.7	98.1	0.3	102.8	4.8	97.6	-5.1	95.5	-2.2	97.9	2.5	85.0	-13.2
1950	79.5	-6.5	97.3	22.4	105.9	8.8	102.6	-3.1	95.6	-6.8	92.5	-3.2	104.9	13.4	108.0	3.0	102.5	-5.1	92.4	-9.9	89.3	-3.4	90.5	1.3
1951	100.4	10.9	111.7	11.3	120.0	7.4	120.9	0.7	114.1	-5.6	111.9	-1.9	108.6	-2.9	106.3	-2.1	102.3	-3.8	94.1	-8.0	91.0	-3.3	95.1	4.5
1952	104.5	9.9	108.5	3.8	102.9	-5.2	97.9	-4.9	89.0	-9.1	92.7	4.2	101.0	9.0	105.1	4.1	105.2	0.1	98.2	-6.7	112.7	14.8	99.1	-12.1
1953	106.2	7.2	105.3	-0.8	107.4	2.0	110.8	3.2	106.0	-4.3	94.4	-10.9	106.7	13.0	102.6	-3.8	99.4	-3.1	93.1	-6.3	91.6	-1.6	82.7	-9.7
1954	91.2	10.3	87.9	-3.6	91.8	4.4	88.4	-3.7	84.3	-4.6	83.6	-0.8	83.0	-0.7	83.3	0.4	77.9	-6.5	72.2	-7.3	70.4	-2.5	66.8	-5.1
1955	79.8	19.5	86.5	8.4	100.5	16.2	96.9	-3.6	91.1	-6.0	92.4	1.4	89.8	-2.8	91.4	1.8	89.0	-2.6	78.6	-11.7	75.4	-4.1	72.1	-4.4
1956	74.1	2.8	78.1	5.4	80.9	3.6	76.1	-5.9	77.4	1.7	72.0	-7.0	75.2	4.4	69.2	-8.0	63.7	-7.9	63.0	-1.1	63.4	0.6	64.3	1.4
1957	63.9	-0.6	68.6	7.4	70.9	3.4	67.6	-4.7	67.7	0.1	69.3	2.4	71.3	2.9	70.8	-0.7	63.7	-10.0	60.2	-5.5	61.9	2.8	60.6	-2.1
1958	68.4	12.9	69.3	1.3	73.7	6.3	65.9	-10.6	71.4	8.3	73.5	2.9	67.7	-7.9	64.0	-5.5	58.2	-9.1	56.1	-3.6	58.4	4.1	55.5	-5.0
1959	62.4	12.4	63.6	1.9	63.0	-0.9	58.2	-7.6	59.0	1.4	58.7	-0.5	58.2	-0.9	54.7	-6.0	55.3	1.1	53.6	-3.1	56.3	5.0	69.1	22.7
1960	64.7	-6.4	66.1	2.2	68.4	3.5	67.8	-0.9	65.6	-3.2	64.7	-1.4	62.7	-3.1	60.1	-4.1	59.2	-1.5	60.1	1.5	60.0	-0.2	60.8	1.3
1961	64.3	5.8	67.4	4.8	63.6	-5.6	58.8	-7.5	56.9	-3.2	46.0	-19.2	46.6	1.3	46.8	0.4	41.3	-11.8	43.5	5.3	44.0	1.1	53.0	20.5
1962	56.2	6.0	57.6	2.5	56.7	-1.6	52.2	-7.9	50.6	-3.1	50.2	-0.8	53.3	6.2	54.0	1.3	57.8	7.0	54.4	-5.9	53.5	-1.7	54.7	2.2
1963	54.6	-0.2	57.7	5.7	57.0	-1.2	57.0	0.0	53.2	-6.7	53.8	1.1	53.8	0.0	51.9	-3.5	52.1	0.4	52.2	0.2	55.0	5.4	48.8	-11.3
1964	53.9	10.5	53.2	-1.3	52.7	-0.9	52.1	-1.1	49.8	-4.4	50.7	1.8	53.8	6.1	51.7	-3.9	52.7	1.9	51.6	-2.1	53.0	2.7	50.7	-4.3
1965	53.2	4.9	54.6	2.6	57.1	4.6	55.3	-3.2	53.7	-2.9	56.0	4.3	56.3	0.5	55.0	-2.3	54.3	-1.3	54.4	0.2	54.1	-0.6	55.5	2.6
1966	58.5	5.4	60.7	3.8	64.2	5.8	60.5	-5.8	64.5	6.6	60.8	-5.7	59.9	-1.5	57.1	-4.7	55.7	-2.5	52.9	-5.0	54.1	2.3	49.1	-9.2
1967	56.1	14.3	61.8	10.2	57.8	-6.5	56.6	-2.1	54.5	-3.7	54.5	0.0	56.6	3.9	49.2	-13.1	46.4	-5.7	47.0	1.3	41.7	-11.3	43.4	4.1
1968	49.8	14.7	55.3	11.0	51.8	-6.3	51.6	-0.4	54.4	5.4	57.0	4.8	59.7	4.7	55.9	-6.4	53.9	-3.6	50.4	-6.5	55.7	10.5	52.7	-5.4
1969	57.5	9.1	59.9	4.2	60.8	1.5	57.9	-4.8	62.7	8.3	61.9	-1.3	65.3	5.5	58.7	-10.1	56.5	-3.7	54.2	-4.1	54.9	1.3	55.2	0.5
1970	60.2	9.1	55.3	-8.1	57.7	4.3	52.7	-8.7	53.2	0.9	49.5	-7.0	52.1	5.3	49.2	-5.6	51.9	5.5	48.7	-6.2	49.6	1.8	41.8	-15.7

[Continued]

Slaughter Poultry
Producer Price Index
Base 1982 = 100
[Continued]

For 1926-1997. Columns headed % show percentile change in the index from the previous period for which an index is available.

Year	Jan Index	%	Feb Index	%	Mar Index	%	Apr Index	%	May Index	%	Jun Index	%	Jul Index	%	Aug Index	%	Sep Index	%	Oct Index	%	Nov Index	%	Dec Index	%
1971	50.1	19.9	52.0	3.8	52.1	0.2	51.8	-0.6	52.8	1.9	56.3	6.6	63.0	11.9	52.5	-16.7	53.5	1.9	48.6	-9.2	48.0	-1.2	45.4	-5.4
1972	49.1	8.1	54.9	11.8	56.1	2.2	49.1	-12.5	50.2	2.2	53.6	6.8	61.7	15.1	55.7	-9.7	58.5	5.0	54.1	-7.5	53.6	-0.9	54.0	0.7
1973	66.6	23.3	71.4	7.2	85.9	20.3	96.8	12.7	93.9	-3.0	96.1	2.3	98.7	2.7	140.5	42.4	118.0	-16.0	98.6	-16.4	80.5	-18.4	75.3	-6.5
1974	74.6	-0.9	93.7	25.6	86.6	-7.6	76.1	-12.1	76.5	0.5	69.2	-9.5	77.2	11.6	78.1	1.2	90.4	15.7	81.8	-9.5	93.2	13.9	87.2	-6.4
1975	90.5	3.8	92.1	1.8	88.6	-3.8	87.7	-1.0	92.5	5.5	99.3	7.4	114.2	15.0	105.5	-7.6	106.3	0.8	109.8	3.3	106.1	-3.4	94.5	-10.9
1976	88.1	-6.8	90.2	2.4	95.2	5.5	86.2	-9.5	90.8	5.3	91.1	0.3	95.9	5.3	93.3	-2.7	85.9	-7.9	78.4	-8.7	72.5	-7.5	75.9	4.7
1977	80.1	5.5	95.7	19.5	92.3	-3.6	95.0	2.9	95.4	0.4	95.2	-0.2	101.0	6.1	91.8	-9.1	94.7	3.2	88.8	-6.2	84.8	-4.5	82.2	-3.1
1978	88.7	7.9	98.4	10.9	97.9	-0.5	102.1	4.3	101.3	-0.8	115.5	14.0	128.5	11.3	106.7	-17.0	110.0	3.1	96.4	-12.4	100.2	3.9	103.5	3.3
1979	107.3	3.7	113.5	5.8	113.4	-0.1	109.1	-3.8	112.7	3.3	95.3	-15.4	95.8	0.5	89.6	-6.5	90.4	0.9	84.4	-6.6	101.9	20.7	101.4	-0.5
1980	101.7	0.3	96.2	-5.4	93.8	-2.5	89.6	-4.5	89.2	-0.4	86.8	-2.7	118.4	36.4	117.0	-1.2	125.6	7.4	116.2	-7.5	115.2	-0.9	114.0	-1.0
1981	111.1	-2.5	115.1	3.6	111.2	-3.4	101.8	-8.5	108.0	6.1	109.4	1.3	112.2	2.6	109.6	-2.3	102.5	-6.5	96.8	-5.6	91.2	-5.8	89.3	-2.1
1982	97.3	9.0	102.8	5.7	103.0	0.2	97.0	-5.8	100.4	3.5	108.0	7.6	110.7	2.5	98.7	-10.8	102.4	3.7	92.3	-9.9	94.6	2.5	92.7	-2.0
1983	92.3	-0.4	104.3	13.0	92.7	-11.1	89.0	-4.0	97.4	9.4	103.9	6.7	111.8	7.6	115.4	3.2	126.2	9.4	108.6	-13.9	124.3	14.5	125.7	1.1
1984	131.6	4.7	131.0	-0.5	134.6	2.7	125.5	-6.8	125.4	-0.1	118.7	-5.3	135.1	13.8	113.9	-15.7	124.9	9.7	114.3	-8.5	128.8	12.7	120.8	-6.2
1985	121.3	0.4	115.9	-4.5	112.3	-3.1	105.4	-6.1	111.8	6.1	116.5	4.2	118.6	1.8	112.6	-5.1	127.4	13.1	117.4	-7.8	132.8	13.1	122.5	-7.8
1986	110.9	-9.5	102.9	-7.2	108.9	5.8	110.1	1.1	113.7	3.3	123.3	8.4	154.6	25.4	177.2	14.6	145.7	-17.8	163.6	12.3	130.8	-20.0	114.5	-12.5
1987	110.6	-3.4	104.1	-5.9	104.0	-0.1	105.3	1.3	112.8	7.1	94.2	-16.5	102.3	8.6	111.2	8.7	100.3	-9.8	88.5	-11.8	93.9	6.1	87.7	-6.6
1988	99.1	13.0	86.9	-12.3	96.9	11.5	97.6	0.7	112.2	15.0	130.4	16.2	156.4	19.9	145.1	-7.2	142.7	-1.7	141.0	-1.2	128.0	-9.2	121.7	-4.9
1989	122.4	0.6	121.5	-0.7	138.5	14.0	138.4	-0.1	155.0	12.0	148.5	-4.2	135.5	-8.8	125.4	-7.5	134.9	7.6	109.0	-19.2	111.8	2.6	104.3	-6.7
1990	108.9	4.4	115.5	6.1	129.1	11.8	117.3	-9.1	128.2	9.3	118.5	-7.6	134.7	13.7	122.1	-9.4	128.9	5.6	110.2	-14.5	108.3	-1.7	104.2	-3.8
1991	110.4	6.0	103.1	-6.6	110.2	6.9	107.3	-2.6	113.9	6.2	112.7	-1.1	119.2	5.8	120.4	1.0	116.7	-3.1	109.1	-6.5	106.8	-2.1	105.1	-1.6
1992	106.9	1.7	102.8	-3.8	105.4	2.5	102.8	-2.5	116.1	12.9	110.7	-4.7	124.1	12.1	120.5	-2.9	111.8	-7.2	119.3	6.7	121.7	2.0	108.8	-10.6
1993	112.0	2.9	110.4	-1.4	116.1	5.2	116.5	0.3	132.3	13.6	118.9	-10.1	124.4	4.6	125.9	1.2	135.1	7.3	126.1	-6.7	127.2	0.9	118.4	-6.9
1994	110.9	-6.3	119.6	7.8	129.5	8.3	126.8	-2.1	138.2	9.0	135.2	-2.2	131.0	-3.1	119.9	-8.5	128.3	7.0	125.0	-2.6	114.4	-8.5	114.2	-0.2
1995	108.6	-4.9	109.3	0.6	113.1	3.5	109.1	-3.5	111.0	1.7	121.1	9.1	130.0	7.3	139.7	7.5	147.2	5.4	135.7	-7.8	150.3	10.8	132.5	-11.8
1996	133.6	0.8	124.0	-7.2	120.0	-3.2	120.9	0.7	140.6	16.3	155.3	10.5	151.3	-2.6	148.6	-1.8	147.4	-0.8	144.3	-2.1	151.3	4.9	149.0	-1.5
1997	138.1	-7.3	130.2	-5.7	117.5	-9.8	127.0	8.1	130.9	3.1	133.4	1.9	146.9	10.1	147.9	0.7	139.9	-5.4	121.7	-13.0	122.3	0.5	115.9	-5.2

Source: U.S. Department of Labor, Bureau of Labor Statistics, Division of Industry Prices and Price Indexes. n.e.c. stands for not elsewhere classified. - indicates no data collected for period or unavailable.

Plant and Animal Fibers
Producer Price Index
Base 1982 = 100

For 1926-1997. Columns headed % show percentile change in the index from the previous period for which an index is available.

Year	Jan Index	%	Feb Index	%	Mar Index	%	Apr Index	%	May Index	%	Jun Index	%	Jul Index	%	Aug Index	%	Sep Index	%	Oct Index	%	Nov Index	%	Dec Index	%
1926	52.6	-	52.1	-1.0	48.5	-6.9	47.0	-3.1	46.4	-1.3	45.9	-1.1	46.2	0.7	48.3	4.5	43.6	-9.7	37.6	-13.8	36.4	-3.2	35.9	-1.4
1927	37.1	3.3	38.3	3.2	39.0	1.8	39.5	1.3	41.8	5.8	42.7	2.2	44.8	4.9	48.4	8.0	51.3	6.0	49.9	-2.7	48.4	-3.0	47.0	-2.9
1928	46.3	-1.5	45.6	-1.5	47.8	4.8	49.1	2.7	51.2	4.3	50.6	-1.2	50.9	0.6	46.8	-8.1	45.4	-3.0	47.1	3.7	47.5	0.8	48.2	1.5
1929	47.6	-1.2	47.7	0.2	48.9	2.5	47.2	-3.5	45.6	-3.4	45.2	-0.9	45.0	-0.4	45.4	0.9	45.6	0.4	44.7	-2.0	42.4	-5.1	41.7	-1.7
1930	41.3	-1.0	38.4	-7.0	37.3	-2.9	38.2	2.4	37.5	-1.8	33.1	-11.7	30.5	-7.9	28.7	-5.9	26.5	-7.7	25.6	-3.4	25.8	0.8	24.2	-6.2
1931	24.7	2.1	25.7	4.0	25.6	-0.4	24.2	-5.5	22.4	-7.4	22.0	-1.8	22.6	2.7	18.9	-16.4	17.5	-7.4	16.9	-3.4	17.3	2.4	16.5	-4.6
1932	16.7	1.2	16.8	0.6	16.4	-2.4	15.0	-8.5	13.7	-8.7	12.7	-7.3	13.6	7.1	16.6	22.1	17.8	7.2	15.9	-10.7	15.0	-5.7	14.3	-4.7
1933	14.5	1.4	13.9	-4.1	15.0	7.9	15.7	4.7	19.2	22.3	21.9	14.1	24.9	13.7	22.4	-10.0	22.5	0.4	22.1	-1.8	22.6	2.3	22.9	1.3
1934	24.7	7.9	26.7	8.1	26.7	0.0	26.0	-2.6	24.9	-4.2	26.2	5.2	26.7	1.9	27.4	2.6	27.0	-1.5	26.2	-3.0	26.5	1.1	26.8	1.1
1935	26.9	0.4	26.5	-1.5	24.4	-7.9	24.8	1.6	25.8	4.0	25.4	-1.6	25.7	1.2	25.1	-2.3	24.5	-2.4	25.7	4.9	27.2	5.8	26.9	-1.1
1936	26.7	-0.7	26.0	-2.6	26.1	0.4	26.2	0.4	26.0	-0.8	26.7	2.7	28.4	6.4	27.4	-3.5	27.4	0.0	27.3	-0.4	27.7	1.5	29.0	4.7
1937	29.8	2.8	29.9	0.3	31.9	6.7	31.6	-0.9	30.0	-5.1	28.9	-3.7	28.6	-1.0	24.9	-12.9	22.5	-9.6	20.8	-7.6	19.8	-4.8	20.0	1.0
1938	20.6	3.0	20.8	1.0	20.7	-0.5	20.5	-1.0	20.0	-2.4	19.8	-1.0	21.0	6.1	20.2	-3.8	19.5	-3.5	20.5	5.1	20.9	2.0	20.4	-2.4
1939	20.8	2.0	21.2	1.9	21.7	2.4	21.5	-0.9	23.1	7.4	23.5	1.7	23.3	-0.9	22.6	-3.0	24.0	6.2	25.3	5.4	26.3	4.0	29.3	11.4
1940	25.8	-11.9	25.0	-3.1	24.5	-2.0	24.0	-2.0	22.8	-5.0	23.5	3.1	22.9	-2.6	21.7	-5.2	21.7	0.0	22.0	1.4	22.8	3.6	23.0	0.9
1941	23.3	1.3	23.4	0.4	24.3	3.8	25.0	2.9	27.7	10.8	29.7	7.2	32.9	10.8	33.6	2.1	35.3	5.1	34.4	-2.5	34.1	-0.9	35.7	4.7
1942	38.7	8.4	38.7	0.0	39.5	2.1	40.4	2.3	40.3	-0.2	38.4	-4.7	39.0	1.6	37.3	-4.4	37.4	0.3	37.6	0.5	38.3	1.9	38.9	1.6
1943	40.1	3.1	40.6	1.2	41.2	1.5	41.3	0.2	41.2	-0.2	41.1	-0.2	40.7	-1.0	40.1	-1.5	40.1	0.0	39.6	-1.2	38.4	-3.0	38.5	0.3
1944	39.2	1.8	40.3	2.8	40.8	1.2	40.6	-0.5	40.7	0.2	41.5	2.0	41.7	0.5	41.1	-1.4	41.2	0.2	41.4	0.5	41.1	-0.7	41.4	0.7
1945	41.5	0.2	41.5	0.0	41.8	0.7	42.4	1.4	43.2	1.9	43.1	-0.2	42.6	-1.2	42.2	-0.9	42.4	0.5	43.5	2.6	44.9	3.2	45.3	0.9
1946	45.5	0.4	47.2	3.7	48.7	3.2	50.1	2.9	49.8	-0.6	52.1	4.6	63.1	21.1	67.5	7.0	68.7	1.8	67.7	-1.5	59.8	-11.7	61.9	3.5
1947	61.0	-1.5	62.9	3.1	65.6	4.3	66.3	1.1	67.5	1.8	69.3	2.7	70.3	1.4	65.7	-6.5	62.0	-5.6	62.7	1.1	65.9	5.1	69.5	5.5
1948	68.7	-1.2	65.7	-4.4	67.7	3.0	72.9	7.7	74.7	2.5	75.6	1.2	71.8	-5.0	67.8	-5.6	67.5	-0.4	67.1	-0.6	67.5	0.6	69.6	3.1
1949	70.7	1.6	70.6	-0.1	70.4	-0.3	70.8	0.6	69.4	-2.0	69.0	-0.6	67.1	-2.8	64.9	-3.3	63.6	-2.0	63.0	-0.9	62.0	-1.6	63.2	1.9
1950	65.0	2.8	67.4	3.7	67.1	-0.4	68.3	1.8	70.0	2.5	72.4	3.4	77.0	6.4	80.5	4.5	90.8	12.8	89.7	-1.2	94.7	5.6	98.0	3.5
1951	108.3	10.5	112.5	3.9	116.4	3.5	112.2	-3.6	107.9	-3.8	105.1	-2.6	92.6	-11.9	80.9	-12.6	77.0	-4.8	80.2	4.2	86.7	8.1	85.6	-1.3
1952	85.8	0.2	81.3	-5.2	80.2	-1.4	80.7	0.6	77.1	-4.5	80.1	3.9	77.9	-2.7	77.7	-0.3	76.5	-1.5	74.0	-3.3	72.3	-2.3	68.7	-5.0
1953	68.2	-0.7	69.3	1.6	70.6	1.9	69.8	-1.1	70.4	0.9	70.2	-0.3	70.9	1.0	70.1	-1.1	69.9	-0.3	69.6	-0.4	69.8	0.3	69.6	-0.3
1954	70.3	1.0	71.9	2.3	71.5	-0.6	71.2	-0.4	72.2	1.4	72.2	0.0	72.4	0.3	72.0	-0.6	72.5	0.7	72.3	-0.3	70.5	-2.5	70.9	0.6
1955	70.5	-0.6	70.4	-0.1	69.4	-1.4	69.3	-0.1	69.8	0.7	69.8	0.0	70.1	0.4	69.4	-1.0	68.1	-1.9	66.9	-1.8	68.2	1.9	68.1	-0.1
1956	68.7	0.9	71.4	3.9	71.2	-0.3	71.4	0.3	71.5	0.1	71.7	0.3	70.4	-1.8	66.3	-5.8	66.4	0.2	67.5	1.7	68.1	0.9	68.4	0.4
1957	69.4	1.5	70.1	1.0	70.2	0.1	70.4	0.3	70.4	0.0	70.8	0.6	70.9	0.1	70.2	-1.0	69.4	-1.1	69.7	0.4	70.7	1.4	70.0	-1.0
1958	69.8	-0.3	69.4	-0.6	68.6	-1.2	68.4	-0.3	68.6	0.3	68.7	0.1	68.7	0.0	68.7	0.0	68.0	-1.0	68.0	0.0	68.0	0.0	67.3	-1.0
1959	67.1	-0.3	66.9	-0.3	67.2	0.4	68.2	1.5	68.7	0.7	68.6	-0.1	67.5	-1.6	64.6	-4.3	64.5	-0.2	63.9	-0.9	63.9	0.0	64.6	1.1
1960	64.7	0.2	64.9	0.3	64.8	-0.2	65.0	0.3	65.2	0.3	65.3	0.2	65.1	-0.3	62.3	-4.3	62.2	-0.2	61.3	-1.4	61.3	0.0	61.3	0.0
1961	61.3	0.0	61.6	0.5	62.7	1.8	63.0	0.5	64.3	2.1	65.0	1.1	65.3	0.5	66.4	1.7	66.6	0.3	67.1	0.8	67.1	0.0	67.1	0.0
1962	67.0	-0.1	67.1	0.1	67.3	0.3	67.6	0.4	67.6	0.0	68.1	0.7	67.9	-0.3	67.3	-0.9	66.6	-1.0	66.6	0.0	66.7	0.2	67.1	0.6
1963	67.9	1.2	68.9	1.5	69.6	1.0	69.7	0.1	69.5	-0.3	69.3	-0.3	68.5	-1.2	68.1	-0.6	68.0	-0.1	68.0	0.0	68.2	0.3	69.3	1.6
1964	69.4	0.1	69.5	0.1	69.8	0.4	69.8	0.0	69.2	-0.9	69.2	0.0	68.0	-1.7	65.6	-3.5	64.5	-1.7	64.1	-0.6	64.2	0.2	63.3	-1.4
1965	63.2	-0.2	62.7	-0.8	62.6	-0.2	62.6	0.0	62.7	0.2	62.9	0.3	62.7	-0.3	61.8	-1.4	61.5	-0.5	61.5	0.0	61.4	-0.2	61.3	-0.2
1966	61.3	0.0	61.2	-0.2	61.3	0.2	61.5	0.3	61.7	0.3	61.7	0.0	61.8	0.2	49.4	-20.1	49.0	-0.8	48.8	-0.4	48.4	-0.8	48.5	-0.2
1967	48.4	-0.2	48.0	-0.8	48.0	0.0	47.8	-0.4	47.8	0.0	48.4	1.3	48.4	0.0	48.8	0.8	49.5	1.4	49.5	0.0	51.2	3.4	55.2	7.8
1968	54.3	-1.6	52.3	-3.7	52.3	0.0	52.0	-0.6	51.8	-0.4	51.9	0.2	51.9	0.0	52.5	1.2	52.7	0.4	50.7	-3.8	48.7	-3.9	47.2	-3.1
1969	47.0	-0.4	46.3	-1.5	46.0	-0.6	46.0	0.0	46.3	0.7	46.3	0.0	46.3	0.0	45.7	-1.3	45.4	-0.7	45.2	-0.4	45.1	-0.2	44.9	-0.4
1970	44.6	-0.7	44.7	0.2	44.4	-0.7	44.7	0.7	44.8	0.2	44.9	0.2	45.2	0.7	45.2	0.0	44.4	-1.8	43.8	-1.4	43.3	-1.1	42.7	-1.4

[Continued]

Plant and Animal Fibers
Producer Price Index
Base 1982 = 100
[Continued]

For 1926-1997. Columns headed % show percentile change in the index from the previous period for which an index is available.

Year	Jan Index	%	Feb Index	%	Mar Index	%	Apr Index	%	May Index	%	Jun Index	%	Jul Index	%	Aug Index	%	Sep Index	%	Oct Index	%	Nov Index	%	Dec Index	%
1971	42.9	0.5	43.4	1.2	43.8	0.9	44.1	0.7	44.5	0.9	45.5	2.2	45.6	0.2	46.0	0.9	46.9	2.0	47.4	1.1	47.9	1.1	50.5	5.4
1972	54.0	6.9	55.8	3.3	56.3	0.9	60.2	6.9	64.1	6.5	62.7	-2.2	61.8	-1.4	59.4	-3.9	53.4	-10.1	52.1	-2.4	55.3	6.1	59.6	7.8
1973	66.1	10.9	69.0	4.4	75.2	9.0	76.2	1.3	84.5	10.9	87.6	3.7	91.9	4.9	112.6	22.5	132.0	17.2	131.3	-0.5	115.3	-12.2	127.8	10.8
1974	135.4	5.9	118.3	-12.6	108.1	-8.6	103.1	-4.6	96.7	-6.2	96.3	-0.4	92.6	-3.8	89.4	-3.5	83.6	-6.5	78.5	-6.1	74.3	-5.4	70.5	-5.1
1975	68.4	-3.0	66.7	-2.5	68.2	2.2	67.8	-0.6	75.5	11.4	71.7	-5.0	75.3	5.0	79.4	5.4	80.8	1.8	81.1	0.4	82.3	1.5	88.5	7.5
1976	95.3	7.7	91.9	-3.6	92.5	0.7	92.4	-0.1	99.3	7.5	116.2	17.0	132.6	14.1	116.1	-12.4	119.4	2.8	123.1	3.1	127.1	3.2	118.0	-7.2
1977	106.7	-9.6	118.3	10.9	124.4	5.2	123.0	-1.1	117.6	-4.4	97.3	-17.3	96.3	-1.0	88.8	-7.8	81.7	-8.0	82.3	0.7	80.9	-1.7	79.3	-2.0
1978	84.3	6.3	86.0	2.0	92.1	7.1	89.2	-3.1	94.5	5.9	95.1	0.6	93.6	-1.6	97.3	4.0	99.2	2.0	103.6	4.4	104.2	0.6	104.9	0.7
1979	105.3	0.4	101.1	-4.0	97.5	-3.6	97.5	0.0	102.3	4.9	108.2	5.8	102.3	-5.5	102.5	0.2	104.1	1.6	104.9	0.8	106.2	1.2	109.4	3.0
1980	117.8	7.7	132.8	12.7	125.6	-5.4	131.6	4.8	134.4	2.1	121.7	-9.4	131.6	8.1	138.4	5.2	145.5	5.1	137.2	-5.7	141.5	3.1	144.9	2.4
1981	140.0	-3.4	132.2	-5.6	133.1	0.7	135.1	1.5	127.3	-5.8	128.0	0.5	123.8	-3.3	114.6	-7.4	101.8	-11.2	104.3	2.5	97.8	-6.2	92.8	-5.1
1982	97.7	5.3	95.4	-2.4	98.3	3.0	102.2	4.0	105.5	3.2	100.1	-5.1	108.8	8.7	102.3	-6.0	97.0	-5.2	97.6	0.6	96.3	-1.3	98.8	2.6
1983	99.4	0.6	101.7	2.3	107.0	5.2	105.3	-1.6	110.3	4.7	113.2	2.6	113.5	0.3	118.6	4.5	117.6	-0.8	115.6	-1.7	120.1	3.9	120.3	0.2
1984	113.0	-6.1	114.7	1.5	123.4	7.6	124.3	0.7	127.7	2.7	124.5	-2.5	116.2	-6.7	104.2	-10.3	103.6	-0.6	100.0	-3.5	99.2	-0.8	100.1	0.9
1985	100.8	0.7	98.9	-1.9	98.8	-0.1	104.1	5.4	99.9	-4.0	98.1	-1.8	99.4	1.3	95.9	-3.5	94.2	-1.8	94.3	0.1	93.5	-0.8	91.9	-1.7
1986	96.8	5.3	97.8	1.0	101.9	4.2	103.8	1.9	106.2	2.3	108.2	1.9	108.7	0.5	46.5	-57.2	53.2	14.4	74.3	39.7	75.9	2.2	87.1	14.8
1987	94.7	8.7	93.1	-1.7	89.9	-3.4	98.4	9.5	108.7	10.5	116.1	6.8	120.1	3.4	123.4	2.7	118.5	-4.0	108.9	-8.1	105.1	-3.5	100.5	-4.4
1988	100.7	0.2	97.8	-2.9	103.2	5.5	103.6	0.4	103.7	0.1	107.6	3.8	99.4	-7.6	98.7	-0.7	89.6	-9.2	89.7	0.1	93.1	3.8	93.9	0.9
1989	95.8	2.0	94.8	-1.0	98.4	3.8	105.0	6.7	108.1	3.0	110.5	2.2	111.5	0.9	116.8	4.8	113.9	-2.5	116.9	2.6	115.3	-1.4	106.3	-7.8
1990	104.8	-1.4	108.7	3.7	114.7	5.5	118.7	3.5	121.9	2.7	125.9	3.3	129.4	2.8	125.1	-3.3	116.6	-6.8	116.4	-0.2	115.0	-1.2	116.9	1.7
1991	115.2	-1.5	126.3	9.6	129.1	2.2	134.0	3.8	139.2	3.9	130.8	-6.0	120.2	-8.1	106.7	-11.2	103.5	-3.0	96.3	-7.0	90.3	-6.2	89.7	-0.7
1992	85.4	-4.8	83.5	-2.2	84.7	1.4	89.0	5.1	93.4	4.9	96.2	3.0	102.0	6.0	96.6	-5.3	93.8	-2.9	82.8	-11.7	83.2	0.5	87.3	4.9
1993	89.5	2.5	89.5	0.0	94.2	5.3	91.5	-2.9	93.3	2.0	90.5	-3.0	90.8	0.3	88.5	-2.5	89.4	1.0	92.0	2.9	88.8	-3.5	98.1	10.5
1994	107.1	9.2	119.0	11.1	120.8	1.5	123.4	2.2	129.2	4.7	129.4	0.2	114.5	-11.5	118.7	3.7	122.1	2.9	111.1	-9.0	120.4	8.4	132.6	10.1
1995	143.5	8.2	149.4	4.1	180.2	20.6	175.2	-2.8	165.7	-5.4	178.9	8.0	163.5	-8.6	139.2	-14.9	147.6	6.0	142.6	-3.4	139.9	-1.9	137.9	-1.4
1996	136.2	-1.2	135.2	-0.7	132.4	-2.1	142.6	7.7	137.4	-3.6	135.7	-1.2	128.2	-5.5	128.3	0.1	122.8	-4.3	119.9	-2.4	113.1	-5.7	120.4	6.5
1997	116.4	-3.3	116.5	0.1	122.5	5.2	115.1	-6.0	116.0	0.8	117.5	1.3	120.0	2.1	121.1	0.9	118.3	-2.3	116.8	-1.3	115.5	-1.1	108.4	-6.1

Source: U.S. Department of Labor, Bureau of Labor Statistics, Division of Industry Prices and Price Indexes. n.e.c. stands for not elsewhere classified. - indicates no data collected for period or unavailable.

967

Fluid Milk
Producer Price Index
Base 1982 = 100

For 1926-1997. Columns headed % show percentile change in the index from the previous period for which an index is available.

Year	Jan Index	%	Feb Index	%	Mar Index	%	Apr Index	%	May Index	%	Jun Index	%	Jul Index	%	Aug Index	%	Sep Index	%	Oct Index	%	Nov Index	%	Dec Index	%
1926	19.6	-	19.6	0.0	19.6	0.0	19.8	1.0	19.2	-3.0	18.9	-1.6	19.1	1.1	19.3	1.0	19.9	3.1	19.8	-0.5	19.7	-0.5	19.7	0.0
1927	19.6	-0.5	19.6	0.0	19.6	0.0	19.4	-1.0	19.2	-1.0	19.2	0.0	19.4	1.0	19.4	0.0	20.9	7.7	20.9	0.0	21.0	0.5	21.0	0.0
1928	20.8	-1.0	20.8	0.0	19.4	-6.7	19.3	-0.5	19.1	-1.0	19.1	0.0	20.0	4.7	20.9	4.5	21.1	1.0	21.0	-0.5	21.0	0.0	21.0	0.0
1929	21.2	1.0	21.1	-0.5	21.1	0.0	21.1	0.0	21.1	0.0	21.4	1.4	21.1	-1.4	21.1	0.0	21.2	0.5	21.4	0.9	21.4	0.0	21.4	0.0
1930	21.1	-1.4	21.1	0.0	21.1	0.0	21.1	0.0	19.8	-6.2	19.8	0.0	19.8	0.0	20.7	4.5	21.1	1.9	21.1	0.0	21.1	0.0	19.8	-6.2
1931	18.7	-5.6	18.5	-1.1	18.5	0.0	18.5	0.0	18.5	0.0	18.9	2.2	19.2	1.6	18.8	-2.1	18.8	0.0	18.8	0.0	17.5	-6.9	17.5	0.0
1932	14.7	-16.0	13.8	-6.1	13.8	0.0	13.8	0.0	13.8	0.0	13.5	-2.2	13.5	0.0	13.5	0.0	13.5	0.0	13.5	0.0	13.5	0.0	11.9	-11.9
1933	11.5	-3.4	11.0	-4.3	10.8	-1.8	10.8	0.0	12.0	11.1	13.5	12.5	13.9	3.0	14.7	5.8	14.7	0.0	14.8	0.7	15.2	2.7	15.5	2.0
1934	15.2	-1.9	14.6	-3.9	14.4	-1.4	14.3	-0.7	15.9	11.2	16.9	6.3	17.3	2.4	17.3	0.0	17.3	0.0	17.5	1.2	17.0	-2.9	17.0	0.0
1935	17.2	1.2	17.4	1.2	17.4	0.0	17.3	-0.6	17.1	-1.2	16.9	-1.2	16.9	0.0	17.1	1.2	16.8	-1.8	16.5	-1.8	16.5	0.0	16.6	0.6
1936	16.5	-0.6	16.6	0.6	15.9	-4.2	15.8	-0.6	15.8	0.0	15.8	0.0	16.4	3.8	17.1	4.3	18.2	6.4	18.3	0.5	18.4	0.5	18.4	0.0
1937	18.4	0.0	18.5	0.5	18.5	0.0	15.1	-18.4	13.3	-11.9	13.3	0.0	14.6	9.8	15.5	6.2	16.7	7.7	16.7	0.0	17.6	5.4	17.8	1.1
1938	16.4	-7.9	15.6	-4.9	15.4	-1.3	14.8	-3.9	14.2	-4.1	14.1	-0.7	14.3	1.4	14.2	-0.7	15.2	7.0	15.2	0.0	15.3	0.7	15.4	0.7
1939	15.2	-1.3	15.1	-0.7	13.0	-13.9	10.9	-16.2	10.9	0.0	11.1	1.8	13.2	18.9	14.6	10.6	15.9	8.9	16.9	6.3	16.9	0.0	16.7	-1.2
1940	16.7	0.0	16.6	-0.6	16.5	-0.6	16.5	0.0	14.8	-10.3	14.8	0.0	15.2	2.7	15.3	0.7	15.1	-1.3	15.4	2.0	16.4	6.5	16.2	-1.2
1941	16.1	-0.6	16.0	-0.6	16.1	0.6	15.5	-3.7	14.6	-5.8	15.4	5.5	16.8	9.1	17.7	5.4	18.2	2.8	19.3	6.0	19.4	0.5	19.4	0.0
1942	19.4	0.0	19.2	-1.0	19.0	-1.0	17.9	-5.8	17.6	-1.7	17.5	-0.6	18.7	6.9	19.0	1.6	20.0	5.3	20.2	1.0	21.1	4.5	21.3	0.9
1943	21.6	1.4	21.6	0.0	21.6	0.0	21.6	0.0	21.6	0.0	21.6	0.0	21.6	0.0	21.6	0.0	21.6	0.0	21.7	0.5	22.5	3.7	22.5	0.0
1944	22.6	0.4	22.6	0.0	22.5	-0.4	22.4	-0.4	22.3	-0.4	22.3	0.0	22.3	0.0	22.4	0.4	22.4	0.0	22.4	0.0	22.5	0.4	22.6	0.4
1945	22.5	0.0	22.5	0.0	22.5	0.0	22.5	0.0	22.4	-0.4	22.4	0.0	22.4	0.0	22.4	0.0	22.4	0.0	22.4	0.0	22.5	0.4	22.6	0.4
1946	22.6	0.0	22.7	0.4	22.7	0.0	22.8	0.4	22.9	0.4	24.8	8.3	28.9	16.5	29.8	3.1	30.5	2.3	32.9	7.9	33.2	0.9	32.8	-1.2
1947	32.3	-1.5	30.6	-5.3	29.8	-2.6	28.4	-4.7	25.8	-9.2	26.1	1.2	27.4	5.0	29.6	8.0	31.0	4.7	32.0	3.2	32.8	2.5	34.0	3.7
1948	35.3	3.8	34.8	-1.4	33.6	-3.4	33.9	0.9	34.0	0.3	35.0	2.9	36.3	3.7	36.2	-0.3	34.9	-3.6	32.6	-6.6	31.5	-3.4	31.4	-0.3
1949	29.7	-5.4	28.5	-4.0	27.6	-3.2	26.7	-3.3	26.3	-1.5	26.3	0.0	26.7	1.5	27.6	3.4	27.8	0.7	27.9	0.4	28.2	1.1	27.9	-1.1
1950	27.3	-2.2	27.2	-0.4	26.9	-1.1	25.9	-3.7	25.3	-2.3	25.0	-1.2	25.8	3.2	26.7	3.5	27.6	3.4	28.4	2.9	29.1	2.5	30.1	3.4
1951	32.5	8.0	32.7	0.6	32.5	-0.6	31.5	-3.1	30.8	-2.2	30.9	0.3	31.3	1.3	31.8	1.6	31.8	0.0	32.2	1.3	32.9	2.2	33.5	1.8
1952	33.7	0.6	33.9	0.6	33.7	-0.6	33.1	-1.8	31.9	-3.6	31.6	-0.9	32.7	3.5	33.7	3.1	34.8	3.3	35.1	0.9	34.5	-1.7	33.3	-3.5
1953	32.2	-3.3	31.5	-2.2	30.7	-2.5	29.6	-3.6	28.6	-3.4	28.5	-0.3	29.5	3.5	29.8	1.0	30.3	1.7	30.8	1.7	31.2	1.3	30.4	-2.6
1954	29.8	-2.0	29.0	-2.7	28.5	-1.7	27.0	-5.3	25.7	-4.8	25.6	-0.4	26.8	4.7	27.4	2.2	28.0	2.2	28.7	2.5	29.1	1.4	28.6	-1.7
1955	28.2	-1.4	28.1	-0.4	27.7	-1.4	27.6	-0.4	26.7	-3.3	26.6	-0.4	27.2	2.3	28.0	2.9	28.6	2.1	29.1	1.7	29.0	-0.3	28.9	-0.3
1956	28.7	-0.7	28.7	0.0	27.7	-3.5	27.5	-0.7	28.4	3.3	28.4	0.0	28.9	1.8	29.1	0.7	29.3	0.7	29.7	1.4	30.2	1.7	30.3	0.3
1957	30.0	-1.0	29.8	-0.7	29.2	-2.0	29.0	-0.7	28.2	-2.8	28.1	-0.4	28.5	1.4	29.0	1.8	29.6	2.1	30.2	2.0	30.4	0.7	30.3	-0.3
1958	30.1	-0.7	29.9	-0.7	29.2	-2.3	28.0	-4.1	27.7	-1.1	27.6	-0.4	28.1	1.8	28.6	1.8	29.3	2.4	29.4	0.3	29.5	0.3	29.4	-0.3
1959	29.2	-0.7	29.2	0.0	28.6	-2.1	28.1	-1.7	27.6	-1.8	27.5	-0.4	28.2	2.5	28.9	2.5	29.3	1.4	29.7	1.4	30.0	1.0	30.1	0.3
1960	30.3	0.7	30.3	0.0	29.9	-1.3	29.2	-2.3	28.4	-2.7	28.5	0.4	29.2	2.5	29.7	1.7	30.5	2.7	31.0	1.6	31.3	1.0	31.3	0.0
1961	30.9	-1.3	30.4	-1.6	30.2	-0.7	29.7	-1.7	29.2	-1.7	29.0	-0.7	30.0	3.4	30.1	0.3	30.4	1.0	30.7	1.0	30.8	0.3	30.6	-0.6
1962	30.6	0.0	30.4	-0.7	29.8	-2.0	28.7	-3.7	28.1	-2.1	28.2	0.4	29.0	2.8	29.3	1.0	29.5	0.7	29.8	1.0	29.7	-0.3	29.6	-0.3
1963	29.4	-0.7	29.3	-0.3	28.9	-1.4	28.5	-1.4	28.2	-1.1	28.4	0.7	29.0	2.1	29.2	0.7	29.6	1.4	29.8	0.7	30.0	0.7	30.0	0.0
1964	29.8	-0.7	29.7	-0.3	29.4	-1.0	28.9	-1.7	28.6	-1.0	28.7	0.3	29.2	1.7	29.6	1.4	30.1	1.7	30.3	0.7	30.6	1.0	30.5	-0.3
1965	30.2	-1.0	30.1	-0.3	29.1	-3.3	29.4	1.0	29.1	-1.0	29.2	0.3	29.7	1.7	30.2	1.7	30.4	0.7	30.8	1.3	31.2	1.3	31.4	0.6
1966	31.5	0.3	32.4	2.9	32.7	0.9	32.5	-0.6	32.2	-0.9	32.7	1.6	34.7	6.1	36.0	3.7	36.4	1.1	36.5	0.3	36.1	-1.1	36.0	-0.3
1967	35.8	-0.6	35.5	-0.8	34.5	-2.8	34.6	0.3	35.0	1.2	35.2	0.6	35.2	0.0	35.1	-0.3	35.9	2.3	35.9	0.0	35.9	0.0	36.1	0.6
1968	36.2	0.3	36.2	0.0	36.0	-0.6	36.7	1.9	37.5	2.2	37.6	0.3	37.9	0.8	37.9	0.0	38.1	0.5	38.4	0.8	38.4	0.0	38.4	0.0
1969	38.3	-0.3	38.5	0.5	38.5	0.0	38.8	0.8	38.9	0.3	39.1	0.5	39.2	0.3	39.2	0.0	39.5	0.8	39.7	0.5	40.0	0.8	40.8	2.0
1970	41.0	0.5	40.9	-0.2	40.6	-0.7	41.0	1.0	40.5	-1.2	40.5	0.0	40.6	0.2	40.5	-0.2	40.7	0.5	40.8	0.2	41.3	1.2	41.6	0.7

[Continued]

Fluid Milk

Producer Price Index
Base 1982 = 100

[Continued]

For 1926-1997. Columns headed % show percentile change in the index from the previous period for which an index is available.

Year	Jan Index	%	Feb Index	%	Mar Index	%	Apr Index	%	May Index	%	Jun Index	%	Jul Index	%	Aug Index	%	Sep Index	%	Oct Index	%	Nov Index	%	Dec Index	%
1971	41.6	0.0	41.7	0.2	41.9	0.5	42.1	0.5	42.0	-0.2	42.2	0.5	42.3	0.2	42.2	-0.2	42.2	0.0	42.2	0.0	42.1	-0.2	42.1	0.0
1972	42.7	1.4	42.6	-0.2	43.1	1.2	43.2	0.2	43.4	0.5	43.1	-0.7	43.2	0.2	43.2	0.0	43.5	0.7	43.8	0.7	43.7	-0.2	43.7	0.0
1973	44.8	2.5	45.5	1.6	46.1	1.3	46.2	0.2	47.0	1.7	47.2	0.4	47.2	0.0	50.8	7.6	56.2	10.6	59.6	6.0	62.7	5.2	62.7	0.0
1974	65.4	4.3	65.9	0.8	65.8	-0.2	65.3	-0.8	63.2	-3.2	58.3	-7.8	55.8	-4.3	56.0	0.4	56.4	0.7	58.8	4.3	61.8	5.1	61.2	-1.0
1975	60.9	-0.5	60.9	0.0	60.1	-1.3	59.3	-1.3	59.0	-0.5	58.6	-0.7	59.7	1.9	62.3	4.4	65.8	5.6	69.9	6.2	73.6	5.3	75.3	2.3
1976	75.2	-0.1	73.5	-2.3	71.4	-2.9	69.7	-2.4	68.7	-1.4	67.3	-2.0	68.4	1.6	71.0	3.8	72.1	1.5	73.2	1.5	72.3	-1.2	71.8	-0.7
1977	70.9	-1.3	70.2	-1.0	69.1	-1.6	70.0	1.3	70.2	0.3	70.6	0.6	71.7	1.6	72.6	1.3	73.2	0.8	74.2	1.4	74.3	0.1	74.4	0.1
1978	73.8	-0.8	74.2	0.5	74.7	0.7	75.1	0.5	75.1	0.0	75.1	0.0	76.6	2.0	78.1	2.0	80.0	2.4	82.1	2.6	83.5	1.7	85.4	2.3
1979	85.6	0.2	86.6	1.2	86.3	-0.3	85.8	-0.6	85.7	-0.1	86.3	0.7	87.7	1.6	88.5	0.9	91.5	3.4	92.3	0.9	92.9	0.7	93.5	0.6
1980	92.8	-0.7	93.4	0.6	93.1	-0.3	93.9	0.9	93.9	0.0	94.0	0.1	94.1	0.1	96.1	2.1	97.5	1.5	99.4	1.9	100.8	1.4	102.8	2.0
1981	102.1	-0.7	102.5	0.4	102.5	0.0	101.7	-0.8	100.4	-1.3	100.9	0.5	100.6	-0.3	100.9	0.3	101.7	0.8	104.2	2.5	102.0	-2.1	101.5	-0.5
1982	101.8	0.3	101.2	-0.6	100.0	-1.2	99.2	-0.8	98.7	-0.5	98.7	0.0	98.8	0.1	98.7	-0.1	99.8	1.1	100.9	1.1	101.2	0.3	101.1	-0.1
1983	100.7	-0.4	100.6	-0.1	100.1	-0.5	99.4	-0.7	99.0	-0.4	98.6	-0.4	98.7	0.1	99.7	1.0	100.7	1.0	100.6	-0.1	100.3	-0.3	99.6	-0.7
1984	98.8	-0.8	97.6	-1.2	97.1	-0.5	96.5	-0.6	96.2	-0.3	96.2	0.0	97.0	0.8	98.0	1.0	99.9	1.9	101.5	1.6	101.8	0.3	101.8	0.0
1985	100.7	-1.1	99.5	-1.2	98.5	-1.0	96.0	-2.5	93.8	-2.3	91.9	-2.0	90.7	-1.3	90.3	-0.4	90.6	0.3	90.6	0.0	91.1	0.6	90.3	-0.9
1986	90.3	0.0	90.2	-0.1	88.9	-1.4	87.9	-1.1	88.2	0.3	88.5	0.3	89.0	0.6	90.7	1.9	91.6	1.0	94.4	3.1	95.7	1.4	96.1	0.4
1987	96.1	0.0	94.6	-1.6	92.2	-2.5	90.7	-1.6	89.4	-1.4	88.1	-1.5	89.7	1.8	91.1	1.6	92.7	1.8	93.2	0.5	93.1	-0.1	91.5	-1.7
1988	90.5	-1.1	89.1	-1.5	86.7	-2.7	85.4	-1.5	85.3	-0.1	83.8	-1.8	84.9	1.3	88.1	3.8	91.2	3.5	94.3	3.4	96.5	2.3	97.0	0.5
1989	96.4	-0.6	94.7	-1.8	91.3	-3.6	90.2	-1.2	89.7	-0.6	91.0	1.4	93.7	3.0	98.1	4.7	103.1	5.1	107.6	4.4	113.1	5.1	116.2	2.7
1990	114.7	-1.3	105.1	-8.4	100.5	-4.4	98.0	-2.5	100.3	2.3	103.1	2.8	105.3	2.1	105.5	0.2	104.6	-0.9	95.4	-8.8	91.8	-3.8	85.8	-6.5
1991	84.4	-1.6	84.1	-0.4	83.1	-1.2	82.9	-0.2	83.4	0.6	85.1	2.0	88.1	3.5	91.8	4.2	94.3	2.7	98.1	4.0	99.3	1.2	99.6	0.3
1992	97.7	-1.9	93.8	-4.0	91.3	-2.7	91.7	0.4	95.3	3.9	98.0	2.8	99.6	1.6	100.1	0.5	99.5	-0.6	98.1	-1.4	95.4	-2.8	92.4	-3.1
1993	91.0	-1.5	89.1	-2.1	89.4	0.3	92.5	3.5	95.9	3.7	96.5	0.6	94.9	-1.7	92.6	-2.4	94.0	1.5	95.6	1.7	98.7	3.2	98.6	-0.1
1994	99.3	0.7	98.2	-1.1	99.3	1.1	99.7	0.4	95.3	-4.4	94.0	-1.4	90.9	-3.3	92.1	1.3	94.9	3.0	95.9	1.1	95.2	-0.7	93.5	-1.8
1995	92.1	-1.5	91.6	-0.5	92.8	1.3	90.7	-2.3	90.8	0.1	89.9	-1.0	89.3	-0.7	92.3	3.4	94.1	2.0	98.0	4.1	100.7	2.8	101.4	0.7
1996	101.4	0.0	101.1	-0.3	99.9	-1.2	101.7	1.8	104.9	3.1	108.0	3.0	113.3	4.9	116.0	2.4	119.6	3.1	116.9	-2.3	109.1	-6.7	102.5	-6.0
1997	97.0	-5.4	97.8	0.8	98.7	0.9	97.6	-1.1	95.6	-2.0	91.0	-4.8	90.6	-0.4	93.7	3.4	97.0	3.5	98.4	1.4	103.0	4.7	104.7	1.7

Source: U.S. Department of Labor, Bureau of Labor Statistics, Division of Industry Prices and Price Indexes. n.e.c. stands for not elsewhere classified. - indicates no data collected for period or unavailable.

Chicken Eggs
Producer Price Index
Base 1982 = 100

For 1926-1997. Columns headed % show percentile change in the index from the previous period for which an index is available.

Year	Jan Index	%	Feb Index	%	Mar Index	%	Apr Index	%	May Index	%	Jun Index	%	Jul Index	%	Aug Index	%	Sep Index	%	Oct Index	%	Nov Index	%	Dec Index	%
1926	-	-	-	-	-	-	-	-	-	-	-	-	-	-	-	-	-	-	-	-	-	-	-	-
1927	-	-	-	-	-	-	-	-	-	-	-	-	-	-	-	-	-	-	-	-	-	-	-	-
1928	-	-	-	-	-	-	-	-	-	-	-	-	-	-	-	-	-	-	-	-	-	-	-	-
1929	-	-	-	-	-	-	-	-	-	-	-	-	-	-	-	-	-	-	-	-	-	-	-	-
1930	-	-	-	-	-	-	-	-	-	-	-	-	-	-	-	-	-	-	-	-	-	-	-	-
1931	-	-	-	-	-	-	-	-	-	-	-	-	-	-	-	-	-	-	-	-	-	-	-	-
1932	-	-	-	-	-	-	-	-	-	-	-	-	-	-	-	-	-	-	-	-	-	-	-	-
1933	-	-	-	-	-	-	-	-	-	-	-	-	-	-	-	-	-	-	-	-	-	-	-	-
1934	-	-	-	-	-	-	-	-	-	-	-	-	-	-	-	-	-	-	-	-	-	-	-	-
1935	-	-	-	-	-	-	-	-	-	-	-	-	-	-	-	-	-	-	-	-	-	-	-	-
1936	-	-	-	-	-	-	-	-	-	-	-	-	-	-	-	-	-	-	-	-	-	-	-	-
1937	48.1	-	43.1	-10.4	44.3	2.8	43.3	-2.3	39.9	-7.9	39.4	-1.3	41.4	5.1	42.1	1.7	46.7	10.9	47.3	1.3	52.7	11.4	50.0	-5.1
1938	43.3	-13.4	35.1	-18.9	34.9	-0.6	35.2	0.9	39.6	12.5	39.7	0.3	42.2	6.3	44.1	4.5	50.5	14.5	52.8	4.6	57.2	8.3	54.3	-5.1
1939	38.6	-28.9	33.9	-12.2	33.2	-2.1	32.8	-1.2	31.7	-3.4	31.1	-1.9	31.8	2.3	32.0	0.6	37.3	16.6	40.9	9.7	46.8	14.4	39.3	-16.0
1940	40.7	3.6	43.4	6.6	33.2	-23.5	32.7	-1.5	32.7	0.0	31.4	-4.0	31.8	1.3	33.3	4.7	39.9	19.8	42.4	6.3	46.0	8.5	49.7	8.0
1941	37.8	-23.9	33.5	-11.4	36.1	7.8	42.5	17.7	44.5	4.7	49.3	10.8	51.8	5.1	54.1	4.4	57.7	6.7	61.0	5.7	69.4	13.8	66.7	-3.9
1942	65.0	-2.5	56.8	-12.6	54.6	-3.9	56.6	3.7	57.5	1.6	59.4	3.3	63.1	6.2	67.3	6.7	70.4	4.6	73.9	5.0	74.5	0.8	74.7	0.3
1943	74.0	-0.9	70.2	-5.1	72.9	3.8	71.6	-1.8	72.9	1.8	75.1	3.0	75.3	0.3	78.9	4.8	82.3	4.3	84.4	2.6	83.7	-0.8	80.2	-4.2
1944	72.6	-9.5	62.8	-13.5	60.2	-4.1	58.5	-2.8	57.5	-1.7	60.7	5.6	66.3	9.2	64.5	-2.7	70.3	9.0	74.5	6.0	82.4	10.6	83.8	1.7
1945	75.8	-9.5	68.2	-10.0	66.8	-2.1	67.0	0.3	67.0	0.0	68.3	1.9	69.9	2.3	74.0	5.9	67.5	-8.8	79.7	18.1	87.1	9.3	85.9	-1.4
1946	70.8	-17.6	65.8	-7.1	65.7	-0.2	64.5	-1.8	65.9	2.2	65.5	-0.6	65.3	-0.3	67.8	3.8	78.6	15.9	83.2	5.9	77.9	-6.4	75.2	-3.5
1947	76.0	1.1	74.5	-2.0	80.8	8.5	82.7	2.4	80.5	-2.7	82.0	1.9	86.6	5.6	84.5	-2.4	91.7	8.5	91.9	0.2	89.0	-3.2	100.7	13.1
1948	86.2	-14.4	83.3	-3.4	82.9	-0.5	83.3	0.5	81.9	-1.7	84.3	2.9	87.2	3.4	95.9	10.0	101.6	5.9	112.4	10.6	110.5	-1.7	96.5	-12.7
1949	85.1	-11.8	77.1	-9.4	79.8	3.5	85.6	7.3	86.0	0.5	87.2	1.4	95.2	9.2	100.6	5.7	108.7	8.1	101.2	-6.9	90.9	-10.2	67.9	-25.3
1950	58.9	-13.3	59.9	1.7	65.0	8.5	62.3	-4.2	58.5	-6.1	62.6	7.0	71.2	13.7	75.5	6.0	88.5	17.2	97.0	9.6	101.8	4.9	102.5	0.7
1951	79.9	-22.0	80.3	0.5	85.6	6.6	85.8	0.2	89.1	3.8	94.1	5.6	94.2	0.1	106.2	12.7	111.4	4.9	115.1	3.3	116.6	1.3	90.3	-22.6
1952	71.6	-20.7	65.9	-8.0	67.9	3.0	72.4	6.6	65.9	-9.0	71.8	9.0	100.1	39.4	101.2	1.1	99.8	-1.4	110.6	10.8	104.3	-5.7	88.3	-15.3
1953	83.3	-5.7	79.0	-5.2	89.2	12.9	90.9	1.9	87.5	-3.7	94.5	8.0	94.2	-0.3	100.9	7.1	108.6	7.6	112.0	3.1	99.0	-11.6	86.2	-12.9
1954	82.2	-4.6	79.5	-3.3	71.0	-10.7	69.1	-2.7	61.2	-11.4	62.8	2.6	74.8	19.1	76.6	2.4	68.5	-10.6	73.1	6.7	74.0	1.2	56.7	-23.4
1955	57.7	1.8	79.9	38.5	72.9	-8.8	69.1	-5.2	63.4	-8.2	66.0	4.1	69.8	5.8	84.6	21.2	91.3	7.9	82.1	-10.1	87.7	6.8	88.0	0.3
1956	76.2	-13.4	72.1	-5.4	75.3	4.4	70.8	-6.0	71.1	0.4	69.8	-1.8	72.8	4.3	68.9	-5.4	80.9	17.4	77.4	-4.3	70.3	-9.2	65.9	-6.3
1957	58.3	-11.5	58.8	0.9	56.6	-3.7	60.7	7.2	51.0	-16.0	54.1	6.1	67.6	25.0	70.7	4.6	80.9	14.4	91.8	13.5	88.7	-3.4	82.8	-6.7
1958	65.5	-20.9	65.8	0.5	83.0	26.1	68.4	-17.6	67.1	-1.9	66.4	-1.0	67.5	1.7	72.3	7.1	87.4	20.9	80.8	-7.6	76.7	-5.1	68.9	-10.2
1959	64.2	-6.8	61.4	-4.4	62.5	1.8	48.3	-22.7	45.3	-6.2	50.1	10.6	58.0	15.8	59.2	2.1	75.7	27.9	61.2	-19.2	56.2	-8.2	55.7	-0.9
1960	50.5	-9.3	51.8	2.6	67.3	29.9	71.1	5.6	61.7	-13.2	57.0	-7.6	58.0	1.8	67.8	16.9	75.8	11.8	87.7	15.7	95.9	9.4	77.8	-18.9
1961	66.7	-14.3	72.0	7.9	67.1	-6.8	58.9	-12.2	56.2	-4.6	56.2	0.0	67.0	19.2	71.6	6.9	67.9	-5.2	70.5	3.8	71.0	0.7	63.7	-10.3
1962	65.0	2.0	64.7	-0.5	60.3	-6.8	60.9	1.0	50.0	-17.9	53.1	6.2	57.2	7.7	65.1	13.8	73.5	12.9	68.4	-6.9	74.6	9.1	65.9	-11.7
1963	66.4	0.8	65.8	-0.9	66.3	0.8	53.9	-18.7	51.2	-5.0	52.6	2.7	58.1	10.5	63.7	9.6	71.6	12.4	65.0	-9.2	68.0	4.6	66.3	-2.5
1964	70.6	6.5	59.5	-15.7	60.1	1.0	52.8	-12.1	51.0	-3.4	58.9	15.5	58.0	-1.5	65.5	12.9	64.3	-1.8	64.9	0.9	60.8	-6.3	56.6	-6.9
1965	52.4	-7.4	50.9	-2.9	57.7	13.4	60.5	4.9	52.4	-13.4	54.4	3.8	56.2	3.3	72.1	10.2	84.9	17.8	76.2	-10.2	80.9	6.2	72.4	-10.5
1966	66.3	-15.5	77.2	16.4	78.7	1.9	67.6	-14.1	57.7	-14.6	60.3	4.5	65.4	8.5	72.1	10.2	61.8	13.4	51.0	-17.5	53.6	5.1	60.3	12.5
1967	66.4	-8.3	55.7	-16.1	60.3	8.3	51.1	-15.3	49.5	-3.1	50.5	2.0	57.1	13.1	54.5	-4.6	84.1	28.8	70.7	-15.9	71.4	1.0	78.2	9.5
1968	49.0	-18.7	53.1	8.4	53.7	1.1	54.9	2.2	48.2	-12.2	58.6	21.6	60.7	3.6	65.3	7.6	84.1	28.8	75.5	-7.1	71.4	1.0	78.2	9.5
1969	81.2	3.8	71.7	-11.7	73.6	2.6	64.6	-12.2	53.5	-17.2	57.0	6.5	77.7	36.3	66.7	-14.2	81.3	21.9	75.5	-7.1	92.8	22.9	103.4	11.4
1970	101.0	-2.3	90.9	-10.0	79.7	-12.3	63.0	-21.0	52.9	-16.0	56.6	7.0	73.8	30.4	59.5	-19.4	78.1	31.3	58.5	-25.1	65.9	12.6	71.2	8.0

[Continued]

Chicken Eggs
Producer Price Index
Base 1982 = 100
[Continued]

For 1926-1997. Columns headed % show percentile change in the index from the previous period for which an index is available.

Year	Jan Index	%	Feb Index	%	Mar Index	%	Apr Index	%	May Index	%	Jun Index	%	Jul Index	%	Aug Index	%	Sep Index	%	Oct Index	%	Nov Index	%	Dec Index	%
1971	63.4	-11.0	54.6	-13.9	56.6	3.7	58.4	3.2	51.7	-11.5	54.8	6.0	50.0	-8.8	61.6	23.2	60.3	-2.1	51.7	-14.3	49.5	-4.3	64.0	29.3
1972	51.8	-19.1	51.4	-0.8	60.3	17.3	48.8	-19.1	50.7	3.9	51.4	1.4	57.2	11.3	55.6	-2.8	64.3	15.6	55.4	-13.8	68.9	24.4	80.5	16.8
1973	88.5	9.9	72.8	-17.7	85.4	17.3	81.1	-5.0	76.7	-5.4	89.2	16.3	86.9	-2.6	117.3	35.0	107.2	-8.6	99.4	-7.3	101.4	2.0	106.6	5.1
1974	110.7	3.8	104.5	-5.6	93.9	-10.1	88.8	-5.4	70.5	-20.6	69.8	-1.0	73.8	5.7	83.7	13.4	95.0	13.5	93.9	-1.2	92.3	-1.7	101.3	9.8
1975	94.4	-6.8	90.9	-3.7	93.0	2.3	78.3	-15.8	81.4	4.0	77.1	-5.3	78.2	1.4	87.7	12.1	97.6	11.3	88.6	-9.2	98.4	11.1	107.6	9.3
1976	101.9	-5.3	99.0	-2.8	89.1	-10.0	91.0	2.1	96.0	5.5	92.8	-3.3	93.9	1.2	104.5	11.3	105.7	1.1	101.1	-4.4	107.9	6.7	119.5	10.8
1977	105.9	-11.4	109.0	2.9	97.1	-10.9	92.4	-4.8	80.8	-12.6	79.1	-2.1	87.6	10.7	90.7	3.5	91.4	0.8	77.0	-15.8	83.6	8.6	93.1	11.4
1978	81.2	-12.8	95.3	17.4	93.6	-1.8	85.2	-9.0	79.0	-7.3	71.3	-9.7	84.1	18.0	88.4	5.1	93.9	6.2	87.5	-6.8	99.6	13.8	105.7	6.1
1979	99.9	-5.5	98.9	-1.0	111.9	13.1	103.8	-7.2	91.7	-11.7	95.5	4.1	93.8	-1.8	93.3	-0.5	98.1	5.1	87.2	-11.1	100.0	14.7	111.0	11.0
1980	92.6	-16.6	84.2	-9.1	103.1	22.4	85.8	-16.8	78.6	-8.4	82.1	4.5	89.2	8.6	99.0	11.0	105.4	6.5	98.0	-7.0	108.6	10.8	121.7	12.1
1981	103.9	-14.6	103.4	-0.5	100.9	-2.4	109.8	8.8	92.3	-15.9	97.7	5.9	103.5	5.9	101.1	-2.3	108.1	6.9	108.4	0.3	117.3	8.2	109.4	-6.7
1982	104.7	-4.3	112.2	7.2	114.2	1.8	107.5	-5.9	91.9	-14.5	89.1	-3.0	96.1	7.9	96.1	0.0	97.0	0.9	99.5	2.6	96.5	-3.0	95.1	-1.5
1983	95.1	0.0	95.1	0.0	95.1	0.0	95.1	0.0	103.6	8.9	94.7	-8.6	99.2	4.8	106.0	6.9	112.0	5.7	-		-		-	
1984	158.0	41.1	157.1	-0.6	132.0	-16.0	147.9	12.0	112.5	-23.9	99.5	-11.6	103.5	4.0	101.4	-2.0	99.4	-2.0	100.7	1.3	98.5	-2.2	104.9	6.5
1985	79.4	-24.3	90.4	13.9	93.8	3.8	98.0	4.5	84.0	-14.3	82.7	-1.5	91.8	11.0	94.5	2.9	105.4	11.5	106.9	1.4	109.2	2.2	111.9	2.5
1986	107.2	-4.2	98.5	-8.1	101.9	3.5	94.9	-6.9	90.7	-4.4	83.4	-8.0	93.6	12.2	107.1	14.4	101.3	-5.4	97.1	-4.1	110.4	13.7	108.5	-1.7
1987	99.0	-8.8	98.2	-0.8	89.7	-8.7	90.1	0.4	84.4	-6.3	80.1	-5.1	85.3	6.5	79.7	-6.6	100.6	26.2	81.1	-19.4	92.6	14.2	70.6	-23.8
1988	76.5	8.4	73.8	-3.5	79.7	8.0	73.1	-8.3	70.8	-3.1	77.1	8.9	95.7	24.1	107.0	11.8	102.1	-4.6	107.4	5.2	99.7	-7.2	100.3	0.6
1989	127.3	26.9	96.7	-24.0	135.8	40.4	110.8	-18.4	107.0	-3.4	104.8	-2.1	111.0	5.9	116.7	5.1	124.6	6.8	124.3	-0.2	134.5	8.2	141.3	5.1
1990	154.8	9.6	114.0	-26.4	128.9	13.1	127.9	-0.8	95.3	-25.5	100.4	5.4	91.6	-8.8	114.4	24.9	112.6	-1.6	121.6	8.0	125.0	2.8	124.5	-0.4
1991	140.0	12.4	110.5	-21.1	131.7	19.2	113.2	-14.0	94.6	-16.4	96.9	2.4	100.7	3.9	109.0	8.2	105.8	-2.9	105.0	-0.8	102.1	-2.8	118.7	16.3
1992	91.9	-22.6	94.1	2.4	92.8	-1.4	90.1	-2.9	86.4	-4.1	84.6	-2.1	83.9	-0.8	87.3	4.1	103.6	18.7	94.7	-8.6	112.4	18.7	107.7	-4.2
1993	102.9	-4.5	107.0	4.0	121.3	13.4	111.1	-8.4	101.6	-8.6	109.5	7.8	95.5	-12.8	110.5	15.7	93.2	-15.7	105.2	12.9	108.6	3.2	103.8	-4.4
1994	100.1	-3.6	109.1	9.0	112.3	2.9	99.0	-11.8	84.2	-14.9	91.1	8.2	89.3	-2.0	100.1	12.1	98.8	-1.3	89.2	-9.7	100.5	12.7	100.0	-0.5
1995	92.6	-7.4	95.8	3.5	97.1	1.4	97.1	0.0	85.4	-12.0	88.8	4.0	97.4	9.7	99.2	1.8	108.9	9.8	111.1	2.0	136.9	23.2	138.8	1.4
1996	123.4	-11.1	126.7	2.7	138.5	9.3	132.1	-4.6	112.4	-14.9	119.2	6.0	116.7	-2.1	130.6	11.9	134.0	2.6	128.8	-3.9	143.9	11.7	161.8	12.4
1997	125.8	-22.2	129.4	2.9	119.7	-7.5	108.2	-9.6	106.2	-1.8	97.4	-8.3	117.7	20.8	107.7	-8.5	120.0	11.4	111.6	-7.0	148.5	33.1	136.2	-8.3

Source: U.S. Department of Labor, Bureau of Labor Statistics, Division of Industry Prices and Price Indexes. n.e.c. stands for not elsewhere classified. - indicates no data collected for period or unavailable.

Hay, Hayseeds and Oilseeds
Producer Price Index
Base 1982 = 100

For 1926-1997. Columns headed % show percentile change in the index from the previous period for which an index is available.

Year	Jan Index	%	Feb Index	%	Mar Index	%	Apr Index	%	May Index	%	Jun Index	%	Jul Index	%	Aug Index	%	Sep Index	%	Oct Index	%	Nov Index	%	Dec Index	%
1926	30.9	-	30.1	-2.6	30.1	0.0	31.9	6.0	31.3	-1.9	27.5	-12.1	28.2	2.5	28.7	1.8	29.0	1.0	28.8	-0.7	28.7	-0.3	28.9	0.7
1927	28.9	0.0	28.6	-1.0	27.6	-3.5	27.4	-0.7	27.3	-0.4	25.1	-8.1	24.0	-4.4	24.9	3.8	24.8	-0.4	25.3	2.0	24.8	-2.0	26.0	4.8
1928	27.0	3.8	26.9	-0.4	28.3	5.2	29.6	4.6	30.5	3.0	27.4	-10.2	26.9	-1.8	27.3	1.5	28.4	4.0	30.2	6.3	31.3	3.6	32.0	2.2
1929	33.1	3.4	33.3	0.6	33.1	-0.6	32.8	-0.9	30.1	-8.2	27.0	-10.3	27.3	1.1	28.1	2.9	29.7	5.7	30.8	3.7	30.4	-1.3	29.8	-2.0
1930	29.7	-0.3	28.7	-3.4	28.2	-1.7	29.0	2.8	28.4	-2.1	25.8	-9.2	25.6	-0.8	27.9	9.0	27.5	-1.4	27.6	0.4	27.6	0.0	26.7	-3.3
1931	25.8	-3.4	24.9	-3.5	24.5	-1.6	24.6	0.4	23.1	-6.1	20.3	-12.1	19.9	-2.0	18.4	-7.5	17.9	-2.7	17.3	-3.4	17.7	2.3	18.4	4.0
1932	18.3	-0.5	17.4	-4.9	18.0	3.4	18.0	0.0	16.2	-10.0	13.9	-14.2	13.5	-2.9	13.7	1.5	13.7	0.0	14.1	2.9	14.1	0.0	13.8	-2.1
1933	13.7	-0.7	13.3	-2.9	13.7	3.0	14.2	3.6	15.6	9.9	15.3	-1.9	16.5	7.8	17.9	8.5	18.0	0.6	17.5	-2.8	17.7	1.1	18.2	2.8
1934	18.8	3.3	19.2	2.1	19.2	0.0	19.7	2.6	20.0	1.5	21.2	6.0	23.3	9.9	26.4	13.3	28.3	7.2	27.6	-2.5	27.0	-2.2	28.3	4.8
1935	28.9	2.1	28.6	-1.0	28.1	-1.7	27.3	-2.8	26.0	-4.8	23.1	-11.2	19.8	-14.3	18.0	-9.1	18.6	3.3	19.3	3.8	19.4	0.5	19.1	-1.5
1936	19.3	1.0	19.3	0.0	18.9	-2.1	20.0	5.8	19.4	-3.0	18.4	-5.2	22.0	19.6	25.0	13.6	25.8	3.2	26.2	1.6	27.3	4.2	27.9	2.2
1937	28.9	3.6	28.9	0.0	28.4	-1.7	28.7	1.1	27.1	-5.6	25.6	-5.5	24.7	-3.5	24.8	0.4	25.5	2.8	26.4	3.5	26.0	-1.5	26.5	1.9
1938	26.8	1.1	26.4	-1.5	25.6	-3.0	24.7	-3.5	23.9	-3.2	22.4	-6.3	22.1	-1.3	20.5	-7.2	18.3	-10.7	19.1	4.4	19.5	2.1	20.1	3.1
1939	21.2	5.5	20.7	-2.4	20.8	0.5	20.7	-0.5	19.9	-3.9	19.6	-1.5	19.0	-3.1	21.5	13.2	20.6	-4.2	21.6	4.9	21.7	0.5	21.9	0.9
1940	22.3	1.8	22.4	0.4	22.1	-1.3	22.0	-0.5	21.8	-0.9	19.9	-8.7	19.4	-2.5	19.7	1.5	18.8	-4.6	18.8	0.0	19.0	1.1	19.4	2.1
1941	19.9	2.6	19.9	0.0	19.7	-1.0	19.9	1.0	20.3	2.0	20.6	1.5	20.9	1.5	21.2	1.4	22.3	5.2	23.5	5.4	25.3	7.7	26.5	4.7
1942	28.1	6.0	29.2	3.9	30.5	4.5	30.9	1.3	30.5	-1.3	29.7	-2.6	29.8	0.3	29.6	-0.7	29.4	-0.7	29.7	1.0	30.4	2.4	31.6	3.9
1943	32.8	3.8	34.3	4.6	35.5	3.5	36.4	2.5	36.5	0.3	34.9	-4.4	34.8	-0.3	34.9	0.3	36.4	4.3	38.9	6.9	41.5	6.7	42.2	1.7
1944	42.1	-0.2	41.7	-1.0	41.0	-1.7	41.0	0.0	41.6	1.5	38.6	-7.2	37.9	-1.8	38.1	0.5	38.7	1.6	41.4	7.0	42.1	1.7	42.2	0.2
1945	43.2	2.4	43.8	1.4	43.5	-0.7	41.8	-3.9	39.2	-6.2	39.4	0.5	39.1	-0.8	37.6	-3.8	37.7	0.3	38.3	1.6	39.7	3.7	39.7	0.0
1946	39.8	0.3	39.6	-0.5	40.4	2.0	40.2	-0.5	40.2	0.0	40.4	0.5	41.1	1.7	41.4	0.7	42.0	1.4	46.7	11.2	54.3	16.3	55.3	1.8
1947	55.7	0.7	55.8	0.2	61.8	10.8	60.2	-2.6	51.8	-14.0	50.9	-1.7	50.9	0.0	50.3	-1.2	51.7	2.8	55.7	7.7	58.8	5.6	61.7	4.9
1948	64.3	4.2	58.6	-8.9	59.4	1.4	60.9	2.5	61.7	1.3	62.1	0.6	59.5	-4.2	53.7	-9.7	51.7	-3.7	49.2	-4.8	50.8	3.3	50.9	0.2
1949	49.3	-3.1	45.9	-6.9	45.3	-1.3	44.7	-1.3	42.2	-5.6	40.8	-3.3	41.0	0.5	45.3	10.5	41.0	-9.5	40.4	-1.5	40.8	1.0	41.7	2.2
1950	42.1	1.0	41.5	-1.4	48.3	16.4	45.0	-6.8	45.3	0.7	45.4	0.2	46.5	2.4	48.1	3.4	46.7	-2.9	45.6	-2.4	51.1	12.1	53.3	4.3
1951	55.6	4.3	57.3	3.1	57.7	0.7	57.3	-0.7	56.3	-1.7	53.2	-5.5	49.7	-6.6	48.4	-2.6	48.5	0.2	50.2	3.5	52.4	4.4	52.9	1.0
1952	52.7	-0.4	52.4	-0.6	50.3	-4.0	49.5	-1.6	49.8	0.6	51.1	2.6	52.1	2.0	51.8	-0.6	50.0	-3.5	50.1	0.2	51.1	2.0	51.0	-0.2
1953	50.4	-1.2	49.2	-2.4	50.6	2.8	49.4	-2.4	48.6	-1.6	46.5	-4.3	44.4	-4.5	44.1	-0.7	42.1	-4.5	43.7	3.8	45.6	4.3	46.5	2.0
1954	46.9	0.9	47.5	1.3	48.4	1.9	50.0	3.3	49.4	-1.2	49.8	0.8	49.2	-1.2	48.8	-0.8	45.3	-7.2	47.6	5.1	47.7	0.2	48.6	1.9
1955	48.9	0.6	48.4	-1.0	48.3	-0.2	46.6	-3.5	46.0	-1.3	45.7	-0.7	44.4	-2.8	42.3	-4.7	38.9	-8.0	39.3	1.0	39.3	0.0	40.2	2.3
1956	40.9	1.7	41.7	2.0	42.8	2.6	45.0	5.1	46.7	3.8	45.3	-3.0	41.8	-7.7	41.5	-0.7	39.7	-4.3	40.7	2.5	43.6	7.1	44.3	1.6
1957	44.9	1.4	43.9	-2.2	44.1	0.5	44.2	0.2	43.8	-0.9	43.2	-1.4	42.7	-1.2	42.2	-1.2	40.4	-4.3	40.1	-0.7	40.2	0.2	40.7	1.2
1958	41.0	0.7	41.0	0.0	41.2	0.5	41.4	0.5	41.4	0.0	41.1	-0.7	39.5	-3.9	39.3	-0.5	37.4	-4.8	38.0	1.6	38.3	0.8	38.9	1.6
1959	39.6	1.8	40.4	2.0	40.7	0.7	41.2	1.2	41.6	1.0	40.4	-2.9	38.9	-3.7	37.9	-2.6	37.9	0.0	39.1	3.2	39.6	1.3	39.6	0.0
1960	40.2	1.5	40.0	-0.5	39.8	-0.5	39.6	-0.5	39.7	0.3	38.6	-2.8	38.1	-1.3	38.2	0.3	37.5	-1.8	37.4	-0.3	37.6	0.5	38.4	2.1
1961	41.2	7.3	42.2	2.4	45.3	7.3	50.0	10.4	47.7	-4.6	43.4	-9.0	43.4	0.0	43.0	-0.9	41.5	-3.5	41.4	-0.2	42.2	1.9	42.3	0.2
1962	42.4	0.2	42.6	0.5	43.0	0.9	43.8	1.9	43.8	0.0	43.3	-1.1	42.9	-0.9	42.9	0.0	40.7	-5.1	42.0	3.2	43.5	3.6	44.1	1.4
1963	45.6	3.4	46.2	1.3	46.3	0.2	45.1	-2.6	45.8	1.6	46.3	1.1	45.3	-2.2	45.3	0.0	45.0	-0.7	46.5	3.3	47.8	2.8	46.7	-2.3
1964	47.0	0.6	46.4	-1.3	45.1	-2.8	43.8	-2.9	42.7	-2.5	42.8	0.2	43.0	0.5	43.1	0.2	44.3	2.8	45.2	2.0	47.1	4.2	45.1	3.2
1965	48.5	2.1	49.1	1.2	48.5	-1.2	48.6	0.2	47.0	-3.3	46.7	-0.6	46.3	-0.9	43.4	-6.3	42.9	-1.2	41.8	-2.6	43.7	4.5	45.1	3.2
1966	46.2	2.4	47.5	2.8	47.1	-0.8	47.6	1.1	49.0	2.9	49.9	1.8	55.1	10.4	56.7	2.9	51.4	-9.3	49.5	-3.7	50.0	1.0	50.7	1.4
1967	50.3	-0.8	49.0	-2.6	49.1	0.2	48.2	-1.8	48.0	-0.4	47.5	-1.0	47.2	-0.6	45.4	-3.8	44.4	-2.2	44.2	-0.5	44.7	1.1	45.9	2.7
1968	46.0	0.2	46.0	0.0	46.5	1.1	46.4	-0.2	46.5	0.2	46.0	-1.1	46.1	0.2	46.0	-0.2	44.6	-3.0	42.9	-3.8	43.7	1.9	44.3	1.4
1969	45.4	2.5	45.8	0.9	45.8	0.0	46.3	1.1	46.9	1.3	45.0	-4.1	45.3	0.7	43.7	-3.5	43.1	-1.4	41.2	-4.4	42.1	2.2	42.8	1.7
1970	43.8	2.3	43.3	-1.1	43.3	0.0	44.7	3.2	45.3	1.3	45.9	1.3	47.6	3.7	47.5	-0.2	48.2	1.5	50.1	3.9	50.8	1.4	50.2	-1.2

[Continued]

Hay, Hayseeds and Oilseeds
Producer Price Index
Base 1982 = 100
[Continued]

For 1926-1997. Columns headed % show percentile change in the index from the previous period for which an index is available.

Year	Jan Index	%	Feb Index	%	Mar Index	%	Apr Index	%	May Index	%	Jun Index	%	Jul Index	%	Aug Index	%	Sep Index	%	Oct Index	%	Nov Index	%	Dec Index	%
1971	51.1	1.8	51.0	-0.2	50.5	-1.0	49.2	-2.6	50.1	1.8	51.6	3.0	53.7	4.1	53.7	0.0	51.1	-4.8	50.7	-0.8	51.4	1.4	51.3	-0.2
1972	51.1	-0.4	51.8	1.4	53.7	3.7	55.7	3.7	54.9	-1.4	54.9	0.0	54.9	0.0	54.5	-0.7	55.4	1.7	54.0	-2.5	58.6	8.5	66.5	13.5
1973	67.6	1.7	83.7	23.8	88.4	5.6	87.8	-0.7	114.2	30.1	140.9	23.4	88.1	-37.5	138.0	56.6	143.1	3.7	99.2	-30.7	91.3	-8.0	98.9	8.3
1974	101.9	3.0	102.5	0.6	102.9	0.4	92.3	-10.3	91.4	-1.0	89.9	-1.6	101.5	12.9	124.4	22.6	117.1	-5.9	126.9	8.4	122.7	-3.3	115.5	-5.9
1975	109.2	-5.5	99.4	-9.0	91.6	-7.8	100.6	9.8	94.1	-6.5	89.4	-5.0	96.2	7.6	100.2	4.2	93.2	-7.0	88.6	-4.9	83.3	-6.0	83.4	0.1
1976	85.3	2.3	86.7	1.6	84.9	-2.1	84.6	-0.4	89.0	5.2	103.1	15.8	112.0	8.6	105.5	-5.8	108.9	3.2	103.4	-5.1	109.0	5.4	113.9	4.5
1977	115.1	1.1	119.6	3.9	130.6	9.2	151.5	16.0	136.2	-10.1	127.0	-6.8	97.6	-23.1	92.1	-5.6	83.8	-9.0	84.0	0.2	90.9	8.2	92.5	1.8
1978	93.3	0.9	90.0	-3.5	98.5	9.4	101.8	3.4	103.2	1.4	103.6	0.4	104.6	1.0	101.2	-3.3	99.9	-1.3	104.0	4.1	107.0	2.9	110.0	2.8
1979	112.8	2.5	115.7	2.6	117.2	1.3	116.7	-0.4	113.1	-3.1	121.4	7.3	122.2	0.7	118.4	-3.1	113.2	-4.4	110.7	-2.2	108.0	-2.4	108.2	0.2
1980	102.5	-5.3	105.6	3.0	101.5	-3.9	96.4	-5.0	97.2	0.8	97.5	0.3	118.1	21.1	122.9	4.1	131.9	7.3	133.7	1.4	140.2	4.9	145.8	4.0
1981	146.5	0.5	138.6	-5.4	136.1	-1.8	139.2	2.3	140.5	0.9	134.1	-4.6	136.3	1.6	133.6	-2.0	125.5	-6.1	108.3	-13.7	103.9	-4.1	102.8	-1.1
1982	102.6	-0.2	102.3	-0.3	100.4	-1.9	104.7	4.3	106.8	2.0	103.1	-3.5	103.4	0.3	96.1	-7.1	94.8	-1.4	91.3	-3.7	96.2	5.4	98.2	2.1
1983	99.8	1.6	102.4	2.6	102.4	0.0	106.4	3.9	106.8	0.4	100.2	-6.2	106.8	6.6	123.5	15.6	139.9	13.3	135.7	-3.0	135.2	-0.4	132.6	-1.9
1984	135.0	1.8	124.7	-7.6	132.2	6.0	132.6	0.3	139.6	5.3	128.0	-8.3	115.5	-9.8	114.0	-1.3	107.3	-5.9	103.0	-4.0	106.8	3.7	106.9	0.1
1985	106.3	-0.6	100.8	-5.2	99.6	-1.2	100.5	0.9	100.3	-0.2	99.0	-1.3	97.2	-1.8	92.5	-4.8	91.3	-1.3	86.8	-4.9	94.0	8.3	93.7	-0.3
1986	94.3	0.6	95.2	1.0	96.0	0.8	91.1	-5.1	91.4	0.3	95.2	4.2	93.7	-1.6	89.4	-4.6	89.2	-0.2	88.0	-1.3	98.4	11.8	93.5	-5.0
1987	94.0	0.5	95.6	1.7	95.4	-0.2	97.7	2.4	104.3	6.8	106.4	2.0	105.1	-1.2	101.9	-3.0	99.7	-2.2	101.0	1.3	104.9	3.9	110.7	5.5
1988	113.7	2.7	114.7	0.9	114.2	-0.4	121.8	6.7	127.8	4.9	150.3	17.6	154.3	2.7	159.2	3.2	163.5	2.7	151.0	-7.6	142.8	-5.4	147.9	3.6
1989	153.2	3.6	144.2	-5.9	149.2	3.5	142.1	-4.8	149.7	5.3	143.8	-3.9	140.3	-2.4	129.8	-7.5	128.3	-1.2	118.2	-7.9	121.0	2.4	124.2	2.6
1990	121.0	-2.6	122.4	1.2	122.0	-0.3	122.6	0.5	116.8	-4.7	118.3	1.3	124.0	4.8	118.7	-4.3	121.4	2.3	128.3	5.7	123.1	-4.1	126.2	2.5
1991	121.3	-3.9	121.9	0.5	117.9	-3.3	116.1	-1.5	110.7	-4.7	114.4	3.3	104.5	-8.7	107.8	3.2	110.3	2.3	106.1	-3.8	106.8	0.7	106.8	0.0
1992	109.2	2.2	107.8	-1.3	111.7	3.6	109.3	-2.1	117.8	7.8	121.3	3.0	111.0	-8.5	107.2	-3.4	109.3	2.0	106.8	-2.3	109.0	2.1	114.5	5.0
1993	116.6	1.8	114.9	-1.5	118.3	3.0	123.2	4.1	128.1	4.0	119.7	-6.6	134.7	12.5	129.4	-3.9	127.3	-1.6	126.1	-0.9	132.9	5.4	142.7	7.4
1994	141.7	-0.7	141.7	0.0	144.7	2.1	143.3	-1.0	138.4	-3.4	141.8	2.5	130.0	-8.3	121.3	-6.7	122.4	0.9	117.2	-4.2	122.5	4.5	123.3	0.7
1995	121.2	-1.7	120.2	-0.8	119.3	-0.7	121.6	1.9	117.3	-3.5	117.4	0.1	120.5	2.6	114.2	-5.2	123.9	8.5	128.8	4.0	132.0	2.5	138.0	4.5
1996	141.3	2.4	138.0	-2.3	139.4	1.0	149.2	7.0	155.2	4.0	149.0	-4.0	149.9	0.6	155.9	4.0	158.1	1.4	140.4	-11.2	140.1	-0.2	138.9	-0.9
1997	147.6	6.3	149.6	1.4	164.2	9.8	164.4	0.1	170.4	3.6	161.5	-5.2	156.2	-3.3	145.4	-6.9	142.2	-2.2	142.5	0.2	146.8	3.0	140.7	-4.2

Source: U.S. Department of Labor, Bureau of Labor Statistics, Division of Industry Prices and Price Indexes. n.e.c. stands for not elsewhere classified. - indicates no data collected for period or unavailable.

Other Farm Products

Producer Price Index
Base 1982 = 100

For 1926-1997. Columns headed % show percentile change in the index from the previous period for which an index is available.

Year	Jan		Feb		Mar		Apr		May		Jun		Jul		Aug		Sep		Oct		Nov		Dec	
	Index	%	Index	%	Index	%	Index	%	Index	%	Index	%	Index	%	Index	%	Index	%	Index	%	Index	%	Index	%
1926	15.7	-	14.6	-7.0	12.8	-12.3	11.8	-7.8	12.3	4.2	12.5	1.6	12.6	0.8	12.6	0.0	12.9	2.4	12.9	0.0	13.6	5.4	14.2	4.4
1927	14.0	-1.4	12.9	-7.9	12.9	0.0	11.4	-11.6	11.0	-3.5	11.4	3.6	11.8	3.5	14.2	20.3	14.2	0.0	13.5	-4.9	13.3	-1.5	16.9	27.1
1928	18.1	7.1	16.8	-7.2	14.5	-13.7	14.4	-0.7	14.3	-0.7	12.4	-13.3	13.3	7.3	14.3	7.5	12.8	-10.5	14.3	11.7	13.3	-7.0	19.1	43.6
1929	20.3	6.3	18.0	-11.3	18.4	2.2	14.5	-21.2	14.2	-2.1	13.0	-8.5	12.8	-1.5	13.0	1.6	13.0	0.0	12.7	-2.3	11.9	-6.3	10.8	-9.2
1930	10.4	-3.7	10.2	-1.9	10.2	0.0	10.2	0.0	10.0	-2.0	9.9	-1.0	9.8	-1.0	9.6	-2.0	9.4	-2.1	9.5	1.1	8.7	-8.4	8.1	-6.9
1931	7.5	-7.4	7.3	-2.7	6.9	-5.5	6.8	-1.4	7.0	2.9	7.1	1.4	7.1	0.0	6.8	-4.2	6.6	-2.9	6.5	-1.5	6.5	0.0	6.3	-3.1
1932	5.9	-6.3	5.8	-1.7	5.8	0.0	5.9	1.7	5.9	0.0	5.8	-1.7	5.8	0.0	6.2	6.9	7.0	12.9	6.5	-7.1	6.1	-6.2	6.2	1.6
1933	6.2	0.0	6.3	1.6	6.3	0.0	6.2	-1.6	6.4	3.2	6.4	0.0	6.5	1.6	6.5	0.0	6.5	0.0	6.7	3.1	7.1	6.0	7.3	2.8
1934	7.6	4.1	7.9	3.9	7.9	0.0	7.8	-1.3	7.8	0.0	7.8	0.0	7.6	-2.6	8.0	5.3	8.5	6.3	9.2	8.2	9.4	2.2	9.4	0.0
1935	9.8	4.3	9.9	1.0	9.8	-1.0	9.7	-1.0	9.6	-1.0	9.5	-1.0	9.5	0.0	9.3	-2.1	8.9	-4.3	8.6	-3.4	8.4	-2.3	8.3	-1.2
1936	8.5	2.4	8.6	1.2	8.5	-1.2	8.4	-1.2	8.4	0.0	8.6	2.4	8.8	2.3	8.8	0.0	9.1	3.4	9.2	1.1	9.5	3.3	10.3	8.4
1937	10.9	5.8	11.1	1.8	11.0	-0.9	10.9	-0.9	10.8	-0.9	10.7	-0.9	10.7	0.0	10.8	0.9	10.7	-0.9	10.8	0.9	10.2	-5.6	9.8	-3.9
1938	9.2	-6.1	9.0	-2.2	8.9	-1.1	8.7	-2.2	8.7	0.0	8.7	0.0	8.9	2.3	9.1	2.2	9.1	0.0	9.0	-1.1	8.9	-1.1	8.8	-1.1
1939	8.8	0.0	8.9	1.1	8.7	-2.2	8.6	-1.1	8.6	0.0	8.6	0.0	8.6	0.0	8.5	-1.2	8.3	-2.4	7.8	-6.0	8.1	3.8	7.9	-2.5
1940	7.9	0.0	7.8	-1.3	7.9	1.3	7.9	0.0	7.7	-2.5	7.6	-1.3	7.5	-1.3	7.4	-1.3	7.5	1.4	7.7	2.7	7.8	1.3	8.1	3.8
1941	8.0	-1.2	8.2	2.5	8.7	6.1	9.0	3.4	9.4	4.4	9.7	3.2	9.8	1.0	10.4	6.1	11.3	8.7	11.8	4.4	12.2	3.4	13.1	7.4
1942	14.1	7.6	14.2	0.7	14.1	-0.7	14.1	0.0	14.1	0.0	14.1	0.0	14.1	0.0	14.5	2.8	15.1	4.1	15.7	4.0	15.9	1.3	16.3	2.5
1943	16.6	1.8	16.2	-2.4	16.3	0.6	16.6	1.8	16.6	0.0	16.6	0.0	16.7	0.6	16.8	0.6	17.0	1.2	16.9	-0.6	17.0	0.6	17.2	1.2
1944	17.4	1.2	17.5	0.6	17.5	0.0	17.5	0.0	17.5	0.0	17.5	0.0	17.4	-0.6	17.5	0.6	17.7	1.1	17.6	-0.6	17.7	0.6	17.7	0.0
1945	17.2	-2.8	17.1	-0.6	17.1	0.0	17.1	0.0	17.2	0.6	17.2	0.0	17.2	0.0	17.3	0.6	17.3	0.0	17.4	0.6	17.4	0.0	17.5	0.6
1946	17.8	1.7	17.7	-0.6	17.7	0.0	17.7	0.0	17.7	0.0	17.7	0.0	19.3	9.0	19.9	3.1	20.3	2.0	22.2	9.4	23.8	7.2	24.8	4.2
1947	25.4	2.4	25.1	-1.2	25.5	1.6	25.0	-2.0	24.2	-3.2	24.8	2.5	25.1	1.2	25.4	1.2	24.9	-2.0	25.7	3.2	25.9	0.8	26.2	1.2
1948	26.1	-0.4	25.9	-0.8	25.5	-1.5	25.2	-1.2	25.2	0.0	25.6	1.6	25.8	0.8	26.4	2.3	26.9	1.9	27.7	3.0	27.8	0.4	27.2	-2.2
1949	26.5	-2.6	26.0	-1.9	25.8	-0.8	25.6	-0.8	25.9	1.2	26.0	0.4	26.3	1.2	26.5	0.8	26.6	0.4	27.9	4.9	31.8	14.0	32.9	3.5
1950	32.4	-1.5	32.1	-0.9	31.3	-2.5	31.5	0.6	31.1	-1.3	32.2	3.5	34.0	5.6	35.2	3.5	36.8	4.5	35.5	-3.5	35.1	-1.1	36.0	2.6
1951	36.9	2.5	37.1	0.5	36.8	-0.8	36.8	0.0	36.7	-0.3	36.5	-0.5	36.1	-1.1	35.8	-0.8	35.7	-0.3	36.5	2.2	35.6	-2.5	36.3	2.0
1952	36.2	-0.3	36.4	0.6	36.4	0.0	35.9	-1.4	36.0	0.3	35.9	-0.3	36.3	1.1	36.2	-0.3	35.9	-0.8	35.7	-0.6	34.8	-2.5	35.4	1.7
1953	35.0	-1.1	35.3	0.9	37.5	6.2	36.0	-4.0	35.6	-1.1	35.9	0.8	37.0	3.1	37.9	2.4	39.2	3.4	38.4	-2.0	38.3	-0.3	38.9	1.6
1954	42.3	8.7	44.2	4.5	47.6	7.7	47.9	0.6	47.6	-0.6	47.7	0.2	48.3	1.3	44.4	-8.1	43.3	-2.5	42.0	-3.0	43.3	3.1	41.5	-4.2
1955	41.1	-1.0	36.7	-10.7	37.6	2.5	37.4	-0.5	36.4	-2.7	37.6	3.3	36.2	-3.7	36.4	0.6	38.4	5.5	38.2	-0.5	36.8	-3.7	36.5	-0.8
1956	36.7	0.5	38.3	4.4	37.7	-1.6	37.7	0.0	38.0	0.8	38.7	1.8	39.2	1.3	39.7	1.3	40.2	1.3	39.4	-2.0	38.7	-1.8	38.9	0.5
1957	39.1	0.5	38.9	-0.5	38.4	-1.3	38.0	-1.0	37.9	-0.3	38.3	1.1	37.6	-1.8	37.6	0.0	37.6	0.0	37.2	-1.1	37.9	1.9	37.5	-1.1
1958	37.7	0.5	37.4	-0.8	37.7	0.8	37.4	-0.8	37.3	-0.3	37.2	-0.3	36.8	-1.1	36.7	-0.3	36.1	-1.6	36.5	1.1	36.2	-0.8	35.8	-1.1
1959	35.3	-1.4	35.4	0.3	35.2	-0.6	35.1	-0.3	35.1	0.0	34.9	-0.6	34.8	-0.3	34.7	-0.3	35.0	0.9	34.6	-1.1	34.6	0.0	33.5	-3.2
1960	33.5	0.0	33.9	1.2	33.6	-0.9	33.8	0.6	33.7	-0.3	33.7	0.0	33.6	-0.3	33.0	-1.8	34.0	3.0	34.3	0.9	34.0	-0.9	34.3	0.9
1961	33.7	-1.7	34.1	1.2	34.1	0.0	34.0	-0.3	34.0	0.0	33.9	-0.3	34.0	0.3	34.0	0.0	34.5	1.5	34.2	-0.9	34.0	-0.6	34.6	1.8
1962	34.2	-1.2	34.2	0.0	34.2	0.0	34.1	-0.3	34.2	0.3	33.8	-1.2	33.8	0.0	32.9	-2.7	33.2	0.9	32.8	-1.2	33.0	0.6	32.6	-1.2
1963	32.0	-1.8	32.6	1.9	32.6	0.0	32.7	0.3	32.8	0.3	32.7	-0.3	32.6	-0.3	32.4	-0.6	32.6	0.6	33.1	1.5	33.2	0.3	33.2	0.0
1964	36.2	9.0	35.3	-2.5	36.8	4.2	36.4	-1.1	36.4	0.0	36.1	-0.8	36.0	-0.3	36.0	0.0	35.4	-1.7	36.3	2.5	36.0	-0.8	36.0	0.0
1965	34.9	-3.1	35.6	2.0	34.8	-2.2	35.0	0.6	34.7	-0.9	35.0	0.9	34.9	-0.3	36.0	3.2	36.9	2.5	36.6	-0.8	36.5	-0.3	37.9	3.8
1966	37.5	-1.1	37.4	-0.3	37.3	-0.3	37.5	0.5	37.1	-1.1	37.0	-0.3	36.5	-1.4	36.7	0.5	36.5	-0.5	36.3	-0.5	36.9	1.7	36.8	-0.3
1967	36.4	-1.1	36.8	1.1	36.4	-1.1	36.3	-0.3	36.5	0.6	36.7	0.5	36.5	-0.5	36.3	-0.5	35.7	-1.7	35.6	-0.3	36.9	3.7	37.1	0.5
1968	37.2	0.3	37.0	-0.5	37.1	0.3	37.3	0.5	37.2	-0.3	37.2	0.0	37.2	0.0	37.7	1.3	38.1	1.1	38.1	0.0	39.1	2.6	39.4	0.8
1969	38.7	-1.8	38.9	0.5	39.1	0.5	38.8	-0.8	38.6	-0.5	38.8	0.5	39.1	0.8	40.0	2.3	40.7	1.7	42.7	4.9	42.4	-0.7	41.4	-2.4
1970	42.6	2.9	42.2	-0.9	42.0	-0.5	42.0	0.0	42.1	0.2	42.0	-0.2	42.6	1.4	43.3	1.6	43.4	0.2	42.8	-1.4	44.2	3.3	43.7	-1.1

[Continued]

Other Farm Products
Producer Price Index
Base 1982 = 100
[Continued]

For 1926-1997. Columns headed % show percentile change in the index from the previous period for which an index is available.

Year	Jan Index	%	Feb Index	%	Mar Index	%	Apr Index	%	May Index	%	Jun Index	%	Jul Index	%	Aug Index	%	Sep Index	%	Oct Index	%	Nov Index	%	Dec Index	%
1971	43.7	0.0	43.6	-0.2	42.3	-3.0	41.7	-1.4	41.4	-0.7	41.4	0.0	41.3	-0.2	41.8	1.2	42.1	0.7	42.1	0.0	41.2	-2.1	42.7	3.6
1972	43.0	0.7	42.5	-1.2	42.8	0.7	43.0	0.5	43.5	1.2	43.7	0.5	44.4	1.6	49.0	10.4	48.3	-1.4	48.2	-0.2	48.8	1.2	49.3	1.0
1973	49.7	0.8	51.2	3.0	52.2	2.0	51.8	-0.8	53.2	2.7	54.0	1.5	55.4	2.6	54.8	-1.1	55.8	1.8	56.3	0.9	55.6	-1.2	54.3	-2.3
1974	55.9	2.9	56.7	1.4	58.0	2.3	59.8	3.1	60.8	1.7	59.5	-2.1	58.3	-2.0	59.2	1.5	60.5	2.2	62.0	2.5	64.0	3.2	63.9	-0.2
1975	62.8	-1.7	63.6	1.3	62.3	-2.0	61.2	-1.8	60.2	-1.6	60.3	0.2	58.3	-3.3	61.2	5.0	61.9	1.1	63.7	2.9	62.8	-1.4	63.5	1.1
1976	64.8	2.0	66.0	1.9	65.6	-0.6	70.6	7.6	75.1	6.4	81.8	8.9	79.7	-2.6	82.9	4.0	92.1	11.1	93.6	1.6	98.8	5.6	105.9	7.2
1977	107.8	1.8	114.4	6.1	134.2	17.3	140.7	4.8	130.6	-7.2	124.5	-4.7	122.1	-1.9	106.4	-12.9	115.5	8.6	107.9	-6.6	110.5	2.4	110.2	-0.3
1978	103.7	-5.9	101.0	-2.6	100.1	-0.9	98.7	-1.4	98.9	0.2	99.3	0.4	97.7	-1.6	95.7	-2.0	103.3	7.9	100.7	-2.5	104.2	3.5	98.7	-5.3
1979	98.3	-0.4	92.4	-6.0	92.7	0.3	92.9	0.2	96.2	3.6	102.4	6.4	113.6	10.9	113.2	-0.4	115.1	1.7	114.2	-0.8	116.0	1.6	116.3	0.3
1980	109.7	-5.7	111.0	1.2	113.5	2.3	111.0	-2.2	113.3	2.1	112.7	-0.5	106.5	-5.5	103.0	-3.3	106.4	3.3	104.1	-2.2	108.1	3.8	107.8	-0.3
1981	107.9	0.1	107.5	-0.4	107.8	0.3	107.8	0.0	94.6	-12.2	88.4	-6.6	91.1	3.1	96.1	5.5	98.0	2.0	95.9	-2.1	99.5	3.8	102.1	2.6
1982	102.0	-0.1	99.7	-2.3	99.5	-0.2	99.9	0.4	99.8	-0.1	99.0	-0.8	96.7	-2.3	100.0	3.4	100.8	0.8	99.8	-1.0	100.7	0.9	102.1	1.4
1983	102.0	-0.1	102.4	0.4	102.1	-0.3	101.7	-0.4	102.4	0.7	103.6	1.2	102.9	-0.7	104.1	1.2	104.7	0.6	103.4	-1.2	103.3	-0.1	100.9	-2.3
1984	102.1	1.2	101.6	-0.5	101.2	-0.4	101.9	0.7	105.0	3.0	101.7	-3.1	101.1	-0.6	103.6	2.5	108.0	4.2	107.1	-0.8	108.5	1.3	107.0	-1.4
1985	105.5	-1.4	104.0	-1.4	104.1	0.1	103.4	-0.7	103.3	-0.1	103.3	0.0	103.2	-0.1	100.0	-3.1	103.0	3.0	102.9	-0.1	103.4	0.5	100.9	-2.4
1986	100.9	0.0	100.3	-0.6	99.1	-1.2	98.5	-0.6	97.9	-0.6	97.9	0.0	97.9	0.0	89.9	-8.2	94.8	5.5	91.1	-3.9	94.0	3.2	94.0	0.0
1987	93.5	-0.5	94.0	0.5	94.0	0.0	93.5	-0.5	93.5	0.0	93.5	0.0	92.0	-1.6	92.0	0.0	96.5	4.9	97.0	0.5	96.5	-0.5	96.5	0.0
1988	95.5	-1.0	95.5	0.0	95.5	0.0	91.5	-4.2	91.5	0.0	91.5	0.0	91.5	0.0	93.0	1.6	98.5	5.9	100.1	1.6	101.1	1.0	99.7	-1.4
1989	99.7	0.0	98.7	-1.0	98.7	0.0	99.2	0.5	99.2	0.0	99.2	0.0	98.7	-0.5	98.1	-0.6	101.2	3.2	114.2	12.8	114.5	0.3	117.8	2.9
1990	117.8	0.0	117.8	0.0	117.8	0.0	119.3	1.3	119.3	0.0	119.3	0.0	117.8	-1.3	117.3	-0.4	121.8	3.8	141.9	16.5	142.4	0.4	150.7	5.8
1991	151.6	0.6	151.6	0.0	151.2	-0.3	151.2	0.0	151.2	0.0	151.2	0.0	151.2	0.0	149.0	-1.5	154.3	3.6	142.7	-7.5	157.2	10.2	156.3	-0.6
1992	152.4	-2.5	152.4	0.0	169.9	11.5	140.8	-17.1	140.8	0.0	140.8	0.0	134.9	-4.2	143.7	6.5	158.2	10.1	157.3	-0.6	158.2	0.6	158.2	0.0
1993	156.3	-1.2	164.1	5.0	162.1	-1.2	145.6	-10.2	136.9	-6.0	136.9	0.0	136.9	0.0	138.8	1.4	150.5	8.4	152.4	1.3	157.3	3.2	157.3	0.0
1994	157.3	0.0	163.1	3.7	136.9	-16.1	147.6	7.8	147.6	0.0	147.6	0.0	130.1	-11.9	135.9	4.5	153.4	12.9	156.3	1.9	158.2	1.2	160.2	1.3
1995	164.7	2.8	167.8	1.9	149.5	-10.9	134.2	-10.2	-	-	-	-	154.3	15.0	152.1	-1.4	160.4	5.5	159.1	-0.8	161.7	1.6	161.7	0.0
1996	166.1	2.7	177.1	6.6	153.0	-13.6	140.7	-8.0	-	-	-	-	140.3	-0.3	153.0	9.1	164.8	7.7	167.9	1.9	168.3	0.2	168.8	0.3
1997	176.2	4.4	180.2	2.3	166.6	-7.5	-	-	-	-	-	-	139.0	-16.6	140.3	0.9	153.9	9.7	157.4	2.3	154.3	-2.0	167.9	8.8

Source: U.S. Department of Labor, Bureau of Labor Statistics, Division of Industry Prices and Price Indexes. n.e.c. stands for not elsewhere classified. - indicates no data collected for period or unavailable.

PROCESSED FOODS AND FEEDS
Producer Price Index
Base 1982 = 100

For 1947-1997. Columns headed % show percentile change in the index from the previous period for which an index is available.

Year	Jan Index	%	Feb Index	%	Mar Index	%	Apr Index	%	May Index	%	Jun Index	%	Jul Index	%	Aug Index	%	Sep Index	%	Oct Index	%	Nov Index	%	Dec Index	%
1947	31.5	-	31.6	0.3	32.9	4.1	32.1	-2.4	31.5	-1.9	31.7	0.6	32.3	1.9	32.8	1.5	34.2	4.3	34.5	0.9	34.9	1.2	35.6	2.0
1948	36.7	3.1	35.0	-4.6	34.9	-0.3	35.4	1.4	35.7	0.8	35.9	0.6	36.1	0.6	35.8	-0.8	35.6	-0.6	34.5	-3.1	34.1	-1.2	33.6	-1.5
1949	32.9	-2.1	32.0	-2.7	32.1	0.3	32.0	-0.3	31.9	-0.3	31.9	0.0	32.1	0.6	32.5	1.2	32.2	-0.9	31.8	-1.2	31.6	-0.6	31.5	-0.3
1950	31.3	-0.6	31.5	0.6	31.7	0.6	31.7	0.0	32.4	2.2	32.4	0.0	34.2	5.6	34.7	1.5	34.9	0.6	34.1	-2.3	34.2	0.3	35.3	3.2
1951	36.4	3.1	37.2	2.2	37.0	-0.5	37.0	0.0	37.0	0.0	36.7	-0.8	36.6	-0.3	36.7	0.3	36.7	0.0	37.0	0.8	37.0	0.0	36.9	-0.3
1952	36.9	0.0	36.8	-0.3	36.6	-0.5	36.3	-0.8	36.4	0.3	36.3	-0.3	36.6	0.8	36.9	0.8	36.9	0.0	36.4	-1.4	36.0	-1.1	35.0	-2.8
1953	35.2	0.6	35.1	-0.3	34.8	-0.9	34.4	-1.1	34.8	1.2	34.2	-1.7	34.8	1.8	34.7	-0.3	35.2	1.4	34.7	-1.4	34.4	-0.9	34.9	1.5
1954	35.5	1.7	35.2	-0.8	35.4	0.6	36.0	1.7	36.2	0.6	35.4	-2.2	35.8	1.1	35.7	-0.3	35.3	-1.1	34.6	-2.0	34.7	0.3	34.6	-0.3
1955	34.7	0.3	34.5	-0.6	34.0	-1.4	34.2	0.6	33.9	-0.9	34.2	0.9	34.2	0.0	33.8	-1.2	33.6	-0.6	33.4	-0.6	32.8	-1.8	32.6	-0.6
1956	32.7	0.3	32.8	0.3	32.8	0.0	33.4	1.8	34.2	2.4	34.0	-0.6	33.8	-0.6	34.0	0.6	34.3	0.9	34.2	-0.3	34.3	0.3	34.2	-0.3
1957	34.6	1.2	34.4	-0.6	34.4	0.0	34.5	0.3	34.5	0.0	34.8	0.9	35.2	1.1	35.1	-0.3	35.0	-0.3	34.6	-1.1	34.8	0.6	35.1	0.9
1958	35.8	2.0	35.9	0.3	36.4	1.4	36.9	1.4	37.1	0.5	37.2	0.3	37.2	0.0	36.6	-1.6	36.4	-0.5	36.1	-0.8	36.1	0.0	36.3	0.6
1959	36.3	0.0	35.9	-1.1	35.8	-0.3	35.9	0.3	35.9	0.0	35.7	-0.6	35.6	-0.3	35.1	-1.4	35.4	0.9	35.2	-0.6	35.0	-0.6	34.9	-0.3
1960	35.2	0.9	35.1	-0.3	35.6	1.4	35.6	0.0	35.4	-0.6	35.5	0.3	35.8	0.8	35.5	-0.8	35.6	0.3	35.9	0.8	35.9	0.0	36.0	0.3
1961	36.5	1.4	36.6	0.3	36.5	-0.3	36.3	-0.5	36.1	-0.6	35.6	-1.4	35.9	0.8	36.0	0.3	36.0	0.0	35.9	-0.3	36.1	0.6	36.4	0.8
1962	36.7	0.8	36.6	-0.3	36.5	-0.3	36.2	-0.8	36.0	-0.6	36.0	0.0	36.5	1.4	36.6	0.3	37.3	1.9	36.7	-1.6	36.7	0.0	36.6	-0.3
1963	36.7	0.3	36.6	-0.3	36.1	-1.4	36.1	0.0	36.7	1.7	36.9	0.5	37.1	0.5	36.8	-0.8	36.9	0.3	37.2	0.8	37.2	0.0	36.7	-1.3
1964	37.3	1.6	36.8	-1.3	36.6	-0.5	36.5	-0.3	36.1	-1.1	36.3	0.6	36.6	0.8	36.5	-0.3	37.1	1.6	36.9	-0.5	36.6	-0.8	36.7	0.3
1965	37.1	1.1	37.0	-0.3	36.9	-0.3	37.1	0.5	37.3	0.5	38.3	2.7	38.5	0.5	38.5	0.0	38.5	0.0	38.5	0.0	38.9	1.0	39.3	1.0
1966	39.7	1.0	40.2	1.3	39.9	-0.7	39.7	-0.5	39.8	0.3	39.9	0.3	40.5	1.5	41.2	1.7	41.1	-0.2	40.6	-1.2	40.1	-1.2	40.2	0.2
1967	40.2	0.0	39.7	-1.2	39.4	-0.8	39.2	-0.5	39.4	0.5	40.1	1.8	40.3	0.5	39.9	-1.0	40.1	0.5	39.8	-0.7	39.5	-0.8	39.7	0.5
1968	40.0	0.8	40.3	0.7	40.2	-0.2	40.2	0.0	40.5	0.7	40.9	1.0	41.3	1.0	41.0	-0.7	41.0	0.0	40.7	-0.7	40.8	0.2	40.9	0.2
1969	41.3	1.0	41.4	0.2	41.5	0.2	41.8	0.7	42.5	1.7	43.3	1.9	43.5	0.5	43.3	-0.5	43.2	-0.2	43.3	0.2	43.3	0.0	43.7	0.9
1970	44.6	2.1	44.7	0.2	44.5	-0.4	44.5	0.0	44.2	-0.7	44.5	0.7	45.1	1.3	44.9	-0.4	45.0	0.2	44.5	-1.1	44.5	0.0	44.0	-1.1
1971	44.5	1.1	45.1	1.3	45.2	0.2	45.2	0.0	45.6	0.9	45.8	0.4	46.2	0.9	46.0	-0.4	45.7	-0.7	45.4	-0.7	45.5	0.2	46.1	1.3
1972	46.6	1.1	47.3	1.5	47.2	-0.2	46.8	-0.8	47.2	0.9	47.6	0.8	48.3	1.5	48.1	-0.4	48.5	0.8	48.5	0.0	48.9	0.8	51.5	5.3
1973	52.6	2.1	54.5	3.6	56.2	3.1	55.6	-1.1	57.7	3.8	60.3	4.5	58.3	-3.3	66.1	13.4	62.2	-5.9	60.9	-2.1	60.4	-0.8	61.9	2.5
1974	64.4	4.0	65.5	1.7	64.8	-1.1	63.3	-2.3	63.2	-0.2	62.6	-0.9	66.6	6.4	71.4	7.2	70.3	-1.5	73.0	3.8	75.4	3.3	74.8	-0.8
1975	74.1	-0.9	72.6	-2.0	70.5	-2.9	71.4	1.3	71.2	-0.3	71.5	0.4	73.4	2.7	74.1	1.0	74.0	-0.1	74.0	0.0	72.6	-1.9	72.0	-0.8
1976	71.3	-1.0	70.2	-1.5	69.9	-0.4	70.8	1.3	71.5	1.0	72.3	1.1	72.6	0.4	70.3	-3.2	70.5	0.3	69.6	-1.3	69.5	-0.1	71.2	2.4
1977	71.3	0.1	72.3	1.4	73.1	1.1	75.0	2.6	76.3	1.7	75.6	-0.9	74.4	-1.6	73.5	-1.2	73.3	-0.3	73.3	0.0	74.3	1.4	75.3	1.3
1978	76.2	1.2	77.5	1.7	78.3	1.0	79.6	1.7	80.5	1.1	81.4	1.1	81.2	-0.2	80.2	-1.2	81.7	1.9	83.1	1.7	82.8	-0.4	84.2	1.7
1979	85.6	1.7	87.1	1.8	87.7	0.7	88.4	0.8	88.3	-0.1	87.7	-0.7	88.8	1.3	87.7	-1.2	89.8	2.4	89.4	-0.4	90.3	1.0	91.2	1.0
1980	90.9	-0.3	92.7	2.0	92.1	-0.6	90.9	-1.3	92.7	2.0	93.0	0.3	96.1	3.3	99.2	3.2	99.3	0.1	101.8	2.5	102.3	0.5	100.0	-2.2
1981	100.7	0.7	99.5	-1.2	98.8	-0.7	98.4	-0.4	98.7	0.3	99.4	0.7	100.3	0.9	99.9	-0.4	99.0	-0.9	98.0	-1.0	97.2	-0.8	96.9	-0.3
1982	98.2	1.3	98.7	0.5	98.7	0.0	99.8	1.1	101.2	1.4	101.7	0.5	101.2	-0.5	100.8	-0.4	100.8	0.0	99.7	-1.1	99.5	-0.2	99.6	0.1
1983	100.1	0.5	101.3	1.2	101.2	-0.1	101.8	0.6	101.8	0.0	101.1	-0.7	101.2	0.1	101.6	0.4	103.2	1.6	102.5	-0.7	102.5	0.0	103.0	0.5
1984	104.9	1.8	104.7	-0.2	106.2	1.4	106.3	0.1	106.4	0.1	105.3	-1.0	106.3	0.9	105.3	-0.9	104.8	-0.5	104.4	-0.4	104.9	0.5	105.2	0.3
1985	105.1	-0.1	104.9	-0.2	104.3	-0.6	103.8	-0.5	103.4	-0.4	102.9	-0.5	103.3	0.4	102.3	-1.0	101.5	-0.8	102.5	1.0	103.9	1.4	104.5	0.6
1986	104.7	0.2	104.0	-0.7	103.7	-0.3	103.3	-0.4	104.3	1.0	104.7	0.4	106.1	1.3	107.2	1.0	107.0	-0.2	106.7	-0.3	106.5	-0.2	106.7	0.2
1987	106.1	-0.6	106.4	0.3	105.9	-0.5	107.2	1.2	109.1	1.8	109.0	-0.1	109.0	0.0	108.2	-0.7	108.9	0.6	108.7	-0.2	108.1	-0.6	108.2	0.1
1988	109.3	1.0	109.1	-0.2	109.6	0.5	110.1	0.5	111.2	1.0	113.5	2.1	115.0	1.3	114.5	-0.4	115.4	0.8	115.0	-0.3	114.8	-0.2	115.0	0.2
1989	116.6	1.4	116.6	0.0	117.5	0.8	117.2	-0.3	117.9	0.6	117.4	-0.4	118.1	0.6	117.9	-0.2	117.9	0.0	117.9	0.0	118.9	0.8	119.3	0.3
1990	120.2	0.8	120.0	-0.2	120.9	0.7	121.2	0.2	123.5	1.9	122.8	-0.6	123.2	0.3	123.0	-0.2	122.4	-0.5	122.2	-0.2	121.7	-0.4	121.7	0.0
1991	122.1	0.3	122.3	0.2	122.6	0.2	122.5	-0.1	122.3	-0.2	121.9	-0.3	121.6	-0.2	121.4	-0.2	121.1	-0.2	121.9	0.7	121.4	-0.4	121.4	0.0

[Continued]

PROCESSED FOODS AND FEEDS
Producer Price Index
Base 1982 = 100
[Continued]

For 1947-1997. Columns headed % show percentile change in the index from the previous period for which an index is available.

Year	Jan Index	%	Feb Index	%	Mar Index	%	Apr Index	%	May Index	%	Jun Index	%	Jul Index	%	Aug Index	%	Sep Index	%	Oct Index	%	Nov Index	%	Dec Index	%
1992	121.3	-0.1	121.7	0.3	121.8	0.1	122.0	0.2	122.5	0.4	123.0	0.4	122.4	-0.5	122.1	-0.2	122.1	0.0	121.8	-0.2	121.6	-0.2	122.4	0.7
1993	122.7	0.2	122.7	0.0	122.9	0.2	123.7	0.7	124.2	0.4	124.0	-0.2	124.3	0.2	124.3	0.0	124.3	0.0	124.5	0.2	124.8	0.2	125.4	0.5
1994	126.0	0.5	126.2	0.2	126.8	0.5	126.6	-0.2	126.1	-0.4	125.4	-0.6	124.9	-0.4	125.2	0.2	125.0	-0.2	124.5	-0.4	124.7	0.2	124.3	-0.3
1995	125.2	0.7	125.9	0.6	126.2	0.2	125.6	-0.5	125.0	-0.5	125.3	0.2	126.7	1.1	127.5	0.6	127.8	0.2	128.9	0.9	130.0	0.9	130.2	0.2
1996	130.0	-0.2	130.3	0.2	130.3	0.0	130.9	0.5	132.7	1.4	134.0	1.0	134.8	0.6	136.1	1.0	136.0	-0.1	136.0	0.0	134.7	-1.0	134.2	-0.4
1997	133.4	-0.6	132.9	-0.4	134.5	1.2	134.5	0.0	135.4	0.7	134.3	-0.8	133.9	-0.3	134.3	0.3	134.1	-0.1	133.5	-0.4	133.7	0.1	132.9	-0.6

Source: U.S. Department of Labor, Bureau of Labor Statistics, Division of Industry Prices and Price Indexes. n.e.c. stands for not elsewhere classified. - indicates no data collected for period or unavailable.

Cereal and Bakery Products
Producer Price Index
Base 1982 = 100

For 1926-1997. Columns headed % show percentile change in the index from the previous period for which an index is available.

Year	Jan Index	%	Feb Index	%	Mar Index	%	Apr Index	%	May Index	%	Jun Index	%	Jul Index	%	Aug Index	%	Sep Index	%	Oct Index	%	Nov Index	%	Dec Index	%
1926	20.1	-	19.8	-1.5	19.5	-1.5	19.3	-1.0	18.9	-2.1	19.0	0.5	18.8	-1.1	18.3	-2.7	18.1	-1.1	18.3	1.1	18.0	-1.6	17.9	-0.6
1927	17.8	-0.6	17.8	0.0	17.6	-1.1	17.6	0.0	18.2	3.4	18.3	0.5	18.2	-0.5	18.0	-1.1	17.5	-2.8	17.5	0.0	17.4	-0.6	17.4	0.0
1928	17.6	1.1	17.6	0.0	17.9	1.7	18.6	3.9	18.9	1.6	18.4	-2.6	17.9	-2.7	17.1	-4.5	17.0	-0.6	16.9	-0.6	16.7	-1.2	16.7	0.0
1929	16.7	0.0	16.9	1.2	16.4	-3.0	16.2	-1.2	15.9	-1.9	16.0	0.6	17.2	7.5	17.0	-1.2	16.9	-0.6	16.6	-1.8	16.5	-0.6	16.5	0.0
1930	16.5	0.0	16.2	-1.8	16.0	-1.2	15.9	-0.6	15.8	-0.6	15.6	-1.3	15.2	-2.6	15.1	-0.7	14.8	-2.0	14.6	-1.4	14.3	-2.1	14.3	0.0
1931	14.3	0.0	14.2	-0.7	14.0	-1.4	13.9	-0.7	14.0	0.7	13.9	-0.7	13.5	-2.9	13.4	-0.7	13.2	-1.5	13.3	0.8	13.7	3.0	13.6	-0.7
1932	13.4	-1.5	13.1	-2.2	12.8	-2.3	12.8	0.0	12.8	0.0	12.6	-1.6	12.4	-1.6	12.4	0.0	12.4	0.0	12.1	-2.4	11.8	-2.5	11.6	-1.7
1933	11.5	-0.9	11.4	-0.9	11.8	3.5	12.4	5.1	13.0	4.8	13.3	2.3	15.7	18.0	16.0	1.9	16.0	0.0	16.0	0.0	16.2	1.3	16.0	-1.2
1934	16.2	1.3	16.2	0.0	16.0	-1.2	16.0	0.0	16.4	2.5	16.7	1.8	16.7	0.0	17.1	2.4	17.3	1.2	17.1	-1.2	17.1	0.0	17.3	1.2
1935	17.3	0.0	17.3	0.0	17.3	0.0	17.5	1.2	17.4	-0.6	17.1	-1.7	17.5	2.3	17.9	2.3	18.2	1.7	18.6	2.2	18.3	-1.6	18.3	0.0
1936	17.3	-5.5	16.7	-3.5	16.2	-3.0	15.8	-2.5	15.5	-1.9	15.4	-0.6	15.9	3.2	16.5	3.8	16.5	0.0	16.5	0.0	16.2	-1.8	16.4	1.2
1937	16.6	1.2	16.8	1.2	16.9	0.6	16.9	0.0	16.7	-1.2	17.0	1.8	17.4	2.4	16.5	-5.2	16.2	-1.8	15.9	-1.9	15.3	-3.8	15.4	0.7
1938	15.6	1.3	15.6	0.0	15.2	-2.6	15.1	-0.7	14.7	-2.6	15.1	2.7	14.9	-1.3	14.5	-2.7	14.3	-1.4	14.1	-1.4	13.9	-1.4	14.1	1.4
1939	13.8	-2.1	13.7	-0.7	13.6	-0.7	13.6	0.0	13.9	2.2	14.3	2.9	13.5	-5.6	13.5	0.0	14.9	10.4	14.7	-1.3	14.7	0.0	15.2	3.4
1940	15.1	-0.7	15.5	2.6	15.5	0.0	15.6	0.6	15.2	-2.6	14.6	-3.9	14.3	-2.1	14.1	-1.4	14.3	1.4	14.5	1.4	14.1	-2.8	13.9	-1.4
1941	14.1	1.4	13.9	-1.4	14.1	1.4	14.5	2.8	14.7	1.4	15.1	2.7	15.1	0.0	15.3	1.3	16.2	5.9	16.2	0.0	16.2	0.0	16.8	3.7
1942	17.1	1.8	17.2	0.6	17.1	-0.6	17.0	-0.6	16.7	-1.8	16.4	-1.8	16.4	0.0	16.5	0.6	16.7	1.2	16.8	0.6	16.9	0.6	16.8	-0.6
1943	17.1	1.8	17.4	1.8	17.6	1.1	17.6	0.0	17.6	0.0	17.6	0.0	17.6	0.0	17.6	0.0	17.8	1.1	17.9	0.6	17.9	0.0	17.9	0.0
1944	17.9	0.0	17.9	0.0	17.9	0.0	17.9	0.0	17.9	0.0	17.9	0.0	17.8	-0.6	17.7	-0.6	17.8	0.6	17.9	0.6	17.9	0.0	17.9	0.0
1945	17.9	0.0	17.9	0.0	17.9	0.0	17.9	0.0	18.0	0.6	18.0	0.0	17.9	-0.6	17.9	0.0	17.9	0.0	17.9	0.0	18.0	0.6	18.0	0.0
1946	18.0	0.0	18.1	0.6	18.1	0.0	18.7	3.3	18.9	1.1	19.2	1.6	23.5	22.4	23.4	-0.4	24.0	2.6	24.2	0.8	25.6	5.8	26.2	2.3
1947	26.6	1.5	26.8	0.8	27.9	4.1	28.4	1.8	28.2	-0.7	27.7	-1.8	28.4	2.5	28.4	0.0	29.1	2.5	30.3	4.1	31.2	3.0	31.1	-0.3
1948	31.1	0.0	29.8	-4.2	29.6	-0.7	29.5	-0.3	29.2	-1.0	29.1	-0.3	29.2	0.3	28.8	-1.4	28.6	-0.7	28.3	-1.0	28.4	0.4	28.4	0.0
1949	28.2	-0.7	28.0	-0.7	28.0	0.0	27.9	-0.4	27.8	-0.4	27.8	0.0	27.9	0.4	27.5	-1.4	27.3	-0.7	27.3	0.0	27.3	0.0	27.3	0.0
1950	27.3	0.0	27.5	0.7	27.6	0.4	27.6	0.0	27.6	0.0	27.5	-0.4	28.4	3.3	29.0	2.1	29.1	0.3	28.8	-1.0	28.8	0.0	29.4	2.1
1951	30.3	3.1	30.7	1.3	30.5	-0.7	30.5	0.0	30.5	0.0	30.3	-0.7	30.3	0.0	30.4	0.3	30.3	-0.3	30.5	0.7	30.7	0.7	30.8	0.3
1952	30.7	-0.3	30.6	-0.3	30.7	0.3	30.6	-0.3	30.5	-0.3	30.4	-0.3	30.3	-0.3	30.3	0.0	30.3	0.0	30.3	0.0	30.5	0.7	30.5	0.0
1953	30.5	0.0	30.7	0.7	31.1	1.3	31.1	0.0	31.1	0.0	30.8	-1.0	30.9	0.3	30.9	0.0	31.6	2.3	31.9	0.9	32.1	0.6	32.0	-0.3
1954	32.0	0.0	32.2	0.6	32.1	-0.3	32.3	0.6	32.3	0.0	32.4	0.3	32.5	0.3	32.3	-0.6	32.4	0.3	32.6	0.6	33.2	1.8	33.3	0.3
1955	33.3	0.0	33.1	-0.6	33.2	0.3	33.3	0.3	33.7	1.2	33.5	-0.6	33.5	0.0	32.8	-2.1	32.6	-0.6	32.7	0.3	32.8	0.3	32.8	0.0
1956	32.8	0.0	32.9	0.3	32.9	0.0	32.9	0.0	32.9	0.0	32.9	0.0	32.7	-0.6	32.6	-0.3	32.7	0.3	32.9	0.6	33.0	0.3	32.9	-0.3
1957	33.0	0.3	33.1	0.3	33.3	0.6	33.3	0.0	33.2	-0.3	33.3	0.3	33.5	0.6	33.3	-0.6	33.3	0.0	33.5	0.6	33.5	0.0	33.7	0.6
1958	33.7	0.0	33.7	0.0	33.6	-0.3	33.8	0.6	33.6	-0.6	33.8	0.6	33.5	-0.9	33.3	-0.6	33.6	0.9	33.7	0.3	33.7	0.0	33.5	-0.6
1959	33.5	0.0	33.5	0.0	33.9	1.2	33.9	0.0	34.0	0.3	34.0	0.0	34.0	0.0	34.0	0.0	34.0	0.0	34.3	0.9	34.3	0.0	34.3	0.0
1960	34.4	0.3	34.4	0.0	34.4	0.0	34.4	0.0	34.6	0.6	34.6	0.0	34.9	0.9	34.8	-0.3	34.9	0.3	35.1	0.6	35.1	0.0	35.2	0.3
1961	35.2	0.0	35.2	0.0	35.2	0.0	35.2	0.0	35.2	0.0	35.3	0.3	35.3	0.0	35.3	0.0	35.4	0.3	35.7	0.8	35.7	0.0	35.7	0.0
1962	36.0	0.8	36.1	0.3	36.1	0.0	36.3	0.6	36.1	-0.6	36.2	0.3	36.3	0.3	36.3	0.0	36.2	-0.3	36.2	0.0	36.3	0.3	36.2	-0.3
1963	36.1	-0.3	36.5	1.1	36.3	-0.5	36.4	0.3	36.2	-0.5	36.0	-0.6	35.8	-0.6	35.7	-0.3	36.0	0.8	36.3	0.8	36.1	-0.6	36.0	-0.3
1964	36.0	0.0	36.1	0.3	35.9	-0.6	36.3	1.1	36.2	-0.3	36.3	0.3	36.5	0.6	36.4	-0.3	36.4	0.0	36.4	0.0	36.4	0.0	36.4	0.0
1965	36.4	0.0	36.3	-0.3	36.4	0.3	36.4	0.0	36.4	0.0	36.5	0.3	36.8	0.8	36.6	-0.5	36.7	0.3	36.8	0.3	37.2	1.1	37.4	0.5
1966	37.6	0.5	37.7	0.3	37.7	0.0	37.9	0.5	38.0	0.3	38.4	1.1	38.9	1.3	40.0	2.8	40.0	0.0	40.0	0.0	40.0	0.0	39.7	-0.7
1967	39.5	-0.5	39.5	0.0	39.4	-0.3	39.4	0.0	39.5	0.3	39.5	0.0	39.3	-0.5	39.3	0.0	39.3	0.0	39.3	0.0	39.4	0.3	39.4	0.0
1968	39.4	0.0	39.5	0.3	39.5	0.0	39.5	0.0	39.4	-0.3	39.4	0.0	39.8	1.0	40.2	1.0	40.0	-0.5	40.2	0.5	40.2	0.0	40.2	0.0
1969	40.2	0.0	40.2	0.0	40.2	0.0	40.2	0.0	40.2	0.0	40.3	0.2	40.4	0.2	40.5	0.2	40.6	0.2	40.8	0.5	41.0	0.5	41.1	0.2
1970	41.1	0.0	41.5	1.0	41.7	0.5	41.9	0.5	41.9	0.0	42.0	0.2	42.4	1.0	42.5	0.2	43.1	1.4	43.3	0.5	43.7	0.9	43.8	0.2

[Continued]

Cereal and Bakery Products
Producer Price Index
Base 1982 = 100
[Continued]

For 1926-1997. Columns headed % show percentile change in the index from the previous period for which an index is available.

Year	Jan Index	%	Feb Index	%	Mar Index	%	Apr Index	%	May Index	%	Jun Index	%	Jul Index	%	Aug Index	%	Sep Index	%	Oct Index	%	Nov Index	%	Dec Index	%
1971	44.0	0.5	44.0	0.0	44.1	0.2	44.1	0.0	44.1	0.0	44.1	0.0	43.9	-0.5	43.9	0.0	43.8	-0.2	43.9	0.2	43.9	0.0	44.0	0.2
1972	44.2	0.5	44.3	0.2	44.4	0.2	44.5	0.2	44.6	0.2	44.6	0.0	44.8	0.4	45.4	1.3	45.7	0.7	46.1	0.9	46.6	1.1	47.3	1.5
1973	47.7	0.8	47.6	-0.2	47.8	0.4	48.7	1.9	49.0	0.6	49.6	1.2	49.5	-0.2	53.7	8.5	58.2	8.4	59.3	1.9	61.5	3.7	63.1	2.6
1974	65.5	3.8	66.8	2.0	67.9	1.6	65.8	-3.1	65.8	0.0	65.4	-0.6	66.6	1.8	66.7	0.2	66.9	0.3	69.4	3.7	70.8	2.0	71.7	1.3
1975	71.8	0.1	72.3	0.7	71.7	-0.8	70.6	-1.5	69.4	-1.7	68.7	-1.0	69.6	1.3	69.3	-0.4	69.7	0.6	70.0	0.4	69.7	-0.4	68.8	-1.3
1976	69.0	0.3	69.1	0.1	68.8	-0.4	68.0	-1.2	68.3	0.4	68.5	0.3	68.4	-0.1	67.1	-1.9	66.9	-0.3	67.0	0.1	66.5	-0.7	66.4	-0.2
1977	66.4	0.0	67.0	0.9	67.6	0.9	67.6	0.0	67.8	0.3	67.4	-0.6	67.7	0.4	67.8	0.1	68.8	1.5	69.2	0.6	70.9	2.5	71.8	1.3
1978	72.6	1.1	72.9	0.4	73.4	0.7	74.4	1.4	74.2	-0.3	74.9	0.9	75.3	0.5	75.8	0.7	75.3	-0.7	76.2	1.2	77.3	1.4	77.5	0.3
1979	77.7	0.3	78.5	1.0	78.8	0.4	80.0	1.5	80.8	1.0	81.3	0.6	83.7	3.0	85.1	1.7	86.2	1.3	86.6	0.5	87.7	1.3	88.1	0.5
1980	88.8	0.8	90.6	2.0	91.3	0.8	91.6	0.3	92.5	1.0	91.9	-0.6	92.5	0.7	92.9	0.4	93.9	1.1	95.1	1.3	96.7	1.7	98.0	1.3
1981	99.1	1.1	99.4	0.3	99.4	0.0	100.0	0.6	101.0	1.0	101.0	0.0	101.8	0.8	101.5	-0.3	101.8	0.3	101.2	-0.6	101.1	-0.1	100.5	-0.6
1982	101.1	0.6	99.8	-1.3	99.8	0.0	99.9	0.1	99.6	-0.3	99.6	0.0	99.7	0.1	99.6	-0.1	100.1	0.5	99.7	-0.4	100.2	0.5	101.0	0.8
1983	101.4	0.4	101.2	-0.2	101.2	0.0	102.0	0.8	102.1	0.1	102.6	0.5	103.0	0.4	103.6	0.6	103.9	0.3	104.3	0.4	104.5	0.2	104.5	0.0
1984	105.1	0.6	105.3	0.2	105.4	0.1	105.7	0.3	105.9	0.2	106.9	0.9	107.3	0.4	107.1	-0.2	107.1	0.0	107.4	0.3	107.8	0.4	107.8	0.0
1985	109.0	1.1	109.4	0.4	109.5	0.1	109.9	0.4	109.6	-0.3	110.3	0.6	110.2	-0.1	110.3	0.1	110.8	0.5	111.4	0.5	111.3	-0.1	111.6	0.3
1986	111.6	0.0	111.6	0.0	111.6	0.0	111.4	-0.2	111.6	0.2	111.1	-0.4	110.7	-0.4	110.9	0.2	110.5	-0.4	110.6	0.1	110.5	-0.1	110.1	-0.4
1987	110.2	0.1	110.8	0.5	111.2	0.4	111.4	0.2	112.0	0.5	111.9	-0.1	111.9	0.0	112.6	0.6	113.0	0.4	114.5	1.3	115.3	0.7	116.7	1.2
1988	118.2	1.3	119.6	1.2	119.8	0.2	120.2	0.3	120.4	0.2	123.2	2.3	124.1	0.7	124.6	0.4	126.4	1.4	126.4	0.0	126.1	-0.2	126.5	0.3
1989	128.2	1.3	129.0	0.6	129.2	0.2	129.1	-0.1	130.8	1.3	131.2	0.3	132.1	0.7	132.9	0.6	132.8	-0.1	132.4	-0.3	132.4	0.0	133.3	0.7
1990	133.2	-0.1	133.8	0.5	133.9	0.1	134.6	0.5	135.1	0.4	134.7	-0.3	134.3	-0.3	134.2	-0.1	133.7	-0.4	134.2	0.4	134.2	0.0	134.6	0.3
1991	135.3	0.5	136.0	0.5	136.6	0.4	137.0	0.3	137.4	0.3	137.8	0.3	137.3	-0.4	138.3	0.7	138.6	0.2	139.9	0.9	140.0	0.1	141.0	0.7
1992	142.1	0.8	143.5	1.0	143.4	-0.1	143.5	0.1	144.0	0.3	145.3	0.9	144.8	-0.3	144.3	-0.3	144.6	0.2	144.9	0.2	145.1	0.1	144.7	-0.3
1993	145.7	0.7	146.5	0.5	146.1	-0.3	146.6	0.3	146.3	-0.2	146.4	0.1	146.6	0.1	147.6	0.7	147.1	-0.3	149.0	1.3	150.6	1.1	152.3	1.1
1994	152.0	-0.2	152.1	0.1	152.0	-0.1	151.5	-0.3	151.7	0.1	150.9	-0.5	150.0	-0.6	149.4	-0.4	150.4	0.7	151.0	0.4	151.1	0.1	151.0	-0.1
1995	151.2	0.1	151.4	0.1	151.1	-0.2	151.3	0.1	152.2	0.6	153.5	0.9	155.1	1.0	156.0	0.6	157.3	0.8	158.9	1.0	158.9	0.0	159.2	0.2
1996	158.4	-0.5	160.2	1.1	159.9	-0.2	160.3	0.3	163.6	2.1	160.9	-1.7	160.2	-0.4	159.6	-0.4	159.0	-0.4	159.6	0.4	158.7	-0.6	158.5	-0.1
1997	158.3	-0.1	158.4	0.1	158.0	-0.3	158.7	0.4	158.8	0.1	158.3	-0.3	157.4	-0.6	157.6	0.1	158.0	0.3	157.9	-0.1	157.9	0.0	157.6	-0.2

Source: U.S. Department of Labor, Bureau of Labor Statistics, Division of Industry Prices and Price Indexes. n.e.c. stands for not elsewhere classified. - indicates no data collected for period or unavailable.

Meats, Poultry, and Fish
Producer Price Index
Base 1982 = 100

For 1926-1997. Columns headed % show percentile change in the index from the previous period for which an index is available.

Year	Jan Index	%	Feb Index	%	Mar Index	%	Apr Index	%	May Index	%	Jun Index	%	Jul Index	%	Aug Index	%	Sep Index	%	Oct Index	%	Nov Index	%	Dec Index	%
1926	17.5	-	17.1	-2.3	17.2	0.6	17.4	1.2	17.5	0.6	17.9	2.3	17.7	-1.1	17.5	-1.1	17.8	1.7	17.7	-0.6	17.3	-2.3	17.2	-0.6
1927	15.6	-9.3	15.7	0.6	15.8	0.6	15.9	0.6	15.7	-1.3	15.5	-1.3	15.8	1.9	15.8	0.0	16.2	2.5	17.5	8.0	17.6	0.6	17.4	-1.1
1928	17.4	0.0	17.1	-1.7	16.6	-2.9	17.4	4.8	18.1	4.0	18.2	0.6	19.7	8.2	20.8	5.6	22.1	6.3	20.4	-7.7	19.0	-6.9	17.9	-5.8
1929	18.4	2.8	17.9	-2.7	19.0	6.1	19.5	2.6	19.5	0.0	19.5	0.0	20.4	4.6	20.3	-0.5	19.8	-2.5	18.6	-6.1	17.9	-3.8	18.1	1.1
1930	18.6	2.8	18.4	-1.1	18.2	-1.1	18.1	-0.5	17.7	-2.2	17.5	-1.1	16.0	-8.6	16.3	1.9	17.4	6.7	16.9	-2.9	16.0	-5.3	15.6	-2.5
1931	15.5	-0.6	14.6	-5.8	14.4	-1.4	14.0	-2.8	13.0	-7.1	12.5	-3.8	12.8	2.4	13.3	3.9	12.9	-3.0	12.5	-3.1	11.8	-5.6	11.1	-5.9
1932	10.8	-2.7	10.4	-3.7	10.7	2.9	10.5	-1.9	9.9	-5.7	9.8	-1.0	10.8	10.2	10.8	0.0	10.6	-1.9	9.9	-6.6	9.4	-5.1	8.6	-8.5
1933	8.7	1.2	8.8	1.1	8.9	1.1	8.8	-1.1	9.2	4.5	9.2	0.0	8.9	-3.3	8.9	0.0	9.0	1.1	8.9	-1.1	8.4	-5.6	8.0	-4.8
1934	8.5	6.3	9.4	10.6	9.9	5.3	10.0	1.0	10.5	5.0	10.9	3.8	11.1	1.8	12.2	9.9	13.4	9.8	12.2	-9.0	12.0	-1.6	12.0	0.0
1935	14.3	19.2	15.3	7.0	16.0	4.6	16.5	3.1	17.0	3.0	16.5	-2.9	16.3	-1.2	17.9	9.8	18.0	0.6	17.0	-5.6	16.5	-2.9	17.0	3.0
1936	16.6	-2.4	16.1	-3.0	15.7	-2.5	15.9	1.3	14.9	-6.3	14.9	0.0	14.8	-0.7	15.1	2.0	15.3	1.3	14.8	-3.3	14.9	0.7	15.2	2.0
1937	15.9	4.6	15.8	-0.6	16.1	1.9	16.6	3.1	16.8	1.2	17.2	2.4	18.5	7.6	19.6	5.9	19.8	1.0	18.8	-5.1	17.2	-8.5	15.5	-9.9
1938	14.4	-7.1	13.7	-4.9	14.3	4.4	14.4	0.7	14.4	0.0	14.8	2.8	15.7	6.1	15.0	-4.5	15.2	1.3	14.6	-3.9	14.3	-2.1	14.0	-2.1
1939	14.3	2.1	14.5	1.4	14.4	-0.7	14.2	-1.4	13.7	-3.5	13.2	-3.6	13.2	0.0	12.9	-2.3	14.2	10.1	13.1	-7.7	12.5	-4.6	12.0	-4.0
1940	12.2	1.7	12.0	-1.6	12.1	0.8	12.5	3.3	12.9	3.2	12.4	-3.9	12.8	3.2	13.3	3.9	13.8	3.8	13.2	-4.3	13.4	1.5	13.5	0.7
1941	14.5	7.4	14.6	0.7	14.6	0.0	15.0	2.7	15.2	1.3	15.9	4.6	16.4	3.1	17.0	3.7	17.4	2.4	16.4	-5.7	15.9	-3.0	16.7	5.0
1942	17.8	6.6	18.2	2.2	19.1	4.9	19.8	3.7	20.1	1.5	19.9	-1.0	19.8	-0.5	20.1	1.5	20.3	1.0	20.2	-0.5	19.6	-3.0	19.9	1.5
1943	20.2	1.5	20.2	0.0	20.2	0.0	20.3	0.5	20.3	0.0	19.5	-3.9	18.5	-5.1	18.5	0.0	18.5	0.0	18.6	0.5	18.6	0.0	18.5	-0.5
1944	18.5	0.0	18.5	0.0	18.5	0.0	18.6	0.5	18.6	0.0	18.5	-0.5	18.5	0.0	18.5	0.0	18.9	0.0	18.9	0.0	18.6	0.0	18.9	0.0
1945	18.6	0.0	18.6	0.0	18.8	1.1	18.9	0.5	19.0	0.5	18.9	-0.5	18.9	0.0	18.9	0.0	18.9	0.0	18.9	0.0	18.9	0.0	18.9	0.0
1946	18.9	0.0	18.9	0.0	19.2	1.6	19.3	0.5	19.3	0.0	19.3	0.0	29.7	53.9	34.6	16.5	22.9	-33.8	33.5	46.3	35.4	5.7	33.0	-6.8
1947	32.1	-2.7	32.8	2.2	34.5	5.2	33.1	-4.1	33.6	1.5	34.6	3.0	35.3	2.0	36.7	4.0	39.2	6.8	37.8	-3.6	36.4	-3.7	37.4	2.7
1948	40.3	7.8	37.8	-6.2	39.0	3.2	40.4	3.6	42.0	4.0	42.3	0.7	44.1	4.3	44.6	1.1	44.4	-0.4	41.0	-7.7	38.8	-5.4	37.7	-2.8
1949	36.6	-2.9	34.9	-4.6	36.5	4.6	36.6	0.3	36.7	0.3	36.8	0.3	36.2	-1.6	35.8	-1.1	36.8	2.8	35.3	-4.1	34.2	-3.1	33.4	-2.3
1950	33.7	0.9	34.6	2.7	34.4	-0.6	34.4	0.0	37.2	8.1	38.3	3.0	41.3	7.8	41.4	0.2	41.8	1.0	38.9	-6.9	38.8	-0.3	40.5	4.4
1951	41.9	3.5	43.9	4.8	43.8	-0.2	43.8	0.0	44.1	0.7	43.8	-0.7	43.7	-0.2	43.9	0.5	44.2	0.7	44.6	0.9	43.3	-2.9	42.4	-2.1
1952	42.4	0.0	41.4	-2.4	41.5	0.2	40.9	-1.4	41.9	2.4	41.2	-1.7	41.3	0.2	42.0	1.7	40.9	-2.6	38.9	-4.9	38.1	-2.1	35.1	-7.9
1953	37.1	5.7	36.7	-1.1	34.1	-7.1	33.3	-2.3	35.1	5.4	34.2	-2.6	36.2	5.8	35.0	-3.3	36.4	4.0	33.2	-8.8	32.2	-3.0	33.5	4.0
1954	36.0	7.5	34.7	-3.6	34.7	0.0	35.3	1.7	36.8	4.2	34.5	-6.3	35.2	2.0	34.4	-2.3	34.4	0.0	32.1	-6.7	32.2	0.3	31.8	-1.2
1955	32.7	2.8	32.5	-0.6	31.1	-4.3	32.1	3.2	32.0	-0.3	34.2	6.9	33.1	-3.2	32.2	-2.7	32.7	1.6	30.5	-6.7	29.1	-4.6	28.1	-3.4
1956	28.3	0.7	28.4	0.4	27.9	-1.8	29.7	6.5	30.7	3.4	31.1	1.3	31.3	0.6	31.8	1.6	33.4	5.0	32.0	-4.2	30.9	-3.4	30.5	-1.3
1957	31.7	3.9	31.4	-0.9	31.6	0.6	33.0	4.4	34.2	3.6	36.1	5.6	37.1	2.8	36.5	-1.6	35.8	-1.9	34.2	-4.5	35.0	2.3	35.7	2.0
1958	38.0	6.4	38.4	1.1	39.6	3.1	40.6	2.5	42.2	3.9	42.6	0.9	41.9	-1.6	40.5	-3.3	40.0	-1.2	38.7	-3.2	38.3	-1.0	37.9	-1.0
1959	38.6	1.8	37.7	-2.3	37.2	-1.3	37.7	1.3	37.9	0.5	38.1	0.5	37.1	-2.6	35.4	-4.6	37.3	5.4	35.5	-4.8	33.9	-4.5	33.8	-0.3
1960	34.6	2.4	34.8	0.6	36.6	5.2	36.1	-1.4	36.8	1.9	36.7	-0.3	37.2	1.4	36.1	-3.0	35.9	-0.6	36.6	1.9	36.1	-1.4	36.4	0.8
1961	36.8	1.1	37.2	1.1	35.9	-3.5	35.3	-1.7	34.3	-2.8	33.6	-2.0	34.6	3.0	35.4	2.3	35.3	-0.3	35.0	-0.8	34.6	-1.1	35.4	2.3
1962	36.7	3.7	36.5	-0.5	36.4	-0.3	35.3	-3.0	35.3	0.0	35.4	0.3	36.6	3.4	37.3	1.9	39.5	5.9	37.0	-6.3	37.0	0.0	36.8	-0.5
1963	36.2	-1.6	35.3	-2.5	33.9	-4.0	33.4	-1.5	34.0	1.8	34.8	2.4	35.6	2.3	35.2	-1.1	34.8	-1.1	34.5	-0.9	33.9	-1.7	32.4	-4.4
1964	33.9	4.6	32.9	-2.9	32.8	-0.3	32.7	-0.3	32.1	-1.8	33.3	3.7	34.5	3.6	34.5	0.0	35.5	2.9	34.5	-2.8	33.2	-3.8	32.8	-1.2
1965	34.0	3.7	34.0	0.0	34.2	0.6	34.6	1.2	36.1	4.3	39.0	8.0	39.3	0.8	39.3	0.0	38.9	-1.0	38.8	-0.3	39.0	0.5	40.8	4.6
1966	41.7	2.2	42.5	1.9	41.9	-1.4	41.0	-2.1	41.0	0.0	40.6	-1.0	40.7	0.2	41.1	1.0	41.5	1.0	40.0	-3.6	38.5	-3.8	38.6	0.3
1967	39.0	1.0	38.7	-0.8	37.6	-2.8	37.2	-1.1	38.4	3.2	40.0	4.2	40.6	1.5	39.7	-2.2	40.1	1.0	38.7	-3.5	37.8	-2.3	38.2	1.1
1968	39.1	2.4	39.8	1.8	39.6	-0.5	39.1	-1.3	39.5	1.0	40.6	2.8	42.0	3.4	40.6	-3.3	41.1	1.2	39.5	-3.9	39.8	0.8	39.7	-0.3
1969	41.1	3.5	41.2	0.2	41.5	0.7	42.2	1.7	44.7	5.9	46.8	4.7	47.1	0.6	46.0	-2.3	45.4	-1.3	44.5	-2.0	44.6	0.2	45.1	1.1
1970	46.6	3.3	46.2	-0.9	47.1	1.9	46.2	-1.9	45.3	-1.9	45.7	0.9	46.7	2.2	45.2	-3.2	44.7	-1.1	43.1	-3.6	42.2	-2.1	40.5	-4.0

[Continued]

Meats, Poultry, and Fish
Producer Price Index
Base 1982 = 100
[Continued]

For 1926-1997. Columns headed % show percentile change in the index from the previous period for which an index is available.

Year	Jan Index	%	Feb Index	%	Mar Index	%	Apr Index	%	May Index	%	Jun Index	%	Jul Index	%	Aug Index	%	Sep Index	%	Oct Index	%	Nov Index	%	Dec Index	%
1971	42.2	4.2	44.7	5.9	43.8	-2.0	44.0	0.5	45.2	2.7	45.3	0.2	46.4	2.4	45.7	-1.5	45.6	-0.2	45.4	-0.4	45.5	0.2	46.8	2.9
1972	48.7	4.1	50.7	4.1	49.4	-2.6	48.0	-2.8	49.2	2.5	51.0	3.7	52.7	3.3	51.3	-2.7	51.1	-0.4	50.6	-1.0	49.7	-1.8	52.9	6.4
1973	56.4	6.6	59.5	5.5	64.1	7.7	63.3	-1.2	63.1	-0.3	64.0	1.4	65.9	3.0	77.0	16.8	72.7	-5.6	66.1	-9.1	64.1	-3.0	64.0	-0.2
1974	69.0	7.8	69.8	1.2	64.3	-7.9	61.2	-4.8	59.5	-2.8	55.0	-7.6	64.9	18.0	65.9	1.5	64.3	-2.4	63.3	-1.6	62.3	-1.6	62.4	0.2
1975	64.3	3.0	63.9	-0.6	63.6	-0.5	67.7	6.4	74.0	9.3	77.5	4.7	81.4	5.0	79.4	-2.5	81.4	2.5	81.7	0.4	78.0	-4.5	76.9	-1.4
1976	75.0	-2.5	72.2	-3.7	70.1	-2.9	73.4	4.7	73.9	0.7	73.8	-0.1	71.9	-2.6	67.8	-5.7	68.4	0.9	65.4	-4.4	65.4	0.0	68.7	5.0
1977	68.6	-0.1	68.9	0.4	67.6	-1.9	67.9	0.4	71.3	5.0	71.2	-0.1	73.6	3.4	70.9	-3.7	71.0	0.1	71.7	1.0	71.2	-0.7	74.1	4.1
1978	75.2	1.5	79.8	6.1	79.5	-0.4	82.2	3.4	85.6	4.1	87.8	2.6	87.1	-0.8	83.8	-3.8	87.1	3.9	88.6	1.7	85.8	-3.2	89.0	3.7
1979	93.3	4.8	96.5	3.4	97.3	0.8	98.2	0.9	97.2	-1.0	93.7	-3.6	92.3	-1.5	87.6	-5.1	93.1	6.3	90.9	-2.4	92.9	2.2	94.3	1.5
1980	93.0	-1.4	93.0	0.0	92.9	-0.1	87.8	-5.5	87.1	-0.8	88.0	1.0	96.5	9.7	100.9	4.6	100.1	-0.8	99.4	-0.7	97.4	-2.0	96.3	-1.1
1981	96.3	0.0	94.6	-1.8	93.9	-0.7	92.8	-1.2	95.2	2.6	96.5	1.4	99.8	3.4	98.8	-1.0	98.3	-0.5	95.7	-2.6	93.2	-2.6	91.7	-1.6
1982	94.6	3.2	96.3	1.8	97.1	0.8	100.2	3.2	103.9	3.7	105.3	1.3	103.3	-1.9	101.8	-1.5	103.2	1.4	99.7	-3.4	97.7	-2.0	97.0	-0.7
1983	97.9	0.9	101.3	3.5	101.2	-0.1	100.6	-0.6	100.1	-0.5	97.1	-3.0	96.0	-1.1	94.4	-1.7	94.3	-0.1	92.0	-2.4	91.1	-1.0	94.1	3.3
1984	99.3	5.5	98.8	-0.5	102.6	3.8	101.6	-1.0	99.8	-1.8	96.1	-3.7	100.5	4.6	97.9	-2.6	96.9	-1.0	95.3	-1.7	97.2	2.0	99.4	2.3
1985	99.6	0.2	99.2	-0.4	97.0	-2.2	95.0	-2.1	94.7	-0.3	92.6	-2.2	94.4	1.9	92.9	-1.6	91.1	-1.9	94.5	3.7	99.1	4.9	100.5	1.4
1986	98.1	-2.4	95.1	-3.1	93.9	-1.3	92.4	-1.6	95.8	3.7	97.2	1.5	103.0	6.0	107.7	4.6	106.4	-1.2	105.2	-1.1	103.7	-1.4	103.6	-0.1
1987	101.9	-1.6	102.5	0.6	100.3	-2.1	104.5	4.2	109.7	5.0	108.9	-0.7	109.5	0.6	106.2	-3.0	108.0	1.7	106.1	-1.8	101.4	-4.4	99.9	-1.5
1988	103.8	3.9	102.7	-1.1	104.0	1.3	104.4	0.4	107.7	3.2	110.0	2.1	109.6	-0.4	107.8	-1.6	109.3	1.4	106.8	-2.3	106.0	-0.7	106.8	0.8
1989	109.8	2.8	109.9	0.1	111.8	1.7	111.4	-0.4	112.7	1.2	111.4	-1.2	111.6	0.2	111.3	-0.3	110.4	-0.8	109.6	-0.7	111.0	1.3	111.5	0.5
1990	114.0	2.2	114.9	0.8	116.9	1.7	118.4	1.3	124.1	4.8	121.5	-2.1	121.6	0.1	121.0	-0.5	119.5	-1.2	121.0	1.3	121.1	0.1	120.9	-0.2
1991	120.0	-0.7	119.6	-0.3	120.6	0.8	120.0	-0.5	121.0	0.8	119.1	-1.6	118.6	-0.4	114.4	-3.5	112.3	-1.8	113.3	0.9	110.9	-2.1	110.0	-0.8
1992	109.0	-0.9	110.8	1.7	112.2	1.3	113.5	1.2	113.7	0.2	113.5	-0.2	112.6	-0.8	111.8	-0.7	111.9	0.1	112.1	0.2	111.0	-1.0	113.8	2.5
1993	114.3	0.4	115.2	0.8	116.7	1.3	118.0	1.1	118.7	0.6	117.6	-0.9	115.0	-2.2	114.3	-0.6	115.2	0.8	114.4	-0.7	113.5	-0.8	112.5	-0.9
1994	113.9	1.2	114.2	0.3	116.7	2.2	116.1	-0.5	114.0	-1.8	112.0	-1.8	110.1	-1.7	112.3	2.0	110.8	-1.3	109.3	-1.4	109.1	-0.2	108.1	-0.9
1995	111.0	2.7	112.8	1.6	112.8	0.0	110.4	-2.1	108.5	-1.7	109.2	0.6	111.9	2.5	112.8	0.8	112.3	-0.4	113.2	0.8	113.8	0.5	112.5	-1.1
1996	111.5	-0.9	112.0	0.4	111.4	-0.5	111.2	-0.2	113.1	1.7	116.6	3.1	118.0	1.2	121.1	2.6	118.9	-1.8	121.0	1.8	121.7	0.6	121.5	-0.2
1997	119.1	-2.0	116.7	-2.0	119.5	2.4	118.9	-0.5	121.6	2.3	119.3	-1.9	119.4	0.1	120.8	1.2	118.9	-1.6	117.9	-0.8	116.9	-0.8	114.7	-1.9

Source: U.S. Department of Labor, Bureau of Labor Statistics, Division of Industry Prices and Price Indexes. n.e.c. stands for not elsewhere classified. - indicates no data collected for period or unavailable.

Dairy Products
Producer Price Index
Base 1982 = 100

For 1926-1997. Columns headed % show percentile change in the index from the previous period for which an index is available.

Year	Jan Index	%	Feb Index	%	Mar Index	%	Apr Index	%	May Index	%	Jun Index	%	Jul Index	%	Aug Index	%	Sep Index	%	Oct Index	%	Nov Index	%	Dec Index	%
1926	17.9	-	17.7	-1.1	17.4	-1.7	17.0	-2.3	16.8	-1.2	16.6	-1.2	16.7	0.6	17.0	1.8	17.6	3.5	18.0	2.3	18.2	1.1	18.7	2.7
1927	18.4	-1.6	18.6	1.1	18.5	-0.5	18.3	-1.1	17.2	-6.0	17.0	-1.2	17.1	0.6	17.2	0.6	18.4	7.0	18.7	1.6	18.8	0.5	19.2	2.1
1928	18.8	-2.1	18.5	-1.6	18.2	-1.6	17.6	-3.3	17.4	-1.1	17.4	0.0	18.0	3.4	18.7	3.9	19.0	1.6	18.8	-1.1	19.0	1.1	19.2	1.1
1929	19.0	-1.0	19.1	0.5	19.0	-0.5	18.5	-2.6	18.2	-1.6	18.4	1.1	18.0	-2.2	18.2	1.1	18.5	1.6	18.5	0.0	18.1	-2.2	17.7	-2.2
1930	17.0	-4.0	17.0	0.0	17.2	1.2	17.3	0.6	16.1	-6.9	15.7	-2.5	16.0	1.9	17.0	6.3	17.4	2.4	17.2	-1.1	16.7	-2.9	15.5	-7.2
1931	14.6	-5.8	14.5	-0.7	14.6	0.7	14.1	-3.4	13.7	-2.8	13.7	0.0	14.1	2.9	14.3	1.4	14.7	2.8	15.0	2.0	14.1	-6.0	13.9	-1.4
1932	11.9	-14.4	11.2	-5.9	11.2	0.0	10.7	-4.5	10.4	-2.8	10.0	-3.8	10.2	2.0	10.5	2.9	10.6	1.0	10.6	0.0	10.8	1.9	10.4	-3.7
1933	9.6	-7.7	9.1	-5.2	8.9	-2.2	9.3	4.5	10.2	9.7	11.0	7.8	11.5	4.5	11.5	0.0	11.5	0.0	11.5	0.0	11.7	1.7	11.4	-2.6
1934	11.4	0.0	12.1	6.1	12.0	-0.8	11.6	-3.3	11.7	0.9	12.7	8.5	13.1	3.1	13.5	3.1	13.3	-1.5	13.5	1.5	13.7	1.5	13.9	1.5
1935	14.6	5.0	15.2	4.1	14.4	-5.3	14.8	2.8	13.6	-8.1	13.0	-4.4	12.9	-0.8	13.2	2.3	13.3	0.8	13.4	0.8	14.2	6.0	14.6	2.8
1936	14.7	0.7	14.9	1.4	14.0	-6.0	13.7	-2.1	13.1	-4.4	13.5	3.1	14.6	8.1	15.3	4.8	15.6	2.0	15.2	-2.6	15.4	1.3	15.5	0.6
1937	15.5	0.0	15.5	0.0	15.7	1.3	13.7	-12.7	12.7	-7.3	12.6	-0.8	13.3	5.6	13.9	4.5	14.8	6.5	14.9	0.7	15.5	4.0	15.7	1.3
1938	14.5	-7.6	13.7	-5.5	13.4	-2.2	12.5	-6.7	12.1	-3.2	12.0	-0.8	12.1	0.8	12.0	-0.8	12.4	3.3	12.5	0.8	12.7	1.6	12.9	1.6
1939	12.5	-3.1	12.5	0.0	11.3	-9.6	10.1	-10.6	10.2	1.0	10.5	2.9	10.4	-1.0	11.9	14.4	13.0	9.2	13.7	5.4	14.0	2.2	14.2	1.4
1940	14.3	0.7	13.9	-2.8	13.7	-1.4	13.5	-1.5	12.7	-5.9	12.6	-0.8	12.9	2.4	12.9	0.0	13.1	1.6	13.5	3.1	14.4	6.7	14.7	2.1
1941	14.0	-4.8	13.9	-0.7	14.0	0.7	14.1	0.7	14.2	0.7	14.7	3.5	15.3	4.1	15.7	2.6	16.2	3.2	16.6	2.5	16.8	1.2	16.7	-0.6
1942	16.8	0.6	16.6	-1.2	16.5	-0.6	16.4	-0.6	16.3	-0.6	16.1	-1.2	16.8	4.3	17.5	4.2	18.4	5.1	19.0	3.3	19.4	2.1	19.5	0.5
1943	19.8	1.5	19.8	0.0	19.8	0.0	19.8	0.0	19.7	-0.5	19.1	-3.0	19.0	-0.5	19.0	0.0	19.0	0.0	19.0	0.0	19.4	2.1	19.3	-0.5
1944	19.3	0.0	19.3	0.0	19.3	0.0	19.2	-0.5	19.2	0.0	19.2	0.0	19.2	0.0	19.3	0.5	19.3	0.0	19.3	0.0	19.3	0.0	19.3	0.0
1945	19.3	0.0	19.3	0.0	19.3	0.0	19.3	0.0	19.3	0.0	19.3	0.0	19.3	0.0	19.3	0.0	19.2	-0.5	19.3	0.5	19.7	2.1	19.8	0.5
1946	20.0	1.0	20.2	1.0	20.3	0.5	20.3	0.0	20.4	0.5	22.2	8.8	27.4	23.4	28.2	2.9	29.5	4.6	32.3	9.5	31.9	-1.2	31.4	-1.6
1947	28.7	-8.6	28.0	-2.4	27.4	-2.1	26.7	-2.6	26.1	-2.2	26.0	-0.4	26.9	3.5	27.8	3.3	28.5	2.5	29.3	2.8	30.3	3.4	30.9	2.0
1948	31.5	1.9	31.5	0.0	30.6	-2.9	30.9	1.0	30.8	-0.3	31.3	1.6	32.2	2.9	32.5	0.9	31.8	-2.2	31.3	-1.6	30.9	-1.3	30.5	-1.3
1949	29.8	-2.3	29.2	-2.0	28.3	-3.1	27.7	-2.1	27.3	-1.4	27.6	1.1	27.7	0.4	28.4	2.5	28.2	-0.7	28.2	0.0	28.0	-0.7	28.1	0.4
1950	27.4	-2.5	27.5	0.4	27.2	-1.1	26.9	-1.1	26.2	-2.6	26.3	0.4	27.0	2.7	27.7	2.6	28.5	2.9	28.9	1.4	29.0	0.3	29.5	1.7
1951	30.9	4.7	31.5	1.9	31.2	-1.0	30.9	-1.0	31.1	0.6	31.1	0.0	31.1	0.0	31.5	1.3	31.0	-1.6	31.7	2.3	32.4	2.2	33.0	1.9
1952	33.1	0.3	33.6	1.5	33.1	-1.5	32.7	-1.2	32.3	-1.2	32.1	-0.6	33.2	3.4	33.3	0.3	34.0	2.1	33.8	-0.6	33.7	-0.3	33.0	-2.1
1953	32.7	-0.9	32.4	-0.9	32.0	-1.2	31.7	-0.9	31.5	-0.6	31.5	0.0	32.1	1.9	32.3	0.6	32.5	0.6	32.9	1.2	33.3	1.2	32.5	-2.4
1954	31.9	-1.8	31.3	-1.9	31.0	-1.0	30.1	-2.9	29.7	-1.3	29.9	0.7	30.7	2.7	30.9	0.7	31.1	0.6	31.7	1.9	31.8	0.3	31.6	-0.6
1955	31.3	-0.9	31.3	0.0	31.3	0.0	31.2	-0.3	30.4	-2.6	30.5	0.3	30.9	1.3	31.5	1.9	30.5	-3.2	30.7	0.7	30.9	0.7	31.3	1.3
1956	31.0	-1.0	31.0	0.0	31.0	0.0	30.9	-0.3	31.5	1.9	31.5	0.0	31.5	0.0	31.8	1.0	32.0	0.6	32.4	1.3	33.1	2.2	32.9	-0.6
1957	32.8	-0.3	32.8	0.0	32.5	-0.9	32.5	0.0	32.3	-0.6	31.5	-2.5	31.6	0.3	32.2	1.9	32.8	1.9	33.2	1.2	33.4	0.6	33.5	0.3
1958	33.3	-0.6	33.3	0.0	33.1	-0.6	32.5	-1.8	32.3	-0.6	32.4	0.3	32.5	0.3	32.7	0.6	33.2	1.5	33.1	-0.3	33.1	0.0	33.1	0.0
1959	33.0	-0.3	33.0	0.0	33.0	0.0	32.7	-0.9	32.6	-0.3	32.7	0.3	33.3	1.8	33.5	0.6	33.9	1.2	34.1	0.6	34.4	0.9	34.5	0.3
1960	34.7	0.6	34.6	-0.3	34.4	-0.6	33.7	-2.0	33.5	-0.6	33.8	0.9	34.2	1.2	34.4	0.6	35.2	2.3	35.4	0.6	35.5	0.3	35.6	0.3
1961	35.4	-0.6	35.0	-1.1	35.2	0.6	35.0	-0.6	34.9	-0.3	35.0	0.3	35.1	0.3	35.3	0.6	35.6	0.8	36.1	1.4	36.1	0.0	36.3	0.6
1962	36.0	-0.8	36.0	0.0	35.6	-1.1	35.0	-1.7	34.4	-1.7	34.6	0.6	34.8	0.6	35.0	0.6	35.0	0.0	35.5	1.4	35.6	0.3	35.6	0.0
1963	35.5	-0.3	35.6	0.3	35.3	-0.8	35.2	-0.3	35.2	0.0	35.1	-0.3	35.4	0.9	35.6	0.6	35.6	0.0	35.4	-0.6	35.6	0.6	35.6	0.0
1964	35.6	0.0	35.4	-0.6	35.4	0.0	35.3	-0.3	35.1	-0.6	35.3	0.6	35.3	0.0	35.4	0.3	35.8	1.1	35.9	0.3	36.1	0.6	35.9	-0.6
1965	35.7	-0.6	35.5	-0.6	35.4	-0.3	35.4	0.0	35.2	-0.6	35.3	0.3	35.5	0.6	35.8	0.8	36.0	0.6	36.0	0.0	36.4	1.1	36.7	0.8
1966	36.6	-0.3	37.2	1.6	37.9	1.9	37.8	-0.3	37.9	0.3	38.4	1.3	39.5	2.9	40.9	3.5	40.9	0.0	41.0	0.2	40.4	-1.5	40.3	-0.2
1967	40.1	-0.5	39.9	-0.5	39.7	-0.5	39.6	-0.3	39.8	0.5	40.2	1.0	40.2	0.0	40.3	0.2	40.5	0.5	40.5	0.0	40.5	0.0	40.9	1.0
1968	40.8	-0.2	40.9	0.2	40.6	-0.7	41.5	2.2	42.5	2.4	42.4	-0.2	42.5	0.2	42.5	0.0	42.5	0.0	42.9	0.9	42.8	-0.2	43.0	0.5
1969	42.9	-0.2	42.9	0.0	43.0	0.2	43.3	0.7	43.6	0.7	43.8	0.5	43.8	0.0	43.8	0.0	44.1	0.7	43.1	-2.3	43.3	0.5	44.2	2.1
1970	44.2	0.0	44.3	0.2	43.9	-0.9	44.5	1.4	44.7	0.4	44.7	0.0	44.8	0.2	44.8	0.0	44.8	0.0	45.1	0.7	45.1	0.0	45.4	0.7

[Continued]

Dairy Products
Producer Price Index
Base 1982 = 100
[Continued]

For 1926-1997. Columns headed % show percentile change in the index from the previous period for which an index is available.

Year	Jan Index	%	Feb Index	%	Mar Index	%	Apr Index	%	May Index	%	Jun Index	%	Jul Index	%	Aug Index	%	Sep Index	%	Oct Index	%	Nov Index	%	Dec Index	%
1971	45.4	0.0	45.2	-0.4	46.2	2.2	46.4	0.4	46.7	0.6	46.7	0.0	46.7	0.0	46.8	0.2	46.8	0.0	46.8	0.0	46.7	-0.2	47.2	1.1
1972	47.1	-0.2	47.2	0.2	47.4	0.4	47.2	-0.4	47.2	0.0	46.3	-1.9	47.3	2.2	47.7	0.8	47.8	0.2	48.2	0.8	48.9	1.5	49.4	1.0
1973	49.7	0.6	49.8	0.2	51.0	2.4	51.1	0.2	50.8	-0.6	51.2	0.8	51.1	-0.2	52.8	3.3	55.1	4.4	56.1	1.8	56.2	0.2	57.2	1.8
1974	58.3	1.9	59.3	1.7	60.8	2.5	61.9	1.8	59.0	-4.7	57.4	-2.7	56.9	-0.9	57.2	0.5	58.2	1.7	58.8	1.0	59.0	0.3	59.0	0.0
1975	59.6	1.0	59.6	0.0	59.7	0.2	59.8	0.2	60.1	0.5	60.5	0.7	61.5	1.7	62.8	2.1	64.6	2.9	66.6	3.1	67.5	1.4	68.8	1.9
1976	68.2	-0.9	65.7	-3.7	67.0	2.0	67.4	0.6	67.2	-0.3	67.2	0.0	68.4	1.8	69.9	2.2	68.5	-2.0	68.2	-0.4	67.6	-0.9	67.2	-0.6
1977	67.0	-0.3	67.0	0.0	67.5	0.7	69.7	3.3	70.0	0.4	70.0	0.0	70.4	0.6	70.5	0.1	70.6	0.1	70.7	0.1	71.1	0.6	71.6	0.7
1978	71.5	-0.1	71.8	0.4	72.4	0.8	74.1	2.3	74.1	0.0	74.5	0.5	74.8	0.4	76.7	2.5	77.5	1.0	79.2	2.2	80.2	1.3	81.5	1.6
1979	81.8	0.4	81.6	-0.2	82.3	0.9	83.2	1.1	83.5	0.4	83.7	0.2	84.0	0.4	86.5	3.0	87.7	1.4	87.6	-0.1	88.1	0.6	88.3	0.2
1980	88.8	0.6	88.7	-0.1	89.6	1.0	91.4	2.0	91.8	0.4	92.2	0.4	92.4	0.2	93.5	1.2	93.9	0.4	95.6	1.8	96.5	0.9	97.4	0.9
1981	98.3	0.9	98.5	0.2	98.5	0.0	98.6	0.1	98.3	-0.3	98.5	0.2	98.5	0.0	98.5	0.0	98.6	0.1	99.2	0.6	99.2	0.0	99.3	0.1
1982	99.5	0.2	99.6	0.1	99.6	0.0	99.8	0.2	99.8	0.0	99.9	0.1	99.9	0.0	100.0	0.1	100.1	0.1	100.4	0.3	100.5	0.1	100.8	0.3
1983	100.7	-0.1	100.8	0.1	100.7	-0.1	100.8	0.1	100.8	0.0	100.6	-0.2	100.6	0.0	100.6	0.0	100.7	0.1	101.0	0.3	101.0	0.0	100.0	-1.0
1984	99.8	-0.2	99.8	0.0	100.0	0.2	100.0	0.0	100.0	0.0	100.3	0.3	101.0	0.7	100.9	-0.1	102.5	1.6	103.0	0.5	103.4	0.4	102.8	-0.6
1985	102.6	-0.2	102.1	-0.5	101.8	-0.3	101.0	-0.8	100.4	-0.6	100.2	-0.2	99.7	-0.5	99.2	-0.5	98.9	-0.3	98.8	-0.1	98.9	0.1	98.9	0.0
1986	98.8	-0.1	98.9	0.1	98.8	-0.1	98.8	0.0	99.2	0.4	99.2	0.0	99.5	0.3	100.3	0.8	100.6	0.3	101.2	0.6	101.8	0.6	102.1	0.3
1987	101.9	-0.2	101.4	-0.5	101.4	0.0	101.2	-0.2	100.9	-0.3	101.1	0.2	101.4	0.3	101.9	0.5	102.7	0.8	102.1	-0.6	102.0	-0.1	101.7	-0.3
1988	101.0	-0.7	100.5	-0.5	100.1	-0.4	100.0	-0.1	100.1	0.1	100.6	0.5	101.2	0.6	102.2	1.0	103.8	1.6	104.9	1.1	105.5	0.6	106.2	0.7
1989	107.1	0.8	106.5	-0.6	106.0	-0.5	105.6	-0.4	105.6	0.0	106.4	0.8	107.9	1.4	110.7	2.6	113.3	2.3	116.4	2.7	120.1	3.2	121.4	1.1
1990	120.5	-0.7	116.9	-3.0	116.1	-0.7	115.1	-0.9	116.6	1.3	118.0	1.2	119.5	1.3	120.2	0.6	119.0	-1.0	117.4	-1.3	114.8	-2.2	112.8	-1.7
1991	112.3	-0.4	112.0	-0.3	111.9	-0.1	111.5	-0.4	111.5	0.0	112.1	0.5	113.6	1.3	115.1	1.3	115.9	0.7	119.3	2.9	119.8	0.4	120.0	0.2
1992	118.3	-1.4	116.0	-1.9	115.0	-0.9	115.4	0.3	116.9	1.3	118.7	1.5	119.4	0.6	120.0	0.5	120.0	0.0	119.4	-0.5	118.7	-0.6	117.4	-1.1
1993	116.4	-0.9	115.4	-0.9	115.0	-0.3	117.2	1.9	118.5	1.1	119.5	0.8	119.2	-0.3	117.9	-1.1	118.4	0.4	119.0	0.5	120.3	1.1	121.0	0.6
1994	120.3	-0.6	119.9	-0.3	120.6	0.6	121.4	0.7	121.2	-0.2	118.7	-2.1	117.1	-1.3	118.2	0.9	118.8	0.5	119.2	0.3	119.4	0.2	118.6	-0.7
1995	117.1	-1.3	117.6	0.4	118.3	0.6	118.1	-0.2	117.7	-0.3	117.2	-0.4	118.0	0.7	119.0	0.8	120.5	1.3	122.6	1.7	125.0	2.0	125.0	0.0
1996	124.1	-0.7	123.4	-0.6	123.1	-0.2	123.2	0.1	126.9	3.0	131.8	3.9	134.6	2.1	137.2	1.9	139.7	1.8	140.7	0.7	132.1	-6.1	128.0	-3.1
1997	126.3	-1.3	127.3	0.8	128.4	0.9	127.8	-0.5	125.9	-1.5	125.3	-0.5	124.5	-0.6	126.0	1.2	127.1	0.9	130.3	2.5	134.1	2.9	134.2	0.1

Source: U.S. Department of Labor, Bureau of Labor Statistics, Division of Industry Prices and Price Indexes. n.e.c. stands for not elsewhere classified. - indicates no data collected for period or unavailable.

Processed Fruits and Vegetables
Producer Price Index
Base 1982 = 100

For 1926-1997. Columns headed % show percentile change in the index from the previous period for which an index is available.

Year	Jan Index	%	Feb Index	%	Mar Index	%	Apr Index	%	May Index	%	Jun Index	%	Jul Index	%	Aug Index	%	Sep Index	%	Oct Index	%	Nov Index	%	Dec Index	%
1926	20.6	-	20.5	-0.5	20.3	-1.0	20.3	0.0	20.1	-1.0	20.2	0.5	20.3	0.5	20.1	-1.0	20.3	1.0	20.5	1.0	20.4	-0.5	20.2	-1.0
1927	20.1	-0.5	20.4	1.5	20.4	0.0	20.0	-2.0	20.0	0.0	20.0	0.0	20.0	0.0	20.0	0.0	19.7	-1.5	19.6	-0.5	20.3	3.6	20.5	1.0
1928	21.4	4.4	21.5	0.5	21.7	0.9	21.8	0.5	21.8	0.0	21.8	0.0	21.6	-0.9	21.0	-2.8	21.1	0.5	21.3	0.9	21.4	0.5	21.5	0.5
1929	21.4	-0.5	21.7	1.4	21.8	0.5	22.1	1.4	22.7	2.7	23.0	1.3	23.5	2.2	22.7	-3.4	22.5	-0.9	22.4	-0.4	22.3	-0.4	22.5	0.9
1930	22.7	0.9	22.6	-0.4	22.5	-0.4	22.2	-1.3	20.7	-6.8	20.5	-1.0	20.4	-0.5	20.4	0.0	20.6	1.0	20.3	-1.5	19.6	-3.4	19.2	-2.0
1931	19.0	-1.0	19.1	0.5	18.6	-2.6	18.3	-1.6	17.7	-3.3	17.5	-1.1	17.5	0.0	17.3	-1.1	17.1	-1.2	16.8	-1.8	16.3	-3.0	16.3	0.0
1932	16.2	-0.6	16.1	-0.6	16.4	1.9	16.4	0.0	16.3	-0.6	16.1	-1.2	15.5	-3.7	15.4	-0.6	15.0	-2.6	15.2	1.3	15.1	-0.7	15.0	-0.7
1933	14.9	-0.7	14.8	-0.7	14.8	0.0	14.9	0.7	15.4	3.4	15.6	1.3	15.9	1.9	16.4	3.1	17.1	4.3	17.2	0.6	17.1	-0.6	17.1	0.0
1934	17.2	0.6	17.5	1.7	17.6	0.6	17.7	0.6	17.6	-0.6	17.6	0.0	17.8	1.1	17.5	-1.7	18.0	2.9	18.7	3.9	18.5	-1.1	18.5	0.0
1935	18.5	0.0	18.7	1.1	18.7	0.0	18.5	-1.1	18.3	-1.1	18.2	-0.5	17.9	-1.6	17.1	-4.5	17.1	0.0	16.9	-1.2	16.8	-0.6	16.8	0.0
1936	16.6	-1.2	16.6	0.0	16.9	1.8	17.1	1.2	17.1	0.0	16.9	-1.2	17.1	1.2	18.1	5.8	18.3	1.1	18.2	-0.5	18.3	0.5	18.4	0.5
1937	18.5	0.5	18.5	0.0	18.5	0.0	18.5	0.0	18.5	0.0	18.7	1.1	18.3	-2.1	17.9	-2.2	17.8	-0.6	17.7	-0.6	17.9	1.1	17.8	-0.6
1938	17.7	-0.6	17.6	-0.6	17.5	-0.6	17.2	-1.7	16.9	-1.7	16.3	-3.6	15.9	-2.5	15.3	-3.8	15.2	-0.7	15.2	0.0	15.1	-0.7	15.1	0.0
1939	15.2	0.7	15.2	0.0	15.3	0.7	15.5	1.3	15.5	0.0	15.6	0.6	15.6	0.0	15.5	-0.6	16.1	3.9	16.4	1.9	16.3	-0.6	16.2	-0.6
1940	16.1	-0.6	16.1	0.0	15.9	-1.2	15.9	0.0	15.9	0.0	16.0	0.6	16.0	0.0	15.8	-1.2	15.7	-0.6	15.7	0.0	15.7	0.0	15.7	0.0
1941	15.9	1.3	16.3	2.5	16.4	0.6	16.8	2.4	17.1	1.8	17.6	2.9	18.9	7.4	19.9	5.3	19.8	-0.5	20.4	3.0	20.7	1.5	21.0	1.4
1942	21.1	0.5	21.2	0.5	21.4	0.9	21.5	0.5	21.5	0.0	22.0	2.3	21.8	-0.9	21.8	0.0	22.0	0.9	22.5	2.3	22.5	0.0	22.5	0.0
1943	22.5	0.0	22.5	0.0	22.5	0.0	22.5	0.0	22.5	0.0	22.5	0.0	22.5	0.0	22.4	-0.4	22.4	0.0	22.5	0.4	22.5	0.0	22.5	0.0
1944	22.6	0.4	22.6	0.0	22.6	0.0	22.6	0.0	22.6	0.0	22.6	0.0	22.6	0.0	22.8	0.9	23.1	1.3	23.0	-0.4	23.0	0.0	23.1	0.4
1945	23.0	-0.4	23.0	0.0	23.0	0.0	23.0	0.0	23.1	0.4	23.1	0.0	23.1	0.0	23.1	0.0	23.1	0.0	23.0	-0.4	23.1	0.4	23.0	-0.4
1946	23.0	0.0	23.0	0.0	23.0	0.0	23.2	0.9	23.4	0.9	23.7	1.3	23.7	0.0	23.4	-1.3	23.5	0.4	23.7	0.9	29.4	24.1	29.4	0.0
1947	31.9	8.5	31.8	-0.3	31.8	0.0	31.8	0.0	32.2	1.3	31.9	-0.9	31.7	-0.6	31.3	-1.3	31.6	1.0	31.6	0.0	31.6	0.0	31.5	-0.3
1948	31.6	0.3	31.6	0.0	31.4	-0.6	31.2	-0.6	31.2	0.0	31.3	0.3	31.5	0.6	32.1	1.9	32.2	0.3	31.8	-1.2	32.0	0.6	31.8	-0.6
1949	31.7	-0.3	31.8	0.3	31.8	0.0	31.8	0.0	32.0	0.6	31.7	-0.9	31.4	-0.9	31.3	-0.3	31.3	0.0	31.3	0.0	31.1	-0.6	30.0	-3.5
1950	30.6	2.0	31.0	1.3	31.0	0.0	30.8	-0.6	30.9	0.3	31.0	0.3	31.2	0.6	32.1	2.9	32.4	0.9	32.6	0.6	32.1	-1.5	32.6	1.6
1951	33.4	2.5	33.7	0.9	33.7	0.0	33.7	0.0	33.4	-0.9	33.0	-1.2	32.7	-0.9	32.6	-0.3	33.1	1.5	33.4	0.9	33.6	0.6	33.6	0.0
1952	33.4	-0.6	33.1	-0.9	33.2	0.3	33.1	-0.3	32.9	-0.6	32.7	-0.6	32.8	0.3	33.2	1.2	33.5	0.9	33.5	0.0	33.5	0.0	33.2	-0.9
1953	33.3	0.3	33.3	0.0	33.2	-0.3	33.0	-0.6	32.9	-0.3	32.8	-0.3	33.2	1.2	33.1	-0.3	33.1	0.0	33.2	0.3	33.1	-0.3	32.8	-0.9
1954	32.8	0.0	32.6	-0.6	32.6	0.0	32.6	0.0	33.0	1.2	33.1	0.3	33.1	0.0	33.1	0.0	33.2	0.3	33.3	0.3	33.3	0.0	33.5	0.6
1955	33.1	-1.2	33.0	-0.3	33.1	0.3	33.1	0.0	32.9	-0.6	33.0	0.3	33.1	0.3	33.2	0.3	33.7	1.5	34.0	0.9	34.0	0.0	34.1	0.3
1956	34.1	0.0	34.4	0.9	34.3	-0.3	34.4	0.3	34.5	0.3	34.7	0.6	34.5	-0.6	33.9	-1.7	33.7	-0.6	33.6	-0.3	33.6	0.0	33.4	-0.6
1957	33.4	0.0	33.5	0.3	33.5	0.0	33.2	-0.9	32.7	-1.5	32.2	-1.5	32.3	0.3	32.2	-0.3	32.4	0.6	32.7	0.9	32.8	0.3	33.1	0.9
1958	33.4	0.9	33.4	0.0	33.7	0.9	34.0	0.9	34.2	0.6	34.9	2.0	35.2	0.9	35.3	0.3	35.2	-0.3	35.4	0.6	35.7	0.8	35.7	0.0
1959	35.0	-2.0	34.9	-0.3	35.2	0.9	34.9	-0.9	34.9	0.0	35.1	0.6	34.9	-0.6	34.1	-2.3	33.8	-0.9	34.0	0.6	33.6	-1.2	33.1	-1.5
1960	33.0	-0.3	33.2	0.6	33.4	0.6	33.4	0.0	33.6	0.6	33.8	0.6	33.9	0.3	33.7	-0.6	34.0	0.9	34.4	1.2	34.6	0.6	34.8	0.6
1961	35.3	1.4	35.4	0.3	35.2	-0.6	35.1	-0.3	34.4	-2.0	34.4	0.0	34.5	0.3	34.0	-1.4	33.9	-0.3	34.1	0.6	34.1	0.0	34.1	0.0
1962	33.7	-1.2	33.9	0.6	33.7	-0.6	33.7	0.0	33.5	-0.6	33.7	0.6	33.6	-0.3	33.0	-1.8	32.8	-0.6	32.8	0.0	32.7	-0.3	32.5	-0.6
1963	34.0	4.6	33.9	-0.3	34.4	1.5	35.0	1.7	35.2	0.6	35.6	1.1	35.9	0.8	35.6	-0.8	35.8	0.6	36.0	0.6	36.2	0.6	36.3	0.3
1964	36.4	0.3	36.5	0.3	36.5	0.0	36.5	0.0	36.1	-1.1	36.1	0.0	35.7	-1.1	34.7	-2.8	34.7	0.0	34.9	0.6	34.8	-0.3	34.7	-0.3
1965	34.7	0.0	34.1	-1.7	34.2	0.3	34.3	0.3	34.1	-0.6	34.5	1.2	34.6	0.3	34.1	-1.4	34.6	1.5	35.6	2.9	35.8	0.6	35.7	-0.3
1966	35.6	-0.3	35.7	0.3	35.6	-0.3	35.6	0.0	35.8	0.6	35.7	-0.3	35.5	-0.6	34.8	-2.0	35.2	1.1	35.9	2.0	36.0	0.3	36.0	0.0
1967	36.0	0.0	35.4	-1.7	35.4	0.0	35.5	0.3	35.7	0.6	36.2	1.4	36.3	0.3	36.4	0.3	36.7	0.8	37.2	1.4	38.1	2.4	38.4	0.8
1968	38.6	0.5	38.7	0.3	38.9	0.5	39.0	0.3	39.1	0.3	39.1	0.0	39.1	0.0	38.6	-1.3	38.6	0.0	38.8	0.5	38.8	0.0	38.6	-0.5
1969	38.7	0.3	39.0	0.8	39.1	0.3	39.3	0.5	39.4	0.3	39.4	0.0	39.7	0.8	39.7	0.0	39.7	0.0	39.5	-0.5	39.6	0.3	39.6	0.0
1970	39.8	0.5	39.9	0.3	39.7	-0.5	39.9	0.5	40.2	0.8	40.3	0.2	40.5	0.5	40.7	0.5	40.8	0.2	40.5	-0.7	40.7	0.5	40.5	-0.5

[Continued]

Processed Fruits and Vegetables
Producer Price Index
Base 1982 = 100
[Continued]

For 1926-1997. Columns headed % show percentile change in the index from the previous period for which an index is available.

Year	Jan Index	%	Feb Index	%	Mar Index	%	Apr Index	%	May Index	%	Jun Index	%	Jul Index	%	Aug Index	%	Sep Index	%	Oct Index	%	Nov Index	%	Dec Index	%
1971	40.6	0.2	40.7	0.2	40.9	0.5	41.2	0.7	41.5	0.7	42.1	1.4	42.3	0.5	42.3	0.0	42.2	-0.2	42.0	-0.5	42.0	0.0	42.2	0.5
1972	42.3	0.2	42.3	0.0	42.5	0.5	43.1	1.4	43.4	0.7	43.5	0.2	43.6	0.2	43.8	0.5	43.7	-0.2	44.4	1.6	45.1	1.6	45.5	0.9
1973	45.7	0.4	45.9	0.4	46.0	0.2	46.1	0.2	46.4	0.7	46.6	0.4	46.5	-0.2	47.1	1.3	47.4	0.6	49.2	3.8	49.7	1.0	50.2	1.0
1974	50.7	1.0	51.3	1.2	51.5	0.4	52.0	1.0	52.9	1.7	54.0	2.1	57.5	6.5	59.3	3.1	60.3	1.7	61.9	2.7	62.3	0.6	62.0	-0.5
1975	62.4	0.6	62.3	-0.2	61.8	-0.8	62.2	0.6	62.3	0.2	62.3	0.0	61.7	-1.0	61.4	-0.5	61.4	0.0	61.7	0.5	61.6	-0.2	61.4	-0.3
1976	61.0	-0.7	60.6	-0.7	60.6	0.0	60.8	0.3	61.2	0.7	61.5	0.5	61.8	0.5	62.3	0.8	62.7	0.6	63.5	1.3	64.0	0.8	64.0	0.0
1977	63.8	-0.3	66.6	4.4	67.1	0.8	67.5	0.6	67.7	0.3	68.4	1.0	68.6	0.3	69.4	1.2	69.6	0.3	69.4	-0.3	70.4	1.4	70.8	0.6
1978	70.8	0.0	70.9	0.1	71.3	0.6	71.6	0.4	71.9	0.4	72.4	0.7	73.0	0.8	74.1	1.5	74.7	0.8	76.6	2.5	78.8	2.9	79.6	1.0
1979	79.6	0.0	80.0	0.5	80.0	0.0	80.3	0.4	80.7	0.5	80.7	0.0	81.5	1.0	81.8	0.4	82.0	0.2	81.4	-0.7	81.0	-0.5	81.1	0.1
1980	81.2	0.1	81.4	0.2	81.5	0.1	81.9	0.5	82.1	0.2	82.8	0.9	83.7	1.1	84.1	0.5	84.3	0.2	85.2	1.1	85.5	0.4	86.2	0.8
1981	86.9	0.8	88.8	2.2	93.0	4.7	94.0	1.1	94.5	0.5	95.6	1.2	96.9	1.4	97.4	0.5	98.4	1.0	99.0	0.6	98.6	-0.4	99.0	0.4
1982	99.5	0.5	100.7	1.2	100.5	-0.2	100.3	-0.2	99.8	-0.5	100.5	0.7	100.0	-0.5	99.9	-0.1	99.4	-0.5	99.6	0.2	99.4	-0.2	100.4	1.0
1983	100.1	-0.3	99.9	-0.2	100.2	0.3	99.7	-0.5	100.3	0.6	101.0	0.7	101.0	0.0	101.4	0.4	101.5	0.1	102.4	0.9	102.3	-0.1	103.1	0.8
1984	104.8	1.6	106.7	1.8	107.6	0.8	107.5	-0.1	108.5	0.9	108.6	0.1	107.9	-0.6	107.8	-0.1	106.3	-1.4	107.8	1.4	106.5	-1.2	106.9	0.4
1985	108.1	1.1	108.1	0.0	109.3	1.1	108.8	-0.5	108.6	-0.2	109.7	1.0	109.2	-0.5	109.3	0.1	107.5	-1.6	106.9	-0.6	105.2	-1.6	105.0	-0.2
1986	104.5	-0.5	104.6	0.1	104.7	0.1	104.1	-0.6	104.3	0.2	105.4	1.1	104.5	-0.9	105.1	0.6	105.1	0.0	104.6	-0.5	105.6	1.0	106.6	0.9
1987	107.3	0.7	107.5	0.2	108.4	0.8	108.3	-0.1	108.4	0.1	109.5	1.0	108.7	-0.7	109.3	0.6	108.5	-0.7	108.4	-0.1	108.8	0.4	110.1	1.2
1988	110.9	0.7	111.4	0.5	111.8	0.4	111.5	-0.3	111.7	0.2	111.6	-0.1	113.4	1.6	115.2	1.6	115.5	0.3	116.5	0.9	117.9	1.2	118.5	0.5
1989	119.0	0.4	118.8	-0.2	119.2	0.3	119.0	-0.2	119.8	0.7	120.5	0.6	120.8	0.2	121.2	0.3	120.7	-0.4	120.0	-0.6	119.9	-0.1	120.4	0.4
1990	122.4	1.7	125.7	2.7	126.9	1.0	126.9	0.0	127.0	0.1	126.5	-0.4	126.1	-0.3	125.8	-0.2	124.9	-0.7	123.6	-1.0	120.9	-2.2	120.2	-0.6
1991	120.0	-0.2	120.2	0.2	119.8	-0.3	119.2	-0.5	119.3	0.1	119.0	-0.3	119.6	0.5	118.7	-0.8	118.6	-0.1	119.2	0.5	120.4	1.0	121.6	1.0
1992	122.1	0.4	122.4	0.2	122.3	-0.1	122.0	-0.2	122.0	0.0	121.0	-0.8	120.6	-0.3	120.5	-0.1	119.8	-0.6	119.1	-0.6	118.9	-0.2	118.4	-0.4
1993	117.5	-0.8	117.0	-0.4	116.4	-0.5	116.1	-0.3	116.7	0.5	117.6	0.8	119.0	1.2	118.7	-0.3	118.9	0.2	119.5	0.5	120.3	0.7	120.4	0.1
1994	120.8	0.3	121.6	0.7	121.4	-0.2	121.7	0.2	122.0	0.2	122.0	0.0	121.9	-0.1	121.6	-0.2	120.6	-0.8	120.6	0.0	120.0	-0.5	119.6	-0.3
1995	120.2	0.5	120.7	0.4	121.3	0.5	120.7	-0.5	122.3	1.3	122.1	-0.2	122.7	0.5	122.9	0.2	122.9	0.0	123.1	0.2	124.3	1.0	125.1	0.6
1996	126.0	0.7	126.0	0.0	126.5	0.4	127.3	0.6	127.6	0.2	127.9	0.2	128.1	0.2	128.2	0.1	128.6	0.3	128.3	-0.2	128.4	0.1	128.1	-0.2
1997	127.8	-0.2	127.8	0.0	127.3	-0.4	127.2	-0.1	126.9	-0.2	126.5	-0.3	126.2	-0.2	125.9	-0.2	125.3	-0.5	125.6	0.2	124.9	-0.6	124.7	-0.2

Source: U.S. Department of Labor, Bureau of Labor Statistics, Division of Industry Prices and Price Indexes. n.e.c. stands for not elsewhere classified. - indicates no data collected for period or unavailable.

Sugar and Confectionery
Producer Price Index
Base 1982 = 100

For 1926-1997. Columns headed % show percentile change in the index from the previous period for which an index is available.

Year	Jan Index	%	Feb Index	%	Mar Index	%	Apr Index	%	May Index	%	Jun Index	%	Jul Index	%	Aug Index	%	Sep Index	%	Oct Index	%	Nov Index	%	Dec Index	%
1926	18.2	-	18.5	1.6	17.7	-4.3	18.3	3.4	19.0	3.8	18.8	-1.1	19.1	1.6	19.3	1.0	19.8	2.6	20.2	2.0	20.6	2.0	22.0	6.8
1927	22.0	0.0	21.4	-2.7	20.9	-2.3	20.9	0.0	21.2	1.4	21.0	-0.9	20.5	-2.4	19.8	-3.4	20.8	5.1	20.4	-1.9	20.1	-1.5	19.9	-1.0
1928	20.0	0.5	19.3	-3.5	20.1	4.1	20.4	1.5	20.5	0.5	20.4	-0.5	19.7	-3.4	19.2	-2.5	19.5	1.6	18.2	-6.7	17.8	-2.2	18.2	2.2
1929	17.7	-2.7	17.2	-2.8	17.0	-1.2	16.9	-0.6	16.9	0.0	16.8	-0.6	17.8	6.0	18.3	2.8	18.4	0.5	18.7	1.6	17.5	-6.4	17.5	0.0
1930	17.6	0.6	17.2	-2.3	16.8	-2.3	16.7	-0.6	16.0	-4.2	15.6	-2.5	15.8	1.3	15.2	-3.8	15.1	-0.7	15.5	2.6	16.1	3.9	15.7	-2.5
1931	15.8	0.6	15.5	-1.9	15.2	-1.9	15.3	0.7	14.9	-2.6	15.3	2.7	16.1	5.2	16.0	-0.6	15.6	-2.5	15.6	0.0	15.5	-0.6	14.6	-5.8
1932	14.3	-2.1	14.2	-0.7	13.5	-4.9	13.0	-3.7	12.5	-3.8	12.9	3.2	13.8	7.0	14.4	4.3	14.4	0.0	14.4	0.0	14.2	-1.4	13.8	-2.8
1933	13.1	-5.1	13.1	0.0	14.0	6.9	14.4	2.9	15.2	5.6	15.6	2.6	15.9	1.9	16.0	0.6	16.2	1.3	15.5	-4.3	15.1	-2.6	15.0	-0.7
1934	14.7	-2.0	15.3	4.1	14.9	-2.6	14.4	-3.4	13.8	-4.2	14.8	7.2	15.6	5.4	15.9	1.9	15.2	-4.4	15.1	-0.7	14.9	-1.3	14.6	-2.0
1935	14.2	-2.7	14.4	1.4	14.8	2.8	16.4	10.8	16.9	3.0	17.0	0.6	17.0	0.6	16.7	-1.8	16.7	0.0	17.0	1.8	17.5	2.9	17.2	-1.7
1936	16.9	1.2	17.0	0.6	16.7	-1.8	17.1	2.4	17.1	0.0	17.1	0.0	16.7	-2.3	16.7	0.0	16.5	-1.2	16.0	-3.0	16.4	2.5	16.9	3.0
1937	17.4	3.0	16.9	-2.9	16.4	-3.0	16.4	0.0	16.3	-0.6	16.1	-1.2	16.3	1.2	16.3	0.0	16.8	3.1	16.0	-4.8	16.1	0.6	15.9	-1.2
1938	15.8	-0.6	15.5	-1.9	15.3	-1.3	14.8	-3.3	14.6	-1.4	14.3	-2.1	14.4	0.7	14.2	-1.4	15.0	5.6	15.3	2.0	15.0	-2.0	14.6	-2.7
1939	14.3	-2.1	14.2	-0.7	14.4	1.4	14.7	2.1	14.7	0.0	14.6	-0.7	14.5	-0.7	14.4	-0.7	18.5	28.5	17.2	-7.0	15.5	-9.9	15.2	-1.9
1940	14.6	-3.9	14.6	0.0	14.5	-0.7	14.6	0.7	14.5	-0.7	14.4	-0.7	14.3	-0.7	14.0	-2.1	14.1	0.7	14.2	0.7	14.4	1.4	14.5	0.7
1941	14.7	1.4	14.9	1.4	16.2	8.7	16.8	3.7	16.7	-0.6	16.8	0.6	16.9	0.6	17.8	5.3	17.7	-0.6	17.3	-2.3	17.3	0.0	17.4	0.6
1942	18.1	4.0	18.2	0.6	18.2	0.0	18.6	2.2	18.6	0.0	18.6	0.0	18.6	0.0	18.6	0.0	18.6	0.0	18.6	0.0	18.6	0.0	18.6	0.0
1943	18.6	0.0	18.6	0.0	18.6	0.0	18.6	0.0	18.6	0.0	18.6	0.0	18.6	0.0	18.6	0.0	18.6	0.0	18.6	0.0	18.6	0.0	18.6	0.0
1944	18.6	0.0	18.6	0.0	18.6	0.0	18.6	0.0	18.6	0.0	18.7	0.5	18.7	0.0	18.7	0.0	18.5	-1.1	18.5	0.0	18.5	0.0	18.5	0.0
1945	18.5	0.0	18.5	0.0	18.5	0.0	18.5	0.0	18.5	0.0	18.5	0.0	18.5	0.0	18.5	0.0	18.5	0.0	18.5	0.0	18.5	0.0	18.5	0.0
1946	18.5	0.0	19.5	5.4	20.2	3.6	20.2	0.0	20.2	0.0	20.2	0.0	20.7	2.5	20.8	0.5	23.5	13.0	26.1	11.1	26.6	1.9	27.2	2.3
1947	27.4	0.7	27.8	1.5	28.1	1.1	28.3	0.7	28.3	0.0	28.4	0.4	28.5	0.4	29.3	2.8	29.4	0.3	29.4	0.0	30.4	3.4	30.6	0.7
1948	30.3	-1.0	30.4	0.3	30.2	-0.7	30.1	-0.3	29.0	-3.7	28.7	-1.0	29.4	2.4	29.5	0.3	29.7	0.7	29.4	-1.0	29.6	0.7	29.2	-1.4
1949	29.4	0.7	28.7	-2.4	27.8	-3.1	27.3	-1.8	26.9	-1.5	26.9	0.0	26.7	-0.7	26.7	0.0	26.9	0.7	27.1	0.7	27.1	0.0	27.0	-0.4
1950	27.1	0.4	26.8	-1.1	26.5	-1.1	26.4	-0.4	26.7	1.1	26.9	0.7	27.7	3.0	28.6	3.2	29.7	3.8	29.6	-0.3	29.6	0.0	29.6	0.0
1951	29.6	0.0	29.6	0.0	29.6	0.0	29.5	-0.3	30.4	3.1	31.3	3.0	31.2	-0.3	30.7	-1.6	30.7	0.0	30.1	-2.0	30.2	0.3	30.1	-0.3
1952	30.1	0.0	30.2	0.3	30.5	1.0	31.2	2.3	31.1	-0.3	31.6	1.6	31.8	0.6	31.5	-0.9	31.5	0.0	31.6	0.3	31.3	-0.9	30.9	-1.3
1953	30.9	0.0	30.9	0.0	31.3	1.3	31.4	0.3	31.3	-0.3	31.4	0.3	31.4	0.0	31.5	0.3	31.4	-0.3	31.5	0.3	31.0	-1.6	31.1	0.3
1954	31.5	1.3	31.5	0.0	32.3	2.5	32.2	-0.3	32.4	0.6	32.4	0.0	32.6	0.6	32.7	0.3	32.3	-1.2	32.1	-0.6	32.1	0.0	31.9	-0.6
1955	31.9	0.0	32.2	0.9	31.7	-1.6	31.7	0.0	31.6	-0.3	31.6	0.0	31.7	0.3	31.5	-0.6	31.4	-0.3	31.5	0.3	31.4	-0.3	31.3	-0.3
1956	31.3	0.0	31.3	0.0	31.4	0.3	30.1	-4.1	31.4	4.3	31.3	-0.3	31.5	0.6	31.4	-0.3	31.5	0.3	31.7	0.6	32.0	0.9	32.1	0.3
1957	32.4	0.9	32.1	-0.9	32.1	0.0	32.1	0.0	32.3	0.6	32.5	0.6	32.7	0.6	32.6	-0.3	32.6	0.0	32.6	0.0	32.7	0.3	32.7	0.0
1958	32.8	0.3	32.7	-0.3	32.4	-0.9	32.7	0.9	33.0	0.9	33.3	0.9	33.3	0.0	33.2	-0.3	33.3	0.3	33.4	0.3	33.3	-0.3	33.5	0.6
1959	33.0	-1.5	32.6	-1.2	32.3	-0.9	32.1	-0.6	32.7	1.9	33.1	1.2	33.0	-0.3	33.0	0.0	33.3	0.9	33.6	0.9	33.4	-0.6	33.1	-0.9
1960	32.4	-2.1	32.6	0.6	32.9	0.9	33.0	0.3	33.1	0.3	33.1	0.0	33.9	2.4	33.9	0.0	34.1	0.6	33.9	-0.6	34.0	0.3	33.7	-0.9
1961	33.7	0.0	33.6	-0.3	33.4	-0.6	33.3	-0.3	33.6	0.9	33.7	0.3	33.3	-1.2	32.8	-1.5	32.7	-0.3	32.7	0.0	32.8	0.3	33.2	1.2
1962	33.2	0.0	33.4	0.6	33.4	0.0	33.6	0.6	33.5	-0.3	33.6	0.3	33.5	-0.3	33.7	0.6	33.5	-0.6	33.8	0.9	33.6	-0.6	33.7	0.3
1963	34.5	2.4	34.5	0.0	34.8	0.9	37.4	7.5	43.8	17.1	43.4	-0.9	39.5	-9.0	36.5	-7.6	36.9	1.1	41.2	11.7	43.1	4.6	41.0	-4.9
1964	42.8	4.4	40.3	-5.8	38.5	-4.5	37.9	-1.6	36.7	-3.2	35.5	-3.3	35.0	-1.4	34.9	-0.3	34.5	-1.1	34.7	0.6	34.4	-0.9	35.2	2.3
1965	36.1	2.6	36.1	0.0	35.5	-1.7	35.5	0.0	35.7	0.6	35.8	0.3	35.8	0.0	35.8	0.3	36.0	0.3	35.9	0.6	35.8	-0.3	35.7	-0.3
1966	35.9	0.6	36.1	0.6	36.0	-0.3	35.9	-0.3	35.9	0.0	35.9	0.0	36.0	0.3	36.4	1.1	36.6	0.5	36.6	0.0	36.8	0.5	36.9	0.3
1967	37.1	0.5	37.0	-0.3	36.9	-0.3	36.7	-0.5	36.7	0.0	37.0	0.8	37.3	0.8	37.4	0.3	37.1	-0.8	37.2	0.3	37.4	0.5	37.0	-1.1
1968	37.2	0.5	37.3	0.3	37.3	0.0	37.4	0.3	37.8	1.1	38.5	1.9	38.6	0.3	38.5	-0.3	38.6	0.3	38.8	0.5	38.7	-0.3	38.9	0.5
1969	39.1	0.5	39.1	0.0	39.2	0.3	39.4	0.5	40.2	2.0	41.5	3.2	41.3	-0.5	41.7	1.0	41.8	0.2	41.9	0.2	42.0	0.2	41.7	-0.7
1970	42.3	1.4	41.9	-0.9	41.8	-0.2	42.2	1.0	42.5	0.7	42.8	0.7	43.5	1.6	43.5	0.0	43.8	0.7	44.0	0.5	43.8	-0.5	43.5	-0.7

[Continued]

Sugar and Confectionery
Producer Price Index
Base 1982 = 100
[Continued]

For 1926-1997. Columns headed % show percentile change in the index from the previous period for which an index is available.

Year	Jan Index	%	Feb Index	%	Mar Index	%	Apr Index	%	May Index	%	Jun Index	%	Jul Index	%	Aug Index	%	Sep Index	%	Oct Index	%	Nov Index	%	Dec Index	%
1971	43.7	0.5	44.2	1.1	44.5	0.7	44.2	-0.7	44.5	0.7	44.4	-0.2	44.5	0.2	44.5	0.0	44.5	0.0	43.7	-1.8	44.2	1.1	44.6	0.9
1972	44.5	-0.2	44.9	0.9	45.2	0.7	44.9	-0.7	44.8	-0.2	45.0	0.4	45.3	0.7	45.0	-0.7	45.1	0.2	45.8	1.6	45.1	-1.5	45.3	0.4
1973	45.0	-0.7	46.1	2.4	46.6	1.1	47.0	0.9	47.8	1.7	48.6	1.7	48.6	0.0	50.3	3.5	50.8	1.0	51.8	2.0	53.3	2.9	52.7	-1.1
1974	56.3	6.8	62.0	10.1	70.5	13.7	70.4	-0.1	80.0	13.6	89.3	11.6	91.5	2.5	100.3	9.6	110.5	10.2	116.9	5.8	155.7	33.2	148.8	-4.4
1975	132.8	-10.8	128.8	-3.0	112.4	-12.7	103.9	-7.6	88.8	-14.5	80.8	-9.0	84.7	4.8	90.2	6.5	81.4	-9.8	77.3	-5.0	77.0	-0.4	73.8	-4.2
1976	75.1	1.8	74.3	-1.1	76.8	3.4	75.1	-2.2	77.4	3.1	73.2	-5.4	74.6	1.9	68.6	-8.0	62.0	-9.6	65.4	5.5	63.6	-2.8	63.2	-0.6
1977	63.8	0.9	65.9	3.3	66.8	1.4	69.1	3.4	68.4	-1.0	65.4	-4.4	63.5	-2.9	66.3	4.4	64.6	-2.6	63.1	-2.3	66.2	4.9	66.4	0.3
1978	68.9	3.8	71.9	4.4	71.5	-0.6	72.7	1.7	72.8	0.1	73.1	0.4	72.6	-0.7	74.3	2.3	75.1	1.1	76.2	1.5	75.1	-1.4	75.8	0.9
1979	75.9	0.1	77.3	1.8	77.3	0.0	77.4	0.1	77.0	-0.5	78.3	1.7	80.0	2.2	80.9	1.1	80.6	-0.4	81.2	0.7	82.7	1.8	86.9	5.1
1980	87.1	0.2	106.6	22.4	98.0	-8.1	102.0	4.1	121.6	19.2	120.7	-0.7	116.3	-3.6	128.7	10.7	126.6	-1.6	150.1	18.6	151.7	1.1	126.0	-16.9
1981	127.8	1.4	119.9	-6.2	112.0	-6.6	105.5	-5.8	97.4	-7.7	101.9	4.6	98.6	-3.2	99.1	0.5	91.5	-7.7	91.5	0.0	90.5	-1.1	91.8	1.4
1982	95.2	3.7	95.4	0.2	94.6	-0.8	94.9	0.3	98.4	3.7	99.8	1.4	102.2	2.4	105.9	3.6	103.3	-2.5	102.5	-0.8	104.0	1.5	103.9	-0.1
1983	104.6	0.7	106.2	1.5	105.2	-0.9	106.6	1.3	107.5	0.8	109.8	2.1	109.9	0.1	110.8	0.8	111.3	0.5	110.5	-0.7	110.4	-0.1	110.3	-0.1
1984	111.2	0.8	111.4	0.2	111.7	0.3	111.9	0.2	112.6	0.6	112.8	0.2	113.1	0.3	112.6	-0.4	112.1	-0.4	111.2	-0.8	110.1	-1.0	109.7	-0.4
1985	108.8	-0.8	107.9	-0.8	108.5	0.6	108.8	0.3	109.2	0.4	109.2	0.0	108.9	-0.3	108.1	-0.7	107.6	-0.5	106.1	-1.4	105.8	-0.3	106.0	0.2
1986	108.0	1.9	108.4	0.4	109.2	0.7	108.8	-0.4	109.0	0.2	109.4	0.4	109.8	0.4	109.8	0.0	110.4	0.5	110.9	0.5	111.1	0.2	111.2	0.1
1987	110.8	-0.4	110.8	0.0	111.2	0.4	111.9	0.6	112.8	0.8	112.9	0.1	113.7	0.7	113.9	0.2	114.0	0.1	113.6	-0.4	113.5	-0.1	113.0	-0.4
1988	112.5	-0.4	112.8	0.3	113.0	0.2	113.3	0.3	113.1	-0.2	113.6	0.4	115.9	2.0	115.9	0.0	115.9	0.0	116.5	0.5	116.8	0.3	117.3	0.4
1989	117.8	0.4	118.3	0.4	118.6	0.3	119.2	0.5	119.6	0.3	120.7	0.9	122.0	1.1	121.3	-0.6	121.6	0.2	120.1	-1.2	120.5	0.3	121.0	0.4
1990	121.1	0.1	121.8	0.6	121.7	-0.1	122.6	0.7	122.8	0.2	123.0	0.2	123.9	0.7	123.7	-0.2	123.9	0.2	123.0	-0.7	124.8	1.5	124.7	-0.1
1991	126.3	1.3	128.4	1.7	127.8	-0.5	128.3	0.4	127.8	-0.4	127.6	-0.2	129.1	1.2	129.4	0.2	129.8	0.3	128.5	-1.0	128.6	0.1	128.8	0.2
1992	128.6	-0.2	127.7	-0.7	127.4	-0.2	127.6	0.2	127.8	0.2	127.7	-0.1	129.0	1.0	129.3	0.2	129.2	-0.1	126.0	-2.5	125.8	-0.2	125.9	0.1
1993	125.4	-0.4	124.5	-0.7	124.6	0.1	124.8	0.2	125.5	0.6	126.6	0.9	129.3	2.1	129.3	0.0	130.6	1.0	131.7	0.8	131.5	-0.2	130.7	-0.6
1994	130.6	-0.1	130.5	-0.1	131.3	0.6	133.2	1.4	133.6	0.3	134.6	0.7	134.7	0.1	134.3	-0.3	133.9	-0.3	130.9	-2.2	131.2	0.2	131.3	0.1
1995	132.0	0.5	133.0	0.8	133.2	0.2	133.5	0.2	133.8	0.2	133.8	0.0	134.6	0.6	134.3	-0.2	134.6	0.2	134.6	0.0	134.9	0.2	135.9	0.7
1996	135.9	0.0	135.9	0.0	136.2	0.2	136.8	0.4	137.3	0.4	138.1	0.6	137.8	-0.2	137.9	0.1	138.5	0.4	138.5	0.0	138.6	0.1	138.8	0.1
1997	138.8	0.0	138.4	-0.3	138.6	0.1	138.4	-0.1	138.4	0.0	138.1	-0.2	138.2	0.1	138.1	-0.1	138.3	0.1	135.0	-2.4	135.0	0.0	133.7	-1.0

Source: U.S. Department of Labor, Bureau of Labor Statistics, Division of Industry Prices and Price Indexes. n.e.c. stands for not elsewhere classified. - indicates no data collected for period or unavailable.

Beverages and Beverage Materials
Producer Price Index
Base 1982 = 100

For 1947-1997. Columns headed % show percentile change in the index from the previous period for which an index is available.

Year	Jan Index	%	Feb Index	%	Mar Index	%	Apr Index	%	May Index	%	Jun Index	%	Jul Index	%	Aug Index	%	Sep Index	%	Oct Index	%	Nov Index	%	Dec Index	%
1947	26.3	-	26.5	0.8	26.6	0.4	26.6	0.0	26.4	-0.8	26.2	-0.8	26.2	0.0	26.4	0.8	26.7	1.1	26.8	0.4	27.0	0.7	27.3	1.1
1948	27.5	0.7	27.7	0.7	27.7	0.0	27.7	0.0	27.7	0.0	27.8	0.4	27.8	0.0	27.8	0.0	27.8	0.0	27.8	0.0	27.9	0.4	27.9	0.0
1949	27.9	0.0	27.9	0.0	27.9	0.0	27.8	-0.4	27.8	0.0	27.8	0.0	27.8	0.0	27.8	0.0	28.0	0.7	28.1	0.4	29.7	5.7	30.2	1.7
1950	30.2	0.0	30.1	-0.3	30.1	0.0	29.7	-1.3	29.6	-0.3	29.7	0.3	30.3	2.0	30.7	1.3	31.0	1.0	31.5	1.6	31.3	-0.6	32.0	2.2
1951	32.5	1.6	32.6	0.3	32.6	0.0	32.6	0.0	32.6	0.0	32.6	0.0	32.5	-0.3	32.5	0.0	32.5	0.0	32.5	0.0	32.5	0.0	32.5	0.0
1952	32.5	0.0	33.3	2.5	33.3	0.0	33.2	-0.3	33.2	0.0	33.2	0.0	33.2	0.0	33.2	0.0	33.2	0.0	33.2	0.0	33.2	0.0	33.2	0.0
1953	33.2	0.0	33.2	0.0	33.6	1.2	33.5	-0.3	33.3	-0.6	33.3	0.0	33.8	1.5	33.8	0.0	34.0	0.6	34.5	1.5	34.6	0.3	34.6	0.0
1954	35.2	1.7	35.6	1.1	36.6	2.8	38.7	5.7	38.7	0.0	38.7	0.0	39.0	0.8	38.7	-0.8	37.6	-2.8	37.6	0.0	37.2	-1.1	37.5	0.8
1955	37.5	0.0	36.6	-2.4	36.2	-1.1	36.2	0.0	36.2	0.0	35.8	-1.1	35.8	0.0	35.9	0.3	36.1	0.6	36.4	0.8	36.1	-0.8	36.1	0.0
1956	36.1	0.0	36.4	0.8	36.9	1.4	36.7	-0.5	36.6	-0.3	36.8	0.5	37.1	0.8	37.4	0.8	37.8	1.1	37.8	0.0	38.0	0.5	37.6	-1.1
1957	37.8	0.5	37.6	-0.5	37.5	-0.3	37.2	-0.8	37.2	0.0	37.2	0.0	37.2	0.0	37.2	0.0	36.9	-0.8	36.6	-0.8	36.6	0.0	36.7	0.3
1958	36.7	0.0	36.7	0.0	36.4	-0.8	36.4	0.0	36.4	0.0	36.4	0.0	36.2	-0.5	36.1	-0.3	36.1	0.0	36.2	0.3	36.2	0.0	36.1	-0.3
1959	35.9	-0.6	35.7	-0.6	36.4	2.0	36.3	-0.3	36.3	0.0	36.3	0.0	36.3	0.0	36.2	-0.3	36.2	0.0	36.2	0.0	36.2	0.0	36.2	0.0
1960	36.2	0.0	36.2	0.0	36.2	0.0	36.2	0.0	36.2	0.0	36.2	0.0	36.1	-0.3	36.1	0.0	36.1	0.0	36.1	0.0	36.1	0.0	36.1	0.0
1961	35.9	-0.6	36.0	0.3	36.0	0.0	35.9	-0.3	35.9	0.0	35.9	0.0	36.1	0.6	36.1	0.0	36.3	0.6	36.1	-0.6	36.2	0.3	36.2	0.0
1962	36.2	0.0	36.2	0.0	36.2	0.0	36.2	0.0	36.2	0.0	36.2	0.0	36.2	0.0	36.3	0.3	36.2	-0.3	36.1	-0.3	36.1	0.0	36.0	-0.3
1963	36.0	0.0	36.0	0.0	36.0	0.0	36.2	0.6	36.3	0.3	36.8	1.4	37.4	1.6	37.5	0.3	37.5	0.0	37.5	0.0	37.7	0.5	37.9	0.5
1964	38.3	1.1	38.5	0.5	38.8	0.8	38.8	0.0	38.9	0.3	38.9	0.0	38.9	0.0	38.9	0.0	38.9	0.0	38.9	0.0	38.9	0.0	38.9	0.0
1965	38.8	-0.3	38.8	0.0	38.5	-0.8	38.6	0.3	38.6	0.0	38.6	0.0	38.6	0.0	38.6	0.0	38.6	0.0	38.6	0.0	38.6	0.0	38.7	0.3
1966	38.7	0.0	38.6	-0.3	38.6	0.0	38.6	0.0	38.6	0.0	38.8	0.5	38.9	0.3	38.9	0.0	38.6	-0.8	38.6	0.0	38.6	0.0	38.7	0.3
1967	38.7	0.0	38.7	0.0	38.6	-0.3	38.7	0.3	38.8	0.3	38.9	0.3	38.9	0.0	39.0	0.3	39.0	0.0	39.2	0.5	39.2	0.0	39.4	0.5
1968	39.4	0.0	39.7	0.8	39.8	0.3	39.9	0.3	40.0	0.3	40.0	0.0	40.0	0.0	40.1	0.2	40.2	0.2	40.4	0.5	40.4	0.0	40.4	0.0
1969	40.5	0.2	40.6	0.2	40.7	0.2	40.7	0.0	40.9	0.5	41.1	0.5	41.2	0.2	41.2	0.0	41.3	0.2	42.1	1.9	42.4	0.7	42.5	0.2
1970	42.9	0.9	43.3	0.9	43.3	0.0	43.4	0.2	44.0	1.4	44.0	0.0	44.1	0.2	44.3	0.5	44.5	0.5	44.6	0.2	44.7	0.2	44.5	-0.4
1971	44.8	0.7	44.9	0.2	44.9	0.0	45.1	0.4	45.1	0.0	45.1	0.0	45.2	0.2	45.3	0.2	45.4	0.2	45.4	0.0	45.4	0.0	45.3	-0.2
1972	45.3	0.0	45.5	0.4	45.4	-0.2	45.6	0.4	45.6	0.0	45.8	0.4	45.9	0.2	46.3	0.9	46.4	0.2	46.2	-0.4	46.5	0.6	46.6	0.2
1973	46.6	0.0	46.7	0.2	47.0	0.6	47.3	0.6	47.5	0.4	47.3	-0.4	47.1	-0.4	47.2	0.2	47.3	0.2	47.9	1.3	48.2	0.6	48.4	0.4
1974	48.9	1.0	49.1	0.4	50.3	2.4	51.5	2.4	52.4	1.7	53.9	2.9	55.9	3.7	56.9	1.8	57.5	1.1	59.4	3.3	60.1	1.2	61.6	2.5
1975	63.3	2.8	63.2	-0.2	63.1	-0.2	63.0	-0.2	62.7	-0.5	62.4	-0.5	62.1	-0.5	62.9	1.3	63.3	0.6	64.3	1.6	64.3	0.0	64.4	0.2
1976	64.3	-0.2	65.1	1.2	65.1	0.0	65.9	1.2	67.1	1.8	67.3	0.3	68.5	1.8	68.4	-0.1	68.7	0.4	69.1	0.6	69.6	0.7	71.6	2.9
1977	71.7	0.1	73.7	2.8	77.7	5.4	78.7	1.3	80.2	1.9	80.9	0.9	79.7	-1.5	80.0	0.4	79.7	-0.4	79.8	0.1	78.5	-1.6	78.4	-0.1
1978	78.7	0.4	78.4	-0.4	77.9	-0.6	77.9	0.0	77.7	-0.3	77.9	0.3	77.3	-0.8	76.6	-0.9	77.0	0.5	78.3	1.7	78.4	0.1	78.3	-0.1
1979	78.2	-0.1	78.3	0.1	78.3	0.0	78.5	0.3	79.9	1.8	81.2	1.6	83.4	2.7	84.3	1.1	84.8	0.6	85.2	0.5	86.1	1.1	86.3	0.2
1980	87.2	1.0	87.5	0.3	88.0	0.6	88.7	0.8	90.0	1.5	91.2	1.3	91.3	0.1	92.3	1.1	91.9	-0.4	93.3	1.5	93.7	0.4	93.6	-0.1
1981	94.6	1.1	95.3	0.7	95.5	0.2	95.8	0.3	96.4	0.6	96.6	0.2	96.9	0.3	97.1	0.2	97.0	-0.1	97.3	0.3	97.9	0.6	98.1	0.2
1982	98.8	0.7	99.3	0.5	99.8	0.5	99.9	0.1	99.9	0.0	99.9	0.0	100.0	0.1	100.4	0.4	100.1	-0.3	100.4	0.3	100.6	0.2	100.8	0.2
1983	101.3	0.5	101.7	0.4	102.0	0.3	102.4	0.4	102.6	0.2	102.4	-0.2	102.7	0.3	102.7	0.0	102.9	0.2	103.3	0.4	103.7	0.4	103.7	0.0
1984	104.6	0.9	105.2	0.6	105.1	-0.1	105.7	0.6	106.5	0.8	106.2	-0.3	106.6	0.4	106.9	0.3	106.9	0.0	107.5	0.6	107.4	-0.1	107.3	-0.1
1985	107.4	0.1	108.0	0.6	107.9	-0.1	107.8	-0.1	107.8	0.0	107.3	-0.5	107.5	0.2	107.1	-0.4	107.1	0.0	107.6	0.5	107.9	0.3	109.0	1.0
1986	112.9	3.6	114.5	1.4	115.0	0.4	115.9	0.8	115.9	0.0	115.5	-0.3	115.5	0.0	114.0	-1.3	113.7	-0.3	114.2	0.4	113.9	-0.3	113.8	-0.1
1987	112.6	-1.1	112.8	0.2	112.9	0.1	113.3	0.4	113.2	-0.1	113.0	-0.2	112.1	-0.8	112.3	0.2	111.6	-0.6	112.3	0.6	112.0	-0.3	112.2	0.2
1988	112.5	0.3	113.0	0.4	113.9	0.8	114.1	0.2	114.1	0.0	114.1	0.0	113.8	-0.3	114.6	0.7	114.7	0.1	115.3	0.5	115.8	0.4	115.8	0.0
1989	116.5	0.6	117.7	1.0	118.7	0.8	119.2	0.4	119.7	0.4	119.6	-0.1	119.4	-0.2	118.3	-0.9	117.1	-1.0	118.1	0.9	118.4	0.3	118.4	0.0
1990	119.7	1.1	120.7	0.8	121.5	0.7	121.5	0.0	121.0	-0.4	120.8	-0.2	120.9	0.1	120.6	-0.2	120.8	0.2	120.3	-0.4	120.5	0.2	121.1	0.5
1991	125.5	3.6	125.5	0.0	125.3	-0.2	125.5	0.2	124.3	-1.0	124.2	-0.1	123.5	-0.6	123.2	-0.2	123.1	-0.1	123.0	-0.1	123.0	0.0	123.2	0.2

[Continued]

Beverages and Beverage Materials
Producer Price Index
Base 1982 = 100
[Continued]

For 1947-1997. Columns headed % show percentile change in the index from the previous period for which an index is available.

Year	Jan Index	%	Feb Index	%	Mar Index	%	Apr Index	%	May Index	%	Jun Index	%	Jul Index	%	Aug Index	%	Sep Index	%	Oct Index	%	Nov Index	%	Dec Index	%
1992	124.8	1.3	125.2	0.3	124.5	-0.6	124.6	0.1	125.1	0.4	125.7	0.5	124.4	-1.0	124.1	-0.2	123.8	-0.2	123.4	-0.3	123.5	0.1	124.0	0.4
1993	124.5	0.4	125.4	0.7	125.4	0.0	125.2	-0.2	125.0	-0.2	124.8	-0.2	124.4	-0.3	124.5	0.1	124.4	-0.1	124.5	0.1	124.3	-0.2	124.6	0.2
1994	125.5	0.7	126.0	0.4	125.2	-0.6	124.8	-0.3	124.8	0.0	125.3	0.4	129.9	3.7	129.7	-0.2	129.7	0.0	130.1	0.3	130.4	0.2	130.5	0.1
1995	131.8	1.0	133.4	1.2	133.8	0.3	134.3	0.4	134.1	-0.1	134.0	-0.1	134.2	0.1	134.4	0.1	133.9	-0.4	134.0	0.1	134.0	0.0	134.3	0.2
1996	134.3	0.0	134.5	0.1	134.3	-0.1	134.8	0.4	134.3	-0.4	134.3	0.0	134.3	0.0	134.6	0.2	134.2	-0.3	135.4	0.9	134.5	-0.7	135.2	0.5
1997	135.3	0.1	135.2	-0.1	137.1	1.4	138.0	0.7	138.9	0.7	139.3	0.3	139.4	0.1	139.4	0.0	138.0	-1.0	137.8	-0.1	136.8	-0.7	136.9	0.1

Source: U.S. Department of Labor, Bureau of Labor Statistics, Division of Industry Prices and Price Indexes. n.e.c. stands for not elsewhere classified. - indicates no data collected for period or unavailable.

Fats and Oils
Producer Price Index
Base 1982 = 100

For 1967-1997. Columns headed % show percentile change in the index from the previous period for which an index is available.

Year	Jan Index	%	Feb Index	%	Mar Index	%	Apr Index	%	May Index	%	Jun Index	%	Jul Index	%	Aug Index	%	Sep Index	%	Oct Index	%	Nov Index	%	Dec Index	%
1967	48.8	-	48.3	-1.0	47.7	-1.2	47.7	0.0	47.6	-0.2	46.6	-2.1	45.3	-2.8	46.2	2.0	45.9	-0.6	44.8	-2.4	44.3	-1.1	44.3	0.0
1968	44.5	0.5	46.6	4.7	46.1	-1.1	45.4	-1.5	46.0	1.3	44.8	-2.6	44.3	-1.1	45.5	2.7	43.9	-3.5	42.3	-3.6	43.8	3.5	43.9	0.2
1969	45.1	2.7	46.6	3.3	46.6	0.0	45.8	-1.7	45.8	0.0	46.0	0.4	45.8	-0.4	45.9	0.2	45.9	0.0	48.6	5.9	50.8	4.5	49.8	-2.0
1970	49.5	-0.6	51.6	4.2	56.3	9.1	55.6	-1.2	54.4	-2.2	53.6	-1.5	53.4	-0.4	55.3	3.6	54.3	-1.8	57.5	5.9	60.7	5.6	58.2	-4.1
1971	57.7	-0.9	59.0	2.3	58.9	-0.2	56.8	-3.6	56.6	-0.4	57.3	1.2	60.2	5.1	62.9	4.5	60.3	-4.1	58.7	-2.7	58.8	0.2	56.4	-4.1
1972	55.6	-1.4	56.3	1.3	56.0	-0.5	56.3	0.5	55.4	-1.6	55.4	0.0	54.5	-1.6	53.5	-1.8	53.2	-0.6	53.2	0.0	52.7	-0.9	52.5	-0.4
1973	52.2	-0.6	57.4	10.0	63.3	10.3	64.0	1.1	68.0	6.3	73.9	8.7	74.2	0.4	103.3	39.2	84.2	-18.5	92.5	9.9	80.4	-13.1	93.7	16.5
1974	96.9	3.4	112.6	16.2	108.2	-3.9	101.3	-6.4	109.2	7.8	107.6	-1.5	119.3	10.9	145.4	21.9	128.0	-12.0	144.6	13.0	143.0	-1.1	129.9	-9.2
1975	127.9	-1.5	117.1	-8.4	110.3	-5.8	108.4	-1.7	98.7	-8.9	94.5	-4.3	108.3	14.6	113.3	4.6	103.5	-8.6	98.9	-4.4	92.0	-7.0	83.2	-9.6
1976	80.4	-3.4	79.8	-0.7	80.3	0.6	77.8	-3.1	76.8	-1.3	78.3	2.0	87.0	11.1	82.5	-5.2	89.8	8.8	85.2	-5.1	88.8	4.2	86.9	-2.1
1977	86.2	-0.8	91.4	6.0	98.3	7.5	109.8	11.7	111.1	1.2	107.1	-3.6	95.5	-10.8	92.5	-3.1	88.4	-4.4	90.2	2.0	90.9	0.8	96.6	6.3
1978	94.3	-2.4	94.5	0.2	104.9	11.0	107.0	2.0	107.9	0.8	105.7	-2.0	106.6	0.9	104.8	-1.7	111.3	6.2	108.2	-2.8	105.8	-2.2	105.8	0.0
1979	106.8	0.9	110.4	3.4	110.9	0.5	114.4	3.2	112.4	-1.7	113.2	0.7	117.7	4.0	117.0	-0.6	117.7	0.6	114.3	-2.9	112.4	-1.7	109.5	-2.6
1980	104.6	-4.5	105.2	0.6	103.5	-1.6	99.7	-3.7	98.5	-1.2	98.9	0.4	105.5	6.7	111.7	5.9	110.8	-0.8	107.4	-3.1	110.6	3.0	108.8	-1.6
1981	107.0	-1.7	106.1	-0.8	106.8	0.7	108.0	1.1	106.1	-1.8	105.7	-0.4	109.1	3.2	106.7	-2.2	104.3	-2.2	103.8	-0.5	102.9	-0.9	101.8	-1.1
1982	100.7	-1.1	100.7	0.0	99.4	-1.3	101.4	2.0	103.3	1.9	103.1	-0.2	102.9	-0.2	100.2	-2.6	98.2	-2.0	99.4	1.2	96.3	-3.1	94.3	-2.1
1983	93.8	-0.5	95.4	1.7	95.8	0.4	99.7	4.1	102.3	2.6	101.9	-0.4	103.3	1.4	114.2	10.6	141.1	23.6	130.9	-7.2	127.6	-2.5	126.3	-1.0
1984	129.4	2.5	127.0	-1.9	133.0	4.7	136.4	2.6	152.7	12.0	152.5	-0.1	145.4	-4.7	142.2	-2.2	138.8	-2.4	140.2	1.0	145.0	3.4	138.3	-4.6
1985	130.4	-5.7	132.6	1.7	135.0	1.8	140.8	4.3	137.6	-2.3	137.8	0.1	132.0	-4.2	118.4	-10.3	113.6	-4.1	110.6	-2.6	109.6	-0.9	106.8	-2.6
1986	107.3	0.5	103.8	-3.3	99.1	-4.5	97.8	-1.3	97.0	-0.8	95.5	-1.5	94.4	-1.2	92.8	-1.7	91.0	-1.9	93.4	2.6	92.9	-0.5	93.3	0.4
1987	95.3	2.1	95.8	0.5	95.6	-0.2	95.4	-0.2	99.2	4.0	97.9	-1.3	97.6	-0.3	96.4	-1.2	97.7	1.3	99.4	1.7	101.1	1.7	103.6	2.5
1988	110.6	6.8	111.1	0.5	109.3	-1.6	111.9	2.4	114.0	1.9	120.1	5.4	132.1	10.0	127.1	-3.8	122.7	-3.5	118.4	-3.5	114.3	-3.5	114.8	0.4
1989	114.1	-0.6	111.6	-2.2	114.7	2.8	113.7	-0.9	117.5	3.3	112.6	-4.2	112.5	-0.1	108.5	-3.6	108.9	0.4	108.3	-0.6	112.5	3.9	110.2	-2.0
1990	111.3	1.0	111.8	0.4	117.8	5.4	116.2	-1.4	124.6	7.2	126.0	1.1	124.6	-1.1	126.3	1.4	124.0	-1.8	118.5	-4.4	115.1	-2.9	116.9	1.6
1991	115.8	-0.9	115.8	0.0	118.2	2.1	116.9	-1.1	111.6	-4.5	110.5	-1.0	107.0	-3.2	110.8	3.6	111.2	0.4	109.8	-1.3	107.9	-1.7	108.9	0.9
1992	108.4	-0.5	108.8	0.4	111.1	2.1	108.6	-2.3	111.1	2.3	113.6	2.3	108.3	-4.7	104.2	-3.8	105.7	1.4	104.9	-0.8	108.5	3.4	111.9	3.1
1993	113.1	1.1	110.7	-2.1	111.5	0.7	112.9	1.3	113.7	0.7	111.4	-2.0	121.5	9.1	119.5	-1.6	118.7	-0.7	117.7	-0.8	120.2	2.1	132.1	9.9
1994	137.3	3.9	136.1	-0.9	137.1	0.7	136.2	-0.7	137.8	1.2	136.9	-0.7	128.5	-6.1	128.3	-0.2	133.6	4.1	132.2	-1.0	141.7	7.2	144.4	1.9
1995	144.3	-0.1	143.3	-0.7	143.2	-0.1	138.2	-3.5	134.3	-2.8	135.2	0.7	138.5	2.4	138.6	0.1	137.3	-0.9	138.4	0.8	136.8	-1.2	134.0	-2.0
1996	130.5	-2.6	129.4	-0.8	127.5	-1.5	131.5	3.1	137.1	4.3	134.8	-1.7	132.3	-1.9	133.3	0.8	133.6	0.2	126.6	-5.2	125.9	-0.6	125.8	-0.1
1997	128.8	2.4	127.8	-0.8	131.3	2.7	128.8	-1.9	130.6	1.4	129.2	-1.1	127.6	-1.2	126.7	-0.7	128.9	1.7	135.2	4.9	139.4	3.1	135.2	-3.0

Source: U.S. Department of Labor, Bureau of Labor Statistics, Division of Industry Prices and Price Indexes. n.e.c. stands for not elsewhere classified. - indicates no data collected for period or unavailable.

Miscellaneous Processed Foods
Producer Price Index
Base 1982 = 100

For 1947-1997. Columns headed % show percentile change in the index from the previous period for which an index is available.

Year	Jan Index	%	Feb Index	%	Mar Index	%	Apr Index	%	May Index	%	Jun Index	%	Jul Index	%	Aug Index	%	Sep Index	%	Oct Index	%	Nov Index	%	Dec Index	%
1947	35.5	-	35.7	0.6	35.6	-0.3	34.7	-2.5	33.9	-2.3	33.7	-0.6	33.8	0.3	33.9	0.3	34.3	1.2	35.5	3.5	35.7	0.6	35.2	-1.4
1948	35.2	0.0	35.0	-0.6	34.8	-0.6	35.1	0.9	35.3	0.6	35.9	1.7	36.2	0.8	37.3	3.0	38.1	2.1	39.0	2.4	38.1	-2.3	37.9	-0.5
1949	37.2	-1.8	36.8	-1.1	38.3	4.1	38.5	0.5	38.4	-0.3	39.6	3.1	40.3	1.8	42.3	5.0	42.0	-0.7	42.6	1.4	42.3	-0.7	42.1	-0.5
1950	41.1	-2.4	42.2	2.7	42.2	0.0	41.8	-0.9	41.4	-1.0	39.5	-4.6	44.2	11.9	52.2	18.1	48.2	-7.7	44.9	-6.8	43.6	-2.9	44.7	2.5
1951	46.1	3.1	47.4	2.8	45.2	-4.6	45.6	0.9	45.8	0.4	45.5	-0.7	45.3	-0.4	45.9	1.3	46.0	0.2	45.3	-1.5	45.1	-0.4	44.3	-1.8
1952	42.5	-4.1	42.8	0.7	43.0	0.5	40.0	-7.0	41.9	4.8	43.9	4.8	47.0	7.1	46.5	-1.1	47.4	1.9	46.1	-2.7	45.3	-1.7	43.4	-4.2
1953	41.9	-3.5	42.4	1.2	44.9	5.9	44.7	-0.4	45.1	0.9	44.6	-1.1	43.5	-2.5	43.3	-0.5	43.3	0.0	43.4	0.2	40.9	-5.8	42.3	3.4
1954	41.4	-2.1	40.4	-2.4	39.5	-2.2	38.2	-3.3	37.6	-1.6	35.9	-4.5	37.6	4.7	40.7	8.2	38.4	-5.7	37.0	-3.6	36.3	-1.9	36.5	0.6
1955	36.4	-0.3	37.4	2.7	37.4	0.0	37.5	0.3	37.5	0.0	37.6	0.3	37.3	-0.8	36.9	-1.1	36.4	-1.4	36.5	0.3	36.2	-0.8	36.3	0.3
1956	36.4	0.3	36.2	-0.5	36.2	0.0	36.3	0.3	36.2	-0.3	36.2	0.0	36.0	-0.6	35.6	-1.1	35.6	0.0	35.4	-0.6	35.5	0.3	35.5	0.0
1957	35.3	-0.6	35.5	0.6	35.3	-0.6	35.3	0.0	35.4	0.3	35.4	0.0	35.2	-0.6	35.3	0.3	35.6	0.8	35.6	0.0	35.8	0.6	35.7	-0.3
1958	35.4	-0.8	35.3	-0.3	35.8	1.4	36.0	0.6	35.9	-0.3	35.9	0.0	36.0	0.3	35.8	-0.6	35.9	0.3	36.0	0.3	36.2	0.6	35.9	-0.8
1959	35.7	-0.6	36.0	0.8	35.5	-1.4	35.4	-0.3	35.6	0.6	35.4	-0.6	35.6	0.6	35.8	0.6	35.9	0.3	35.9	0.0	36.5	1.7	37.1	1.6
1960	38.5	3.8	37.7	-2.1	37.7	0.0	38.1	1.1	37.9	-0.5	38.5	1.6	38.3	-0.5	37.7	-1.6	37.6	-0.3	37.3	-0.8	38.1	2.1	37.4	-1.8
1961	38.1	1.9	37.9	-0.5	38.3	1.1	38.0	-0.8	38.1	0.3	38.3	0.5	38.1	-0.5	37.9	-0.5	37.9	0.0	37.6	-0.8	36.9	-1.9	36.6	-0.8
1962	36.5	-0.3	36.4	-0.3	36.7	0.8	36.2	-1.4	36.0	-0.6	36.4	1.1	36.1	-0.8	36.1	0.0	36.7	1.7	37.4	1.9	36.2	-3.2	35.9	-0.8
1963	35.8	-0.3	36.2	1.1	36.2	0.0	36.2	0.0	36.4	0.6	37.1	1.9	37.3	0.5	38.1	2.1	38.1	0.0	38.8	1.8	38.5	-0.8	38.4	-0.3
1964	38.4	0.0	38.1	-0.8	38.5	1.0	39.3	2.1	38.9	-1.0	38.7	-0.5	38.9	0.5	38.9	0.0	39.1	0.5	39.0	-0.3	39.4	1.0	39.7	0.8
1965	40.9	3.0	40.9	0.0	40.2	-1.7	39.9	-0.7	40.1	0.5	40.3	0.5	40.5	0.5	41.0	1.2	40.8	-0.5	40.8	0.0	40.8	0.0	40.8	0.0
1966	40.7	-0.2	40.8	0.2	40.9	0.2	40.7	-0.5	40.4	-0.7	40.2	-0.5	40.7	1.2	40.8	0.2	40.8	0.0	41.1	0.7	41.0	-0.2	40.6	-1.0
1967	40.2	-1.0	39.8	-1.0	40.0	0.5	40.4	1.0	40.2	-0.5	40.2	0.0	40.4	0.5	40.1	-0.7	40.2	0.2	40.2	0.0	40.4	0.5	40.6	0.5
1968	40.8	0.5	40.8	0.0	40.8	0.0	40.8	0.0	40.7	-0.2	40.9	0.5	41.0	0.2	41.0	0.0	41.8	2.0	42.3	1.2	42.3	0.0	42.2	-0.2
1969	42.2	0.0	42.6	0.9	42.6	0.0	42.4	-0.5	42.4	0.0	42.4	0.0	42.7	0.7	42.8	0.2	43.3	1.2	47.0	8.5	45.5	-3.2	45.2	-0.7
1970	45.2	0.0	45.5	0.7	45.4	-0.2	44.9	-1.1	44.3	-1.3	45.3	2.3	45.8	1.1	45.9	0.2	46.3	0.9	45.9	-0.9	45.5	-0.9	45.3	-0.4
1971	45.0	-0.7	45.0	0.0	45.7	1.6	46.0	0.7	45.8	-0.4	45.8	0.0	45.8	0.0	45.8	0.0	45.5	-0.7	45.4	-0.2	45.5	0.2	45.5	0.0
1972	45.7	0.4	45.8	0.2	45.7	-0.2	45.8	0.2	46.3	1.1	46.0	-0.6	46.0	0.0	45.8	-0.4	46.8	2.2	47.0	0.4	46.7	-0.6	46.6	-0.2
1973	46.9	0.6	47.2	0.6	47.8	1.3	47.7	-0.2	47.8	0.2	48.3	1.0	49.7	2.9	51.7	4.0	51.5	-0.4	52.0	1.0	52.0	0.0	52.6	1.2
1974	54.0	2.7	56.3	4.3	59.1	5.0	60.1	1.7	61.5	2.3	63.0	2.4	64.5	2.4	66.4	2.9	68.5	3.2	69.0	0.7	71.1	3.0	72.1	1.4
1975	73.2	1.5	72.9	-0.4	72.3	-0.8	72.5	0.3	72.0	-0.7	71.4	-0.8	70.8	-0.8	71.6	1.1	71.8	0.3	71.3	-0.7	70.9	-0.6	70.4	-0.7
1976	69.5	-1.3	68.8	-1.0	68.8	0.0	69.8	1.5	69.9	0.1	69.5	-0.6	69.6	0.1	69.9	0.4	70.6	1.0	71.5	1.3	71.7	0.3	73.5	2.5
1977	73.3	-0.3	74.0	1.0	74.0	0.0	74.3	0.4	77.4	4.2	77.6	0.3	78.2	0.8	78.2	0.0	78.1	-0.1	78.0	-0.1	77.2	-1.0	77.2	0.0
1978	77.8	0.8	78.1	0.4	78.8	0.9	80.2	1.8	80.6	0.5	80.4	-0.2	81.5	1.4	79.2	-2.8	79.4	0.3	80.6	1.5	82.0	1.7	82.1	0.1
1979	83.1	1.2	83.7	0.7	87.5	4.5	88.2	0.8	88.6	0.5	84.9	-4.2	85.6	0.8	87.6	2.3	88.1	0.6	88.8	0.8	89.4	0.7	89.7	0.3
1980	90.7	1.1	89.9	-0.9	90.4	0.6	90.6	0.2	90.0	-0.7	89.9	-0.1	89.9	0.0	90.1	0.2	91.2	1.2	92.8	1.8	94.6	1.9	96.7	2.2
1981	98.2	1.6	99.8	1.6	100.2	0.4	100.6	0.4	101.0	0.4	101.2	0.2	101.5	0.3	101.4	-0.1	101.8	0.4	100.5	-1.3	100.6	0.1	100.6	0.0
1982	101.0	0.4	100.9	-0.1	100.4	-0.5	100.4	0.0	99.8	-0.6	100.0	0.2	99.8	-0.2	98.9	-0.9	99.4	0.5	99.7	0.3	99.7	0.0	100.0	0.3
1983	100.1	0.1	100.3	0.2	100.0	-0.3	100.5	0.5	100.5	0.0	101.2	0.7	102.6	1.4	101.7	-0.9	104.0	2.3	105.4	1.3	106.5	1.0	107.1	0.6
1984	107.3	0.2	110.8	3.3	110.7	-0.1	111.2	0.5	111.1	-0.1	112.6	1.4	113.2	0.5	112.8	-0.4	113.1	0.3	113.1	0.0	113.0	-0.1	113.0	0.0
1985	113.2	0.2	113.2	0.0	113.2	0.0	113.5	0.3	114.1	0.5	114.1	0.0	114.5	0.4	115.1	0.5	114.5	-0.5	114.5	0.0	114.6	0.1	114.6	0.0
1986	115.4	0.7	115.1	-0.3	115.2	0.1	115.1	-0.1	115.4	0.3	115.7	0.3	116.1	0.3	116.4	0.3	116.6	0.2	117.4	0.7	117.7	0.3	118.3	0.5
1987	118.9	0.5	119.5	0.5	119.8	0.3	120.0	0.2	120.0	0.0	119.5	-0.4	119.5	0.0	119.7	0.2	119.6	-0.1	119.9	0.3	120.3	0.3	120.5	0.2
1988	119.9	-0.5	120.5	0.5	120.7	0.2	121.4	0.6	121.5	0.1	121.3	-0.2	122.7	1.2	123.4	0.6	123.8	0.3	124.3	0.4	125.1	0.6	125.3	0.2
1989	126.2	0.7	127.5	1.0	128.1	0.5	128.6	0.4	129.3	0.5	129.3	0.0	129.4	0.1	130.0	0.5	130.3	0.2	130.6	0.2	131.1	0.4	131.8	0.5
1990	131.6	-0.2	132.2	0.5	132.9	0.5	133.1	0.2	133.8	0.5	133.7	-0.1	134.1	0.3	134.8	0.5	135.0	0.1	134.8	-0.1	136.7	1.4	137.4	0.5
1991	137.6	0.1	137.9	0.2	137.8	-0.1	138.2	0.3	137.3	-0.7	137.8	0.4	137.9	0.1	139.0	0.8	138.8	-0.1	139.2	0.3	138.9	-0.2	138.8	-0.1

[Continued]

Miscellaneous Processed Foods
Producer Price Index
Base 1982 = 100
[Continued]

For 1947-1997. Columns headed % show percentile change in the index from the previous period for which an index is available.

Year	Jan Index	%	Feb Index	%	Mar Index	%	Apr Index	%	May Index	%	Jun Index	%	Jul Index	%	Aug Index	%	Sep Index	%	Oct Index	%	Nov Index	%	Dec Index	%
1992	139.1	0.2	139.1	0.0	138.8	-0.2	138.7	-0.1	138.7	0.0	138.4	-0.2	138.9	0.4	139.4	0.4	139.5	0.1	139.4	-0.1	140.2	0.6	140.2	0.0
1993	140.7	0.4	141.2	0.4	141.8	0.4	141.9	0.1	142.1	0.1	142.2	0.1	142.5	0.2	143.1	0.4	142.8	-0.2	143.1	0.2	143.3	0.1	143.4	0.1
1994	143.5	0.1	144.2	0.5	144.1	-0.1	144.1	0.0	144.0	-0.1	144.1	0.1	144.2	0.1	144.3	0.1	144.3	0.0	144.7	0.3	145.0	0.2	145.3	0.2
1995	145.6	0.2	145.0	-0.4	145.2	0.1	145.4	0.1	145.3	-0.1	145.3	0.0	146.2	0.6	146.6	0.3	146.8	0.1	147.4	0.4	147.6	0.1	147.8	0.1
1996	148.1	0.2	148.6	0.3	148.7	0.1	148.8	0.1	149.3	0.3	149.6	0.2	150.2	0.4	150.6	0.3	151.1	0.3	151.0	-0.1	151.5	0.3	151.9	0.3
1997	152.3	0.3	152.3	0.0	152.4	0.1	152.7	0.2	152.6	-0.1	152.7	0.1	153.3	0.4	153.4	0.1	153.3	-0.1	153.4	0.1	153.4	0.0	153.6	0.1

Source: U.S. Department of Labor, Bureau of Labor Statistics, Division of Industry Prices and Price Indexes. n.e.c. stands for not elsewhere classified. - indicates no data collected for period or unavailable.

Prepared Animal Feeds
Producer Price Index
Base 1982 = 100

For 1947-1997. Columns headed % show percentile change in the index from the previous period for which an index is available.

Year	Jan Index	%	Feb Index	%	Mar Index	%	Apr Index	%	May Index	%	Jun Index	%	Jul Index	%	Aug Index	%	Sep Index	%	Oct Index	%	Nov Index	%	Dec Index	%
1947	45.3	-	42.0	-7.3	50.8	21.0	47.5	-6.5	48.7	2.5	52.8	8.4	57.3	8.5	58.4	1.9	65.4	12.0	63.8	-2.4	63.3	-0.8	67.9	7.3
1948	74.2	9.3	61.1	-17.7	60.2	-1.5	60.9	1.2	58.7	-3.6	60.3	2.7	55.4	-8.1	47.7	-13.9	48.5	1.7	44.9	-7.4	50.0	11.4	50.5	1.0
1949	49.5	-2.0	45.2	-8.7	47.4	4.9	50.5	6.5	48.7	-3.6	48.8	0.2	52.6	7.8	56.0	6.5	49.8	-11.1	47.5	-4.6	45.7	-3.8	46.5	1.8
1950	44.7	-3.9	43.8	-2.0	47.2	7.8	49.4	4.7	53.7	8.7	50.1	-6.7	56.7	13.2	49.2	-13.2	47.7	-3.0	45.5	-4.6	47.9	5.3	50.2	4.8
1951	51.4	2.4	52.7	2.5	52.9	0.4	54.4	2.8	51.7	-5.0	51.4	-0.6	52.4	1.9	51.2	-2.3	53.8	5.1	55.8	3.7	57.9	3.8	58.8	1.6
1952	60.2	2.4	60.7	0.8	58.5	-3.6	58.9	0.7	57.9	-1.7	57.7	-0.3	54.9	-4.9	58.5	6.6	57.9	-1.0	57.9	0.0	55.2	-4.7	54.6	-1.1
1953	52.3	-4.2	50.5	-3.4	50.8	0.6	47.4	-6.7	48.7	2.7	44.7	-8.2	44.2	-1.1	45.4	2.7	43.6	-4.0	43.3	-0.7	42.1	-2.8	49.3	17.1
1954	50.2	1.8	52.0	3.6	54.0	3.8	59.4	10.0	58.3	-1.9	53.8	-7.7	52.5	-2.4	50.9	-3.0	47.6	-6.5	45.1	-5.3	45.4	0.7	46.4	2.2
1955	45.3	-2.4	45.9	1.3	44.3	-3.5	42.8	-3.4	40.1	-6.3	37.8	-5.7	39.5	4.5	38.3	-3.0	38.8	1.3	39.9	2.8	36.3	-9.0	36.8	1.4
1956	37.3	1.4	36.4	-2.4	35.9	-1.4	39.8	10.9	43.7	9.8	40.6	-7.1	38.9	-4.2	38.5	-1.0	37.2	-3.4	36.4	-2.2	38.4	5.5	38.8	1.0
1957	39.8	2.6	38.9	-2.3	38.5	-1.0	38.0	-1.3	35.9	-5.5	33.9	-5.6	35.3	4.1	36.4	3.1	35.5	-2.5	33.7	-5.1	32.8	-2.7	33.2	1.2
1958	34.2	3.0	35.1	2.6	39.9	13.7	43.2	8.3	41.7	-3.5	39.2	-6.0	42.6	8.7	41.0	-3.8	38.2	-6.8	36.9	-3.4	38.8	5.1	46.2	19.1
1959	46.1	-0.2	43.9	-4.8	42.5	-3.2	44.3	4.2	40.9	-7.7	36.9	-9.8	38.6	4.6	37.8	-2.1	34.5	-8.7	37.6	9.0	39.4	4.8	39.6	0.5
1960	40.4	2.0	38.6	-4.5	39.1	1.3	40.4	3.3	36.3	-10.1	36.1	-0.6	36.0	-0.3	35.1	-2.5	36.2	3.1	35.4	-2.2	35.7	0.8	37.4	4.8
1961	39.9	6.7	39.6	-0.8	40.7	2.8	41.4	1.7	42.9	3.6	40.1	-6.5	39.9	-0.5	39.7	-0.5	39.7	0.0	38.0	-4.3	41.0	7.9	42.0	2.4
1962	42.4	1.0	41.6	-1.9	41.6	0.0	41.8	0.5	41.8	0.0	41.4	-1.0	42.9	3.6	42.6	-0.7	43.9	3.1	43.6	-0.7	44.4	1.8	44.7	0.7
1963	45.7	2.2	45.7	0.0	45.2	-1.1	43.2	-4.4	43.0	-0.5	43.3	0.7	44.9	3.7	45.5	1.3	46.0	1.1	45.5	-1.1	45.3	-0.4	46.2	2.0
1964	46.5	0.6	45.3	-2.6	44.5	-1.8	44.3	-0.4	42.7	-3.6	42.4	-0.7	42.8	0.9	42.6	-0.5	43.9	3.1	44.5	1.4	43.4	-2.5	45.0	3.7
1965	44.5	-1.1	44.2	-0.7	44.1	-0.2	44.6	1.1	43.6	-2.2	45.1	3.4	45.9	1.8	45.2	-1.5	45.1	-0.2	44.9	-0.4	46.3	3.1	45.8	-1.1
1966	47.0	2.6	48.2	2.6	46.2	-4.1	46.1	-0.2	47.6	3.3	47.9	0.6	51.2	6.9	51.6	0.8	51.1	-1.0	49.5	-3.1	49.6	0.2	51.0	2.8
1967	51.0	0.0	48.7	-4.5	48.2	-1.0	47.5	-1.5	45.9	-3.4	47.3	3.1	47.6	0.6	46.2	-2.9	47.0	1.7	46.6	-0.9	45.9	-1.5	46.2	0.7
1968	46.5	0.6	46.2	-0.6	46.0	-0.4	45.3	-1.5	45.5	0.4	46.2	1.5	46.2	0.0	45.8	-0.9	45.4	-0.9	45.4	0.0	45.3	-0.2	45.7	0.9
1969	45.7	0.0	45.4	-0.7	44.7	-1.5	45.8	2.5	44.4	-3.1	45.2	1.8	45.9	1.5	45.7	-0.4	46.1	0.9	46.4	0.7	46.2	-0.4	47.1	1.9
1970	51.0	8.3	50.9	-0.2	46.1	-9.4	46.9	1.7	46.3	-1.3	46.9	1.3	49.3	5.1	49.5	0.4	50.7	2.4	49.4	-2.6	50.0	1.2	51.7	3.4
1971	51.1	-1.2	49.7	-2.7	50.8	2.2	49.4	-2.8	49.5	0.2	50.9	2.8	50.6	-0.6	49.6	-2.0	48.0	-3.2	46.7	-2.7	47.5	1.7	49.5	4.2
1972	49.1	-0.8	49.1	0.0	51.4	4.7	51.3	-0.2	51.3	0.0	51.0	-0.6	52.5	2.9	52.9	0.8	55.8	5.5	55.1	-1.3	61.7	12.0	77.4	25.4
1973	78.7	1.7	86.4	9.8	86.3	-0.1	78.9	-8.6	100.0	26.7	122.0	22.0	93.3	-23.5	123.9	32.8	90.0	-27.4	87.3	-3.0	86.8	-0.6	95.1	9.6
1974	96.2	1.2	90.3	-6.1	85.7	-5.1	78.7	-8.2	73.4	-6.7	72.2	-1.6	73.9	2.4	102.8	39.1	87.4	-15.0	100.0	14.4	92.6	-7.4	92.1	-0.5
1975	87.8	-4.7	79.3	-9.7	75.4	-4.9	81.1	7.6	78.0	-3.8	80.0	2.6	80.2	0.2	84.0	4.7	83.9	-0.1	84.0	0.1	81.3	-3.2	82.6	1.6
1976	83.6	1.2	82.9	-0.8	82.9	0.0	82.2	-0.8	85.8	4.4	100.8	17.5	102.3	1.5	93.2	-8.9	100.1	7.4	94.6	-5.5	94.7	0.1	100.9	6.5
1977	103.6	2.7	103.6	0.0	105.0	1.4	115.0	9.5	113.3	-1.5	106.7	-5.8	89.1	-16.5	83.2	-6.6	82.7	-0.6	79.7	-3.6	91.7	15.1	88.6	-3.4
1978	92.0	3.8	88.4	-3.9	94.9	7.4	93.5	-1.5	91.7	-1.9	93.6	2.1	92.9	-0.7	89.9	-3.2	91.7	2.0	95.2	3.8	97.2	2.1	100.3	3.2
1979	100.0	-0.3	102.8	2.8	102.1	-0.7	102.0	-0.1	99.8	-2.2	104.3	4.5	111.2	6.6	102.3	-8.0	103.8	1.5	106.0	2.1	105.3	-0.7	106.5	1.1
1980	104.0	-2.3	104.0	0.0	102.5	-1.4	97.0	-5.4	98.0	1.0	97.0	-1.0	106.0	9.3	110.0	3.8	115.2	4.7	116.8	1.4	120.5	3.2	116.9	-3.0
1981	117.8	0.8	111.6	-5.3	109.4	-2.0	112.5	2.8	114.1	1.4	110.9	-2.8	109.9	-0.9	108.4	-1.4	105.5	-2.7	103.2	-2.2	101.6	-1.6	102.8	1.2
1982	102.9	0.1	101.7	-1.2	100.0	-1.7	102.4	2.4	102.9	0.5	102.4	-0.5	101.3	-1.1	98.2	-3.1	96.7	-1.5	94.6	-2.2	97.5	3.1	99.4	1.9
1983	100.2	0.8	100.5	0.3	100.5	0.0	105.5	5.0	104.8	-0.7	102.8	-1.9	104.1	1.3	110.3	6.0	118.0	7.0	117.7	-0.3	119.3	1.4	116.2	-2.6
1984	116.1	-0.1	109.4	-5.8	111.4	1.8	111.8	0.4	109.9	-1.7	106.7	-2.9	102.5	-3.9	101.3	-1.2	99.0	-2.3	95.8	-3.2	94.5	-1.4	94.1	-0.4
1985	93.7	-0.4	91.6	-2.2	89.7	-2.1	88.1	-1.8	86.3	-2.0	87.0	0.8	88.0	1.1	88.4	0.5	89.1	0.8	91.0	2.1	93.2	2.4	94.5	1.4
1986	95.6	1.2	94.1	-1.6	95.0	1.0	95.5	0.5	95.2	-0.3	95.5	0.3	94.4	-1.2	93.5	-1.0	95.7	2.4	92.5	-3.3	93.9	1.5	94.5	0.6
1987	93.8	-0.7	94.1	0.3	92.4	-1.8	93.8	1.5	98.4	4.9	99.9	1.5	99.4	-0.5	98.4	-1.0	99.9	1.5	100.3	0.4	104.8	4.5	107.3	2.4
1988	105.8	-1.4	102.9	-2.7	104.0	1.1	106.0	1.9	107.1	1.0	120.2	12.2	127.3	5.9	123.6	-2.9	125.4	1.5	125.5	0.1	123.3	-1.8	120.9	-1.9
1989	124.3	2.8	121.1	-2.6	122.0	0.7	119.0	-2.5	117.8	-1.0	114.9	-2.5	117.6	2.3	114.2	-2.9	115.3	1.0	112.3	-2.6	110.9	-1.2	110.3	-0.5
1990	110.7	0.4	106.1	-4.2	105.9	-0.2	106.2	0.3	109.1	2.7	107.4	-1.6	109.3	1.8	107.4	-1.7	107.7	0.3	108.0	0.3	105.6	-2.2	105.9	0.3
1991	104.5	-1.3	105.1	0.6	106.3	1.1	105.9	-0.4	105.8	-0.1	106.0	0.2	104.1	-1.8	107.9	3.7	109.0	1.0	108.7	-0.3	109.4	0.6	109.0	-0.4

[Continued]

Prepared Animal Feeds
Producer Price Index
Base 1982 = 100
[Continued]

For 1947-1997. Columns headed % show percentile change in the index from the previous period for which an index is available.

Year	Jan Index	%	Feb Index	%	Mar Index	%	Apr Index	%	May Index	%	Jun Index	%	Jul Index	%	Aug Index	%	Sep Index	%	Oct Index	%	Nov Index	%	Dec Index	%
1992	108.7	-0.3	108.9	0.2	109.3	0.4	107.9	-1.3	108.7	0.7	109.3	0.6	107.7	-1.5	106.9	-0.7	107.9	0.9	107.3	-0.6	107.3	0.0	109.6	2.1
1993	110.0	0.4	107.9	-1.9	107.0	-0.8	108.2	1.1	108.5	0.3	107.9	-0.6	113.2	4.9	114.9	1.5	112.6	-2.0	111.7	-0.8	113.3	1.4	116.2	2.6
1994	115.9	-0.3	116.6	0.6	116.0	-0.5	113.8	-1.9	113.2	-0.5	114.3	1.0	112.1	-1.9	109.4	-2.4	109.0	-0.4	107.1	-1.7	104.7	-2.2	103.9	-0.8
1995	104.1	0.2	102.8	-1.2	103.9	1.1	105.2	1.3	103.7	-1.4	104.7	1.0	105.7	1.0	108.4	2.6	110.3	1.8	114.7	4.0	120.6	5.1	125.3	3.9
1996	129.1	3.0	129.4	0.2	131.4	1.5	134.8	2.6	138.6	2.8	138.1	-0.4	139.8	1.2	140.2	0.3	142.8	1.9	135.3	-5.3	131.7	-2.7	132.1	0.3
1997	131.2	-0.7	131.7	0.4	136.1	3.3	137.5	1.0	139.7	1.6	136.6	-2.2	132.6	-2.9	131.7	-0.7	135.0	2.5	126.8	-6.1	128.0	0.9	127.7	-0.2

Source: U.S. Department of Labor, Bureau of Labor Statistics, Division of Industry Prices and Price Indexes. n.e.c. stands for not elsewhere classified. - indicates no data collected for period or unavailable.

TEXTILE PRODUCTS AND APPAREL
Producer Price Index
Base 1982 = 100

For 1947-1997. Columns headed % show percentile change in the index from the previous period for which an index is available.

Year	Jan Index	%	Feb Index	%	Mar Index	%	Apr Index	%	May Index	%	Jun Index	%	Jul Index	%	Aug Index	%	Sep Index	%	Oct Index	%	Nov Index	%	Dec Index	%
1947	49.8	-	50.1	0.6	50.3	0.4	50.3	0.0	50.2	-0.2	50.0	-0.4	50.2	0.4	50.4	0.4	51.0	1.2	51.2	0.4	51.7	1.0	52.6	1.7
1948	53.2	1.1	53.5	0.6	53.4	-0.2	52.9	-0.9	53.1	0.4	52.8	-0.6	52.9	0.2	52.9	0.0	52.8	-0.2	52.6	-0.4	52.2	-0.8	52.1	-0.2
1949	51.0	-2.1	50.5	-1.0	49.8	-1.4	48.9	-1.8	47.8	-2.2	47.5	-0.6	47.3	-0.4	47.3	0.0	47.4	0.2	47.6	0.4	47.7	0.2	47.7	0.0
1950	47.7	0.0	47.8	0.2	47.7	-0.2	47.1	-1.3	47.0	-0.2	47.3	0.6	48.7	3.0	50.8	4.3	52.8	3.9	54.4	3.0	55.2	1.5	56.4	2.2
1951	58.0	2.8	58.6	1.0	58.7	0.2	58.5	-0.3	58.1	-0.7	57.2	-1.5	56.5	-1.2	54.9	-2.8	53.6	-2.4	52.6	-1.9	52.6	0.0	52.6	0.0
1952	52.3	-0.6	51.7	-1.1	50.9	-1.5	50.6	-0.6	50.3	-0.6	50.1	-0.4	50.1	0.0	50.2	0.2	50.4	0.4	50.2	-0.4	50.0	-0.4	49.8	-0.4
1953	50.1	0.6	49.9	-0.4	49.4	-1.0	49.3	-0.2	49.4	0.2	49.3	-0.2	49.4	0.2	49.4	0.0	49.1	-0.6	48.9	-0.4	48.7	-0.4	48.5	-0.4
1954	48.6	0.2	48.2	-0.8	48.1	-0.2	48.0	-0.2	48.0	0.0	48.1	0.2	48.2	0.2	48.2	0.0	48.2	0.0	48.3	0.2	48.2	-0.2	48.2	0.0
1955	48.2	0.0	48.2	0.0	48.2	0.0	48.1	-0.2	48.1	0.0	48.2	0.2	48.2	0.0	48.2	0.0	48.3	0.2	48.3	0.0	48.4	0.2	48.4	0.0
1956	48.4	0.0	48.6	0.4	48.5	-0.2	48.2	-0.6	48.1	-0.2	48.1	0.0	48.1	0.0	48.0	-0.2	48.0	0.0	48.2	0.4	48.3	0.2	48.4	0.2
1957	48.5	0.2	48.4	-0.2	48.3	-0.2	48.2	-0.2	48.3	0.2	48.3	0.0	48.3	0.0	48.3	0.0	48.3	0.0	48.2	-0.2	48.1	-0.2	48.1	0.0
1958	47.9	-0.4	47.7	-0.4	47.6	-0.2	47.5	-0.2	47.4	-0.2	47.3	-0.2	47.3	0.0	47.3	0.0	47.3	0.0	47.2	-0.2	47.2	0.0	47.3	0.2
1959	47.3	0.0	47.5	0.4	47.6	0.2	47.7	0.2	47.8	0.2	48.1	0.6	48.2	0.2	48.4	0.4	48.5	0.2	48.5	0.0	48.7	0.4	49.0	0.6
1960	48.9	-0.2	48.9	0.0	48.7	-0.4	48.7	0.0	48.7	0.0	48.7	0.0	48.7	0.0	48.6	-0.2	48.5	-0.2	48.5	0.0	48.3	-0.4	48.2	-0.2
1961	48.0	-0.4	48.0	0.0	47.8	-0.4	47.7	-0.2	47.6	-0.2	47.5	-0.2	47.6	0.2	47.7	0.2	47.8	0.2	48.0	0.4	48.0	0.0	48.1	0.2
1962	48.1	0.0	48.1	0.0	48.2	0.2	48.2	0.0	48.2	0.0	48.3	0.2	48.3	0.0	48.3	0.0	48.2	-0.2	48.2	0.0	48.2	0.0	48.2	0.0
1963	48.1	-0.2	48.1	0.0	48.0	-0.2	48.0	0.0	48.0	0.0	48.1	0.2	48.1	0.0	48.1	0.0	48.2	0.2	48.2	0.0	48.4	0.4	48.5	0.2
1964	48.5	0.0	48.5	0.0	48.5	0.0	48.4	-0.2	48.5	0.2	48.4	-0.2	48.4	0.0	48.5	0.2	48.5	0.0	48.6	0.2	48.6	0.0	48.6	0.0
1965	48.6	0.0	48.6	0.0	48.6	0.0	48.6	0.0	48.7	0.2	48.8	0.2	48.8	0.0	48.8	0.0	48.9	0.2	48.9	0.0	48.8	-0.2	48.9	0.2
1966	48.8	-0.2	48.9	0.2	48.9	0.0	49.0	0.2	49.0	0.0	49.0	0.0	49.1	0.2	49.1	0.0	49.0	-0.2	49.0	0.0	48.9	-0.2	48.8	-0.2
1967	48.9	0.2	48.9	0.0	48.8	-0.2	48.7	-0.2	48.6	-0.2	48.6	0.0	48.6	0.0	48.6	0.0	48.8	0.4	48.9	0.2	49.3	0.8	49.7	0.8
1968	50.0	0.6	50.1	0.2	50.2	0.2	50.2	0.0	50.3	0.2	50.5	0.4	50.7	0.4	50.9	0.4	51.1	0.4	51.3	0.4	51.5	0.4	51.4	-0.2
1969	51.6	0.4	51.5	-0.2	51.4	-0.2	51.4	0.0	51.4	0.0	51.7	0.6	51.9	0.4	52.1	0.4	52.1	0.0	52.2	0.2	52.3	0.2	52.2	-0.2
1970	52.4	0.4	52.3	-0.2	52.4	0.2	52.4	0.0	52.3	-0.2	52.4	0.2	52.4	0.0	52.4	0.0	52.4	0.0	52.3	-0.2	52.2	-0.2	52.2	0.0
1971	52.2	0.0	52.3	0.2	52.4	0.2	52.7	0.6	52.8	0.2	53.4	1.1	53.6	0.4	53.9	0.6	53.8	-0.2	53.8	0.0	53.9	0.2	54.3	0.7
1972	54.4	0.2	54.7	0.6	54.8	0.2	55.0	0.4	55.4	0.7	55.5	0.2	55.7	0.4	55.8	0.2	55.9	0.2	56.1	0.4	56.3	0.4	56.5	0.4
1973	57.0	0.9	57.4	0.7	58.2	1.4	59.0	1.4	59.8	1.4	60.5	1.2	60.7	0.3	61.2	0.8	62.0	1.3	62.8	1.3	63.5	1.1	64.2	1.1
1974	65.4	1.9	66.1	1.1	66.5	0.6	67.2	1.1	68.0	1.2	69.3	1.9	69.5	0.3	69.6	0.1	69.5	-0.1	68.7	-1.2	68.3	-0.6	67.7	-0.9
1975	67.2	-0.7	66.7	-0.7	65.7	-1.5	65.7	0.0	66.1	0.6	66.4	0.5	66.9	0.8	67.3	0.6	67.6	0.4	69.1	2.2	70.0	1.3	70.4	0.6
1976	71.2	1.1	71.5	0.4	71.7	0.3	72.0	0.4	72.0	0.0	72.5	0.7	72.8	0.4	73.1	0.4	72.8	-0.4	73.0	0.3	73.4	0.5	73.3	-0.1
1977	73.7	0.5	74.2	0.7	74.5	0.4	75.1	0.8	75.3	0.3	75.6	0.4	75.5	-0.1	75.6	0.1	75.8	0.3	75.9	0.1	75.9	0.0	76.2	0.4
1978	76.5	0.4	76.8	0.4	76.9	0.1	77.2	0.4	77.5	0.4	77.8	0.4	78.2	0.5	78.5	0.4	78.9	0.5	79.3	0.5	79.8	0.6	80.0	0.3
1979	80.2	0.2	80.3	0.1	80.8	0.6	81.4	0.7	81.7	0.4	82.3	0.7	82.8	0.6	83.4	0.7	83.7	0.4	84.1	0.5	84.5	0.5	84.6	0.1
1980	85.7	1.3	86.3	0.7	87.6	1.5	88.6	1.1	89.0	0.5	89.4	0.4	90.3	1.0	90.7	0.4	91.2	0.6	92.0	0.9	92.7	0.8	93.1	0.4
1981	94.4	1.4	94.8	0.4	95.4	0.6	96.6	1.3	97.4	0.8	97.8	0.4	98.4	0.6	98.9	0.5	99.2	0.3	99.7	0.5	99.5	-0.2	99.4	-0.1
1982	100.2	0.8	100.5	0.3	100.2	-0.3	100.4	0.2	100.4	0.0	100.2	-0.2	99.8	-0.4	99.8	0.0	99.9	0.1	99.8	-0.1	99.7	-0.1	99.0	-0.7
1983	99.1	0.1	99.0	-0.1	99.4	0.4	99.5	0.1	99.9	0.4	100.1	0.2	100.4	0.3	100.7	0.3	100.8	0.1	101.2	0.4	101.5	0.3	101.6	0.1
1984	101.8	0.2	102.5	0.7	102.6	0.1	102.6	0.0	102.9	0.3	102.8	-0.1	102.9	0.1	102.7	-0.2	103.0	0.3	102.9	-0.1	102.7	-0.2	102.6	-0.1
1985	102.8	0.2	103.0	0.2	102.9	-0.1	103.0	0.1	102.9	-0.1	102.8	-0.1	102.7	-0.1	102.9	0.2	102.8	-0.1	102.7	-0.1	102.9	0.2	103.0	0.1
1986	103.0	0.0	103.1	0.1	103.3	0.2	103.2	-0.1	103.2	0.0	103.2	0.0	103.3	0.1	103.2	-0.1	103.2	0.0	103.2	0.0	103.3	0.1	103.4	0.1
1987	103.6	0.2	103.7	0.1	103.9	0.2	104.2	0.3	104.4	0.2	104.8	0.4	105.3	0.5	105.6	0.3	106.0	0.4	106.4	0.4	106.6	0.2	107.0	0.4
1988	107.6	0.6	108.1	0.5	108.4	0.3	108.7	0.3	108.9	0.2	109.3	0.4	109.5	0.2	109.6	0.1	109.8	0.2	110.0	0.2	110.2	0.2	110.5	0.3
1989	111.0	0.5	111.3	0.3	111.2	-0.1	111.6	0.4	111.8	0.2	112.2	0.4	112.6	0.4	112.9	0.3	113.0	0.1	113.3	0.3	113.5	0.2	113.6	0.1
1990	114.6	0.9	114.6	0.0	114.7	0.1	114.9	0.2	114.8	-0.1	115.0	0.2	115.1	0.1	115.1	0.0	115.1	0.0	115.1	0.0	115.3	0.2	115.2	-0.1
1991	115.7	0.4	115.8	0.1	115.9	0.1	116.0	0.1	116.0	0.0	116.2	0.2	116.3	0.1	116.5	0.2	116.6	0.1	116.7	0.1	116.8	0.1	116.9	0.1

[Continued]

TEXTILE PRODUCTS AND APPAREL
Producer Price Index
Base 1982 = 100
[Continued]

For 1947-1997. Columns headed % show percentile change in the index from the previous period for which an index is available.

Year	Jan		Feb		Mar		Apr		May		Jun		Jul		Aug		Sep		Oct		Nov		Dec	
	Index	%	Index	%	Index	%	Index	%	Index	%	Index	%	Index	%	Index	%	Index	%	Index	%	Index	%	Index	%
1992	117.4	0.4	117.6	0.2	117.7	0.1	117.8	0.1	117.7	-0.1	117.9	0.2	117.8	-0.1	117.8	0.0	118.0	0.2	118.1	0.1	118.0	-0.1	118.0	0.0
1993	118.0	0.0	117.9	-0.1	117.9	0.0	118.1	0.2	118.0	-0.1	118.0	0.0	118.2	0.2	118.3	0.1	118.1	-0.2	118.1	0.0	118.0	-0.1	117.9	-0.1
1994	117.9	0.0	117.9	0.0	117.9	0.0	117.9	0.0	118.0	0.1	118.1	0.1	118.4	0.3	118.5	0.1	118.7	0.2	118.6	-0.1	118.6	0.0	118.8	0.2
1995	119.4	0.5	119.9	0.4	120.1	0.2	120.4	0.2	120.8	0.3	120.8	0.0	121.0	0.2	121.1	0.1	121.5	0.3	121.6	0.1	121.3	-0.2	121.3	0.0
1996	121.8	0.4	121.9	0.1	122.0	0.1	122.0	0.0	122.3	0.2	122.3	0.0	122.6	0.2	122.5	-0.1	123.0	0.4	122.9	-0.1	122.7	-0.2	122.7	0.0
1997	122.6	-0.1	122.5	-0.1	122.6	0.1	122.5	-0.1	122.6	0.1	122.6	0.0	122.6	0.0	122.6	0.0	122.7	0.1	122.5	-0.2	122.5	0.0	122.5	0.0

Source: U.S. Department of Labor, Bureau of Labor Statistics, Division of Industry Prices and Price Indexes. n.e.c. stands for not elsewhere classified. - indicates no data collected for period or unavailable.

Synthetic Fibers
Producer Price Index
Base 1982 = 100

For 1975-1997. Columns headed % show percentile change in the index from the previous period for which an index is available.

Year	Jan Index	%	Feb Index	%	Mar Index	%	Apr Index	%	May Index	%	Jun Index	%	Jul Index	%	Aug Index	%	Sep Index	%	Oct Index	%	Nov Index	%	Dec Index	%
1975	-	-	-	-	-	-	-	-	-	-	-	-	-	-	-	-	-	-	-	-	-	-	61.7	-
1976	62.8	1.8	63.1	0.5	63.0	-0.2	63.5	0.8	63.4	-0.2	63.2	-0.3	63.3	0.2	63.7	0.6	63.6	-0.2	62.8	-1.3	62.7	-0.2	62.7	0.0
1977	63.2	0.8	63.8	0.9	63.7	-0.2	65.7	3.1	66.1	0.6	67.4	2.0	67.2	-0.3	67.4	0.3	67.5	0.1	67.4	-0.1	67.4	0.0	67.4	0.0
1978	67.9	0.7	67.8	-0.1	67.8	0.0	67.4	-0.6	67.6	0.3	67.2	-0.6	67.2	0.0	67.3	0.1	67.3	0.0	67.5	0.3	68.2	1.0	68.2	0.0
1979	69.7	2.2	70.0	0.4	70.1	0.1	71.0	1.3	72.4	2.0	73.1	1.0	73.8	1.0	74.4	0.8	76.2	2.4	76.9	0.9	76.6	-0.4	76.9	0.4
1980	78.4	2.0	78.5	0.1	79.6	1.4	80.5	1.1	82.2	2.1	83.0	1.0	83.9	1.1	84.8	1.1	86.1	1.5	86.5	0.5	86.8	0.3	86.9	0.1
1981	90.4	4.0	90.7	0.3	91.9	1.3	93.5	1.7	96.5	3.2	97.4	0.9	98.5	1.1	99.5	1.0	99.3	-0.2	100.4	1.1	99.7	-0.7	99.6	-0.1
1982	100.5	0.9	100.7	0.2	99.5	-1.2	100.6	1.1	100.8	0.2	100.5	-0.3	99.6	-0.9	100.1	0.5	100.3	0.2	99.4	-0.9	99.5	0.1	98.5	-1.0
1983	96.7	-1.8	94.5	-2.3	95.0	0.5	94.9	-0.1	96.0	1.2	96.2	0.2	97.7	1.6	97.2	-0.5	97.5	0.3	99.1	1.6	98.3	-0.8	97.5	-0.8
1984	98.3	0.8	99.6	1.3	99.2	-0.4	99.1	-0.1	99.1	0.0	99.0	-0.1	98.8	-0.2	98.7	-0.1	98.2	-0.5	97.6	-0.6	97.2	-0.4	97.3	0.1
1985	97.2	-0.1	97.2	0.0	96.6	-0.6	97.1	0.5	96.9	-0.2	96.5	-0.4	95.4	-1.1	95.5	0.1	95.6	0.1	92.4	-3.3	92.8	0.4	93.0	0.2
1986	93.6	0.6	93.5	-0.1	93.5	0.0	92.4	-1.2	92.3	-0.1	92.1	-0.2	92.5	0.4	92.3	-0.2	92.2	-0.1	91.7	-0.5	91.7	0.0	91.6	-0.1
1987	92.1	0.5	91.4	-0.8	91.3	-0.1	90.8	-0.5	90.8	0.0	91.0	0.2	91.4	0.4	91.7	0.3	91.9	0.2	92.8	1.0	93.3	0.5	93.6	0.3
1988	94.4	0.9	94.7	0.3	95.1	0.4	96.3	1.3	97.0	0.7	96.6	-0.4	97.6	1.0	98.0	0.4	98.6	0.6	99.4	0.8	99.4	0.0	99.9	0.5
1989	100.6	0.7	101.1	0.5	101.6	0.5	104.1	2.5	105.0	0.9	106.2	1.1	106.5	0.3	106.2	-0.3	105.9	-0.3	107.1	1.1	106.7	-0.4	106.9	0.2
1990	106.9	0.0	107.3	0.4	107.4	0.1	106.6	-0.7	106.7	0.1	106.4	-0.3	107.5	1.0	107.1	-0.4	107.2	0.1	105.4	-1.7	105.8	0.4	106.0	0.2
1991	106.8	0.8	106.9	0.1	106.6	-0.3	105.5	-1.0	105.3	-0.2	105.3	0.0	105.1	-0.2	105.0	-0.1	105.0	0.0	104.2	-0.8	104.0	-0.2	103.5	-0.5
1992	103.1	-0.4	103.6	0.5	103.5	-0.1	104.2	0.7	103.4	-0.8	103.9	0.5	103.9	0.0	103.6	-0.3	103.2	-0.4	103.3	0.1	102.4	-0.9	102.5	0.1
1993	102.6	0.1	102.3	-0.3	102.4	0.1	102.8	0.4	102.9	0.1	103.5	0.6	103.8	0.3	105.1	1.3	104.5	-0.6	104.4	-0.1	104.2	-0.2	104.2	0.0
1994	103.8	-0.4	103.5	-0.3	103.1	-0.4	103.0	-0.1	103.2	0.2	103.4	0.2	104.6	1.2	105.6	1.0	105.9	0.3	104.8	-1.0	104.2	-0.6	104.3	0.1
1995	106.8	2.4	107.0	0.2	106.4	-0.6	108.4	1.9	108.6	0.2	108.4	-0.2	109.6	1.1	111.0	1.3	111.6	0.5	112.4	0.7	111.8	-0.5	110.9	-0.8
1996	111.0	0.1	111.2	0.2	111.2	0.0	111.2	0.0	111.0	-0.2	109.5	-1.4	111.7	2.0	111.8	0.1	112.1	0.3	112.0	-0.1	111.7	-0.3	111.6	-0.1
1997	112.7	1.0	111.4	-1.2	111.4	0.0	111.5	0.1	111.3	-0.2	111.0	-0.3	110.9	-0.1	111.0	0.1	110.5	-0.5	110.6	0.1	110.5	-0.1	110.2	-0.3

Source: U.S. Department of Labor, Bureau of Labor Statistics, Division of Industry Prices and Price Indexes. n.e.c. stands for not elsewhere classified. - indicates no data collected for period or unavailable.

Processed Yarns and Threads
Producer Price Index
Base 1982 = 100

For 1975-1997. Columns headed % show percentile change in the index from the previous period for which an index is available.

Year	Jan Index	%	Feb Index	%	Mar Index	%	Apr Index	%	May Index	%	Jun Index	%	Jul Index	%	Aug Index	%	Sep Index	%	Oct Index	%	Nov Index	%	Dec Index	%
1975	-	-	-	-	-	-	-	-	-	-	-	-	-	-	-	-	-	-	-	-	-	-	72.3	-
1976	73.4	1.5	73.3	-0.1	72.8	-0.7	71.8	-1.4	71.6	-0.3	72.1	0.7	73.1	1.4	72.1	-1.4	71.5	-0.8	70.9	-0.8	70.5	-0.6	70.3	-0.3
1977	70.0	-0.4	70.5	0.7	71.4	1.3	73.4	2.8	74.0	0.8	74.8	1.1	74.8	0.0	74.3	-0.7	73.8	-0.7	73.2	-0.8	72.6	-0.8	72.7	0.1
1978	72.8	0.1	73.1	0.4	73.2	0.1	73.1	-0.1	73.0	-0.1	73.5	0.7	73.7	0.3	74.0	0.4	74.7	0.9	75.2	0.7	76.2	1.3	75.7	-0.7
1979	76.2	0.7	76.2	0.0	77.4	1.6	77.2	-0.3	78.0	1.0	78.5	0.6	79.2	0.9	80.0	1.0	80.8	1.0	81.0	0.2	81.4	0.5	81.5	0.1
1980	82.8	1.6	85.3	3.0	86.3	1.2	88.3	2.3	89.8	1.7	88.8	-1.1	88.5	-0.3	89.1	0.7	89.9	0.9	90.5	0.7	91.0	0.6	92.7	1.9
1981	93.9	1.3	94.2	0.3	97.3	3.3	97.6	0.3	100.2	2.7	100.7	0.5	101.5	0.8	102.7	1.2	102.9	0.2	104.4	1.5	101.5	-2.8	101.0	-0.5
1982	100.7	-0.3	101.7	1.0	101.6	-0.1	101.6	0.0	101.9	0.3	100.8	-1.1	98.3	-2.5	98.3	0.0	98.8	0.5	98.7	-0.1	98.9	0.2	98.9	0.0
1983	97.4	-1.5	97.7	0.3	98.2	0.5	98.3	0.1	99.3	1.0	99.5	0.2	100.2	0.7	101.4	1.2	101.4	0.0	102.2	0.8	102.5	0.3	103.3	0.8
1984	102.9	-0.4	104.1	1.2	104.1	0.0	103.8	-0.3	104.3	0.5	104.0	-0.3	103.9	-0.1	102.8	-1.1	102.8	0.0	102.3	-0.5	101.8	-0.5	101.8	0.0
1985	102.2	0.4	102.6	0.4	102.3	-0.3	102.2	-0.1	102.2	0.0	102.1	-0.1	102.2	0.1	101.9	-0.3	101.8	-0.1	101.8	0.0	101.8	0.0	101.6	-0.2
1986	101.3	-0.3	101.2	-0.1	101.3	0.1	101.9	0.6	101.7	-0.2	101.5	-0.2	101.7	0.2	102.1	0.4	102.3	0.2	101.9	-0.4	101.6	-0.3	102.1	0.5
1987	101.5	-0.6	101.3	-0.2	101.1	-0.2	101.6	0.5	102.6	1.0	103.4	0.8	104.3	0.9	104.8	0.5	105.3	0.5	106.2	0.9	106.4	0.2	106.9	0.5
1988	107.6	0.7	107.8	0.2	107.8	0.0	107.9	0.1	107.8	-0.1	108.1	0.3	108.2	0.1	108.0	-0.2	108.1	0.1	108.3	0.2	108.2	-0.1	108.5	0.3
1989	108.5	0.0	108.9	0.4	109.6	0.6	110.0	0.4	110.2	0.2	110.5	0.3	110.8	0.3	111.2	0.4	111.1	-0.1	111.4	0.3	111.7	0.3	111.4	-0.3
1990	113.1	1.5	113.4	0.3	113.4	0.0	113.6	0.2	113.6	0.0	113.8	0.2	112.4	-1.2	111.3	-1.0	111.2	-0.1	111.2	0.0	112.2	0.9	112.4	0.2
1991	112.8	0.4	112.7	-0.1	112.8	0.1	112.9	0.1	112.6	-0.3	113.1	0.4	113.1	0.0	112.4	-0.6	112.1	-0.3	112.0	-0.1	112.2	0.2	112.0	-0.2
1992	111.8	-0.2	111.6	-0.2	111.7	0.1	111.7	0.0	111.6	-0.1	111.7	0.1	110.1	-1.4	110.2	0.1	109.8	-0.4	109.7	-0.1	109.8	0.1	109.6	-0.2
1993	108.5	-1.0	108.2	-0.3	108.0	-0.2	107.9	-0.1	107.7	-0.2	107.9	0.2	107.9	0.0	107.7	-0.2	107.8	0.1	107.7	-0.1	107.3	-0.4	107.1	-0.2
1994	107.1	0.0	107.0	-0.1	107.1	0.1	107.2	0.1	107.3	0.1	108.4	1.0	109.1	0.6	108.9	-0.2	109.0	0.1	109.4	0.4	109.8	0.4	109.9	0.1
1995	110.6	0.6	111.1	0.5	112.0	0.8	112.2	0.2	113.1	0.8	113.2	0.1	112.9	-0.3	113.5	0.5	113.4	-0.1	113.5	0.1	113.9	0.4	113.8	-0.1
1996	114.4	0.5	114.5	0.1	114.1	-0.3	114.7	0.5	114.5	-0.2	114.6	0.1	114.5	-0.1	114.3	-0.2	116.4	1.8	114.9	-1.3	114.8	-0.1	114.6	-0.2
1997	114.2	-0.3	114.4	0.2	114.4	0.0	114.0	-0.3	113.9	-0.1	113.7	-0.2	113.5	-0.2	113.6	0.1	113.7	0.1	113.9	0.2	113.6	-0.3	113.3	-0.3

Source: U.S. Department of Labor, Bureau of Labor Statistics, Division of Industry Prices and Price Indexes. n.e.c. stands for not elsewhere classified. - indicates no data collected for period or unavailable.

Gray Fabrics
Producer Price Index
Base 1982 = 100

For 1975-1997. Columns headed % show percentile change in the index from the previous period for which an index is available.

Year	Jan Index	%	Feb Index	%	Mar Index	%	Apr Index	%	May Index	%	Jun Index	%	Jul Index	%	Aug Index	%	Sep Index	%	Oct Index	%	Nov Index	%	Dec Index	%
1975	-	-	-		-		-		-		-		-		-		-		-		-		68.8	-
1976	70.3	2.2	71.2	1.3	71.2	0.0	71.6	0.6	72.4	1.1	73.4	1.4	74.7	1.8	74.7	0.0	73.7	-1.3	73.9	0.3	75.1	1.6	74.1	-1.3
1977	73.0	-1.5	72.1	-1.2	71.9	-0.3	72.3	0.6	72.0	-0.4	71.9	-0.1	72.2	0.4	71.1	-1.5	70.9	-0.3	71.4	0.7	72.4	1.4	73.8	1.9
1978	75.0	1.6	75.7	0.9	77.2	2.0	78.4	1.6	80.7	2.9	81.1	0.5	82.0	1.1	83.2	1.5	85.5	2.8	87.1	1.9	87.2	0.1	86.7	-0.6
1979	86.4	-0.3	84.8	-1.9	84.7	-0.1	85.7	1.2	85.8	0.1	86.3	0.6	88.3	2.3	88.6	0.3	88.6	0.0	89.2	0.7	89.9	0.8	91.1	1.3
1980	91.3	0.2	91.1	-0.2	94.1	3.3	94.3	0.2	93.9	-0.4	92.7	-1.3	93.4	0.8	94.6	1.3	97.0	2.5	98.7	1.8	99.8	1.1	99.1	-0.7
1981	98.8	-0.3	99.1	0.3	99.6	0.5	100.9	1.3	100.4	-0.5	101.5	1.1	102.0	0.5	102.5	0.5	102.6	0.1	101.9	-0.7	101.4	-0.5	101.3	-0.1
1982	102.0	0.7	101.4	-0.6	100.9	-0.5	100.7	-0.2	100.4	-0.3	100.5	0.1	99.7	-0.8	99.5	-0.2	98.8	-0.7	98.9	0.1	98.5	-0.4	98.6	0.1
1983	99.4	0.8	99.3	-0.1	99.8	0.5	100.3	0.5	100.6	0.3	100.4	-0.2	100.6	0.2	101.0	0.4	101.4	0.4	102.9	1.5	104.2	1.3	104.6	0.4
1984	104.0	-0.6	105.2	1.2	105.4	0.2	105.3	-0.1	105.8	0.5	106.2	0.4	106.2	0.0	106.3	0.1	106.4	0.1	106.5	0.1	105.8	-0.7	106.0	0.2
1985	105.8	-0.2	105.0	-0.8	104.6	-0.4	104.4	-0.2	104.7	0.3	104.4	-0.3	104.0	-0.4	103.5	-0.5	103.5	0.0	104.0	0.5	104.2	0.2	104.3	0.1
1986	104.2	-0.1	104.1	-0.1	103.9	-0.2	104.1	0.2	103.9	-0.2	104.0	0.1	104.2	0.2	103.5	-0.7	102.9	-0.6	103.2	0.3	103.3	0.1	103.2	-0.1
1987	103.7	0.5	103.7	0.0	103.9	0.2	105.4	1.4	105.8	0.4	106.7	0.9	108.0	1.2	107.9	-0.1	109.3	1.3	110.3	0.9	110.8	0.5	111.1	0.3
1988	111.8	0.6	112.8	0.9	113.2	0.4	113.9	0.6	114.2	0.3	114.6	0.4	114.9	0.3	115.1	0.2	114.3	-0.7	114.2	-0.1	114.5	0.3	115.0	0.4
1989	115.5	0.4	113.9	-1.4	114.0	0.1	114.0	0.0	113.9	-0.1	114.5	0.5	115.5	0.9	115.7	0.2	115.8	0.1	116.5	0.6	116.5	0.0	116.7	0.2
1990	117.2	0.4	117.3	0.1	117.2	-0.1	117.3	0.1	117.2	-0.1	116.4	-0.7	117.6	1.0	117.2	-0.3	116.7	-0.4	116.8	0.1	117.5	0.6	117.8	0.3
1991	117.2	-0.5	116.7	-0.4	116.6	-0.1	116.6	0.0	116.8	0.2	116.6	-0.2	117.1	0.4	117.9	0.7	118.0	0.1	118.1	0.1	118.3	0.2	119.2	0.8
1992	119.8	0.5	120.2	0.3	120.3	0.1	120.7	0.3	121.2	0.4	121.5	0.2	121.5	0.0	121.2	-0.2	121.0	-0.2	120.5	-0.4	119.8	-0.6	120.1	0.3
1993	120.1	0.0	119.8	-0.2	119.5	-0.3	119.6	0.1	118.4	-1.0	119.0	0.5	118.8	-0.2	118.8	0.0	117.5	-1.1	118.1	0.5	117.0	-0.9	116.9	-0.1
1994	116.5	-0.3	116.3	-0.2	116.4	0.1	116.6	0.2	116.4	-0.2	116.4	0.0	116.3	-0.1	117.2	0.8	117.6	0.3	116.5	-0.9	117.2	0.6	117.7	0.4
1995	118.6	0.8	120.5	1.6	120.7	0.2	121.0	0.2	121.7	0.6	122.0	0.2	121.4	-0.5	121.4	0.0	122.5	0.9	121.8	-0.6	120.9	-0.7	121.6	0.6
1996	120.8	-0.7	120.8	0.0	121.9	0.9	122.4	0.4	121.6	-0.7	120.9	-0.6	121.1	0.2	121.4	0.2	121.3	-0.1	121.6	0.2	121.2	-0.3	121.5	0.2
1997	121.4	-0.1	121.7	0.2	121.6	-0.1	121.4	-0.2	121.8	0.3	121.9	0.1	121.9	0.0	121.7	-0.2	122.4	0.6	122.1	-0.2	121.4	-0.6	121.8	0.3

Source: U.S. Department of Labor, Bureau of Labor Statistics, Division of Industry Prices and Price Indexes. n.e.c. stands for not elsewhere classified. - indicates no data collected for period or unavailable.

Finished Fabrics
Producer Price Index
Base 1982 = 100

For 1975-1997. Columns headed % show percentile change in the index from the previous period for which an index is available.

Year	Jan Index	%	Feb Index	%	Mar Index	%	Apr Index	%	May Index	%	Jun Index	%	Jul Index	%	Aug Index	%	Sep Index	%	Oct Index	%	Nov Index	%	Dec Index	%
1975	-	-	-	-	-	-	-	-	-	-	-	-	-	-	-	-	-	-	-	-	-	-	80.3	-
1976	79.8	-0.6	80.9	1.4	81.7	1.0	82.4	0.9	81.8	-0.7	81.4	-0.5	81.1	-0.4	81.2	0.1	80.7	-0.6	80.5	-0.2	81.4	1.1	81.5	0.1
1977	80.9	-0.7	81.7	1.0	82.7	1.2	83.7	1.2	84.3	0.7	84.2	-0.1	83.9	-0.4	83.9	0.0	83.8	-0.1	83.7	-0.1	83.1	-0.7	83.2	0.1
1978	83.2	0.0	83.3	0.1	82.7	-0.7	82.8	0.1	82.9	0.1	82.8	-0.1	82.9	0.1	83.0	0.1	83.6	0.7	83.9	0.4	84.2	0.4	85.1	1.1
1979	83.1	-2.4	83.6	0.6	84.6	1.2	85.0	0.5	85.9	1.1	86.4	0.6	86.9	0.6	87.5	0.7	87.6	0.1	87.4	-0.2	88.1	0.8	88.2	0.1
1980	88.7	0.6	89.2	0.6	90.9	1.9	91.9	1.1	92.6	0.8	93.0	0.4	93.6	0.6	93.8	0.2	93.9	0.1	95.0	1.2	95.6	0.6	96.5	0.9
1981	98.1	1.7	98.7	0.6	98.9	0.2	100.3	1.4	100.9	0.6	100.8	-0.1	101.1	0.3	101.8	0.7	101.8	0.0	101.7	-0.1	101.6	-0.1	100.8	-0.8
1982	101.8	1.0	102.1	0.3	100.8	-1.3	100.6	-0.2	100.5	-0.1	99.5	-1.0	99.4	-0.1	99.8	0.4	99.3	-0.5	98.9	-0.4	98.7	-0.2	98.6	-0.1
1983	98.1	-0.5	98.2	0.1	98.3	0.1	98.9	0.6	98.6	-0.3	98.3	-0.3	98.3	0.0	99.2	0.9	99.0	-0.2	99.4	0.4	99.9	0.5	100.2	0.3
1984	100.2	0.0	101.4	1.2	101.9	0.5	101.9	0.0	102.2	0.3	102.0	-0.2	101.9	-0.1	102.1	0.2	102.2	0.1	101.8	-0.4	101.7	-0.1	101.6	-0.1
1985	101.6	0.0	102.0	0.4	102.0	0.0	102.1	0.1	101.0	-1.1	100.9	-0.1	100.8	-0.1	101.1	0.3	101.3	0.2	101.3	0.0	101.2	-0.1	101.1	-0.1
1986	101.3	0.2	101.1	-0.2	101.3	0.2	101.3	0.0	101.5	0.2	101.5	0.0	101.6	0.1	101.6	0.0	101.4	-0.2	101.3	-0.1	101.3	0.0	101.3	0.0
1987	102.7	1.4	103.0	0.3	103.1	0.1	103.4	0.3	103.7	0.3	104.0	0.3	104.0	0.0	104.6	0.6	104.7	0.1	105.5	0.8	105.9	0.4	106.2	0.3
1988	106.9	0.7	108.2	1.2	109.0	0.7	109.2	0.2	109.3	0.1	109.6	0.3	109.4	-0.2	109.4	0.0	109.9	0.5	110.1	0.2	111.0	0.8	110.8	-0.2
1989	111.7	0.8	112.1	0.4	112.6	0.4	112.9	0.3	113.5	0.5	113.8	0.3	113.9	0.1	114.1	0.2	114.2	0.1	114.6	0.4	114.9	0.3	115.0	0.1
1990	115.5	0.4	115.6	0.1	115.7	0.1	116.0	0.3	115.9	-0.1	116.0	0.1	115.8	-0.2	115.8	0.0	115.8	0.0	116.4	0.5	116.4	0.0	116.5	0.1
1991	116.7	0.2	117.1	0.3	117.3	0.2	117.4	0.1	117.5	0.1	117.4	-0.1	117.6	0.2	117.8	0.2	118.0	0.2	117.9	-0.1	118.0	0.1	117.8	-0.2
1992	118.1	0.3	118.4	0.3	118.4	0.0	118.6	0.2	118.7	0.1	119.1	0.3	118.9	-0.2	119.0	0.1	119.0	0.0	119.2	0.2	119.3	0.1	119.2	-0.1
1993	119.4	0.2	119.4	0.0	119.4	0.0	119.5	0.1	120.0	0.4	119.8	-0.2	119.6	-0.2	119.5	-0.1	119.4	-0.1	119.4	0.0	119.3	-0.1	119.1	-0.2
1994	119.2	0.1	118.9	-0.3	118.9	0.0	119.2	0.3	119.2	0.0	119.2	0.0	119.1	-0.1	119.1	0.0	119.1	0.0	119.5	0.3	119.6	0.1	119.5	-0.1
1995	120.0	0.4	120.6	0.5	121.0	0.3	121.3	0.2	121.7	0.3	121.8	0.1	122.0	0.2	122.3	0.2	122.3	0.0	122.4	0.1	122.3	-0.1	122.3	0.0
1996	123.1	0.7	123.2	0.1	123.1	-0.1	123.6	0.4	123.5	-0.1	123.7	0.2	123.7	0.0	123.9	0.2	123.8	-0.1	123.7	-0.1	123.9	0.2	123.6	-0.2
1997	123.7	0.1	123.8	0.1	123.6	-0.2	123.9	0.2	124.0	0.1	123.9	-0.1	123.9	0.0	123.8	-0.1	123.9	0.1	124.1	0.2	124.0	-0.1	123.7	-0.2

Source: U.S. Department of Labor, Bureau of Labor Statistics, Division of Industry Prices and Price Indexes. n.e.c. stands for not elsewhere classified. - indicates no data collected for period or unavailable.

Apparel & Other Fabricated Textile Products
Producer Price Index
Base 1982 = 100

For 1977-1997. Columns headed % show percentile change in the index from the previous period for which an index is available.

Year	Jan Index	%	Feb Index	%	Mar Index	%	Apr Index	%	May Index	%	Jun Index	%	Jul Index	%	Aug Index	%	Sep Index	%	Oct Index	%	Nov Index	%	Dec Index	%
1977	-	-	-	-	-	-	-	-	-	-	-	-	-	-	-	-	-	-	-	-	-	-	76.2	-
1978	76.5	0.4	76.7	0.3	76.9	0.3	77.1	0.3	77.3	0.3	77.8	0.6	78.2	0.5	78.4	0.3	78.3	-0.1	78.6	0.4	79.1	0.6	79.4	0.4
1979	80.1	0.9	80.4	0.4	80.8	0.5	81.4	0.7	81.4	0.0	82.1	0.9	82.2	0.1	82.8	0.7	83.1	0.4	83.4	0.4	83.8	0.5	83.7	-0.1
1980	85.0	1.6	85.6	0.7	86.6	1.2	87.5	1.0	87.6	0.1	88.6	1.1	89.7	1.2	90.0	0.3	90.1	0.1	90.6	0.6	91.3	0.8	91.6	0.3
1981	92.9	1.4	93.3	0.4	93.6	0.3	94.8	1.3	95.3	0.5	95.7	0.4	96.3	0.6	96.6	0.3	97.0	0.4	97.8	0.8	98.2	0.4	98.3	0.1
1982	99.3	1.0	99.6	0.3	99.8	0.2	100.1	0.3	100.1	0.0	100.3	0.2	100.1	-0.2	100.2	0.1	100.4	0.2	100.5	0.1	100.3	-0.2	99.4	-0.9
1983	100.0	0.6	100.1	0.1	100.5	0.4	100.3	-0.2	100.8	0.5	101.2	0.4	101.4	0.2	101.5	0.1	101.6	0.1	101.5	-0.1	101.8	0.3	101.7	-0.1
1984	102.2	0.5	102.4	0.2	102.5	0.1	102.6	0.1	102.8	0.2	102.6	-0.2	102.9	0.3	102.8	-0.1	103.3	0.5	103.3	0.0	103.4	0.1	103.2	-0.2
1985	103.5	0.3	103.7	0.2	103.8	0.1	104.0	0.2	104.0	0.0	104.0	0.0	104.2	0.2	104.5	0.3	104.4	-0.1	104.5	0.1	104.8	0.3	105.0	0.2
1986	105.0	0.0	105.3	0.3	105.6	0.3	105.4	-0.2	105.5	0.1	105.5	0.0	105.6	0.1	105.5	-0.1	105.6	0.1	105.8	0.2	105.9	0.1	105.9	0.0
1987	106.0	0.1	106.2	0.2	106.5	0.3	106.7	0.2	106.7	0.0	107.0	0.3	107.4	0.4	107.7	0.3	108.0	0.3	108.1	0.1	108.1	0.0	108.6	0.5
1988	109.1	0.5	109.3	0.2	109.6	0.3	109.7	0.1	109.9	0.2	110.4	0.5	110.7	0.3	110.8	0.1	111.1	0.3	111.2	0.1	111.3	0.1	111.6	0.3
1989	112.1	0.4	112.5	0.4	112.2	-0.3	112.4	0.2	112.5	0.1	112.6	0.1	113.0	0.4	113.4	0.4	113.6	0.2	113.7	0.1	114.0	0.3	114.2	0.2
1990	115.3	1.0	115.3	0.0	115.4	0.1	115.7	0.3	115.7	0.0	116.0	0.3	116.1	0.1	116.4	0.3	116.5	0.1	116.6	0.1	116.6	0.0	116.3	-0.3
1991	116.9	0.5	117.3	0.3	117.5	0.2	117.8	0.3	117.8	0.0	118.1	0.3	118.2	0.1	118.4	0.2	118.5	0.1	118.7	0.2	118.9	0.2	119.0	0.1
1992	119.8	0.7	120.0	0.2	120.2	0.2	120.2	0.0	120.1	-0.1	120.2	0.1	120.3	0.1	120.5	0.2	120.8	0.2	121.0	0.2	121.1	0.1	121.1	0.0
1993	121.3	0.2	121.3	0.0	121.4	0.1	121.5	0.1	121.6	0.1	121.3	-0.2	121.7	0.3	121.7	0.0	121.7	0.0	121.7	0.0	121.7	0.0	121.6	-0.1
1994	121.8	0.2	121.9	0.1	122.0	0.1	121.8	-0.2	122.0	0.2	121.8	-0.2	122.2	0.3	122.1	-0.1	122.2	0.1	122.3	0.1	122.2	-0.1	122.4	0.2
1995	122.6	0.2	122.8	0.2	123.1	0.2	122.9	-0.2	123.1	0.2	123.1	0.0	123.4	0.2	123.2	-0.2	123.6	0.3	123.8	0.2	123.4	-0.3	123.5	0.1
1996	124.2	0.6	124.3	0.1	124.4	0.1	124.2	-0.2	124.9	0.6	125.1	0.2	125.4	0.2	125.1	-0.2	125.6	0.4	125.8	0.2	125.5	-0.2	125.7	0.2
1997	125.5	-0.2	125.3	-0.2	125.6	0.2	125.4	-0.2	125.6	0.2	125.7	0.1	125.7	0.0	125.8	0.1	125.9	0.1	125.5	-0.3	125.8	0.2	125.9	0.1

Source: U.S. Department of Labor, Bureau of Labor Statistics, Division of Industry Prices and Price Indexes. n.e.c. stands for not elsewhere classified. - indicates no data collected for period or unavailable.

Miscellaneous Textile Products/Services
Producer Price Index
Base 1982 = 100

For 1985-1997. Columns headed % show percentile change in the index from the previous period for which an index is available.

Year	Jan Index	%	Feb Index	%	Mar Index	%	Apr Index	%	May Index	%	Jun Index	%	Jul Index	%	Aug Index	%	Sep Index	%	Oct Index	%	Nov Index	%	Dec Index	%
1985	-	-	-	-	-	-	-	-	-	-	100.0	-	99.7	-0.3	99.3	-0.4	99.2	-0.1	99.2	0.0	99.2	0.0	97.7	-1.5
1986	97.8	0.1	98.2	0.4	98.3	0.1	96.4	-1.9	96.6	0.2	96.5	-0.1	95.4	-1.1	94.1	-1.4	94.0	-0.1	95.2	1.3	96.2	1.1	97.5	1.4
1987	97.2	-0.3	97.8	0.6	97.8	0.0	97.8	0.0	97.7	-0.1	98.1	0.4	98.5	0.4	99.2	0.7	99.8	0.6	99.8	0.0	100.1	0.3	100.7	0.6
1988	102.7	2.0	103.4	0.7	104.3	0.9	104.9	0.6	105.0	0.1	105.2	0.2	105.3	0.1	105.3	0.0	105.2	-0.1	106.2	1.0	107.8	1.5	107.9	0.1
1989	109.3	1.3	109.8	0.5	109.6	-0.2	109.4	-0.2	109.5	0.1	110.9	1.3	113.6	2.4	113.8	0.2	113.9	0.1	113.7	-0.2	113.8	0.1	113.7	-0.1
1990	113.7	0.0	113.9	0.2	114.0	0.1	113.9	-0.1	113.6	-0.3	114.0	0.4	114.0	0.0	114.1	0.1	113.9	-0.2	113.9	0.0	114.3	0.4	114.3	0.0
1991	115.9	1.4	112.6	-2.8	112.0	-0.5	111.4	-0.5	111.7	0.3	111.9	0.2	111.7	-0.2	115.2	3.1	115.1	-0.1	114.6	-0.4	115.0	0.3	114.2	-0.7
1992	114.4	0.2	114.5	0.1	114.7	0.2	114.5	-0.2	114.7	0.2	114.8	0.1	114.8	0.0	114.8	0.0	115.3	0.4	115.3	0.0	115.3	0.0	115.3	0.0
1993	115.6	0.3	115.4	-0.2	115.5	0.1	115.9	0.3	115.7	-0.2	116.0	0.3	116.1	0.1	115.9	-0.2	116.2	0.3	116.4	0.2	116.2	-0.2	116.2	0.0
1994	116.4	0.2	116.6	0.2	117.1	0.4	117.0	-0.1	117.8	0.7	118.8	0.8	118.6	-0.2	118.3	-0.3	118.4	0.1	118.8	0.3	119.4	0.5	119.6	0.2
1995	120.2	0.5	120.8	0.5	122.2	1.2	123.0	0.7	124.1	0.9	124.1	0.0	124.3	0.2	124.6	0.2	124.2	-0.3	125.3	0.9	125.3	0.0	124.9	-0.3
1996	124.6	-0.2	124.8	0.2	124.5	-0.2	124.4	-0.1	124.0	-0.3	123.6	-0.3	123.6	0.0	123.4	-0.2	122.7	-0.6	122.2	-0.4	122.1	-0.1	122.0	-0.1
1997	121.7	-0.2	121.2	-0.4	121.0	-0.2	121.2	0.2	121.1	-0.1	121.1	0.0	120.3	-0.7	119.7	-0.5	119.1	-0.5	118.5	-0.5	118.3	-0.2	118.3	0.0

Source: U.S. Department of Labor, Bureau of Labor Statistics, Division of Industry Prices and Price Indexes. n.e.c. stands for not elsewhere classified. - indicates no data collected for period or unavailable.

HIDES, SKINS, LEATHER, AND RELATED PRODUCTS
Producer Price Index
Base 1982 = 100

For 1926-1997. Columns headed % show percentile change in the index from the previous period for which an index is available.

Year	Jan Index	%	Feb Index	%	Mar Index	%	Apr Index	%	May Index	%	Jun Index	%	Jul Index	%	Aug Index	%	Sep Index	%	Oct Index	%	Nov Index	%	Dec Index	%
1926	17.6	-	17.3	-1.7	17.1	-1.2	16.9	-1.2	16.9	0.0	16.9	0.0	16.9	0.0	17.0	0.6	16.9	-0.6	17.2	1.8	17.1	-0.6	17.1	0.0
1927	17.2	0.6	17.1	-0.6	17.1	0.0	17.4	1.8	17.7	1.7	18.3	3.4	19.0	3.8	19.0	0.0	19.2	1.1	19.2	0.0	19.4	1.0	19.9	2.6
1928	20.6	3.5	21.1	2.4	21.1	0.0	21.6	2.4	21.5	-0.5	21.1	-1.9	21.1	0.0	20.6	-2.4	20.6	0.0	20.0	-2.9	19.7	-1.5	19.7	0.0
1929	19.3	-2.0	18.6	-3.6	18.4	-1.1	18.4	0.0	18.2	-1.1	18.4	1.1	18.6	1.1	18.7	0.5	18.9	1.1	18.8	-0.5	18.5	-1.6	18.4	-0.5
1930	17.9	-2.7	17.7	-1.1	17.6	-0.6	17.5	-0.6	17.5	0.0	17.5	0.0	17.2	-1.7	16.9	-1.7	17.0	0.6	16.5	-2.9	16.1	-2.4	15.6	-3.1
1931	15.1	-3.2	14.8	-2.0	14.9	0.7	14.9	0.0	14.9	0.0	15.0	0.7	15.3	2.0	15.1	-1.3	14.5	-4.0	14.1	-2.8	13.9	-1.4	13.6	-2.2
1932	13.5	-0.7	13.4	-0.7	13.2	-1.5	12.8	-3.0	12.4	-3.1	12.1	-2.4	11.7	-3.3	11.9	1.7	12.3	3.4	12.4	0.8	12.2	-1.6	11.9	-2.5
1933	11.8	-0.8	11.6	-1.7	11.6	0.0	11.8	1.7	13.1	11.0	14.1	7.6	14.7	4.3	15.6	6.1	15.8	1.3	15.2	-3.8	15.1	-0.7	15.2	0.7
1934	15.3	0.7	15.3	0.0	15.1	-1.3	15.2	0.7	15.0	-1.3	14.9	-0.7	14.7	-1.3	14.3	-2.7	14.4	0.7	14.3	-0.7	14.4	0.7	14.5	0.7
1935	14.7	1.4	14.7	0.0	14.6	-0.7	14.7	0.7	15.1	2.7	15.2	0.7	15.2	0.0	15.3	0.7	15.5	1.3	16.0	3.2	16.3	1.9	16.3	0.0
1936	16.6	1.8	16.4	-1.2	16.2	-1.2	16.1	-0.6	16.0	-0.6	16.0	0.0	16.0	0.0	16.0	0.0	16.1	0.6	16.3	1.2	16.5	1.2	17.0	3.0
1937	17.4	2.4	17.5	0.6	17.7	1.1	18.2	2.8	18.2	0.0	18.2	0.0	18.2	0.0	18.4	1.1	18.4	0.0	18.2	-1.1	17.3	-4.9	16.7	-3.5
1938	16.5	-1.2	16.2	-1.8	16.0	-1.2	15.7	-1.9	15.6	-0.6	15.4	-1.3	15.6	1.3	15.7	0.6	15.7	0.0	16.0	1.9	16.1	0.6	15.9	-1.2
1939	15.9	0.0	15.7	-1.3	15.6	-0.6	15.5	-0.6	15.6	0.6	15.8	1.3	15.8	0.0	15.8	0.0	16.8	6.3	17.9	6.5	17.7	-1.1	17.7	0.0
1940	17.7	0.0	17.5	-1.1	17.4	-0.6	17.4	0.0	17.3	-0.6	16.9	-2.3	16.9	0.0	16.5	-2.4	16.8	1.8	17.1	1.8	17.5	2.3	17.5	0.0
1941	17.5	0.0	17.4	-0.6	17.5	0.6	17.7	1.1	18.2	2.8	18.4	1.1	18.7	1.6	18.8	0.5	19.0	1.1	19.2	1.1	19.5	1.6	19.6	0.5
1942	19.6	0.0	19.7	0.5	19.9	1.0	20.4	2.5	20.3	-0.5	20.2	-0.5	20.2	0.0	20.2	0.0	20.1	-0.5	20.1	0.0	20.1	0.0	20.1	0.0
1943	20.1	0.0	20.1	0.0	20.1	0.0	20.1	0.0	20.1	0.0	20.1	0.0	20.1	0.0	20.1	0.0	20.1	0.0	20.1	0.0	19.9	-1.0	20.0	0.5
1944	20.0	0.0	20.0	0.0	20.0	0.0	20.0	0.0	20.0	0.0	20.0	0.0	19.9	-0.5	19.8	-0.5	19.8	0.0	19.8	0.0	19.8	0.0	20.0	1.0
1945	20.1	0.5	20.1	0.0	20.1	0.0	20.1	0.0	20.1	0.0	20.1	0.0	20.1	0.0	20.1	0.0	20.3	1.0	20.3	0.0	20.3	0.0	20.3	0.0
1946	20.4	0.5	20.4	0.0	20.4	0.0	20.4	0.0	20.6	1.0	20.9	1.5	24.1	15.3	23.7	-1.7	24.2	2.1	24.3	0.4	29.4	21.0	30.2	2.7
1947	30.1	-0.3	30.3	0.7	30.5	0.7	30.2	-1.0	30.0	-0.7	30.2	0.7	31.0	2.6	31.9	2.9	32.2	0.9	34.0	5.6	35.2	3.5	35.0	-0.6
1948	34.2	-2.3	32.6	-4.7	31.3	-4.0	31.7	1.3	32.2	1.6	32.1	-0.3	32.4	0.9	31.9	-1.5	31.6	-0.9	31.3	-0.9	31.9	1.9	31.6	-0.9
1949	31.5	-0.3	30.7	-2.5	30.2	-1.6	30.1	-0.3	30.0	-0.3	30.0	0.0	29.7	-1.0	30.0	1.0	30.4	1.3	30.7	1.0	30.8	0.3	30.7	-0.3
1950	30.2	-1.6	30.2	0.0	30.5	1.0	30.5	0.0	30.8	1.0	31.1	1.0	32.5	4.5	33.4	2.8	34.7	3.9	35.4	2.0	36.6	3.4	38.1	4.1
1951	39.9	4.7	40.1	0.5	39.8	-0.7	39.7	-0.3	39.6	-0.3	39.1	-1.3	38.4	-1.8	37.0	-3.6	37.0	0.0	35.7	-3.5	33.6	-5.9	33.0	-1.8
1952	32.1	-2.7	31.2	-2.8	30.8	-1.3	29.5	-4.2	29.7	0.7	30.1	1.3	30.2	0.3	30.3	0.3	30.3	0.0	30.3	0.0	30.7	1.3	31.1	1.3
1953	30.5	-1.9	30.8	1.0	30.8	0.0	30.7	-0.3	31.5	2.6	31.7	0.6	31.4	-0.9	31.4	0.0	31.3	-0.3	30.5	-2.6	30.5	0.0	30.0	-1.6
1954	29.9	-0.3	29.8	-0.3	29.7	-0.3	29.7	0.0	30.1	1.3	30.0	-0.3	29.8	-0.7	29.5	-1.0	29.2	-1.0	29.0	-0.7	29.1	0.3	28.8	-1.0
1955	28.8	0.0	29.0	0.7	28.9	-0.3	29.3	1.4	29.2	-0.3	29.2	0.0	29.4	0.7	29.4	0.0	29.5	0.3	29.9	1.4	30.2	1.0	30.3	0.3
1956	30.3	0.0	30.5	0.7	30.7	0.7	31.6	2.9	31.4	-0.6	31.4	0.0	31.4	0.0	31.4	0.0	31.4	0.0	31.3	-0.3	31.3	0.0	31.1	-0.6
1957	30.9	-0.6	30.8	-0.3	30.9	0.3	31.0	0.3	31.0	0.3	31.3	1.0	31.6	1.0	31.5	-0.3	31.4	-0.3	31.4	0.0	31.4	0.0	31.2	-0.6
1958	31.2	0.0	31.3	0.3	31.2	-0.3	31.3	0.3	31.4	0.3	31.5	0.3	31.5	0.0	31.5	0.0	31.4	-0.3	31.8	1.3	32.1	0.9	32.5	1.2
1959	32.7	0.6	33.1	1.2	34.1	3.0	37.0	8.5	37.2	0.5	37.3	0.3	37.5	0.5	37.6	0.3	37.4	-0.5	36.5	-2.4	35.1	-3.8	35.3	0.6
1960	35.4	0.3	35.1	-0.8	35.1	0.0	35.2	0.3	34.9	-0.9	34.6	-0.9	34.6	0.0	34.1	-1.4	33.9	-0.6	34.1	0.6	34.1	0.0	34.2	0.3
1961	34.0	-0.6	33.9	-0.3	34.3	1.2	34.5	0.6	34.8	0.9	34.6	-0.6	34.9	0.9	35.5	1.7	35.6	0.3	35.8	0.6	35.7	-0.3	35.6	-0.3
1962	35.6	0.0	35.4	-0.6	35.3	-0.3	35.1	-0.6	35.3	0.6	35.5	0.6	35.3	-0.6	35.2	-0.3	35.3	0.3	35.3	0.0	35.3	0.0	35.1	-0.6
1963	34.8	-0.9	34.6	-0.6	34.6	0.0	34.3	-0.9	34.5	0.6	34.3	-0.6	34.3	0.0	34.1	-0.6	33.9	-0.6	34.0	0.3	34.0	0.0	33.8	-0.6
1964	33.8	0.0	33.7	-0.3	33.7	0.0	34.3	1.8	34.4	0.3	34.5	0.3	34.6	0.3	34.7	0.3	34.6	-0.3	34.8	0.6	34.7	-0.3	34.6	-0.3
1965	34.5	-0.3	34.6	0.3	34.8	0.6	35.0	0.6	35.3	0.9	35.4	0.3	35.8	1.1	36.9	3.1	36.6	-0.8	37.2	1.6	37.4	0.5	37.7	0.8
1966	38.2	1.3	38.7	1.3	39.0	0.8	39.6	1.5	40.4	2.0	40.4	0.0	40.4	0.0	39.9	-1.2	39.4	-1.3	39.0	-1.0	38.6	-1.0	38.6	0.0
1967	38.8	0.5	38.8	0.0	38.5	-0.8	38.0	-1.3	37.9	-0.3	38.0	0.3	37.9	-0.3	37.5	-1.1	37.7	0.5	37.7	0.0	38.0	0.8	38.2	0.5
1968	38.3	0.3	38.4	0.3	38.8	1.0	38.9	0.3	39.1	0.5	39.0	-0.3	39.3	0.8	39.3	0.0	39.7	1.0	40.2	1.3	40.2	0.0	40.4	0.5
1969	40.6	0.5	40.6	0.0	40.6	0.0	41.5	2.2	41.5	0.0	41.3	-0.5	41.6	0.7	41.7	0.2	42.3	1.4	42.0	-0.7	42.0	0.0	41.8	-0.5
1970	42.0	0.5	42.0	0.0	42.0	0.0	42.3	0.7	42.1	-0.5	41.8	-0.7	41.8	0.0	41.8	0.0	41.8	0.0	42.0	0.5	42.2	0.5	42.0	-0.5

[Continued]

HIDES, SKINS, LEATHER, AND RELATED PRODUCTS
Producer Price Index
Base 1982 = 100
[Continued]

For 1926-1997. Columns headed % show percentile change in the index from the previous period for which an index is available.

Year	Jan Index	%	Feb Index	%	Mar Index	%	Apr Index	%	May Index	%	Jun Index	%	Jul Index	%	Aug Index	%	Sep Index	%	Oct Index	%	Nov Index	%	Dec Index	%
1971	42.6	1.4	42.8	0.5	42.8	0.0	43.4	1.4	43.6	0.5	43.5	-0.2	43.5	0.0	43.6	0.2	43.7	0.2	43.7	0.0	43.8	0.2	44.2	0.9
1972	44.9	1.6	45.4	1.1	46.8	3.1	48.4	3.4	49.3	1.9	49.8	1.0	50.1	0.6	51.3	2.4	51.7	0.8	53.2	2.9	54.8	3.0	54.1	-1.3
1973	54.8	1.3	55.2	0.7	54.6	-1.1	55.2	1.1	54.1	-2.0	53.6	-0.9	53.8	0.4	54.4	1.1	54.7	0.6	54.7	0.0	54.5	-0.4	54.0	-0.9
1974	54.3	0.6	54.6	0.6	54.6	0.0	55.4	1.5	55.7	0.5	55.6	-0.2	55.8	0.4	55.7	-0.2	56.4	1.3	55.3	-2.0	55.0	-0.5	54.5	-0.9
1975	54.1	-0.7	54.0	-0.2	54.5	0.9	56.2	3.1	56.2	0.0	56.6	0.7	56.8	0.4	56.9	0.2	57.6	1.2	58.0	0.7	58.8	1.4	58.9	0.2
1976	60.2	2.2	61.2	1.7	62.0	1.3	63.3	2.1	64.8	2.4	64.0	-1.2	64.9	1.4	65.3	0.6	66.1	1.2	65.1	-1.5	64.6	-0.8	65.3	1.1
1977	66.8	2.3	67.3	0.7	67.7	0.6	68.5	1.2	69.3	1.2	68.3	-1.4	68.5	0.3	68.6	0.1	68.4	-0.3	68.2	-0.3	68.5	0.4	69.1	0.9
1978	70.8	2.5	71.3	0.7	71.5	0.3	73.1	2.2	73.7	0.8	74.3	0.8	75.1	1.1	78.1	4.0	80.2	2.7	81.1	1.1	82.1	1.2	82.3	0.2
1979	85.1	3.4	88.4	3.9	96.5	9.2	98.6	2.2	102.6	4.1	102.0	-0.6	99.7	-2.3	98.2	-1.5	95.6	-2.6	96.7	1.2	94.8	-2.0	94.9	0.1
1980	97.3	2.5	95.5	-1.8	94.0	-1.6	92.7	-1.4	91.6	-1.2	91.7	0.1	93.3	1.7	95.7	2.6	94.3	-1.5	95.6	1.4	97.2	1.7	97.8	0.6
1981	98.3	0.5	98.1	-0.2	99.4	1.3	100.3	0.9	100.4	0.1	99.6	-0.8	99.4	-0.2	99.5	0.1	99.6	0.1	99.0	-0.6	98.9	-0.1	99.2	0.3
1982	99.7	0.5	99.6	-0.1	99.2	-0.4	100.3	1.1	100.2	-0.1	99.7	-0.5	100.2	0.5	99.8	-0.4	100.3	0.5	100.2	-0.1	100.2	0.0	100.6	0.4
1983	101.5	0.9	100.6	-0.9	100.9	0.3	101.8	0.9	102.6	0.8	103.3	0.7	103.7	0.4	104.6	0.9	104.5	-0.1	104.2	-0.3	105.5	1.2	105.6	0.1
1984	106.3	0.7	107.9	1.5	109.2	1.2	109.2	0.0	109.9	0.6	110.5	0.5	110.0	-0.5	109.9	-0.1	109.9	0.0	109.5	-0.4	108.1	-1.3	108.0	-0.1
1985	108.0	0.0	108.0	0.0	107.5	-0.5	108.4	0.8	108.2	-0.2	108.7	0.5	108.4	-0.3	109.0	0.6	109.3	0.3	109.9	0.5	110.4	0.5	111.3	0.8
1986	111.8	0.4	112.0	0.2	111.8	-0.2	112.3	0.4	112.9	0.5	113.4	0.4	113.2	-0.2	113.1	-0.1	112.9	-0.2	113.4	0.4	114.0	0.5	114.8	0.7
1987	114.9	0.1	115.0	0.1	116.5	1.3	118.3	1.5	120.7	2.0	120.2	-0.4	121.0	0.7	121.3	0.2	123.0	1.4	124.1	0.9	124.3	0.2	125.7	1.1
1988	128.4	2.1	129.1	0.5	132.6	2.7	134.2	1.2	134.6	0.3	131.2	-2.5	130.1	-0.8	131.6	1.2	132.5	0.7	131.9	-0.5	130.4	-1.1	130.1	-0.2
1989	131.2	0.8	133.2	1.5	136.8	2.7	136.1	-0.5	134.8	-1.0	135.2	0.3	136.9	1.3	137.2	0.2	138.0	0.6	138.2	0.1	138.0	-0.1	139.5	1.1
1990	138.9	-0.4	141.7	2.0	141.6	-0.1	142.9	0.9	143.7	0.6	143.0	-0.5	142.8	-0.1	142.2	-0.4	141.4	-0.6	140.9	-0.4	140.5	-0.3	140.6	0.1
1991	140.2	-0.3	140.0	-0.1	140.4	0.3	141.1	0.5	140.4	-0.5	140.0	-0.3	138.3	-1.2	138.1	-0.1	136.6	-1.1	136.3	-0.2	137.1	0.6	137.6	0.4
1992	138.6	0.7	139.0	0.3	139.8	0.6	139.9	0.1	140.7	0.6	140.8	0.1	140.1	-0.5	140.8	0.5	140.9	0.1	141.0	0.1	140.6	-0.3	142.0	1.0
1993	143.6	1.1	142.5	-0.8	142.9	0.3	143.6	0.5	143.8	0.1	143.7	-0.1	143.5	-0.1	143.9	0.3	144.1	0.1	143.7	-0.3	144.1	0.3	144.4	0.2
1994	145.1	0.5	143.8	-0.9	144.6	0.6	146.1	1.0	146.7	0.4	147.2	0.3	148.7	1.0	149.0	0.2	150.8	1.2	153.2	1.6	153.7	0.3	153.5	-0.1
1995	154.1	0.4	155.2	0.7	156.2	0.6	156.1	-0.1	157.8	1.1	155.0	-1.8	154.9	-0.1	153.2	-1.1	152.0	-0.8	150.6	-0.9	149.5	-0.7	149.5	0.0
1996	149.0	-0.3	149.3	0.2	149.7	0.3	148.4	-0.9	149.2	0.5	149.2	0.0	149.4	0.1	150.3	0.6	150.2	-0.1	153.1	1.9	153.6	0.3	154.4	0.5
1997	155.3	0.6	156.2	0.6	156.8	0.4	157.5	0.4	156.1	-0.9	153.6	-1.6	151.6	-1.3	152.2	0.4	151.5	-0.5	152.5	0.7	154.3	1.2	153.5	-0.5

Source: U.S. Department of Labor, Bureau of Labor Statistics, Division of Industry Prices and Price Indexes. n.e.c. stands for not elsewhere classified. - indicates no data collected for period or unavailable.

Hides and Skins
Producer Price Index
Base 1982 = 100

For 1926-1997. Columns headed % show percentile change in the index from the previous period for which an index is available.

Year	Jan Index	%	Feb Index	%	Mar Index	%	Apr Index	%	May Index	%	Jun Index	%	Jul Index	%	Aug Index	%	Sep Index	%	Oct Index	%	Nov Index	%	Dec Index	%
1926	23.1	-	21.3	-7.8	20.0	-6.1	18.7	-6.5	19.4	3.7	19.3	-0.5	19.9	3.1	20.6	3.5	19.6	-4.9	21.7	10.7	21.1	-2.8	21.1	0.0
1927	21.5	1.9	20.8	-3.3	20.9	0.5	22.1	5.7	23.4	5.9	25.3	8.1	27.3	7.9	26.8	-1.8	26.3	-1.9	26.2	-0.4	26.9	2.7	27.9	3.7
1928	30.9	10.8	32.4	4.9	32.2	-0.6	34.2	6.2	33.6	-1.8	31.7	-5.7	31.8	0.3	28.8	-9.4	29.0	0.7	26.6	-8.3	26.6	0.0	26.8	0.8
1929	25.4	-5.2	21.7	-14.6	22.1	1.8	22.1	0.0	21.4	-3.2	22.6	5.6	23.4	3.5	24.0	2.6	24.8	3.3	24.1	-2.8	22.3	-7.5	22.0	-1.3
1930	21.3	-3.2	20.2	-5.2	19.6	-3.0	19.6	0.0	19.8	1.0	20.2	2.0	19.2	-5.0	18.6	-3.1	19.2	3.2	17.1	-10.9	15.4	-9.9	14.1	-8.4
1931	13.2	-6.4	11.8	-10.6	12.7	7.6	12.7	0.0	12.8	0.8	13.4	4.7	14.9	11.2	14.1	-5.4	12.0	-14.9	10.2	-15.0	10.0	-2.0	10.0	0.0
1932	10.0	0.0	9.5	-5.0	9.1	-4.2	8.3	-8.8	7.3	-12.0	6.6	-9.6	6.9	4.5	8.0	15.9	9.9	23.7	10.1	2.0	9.5	-5.9	8.5	-10.5
1933	8.8	3.5	8.4	-4.5	8.5	1.2	9.4	10.6	13.8	46.8	16.6	20.3	18.1	9.0	18.7	3.3	17.2	-8.0	14.5	-15.7	14.4	-0.7	15.2	5.6
1934	15.8	3.9	16.0	1.3	15.0	-6.3	15.7	4.7	15.0	-4.5	14.3	-4.7	13.6	-4.9	11.7	-14.0	12.3	5.1	12.2	-0.8	12.9	5.7	13.8	7.0
1935	14.5	5.1	14.2	-2.1	13.6	-4.2	14.5	6.6	15.6	7.6	16.0	2.6	16.3	1.9	16.4	0.6	17.1	4.3	19.0	11.1	19.7	3.7	19.7	0.0
1936	20.6	4.6	19.8	-3.9	18.6	-6.1	18.4	-1.1	17.8	-3.3	18.2	2.2	17.9	-1.6	18.4	2.8	19.1	3.8	19.8	3.7	20.7	4.5	22.6	9.2
1937	23.7	4.9	23.5	-0.8	24.2	3.0	24.8	2.5	24.0	-3.2	23.4	-2.5	23.8	1.7	24.9	4.6	24.6	-1.2	24.0	-2.4	19.3	-19.6	17.5	-9.3
1938	16.8	-4.0	15.3	-8.9	14.2	-7.2	12.8	-9.9	13.0	1.6	12.8	-1.5	14.5	13.3	15.4	6.2	15.5	0.6	16.8	8.4	17.5	4.2	16.1	-8.0
1939	16.0	-0.6	14.9	-6.9	15.1	1.3	14.0	-7.3	14.7	5.0	15.4	4.8	15.8	2.6	15.8	0.0	19.9	25.9	23.0	15.6	21.3	-7.4	21.5	0.9
1940	21.0	-2.3	19.8	-5.7	19.3	-2.5	19.4	0.5	18.8	-3.1	16.7	-11.2	17.3	3.6	15.8	-8.7	17.2	8.9	19.2	11.6	20.7	7.8	20.3	-1.9
1941	20.2	-0.5	19.4	-4.0	20.3	4.6	21.4	5.4	22.6	5.6	23.0	1.8	23.0	0.0	22.9	-0.4	22.9	0.0	23.1	0.9	23.3	0.9	23.7	1.7
1942	23.6	-0.4	23.6	0.0	23.8	0.8	25.3	6.3	24.8	-2.0	24.2	-2.4	24.2	0.0	24.3	0.4	24.1	-0.8	23.7	-1.7	23.7	0.0	23.7	0.0
1943	23.7	0.0	23.7	0.0	23.7	0.0	23.7	0.0	23.7	0.0	23.7	0.0	23.7	0.0	23.7	0.0	23.7	0.0	23.7	0.0	22.2	-6.3	22.8	2.7
1944	23.1	1.3	22.7	-1.7	22.7	0.0	22.7	0.0	22.9	0.9	22.2	-3.1	21.9	-1.4	21.6	-1.4	21.7	0.5	22.0	1.4	21.9	-0.5	23.3	6.4
1945	23.5	0.9	23.6	0.4	23.8	0.8	23.9	0.4	23.9	0.0	24.0	0.4	24.0	0.0	24.1	0.4	24.1	0.0	24.0	-0.4	24.0	0.0	24.0	0.0
1946	24.0	0.0	24.0	0.0	24.0	0.0	24.0	0.0	24.7	2.9	24.8	0.4	34.6	39.5	31.8	-8.1	31.0	-2.5	31.3	1.0	45.2	44.4	44.2	-2.2
1947	40.6	-8.1	42.7	5.2	43.8	2.6	41.4	-5.5	39.9	-3.6	41.7	4.5	46.1	10.6	49.6	7.6	50.4	1.6	55.6	10.3	60.5	8.8	58.7	-3.0
1948	53.7	-8.5	46.8	-12.8	39.3	-16.0	42.0	6.9	45.0	7.1	44.6	-0.9	46.6	4.5	44.4	-4.7	42.9	-3.4	41.3	-3.7	44.6	8.0	43.1	-3.4
1949	43.2	0.2	38.7	-10.4	37.0	-4.4	37.2	0.5	37.2	0.0	37.7	1.3	36.0	-4.5	38.0	5.6	40.0	5.3	40.8	2.0	40.5	-0.7	38.9	-4.0
1950	37.4	-3.9	37.0	-1.1	38.4	3.8	38.1	-0.8	39.0	2.4	41.2	5.6	45.1	9.5	46.6	3.3	52.6	12.9	52.5	-0.2	54.7	4.2	57.1	4.4
1951	61.5	7.7	58.8	-4.4	58.5	-0.5	57.0	-2.6	56.8	-0.4	56.5	-0.5	54.1	-4.2	49.5	-8.5	48.6	-1.8	47.8	-1.6	38.2	-20.1	35.7	-6.5
1952	30.4	-14.8	27.8	-8.6	26.0	-6.5	21.7	-16.5	25.4	17.1	26.0	2.4	27.0	3.8	28.1	4.1	28.1	0.0	28.4	1.1	30.2	6.3	30.8	2.0
1953	27.1	-12.0	29.0	7.0	28.3	-2.4	29.0	2.5	32.6	12.4	33.3	2.1	32.0	-3.9	32.6	1.9	32.4	-0.6	28.1	-13.3	28.0	-0.4	25.2	-10.0
1954	24.8	-1.6	24.2	-2.4	24.4	0.8	24.6	0.8	27.3	11.0	26.5	-2.9	25.4	-4.2	24.4	-3.9	22.5	-7.8	21.6	-4.0	23.0	6.5	20.7	-10.0
1955	21.6	4.3	22.5	4.2	22.1	-1.8	24.8	12.2	23.2	-6.5	24.3	4.7	25.4	4.5	25.7	1.2	26.6	3.5	27.2	2.3	26.3	-3.3	26.7	1.5
1956	24.7	-7.5	25.4	2.8	25.5	0.4	27.0	5.9	25.8	-4.4	26.7	3.5	26.4	-1.1	26.4	0.0	27.6	4.5	25.2	-8.7	25.8	2.4	23.5	-8.9
1957	22.7	-3.4	21.9	-3.5	22.2	1.4	22.6	1.8	24.4	8.0	25.9	6.1	27.1	4.6	26.8	-1.1	25.4	-5.2	24.8	-2.4	23.5	-5.2	22.0	-6.4
1958	22.1	0.5	22.3	0.9	22.3	0.0	23.2	4.0	24.2	4.3	24.9	2.9	25.4	2.0	26.4	3.9	25.8	-2.3	27.0	4.7	28.4	5.2	29.0	2.1
1959	30.0	3.4	31.8	6.0	38.3	20.4	47.4	23.8	43.0	-9.3	46.6	8.4	47.0	0.9	46.6	-0.9	44.7	-4.1	38.2	-14.5	29.3	-23.3	32.2	9.9
1960	32.2	0.0	30.4	-5.6	31.4	3.3	32.1	2.2	31.8	-0.9	29.3	-7.9	29.7	1.4	27.8	-6.4	27.2	-2.2	28.0	2.9	28.7	2.5	28.3	-1.4
1961	26.9	-4.9	26.4	-1.9	30.0	13.6	29.7	-1.0	31.0	4.4	29.7	-4.2	33.3	12.1	36.2	8.7	36.0	-0.6	35.9	-0.3	34.7	-3.3	33.3	-4.0
1962	32.6	-2.1	31.2	-4.3	30.7	-1.6	30.6	-0.3	31.2	2.0	32.1	2.9	30.8	-4.0	31.1	1.0	32.8	5.5	32.2	-1.8	31.7	-1.6	30.1	-5.0
1963	28.2	-6.3	25.4	-9.9	26.1	2.8	25.1	-3.8	25.9	3.2	25.4	-1.9	24.7	-2.8	23.8	-3.6	22.9	-3.8	23.8	3.9	24.5	2.9	22.6	-7.8
1964	22.5	-0.4	21.9	-2.7	22.4	2.3	26.1	16.5	25.4	-2.7	26.7	5.1	27.4	2.6	28.4	3.6	28.3	-0.4	28.2	-0.4	26.8	-5.0	26.7	-0.4
1965	25.6	-4.1	26.7	4.3	27.3	2.2	28.5	4.4	31.3	9.8	30.5	-2.6	34.7	13.8	39.5	13.8	37.0	-6.3	37.2	0.5	37.4	0.5	39.1	4.5
1966	41.4	5.9	45.2	9.2	43.7	-3.3	44.0	0.7	48.2	9.5	47.6	-1.2	46.3	-2.7	41.8	-9.7	39.7	-5.0	35.7	-10.1	33.8	-5.3	32.3	-4.4
1967	32.6	0.9	31.9	-2.1	29.3	-8.2	26.1	-10.9	25.8	-1.1	28.4	10.1	27.7	-2.5	25.7	-7.2	27.6	7.4	25.7	-6.9	26.9	4.7	26.8	-0.4
1968	26.1	-2.6	26.8	2.7	29.7	10.8	28.3	-4.7	29.0	2.5	28.2	-2.8	30.0	6.4	30.4	1.3	31.6	3.9	31.2	-1.3	31.7	1.6	31.6	-0.3
1969	32.3	2.2	31.4	-2.8	32.3	2.9	37.2	15.2	36.3	-2.4	34.7	-4.4	36.4	4.9	36.4	0.0	38.1	4.7	34.9	-8.4	32.7	-6.3	32.2	-1.5
1970	30.4	-5.6	29.9	-1.6	29.4	-1.7	31.6	7.5	30.1	-4.7	27.8	-7.6	26.9	-3.2	27.4	1.9	27.8	1.5	28.8	3.6	30.4	5.6	28.4	-6.6

[Continued]

Hides and Skins
Producer Price Index
Base 1982 = 100
[Continued]

For 1926-1997. Columns headed % show percentile change in the index from the previous period for which an index is available.

Year	Jan Index	%	Feb Index	%	Mar Index	%	Apr Index	%	May Index	%	Jun Index	%	Jul Index	%	Aug Index	%	Sep Index	%	Oct Index	%	Nov Index	%	Dec Index	%
1971	27.6	-2.8	29.3	6.2	29.4	0.3	33.8	15.0	33.9	0.3	31.8	-6.2	31.8	0.0	31.9	0.3	32.8	2.8	32.7	-0.3	34.3	4.9	35.8	4.4
1972	37.9	5.9	41.5	9.5	48.5	16.9	52.6	8.5	55.8	6.1	56.9	2.0	59.2	4.0	67.7	14.4	68.0	0.4	75.5	11.0	80.0	6.0	71.1	-11.1
1973	76.4	7.5	76.0	-0.5	68.7	-9.6	75.3	9.6	70.7	-6.1	67.3	-4.8	68.7	2.1	72.9	6.1	71.7	-1.6	71.4	-0.4	66.8	-6.4	63.4	-5.1
1974	61.6	-2.8	61.9	0.5	56.2	-9.2	58.9	4.8	60.9	3.4	57.7	-5.3	60.1	4.2	57.0	-5.2	54.3	-4.7	44.9	-17.3	43.6	-2.9	38.1	-12.6
1975	34.8	-8.7	34.1	-2.0	38.6	13.2	48.5	25.6	47.6	-1.9	50.9	6.9	52.1	2.4	52.0	-0.2	53.6	3.1	56.0	4.5	58.3	4.1	57.2	-1.9
1976	62.6	9.4	64.0	2.2	66.8	4.4	75.4	12.9	79.7	5.7	72.8	-8.7	77.7	6.7	79.4	2.2	81.4	2.5	70.1	-13.9	64.6	-7.8	70.0	8.4
1977	77.8	11.1	78.8	1.3	79.7	1.1	85.0	6.6	87.3	2.7	80.5	-7.8	81.3	1.0	80.4	-1.1	76.5	-4.9	74.3	-2.9	76.2	2.6	81.4	6.8
1978	83.7	2.8	83.1	-0.7	82.5	-0.7	89.4	8.4	89.7	0.3	96.6	7.7	100.5	4.0	111.7	11.1	121.4	8.7	119.3	-1.7	116.2	-2.6	111.9	-3.7
1979	126.2	12.8	138.8	10.0	178.3	28.5	179.0	0.4	185.9	3.9	170.3	-8.4	157.9	-7.3	142.7	-9.6	129.7	-9.1	133.5	2.9	124.8	-6.5	123.7	-0.9
1980	130.7	5.7	112.9	-13.6	97.2	-13.9	91.6	-5.8	80.8	-11.8	88.0	8.9	99.4	13.0	111.1	11.8	99.3	-10.6	106.4	7.2	114.0	7.1	109.5	-3.9
1981	105.2	-3.9	102.4	-2.7	-	-	-	-	107.4	4.9	102.6	-4.5	100.8	-1.8	102.0	1.2	103.5	1.5	103.5	0.0	103.0	-0.5	105.9	2.8
1982	107.7	1.7	107.5	-0.2	102.4	-4.7	104.5	2.1	104.7	0.2	103.2	-1.4	99.3	-3.8	96.7	-2.6	95.6	-1.1	92.7	-3.0	90.2	-2.7	95.4	5.8
1983	95.3	-0.1	94.3	-1.0	94.5	0.2	99.3	5.1	109.2	10.0	109.1	-0.1	110.8	1.6	116.9	5.5	116.4	-0.4	115.1	-1.1	127.1	10.4	130.0	2.3
1984	134.1	3.2	141.4	5.4	146.3	3.5	145.8	-0.3	150.0	2.9	150.9	0.6	150.2	-0.5	149.1	-0.7	150.6	1.0	145.0	-3.7	129.7	-10.6	133.0	2.5
1985	125.4	-5.7	119.3	-4.9	114.3	-4.2	125.6	9.9	126.4	0.6	123.6	-2.2	120.5	-2.5	124.8	3.6	124.8	0.0	129.6	3.8	133.7	3.2	144.8	8.3
1986	144.4	-0.3	145.0	0.4	143.4	-1.1	148.3	3.4	149.7	0.9	151.6	1.3	150.0	-1.1	144.5	-3.7	142.0	-1.7	146.6	3.2	151.7	3.5	154.7	2.0
1987	152.5	-1.4	153.6	0.7	160.7	4.6	171.8	6.9	189.2	10.1	185.4	-2.0	182.9	-1.3	183.3	0.2	188.0	2.6	195.2	3.8	196.4	0.6	199.9	1.8
1988	210.2	5.2	208.7	-0.7	225.6	8.1	234.2	3.8	234.6	0.2	208.6	-11.1	188.8	-9.5	199.5	5.7	205.0	2.8	193.9	-5.4	181.9	-6.2	178.0	-2.1
1989	181.2	1.8	190.3	5.0	228.1	19.9	222.3	-2.5	207.8	-6.5	211.2	1.6	221.3	4.8	214.3	-3.2	217.1	1.3	218.8	0.8	216.9	-0.9	225.8	4.1
1990	203.8	-9.7	227.4	11.6	220.1	-3.2	234.4	6.5	233.0	-0.6	227.8	-2.2	227.4	-0.2	217.2	-4.5	210.3	-3.2	207.2	-1.5	204.0	-1.5	202.6	-0.7
1991	196.8	-2.9	190.6	-3.2	188.1	-1.3	198.1	5.3	184.0	-7.1	174.2	-5.3	166.6	-4.4	161.4	-3.1	152.1	-5.8	154.4	1.5	160.1	3.7	163.9	2.4
1992	164.5	0.4	168.5	2.4	168.4	-0.1	175.3	4.1	180.2	2.8	174.8	-3.0	171.5	-1.9	171.7	0.1	176.8	3.0	178.2	0.8	175.2	-1.7	183.0	4.5
1993	188.1	2.8	178.1	-5.3	180.6	1.4	185.8	2.9	186.6	0.4	181.6	-2.7	185.1	1.9	178.9	-3.3	187.1	4.6	183.9	-1.7	186.3	1.3	188.1	1.0
1994	184.6	-1.9	180.3	-2.3	183.4	1.7	196.4	7.1	199.1	1.4	198.1	-0.5	207.8	4.9	210.0	1.1	217.2	3.4	235.9	8.6	234.1	-0.8	229.1	-2.1
1995	227.1	-0.9	229.6	1.1	238.1	3.7	229.7	-3.5	243.0	5.8	222.6	-8.4	223.3	0.3	212.4	-4.9	205.4	-3.3	191.0	-7.0	181.7	-4.9	182.4	0.4
1996	177.7	-2.6	180.7	1.7	182.1	0.8	180.7	-0.8	183.1	1.3	186.3	1.7	191.5	2.8	196.3	2.5	191.8	-2.3	210.5	9.7	210.1	-0.2	211.1	0.5
1997	213.2	1.0	215.2	0.9	217.5	1.1	217.7	0.1	214.8	-1.3	204.5	-4.8	185.6	-9.2	191.7	3.3	185.8	-3.1	188.4	1.4	196.6	4.4	192.8	-1.9

Source: U.S. Department of Labor, Bureau of Labor Statistics, Division of Industry Prices and Price Indexes. n.e.c. stands for not elsewhere classified. - indicates no data collected for period or unavailable.

Leather
Producer Price Index
Base 1982 = 100

For 1926-1997. Columns headed % show percentile change in the index from the previous period for which an index is available.

Year	Jan Index	%	Feb Index	%	Mar Index	%	Apr Index	%	May Index	%	Jun Index	%	Jul Index	%	Aug Index	%	Sep Index	%	Oct Index	%	Nov Index	%	Dec Index	%
1926	16.4	-	16.4	0.0	16.4	0.0	16.4	0.0	16.1	-1.8	16.1	0.0	16.0	-0.6	16.0	0.0	16.1	0.6	16.1	0.0	16.1	0.0	16.1	0.0
1927	16.1	0.0	16.1	0.0	16.2	0.6	16.2	0.0	16.7	3.1	17.4	4.2	18.3	5.2	18.5	1.1	18.7	1.1	18.9	1.1	18.9	0.0	19.8	4.8
1928	20.0	1.0	20.9	4.5	20.9	0.0	21.0	0.5	21.0	0.0	20.6	-1.9	20.8	1.0	20.8	0.0	20.4	-1.9	20.1	-1.5	19.2	-4.5	19.3	0.5
1929	19.5	1.0	18.9	-3.1	18.2	-3.7	18.0	-1.1	17.9	-0.6	17.9	0.0	18.1	1.1	18.0	-0.6	18.2	1.1	18.5	1.6	18.3	-1.1	17.9	-2.2
1930	17.5	-2.2	17.4	-0.6	17.4	0.0	17.0	-2.3	16.9	-0.6	16.6	-1.8	16.2	-2.4	16.2	0.0	15.9	-1.9	15.6	-1.9	15.1	-3.2	14.8	-2.0
1931	14.7	-0.7	14.4	-2.0	14.3	-0.7	14.3	0.0	14.2	-0.7	14.2	0.0	14.5	2.1	14.6	0.7	13.5	-7.5	13.0	-3.7	12.7	-2.3	12.7	0.0
1932	12.5	-1.6	12.4	-0.8	11.9	-4.0	10.9	-8.4	9.8	-10.1	9.5	-3.1	9.7	2.1	9.7	0.0	10.2	5.2	10.4	2.0	10.0	-3.8	9.5	-5.0
1933	9.2	-3.2	8.9	-3.3	9.0	1.1	9.2	2.2	11.0	19.6	12.0	9.1	12.6	5.0	13.3	5.6	13.8	3.8	13.5	-2.2	12.8	-5.2	12.9	0.8
1934	12.9	0.0	12.9	0.0	12.9	0.0	12.7	-1.6	12.3	-3.1	12.2	-0.8	12.1	-0.8	11.5	-5.0	11.4	-0.9	11.4	0.0	11.5	0.9	11.6	0.9
1935	12.0	3.4	12.0	0.0	12.0	0.0	12.1	0.8	12.9	6.6	13.0	0.8	13.0	0.0	13.0	0.0	13.4	3.1	14.0	4.5	14.2	1.4	14.2	0.0
1936	14.1	-0.7	13.9	-1.4	13.7	-1.4	13.6	-0.7	13.6	0.0	13.5	-0.7	13.4	-0.7	13.3	-0.7	13.6	2.3	13.8	1.5	14.3	3.6	15.0	4.9
1937	15.2	1.3	15.4	1.3	15.7	1.9	16.3	3.8	16.3	0.0	16.0	-1.8	16.0	0.0	16.2	1.3	16.0	-1.2	15.7	-1.9	15.0	-4.5	14.0	-6.7
1938	14.0	0.0	13.6	-2.9	13.5	-0.7	13.3	-1.5	13.3	0.0	13.2	-0.8	13.3	0.8	13.3	0.0	13.3	0.0	13.7	3.0	14.0	2.2	13.9	-0.7
1939	13.7	-1.4	13.6	-0.7	13.4	-1.5	13.4	0.0	13.4	0.0	13.6	1.5	13.6	0.0	13.6	0.0	14.9	9.6	15.8	6.0	15.8	0.0	15.4	-2.5
1940	15.5	0.6	15.2	-1.9	15.1	-0.7	15.1	0.0	15.1	0.0	14.9	-1.3	14.8	-0.7	14.3	-3.4	14.4	0.7	14.7	2.1	15.1	2.7	15.2	0.7
1941	15.3	0.7	15.3	0.0	15.3	0.0	15.4	0.7	15.7	1.9	15.8	0.6	15.9	0.6	15.9	0.0	16.2	1.9	16.3	0.6	16.4	0.6	16.4	0.0
1942	16.4	0.0	16.4	0.0	16.4	0.0	16.4	0.0	16.4	0.0	16.4	0.0	16.4	0.0	16.4	0.0	16.4	0.0	16.4	0.0	16.4	0.0	16.4	0.0
1943	16.4	0.0	16.4	0.0	16.4	0.0	16.4	0.0	16.4	0.0	16.4	0.0	16.4	0.0	16.4	0.0	16.4	0.0	16.4	0.0	16.4	0.0	16.4	0.0
1944	16.4	0.0	16.4	0.0	16.4	0.0	16.4	0.0	16.4	0.0	16.4	0.0	16.4	0.0	16.4	0.0	16.4	0.0	16.4	0.0	16.4	0.0	16.4	0.0
1945	16.4	0.0	16.4	0.0	16.4	0.0	16.4	0.0	16.4	0.0	16.4	0.0	16.4	0.0	16.4	0.0	16.8	2.4	16.8	0.0	16.8	0.0	16.8	0.0
1946	16.8	0.0	16.8	0.0	16.8	0.0	16.8	0.0	16.8	0.0	17.9	6.5	21.5	20.1	21.6	0.5	22.4	3.7	22.4	0.0	28.8	28.6	29.9	3.8
1947	29.2	-2.3	29.5	1.0	29.8	1.0	29.6	-0.7	29.2	-1.4	29.6	1.4	30.1	1.7	30.7	2.0	31.9	3.9	35.6	11.6	36.5	2.5	35.2	-3.6
1948	33.6	-4.5	30.5	-9.2	29.2	-4.3	29.7	1.7	30.3	2.0	30.4	0.3	30.4	0.0	29.1	-4.3	28.5	-2.1	28.5	0.0	29.8	4.6	29.2	-2.0
1949	29.2	0.0	27.9	-4.5	27.4	-1.8	27.1	-1.1	27.0	-0.4	27.1	0.4	26.7	-1.5	27.2	1.9	27.8	2.2	28.5	2.5	28.5	0.0	28.4	-0.4
1950	28.1	-1.1	27.9	-0.7	28.3	1.4	28.5	0.7	28.8	1.1	29.2	1.4	32.5	11.3	33.2	2.2	34.5	3.9	35.1	1.7	36.3	3.4	38.8	6.9
1951	40.8	5.2	40.9	0.2	40.9	0.0	40.9	0.0	40.8	-0.2	39.4	-3.4	37.9	-3.8	35.2	-7.1	35.7	1.4	32.7	-8.4	29.8	-8.9	29.3	-1.7
1952	28.8	-1.7	26.6	-7.6	26.0	-2.3	25.1	-3.5	25.1	0.0	26.4	5.2	26.5	0.4	26.5	0.0	26.5	0.0	26.7	0.8	26.8	0.4	27.6	3.0
1953	27.3	-1.1	27.3	0.0	27.7	1.5	27.5	-0.7	28.9	5.1	29.1	0.7	28.5	-2.1	28.2	-1.1	28.1	-0.4	26.8	-4.6	26.8	0.0	26.3	-1.9
1954	26.1	-0.8	26.0	-0.4	25.6	-1.5	25.5	-0.4	26.0	2.0	26.0	0.0	25.7	-1.2	25.1	-2.3	24.6	-2.0	24.4	-0.8	24.3	-0.4	24.2	-0.4
1955	24.1	-0.4	24.4	1.2	24.4	0.0	24.8	1.6	25.2	1.6	24.9	-1.2	25.3	1.6	25.2	-0.4	25.3	0.4	25.6	1.2	26.0	1.6	26.2	0.8
1956	26.6	1.5	26.7	0.4	27.0	1.1	28.1	4.1	27.6	-1.8	27.2	-1.4	27.2	0.0	27.0	-0.7	27.0	0.0	27.0	0.0	26.9	-0.4	27.0	0.4
1957	26.2	-3.0	26.0	-0.8	26.3	1.2	26.3	0.0	26.3	0.0	27.0	2.7	27.4	1.5	27.2	-0.7	27.2	0.0	27.1	-0.4	27.1	0.0	27.0	-0.4
1958	26.9	-0.4	26.9	0.0	27.0	0.4	27.0	0.0	27.0	0.0	27.3	1.1	27.2	-0.4	27.2	0.0	27.1	-0.4	27.6	1.8	28.1	1.8	29.5	5.0
1959	29.5	0.0	30.0	1.7	30.7	2.3	35.7	16.3	37.0	3.6	35.7	-3.5	35.2	-1.4	34.8	-1.1	34.8	0.0	33.3	-4.3	30.8	-7.5	30.7	-0.3
1960	31.3	2.0	31.1	-0.6	30.5	-1.9	31.1	2.0	30.7	-1.3	30.6	-0.3	30.4	-0.7	29.4	-3.3	28.9	-1.7	29.1	0.7	28.8	-1.0	29.5	2.4
1961	29.0	-1.7	28.9	-0.3	29.8	3.1	30.4	2.0	30.9	1.6	30.4	-1.6	30.4	0.0	31.6	3.9	32.0	1.3	32.5	1.6	32.2	-0.9	32.2	0.0
1962	32.3	0.3	32.2	-0.3	31.9	-0.9	31.9	0.0	32.2	0.9	32.0	-0.6	31.6	-1.2	31.1	-1.6	31.0	-0.3	31.0	0.0	31.1	0.3	30.9	-0.6
1963	30.6	-1.0	30.5	-0.3	30.2	-1.0	29.9	-1.0	30.1	0.7	29.8	-1.0	29.8	0.0	29.2	-2.0	29.0	-0.7	29.0	0.0	29.0	0.0	29.0	0.0
1964	29.0	0.0	29.0	0.0	29.0	0.0	29.7	2.4	30.4	2.4	30.1	-1.0	30.5	1.3	30.4	-0.3	30.3	-0.3	30.5	0.7	30.3	-0.7	30.3	0.0
1965	30.4	0.3	30.1	-1.0	30.8	2.3	30.2	-1.9	30.4	0.7	31.3	3.0	30.8	-1.6	32.8	6.5	32.3	-1.5	32.6	0.9	33.0	1.2	33.2	0.6
1966	33.9	2.1	34.4	1.5	35.9	4.4	35.6	-0.8	36.4	2.2	36.9	1.4	36.7	-0.5	36.4	-0.8	35.5	-2.5	34.2	-3.7	33.2	-2.9	33.8	1.8
1967	34.0	0.6	33.9	-0.3	33.4	-1.5	32.9	-1.5	32.3	-1.8	32.1	-0.6	31.9	-0.6	31.1	-2.5	30.7	-1.3	30.5	-0.7	31.0	1.6	31.8	2.6
1968	31.6	-0.6	31.7	0.3	32.1	1.3	32.5	1.2	32.8	0.9	32.9	0.3	33.1	0.6	33.1	0.0	33.2	0.3	33.5	0.9	33.1	-1.2	33.7	1.8
1969	34.0	0.9	33.9	-0.3	33.9	0.0	35.6	5.0	35.4	-0.6	35.4	0.0	35.3	-0.3	35.2	-0.3	35.4	0.6	35.0	-1.1	34.8	-0.6	34.8	0.0
1970	34.8	0.0	34.1	-2.0	34.4	0.9	35.1	2.0	35.1	0.0	34.9	-0.6	34.9	0.0	34.6	-0.9	34.0	-1.7	34.4	1.2	34.5	0.3	34.5	0.0

[Continued]

Leather

Producer Price Index
Base 1982 = 100

[Continued]

For 1926-1997. Columns headed % show percentile change in the index from the previous period for which an index is available.

Year	Jan Index	%	Feb Index	%	Mar Index	%	Apr Index	%	May Index	%	Jun Index	%	Jul Index	%	Aug Index	%	Sep Index	%	Oct Index	%	Nov Index	%	Dec Index	%
1971	34.8	0.9	34.9	0.3	34.9	0.0	35.6	2.0	36.3	2.0	36.7	1.1	36.7	0.0	36.7	0.0	36.6	-0.3	36.7	0.3	36.7	0.0	37.8	3.0
1972	38.5	1.9	38.7	0.5	41.3	6.7	44.4	7.5	44.3	-0.2	44.5	0.5	44.3	-0.4	45.1	1.8	46.1	2.2	49.2	6.7	52.2	6.1	52.1	-0.2
1973	52.3	0.4	52.3	0.0	52.8	1.0	51.8	-1.9	51.3	-1.0	50.2	-2.1	50.4	0.4	50.6	0.4	52.3	3.4	51.6	-1.3	51.5	-0.2	50.1	-2.7
1974	50.0	-0.2	49.8	-0.4	50.3	1.0	50.9	1.2	51.2	0.6	50.3	-1.8	49.9	-0.8	49.6	-0.6	49.9	0.6	48.7	-2.4	47.4	-2.7	46.7	-1.5
1975	45.3	-3.0	44.6	-1.5	45.5	2.0	48.7	7.0	49.2	1.0	49.2	0.0	49.0	-0.4	48.7	-0.6	49.5	1.6	49.8	0.6	52.2	4.8	52.3	0.2
1976	53.0	1.3	55.5	4.7	57.5	3.6	59.0	2.6	65.3	10.7	61.4	-6.0	61.7	0.5	63.1	2.3	63.4	0.5	62.0	-2.2	61.5	-0.8	61.6	0.2
1977	64.1	4.1	64.7	0.9	64.7	0.0	65.6	1.4	67.7	3.2	65.0	-4.0	63.8	-1.8	64.3	0.8	64.4	0.2	63.1	-2.0	63.2	0.2	64.4	1.9
1978	67.7	5.1	68.1	0.6	69.1	1.5	69.8	1.0	69.8	0.0	69.8	0.0	72.1	3.3	80.9	12.2	86.5	6.9	86.5	0.0	89.5	3.5	89.8	0.3
1979	94.0	4.7	99.3	5.6	119.4	20.2	126.4	5.9	137.9	9.1	133.2	-3.4	123.7	-7.1	117.5	-5.0	106.0	-9.8	110.3	4.1	102.7	-6.9	104.3	1.6
1980	111.6	7.0	109.3	-2.1	99.9	-8.6	95.6	-4.3	93.3	-2.4	91.3	-2.1	93.8	2.7	100.9	7.6	95.7	-5.2	97.0	1.4	101.9	5.1	106.8	4.8
1981	106.8	0.0	99.6	-6.7	103.6	4.0	108.5	4.7	106.0	-2.3	103.1	-2.7	102.4	-0.7	100.8	-1.6	100.6	-0.2	100.7	0.1	100.0	-0.7	100.3	0.3
1982	102.5	2.2	102.0	-0.5	100.6	-1.4	99.7	-0.9	99.5	-0.2	98.8	-0.7	98.7	-0.1	97.9	-0.8	99.3	1.4	99.4	0.1	100.5	1.1	101.0	0.5
1983	101.0	0.0	100.5	-0.5	101.6	1.1	102.9	1.3	104.9	1.9	107.9	2.9	108.5	0.6	110.3	1.7	109.0	-1.2	108.1	-0.8	109.4	1.2	110.5	1.0
1984	111.2	0.6	116.3	4.6	121.4	4.4	124.2	2.3	125.5	1.0	124.6	-0.7	123.1	-1.2	121.4	-1.4	119.3	-1.7	118.6	-0.6	115.5	-2.6	113.8	-1.5
1985	115.0	1.1	113.2	-1.6	111.9	-1.1	112.5	0.5	112.6	0.1	112.1	-0.4	112.0	-0.1	112.5	0.4	113.0	0.4	114.0	0.9	115.6	1.4	116.3	0.6
1986	118.4	1.8	118.4	0.0	118.5	0.1	118.9	0.3	123.2	3.6	126.6	2.8	125.4	-0.9	125.8	0.3	124.7	-0.9	122.7	-1.6	124.2	1.2	127.8	2.9
1987	128.1	0.2	129.4	1.0	131.9	1.9	137.5	4.2	140.5	2.2	143.1	1.9	142.3	-0.6	141.0	-0.9	145.6	3.3	148.6	2.1	149.6	0.7	153.0	2.3
1988	158.0	3.3	160.1	1.3	171.1	6.9	175.1	2.3	176.4	0.7	165.0	-6.5	165.7	0.4	168.2	1.5	168.8	0.4	170.7	1.1	166.0	-2.8	164.9	-0.7
1989	166.6	1.0	169.4	1.7	170.2	0.5	168.2	-1.2	166.7	-0.9	168.0	0.8	171.4	2.0	171.5	0.1	172.5	0.6	172.9	0.2	173.0	0.1	174.0	0.6
1990	176.6	1.5	178.0	0.8	177.7	-0.2	179.5	1.0	181.2	0.9	179.6	-0.9	179.0	-0.3	177.3	-0.9	176.5	-0.5	175.4	-0.6	174.9	-0.3	174.7	-0.1
1991	174.3	-0.2	173.7	-0.3	172.6	-0.6	172.1	-0.3	172.7	0.3	171.7	-0.6	167.7	-2.3	165.8	-1.1	163.4	-1.4	161.5	-1.2	162.4	0.6	162.8	0.2
1992	161.3	-0.9	161.8	0.3	163.4	1.0	162.8	-0.4	163.9	0.7	164.0	0.1	164.7	0.4	163.7	-0.6	164.8	0.7	165.1	0.2	164.0	-0.7	165.1	0.7
1993	166.6	0.9	169.0	1.4	169.0	0.0	168.3	-0.4	169.7	0.8	168.7	-0.6	167.2	-0.9	168.7	0.9	169.0	0.2	168.6	-0.2	168.9	0.2	169.1	0.1
1994	171.2	1.2	171.0	-0.1	172.9	1.1	173.6	0.4	174.9	0.7	178.5	2.1	180.7	1.2	181.2	0.3	184.4	1.8	186.8	1.3	189.4	1.4	190.4	0.5
1995	192.2	0.9	194.7	1.3	195.2	0.3	198.4	1.6	199.5	0.6	195.3	-2.1	193.9	-0.7	190.0	-2.0	186.5	-1.8	184.6	-1.0	183.5	-0.6	182.4	-0.6
1996	182.3	-0.1	181.0	-0.7	181.2	0.1	176.1	-2.8	178.1	1.1	175.2	-1.6	172.7	-1.4	173.4	0.4	176.0	1.5	177.4	0.8	179.4	1.1	182.5	1.7
1997	183.2	0.4	185.3	1.1	185.5	0.1	188.1	1.4	183.6	-2.4	180.2	-1.9	179.7	-0.3	178.0	-0.9	178.4	0.2	181.3	1.6	184.7	1.9	182.9	-1.0

Source: U.S. Department of Labor, Bureau of Labor Statistics, Division of Industry Prices and Price Indexes. n.e.c. stands for not elsewhere classified. - indicates no data collected for period or unavailable.

Footwear
Producer Price Index
Base 1982 = 100

For 1926-1997. Columns headed % show percentile change in the index from the previous period for which an index is available.

Year	Jan Index	%	Feb Index	%	Mar Index	%	Apr Index	%	May Index	%	Jun Index	%	Jul Index	%	Aug Index	%	Sep Index	%	Oct Index	%	Nov Index	%	Dec Index	%
1926	14.7	-	14.7	0.0	14.7	0.0	14.7	0.0	14.7	0.0	14.7	0.0	14.5	-1.4	14.5	0.0	14.5	0.0	14.5	0.0	14.5	0.0	14.5	0.0
1927	14.5	0.0	14.5	0.0	14.5	0.0	14.5	0.0	14.6	0.7	14.7	0.7	15.0	2.0	15.1	0.7	15.4	2.0	15.4	0.0	15.5	0.6	15.6	0.6
1928	15.8	1.3	15.9	0.6	16.0	0.6	16.1	0.6	16.1	0.0	16.2	0.6	16.2	0.0	16.2	0.0	16.2	0.0	16.1	-0.6	15.9	-1.2	15.8	-0.6
1929	15.6	-1.3	15.6	0.0	15.6	0.0	15.6	0.0	15.5	-0.6	15.5	0.0	15.5	0.0	15.5	0.0	15.5	0.0	15.5	0.0	15.5	0.0	15.5	0.0
1930	15.1	-2.6	15.1	0.0	15.1	0.0	15.1	0.0	15.1	0.0	15.0	-0.7	15.0	0.0	14.7	-2.0	14.7	0.0	14.7	0.0	14.7	0.0	14.3	-2.7
1931	13.9	-2.8	13.8	-0.7	13.8	0.0	13.8	0.0	13.8	0.0	13.8	0.0	13.6	-1.4	13.6	0.0	13.6	0.0	13.6	0.0	13.5	-0.7	13.0	-3.7
1932	12.9	-0.8	12.9	0.0	12.9	0.0	12.9	0.0	12.9	0.0	12.7	-1.6	12.3	-3.1	12.3	0.0	12.3	0.0	12.3	0.0	12.3	0.0	12.2	-0.8
1933	12.2	0.0	12.1	-0.8	12.1	0.0	12.1	0.0	12.2	0.8	12.4	1.6	12.9	4.0	14.0	8.5	14.4	2.9	14.4	0.0	14.4	0.0	14.4	0.0
1934	14.4	0.0	14.4	0.0	14.4	0.0	14.4	0.0	14.4	0.0	14.4	0.0	14.3	-0.7	14.3	0.0	14.3	0.0	14.3	0.0	14.2	-0.7	14.2	0.0
1935	14.1	-0.7	14.2	0.7	14.2	0.0	14.2	0.0	14.2	0.0	14.2	0.0	14.3	0.7	14.3	0.0	14.3	0.0	14.4	0.7	14.5	0.7	14.6	0.7
1936	14.7	0.7	14.7	0.0	14.7	0.0	14.7	0.0	14.6	-0.7	14.5	-0.7	14.5	0.0	14.5	0.0	14.5	0.0	14.5	0.0	14.5	0.0	14.5	0.0
1937	14.5	0.0	14.8	2.1	14.9	0.7	15.1	1.3	15.5	2.6	15.7	1.3	15.6	-0.6	15.6	0.0	15.7	0.6	15.7	0.0	15.6	-0.6	15.4	-1.3
1938	15.3	-0.6	15.2	-0.7	15.2	0.0	15.2	0.0	14.9	-2.0	14.9	0.0	14.8	-0.7	14.7	-0.7	14.7	0.0	14.7	0.0	14.7	0.0	14.7	0.0
1939	14.8	0.7	14.7	-0.7	14.8	0.7	14.8	0.0	14.8	0.0	14.8	0.0	14.7	-0.7	14.7	0.0	14.9	1.4	15.4	3.4	15.6	1.3	15.7	0.6
1940	15.7	0.0	15.8	0.6	15.8	0.0	15.8	0.0	15.8	0.0	15.8	0.0	15.6	-1.3	15.6	0.0	15.6	0.0	15.6	0.0	15.6	0.0	15.6	0.0
1941	15.6	0.0	15.6	0.0	15.6	0.0	15.8	1.3	16.0	1.3	16.3	1.9	16.7	2.5	16.9	1.2	17.1	1.2	17.3	1.2	17.6	1.7	17.6	0.0
1942	17.7	0.6	17.8	0.6	18.1	1.7	18.5	2.2	18.5	0.0	18.4	-0.5	18.4	0.0	18.4	0.0	18.4	0.0	18.4	0.0	18.4	0.0	18.4	0.0
1943	18.4	0.0	18.4	0.0	18.4	0.0	18.4	0.0	18.4	0.0	18.4	0.0	18.4	0.0	18.4	0.0	18.4	0.0	18.4	0.0	18.4	0.0	18.4	0.0
1944	18.4	0.0	18.4	0.0	18.4	0.0	18.4	0.0	18.4	0.0	18.4	0.0	18.4	0.0	18.4	0.0	18.4	0.0	18.4	0.0	18.4	0.0	18.4	0.0
1945	18.4	0.0	18.4	0.0	18.4	0.0	18.4	0.0	18.4	0.0	18.4	0.0	18.4	0.0	18.4	0.0	18.4	0.0	18.4	0.0	18.5	0.5	18.5	0.0
1946	18.7	1.1	18.7	0.0	18.7	0.0	18.7	0.0	18.8	0.5	18.9	0.5	20.5	8.5	20.5	0.0	21.1	2.9	21.1	0.0	23.8	12.8	24.8	4.2
1947	25.3	2.0	25.3	0.0	25.3	0.0	25.4	0.4	25.6	0.8	25.6	0.0	25.7	0.4	26.0	1.2	25.8	-0.8	26.1	1.2	26.5	1.5	27.2	2.6
1948	27.4	0.7	27.4	0.0	27.6	0.7	27.8	0.7	27.6	-0.7	27.5	-0.4	27.6	0.4	27.8	0.7	27.9	0.4	27.8	-0.4	27.5	-1.1	27.5	0.0
1949	27.4	-0.4	27.4	0.0	27.4	0.0	27.3	-0.4	27.1	-0.7	27.1	0.0	27.1	0.0	27.1	0.0	27.1	0.0	27.1	0.0	27.3	0.7	27.5	0.7
1950	27.3	-0.7	27.3	0.0	27.4	0.4	27.4	0.0	27.6	0.7	27.6	0.0	27.8	0.7	28.7	3.2	29.1	1.4	30.1	3.4	31.2	3.7	32.2	3.2
1951	32.9	2.2	33.5	1.8	33.1	-1.2	33.1	0.0	33.1	0.0	33.0	-0.3	32.9	-0.3	32.8	-0.3	32.8	0.0	32.1	-2.1	31.8	-0.9	31.3	-1.6
1952	31.2	-0.3	31.2	0.0	31.2	0.0	30.4	-2.6	29.9	-1.6	29.8	-0.3	29.8	0.0	29.8	0.0	29.8	0.0	29.8	0.0	29.8	0.0	30.1	1.0
1953	30.1	0.0	30.2	0.3	30.2	0.0	30.0	-0.7	30.0	0.0	30.0	0.0	30.0	0.0	30.1	0.3	30.1	0.0	30.0	-0.3	30.1	0.3	30.1	0.0
1954	30.1	0.0	30.1	0.0	30.1	0.0	30.1	0.0	30.1	0.0	30.1	0.0	30.1	0.0	30.1	0.0	30.1	0.0	30.1	0.0	30.0	-0.3	30.0	0.0
1955	30.0	0.0	30.0	0.0	30.0	0.0	30.0	0.0	30.0	0.0	30.0	0.0	30.0	0.0	30.0	0.0	30.0	0.0	30.5	1.7	31.1	2.0	31.1	0.0
1956	31.1	0.0	31.1	0.0	31.3	0.6	32.2	2.9	32.3	0.3	32.4	0.3	32.4	0.0	32.4	0.0	32.4	0.0	32.5	0.3	32.5	0.0	32.5	0.0
1957	32.5	0.0	32.5	0.0	32.5	0.0	32.6	0.3	32.5	-0.3	32.5	0.0	32.6	0.3	32.6	0.0	32.6	0.0	32.8	0.6	32.9	0.3	32.7	-0.6
1958	32.8	0.3	32.8	0.0	32.8	0.0	32.7	-0.3	32.8	0.3	32.8	0.0	32.8	0.0	32.8	0.0	32.8	0.0	33.0	0.6	33.1	0.3	33.1	0.0
1959	33.1	0.0	33.1	0.0	33.3	0.6	34.5	3.6	34.8	0.9	35.0	0.6	35.1	0.3	35.6	1.4	35.6	0.0	35.9	0.8	36.0	0.3	36.1	0.3
1960	36.1	0.0	36.1	0.0	36.1	0.0	35.9	-0.6	35.6	-0.8	35.6	0.0	35.6	0.0	35.6	0.0	35.6	0.0	35.6	0.0	35.6	0.0	35.6	0.0
1961	35.7	0.3	35.7	0.0	35.7	0.0	35.7	0.0	35.8	0.3	35.8	0.0	35.8	0.0	35.9	0.3	36.0	0.3	36.2	0.6	36.3	0.3	36.3	0.0
1962	36.3	0.0	36.3	0.0	36.3	0.0	36.3	0.0	36.3	0.0	36.3	0.0	36.4	0.3	36.4	0.0	36.4	0.0	36.2	-0.5	36.2	0.0	36.3	0.3
1963	36.2	-0.3	36.2	0.0	36.2	0.0	36.2	0.0	36.2	0.0	36.2	0.0	36.2	0.0	36.2	0.0	36.2	0.0	36.2	0.0	36.2	0.0	36.2	0.0
1964	36.2	0.0	36.2	0.0	36.2	0.0	36.2	0.0	36.2	0.0	36.2	0.0	36.2	0.0	36.2	0.0	36.2	0.0	36.5	0.8	36.5	0.0	36.5	0.0
1965	36.5	0.0	36.5	0.0	36.5	0.0	36.7	0.5	36.7	0.0	36.7	0.0	36.8	0.3	36.9	0.3	36.9	0.0	38.0	3.0	38.0	0.0	38.0	0.0
1966	38.3	0.8	38.5	0.5	38.6	0.3	39.5	2.3	39.8	0.8	39.8	0.0	39.8	0.0	39.8	0.0	39.8	0.0	40.2	1.0	40.2	0.0	40.2	0.0
1967	40.5	0.7	40.7	0.5	40.7	0.0	40.6	-0.2	40.6	0.0	40.6	0.0	40.6	0.0	40.5	-0.2	40.7	0.5	41.3	1.5	41.3	0.0	41.6	0.7
1968	42.0	1.0	42.0	0.0	42.0	0.0	42.3	0.7	42.5	0.5	42.5	0.0	42.6	0.2	42.5	-0.2	43.1	1.4	43.9	1.9	44.0	0.2	44.0	0.0
1969	44.2	0.5	44.2	0.0	44.0	-0.5	44.1	0.2	44.2	0.2	44.2	0.0	44.4	0.5	44.5	0.2	45.3	1.8	45.6	0.7	45.8	0.4	45.7	-0.2
1970	46.1	0.9	46.4	0.7	46.4	0.0	46.2	-0.4	46.1	-0.2	46.1	0.0	46.1	0.0	46.1	0.0	46.4	0.7	46.5	0.2	46.5	0.0	46.5	0.0

[Continued]

Footwear
Producer Price Index
Base 1982 = 100
[Continued]

For 1926-1997. Columns headed % show percentile change in the index from the previous period for which an index is available.

Year	Jan Index	%	Feb Index	%	Mar Index	%	Apr Index	%	May Index	%	Jun Index	%	Jul Index	%	Aug Index	%	Sep Index	%	Oct Index	%	Nov Index	%	Dec Index	%
1971	47.5	2.2	47.5	0.0	47.5	0.0	47.6	0.2	47.7	0.2	47.7	0.0	47.7	0.0	47.7	0.0	47.7	0.0	47.7	0.0	47.7	0.0	47.8	0.2
1972	48.2	0.8	48.4	0.4	49.0	1.2	50.0	2.0	50.9	1.8	51.4	1.0	51.6	0.4	51.6	0.0	51.7	0.2	51.8	0.2	52.4	1.2	52.5	0.2
1973	52.6	0.2	53.4	1.5	53.5	0.2	53.7	0.4	52.8	-1.7	52.8	0.0	52.9	0.2	52.9	0.0	53.2	0.6	53.5	0.6	53.8	0.6	54.1	0.6
1974	54.7	1.1	55.1	0.7	55.5	0.7	56.4	1.6	56.6	0.4	56.9	0.5	57.1	0.4	57.4	0.5	58.8	2.4	58.9	0.2	59.1	0.3	59.1	0.0
1975	59.3	0.3	59.6	0.5	59.6	0.0	59.9	0.5	59.9	0.0	60.0	0.2	60.1	0.2	60.2	0.2	61.0	1.3	61.3	0.5	61.3	0.0	61.4	0.2
1976	62.1	1.1	62.8	1.1	63.2	0.6	63.8	0.9	64.0	0.3	64.8	1.3	65.6	1.2	65.8	0.3	66.3	0.8	66.4	0.2	66.5	0.2	66.8	0.5
1977	67.1	0.4	67.5	0.6	67.9	0.6	68.2	0.4	68.6	0.6	68.6	0.0	69.3	1.0	69.4	0.1	69.4	0.0	69.9	0.7	70.0	0.1	70.1	0.1
1978	70.8	1.0	71.7	1.3	71.7	0.0	73.5	2.5	73.8	0.4	73.9	0.1	74.1	0.3	75.1	1.3	75.9	1.1	77.8	2.5	78.4	0.8	79.3	1.1
1979	80.2	1.1	82.8	3.2	85.7	3.5	86.6	1.1	88.3	2.0	90.3	2.3	90.5	0.2	92.0	1.7	92.6	0.7	92.9	0.3	93.0	0.1	93.0	0.0
1980	93.5	0.5	93.1	-0.4	94.6	1.6	94.7	0.1	94.7	0.0	94.7	0.0	95.0	0.3	95.4	0.4	96.1	0.7	96.6	0.5	97.0	0.4	96.7	-0.3
1981	97.3	0.6	98.2	0.9	98.1	-0.1	98.4	0.3	98.5	0.1	98.6	0.1	98.9	0.3	99.0	0.1	99.1	0.1	97.8	-1.3	97.9	0.1	98.0	0.1
1982	97.5	-0.5	97.4	-0.1	97.9	0.5	99.9	2.0	99.8	-0.1	99.7	-0.1	101.0	1.3	101.1	0.1	101.3	0.2	101.6	0.3	101.7	0.1	101.1	-0.6
1983	102.7	1.6	101.1	-1.6	101.3	0.2	102.1	0.8	101.5	-0.6	102.0	0.5	102.0	0.0	102.4	0.4	102.7	0.3	102.6	-0.1	102.6	0.0	102.2	-0.4
1984	102.4	0.2	103.1	0.7	103.5	0.4	102.7	-0.8	102.6	-0.1	102.3	-0.3	102.1	-0.2	102.4	0.3	102.8	0.4	102.9	0.1	103.0	0.1	103.1	0.1
1985	103.2	0.1	104.5	1.3	104.2	-0.3	104.1	-0.1	103.6	-0.5	104.9	1.3	104.9	0.0	105.3	0.4	105.7	0.4	105.7	0.0	105.5	-0.2	105.5	0.0
1986	105.9	0.4	106.3	0.4	106.8	0.5	107.1	0.3	106.8	-0.3	106.4	-0.4	106.5	0.1	106.8	0.3	107.0	0.2	107.5	0.5	107.5	0.0	107.8	0.3
1987	108.0	0.2	107.5	-0.5	108.4	0.8	108.2	-0.2	108.9	0.6	107.5	-1.3	109.7	2.0	110.3	0.5	111.0	0.6	110.9	-0.1	110.6	-0.3	111.4	0.7
1988	112.7	1.2	113.7	0.9	114.0	0.3	114.1	0.1	114.2	0.1	114.8	0.5	115.5	0.6	116.0	0.4	116.2	0.2	116.4	0.2	116.9	0.4	117.2	0.3
1989	118.1	0.8	119.5	1.2	119.8	0.3	120.0	0.2	119.9	-0.1	119.9	0.0	120.4	0.4	121.8	1.2	122.3	0.4	122.5	0.2	122.5	0.0	123.1	0.5
1990	124.2	0.9	125.3	0.9	125.5	0.2	125.4	-0.1	125.8	0.3	125.5	-0.2	125.6	0.1	126.0	0.3	126.1	0.1	126.2	0.1	125.9	-0.2	126.1	0.2
1991	126.3	0.2	127.1	0.6	128.0	0.7	128.3	0.2	128.7	0.3	128.8	0.1	129.2	0.3	129.3	0.1	129.5	0.2	129.1	-0.3	129.3	0.2	129.6	0.2
1992	130.6	0.8	131.8	0.9	131.4	-0.3	131.5	0.1	131.6	0.1	131.9	0.2	132.1	0.2	132.5	0.3	132.8	0.2	132.4	-0.3	132.4	0.0	133.3	0.7
1993	133.5	0.2	133.8	0.2	133.9	0.1	134.5	0.4	134.1	-0.3	134.2	0.1	134.8	0.4	134.8	0.0	134.9	0.1	134.7	-0.1	134.9	0.1	135.1	0.1
1994	135.5	0.3	135.1	-0.3	135.4	0.2	135.2	-0.1	135.4	0.1	135.2	-0.1	135.3	0.1	135.3	0.0	135.6	0.2	135.8	0.1	136.1	0.2	136.6	0.4
1995	137.5	0.7	138.6	0.8	138.7	0.1	138.8	0.1	138.9	0.1	139.0	0.1	139.2	0.1	139.3	0.1	139.3	0.0	140.1	0.6	140.4	0.2	140.5	0.1
1996	140.6	0.1	141.1	0.4	141.3	0.1	141.2	-0.1	141.2	0.0	141.6	0.3	141.7	0.1	142.0	0.2	142.0	0.0	142.2	0.1	142.2	0.0	142.3	0.1
1997	143.1	0.6	143.3	0.1	143.5	0.1	143.5	0.0	143.7	0.1	142.2	-1.0	144.1	1.3	144.3	0.1	144.4	0.1	144.4	0.0	144.2	-0.1	144.2	0.0

Source: U.S. Department of Labor, Bureau of Labor Statistics, Division of Industry Prices and Price Indexes. n.e.c. stands for not elsewhere classified. - indicates no data collected for period or unavailable.

Other Leather and Related Products
Producer Price Index
Base 1982 = 100

For 1947-1997. Columns headed % show percentile change in the index from the previous period for which an index is available.

Year	Jan Index	%	Feb Index	%	Mar Index	%	Apr Index	%	May Index	%	Jun Index	%	Jul Index	%	Aug Index	%	Sep Index	%	Oct Index	%	Nov Index	%	Dec Index	%
1947	35.0	-	34.4	-1.7	34.4	0.0	34.2	-0.6	33.6	-1.8	33.5	-0.3	34.5	3.0	35.0	1.4	35.4	1.1	36.0	1.7	37.6	4.4	37.8	0.5
1948	37.7	-0.3	37.2	-1.3	36.2	-2.7	35.7	-1.4	35.8	0.3	35.9	0.3	36.1	0.6	36.0	-0.3	35.5	-1.4	35.2	-0.8	35.3	0.3	35.6	0.8
1949	35.5	-0.3	35.4	-0.3	34.8	-1.7	34.3	-1.4	34.4	0.3	34.2	-0.6	34.0	-0.6	33.9	-0.3	33.8	-0.3	33.9	0.3	33.8	-0.3	34.0	0.6
1950	33.6	-1.2	33.6	0.0	33.6	0.0	33.6	0.0	33.7	0.3	33.5	-0.6	34.0	1.5	34.8	2.4	35.2	1.1	35.7	1.4	36.1	1.1	36.9	2.2
1951	40.0	8.4	40.6	1.5	40.6	0.0	40.9	0.7	40.7	-0.5	40.5	-0.5	40.1	-1.0	39.0	-2.7	39.0	0.0	37.6	-3.6	37.2	-1.1	37.2	0.0
1952	36.6	-1.6	36.3	-0.8	35.8	-1.4	35.2	-1.7	35.3	0.3	35.4	0.3	35.3	-0.3	35.2	-0.3	35.1	-0.3	34.8	-0.9	35.0	0.6	35.3	0.9
1953	34.8	-1.4	34.8	0.0	34.8	0.0	34.9	0.3	35.1	0.6	35.3	0.6	35.0	-0.8	35.0	0.0	34.8	-0.6	34.8	0.0	34.7	-0.3	34.5	-0.6
1954	34.5	0.0	34.4	-0.3	34.3	-0.3	34.2	-0.3	34.2	0.0	34.2	0.0	34.1	-0.3	34.0	-0.3	33.9	-0.3	33.8	-0.3	33.8	0.0	33.7	-0.3
1955	33.7	0.0	33.7	0.0	33.6	-0.3	33.7	0.3	33.4	-0.9	33.4	0.0	33.9	1.5	33.9	0.0	33.8	-0.3	33.8	0.0	33.8	0.0	34.0	0.6
1956	34.3	0.9	34.5	0.6	34.5	0.0	34.8	0.9	34.8	0.0	34.8	0.0	34.7	-0.3	34.8	0.3	34.6	-0.6	34.6	0.0	34.6	0.0	34.5	-0.3
1957	34.4	-0.3	34.2	-0.6	34.4	0.6	34.4	0.0	34.2	-0.6	34.2	0.0	34.6	1.2	34.5	-0.3	34.6	0.3	34.6	0.0	34.7	0.3	34.6	-0.3
1958	34.6	0.0	34.6	0.0	34.2	-1.2	34.3	0.3	34.2	-0.3	34.2	0.0	34.2	0.0	34.0	-0.6	34.0	0.0	34.2	0.6	34.2	0.0	34.5	0.9
1959	34.8	0.9	35.4	1.7	36.3	2.5	38.7	6.6	39.5	2.1	39.4	-0.3	40.0	1.5	40.1	0.2	40.0	-0.2	39.1	-2.3	38.4	-1.8	37.9	-1.3
1960	38.0	0.3	37.7	-0.8	37.7	0.0	37.7	0.0	37.5	-0.5	37.4	-0.3	37.1	-0.8	36.8	-0.8	36.5	-0.8	36.5	0.0	36.6	0.3	36.5	-0.3
1961	36.6	0.3	36.5	-0.3	36.4	-0.3	36.6	0.5	36.7	0.3	36.7	0.0	36.6	-0.3	36.9	0.8	37.0	0.3	36.9	-0.3	37.2	0.8	37.2	0.0
1962	37.4	0.5	37.3	-0.3	37.3	0.0	36.6	-1.9	36.3	-0.8	37.4	3.0	37.5	0.3	37.1	-1.1	37.1	0.0	37.4	0.8	37.5	0.3	37.6	0.3
1963	37.4	-0.5	37.4	0.0	37.4	0.0	37.3	-0.3	37.2	-0.3	37.2	0.0	37.1	-0.3	36.9	-0.5	36.9	0.0	36.9	0.0	36.8	-0.3	36.9	0.3
1964	36.3	-1.6	36.3	0.0	36.2	-0.3	37.0	2.2	36.9	-0.3	36.8	-0.3	37.1	0.8	37.0	-0.3	36.9	-0.3	36.9	0.0	37.1	0.5	37.1	0.0
1965	36.6	-1.3	36.7	0.3	36.7	0.0	37.2	1.4	37.4	0.5	37.4	0.0	37.6	0.5	38.8	3.2	39.0	0.5	38.9	-0.3	38.9	0.0	39.3	1.0
1966	39.4	0.3	39.8	1.0	40.1	0.8	40.8	1.7	41.2	1.0	41.3	0.2	41.6	0.7	41.4	-0.5	41.1	-0.7	41.2	0.2	41.1	-0.2	40.7	-1.0
1967	41.0	0.7	41.0	0.0	40.9	-0.2	40.9	0.0	40.8	-0.2	40.4	-1.0	40.3	-0.2	40.3	0.0	40.0	-0.7	39.9	-0.2	39.9	0.0	39.8	-0.3
1968	40.0	0.5	40.0	0.0	40.1	0.2	40.1	0.0	40.1	0.0	40.1	0.0	40.2	0.2	40.2	0.0	40.2	0.0	40.5	0.7	40.5	0.0	40.6	0.2
1969	41.0	1.0	41.0	0.0	41.2	0.5	41.5	0.7	41.7	0.5	41.8	0.2	42.0	0.5	41.9	-0.2	42.1	0.5	42.2	0.2	42.4	0.5	42.3	-0.2
1970	42.6	0.7	42.7	0.2	42.8	0.2	42.8	0.0	43.1	0.7	43.1	0.0	43.2	0.2	43.2	0.0	43.2	0.0	43.2	0.0	43.2	0.0	43.2	0.0
1971	43.4	0.5	43.5	0.2	43.5	0.0	43.5	0.0	43.6	0.2	43.7	0.2	43.8	0.2	44.0	0.5	44.1	0.2	44.1	0.0	44.1	0.0	44.4	0.7
1972	44.7	0.7	44.9	0.4	45.2	0.7	46.0	1.8	46.6	1.3	47.2	1.3	47.1	-0.2	48.0	1.9	48.7	1.5	50.0	2.7	51.4	2.8	51.9	1.0
1973	52.3	0.8	52.3	0.0	52.3	0.0	52.5	0.4	52.2	-0.6	52.1	-0.2	52.2	0.2	52.8	1.1	52.7	-0.2	52.8	0.2	52.6	-0.4	52.7	0.2
1974	53.3	1.1	53.8	0.9	54.8	1.9	54.7	-0.2	54.6	-0.2	55.3	1.3	55.4	0.2	55.4	0.0	56.3	1.6	56.0	-0.5	56.0	0.0	56.5	0.9
1975	56.6	0.2	56.4	-0.4	56.2	-0.4	56.2	0.0	56.4	0.4	56.8	0.7	57.0	0.4	57.2	0.4	57.3	0.2	57.4	0.2	58.0	1.0	58.3	0.5
1976	60.3	3.4	61.0	1.2	61.1	0.2	61.2	0.2	61.5	0.5	61.5	0.0	61.6	0.2	61.7	0.2	62.7	1.6	63.0	0.5	63.0	0.0	63.1	0.2
1977	64.5	2.2	65.3	1.2	65.7	0.6	66.0	0.5	66.2	0.3	66.2	0.0	66.2	0.0	66.4	0.3	66.5	0.2	66.5	0.0	66.6	0.2	66.6	0.0
1978	68.8	3.3	68.9	0.1	69.4	0.7	69.5	0.1	71.2	2.4	71.4	0.3	71.5	0.1	72.3	1.1	72.7	0.6	72.9	0.3	74.8	2.6	74.9	0.1
1979	77.1	2.9	77.7	0.8	79.2	1.9	81.2	2.5	84.5	4.1	85.8	1.5	85.7	-0.1	85.3	-0.5	84.9	-0.5	84.8	-0.1	84.3	-0.6	84.1	-0.2
1980	86.1	2.4	86.8	0.8	88.0	1.4	87.4	-0.7	87.9	0.6	87.3	-0.7	87.9	0.7	88.4	0.6	88.5	0.1	89.7	1.4	90.0	0.3	91.1	1.2
1981	93.0	2.1	95.8	3.0	96.4	0.6	96.4	0.0	98.7	2.4	98.8	0.1	98.2	-0.6	99.1	0.9	99.0	-0.1	99.0	0.0	99.2	0.2	99.2	0.0
1982	100.1	0.9	100.3	0.2	100.3	0.0	100.3	0.0	100.3	0.0	99.3	-1.0	99.8	0.5	99.0	-0.8	100.1	1.1	99.9	-0.2	99.9	0.0	100.7	0.8
1983	101.4	0.7	101.5	0.1	101.4	-0.1	101.5	0.1	101.7	0.2	101.7	0.0	102.5	0.8	102.6	0.1	102.5	-0.1	102.5	0.0	103.4	0.9	103.3	-0.1
1984	104.0	0.7	104.0	0.0	104.0	0.0	104.3	0.3	105.0	0.7	108.3	3.1	108.0	-0.3	108.2	0.2	108.2	0.0	108.4	0.2	108.3	-0.1	107.9	-0.4
1985	109.2	1.2	109.3	0.1	110.1	0.7	110.2	0.1	110.3	0.1	110.5	0.2	110.2	-0.3	110.2	0.0	110.6	0.4	110.8	0.2	111.3	0.5	111.3	0.0
1986	111.5	0.2	111.0	-0.4	109.7	-1.2	109.5	-0.2	109.5	0.0	109.9	0.4	109.9	0.0	110.0	0.1	110.2	0.2	111.0	0.7	111.0	0.0	111.1	0.1
1987	111.5	0.4	111.4	-0.1	111.6	0.2	111.6	0.0	112.2	0.5	112.5	0.3	112.9	0.4	113.4	0.4	114.2	0.7	114.4	0.2	114.8	0.3	115.2	0.3
1988	116.6	1.2	116.8	0.2	117.1	0.3	117.7	0.5	118.2	0.4	119.5	1.1	119.9	0.3	120.0	0.1	120.6	0.5	120.6	0.0	120.7	0.1	120.9	0.2
1989	121.4	0.4	121.9	0.4	122.2	0.2	122.4	0.2	123.2	0.7	122.9	-0.2	122.9	0.0	123.7	0.7	124.4	0.6	123.9	-0.4	123.7	-0.2	124.8	0.9
1990	126.0	1.0	126.3	0.2	127.9	1.3	127.6	-0.2	129.2	1.3	129.7	0.4	129.4	-0.2	130.6	0.9	130.1	-0.4	129.6	-0.4	130.0	0.3	130.8	0.6
1991	130.8	0.0	131.3	0.4	132.4	0.8	131.9	-0.4	132.7	0.6	134.4	1.3	132.4	-1.5	134.3	1.4	132.8	-1.1	132.8	0.0	132.9	0.1	133.0	0.1

[Continued]

Other Leather and Related Products
Producer Price Index
Base 1982 = 100
[Continued]

For 1947-1997. Columns headed % show percentile change in the index from the previous period for which an index is available.

Year	Jan		Feb		Mar		Apr		May		Jun		Jul		Aug		Sep		Oct		Nov		Dec	
	Index	%	Index	%	Index	%	Index	%	Index	%	Index	%	Index	%	Index	%	Index	%	Index	%	Index	%	Index	%
1992	135.7	2.0	133.7	-1.5	136.2	1.9	134.0	-1.6	134.4	0.3	136.2	1.3	134.2	1.5	136.6	1.8	134.2	-1.8	134.3	0.1	134.6	0.2	134.6	0.0
1993	137.1	1.9	135.2	-1.4	135.3	0.1	135.7	0.3	135.8	0.1	137.8	1.5	135.9	-1.4	138.3	1.8	135.9	-1.7	136.1	0.1	136.1	0.0	136.1	0.0
1994	137.8	1.2	135.6	-1.6	135.8	0.1	136.0	0.1	136.2	0.1	136.3	0.1	136.4	0.1	136.5	0.1	137.5	0.7	137.6	0.1	137.8	0.1	137.6	-0.1
1995	138.2	0.4	138.0	-0.1	138.1	0.1	138.4	0.2	138.6	0.1	138.9	0.2	138.9	0.0	139.1	0.1	139.5	0.3	139.9	0.3	139.7	-0.1	140.1	0.3
1996	140.3	0.1	140.6	0.2	140.7	0.1	140.9	0.1	141.2	0.2	141.2	0.0	141.5	0.2	141.2	-0.2	141.2	0.0	141.2	0.0	141.3	0.1	141.3	0.0
1997	142.0	0.5	142.3	0.2	143.0	0.5	143.2	0.1	143.3	0.1	143.8	0.3	143.8	0.0	144.2	0.3	144.2	0.0	143.9	-0.2	144.0	0.1	144.5	0.3

Source: U.S. Department of Labor, Bureau of Labor Statistics, Division of Industry Prices and Price Indexes. n.e.c. stands for not elsewhere classified. - indicates no data collected for period or unavailable.

FUELS AND RELATED PRODUCTS AND POWER
Producer Price Index
Base 1982 = 100

For 1926-1997. Columns headed % show percentile change in the index from the previous period for which an index is available.

Year	Jan Index	%	Feb Index	%	Mar Index	%	Apr Index	%	May Index	%	Jun Index	%	Jul Index	%	Aug Index	%	Sep Index	%	Oct Index	%	Nov Index	%	Dec Index	%
1926	10.2	-	10.2	0.0	10.2	0.0	10.1	-1.0	10.4	3.0	10.4	0.0	10.3	-1.0	10.4	1.0	10.4	0.0	10.4	0.0	10.5	1.0	10.2	-2.9
1927	10.1	-1.0	10.0	-1.0	9.4	-6.0	9.0	-4.3	8.9	-1.1	8.9	0.0	8.9	0.0	8.9	0.0	8.9	0.0	8.9	0.0	8.8	-1.1	8.7	-1.1
1928	8.6	-1.1	8.6	0.0	8.5	-1.2	8.6	1.2	8.6	0.0	8.7	1.2	8.7	0.0	8.9	2.3	8.9	0.0	8.9	0.0	8.9	0.0	8.8	-1.1
1929	8.7	-1.1	8.6	-1.1	8.5	-1.2	8.5	0.0	8.5	0.0	8.7	2.4	8.6	-1.1	8.5	-1.2	8.5	0.0	8.6	1.2	8.6	0.0	8.6	0.0
1930	8.4	-2.3	8.4	0.0	8.2	-2.4	8.2	0.0	8.3	1.2	8.2	-1.2	8.1	-1.2	8.0	-1.2	8.2	2.5	8.0	-2.4	7.8	-2.5	7.6	-2.6
1931	7.6	0.0	7.5	-1.3	7.0	-6.7	6.8	-2.9	6.7	-1.5	6.5	-3.0	6.5	0.0	6.9	6.2	7.0	1.4	7.0	0.0	7.2	2.9	7.0	-2.8
1932	7.0	0.0	7.0	0.0	7.0	0.0	7.2	2.9	7.3	1.4	7.4	1.4	7.5	1.4	7.4	-1.3	7.3	-1.4	7.3	0.0	7.4	1.4	7.2	-2.7
1933	6.8	-5.6	6.6	-2.9	6.5	-1.5	6.3	-3.1	6.2	-1.6	6.3	1.6	6.7	6.3	6.8	1.5	7.3	7.4	7.6	4.1	7.6	0.0	7.6	0.0
1934	7.5	-1.3	7.5	0.0	7.4	-1.3	7.4	0.0	7.5	1.4	7.5	0.0	7.6	1.3	7.7	1.3	7.7	0.0	7.7	0.0	7.7	0.0	7.6	-1.3
1935	7.5	-1.3	7.5	0.0	7.5	0.0	7.5	0.0	7.5	0.0	7.7	2.7	7.7	0.0	7.6	-1.3	7.5	-1.3	7.6	1.3	7.7	1.3	7.7	0.0
1936	7.8	1.3	7.8	0.0	7.9	1.3	7.9	0.0	7.8	-1.3	7.8	0.0	7.9	1.3	7.9	0.0	7.8	-1.3	7.9	1.3	7.9	0.0	7.9	0.0
1937	7.9	0.0	7.9	0.0	7.9	0.0	7.9	0.0	8.0	1.3	8.0	0.0	8.1	1.3	8.1	0.0	8.1	0.0	8.1	0.0	8.1	0.0	8.1	0.0
1938	8.1	0.0	8.1	0.0	8.0	-1.2	7.9	-1.2	7.9	0.0	7.9	0.0	7.9	0.0	7.9	0.0	7.9	0.0	7.8	-1.3	7.6	-2.6	7.6	0.0
1939	7.5	-1.3	7.5	0.0	7.5	0.0	7.6	1.3	7.6	0.0	7.5	-1.3	7.5	0.0	7.5	0.0	7.5	0.0	7.6	1.3	7.6	0.0	7.5	-1.3
1940	7.5	0.0	7.5	0.0	7.4	-1.3	7.4	0.0	7.4	0.0	7.4	0.0	7.3	-1.4	7.3	0.0	7.3	0.0	7.4	1.4	7.4	0.0	7.4	0.0
1941	7.4	0.0	7.4	0.0	7.4	0.0	7.5	1.4	7.8	4.0	8.0	2.6	8.1	1.3	8.2	1.2	8.2	0.0	8.2	0.0	8.1	-1.2	8.1	0.0
1942	8.1	0.0	8.0	-1.2	8.0	0.0	8.0	0.0	8.0	0.0	8.1	1.3	8.2	1.2	8.2	0.0	8.2	0.0	8.2	0.0	8.2	0.0	8.2	0.0
1943	8.2	0.0	8.2	0.0	8.3	1.2	8.3	0.0	8.3	0.0	8.4	1.2	8.4	0.0	8.4	0.0	8.4	0.0	8.4	0.0	8.4	0.0	8.5	1.2
1944	8.5	0.0	8.6	1.2	8.6	0.0	8.6	0.0	8.6	0.0	8.6	0.0	8.6	0.0	8.6	0.0	8.6	0.0	8.6	0.0	8.6	0.0	8.6	0.0
1945	8.6	0.0	8.6	0.0	8.6	0.0	8.6	0.0	8.6	0.0	8.7	1.2	8.7	0.0	8.8	1.1	8.7	-1.1	8.7	0.0	8.7	0.0	8.7	0.0
1946	8.8	1.1	8.8	0.0	8.8	0.0	8.9	1.1	8.9	0.0	9.1	2.2	9.3	2.2	9.8	5.4	9.7	-1.0	9.7	0.0	9.8	1.0	9.9	1.0
1947	10.1	2.0	10.2	1.0	10.5	2.9	10.8	2.9	10.8	0.0	10.8	0.0	11.2	3.7	11.4	1.8	11.5	0.9	11.6	0.9	11.9	2.6	12.4	4.2
1948	12.9	4.0	13.0	0.8	13.0	0.0	13.0	0.0	13.0	0.0	13.0	0.0	13.2	1.5	13.1	-0.8	13.1	0.0	13.2	0.8	13.2	0.0	13.1	-0.8
1949	13.1	0.0	12.9	-1.5	12.7	-1.6	12.4	-2.4	12.3	-0.8	12.2	-0.8	12.2	0.0	12.2	0.0	12.2	0.0	12.3	0.8	12.3	0.0	12.3	0.0
1950	12.4	0.8	12.4	0.0	12.4	0.0	12.3	-0.8	12.4	0.8	12.5	0.8	12.6	0.8	12.7	0.8	12.7	0.0	12.8	0.8	12.9	0.8	12.8	-0.8
1951	13.0	1.6	13.1	0.8	13.1	0.0	13.0	-0.8	13.0	0.0	13.0	0.0	13.0	0.0	13.0	0.0	13.0	0.0	13.0	0.0	13.0	0.0	13.1	0.8
1952	13.1	0.0	13.1	0.0	13.1	0.0	13.0	-0.8	12.9	-0.8	12.9	0.0	12.9	0.0	12.9	0.0	13.0	0.8	13.0	0.0	13.0	0.0	13.1	0.8
1953	13.1	0.0	13.2	0.8	13.2	0.0	13.1	-0.8	13.1	0.0	13.2	0.8	13.5	2.3	13.5	0.0	13.5	0.0	13.6	0.7	13.6	0.0	13.5	-0.7
1954	13.5	0.0	13.5	0.0	13.3	-1.5	13.2	-0.8	13.2	0.0	13.1	-0.8	13.0	-0.8	13.0	0.0	13.0	0.0	13.0	0.0	13.1	0.8	13.1	0.0
1955	13.2	0.8	13.3	0.8	13.2	-0.8	13.1	-0.8	13.0	-0.8	13.0	0.0	13.0	0.0	13.1	0.8	13.2	0.8	13.2	0.0	13.2	0.0	13.3	0.8
1956	13.5	1.5	13.6	0.7	13.5	-0.7	13.5	0.0	13.5	0.0	13.5	0.0	13.5	0.0	13.5	0.0	13.5	0.0	13.6	0.7	13.6	0.0	13.9	2.2
1957	14.2	2.2	14.6	2.8	14.5	-0.7	14.6	0.7	14.5	-0.7	14.3	-1.4	14.2	-0.7	14.2	0.0	14.2	0.0	14.1	-0.7	14.1	0.0	14.2	0.7
1958	14.2	0.0	13.8	-2.8	13.7	-0.7	13.5	-1.5	13.4	-0.7	13.5	0.7	13.6	0.7	13.9	2.2	13.9	0.0	13.8	-0.7	13.7	-0.7	13.8	0.7
1959	13.9	0.7	14.0	0.7	14.0	0.0	13.9	-0.7	13.8	-0.7	13.6	-1.4	13.5	-0.7	13.7	1.5	13.6	-0.7	13.6	0.0	13.6	0.0	13.6	0.0
1960	13.6	0.0	13.7	0.7	13.7	0.0	13.7	0.0	13.5	-1.5	13.7	1.5	13.9	1.5	14.1	1.4	14.2	0.7	14.2	0.0	14.2	0.0	14.2	0.0
1961	14.3	0.7	14.4	0.7	14.3	-0.7	14.1	-1.4	13.8	-2.1	13.9	0.7	14.0	0.7	14.0	0.0	14.0	0.0	13.9	-0.7	13.8	-0.7	13.9	0.7	14.0	0.7
1962	14.1	0.7	14.0	-0.7	13.8	-1.4	14.0	1.4	13.9	-0.7	13.9	0.0	13.9	0.0	13.8	-0.7	14.0	1.4	14.0	0.0	14.0	0.0	14.0	0.0
1963	14.0	0.0	14.0	0.0	14.0	0.0	14.0	0.0	14.0	0.0	14.1	0.7	14.0	-0.7	13.8	-1.4	13.8	0.0	13.8	0.0	13.6	-1.4	13.8	1.5
1964	13.8	0.0	13.8	0.0	13.5	-2.2	13.4	-0.7	13.4	0.0	13.4	0.0	13.5	0.7	13.4	-0.7	13.3	-0.7	13.5	1.5	13.6	0.7	13.7	0.7
1965	13.7	0.0	13.6	-0.7	13.6	0.0	13.6	0.0	13.7	0.7	13.7	0.0	13.7	0.0	13.8	0.7	13.8	0.0	13.8	0.0	14.0	1.4	14.0	0.0
1966	14.0	0.0	14.0	0.0	13.9	-0.7	13.9	0.0	14.0	0.7	14.1	0.7	14.1	0.0	14.2	0.7	14.2	0.0	14.3	0.7	14.3	0.0	14.3	0.0
1967	14.3	0.0	14.4	0.7	14.4	0.0	14.4	0.0	14.5	0.7	14.5	0.0	14.5	0.0	14.6	0.7	14.6	0.0	14.4	-1.4	14.3	-0.7	14.3	0.0
1968	14.2	-0.7	14.3	0.7	14.2	-0.7	14.3	0.7	14.3	0.0	14.4	0.7	14.4	0.0	14.3	-0.7	14.3	0.0	14.2	-0.7	14.2	0.0	14.2	0.0
1969	14.2	0.0	14.3	0.7	14.5	1.4	14.5	0.0	14.5	0.0	14.6	0.7	14.6	0.0	14.6	0.0	14.6	0.0	14.7	0.7	14.7	0.0	14.8	0.7
1970	14.7	-0.7	14.8	0.7	14.8	0.0	15.0	1.4	15.1	0.7	15.1	0.0	15.2	0.7	15.3	0.7	15.6	2.0	15.8	1.3	15.9	0.6	16.4	3.1

[Continued]

FUELS AND RELATED PRODUCTS AND POWER

Producer Price Index
Base 1982 = 100

[Continued]

For 1926-1997. Columns headed % show percentile change in the index from the previous period for which an index is available.

Year	Jan Index	%	Feb Index	%	Mar Index	%	Apr Index	%	May Index	%	Jun Index	%	Jul Index	%	Aug Index	%	Sep Index	%	Oct Index	%	Nov Index	%	Dec Index	%
1971	16.5	0.6	16.5	0.0	16.4	-0.6	16.4	0.0	16.6	1.2	16.6	0.0	16.7	0.6	16.8	0.6	16.8	0.0	16.7	-0.6	16.7	0.0	16.9	1.2
1972	16.7	-1.2	16.7	0.0	16.8	0.6	16.9	0.6	16.9	0.0	17.0	0.6	17.1	0.6	17.3	1.2	17.4	0.6	17.4	0.0	17.5	0.6	17.6	0.6
1973	17.6	0.0	18.2	3.4	18.4	1.1	18.6	1.1	18.9	1.6	19.2	1.6	19.4	1.0	19.5	0.5	19.8	1.5	20.1	1.5	20.8	3.5	21.9	5.3
1974	23.4	6.8	25.6	9.4	27.3	6.6	28.5	4.4	29.5	3.5	30.4	3.1	32.0	5.3	32.6	1.9	32.5	-0.3	33.0	1.5	32.8	-0.6	33.0	0.6
1975	33.5	1.5	33.5	0.0	33.6	0.3	34.1	1.5	34.4	0.9	35.0	1.7	35.6	1.7	36.4	2.2	36.8	1.1	37.0	0.5	37.1	0.3	37.2	0.3
1976	37.1	-0.3	36.9	-0.5	36.9	0.0	37.1	0.5	37.1	0.0	37.6	1.3	38.3	1.9	38.8	1.3	39.1	0.8	40.0	2.3	40.6	1.5	40.3	-0.7
1977	40.2	-0.2	41.7	3.7	42.4	1.7	43.1	1.7	43.6	1.2	43.9	0.7	44.3	0.9	44.7	0.9	44.7	0.0	44.8	0.2	44.8	0.0	45.0	0.4
1978	45.1	0.2	45.1	0.0	45.5	0.9	45.8	0.7	46.1	0.7	46.6	1.1	46.8	0.4	46.9	0.2	47.1	0.4	47.4	0.6	47.6	0.4	48.2	1.3
1979	48.8	1.2	49.4	1.2	50.6	2.4	52.2	3.2	54.5	4.4	56.8	4.2	59.4	4.6	62.4	5.1	65.6	5.1	67.6	3.0	68.8	1.8	70.4	2.3
1980	73.3	4.1	76.8	4.8	79.9	4.0	81.7	2.3	82.5	1.0	83.2	0.8	84.5	1.6	85.2	0.8	85.6	0.5	85.5	-0.1	86.6	1.3	88.8	2.5
1981	91.5	3.0	96.3	5.2	100.5	4.4	102.0	1.5	102.3	0.3	102.1	-0.2	101.7	-0.4	101.6	-0.1	101.5	-0.1	100.7	-0.8	100.7	0.0	101.3	0.6
1982	101.7	0.4	100.7	-1.0	99.5	-1.2	96.7	-2.8	95.5	-1.2	97.7	2.3	101.1	3.5	101.8	0.7	101.0	-0.8	100.8	-0.2	101.9	1.1	101.5	-0.4
1983	98.6	-2.9	96.5	-2.1	94.9	-1.7	93.0	-2.0	94.0	1.1	96.0	2.1	96.5	0.5	96.9	0.4	97.0	0.1	96.6	-0.4	95.7	-0.9	94.9	-0.8
1984	94.1	-0.8	94.6	0.5	95.0	0.4	94.4	-0.6	95.3	1.0	96.1	0.8	95.9	-0.2	94.9	-1.0	94.1	-0.8	94.4	0.3	94.5	0.1	93.6	-1.0
1985	91.9	-1.8	90.2	-1.8	90.2	0.0	91.4	1.3	93.4	2.2	92.4	-1.1	91.7	-0.8	90.5	-1.3	90.7	0.2	90.6	-0.1	91.6	1.1	92.3	0.8
1986	89.5	-3.0	81.8	-8.6	73.9	-9.7	69.6	-5.8	69.8	0.3	69.9	0.1	64.1	-8.3	63.2	-1.4	65.3	3.3	63.3	-3.1	63.3	0.0	63.4	0.2
1987	66.6	5.0	68.0	2.1	68.3	0.4	69.1	1.2	69.7	0.9	71.1	2.0	72.6	2.1	73.8	1.7	72.2	-2.2	71.1	-1.5	70.8	-0.4	69.5	-1.8
1988	67.2	-3.3	66.7	-0.7	65.9	-1.2	67.6	2.6	68.4	1.2	68.6	0.3	68.0	-0.9	67.6	-0.6	66.1	-2.2	64.5	-2.4	64.4	-0.2	65.6	1.9
1989	68.1	3.8	68.9	1.2	69.9	1.5	74.2	6.2	76.0	2.4	75.8	-0.3	75.5	-0.4	72.0	-4.6	73.9	2.6	73.7	-0.3	72.8	-1.2	73.7	1.2
1990	79.8	8.3	77.0	-3.5	74.6	-3.1	73.4	-1.6	74.1	1.0	72.8	-1.8	72.7	-0.1	82.4	13.3	91.3	10.8	101.0	10.6	97.4	-3.6	90.5	-7.1
1991	90.1	-0.4	83.0	-7.9	78.5	-5.4	78.1	-0.5	80.2	2.7	80.3	0.1	80.1	-0.2	81.3	1.5	81.4	0.1	81.3	-0.1	81.2	-0.1	79.1	-2.6
1992	76.3	-3.5	76.8	0.7	75.8	-1.3	77.1	1.7	79.7	3.4	83.2	4.4	83.3	0.1	82.8	-0.6	84.4	1.9	83.2	-1.4	82.1	-1.3	79.7	-2.9
1993	79.4	-0.4	79.2	-0.3	79.7	0.6	80.3	0.8	81.9	2.0	83.2	1.6	81.0	-2.6	80.2	-1.0	80.9	0.9	81.2	0.4	78.3	-3.6	74.7	-4.6
1994	75.4	0.9	75.4	0.0	76.0	0.8	76.4	0.5	77.2	1.0	79.5	3.0	80.6	1.4	82.0	1.7	79.9	-2.6	77.4	-3.1	77.5	0.1	76.6	-1.2
1995	76.8	0.3	76.8	0.0	76.8	0.0	78.5	2.2	80.0	1.9	81.0	1.3	79.2	-2.2	78.3	-1.1	78.3	0.0	76.8	-1.9	75.9	-1.2	77.9	2.6
1996	80.6	3.5	80.9	0.4	82.0	1.4	86.2	5.1	86.6	0.5	85.2	-1.6	85.9	0.8	86.8	1.0	87.1	0.3	86.8	-0.3	88.5	2.0	93.3	5.4
1997	96.1	3.0	90.3	-6.0	83.4	-7.6	82.2	-1.4	83.4	1.5	84.5	1.3	83.9	-0.7	84.9	1.2	86.5	1.9	86.7	0.2	87.0	0.3	82.8	-4.8

Source: U.S. Department of Labor, Bureau of Labor Statistics, Division of Industry Prices and Price Indexes. n.e.c. stands for not elsewhere classified. - indicates no data collected for period or unavailable.

Coal
Producer Price Index
Base 1982 = 100

For 1926-1997. Columns headed % show percentile change in the index from the previous period for which an index is available.

Year	Jan Index	%	Feb Index	%	Mar Index	%	Apr Index	%	May Index	%	Jun Index	%	Jul Index	%	Aug Index	%	Sep Index	%	Oct Index	%	Nov Index	%	Dec Index	%
1926	8.7	-	8.4	-3.4	8.3	-1.2	8.1	-2.4	8.1	0.0	8.1	0.0	8.1	0.0	8.2	1.2	8.3	1.2	8.7	4.8	9.4	8.0	8.9	-5.3
1927	8.7	-2.2	8.5	-2.3	8.4	-1.2	8.3	-1.2	8.3	0.0	8.3	0.0	8.3	0.0	8.4	1.2	8.5	1.2	8.3	-2.4	8.2	-1.2	8.2	0.0
1928	8.1	-1.2	8.1	0.0	8.0	-1.2	7.8	-2.5	7.7	-1.3	7.8	1.3	7.7	-1.3	7.8	1.3	7.8	0.0	7.9	1.3	7.9	0.0	7.8	-1.3
1929	7.9	1.3	7.9	0.0	7.8	-1.3	7.5	-3.8	7.5	0.0	7.5	0.0	7.6	1.3	7.6	0.0	7.7	1.3	7.7	0.0	7.7	0.0	7.8	1.3
1930	7.7	-1.3	7.7	0.0	7.6	-1.3	7.5	-1.3	7.4	-1.3	7.4	0.0	7.4	0.0	7.5	1.4	7.5	0.0	7.6	1.3	7.5	-1.3	7.5	0.0
1931	7.5	0.0	7.4	-1.3	7.3	-1.4	7.2	-1.4	7.2	0.0	7.2	0.0	7.2	0.0	7.3	1.4	7.3	0.0	7.3	0.0	7.3	0.0	7.3	0.0
1932	7.4	1.4	7.3	-1.4	7.2	-1.4	7.1	-1.4	7.0	-1.4	7.0	0.0	7.0	0.0	7.0	0.0	7.0	0.0	7.0	0.0	7.0	0.0	7.0	0.0
1933	7.0	0.0	6.9	-1.4	6.9	0.0	6.7	-2.9	6.6	-1.5	6.6	0.0	6.8	3.0	7.0	2.9	7.1	1.4	7.4	4.2	7.5	1.4	7.5	0.0
1934	7.5	0.0	7.5	0.0	7.5	0.0	7.6	1.3	7.6	0.0	7.6	0.0	7.7	1.3	7.8	1.3	7.8	0.0	7.8	0.0	7.8	0.0	7.8	0.0
1935	7.8	0.0	7.8	0.0	7.8	0.0	7.6	-2.6	7.6	0.0	7.6	0.0	7.7	1.3	7.7	0.0	7.8	1.3	7.9	1.3	8.0	1.3	8.0	0.0
1936	8.0	0.0	8.1	1.3	8.0	-1.2	7.8	-2.5	7.7	-1.3	7.7	0.0	7.7	0.0	7.8	1.3	7.8	0.0	7.9	1.3	7.9	0.0	7.9	0.0
1937	7.9	0.0	7.9	0.0	7.8	-1.3	7.7	-1.3	7.8	1.3	7.8	0.0	7.8	0.0	7.9	1.3	7.9	0.0	7.9	0.0	7.9	0.0	8.1	2.5
1938	8.2	1.2	8.2	0.0	7.9	-3.7	7.8	-1.3	7.7	-1.3	7.7	0.0	7.8	1.3	7.8	0.0	7.9	1.3	7.9	0.0	7.9	0.0	7.9	0.0
1939	7.9	0.0	7.9	0.0	7.9	0.0	7.8	-1.3	7.8	0.0	7.6	-2.6	7.6	0.0	7.6	0.0	7.6	0.0	7.8	2.6	7.8	0.0	7.8	0.0
1940	7.9	1.3	7.9	0.0	7.8	-1.3	7.7	-1.3	7.6	-1.3	7.7	1.3	7.7	0.0	7.7	0.0	7.8	1.3	8.0	2.6	8.0	0.0	8.1	1.3
1941	8.1	0.0	8.1	0.0	8.0	-1.2	8.0	0.0	8.2	2.5	8.3	1.2	8.4	1.2	8.5	1.2	8.6	1.2	8.6	0.0	8.6	0.0	8.6	0.0
1942	8.7	1.2	8.7	0.0	8.7	0.0	8.6	-1.1	8.7	1.2	8.7	0.0	8.7	0.0	8.8	1.1	8.8	0.0	8.8	0.0	8.8	0.0	8.9	1.1
1943	9.0	1.1	9.1	1.1	9.2	1.1	9.2	0.0	9.2	0.0	9.2	0.0	9.3	1.1	9.3	0.0	9.3	0.0	9.3	0.0	9.3	0.0	9.5	2.2
1944	9.6	1.1	9.6	0.0	9.6	0.0	9.6	0.0	9.6	0.0	9.6	0.0	9.6	0.0	9.6	0.0	9.6	0.0	9.6	0.0	9.6	0.0	9.6	0.0
1945	9.6	0.0	9.6	0.0	9.6	0.0	9.6	0.0	9.8	2.1	9.9	1.0	10.0	1.0	10.0	0.0	10.0	0.0	10.0	0.0	10.0	0.0	10.1	1.0
1946	10.1	0.0	10.1	0.0	10.1	0.0	10.1	0.0	10.1	0.0	10.6	5.0	11.0	3.8	11.1	0.9	11.1	0.0	11.1	0.0	11.1	0.0	11.2	0.9
1947	11.5	2.7	11.5	0.0	11.5	0.0	11.6	0.9	11.6	0.0	11.6	0.0	13.5	16.4	14.3	5.9	14.4	0.7	14.5	0.7	14.5	0.0	14.6	0.7
1948	14.7	0.7	14.7	0.0	14.7	0.0	14.8	0.7	15.0	1.4	15.1	0.7	16.3	7.9	16.4	0.6	16.4	0.0	16.3	-0.6	16.3	0.0	16.3	0.0
1949	16.3	0.0	16.2	-0.6	16.0	-1.2	15.4	-3.8	15.2	-1.3	15.2	0.0	15.3	0.7	15.3	0.0	15.3	0.0	15.3	0.0	15.5	1.3	15.6	0.6
1950	15.7	0.6	15.8	0.6	16.0	1.3	15.5	-3.1	15.4	-0.6	15.4	0.0	15.4	0.0	15.5	0.6	15.6	0.6	15.6	0.0	15.6	0.0	15.6	0.0
1951	15.6	0.0	16.2	3.8	16.2	0.0	15.9	-1.9	15.8	-0.6	15.9	0.6	15.7	-1.3	15.8	0.6	15.9	0.6	16.0	0.6	16.0	0.0	16.0	0.0
1952	16.0	0.0	16.0	0.0	16.0	0.0	15.4	-3.8	15.4	0.0	15.5	0.6	15.6	0.6	15.6	0.0	15.8	1.3	16.6	5.1	16.7	0.6	17.0	1.8
1953	17.1	0.6	17.0	-0.6	16.8	-1.2	16.3	-3.0	16.3	0.0	16.3	0.0	16.4	0.6	16.4	0.0	16.5	0.6	16.5	0.0	16.5	0.0	16.5	0.0
1954	16.4	-0.6	16.3	-0.6	15.8	-3.1	15.3	-3.2	15.4	0.7	15.4	0.0	15.4	0.0	15.4	0.0	15.5	0.6	15.4	-0.6	15.4	0.0	15.4	0.0
1955	15.4	0.0	15.4	0.0	15.4	0.0	15.0	-2.6	14.7	-2.0	14.8	0.7	14.9	0.7	15.0	0.7	15.9	6.0	16.0	0.6	16.0	0.0	16.1	0.6
1956	16.1	0.0	16.1	0.0	16.2	0.6	16.4	1.2	16.4	0.0	16.5	0.6	16.6	0.6	16.7	0.6	16.8	0.6	17.8	6.0	17.9	0.6	18.1	1.1
1957	18.2	0.6	18.2	0.0	18.1	-0.5	18.1	0.0	18.1	0.0	18.1	0.0	18.2	0.6	18.3	0.5	18.3	0.0	18.4	0.5	18.5	0.5	18.5	0.0
1958	18.5	0.0	18.5	0.0	18.5	0.0	17.6	-4.9	17.6	0.0	17.7	0.6	17.8	0.6	17.9	0.6	18.0	0.6	18.2	1.1	18.2	0.0	18.2	0.0
1959	18.4	1.1	18.5	0.5	18.3	-1.1	17.5	-4.4	17.4	-0.6	17.6	1.1	17.8	1.1	17.9	0.6	18.0	0.6	18.1	0.6	18.2	0.6	18.2	0.0
1960	18.2	0.0	18.2	0.0	18.2	0.0	17.5	-3.8	17.4	-0.6	17.5	0.6	17.7	1.1	17.8	0.6	18.0	1.1	18.0	0.0	18.0	0.0	18.1	0.6
1961	18.1	0.0	18.1	0.0	18.0	-0.6	17.6	-2.2	17.2	-2.3	17.3	0.6	17.4	0.6	17.5	0.6	17.6	0.6	17.7	0.6	17.8	0.6	17.9	0.6
1962	17.9	0.0	17.9	0.0	17.9	0.0	17.3	-3.4	17.1	-1.2	17.1	0.0	17.3	1.2	17.3	0.0	17.5	1.2	17.6	0.6	17.7	0.6	17.8	0.6
1963	17.8	0.0	17.8	0.0	17.8	0.0	17.2	-3.4	17.1	-0.6	17.2	0.6	17.3	0.6	17.4	0.6	17.6	1.1	17.7	0.6	17.8	0.6	17.8	0.0
1964	17.8	0.0	17.8	0.0	17.6	-1.1	17.2	-2.3	17.2	0.0	17.3	0.6	17.4	0.6	17.5	0.6	17.6	0.6	17.7	0.6	17.7	0.0	17.8	0.6
1965	17.8	0.0	17.8	0.0	17.6	-1.1	17.1	-2.8	17.1	0.0	17.1	0.0	17.2	0.6	17.3	0.6	17.5	1.2	17.6	0.6	17.7	0.6	17.7	0.0
1966	17.8	0.6	17.8	0.0	17.7	-0.6	17.2	-2.8	17.5	1.7	17.6	0.6	17.7	0.6	17.8	0.6	18.0	1.1	18.2	1.1	18.4	1.1	18.5	0.5
1967	18.5	0.0	18.5	0.0	18.5	0.0	18.6	0.5	18.6	0.0	18.6	0.0	18.6	0.0	18.8	1.1	18.8	0.0	18.9	0.5	19.0	0.5	19.0	0.0
1968	19.0	0.0	19.0	0.0	19.1	0.5	19.2	0.5	19.1	-0.5	19.1	0.0	19.2	0.5	19.2	0.0	19.2	0.0	19.9	3.6	20.2	1.5	20.4	1.0
1969	20.4	0.0	20.4	0.0	20.4	0.0	20.6	1.0	20.5	-0.5	20.7	1.0	20.9	1.0	20.9	0.0	21.0	0.5	22.0	4.8	22.4	1.8	22.5	0.4
1970	22.7	0.9	23.8	4.8	24.1	1.3	26.4	9.5	26.6	0.8	27.8	4.5	28.4	2.2	28.8	1.4	30.1	4.5	32.8	9.0	32.9	0.3	32.9	0.0

[Continued]

Coal

Producer Price Index
Base 1982 = 100
[Continued]

For 1926-1997. Columns headed % show percentile change in the index from the previous period for which an index is available.

Year	Jan Index	%	Feb Index	%	Mar Index	%	Apr Index	%	May Index	%	Jun Index	%	Jul Index	%	Aug Index	%	Sep Index	%	Oct Index	%	Nov Index	%	Dec Index	%
1971	32.9	0.0	32.9	0.0	32.9	0.0	34.4	4.6	34.2	-0.6	34.1	-0.3	34.2	0.3	34.2	0.0	34.2	0.0	34.2	0.0	34.2	0.0	36.0	5.3
1972	36.0	0.0	36.0	0.0	36.0	0.0	35.8	-0.6	35.8	0.0	35.8	0.0	35.8	0.0	35.8	0.0	35.9	0.3	36.0	0.3	37.6	4.4	38.4	2.1
1973	38.4	0.0	38.7	0.8	38.8	0.3	40.0	3.1	40.1	0.2	40.2	0.2	40.0	-0.5	40.1	0.2	41.6	3.7	41.9	0.7	44.7	6.7	45.0	0.7
1974	46.6	3.6	47.3	1.5	48.5	2.5	56.8	17.1	57.6	1.4	60.1	4.3	64.3	7.0	66.9	4.0	69.5	3.9	73.7	6.0	74.4	0.9	80.1	7.7
1975	80.2	0.1	76.6	-4.5	72.6	-5.2	72.4	-0.3	72.8	0.6	72.2	-0.8	71.5	-1.0	70.7	-1.1	69.8	-1.3	69.4	-0.6	68.2	-1.7	69.4	1.8
1976	69.2	-0.3	69.0	-0.3	68.8	-0.3	68.7	-0.1	68.7	0.0	68.6	-0.1	68.8	0.3	68.8	0.0	68.8	0.0	68.9	0.1	69.0	0.1	69.9	1.3
1977	70.3	0.6	70.6	0.4	70.8	0.3	71.0	0.3	72.3	1.8	73.0	1.0	73.5	0.7	73.7	0.3	73.9	0.3	74.5	0.8	74.9	0.5	75.2	0.4
1978	75.5	0.4	75.7	0.3	76.1	0.5	79.7	4.7	80.9	1.5	81.3	0.5	81.7	0.5	82.6	1.1	82.8	0.2	83.0	0.2	82.7	-0.4	83.0	0.4
1979	83.0	0.0	83.0	0.0	83.3	0.4	83.6	0.4	84.3	0.8	84.5	0.2	84.6	0.1	84.9	0.4	84.6	-0.4	85.0	0.5	85.1	0.1	85.8	0.8
1980	85.9	0.1	86.0	0.1	86.3	0.3	87.0	0.8	87.2	0.2	87.2	0.0	87.4	0.2	87.6	0.2	88.1	0.6	88.0	-0.1	88.9	1.0	88.9	0.0
1981	89.4	0.6	89.9	0.6	90.0	0.1	90.9	1.0	91.1	0.2	91.9	0.9	94.5	2.8	94.8	0.3	95.4	0.6	95.5	0.1	95.9	0.4	96.4	0.5
1982	98.2	1.9	99.1	0.9	99.0	-0.1	99.6	0.6	99.9	0.3	99.8	-0.1	100.6	0.8	100.8	0.2	100.7	-0.1	100.6	-0.1	100.9	0.3	100.7	-0.2
1983	100.2	-0.5	99.7	-0.5	100.7	1.0	100.6	-0.1	100.1	-0.5	99.9	-0.2	100.0	0.1	100.3	0.3	100.6	0.3	100.7	0.1	101.4	0.7	101.7	0.3
1984	101.2	-0.5	101.9	0.7	102.1	0.2	101.4	-0.7	102.4	1.0	101.8	-0.6	102.5	0.7	102.9	0.4	102.7	-0.2	102.7	0.0	102.6	-0.1	102.4	-0.2
1985	102.5	0.1	102.8	0.3	102.6	-0.2	102.4	-0.2	102.5	0.1	102.4	-0.1	102.8	0.4	102.9	0.1	102.6	-0.3	101.7	-0.9	100.6	-1.1	101.1	0.5
1986	101.3	0.2	100.9	-0.4	101.5	0.6	101.1	-0.4	100.9	-0.2	100.8	-0.1	100.9	0.1	100.7	-0.2	100.5	-0.2	100.5	0.0	100.1	-0.4	100.0	-0.1
1987	100.1	0.1	99.3	-0.8	99.0	-0.3	97.2	-1.8	96.8	-0.4	96.5	-0.3	96.1	-0.4	96.1	0.0	95.8	-0.3	96.0	0.2	96.4	0.4	95.9	-0.5
1988	95.6	-0.3	96.3	0.7	95.8	-0.5	95.5	-0.3	95.2	-0.3	95.2	0.0	95.7	0.5	95.1	-0.6	95.4	0.3	95.5	0.1	94.7	-0.8	94.6	-0.1
1989	94.1	-0.5	93.6	-0.5	93.6	0.0	94.2	0.6	94.6	0.4	94.9	0.3	96.2	1.4	96.6	0.4	96.5	-0.1	97.1	0.6	97.7	0.6	97.2	-0.5
1990	97.8	0.6	96.3	-1.5	96.4	0.1	96.7	0.3	97.7	1.0	97.9	0.2	98.0	0.1	96.9	-1.1	97.5	0.6	98.2	0.7	98.8	0.6	97.9	-0.9
1991	98.5	0.6	98.2	-0.3	97.4	-0.8	97.3	-0.1	97.1	-0.2	98.0	0.9	97.6	-0.4	96.6	-1.0	96.6	0.0	95.9	-0.7	97.1	1.3	96.3	-0.8
1992	93.7	-2.7	94.5	0.9	93.8	-0.7	94.8	1.1	95.0	0.2	96.0	1.1	95.3	-0.7	95.1	-0.2	95.1	0.0	95.7	0.6	94.8	-0.9	96.5	1.8
1993	95.6	-0.9	94.9	-0.7	94.9	0.0	94.6	-0.3	94.1	-0.5	94.1	0.0	94.4	0.3	95.5	1.2	97.8	2.4	100.3	2.6	99.5	-0.8	97.5	-2.0
1994	97.3	-0.2	96.1	-1.2	96.2	0.1	96.5	0.3	96.8	0.3	95.5	-1.3	95.6	0.1	96.2	0.6	97.8	1.7	98.4	0.6	98.3	-0.1	95.5	-2.8
1995	91.9	-3.8	94.6	2.9	96.9	2.4	95.9	-1.0	93.9	-2.1	94.3	0.4	96.0	1.8	95.3	-0.7	95.2	-0.1	96.4	1.3	94.8	-1.7	94.7	-0.1
1996	92.1	-2.7	95.3	3.5	95.7	0.4	94.3	-1.5	97.0	2.9	95.0	-2.1	93.3	-1.8	96.4	3.3	93.6	-2.9	93.3	-0.3	94.6	1.4	93.7	-1.0
1997	97.3	3.8	94.6	-2.8	96.7	2.2	100.3	3.7	95.2	-5.1	96.9	1.8	94.9	-2.1	95.4	0.5	96.2	0.8	95.0	-1.2	94.3	-0.7	96.2	2.0

Source: U.S. Department of Labor, Bureau of Labor Statistics, Division of Industry Prices and Price Indexes. n.e.c. stands for not elsewhere classified. - indicates no data collected for period or unavailable.

Coke Oven Products

Producer Price Index
Base 1982 = 100

For 1926-1997. Columns headed % show percentile change in the index from the previous period for which an index is available.

Year	Jan Index	%	Feb Index	%	Mar Index	%	Apr Index	%	May Index	%	Jun Index	%	Jul Index	%	Aug Index	%	Sep Index	%	Oct Index	%	Nov Index	%	Dec Index	%
1926	6.8	-	6.8	0.0	6.1	-10.3	5.6	-8.2	5.5	-1.8	5.6	1.8	5.6	0.0	5.6	0.0	5.7	1.8	5.7	0.0	6.3	10.5	6.1	-3.2
1927	5.8	-4.9	5.7	-1.7	5.7	0.0	5.7	0.0	5.6	-1.8	5.6	0.0	5.6	0.0	5.6	0.0	5.6	0.0	5.6	0.0	5.5	-1.8	5.5	0.0
1928	5.1	-7.3	5.0	-2.0	5.0	0.0	4.9	-2.0	5.0	2.0	5.0	0.0	5.0	0.0	5.0	0.0	5.0	0.0	5.0	0.0	5.0	0.0	5.0	0.0
1929	5.0	0.0	5.0	0.0	5.1	2.0	5.0	-2.0	5.0	0.0	5.0	0.0	5.0	0.0	5.0	0.0	5.0	0.0	5.0	0.0	5.0	0.0	5.0	0.0
1930	5.0	0.0	5.0	0.0	5.0	0.0	5.0	0.0	5.0	0.0	5.0	0.0	5.0	0.0	5.0	0.0	5.0	0.0	5.0	0.0	5.0	0.0	5.0	0.0
1931	5.0	0.0	5.0	0.0	5.0	0.0	5.0	0.0	5.0	0.0	4.9	-2.0	4.9	0.0	4.9	0.0	4.9	0.0	4.9	0.0	4.8	-2.0	4.8	0.0
1932	4.8	0.0	4.8	0.0	4.8	0.0	4.7	-2.1	4.6	-2.1	4.6	0.0	4.5	-2.2	4.6	2.2	4.6	0.0	4.6	0.0	4.5	-2.2	4.5	0.0
1933	4.5	0.0	4.5	0.0	4.5	0.0	4.5	0.0	4.5	0.0	4.5	0.0	4.5	0.0	4.6	2.2	4.7	2.2	4.9	4.3	5.0	0.0	5.0	0.0
1934	5.0	0.0	5.0	0.0	5.0	0.0	5.0	0.0	5.0	0.0	5.0	0.0	5.1	2.0	5.1	0.0	5.1	0.0	5.1	0.0	5.1	0.0	5.1	0.0
1935	5.1	0.0	5.3	3.9	5.3	0.0	5.3	0.0	5.3	0.0	5.3	0.0	5.3	0.0	5.3	0.0	5.3	0.0	5.3	0.0	5.3	0.0	5.3	0.0
1936	5.5	3.8	5.6	1.8	5.6	0.0	5.6	0.0	5.6	0.0	5.6	0.0	5.6	0.0	5.6	0.0	5.6	0.0	5.8	3.6	5.8	0.0	5.8	0.0
1937	5.8	0.0	5.8	0.0	5.8	0.0	6.1	5.2	6.2	1.6	6.2	0.0	6.2	0.0	6.2	0.0	6.2	0.0	6.2	0.0	6.3	1.6	6.3	0.0
1938	6.3	0.0	6.3	0.0	6.3	0.0	6.3	0.0	6.3	0.0	6.2	-1.6	6.2	0.0	6.2	0.0	6.2	0.0	6.2	0.0	6.2	0.0	6.2	0.0
1939	6.2	0.0	6.2	0.0	6.2	0.0	6.2	0.0	6.2	0.0	6.2	0.0	6.2	0.0	6.2	0.0	6.2	0.0	6.4	3.2	6.6	3.1	6.5	-1.5
1940	6.5	0.0	6.5	0.0	6.5	0.0	6.5	0.0	6.5	0.0	6.5	0.0	6.5	0.0	6.5	0.0	6.5	0.0	6.5	0.0	6.7	3.1	6.8	1.5
1941	6.8	0.0	6.8	0.0	6.8	0.0	6.8	0.0	7.1	4.4	7.3	2.8	7.3	0.0	7.3	0.0	7.3	0.0	7.3	0.0	7.3	0.0	7.3	0.0
1942	7.3	0.0	7.3	0.0	7.3	0.0	7.3	0.0	7.3	0.0	7.3	0.0	7.3	0.0	7.3	0.0	7.3	0.0	7.3	0.0	7.3	0.0	7.3	0.0
1943	7.3	0.0	7.3	0.0	7.3	0.0	7.3	0.0	7.3	0.0	7.3	0.0	7.3	0.0	7.3	0.0	7.3	0.0	7.3	0.0	7.4	1.4	7.4	0.0
1944	7.5	1.4	7.8	4.0	7.8	0.0	7.8	0.0	7.8	0.0	7.8	0.0	7.8	0.0	7.8	0.0	7.8	0.0	7.8	0.0	7.8	0.0	7.8	0.0
1945	7.8	0.0	7.8	0.0	7.8	0.0	7.8	0.0	7.8	0.0	7.8	0.0	7.8	0.0	8.0	2.6	8.0	0.0	8.0	0.0	8.0	0.0	8.0	0.0
1946	8.0	0.0	8.0	0.0	8.0	0.0	7.9	-1.2	7.9	0.0	7.9	0.0	8.8	11.4	8.8	0.0	8.8	0.0	8.8	0.0	8.8	0.0	8.8	0.0
1947	9.1	3.4	9.2	1.1	9.2	0.0	9.3	1.1	9.3	0.0	9.4	1.1	9.6	2.1	10.4	8.3	10.7	2.9	10.7	0.0	10.8	0.9	10.9	0.9
1948	11.3	3.7	11.4	0.9	11.4	0.0	11.5	0.9	12.1	5.2	12.4	2.5	12.6	1.6	12.9	2.4	12.9	0.0	12.9	0.0	12.9	0.0	12.9	0.0
1949	13.1	1.6	13.2	0.8	13.2	0.0	13.2	0.0	13.1	-0.8	13.1	0.0	13.1	0.0	13.1	0.0	13.1	0.0	13.1	0.0	13.1	0.0	13.1	0.0
1950	13.1	0.0	13.3	1.5	13.5	1.5	13.6	0.7	13.6	0.0	13.6	0.0	13.6	0.0	13.6	0.0	13.6	0.0	13.8	1.5	14.2	2.9	14.3	0.7
1951	14.5	1.4	14.5	0.0	14.5	0.0	14.6	0.7	14.6	0.0	14.6	0.0	14.6	0.0	14.6	0.0	14.6	0.0	14.6	0.0	14.6	0.0	14.6	0.0
1952	14.6	0.0	14.6	0.0	14.6	0.0	14.6	0.0	14.6	0.0	14.6	0.0	14.6	0.0	14.6	0.0	14.6	0.0	14.6	0.0	14.6	0.0	15.2	4.1
1953	15.5	2.0	15.5	0.0	15.5	0.0	15.5	0.0	15.5	0.0	15.5	0.0	15.5	0.0	15.5	0.0	15.5	0.0	15.6	0.6	15.6	0.0	15.6	0.0
1954	15.6	0.0	15.6	0.0	15.6	0.0	15.6	0.0	15.6	0.0	15.6	0.0	15.6	0.0	15.6	0.0	15.6	0.0	15.6	0.0	15.6	0.0	15.6	0.0
1955	15.6	0.0	15.6	0.0	15.6	0.0	15.7	0.6	15.7	0.0	15.7	0.0	15.7	0.0	16.2	3.2	16.1	-0.6	16.3	1.2	16.3	0.0	16.3	0.0
1956	17.1	4.9	17.1	0.0	17.1	0.0	17.1	0.0	17.1	0.0	17.1	0.0	17.1	0.0	18.0	5.3	18.4	2.2	18.4	0.0	18.4	0.0	18.4	0.0
1957	18.7	1.6	19.1	2.1	19.0	-0.5	19.0	0.0	19.0	0.0	19.0	0.0	19.0	0.0	19.0	0.0	19.0	0.0	19.0	0.0	19.0	0.0	19.0	0.0
1958	19.0	0.0	19.0	0.0	19.0	0.0	19.0	0.0	19.0	0.0	19.0	0.0	19.0	0.0	19.0	0.0	19.0	0.0	19.0	0.0	19.0	0.0	19.0	0.0
1959	19.2	1.1	20.0	4.2	20.0	0.0	20.0	0.0	20.0	0.0	20.0	0.0	20.0	0.0	20.0	0.0	20.0	0.0	20.0	0.0	20.0	0.0	20.0	0.0
1960	20.0	0.0	20.0	0.0	20.0	0.0	20.0	0.0	20.0	0.0	20.0	0.0	20.0	0.0	20.0	0.0	20.0	0.0	20.0	0.0	20.0	0.0	20.0	0.0
1961	20.0	0.0	20.0	0.0	20.0	0.0	20.0	0.0	20.0	0.0	20.0	0.0	20.0	0.0	20.0	0.0	20.0	0.0	20.0	0.0	20.0	0.0	20.0	0.0
1962	20.0	0.0	20.0	0.0	20.0	0.0	20.0	0.0	20.0	0.0	20.0	0.0	20.0	0.0	20.0	0.0	20.0	0.0	20.0	0.0	20.0	0.0	20.0	0.0
1963	20.0	0.0	20.0	0.0	20.0	0.0	20.0	0.0	20.0	0.0	20.0	0.0	20.0	0.0	20.0	0.0	20.0	0.0	20.0	0.0	20.0	0.0	20.0	0.0
1964	20.0	0.0	20.0	0.0	20.0	0.0	20.5	2.5	20.8	1.5	20.8	0.0	20.8	0.0	20.8	0.0	20.8	0.0	20.8	0.0	20.8	0.0	20.8	0.0
1965	20.8	-	20.8	0.0	20.8	0.0	20.8	0.0	20.8	0.0	20.8	0.0	20.8	0.0	20.8	0.0	20.8	0.0	20.8	0.0	20.8	0.0	20.8	0.0
1966	20.8	0.0	20.8	0.0	20.8	0.0	20.8	0.0	20.8	0.0	21.2	1.9	21.7	2.4	21.7	0.0	21.7	0.0	21.7	0.0	21.7	0.0	21.7	0.0
1967	21.7	0.0	21.7	0.0	21.7	0.0	21.7	0.0	21.7	0.0	21.7	0.0	21.7	0.0	21.7	0.0	21.7	0.0	21.7	0.0	21.7	0.0	21.7	0.0
1968	21.7	0.0	21.7	0.0	21.7	0.0	22.6	4.1	22.6	0.0	22.6	0.0	22.6	0.0	22.6	0.0	22.6	0.0	22.6	0.0	22.6	0.0	23.3	3.1
1969	23.3	0.0	23.3	0.0	23.3	0.0	23.3	0.0	23.3	0.0	23.3	0.0	23.3	0.0	23.3	0.0	23.3	0.0	24.5	5.2	24.5	0.0	24.5	0.0
1970	24.5	0.0	24.5	0.0	24.5	0.0	27.0	10.2	27.0	0.0	27.0	0.0	27.3	1.1	27.3	0.0	27.3	0.0	31.6	15.8	31.6	0.0	31.6	0.0

[Continued]

Coke Oven Products
Producer Price Index
Base 1982 = 100
[Continued]

For 1926-1997. Columns headed % show percentile change in the index from the previous period for which an index is available.

Year	Jan Index	%	Feb Index	%	Mar Index	%	Apr Index	%	May Index	%	Jun Index	%	Jul Index	%	Aug Index	%	Sep Index	%	Oct Index	%	Nov Index	%	Dec Index	%
1971	31.6	0.0	31.6	0.0	31.6	0.0	31.6	0.0	32.2	1.9	32.6	1.2	32.6	0.0	32.6	0.0	32.6	0.0	32.6	0.0	32.6	0.0	32.6	0.0
1972	32.6	0.0	33.6	3.1	33.6	0.0	33.6	0.0	33.6	0.0	33.6	0.0	33.6	0.0	33.6	0.0	33.6	0.0	34.0	1.2	34.0	0.0	34.6	1.8
1973	35.2	1.7	35.7	1.4	35.7	0.0	36.2	1.4	36.2	0.0	36.2	0.0	36.2	0.0	36.2	0.0	36.2	0.0	36.2	0.0	36.2	0.0	36.8	1.7
1974	37.7	2.4	37.6	-0.3	40.1	6.6	46.6	16.2	52.4	12.4	53.9	2.9	55.4	2.8	58.5	5.6	60.8	3.9	66.1	8.7	67.2	1.7	67.6	0.6
1975	71.6	5.9	71.6	0.0	71.6	0.0	72.0	0.6	72.0	0.0	72.0	0.0	71.4	-0.8	71.1	-0.4	71.7	0.8	71.7	0.0	71.7	0.0	71.7	0.0
1976	71.6	-0.1	74.9	4.6	75.0	0.1	75.0	0.0	75.0	0.0	75.0	0.0	75.0	0.0	75.0	0.0	75.0	0.0	75.8	1.1	75.8	0.0	78.7	3.8
1977	79.6	1.1	79.6	0.0	79.6	0.0	80.8	1.5	81.3	0.6	83.6	2.8	83.6	0.0	83.6	0.0	83.6	0.0	83.6	0.0	83.6	0.0	83.6	0.0
1978	84.1	0.6	86.8	3.2	86.8	0.0	86.8	0.0	90.7	4.5	90.7	0.0	90.7	0.0	90.7	0.0	90.7	0.0	90.7	0.0	90.7	0.0	90.7	0.0
1979	91.2	0.6	91.8	0.7	92.8	1.1	93.2	0.4	93.3	0.1	93.3	0.0	93.3	0.0	93.3	0.0	93.3	0.0	93.4	0.1	93.4	0.0	93.4	0.0
1980	93.3	-0.1	93.3	0.0	93.3	0.0	93.3	0.0	93.3	0.0	93.3	0.0	93.3	0.0	93.3	0.0	93.3	0.0	93.3	0.0	93.3	0.0	93.2	-0.1
1981	93.2	0.0	93.2	0.0	93.2	0.0	93.2	0.0	101.3	8.7	101.7	0.4	101.7	0.0	101.7	0.0	101.7	0.0	101.7	0.0	101.7	0.0	101.7	0.0
1982	101.7	0.0	101.7	0.0	101.3	-0.4	101.3	0.0	101.3	0.0	100.1	-1.2	99.7	-0.4	99.4	-0.3	99.6	0.2	98.0	-1.6	98.0	0.0	98.0	0.0
1983	97.7	-0.3	97.7	0.0	96.9	-0.8	96.9	0.0	95.0	-2.0	95.0	0.0	93.5	-1.6	98.3	5.1	98.3	0.0	98.1	-0.2	98.3	0.2	90.0	-8.4
1984	90.6	0.7	94.8	4.6	95.1	0.3	95.9	0.8	95.6	-0.3	95.8	0.2	95.7	-0.1	94.7	-1.0	94.4	-0.3	93.7	-0.7	93.7	0.0	94.2	0.5
1985	95.2	1.1	95.2	0.0	93.8	-1.5	93.2	-0.6	93.0	-0.2	93.0	0.0	92.8	-0.2	92.8	0.0	92.8	0.0	92.5	-0.3	92.5	0.0	91.8	-0.8
1986	90.2	-1.7	90.4	0.2	90.3	-0.1	89.1	-1.3	89.0	-0.1	88.1	-1.0	88.0	-0.1	87.9	-0.1	88.0	0.1	87.4	-0.7	84.0	-3.9	84.0	0.0
1987	81.9	-2.5	80.9	-1.2	82.3	1.7	83.2	1.1	84.0	1.0	82.5	-1.8	82.4	-0.1	82.5	0.1	82.3	-0.2	83.5	1.5	83.5	0.0	84.2	0.8
1988	84.3	0.1	84.6	0.4	85.0	0.5	85.0	0.0	85.0	0.0	85.0	0.0	85.0	0.0	85.0	0.0	85.0	0.0	85.0	0.0	85.0	0.0	85.0	0.0
1989	88.8	4.5	88.9	0.1	89.1	0.2	88.5	-0.7	90.5	2.3	90.4	-0.1	90.6	0.2	90.8	0.2	90.7	-0.1	91.0	0.3	89.8	-1.3	89.8	0.0
1990	90.4	0.7	94.1	4.1	91.1	-3.2	90.9	-0.2	90.7	-0.2	90.9	0.2	90.1	-0.9	91.2	1.2	91.0	-0.2	92.7	1.9	92.3	-0.4	91.7	-0.7
1991	90.7	-1.1	93.7	3.3	94.5	0.9	95.0	0.5	94.6	-0.4	94.6	0.0	94.6	0.0	93.1	-1.6	94.1	1.1	93.9	-0.2	94.2	0.3	93.8	-0.4
1992	94.4	0.6	94.3	-0.1	92.1	-2.3	91.8	-0.3	90.9	-1.0	89.5	-1.5	90.5	1.1	90.3	-0.2	90.1	-0.2	90.1	0.0	91.1	1.1	90.9	-0.2
1993	91.3	0.4	88.6	-3.0	88.7	0.1	88.8	0.1	88.2	-0.7	88.0	-0.2	88.7	0.8	89.8	1.2	90.7	1.0	89.7	-1.1	88.5	-1.3	88.9	0.5
1994	87.9	-1.1	88.3	0.5	88.7	0.5	90.4	1.9	90.1	-0.3	90.1	0.0	90.3	0.2	87.7	-2.9	87.5	-0.2	87.9	0.5	87.3	-0.7	87.0	-0.3
1995	87.9	1.0	91.7	4.3	91.7	0.0	91.5	-0.2	91.9	0.4	92.3	0.4	91.6	-0.8	91.8	0.2	93.0	1.3	93.5	0.5	93.5	0.0	93.8	0.3
1996	94.0	0.2	94.1	0.1	97.5	3.6	97.4	-0.1	97.4	0.0	97.3	-0.1	95.6	-1.7	95.7	0.1	95.4	-0.3	95.5	0.1	95.7	0.2	94.0	-1.8
1997	94.6	0.6	94.5	-0.1	94.8	0.3	94.5	-0.3	94.6	0.1	94.6	0.0	94.2	-0.4	94.6	0.4	94.9	0.3	94.8	-0.1	97.4	2.7	97.4	0.0

Source: U.S. Department of Labor, Bureau of Labor Statistics, Division of Industry Prices and Price Indexes. n.e.c. stands for not elsewhere classified. - indicates no data collected for period or unavailable.

Gas Fuels
Producer Price Index
Base 1982 = 100

For 1958-1997. Columns headed % show percentile change in the index from the previous period for which an index is available.

Year	Jan Index	%	Feb Index	%	Mar Index	%	Apr Index	%	May Index	%	Jun Index	%	Jul Index	%	Aug Index	%	Sep Index	%	Oct Index	%	Nov Index	%	Dec Index	%
1958	7.1	-	7.2	1.4	7.1	-1.4	6.9	-2.8	6.9	0.0	6.9	0.0	6.9	0.0	7.2	4.3	7.3	1.4	7.5	2.7	7.5	0.0	7.6	1.3
1959	7.9	3.9	7.9	0.0	8.0	1.3	7.7	-3.8	7.7	0.0	7.5	-2.6	7.5	0.0	7.7	2.7	8.0	3.9	7.8	-2.5	8.0	2.6	8.1	1.3
1960	8.2	1.2	8.1	-1.2	8.2	1.2	8.2	0.0	7.9	-3.7	7.9	0.0	8.1	2.5	8.2	1.2	8.5	3.7	8.5	0.0	8.5	0.0	8.5	0.0
1961	8.5	0.0	8.6	1.2	8.6	0.0	8.3	-3.5	8.4	1.2	8.1	-3.6	8.2	1.2	8.2	0.0	8.2	0.0	8.4	2.4	8.4	0.0	8.4	0.0
1962	8.3	-1.2	8.6	3.6	8.4	-2.3	8.1	-3.6	8.2	1.2	8.0	-2.4	8.4	5.0	8.3	-1.2	8.5	2.4	8.7	2.4	8.6	-1.1	8.7	1.2
1963	8.5	-2.3	9.0	5.9	9.0	0.0	8.7	-3.3	8.5	-2.3	8.5	0.0	8.5	0.0	8.5	0.0	8.6	1.2	8.6	0.0	8.6	0.0	8.8	2.3
1964	8.8	0.0	8.9	1.1	8.7	-2.2	8.5	-2.3	8.2	-3.5	8.2	0.0	8.5	3.7	8.5	0.0	8.4	-1.2	8.5	1.2	8.7	2.4	8.7	0.0
1965	8.6	-1.1	8.7	1.2	8.7	0.0	8.6	-1.1	8.6	0.0	8.7	1.2	8.6	-1.1	8.7	1.2	8.8	1.1	8.9	1.1	8.9	0.0	9.1	2.2
1966	9.0	-1.1	9.1	1.1	9.0	-1.1	9.1	1.1	9.0	-1.1	9.1	1.1	9.0	-1.1	9.1	1.1	9.1	0.0	9.2	1.1	9.2	0.0	9.3	1.1
1967	9.5	2.2	9.5	0.0	9.5	0.0	9.5	0.0	9.5	0.0	9.5	0.0	9.3	-2.1	9.4	1.1	9.4	0.0	9.4	0.0	9.4	0.0	9.4	0.0
1968	9.2	-2.1	9.4	2.2	8.9	-5.3	8.8	-1.1	8.7	-1.1	8.7	0.0	8.5	-2.3	8.5	0.0	8.5	0.0	8.5	0.0	8.5	0.0	8.6	1.2
1969	8.7	1.2	8.8	1.1	8.8	0.0	8.6	-2.3	8.6	0.0	8.6	0.0	8.6	0.0	8.7	1.2	8.7	0.0	9.1	4.6	9.1	0.0	9.3	2.2
1970	9.3	0.0	9.5	2.2	9.6	1.1	9.6	0.0	9.6	0.0	9.7	1.0	9.7	0.0	9.7	0.0	10.1	4.1	10.0	-1.0	10.1	1.0	10.3	2.0
1971	10.2	-1.0	10.3	1.0	10.4	1.0	10.1	-2.9	10.1	0.0	10.1	0.0	10.1	0.0	10.2	1.0	10.3	1.0	10.3	0.0	10.3	0.0	10.4	1.0
1972	10.4	0.0	10.4	0.0	10.5	1.0	10.6	1.0	10.7	0.9	10.6	-0.9	10.7	0.9	10.8	0.9	11.0	1.9	11.1	0.9	11.2	0.9	11.2	0.0
1973	11.2	0.0	11.2	0.0	11.2	0.0	11.3	0.9	11.4	0.9	12.1	6.1	12.1	0.0	12.3	1.7	12.5	1.6	12.6	0.8	12.5	-0.8	13.0	4.0
1974	12.9	-0.8	13.8	7.0	14.0	1.4	14.0	0.0	14.1	0.7	14.3	1.4	17.7	23.8	17.9	1.1	15.7	-12.3	15.8	0.6	16.5	4.4	16.7	1.2
1975	17.1	2.4	17.8	4.1	17.7	-0.6	19.5	10.2	20.6	5.6	20.7	0.5	21.3	2.9	21.4	0.5	21.8	1.9	21.8	0.0	22.2	1.8	23.1	4.1
1976	23.0	-0.4	23.3	1.3	24.0	3.0	25.1	4.6	25.2	0.4	26.0	3.2	26.1	0.4	27.0	3.4	27.3	1.1	31.2	14.3	34.4	10.3	31.8	-7.6
1977	30.4	-4.4	34.3	12.8	35.0	2.0	35.7	2.0	36.8	3.1	36.4	-1.1	36.9	1.4	37.8	2.4	38.2	1.1	38.3	0.3	39.0	1.8	39.8	2.1
1978	39.6	-0.5	39.4	-0.5	40.0	1.5	40.4	1.0	40.4	0.0	40.4	0.0	40.6	0.5	40.1	-1.2	40.7	1.5	40.5	-0.5	40.9	1.0	41.9	2.4
1979	42.4	1.2	43.2	1.9	44.4	2.8	45.0	1.4	47.8	6.2	49.2	2.9	51.7	5.1	54.0	4.4	56.9	5.4	58.4	2.6	60.0	2.7	62.4	4.0
1980	63.9	2.4	67.6	5.8	67.5	-0.1	68.8	1.9	70.2	2.0	70.6	0.6	71.8	1.7	72.8	1.4	74.1	1.8	75.6	2.0	77.8	2.9	79.6	2.3
1981	80.8	1.5	83.1	2.8	83.9	1.0	85.6	2.0	88.0	2.8	90.0	2.3	91.4	1.6	89.5	-2.1	92.1	2.9	91.0	-1.2	92.7	1.9	94.6	2.0
1982	93.1	-1.6	93.1	0.0	93.4	0.3	93.6	0.2	94.4	0.9	96.9	2.6	99.4	2.6	101.3	1.9	104.8	3.5	106.5	1.6	112.2	5.4	111.3	-0.8
1983	108.1	-2.9	108.8	0.6	111.2	2.2	109.0	-2.0	109.0	0.0	108.9	-0.1	108.3	-0.6	108.0	-0.3	108.1	0.1	106.4	-1.6	105.8	-0.6	105.6	-0.2
1984	105.9	0.3	105.4	-0.5	102.8	-2.5	103.9	1.1	104.1	0.2	104.6	0.5	104.7	0.1	105.3	0.6	104.1	-1.1	104.9	0.8	105.0	0.1	104.0	-1.0
1985	101.2	-2.7	100.6	-0.6	98.4	-2.2	98.9	0.5	101.7	2.8	99.7	-2.0	99.0	-0.7	96.7	-2.3	97.2	0.5	97.4	0.2	96.5	-0.9	97.1	0.6
1986	97.5	0.4	94.0	-3.6	94.2	0.2	88.6	-5.9	86.8	-2.0	85.2	-1.8	79.4	-6.8	76.3	-3.9	73.2	-4.1	74.4	1.6	74.9	0.7	73.6	-1.7
1987	73.6	0.0	73.0	-0.8	76.2	4.4	75.5	-0.9	74.4	-1.5	74.0	-0.5	74.1	0.1	74.8	0.9	75.4	0.8	73.1	-3.1	71.6	-2.1	73.8	3.1
1988	73.3	-0.7	71.7	-2.2	72.3	0.8	74.5	3.0	72.0	-3.4	69.8	-3.1	71.1	1.9	68.7	-3.4	69.0	0.4	71.7	3.9	70.5	-1.7	71.7	1.7
1989	75.2	4.9	77.3	2.8	74.0	-4.3	75.2	1.6	77.1	2.5	76.3	-1.0	76.2	-0.1	72.8	-4.5	75.4	3.6	73.7	-2.3	74.2	0.7	76.0	2.4
1990	82.5	8.6	81.8	-0.8	76.8	-6.1	74.3	-3.3	73.9	-0.5	71.8	-2.8	76.4	6.4	71.8	-6.0	76.5	6.5	80.7	5.5	85.9	6.4	88.4	2.9
1991	86.8	-1.8	80.5	-7.3	78.3	-2.7	74.6	-4.7	77.2	3.5	75.0	-2.8	73.2	-2.4	74.2	1.4	71.5	-3.6	74.3	3.9	78.4	5.5	80.6	2.8
1992	76.1	-5.6	73.7	-3.2	70.5	-4.3	70.1	-0.6	71.0	1.3	70.2	-1.1	75.9	8.1	75.3	-0.8	81.0	7.6	78.7	-2.8	86.2	9.5	82.5	-4.3
1993	82.2	-0.4	75.8	-7.8	74.0	-2.4	75.0	1.4	81.3	8.4	85.9	5.7	77.1	-10.2	75.7	-1.8	78.6	3.8	81.1	3.2	77.9	-3.9	77.5	-0.5
1994	82.7	6.7	75.6	-8.6	80.3	6.2	78.0	-2.9	72.7	-6.8	72.4	-0.4	69.1	-4.6	71.7	3.8	69.8	-2.6	66.1	-5.3	65.3	-1.2	70.3	7.7
1995	69.6	-1.0	66.0	-5.2	64.3	-2.6	65.2	1.4	66.0	1.2	67.8	2.7	65.5	-3.4	59.2	-9.6	60.3	1.9	62.7	4.0	65.6	4.6	70.7	7.8
1996	79.7	12.7	89.9	12.8	82.5	-8.2	88.5	7.3	83.8	-5.3	76.8	-8.4	83.2	8.3	85.1	2.3	78.7	-7.5	79.5	1.0	99.8	25.5	132.1	32.4
1997	145.8	10.4	113.9	-21.9	79.5	-30.2	75.7	-4.8	80.0	5.7	84.5	5.6	81.4	-3.7	83.0	2.0	91.3	10.0	102.3	12.0	111.7	9.2	94.2	-15.7

Source: U.S. Department of Labor, Bureau of Labor Statistics, Division of Industry Prices and Price Indexes. n.e.c. stands for not elsewhere classified. - indicates no data collected for period or unavailable.

Electric Power
Producer Price Index
Base 1982 = 100

For 1958-1997. Columns headed % show percentile change in the index from the previous period for which an index is available.

Year	Jan Index	%	Feb Index	%	Mar Index	%	Apr Index	%	May Index	%	Jun Index	%	Jul Index	%	Aug Index	%	Sep Index	%	Oct Index	%	Nov Index	%	Dec Index	%
1958	24.4	-	24.5	0.4	24.5	0.0	24.4	-0.4	24.4	0.0	24.5	0.4	24.5	0.0	24.6	0.4	24.6	0.0	24.6	0.0	24.6	0.0	24.6	0.0
1959	24.6	0.0	24.6	0.0	24.6	0.0	24.6	0.0	24.6	0.0	24.6	0.0	24.6	0.0	24.6	0.0	24.6	0.0	24.6	0.0	24.6	0.0	24.7	0.4
1960	24.7	0.0	24.9	0.8	24.9	0.0	24.9	0.0	24.8	-0.4	24.9	0.4	24.9	0.0	24.9	0.0	24.9	0.0	24.9	0.0	25.0	0.4	25.0	0.0
1961	25.0	0.0	25.0	0.0	25.0	0.0	25.0	0.0	25.0	0.0	25.0	0.0	25.0	0.0	25.0	0.0	25.0	0.0	25.0	0.0	25.1	0.4	25.0	-0.4
1962	25.0	0.0	25.2	0.8	25.2	0.0	25.2	0.0	25.1	-0.4	25.1	0.0	25.1	0.0	25.1	0.0	25.1	0.0	25.1	0.0	25.1	0.0	25.1	0.0
1963	25.0	-0.4	25.0	0.0	25.0	0.0	25.0	0.0	25.0	0.0	25.0	0.0	24.9	-0.4	24.9	0.0	24.9	0.0	24.8	-0.4	24.7	-0.4	24.7	0.0
1964	24.7	0.0	24.7	0.0	24.3	-1.6	24.7	1.6	24.7	0.0	24.6	-0.4	24.6	0.0	24.8	0.8	24.8	0.0	24.8	0.0	24.8	0.0	24.7	-0.4
1965	24.7	0.0	24.6	-0.4	24.6	0.0	24.6	0.0	24.6	0.0	24.6	0.0	24.6	0.0	24.6	0.0	24.6	0.0	24.6	0.0	24.6	0.0	24.6	0.0
1966	24.5	-0.4	24.5	0.0	24.5	0.0	24.5	0.0	24.5	0.0	24.5	0.0	24.5	0.0	24.5	0.0	24.5	0.0	24.5	0.0	24.5	0.0	24.6	0.4
1967	24.6	0.0	24.6	0.0	24.6	0.0	24.6	0.0	24.6	0.0	24.6	0.0	24.6	0.0	24.6	0.0	24.6	0.0	24.6	0.0	24.6	0.0	24.7	0.4
1968	24.7	0.0	24.7	0.0	24.7	0.0	24.7	0.0	24.7	0.0	24.7	0.0	24.9	0.8	24.9	0.0	24.9	0.0	24.9	0.0	24.9	0.0	24.9	0.0
1969	24.8	-0.4	24.8	0.0	24.9	0.4	24.9	0.0	24.9	0.0	24.9	0.0	24.9	0.0	25.1	0.8	25.3	0.8	25.3	0.0	25.3	0.0	25.3	0.0
1970	25.3	0.0	25.3	0.0	25.3	0.0	25.3	0.0	25.5	0.8	25.6	0.4	26.0	1.6	26.2	0.8	26.6	1.5	26.9	1.1	27.0	0.4	27.4	1.5
1971	27.5	0.4	27.8	1.1	28.1	1.1	28.1	0.0	28.2	0.4	28.4	0.7	28.8	1.4	29.1	1.0	29.1	0.0	29.0	-0.3	29.1	0.3	29.8	2.4
1972	29.2	-2.0	29.5	1.0	29.5	0.0	29.6	0.3	29.8	0.7	29.9	0.3	30.0	0.3	30.0	0.0	30.2	0.7	30.3	0.3	30.2	-0.3	30.2	0.0
1973	30.5	1.0	31.0	1.6	31.2	0.6	31.4	0.6	31.5	0.3	31.6	0.3	31.7	0.3	31.8	0.3	32.2	1.3	32.5	0.9	32.8	0.9	33.4	1.8
1974	33.8	1.2	35.0	3.6	36.6	4.6	37.7	3.0	39.3	4.2	40.5	3.1	41.2	1.7	42.0	1.9	42.8	1.9	43.9	2.6	44.2	0.7	44.4	0.5
1975	45.1	1.6	45.9	1.8	47.0	2.4	47.9	1.9	47.4	-1.0	46.9	-1.1	47.4	1.1	48.0	1.3	48.6	1.2	49.1	1.0	49.0	-0.2	48.6	-0.8
1976	48.8	0.4	49.0	0.4	49.6	1.2	50.3	1.4	50.4	0.2	50.8	0.8	51.7	1.8	52.5	1.5	52.8	0.6	52.4	-0.8	52.6	0.4	52.0	-1.1
1977	52.6	1.2	54.0	2.7	55.0	1.9	56.4	2.5	56.7	0.5	57.6	1.6	58.8	2.1	60.2	2.4	59.7	-0.8	59.6	-0.2	58.5	-1.8	58.3	-0.3
1978	58.9	1.0	59.7	1.4	61.5	3.0	61.7	0.3	62.2	0.8	63.2	1.6	62.7	-0.8	62.4	-0.5	62.1	-0.5	62.2	0.2	61.6	-1.0	61.7	0.2
1979	61.7	0.0	61.8	0.2	63.3	2.4	64.1	1.3	65.4	2.0	66.4	1.5	67.6	1.8	68.6	1.5	69.0	0.6	69.7	1.0	69.3	-0.6	70.6	1.9
1980	71.5	1.3	73.6	2.9	75.2	2.2	76.3	1.5	77.9	2.1	80.2	3.0	81.5	1.6	82.1	0.7	83.2	1.3	83.0	-0.2	82.1	-1.1	83.1	1.2
1981	84.0	1.1	85.2	1.4	86.4	1.4	87.4	1.2	88.7	1.5	90.2	1.7	92.2	2.2	94.9	2.9	94.4	-0.5	93.1	-1.4	93.1	0.0	94.5	1.5
1982	96.6	2.2	96.6	0.0	99.3	2.8	99.9	0.6	100.1	0.2	99.8	-0.3	102.3	2.5	102.1	-0.2	102.1	0.0	100.6	-1.5	99.6	-1.0	100.8	1.2
1983	101.1	0.3	101.1	0.0	101.2	0.1	100.7	-0.5	101.4	0.7	103.2	1.8	104.9	1.6	105.1	0.2	105.3	0.2	104.2	-1.0	103.0	-1.2	102.7	-0.3
1984	103.4	0.7	104.3	0.9	105.0	0.7	106.2	1.1	106.6	0.4	109.9	3.1	111.6	1.5	112.4	0.7	112.3	-0.1	109.6	-2.4	109.0	-0.5	108.4	-0.6
1985	109.7	1.2	109.7	0.0	110.1	0.4	110.5	0.4	110.2	-0.3	113.2	2.7	113.7	0.4	114.0	0.3	113.7	-0.3	112.0	-1.5	111.4	-0.5	111.0	-0.4
1986	112.3	1.2	113.2	0.8	112.7	-0.4	111.5	-1.1	112.1	0.5	114.0	1.7	114.8	0.7	114.8	0.0	114.8	0.0	111.0	-3.3	110.2	-0.7	109.9	-0.3
1987	108.4	-1.4	108.3	-0.1	108.7	0.4	108.0	-0.6	109.9	1.8	113.2	3.0	114.8	1.4	114.6	-0.2	114.1	-0.4	110.4	-3.2	108.1	-2.1	108.4	0.3
1988	107.8	-0.6	108.0	0.2	107.7	-0.3	107.6	-0.1	107.6	0.0	115.6	7.4	116.8	1.0	116.8	0.0	117.1	0.3	112.8	-3.7	107.8	-4.4	109.1	1.2
1989	110.6	1.4	110.8	0.2	110.9	0.1	111.1	0.2	112.6	1.4	119.3	6.0	120.8	1.3	120.7	-0.1	120.7	0.0	115.2	-4.6	111.8	-3.0	112.6	0.7
1990	113.1	0.4	113.6	0.4	113.8	0.2	113.7	-0.1	115.5	1.6	121.7	5.4	121.9	0.2	122.1	0.2	122.4	0.2	119.1	-2.7	117.6	-1.3	116.8	-0.7
1991	120.5	3.2	120.4	-0.1	120.2	-0.2	120.2	0.0	123.1	2.4	128.8	4.6	130.4	1.2	130.4	0.0	130.5	0.1	124.7	-4.4	120.2	-3.6	121.9	1.4
1992	122.2	0.2	121.8	-0.3	122.1	0.2	121.4	-0.6	124.5	2.6	131.7	5.8	132.7	0.8	132.4	-0.2	132.7	0.2	127.4	-4.0	122.8	-3.6	123.7	0.7
1993	124.2	0.4	123.9	-0.2	124.0	0.1	124.6	0.5	125.7	0.9	134.8	7.2	135.1	0.2	135.3	0.1	135.8	0.4	129.7	-4.5	125.3	-3.4	125.1	-0.2
1994	125.2	0.1	125.2	0.0	125.1	-0.1	124.8	-0.2	125.7	0.7	133.0	5.8	133.9	0.7	134.1	0.1	134.1	0.0	128.6	-4.1	127.0	-1.2	127.4	0.3
1995	127.5	0.1	127.7	0.2	127.9	0.2	126.3	-1.3	129.6	2.6	135.9	4.9	137.0	0.8	137.0	0.0	134.9	-1.5	131.2	-2.7	127.8	-2.6	127.9	0.1
1996	128.0	0.1	126.9	-0.9	127.7	0.6	128.1	0.3	131.4	2.6	137.2	4.4	137.0	-0.1	137.4	0.3	137.3	-0.1	131.9	-3.9	127.8	-3.1	128.2	0.3
1997	128.5	0.2	128.4	-0.1	128.4	0.0	127.9	-0.4	129.8	1.5	136.5	5.2	137.1	0.4	136.0	-0.8	137.2	0.9	131.7	-4.0	128.2	-2.7	128.5	0.2

Source: U.S. Department of Labor, Bureau of Labor Statistics, Division of Industry Prices and Price Indexes. n.e.c. stands for not elsewhere classified. - indicates no data collected for period or unavailable.

Utility Natural Gas
Producer Price Index
Base 1982 = 100

For 1990-1997. Columns headed % show percentile change in the index from the previous period for which an index is available.

Year	Jan Index	%	Feb Index	%	Mar Index	%	Apr Index	%	May Index	%	Jun Index	%	Jul Index	%	Aug Index	%	Sep Index	%	Oct Index	%	Nov Index	%	Dec Index	%
1990	-		-		-		-		-		-		-		-		-		-		-		100.0	-
1991	101.2	1.2	99.5	-1.7	97.7	-1.8	97.1	-0.6	96.2	-0.9	95.2	-1.0	95.0	-0.2	94.7	-0.3	95.1	0.4	96.2	1.2	98.6	2.5	99.8	1.2
1992	100.1	0.3	98.0	-2.1	96.9	-1.1	96.0	-0.9	95.5	-0.5	96.0	0.5	96.1	0.1	96.9	0.8	98.3	1.4	101.2	3.0	103.7	2.5	104.2	0.5
1993	104.0	-0.2	102.8	-1.2	102.2	-0.6	101.9	-0.3	103.9	2.0	103.5	-0.4	103.2	-0.3	104.0	0.8	105.0	1.0	104.9	-0.1	106.4	1.4	107.6	1.1
1994	107.6	0.0	107.7	0.1	108.1	0.4	106.7	-1.3	105.5	-1.1	103.0	-2.4	102.1	-0.9	102.2	0.1	101.9	-0.3	101.1	-0.8	103.1	2.0	103.7	0.6
1995	104.0	0.3	102.5	-1.4	101.2	-1.3	99.9	-1.3	97.5	-2.4	97.6	0.1	97.0	-0.6	96.2	-0.8	96.1	-0.1	95.8	-0.3	97.6	1.9	100.6	3.1
1996	102.5	1.9	103.6	1.1	104.9	1.3	104.4	-0.5	103.9	-0.5	104.1	0.2	104.5	0.4	105.6	1.1	103.5	-2.0	102.9	-0.6	108.4	5.3	114.3	5.4
1997	122.1	6.8	120.1	-1.6	111.8	-6.9	105.8	-5.4	105.4	-0.4	106.6	1.1	107.5	0.8	107.0	-0.5	108.4	1.3	112.9	4.2	119.8	6.1	116.3	-2.9

Source: U.S. Department of Labor, Bureau of Labor Statistics, Division of Industry Prices and Price Indexes. n.e.c. stands for not elsewhere classified. - indicates no data collected for period or unavailable.

Crude Petroleum (domestic production)
Producer Price Index
Base 1982 = 100

For 1991-1997. Columns headed % show percentile change in the index from the previous period for which an index is available.

Year	Jan Index	%	Feb Index	%	Mar Index	%	Apr Index	%	May Index	%	Jun Index	%	Jul Index	%	Aug Index	%	Sep Index	%	Oct Index	%	Nov Index	%	Dec Index	%
1991	-	-	-	-	-	-	-	-	-	-	-	-	59.3	-	60.4	1.9	60.4	0.0	66.3	9.8	64.0	-3.5	55.1	-13.9
1992	51.3	-6.9	53.5	4.3	51.0	-4.7	56.0	9.8	59.2	5.7	64.3	8.6	61.9	-3.7	60.5	-2.3	63.1	4.3	63.4	0.5	58.5	-7.7	53.8	-8.0
1993	52.0	-3.3	56.1	7.9	58.1	3.6	57.7	-0.7	57.9	0.3	52.9	-8.6	50.2	-5.1	48.3	-3.8	46.5	-3.7	51.8	11.4	46.0	-11.2	38.9	-15.4
1994	39.3	1.0	37.8	-3.8	39.6	4.8	42.7	7.8	48.9	14.5	52.9	8.2	56.2	6.2	54.4	-3.2	48.3	-11.2	49.3	2.1	49.1	-0.4	47.1	-4.1
1995	48.4	2.8	51.0	5.4	50.6	-0.8	55.3	9.3	56.0	1.3	53.3	-4.8	48.3	-9.4	49.1	1.7	51.4	4.7	48.3	-6.0	49.0	1.4	52.2	6.5
1996	56.0	7.3	52.8	-5.7	57.7	9.3	66.0	14.4	61.0	-7.6	57.7	-5.4	59.9	3.8	62.0	3.5	67.2	8.4	72.0	7.1	68.5	-4.9	70.9	3.5
1997	73.4	3.5	64.5	-12.1	56.3	-12.7	56.1	-0.4	60.2	7.3	51.8	-14.0	54.9	6.0	54.9	0.0	53.3	-2.9	57.3	7.5	56.4	-1.6	50.8	-9.9

Source: U.S. Department of Labor, Bureau of Labor Statistics, Division of Industry Prices and Price Indexes. n.e.c. stands for not elsewhere classified. - indicates no data collected for period or unavailable.

Petroleum Products, Refined

Producer Price Index
Base 1982 = 100

For 1947-1997. Columns headed % show percentile change in the index from the previous period for which an index is available.

Year	Jan Index	%	Feb Index	%	Mar Index	%	Apr Index	%	May Index	%	Jun Index	%	Jul Index	%	Aug Index	%	Sep Index	%	Oct Index	%	Nov Index	%	Dec Index	%
1947	8.3	-	8.4	1.2	9.0	7.1	9.6	6.7	9.6	0.0	9.7	1.0	9.9	2.1	10.1	2.0	10.1	0.0	10.2	1.0	10.7	4.9	11.3	5.6
1948	12.1	7.1	12.3	1.7	12.3	0.0	12.3	0.0	12.3	0.0	12.3	0.0	12.3	0.0	12.2	-0.8	12.1	-0.8	12.2	0.8	12.1	-0.8	11.9	-1.7
1949	11.7	-1.7	11.2	-4.3	11.0	-1.8	10.7	-2.7	10.5	-1.9	10.4	-1.0	10.3	-1.0	10.4	1.0	10.5	1.0	10.6	1.0	10.4	-1.9	10.4	0.0
1950	10.5	1.0	10.5	0.0	10.5	0.0	10.6	1.0	10.9	2.8	11.1	1.8	11.3	1.8	11.6	2.7	11.7	0.9	11.8	0.9	11.8	0.0	11.8	0.0
1951	12.0	1.7	12.0	0.0	12.1	0.8	12.1	0.0	12.0	-0.8	12.1	0.8	12.1	0.0	12.1	0.0	12.1	0.0	12.1	0.0	12.1	0.0	12.1	0.0
1952	12.1	0.0	12.0	-0.8	12.1	0.8	11.9	-1.7	12.0	0.8	11.9	-0.8	11.9	0.0	11.8	-0.8	11.8	0.0	11.8	0.0	11.7	-0.8	11.7	0.0
1953	11.7	0.0	11.6	-0.9	11.8	1.7	11.8	0.0	11.9	0.8	11.9	0.0	12.6	5.9	12.6	0.0	12.6	0.0	12.6	0.0	12.6	0.0	12.4	-1.6
1954	12.3	-0.8	12.2	-0.8	11.9	-2.5	12.0	0.8	12.0	0.0	11.9	-0.8	11.5	-3.4	11.6	0.9	11.7	0.9	11.6	-0.9	11.7	0.9	11.8	0.9
1955	11.9	0.8	11.9	0.0	12.0	0.8	11.9	-0.8	11.9	0.0	11.9	0.0	11.9	0.0	12.1	1.7	12.2	0.8	12.3	0.8	12.3	0.0	12.4	0.8
1956	12.6	1.6	12.7	0.8	12.6	-0.8	12.7	0.8	12.8	0.8	12.8	0.0	12.8	0.0	12.8	0.0	12.8	0.0	12.8	0.0	12.7	-0.8	13.1	3.1
1957	13.5	3.1	14.2	5.2	14.1	-0.7	14.1	0.0	14.0	-0.7	13.8	-1.4	13.6	-1.4	13.5	-0.7	13.5	0.0	13.4	-0.7	13.2	-1.5	13.2	0.0
1958	13.1	-0.8	12.6	-3.8	12.4	-1.6	12.2	-1.6	12.1	-0.8	12.2	0.8	12.4	1.6	12.7	2.4	12.7	0.0	12.5	-1.6	12.4	-0.8	12.4	0.0
1959	12.6	1.6	12.8	1.6	12.8	0.0	12.8	0.0	12.6	-1.6	12.2	-3.2	12.2	0.0	12.3	0.8	12.2	-0.8	12.2	0.0	12.1	-0.8	12.1	0.0
1960	12.2	0.8	12.2	0.0	12.2	0.0	12.3	0.8	12.0	-2.4	12.3	2.5	12.6	2.4	12.8	1.6	13.0	1.6	13.0	0.0	12.9	-0.8	13.0	0.8
1961	13.2	1.5	13.3	0.8	13.2	-0.8	12.8	-3.0	12.5	-2.3	12.7	1.6	12.8	0.8	12.7	-0.8	12.5	-1.6	12.3	-1.6	12.5	1.6	12.7	1.6
1962	12.8	0.8	12.6	-1.6	12.2	-3.2	12.7	4.1	12.6	-0.8	12.6	0.0	12.6	0.0	12.5	-0.8	12.8	2.4	12.7	-0.8	12.7	0.0	12.7	0.0
1963	12.6	-0.8	12.5	-0.8	12.6	0.8	12.6	0.0	12.7	0.8	12.8	0.8	12.7	-0.8	12.3	-3.1	12.3	0.0	12.3	0.0	12.1	-1.6	12.3	1.7
1964	12.4	0.8	12.2	-1.6	11.9	-2.5	11.7	-1.7	11.8	0.9	11.9	0.8	11.9	0.0	11.7	-1.7	11.5	-1.7	11.8	2.6	12.0	1.7	12.1	0.8
1965	12.2	0.8	12.1	-0.8	12.1	0.0	12.1	0.0	12.3	1.7	12.3	0.0	12.3	0.0	12.4	0.8	12.4	0.0	12.4	0.0	12.6	1.6	12.7	0.8
1966	12.6	-0.8	12.6	0.0	12.5	-0.8	12.6	0.8	12.7	0.8	12.9	1.6	12.8	-0.8	12.9	0.8	13.0	0.8	13.0	0.0	13.0	0.0	12.9	-0.8
1967	12.9	0.0	13.1	1.6	13.2	0.8	13.1	-0.8	13.3	1.5	13.3	0.0	13.3	0.0	13.4	0.8	13.4	0.0	13.0	-3.0	12.9	-0.8	12.8	-0.8
1968	12.7	-0.8	12.8	0.8	12.8	0.0	12.9	0.8	12.9	0.0	13.3	3.1	13.2	-0.8	13.0	-1.5	13.0	0.0	12.8	-1.5	12.8	0.0	12.7	-0.8
1969	12.7	0.0	12.8	0.8	13.1	2.3	13.2	0.8	13.2	0.0	13.3	0.0	13.3	0.0	13.2	-0.8	13.1	-0.8	13.1	0.0	13.1	0.0	13.1	0.0
1970	13.0	-0.8	13.0	0.0	13.0	0.0	13.0	0.0	13.3	2.3	13.1	-1.5	13.2	0.8	13.3	0.8	13.3	0.0	13.3	0.0	13.5	1.5	14.2	5.2
1971	14.2	0.0	14.1	-0.7	14.0	-0.7	13.8	-1.4	14.1	2.2	14.1	0.0	14.2	0.7	14.2	0.0	14.2	0.0	14.1	-0.7	14.0	-0.7	14.0	0.0
1972	13.9	-0.7	13.9	0.0	14.0	0.7	14.0	0.0	14.1	0.7	14.3	1.4	14.3	0.0	14.5	1.4	14.6	0.7	14.6	0.0	14.7	0.7	14.7	0.0
1973	14.7	0.0	15.6	6.1	15.9	1.9	16.1	1.3	16.4	1.9	16.8	2.4	17.1	1.8	17.1	0.0	17.2	0.6	17.6	2.3	18.4	4.5	19.9	8.2
1974	21.9	10.1	24.7	12.8	27.1	9.7	28.3	4.4	29.5	4.2	30.5	3.4	31.5	3.3	32.0	1.6	31.9	-0.3	32.1	0.6	31.3	-2.5	31.3	0.0
1975	31.8	1.6	31.6	-0.6	31.8	0.6	32.0	0.6	32.3	0.9	33.1	2.5	34.0	2.7	35.3	3.8	35.7	1.1	36.0	0.8	36.1	0.3	36.1	0.0
1976	35.8	-0.8	35.8	0.0	35.4	-1.1	35.1	-0.8	35.1	0.0	35.5	1.1	36.4	2.5	36.9	1.4	37.3	1.1	37.4	0.3	37.5	0.3	37.8	0.8
1977	38.0	0.5	38.8	2.1	39.7	2.3	40.3	1.5	40.8	1.2	41.0	0.5	41.2	0.5	41.1	-0.2	41.1	0.0	41.3	0.5	41.2	-0.2	41.2	0.0
1978	41.3	0.2	41.1	-0.5	40.8	-0.7	40.9	0.2	41.3	1.0	41.8	1.2	42.2	1.0	42.5	0.7	42.8	0.7	43.3	1.2	43.6	0.7	44.4	1.8
1979	45.2	1.8	46.0	1.8	47.3	2.8	49.7	5.1	52.5	5.6	55.6	5.9	59.1	6.3	63.4	7.3	67.5	6.5	70.1	3.9	71.7	2.3	72.9	1.7
1980	76.6	5.1	81.5	6.4	86.6	6.3	89.1	2.9	89.4	0.3	89.5	0.1	91.1	1.8	91.6	0.5	91.5	-0.1	90.7	-0.9	91.6	1.0	94.2	2.8
1981	96.8	2.8	101.1	4.4	108.4	7.2	110.5	1.9	109.7	-0.7	108.8	-0.8	107.2	-1.5	106.9	-0.3	105.9	-0.9	105.4	-0.5	104.9	-0.5	104.9	0.0
1982	105.3	0.4	103.7	-1.5	101.2	-2.4	96.4	-4.7	93.7	-2.8	97.1	3.6	102.0	5.0	102.7	0.7	100.0	-2.6	99.1	-0.9	99.6	0.5	99.1	-0.5
1983	94.7	-4.4	91.0	-3.9	87.6	-3.7	84.8	-3.2	86.6	2.1	89.9	3.8	90.5	0.7	91.3	0.9	91.3	0.0	91.5	0.2	90.4	-1.2	89.1	-1.4
1984	87.1	-2.2	88.0	1.0	89.4	1.6	87.6	-2.0	89.0	1.6	89.3	0.3	88.4	-1.0	86.0	-2.7	84.9	-1.3	86.1	1.4	86.9	0.9	85.7	-1.4
1985	83.5	-2.6	80.9	-3.1	81.5	0.7	83.6	2.6	86.4	3.3	84.3	-2.4	82.8	-1.8	81.5	-1.6	81.7	0.2	82.1	0.5	84.3	2.7	85.4	1.3
1986	79.9	-6.4	68.9	-13.8	56.7	-17.7	52.0	-8.3	53.3	2.5	53.3	0.0	44.7	-16.1	44.3	-0.9	48.2	8.8	45.4	-5.8	45.5	0.2	46.4	2.0
1987	50.8	9.5	53.9	6.1	52.9	-1.9	55.4	4.7	56.1	1.3	57.7	2.9	59.3	2.9	61.5	3.7	58.9	-4.2	59.0	0.2	59.8	1.4	56.8	-5.0
1988	53.7	-5.5	52.9	-1.5	52.1	-1.5	54.4	4.4	56.4	3.7	55.4	-1.8	55.3	-0.2	55.8	0.9	52.9	-5.2	51.1	-3.4	53.5	4.7	52.9	-1.1
1989	54.4	2.8	55.0	1.1	57.1	3.8	64.9	13.7	67.7	4.3	65.6	-3.1	63.1	-3.8	58.9	-6.7	61.4	4.2	63.0	2.6	61.6	-2.2	61.9	0.5
1990	71.8	16.0	64.5	-10.2	63.3	-1.9	65.1	2.8	65.3	0.3	63.9	-2.1	62.3	-2.5	74.5	19.6	86.7	16.4	96.9	11.8	96.4	-0.5	87.0	-9.8
1991	79.1	-9.1	71.5	-9.6	64.0	-10.5	63.6	-0.6	66.4	4.4	65.4	-1.5	63.3	-3.2	66.4	4.9	67.9	2.3	66.9	-1.5	67.8	1.3	63.4	-6.5

[Continued]

Petroleum Products, Refined

Producer Price Index
Base 1982 = 100

[Continued]

For 1947-1997. Columns headed % show percentile change in the index from the previous period for which an index is available.

Year	Jan Index	%	Feb Index	%	Mar Index	%	Apr Index	%	May Index	%	Jun Index	%	Jul Index	%	Aug Index	%	Sep Index	%	Oct Index	%	Nov Index	%	Dec Index	%
1992	57.7	-9.0	59.7	3.5	59.2	-0.8	61.9	4.6	66.2	6.9	69.9	5.6	68.1	-2.6	67.5	-0.9	68.6	1.6	68.5	-0.1	67.0	-2.2	62.1	-7.3
1993	61.6	-0.8	62.5	1.5	63.9	2.2	65.1	1.9	66.5	2.2	64.5	-3.0	62.0	-3.9	60.3	-2.7	61.1	1.3	63.1	3.3	60.5	-4.1	52.9	-12.6
1994	52.9	0.0	56.4	6.6	55.8	-1.1	57.0	2.2	58.1	1.9	59.3	2.1	62.0	4.6	66.1	6.6	63.0	-4.7	60.0	-4.8	61.6	2.7	57.5	-6.7
1995	58.1	1.0	58.2	0.2	59.0	1.4	63.1	6.9	66.1	4.8	64.8	-2.0	61.4	-5.2	60.9	-0.8	61.1	0.3	59.3	-2.9	57.8	-2.5	59.8	3.5
1996	63.2	5.7	61.1	-3.3	65.3	6.9	73.2	12.1	75.1	2.6	69.9	-6.9	69.0	-1.3	69.4	0.6	72.1	3.9	74.2	2.9	74.6	0.5	74.5	-0.1
1997	74.3	-0.3	72.9	-1.9	69.5	-4.7	68.2	-1.9	67.9	-0.4	66.3	-2.4	64.3	-3.0	67.8	5.4	68.5	1.0	67.0	-2.2	66.3	-1.0	62.1	-6.3

Source: U.S. Department of Labor, Bureau of Labor Statistics, Division of Industry Prices and Price Indexes. n.e.c. stands for not elsewhere classified. - indicates no data collected for period or unavailable.

Petroleum and Coal Products, n.e.c.
Producer Price Index
Base 1982 = 100

For 1984-1997. Columns headed % show percentile change in the index from the previous period for which an index is available.

Year	Jan Index	%	Feb Index	%	Mar Index	%	Apr Index	%	May Index	%	Jun Index	%	Jul Index	%	Aug Index	%	Sep Index	%	Oct Index	%	Nov Index	%	Dec Index	%
1984	-	-	-	-	-	-	-	-	-	-	-	-	-	-	-	-	-	-	-	-	-	-	100.0	-
1985	100.0	0.0	99.9	-0.1	99.9	0.0	99.9	0.0	99.9	0.0	99.9	0.0	105.2	5.3	103.6	-1.5	103.1	-0.5	95.0	-7.9	100.2	5.5	99.2	-1.0
1986	95.2	-4.0	95.2	0.0	92.9	-2.4	90.8	-2.3	81.7	-10.0	78.7	-3.7	70.5	-10.4	70.8	0.4	63.4	-10.5	63.5	0.2	65.3	2.8	57.3	-12.3
1987	61.8	7.9	60.4	-2.3	63.7	5.5	63.6	-0.2	60.4	-5.0	62.4	3.3	62.8	0.6	63.7	1.4	64.6	1.4	65.6	1.5	66.0	0.6	69.9	5.9
1988	62.7	-10.3	70.8	12.9	62.6	-11.6	68.0	8.6	69.6	2.4	67.4	-3.2	69.4	3.0	69.9	0.7	68.1	-2.6	61.8	-9.3	63.7	3.1	62.7	-1.6
1989	59.1	-5.7	60.3	2.0	65.6	8.8	65.8	0.3	64.4	-2.1	63.5	-1.4	68.1	7.2	69.2	1.6	67.5	-2.5	67.1	-0.6	69.4	3.4	60.0	-13.5
1990	61.9	3.2	63.5	2.6	63.3	-0.3	64.2	1.4	67.6	5.3	68.3	1.0	66.6	-2.5	68.0	2.1	70.1	3.1	70.2	0.1	69.8	-0.6	74.2	6.3
1991	71.7	-3.4	76.3	6.4	67.0	-12.2	68.4	2.1	64.9	-5.1	68.4	5.4	61.4	-10.2	61.9	0.8	61.1	-1.3	61.9	1.3	55.9	-9.7	44.5	-20.4
1992	58.1	30.6	58.4	0.5	59.6	2.1	60.7	1.8	58.2	-4.1	54.7	-6.0	57.7	5.5	58.5	1.4	54.7	-6.5	61.1	11.7	63.1	3.3	60.5	-4.1
1993	67.0	10.7	66.8	-0.3	66.0	-1.2	69.3	5.0	68.0	-1.9	63.1	-7.2	69.0	9.4	65.8	-4.6	66.4	0.9	64.1	-3.5	67.3	5.0	64.0	-4.9
1994	65.0	1.6	65.2	0.3	61.6	-5.5	62.2	1.0	69.1	11.1	67.0	-3.0	68.4	2.1	65.3	-4.5	64.0	-2.0	66.5	3.9	68.1	2.4	66.9	-1.8
1995	67.5	0.9	67.9	0.6	68.1	0.3	76.7	12.6	71.8	-6.4	69.1	-3.8	69.5	0.6	70.9	2.0	73.9	4.2	72.1	-2.4	66.9	-7.2	63.5	-5.1
1996	67.4	6.1	68.9	2.2	66.9	-2.9	68.1	1.8	68.3	0.3	73.1	7.0	75.2	2.9	74.2	-1.3	73.0	-1.6	70.7	-3.2	70.6	-0.1	66.5	-5.8
1997	75.3	13.2	72.2	-4.1	71.4	-1.1	70.1	-1.8	73.1	4.3	73.1	0.0	70.5	-3.6	72.5	2.8	73.6	1.5	75.8	3.0	72.5	-4.4	69.6	-4.0

Source: U.S. Department of Labor, Bureau of Labor Statistics, Division of Industry Prices and Price Indexes. n.e.c. stands for not elsewhere classified. - indicates no data collected for period or unavailable.

CHEMICALS AND ALLIED PRODUCTS
Producer Price Index
Base 1982 = 100

For 1933-1997. Columns headed % show percentile change in the index from the previous period for which an index is available.

Year	Jan Index	%	Feb Index	%	Mar Index	%	Apr Index	%	May Index	%	Jun Index	%	Jul Index	%	Aug Index	%	Sep Index	%	Oct Index	%	Nov Index	%	Dec Index	%
1933	15.7	-	15.6	-0.6	15.7	0.6	15.7	0.0	16.0	1.9	16.2	1.3	16.6	2.5	16.7	0.6	16.6	-0.6	16.5	-0.6	16.5	0.0	16.6	0.6
1934	16.8	1.2	17.0	1.2	17.0	0.0	17.0	0.0	16.9	-0.6	16.9	0.0	16.9	0.0	16.9	0.0	17.0	0.6	17.1	0.6	17.0	-0.6	17.1	0.6
1935	17.2	0.6	17.3	0.6	17.6	1.7	17.6	0.0	17.7	0.6	17.8	0.6	17.6	-1.1	17.6	0.0	17.9	1.7	18.0	0.6	17.9	-0.6	17.9	0.0
1936	17.8	-0.6	17.7	-0.6	17.6	-0.6	17.6	0.0	17.4	-1.1	17.4	0.0	17.6	1.1	17.8	1.1	17.9	0.6	18.0	0.6	18.1	0.6	18.6	2.8
1937	18.9	1.6	19.0	0.5	19.0	0.0	19.0	0.0	18.7	-1.6	18.6	-0.5	18.7	0.5	18.6	-0.5	18.5	-0.5	18.4	-0.5	18.1	-1.6	17.9	-1.1
1938	18.1	1.1	18.1	0.0	18.0	-0.6	17.9	-0.6	17.7	-1.1	17.5	-1.1	17.5	0.0	17.6	0.6	17.6	0.0	17.6	0.0	17.6	0.0	17.5	-0.6
1939	17.5	0.0	17.4	-0.6	17.5	0.6	17.5	0.0	17.5	0.0	17.5	0.0	17.4	-0.6	17.3	-0.6	17.9	3.5	18.1	1.1	18.0	-0.6	18.1	0.6
1940	18.2	0.6	18.1	-0.5	18.1	0.0	18.3	1.1	17.9	-2.2	17.8	-0.6	17.8	0.0	17.7	-0.6	17.7	0.0	17.8	0.6	17.9	0.6	17.9	0.0
1941	18.1	1.1	18.1	0.0	18.4	1.7	18.8	2.2	19.2	2.1	19.4	1.0	19.7	1.5	19.9	1.0	20.3	2.0	20.6	1.5	20.6	0.0	20.8	1.0
1942	18.6	-10.6	21.9	17.7	22.1	0.9	22.1	0.0	22.1	0.0	22.0	-0.5	22.0	0.0	21.8	-0.9	21.9	0.5	21.9	0.0	21.8	-0.5	21.7	-0.5
1943	21.8	0.5	21.9	0.5	21.9	0.0	22.0	0.5	21.9	-0.5	21.9	0.0	21.9	0.0	22.0	0.5	22.0	0.0	22.0	0.0	22.0	0.0	22.0	0.0
1944	22.1	0.5	22.1	0.0	22.1	0.0	22.2	0.5	22.2	0.0	22.2	0.0	22.2	0.0	22.2	0.0	22.1	-0.5	22.2	0.5	22.2	0.0	22.2	0.0
1945	22.2	0.0	22.2	0.0	22.2	0.0	22.2	0.0	22.2	0.0	22.2	0.0	22.2	0.0	22.3	0.5	22.4	0.4	22.4	0.0	22.5	0.4	22.5	0.0
1946	22.5	0.0	22.5	0.0	22.5	0.0	22.5	0.0	22.6	0.4	22.6	0.0	23.5	4.0	23.3	-0.9	23.4	0.4	23.8	1.7	29.5	23.9	31.0	5.1
1947	32.1	3.5	32.4	0.9	32.9	1.5	32.8	-0.3	31.7	-3.4	31.2	-1.6	30.8	-1.3	30.5	-1.0	31.1	2.0	32.3	3.9	33.3	3.1	33.4	0.3
1948	33.8	1.2	33.3	-1.5	33.1	-0.6	33.0	-0.3	32.6	-1.2	32.8	0.6	32.9	0.3	32.7	-0.6	32.7	0.0	32.6	-0.3	32.4	-0.6	32.0	-1.2
1949	31.5	-1.6	31.1	-1.3	30.7	-1.3	30.1	-2.0	30.0	-0.3	29.9	-0.3	29.6	-1.0	29.6	0.0	29.5	-0.3	29.3	-0.7	29.3	0.0	29.2	-0.3
1950	29.2	0.0	29.1	-0.3	29.1	0.0	29.1	0.0	29.1	0.0	29.1	0.0	29.5	1.4	30.3	2.7	31.5	4.0	32.3	2.5	32.7	1.2	34.0	4.0
1951	35.2	3.5	35.6	1.1	35.4	-0.6	35.2	-0.6	35.2	0.0	34.8	-1.1	34.4	-1.1	34.3	-0.3	34.3	0.0	34.4	0.3	34.3	-0.3	34.3	0.0
1952	33.7	-1.7	33.5	-0.6	33.3	-0.6	33.1	-0.6	32.9	-0.6	32.9	0.0	32.9	0.0	32.9	0.0	32.9	0.0	32.8	-0.3	32.7	-0.3	32.6	-0.3
1953	32.7	0.3	32.7	0.0	32.9	0.6	33.4	1.5	33.4	0.0	33.4	0.0	33.6	0.6	33.6	0.0	33.7	0.3	33.7	0.0	33.9	0.6	33.9	0.0
1954	33.9	0.0	34.0	0.3	34.0	0.0	33.9	-0.3	33.9	0.0	33.8	-0.3	33.7	-0.3	33.8	0.3	33.8	0.0	33.8	0.0	33.8	0.0	33.8	0.0
1955	33.9	0.3	33.9	0.0	33.8	-0.3	33.9	0.3	33.8	-0.3	33.8	0.0	33.5	-0.9	33.5	0.0	33.5	0.0	33.7	0.6	33.7	0.0	33.7	0.0
1956	33.6	-0.3	33.6	0.0	33.7	0.3	33.8	0.3	33.8	0.0	33.9	0.3	33.9	0.0	33.9	0.0	33.9	0.0	34.0	0.3	34.2	0.6	34.2	0.0
1957	34.3	0.3	34.4	0.3	34.4	0.0	34.5	0.3	34.5	0.0	34.6	0.3	34.6	0.0	34.7	0.3	34.8	0.3	34.9	0.3	34.9	0.0	35.0	0.3
1958	35.0	0.0	35.0	0.0	35.0	0.0	35.1	0.3	35.0	-0.3	35.0	0.0	34.9	-0.3	34.8	-0.3	34.7	-0.3	34.8	0.3	34.8	0.0	34.8	0.0
1959	34.8	0.0	34.7	-0.3	34.7	0.0	34.8	0.3	34.8	0.0	34.8	0.0	34.7	-0.3	34.7	0.0	34.7	0.0	34.8	0.3	34.8	0.0	34.8	0.0
1960	34.7	-0.3	34.8	0.3	34.8	0.0	34.8	0.0	34.8	0.0	34.8	0.0	34.9	0.3	34.9	0.0	34.9	0.0	34.8	-0.3	34.8	0.0	34.8	0.0
1961	34.7	-0.3	34.8	0.3	34.8	0.0	34.8	0.0	34.7	-0.3	34.6	-0.3	34.4	-0.6	34.3	-0.3	34.2	-0.3	34.1	-0.3	34.1	0.0	34.1	0.0
1962	34.2	0.3	34.1	-0.3	34.1	0.0	34.0	-0.3	34.0	0.0	33.9	-0.3	33.8	-0.3	33.7	-0.3	33.7	0.0	33.8	0.3	33.7	-0.3	33.7	0.0
1963	33.7	0.0	33.6	-0.3	33.7	0.3	33.5	-0.6	33.5	0.0	33.5	0.0	33.4	-0.3	33.4	0.0	33.4	0.0	33.5	0.3	33.5	0.0	33.5	0.0
1964	33.5	0.0	33.5	0.0	33.6	0.3	33.6	0.0	33.6	0.0	33.6	0.0	33.6	0.0	33.6	0.0	33.6	0.0	33.7	0.3	33.8	0.3	33.8	0.0
1965	33.8	0.0	33.9	0.3	33.9	0.0	33.9	0.0	33.9	0.0	33.9	0.0	33.9	0.0	33.8	-0.3	33.8	0.0	33.9	0.3	33.9	0.0	33.9	0.0
1966	33.9	0.0	33.9	0.0	33.9	0.0	33.9	0.0	34.0	0.3	33.9	-0.3	34.0	0.3	34.0	0.0	34.1	0.3	34.0	-0.3	34.1	0.3	34.1	0.0
1967	34.2	0.3	34.2	0.0	34.2	0.0	34.3	0.3	34.3	0.0	34.2	-0.3	34.2	0.0	34.1	-0.3	34.0	-0.3	34.1	0.3	34.1	0.0	34.2	0.3
1968	34.1	-0.3	34.1	0.0	34.3	0.6	34.3	0.0	34.3	0.0	34.2	-0.3	34.1	-0.3	34.1	0.0	34.0	-0.3	34.0	0.0	34.0	0.0	34.0	0.0
1969	33.9	-0.3	34.0	0.3	34.1	0.3	34.0	-0.3	34.1	0.3	34.2	0.3	34.1	-0.3	34.3	0.6	34.4	0.3	34.3	-0.3	34.4	0.3	34.3	-0.3
1970	34.5	0.6	34.6	0.3	34.7	0.3	34.9	0.6	35.0	0.3	35.0	0.0	35.1	0.3	35.1	0.0	35.1	0.0	35.3	0.6	35.3	0.0	35.2	-0.3
1971	35.5	0.9	35.7	0.6	35.7	0.0	35.8	0.3	35.7	-0.3	35.7	0.0	35.7	0.0	35.6	-0.3	35.6	0.0	35.6	0.0	35.5	-0.3	35.4	-0.3
1972	35.4	0.0	35.4	0.0	35.4	0.0	35.6	0.6	35.7	0.3	35.7	0.0	35.6	-0.3	35.7	0.3	35.7	0.0	35.7	0.0	35.8	0.3	35.9	0.3
1973	36.0	0.3	36.1	0.3	36.5	1.1	36.8	0.8	37.4	1.6	37.8	1.1	37.9	0.3	38.0	0.3	38.1	0.3	38.6	1.3	38.8	0.5	39.6	2.1
1974	40.4	2.0	41.1	1.7	43.5	5.8	45.3	4.1	46.9	3.5	48.9	4.3	50.8	3.9	54.2	6.7	55.3	2.0	57.7	4.3	59.2	2.6	59.5	0.5
1975	60.2	1.2	60.9	1.2	62.2	2.1	62.4	0.3	62.3	-0.2	62.0	-0.5	62.1	0.2	62.3	0.3	62.3	0.0	62.4	0.2	62.6	0.3	62.7	0.2
1976	63.1	0.6	63.3	0.3	63.6	0.5	64.0	0.6	64.0	0.0	64.1	0.2	64.0	-0.2	64.3	0.5	64.5	0.3	64.5	0.0	64.5	0.0	64.4	-0.2
1977	64.6	0.3	65.0	0.6	65.4	0.6	66.0	0.9	66.4	0.6	66.4	0.0	66.2	-0.3	66.2	0.0	66.1	-0.2	66.3	0.3	66.4	0.2	66.4	0.0

[Continued]

CHEMICALS AND ALLIED PRODUCTS
Producer Price Index
Base 1982 = 100
[Continued]

For 1933-1997. Columns headed % show percentile change in the index from the previous period for which an index is available.

Year	Jan Index	%	Feb Index	%	Mar Index	%	Apr Index	%	May Index	%	Jun Index	%	Jul Index	%	Aug Index	%	Sep Index	%	Oct Index	%	Nov Index	%	Dec Index	%
1978	66.4	0.0	66.8	0.6	67.1	0.4	67.3	0.3	68.0	1.0	68.1	0.1	68.4	0.4	68.3	-0.1	68.5	0.3	69.0	0.7	69.2	0.3	69.2	0.0
1979	70.1	1.3	70.9	1.1	71.8	1.3	73.6	2.5	74.6	1.4	75.0	0.5	77.0	2.7	78.2	1.6	79.0	1.0	80.1	1.4	80.7	0.7	81.5	1.0
1980	84.2	3.3	85.1	1.1	86.5	1.6	88.9	2.8	89.8	1.0	89.9	0.1	90.1	0.2	90.5	0.4	90.1	-0.4	90.6	0.6	91.2	0.7	91.7	0.5
1981	93.9	2.4	95.0	1.2	95.9	0.9	97.8	2.0	98.7	0.9	99.4	0.7	99.7	0.3	100.3	0.6	100.4	0.1	100.1	-0.3	99.9	-0.2	99.8	-0.1
1982	100.2	0.4	100.5	0.3	100.8	0.3	100.7	-0.1	100.9	0.2	100.3	-0.6	99.7	-0.6	99.8	0.1	99.5	-0.3	99.2	-0.3	99.4	0.2	99.1	-0.3
1983	99.0	-0.1	99.4	0.4	99.2	-0.2	99.7	0.5	99.6	-0.1	99.5	-0.1	100.5	1.0	100.7	0.2	101.2	0.5	101.1	-0.1	101.4	0.3	101.9	0.5
1984	102.0	0.1	101.5	-0.5	102.7	1.2	103.3	0.6	103.6	0.3	103.4	-0.2	103.5	0.1	103.0	-0.5	103.0	0.0	103.1	0.1	103.2	0.1	102.9	-0.3
1985	103.2	0.3	103.4	0.2	103.5	0.1	103.8	0.3	103.7	-0.1	103.9	0.2	104.2	0.3	104.2	0.0	104.2	0.0	103.7	-0.5	103.5	-0.2	103.3	-0.2
1986	104.4	1.1	103.9	-0.5	104.0	0.1	102.7	-1.3	102.1	-0.6	102.1	0.0	102.1	0.0	101.6	-0.5	101.8	0.2	102.0	0.2	102.2	0.2	102.0	-0.2
1987	103.0	1.0	103.6	0.6	104.3	0.7	105.2	0.9	105.9	0.7	107.1	1.1	107.0	-0.1	107.1	0.1	107.5	0.4	108.2	0.7	108.8	0.6	109.1	0.3
1988	110.6	1.4	111.6	0.9	112.7	1.0	113.8	1.0	114.6	0.7	115.3	0.6	117.4	1.8	118.2	0.7	119.1	0.8	119.9	0.7	121.1	1.0	121.7	0.5
1989	123.7	1.6	124.3	0.5	124.5	0.2	124.9	0.3	124.9	0.0	124.1	-0.6	123.1	-0.8	121.9	-1.0	121.4	-0.4	121.4	0.0	121.0	-0.3	121.0	0.0
1990	121.2	0.2	121.7	0.4	121.8	0.1	121.9	0.1	122.3	0.3	122.2	-0.1	122.4	0.2	122.5	0.1	124.5	1.6	126.5	1.6	128.2	1.3	127.9	-0.2
1991	128.3	0.3	128.1	-0.2	126.0	-1.6	126.0	0.0	125.3	-0.6	125.0	-0.2	124.4	-0.5	124.5	0.1	124.5	0.0	124.9	0.3	124.9	0.0	125.0	0.1
1992	124.6	-0.3	124.5	-0.1	124.4	-0.1	124.8	0.3	125.2	0.3	126.0	0.6	126.4	0.3	126.7	0.2	127.0	0.2	127.1	0.1	127.5	0.3	127.0	-0.4
1993	127.6	0.5	128.1	0.4	127.8	-0.2	128.6	0.6	128.2	-0.3	128.5	0.2	128.2	-0.2	128.3	0.1	128.1	-0.2	128.2	0.1	128.5	0.2	127.9	-0.5
1994	128.3	0.3	128.2	-0.1	128.3	0.1	129.3	0.8	130.2	0.7	130.7	0.4	131.2	0.4	132.6	1.1	134.8	1.7	136.4	1.2	137.2	0.6	138.4	0.9
1995	140.4	1.4	141.8	1.0	142.5	0.5	144.1	1.1	144.4	0.2	143.8	-0.4	143.6	-0.1	142.9	-0.5	142.6	-0.2	141.8	-0.6	141.0	-0.6	140.7	-0.2
1996	140.8	0.1	140.9	0.1	141.1	0.1	141.4	0.2	142.2	0.6	142.2	0.0	142.0	-0.1	142.5	0.4	143.3	0.6	143.0	-0.2	142.8	-0.1	143.2	0.3
1997	143.6	0.3	143.8	0.1	143.7	-0.1	143.5	-0.1	143.5	0.0	143.4	-0.1	143.7	0.2	143.7	0.0	143.5	-0.1	144.0	0.3	143.9	-0.1	143.5	-0.3

Source: U.S. Department of Labor, Bureau of Labor Statistics, Division of Industry Prices and Price Indexes. n.e.c. stands for not elsewhere classified. - indicates no data collected for period or unavailable.

Industrial Chemicals
Producer Price Index
Base 1982 = 100

For 1926-1997. Columns headed % show percentile change in the index from the previous period for which an index is available.

Year	Jan Index	%	Feb Index	%	Mar Index	%	Apr Index	%	May Index	%	Jun Index	%	Jul Index	%	Aug Index	%	Sep Index	%	Oct Index	%	Nov Index	%	Dec Index	%
1926	-	-	-	-	-	-	-	-	-	-	-	-	-	-	-	-	-	-	-	-	-	-	-	-
1927	-	-	-	-	-	-	-	-	-	-	-	-	-	-	-	-	-	-	-	-	-	-	-	-
1928	-	-	-	-	-	-	-	-	-	-	-	-	-	-	-	-	-	-	-	-	-	-	-	-
1929	-	-	-	-	-	-	-	-	-	-	-	-	-	-	-	-	-	-	-	-	-	-	-	-
1930	-	-	-	-	-	-	-	-	-	-	-	-	-	-	-	-	-	-	-	-	-	-	-	-
1931	-	-	-	-	-	-	-	-	-	-	-	-	-	-	-	-	-	-	-	-	-	-	-	-
1932	-	-	-	-	-	-	-	-	-	-	-	-	-	-	-	-	-	-	-	-	-	-	-	-
1933	17.4	-	17.4	0.0	17.2	-1.1	17.2	0.0	17.3	0.6	17.3	0.0	17.2	-0.6	17.2	0.0	17.2	0.0	17.2	0.0	17.4	1.2	17.4	0.0
1934	17.4	0.0	17.4	0.0	17.4	0.0	17.3	-0.6	17.3	0.0	17.3	0.0	17.1	-1.2	17.2	0.6	17.2	0.0	17.2	0.0	17.2	0.0	17.3	0.6
1935	17.3	0.0	17.4	0.6	17.4	0.0	17.4	0.0	17.5	0.6	17.5	0.0	17.5	0.0	17.9	2.3	17.9	0.0	17.9	0.0	17.9	0.0	17.9	0.0
1936	17.8	-0.6	17.8	0.0	17.6	-1.1	17.6	0.0	17.5	-0.6	17.5	0.0	17.4	-0.6	17.3	-0.6	17.3	0.0	17.4	0.6	17.3	-0.6	17.4	0.6
1937	17.4	0.0	17.6	1.1	17.6	0.0	17.6	0.0	17.6	0.0	17.6	0.0	17.8	1.1	17.5	-1.7	17.5	0.0	17.4	-0.6	17.4	0.0	17.4	0.0
1938	17.4	0.0	17.4	0.0	17.3	-0.6	17.3	0.0	17.2	-0.6	17.2	0.0	17.2	0.0	17.1	-0.6	17.1	0.0	17.1	0.0	17.0	-0.6	17.0	0.0
1939	17.0	0.0	16.9	-0.6	16.8	-0.6	16.8	0.0	16.8	0.0	16.7	-0.6	16.7	0.0	16.7	0.0	16.8	0.6	17.0	1.2	17.0	0.0	17.0	0.0
1940	17.0	0.0	17.0	0.0	17.0	0.0	16.9	-0.6	17.0	0.6	17.0	0.0	16.9	-0.6	16.8	-0.6	16.8	0.0	16.9	0.6	17.0	0.6	17.0	0.0
1941	17.0	0.0	17.1	0.6	17.1	0.0	17.2	0.6	17.3	0.6	17.3	0.0	17.4	0.6	17.4	0.0	17.6	1.1	17.6	0.0	17.6	0.0	17.6	0.0
1942	18.9	7.4	19.2	1.6	19.2	0.0	19.2	0.0	19.2	0.0	19.2	0.0	19.2	0.0	19.2	0.0	19.2	0.0	19.2	0.0	19.2	0.0	19.1	-0.5
1943	19.3	1.0	19.3	0.0	19.2	-0.5	19.2	0.0	19.2	0.0	19.2	0.0	19.2	0.0	19.2	0.0	19.2	0.0	19.2	0.0	19.2	0.0	19.2	0.0
1944	19.2	0.0	19.2	0.0	19.2	0.0	19.2	0.0	19.2	0.0	19.2	0.0	19.2	0.0	19.2	0.0	19.1	-0.5	19.1	0.0	19.0	-0.5	19.0	0.0
1945	19.0	0.0	19.0	0.0	19.0	0.0	19.0	0.0	19.0	0.0	19.1	0.5	19.1	0.0	19.1	0.0	19.1	0.0	19.2	0.5	19.3	0.5	19.3	0.0
1946	19.3	0.0	19.3	0.0	19.3	0.0	19.3	0.0	19.5	1.0	19.5	0.0	19.6	0.5	19.6	0.0	19.6	0.0	19.7	0.5	21.2	7.6	22.2	4.7
1947	22.5	1.4	22.7	0.9	23.0	1.3	23.6	2.6	23.3	-1.3	23.4	0.4	23.2	-0.9	22.8	-1.7	23.0	0.9	23.6	2.6	24.1	2.1	24.2	0.4
1948	24.5	1.2	24.7	0.8	24.8	0.4	24.9	0.4	24.8	-0.4	24.8	0.0	25.2	1.6	24.9	-1.2	24.8	-0.4	24.9	0.4	24.4	-2.0	24.1	-1.2
1949	23.9	-0.8	23.3	-2.5	23.0	-1.3	22.6	-1.7	22.5	-0.4	22.4	-0.4	22.5	0.4	22.5	0.0	22.4	-0.4	22.3	-0.4	22.2	-0.4	22.2	0.0
1950	22.3	0.5	22.3	0.0	22.2	-0.4	22.4	0.9	22.4	0.0	22.7	1.3	23.1	1.8	23.7	2.6	24.8	4.6	26.1	5.2	26.3	0.8	27.5	4.6
1951	28.3	2.9	28.4	0.4	28.4	0.0	28.5	0.4	28.5	0.0	28.5	0.0	28.4	-0.4	28.4	0.0	28.4	0.0	28.5	0.4	28.5	0.0	28.4	-0.4
1952	27.8	-2.1	27.7	-0.4	27.5	-0.7	27.5	0.0	27.1	-1.5	27.1	0.0	27.0	-0.4	27.0	0.0	26.9	-0.4	26.8	-0.4	26.5	-1.1	26.4	-0.4
1953	26.5	0.4	26.6	0.4	26.8	0.8	27.5	2.6	27.8	1.1	28.1	1.1	28.3	0.7	28.3	0.0	28.3	0.0	28.2	-0.4	28.1	-0.4	27.9	-0.7
1954	27.9	0.0	27.9	0.0	27.8	-0.4	27.7	-0.4	27.6	-0.4	27.5	-0.4	27.6	0.4	27.7	0.4	27.7	0.0	27.7	0.0	27.7	0.0	27.7	0.0
1955	27.6	-0.4	27.7	0.4	27.7	0.0	27.8	0.4	27.7	-0.4	27.7	0.0	27.9	0.7	27.8	-0.4	27.9	0.4	28.0	0.4	28.1	0.4	28.1	0.0
1956	28.3	0.7	28.3	0.0	28.3	0.0	28.5	0.7	28.4	-0.4	28.5	0.4	28.8	1.1	28.8	0.0	28.7	-0.3	28.9	0.7	28.8	-0.3	28.8	0.0
1957	29.1	1.0	29.0	-0.3	29.0	0.0	29.1	0.3	29.1	0.0	29.2	0.3	29.1	-0.3	29.1	0.0	29.1	0.0	29.1	0.0	29.1	0.0	29.2	0.3
1958	29.2	0.0	29.1	-0.3	29.2	0.3	29.3	0.3	29.2	-0.3	29.1	-0.3	29.0	-0.3	28.9	-0.3	28.9	0.0	29.1	0.7	29.1	0.0	29.2	0.3
1959	29.2	0.0	29.2	0.0	29.1	-0.3	29.2	0.3	29.2	0.0	29.2	0.0	29.2	0.0	29.2	0.0	29.2	0.0	29.2	0.0	29.2	0.0	29.2	0.0
1960	29.2	0.0	29.3	0.3	29.3	0.0	29.3	0.0	29.4	0.3	29.4	0.0	29.4	0.0	29.4	0.0	29.3	-0.3	29.1	-0.7	29.1	0.0	29.1	0.0
1961	29.0	-0.3	29.0	0.0	29.0	0.0	29.0	0.0	28.9	-0.3	28.8	-0.3	28.5	-1.0	28.4	-0.4	28.4	0.0	28.3	-0.4	28.3	0.0	28.3	0.0
1962	28.3	0.0	28.2	-0.4	28.1	-0.4	28.1	0.0	28.1	0.0	28.0	-0.4	28.0	0.0	27.9	-0.4	27.9	0.0	28.0	0.4	27.9	-0.4	27.9	0.0
1963	28.0	0.4	27.7	-1.1	27.8	0.4	27.7	-0.4	27.7	0.0	27.7	0.0	27.5	-0.4	27.5	0.0	27.3	-0.7	27.3	0.0	27.5	0.7	27.4	-0.4	27.5	0.4
1964	27.5	0.0	27.4	-0.4	27.5	0.4	27.5	0.0	27.5	0.0	27.6	0.0	27.7	0.4	27.7	0.0	27.7	0.0	27.8	0.4	27.8	0.0	27.8	0.0
1965	27.5	0.4	27.6	0.4	27.5	-0.4	27.6	0.4	27.6	0.0	27.6	0.0	27.9	0.4	27.9	0.0	27.9	0.0	27.9	0.0	28.0	0.4	28.1	0.4
1966	27.7	-0.4	27.7	0.0	27.7	0.0	27.9	0.7	28.0	0.4	27.9	-0.4	28.3	0.0	28.3	0.0	28.3	0.0	28.6	1.1	28.6	0.0	28.6	0.0
1967	28.1	0.0	28.2	0.4	28.3	0.4	28.4	0.4	28.4	0.0	28.3	-0.4	28.3	0.0	28.3	0.0	28.3	0.0	28.6	1.1	28.6	0.0	28.6	0.0
1968	28.7	0.3	28.7	0.0	28.7	0.0	28.8	0.3	28.8	0.0	28.7	-0.3	28.6	-0.3	28.6	0.0	28.5	-0.3	28.5	0.0	28.5	0.0	28.5	0.0
1969	28.6	0.4	28.6	0.0	28.5	-0.3	28.2	-1.1	28.2	0.0	28.3	0.4	28.4	0.4	28.6	0.7	28.6	0.0	28.4	-0.7	28.5	0.4	28.5	0.0
1970	28.5	0.0	28.4	-0.4	28.3	-0.4	28.5	0.7	28.6	0.4	28.6	0.0	28.8	0.7	28.7	-0.3	28.7	0.0	28.8	0.3	28.8	0.0	28.7	-0.3

[Continued]

Industrial Chemicals
Producer Price Index
Base 1982 = 100
[Continued]

For 1926-1997. Columns headed % show percentile change in the index from the previous period for which an index is available.

Year	Jan Index	%	Feb Index	%	Mar Index	%	Apr Index	%	May Index	%	Jun Index	%	Jul Index	%	Aug Index	%	Sep Index	%	Oct Index	%	Nov Index	%	Dec Index	%
1971	28.9	0.7	28.9	0.0	29.0	0.3	28.9	-0.3	28.9	0.0	29.0	0.3	29.1	0.3	29.0	-0.3	29.1	0.3	29.1	0.0	28.8	-1.0	28.7	-0.3
1972	28.8	0.3	28.8	0.0	28.6	-0.7	28.8	0.7	28.8	0.0	28.8	0.0	28.8	0.0	28.7	-0.3	28.7	0.0	28.6	-0.3	28.6	0.0	28.6	0.0
1973	28.7	0.3	28.9	0.7	28.9	0.0	29.1	0.7	29.1	0.0	29.2	0.3	29.3	0.3	29.4	0.3	29.6	0.7	29.9	1.0	29.9	0.0	30.0	0.3
1974	30.7	2.3	31.3	2.0	34.6	10.5	37.1	7.2	39.2	5.7	41.7	6.4	44.1	5.8	47.6	7.9	49.5	4.0	51.6	4.2	53.9	4.5	55.2	2.4
1975	55.8	1.1	57.3	2.7	58.9	2.8	58.8	-0.2	59.2	0.7	58.7	-0.8	58.5	-0.3	58.8	0.5	59.1	0.5	59.3	0.3	59.7	0.7	59.9	0.3
1976	60.6	1.2	61.4	1.3	61.8	0.7	61.9	0.2	62.0	0.2	62.0	0.0	62.2	0.3	62.7	0.8	62.9	0.3	63.0	0.2	63.1	0.2	62.8	-0.5
1977	62.9	0.2	63.2	0.5	63.1	-0.2	63.4	0.5	63.6	0.3	63.6	0.0	63.7	0.2	63.7	0.0	63.6	-0.2	63.8	0.3	63.8	0.0	63.9	0.2
1978	63.6	-0.5	63.6	0.0	63.6	0.0	63.6	0.0	63.5	-0.2	63.5	0.0	63.8	0.5	64.2	0.6	64.2	0.0	64.7	0.8	64.5	-0.3	65.0	0.8
1979	66.4	2.2	67.3	1.4	68.0	1.0	70.4	3.5	72.5	3.0	73.5	1.4	76.7	4.4	78.6	2.5	79.4	1.0	81.0	2.0	81.8	1.0	82.9	1.3
1980	85.9	3.6	87.3	1.6	88.9	1.8	91.4	2.8	93.2	2.0	93.5	0.3	93.2	-0.3	93.6	0.4	92.9	-0.7	93.6	0.8	94.4	0.9	94.9	0.5
1981	97.7	3.0	99.9	2.3	100.5	0.6	102.8	2.3	104.5	1.7	104.9	0.4	105.1	0.2	105.4	0.3	105.5	0.1	104.3	-1.1	103.1	-1.2	102.9	-0.2
1982	102.9	0.0	102.7	-0.2	102.5	-0.2	101.5	-1.0	101.3	-0.2	99.6	-1.7	99.0	-0.6	99.0	0.0	98.3	-0.7	98.1	-0.2	97.9	-0.2	97.1	-0.8
1983	96.2	-0.9	96.5	0.3	96.1	-0.4	96.1	0.0	96.1	0.0	96.0	-0.1	98.4	2.5	98.6	0.2	98.0	-0.6	97.8	-0.2	98.2	0.4	99.1	0.9
1984	98.5	-0.6	95.8	-2.7	97.8	2.1	98.0	0.2	97.9	-0.1	98.0	0.1	98.0	0.0	96.7	-1.3	95.8	-0.9	95.3	-0.5	94.9	-0.4	95.0	0.1
1985	95.5	0.5	95.5	0.0	95.5	0.0	95.3	-0.2	95.5	0.2	96.3	0.8	96.4	0.1	97.5	1.1	97.1	-0.4	95.9	-1.2	95.4	-0.5	95.6	0.2
1986	96.9	1.4	95.0	-2.0	95.4	0.4	91.8	-3.8	90.2	-1.7	89.8	-0.4	89.7	-0.1	89.5	-0.2	89.9	0.4	90.2	0.3	89.8	-0.4	90.2	0.4
1987	92.0	2.0	92.8	0.9	93.7	1.0	94.1	0.4	95.2	1.2	97.8	2.7	96.3	-1.5	95.6	-0.7	95.5	-0.1	96.8	1.4	97.6	0.8	98.2	0.6
1988	99.4	1.2	100.3	0.9	102.1	1.8	103.3	1.2	104.3	1.0	105.8	1.4	108.6	2.6	109.4	0.7	110.0	0.5	111.4	1.3	112.8	1.3	114.2	1.2
1989	117.2	2.6	117.6	0.3	116.7	-0.8	117.5	0.7	117.8	0.3	115.6	-1.9	114.1	-1.3	113.4	-0.6	112.4	-0.9	112.5	0.1	111.7	-0.7	111.6	-0.1
1990	111.4	-0.2	111.3	-0.1	110.7	-0.5	110.4	-0.3	110.8	0.4	111.1	0.3	111.1	0.0	110.7	-0.4	114.9	3.8	118.4	3.0	120.1	1.4	117.8	-1.9
1991	117.5	-0.3	116.7	-0.7	113.2	-3.0	112.9	-0.3	111.9	-0.9	111.7	-0.2	109.7	-1.8	109.1	-0.5	109.7	0.5	109.7	0.0	109.7	0.0	109.9	0.2
1992	108.4	-1.4	107.3	-1.0	107.2	-0.1	107.5	0.3	107.7	0.2	109.9	2.0	110.2	0.3	110.5	0.3	111.0	0.5	110.7	-0.3	111.4	0.6	109.4	-1.8
1993	109.8	0.4	110.7	0.8	110.0	-0.6	111.9	1.7	111.1	-0.7	111.3	0.2	110.6	-0.6	110.4	-0.2	110.3	-0.1	110.2	-0.1	110.5	0.3	108.7	-1.6
1994	108.6	-0.1	108.1	-0.5	108.4	0.3	109.6	1.1	110.8	1.1	111.7	0.8	112.9	1.1	115.2	2.0	119.8	4.0	121.2	1.2	122.0	0.7	123.0	0.8
1995	125.6	2.1	127.9	1.8	128.5	0.5	131.5	2.3	132.0	0.4	130.3	-1.3	130.4	0.1	129.6	-0.6	128.8	-0.6	127.3	-1.2	124.6	-2.1	124.4	-0.2
1996	124.7	0.2	125.1	0.3	125.1	0.0	126.9	1.4	127.7	0.6	127.6	-0.1	126.8	-0.6	127.2	0.3	127.9	0.6	126.9	-0.8	127.1	0.2	127.5	0.3
1997	127.9	0.3	127.7	-0.2	126.7	-0.8	126.2	-0.4	125.8	-0.3	125.2	-0.5	125.8	0.5	126.7	0.7	126.8	0.1	127.2	0.3	127.3	0.1	127.0	-0.2

Source: U.S. Department of Labor, Bureau of Labor Statistics, Division of Industry Prices and Price Indexes. n.e.c. stands for not elsewhere classified. - indicates no data collected for period or unavailable.

Paints and Allied Products
Producer Price Index
Base 1982 = 100

For 1971-1997. Columns headed % show percentile change in the index from the previous period for which an index is available.

Year	Jan Index	%	Feb Index	%	Mar Index	%	Apr Index	%	May Index	%	Jun Index	%	Jul Index	%	Aug Index	%	Sep Index	%	Oct Index	%	Nov Index	%	Dec Index	%
1971	39.5	-	39.5	0.0	39.6	0.3	39.8	0.5	39.8	0.0	39.3	-1.3	39.4	0.3	39.4	0.0	39.4	0.0	39.4	0.0	39.4	0.0	39.6	0.5
1972	39.8	0.5	40.0	0.5	40.2	0.5	40.3	0.2	40.4	0.2	40.4	0.0	40.5	0.2	40.6	0.2	40.6	0.0	40.5	-0.2	40.5	0.0	40.7	0.5
1973	41.0	0.7	41.1	0.2	41.2	0.2	41.5	0.7	41.8	0.7	42.1	0.7	42.3	0.5	42.4	0.2	42.5	0.2	43.7	2.8	44.3	1.4	45.1	1.8
1974	46.1	2.2	46.5	0.9	47.9	3.0	49.3	2.9	49.6	0.6	52.2	5.2	53.9	3.3	54.5	1.1	55.3	1.5	56.8	2.7	59.2	4.2	59.2	0.0
1975	59.6	0.7	59.5	-0.2	60.4	1.5	60.3	-0.2	60.8	0.8	60.2	-1.0	60.4	0.3	60.3	-0.2	61.2	1.5	61.1	-0.2	61.0	-0.2	61.0	0.0
1976	60.8	-0.3	61.1	0.5	60.9	-0.3	64.1	5.3	64.2	0.2	64.3	0.2	65.0	1.1	65.5	0.8	66.1	0.9	66.2	0.2	66.6	0.6	66.6	0.0
1977	66.6	0.0	66.9	0.5	67.9	1.5	68.7	1.2	69.1	0.6	69.0	-0.1	68.9	-0.1	68.9	0.0	68.8	-0.1	68.6	-0.3	69.0	0.6	69.2	0.3
1978	69.0	-0.3	69.5	0.7	70.1	0.9	70.7	0.9	71.2	0.7	71.4	0.3	71.6	0.3	71.8	0.3	72.2	0.6	72.6	0.6	73.4	1.1	74.0	0.8
1979	74.3	0.4	75.2	1.2	75.7	0.7	76.7	1.3	77.1	0.5	77.7	0.8	79.6	2.4	79.8	0.3	80.6	1.0	81.0	0.5	82.0	1.2	82.3	0.4
1980	85.1	3.4	85.7	0.7	87.4	2.0	88.7	1.5	90.4	1.9	90.6	0.2	90.9	0.3	91.1	0.2	91.3	0.2	91.4	0.1	91.8	0.4	92.1	0.3
1981	92.9	0.9	94.0	1.2	94.6	0.6	95.7	1.2	96.9	1.3	-	-	-	-	-	-	-	-	98.4	1.5	99.1	0.7	99.0	-0.1
1982	99.6	0.6	99.6	0.0	99.7	0.1	99.6	-0.1	100.7	1.1	100.4	-0.3	100.3	-0.1	100.0	-0.3	100.1	0.1	100.1	0.0	100.0	-0.1	99.9	-0.1
1983	99.8	-0.1	99.5	-0.3	99.3	-0.2	99.6	0.3	99.6	0.0	99.5	-0.1	99.8	0.3	100.5	0.7	101.7	1.2	101.7	0.0	101.7	0.0	101.7	0.0
1984	102.0	0.3	102.6	0.6	102.5	-0.1	104.2	1.7	105.4	1.2	105.7	0.3	106.1	0.4	106.5	0.4	106.4	-0.1	106.6	0.2	106.6	0.0	106.8	0.2
1985	106.8	0.0	106.2	-0.6	106.4	0.2	106.7	0.3	107.0	0.3	107.2	0.2	107.1	-0.1	106.9	-0.2	106.5	-0.4	106.5	0.0	106.3	-0.2	106.6	0.3
1986	106.9	0.3	106.8	-0.1	107.0	0.2	105.4	-1.5	105.3	-0.1	105.3	0.0	105.9	0.6	105.5	-0.4	105.5	0.0	104.9	-0.6	105.0	0.1	105.1	0.1
1987	105.5	0.4	105.4	-0.1	105.7	0.3	106.8	1.0	106.9	0.1	107.9	0.9	108.1	0.2	108.7	0.6	108.8	0.1	108.8	0.0	107.6	-1.1	108.4	0.7
1988	109.6	1.1	109.8	0.2	110.6	0.7	111.2	0.5	111.5	0.3	112.2	0.6	113.7	1.3	114.1	0.4	114.7	0.5	115.4	0.6	117.0	1.4	117.2	0.2
1989	119.7	2.1	121.4	1.4	121.7	0.2	123.0	1.1	123.1	0.1	124.0	0.7	124.4	0.3	122.4	-1.6	123.0	0.5	123.3	0.2	122.2	-0.9	122.4	0.2
1990	122.8	0.3	125.3	2.0	125.5	0.2	126.1	0.5	126.4	0.2	127.0	0.5	127.3	0.2	127.5	0.2	131.8	3.4	132.3	0.4	134.7	1.8	134.7	0.0
1991	135.8	0.8	136.3	0.4	130.6	-4.2	130.7	0.1	130.7	0.0	131.3	0.5	131.4	0.1	131.3	-0.1	130.1	-0.9	130.1	0.0	130.5	0.3	130.4	-0.1
1992	130.3	-0.1	130.5	0.2	130.6	0.1	130.9	0.2	131.1	0.2	131.1	0.0	131.5	0.3	131.4	-0.1	131.2	-0.2	131.3	0.1	131.3	0.0	131.3	0.0
1993	131.7	0.3	132.0	0.2	131.9	-0.1	132.5	0.5	132.3	-0.2	132.2	-0.1	132.3	0.1	132.2	-0.1	132.2	0.0	132.1	-0.1	132.4	0.2	132.4	0.0
1994	132.6	0.2	133.0	0.3	133.1	0.1	133.1	0.0	133.3	0.2	133.5	0.2	133.8	0.2	134.1	0.2	134.4	0.2	134.7	0.2	135.3	0.4	135.8	0.4
1995	137.5	1.3	138.5	0.7	138.8	0.2	140.4	1.2	141.3	0.6	141.1	-0.1	141.5	0.3	142.1	0.4	142.2	0.1	142.5	0.2	143.1	0.4	142.8	-0.2
1996	143.5	0.5	143.6	0.1	144.4	0.6	144.6	0.1	144.5	-0.1	144.5	0.0	144.3	-0.1	145.7	1.0	145.5	-0.1	145.5	0.0	145.9	0.3	145.9	0.0
1997	146.2	0.2	146.9	0.5	147.0	0.1	148.2	0.8	148.1	-0.1	148.3	0.1	148.4	0.1	148.6	0.1	148.4	-0.1	148.9	0.3	148.7	-0.1	148.7	0.0

Source: U.S. Department of Labor, Bureau of Labor Statistics, Division of Industry Prices and Price Indexes. n.e.c. stands for not elsewhere classified. - indicates no data collected for period or unavailable.

Drugs and Pharmaceuticals
Producer Price Index
Base 1982 = 100

For 1947-1997. Columns headed % show percentile change in the index from the previous period for which an index is available.

Year	Jan Index	%	Feb Index	%	Mar Index	%	Apr Index	%	May Index	%	Jun Index	%	Jul Index	%	Aug Index	%	Sep Index	%	Oct Index	%	Nov Index	%	Dec Index	%
1947	59.3	-	59.3	0.0	58.7	-1.0	56.7	-3.4	56.8	0.2	56.5	-0.5	56.3	-0.4	55.6	-1.2	55.4	-0.4	55.6	0.4	56.5	1.6	57.5	1.8
1948	56.3	-2.1	56.3	0.0	55.4	-1.6	55.2	-0.4	55.0	-0.4	55.0	0.0	54.8	-0.4	55.3	0.9	54.6	-1.3	52.8	-3.3	52.9	0.2	52.9	0.0
1949	51.6	-2.5	51.9	0.6	51.5	-0.8	50.9	-1.2	50.9	0.0	50.9	0.0	50.5	-0.8	50.1	-0.8	50.1	0.0	50.1	0.0	50.0	-0.2	49.9	-0.2
1950	49.7	-0.4	49.5	-0.4	49.4	-0.2	49.4	0.0	49.4	0.0	49.4	0.0	49.5	0.2	50.2	1.4	50.5	0.6	50.8	0.6	51.3	1.0	51.7	0.8
1951	51.9	0.4	51.9	0.0	51.9	0.0	51.9	0.0	51.7	-0.4	51.8	0.2	51.7	-0.2	51.7	0.0	51.7	0.0	51.7	0.0	51.5	-0.4	51.6	0.2
1952	51.4	-0.4	50.6	-1.6	50.5	-0.2	50.2	-0.6	49.9	-0.6	49.9	0.0	49.9	0.0	49.9	0.0	49.9	0.0	49.8	-0.2	49.8	0.0	49.4	-0.8
1953	49.6	0.4	49.5	-0.2	49.6	0.2	50.4	1.6	50.5	0.2	50.5	0.0	50.5	0.0	50.7	0.4	50.6	-0.2	50.6	0.0	50.6	0.0	50.8	0.4
1954	50.8	0.0	50.8	0.0	50.8	0.0	50.9	0.2	50.9	0.0	50.9	0.0	50.9	0.0	50.9	0.0	50.9	0.0	50.7	-0.4	50.7	0.0	50.7	0.0
1955	50.7	0.0	50.6	-0.2	50.5	-0.2	50.5	0.0	50.5	0.0	50.4	-0.2	50.3	-0.2	50.0	-0.6	50.0	0.0	50.0	0.0	50.0	0.0	50.0	0.0
1956	50.1	0.2	49.8	-0.6	49.8	0.0	49.8	0.0	49.9	0.2	49.9	0.0	49.9	0.0	49.9	0.0	49.8	-0.2	49.8	0.0	50.0	0.4	50.1	0.2
1957	50.1	0.0	50.5	0.8	50.5	0.0	50.6	0.2	50.6	0.0	50.6	0.0	50.6	0.0	50.6	0.0	50.6	0.0	50.6	0.0	50.6	0.0	50.6	0.0
1958	50.7	0.2	50.7	0.0	50.9	0.4	50.9	0.0	51.1	0.4	51.2	0.2	51.1	-0.2	51.1	0.0	51.1	0.0	50.8	-0.6	50.5	-0.6	50.5	0.0
1959	50.5	0.0	50.5	0.0	50.3	-0.4	50.3	0.0	50.5	0.4	50.5	0.0	50.6	0.2	50.6	0.0	50.6	0.0	50.6	0.0	50.6	0.0	50.6	0.0
1960	50.6	0.0	50.6	0.0	50.6	0.0	50.7	0.2	50.9	0.4	51.1	0.4	51.1	0.0	51.1	0.0	50.7	-0.8	50.5	-0.4	50.3	-0.4	50.3	0.0
1961	50.2	-0.2	50.2	0.0	50.1	-0.2	50.1	0.0	50.0	-0.2	50.0	0.0	50.1	0.2	49.4	-1.4	49.1	-0.6	49.2	0.2	49.3	0.2	49.3	0.0
1962	49.2	-0.2	49.2	0.0	49.2	0.0	49.1	-0.2	49.1	0.0	49.1	0.0	48.2	-1.8	48.1	-0.2	48.1	0.0	48.2	0.2	48.2	0.0	48.0	-0.4
1963	48.2	0.4	48.2	0.0	48.2	0.0	48.2	0.0	48.2	0.0	48.2	0.0	48.2	0.0	48.1	-0.2	48.1	0.0	48.1	0.0	48.1	0.0	48.1	0.0
1964	48.3	0.4	48.3	0.0	48.2	-0.2	48.3	0.2	48.4	0.2	47.9	-1.0	48.0	0.2	47.9	-0.2	47.9	0.0	47.9	0.0	47.9	0.0	47.9	0.0
1965	47.8	-0.2	47.9	0.2	47.9	0.0	48.0	0.2	48.1	0.2	47.6	-1.0	47.6	0.0	47.6	0.0	47.6	0.0	47.6	0.0	47.9	0.6	47.9	0.0
1966	47.8	-0.2	47.8	0.0	47.8	0.0	47.6	-0.4	47.6	0.0	47.7	0.2	47.8	0.2	47.9	0.2	48.0	0.2	48.1	0.2	48.1	0.0	47.9	-0.4
1967	47.9	0.0	47.7	-0.4	47.8	0.2	47.6	-0.4	47.6	0.0	47.6	0.0	47.6	0.0	47.4	-0.4	47.4	0.0	47.4	0.0	47.5	0.2	47.5	0.0
1968	47.0	-1.1	47.1	0.2	47.3	0.4	47.3	0.0	47.3	0.0	47.4	0.2	47.3	-0.2	47.1	-0.4	47.0	-0.2	47.3	0.6	47.4	0.2	47.4	0.0
1969	47.4	0.0	47.4	0.0	47.4	0.0	47.5	0.2	47.6	0.2	47.5	-0.2	47.6	0.2	47.6	0.0	47.6	0.0	47.6	0.0	47.7	0.2	47.9	0.4
1970	47.8	-0.2	47.9	0.2	48.2	0.6	47.9	-0.6	48.0	0.2	48.1	0.2	48.2	0.2	48.4	0.4	48.1	-0.6	48.2	0.2	48.4	0.4	48.5	0.2
1971	48.5	0.0	48.7	0.4	48.8	0.2	48.6	-0.4	48.6	0.0	48.7	0.2	48.9	0.4	48.9	0.0	48.9	0.0	48.9	0.0	48.8	-0.2	48.8	0.0
1972	48.7	-0.2	48.7	0.0	48.8	0.2	48.8	0.0	48.9	0.2	49.1	0.4	49.1	0.0	49.2	0.2	49.1	-0.2	49.2	0.2	49.3	0.2	49.3	0.0
1973	49.3	0.0	49.3	0.0	49.4	0.2	49.4	0.0	49.5	0.2	49.7	0.4	49.7	0.0	49.7	0.0	49.8	0.2	49.8	0.0	49.9	0.2	50.0	0.2
1974	50.1	0.2	50.3	0.4	50.6	0.6	51.2	1.2	51.9	1.4	53.0	2.1	53.7	1.3	54.9	2.2	55.7	1.5	56.7	1.8	57.6	1.6	58.0	0.7
1975	58.9	1.6	59.1	0.3	59.3	0.3	59.9	1.0	59.9	0.0	60.2	0.5	60.7	0.8	60.7	0.0	60.6	-0.2	61.2	1.0	61.3	0.2	61.5	0.3
1976	62.3	1.3	62.7	0.6	62.9	0.3	63.3	0.6	63.4	0.2	64.0	0.9	64.1	0.2	64.3	0.3	64.5	0.3	64.5	0.0	64.7	0.3	64.9	0.3
1977	65.5	0.9	65.9	0.6	66.2	0.5	66.4	0.3	66.5	0.2	67.0	0.7	67.2	0.3	67.2	0.0	67.3	0.1	67.5	0.3	67.7	0.3	68.0	0.4
1978	68.6	0.9	69.0	0.6	69.2	0.3	69.6	0.6	69.8	0.3	70.3	0.7	70.7	0.6	70.9	0.3	71.2	0.4	71.5	0.4	72.4	1.3	72.9	0.7
1979	73.9	1.4	74.4	0.7	74.6	0.3	75.0	0.5	75.1	0.1	75.7	0.8	75.8	0.1	76.0	0.3	76.7	0.9	77.5	1.0	77.6	0.1	78.3	0.9
1980	79.3	1.3	79.8	0.6	80.4	0.8	82.2	2.2	82.3	0.1	83.0	0.9	83.6	0.7	83.8	0.2	84.2	0.5	84.9	0.8	86.2	1.5	86.9	0.8
1981	87.9	1.2	89.2	1.5	90.1	1.0	90.9	0.9	91.6	0.8	91.9	0.3	93.1	1.3	92.8	-0.3	94.2	1.5	94.5	0.3	94.3	-0.2	94.7	0.4
1982	96.2	1.6	97.3	1.1	98.0	0.7	99.4	1.4	99.9	0.5	99.8	-0.1	100.0	0.2	100.5	0.5	101.1	0.6	102.3	1.2	102.6	0.3	102.8	0.2
1983	104.1	1.3	105.7	1.5	106.1	0.4	107.2	1.0	107.2	0.0	107.2	0.0	108.3	1.0	108.2	-0.1	108.2	0.0	109.1	0.8	110.0	0.8	109.9	-0.1
1984	110.9	0.9	111.6	0.6	113.1	1.3	114.2	1.0	114.3	0.1	112.9	-1.2	114.5	1.4	114.6	0.1	114.1	-0.4	116.5	2.1	117.5	0.9	116.6	-0.8
1985	117.8	1.0	119.1	1.1	120.1	0.8	121.0	0.7	121.7	0.6	121.0	-0.6	123.6	2.1	122.9	-0.6	123.4	0.4	124.4	0.8	125.1	0.6	124.1	-0.8
1986	126.6	2.0	126.5	-0.1	128.0	1.2	129.2	0.9	129.6	0.3	129.8	0.2	130.3	0.4	130.7	0.3	131.5	0.6	132.5	0.8	133.2	0.5	133.2	0.0
1987	134.7	1.1	135.8	0.8	137.3	1.1	138.2	0.7	139.5	0.9	138.9	-0.4	139.2	0.2	139.5	0.2	141.0	1.1	140.0	-0.7	142.6	1.9	142.4	-0.1
1988	143.3	0.6	143.6	0.2	145.5	1.3	146.0	0.3	147.4	1.0	147.4	0.0	149.2	1.2	149.2	0.0	150.8	1.1	151.5	0.5	153.3	1.2	153.1	-0.1
1989	155.5	1.6	155.6	0.1	157.7	1.3	158.6	0.6	158.6	0.0	160.1	0.9	160.7	0.4	161.9	0.7	161.3	-0.4	162.3	0.6	163.6	0.8	164.3	0.4
1990	166.0	1.0	167.5	0.9	168.7	0.7	169.8	0.7	170.5	0.4	170.1	-0.2	171.0	0.5	171.7	0.4	171.6	-0.1	172.9	0.8	174.5	0.9	175.1	0.3
1991	176.3	0.7	178.0	1.0	178.3	0.2	181.1	1.6	181.7	0.3	182.6	0.5	184.7	1.2	185.5	0.4	184.0	-0.8	186.1	1.1	186.1	0.0	186.5	0.2

[Continued]

Drugs and Pharmaceuticals

Producer Price Index
Base 1982 = 100
[Continued]

For 1947-1997. Columns headed % show percentile change in the index from the previous period for which an index is available.

Year	Jan Index	%	Feb Index	%	Mar Index	%	Apr Index	%	May Index	%	Jun Index	%	Jul Index	%	Aug Index	%	Sep Index	%	Oct Index	%	Nov Index	%	Dec Index	%
1992	187.2	0.4	188.8	0.9	189.6	0.4	191.3	0.9	191.9	0.3	192.2	0.2	192.8	0.3	193.8	0.5	193.7	-0.1	194.8	0.6	194.6	-0.1	196.0	0.7
1993	197.9	1.0	199.1	0.6	199.2	0.1	200.5	0.7	200.3	-0.1	201.0	0.3	201.5	0.2	202.3	0.4	202.1	-0.1	202.6	0.2	202.2	-0.2	202.3	0.0
1994	204.6	1.1	204.5	-0.0	204.7	0.1	205.3	0.3	206.2	0.4	206.2	0.0	206.0	-0.1	206.3	0.1	206.6	0.1	206.4	-0.1	207.3	0.4	207.3	0.0
1995	207.8	0.2	208.9	0.5	208.9	0.0	210.4	0.7	210.4	0.0	210.2	-0.1	210.8	0.3	210.9	0.0	211.9	0.5	213.1	0.6	213.4	0.1	213.8	0.2
1996	213.5	-0.1	213.4	-0.0	214.4	0.5	214.1	-0.1	214.8	0.3	215.0	0.1	215.4	0.2	215.1	-0.1	215.1	0.0	215.4	0.1	214.8	-0.3	215.4	0.3
1997	217.4	0.9	218.2	0.4	218.6	0.2	217.7	-0.4	218.3	0.3	218.6	0.1	219.1	0.2	219.3	0.1	219.3	0.0	220.1	0.4	220.6	0.2	220.8	0.1

Source: U.S. Department of Labor, Bureau of Labor Statistics, Division of Industry Prices and Price Indexes. n.e.c. stands for not elsewhere classified. - indicates no data collected for period or unavailable.

Fats and Oils, Inedible
Producer Price Index
Base 1982 = 100

For 1926-1997. Columns headed % show percentile change in the index from the previous period for which an index is available.

Year	Jan Index	%	Feb Index	%	Mar Index	%	Apr Index	%	May Index	%	Jun Index	%	Jul Index	%	Aug Index	%	Sep Index	%	Oct Index	%	Nov Index	%	Dec Index	%
1926	-	-	-	-	-	-	-	-	-	-	-	-	-	-	-	-	-	-	-	-	-	-	-	-
1927	-	-	-	-	-	-	-	-	-	-	-	-	-	-	-	-	-	-	-	-	-	-	-	-
1928	-	-	-	-	-	-	-	-	-	-	-	-	-	-	-	-	-	-	-	-	-	-	-	-
1929	-	-	-	-	-	-	-	-	-	-	-	-	-	-	-	-	-	-	-	-	-	-	-	-
1930	-	-	-	-	-	-	-	-	-	-	-	-	-	-	-	-	-	-	-	-	-	-	-	-
1931	-	-	-	-	-	-	-	-	-	-	-	-	-	-	-	-	-	-	-	-	-	-	-	-
1932	-	-	-	-	-	-	-	-	-	-	-	-	-	-	-	-	-	-	-	-	-	-	-	-
1933	19.3	-	18.6	-3.6	18.8	1.1	19.1	1.6	22.2	16.2	23.4	5.4	23.0	-1.7	22.7	-1.3	21.0	-7.5	20.9	-0.5	21.1	1.0	20.3	-3.8
1934	19.5	-3.9	19.9	2.1	20.2	1.5	20.1	-0.5	20.4	1.5	19.8	-2.9	20.1	1.5	21.3	6.0	23.1	8.5	24.6	6.5	23.8	-3.3	25.4	6.7
1935	29.7	16.9	33.3	12.1	36.3	9.0	34.6	-4.7	35.3	2.0	33.0	-6.5	29.5	-10.6	29.4	-0.3	31.1	5.8	33.7	8.4	33.1	-1.8	32.8	-0.9
1936	32.8	0.0	31.8	-3.0	30.3	-4.7	29.4	-3.0	26.7	-9.2	27.4	2.6	30.8	12.4	32.6	5.8	36.8	12.9	37.6	2.2	39.8	5.9	45.7	14.8
1937	51.4	12.5	50.5	-1.8	50.1	-0.8	47.8	-4.6	42.8	-10.5	40.5	-5.4	39.4	-2.7	36.9	-6.3	34.4	-6.8	33.2	-3.5	31.2	-6.0	29.7	-4.8
1938	30.4	2.4	29.4	-3.3	28.5	-3.1	26.1	-8.4	25.2	-3.4	24.6	-2.4	26.1	6.1	25.6	-1.9	25.1	-2.0	25.0	-0.4	24.6	-1.6	24.5	-0.4
1939	24.6	0.4	24.3	-1.2	25.0	2.9	24.3	-2.8	24.7	1.6	24.5	-0.8	22.9	-6.5	21.5	-6.1	28.7	33.5	30.3	5.6	29.0	-4.3	28.2	-2.8
1940	27.8	-1.4	27.0	-2.9	25.4	-5.9	24.8	-2.4	24.4	-1.6	23.9	-2.0	22.8	-4.6	20.7	-9.2	21.1	1.9	21.0	-0.5	22.4	6.7	22.4	0.0
1941	24.5	9.4	24.8	1.2	29.5	19.0	36.7	24.4	42.7	16.3	42.7	0.0	44.4	4.0	46.2	4.1	48.4	4.8	49.4	2.1	49.2	-0.4	54.0	9.8
1942	56.3	4.3	57.3	1.8	57.6	0.5	57.7	0.2	57.5	-0.3	57.4	-0.2	55.2	-3.8	53.8	-2.5	53.8	0.0	53.8	0.0	53.8	0.0	53.8	0.0
1943	53.8	0.0	53.8	0.0	53.8	0.0	53.8	0.0	54.0	0.4	54.0	0.0	54.0	0.0	54.0	0.0	54.0	0.0	54.0	0.0	54.0	0.0	54.0	0.0
1944	54.0	0.0	54.0	0.0	54.0	0.0	54.0	0.0	54.0	0.0	54.0	0.0	54.0	0.0	54.0	0.0	54.0	0.0	54.0	0.0	54.0	0.0	54.0	0.0
1945	54.0	0.0	54.0	0.0	54.0	0.0	54.0	0.0	54.0	0.0	54.0	0.0	54.0	0.0	54.0	0.0	54.0	0.0	54.0	0.0	54.0	0.0	54.0	0.0
1946	53.8	-0.4	53.9	0.2	54.1	0.4	54.1	0.0	54.1	0.0	54.1	0.0	60.4	11.6	54.3	-10.1	54.7	0.7	58.8	7.5	101.1	71.9	107.5	6.3
1947	111.5	3.7	114.9	3.0	128.8	12.1	116.8	-9.3	86.3	-26.1	67.5	-21.8	64.5	-4.4	62.6	-2.9	82.4	31.6	103.6	25.7	121.2	17.0	111.0	-8.4
1948	120.6	8.6	96.0	-20.4	100.0	4.2	96.0	-4.0	85.6	-10.8	92.6	8.2	87.4	-5.6	77.9	-10.9	80.8	3.7	77.8	-3.7	79.0	1.5	70.2	-11.1
1949	56.2	-19.9	49.8	-11.4	44.8	-10.0	39.8	-11.2	42.0	5.5	40.1	-4.5	39.2	-2.2	46.1	17.6	41.7	-9.5	39.7	-4.8	39.7	0.0	39.9	0.5
1950	42.5	6.5	41.7	-1.9	43.4	4.1	43.3	-0.2	41.8	-3.5	37.3	-10.8	44.2	18.5	53.0	19.9	66.5	25.5	65.3	-1.8	71.5	9.5	80.1	12.0
1951	88.9	11.0	94.4	6.2	87.8	-7.0	82.3	-6.3	79.3	-3.6	67.7	-14.6	53.6	-20.8	53.8	0.4	55.8	3.7	54.9	-1.6	49.9	-9.1	47.0	-5.8
1952	43.4	-7.7	39.2	-9.7	36.2	-7.7	32.6	-9.9	36.1	10.7	39.8	10.2	38.1	-4.3	36.3	-4.7	37.4	3.0	39.0	4.3	40.6	4.1	40.4	-0.5
1953	40.9	1.2	40.3	-1.5	45.1	11.9	42.7	-5.3	38.2	-10.5	35.6	-6.8	35.7	0.3	35.9	0.6	39.1	8.9	40.8	4.3	44.4	8.8	44.8	0.9
1954	46.8	4.5	48.6	3.8	46.3	-4.7	45.7	-1.3	45.4	-0.7	42.6	-6.2	39.8	-6.6	40.9	2.8	41.3	1.0	43.2	4.6	44.2	2.3	45.4	2.7
1955	47.3	4.2	46.7	-1.3	42.4	-9.2	42.2	-0.5	40.7	-3.6	41.1	1.0	42.7	3.9	41.8	-2.1	42.7	2.2	44.5	4.2	44.1	-0.9	43.3	-1.8
1956	42.5	-1.8	41.6	-2.1	42.1	1.2	44.4	5.5	46.1	3.8	42.1	-8.7	41.1	-2.4	41.1	0.0	42.4	3.2	42.7	0.7	44.2	3.5	45.4	2.7
1957	44.9	-1.1	44.4	-1.1	44.3	-0.2	44.5	0.5	45.3	1.8	46.1	1.8	46.7	1.3	48.5	3.9	49.3	1.6	49.5	0.4	49.9	0.8	50.0	0.2
1958	48.3	-3.4	48.1	-0.4	49.1	2.1	47.6	-3.1	47.0	-1.3	47.3	0.6	47.8	1.1	47.8	0.0	47.2	-1.3	47.9	1.5	49.5	3.3	47.0	-5.1
1959	45.8	-2.6	45.0	-1.7	46.1	2.4	46.2	0.2	46.2	0.0	44.7	-3.2	42.3	-5.4	41.1	-2.8	42.1	2.4	41.7	-1.0	39.9	-4.3	38.9	-2.5
1960	37.6	-3.3	37.8	0.5	38.7	2.4	39.6	2.3	38.4	-3.0	36.6	-4.7	36.6	0.0	37.4	2.2	36.5	-2.4	36.6	0.3	37.4	2.2	37.1	-0.8
1961	38.4	3.5	41.8	8.9	44.1	5.5	47.5	7.7	47.0	-1.1	41.4	-11.9	39.9	-3.6	39.1	-2.0	37.3	-4.6	36.0	-3.5	35.2	-2.2	36.1	2.6
1962	38.2	5.8	35.5	-7.1	37.4	5.4	36.5	-2.4	35.5	-2.7	33.8	-4.8	33.9	0.3	33.6	-0.9	33.3	-0.9	35.3	6.0	35.0	-0.8	33.5	-4.3
1963	33.0	-1.5	33.5	1.5	34.3	2.4	35.8	4.4	36.2	1.1	37.1	2.5	37.5	1.1	37.6	0.3	37.4	-0.5	40.8	9.1	41.5	1.7	39.2	-5.5
1964	38.3	-2.3	38.3	0.0	39.5	3.1	40.2	1.8	40.8	1.5	42.9	5.1	44.2	3.0	46.7	5.7	48.9	4.7	49.6	1.4	51.9	4.6	53.8	3.7
1965	52.2	-3.0	54.5	4.4	54.7	0.4	55.8	2.0	53.7	-3.8	52.5	-2.2	50.8	-3.2	48.1	-5.3	49.9	3.7	50.7	1.6	49.1	-3.2	50.7	3.3
1966	52.1	2.8	50.7	-2.7	49.0	-3.4	47.9	-2.2	47.2	-1.5	46.8	-0.8	48.5	3.6	48.6	0.2	47.8	-1.6	43.5	-9.0	42.2	-3.0	43.8	3.8
1967	42.5	-3.0	41.0	-3.5	37.5	-8.5	39.3	4.8	38.2	-2.8	36.6	-4.2	35.5	-3.0	35.6	0.3	35.5	-0.3	36.2	2.0	35.9	-0.8	35.6	-0.8
1968	35.2	-1.1	35.3	0.3	36.8	4.2	37.2	1.1	36.1	-3.0	33.5	-7.2	31.8	-5.1	32.8	3.1	31.6	-3.7	32.2	1.9	33.8	5.0	32.2	-4.7
1969	33.3	3.4	33.9	1.8	37.0	9.1	38.6	4.3	38.4	-0.5	40.0	4.2	41.7	4.2	45.7	9.6	46.9	2.6	45.5	-3.0	46.3	1.8	42.7	-7.8
1970	43.8	2.6	43.4	-0.9	47.2	8.8	49.5	4.9	49.2	-0.6	49.8	1.2	49.6	-0.4	51.6	4.0	48.1	-6.8	54.1	12.5	56.7	4.8	53.8	-5.1

[Continued]

Fats and Oils, Inedible
Producer Price Index
Base 1982 = 100
[Continued]

For 1926-1997. Columns headed % show percentile change in the index from the previous period for which an index is available.

Year	Jan Index	%	Feb Index	%	Mar Index	%	Apr Index	%	May Index	%	Jun Index	%	Jul Index	%	Aug Index	%	Sep Index	%	Oct Index	%	Nov Index	%	Dec Index	%
1971	50.1	-6.9	53.4	6.6	54.0	1.1	53.6	-0.7	52.0	-3.0	49.4	-5.0	49.0	-0.8	50.2	2.4	49.8	-0.8	48.3	-3.0	46.9	-2.9	43.4	-7.5
1972	41.7	-3.9	41.4	-0.7	38.7	-6.5	42.0	8.5	43.4	3.3	43.4	0.0	42.4	-2.3	45.4	7.1	43.6	-4.0	43.9	0.7	46.1	5.0	48.0	4.1
1973	48.8	1.7	52.1	6.8	65.1	25.0	68.9	5.8	86.9	26.1	98.7	13.6	98.5	-0.2	102.3	3.9	104.7	2.3	102.2	-2.4	90.6	-11.4	107.1	18.2
1974	111.6	4.2	125.7	12.6	139.4	10.9	144.3	3.5	134.5	-6.8	135.3	0.6	130.1	-3.8	142.4	9.5	121.8	-14.5	122.9	0.9	112.8	-8.2	99.0	-12.2
1975	88.1	-11.0	86.7	-1.6	81.7	-5.8	97.9	19.8	93.8	-4.2	92.4	-1.5	97.5	5.5	107.0	9.7	108.5	1.4	99.0	-8.8	97.6	-1.4	96.3	-1.3
1976	92.3	-4.2	91.8	-0.5	95.9	4.5	91.2	-4.9	88.2	-3.3	91.2	3.4	97.0	6.4	93.4	-3.7	98.4	5.4	94.1	-4.4	94.1	0.0	95.3	1.3
1977	95.5	0.2	100.4	5.1	102.5	2.1	114.2	11.4	126.4	10.7	119.4	-5.5	105.6	-11.6	100.7	-4.6	92.4	-8.2	97.7	5.7	99.4	1.7	99.7	0.3
1978	98.6	-1.1	105.4	6.9	110.3	4.6	112.8	2.3	118.0	4.6	117.3	-0.6	125.7	7.2	117.2	-6.8	126.7	8.1	127.3	0.5	135.3	6.3	124.7	-7.8
1979	125.9	1.0	137.8	9.5	149.2	8.3	168.0	12.6	156.6	-6.8	140.1	-10.5	142.9	2.0	140.9	-1.4	142.3	1.0	137.4	-3.4	128.9	-6.2	122.5	-5.0
1980	121.9	-0.5	113.2	-7.1	112.3	-0.8	111.7	-0.5	110.4	-1.2	95.8	-13.2	97.4	1.7	115.2	18.3	114.0	-1.0	113.1	-0.8	115.4	2.0	118.8	2.9
1981	116.3	-2.1	108.5	-6.7	110.7	2.0	117.1	5.8	116.9	-0.2	113.5	-2.9	108.9	-4.1	114.4	5.1	106.9	-6.6	104.0	-2.7	105.8	1.7	105.0	-0.8
1982	102.1	-2.8	102.7	0.6	108.6	5.7	105.8	-2.6	108.0	2.1	107.6	-0.4	104.2	-3.2	95.2	-8.6	95.1	-0.1	90.7	-4.6	89.7	-1.1	90.2	0.6
1983	90.6	0.4	94.9	4.7	98.2	3.5	104.2	6.1	107.5	3.2	103.7	-3.5	97.7	-5.8	104.1	6.6	123.2	18.3	119.3	-3.2	120.4	0.9	119.4	-0.8
1984	125.2	4.9	130.7	4.4	137.3	5.0	143.5	4.5	149.5	4.2	155.1	3.7	141.8	-8.6	131.1	-7.5	134.6	2.7	136.7	1.6	142.3	4.1	141.1	-0.8
1985	129.7	-8.1	130.0	0.2	129.7	-0.2	130.7	0.8	124.0	-5.1	111.7	-9.9	104.8	-6.2	97.6	-6.9	92.6	-5.1	93.6	1.1	90.7	-3.1	91.9	1.3
1986	94.5	2.8	95.9	1.5	86.4	-9.9	81.6	-5.6	76.9	-5.8	71.5	-7.0	69.9	-2.2	71.2	1.9	72.2	1.4	76.9	6.5	80.2	4.3	84.1	4.9
1987	94.5	12.4	95.1	0.6	91.3	-4.0	83.0	-9.1	91.0	9.6	94.9	4.3	92.5	-2.5	93.0	0.5	95.5	2.7	94.8	-0.7	93.3	-1.6	93.4	0.1
1988	110.5	18.3	110.8	0.3	110.1	-0.6	109.6	-0.5	105.9	-3.4	115.1	8.7	123.0	6.9	122.0	-0.8	111.6	-8.5	107.2	-3.9	100.7	-6.1	103.7	3.0
1989	103.2	-0.5	102.4	-0.8	101.8	-0.6	99.1	-2.7	96.2	-2.9	99.2	3.1	94.5	-4.7	85.9	-9.1	86.8	1.0	93.9	8.2	92.2	-1.8	90.7	-1.6
1990	88.3	-2.6	94.2	6.7	90.6	-3.8	85.6	-5.5	86.8	1.4	88.5	2.0	88.4	-0.1	83.0	-6.1	82.4	-0.7	87.0	5.6	89.6	3.0	92.8	3.6
1991	96.6	4.1	89.5	-7.3	86.2	-3.7	86.5	0.3	83.5	-3.5	82.1	-1.7	80.5	-1.9	86.9	8.0	87.7	0.9	87.1	-0.7	88.3	1.4	87.0	-1.5
1992	88.9	2.2	86.5	-2.7	83.0	-4.0	84.6	1.9	87.2	3.1	91.7	5.2	94.7	3.3	98.1	3.6	99.4	1.3	98.8	-0.6	102.7	3.9	100.9	-1.8
1993	100.6	-0.3	97.5	-3.1	97.5	0.0	100.7	3.3	99.9	-0.8	96.5	-3.4	93.5	-3.1	94.7	1.3	91.2	-3.7	90.2	-1.1	90.1	-0.1	94.7	5.1
1994	99.9	5.5	102.8	2.9	101.7	-1.1	99.0	-2.7	99.3	0.3	105.0	5.7	106.6	1.5	112.6	5.6	116.1	3.1	118.4	2.0	125.2	5.7	140.2	12.0
1995	142.8	1.9	121.9	-14.6	124.1	1.8	122.0	-1.7	119.7	-1.9	121.8	1.8	125.7	3.2	124.8	-0.7	124.3	-0.4	125.5	1.0	135.0	7.6	134.8	-0.1
1996	132.3	-1.9	121.4	-8.2	115.8	-4.6	116.1	0.3	130.7	12.6	132.7	1.5	136.3	2.7	147.2	8.0	160.8	9.2	143.8	-10.6	125.3	-12.9	137.6	9.8
1997	150.3	9.2	146.4	-2.6	132.5	-9.5	115.8	-12.6	122.2	5.5	127.4	4.3	124.3	-2.4	121.7	-2.1	124.9	2.6	135.1	8.2	143.7	6.4	143.1	-0.4

Source: U.S. Department of Labor, Bureau of Labor Statistics, Division of Industry Prices and Price Indexes. n.e.c. stands for not elsewhere classified. - indicates no data collected for period or unavailable.

Agricultural Chemicals and Chemical Products
Producer Price Index
Base 1982 = 100

For 1947-1997. Columns headed % show percentile change in the index from the previous period for which an index is available.

Year	Jan Index	%	Feb Index	%	Mar Index	%	Apr Index	%	May Index	%	Jun Index	%	Jul Index	%	Aug Index	%	Sep Index	%	Oct Index	%	Nov Index	%	Dec Index	%
1947	28.3	-	28.3	0.0	28.9	2.1	29.0	0.3	29.0	0.0	28.8	-0.7	28.9	0.3	28.9	0.0	29.0	0.3	29.3	1.0	29.5	0.7	29.7	0.7
1948	29.9	0.7	29.8	-0.3	29.9	0.3	29.8	-0.3	29.7	-0.3	29.7	0.0	30.2	1.7	30.6	1.3	30.9	1.0	31.1	0.6	31.3	0.6	31.3	0.0
1949	31.6	1.0	31.5	-0.3	31.5	0.0	31.5	0.0	31.5	0.0	31.3	-0.6	31.5	0.6	31.4	-0.3	31.4	0.0	31.4	0.0	31.0	-1.3	30.9	-0.3
1950	30.8	-0.3	30.6	-0.6	30.7	0.3	30.8	0.3	30.8	0.0	30.1	-2.3	30.1	0.0	30.2	0.3	30.2	0.0	30.2	0.0	30.6	1.3	31.6	3.3
1951	32.1	1.6	32.1	0.0	32.1	0.0	32.1	0.0	32.1	0.0	31.9	-0.6	32.5	1.9	32.6	0.3	32.8	0.6	32.9	0.3	32.9	0.0	33.0	0.3
1952	33.0	0.0	33.1	0.3	33.3	0.6	33.3	0.0	33.5	0.6	32.9	-1.8	33.0	0.3	33.0	0.0	33.0	0.0	33.0	0.0	33.0	0.0	33.0	0.0
1953	32.9	-0.3	32.8	-0.3	32.8	0.0	32.9	0.3	33.0	0.3	32.7	-0.9	33.1	1.2	33.2	0.3	33.2	0.0	33.1	-0.3	33.3	0.6	33.4	0.3
1954	33.2	-0.6	33.4	0.6	33.4	0.0	33.4	0.0	33.4	0.0	33.1	-0.9	33.1	0.0	33.2	0.3	33.1	-0.3	33.0	-0.3	33.0	0.0	33.1	0.3
1955	33.2	0.3	33.2	0.0	33.2	0.0	33.1	-0.3	33.1	0.0	32.8	-0.9	32.9	0.3	33.0	0.3	32.9	-0.3	33.0	0.3	32.9	-0.3	32.9	0.0
1956	33.0	0.3	32.8	-0.6	32.8	0.0	32.8	0.0	32.3	-1.5	32.3	0.0	32.2	-0.3	32.3	0.3	32.2	-0.3	32.1	-0.3	32.3	0.6	32.3	0.0
1957	32.5	0.6	32.3	-0.6	32.3	0.0	32.5	0.6	32.4	-0.3	32.3	-0.3	32.3	0.0	32.5	0.6	32.7	0.6	32.8	0.3	32.8	0.0	33.1	0.9
1958	33.4	0.9	33.3	-0.3	33.4	0.3	33.6	0.6	33.6	0.0	33.6	0.0	33.4	-0.6	32.9	-1.5	32.8	-0.3	33.0	0.6	32.9	-0.3	32.9	0.0
1959	33.4	1.5	33.4	0.0	33.4	0.0	33.3	-0.3	33.2	-0.3	33.3	0.3	33.2	-0.3	33.0	-0.6	33.1	0.3	33.2	0.3	33.2	0.0	33.3	0.3
1960	33.4	0.3	33.5	0.3	33.5	0.0	33.5	0.0	33.5	0.0	33.5	0.0	33.7	0.6	33.7	0.0	33.8	0.3	34.0	0.6	34.0	0.0	33.9	-0.3
1961	34.0	0.3	34.0	0.0	34.0	0.0	34.0	0.0	34.0	0.0	33.8	-0.6	33.8	0.0	33.6	-0.6	33.8	0.6	33.4	-1.2	33.6	0.6	33.5	-0.3
1962	34.2	2.1	34.3	0.3	34.0	-0.9	34.0	0.0	33.9	-0.3	33.9	0.0	33.6	-0.9	33.2	-1.2	33.2	0.0	33.2	0.0	33.2	0.0	33.2	0.0
1963	33.4	0.6	33.2	-0.6	33.2	0.0	33.4	0.6	33.4	0.0	33.2	-0.6	33.1	-0.3	32.7	-1.2	32.8	0.3	32.8	0.0	32.9	0.3	32.7	-0.6
1964	32.8	0.3	32.9	0.3	32.9	0.0	32.9	0.0	32.9	0.0	32.9	0.0	33.0	0.3	32.8	-0.6	32.7	-0.3	32.8	0.3	33.0	0.6	33.0	0.0
1965	33.2	0.6	33.5	0.9	33.6	0.3	33.5	-0.3	33.5	0.0	33.6	0.3	33.7	0.3	33.6	-0.3	33.7	0.3	33.8	0.3	33.8	0.0	33.8	0.0
1966	33.8	0.0	33.9	0.3	33.9	0.0	34.1	0.6	34.2	0.3	34.0	-0.6	33.9	-0.3	33.6	-0.9	33.7	0.3	33.9	0.6	34.1	0.6	34.0	-0.3
1967	34.4	1.2	34.8	1.2	34.9	0.3	34.7	-0.6	34.7	0.0	34.7	0.0	34.2	-1.4	33.6	-1.8	33.4	-0.6	33.5	0.3	33.6	0.3	33.7	0.3
1968	32.8	-2.7	33.2	1.2	33.4	0.6	33.5	0.3	33.5	0.0	33.4	-0.3	33.4	0.0	32.7	-2.1	32.5	-0.6	32.3	-0.6	31.8	-1.5	31.8	0.0
1969	30.6	-3.8	30.4	-0.7	30.5	0.3	30.4	-0.3	30.4	0.0	30.4	0.0	29.2	-3.9	29.2	0.0	28.9	-1.0	28.5	-1.4	28.6	0.4	28.6	0.0
1970	28.9	1.0	30.2	4.5	30.4	0.7	30.5	0.3	30.3	-0.7	30.3	0.0	30.0	-1.0	30.2	0.7	30.4	0.7	30.6	0.7	30.6	0.0	30.6	0.0
1971	31.5	2.9	31.8	1.0	32.2	1.3	32.3	0.3	32.2	-0.3	32.2	0.0	31.5	-2.2	30.9	-1.9	30.9	0.0	30.9	0.0	30.9	0.0	30.9	0.0
1972	30.9	0.0	30.8	-0.3	31.0	0.6	31.5	1.6	31.5	0.0	31.6	0.3	31.4	-0.6	31.5	0.3	31.5	0.0	31.5	0.0	31.6	0.3	31.6	0.0
1973	31.8	0.6	31.8	0.0	32.0	0.6	32.3	0.9	32.4	0.3	32.5	0.3	33.1	1.8	32.8	-0.9	32.8	0.0	32.8	0.0	35.9	9.5	36.3	1.1
1974	38.4	5.8	38.7	0.8	40.4	4.4	40.4	0.0	40.4	0.0	41.1	1.7	44.8	9.0	48.6	8.5	49.7	2.3	58.3	17.3	61.9	6.2	62.3	0.6
1975	65.0	4.3	65.9	1.4	72.4	9.9	72.6	0.3	72.5	-0.1	72.2	-0.4	71.9	-0.4	70.6	-1.8	68.8	-2.5	68.4	-0.6	67.6	-1.2	67.7	0.1
1976	67.7	0.0	65.4	-3.4	65.1	-0.5	64.9	-0.3	64.9	0.0	64.3	-0.9	63.1	-1.9	63.7	1.0	63.9	0.3	63.9	0.0	63.0	-1.4	62.7	-0.5
1977	62.3	-0.6	62.9	1.0	64.0	1.7	64.6	0.9	64.5	-0.2	64.6	0.2	64.5	-0.2	64.8	0.5	65.0	0.3	65.0	0.0	64.4	-0.9	64.0	-0.6
1978	64.1	0.2	64.7	0.9	65.3	0.9	65.7	0.6	69.6	5.9	69.3	-0.4	69.1	-0.3	69.1	0.0	69.3	0.3	69.6	0.4	69.2	-0.6	69.1	-0.1
1979	69.0	-0.1	69.4	0.6	70.5	1.6	71.7	1.7	71.8	0.1	71.5	-0.4	72.2	1.0	73.6	1.9	75.0	1.9	76.7	2.3	78.5	2.3	79.6	1.4
1980	82.7	3.9	84.8	2.5	87.6	3.3	88.4	0.9	88.4	0.0	88.1	-0.3	88.5	0.5	88.9	0.5	89.1	0.2	89.1	0.0	89.3	0.2	90.0	0.8
1981	91.5	1.7	92.9	1.5	94.3	1.5	95.0	0.7	95.4	0.4	98.8	3.6	98.8	0.0	100.3	1.5	100.1	-0.2	100.2	0.1	101.1	0.9	100.8	-0.3
1982	101.5	0.7	101.9	0.4	101.6	-0.3	101.1	-0.5	100.8	-0.3	100.6	-0.2	99.7	-0.9	99.5	-0.2	99.1	-0.4	98.7	-0.4	98.0	-0.7	97.5	-0.5
1983	96.8	-0.7	96.9	0.1	97.2	0.3	96.7	-0.5	96.6	-0.1	96.0	-0.6	95.1	-0.9	94.8	-0.3	94.4	-0.4	94.5	0.1	95.9	1.5	96.4	0.5
1984	95.2	-1.2	97.7	2.6	98.5	0.8	98.6	0.1	98.1	-0.5	98.0	-0.1	97.4	-0.6	96.8	-0.6	97.4	0.6	97.6	0.2	96.6	-1.0	96.6	0.0
1985	96.7	0.1	96.3	-0.4	96.4	0.1	96.7	0.3	96.8	0.1	96.3	-0.5	96.4	0.1	96.5	0.1	96.4	-0.1	95.8	-0.6	95.7	-0.1	94.6	-1.1
1986	94.1	-0.5	95.1	1.1	95.6	0.5	95.5	-0.1	95.4	-0.1	95.7	0.3	95.1	-0.6	93.7	-1.5	93.5	-0.2	92.2	-1.4	92.4	0.2	92.2	-0.2
1987	92.1	-0.1	93.8	1.8	94.8	1.1	97.2	2.5	96.4	-0.8	96.5	0.1	96.8	0.3	97.3	0.5	97.8	0.5	97.7	-0.1	98.0	0.3	98.3	0.3
1988	101.1	2.8	103.1	2.0	104.3	1.2	104.5	0.2	103.9	-0.6	102.9	-1.0	103.4	0.5	103.8	0.4	104.4	0.6	105.5	1.1	107.6	2.0	109.2	1.5
1989	112.0	2.6	113.4	1.3	114.3	0.8	113.4	-0.8	112.2	-1.1	109.8	-2.1	106.5	-3.0	105.0	-1.4	104.7	-0.3	103.7	-1.0	104.4	0.7	104.5	0.1
1990	104.4	-0.1	105.8	1.3	105.7	-0.1	106.8	1.0	106.5	-0.3	105.3	-1.1	105.7	0.4	106.4	0.7	108.0	1.5	109.9	1.8	111.8	1.7	112.0	0.2
1991	112.0	0.0	112.3	0.3	112.3	0.0	112.2	-0.1	111.7	-0.4	111.2	-0.4	111.8	0.5	112.1	0.3	111.8	-0.3	111.5	-0.3	110.7	-0.7	110.9	0.2

[Continued]

Agricultural Chemicals and Chemical Products
Producer Price Index
Base 1982 = 100
[Continued]

For 1947-1997. Columns headed % show percentile change in the index from the previous period for which an index is available.

Year	Jan Index	%	Feb Index	%	Mar Index	%	Apr Index	%	May Index	%	Jun Index	%	Jul Index	%	Aug Index	%	Sep Index	%	Oct Index	%	Nov Index	%	Dec Index	%
1992	110.7	-0.2	110.9	0.2	111.2	0.3	111.3	0.1	111.7	0.4	111.6	-0.1	110.2	-1.3	109.3	-0.8	109.1	-0.2	109.3	0.2	109.4	0.1	109.3	-0.1
1993	110.6	1.2	110.2	-0.4	110.3	0.1	109.6	-0.6	109.3	-0.3	109.6	0.3	109.3	-0.3	107.7	-1.5	108.0	0.3	109.2	1.1	113.0	3.5	112.1	-0.8
1994	113.8	1.5	115.6	1.6	116.3	0.6	119.0	2.3	120.3	1.1	119.8	-0.4	120.5	0.6	120.1	-0.3	121.4	1.1	123.5	1.7	124.4	0.7	124.7	0.2
1995	126.9	1.8	129.6	2.1	131.5	1.5	132.5	0.8	132.1	-0.3	131.1	-0.8	129.4	-1.3	127.9	-1.2	128.2	0.2	128.7	0.4	130.7	1.6	132.7	1.5
1996	135.2	1.9	136.3	0.8	138.2	1.4	136.9	-0.9	134.9	-1.5	132.9	-1.5	129.9	-2.3	129.9	0.0	131.1	0.9	132.2	0.8	132.7	0.4	133.7	0.8
1997	134.1	0.3	133.8	-0.2	134.1	0.2	134.6	0.4	134.3	-0.2	132.7	-1.2	132.0	-0.5	132.0	0.0	131.7	-0.2	131.9	0.2	132.1	0.2	130.9	-0.9

Source: U.S. Department of Labor, Bureau of Labor Statistics, Division of Industry Prices and Price Indexes. n.e.c. stands for not elsewhere classified. - indicates no data collected for period or unavailable.

Plastic Resins and Materials

Producer Price Index

Base 1982 = 100

For 1947-1997. Columns headed % show percentile change in the index from the previous period for which an index is available.

Year	Jan Index	%	Feb Index	%	Mar Index	%	Apr Index	%	May Index	%	Jun Index	%	Jul Index	%	Aug Index	%	Sep Index	%	Oct Index	%	Nov Index	%	Dec Index	%
1947	37.3	-	37.3	0.0	37.3	0.0	37.3	0.0	37.5	0.5	37.5	0.0	37.5	0.0	37.5	0.0	37.5	0.0	37.5	0.0	37.2	-0.8	37.2	0.0
1948	37.6	1.1	37.2	-1.1	36.6	-1.6	36.6	0.0	36.6	0.0	36.6	0.0	37.5	2.5	37.4	-0.3	37.5	0.3	37.6	0.3	37.6	0.0	37.6	0.0
1949	38.1	1.3	38.1	0.0	37.6	-1.3	37.6	0.0	37.6	0.0	37.6	0.0	37.6	0.0	37.6	0.0	37.6	0.0	37.6	0.0	37.7	0.3	37.7	0.0
1950	37.5	-0.5	38.0	1.3	37.5	-1.3	37.5	0.0	37.3	-0.5	37.3	0.0	37.3	0.0	37.3	0.0	38.4	2.9	38.5	0.3	39.2	1.8	39.3	0.3
1951	45.9	16.8	46.9	2.2	47.4	1.1	47.4	0.0	47.4	0.0	47.4	0.0	47.4	0.0	47.4	0.0	47.6	0.4	47.6	0.0	47.7	0.2	47.7	0.0
1952	47.7	0.0	47.2	-1.0	47.0	-0.4	47.0	0.0	47.0	0.0	47.0	0.0	46.9	-0.2	46.9	0.0	46.9	0.0	46.9	0.0	46.9	0.0	47.0	0.2
1953	47.0	0.0	47.0	0.0	47.0	0.0	47.0	0.0	47.0	0.0	47.0	0.0	47.0	0.0	47.2	0.4	47.4	0.4	47.4	0.0	47.4	0.0	47.4	0.0
1954	47.0	-0.8	46.8	-0.4	46.8	0.0	46.8	0.0	46.8	0.0	46.8	0.0	46.8	0.0	46.8	0.0	46.8	0.0	46.8	0.0	46.5	-0.6	46.5	0.0
1955	46.3	-0.4	46.3	0.0	46.3	0.0	46.3	0.0	46.3	0.0	46.3	0.0	46.3	0.0	42.9	-7.3	42.9	0.0	42.9	0.0	42.9	0.0	42.9	0.0
1956	40.7	-5.1	40.7	0.0	40.7	0.0	40.6	-0.2	40.6	0.0	40.6	0.0	40.6	0.0	40.6	0.0	40.3	-0.7	40.3	0.0	40.3	0.0	40.4	0.2
1957	40.4	0.0	40.6	0.5	40.6	0.0	40.6	0.0	40.6	0.0	40.5	-0.2	40.5	0.0	40.7	0.5	40.7	0.0	40.7	0.0	40.5	-0.5	40.7	0.5
1958	40.7	0.0	40.7	0.0	40.5	-0.5	40.5	0.0	40.5	0.0	40.5	0.0	40.2	-0.7	39.4	-2.0	39.4	0.0	39.4	0.0	39.4	0.0	38.9	-1.3
1959	38.9	0.0	38.9	0.0	38.2	-1.8	38.2	0.0	38.2	0.0	38.2	0.0	38.2	0.0	38.2	0.0	38.2	0.0	38.2	0.0	38.2	0.0	38.2	0.0
1960	38.2	0.0	38.2	0.0	38.2	0.0	38.2	0.0	38.2	0.0	38.2	0.0	38.2	0.0	38.2	0.0	38.2	0.0	38.2	0.0	38.2	0.0	38.1	-0.3
1961	36.5	-4.2	36.5	0.0	36.5	0.0	36.5	0.0	36.5	0.0	36.5	0.0	36.4	-0.3	36.4	0.0	36.4	0.0	36.3	-0.3	36.3	0.0	36.3	0.0
1962	36.3	0.0	36.3	0.0	36.3	0.0	36.3	0.0	36.3	0.0	36.3	0.0	36.3	0.0	36.3	0.0	36.3	0.0	36.3	0.0	36.3	0.0	36.3	0.0
1963	36.3	0.0	36.3	0.0	36.3	0.0	35.3	-2.8	35.3	0.0	35.3	0.0	35.3	0.0	35.3	0.0	35.3	0.0	35.3	0.0	35.3	0.0	35.3	0.0
1964	35.3	0.0	35.3	0.0	35.3	0.0	35.3	0.0	35.3	0.0	35.3	0.0	35.3	0.0	35.3	0.0	35.3	0.0	35.3	0.0	35.0	-0.8	35.0	0.0
1965	35.0	0.0	35.0	0.0	35.0	0.0	35.0	0.0	35.0	0.0	35.0	0.0	35.0	0.0	35.0	0.0	35.0	0.0	35.0	0.0	35.0	0.0	35.0	0.0
1966	35.0	0.0	35.0	0.0	35.0	0.0	35.0	0.0	35.0	0.0	35.0	0.0	35.0	0.0	35.3	0.9	35.6	0.8	35.7	0.3	35.7	0.0	35.7	0.0
1967	35.7	0.0	35.8	0.3	35.8	0.0	35.8	0.0	36.0	0.6	35.7	-0.8	35.6	-0.3	35.5	-0.3	34.7	-2.3	34.0	-2.0	34.3	0.9	34.4	0.3
1968	34.0	-1.2	33.0	-2.9	32.8	-0.6	32.9	0.3	32.5	-1.2	32.2	-0.9	32.0	-0.6	31.9	-0.3	32.0	0.3	32.1	0.3	32.0	-0.3	31.9	-0.3
1969	31.9	0.0	32.1	0.6	32.1	0.0	32.0	-0.3	32.0	0.0	32.0	0.0	31.8	-0.6	32.0	0.6	32.1	0.3	31.7	-1.2	31.5	-0.6	31.7	0.6
1970	31.7	0.0	31.9	0.6	31.9	0.0	32.1	0.6	31.8	-0.9	31.7	-0.3	32.1	1.3	32.0	-0.3	32.1	0.3	32.3	0.6	32.0	-0.9	31.8	-0.6
1971	31.6	-0.6	31.4	-0.6	30.8	-1.9	31.1	1.0	31.1	0.0	31.0	-0.3	31.2	0.6	31.4	0.6	31.5	0.3	31.7	0.6	31.4	-0.9	31.4	0.0
1972	31.3	-0.3	31.5	0.6	31.4	-0.3	31.2	-0.6	31.3	0.3	31.0	-1.0	31.0	0.0	31.1	0.3	31.4	1.0	31.5	0.3	31.6	0.3	31.5	-0.3
1973	31.6	0.3	31.8	0.6	31.9	0.3	32.2	0.9	32.6	1.2	32.7	0.3	32.9	0.6	32.9	0.0	32.9	0.0	32.6	-0.9	32.8	0.6	32.8	0.0
1974	33.1	0.9	34.0	2.7	40.9	20.3	43.7	6.8	45.2	3.4	49.7	10.0	52.0	4.6	56.7	9.0	61.6	8.6	63.2	2.6	64.0	1.3	64.6	0.9
1975	64.6	0.0	64.3	-0.5	64.2	-0.2	64.3	0.2	62.2	-3.3	62.1	-0.2	62.5	0.6	62.6	0.2	63.2	1.0	64.9	2.7	65.2	0.5	65.8	0.9
1976	66.1	0.5	67.2	1.7	67.1	-0.1	68.4	1.9	68.5	0.1	68.9	0.6	69.7	1.2	69.6	-0.1	69.1	-0.7	69.0	-0.1	68.9	-0.1	68.8	-0.1
1977	68.3	-0.7	68.1	-0.3	68.7	0.9	69.1	0.6	69.4	0.4	69.7	0.4	70.6	1.3	70.6	0.0	70.6	0.0	70.5	-0.1	70.4	-0.1	70.1	-0.4
1978	70.1	0.0	70.0	-0.1	70.2	0.3	70.2	0.0	70.8	0.9	70.9	0.1	71.0	0.1	70.6	-0.6	70.6	0.0	70.4	-0.3	70.3	-0.1	71.0	1.0
1979	72.1	1.5	72.8	1.0	74.4	2.2	77.8	4.6	80.6	3.6	81.2	0.7	86.3	6.3	88.2	2.2	88.9	0.8	91.7	3.1	92.2	0.5	92.6	0.4
1980	95.4	3.0	96.0	0.6	96.8	0.8	101.5	4.9	101.8	0.3	101.5	-0.3	100.8	-0.7	99.3	-1.5	97.6	-1.7	97.4	-0.2	97.5	0.1	96.7	-0.8
1981	96.9	0.2	97.4	0.5	98.6	1.2	100.6	2.0	101.6	1.0	102.3	0.7	104.4	2.1	105.0	0.6	104.7	-0.3	105.7	1.0	103.4	-2.2	103.8	0.4
1982	100.9	-2.8	101.4	0.5	100.7	-0.7	100.9	0.2	99.9	-1.0	99.5	-0.4	99.1	-0.4	99.6	0.5	99.3	-0.3	99.3	0.0	99.6	0.3	99.7	0.1
1983	100.2	0.5	99.9	-0.3	99.5	-0.4	100.7	1.2	101.6	0.9	102.0	0.4	102.8	0.8	103.6	0.8	106.8	3.1	105.5	-1.2	105.1	-0.4	106.4	1.2
1984	107.7	1.2	107.6	-0.1	108.0	0.4	108.6	0.6	109.6	0.9	109.8	0.2	109.6	-0.2	109.5	-0.1	110.0	0.5	109.2	-0.7	109.0	-0.2	108.1	-0.8
1985	107.7	-0.4	108.3	0.6	108.1	-0.2	108.0	-0.1	107.8	-0.2	108.4	0.6	108.5	0.1	108.1	-0.4	107.7	-0.4	106.1	-1.5	106.0	-0.1	105.6	-0.4
1986	106.2	0.6	106.7	0.5	106.5	-0.2	104.7	-1.7	104.3	-0.4	104.2	-0.1	104.7	0.5	103.9	-0.8	102.4	-1.4	103.4	1.0	104.1	0.7	102.4	-1.6
1987	102.6	0.2	102.4	-0.2	103.2	0.8	106.3	3.0	107.0	0.7	109.7	2.5	112.8	2.8	113.1	0.3	114.2	1.0	116.8	2.3	117.4	0.5	117.7	0.3
1988	121.5	3.2	123.5	1.6	124.4	0.7	127.6	2.6	130.1	2.0	131.2	0.8	134.8	2.7	136.9	1.6	138.9	1.5	139.8	0.6	140.2	0.3	140.1	-0.1
1989	140.3	0.1	141.1	0.6	140.6	-0.4	140.7	0.1	139.8	-0.6	138.0	-1.3	135.3	-2.0	127.7	-5.6	126.1	-1.3	124.7	-1.1	123.7	-0.8	123.3	-0.3
1990	122.2	-0.9	121.6	-0.5	122.2	0.5	123.0	0.7	123.5	0.4	123.0	-0.4	122.3	-0.6	122.3	0.0	122.0	-0.2	125.9	3.2	129.1	2.5	132.1	2.3
1991	131.1	-0.8	128.7	-1.8	126.1	-2.0	122.9	-2.5	120.6	-1.9	117.0	-3.0	115.0	-1.7	114.9	-0.1	114.9	0.0	116.4	1.3	116.4	0.0	116.0	-0.3

[Continued]

Plastic Resins and Materials
Producer Price Index
Base 1982 = 100
[Continued]

For 1947-1997. Columns headed % show percentile change in the index from the previous period for which an index is available.

Year	Jan Index	%	Feb Index	%	Mar Index	%	Apr Index	%	May Index	%	Jun Index	%	Jul Index	%	Aug Index	%	Sep Index	%	Oct Index	%	Nov Index	%	Dec Index	%
1992	115.5	-0.4	115.6	0.1	114.2	-1.2	114.2	0.0	114.7	0.4	115.2	0.4	116.9	1.5	117.7	0.7	118.0	0.3	118.2	0.2	118.1	-0.1	118.1	0.0
1993	118.3	0.2	118.0	-0.3	117.6	-0.3	117.1	-0.4	116.3	-0.7	116.9	0.5	116.9	0.0	117.6	0.6	117.4	-0.2	116.9	-0.4	116.2	-0.6	116.2	0.0
1994	115.0	-1.0	114.7	-0.3	114.5	-0.2	116.5	1.7	117.7	1.0	119.1	1.2	119.6	0.4	121.5	1.6	126.3	4.0	131.9	4.4	134.1	1.7	138.1	3.0
1995	142.5	3.2	145.8	2.3	146.1	0.2	148.5	1.6	149.0	0.3	148.9	-0.1	147.0	-1.3	144.8	-1.5	142.7	-1.5	139.2	-2.5	135.8	-2.4	132.2	-2.7
1996	129.9	-1.7	128.4	-1.2	128.4	0.0	127.7	-0.5	130.6	2.3	132.1	1.1	133.2	0.8	135.2	1.5	137.9	2.0	138.0	0.1	138.0	0.0	137.7	-0.2
1997	137.0	-0.5	137.5	0.4	138.7	0.9	138.9	0.1	139.1	0.1	139.6	0.4	139.3	-0.2	137.4	-1.4	136.0	-1.0	136.7	0.5	134.3	-1.8	133.2	-0.8

Source: U.S. Department of Labor, Bureau of Labor Statistics, Division of Industry Prices and Price Indexes. n.e.c. stands for not elsewhere classified. - indicates no data collected for period or unavailable.

Other Chemicals and Allied Products

Producer Price Index
Base 1982 = 100

For 1947-1997. Columns headed % show percentile change in the index from the previous period for which an index is available.

Year	Jan Index	%	Feb Index	%	Mar Index	%	Apr Index	%	May Index	%	Jun Index	%	Jul Index	%	Aug Index	%	Sep Index	%	Oct Index	%	Nov Index	%	Dec Index	%
1947	31.7	-	31.8	0.3	32.2	1.3	32.7	1.6	31.1	-4.9	30.8	-1.0	30.0	-2.6	30.0	0.0	30.1	0.3	32.1	6.6	33.4	4.0	34.2	2.4
1948	34.4	0.6	33.9	-1.5	33.2	-2.1	33.1	-0.3	32.2	-2.7	31.7	-1.6	32.1	1.3	32.2	0.3	32.1	-0.3	31.9	-0.6	31.8	-0.3	31.3	-1.6
1949	30.8	-1.6	30.0	-2.6	29.7	-1.0	29.0	-2.4	28.5	-1.7	28.5	0.0	28.0	-1.8	27.7	-1.1	27.8	0.4	27.8	0.0	27.8	0.0	27.7	-0.4
1950	27.3	-1.4	27.3	0.0	27.3	0.0	27.3	0.0	27.3	0.0	27.2	-0.4	27.2	0.0	28.5	4.8	29.7	4.2	30.2	1.7	30.7	1.7	32.0	4.2
1951	32.8	2.5	33.4	1.8	32.6	-2.4	32.4	-0.6	32.4	0.0	32.3	-0.3	31.7	-1.9	31.1	-1.9	30.7	-1.3	30.7	0.0	30.7	0.0	30.5	-0.7
1952	30.1	-1.3	30.1	0.0	30.1	0.0	29.7	-1.3	29.7	0.0	29.7	0.0	29.7	0.0	29.7	0.0	29.7	0.0	29.6	-0.3	29.5	-0.3	29.6	0.3
1953	29.6	0.0	29.5	-0.3	29.5	0.0	29.6	0.3	29.6	0.0	29.5	-0.3	29.5	0.0	29.4	-0.3	29.5	0.3	29.6	0.3	30.1	1.7	30.2	0.3
1954	30.4	0.7	31.0	2.0	31.4	1.3	31.4	0.0	31.4	0.0	31.3	-0.3	31.4	0.3	31.2	-0.6	31.3	0.3	31.4	0.3	31.4	0.0	31.5	0.3
1955	31.5	0.0	31.7	0.6	31.5	-0.6	31.4	-0.3	31.4	0.0	31.4	0.0	31.4	0.0	31.4	0.0	31.4	0.0	31.7	1.0	31.7	0.0	31.7	0.0
1956	31.8	0.3	31.8	0.0	31.7	-0.3	31.8	0.3	31.9	0.3	32.7	2.5	32.7	0.0	32.6	-0.3	32.6	0.0	32.8	0.6	33.0	0.6	33.0	0.0
1957	33.1	0.3	33.3	0.6	33.3	0.0	33.3	0.0	33.3	0.0	33.2	-0.3	33.5	0.9	33.5	0.0	34.1	1.8	34.1	0.0	34.1	0.0	34.2	0.3
1958	34.1	-0.3	34.1	0.0	34.1	0.0	34.4	0.9	34.4	0.0	34.4	0.0	34.4	0.0	34.4	0.0	34.5	0.3	34.4	-0.3	34.4	0.0	34.4	0.0
1959	34.6	0.6	34.5	-0.3	34.5	0.0	34.5	0.0	34.6	0.3	34.6	0.0	34.7	0.3	34.7	0.0	34.7	0.0	34.7	0.0	34.7	0.0	34.8	0.3
1960	34.6	-0.6	34.6	0.0	34.6	0.0	34.6	0.0	34.6	0.0	34.6	0.0	34.6	0.0	34.7	0.3	34.8	0.3	35.1	0.9	35.0	-0.3	35.0	0.0
1961	34.9	-0.3	35.0	0.3	35.0	0.0	35.0	0.0	35.1	0.3	35.1	0.0	35.1	0.0	34.9	-0.6	34.9	0.0	34.9	0.0	34.9	0.0	34.9	0.0
1962	34.9	0.0	34.8	-0.3	34.9	0.3	34.9	0.0	34.8	-0.3	34.9	0.3	34.9	0.0	34.8	-0.3	34.9	0.3	35.0	0.3	35.0	0.0	35.0	0.0
1963	35.1	0.3	35.1	0.0	35.2	0.3	35.3	0.3	35.3	0.0	35.3	0.0	35.3	0.0	35.4	0.3	35.4	0.0	35.5	0.3	35.5	0.0	35.5	0.0
1964	35.5	0.0	35.5	0.0	35.5	0.0	35.6	0.3	35.7	0.3	35.7	0.0	35.7	0.0	35.7	0.0	35.7	0.0	35.7	0.0	35.7	0.0	35.7	0.0
1965	35.8	0.3	35.9	0.3	35.9	0.0	35.9	0.0	35.9	0.0	35.9	0.0	35.9	0.0	36.0	0.3	36.1	0.3	36.2	0.3	36.3	0.3	36.2	-0.3
1966	36.4	0.6	36.4	0.0	36.4	0.0	36.4	0.0	36.4	0.0	36.3	-0.3	36.4	0.3	36.5	0.3	36.5	0.0	36.5	0.0	36.5	0.0	36.6	0.3
1967	36.8	0.5	36.8	0.0	36.8	0.0	37.1	0.8	37.1	0.0	37.1	0.0	37.1	0.0	37.2	0.3	37.1	-0.3	37.2	0.3	37.1	-0.3	37.1	0.0
1968	37.1	0.0	37.2	0.3	37.4	0.5	37.5	0.3	37.6	0.3	37.8	0.5	37.8	0.0	37.8	0.0	37.9	0.3	37.7	-0.5	37.7	0.0	37.7	0.0
1969	37.7	0.0	38.0	0.8	38.1	0.3	38.4	0.8	38.5	0.3	38.6	0.3	38.6	0.0	38.6	0.0	38.9	0.8	39.1	0.5	39.3	0.5	39.4	0.3
1970	39.5	0.3	39.5	0.0	39.8	0.8	39.9	0.3	40.2	0.8	40.3	0.2	40.5	0.5	40.5	0.0	40.5	0.0	40.5	0.0	40.5	0.0	40.4	-0.2
1971	41.1	1.7	41.2	0.2	41.3	0.2	41.3	0.0	41.5	0.5	41.6	0.2	41.6	0.0	41.6	0.0	41.6	0.0	41.6	0.0	41.6	0.0	41.6	0.0
1972	41.6	0.0	41.7	0.2	41.7	0.0	42.0	0.7	42.2	0.5	42.1	-0.2	41.9	-0.5	42.0	0.2	42.1	0.2	42.2	0.2	42.2	0.0	42.2	0.0
1973	42.2	0.0	42.3	0.2	42.6	0.7	43.1	1.2	43.6	1.2	43.7	0.2	43.7	0.0	43.8	0.2	43.8	0.0	44.9	2.5	45.2	0.7	46.1	2.0
1974	47.0	2.0	47.1	0.2	47.5	0.8	48.7	2.5	52.3	7.4	53.6	2.5	55.0	2.6	59.4	8.0	60.2	1.3	61.3	1.8	61.5	0.3	61.6	0.2
1975	62.8	1.9	63.1	0.5	63.1	0.0	62.2	-1.4	62.0	-0.3	62.0	0.0	61.9	-0.2	62.0	0.2	62.1	0.2	62.1	0.0	62.7	1.0	63.0	0.5
1976	63.5	0.8	63.4	-0.2	63.7	0.5	63.7	0.0	63.8	0.2	63.8	0.0	62.5	-2.0	62.6	0.2	62.7	0.2	62.9	0.3	62.9	0.0	62.7	-0.3
1977	63.8	1.8	64.2	0.6	64.6	0.6	64.9	0.5	65.1	0.3	65.2	0.2	65.1	-0.2	65.3	0.3	65.4	0.2	65.4	0.0	65.7	0.5	65.9	0.3
1978	66.1	0.3	66.8	1.1	67.1	0.4	67.2	0.1	67.3	0.1	67.5	0.3	67.6	0.1	67.1	-0.7	67.1	0.0	68.1	1.5	68.2	0.1	67.5	-1.0
1979	68.2	1.0	68.4	0.3	69.0	0.9	69.2	0.3	69.9	1.0	70.5	0.9	71.0	0.7	72.0	1.4	72.5	0.7	72.9	0.6	73.6	1.0	74.6	1.4
1980	77.5	3.9	78.2	0.9	79.6	1.8	82.6	3.8	83.2	0.7	84.0	1.0	84.6	0.7	84.8	0.2	84.8	0.0	85.5	0.8	86.0	0.6	86.7	0.8
1981	90.5	4.4	90.7	0.2	91.9	1.3	94.5	2.8	94.3	-0.2	94.9	0.6	94.3	-0.6	95.3	1.1	95.3	0.0	95.1	-0.2	96.2	1.2	96.2	0.0
1982	97.7	1.6	98.1	0.4	99.4	1.3	100.0	0.6	101.0	1.0	101.4	0.4	100.4	-1.0	100.8	0.4	100.4	-0.4	99.5	-0.9	100.8	1.3	100.7	-0.1
1983	101.0	0.3	101.6	0.6	100.7	-0.9	101.7	1.0	100.7	-1.0	100.9	0.2	101.5	0.6	101.5	0.0	101.6	0.1	101.6	0.0	101.4	-0.2	101.3	-0.1
1984	101.8	0.5	101.2	-0.6	101.9	0.7	102.6	0.7	102.6	0.0	102.1	-0.5	102.7	0.6	103.0	0.3	103.5	0.5	103.5	0.0	104.1	0.6	103.7	-0.4
1985	104.4	0.7	104.7	0.3	104.8	0.1	105.4	0.6	104.9	-0.5	105.4	0.5	105.5	0.1	105.1	-0.4	106.0	0.9	105.6	-0.4	105.8	0.2	105.4	-0.1
1986	106.7	1.2	106.4	-0.3	105.5	-0.8	105.9	0.4	105.6	-0.3	106.0	0.4	105.8	-0.2	105.0	-0.8	105.5	0.5	105.8	0.3	105.8	0.0	105.3	-0.5
1987	105.9	0.6	106.0	0.1	106.2	0.2	106.1	-0.1	106.7	0.6	106.8	0.1	106.7	-0.1	107.4	0.7	107.7	0.3	107.9	0.2	108.2	0.3	108.1	-0.1
1988	108.6	0.5	109.3	0.6	109.4	0.1	110.1	0.6	110.6	0.5	111.0	0.4	112.5	1.4	113.4	0.8	114.2	0.7	114.1	-0.1	114.8	0.6	115.1	0.3
1989	115.7	0.5	116.1	0.3	116.8	0.6	117.1	0.3	117.3	0.2	117.6	0.3	117.7	0.1	118.0	0.3	118.0	0.0	118.1	0.1	117.6	-0.4	117.3	-0.3
1990	118.0	0.6	118.1	0.1	118.3	0.2	118.0	-0.3	118.1	0.1	118.1	0.0	118.5	0.3	118.8	0.3	119.6	0.7	119.7	0.1	120.4	0.6	120.6	0.2
1991	121.7	0.9	121.9	0.2	121.3	-0.5	121.4	0.1	121.1	-0.2	121.0	-0.1	120.9	-0.1	121.2	0.2	122.0	0.7	121.8	-0.2	122.1	0.2	122.1	0.0

[Continued]

Other Chemicals and Allied Products
Producer Price Index
Base 1982 = 100
[Continued]

For 1947-1997. Columns headed % show percentile change in the index from the previous period for which an index is available.

Year	Jan Index	%	Feb Index	%	Mar Index	%	Apr Index	%	May Index	%	Jun Index	%	Jul Index	%	Aug Index	%	Sep Index	%	Oct Index	%	Nov Index	%	Dec Index	%
1992	122.3	0.2	122.4	0.1	122.3	-0.1	122.7	0.3	123.0	0.2	123.1	0.1	123.3	0.2	123.4	0.1	123.8	0.3	124.0	0.2	124.4	0.3	124.3	-0.1
1993	124.9	0.5	125.3	0.3	125.1	-0.2	125.5	0.3	125.6	0.1	125.7	0.1	125.6	-0.1	125.6	0.0	125.5	-0.1	125.6	0.1	125.6	0.0	125.8	0.2
1994	126.0	0.2	126.1	0.1	125.9	-0.2	126.0	0.1	126.6	0.5	126.5	-0.1	126.6	0.1	127.9	1.0	127.6	-0.2	128.4	0.6	128.3	-0.1	129.1	0.6
1995	129.8	0.5	129.5	-0.2	130.6	0.8	130.5	-0.1	130.7	0.2	130.7	0.0	130.8	0.1	130.3	-0.4	130.8	0.4	130.6	-0.2	131.4	0.6	131.5	0.1
1996	132.1	0.5	132.5	0.3	132.1	-0.3	132.2	0.1	132.5	0.2	132.4	-0.1	132.5	0.1	132.3	-0.2	132.7	0.3	132.8	0.1	132.3	-0.4	132.3	0.0
1997	132.4	0.1	132.6	0.2	132.6	0.0	132.9	0.2	133.0	0.1	133.4	0.3	133.7	0.2	133.5	-0.1	133.6	0.1	133.7	0.1	134.1	0.3	133.8	-0.2

Source: U.S. Department of Labor, Bureau of Labor Statistics, Division of Industry Prices and Price Indexes. n.e.c. stands for not elsewhere classified. - indicates no data collected for period or unavailable.

RUBBER AND PLASTIC PRODUCTS
Producer Price Index
Base 1982 = 100

For 1926-1997. Columns headed % show percentile change in the index from the previous period for which an index is available.

Year	Jan Index	%	Feb Index	%	Mar Index	%	Apr Index	%	May Index	%	Jun Index	%	Jul Index	%	Aug Index	%	Sep Index	%	Oct Index	%	Nov Index	%	Dec Index	%
1926	59.1	-	53.7	-9.1	52.8	-1.7	51.0	-3.4	50.5	-1.0	49.4	-2.2	44.0	-10.9	42.7	-3.0	42.6	-0.2	43.0	0.9	39.1	-9.1	37.0	-5.4
1927	36.6	-1.1	36.3	-0.8	36.9	1.7	36.8	-0.3	36.9	0.3	36.0	-2.4	35.6	-1.1	35.5	-0.3	35.2	-0.8	34.3	-2.6	33.8	-1.5	34.5	2.1
1928	34.3	-0.6	32.5	-5.2	31.5	-3.1	30.1	-4.4	29.7	-1.3	27.2	-8.4	26.3	-3.3	26.3	0.0	26.1	-0.8	25.6	-1.9	25.0	-2.3	24.9	-0.4
1929	25.2	1.2	25.6	1.6	25.7	0.4	25.1	-2.3	24.9	-0.8	24.7	-0.8	24.8	0.4	24.6	-0.8	24.5	-0.4	24.2	-1.2	23.2	-4.1	23.1	-0.4
1930	22.9	-0.9	23.0	0.4	22.9	-0.4	22.8	-0.4	22.7	-0.4	21.3	-6.2	21.0	-1.4	20.6	-1.9	20.2	-1.9	20.2	0.0	20.5	1.5	20.4	-0.5
1931	19.2	-5.9	19.0	-1.0	19.0	0.0	18.7	-1.6	18.7	0.0	18.4	-1.6	18.4	0.0	18.1	-1.6	18.1	0.0	18.1	0.0	17.9	-1.1	16.1	-10.1
1932	15.7	-2.5	15.5	-1.3	15.2	-1.9	15.1	-0.7	15.1	0.0	15.2	0.7	15.4	1.3	15.6	1.3	16.5	5.8	17.1	3.6	17.1	0.0	17.1	0.0
1933	17.0	-0.6	16.2	-4.7	15.8	-2.5	14.5	-8.2	14.9	2.8	16.1	8.1	17.1	6.2	17.5	2.3	17.5	0.0	17.6	0.6	17.9	1.7	17.9	0.0
1934	18.0	0.6	18.4	2.2	18.9	2.7	19.1	1.1	19.5	2.1	19.5	0.0	19.7	1.0	20.0	1.5	19.9	-0.5	19.6	-1.5	20.3	3.6	20.3	0.0
1935	20.3	0.0	20.3	0.0	19.7	-3.0	19.6	-0.5	19.3	-1.5	19.4	0.5	19.3	-0.5	19.3	0.0	19.2	-0.5	19.5	1.6	19.6	0.5	19.6	0.0
1936	19.9	1.5	20.1	1.0	20.2	0.5	20.3	0.5	21.1	3.9	21.2	0.5	21.3	0.5	21.3	0.0	21.3	0.0	21.3	0.0	22.5	5.6	23.0	2.2
1937	23.9	3.9	24.4	2.1	25.8	5.7	26.1	1.2	25.6	-1.9	25.2	-1.6	25.0	-0.8	24.9	-0.4	24.9	0.0	24.3	-2.4	24.0	-1.2	24.0	0.0
1938	24.3	1.2	24.3	0.0	24.1	-0.8	23.7	-1.7	23.6	-0.4	23.9	1.3	24.4	2.1	24.6	0.8	24.6	0.0	24.9	1.2	25.2	1.2	25.2	0.0
1939	25.1	-0.4	25.3	0.8	25.5	0.8	25.4	-0.4	25.5	0.4	25.5	0.0	25.5	0.0	25.5	0.0	27.0	5.9	26.4	-2.2	23.5	-11.0	24.4	3.8
1940	24.2	-0.8	24.0	-0.8	24.0	0.0	23.0	-4.2	23.5	2.2	23.8	1.3	23.7	-0.4	23.3	-1.7	23.1	-0.9	23.4	1.3	23.6	0.9	24.3	3.0
1941	24.2	-0.4	24.3	0.4	24.6	1.2	24.7	0.4	24.7	0.0	24.2	-2.0	24.5	1.2	25.8	5.3	25.7	-0.4	27.3	6.2	27.9	2.2	27.9	0.0
1942	27.8	-0.4	27.8	0.0	27.8	0.0	28.4	2.2	30.5	7.4	30.5	0.0	30.5	0.0	30.5	0.0	30.5	0.0	30.5	0.0	30.5	0.0	30.5	0.0
1943	30.5	0.0	30.5	0.0	30.5	0.0	30.5	0.0	30.5	0.0	30.5	0.0	30.5	0.0	30.5	0.0	30.5	0.0	30.5	0.0	30.5	0.0	30.5	0.0
1944	30.5	0.0	30.6	0.3	30.6	0.0	30.6	0.0	29.8	-2.6	29.8	0.0	29.8	0.0	29.8	0.0	29.8	0.0	29.8	0.0	29.8	0.0	29.8	0.0
1945	29.9	0.3	29.9	0.0	29.9	0.0	29.4	-1.7	28.9	-1.7	28.9	0.0	28.9	0.0	28.9	0.0	28.9	0.0	28.9	0.0	28.9	0.0	28.9	0.0
1946	28.9	0.0	28.9	0.0	28.9	0.0	28.9	0.0	28.9	0.0	29.2	1.0	29.5	1.0	29.6	0.3	29.7	0.3	29.7	0.0	29.7	0.0	29.9	0.7
1947	30.4	1.7	30.5	0.3	30.5	0.0	30.4	-0.3	29.9	-1.6	28.4	-5.0	27.8	-2.1	27.8	0.0	28.0	0.7	28.5	1.8	29.0	1.8	29.4	1.4
1948	29.6	0.7	29.5	-0.3	29.5	0.0	29.7	0.7	29.8	0.3	29.8	0.0	30.7	3.0	30.7	0.0	30.7	0.0	30.7	0.0	30.5	-0.7	30.3	-0.7
1949	30.2	-0.3	30.0	-0.7	30.0	0.0	29.7	-1.0	29.6	-0.3	28.8	-2.7	28.4	-1.4	28.3	-0.4	28.4	0.4	28.3	-0.4	28.8	1.8	29.5	2.4
1950	29.7	0.7	29.9	0.7	29.9	0.0	30.6	2.3	31.5	2.9	32.3	2.5	34.1	5.6	38.2	12.0	39.9	4.5	41.5	4.0	44.0	6.0	44.9	2.0
1951	45.2	0.7	45.0	-0.4	45.0	0.0	44.7	-0.7	44.6	-0.2	43.8	-1.8	42.6	-2.7	42.6	0.0	42.7	0.2	42.7	0.0	42.7	0.0	42.6	-0.2
1952	42.5	-0.2	42.3	-0.5	41.9	-0.9	41.5	-1.0	41.4	-0.2	39.4	-4.8	38.4	-2.5	37.7	-1.8	37.3	-1.1	37.2	-0.3	37.3	0.3	37.7	1.1
1953	37.6	-0.3	37.2	-1.1	37.1	-0.3	36.8	-0.8	37.0	0.5	36.9	-0.3	36.8	-0.3	36.4	-1.1	36.6	0.5	36.6	0.0	36.7	0.3	36.8	0.3
1954	36.8	0.0	36.8	0.0	36.9	0.3	36.9	0.0	36.9	0.0	37.2	0.8	37.4	0.5	37.3	-0.3	37.5	0.5	37.9	1.1	38.8	2.4	38.9	0.3
1955	40.4	3.9	41.5	2.7	40.7	-1.9	40.8	0.2	40.7	-0.2	41.4	1.7	42.3	2.2	43.9	3.8	44.7	1.8	43.6	-2.5	44.4	1.8	44.5	0.2
1956	43.8	-1.6	43.4	-0.9	43.1	-0.7	42.8	-0.7	42.3	-1.2	42.2	-0.2	42.3	0.2	43.3	2.4	43.0	-0.7	43.0	0.0	43.3	0.7	43.7	0.9
1957	42.8	-2.1	42.5	-0.7	42.6	0.2	42.6	0.0	42.7	0.2	42.8	0.2	42.8	0.0	43.3	1.2	43.2	-0.2	43.1	-0.2	42.7	-0.9	43.0	0.7
1958	42.8	-0.5	42.7	-0.2	42.7	0.0	42.6	-0.2	42.4	-0.5	42.6	0.5	42.7	0.2	42.7	0.0	42.9	0.5	43.2	0.7	43.3	0.2	43.0	-0.7
1959	42.8	-0.5	42.9	0.2	43.1	0.5	43.3	0.5	43.7	0.9	43.1	-1.4	43.1	0.0	41.5	-3.7	41.8	0.7	41.8	0.0	42.6	1.9	41.9	-1.6
1960	42.3	1.0	42.7	0.9	42.7	0.0	42.7	0.0	43.2	1.2	43.3	0.2	43.3	0.0	42.9	-0.9	42.8	-0.2	42.7	-0.2	42.4	-0.7	41.6	-1.9
1961	41.2	-1.0	41.2	0.0	41.3	0.2	41.3	0.0	41.4	0.2	41.2	-0.5	41.0	-0.5	41.1	0.2	41.2	0.2	41.1	-0.2	40.9	-0.5	40.4	-1.2
1962	40.2	-0.5	40.0	-0.5	40.0	0.0	39.7	-0.7	39.9	0.5	39.8	-0.3	39.7	-0.3	39.7	0.0	39.7	0.0	39.8	0.3	40.1	0.8	40.4	0.7
1963	40.3	-0.2	40.3	0.0	40.2	-0.2	40.2	0.0	39.9	-0.7	39.8	-0.3	39.8	0.0	40.1	0.8	39.9	-0.5	40.3	1.0	40.3	0.0	40.1	-0.5
1964	40.1	0.0	40.0	-0.2	40.1	0.2	39.8	-0.7	39.6	-0.5	39.2	-1.0	39.2	0.0	39.2	0.0	39.3	0.3	39.4	0.3	39.4	0.0	39.4	0.0
1965	39.5	0.3	39.4	-0.3	39.4	0.0	39.5	0.3	39.7	0.5	39.8	0.3	39.8	0.0	39.9	0.3	39.9	0.0	39.9	0.0	40.0	0.3	40.0	0.0
1966	40.1	0.2	40.2	0.2	40.3	0.2	40.8	1.2	40.8	0.0	40.8	0.0	40.6	-0.5	40.6	0.0	40.5	-0.2	40.4	-0.2	40.6	0.5	40.6	0.0
1967	40.9	0.7	41.0	0.2	41.0	0.0	41.0	0.0	40.9	-0.2	40.9	0.0	40.9	0.0	41.8	2.2	42.0	0.5	42.2	0.5	42.4	0.5	42.4	0.0
1968	42.4	0.0	42.5	0.2	42.5	0.0	42.5	0.0	42.6	0.2	42.7	0.2	42.9	0.5	43.1	0.5	43.1	0.0	43.2	0.2	43.2	0.0	43.3	0.2
1969	42.8	-1.2	43.0	0.5	43.1	0.2	43.3	0.5	43.2	-0.2	43.2	0.0	43.8	1.4	44.0	0.5	43.8	-0.5	44.2	0.9	44.5	0.7	44.5	0.0
1970	44.7	0.4	44.6	-0.2	44.6	0.0	44.5	-0.2	44.4	-0.2	44.4	0.0	45.0	1.4	45.2	0.4	45.2	0.0	45.2	0.0	45.2	0.0	45.2	0.0

[Continued]

RUBBER AND PLASTIC PRODUCTS
Producer Price Index
Base 1982 = 100
[Continued]

For 1926-1997. Columns headed % show percentile change in the index from the previous period for which an index is available.

Year	Jan Index	%	Feb Index	%	Mar Index	%	Apr Index	%	May Index	%	Jun Index	%	Jul Index	%	Aug Index	%	Sep Index	%	Oct Index	%	Nov Index	%	Dec Index	%
1971	44.9	-0.7	45.1	0.4	45.1	0.0	45.1	0.0	45.0	-0.2	45.0	0.0	45.3	0.7	45.5	0.4	45.4	-0.2	45.3	-0.2	45.3	0.0	45.3	0.0
1972	45.4	0.2	45.3	-0.2	45.1	-0.4	45.1	0.0	45.1	0.0	45.1	0.0	45.3	0.4	45.4	0.2	45.4	0.0	45.4	0.0	45.5	0.2	45.5	0.0
1973	45.6	0.2	45.6	0.0	45.7	0.2	45.8	0.2	46.2	0.9	46.6	0.9	46.8	0.4	46.9	0.2	46.7	-0.4	47.2	1.1	47.6	0.8	48.3	1.5
1974	48.8	1.0	49.6	1.6	51.3	3.4	53.6	4.5	55.4	3.4	56.2	1.4	57.8	2.8	59.4	2.8	60.3	1.5	61.1	1.3	61.5	0.7	61.9	0.7
1975	62.0	0.2	62.2	0.3	62.0	-0.3	61.9	-0.2	61.7	-0.3	61.6	-0.2	62.2	1.0	62.2	0.0	62.5	0.5	62.8	0.5	62.9	0.2	62.9	0.0
1976	63.1	0.3	63.9	1.3	64.4	0.8	64.9	0.8	65.1	0.3	65.1	0.0	65.6	0.8	66.7	1.7	67.9	1.8	68.2	0.4	68.3	0.1	68.2	-0.1
1977	68.2	0.0	68.0	-0.3	68.2	0.3	68.7	0.7	68.9	0.3	69.4	0.7	70.0	0.9	70.1	0.1	70.2	0.1	70.5	0.4	70.5	0.0	70.5	0.0
1978	70.5	0.0	70.5	0.0	71.0	0.7	71.6	0.8	72.0	0.6	72.3	0.4	72.5	0.3	72.8	0.4	73.2	0.5	73.8	0.8	74.3	0.7	74.4	0.1
1979	74.9	0.7	75.9	1.3	77.0	1.4	78.2	1.6	79.0	1.0	80.0	1.3	81.0	1.3	82.4	1.7	83.1	0.8	84.1	1.2	84.9	1.0	85.3	0.5
1980	86.1	0.9	87.3	1.4	88.1	0.9	88.7	0.7	89.1	0.5	90.0	1.0	90.7	0.8	91.3	0.7	92.0	0.8	92.3	0.3	92.6	0.3	92.5	-0.1
1981	93.2	0.8	93.8	0.6	94.6	0.9	95.6	1.1	96.1	0.5	96.7	0.6	96.2	-0.5	97.0	0.8	97.7	0.7	98.3	0.6	98.6	0.3	98.7	0.1
1982	98.3	-0.4	99.2	0.9	99.8	0.6	99.9	0.1	100.3	0.4	100.5	0.2	100.3	-0.2	100.5	0.2	100.5	0.0	100.4	-0.1	100.1	-0.3	100.3	0.2
1983	100.6	0.3	100.4	-0.2	100.2	-0.2	100.7	0.5	100.8	0.1	100.7	-0.1	100.8	0.1	101.0	0.2	100.8	-0.2	101.2	0.4	100.9	-0.3	101.0	0.1
1984	101.4	0.4	102.0	0.6	102.1	0.1	102.4	0.3	102.5	0.1	102.6	0.1	102.6	0.0	102.6	0.0	102.9	0.3	102.2	-0.7	102.0	-0.2	101.9	-0.1
1985	102.2	0.3	102.1	-0.1	102.1	0.0	102.2	0.1	102.1	-0.1	102.0	-0.1	101.9	-0.1	101.4	-0.5	101.5	0.1	101.6	0.1	101.7	0.1	101.9	0.2
1986	102.3	0.4	102.5	0.2	102.2	-0.3	102.2	0.0	102.0	-0.2	102.0	0.0	101.7	-0.3	102.0	0.3	101.8	-0.2	101.5	-0.3	101.3	-0.2	101.2	-0.1
1987	101.5	0.3	101.6	0.1	101.4	-0.2	101.8	0.4	102.0	0.2	102.3	0.3	102.9	0.6	103.2	0.3	103.7	0.5	104.4	0.7	105.1	0.7	105.5	0.4
1988	106.2	0.7	106.9	0.7	107.7	0.7	108.2	0.5	108.8	0.6	109.1	0.3	109.8	0.6	110.6	0.7	111.0	0.4	111.1	0.1	111.2	0.1	111.3	0.1
1989	111.9	0.5	112.2	0.3	112.7	0.4	113.0	0.3	113.0	0.0	112.8	-0.2	112.8	0.0	112.6	-0.2	112.7	0.1	112.5	-0.2	112.5	0.0	112.9	0.4
1990	113.2	0.3	112.9	-0.3	113.3	0.4	113.3	0.0	113.5	0.2	113.2	-0.3	113.1	-0.1	113.2	0.1	113.4	0.2	114.2	0.7	115.0	0.7	115.4	0.3
1991	116.0	0.5	116.0	0.0	115.8	-0.2	115.5	-0.3	115.2	-0.3	115.0	-0.2	114.8	-0.2	114.7	-0.1	114.6	-0.1	114.7	0.1	114.6	-0.1	114.7	0.1
1992	114.7	0.0	114.3	-0.3	114.3	0.0	114.6	0.3	114.9	0.3	115.0	0.1	115.2	0.2	115.3	0.1	115.5	0.2	115.7	0.2	115.8	0.1	115.7	-0.1
1993	115.7	0.0	115.7	0.0	115.6	-0.1	116.0	0.3	115.8	-0.2	115.9	0.1	115.9	0.0	116.0	0.1	116.4	0.3	116.5	0.1	116.4	-0.1	116.5	0.1
1994	116.2	-0.3	116.2	0.0	116.2	0.0	116.2	0.0	116.5	0.3	116.7	0.2	117.1	0.3	117.4	0.3	118.5	0.9	119.6	0.9	120.3	0.6	120.9	0.5
1995	122.1	1.0	122.7	0.5	123.4	0.6	124.1	0.6	124.7	0.5	125.1	0.3	125.2	0.1	125.3	0.1	125.3	0.0	125.1	-0.2	124.7	-0.3	124.3	-0.3
1996	123.9	-0.3	123.7	-0.2	123.6	-0.1	123.4	-0.2	123.7	0.2	123.8	0.1	123.9	0.1	124.2	0.2	124.1	-0.1	123.7	-0.3	123.7	0.0	123.7	0.0
1997	123.2	-0.4	123.1	-0.1	122.9	-0.2	123.2	0.2	123.3	0.1	123.2	-0.1	123.3	0.1	123.4	0.1	123.3	-0.1	123.2	-0.1	123.2	0.0	123.1	-0.1

Source: U.S. Department of Labor, Bureau of Labor Statistics, Division of Industry Prices and Price Indexes. n.e.c. stands for not elsewhere classified. - indicates no data collected for period or unavailable.

Rubber and Rubber Products
Producer Price Index
Base 1982 = 100

For 1967-1997. Columns headed % show percentile change in the index from the previous period for which an index is available.

Year	Jan Index	%	Feb Index	%	Mar Index	%	Apr Index	%	May Index	%	Jun Index	%	Jul Index	%	Aug Index	%	Sep Index	%	Oct Index	%	Nov Index	%	Dec Index	%
1967	36.9	-	36.9	0.0	37.0	0.3	37.0	0.0	36.9	-0.3	36.9	0.0	36.9	0.0	37.6	1.9	37.8	0.5	38.1	0.8	38.2	0.3	38.2	0.0
1968	38.2	0.0	38.3	0.3	38.3	0.0	38.3	0.0	38.4	0.3	38.5	0.3	38.7	0.5	38.8	0.3	38.8	0.0	38.9	0.3	38.9	0.0	39.0	0.3
1969	38.5	-1.3	38.8	0.8	38.9	0.3	39.0	0.3	38.9	-0.3	38.9	0.0	39.5	1.5	39.6	0.3	39.5	-0.3	39.8	0.8	40.1	0.8	40.1	0.0
1970	40.3	0.5	40.4	0.2	40.3	-0.2	40.4	0.2	40.4	0.0	40.4	0.0	41.3	2.2	41.7	1.0	41.9	0.5	42.0	0.2	42.0	0.0	42.0	0.0
1971	41.5	-1.2	41.5	0.0	41.5	0.0	41.4	-0.2	41.4	0.0	41.5	0.2	42.3	1.9	42.5	0.5	42.4	-0.2	42.3	-0.2	42.3	0.0	42.3	0.0
1972	42.4	0.2	42.2	-0.5	42.2	0.0	42.2	0.0	42.2	0.0	42.3	0.2	42.5	0.5	42.7	0.5	42.7	0.0	42.7	0.0	42.8	0.2	42.8	0.0
1973	42.9	0.2	43.0	0.2	43.1	0.2	43.2	0.2	43.7	1.2	44.1	0.9	44.3	0.5	44.4	0.2	44.2	-0.5	44.9	1.6	45.3	0.9	46.1	1.8
1974	46.6	1.1	47.4	1.7	49.1	3.6	49.7	1.2	50.7	2.0	51.1	0.8	52.4	2.5	53.5	2.1	53.8	0.6	54.4	1.1	54.6	0.4	55.2	1.1
1975	55.5	0.5	55.9	0.7	56.0	0.2	56.1	0.2	56.1	0.0	56.1	0.0	57.2	2.0	57.2	0.0	57.3	0.2	57.5	0.3	57.7	0.3	57.8	0.2
1976	58.0	0.3	58.4	0.7	59.2	1.4	59.3	0.2	59.4	0.2	59.5	0.2	59.9	0.7	62.1	3.7	63.4	2.1	64.0	0.9	64.0	0.0	64.0	0.0
1977	63.9	-0.2	63.0	-1.4	63.2	0.3	64.2	1.6	64.2	0.0	64.6	0.6	65.3	1.1	65.5	0.3	65.8	0.5	66.2	0.6	66.2	0.0	66.3	0.2
1978	66.5	0.3	66.5	0.0	66.9	0.6	68.0	1.6	68.9	1.3	69.3	0.6	69.5	0.3	69.8	0.4	70.2	0.6	71.1	1.3	71.9	1.1	72.0	0.1
1979	72.7	1.0	73.8	1.5	74.5	0.9	75.1	0.8	75.7	0.8	76.5	1.1	78.3	2.4	80.1	2.3	81.1	1.2	82.3	1.5	83.5	1.5	83.8	0.4
1980	84.5	0.8	86.4	2.2	86.5	0.1	87.1	0.7	87.6	0.6	88.4	0.9	89.3	1.0	89.7	0.4	90.6	1.0	91.3	0.8	91.5	0.2	91.5	0.0
1981	91.9	0.4	92.8	1.0	94.1	1.4	94.5	0.4	95.0	0.5	95.9	0.9	95.1	-0.8	95.9	0.8	97.2	1.4	98.2	1.0	98.7	0.5	98.8	0.1
1982	98.0	-0.8	99.3	1.3	99.6	0.3	99.6	0.0	100.5	0.9	100.6	0.1	100.4	-0.2	100.9	0.5	100.6	-0.3	100.4	-0.2	100.0	-0.4	100.2	0.2
1983	100.7	0.5	100.2	-0.5	99.8	-0.4	99.7	-0.1	99.7	0.0	99.2	-0.5	99.0	-0.2	99.0	0.0	98.5	-0.5	98.9	0.4	98.7	-0.2	98.8	0.1
1984	99.5	0.7	99.6	0.1	99.1	-0.5	99.8	0.7	99.4	-0.4	99.5	0.1	99.5	0.0	99.9	0.4	100.1	0.2	98.9	-1.2	98.5	-0.4	98.5	0.0
1985	98.7	0.2	99.1	0.4	99.0	-0.1	98.9	-0.1	99.0	0.1	98.7	-0.3	98.9	0.2	98.5	-0.4	98.6	0.1	98.5	-0.1	98.7	0.2	98.4	-0.3
1986	98.7	0.3	99.0	0.3	98.9	-0.1	98.8	-0.1	98.6	-0.2	98.5	-0.1	97.9	-0.6	97.8	-0.1	97.6	-0.2	97.6	0.0	97.0	-0.6	97.0	0.0
1987	97.5	0.5	97.5	0.0	97.4	-0.1	98.1	0.7	98.5	0.4	99.0	0.5	100.1	1.1	100.2	0.1	100.4	0.2	100.9	0.5	101.1	0.2	101.8	0.7
1988	102.3	0.5	102.5	0.2	102.6	0.1	102.9	0.3	102.6	-0.3	103.1	0.5	103.7	0.6	104.4	0.7	104.6	0.2	104.5	-0.1	104.5	0.0	104.9	0.4
1989	105.8	0.9	106.4	0.6	106.8	0.4	107.1	0.3	107.4	0.3	107.4	0.0	107.3	-0.1	107.1	-0.2	106.9	-0.2	107.2	0.3	107.4	0.2	107.7	0.3
1990	107.9	0.2	107.6	-0.3	108.5	0.8	108.1	-0.4	108.2	0.1	108.1	-0.1	108.1	0.0	108.5	0.4	108.6	0.1	109.2	0.6	110.1	0.8	110.4	0.3
1991	110.6	0.2	110.6	0.0	110.4	-0.2	109.9	-0.5	109.8	-0.1	109.7	-0.1	109.1	-0.5	108.8	-0.3	108.6	-0.2	109.1	0.5	109.1	0.0	109.0	-0.1
1992	109.2	0.2	109.1	-0.1	109.0	-0.1	108.9	-0.1	109.0	0.1	109.8	0.7	109.8	0.0	110.0	0.2	110.3	0.3	110.3	0.0	111.0	0.6	111.0	0.0
1993	110.4	-0.5	110.3	-0.1	110.4	0.1	110.9	0.5	110.9	0.0	111.0	0.1	111.0	0.0	110.9	-0.1	111.1	0.2	111.1	0.0	111.0	-0.1	111.0	0.0
1994	110.9	-0.1	110.8	-0.1	110.9	0.1	111.2	0.3	111.4	0.2	111.8	0.4	112.0	0.2	112.0	0.0	112.2	0.2	113.0	0.7	113.4	0.4	113.5	0.1
1995	114.5	0.9	115.1	0.5	116.1	0.9	116.5	0.3	116.9	0.3	117.7	0.7	118.2	0.4	118.3	0.1	118.3	0.0	118.3	0.0	118.2	-0.1	117.5	-0.6
1996	116.8	-0.6	116.4	-0.3	116.3	-0.1	116.5	0.2	116.6	0.1	116.0	-0.5	116.1	0.1	116.5	0.3	116.5	0.0	116.1	-0.3	115.9	-0.2	116.5	0.5
1997	116.5	0.0	116.1	-0.3	116.0	-0.1	116.3	0.3	116.2	-0.1	115.8	-0.3	115.4	-0.3	115.6	0.2	115.8	0.2	115.8	0.0	115.3	-0.4	115.3	0.0

Source: U.S. Department of Labor, Bureau of Labor Statistics, Division of Industry Prices and Price Indexes. n.e.c. stands for not elsewhere classified. - indicates no data collected for period or unavailable.

Plastic Products
Producer Price Index
Base 1982 = 100

For 1971-1997. Columns headed % show percentile change in the index from the previous period for which an index is available.

Year	Jan Index	%	Feb Index	%	Mar Index	%	Apr Index	%	May Index	%	Jun Index	%	Jul Index	%	Aug Index	%	Sep Index	%	Oct Index	%	Nov Index	%	Dec Index	%
1971	48.4	-	49.3	1.9	49.2	-0.2	49.2	0.0	48.9	-0.6	48.8	-0.2	48.2	-1.2	48.2	0.0	48.2	0.0	48.1	-0.2	48.1	0.0	48.0	-0.2
1972	48.1	0.2	48.1	0.0	47.7	-0.8	47.6	-0.2	47.6	0.0	47.4	-0.4	47.5	0.2	47.5	0.0	47.5	0.0	47.5	0.0	47.6	0.2	47.6	0.0
1973	47.6	0.0	47.6	0.0	47.6	0.0	47.7	0.2	47.8	0.2	48.5	1.5	48.4	-0.2	48.4	0.0	48.4	0.0	48.5	0.2	48.7	0.4	49.1	0.8
1974	49.7	1.2	50.5	1.6	52.0	3.0	57.4	10.4	60.7	5.7	62.1	2.3	64.2	3.4	66.7	3.9	68.8	3.1	70.0	1.7	70.8	1.1	70.6	-0.3
1975	70.3	-0.4	70.0	-0.4	69.4	-0.9	68.9	-0.7	68.4	-0.7	67.9	-0.7	67.6	-0.4	67.4	-0.3	68.2	1.2	68.6	0.6	68.7	0.1	68.6	-0.1
1976	68.7	0.1	69.9	1.7	70.1	0.3	71.1	1.4	71.4	0.4	71.2	-0.3	71.8	0.8	71.9	0.1	72.8	1.3	72.8	0.0	72.9	0.1	72.9	0.0
1977	72.9	0.0	73.6	1.0	73.7	0.1	73.6	-0.1	74.0	0.5	74.6	0.8	75.1	0.7	75.2	0.1	75.1	-0.1	75.3	0.3	75.2	-0.1	75.1	-0.1
1978	74.9	-0.3	75.0	0.1	75.5	0.7	75.6	0.1	75.4	-0.3	75.6	0.3	75.7	0.1	76.1	0.5	76.6	0.7	76.7	0.1	77.0	0.4	77.1	0.1
1979	77.3	0.3	78.2	1.2	79.9	2.2	81.6	2.1	82.7	1.3	83.9	1.5	84.0	0.1	84.8	1.0	85.4	0.7	86.1	0.8	86.4	0.3	87.0	0.7
1980	87.9	1.0	88.2	0.3	89.9	1.9	90.4	0.6	90.7	0.3	91.8	1.2	92.2	0.4	93.1	1.0	93.5	0.4	93.4	-0.1	93.7	0.3	93.6	-0.1
1981	94.5	1.0	94.9	0.4	95.2	0.3	96.9	1.8	97.2	0.3	97.6	0.4	97.3	-0.3	98.1	0.8	98.2	0.1	98.5	0.3	98.5	0.0	98.7	0.2
1982	98.6	-0.1	99.0	0.4	100.0	1.0	100.3	0.3	100.1	-0.2	100.4	0.3	100.1	-0.3	100.2	0.1	100.3	0.1	100.3	0.0	100.3	0.0	100.5	0.2
1983	100.6	0.1	100.6	0.0	100.7	0.1	101.7	1.0	101.9	0.2	102.4	0.5	102.8	0.4	103.1	0.3	103.2	0.1	103.8	0.6	103.3	-0.5	103.4	0.1
1984	103.5	0.1	104.6	1.1	105.4	0.8	105.4	0.0	106.0	0.6	105.9	-0.1	106.0	0.1	105.6	-0.4	105.9	0.3	105.9	0.0	105.8	-0.1	105.7	-0.1
1985	106.1	0.4	105.4	-0.7	105.6	0.2	105.9	0.3	105.6	-0.3	105.7	0.1	105.2	-0.5	104.7	-0.5	104.8	0.1	105.0	0.2	105.1	0.1	105.8	0.7
1986	106.3	0.5	106.5	0.2	106.0	-0.5	106.0	0.0	105.9	-0.1	105.9	0.0	105.9	0.0	106.7	0.8	106.5	-0.2	105.9	-0.6	106.0	0.1	105.8	-0.2
1987	106.1	0.3	106.1	0.0	106.0	-0.1	106.1	0.1	106.2	0.1	106.4	0.2	106.7	0.3	107.3	0.6	107.9	0.6	108.7	0.7	109.6	0.8	109.9	0.3
1988	110.8	0.8	111.7	0.8	112.9	1.1	113.5	0.5	114.6	1.0	114.9	0.3	115.6	0.6	116.5	0.8	117.0	0.4	117.3	0.3	117.4	0.1	117.4	0.0
1989	117.8	0.3	118.0	0.2	118.5	0.4	118.8	0.3	118.7	-0.1	118.4	-0.3	118.4	0.0	118.2	-0.2	118.5	0.3	117.9	-0.5	117.9	0.0	118.3	0.3
1990	118.7	0.3	118.4	-0.3	118.5	0.1	118.7	0.2	119.0	0.3	118.6	-0.3	118.4	-0.2	118.4	0.0	118.7	0.3	119.5	0.7	120.3	0.7	120.8	0.4
1991	121.6	0.7	121.6	0.0	121.5	-0.1	121.2	-0.2	120.8	-0.3	120.6	-0.2	120.6	0.0	120.6	0.0	120.6	0.0	120.3	-0.2	120.3	0.0	120.5	0.2
1992	120.4	-0.1	119.8	-0.5	119.9	0.1	120.4	0.4	120.7	0.2	120.5	-0.2	120.8	0.2	120.9	0.1	121.1	0.2	121.3	0.2	121.3	0.0	121.0	-0.2
1993	121.3	0.2	121.3	0.0	121.2	-0.1	121.5	0.2	121.3	-0.2	121.3	0.0	121.3	0.0	121.5	0.2	122.0	0.4	122.1	0.1	122.1	0.0	122.2	0.1
1994	121.8	-0.3	121.9	0.1	121.8	-0.1	121.8	0.0	122.0	0.2	122.2	0.2	122.6	0.3	123.1	0.4	124.6	1.2	125.9	1.0	126.8	0.7	127.5	0.6
1995	129.0	1.2	129.5	0.4	130.2	0.5	131.0	0.6	131.6	0.5	131.9	0.2	131.9	0.0	132.0	0.1	131.9	-0.1	131.7	-0.2	131.1	-0.5	130.8	-0.2
1996	130.5	-0.2	130.3	-0.2	130.3	0.0	129.9	-0.3	130.3	0.3	130.7	0.3	130.8	0.1	131.1	0.2	131.0	-0.1	130.5	-0.4	130.7	0.2	130.4	-0.2
1997	129.7	-0.5	129.7	0.0	129.5	-0.2	129.7	0.2	129.9	0.2	129.9	0.0	130.2	0.2	130.3	0.1	130.0	-0.2	130.0	0.0	130.1	0.1	130.0	-0.1

Source: U.S. Department of Labor, Bureau of Labor Statistics, Division of Industry Prices and Price Indexes. n.e.c. stands for not elsewhere classified. - indicates no data collected for period or unavailable.

LUMBER AND WOOD PRODUCTS
Producer Price Index
Base 1982 = 100

For 1926-1997. Columns headed % show percentile change in the index from the previous period for which an index is available.

Year	Jan Index	%	Feb Index	%	Mar Index	%	Apr Index	%	May Index	%	Jun Index	%	Jul Index	%	Aug Index	%	Sep Index	%	Oct Index	%	Nov Index	%	Dec Index	%
1926	9.6	-	9.5	-1.0	9.5	0.0	9.4	-1.1	9.3	-1.1	9.2	-1.1	9.2	0.0	9.2	0.0	9.2	0.0	9.1	-1.1	9.3	2.2	9.2	-1.1
1927	9.0	-2.2	9.0	0.0	8.9	-1.1	8.9	0.0	8.9	0.0	8.9	0.0	8.8	-1.1	8.7	-1.1	8.6	-1.1	8.6	0.0	8.5	-1.2	8.4	-1.2
1928	8.4	0.0	8.4	0.0	8.4	0.0	8.3	-1.2	8.3	0.0	8.3	0.0	8.4	1.2	8.5	1.2	8.6	1.2	8.6	0.0	8.7	1.2	8.8	1.1
1929	8.7	-1.1	8.9	2.3	9.0	1.1	8.9	-1.1	8.8	-1.1	8.8	0.0	8.7	-1.1	8.8	1.1	8.9	1.1	8.9	0.0	8.6	-3.4	8.6	0.0
1930	8.6	0.0	8.6	0.0	8.6	0.0	8.6	0.0	8.4	-2.3	8.1	-3.6	7.8	-3.7	7.7	-1.3	7.7	0.0	7.5	-2.6	7.5	0.0	7.3	-2.7
1931	7.2	-1.4	6.9	-4.2	7.0	1.4	6.8	-2.9	6.6	-2.9	6.5	-1.5	6.4	-1.5	6.3	-1.6	6.3	0.0	6.1	-3.2	6.2	1.6	6.2	0.0
1932	6.2	0.0	6.0	-3.2	5.9	-1.7	5.8	-1.7	5.7	-1.7	5.5	-3.5	5.5	0.0	5.3	-3.6	5.4	1.9	5.4	0.0	5.4	0.0	5.4	0.0
1933	5.3	-1.9	5.4	1.9	5.5	1.9	5.5	0.0	5.7	3.6	6.4	12.3	7.1	10.9	7.4	4.2	7.7	4.1	7.9	2.6	8.1	2.5	8.1	0.0
1934	8.1	0.0	8.1	0.0	8.0	-1.2	8.1	1.3	8.0	-1.2	8.0	0.0	7.8	-2.5	7.6	-2.6	7.6	0.0	7.6	0.0	7.5	-1.3	7.5	0.0
1935	7.4	-1.3	7.5	1.4	7.4	-1.3	7.4	0.0	7.4	0.0	7.5	1.4	7.6	1.3	7.7	1.3	7.7	0.0	7.7	0.0	7.7	0.0	7.6	-1.3
1936	7.7	1.3	7.7	0.0	7.7	0.0	7.8	1.3	7.8	0.0	7.7	-1.3	7.8	1.3	7.8	0.0	8.0	2.6	8.0	0.0	8.1	1.3	8.4	3.7
1937	8.7	3.6	9.2	5.7	9.5	3.3	9.6	1.1	9.7	1.0	9.7	0.0	9.5	-2.1	9.4	-1.1	9.3	-1.1	9.2	-1.1	8.9	-3.3	8.9	0.0
1938	8.7	-2.2	8.6	-1.1	8.6	0.0	8.6	0.0	8.3	-3.5	8.3	0.0	8.3	0.0	8.4	1.2	8.5	1.2	8.4	-1.2	8.4	0.0	8.5	1.2
1939	8.6	1.2	8.6	0.0	8.6	0.0	8.5	-1.2	8.5	0.0	8.5	0.0	8.6	1.2	8.6	0.0	8.7	1.2	9.1	4.6	9.2	1.1	9.1	-1.1
1940	9.1	0.0	9.1	0.0	9.1	0.0	9.0	-1.1	9.0	0.0	9.0	0.0	9.0	0.0	9.3	3.3	10.1	8.6	10.7	5.9	11.0	2.8	11.1	0.9
1941	11.1	0.0	11.0	-0.9	11.0	0.0	11.0	0.0	11.0	0.0	11.0	0.0	11.4	3.6	11.9	4.4	12.0	0.8	12.2	1.7	12.1	-0.8	12.2	0.8
1942	12.4	1.6	12.5	0.8	12.5	0.0	12.4	-0.8	12.4	0.0	12.4	0.0	12.5	0.8	12.5	0.0	12.5	0.0	12.5	0.0	12.6	0.8	12.7	0.8
1943	12.7	0.0	12.8	0.8	12.8	0.0	12.8	0.0	12.9	0.8	13.0	0.8	13.1	0.8	13.5	3.1	13.7	1.5	13.7	0.0	13.8	0.7	13.8	0.0
1944	13.8	0.0	13.9	0.7	14.1	1.4	14.3	1.4	14.4	0.7	14.4	0.0	14.4	0.0	14.4	0.0	14.4	0.0	14.4	0.0	14.4	0.0	14.4	0.0
1945	14.4	0.0	14.4	0.0	14.4	0.0	14.4	0.0	14.4	0.0	14.4	0.0	14.5	0.7	14.5	0.0	14.5	0.0	14.5	0.0	14.5	0.0	14.6	0.7
1946	14.7	0.7	14.9	1.4	15.5	4.0	15.9	2.6	16.1	1.3	16.4	1.9	16.5	0.6	16.5	0.0	16.6	0.6	16.8	1.2	17.9	6.5	20.9	16.8
1947	23.4	12.0	23.9	2.1	24.7	3.3	25.4	2.8	25.5	0.4	25.4	-0.4	25.5	0.4	26.0	2.0	26.6	2.3	27.0	1.5	27.7	2.6	28.2	1.8
1948	28.7	1.8	28.9	0.7	29.2	1.0	29.3	0.3	29.6	1.0	29.8	0.7	30.0	0.7	30.2	0.7	30.1	-0.3	29.7	-1.3	29.5	-0.7	29.0	-1.7
1949	28.7	-1.0	28.3	-1.4	28.1	-0.7	27.8	-1.1	27.4	-1.4	27.0	-1.5	26.6	-1.5	26.3	-1.1	26.4	0.4	26.7	1.1	27.0	1.1	27.3	1.1
1950	27.7	1.5	28.3	2.2	28.9	2.1	29.3	1.4	30.3	3.4	30.9	2.0	31.7	2.6	33.1	4.4	34.3	3.6	34.0	-0.9	33.8	-0.6	33.9	0.3
1951	34.6	2.1	34.8	0.6	34.9	0.3	34.9	0.0	34.8	-0.3	34.3	-1.4	34.1	-0.6	33.7	-1.2	33.5	-0.6	33.5	0.0	33.4	-0.3	33.2	-0.6
1952	33.1	-0.3	33.2	0.3	33.2	0.0	33.3	0.3	33.3	0.0	33.1	-0.6	33.2	0.3	33.2	0.0	33.2	0.0	33.1	-0.3	33.0	-0.3	33.0	0.0
1953	33.2	0.6	33.4	0.6	33.5	0.3	33.7	0.6	33.6	-0.3	33.5	-0.3	33.4	-0.3	33.2	-0.6	32.8	-1.2	32.6	-0.6	32.3	-0.9	32.3	0.0
1954	32.2	-0.3	32.2	0.0	32.2	0.0	32.0	-0.6	32.0	0.0	32.1	0.3	32.8	2.2	32.8	0.0	32.9	0.3	33.0	0.3	33.0	0.0	33.1	0.3
1955	33.2	0.3	33.4	0.6	33.5	0.3	33.8	0.9	34.1	0.9	34.1	0.0	34.2	0.3	34.5	0.9	34.7	0.6	34.6	-0.3	34.5	-0.3	34.5	0.0
1956	34.8	0.9	34.9	0.3	35.3	1.1	35.4	0.3	35.3	-0.3	35.1	-0.6	34.9	-0.6	34.5	-1.1	34.1	-1.2	33.6	-1.5	33.5	-0.3	33.4	-0.3
1957	33.5	0.3	33.3	-0.6	33.1	-0.6	33.2	0.3	33.0	-0.6	33.0	0.0	33.0	0.0	32.9	-0.3	32.7	-0.6	32.5	-0.6	32.3	-0.6	32.2	-0.3	32.1	-0.3
1958	32.1	0.0	31.9	-0.6	31.8	-0.3	31.9	0.3	32.0	0.3	32.1	0.3	32.2	0.3	32.7	1.6	33.2	1.5	33.3	0.3	33.1	-0.6	33.0	-0.3
1959	33.2	0.6	33.8	1.8	34.2	1.2	34.8	1.8	35.3	1.4	35.5	0.6	35.4	-0.3	35.4	0.0	35.1	-0.8	34.8	-0.9	34.3	-1.4	34.4	0.3
1960	34.5	0.3	34.4	-0.3	34.3	-0.3	34.2	-0.3	34.1	-0.3	33.8	-0.9	33.5	-0.9	32.9	-1.8	32.8	-0.3	32.5	-0.9	32.2	-0.9	32.2	0.0
1961	31.9	-0.9	31.6	-0.9	31.8	0.6	32.5	2.2	32.4	-0.3	32.5	0.3	32.3	-0.6	32.0	-0.9	31.9	-0.3	31.6	-0.9	31.6	0.0	31.5	-0.3
1962	31.5	0.0	31.7	0.6	32.1	1.3	32.2	0.3	32.3	0.3	32.4	0.3	32.5	0.3	32.5	0.0	32.3	-0.6	32.2	-0.3	32.1	-0.3	31.9	-0.6
1963	32.0	0.3	32.0	0.0	32.2	0.6	32.3	0.3	32.5	0.6	32.8	0.9	33.9	3.4	34.2	0.9	33.3	-2.6	33.0	-0.9	33.0	0.0	33.0	0.0
1964	33.0	0.0	33.3	0.9	33.6	0.9	33.9	0.9	33.9	0.0	33.8	-0.3	33.7	-0.3	33.6	-0.3	33.5	-0.3	33.4	-0.3	33.2	-0.6	33.1	-0.3
1965	33.6	1.5	33.6	0.0	33.5	-0.3	33.5	0.0	33.5	0.0	33.4	-0.3	33.5	0.3	33.9	1.2	34.0	0.3	33.9	-0.3	33.9	0.0	34.0	0.3
1966	34.2	0.6	34.6	1.2	35.2	1.7	36.1	2.6	36.5	1.1	35.9	-1.6	35.5	-1.1	35.4	-0.3	35.3	-0.3	34.9	-1.1	34.3	-1.7	34.1	-0.6
1967	34.2	0.3	34.6	1.2	34.5	-0.3	34.7	0.6	34.7	0.0	34.9	0.6	35.1	0.6	35.4	0.9	36.2	2.3	35.7	-1.4	35.5	-0.6	35.9	1.1
1968	36.2	0.8	37.2	2.8	38.0	2.2	38.6	1.6	39.0	1.0	39.1	0.3	39.7	1.5	40.1	1.0	40.9	2.0	41.7	2.0	42.3	1.4	44.5	5.2
1969	45.9	3.1	48.2	5.0	49.8	3.3	47.8	-4.0	45.9	-4.0	43.3	-5.7	41.8	-3.5	41.3	-1.2	41.1	-0.5	40.9	-0.5	41.3	1.0	40.8	-1.2
1970	40.5	-0.7	40.0	-1.2	39.7	-0.7	40.0	0.8	40.3	0.7	40.0	-0.7	39.9	-0.2	40.1	0.5	40.1	0.0	39.7	-1.0	39.3	-1.0	39.0	-0.8

[Continued]

LUMBER AND WOOD PRODUCTS
Producer Price Index
Base 1982 = 100
[Continued]

For 1926-1997. Columns headed % show percentile change in the index from the previous period for which an index is available.

Year	Jan Index	%	Feb Index	%	Mar Index	%	Apr Index	%	May Index	%	Jun Index	%	Jul Index	%	Aug Index	%	Sep Index	%	Oct Index	%	Nov Index	%	Dec Index	%
1971	39.4	1.0	41.2	4.6	43.4	5.3	43.9	1.2	44.0	0.2	44.4	0.9	46.0	3.6	47.5	3.3	47.3	-0.4	46.4	-1.9	46.2	-0.4	46.7	1.1
1972	47.4	1.5	48.4	2.1	49.0	1.2	49.6	1.2	50.1	1.0	50.6	1.0	51.3	1.4	52.0	1.4	52.1	0.2	52.4	0.6	52.5	0.2	52.6	0.2
1973	53.0	0.8	56.5	6.6	60.8	7.6	63.9	5.1	65.6	2.7	64.3	-2.0	62.4	-3.0	62.8	0.6	63.9	1.8	63.3	-0.9	64.9	2.5	65.4	0.8
1974	64.5	-1.4	64.6	0.2	67.2	4.0	70.3	4.6	69.5	-1.1	67.5	-2.9	66.2	-1.9	64.5	-2.6	63.4	-1.7	59.5	-6.2	58.2	-2.2	58.1	-0.2
1975	57.9	-0.3	59.5	2.8	59.6	0.2	61.4	3.0	64.3	4.7	63.6	-1.1	63.1	-0.8	63.1	0.0	63.2	0.2	62.9	-0.5	62.6	-0.5	64.3	2.7
1976	67.0	4.2	68.9	2.8	71.1	3.2	71.4	0.4	71.1	-0.4	70.2	-1.3	71.5	1.9	72.9	2.0	74.7	2.5	75.0	0.4	75.3	0.4	77.3	2.7
1977	78.2	1.2	78.8	0.8	80.4	2.0	80.7	0.4	80.6	-0.1	80.3	-0.4	82.7	3.0	85.3	3.1	88.8	4.1	87.0	-2.0	85.5	-1.7	87.5	2.3
1978	90.0	2.9	92.6	2.9	93.5	1.0	94.7	1.3	96.0	1.4	97.8	1.9	97.4	-0.4	98.9	1.5	99.3	0.4	99.8	0.5	101.9	2.1	101.4	-0.5
1979	101.9	0.5	103.2	1.3	105.5	2.2	107.1	1.5	106.4	-0.7	105.3	-1.0	105.4	0.1	107.0	1.5	108.8	1.7	108.5	-0.3	105.0	-3.2	101.9	-3.0
1980	101.9	0.0	103.5	1.6	103.6	0.1	96.8	-6.6	95.5	-1.3	98.3	2.9	101.6	3.4	104.0	2.4	102.6	-1.3	101.5	-1.1	103.0	1.5	105.2	2.1
1981	104.1	-1.0	103.5	-0.6	103.4	-0.1	105.1	1.6	104.8	-0.3	104.7	-0.1	104.1	-0.6	103.4	-0.7	101.6	-1.7	99.8	-1.8	99.1	-0.7	100.2	1.1
1982	100.3	0.1	100.2	-0.1	100.2	0.0	100.6	0.4	99.9	-0.7	101.5	1.6	101.4	-0.1	99.8	-1.6	99.4	-0.4	98.1	-1.3	98.3	0.2	100.3	2.0
1983	103.0	2.7	106.4	3.3	107.4	0.9	107.9	0.5	108.2	0.3	110.6	2.2	110.5	-0.1	110.3	-0.2	107.3	-2.7	107.3	0.0	107.1	-0.2	108.4	1.2
1984	108.6	0.2	110.9	2.1	111.3	0.4	110.7	-0.5	108.3	-2.2	107.9	-0.4	106.9	-0.9	107.0	0.1	106.5	-0.5	105.5	-0.9	105.7	0.2	106.4	0.7
1985	106.9	0.5	106.5	-0.4	106.4	-0.1	105.9	-0.5	107.7	1.7	110.0	2.1	108.9	-1.0	107.3	-1.5	105.5	-1.7	105.2	-0.3	104.3	-0.9	104.7	0.4
1986	105.0	0.3	104.3	-0.7	105.8	1.4	108.4	2.5	108.2	-0.2	107.5	-0.6	107.8	0.3	107.9	0.1	108.4	0.5	107.9	-0.5	108.0	0.1	107.8	-0.2
1987	108.1	0.3	109.4	1.2	110.6	1.1	110.7	0.1	110.7	0.0	111.4	0.6	112.4	0.9	113.7	1.2	116.2	2.2	116.1	-0.1	116.9	0.7	117.1	0.2
1988	117.8	0.6	118.4	0.5	118.9	0.4	119.2	0.3	119.1	-0.1	119.3	0.2	120.0	0.6	118.8	-1.0	118.9	0.1	118.7	-0.2	118.8	0.1	119.0	0.2
1989	120.1	0.9	122.0	1.6	123.2	1.0	125.2	1.6	126.5	1.0	127.4	0.7	128.9	1.2	129.0	0.1	129.0	0.0	130.9	1.5	130.0	-0.7	128.5	-1.2
1990	129.0	0.4	129.7	0.5	130.5	0.6	132.4	1.5	132.0	-0.3	130.7	-1.0	131.3	0.5	130.2	-0.8	129.3	-0.7	127.5	-1.4	126.9	-0.5	126.8	-0.1
1991	127.6	0.6	127.2	-0.3	127.8	0.5	129.2	1.1	132.3	2.4	136.2	2.9	136.9	0.5	133.3	-2.6	133.4	0.1	133.2	-0.1	133.4	0.2	134.6	0.9
1992	137.6	2.2	142.9	3.9	145.7	2.0	147.5	1.2	147.6	0.1	146.3	-0.9	145.3	-0.7	145.4	0.1	148.7	2.3	148.7	0.0	149.5	0.5	154.4	3.3
1993	160.2	3.8	169.3	5.7	176.9	4.5	181.2	2.4	179.8	-0.8	174.1	-3.2	171.7	-1.4	171.1	-0.3	173.2	1.2	174.0	0.5	177.3	1.9	179.6	1.3
1994	184.6	2.8	183.3	-0.7	184.2	0.5	180.3	-2.1	178.2	-1.2	179.4	0.7	177.4	-1.1	177.7	0.2	178.3	0.3	177.8	-0.3	179.4	0.9	179.2	-0.1
1995	179.6	0.2	179.5	-0.1	180.6	0.6	180.4	-0.1	179.7	-0.4	178.0	-0.9	178.2	0.1	177.8	-0.2	178.9	0.6	177.2	-1.0	174.2	-1.7	173.5	-0.4
1996	172.9	-0.3	173.0	0.1	172.8	-0.1	171.9	-0.5	175.8	2.3	176.8	0.6	175.0	-1.0	177.0	1.1	180.2	1.8	177.8	-1.3	180.2	1.3	179.7	-0.3
1997	180.6	0.5	183.4	1.6	184.8	0.8	185.4	0.3	186.8	0.8	185.4	-0.7	185.9	0.3	185.0	-0.5	183.7	-0.7	180.8	-1.6	181.9	0.6	181.9	0.0

Source: U.S. Department of Labor, Bureau of Labor Statistics, Division of Industry Prices and Price Indexes. n.e.c. stands for not elsewhere classified. - indicates no data collected for period or unavailable.

Lumber
Producer Price Index
Base 1982 = 100

For 1926-1997. Columns headed % show percentile change in the index from the previous period for which an index is available.

Year	Jan Index	%	Feb Index	%	Mar Index	%	Apr Index	%	May Index	%	Jun Index	%	Jul Index	%	Aug Index	%	Sep Index	%	Oct Index	%	Nov Index	%	Dec Index	%
1926	8.3	-	8.3	0.0	8.3	0.0	8.2	-1.2	8.1	-1.2	8.0	-1.2	8.0	0.0	7.9	-1.2	7.9	0.0	7.9	0.0	8.1	2.5	8.0	-1.2
1927	7.9	-1.2	7.8	-1.3	7.7	-1.3	7.7	0.0	7.7	0.0	7.7	0.0	7.6	-1.3	7.5	-1.3	7.4	-1.3	7.4	0.0	7.3	-1.4	7.2	-1.4
1928	7.2	0.0	7.2	0.0	7.2	0.0	7.1	-1.4	7.1	0.0	7.2	1.4	7.2	0.0	7.3	1.4	7.4	1.4	7.5	1.4	7.5	0.0	7.6	1.3
1929	7.5	-1.3	7.7	2.7	7.8	1.3	7.7	-1.3	7.6	-1.3	7.6	0.0	7.5	-1.3	7.5	0.0	7.7	2.7	7.8	1.3	7.4	-5.1	7.4	0.0
1930	7.5	1.4	7.4	-1.3	7.4	0.0	7.4	0.0	7.2	-2.7	6.9	-4.2	6.8	-1.4	6.6	-2.9	6.6	0.0	6.4	-3.0	6.5	1.6	6.3	-3.1
1931	6.2	-1.6	6.0	-3.2	6.0	0.0	6.0	0.0	5.6	-6.7	5.6	0.0	5.4	-3.6	5.4	0.0	5.4	0.0	5.3	-1.9	5.3	0.0	5.3	0.0
1932	5.3	0.0	5.1	-3.8	5.0	-2.0	4.8	-4.0	4.8	0.0	4.7	-2.1	4.6	-2.1	4.5	-2.2	4.5	0.0	4.6	2.2	4.6	0.0	4.6	0.0
1933	4.5	-2.2	4.5	0.0	4.7	4.4	4.7	0.0	4.8	2.1	5.5	14.6	6.1	10.9	6.4	4.9	6.6	3.1	6.8	3.0	7.0	2.9	7.1	1.4
1934	7.1	0.0	7.1	0.0	7.0	-1.4	7.1	1.4	7.0	-1.4	7.0	0.0	6.9	-1.4	6.6	-4.3	6.7	1.5	6.6	-1.5	6.6	0.0	6.6	0.0
1935	6.4	-3.0	6.4	0.0	6.3	-1.6	6.3	0.0	6.5	3.2	6.7	3.1	6.9	3.0	6.9	0.0	6.8	-1.4	6.7	-1.5	6.6	-1.5	6.7	1.5
1936	6.8	1.5	6.8	0.0	7.0	2.9	7.1	1.4	7.1	0.0	7.1	0.0	7.0	-1.4	7.0	0.0	7.0	0.0	7.1	1.4	7.1	0.0	7.4	4.2
1937	7.8	5.4	8.3	6.4	8.6	3.6	8.6	0.0	8.5	-1.2	8.3	-2.4	8.1	-2.4	8.0	-1.2	8.0	0.0	7.8	-2.5	7.5	-3.8	7.2	-4.0
1938	7.1	-1.4	7.1	0.0	7.1	0.0	7.0	-1.4	7.0	0.0	6.8	-2.9	6.8	0.0	7.0	2.9	7.1	1.4	7.1	0.0	7.2	1.4	7.4	2.8
1939	7.4	0.0	7.4	0.0	7.4	0.0	7.4	0.0	7.3	-1.4	7.2	-1.4	7.2	0.0	7.3	1.4	7.6	4.1	8.0	5.3	8.1	1.3	8.0	-1.2
1940	8.0	0.0	7.9	-1.2	7.9	0.0	7.8	-1.3	7.8	0.0	7.7	-1.3	7.7	0.0	7.9	2.6	8.7	10.1	9.3	6.9	9.5	2.2	9.6	1.1
1941	9.6	0.0	9.5	-1.0	9.4	-1.1	9.4	0.0	9.4	0.0	9.5	1.1	9.9	4.2	10.3	4.0	10.5	1.9	10.5	0.0	10.4	-1.0	10.5	1.0
1942	10.6	1.0	10.7	0.9	10.7	0.0	10.7	0.0	10.6	-0.9	10.6	0.0	10.7	0.9	10.7	0.0	10.7	0.0	10.5	-1.9	10.9	3.8	10.9	0.0
1943	10.9	0.0	11.0	0.9	11.0	0.0	11.0	0.0	11.2	1.8	11.2	0.0	11.3	0.9	11.7	3.5	11.8	0.9	11.9	0.8	12.0	0.8	12.0	0.0
1944	12.0	0.0	12.1	0.8	12.2	0.8	12.5	2.5	12.5	0.0	12.5	0.0	12.5	0.0	12.5	0.0	12.5	0.0	12.5	0.0	12.5	0.0	12.5	0.0
1945	12.5	0.0	12.5	0.0	12.5	0.0	12.5	0.0	12.5	0.0	12.5	0.0	12.5	0.0	12.5	0.0	12.5	0.0	12.5	0.0	12.5	0.0	12.8	2.4
1946	12.8	0.0	12.9	0.8	13.6	5.4	13.9	2.2	14.0	0.7	14.2	1.4	14.4	1.4	14.4	0.0	14.4	0.0	14.4	0.0	15.5	7.6	18.4	18.7
1947	20.6	12.0	21.1	2.4	22.0	4.3	22.7	3.2	22.7	0.0	22.6	-0.4	22.8	0.9	23.2	1.8	23.9	3.0	24.2	1.3	24.9	2.9	25.4	2.0
1948	25.6	0.8	25.8	0.8	26.0	0.8	26.0	0.0	26.4	1.5	26.4	0.0	26.5	0.4	26.7	0.8	26.5	-0.7	26.2	-1.1	25.8	-1.5	25.5	-1.2
1949	25.2	-1.2	24.9	-1.2	24.7	-0.8	24.4	-1.2	24.0	-1.6	23.6	-1.7	23.3	-1.3	22.9	-1.7	23.0	0.4	23.3	1.3	23.6	1.3	23.9	1.3
1950	24.3	1.7	24.9	2.5	25.5	2.4	25.9	1.6	27.0	4.2	27.6	2.2	28.4	2.9	29.6	4.2	30.7	3.7	30.2	-1.6	30.1	-0.3	30.2	0.3
1951	30.6	1.3	30.8	0.7	30.9	0.3	30.9	0.0	30.8	-0.3	30.3	-1.6	30.0	-1.0	29.7	-1.0	29.5	-0.7	29.5	0.0	29.5	0.0	29.4	-0.3
1952	29.3	-0.3	29.4	0.3	29.4	0.0	29.6	0.7	29.5	-0.3	29.3	-0.7	29.4	0.3	29.4	0.0	29.4	0.0	29.3	-0.3	29.3	0.0	29.2	-0.3
1953	29.3	0.3	29.3	0.0	29.5	0.7	29.7	0.7	29.5	-0.7	29.4	-0.3	29.3	-0.3	29.1	-0.7	28.9	-0.7	28.6	-1.0	28.4	-0.7	28.4	0.0
1954	28.3	-0.4	28.2	-0.4	28.2	0.0	28.1	-0.4	28.1	0.0	28.2	0.4	28.9	2.5	28.9	0.0	29.0	0.3	29.2	0.7	29.2	0.0	29.2	0.0
1955	29.3	0.3	29.6	1.0	29.7	0.3	30.0	1.0	30.3	1.0	30.4	0.3	30.5	0.3	30.9	1.3	31.0	0.3	31.0	0.0	30.9	-0.3	30.8	-0.3
1956	31.2	1.3	31.3	0.3	31.7	1.3	31.9	0.6	31.9	0.0	31.6	-0.9	31.4	-0.6	31.0	-1.3	30.6	-1.3	30.2	-1.3	30.1	-0.3	29.9	-0.7
1957	30.0	0.3	29.8	-0.7	29.6	-0.7	29.6	0.0	29.4	-0.7	29.4	0.0	29.3	-0.3	29.2	-0.3	28.9	-1.0	28.7	-0.7	28.6	-0.3	28.4	-0.7
1958	28.5	0.4	28.3	-0.7	28.3	0.0	28.3	0.0	28.5	0.7	28.5	0.0	28.5	0.0	29.1	2.1	29.5	1.4	29.5	0.0	29.3	-0.7	29.3	0.0
1959	29.5	0.7	30.1	2.0	30.6	1.7	30.9	1.0	31.5	1.9	31.8	1.0	31.7	-0.3	31.8	0.3	31.6	-0.6	31.2	-1.3	30.7	-1.6	30.8	0.3
1960	30.8	0.0	30.8	0.0	30.7	-0.3	30.7	0.0	30.5	-0.7	30.1	-1.3	29.7	-1.3	29.1	-2.0	28.8	-1.0	28.4	-1.4	28.1	-1.1	28.1	0.0
1961	27.9	-0.7	27.7	-0.7	27.9	0.7	28.4	1.8	28.5	0.4	28.5	0.0	28.5	0.0	28.2	-1.1	28.1	-0.4	27.9	-0.7	27.8	-0.4	27.8	0.0
1962	27.9	0.4	28.2	1.1	28.4	0.7	28.7	1.1	28.9	0.7	29.0	0.3	29.1	0.3	29.0	-0.3	28.9	-0.3	28.7	-0.7	28.6	-0.3	28.4	-0.7
1963	28.5	0.4	28.5	0.0	28.7	0.7	29.0	1.0	29.2	0.7	29.4	0.7	30.3	3.1	30.5	0.7	29.9	-2.0	29.5	-1.3	29.5	0.0	29.4	-0.3
1964	29.4	0.0	29.8	1.4	30.1	1.0	30.3	0.7	30.3	0.0	30.2	-0.3	30.1	-0.3	30.0	-0.3	29.9	-0.3	29.8	-0.3	29.4	-1.3	29.4	0.0
1965	29.9	1.7	30.1	0.7	30.1	0.0	30.0	-0.3	30.0	0.0	30.0	0.0	30.1	0.3	30.4	1.0	30.6	0.7	30.6	0.0	30.6	0.0	30.7	0.3
1966	31.0	1.0	31.3	1.0	31.8	1.6	32.9	3.5	33.6	2.1	33.2	-1.2	32.8	-1.2	32.7	-0.3	32.5	-0.6	32.0	-1.5	31.3	-2.2	31.0	-1.0
1967	31.0	0.0	31.3	1.0	31.5	0.6	31.6	0.3	31.8	0.6	32.0	0.6	32.1	0.3	32.6	1.6	33.3	2.1	33.0	-0.9	32.8	-0.6	33.2	1.2
1968	33.9	2.1	34.8	2.7	35.7	2.6	36.7	2.8	37.2	1.4	37.1	-0.3	37.9	2.2	38.5	1.6	39.0	1.3	39.6	1.5	40.4	2.0	42.2	4.5
1969	43.9	4.0	46.3	5.5	48.9	5.6	49.0	0.2	46.3	-5.5	42.3	-8.6	39.6	-6.4	38.9	-1.8	38.5	-1.0	38.0	-1.3	38.4	1.1	38.1	-0.8
1970	37.7	-1.0	36.9	-2.1	36.5	-1.1	36.7	0.5	36.9	0.5	36.5	-1.1	36.2	-0.8	36.5	0.8	36.8	0.8	36.6	-0.5	36.1	-1.4	35.7	-1.1

[Continued]

Lumber
Producer Price Index
Base 1982 = 100
[Continued]

For 1926-1997. Columns headed % show percentile change in the index from the previous period for which an index is available.

Year	Jan Index	%	Feb Index	%	Mar Index	%	Apr Index	%	May Index	%	Jun Index	%	Jul Index	%	Aug Index	%	Sep Index	%	Oct Index	%	Nov Index	%	Dec Index	%
1971	36.4	2.0	38.7	6.3	41.5	7.2	42.5	2.4	42.9	0.9	43.5	1.4	46.1	6.0	47.6	3.3	47.5	-0.2	46.1	-2.9	45.8	-0.7	46.4	1.3
1972	47.3	1.9	48.4	2.3	49.0	1.2	49.9	1.8	50.5	1.2	51.2	1.4	52.0	1.6	52.8	1.5	53.1	0.6	53.5	0.8	53.7	0.4	54.0	0.6
1973	54.4	0.7	58.7	7.9	63.0	7.3	66.7	5.9	69.3	3.9	69.1	-0.3	67.4	-2.5	67.8	0.6	69.8	2.9	69.0	-1.1	67.9	-1.6	69.1	1.8
1974	68.6	-0.7	68.4	-0.3	71.2	4.1	74.3	4.4	73.1	-1.6	70.9	-3.0	68.9	-2.8	66.5	-3.5	64.2	-3.5	59.1	-7.9	57.3	-3.0	57.0	-0.5
1975	56.8	-0.4	58.3	2.6	58.7	0.7	60.9	3.7	64.6	6.1	64.2	-0.6	63.3	-1.4	63.7	0.6	63.3	-0.6	63.1	-0.3	62.1	-1.6	64.4	3.7
1976	67.6	5.0	70.7	4.6	74.1	4.8	74.2	0.1	73.1	-1.5	72.2	-1.2	74.4	3.0	76.0	2.2	78.6	3.4	79.0	0.5	78.6	-0.5	81.1	3.2
1977	83.0	2.3	83.5	0.6	85.7	2.6	86.5	0.9	86.3	-0.2	85.2	-1.3	88.8	4.2	92.1	3.7	97.1	5.4	94.1	-3.1	91.6	-2.7	93.6	2.2
1978	96.7	3.3	99.3	2.7	100.5	1.2	101.9	1.4	101.8	-0.1	103.2	1.4	102.7	-0.5	105.1	2.3	106.9	1.7	107.6	0.7	110.0	2.2	109.1	-0.8
1979	108.3	-0.7	109.4	1.0	112.8	3.1	114.3	1.3	114.2	-0.1	114.2	0.0	114.2	0.0	117.5	2.9	120.3	2.4	119.2	-0.9	114.4	-4.0	109.2	-4.5
1980	108.2	-0.9	109.9	1.6	109.6	-0.3	99.8	-8.9	97.0	-2.8	100.7	3.8	105.3	4.6	107.4	2.0	105.6	-1.7	103.2	-2.3	104.6	1.4	107.1	2.4
1981	106.6	-0.5	105.2	-1.3	104.9	-0.3	107.4	2.4	108.2	0.7	108.0	-0.2	107.0	-0.9	106.2	-0.7	103.0	-3.0	100.3	-2.6	98.7	-1.6	99.7	1.0
1982	99.7	0.0	99.1	-0.6	99.2	0.1	100.5	1.3	99.9	-0.6	101.6	1.7	102.7	1.1	100.3	-2.3	99.8	-0.5	98.3	-1.5	98.2	-0.1	100.6	2.4
1983	105.2	4.6	110.9	5.4	112.4	1.4	114.0	1.4	115.4	1.2	120.0	4.0	120.1	0.1	118.0	-1.7	111.5	-5.5	110.9	-0.5	110.3	-0.5	113.0	2.4
1984	113.5	0.4	117.4	3.4	119.2	1.5	118.9	-0.3	114.4	-3.8	112.8	-1.4	110.2	-2.3	110.1	-0.1	108.8	-1.2	107.6	-1.1	108.3	0.7	109.2	0.8
1985	110.4	1.1	110.4	0.0	110.7	0.3	109.4	-1.2	112.4	2.7	116.8	3.9	114.1	-2.3	110.0	-3.6	107.0	-2.7	105.3	-1.6	103.8	-1.4	104.8	1.0
1986	106.0	1.1	105.7	-0.3	108.3	2.5	113.3	4.6	113.0	-0.3	110.4	-2.3	111.1	0.6	111.3	0.2	112.9	1.4	111.1	-1.6	112.0	0.8	111.3	-0.6
1987	111.9	0.5	114.4	2.2	116.0	1.4	116.8	0.7	116.9	0.1	117.9	0.9	119.7	1.5	120.2	0.4	123.3	2.6	120.5	-2.3	120.4	-0.1	120.3	-0.1
1988	120.8	0.4	121.5	0.6	123.0	1.2	123.9	0.7	123.8	-0.1	124.4	0.5	125.1	0.6	123.2	-1.5	120.9	-1.9	120.0	-0.7	119.9	-0.1	118.8	-0.9
1989	119.8	0.8	122.3	2.1	123.4	0.9	126.5	2.5	128.5	1.6	128.7	0.2	130.0	1.0	128.8	-0.9	127.0	-1.4	127.3	0.2	123.2	-3.2	123.1	-0.1
1990	124.5	1.1	125.8	1.0	127.4	1.3	129.3	1.5	128.0	-1.0	125.9	-1.6	126.5	0.5	124.8	-1.3	123.5	-1.0	120.5	-2.4	119.4	-0.9	119.3	-0.1
1991	120.0	0.6	118.8	-1.0	119.6	0.7	121.6	1.7	125.2	3.0	132.7	6.0	133.2	0.4	125.1	-6.1	125.0	-0.1	124.5	-0.4	125.4	0.7	128.2	2.2
1992	132.3	3.2	140.9	6.5	146.4	3.9	148.6	1.5	148.7	0.1	144.1	-3.1	142.8	-0.9	142.0	-0.6	144.8	2.0	143.8	-0.7	146.9	2.2	155.5	5.9
1993	164.6	5.9	181.1	10.0	196.4	8.4	197.3	0.5	189.0	-4.2	178.7	-5.4	172.9	-3.2	175.9	1.7	179.0	1.8	181.5	1.4	188.6	3.9	195.9	3.9
1994	202.0	3.1	196.6	-2.7	197.4	0.4	188.2	-4.7	185.7	-1.3	189.7	2.2	184.4	-2.8	185.5	0.6	184.7	-0.4	181.4	-1.8	183.4	1.1	181.7	-0.9
1995	182.1	0.2	177.8	-2.4	179.3	0.8	175.7	-2.0	173.4	-1.3	169.9	-2.0	173.0	1.8	172.2	-0.5	174.1	1.1	171.0	-1.8	167.0	-2.3	165.7	-0.8
1996	165.7	0.0	166.8	0.7	169.6	1.7	172.2	1.5	181.3	5.3	184.7	1.9	181.0	-2.0	184.4	1.9	189.6	2.8	182.8	-3.6	190.3	4.1	189.3	-0.5
1997	190.2	0.5	195.3	2.7	196.4	0.6	199.9	1.8	203.3	1.7	197.9	-2.7	199.0	0.6	196.8	-1.1	192.2	-2.3	186.5	-3.0	189.0	1.3	189.1	0.1

Source: U.S. Department of Labor, Bureau of Labor Statistics, Division of Industry Prices and Price Indexes. n.e.c. stands for not elsewhere classified. - indicates no data collected for period or unavailable.

Millwork
Producer Price Index
Base 1982 = 100

For 1926-1997. Columns headed % show percentile change in the index from the previous period for which an index is available.

Year	Jan Index	%	Feb Index	%	Mar Index	%	Apr Index	%	May Index	%	Jun Index	%	Jul Index	%	Aug Index	%	Sep Index	%	Oct Index	%	Nov Index	%	Dec Index	%
1926	10.7	-	10.7	0.0	10.7	0.0	10.7	0.0	10.7	0.0	10.7	0.0	10.7	0.0	10.7	0.0	10.7	0.0	10.7	0.0	10.7	0.0	10.7	0.0
1927	10.7	0.0	10.7	0.0	10.7	0.0	10.7	0.0	10.7	0.0	10.7	0.0	10.7	0.0	10.7	0.0	10.7	0.0	10.7	0.0	10.7	0.0	10.7	0.0
1928	10.7	0.0	10.7	0.0	10.7	0.0	10.7	0.0	10.7	0.0	10.7	0.0	10.7	0.0	10.7	0.0	10.7	0.0	10.7	0.0	10.7	0.0	10.7	0.0
1929	10.8	0.9	10.8	0.0	10.8	0.0	10.8	0.0	10.8	0.0	10.8	0.0	10.7	-0.9	10.7	0.0	10.7	0.0	10.7	0.0	10.7	0.0	10.7	0.0
1930	10.7	0.0	10.7	0.0	10.7	0.0	10.7	0.0	10.6	-0.9	10.6	0.0	9.9	-6.6	9.9	0.0	9.9	0.0	9.4	-5.1	9.4	0.0	9.1	-3.2
1931	8.9	-2.2	8.7	-2.2	8.7	0.0	8.7	0.0	8.7	0.0	8.7	0.0	8.7	0.0	8.7	0.0	8.4	-3.4	8.1	-3.6	8.1	0.0	8.1	0.0
1932	8.7	7.4	8.7	0.0	8.7	0.0	8.7	0.0	8.7	0.0	8.7	0.0	8.3	-4.6	8.3	0.0	8.3	0.0	7.8	-6.0	7.8	0.0	7.8	0.0
1933	7.8	0.0	7.8	0.0	8.3	6.4	8.3	0.0	8.3	0.0	8.4	1.2	8.9	6.0	9.7	9.0	9.7	0.0	9.7	0.0	9.7	0.0	9.5	-2.1
1934	9.5	0.0	9.5	0.0	9.5	0.0	9.6	1.1	9.7	1.0	9.7	0.0	9.2	-5.2	8.7	-5.4	8.7	0.0	8.7	0.0	8.7	0.0	8.7	0.0
1935	8.7	0.0	8.7	0.0	8.7	0.0	8.7	0.0	8.7	0.0	8.7	0.0	8.9	2.3	9.6	7.9	9.6	0.0	9.6	0.0	9.6	0.0	9.6	0.0
1936	9.6	0.0	9.6	0.0	9.6	0.0	9.6	0.0	9.6	0.0	9.8	2.1	9.8	0.0	9.8	0.0	9.8	0.0	9.8	0.0	9.8	0.0	10.1	3.1
1937	10.2	1.0	10.7	4.9	10.7	0.0	10.7	0.0	12.7	18.7	12.7	0.0	12.3	-3.1	12.1	-1.6	12.1	0.0	12.1	0.0	12.0	-0.8	11.9	-0.8
1938	11.1	-6.7	11.1	0.0	11.1	0.0	11.1	0.0	10.2	-8.1	10.2	0.0	10.1	-1.0	10.1	0.0	10.1	0.0	10.2	1.0	10.2	0.0	10.2	0.0
1939	10.2	0.0	10.2	0.0	10.2	0.0	10.2	0.0	10.2	0.0	10.2	0.0	10.2	0.0	10.2	0.0	10.2	0.0	10.2	0.0	10.7	4.9	10.7	0.0
1940	10.7	0.0	10.7	0.0	10.7	0.0	10.7	0.0	10.7	0.0	11.3	5.6	11.5	1.8	11.5	0.0	11.5	0.0	11.5	0.0	12.1	5.2	12.1	0.0
1941	12.1	0.0	12.1	0.0	12.2	0.8	12.3	0.8	12.5	1.6	12.5	0.0	12.6	0.8	12.8	1.6	12.8	0.0	13.9	8.6	14.0	0.7	14.0	0.0
1942	14.0	0.0	14.0	0.0	14.0	0.0	14.0	0.0	14.0	0.0	14.0	0.0	14.0	0.0	14.0	0.0	14.0	0.0	14.0	0.0	14.0	0.0	14.0	0.0
1943	14.0	0.0	14.0	0.0	14.0	0.0	14.0	0.0	14.0	0.0	14.0	0.0	14.0	0.0	14.0	0.0	14.0	0.0	14.4	2.9	14.4	0.0	14.4	0.0
1944	14.4	0.0	14.4	0.0	14.4	0.0	14.4	0.0	14.7	2.1	14.7	0.0	14.7	0.0	14.7	0.0	14.7	0.0	14.7	0.0	14.7	0.0	14.7	0.0
1945	14.7	0.0	14.7	0.0	14.7	0.0	14.7	0.0	14.7	0.0	14.7	0.0	14.7	0.0	14.7	0.0	14.7	0.0	14.7	0.0	14.7	0.0	14.7	0.0
1946	14.7	0.0	14.7	0.0	14.7	0.0	14.7	0.0	17.0	15.6	17.0	0.0	17.0	0.0	17.0	0.0	17.5	2.9	18.3	4.6	18.4	0.5	18.4	0.0
1947	19.5	6.0	19.9	2.1	20.1	1.0	20.3	1.0	20.6	1.5	21.0	1.9	21.4	1.9	21.6	0.9	22.2	2.8	22.8	2.7	23.0	0.9	23.0	0.0
1948	23.7	3.0	23.9	0.8	24.7	3.3	24.8	0.4	24.8	0.0	25.5	2.8	26.4	3.5	26.7	1.1	26.8	0.4	26.8	0.0	26.8	0.0	26.8	0.0
1949	26.6	-0.7	26.6	0.0	26.5	-0.4	26.4	-0.4	26.4	0.0	26.3	-0.4	26.2	-0.4	26.1	-0.4	26.0	-0.4	26.0	0.0	26.0	0.0	26.1	0.4
1950	26.4	1.1	26.6	0.8	26.6	0.0	26.8	0.8	26.9	0.4	27.1	0.7	27.6	1.8	28.4	2.9	29.5	3.9	29.8	1.0	29.9	0.3	29.9	0.0
1951	31.5	5.4	32.0	1.6	31.9	-0.3	32.0	0.3	32.0	0.0	31.9	-0.3	31.8	-0.3	31.6	-0.6	31.6	0.0	31.6	0.0	31.5	-0.3	31.4	-0.3
1952	31.0	-1.3	30.8	-0.6	30.9	0.3	30.8	-0.3	30.8	0.0	30.8	0.0	30.9	0.3	31.0	0.3	31.0	0.0	31.1	0.3	31.1	0.0	31.3	0.6
1953	31.5	0.6	32.1	1.9	32.1	0.0	32.2	0.3	32.2	0.0	32.2	0.0	32.1	-0.3	32.1	0.0	32.1	0.0	32.0	-0.3	32.0	0.0	32.0	0.0
1954	32.0	0.0	32.0	0.0	32.0	0.0	31.9	-0.3	31.9	0.0	31.9	0.0	31.9	0.0	31.6	-0.9	31.7	0.3	31.7	0.0	31.7	0.0	31.8	0.3
1955	31.8	0.0	31.5	-0.9	31.4	-0.3	31.5	0.3	31.5	0.0	31.3	-0.6	31.3	0.0	31.3	0.0	31.2	-0.3	31.2	0.0	31.2	0.0	31.4	0.6
1956	31.5	0.3	31.5	0.0	31.5	0.0	31.5	0.0	31.5	0.0	31.6	0.3	31.6	0.0	31.6	0.0	31.5	-0.3	31.4	-0.3	31.3	-0.3	31.3	0.0
1957	31.4	0.3	31.4	0.0	31.4	0.0	31.3	-0.3	31.3	0.0	31.3	0.0	31.3	0.0	31.3	0.0	31.3	0.0	31.3	0.0	31.2	-0.3	31.1	-0.3
1958	31.1	0.0	31.1	0.0	31.1	0.0	31.1	0.0	31.0	-0.3	31.0	0.0	31.0	0.0	30.9	-0.3	31.1	0.6	31.8	2.3	31.8	0.0	31.8	0.0
1959	31.7	-0.3	31.7	0.0	31.7	0.0	33.0	4.1	33.5	1.5	33.5	0.0	33.6	0.3	33.8	0.6	33.8	0.0	33.8	0.0	33.7	-0.3	33.6	-0.3
1960	33.6	0.0	33.6	0.0	33.6	0.0	33.4	-0.6	33.4	0.0	33.4	0.0	33.5	0.3	33.3	-0.6	33.0	-0.9	33.0	0.0	33.1	0.3	33.0	-0.3
1961	33.1	0.3	32.9	-0.6	32.9	0.0	32.9	0.0	32.5	-1.2	32.7	0.6	32.2	-1.5	31.9	-0.9	32.3	1.3	32.3	0.0	32.2	-0.3	32.2	0.0
1962	32.2	0.0	32.1	-0.3	32.2	0.3	32.3	0.3	32.5	0.6	32.5	0.0	32.6	0.3	32.7	0.3	32.6	-0.3	32.6	0.0	32.6	0.0	32.6	0.0
1963	32.6	0.0	32.6	0.0	32.7	0.3	32.7	0.0	32.7	0.0	32.9	0.6	33.2	0.9	33.5	0.9	33.7	0.6	33.9	0.6	33.9	0.0	33.9	0.0
1964	34.0	0.3	34.1	0.3	34.2	0.3	34.7	1.5	34.8	0.3	34.8	0.0	34.8	0.0	34.8	0.0	34.8	0.0	34.8	0.0	34.8	0.0	34.8	0.0
1965	34.4	-1.1	34.3	-0.3	34.3	0.0	34.3	0.0	34.4	0.3	34.4	0.0	34.4	0.0	34.4	0.0	34.4	0.0	34.4	0.0	34.4	0.0	34.4	0.0
1966	34.4	0.0	34.6	0.6	34.9	0.9	35.0	0.3	35.2	0.6	35.3	0.3	35.3	0.0	35.4	0.3	35.4	0.0	35.4	0.0	35.2	-0.6	35.2	0.0
1967	35.2	0.0	35.5	0.9	35.5	0.0	35.6	0.3	35.6	0.0	35.6	0.0	35.8	0.6	35.9	0.3	36.1	0.6	36.2	0.3	36.2	0.0	36.3	0.3
1968	36.4	0.3	36.6	0.5	36.9	0.8	37.2	0.8	37.6	1.1	37.8	0.5	37.8	0.0	38.0	0.5	38.5	1.3	38.8	0.8	39.2	1.0	39.5	0.8
1969	39.9	1.0	40.5	1.5	41.1	1.5	42.2	2.7	42.6	0.9	43.4	1.9	43.3	-0.2	43.1	-0.5	42.9	-0.5	42.7	-0.5	42.5	-0.5	42.0	-1.2
1970	41.9	-0.2	41.7	-0.5	41.7	0.0	41.7	0.0	41.8	0.2	41.8	0.0	41.8	0.0	41.8	0.0	41.4	-1.0	40.9	-1.2	40.9	0.0	40.8	-0.2

[Continued]

Millwork
Producer Price Index
Base 1982 = 100
[Continued]

For 1926-1997. Columns headed % show percentile change in the index from the previous period for which an index is available.

Year	Jan Index	%	Feb Index	%	Mar Index	%	Apr Index	%	May Index	%	Jun Index	%	Jul Index	%	Aug Index	%	Sep Index	%	Oct Index	%	Nov Index	%	Dec Index	%
1971	40.9	0.2	41.3	1.0	41.6	0.7	42.5	2.2	43.1	1.4	43.7	1.4	44.0	0.7	44.4	0.9	44.3	-0.2	44.3	0.0	44.3	0.0	44.5	0.5
1972	44.7	0.4	44.9	0.4	45.0	0.2	45.3	0.7	45.7	0.9	46.0	0.7	46.4	0.9	46.5	0.2	46.6	0.2	46.8	0.4	46.8	0.0	46.8	0.0
1973	47.0	0.4	47.7	1.5	48.3	1.3	50.5	4.6	52.4	3.8	52.9	1.0	53.1	0.4	53.1	0.0	53.3	0.4	53.5	0.4	53.5	0.0	53.8	0.6
1974	54.2	0.7	54.3	0.2	54.9	1.1	56.1	2.2	57.5	2.5	58.4	1.6	57.9	-0.9	57.7	-0.3	57.5	-0.3	56.2	-2.3	55.0	-2.1	54.9	-0.2
1975	55.1	0.4	55.5	0.7	55.5	0.0	56.0	0.9	57.4	2.5	57.9	0.9	58.3	0.7	58.4	0.2	58.5	0.2	58.7	0.3	58.7	0.0	59.0	0.5
1976	59.8	1.4	60.5	1.2	61.7	2.0	62.7	1.6	63.6	1.4	63.7	0.2	63.5	-0.3	63.8	0.5	64.5	1.1	65.0	0.8	65.5	0.8	65.5	0.0
1977	65.7	0.3	66.6	1.4	67.4	1.2	68.2	1.2	68.5	0.4	68.9	0.6	68.8	-0.1	69.7	1.3	70.8	1.6	71.8	1.4	72.5	1.0	73.1	0.8
1978	74.9	2.5	78.5	4.8	80.8	2.9	83.7	3.6	86.1	2.9	87.7	1.9	88.3	0.7	86.5	-2.0	86.0	-0.6	85.8	-0.2	86.4	0.7	86.5	0.1
1979	87.5	1.2	90.0	2.9	92.3	2.6	95.2	3.1	93.6	-1.7	92.7	-1.0	90.4	-2.5	89.3	-1.2	89.8	0.6	91.5	1.9	90.3	-1.3	89.6	-0.8
1980	90.9	1.5	92.3	1.5	93.8	1.6	92.2	-1.7	90.1	-2.3	90.5	0.4	91.6	1.2	93.2	1.7	94.6	1.5	94.7	0.1	96.6	2.0	97.8	1.2
1981	97.9	0.1	98.0	0.1	98.7	0.7	99.0	0.3	98.4	-0.6	97.4	-1.0	97.9	0.5	97.5	-0.4	97.1	-0.4	97.1	0.0	97.3	0.2	97.9	0.6
1982	99.2	1.3	99.7	0.5	98.9	-0.8	99.0	0.1	98.9	-0.1	100.4	1.5	101.0	0.6	100.3	-0.7	100.0	-0.3	99.7	-0.3	100.3	0.6	102.5	2.2
1983	105.1	2.5	107.5	2.3	108.8	1.2	108.4	-0.4	107.0	-1.3	105.5	-1.4	106.0	0.5	109.7	3.5	109.5	-0.2	110.0	0.5	110.2	0.2	110.4	0.2
1984	110.4	0.0	110.5	0.1	110.9	0.4	109.9	-0.9	108.9	-0.9	109.2	0.3	109.8	0.5	109.9	0.1	110.0	0.1	109.9	-0.1	110.8	0.8	111.5	0.6
1985	111.9	0.4	111.5	-0.4	111.0	-0.4	110.8	-0.2	111.1	0.3	111.6	0.5	112.2	0.5	112.3	0.1	112.3	0.0	112.0	-0.3	111.9	-0.1	111.8	-0.1
1986	111.6	-0.2	111.7	0.1	112.1	0.4	112.8	0.6	113.3	0.4	114.4	1.0	114.8	0.3	115.1	0.3	115.1	0.0	114.5	-0.5	114.2	-0.3	114.2	0.0
1987	114.7	0.4	115.0	0.3	116.1	1.0	116.9	0.7	117.4	0.4	118.1	0.6	118.5	0.3	118.8	0.3	118.9	0.1	119.3	0.3	119.4	0.1	119.5	0.1
1988	119.7	0.2	120.3	0.5	120.8	0.4	121.2	0.3	121.6	0.3	121.9	0.2	122.4	0.4	122.5	0.1	122.7	0.2	123.3	0.5	122.9	-0.3	123.0	0.1
1989	123.5	0.4	125.1	1.3	126.3	1.0	127.4	0.9	128.0	0.5	128.3	0.2	127.9	-0.3	128.0	0.1	127.9	-0.1	128.2	0.2	128.3	0.1	128.7	0.3
1990	128.9	0.2	129.5	0.5	130.0	0.4	130.6	0.5	130.9	0.2	130.4	-0.4	130.5	0.1	130.5	0.0	130.6	0.1	130.5	-0.1	130.8	0.2	131.0	0.2
1991	131.5	0.4	131.6	0.1	131.9	0.2	133.6	1.3	134.3	0.5	135.8	1.1	136.9	0.8	137.6	0.5	137.6	0.0	138.0	0.3	138.1	0.1	139.3	0.9
1992	140.3	0.7	142.2	1.4	142.9	0.5	144.0	0.8	144.0	0.0	144.0	0.0	143.3	-0.5	142.3	-0.7	143.3	0.7	143.6	0.2	143.7	0.1	145.7	1.4
1993	148.0	1.6	151.8	2.6	155.9	2.7	158.8	1.9	158.2	-0.4	156.6	-1.0	155.7	-0.6	156.1	0.3	158.7	1.7	159.1	0.3	159.9	0.5	160.7	0.5
1994	162.8	1.3	163.4	0.4	163.2	-0.1	162.4	-0.5	161.5	-0.6	161.7	0.1	161.5	-0.1	161.3	-0.1	161.6	0.2	162.6	0.6	163.3	0.4	163.3	0.0
1995	163.9	0.4	163.4	-0.3	163.8	0.2	163.8	0.0	163.7	-0.1	163.7	0.0	163.9	0.1	164.0	0.1	164.2	0.1	164.0	-0.1	163.4	-0.4	163.6	0.1
1996	163.6	0.0	163.8	0.1	164.1	0.2	164.6	0.3	165.8	0.7	166.7	0.5	167.0	0.2	167.9	0.5	168.7	0.5	168.7	0.0	169.3	0.4	169.3	0.0
1997	170.1	0.5	170.3	0.1	170.4	0.1	170.8	0.2	171.2	0.2	171.4	0.1	171.5	0.1	171.4	-0.1	171.3	-0.1	171.0	-0.2	170.6	-0.2	170.8	0.1

Source: U.S. Department of Labor, Bureau of Labor Statistics, Division of Industry Prices and Price Indexes. n.e.c. stands for not elsewhere classified. - indicates no data collected for period or unavailable.

Plywood
Producer Price Index
Base 1982 = 100

For 1947-1997. Columns headed % show percentile change in the index from the previous period for which an index is available.

Year	Jan Index	%	Feb Index	%	Mar Index	%	Apr Index	%	May Index	%	Jun Index	%	Jul Index	%	Aug Index	%	Sep Index	%	Oct Index	%	Nov Index	%	Dec Index	%
1947	47.9	-	48.2	0.6	48.2	0.0	48.6	0.8	48.7	0.2	48.7	0.0	45.7	-6.2	45.7	0.0	45.7	0.0	45.7	0.0	45.8	0.2	46.9	2.4
1948	51.8	10.4	51.8	0.0	52.1	0.6	52.2	0.2	53.0	1.5	53.9	1.7	54.6	1.3	54.8	0.4	54.8	0.0	54.8	0.0	54.8	0.0	54.3	-0.9
1949	49.6	-8.7	49.0	-1.2	49.0	0.0	48.7	-0.6	47.0	-3.5	45.1	-4.0	44.5	-1.3	45.2	1.6	45.0	-0.4	45.5	1.1	46.1	1.3	47.0	2.0
1950	48.3	2.8	49.2	1.9	49.5	0.6	49.5	0.0	49.6	0.2	50.0	0.8	51.1	2.2	54.3	6.3	56.0	3.1	56.7	1.3	56.7	0.0	57.4	1.2
1951	57.7	0.5	57.9	0.3	57.9	0.0	57.9	0.0	57.9	0.0	57.9	0.0	57.5	-0.7	57.5	0.0	56.5	-1.7	56.2	-0.5	53.8	-4.3	50.5	-6.1
1952	51.2	1.4	51.5	0.6	51.9	0.8	51.9	0.0	51.9	0.0	52.0	0.2	52.0	0.0	52.1	0.2	52.1	0.0	52.2	0.2	50.3	-3.6	50.3	0.0
1953	53.4	6.2	54.5	2.1	55.1	1.1	55.1	0.0	55.3	0.4	55.3	0.0	55.4	0.2	55.3	-0.2	52.5	-5.1	51.5	-1.9	50.7	-1.6	51.1	0.8
1954	50.9	-0.4	51.6	1.4	50.6	-1.9	49.5	-2.2	49.8	0.6	49.0	-1.6	50.7	3.5	51.8	2.2	50.7	-2.1	51.3	1.2	51.3	0.0	51.3	0.0
1955	51.5	0.4	51.5	0.0	51.5	0.0	51.5	0.0	51.9	0.8	51.9	0.0	52.0	0.2	52.0	0.0	52.2	0.4	52.2	0.0	52.1	-0.2	52.0	-0.2
1956	52.8	1.5	52.8	0.0	52.8	0.0	52.6	-0.4	50.5	-4.0	49.6	-1.8	50.8	2.4	48.8	-3.9	48.8	0.0	47.2	-3.3	46.6	-1.3	46.5	-0.2
1957	47.7	2.6	47.4	-0.6	47.3	-0.2	47.5	0.4	47.6	0.2	48.0	0.8	47.6	-0.8	46.8	-1.7	46.6	-0.4	47.6	2.1	47.4	-0.4	47.0	-0.8
1958	47.0	0.0	46.0	-2.1	45.7	-0.7	46.4	1.5	45.4	-2.2	46.7	2.9	48.3	3.4	49.2	1.9	50.1	1.8	50.5	0.8	49.2	-2.6	48.7	-1.0
1959	49.0	0.6	51.0	4.1	51.1	0.2	52.4	2.5	52.4	0.0	51.7	-1.3	50.3	-2.7	49.6	-1.4	47.5	-4.2	47.4	-0.2	46.4	-2.1	47.8	3.0
1960	48.3	1.0	47.7	-1.2	47.1	-1.3	47.2	0.2	47.0	-0.4	47.0	0.0	47.0	0.0	46.6	-0.9	47.4	1.7	47.7	0.6	47.2	-1.0	46.7	-1.1
1961	45.1	-3.4	44.6	-1.1	45.2	1.3	48.7	7.7	47.8	-1.8	47.8	0.0	47.8	0.0	46.8	-2.1	46.1	-1.5	44.7	-3.0	45.0	0.7	44.8	-0.4
1962	44.5	-0.7	44.8	0.7	45.5	1.6	45.5	0.0	44.5	-2.2	44.8	0.7	44.6	-0.4	44.5	-0.2	44.5	0.0	44.4	-0.2	44.2	-0.5	43.6	-1.4
1963	43.7	0.2	43.7	0.0	44.0	0.7	43.9	-0.2	43.9	0.0	44.7	1.8	48.7	8.9	50.3	3.3	44.7	-11.1	44.6	-0.2	44.7	0.2	44.6	-0.2
1964	44.0	-1.3	44.5	1.1	45.7	2.7	45.8	0.2	45.5	-0.7	44.7	-1.8	44.6	-0.2	44.3	-0.7	44.3	0.0	44.0	-0.7	43.8	-0.5	43.6	-0.5
1965	45.6	4.6	44.9	-1.5	44.5	-0.9	44.4	-0.2	44.1	-0.7	43.7	-0.9	43.9	0.5	45.7	4.1	45.1	-1.3	44.2	-2.0	44.3	0.2	44.5	0.5
1966	45.4	2.0	45.4	0.0	47.2	4.0	49.5	4.9	48.4	-2.2	44.5	-8.1	44.2	-0.7	43.5	-1.6	43.1	-0.9	42.6	-1.2	42.0	-1.4	42.2	0.5
1967	42.2	0.0	43.1	2.1	42.3	-1.9	42.4	0.2	42.3	-0.2	42.3	0.0	43.2	2.1	43.9	1.6	46.2	5.2	43.4	-6.1	42.4	-2.3	43.6	2.8
1968	43.4	-0.5	45.7	5.3	47.0	2.8	47.0	0.0	47.0	0.0	47.4	0.9	48.9	3.2	49.2	0.6	51.5	4.7	54.0	4.9	54.4	0.7	62.3	14.5
1969	65.2	4.7	70.7	8.4	71.0	0.4	53.6	-24.5	50.0	-6.7	45.5	-9.0	45.4	-0.2	45.2	-0.4	45.6	0.9	46.4	1.8	48.1	3.7	46.8	-2.7
1970	45.9	-1.9	46.4	1.1	45.5	-1.9	47.0	3.3	47.9	1.9	47.4	-1.0	47.6	0.4	48.0	0.8	47.7	-0.6	46.5	-2.5	45.5	-2.2	45.1	-0.9
1971	45.2	0.2	48.4	7.1	51.8	7.0	49.9	-3.7	47.6	-4.6	47.5	-0.2	48.1	1.3	51.9	7.9	51.2	-1.3	49.9	-2.5	50.0	0.2	50.8	1.6
1972	51.8	2.0	53.9	4.1	55.5	3.0	55.5	0.0	56.1	1.1	56.7	1.1	57.3	1.1	58.5	2.1	58.0	-0.9	58.0	0.0	57.4	-1.0	57.0	-0.7
1973	57.8	1.4	64.4	11.4	76.2	18.3	78.6	3.1	76.6	-2.5	66.7	-12.9	59.4	-10.9	60.3	1.5	59.5	-1.3	58.0	-2.5	73.2	26.2	71.5	-2.3
1974	66.7	-6.7	68.0	1.9	73.6	8.2	81.5	10.7	77.3	-5.2	70.2	-9.2	69.4	-1.1	66.9	-3.6	68.1	1.8	63.4	-6.9	63.7	0.5	64.2	0.8
1975	63.1	-1.7	67.9	7.6	67.5	-0.6	71.1	5.3	74.4	4.6	69.9	-6.0	69.4	-0.7	68.3	-1.6	69.8	2.2	68.6	-1.7	70.2	2.3	73.1	4.1
1976	77.9	6.6	79.2	1.7	79.8	0.8	79.7	-0.1	78.8	-1.1	76.1	-3.4	78.0	2.5	80.8	3.6	82.5	2.1	82.0	-0.6	83.8	2.2	88.4	5.5
1977	88.2	-0.2	88.2	0.0	89.6	1.6	87.3	-2.6	86.2	-1.3	87.3	1.3	91.3	4.6	94.7	3.7	99.3	4.9	95.5	-3.8	92.0	-3.7	97.3	5.8
1978	99.9	2.7	100.5	0.6	97.5	-3.0	94.9	-2.7	98.4	3.7	101.7	3.4	99.7	-2.0	104.5	4.8	102.6	-1.8	103.5	0.9	107.7	4.1	107.3	-0.4
1979	110.9	3.4	110.8	-0.1	109.7	-1.0	108.7	-0.9	107.4	-1.2	102.8	-4.3	107.6	4.7	109.6	1.9	111.1	1.4	109.4	-1.5	104.3	-4.7	102.5	-1.7
1980	102.6	0.1	104.9	2.2	103.4	-1.4	94.7	-8.4	99.4	5.0	104.1	4.7	108.9	4.6	114.6	5.2	108.8	-5.1	109.0	0.2	110.6	1.5	113.5	2.6
1981	108.2	-4.7	108.2	0.0	107.2	-0.9	110.3	2.9	107.0	-3.0	108.4	1.3	106.7	-1.6	105.8	-0.8	103.8	-1.9	100.9	-2.8	100.6	-0.3	103.3	2.7
1982	102.3	-1.0	101.3	-1.0	101.9	0.6	100.8	-1.1	99.3	-1.5	103.0	3.7	100.1	-2.8	98.7	-1.4	98.4	-0.3	96.5	-1.9	98.2	1.8	99.6	1.4
1983	101.4	1.8	103.2	1.8	102.9	-0.3	103.1	0.2	103.9	0.8	110.1	6.0	108.8	-1.2	106.1	-2.5	104.3	-1.7	106.2	1.8	105.4	-0.8	106.5	1.0
1984	106.9	0.4	107.5	0.6	107.1	-0.4	104.9	-2.1	101.4	-3.3	101.8	0.4	102.2	0.4	106.0	3.7	104.9	-1.0	103.4	-1.4	101.2	-2.1	101.6	0.4
1985	100.9	-0.7	97.6	-3.3	96.3	-1.3	96.0	-0.3	100.1	4.3	102.2	2.1	102.0	-0.2	102.4	0.4	99.2	-3.1	100.8	1.6	99.0	-1.8	99.4	0.4
1986	98.9	-0.5	98.5	-0.4	100.6	2.1	105.3	4.7	103.3	-1.9	101.5	-1.7	101.6	0.1	101.3	-0.3	101.6	0.3	101.9	0.3	101.3	-0.6	100.6	-0.7
1987	100.5	-0.1	102.3	1.8	103.4	1.1	101.1	-2.2	99.3	-1.8	98.8	-0.5	100.3	1.5	102.8	2.5	107.4	4.5	104.6	-2.6	105.9	1.2	104.2	-1.6
1988	105.3	1.1	104.4	-0.9	103.4	-1.0	102.1	-1.3	100.3	-1.8	102.2	1.9	105.3	3.0	100.3	-4.7	106.3	6.0	103.1	-3.0	103.6	0.5	104.7	1.1
1989	105.9	1.1	109.9	3.8	111.1	1.1	111.3	0.2	113.4	1.9	113.4	0.0	118.4	4.4	115.2	-2.7	118.5	2.9	127.6	7.7	128.7	0.9	116.9	-9.2
1990	114.3	-2.2	115.8	1.3	116.1	0.3	125.3	7.9	122.7	-2.1	115.8	-5.6	117.6	1.6	112.6	-4.3	111.3	-1.2	106.8	-4.0	105.7	-1.0	106.7	0.9
1991	104.0	-2.5	102.7	-1.3	105.4	2.6	106.9	1.4	118.9	11.2	129.3	8.7	130.0	0.5	114.4	-12.0	116.2	1.6	112.6	-3.1	114.3	1.5	116.4	1.8

[Continued]

Plywood

Producer Price Index
Base 1982 = 100

[Continued]

For 1947-1997. Columns headed % show percentile change in the index from the previous period for which an index is available.

Year	Jan Index	%	Feb Index	%	Mar Index	%	Apr Index	%	May Index	%	Jun Index	%	Jul Index	%	Aug Index	%	Sep Index	%	Oct Index	%	Nov Index	%	Dec Index	%
1992	119.5	2.7	132.2	10.6	135.3	2.3	132.2	-2.3	130.1	-1.6	128.8	-1.0	125.2	-2.8	128.8	2.9	143.5	11.4	140.3	-2.2	138.0	-1.6	145.8	5.7
1993	154.9	6.2	164.8	6.4	168.9	2.5	158.7	-6.0	148.5	-6.4	144.0	-3.0	143.3	-0.5	146.4	2.2	149.6	2.2	147.9	-1.1	150.8	2.0	155.5	3.1
1994	159.7	2.7	153.8	-3.7	152.5	-0.8	147.8	-3.1	149.2	0.9	153.8	3.1	153.7	-0.1	157.6	2.5	165.7	5.1	164.6	-0.7	172.5	4.8	172.0	-0.3
1995	166.0	-3.5	162.8	-1.9	164.5	1.0	164.0	-0.3	165.2	0.7	159.3	-3.6	167.6	5.2	171.1	2.1	173.4	1.3	169.9	-2.0	161.7	-4.8	157.4	-2.7
1996	154.0	-2.2	154.2	0.1	152.1	-1.4	151.6	-0.3	158.3	4.4	155.8	-1.6	154.0	-1.2	157.4	2.2	166.7	5.9	160.1	-4.0	157.9	-1.4	155.3	-1.6
1997	154.5	-0.5	158.8	2.8	163.6	3.0	159.1	-2.8	158.2	-0.6	162.7	2.8	162.6	-0.1	161.6	-0.6	162.6	0.6	156.0	-4.1	157.9	1.2	153.9	-2.5

Source: U.S. Department of Labor, Bureau of Labor Statistics, Division of Industry Prices and Price Indexes. n.e.c. stands for not elsewhere classified. - indicates no data collected for period or unavailable.

Other Wood Products

Producer Price Index
Base 1982 = 100

For 1966-1997. Columns headed % show percentile change in the index from the previous period for which an index is available.

Year	Jan Index	%	Feb Index	%	Mar Index	%	Apr Index	%	May Index	%	Jun Index	%	Jul Index	%	Aug Index	%	Sep Index	%	Oct Index	%	Nov Index	%	Dec Index	%
1966	-	-	-	-	-	-	-	-	-	-	-	-	-	-	-	-	-	-	-	-	-	-	41.6	-
1967	42.4	1.9	42.4	0.0	42.4	0.0	42.4	0.0	42.4	0.0	42.4	0.0	42.4	0.0	42.3	-0.2	42.1	-0.5	42.2	0.2	42.2	0.0	42.2	0.0
1968	42.5	0.7	44.0	3.5	44.0	0.0	44.1	0.2	44.2	0.2	44.2	0.0	44.3	0.2	44.3	0.0	44.7	0.9	44.8	0.2	45.4	1.3	45.9	1.1
1969	46.0	0.2	46.2	0.4	46.7	1.1	46.8	0.2	47.6	1.7	47.8	0.4	48.0	0.4	48.5	1.0	48.4	-0.2	48.5	0.2	48.5	0.0	49.2	1.4
1970	49.7	1.0	49.7	0.0	49.7	0.0	49.6	-0.2	49.6	0.0	49.6	0.0	49.7	0.2	49.7	0.0	49.6	-0.2	49.6	0.0	49.6	0.0	49.9	0.6
1971	49.9	0.0	50.0	0.2	50.1	0.2	50.5	0.8	50.5	0.0	50.4	-0.2	50.4	0.0	50.4	0.0	50.4	0.0	50.4	0.0	50.4	0.0	50.4	0.0
1972	50.6	0.4	50.8	0.4	50.9	0.2	51.3	0.8	51.9	1.2	52.2	0.6	53.2	1.9	53.7	0.9	54.0	0.6	54.3	0.6	55.1	1.5	55.2	0.2
1973	56.4	2.2	57.2	1.4	59.7	4.4	62.4	4.5	63.4	1.6	64.3	1.4	64.7	0.6	64.9	0.3	66.0	1.7	67.0	1.5	67.3	0.4	67.4	0.1
1974	67.4	0.0	68.5	1.6	69.2	1.0	69.5	0.4	70.8	1.9	71.3	0.7	71.6	0.4	71.8	0.3	72.1	0.4	71.7	-0.6	71.3	-0.6	71.1	-0.3
1975	70.4	-1.0	70.2	-0.3	69.5	-1.0	68.9	-0.9	68.7	-0.3	68.4	-0.4	68.0	-0.6	68.1	0.1	68.0	-0.1	67.8	-0.3	67.7	-0.1	66.9	-1.2
1976	67.8	1.3	68.7	1.3	68.9	0.3	69.2	0.4	69.3	0.1	70.0	1.0	70.3	0.4	70.4	0.1	71.9	2.1	72.1	0.3	72.5	0.6	73.0	0.7
1977	73.4	0.5	74.7	1.8	75.8	1.5	76.7	1.2	78.1	1.8	78.5	0.5	78.6	0.1	79.0	0.5	80.3	1.6	80.3	0.0	80.4	0.1	80.9	0.6
1978	82.4	1.9	84.3	2.3	85.6	1.5	86.7	1.3	88.4	2.0	90.6	2.5	92.0	1.5	92.0	0.0	92.8	0.9	93.4	0.6	93.8	0.4	94.0	0.2
1979	94.5	0.5	95.8	1.4	98.3	2.6	99.7	1.4	100.9	1.2	101.0	0.1	100.6	-0.4	100.5	-0.1	100.8	0.3	100.7	-0.1	101.6	0.9	101.8	0.2
1980	102.6	0.8	103.0	0.4	102.9	-0.1	102.3	-0.6	101.9	-0.4	101.1	-0.8	100.3	-0.8	100.0	-0.3	100.3	0.3	100.2	-0.1	100.2	0.0	100.0	-0.2
1981	101.0	1.0	100.8	-0.2	100.3	-0.5	100.9	0.6	100.9	0.0	101.5	0.6	101.9	0.4	101.5	-0.4	101.8	0.3	101.6	-0.2	101.3	-0.3	101.4	0.1
1982	100.9	-0.5	101.1	0.2	101.0	-0.1	100.7	-0.3	100.5	-0.2	99.9	-0.6	99.9	0.0	99.8	-0.1	99.8	0.0	99.8	0.0	98.7	-1.1	97.9	-0.8
1983	98.2	0.3	98.7	0.5	98.1	-0.6	97.7	-0.4	97.9	0.2	97.2	-0.7	97.3	0.1	97.1	-0.2	97.1	0.0	97.2	0.1	97.3	0.1	97.6	0.3
1984	97.4	-0.2	97.7	0.3	98.2	0.5	98.8	0.6	99.4	0.6	99.5	0.1	99.6	0.1	100.1	0.5	99.9	-0.2	100.2	0.3	100.2	0.0	100.8	0.6
1985	100.7	-0.1	100.7	0.0	101.0	0.3	101.2	0.2	100.1	-1.1	99.9	-0.2	99.9	0.0	99.7	-0.2	99.6	-0.1	99.7	0.1	99.5	-0.2	99.5	0.0
1986	99.7	0.2	99.6	-0.1	99.6	0.0	99.6	0.0	99.8	0.2	100.8	1.0	101.4	0.6	101.0	-0.4	101.1	0.1	102.0	0.9	102.7	0.7	102.9	0.2
1987	103.0	0.1	102.9	-0.1	103.0	0.1	103.2	0.2	103.3	0.1	103.5	0.2	103.5	0.0	103.8	0.3	104.1	0.3	104.6	0.5	104.6	0.0	105.0	0.4
1988	105.4	0.4	105.8	0.4	106.2	0.4	106.5	0.3	106.5	0.0	107.1	0.6	107.5	0.4	107.7	0.2	107.9	0.2	108.3	0.4	108.6	0.3	108.3	-0.3
1989	108.5	0.2	109.4	0.8	110.2	0.7	111.4	1.1	112.4	0.9	113.7	1.2	114.2	0.4	115.6	1.2	116.2	0.5	115.1	-0.9	115.2	0.1	114.9	-0.3
1990	114.6	-0.3	114.4	-0.2	114.1	-0.3	114.4	0.3	114.5	0.1	114.9	0.3	114.8	-0.1	115.1	0.3	115.0	-0.1	115.3	0.3	114.9	-0.3	114.8	-0.1
1991	115.4	0.5	116.1	0.6	117.0	0.8	117.9	0.8	118.3	0.3	119.1	0.7	120.4	1.1	119.3	-0.9	120.5	1.0	119.7	-0.7	119.9	0.2	119.9	0.0
1992	119.9	0.0	119.8	-0.1	121.7	1.6	122.4	0.6	125.1	2.2	125.6	0.4	125.4	-0.2	125.4	0.0	126.0	0.5	126.8	0.6	127.7	0.7	127.6	-0.1
1993	129.7	1.6	131.4	1.3	133.6	1.7	135.1	1.1	137.1	1.5	136.2	-0.7	136.4	0.1	135.6	-0.6	136.9	1.0	136.4	-0.4	136.4	0.0	138.1	1.2
1994	137.2	-0.7	137.7	0.4	137.6	-0.1	138.4	0.6	138.9	0.4	137.4	-1.1	137.8	0.3	137.5	-0.2	137.1	-0.3	137.8	0.5	138.0	0.1	137.5	-0.4
1995	139.0	1.1	141.5	1.8	141.6	0.1	141.8	0.1	144.0	1.6	142.8	-0.8	143.5	0.5	145.2	1.2	148.5	2.3	147.6	-0.6	144.9	-1.8	144.2	-0.5
1996	137.8	-4.4	135.8	-1.5	133.8	-1.5	130.7	-2.3	126.6	-3.1	126.1	-0.4	122.5	-2.9	122.7	0.2	123.2	0.4	123.4	0.2	123.7	0.2	123.6	-0.1
1997	123.3	-0.2	123.4	0.1	127.1	3.0	127.1	0.0	127.1	0.0	127.3	0.2	128.2	0.7	128.7	0.4	129.2	0.4	131.2	1.5	132.8	1.2	134.3	1.1

Source: U.S. Department of Labor, Bureau of Labor Statistics, Division of Industry Prices and Price Indexes. n.e.c. stands for not elsewhere classified. - indicates no data collected for period or unavailable.

Logs, Bolts, Timber and Pulpwood
Producer Price Index
Base 1982 = 100

For 1981-1997. Columns headed % show percentile change in the index from the previous period for which an index is available.

Year	Jan Index	%	Feb Index	%	Mar Index	%	Apr Index	%	May Index	%	Jun Index	%	Jul Index	%	Aug Index	%	Sep Index	%	Oct Index	%	Nov Index	%	Dec Index	%
1981	-	-	-	-	-	-	-	-	-	-	-	-	-	-	-	-	-	-	-	-	-	-	103.1	-
1982	102.0	-1.1	103.3	1.3	104.4	1.1	104.8	0.4	103.3	-1.4	102.7	-0.6	99.8	-2.8	98.6	-1.2	97.1	-1.5	94.4	-2.8	93.7	-0.7	95.9	2.3
1983	94.8	-1.1	96.0	1.3	96.9	0.9	96.6	-0.3	96.2	-0.4	96.9	0.7	96.5	-0.4	97.3	0.8	97.9	0.6	96.2	-1.7	97.1	0.9	96.5	-0.6
1984	95.9	-0.6	100.8	5.1	96.9	-3.9	97.9	1.0	100.2	2.3	100.5	0.3	99.1	-1.4	94.7	-4.4	96.5	1.9	93.4	-3.2	93.7	0.3	93.8	0.1
1985	94.4	0.6	96.5	2.2	96.8	0.3	97.3	0.5	97.2	-0.1	97.5	0.3	96.5	-1.0	95.5	-1.0	94.4	-1.2	95.4	1.1	95.3	-0.1	95.3	0.0
1986	94.5	-0.8	90.6	-4.1	91.6	1.1	91.9	0.3	92.4	0.5	92.9	0.5	91.8	-1.2	92.3	0.5	92.0	-0.3	92.4	0.4	92.2	-0.2	92.6	0.4
1987	93.2	0.6	94.8	1.7	96.2	1.5	95.9	-0.3	96.0	0.1	97.3	1.4	98.5	1.2	102.1	3.7	107.2	5.0	111.0	3.5	114.0	2.7	115.6	1.4
1988	117.3	1.5	118.2	0.8	118.6	0.3	119.1	0.4	118.9	-0.2	117.5	-1.2	117.3	-0.2	116.6	-0.6	116.4	-0.2	116.8	0.3	117.4	0.5	118.7	1.1
1989	120.8	1.8	122.2	1.2	123.6	1.1	127.2	2.9	128.2	0.8	131.1	2.3	133.7	2.0	137.2	2.6	137.3	0.1	140.7	2.5	140.8	0.1	140.4	-0.3
1990	142.1	1.2	142.1	0.0	143.3	0.8	143.7	0.3	144.2	0.3	144.8	0.4	146.1	0.9	145.2	-0.6	143.3	-1.3	140.9	-1.7	139.5	-1.0	138.6	-0.6
1991	141.9	2.4	142.1	0.1	141.0	-0.8	141.6	0.4	144.3	1.9	144.0	-0.2	144.4	0.3	146.3	1.3	145.4	-0.6	147.5	1.4	145.8	-1.2	145.4	-0.3
1992	151.6	4.3	155.8	2.8	158.8	1.9	164.1	3.3	164.9	0.5	165.1	0.1	165.1	0.0	165.9	0.5	168.1	1.3	170.7	1.5	171.4	0.4	176.4	2.9
1993	183.2	3.9	193.8	5.8	200.9	3.7	222.6	10.8	233.5	4.9	224.9	-3.7	222.5	-1.1	212.6	-4.4	212.6	0.0	212.9	0.1	215.6	1.3	212.4	-1.5
1994	223.7	5.3	226.5	1.3	230.7	1.9	227.2	-1.5	220.7	-2.9	218.1	-1.2	215.5	-1.2	213.5	-0.9	212.6	-0.4	213.3	0.3	212.8	-0.2	214.5	0.8
1995	218.1	1.7	224.5	2.9	225.9	0.6	229.3	1.5	228.4	-0.4	228.8	0.2	219.9	-3.9	216.0	-1.8	216.0	0.0	214.6	-0.6	211.5	-1.4	212.3	0.4
1996	214.5	1.0	214.0	-0.2	209.3	-2.2	200.2	-4.3	202.8	1.3	201.5	-0.6	201.7	0.1	203.6	0.9	206.0	1.2	208.8	1.4	209.8	0.5	209.5	-0.1
1997	213.0	1.7	215.9	1.4	216.2	0.1	215.7	-0.2	216.6	0.4	215.2	-0.6	215.4	0.1	214.8	-0.3	214.7	-0.0	211.5	-1.5	212.0	0.2	212.5	0.2

Source: U.S. Department of Labor, Bureau of Labor Statistics, Division of Industry Prices and Price Indexes. n.e.c. stands for not elsewhere classified. - indicates no data collected for period or unavailable.

Prefabricated Wood Buildings & Components
Producer Price Index
Base 1982 = 100

For 1984-1997. Columns headed % show percentile change in the index from the previous period for which an index is available.

Year	Jan Index	%	Feb Index	%	Mar Index	%	Apr Index	%	May Index	%	Jun Index	%	Jul Index	%	Aug Index	%	Sep Index	%	Oct Index	%	Nov Index	%	Dec Index	%
1984	-	-	-	-	-	-	-	-	-	-	-	-	-	-	-	-	-	-	-	-	-	-	100.0	-
1985	100.4	0.4	100.2	-0.2	100.6	0.4	100.7	0.1	101.1	0.4	101.6	0.5	101.9	0.3	102.1	0.2	102.2	0.1	102.2	0.0	102.1	-0.1	102.1	0.0
1986	102.7	0.6	103.1	0.4	103.3	0.2	104.1	0.8	104.4	0.3	104.4	0.0	104.3	-0.1	104.4	0.1	104.7	0.3	104.7	0.0	104.7	0.0	104.8	0.1
1987	104.8	0.0	104.9	0.1	104.5	-0.4	105.4	0.9	105.5	0.1	105.2	-0.3	105.7	0.5	105.8	0.1	105.8	0.0	105.8	0.0	106.1	0.3	106.1	0.0
1988	106.2	0.1	107.3	1.0	107.8	0.5	107.9	0.1	107.6	-0.3	108.1	0.5	108.5	0.4	108.5	0.0	108.5	0.0	109.2	0.6	109.2	0.0	109.2	0.0
1989	109.8	0.5	109.8	0.0	110.5	0.6	110.7	0.2	110.7	0.0	110.7	0.0	111.0	0.3	111.0	0.0	111.0	0.0	111.0	0.0	110.8	-0.2	111.0	0.2
1990	111.3	0.3	111.8	0.4	111.6	-0.2	111.9	0.3	112.8	0.8	113.1	0.3	113.2	0.1	113.8	0.5	113.9	0.1	114.7	0.7	114.7	0.0	114.7	0.0
1991	115.7	0.9	115.7	0.0	115.9	0.2	117.2	1.1	117.5	0.3	119.6	1.8	119.7	0.1	120.1	0.3	120.2	0.1	119.0	-1.0	118.9	-0.1	118.9	0.0
1992	119.3	0.3	120.3	0.8	120.6	0.2	122.8	1.8	122.9	0.1	123.0	0.1	122.9	-0.1	123.1	0.2	123.2	0.1	124.5	1.1	125.2	0.6	125.4	0.2
1993	125.7	0.2	128.3	2.1	130.1	1.4	132.1	1.5	134.7	2.0	134.4	-0.2	134.0	-0.3	133.2	-0.6	132.9	-0.2	133.6	0.5	134.5	0.7	136.3	1.3
1994	135.3	-0.7	138.5	2.4	139.6	0.8	141.8	1.6	141.9	0.1	142.4	0.4	142.5	0.1	142.7	0.1	143.1	0.3	144.0	0.6	143.9	-0.1	144.0	0.1
1995	145.3	0.9	146.1	0.6	146.5	0.3	148.2	1.2	148.5	0.2	148.8	0.2	148.4	-0.3	148.4	0.0	148.4	0.0	148.2	-0.1	148.2	0.0	148.2	0.0
1996	148.9	0.5	149.2	0.2	149.7	0.3	150.0	0.2	150.6	0.4	150.7	0.1	151.3	0.4	150.8	-0.3	151.1	0.2	151.5	0.3	151.6	0.1	153.3	1.1
1997	153.5	0.1	153.8	0.2	154.3	0.3	155.1	0.5	157.1	1.3	157.2	0.1	157.2	0.0	157.1	-0.1	157.9	0.5	158.0	0.1	158.0	0.0	157.8	-0.1

Source: U.S. Department of Labor, Bureau of Labor Statistics, Division of Industry Prices and Price Indexes. n.e.c. stands for not elsewhere classified. - indicates no data collected for period or unavailable.

Treated Wood and Contract Wood Preserving
Producer Price Index
Base 1982 = 100

For 1985-1997. Columns headed % show percentile change in the index from the previous period for which an index is available.

Year	Jan Index	%	Feb Index	%	Mar Index	%	Apr Index	%	May Index	%	Jun Index	%	Jul Index	%	Aug Index	%	Sep Index	%	Oct Index	%	Nov Index	%	Dec Index	%
1985	-	-	-	-	-	-	-	-	-	-	100.0	-	99.5	-0.5	99.0	-0.5	99.0	0.0	98.9	-0.1	98.9	0.0	98.8	-0.1
1986	98.8	0.0	98.3	-0.5	98.9	0.6	98.1	-0.8	98.2	0.1	98.0	-0.2	97.7	-0.3	97.8	0.1	97.6	-0.2	97.7	0.1	97.3	-0.4	97.4	0.1
1987	97.0	-0.4	97.7	0.7	98.0	0.3	98.5	0.5	98.9	0.4	100.0	1.1	99.4	-0.6	99.5	0.1	99.4	-0.1	98.9	-0.5	98.9	0.0	99.1	0.2
1988	100.0	0.9	100.9	0.9	100.9	0.0	101.0	0.1	101.4	0.4	102.2	0.8	102.6	0.4	102.1	-0.5	101.8	-0.3	103.9	2.1	104.6	0.7	104.8	0.2
1989	106.6	1.7	107.9	1.2	108.3	0.4	108.9	0.6	110.6	1.6	110.9	0.3	111.2	0.3	111.1	-0.1	110.9	-0.2	110.1	-0.7	109.9	-0.2	110.0	0.1
1990	110.3	0.3	111.7	1.3	111.9	0.2	112.3	0.4	113.3	0.9	113.2	-0.1	113.5	0.3	113.6	0.1	112.7	-0.8	112.0	-0.6	113.3	1.2	113.3	0.0
1991	113.5	0.2	113.4	-0.1	114.4	0.9	114.8	0.3	114.6	-0.2	118.9	3.8	119.6	0.6	115.5	-3.4	115.3	-0.2	115.0	-0.3	115.9	0.8	116.7	0.7
1992	118.9	1.9	122.6	3.1	123.2	0.5	123.4	0.2	124.0	0.5	122.4	-1.3	122.2	-0.2	123.2	0.8	125.5	1.9	124.3	-1.0	124.4	0.1	127.6	2.6
1993	131.1	2.7	135.9	3.7	141.7	4.3	142.4	0.5	138.3	-2.9	132.4	-4.3	132.1	-0.2	134.3	1.7	136.7	1.8	139.2	1.8	146.1	5.0	147.3	0.8
1994	152.0	3.2	149.8	-1.4	151.4	1.1	148.2	-2.1	145.6	-1.8	149.2	2.5	148.4	-0.5	149.3	0.6	148.4	-0.6	147.0	-0.9	149.6	1.8	148.7	-0.6
1995	148.9	0.1	151.3	1.6	151.9	0.4	152.9	0.7	149.7	-2.1	147.5	-1.5	148.9	0.9	149.2	0.2	148.7	-0.3	147.6	-0.7	146.7	-0.6	147.3	0.4
1996	147.1	-0.1	147.0	-0.1	148.8	1.2	151.0	1.5	157.4	4.2	162.7	3.4	156.8	-3.6	158.4	1.0	159.7	0.8	154.8	-3.1	157.6	1.8	157.1	-0.3
1997	157.2	0.1	163.4	3.9	165.7	1.4	168.5	1.7	171.3	1.7	167.4	-2.3	166.9	-0.3	165.5	-0.8	162.3	-1.9	159.0	-2.0	159.1	0.1	162.6	2.2

Source: U.S. Department of Labor, Bureau of Labor Statistics, Division of Industry Prices and Price Indexes. n.e.c. stands for not elsewhere classified. - indicates no data collected for period or unavailable.

PULP, PAPER, AND ALLIED PRODUCTS
Producer Price Index
Base 1982 = 100

For 1947-1997. Columns headed % show percentile change in the index from the previous period for which an index is available.

Year	Jan Index	%	Feb Index	%	Mar Index	%	Apr Index	%	May Index	%	Jun Index	%	Jul Index	%	Aug Index	%	Sep Index	%	Oct Index	%	Nov Index	%	Dec Index	%
1947	24.5	-	24.7	0.8	24.8	0.4	25.1	1.2	25.1	0.0	25.1	0.0	25.1	0.0	25.2	0.4	25.3	0.4	25.5	0.8	25.5	0.0	25.8	1.2
1948	26.0	0.8	26.3	1.2	26.2	-0.4	26.1	-0.4	26.1	0.0	26.1	0.0	26.2	0.4	26.3	0.4	26.4	0.4	26.4	0.0	26.3	-0.4	26.3	0.0
1949	26.3	0.0	26.2	-0.4	26.0	-0.8	25.7	-1.2	25.3	-1.6	24.8	-2.0	24.5	-1.2	24.4	-0.4	24.5	0.4	24.5	0.0	24.6	0.4	24.6	0.0
1950	24.6	0.0	24.5	-0.4	24.5	0.0	24.5	0.0	24.4	-0.4	24.5	0.4	24.9	1.6	25.9	4.0	26.4	1.9	27.4	3.8	28.0	2.2	29.2	4.3
1951	30.6	4.8	30.7	0.3	30.7	0.0	30.5	-0.7	30.5	0.0	30.6	0.3	30.6	0.0	30.5	-0.3	30.4	-0.3	30.3	-0.3	30.2	-0.3	30.2	0.0
1952	30.1	-0.3	30.2	0.3	30.0	-0.7	29.9	-0.3	29.8	-0.3	29.7	-0.3	29.4	-1.0	29.5	0.3	29.5	0.0	29.4	-0.3	29.4	0.0	29.5	0.3
1953	29.5	0.0	29.4	-0.3	29.3	-0.3	29.4	0.3	29.4	0.0	29.5	0.3	29.5	0.0	29.6	0.3	29.8	0.7	30.0	0.7	29.9	-0.3	29.8	-0.3
1954	29.8	0.0	29.8	0.0	29.7	-0.3	29.6	-0.3	29.5	-0.3	29.5	0.0	29.6	0.3	29.6	0.0	29.6	0.0	29.6	0.0	29.6	0.0	29.5	-0.3
1955	29.6	0.3	29.7	0.3	29.8	0.3	29.9	0.3	30.0	0.3	30.2	0.7	30.3	0.3	30.5	0.7	30.7	0.7	31.3	2.0	31.4	0.3	31.5	0.3
1956	31.8	1.0	32.0	0.6	32.3	0.9	32.5	0.6	32.4	-0.3	32.5	0.3	32.5	0.0	32.6	0.3	32.6	0.0	32.7	0.3	32.6	-0.3	32.6	0.0
1957	32.8	0.6	32.8	0.0	32.8	0.0	32.8	0.0	32.9	0.3	32.9	0.0	33.0	0.3	33.1	0.3	33.2	0.3	33.4	0.6	33.4	0.0	33.4	0.0
1958	33.3	-0.3	33.3	0.0	33.3	0.0	33.3	0.0	33.3	0.0	33.3	0.0	33.4	0.3	33.4	0.0	33.6	0.6	33.6	0.0	33.6	0.0	33.5	-0.3
1959	33.5	0.0	33.6	0.3	33.6	0.0	33.7	0.3	33.6	-0.3	33.7	0.3	33.7	0.0	33.7	0.0	33.7	0.0	33.8	0.3	33.7	-0.3	33.7	0.0
1960	34.1	1.2	33.9	-0.6	33.9	0.0	33.9	0.0	34.0	0.3	34.0	0.0	34.0	0.0	33.9	-0.3	33.9	0.0	34.0	0.3	33.9	-0.3	33.7	-0.6
1961	33.7	0.0	33.7	0.0	33.5	-0.6	33.4	-0.3	32.1	-3.9	32.2	0.3	32.2	0.0	32.2	0.0	33.0	2.5	33.3	0.9	33.1	-0.6	33.3	0.6
1962	33.3	0.0	33.3	0.0	33.7	1.2	33.8	0.3	33.6	-0.6	33.5	-0.3	33.4	-0.3	33.3	-0.3	33.2	-0.3	33.1	-0.3	33.1	0.0	33.0	-0.3
1963	33.0	0.0	33.1	0.3	33.0	-0.3	33.0	0.0	33.1	0.3	33.2	0.3	33.0	-0.6	33.1	0.3	33.1	0.0	33.2	0.3	33.2	0.0	33.2	0.0
1964	33.3	0.3	33.3	0.0	33.1	-0.6	33.1	0.0	32.9	-0.6	32.9	0.0	32.9	0.0	32.9	0.0	32.9	0.0	33.1	0.6	33.0	-0.3	33.0	0.0
1965	33.0	0.0	33.0	0.0	33.2	0.6	33.3	0.3	33.4	0.3	33.4	0.0	33.3	-0.3	33.3	0.0	33.4	0.3	33.5	0.3	33.6	0.3	33.7	0.3
1966	33.8	0.3	33.8	0.0	34.0	0.6	34.2	0.6	34.3	0.3	34.4	0.3	34.4	0.0	34.4	0.0	34.4	0.0	34.4	0.0	34.4	0.0	34.4	0.0
1967	34.4	0.0	34.4	0.0	34.5	0.3	34.6	0.3	34.6	0.0	34.6	0.0	34.7	0.3	34.6	-0.3	34.6	0.0	34.7	0.3	34.8	0.3	34.9	0.3
1968	34.9	0.0	35.1	0.6	35.1	0.0	35.1	0.0	35.1	0.0	34.9	-0.6	35.0	0.3	34.9	-0.3	35.0	0.3	35.1	0.3	35.1	0.0	35.1	0.0
1969	35.4	0.9	35.6	0.6	35.8	0.6	35.9	0.3	36.0	0.3	36.0	0.0	36.0	0.0	36.2	0.6	36.3	0.3	36.4	0.3	36.5	0.3	36.6	0.3
1970	37.2	1.6	37.3	0.3	37.4	0.3	37.5	0.3	37.4	-0.3	37.4	0.0	37.5	0.3	37.4	-0.3	37.5	0.3	37.7	0.5	37.7	0.0	37.6	-0.3
1971	37.8	0.5	37.8	0.0	37.9	0.3	38.0	0.3	38.1	0.3	38.2	0.3	38.3	0.3	38.3	0.0	38.3	0.0	38.3	0.0	38.3	0.0	38.4	0.3
1972	38.4	0.0	38.7	0.8	38.9	0.5	39.1	0.5	39.2	0.3	39.3	0.3	39.4	0.3	39.5	0.3	39.6	0.3	39.7	0.3	39.8	0.3	39.9	0.3
1973	40.1	0.5	40.4	0.7	41.0	1.5	41.5	1.2	41.8	0.7	42.3	1.2	42.4	0.2	42.7	0.7	43.1	0.9	43.6	1.2	44.2	1.4	44.6	0.9
1974	45.6	2.2	46.0	0.9	47.5	3.3	50.0	5.3	50.8	1.6	51.1	0.6	53.1	3.9	56.4	6.2	56.9	0.9	57.5	1.1	57.8	0.5	57.9	0.2
1975	58.8	1.6	58.8	0.0	58.9	0.2	58.8	-0.2	58.8	0.0	58.8	0.0	58.9	0.2	58.9	0.0	59.0	0.2	59.2	0.3	59.3	0.2	59.9	1.0
1976	60.5	1.0	60.9	0.7	61.3	0.7	61.9	1.0	62.1	0.3	62.2	0.2	62.5	0.5	62.7	0.3	62.9	0.3	62.9	0.0	62.9	0.0	63.0	0.2
1977	63.4	0.6	63.4	0.0	63.6	0.3	64.2	0.9	64.5	0.5	64.9	0.6	65.0	0.2	65.1	0.2	65.2	0.2	65.3	0.2	65.2	-0.2	65.0	-0.3
1978	65.1	0.2	65.3	0.3	65.7	0.6	66.5	1.2	66.9	0.6	67.0	0.1	67.7	1.0	67.8	0.1	68.9	1.6	70.1	1.7	70.6	0.7	71.1	0.7
1979	71.7	0.8	72.3	0.8	73.5	1.7	74.5	1.4	74.9	0.5	75.0	0.1	75.6	0.8	77.0	1.9	77.2	0.3	78.8	2.1	79.5	0.9	80.3	1.0
1980	82.2	2.4	82.8	0.7	84.0	1.4	85.8	2.1	86.3	0.6	87.0	0.8	87.2	0.2	87.4	0.2	87.5	0.1	88.1	0.7	88.3	0.2	88.9	0.7
1981	91.6	3.0	92.5	1.0	93.2	0.8	94.0	0.9	94.3	0.3	94.5	0.2	95.2	0.7	95.6	0.4	96.2	0.6	96.7	0.5	97.1	0.4	97.3	0.2
1982	98.9	1.6	99.2	0.3	99.5	0.3	99.9	0.4	100.3	0.4	100.3	0.0	100.1	-0.2	100.2	0.1	100.2	0.0	100.4	0.2	100.4	0.0	100.6	0.2
1983	101.7	1.1	101.9	0.2	102.1	0.2	102.3	0.2	102.5	0.2	102.9	0.4	103.2	0.3	103.5	0.3	103.9	0.4	104.7	0.8	105.2	0.5	105.3	0.1
1984	107.0	1.6	108.1	1.0	108.8	0.6	109.5	0.6	110.1	0.5	110.3	0.2	110.8	0.5	111.3	0.5	111.5	0.2	111.9	0.4	112.2	0.3	112.3	0.1
1985	113.3	0.9	113.5	0.2	113.5	0.0	113.5	0.0	113.4	-0.1	113.3	-0.1	113.2	-0.1	113.2	0.0	113.1	-0.1	113.3	0.2	113.4	0.1	113.4	0.0
1986	114.5	1.0	114.7	0.2	114.7	0.0	115.3	0.5	115.6	0.3	115.8	0.2	116.1	0.3	116.5	0.3	117.0	0.4	117.6	0.5	117.9	0.3	118.1	0.2
1987	119.5	1.2	120.3	0.7	120.6	0.2	120.9	0.2	121.0	0.1	121.2	0.2	121.6	0.3	122.2	0.5	122.9	0.6	123.8	0.7	123.9	0.1	124.2	0.2
1988	126.6	1.9	127.3	0.6	128.0	0.5	128.9	0.7	129.6	0.5	130.0	0.3	131.0	0.8	131.3	0.2	132.1	0.6	132.8	0.5	133.1	0.2	133.5	0.3
1989	135.1	1.2	136.3	0.9	136.9	0.4	137.4	0.4	137.8	0.3	137.9	0.1	138.0	0.1	138.4	0.3	138.6	0.1	139.1	0.4	139.3	0.1	139.2	-0.1
1990	140.3	0.8	140.5	0.1	140.7	0.1	140.9	0.1	141.1	0.1	141.0	-0.1	141.1	0.1	141.1	0.0	141.3	0.1	142.0	0.5	142.3	0.2	142.3	0.0
1991	143.6	0.9	143.8	0.1	143.7	-0.1	143.2	-0.3	143.0	-0.1	142.7	-0.2	142.3	-0.3	142.2	-0.1	142.3	0.1	142.6	0.2	142.8	0.1	142.7	-0.1

[Continued]

PULP, PAPER, AND ALLIED PRODUCTS
Producer Price Index
Base 1982 = 100
[Continued]

For 1947-1997. Columns headed % show percentile change in the index from the previous period for which an index is available.

Year	Jan Index	%	Feb Index	%	Mar Index	%	Apr Index	%	May Index	%	Jun Index	%	Jul Index	%	Aug Index	%	Sep Index	%	Oct Index	%	Nov Index	%	Dec Index	%
1992	144.1	1.0	144.2	0.1	144.4	0.1	144.9	0.3	145.2	0.2	145.1	-0.1	145.2	0.1	145.4	0.1	145.8	0.3	146.1	0.2	145.9	-0.1	145.9	0.0
1993	147.0	0.8	147.1	0.1	147.3	0.1	147.7	0.3	147.7	0.0	147.1	-0.4	147.1	0.0	147.1	0.0	147.1	0.0	147.6	0.3	147.6	0.0	147.8	0.1
1994	148.6	0.5	148.8	0.1	149.2	0.3	149.4	0.1	150.1	0.5	151.0	0.6	152.0	0.7	153.1	0.7	154.5	0.9	156.2	1.1	158.0	1.2	159.5	0.9
1995	163.2	2.3	165.9	1.7	168.1	1.3	170.6	1.5	172.7	1.2	174.5	1.0	175.4	0.5	175.6	0.1	175.4	-0.1	175.4	0.0	175.2	-0.1	174.7	-0.3
1996	174.1	-0.3	173.2	-0.5	171.1	-1.2	169.2	-1.1	168.0	-0.7	167.5	-0.3	167.0	-0.3	166.6	-0.2	166.9	0.2	166.9	0.0	166.9	0.0	167.2	0.2
1997	167.6	0.2	167.1	-0.3	166.5	-0.4	166.3	-0.1	166.1	-0.1	166.4	0.2	166.9	0.3	167.8	0.5	168.7	0.5	169.5	0.5	170.4	0.5	171.2	0.5

Source: U.S. Department of Labor, Bureau of Labor Statistics, Division of Industry Prices and Price Indexes. n.e.c. stands for not elsewhere classified. - indicates no data collected for period or unavailable.

Pulp, Paper, and Products, ex. Building Paper
Producer Price Index
Base 1982 = 100

For 1947-1997. Columns headed % show percentile change in the index from the previous period for which an index is available.

Year	Jan Index	%	Feb Index	%	Mar Index	%	Apr Index	%	May Index	%	Jun Index	%	Jul Index	%	Aug Index	%	Sep Index	%	Oct Index	%	Nov Index	%	Dec Index	%
1947	25.8	-	26.0	0.8	26.2	0.8	26.6	1.5	26.5	-0.4	26.5	0.0	26.5	0.0	26.7	0.8	26.8	0.4	26.9	0.4	26.9	0.0	27.3	1.5
1948	27.5	0.7	27.7	0.7	27.7	0.0	27.6	-0.4	27.6	0.0	27.6	0.0	27.7	0.4	27.8	0.4	27.8	0.0	27.8	0.0	27.8	0.0	27.7	-0.4
1949	27.7	0.0	27.6	-0.4	27.5	-0.4	27.1	-1.5	26.6	-1.8	26.1	-1.9	25.8	-1.1	25.7	-0.4	25.8	0.4	25.8	0.0	25.9	0.4	25.9	0.0
1950	25.9	0.0	25.8	-0.4	25.8	0.0	25.8	0.0	25.7	-0.4	25.7	0.0	26.2	1.9	27.3	4.2	27.8	1.8	28.8	3.6	29.6	2.8	30.8	4.1
1951	32.4	5.2	32.5	0.3	32.4	-0.3	32.2	-0.6	32.2	0.0	32.4	0.6	32.4	0.0	32.2	-0.6	32.1	-0.3	32.0	-0.3	31.9	-0.3	31.9	0.0
1952	31.8	-0.3	31.8	0.0	31.7	-0.3	31.6	-0.3	31.5	-0.3	31.4	-0.3	31.0	-1.3	31.1	0.3	31.1	0.0	31.1	0.0	31.0	-0.3	31.1	0.3
1953	31.1	0.0	31.0	-0.3	30.9	-0.3	31.0	0.3	31.0	0.0	31.1	0.3	31.1	0.0	31.2	0.3	31.4	0.6	31.6	0.6	31.5	-0.3	31.4	-0.3
1954	31.4	0.0	31.4	0.0	31.3	-0.3	31.2	-0.3	31.1	-0.3	31.1	0.0	31.2	0.3	31.2	0.0	31.2	0.0	31.2	0.0	31.1	-0.3	31.1	0.0
1955	31.2	0.3	31.3	0.3	31.3	0.0	31.5	0.6	31.6	0.3	31.8	0.6	32.0	0.6	32.1	0.3	32.4	0.9	32.9	1.5	33.1	0.6	33.2	0.3
1956	33.5	0.9	33.7	0.6	34.1	1.2	34.2	0.3	34.2	0.0	34.2	0.0	34.3	0.3	34.4	0.3	34.3	-0.3	34.4	0.3	34.3	-0.3	34.4	0.3
1957	34.5	0.3	34.5	0.0	34.6	0.3	34.5	-0.3	34.6	0.3	34.6	0.0	34.7	0.3	34.9	0.6	35.0	0.3	35.1	0.3	35.2	0.3	35.2	0.0
1958	35.1	-0.3	35.1	0.0	35.0	-0.3	35.0	0.0	35.0	0.0	35.0	0.0	35.1	0.3	35.2	0.3	35.3	0.3	35.4	0.3	35.4	0.0	35.0	-1.1
1959	35.3	0.9	35.3	0.0	35.4	0.3	35.5	0.3	35.4	-0.3	35.5	0.3	35.5	0.0	35.5	0.0	35.5	0.0	35.5	0.0	35.5	0.0	35.5	0.0
1960	35.9	1.1	35.7	-0.6	35.7	0.0	35.7	0.0	35.8	0.3	35.8	0.0	35.9	0.3	35.7	-0.6	35.7	0.0	35.8	0.3	35.7	-0.3	35.5	-0.6
1961	35.5	0.0	35.4	-0.3	35.3	-0.3	35.1	-0.6	33.8	-3.7	33.9	0.3	33.8	-0.3	33.8	0.0	34.7	2.7	35.0	0.9	34.8	-0.6	35.0	0.6
1962	35.1	0.3	35.1	0.0	35.5	1.1	35.7	0.6	35.5	-0.6	35.4	-0.3	35.2	-0.6	35.1	-0.3	35.0	-0.3	34.9	-0.3	34.8	-0.3	34.8	0.0
1963	34.8	0.0	34.9	0.3	34.8	-0.3	34.8	0.0	34.8	0.0	35.0	0.6	34.8	-0.6	34.8	0.0	34.8	0.0	35.0	0.6	35.0	0.0	35.0	0.0
1964	35.1	0.3	35.2	0.3	35.0	-0.6	34.9	-0.3	34.7	-0.6	34.7	0.0	34.7	0.0	34.7	0.0	34.7	0.0	34.9	0.6	34.8	-0.3	34.8	0.0
1965	34.8	0.0	34.9	0.3	35.1	0.6	35.2	0.3	35.2	0.0	35.2	0.0	35.2	0.0	35.2	0.0	35.2	0.0	35.4	0.6	35.5	0.3	35.5	0.0
1966	35.7	0.6	35.7	0.0	35.9	0.6	36.1	0.6	36.2	0.3	36.3	0.3	36.4	0.3	36.4	0.0	36.4	0.0	36.3	-0.3	36.3	0.0	36.3	0.0
1967	36.3	0.0	36.4	0.3	36.5	0.3	36.6	0.3	36.6	0.0	36.6	0.0	36.7	0.3	36.6	-0.3	36.6	0.0	36.7	0.3	36.9	0.5	36.9	0.0
1968	37.0	0.3	37.1	0.3	37.0	-0.3	37.0	0.0	37.1	0.3	36.9	-0.5	37.0	0.3	36.9	-0.3	37.0	0.3	37.0	0.0	37.0	0.0	37.0	0.0
1969	37.4	1.1	37.6	0.5	37.8	0.5	37.9	0.3	37.9	0.0	38.0	0.3	38.1	0.3	38.3	0.5	38.4	0.3	38.5	0.3	38.7	0.5	38.7	0.0
1970	39.4	1.8	39.5	0.3	39.6	0.3	39.7	0.3	39.6	-0.3	39.6	0.0	39.7	0.3	39.7	0.0	39.7	0.0	39.9	0.5	39.9	0.0	39.9	0.0
1971	40.1	0.5	40.0	-0.2	40.1	0.2	40.2	0.2	40.3	0.2	40.5	0.5	40.6	0.2	40.6	0.0	40.6	0.0	40.6	0.0	40.6	0.0	40.6	0.0
1972	40.7	0.2	41.0	0.7	41.2	0.5	41.4	0.5	41.5	0.2	41.6	0.2	41.7	0.2	41.9	0.5	41.9	0.0	42.1	0.5	42.2	0.2	42.3	0.2
1973	42.5	0.5	42.8	0.7	43.4	1.4	44.0	1.4	44.3	0.7	44.8	1.1	44.9	0.2	45.3	0.9	45.7	0.9	46.2	1.1	46.8	1.3	47.2	0.9
1974	48.4	2.5	48.8	0.8	50.4	3.3	53.1	5.4	53.9	1.5	54.3	0.7	56.5	4.1	60.1	6.4	60.6	0.8	61.3	1.2	61.7	0.7	61.8	0.2
1975	62.7	1.5	62.8	0.2	62.8	0.0	62.7	-0.2	62.7	0.0	62.7	0.0	62.8	0.2	62.8	0.0	62.9	0.2	63.1	0.3	63.2	0.2	63.9	1.1
1976	64.6	1.1	64.9	0.5	65.3	0.6	65.9	0.9	66.2	0.5	66.2	0.0	66.6	0.6	66.7	0.2	67.0	0.4	67.0	0.0	66.9	-0.1	67.0	0.1
1977	67.4	0.6	67.5	0.1	67.7	0.3	68.3	0.9	68.6	0.4	69.0	0.6	69.1	0.1	69.0	-0.1	69.1	0.1	69.2	0.1	69.1	-0.1	68.8	-0.4
1978	68.9	0.1	69.0	0.1	69.3	0.4	70.2	1.3	70.6	0.6	70.7	0.1	71.5	1.1	71.7	0.3	72.9	1.7	74.2	1.8	74.8	0.8	75.3	0.7
1979	76.0	0.9	76.7	0.9	78.0	1.7	79.0	1.3	79.5	0.6	79.7	0.3	80.4	0.9	81.9	1.9	82.1	0.2	83.8	2.1	84.6	1.0	85.4	0.9
1980	87.5	2.5	88.1	0.7	89.3	1.4	91.3	2.2	91.7	0.4	92.4	0.8	92.6	0.2	92.9	0.3	93.0	0.1	93.6	0.6	93.8	0.2	94.4	0.6
1981	95.5	1.2	96.8	1.4	97.7	0.9	98.3	0.6	98.8	0.5	99.3	0.5	99.6	0.3	100.2	0.6	100.6	0.4	100.9	0.3	100.9	0.0	100.9	0.0
1982	101.0	0.1	101.3	0.3	101.3	0.0	100.8	-0.5	100.6	-0.2	100.3	-0.3	99.8	-0.5	99.6	-0.2	99.4	-0.2	98.9	-0.5	98.6	-0.3	98.4	-0.2
1983	98.4	0.0	98.4	0.0	98.4	0.0	98.3	-0.1	98.3	0.0	98.5	0.2	98.9	0.4	99.2	0.3	100.0	0.8	100.7	0.7	101.4	0.7	101.5	0.1
1984	102.8	1.3	104.3	1.5	105.5	1.2	106.7	1.1	107.1	0.4	107.4	0.3	108.2	0.7	108.5	0.3	108.9	0.4	109.6	0.6	109.7	0.1	109.4	-0.3
1985	109.1	-0.3	108.7	-0.4	108.2	-0.5	107.8	-0.4	107.4	-0.4	107.0	-0.4	106.3	-0.7	106.0	-0.3	105.7	-0.3	105.6	-0.1	105.4	-0.2	105.4	0.0
1986	105.4	0.0	105.5	0.1	105.9	0.4	106.3	0.4	106.7	0.4	106.9	0.2	107.6	0.7	108.2	0.6	108.7	0.5	109.3	0.6	109.8	0.5	110.0	0.2
1987	111.3	1.2	112.4	1.0	112.6	0.2	113.2	0.5	113.1	-0.1	113.4	0.3	114.0	0.5	114.8	0.7	115.7	0.8	116.7	0.9	117.1	0.3	117.6	0.4
1988	119.9	2.0	120.5	0.5	121.6	0.9	123.1	1.2	124.1	0.8	124.6	0.4	125.8	1.0	126.4	0.5	127.6	0.9	128.1	0.4	128.3	0.2	128.5	0.2
1989	129.5	0.8	131.1	1.2	131.8	0.5	132.4	0.5	132.9	0.4	132.8	-0.1	132.5	-0.2	132.8	0.2	132.8	0.0	133.6	0.6	133.6	0.0	133.4	-0.1
1990	133.4	0.0	133.3	-0.1	133.2	-0.1	133.4	0.2	133.1	-0.2	132.8	-0.2	132.6	-0.2	132.5	-0.1	132.3	-0.2	132.7	0.3	132.8	0.1	132.8	0.0
1991	132.6	-0.2	132.4	-0.2	131.8	-0.5	130.8	-0.8	129.8	-0.8	129.1	-0.5	128.6	-0.4	128.1	-0.4	128.5	0.3	128.4	-0.1	128.6	0.2	128.5	-0.1

[Continued]

Pulp, Paper, and Products, ex. Building Paper
Producer Price Index
Base 1982 = 100
[Continued]

For 1947-1997. Columns headed % show percentile change in the index from the previous period for which an index is available.

Year	Jan Index	%	Feb Index	%	Mar Index	%	Apr Index	%	May Index	%	Jun Index	%	Jul Index	%	Aug Index	%	Sep Index	%	Oct Index	%	Nov Index	%	Dec Index	%
1992	128.5	0.0	128.6	0.1	128.6	0.0	129.4	0.6	129.5	0.1	129.4	-0.1	129.4	0.0	129.4	0.0	129.9	0.4	129.6	-0.2	129.2	-0.3	128.8	-0.3
1993	128.3	-0.4	128.0	-0.2	128.2	0.2	128.3	0.1	128.2	-0.1	128.0	-0.2	127.5	-0.4	127.0	-0.4	126.6	-0.3	126.9	0.2	126.9	0.0	126.9	0.0
1994	126.7	-0.2	127.0	0.2	127.3	0.2	127.9	0.5	128.6	0.5	130.5	1.5	132.3	1.4	134.2	1.4	136.3	1.6	139.5	2.3	142.0	1.8	144.4	1.7
1995	149.2	3.3	154.0	3.2	157.8	2.5	162.2	2.8	165.8	2.2	168.4	1.6	169.1	0.4	169.2	0.1	168.3	-0.5	166.9	-0.8	165.4	-0.9	164.2	-0.7
1996	161.6	-1.6	159.4	-1.4	155.1	-2.7	151.2	-2.5	148.4	-1.9	147.4	-0.7	146.6	-0.5	145.4	-0.8	145.2	-0.1	145.2	0.0	145.0	-0.1	145.4	0.3
1997	145.1	-0.2	144.1	-0.7	143.1	-0.7	142.1	-0.7	142.1	0.0	142.5	0.3	143.2	0.5	144.8	1.1	146.2	1.0	146.7	0.3	147.7	0.7	148.9	0.8

Source: U.S. Department of Labor, Bureau of Labor Statistics, Division of Industry Prices and Price Indexes. n.e.c. stands for not elsewhere classified. - indicates no data collected for period or unavailable.

Building Paper & Building Board Mill Products
Producer Price Index
Base 1982 = 100

For 1947-1997. Columns headed % show percentile change in the index from the previous period for which an index is available.

Year	Jan Index	%	Feb Index	%	Mar Index	%	Apr Index	%	May Index	%	Jun Index	%	Jul Index	%	Aug Index	%	Sep Index	%	Oct Index	%	Nov Index	%	Dec Index	%
1947	29.0	-	29.0	0.0	29.1	0.3	29.1	0.0	29.1	0.0	29.1	0.0	29.1	0.0	29.0	-0.3	29.0	0.0	29.5	1.7	30.9	4.7	30.9	0.0
1948	31.1	0.6	31.4	1.0	31.4	0.0	31.4	0.0	31.8	1.3	33.1	4.1	33.4	0.9	33.4	0.0	33.4	0.0	33.4	0.0	33.4	0.0	33.4	0.0
1949	33.3	-0.3	33.2	-0.3	33.2	0.0	33.2	0.0	32.9	-0.9	32.8	-0.3	32.8	0.0	32.8	0.0	32.8	0.0	32.8	0.0	32.8	0.0	32.8	0.0
1950	32.8	0.0	32.8	0.0	32.8	0.0	32.8	0.0	32.8	0.0	32.8	0.0	33.6	2.4	34.4	2.4	34.4	0.0	34.7	0.9	35.6	2.6	35.9	0.8
1951	35.9	0.0	35.9	0.0	35.9	0.0	35.9	0.0	35.9	0.0	35.9	0.0	35.9	0.0	35.9	0.0	35.9	0.0	35.9	0.0	35.9	0.0	35.9	0.0
1952	35.9	0.0	35.9	0.0	35.9	0.0	36.0	0.3	36.6	1.7	36.6	0.0	36.6	0.0	36.6	0.0	36.6	0.0	36.6	0.0	37.3	1.9	37.3	0.0
1953	37.3	0.0	37.3	0.0	37.3	0.0	37.3	0.0	38.9	4.3	38.9	0.0	38.9	0.0	38.9	0.0	38.9	0.0	38.9	0.0	38.9	0.0	38.9	0.0
1954	40.4	3.9	40.4	0.0	40.4	0.0	40.4	0.0	40.4	0.0	40.4	0.0	40.4	0.0	40.4	0.0	40.3	-0.2	40.3	0.0	40.3	0.0	40.3	0.0
1955	40.3	0.0	40.9	1.5	41.0	0.2	41.0	0.0	41.0	0.0	41.0	0.0	41.0	0.0	41.9	2.2	41.9	0.0	42.2	0.7	42.2	0.0	42.2	0.0
1956	42.2	0.0	42.2	0.0	42.2	0.0	43.7	3.6	43.7	0.0	43.7	0.0	43.7	0.0	43.7	0.0	43.7	0.0	43.7	0.0	43.7	0.0	43.7	0.0
1957	44.6	2.1	44.6	0.0	44.6	0.0	44.8	0.4	44.8	0.0	44.8	0.0	44.8	0.0	44.8	0.0	44.8	0.0	44.8	0.0	44.8	0.0	44.8	0.0
1958	44.8	0.0	44.8	0.0	45.1	0.7	45.6	1.1	45.6	0.0	45.6	0.0	45.6	0.0	45.3	-0.7	45.3	0.0	45.3	0.0	45.3	0.0	45.4	0.2
1959	45.5	0.2	45.6	0.2	45.6	0.0	45.8	0.4	46.4	1.3	46.4	0.0	46.6	0.4	46.7	0.2	46.7	0.0	46.7	0.0	46.7	0.0	46.7	0.0
1960	46.7	0.0	46.7	0.0	46.3	-0.9	45.9	-0.9	45.9	0.0	45.9	0.0	45.6	-0.7	46.0	0.9	45.9	-0.2	46.1	0.4	46.0	-0.2	46.0	0.0
1961	46.0	0.0	46.2	0.4	46.1	-0.2	45.9	-0.4	45.7	-0.4	45.8	0.2	45.8	0.0	45.8	0.0	45.8	0.0	45.8	0.0	45.5	-0.7	45.3	-0.4
1962	44.8	-1.1	44.7	-0.2	44.6	-0.2	44.5	-0.2	44.4	-0.2	43.4	-2.3	43.8	0.9	44.1	0.7	44.1	0.0	43.7	-0.9	43.8	0.2	43.6	-0.5
1963	43.3	-0.7	43.3	0.0	42.7	-1.4	43.3	1.4	43.6	0.7	44.2	1.4	44.2	0.0	44.2	0.0	44.3	0.2	43.9	-0.9	43.1	-1.8	43.2	0.2
1964	43.2	0.0	43.0	-0.5	42.5	-1.2	42.4	-0.2	42.8	0.9	42.8	0.0	42.8	0.0	42.7	-0.2	42.8	0.2	42.8	0.0	42.6	-0.5	42.3	-0.7
1965	42.3	0.0	41.8	-1.2	41.8	0.0	41.8	0.0	42.0	0.5	42.0	0.0	42.3	0.7	42.3	0.0	42.3	0.0	42.5	0.5	42.3	-0.5	42.0	-0.7
1966	42.0	0.0	42.0	0.0	42.0	0.0	42.0	0.0	42.0	0.0	42.0	0.0	42.1	0.2	42.2	0.2	42.1	-0.2	42.3	0.5	42.3	0.0	42.1	-0.5
1967	42.0	-0.2	42.2	0.5	41.9	-0.7	41.9	0.0	41.7	-0.5	41.5	-0.5	41.5	0.0	41.3	-0.5	41.5	0.5	41.8	0.7	41.8	0.0	41.7	-0.2
1968	41.7	0.0	41.6	-0.2	41.7	0.2	41.8	0.2	41.9	0.2	41.8	-0.2	41.8	0.0	42.3	1.2	42.4	0.2	42.5	0.2	42.6	0.2	43.0	0.9
1969	44.2	2.8	44.6	0.9	45.2	1.3	45.6	0.9	45.8	0.4	45.1	-1.5	43.5	-3.5	43.2	-0.7	43.2	0.0	42.9	-0.7	42.9	0.0	42.7	-0.5
1970	42.3	-0.9	42.2	-0.2	42.1	-0.2	42.4	0.7	42.3	-0.2	42.3	0.0	42.2	-0.2	42.1	-0.2	42.0	-0.2	42.0	0.0	42.0	0.0	41.8	-0.5
1971	41.7	-0.2	41.7	0.0	42.2	1.2	42.5	0.7	42.9	0.9	43.2	0.7	43.2	0.0	43.5	0.7	43.5	0.0	43.6	0.2	43.6	0.0	43.6	0.0
1972	43.7	0.2	43.7	0.0	44.1	0.9	44.3	0.5	44.5	0.5	44.5	0.0	44.6	0.2	44.7	0.2	44.8	0.2	44.8	0.0	44.8	0.0	44.8	0.0
1973	44.7	-0.2	45.1	0.9	45.3	0.4	45.6	0.7	46.3	1.5	46.7	0.9	46.8	0.2	47.1	0.6	48.4	2.8	49.2	1.7	49.6	0.8	50.2	1.2
1974	50.8	1.2	50.9	0.2	51.5	1.2	51.6	0.2	52.4	1.6	52.2	-0.4	51.9	-0.6	52.2	0.6	52.3	0.2	51.8	-1.0	50.5	-2.5	50.6	0.2
1975	51.8	2.4	51.9	0.2	51.6	-0.6	51.5	-0.2	52.5	1.9	52.7	0.4	53.2	0.9	53.3	0.2	53.8	0.9	54.8	1.9	54.9	0.2	55.0	0.2
1976	54.8	-0.4	55.6	1.5	57.2	2.9	56.9	-0.5	56.9	0.0	58.3	2.5	59.0	1.2	58.7	-0.5	59.2	0.9	58.9	-0.5	59.4	0.8	60.2	1.3
1977	60.6	0.7	60.3	-0.5	60.9	1.0	62.1	2.0	63.2	1.8	64.2	1.6	65.9	2.6	67.8	2.9	69.6	2.7	70.5	1.3	70.3	-0.3	71.3	1.4
1978	73.1	2.5	75.2	2.9	77.9	3.6	78.8	1.2	79.7	1.1	80.3	0.8	80.6	0.4	79.3	-1.6	78.1	-1.5	79.1	1.3	78.8	-0.4	77.9	-1.1
1979	76.9	-1.3	76.7	-0.3	76.2	-0.7	76.6	0.5	76.5	-0.1	75.5	-1.3	74.3	-1.6	74.8	0.7	76.3	2.0	76.6	0.4	76.7	0.1	77.1	0.5
1980	77.7	0.8	80.0	3.0	83.0	3.8	84.0	1.2	86.4	2.9	87.2	0.9	88.4	1.4	87.8	-0.7	87.8	0.0	88.8	1.1	90.4	1.8	91.7	1.4
1981	91.7	0.0	94.3	2.8	95.2	1.0	97.1	2.0	99.1	2.1	99.1	0.0	98.3	-0.8	97.8	-0.5	97.8	0.0	97.4	-0.4	96.9	-0.5	96.2	-0.7
1982	97.6	1.5	96.6	-1.0	100.1	3.6	98.7	-1.4	100.3	1.6	100.2	-0.1	100.1	-0.1	102.1	2.0	101.6	-0.5	101.1	-0.5	100.6	-0.5	101.1	0.5
1983	100.7	-0.4	100.8	0.1	102.0	1.2	103.1	1.1	104.1	1.0	106.8	2.6	107.0	0.2	105.3	-1.6	105.5	0.2	106.3	0.8	106.4	0.1	104.6	-1.7
1984	105.2	0.6	106.5	1.2	108.0	1.4	111.0	2.8	110.7	-0.3	110.7	0.0	109.8	-0.8	108.5	-1.2	108.3	-0.2	107.6	-0.6	105.9	-1.6	105.8	-0.1
1985	106.6	0.8	107.0	0.4	107.0	0.0	107.5	0.5	108.0	0.5	108.5	0.5	108.5	0.0	108.0	-0.5	108.6	0.6	106.5	-1.9	106.4	-0.1	105.9	-0.5
1986	105.8	-0.1	106.4	0.6	107.4	0.9	108.9	1.4	109.6	0.6	109.6	0.0	109.5	-0.1	109.5	0.0	109.7	0.2	110.7	0.9	109.7	-0.9	109.4	-0.3
1987	109.6	0.2	109.3	-0.3	109.2	-0.1	109.1	-0.1	109.8	0.6	110.2	0.4	111.1	0.8	112.2	1.0	113.2	0.9	113.8	0.5	113.4	-0.4	113.7	0.3
1988	113.7	0.0	114.0	0.3	113.1	-0.8	113.3	0.2	113.4	0.1	114.2	0.7	113.9	-0.3	112.7	-1.1	112.5	-0.2	112.5	0.0	112.7	0.2	113.3	0.5
1989	112.9	-0.4	113.8	0.8	114.2	0.4	115.1	0.8	115.5	0.3	115.8	0.3	116.4	0.5	116.2	-0.2	116.3	0.1	116.6	0.3	117.0	0.3	116.9	-0.1
1990	116.6	-0.3	116.0	-0.5	115.5	-0.4	113.7	-1.6	113.4	-0.3	111.9	-1.3	111.2	-0.6	110.3	-0.8	109.8	-0.5	109.4	-0.4	109.1	-0.3	108.9	-0.2
1991	109.3	0.4	109.8	0.5	111.3	1.4	112.7	1.3	113.5	0.7	113.4	-0.1	114.6	1.1	112.8	-1.6	112.2	-0.5	110.9	-1.2	110.6	-0.3	110.9	0.3

[Continued]

Building Paper & Building Board Mill Products
Producer Price Index
Base 1982 = 100
[Continued]

For 1947-1997. Columns headed % show percentile change in the index from the previous period for which an index is available.

Year	Jan Index	%	Feb Index	%	Mar Index	%	Apr Index	%	May Index	%	Jun Index	%	Jul Index	%	Aug Index	%	Sep Index	%	Oct Index	%	Nov Index	%	Dec Index	%
1992	112.5	1.4	117.1	4.1	119.2	1.8	118.5	-0.6	119.1	0.5	118.9	-0.2	118.8	-0.1	120.0	1.0	123.7	3.1	123.5	-0.2	121.8	-1.4	121.7	-0.1
1993	124.9	2.6	129.0	3.3	133.9	3.8	135.4	1.1	133.8	-1.2	132.0	-1.3	131.2	-0.6	131.6	0.3	134.7	2.4	133.8	-0.7	135.1	1.0	137.5	1.8
1994	138.7	0.9	139.2	0.4	140.4	0.9	140.9	0.4	142.3	1.0	142.9	0.4	143.2	0.2	146.0	2.0	148.6	1.8	146.9	-1.1	149.8	2.0	149.6	-0.1
1995	147.3	-1.5	148.0	0.5	147.3	-0.5	146.6	-0.5	145.4	-0.8	141.3	-2.8	141.4	0.1	142.3	0.6	145.8	2.5	146.3	0.3	145.5	-0.5	141.9	-2.5
1996	138.5	-2.4	138.2	-0.2	136.3	-1.4	136.2	-0.1	137.9	1.2	135.9	-1.5	137.4	1.1	137.3	-0.1	140.5	2.3	138.7	-1.3	136.2	-1.8	133.7	-1.8
1997	132.4	-1.0	130.9	-1.1	130.9	0.0	129.1	-1.4	128.1	-0.8	128.7	0.5	127.4	-1.0	127.0	-0.3	128.4	1.1	127.1	-1.0	135.2	6.4	134.6	-0.4

Source: U.S. Department of Labor, Bureau of Labor Statistics, Division of Industry Prices and Price Indexes. n.e.c. stands for not elsewhere classified. - indicates no data collected for period or unavailable.

Publications, Printed Matter & Printing Materials
Producer Price Index
Base 1982 = 100

For 1980-1997. Columns headed % show percentile change in the index from the previous period for which an index is available.

Year	Jan Index	%	Feb Index	%	Mar Index	%	Apr Index	%	May Index	%	Jun Index	%	Jul Index	%	Aug Index	%	Sep Index	%	Oct Index	%	Nov Index	%	Dec Index	%
1980	-		-		-		-		-		-		-		-		-		-		-		84.5	-
1981	88.5	4.7	89.1	0.7	89.5	0.4	90.5	1.1	90.5	0.0	90.6	0.1	91.6	1.1	91.8	0.2	92.7	1.0	93.3	0.6	94.1	0.9	94.5	0.4
1982	97.2	2.9	97.5	0.3	98.2	0.7	99.3	1.1	100.1	0.8	100.2	0.1	100.4	0.2	100.6	0.2	100.9	0.3	101.5	0.6	101.7	0.2	102.4	0.7
1983	104.4	2.0	104.7	0.3	105.1	0.4	105.5	0.4	105.8	0.3	106.2	0.4	106.4	0.2	106.8	0.4	106.9	0.1	107.8	0.8	108.1	0.3	108.3	0.2
1984	110.5	2.0	111.1	0.5	111.4	0.3	111.8	0.4	112.3	0.4	112.6	0.3	112.8	0.2	113.6	0.7	113.7	0.1	113.9	0.2	114.4	0.4	114.7	0.3
1985	116.8	1.8	117.4	0.5	118.0	0.5	118.2	0.2	118.3	0.1	118.5	0.2	118.8	0.3	119.2	0.3	119.2	0.0	119.8	0.5	120.0	0.2	120.0	0.0
1986	122.0	1.7	122.2	0.2	122.1	-0.1	122.7	0.5	122.9	0.2	123.0	0.1	123.2	0.2	123.4	0.2	123.9	0.4	124.4	0.4	124.7	0.2	124.8	0.1
1987	126.4	1.3	127.0	0.5	127.3	0.2	127.4	0.1	127.6	0.2	127.8	0.2	128.0	0.2	128.4	0.3	128.8	0.3	129.5	0.5	129.4	-0.1	129.6	0.2
1988	132.2	2.0	132.8	0.5	133.3	0.4	133.6	0.2	134.0	0.3	134.3	0.2	135.1	0.6	135.2	0.1	135.6	0.3	136.5	0.7	136.9	0.3	137.3	0.3
1989	139.7	1.7	140.5	0.6	140.9	0.3	141.3	0.3	141.5	0.1	142.0	0.4	142.4	0.3	142.9	0.4	143.3	0.3	143.5	0.1	143.8	0.2	143.9	0.1
1990	146.0	1.5	146.6	0.4	147.0	0.3	147.4	0.3	148.0	0.4	148.0	0.0	148.4	0.3	148.7	0.2	149.3	0.4	150.2	0.6	150.7	0.3	150.9	0.1
1991	153.5	1.7	154.1	0.4	154.5	0.3	154.4	-0.1	154.9	0.3	155.0	0.1	154.7	-0.2	155.0	0.2	154.9	-0.1	155.5	0.4	155.8	0.2	155.7	-0.1
1992	158.4	1.7	158.3	-0.1	158.7	0.3	159.0	0.2	159.4	0.3	159.2	-0.1	159.5	0.2	159.8	0.2	160.1	0.2	161.0	0.6	161.0	0.0	161.3	0.2
1993	163.8	1.5	164.3	0.3	164.3	0.0	164.8	0.3	164.9	0.1	164.2	-0.4	164.5	0.2	165.1	0.4	165.2	0.1	166.0	0.5	165.9	-0.1	166.3	0.2
1994	168.0	1.0	168.1	0.1	168.5	0.2	168.5	0.0	169.0	0.3	169.1	0.1	169.3	0.1	169.6	0.2	170.3	0.4	170.8	0.3	171.8	0.6	172.6	0.5
1995	175.3	1.6	176.3	0.6	177.0	0.4	177.9	0.5	178.6	0.4	179.8	0.7	180.8	0.6	181.1	0.2	181.6	0.3	182.7	0.6	183.8	0.6	184.0	0.1
1996	185.7	0.9	186.1	0.2	186.1	0.0	186.4	0.2	186.7	0.2	186.8	0.1	186.5	-0.2	186.8	0.2	187.5	0.4	187.7	0.1	188.1	0.2	188.3	0.1
1997	189.5	0.6	189.5	0.0	189.3	-0.1	189.9	0.3	189.6	-0.2	189.8	0.1	190.1	0.2	190.3	0.1	190.7	0.2	192.0	0.7	192.4	0.2	192.9	0.3

Source: U.S. Department of Labor, Bureau of Labor Statistics, Division of Industry Prices and Price Indexes. n.e.c. stands for not elsewhere classified. - indicates no data collected for period or unavailable.

METALS AND METAL PRODUCTS
Producer Price Index
Base 1982 = 100

For 1926-1997. Columns headed % show percentile change in the index from the previous period for which an index is available.

Year	Jan Index	%	Feb Index	%	Mar Index	%	Apr Index	%	May Index	%	Jun Index	%	Jul Index	%	Aug Index	%	Sep Index	%	Oct Index	%	Nov Index	%	Dec Index	%
1926	13.9	-	13.8	-0.7	13.8	0.0	13.7	-0.7	13.6	-0.7	13.6	0.0	13.6	0.0	13.7	0.7	13.8	0.7	13.8	0.0	13.7	-0.7	13.7	0.0
1927	13.2	-3.6	13.0	-1.5	13.0	0.0	13.0	0.0	12.9	-0.8	12.8	-0.8	12.8	0.0	12.9	0.8	12.8	-0.8	12.7	-0.8	12.7	0.0	12.7	0.0
1928	12.7	0.0	12.8	0.8	12.8	0.0	12.8	0.0	12.8	0.0	12.8	0.0	12.8	0.0	12.8	0.0	12.9	0.8	13.0	0.8	13.1	0.8	13.1	0.0
1929	13.2	0.8	13.3	0.8	13.7	3.0	13.6	-0.7	13.4	-1.5	13.4	0.0	13.3	-0.7	13.3	0.0	13.3	0.0	13.3	0.0	13.2	-0.8	13.1	-0.8
1930	12.9	-1.5	12.8	-0.8	12.8	0.0	12.5	-2.3	12.2	-2.4	11.9	-2.5	11.7	-1.7	11.6	-0.9	11.6	0.0	11.4	-1.7	11.4	0.0	11.4	0.0
1931	11.2	-1.8	11.2	0.0	11.2	0.0	11.1	-0.9	10.9	-1.8	10.8	-0.9	10.7	-0.9	10.6	-0.9	10.6	0.0	10.4	-1.9	10.4	0.0	10.3	-1.0
1932	10.2	-1.0	10.0	-2.0	9.9	-1.0	9.9	0.0	9.9	0.0	9.9	0.0	9.6	-3.0	9.8	2.1	10.0	2.0	10.1	1.0	9.9	-2.0	9.8	-1.0
1933	9.7	-1.0	9.5	-2.1	9.5	0.0	9.5	0.0	9.7	2.1	10.0	3.1	10.3	3.0	10.4	1.0	10.6	1.9	10.8	1.9	10.7	-0.9	10.9	1.9
1934	10.9	0.0	11.1	1.8	11.2	0.9	11.3	0.9	11.6	2.7	11.4	-1.7	11.2	-1.8	11.2	0.0	11.2	0.0	11.1	-0.9	11.1	0.0	11.1	0.0
1935	11.1	0.0	11.1	0.0	11.1	0.0	11.1	0.0	11.2	0.9	11.2	0.0	11.2	0.0	11.2	0.0	11.2	0.0	11.3	0.9	11.3	0.0	11.3	0.0
1936	11.3	0.0	11.3	0.0	11.2	-0.9	11.2	0.0	11.2	0.0	11.2	0.0	11.4	1.8	11.4	0.0	11.5	0.9	11.6	0.9	11.7	0.9	12.0	2.6
1937	12.3	2.5	12.4	0.8	13.4	8.1	13.5	0.7	13.3	-1.5	13.3	0.0	13.3	0.0	13.4	0.8	13.3	-0.7	13.1	-1.5	12.8	-2.3	12.7	-0.8
1938	12.8	0.8	12.6	-1.6	12.6	0.0	12.7	0.8	12.8	0.8	12.6	-1.6	12.4	-1.6	12.5	0.8	12.5	0.0	12.5	0.0	12.6	0.8	12.5	-0.8
1939	12.5	0.0	12.5	0.0	12.5	0.0	12.4	-0.8	12.3	-0.8	12.3	0.0	12.3	0.0	12.3	0.0	12.6	2.4	12.7	0.8	12.7	0.0	12.7	0.0
1940	12.7	0.0	12.6	-0.8	12.6	0.0	12.4	-1.6	12.4	0.0	12.4	0.0	12.4	0.0	12.4	0.0	12.5	0.8	12.6	0.8	12.6	0.0	12.6	0.0
1941	12.6	0.0	12.6	0.0	12.7	0.8	12.7	0.0	12.7	0.0	12.8	0.8	12.8	0.0	12.8	0.0	12.8	0.0	12.8	0.0	12.9	0.8	12.9	0.0
1942	12.9	0.0	12.9	0.0	13.0	0.8	13.0	0.0	13.0	0.0	13.0	0.0	12.9	-0.8	12.9	0.0	13.0	0.8	13.0	0.0	13.0	0.0	12.9	-0.8
1943	12.9	0.0	12.9	0.0	12.9	0.0	12.9	0.0	12.9	0.0	13.0	0.8	12.9	-0.8	12.9	0.0	12.9	0.0	12.9	0.0	12.9	0.0	12.9	0.0
1944	12.9	0.0	12.9	0.0	13.0	0.8	13.0	0.0	12.9	-0.8	12.9	0.0	12.9	0.0	12.9	0.0	12.9	0.0	12.9	0.0	12.9	0.0	12.9	0.0
1945	13.0	0.8	13.0	0.0	13.0	0.0	13.0	0.0	13.0	0.0	13.1	0.8	13.1	0.0	13.1	0.0	13.2	0.8	13.2	0.0	13.3	0.8	13.3	0.0
1946	13.3	0.0	13.5	1.5	13.9	3.0	14.0	0.7	14.1	0.7	14.7	4.3	15.0	2.0	15.1	0.7	15.1	0.0	15.2	0.7	15.7	3.3	16.4	4.5
1947	17.5	6.7	17.6	0.6	17.9	1.7	18.0	0.6	17.8	-1.1	17.9	0.6	18.1	1.1	18.5	2.2	18.6	0.5	18.7	0.5	18.8	0.5	18.9	0.5
1948	19.3	2.1	19.5	1.0	19.7	1.0	20.1	2.0	20.0	-0.5	20.1	0.5	20.5	2.0	21.6	5.4	21.8	0.9	21.9	0.5	22.0	0.5	22.1	0.5
1949	22.2	0.5	21.9	-1.4	21.7	-0.9	21.1	-2.8	20.6	-2.4	20.3	-1.5	20.3	0.0	20.4	0.5	20.5	0.5	20.5	0.0	20.6	0.5	20.6	0.0
1950	20.8	1.0	20.9	0.5	20.9	0.0	21.0	0.5	21.3	1.4	21.7	1.9	21.8	0.5	22.1	1.4	22.6	2.3	23.1	2.2	23.5	1.7	24.3	3.4
1951	24.7	1.6	24.7	0.0	24.6	-0.4	24.6	0.0	24.6	0.0	24.4	-0.8	24.4	0.0	24.3	-0.4	24.3	0.0	24.4	0.4	24.4	0.0	24.4	0.0
1952	24.4	0.0	24.4	0.0	24.4	0.0	24.4	0.0	24.3	-0.4	24.1	-0.8	24.3	0.8	24.7	1.6	24.8	0.4	24.7	-0.4	24.7	0.0	24.7	0.0
1953	24.7	0.0	24.8	0.4	25.0	0.8	24.9	-0.4	25.0	0.4	25.3	1.2	25.8	2.0	25.8	0.0	25.6	-0.8	25.5	-0.4	25.5	0.0	25.4	-0.4
1954	25.4	0.0	25.2	-0.8	25.2	0.0	25.3	0.4	25.3	0.0	25.3	0.0	25.5	0.8	25.6	0.4	25.7	0.4	25.9	0.8	25.9	0.0	25.9	0.0
1955	25.9	0.0	26.2	1.2	26.3	0.4	26.5	0.8	26.4	-0.4	26.4	0.0	27.3	3.4	27.8	1.8	28.3	1.8	28.4	0.4	28.5	0.4	28.7	0.7
1956	28.9	0.7	28.9	0.0	29.2	1.0	29.4	0.7	29.2	-0.7	29.1	-0.3	28.9	-0.7	29.9	3.5	30.3	1.3	30.3	0.0	30.3	0.0	30.4	0.3
1957	30.3	-0.3	30.2	-0.3	30.1	-0.3	29.9	-0.7	29.9	0.0	30.0	0.3	30.4	1.3	30.5	0.3	30.3	-0.7	30.1	-0.7	30.0	-0.3	30.0	0.0
1958	29.9	-0.3	29.9	0.0	29.9	0.0	29.6	-1.0	29.6	0.0	29.6	0.0	29.6	0.0	30.1	1.7	30.2	0.3	30.3	0.3	30.5	0.7	30.5	0.0
1959	30.5	0.0	30.6	0.3	30.6	0.0	30.5	-0.3	30.5	0.0	30.6	0.3	30.4	-0.7	30.5	0.3	30.6	0.3	30.8	0.7	31.1	1.0	30.9	-0.6
1960	31.0	0.3	30.9	-0.3	30.8	-0.3	30.8	0.0	30.7	-0.3	30.6	-0.3	30.6	0.0	30.6	0.0	30.6	0.0	30.5	-0.3	30.4	-0.3	30.3	-0.3
1961	30.3	0.0	30.4	0.3	30.4	0.0	30.4	0.0	30.5	0.3	30.5	0.0	30.5	0.0	30.6	0.3	30.6	0.0	30.5	-0.3	30.4	-0.3	30.4	0.0
1962	30.5	0.3	30.4	-0.3	30.4	0.0	30.3	-0.3	30.3	0.0	30.2	-0.3	30.2	0.0	30.2	0.0	30.2	0.0	30.1	-0.3	30.0	-0.3	30.0	0.0
1963	30.1	0.3	30.1	0.0	30.1	0.0	30.1	0.0	30.2	0.3	30.2	0.0	30.2	0.0	30.3	0.3	30.3	0.0	30.5	0.7	30.6	0.3	30.6	0.0
1964	30.8	0.7	30.8	0.0	30.9	0.3	30.9	0.0	30.9	0.0	30.9	0.0	31.0	0.3	31.2	0.6	31.2	0.0	31.4	0.6	31.6	0.6	31.7	0.3
1965	31.6	-0.3	31.6	0.0	31.7	0.3	31.8	0.3	32.0	0.6	32.0	0.0	32.0	0.0	32.1	0.3	32.1	0.0	32.2	0.3	32.3	0.3	32.3	0.0
1966	32.4	0.3	32.5	0.3	32.7	0.6	32.7	0.0	32.8	0.3	32.9	0.3	32.9	0.0	32.8	-0.3	32.8	0.0	32.9	0.3	33.0	0.3	33.0	0.0
1967	33.1	0.3	33.2	0.3	33.1	-0.3	33.0	-0.3	33.0	0.0	33.0	0.0	33.0	0.0	33.0	0.0	33.2	0.6	33.3	0.3	33.6	0.9	33.7	0.3
1968	34.0	0.9	34.3	0.9	34.4	0.3	34.2	-0.6	33.8	-1.2	33.8	0.0	33.7	-0.3	33.7	0.0	33.9	0.6	34.0	0.3	34.0	0.0	34.1	0.3
1969	34.6	1.5	34.8	0.6	35.0	0.6	35.2	0.6	35.5	0.9	35.7	0.6	35.9	0.6	36.4	1.4	36.8	1.1	37.0	0.5	37.1	0.3	37.5	1.1
1970	37.8	0.8	38.2	1.1	38.4	0.5	38.7	0.8	38.9	0.5	39.1	0.5	39.0	-0.3	38.9	-0.3	38.9	0.0	39.0	0.3	38.7	-0.8	38.5	-0.5

[Continued]

METALS AND METAL PRODUCTS
Producer Price Index
Base 1982 = 100
[Continued]

For 1926-1997. Columns headed % show percentile change in the index from the previous period for which an index is available.

Year	Jan Index	%	Feb Index	%	Mar Index	%	Apr Index	%	May Index	%	Jun Index	%	Jul Index	%	Aug Index	%	Sep Index	%	Oct Index	%	Nov Index	%	Dec Index	%
1971	38.6	0.3	38.5	-0.3	38.5	0.0	38.9	1.0	39.1	0.5	39.2	0.3	39.5	0.8	40.1	1.5	40.1	0.0	40.0	-0.2	40.0	0.0	39.9	-0.2
1972	40.3	1.0	40.6	0.7	40.9	0.7	40.9	0.0	41.0	0.2	41.0	0.0	40.9	-0.2	41.0	0.2	41.1	0.2	41.1	0.0	41.2	0.2	41.2	0.0
1973	41.6	1.0	42.1	1.2	42.8	1.7	43.3	1.2	43.7	0.9	43.9	0.5	44.0	0.2	44.3	0.7	44.5	0.5	45.1	1.3	45.9	1.8	47.0	2.4
1974	48.1	2.3	49.1	2.1	51.3	4.5	53.4	4.1	55.9	4.7	57.7	3.2	59.8	3.6	61.5	2.8	62.0	0.8	62.0	0.0	61.9	-0.2	61.2	-1.1
1975	61.5	0.5	61.8	0.5	61.7	-0.2	61.6	-0.2	61.4	-0.3	61.2	-0.3	60.8	-0.7	61.1	0.5	61.5	0.7	62.1	1.0	62.0	-0.2	62.0	0.0
1976	62.3	0.5	62.7	0.6	63.2	0.8	64.0	1.3	64.4	0.6	65.2	1.2	65.9	1.1	66.2	0.5	66.3	0.2	66.3	0.0	66.3	0.0	66.6	0.5
1977	67.0	0.6	67.4	0.6	68.5	1.6	69.0	0.7	69.1	0.1	68.9	-0.3	69.8	1.3	70.2	0.6	70.5	0.4	70.2	-0.4	70.3	0.1	70.7	0.6
1978	71.4	1.0	72.6	1.7	73.3	1.0	74.2	1.2	74.5	0.4	74.9	0.5	75.4	0.7	76.6	1.6	76.7	0.1	77.6	1.2	78.1	0.6	78.5	0.5
1979	80.2	2.2	82.0	2.2	83.5	1.8	84.9	1.7	84.9	0.0	85.6	0.8	86.5	1.1	86.8	0.3	87.4	0.7	89.4	2.3	89.9	0.6	90.7	0.9
1980	94.3	4.0	95.8	1.6	95.1	-0.7	94.3	-0.8	93.4	-1.0	93.5	0.1	93.7	0.2	94.5	0.9	95.3	0.8	96.8	1.6	96.5	-0.3	96.4	-0.1
1981	97.5	1.1	97.5	0.0	98.3	0.8	99.1	0.8	99.2	0.1	98.9	-0.3	100.1	1.2	100.8	0.7	101.1	0.3	101.2	0.1	100.9	-0.3	100.5	-0.4
1982	101.0	0.5	100.9	-0.1	100.4	-0.5	100.5	0.1	100.4	-0.1	99.2	-1.2	99.3	0.1	99.2	-0.1	100.0	0.8	100.0	0.0	99.6	-0.4	99.4	-0.2
1983	99.6	0.2	101.0	1.4	100.9	-0.1	101.0	0.1	101.5	0.5	101.5	0.0	101.9	0.4	102.2	0.3	103.0	0.8	103.1	0.1	103.1	0.0	103.4	0.3
1984	103.7	0.3	104.4	0.7	105.0	0.6	105.4	0.4	105.2	-0.2	105.2	0.0	104.8	-0.4	104.8	0.0	104.7	-0.1	104.8	0.1	104.9	0.1	104.6	-0.3
1985	104.4	-0.2	104.6	0.2	104.6	0.0	105.0	0.4	104.9	-0.1	104.4	-0.5	104.3	-0.1	104.3	0.0	104.2	-0.1	104.2	0.0	103.9	-0.3	103.9	0.0
1986	103.1	-0.8	103.2	0.1	103.2	0.0	103.1	-0.1	103.0	-0.1	103.0	0.0	102.9	-0.1	103.1	0.2	103.3	0.2	103.4	0.1	103.4	0.0	103.3	-0.1
1987	103.7	0.4	103.8	0.1	104.0	0.2	104.4	0.4	105.2	0.8	105.8	0.6	106.7	0.9	107.7	0.9	108.8	1.0	110.8	1.8	111.7	0.8	112.9	1.1
1988	114.4	1.3	114.7	0.3	115.4	0.6	116.9	1.3	117.4	0.4	118.0	0.5	119.2	1.0	119.8	0.5	120.2	0.3	121.4	1.0	122.8	1.2	124.0	1.0
1989	125.3	1.0	125.1	-0.2	125.6	0.4	125.6	0.0	125.2	-0.3	124.0	-1.0	123.0	-0.8	123.0	0.0	123.7	0.6	123.9	0.2	122.8	-0.9	121.7	-0.9
1990	121.7	0.0	120.9	-0.7	122.0	0.9	122.9	0.7	123.1	0.2	122.6	-0.4	122.9	0.2	124.2	1.1	124.6	0.3	124.5	-0.1	123.3	-1.0	122.4	-0.7
1991	122.4	0.0	121.9	-0.4	121.5	-0.3	121.3	-0.2	120.5	-0.7	119.7	-0.7	119.6	-0.1	119.5	-0.1	119.5	0.0	119.3	-0.2	118.9	-0.3	118.7	-0.2
1992	118.2	-0.4	118.9	0.6	119.4	0.4	119.6	0.2	119.5	-0.1	119.6	0.1	120.0	0.3	120.2	0.2	119.6	-0.5	118.8	-0.7	118.2	-0.5	118.5	0.3
1993	118.9	0.3	119.2	0.3	119.0	-0.2	118.7	-0.3	118.4	-0.3	118.9	0.4	119.5	0.5	119.5	0.0	119.5	0.0	119.4	-0.1	119.6	0.2	120.2	0.5
1994	120.7	0.4	121.7	0.8	122.3	0.5	122.5	0.2	122.7	0.2	123.5	0.7	124.7	1.0	125.5	0.6	126.5	0.8	127.3	0.6	129.4	1.6	130.6	0.9
1995	133.4	2.1	134.6	0.9	134.7	0.1	135.2	0.4	134.7	-0.4	134.8	0.1	135.2	0.3	135.5	0.2	135.0	-0.4	134.1	-0.7	133.7	-0.3	133.4	-0.2
1996	132.8	-0.4	131.8	-0.8	131.8	0.0	132.0	0.2	132.4	0.3	131.9	-0.4	130.4	-1.1	130.0	-0.3	130.0	0.0	129.4	-0.5	129.4	0.0	129.9	0.4
1997	131.0	0.8	131.6	0.5	132.2	0.5	131.8	-0.3	132.2	0.3	132.5	0.2	132.0	-0.4	132.2	0.2	132.0	-0.2	131.9	-0.1	131.3	-0.5	130.6	-0.5

Source: U.S. Department of Labor, Bureau of Labor Statistics, Division of Industry Prices and Price Indexes. n.e.c. stands for not elsewhere classified. - indicates no data collected for period or unavailable.

Iron and Steel
Producer Price Index
Base 1982 = 100

For 1926-1997. Columns headed % show percentile change in the index from the previous period for which an index is available.

Year	Jan Index	%	Feb Index	%	Mar Index	%	Apr Index	%	May Index	%	Jun Index	%	Jul Index	%	Aug Index	%	Sep Index	%	Oct Index	%	Nov Index	%	Dec Index	%
1926	11.4	-	11.4	0.0	11.4	0.0	11.3	-0.9	11.3	0.0	11.2	-0.9	11.2	0.0	11.2	0.0	11.3	0.9	11.3	0.0	11.3	0.0	11.2	-0.9
1927	10.9	-2.7	10.7	-1.8	10.7	0.0	10.7	0.0	10.7	0.0	10.7	0.0	10.7	0.0	10.6	-0.9	10.6	0.0	10.6	0.0	10.5	-0.9	10.5	0.0	10.4	-1.0
1928	10.5	1.0	10.6	1.0	10.6	0.0	10.6	0.0	10.6	0.0	10.5	-0.9	10.5	0.0	10.5	0.0	10.5	0.0	10.6	1.0	10.6	0.0	10.7	0.9
1929	10.7	0.0	10.7	0.0	10.7	0.0	10.8	0.9	10.8	0.0	10.8	0.0	10.8	0.0	10.8	0.0	10.7	-0.9	10.7	0.0	10.7	0.0	10.6	-0.9	10.6	0.0
1930	10.4	-1.9	10.3	-1.0	10.3	0.0	10.2	-1.0	10.2	0.0	10.1	-1.0	10.0	-1.0	9.9	-1.0	9.9	0.0	9.9	0.0	9.8	-1.0	9.8	0.0
1931	9.6	-2.0	9.7	1.0	9.6	-1.0	9.5	-1.0	9.5	0.0	9.4	-1.1	9.4	0.0	9.3	-1.1	9.3	0.0	9.2	-1.1	9.2	0.0	9.1	-1.1
1932	9.0	-1.1	9.0	0.0	9.0	0.0	9.1	1.1	9.0	-1.1	9.0	0.0	8.7	-3.3	8.9	2.3	9.0	1.1	9.1	1.1	9.0	-1.1	8.9	-1.1
1933	8.8	-1.1	8.7	-1.1	8.6	-1.1	8.6	0.0	8.5	-1.2	8.6	1.2	8.8	2.3	8.9	1.1	9.1	2.2	9.3	2.2	9.2	-1.1	9.4	2.2
1934	9.4	0.0	9.7	3.2	9.8	1.0	9.9	1.0	10.2	3.0	10.0	-2.0	9.8	-2.0	9.8	0.0	9.8	0.0	9.7	-1.0	9.7	0.0	9.7	0.0
1935	9.7	0.0	9.7	0.0	9.7	0.0	9.7	0.0	9.8	1.0	9.9	1.0	9.8	-1.0	9.9	1.0	9.8	-1.0	9.8	0.0	9.8	0.0	9.8	0.0
1936	9.9	1.0	9.8	-1.0	9.8	0.0	9.8	0.0	9.7	-1.0	9.7	0.0	9.9	2.1	9.9	0.0	10.0	1.0	10.1	1.0	10.1	0.0	10.2	1.0
1937	10.4	2.0	10.4	0.0	11.0	5.8	11.2	1.8	11.2	0.0	11.2	0.0	11.3	0.9	11.3	0.0	11.3	0.0	11.2	-0.9	11.2	0.0	11.2	0.0
1938	11.2	0.0	11.2	0.0	11.2	0.0	11.3	0.9	11.5	1.8	11.4	-0.9	11.0	-3.5	11.0	0.0	11.0	0.0	10.9	-0.9	11.0	0.9	10.9	-0.9
1939	10.9	0.0	10.9	0.0	10.9	0.0	10.9	0.0	10.8	-0.9	10.7	-0.9	10.7	0.0	10.7	0.0	10.8	0.9	10.9	0.9	10.9	0.0	10.9	0.0
1940	10.9	0.0	10.9	0.0	10.9	0.0	10.6	-2.8	10.6	0.0	10.6	0.0	10.7	0.9	10.7	0.0	10.7	0.0	10.7	0.0	10.8	0.9	10.8	0.0
1941	10.8	0.0	10.8	0.0	10.8	0.0	10.8	0.0	10.9	0.9	10.9	0.0	10.9	0.0	11.0	0.9	11.0	0.0	11.0	0.0	11.0	0.0	11.0	0.0
1942	11.0	0.0	11.0	0.0	11.0	0.0	11.0	0.0	11.0	0.0	11.0	0.0	11.0	0.0	11.0	0.0	11.0	0.0	11.0	0.0	11.0	0.0	11.0	0.0
1943	11.0	0.0	11.0	0.0	11.0	0.0	11.0	0.0	11.0	0.0	11.0	0.0	11.0	0.0	11.0	0.0	11.0	0.0	11.0	0.0	11.0	0.0	11.0	0.0
1944	11.0	0.0	11.0	0.0	11.0	0.0	11.0	0.0	11.0	0.0	11.0	0.0	11.0	0.0	11.0	0.0	11.0	0.0	11.0	0.0	11.0	0.0	11.0	0.0
1945	11.1	0.9	11.1	0.0	11.1	0.0	11.1	0.0	11.1	0.0	11.2	0.9	11.2	0.0	11.2	0.0	11.2	0.0	11.3	0.9	11.3	0.0	11.4	0.9
1946	11.4	0.0	11.7	2.6	12.1	3.4	12.1	0.0	12.2	0.8	12.4	1.6	12.6	1.6	12.8	1.6	12.8	0.0	12.8	0.0	12.9	0.8	13.3	3.1
1947	14.4	8.3	14.5	0.7	14.7	1.4	14.7	0.0	14.4	-2.0	14.5	0.7	14.9	2.8	15.8	6.0	15.7	-0.6	15.9	1.3	15.9	0.0	16.0	0.6
1948	16.5	3.1	16.7	1.2	16.8	0.6	16.9	0.6	16.8	-0.6	16.8	0.0	17.2	2.4	18.5	7.6	18.5	0.0	18.6	0.5	18.7	0.5	18.8	0.5
1949	18.8	0.0	18.4	-2.1	18.3	-0.5	17.7	-3.3	17.4	-1.7	17.4	0.0	17.3	-0.6	17.4	0.6	17.7	1.7	17.8	0.6	17.9	0.6	18.1	1.1
1950	18.3	1.1	18.5	1.1	18.5	0.0	18.5	0.0	18.7	1.1	19.1	2.1	19.0	-0.5	19.2	1.1	19.3	0.5	19.4	0.5	19.6	1.0	20.6	5.1
1951	21.0	1.9	20.8	-1.0	20.7	-0.5	20.7	0.0	20.7	0.0	20.7	0.0	20.7	0.0	20.7	0.0	20.7	0.0	20.7	0.0	20.7	0.0	20.7	0.0
1952	20.7	0.0	20.8	0.5	20.8	0.0	20.7	-0.5	20.7	0.0	20.6	-0.5	20.6	0.0	21.4	3.9	21.5	0.5	21.4	-0.5	21.4	0.0	21.4	0.0
1953	21.4	0.0	21.5	0.5	21.5	0.0	21.5	0.0	21.7	0.9	22.0	1.4	22.9	4.1	22.9	0.0	22.7	-0.9	22.5	-0.9	22.5	0.0	22.4	-0.4
1954	22.2	-0.9	22.1	-0.5	22.0	-0.5	22.1	0.5	22.2	0.5	22.2	0.0	22.5	1.4	22.5	0.0	22.6	0.4	22.7	0.4	22.8	0.4	22.7	-0.4
1955	22.9	0.9	22.9	0.0	22.9	0.0	23.0	0.4	22.8	-0.9	22.9	0.4	24.1	5.2	24.4	1.2	24.4	0.0	24.5	0.4	24.6	0.4	24.8	0.8
1956	25.2	1.6	25.1	-0.4	25.2	0.4	25.4	0.8	25.4	0.0	25.2	-0.8	25.2	0.0	26.8	6.3	27.2	1.5	27.1	-0.4	27.4	1.1	27.5	0.4
1957	27.7	0.7	27.6	-0.4	27.6	0.0	27.3	-1.1	27.5	0.7	27.9	1.5	28.7	2.9	28.8	0.3	28.7	-0.3	28.3	-1.4	28.1	-0.7	28.1	0.0
1958	28.1	0.0	28.3	0.7	28.2	-0.4	28.1	-0.4	28.0	-0.4	28.1	0.4	28.1	0.0	28.9	2.8	28.9	0.0	28.9	0.0	29.0	0.3	28.9	-0.3
1959	29.0	0.3	29.1	0.3	29.0	-0.3	28.8	-0.7	28.7	-0.3	28.9	0.7	28.9	0.0	29.0	0.3	29.1	0.3	29.1	0.0	29.2	0.3	29.0	-0.7
1960	29.1	0.3	28.9	-0.7	28.7	-0.7	28.7	0.0	28.7	0.0	28.6	-0.3	28.6	0.0	28.6	0.0	28.6	0.0	28.4	-0.7	28.4	0.0	28.4	0.0
1961	28.5	0.4	28.6	0.4	28.7	0.3	28.8	0.3	28.7	-0.3	28.7	0.0	28.6	-0.3	28.7	0.3	28.8	0.3	28.7	-0.3	28.5	-0.7	28.5	0.0
1962	28.6	0.4	28.6	0.0	28.4	-0.7	28.3	-0.4	28.3	0.0	28.2	-0.4	28.2	0.0	28.2	0.0	28.2	0.0	28.1	-0.4	28.0	-0.4	28.1	0.4
1963	28.1	0.0	28.1	0.0	28.0	-0.4	28.1	0.4	28.3	0.7	28.2	-0.4	28.2	0.0	28.2	0.0	28.2	0.0	28.4	0.7	28.4	0.0	28.5	0.4
1964	28.5	0.0	28.5	0.0	28.5	0.0	28.5	0.0	28.6	0.4	28.6	0.0	28.7	0.3	28.8	0.3	28.6	-0.7	28.7	0.3	28.7	0.0	28.8	0.3
1965	28.9	0.3	28.8	-0.3	28.8	0.0	28.9	0.3	28.9	0.0	28.8	-0.3	28.9	0.3	28.9	0.0	28.8	-0.3	28.8	0.0	28.8	0.0	29.0	0.7
1966	29.1	0.3	29.1	0.0	29.1	0.0	29.1	0.0	29.0	-0.3	29.1	0.3	29.1	0.0	29.2	0.3	29.2	0.0	29.2	0.0	29.3	0.3	29.3	0.0
1967	29.4	0.3	29.4	0.0	29.5	0.3	29.4	-0.3	29.4	0.0	29.4	0.0	29.4	0.0	29.4	0.0	29.6	0.7	29.6	0.0	29.7	0.3	29.8	0.3
1968	30.1	1.0	30.1	0.0	30.0	-0.3	29.9	-0.3	29.9	0.0	29.9	0.0	29.9	0.0	29.9	0.0	30.4	1.7	30.4	0.0	30.2	-0.7	30.2	0.0
1969	30.6	1.3	30.7	0.3	30.9	0.7	31.0	0.3	31.3	1.0	31.4	0.3	31.6	0.6	32.1	1.6	32.2	0.3	32.4	0.6	32.4	0.0	32.5	0.3
1970	32.7	0.6	33.3	1.8	33.5	0.6	33.4	-0.3	33.9	1.5	34.3	1.2	34.3	0.0	34.2	-0.3	34.4	0.6	34.6	0.6	34.3	-0.9	34.3	0.0

[Continued]

Iron and Steel

Producer Price Index
Base 1982 = 100

[Continued]

For 1926-1997. Columns headed % show percentile change in the index from the previous period for which an index is available.

Year	Jan Index	%	Feb Index	%	Mar Index	%	Apr Index	%	May Index	%	Jun Index	%	Jul Index	%	Aug Index	%	Sep Index	%	Oct Index	%	Nov Index	%	Dec Index	%
1971	34.6	0.9	34.8	0.6	34.8	0.0	34.9	0.3	35.4	1.4	35.5	0.3	36.0	1.4	37.0	2.8	37.1	0.3	37.1	0.0	37.0	-0.3	37.0	0.0
1972	37.4	1.1	37.8	1.1	37.9	0.3	37.8	-0.3	37.8	0.0	37.8	0.0	37.8	0.0	37.9	0.3	38.0	0.3	38.0	0.0	38.1	0.3	38.2	0.3
1973	38.9	1.8	39.2	0.8	39.3	0.3	39.5	0.5	39.9	1.0	40.1	0.5	40.1	0.0	40.1	0.0	40.3	0.5	40.9	1.5	41.8	2.2	42.0	0.5
1974	42.7	1.7	43.9	2.8	46.5	5.9	48.6	4.5	49.9	2.7	52.5	5.2	56.2	7.0	57.7	2.7	58.4	1.2	58.7	0.5	58.9	0.3	58.0	-1.5
1975	58.8	1.4	59.1	0.5	59.2	0.2	59.3	0.2	59.2	-0.2	58.8	-0.7	58.2	-1.0	58.5	0.5	59.1	1.0	60.4	2.2	60.2	-0.3	60.3	0.2
1976	60.8	0.8	61.8	1.6	62.4	1.0	62.9	0.8	62.9	0.0	64.4	2.4	64.9	0.8	64.9	0.0	64.5	-0.6	64.5	0.0	64.6	0.2	65.7	1.7
1977	66.1	0.6	66.3	0.3	67.1	1.2	67.3	0.3	67.2	-0.1	66.9	-0.4	68.5	2.4	68.8	0.4	69.6	1.2	69.1	-0.7	68.9	-0.3	69.5	0.9
1978	70.2	1.0	72.2	2.8	73.0	1.1	74.3	1.8	74.3	0.0	74.5	0.3	74.9	0.5	76.3	1.9	76.3	0.0	76.7	0.5	77.2	0.7	77.6	0.5
1979	80.3	3.5	81.1	1.0	82.6	1.8	82.6	0.0	82.4	-0.2	83.5	1.3	84.6	1.3	84.4	-0.2	84.2	-0.2	85.3	1.3	86.1	0.9	86.4	0.3
1980	87.7	1.5	88.6	1.0	89.0	0.5	90.6	1.8	89.9	-0.8	89.5	-0.4	88.7	-0.9	89.3	0.7	89.8	0.6	91.6	2.0	92.2	0.7	93.3	1.2
1981	95.3	2.1	95.3	0.0	96.8	1.6	97.6	0.8	97.5	-0.1	97.4	-0.1	99.9	2.6	100.3	0.4	100.2	-0.1	100.7	0.5	100.3	-0.4	100.3	0.0
1982	101.2	0.9	101.1	-0.1	101.0	-0.1	101.1	0.1	100.7	-0.4	99.8	-0.9	99.5	-0.3	99.4	-0.1	99.3	-0.1	99.6	0.3	99.1	-0.5	98.2	-0.9
1983	98.3	0.1	100.3	2.0	100.8	0.5	100.7	-0.1	100.6	-0.1	100.7	0.1	100.9	0.2	101.2	0.3	102.7	1.5	102.8	0.1	103.1	0.3	103.5	0.4
1984	104.4	0.9	105.1	0.7	105.1	0.0	105.1	0.0	105.4	0.3	105.3	-0.1	105.4	0.1	105.4	0.0	105.6	0.2	105.7	0.1	105.5	-0.2	105.3	-0.2
1985	105.3	0.0	105.4	0.1	105.5	0.1	105.4	-0.1	105.0	-0.4	104.6	-0.4	104.5	-0.1	104.6	0.1	104.6	0.0	104.5	-0.1	104.1	-0.4	104.1	0.0
1986	101.0	-3.0	101.1	0.1	100.8	-0.3	101.0	0.2	101.2	0.2	101.1	-0.1	101.1	0.0	101.2	0.1	101.4	0.2	101.4	0.0	101.3	-0.1	101.3	0.0
1987	102.0	0.7	102.3	0.3	101.9	-0.4	101.9	0.0	102.2	0.3	102.5	0.3	103.1	0.6	103.7	0.6	105.4	1.6	109.5	3.9	110.4	0.8	109.9	-0.5
1988	110.9	0.9	113.0	1.9	113.6	0.5	114.8	1.1	115.0	0.2	114.9	-0.1	117.0	1.8	118.0	0.9	117.4	-0.5	118.3	0.8	117.6	-0.6	117.6	0.0
1989	119.7	1.8	120.6	0.8	120.7	0.1	120.8	0.1	120.6	-0.2	119.8	-0.7	119.0	-0.7	118.4	-0.5	118.1	-0.3	117.8	-0.3	116.9	-0.8	116.5	-0.3
1990	116.7	0.2	116.2	-0.4	116.5	0.3	117.1	0.5	117.9	0.7	117.4	-0.4	117.5	0.1	118.2	0.6	117.9	-0.3	117.5	-0.3	116.9	-0.5	116.8	-0.1
1991	117.0	0.2	116.6	-0.3	115.8	-0.7	115.4	-0.3	114.5	-0.8	113.5	-0.9	113.3	-0.2	113.0	-0.3	112.8	-0.2	112.4	-0.4	112.3	-0.1	112.3	0.0
1992	112.1	-0.2	112.3	0.2	112.7	0.4	112.3	-0.4	112.2	-0.1	111.4	-0.7	111.4	0.0	111.2	-0.2	111.0	-0.2	110.3	-0.6	110.1	-0.2	110.6	0.5
1993	111.9	1.2	113.1	1.1	113.4	0.3	113.5	0.1	114.2	0.6	115.6	1.2	116.5	0.8	116.7	0.2	117.3	0.5	119.0	1.4	119.9	0.8	120.8	0.8
1994	121.3	0.4	122.0	0.6	121.8	-0.2	121.4	-0.3	120.6	-0.7	118.8	-1.5	120.4	1.3	122.3	1.6	123.1	0.7	123.1	0.0	124.1	0.8	124.7	0.5
1995	127.2	2.0	128.4	0.9	129.1	0.5	129.8	0.5	129.9	0.1	129.7	-0.2	129.9	0.2	130.4	0.4	129.4	-0.8	128.4	-0.8	126.9	-1.2	126.6	-0.2
1996	127.0	0.3	126.3	-0.6	125.7	-0.5	125.9	0.2	126.3	0.3	126.2	-0.1	125.8	-0.3	126.2	0.3	126.4	0.2	125.5	-0.7	124.3	-1.0	124.2	-0.1
1997	125.5	1.0	126.6	0.9	126.2	-0.3	125.8	-0.3	126.0	0.2	126.1	0.1	126.7	0.5	126.8	0.1	126.8	0.0	127.1	0.2	127.6	0.4	127.1	-0.4

Source: U.S. Department of Labor, Bureau of Labor Statistics, Division of Industry Prices and Price Indexes. n.e.c. stands for not elsewhere classified. - indicates no data collected for period or unavailable.

Nonferrous Metals
Producer Price Index
Base 1982 = 100

For 1926-1997. Columns headed % show percentile change in the index from the previous period for which an index is available.

Year	Jan Index	%	Feb Index	%	Mar Index	%	Apr Index	%	May Index	%	Jun Index	%	Jul Index	%	Aug Index	%	Sep Index	%	Oct Index	%	Nov Index	%	Dec Index	%
1926	16.8	-	16.8	0.0	16.6	-1.2	16.2	-2.4	16.0	-1.2	16.1	0.6	16.5	2.5	16.8	1.8	16.8	0.0	16.6	-1.2	16.4	-1.2	16.0	-2.4
1927	15.7	-1.9	15.5	-1.3	15.8	1.9	15.5	-1.9	15.2	-1.9	15.0	-1.3	14.9	-0.7	15.4	3.4	15.1	-1.9	15.0	-0.7	15.1	0.7	15.4	2.0
1928	15.3	-0.6	15.1	-1.3	15.0	-0.7	15.2	1.3	15.3	0.7	15.4	0.7	15.4	0.0	15.4	0.0	15.6	1.3	15.9	1.9	16.2	1.9	16.2	0.0
1929	16.7	3.1	17.4	4.2	19.3	10.9	18.6	-3.6	17.4	-6.5	17.4	0.0	17.4	0.0	17.4	0.0	17.3	-0.6	17.3	0.0	17.0	-1.7	16.8	-1.2
1930	16.7	-0.6	16.7	0.0	16.4	-1.8	15.1	-7.9	13.5	-10.6	13.2	-2.2	12.4	-6.1	12.3	-0.8	12.1	-1.6	11.5	-5.0	11.6	0.9	11.8	1.7
1931	11.5	-2.5	11.3	-1.7	11.4	0.9	11.1	-2.6	10.4	-6.3	10.1	-2.9	10.1	0.0	9.9	-2.0	9.7	-2.0	9.1	-6.2	9.0	-1.1	8.9	-1.1
1932	9.1	2.2	8.7	-4.4	8.3	-4.6	8.1	-2.4	7.9	-2.5	7.9	0.0	7.7	-2.5	8.0	3.9	8.5	6.3	8.3	-2.4	8.1	-2.4	7.9	-2.5
1933	7.7	-2.5	7.6	-1.3	7.9	3.9	8.1	2.5	9.3	14.8	10.4	11.8	11.2	7.7	11.2	0.0	11.3	0.9	11.0	-2.7	11.2	1.8	11.0	-1.8
1934	10.9	-0.9	10.8	-0.9	10.9	0.9	11.2	2.8	11.2	0.0	11.3	0.9	11.3	0.0	11.3	0.0	11.3	0.0	11.2	-0.9	11.2	0.0	11.1	-0.9
1935	11.2	0.9	11.1	-0.9	11.1	0.0	11.2	0.9	11.4	1.8	11.4	0.0	10.9	-4.4	11.0	0.9	11.3	2.7	11.7	3.5	11.8	0.9	11.6	-1.7
1936	11.5	-0.9	11.5	0.0	11.5	0.0	11.6	0.9	11.7	0.9	11.5	-1.7	11.6	0.9	11.7	0.9	11.8	0.9	11.8	0.0	12.4	5.1	13.0	4.8
1937	14.0	7.7	14.8	5.7	16.7	12.8	16.0	-4.2	15.1	-5.6	15.1	0.0	15.3	1.3	15.4	0.7	15.3	-0.6	14.1	-7.8	12.9	-8.5	12.4	-3.9
1938	12.4	0.0	11.9	-4.0	11.8	-0.8	11.7	-0.8	11.3	-3.4	11.1	-1.8	11.8	6.3	12.0	1.7	12.1	0.8	12.6	4.1	12.8	1.6	12.7	-0.8
1939	12.6	-0.8	12.6	0.0	12.6	0.0	12.3	-2.4	12.1	-1.6	12.0	-0.8	12.1	0.8	12.3	1.7	14.0	13.8	14.1	0.7	14.0	-0.7	13.9	-0.7
1940	13.6	-2.2	13.0	-4.4	13.2	1.5	13.0	-1.5	13.2	1.5	13.4	1.5	13.4	0.0	13.0	-3.0	13.3	2.3	13.8	3.8	13.8	0.0	13.7	-0.7
1941	13.8	0.7	13.8	0.0	13.9	0.7	13.9	0.0	13.9	0.0	13.9	0.0	14.0	0.7	13.9	-0.7	13.9	0.0	13.9	0.0	14.0	0.7	14.0	0.0
1942	14.1	0.7	14.1	0.0	14.1	0.0	14.1	0.0	14.1	0.0	14.1	0.0	14.1	0.0	14.1	0.0	14.1	0.0	14.2	0.7	14.2	0.0	14.2	0.0
1943	14.2	0.0	14.2	0.0	14.2	0.0	14.2	0.0	14.2	0.0	14.2	0.0	14.2	0.0	14.2	0.0	14.2	0.0	14.2	0.0	14.2	0.0	14.2	0.0
1944	14.1	-0.7	14.1	0.0	14.1	0.0	14.1	0.0	14.1	0.0	14.1	0.0	14.1	0.0	14.1	0.0	14.1	0.0	14.1	0.0	14.1	0.0	14.1	0.0
1945	14.1	0.0	14.2	0.7	14.1	-0.7	14.1	0.0	14.1	0.0	14.1	0.0	14.1	0.0	14.1	0.0	14.1	0.0	14.1	0.0	14.1	0.0	14.1	0.0
1946	14.1	0.0	14.1	0.0	14.2	0.7	14.4	1.4	14.6	1.4	16.4	12.3	16.9	3.0	16.7	-1.2	16.7	0.0	16.8	0.6	19.5	16.1	21.3	9.2
1947	21.5	0.9	21.7	0.9	22.6	4.1	22.8	0.9	22.8	0.0	22.7	-0.4	22.5	-0.9	22.5	0.0	22.5	0.0	22.5	0.0	22.5	0.0	22.8	1.3
1948	23.0	0.9	23.2	0.9	23.2	0.0	23.6	1.7	23.6	0.0	23.9	1.3	24.6	2.9	26.1	6.1	26.1	0.0	26.3	0.8	27.0	2.7	27.1	0.4
1949	27.0	-0.4	26.8	-0.7	26.1	-2.6	24.4	-6.5	22.4	-8.2	21.2	-5.4	21.4	0.9	21.9	2.3	21.9	0.0	21.5	-1.8	21.7	0.9	21.4	-1.4
1950	21.4	0.0	21.3	-0.5	21.2	-0.5	21.4	0.9	22.4	4.7	23.9	6.7	24.1	0.8	24.9	3.3	26.4	6.0	27.9	5.7	28.9	3.6	29.1	0.7
1951	29.6	1.7	29.7	0.3	29.4	-1.0	29.5	0.3	29.4	-0.3	28.9	-1.7	28.5	-1.4	28.5	0.0	28.6	0.4	29.1	1.7	29.1	0.0	29.1	0.0
1952	29.1	0.0	29.3	0.7	29.3	0.0	29.3	0.0	28.6	-2.4	28.1	-1.7	29.1	3.6	29.2	0.3	29.2	0.0	28.8	-1.4	28.8	0.0	28.7	-0.3
1953	28.8	0.3	29.2	1.4	30.8	5.5	30.1	-2.3	29.7	-1.3	29.9	0.7	29.7	-0.7	29.2	-1.7	28.8	-1.4	28.6	-0.7	28.7	0.3	28.6	-0.3
1954	28.5	-0.3	28.1	-1.4	28.4	1.1	28.9	1.8	29.0	0.3	29.0	0.0	29.1	0.3	29.3	0.7	29.6	1.0	29.9	1.0	29.9	0.0	29.9	0.0
1955	30.0	0.3	31.4	4.7	31.5	0.3	32.4	2.9	32.3	-0.3	32.3	0.0	32.7	1.2	34.0	4.0	36.2	6.5	36.1	-0.3	36.1	0.0	36.6	1.4
1956	36.8	0.5	36.9	0.3	38.0	3.0	38.3	0.8	37.5	-2.1	37.1	-1.1	35.8	-3.5	36.5	2.0	36.3	-0.5	36.2	-0.3	35.1	-3.0	35.1	0.0
1957	34.9	-0.6	34.1	-2.3	33.6	-1.5	33.4	-0.6	32.8	-1.8	32.4	-1.2	31.5	-2.8	31.6	0.3	30.9	-2.2	30.5	-1.3	30.7	0.7	30.6	-0.3
1958	30.2	-1.3	30.0	-0.7	29.8	-0.7	29.1	-2.3	29.1	0.0	29.3	0.7	29.3	0.0	29.6	1.0	29.9	1.0	30.7	2.7	31.4	2.3	31.3	-0.3
1959	31.3	0.0	31.5	0.6	31.9	1.3	31.6	-0.9	31.9	0.9	31.9	0.0	31.4	-1.6	31.4	0.0	31.9	1.6	32.2	0.9	33.1	2.8	33.0	-0.3
1960	33.5	1.5	33.5	0.0	33.0	-1.5	32.9	-0.3	32.9	0.0	32.6	-0.9	32.5	-0.3	32.5	0.0	32.5	0.0	32.2	-0.9	31.8	-1.2	31.4	-1.3
1961	31.0	-1.3	31.0	0.0	31.0	0.0	31.1	0.3	31.5	1.3	31.7	0.6	31.9	0.6	31.9	0.0	32.0	0.3	31.7	-0.9	31.4	-0.9	31.6	0.6
1962	31.5	-0.3	31.5	0.0	31.4	-0.3	31.3	-0.3	31.3	0.0	31.1	-0.6	31.1	0.0	31.1	0.0	31.0	-0.3	30.7	-1.0	30.8	0.3	30.7	-0.3
1963	30.8	0.3	30.8	0.0	30.8	0.0	30.8	0.0	31.0	0.6	31.0	0.0	31.1	0.3	31.2	0.3	31.3	0.3	31.3	0.0	31.4	0.3	31.7	1.0
1964	31.8	0.3	31.9	0.3	32.2	0.9	32.6	1.2	32.6	0.0	32.6	0.0	32.8	0.6	33.2	1.2	33.6	1.2	34.6	3.0	35.1	1.4	35.5	1.1
1965	35.0	-1.4	35.1	0.3	35.2	0.3	35.6	1.1	36.2	1.7	36.5	0.8	36.2	-0.8	36.6	1.1	36.7	0.3	36.8	0.3	37.3	1.4	36.8	-1.3
1966	37.1	0.8	37.5	1.1	37.9	1.1	38.3	1.1	38.4	0.3	38.7	0.8	38.6	-0.3	37.8	-2.1	37.6	-0.5	37.7	0.3	38.0	0.8	37.8	-0.5
1967	38.2	1.1	38.4	0.5	38.0	-1.0	37.7	-0.8	37.3	-1.1	37.3	0.0	37.2	-0.3	37.3	0.3	37.5	0.5	38.0	1.3	39.0	2.6	39.5	1.3
1968	40.0	1.3	41.1	2.8	41.8	1.7	40.9	-2.2	38.8	-5.1	38.7	-0.3	38.3	-1.0	38.1	-0.5	38.0	-0.3	38.2	0.5	38.3	0.3	38.7	1.0
1969	39.8	2.8	40.4	1.5	40.7	0.7	41.5	2.0	42.0	1.2	42.5	1.2	42.6	0.2	43.7	2.6	45.0	3.0	45.4	0.9	45.9	1.1	47.0	2.4
1970	48.0	2.1	48.0	0.0	48.2	0.4	49.3	2.3	49.3	0.0	48.6	-1.4	47.8	-1.6	47.2	-1.3	46.4	-1.7	46.1	-0.6	45.0	-2.4	44.0	-2.2

[Continued]

Nonferrous Metals
Producer Price Index
Base 1982 = 100
[Continued]

For 1926-1997. Columns headed % show percentile change in the index from the previous period for which an index is available.

Year	Jan Index	%	Feb Index	%	Mar Index	%	Apr Index	%	May Index	%	Jun Index	%	Jul Index	%	Aug Index	%	Sep Index	%	Oct Index	%	Nov Index	%	Dec Index	%
1971	43.3	-1.6	42.8	-1.2	42.6	-0.5	44.0	3.3	43.9	-0.2	43.6	-0.7	43.7	0.2	43.9	0.5	43.7	-0.5	43.6	-0.2	43.5	-0.2	43.1	-0.9
1972	43.4	0.7	43.6	0.5	44.5	2.1	44.6	0.2	44.7	0.2	44.6	-0.2	44.3	-0.7	44.3	0.0	44.5	0.5	44.5	0.0	44.5	0.0	44.5	0.0
1973	44.7	0.4	45.9	2.7	48.7	6.1	49.8	2.3	50.5	1.4	51.2	1.4	51.5	0.6	52.3	1.6	52.6	0.6	53.4	1.5	55.0	3.0	59.0	7.3
1974	61.1	3.6	62.6	2.5	66.9	6.9	70.8	5.8	76.0	7.3	76.0	0.0	75.3	-0.9	76.0	0.9	74.7	-1.7	72.4	-3.1	71.0	-1.9	69.0	-2.8
1975	67.8	-1.7	66.8	-1.5	66.0	-1.2	65.3	-1.1	64.9	-0.6	64.2	-1.1	63.6	-0.9	64.2	0.9	64.8	0.9	64.8	0.0	64.5	-0.5	64.3	-0.3
1976	64.1	-0.3	64.4	0.5	65.2	1.2	67.4	3.4	68.9	2.2	69.5	0.9	71.0	2.2	71.3	0.4	72.0	1.0	71.5	-0.7	71.1	-0.6	70.2	-1.3
1977	70.7	0.7	71.9	1.7	74.3	3.3	75.9	2.2	76.2	0.4	74.8	-1.8	75.1	0.4	75.3	0.3	74.0	-1.7	73.4	-0.8	73.7	0.4	74.0	0.4
1978	75.1	1.5	75.8	0.9	76.3	0.7	77.0	0.9	77.1	0.1	77.9	1.0	78.1	0.3	80.1	2.6	80.2	0.1	82.4	2.7	82.8	0.5	83.1	0.4
1979	84.8	2.0	90.7	7.0	93.6	3.2	98.5	5.2	98.0	-0.5	98.5	0.5	99.5	1.0	99.8	0.3	102.2	2.4	107.4	5.1	107.8	0.4	110.7	2.7
1980	123.8	11.8	128.1	3.5	121.9	-4.8	113.2	-7.1	109.9	-2.9	109.6	-0.3	111.0	1.3	113.2	2.0	114.6	1.2	117.4	2.4	114.6	-2.4	111.3	-2.9
1981	110.8	-0.4	109.0	-1.6	108.7	-0.3	109.4	0.6	109.1	-0.3	107.9	-1.1	107.3	-0.6	109.0	1.6	109.8	0.7	108.3	-1.4	106.6	-1.6	105.1	-1.4
1982	104.1	-1.0	103.8	-0.3	101.4	-2.3	100.9	-0.5	100.0	-0.9	96.1	-3.9	97.3	1.2	97.0	-0.3	100.6	3.7	99.7	-0.9	99.3	-0.4	99.8	0.5
1983	101.3	1.5	104.6	3.3	102.6	-1.9	103.1	0.5	105.3	2.1	104.6	-0.7	105.6	1.0	106.1	0.5	107.0	0.8	106.0	-0.9	104.9	-1.0	105.5	0.6
1984	105.0	-0.5	106.3	1.2	108.6	2.2	109.7	1.0	107.8	-1.7	107.3	-0.5	105.1	-2.1	104.4	-0.7	103.1	-1.2	101.2	-1.8	102.2	1.0	100.9	-1.3
1985	99.9	-1.0	100.5	0.6	99.6	-0.9	101.8	2.2	101.7	-0.1	100.0	-1.7	99.2	-0.8	99.2	0.0	98.9	-0.3	98.6	-0.3	97.8	-0.8	97.6	-0.2
1986	98.5	0.9	98.6	0.1	99.3	0.7	98.5	-0.8	97.9	-0.6	98.2	0.3	97.6	-0.6	98.2	0.6	98.7	0.5	99.0	0.3	98.9	-0.1	98.5	-0.4
1987	99.1	0.6	99.1	0.0	100.2	1.1	101.8	1.6	104.6	2.8	106.0	1.3	109.1	2.9	112.0	2.7	114.2	2.0	116.7	2.2	118.5	1.5	124.1	4.7
1988	127.5	2.7	124.8	-2.1	125.7	0.7	128.9	2.5	129.3	0.3	131.7	1.9	132.8	0.8	132.9	0.1	134.8	1.4	137.8	2.2	144.0	4.5	148.3	3.0
1989	149.9	1.1	147.1	-1.9	148.2	0.7	147.2	-0.7	144.6	-1.8	140.1	-3.1	136.3	-2.7	136.9	0.4	139.5	1.9	140.2	0.5	136.5	-2.6	131.9	-3.4
1990	130.9	-0.8	127.9	-2.3	131.8	3.0	134.5	2.0	134.0	-0.4	132.1	-1.4	133.2	0.8	137.3	3.1	139.0	1.2	139.2	0.1	134.8	-3.2	130.6	-3.1
1991	129.6	-0.8	128.1	-1.2	127.2	-0.7	126.5	-0.6	124.2	-1.8	121.6	-2.1	120.9	-0.6	121.2	0.2	121.3	0.1	121.1	-0.2	120.2	-0.7	118.9	-1.1
1992	117.1	-1.5	119.4	2.0	121.0	1.3	121.5	0.4	121.6	0.1	122.8	1.0	124.0	1.0	125.2	1.0	122.9	-1.8	120.0	-2.4	117.6	-2.0	117.9	0.3
1993	119.1	1.0	118.8	-0.3	117.5	-1.1	115.7	-1.5	113.2	-2.2	113.5	0.3	114.6	1.0	114.7	0.1	113.4	-1.1	111.1	-2.0	110.2	-0.8	111.5	1.2
1994	112.8	1.2	116.2	3.0	118.5	2.0	119.1	0.5	120.5	1.2	125.2	3.9	128.1	2.3	128.8	0.5	131.2	1.9	134.0	2.1	140.5	4.9	144.5	2.8
1995	151.2	4.6	152.8	1.1	151.5	-0.9	152.1	0.4	149.1	-2.0	149.4	0.2	150.3	0.6	150.8	0.3	149.3	-1.0	146.6	-1.8	146.4	-0.1	145.4	-0.7
1996	142.7	-1.9	140.3	-1.7	140.5	0.1	140.5	0.0	141.8	0.9	139.8	-1.4	133.9	-4.2	131.8	-1.6	131.3	-0.4	130.1	-0.9	131.4	1.0	133.4	1.5
1997	136.0	1.9	137.0	0.7	139.7	2.0	138.2	-1.1	139.1	0.7	139.7	0.4	136.9	-2.0	137.4	0.4	136.4	-0.7	135.4	-0.7	132.7	-2.0	130.4	-1.7

Source: U.S. Department of Labor, Bureau of Labor Statistics, Division of Industry Prices and Price Indexes. n.e.c. stands for not elsewhere classified. - indicates no data collected for period or unavailable.

Metal Containers
Producer Price Index
Base 1982 = 100

For 1926-1997. Columns headed % show percentile change in the index from the previous period for which an index is available.

Year	Jan Index	%	Feb Index	%	Mar Index	%	Apr Index	%	May Index	%	Jun Index	%	Jul Index	%	Aug Index	%	Sep Index	%	Oct Index	%	Nov Index	%	Dec Index	%
1926	15.2	-	15.2	0.0	15.2	0.0	15.2	0.0	15.2	0.0	15.2	0.0	15.2	0.0	15.2	0.0	15.2	0.0	15.2	0.0	15.2	0.0	15.2	0.0
1927	15.2	0.0	15.2	0.0	15.2	0.0	15.2	0.0	15.2	0.0	15.2	0.0	15.2	0.0	15.2	0.0	15.2	0.0	15.2	0.0	15.2	0.0	15.2	0.0
1928	14.7	-3.3	14.7	0.0	14.7	0.0	14.7	0.0	14.7	0.0	14.7	0.0	14.7	0.0	14.7	0.0	14.7	0.0	14.7	0.0	14.7	0.0	14.7	0.0
1929	14.9	1.4	14.9	0.0	14.9	0.0	14.9	0.0	14.9	0.0	14.9	0.0	14.9	0.0	14.9	0.0	14.9	0.0	14.9	0.0	14.9	0.0	14.9	0.0
1930	14.7	-1.3	14.7	0.0	14.7	0.0	14.7	0.0	14.7	0.0	14.7	0.0	14.7	0.0	14.7	0.0	14.6	-0.7	14.6	0.0	14.6	0.0	14.6	0.0
1931	14.2	-2.7	14.2	0.0	14.1	-0.7	14.1	0.0	14.1	0.0	14.1	0.0	14.0	-0.7	14.0	0.0	14.0	0.0	14.0	0.0	14.0	0.0	14.0	0.0
1932	13.5	-3.6	13.5	0.0	13.5	0.0	13.5	0.0	13.5	0.0	13.5	0.0	13.5	0.0	13.5	0.0	13.5	0.0	13.5	0.0	13.5	0.0	13.5	0.0
1933	12.6	-6.7	12.6	0.0	12.6	0.0	12.6	0.0	12.6	0.0	12.6	0.0	12.6	0.0	12.6	0.0	12.6	0.0	12.7	0.8	12.7	0.0	12.7	0.0
1934	14.4	13.4	14.4	0.0	14.4	0.0	14.5	0.7	14.5	0.0	14.5	0.0	14.5	0.0	14.5	0.0	14.5	0.0	14.5	0.0	14.5	0.0	14.5	0.0
1935	14.4	-0.7	14.4	0.0	14.4	0.0	14.4	0.0	14.4	0.0	14.4	0.0	14.4	0.0	14.4	0.0	14.4	0.0	14.4	0.0	14.4	0.0	14.4	0.0
1936	14.4	0.0	14.4	0.0	14.4	0.0	14.4	0.0	14.4	0.0	14.4	0.0	14.4	0.0	14.4	0.0	14.4	0.0	14.6	1.4	14.6	0.0	14.6	0.0
1937	13.4	-8.2	13.4	0.0	13.4	0.0	13.5	0.7	13.5	0.0	13.5	0.0	13.5	0.0	13.5	0.0	13.5	0.0	13.5	0.0	13.5	0.0	13.5	0.0
1938	14.4	6.7	14.4	0.0	14.4	0.0	14.4	0.0	14.4	0.0	14.4	0.0	14.4	0.0	14.4	0.0	14.4	0.0	14.4	0.0	14.4	0.0	14.4	0.0
1939	13.8	-4.2	13.8	0.0	13.8	0.0	13.8	0.0	13.8	0.0	13.8	0.0	13.8	0.0	13.8	0.0	13.8	0.0	13.8	0.0	13.8	0.0	13.8	0.0
1940	13.5	-2.2	13.5	0.0	13.5	0.0	13.5	0.0	13.5	0.0	13.5	0.0	13.5	0.0	13.5	0.0	13.5	0.0	13.5	0.0	13.5	0.0	13.5	0.0
1941	13.5	0.0	13.5	0.0	13.5	0.0	13.5	0.0	13.5	0.0	13.5	0.0	13.6	0.7	13.6	0.0	13.6	0.0	13.6	0.0	13.6	0.0	13.6	0.0
1942	13.8	1.5	13.8	0.0	13.8	0.0	13.8	0.0	13.8	0.0	13.8	0.0	13.8	0.0	13.8	0.0	13.8	0.0	13.8	0.0	13.8	0.0	13.8	0.0
1943	13.8	0.0	13.8	0.0	13.8	0.0	13.8	0.0	13.8	0.0	13.8	0.0	13.8	0.0	13.8	0.0	13.8	0.0	13.8	0.0	13.8	0.0	13.8	0.0
1944	13.8	0.0	13.8	0.0	13.8	0.0	13.8	0.0	13.8	0.0	13.8	0.0	13.8	0.0	13.8	0.0	13.8	0.0	13.8	0.0	13.8	0.0	13.8	0.0
1945	13.8	0.0	13.8	0.0	13.8	0.0	13.8	0.0	13.8	0.0	13.8	0.0	13.8	0.0	13.8	0.0	13.8	0.0	13.8	0.0	13.8	0.0	13.8	0.0
1946	13.8	0.0	13.8	0.0	13.8	0.0	13.8	0.0	14.3	3.6	14.3	0.0	14.3	0.0	14.3	0.0	14.3	0.0	14.3	0.0	14.3	0.0	14.3	0.0
1947	15.9	11.2	15.9	0.0	15.9	0.0	15.9	0.0	15.9	0.0	15.9	0.0	15.9	0.0	16.3	2.5	16.3	0.0	16.3	0.0	16.3	0.0	16.3	0.0
1948	17.8	9.2	17.8	0.0	17.8	0.0	17.8	0.0	17.7	-0.6	17.7	0.0	17.8	0.6	17.9	0.6	17.9	0.0	17.9	0.0	17.9	0.0	17.9	0.0
1949	19.3	7.8	19.3	0.0	19.3	0.0	19.3	0.0	19.3	0.0	19.3	0.0	19.3	0.0	19.3	0.0	19.3	0.0	19.3	0.0	19.3	0.0	19.3	0.0
1950	19.4	0.5	19.4	0.0	19.3	-0.5	19.3	0.0	19.3	0.0	19.3	0.0	19.3	0.0	19.3	0.0	19.3	0.0	19.3	0.0	19.3	0.0	19.6	1.6
1951	21.5	9.7	21.5	0.0	21.5	0.0	21.5	0.0	21.5	0.0	21.5	0.0	21.5	0.0	21.5	0.0	21.5	0.0	21.5	0.0	21.5	0.0	21.5	0.0
1952	21.4	-0.5	21.4	0.0	21.4	0.0	21.4	0.0	21.4	0.0	21.4	0.0	21.4	0.0	21.4	0.0	22.0	2.8	22.2	0.9	22.2	0.0	22.2	0.0
1953	22.2	0.0	22.2	0.0	22.2	0.0	22.4	0.9	22.4	0.0	22.4	0.0	22.8	1.8	22.8	0.0	22.8	0.0	22.8	0.0	22.8	0.0	22.8	0.0
1954	23.0	0.9	23.0	0.0	23.0	0.0	23.0	0.0	23.0	0.0	23.0	0.0	23.1	0.4	23.2	0.4	23.2	0.0	23.2	0.0	23.3	0.4	23.3	0.0
1955	23.3	0.0	23.3	0.0	23.3	0.0	23.3	0.0	23.3	0.0	23.3	0.0	23.3	0.0	23.5	0.9	23.5	0.0	23.5	0.0	24.4	3.8	24.4	0.0
1956	24.4	0.0	24.4	0.0	24.4	0.0	24.4	0.0	25.0	2.5	25.0	0.0	25.0	0.0	25.1	0.4	25.4	1.2	25.4	0.0	26.1	2.8	26.1	0.0
1957	26.1	0.0	26.1	0.0	26.2	0.4	26.2	0.0	27.0	3.1	27.0	0.0	27.1	0.4	27.1	0.0	27.1	0.0	27.1	0.0	27.1	0.0	27.1	0.0
1958	27.1	0.0	27.1	0.0	27.6	1.8	27.6	0.0	27.6	0.0	27.6	0.0	27.6	0.0	27.6	0.0	27.7	0.4	27.7	0.0	27.7	0.0	28.3	2.2
1959	27.7	-2.1	27.7	0.0	27.7	0.0	27.1	-2.2	27.1	0.0	27.1	0.0	27.1	0.0	27.1	0.0	27.1	0.0	27.1	0.0	27.1	0.0	27.1	0.0
1960	27.1	0.0	27.4	1.1	27.4	0.0	27.4	0.0	27.4	0.0	27.2	-0.7	27.2	0.0	27.2	0.0	27.2	0.0	27.2	0.0	27.2	0.0	27.2	0.0
1961	27.8	2.2	27.8	0.0	27.8	0.0	27.8	0.0	27.8	0.0	27.8	0.0	27.8	0.0	27.8	0.0	27.8	0.0	27.8	0.0	27.8	0.0	27.8	0.0
1962	28.2	1.4	28.2	0.0	28.2	0.0	28.2	0.0	28.2	0.0	28.2	0.0	28.2	0.0	28.2	0.0	28.2	0.0	28.2	0.0	28.2	0.0	28.2	0.0
1963	28.4	0.7	28.4	0.0	28.4	0.0	28.4	0.0	28.5	0.4	28.5	0.0	28.6	0.4	28.6	0.0	28.5	-0.3	28.5	0.0	28.5	0.0	28.5	0.0
1964	28.5	0.0	28.7	0.7	28.7	0.0	28.7	0.0	28.7	0.0	28.7	0.0	28.7	0.0	28.7	0.0	28.7	0.0	28.7	0.0	28.7	0.0	28.7	0.0
1965	28.8	0.3	28.8	0.0	28.8	0.0	28.8	0.0	29.5	2.4	29.5	0.0	29.5	0.0	29.5	0.0	29.5	0.0	29.5	0.0	29.5	0.0	29.9	1.4
1966	29.9	0.0	29.9	0.0	29.9	0.0	29.9	0.0	30.0	0.3	30.0	0.0	30.4	0.0	30.4	0.0	30.4	0.0	30.4	0.0	30.4	0.0	30.7	0.0
1967	30.3	1.0	30.3	0.0	30.3	0.0	30.4	0.3	30.4	0.0	30.4	0.0	30.4	0.0	30.4	0.0	30.4	0.0	30.4	0.0	30.7	1.0	30.7	0.0
1968	30.7	0.0	30.8	0.3	30.8	0.0	31.8	3.2	31.8	0.0	31.8	0.0	31.8	0.0	31.8	0.0	31.8	0.0	31.9	0.3	31.9	0.0	31.8	-0.3
1969	31.8	0.0	32.4	1.9	32.4	0.0	32.5	0.3	32.5	0.0	32.5	0.0	32.5	0.0	32.5	0.0	32.7	0.6	32.8	0.3	32.8	0.0	32.8	0.0
1970	32.8	0.0	34.0	3.7	34.0	0.0	34.0	0.0	34.0	0.0	34.0	0.0	34.3	0.9	34.3	0.0	34.3	0.0	35.2	2.6	35.2	0.0	35.2	0.0

[Continued]

Metal Containers

Producer Price Index

Base 1982 = 100

[Continued]

For 1926-1997. Columns headed % show percentile change in the index from the previous period for which an index is available.

Year	Jan Index	%	Feb Index	%	Mar Index	%	Apr Index	%	May Index	%	Jun Index	%	Jul Index	%	Aug Index	%	Sep Index	%	Oct Index	%	Nov Index	%	Dec Index	%
1971	35.2	0.0	35.2	0.0	35.2	0.0	37.5	6.5	37.5	0.0	37.5	0.0	37.5	0.0	37.8	0.8	37.8	0.0	37.8	0.0	37.8	0.0	37.8	0.0
1972	37.8	0.0	38.7	2.4	38.7	0.0	38.7	0.0	38.8	0.3	39.2	1.0	39.5	0.8	39.8	0.8	39.9	0.3	39.9	0.0	39.9	0.0	39.9	0.0
1973	39.9	0.0	39.8	-0.3	41.3	3.8	41.3	0.0	41.3	0.0	41.3	0.0	41.3	0.0	41.3	0.0	41.3	0.0	41.0	-0.7	41.0	0.0	41.0	0.0
1974	42.2	2.9	42.3	0.2	42.5	0.5	44.7	5.2	46.3	3.6	50.3	8.6	52.0	3.4	56.1	7.9	56.2	0.2	56.4	0.4	56.4	0.0	56.4	0.0
1975	56.4	0.0	60.0	6.4	59.6	-0.7	59.6	0.0	58.2	-2.3	58.2	0.0	58.2	0.0	58.1	-0.2	58.2	0.2	58.2	0.0	58.4	0.3	58.7	0.5
1976	58.6	-0.2	58.7	0.2	61.9	5.5	61.9	0.0	61.9	0.0	61.9	0.0	62.3	0.6	62.2	-0.2	62.2	0.0	62.2	0.0	62.3	0.2	62.3	0.0
1977	62.3	0.0	62.3	0.0	66.0	5.9	66.1	0.2	66.0	-0.2	66.0	0.0	66.2	0.3	66.4	0.3	68.5	3.2	69.0	0.7	69.1	0.1	69.1	0.0
1978	69.2	0.1	71.1	2.7	72.1	1.4	72.1	0.0	73.9	2.5	74.0	0.1	74.3	0.4	75.0	0.9	74.9	-0.1	77.5	3.5	77.5	0.0	77.4	-0.1
1979	78.2	1.0	78.2	0.0	80.5	2.9	82.2	2.1	81.7	-0.6	81.4	-0.4	81.3	-0.1	81.7	0.5	81.8	0.1	85.2	4.2	85.5	0.4	85.5	0.0
1980	86.2	0.8	86.6	0.5	87.8	1.4	91.6	4.3	92.1	0.5	92.1	0.0	92.2	0.1	92.3	0.1	92.3	0.0	92.7	0.4	92.3	-0.4	92.3	0.0
1981	94.8	2.7	95.5	0.7	95.6	0.1	95.6	0.0	95.6	0.0	95.6	0.0	96.0	0.4	97.0	1.0	97.0	0.0	96.9	-0.1	96.8	-0.1	96.4	-0.4
1982	98.7	2.4	99.3	0.6	99.6	0.3	100.5	0.9	100.5	0.0	100.4	-0.1	100.5	0.1	100.1	-0.4	100.1	0.0	100.3	0.2	100.1	-0.2	99.9	-0.2
1983	99.8	-0.1	100.8	1.0	100.9	0.1	101.0	0.1	102.6	1.6	102.7	0.1	102.4	-0.3	102.5	0.1	103.0	0.5	103.0	0.0	102.9	-0.1	103.6	0.7
1984	104.7	1.1	104.9	0.2	105.1	0.2	105.1	0.0	105.9	0.8	105.9	0.0	105.9	0.0	107.2	1.2	107.2	0.0	108.8	1.5	108.8	0.0	108.7	-0.1
1985	108.8	0.1	109.0	0.2	108.9	-0.1	108.9	0.0	109.0	0.1	109.0	0.0	109.0	0.0	108.9	-0.1	108.9	0.0	108.9	0.0	109.0	0.1	109.9	0.8
1986	110.2	0.3	110.1	-0.1	110.2	0.1	110.1	-0.1	110.0	-0.1	110.0	0.0	110.3	0.3	110.4	0.1	110.4	0.0	110.4	0.0	110.4	0.0	110.4	0.0
1987	109.9	-0.5	110.0	0.1	109.8	-0.2	109.8	0.0	109.6	-0.2	109.7	0.1	109.0	-0.6	109.1	0.1	109.8	0.6	109.6	-0.2	109.8	0.2	108.0	-1.6
1988	108.3	0.3	108.9	0.6	109.5	0.6	110.1	0.5	110.4	0.3	110.3	-0.1	110.1	-0.2	110.9	0.7	111.3	0.4	111.1	-0.2	111.0	-0.1	110.1	-0.8
1989	110.1	0.0	109.7	-0.4	109.7	0.0	110.3	0.5	111.3	0.9	111.5	0.2	112.5	0.9	112.0	-0.4	112.2	0.2	113.0	0.7	113.1	0.1	112.6	-0.4
1990	113.6	0.9	113.5	-0.1	113.8	0.3	113.8	0.0	114.2	0.4	114.1	-0.1	114.2	0.1	114.1	-0.1	114.2	0.1	114.1	-0.1	114.1	0.0	113.9	-0.2
1991	114.7	0.7	114.9	0.2	114.6	-0.3	114.7	0.1	114.9	0.2	114.9	0.0	116.1	1.0	116.3	0.2	116.2	-0.1	116.4	0.2	116.3	-0.1	116.2	-0.1
1992	113.8	-2.1	114.3	0.4	113.9	-0.3	114.0	0.1	113.8	-0.2	114.0	0.2	113.9	-0.1	113.7	-0.2	113.9	0.2	113.9	0.0	113.9	0.0	114.0	0.1
1993	109.9	-3.6	110.2	0.3	109.5	-0.6	109.2	-0.3	109.1	-0.1	109.1	0.0	109.2	0.1	108.8	-0.4	109.8	0.9	110.1	0.3	111.0	0.8	110.1	-0.8
1994	109.0	-1.0	108.5	-0.5	107.7	-0.7	108.0	0.3	108.0	0.0	106.6	-1.3	106.9	0.3	108.1	1.1	108.2	0.1	108.6	0.4	108.8	0.2	108.9	0.1
1995	109.6	0.6	117.8	7.5	117.8	0.0	118.1	0.3	118.1	0.0	118.3	0.2	118.0	-0.3	118.0	0.0	117.8	-0.2	117.9	0.1	117.7	-0.2	117.8	0.1
1996	115.1	-2.3	110.5	-4.0	110.5	0.0	110.5	0.0	109.7	-0.7	109.5	-0.2	109.6	0.1	109.6	0.0	109.5	-0.1	108.5	-0.9	108.4	-0.1	109.1	0.6
1997	108.0	-1.0	108.0	0.0	108.2	0.2	107.9	-0.3	107.9	0.0	107.8	-0.1	107.6	-0.2	107.8	0.2	107.7	-0.1	107.8	0.1	107.7	-0.1	107.7	0.0

Source: U.S. Department of Labor, Bureau of Labor Statistics, Division of Industry Prices and Price Indexes. n.e.c. stands for not elsewhere classified. - indicates no data collected for period or unavailable.

Hardware
Producer Price Index
Base 1982 = 100

For 1947-1997. Columns headed % show percentile change in the index from the previous period for which an index is available.

Year	Jan Index	%	Feb Index	%	Mar Index	%	Apr Index	%	May Index	%	Jun Index	%	Jul Index	%	Aug Index	%	Sep Index	%	Oct Index	%	Nov Index	%	Dec Index	%
1947	16.7	-	16.9	1.2	16.9	0.0	16.9	0.0	17.0	0.6	17.0	0.0	17.1	0.6	17.2	0.6	17.4	1.2	17.6	1.1	17.7	0.6	17.7	0.0
1948	17.7	0.0	17.8	0.6	17.9	0.6	17.9	0.0	18.2	1.7	18.3	0.5	18.3	0.0	19.1	4.4	19.7	3.1	19.8	0.5	19.9	0.5	19.9	0.0
1949	19.9	0.0	19.9	0.0	19.9	0.0	19.7	-1.0	19.7	0.0	19.7	0.0	19.7	0.0	19.7	0.0	19.5	-1.0	19.2	-1.5	19.2	0.0	19.2	0.0
1950	19.6	2.1	20.1	2.6	20.2	0.5	20.3	0.5	20.5	1.0	20.6	0.5	20.9	1.5	21.4	2.4	21.8	1.9	22.2	1.8	22.9	3.2	23.2	1.3
1951	23.3	0.4	23.3	0.0	23.3	0.0	23.3	0.0	23.3	0.0	23.3	0.0	23.3	0.0	23.3	0.0	23.3	0.0	23.3	0.0	23.3	0.0	23.3	0.0
1952	23.3	0.0	23.3	0.0	23.4	0.4	23.4	0.0	23.4	0.0	22.9	-2.1	22.9	0.0	22.9	0.0	22.9	0.0	23.2	1.3	23.2	0.0	23.3	0.4
1953	23.3	0.0	23.3	0.0	23.3	0.0	23.7	1.7	24.7	4.2	24.9	0.8	24.9	0.0	25.1	0.8	25.3	0.8	25.4	0.4	25.4	0.0	25.4	0.0
1954	25.4	0.0	25.5	0.4	25.5	0.0	25.6	0.4	25.5	-0.4	25.5	0.0	25.5	0.0	25.7	0.8	26.0	1.2	26.2	0.8	26.3	0.4	26.3	0.0
1955	26.4	0.4	26.5	0.4	26.7	0.8	26.7	0.0	26.7	0.0	26.7	0.0	26.8	0.4	27.0	0.7	27.3	1.1	28.0	2.6	28.0	0.0	28.0	0.0
1956	28.0	0.0	28.0	0.0	28.3	1.1	28.5	0.7	28.5	0.0	28.6	0.4	28.7	0.3	29.3	2.1	29.3	0.0	29.5	0.7	29.6	0.3	29.6	0.0
1957	29.9	1.0	29.9	0.0	30.0	0.3	30.2	0.7	30.4	0.7	30.4	0.0	30.4	0.0	30.7	1.0	30.9	0.7	30.9	0.0	30.9	0.0	31.1	0.6
1958	31.2	0.3	31.2	0.0	31.2	0.0	31.3	0.3	31.6	1.0	31.8	0.6	31.8	0.0	31.8	0.0	31.8	0.0	31.8	0.0	31.9	0.3	31.9	0.0
1959	31.9	0.0	32.0	0.3	32.0	0.0	32.0	0.0	32.0	0.0	32.0	0.0	32.0	0.0	32.0	0.0	32.0	0.0	32.0	0.0	32.0	0.0	32.0	0.0
1960	32.1	0.3	32.1	0.0	32.1	0.0	32.2	0.3	32.2	0.0	32.3	0.3	32.3	0.0	32.3	0.0	32.3	0.0	32.3	0.0	32.3	0.0	32.3	0.0
1961	32.3	0.0	32.4	0.3	32.4	0.0	32.4	0.0	32.6	0.6	32.6	0.0	32.6	0.0	32.6	0.0	32.7	0.3	32.7	0.0	32.7	0.0	32.7	0.0
1962	32.8	0.3	32.7	-0.3	32.7	0.0	32.6	-0.3	32.6	0.0	32.7	0.3	32.5	-0.6	32.5	0.0	32.5	0.0	32.5	0.0	32.5	0.0	32.5	0.0
1963	32.5	0.0	32.6	0.3	32.6	0.0	32.6	0.0	32.6	0.0	32.6	0.0	32.6	0.0	32.6	0.0	32.7	0.3	32.7	0.0	32.7	0.0	32.7	0.0
1964	32.8	0.3	32.8	0.0	32.9	0.3	32.9	0.0	32.9	0.0	32.9	0.0	32.9	0.0	32.9	0.0	32.9	0.0	32.9	0.0	32.9	0.0	32.9	0.0
1965	32.9	0.0	32.9	0.0	33.0	0.3	33.0	0.0	33.2	0.6	33.2	0.0	33.3	0.3	33.4	0.3	33.4	0.0	33.5	0.3	33.5	0.0	33.6	0.3
1966	33.6	0.0	33.7	0.3	34.0	0.9	34.0	0.0	34.4	1.2	34.4	0.0	34.4	0.0	34.5	0.3	34.6	0.3	34.8	0.6	35.0	0.6	35.1	0.3
1967	35.0	-0.3	35.0	0.0	35.3	0.9	35.3	0.0	35.4	0.3	35.4	0.0	35.7	0.8	36.1	1.1	36.1	0.0	36.2	0.3	36.3	0.3	36.4	0.3
1968	36.4	0.0	36.6	0.5	36.5	-0.3	36.5	0.0	36.6	0.3	36.6	0.0	36.6	0.0	36.6	0.0	36.7	0.3	36.8	0.3	36.8	0.0	37.1	0.8
1969	37.3	0.5	37.4	0.3	37.5	0.3	37.5	0.0	37.6	0.3	37.6	0.0	37.8	0.5	37.8	0.0	37.9	0.3	38.4	1.3	38.6	0.5	38.6	0.0
1970	39.0	1.0	39.1	0.3	39.2	0.3	39.3	0.3	39.4	0.3	39.5	0.3	39.7	0.5	39.9	0.5	40.1	0.5	40.3	0.5	41.0	1.7	41.1	0.2
1971	41.2	0.2	41.3	0.2	41.3	0.0	41.3	0.0	41.3	0.0	41.4	0.2	41.7	0.7	42.0	0.7	42.0	0.0	42.0	0.0	42.1	0.2	42.2	0.2
1972	42.3	0.2	42.5	0.5	42.5	0.0	42.7	0.5	42.9	0.5	43.0	0.2	43.0	0.0	43.1	0.2	43.1	0.0	43.2	0.2	43.3	0.2	43.3	0.0
1973	43.4	0.2	43.5	0.2	43.6	0.2	43.8	0.5	44.0	0.5	44.3	0.7	44.4	0.2	44.4	0.0	45.2	1.8	45.6	0.9	45.7	0.2	46.1	0.9
1974	46.5	0.9	46.7	0.4	46.9	0.4	47.1	0.4	48.4	2.8	49.3	1.9	49.9	1.2	51.0	2.2	52.5	2.9	53.9	2.7	55.0	2.0	55.5	0.9
1975	56.0	0.9	56.5	0.9	57.7	2.1	57.7	0.0	58.1	0.7	58.2	0.2	58.3	0.2	58.4	0.2	58.6	0.3	59.3	1.2	59.5	0.3	59.6	0.2
1976	60.2	1.0	60.5	0.5	60.7	0.3	60.9	0.3	61.5	1.0	61.7	0.3	61.8	0.2	61.9	0.2	62.2	0.5	62.6	0.6	63.2	1.0	63.9	1.1
1977	64.8	1.4	65.1	0.5	65.4	0.5	65.5	0.2	65.6	0.2	65.9	0.5	66.7	1.2	66.7	0.0	66.9	0.3	66.7	-0.3	67.1	0.6	67.6	0.7
1978	69.0	2.1	69.2	0.3	69.4	0.3	70.2	1.2	70.7	0.7	70.8	0.1	71.5	1.0	71.9	0.6	72.2	0.4	73.5	1.8	74.4	1.2	75.2	1.1
1979	75.5	0.4	76.1	0.8	76.4	0.4	77.0	0.8	77.4	0.5	77.5	0.1	78.0	0.6	78.5	0.6	79.0	0.6	79.9	1.1	80.5	0.8	80.7	0.2
1980	81.4	0.9	82.2	1.0	82.6	0.5	84.7	2.5	85.1	0.5	85.8	0.8	86.6	0.9	86.8	0.2	87.7	1.0	88.0	0.3	89.1	1.2	89.8	0.8
1981	90.8	1.1	92.1	1.4	92.3	0.2	92.2	-0.1	92.6	0.4	92.6	0.0	94.1	1.6	94.7	0.6	95.6	1.0	96.2	0.6	96.9	0.7	97.1	0.2
1982	97.8	0.7	98.0	0.2	99.3	1.3	99.4	0.1	99.5	0.1	100.0	0.5	100.3	0.3	100.8	0.5	100.9	0.1	101.0	0.1	101.0	0.0	102.0	1.0
1983	102.5	0.5	102.7	0.2	102.8	0.1	103.0	0.2	103.0	0.0	104.0	1.0	104.2	0.2	104.3	0.1	104.4	0.1	104.5	0.1	104.6	0.1	104.7	0.1
1984	104.7	0.0	104.9	0.2	105.1	0.2	105.1	0.0	105.4	0.3	105.7	0.3	106.0	0.3	106.3	0.3	106.7	0.4	107.0	0.3	107.0	0.0	107.4	0.4
1985	108.0	0.6	108.2	0.2	108.8	0.6	109.1	0.3	109.1	0.0	109.1	0.0	109.2	0.1	109.4	0.2	109.4	0.0	109.6	0.2	109.7	0.1	109.9	0.2
1986	110.8	0.8	110.9	0.1	109.1	-1.6	109.2	0.1	109.3	0.1	109.3	0.0	109.4	0.1	109.5	0.1	109.2	-0.3	109.4	0.2	108.7	-0.6	108.9	0.2
1987	108.5	-0.4	108.9	0.4	109.0	0.1	109.2	0.2	109.6	0.4	109.8	0.2	109.6	-0.2	109.7	0.1	109.8	0.1	110.1	0.3	110.2	0.1	111.0	0.7
1988	111.5	0.5	111.9	0.4	112.2	0.3	112.8	0.5	113.0	0.2	112.9	-0.1	113.6	0.6	114.0	0.4	114.3	0.3	115.6	1.1	116.1	0.4	116.7	0.5
1989	117.3	0.5	118.4	0.9	119.1	0.6	119.2	0.1	119.7	0.4	119.9	0.2	120.5	0.5	120.7	0.2	121.2	0.4	122.3	0.9	122.8	0.4	123.2	0.3
1990	124.0	0.6	124.8	0.6	125.0	0.2	125.5	0.4	125.6	0.1	125.7	0.1	126.0	0.2	126.2	0.2	126.5	0.2	126.9	0.3	127.0	0.1	127.7	0.6
1991	129.4	1.3	129.7	0.2	129.9	0.2	129.9	0.0	130.0	0.1	130.1	0.1	130.1	0.0	130.2	0.1	130.3	0.1	130.7	0.3	130.6	-0.1	131.2	0.5

[Continued]

Hardware
Producer Price Index
Base 1982 = 100
[Continued]

For 1947-1997. Columns headed % show percentile change in the index from the previous period for which an index is available.

Year	Jan Index	%	Feb Index	%	Mar Index	%	Apr Index	%	May Index	%	Jun Index	%	Jul Index	%	Aug Index	%	Sep Index	%	Oct Index	%	Nov Index	%	Dec Index	%
1992	131.6	0.3	132.0	0.3	132.2	0.2	132.5	0.2	132.6	0.1	132.6	0.0	132.8	0.2	133.0	0.2	133.1	0.1	133.2	0.1	133.5	0.2	133.8	0.2
1993	134.1	0.2	134.3	0.1	134.6	0.2	134.8	0.1	134.8	0.0	135.2	0.3	135.3	0.1	135.5	0.1	135.6	0.1	135.7	0.1	135.9	0.1	136.2	0.2
1994	136.4	0.1	136.5	0.1	136.7	0.1	137.2	0.4	137.4	0.1	137.5	0.1	137.6	0.1	137.8	0.1	138.0	0.1	138.1	0.1	138.5	0.3	138.6	0.1
1995	139.4	0.6	139.7	0.2	140.4	0.5	140.8	0.3	140.9	0.1	141.4	0.4	141.5	0.1	141.6	0.1	141.7	0.1	141.7	0.0	141.9	0.1	142.2	0.2
1996	142.8	0.4	143.1	0.2	143.5	0.3	143.5	0.0	143.6	0.1	143.7	0.1	143.7	0.0	144.2	0.3	144.2	0.0	144.6	0.3	144.1	-0.3	144.2	0.1
1997	144.9	0.5	144.7	-0.1	145.2	0.3	145.4	0.1	145.5	0.1	145.7	0.1	145.2	-0.3	145.9	0.5	145.9	0.0	146.4	0.3	145.9	-0.3	146.1	0.1

Source: U.S. Department of Labor, Bureau of Labor Statistics, Division of Industry Prices and Price Indexes. n.e.c. stands for not elsewhere classified. - indicates no data collected for period or unavailable.

Plumbing Fixtures and Brass Fittings
Producer Price Index
Base 1982 = 100

For 1926-1997. Columns headed % show percentile change in the index from the previous period for which an index is available.

Year	Jan Index	%	Feb Index	%	Mar Index	%	Apr Index	%	May Index	%	Jun Index	%	Jul Index	%	Aug Index	%	Sep Index	%	Oct Index	%	Nov Index	%	Dec Index	%
1926	26.4	-	26.4	0.0	26.4	0.0	26.4	0.0	26.3	-0.4	25.9	-1.5	25.8	-0.4	26.0	0.8	26.2	0.8	26.2	0.0	26.1	-0.4	26.2	0.4
1927	26.2	0.0	25.5	-2.7	23.5	-7.8	23.5	0.0	23.1	-1.7	22.8	-1.3	22.8	0.0	22.8	0.0	22.9	0.4	22.9	0.0	22.9	0.0	22.7	-0.9
1928	22.7	0.0	22.7	0.0	23.4	3.1	23.5	0.4	23.6	0.4	24.3	3.0	24.3	0.0	24.3	0.0	24.3	0.0	24.3	0.0	24.4	0.4	24.4	0.0
1929	24.1	-1.2	22.4	-7.1	22.4	0.0	22.6	0.9	22.6	0.0	22.6	0.0	22.1	-2.2	22.5	1.8	22.5	0.0	22.1	-1.8	22.1	0.0	22.1	0.0
1930	22.1	0.0	22.7	2.7	23.0	1.3	24.1	4.8	24.1	0.0	20.8	-13.7	19.9	-4.3	19.9	0.0	19.8	-0.5	19.8	0.0	19.7	-0.5	20.5	4.1
1931	20.6	0.5	20.2	-1.9	20.2	0.0	20.2	0.0	20.2	0.0	20.2	0.0	20.2	0.0	20.2	0.0	20.0	-1.0	20.1	0.5	20.0	-0.5	19.3	-3.5
1932	16.4	-15.0	16.2	-1.2	15.6	-3.7	15.6	0.0	15.6	0.0	16.6	6.4	16.8	1.2	16.8	0.0	16.8	0.0	16.8	0.0	16.8	0.0	16.8	0.0
1933	14.5	-13.7	12.8	-11.7	12.8	0.0	12.8	0.0	13.8	7.8	16.2	17.4	16.7	3.1	16.9	1.2	19.1	13.0	19.1	0.0	19.1	0.0	19.0	-0.5
1934	19.0	0.0	18.8	-1.1	18.8	0.0	18.8	0.0	17.9	-4.8	16.9	-5.6	16.9	0.0	17.0	0.6	15.5	-8.8	14.0	-9.7	13.9	-0.7	13.9	0.0
1935	13.9	0.0	14.0	0.7	14.1	0.7	14.0	-0.7	14.0	0.0	14.0	0.0	14.9	6.4	15.5	4.0	15.5	0.0	15.5	0.0	15.5	0.0	15.5	0.0
1936	15.8	1.9	16.9	7.0	16.9	0.0	16.9	0.0	16.9	0.0	16.9	0.0	16.9	0.0	16.9	0.0	16.9	0.0	16.9	0.0	16.9	0.0	16.9	0.0
1937	16.9	0.0	16.9	0.0	17.0	0.6	17.2	1.2	17.2	0.0	17.2	0.0	17.2	0.0	17.2	0.0	17.2	0.0	17.2	0.0	17.2	0.0	17.2	0.0
1938	17.1	-0.6	17.1	0.0	17.0	-0.6	17.0	0.0	17.0	0.0	17.0	0.0	17.0	0.0	17.0	0.0	16.6	-2.4	16.6	0.0	16.6	0.0	16.6	0.0
1939	16.6	0.0	16.9	1.8	16.9	0.0	16.9	0.0	16.9	0.0	16.9	0.0	16.9	0.0	16.9	0.0	16.9	0.0	16.9	0.0	16.9	0.0	16.9	0.0
1940	17.0	0.6	17.2	1.2	18.1	5.2	18.1	0.0	18.1	0.0	18.1	0.0	18.1	0.0	18.1	0.0	18.1	0.0	18.1	0.0	18.1	0.0	18.1	0.0
1941	18.1	0.0	18.1	0.0	18.0	-0.6	18.0	0.0	18.0	0.0	18.0	0.0	18.1	0.6	18.3	1.1	18.5	1.1	18.6	0.5	18.7	0.5	19.2	2.7
1942	21.2	10.4	21.1	-0.5	20.5	-2.8	20.6	0.5	20.6	0.0	20.6	0.0	19.8	-3.9	19.8	0.0	19.8	0.0	19.7	-0.5	19.7	0.0	19.7	0.0
1943	19.8	0.0	19.8	0.0	19.8	0.0	19.8	0.0	19.8	0.0	19.8	0.0	19.8	0.0	19.8	0.0	19.7	-0.5	19.7	0.0	19.7	0.0	19.7	0.0
1944	19.7	0.0	19.7	0.0	19.7	0.0	19.7	0.0	18.6	-5.6	18.6	0.0	18.6	0.0	18.6	0.0	18.6	0.0	18.6	0.0	18.6	0.0	18.6	0.0
1945	18.6	0.0	18.6	0.0	18.6	0.0	18.7	0.5	18.7	0.0	18.7	0.0	18.7	0.0	18.9	1.1	19.1	1.1	19.1	0.0	19.1	0.0	19.1	0.0
1946	19.1	0.0	19.1	0.0	19.6	2.6	19.9	1.5	19.9	0.0	19.8	-0.5	19.8	0.0	20.0	1.0	20.4	2.0	20.4	0.0	20.4	0.0	22.8	11.8
1947	22.9	0.4	23.6	3.1	23.8	0.8	23.8	0.0	23.8	0.0	23.8	0.0	23.9	0.4	24.1	0.8	24.6	2.1	24.6	0.0	24.7	0.4	24.7	0.0
1948	25.2	2.0	25.7	2.0	25.7	0.0	25.7	0.0	25.7	0.0	25.7	0.0	25.8	0.4	26.6	3.1	26.7	0.4	26.7	0.0	26.7	0.0	26.6	-0.4
1949	26.5	-0.4	26.3	-0.8	26.2	-0.4	26.2	0.0	25.9	-1.1	25.9	0.0	25.9	0.0	25.9	0.0	25.9	0.0	25.9	0.0	25.9	0.0	25.8	-0.4
1950	25.8	0.0	25.8	0.0	25.8	0.0	25.9	0.4	26.2	1.2	26.2	0.0	26.2	0.0	27.8	6.1	28.1	1.1	29.6	5.3	30.8	4.1	31.3	1.6
1951	31.3	0.0	31.3	0.0	31.3	0.0	31.3	0.0	31.3	0.0	31.2	-0.3	31.1	-0.3	31.0	-0.3	30.9	-0.3	30.8	-0.3	30.8	0.0	30.7	-0.3
1952	29.6	-3.6	29.6	0.0	29.6	0.0	29.5	-0.3	29.4	-0.3	29.9	1.7	30.0	0.3	30.0	0.0	30.0	0.0	30.0	0.0	30.0	0.0	30.0	0.0
1953	28.8	-4.0	29.0	0.7	29.0	0.0	28.9	-0.3	28.9	0.0	28.8	-0.3	29.5	2.4	30.1	2.0	30.1	0.0	30.0	-0.3	30.0	0.0	30.0	0.0
1954	30.0	0.0	30.0	0.0	30.0	0.0	30.0	0.0	30.0	0.0	30.1	0.3	30.1	0.0	30.1	0.0	30.1	0.0	30.1	0.0	30.1	0.0	30.1	0.0
1955	30.1	0.0	30.1	0.0	31.2	3.7	31.3	0.3	31.3	0.0	31.3	0.0	31.3	0.0	32.5	3.8	32.5	0.0	32.8	0.9	33.8	3.0	33.8	0.0
1956	33.8	0.0	33.8	0.0	33.8	0.0	34.0	0.6	34.3	0.9	34.0	-0.9	34.0	0.0	34.0	0.0	34.0	0.0	34.0	0.0	34.0	0.0	34.0	0.0
1957	33.8	-0.6	33.8	0.0	33.5	-0.9	33.4	-0.3	33.0	-1.2	32.8	-0.6	32.8	0.0	32.7	-0.3	32.7	0.0	32.6	-0.3	32.6	0.0	32.6	0.0
1958	32.3	-0.9	31.9	-1.2	31.6	-0.9	31.4	-0.6	31.1	-1.0	31.1	0.0	30.4	-2.3	30.4	0.0	31.4	3.3	31.6	0.6	31.6	0.0	31.6	0.0
1959	31.7	0.3	31.9	0.6	32.8	2.8	32.9	0.3	33.2	0.9	33.2	0.0	33.2	0.0	33.2	0.0	33.2	0.0	33.2	0.0	33.6	1.2	33.8	0.6
1960	34.0	0.6	34.0	0.0	34.0	0.0	33.5	-1.5	33.7	0.6	33.3	-1.2	33.3	0.0	33.3	0.0	33.3	0.0	33.1	-0.6	33.1	0.0	33.1	0.0
1961	33.2	0.3	33.2	0.0	33.2	0.0	33.2	0.0	33.3	0.3	33.5	0.6	33.6	0.3	33.8	0.6	33.8	0.0	33.9	0.3	33.9	0.0	33.8	-0.3
1962	33.8	0.0	33.8	0.0	33.7	-0.3	33.7	0.0	33.7	0.0	32.0	-5.0	31.5	-1.6	31.4	-0.3	31.4	0.0	31.5	0.3	31.6	0.3	31.6	0.0
1963	31.6	0.0	32.8	3.8	32.8	0.0	32.7	-0.3	32.7	0.0	32.6	-0.3	32.5	-0.3	32.5	0.0	32.5	0.0	32.5	0.0	32.5	0.0	32.5	0.0
1964	32.4	-0.3	32.4	0.0	32.3	-0.3	32.3	0.0	32.3	0.0	32.3	0.0	32.6	0.9	33.1	1.5	33.1	0.0	33.4	0.9	33.4	0.0	33.4	0.0
1965	33.3	-0.3	33.3	0.0	33.3	0.0	33.3	0.0	33.3	0.0	33.3	0.0	33.3	0.0	33.6	0.9	33.6	0.0	33.6	0.0	33.7	0.3	34.1	1.2
1966	34.0	-0.3	34.1	0.3	34.3	0.6	34.8	1.5	35.0	0.6	35.2	0.6	35.7	1.4	35.7	0.0	35.9	0.6	35.9	0.0	35.9	0.0	35.9	0.0
1967	35.9	0.0	36.0	0.3	36.0	0.0	36.0	0.0	36.0	0.0	36.0	0.0	35.7	-0.8	35.7	0.0	35.7	0.0	35.7	0.0	35.7	0.0	35.9	0.6
1968	36.0	0.3	37.0	2.8	37.1	0.3	37.2	0.3	37.2	0.0	37.0	-0.5	37.0	0.0	37.1	0.3	37.1	0.0	37.2	0.3	37.4	0.5	37.4	0.0
1969	37.6	0.5	37.7	0.3	37.8	0.3	37.8	0.0	38.0	0.5	38.3	0.8	38.8	1.3	38.8	0.0	39.1	0.8	39.2	0.3	39.6	1.0	39.4	-0.5
1970	39.2	-0.5	39.2	0.0	39.2	0.0	40.0	2.0	39.6	-1.0	39.8	0.5	40.0	0.5	39.8	-0.5	40.6	2.0	40.5	-0.2	40.4	-0.2	40.6	0.5

[Continued]

Plumbing Fixtures and Brass Fittings
Producer Price Index
Base 1982 = 100
[Continued]

For 1926-1997. Columns headed % show percentile change in the index from the previous period for which an index is available.

Year	Jan Index	%	Feb Index	%	Mar Index	%	Apr Index	%	May Index	%	Jun Index	%	Jul Index	%	Aug Index	%	Sep Index	%	Oct Index	%	Nov Index	%	Dec Index	%
1971	40.7	0.2	40.7	0.0	40.7	0.0	41.3	1.5	41.6	0.7	42.0	1.0	42.3	0.7	42.4	0.2	42.4	0.0	42.4	0.0	42.4	0.0	42.5	0.2
1972	42.4	-0.2	42.6	0.5	42.6	0.0	42.7	0.2	42.7	0.0	42.9	0.5	43.0	0.2	43.1	0.2	43.2	0.2	43.3	0.2	43.3	0.0	43.3	0.0
1973	43.4	0.2	43.6	0.5	44.2	1.4	44.8	1.4	45.1	0.7	45.3	0.4	45.3	0.0	45.4	0.2	45.6	0.4	45.8	0.4	46.3	1.1	46.7	0.9
1974	47.9	2.6	48.3	0.8	48.8	1.0	50.5	3.5	52.2	3.4	53.1	1.7	54.6	2.8	56.6	3.7	57.2	1.1	57.4	0.3	57.7	0.5	57.9	0.3
1975	58.3	0.7	58.4	0.2	58.7	0.5	58.3	-0.7	58.1	-0.3	58.0	-0.2	57.7	-0.5	57.6	-0.2	57.8	0.3	58.6	1.4	58.7	0.2	58.7	0.0
1976	59.0	0.5	60.4	2.4	60.5	0.2	60.9	0.7	61.4	0.8	62.8	2.3	63.8	1.6	63.8	0.0	64.2	0.6	64.2	0.0	64.3	0.2	64.3	0.0
1977	64.4	0.2	64.5	0.2	65.4	1.4	65.6	0.3	66.4	1.2	66.8	0.6	67.9	1.6	68.1	0.3	68.5	0.6	68.5	0.0	68.6	0.1	68.9	0.4
1978	69.0	0.1	69.9	1.3	70.3	0.6	70.9	0.9	71.1	0.3	71.4	0.4	71.7	0.4	72.2	0.7	72.4	0.3	72.6	0.3	72.6	0.0	73.1	0.7
1979	73.3	0.3	74.6	1.8	75.2	0.8	76.1	1.2	76.7	0.8	77.8	1.4	78.8	1.3	79.8	1.3	80.0	0.3	80.2	0.2	80.9	0.9	81.3	0.5
1980	83.5	2.7	84.9	1.7	87.0	2.5	87.5	0.6	88.8	1.5	89.2	0.5	89.6	0.4	89.9	0.3	89.9	0.0	89.9	0.0	90.5	0.7	91.5	1.1
1981	92.1	0.7	93.0	1.0	93.1	0.1	95.2	2.3	95.5	0.3	96.5	1.0	97.2	0.7	97.3	0.1	97.4	0.1	97.9	0.5	98.0	0.1	98.3	0.3
1982	98.5	0.2	99.2	0.7	100.2	1.0	100.6	0.4	100.8	0.2	101.4	0.6	101.6	0.2	98.5	-3.1	99.4	0.9	99.7	0.3	99.9	0.2	100.2	0.3
1983	100.7	0.5	101.7	1.0	102.5	0.8	103.2	0.7	103.7	0.5	104.3	0.6	104.2	-0.1	104.1	-0.1	104.9	0.8	105.0	0.1	105.5	0.5	105.5	0.0
1984	105.5	0.0	106.3	0.8	107.6	1.2	108.2	0.6	108.2	0.0	108.5	0.3	108.6	0.1	109.3	0.6	109.2	-0.1	109.9	0.6	110.9	0.9	111.0	0.1
1985	109.9	-1.0	110.1	0.2	110.4	0.3	111.7	1.2	112.1	0.4	112.3	0.2	112.3	0.0	112.4	0.1	112.6	0.2	113.0	0.4	113.0	0.0	112.9	-0.1
1986	113.0	0.1	113.5	0.4	115.7	1.9	115.8	0.1	115.9	0.1	116.3	0.3	116.2	-0.1	115.9	-0.3	116.1	0.2	115.9	-0.2	115.8	-0.1	115.6	-0.2
1987	116.2	0.5	118.4	1.9	118.3	-0.1	118.7	0.3	120.0	1.1	120.1	0.1	120.2	0.1	120.5	0.2	120.6	0.1	120.9	0.2	121.2	0.2	121.7	0.4
1988	121.9	0.2	123.6	1.4	127.6	3.2	127.9	0.2	128.4	0.4	128.7	0.2	129.0	0.2	130.6	1.2	130.8	0.2	131.6	0.6	131.8	0.2	132.2	0.3
1989	133.8	1.2	135.6	1.3	135.8	0.1	136.7	0.7	137.5	0.6	137.7	0.1	138.0	0.2	138.7	0.5	139.5	0.6	139.5	0.0	139.9	0.3	139.9	0.0
1990	141.2	0.9	141.9	0.5	142.7	0.6	143.5	0.6	144.0	0.3	144.1	0.1	144.3	0.1	144.5	0.1	145.9	1.0	146.3	0.3	146.5	0.1	146.6	0.1
1991	146.5	-0.1	149.0	1.7	149.4	0.3	150.0	0.4	150.1	0.1	150.1	0.0	150.3	0.1	150.3	0.0	150.0	-0.2	150.2	0.1	150.3	0.1	150.5	0.1
1992	150.7	0.1	151.0	0.2	152.1	0.7	153.4	0.9	153.7	0.2	153.9	0.1	154.1	0.1	154.2	0.1	152.9	-0.8	153.8	0.6	153.5	-0.2	153.8	0.2
1993	153.7	-0.1	153.3	-0.3	155.2	1.2	156.2	0.6	156.3	0.1	156.5	0.1	155.9	-0.4	156.5	0.4	156.5	0.0	156.8	0.2	156.9	0.1	156.8	-0.1
1994	157.4	0.4	157.8	0.3	158.6	0.5	159.2	0.4	159.3	0.1	160.3	0.6	159.7	-0.4	160.3	0.4	160.3	0.0	160.5	0.1	161.1	0.4	161.1	0.0
1995	161.7	0.4	164.8	1.9	165.7	0.5	165.9	0.1	166.5	0.4	166.5	0.0	166.5	0.0	166.7	0.1	166.8	0.1	167.2	0.2	166.7	-0.3	166.6	-0.1
1996	167.6	0.6	170.2	1.6	170.9	0.4	171.0	0.1	171.5	0.3	171.8	0.2	171.6	-0.1	171.5	-0.1	171.6	0.1	171.6	0.0	171.8	0.1	171.4	-0.2
1997	171.9	0.3	174.3	1.4	174.5	0.1	174.7	0.1	175.0	0.2	175.1	0.1	174.8	-0.2	174.9	0.1	174.6	-0.2	175.2	0.3	175.0	-0.1	174.7	-0.2

Source: U.S. Department of Labor, Bureau of Labor Statistics, Division of Industry Prices and Price Indexes. n.e.c. stands for not elsewhere classified. - indicates no data collected for period or unavailable.

Heating Equipment
Producer Price Index
Base 1982 = 100

For 1947-1997. Columns headed % show percentile change in the index from the previous period for which an index is available.

Year	Jan Index	%	Feb Index	%	Mar Index	%	Apr Index	%	May Index	%	Jun Index	%	Jul Index	%	Aug Index	%	Sep Index	%	Oct Index	%	Nov Index	%	Dec Index	%
1947	35.3	-	35.3	0.0	35.3	0.0	35.3	0.0	35.4	0.3	35.2	-0.6	35.5	0.9	35.7	0.6	36.3	1.7	36.5	0.6	36.6	0.3	36.7	0.3
1948	36.6	-0.3	36.8	0.5	36.8	0.0	37.0	0.5	37.1	0.3	37.1	0.0	37.2	0.3	38.6	3.8	39.7	2.8	39.7	0.0	39.7	0.0	39.7	0.0
1949	39.7	0.0	39.7	0.0	39.4	-0.8	39.3	-0.3	39.2	-0.3	38.9	-0.8	38.6	-0.8	38.5	-0.3	38.4	-0.3	38.4	0.0	38.3	-0.3	38.3	0.0
1950	38.2	-0.3	38.3	0.3	38.3	0.0	38.3	0.0	38.4	0.3	38.3	-0.3	38.6	0.8	39.6	2.6	40.3	1.8	41.2	2.2	41.5	0.7	42.4	2.2
1951	43.0	1.4	43.1	0.2	43.1	0.0	43.1	0.0	43.1	0.0	43.0	-0.2	42.9	-0.2	43.0	0.2	43.0	0.0	43.0	0.0	42.9	-0.2	43.0	0.2
1952	42.8	-0.5	42.8	0.0	42.8	0.0	42.7	-0.2	42.7	0.0	42.6	-0.2	42.7	0.2	42.7	0.0	42.7	0.0	42.7	0.0	42.7	0.0	42.7	0.0
1953	42.7	0.0	42.7	0.0	42.7	0.0	42.7	0.0	42.9	0.5	43.0	0.2	43.2	0.5	43.4	0.5	43.5	0.2	43.5	0.0	43.5	0.0	43.4	-0.2
1954	43.3	-0.2	43.1	-0.5	42.9	-0.5	43.0	0.2	42.7	-0.7	42.7	0.0	42.8	0.2	42.8	0.0	42.8	0.0	42.9	0.2	42.9	0.0	42.9	0.0
1955	42.7	-0.5	42.7	0.0	42.7	0.0	42.7	0.0	42.6	-0.2	42.6	0.0	42.7	0.2	43.5	1.9	44.0	1.1	44.0	0.0	44.1	0.2	44.0	-0.2
1956	44.0	0.0	44.0	0.0	44.0	0.0	44.0	0.0	44.0	0.0	44.1	0.2	44.3	0.5	44.7	0.9	45.4	1.6	45.7	0.7	45.8	0.2	45.8	0.0
1957	46.0	0.4	46.0	0.0	45.5	-1.1	45.5	0.0	45.4	-0.2	45.6	0.4	46.0	0.9	45.7	-0.7	45.7	0.0	45.7	0.0	45.7	0.0	45.5	-0.4
1958	45.4	-0.2	45.3	-0.2	45.1	-0.4	45.1	0.0	45.1	0.0	45.2	0.2	45.3	0.2	45.3	0.0	45.4	0.2	45.4	0.0	45.4	0.0	45.5	0.2
1959	45.5	0.0	45.6	0.2	45.5	-0.2	45.5	0.0	45.5	0.0	45.5	0.0	45.5	0.0	45.4	-0.2	45.4	0.0	45.4	0.0	45.4	0.0	45.4	0.0
1960	45.2	-0.4	44.9	-0.7	44.9	0.0	44.9	0.0	44.9	0.0	44.9	0.0	44.3	-1.3	44.4	0.2	44.6	0.5	44.6	0.0	44.3	-0.7	43.6	-1.6
1961	42.9	-1.6	42.9	0.0	42.7	-0.5	43.0	0.7	43.1	0.2	43.1	0.0	43.1	0.0	43.2	0.2	43.0	-0.5	42.9	-0.2	42.7	-0.5	42.9	0.5
1962	42.7	-0.5	42.7	0.0	42.6	-0.2	42.6	0.0	42.3	-0.7	42.2	-0.2	42.2	0.0	42.2	0.0	42.1	-0.2	42.2	0.2	42.2	0.0	42.4	0.5
1963	42.1	-0.7	42.0	-0.2	42.1	0.2	42.2	0.2	42.3	0.2	42.4	0.2	42.4	0.0	42.3	-0.2	42.3	0.0	42.3	0.0	42.2	-0.2	42.2	0.0
1964	41.8	-0.9	41.7	-0.2	41.9	0.5	41.9	0.0	41.8	-0.2	42.0	0.5	41.8	-0.5	41.7	-0.2	41.7	0.0	41.7	0.0	41.8	0.2	41.9	0.2
1965	41.5	-1.0	41.6	0.2	41.7	0.2	41.8	0.2	41.7	-0.2	41.8	0.2	41.7	-0.2	41.8	0.2	41.8	0.0	41.8	0.0	41.7	-0.2	41.7	0.0
1966	41.6	-0.2	41.7	0.2	41.7	0.0	41.9	0.5	41.9	0.0	42.1	0.5	42.2	0.2	42.1	-0.2	42.2	0.2	42.4	0.5	42.5	0.2	42.5	0.0
1967	42.1	-0.9	41.8	-0.7	41.9	0.2	41.9	0.0	41.9	0.0	42.2	0.7	42.2	0.0	42.1	-0.2	42.2	0.2	42.3	0.2	42.5	0.5	42.6	0.2
1968	42.5	-0.2	42.7	0.5	42.9	0.5	43.1	0.5	43.3	0.5	43.4	0.2	43.5	0.2	43.5	0.0	43.5	0.0	43.5	0.0	43.6	0.2	43.8	0.5
1969	43.7	-0.2	43.8	0.2	43.9	0.2	44.1	0.5	44.1	0.0	44.3	0.5	44.4	0.2	44.5	0.2	44.6	0.2	44.9	0.7	45.4	1.1	45.4	0.0
1970	45.4	0.0	45.5	0.2	45.7	0.4	46.1	0.9	46.2	0.2	46.6	0.9	47.0	0.9	47.0	0.0	47.1	0.2	47.4	0.6	47.6	0.4	47.7	0.2
1971	47.8	0.2	48.1	0.6	48.1	0.0	48.3	0.4	48.6	0.6	48.5	-0.2	48.8	0.6	49.0	0.4	49.0	0.0	49.0	0.0	49.0	0.0	49.0	0.0
1972	48.9	-0.2	49.0	0.2	49.3	0.6	49.7	0.8	49.8	0.2	50.0	0.4	50.2	0.4	50.2	0.0	50.3	0.2	50.2	-0.2	50.3	0.2	50.2	-0.2
1973	50.1	-0.2	50.3	0.4	50.4	0.2	50.8	0.8	50.7	-0.2	50.9	0.4	51.0	0.2	50.9	-0.2	50.9	0.0	50.9	0.0	51.0	0.2	51.3	0.6
1974	51.8	1.0	52.1	0.6	52.5	0.8	53.8	2.5	54.8	1.9	56.0	2.2	57.8	3.2	59.0	2.1	59.6	1.0	61.1	2.5	62.0	1.5	62.6	1.0
1975	62.5	-0.2	62.8	0.5	63.0	0.3	63.1	0.2	63.3	0.3	63.5	0.3	63.3	-0.3	63.4	0.2	63.4	0.0	64.1	1.1	64.5	0.6	65.4	1.4
1976	65.5	0.2	65.5	0.0	65.4	-0.2	65.7	0.5	66.1	0.6	66.2	0.2	66.8	0.9	67.2	0.6	67.6	0.6	67.5	-0.1	67.8	0.4	68.2	0.6
1977	68.7	0.7	68.8	0.1	69.0	0.3	68.9	-0.1	69.1	0.3	69.4	0.4	69.7	0.4	70.0	0.4	70.3	0.4	70.8	0.7	70.9	0.1	71.4	0.7
1978	72.2	1.1	72.0	-0.3	72.2	0.3	72.8	0.8	73.1	0.4	73.3	0.3	73.5	0.3	74.3	1.1	74.2	-0.1	74.6	0.5	74.7	0.1	75.5	1.1
1979	75.9	0.5	76.3	0.5	77.3	1.3	77.5	0.3	78.3	1.0	78.1	-0.3	78.4	0.4	79.3	1.1	80.7	1.8	81.0	0.4	81.4	0.5	82.4	1.2
1980	84.1	2.1	85.4	1.5	85.4	0.0	86.1	0.8	86.0	-0.1	86.4	0.5	86.9	0.6	87.7	0.9	88.0	0.3	88.8	0.9	89.4	0.7	90.2	0.9
1981	91.3	1.2	91.7	0.4	92.5	0.9	92.7	0.2	93.7	1.1	94.2	0.5	95.4	1.3	96.1	0.7	96.3	0.2	96.5	0.2	96.5	0.0	96.9	0.4
1982	98.4	1.5	98.3	-0.1	99.3	1.0	99.5	0.2	100.0	0.5	100.5	0.5	100.7	0.2	100.5	-0.2	100.8	0.3	100.5	-0.3	100.7	0.2	100.9	0.2
1983	101.5	0.6	101.5	0.0	101.6	0.1	102.2	0.6	102.3	0.1	102.4	0.1	103.2	0.8	103.3	0.1	104.0	0.7	103.4	-0.6	103.5	0.1	103.6	0.1
1984	104.2	0.6	104.6	0.4	104.8	0.2	105.5	0.7	106.4	0.9	106.5	0.1	107.6	1.0	107.7	0.1	107.8	0.1	107.9	0.1	107.9	0.0	108.1	0.2
1985	108.0	-0.1	108.5	0.5	108.6	0.1	108.7	0.1	109.4	0.6	109.5	0.1	109.6	0.1	110.0	0.4	110.3	0.3	110.2	-0.1	110.3	0.1	110.5	0.2
1986	111.6	1.0	111.7	0.1	111.6	-0.1	112.5	0.8	112.3	-0.2	113.0	0.6	113.1	0.1	113.5	0.4	113.4	-0.1	114.3	0.8	114.4	0.1	114.5	0.1
1987	115.3	0.7	115.4	0.1	115.7	0.3	115.6	-0.1	115.6	0.0	115.1	-0.4	115.5	0.3	115.6	0.1	115.5	-0.1	115.7	0.2	117.1	1.2	114.1	-2.6
1988	115.9	1.6	118.4	2.2	118.4	0.0	118.5	0.1	118.8	0.3	118.5	-0.3	119.9	1.2	120.1	0.2	120.0	-0.1	120.5	0.4	120.8	0.2	121.0	0.2
1989	121.8	0.7	123.2	1.1	123.7	0.4	124.6	0.7	124.7	0.1	124.3	-0.3	124.8	0.4	125.1	0.2	126.9	1.4	126.9	0.0	127.3	0.3	127.6	0.2
1990	129.9	1.8	130.8	0.7	130.9	0.1	130.7	-0.2	130.7	0.0	130.6	-0.1	131.7	0.8	131.8	0.1	132.0	0.2	133.3	1.0	133.3	0.0	133.3	0.0
1991	134.0	0.5	134.3	0.2	134.1	-0.1	133.2	-0.7	133.5	0.2	133.5	0.0	134.1	0.4	134.4	0.2	134.0	-0.3	134.8	0.6	134.8	0.0	134.6	-0.1

[Continued]

Heating Equipment
Producer Price Index
Base 1982 = 100
[Continued]

For 1947-1997. Columns headed % show percentile change in the index from the previous period for which an index is available.

Year	Jan Index	%	Feb Index	%	Mar Index	%	Apr Index	%	May Index	%	Jun Index	%	Jul Index	%	Aug Index	%	Sep Index	%	Oct Index	%	Nov Index	%	Dec Index	%
1992	136.2	1.2	136.6	0.3	137.2	0.4	137.1	-0.1	137.6	0.4	137.4	-0.1	137.6	0.1	137.4	-0.1	137.3	-0.1	137.6	0.2	137.0	-0.4	138.1	0.8
1993	139.2	0.8	139.3	0.1	139.4	0.1	140.6	0.9	140.7	0.1	141.2	0.4	140.9	-0.2	140.7	-0.1	140.4	-0.2	140.6	0.1	140.7	0.1	140.7	0.0
1994	141.2	0.4	141.8	0.4	142.1	0.2	142.4	0.2	142.6	0.1	142.4	-0.1	142.6	0.1	142.9	0.2	143.0	0.1	143.0	0.0	143.1	0.1	143.3	0.1
1995	145.3	1.4	146.5	0.8	147.0	0.3	147.2	0.1	147.4	0.1	147.6	0.1	147.7	0.1	148.1	0.3	148.2	0.1	148.4	0.1	148.4	0.0	148.5	0.1
1996	150.1	1.1	150.5	0.3	150.5	0.0	150.6	0.1	150.8	0.1	151.1	0.2	151.5	0.3	151.8	0.2	151.8	0.0	151.8	0.0	151.8	0.0	151.9	0.1
1997	152.0	0.1	152.0	0.0	152.0	0.0	152.2	0.1	151.7	-0.3	152.1	0.3	152.7	0.4	152.8	0.1	152.9	0.1	153.0	0.1	153.3	0.2	153.9	0.4

Source: U.S. Department of Labor, Bureau of Labor Statistics, Division of Industry Prices and Price Indexes. n.e.c. stands for not elsewhere classified. - indicates no data collected for period or unavailable.

Fabricated Structural Metal Products
Producer Price Index
Base 1982 = 100

For 1947-1997. Columns headed % show percentile change in the index from the previous period for which an index is available.

Year	Jan Index	%	Feb Index	%	Mar Index	%	Apr Index	%	May Index	%	Jun Index	%	Jul Index	%	Aug Index	%	Sep Index	%	Oct Index	%	Nov Index	%	Dec Index	%
1947	22.2	-	22.2	0.0	22.4	0.9	22.4	0.0	22.3	-0.4	22.3	0.0	22.3	0.0	22.3	0.0	22.9	2.7	23.0	0.4	23.1	0.4	23.1	0.0
1948	23.2	0.4	23.2	0.0	23.3	0.4	23.4	0.4	23.2	-0.9	23.2	0.0	23.4	0.9	24.5	4.7	24.7	0.8	24.7	0.0	24.7	0.0	24.7	0.0
1949	24.6	-0.4	24.5	-0.4	24.4	-0.4	24.0	-1.6	23.7	-1.2	23.4	-1.3	23.4	0.0	22.8	-2.6	22.7	-0.4	22.7	0.0	22.8	0.4	22.9	0.4
1950	23.0	0.4	23.4	1.7	23.4	0.0	23.3	-0.4	23.3	0.0	23.3	0.0	23.9	2.6	24.2	1.3	24.6	1.7	25.7	4.5	26.0	1.2	27.2	4.6
1951	27.6	1.5	27.8	0.7	27.7	-0.4	27.7	0.0	27.7	0.0	27.7	0.0	27.3	-1.4	27.1	-0.7	27.1	0.0	27.0	-0.4	27.0	0.0	27.0	0.0
1952	27.0	0.0	26.9	-0.4	26.9	0.0	26.9	0.0	26.9	0.0	26.9	0.0	26.9	0.0	26.9	0.0	26.9	0.0	26.6	-1.1	26.6	0.0	26.5	-0.4
1953	26.5	0.0	26.5	0.0	26.5	0.0	26.5	0.0	26.5	0.0	26.7	0.8	27.4	2.6	27.5	0.4	27.5	0.0	27.4	-0.4	27.4	0.0	27.3	-0.4
1954	27.4	0.4	27.2	-0.7	27.2	0.0	27.2	0.0	27.1	-0.4	27.0	-0.4	27.0	0.0	27.4	1.5	27.5	0.4	27.5	0.0	27.4	-0.4	27.5	0.4
1955	27.5	0.0	27.5	0.0	27.5	0.0	27.6	0.4	27.7	0.4	27.7	0.0	28.8	4.0	29.5	2.4	29.6	0.3	29.7	0.3	29.7	0.0	29.8	0.3
1956	30.0	0.7	30.0	0.0	30.2	0.7	30.6	1.3	30.1	-1.6	30.1	0.0	30.2	0.3	31.3	3.6	31.9	1.9	31.9	0.0	32.0	0.3	32.0	0.0
1957	31.2	-2.5	31.1	-0.3	31.1	0.0	30.9	-0.6	30.8	-0.3	30.7	-0.3	31.3	2.0	31.6	1.0	31.4	-0.6	31.4	0.0	31.4	0.0	31.4	0.0
1958	31.4	0.0	31.4	0.0	31.3	-0.3	31.3	0.0	31.3	0.0	31.2	-0.3	31.0	-0.6	31.1	0.3	31.0	-0.3	31.1	0.3	31.2	0.3	31.2	0.0
1959	31.2	0.0	31.2	0.0	30.8	-1.3	30.8	0.0	30.8	0.0	30.8	0.0	30.8	0.0	30.8	0.0	31.3	1.6	31.3	0.0	31.6	1.0	31.6	0.0
1960	31.6	0.0	31.6	0.0	31.7	0.3	31.5	-0.6	31.4	-0.3	31.4	0.0	31.4	0.0	31.4	0.0	31.3	-0.3	31.2	-0.3	31.2	0.0	31.2	0.0
1961	31.1	-0.3	31.1	0.0	30.9	-0.6	30.9	0.0	30.8	-0.3	30.8	0.0	30.8	0.0	30.8	0.0	30.7	-0.3	30.7	0.0	30.7	0.0	30.7	0.0
1962	30.6	-0.3	30.6	0.0	30.6	0.0	30.6	0.0	30.6	0.0	30.6	0.0	30.6	0.0	30.6	0.0	30.6	0.0	30.6	0.0	30.6	0.0	30.6	0.0
1963	30.6	0.0	30.5	-0.3	30.5	0.0	30.4	-0.3	30.5	0.3	30.6	0.3	30.6	0.0	30.6	0.0	30.7	0.3	30.7	0.0	30.8	0.3	30.8	0.0
1964	30.8	0.0	30.9	0.3	30.7	-0.6	30.8	0.3	30.7	-0.3	30.9	0.7	30.9	0.0	31.0	0.3	31.0	0.0	31.0	0.0	31.1	0.3	31.2	0.3
1965	31.3	0.3	31.2	-0.3	31.3	0.3	31.4	0.3	31.5	0.3	31.5	0.0	31.6	0.3	31.7	0.3	31.7	0.0	31.7	0.0	31.8	0.3	31.8	0.0
1966	31.9	0.3	32.0	0.3	32.1	0.3	32.3	0.6	32.3	0.0	32.4	0.3	32.5	0.3	32.5	0.0	32.5	0.0	32.6	0.3	32.6	0.0	32.7	0.3
1967	32.6	-0.3	32.6	0.0	32.6	0.0	32.7	0.3	32.7	0.0	32.7	0.0	32.8	0.3	32.9	0.3	32.9	0.0	33.0	0.3	33.0	0.0	33.0	0.0
1968	33.1	0.3	33.1	0.0	33.3	0.6	33.3	0.0	33.2	-0.3	33.5	0.9	33.5	0.0	33.7	0.6	33.8	0.3	33.9	0.3	33.9	0.0	34.0	0.3
1969	34.0	0.0	34.1	0.3	34.1	0.0	34.3	0.6	34.5	0.6	34.8	0.9	34.9	0.3	35.1	0.6	35.2	0.3	35.3	0.3	35.4	0.3	35.4	0.0
1970	35.6	0.6	35.8	0.6	36.2	1.1	36.3	0.3	36.5	0.6	36.8	0.8	37.1	0.8	37.2	0.3	37.3	0.3	37.3	0.0	37.3	0.0	37.5	0.5
1971	37.7	0.5	37.9	0.5	38.2	0.8	38.3	0.3	38.4	0.3	38.6	0.5	38.8	0.5	39.5	1.8	39.4	-0.3	39.4	0.0	39.4	0.0	39.4	0.0
1972	39.9	1.3	40.0	0.3	40.1	0.2	40.1	0.0	40.0	-0.2	40.1	0.2	40.1	0.0	40.2	0.2	40.2	0.0	40.4	0.5	40.4	0.0	40.5	0.2
1973	40.8	0.7	40.9	0.2	41.0	0.2	41.2	0.5	41.6	1.0	41.6	0.0	41.7	0.2	41.9	0.5	42.2	0.7	42.5	0.7	42.9	0.9	43.2	0.7
1974	44.4	2.8	44.9	1.1	46.0	2.4	47.2	2.6	49.8	5.5	52.1	4.6	54.2	4.0	57.5	6.1	59.0	2.6	59.7	1.2	59.9	0.3	60.0	0.2
1975	60.8	1.3	62.2	2.3	62.3	0.2	61.8	-0.8	61.9	0.2	61.9	0.0	61.8	-0.2	62.0	0.3	62.1	0.2	62.4	0.5	62.3	-0.2	62.6	0.5
1976	62.5	-0.2	62.4	-0.2	62.6	0.3	62.5	-0.2	62.6	0.2	63.0	0.6	63.5	0.8	64.1	0.9	64.6	0.8	64.8	0.3	65.0	0.3	65.3	0.5
1977	65.4	0.2	65.7	0.5	66.2	0.8	66.6	0.6	67.0	0.6	67.2	0.3	68.2	1.5	68.9	1.0	69.5	0.9	69.5	0.0	69.6	0.1	70.0	0.6
1978	70.4	0.6	71.8	2.0	72.6	1.1	73.7	1.5	73.9	0.3	74.1	0.3	74.8	0.9	75.5	0.9	75.7	0.3	76.0	0.4	76.2	0.3	76.6	0.5
1979	78.2	2.1	78.9	0.9	79.2	0.4	80.0	1.0	81.0	1.3	81.4	0.5	82.2	1.0	82.7	0.6	83.2	0.6	84.1	1.1	84.2	0.1	84.5	0.4
1980	84.9	0.5	85.2	0.4	87.0	2.1	88.3	1.5	88.5	0.2	88.6	0.1	89.3	0.8	89.6	0.3	89.9	0.3	90.9	1.1	91.2	0.3	91.6	0.4
1981	92.9	1.4	93.6	0.8	95.0	1.5	96.1	1.2	96.4	0.3	96.8	0.4	97.7	0.9	98.2	0.5	98.4	0.2	99.3	0.9	99.5	0.2	99.4	-0.1
1982	99.6	0.2	99.7	0.1	99.9	0.2	100.1	0.2	100.0	-0.1	100.2	0.2	99.7	-0.5	99.8	0.1	100.5	0.7	100.4	-0.1	100.2	-0.2	100.0	-0.2
1983	99.6	-0.4	99.4	-0.2	99.6	0.2	99.2	-0.4	99.1	-0.1	99.1	0.0	99.2	0.1	99.4	0.2	99.8	0.4	99.8	0.0	100.2	0.4	100.4	0.2
1984	100.6	0.2	100.7	0.1	101.2	0.5	101.5	0.3	101.9	0.4	102.1	0.2	102.3	0.2	102.4	0.1	102.4	0.0	102.9	0.5	102.6	-0.3	102.8	0.2
1985	102.9	0.1	102.9	0.0	103.2	0.3	103.2	0.0	103.2	0.0	103.2	0.0	103.2	0.0	103.4	0.2	103.3	-0.1	103.5	0.2	103.3	-0.2	103.3	0.0
1986	103.3	0.0	103.5	0.2	103.4	-0.1	103.4	0.0	103.3	-0.1	103.5	0.2	103.5	0.0	103.7	0.2	103.7	0.0	103.6	-0.1	104.1	0.5	103.8	-0.3
1987	103.6	-0.2	103.8	0.2	104.0	0.2	104.2	0.2	104.4	0.2	104.9	0.5	105.2	0.3	105.6	0.4	106.1	0.5	107.0	0.8	107.8	0.7	108.6	0.7
1988	110.2	1.5	110.8	0.5	111.7	0.8	112.9	1.1	113.8	0.8	114.4	0.5	115.4	0.9	115.8	0.3	116.2	0.3	116.5	0.3	116.8	0.3	117.4	0.5
1989	118.2	0.7	118.9	0.6	119.4	0.4	119.8	0.3	120.5	0.6	120.5	0.0	120.7	0.2	120.8	0.1	120.9	0.1	121.0	0.1	121.2	0.2	121.1	-0.1
1990	121.1	0.0	121.2	0.1	121.3	0.1	121.4	0.1	121.9	0.4	122.0	0.1	122.0	0.0	122.1	0.1	122.1	0.0	122.2	0.1	122.1	-0.1	122.4	0.2
1991	122.7	0.2	122.5	-0.2	122.5	0.0	122.9	0.3	122.7	-0.2	122.6	-0.1	122.5	-0.1	122.6	0.1	122.5	-0.1	122.0	-0.4	121.7	-0.2	121.7	0.0

[Continued]

Fabricated Structural Metal Products
Producer Price Index
Base 1982 = 100
[Continued]

For 1947-1997. Columns headed % show percentile change in the index from the previous period for which an index is available.

Year	Jan Index	%	Feb Index	%	Mar Index	%	Apr Index	%	May Index	%	Jun Index	%	Jul Index	%	Aug Index	%	Sep Index	%	Oct Index	%	Nov Index	%	Dec Index	%
1992	122.0	0.2	121.8	-0.2	122.0	0.2	122.2	0.2	122.0	-0.2	122.0	0.0	122.2	0.2	122.3	0.1	122.1	-0.2	122.2	0.1	122.2	0.0	122.2	0.0
1993	121.8	-0.3	122.1	0.2	122.4	0.2	122.7	0.2	122.9	0.2	123.1	0.2	123.4	0.2	123.6	0.2	123.8	0.2	124.1	0.2	124.4	0.2	124.6	0.2
1994	124.9	0.2	125.0	0.1	125.2	0.2	125.7	0.4	126.3	0.5	127.1	0.6	127.4	0.2	128.0	0.5	128.7	0.5	129.2	0.4	130.1	0.7	130.4	0.2
1995	131.9	1.2	132.5	0.5	133.6	0.8	134.4	0.6	134.6	0.1	135.2	0.4	135.8	0.4	136.0	0.1	136.5	0.4	136.6	0.1	136.7	0.1	136.7	0.0
1996	136.8	0.1	136.9	0.1	137.1	0.1	137.2	0.1	137.5	0.2	138.0	0.4	138.0	0.0	138.2	0.1	138.4	0.1	138.6	0.1	138.6	0.0	138.6	0.0
1997	139.0	0.3	139.1	0.1	139.2	0.1	139.8	0.4	140.2	0.3	140.4	0.1	140.6	0.1	140.8	0.1	141.0	0.1	141.1	0.1	141.5	0.3	141.3	-0.1

Source: U.S. Department of Labor, Bureau of Labor Statistics, Division of Industry Prices and Price Indexes. n.e.c. stands for not elsewhere classified. - indicates no data collected for period or unavailable.

Miscellaneous Metal Products
Producer Price Index
Base 1982 = 100

For 1947-1997. Columns headed % show percentile change in the index from the previous period for which an index is available.

Year	Jan Index	%	Feb Index	%	Mar Index	%	Apr Index	%	May Index	%	Jun Index	%	Jul Index	%	Aug Index	%	Sep Index	%	Oct Index	%	Nov Index	%	Dec Index	%
1947	17.4	-	17.4	0.0	17.7	1.7	17.9	1.1	17.9	0.0	18.0	0.6	18.1	0.6	18.2	0.6	18.2	0.0	18.5	1.6	18.6	0.5	18.6	0.0
1948	18.6	0.0	18.9	1.6	20.0	5.8	22.5	12.5	22.5	0.0	22.6	0.4	22.6	0.0	23.6	4.4	23.8	0.8	23.8	0.0	23.9	0.4	23.9	0.0
1949	23.9	0.0	23.9	0.0	23.9	0.0	24.0	0.4	24.0	0.0	23.9	-0.4	23.9	0.0	23.8	-0.4	23.8	0.0	23.8	0.0	23.7	-0.4	23.6	-0.4
1950	24.0	1.7	24.1	0.4	24.2	0.4	24.2	0.0	24.2	0.0	24.2	0.0	24.3	0.4	24.4	0.4	25.1	2.9	25.7	2.4	25.8	0.4	26.4	2.3
1951	26.9	1.9	26.9	0.0	26.9	0.0	26.9	0.0	26.9	0.0	26.9	0.0	26.9	0.0	26.8	-0.4	26.6	-0.7	26.6	0.0	26.6	0.0	26.6	0.0
1952	26.6	0.0	26.6	0.0	26.6	0.0	26.6	0.0	26.6	0.0	26.6	0.0	26.6	0.0	26.6	0.0	26.8	0.8	26.9	0.4	26.9	0.0	27.0	0.4
1953	27.0	0.0	27.1	0.4	26.1	-3.7	26.2	0.4	26.5	1.1	26.5	0.0	26.8	1.1	27.0	0.7	27.1	0.4	27.2	0.4	27.2	0.0	27.2	0.0
1954	27.2	0.0	27.0	-0.7	27.0	0.0	26.8	-0.7	26.8	0.0	26.8	0.0	26.8	0.0	26.9	0.4	26.9	0.0	26.9	0.0	27.0	0.4	26.9	-0.4
1955	26.9	0.0	26.9	0.0	26.9	0.0	26.9	0.0	26.9	0.0	26.9	0.0	27.1	0.7	27.7	2.2	27.9	0.7	28.1	0.7	28.2	0.4	28.3	0.4
1956	28.3	0.0	28.3	0.0	28.4	0.4	28.3	-0.4	28.3	0.0	28.3	0.0	28.3	0.0	28.5	0.7	29.3	2.8	30.2	3.1	30.2	0.0	30.2	0.0
1957	30.2	0.0	30.4	0.7	30.5	0.3	30.6	0.3	30.6	0.0	30.6	0.0	31.1	1.6	31.3	0.6	31.5	0.6	31.5	0.0	31.4	-0.3	31.6	0.6
1958	31.4	-0.6	31.3	-0.3	31.3	0.0	31.2	-0.3	31.2	0.0	31.0	-0.6	31.0	0.0	31.1	0.3	31.1	0.0	31.1	0.0	31.0	-0.3	31.0	0.0
1959	31.1	0.3	31.2	0.3	31.2	0.0	31.2	0.0	31.2	0.0	31.2	0.0	31.1	-0.3	31.0	-0.3	31.2	0.6	31.3	0.3	31.5	0.6	31.3	-0.6
1960	31.3	0.0	31.3	0.0	31.2	-0.3	31.2	0.0	31.2	0.0	31.2	0.0	31.2	0.0	31.2	0.0	31.2	0.0	31.2	0.0	31.2	0.0	31.3	0.3	31.7	1.3
1961	32.0	0.9	32.0	0.0	32.0	0.0	32.1	0.3	32.1	0.0	32.0	-0.3	31.9	-0.3	32.2	0.9	32.2	0.0	32.2	0.0	32.1	-0.3	32.1	0.0
1962	32.1	0.0	32.1	0.0	32.4	0.9	32.5	0.3	32.4	-0.3	32.3	-0.3	32.3	0.0	32.3	0.0	32.3	0.0	32.3	0.0	32.3	0.0	32.3	0.0
1963	32.2	-0.3	32.2	0.0	32.2	0.0	32.3	0.3	32.3	0.0	32.6	0.9	32.7	0.3	32.7	0.0	32.7	0.0	33.3	1.8	33.3	0.0	33.6	0.9
1964	34.0	1.2	34.0	0.0	33.9	-0.3	33.9	0.0	33.6	-0.9	33.7	0.3	33.6	-0.3	33.6	0.0	33.6	0.0	33.6	0.0	33.6	0.0	33.7	0.3
1965	33.7	0.0	33.9	0.6	33.9	0.0	34.0	0.3	34.0	0.0	34.0	0.0	34.0	0.0	33.9	-0.3	34.2	0.9	34.2	0.0	34.1	-0.3	34.1	0.0	34.1	0.0
1966	34.2	0.3	34.4	0.6	34.5	0.3	34.5	0.0	34.5	0.0	34.6	0.3	34.6	0.0	34.9	0.9	35.0	0.3	35.0	0.0	35.2	0.6	35.2	0.0
1967	35.3	0.3	35.3	0.0	35.3	0.0	35.3	0.0	35.3	0.0	35.3	0.0	35.4	0.3	35.5	0.3	35.5	0.0	35.5	0.0	35.5	0.0	35.6	0.3
1968	35.7	0.3	35.9	0.6	35.9	0.0	35.9	0.0	35.9	0.0	35.9	0.0	36.0	0.3	36.0	0.0	36.3	0.8	36.6	0.8	36.6	0.0	36.8	0.5
1969	37.2	1.1	37.4	0.5	37.5	0.3	37.5	0.0	37.5	0.0	37.6	0.3	38.0	1.1	38.5	1.3	38.7	0.5	38.7	0.0	38.7	0.0	38.8	0.3
1970	38.9	0.3	39.0	0.3	39.6	1.5	39.6	0.0	39.9	0.8	40.6	1.8	40.8	0.5	40.9	0.2	41.5	1.5	41.6	0.2	41.7	0.2	41.7	0.0
1971	41.6	-0.2	41.7	0.2	41.7	0.0	41.8	0.2	41.8	0.0	42.0	0.5	42.3	0.7	42.4	0.2	42.4	0.0	42.3	-0.2	42.3	0.0	42.8	1.2
1972	43.0	0.5	43.6	1.4	44.0	0.9	44.0	0.0	44.0	0.0	44.1	0.2	44.0	-0.2	44.2	0.5	44.2	0.0	44.2	0.0	44.2	0.0	44.2	0.0
1973	44.4	0.5	44.5	0.2	44.8	0.7	45.1	0.7	45.4	0.7	45.6	0.4	45.7	0.2	46.4	1.5	46.5	0.2	46.8	0.6	47.4	1.3	47.7	0.6
1974	48.5	1.7	49.1	1.2	49.5	0.8	50.7	2.4	53.2	4.9	54.6	2.6	57.1	4.6	59.0	3.3	60.5	2.5	61.7	2.0	62.2	0.8	62.6	0.6
1975	63.1	0.8	63.3	0.3	63.7	0.6	63.8	0.2	63.5	-0.5	64.3	1.3	64.5	0.3	64.5	0.0	64.5	0.0	64.6	0.2	64.7	0.2	64.7	0.0
1976	65.0	0.5	65.0	0.0	64.9	-0.2	65.2	0.5	65.5	0.5	65.7	0.3	66.3	0.9	67.0	1.1	67.2	0.3	67.4	0.3	67.7	0.4	67.5	-0.3
1977	67.8	0.4	68.0	0.3	68.1	0.1	68.1	0.0	68.3	0.3	68.9	0.9	69.7	1.2	70.2	0.7	70.8	0.9	71.0	0.3	71.4	0.6	71.6	0.3
1978	71.8	0.3	72.2	0.6	72.8	0.8	73.3	0.7	73.9	0.8	74.8	1.2	75.6	1.1	76.4	1.1	77.0	0.8	77.3	0.4	77.9	0.8	78.2	0.4
1979	78.6	0.5	79.1	0.6	79.8	0.9	80.4	0.8	80.9	0.6	81.5	0.7	82.1	0.7	83.4	1.6	83.8	0.5	84.5	0.8	84.5	0.0	84.7	0.2
1980	85.2	0.6	85.6	0.5	86.5	1.1	87.2	0.8	87.4	0.2	88.7	1.5	88.9	0.2	89.7	0.9	90.3	0.7	90.8	0.6	91.0	0.2	91.2	0.2
1981	92.3	1.2	93.2	1.0	93.8	0.6	94.6	0.9	95.5	1.0	95.4	-0.1	96.3	0.9	96.7	0.4	96.9	0.2	97.8	0.9	98.5	0.7	98.6	0.1
1982	99.6	1.0	98.7	-0.9	98.8	0.1	99.1	0.3	100.8	1.7	100.6	-0.2	100.3	-0.3	100.4	0.1	100.5	0.1	100.6	0.1	100.4	-0.2	100.3	-0.1
1983	98.9	-1.4	98.8	-0.1	99.3	0.5	99.4	0.1	99.5	0.1	100.4	0.9	100.5	0.1	100.6	0.1	100.7	0.1	102.3	1.6	102.6	0.3	102.6	0.0
1984	102.8	0.2	103.1	0.3	103.5	0.4	103.8	0.3	103.9	0.1	104.2	0.3	104.2	0.0	104.5	0.3	104.8	0.3	106.8	1.9	106.8	0.0	106.9	0.1
1985	106.9	0.0	107.0	0.1	107.0	0.0	107.0	0.0	107.0	0.0	107.2	0.2	107.3	0.1	107.2	-0.1	107.1	-0.1	107.0	-0.1	107.1	0.1	107.0	-0.1
1986	107.1	0.1	107.2	0.1	107.2	0.0	107.2	0.0	106.8	-0.4	106.8	0.0	106.6	-0.2	106.7	0.1	106.9	0.2	107.1	0.2	107.2	0.1	107.3	0.1
1987	107.5	0.2	107.6	0.1	107.6	0.0	107.5	-0.1	107.5	0.0	107.6	0.1	107.8	0.2	107.7	-0.1	107.7	0.0	108.2	0.5	108.4	0.2	108.8	0.4
1988	109.2	0.4	109.7	0.5	110.3	0.5	111.3	0.9	112.0	0.6	111.9	-0.1	112.3	0.4	113.1	0.7	113.4	0.3	113.8	0.4	114.2	0.4	114.5	0.3
1989	115.3	0.7	115.7	0.3	115.9	0.2	116.5	0.5	116.9	0.3	117.0	0.1	117.1	0.1	117.6	0.4	117.7	0.1	117.8	0.1	118.0	0.2	118.3	0.3
1990	118.6	0.3	118.8	0.2	118.9	0.1	119.1	0.2	119.2	0.1	119.4	0.2	119.3	-0.1	119.6	0.3	119.9	0.3	119.8	-0.1	119.9	0.1	119.8	-0.1
1991	120.1	0.3	120.1	0.0	120.2	0.1	120.1	-0.1	120.4	0.2	120.6	0.2	120.9	0.2	120.7	-0.2	120.7	0.0	120.6	-0.1	120.4	-0.2	120.6	0.2

[Continued]

Miscellaneous Metal Products
Producer Price Index
Base 1982 = 100
[Continued]

For 1947-1997. Columns headed % show percentile change in the index from the previous period for which an index is available.

Year	Jan Index	%	Feb Index	%	Mar Index	%	Apr Index	%	May Index	%	Jun Index	%	Jul Index	%	Aug Index	%	Sep Index	%	Oct Index	%	Nov Index	%	Dec Index	%
1992	120.9	0.2	121.0	0.1	121.1	0.1	121.2	0.1	121.2	0.0	121.2	0.0	121.3	0.1	121.3	0.0	121.5	0.2	121.9	0.3	121.9	0.0	121.9	0.0
1993	121.8	-0.1	122.0	0.2	122.0	0.0	122.2	0.2	122.3	0.1	122.3	0.0	122.5	0.2	122.3	-0.2	122.4	0.1	122.4	0.0	122.7	0.2	122.8	0.1
1994	123.0	0.2	123.0	0.0	123.2	0.2	123.3	0.1	123.4	0.1	123.5	0.1	123.5	0.0	123.6	0.1	123.8	0.2	124.0	0.2	124.2	0.2	124.4	0.2
1995	125.0	0.5	125.3	0.2	125.4	0.1	125.5	0.1	125.8	0.2	125.9	0.1	126.0	0.1	126.3	0.2	126.4	0.1	126.3	-0.1	126.4	0.1	126.3	-0.1
1996	126.5	0.2	126.5	0.0	126.7	0.2	126.8	0.1	127.0	0.2	126.9	-0.1	127.0	0.1	127.0	0.0	127.1	0.1	127.1	0.0	127.0	-0.1	127.1	0.1
1997	127.3	0.2	127.4	0.1	127.4	0.0	127.3	-0.1	127.6	0.2	127.6	0.0	127.8	0.2	127.8	0.0	127.8	0.0	127.9	0.1	127.9	0.0	128.0	0.1

Source: U.S. Department of Labor, Bureau of Labor Statistics, Division of Industry Prices and Price Indexes. n.e.c. stands for not elsewhere classified. - indicates no data collected for period or unavailable.

Metal Treatment Services
Producer Price Index
Base 1982 = 100

For 1984-1997. Columns headed % show percentile change in the index from the previous period for which an index is available.

Year	Jan Index	%	Feb Index	%	Mar Index	%	Apr Index	%	May Index	%	Jun Index	%	Jul Index	%	Aug Index	%	Sep Index	%	Oct Index	%	Nov Index	%	Dec Index	%
1984	-		-		-		-		-		-		-		-		-		-		-		100.0	-
1985	100.4	0.4	100.9	0.5	100.8	-0.1	101.4	0.6	102.2	0.8	102.2	0.0	102.7	0.5	103.4	0.7	103.4	0.0	103.4	0.0	103.8	0.4	104.0	0.2
1986	104.5	0.5	104.2	-0.3	104.3	0.1	104.4	0.1	104.4	0.0	104.5	0.1	104.7	0.2	104.9	0.2	105.0	0.1	105.1	0.1	105.2	0.1	105.1	-0.1
1987	105.5	0.4	105.6	0.1	105.7	0.1	105.8	0.1	106.1	0.3	106.1	0.0	106.0	-0.1	106.5	0.5	106.2	-0.3	106.7	0.5	106.8	0.1	107.4	0.6
1988	107.5	0.1	107.7	0.2	107.8	0.1	108.7	0.8	108.3	-0.4	109.1	0.7	110.0	0.8	110.3	0.3	111.8	1.4	112.1	0.3	112.2	0.1	112.6	0.4
1989	113.3	0.6	113.6	0.3	114.0	0.4	114.6	0.5	114.6	0.0	114.7	0.1	114.6	-0.1	114.7	0.1	114.9	0.2	115.0	0.1	115.0	0.0	115.2	0.2
1990	115.5	0.3	115.6	0.1	115.7	0.1	115.7	0.0	115.8	0.1	115.9	0.1	116.7	0.7	116.8	0.1	116.9	0.1	117.1	0.2	116.9	-0.2	116.9	0.0
1991	117.5	0.5	117.6	0.1	117.5	-0.1	117.4	-0.1	117.3	-0.1	117.3	0.0	117.3	0.0	117.3	0.0	117.3	0.0	117.7	0.3	117.7	0.0	117.5	-0.2
1992	117.7	0.2	117.8	0.1	117.9	0.1	118.0	0.1	118.1	0.1	118.1	0.0	118.3	0.2	118.4	0.1	118.5	0.1	118.5	0.0	118.5	0.0	118.7	0.2
1993	119.1	0.3	119.3	0.2	119.4	0.1	119.6	0.2	119.6	0.0	119.7	0.1	119.9	0.2	120.1	0.2	120.1	0.0	120.3	0.2	120.3	0.0	120.3	0.0
1994	120.6	0.2	121.0	0.3	121.0	0.0	121.1	0.1	121.2	0.1	121.3	0.1	121.5	0.2	121.7	0.2	121.6	-0.1	121.6	0.0	122.2	0.5	122.2	0.0
1995	122.5	0.2	122.7	0.2	123.1	0.3	123.2	0.1	123.3	0.1	123.1	-0.2	123.6	0.4	123.6	0.0	124.1	0.4	124.3	0.2	124.3	0.0	124.3	0.0
1996	124.4	0.1	124.6	0.2	124.6	0.0	124.7	0.1	124.7	0.0	124.8	0.1	124.9	0.1	125.0	0.1	125.0	0.0	125.1	0.1	125.2	0.1	125.1	-0.1
1997	125.2	0.1	125.3	0.1	125.5	0.2	125.7	0.2	125.7	0.0	125.9	0.2	126.1	0.2	126.7	0.5	126.9	0.2	126.8	-0.1	126.3	-0.4	126.4	0.1

Source: U.S. Department of Labor, Bureau of Labor Statistics, Division of Industry Prices and Price Indexes. n.e.c. stands for not elsewhere classified. - indicates no data collected for period or unavailable.

MACHINERY AND EQUIPMENT
Producer Price Index
Base 1982 = 100

For 1939-1997. Columns headed % show percentile change in the index from the previous period for which an index is available.

Year	Jan Index	%	Feb Index	%	Mar Index	%	Apr Index	%	May Index	%	Jun Index	%	Jul Index	%	Aug Index	%	Sep Index	%	Oct Index	%	Nov Index	%	Dec Index	%
1939	14.9	-	14.9	0.0	14.9	0.0	14.8	-0.7	14.8	0.0	14.8	0.0	14.8	0.0	14.8	0.0	14.8	0.0	14.8	0.0	14.8	0.0	14.8	0.0
1940	14.9	0.7	14.9	0.0	14.9	0.0	14.9	0.0	14.8	-0.7	14.9	0.7	14.9	0.0	14.9	0.0	14.9	0.0	14.9	0.0	14.9	0.0	14.9	0.0
1941	14.9	0.0	15.0	0.7	15.0	0.0	15.0	0.0	15.0	0.0	15.1	0.7	15.1	0.0	15.1	0.0	15.2	0.7	15.2	0.0	15.4	1.3	15.4	0.0
1942	15.4	0.0	15.4	0.0	15.4	0.0	15.4	0.0	15.4	0.0	15.4	0.0	15.4	0.0	15.3	-0.6	15.2	-0.7	15.2	0.0	15.2	0.0	15.2	0.0
1943	15.2	0.0	15.2	0.0	15.2	0.0	15.2	0.0	15.2	0.0	15.2	0.0	15.2	0.0	15.2	0.0	15.2	0.0	15.2	0.0	15.2	0.0	15.1	-0.7
1944	15.2	0.7	15.2	0.0	15.2	0.0	15.2	0.0	15.2	0.0	15.1	-0.7	15.1	0.0	15.1	0.0	15.1	0.0	15.1	0.0	15.1	0.0	15.1	0.0
1945	15.1	0.0	15.1	0.0	15.1	0.0	15.1	0.0	15.1	0.0	15.2	0.7	15.2	0.0	15.2	0.0	15.2	0.0	15.2	0.0	15.2	0.0	15.2	0.0
1946	15.3	0.7	15.4	0.7	15.4	0.0	15.6	1.3	16.3	4.5	16.6	1.8	16.9	1.8	17.1	1.2	17.4	1.8	17.5	0.6	17.9	2.3	18.4	2.8
1947	18.6	1.1	18.7	0.5	18.7	0.0	18.8	0.5	19.2	2.1	19.3	0.5	19.3	0.0	19.4	0.5	19.6	1.0	19.7	0.5	19.9	1.0	19.9	0.0
1948	20.1	1.0	20.1	0.0	20.2	0.5	20.2	0.0	20.2	0.0	20.4	1.0	20.7	1.5	21.2	2.4	21.6	1.9	21.8	0.9	21.9	0.5	22.0	0.5
1949	22.0	0.0	22.1	0.5	22.0	-0.5	22.0	0.0	21.9	-0.5	21.8	-0.5	21.8	0.0	21.8	0.0	21.8	0.0	21.7	-0.5	21.7	0.0	21.7	0.0
1950	21.7	0.0	21.7	0.0	21.7	0.0	21.8	0.5	21.8	0.0	22.0	0.9	22.2	0.9	22.8	2.7	23.2	1.8	23.6	1.7	23.9	1.3	24.8	3.8
1951	25.2	1.6	25.3	0.4	25.3	0.0	25.3	0.0	25.3	0.0	25.3	0.0	25.3	0.0	25.3	0.0	25.3	0.0	25.4	0.4	25.4	0.0	25.4	0.0
1952	25.4	0.0	25.4	0.0	25.4	0.0	25.4	0.0	25.4	0.0	25.3	-0.4	25.3	0.0	25.3	0.0	25.3	0.0	25.3	0.0	25.3	0.0	25.3	0.0
1953	25.3	0.0	25.3	0.0	25.4	0.4	25.6	0.8	25.7	0.4	25.9	0.8	26.0	0.4	26.2	0.8	26.3	0.4	26.3	0.0	26.3	0.0	26.3	0.0
1954	26.3	0.0	26.4	0.4	26.4	0.0	26.3	-0.4	26.3	0.0	26.3	0.0	26.3	0.0	26.3	0.0	26.3	0.0	26.3	0.0	26.4	0.4	26.4	0.0
1955	26.5	0.4	26.6	0.4	26.6	0.0	26.6	0.0	26.7	0.4	26.8	0.4	27.0	0.7	27.3	1.1	27.8	1.8	27.9	0.4	28.1	0.7	28.2	0.4
1956	28.3	0.4	28.4	0.4	28.5	0.4	28.8	1.1	29.1	1.0	29.1	0.0	29.2	0.3	29.4	0.7	30.0	2.0	30.3	1.0	30.6	1.0	30.7	0.3
1957	30.9	0.7	31.0	0.3	31.1	0.3	31.1	0.0	31.2	0.3	31.2	0.0	31.4	0.6	31.5	0.3	31.7	0.6	31.9	0.6	32.0	0.3	32.0	0.0
1958	32.1	0.3	32.0	-0.3	32.0	0.0	32.1	0.3	32.1	0.0	32.1	0.0	32.1	0.0	32.1	0.0	32.1	0.0	32.1	0.0	32.2	0.3	32.3	0.3
1959	32.4	0.3	32.4	0.0	32.5	0.3	32.5	0.0	32.6	0.3	32.7	0.3	32.9	0.6	33.0	0.3	33.0	0.0	33.0	0.0	33.1	0.3	33.1	0.0
1960	33.1	0.0	33.1	0.0	33.1	0.0	33.1	0.0	33.0	-0.3	33.0	0.0	33.0	0.0	33.0	0.0	33.0	0.0	33.0	0.0	33.0	0.0	33.0	0.0
1961	33.1	0.3	33.1	0.0	33.1	0.0	33.0	-0.3	33.0	0.0	33.0	0.0	33.0	0.0	32.9	-0.3	32.9	0.0	33.0	0.3	33.0	0.0	33.0	0.0
1962	33.0	0.0	33.0	0.0	33.1	0.3	33.1	0.0	33.1	0.0	33.0	-0.3	33.0	0.0	33.0	0.0	33.0	0.0	33.0	0.0	33.0	0.0	33.0	0.0
1963	33.0	0.0	33.0	0.0	32.9	-0.3	33.0	0.3	33.0	0.0	33.1	0.3	33.0	-0.3	33.0	0.0	33.1	0.3	33.1	0.0	33.2	0.3	33.3	0.3
1964	33.2	-0.3	33.3	0.3	33.3	0.0	33.4	0.3	33.4	0.0	33.3	-0.3	33.3	0.0	33.3	0.0	33.3	0.0	33.3	0.0	33.4	0.3	33.4	0.0
1965	33.5	0.3	33.5	0.0	33.5	0.0	33.6	0.3	33.6	0.0	33.7	0.3	33.6	-0.3	33.7	0.3	33.7	0.0	33.8	0.3	33.9	0.3	33.9	0.0
1966	34.0	0.3	34.2	0.6	34.3	0.3	34.4	0.3	34.6	0.6	34.7	0.3	34.8	0.3	34.8	0.0	34.9	0.3	35.1	0.6	35.4	0.9	35.5	0.3
1967	35.7	0.6	35.7	0.0	35.7	0.0	35.8	0.3	35.8	0.0	35.8	0.0	35.8	0.0	35.9	0.3	35.9	0.0	36.0	0.3	36.2	0.6	36.3	0.3
1968	36.6	0.8	36.7	0.3	36.7	0.0	36.9	0.5	37.0	0.3	37.0	0.0	37.1	0.3	37.1	0.0	37.2	0.3	37.3	0.3	37.4	0.3	37.5	0.3
1969	37.6	0.3	37.7	0.3	37.8	0.3	37.9	0.3	38.0	0.3	38.1	0.3	38.2	0.3	38.2	0.0	38.5	0.8	38.7	0.5	38.9	0.5	39.1	0.5
1970	39.4	0.8	39.4	0.0	39.5	0.3	39.6	0.3	39.7	0.3	39.8	0.3	40.0	0.5	40.0	0.0	40.2	0.5	40.4	0.5	40.6	0.5	40.8	0.5
1971	41.0	0.5	41.1	0.2	41.2	0.2	41.3	0.2	41.4	0.2	41.4	0.0	41.6	0.5	41.7	0.2	41.6	-0.2	41.6	0.0	41.6	0.0	41.7	0.2
1972	41.8	0.2	42.0	0.5	42.1	0.2	42.2	0.2	42.3	0.2	42.4	0.2	42.4	0.0	42.4	0.0	42.4	0.0	42.5	0.2	42.5	0.0	42.5	0.0
1973	42.6	0.2	42.8	0.5	43.0	0.5	43.3	0.7	43.6	0.7	43.7	0.2	43.8	0.2	43.9	0.2	44.0	0.2	44.2	0.5	44.4	0.5	44.7	0.7
1974	45.2	1.1	45.6	0.9	46.3	1.5	46.9	1.3	48.1	2.6	49.2	2.3	50.3	2.2	51.8	3.0	52.7	1.7	53.8	2.1	54.8	1.9	55.2	0.7
1975	56.2	1.8	56.6	0.7	57.0	0.7	57.3	0.5	57.5	0.3	57.7	0.3	58.0	0.5	58.2	0.3	58.5	0.5	58.9	0.7	59.3	0.7	59.5	0.3
1976	60.0	0.8	60.2	0.3	60.4	0.3	60.7	0.5	60.9	0.3	61.1	0.3	61.4	0.5	61.6	0.3	62.0	0.6	62.4	0.6	62.6	0.3	62.9	0.5
1977	63.4	0.8	63.7	0.5	63.9	0.3	64.2	0.5	64.6	0.6	64.8	0.3	65.2	0.6	65.6	0.6	65.9	0.5	66.6	1.1	67.0	0.6	67.3	0.4
1978	67.9	0.9	68.3	0.6	68.7	0.6	69.1	0.6	69.6	0.7	70.1	0.7	70.5	0.6	70.9	0.6	71.3	0.6	71.9	0.8	72.7	1.1	73.1	0.6
1979	73.6	0.7	74.1	0.7	74.6	0.7	75.2	0.8	75.8	0.8	76.2	0.5	77.0	1.0	77.5	0.6	78.1	0.8	78.9	1.0	79.4	0.6	80.1	0.9
1980	81.6	1.9	82.6	1.2	83.4	1.0	84.8	1.7	85.2	0.5	85.8	0.7	86.6	0.9	87.0	0.5	87.8	0.9	88.5	0.8	89.1	0.7	89.6	0.6
1981	90.9	1.5	91.6	0.8	92.4	0.9	93.1	0.8	93.5	0.4	94.0	0.5	95.0	1.1	95.5	0.5	96.2	0.7	96.6	0.4	97.0	0.4	97.6	0.6
1982	98.3	0.7	98.8	0.5	99.1	0.3	99.6	0.5	99.8	0.2	99.9	0.1	100.3	0.4	100.4	0.1	100.5	0.1	100.8	0.3	101.1	0.3	101.3	0.2
1983	101.6	0.3	102.0	0.4	102.1	0.1	102.4	0.3	102.6	0.2	102.7	0.1	103.1	0.4	103.1	0.0	103.3	0.2	103.2	-0.1	103.3	0.1	103.6	0.3

[Continued]

MACHINERY AND EQUIPMENT
Producer Price Index
Base 1982 = 100
[Continued]

For 1939-1997. Columns headed % show percentile change in the index from the previous period for which an index is available.

Year	Jan Index	%	Feb Index	%	Mar Index	%	Apr Index	%	May Index	%	Jun Index	%	Jul Index	%	Aug Index	%	Sep Index	%	Oct Index	%	Nov Index	%	Dec Index	%
1984	103.9	0.3	104.1	0.2	104.4	0.3	104.8	0.4	105.0	0.2	105.2	0.2	105.5	0.3	105.5	0.0	105.6	0.1	105.8	0.2	105.9	0.1	106.0	0.1
1985	106.5	0.5	106.8	0.3	106.8	0.0	106.9	0.1	107.1	0.2	107.2	0.1	107.3	0.1	107.5	0.2	107.6	0.1	107.6	0.0	107.7	0.1	107.8	0.1
1986	108.0	0.2	108.2	0.2	108.3	0.1	108.6	0.3	108.6	0.0	108.7	0.1	109.0	0.3	109.1	0.1	109.1	0.0	109.2	0.1	109.4	0.2	109.5	0.1
1987	109.8	0.3	109.9	0.1	110.0	0.1	110.0	0.0	110.2	0.2	110.1	-0.1	110.4	0.3	110.6	0.2	110.6	0.0	110.9	0.3	111.0	0.1	111.3	0.3
1988	111.9	0.5	112.2	0.3	112.3	0.1	112.5	0.2	112.9	0.4	112.9	0.0	113.2	0.3	113.6	0.4	113.9	0.3	114.2	0.3	114.5	0.3	114.8	0.3
1989	115.6	0.7	116.0	0.3	116.3	0.3	116.5	0.2	116.9	0.3	117.3	0.3	117.8	0.4	118.0	0.2	118.2	0.2	118.5	0.3	118.7	0.2	118.9	0.2
1990	119.6	0.6	119.7	0.1	120.0	0.3	120.2	0.2	120.4	0.2	120.5	0.1	120.8	0.2	120.9	0.1	121.2	0.2	121.4	0.2	121.7	0.2	122.0	0.2
1991	122.6	0.5	122.9	0.2	123.0	0.1	123.1	0.1	123.1	0.0	123.1	0.0	123.0	-0.1	123.0	0.0	123.0	0.0	123.0	0.0	123.1	0.1	123.2	0.1
1992	123.3	0.1	123.5	0.2	123.6	0.1	123.4	-0.2	123.4	0.0	123.2	-0.2	123.1	-0.1	123.2	0.1	123.2	0.0	123.3	0.1	123.4	0.1	123.5	0.1
1993	123.9	0.3	123.9	0.0	123.9	0.0	124.0	0.1	123.9	-0.1	124.0	0.1	124.0	0.0	124.0	0.0	124.1	0.1	124.2	0.1	124.2	0.0	124.2	0.0
1994	124.6	0.3	124.7	0.1	124.9	0.2	125.1	0.2	125.2	0.1	125.2	0.0	125.3	0.1	125.2	-0.1	125.2	0.0	125.2	0.0	125.3	0.1	125.4	0.1
1995	125.9	0.4	126.2	0.2	126.2	0.0	126.4	0.2	126.5	0.1	126.5	0.0	126.6	0.1	126.5	-0.1	126.7	0.2	127.0	0.2	127.2	0.2	127.0	-0.2
1996	127.3	0.2	127.3	0.0	127.0	-0.2	126.6	-0.3	126.4	-0.2	126.2	-0.2	126.3	0.1	126.4	0.1	126.3	-0.1	126.2	-0.1	126.2	0.0	126.2	0.0
1997	126.4	0.2	126.3	-0.1	126.3	0.0	126.2	-0.1	125.9	-0.2	125.9	0.0	126.0	0.1	125.7	-0.2	125.6	-0.1	125.6	0.0	125.6	0.0	125.4	-0.2

Source: U.S. Department of Labor, Bureau of Labor Statistics, Division of Industry Prices and Price Indexes. n.e.c. stands for not elsewhere classified. - indicates no data collected for period or unavailable.

Agricultural Machinery and Equipment
Producer Price Index
Base 1982 = 100

For 1926-1997. Columns headed % show percentile change in the index from the previous period for which an index is available.

Year	Jan Index	%	Feb Index	%	Mar Index	%	Apr Index	%	May Index	%	Jun Index	%	Jul Index	%	Aug Index	%	Sep Index	%	Oct Index	%	Nov Index	%	Dec Index	%
1926	14.1	-	14.1	0.0	14.1	0.0	14.1	0.0	14.1	0.0	14.1	0.0	14.1	0.0	14.1	0.0	14.1	0.0	14.1	0.0	14.1	0.0	14.1	0.0
1927	14.1	0.0	14.1	0.0	14.1	0.0	14.1	0.0	14.1	0.0	14.1	0.0	14.1	0.0	14.1	0.0	14.1	0.0	14.0	-0.7	14.0	0.0	14.0	0.0
1928	14.0	0.0	14.0	0.0	14.0	0.0	14.0	0.0	14.0	0.0	14.0	0.0	14.0	0.0	14.0	0.0	14.0	0.0	14.0	0.0	14.0	0.0	14.0	0.0
1929	14.0	0.0	14.0	0.0	14.0	0.0	14.0	0.0	14.0	0.0	14.0	0.0	14.0	0.0	14.0	0.0	14.0	0.0	13.8	-1.4	13.8	0.0	13.7	-0.7
1930	13.7	0.0	13.7	0.0	13.5	-1.5	13.3	-1.5	13.3	0.0	13.3	0.0	13.3	0.0	13.3	0.0	13.3	0.0	13.3	0.0	13.3	0.0	13.3	0.0
1931	13.3	0.0	13.3	0.0	13.3	0.0	13.3	0.0	13.3	0.0	13.3	0.0	13.3	0.0	13.3	0.0	13.3	0.0	12.1	-9.0	12.1	0.0	12.1	0.0
1932	12.1	0.0	12.0	-0.8	12.0	0.0	12.0	0.0	12.0	0.0	12.0	0.0	12.0	0.0	12.0	0.0	12.0	0.0	12.0	0.0	12.0	0.0	11.9	-0.8
1933	11.9	0.0	11.7	-1.7	11.7	0.0	11.7	0.0	11.7	0.0	11.7	0.0	11.7	0.0	11.7	0.0	11.7	0.0	11.8	0.9	11.8	0.0	12.0	1.7
1934	12.0	0.0	12.0	0.0	12.0	0.0	12.0	0.0	12.9	7.5	12.9	0.0	13.0	0.8	13.0	0.0	13.0	0.0	13.0	0.0	13.0	0.0	13.1	0.8
1935	13.1	0.0	13.2	0.8	13.2	0.0	13.2	0.0	13.2	0.0	13.2	0.0	13.2	0.0	13.2	0.0	13.2	0.0	13.2	0.0	13.3	0.8	13.3	0.0
1936	13.3	0.0	13.4	0.8	13.3	-0.7	13.3	0.0	13.3	0.0	13.3	0.0	13.3	0.0	13.3	0.0	13.3	0.0	13.3	0.0	13.1	-1.5	13.1	0.0
1937	13.1	0.0	13.1	0.0	13.1	0.0	13.0	-0.8	13.2	1.5	13.3	0.8	13.3	0.0	13.3	0.0	13.3	0.0	13.3	0.0	13.6	2.3	13.6	0.0
1938	13.6	0.0	13.6	0.0	13.6	0.0	13.6	0.0	13.6	0.0	13.6	0.0	13.6	0.0	13.5	-0.7	13.5	0.0	13.5	0.0	13.2	-2.2	13.2	0.0
1939	13.2	0.0	13.1	-0.8	13.1	0.0	13.2	0.8	13.2	0.0	13.2	0.0	13.2	0.0	13.2	0.0	13.2	0.0	13.2	0.0	13.2	0.0	13.2	0.0
1940	13.2	0.0	13.2	0.0	13.2	0.0	13.2	0.0	13.1	-0.8	13.1	0.0	13.0	-0.8	13.0	0.0	13.1	0.8	13.1	0.0	13.1	0.0	13.1	0.0
1941	13.1	0.0	13.1	0.0	13.1	0.0	13.0	-0.8	13.1	0.8	13.1	0.0	13.1	0.0	13.1	0.0	13.2	0.8	13.2	0.0	13.6	3.0	13.6	0.0
1942	13.6	0.0	13.7	0.7	13.7	0.0	13.7	0.0	13.7	0.0	13.7	0.0	13.7	0.0	13.7	0.0	13.7	0.0	13.7	0.0	13.7	0.0	13.7	0.0
1943	13.7	0.0	13.7	0.0	13.7	0.0	13.7	0.0	13.7	0.0	13.7	0.0	13.7	0.0	13.7	0.0	13.7	0.0	13.7	0.0	13.7	0.0	13.7	0.0
1944	13.7	0.0	13.7	0.0	13.7	0.0	13.7	0.0	13.7	0.0	13.7	0.0	13.7	0.0	13.8	0.7	13.8	0.0	13.8	0.0	13.8	0.0	13.8	0.0
1945	13.8	0.0	13.8	0.0	13.8	0.0	13.8	0.0	13.8	0.0	13.8	0.0	13.8	0.0	13.8	0.0	13.8	0.0	13.8	0.0	13.9	0.7	13.9	0.0
1946	13.8	-0.7	13.8	0.0	13.8	0.0	13.9	0.7	14.4	3.6	14.8	2.8	14.8	0.0	15.2	2.7	15.3	0.7	15.3	0.0	15.8	3.3	16.7	5.7
1947	16.8	0.6	16.8	0.0	16.8	0.0	16.8	0.0	16.9	0.6	16.9	0.0	16.9	0.0	17.0	0.6	17.1	0.6	17.3	1.2	17.7	2.3	18.1	2.3
1948	18.2	0.6	18.3	0.5	18.4	0.5	18.5	0.5	18.6	0.5	18.8	1.1	19.1	1.6	19.3	1.0	20.0	3.6	20.3	1.5	20.5	1.0	20.5	0.0
1949	20.5	0.0	20.5	0.0	20.5	0.0	20.5	0.0	20.5	0.0	20.5	0.0	20.5	0.0	20.5	0.0	20.5	0.0	20.5	0.0	20.4	-0.5	20.4	0.0
1950	20.4	0.0	20.4	0.0	20.4	0.0	20.5	0.5	20.5	0.0	20.5	0.0	20.5	0.0	20.8	1.5	21.4	2.9	21.7	1.4	21.9	0.9	22.4	2.3
1951	22.4	0.0	22.8	1.8	22.8	0.0	22.8	0.0	22.8	0.0	22.8	0.0	22.8	0.0	22.8	0.0	22.8	0.0	22.8	0.0	22.8	0.0	22.8	0.0
1952	23.0	0.9	23.0	0.0	23.0	0.0	23.0	0.0	23.0	0.0	23.0	0.0	23.0	0.0	23.0	0.0	23.0	0.0	23.0	0.0	23.0	0.0	23.0	0.0
1953	23.0	0.0	23.0	0.0	23.1	0.4	23.2	0.4	23.2	0.0	23.2	0.0	23.2	0.0	23.2	0.0	23.2	0.0	23.2	0.0	23.2	0.0	23.2	0.0
1954	23.2	0.0	23.3	0.4	23.2	-0.4	23.2	0.0	23.2	0.0	23.2	0.0	23.2	0.0	23.1	-0.4	23.1	0.0	23.1	0.0	23.0	-0.4	23.0	0.0
1955	23.0	0.0	23.0	0.0	23.0	0.0	23.0	0.0	23.0	0.0	23.0	0.0	23.0	0.0	23.2	0.9	23.9	3.0	24.0	0.4	23.9	-0.4	23.9	0.0
1956	24.0	0.4	24.0	0.0	23.9	-0.4	23.9	0.0	23.9	0.0	24.0	0.4	24.0	0.0	24.0	0.0	24.1	0.4	24.5	1.7	24.8	1.2	24.8	0.0
1957	24.9	0.4	25.0	0.4	25.0	0.0	25.0	0.0	25.0	0.0	25.0	0.0	25.0	0.0	25.1	0.4	25.3	0.8	25.8	2.0	26.0	0.8	26.2	0.8
1958	26.2	0.0	26.2	0.0	26.2	0.0	26.2	0.0	26.2	0.0	26.2	0.0	26.2	0.0	26.1	-0.4	26.3	0.8	26.4	0.4	26.9	1.9	27.1	0.7
1959	27.1	0.0	27.1	0.0	27.1	0.0	27.1	0.0	27.2	0.4	27.2	0.0	27.2	0.0	27.2	0.0	27.2	0.0	27.2	0.0	27.3	0.4	27.3	0.0
1960	27.3	0.0	27.5	0.7	27.5	0.0	27.6	0.4	27.6	0.0	27.6	0.0	27.6	0.0	27.7	0.4	27.7	0.0	27.8	0.4	28.1	1.1	28.0	-0.4
1961	28.1	0.4	28.1	0.0	28.1	0.0	28.2	0.4	28.2	0.0	28.2	0.0	28.2	0.0	28.2	0.0	28.2	0.0	28.2	0.0	28.3	0.4	28.5	0.7
1962	28.6	0.4	28.7	0.3	28.7	0.0	28.7	0.0	28.7	0.0	28.8	0.3	28.8	0.0	28.7	-0.3	28.7	0.0	28.8	0.3	28.8	0.0	28.9	0.3
1963	29.1	0.7	29.1	0.0	29.2	0.3	29.1	-0.3	29.1	0.0	29.2	0.3	29.1	-0.3	29.1	0.0	29.1	0.0	29.2	0.3	29.3	0.3	29.4	0.3
1964	29.4	0.0	29.5	0.3	29.6	0.3	29.6	0.0	29.6	0.0	29.6	0.0	29.6	0.0	29.7	0.3	29.7	0.0	29.6	-0.3	29.9	1.0	30.0	0.3
1965	30.0	0.0	30.1	0.3	30.1	0.0	30.1	0.0	30.1	0.0	30.1	0.0	30.2	0.3	30.2	0.0	30.2	0.0	30.2	0.0	30.7	1.7	30.7	0.0
1966	30.8	0.3	30.9	0.3	31.0	0.3	31.0	0.0	31.1	0.3	31.1	0.0	31.1	0.0	31.1	0.0	31.1	0.0	31.1	0.0	31.6	1.6	31.7	0.3
1967	31.9	0.6	32.0	0.3	32.0	0.0	32.0	0.0	32.0	0.0	32.0	0.0	32.1	0.3	32.1	0.0	32.1	0.0	32.1	0.0	32.7	1.9	32.9	0.6
1968	33.0	0.3	33.1	0.3	33.1	0.0	33.1	0.0	33.1	0.0	33.2	0.3	33.3	0.3	33.4	0.3	33.5	0.3	33.7	0.6	34.0	0.9	34.2	0.6
1969	34.5	0.9	34.6	0.3	34.6	0.0	34.6	0.0	34.6	0.0	34.7	0.3	34.8	0.3	34.8	0.0	34.9	0.3	35.1	0.6	35.6	1.4	35.8	0.6
1970	35.9	0.3	36.1	0.6	36.1	0.0	36.1	0.0	36.2	0.3	36.1	-0.3	36.2	0.3	36.2	0.0	36.4	0.6	36.6	0.5	37.4	2.2	37.5	0.3

[Continued]

Agricultural Machinery and Equipment
Producer Price Index
Base 1982 = 100
[Continued]

For 1926-1997. Columns headed % show percentile change in the index from the previous period for which an index is available.

Year	Jan Index	%	Feb Index	%	Mar Index	%	Apr Index	%	May Index	%	Jun Index	%	Jul Index	%	Aug Index	%	Sep Index	%	Oct Index	%	Nov Index	%	Dec Index	%
1971	37.5	0.0	37.5	0.0	37.5	0.0	37.6	0.3	37.6	0.0	37.7	0.3	37.8	0.3	37.9	0.3	37.9	0.0	37.9	0.0	37.9	0.0	38.2	0.8
1972	38.5	0.8	39.1	1.6	39.2	0.3	39.3	0.3	39.3	0.0	39.4	0.3	39.4	0.0	39.5	0.3	39.4	-0.3	39.4	0.0	39.5	0.3	39.5	0.0
1973	39.7	0.5	40.0	0.8	40.1	0.2	40.1	0.0	40.2	0.2	40.3	0.2	40.3	0.0	40.4	0.2	40.4	0.0	41.0	1.5	41.4	1.0	41.6	0.5
1974	42.1	1.2	42.2	0.2	42.6	0.9	42.9	0.7	44.3	3.3	45.3	2.3	46.3	2.2	47.6	2.8	48.9	2.7	49.8	1.8	51.3	3.0	51.5	0.4
1975	52.6	2.1	52.8	0.4	53.4	1.1	53.6	0.4	53.8	0.4	53.9	0.2	54.2	0.6	54.3	0.2	54.4	0.2	55.1	1.3	56.0	1.6	56.3	0.5
1976	56.9	1.1	57.2	0.5	57.6	0.7	57.8	0.3	58.2	0.7	58.5	0.5	58.8	0.5	59.1	0.5	59.7	1.0	59.9	0.3	60.7	1.3	61.3	1.0
1977	61.8	0.8	62.2	0.6	62.5	0.5	62.6	0.2	62.8	0.3	63.0	0.3	63.2	0.3	63.8	0.9	64.4	0.9	64.7	0.5	66.0	2.0	66.3	0.5
1978	66.4	0.2	66.8	0.6	66.9	0.1	67.2	0.4	67.4	0.3	67.8	0.6	68.2	0.6	68.8	0.9	70.0	1.7	70.3	0.4	70.9	0.9	71.3	0.6
1979	71.6	0.4	72.0	0.6	72.3	0.4	72.8	0.7	73.4	0.8	73.7	0.4	74.3	0.8	75.0	0.9	76.3	1.7	77.1	1.0	78.2	1.4	78.5	0.4
1980	79.8	1.7	80.3	0.6	81.0	0.9	81.8	1.0	82.4	0.7	82.7	0.4	83.1	0.5	83.5	0.5	84.8	1.6	85.3	0.6	87.3	2.3	87.7	0.5
1981	88.8	1.3	89.5	0.8	90.0	0.6	90.8	0.9	91.8	1.1	92.2	0.4	92.6	0.4	93.3	0.8	94.1	0.9	95.0	1.0	96.7	1.8	97.3	0.6
1982	97.4	0.1	97.9	0.5	98.5	0.6	98.6	0.1	99.1	0.5	99.6	0.5	100.0	0.4	100.4	0.4	101.0	0.6	102.1	1.1	102.5	0.4	103.1	0.6
1983	103.6	0.5	103.9	0.3	104.0	0.1	104.1	0.1	104.9	0.8	104.9	0.0	105.1	0.2	105.2	0.1	105.6	0.4	105.4	-0.2	105.6	0.2	106.1	0.5
1984	106.4	0.3	106.5	0.1	107.0	0.5	107.9	0.8	108.7	0.7	108.6	-0.1	108.9	0.3	108.9	0.0	108.4	-0.5	108.4	0.0	108.3	-0.1	108.5	0.2
1985	108.8	0.3	108.7	-0.1	108.8	0.1	108.7	-0.1	108.8	0.1	108.9	0.1	108.9	0.0	108.7	-0.2	108.4	-0.3	108.5	0.1	108.6	0.1	108.7	0.1
1986	108.8	0.1	108.8	0.0	109.0	0.2	109.1	0.1	109.1	0.0	109.2	0.1	109.3	0.1	109.4	0.1	109.3	-0.1	109.6	0.3	109.7	0.1	109.6	-0.1
1987	108.9	-0.6	109.0	0.1	109.1	0.1	109.6	0.5	109.9	0.3	109.9	0.0	110.0	0.1	109.8	-0.2	109.7	-0.1	109.8	0.1	109.9	0.1	109.9	0.0
1988	111.4	1.4	111.5	0.1	112.2	0.6	112.3	0.1	112.5	0.2	111.8	-0.6	112.4	0.5	113.2	0.7	113.3	0.1	113.3	0.0	114.0	0.6	114.2	0.2
1989	114.2	0.0	116.5	2.0	116.5	0.0	116.9	0.3	117.7	0.7	117.6	-0.1	117.9	0.3	118.3	0.3	118.7	0.3	118.5	-0.2	119.5	0.8	120.1	0.5
1990	120.4	0.2	120.5	0.1	120.7	0.2	121.2	0.4	121.3	0.1	121.4	0.1	121.5	0.1	122.3	0.7	122.6	0.2	122.3	-0.2	122.8	0.4	123.4	0.5
1991	123.7	0.2	124.4	0.6	124.7	0.2	124.9	0.2	125.1	0.2	125.4	0.2	125.6	0.2	126.2	0.5	126.5	0.2	126.6	0.1	127.7	0.9	127.7	0.0
1992	127.9	0.2	128.3	0.3	128.5	0.2	128.7	0.2	128.7	0.0	128.8	0.1	128.9	0.1	129.1	0.2	131.3	1.7	131.4	0.1	131.4	0.0	131.5	0.1
1993	131.7	0.2	132.1	0.3	132.3	0.2	133.1	0.6	133.5	0.3	133.6	0.1	133.6	0.0	133.7	0.1	134.5	0.6	134.7	0.1	134.9	0.1	135.3	0.3
1994	135.8	0.4	136.0	0.1	136.1	0.1	136.4	0.2	136.5	0.1	136.6	0.1	136.7	0.1	136.8	0.1	137.5	0.5	138.2	0.5	138.4	0.1	139.0	0.4
1995	140.3	0.9	140.4	0.1	140.7	0.2	141.1	0.3	143.0	1.3	143.2	0.1	143.3	0.1	143.5	0.1	144.0	0.3	144.6	0.4	145.5	0.6	145.6	0.1
1996	146.0	0.3	146.7	0.5	147.0	0.2	147.4	0.3	146.1	-0.9	146.1	0.0	146.3	0.1	146.7	0.3	147.0	0.2	147.4	0.3	147.7	0.2	147.7	0.0
1997	148.2	0.3	148.5	0.2	148.9	0.3	149.1	0.1	148.8	-0.2	148.5	-0.2	148.9	0.3	149.1	0.1	149.2	0.1	148.3	-0.6	148.4	0.1	148.3	-0.1

Source: U.S. Department of Labor, Bureau of Labor Statistics, Division of Industry Prices and Price Indexes. n.e.c. stands for not elsewhere classified. - indicates no data collected for period or unavailable.

Construction Machinery and Equipment
Producer Price Index
Base 1982 = 100

For 1939-1997. Columns headed % show percentile change in the index from the previous period for which an index is available.

Year	Jan Index	%	Feb Index	%	Mar Index	%	Apr Index	%	May Index	%	Jun Index	%	Jul Index	%	Aug Index	%	Sep Index	%	Oct Index	%	Nov Index	%	Dec Index	%
1939	-	-	-	-	-	-	-	-	-	-	-	-	-	-	9.3	-	9.3	0.0	9.3	0.0	9.4	1.1	9.4	0.0
1940	9.4	0.0	9.4	0.0	9.4	0.0	9.4	0.0	9.4	0.0	9.4	0.0	9.5	1.1	9.5	0.0	9.5	0.0	9.5	0.0	9.5	0.0	9.5	0.0
1941	9.6	1.1	9.7	1.0	9.7	0.0	9.8	1.0	9.8	0.0	9.9	1.0	9.9	0.0	10.1	2.0	10.2	1.0	10.3	1.0	10.3	0.0	10.3	0.0
1942	10.3	0.0	10.3	0.0	10.3	0.0	10.3	0.0	10.3	0.0	10.3	0.0	10.3	0.0	10.3	0.0	10.3	0.0	10.3	0.0	10.3	0.0	10.3	0.0
1943	10.3	0.0	10.3	0.0	10.3	0.0	10.3	0.0	10.3	0.0	10.3	0.0	10.3	0.0	10.3	0.0	10.3	0.0	10.3	0.0	10.3	0.0	10.3	0.0
1944	10.3	0.0	10.3	0.0	10.3	0.0	10.3	0.0	10.3	0.0	10.3	0.0	10.3	0.0	10.3	0.0	10.3	0.0	10.3	0.0	10.3	0.0	10.4	1.0
1945	10.4	0.0	10.4	0.0	10.4	0.0	10.4	0.0	10.4	0.0	10.4	0.0	10.4	0.0	10.4	0.0	10.4	0.0	10.4	0.0	10.5	1.0	10.6	1.0
1946	10.6	0.0	10.7	0.9	10.7	0.0	11.0	2.8	11.2	1.8	11.4	1.8	11.4	0.0	11.4	0.0	11.5	0.9	11.7	1.7	11.7	0.0	12.0	2.6
1947	12.3	2.5	12.4	0.8	12.4	0.0	12.4	0.0	12.6	1.6	12.7	0.8	12.9	1.6	12.9	0.0	13.0	0.8	13.1	0.8	13.3	1.5	13.5	1.5
1948	13.6	0.7	13.7	0.7	13.8	0.7	13.9	0.7	13.9	0.0	14.2	2.2	14.4	1.4	14.8	2.8	15.2	2.7	15.4	1.3	15.4	0.0	15.5	0.6
1949	15.5	0.0	15.5	0.0	15.4	-0.6	15.4	0.0	15.4	0.0	15.4	0.0	15.4	0.0	15.4	0.0	15.4	0.0	15.4	0.0	15.4	0.0	15.4	0.0
1950	15.4	0.0	15.4	0.0	15.4	0.0	15.4	0.0	15.4	0.0	15.4	0.0	15.5	0.6	16.0	3.2	16.3	1.9	16.5	1.2	16.5	0.0	17.3	4.8
1951	17.5	1.2	17.6	0.6	17.6	0.0	17.6	0.0	17.6	0.0	17.6	0.0	17.6	0.0	17.6	0.0	17.6	0.0	17.6	0.0	17.6	0.0	17.6	0.0
1952	17.7	0.6	17.8	0.6	17.8	0.0	17.8	0.0	17.8	0.0	17.9	0.6	17.9	0.0	17.8	-0.6	17.9	0.6	17.9	0.0	18.0	0.6	18.0	0.0
1953	18.0	0.0	18.0	0.0	18.1	0.6	18.3	1.1	18.3	0.0	18.4	0.5	18.6	1.1	18.6	0.0	18.6	0.0	18.6	0.0	18.6	0.0	18.6	0.0
1954	18.7	0.5	18.7	0.0	18.7	0.0	18.7	0.0	18.7	0.0	18.7	0.0	18.7	0.0	18.7	0.0	18.7	0.0	18.7	0.0	18.7	0.0	18.9	1.1
1955	19.0	0.5	19.0	0.0	19.0	0.0	19.1	0.5	19.1	0.0	19.2	0.5	19.2	0.0	19.7	2.6	20.0	1.5	20.2	1.0	20.2	0.0	20.3	0.5
1956	20.4	0.5	20.4	0.0	20.4	0.0	20.6	1.0	20.8	1.0	20.8	0.0	21.0	1.0	21.3	1.4	21.5	0.9	22.0	2.3	22.1	0.5	22.2	0.5
1957	22.2	0.0	22.2	0.0	22.2	0.0	22.4	0.9	22.4	0.0	22.4	0.0	22.4	0.0	22.9	2.2	23.1	0.9	23.4	1.3	23.5	0.4	23.5	0.0
1958	23.5	0.0	23.5	0.0	23.5	0.0	23.5	0.0	23.5	0.0	23.5	0.0	23.5	0.0	23.5	0.0	23.6	0.4	23.7	0.4	23.9	0.8	24.2	1.3
1959	24.3	0.4	24.4	0.4	24.4	0.0	24.4	0.0	24.4	0.0	24.4	0.0	24.4	0.0	24.5	0.4	24.5	0.0	24.5	0.0	24.6	0.4	24.6	0.0
1960	24.7	0.4	24.7	0.0	24.8	0.4	24.9	0.4	24.9	0.0	24.9	0.0	25.0	0.4	25.1	0.4	25.1	0.0	25.1	0.0	25.2	0.4	25.2	0.0
1961	25.3	0.4	25.4	0.4	25.4	0.0	25.4	0.0	25.4	0.0	25.4	0.0	25.4	0.0	25.4	0.0	25.4	0.0	25.4	0.0	25.4	0.0	25.4	0.0
1962	25.4	0.0	25.4	0.0	25.4	0.0	25.4	0.0	25.4	0.0	25.4	0.0	25.4	0.0	25.4	0.0	25.4	0.0	25.5	0.4	25.5	0.0	25.6	0.4
1963	25.6	0.0	25.6	0.0	25.7	0.4	25.7	0.0	25.8	0.4	25.9	0.4	25.9	0.0	26.0	0.4	26.0	0.0	26.1	0.4	26.2	0.4	26.3	0.4
1964	26.4	0.4	26.4	0.0	26.4	0.0	26.5	0.4	26.5	0.0	26.5	0.0	26.5	0.0	26.5	0.0	26.5	0.0	26.5	0.0	26.8	1.1	26.8	0.0
1965	26.9	0.4	27.0	0.4	27.0	0.0	27.1	0.4	27.2	0.4	27.2	0.0	27.2	0.0	27.3	0.4	27.3	0.0	27.3	0.0	27.5	0.7	27.5	0.0
1966	27.6	0.4	27.7	0.4	27.8	0.4	28.0	0.7	28.1	0.4	28.1	0.0	28.1	0.0	28.1	0.0	28.2	0.4	28.3	0.4	28.5	0.7	28.6	0.4
1967	28.6	0.0	28.7	0.3	28.8	0.3	28.8	0.0	28.9	0.3	28.9	0.0	29.0	0.3	29.0	0.0	29.0	0.0	29.4	1.4	29.7	1.0	29.9	0.7
1968	30.2	1.0	30.3	0.3	30.4	0.3	30.5	0.3	30.6	0.3	30.6	0.0	30.6	0.0	30.6	0.0	30.9	1.0	31.1	0.6	31.4	1.0	31.4	0.0
1969	31.6	0.6	31.7	0.3	31.8	0.3	31.8	0.0	31.8	0.0	31.9	0.3	32.0	0.3	32.0	0.0	32.3	0.9	32.7	1.2	32.9	0.6	33.1	0.6
1970	33.1	0.0	33.2	0.3	33.2	0.0	33.2	0.0	33.4	0.6	33.4	0.0	33.4	0.0	33.6	0.6	33.7	0.3	34.4	2.1	34.7	0.9	35.0	0.9
1971	35.1	0.3	35.2	0.3	35.2	0.0	35.3	0.3	35.3	0.0	35.3	0.0	35.5	0.6	35.5	0.0	35.5	0.0	35.5	0.0	35.5	0.0	35.9	1.1
1972	36.1	0.6	36.3	0.6	36.3	0.0	36.5	0.6	36.5	0.0	36.6	0.3	36.6	0.0	36.7	0.3	36.7	0.0	36.7	0.0	36.7	0.0	36.7	0.0
1973	36.8	0.3	37.0	0.5	37.4	1.1	37.9	1.3	38.1	0.5	38.2	0.3	38.2	0.0	38.2	0.0	38.2	0.0	38.5	0.8	38.6	0.3	39.0	1.0
1974	39.4	1.0	39.8	1.0	40.3	1.3	40.7	1.0	42.2	3.7	43.3	2.6	44.0	1.6	46.9	6.6	47.5	1.3	48.6	2.3	49.1	1.0	49.4	0.6
1975	51.6	4.5	52.4	1.6	52.9	1.0	53.5	1.1	53.5	0.0	53.6	0.2	53.8	0.4	53.9	0.2	54.5	1.1	54.8	0.6	55.6	1.5	56.0	0.7
1976	56.2	0.4	56.6	0.7	56.7	0.2	56.8	0.2	57.1	0.5	57.5	0.7	58.1	1.0	58.3	0.3	58.4	0.2	58.9	0.9	59.5	1.0	59.9	0.7
1977	60.2	0.5	60.5	0.5	60.6	0.2	61.1	0.8	61.6	0.8	61.7	0.2	62.2	0.8	62.6	0.6	62.4	-0.3	63.2	1.3	64.2	1.6	64.9	1.1
1978	65.0	0.2	65.4	0.6	65.6	0.3	66.4	1.2	67.0	0.9	67.2	0.3	67.7	0.7	68.2	0.7	68.9	1.0	69.9	1.5	70.5	0.9	70.9	0.6
1979	71.4	0.7	72.1	1.0	72.3	0.3	73.2	1.2	73.8	0.8	73.9	0.1	74.7	1.1	75.2	0.7	75.3	0.1	76.7	1.9	77.2	0.7	78.2	1.3
1980	80.3	2.7	80.9	0.7	81.3	0.5	82.6	1.6	83.1	0.6	83.6	0.6	84.8	1.4	85.3	0.6	86.0	0.8	87.0	1.2	87.3	0.3	87.6	0.3
1981	88.9	1.5	90.1	1.3	90.9	0.9	92.2	1.4	92.6	0.4	93.1	0.5	94.2	1.2	94.5	0.3	94.9	0.4	95.5	0.6	95.9	0.4	96.5	0.6
1982	98.0	1.6	98.3	0.3	98.6	0.3	99.3	0.7	99.9	0.6	100.0	0.1	100.6	0.6	100.8	0.2	101.1	0.3	101.1	0.0	101.2	0.1	101.2	0.0
1983	101.3	0.1	101.6	0.3	101.7	0.1	102.0	0.3	102.4	0.4	102.5	0.1	102.6	0.1	102.6	0.0	102.8	0.2	102.8	0.0	102.9	0.1	102.8	-0.1

[Continued]

Construction Machinery and Equipment
Producer Price Index
Base 1982 = 100
[Continued]

For 1939-1997. Columns headed % show percentile change in the index from the previous period for which an index is available.

Year	Jan Index	%	Feb Index	%	Mar Index	%	Apr Index	%	May Index	%	Jun Index	%	Jul Index	%	Aug Index	%	Sep Index	%	Oct Index	%	Nov Index	%	Dec Index	%
1984	103.0	0.2	103.5	0.5	103.3	-0.2	104.0	0.7	104.0	0.0	104.1	0.1	104.2	0.1	103.8	-0.4	103.9	0.1	104.0	0.1	104.0	0.0	104.0	0.0
1985	105.3	1.3	105.6	0.3	105.4	-0.2	105.2	-0.2	105.2	0.0	105.3	0.1	105.3	0.0	105.4	0.1	105.5	0.1	105.6	0.1	105.7	0.1	105.7	0.0
1986	106.2	0.5	106.3	0.1	106.3	0.0	106.4	0.1	106.5	0.1	106.7	0.2	106.7	0.0	106.7	0.0	106.7	0.0	106.7	0.0	107.5	0.7	107.5	0.0
1987	107.7	0.2	107.9	0.2	108.4	0.5	108.5	0.1	109.2	0.6	109.2	0.0	109.1	-0.1	109.2	0.1	109.3	0.1	109.4	0.1	109.5	0.1	109.7	0.2
1988	110.6	0.8	111.0	0.4	111.0	0.0	111.1	0.1	111.1	0.0	111.2	0.1	111.9	0.6	112.3	0.4	112.3	0.0	112.3	0.0	113.0	0.6	113.2	0.2
1989	115.1	1.7	115.3	0.2	115.8	0.4	116.1	0.3	116.3	0.2	117.6	1.1	117.9	0.3	118.2	0.3	118.3	0.1	118.2	-0.1	118.5	0.3	118.6	0.1
1990	119.7	0.9	120.5	0.7	120.5	0.0	120.5	0.0	120.8	0.2	121.3	0.4	122.4	0.9	122.7	0.2	122.5	-0.2	122.6	0.1	122.8	0.2	123.1	0.2
1991	123.7	0.5	124.2	0.4	124.4	0.2	124.5	0.1	124.6	0.1	124.7	0.1	125.7	0.8	125.8	0.1	125.8	0.0	125.8	0.0	126.3	0.4	126.6	0.2
1992	126.8	0.2	127.3	0.4	127.4	0.1	127.7	0.2	127.7	0.0	128.2	0.4	129.4	0.9	129.6	0.2	129.7	0.1	129.8	0.1	130.2	0.3	130.5	0.2
1993	131.6	0.8	132.3	0.5	132.3	0.0	132.0	-0.2	132.1	0.1	132.2	0.1	132.2	0.0	132.3	0.1	131.4	-0.7	131.7	0.2	131.9	0.2	132.0	0.1
1994	133.4	1.1	133.4	0.0	133.3	-0.1	133.4	0.1	133.5	0.1	133.3	-0.1	133.6	0.2	133.6	0.0	133.8	0.1	134.1	0.2	134.3	0.1	134.6	0.2
1995	135.6	0.7	136.0	0.3	136.1	0.1	136.2	0.1	136.6	0.3	136.6	0.0	136.7	0.1	136.7	0.0	137.1	0.3	137.3	0.1	137.3	0.0	137.9	0.4
1996	138.8	0.7	139.4	0.4	139.4	0.0	139.5	0.1	139.7	0.1	139.9	0.1	140.0	0.1	140.1	0.1	140.1	0.0	140.3	0.1	140.5	0.1	140.4	-0.1
1997	142.0	1.1	142.0	0.0	141.9	-0.1	142.0	0.1	142.0	0.0	142.0	0.0	142.0	0.0	142.1	0.1	142.2	0.1	142.9	0.5	142.8	-0.1	142.8	0.0

Source: U.S. Department of Labor, Bureau of Labor Statistics, Division of Industry Prices and Price Indexes. n.e.c. stands for not elsewhere classified. - indicates no data collected for period or unavailable.

Metalworking Machinery and Equipment
Producer Price Index
Base 1982 = 100

For 1947-1997. Columns headed % show percentile change in the index from the previous period for which an index is available.

Year	Jan Index	%	Feb Index	%	Mar Index	%	Apr Index	%	May Index	%	Jun Index	%	Jul Index	%	Aug Index	%	Sep Index	%	Oct Index	%	Nov Index	%	Dec Index	%
1947	13.9	-	13.9	0.0	13.9	0.0	14.0	0.7	14.2	1.4	14.3	0.7	14.3	0.0	14.5	1.4	14.5	0.0	14.7	1.4	14.8	0.7	14.8	0.0
1948	15.0	1.4	15.0	0.0	15.0	0.0	15.1	0.7	15.1	0.0	15.1	0.0	15.2	0.7	15.6	2.6	15.9	1.9	16.0	0.6	16.0	0.0	16.1	0.6
1949	16.2	0.6	16.2	0.0	16.2	0.0	16.2	0.0	16.2	0.0	16.2	0.0	16.2	0.0	16.1	-0.6	16.1	0.0	16.1	0.0	16.1	0.0	16.1	0.0
1950	16.3	1.2	16.3	0.0	16.3	0.0	16.6	1.8	16.7	0.6	16.7	0.0	16.9	1.2	17.4	3.0	17.7	1.7	17.9	1.1	18.2	1.7	18.8	3.3
1951	19.1	1.6	19.1	0.0	19.1	0.0	19.1	0.0	19.1	0.0	19.0	-0.5	19.0	0.0	19.0	0.0	19.2	1.1	19.4	1.0	19.5	0.5	19.6	0.5
1952	19.5	-0.5	19.5	0.0	19.5	0.0	19.5	0.0	19.5	0.0	19.5	0.0	19.5	0.0	19.5	0.0	19.5	0.0	19.5	0.0	19.5	0.0	19.5	0.0
1953	19.5	0.0	19.5	0.0	19.5	0.0	19.6	0.5	19.7	0.5	19.8	0.5	19.9	0.5	19.9	0.0	20.0	0.5	20.0	0.0	20.0	0.0	20.0	0.0
1954	20.0	0.0	20.1	0.5	20.1	0.0	20.0	-0.5	20.0	0.0	20.0	0.0	20.0	0.0	20.1	0.5	20.1	0.0	20.2	0.5	20.2	0.0	20.2	0.0
1955	20.3	0.5	20.4	0.5	20.4	0.0	20.5	0.5	20.8	1.5	21.2	1.9	21.5	1.4	21.6	0.5	21.7	0.5	21.8	0.5	21.9	0.5	22.0	0.5
1956	22.2	0.9	22.3	0.5	22.6	1.3	22.8	0.9	22.9	0.4	23.0	0.4	23.0	0.0	23.2	0.9	23.7	2.2	24.0	1.3	24.0	0.0	24.1	0.4
1957	24.1	0.0	24.2	0.4	24.3	0.4	24.3	0.0	24.3	0.0	24.3	0.0	24.5	0.8	24.6	0.4	24.8	0.8	25.1	1.2	25.2	0.4	25.2	0.0
1958	25.2	0.0	25.2	0.0	25.2	0.0	25.2	0.0	25.1	-0.4	25.1	0.0	25.1	0.0	25.1	0.0	25.1	0.0	25.2	0.4	25.2	0.0	25.2	0.0
1959	25.3	0.4	25.4	0.4	25.6	0.8	25.6	0.0	25.6	0.0	25.6	0.0	25.7	0.4	25.7	0.0	26.0	1.2	26.1	0.4	26.1	0.0	26.1	0.0
1960	26.1	0.0	26.2	0.4	26.3	0.4	26.3	0.0	26.4	0.4	26.5	0.4	26.5	0.0	26.5	0.0	26.6	0.4	26.7	0.4	26.8	0.4	26.8	0.0
1961	26.8	0.0	26.8	0.0	26.8	0.0	26.6	-0.7	26.6	0.0	26.6	0.0	26.6	0.0	26.6	0.0	26.7	0.4	26.8	0.4	26.9	0.4	27.0	0.4
1962	27.1	0.4	27.1	0.0	27.2	0.4	27.2	0.0	27.2	0.0	27.3	0.4	27.3	0.0	27.3	0.0	27.3	0.0	27.3	0.0	27.3	0.0	27.2	-0.4
1963	27.2	0.0	27.2	0.0	27.2	0.0	27.2	0.0	27.2	0.0	27.3	0.4	27.3	0.0	27.4	0.4	27.4	0.0	27.4	0.0	27.4	0.0	27.5	0.4
1964	27.5	0.0	27.5	0.0	27.5	0.0	27.6	0.4	27.7	0.4	27.8	0.4	28.0	0.7	28.0	0.0	28.0	0.0	28.1	0.4	28.1	0.0	28.1	0.0
1965	28.3	0.7	28.4	0.4	28.4	0.0	28.4	0.0	28.5	0.4	28.5	0.0	28.5	0.0	28.7	0.7	28.8	0.3	28.9	0.3	28.9	0.0	29.0	0.3
1966	29.1	0.3	29.3	0.7	29.4	0.3	29.4	0.0	29.7	1.0	29.9	0.7	29.9	0.0	30.1	0.7	30.3	0.7	30.5	0.7	30.6	0.3	30.7	0.3
1967	30.7	0.0	30.8	0.3	30.9	0.3	30.9	0.0	31.1	0.6	31.1	0.0	31.2	0.3	31.3	0.3	31.3	0.0	31.4	0.3	31.6	0.6	31.7	0.3
1968	31.8	0.3	31.9	0.3	32.0	0.3	32.2	0.6	32.3	0.3	32.3	0.0	32.5	0.6	32.6	0.3	32.7	0.3	32.7	0.0	32.8	0.3	32.9	0.3
1969	33.0	0.3	33.1	0.3	33.1	0.0	33.2	0.3	33.3	0.3	33.3	0.0	33.6	0.9	33.7	0.3	33.9	0.6	34.1	0.6	34.5	1.2	34.8	0.9
1970	35.1	0.9	35.2	0.3	35.3	0.3	35.3	0.0	35.7	1.1	35.8	0.3	35.9	0.3	35.5	-1.1	35.6	0.3	35.7	0.3	35.8	0.3	35.9	0.3
1971	36.0	0.3	36.2	0.6	36.2	0.0	36.4	0.6	36.6	0.5	36.8	0.5	36.9	0.3	37.0	0.3	37.0	0.0	37.0	0.0	37.0	0.0	37.0	0.0
1972	36.9	-0.3	37.1	0.5	37.2	0.3	37.3	0.3	37.4	0.3	37.4	0.0	37.5	0.3	37.6	0.3	37.7	0.3	37.8	0.3	37.8	0.0	37.8	0.0
1973	38.0	0.5	38.1	0.3	38.5	1.0	38.8	0.8	39.0	0.5	39.2	0.5	39.2	0.0	39.2	0.0	39.5	0.8	39.7	0.5	39.9	0.5	40.2	0.8
1974	40.9	1.7	41.2	0.7	41.8	1.5	42.6	1.9	43.9	3.1	45.1	2.7	46.5	3.1	47.6	2.4	48.6	2.1	49.8	2.5	50.4	1.2	50.8	0.8
1975	51.4	1.2	52.1	1.4	52.6	1.0	52.9	0.6	53.0	0.2	53.6	1.1	53.8	0.4	53.9	0.2	53.9	0.0	54.6	1.3	54.9	0.5	55.1	0.4
1976	55.5	0.7	55.7	0.4	55.9	0.4	56.3	0.7	56.5	0.4	56.7	0.4	56.9	0.4	57.2	0.5	57.5	0.5	57.9	0.7	58.4	0.9	58.8	0.7
1977	59.5	1.2	60.0	0.8	60.4	0.7	60.7	0.5	61.0	0.5	61.7	1.1	62.1	0.6	62.6	0.8	62.9	0.5	63.4	0.8	63.9	0.8	64.2	0.5
1978	64.9	1.1	65.3	0.6	65.7	0.6	66.1	0.6	66.7	0.9	67.2	0.7	67.5	0.4	68.0	0.7	68.7	1.0	69.7	1.5	70.5	1.1	71.1	0.9
1979	71.8	1.0	72.3	0.7	72.6	0.4	73.3	1.0	74.1	1.1	74.5	0.5	75.2	0.9	75.9	0.9	76.8	1.2	77.8	1.3	78.6	1.0	79.3	0.9
1980	80.7	1.8	81.6	1.1	82.3	0.9	84.2	2.3	85.0	1.0	85.8	0.9	86.6	0.9	86.9	0.3	87.3	0.5	88.0	0.8	88.5	0.6	89.0	0.6
1981	90.3	1.5	90.9	0.7	91.9	1.1	93.1	1.3	93.5	0.4	93.9	0.4	94.4	0.5	94.6	0.2	95.1	0.5	95.5	0.4	95.9	0.4	97.5	1.7
1982	98.4	0.9	98.9	0.5	99.0	0.1	99.6	0.6	99.9	0.3	100.1	0.2	100.5	0.4	100.6	0.1	100.7	0.1	100.7	0.0	100.8	0.1	100.8	0.0
1983	101.0	0.2	101.3	0.3	101.4	0.1	101.7	0.3	101.8	0.1	101.9	0.1	101.8	-0.1	101.7	-0.1	101.8	0.1	101.9	0.1	102.0	0.1	102.4	0.4
1984	102.6	0.2	102.9	0.3	103.0	0.1	103.6	0.6	103.9	0.3	103.9	0.0	104.1	0.2	104.3	0.2	104.6	0.3	105.0	0.4	105.4	0.4	105.5	0.1
1985	105.5	0.0	105.8	0.3	106.0	0.2	106.2	0.2	106.3	0.1	106.5	0.2	106.6	0.1	107.1	0.5	107.1	0.0	107.2	0.1	107.2	0.0	107.2	0.0
1986	107.6	0.4	107.8	0.2	107.9	0.1	108.1	0.2	108.2	0.1	108.5	0.3	108.7	0.2	108.7	0.0	108.7	0.0	108.9	0.2	109.0	0.1	109.2	0.2
1987	109.3	0.1	109.4	0.1	109.6	0.2	109.8	0.2	109.9	0.1	109.8	-0.1	110.3	0.5	110.3	0.0	110.5	0.2	110.6	0.1	110.8	0.2	111.0	0.2
1988	111.4	0.4	111.7	0.3	112.4	0.6	112.7	0.3	113.0	0.3	113.2	0.2	113.6	0.4	114.2	0.5	114.5	0.3	114.7	0.2	115.0	0.3	115.3	0.3
1989	116.0	0.6	116.4	0.3	116.9	0.4	117.4	0.4	117.8	0.3	118.1	0.3	118.5	0.3	118.8	0.3	119.0	0.2	119.3	0.3	119.9	0.5	120.1	0.2
1990	120.7	0.5	121.4	0.6	122.2	0.7	122.4	0.2	122.7	0.2	122.8	0.1	122.9	0.1	123.1	0.2	123.6	0.4	124.3	0.6	124.6	0.2	124.8	0.2
1991	126.4	1.3	126.7	0.2	127.1	0.3	127.2	0.1	127.3	0.1	127.8	0.4	128.0	0.2	128.0	0.0	128.1	0.1	128.2	0.1	128.4	0.2	128.5	0.1

[Continued]

Metalworking Machinery and Equipment
Producer Price Index
Base 1982 = 100
[Continued]

For 1947-1997. Columns headed % show percentile change in the index from the previous period for which an index is available.

Year	Jan Index	%	Feb Index	%	Mar Index	%	Apr Index	%	May Index	%	Jun Index	%	Jul Index	%	Aug Index	%	Sep Index	%	Oct Index	%	Nov Index	%	Dec Index	%
1992	129.4	0.7	129.7	0.2	130.2	0.4	130.6	0.3	130.8	0.2	130.8	0.0	131.0	0.2	131.5	0.4	131.6	0.1	131.7	0.1	131.6	-0.1	131.7	0.1
1993	132.4	0.5	132.5	0.1	133.0	0.4	132.8	-0.2	133.0	0.2	133.3	0.2	133.7	0.3	133.8	0.1	134.3	0.4	134.4	0.1	134.5	0.1	134.6	0.1
1994	134.8	0.1	135.0	0.1	135.4	0.3	136.5	0.8	136.7	0.1	136.5	-0.1	136.7	0.1	136.8	0.1	137.0	0.1	137.1	0.1	137.4	0.2	137.4	0.0
1995	137.9	0.4	138.6	0.5	138.9	0.2	139.2	0.2	139.7	0.4	139.8	0.1	140.4	0.4	140.5	0.1	140.5	0.0	140.6	0.1	140.8	0.1	140.9	0.1
1996	142.0	0.8	142.2	0.1	142.5	0.2	142.7	0.1	143.1	0.3	143.3	0.1	143.3	0.0	143.4	0.1	143.5	0.1	143.6	0.1	144.0	0.3	144.1	0.1
1997	144.3	0.1	144.6	0.2	144.7	0.1	145.0	0.2	145.3	0.2	145.4	0.1	145.5	0.1	145.7	0.1	145.8	0.1	146.0	0.1	145.9	-0.1	145.9	0.0

Source: U.S. Department of Labor, Bureau of Labor Statistics, Division of Industry Prices and Price Indexes. n.e.c. stands for not elsewhere classified. - indicates no data collected for period or unavailable.

General Purpose Machinery and Equipment
Producer Price Index
Base 1982 = 100

For 1939-1997. Columns headed % show percentile change in the index from the previous period for which an index is available.

Year	Jan Index	%	Feb Index	%	Mar Index	%	Apr Index	%	May Index	%	Jun Index	%	Jul Index	%	Aug Index	%	Sep Index	%	Oct Index	%	Nov Index	%	Dec Index	%
1939	13.4	-	13.3	-0.7	13.3	0.0	13.3	0.0	13.3	0.0	13.3	0.0	13.3	0.0	13.3	0.0	13.3	0.0	13.3	0.0	13.3	0.0	13.3	0.0
1940	13.3	0.0	13.3	0.0	13.3	0.0	13.3	0.0	13.3	0.0	13.3	0.0	13.3	0.0	13.3	0.0	13.3	0.0	13.3	0.0	13.3	0.0	13.3	0.0
1941	13.4	0.8	13.4	0.0	13.4	0.0	13.4	0.0	13.4	0.0	13.6	1.5	13.6	0.0	13.7	0.7	13.7	0.0	13.7	0.0	13.7	0.0	13.8	0.7
1942	13.9	0.7	13.8	-0.7	13.8	0.0	13.8	0.0	13.8	0.0	13.8	0.0	13.8	0.0	13.6	-1.4	13.6	0.0	13.6	0.0	13.5	-0.7	13.5	0.0
1943	13.5	0.0	13.5	0.0	13.5	0.0	13.5	0.0	13.4	-0.7	13.4	0.0	13.4	0.0	13.4	0.0	13.4	0.0	13.4	0.0	13.4	0.0	13.4	0.0
1944	13.4	0.0	13.4	0.0	13.4	0.0	13.4	0.0	13.4	0.0	13.4	0.0	13.4	0.0	13.4	0.0	13.4	0.0	13.4	0.0	13.4	0.0	13.4	0.0
1945	13.4	0.0	13.4	0.0	13.4	0.0	13.4	0.0	13.4	0.0	13.4	0.0	13.4	0.0	13.4	0.0	13.4	0.0	13.4	0.0	13.4	0.0	13.4	0.0
1946	13.4	0.0	13.5	0.7	13.5	0.0	13.5	0.0	13.8	2.2	14.0	1.4	14.4	2.9	14.7	2.1	15.2	3.4	15.3	0.7	15.6	2.0	16.0	2.6
1947	16.2	1.3	16.3	0.6	16.3	0.0	16.3	0.0	16.4	0.6	16.6	1.2	16.6	0.0	16.7	0.6	17.0	1.8	17.2	1.2	17.2	0.0	17.3	0.6
1948	17.4	0.6	17.4	0.0	17.5	0.6	17.5	0.0	17.6	0.6	17.6	0.0	17.9	1.7	18.5	3.4	18.8	1.6	19.1	1.6	19.1	0.0	19.1	0.0
1949	19.2	0.5	19.3	0.5	19.2	-0.5	19.2	0.0	19.2	0.0	19.2	0.0	19.1	-0.5	19.1	0.0	19.1	0.0	19.1	0.0	19.1	0.0	19.1	0.0
1950	19.0	-0.5	19.1	0.5	19.1	0.0	19.2	0.5	19.2	0.0	19.2	0.0	19.5	1.6	20.0	2.6	20.4	2.0	20.7	1.5	21.0	1.4	21.9	4.3
1951	22.2	1.4	22.2	0.0	22.2	0.0	22.2	0.0	22.2	0.0	22.2	0.0	22.2	0.0	22.2	0.0	22.2	0.0	22.3	0.5	22.3	0.0	22.2	-0.4
1952	22.2	0.0	22.2	0.0	22.1	-0.5	22.1	0.0	22.1	0.0	22.0	-0.5	22.0	0.0	22.0	0.0	22.0	0.0	21.9	-0.5	21.9	0.0	21.9	0.0
1953	21.9	0.0	21.9	0.0	22.0	0.5	22.2	0.9	22.3	0.5	22.5	0.9	22.6	0.4	22.8	0.9	23.0	0.9	23.1	0.4	23.1	0.0	23.1	0.0
1954	23.1	0.0	23.1	0.0	23.1	0.0	23.1	0.0	23.1	0.0	23.1	0.0	23.0	-0.4	23.0	0.0	23.1	0.4	23.1	0.0	23.1	0.0	23.1	0.0
1955	23.1	0.0	23.5	1.7	23.5	0.0	23.6	0.4	23.6	0.0	23.7	0.4	23.8	0.4	24.2	1.7	24.6	1.7	24.9	1.2	25.3	1.6	25.5	0.8
1956	25.5	0.0	25.5	0.0	25.7	0.8	25.9	0.8	26.3	1.5	26.2	-0.4	26.3	0.4	26.8	1.9	27.3	1.9	27.5	0.7	27.7	0.7	27.8	0.4
1957	28.0	0.7	28.0	0.0	28.1	0.4	28.1	0.0	28.1	0.0	28.2	0.4	28.3	0.4	28.4	0.4	28.5	0.4	28.7	0.7	28.9	0.7	28.9	0.0
1958	28.9	0.0	28.7	-0.7	28.7	0.0	28.7	0.0	28.7	0.0	28.8	0.3	28.7	-0.3	28.6	-0.3	28.7	0.3	28.8	0.3	29.1	1.0	29.2	0.3
1959	29.3	0.3	29.5	0.7	29.4	-0.3	29.3	-0.3	29.3	0.0	29.8	1.7	29.9	0.3	29.9	0.0	30.0	0.3	30.1	0.3	30.1	0.0	30.2	0.3
1960	30.1	-0.3	30.2	0.3	30.1	-0.3	30.2	0.3	30.1	-0.3	29.9	-0.7	29.9	0.0	29.9	0.0	30.0	0.3	29.9	-0.3	29.9	0.0	29.9	0.0
1961	29.9	0.0	29.9	0.0	29.9	0.0	29.8	-0.3	29.8	0.0	29.9	0.3	29.8	-0.3	29.7	-0.3	29.7	0.0	29.6	-0.3	29.7	0.3	29.7	0.0
1962	29.8	0.3	29.8	0.0	29.9	0.3	29.9	0.0	29.9	0.0	29.9	0.0	29.8	-0.3	29.9	0.3	30.0	0.3	30.0	0.0	30.0	0.0	30.1	0.3
1963	30.1	0.0	30.0	-0.3	29.9	-0.3	29.9	0.0	29.9	0.0	30.0	0.3	30.0	0.0	30.0	0.0	30.1	0.3	30.2	0.3	30.2	0.0	30.3	0.3
1964	30.3	0.0	30.3	0.0	30.4	0.3	30.3	-0.3	30.4	0.3	30.3	-0.3	30.2	-0.3	30.0	-0.7	30.0	0.0	30.3	1.0	30.3	0.0	30.4	0.3
1965	30.1	-1.0	30.2	0.3	30.2	0.0	30.2	0.0	30.3	0.3	30.3	0.0	30.3	0.0	30.5	0.7	30.6	0.3	30.8	0.7	30.9	0.3	30.9	0.0
1966	30.9	0.0	30.9	0.0	31.1	0.6	31.4	1.0	31.6	0.6	31.8	0.6	31.8	0.0	32.0	0.6	32.2	0.6	32.4	0.6	32.5	0.3	32.5	0.0
1967	32.7	0.6	32.8	0.3	32.8	0.0	32.8	0.0	32.8	0.0	32.7	-0.3	32.8	0.3	32.9	0.3	33.0	0.3	33.1	0.3	33.2	0.3	33.3	0.3
1968	33.4	0.3	33.6	0.6	33.7	0.3	33.8	0.3	33.9	0.3	34.0	0.3	34.0	0.0	34.1	0.3	34.2	0.3	34.3	0.3	34.2	-0.3	34.3	0.3
1969	34.4	0.3	34.5	0.3	34.7	0.6	34.8	0.3	34.9	0.3	35.1	0.6	35.2	0.3	35.3	0.3	35.6	0.8	35.8	0.6	35.9	0.3	36.2	0.8
1970	36.6	1.1	36.6	0.0	36.8	0.5	36.9	0.3	37.1	0.5	37.1	0.0	37.5	1.1	37.6	0.3	37.8	0.5	38.1	0.8	38.2	0.3	38.5	0.8
1971	38.5	0.0	38.6	0.3	38.8	0.5	39.0	0.5	39.2	0.5	39.3	0.3	39.5	0.5	39.6	0.3	39.6	0.0	39.6	0.0	39.6	0.0	39.7	0.3
1972	39.7	0.0	39.9	0.5	40.0	0.3	40.1	0.2	40.2	0.2	40.4	0.5	40.4	0.0	40.4	0.0	40.5	0.2	40.5	0.0	40.6	0.2	40.6	0.0
1973	40.7	0.2	40.9	0.5	41.1	0.5	41.3	0.5	41.6	0.7	41.8	0.5	41.9	0.2	41.9	0.0	42.0	0.2	42.2	0.5	42.9	1.7	43.0	0.2
1974	43.6	1.4	44.0	0.9	44.7	1.6	45.9	2.7	47.5	3.5	49.1	3.4	50.5	2.9	52.0	3.0	53.2	2.3	54.7	2.8	55.6	1.6	56.2	1.1
1975	56.8	1.1	57.2	0.7	57.5	0.5	57.9	0.7	58.4	0.9	58.6	0.3	59.1	0.9	59.3	0.3	59.6	0.5	59.8	0.3	60.1	0.5	60.4	0.5
1976	60.7	0.5	61.0	0.5	61.2	0.3	61.6	0.7	62.0	0.6	62.5	0.8	62.6	0.2	62.8	0.3	63.3	0.8	63.7	0.6	63.7	0.0	64.0	0.5
1977	64.4	0.6	64.7	0.5	65.0	0.5	65.2	0.3	65.9	1.1	66.4	0.8	66.7	0.5	67.0	0.4	67.3	0.4	67.6	0.4	68.0	0.6	68.2	0.3
1978	68.7	0.7	69.1	0.6	69.5	0.6	69.9	0.6	70.5	0.9	71.0	0.7	71.5	0.7	71.8	0.4	72.3	0.7	72.9	0.8	73.6	1.0	74.0	0.5
1979	74.5	0.7	74.9	0.5	75.8	1.2	76.5	0.9	77.0	0.7	77.3	0.4	78.0	0.9	78.4	0.5	79.0	0.8	79.9	1.1	80.3	0.5	81.4	1.4
1980	82.6	1.5	83.3	0.8	84.4	1.3	85.9	1.8	86.4	0.6	87.1	0.8	87.5	0.5	87.8	0.3	88.8	1.1	89.6	0.9	90.2	0.7	90.7	0.6
1981	91.6	1.0	92.2	0.7	92.9	0.8	93.5	0.6	94.1	0.6	94.4	0.3	95.6	1.3	96.1	0.5	96.7	0.6	97.1	0.4	97.4	0.3	98.0	0.6
1982	98.7	0.7	99.1	0.4	99.3	0.2	99.8	0.5	99.9	0.1	99.8	-0.1	100.3	0.5	100.3	0.0	100.3	0.0	100.6	0.3	100.8	0.2	101.0	0.2
1983	101.1	0.1	101.3	0.2	101.2	-0.1	101.4	0.2	101.5	0.1	101.5	0.0	101.5	0.0	101.3	-0.2	101.4	0.1	101.3	-0.1	101.5	0.2	101.9	0.4

[Continued]

General Purpose Machinery and Equipment
Producer Price Index
Base 1982 = 100
[Continued]

For 1939-1997. Columns headed % show percentile change in the index from the previous period for which an index is available.

Year	Jan Index	%	Feb Index	%	Mar Index	%	Apr Index	%	May Index	%	Jun Index	%	Jul Index	%	Aug Index	%	Sep Index	%	Oct Index	%	Nov Index	%	Dec Index	%
1984	102.2	0.3	102.3	0.1	102.5	0.2	103.0	0.5	103.0	0.0	103.3	0.3	103.7	0.4	103.8	0.1	103.9	0.1	103.9	0.0	104.1	0.2	104.2	0.1
1985	104.7	0.5	104.9	0.2	105.2	0.3	105.4	0.2	105.7	0.3	105.8	0.1	106.0	0.2	106.1	0.1	106.0	-0.1	106.1	0.1	106.2	0.1	106.2	0.0
1986	106.4	0.2	106.7	0.3	106.9	0.2	107.2	0.3	107.2	0.0	107.2	0.0	107.3	0.1	107.4	0.1	107.4	0.0	107.5	0.1	107.5	0.0	107.6	0.1
1987	107.8	0.2	107.8	0.0	107.9	0.1	107.9	0.0	108.0	0.1	108.1	0.1	108.2	0.1	108.3	0.1	108.6	0.3	108.6	0.0	108.9	0.3	109.4	0.5
1988	110.2	0.7	110.7	0.5	111.3	0.5	111.7	0.4	112.0	0.3	112.3	0.3	112.9	0.5	113.3	0.4	113.9	0.5	114.3	0.4	115.1	0.7	115.8	0.6
1989	116.6	0.7	117.0	0.3	117.7	0.6	118.0	0.3	118.6	0.5	119.1	0.4	119.3	0.2	119.6	0.3	120.2	0.5	120.5	0.2	120.7	0.2	121.0	0.2
1990	121.8	0.7	122.3	0.4	122.9	0.5	123.0	0.1	123.3	0.2	123.5	0.2	123.8	0.2	124.1	0.2	124.3	0.2	124.7	0.3	124.8	0.1	125.4	0.5
1991	126.3	0.7	126.9	0.5	127.2	0.2	127.3	0.1	127.7	0.3	128.0	0.2	128.0	0.0	128.1	0.1	128.2	0.1	128.4	0.2	128.5	0.1	128.6	0.1
1992	129.2	0.5	129.4	0.2	129.7	0.2	130.0	0.2	130.1	0.1	129.5	-0.5	129.8	0.2	130.0	0.2	130.2	0.2	130.2	0.0	130.3	0.1	130.3	0.0
1993	131.2	0.7	131.4	0.2	131.5	0.1	131.7	0.2	131.8	0.1	132.1	0.2	132.3	0.2	132.6	0.2	132.7	0.1	132.8	0.1	133.0	0.2	133.2	0.2
1994	133.6	0.3	133.7	0.1	134.1	0.3	134.2	0.1	134.3	0.1	134.6	0.2	134.9	0.2	135.1	0.1	135.2	0.1	135.7	0.4	135.9	0.1	136.1	0.1
1995	136.9	0.6	137.7	0.6	138.1	0.3	138.5	0.3	138.7	0.1	138.9	0.1	139.3	0.3	139.5	0.1	139.7	0.1	140.0	0.2	140.5	0.4	140.8	0.2
1996	141.6	0.6	141.9	0.2	142.2	0.2	142.3	0.1	142.3	0.0	142.4	0.1	142.6	0.1	142.7	0.1	142.7	0.0	143.0	0.2	143.3	0.2	143.4	0.1
1997	143.8	0.3	144.0	0.1	144.5	0.3	144.9	0.3	144.9	0.0	145.0	0.1	145.2	0.1	145.3	0.1	145.4	0.1	145.5	0.1	145.5	0.0	145.6	0.1

Source: U.S. Department of Labor, Bureau of Labor Statistics, Division of Industry Prices and Price Indexes. n.e.c. stands for not elsewhere classified. - indicates no data collected for period or unavailable.

Electronic Computers and Computer Equipment
Producer Price Index
Base 1982 = 100

For 1990-1997. Columns headed % show percentile change in the index from the previous period for which an index is available.

Year	Jan		Feb		Mar		Apr		May		Jun		Jul		Aug		Sep		Oct		Nov		Dec	
	Index	%	Index	%	Index	%	Index	%	Index	%	Index	%	Index	%	Index	%	Index	%	Index	%	Index	%	Index	%
1990	-	-	-	-	-	-	-	-	-	-	-	-	-	-	-	-	-	-	-	-	-	-	100.0	-
1991	97.9	-2.1	97.2	-0.7	96.2	-1.0	95.7	-0.5	93.1	-2.7	89.7	-3.7	86.1	-4.0	83.5	-3.0	83.2	-0.4	82.0	-1.4	81.6	-0.5	80.6	-1.2
1992	79.7	-1.1	78.9	-1.0	77.7	-1.5	75.7	-2.6	75.0	-0.9	73.1	-2.5	71.1	-2.7	70.8	-0.4	69.7	-1.6	68.9	-1.1	68.8	-0.1	68.6	-0.3
1993	67.6	-1.5	66.1	-2.2	64.9	-1.8	63.5	-2.2	62.9	-0.9	62.0	-1.4	61.3	-1.1	60.3	-1.6	60.3	0.0	59.2	-1.8	59.2	0.0	58.9	-0.5
1994	58.4	-0.8	57.8	-1.0	58.1	0.5	57.8	-0.5	57.5	-0.5	57.4	-0.2	57.0	-0.7	56.6	-0.7	56.7	0.2	55.8	-1.6	55.2	-1.1	55.2	0.0
1995	54.7	-0.9	53.8	-1.6	53.4	-0.7	53.5	0.2	53.2	-0.6	52.6	-1.1	52.2	-0.8	51.4	-1.5	50.9	-1.0	50.6	-0.6	50.2	-0.8	50.0	-0.4
1996	49.2	-1.6	48.1	-2.2	47.5	-1.2	46.3	-2.5	45.9	-0.9	45.4	-1.1	44.9	-1.1	44.7	-0.4	44.3	-0.9	43.7	-1.4	43.1	-1.4	42.5	-1.4
1997	42.1	-0.9	41.7	-1.0	41.3	-1.0	40.8	-1.2	39.5	-3.2	39.0	-1.3	38.6	-1.0	38.1	-1.3	37.7	-1.0	37.5	-0.5	37.0	-1.3	36.8	-0.5

Source: U.S. Department of Labor, Bureau of Labor Statistics, Division of Industry Prices and Price Indexes. n.e.c. stands for not elsewhere classified. - indicates no data collected for period or unavailable.

Special Industry Machinery and Equipment
Producer Price Index
Base 1982 = 100

For 1961-1997. Columns headed % show percentile change in the index from the previous period for which an index is available.

Year	Jan Index	%	Feb Index	%	Mar Index	%	Apr Index	%	May Index	%	Jun Index	%	Jul Index	%	Aug Index	%	Sep Index	%	Oct Index	%	Nov Index	%	Dec Index	%
1961	26.4	-	26.4	0.0	26.4	0.0	26.4	0.0	26.5	0.4	26.5	0.0	26.5	0.0	26.5	0.0	26.5	0.0	26.5	0.0	26.5	0.0	26.6	0.4
1962	26.7	0.4	26.8	0.4	26.8	0.0	26.8	0.0	26.8	0.0	26.8	0.0	26.9	0.4	26.9	0.0	26.9	0.0	26.9	0.0	27.0	0.4	27.1	0.4
1963	27.1	0.0	27.2	0.4	27.2	0.0	27.4	0.7	27.4	0.0	27.4	0.0	27.4	0.0	27.5	0.4	27.6	0.4	27.6	0.0	27.6	0.0	27.7	0.4
1964	27.7	0.0	27.7	0.0	27.9	0.7	27.9	0.0	27.9	0.0	27.9	0.0	27.9	0.0	27.9	0.0	27.9	0.0	27.9	0.0	28.1	0.7	28.1	0.0
1965	28.3	0.7	28.3	0.0	28.4	0.4	28.4	0.0	28.4	0.0	28.4	0.0	28.4	0.0	28.4	0.0	28.5	0.4	28.5	0.0	28.7	0.7	28.7	0.0
1966	28.8	0.3	28.8	0.0	29.0	0.7	29.0	0.0	29.2	0.7	29.5	1.0	29.6	0.3	29.7	0.3	29.8	0.3	30.0	0.7	30.1	0.3	30.1	0.0
1967	30.4	1.0	30.5	0.3	30.5	0.0	30.5	0.0	30.7	0.7	30.7	0.0	30.7	0.0	30.8	0.3	30.8	0.0	31.2	1.3	31.2	0.0	31.4	0.6
1968	31.8	1.3	31.8	0.0	31.8	0.0	32.2	1.3	32.3	0.3	32.4	0.3	32.5	0.3	32.5	0.0	32.6	0.3	32.7	0.3	32.9	0.6	32.9	0.0
1969	33.0	0.3	33.3	0.9	33.4	0.3	33.5	0.3	33.6	0.3	33.7	0.3	34.0	0.9	34.0	0.0	34.1	0.3	34.2	0.3	34.4	0.6	34.9	1.5
1970	35.1	0.6	35.1	0.0	35.2	0.3	35.2	0.0	35.3	0.3	35.4	0.3	35.6	0.6	35.6	0.0	35.8	0.6	36.1	0.8	36.1	0.0	36.4	0.8
1971	36.7	0.8	36.8	0.3	36.8	0.0	36.9	0.3	37.0	0.3	37.2	0.5	37.4	0.5	37.4	0.0	37.5	0.3	37.5	0.0	37.5	0.0	37.5	0.0
1972	37.7	0.5	37.9	0.5	37.8	-0.3	37.9	0.3	38.0	0.3	38.1	0.3	38.1	0.0	38.1	0.0	38.1	0.0	38.2	0.3	38.3	0.3	38.3	0.0
1973	38.4	0.3	38.9	1.3	39.1	0.5	39.5	1.0	39.7	0.5	40.0	0.8	40.0	0.0	40.5	1.3	40.8	0.7	40.9	0.2	41.0	0.2	41.5	1.2
1974	41.8	0.7	42.5	1.7	43.6	2.6	44.1	1.1	45.2	2.5	45.8	1.3	46.2	0.9	48.0	3.9	48.8	1.7	49.8	2.0	50.4	1.2	51.0	1.2
1975	51.8	1.6	52.2	0.8	53.1	1.7	53.3	0.4	53.3	0.0	53.6	0.6	54.0	0.7	54.3	0.6	54.3	0.0	54.9	1.1	55.2	0.5	55.7	0.9
1976	56.3	1.1	56.5	0.4	56.8	0.5	57.5	1.2	57.5	0.0	57.8	0.5	58.3	0.9	58.4	0.2	58.7	0.5	59.0	0.5	59.0	0.0	59.6	1.0
1977	60.1	0.8	60.4	0.5	60.7	0.5	61.2	0.8	61.7	0.8	62.1	0.6	62.4	0.5	62.7	0.5	62.8	0.2	64.4	2.5	64.6	0.3	65.1	0.8
1978	65.7	0.9	65.9	0.3	66.6	1.1	67.1	0.8	67.4	0.4	68.3	1.3	68.7	0.6	69.2	0.7	69.8	0.9	70.8	1.4	71.6	1.1	71.9	0.4
1979	72.7	1.1	72.9	0.3	73.5	0.8	74.9	1.9	75.4	0.7	75.7	0.4	76.8	1.5	77.2	0.5	77.2	0.0	78.1	1.2	78.4	0.4	78.8	0.5
1980	80.1	1.6	80.9	1.0	81.6	0.9	83.6	2.5	84.0	0.5	84.4	0.5	85.1	0.8	85.2	0.1	87.0	2.1	88.0	1.1	88.5	0.6	89.5	1.1
1981	90.9	1.6	92.0	1.2	92.6	0.7	93.3	0.8	94.5	1.3	95.0	0.5	95.6	0.6	95.4	-0.2	96.2	0.8	96.8	0.6	96.9	0.1	97.3	0.4
1982	98.6	1.3	98.6	0.0	98.8	0.2	99.3	0.5	99.6	0.3	100.0	0.4	100.6	0.6	100.5	-0.1	100.5	0.0	100.8	0.3	101.2	0.4	101.5	0.3
1983	102.1	0.6	102.3	0.2	102.6	0.3	102.9	0.3	103.3	0.4	103.5	0.2	103.9	0.4	104.3	0.4	104.5	0.2	104.7	0.2	104.9	0.2	105.2	0.3
1984	105.2	0.0	105.5	0.3	106.0	0.5	106.7	0.7	107.1	0.4	107.2	0.1	108.2	0.9	108.5	0.3	108.0	-0.5	108.1	0.1	108.2	0.1	108.4	0.2
1985	109.4	0.9	109.8	0.4	110.0	0.2	110.2	0.2	110.4	0.2	110.7	0.3	111.0	0.3	111.2	0.2	111.4	0.2	111.5	0.1	111.8	0.3	112.2	0.4
1986	112.6	0.4	112.9	0.3	113.0	0.1	113.3	0.3	113.6	0.3	114.2	0.5	114.4	0.2	114.8	0.3	115.2	0.3	115.2	0.0	115.4	0.2	115.8	0.3
1987	116.2	0.3	116.6	0.3	116.7	0.1	116.8	0.1	117.0	0.2	117.0	0.0	117.3	0.3	117.3	0.0	117.5	0.2	118.1	0.5	118.4	0.3	118.8	0.3
1988	119.3	0.4	119.8	0.4	120.1	0.3	120.7	0.5	121.0	0.2	121.5	0.4	122.0	0.4	122.3	0.2	122.6	0.2	123.2	0.5	123.9	0.6	124.1	0.2
1989	124.7	0.5	125.4	0.6	125.7	0.2	126.2	0.4	126.7	0.4	127.1	0.3	127.3	0.2	127.6	0.2	127.9	0.2	128.1	0.2	128.3	0.2	128.6	0.2
1990	129.2	0.5	129.8	0.5	130.1	0.2	131.0	0.7	131.2	0.2	131.5	0.2	131.8	0.2	131.9	0.1	132.4	0.4	132.7	0.2	133.1	0.3	133.4	0.2
1991	134.7	1.0	134.9	0.1	135.2	0.2	135.6	0.3	136.0	0.3	136.1	0.1	136.1	0.0	136.1	0.0	136.4	0.2	136.7	0.2	136.8	0.1	136.9	0.1
1992	137.6	0.5	138.1	0.4	138.3	0.1	138.8	0.4	139.2	0.3	139.3	0.1	139.4	0.1	139.5	0.1	140.5	0.7	140.7	0.1	141.0	0.2	141.2	0.1
1993	141.9	0.5	142.6	0.5	143.0	0.3	143.3	0.2	143.4	0.1	143.7	0.2	143.9	0.1	143.9	0.0	144.1	0.1	144.5	0.3	144.7	0.1	144.7	0.0
1994	145.1	0.3	145.5	0.3	145.7	0.1	145.9	0.1	146.0	0.1	146.2	0.1	146.4	0.1	146.4	0.0	146.5	0.1	146.6	0.1	146.8	0.1	147.0	0.1
1995	148.1	0.7	148.6	0.3	149.0	0.3	149.3	0.2	149.7	0.3	150.0	0.2	150.2	0.1	150.3	0.1	150.5	0.1	150.7	0.1	150.8	0.1	151.0	0.1
1996	152.0	0.7	152.4	0.3	152.7	0.2	152.9	0.1	153.0	0.1	153.2	0.1	153.4	0.1	153.8	0.3	153.9	0.1	154.0	0.1	154.4	0.3	154.4	0.0
1997	155.3	0.6	156.1	0.5	156.3	0.1	156.4	0.1	156.4	0.0	156.5	0.1	156.7	0.1	157.1	0.3	157.2	0.1	157.1	-0.1	157.4	0.2	157.5	0.1

Source: U.S. Department of Labor, Bureau of Labor Statistics, Division of Industry Prices and Price Indexes. n.e.c. stands for not elsewhere classified. - indicates no data collected for period or unavailable.

Electrical Machinery and Equipment
Producer Price Index
Base 1982 = 100

For 1939-1997. Columns headed % show percentile change in the index from the previous period for which an index is available.

Year	Jan Index	%	Feb Index	%	Mar Index	%	Apr Index	%	May Index	%	Jun Index	%	Jul Index	%	Aug Index	%	Sep Index	%	Oct Index	%	Nov Index	%	Dec Index	%
1939	19.6	-	19.6	0.0	19.6	0.0	19.6	0.0	19.6	0.0	19.6	0.0	19.5	-0.5	19.5	0.0	19.5	0.0	19.5	0.0	19.5	0.0	19.5	0.0
1940	19.5	0.0	19.5	0.0	19.5	0.0	19.5	0.0	19.5	0.0	19.5	0.0	19.5	0.0	19.5	0.0	19.5	0.0	19.5	0.0	19.5	0.0	19.5	0.0
1941	19.5	0.0	19.5	0.0	19.5	0.0	19.5	0.0	19.5	0.0	19.5	0.0	19.5	0.0	19.6	0.5	19.7	0.5	19.7	0.0	19.8	0.5	19.8	0.0
1942	19.8	0.0	19.8	0.0	19.7	-0.5	19.6	-0.5	19.6	0.0	19.6	0.0	19.6	0.0	19.6	0.0	19.6	0.0	19.6	0.0	19.5	-0.5	19.5	0.0
1943	19.5	0.0	19.5	0.0	19.5	0.0	19.5	0.0	19.5	0.0	19.5	0.0	19.5	0.0	19.4	-0.5	19.4	0.0	19.4	0.0	19.4	0.0	19.4	0.0
1944	19.4	0.0	19.4	0.0	19.4	0.0	19.4	0.0	19.4	0.0	19.1	-1.5	19.0	-0.5	19.0	0.0	19.0	0.0	19.0	0.0	19.0	0.0	19.0	0.0
1945	19.0	0.0	19.0	0.0	19.0	0.0	19.0	0.0	19.2	1.1	19.3	0.5	19.3	0.0	19.3	0.0	19.3	0.0	19.4	0.5	19.5	0.5	19.5	0.0
1946	19.6	0.5	19.6	0.0	19.6	0.0	20.5	4.6	21.9	6.8	22.3	1.8	22.5	0.9	22.6	0.4	22.8	0.9	23.3	2.2	24.4	4.7	25.3	3.7
1947	25.5	0.8	25.6	0.4	25.7	0.4	26.0	1.2	27.3	5.0	27.5	0.7	27.4	-0.4	27.5	0.4	27.6	0.4	27.5	-0.4	27.5	0.0	27.6	0.4
1948	27.4	-0.7	27.3	-0.4	27.3	0.0	27.3	0.0	27.2	-0.4	27.3	0.4	27.9	2.2	28.8	3.2	29.1	1.0	29.2	0.3	29.4	0.7	29.5	0.3
1949	29.7	0.7	29.8	0.3	29.8	0.0	29.2	-2.0	28.8	-1.4	28.5	-1.0	28.4	-0.4	28.4	0.0	28.4	0.0	28.4	0.0	28.4	0.0	28.4	0.0
1950	28.2	-0.7	28.0	-0.7	28.1	0.4	28.1	0.0	28.1	0.0	28.5	1.4	29.1	2.1	30.4	4.5	30.9	1.6	31.9	3.2	32.0	0.3	33.5	4.7
1951	34.0	1.5	34.0	0.0	34.0	0.0	34.0	0.0	34.0	0.0	34.0	0.0	34.2	0.6	34.1	-0.3	34.1	0.0	34.0	-0.3	34.1	0.3	34.0	-0.3
1952	33.9	-0.3	34.0	0.3	33.9	-0.3	33.8	-0.3	33.8	0.0	33.5	-0.9	33.5	0.0	33.5	0.0	33.4	-0.3	33.3	-0.3	33.4	0.3	33.4	0.0
1953	33.4	0.0	33.4	0.0	33.5	0.3	33.9	1.2	34.2	0.9	34.7	1.5	34.9	0.6	35.1	0.6	35.2	0.3	35.3	0.3	35.4	0.3	35.4	0.0
1954	35.4	0.0	35.4	0.0	35.4	0.0	35.3	-0.3	35.2	-0.3	35.2	0.0	35.2	0.0	35.1	-0.3	35.1	0.0	35.0	-0.3	35.4	1.1	35.4	0.0
1955	35.4	0.0	35.4	0.0	35.3	-0.3	35.3	0.0	35.3	0.0	35.3	0.0	35.4	0.3	35.7	0.8	36.5	2.2	36.5	0.0	36.7	0.5	36.9	0.5
1956	37.0	0.3	37.2	0.5	37.3	0.3	37.9	1.6	38.3	1.1	38.4	0.3	38.4	0.0	38.6	0.5	39.6	2.6	40.0	1.0	40.6	1.5	40.6	0.0
1957	40.8	0.5	41.1	0.7	41.2	0.2	41.3	0.2	41.4	0.2	41.4	0.0	41.8	1.0	41.8	0.0	42.2	1.0	42.1	-0.2	42.2	0.2	42.2	0.0
1958	42.2	0.0	42.2	0.0	42.2	0.0	42.4	0.5	42.5	0.2	42.6	0.2	42.6	0.0	42.7	0.2	42.7	0.0	42.7	0.0	42.5	-0.5	42.5	0.0
1959	42.5	0.0	42.5	0.0	42.7	0.5	42.7	0.0	43.0	0.7	43.0	0.0	43.5	1.2	43.4	-0.2	43.5	0.2	43.6	0.2	43.6	0.0	43.4	-0.5
1960	43.5	0.2	43.5	0.0	43.5	0.0	43.3	-0.5	42.8	-1.2	42.8	0.0	42.9	0.2	42.8	-0.2	42.7	-0.2	42.6	-0.2	42.6	0.0	42.6	0.0
1961	42.9	0.7	42.9	0.0	42.9	0.0	42.4	-1.2	42.4	0.0	42.4	0.0	42.4	0.0	42.0	-0.9	42.0	0.0	42.2	0.5	42.2	0.0	42.1	-0.2
1962	41.9	-0.5	41.9	0.0	41.9	0.0	41.8	-0.2	41.8	0.0	41.8	0.0	41.6	-0.5	41.6	0.0	41.8	0.5	41.8	0.0	41.6	-0.5	41.6	0.0
1963	41.5	-0.2	41.5	0.0	41.1	-1.0	41.2	0.2	41.4	0.5	41.5	0.2	41.2	-0.7	41.2	0.0	41.2	0.0	41.3	0.2	41.4	0.2	41.5	0.2
1964	41.0	-1.2	41.1	0.2	41.2	0.2	41.5	0.7	41.5	0.0	40.9	-1.4	40.9	0.0	41.0	0.2	40.9	-0.2	40.9	0.0	40.9	0.0	40.9	0.0
1965	41.0	0.2	41.1	0.2	41.1	0.0	41.2	0.2	41.2	0.0	41.1	-0.2	41.2	0.2	41.0	-0.5	41.0	0.0	41.0	0.0	40.9	-0.2	41.0	0.2
1966	41.2	0.5	41.5	0.7	41.7	0.5	41.8	0.2	42.0	0.5	41.9	-0.2	42.0	0.2	42.0	0.0	42.1	0.2	42.2	0.2	42.7	1.2	43.1	0.9
1967	43.2	0.2	43.2	0.0	43.2	0.0	43.2	0.0	43.2	0.0	43.2	0.0	43.2	0.0	43.1	-0.2	43.1	0.0	43.0	-0.2	43.1	0.2	43.4	0.7
1968	43.5	0.2	43.6	0.2	43.6	0.0	43.6	0.0	43.7	0.2	43.7	0.0	43.7	0.0	43.7	0.0	43.9	0.5	43.9	0.0	44.0	0.2	43.9	-0.2
1969	43.9	0.0	44.2	0.7	44.2	0.0	44.2	0.0	44.3	0.2	44.4	0.2	44.4	0.0	44.4	0.0	44.7	0.7	44.8	0.2	45.0	0.4	45.1	0.2
1970	45.3	0.4	45.2	-0.2	45.4	0.4	45.5	0.2	45.6	0.2	45.9	0.7	46.1	0.4	46.2	0.2	46.4	0.4	46.4	0.0	46.6	0.4	46.7	0.2
1971	46.9	0.4	47.1	0.4	47.2	0.2	47.1	-0.2	47.1	0.0	47.1	0.0	47.2	0.2	47.3	0.2	47.2	-0.2	47.2	0.0	47.1	-0.2	47.1	0.0
1972	47.3	0.4	47.5	0.4	47.6	0.2	47.6	0.0	47.7	0.2	47.8	0.2	47.8	0.0	47.8	0.0	47.7	-0.2	47.7	0.0	47.8	0.2	47.8	0.0
1973	47.9	0.2	47.9	0.0	48.1	0.4	48.2	0.2	48.5	0.6	48.7	0.4	48.7	0.0	48.7	0.0	48.7	0.0	48.8	0.2	48.9	0.2	49.2	0.6
1974	49.7	1.0	50.0	0.6	50.5	1.0	51.2	1.4	52.1	1.8	53.3	2.3	54.5	2.3	55.5	1.8	56.3	1.4	57.2	1.6	58.5	2.3	59.0	0.9
1975	59.6	1.0	59.9	0.5	60.1	0.3	60.2	0.2	60.5	0.5	60.6	0.2	60.8	0.3	60.9	0.2	61.2	0.5	61.5	0.5	61.8	0.5	61.8	0.0
1976	62.3	0.8	62.5	0.3	62.6	0.2	62.7	0.2	62.8	0.2	63.1	0.5	63.2	0.2	63.3	0.2	64.0	1.1	64.4	0.6	64.6	0.3	64.8	0.3
1977	65.1	0.5	65.4	0.5	65.6	0.3	65.7	0.2	66.0	0.5	66.1	0.2	66.5	0.6	66.7	0.3	67.2	0.7	67.9	1.0	68.2	0.4	68.2	0.0
1978	69.1	1.3	69.4	0.4	69.9	0.7	70.3	0.6	70.6	0.4	71.1	0.7	71.4	0.4	71.6	0.3	71.9	0.4	72.3	0.6	73.2	1.2	73.6	0.5
1979	73.9	0.4	74.6	0.9	75.1	0.7	75.6	0.7	76.2	0.8	76.7	0.7	77.7	1.3	78.2	0.6	78.8	0.8	79.6	1.0	79.8	0.3	80.6	1.0
1980	82.3	2.1	83.9	1.9	84.9	1.2	85.9	1.2	86.3	0.5	87.1	0.9	88.0	1.0	88.5	0.6	89.0	0.6	89.4	0.4	89.6	0.2	90.2	0.7
1981	91.5	1.4	92.3	0.9	93.3	1.1	93.9	0.6	93.9	0.0	94.7	0.9	95.5	0.8	96.2	0.7	96.8	0.6	97.3	0.5	97.6	0.3	98.0	0.4
1982	98.8	0.8	99.1	0.3	99.5	0.4	100.0	0.5	99.9	-0.1	100.0	0.1	100.0	0.0	100.1	0.1	100.1	0.0	100.5	0.4	100.9	0.4	101.2	0.3
1983	101.6	0.4	102.4	0.8	102.6	0.2	102.9	0.3	103.0	0.1	103.1	0.1	104.4	1.3	104.4	0.0	104.9	0.5	104.8	-0.1	104.9	0.1	105.3	0.4

[Continued]

Electrical Machinery and Equipment
Producer Price Index
Base 1982 = 100
[Continued]

For 1939-1997. Columns headed % show percentile change in the index from the previous period for which an index is available.

Year	Jan Index	%	Feb Index	%	Mar Index	%	Apr Index	%	May Index	%	Jun Index	%	Jul Index	%	Aug Index	%	Sep Index	%	Oct Index	%	Nov Index	%	Dec Index	%
1984	105.7	0.4	106.1	0.4	106.5	0.4	107.0	0.5	107.1	0.1	107.6	0.5	107.7	0.1	107.7	0.0	107.9	0.2	108.3	0.4	108.6	0.3	108.7	0.1
1985	109.3	0.6	109.6	0.3	109.6	0.0	109.3	-0.3	109.5	0.2	109.4	-0.1	109.6	0.2	109.7	0.1	109.8	0.1	109.9	0.1	109.8	-0.1	110.0	0.2
1986	110.3	0.3	110.6	0.3	110.8	0.2	111.0	0.2	111.0	0.0	110.9	-0.1	111.5	0.5	111.5	0.0	111.7	0.2	111.7	0.0	111.8	0.1	111.9	0.1
1987	112.3	0.4	112.4	0.1	112.3	-0.1	112.2	-0.1	112.3	0.1	112.2	-0.1	112.7	0.4	112.9	0.2	112.7	-0.2	113.1	0.4	113.2	0.1	113.4	0.2
1988	113.7	0.3	114.1	0.4	113.7	-0.4	113.8	0.1	114.4	0.5	114.2	-0.2	114.4	0.2	114.7	0.3	114.8	0.1	115.1	0.3	115.2	0.1	115.4	0.2
1989	116.2	0.7	116.6	0.3	116.7	0.1	116.8	0.1	117.0	0.2	117.5	0.4	117.9	0.3	118.0	0.1	117.9	-0.1	118.4	0.4	118.3	-0.1	118.4	0.1
1990	118.9	0.4	118.6	-0.3	118.9	0.3	119.0	0.1	119.0	0.0	119.2	0.2	119.5	0.3	119.4	-0.1	119.5	0.1	119.6	0.1	119.8	0.2	119.9	0.1
1991	120.5	0.5	120.6	0.1	120.7	0.1	120.9	0.2	120.7	-0.2	120.8	0.1	120.9	0.1	120.9	0.0	120.8	-0.1	120.8	0.0	120.9	0.1	120.9	0.0
1992	120.9	0.0	121.2	0.2	121.4	0.2	121.2	-0.2	121.3	0.1	121.2	-0.1	121.2	0.0	121.2	0.0	121.2	0.0	121.4	0.2	121.6	0.2	121.7	0.1
1993	122.0	0.2	122.2	0.2	122.2	0.0	122.6	0.3	122.4	-0.2	122.4	0.0	122.4	0.0	122.5	0.1	122.6	0.1	122.7	0.1	122.8	0.1	122.7	-0.1
1994	123.1	0.3	123.2	0.1	123.3	0.1	123.6	0.2	123.7	0.1	123.7	0.0	123.8	0.1	123.5	-0.2	123.4	-0.1	123.2	-0.2	123.4	0.2	123.4	0.0
1995	123.9	0.4	124.2	0.2	124.1	-0.1	124.2	0.1	124.2	0.0	124.1	-0.1	124.0	-0.1	124.0	0.0	124.2	0.2	124.8	0.5	124.9	0.1	124.3	-0.5
1996	124.6	0.2	124.6	0.0	124.1	-0.4	123.6	-0.4	123.2	-0.3	122.9	-0.2	123.1	0.2	123.2	0.1	123.2	0.0	122.9	-0.2	122.9	0.0	123.2	0.2
1997	123.0	-0.2	122.9	-0.1	122.7	-0.2	122.6	-0.1	122.4	-0.2	122.4	0.0	122.6	0.2	122.1	-0.4	122.0	-0.1	121.9	-0.1	122.1	0.2	121.8	-0.2

Source: U.S. Department of Labor, Bureau of Labor Statistics, Division of Industry Prices and Price Indexes. n.e.c. stands for not elsewhere classified. - indicates no data collected for period or unavailable.

Miscellaneous Instruments
Producer Price Index
Base 1982 = 100

For 1980-1997. Columns headed % show percentile change in the index from the previous period for which an index is available.

Year	Jan Index	%	Feb Index	%	Mar Index	%	Apr Index	%	May Index	%	Jun Index	%	Jul Index	%	Aug Index	%	Sep Index	%	Oct Index	%	Nov Index	%	Dec Index	%
1980	-	-	-	-	-	-	-	-	-	-	86.1	-	86.4	0.3	86.3	-0.1	87.4	1.3	89.1	1.9	90.3	1.3	91.6	1.4
1981	89.9	-1.9	89.1	-0.9	88.5	-0.7	88.8	0.3	88.9	0.1	89.8	1.0	91.0	1.3	94.4	3.7	95.8	1.5	95.2	-0.6	95.8	0.6	95.8	0.0
1982	96.2	0.4	98.7	2.6	98.2	-0.5	99.3	1.1	99.4	0.1	99.3	-0.1	99.6	0.3	98.0	-1.6	100.8	2.9	103.1	2.3	101.9	-1.2	105.4	3.4
1983	106.1	0.7	107.1	0.9	106.9	-0.2	106.3	-0.6	105.9	-0.4	104.7	-1.1	104.6	-0.1	104.7	0.1	105.0	0.3	105.1	0.1	104.9	-0.2	104.6	-0.3
1984	104.9	0.3	105.4	0.5	105.6	0.2	105.0	-0.6	105.2	0.2	105.7	0.5	106.5	0.8	108.1	1.5	108.4	0.3	108.3	-0.1	108.0	-0.3	108.8	0.7
1985	109.4	0.6	109.5	0.1	109.0	-0.5	108.3	-0.6	108.8	0.5	109.6	0.7	110.5	0.8	110.1	-0.4	110.4	0.3	110.6	0.2	110.9	0.3	110.8	-0.1
1986	111.4	0.5	111.7	0.3	111.4	-0.3	111.7	0.3	111.9	0.2	112.3	0.4	113.2	0.8	113.7	0.4	113.7	0.0	113.9	0.2	114.0	0.1	114.2	0.2
1987	114.8	0.5	115.3	0.4	115.3	0.0	115.4	0.1	115.5	0.1	115.1	-0.3	115.7	0.5	115.9	0.2	116.1	0.2	116.3	0.2	116.4	0.1	116.8	0.3
1988	117.6	0.7	118.2	0.5	118.9	0.6	118.6	-0.3	118.6	0.0	118.6	0.0	118.9	0.3	119.2	0.3	119.2	0.0	119.3	0.1	119.9	0.5	119.9	0.0
1989	121.0	0.9	121.4	0.3	121.5	0.1	121.9	0.3	122.1	0.2	122.4	0.2	122.8	0.3	123.1	0.2	123.2	0.1	123.1	-0.1	123.4	0.2	123.9	0.4
1990	125.0	0.9	125.5	0.4	125.9	0.3	126.1	0.2	126.5	0.3	126.2	-0.2	126.9	0.6	127.1	0.2	127.2	0.1	127.5	0.2	128.1	0.5	128.3	0.2
1991	129.1	0.6	129.5	0.3	129.5	0.0	129.8	0.2	129.7	-0.1	129.9	0.2	130.5	0.5	130.6	0.1	130.8	0.2	131.4	0.5	131.3	-0.1	131.5	0.2
1992	132.4	0.7	132.6	0.2	132.6	0.0	132.9	0.2	132.9	0.0	133.4	0.4	134.0	0.4	134.2	0.1	134.4	0.1	135.0	0.4	135.1	0.1	135.2	0.1
1993	136.7	1.1	136.8	0.1	136.9	0.1	137.5	0.4	137.5	0.0	137.8	0.2	138.2	0.3	138.3	0.1	138.3	0.0	138.4	0.1	138.3	-0.1	138.5	0.1
1994	138.9	0.3	139.1	0.1	139.2	0.1	139.4	0.1	139.5	0.1	139.6	0.1	139.8	0.1	140.0	0.1	139.8	-0.1	139.8	0.0	140.1	0.2	139.6	-0.4
1995	139.9	0.2	140.2	0.2	140.2	0.0	140.4	0.1	140.6	0.1	140.9	0.2	141.6	0.5	141.3	-0.2	141.5	0.1	141.7	0.1	142.0	0.2	141.9	-0.1
1996	142.7	0.6	142.9	0.1	142.9	0.0	142.8	-0.1	143.1	0.2	143.3	0.1	143.5	0.1	143.6	0.1	143.4	-0.1	143.4	0.0	143.6	0.1	144.0	0.3
1997	145.3	0.9	145.4	0.1	145.6	0.1	146.0	0.3	146.0	0.0	146.0	0.0	146.3	0.2	146.5	0.1	146.6	0.1	145.8	-0.5	146.2	0.3	145.9	-0.2

Source: U.S. Department of Labor, Bureau of Labor Statistics, Division of Industry Prices and Price Indexes. n.e.c. stands for not elsewhere classified. - indicates no data collected for period or unavailable.

Miscellaneous Machinery
Producer Price Index
Base 1982 = 100

For 1947-1997. Columns headed % show percentile change in the index from the previous period for which an index is available.

Year	Jan Index	%	Feb Index	%	Mar Index	%	Apr Index	%	May Index	%	Jun Index	%	Jul Index	%	Aug Index	%	Sep Index	%	Oct Index	%	Nov Index	%	Dec Index	%
1947	21.2	-	21.3	0.5	21.4	0.5	21.4	0.0	21.5	0.5	21.6	0.5	21.6	0.0	21.7	0.5	21.8	0.5	22.0	0.9	22.2	0.9	22.4	0.9
1948	22.5	0.4	22.6	0.4	22.7	0.4	22.8	0.4	22.8	0.0	22.9	0.4	23.4	2.2	23.8	1.7	24.0	0.8	24.2	0.8	24.3	0.4	24.3	0.0
1949	24.3	0.0	24.3	0.0	24.3	0.0	24.3	0.0	24.3	0.0	24.3	0.0	24.3	0.0	24.3	0.0	24.3	0.0	24.3	0.0	24.3	0.0	24.2	-0.4
1950	24.2	0.0	24.3	0.4	24.3	0.0	24.3	0.0	24.3	0.0	24.3	0.0	24.4	0.4	24.9	2.0	25.2	1.2	25.5	1.2	25.8	1.2	26.5	2.7
1951	27.5	3.8	27.5	0.0	27.5	0.0	27.5	0.0	27.5	0.0	27.5	0.0	27.6	0.4	27.6	0.0	27.6	0.0	27.6	0.0	27.6	0.0	27.8	0.7
1952	27.8	0.0	27.8	0.0	27.6	-0.7	27.6	0.0	27.5	-0.4	27.5	0.0	27.5	0.0	27.5	0.0	27.5	0.0	27.6	0.1	27.6	0.0	27.6	0.0
1953	27.6	0.0	27.8	0.7	27.8	0.0	27.8	0.0	28.2	1.4	28.3	0.4	28.5	0.7	28.7	0.7	28.7	0.0	28.7	0.0	28.7	0.0	28.8	0.3
1954	28.8	0.0	28.8	0.0	28.9	0.3	28.9	0.0	28.9	0.0	29.0	0.3	29.0	0.0	29.0	0.0	29.1	0.3	29.1	0.0	29.1	0.0	29.1	0.0
1955	29.2	0.3	29.2	0.0	29.3	0.3	29.3	0.0	29.4	0.3	29.4	0.0	29.4	0.0	30.1	2.4	30.5	1.3	30.7	0.7	30.8	0.3	30.8	0.0
1956	30.8	0.0	30.9	0.3	31.0	0.3	31.0	0.0	31.2	0.6	31.3	0.3	31.6	1.0	31.7	0.3	32.1	1.3	32.5	1.2	32.8	0.9	32.9	0.3
1957	32.9	0.0	33.0	0.3	33.1	0.3	33.2	0.3	33.2	0.0	33.2	0.0	33.4	0.6	33.8	1.2	34.0	0.6	34.1	0.3	34.2	0.3	34.3	0.3
1958	34.4	0.3	34.4	0.0	34.4	0.0	34.4	0.0	34.1	-0.9	34.1	0.0	34.1	0.0	34.1	0.0	34.1	0.0	34.1	0.0	34.2	0.3	34.3	0.3
1959	34.3	0.0	34.4	0.3	34.5	0.3	34.5	0.0	34.5	0.0	34.5	0.0	34.5	0.0	34.6	0.3	34.5	-0.3	34.6	0.3	34.6	0.0	34.6	0.0
1960	34.6	0.0	34.6	0.0	34.7	0.3	34.7	0.0	34.7	0.0	34.7	0.0	34.7	0.0	34.7	0.0	34.7	0.0	34.7	0.0	34.8	0.3	34.9	0.3
1961	34.9	0.0	34.9	0.0	34.9	0.0	35.0	0.3	35.0	0.0	35.0	0.0	35.1	0.3	35.1	0.0	35.1	0.0	35.0	-0.3	35.0	0.0	35.1	0.3
1962	35.1	0.0	35.1	0.0	35.2	0.3	35.1	-0.3	35.1	0.0	35.2	0.3	35.2	0.0	35.3	0.3	35.2	-0.3	35.2	0.0	35.2	0.0	35.2	0.0
1963	35.2	0.0	35.2	0.0	35.4	0.6	35.2	-0.6	35.2	0.0	35.2	0.0	35.2	0.0	35.2	0.0	35.3	0.3	35.3	0.0	35.4	0.3	35.4	0.0
1964	35.5	0.3	35.5	0.0	35.5	0.0	35.6	0.3	35.6	0.0	35.6	0.0	35.6	0.0	35.7	0.3	35.7	0.0	35.8	0.3	35.8	0.0	35.5	-0.8
1965	35.8	0.8	35.8	0.0	35.8	0.0	35.9	0.3	35.9	0.0	36.0	0.3	35.8	-0.6	35.8	0.0	35.8	0.0	35.8	0.0	35.9	0.3	35.9	0.0
1966	35.9	0.0	36.0	0.3	36.1	0.3	36.0	-0.3	36.1	0.3	36.1	0.0	36.3	0.6	36.3	0.0	36.4	0.3	36.6	0.5	36.7	0.3	36.8	0.3
1967	37.0	0.5	37.1	0.3	37.1	0.0	37.1	0.0	37.1	0.0	37.2	0.3	37.2	0.0	37.2	0.0	37.3	0.3	37.4	0.3	37.6	0.5	37.7	0.3
1968	38.2	1.3	38.4	0.5	38.5	0.3	38.6	0.3	38.9	0.8	38.9	0.0	38.9	0.0	38.9	0.0	39.0	0.3	39.3	0.8	39.3	0.0	39.4	0.3
1969	39.5	0.3	39.6	0.3	39.7	0.3	39.9	0.5	40.1	0.5	40.1	0.0	40.3	0.5	40.4	0.2	40.6	0.5	40.8	0.5	41.0	0.5	41.2	0.5
1970	41.3	0.2	41.4	0.2	41.6	0.5	41.9	0.7	41.8	-0.2	41.9	0.2	41.9	0.0	41.9	0.0	42.3	1.0	42.5	0.5	42.7	0.5	43.1	0.9
1971	43.3	0.5	43.3	0.0	43.4	0.2	43.7	0.7	43.8	0.2	43.7	-0.2	43.8	0.2	44.0	0.5	43.9	-0.2	43.9	0.0	43.9	0.0	44.0	0.2
1972	44.1	0.2	44.3	0.5	44.3	0.0	44.6	0.7	44.8	0.4	45.0	0.4	45.0	0.0	45.0	0.0	45.0	0.0	45.1	0.2	45.0	-0.2	45.1	0.2
1973	45.1	0.0	45.3	0.4	45.6	0.7	45.9	0.7	46.4	1.1	46.4	0.0	46.4	0.0	46.5	0.2	46.6	0.2	46.6	0.0	46.8	0.4	47.0	0.4
1974	47.6	1.3	47.9	0.6	48.7	1.7	49.3	1.2	50.0	1.4	51.0	2.0	52.0	2.0	53.5	2.9	54.0	0.9	55.7	3.1	56.9	2.2	57.1	0.4
1975	58.9	3.2	59.1	0.3	59.0	-0.2	59.7	1.2	60.2	0.8	60.2	0.0	60.3	0.2	60.8	0.8	61.5	1.2	61.8	0.5	62.1	0.5	62.2	0.2
1976	62.9	1.1	63.2	0.5	63.5	0.5	63.7	0.3	63.7	0.0	63.8	0.2	64.2	0.6	64.1	-0.2	64.4	0.5	65.0	0.9	65.0	0.0	65.2	0.3
1977	65.6	0.6	65.9	0.5	66.1	0.3	66.3	0.3	66.8	0.8	67.0	0.3	67.3	0.4	67.8	0.7	68.3	0.7	68.6	0.4	69.0	0.6	69.3	0.4
1978	70.1	1.2	70.5	0.6	71.2	1.0	71.4	0.3	71.8	0.6	72.3	0.7	72.9	0.8	73.3	0.5	73.6	0.4	73.9	0.4	74.6	0.9	74.7	0.1
1979	75.5	1.1	75.8	0.4	76.0	0.3	76.5	0.7	77.1	0.8	77.3	0.3	78.1	1.0	78.1	0.0	79.0	1.2	79.6	0.8	80.1	0.6	80.6	0.6
1980	82.1	1.9	82.4	0.4	83.2	1.0	84.7	1.8	84.7	0.0	85.0	0.4	86.1	1.3	86.5	0.5	87.0	0.6	88.1	1.3	88.9	0.9	89.3	0.4
1981	90.7	1.6	91.3	0.7	92.0	0.8	92.6	0.7	92.7	0.1	93.2	0.5	94.7	1.6	95.4	0.7	96.3	0.9	96.5	0.2	96.8	0.3	97.0	0.2
1982	97.4	0.4	98.4	1.0	98.7	0.3	99.2	0.5	99.8	0.6	100.1	0.3	100.4	0.3	100.9	0.5	101.1	0.2	101.2	0.1	101.4	0.2	101.5	0.1
1983	101.7	0.2	101.6	-0.1	102.0	0.4	102.1	0.1	102.6	0.5	102.5	-0.1	102.5	0.0	102.6	0.1	102.3	-0.3	101.8	-0.5	102.0	0.2	102.0	0.0
1984	102.7	0.7	102.2	-0.5	102.3	0.1	102.3	0.0	102.0	-0.3	102.1	0.1	102.2	0.1	102.1	-0.1	102.3	0.2	102.2	-0.1	102.4	0.2	102.3	-0.1
1985	102.5	0.2	102.6	0.1	102.6	0.0	103.1	0.5	103.0	-0.1	103.5	0.5	103.5	0.0	103.6	0.1	103.7	0.1	103.6	-0.1	103.7	0.1	103.7	0.0
1986	103.8	0.1	103.7	-0.1	103.8	0.1	104.2	0.4	104.3	0.1	104.3	0.0	104.3	0.0	104.3	0.0	104.0	-0.3	104.2	0.2	104.3	0.1	104.6	0.3
1987	105.1	0.5	105.2	0.1	105.4	0.2	105.5	0.1	105.6	0.1	105.4	-0.2	105.3	-0.1	105.9	0.6	105.9	0.0	106.1	0.2	106.6	0.5	106.9	0.3
1988	107.5	0.6	107.5	0.0	107.7	0.2	107.9	0.2	108.0	0.1	108.1	0.1	108.5	0.4	109.1	0.6	109.5	0.4	109.5	0.0	109.7	0.2	110.2	0.5
1989	110.7	0.5	110.8	0.1	111.1	0.3	111.3	0.2	111.7	0.4	112.2	0.4	113.1	0.8	113.5	0.4	114.2	0.6	114.4	0.2	114.6	0.2	114.7	0.1
1990	115.7	0.9	115.7	0.0	115.9	0.2	116.0	0.1	116.1	0.1	116.2	0.1	116.3	0.1	116.8	0.4	117.5	0.6	117.6	0.1	118.4	0.7	118.3	-0.1
1991	119.1	0.7	119.4	0.3	119.8	0.3	119.8	0.0	120.0	0.2	120.1	0.1	120.4	0.2	120.8	0.3	121.0	0.2	120.9	-0.1	121.0	0.1	121.2	0.2

[Continued]

Miscellaneous Machinery
Producer Price Index
Base 1982 = 100
[Continued]

For 1947-1997. Columns headed % show percentile change in the index from the previous period for which an index is available.

Year	Jan Index	%	Feb Index	%	Mar Index	%	Apr Index	%	May Index	%	Jun Index	%	Jul Index	%	Aug Index	%	Sep Index	%	Oct Index	%	Nov Index	%	Dec Index	%
1992	121.5	0.2	121.5	0.0	121.4	-0.1	121.3	-0.1	121.5	0.2	121.6	0.1	121.7	0.1	121.9	0.2	121.9	0.0	121.9	0.0	122.0	0.1	122.0	0.0
1993	122.3	0.2	122.4	0.1	122.5	0.1	122.4	-0.1	122.5	0.1	122.4	-0.1	122.6	0.2	122.9	0.2	123.0	0.1	123.2	0.2	123.1	-0.1	123.3	0.2
1994	123.9	0.5	124.2	0.2	124.2	0.0	124.2	0.0	124.2	0.0	124.4	0.2	124.5	0.1	124.7	0.2	125.2	0.4	125.5	0.2	125.6	0.1	125.7	0.1
1995	126.2	0.4	126.4	0.2	126.4	0.0	126.6	0.2	126.7	0.1	126.8	0.1	127.2	0.3	127.2	0.0	127.3	0.1	127.4	0.1	127.6	0.2	127.7	0.1
1996	128.2	0.4	128.6	0.3	128.7	0.1	128.8	0.1	128.8	0.0	128.9	0.1	129.5	0.5	129.5	0.0	129.8	0.2	129.8	0.0	129.9	0.1	130.1	0.2
1997	130.4	0.2	130.3	-0.1	130.6	0.2	130.7	0.1	130.7	0.0	130.7	0.0	131.0	0.2	131.1	0.1	131.1	0.0	131.1	0.0	131.3	0.2	131.3	0.0

Source: U.S. Department of Labor, Bureau of Labor Statistics, Division of Industry Prices and Price Indexes. n.e.c. stands for not elsewhere classified. - indicates no data collected for period or unavailable.

FURNITURE AND HOUSEHOLD DURABLES
Producer Price Index
Base 1982 = 100

For 1926-1997. Columns headed % show percentile change in the index from the previous period for which an index is available.

Year	Jan Index	%	Feb Index	%	Mar Index	%	Apr Index	%	May Index	%	Jun Index	%	Jul Index	%	Aug Index	%	Sep Index	%	Oct Index	%	Nov Index	%	Dec Index	%
1926	28.8	-	28.8	0.0	28.8	0.0	28.7	-0.3	28.6	-0.3	28.6	0.0	28.6	0.0	28.6	0.0	28.5	-0.3	28.5	0.0	28.5	0.0	28.2	-1.1
1927	28.0	-0.7	28.0	0.0	27.9	-0.4	27.9	0.0	27.9	0.0	28.0	0.4	27.9	-0.4	27.9	0.0	27.6	-1.1	27.8	0.7	27.9	0.4	27.9	0.0
1928	27.6	-1.1	27.6	0.0	27.4	-0.7	27.3	-0.4	27.4	0.4	27.1	-1.1	27.1	0.0	27.1	0.0	27.1	0.0	26.9	-0.7	26.9	0.0	26.9	0.0
1929	26.9	0.0	26.8	-0.4	26.8	0.0	26.9	0.4	26.9	0.0	27.1	0.7	27.0	-0.4	27.0	0.0	27.0	0.0	27.1	0.4	27.1	0.0	27.1	0.0
1930	26.8	-1.1	26.8	0.0	26.8	0.0	26.8	0.0	26.8	0.0	26.8	0.0	26.6	-0.7	26.6	0.0	26.4	-0.8	26.4	0.0	26.2	-0.8	25.4	-3.1
1931	25.4	0.0	25.4	0.0	25.3	-0.4	25.3	0.0	24.9	-1.6	24.8	-0.4	24.6	-0.8	24.4	-0.8	23.7	-2.9	23.2	-2.1	23.2	0.0	22.5	-3.0
1932	22.3	-0.9	22.2	-0.4	22.1	-0.5	21.9	-0.9	21.4	-2.3	21.4	0.0	21.2	-0.9	21.2	0.0	21.1	-0.5	21.2	0.5	21.2	0.0	21.2	0.0
1933	20.8	-1.9	20.6	-1.0	20.6	0.0	20.5	-0.5	20.6	0.5	21.0	1.9	21.4	1.9	21.8	1.9	22.3	2.3	23.0	3.1	23.0	0.0	23.0	0.0
1934	23.1	0.4	23.2	0.4	23.3	0.4	23.4	0.4	23.6	0.9	23.6	0.0	23.5	-0.4	23.5	0.0	23.6	0.4	23.5	-0.4	23.4	-0.4	23.4	0.0
1935	23.2	-0.9	23.2	0.0	23.3	0.4	23.2	-0.4	23.3	0.4	23.2	-0.4	23.2	0.0	23.2	0.0	23.2	0.0	23.2	0.0	23.2	0.0	23.2	0.0
1936	23.5	1.3	23.5	0.0	23.5	0.0	23.5	0.0	23.5	0.0	23.5	0.0	23.4	-0.4	23.5	0.4	23.6	0.4	23.7	0.4	23.8	0.4	24.1	1.3
1937	25.4	5.4	25.7	1.2	25.8	0.4	25.8	0.0	25.9	0.4	26.1	0.8	26.1	0.0	26.4	1.1	26.6	0.8	26.6	0.0	26.4	-0.8	26.2	-0.8
1938	25.8	-1.5	25.8	0.0	25.8	0.0	25.7	-0.4	25.7	0.0	25.7	0.0	25.4	-1.2	25.4	0.0	25.3	-0.4	25.2	-0.4	25.2	0.0	25.3	0.4
1939	25.2	-0.4	25.2	0.0	25.2	0.0	25.2	0.0	25.2	0.0	25.3	0.4	25.3	0.0	25.3	0.0	25.5	0.8	25.9	1.6	25.9	0.0	25.9	0.0
1940	25.8	-0.4	25.9	0.4	25.9	0.0	26.0	0.4	26.0	0.0	26.0	0.0	26.0	0.0	26.0	0.0	26.0	0.0	26.0	0.0	26.0	0.0	26.1	0.4
1941	26.1	0.0	26.1	0.0	26.4	1.1	26.6	0.8	26.8	0.8	27.4	2.2	27.8	1.5	28.0	0.7	28.5	1.8	29.1	2.1	29.3	0.7	29.6	1.0
1942	29.8	0.7	29.8	0.0	29.8	0.0	29.9	0.3	29.9	0.0	29.9	0.0	29.9	0.0	29.9	0.0	29.9	0.0	29.9	0.0	29.9	0.0	29.9	0.0
1943	29.7	-0.7	29.7	0.0	29.7	0.0	29.7	0.0	29.7	0.0	29.7	0.0	29.7	0.0	29.7	0.0	29.7	0.0	29.7	0.0	29.7	0.0	29.7	0.0
1944	30.5	2.7	30.4	-0.3	30.4	0.0	30.4	0.0	30.4	0.0	30.4	0.0	30.4	0.0	30.5	0.3	30.5	0.0	30.5	0.0	30.5	0.0	30.5	0.0
1945	30.5	0.0	30.5	0.0	30.5	0.0	30.5	0.0	30.5	0.0	30.5	0.0	30.5	0.0	30.5	0.0	30.5	0.0	30.5	0.0	30.5	0.0	30.5	0.0
1946	30.8	1.0	30.9	0.3	31.0	0.3	31.2	0.6	31.6	1.3	32.2	1.9	32.4	0.6	32.5	0.3	32.9	1.2	33.2	0.9	34.2	3.0	35.9	5.0
1947	36.5	1.7	36.6	0.3	36.6	0.0	36.8	0.5	36.8	0.0	36.9	0.3	37.2	0.8	37.3	0.3	37.5	0.5	37.8	0.8	37.9	0.3	38.1	0.5
1948	38.4	0.8	38.4	0.0	38.5	0.3	38.8	0.8	38.8	0.0	38.9	0.3	39.2	0.8	39.5	0.8	40.0	1.3	40.8	2.0	40.9	0.2	40.9	0.0
1949	40.7	-0.5	40.7	0.0	40.6	-0.2	40.5	-0.2	40.3	-0.5	40.2	-0.2	39.8	-1.0	39.7	-0.3	39.6	-0.3	39.5	-0.3	39.6	0.3	39.7	0.3
1950	39.7	0.0	39.8	0.3	39.8	0.0	39.9	0.3	40.1	0.5	40.1	0.0	40.3	0.5	40.8	1.2	41.6	2.0	42.6	2.4	43.1	1.2	43.6	1.2
1951	44.4	1.8	44.6	0.5	44.7	0.2	44.9	0.4	44.8	-0.2	44.7	-0.2	44.5	-0.4	44.1	-0.9	44.0	-0.2	43.9	-0.2	43.8	-0.2	43.8	0.0
1952	43.7	-0.2	43.7	0.0	43.5	-0.5	43.6	0.2	43.4	-0.5	43.4	0.0	43.4	0.0	43.3	-0.2	43.5	0.5	43.5	0.0	43.6	0.2	43.7	0.2
1953	43.8	0.2	43.9	0.2	44.0	0.2	44.3	0.7	44.4	0.2	44.5	0.2	44.6	0.2	44.6	0.0	44.7	0.2	44.6	-0.2	44.7	0.2	44.7	0.0
1954	44.8	0.2	44.7	-0.2	44.7	0.0	44.9	0.4	44.9	0.0	44.9	0.0	44.8	-0.2	44.8	0.0	44.8	0.0	44.9	0.2	44.9	0.0	45.0	0.2
1955	44.9	-0.2	44.9	0.0	44.7	-0.4	44.7	0.0	44.7	0.0	44.8	0.2	44.9	0.2	45.1	0.4	45.3	0.4	45.5	0.4	45.6	0.2	45.6	0.0
1956	45.9	0.7	46.0	0.2	46.0	0.0	45.9	-0.2	45.9	0.0	46.0	0.2	46.0	0.0	46.3	0.7	46.5	0.4	47.0	1.1	47.1	0.2	47.1	0.0
1957	47.4	0.6	47.4	0.0	47.4	0.0	47.2	-0.4	47.3	0.2	47.3	0.0	47.5	0.4	47.6	0.2	47.5	-0.2	47.6	0.2	47.7	0.2	48.0	0.6
1958	48.1	0.2	48.0	-0.2	48.0	0.0	48.0	0.0	47.9	-0.2	47.8	-0.2	47.9	0.2	47.8	-0.2	47.8	0.0	47.8	0.0	47.7	-0.2	47.7	0.0
1959	47.9	0.4	47.9	0.0	48.0	0.2	48.0	0.0	48.0	0.0	48.0	0.0	48.1	0.2	48.0	-0.2	48.0	0.0	47.9	-0.2	47.9	0.0	47.9	0.0
1960	48.0	0.2	48.0	0.0	48.1	0.2	48.0	-0.2	47.9	-0.2	47.8	-0.2	47.8	0.0	47.8	0.0	47.7	-0.2	47.7	0.0	47.6	-0.2	47.6	0.0
1961	47.5	-0.2	47.5	0.0	47.5	0.0	47.6	0.2	47.6	0.0	47.6	0.0	47.5	-0.2	47.5	0.0	47.5	0.0	47.5	0.0	47.5	0.0	47.5	0.0
1962	47.5	0.0	47.4	-0.2	47.3	-0.2	47.3	0.0	47.3	0.0	47.3	0.0	47.2	-0.2	47.2	0.0	47.1	-0.2	47.1	0.0	47.1	0.0	47.0	-0.2
1963	47.0	0.0	46.9	-0.2	46.9	0.0	46.9	0.0	46.8	-0.2	46.9	0.2	46.8	-0.2	46.9	0.2	46.9	0.0	46.9	0.0	46.9	0.0	47.0	-0.2
1964	47.0	0.4	47.1	0.2	47.1	0.0	47.1	0.0	47.1	0.0	47.1	0.0	47.1	0.0	47.1	0.0	47.1	0.0	47.1	0.0	46.8	0.2	46.9	0.0
1965	47.0	0.0	46.9	-0.2	47.0	0.0	46.8	-0.4	46.8	0.0	46.8	0.0	46.7	-0.2	46.7	0.0	46.7	0.0	46.7	0.0	46.8	0.2	48.0	0.0
1966	47.0	0.2	47.0	0.0	47.0	0.0	47.1	0.2	47.3	0.4	47.3	0.0	47.3	0.0	47.4	0.2	47.4	0.0	47.6	0.4	47.9	0.6	48.0	0.0
1967	48.0	0.0	48.0	0.0	48.0	0.0	48.1	0.2	48.2	0.2	48.2	0.0	48.2	0.0	48.3	0.2	48.4	0.2	48.6	0.4	48.8	0.4	48.9	0.2
1968	49.2	0.6	49.4	0.4	49.5	0.2	49.6	0.2	49.7	0.2	49.6	-0.2	49.7	0.2	49.8	0.2	49.8	0.0	49.9	0.2	49.9	0.0	50.1	0.4
1969	50.4	0.6	50.4	0.0	50.5	0.2	50.5	0.0	50.5	0.0	50.5	0.0	50.6	0.2	50.7	0.2	50.8	0.2	50.9	0.2	51.0	0.2	51.2	0.4
1970	51.4	0.4	51.6	0.4	51.6	0.0	51.8	0.4	51.7	-0.2	51.8	0.2	52.0	0.4	52.0	0.0	52.1	0.2	52.2	0.2	52.4	0.4	52.5	0.2

[Continued]

FURNITURE AND HOUSEHOLD DURABLES
Producer Price Index
Base 1982 = 100
[Continued]

For 1926-1997. Columns headed % show percentile change in the index from the previous period for which an index is available.

Year	Jan Index	%	Feb Index	%	Mar Index	%	Apr Index	%	May Index	%	Jun Index	%	Jul Index	%	Aug Index	%	Sep Index	%	Oct Index	%	Nov Index	%	Dec Index	%
1971	52.8	0.6	53.0	0.4	53.0	0.0	53.0	0.0	53.1	0.2	53.1	0.0	53.3	0.4	53.3	0.0	53.3	0.0	53.3	0.0	53.2	-0.2	53.2	0.0
1972	53.3	0.2	53.5	0.4	53.6	0.2	53.6	0.0	53.7	0.2	53.7	0.0	53.8	0.2	54.0	0.4	54.1	0.2	54.1	0.0	54.3	0.4	54.3	0.0
1973	54.4	0.2	54.6	0.4	54.8	0.4	55.1	0.5	55.6	0.9	55.7	0.2	55.7	0.0	56.0	0.5	56.1	0.2	56.3	0.4	56.6	0.5	56.8	0.4
1974	57.5	1.2	58.1	1.0	58.6	0.9	59.4	1.4	60.2	1.3	60.9	1.2	62.0	1.8	62.7	1.1	64.2	2.4	65.5	2.0	66.2	1.1	66.5	0.5
1975	67.1	0.9	67.2	0.1	66.9	-0.4	66.9	0.0	67.0	0.1	67.2	0.3	67.3	0.1	67.6	0.4	67.7	0.1	68.2	0.7	68.4	0.3	68.6	0.3
1976	69.3	1.0	69.4	0.1	69.6	0.3	69.8	0.3	70.0	0.3	70.2	0.3	70.4	0.3	70.6	0.3	70.9	0.4	71.1	0.3	71.3	0.3	71.5	0.3
1977	71.9	0.6	72.1	0.3	72.3	0.3	72.5	0.3	72.8	0.4	73.2	0.5	73.2	0.0	73.7	0.7	73.8	0.1	74.0	0.3	74.3	0.4	74.5	0.3
1978	75.6	1.5	75.7	0.1	76.2	0.7	76.5	0.4	76.9	0.5	77.1	0.3	78.0	1.2	78.2	0.3	78.3	0.1	78.7	0.5	79.0	0.4	79.5	0.6
1979	80.5	1.3	81.1	0.7	81.3	0.2	81.5	0.2	82.0	0.6	82.2	0.2	82.5	0.4	82.9	0.5	83.5	0.7	84.6	1.3	85.2	0.7	86.0	0.9
1980	88.6	3.0	89.7	1.2	89.7	0.0	89.1	-0.7	89.6	0.6	90.1	0.6	90.8	0.8	91.3	0.6	91.6	0.3	92.2	0.7	92.5	0.3	93.3	0.9
1981	93.7	0.4	94.3	0.6	94.6	0.3	94.9	0.3	95.4	0.5	95.3	-0.1	96.4	1.2	96.4	0.0	97.1	0.7	97.3	0.2	97.6	0.3	98.1	0.5
1982	98.3	0.2	98.9	0.6	99.3	0.4	99.6	0.3	99.8	0.2	100.0	0.2	100.0	0.0	100.5	0.5	100.7	0.2	101.0	0.3	100.9	-0.1	101.1	0.2
1983	101.8	0.7	102.7	0.9	102.6	-0.1	102.8	0.2	103.2	0.4	103.4	0.2	103.8	0.4	103.9	0.1	104.1	0.2	104.0	-0.1	104.2	0.2	104.2	0.0
1984	104.7	0.5	105.0	0.3	105.1	0.1	105.4	0.3	105.9	0.5	105.9	0.0	105.9	0.0	105.9	0.0	105.8	-0.1	105.9	0.1	106.3	0.4	106.3	0.0
1985	106.4	0.1	106.7	0.3	106.8	0.1	107.1	0.3	107.1	0.0	107.1	0.0	107.3	0.2	107.3	0.0	107.2	-0.1	107.2	0.0	107.4	0.2	107.5	0.1
1986	107.6	0.1	107.7	0.1	107.9	0.2	108.1	0.2	108.3	0.2	108.4	0.1	108.3	-0.1	108.4	0.1	108.3	-0.1	108.5	0.2	108.7	0.2	108.7	0.0
1987	109.0	0.3	109.1	0.1	109.2	0.1	109.6	0.4	109.8	0.2	109.9	0.1	110.0	0.1	110.3	0.3	110.3	0.0	110.5	0.2	110.7	0.2	110.9	0.2
1988	111.6	0.6	111.9	0.3	112.3	0.4	112.5	0.2	112.8	0.3	112.7	-0.1	113.1	0.4	113.4	0.3	113.7	0.3	113.9	0.2	114.3	0.4	114.5	0.2
1989	115.0	0.4	115.3	0.3	115.7	0.3	116.2	0.4	116.5	0.3	117.0	0.4	117.5	0.4	117.9	0.3	117.9	0.0	117.7	-0.2	117.8	0.1	117.9	0.1
1990	118.4	0.4	118.7	0.3	118.7	0.0	119.0	0.2	119.0	0.0	119.2	0.2	119.1	-0.1	119.2	0.1	119.3	0.1	119.5	0.2	119.8	0.3	120.0	0.2
1991	120.6	0.5	120.9	0.2	121.0	0.1	121.2	0.2	121.2	0.0	121.2	0.0	121.2	0.0	121.2	0.0	121.2	0.0	121.4	0.2	121.4	0.0	121.5	0.1
1992	121.8	0.2	121.8	0.0	121.9	0.1	122.0	0.1	122.1	0.1	122.2	0.1	122.2	0.0	122.2	0.0	122.4	0.2	122.3	-0.1	122.6	0.2	122.6	0.0
1993	122.6	0.0	122.9	0.2	123.0	0.1	123.2	0.2	123.4	0.2	123.6	0.2	123.8	0.2	124.0	0.2	124.0	0.0	124.5	0.4	124.8	0.2	124.8	0.0
1994	125.2	0.3	125.4	0.2	125.5	0.1	125.8	0.2	126.1	0.2	126.2	0.1	126.4	0.2	126.3	-0.1	126.2	-0.1	126.4	0.2	126.7	0.2	126.7	0.0
1995	127.2	0.4	127.5	0.2	127.5	0.0	127.8	0.2	128.0	0.2	128.1	0.1	128.2	0.1	128.4	0.2	128.5	0.1	128.9	0.3	129.3	0.3	129.3	0.0
1996	129.6	0.2	129.9	0.2	129.9	0.0	130.0	0.1	130.3	0.2	130.2	-0.1	130.6	0.3	130.5	-0.1	130.6	0.1	130.9	0.2	130.9	0.0	130.9	0.0
1997	130.9	0.0	130.9	0.0	131.0	0.1	130.7	-0.2	130.9	0.2	130.9	0.0	130.9	0.0	130.7	-0.2	130.7	0.0	130.9	0.2	130.6	-0.2	130.7	0.1

Source: U.S. Department of Labor, Bureau of Labor Statistics, Division of Industry Prices and Price Indexes. n.e.c. stands for not elsewhere classified. - indicates no data collected for period or unavailable.

Household Furniture

Producer Price Index
Base 1982 = 100

For 1926-1997. Columns headed % show percentile change in the index from the previous period for which an index is available.

Year	Jan Index	%	Feb Index	%	Mar Index	%	Apr Index	%	May Index	%	Jun Index	%	Jul Index	%	Aug Index	%	Sep Index	%	Oct Index	%	Nov Index	%	Dec Index	%
1926	23.2	-	23.1	-0.4	23.1	0.0	23.0	-0.4	22.9	-0.4	22.8	-0.4	22.8	0.0	22.8	0.0	22.8	0.0	22.8	0.0	22.8	0.0	22.8	0.0
1927	22.4	-1.8	22.4	0.0	22.4	0.0	22.4	0.0	22.4	0.0	22.4	0.0	22.4	0.0	22.4	0.0	22.4	0.0	22.2	-0.9	22.3	0.5	22.2	-0.4
1928	22.3	0.5	22.3	0.0	22.2	-0.4	22.2	0.0	22.2	0.0	22.2	0.0	22.2	0.0	22.2	0.0	22.2	0.0	21.8	-1.8	21.8	0.0	21.8	0.0
1929	21.6	-0.9	21.6	0.0	21.6	0.0	21.6	0.0	21.6	0.0	21.8	0.9	21.8	0.0	21.8	0.0	21.8	0.0	21.5	-1.4	21.8	1.4	21.8	0.0
1930	21.7	-0.5	21.7	0.0	21.7	0.0	21.7	0.0	21.7	0.0	21.6	-0.5	21.5	-0.5	21.5	0.0	21.4	-0.5	21.4	0.0	21.4	0.0	21.1	-1.4
1931	21.1	0.0	21.1	0.0	21.1	0.0	21.1	0.0	20.7	-1.9	20.5	-1.0	20.4	-0.5	20.3	-0.5	19.4	-4.4	18.8	-3.1	18.8	0.0	18.4	-2.1
1932	18.2	-1.1	18.2	0.0	18.1	-0.5	17.7	-2.2	17.0	-4.0	16.9	-0.6	16.7	-1.2	16.6	-0.6	16.7	0.6	16.7	0.0	16.7	0.0	16.6	-0.6
1933	16.5	-0.6	16.4	-0.6	16.4	0.0	16.4	0.0	16.4	0.0	16.8	2.4	17.1	1.8	17.5	2.3	17.9	2.3	18.2	1.7	18.2	0.0	18.1	-0.5
1934	18.1	0.0	18.1	0.0	18.2	0.6	18.3	0.5	18.3	0.0	18.1	-1.1	18.0	-0.6	18.1	0.6	18.1	0.0	18.1	0.0	18.0	-0.6	17.9	-0.6
1935	17.9	0.0	17.7	-1.1	17.7	0.0	17.7	0.0	17.7	0.0	17.7	0.0	17.6	-0.6	17.6	0.0	17.6	0.0	17.6	0.0	17.7	0.6	17.7	0.0
1936	17.8	0.6	17.8	0.0	17.8	0.0	17.8	0.0	17.8	0.0	17.7	-0.6	17.7	0.0	17.7	0.0	17.8	0.6	17.9	0.6	18.1	1.1	18.2	0.6
1937	19.2	5.5	19.4	1.0	19.4	0.0	19.6	1.0	19.7	0.5	19.8	0.5	19.8	0.0	19.9	0.5	19.9	0.0	19.9	0.0	19.7	-1.0	19.7	0.0
1938	19.1	-3.0	19.1	0.0	19.1	0.0	19.1	0.0	19.1	0.0	19.1	0.0	18.8	-1.6	18.8	0.0	18.8	0.0	18.8	0.0	18.7	-0.5	18.7	0.0
1939	18.4	-1.6	18.4	0.0	18.4	0.0	18.5	0.5	18.5	0.0	18.5	0.0	18.5	0.0	18.5	0.0	18.6	0.5	18.7	0.5	18.8	0.5	18.8	0.0
1940	18.7	-0.5	18.7	0.0	18.7	0.0	18.7	0.0	18.7	0.0	18.7	0.0	18.7	0.0	18.7	0.0	18.7	0.0	18.7	0.0	18.7	0.0	18.8	0.5
1941	18.9	0.5	18.9	0.0	19.0	0.5	19.1	0.5	19.3	1.0	19.9	3.1	20.4	2.5	20.5	0.5	21.1	2.9	21.6	2.4	21.9	1.4	22.1	0.9
1942	22.3	0.9	22.3	0.0	22.3	0.0	22.3	0.0	22.3	0.0	22.3	0.0	22.3	0.0	22.3	0.0	22.3	0.0	22.4	0.0	22.4	0.0	22.6	0.9
1943	22.4	0.4	22.4	0.0	22.4	0.0	22.4	0.0	22.4	0.0	22.4	0.0	22.4	0.0	22.4	0.0	22.4	0.0	22.4	0.0	22.4	0.0	22.6	0.9
1944	22.9	1.3	23.1	0.9	23.1	0.0	23.1	0.0	23.1	0.0	23.1	0.0	23.1	0.0	23.1	0.0	23.1	0.0	23.1	0.0	23.2	0.4	23.2	0.0
1945	23.2	0.0	23.2	0.0	23.2	0.0	23.2	0.0	23.2	0.0	23.5	1.3	23.5	0.0	23.5	0.0	23.5	0.0	23.5	0.0	23.5	0.0	23.5	0.0
1946	23.9	1.7	24.0	0.4	24.0	0.0	24.1	0.4	24.5	1.7	24.8	1.2	24.9	0.4	25.2	1.2	25.4	0.8	25.8	1.6	26.3	1.9	26.9	2.3
1947	29.4	9.3	29.4	0.0	29.4	0.0	29.5	0.3	29.5	0.0	29.5	0.0	29.7	0.7	29.9	0.7	30.3	1.3	30.7	1.3	30.8	0.3	31.1	1.0
1948	31.9	2.6	31.9	0.0	31.9	0.0	32.0	0.3	31.9	-0.3	32.0	0.3	32.0	0.0	32.3	0.9	32.5	0.6	32.5	0.0	32.5	0.0	32.5	0.0
1949	32.3	-0.6	32.3	0.0	32.3	0.0	32.3	0.0	32.0	-0.9	31.9	-0.3	31.2	-2.2	31.3	0.3	31.3	0.0	31.3	0.0	31.3	0.0	31.4	0.3
1950	31.5	0.3	31.5	0.0	31.5	0.0	31.6	0.3	31.6	0.0	31.8	0.6	32.2	1.3	33.2	3.1	34.2	3.0	34.8	1.8	35.2	1.1	35.9	2.0
1951	36.7	2.2	36.8	0.3	36.8	0.0	36.8	0.0	36.7	-0.3	36.5	-0.5	36.2	-0.8	36.2	0.0	36.2	0.0	36.1	-0.3	36.2	0.3	36.0	-0.6
1952	35.5	-1.4	35.5	0.0	35.5	0.0	35.5	0.0	35.4	-0.3	35.2	-0.6	35.2	0.0	35.2	0.0	35.2	0.0	35.2	0.0	35.3	0.3	35.3	0.0
1953	35.4	0.3	35.5	0.3	35.5	0.0	35.6	0.3	35.6	0.0	35.7	0.3	35.6	-0.3	35.6	0.0	35.7	0.3	35.7	0.0	35.7	0.0	35.7	0.0
1954	35.7	0.0	35.6	-0.3	35.6	0.0	35.5	-0.3	35.5	0.0	35.4	-0.3	35.3	-0.3	35.3	0.0	35.3	0.0	35.3	0.0	35.3	0.0	35.3	0.0
1955	35.2	-0.3	35.2	0.0	35.2	0.0	35.3	0.3	35.4	0.3	35.3	-0.3	35.4	0.3	35.8	1.1	36.0	0.6	36.2	0.6	36.4	0.6	36.5	0.3
1956	36.7	0.5	36.7	0.0	36.8	0.3	36.9	0.3	36.9	0.0	36.9	0.0	37.3	1.1	37.4	0.3	37.6	0.5	37.8	0.5	37.9	0.3	37.9	0.0
1957	38.2	0.8	38.2	0.0	38.2	0.0	38.3	0.3	38.3	0.0	38.3	0.0	38.4	0.3	38.5	0.3	38.3	-0.5	38.3	0.0	38.4	0.3	38.4	0.0
1958	38.5	0.3	38.6	0.3	38.4	-0.5	38.4	0.0	38.4	0.0	38.3	-0.3	38.3	0.0	38.3	0.0	38.4	0.3	38.5	0.3	38.7	0.5	38.8	0.3
1959	38.8	0.0	38.8	0.0	38.8	0.0	38.6	-0.5	38.7	0.3	38.8	0.3	38.9	0.3	38.9	0.0	38.8	-0.3	38.9	0.3	38.9	0.0	38.9	0.0
1960	39.0	0.3	39.1	0.3	39.1	0.0	39.1	0.0	39.1	0.0	39.1	0.0	39.1	0.0	39.1	0.0	39.1	0.0	39.3	0.5	39.3	0.0	39.3	0.0
1961	39.5	0.5	39.5	0.0	39.5	0.0	39.5	0.0	39.6	0.3	39.6	0.0	39.6	0.0	39.6	0.0	39.6	0.0	39.7	0.3	39.9	0.5	39.8	-0.3
1962	39.9	0.3	39.9	0.0	39.9	0.0	39.9	0.0	40.0	0.3	40.0	0.0	40.1	0.2	40.1	0.0	40.0	-0.2	40.1	0.2	40.1	0.0	40.2	0.2
1963	40.3	0.2	40.3	0.0	40.3	0.0	40.2	-0.2	40.2	0.0	40.3	0.2	40.3	0.0	40.3	0.0	40.4	0.2	40.4	0.0	40.4	0.0	40.3	-0.2
1964	40.5	0.5	40.5	0.0	40.5	0.0	40.6	0.2	40.6	0.0	40.5	-0.2	40.6	0.2	40.6	0.0	40.6	0.0	40.6	0.0	40.7	0.2	40.7	0.0
1965	40.9	0.5	40.9	0.0	40.9	0.0	40.9	0.0	40.9	0.0	40.8	-0.2	40.8	0.0	40.9	0.2	40.9	0.0	41.0	0.2	41.1	0.2	41.1	0.0
1966	41.2	0.2	41.3	0.2	41.3	0.0	41.7	1.0	42.0	0.7	42.0	0.0	42.0	0.0	42.2	0.5	42.3	0.2	42.5	0.5	43.0	1.2	43.1	0.2
1967	43.1	0.0	43.2	0.2	43.3	0.2	43.3	0.0	43.3	0.0	43.3	0.0	43.4	0.2	43.6	0.5	43.6	0.0	43.7	0.2	44.0	0.7	44.0	0.0
1968	44.4	0.9	44.6	0.5	44.7	0.2	44.8	0.2	45.1	0.7	45.2	0.2	45.3	0.2	45.3	0.0	45.4	0.2	45.7	0.7	45.9	0.4	46.0	0.2
1969	46.6	1.3	46.7	0.2	46.8	0.2	46.8	0.0	47.0	0.4	47.1	0.2	47.4	0.6	47.4	0.0	47.5	0.2	47.6	0.2	47.7	0.2	47.6	-0.2
1970	47.9	0.6	48.3	0.8	48.4	0.2	48.4	0.0	48.6	0.4	48.6	0.0	48.7	0.2	48.8	0.2	48.8	0.0	48.8	0.0	48.9	0.2	49.0	0.2

[Continued]

Household Furniture
Producer Price Index
Base 1982 = 100
[Continued]

For 1926-1997. Columns headed % show percentile change in the index from the previous period for which an index is available.

Year	Jan Index	%	Feb Index	%	Mar Index	%	Apr Index	%	May Index	%	Jun Index	%	Jul Index	%	Aug Index	%	Sep Index	%	Oct Index	%	Nov Index	%	Dec Index	%
1971	49.2	0.4	49.7	1.0	49.7	0.0	49.7	0.0	50.1	0.8	50.1	0.0	50.2	0.2	50.3	0.2	50.3	0.0	50.3	0.0	50.0	-0.6	50.0	0.0
1972	50.5	1.0	50.8	0.6	50.8	0.0	50.9	0.2	51.0	0.2	51.0	0.0	51.1	0.2	51.3	0.4	51.2	-0.2	51.2	0.0	51.4	0.4	51.6	0.4
1973	51.8	0.4	51.9	0.2	52.2	0.6	53.0	1.5	53.2	0.4	53.6	0.8	53.6	0.0	53.8	0.4	54.1	0.6	54.5	0.7	55.1	1.1	55.3	0.4
1974	56.1	1.4	56.5	0.7	56.7	0.4	57.8	1.9	58.7	1.6	58.9	0.3	59.5	1.0	60.0	0.8	60.9	1.5	62.1	2.0	62.9	1.3	62.9	0.0
1975	63.3	0.6	63.3	0.0	63.2	-0.2	63.3	0.2	63.2	-0.2	63.2	0.0	63.3	0.2	63.3	0.0	63.6	0.5	64.3	1.1	64.6	0.5	65.1	0.8
1976	65.6	0.8	65.5	-0.2	65.6	0.2	65.8	0.3	66.1	0.5	66.6	0.8	66.8	0.3	66.9	0.1	67.4	0.7	68.1	1.0	68.5	0.6	69.0	0.7
1977	69.1	0.1	69.1	0.0	69.5	0.6	69.9	0.6	70.1	0.3	70.6	0.7	70.9	0.4	71.0	0.1	71.1	0.1	71.4	0.4	71.8	0.6	72.4	0.8
1978	73.2	1.1	73.4	0.3	73.7	0.4	73.9	0.3	74.3	0.5	75.0	0.9	76.0	1.3	76.4	0.5	76.6	0.3	77.4	1.0	77.8	0.5	78.0	0.3
1979	78.8	1.0	78.9	0.1	79.1	0.3	79.5	0.5	80.4	1.1	80.6	0.2	80.8	0.2	81.0	0.2	82.0	1.2	82.7	0.9	84.0	1.6	84.8	1.0
1980	85.9	1.3	86.4	0.6	86.6	0.2	87.2	0.7	88.3	1.3	88.8	0.6	89.8	1.1	90.5	0.8	90.7	0.2	91.3	0.7	91.8	0.5	92.3	0.5
1981	92.6	0.3	93.0	0.4	93.3	0.3	94.2	1.0	94.1	-0.1	95.1	1.1	95.7	0.6	96.0	0.3	96.7	0.7	96.9	0.2	97.9	1.0	98.6	0.7
1982	99.0	0.4	98.9	-0.1	99.0	0.1	99.9	0.9	100.1	0.2	100.2	0.1	100.1	-0.1	100.2	0.1	100.4	0.2	100.6	0.2	100.7	0.1	100.9	0.2
1983	100.9	0.0	101.2	0.3	100.6	-0.6	100.8	0.2	102.0	1.2	102.2	0.2	102.4	0.2	102.8	0.2	102.9	0.1	103.1	0.2	103.3	0.2	103.2	-0.1
1984	103.5	0.3	104.0	0.5	104.4	0.4	104.8	0.4	105.1	0.3	105.4	0.3	105.4	0.0	105.6	0.2	105.9	0.3	106.3	0.4	106.6	0.3	106.8	0.2
1985	107.4	0.6	107.7	0.3	107.7	0.0	108.3	0.6	108.8	0.5	109.0	0.2	108.7	-0.3	108.8	0.1	108.8	0.0	108.7	-0.1	108.9	0.2	109.0	0.1
1986	109.3	0.3	109.8	0.5	110.0	0.2	109.8	-0.2	110.3	0.5	110.2	-0.1	110.1	-0.1	110.6	0.5	110.4	-0.2	110.7	0.3	110.8	0.1	111.0	0.2
1987	111.2	0.2	111.7	0.4	112.0	0.3	112.5	0.4	112.8	0.3	112.8	0.0	112.8	0.0	113.1	0.3	113.6	0.4	113.6	0.0	114.2	0.5	115.2	0.9
1988	115.8	0.5	116.2	0.3	116.8	0.5	117.0	0.2	117.2	0.2	117.4	0.2	117.8	0.3	118.1	0.3	118.1	0.0	118.6	0.4	119.0	0.3	119.5	0.4
1989	119.6	0.1	120.2	0.5	120.7	0.4	121.3	0.5	121.6	0.2	121.7	0.1	121.9	0.2	122.3	0.3	122.5	0.2	123.1	0.5	123.4	0.2	123.5	0.1
1990	123.6	0.1	123.9	0.2	124.0	0.1	124.4	0.3	124.9	0.4	125.1	0.2	125.2	0.1	125.3	0.1	125.5	0.2	126.0	0.4	126.5	0.4	126.6	0.1
1991	126.9	0.2	127.3	0.3	127.7	0.3	127.8	0.1	127.9	0.1	127.9	0.0	128.0	0.1	128.1	0.1	128.3	0.2	128.7	0.3	128.9	0.2	128.9	0.0
1992	129.2	0.2	129.4	0.2	129.6	0.2	129.7	0.1	129.7	0.0	129.9	0.2	130.0	0.1	130.1	0.1	130.4	0.2	130.5	0.1	130.9	0.3	131.0	0.1
1993	131.2	0.2	131.6	0.3	131.7	0.1	132.2	0.4	132.6	0.3	133.0	0.3	133.2	0.2	133.3	0.1	133.6	0.2	135.8	1.6	136.4	0.4	135.8	-0.4
1994	136.1	0.2	136.9	0.6	137.2	0.2	137.4	0.1	137.8	0.3	138.0	0.1	138.1	0.1	138.1	0.0	138.6	0.4	138.9	0.2	139.2	0.2	139.4	0.1
1995	140.0	0.4	140.4	0.3	140.7	0.2	141.0	0.2	141.6	0.4	141.8	0.1	142.0	0.1	142.2	0.1	142.5	0.2	142.7	0.1	143.2	0.4	143.2	0.0
1996	143.6	0.3	143.8	0.1	144.1	0.2	144.2	0.1	144.4	0.1	144.5	0.1	144.6	0.1	144.5	-0.1	144.7	0.1	144.9	0.1	145.2	0.2	145.2	0.0
1997	145.4	0.1	145.7	0.2	145.9	0.1	146.0	0.1	146.0	0.0	146.1	0.1	146.4	0.2	146.3	-0.1	146.6	0.2	146.5	-0.1	146.8	0.2	146.8	0.0

Source: U.S. Department of Labor, Bureau of Labor Statistics, Division of Industry Prices and Price Indexes. n.e.c. stands for not elsewhere classified. - indicates no data collected for period or unavailable.

Commercial Furniture
Producer Price Index
Base 1982 = 100

For 1947-1997. Columns headed % show percentile change in the index from the previous period for which an index is available.

Year	Jan Index	%	Feb Index	%	Mar Index	%	Apr Index	%	May Index	%	Jun Index	%	Jul Index	%	Aug Index	%	Sep Index	%	Oct Index	%	Nov Index	%	Dec Index	%
1947	19.5	-	19.5	0.0	19.6	0.5	20.1	2.6	20.3	1.0	20.3	0.0	20.3	0.0	20.3	0.0	20.4	0.5	20.5	0.5	20.5	0.0	20.7	1.0
1948	20.9	1.0	21.0	0.5	21.1	0.5	21.1	0.0	21.1	0.0	21.1	0.0	21.2	0.5	21.9	3.3	22.0	0.5	22.3	1.4	22.3	0.0	22.3	0.0
1949	22.3	0.0	22.3	0.0	22.3	0.0	22.3	0.0	22.2	-0.4	22.2	0.0	22.2	0.0	22.2	0.0	22.2	0.0	22.2	0.0	22.2	0.0	22.2	0.0
1950	22.2	0.0	22.2	0.0	22.2	0.0	22.2	0.0	22.5	1.4	22.6	0.4	23.0	1.8	23.7	3.0	23.8	0.4	24.5	2.9	25.4	3.7	26.0	2.4
1951	26.6	2.3	26.6	0.0	26.6	0.0	26.6	0.0	26.6	0.0	26.6	0.0	26.6	0.0	26.6	0.0	26.6	0.0	26.4	-0.8	26.1	-1.1	26.1	0.0
1952	26.1	0.0	26.1	0.0	26.2	0.4	26.2	0.0	26.2	0.0	26.2	0.0	26.2	0.0	26.1	-0.4	26.1	0.0	26.2	0.4	26.2	0.0	26.2	0.0
1953	26.2	0.0	26.2	0.0	26.2	0.0	26.2	0.0	26.5	1.1	26.8	1.1	26.8	0.0	26.8	0.0	26.8	0.0	26.8	0.0	26.9	0.4	26.9	0.0
1954	26.9	0.0	26.9	0.0	26.9	0.0	26.9	0.0	26.9	0.0	26.9	0.0	26.9	0.0	26.9	0.0	26.9	0.0	27.1	0.7	27.4	1.1	27.4	0.0
1955	27.4	0.0	27.4	0.0	27.4	0.0	27.4	0.0	27.4	0.0	27.6	0.7	27.7	0.4	28.6	3.2	29.0	1.4	29.2	0.7	29.2	0.0	29.2	0.0
1956	29.3	0.3	29.5	0.7	29.5	0.0	29.5	0.0	29.5	0.0	29.5	0.0	29.6	0.3	31.1	5.1	31.3	0.6	31.3	0.0	31.3	0.0	31.3	0.0
1957	31.3	0.0	31.3	0.0	31.3	0.0	31.4	0.3	31.4	0.0	31.4	0.0	32.7	4.1	32.7	0.0	32.7	0.0	32.7	0.0	32.8	0.3	32.8	0.0
1958	32.8	0.0	32.8	0.0	32.8	0.0	32.8	0.0	32.8	0.0	32.8	0.0	33.0	0.6	33.0	0.0	33.0	0.0	33.0	0.0	33.0	0.0	33.0	0.0
1959	33.0	0.0	33.0	0.0	33.0	0.0	33.0	0.0	33.0	0.0	33.0	0.0	33.1	0.3	33.1	0.0	33.1	0.0	33.1	0.0	33.1	0.0	33.1	0.0
1960	33.2	0.3	33.2	0.0	33.4	0.6	33.4	0.0	33.4	0.0	33.4	0.0	33.5	0.3	33.5	0.0	33.5	0.0	33.5	0.0	33.5	0.0	33.5	0.0
1961	33.2	-0.9	33.2	0.0	33.2	0.0	33.2	0.0	33.2	0.0	33.2	0.0	33.2	0.0	33.2	0.0	33.4	0.6	33.4	0.0	33.4	0.0	33.4	0.0
1962	33.4	0.0	33.4	0.0	33.4	0.0	33.4	0.0	33.4	0.0	33.4	0.0	33.5	0.3	33.5	0.0	33.5	0.0	33.5	0.0	33.5	0.0	33.4	-0.3
1963	33.4	0.0	33.4	0.0	33.4	0.0	33.4	0.0	33.4	0.0	33.6	0.0	33.6	0.0	33.7	0.3	33.7	0.0	33.7	0.0	33.7	0.0	33.7	0.0
1964	33.7	0.0	33.7	0.0	33.7	0.0	33.7	0.0	33.7	0.0	33.7	0.0	33.7	0.0	33.7	0.0	33.7	0.0	33.7	0.0	33.7	0.0	33.8	0.3
1965	33.8	0.0	33.8	0.0	33.8	0.0	33.8	0.0	33.9	0.3	33.9	0.0	33.9	0.0	33.9	0.0	33.9	0.0	33.9	0.0	34.0	0.3	34.0	0.0
1966	34.0	0.0	34.0	0.0	34.0	0.0	34.0	0.0	34.4	1.2	34.4	0.0	34.6	0.6	34.6	0.0	34.6	0.0	35.1	1.4	35.3	0.6	35.5	0.6
1967	35.5	0.0	35.7	0.6	35.7	0.0	35.7	0.0	36.6	2.5	36.6	0.0	36.6	0.0	36.6	0.0	36.6	0.0	36.6	0.0	36.7	0.3	36.8	0.3
1968	37.1	0.8	37.1	0.0	37.2	0.3	37.4	0.5	37.6	0.5	37.8	0.5	37.9	0.3	37.9	0.0	37.9	0.0	38.1	0.5	38.1	0.0	38.2	0.3
1969	38.2	0.0	38.3	0.3	38.5	0.5	38.5	0.0	38.9	1.0	39.0	0.3	39.1	0.3	39.1	0.0	39.8	1.8	40.0	0.5	40.5	1.3	40.5	0.0
1970	40.7	0.5	40.7	0.0	40.9	0.5	40.9	0.0	40.9	0.0	41.7	2.0	41.7	0.0	42.0	0.7	42.0	0.0	42.1	0.2	42.7	1.4	42.7	0.0
1971	42.7	0.0	42.9	0.5	42.9	0.0	42.9	0.0	42.9	0.0	42.9	0.0	42.9	0.0	42.9	0.0	42.9	0.0	42.9	0.0	42.9	0.0	42.9	0.0
1972	42.9	0.0	42.9	0.0	43.1	0.5	43.3	0.5	43.3	0.0	43.4	0.2	43.5	0.2	43.5	0.0	44.0	1.1	44.2	0.5	44.8	1.4	44.8	0.0
1973	44.9	0.2	44.9	0.0	44.9	0.0	44.9	0.0	47.4	5.6	47.4	0.0	47.4	0.0	48.0	1.3	48.2	0.4	48.5	0.6	48.6	0.2	48.6	0.0
1974	49.5	1.9	50.5	2.0	51.0	1.0	51.4	0.8	52.3	1.8	53.5	2.3	55.5	3.7	56.7	2.2	60.4	6.5	60.6	0.3	61.3	1.2	61.3	0.0
1975	60.5	-1.3	60.4	-0.2	60.3	-0.2	60.3	0.0	60.3	0.0	60.3	0.0	60.3	0.0	60.8	0.8	60.8	0.0	61.3	0.8	60.6	-1.1	60.6	0.0
1976	60.9	0.5	61.5	1.0	61.6	0.2	62.5	1.5	63.0	0.8	63.3	0.5	63.5	0.3	63.7	0.3	63.7	0.0	64.0	0.5	64.0	0.0	64.0	0.0
1977	64.3	0.5	64.7	0.6	64.9	0.3	66.5	2.5	67.1	0.9	67.8	1.0	66.9	-1.3	69.3	3.6	69.2	-0.1	69.2	0.0	69.8	0.9	69.8	0.0
1978	70.7	1.3	70.8	0.1	72.2	2.0	72.8	0.8	72.8	0.0	72.8	0.0	73.7	1.2	74.0	0.4	73.9	-0.1	74.2	0.4	74.4	0.3	75.2	1.1
1979	77.8	3.5	80.3	3.2	80.3	0.0	80.5	0.2	80.5	0.0	80.5	0.0	80.8	0.4	80.8	0.0	80.8	0.0	81.1	0.4	81.1	0.0	81.7	0.7
1980	82.4	0.9	84.0	1.9	84.5	0.6	84.8	0.4	84.9	0.1	85.5	0.7	86.1	0.7	86.1	0.0	86.3	0.2	87.6	1.5	87.9	0.3	88.0	0.1
1981	89.6	1.8	91.3	1.9	92.0	0.8	92.4	0.4	93.5	1.2	93.6	0.1	93.9	0.3	94.1	0.2	94.9	0.9	95.2	0.3	95.6	0.4	95.8	0.2
1982	96.8	1.0	98.4	1.7	99.3	0.9	99.5	0.2	99.9	0.4	100.2	0.3	100.7	0.5	100.9	0.2	101.0	0.1	101.0	0.0	101.1	0.1	101.1	0.0
1983	102.0	0.9	102.4	0.4	103.5	1.1	103.9	0.4	103.8	-0.1	104.1	0.3	104.3	0.2	104.0	-0.3	104.3	0.3	104.3	0.0	105.2	0.9	105.1	-0.1
1984	106.5	1.3	107.0	0.5	107.0	0.0	107.5	0.5	107.9	0.4	107.8	-0.1	108.2	0.4	108.3	0.1	108.0	-0.3	107.9	-0.1	109.1	1.1	108.8	-0.3
1985	109.0	0.2	109.9	0.8	110.2	0.3	111.2	0.9	111.4	0.2	111.7	0.3	112.5	0.7	112.9	0.4	113.1	0.2	112.9	-0.2	113.9	0.9	113.9	0.0
1986	114.2	0.3	114.2	0.0	114.2	0.0	114.9	0.6	114.9	0.0	115.3	0.3	115.5	0.2	115.4	-0.1	115.5	0.1	116.2	0.6	116.7	0.4	116.5	-0.2
1987	116.9	0.3	117.1	0.2	117.5	0.3	118.2	0.6	118.4	0.2	118.6	0.2	118.6	0.0	118.9	0.3	119.1	0.2	119.7	0.5	119.9	0.2	120.0	0.1
1988	121.2	1.0	121.4	0.2	122.7	1.1	123.5	0.7	123.8	0.2	123.8	0.0	125.0	1.0	125.2	0.2	125.8	0.5	125.7	-0.1	125.9	0.2	126.5	0.5
1989	126.9	0.3	126.9	0.0	127.4	0.4	127.7	0.2	128.2	0.4	128.6	0.3	129.3	0.5	130.1	0.6	130.8	0.5	130.6	-0.2	130.8	0.2	130.8	0.0
1990	131.8	0.8	132.4	0.5	132.4	0.0	132.7	0.2	133.2	0.4	133.4	0.2	133.5	0.1	133.7	0.1	133.9	0.1	134.3	0.3	134.6	0.2	135.4	0.6
1991	135.9	0.4	136.4	0.4	135.9	-0.4	135.8	-0.1	136.1	0.2	136.1	0.0	136.2	0.1	136.2	0.0	136.3	0.1	136.5	0.1	136.6	0.1	136.6	0.0

[Continued]

Commercial Furniture
Producer Price Index
Base 1982 = 100
[Continued]

For 1947-1997. Columns headed % show percentile change in the index from the previous period for which an index is available.

Year	Jan Index	%	Feb Index	%	Mar Index	%	Apr Index	%	May Index	%	Jun Index	%	Jul Index	%	Aug Index	%	Sep Index	%	Oct Index	%	Nov Index	%	Dec Index	%
1992	137.0	0.3	137.2	0.1	137.3	0.1	137.9	0.4	138.0	0.1	138.1	0.1	137.8	-0.2	138.2	0.3	138.5	0.2	138.5	0.0	139.1	0.4	139.3	0.1
1993	139.2	-0.1	139.8	0.4	139.6	-0.1	140.1	0.4	140.3	0.1	140.5	0.1	140.8	0.2	141.0	0.1	140.7	-0.2	140.8	0.1	141.0	0.1	141.8	0.6
1994	143.2	1.0	143.5	0.2	143.6	0.1	144.5	0.6	145.3	0.6	145.2	-0.1	145.6	0.3	145.3	-0.2	144.8	-0.3	144.5	-0.2	145.2	0.5	145.4	0.1
1995	146.2	0.6	146.6	0.3	146.6	0.0	147.8	0.8	147.4	-0.3	148.1	0.5	148.0	-0.1	148.9	0.6	148.5	-0.3	149.6	0.7	150.2	0.4	150.4	0.1
1996	150.6	0.1	151.4	0.5	150.9	-0.3	151.3	0.3	150.7	-0.4	151.1	0.3	151.8	0.5	151.5	-0.2	151.8	0.2	153.0	0.8	153.2	0.1	153.4	0.1
1997	153.6	0.1	153.4	-0.1	153.2	-0.1	153.9	0.5	154.3	0.3	154.2	-0.1	154.7	0.3	154.3	-0.3	154.7	0.3	154.4	-0.2	155.0	0.4	155.1	0.1

Source: U.S. Department of Labor, Bureau of Labor Statistics, Division of Industry Prices and Price Indexes. n.e.c. stands for not elsewhere classified. - indicates no data collected for period or unavailable.

Floor Coverings
Producer Price Index
Base 1982 = 100

For 1926-1997. Columns headed % show percentile change in the index from the previous period for which an index is available.

Year	Jan Index	%	Feb Index	%	Mar Index	%	Apr Index	%	May Index	%	Jun Index	%	Jul Index	%	Aug Index	%	Sep Index	%	Oct Index	%	Nov Index	%	Dec Index	%
1926	31.9	-	31.9	0.0	31.9	0.0	31.9	0.0	31.9	0.0	31.7	-0.6	31.7	0.0	31.7	0.0	31.7	0.0	31.7	0.0	31.7	0.0	30.3	-4.4
1927	30.3	0.0	30.3	0.0	30.1	-0.7	30.1	0.0	30.1	0.0	30.3	0.7	30.3	0.0	30.3	0.0	30.3	0.0	30.3	0.0	30.3	0.0	30.4	0.3
1928	30.4	0.0	30.4	0.0	30.4	0.0	30.4	0.0	30.4	0.0	29.1	-4.3	29.1	0.0	29.1	0.0	29.1	0.0	29.1	0.0	29.4	1.0	29.4	0.0
1929	29.4	0.0	29.4	0.0	29.4	0.0	29.4	0.0	29.4	0.0	29.4	0.0	29.7	1.0	29.7	0.0	29.7	0.0	30.2	1.7	30.2	0.0	30.3	0.3
1930	30.6	1.0	30.6	0.0	30.6	0.0	30.6	0.0	30.6	0.0	30.6	0.0	30.6	0.0	30.6	0.0	29.9	-2.3	29.9	0.0	29.9	0.0	25.6	-14.4
1931	25.6	0.0	25.6	0.0	25.6	0.0	25.6	0.0	25.6	0.0	25.6	0.0	25.6	0.0	25.6	0.0	25.6	0.0	25.6	0.0	25.6	0.0	22.7	-11.3
1932	22.7	0.0	22.7	0.0	22.7	0.0	22.7	0.0	22.9	0.9	23.0	0.4	22.8	-0.9	22.7	-0.4	22.7	0.0	22.7	0.0	22.7	0.0	22.7	0.0
1933	22.7	0.0	22.7	0.0	22.7	0.0	22.7	0.0	22.7	0.0	23.2	2.2	23.5	1.3	24.0	2.1	24.3	1.2	24.7	1.6	24.7	0.0	24.7	0.0
1934	24.7	0.0	24.7	0.0	24.7	0.0	24.7	0.0	25.4	2.8	26.7	5.1	26.7	0.0	26.7	0.0	26.7	0.0	26.1	-2.2	26.1	0.0	26.1	0.0
1935	26.2	0.4	26.2	0.0	26.2	0.0	26.2	0.0	26.2	0.0	26.2	0.0	26.2	0.0	26.2	0.0	26.2	0.0	26.2	0.0	26.2	0.0	26.2	0.0
1936	26.3	0.4	26.3	0.0	26.3	0.0	26.3	0.0	26.3	0.0	26.4	0.4	26.0	-1.5	26.0	0.0	26.1	0.4	26.3	0.8	26.3	0.0	27.1	3.0
1937	27.4	1.1	28.9	5.5	28.9	0.0	28.9	0.0	28.9	0.0	28.9	0.0	29.8	3.1	30.7	3.0	30.7	0.0	30.7	0.0	30.7	0.0	29.6	-3.6
1938	29.1	-1.7	29.1	0.0	28.7	-1.4	28.4	-1.0	28.4	0.0	28.4	0.0	28.2	-0.7	28.2	0.0	27.9	-1.1	27.0	-3.2	27.3	1.1	27.9	2.2
1939	28.1	0.7	28.1	0.0	28.1	0.0	28.1	0.0	28.1	0.0	28.1	0.0	28.0	-0.4	28.0	0.0	29.5	5.4	30.9	4.7	31.1	0.6	31.1	0.0
1940	30.8	-1.0	30.8	0.0	30.8	0.0	31.2	1.3	31.3	0.3	31.3	0.0	31.3	0.0	31.3	0.0	31.3	0.0	31.3	0.0	31.3	0.0	31.3	0.0
1941	31.3	0.0	31.3	0.0	31.5	0.6	32.0	1.6	32.2	0.6	32.5	0.9	32.5	0.0	32.5	0.0	32.5	0.0	32.5	0.0	32.5	0.0	32.5	0.0
1942	33.1	1.8	33.2	0.3	33.2	0.0	33.2	0.0	33.2	0.0	33.2	0.0	33.2	0.0	33.2	0.0	33.2	0.0	33.2	0.0	33.2	0.0	33.2	0.0
1943	33.2	0.0	33.2	0.0	33.2	0.0	33.2	0.0	33.2	0.0	33.2	0.0	33.2	0.0	33.2	0.0	33.2	0.0	33.2	0.0	33.2	0.0	33.2	0.0
1944	33.2	0.0	33.2	0.0	33.2	0.0	33.2	0.0	33.2	0.0	33.2	0.0	33.2	0.0	33.2	0.0	33.2	0.0	33.2	0.0	33.2	0.0	33.2	0.0
1945	33.1	-0.3	33.1	0.0	33.1	0.0	33.1	0.0	33.1	0.0	33.1	0.0	33.1	0.0	33.1	0.0	33.1	0.0	33.1	0.0	33.1	0.0	33.1	0.0
1946	34.3	3.6	34.8	1.5	35.3	1.4	36.3	2.8	37.0	1.9	37.0	0.0	37.0	0.0	37.0	0.0	37.3	0.8	37.4	0.3	39.0	4.3	39.9	2.3
1947	42.7	7.0	42.7	0.0	42.8	0.2	42.9	0.2	42.9	0.0	43.1	0.5	44.0	2.1	44.0	0.0	44.1	0.2	44.1	0.0	44.1	0.0	45.3	2.7
1948	45.5	0.4	45.6	0.2	45.6	0.0	45.6	0.0	45.6	0.0	46.2	1.3	46.5	0.6	46.6	0.2	47.2	1.3	47.4	0.4	47.4	0.0	47.4	0.0
1949	47.8	0.8	47.9	0.2	48.0	0.2	47.3	-1.5	47.3	0.0	46.5	-1.7	45.6	-1.9	45.6	0.0	45.5	-0.2	45.6	0.2	46.0	0.9	46.8	1.7
1950	47.4	1.3	48.2	1.7	48.4	0.4	48.5	0.2	49.6	2.3	49.6	0.0	50.4	1.6	53.9	6.9	55.3	2.6	57.9	4.7	58.3	0.7	60.3	3.4
1951	63.0	4.5	64.0	1.6	66.6	4.1	68.0	2.1	68.0	0.0	66.9	-1.6	64.8	-3.1	60.8	-6.2	58.4	-3.9	57.7	-1.2	57.1	-1.0	57.5	0.7
1952	57.5	0.0	57.6	0.2	57.4	-0.3	57.7	0.5	55.0	-4.7	54.2	-1.5	54.2	0.0	54.1	-0.2	55.7	3.0	55.7	0.0	55.7	0.0	55.9	0.4
1953	56.5	1.1	56.5	0.0	56.5	0.0	56.5	0.0	56.9	0.7	56.8	-0.2	57.0	0.4	57.0	0.0	57.0	0.0	57.0	0.0	56.9	-0.2	56.8	-0.2
1954	55.8	-1.8	55.7	-0.2	55.8	0.2	55.8	0.0	55.8	0.0	55.8	0.0	55.9	0.2	56.2	0.5	56.6	0.7	56.4	-0.4	56.4	0.0	56.4	0.0
1955	56.5	0.2	56.6	0.2	56.6	0.0	56.9	0.5	56.9	0.0	57.5	1.1	57.7	0.3	57.7	0.0	58.3	1.0	58.6	0.5	58.6	0.0	58.8	0.3
1956	59.4	1.0	59.4	0.0	59.4	0.0	59.4	0.0	59.4	0.0	59.4	0.0	59.8	0.7	59.8	0.0	60.1	0.5	60.0	-0.2	60.1	0.2	60.1	0.0
1957	61.4	2.2	61.1	-0.5	61.1	0.0	60.9	-0.3	60.9	0.0	60.9	0.0	60.3	-1.0	60.3	0.0	60.3	0.0	60.3	0.0	60.3	0.0	60.3	0.0
1958	59.8	-0.8	59.1	-1.2	58.8	-0.5	58.5	-0.5	58.5	0.0	58.2	-0.5	57.7	-0.9	57.7	0.0	57.5	-0.3	57.4	-0.2	57.4	0.0	57.4	0.0
1959	57.4	0.0	57.5	0.2	57.9	0.7	58.1	0.3	58.1	0.0	58.3	0.3	58.5	0.3	58.5	0.0	58.7	0.3	58.8	0.2	58.8	0.0	58.7	-0.2
1960	59.0	0.5	59.0	0.0	59.5	0.8	59.5	0.0	59.5	0.0	59.5	0.0	59.5	0.0	59.5	0.0	59.5	0.0	59.4	-0.2	59.4	0.0	59.3	-0.2	59.3	0.0
1961	58.6	-1.2	58.5	-0.2	58.5	0.0	58.5	0.0	58.5	0.0	58.5	0.0	58.8	0.5	58.8	0.0	58.8	0.0	58.7	-0.2	58.7	0.0	58.6	-0.2
1962	58.4	-0.3	57.2	-2.1	57.2	0.0	57.2	0.0	57.2	0.0	57.2	0.0	57.1	-0.2	57.1	0.0	57.1	0.0	57.1	0.0	57.1	0.0	56.9	-0.4
1963	56.8	-0.2	56.6	-0.4	56.7	0.2	56.6	-0.2	56.5	-0.2	56.6	0.2	57.0	0.7	57.0	0.0	57.1	0.2	57.5	0.7	57.8	0.5	57.9	0.2
1964	59.1	2.1	59.1	0.0	59.1	0.0	59.1	0.0	58.9	-0.3	58.2	-1.2	58.5	0.5	58.5	0.0	58.5	0.0	58.5	0.0	58.5	0.0	58.5	0.0
1965	57.9	-1.0	57.9	0.0	57.8	-0.2	57.7	-0.2	57.7	0.0	57.7	0.0	57.7	0.0	57.6	-0.2	57.6	0.0	57.5	-0.2	57.5	0.0	57.6	0.2
1966	57.7	0.2	57.7	0.0	57.6	-0.2	57.6	0.0	57.6	0.0	57.4	-0.3	57.1	-0.5	57.0	-0.2	57.0	0.0	57.0	0.0	57.0	0.0	56.8	-0.4
1967	55.5	-2.3	55.0	-0.9	55.2	0.4	54.9	-0.5	54.9	0.0	54.9	0.0	54.5	-0.7	54.5	0.0	55.0	0.9	55.9	1.6	55.9	0.0	56.1	0.4
1968	56.1	0.0	56.0	-0.2	56.0	0.0	56.0	0.0	56.0	0.0	55.8	-0.4	55.7	-0.5	55.8	0.2	56.0	0.4	55.9	-0.2	55.9	0.0	55.9	0.0
1969	56.3	0.7	56.4	0.2	56.3	-0.2	56.0	-0.5	55.8	-0.4	55.3	-0.9	54.9	-0.7	54.9	0.0	54.9	0.0	54.9	0.0	54.9	0.0	54.9	0.0
1970	55.1	0.4	55.1	0.0	55.0	-0.2	55.0	0.0	54.7	-0.5	54.5	-0.4	54.9	0.7	54.7	-0.4	54.7	0.0	54.9	0.4	54.9	0.0	55.0	0.2

[Continued]

Floor Coverings
Producer Price Index
Base 1982 = 100
[Continued]

For 1926-1997. Columns headed % show percentile change in the index from the previous period for which an index is available.

Year	Jan Index	%	Feb Index	%	Mar Index	%	Apr Index	%	May Index	%	Jun Index	%	Jul Index	%	Aug Index	%	Sep Index	%	Oct Index	%	Nov Index	%	Dec Index	%
1971	55.7	1.3	55.5	-0.4	55.4	-0.2	55.2	-0.4	55.2	0.0	54.2	-1.8	54.2	0.0	53.9	-0.6	53.9	0.0	53.9	0.0	53.9	0.0	54.1	0.4
1972	54.2	0.2	54.2	0.0	54.2	0.0	54.2	0.0	54.2	0.0	54.4	0.4	54.5	0.2	54.5	0.0	54.7	0.4	54.7	0.0	54.7	0.0	54.7	0.0
1973	55.0	0.5	55.7	1.3	55.8	0.2	56.1	0.5	56.6	0.9	56.7	0.2	56.7	0.0	56.7	0.0	56.6	-0.2	57.1	0.9	57.1	0.0	57.2	0.2
1974	58.6	2.4	59.0	0.7	59.4	0.7	61.0	2.7	61.4	0.7	63.2	2.9	64.0	1.3	65.8	2.8	67.6	2.7	68.1	0.7	68.2	0.1	68.6	0.6
1975	68.4	-0.3	68.2	-0.3	68.2	0.0	68.1	-0.1	67.9	-0.3	67.9	0.0	68.4	0.7	69.9	2.2	70.0	0.1	70.0	0.0	70.0	0.0	70.2	0.3
1976	72.1	2.7	72.4	0.4	72.4	0.0	72.4	0.0	72.4	0.0	72.5	0.1	72.5	0.0	72.6	0.1	72.6	0.0	72.6	0.0	72.6	0.0	72.8	0.3
1977	74.8	2.7	74.8	0.0	74.8	0.0	74.8	0.0	74.8	0.0	75.0	0.3	75.2	0.3	75.4	0.3	75.4	0.0	75.7	0.4	76.3	0.8	76.4	0.1
1978	77.2	1.0	77.2	0.0	77.3	0.1	78.2	1.2	78.3	0.1	78.6	0.4	78.7	0.1	78.7	0.0	78.6	-0.1	78.4	-0.3	78.4	0.0	78.5	0.1
1979	79.1	0.8	79.3	0.3	79.5	0.3	79.7	0.3	80.6	1.1	80.9	0.4	82.3	1.7	82.8	0.6	83.0	0.2	84.0	1.2	84.4	0.5	84.4	0.0
1980	87.8	4.0	87.5	-0.3	88.8	1.5	89.5	0.8	89.4	-0.1	89.5	0.1	90.1	0.7	90.4	0.3	90.5	0.1	90.7	0.2	91.4	0.8	94.2	3.1
1981	95.1	1.0	94.9	-0.2	96.1	1.3	96.8	0.7	99.1	2.4	99.8	0.7	100.9	1.1	100.4	-0.5	100.3	-0.1	99.9	-0.4	100.6	0.7	100.2	-0.4
1982	99.5	-0.7	99.7	0.2	99.7	0.0	100.0	0.3	100.1	0.1	100.4	0.3	100.0	-0.4	99.9	-0.1	100.2	0.3	100.2	0.0	100.1	-0.1	100.2	0.1
1983	100.6	0.4	100.5	-0.1	100.4	-0.1	100.6	0.2	100.5	-0.1	100.2	-0.3	103.0	2.8	104.3	1.3	104.6	0.3	104.6	0.0	104.5	-0.1	104.5	0.0
1984	103.9	-0.6	104.0	0.1	103.9	-0.1	103.9	0.0	105.8	1.8	106.4	0.6	106.4	0.0	106.3	-0.1	106.3	0.0	106.5	0.2	106.5	0.0	106.7	0.2
1985	106.9	0.2	106.2	-0.7	106.4	0.2	106.5	0.1	105.7	-0.8	104.8	-0.9	105.2	0.4	104.9	-0.3	105.2	0.3	104.9	-0.3	105.2	0.3	105.3	0.1
1986	107.4	2.0	107.7	0.3	107.7	0.0	107.8	0.1	108.1	0.3	108.6	0.5	108.1	-0.5	108.3	0.2	108.4	0.1	109.0	0.6	109.3	0.3	109.2	-0.1
1987	109.9	0.6	109.8	-0.1	109.2	-0.5	109.4	0.2	109.9	0.5	110.2	0.3	111.1	0.8	111.5	0.4	111.6	0.1	112.0	0.4	111.9	-0.1	111.6	-0.3
1988	112.7	1.0	113.1	0.4	112.9	-0.2	113.6	0.6	114.0	0.4	113.8	-0.2	114.7	0.8	115.4	0.6	116.0	0.5	116.5	0.4	117.1	0.5	117.0	-0.1
1989	117.5	0.4	116.7	-0.7	117.3	0.5	117.3	0.0	116.9	-0.3	117.9	0.9	118.6	0.6	119.0	0.3	117.5	-1.3	117.0	-0.4	117.4	0.3	117.7	0.3
1990	117.7	0.0	118.3	0.5	119.3	0.8	119.5	0.2	119.6	0.1	119.4	-0.2	119.4	0.0	119.2	-0.2	118.8	-0.3	118.6	-0.2	119.1	0.4	119.5	0.3
1991	120.3	0.7	121.4	0.9	120.9	-0.4	120.7	-0.2	120.5	-0.2	120.1	-0.3	120.1	0.0	120.1	0.0	119.9	-0.2	120.2	0.3	120.4	0.2	120.3	-0.1
1992	120.1	-0.2	120.1	0.0	119.5	-0.5	119.7	0.2	120.4	0.6	120.8	0.3	121.0	0.2	120.7	-0.2	120.5	-0.2	120.5	0.0	120.2	-0.2	120.2	0.0
1993	119.4	-0.7	119.5	0.1	119.5	0.0	119.4	-0.1	119.2	-0.2	119.1	-0.1	120.0	0.8	120.8	0.7	121.2	0.3	121.3	0.1	121.4	0.1	121.2	-0.2
1994	121.4	0.2	121.3	-0.1	120.9	-0.3	121.1	0.2	121.0	-0.1	121.3	0.2	121.9	0.5	121.8	-0.1	121.2	-0.5	121.7	0.4	122.4	0.6	122.2	-0.2
1995	122.6	0.3	122.9	0.2	122.7	-0.2	123.1	0.3	123.8	0.6	123.3	-0.4	123.5	0.2	123.6	0.1	124.0	0.3	125.1	0.9	124.8	-0.2	125.0	0.2
1996	124.9	-0.1	125.2	0.2	125.8	0.5	124.8	-0.8	126.4	1.3	125.6	-0.6	126.8	1.0	127.3	0.4	128.0	0.5	128.1	0.1	128.2	0.1	127.8	-0.3
1997	127.8	0.0	128.8	0.8	129.0	0.2	125.8	-2.5	126.7	0.7	126.9	0.2	128.5	1.3	128.5	0.0	128.4	-0.1	127.9	-0.4	127.2	-0.5	127.6	0.3

Source: U.S. Department of Labor, Bureau of Labor Statistics, Division of Industry Prices and Price Indexes. n.e.c. stands for not elsewhere classified. - indicates no data collected for period or unavailable.

Household Appliances
Producer Price Index
Base 1982 = 100

For 1947-1997. Columns headed % show percentile change in the index from the previous period for which an index is available.

Year	Jan Index	%	Feb Index	%	Mar Index	%	Apr Index	%	May Index	%	Jun Index	%	Jul Index	%	Aug Index	%	Sep Index	%	Oct Index	%	Nov Index	%	Dec Index	%
1947	50.3	-	50.4	0.2	50.5	0.2	50.6	0.2	50.8	0.4	51.1	0.6	51.5	0.8	51.7	0.4	52.3	1.2	52.7	0.8	52.9	0.4	53.2	0.6
1948	53.1	-0.2	53.1	0.0	53.1	0.0	53.2	0.2	53.0	-0.4	53.1	0.2	54.0	1.7	54.3	0.6	54.7	0.7	55.4	1.3	55.5	0.2	55.5	0.0
1949	54.6	-1.6	54.6	0.0	54.4	-0.4	54.1	-0.6	53.7	-0.7	53.5	-0.4	53.4	-0.2	53.2	-0.4	53.2	0.0	53.1	-0.2	53.1	0.0	53.1	0.0
1950	53.1	0.0	53.0	-0.2	53.0	0.0	53.2	0.4	53.2	0.0	53.1	-0.2	53.2	0.2	53.8	1.1	54.7	1.7	55.5	1.5	56.0	0.9	56.7	1.3
1951	57.1	0.7	57.3	0.4	57.3	0.0	57.3	0.0	57.3	0.0	57.4	0.2	57.1	-0.5	57.1	0.0	57.3	0.4	57.3	0.0	57.3	0.0	57.4	0.2
1952	57.3	-0.2	57.3	0.0	57.0	-0.5	57.2	0.4	56.9	-0.5	56.7	-0.4	56.7	0.0	56.7	0.0	56.9	0.4	56.9	0.0	56.9	0.0	57.0	0.2
1953	57.0	0.0	57.0	0.0	57.3	0.5	57.3	0.0	57.4	0.2	57.4	0.0	57.8	0.7	57.8	0.0	57.9	0.2	57.9	0.0	57.9	0.0	57.9	0.0
1954	58.1	0.3	58.2	0.2	58.1	-0.2	58.3	0.3	58.3	0.0	58.3	0.0	58.2	-0.2	58.2	0.0	58.0	-0.3	58.1	0.2	57.9	-0.3	58.0	0.2
1955	57.7	-0.5	57.6	-0.2	56.9	-1.2	56.9	0.0	56.5	-0.7	56.5	0.0	56.5	0.0	56.6	0.2	56.4	-0.4	56.3	-0.2	56.4	0.2	56.2	-0.4
1956	56.0	-0.4	56.1	0.2	55.9	-0.4	55.8	-0.2	55.8	0.0	55.8	0.0	55.4	-0.7	55.8	0.7	56.0	0.4	56.5	0.9	56.5	0.0	56.2	-0.5
1957	56.5	0.5	56.7	0.4	56.7	0.0	55.9	-1.4	55.8	-0.2	55.8	0.0	55.7	-0.2	55.6	-0.2	55.5	-0.2	55.9	0.7	55.8	-0.2	55.9	0.2
1958	55.9	0.0	55.9	0.0	55.9	0.0	55.9	0.0	55.7	-0.4	55.7	0.0	55.7	0.0	55.6	-0.2	55.2	-0.7	55.3	0.2	55.1	-0.4	55.1	0.0
1959	55.8	1.3	55.8	0.0	55.8	0.0	55.8	0.0	55.8	0.0	55.8	0.0	55.4	-0.7	55.4	0.0	55.4	0.0	55.2	-0.4	55.3	0.2	55.0	-0.5
1960	54.8	-0.4	54.8	0.0	54.7	-0.2	54.7	0.0	54.2	-0.9	53.9	-0.6	53.9	0.0	53.6	-0.6	53.5	-0.2	53.5	0.0	53.4	-0.2	53.3	-0.2
1961	53.2	-0.2	53.2	0.0	53.1	-0.2	53.1	0.0	53.0	-0.2	52.9	-0.2	52.9	0.0	52.9	0.0	52.9	0.0	53.0	0.2	52.9	-0.2	52.8	-0.2
1962	52.9	0.2	52.9	0.0	52.8	-0.2	52.7	-0.2	52.5	-0.4	52.5	0.0	52.3	-0.4	52.0	-0.6	51.9	-0.2	51.8	-0.2	51.8	0.0	51.8	0.0
1963	51.4	-0.8	51.4	0.0	51.4	0.0	51.3	-0.2	51.2	-0.2	51.2	0.0	51.1	-0.2	51.1	0.0	50.9	-0.4	50.8	-0.2	50.8	0.0	50.7	-0.2
1964	50.9	0.4	51.1	0.4	51.1	0.0	51.0	-0.2	51.0	0.0	50.8	-0.4	50.8	0.0	50.8	0.0	50.7	-0.2	50.8	0.2	50.5	-0.6	50.4	-0.2
1965	50.2	-0.4	50.1	-0.2	50.1	0.0	49.8	-0.6	49.7	-0.2	49.8	0.2	49.7	-0.2	49.3	-0.8	49.3	0.0	49.3	0.0	49.3	0.0	49.4	0.2
1966	49.6	0.4	49.6	0.0	49.6	0.0	49.7	0.2	49.8	0.2	49.8	0.0	49.6	-0.4	49.4	-0.4	49.4	0.0	49.5	0.2	49.7	0.4	49.7	0.0
1967	49.9	0.4	50.0	0.2	50.0	0.0	50.1	0.2	50.0	-0.2	50.2	0.4	50.3	0.2	50.2	-0.2	50.3	0.2	50.4	0.2	50.6	0.4	50.6	0.0
1968	50.7	0.2	50.9	0.4	51.1	0.4	51.2	0.2	51.1	-0.2	51.0	-0.2	51.2	0.4	51.3	0.2	51.3	0.0	51.4	0.2	51.2	-0.4	51.3	0.2
1969	51.4	0.2	51.6	0.4	51.6	0.0	51.6	0.0	51.6	0.0	51.6	0.0	51.6	0.0	51.6	0.0	51.8	0.4	51.9	0.2	51.9	0.0	52.1	0.4
1970	52.7	1.2	52.6	-0.2	52.6	0.0	52.8	0.4	52.7	-0.2	52.7	0.0	52.8	0.2	52.9	0.2	52.9	0.0	53.2	0.6	53.3	0.2	53.3	0.0
1971	53.8	0.9	53.9	0.2	54.0	0.2	53.9	-0.2	53.9	0.0	53.9	0.0	54.1	0.4	54.2	0.2	54.2	0.0	54.2	0.0	54.1	-0.2	54.1	0.0
1972	53.7	-0.7	54.0	0.6	53.9	-0.2	54.0	0.2	53.9	-0.2	53.8	-0.2	53.9	0.2	54.1	0.4	54.3	0.4	54.2	-0.2	54.2	0.0	54.2	0.0
1973	54.1	-0.2	54.3	0.4	54.4	0.2	54.4	0.0	54.2	-0.4	53.9	-0.6	54.1	0.4	54.7	1.1	54.7	0.0	54.8	0.2	55.0	0.4	55.2	0.4
1974	55.9	1.3	56.1	0.4	56.5	0.7	56.9	0.7	57.3	0.7	58.0	1.2	58.6	1.0	59.4	1.4	60.7	2.2	62.8	3.5	63.7	1.4	64.6	1.4
1975	65.3	1.1	65.6	0.5	65.3	-0.5	65.6	0.5	65.8	0.3	66.4	0.9	66.4	0.0	66.5	0.2	67.1	0.9	67.4	0.4	68.0	0.9	68.2	0.3
1976	68.5	0.4	69.0	0.7	69.5	0.7	69.7	0.3	69.7	0.0	69.9	0.3	70.2	0.4	70.3	0.1	70.4	0.1	70.5	0.1	70.6	0.1	70.8	0.3
1977	71.0	0.3	71.4	0.6	71.8	0.6	72.0	0.3	72.0	0.0	72.7	1.0	73.2	0.7	73.6	0.5	74.1	0.7	74.2	0.1	74.3	0.1	74.3	0.0
1978	75.1	1.1	75.2	0.1	75.9	0.9	76.5	0.8	76.6	0.1	76.7	0.1	77.1	0.5	77.4	0.4	77.4	0.0	77.6	0.3	78.2	0.8	78.2	0.0
1979	78.9	0.9	79.5	0.8	79.8	0.4	79.7	-0.1	80.0	0.4	80.4	0.5	80.9	0.6	81.5	0.7	81.7	0.2	82.0	0.4	82.6	0.7	83.0	0.5
1980	83.6	0.7	84.8	1.4	85.3	0.6	85.9	0.7	87.0	1.3	88.1	1.3	88.3	0.2	88.5	0.2	89.0	0.6	89.2	0.2	89.6	0.4	90.1	0.6
1981	91.5	1.6	92.2	0.8	92.5	0.3	93.0	0.5	93.2	0.2	93.5	0.3	94.8	1.4	95.0	0.2	95.5	0.5	95.8	0.3	95.9	0.1	96.1	0.2
1982	97.1	1.0	98.1	1.0	99.1	1.0	99.3	0.2	99.9	0.6	100.2	0.3	100.6	0.4	101.0	0.4	101.1	0.1	101.1	0.0	101.1	0.0	101.3	0.2
1983	102.4	1.1	102.9	0.5	103.0	0.1	103.6	0.6	104.2	0.6	104.2	0.0	104.4	0.2	104.3	-0.1	104.5	0.2	104.3	-0.2	104.5	0.2	104.7	0.2
1984	105.4	0.7	105.8	0.4	106.0	0.2	105.9	-0.1	105.9	0.0	106.1	0.2	106.2	0.1	106.5	0.3	106.3	-0.2	106.0	-0.3	106.0	0.0	106.1	0.1
1985	106.1	0.0	106.1	0.0	106.3	0.2	106.5	0.2	106.7	0.2	106.8	0.1	107.1	0.3	107.2	0.1	107.0	-0.2	107.0	0.0	106.9	-0.1	106.6	-0.3
1986	105.5	-1.0	105.6	0.1	105.8	0.2	106.1	0.3	106.4	0.3	105.9	-0.5	105.9	0.0	105.6	-0.3	105.5	-0.1	105.4	-0.1	105.2	-0.2	105.0	-0.2
1987	105.2	0.2	105.3	0.1	105.6	0.3	105.7	0.1	105.8	0.1	105.8	0.0	106.0	0.2	105.8	-0.2	105.5	-0.3	105.4	-0.1	105.7	0.3	105.2	-0.5
1988	105.5	0.3	106.0	0.5	106.2	0.2	106.2	0.0	106.3	0.1	106.1	-0.2	105.6	-0.5	105.6	0.0	105.8	0.2	106.0	0.2	106.5	0.5	106.2	-0.3
1989	107.0	0.8	107.3	0.3	107.6	0.3	107.7	0.1	108.1	0.4	108.5	0.4	109.2	0.6	109.3	0.1	109.7	0.4	110.0	0.3	110.0	0.0	110.1	0.1
1990	110.5	0.4	110.6	0.1	110.7	0.1	110.9	0.2	110.4	-0.5	111.0	0.5	110.7	-0.3	110.8	0.1	110.9	0.1	110.9	0.0	111.0	0.1	110.9	-0.1
1991	111.6	0.6	111.3	-0.3	111.3	0.0	111.4	0.1	111.5	0.1	111.3	-0.2	111.3	0.0	111.4	0.1	111.3	-0.1	111.3	0.0	111.2	-0.1	111.0	-0.2

[Continued]

Household Appliances
Producer Price Index
Base 1982 = 100
[Continued]

For 1947-1997. Columns headed % show percentile change in the index from the previous period for which an index is available.

Year	Jan		Feb		Mar		Apr		May		Jun		Jul		Aug		Sep		Oct		Nov		Dec	
	Index	%	Index	%	Index	%	Index	%	Index	%	Index	%	Index	%	Index	%	Index	%	Index	%	Index	%	Index	%
1992	111.2	0.2	111.1	-0.1	111.1	0.0	111.4	0.3	111.3	-0.1	111.2	-0.1	111.2	0.0	111.2	0.0	111.3	0.1	111.6	0.3	112.3	0.6	111.8	-0.4
1993	112.0	0.2	112.3	0.3	112.5	0.2	112.8	0.3	113.0	0.2	113.4	0.4	113.4	0.0	113.4	0.0	113.4	0.0	113.0	-0.4	113.0	0.0	112.7	-0.3
1994	112.8	0.1	112.8	0.0	113.0	0.2	113.1	0.1	113.2	0.1	112.9	-0.3	112.9	0.0	112.7	-0.2	112.7	0.0	112.9	0.2	112.7	-0.2	112.4	-0.3
1995	112.3	-0.1	112.3	0.0	112.1	-0.2	112.4	0.3	112.4	0.0	112.2	-0.2	112.3	0.1	112.2	-0.1	112.6	0.4	112.6	0.0	112.7	0.1	112.5	-0.2
1996	112.4	-0.1	112.5	0.1	112.6	0.1	113.0	0.4	113.1	0.1	113.1	0.0	113.0	-0.1	113.0	0.0	112.5	-0.4	112.4	-0.1	112.4	0.0	111.9	-0.4
1997	111.5	-0.4	111.0	-0.4	111.1	0.1	110.4	-0.6	110.5	0.1	110.4	-0.1	110.0	-0.4	109.7	-0.3	109.4	-0.3	109.4	0.0	109.3	-0.1	109.0	-0.3

Source: U.S. Department of Labor, Bureau of Labor Statistics, Division of Industry Prices and Price Indexes. n.e.c. stands for not elsewhere classified. - indicates no data collected for period or unavailable.

Home Electronic Equipment
Producer Price Index
Base 1982 = 100

For 1947-1997. Columns headed % show percentile change in the index from the previous period for which an index is available.

Year	Jan Index	%	Feb Index	%	Mar Index	%	Apr Index	%	May Index	%	Jun Index	%	Jul Index	%	Aug Index	%	Sep Index	%	Oct Index	%	Nov Index	%	Dec Index	%
1947	140.1	-	140.5	0.3	140.5	0.0	140.5	0.0	140.5	0.0	140.5	0.0	140.5	0.0	140.8	0.2	142.3	1.1	142.3	0.0	142.3	0.0	142.3	0.0
1948	142.1	-0.1	142.1	0.0	142.1	0.0	141.6	-0.4	141.6	0.0	143.8	1.6	143.8	0.0	143.8	0.0	152.6	6.1	155.5	1.9	155.5	0.0	155.3	-0.1
1949	154.6	-0.5	154.6	0.0	154.6	0.0	154.4	-0.1	154.4	0.0	154.2	-0.1	153.5	-0.5	149.9	-2.3	149.9	0.0	146.9	-2.0	146.9	0.0	146.7	-0.1
1950	146.2	-0.3	146.7	0.3	146.7	0.0	146.7	0.0	146.7	0.0	146.4	-0.2	141.8	-3.1	131.4	-7.3	134.9	2.7	139.1	3.1	139.0	-0.1	136.4	-1.9
1951	135.7	-0.5	135.7	0.0	135.7	0.0	135.7	0.0	135.7	0.0	135.7	0.0	137.1	1.0	136.5	-0.4	136.2	-0.2	136.3	0.1	136.3	0.0	136.3	0.0
1952	136.4	0.1	136.4	0.0	132.8	-2.6	132.8	0.0	132.8	0.0	137.3	3.4	137.3	0.0	137.2	-0.1	137.2	0.0	137.2	0.0	137.3	0.1	137.3	0.0
1953	-		-		-		-		-		-		-		-		-		-		-		-	
1954	-		-		-		-		-		-		-		-		-		-		-		-	
1955	137.0	-0.2	136.5	-0.4	136.4	-0.1	136.4	0.0	136.6	0.1	136.5	-0.1	136.4	-0.1	134.9	-1.1	135.7	0.6	135.8	0.1	135.9	0.1	136.4	0.4
1956	136.4	0.0	136.6	0.1	136.6	0.0	135.9	-0.5	135.7	-0.1	135.2	-0.4	136.2	0.7	136.5	0.2	137.2	0.5	137.0	-0.1	137.0	0.0	136.6	-0.3
1957	137.0	0.3	137.0	0.0	136.4	-0.4	136.4	0.0	136.4	0.0	136.8	0.3	138.9	1.5	140.1	0.9	140.1	0.0	140.1	0.0	140.1	0.0	140.4	0.2
1958	139.7	-0.5	138.8	-0.6	138.8	0.0	138.8	0.0	138.2	-0.4	137.2	-0.7	139.1	1.4	139.0	-0.1	139.0	0.0	139.0	0.0	135.8	-2.3	135.6	-0.1
1959	136.5	0.7	136.5	0.0	135.9	-0.4	135.9	0.0	135.9	0.0	136.2	0.2	138.2	1.5	136.6	-1.2	135.8	-0.6	134.9	-0.7	134.5	-0.3	134.6	0.1
1960	134.3	-0.2	134.5	0.1	134.5	0.0	134.3	-0.1	134.3	0.0	133.9	-0.3	133.9	0.0	133.5	-0.3	133.5	0.0	132.5	-0.7	132.5	0.0	133.7	0.9
1961	133.1	-0.4	132.5	-0.5	132.8	0.2	132.8	0.0	131.6	-0.9	131.8	0.2	131.8	0.0	129.9	-1.4	129.3	-0.5	128.8	-0.4	129.0	0.2	129.0	0.0
1962	127.1	-1.5	126.1	-0.8	125.7	-0.3	125.4	-0.2	126.8	1.1	124.9	-1.5	124.8	-0.1	124.8	0.0	124.7	-0.1	124.7	0.0	124.2	-0.4	124.2	0.0
1963	123.9	-0.2	123.9	0.0	122.9	-0.8	122.9	0.0	122.2	-0.6	122.2	0.0	120.6	-1.3	120.6	0.0	120.7	0.1	120.7	0.0	120.7	0.0	120.0	-0.6
1964	119.9	-0.1	119.9	0.0	119.9	0.0	120.0	0.1	120.0	0.0	120.0	0.0	120.0	0.0	120.0	0.0	120.0	0.0	120.0	0.0	119.9	-0.1	119.0	-0.8
1965	118.8	-0.2	118.1	-0.6	118.1	0.0	118.1	0.0	118.1	0.0	118.1	0.0	116.3	-1.5	116.1	-0.2	116.1	0.0	116.2	0.1	116.2	0.0	116.2	0.0
1966	115.4	-0.7	115.3	-0.1	114.8	-0.4	114.8	0.0	114.8	0.0	114.8	0.0	114.8	0.0	114.2	-0.5	114.5	0.3	115.3	0.7	115.3	0.0	115.3	0.0
1967	114.9	-0.3	114.5	-0.3	114.5	0.0	114.5	0.0	114.0	-0.4	112.8	-1.1	112.4	-0.4	112.4	0.0	112.2	-0.2	113.4	1.1	113.6	0.2	112.9	-0.6
1968	112.9	0.0	113.0	0.1	112.7	-0.3	112.3	-0.4	112.4	0.1	111.2	-1.1	110.9	-0.3	110.9	0.0	110.8	-0.1	110.3	-0.5	109.7	-0.5	109.7	0.0
1969	108.2	-1.4	108.2	0.0	108.1	-0.1	107.8	-0.3	107.2	-0.6	107.0	-0.2	107.0	0.0	107.0	0.0	107.0	0.0	107.0	0.0	106.6	-0.4	106.6	0.0
1970	105.8	-0.8	105.8	0.0	105.8	0.0	105.8	0.0	105.6	-0.2	105.5	-0.1	105.8	0.3	106.0	0.2	106.2	0.2	106.4	0.2	107.0	0.6	106.5	-0.5
1971	106.6	0.1	106.3	-0.3	106.2	-0.1	106.1	-0.1	106.1	0.0	106.2	0.1	106.3	0.1	105.9	-0.4	105.8	-0.1	105.8	0.0	105.8	0.0	105.8	0.0
1972	105.9	0.1	105.5	-0.4	105.6	0.1	105.4	-0.2	105.5	0.1	105.2	-0.3	104.9	-0.3	104.9	0.0	105.5	0.6	105.5	0.0	105.0	-0.5	104.8	-0.2
1973	104.9	0.1	104.9	0.0	104.7	-0.2	104.7	0.0	104.7	0.0	104.0	-0.7	104.0	0.0	104.4	0.4	103.9	-0.5	103.9	0.0	103.9	0.0	103.4	-0.5
1974	103.7	0.3	103.8	0.1	104.7	0.9	104.7	0.0	105.0	0.3	105.7	0.7	106.3	0.6	106.3	0.0	106.8	0.5	106.8	0.0	107.3	0.5	107.5	0.2
1975	108.3	0.7	108.6	0.3	108.4	-0.2	104.4	-3.7	104.4	0.0	105.6	1.1	105.9	0.3	107.4	1.4	105.4	-1.9	105.4	0.0	105.4	0.0	105.4	0.0
1976	104.8	-0.6	104.1	-0.7	103.7	-0.4	103.7	0.0	103.7	0.0	103.6	-0.1	103.6	0.0	103.6	0.0	103.6	0.0	103.6	0.0	103.3	-0.3	103.2	-0.1
1977	101.8	-1.4	101.5	-0.3	101.5	0.0	100.2	-1.3	100.3	0.1	100.4	0.1	98.6	-1.8	98.6	0.0	98.1	-0.5	97.9	-0.2	98.3	0.4	98.2	-0.1
1978	101.0	2.9	100.7	-0.3	101.1	0.4	100.7	-0.4	102.2	1.5	100.5	-1.7	103.2	2.7	103.1	-0.1	104.0	0.9	103.7	-0.3	103.9	0.2	104.9	1.0
1979	104.7	-0.2	104.8	0.1	104.8	0.0	104.8	0.0	105.0	0.2	105.4	0.4	102.4	-2.8	102.4	0.0	102.5	0.1	102.5	0.0	102.6	0.1	102.8	0.2
1980	103.3	0.5	103.5	0.2	103.6	0.1	103.8	0.2	104.5	0.7	104.3	-0.2	104.1	-0.2	103.7	-0.4	104.1	0.4	103.9	-0.2	103.6	-0.3	103.4	-0.2
1981	103.4	0.0	103.7	0.3	103.7	0.0	103.3	-0.4	103.1	-0.2	98.4	-4.6	99.3	0.9	99.4	0.1	99.7	0.3	100.0	0.3	99.9	-0.1	101.8	1.9
1982	101.4	-0.4	101.7	0.3	101.2	-0.5	99.8	-1.4	100.0	0.2	100.4	0.4	99.1	-1.3	99.9	0.8	99.2	-0.7	99.7	0.5	98.8	-0.9	98.9	0.1
1983	99.2	0.3	98.8	-0.4	98.8	0.0	98.3	-0.5	98.1	-0.2	98.2	0.1	97.6	-0.6	97.1	-0.5	97.4	0.3	97.4	0.0	96.7	-0.7	95.9	-0.8
1984	95.9	0.0	95.5	-0.4	95.4	-0.1	96.4	1.0	96.0	-0.4	95.3	-0.7	95.6	0.3	95.2	-0.4	94.3	-0.9	94.4	0.1	94.3	-0.1	93.9	-0.4
1985	91.8	-2.2	93.0	1.3	92.0	-1.1	91.8	-0.2	90.8	-1.1	90.1	-0.8	90.9	0.9	90.4	-0.6	89.7	-0.8	89.4	-0.3	89.4	0.0	90.3	1.0
1986	89.8	-0.6	89.8	0.0	89.8	0.0	89.8	0.0	89.8	0.0	90.5	0.8	90.1	-0.4	89.9	-0.2	89.9	0.0	89.9	0.0	89.9	0.0	89.9	0.0
1987	89.1	-0.9	88.5	-0.7	88.9	0.5	89.1	0.2	88.9	-0.2	88.8	-0.1	88.7	-0.1	89.0	0.3	88.9	-0.1	88.7	-0.2	88.7	0.0	88.7	0.0
1988	88.5	-0.2	89.0	0.6	88.2	-0.9	87.1	-1.2	87.2	0.1	86.3	-1.0	86.7	0.5	86.6	-0.1	86.7	0.1	86.6	-0.1	86.8	0.2	86.7	-0.1
1989	88.0	1.5	88.0	0.0	88.0	0.0	88.3	0.3	88.3	0.0	88.4	0.1	88.4	0.0	88.0	-0.5	87.5	-0.6	83.2	-4.9	83.2	0.0	83.0	-0.2
1990	83.0	0.0	82.9	-0.1	82.8	-0.1	82.7	-0.1	82.6	-0.1	82.6	0.0	82.6	0.0	82.6	0.0	82.6	0.0	82.6	0.0	82.7	0.1	82.8	0.1	82.8	0.0
1991	82.9	0.1	83.1	0.2	83.1	0.0	83.1	0.0	83.5	0.5	83.6	0.1	83.5	-0.1	83.0	-0.6	83.0	0.0	83.1	0.1	83.0	-0.1	83.0	0.0

[Continued]

Home Electronic Equipment
Producer Price Index
Base 1982 = 100
[Continued]

For 1947-1997. Columns headed % show percentile change in the index from the previous period for which an index is available.

Year	Jan Index	%	Feb Index	%	Mar Index	%	Apr Index	%	May Index	%	Jun Index	%	Jul Index	%	Aug Index	%	Sep Index	%	Oct Index	%	Nov Index	%	Dec Index	%
1992	83.0	0.0	82.8	-0.2	82.8	0.0	82.6	-0.2	82.3	-0.4	81.9	-0.5	81.9	0.0	81.9	0.0	81.6	-0.4	81.0	-0.7	80.8	-0.2	80.8	0.0
1993	80.6	-0.2	80.7	0.1	80.5	-0.2	80.4	-0.1	80.2	-0.2	79.9	-0.4	80.0	0.1	79.8	-0.2	79.4	-0.5	79.6	0.3	80.8	1.5	80.7	-0.1
1994	80.7	0.0	80.7	0.0	80.6	-0.1	80.7	0.1	80.1	-0.7	80.0	-0.1	80.0	0.0	80.0	0.0	79.9	-0.1	80.2	0.4	80.1	-0.1	80.1	0.0
1995	80.2	0.1	80.2	0.0	79.5	-0.9	79.1	-0.5	78.3	-1.0	78.3	0.0	78.4	0.1	78.4	0.0	77.9	-0.6	77.9	0.0	79.4	1.9	79.3	-0.1
1996	79.4	0.1	79.3	-0.1	79.0	-0.4	79.0	0.0	79.1	0.1	79.0	-0.1	79.2	0.3	79.0	-0.3	79.0	0.0	78.7	-0.4	78.3	-0.5	78.3	0.0
1997	78.2	-0.1	78.3	0.1	78.2	-0.1	78.3	0.1	78.3	0.0	78.3	0.0	76.0	-2.9	76.1	0.1	76.1	0.0	78.3	2.9	76.0	-2.9	76.0	0.0

Source: U.S. Department of Labor, Bureau of Labor Statistics, Division of Industry Prices and Price Indexes. n.e.c. stands for not elsewhere classified. - indicates no data collected for period or unavailable.

Other Household Durable Goods
Producer Price Index
Base 1982 = 100

For 1947-1997. Columns headed % show percentile change in the index from the previous period for which an index is available.

Year	Jan Index	%	Feb Index	%	Mar Index	%	Apr Index	%	May Index	%	Jun Index	%	Jul Index	%	Aug Index	%	Sep Index	%	Oct Index	%	Nov Index	%	Dec Index	%
1947	19.5	-	19.4	-0.5	19.5	0.5	19.5	0.0	19.5	0.0	19.5	0.0	19.4	-0.5	19.4	0.0	19.5	0.5	19.5	0.0	19.5	0.0	19.6	0.5
1948	19.5	-0.5	19.5	0.0	19.5	0.0	19.5	0.0	19.6	0.5	19.6	0.0	19.9	1.5	20.2	1.5	20.2	0.0	20.5	1.5	20.8	1.5	21.0	1.0
1949	21.1	0.5	21.1	0.0	21.1	0.0	21.1	0.0	21.0	-0.5	21.0	0.0	20.9	-0.5	20.9	0.0	20.8	-0.5	20.8	0.0	20.8	0.0	20.8	0.0
1950	21.0	1.0	21.0	0.0	21.0	0.0	21.0	0.0	21.0	0.0	21.1	0.5	21.2	0.5	21.4	0.9	21.7	1.4	22.0	1.4	22.3	1.4	22.7	1.8
1951	23.0	1.3	23.1	0.4	23.1	0.0	23.1	0.0	23.1	0.0	23.1	0.0	23.1	0.0	23.1	0.0	23.2	0.4	23.2	0.0	23.2	0.0	23.2	0.0
1952	23.2	0.0	23.2	0.0	23.2	0.0	23.3	0.4	23.2	-0.4	23.2	0.0	23.3	0.4	23.3	0.0	23.3	0.0	23.3	0.0	23.3	0.0	23.4	0.4
1953	23.8	1.7	24.0	0.8	24.0	0.0	24.0	0.0	24.0	0.0	24.0	0.0	24.4	1.7	24.4	0.0	24.4	0.0	24.5	0.4	24.7	0.8	24.8	0.4
1954	24.9	0.4	24.9	0.0	24.9	0.0	25.0	0.4	25.0	0.0	25.0	0.0	25.0	0.0	25.0	0.0	25.0	0.0	25.2	0.8	25.3	0.4	25.3	0.0
1955	25.4	0.4	25.4	0.0	25.4	0.0	25.4	0.0	25.4	0.0	25.5	0.4	25.8	1.2	26.1	1.2	26.1	0.0	26.4	1.1	26.5	0.4	26.7	0.8
1956	26.9	0.7	27.1	0.7	27.1	0.0	27.0	-0.4	27.1	0.4	27.1	0.0	27.1	0.0	27.2	0.4	27.3	0.4	27.8	1.8	27.8	0.0	28.3	1.8
1957	28.3	0.0	28.4	0.4	28.4	0.0	28.4	0.0	28.6	0.7	28.7	0.3	28.7	0.0	28.7	0.0	28.8	0.3	28.9	0.3	29.0	0.3	29.3	1.0
1958	29.8	1.7	29.8	0.0	29.8	0.0	29.8	0.0	29.8	0.0	29.9	0.3	29.8	-0.3	29.7	-0.3	29.8	0.3	29.8	0.0	29.8	0.0	30.0	0.7
1959	30.0	0.0	30.1	0.3	30.1	0.0	30.1	0.0	30.2	0.3	30.2	0.0	30.3	0.3	30.2	-0.3	30.2	0.0	30.2	0.0	30.2	0.0	30.2	0.0
1960	30.7	1.7	30.8	0.3	30.8	0.0	30.8	0.0	30.8	0.0	30.8	0.0	30.9	0.3	30.9	0.0	30.9	0.0	30.9	0.0	30.9	0.0	30.9	0.0
1961	30.8	-0.3	30.7	-0.3	30.7	0.0	30.7	0.0	30.8	0.3	30.8	0.0	30.8	0.0	30.8	0.0	30.8	0.0	30.8	0.0	30.9	0.3	31.0	0.3
1962	31.3	1.0	31.2	-0.3	31.4	0.6	31.4	0.0	31.4	0.0	31.4	0.0	31.3	-0.3	31.2	-0.3	31.4	0.6	31.2	-0.6	31.2	0.0	31.2	0.0
1963	31.2	0.0	31.2	0.0	31.2	0.0	31.4	0.6	31.3	-0.3	31.5	0.6	31.6	0.3	31.5	-0.3	31.6	0.3	31.6	0.0	31.6	0.0	31.5	-0.3
1964	31.7	0.6	31.7	0.0	31.7	0.0	31.7	0.0	31.8	0.3	31.8	0.0	31.8	0.0	31.8	0.0	31.8	0.0	31.8	0.0	31.8	0.0	32.0	0.6
1965	32.2	0.6	32.2	0.0	32.2	0.0	32.2	0.0	32.2	0.0	32.2	0.0	32.2	0.0	32.1	-0.3	32.2	0.3	32.2	0.0	32.2	0.0	32.2	0.0
1966	32.5	0.9	32.6	0.3	32.6	0.0	32.6	0.0	32.6	0.0	32.6	0.0	33.1	1.5	33.1	0.0	33.3	0.6	33.6	0.9	33.6	0.0	33.7	0.3
1967	33.9	0.6	33.9	0.0	34.0	0.3	34.2	0.6	34.3	0.3	34.3	0.0	34.5	0.6	34.9	1.2	35.0	0.3	35.2	0.6	35.2	0.0	35.3	0.3
1968	36.5	3.4	36.6	0.3	36.7	0.3	36.8	0.3	36.7	-0.3	36.7	0.0	36.9	0.5	37.0	0.3	37.1	0.3	37.1	0.0	37.2	0.3	37.9	1.9
1969	38.1	0.5	38.2	0.3	38.3	0.3	38.4	0.3	38.4	0.0	38.5	0.3	38.7	0.5	38.7	0.0	38.8	0.3	38.9	0.3	38.8	-0.3	39.5	1.8
1970	39.5	0.0	39.9	1.0	39.8	-0.3	40.1	0.8	40.0	-0.2	40.1	0.2	40.1	0.0	40.1	0.0	40.4	0.7	40.3	-0.2	40.4	0.2	40.6	0.5
1971	41.2	1.5	41.4	0.5	41.4	0.0	41.5	0.2	41.5	0.0	41.5	0.0	42.1	1.4	42.2	0.2	42.2	0.0	42.1	-0.2	42.1	0.0	42.2	0.2
1972	42.3	0.2	42.9	1.4	43.0	0.2	43.0	0.0	43.2	0.5	43.4	0.5	43.7	0.7	43.8	0.2	43.9	0.2	43.9	0.0	43.9	0.0	43.9	0.0
1973	43.9	0.0	44.3	0.9	44.6	0.7	45.0	0.9	45.2	0.4	45.3	0.2	45.2	-0.2	45.2	0.0	45.1	-0.2	45.4	0.7	45.6	0.4	45.9	0.7
1974	46.3	0.9	47.2	1.9	48.1	1.9	49.2	2.3	50.2	2.0	50.8	1.2	52.3	3.0	52.6	0.6	53.3	1.3	55.1	3.4	55.5	0.7	56.1	1.1
1975	57.7	2.9	58.1	0.7	57.4	-1.2	58.1	1.2	58.1	0.0	58.1	0.0	58.1	0.0	58.0	-0.2	58.1	0.2	58.7	1.0	59.1	0.7	59.4	0.5
1976	60.6	2.0	60.9	0.5	61.0	0.2	61.1	0.2	61.4	0.5	61.4	0.0	61.7	0.5	62.1	0.6	62.9	1.3	62.9	0.0	63.2	0.5	63.4	0.3
1977	64.8	2.2	65.0	0.3	65.1	0.2	64.9	-0.3	65.5	0.9	65.6	0.2	65.9	0.5	66.1	0.3	66.1	0.0	66.3	0.3	66.5	0.3	66.9	0.6
1978	68.5	2.4	68.5	0.0	68.4	-0.1	68.4	0.0	69.3	1.3	69.9	0.9	70.9	1.4	70.7	-0.3	70.7	0.0	71.9	1.7	72.1	0.3	73.4	1.8
1979	74.7	1.8	74.9	0.3	75.3	0.5	75.6	0.4	75.9	0.4	76.3	0.5	77.3	1.3	78.3	1.3	79.8	1.9	84.9	6.4	85.8	1.1	87.9	2.4
1980	99.3	13.0	102.1	2.8	99.6	-2.4	92.4	-7.2	91.8	-0.6	92.1	0.3	93.8	1.8	95.4	1.7	95.5	0.1	97.4	2.0	97.2	-0.2	98.7	1.5
1981	96.4	-2.3	97.0	0.6	96.1	-0.9	95.2	-0.9	95.6	0.4	95.5	-0.1	97.5	2.1	97.1	-0.4	98.8	1.8	98.8	0.0	98.6	-0.2	98.9	0.3
1982	98.0	-0.9	98.1	0.1	98.5	0.4	98.8	0.3	98.7	-0.1	98.9	0.2	98.6	-0.3	100.9	2.3	101.4	0.5	102.5	1.1	102.7	0.2	103.1	0.4
1983	104.7	1.6	108.8	3.9	108.1	-0.6	107.8	-0.3	108.1	0.3	108.6	0.5	108.8	0.2	108.5	-0.3	108.7	0.2	108.5	-0.2	108.9	0.4	108.9	0.0
1984	109.9	0.9	109.5	-0.4	109.5	0.0	110.3	0.7	111.2	0.8	110.6	-0.5	110.1	-0.5	109.5	-0.5	109.5	0.0	109.8	0.3	110.8	0.9	110.8	0.0
1985	111.5	0.6	111.5	0.0	112.0	0.4	111.9	-0.1	111.7	-0.2	111.9	0.2	111.5	-0.4	111.4	-0.1	111.2	-0.2	111.9	0.6	111.8	-0.1	112.0	0.2
1986	112.6	0.5	112.1	-0.4	112.3	0.2	112.6	0.3	112.6	0.0	112.9	0.3	113.0	0.1	112.9	-0.1	113.1	0.2	113.1	0.0	113.3	0.2	113.6	0.3
1987	114.6	0.9	114.5	-0.1	114.7	0.2	114.7	0.0	115.2	0.4	115.3	0.1	115.6	0.3	115.8	0.2	115.8	0.0	116.2	0.3	116.3	0.1	116.6	0.3
1988	117.8	1.0	118.1	0.3	118.4	0.3	118.8	0.3	119.4	0.5	119.3	-0.1	119.8	0.4	120.5	0.6	120.9	0.3	121.2	0.2	121.4	0.2	121.8	0.3
1989	122.7	0.7	123.5	0.7	124.1	0.5	126.2	1.7	126.7	0.4	127.9	0.9	128.5	0.5	129.0	0.4	129.2	0.2	129.7	0.4	129.6	-0.1	129.7	0.1
1990	130.9	0.9	131.5	0.5	130.5	-0.8	131.1	0.5	130.7	-0.3	130.9	0.2	130.0	-0.7	130.4	0.3	130.7	0.2	130.8	0.1	130.7	-0.1	130.7	0.0
1991	132.1	1.1	132.6	0.4	133.5	0.7	134.6	0.8	134.5	-0.1	134.6	0.1	134.8	0.1	134.8	0.0	134.7	-0.1	134.7	0.0	134.8	0.1	135.2	0.3

[Continued]

Other Household Durable Goods
Producer Price Index
Base 1982 = 100
[Continued]

For 1947-1997. Columns headed % show percentile change in the index from the previous period for which an index is available.

Year	Jan Index	%	Feb Index	%	Mar Index	%	Apr Index	%	May Index	%	Jun Index	%	Jul Index	%	Aug Index	%	Sep Index	%	Oct Index	%	Nov Index	%	Dec Index	%
1992	136.1	0.7	136.6	0.4	137.2	0.4	136.1	-0.8	136.2	0.1	136.5	0.2	136.5	0.0	136.7	0.1	136.9	0.1	136.6	-0.2	136.5	-0.1	136.7	0.1
1993	137.3	0.4	137.4	0.1	137.8	0.3	137.9	0.1	137.8	-0.1	137.8	0.0	137.8	0.0	138.0	0.1	138.2	0.1	138.5	0.2	138.6	0.1	138.7	0.1
1994	139.4	0.5	139.4	0.0	139.7	0.2	139.6	-0.1	140.0	0.3	140.9	0.6	141.1	0.1	141.5	0.3	141.5	0.0	141.9	0.3	142.2	0.2	142.4	0.1
1995	143.4	0.7	144.1	0.5	144.5	0.3	144.5	0.0	144.8	0.2	144.8	0.0	145.0	0.1	145.1	0.1	145.2	0.1	145.3	0.1	145.6	0.2	145.7	0.1
1996	146.9	0.8	147.3	0.3	147.6	0.2	147.7	0.1	148.3	0.4	148.4	0.1	148.4	0.0	148.4	0.0	148.4	0.0	148.4	0.0	148.5	0.1	148.9	0.3
1997	149.2	0.2	149.3	0.1	149.7	0.3	150.0	0.2	150.2	0.1	150.2	0.0	149.9	-0.2	150.1	0.1	149.4	-0.5	149.3	-0.1	149.4	0.1	149.6	0.1

Source: U.S. Department of Labor, Bureau of Labor Statistics, Division of Industry Prices and Price Indexes. n.e.c. stands for not elsewhere classified. - indicates no data collected for period or unavailable.

NONMETALLIC MINERAL PRODUCTS
Producer Price Index
Base 1982 = 100

For 1926-1997. Columns headed % show percentile change in the index from the previous period for which an index is available.

Year	Jan Index	%	Feb Index	%	Mar Index	%	Apr Index	%	May Index	%	Jun Index	%	Jul Index	%	Aug Index	%	Sep Index	%	Oct Index	%	Nov Index	%	Dec Index	%
1926	16.4	-	16.4	0.0	16.5	0.6	16.5	0.0	16.4	-0.6	16.4	0.0	16.4	0.0	16.3	-0.6	16.2	-0.6	16.4	1.2	16.4	0.0	16.4	0.0
1927	16.1	-1.8	15.9	-1.2	15.8	-0.6	15.8	0.0	15.8	0.0	15.8	0.0	15.8	0.0	15.7	-0.6	15.6	-0.6	15.6	0.0	15.3	-1.9	15.4	0.7
1928	15.5	0.6	15.4	-0.6	15.2	-1.3	16.0	5.3	16.3	1.9	16.6	1.8	16.6	0.0	16.6	0.0	16.6	0.0	16.6	0.0	16.6	0.0	16.3	-1.8
1929	16.1	-1.2	16.1	0.0	16.0	-0.6	16.1	0.6	16.1	0.0	16.0	-0.6	16.1	0.6	16.0	-0.6	15.8	-1.2	15.7	-0.6	15.8	0.6	16.1	1.9
1930	16.1	0.0	16.1	0.0	16.1	0.0	16.1	0.0	16.0	-0.6	15.7	-1.9	15.8	0.6	15.8	0.0	15.8	0.0	15.9	0.6	16.0	0.6	15.8	-1.2
1931	15.6	-1.3	15.6	0.0	15.3	-1.9	15.1	-1.3	15.0	-0.7	14.9	-0.7	14.5	-2.7	14.6	0.7	14.6	0.0	14.6	0.0	14.5	-0.7	14.3	-1.4
1932	14.1	-1.4	14.0	-0.7	14.0	0.0	13.9	-0.7	13.5	-2.9	13.4	-0.7	13.7	2.2	13.8	0.7	14.1	2.2	14.1	0.0	14.2	0.7	14.3	0.7
1933	14.2	-0.7	14.1	-0.7	14.1	0.0	14.1	0.0	14.2	0.7	14.4	1.4	14.8	2.8	15.1	2.0	15.2	0.7	15.5	2.0	15.6	0.6	15.6	0.0
1934	15.8	1.3	15.8	0.0	15.7	-0.6	15.6	-0.6	15.6	0.0	15.8	1.3	15.8	0.0	15.7	-0.6	15.7	0.0	15.7	0.0	15.7	0.0	15.7	0.0
1935	15.8	0.6	15.7	-0.6	15.7	0.0	15.7	0.0	15.8	0.6	15.8	0.0	15.8	0.0	15.7	-0.6	15.7	0.0	15.7	0.0	15.7	0.0	15.6	-0.6
1936	15.6	0.0	15.6	0.0	15.6	0.0	15.7	0.6	15.8	0.6	15.8	0.0	15.8	0.0	15.8	0.0	15.8	0.0	15.8	0.0	15.9	0.6	16.0	0.6
1937	16.0	0.0	16.1	0.6	16.1	0.0	16.2	0.6	16.3	0.6	16.2	-0.6	16.3	0.6	16.3	0.0	16.1	-1.2	16.1	0.0	16.0	-0.6	15.8	-1.2
1938	15.8	0.0	15.8	0.0	15.6	-1.3	15.6	0.0	15.6	0.0	15.6	0.0	15.7	0.6	15.6	-0.6	15.6	0.0	15.7	0.6	15.3	-2.5	15.4	0.7
1939	15.3	-0.6	15.3	0.0	15.3	0.0	15.4	0.7	15.3	-0.6	15.3	0.0	15.3	0.0	15.2	-0.7	15.3	0.7	15.3	0.0	15.3	0.0	15.4	0.7
1940	15.4	0.0	15.4	0.0	15.4	0.0	15.3	-0.6	15.3	0.0	15.3	0.0	15.3	0.0	15.3	0.0	15.3	0.0	15.3	0.0	15.3	0.0	15.3	0.0
1941	15.4	0.7	15.4	0.0	15.4	0.0	15.4	0.0	15.5	0.6	15.6	0.6	15.6	0.0	15.8	1.3	15.8	0.0	16.0	1.3	16.3	1.9	16.2	-0.6
1942	16.2	0.0	16.2	0.0	16.3	0.6	16.3	0.0	16.3	0.0	16.3	0.0	16.3	0.0	16.3	0.0	16.3	0.0	16.3	0.0	16.3	0.0	16.3	0.0
1943	16.3	0.0	16.3	0.0	16.3	0.0	16.3	0.0	16.3	0.0	16.3	0.0	16.3	0.0	16.3	0.0	16.5	1.2	16.5	0.0	16.5	0.0	16.5	0.0
1944	16.5	0.0	16.5	0.0	16.5	0.0	16.5	0.0	16.6	0.6	16.6	0.0	16.7	0.6	16.7	0.0	16.8	0.6	17.0	1.2	17.0	0.0	17.0	0.0
1945	17.2	1.2	17.3	0.6	17.3	0.0	17.3	0.0	17.3	0.0	17.3	0.0	17.4	0.6	17.4	0.0	17.5	0.6	17.6	0.6	17.7	0.6	17.7	0.0
1946	17.9	1.1	17.9	0.0	18.0	0.6	18.1	0.6	18.2	0.6	18.3	0.5	18.5	1.1	18.8	1.6	18.9	0.5	19.0	0.5	19.2	1.1	19.5	1.6
1947	20.0	2.6	20.1	0.5	20.4	1.5	20.6	1.0	20.6	0.0	20.6	0.0	20.7	0.5	20.7	0.0	20.8	0.5	21.0	1.0	21.2	1.0	21.4	0.9
1948	21.8	1.9	21.9	0.5	21.9	0.0	22.0	0.5	22.0	0.0	22.1	0.5	22.6	2.3	22.8	0.9	22.8	0.0	22.9	0.4	22.9	0.0	22.9	0.0
1949	23.0	0.4	23.0	0.0	23.0	0.0	23.0	0.0	23.0	0.0	23.0	0.0	22.9	-0.4	23.0	0.4	23.0	0.0	23.0	0.0	23.0	0.0	23.0	0.0
1950	23.1	0.4	23.1	0.0	23.2	0.4	23.2	0.0	23.1	-0.4	23.2	0.4	23.2	0.0	23.4	0.9	23.6	0.9	24.1	2.1	24.4	1.2	24.6	0.8
1951	25.0	1.6	25.0	0.0	25.0	0.0	25.0	0.0	25.0	0.0	25.0	0.0	25.0	0.0	25.0	0.0	25.0	0.0	25.0	0.0	25.0	0.0	24.8	-0.8
1952	24.9	0.4	24.9	0.0	24.9	0.0	24.8	-0.4	24.9	0.4	25.0	0.4	25.0	0.0	25.0	0.0	25.0	0.0	25.2	0.8	25.2	0.0	25.2	0.0
1953	25.2	0.0	25.2	0.0	25.3	0.4	25.7	1.6	25.8	0.4	26.0	0.8	26.3	1.2	26.3	0.0	26.5	0.8	26.5	0.0	26.6	0.4	26.6	0.0
1954	26.6	0.0	26.6	0.0	26.6	0.0	26.6	0.0	26.3	-1.1	26.2	-0.4	26.5	1.1	26.5	0.0	26.8	1.1	26.8	0.0	26.8	0.0	26.8	0.0
1955	26.9	0.4	26.8	-0.4	26.8	0.0	26.9	0.4	27.1	0.7	27.2	0.4	27.6	1.5	27.8	0.7	27.8	0.0	27.9	0.4	27.5	-1.4	27.6	0.4
1956	28.0	1.4	28.0	0.0	28.1	0.4	28.3	0.7	28.3	0.0	28.4	0.4	28.7	1.1	28.8	0.3	28.9	0.3	28.9	0.0	28.9	0.0	28.9	0.0
1957	29.0	0.3	29.2	0.7	29.3	0.3	29.6	1.0	29.7	0.3	29.7	0.0	29.8	0.3	29.8	0.0	29.8	0.0	29.8	0.0	29.8	0.0	29.9	0.3
1958	30.0	0.3	30.0	0.0	29.8	-0.7	29.8	0.0	29.8	0.0	29.8	0.0	29.8	0.0	29.8	0.0	30.1	1.0	30.1	0.0	30.1	0.0	30.1	0.0
1959	30.2	0.3	30.3	0.3	30.3	0.0	30.4	0.3	30.4	0.0	30.2	-0.7	30.3	0.3	30.2	-0.3	30.3	0.3	30.3	0.0	30.3	0.0	30.3	0.0
1960	30.4	0.3	30.4	0.0	30.4	0.0	30.4	0.0	30.3	-0.3	30.3	0.0	30.3	0.0	30.3	0.0	30.3	0.0	30.4	0.3	30.4	0.0	30.3	-0.3	30.3	0.0
1961	30.5	0.7	30.4	-0.3	30.5	0.3	30.5	0.0	30.5	0.0	30.5	0.0	30.4	-0.3	30.4	0.0	30.5	0.3	30.6	0.3	30.5	-0.3	30.4	-0.3
1962	30.5	0.3	30.6	0.3	30.6	0.0	30.7	0.3	30.6	-0.3	30.5	-0.3	30.4	-0.3	30.3	-0.3	30.3	0.0	30.3	0.0	30.3	0.0	30.3	0.0
1963	30.4	0.0	30.4	0.0	30.4	0.0	30.4	0.0	30.3	-0.3	30.3	0.0	30.4	0.3	30.4	0.0	30.5	0.3	30.5	0.0	30.5	0.0	30.4	-0.3
1964	30.3	0.0	30.3	0.0	30.3	0.0	30.3	0.0	30.3	0.0	30.5	0.0	30.4	-0.3	30.4	0.0	30.4	0.0	30.4	0.0	30.4	0.0	30.4	0.0
1965	30.4	0.0	30.5	0.3	30.5	0.0	30.5	0.0	30.5	0.0	30.5	0.0	30.5	0.0	30.4	-0.3	30.4	0.0	30.4	0.0	30.4	0.0	30.4	0.0
1966	30.5	0.3	30.6	0.3	30.6	0.0	30.6	0.0	30.7	0.3	30.7	0.0	30.8	0.3	30.8	0.0	30.9	0.3	30.9	0.0	30.9	0.0	30.9	0.0
1967	31.1	0.6	31.1	0.0	31.1	0.0	31.2	0.3	31.0	-0.6	31.1	0.3	31.2	0.3	31.3	0.3	31.3	0.0	31.4	0.3	31.5	0.3	31.6	0.3
1968	31.9	0.9	32.0	0.3	32.2	0.6	32.2	0.0	32.3	0.3	32.4	0.3	32.5	0.3	32.5	0.0	32.5	0.0	32.6	0.3	32.7	0.3	32.7	0.0
1969	33.1	1.2	33.3	0.6	33.3	0.0	33.5	0.6	33.6	0.3	33.6	0.0	33.7	0.3	33.7	0.0	33.8	0.3	33.9	0.3	33.9	0.0	34.1	0.6
1970	34.8	2.1	34.9	0.3	34.9	0.0	35.3	1.1	35.1	-0.6	35.1	0.0	35.2	0.3	35.3	0.3	35.3	0.0	35.5	0.6	35.8	0.8	36.0	0.6

[Continued]

NONMETALLIC MINERAL PRODUCTS
Producer Price Index
Base 1982 = 100
[Continued]

For 1926-1997. Columns headed % show percentile change in the index from the previous period for which an index is available.

Year	Jan Index	%	Feb Index	%	Mar Index	%	Apr Index	%	May Index	%	Jun Index	%	Jul Index	%	Aug Index	%	Sep Index	%	Oct Index	%	Nov Index	%	Dec Index	%
1971	37.1	3.1	37.2	0.3	37.8	1.6	38.0	0.5	38.1	0.3	38.3	0.5	38.5	0.5	38.7	0.5	38.7	0.0	38.7	0.0	38.7	0.0	38.8	0.3
1972	38.8	0.0	38.9	0.3	39.0	0.3	39.2	0.5	39.3	0.3	39.3	0.0	39.4	0.3	39.6	0.5	39.6	0.0	39.7	0.3	39.8	0.3	39.8	0.0
1973	40.0	0.5	40.1	0.2	40.3	0.5	40.6	0.7	40.7	0.2	40.9	0.5	40.6	-0.7	40.6	0.0	40.6	0.0	40.9	0.7	41.1	0.5	41.4	0.7
1974	43.3	4.6	44.4	2.5	45.0	1.4	45.8	1.8	47.1	2.8	47.6	1.1	48.8	2.5	49.2	0.8	49.9	1.4	50.7	1.6	51.0	0.6	51.3	0.6
1975	52.6	2.5	53.2	1.1	53.4	0.4	54.0	1.1	54.1	0.2	54.1	0.0	54.6	0.9	54.9	0.5	55.0	0.2	55.3	0.5	55.5	0.4	55.6	0.2
1976	56.6	1.8	56.7	0.2	57.1	0.7	57.9	1.4	58.1	0.3	58.2	0.2	58.5	0.5	58.7	0.3	58.9	0.3	59.1	0.3	59.2	0.2	59.2	0.0
1977	60.1	1.5	60.5	0.7	60.9	0.7	62.0	1.8	62.2	0.3	62.6	0.6	63.0	0.6	63.3	0.5	63.8	0.8	64.1	0.5	64.2	0.2	64.5	0.5
1978	66.5	3.1	67.2	1.1	67.4	0.3	68.2	1.2	68.5	0.4	69.3	1.2	70.2	1.3	71.0	1.1	71.3	0.4	71.6	0.4	71.8	0.3	72.2	0.6
1979	74.4	3.0	75.1	0.9	75.2	0.1	76.0	1.1	76.7	0.9	77.1	0.5	77.9	1.0	78.1	0.3	79.5	1.8	80.0	0.6	80.4	0.5	81.1	0.9
1980	83.8	3.3	85.6	2.1	86.4	0.9	88.6	2.5	88.7	0.1	88.5	-0.2	88.9	0.5	89.3	0.4	89.6	0.3	90.1	0.6	90.2	0.1	90.9	0.8
1981	92.6	1.9	93.1	0.5	94.0	1.0	97.0	3.2	97.4	0.4	97.9	0.5	98.2	0.3	98.1	-0.1	97.8	-0.3	97.8	0.0	98.0	0.2	97.9	-0.1
1982	98.6	0.7	99.6	1.0	99.9	0.3	100.0	0.1	100.3	0.3	100.2	-0.1	100.3	0.1	100.1	-0.2	100.3	0.2	100.3	0.0	100.3	0.0	100.1	-0.2
1983	100.4	0.3	100.7	0.3	100.6	-0.1	101.2	0.6	101.2	0.0	101.4	0.2	101.5	0.1	101.9	0.4	102.2	0.3	102.4	0.2	102.7	0.3	102.7	0.0
1984	103.1	0.4	103.7	0.6	104.1	0.4	104.9	0.8	105.4	0.5	105.6	0.2	106.1	0.5	106.4	0.3	106.3	-0.1	106.2	-0.1	106.0	-0.2	106.2	0.2
1985	106.7	0.5	107.0	0.3	107.4	0.4	107.9	0.5	108.7	0.7	109.1	0.4	109.2	0.1	109.4	0.2	109.3	-0.1	109.5	0.2	109.5	0.0	109.6	0.1
1986	110.1	0.5	110.0	-0.1	110.1	0.1	110.2	0.1	110.4	0.2	110.2	-0.2	110.2	0.0	109.9	-0.3	109.7	-0.2	109.7	0.0	109.7	0.0	109.3	-0.4
1987	109.3	0.0	109.6	0.3	109.7	0.1	109.9	0.2	109.9	0.0	110.1	0.2	110.1	0.0	109.9	-0.2	110.0	0.1	110.4	0.4	110.5	0.1	110.4	-0.1
1988	110.8	0.4	110.9	0.1	110.9	0.0	111.0	0.1	111.2	0.2	111.3	0.1	111.1	-0.2	111.1	0.0	111.3	0.2	111.4	0.1	111.5	0.1	111.7	0.2
1989	111.8	0.1	111.8	0.0	112.0	0.2	112.6	0.5	112.7	0.1	112.8	0.1	112.8	0.0	112.8	0.0	112.9	0.1	113.0	0.1	113.1	0.1	113.2	0.1
1990	113.8	0.5	113.9	0.1	114.2	0.3	114.3	0.1	114.5	0.2	114.6	0.1	114.6	0.0	114.7	0.1	115.0	0.3	115.3	0.3	115.8	0.4	115.8	0.0
1991	116.9	0.9	117.2	0.3	117.4	0.2	117.3	-0.1	117.3	0.0	117.3	0.0	117.2	-0.1	117.1	-0.1	117.2	0.1	117.4	0.2	117.2	-0.2	117.1	-0.1
1992	117.2	0.1	117.1	-0.1	117.3	0.2	116.9	-0.3	116.9	0.0	117.0	0.1	117.1	0.1	117.4	0.3	117.4	0.0	117.4	0.0	117.7	0.3	117.8	0.1
1993	118.4	0.5	118.6	0.2	118.9	0.3	119.6	0.6	119.7	0.1	120.0	0.3	120.2	0.2	120.5	0.2	120.8	0.2	121.0	0.2	121.2	0.2	121.4	0.2
1994	121.8	0.3	122.2	0.3	122.9	0.6	123.4	0.4	123.7	0.2	124.3	0.5	124.5	0.2	124.8	0.2	125.1	0.2	125.5	0.3	125.8	0.2	126.0	0.2
1995	126.9	0.7	127.5	0.5	128.2	0.5	129.3	0.9	129.4	0.1	129.3	-0.1	129.3	0.0	129.4	0.1	129.6	0.2	129.5	-0.1	129.8	0.2	129.7	-0.1
1996	130.0	0.2	130.2	0.2	130.2	0.0	130.5	0.2	130.8	0.2	130.9	0.1	131.2	0.2	131.2	0.0	131.6	0.3	131.7	0.1	132.0	0.2	131.9	-0.1
1997	132.3	0.3	132.5	0.2	132.6	0.1	133.3	0.5	133.3	0.0	133.4	0.1	133.4	0.0	133.5	0.1	133.5	0.0	133.6	0.1	133.7	0.1	133.7	0.0

Source: U.S. Department of Labor, Bureau of Labor Statistics, Division of Industry Prices and Price Indexes. n.e.c. stands for not elsewhere classified. - indicates no data collected for period or unavailable.

Glass
Producer Price Index
Base 1982 = 100

For 1947-1997. Columns headed % show percentile change in the index from the previous period for which an index is available.

Year	Jan Index	%	Feb Index	%	Mar Index	%	Apr Index	%	May Index	%	Jun Index	%	Jul Index	%	Aug Index	%	Sep Index	%	Oct Index	%	Nov Index	%	Dec Index	%
1947	28.9	-	28.9	0.0	30.0	3.8	30.5	1.7	30.5	0.0	30.5	0.0	30.5	0.0	30.5	0.0	30.5	0.0	30.5	0.0	30.5	0.0	30.5	0.0
1948	30.7	0.7	30.5	-0.7	30.5	0.0	30.7	0.7	30.5	-0.7	30.5	0.0	31.8	4.3	33.1	4.1	33.1	0.0	33.3	0.6	33.5	0.6	33.5	0.0
1949	33.5	0.0	33.5	0.0	33.4	-0.3	33.3	-0.3	33.3	0.0	33.3	0.0	33.3	0.0	33.3	0.0	33.3	0.0	33.3	0.0	33.3	0.0	33.3	0.0
1950	33.3	0.0	33.1	-0.6	33.9	2.4	34.0	0.3	33.6	-1.2	33.6	0.0	33.6	0.0	33.6	0.0	33.6	0.0	35.0	4.2	36.3	3.7	36.3	0.0
1951	36.3	0.0	36.3	0.0	36.3	0.0	36.3	0.0	36.3	0.0	36.3	0.0	36.3	0.0	36.3	0.0	36.3	0.0	36.3	0.0	36.3	0.0	36.3	0.0
1952	36.3	0.0	36.3	0.0	36.3	0.0	36.3	0.0	36.3	0.0	36.3	0.0	36.3	0.0	36.3	0.0	36.3	0.0	36.3	0.0	36.3	0.0	36.3	0.0
1953	36.3	0.0	36.3	0.0	37.0	1.9	37.0	0.0	37.0	0.0	39.1	5.7	39.6	1.3	39.6	0.0	39.6	0.0	39.6	0.0	39.6	0.0	39.6	0.0
1954	39.6	0.0	39.6	0.0	39.6	0.0	39.6	0.0	39.6	0.0	39.6	0.0	39.6	0.0	39.6	0.0	39.4	-0.5	39.4	0.0	39.4	0.0	39.4	0.0
1955	39.4	0.0	39.4	0.0	39.4	0.0	39.7	0.8	39.7	0.0	40.1	1.0	41.7	4.0	41.7	0.0	41.7	0.0	42.3	1.4	41.7	-1.4	41.7	0.0
1956	41.7	0.0	41.7	0.0	41.7	0.0	41.7	0.0	41.7	0.0	41.9	0.5	42.9	2.4	43.1	0.5	43.1	0.0	43.1	0.0	43.1	0.0	43.1	0.0
1957	43.1	0.0	43.1	0.0	43.1	0.0	43.1	0.0	43.1	0.0	43.1	0.0	43.1	0.0	43.1	0.0	43.1	0.0	43.1	0.0	43.1	0.0	43.1	0.0
1958	43.1	0.0	43.1	0.0	43.1	0.0	43.1	0.0	43.1	0.0	43.1	0.0	43.1	0.0	43.0	-0.2	42.9	-0.2	42.9	0.0	42.9	0.0	42.9	0.0
1959	42.9	0.0	42.9	0.0	42.9	0.0	42.9	0.0	42.9	0.0	43.0	0.2	43.0	0.0	43.0	0.0	43.0	0.0	43.0	0.0	43.0	0.0	43.0	0.0
1960	43.0	0.0	43.0	0.0	43.0	0.0	43.0	0.0	41.4	-3.7	41.4	0.0	41.4	0.0	41.4	0.0	41.4	0.0	41.4	0.0	41.4	0.0	41.4	0.0
1961	42.0	0.0	42.0	0.0	42.0	0.0	42.0	0.0	42.0	0.0	41.4	-1.4	41.4	0.0	41.4	0.0	41.4	0.0	41.4	0.0	41.4	0.0	41.4	0.0
1962	41.4	0.0	41.4	0.0	41.4	0.0	42.1	1.7	42.2	0.2	42.2	0.0	42.2	0.0	41.6	-1.4	41.6	0.0	41.6	0.0	41.6	0.0	41.6	0.0
1963	41.6	0.0	41.6	0.0	41.6	0.0	41.6	0.0	41.6	0.0	41.6	0.0	41.6	0.0	42.6	2.4	43.0	0.9	43.8	1.9	43.5	-0.7	43.5	0.0
1964	43.5	0.0	43.5	0.0	43.8	0.7	44.2	0.9	44.1	-0.2	44.1	0.0	44.1	0.0	44.4	0.7	44.4	0.0	44.4	0.0	44.4	0.0	43.9	-1.1
1965	43.9	0.0	43.8	-0.2	43.8	0.0	43.8	0.0	43.8	0.0	43.8	0.0	43.8	0.0	43.1	-1.6	43.1	0.0	43.0	-0.2	43.0	0.0	43.0	0.0
1966	43.0	0.0	43.0	0.0	42.7	-0.7	42.9	0.5	43.1	0.5	43.1	0.0	43.2	0.2	42.9	-0.7	43.3	0.9	43.9	1.4	44.5	1.4	44.5	0.0
1967	-	-	-	-	-	-	-	-	-	-	-	-	-	-	-	-	-	-	-	-	-	-	-	-
1968	-	-	-	-	-	-	-	-	-	-	-	-	-	-	-	-	-	-	-	-	-	-	-	-
1969	-	-	-	-	-	-	-	-	-	-	-	-	-	-	-	-	-	-	-	-	-	-	-	-
1970	-	-	-	-	-	-	-	-	-	-	-	-	-	-	-	-	-	-	-	-	-	-	-	-
1971	55.6	24.9	55.6	0.0	56.6	1.8	57.0	0.7	55.3	-3.0	55.3	0.0	55.3	0.0	55.3	0.0	55.3	0.0	55.3	0.0	55.3	0.0	55.4	0.2
1972	55.8	0.7	55.8	0.0	55.3	-0.9	54.7	-1.1	54.9	0.4	54.7	-0.4	55.0	0.5	55.5	0.9	55.5	0.0	55.3	-0.4	55.3	0.0	55.3	0.0
1973	55.3	0.0	55.3	0.0	56.0	1.3	56.0	0.0	56.2	0.4	55.2	-1.8	53.2	-3.6	53.2	0.0	53.4	0.4	53.4	0.0	54.5	2.1	55.8	2.4
1974	56.3	0.9	56.3	0.0	56.3	0.0	56.3	0.0	56.6	0.5	57.8	2.1	58.1	0.5	58.1	0.0	60.1	3.4	60.6	0.8	60.5	-0.2	60.9	0.7
1975	60.9	0.0	60.9	0.0	60.9	0.0	62.5	2.6	62.3	-0.3	61.4	-1.4	63.3	3.1	63.8	0.8	63.8	0.0	64.8	1.6	64.7	-0.2	64.7	0.0
1976	64.7	0.0	64.7	0.0	65.7	1.5	67.6	2.9	67.6	0.0	68.3	1.0	69.0	1.0	69.0	0.0	69.0	0.0	69.0	0.0	68.9	-0.1	68.9	0.0
1977	69.1	0.3	72.0	4.2	72.0	0.0	72.0	0.0	72.2	0.3	73.0	1.1	72.3	-1.0	72.8	0.7	72.8	0.0	73.4	0.8	74.1	1.0	76.0	2.6
1978	76.0	0.0	76.9	1.2	76.9	0.0	78.0	1.4	78.0	0.0	78.0	0.0	78.2	0.3	78.4	0.3	78.4	0.0	78.4	0.0	78.5	0.1	80.8	2.9
1979	81.8	1.2	82.7	1.1	82.7	0.0	82.7	0.0	82.7	0.0	83.1	0.5	83.1	0.0	83.1	0.0	83.3	0.2	83.4	0.1	83.7	0.4	84.2	0.6
1980	86.3	2.5	86.3	0.0	86.4	0.1	88.2	2.1	88.2	0.0	87.4	-0.9	87.7	0.3	90.1	2.7	90.2	0.1	90.6	0.4	91.7	1.2	91.7	0.0
1981	92.1	0.4	92.3	0.2	92.5	0.2	94.9	2.6	94.9	0.0	94.9	0.0	98.6	3.9	98.6	0.0	98.6	0.0	98.6	0.0	98.6	0.0	97.6	-1.0
1982	97.6	0.0	97.6	0.0	97.6	0.0	97.6	0.0	102.2	4.7	102.2	0.0	102.1	-0.1	99.8	-2.3	99.8	0.0	99.8	0.0	101.7	1.9	101.7	0.0
1983	103.7	2.0	103.7	0.0	103.7	0.0	103.7	0.0	103.7	0.0	103.7	0.0	103.7	0.0	103.7	0.0	103.8	0.1	104.5	0.7	104.8	0.3	104.7	-0.1
1984	107.0	2.2	107.1	0.1	106.8	-0.3	107.1	0.3	105.9	-1.1	106.0	0.1	106.0	0.0	103.9	-2.0	104.2	0.3	104.3	0.1	104.1	-0.2	104.2	0.1
1985	103.4	-0.8	103.3	-0.1	103.3	0.0	103.8	0.5	104.6	0.8	104.5	-0.1	105.1	0.6	105.4	0.3	105.2	-0.2	105.8	0.6	106.0	0.2	106.2	0.2
1986	106.8	0.6	106.8	0.0	106.8	0.0	107.0	0.2	106.9	-0.1	106.9	0.0	108.1	1.1	107.8	-0.3	107.8	0.0	107.8	0.0	108.1	0.3	108.2	0.1
1987	108.2	0.0	108.3	0.1	109.1	0.7	109.2	0.1	109.0	-0.2	109.5	0.5	109.7	0.2	109.8	0.1	109.6	-0.2	110.1	0.5	110.0	-0.1	110.7	0.6
1988	110.8	0.1	111.2	0.4	111.7	0.4	111.9	0.2	112.3	0.4	111.9	-0.4	112.3	0.4	112.7	0.4	113.1	0.4	113.0	-0.1	113.2	0.2	113.9	0.6
1989	113.4	-0.4	113.1	-0.3	112.6	-0.4	112.8	0.2	113.7	0.8	113.2	-0.4	113.3	0.1	113.0	-0.3	113.2	0.2	113.5	0.3	113.2	-0.3	113.7	0.4
1990	114.8	1.0	114.5	-0.3	114.3	-0.2	114.0	-0.3	114.1	0.1	113.9	-0.2	113.6	-0.3	113.2	-0.4	113.3	0.1	113.4	0.1	113.4	0.0	113.3	-0.1
1991	113.9	0.5	113.9	0.0	114.4	0.4	114.2	-0.2	114.3	0.1	113.7	-0.5	113.4	-0.3	114.0	0.5	115.0	0.9	115.8	0.7	115.2	-0.5	115.1	-0.1

[Continued]

Glass
Producer Price Index
Base 1982 = 100
[Continued]

For 1947-1997. Columns headed % show percentile change in the index from the previous period for which an index is available.

Year	Jan		Feb		Mar		Apr		May		Jun		Jul		Aug		Sep		Oct		Nov		Dec	
	Index	%	Index	%	Index	%	Index	%	Index	%	Index	%	Index	%	Index	%	Index	%	Index	%	Index	%	Index	%
1992	115.4	0.3	114.8	-0.5	114.9	0.1	115.3	0.3	115.3	0.0	115.2	-0.1	115.2	0.0	116.6	1.2	116.4	-0.2	116.0	-0.3	116.1	0.1	117.1	0.9
1993	116.3	-0.7	116.8	0.4	116.6	-0.2	116.9	0.3	117.0	0.1	117.1	0.1	117.0	-0.1	117.4	0.3	117.2	-0.2	116.5	-0.6	117.1	0.5	117.2	0.1
1994	117.6	0.3	118.2	0.5	118.6	0.3	118.7	0.1	119.7	0.8	120.5	0.7	120.7	0.2	121.1	0.3	120.8	-0.2	121.3	0.4	122.6	1.1	121.4	-1.0
1995	122.4	0.8	123.2	0.7	123.8	0.5	124.7	0.7	124.7	0.0	122.4	-1.8	122.6	0.2	122.3	-0.2	122.3	0.0	122.2	-0.1	122.0	-0.2	121.7	-0.2
1996	122.1	0.3	122.1	0.0	121.3	-0.7	120.9	-0.3	120.4	-0.4	120.4	0.0	120.5	0.1	120.4	-0.1	120.3	-0.1	120.3	0.0	120.6	0.2	120.9	0.2
1997	120.6	-0.2	120.4	-0.2	120.1	-0.2	120.2	0.1	120.1	-0.1	120.2	0.1	120.3	0.1	120.5	0.2	120.3	-0.2	120.6	0.2	120.7	0.1	120.6	-0.1

Source: U.S. Department of Labor, Bureau of Labor Statistics, Division of Industry Prices and Price Indexes. n.e.c. stands for not elsewhere classified. - indicates no data collected for period or unavailable.

Concrete Ingredients and Related Products
Producer Price Index
Base 1982 = 100

For 1926-1997. Columns headed % show percentile change in the index from the previous period for which an index is available.

Year	Jan Index	%	Feb Index	%	Mar Index	%	Apr Index	%	May Index	%	Jun Index	%	Jul Index	%	Aug Index	%	Sep Index	%	Oct Index	%	Nov Index	%	Dec Index	%
1926	15.0	-	15.0	0.0	15.0	0.0	14.9	-0.7	14.9	0.0	14.9	0.0	14.9	0.0	14.8	-0.7	14.8	0.0	14.9	0.7	14.9	0.0	15.0	0.7
1927	14.9	-0.7	14.6	-2.0	14.6	0.0	14.6	0.0	14.6	0.0	14.6	0.0	14.6	0.0	14.4	-1.4	14.4	0.0	14.4	0.0	14.4	0.0	14.5	0.7
1928	14.6	0.7	14.6	0.0	14.5	-0.7	16.5	13.8	17.1	3.6	17.1	0.0	17.0	-0.6	17.1	0.6	16.9	-1.2	16.8	-0.6	16.9	0.6	17.0	0.6
1929	17.0	0.0	17.0	0.0	16.7	-1.8	16.6	-0.6	16.6	0.0	16.6	0.0	16.6	0.0	16.4	-1.2	15.8	-3.7	15.7	-0.6	15.9	1.3	16.4	3.1
1930	16.5	0.6	16.7	1.2	16.6	-0.6	16.6	0.0	16.6	0.0	16.6	0.0	16.2	-2.4	16.6	2.5	16.6	0.0	16.6	0.0	16.6	0.0	16.5	-0.6
1931	16.5	0.0	16.2	-1.8	15.9	-1.9	15.6	-1.9	15.4	-1.3	15.2	-1.3	14.4	-5.3	14.6	1.4	14.6	0.0	14.5	-0.7	14.5	0.0	14.2	-2.1
1932	13.9	-2.1	13.9	0.0	13.9	0.0	13.7	-1.4	13.6	-0.7	13.8	1.5	14.7	6.5	14.8	0.7	14.8	0.0	14.8	0.0	14.9	0.7	15.1	1.3
1933	15.1	0.0	15.2	0.7	15.2	0.0	15.2	0.0	15.2	0.0	15.2	0.0	15.8	3.9	16.1	1.9	16.1	0.0	16.2	0.6	16.2	0.0	16.3	0.6
1934	16.6	1.8	16.7	0.6	16.6	-0.6	16.2	-2.4	16.2	0.0	16.6	2.5	16.6	0.0	16.6	0.0	16.6	0.0	16.6	0.0	16.6	0.0	16.6	0.0
1935	16.6	0.0	16.6	0.0	16.6	0.0	16.7	0.6	16.6	-0.6	16.6	0.0	16.6	0.0	16.6	0.0	16.6	0.0	16.6	0.0	16.7	0.6	16.7	0.0
1936	16.6	-0.6	16.7	0.6	16.6	-0.6	16.6	0.0	16.7	0.6	16.7	0.0	16.7	0.0	16.7	0.0	16.7	0.0	16.7	0.0	16.7	0.0	16.7	0.0
1937	16.7	0.0	16.6	-0.6	16.6	0.0	16.6	0.0	16.6	0.0	16.6	0.0	16.6	0.0	16.7	0.6	16.7	0.0	16.3	-2.4	16.7	2.5	16.7	0.0
1938	16.7	0.0	16.7	0.0	16.7	0.0	16.7	0.0	16.7	0.0	16.6	-0.6	16.8	1.2	16.7	-0.6	16.6	-0.6	16.7	0.6	16.9	1.2	16.9	0.0
1939	16.7	-1.2	16.7	0.0	16.7	0.0	16.7	0.0	16.7	0.0	16.7	0.0	16.7	0.0	16.7	0.0	16.7	0.0	16.7	0.0	16.7	0.0	16.7	0.0
1940	16.7	0.0	16.7	0.0	16.7	0.0	16.6	-0.6	16.6	0.0	16.6	0.0	16.6	0.0	16.6	0.0	16.6	0.0	16.6	0.0	16.6	0.0	16.6	0.0
1941	16.6	0.0	16.6	0.0	16.6	0.0	16.6	0.0	16.7	0.6	16.7	0.0	16.8	0.6	16.8	0.0	16.9	0.6	16.9	0.0	17.0	0.6	17.1	0.6
1942	17.1	0.0	17.2	0.6	17.2	0.0	17.3	0.6	17.3	0.0	17.3	0.0	17.3	0.0	17.3	0.0	17.3	0.0	17.3	0.0	17.3	0.0	17.3	0.0
1943	17.3	0.0	17.3	0.0	17.3	0.0	17.3	0.0	17.3	0.0	17.2	-0.6	17.2	0.0	17.3	0.6	17.3	0.0	17.2	-0.6	17.2	0.0	17.2	0.0
1944	17.2	0.0	17.2	0.0	17.2	0.0	17.3	0.6	17.6	1.7	17.6	0.0	17.6	0.0	17.6	0.0	17.6	0.0	17.7	0.6	17.7	0.0	17.7	0.0
1945	17.7	0.0	17.9	1.1	17.9	0.0	17.9	0.0	17.9	0.0	17.9	0.0	17.9	0.0	17.9	0.0	18.0	0.6	18.1	0.6	18.1	0.0	18.1	0.0
1946	18.4	1.7	18.4	0.0	18.5	0.5	18.5	0.0	18.5	0.0	18.6	0.5	18.7	0.5	18.9	1.1	19.0	0.5	19.0	0.0	19.1	0.5	19.2	0.5
1947	19.6	2.1	19.9	1.5	20.0	0.5	20.2	1.0	20.2	0.0	20.3	0.5	20.4	0.5	20.7	1.5	20.9	1.0	21.0	0.5	21.1	0.5	21.1	0.0
1948	21.7	2.8	21.9	0.9	22.0	0.5	22.1	0.5	22.1	0.0	22.2	0.5	22.7	2.3	22.7	0.0	22.8	0.4	22.8	0.0	22.9	0.4	23.0	0.4
1949	23.1	0.4	23.2	0.4	23.2	0.0	23.2	0.0	23.2	0.0	23.2	0.0	23.1	-0.4	23.1	0.0	23.1	0.0	23.2	0.4	23.2	0.0	23.2	0.0
1950	23.3	0.4	23.3	0.0	23.3	0.0	23.3	0.0	23.3	0.0	23.3	0.0	23.3	0.0	23.4	0.4	23.5	0.4	23.9	1.7	24.0	0.4	24.1	0.4
1951	24.9	3.3	24.9	0.0	24.9	0.0	24.9	0.0	24.9	0.0	24.9	0.0	24.9	0.0	24.9	0.0	24.9	0.0	24.9	0.0	24.9	0.0	24.9	0.0
1952	24.9	0.0	24.9	0.0	24.9	0.0	24.9	0.0	24.9	0.0	24.9	0.0	24.9	0.0	24.9	0.0	24.9	0.0	24.9	0.0	24.9	0.0	24.9	0.0
1953	24.9	0.0	24.9	0.0	25.0	0.4	25.9	3.6	26.0	0.4	26.0	0.0	26.0	0.0	26.1	0.4	26.3	0.8	26.3	0.0	26.3	0.0	26.3	0.0
1954	26.4	0.4	26.4	0.0	26.4	0.0	26.4	0.0	26.4	0.0	26.5	0.4	26.9	1.5	26.9	0.0	26.9	0.0	26.9	0.0	26.9	0.0	26.9	0.0
1955	27.1	0.7	27.3	0.7	27.3	0.0	27.5	0.7	27.5	0.0	27.5	0.0	27.5	0.0	27.6	0.4	27.6	0.0	27.6	0.0	27.6	0.0	27.7	0.4
1956	28.6	3.2	28.6	0.0	28.6	0.0	28.6	0.0	28.6	0.0	28.7	0.3	28.7	0.0	28.7	0.0	28.7	0.0	29.0	1.0	29.0	0.0	29.0	0.0
1957	29.6	2.1	29.7	0.3	29.7	0.0	29.8	0.3	29.8	0.0	29.9	0.3	30.0	0.3	30.0	0.0	30.1	0.3	30.1	0.0	30.1	0.0	30.1	0.0
1958	30.6	1.7	30.6	0.0	30.5	-0.3	30.6	0.3	30.6	0.0	30.6	0.0	30.6	0.0	30.6	0.0	30.6	0.0	30.6	0.0	30.6	0.0	30.6	0.0
1959	30.9	1.0	30.9	0.0	30.9	0.0	30.9	0.0	30.9	0.0	30.8	-0.3	30.9	0.3	30.9	0.0	30.9	0.0	30.9	0.0	30.9	0.0	30.9	0.0
1960	31.3	1.3	31.3	0.0	31.3	0.0	31.3	0.0	31.3	0.0	31.3	0.0	31.3	0.0	31.3	0.0	31.3	0.0	31.3	0.0	31.3	0.0	31.3	0.0
1961	31.3	0.0	31.3	0.0	31.4	0.3	31.4	0.0	31.4	0.0	31.4	0.0	31.4	0.0	31.4	0.0	31.4	0.0	31.4	0.0	31.2	-0.6	31.0	-0.6
1962	31.3	1.0	31.4	0.3	31.4	0.0	31.4	0.0	31.4	0.0	31.5	0.3	31.5	0.0	31.5	0.0	31.5	0.0	31.5	0.0	31.5	0.0	31.5	0.0
1963	31.3	-0.6	31.4	0.3	31.4	0.0	31.4	0.0	31.4	0.0	31.5	0.3	31.5	0.0	31.4	-0.3	31.4	0.0	31.4	0.0	31.4	0.0	31.4	0.0
1964	31.3	-0.3	31.3	0.0	31.3	0.0	31.3	0.0	31.3	0.0	31.3	0.0	31.3	0.0	31.3	0.0	31.3	0.0	31.3	0.0	31.4	0.3	31.4	0.0
1965	31.5	0.3	31.5	0.0	31.5	0.0	31.5	0.0	31.6	0.0	31.6	0.0	31.6	0.0	31.6	0.0	31.6	0.0	31.6	0.0	31.6	0.0	31.5	0.0
1966	31.6	0.3	31.6	0.0	31.6	0.0	31.6	0.0	31.6	0.0	31.6	0.0	31.6	0.0	31.6	0.0	31.6	0.0	31.6	0.0	31.8	0.6	31.7	-0.3	31.8	0.3
1967	32.2	1.3	32.2	0.0	32.2	0.0	32.3	0.3	32.2	-0.3	32.2	0.0	32.2	0.0	32.3	0.3	32.3	0.0	32.4	0.3	32.4	0.0	32.5	0.3
1968	32.9	1.2	33.1	0.6	33.1	0.0	33.2	0.3	33.2	0.0	33.3	0.3	33.4	0.3	33.4	0.0	33.4	0.0	33.4	0.0	33.6	0.6	33.6	0.0
1969	34.3	2.1	34.2	-0.3	34.3	0.3	34.3	0.0	34.3	0.0	34.4	0.3	34.5	0.3	34.5	0.0	34.6	0.3	34.6	0.0	34.6	0.0	34.6	0.0
1970	35.9	3.8	36.1	0.6	36.1	0.0	37.1	2.8	36.2	-2.4	36.3	0.3	36.3	0.0	36.3	0.0	36.3	0.0	36.4	0.3	36.4	0.0	36.4	0.0

[Continued]

Concrete Ingredients and Related Products
Producer Price Index
Base 1982 = 100
[Continued]

For 1926-1997. Columns headed % show percentile change in the index from the previous period for which an index is available.

Year	Jan Index	Jan %	Feb Index	Feb %	Mar Index	Mar %	Apr Index	Apr %	May Index	May %	Jun Index	Jun %	Jul Index	Jul %	Aug Index	Aug %	Sep Index	Sep %	Oct Index	Oct %	Nov Index	Nov %	Dec Index	Dec %
1971	37.7	3.6	37.8	0.3	38.9	2.9	39.0	0.3	39.1	0.3	39.2	0.3	39.8	1.5	40.0	0.5	40.1	0.2	40.1	0.0	40.1	0.0	40.1	0.0
1972	40.1	0.0	40.2	0.2	40.2	0.0	40.8	1.5	40.9	0.2	40.9	0.0	40.9	0.0	41.3	1.0	41.4	0.2	41.4	0.0	41.4	0.0	41.4	0.0
1973	41.6	0.5	41.7	0.2	41.9	0.5	42.5	1.4	42.4	-0.2	42.5	0.2	42.5	0.0	42.5	0.0	42.5	0.0	42.6	0.2	42.6	0.0	42.6	0.0
1974	44.8	5.2	45.1	0.7	45.3	0.4	46.2	2.0	46.9	1.5	47.1	0.4	49.5	5.1	49.7	0.4	49.8	0.2	50.2	0.8	50.4	0.4	50.5	0.2
1975	53.9	6.7	54.4	0.9	54.7	0.6	55.3	1.1	55.5	0.4	55.6	0.2	56.1	0.9	56.1	0.0	56.5	0.7	56.4	-0.2	56.4	0.0	56.4	0.0
1976	58.2	3.2	58.4	0.3	58.6	0.3	60.3	2.9	60.4	0.2	60.5	0.2	60.9	0.7	60.9	0.0	61.0	0.2	61.1	0.2	61.0	-0.2	61.1	0.2
1977	62.6	2.5	62.7	0.2	63.0	0.5	64.0	1.6	64.4	0.6	64.5	0.2	64.7	0.3	64.8	0.2	64.9	0.2	64.9	0.0	65.0	0.2	65.0	0.0
1978	67.7	4.2	68.0	0.4	68.4	0.6	69.9	2.2	70.0	0.1	70.2	0.3	70.7	0.7	71.0	0.4	71.3	0.4	71.6	0.4	72.1	0.7	72.1	0.0
1979	76.1	5.5	76.9	1.1	77.4	0.7	78.1	0.9	78.2	0.1	78.5	0.4	79.1	0.8	79.3	0.3	79.6	0.4	80.1	0.6	80.5	0.5	81.0	0.6
1980	85.5	5.6	86.0	0.6	86.3	0.3	87.7	1.6	87.9	0.2	88.1	0.2	89.0	1.0	89.9	1.0	90.0	0.1	90.0	0.0	90.1	0.1	90.2	0.1
1981	93.5	3.7	94.0	0.5	94.4	0.4	96.0	1.7	96.0	0.0	96.0	0.0	96.1	0.1	96.1	0.0	96.3	0.2	96.3	0.0	96.3	0.0	96.4	0.1
1982	98.8	2.5	99.5	0.7	99.9	0.4	99.8	-0.1	100.8	1.0	100.9	0.1	100.6	-0.3	100.4	-0.2	100.3	-0.1	100.0	-0.3	100.0	0.0	98.9	-1.1
1983	99.1	0.2	100.0	0.9	99.5	-0.5	100.9	1.4	101.2	0.3	101.4	0.2	101.3	-0.1	102.1	0.8	102.3	0.2	102.2	-0.1	101.6	-0.6	101.5	-0.1
1984	101.8	0.3	103.2	1.4	104.6	1.4	104.6	0.0	105.8	1.1	105.4	-0.4	105.5	0.1	106.0	0.5	105.9	-0.1	105.7	-0.2	106.0	0.3	106.3	0.3
1985	106.8	0.5	107.6	0.7	108.2	0.6	108.5	0.3	109.3	0.7	109.3	0.0	108.9	-0.4	109.1	0.2	108.7	-0.4	108.6	-0.1	108.1	-0.5	108.4	0.3
1986	109.4	0.9	109.4	0.0	109.7	0.3	110.1	0.4	109.7	-0.4	109.5	-0.2	109.4	-0.1	109.3	-0.1	109.4	0.1	109.5	0.1	109.5	0.0	108.2	-1.2
1987	109.1	0.8	109.6	0.5	110.1	0.5	110.4	0.3	110.7	0.3	110.8	0.1	110.8	0.0	110.8	0.0	110.8	0.0	110.8	0.0	110.8	0.0	110.6	-0.2
1988	111.3	0.6	111.6	0.3	111.6	0.0	112.3	0.6	112.6	0.3	112.3	-0.3	112.1	-0.2	112.2	0.1	112.0	-0.2	111.9	-0.1	111.9	0.0	111.9	0.0
1989	112.3	0.4	112.3	0.0	112.3	0.0	113.1	0.7	113.3	0.2	113.3	0.0	113.3	0.0	113.2	-0.1	113.7	0.4	113.8	0.1	113.6	-0.2	113.6	0.0
1990	113.9	0.3	114.3	0.4	114.8	0.4	115.2	0.3	115.5	0.3	115.5	0.0	115.3	-0.2	115.5	0.2	115.8	0.3	115.8	0.0	116.0	0.2	115.9	-0.1
1991	117.1	1.0	118.3	1.0	118.3	0.0	118.6	0.3	118.8	0.2	118.9	0.1	118.7	-0.2	118.8	0.1	118.5	-0.3	118.5	0.0	118.3	-0.2	118.2	-0.1
1992	118.8	0.5	118.8	0.0	119.4	0.5	119.3	-0.1	119.4	0.1	119.4	0.0	119.4	0.0	119.5	0.1	119.4	-0.1	119.6	0.2	119.7	0.1	119.9	0.2
1993	120.9	0.8	121.1	0.2	121.4	0.2	123.2	1.5	123.2	0.0	123.5	0.2	123.7	0.2	123.8	0.1	124.5	0.6	125.5	0.8	125.2	-0.2	125.3	0.1
1994	126.2	0.7	126.6	0.3	127.0	0.3	128.4	1.1	128.4	0.0	129.0	0.5	129.2	0.2	129.7	0.4	129.8	0.1	130.2	0.3	130.2	0.0	130.2	0.0
1995	131.6	1.1	132.1	0.4	132.4	0.2	134.5	1.6	134.8	0.2	135.2	0.3	135.7	0.4	135.7	0.0	135.9	0.1	135.8	-0.1	136.0	0.1	135.9	-0.1
1996	136.5	0.4	136.7	0.1	137.0	0.2	138.6	1.2	139.2	0.4	139.2	0.0	139.4	0.1	139.3	-0.1	140.0	0.5	140.0	0.0	140.2	0.1	140.0	-0.1
1997	140.7	0.5	140.7	0.0	140.8	0.1	142.3	1.1	142.7	0.3	143.0	0.2	143.2	0.1	143.3	0.1	143.2	-0.1	143.2	0.0	143.2	0.0	143.4	0.1

Source: U.S. Department of Labor, Bureau of Labor Statistics, Division of Industry Prices and Price Indexes. n.e.c. stands for not elsewhere classified. - indicates no data collected for period or unavailable.

Concrete Products
Producer Price Index
Base 1982 = 100

For 1926-1997. Columns headed % show percentile change in the index from the previous period for which an index is available.

Year	Jan Index	%	Feb Index	%	Mar Index	%	Apr Index	%	May Index	%	Jun Index	%	Jul Index	%	Aug Index	%	Sep Index	%	Oct Index	%	Nov Index	%	Dec Index	%
1926	23.7	-	23.7	0.0	23.7	0.0	23.7	0.0	23.7	0.0	23.7	0.0	23.7	0.0	23.7	0.0	23.7	0.0	23.7	0.0	23.7	0.0	23.7	0.0
1927	23.7	0.0	23.7	0.0	23.7	0.0	23.7	0.0	23.7	0.0	23.7	0.0	23.7	0.0	23.7	0.0	23.7	0.0	23.7	0.0	23.7	0.0	23.7	0.0
1928	23.7	0.0	23.7	0.0	23.7	0.0	23.7	0.0	23.7	0.0	23.7	0.0	23.7	0.0	23.7	0.0	23.7	0.0	23.7	0.0	23.7	0.0	23.7	0.0
1929	23.7	0.0	23.7	0.0	23.7	0.0	23.7	0.0	23.7	0.0	23.7	0.0	23.7	0.0	23.0	-3.0	23.0	0.0	23.0	0.0	23.0	0.0	23.0	0.0
1930	23.0	0.0	23.0	0.0	23.0	0.0	23.0	0.0	22.6	-1.7	22.6	0.0	23.0	1.8	23.7	3.0	25.0	5.5	25.0	0.0	25.0	0.0	25.0	0.0
1931	24.6	-1.6	23.2	-5.7	22.6	-2.6	22.6	0.0	22.6	0.0	22.6	0.0	22.5	-0.4	21.3	-5.3	21.3	0.0	21.3	0.0	21.3	0.0	21.3	0.0
1932	21.3	0.0	21.2	-0.5	21.2	0.0	20.0	-5.7	20.0	0.0	20.0	0.0	20.0	0.0	20.0	0.0	20.0	0.0	20.9	4.5	20.9	0.0	20.9	0.0
1933	20.9	0.0	20.9	0.0	20.9	0.0	20.9	0.0	20.9	0.0	20.9	0.0	20.9	0.0	20.9	0.0	20.9	0.0	20.9	0.0	20.9	0.0	20.9	0.0
1934	20.9	0.0	20.9	0.0	20.9	0.0	20.9	0.0	20.9	0.0	20.9	0.0	20.9	0.0	20.9	0.0	20.9	0.0	20.9	0.0	20.9	0.0	20.9	0.0
1935	20.9	0.0	20.9	0.0	19.7	-5.7	18.6	-5.6	18.6	0.0	18.6	0.0	18.6	0.0	18.6	0.0	18.6	0.0	18.6	0.0	18.6	0.0	18.6	0.0
1936	20.9	12.4	20.9	0.0	20.9	0.0	20.9	0.0	20.9	0.0	20.9	0.0	20.9	0.0	20.9	0.0	20.4	-2.4	18.6	-8.8	18.6	0.0	18.6	0.0
1937	18.6	0.0	18.6	0.0	18.6	0.0	21.2	14.0	21.2	0.0	21.2	0.0	21.2	0.0	21.2	0.0	21.2	0.0	21.2	0.0	21.2	0.0	19.2	-9.4
1938	18.6	-3.1	18.6	0.0	18.6	0.0	18.6	0.0	18.6	0.0	18.6	0.0	18.6	0.0	18.6	0.0	18.6	0.0	18.6	0.0	18.6	0.0	19.9	7.0
1939	21.2	6.5	21.2	0.0	21.2	0.0	21.2	0.0	18.0	-15.1	15.9	-11.7	15.9	0.0	15.9	0.0	17.2	8.2	18.6	8.1	18.6	0.0	18.6	0.0
1940	18.6	0.0	18.6	0.0	16.6	-10.8	15.9	-4.2	15.9	0.0	15.9	0.0	15.9	0.0	15.9	0.0	15.9	0.0	15.9	0.0	15.9	0.0	18.0	13.2
1941	18.6	3.3	18.6	0.0	18.6	0.0	18.6	0.0	18.6	0.0	18.9	1.6	19.9	5.3	19.9	0.0	19.9	0.0	19.9	0.0	19.9	0.0	19.9	0.0
1942	19.9	0.0	19.9	0.0	19.9	0.0	19.9	0.0	19.9	0.0	19.9	0.0	19.9	0.0	19.9	0.0	19.9	0.0	19.9	0.0	19.9	0.0	19.9	0.0
1943	19.9	0.0	19.9	0.0	19.9	0.0	19.9	0.0	19.9	0.0	19.9	0.0	19.9	0.0	19.9	0.0	19.9	0.0	19.9	0.0	19.9	0.0	19.9	0.0
1944	19.9	0.0	19.9	0.0	19.9	0.0	19.9	0.0	19.9	0.0	19.9	0.0	19.9	0.0	19.9	0.0	19.9	0.0	19.9	0.0	19.9	0.0	19.9	0.0
1945	19.9	0.0	19.9	0.0	19.9	0.0	19.9	0.0	19.9	0.0	19.9	0.0	19.9	0.0	19.9	0.0	19.9	0.0	19.9	0.0	19.9	0.0	19.9	0.0
1946	19.9	0.0	19.9	0.0	19.9	0.0	19.9	0.0	20.2	1.5	21.2	5.0	22.0	3.8	21.2	-3.6	21.2	0.0	21.2	0.0	22.5	6.1	23.9	6.2
1947	23.9	0.0	23.9	0.0	23.9	0.0	23.9	0.0	23.9	0.0	23.9	0.0	24.0	0.4	23.8	-0.8	23.6	-0.8	24.0	1.7	24.2	0.8	24.2	0.0
1948	24.7	2.1	24.8	0.4	24.8	0.0	24.8	0.0	24.8	0.0	24.8	0.0	25.0	0.8	25.4	1.6	25.4	0.0	25.4	0.0	25.4	0.0	25.4	0.0
1949	25.4	0.0	25.4	0.0	25.6	0.8	25.6	0.0	25.6	0.0	25.6	0.0	25.6	0.0	25.8	0.8	25.8	0.0	25.8	0.0	25.8	0.0	25.8	0.0
1950	25.8	0.0	25.8	0.0	25.8	0.0	25.8	0.0	25.9	0.4	26.0	0.4	26.0	0.0	26.2	0.8	26.6	1.5	27.0	1.5	27.0	0.0	27.2	0.7
1951	27.9	2.6	28.0	0.4	28.0	0.0	28.0	0.0	28.0	0.0	28.0	0.0	28.0	0.0	28.0	0.0	28.0	0.0	28.0	0.0	28.0	0.0	28.0	0.0
1952	28.0	0.0	28.0	0.0	28.0	0.0	28.0	0.0	28.0	0.0	28.0	0.0	28.0	0.0	28.0	0.0	28.0	0.0	28.0	0.0	28.0	0.0	28.0	0.0
1953	28.1	0.4	28.1	0.0	28.1	0.0	28.4	1.1	28.7	1.1	28.7	0.0	28.8	0.3	28.9	0.3	29.2	1.0	29.2	0.0	29.2	0.0	29.1	-0.3
1954	29.1	0.0	29.2	0.3	29.2	0.0	29.2	0.0	29.2	0.0	29.2	0.0	29.3	0.3	29.3	0.0	29.3	0.0	29.3	0.0	29.2	-0.3	29.2	0.0
1955	29.0	-0.7	29.1	0.3	29.4	1.0	29.4	0.0	29.4	0.0	29.4	0.0	29.4	0.0	29.5	0.3	29.8	1.0	29.9	0.3	29.9	0.0	29.9	0.0
1956	30.2	1.0	30.2	0.0	30.2	0.0	30.3	0.3	30.3	0.0	30.3	0.0	30.6	1.0	30.7	0.3	31.1	1.3	31.1	0.0	31.2	0.3	31.2	0.0
1957	31.3	0.3	31.3	0.0	31.3	0.0	31.5	0.6	31.5	0.0	31.5	0.0	31.4	-0.3	31.4	0.0	31.4	0.0	31.5	0.3	31.5	0.0	31.6	0.3
1958	31.8	0.6	31.8	0.0	31.8	0.0	31.8	0.0	31.9	0.3	31.9	0.0	32.0	0.3	31.9	-0.3	31.8	-0.3	31.9	0.3	31.9	0.0	32.0	0.3
1959	32.0	0.0	32.1	0.3	32.2	0.3	32.2	0.0	32.3	0.3	32.3	0.0	32.3	0.0	32.3	0.0	32.4	0.3	32.4	0.0	32.4	0.0	32.4	0.0
1960	32.5	0.3	32.6	0.3	32.6	0.0	32.6	0.0	32.7	0.3	32.6	-0.3	32.6	0.0	32.6	0.0	32.6	0.0	32.6	0.0	32.6	0.0	32.6	0.0
1961	32.6	0.0	32.6	0.0	32.6	0.0	32.6	0.0	32.6	0.0	32.6	0.0	32.6	0.0	32.6	0.0	32.7	0.3	32.7	0.0	32.6	-0.3	32.6	0.0
1962	32.6	0.0	32.7	0.3	32.7	0.0	32.7	0.0	32.6	-0.3	32.6	0.0	32.7	0.3	32.7	0.0	32.7	0.0	32.7	0.0	32.7	0.0	32.6	-0.3
1963	32.6	0.0	32.6	0.0	32.6	0.0	32.6	0.0	32.5	-0.3	32.5	0.0	32.2	-0.9	32.2	0.0	32.3	0.3	32.3	0.0	32.3	0.0	32.2	0.0
1964	32.2	-0.3	32.2	0.0	32.1	-0.3	32.0	-0.3	32.0	0.0	32.1	0.3	32.1	0.0	32.1	0.0	32.3	-0.3	32.4	0.3	32.4	0.0	32.4	0.0
1965	32.3	0.3	32.2	-0.3	32.2	0.0	32.3	0.3	32.3	0.0	32.4	0.3	32.4	0.0	32.9	-0.3	33.0	0.3	33.0	0.0	33.0	0.0	33.1	0.3
1966	32.5	0.3	32.5	0.0	32.6	0.3	32.7	0.3	32.7	0.0	32.8	0.3	32.8	0.0	32.9	0.3	33.0	0.3	33.0	0.0	33.0	0.0	33.1	0.3
1967	33.3	0.6	33.4	0.3	33.4	0.0	33.5	0.3	33.5	0.0	33.6	0.3	33.6	0.0	33.7	0.3	33.7	0.0	33.7	0.0	33.7	0.0	33.7	0.0
1968	33.9	0.6	34.0	0.3	34.1	0.3	34.3	0.6	34.3	0.0	34.5	0.6	34.5	0.0	34.6	0.3	34.6	0.0	34.8	0.6	34.8	0.0	34.9	0.3
1969	35.3	1.1	35.4	0.3	35.5	0.3	35.6	0.3	35.6	0.0	35.6	0.0	35.8	0.6	35.9	0.3	36.1	0.6	36.2	0.3	36.2	0.0	36.4	0.6
1970	37.0	1.6	37.1	0.3	37.3	0.5	37.3	0.0	37.4	0.3	37.6	0.5	37.7	0.3	37.8	0.3	38.1	0.8	38.1	0.0	38.2	0.3	38.4	0.5

[Continued]

Concrete Products
Producer Price Index
Base 1982 = 100
[Continued]

For 1926-1997. Columns headed % show percentile change in the index from the previous period for which an index is available.

Year	Jan Index	%	Feb Index	%	Mar Index	%	Apr Index	%	May Index	%	Jun Index	%	Jul Index	%	Aug Index	%	Sep Index	%	Oct Index	%	Nov Index	%	Dec Index	%
1971	39.3	2.3	39.5	0.5	39.8	0.8	40.1	0.8	40.1	0.0	40.3	0.5	40.8	1.2	41.2	1.0	41.1	-0.2	41.1	0.0	41.1	0.0	41.3	0.5
1972	41.4	0.2	41.6	0.5	41.8	0.5	42.0	0.5	42.0	0.0	42.1	0.2	42.3	0.5	42.3	0.0	42.4	0.2	42.7	0.7	42.7	0.0	42.8	0.2
1973	43.1	0.7	43.3	0.5	43.5	0.5	43.9	0.9	44.1	0.5	44.4	0.7	44.4	0.0	44.4	0.0	44.5	0.2	44.9	0.9	45.0	0.2	45.2	0.4
1974	47.0	4.0	47.8	1.7	48.6	1.7	48.8	0.4	49.6	1.6	50.3	1.4	52.1	3.6	52.5	0.8	52.8	0.6	53.6	1.5	53.9	0.6	54.3	0.7
1975	56.1	3.3	56.4	0.5	56.8	0.7	57.0	0.4	57.1	0.2	57.2	0.2	57.5	0.5	57.5	0.0	57.5	0.0	57.8	0.5	57.9	0.2	58.1	0.3
1976	59.6	2.6	59.8	0.3	59.8	0.0	59.9	0.2	60.2	0.5	60.3	0.2	60.8	0.8	60.9	0.2	60.9	0.0	60.9	0.0	61.2	0.5	61.5	0.5
1977	62.9	2.3	63.1	0.3	63.2	0.2	63.8	0.9	64.0	0.3	64.1	0.2	64.7	0.9	65.0	0.5	65.1	0.2	65.5	0.6	65.6	0.2	65.7	0.2
1978	68.1	3.7	68.9	1.2	69.2	0.4	69.8	0.9	70.4	0.9	71.1	1.0	72.0	1.3	73.8	2.5	74.4	0.8	74.6	0.3	74.8	0.3	75.3	0.7
1979	79.1	5.0	79.4	0.4	79.8	0.5	80.7	1.1	81.1	0.5	81.8	0.9	82.3	0.6	82.7	0.5	83.5	1.0	84.0	0.6	84.1	0.1	85.0	1.1
1980	89.1	4.8	89.6	0.6	90.3	0.8	91.6	1.4	92.4	0.9	92.6	0.2	92.6	0.0	92.7	0.1	93.1	0.4	93.2	0.1	93.3	0.1	93.2	-0.1
1981	96.1	3.1	96.2	0.1	96.3	0.1	97.3	1.0	97.8	0.5	98.5	0.7	98.5	0.0	98.5	0.0	98.4	-0.1	98.5	0.1	98.5	0.0	98.6	0.1
1982	99.2	0.6	99.3	0.1	99.5	0.2	100.0	0.5	100.1	0.1	100.2	0.1	100.3	0.1	100.4	0.1	100.3	-0.1	100.3	0.0	100.1	-0.2	100.2	0.1
1983	100.5	0.3	100.8	0.3	100.9	0.1	101.1	0.2	101.1	0.0	101.3	0.2	101.5	0.2	101.7	0.2	101.9	0.2	101.9	0.0	102.1	0.2	102.2	0.1
1984	102.4	0.2	102.7	0.3	102.8	0.1	103.7	0.9	103.9	0.2	104.1	0.2	104.3	0.2	104.5	0.2	104.7	0.2	104.8	0.1	104.7	-0.1	104.8	0.1
1985	105.6	0.8	105.6	0.0	106.0	0.4	106.3	0.3	107.5	1.1	107.9	0.4	107.9	0.0	108.4	0.5	108.5	0.1	108.4	-0.1	108.6	0.2	108.8	0.2
1986	109.1	0.3	109.1	0.0	109.1	0.0	109.6	0.5	109.6	0.0	109.3	-0.3	109.4	0.1	109.2	-0.2	109.1	-0.1	108.9	-0.2	108.9	0.0	109.1	0.2
1987	109.4	0.3	109.4	0.0	109.2	-0.2	109.3	0.1	109.4	0.1	109.3	-0.1	109.4	0.1	109.3	-0.1	109.4	0.1	109.4	0.0	109.6	0.2	109.4	-0.2
1988	109.7	0.3	109.8	0.1	109.8	0.0	109.7	-0.1	109.9	0.2	110.1	0.2	110.1	0.0	110.1	0.0	109.9	-0.2	109.9	0.0	110.2	0.3	110.3	0.1
1989	110.4	0.1	110.7	0.3	110.7	0.0	110.7	0.0	110.8	0.1	111.2	0.4	111.4	0.2	111.7	0.3	111.6	-0.1	111.6	0.0	111.6	0.0	111.9	0.3
1990	112.1	0.2	112.2	0.1	112.8	0.5	112.6	-0.2	113.1	0.4	113.3	0.2	113.7	0.4	113.9	0.2	114.2	0.3	114.2	0.0	114.8	0.5	115.0	0.2
1991	116.0	0.9	116.2	0.2	116.5	0.3	116.3	-0.2	116.5	0.2	116.9	0.3	117.0	0.1	116.9	-0.1	116.7	-0.2	116.7	0.0	116.7	0.0	116.9	0.2
1992	117.1	0.2	117.2	0.1	117.2	0.0	116.9	-0.3	117.1	0.2	117.0	-0.1	117.1	0.1	117.3	0.2	117.1	-0.2	117.2	0.1	117.7	0.4	118.0	0.3
1993	118.7	0.6	118.9	0.2	119.2	0.3	119.5	0.3	119.7	0.2	120.0	0.3	120.2	0.2	120.3	0.1	120.7	0.3	121.0	0.2	121.7	0.6	122.1	0.3
1994	122.5	0.3	122.7	0.2	123.4	0.6	123.7	0.2	124.0	0.2	124.2	0.2	124.7	0.4	125.1	0.3	125.3	0.2	125.8	0.4	126.5	0.6	127.0	0.4
1995	127.8	0.6	128.1	0.2	128.5	0.3	129.1	0.5	129.3	0.2	129.3	0.0	129.6	0.2	129.7	0.1	130.0	0.2	130.2	0.2	130.8	0.5	131.0	0.2
1996	131.5	0.4	132.0	0.4	132.4	0.3	132.8	0.3	133.0	0.2	133.2	0.2	133.6	0.3	133.5	-0.1	133.8	0.2	133.8	0.0	134.5	0.5	134.7	0.1
1997	135.0	0.2	135.2	0.1	135.4	0.1	135.9	0.4	136.1	0.1	135.8	-0.2	136.2	0.3	136.1	-0.1	136.1	0.0	136.4	0.2	136.8	0.3	136.8	0.0

Source: U.S. Department of Labor, Bureau of Labor Statistics, Division of Industry Prices and Price Indexes. n.e.c. stands for not elsewhere classified. - indicates no data collected for period or unavailable.

Clay Construction Products ex. Refractories
Producer Price Index
Base 1982 = 100

For 1947-1997. Columns headed % show percentile change in the index from the previous period for which an index is available.

Year	Jan Index	%	Feb Index	%	Mar Index	%	Apr Index	%	May Index	%	Jun Index	%	Jul Index	%	Aug Index	%	Sep Index	%	Oct Index	%	Nov Index	%	Dec Index	%
1947	23.5	-	23.5	0.0	23.6	0.4	23.6	0.0	23.7	0.4	23.7	0.0	23.7	0.0	24.0	1.3	24.2	0.8	24.3	0.4	24.5	0.8	24.5	0.0
1948	24.9	1.6	25.1	0.8	25.2	0.4	25.3	0.4	25.5	0.8	25.7	0.8	25.9	0.8	26.0	0.4	26.1	0.4	26.3	0.8	26.3	0.0	26.3	0.0
1949	26.5	0.8	26.5	0.0	26.5	0.0	26.5	0.0	26.5	0.0	26.5	0.0	26.5	0.0	26.4	-0.4	26.3	-0.4	26.3	0.0	26.4	0.4	26.4	0.0
1950	26.5	0.4	26.6	0.4	26.7	0.4	26.7	0.0	27.0	1.1	27.2	0.7	27.6	1.5	28.1	1.8	28.4	1.1	28.7	1.1	28.9	0.7	29.4	1.7
1951	29.8	1.4	29.9	0.3	29.9	0.0	29.9	0.0	29.9	0.0	29.9	0.0	29.9	0.0	29.9	0.0	29.9	0.0	29.9	0.0	29.9	0.0	29.9	0.0
1952	29.9	0.0	29.9	0.0	29.9	0.0	29.8	-0.3	29.9	0.3	29.9	0.0	29.8	-0.3	29.8	0.0	29.8	0.0	29.8	0.0	29.8	0.0	29.8	0.0
1953	29.8	0.0	29.8	0.0	29.9	0.3	30.1	0.7	30.1	0.0	30.3	0.7	30.4	0.3	30.6	0.7	30.8	0.7	30.8	0.0	30.8	0.0	30.8	0.0
1954	30.8	0.0	30.8	0.0	30.8	0.0	30.8	0.0	30.8	0.0	30.8	0.0	30.8	0.0	30.9	0.3	31.0	0.3	31.0	0.0	31.0	0.0	31.0	0.0
1955	31.2	0.6	31.3	0.3	31.5	0.6	31.6	0.3	31.7	0.3	31.9	0.6	32.0	0.3	32.3	0.9	32.8	1.5	33.0	0.6	33.0	0.0	33.1	0.3
1956	33.4	0.9	33.5	0.3	33.6	0.3	33.7	0.3	33.7	0.0	33.9	0.6	33.9	0.0	33.9	0.0	33.9	0.0	33.9	0.0	34.1	0.6	34.1	0.0
1957	34.2	0.3	34.2	0.0	34.3	0.3	34.3	0.0	34.3	0.0	34.4	0.3	34.4	0.0	34.3	-0.3	34.3	0.0	34.3	0.0	34.3	0.0	34.4	0.3
1958	34.5	0.3	34.5	0.0	34.5	0.0	34.5	0.0	34.5	0.0	34.5	0.0	34.5	0.0	34.5	0.0	34.6	0.3	34.6	0.0	34.7	0.3	34.9	0.6
1959	35.0	0.3	35.2	0.6	35.2	0.0	35.2	0.0	35.3	0.3	35.4	0.3	35.5	0.3	35.5	0.0	35.5	0.0	35.5	0.0	35.5	0.0	35.6	0.3
1960	35.8	0.6	35.9	0.3	35.9	0.0	35.9	0.0	35.9	0.0	35.9	0.0	35.9	0.0	36.0	0.3	36.1	0.3	36.1	0.0	36.1	0.0	36.1	0.0
1961	36.0	-0.3	36.0	0.0	36.0	0.0	36.0	0.0	36.1	0.3	36.1	0.0	36.1	0.0	36.2	0.3	36.2	0.0	36.3	0.3	36.3	0.0	36.3	0.0
1962	36.3	0.0	36.4	0.3	36.4	0.0	36.5	0.3	36.5	0.0	36.5	0.0	36.5	0.0	36.5	0.0	36.5	0.0	36.4	-0.3	36.4	0.0	36.4	0.0
1963	36.5	0.3	36.5	0.0	36.5	0.0	36.6	0.3	36.7	0.3	36.7	0.0	36.7	0.0	36.7	0.0	36.6	-0.3	36.6	0.0	36.7	0.3	36.7	0.0
1964	36.5	-0.5	36.7	0.5	36.7	0.0	36.8	0.3	36.8	0.0	36.7	-0.3	36.7	0.0	36.7	0.0	36.8	0.3	36.8	0.0	36.8	0.0	36.9	0.3
1965	36.9	0.0	36.9	0.0	36.9	0.0	36.9	0.0	36.9	0.0	36.9	0.0	36.9	0.0	37.1	0.5	37.2	0.3	37.2	0.0	37.2	0.0	37.3	0.3
1966	37.3	0.0	37.4	0.3	37.5	0.3	37.5	0.0	37.5	0.0	37.7	0.5	37.7	0.0	37.8	0.3	37.8	0.0	37.8	0.0	38.0	0.5	37.9	-0.3
1967	38.0	0.3	38.0	0.0	38.1	0.3	38.1	0.0	38.2	0.3	38.2	0.0	38.5	0.8	38.5	0.0	38.6	0.3	38.6	0.0	38.6	0.0	38.8	0.5
1968	38.9	0.3	38.9	0.0	39.0	0.3	39.0	0.0	39.2	0.5	39.0	-0.5	39.1	0.3	39.6	1.3	39.6	0.0	39.7	0.3	40.1	1.0	40.1	0.0
1969	40.3	0.5	40.3	0.0	40.3	0.0	40.6	0.7	40.6	0.0	40.6	0.0	40.6	0.0	40.7	0.2	40.9	0.5	41.0	0.2	41.2	0.5	41.2	0.0
1970	41.5	0.7	41.5	0.0	41.7	0.5	42.0	0.7	42.1	0.2	42.1	0.0	42.2	0.2	42.2	0.0	42.4	0.5	42.5	0.2	42.5	0.0	42.6	0.2
1971	43.0	0.9	43.5	1.2	43.8	0.7	44.0	0.5	44.0	0.0	44.1	0.2	44.1	0.0	44.3	0.5	44.0	-0.7	44.0	0.0	44.0	0.0	44.3	0.7
1972	44.0	-0.7	44.5	1.1	44.6	0.2	44.9	0.7	45.0	0.2	45.0	0.0	45.1	0.2	45.1	0.0	45.1	0.0	45.4	0.7	45.5	0.2	45.6	0.2
1973	46.1	1.1	46.6	1.1	46.9	0.6	47.2	0.6	47.4	0.4	47.5	0.2	47.5	0.0	47.5	0.0	47.5	0.0	47.8	0.6	47.8	0.0	47.9	0.2
1974	48.8	1.9	49.2	0.8	50.1	1.8	50.4	0.6	50.9	1.0	51.4	1.0	51.9	1.0	52.6	1.3	53.4	1.5	54.2	1.5	54.2	0.0	54.9	1.3
1975	55.7	1.5	56.3	1.1	56.3	0.0	57.0	1.2	57.2	0.4	57.9	1.2	58.0	0.2	58.4	0.7	59.1	1.2	59.7	1.0	59.9	0.3	59.9	0.0
1976	61.0	1.8	61.4	0.7	61.6	0.3	61.9	0.5	62.0	0.2	62.2	0.3	62.5	0.5	63.2	1.1	63.7	0.8	63.7	0.0	64.5	1.3	64.7	0.3
1977	65.2	0.8	64.6	-0.9	65.4	1.2	68.1	4.1	68.5	0.6	69.1	0.9	70.5	2.0	70.8	0.4	71.2	0.6	72.0	1.1	71.0	-1.4	71.2	0.3
1978	72.7	2.1	73.0	0.4	73.9	1.2	74.3	0.5	74.5	0.3	75.0	0.7	75.4	0.5	75.8	0.5	77.6	2.4	77.6	0.0	78.4	1.0	79.2	1.0
1979	80.4	1.5	80.8	0.5	81.6	1.0	82.4	1.0	82.7	0.4	83.0	0.4	84.5	1.8	85.3	0.9	85.8	0.6	84.8	-1.2	84.8	0.0	86.9	2.5
1980	88.0	1.3	88.6	0.7	88.7	0.1	90.1	1.6	88.2	-2.1	88.2	0.0	88.2	0.0	88.1	-0.1	88.2	0.1	89.5	1.5	89.6	0.1	89.6	0.0
1981	91.8	2.5	92.0	0.2	93.8	2.0	94.3	0.5	95.9	1.7	96.1	0.2	96.2	0.1	96.2	0.0	97.9	1.8	98.2	0.3	98.4	0.2	98.7	0.3
1982	98.7	0.0	98.8	0.1	98.8	0.0	99.0	0.2	99.2	0.2	99.3	0.1	99.4	0.1	101.2	1.8	101.2	0.0	101.2	0.0	101.5	0.3	101.5	0.0
1983	101.6	0.1	101.3	-0.3	103.8	2.5	105.7	1.8	106.5	0.8	107.9	1.3	108.3	0.4	108.3	0.0	108.3	0.0	108.7	0.4	108.9	0.2	109.0	0.1
1984	109.0	0.0	108.8	-0.2	109.0	0.2	109.3	0.3	109.5	0.2	109.8	0.3	109.8	0.0	110.5	0.6	111.0	0.5	111.0	0.0	111.0	0.0	111.1	0.1
1985	111.7	0.5	111.8	0.1	111.9	0.1	112.1	0.2	112.3	0.2	113.9	1.4	113.8	-0.1	114.2	0.4	114.5	0.3	114.7	0.2	114.9	0.2	115.8	0.8
1986	116.8	0.9	115.5	-1.1	116.8	1.1	117.6	0.7	117.7	0.1	118.3	0.5	119.2	0.8	119.0	-0.2	118.9	-0.1	119.6	0.6	118.6	-0.8	118.3	-0.3
1987	119.6	1.1	119.5	-0.1	119.8	0.3	120.9	0.9	121.4	0.4	121.8	0.3	121.5	-0.2	122.4	0.7	122.2	-0.2	122.5	0.2	122.7	0.2	122.7	0.0
1988	123.1	0.3	124.0	0.7	124.0	0.0	123.7	-0.2	124.4	0.6	125.4	0.8	125.9	0.4	125.1	-0.6	125.2	0.1	125.5	0.2	125.7	0.2	126.2	0.4
1989	126.1	-0.1	125.6	-0.4	126.3	0.6	126.5	0.2	125.7	-0.6	126.9	1.0	126.8	-0.1	127.5	0.6	127.7	0.2	127.9	0.2	128.2	0.2	128.6	0.3
1990	128.5	-0.1	128.6	0.1	129.4	0.6	129.4	0.0	129.6	0.2	130.0	0.3	130.5	0.4	130.4	-0.1	130.4	0.0	130.5	0.1	130.2	-0.2	130.7	0.4
1991	129.5	-0.9	129.7	0.2	129.9	0.2	130.4	0.4	130.6	0.2	130.2	-0.3	130.1	-0.1	130.0	-0.1	130.3	0.2	130.4	0.1	130.3	-0.1	130.4	0.1

[Continued]

Clay Construction Products ex. Refractories
Producer Price Index
Base 1982 = 100
[Continued]

For 1947-1997. Columns headed % show percentile change in the index from the previous period for which an index is available.

Year	Jan Index	%	Feb Index	%	Mar Index	%	Apr Index	%	May Index	%	Jun Index	%	Jul Index	%	Aug Index	%	Sep Index	%	Oct Index	%	Nov Index	%	Dec Index	%
1992	130.3	-0.1	130.7	0.3	131.2	0.4	131.0	-0.2	132.0	0.8	132.4	0.3	132.5	0.1	132.7	0.2	132.6	-0.1	132.8	0.2	132.9	0.1	132.8	-0.1
1993	133.4	0.5	134.1	0.5	134.0	-0.1	134.7	0.5	134.9	0.1	135.3	0.3	135.5	0.1	135.8	0.2	135.9	0.1	136.1	0.1	136.1	0.0	135.7	-0.3
1994	135.9	0.1	136.7	0.6	138.2	1.1	138.1	-0.1	138.5	0.3	138.7	0.1	138.8	0.1	138.8	0.0	138.8	0.0	138.9	0.1	138.8	-0.1	138.9	0.1
1995	139.3	0.3	139.7	0.3	140.6	0.6	141.2	0.4	141.4	0.1	141.8	0.3	141.9	0.1	142.0	0.1	142.0	0.0	142.0	0.0	142.0	0.0	142.1	0.1
1996	142.3	0.1	141.9	-0.3	141.9	0.0	142.0	0.1	142.0	0.0	142.4	0.3	142.6	0.1	142.6	0.0	142.6	0.0	142.7	0.1	142.7	0.0	142.6	-0.1
1997	142.4	-0.1	142.4	0.0	142.9	0.4	143.3	0.3	143.3	0.0	143.2	-0.1	143.3	0.1	143.9	0.4	144.1	0.1	144.1	0.0	144.1	0.0	144.1	0.0

Source: U.S. Department of Labor, Bureau of Labor Statistics, Division of Industry Prices and Price Indexes. n.e.c. stands for not elsewhere classified. - indicates no data collected for period or unavailable.

Refractories
Producer Price Index
Base 1982 = 100

For 1947-1997. Columns headed % show percentile change in the index from the previous period for which an index is available.

Year	Jan Index	%	Feb Index	%	Mar Index	%	Apr Index	%	May Index	%	Jun Index	%	Jul Index	%	Aug Index	%	Sep Index	%	Oct Index	%	Nov Index	%	Dec Index	%
1947	13.4	-	13.4	0.0	13.4	0.0	14.5	8.2	14.5	0.0	14.5	0.0	14.5	0.0	14.5	0.0	14.5	0.0	14.5	0.0	15.0	3.4	15.1	0.7
1948	15.1	0.0	15.1	0.0	15.1	0.0	15.1	0.0	15.1	0.0	15.1	0.0	16.1	6.6	16.5	2.5	16.5	0.0	16.5	0.0	16.5	0.0	16.5	0.0
1949	16.5	0.0	16.5	0.0	16.5	0.0	16.5	0.0	16.5	0.0	16.5	0.0	16.5	0.0	16.5	0.0	16.5	0.0	16.5	0.0	16.5	0.0	16.5	0.0
1950	17.6	6.7	17.8	1.1	17.8	0.0	17.8	0.0	17.8	0.0	17.8	0.0	17.8	0.0	17.8	0.0	17.8	0.0	19.1	7.3	19.6	2.6	19.6	0.0
1951	19.6	0.0	19.6	0.0	19.6	0.0	19.6	0.0	19.6	0.0	19.6	0.0	19.6	0.0	19.6	0.0	19.6	0.0	19.6	0.0	19.6	0.0	19.6	0.0
1952	19.6	0.0	19.6	0.0	19.6	0.0	19.6	0.0	19.6	0.0	19.6	0.0	19.6	0.0	19.6	0.0	19.6	0.0	20.5	4.6	20.5	0.0	20.5	0.0
1953	20.5	0.0	20.5	0.0	20.5	0.0	20.5	0.0	20.5	0.0	20.5	0.0	22.5	9.8	22.5	0.0	22.5	0.0	22.5	0.0	22.5	0.0	22.5	0.0
1954	22.5	0.0	22.5	0.0	22.5	0.0	22.5	0.0	22.5	0.0	22.5	0.0	22.5	0.0	22.5	0.0	23.6	4.9	23.6	0.0	23.6	0.0	23.6	0.0
1955	23.6	0.0	23.6	0.0	23.6	0.0	23.6	0.0	23.6	0.0	23.6	0.0	24.9	5.5	25.2	1.2	25.2	0.0	25.2	0.0	25.2	0.0	25.2	0.0
1956	25.2	0.0	25.2	0.0	25.2	0.0	25.2	0.0	25.2	0.0	25.2	0.0	26.2	4.0	26.5	1.1	26.5	0.0	26.5	0.0	26.5	0.0	26.5	0.0
1957	26.5	0.0	26.5	0.0	26.5	0.0	27.9	5.3	27.9	0.0	27.9	0.0	27.9	0.0	27.9	0.0	27.9	0.0	27.9	0.0	27.9	0.0	27.9	0.0
1958	27.9	0.0	27.9	0.0	27.9	0.0	27.9	0.0	27.9	0.0	27.9	0.0	27.9	0.0	27.9	0.0	29.0	3.9	29.0	0.0	29.0	0.0	29.0	0.0
1959	29.0	0.0	29.0	0.0	29.0	0.0	29.0	0.0	29.0	0.0	29.0	0.0	29.0	0.0	29.0	0.0	29.0	0.0	29.0	0.0	29.0	0.0	29.0	0.0
1960	29.0	0.0	29.0	0.0	29.0	0.0	29.0	0.0	29.0	0.0	29.0	0.0	29.0	0.0	29.0	0.0	29.0	0.0	29.0	0.0	29.0	0.0	29.0	0.0
1961	29.0	0.0	29.0	0.0	29.0	0.0	29.0	0.0	28.7	-1.0	28.7	0.0	28.7	0.0	28.7	0.0	28.7	0.0	28.7	0.0	28.7	0.0	28.7	0.0
1962	28.7	0.0	28.7	0.0	28.7	0.0	28.7	0.0	28.7	0.0	28.7	0.0	28.7	0.0	28.7	0.0	28.7	0.0	28.7	0.0	28.7	0.0	28.7	0.0
1963	28.7	0.0	28.7	0.0	28.7	0.0	28.7	0.0	28.7	0.0	28.7	0.0	28.4	-1.0	28.4	0.0	28.4	0.0	28.4	0.0	28.4	0.0	28.4	0.0
1964	28.4	0.0	28.4	0.0	28.4	0.0	28.9	1.8	28.9	0.0	28.9	0.0	28.9	0.0	28.9	0.0	28.9	0.0	29.0	0.3	29.1	0.3	29.1	0.0
1965	29.1	0.0	29.1	0.0	29.1	0.0	29.1	0.0	29.1	0.0	29.1	0.0	29.1	0.0	29.1	0.0	29.1	0.0	29.1	0.0	29.1	0.0	29.1	0.0
1966	29.1	0.0	29.1	0.0	29.1	0.0	29.2	0.3	29.4	0.7	29.4	0.0	29.4	0.0	29.4	0.0	29.4	0.0	29.4	0.0	29.4	0.0	29.4	0.0
1967	29.6	0.7	29.6	0.0	29.6	0.0	29.6	0.0	29.6	0.0	29.6	0.0	29.6	0.0	29.6	0.0	29.6	0.0	29.6	0.0	29.9	1.0	29.9	0.0
1968	30.1	0.7	31.7	5.3	31.8	0.3	31.8	0.0	31.8	0.0	31.8	0.0	31.8	0.0	31.8	0.0	31.8	0.0	31.8	0.0	31.8	0.0	31.8	0.0
1969	31.8	0.0	31.8	0.0	31.8	0.0	32.1	0.9	32.1	0.0	32.1	0.0	32.1	0.0	33.0	2.8	33.1	0.3	33.1	0.0	33.1	0.0	34.1	3.0
1970	34.9	2.3	35.3	1.1	35.4	0.3	35.6	0.6	35.6	0.0	35.5	-0.3	35.6	0.3	35.6	0.0	35.6	0.0	35.6	0.0	37.6	5.6	37.6	0.0
1971	37.6	0.0	37.6	0.0	37.6	0.0	37.6	0.0	37.6	0.0	37.7	0.3	37.7	0.0	37.7	0.0	37.7	0.0	37.7	0.0	37.7	0.0	37.7	0.0
1972	37.7	0.0	37.7	0.0	37.7	0.0	37.7	0.0	37.7	0.0	37.7	0.0	37.7	0.0	38.5	2.1	39.2	1.8	39.2	0.0	39.2	0.0	39.2	0.0
1973	40.4	3.1	40.4	0.0	40.4	0.0	40.4	0.0	40.4	0.0	40.4	0.0	40.4	0.0	40.4	0.0	40.4	0.0	40.4	0.0	40.4	0.0	40.4	0.0
1974	40.4	0.0	40.4	0.0	40.4	0.0	40.4	0.0	40.4	0.0	40.4	0.0	40.9	1.2	40.9	0.0	45.5	11.2	46.6	2.4	46.8	0.4	47.6	1.7
1975	47.8	0.4	48.4	1.3	48.5	0.2	48.5	0.0	48.6	0.2	48.6	0.0	48.6	0.0	48.6	0.0	48.7	0.2	48.7	0.0	52.5	7.8	53.3	1.5
1976	53.3	0.0	53.3	0.0	53.4	0.2	53.5	0.2	53.5	0.0	53.5	0.0	53.6	0.2	53.8	0.4	56.0	4.1	56.7	1.3	57.2	0.9	57.2	0.0
1977	57.3	0.2	57.3	0.0	57.3	0.0	57.3	0.0	57.6	0.5	58.3	1.2	58.5	0.3	58.9	0.7	61.4	4.2	61.8	0.7	62.1	0.5	62.1	0.0
1978	62.2	0.2	62.3	0.2	62.3	0.0	62.4	0.2	62.5	0.2	62.5	0.0	63.2	1.1	66.0	4.4	66.4	0.6	66.9	0.8	67.1	0.3	67.1	0.0
1979	67.5	0.6	67.6	0.1	67.7	0.1	67.8	0.1	67.8	0.0	69.0	1.8	71.4	3.5	71.7	0.4	71.9	0.3	72.6	1.0	73.4	1.1	73.6	0.3
1980	73.7	0.1	74.5	1.1	75.3	1.1	77.6	3.1	78.4	1.0	78.9	0.6	79.7	1.0	80.3	0.8	80.3	0.0	81.1	1.0	81.1	0.0	81.1	0.0
1981	83.8	3.3	87.1	3.9	87.9	0.9	87.9	0.0	90.2	2.6	91.1	1.0	91.1	0.0	91.1	0.0	91.1	0.0	91.3	0.2	91.6	0.3	92.4	0.9
1982	94.0	1.7	99.4	5.7	100.1	0.7	100.5	0.4	100.7	0.2	101.0	0.3	101.0	0.0	101.1	0.1	101.1	0.0	101.1	0.0	100.0	-1.1	100.0	0.0
1983	100.2	0.2	100.2	0.0	100.2	0.0	100.3	0.1	100.3	0.0	99.9	-0.4	100.3	0.4	100.7	0.4	100.9	0.2	102.3	1.4	104.8	2.4	104.8	0.0
1984	105.0	0.2	105.6	0.6	107.1	1.4	107.3	0.2	107.3	0.0	107.3	0.0	107.3	0.0	107.3	0.0	107.3	0.0	107.3	0.0	108.4	1.0	108.4	0.0
1985	108.6	0.2	108.6	0.0	108.9	0.3	109.5	0.6	110.1	0.5	110.1	0.0	110.1	0.0	110.1	0.0	110.1	0.0	110.1	0.0	110.1	0.0	110.2	0.1
1986	110.2	0.0	110.2	0.0	110.2	0.0	110.3	0.1	110.5	0.2	110.5	0.0	110.5	0.0	110.5	0.0	110.4	-0.1	109.9	-0.5	109.3	-0.5	109.7	0.4
1987	109.9	0.2	109.9	0.0	109.9	0.0	110.0	0.1	110.0	0.0	110.4	0.4	110.6	0.2	110.8	0.2	110.9	0.1	110.9	0.0	111.1	0.2	111.9	0.7
1988	112.6	0.6	112.6	0.0	112.5	-0.1	113.5	0.9	113.7	0.2	113.8	0.1	113.8	0.0	113.8	0.0	114.1	0.3	115.1	0.9	115.2	0.1	115.4	0.2
1989	118.1	2.3	119.0	0.8	119.2	0.2	119.6	0.3	119.6	0.0	119.6	0.0	119.8	0.2	119.3	-0.4	119.4	0.1	119.6	0.2	119.6	0.0	119.6	0.0
1990	120.3	0.6	120.9	0.5	121.5	0.5	122.0	0.4	122.1	0.1	122.8	0.6	122.8	0.0	122.9	0.1	122.7	-0.2	122.8	0.1	123.4	0.5	123.4	0.0
1991	124.7	1.1	125.1	0.3	125.3	0.2	125.4	0.1	125.8	0.3	125.3	-0.4	125.3	0.0	125.4	0.1	125.5	0.1	125.5	0.0	125.5	0.0	125.9	0.3

[Continued]

Refractories
Producer Price Index
Base 1982 = 100
[Continued]

For 1947-1997. Columns headed % show percentile change in the index from the previous period for which an index is available.

Year	Jan		Feb		Mar		Apr		May		Jun		Jul		Aug		Sep		Oct		Nov		Dec	
	Index	%	Index	%	Index	%	Index	%	Index	%	Index	%	Index	%	Index	%	Index	%	Index	%	Index	%	Index	%
1992	126.1	0.2	125.6	-0.4	126.8	1.0	126.7	-0.1	126.7	0.0	126.8	0.1	126.3	-0.4	127.6	1.0	126.3	-1.0	126.3	0.0	125.2	-0.9	125.8	0.5
1993	126.1	0.2	126.1	0.0	126.5	0.3	126.5	0.0	127.2	0.6	127.4	0.2	127.7	0.2	127.9	0.2	127.6	-0.2	127.9	0.2	127.5	-0.3	127.4	-0.1
1994	128.5	0.9	128.0	-0.4	127.7	-0.2	127.8	0.1	127.7	-0.1	127.9	0.2	128.3	0.3	127.8	-0.4	128.4	0.5	128.4	0.0	128.9	0.4	128.9	0.0
1995	128.8	-0.1	129.8	0.8	131.5	1.3	132.4	0.7	132.4	0.0	132.5	0.1	132.5	0.0	132.3	-0.2	133.0	0.5	132.9	-0.1	132.9	0.0	133.9	0.8
1996	134.2	0.2	136.0	1.3	136.4	0.3	136.9	0.4	136.8	-0.1	137.0	0.1	137.5	0.4	137.3	-0.1	137.7	0.3	137.3	-0.3	137.3	0.0	137.2	-0.1
1997	137.4	0.1	138.3	0.7	138.2	-0.1	138.8	0.4	138.6	-0.1	137.8	-0.6	138.1	0.2	139.3	0.9	139.4	0.1	139.5	0.1	139.6	0.1	139.7	0.1

Source: U.S. Department of Labor, Bureau of Labor Statistics, Division of Industry Prices and Price Indexes. n.e.c. stands for not elsewhere classified. - indicates no data collected for period or unavailable.

Asphalt Felts and Coatings
Producer Price Index
Base 1982 = 100

For 1926-1997. Columns headed % show percentile change in the index from the previous period for which an index is available.

Year	Jan Index	%	Feb Index	%	Mar Index	%	Apr Index	%	May Index	%	Jun Index	%	Jul Index	%	Aug Index	%	Sep Index	%	Oct Index	%	Nov Index	%	Dec Index	%
1926	20.6	-	20.5	-0.5	20.8	1.5	21.0	1.0	21.2	1.0	21.3	0.5	21.4	0.5	21.4	0.0	21.4	0.0	21.4	0.0	21.4	0.0	21.3	-0.5
1927	20.8	-2.3	20.8	0.0	20.5	-1.4	20.1	-2.0	20.3	1.0	20.3	0.0	20.2	-0.5	20.3	0.5	20.3	0.0	20.3	0.0	17.7	-12.8	17.8	0.6
1928	18.0	1.1	17.6	-2.2	15.6	-11.4	15.8	1.3	15.8	0.0	18.9	19.6	19.2	1.6	19.2	0.0	19.3	0.5	19.4	0.5	19.4	0.0	15.9	-18.0
1929	14.4	-9.4	14.3	-0.7	14.3	0.0	15.4	7.7	16.1	4.5	16.2	0.6	16.4	1.2	16.4	0.0	16.4	0.0	16.4	0.0	16.4	0.0	16.4	0.0
1930	15.6	-4.9	15.6	0.0	15.6	0.0	15.6	0.0	15.6	0.0	15.6	0.0	15.6	0.0	15.6	0.0	15.8	1.3	16.4	3.8	17.3	5.5	17.3	0.0
1931	16.7	-3.5	16.7	0.0	16.7	0.0	16.7	0.0	16.7	0.0	16.7	0.0	16.7	0.0	16.7	0.0	16.7	0.0	16.7	0.0	16.7	0.0	16.7	0.0
1932	15.8	-5.4	15.3	-3.2	15.5	1.3	15.6	0.6	15.3	-1.9	14.3	-6.5	13.2	-7.7	13.6	3.0	15.1	11.0	16.1	6.6	17.0	5.6	16.9	-0.6
1933	15.7	-7.1	13.7	-12.7	13.8	0.7	13.9	0.7	15.1	8.6	15.8	4.6	16.0	1.3	16.4	2.5	16.5	0.6	16.9	2.4	17.1	1.2	17.1	0.0
1934	17.2	0.6	16.2	-5.8	15.2	-6.2	15.4	1.3	16.2	5.2	16.6	2.5	17.0	2.4	17.5	2.9	17.7	1.1	17.7	0.0	17.7	0.0	17.8	0.6
1935	17.9	0.6	17.8	-0.6	17.7	-0.6	17.7	0.0	18.0	1.7	18.1	0.6	18.0	-0.6	17.5	-2.8	17.5	0.0	17.7	1.1	17.8	0.6	16.7	-6.2
1936	16.5	-1.2	16.4	-0.6	16.4	0.0	17.2	4.9	17.5	1.7	17.5	0.0	17.5	0.0	17.6	0.6	17.7	0.6	18.3	3.4	18.4	0.5	18.4	0.0
1937	18.5	0.5	18.7	1.1	19.3	3.2	19.3	0.0	19.8	2.6	20.0	1.0	20.0	0.0	20.0	0.0	19.6	-2.0	19.1	-2.6	18.3	-4.2	16.3	-10.9
1938	16.1	-1.2	15.9	-1.2	15.0	-5.7	15.2	1.3	15.3	0.7	15.3	0.0	15.3	0.0	15.3	0.0	15.3	0.0	15.3	0.0	15.3	0.0	15.3	0.0
1939	15.5	1.3	15.5	0.0	15.5	0.0	15.6	0.6	15.9	1.9	15.9	0.0	15.9	0.0	16.0	0.6	16.2	1.3	16.3	0.6	16.3	0.0	16.6	1.8
1940	17.0	2.4	17.0	0.0	17.5	2.9	17.8	1.7	17.8	0.0	17.8	0.0	17.7	-0.6	17.4	-1.7	17.3	-0.6	17.1	-1.2	17.1	0.0	17.1	0.0
1941	17.2	0.6	17.2	0.0	16.9	-1.7	16.7	-1.2	17.0	1.8	17.5	2.9	18.0	2.9	18.5	2.8	18.8	1.6	19.5	3.7	19.5	0.0	18.3	-6.2
1942	17.5	-4.4	17.5	0.0	17.5	0.0	17.5	0.0	17.5	0.0	17.5	0.0	17.5	0.0	17.5	0.0	17.5	0.0	17.5	0.0	17.5	0.0	17.5	0.0
1943	17.5	0.0	17.5	0.0	17.5	0.0	17.5	0.0	17.5	0.0	17.5	0.0	17.5	0.0	17.5	0.0	17.5	0.0	17.5	0.0	17.5	0.0	17.5	0.0
1944	17.5	0.0	17.5	0.0	17.5	0.0	17.5	0.0	17.5	0.0	17.5	0.0	17.5	0.0	17.6	0.6	17.9	1.7	18.0	0.6	18.0	0.0	18.0	0.0
1945	18.0	0.0	18.0	0.0	18.0	0.0	18.0	0.0	18.0	0.0	18.0	0.0	18.0	0.0	18.0	0.0	18.0	0.0	18.0	0.0	18.0	0.0	18.0	0.0
1946	18.0	0.0	18.0	0.0	18.0	0.0	18.0	0.0	18.5	2.8	18.9	2.2	19.0	0.5	19.1	0.5	19.1	0.0	19.2	0.5	19.3	0.5	20.7	7.3
1947	20.5	-1.0	20.6	0.5	21.4	3.9	21.6	0.9	21.6	0.0	21.6	0.0	21.6	0.0	21.5	-0.5	21.5	0.0	21.5	0.0	21.5	0.0	22.6	5.1
1948	23.2	2.7	23.2	0.0	23.2	0.0	23.2	0.0	23.2	0.0	23.6	1.7	24.2	2.5	23.6	-2.5	23.6	0.0	23.6	0.0	23.6	0.0	23.6	0.0
1949	23.6	0.0	23.6	0.0	23.6	0.0	23.6	0.0	23.6	0.0	23.6	0.0	23.4	-0.8	23.4	0.0	23.4	0.0	23.2	-0.9	23.2	0.0	23.2	0.0
1950	23.2	0.0	23.2	0.0	23.2	0.0	22.9	-1.3	22.5	-1.7	22.5	0.0	22.5	0.0	22.9	1.8	22.9	0.0	23.2	1.3	24.0	3.4	24.0	0.0
1951	24.0	0.0	24.0	0.0	24.0	0.0	24.0	0.0	24.0	0.0	24.0	0.0	24.0	0.0	24.0	0.0	24.0	0.0	24.0	0.0	24.0	0.0	22.5	-6.3
1952	22.5	0.0	22.5	0.0	22.5	0.0	22.5	0.0	22.5	0.0	24.2	7.6	24.2	0.0	24.2	0.0	24.2	0.0	24.2	0.0	24.2	0.0	24.2	0.0
1953	24.2	0.0	24.2	0.0	24.2	0.0	24.2	0.0	24.2	0.0	24.2	0.0	24.1	-0.4	24.1	0.0	25.0	3.7	25.1	0.4	25.1	0.0	25.1	0.0
1954	25.1	0.0	25.1	0.0	25.1	0.0	24.7	-1.6	21.9	-11.3	21.5	-1.8	22.5	4.7	22.5	0.0	23.7	5.3	24.2	2.1	24.2	0.0	24.2	0.0
1955	24.2	0.0	22.9	-5.4	22.5	-1.7	22.5	0.0	24.1	7.1	24.3	0.8	25.3	4.1	26.1	3.2	26.1	0.0	26.1	0.0	23.0	-11.9	23.0	0.0
1956	22.7	-1.3	22.7	0.0	24.3	7.0	25.5	4.9	25.5	0.0	25.5	0.0	26.9	5.5	26.8	-0.4	26.8	0.0	26.8	0.0	26.1	-2.6	26.1	0.0
1957	25.4	-2.7	26.3	3.5	26.9	2.3	27.7	3.0	28.7	3.6	28.7	0.0	28.7	0.0	28.7	0.0	28.4	-1.0	28.4	0.0	28.4	0.0	28.4	0.0
1958	28.4	0.0	28.4	0.0	24.4	-14.1	24.4	0.0	24.2	-0.8	23.5	-2.9	23.5	0.0	23.5	0.0	27.0	14.9	27.0	0.0	27.0	0.0	27.0	0.0
1959	27.0	0.0	27.3	1.1	27.2	-0.4	28.8	5.9	28.8	0.0	25.9	-10.1	25.5	-1.5	25.5	0.0	25.3	-0.8	25.3	0.0	25.9	2.4	25.9	0.0
1960	25.9	0.0	24.5	-5.4	24.5	0.0	24.3	-0.8	24.3	0.0	24.3	0.0	24.3	0.0	24.3	0.0	24.3	0.0	24.3	0.0	24.3	0.0	24.3	0.0
1961	26.0	7.0	26.0	0.0	26.0	0.0	26.0	0.0	25.8	-0.8	25.8	0.0	26.0	0.8	26.0	0.0	26.0	0.0	27.5	5.8	27.5	0.0	27.5	0.0
1962	27.3	-0.7	27.1	-0.7	27.1	0.0	27.1	0.0	26.4	-2.6	25.5	-3.4	23.9	-6.3	23.9	0.0	23.9	0.0	23.9	0.0	23.9	0.0	23.9	0.0
1963	23.9	0.0	25.1	5.0	25.1	0.0	25.1	0.0	24.7	-1.6	23.8	-3.6	23.5	-1.3	23.5	0.0	23.5	0.0	23.3	-0.9	23.3	0.0	23.3	0.0
1964	23.3	0.0	23.3	0.0	23.1	-0.9	23.1	0.0	23.1	0.0	23.1	0.0	23.7	2.6	24.3	2.5	24.3	0.0	24.3	0.0	24.3	0.0	24.3	0.0
1965	24.3	0.0	24.3	0.0	24.5	0.8	24.6	0.4	24.6	0.0	24.6	0.0	24.6	0.0	24.6	0.0	25.4	3.3	25.3	-0.4	25.3	0.0	25.3	-0.5
1966	25.3	0.0	25.3	0.0	25.3	0.0	25.3	0.0	25.2	-0.4	25.2	0.0	26.1	3.6	26.1	0.0	26.1	0.0	26.1	0.0	26.1	0.0	25.6	-1.9
1967	25.6	0.0	25.3	-1.2	25.3	0.0	25.3	0.0	23.6	-6.7	23.6	0.0	24.4	3.4	24.4	0.0	25.3	3.7	25.3	0.0	26.5	4.7	26.5	0.0
1968	26.6	0.4	26.2	-1.5	26.2	0.0	26.1	-0.4	26.1	0.0	25.8	-1.1	26.1	1.2	26.1	0.0	25.4	-2.7	25.4	0.0	25.4	0.0	25.4	0.0
1969	25.4	0.0	26.1	2.8	26.0	-0.4	26.0	0.0	25.6	-1.5	26.3	2.7	26.6	1.1	25.1	-5.6	25.1	0.0	25.1	0.0	25.1	0.0	27.1	8.0
1970	27.2	0.4	26.9	-1.1	26.1	-3.0	25.4	-2.7	25.4	0.0	24.5	-3.5	24.3	-0.8	24.9	2.5	25.4	2.0	25.6	0.8	26.5	3.5	26.9	1.5

[Continued]

Asphalt Felts and Coatings
Producer Price Index
Base 1982 = 100
[Continued]

For 1926-1997. Columns headed % show percentile change in the index from the previous period for which an index is available.

Year	Jan Index	%	Feb Index	%	Mar Index	%	Apr Index	%	May Index	%	Jun Index	%	Jul Index	%	Aug Index	%	Sep Index	%	Oct Index	%	Nov Index	%	Dec Index	%
1971	27.3	1.5	27.3	0.0	31.0	13.6	31.0	0.0	31.0	0.0	32.8	5.8	32.9	0.3	32.9	0.0	32.9	0.0	32.9	0.0	32.9	0.0	32.9	0.0
1972	32.9	0.0	32.9	0.0	32.9	0.0	32.9	0.0	32.9	0.0	32.9	0.0	32.9	0.0	32.9	0.0	32.9	0.0	32.9	0.0	32.9	0.0	32.9	0.0
1973	32.9	0.0	32.9	0.0	32.9	0.0	33.7	2.4	34.3	1.8	34.3	0.0	34.2	-0.3	34.2	0.0	34.2	0.0	34.3	0.3	35.1	2.3	35.1	0.0
1974	37.7	7.4	40.1	6.4	43.0	7.2	48.2	12.1	50.2	4.1	50.8	1.2	51.8	2.0	52.9	2.1	52.9	0.0	54.1	2.3	54.3	0.4	54.3	0.0
1975	54.3	0.0	54.7	0.7	54.7	0.0	57.2	4.6	57.2	0.0	57.2	0.0	57.5	0.5	56.9	-1.0	57.4	0.9	58.1	1.2	57.5	-1.0	57.5	0.0
1976	57.5	0.0	57.6	0.2	59.3	3.0	60.1	1.3	59.6	-0.8	59.6	0.0	59.6	0.0	62.1	4.2	61.6	-0.8	61.7	0.2	60.1	-2.6	58.9	-2.0
1977	57.9	-1.7	57.9	0.0	61.0	5.4	61.0	0.0	61.0	0.0	61.8	1.3	63.6	2.9	63.6	0.0	67.0	5.3	69.1	3.1	69.1	0.0	69.1	0.0
1978	69.6	0.7	69.6	0.0	69.7	0.1	72.2	3.6	72.2	0.0	72.6	0.6	74.2	2.2	74.7	0.7	74.8	0.1	76.6	2.4	76.6	0.0	76.6	0.0
1979	77.0	0.5	79.8	3.6	76.1	-4.6	79.4	4.3	79.8	0.5	81.1	1.6	82.4	1.6	81.8	-0.7	83.6	2.2	84.7	1.3	87.2	3.0	87.0	-0.2
1980	89.5	2.9	93.5	4.5	97.6	4.4	102.6	5.1	100.7	-1.9	100.6	-0.1	103.9	3.3	103.2	-0.7	102.4	-0.8	102.5	0.1	99.7	-2.7	99.1	-0.6
1981	99.1	0.0	97.8	-1.3	98.0	0.2	104.4	6.5	102.3	-2.0	107.6	5.2	105.9	-1.6	105.6	-0.3	100.8	-4.5	101.1	0.3	103.0	1.9	101.8	-1.2
1982	100.7	-1.1	100.5	-0.2	99.0	-1.5	97.1	-1.9	96.8	-0.3	99.5	2.8	100.4	0.9	100.4	0.0	103.8	3.4	102.1	-1.6	100.2	-1.9	99.6	-0.6
1983	98.8	-0.8	95.5	-3.3	94.0	-1.6	96.4	2.6	95.4	-1.0	95.3	-0.1	96.7	1.5	96.2	-0.5	97.2	1.0	97.4	0.2	97.3	-0.1	96.4	-0.9
1984	96.6	0.2	98.5	2.0	96.8	-1.7	99.4	2.7	100.1	0.7	99.0	-1.1	99.0	0.0	102.5	3.5	102.4	-0.1	102.7	0.3	102.9	0.2	103.4	0.5
1985	102.8	-0.6	102.3	-0.5	101.9	-0.4	103.4	1.5	103.6	0.2	103.0	-0.6	103.0	0.0	102.5	-0.5	102.1	-0.4	101.7	-0.4	102.7	1.0	102.2	-0.5
1986	101.8	-0.4	101.8	0.0	100.6	-1.2	99.3	-1.3	99.3	0.0	97.3	-2.0	97.1	-0.2	97.3	0.2	96.6	-0.7	95.6	-1.0	94.6	-1.0	94.0	-0.6
1987	91.8	-2.3	91.5	-0.3	90.8	-0.8	91.4	0.7	91.3	-0.1	90.9	-0.4	90.6	-0.3	92.8	2.4	93.4	0.6	94.4	1.1	94.9	0.5	94.8	-0.1
1988	93.8	-1.1	92.7	-1.2	93.4	0.8	92.7	-0.7	93.1	0.4	94.6	1.6	95.8	1.3	95.6	-0.2	96.3	0.7	97.1	0.8	96.0	-1.1	95.4	-0.6
1989	95.0	-0.4	94.9	-0.1	94.2	-0.7	96.0	1.9	95.7	-0.3	95.9	0.2	95.8	-0.1	95.7	-0.1	96.2	0.5	96.6	0.4	96.7	0.1	97.1	0.4
1990	97.1	0.0	95.8	-1.3	95.7	-0.1	96.0	0.3	95.6	-0.4	94.9	-0.7	94.3	-0.6	95.9	1.7	96.5	0.6	100.4	4.0	101.5	1.1	101.7	0.2
1991	100.5	-1.2	100.0	-0.5	100.4	0.4	99.3	-1.1	97.9	-1.4	98.4	0.5	98.4	0.0	97.0	-1.4	97.2	0.2	97.1	-0.1	96.5	-0.6	96.0	-0.5
1992	96.0	0.0	95.6	-0.4	95.4	-0.2	95.1	-0.3	95.6	0.5	95.9	0.3	96.3	0.4	96.2	-0.1	96.0	-0.2	97.1	1.1	98.1	1.0	97.8	-0.3
1993	98.2	0.4	97.3	-0.9	97.6	0.3	96.9	-0.7	96.7	-0.2	96.8	0.1	97.0	0.2	97.1	0.1	96.5	-0.6	96.1	-0.4	95.6	-0.5	95.8	0.2
1994	95.8	0.0	94.9	-0.9	94.5	-0.4	94.6	0.1	94.9	0.3	95.2	0.3	95.2	0.0	95.8	0.6	95.6	-0.2	95.7	0.1	95.8	0.1	95.8	0.0
1995	96.1	0.3	96.6	0.5	97.7	1.1	99.8	2.1	100.9	1.1	101.4	0.5	101.6	0.2	101.1	-0.5	101.1	0.0	101.3	0.2	101.1	-0.2	100.8	-0.3
1996	100.8	0.0	100.4	-0.4	100.3	-0.1	99.9	-0.4	100.2	0.3	99.3	-0.9	99.7	0.4	99.8	0.1	100.1	0.3	100.1	0.0	100.4	0.3	99.7	-0.7
1997	99.6	-0.1	99.9	0.3	99.4	-0.5	100.3	0.9	100.2	-0.1	100.6	0.4	100.3	-0.3	100.4	0.1	100.2	-0.2	99.3	-0.9	99.2	-0.1	98.8	-0.4

Source: U.S. Department of Labor, Bureau of Labor Statistics, Division of Industry Prices and Price Indexes. n.e.c. stands for not elsewhere classified. - indicates no data collected for period or unavailable.

Gypsum Products
Producer Price Index
Base 1982 = 100

For 1947-1997. Columns headed % show percentile change in the index from the previous period for which an index is available.

Year	Jan Index	%	Feb Index	%	Mar Index	%	Apr Index	%	May Index	%	Jun Index	%	Jul Index	%	Aug Index	%	Sep Index	%	Oct Index	%	Nov Index	%	Dec Index	%
1947	26.9	-	26.9	0.0	26.9	0.0	26.9	0.0	26.9	0.0	26.9	0.0	26.9	0.0	26.9	0.0	26.9	0.0	28.6	6.3	29.4	2.8	29.4	0.0
1948	29.4	0.0	29.4	0.0	29.4	0.0	29.6	0.7	30.2	2.0	30.2	0.0	30.2	0.0	30.2	0.0	30.2	0.0	30.2	0.0	30.2	0.0	30.1	-0.3
1949	29.8	-1.0	29.7	-0.3	29.7	0.0	29.7	0.0	29.7	0.0	29.7	0.0	29.7	0.0	29.7	0.0	29.7	0.0	29.7	0.0	29.7	0.0	29.7	0.0
1950	29.7	0.0	29.7	0.0	29.7	0.0	29.7	0.0	29.7	0.0	29.7	0.0	29.7	0.0	29.7	0.0	30.4	2.4	31.1	2.3	31.1	0.0	31.1	0.0	32.9	5.8
1951	34.1	3.6	34.1	0.0	34.1	0.0	34.1	0.0	34.1	0.0	34.1	0.0	34.1	0.0	34.1	0.0	34.1	0.0	34.1	0.0	34.2	0.3	34.2	0.0
1952	34.2	0.0	34.2	0.0	34.2	0.0	34.2	0.0	34.2	0.0	34.2	0.0	34.2	0.0	34.2	0.0	34.2	0.0	34.2	0.0	34.2	0.0	34.2	0.0
1953	34.2	0.0	34.2	0.0	34.4	0.6	35.5	3.2	35.5	0.0	35.5	0.0	35.5	0.0	35.5	0.0	35.5	0.0	35.5	0.0	35.5	0.0	35.5	0.0
1954	35.5	0.0	35.5	0.0	35.5	0.0	35.5	0.0	35.5	0.0	35.5	0.0	35.5	0.0	35.5	0.0	35.5	0.0	35.5	0.0	35.5	0.0	35.5	0.0
1955	35.5	0.0	35.5	0.0	35.5	0.0	35.5	0.0	35.5	0.0	35.5	0.0	35.5	0.0	35.5	0.0	35.5	0.0	35.5	0.0	35.5	0.0	35.5	0.0
1956	36.9	3.9	36.9	0.0	36.9	0.0	36.9	0.0	36.9	0.0	36.9	0.0	36.9	0.0	36.9	0.0	36.9	0.0	36.9	0.0	36.9	0.0	36.9	0.0
1957	36.9	0.0	36.9	0.0	36.9	0.0	36.9	0.0	36.9	0.0	36.9	0.0	36.9	0.0	36.9	0.0	36.9	0.0	36.9	0.0	36.9	0.0	36.9	0.0
1958	36.9	0.0	36.9	0.0	38.7	4.9	38.7	0.0	38.7	0.0	38.7	0.0	38.7	0.0	38.7	0.0	38.7	0.0	38.7	0.0	38.7	0.0	38.7	0.0
1959	38.7	0.0	38.7	0.0	38.7	0.0	38.7	0.0	38.7	0.0	38.7	0.0	38.7	0.0	38.7	0.0	38.7	0.0	38.7	0.0	38.7	0.0	38.7	0.0
1960	38.7	0.0	38.7	0.0	38.7	0.0	38.7	0.0	38.7	0.0	38.7	0.0	38.7	0.0	38.7	0.0	38.7	0.0	38.7	0.0	38.7	0.0	38.7	0.0
1961	39.1	1.0	39.1	0.0	39.1	0.0	39.1	0.0	39.1	0.0	39.1	0.0	39.1	0.0	39.9	2.0	39.9	0.0	39.9	0.0	39.9	0.0	39.9	0.0
1962	39.9	0.0	39.9	0.0	39.9	0.0	39.9	0.0	39.9	0.0	39.9	0.0	39.9	0.0	39.9	0.0	39.9	0.0	39.9	0.0	39.9	0.0	39.9	0.0
1963	39.9	0.0	39.9	0.0	39.9	0.0	39.9	0.0	39.9	0.0	39.9	0.0	39.9	0.0	40.2	0.8	40.3	0.2	40.3	0.0	40.3	0.0	40.3	0.0
1964	40.3	0.0	41.2	2.2	41.2	0.0	41.2	0.0	41.2	0.0	41.2	0.0	41.2	0.0	41.2	0.0	41.2	0.0	41.2	0.0	41.2	0.0	40.5	-1.7
1965	40.5	0.0	40.9	1.0	41.2	0.7	41.1	-0.2	41.1	0.0	40.9	-0.5	40.1	-2.0	38.2	-4.7	38.0	-0.5	37.6	-1.1	37.5	-0.3	37.0	-1.3
1966	38.5	4.1	38.5	0.0	38.5	0.0	38.5	0.0	38.8	0.8	39.0	0.5	39.0	0.0	39.0	0.0	39.0	0.0	39.0	0.0	39.3	0.8	39.3	0.0
1967	39.4	0.3	39.4	0.0	38.9	-1.3	38.9	0.0	38.9	0.0	38.4	-1.3	38.3	-0.3	38.3	0.0	38.3	0.0	40.1	4.7	40.1	0.0	40.1	0.0
1968	40.1	0.0	40.5	1.0	40.5	0.0	40.5	0.0	40.5	0.0	40.5	0.0	40.5	0.0	40.5	0.0	40.5	0.0	40.3	-0.5	40.3	0.0	40.3	0.0
1969	40.3	0.0	40.3	0.0	40.3	0.0	40.3	0.0	41.7	3.5	40.2	-3.6	40.2	0.0	39.6	-1.5	40.2	1.5	40.9	1.7	41.6	1.7	39.5	-5.0
1970	40.7	3.0	41.2	1.2	40.6	-1.5	40.1	-1.2	39.5	-1.5	38.3	-3.0	38.1	-0.5	38.7	1.6	37.7	-2.6	37.9	0.5	37.5	-1.1	37.1	-1.1
1971	38.0	2.4	39.4	3.7	40.4	2.5	41.4	2.5	42.6	2.9	43.4	1.9	44.0	1.4	44.7	1.6	45.0	0.7	44.7	-0.7	44.1	-1.3	44.8	1.6
1972	44.3	-1.1	44.1	-0.5	45.0	2.0	44.9	-0.2	44.3	-1.3	44.5	0.5	45.2	1.6	45.4	0.4	45.0	-0.9	45.1	0.2	44.9	-0.4	44.9	0.0
1973	45.8	2.0	45.2	-1.3	46.1	2.0	46.7	1.3	47.0	0.6	48.5	3.2	48.0	-1.0	47.8	-0.4	47.6	-0.4	47.8	0.4	47.7	-0.2	48.1	0.8
1974	49.9	3.7	50.8	1.8	50.6	-0.4	51.8	2.4	52.1	0.6	53.7	3.1	54.2	0.9	55.8	3.0	56.9	2.0	56.5	-0.7	56.2	-0.5	56.4	0.4
1975	56.1	-0.5	56.1	0.0	56.9	1.4	56.2	-1.2	56.0	-0.4	56.0	0.0	55.0	-1.8	55.9	1.6	56.2	0.5	56.7	0.9	57.4	1.2	56.4	-1.7
1976	58.7	4.1	58.0	-1.2	58.7	1.2	58.9	0.3	60.0	1.9	59.9	-0.2	59.9	0.0	60.6	1.2	61.6	1.7	62.1	0.8	62.5	0.6	62.5	0.0
1977	62.8	0.5	63.5	1.1	64.1	0.9	67.2	4.8	68.7	2.2	73.1	6.4	72.9	-0.3	74.1	1.6	75.6	2.0	78.7	4.1	79.4	0.9	80.0	0.8
1978	81.9	2.4	84.3	2.9	84.8	0.6	86.4	1.9	89.1	3.1	89.9	0.9	91.4	1.7	92.1	0.8	92.2	0.1	92.5	0.3	94.5	2.2	94.8	0.3
1979	96.7	2.0	97.9	1.2	98.0	0.1	98.5	0.5	97.2	-1.3	98.2	1.0	98.3	0.1	98.5	0.2	99.6	1.1	99.7	0.1	100.1	0.4	99.6	-0.5
1980	99.7	0.1	102.4	2.7	104.5	2.1	103.1	-1.3	100.2	-2.8	100.4	0.2	98.9	-1.5	98.4	-0.5	98.3	-0.1	97.5	-0.8	98.9	1.4	98.7	-0.2
1981	101.4	2.7	100.5	-0.9	100.6	0.1	100.3	-0.3	102.0	1.7	101.8	-0.2	101.4	-0.4	99.7	-1.7	98.8	-0.9	98.6	-0.2	98.2	-0.4	97.5	-0.7
1982	97.8	0.3	99.6	1.8	101.8	2.2	102.8	1.0	101.3	-1.5	100.1	-1.2	99.9	-0.2	99.2	-0.7	99.2	0.0	99.6	0.4	99.6	0.0	99.2	-0.4
1983	102.7	3.5	104.4	1.7	103.9	-0.5	106.2	2.2	107.7	1.4	106.9	-0.7	107.8	0.8	113.0	4.8	116.3	2.9	122.2	5.1	123.1	0.7	126.0	2.4
1984	128.3	1.8	132.6	3.4	132.6	0.0	137.9	4.0	140.9	2.2	140.7	-0.1	140.5	-0.1	140.4	-0.1	138.8	-1.1	132.4	-4.6	130.6	-1.4	129.1	-1.1
1985	128.3	-0.6	134.5	4.8	131.4	-2.3	130.2	-0.9	130.1	-0.1	132.0	1.5	132.2	0.2	132.1	-0.1	129.4	-2.0	132.7	2.6	135.9	2.4	139.2	2.4
1986	140.7	1.1	141.4	0.5	137.4	-2.8	135.2	-1.6	140.7	4.1	138.3	-1.7	136.5	-1.3	134.3	-1.6	133.2	-0.8	134.0	0.6	137.0	2.2	135.7	-0.9
1987	133.9	-1.3	131.8	-1.6	127.1	-3.6	127.2	0.1	129.5	1.8	128.0	-1.2	124.0	-3.1	119.5	-3.6	118.8	-0.6	119.8	0.8	120.8	0.8	121.5	0.6
1988	120.9	-0.5	116.7	-3.5	113.3	-2.9	111.7	-1.4	112.7	0.9	110.4	-2.0	108.6	-1.6	108.0	-0.6	110.6	2.4	113.6	2.7	114.6	0.9	113.9	-0.6
1989	111.3	-2.3	110.8	-0.4	110.1	-0.6	110.3	0.2	110.6	0.3	110.4	-0.2	109.8	-0.5	107.9	-1.7	108.9	0.9	109.5	0.6	111.5	1.8	109.4	-1.9
1990	106.9	-2.3	106.0	-0.8	106.3	0.3	106.8	0.5	107.0	0.2	106.2	-0.7	105.4	-0.8	102.4	-2.8	104.0	1.6	103.4	-0.6	104.5	1.1	103.3	-1.1
1991	102.8	-0.5	105.4	2.5	104.8	-0.6	101.4	-3.2	100.3	-1.1	97.0	-3.3	96.0	-1.0	95.0	-1.0	97.5	2.6	98.2	0.7	96.8	-1.4	96.9	0.1

[Continued]

Gypsum Products

Producer Price Index
Base 1982 = 100

[Continued]

For 1947-1997. Columns headed % show percentile change in the index from the previous period for which an index is available.

Year	Jan Index	%	Feb Index	%	Mar Index	%	Apr Index	%	May Index	%	Jun Index	%	Jul Index	%	Aug Index	%	Sep Index	%	Oct Index	%	Nov Index	%	Dec Index	%
1992	94.8	-2.2	92.8	-2.1	96.0	3.4	96.6	0.6	100.5	4.0	100.4	-0.1	100.4	0.0	103.0	2.6	105.4	2.3	104.1	-1.2	104.0	-0.1	101.2	-2.7
1993	99.4	-1.8	102.0	2.6	103.4	1.4	108.8	5.2	108.2	-0.6	107.6	-0.6	106.7	-0.8	110.2	3.3	112.5	2.1	112.6	0.1	114.2	1.4	114.2	0.0
1994	113.0	-1.1	117.9	4.3	128.8	9.2	130.7	1.5	131.3	0.5	139.5	6.2	139.8	0.2	140.7	0.6	146.2	3.9	149.0	1.9	146.3	-1.8	149.4	2.1
1995	148.4	-0.7	151.9	2.4	157.6	3.8	161.2	2.3	159.9	-0.8	158.7	-0.8	154.8	-2.5	153.5	-0.8	152.7	-0.5	152.5	-0.1	151.5	-0.7	150.9	-0.4
1996	149.8	-0.7	149.5	-0.2	146.4	-2.1	145.3	-0.8	148.0	1.9	152.3	2.9	152.5	0.1	157.4	3.2	159.3	1.2	162.2	1.8	165.0	1.7	160.8	-2.5
1997	169.0	5.1	168.3	-0.4	168.2	-0.1	171.3	1.8	173.6	1.3	172.0	-0.9	169.4	-1.5	168.9	-0.3	169.6	0.4	173.8	2.5	172.8	-0.6	172.0	-0.5

Source: U.S. Department of Labor, Bureau of Labor Statistics, Division of Industry Prices and Price Indexes. n.e.c. stands for not elsewhere classified. - indicates no data collected for period or unavailable.

Glass Containers
Producer Price Index
Base 1982 = 100

For 1947-1997. Columns headed % show percentile change in the index from the previous period for which an index is available.

Year	Jan Index	%	Feb Index	%	Mar Index	%	Apr Index	%	May Index	%	Jun Index	%	Jul Index	%	Aug Index	%	Sep Index	%	Oct Index	%	Nov Index	%	Dec Index	%
1947	14.1	-	14.5	2.8	14.5	0.0	14.5	0.0	14.5	0.0	14.5	0.0	14.9	2.8	14.9	0.0	14.9	0.0	14.9	0.0	14.9	0.0	14.9	0.0
1948	14.9	0.0	14.9	0.0	14.9	0.0	16.9	13.4	16.9	0.0	16.9	0.0	16.9	0.0	16.9	0.0	16.9	0.0	19.2	13.6	19.2	0.0	19.2	0.0
1949	19.2	0.0	19.2	0.0	19.2	0.0	19.2	0.0	19.2	0.0	19.0	-1.0	19.0	0.0	19.0	0.0	19.0	0.0	19.0	0.0	19.0	0.0	19.0	0.0
1950	18.7	-1.6	18.7	0.0	18.7	0.0	18.7	0.0	18.7	0.0	18.7	0.0	18.7	0.0	18.7	0.0	18.7	0.0	20.0	7.0	20.0	0.0	20.0	0.0
1951	20.6	3.0	20.6	0.0	20.6	0.0	20.6	0.0	20.6	0.0	20.6	0.0	20.6	0.0	20.6	0.0	20.6	0.0	20.6	0.0	20.6	0.0	20.6	0.0
1952	20.6	0.0	20.6	0.0	20.6	0.0	20.6	0.0	21.4	3.9	21.4	0.0	21.4	0.0	21.4	0.0	21.4	0.0	21.4	0.0	21.4	0.0	21.4	0.0
1953	21.4	0.0	21.4	0.0	21.4	0.0	23.2	8.4	23.2	0.0	23.2	0.0	23.2	0.0	23.2	0.0	23.2	0.0	23.0	-0.9	23.0	0.0	23.0	0.0
1954	23.0	0.0	23.0	0.0	23.0	0.0	24.1	4.8	24.1	0.0	24.1	0.0	24.1	0.0	24.1	0.0	24.1	0.0	24.1	0.0	24.1	0.0	24.1	0.0
1955	24.1	0.0	24.1	0.0	24.1	0.0	24.1	0.0	24.1	0.0	24.1	0.0	24.1	0.0	24.1	0.0	24.1	0.0	24.3	0.8	24.3	0.0	24.3	0.0
1956	24.9	2.5	24.9	0.0	24.9	0.0	24.9	0.0	24.9	0.0	24.9	0.0	24.9	0.0	24.9	0.0	24.9	0.0	26.7	7.2	26.7	0.0	26.7	0.0
1957	26.7	0.0	26.7	0.0	26.7	0.0	26.7	0.0	26.7	0.0	26.7	0.0	26.7	0.0	26.7	0.0	26.7	0.0	26.7	0.0	26.9	0.7	28.3	5.2
1958	28.3	0.0	28.3	0.0	28.3	0.0	28.3	0.0	28.3	0.0	28.3	0.0	28.3	0.0	28.3	0.0	28.3	0.0	28.3	0.0	28.3	0.0	28.3	0.0
1959	28.3	0.0	28.3	0.0	28.3	0.0	28.3	0.0	28.3	0.0	28.3	0.0	28.3	0.0	28.3	0.0	28.3	0.0	28.3	0.0	28.3	0.0	28.3	0.0
1960	28.2	-0.4	28.2	0.0	28.2	0.0	27.5	-2.5	27.5	0.0	27.5	0.0	27.5	0.0	27.5	0.0	27.5	0.0	27.0	-1.8	27.0	0.0	27.0	0.0
1961	27.0	0.0	27.0	0.0	27.0	0.0	27.8	3.0	27.8	0.0	27.8	0.0	27.4	-1.4	27.4	0.0	27.4	0.0	27.4	0.0	27.4	0.0	26.9	-1.8
1962	26.9	0.0	26.9	0.0	26.9	0.0	26.9	0.0	26.9	0.0	26.9	0.0	26.9	0.0	26.9	0.0	26.9	0.0	26.9	0.0	26.9	0.0	26.9	0.0
1963	26.9	0.0	26.9	0.0	26.9	0.0	26.9	0.0	26.9	0.0	26.8	-0.4	26.8	0.0	26.8	0.0	26.8	0.0	26.8	0.0	26.8	0.0	26.8	0.0
1964	26.8	0.0	26.8	0.0	26.8	0.0	27.1	1.1	27.1	0.0	27.1	0.0	27.1	0.0	27.1	0.0	27.1	0.0	27.1	0.0	27.1	0.0	27.1	0.0
1965	27.1	0.0	27.1	0.0	27.1	0.0	27.1	0.0	27.1	0.0	27.2	0.4	27.2	0.0	27.3	0.4	27.3	0.0	27.3	0.0	27.8	1.8	27.8	0.0
1966	27.8	0.0	27.9	0.4	27.8	-0.4	27.6	-0.7	27.6	0.0	27.6	0.0	27.6	0.0	27.6	0.0	28.1	1.8	28.1	0.0	28.1	0.0	28.1	0.0
1967	28.1	0.0	28.1	0.0	28.1	0.0	28.1	0.0	28.1	0.0	28.1	0.0	28.1	0.0	28.1	0.0	28.1	0.0	28.1	0.0	28.1	0.0	28.1	0.0
1968	29.3	4.3	29.6	1.0	29.6	0.0	29.6	0.0	30.5	3.0	30.5	0.0	30.5	0.0	30.5	0.0	30.5	0.0	30.7	0.7	30.7	0.0	30.7	0.0
1969	32.3	5.2	32.3	0.0	32.3	0.0	32.3	0.0	32.3	0.0	32.3	0.0	32.3	0.0	32.3	0.0	32.3	0.0	32.3	0.0	32.3	0.0	32.3	0.0
1970	33.6	4.0	33.6	0.0	33.6	0.0	33.6	0.0	33.6	0.0	33.6	0.0	33.6	0.0	33.6	0.0	33.6	0.0	33.6	0.0	35.0	4.2	35.0	0.0
1971	37.1	6.0	37.0	-0.3	37.0	0.0	37.0	0.0	37.0	0.0	37.0	0.0	37.0	0.0	37.0	0.0	37.0	0.0	37.0	0.0	37.0	0.0	37.0	0.0
1972	37.0	0.0	37.0	0.0	37.0	0.0	38.3	3.5	38.3	0.0	38.3	0.0	38.4	0.3	38.4	0.0	38.4	0.0	38.4	0.0	38.4	0.0	38.4	0.0
1973	38.4	0.0	38.4	0.0	38.4	0.0	38.5	0.3	38.5	0.0	39.8	3.4	38.6	-3.0	38.6	0.0	38.6	0.0	40.4	4.7	40.4	0.0	40.4	0.0
1974	40.4	0.0	40.4	0.0	41.0	1.5	41.3	0.7	44.2	7.0	44.3	0.2	44.3	0.0	44.3	0.0	44.3	0.0	46.7	5.4	46.7	0.0	46.7	0.0
1975	46.7	0.0	49.8	6.6	49.8	0.0	49.8	0.0	49.8	0.0	49.8	0.0	49.8	0.0	52.3	5.0	52.2	-0.2	52.2	0.0	52.2	0.0	52.2	0.0
1976	52.1	-0.2	52.1	0.0	52.1	0.0	55.3	6.1	55.5	0.4	55.5	0.0	55.5	0.0	55.5	0.0	55.5	0.0	56.8	2.3	56.8	0.0	56.8	0.0
1977	56.8	0.0	56.8	0.0	56.8	0.0	61.3	7.9	61.3	0.0	61.3	0.0	61.3	0.0	61.3	0.0	61.3	0.0	61.5	0.3	61.5	0.0	61.5	0.0
1978	66.5	8.1	66.5	0.0	66.5	0.0	66.5	0.0	66.5	0.0	70.0	5.3	70.0	0.0	70.5	0.7	70.5	0.0	70.5	0.0	70.5	0.0	70.5	0.0
1979	70.5	0.0	70.5	0.0	70.5	0.0	70.5	0.0	74.6	5.8	74.6	0.0	74.6	0.0	74.6	0.0	74.6	0.0	74.6	0.0	74.6	0.0	77.1	3.4
1980	77.1	0.0	77.1	0.0	77.1	0.0	82.8	7.4	82.8	0.0	82.8	0.0	82.8	0.0	82.8	0.0	82.8	0.0	86.1	4.0	86.1	0.0	87.6	1.7
1981	87.6	0.0	87.6	0.0	87.6	0.0	91.9	4.9	94.3	2.6	94.3	0.0	94.4	0.1	94.4	0.0	94.4	0.0	94.4	0.0	94.4	0.0	94.4	0.0
1982	94.3	-0.1	99.1	5.1	100.1	1.0	100.7	0.6	100.7	0.0	100.7	0.0	100.7	0.0	100.7	0.0	100.9	0.2	100.8	-0.1	100.6	-0.2	100.6	0.0
1983	100.3	-0.3	100.1	-0.2	99.6	-0.5	99.4	-0.2	99.0	-0.4	98.9	-0.1	98.9	0.0	98.8	-0.1	98.8	0.0	98.5	-0.3	98.5	0.0	98.6	0.1
1984	98.6	0.0	98.6	0.0	98.9	0.3	100.7	1.8	101.8	1.1	102.7	0.9	103.0	0.3	103.0	0.0	102.5	-0.5	102.6	0.1	102.4	-0.2	102.4	0.0
1985	102.3	-0.1	102.5	0.2	105.2	2.6	105.3	0.1	105.9	0.6	107.4	1.4	108.8	1.3	108.9	0.1	108.8	-0.1	109.2	0.4	108.8	-0.4	108.8	0.0
1986	109.5	0.6	109.5	0.0	111.0	1.4	111.1	0.1	112.2	1.0	112.6	0.4	112.8	0.2	113.1	0.3	113.1	0.0	112.7	-0.4	112.7	0.0	112.5	-0.2
1987	112.5	0.0	113.4	0.8	113.7	0.3	113.8	0.1	113.2	-0.5	113.3	0.1	113.0	-0.3	112.9	-0.1	112.9	0.0	112.7	-0.2	112.5	-0.2	112.5	0.0
1988	112.3	-0.2	112.2	-0.1	112.2	0.0	112.1	-0.1	112.1	0.0	112.2	0.1	112.2	0.0	112.5	0.3	112.3	-0.2	112.3	0.0	112.3	0.0	112.3	0.0
1989	112.3	0.0	112.3	0.0	113.8	1.3	116.9	2.7	116.4	-0.4	115.9	-0.4	115.9	0.0	115.9	0.0	115.7	-0.2	115.7	0.0	115.7	0.0	115.7	0.0
1990	118.9	2.8	119.5	0.5	120.0	0.4	120.2	0.2	120.4	0.2	120.7	0.2	120.7	0.0	120.7	0.0	121.0	0.2	121.0	0.0	121.0	0.0	121.0	0.0
1991	124.8	3.1	124.9	0.1	125.0	0.1	125.3	0.2	125.6	0.2	125.6	0.0	125.6	0.0	125.5	-0.1	125.7	0.2	125.7	0.0	125.7	0.0	125.7	0.0

[Continued]

Glass Containers
Producer Price Index
Base 1982 = 100
[Continued]

For 1947-1997. Columns headed % show percentile change in the index from the previous period for which an index is available.

Year	Jan Index	%	Feb Index	%	Mar Index	%	Apr Index	%	May Index	%	Jun Index	%	Jul Index	%	Aug Index	%	Sep Index	%	Oct Index	%	Nov Index	%	Dec Index	%
1992	125.5	-0.2	125.5	0.0	125.4	-0.1	125.3	-0.1	125.0	-0.2	125.1	0.1	125.1	0.0	125.0	-0.1	124.9	-0.1	124.9	0.0	124.7	-0.2	124.7	0.0
1993	124.5	-0.2	124.9	0.3	125.0	0.1	124.9	-0.1	125.4	0.4	126.0	0.5	126.4	0.3	126.5	0.1	126.7	0.2	126.7	0.0	126.6	-0.1	126.5	-0.1
1994	126.6	0.1	126.4	-0.2	126.4	0.0	126.4	0.0	127.9	1.2	127.9	0.0	127.9	0.0	127.9	0.0	128.2	0.2	128.2	0.0	128.2	0.0	128.3	0.1
1995	128.7	0.3	128.6	-0.1	130.1	1.2	129.9	-0.2	130.7	0.6	130.7	0.0	131.0	0.2	131.0	0.0	131.2	0.2	131.2	0.0	131.2	0.0	131.2	0.0
1996	130.2	-0.8	130.2	0.0	129.2	-0.8	129.7	0.4	129.6	-0.1	129.6	0.0	129.6	0.0	129.6	0.0	129.3	-0.2	127.4	-1.5	127.4	0.0	127.4	0.0
1997	126.0	-1.1	126.0	0.0	125.9	-0.1	125.9	0.0	125.5	-0.3	125.5	0.0	125.5	0.0	125.5	0.0	125.7	0.2	125.7	0.0	125.9	0.2	125.9	0.0

Source: U.S. Department of Labor, Bureau of Labor Statistics, Division of Industry Prices and Price Indexes. n.e.c. stands for not elsewhere classified. - indicates no data collected for period or unavailable.

Other Nonmetallic Minerals

Producer Price Index
Base 1982 = 100

For 1947-1997. Columns headed % show percentile change in the index from the previous period for which an index is available.

Year	Jan Index	%	Feb Index	%	Mar Index	%	Apr Index	%	May Index	%	Jun Index	%	Jul Index	%	Aug Index	%	Sep Index	%	Oct Index	%	Nov Index	%	Dec Index	%
1947	14.4	-	14.6	1.4	14.7	0.7	14.8	0.7	14.9	0.7	14.9	0.0	14.9	0.0	14.9	0.0	15.0	0.7	15.0	0.0	15.5	3.3	15.7	1.3
1948	15.9	1.3	16.0	0.6	16.0	0.0	16.1	0.6	16.1	0.0	16.3	1.2	16.6	1.8	16.6	0.0	16.6	0.0	16.6	0.0	16.5	-0.6	16.7	1.2
1949	16.6	-0.6	16.6	0.0	16.6	0.0	16.6	0.0	16.6	0.0	16.6	0.0	16.5	-0.6	16.4	-0.6	16.4	0.0	16.3	-0.6	16.3	0.0	16.3	0.0
1950	16.3	0.0	16.7	2.5	16.8	0.6	16.8	0.0	16.8	0.0	16.8	0.0	16.9	0.6	17.1	1.2	17.3	1.2	17.3	0.0	17.4	0.6	17.7	1.7
1951	17.7	0.0	17.7	0.0	17.7	0.0	17.7	0.0	17.7	0.0	17.7	0.0	17.7	0.0	17.7	0.0	17.7	0.0	17.7	0.0	17.7	0.0	17.7	0.0
1952	17.7	0.0	17.7	0.0	17.7	0.0	17.8	0.6	17.8	0.0	17.8	0.0	17.8	0.0	17.8	0.0	17.8	0.0	17.9	0.6	18.3	2.2	18.4	0.5
1953	18.4	0.0	18.4	0.0	18.4	0.0	18.4	0.0	18.4	0.0	18.5	0.5	18.7	1.1	18.8	0.5	18.8	0.0	18.8	0.0	18.9	0.5	18.9	0.0
1954	19.1	1.1	19.1	0.0	19.1	0.0	19.1	0.0	19.1	0.0	19.1	0.0	19.1	0.0	19.2	0.5	19.2	0.0	19.2	0.0	19.0	-1.0	19.0	0.0
1955	19.0	0.0	19.0	0.0	19.0	0.0	19.0	0.0	19.3	1.6	19.5	1.0	19.5	0.0	19.5	0.0	19.6	0.5	19.6	0.0	19.4	-1.0	19.4	0.0
1956	19.4	0.0	19.6	1.0	19.5	-0.5	19.6	0.5	19.6	0.0	19.6	0.0	19.7	0.5	19.7	0.0	19.7	0.0	19.8	0.5	19.8	0.0	19.8	0.0
1957	19.8	0.0	20.1	1.5	20.3	1.0	20.4	0.5	20.4	0.0	20.4	0.0	20.4	0.0	20.5	0.5	20.5	0.0	20.5	0.0	20.5	0.0	20.9	2.0
1958	20.9	0.0	20.9	0.0	20.9	0.0	20.9	0.0	20.9	0.0	20.9	0.0	20.9	0.0	20.9	0.0	20.9	0.0	20.9	0.0	20.9	0.0	20.9	0.0
1959	20.9	0.0	21.0	0.5	21.1	0.5	21.1	0.0	21.1	0.0	21.1	0.0	21.1	0.0	21.1	0.0	21.1	0.0	21.1	0.0	21.1	0.0	21.1	0.0
1960	21.1	0.0	21.3	0.9	21.3	0.0	21.4	0.5	21.4	0.0	21.4	0.0	21.4	0.0	21.4	0.0	21.4	0.0	21.5	0.5	21.3	-0.9	21.3	0.0
1961	21.3	0.0	21.2	-0.5	21.3	0.5	21.3	0.0	21.3	0.0	21.3	0.0	21.3	0.0	21.3	0.0	21.2	-0.5	21.2	0.0	21.2	0.0	21.1	-0.5
1962	21.1	0.0	21.4	1.4	21.4	0.0	21.4	0.0	21.2	-0.9	21.2	0.0	21.1	-0.5	21.1	0.0	21.1	0.0	21.2	0.5	21.3	0.5	21.3	0.0
1963	21.2	-0.5	21.1	-0.5	21.1	0.0	21.1	0.0	21.1	0.0	21.0	-0.5	21.0	0.0	20.9	-0.5	21.0	0.5	21.1	0.5	21.1	0.0	21.1	0.0
1964	21.0	-0.5	21.0	0.0	21.0	0.0	21.0	0.0	21.0	0.0	21.1	0.5	21.2	0.5	21.2	0.0	21.1	-0.5	21.1	0.0	21.1	0.0	21.0	-0.5
1965	21.0	0.0	21.0	0.0	21.1	0.5	21.1	0.0	21.1	0.0	21.1	0.0	21.1	0.0	21.1	0.0	21.0	-0.5	21.0	0.0	21.0	0.0	21.0	0.0
1966	21.2	1.0	21.1	-0.5	21.2	0.5	21.2	0.0	21.1	-0.5	21.0	-0.5	21.1	0.5	21.2	0.5	21.2	0.0	21.2	0.0	21.0	-0.9	21.0	0.0
1967	21.1	0.5	21.1	0.0	21.3	0.9	21.2	-0.5	21.2	0.0	21.2	0.0	21.2	0.0	21.2	0.0	21.1	-0.5	21.2	0.5	21.2	0.0	21.3	0.5
1968	21.6	1.4	21.6	0.0	21.6	0.0	21.6	0.0	21.6	0.0	21.9	1.4	22.0	0.5	22.0	0.0	22.0	0.0	22.2	0.9	22.2	0.0	22.2	0.0
1969	22.3	0.5	22.4	0.4	22.4	0.0	22.7	1.3	22.7	0.0	22.7	0.0	22.7	0.0	22.7	0.0	22.8	0.4	23.0	0.9	23.0	0.0	23.0	0.0
1970	23.0	0.0	23.1	0.4	23.4	1.3	23.6	0.9	23.6	0.0	23.6	0.0	23.7	0.4	23.8	0.4	23.8	0.0	24.4	2.5	24.4	0.0	24.9	2.0
1971	25.6	2.8	25.7	0.4	25.7	0.0	25.9	0.8	26.5	2.3	26.5	0.0	26.6	0.4	26.6	0.0	26.6	0.0	26.6	0.0	26.6	0.0	26.6	0.0
1972	26.6	0.0	26.7	0.4	26.8	0.4	26.8	0.0	27.2	1.5	27.0	-0.7	26.9	-0.4	26.9	0.0	27.0	0.4	27.0	0.0	27.0	0.0	27.0	0.0
1973	27.1	0.4	27.1	0.0	27.2	0.4	27.2	0.0	27.4	0.7	27.5	0.4	27.1	-1.5	27.1	0.0	27.0	-0.4	27.0	0.0	27.1	0.4	27.9	3.0
1974	31.9	14.3	35.4	11.0	36.2	2.3	37.5	3.6	40.1	6.9	40.4	0.7	41.4	2.5	42.0	1.4	42.8	1.9	43.1	0.7	44.4	3.0	44.5	0.2
1975	45.2	1.6	45.3	0.2	45.3	0.0	46.4	2.4	46.4	0.0	46.6	0.4	47.3	1.5	47.4	0.2	47.3	-0.2	47.7	0.8	47.6	-0.2	47.7	0.2
1976	48.5	1.7	48.5	0.0	49.3	1.6	49.0	-0.6	49.2	0.4	49.2	0.0	49.3	0.2	49.2	-0.2	49.7	1.0	49.8	0.2	49.8	0.0	49.8	0.0
1977	51.0	2.4	51.2	0.4	52.0	1.6	52.5	1.0	52.5	0.0	53.1	1.1	53.3	0.4	53.8	0.9	54.6	1.5	54.3	-0.5	54.3	0.0	54.5	0.4
1978	55.3	1.5	56.7	2.5	56.9	0.4	57.0	0.2	57.2	0.4	58.1	1.6	59.9	3.1	59.8	-0.2	59.8	0.0	60.0	0.3	60.1	0.2	60.1	0.0
1979	61.2	1.8	62.3	1.8	62.4	0.2	63.6	1.9	64.2	0.9	64.0	-0.3	65.8	2.8	65.7	-0.2	71.2	8.4	72.3	1.5	72.5	0.3	72.5	0.0
1980	74.6	2.9	80.9	8.4	82.0	1.4	84.7	3.3	84.9	0.2	83.7	-1.4	84.1	0.5	84.2	0.1	84.9	0.8	85.4	0.6	85.5	0.1	88.8	3.9
1981	88.7	-0.1	90.0	1.5	93.6	4.0	101.5	8.4	101.2	-0.3	101.1	-0.1	100.9	-0.2	100.7	-0.2	100.5	-0.2	100.3	-0.2	100.4	0.1	100.6	0.2
1982	100.6	0.0	101.5	0.9	101.6	0.1	101.5	-0.1	99.9	-1.6	98.6	-1.3	98.9	0.3	98.8	-0.1	99.1	0.3	99.7	0.6	99.9	0.2	99.8	-0.1
1983	99.9	0.1	100.9	1.0	101.0	0.1	101.5	0.5	101.4	-0.1	101.6	0.2	101.7	0.1	102.1	0.4	102.3	0.2	102.4	0.1	103.3	0.9	103.2	0.1
1984	103.1	-0.1	103.4	0.3	104.0	0.6	104.1	0.1	104.9	0.8	105.8	0.9	107.5	1.6	108.4	0.8	108.0	-0.4	107.9	-0.1	107.2	-0.6	107.5	0.3
1985	109.0	1.4	109.0	0.0	109.0	0.0	110.0	0.9	110.9	0.8	111.0	0.1	111.0	0.0	111.1	0.1	111.1	0.0	111.5	0.4	111.0	-0.4	110.9	-0.1
1986	111.1	0.2	110.9	-0.2	110.8	-0.1	110.6	-0.2	111.0	0.4	111.0	0.0	110.4	-0.5	109.5	-0.8	109.3	-0.2	109.6	0.3	109.4	-0.2	109.0	-0.4
1987	108.6	-0.4	109.1	0.5	109.6	0.5	109.8	0.2	109.6	-0.2	110.3	0.6	110.9	0.5	110.1	-0.7	110.6	0.5	111.8	1.1	111.9	0.1	111.3	-0.5
1988	112.5	1.1	112.8	0.3	112.9	0.1	113.1	0.2	113.2	0.1	113.4	0.2	112.4	-0.9	112.3	-0.1	112.7	0.4	112.8	0.1	113.0	0.2	113.2	0.2
1989	113.6	0.4	113.5	-0.1	113.9	0.4	114.3	0.4	114.1	-0.2	114.2	0.1	114.5	0.3	114.4	-0.1	114.4	0.0	114.3	-0.1	114.5	0.2	114.7	0.2
1990	115.2	0.4	115.4	0.2	115.4	0.0	115.5	0.1	115.5	0.0	115.6	0.1	115.6	0.0	115.8	0.2	116.5	0.6	116.6	0.1	117.6	0.9	117.7	0.1
1991	118.5	0.7	118.4	-0.1	118.3	-0.1	118.5	0.2	118.6	0.1	118.5	-0.1	118.4	-0.1	118.4	0.0	118.4	0.0	118.5	0.1	118.5	0.0	118.1	-0.3

[Continued]

Other Nonmetallic Minerals
Producer Price Index
Base 1982 = 100
[Continued]

For 1947-1997. Columns headed % show percentile change in the index from the previous period for which an index is available.

Year	Jan Index	%	Feb Index	%	Mar Index	%	Apr Index	%	May Index	%	Jun Index	%	Jul Index	%	Aug Index	%	Sep Index	%	Oct Index	%	Nov Index	%	Dec Index	%
1992	117.8	-0.3	118.0	0.2	117.8	-0.2	116.1	-1.4	115.0	-0.9	115.5	0.4	115.8	0.3	116.0	0.2	116.0	0.0	116.0	0.0	116.2	0.2	116.3	0.1
1993	117.6	1.1	117.8	0.2	118.0	0.2	118.5	0.4	118.7	0.2	119.2	0.4	119.7	0.4	119.8	0.1	120.1	0.3	120.2	0.1	120.0	-0.2	120.3	0.3
1994	120.7	0.3	121.3	0.5	121.4	0.1	121.5	0.1	121.5	0.0	121.5	0.0	121.5	0.0	121.7	0.2	121.7	0.0	121.9	0.2	122.0	0.1	122.3	0.2
1995	123.6	1.1	124.3	0.6	124.7	0.3	125.4	0.6	125.1	-0.2	125.6	0.4	125.2	-0.3	125.9	0.6	126.3	0.3	126.0	-0.2	126.3	0.2	126.3	0.0
1996	126.7	0.3	126.7	0.0	127.3	0.5	127.0	-0.2	127.7	0.6	127.4	-0.2	127.9	0.4	127.5	-0.3	128.4	0.7	128.6	0.2	128.6	0.0	128.5	-0.1
1997	128.9	0.3	129.8	0.7	130.2	0.3	130.5	0.2	130.2	-0.2	130.6	0.3	130.5	-0.1	130.8	0.2	130.5	-0.2	130.3	-0.2	130.2	-0.1	130.2	0.0

Source: U.S. Department of Labor, Bureau of Labor Statistics, Division of Industry Prices and Price Indexes. n.e.c. stands for not elsewhere classified. - indicates no data collected for period or unavailable.

TRANSPORTATION EQUIPMENT
Producer Price Index
Base 1982 = 100

For 1969-1997. Columns headed % show percentile change in the index from the previous period for which an index is available.

Year	Jan Index	%	Feb Index	%	Mar Index	%	Apr Index	%	May Index	%	Jun Index	%	Jul Index	%	Aug Index	%	Sep Index	%	Oct Index	%	Nov Index	%	Dec Index	%
1969	40.1	-	40.1	0.0	40.1	0.0	40.1	0.0	40.1	0.0	40.2	0.2	40.2	0.0	40.1	-0.2	40.1	0.0	41.0	2.2	41.2	0.5	41.2	0.0
1970	41.3	0.2	41.2	-0.2	41.4	0.5	41.3	-0.2	41.4	0.2	41.4	0.0	41.4	0.0	41.5	0.2	41.5	0.0	43.3	4.3	43.5	0.5	43.5	0.0
1971	43.7	0.5	43.9	0.5	44.0	0.2	44.0	0.0	44.1	0.2	44.1	0.0	44.3	0.5	44.3	0.0	43.9	-0.9	44.4	1.1	44.4	0.0	45.2	1.8
1972	45.4	0.4	45.5	0.2	45.5	0.0	45.6	0.2	45.6	0.0	45.7	0.2	45.7	0.0	45.7	0.0	45.7	0.0	45.2	-1.1	45.3	0.2	45.7	0.9
1973	45.7	0.0	45.7	0.0	45.9	0.4	46.0	0.2	46.1	0.2	46.0	-0.2	46.1	0.2	46.1	0.0	45.9	-0.4	46.4	1.1	46.5	0.2	47.0	1.1
1974	47.5	1.1	47.6	0.2	47.7	0.2	47.8	0.2	48.6	1.7	49.2	1.2	50.1	1.8	50.8	1.4	51.1	0.6	53.8	5.3	54.1	0.6	54.9	1.5
1975	54.9	0.0	55.4	0.9	55.9	0.9	56.0	0.2	56.0	0.0	56.1	0.2	56.1	0.0	56.3	0.4	56.5	0.4	58.7	3.9	59.0	0.5	59.1	0.2
1976	59.6	0.8	59.6	0.0	59.7	0.2	59.7	0.0	59.7	0.0	59.8	0.2	59.8	0.0	60.2	0.7	60.5	0.5	62.5	3.3	62.6	0.2	62.9	0.5
1977	62.9	0.0	63.0	0.2	63.4	0.6	63.6	0.3	63.7	0.2	63.9	0.3	63.9	0.0	64.4	0.8	64.7	0.5	67.2	3.9	67.3	0.1	67.4	0.1
1978	67.7	0.4	67.9	0.3	67.9	0.0	68.3	0.6	68.9	0.9	69.1	0.3	69.2	0.1	69.3	0.1	69.5	0.3	71.8	3.3	72.1	0.4	72.3	0.3
1979	73.2	1.2	73.5	0.4	73.6	0.1	74.8	1.6	75.0	0.3	75.1	0.1	75.4	0.4	74.5	-1.2	74.8	0.4	77.8	4.0	78.0	0.3	78.3	0.4
1980	79.6	1.7	79.4	-0.3	79.6	0.3	81.4	2.3	81.1	-0.4	81.4	0.4	82.6	1.5	83.6	1.2	81.9	-2.0	87.1	6.3	87.2	0.1	89.8	3.0
1981	91.1	1.4	91.8	0.8	91.4	-0.4	92.9	1.6	93.6	0.8	93.8	0.2	94.1	0.3	94.5	0.4	92.8	-1.8	97.9	5.5	98.7	0.8	98.9	0.2
1982	99.6	0.7	98.2	-1.4	98.2	0.0	98.4	0.2	99.1	0.7	99.8	0.7	100.1	0.3	100.4	0.3	97.9	-2.5	102.5	4.7	102.6	0.1	103.1	0.5
1983	102.7	-0.4	102.5	-0.2	102.2	-0.3	102.4	0.2	102.5	0.1	102.6	0.1	102.6	0.0	102.9	0.3	100.3	-2.5	104.4	4.1	104.4	0.0	104.4	0.0
1984	104.8	0.4	105.0	0.2	105.1	0.1	105.2	0.1	105.1	-0.1	105.0	-0.1	105.1	0.1	105.0	-0.1	103.2	-1.7	106.1	2.8	106.4	0.3	106.2	-0.2
1985	106.9	0.7	107.4	0.5	107.2	-0.2	107.4	0.2	107.8	0.4	107.9	0.1	108.1	0.2	108.1	0.0	104.1	-3.7	110.2	5.9	110.2	0.0	109.8	-0.4
1986	109.5	-0.3	109.7	0.2	109.5	-0.2	110.3	0.7	110.2	-0.1	110.3	0.1	110.4	0.1	110.0	-0.4	107.5	-2.3	113.2	5.3	113.1	-0.1	112.8	-0.3
1987	113.1	0.3	112.1	-0.9	112.4	0.3	113.0	0.5	112.4	-0.5	112.3	-0.1	112.2	-0.1	111.9	-0.3	110.9	-0.9	113.8	2.6	113.5	-0.3	112.5	-0.9
1988	113.2	0.6	113.2	0.0	113.1	-0.1	113.5	0.4	113.7	0.2	114.0	0.3	113.9	-0.1	114.0	0.1	113.2	-0.7	116.6	3.0	116.3	-0.3	116.3	0.0
1989	116.8	0.4	117.1	0.3	116.8	-0.3	116.4	-0.3	117.2	0.7	117.6	0.3	116.9	-0.6	117.1	0.2	116.6	-0.4	120.0	2.9	120.0	0.0	119.8	-0.2
1990	119.7	-0.1	120.2	0.4	120.3	0.1	120.5	0.2	120.4	-0.1	121.0	0.5	121.2	0.2	121.1	-0.1	121.0	-0.1	124.0	2.5	124.2	0.2	124.2	0.0
1991	125.2	0.8	125.7	0.4	125.7	0.0	125.5	-0.2	125.6	0.1	125.6	0.0	125.7	0.1	126.0	0.2	125.2	-0.6	129.1	3.1	128.9	-0.2	129.0	0.1
1992	129.8	0.6	129.7	-0.1	130.0	0.2	130.2	0.2	130.2	0.0	130.1	-0.1	130.2	0.1	130.0	-0.2	128.5	-1.2	132.3	3.0	132.2	-0.1	132.1	-0.1
1993	132.7	0.5	133.1	0.3	133.3	0.2	133.4	0.1	133.3	-0.1	133.3	0.0	133.6	0.2	133.5	-0.1	131.7	-1.3	135.2	2.7	135.5	0.2	135.6	0.1
1994	136.5	0.7	136.6	0.1	136.6	0.0	136.7	0.1	137.1	0.3	137.0	-0.1	137.2	0.1	137.2	0.0	135.6	-1.2	138.5	2.1	138.3	-0.1	138.7	0.3
1995	139.6	0.6	139.6	0.0	139.4	-0.1	139.3	-0.1	139.3	0.0	139.0	-0.2	139.0	0.0	138.9	-0.1	137.1	-1.3	141.1	2.9	141.7	0.4	141.7	0.0
1996	141.7	0.0	141.7	0.0	141.8	0.1	141.6	-0.1	141.6	0.0	141.7	0.1	141.3	-0.3	141.4	0.1	140.0	-1.0	142.9	2.1	142.7	-0.1	142.6	-0.1
1997	142.9	0.2	142.8	-0.1	142.7	-0.1	142.3	-0.3	141.5	-0.6	141.4	-0.1	140.5	-0.6	140.5	0.0	139.5	-0.7	142.5	2.2	142.0	-0.4	141.5	-0.4

Source: U.S. Department of Labor, Bureau of Labor Statistics, Division of Industry Prices and Price Indexes. n.e.c. stands for not elsewhere classified. - indicates no data collected for period or unavailable.

Motor Vehicles and Equipment
Producer Price Index
Base 1982 = 100

For 1926-1997. Columns headed % show percentile change in the index from the previous period for which an index is available.

Year	Jan Index	%	Feb Index	%	Mar Index	%	Apr Index	%	May Index	%	Jun Index	%	Jul Index	%	Aug Index	%	Sep Index	%	Oct Index	%	Nov Index	%	Dec Index	%
1926	-	-	-	-	-	-	-	-	-	-	-	-	-	-	-	-	-	-	-	-	-	-	-	-
1927	-	-	-	-	-	-	-	-	-	-	-	-	-	-	-	-	-	-	-	-	-	-	-	-
1928	-	-	-	-	-	-	-	-	-	-	-	-	-	-	-	-	-	-	-	-	-	-	-	-
1929	-	-	-	-	-	-	-	-	-	-	-	-	-	-	-	-	-	-	-	-	-	-	-	-
1930	-	-	-	-	-	-	-	-	-	-	-	-	-	-	-	-	-	-	-	-	-	-	-	-
1931	-	-	-	-	-	-	-	-	-	-	-	-	-	-	-	-	-	-	-	-	-	-	-	-
1932	-	-	-	-	-	-	-	-	-	-	-	-	-	-	-	-	-	-	-	-	-	-	-	-
1933	-	-	-	-	-	-	-	-	-	-	-	-	-	-	-	-	-	-	-	-	-	-	-	-
1934	-	-	-	-	-	-	-	-	-	-	-	-	-	-	-	-	-	-	-	-	-	-	-	-
1935	-	-	-	-	-	-	-	-	-	-	-	-	-	-	-	-	-	-	-	-	-	-	-	-
1936	-	-	-	-	-	-	-	-	-	-	-	-	-	-	-	-	-	-	-	-	-	-	-	-
1937	14.4	-	14.4	0.0	14.4	0.0	14.5	0.7	14.5	0.0	14.5	0.0	14.5	0.0	15.0	3.4	15.2	1.3	15.4	1.3	15.9	3.2	15.9	0.0
1938	15.9	0.0	15.9	0.0	15.9	0.0	15.9	0.0	16.0	0.6	16.0	0.0	16.0	0.0	16.0	0.0	16.0	0.0	15.8	-1.2	15.6	-1.3	15.6	0.0
1939	15.6	0.0	15.6	0.0	15.6	0.0	15.6	0.0	15.5	-0.6	15.5	0.0	15.5	0.0	15.4	-0.6	15.4	0.0	15.6	1.3	15.8	1.3	15.8	0.0
1940	15.8	0.0	15.8	0.0	15.8	0.0	15.8	0.0	15.8	0.0	15.8	0.0	15.9	0.6	15.9	0.0	16.0	0.6	16.7	4.4	16.7	0.0	16.7	0.0
1941	16.7	0.0	16.6	-0.6	16.6	0.0	16.7	0.6	16.7	0.0	16.7	0.0	16.8	0.6	16.8	0.0	16.8	0.0	18.7	11.3	18.7	0.0	18.7	0.0
1942	18.7	0.0	18.7	0.0	18.8	0.5	18.8	0.0	18.8	0.0	18.8	0.0	18.8	0.0	18.8	0.0	18.8	0.0	18.8	0.0	18.8	0.0	18.8	0.0
1943	18.8	0.0	18.8	0.0	18.8	0.0	18.8	0.0	18.8	0.0	18.8	0.0	18.8	0.0	18.8	0.0	18.8	0.0	18.8	0.0	18.8	0.0	18.8	0.0
1944	18.8	0.0	18.8	0.0	18.8	0.0	18.8	0.0	18.8	0.0	18.9	0.5	18.9	0.0	18.9	0.0	18.9	0.0	18.9	0.0	19.0	0.5	19.0	0.0
1945	19.0	0.0	19.0	0.0	19.1	0.5	19.1	0.0	19.2	0.5	19.3	0.5	19.3	0.0	19.3	0.0	19.3	0.0	19.3	0.0	19.5	1.0	19.5	0.0
1946	19.7	1.0	20.1	2.0	20.4	1.5	20.9	2.5	21.9	4.8	22.6	3.2	22.6	0.0	23.1	2.2	23.4	1.3	23.6	0.9	24.3	3.0	24.8	2.1
1947	24.9	0.4	24.9	0.0	24.9	0.0	24.8	-0.4	24.9	0.4	25.0	0.4	25.0	0.0	25.9	3.6	26.4	1.9	26.4	0.0	26.5	0.4	26.6	0.4
1948	26.8	0.8	26.7	-0.4	26.7	0.0	26.7	0.0	26.8	0.4	27.8	3.7	28.5	2.5	29.4	3.2	29.6	0.7	29.6	0.0	29.7	0.3	29.9	0.7
1949	30.0	0.3	30.3	1.0	30.4	0.3	30.2	-0.7	30.1	-0.3	30.0	-0.3	30.1	0.3	30.1	0.0	30.1	0.0	30.1	0.0	30.1	0.0	30.1	0.0
1950	30.0	-0.3	29.9	-0.3	29.8	-0.3	29.8	0.0	29.9	0.3	29.9	0.0	29.9	0.0	29.9	0.0	30.1	0.7	30.1	0.0	30.1	0.0	30.4	1.0
1951	30.5	0.3	30.6	0.3	31.4	2.6	31.4	0.0	31.4	0.0	31.4	0.0	31.4	0.0	31.6	0.6	31.9	0.9	32.4	1.6	32.5	0.3	32.6	0.3
1952	32.7	0.3	33.5	2.4	33.5	0.0	33.5	0.0	33.5	0.0	33.5	0.0	33.5	0.0	33.5	0.0	33.5	0.0	33.5	0.0	33.5	0.0	33.5	0.0
1953	33.5	0.0	33.5	0.0	33.5	0.0	33.2	-0.9	33.2	0.0	33.2	0.0	33.2	0.0	33.2	0.0	33.2	0.0	33.2	0.0	33.2	0.0	33.2	0.0
1954	33.2	0.0	33.2	0.0	33.2	0.0	33.2	0.0	33.2	0.0	33.2	0.0	33.2	0.0	33.2	0.0	33.2	0.0	33.2	0.0	33.8	1.8	34.0	0.6
1955	34.0	0.0	34.0	0.0	34.0	0.0	34.1	0.3	34.1	0.0	34.1	0.0	34.1	0.0	34.1	0.0	34.1	0.0	34.9	2.3	35.3	1.1	35.4	0.3
1956	35.4	0.0	35.6	0.6	36.1	1.4	36.1	0.0	36.1	0.0	36.1	0.0	36.1	0.0	36.1	0.0	36.2	0.3	36.6	1.1	37.5	2.5	37.5	0.0
1957	37.5	0.0	37.6	0.3	37.6	0.0	37.7	0.3	37.7	0.0	37.7	0.0	37.7	0.0	37.7	0.0	37.7	0.0	37.9	0.5	38.8	2.4	38.9	0.3
1958	38.9	0.0	38.9	0.0	38.9	0.0	38.9	0.0	38.9	0.0	38.9	0.0	38.9	0.0	38.9	0.0	38.9	0.0	39.0	0.3	39.9	2.3	40.0	0.3
1959	40.0	0.0	40.0	0.0	40.0	0.0	40.0	0.0	40.0	0.0	40.0	0.0	40.0	0.0	40.0	0.0	40.0	0.0	39.6	-1.0	39.6	0.0	39.6	0.0
1960	39.6	0.0	39.6	0.0	39.6	0.0	39.6	0.0	39.6	0.0	39.6	0.0	39.6	0.0	39.6	0.0	37.9	-4.3	39.2	3.4	39.2	0.0	39.3	0.3
1961	39.4	0.3	39.2	-0.5	39.2	0.0	39.2	0.0	39.2	0.0	39.2	0.0	39.2	0.0	39.2	0.0	39.2	0.0	39.2	0.0	39.2	0.0	39.2	0.0
1962	39.2	0.0	39.1	-0.3	39.1	0.0	39.1	0.0	39.1	0.0	39.4	0.8	39.4	0.0	39.4	0.0	39.4	0.0	39.2	-0.5	39.2	0.0	39.2	0.0
1963	39.2	0.0	39.2	0.0	39.2	0.0	39.0	-0.5	38.9	-0.3	38.7	-0.5	38.9	0.5	38.8	-0.3	38.7	-0.3	38.9	0.5	38.9	0.0	38.9	0.0
1964	38.9	0.0	38.9	0.0	38.9	0.0	38.9	0.0	39.4	1.3	39.3	-0.3	39.3	0.0	39.2	-0.3	39.1	-0.3	39.2	0.3	39.2	0.0	39.2	0.0
1965	39.2	0.0	39.3	0.3	39.2	-0.3	39.2	0.0	39.2	0.0	39.2	0.0	39.2	0.0	39.2	0.0	39.1	-0.3	39.1	0.0	39.1	0.0	39.1	0.0
1966	39.1	0.0	39.1	0.0	39.0	-0.3	39.0	0.0	39.3	0.8	39.2	-0.3	39.2	0.0	39.1	-0.3	39.0	-0.3	39.6	1.5	39.6	0.0	39.6	0.0
1967	39.6	0.0	39.6	0.0	39.6	0.0	39.6	0.0	39.4	-0.5	39.5	0.3	39.4	-0.3	39.6	0.5	39.6	0.0	40.6	2.5	40.6	0.0	40.6	0.0
1968	40.7	0.2	40.7	0.0	40.7	0.0	40.7	0.0	40.6	-0.2	40.8	0.5	40.7	-0.2	40.7	0.0	40.7	0.0	41.6	2.2	41.6	0.0	41.6	0.0
1969	41.5	-0.2	41.5	0.0	41.4	-0.2	41.5	0.2	41.5	0.0	41.6	0.2	41.5	-0.2	41.4	-0.2	41.4	0.0	42.3	2.2	42.5	0.5	42.5	0.0
1970	42.5	0.0	42.5	0.0	42.7	0.5	42.5	-0.5	42.7	0.5	42.7	0.0	42.7	0.0	42.7	0.0	42.8	0.2	44.9	4.9	45.0	0.2	45.0	0.0

[Continued]

Motor Vehicles and Equipment
Producer Price Index
Base 1982 = 100
[Continued]

For 1926-1997. Columns headed % show percentile change in the index from the previous period for which an index is available.

Year	Jan Index	%	Feb Index	%	Mar Index	%	Apr Index	%	May Index	%	Jun Index	%	Jul Index	%	Aug Index	%	Sep Index	%	Oct Index	%	Nov Index	%	Dec Index	%
1971	45.2	0.4	45.4	0.4	45.5	0.2	45.6	0.2	45.6	0.0	45.7	0.2	45.8	0.2	45.8	0.0	45.3	-1.1	46.0	1.5	46.0	0.0	46.9	2.0
1972	46.9	0.0	47.0	0.2	46.9	-0.2	47.0	0.2	47.0	0.0	47.2	0.4	47.1	-0.2	47.1	0.0	47.1	0.0	46.5	-1.3	46.6	0.2	47.1	1.1
1973	47.0	-0.2	47.1	0.2	47.2	0.2	47.4	0.4	47.4	0.0	47.3	-0.2	47.4	0.2	47.4	0.0	47.1	-0.6	47.7	1.3	47.8	0.2	48.3	1.0
1974	48.9	1.2	49.0	0.2	49.0	0.0	49.1	0.2	49.7	1.2	50.2	1.0	51.1	1.8	51.8	1.4	52.0	0.4	55.0	5.8	55.3	0.5	56.0	1.3
1975	55.8	-0.4	56.3	0.9	56.9	1.1	56.9	0.0	56.9	0.0	57.0	0.2	56.9	-0.2	57.1	0.4	57.3	0.4	59.7	4.2	59.9	0.3	60.0	0.2
1976	60.2	0.3	60.2	0.0	60.4	0.3	60.4	0.0	60.3	-0.2	60.4	0.2	60.4	0.0	60.8	0.7	61.1	0.5	63.3	3.6	63.4	0.2	63.5	0.2
1977	63.4	-0.2	63.5	0.2	64.0	0.8	64.1	0.2	64.3	0.3	64.4	0.2	64.4	0.0	64.9	0.8	65.2	0.5	68.0	4.3	67.9	-0.1	68.0	0.1
1978	68.2	0.3	68.4	0.3	68.4	0.0	68.8	0.6	69.5	1.0	69.7	0.3	69.8	0.1	70.0	0.3	70.0	0.0	72.4	3.4	72.6	0.3	72.8	0.3
1979	73.6	1.1	74.0	0.5	74.1	0.1	75.4	1.8	75.6	0.3	75.7	0.1	76.0	0.4	74.7	-1.7	75.0	0.4	78.4	4.5	78.6	0.3	78.9	0.4
1980	79.9	1.3	79.6	-0.4	79.9	0.4	81.8	2.4	81.4	-0.5	81.7	0.4	83.0	1.6	84.2	1.4	81.8	-2.9	86.9	6.2	87.0	0.1	90.0	3.4
1981	91.1	1.2	91.9	0.9	91.4	-0.5	93.1	1.9	93.9	0.9	94.2	0.3	94.5	0.3	94.9	0.4	92.7	-2.3	98.6	6.4	99.1	0.5	99.3	0.2
1982	99.8	0.5	98.2	-1.6	98.2	0.0	98.4	0.2	99.2	0.8	99.9	0.7	100.3	0.4	100.6	0.3	97.4	-3.2	102.6	5.3	102.6	0.0	102.7	0.1
1983	102.3	-0.4	102.0	-0.3	101.7	-0.3	101.8	0.1	102.0	0.2	102.1	0.1	102.1	0.0	102.2	0.1	99.2	-2.9	103.7	4.5	103.7	0.0	103.7	0.0
1984	103.9	0.2	104.0	0.1	104.1	0.1	104.2	0.1	104.1	-0.1	103.9	-0.2	104.0	0.1	103.9	-0.1	101.6	-2.2	105.0	3.3	105.2	0.2	104.9	-0.3
1985	105.5	0.6	106.1	0.6	105.9	-0.2	106.0	0.1	106.4	0.4	106.5	0.1	106.5	0.0	106.5	0.0	101.4	-4.8	108.8	7.3	108.8	0.0	108.2	-0.6
1986	107.6	-0.6	107.8	0.2	107.5	-0.3	108.6	1.0	108.5	-0.1	108.7	0.2	108.8	0.1	108.3	-0.5	105.2	-2.9	113.1	7.5	113.0	-0.1	112.5	-0.4
1987	112.6	0.1	110.9	-1.5	111.1	0.2	112.3	1.1	111.8	-0.4	111.5	-0.3	111.4	-0.1	110.8	-0.5	108.9	-1.7	114.2	4.9	113.3	-0.8	111.8	-1.3
1988	112.0	0.2	111.9	-0.1	111.8	-0.1	112.0	0.2	112.3	0.3	112.4	0.1	112.6	0.2	112.8	0.2	110.9	-1.7	116.9	5.4	116.1	-0.7	116.0	-0.1
1989	116.2	0.2	116.5	0.3	115.5	-0.9	114.8	-0.6	115.6	0.7	115.9	0.3	114.5	-1.2	114.5	0.0	113.8	-0.6	119.6	5.1	118.8	-0.7	118.6	-0.2
1990	117.2	-1.2	117.3	0.1	117.0	-0.3	116.9	-0.1	116.6	-0.3	117.6	0.9	117.8	0.2	117.2	-0.5	116.7	-0.4	121.6	4.2	121.5	-0.1	121.5	0.0
1991	121.9	0.3	122.4	0.4	122.2	-0.2	121.5	-0.6	120.7	-0.7	120.6	-0.1	120.5	-0.1	120.6	0.1	119.2	-1.2	125.8	5.5	125.4	-0.3	124.9	-0.4
1992	124.8	-0.1	124.6	-0.2	124.9	0.2	124.8	-0.1	124.7	-0.1	124.3	-0.3	124.4	0.1	123.9	-0.4	121.3	-2.1	127.1	4.8	127.1	0.0	126.9	-0.2
1993	127.1	0.2	127.8	0.6	127.8	0.0	127.7	-0.1	127.6	-0.1	127.7	0.1	127.8	0.1	127.7	-0.1	124.9	-2.2	129.7	3.8	129.9	0.2	130.0	0.1
1994	130.7	0.5	130.9	0.2	130.8	-0.1	130.8	0.0	131.4	0.5	131.3	-0.1	131.5	0.2	131.6	0.1	129.0	-2.0	132.8	2.9	132.5	-0.2	133.0	0.4
1995	133.4	0.3	133.3	-0.1	133.1	-0.2	132.9	-0.2	132.7	-0.2	132.2	-0.4	132.2	0.0	131.9	-0.2	129.1	-2.1	134.8	4.4	135.5	0.5	135.4	-0.1
1996	134.5	-0.7	134.5	0.0	134.5	0.0	134.1	-0.3	134.1	0.0	134.2	0.1	133.5	-0.5	133.3	-0.1	131.0	-1.7	135.2	3.2	134.9	-0.2	134.8	-0.1
1997	134.6	-0.1	134.5	-0.1	134.3	-0.1	133.7	-0.4	132.5	-0.9	132.3	-0.2	131.0	-1.0	131.0	0.0	129.6	-1.1	134.3	3.6	133.5	-0.6	132.6	-0.7

Source: U.S. Department of Labor, Bureau of Labor Statistics, Division of Industry Prices and Price Indexes. n.e.c. stands for not elsewhere classified. - indicates no data collected for period or unavailable.

Aircraft and Aircraft Equipment
Producer Price Index
Base 1982 = 100

For 1971-1997. Columns headed % show percentile change in the index from the previous period for which an index is available.

Year	Jan Index	%	Feb Index	%	Mar Index	%	Apr Index	%	May Index	%	Jun Index	%	Jul Index	%	Aug Index	%	Sep Index	%	Oct Index	%	Nov Index	%	Dec Index	%
1971	36.7	-	36.7	0.0	36.7	0.0	36.7	0.0	36.7	0.0	36.7	0.0	36.7	0.0	36.7	0.0	36.7	0.0	36.1	-1.6	36.1	0.0	37.0	2.5
1972	38.4	3.8	38.4	0.0	38.4	0.0	38.4	0.0	38.4	0.0	38.4	0.0	38.4	0.0	38.4	0.0	38.4	0.0	38.6	0.5	38.6	0.0	38.6	0.0
1973	38.6	0.0	38.8	0.5	39.0	0.5	39.0	0.0	39.0	0.0	39.0	0.0	39.0	0.0	39.0	0.0	39.0	0.0	39.0	0.0	39.1	0.3	39.2	0.3
1974	39.2	0.0	39.2	0.0	39.2	0.0	39.7	1.3	41.8	5.3	41.8	0.0	42.0	0.5	42.0	0.0	43.3	3.1	43.9	1.4	44.3	0.9	45.1	1.8
1975	46.1	2.2	46.1	0.0	46.3	0.4	48.2	4.1	48.2	0.0	48.2	0.0	48.2	0.0	48.2	0.0	49.4	2.5	50.9	3.0	50.9	0.0	50.9	0.0
1976	53.9	5.9	53.8	-0.2	53.8	0.0	53.8	0.0	53.8	0.0	53.8	0.0	53.8	0.0	53.8	0.0	54.7	1.7	55.7	1.8	55.7	0.0	57.6	3.4
1977	58.3	1.2	58.3	0.0	58.3	0.0	58.4	0.2	58.4	0.0	58.4	0.0	58.4	0.0	58.4	0.0	59.2	1.4	60.8	2.7	62.0	2.0	62.0	0.0
1978	63.1	1.8	63.1	0.0	63.1	0.0	63.1	0.0	63.1	0.0	63.1	0.0	63.1	0.0	63.1	0.0	64.3	1.9	65.9	2.5	67.3	2.1	67.4	0.1
1979	68.4	1.5	68.4	0.0	68.8	0.6	69.0	0.3	69.2	0.3	69.3	0.1	69.5	0.3	70.3	1.2	70.3	0.0	71.0	1.0	71.8	1.1	72.3	0.7
1980	75.3	4.1	75.3	0.0	75.3	0.0	75.9	0.8	75.9	0.0	75.9	0.0	76.1	0.3	76.1	0.0	78.9	3.7	87.0	10.3	87.0	0.0	87.4	0.5
1981	89.4	2.3	89.4	0.0	89.9	0.6	90.0	0.1	90.0	0.0	90.3	0.3	90.3	0.0	90.3	0.0	92.7	2.7	92.4	-0.3	95.5	3.4	95.5	0.0
1982	97.3	1.9	97.3	0.0	97.3	0.0	98.6	1.3	98.6	0.0	98.6	0.0	98.6	0.0	98.6	0.0	101.5	2.9	102.5	1.0	103.6	1.1	107.4	3.7
1983	106.3	-1.0	106.7	0.4	107.1	0.4	107.1	0.0	107.1	0.0	107.1	0.0	107.1	0.0	108.7	1.5	108.7	0.0	111.1	2.2	111.1	0.0	111.1	0.0
1984	112.5	1.3	114.4	1.7	114.4	0.0	114.4	0.0	114.4	0.0	114.4	0.0	114.6	0.2	114.6	0.0	116.1	1.3	116.2	0.1	117.2	0.9	117.2	0.0
1985	118.2	0.9	118.2	0.0	118.2	0.0	119.9	1.4	120.0	0.1	120.0	0.0	121.4	1.2	121.5	0.1	-	-	-	-	-	-	-	-
1986	124.1	2.1	124.4	0.2	124.4	0.0	124.6	0.2	124.3	-0.2	124.3	0.0	124.5	0.2	124.6	0.1	122.6	-1.6	122.8	0.2	122.8	0.0	122.7	-0.1
1987	123.5	0.7	123.5	0.0	123.9	0.3	123.9	0.0	122.8	-0.9	122.9	0.1	122.9	0.0	122.9	0.0	123.1	0.2	123.1	0.0	123.4	0.2	123.3	-0.1
1988	125.1	1.5	125.2	0.1	125.3	0.1	126.2	0.7	126.0	-0.2	126.7	0.6	125.8	-0.7	126.0	0.2	126.4	0.3	126.3	-0.1	126.6	0.2	126.7	0.1
1989	127.9	0.9	128.1	0.2	128.9	0.6	129.3	0.3	129.4	0.1	129.6	0.2	129.9	0.2	130.4	0.4	130.4	0.0	130.7	0.2	132.0	1.0	132.2	0.2
1990	134.3	1.6	134.9	0.4	135.4	0.4	136.1	0.5	136.3	0.1	136.4	0.1	136.7	0.2	137.5	0.6	137.6	0.1	138.4	0.6	138.9	0.4	139.1	0.1
1991	141.7	1.9	142.0	0.2	142.3	0.2	142.8	0.4	144.2	1.0	144.3	0.1	144.7	0.3	145.5	0.6	145.6	0.1	146.0	0.3	146.2	0.1	146.4	0.1
1992	149.5	2.1	149.7	0.1	149.9	0.1	150.6	0.5	150.9	0.2	151.4	0.3	151.4	0.0	152.0	0.4	152.5	0.3	152.8	0.2	152.5	-0.2	152.6	0.1
1993	153.5	0.6	153.5	0.0	153.9	0.3	154.6	0.5	154.7	0.1	154.0	-0.5	154.7	0.5	155.1	0.3	154.8	-0.2	156.4	1.0	156.8	0.3	156.9	0.1
1994	158.4	1.0	158.6	0.1	158.5	-0.1	158.7	0.1	158.7	0.0	158.7	0.0	158.8	0.1	158.9	0.1	159.0	0.1	160.5	0.9	160.8	0.2	160.8	0.0
1995	163.1	1.4	163.1	0.0	162.9	-0.1	162.8	-0.1	163.0	0.1	163.3	0.2	163.4	0.1	163.5	0.1	163.5	0.0	164.8	0.8	165.2	0.2	165.3	0.1
1996	167.0	1.0	167.1	0.1	167.3	0.1	167.1	-0.1	167.3	0.1	167.6	0.2	167.7	0.1	168.1	0.2	168.4	0.2	168.6	0.1	168.8	0.1	169.0	0.1
1997	170.1	0.7	170.0	-0.1	170.3	0.2	169.8	-0.3	170.0	0.1	170.1	0.1	169.9	-0.1	169.7	-0.1	169.4	-0.2	169.4	0.0	169.1	-0.2	169.4	0.2

Source: U.S. Department of Labor, Bureau of Labor Statistics, Division of Industry Prices and Price Indexes. n.e.c. stands for not elsewhere classified. - indicates no data collected for period or unavailable.

Ships and Boats
Producer Price Index
Base 1982 = 100

For 1981-1997. Columns headed % show percentile change in the index from the previous period for which an index is available.

Year	Jan Index	%	Feb Index	%	Mar Index	%	Apr Index	%	May Index	%	Jun Index	%	Jul Index	%	Aug Index	%	Sep Index	%	Oct Index	%	Nov Index	%	Dec Index	%
1981	-	-	-	-	-	-	-	-	-	-	-	-	-	-	-	-	-	-	-	-	-	-	97.5	-
1982	98.1	0.6	98.9	0.8	99.2	0.3	99.7	0.5	99.8	0.1	100.3	0.5	100.1	-0.2	100.4	0.3	100.6	0.2	100.9	0.3	101.0	0.1	100.9	-0.1
1983	101.0	0.1	101.4	0.4	101.5	0.1	102.4	0.9	102.7	0.3	102.9	0.2	103.1	0.2	103.2	0.1	104.1	0.9	104.5	0.4	104.4	-0.1	105.2	0.8
1984	106.1	0.9	106.3	0.2	106.5	0.2	106.6	0.1	108.1	1.4	108.0	-0.1	108.6	0.6	108.0	-0.6	107.0	-0.9	107.3	0.3	107.6	0.3	108.1	0.5
1985	108.6	0.5	109.0	0.4	109.1	0.1	110.0	0.8	110.0	0.0	110.0	0.0	109.7	-0.3	110.4	0.6	110.5	0.1	111.6	1.0	112.0	0.4	112.4	0.4
1986	113.2	0.7	113.2	0.0	113.3	0.1	113.4	0.1	113.6	0.2	113.6	0.0	113.5	-0.1	113.4	-0.1	113.4	0.0	113.6	0.2	113.6	0.0	113.6	0.0
1987	113.8	0.2	113.9	0.1	114.0	0.1	114.1	0.1	114.1	0.0	114.1	0.0	114.1	0.0	114.1	0.0	114.2	0.1	114.2	0.0	114.2	0.0	114.3	0.1
1988	114.4	0.1	114.5	0.1	114.1	-0.3	114.1	0.0	114.2	0.1	114.2	0.0	114.5	0.3	114.6	0.1	116.5	1.7	116.3	-0.2	116.8	0.4	116.7	-0.1
1989	116.9	0.2	117.2	0.3	117.2	0.0	114.8	-2.0	119.9	4.4	122.1	1.8	122.4	0.2	124.0	1.3	122.1	-1.5	122.0	-0.1	122.1	0.1	120.6	-1.2
1990	120.9	0.2	123.5	2.2	125.0	1.2	125.1	0.1	125.1	0.0	125.2	0.1	125.3	0.1	125.9	0.5	127.0	0.9	127.4	0.3	127.2	-0.2	127.3	0.1
1991	127.5	0.2	127.7	0.2	128.7	0.8	128.7	0.0	130.6	1.5	130.6	0.0	130.8	0.2	130.8	0.0	130.8	0.0	131.3	0.4	131.3	0.0	134.9	2.7
1992	135.0	0.1	135.2	0.1	137.2	1.5	137.8	0.4	137.9	0.1	137.9	0.0	137.9	0.0	137.6	-0.2	137.9	0.2	137.9	0.0	138.0	0.1	138.1	0.1
1993	142.5	3.2	142.9	0.3	143.1	0.1	143.5	0.3	143.5	0.0	143.5	0.0	143.5	0.0	143.1	-0.3	143.4	0.2	143.5	0.1	143.5	0.0	143.5	0.0
1994	144.6	0.8	144.8	0.1	145.6	0.6	145.8	0.1	145.8	0.0	145.8	0.0	145.0	-0.5	145.1	0.1	145.3	0.1	145.5	0.1	145.5	0.0	145.6	0.1
1995	146.4	0.5	147.7	0.9	147.7	0.0	147.9	0.1	147.9	0.0	148.0	0.1	147.7	-0.2	147.8	0.1	148.1	0.2	148.2	0.1	148.3	0.1	148.4	0.1
1996	150.5	1.4	150.7	0.1	150.7	0.0	153.7	2.0	153.3	-0.3	153.5	0.1	153.9	0.3	155.1	0.8	155.0	-0.1	159.5	2.9	156.3	-2.0	156.6	0.2
1997	158.2	1.0	158.2	0.0	158.4	0.1	160.8	1.5	157.5	-2.1	157.5	0.0	158.9	0.9	160.4	0.9	160.5	0.1	160.2	-0.2	161.1	0.6	161.1	0.0

Source: U.S. Department of Labor, Bureau of Labor Statistics, Division of Industry Prices and Price Indexes. n.e.c. stands for not elsewhere classified. - indicates no data collected for period or unavailable.

Railroad Equipment

Producer Price Index
Base 1982 = 100

For 1961-1997. Columns headed % show percentile change in the index from the previous period for which an index is available.

Year	Jan Index	%	Feb Index	%	Mar Index	%	Apr Index	%	May Index	%	Jun Index	%	Jul Index	%	Aug Index	%	Sep Index	%	Oct Index	%	Nov Index	%	Dec Index	%
1961	27.9	-	27.9	0.0	27.9	0.0	27.9	0.0	27.9	0.0	27.9	0.0	27.9	0.0	27.9	0.0	27.9	0.0	28.0	0.4	28.0	0.0	28.0	0.0
1962	28.0	0.0	28.0	0.0	28.0	0.0	28.0	0.0	28.0	0.0	28.0	0.0	28.0	0.0	28.0	0.0	28.0	0.0	28.0	0.0	28.0	0.0	28.0	0.0
1963	28.0	0.0	28.0	0.0	28.0	0.0	28.0	0.0	28.0	0.0	28.0	0.0	28.0	0.0	28.0	0.0	28.0	0.0	28.0	0.0	28.0	0.0	28.0	0.0
1964	28.0	0.0	28.0	0.0	28.0	0.0	27.9	-0.4	27.9	0.0	27.9	0.0	28.0	0.4	28.0	0.0	28.0	0.0	28.0	0.0	28.0	0.0	28.0	0.0
1965	28.0	0.0	28.0	0.0	28.0	0.0	28.0	0.0	28.0	0.0	28.1	0.4	28.1	0.0	28.1	0.0	28.1	0.0	28.1	0.0	28.1	0.0	28.1	0.0
1966	28.1	0.0	28.1	0.0	28.1	0.0	28.1	0.0	28.1	0.0	28.1	0.0	28.1	0.0	28.1	0.0	28.1	0.0	28.1	0.0	28.1	0.0	28.6	1.8
1967	28.7	0.3	28.7	0.0	28.7	0.0	28.7	0.0	28.7	0.0	28.7	0.0	28.7	0.0	28.7	0.0	28.7	0.0	29.2	1.7	29.3	0.3	29.3	0.0
1968	29.4	0.3	29.4	0.0	29.4	0.0	29.4	0.0	29.4	0.0	29.4	0.0	29.8	1.4	29.9	0.3	29.9	0.0	30.3	1.3	30.3	0.0	30.3	0.0
1969	30.3	0.0	30.3	0.0	30.8	1.7	30.8	0.0	31.0	0.6	31.2	0.6	31.9	2.2	32.0	0.3	32.0	0.0	32.2	0.6	32.2	0.0	32.3	0.3
1970	32.7	1.2	32.8	0.3	33.0	0.6	33.1	0.3	33.1	0.0	33.2	0.3	33.2	0.0	33.2	0.0	33.3	0.3	33.5	0.6	33.5	0.0	33.7	0.6
1971	34.3	1.8	34.3	0.0	34.5	0.6	34.5	0.0	34.7	0.6	34.8	0.3	35.2	1.1	35.3	0.3	35.3	0.0	35.3	0.0	35.3	0.0	35.3	0.0
1972	35.7	1.1	35.8	0.3	36.7	2.5	37.1	1.1	37.4	0.8	37.4	0.0	37.6	0.5	37.6	0.0	37.6	0.0	37.6	0.0	37.6	0.0	37.8	0.5
1973	38.0	0.5	38.2	0.5	38.3	0.3	38.5	0.5	38.8	0.8	38.9	0.3	38.9	0.0	39.0	0.3	39.3	0.8	39.3	0.0	39.4	0.3	40.0	1.5
1974	40.5	1.3	40.7	0.5	41.8	2.7	42.9	2.6	44.4	3.5	47.2	6.3	48.5	2.8	50.4	3.9	51.4	2.0	52.2	1.6	53.1	1.7	54.2	2.1
1975	56.7	4.6	56.9	0.4	57.2	0.5	57.2	0.0	57.6	0.7	57.5	-0.2	58.4	1.6	58.2	-0.3	58.4	0.3	59.1	1.2	59.7	1.0	60.0	0.5
1976	60.4	0.7	61.2	1.3	61.2	0.0	61.7	0.8	61.7	0.0	62.2	0.8	62.6	0.6	63.2	1.0	63.2	0.0	64.3	1.7	64.3	0.0	64.4	0.2
1977	65.8	2.2	65.8	0.0	66.4	0.9	66.7	0.5	66.7	0.0	66.9	0.3	67.6	1.0	67.9	0.4	67.9	0.0	68.9	1.5	68.9	0.0	69.2	0.4
1978	70.3	1.6	70.6	0.4	70.6	0.0	72.2	2.3	72.4	0.3	72.4	0.0	73.2	1.1	73.4	0.3	74.1	1.0	75.1	1.3	75.5	0.5	75.6	0.1
1979	76.9	1.7	77.4	0.7	77.6	0.3	78.4	1.0	78.4	0.0	79.3	1.1	81.0	2.1	81.1	0.1	81.3	0.2	82.6	1.6	83.2	0.7	83.4	0.2
1980	85.9	3.0	86.4	0.6	87.2	0.9	89.4	2.5	89.6	0.2	90.1	0.6	91.3	1.3	91.8	0.5	92.4	0.7	93.3	1.0	93.4	0.1	93.5	0.1
1981	96.0	2.7	96.0	0.0	96.4	0.4	96.9	0.5	95.6	-1.3	95.7	0.1	97.6	2.0	97.8	0.2	97.8	0.0	97.8	0.0	98.5	0.7	98.2	-0.3
1982	99.8	1.6	99.8	0.0	99.9	0.1	99.1	-0.8	98.9	-0.2	98.9	0.0	98.9	0.0	100.4	1.5	100.4	0.0	101.2	0.8	101.2	0.0	101.2	0.0
1983	101.3	0.1	101.2	-0.1	101.1	-0.1	101.0	-0.1	101.1	0.1	101.0	-0.1	101.4	0.4	101.3	-0.1	101.2	-0.1	100.6	-0.6	100.6	0.0	101.2	0.6
1984	101.5	0.3	101.5	0.0	101.6	0.1	102.3	0.7	102.3	0.0	102.3	0.0	102.9	0.6	103.2	0.3	103.2	0.0	103.6	0.4	103.6	0.0	103.6	0.0
1985	103.9	0.3	104.4	0.5	104.7	0.3	104.8	0.1	104.6	-0.2	105.0	0.4	105.1	0.1	105.2	0.1	105.2	0.0	105.2	0.0	105.1	-0.1	105.2	0.1
1986	105.9	0.7	105.5	-0.4	105.6	0.1	105.6	0.0	105.3	-0.3	105.3	0.0	106.1	0.8	104.9	-1.1	105.2	0.3	105.2	0.0	105.2	0.0	105.3	0.1
1987	105.2	-0.1	104.6	-0.6	104.7	0.1	104.6	-0.1	104.5	-0.1	104.4	-0.1	104.7	0.3	104.8	0.1	104.8	0.0	104.6	-0.2	105.0	0.4	105.0	0.0
1988	105.3	0.3	104.8	-0.5	105.5	0.7	106.2	0.7	107.0	0.8	108.1	1.0	108.2	0.1	108.6	0.4	108.8	0.2	108.8	0.0	109.0	0.2	110.2	1.1
1989	111.8	1.5	112.2	0.4	112.2	0.0	114.2	1.8	114.2	0.0	114.3	0.1	114.6	0.3	114.6	0.0	114.7	0.1	114.8	0.1	114.9	0.1	115.6	0.6
1990	116.3	0.6	117.5	1.0	117.4	-0.1	117.6	0.2	117.7	0.1	118.5	0.7	118.5	0.0	118.5	0.0	119.9	1.2	119.9	0.0	120.9	0.8	120.9	0.0
1991	122.0	0.9	121.9	-0.1	122.2	0.2	122.1	-0.1	122.2	0.1	122.2	0.0	122.6	0.3	122.8	0.2	122.8	0.0	122.3	-0.4	121.9	-0.3	121.8	-0.1
1992	122.5	0.6	123.2	0.6	123.6	0.3	123.6	0.0	123.7	0.1	123.9	0.2	124.0	0.1	123.9	-0.1	124.2	0.2	124.2	0.0	123.8	-0.3	123.3	-0.4
1993	123.6	0.2	124.2	0.5	124.3	0.1	124.5	0.2	124.5	0.0	124.6	0.1	125.0	0.3	125.8	0.6	126.1	0.2	125.7	-0.3	125.7	0.0	127.6	1.5
1994	127.9	0.2	128.1	0.2	128.5	0.3	128.5	0.0	128.7	0.2	129.0	0.2	129.1	0.1	129.8	0.5	129.9	0.1	130.0	0.1	130.1	0.1	130.2	0.1
1995	130.9	0.5	132.7	1.4	133.2	0.4	134.2	0.8	134.7	0.4	135.2	0.4	135.5	0.2	135.7	0.1	135.6	-0.1	136.1	0.4	136.6	0.4	136.9	0.2
1996	136.7	-0.1	137.7	0.7	137.6	-0.1	137.8	0.1	137.7	-0.1	137.3	-0.3	137.3	0.0	137.2	-0.1	137.0	-0.1	137.0	0.0	136.5	-0.4	136.3	-0.1
1997	142.4	4.5	136.6	-4.1	132.2	-3.2	131.6	-0.5	134.2	2.0	134.3	0.1	133.8	-0.4	133.5	-0.2	134.2	0.5	134.8	0.4	135.6	0.6	134.7	-0.7

Source: U.S. Department of Labor, Bureau of Labor Statistics, Division of Industry Prices and Price Indexes. n.e.c. stands for not elsewhere classified. - indicates no data collected for period or unavailable.

Transportation Equipment, n.e.c.
Producer Price Index
Base 1982 = 100

For 1985-1997. Columns headed % show percentile change in the index from the previous period for which an index is available.

Year	Jan Index	%	Feb Index	%	Mar Index	%	Apr Index	%	May Index	%	Jun Index	%	Jul Index	%	Aug Index	%	Sep Index	%	Oct Index	%	Nov Index	%	Dec Index	%
1985	-	-	-	-	-	-	-	-	-	-	100.0	-	100.0	0.0	99.5	-0.5	99.3	-0.2	99.3	0.0	99.3	0.0	99.3	0.0
1986	99.0	-0.3	99.4	0.4	100.1	0.7	100.0	-0.1	99.9	-0.1	100.0	0.1	100.1	0.1	100.6	0.5	100.2	-0.4	100.3	0.1	101.1	0.8	101.1	0.0
1987	101.1	0.0	101.2	0.1	101.2	0.0	101.2	0.0	101.6	0.4	101.8	0.2	102.0	0.2	102.1	0.1	102.8	0.7	103.2	0.4	103.1	-0.1	103.1	0.0
1988	103.3	0.2	103.9	0.6	104.0	0.1	105.4	1.3	105.4	0.0	105.3	-0.1	106.5	1.1	106.6	0.1	108.0	1.3	108.0	0.0	108.3	0.3	108.2	-0.1
1989	108.7	0.5	109.0	0.3	109.1	0.1	109.4	0.3	109.4	0.0	109.2	-0.2	109.4	0.2	109.7	0.3	110.3	0.5	110.9	0.5	111.1	0.2	111.2	0.1
1990	111.2	0.0	111.2	0.0	111.0	-0.2	111.7	0.6	111.7	0.0	111.7	0.0	111.8	0.1	111.8	0.0	111.8	0.0	111.7	-0.1	112.0	0.3	111.8	-0.2
1991	112.4	0.5	112.6	0.2	113.1	0.4	113.3	0.2	113.7	0.4	113.8	0.1	113.8	0.0	113.9	0.1	114.3	0.4	114.2	-0.1	114.2	0.0	114.2	0.0
1992	114.8	0.5	114.9	0.1	114.7	-0.2	114.7	0.0	114.7	0.0	114.8	0.1	114.6	-0.2	114.6	0.0	114.6	0.0	114.8	0.2	114.8	0.0	114.8	0.0
1993	115.0	0.2	115.5	0.4	115.4	-0.1	115.5	0.1	115.5	0.0	115.5	0.0	115.6	0.1	115.8	0.2	116.0	0.2	115.8	-0.2	116.3	0.4	116.3	0.0
1994	116.4	0.1	116.6	0.2	116.6	0.0	116.8	0.2	117.1	0.3	117.4	0.3	117.5	0.1	117.5	0.0	117.8	0.3	118.3	0.4	118.4	0.1	119.0	0.5
1995	119.9	0.8	120.5	0.5	121.1	0.5	121.2	0.1	121.1	-0.1	121.3	0.2	121.2	-0.1	121.6	0.3	122.2	0.5	122.6	0.3	122.9	0.2	122.9	0.0
1996	123.1	0.2	124.3	1.0	124.7	0.3	125.0	0.2	124.9	-0.1	125.2	0.2	125.1	-0.1	124.9	-0.2	124.9	0.0	124.9	0.0	125.4	0.4	126.0	0.5
1997	126.1	0.1	126.2	0.1	126.8	0.5	126.9	0.1	126.9	0.0	126.9	0.0	126.8	-0.1	126.9	0.1	127.1	0.2	126.8	-0.2	128.9	1.7	128.9	0.0

Source: U.S. Department of Labor, Bureau of Labor Statistics, Division of Industry Prices and Price Indexes. n.e.c. stands for not elsewhere classified. - indicates no data collected for period or unavailable.

MISCELLANEOUS PRODUCTS
Producer Price Index
Base 1982 = 100

For 1947-1997. Columns headed % show percentile change in the index from the previous period for which an index is available.

Year	Jan Index	%	Feb Index	%	Mar Index	%	Apr Index	%	May Index	%	Jun Index	%	Jul Index	%	Aug Index	%	Sep Index	%	Oct Index	%	Nov Index	%	Dec Index	%
1947	26.5	-	26.5	0.0	26.5	0.0	26.6	0.4	26.7	0.4	26.6	-0.4	26.4	-0.8	26.6	0.8	26.6	0.0	26.6	0.0	26.8	0.8	26.8	0.0
1948	27.0	0.7	27.1	0.4	27.2	0.4	27.2	0.0	27.3	0.4	27.3	0.0	27.3	0.0	28.2	3.3	28.3	0.4	28.3	0.0	28.4	0.4	28.5	0.4
1949	28.5	0.0	28.5	0.0	28.5	0.0	28.2	-1.1	28.2	0.0	28.1	-0.4	28.1	0.0	28.0	-0.4	28.0	0.0	28.0	0.0	28.1	0.4	28.2	0.4
1950	28.1	-0.4	28.1	0.0	28.1	0.0	28.1	0.0	28.1	0.0	28.1	0.0	28.2	0.4	29.0	2.8	29.2	0.7	29.4	0.7	29.6	0.7	29.9	1.0
1951	30.3	1.3	30.3	0.0	30.3	0.0	30.4	0.3	30.4	0.0	30.3	-0.3	30.4	0.3	30.4	0.0	30.4	0.0	30.4	0.0	30.3	-0.3	30.3	0.0
1952	30.3	0.0	30.3	0.0	30.2	-0.3	30.2	0.0	30.2	0.0	30.1	-0.3	30.1	0.0	30.1	0.0	30.1	0.0	30.1	0.0	30.1	0.0	30.1	0.0
1953	30.1	0.0	30.1	0.0	31.1	3.3	31.1	0.0	31.1	0.0	31.1	0.0	31.1	0.0	31.1	0.0	31.1	0.0	31.1	0.0	31.1	0.0	31.1	0.0
1954	31.1	0.0	31.1	0.0	31.1	0.0	31.3	0.6	31.2	-0.3	31.3	0.3	31.3	0.0	31.3	0.0	31.3	0.0	31.3	0.0	31.3	0.0	31.3	0.0
1955	31.2	-0.3	31.1	-0.3	31.1	0.0	31.2	0.3	31.2	0.0	31.2	0.0	31.2	0.0	31.3	0.3	31.3	0.0	31.3	0.0	31.4	0.3	31.5	0.3
1956	31.6	0.3	31.6	0.0	31.6	0.0	31.7	0.3	31.7	0.0	31.7	0.0	31.7	0.0	31.7	0.0	31.8	0.3	31.8	0.0	31.9	0.3	31.9	0.0
1957	32.1	0.6	32.2	0.3	32.2	0.0	32.2	0.0	32.2	0.0	32.2	0.0	33.0	2.5	33.0	0.0	33.1	0.3	33.1	0.0	33.2	0.3	33.2	0.0
1958	33.2	0.0	33.2	0.0	33.2	0.0	33.2	0.0	33.2	0.0	33.4	0.6	33.3	-0.3	33.4	0.3	33.3	-0.3	33.3	0.0	33.3	0.0	33.3	0.0
1959	33.3	0.0	33.3	0.0	33.4	0.3	33.4	0.0	33.4	0.0	33.4	0.0	33.4	0.0	33.4	0.0	33.4	0.0	33.4	0.0	33.4	0.0	33.5	0.3
1960	33.6	0.3	33.6	0.0	33.6	0.0	33.6	0.0	33.6	0.0	33.6	0.0	33.6	0.0	33.7	0.3	33.7	0.0	33.7	0.0	33.7	0.0	33.7	0.0
1961	33.7	0.0	33.7	0.0	33.7	0.0	33.7	0.0	33.7	0.0	33.7	0.0	33.7	0.0	33.8	0.3	33.8	0.0	33.9	0.3	33.9	0.0	33.9	0.0
1962	33.8	-0.3	33.9	0.3	33.9	0.0	33.9	0.0	33.9	0.0	33.9	0.0	33.9	0.0	33.9	0.0	33.9	0.0	34.0	0.3	34.0	0.0	34.0	0.0
1963	34.0	0.0	34.0	0.0	33.9	-0.3	33.9	0.0	34.1	0.6	34.3	0.6	34.3	0.0	34.3	0.0	34.3	0.0	34.4	0.3	34.4	0.0	34.4	0.0
1964	34.4	0.0	34.4	0.0	34.4	0.0	34.4	0.0	34.4	0.0	34.4	0.0	34.4	0.0	34.5	0.3	34.5	0.0	34.5	0.0	34.5	0.0	34.5	0.0
1965	34.5	0.0	34.5	0.0	34.5	0.0	34.7	0.6	34.8	0.3	34.6	-0.6	34.8	0.6	34.8	0.0	34.8	0.0	34.8	0.0	34.8	0.0	34.8	0.0
1966	34.9	0.3	34.9	0.0	35.2	0.9	35.3	0.3	35.3	0.0	35.4	0.3	35.4	0.0	35.4	0.0	35.4	0.0	35.5	0.3	35.6	0.3	35.6	0.0
1967	35.7	0.3	35.7	0.0	35.7	0.0	35.7	0.0	35.8	0.3	36.3	1.4	36.4	0.3	36.4	0.0	36.5	0.3	36.6	0.3	36.6	0.0	36.7	0.3
1968	36.7	0.0	36.8	0.3	36.8	0.0	36.9	0.3	36.9	0.0	36.9	0.0	36.9	0.0	37.0	0.3	37.0	0.0	37.1	0.3	37.3	0.5	37.3	0.0
1969	37.3	0.0	37.3	0.0	37.3	0.0	37.4	0.3	37.4	0.0	38.2	2.1	38.4	0.5	38.5	0.3	38.6	0.3	38.7	0.3	38.7	0.0	38.7	0.0
1970	38.9	0.5	39.0	0.3	39.1	0.3	39.0	-0.3	39.2	0.5	40.1	2.3	40.2	0.2	40.2	0.0	40.3	0.2	40.3	0.0	40.3	0.0	40.4	0.2
1971	40.6	0.5	40.7	0.2	40.7	0.0	40.7	0.0	40.8	0.2	40.8	0.0	40.9	0.2	41.0	0.2	41.0	0.0	41.0	0.0	41.0	0.0	41.0	0.0
1972	41.1	0.2	41.2	0.2	41.3	0.2	41.3	0.0	41.3	0.0	41.3	0.0	41.6	0.7	41.6	0.0	41.7	0.2	41.6	-0.2	41.6	0.0	41.6	0.0
1973	41.9	0.7	42.4	1.2	42.7	0.7	42.9	0.5	43.2	0.7	43.5	0.7	43.7	0.5	43.8	0.2	43.8	0.0	43.8	0.0	43.9	0.2	44.0	0.2
1974	44.7	1.6	45.1	0.9	45.5	0.9	46.4	2.0	48.2	3.9	48.6	0.8	48.9	0.6	49.0	0.2	49.3	0.6	49.6	0.6	50.9	2.6	51.5	1.2
1975	52.6	2.1	52.9	0.6	53.1	0.4	53.3	0.4	53.3	0.0	53.4	0.2	53.4	0.0	53.4	0.0	53.6	0.4	53.4	-0.4	53.8	0.7	54.7	1.7
1976	54.9	0.4	55.1	0.4	55.2	0.2	55.2	0.0	55.2	0.0	55.8	1.1	55.6	-0.4	55.5	-0.2	55.7	0.4	55.7	0.0	56.4	1.3	56.8	0.7
1977	57.9	1.9	58.1	0.3	58.2	0.2	58.8	1.0	59.0	0.3	59.1	0.2	59.3	0.3	59.4	0.2	60.1	1.2	60.9	1.3	61.1	0.3	61.4	0.5
1978	62.1	1.1	62.0	-0.2	62.4	0.6	65.6	5.1	66.1	0.8	66.7	0.9	68.6	2.8	69.2	0.9	69.8	0.9	69.0	-1.1	68.4	-0.9	70.0	2.3
1979	71.5	2.1	72.3	1.1	72.6	0.4	72.9	0.4	73.6	1.0	74.2	0.8	74.9	0.9	75.6	0.9	77.1	2.0	79.2	2.7	80.1	1.1	82.3	2.7
1980	87.9	6.8	95.1	8.2	92.6	-2.6	91.4	-1.3	91.0	-0.4	93.3	2.5	94.6	1.4	94.1	-0.5	95.9	1.9	96.2	0.3	95.4	-0.8	96.0	0.6
1981	95.6	-0.4	95.8	0.2	95.5	-0.3	96.2	0.7	96.5	0.3	96.3	-0.2	95.2	-1.1	95.0	-0.2	96.6	1.7	97.1	0.5	96.8	-0.3	96.8	0.0
1982	97.1	0.3	98.9	1.9	98.7	-0.2	98.8	0.1	98.5	-0.3	98.2	-0.3	98.9	0.7	98.4	-0.5	101.1	2.7	103.3	2.2	103.1	-0.2	105.0	1.8
1983	103.3	-1.6	104.4	1.1	104.0	-0.4	104.0	0.0	103.8	-0.2	104.2	0.4	105.5	1.2	105.6	0.1	105.4	-0.2	105.5	0.1	105.5	0.0	105.9	0.4
1984	106.5	0.6	106.7	0.2	106.7	0.0	106.6	-0.1	106.4	-0.2	107.0	0.6	107.5	0.5	107.9	0.4	107.3	-0.6	107.2	-0.1	107.2	0.0	107.3	0.1
1985	108.2	0.8	108.8	0.6	108.7	-0.1	109.1	0.4	109.0	-0.1	109.0	0.0	109.8	0.7	109.8	0.0	109.9	0.1	110.0	0.1	110.1	0.1	109.9	-0.2
1986	111.2	1.2	111.0	-0.2	111.1	0.1	111.2	0.1	111.1	-0.1	111.0	-0.1	111.9	0.8	112.0	0.1	112.1	0.1	112.3	0.2	112.4	0.1	112.2	-0.2
1987	113.1	0.8	113.1	0.0	113.3	0.2	113.9	0.5	114.0	0.1	114.0	0.0	115.1	1.0	115.5	0.3	115.8	0.3	116.2	0.3	116.7	0.4	117.7	0.9
1988	118.7	0.8	119.2	0.4	119.1	-0.1	119.4	0.3	119.4	0.0	119.4	0.0	120.9	1.3	120.7	-0.2	120.7	0.0	121.1	0.3	121.2	0.1	122.6	1.2
1989	124.0	1.1	124.2	0.2	124.5	0.2	124.6	0.1	125.2	0.5	126.7	1.2	127.2	0.4	127.4	0.2	127.6	0.2	128.2	0.5	128.4	0.2	130.0	1.2
1990	131.2	0.9	131.9	0.5	132.0	0.1	132.3	0.2	133.2	0.7	134.4	0.9	134.6	0.1	134.9	0.2	135.3	0.3	135.9	0.4	136.9	0.7	138.2	0.9
1991	139.1	0.7	138.9	-0.1	139.4	0.4	140.0	0.4	140.1	0.1	140.9	0.6	141.8	0.6	141.7	-0.1	141.5	-0.1	141.4	-0.1	141.8	0.3	143.4	1.1

[Continued]

MISCELLANEOUS PRODUCTS
Producer Price Index
Base 1982 = 100
[Continued]

For 1947-1997. Columns headed % show percentile change in the index from the previous period for which an index is available.

Year	Jan Index	%	Feb Index	%	Mar Index	%	Apr Index	%	May Index	%	Jun Index	%	Jul Index	%	Aug Index	%	Sep Index	%	Oct Index	%	Nov Index	%	Dec Index	%
1992	143.9	0.3	143.9	0.0	144.0	0.1	144.8	0.6	146.4	1.1	146.2	-0.1	146.3	0.1	143.8	-1.7	145.3	1.0	145.5	0.1	145.8	0.2	147.3	1.0
1993	148.6	0.9	149.4	0.5	149.4	0.0	150.4	0.7	150.7	0.2	149.6	-0.7	149.6	0.0	138.9	-7.2	138.9	0.0	138.8	-0.1	139.1	0.2	140.9	1.3
1994	141.9	0.7	141.8	-0.1	141.6	-0.1	141.7	0.1	141.5	-0.1	141.6	0.1	141.8	0.1	141.8	0.0	141.8	0.0	142.0	0.1	142.4	0.3	142.4	0.0
1995	143.0	0.4	143.6	0.4	143.8	0.1	144.3	0.3	145.2	0.6	145.3	0.1	145.7	0.3	146.6	0.6	146.6	0.0	147.0	0.3	147.0	0.0	146.9	-0.1
1996	147.7	0.5	146.6	-0.7	146.4	-0.1	146.4	0.0	147.8	1.0	147.8	0.0	148.3	0.3	148.1	-0.1	147.9	-0.1	148.3	0.3	148.4	0.1	148.5	0.1
1997	148.7	0.1	148.9	0.1	149.5	0.4	150.6	0.7	150.9	0.2	150.9	0.0	151.0	0.1	151.0	0.0	152.2	0.8	152.3	0.1	152.3	0.0	152.7	0.3

Source: U.S. Department of Labor, Bureau of Labor Statistics, Division of Industry Prices and Price Indexes. n.e.c. stands for not elsewhere classified. - indicates no data collected for period or unavailable.

Toys, Sporting Goods, Small Arms, etc.
Producer Price Index
Base 1982 = 100

For 1947-1997. Columns headed % show percentile change in the index from the previous period for which an index is available.

Year	Jan Index	%	Feb Index	%	Mar Index	%	Apr Index	%	May Index	%	Jun Index	%	Jul Index	%	Aug Index	%	Sep Index	%	Oct Index	%	Nov Index	%	Dec Index	%
1947	34.8	-	34.8	0.0	34.9	0.3	35.1	0.6	35.1	0.0	35.1	0.0	35.3	0.6	35.3	0.0	35.1	-0.6	35.1	0.0	35.1	0.0	35.3	0.6
1948	36.0	2.0	36.1	0.3	36.3	0.6	36.5	0.6	36.6	0.3	36.6	0.0	36.6	0.0	37.0	1.1	37.0	0.0	37.0	0.0	37.1	0.3	37.1	0.0
1949	36.6	-1.3	36.8	0.5	36.9	0.3	36.9	0.0	36.8	-0.3	36.8	0.0	36.6	-0.5	36.5	-0.3	36.4	-0.3	36.5	0.3	36.9	1.1	36.9	0.0
1950	37.6	1.9	37.7	0.3	37.7	0.0	37.8	0.3	37.8	0.0	37.9	0.3	38.2	0.8	38.5	0.8	39.6	2.9	40.1	1.3	40.2	0.2	41.0	2.0
1951	41.8	2.0	42.0	0.5	42.2	0.5	42.2	0.0	42.2	0.0	42.2	0.0	42.1	-0.2	42.1	0.0	42.0	-0.2	42.0	0.0	41.7	-0.7	41.7	0.0
1952	41.5	-0.5	41.4	-0.2	41.1	-0.7	41.0	-0.2	41.0	0.0	41.0	0.0	41.0	0.0	40.9	-0.2	40.9	0.0	40.9	0.0	40.9	0.0	40.9	0.0
1953	40.8	-0.2	40.8	0.0	40.8	0.0	41.1	0.7	41.3	0.5	41.2	-0.2	41.2	0.0	41.2	0.0	41.2	0.0	41.2	0.0	41.2	0.0	40.9	-0.7
1954	40.9	0.0	40.9	0.0	40.9	0.0	41.0	0.2	41.0	0.0	41.0	0.0	41.0	0.0	41.0	0.0	40.8	-0.5	40.8	0.0	40.8	0.0	40.8	0.0
1955	40.9	0.2	40.9	0.0	40.9	0.0	40.9	0.0	40.9	0.0	40.9	0.0	40.9	0.0	41.0	0.2	41.0	0.0	41.1	0.2	41.3	0.5	41.6	0.7
1956	41.9	0.7	41.9	0.0	41.8	-0.2	41.9	0.2	41.9	0.0	41.9	0.0	41.8	-0.2	42.0	0.5	42.2	0.5	42.2	0.0	42.2	0.0	42.3	0.2
1957	42.4	0.2	42.4	0.0	42.4	0.0	42.4	0.0	42.4	0.0	42.4	0.0	42.4	0.0	42.6	0.5	42.7	0.2	42.6	-0.2	42.6	0.0	42.6	0.0
1958	43.2	1.4	43.2	0.0	43.1	-0.2	43.1	0.0	43.1	0.0	43.1	0.0	43.1	0.0	43.1	0.0	42.9	-0.5	42.9	0.0	42.9	0.0	42.9	0.0
1959	42.6	-0.7	42.6	0.0	42.4	-0.5	42.3	-0.2	42.3	0.0	42.3	0.0	42.4	0.2	42.5	0.2	42.5	0.0	42.5	0.0	42.5	0.0	42.6	0.2
1960	42.5	-0.2	42.6	0.2	42.6	0.0	42.8	0.5	42.8	0.0	42.8	0.0	42.9	0.2	42.9	0.0	42.9	0.0	42.9	0.0	42.9	0.0	42.9	0.0
1961	42.8	-0.2	42.8	0.0	43.0	0.5	43.0	0.0	43.0	0.0	43.0	0.0	43.0	0.0	43.3	0.7	43.2	-0.2	43.4	0.5	43.4	0.0	43.1	-0.7
1962	42.9	-0.5	42.8	-0.2	42.9	0.2	42.9	0.0	42.9	0.0	43.0	0.2	43.1	0.2	43.1	0.0	43.2	0.2	43.2	0.0	43.2	0.0	43.2	0.0
1963	43.2	0.0	43.2	0.0	42.9	-0.7	43.0	0.2	43.0	0.0	43.0	0.0	43.1	0.2	43.2	0.2	43.2	0.0	43.2	0.0	43.1	-0.2	43.2	0.2
1964	43.1	-0.2	43.1	0.0	43.2	0.2	43.0	-0.5	43.0	0.0	43.1	0.2	43.1	0.0	43.1	0.0	43.2	0.2	43.2	0.0	43.2	0.0	43.2	0.0
1965	43.6	0.9	43.6	0.0	43.6	0.0	43.7	0.2	43.8	0.2	43.8	0.0	43.9	0.2	43.8	-0.2	44.0	0.5	44.0	0.0	44.0	0.0	44.0	0.0
1966	44.0	0.0	44.1	0.2	44.1	0.0	44.3	0.5	44.3	0.0	44.3	0.0	44.6	0.7	44.8	0.4	44.8	0.0	44.8	0.0	44.8	0.0	44.8	0.0
1967	45.0	0.4	45.0	0.0	44.9	-0.2	45.0	0.2	45.0	0.0	45.1	0.2	45.2	0.2	45.2	0.0	45.3	0.2	45.4	0.2	45.4	0.0	45.4	0.0
1968	45.6	0.4	45.5	-0.2	46.1	1.3	46.1	0.0	46.2	0.2	46.2	0.0	46.3	0.2	46.4	0.2	46.5	0.2	46.5	0.0	46.6	0.2	46.6	0.0
1969	47.1	1.1	47.1	0.0	47.2	0.2	47.2	0.0	47.3	0.2	47.3	0.0	47.5	0.4	47.8	0.6	47.9	0.2	48.0	0.2	48.1	0.2	48.2	0.2
1970	48.9	1.5	49.0	0.2	49.6	1.2	49.1	-1.0	49.4	0.6	49.4	0.0	49.5	0.2	49.6	0.2	49.9	0.6	49.9	0.0	49.9	0.0	50.0	0.2
1971	50.8	1.6	50.8	0.0	51.0	0.4	50.8	-0.4	50.8	0.0	51.0	0.4	51.0	0.0	50.9	-0.2	50.9	0.0	50.9	0.0	51.0	0.2	51.0	0.0
1972	51.3	0.6	51.5	0.4	51.7	0.4	51.5	-0.4	51.5	0.0	51.6	0.2	51.7	0.2	51.7	0.0	51.8	0.2	51.9	0.2	51.9	0.0	52.0	0.2
1973	52.5	1.0	52.6	0.2	52.9	0.6	52.9	0.0	53.0	0.2	53.1	0.2	53.1	0.0	53.2	0.2	53.4	0.4	53.8	0.7	54.1	0.6	54.2	0.2
1974	56.2	3.7	57.0	1.4	57.5	0.9	57.8	0.5	58.4	1.0	59.0	1.0	59.6	1.0	61.3	2.9	61.8	0.8	62.4	1.0	63.0	1.0	63.0	0.0
1975	65.4	3.8	65.9	0.8	66.0	0.2	65.8	-0.3	65.8	0.0	65.9	0.2	65.9	0.0	65.9	0.0	65.9	0.0	66.1	0.3	66.3	0.3	66.3	0.0
1976	66.9	0.9	67.1	0.3	67.5	0.6	67.4	-0.1	67.6	0.3	67.9	0.4	68.0	0.1	67.9	-0.1	68.1	0.3	68.1	0.0	68.2	0.1	68.2	0.0
1977	69.4	1.8	69.6	0.3	69.8	0.3	69.7	-0.1	69.8	0.1	69.9	0.1	70.1	0.3	70.3	0.3	70.2	-0.1	70.7	0.7	70.8	0.1	70.9	0.1
1978	72.1	1.7	72.9	1.1	73.3	0.5	73.5	0.3	73.3	-0.3	73.7	0.5	73.7	0.0	74.0	0.4	74.1	0.1	74.5	0.5	74.6	0.1	74.4	-0.3
1979	76.9	3.4	77.2	0.4	77.5	0.4	78.2	0.9	78.7	0.6	78.9	0.3	79.9	1.3	80.2	0.4	81.2	1.2	81.8	0.7	81.8	0.0	82.6	1.0
1980	86.2	4.4	87.4	1.4	87.8	0.5	88.2	0.5	88.5	0.3	89.2	0.8	90.4	1.3	90.9	0.6	91.4	0.6	91.5	0.1	91.6	0.1	92.9	1.4
1981	94.1	1.3	95.1	1.1	95.3	0.2	95.4	0.1	95.4	0.0	95.4	0.0	96.3	0.9	96.0	-0.3	96.5	0.5	96.2	-0.3	96.1	-0.1	96.3	0.2
1982	98.6	2.4	99.4	0.8	99.6	0.2	99.8	0.2	100.2	0.4	100.2	0.0	100.3	0.1	100.9	0.6	100.1	-0.8	99.9	-0.2	100.0	0.1	101.0	1.0
1983	100.6	-0.4	101.7	1.1	101.9	0.2	102.2	0.3	102.1	-0.1	102.0	-0.1	101.3	-0.7	101.4	0.1	101.5	0.1	102.0	0.5	101.7	-0.3	101.7	0.0
1984	102.7	1.0	102.9	0.2	102.8	-0.1	102.3	-0.5	102.4	0.1	102.3	-0.1	102.3	0.0	102.3	0.0	102.5	0.2	102.7	0.2	102.8	0.1	102.8	0.0
1985	103.0	0.2	104.3	1.3	104.5	0.2	104.4	-0.1	104.4	0.0	104.3	-0.1	104.2	-0.1	104.2	0.0	104.4	0.2	105.7	1.2	105.9	0.2	105.2	-0.7
1986	105.7	0.5	106.1	0.4	106.3	0.2	106.4	0.1	106.5	0.1	106.6	0.1	106.8	0.2	106.9	0.1	106.8	-0.1	107.1	0.3	107.1	0.0	106.6	-0.5
1987	106.5	-0.1	107.3	0.8	107.1	-0.2	107.4	0.3	107.4	0.0	107.6	0.2	107.7	0.1	107.7	0.0	108.3	0.6	108.6	0.3	108.8	0.2	109.0	0.2
1988	110.1	1.0	110.9	0.7	111.0	0.1	111.1	0.1	111.2	0.1	111.5	0.3	112.0	0.4	112.2	0.2	112.3	0.1	112.7	0.4	112.9	0.2	113.2	0.3
1989	114.7	1.3	115.5	0.7	115.9	0.3	116.0	0.1	116.2	0.2	116.7	0.4	116.9	0.2	117.4	0.4	117.6	0.2	118.0	0.3	117.7	-0.3	118.1	0.3
1990	118.5	0.3	119.1	0.5	119.1	0.0	119.2	0.1	119.3	0.1	119.4	0.1	119.3	-0.1	119.6	0.3	119.5	-0.1	120.8	1.1	120.6	-0.2	120.8	0.2
1991	121.3	0.4	121.6	0.2	121.9	0.2	122.0	0.1	122.2	0.2	122.6	0.3	122.7	0.1	123.1	0.3	123.2	0.1	123.6	0.3	123.3	-0.2	123.2	-0.1

[Continued]

Toys, Sporting Goods, Small Arms, etc.
Producer Price Index
Base 1982 = 100
[Continued]

For 1947-1997. Columns headed % show percentile change in the index from the previous period for which an index is available.

Year	Jan Index	%	Feb Index	%	Mar Index	%	Apr Index	%	May Index	%	Jun Index	%	Jul Index	%	Aug Index	%	Sep Index	%	Oct Index	%	Nov Index	%	Dec Index	%
1992	123.8	0.5	124.1	0.2	123.9	-0.2	124.0	0.1	124.4	0.3	124.6	0.2	124.6	0.0	124.7	0.1	125.9	1.0	125.9	0.0	124.6	-1.0	124.2	-0.3
1993	125.0	0.6	125.2	0.2	125.1	-0.1	125.2	0.1	125.3	0.1	125.3	0.0	125.3	0.0	125.9	0.5	125.8	-0.1	126.0	0.2	125.9	-0.1	126.0	0.1
1994	126.5	0.4	126.5	0.0	126.4	-0.1	126.5	0.1	126.7	0.2	126.8	0.1	127.4	0.5	127.3	-0.1	127.3	0.0	127.2	-0.1	127.5	0.2	127.7	0.2
1995	128.1	0.3	128.5	0.3	128.7	0.2	129.0	0.2	128.8	-0.2	128.9	0.1	129.4	0.4	129.3	-0.1	129.4	0.1	129.5	0.1	129.5	0.0	129.6	0.1
1996	129.7	0.1	130.2	0.4	130.2	0.0	130.3	0.1	130.4	0.1	130.5	0.1	130.5	0.0	130.7	0.2	130.8	0.1	130.8	0.0	130.6	-0.2	130.3	-0.2
1997	130.7	0.3	130.9	0.2	131.5	0.5	131.7	0.2	131.6	-0.1	131.3	-0.2	131.4	0.1	131.8	0.3	131.9	0.1	132.1	0.2	131.8	-0.2	131.7	-0.1

Source: U.S. Department of Labor, Bureau of Labor Statistics, Division of Industry Prices and Price Indexes. n.e.c. stands for not elsewhere classified. - indicates no data collected for period or unavailable.

Tobacco Products, incl. Stemmed & Redried
Producer Price Index
Base 1982 = 100

For 1947-1997. Columns headed % show percentile change in the index from the previous period for which an index is available.

Year	Jan Index	%	Feb Index	%	Mar Index	%	Apr Index	%	May Index	%	Jun Index	%	Jul Index	%	Aug Index	%	Sep Index	%	Oct Index	%	Nov Index	%	Dec Index	%
1947	20.4	-	20.4	0.0	20.4	0.0	20.5	0.5	20.5	0.0	20.5	0.0	20.5	0.0	20.5	0.0	20.5	0.0	20.5	0.0	20.5	0.0	20.5	0.0
1948	20.5	0.0	20.5	0.0	20.5	0.0	20.5	0.0	20.5	0.0	20.5	0.0	20.6	0.5	22.3	8.3	22.3	0.0	22.3	0.0	22.3	0.0	22.3	0.0
1949	22.3	0.0	22.3	0.0	22.3	0.0	22.3	0.0	22.3	0.0	22.3	0.0	22.3	0.0	22.4	0.4	22.4	0.0	22.4	0.0	22.4	0.0	22.4	0.0
1950	22.4	0.0	22.4	0.0	22.4	0.0	22.4	0.0	22.4	0.0	22.4	0.0	22.4	0.0	22.4	0.0	23.3	4.0	23.3	0.0	23.4	0.4	23.4	0.0
1951	23.4	0.0	23.4	0.0	23.4	0.0	23.4	0.0	23.4	0.0	23.4	0.0	23.4	0.0	23.4	0.0	23.4	0.0	23.4	0.0	23.6	0.9	23.6	0.0
1952	23.6	0.0	23.6	0.0	23.6	0.0	23.6	0.0	23.6	0.0	23.6	0.0	23.6	0.0	23.6	0.0	23.6	0.0	23.6	0.0	23.6	0.0	23.6	0.0
1953	23.7	0.4	23.7	0.0	25.6	8.0	25.6	0.0	25.6	0.0	25.6	0.0	25.6	0.0	25.6	0.0	25.6	0.0	25.6	0.0	25.6	0.0	25.6	0.0
1954	25.6	0.0	25.6	0.0	25.6	0.0	25.6	0.0	25.6	0.0	25.6	0.0	25.6	0.0	25.6	0.0	25.6	0.0	25.6	0.0	25.6	0.0	25.6	0.0
1955	25.6	0.0	25.6	0.0	25.6	0.0	25.6	0.0	25.6	0.0	25.6	0.0	25.6	0.0	25.6	0.0	25.6	0.0	25.6	0.0	25.6	0.0	25.6	0.0
1956	25.6	0.0	25.6	0.0	25.6	0.0	25.6	0.0	25.6	0.0	25.6	0.0	25.6	0.0	25.6	0.0	25.6	0.0	25.6	0.0	25.6	0.0	25.7	0.4
1957	25.7	0.0	25.7	0.0	25.7	0.0	25.7	0.0	25.8	0.4	25.8	0.0	27.7	7.4	27.7	0.0	27.7	0.0	27.7	0.0	27.7	0.0	27.7	0.0
1958	27.7	0.0	27.7	0.0	27.7	0.0	27.7	0.0	27.7	0.0	27.7	0.0	27.7	0.0	27.7	0.0	27.7	0.0	27.7	0.0	27.7	0.0	27.7	0.0
1959	27.7	0.0	27.8	0.4	27.9	0.4	27.9	0.0	27.9	0.0	27.9	0.0	27.9	0.0	27.9	0.0	27.9	0.0	27.9	0.0	27.9	0.0	27.9	0.0
1960	27.9	0.0	27.9	0.0	27.9	0.0	27.9	0.0	27.9	0.0	27.9	0.0	27.9	0.0	27.9	0.0	27.9	0.0	27.9	0.0	27.9	0.0	27.9	0.0
1961	27.9	0.0	27.9	0.0	27.9	0.0	27.9	0.0	27.9	0.0	27.9	0.0	27.9	0.0	27.9	0.0	27.9	0.0	27.9	0.0	27.9	0.0	27.9	0.0
1962	27.9	0.0	27.9	0.0	27.9	0.0	27.9	0.0	27.9	0.0	27.9	0.0	27.9	0.0	27.9	0.0	27.9	0.0	28.0	0.4	28.0	0.0	28.0	0.0
1963	28.0	0.0	28.0	0.0	28.0	0.0	28.0	0.0	28.7	2.5	29.0	1.0	29.0	0.0	29.0	0.0	29.0	0.0	29.0	0.0	29.0	0.0	29.0	0.0
1964	29.0	0.0	29.0	0.0	29.1	0.3	29.1	0.0	29.1	0.0	29.1	0.0	29.1	0.0	29.1	0.0	29.1	0.0	29.1	0.0	29.1	0.0	29.1	0.0
1965	29.1	0.0	29.1	0.0	29.1	0.0	29.2	0.3	29.4	0.7	29.1	-1.0	29.1	0.0	29.1	0.0	29.1	0.0	29.1	0.0	29.1	0.0	29.1	0.0
1966	29.2	0.3	29.2	0.0	30.1	3.1	30.2	0.3	30.2	0.0	30.2	0.0	30.2	0.0	30.2	0.0	30.2	0.0	30.2	0.0	30.2	0.0	30.2	0.0
1967	30.2	0.0	30.2	0.0	30.2	0.0	30.2	0.0	30.2	0.0	31.5	4.3	31.5	0.0	31.5	0.0	31.5	0.0	31.5	0.0	31.5	0.0	31.5	0.0
1968	31.5	0.0	31.5	0.0	31.5	0.0	31.5	0.0	31.5	0.0	31.5	0.0	31.5	0.0	31.5	0.0	31.5	0.0	31.6	0.3	32.0	1.3	32.0	0.0
1969	32.0	0.0	32.0	0.0	32.0	0.0	32.1	0.3	32.1	0.0	33.8	5.3	33.9	0.3	33.9	0.0	34.0	0.3	34.0	0.0	34.0	0.0	34.0	0.0
1970	34.0	0.0	34.0	0.0	34.0	0.0	34.0	0.0	34.0	0.0	36.3	6.8	36.0	-0.8	35.9	-0.3	35.9	0.0	35.9	0.0	35.9	0.0	35.9	0.0
1971	36.0	0.3	36.1	0.3	36.1	0.0	36.1	0.0	36.1	0.0	36.1	0.0	36.1	0.0	36.1	0.0	36.1	0.0	36.1	0.0	36.1	0.0	36.1	0.0
1972	36.3	0.6	36.3	0.0	36.3	0.0	36.3	0.0	36.4	0.3	36.4	0.0	36.4	0.0	36.4	0.0	36.4	0.0	36.4	0.0	36.4	0.0	36.4	0.0
1973	36.4	0.0	37.5	3.0	37.7	0.5	37.7	0.0	37.9	0.5	37.9	0.0	37.9	0.0	37.9	0.0	37.9	0.0	38.0	0.3	38.0	0.0	38.1	0.3
1974	38.1	0.0	38.2	0.3	38.2	0.0	38.3	0.3	41.2	7.6	41.7	1.2	41.7	0.0	41.9	0.5	41.9	0.0	41.9	0.0	44.8	6.9	45.4	1.3
1975	45.6	0.4	45.8	0.4	45.9	0.2	46.0	0.2	46.0	0.0	46.0	0.0	46.0	0.0	46.0	0.0	46.1	0.2	46.2	0.2	46.8	1.3	49.2	5.1
1976	49.2	0.0	49.2	0.0	49.3	0.2	50.2	1.8	50.1	-0.2	50.1	0.0	50.1	0.0	50.1	0.0	50.2	0.2	50.3	0.2	53.3	6.0	53.3	0.0
1977	54.1	1.5	54.1	0.0	54.1	0.0	54.2	0.2	54.2	0.0	54.3	0.2	54.4	0.2	54.4	0.0	57.8	6.3	58.7	1.6	58.7	0.0	58.8	0.2
1978	59.0	0.3	59.2	0.3	59.2	0.0	59.3	0.2	59.3	0.0	61.3	3.4	63.6	3.8	63.6	0.0	63.6	0.0	63.1	-0.8	63.1	0.0	63.1	0.0
1979	66.1	4.8	66.1	0.0	66.2	0.2	66.4	0.3	66.4	0.0	66.4	0.0	66.5	0.2	68.5	3.0	68.7	0.3	68.8	0.1	68.8	0.0	70.1	1.9
1980	73.2	4.4	73.4	0.3	73.5	0.1	73.7	0.3	76.7	4.1	76.8	0.1	76.8	0.0	76.8	0.0	76.8	0.0	77.2	0.5	78.8	2.1	78.9	0.1
1981	78.9	0.0	79.3	0.5	79.3	0.0	83.2	4.9	83.2	0.0	83.2	0.0	83.2	0.0	83.2	0.0	85.0	2.2	86.1	1.3	86.1	0.0	86.1	0.0
1982	86.1	0.0	94.9	10.2	94.9	0.0	94.9	0.0	95.0	0.1	95.0	0.0	96.4	1.5	96.4	0.0	101.9	5.7	113.1	11.0	112.8	-0.3	118.5	5.1
1983	110.2	-7.0	110.3	0.1	109.5	-0.7	109.6	0.1	109.5	-0.1	109.0	-0.5	115.6	6.1	116.6	0.9	116.6	0.0	116.6	0.0	116.7	0.1	116.7	0.0
1984	120.5	3.3	120.8	0.2	120.8	0.0	120.8	0.0	120.9	0.1	123.9	2.5	126.5	2.1	125.9	-0.5	125.9	0.0	124.5	-1.1	124.6	0.1	124.7	0.1
1985	130.0	4.3	130.2	0.2	130.2	0.0	130.2	0.0	130.2	0.0	130.2	0.0	134.9	3.6	134.9	0.0	134.9	0.0	134.7	-0.1	134.8	0.1	134.8	0.0
1986	139.6	3.6	139.7	0.1	139.8	0.1	139.7	-0.1	139.8	0.1	139.8	0.0	145.2	3.9	145.2	0.0	145.2	0.0	145.2	0.0	145.2	0.1	145.2	0.0
1987	150.8	3.9	150.8	0.0	150.8	0.0	150.9	0.1	150.9	0.0	150.9	0.0	157.5	4.4	157.6	0.1	157.6	0.0	157.5	-0.1	157.6	0.1	163.3	3.6
1988	166.6	2.0	166.7	0.1	166.7	0.0	166.8	0.1	166.8	0.0	166.8	0.0	175.4	5.2	175.4	0.0	175.4	0.0	175.6	0.1	175.5	-0.1	184.7	5.2
1989	187.2	1.4	187.3	0.1	187.3	0.0	187.3	0.0	187.4	0.1	196.8	5.0	197.9	0.6	198.1	0.1	198.1	0.0	200.4	1.2	200.4	0.0	209.6	4.6
1990	212.3	1.3	212.8	0.2	212.8	0.0	212.8	0.0	217.4	2.2	224.1	3.1	224.3	0.1	224.3	0.0	225.0	0.3	224.9	-0.0	230.4	2.4	236.1	2.5
1991	237.4	0.6	237.4	0.0	239.6	0.9	243.3	1.5	243.4	0.0	249.1	2.3	254.4	2.1	255.0	0.2	254.9	-0.0	255.0	0.0	259.8	1.9	267.2	2.8

[Continued]

Tobacco Products, incl. Stemmed & Redried
Producer Price Index
Base 1982 = 100
[Continued]

For 1947-1997. Columns headed % show percentile change in the index from the previous period for which an index is available.

Year	Jan Index	%	Feb Index	%	Mar Index	%	Apr Index	%	May Index	%	Jun Index	%	Jul Index	%	Aug Index	%	Sep Index	%	Oct Index	%	Nov Index	%	Dec Index	%
1992	268.1	0.3	268.2	0.0	268.2	0.0	273.7	2.1	283.2	3.5	283.2	0.0	283.4	0.1	265.9	-6.2	274.1	3.1	274.2	0.0	276.5	0.8	285.1	3.1
1993	291.8	2.4	292.2	0.1	292.2	0.0	296.2	1.4	296.9	0.2	289.2	-2.6	287.2	-0.7	213.3	-25.7	213.2	-0.0	213.5	0.1	213.6	0.0	224.2	5.0
1994	224.7	0.2	224.7	0.0	224.7	0.0	224.7	0.0	224.7	0.0	224.7	0.0	224.7	0.0	224.1	-0.3	224.9	0.4	224.6	-0.1	225.1	0.2	225.2	0.0
1995	225.4	0.1	226.0	0.3	228.1	0.9	228.5	0.2	233.7	2.3	233.6	-0.0	233.5	-0.0	233.6	0.0	233.4	-0.1	233.5	0.0	233.5	0.0	233.2	-0.1
1996	233.2	0.0	233.2	0.0	233.2	0.0	233.3	0.0	240.0	2.9	239.9	-0.0	240.1	0.1	240.4	0.1	238.2	-0.9	239.1	0.4	238.8	-0.1	239.2	0.2
1997	239.4	0.1	239.2	-0.1	241.4	0.9	247.2	2.4	248.2	0.4	248.5	0.1	248.4	-0.0	247.8	-0.2	256.4	3.5	255.7	-0.3	256.0	0.1	257.9	0.7

Source: U.S. Department of Labor, Bureau of Labor Statistics, Division of Industry Prices and Price Indexes. n.e.c. stands for not elsewhere classified. - indicates no data collected for period or unavailable.

Notions

Producer Price Index
Base 1982 = 100

For 1947-1997. Columns headed % show percentile change in the index from the previous period for which an index is available.

Year	Jan Index	%	Feb Index	%	Mar Index	%	Apr Index	%	May Index	%	Jun Index	%	Jul Index	%	Aug Index	%	Sep Index	%	Oct Index	%	Nov Index	%	Dec Index	%
1947	37.9	-	37.9	0.0	37.9	0.0	37.9	0.0	37.9	0.0	37.9	0.0	37.9	0.0	37.9	0.0	37.6	-0.8	37.5	-0.3	37.5	0.0	37.5	0.0
1948	37.9	1.1	37.9	0.0	37.9	0.0	37.9	0.0	37.9	0.0	37.9	0.0	38.0	0.3	38.0	0.0	38.3	0.8	37.8	-1.3	37.8	0.0	37.5	-0.8
1949	37.5	0.0	37.5	0.0	37.1	-1.1	33.4	-10.0	33.0	-1.2	33.0	0.0	33.0	0.0	33.0	0.0	33.0	0.0	33.0	0.0	33.0	0.0	33.0	0.0
1950	33.0	0.0	33.0	0.0	33.0	0.0	33.0	0.0	32.5	-1.5	32.5	0.0	32.3	-0.6	33.6	4.0	34.6	3.0	34.9	0.9	35.8	2.6	36.1	0.8
1951	36.4	0.8	37.1	1.9	37.1	0.0	37.1	0.0	37.1	0.0	37.1	0.0	37.1	0.0	37.1	0.0	37.1	0.0	37.1	0.0	37.1	0.0	37.1	0.0
1952	36.7	-1.1	36.7	0.0	36.0	-1.9	35.2	-2.2	33.5	-4.8	33.5	0.0	33.5	0.0	33.2	-0.9	33.2	0.0	33.3	0.3	33.4	0.3	34.0	1.8
1953	34.0	0.0	34.0	0.0	34.5	1.5	34.1	-1.2	34.1	0.0	34.1	0.0	34.1	0.0	34.2	0.3	34.2	0.0	34.2	0.0	34.2	0.0	34.2	0.0
1954	34.2	0.0	34.2	0.0	34.2	0.0	34.2	0.0	34.2	0.0	35.2	2.9	35.2	0.0	35.2	0.0	35.1	-0.3	35.1	0.0	35.1	0.0	35.1	0.0
1955	35.1	0.0	33.8	-3.7	33.8	0.0	33.8	0.0	34.0	0.6	34.0	0.0	33.3	-2.1	33.3	0.0	33.3	0.0	33.3	0.0	33.3	0.0	33.3	0.0
1956	33.9	1.8	33.9	0.0	34.4	1.5	34.9	1.5	35.0	0.3	35.0	0.0	35.0	0.0	35.1	0.3	35.3	0.6	35.3	0.0	35.3	0.0	35.3	0.0
1957	35.4	0.3	35.4	0.0	35.4	0.0	35.6	0.6	35.6	0.0	35.6	0.0	35.6	0.0	35.6	0.0	35.6	0.0	35.6	0.0	35.8	0.6	36.0	0.6
1958	35.6	-1.1	35.7	0.3	35.7	0.0	35.7	0.0	35.7	0.0	35.7	0.0	35.7	0.0	35.7	0.0	35.7	0.0	35.7	0.0	35.7	0.0	35.7	0.0
1959	35.7	0.0	35.7	0.0	35.7	0.0	35.7	0.0	35.7	0.0	35.7	0.0	35.7	0.0	35.2	-1.4	35.2	0.0	35.7	1.4	35.7	0.0	35.7	0.0
1960	35.7	0.0	35.7	0.0	35.7	0.0	35.6	-0.3	35.3	-0.8	35.3	0.0	35.6	0.8	35.6	0.0	35.3	-0.8	35.3	0.0	35.3	0.0	35.3	0.0
1961	35.3	0.0	35.3	0.0	35.3	0.0	35.3	0.0	35.2	-0.3	35.2	0.0	35.2	0.0	35.2	0.0	35.2	0.0	35.2	0.0	35.2	0.0	35.2	0.0
1962	35.2	0.0	35.2	0.0	35.2	0.0	35.2	0.0	35.2	0.0	35.2	0.0	35.2	0.0	35.2	0.0	35.2	0.0	35.2	0.0	35.2	0.0	35.2	0.0
1963	35.2	0.0	35.2	0.0	35.2	0.0	35.2	0.0	35.2	0.0	35.2	0.0	35.2	0.0	35.2	0.0	35.3	0.3	35.3	0.0	35.3	0.0	35.3	0.0
1964	35.3	0.0	35.3	0.0	35.3	0.0	35.3	0.0	35.3	0.0	35.3	0.0	35.3	0.0	35.3	0.0	35.3	0.0	35.3	0.0	35.3	0.0	35.3	0.0
1965	35.3	0.0	35.3	0.0	35.3	0.0	35.3	0.0	35.3	0.0	35.3	0.0	35.3	0.0	35.3	0.0	35.3	0.0	35.3	0.0	35.3	0.0	35.3	0.0
1966	35.3	0.0	35.6	0.8	35.6	0.0	35.6	0.0	35.9	0.8	36.3	1.1	35.9	-1.1	35.9	0.0	35.9	0.0	35.9	0.0	35.9	0.0	35.9	0.0
1967	35.9	0.0	35.9	0.0	35.9	0.0	35.9	0.0	35.9	0.0	35.9	0.0	35.9	0.0	35.9	0.0	35.9	0.0	35.7	-0.6	37.0	3.6	37.0	0.0
1968	37.0	0.0	38.2	3.2	35.7	-6.5	35.7	0.0	35.7	0.0	35.7	0.0	35.7	0.0	35.8	0.3	35.8	0.0	36.0	0.6	36.0	0.0	36.0	0.0
1969	36.0	0.0	36.0	0.0	36.0	0.0	36.0	0.0	36.5	1.4	36.7	0.5	36.7	0.0	38.3	4.4	38.3	0.0	38.3	0.0	38.3	0.0	38.3	0.0
1970	38.3	0.0	39.0	1.8	39.0	0.0	38.8	-0.5	39.0	0.5	39.1	0.3	39.2	0.3	39.2	0.0	39.5	0.8	39.5	0.0	39.5	0.0	39.7	0.5
1971	40.4	1.8	40.4	0.0	40.4	0.0	40.4	0.0	40.4	0.0	40.4	0.0	40.4	0.0	40.4	0.0	40.4	0.0	40.4	0.0	40.4	0.0	40.4	0.0
1972	40.3	-0.2	40.3	0.0	40.3	0.0	40.3	0.0	40.3	0.0	40.3	0.0	40.3	0.0	40.3	0.0	40.8	1.2	40.8	0.0	40.8	0.0	40.8	0.0
1973	40.8	0.0	40.8	0.0	40.8	0.0	40.8	0.0	41.4	1.5	41.4	0.0	40.8	-1.4	41.0	0.5	41.0	0.0	41.7	1.7	42.3	1.4	42.6	0.7
1974	42.9	0.7	42.9	0.0	44.0	2.6	45.5	3.4	49.5	8.8	50.9	2.8	51.9	2.0	52.5	1.2	53.8	2.5	53.8	0.0	53.8	0.0	53.8	0.0
1975	54.2	0.7	54.2	0.0	54.2	0.0	54.2	0.0	54.2	0.0	54.2	0.0	54.2	0.0	54.2	0.0	54.2	0.0	54.7	0.9	55.7	1.8	56.5	1.4
1976	56.5	0.0	56.5	0.0	57.1	1.1	57.4	0.5	58.4	1.7	59.4	1.7	59.4	0.0	59.7	0.5	59.7	0.0	59.7	0.0	59.7	0.0	59.8	0.2
1977	61.3	2.5	62.3	1.6	62.3	0.0	62.3	0.0	62.3	0.0	62.3	0.0	62.3	0.0	62.4	0.2	62.4	0.0	62.4	0.0	62.4	0.0	62.4	0.0
1978	65.3	4.6	65.3	0.0	65.5	0.3	65.5	0.0	65.5	0.0	65.5	0.0	65.5	0.0	65.6	0.2	66.2	0.9	66.2	0.0	66.2	0.0	66.2	0.0
1979	67.9	2.6	67.9	0.0	68.7	1.2	68.7	0.0	68.8	0.1	68.8	0.0	69.3	0.7	69.3	0.0	69.3	0.0	70.6	1.9	70.7	0.1	71.0	0.4
1980	73.3	3.2	73.4	0.1	74.8	1.9	78.3	4.7	78.4	0.1	78.4	0.0	80.0	2.0	80.8	1.0	80.8	0.0	80.9	0.1	80.9	0.0	81.2	0.4
1981	82.0	1.0	89.3	8.9	89.3	0.0	89.7	0.4	96.7	7.8	96.7	0.0	96.6	-0.1	96.7	0.1	96.7	0.0	97.4	0.7	97.4	0.0	97.4	0.0
1982	97.6	0.2	97.6	0.0	98.0	0.4	98.0	0.0	101.1	3.2	101.1	0.0	101.1	0.0	101.1	0.0	101.1	0.0	101.1	0.0	101.0	-0.1	101.0	0.0
1983	101.3	0.3	101.3	0.0	101.3	0.0	101.2	-0.1	101.2	0.0	101.2	0.0	101.2	0.0	101.0	-0.2	101.0	0.0	101.0	0.0	100.9	-0.1	101.1	0.2
1984	101.6	0.5	101.9	0.3	101.9	0.0	102.2	0.3	102.5	0.3	102.5	0.0	102.5	0.0	102.5	0.0	102.5	0.0	102.3	-0.2	102.3	0.0	102.4	0.1
1985	102.4	0.0	102.6	0.2	102.6	0.0	103.1	0.5	103.1	0.0	103.1	0.0	103.1	0.0	103.0	-0.1	103.0	0.0	103.0	0.0	103.0	0.0	102.9	-0.1
1986	103.0	0.1	103.8	0.8	103.6	-0.2	103.8	0.2	103.9	0.1	103.8	-0.1	103.8	0.0	103.8	0.0	103.7	-0.1	103.7	0.0	103.9	0.2	103.9	0.0
1987	103.6	-0.3	104.8	1.2	105.0	0.2	105.0	0.0	105.1	0.1	105.2	0.1	105.5	0.3	105.7	0.2	105.7	0.0	105.8	0.1	105.5	-0.3	105.9	0.4
1988	106.3	0.4	106.6	0.3	106.5	-0.1	107.4	0.8	107.4	0.0	108.1	0.7	108.2	0.1	108.5	0.3	108.9	0.4	108.9	0.0	109.1	0.2	109.2	0.1
1989	109.9	0.6	110.6	0.6	111.1	0.5	111.5	0.4	112.0	0.4	112.2	0.2	112.1	-0.1	112.1	0.0	113.8	1.5	114.7	0.8	114.6	-0.1	114.7	0.1
1990	114.9	0.2	115.2	0.3	115.3	0.1	115.4	0.1	115.3	-0.1	115.7	0.3	115.7	0.0	115.7	0.0	115.9	0.2	116.5	0.5	116.5	0.0	116.9	0.3
1991	117.0	0.1	116.8	-0.2	116.9	0.1	116.9	0.0	117.5	0.5	118.2	0.6	118.4	0.2	118.7	0.3	118.5	-0.2	118.1	-0.3	118.2	0.1	119.1	0.8

[Continued]

Notions
Producer Price Index
Base 1982 = 100
[Continued]

For 1947-1997. Columns headed % show percentile change in the index from the previous period for which an index is available.

Year	Jan Index	%	Feb Index	%	Mar Index	%	Apr Index	%	May Index	%	Jun Index	%	Jul Index	%	Aug Index	%	Sep Index	%	Oct Index	%	Nov Index	%	Dec Index	%
1992	119.1	0.0	119.1	0.0	119.1	0.0	119.0	-0.1	119.3	0.3	119.4	0.1	119.6	0.2	119.0	-0.5	118.7	-0.3	119.4	0.6	120.1	0.6	119.3	-0.7
1993	119.6	0.3	120.4	0.7	119.8	-0.5	120.1	0.3	120.4	0.2	120.6	0.2	120.5	-0.1	120.4	-0.1	120.9	0.4	120.9	0.0	121.1	0.2	121.1	0.0
1994	121.0	-0.1	121.8	0.7	121.5	-0.2	121.6	0.1	121.9	0.2	121.9	0.0	121.5	-0.3	121.8	0.2	122.0	0.2	121.7	-0.2	122.1	0.3	122.4	0.2
1995	122.7	0.2	123.4	0.6	124.0	0.5	123.6	-0.3	123.6	0.0	123.3	-0.2	123.8	0.4	123.7	-0.1	123.8	0.1	124.3	0.4	124.7	0.3	125.4	0.6
1996	125.6	0.2	125.7	0.1	126.0	0.2	125.8	-0.2	124.9	-0.7	125.2	0.2	125.2	0.0	125.4	0.2	125.3	-0.1	126.6	1.0	126.6	0.0	126.6	0.0
1997	126.8	0.2	127.0	0.2	126.5	-0.4	125.2	-1.0	125.5	0.2	125.7	0.2	125.7	0.0	125.2	-0.4	125.2	0.0	125.3	0.1	125.6	0.2	125.4	-0.2

Source: U.S. Department of Labor, Bureau of Labor Statistics, Division of Industry Prices and Price Indexes. n.e.c. stands for not elsewhere classified. - indicates no data collected for period or unavailable.

Photographic Equipment and Supplies
Producer Price Index
Base 1982 = 100

For 1947-1997. Columns headed % show percentile change in the index from the previous period for which an index is available.

Year	Jan Index	%	Feb Index	%	Mar Index	%	Apr Index	%	May Index	%	Jun Index	%	Jul Index	%	Aug Index	%	Sep Index	%	Oct Index	%	Nov Index	%	Dec Index	%
1947	31.5	-	31.5	0.0	31.6	0.3	31.6	0.0	31.8	0.6	31.9	0.3	31.9	0.0	32.9	3.1	32.9	0.0	32.9	0.0	33.0	0.3	33.4	1.2
1948	34.4	3.0	34.6	0.6	34.7	0.3	34.8	0.3	34.9	0.3	35.0	0.3	35.0	0.0	35.3	0.9	35.5	0.6	35.8	0.8	36.4	1.7	36.7	0.8
1949	36.7	0.0	37.5	2.2	37.1	-1.1	37.0	-0.3	36.7	-0.8	36.5	-0.5	36.5	0.0	36.5	0.0	36.5	0.0	36.3	-0.5	36.3	0.0	36.3	0.0
1950	36.3	0.0	36.2	-0.3	35.9	-0.8	35.9	0.0	36.0	0.3	36.0	0.0	36.0	0.0	36.0	0.0	36.4	1.1	36.9	1.4	36.9	0.0	37.1	0.5
1951	37.2	0.3	37.2	0.0	37.2	0.0	37.2	0.0	37.2	0.0	37.2	0.0	37.8	1.6	37.8	0.0	37.8	0.0	37.8	0.0	37.9	0.3	37.9	0.0
1952	37.7	-0.5	38.0	0.8	38.0	0.0	38.0	0.0	38.0	0.0	38.0	0.0	38.0	0.0	38.0	0.0	38.0	0.0	38.0	0.0	38.0	0.0	38.0	0.0
1953	38.0	0.0	38.0	0.0	38.1	0.3	38.1	0.0	38.2	0.3	38.4	0.5	38.4	0.0	38.3	-0.3	38.5	0.5	38.5	0.0	38.5	0.0	38.5	0.0
1954	38.5	0.0	38.5	0.0	38.5	0.0	38.7	0.5	38.7	0.0	38.7	0.0	38.8	0.3	38.7	-0.3	38.7	0.0	38.7	0.0	38.7	0.0	38.7	0.0
1955	38.6	-0.3	38.6	0.0	38.7	0.3	39.0	0.8	39.0	0.0	39.0	0.0	39.2	0.5	39.3	0.3	39.3	0.0	39.4	0.3	39.5	0.3	39.5	0.0
1956	39.6	0.3	39.7	0.3	39.7	0.0	39.6	-0.3	39.6	0.0	39.8	0.5	39.8	0.0	39.8	0.0	39.8	0.0	39.8	0.0	40.5	1.8	40.5	0.0
1957	41.1	1.5	41.1	0.0	41.2	0.2	41.3	0.2	41.3	0.0	41.3	0.0	41.3	0.0	41.8	1.2	42.2	1.0	42.2	0.0	42.2	0.0	42.3	0.2
1958	42.3	0.0	42.4	0.2	42.4	0.0	42.4	0.0	42.4	0.0	42.8	0.9	42.8	0.0	42.7	-0.2	42.7	0.0	42.7	0.0	42.8	0.2	42.8	0.0
1959	43.3	1.2	43.3	0.0	44.0	1.6	44.1	0.2	44.1	0.0	44.1	0.0	44.1	0.0	44.2	0.2	44.3	0.2	44.3	0.0	44.3	0.0	44.3	0.0
1960	44.2	-0.2	44.2	0.0	44.2	0.0	44.2	0.0	44.2	0.0	44.2	0.0	44.2	0.0	44.4	0.5	44.4	0.0	44.6	0.5	44.9	0.7	44.9	0.0
1961	44.8	-0.2	44.9	0.2	44.8	-0.2	44.8	0.0	44.5	-0.7	44.4	-0.2	44.5	0.2	45.0	1.1	45.2	0.4	45.4	0.4	45.5	0.2	45.7	0.4
1962	45.7	0.0	46.0	0.7	46.0	0.0	45.9	-0.2	46.0	0.2	46.1	0.2	46.1	0.0	46.2	0.2	46.1	-0.2	46.1	0.0	46.1	0.0	46.1	0.0
1963	46.2	0.2	46.2	0.0	45.9	-0.6	45.9	0.0	46.0	0.2	46.1	0.2	46.2	0.2	45.9	-0.6	45.8	-0.2	45.9	0.2	45.9	0.0	46.1	0.4
1964	46.2	0.2	46.2	0.0	46.2	0.0	46.2	0.0	46.2	0.0	46.2	0.0	46.3	0.2	46.3	0.0	46.3	0.0	46.5	0.4	46.5	0.0	46.5	0.0
1965	46.5	0.0	46.5	0.0	46.6	0.2	46.8	0.4	46.8	0.0	46.7	-0.2	46.7	0.0	46.7	0.0	46.7	0.0	46.7	0.0	46.7	0.0	46.7	0.0
1966	46.6	-0.2	46.6	0.0	46.6	0.0	46.5	-0.2	46.5	0.0	46.5	0.0	46.5	0.0	46.4	-0.2	46.3	-0.2	46.3	0.0	46.9	1.3	47.0	0.2
1967	47.1	0.2	47.1	0.0	47.1	0.0	47.1	0.0	47.1	0.0	47.1	0.0	47.1	0.0	47.6	1.1	47.7	0.2	48.6	1.9	48.6	0.0	48.6	0.0
1968	48.0	-1.2	48.6	1.2	48.6	0.0	48.6	0.0	49.0	0.8	49.0	0.0	48.5	-1.0	48.5	0.0	48.5	0.0	48.6	0.2	48.6	0.0	48.6	0.0
1969	48.4	-0.4	48.4	0.0	48.1	-0.6	48.2	0.2	48.4	0.4	48.4	0.0	48.7	0.6	48.7	0.0	49.0	0.6	49.1	0.2	49.2	0.2	49.3	0.2
1970	49.4	0.2	49.5	0.2	49.5	0.0	49.7	0.4	49.7	0.0	49.5	-0.4	50.1	1.2	50.2	0.2	50.1	-0.2	50.1	0.0	50.2	0.2	50.2	0.0
1971	50.3	0.2	50.4	0.2	50.4	0.0	50.4	0.0	50.4	0.0	50.5	0.2	50.6	0.2	50.6	0.0	50.6	0.0	50.6	0.0	50.6	0.0	50.6	0.0
1972	50.6	0.0	50.7	0.2	50.8	0.2	50.5	-0.6	50.5	0.0	50.5	0.0	50.5	0.0	50.8	0.6	50.8	0.0	50.8	0.0	50.8	0.0	50.8	0.0
1973	51.0	0.4	51.1	0.2	51.6	1.0	51.5	-0.2	51.4	-0.2	51.5	0.2	51.6	0.2	51.6	0.0	51.6	0.0	51.6	0.0	51.7	0.2	51.9	0.4
1974	51.9	0.0	52.3	0.8	52.5	0.4	52.6	0.2	55.6	5.7	55.6	0.0	56.4	1.4	56.4	0.0	57.4	1.8	57.6	0.3	58.0	0.7	59.9	3.3
1975	60.3	0.7	60.5	0.3	61.1	1.0	61.8	1.1	61.9	0.2	62.2	0.5	62.3	0.2	62.4	0.2	62.8	0.6	63.4	1.0	63.5	0.2	62.7	-1.3
1976	63.2	0.8	64.0	1.3	64.1	0.2	64.2	0.2	64.2	0.0	65.2	1.6	65.1	-0.2	65.1	0.0	65.1	0.0	65.1	0.0	65.2	0.2	66.2	1.5
1977	65.7	-0.8	65.8	0.2	65.8	0.0	65.6	-0.3	66.5	1.4	66.7	0.3	67.1	0.6	67.0	-0.1	66.8	-0.3	66.9	0.1	66.9	0.0	67.2	0.4
1978	67.6	0.6	67.8	0.3	67.8	0.0	68.7	1.3	68.8	0.1	69.4	0.9	69.4	0.0	69.6	0.3	70.2	0.9	70.7	0.7	70.7	0.0	70.7	0.0
1979	71.4	1.0	71.4	0.0	71.4	0.0	71.3	-0.1	71.6	0.4	72.1	0.7	72.2	0.1	72.3	0.1	73.3	1.4	74.8	2.0	76.6	2.4	78.1	2.0
1980	78.9	1.0	103.9	31.7	104.1	0.2	100.9	-3.1	94.9	-5.9	95.9	1.1	95.8	-0.1	95.5	-0.3	95.5	0.0	95.4	-0.1	98.2	2.9	98.2	0.0
1981	98.6	0.4	99.6	1.0	100.4	0.8	100.9	0.5	101.0	0.1	101.0	0.0	100.5	-0.5	98.4	-2.1	99.2	0.8	99.3	0.1	99.4	0.1	99.4	0.0
1982	99.8	0.4	100.0	0.2	100.8	0.8	101.8	1.0	100.1	-1.7	100.0	-0.1	99.3	-0.7	99.3	0.0	99.8	0.5	99.7	-0.1	99.7	0.0	99.8	0.1
1983	99.8	0.0	100.7	0.9	102.9	2.2	103.0	0.1	103.0	0.0	102.9	-0.1	102.9	0.0	102.9	0.0	102.9	0.0	103.0	0.1	103.0	0.0	103.0	0.0
1984	103.1	0.1	103.6	0.5	101.1	-2.4	101.5	0.4	101.5	0.0	101.5	0.0	101.6	0.1	102.4	0.8	102.4	0.0	102.5	0.1	101.2	-1.3	101.3	0.1
1985	101.5	0.2	101.6	0.1	102.6	1.0	102.6	0.0	102.5	-0.1	102.6	0.1	102.5	-0.1	102.5	0.0	103.0	0.5	103.0	0.0	103.1	0.1	103.2	0.1
1986	103.2	0.0	103.2	0.0	103.9	0.7	103.8	-0.1	104.7	0.9	104.1	-0.6	104.1	0.0	104.1	0.0	104.1	0.0	104.2	0.1	104.2	0.0	104.1	-0.1
1987	104.2	0.1	104.4	0.2	104.3	-0.1	105.4	1.1	105.6	0.2	105.7	0.1	105.7	0.0	105.7	0.0	105.9	0.2	106.1	0.2	106.1	0.0	105.8	-0.3
1988	105.8	0.0	105.8	0.0	105.8	0.0	106.5	0.7	106.5	0.0	107.1	0.6	107.1	0.0	107.3	0.2	107.3	0.0	108.9	1.5	109.1	0.2	108.7	-0.4
1989	111.8	2.9	111.9	0.1	112.7	0.7	113.1	0.4	114.4	1.1	114.4	0.0	114.4	0.0	114.5	0.1	115.8	1.1	116.2	0.3	116.2	0.0	116.2	0.0
1990	117.5	1.1	117.8	0.3	117.8	0.0	117.8	0.0	117.9	0.1	117.9	0.0	118.9	0.8	118.8	-0.1	119.0	0.2	118.9	-0.1	118.9	0.0	119.5	0.5
1991	119.6	0.1	117.6	-1.7	117.7	0.1	118.0	0.3	117.9	-0.1	117.9	0.0	117.9	0.0	117.9	0.0	117.9	0.0	118.3	0.3	118.4	0.1	118.5	0.1

[Continued]

Photographic Equipment and Supplies
Producer Price Index
Base 1982 = 100
[Continued]

For 1947-1997. Columns headed % show percentile change in the index from the previous period for which an index is available.

Year	Jan Index	%	Feb Index	%	Mar Index	%	Apr Index	%	May Index	%	Jun Index	%	Jul Index	%	Aug Index	%	Sep Index	%	Oct Index	%	Nov Index	%	Dec Index	%
1992	118.6	0.1	118.7	0.1	118.2	-0.4	118.2	0.0	118.4	0.2	118.7	0.3	118.7	0.0	118.7	0.0	118.9	0.2	118.8	-0.1	118.9	0.1	118.9	0.0
1993	117.7	-1.0	117.8	0.1	117.8	0.0	117.9	0.1	117.9	0.0	117.9	0.0	118.3	0.3	118.8	0.4	118.6	-0.2	117.1	-1.3	118.0	0.8	117.1	-0.8
1994	120.3	2.7	119.1	-1.0	118.0	-0.9	118.2	0.2	116.9	-1.1	116.2	-0.6	116.4	0.2	116.2	-0.2	114.5	-1.5	115.4	0.8	115.6	0.2	115.6	0.0
1995	116.6	0.9	117.9	1.1	117.6	-0.3	118.5	0.8	118.4	-0.1	118.5	0.1	119.5	0.8	120.0	0.4	117.9	-1.7	119.6	1.4	118.4	-1.0	118.3	-0.1
1996	120.3	1.7	120.8	0.4	120.1	-0.6	119.4	-0.6	120.3	0.8	119.8	-0.4	119.9	0.1	119.5	-0.3	119.7	0.2	120.4	0.6	119.6	-0.7	118.9	-0.6
1997	118.6	-0.3	118.6	0.0	119.6	0.8	119.6	0.0	119.8	0.2	118.0	-1.5	118.0	0.0	118.0	0.0	118.6	0.5	118.1	-0.4	118.0	-0.1	118.5	0.4

Source: U.S. Department of Labor, Bureau of Labor Statistics, Division of Industry Prices and Price Indexes. n.e.c. stands for not elsewhere classified. - indicates no data collected for period or unavailable.

Mobile Homes
Producer Price Index
Base 1982 = 100

For 1981-1997. Columns headed % show percentile change in the index from the previous period for which an index is available.

Year	Jan Index	%	Feb Index	%	Mar Index	%	Apr Index	%	May Index	%	Jun Index	%	Jul Index	%	Aug Index	%	Sep Index	%	Oct Index	%	Nov Index	%	Dec Index	%
1981	94.5	-	94.6	0.1	95.8	1.3	96.2	0.4	96.3	0.1	96.4	0.1	97.7	1.3	97.8	0.1	98.0	0.2	98.3	0.3	98.4	0.1	98.4	0.0
1982	98.5	0.1	98.6	0.1	100.0	1.4	100.2	0.2	100.4	0.2	100.3	-0.1	100.5	0.2	100.6	0.1	100.6	0.0	100.5	-0.1	99.9	-0.6	99.9	0.0
1983	100.0	0.1	99.9	-0.1	100.6	0.7	100.3	-0.3	100.3	0.0	100.8	0.5	101.0	0.2	101.2	0.2	101.5	0.3	101.8	0.3	101.9	0.1	102.0	0.1
1984	100.1	-1.9	100.3	0.2	100.4	0.1	101.2	0.8	101.1	-0.1	100.5	-0.6	100.7	0.2	100.8	0.1	101.1	0.3	101.1	0.0	101.6	0.5	101.5	-0.1
1985	101.5	0.0	101.6	0.1	101.5	-0.1	101.5	0.0	101.5	0.0	101.8	0.3	101.7	-0.1	101.8	0.1	102.0	0.2	101.8	-0.2	101.9	0.1	101.9	0.0
1986	102.2	0.3	100.9	-1.3	101.1	0.2	102.8	1.7	102.9	0.1	103.1	0.2	103.1	0.0	103.2	0.1	103.2	0.0	103.3	0.1	103.5	0.2	103.6	0.1
1987	103.7	0.1	103.7	0.0	103.7	0.0	103.5	-0.2	104.0	0.5	104.0	0.0	104.4	0.4	103.9	-0.5	104.7	0.8	105.0	0.3	105.1	0.1	106.2	1.0
1988	106.5	0.3	107.0	0.5	107.7	0.7	108.2	0.5	108.9	0.6	109.3	0.4	109.8	0.5	109.9	0.1	110.4	0.5	110.7	0.3	111.6	0.8	111.4	-0.2
1989	111.6	0.2	111.9	0.3	112.1	0.2	112.5	0.4	113.9	1.2	113.9	0.0	114.3	0.4	114.8	0.4	115.2	0.3	115.5	0.3	115.8	0.3	115.9	0.1
1990	115.9	0.0	116.2	0.3	116.2	0.0	116.4	0.2	116.9	0.4	117.5	0.5	117.7	0.2	118.0	0.3	118.2	0.2	118.4	0.2	119.3	0.8	119.3	0.0
1991	119.3	0.0	119.5	0.2	119.5	0.0	119.6	0.1	120.1	0.4	120.4	0.2	120.8	0.3	121.1	0.2	121.0	-0.1	121.0	0.0	121.2	0.2	121.2	0.0
1992	120.4	-0.7	120.4	0.0	120.4	0.0	120.9	0.4	121.3	0.3	121.4	0.1	121.7	0.2	122.0	0.2	122.1	0.1	123.0	0.7	123.5	0.4	123.5	0.0
1993	123.5	0.0	124.6	0.9	125.5	0.7	126.6	0.9	127.3	0.6	127.6	0.2	129.2	1.3	129.2	0.0	129.1	-0.1	129.3	0.2	130.7	1.1	131.1	0.3
1994	132.6	1.1	132.6	0.0	135.7	2.3	135.8	0.1	135.8	0.0	137.0	0.9	137.2	0.1	137.3	0.1	138.0	0.5	139.1	0.8	141.0	1.4	142.0	0.7
1995	143.9	1.3	144.7	0.6	144.7	0.0	144.9	0.1	144.9	0.0	145.9	0.7	146.1	0.1	144.9	-0.8	145.2	0.2	145.6	0.3	148.6	2.1	148.5	-0.1
1996	148.5	0.0	148.6	0.1	148.8	0.1	148.9	0.1	149.3	0.3	149.9	0.4	150.2	0.2	150.2	0.0	150.4	0.1	150.5	0.1	150.8	0.2	151.4	0.4
1997	151.1	-0.2	151.1	0.0	151.3	0.1	152.1	0.5	152.1	0.0	152.2	0.1	152.7	0.3	152.7	0.0	152.5	-0.1	152.6	0.1	153.1	0.3	152.8	-0.2

Source: U.S. Department of Labor, Bureau of Labor Statistics, Division of Industry Prices and Price Indexes. n.e.c. stands for not elsewhere classified. - indicates no data collected for period or unavailable.

Medical, Surgical & Personal Aid Devices
Producer Price Index
Base 1982 = 100

For 1978-1997. Columns headed % show percentile change in the index from the previous period for which an index is available.

Year	Jan Index	%	Feb Index	%	Mar Index	%	Apr Index	%	May Index	%	Jun Index	%	Jul Index	%	Aug Index	%	Sep Index	%	Oct Index	%	Nov Index	%	Dec Index	%
1978	-	-	-	-	-	-	-	-	-	-	86.5	-	86.4	-0.1	86.9	0.6	86.9	0.0	87.4	0.6	87.4	0.0	88.3	1.0
1979	88.6	0.3	88.6	0.0	88.6	0.0	88.6	0.0	89.1	0.6	89.6	0.6	89.8	0.2	90.2	0.4	90.2	0.0	90.2	0.0	90.3	0.1	90.3	0.0
1980	90.1	-0.2	90.5	0.4	92.9	2.7	92.9	0.0	94.2	1.4	94.2	0.0	94.2	0.0	94.2	0.0	94.7	0.5	93.8	-1.0	93.8	0.0	93.8	0.0
1981	93.8	0.0	94.0	0.2	94.9	1.0	97.4	2.6	98.2	0.8	98.2	0.0	98.2	0.0	98.2	0.0	98.2	0.0	98.2	0.0	98.2	0.0	98.2	0.0
1982	98.7	0.5	98.7	0.0	98.7	0.0	98.7	0.0	99.0	0.3	99.0	0.0	100.5	1.5	100.5	0.0	101.4	0.9	101.6	0.2	101.6	0.0	101.6	0.0
1983	102.7	1.1	101.7	-1.0	102.6	0.9	102.4	-0.2	102.6	0.2	102.8	0.2	104.4	1.6	104.7	0.3	104.5	-0.2	105.2	0.7	105.9	0.7	105.9	0.0
1984	107.6	1.6	107.7	0.1	107.8	0.1	108.3	0.5	108.2	-0.1	108.2	0.0	108.4	0.2	108.9	0.5	108.4	-0.5	108.6	0.2	108.7	0.1	108.7	0.0
1985	109.4	0.6	109.2	-0.2	109.3	0.1	109.2	-0.1	109.2	0.0	109.2	0.0	108.7	-0.5	108.7	0.0	108.7	0.0	108.9	0.2	108.9	0.0	109.0	0.1
1986	110.4	1.3	110.5	0.1	110.8	0.3	111.0	0.2	111.0	0.0	111.2	0.2	111.5	0.3	111.6	0.1	111.8	0.2	112.4	0.5	114.7	2.0	114.3	-0.3
1987	114.1	-0.2	114.2	0.1	114.6	0.4	117.8	2.8	117.6	-0.2	117.8	0.2	117.6	-0.2	117.9	0.3	117.7	-0.2	117.8	0.1	118.4	0.5	118.2	-0.2
1988	119.1	0.8	119.2	0.1	119.4	0.2	119.5	0.1	119.8	0.3	117.8	-1.7	118.0	0.2	118.1	0.1	118.1	0.0	119.3	1.0	119.4	0.1	119.4	0.0
1989	121.2	1.5	121.5	0.2	121.8	0.2	122.1	0.2	123.1	0.8	123.1	0.0	122.9	-0.2	123.0	0.1	123.8	0.7	124.4	0.5	124.5	0.1	124.8	0.2
1990	125.9	0.9	126.0	0.1	126.3	0.2	126.9	0.5	127.2	0.2	127.3	0.1	127.4	0.1	127.8	0.3	128.0	0.2	128.4	0.3	128.3	-0.1	128.5	0.2
1991	129.3	0.6	129.5	0.2	129.7	0.2	130.0	0.2	130.0	0.0	130.2	0.2	130.4	0.2	130.6	0.2	131.2	0.5	130.9	-0.2	131.1	0.2	130.9	-0.2
1992	132.4	1.1	132.8	0.3	133.5	0.5	133.6	0.1	133.8	0.1	133.9	0.1	133.5	-0.3	134.4	0.7	134.3	-0.1	134.8	0.4	134.7	-0.1	134.6	-0.1
1993	136.0	1.0	137.5	1.1	137.9	0.3	137.8	-0.1	138.5	0.5	137.9	-0.4	137.5	-0.3	138.3	0.6	137.7	-0.4	138.0	0.2	138.1	0.1	138.7	0.4
1994	139.3	0.4	140.3	0.7	140.6	0.2	140.4	-0.1	140.1	-0.2	140.3	0.1	140.7	0.3	140.5	-0.1	140.7	0.1	140.7	0.0	140.7	0.0	140.1	-0.4
1995	140.2	0.1	141.0	0.6	140.9	-0.1	140.6	-0.2	140.9	0.2	141.0	0.1	141.3	0.2	141.1	-0.1	142.0	0.6	142.2	0.1	142.0	-0.1	142.2	0.1
1996	143.5	0.9	143.4	-0.1	143.6	0.1	143.4	-0.1	143.5	0.1	143.4	-0.1	143.6	0.1	142.2	-1.0	142.1	-0.1	142.4	0.2	142.7	0.2	142.9	0.1
1997	142.9	0.0	142.9	0.0	142.8	-0.1	143.1	0.2	143.1	0.0	143.3	0.1	143.4	0.1	143.2	-0.1	143.1	-0.1	143.0	-0.1	142.8	-0.1	142.8	0.0

Source: U.S. Department of Labor, Bureau of Labor Statistics, Division of Industry Prices and Price Indexes. n.e.c. stands for not elsewhere classified. - indicates no data collected for period or unavailable.

Industrial Safety Equipment
Producer Price Index
Base 1982 = 100

For 1978-1997. Columns headed % show percentile change in the index from the previous period for which an index is available.

Year	Jan Index	%	Feb Index	%	Mar Index	%	Apr Index	%	May Index	%	Jun Index	%	Jul Index	%	Aug Index	%	Sep Index	%	Oct Index	%	Nov Index	%	Dec Index	%
1978	-	-	-	-	-	-	-	-	-	-	77.3	-	77.5	0.3	77.5	0.0	77.8	0.4	78.5	0.9	79.0	0.6	79.6	0.8
1979	80.2	0.8	81.0	1.0	81.6	0.7	82.5	1.1	82.9	0.5	83.1	0.2	83.7	0.7	83.9	0.2	84.2	0.4	84.5	0.4	86.3	2.1	86.1	-0.2
1980	87.4	1.5	88.2	0.9	88.6	0.5	89.0	0.5	89.5	0.6	89.9	0.4	90.2	0.3	90.2	0.0	90.2	0.0	90.5	0.3	90.5	0.0	91.1	0.7
1981	93.0	2.1	94.4	1.5	94.7	0.3	95.0	0.3	94.9	-0.1	94.9	0.0	95.7	0.8	96.1	0.4	96.1	0.0	96.3	0.2	96.4	0.1	96.6	0.2
1982	98.1	1.6	99.2	1.1	99.6	0.4	99.6	0.0	99.8	0.2	100.2	0.4	100.2	0.0	100.6	0.4	100.5	-0.1	100.7	0.2	100.7	0.0	100.7	0.0
1983	101.9	1.2	102.0	0.1	102.5	0.5	102.9	0.4	102.9	0.0	103.0	0.1	103.6	0.6	103.6	0.0	103.6	0.0	103.2	-0.4	103.2	0.0	104.2	1.0
1984	103.6	-0.6	103.6	0.0	103.6	0.0	103.6	0.0	103.8	0.2	109.5	5.5	108.1	-1.3	110.1	1.9	109.2	-0.8	109.2	0.0	109.0	-0.2	109.8	0.7
1985	111.1	1.2	111.2	0.1	111.0	-0.2	111.2	0.2	111.1	-0.1	110.9	-0.2	110.9	0.0	110.7	-0.2	111.1	0.4	111.1	0.0	112.1	0.9	113.4	1.2
1986	117.5	3.6	117.6	0.1	118.1	0.4	120.8	2.3	120.7	-0.1	120.7	0.0	120.8	0.1	121.7	0.7	121.9	0.2	123.2	1.1	124.4	1.0	125.0	0.5
1987	125.1	0.1	128.0	2.3	128.0	0.0	128.4	0.3	127.9	-0.4	128.7	0.6	129.3	0.5	130.0	0.5	130.2	0.2	130.9	0.5	131.0	0.1	131.1	0.1
1988	132.0	0.7	132.1	0.1	133.8	1.3	136.5	2.0	136.5	0.0	136.7	0.1	137.6	0.7	137.7	0.1	137.7	0.0	137.8	0.1	140.9	2.2	140.9	0.0
1989	140.9	0.0	140.9	0.0	142.0	0.8	144.6	1.8	144.6	0.0	144.8	0.1	144.9	0.1	144.9	0.0	144.8	-0.1	146.1	0.9	145.9	-0.1	146.0	0.1
1990	146.1	0.1	146.1	0.0	146.1	0.0	149.5	2.3	150.2	0.5	150.7	0.3	150.4	-0.2	150.4	0.0	151.0	0.4	151.5	0.3	151.2	-0.2	152.7	1.0
1991	154.6	1.2	153.7	-0.6	156.4	1.8	157.0	0.4	156.7	-0.2	156.9	0.1	158.5	1.0	159.9	0.9	159.8	-0.1	161.1	0.8	158.8	-1.4	159.5	0.4
1992	159.7	0.1	159.8	0.1	160.0	0.1	163.1	1.9	163.7	0.4	163.6	-0.1	166.3	1.7	166.3	0.0	165.5	-0.5	165.5	0.0	164.8	-0.4	164.7	-0.1
1993	165.0	0.2	166.0	0.6	165.3	-0.4	165.0	-0.2	165.5	0.3	166.0	0.3	166.1	0.1	166.7	0.4	166.6	-0.1	166.9	0.2	169.5	1.6	169.9	0.2
1994	169.9	0.0	172.1	1.3	172.2	0.1	172.2	0.0	172.4	0.1	172.6	0.1	173.2	0.3	173.2	0.0	173.2	0.0	173.7	0.3	173.7	0.0	172.9	-0.5
1995	173.6	0.4	173.7	0.1	179.6	3.4	179.7	0.1	179.7	0.0	180.4	0.4	180.4	0.0	180.3	-0.1	180.0	-0.2	177.8	-1.2	178.2	0.2	178.3	0.1
1996	178.4	0.1	182.7	2.4	183.3	0.3	182.1	-0.7	180.2	-1.0	184.7	2.5	183.4	-0.7	183.4	0.0	183.4	0.0	183.8	0.2	183.5	-0.2	183.9	0.2
1997	184.0	0.1	184.6	0.3	186.3	0.9	186.3	0.0	186.4	0.1	186.6	0.1	186.6	0.0	186.8	0.1	186.8	0.0	186.4	-0.2	186.4	0.0	186.5	0.1

Source: U.S. Department of Labor, Bureau of Labor Statistics, Division of Industry Prices and Price Indexes. n.e.c. stands for not elsewhere classified. - indicates no data collected for period or unavailable.

Mining Services
Producer Price Index
Base 1982 = 100

For 1985-1997. Columns headed % show percentile change in the index from the previous period for which an index is available.

Year	Jan Index	%	Feb Index	%	Mar Index	%	Apr Index	%	May Index	%	Jun Index	%	Jul Index	%	Aug Index	%	Sep Index	%	Oct Index	%	Nov Index	%	Dec Index	%
1985	-	-	-	-	-	-	-	-	-	-	100.0	-	99.6	-0.4	99.6	0.0	99.6	0.0	99.5	-0.1	99.2	-0.3	99.0	-0.2
1986	98.8	-0.2	97.0	-1.8	95.9	-1.1	93.7	-2.3	91.7	-2.1	90.7	-1.1	89.6	-1.2	88.8	-0.9	88.7	-0.1	87.6	-1.2	86.9	-0.8	86.7	-0.2
1987	86.5	-0.2	86.2	-0.3	86.4	0.2	86.5	0.1	86.5	0.0	86.3	-0.2	86.5	0.2	87.2	0.8	87.8	0.7	88.5	0.8	89.5	1.1	90.0	0.6
1988	90.6	0.7	91.6	1.1	91.1	-0.5	91.2	0.1	91.0	-0.2	91.0	0.0	90.9	-0.1	90.0	-1.0	89.9	-0.1	89.8	-0.1	89.8	0.0	89.8	0.0
1989	90.4	0.7	90.3	-0.1	90.3	0.0	90.0	-0.3	90.5	0.6	90.7	0.2	91.3	0.7	91.6	0.3	91.2	-0.4	91.4	0.2	91.7	0.3	91.9	0.2
1990	92.8	1.0	93.8	1.1	93.8	0.0	94.4	0.6	94.7	0.3	95.0	0.3	95.0	0.0	95.7	0.7	96.4	0.7	97.4	1.0	97.8	0.4	98.7	0.9
1991	99.6	0.9	99.6	0.0	99.8	0.2	99.5	-0.3	99.6	0.1	99.2	-0.4	99.0	-0.2	98.3	-0.7	97.9	-0.4	97.0	-0.9	96.3	-0.7	97.5	1.2
1992	97.0	-0.5	96.6	-0.4	96.8	0.2	95.6	-1.2	95.7	0.1	93.7	-2.1	94.2	0.5	93.3	-1.0	94.0	0.8	94.3	0.3	94.7	0.4	95.8	1.2
1993	96.3	0.5	98.4	2.2	98.3	-0.1	99.2	0.9	99.2	0.0	99.8	0.6	100.4	0.6	100.5	0.1	101.6	1.1	101.6	0.0	101.7	0.1	102.6	0.9
1994	103.3	0.7	103.3	0.0	102.2	-1.1	101.9	-0.3	101.7	-0.2	102.3	0.6	102.3	0.0	103.1	0.8	103.6	0.5	103.4	-0.2	104.1	0.7	103.9	-0.2
1995	103.6	-0.3	103.5	-0.1	102.7	-0.8	103.0	0.3	103.0	0.0	102.9	-0.1	103.1	0.2	109.0	5.7	110.2	1.1	110.5	0.3	110.5	0.0	110.7	0.2
1996	111.2	0.5	101.9	-8.4	101.9	0.0	103.0	1.1	105.4	2.3	105.6	0.2	108.7	2.9	109.4	0.6	110.0	0.5	110.6	0.5	111.5	0.8	112.2	0.6
1997	113.7	1.3	114.5	0.7	115.3	0.7	116.6	1.1	118.2	1.4	119.5	1.1	120.0	0.4	120.5	0.4	120.8	0.2	121.9	0.9	122.5	0.5	123.3	0.7

Source: U.S. Department of Labor, Bureau of Labor Statistics, Division of Industry Prices and Price Indexes. n.e.c. stands for not elsewhere classified. - indicates no data collected for period or unavailable.

Other Miscellaneous Products
Producer Price Index
Base 1982 = 100

For 1947-1997. Columns headed % show percentile change in the index from the previous period for which an index is available.

Year	Jan Index	%	Feb Index	%	Mar Index	%	Apr Index	%	May Index	%	Jun Index	%	Jul Index	%	Aug Index	%	Sep Index	%	Oct Index	%	Nov Index	%	Dec Index	%
1947	23.2	-	23.2	0.0	23.2	0.0	23.4	0.9	23.4	0.0	23.1	-1.3	22.9	-0.9	22.9	0.0	23.0	0.4	23.2	0.9	23.4	0.9	23.4	0.0
1948	23.5	0.4	23.7	0.9	23.7	0.0	23.7	0.0	23.7	0.0	23.8	0.4	23.8	0.0	23.9	0.4	23.9	0.0	23.9	0.0	24.0	0.4	24.2	0.8
1949	24.2	0.0	24.2	0.0	24.2	0.0	23.8	-1.7	23.9	0.4	23.9	0.0	23.7	-0.8	23.7	0.0	23.7	0.0	23.7	0.0	23.9	0.8	23.9	0.0
1950	23.6	-1.3	23.6	0.0	23.6	0.0	23.7	0.4	23.7	0.0	23.6	-0.4	23.7	0.4	24.3	2.5	24.2	-0.4	24.6	1.7	24.7	0.4	25.2	2.0
1951	25.7	2.0	25.7	0.0	25.7	0.0	25.7	0.0	25.7	0.0	25.7	0.0	25.7	0.0	25.7	0.0	25.7	0.0	25.7	0.0	25.7	0.0	25.7	0.0
1952	25.7	0.0	25.7	0.0	25.7	0.0	25.7	0.0	25.7	0.0	25.7	0.0	25.7	0.0	25.7	0.0	25.7	0.0	25.7	0.0	25.7	0.0	25.7	0.0
1953	25.7	0.0	25.7	0.0	25.8	0.4	25.8	0.0	25.7	-0.4	25.7	0.0	25.7	0.0	25.7	0.0	25.7	0.0	25.7	0.0	25.7	0.0	25.7	0.0
1954	25.7	0.0	25.8	0.4	25.9	0.4	26.0	0.4	25.9	-0.4	26.0	0.4	26.0	0.0	26.0	0.0	26.0	0.0	26.1	0.4	26.1	0.0	26.1	0.0
1955	26.0	-0.4	26.0	0.0	26.0	0.0	26.0	0.0	26.0	0.0	26.0	0.0	26.1	0.4	26.2	0.4	26.2	0.0	26.2	0.0	26.3	0.4	26.4	0.4
1956	26.4	0.0	26.4	0.0	26.4	0.0	26.5	0.4	26.5	0.0	26.5	0.0	26.5	0.0	26.5	0.0	26.6	0.4	26.6	0.0	26.7	0.4	26.7	0.0
1957	27.0	1.1	27.1	0.4	27.1	0.0	27.1	0.0	27.1	0.0	27.0	-0.4	27.1	0.4	27.1	0.0	27.2	0.4	27.3	0.4	27.3	0.0	27.3	0.0
1958	27.2	-0.4	27.3	0.4	27.3	0.0	27.3	0.0	27.3	0.0	27.5	0.7	27.4	-0.4	27.4	0.0	27.4	0.0	27.4	0.0	27.4	0.0	27.5	0.4
1959	27.5	0.0	27.5	0.0	27.5	0.0	27.5	0.0	27.5	0.0	27.4	-0.4	27.4	0.0	27.5	0.4	27.5	0.0	27.5	0.0	27.5	0.0	27.7	0.7
1960	27.9	0.7	27.9	0.0	27.9	0.0	27.9	0.0	28.0	0.4	27.9	-0.4	28.0	0.4	28.0	0.0	28.0	0.0	28.0	0.0	27.9	-0.4	28.0	0.4
1961	28.1	0.4	28.1	0.0	28.0	-0.4	27.9	-0.4	28.0	0.4	28.0	0.0	28.0	0.0	28.1	0.4	28.1	0.0	28.1	0.0	28.1	0.0	28.1	0.0
1962	28.0	-0.4	28.0	0.0	28.0	0.0	28.1	0.4	28.1	0.0	28.1	0.0	28.1	0.0	28.1	0.0	28.1	0.0	28.1	0.0	28.2	0.4	28.1	-0.4
1963	28.1	0.0	28.1	0.0	28.1	0.0	28.0	-0.4	28.0	0.0	28.0	0.0	28.0	0.0	28.0	0.0	28.0	0.0	28.0	0.0	28.0	0.0	28.0	0.0
1964	28.1	0.4	28.0	-0.4	28.1	0.4	28.1	0.0	28.1	0.0	28.0	-0.4	28.2	0.7	28.2	0.0	28.2	0.0	28.2	0.0	28.2	0.0	28.2	0.0
1965	28.1	-0.4	28.1	0.0	28.1	0.0	28.1	0.0	28.1	0.0	28.3	0.7	28.6	1.1	28.6	0.0	28.6	0.0	28.6	0.0	28.6	0.0	28.6	0.0
1966	28.7	0.3	28.7	0.0	28.6	-0.3	28.7	0.3	28.7	0.0	28.7	0.0	28.8	0.3	28.9	0.3	28.9	0.0	28.9	0.0	29.0	0.3	29.0	0.0
1967	29.3	1.0	29.3	0.0	29.4	0.3	29.4	0.0	29.5	0.3	29.6	0.3	29.7	0.3	29.7	0.0	29.7	0.0	29.7	0.0	29.8	0.3	29.9	0.3
1968	30.1	0.7	30.1	0.0	30.1	0.0	30.2	0.3	30.2	0.0	30.2	0.0	30.3	0.3	30.4	0.3	30.5	0.3	30.6	0.3	30.6	0.0	30.6	0.0
1969	30.4	-0.7	30.4	0.0	30.5	0.3	30.5	0.0	30.6	0.3	30.9	1.0	31.2	1.0	31.2	0.0	31.3	0.3	31.4	0.3	31.4	0.0	31.4	0.0
1970	31.5	0.3	31.5	0.0	31.5	0.0	31.5	0.0	32.0	1.6	32.1	0.3	32.5	1.2	32.5	0.0	32.6	0.3	32.6	0.0	32.7	0.3	32.7	0.0
1971	32.9	0.6	33.0	0.3	32.9	-0.3	33.1	0.6	33.2	0.3	33.3	0.3	33.5	0.6	33.5	0.0	33.5	0.0	33.5	0.0	33.5	0.0	33.5	0.0
1972	33.7	0.6	33.8	0.3	33.8	0.0	34.0	0.6	34.0	0.0	34.1	0.3	34.7	1.8	34.8	0.3	34.8	0.0	34.6	-0.6	34.5	-0.3	34.6	0.3
1973	35.1	1.4	35.2	0.3	35.4	0.6	36.1	2.0	36.9	2.2	37.6	1.9	38.3	1.9	38.3	0.0	38.3	0.0	37.8	-1.3	37.9	0.3	38.0	0.3
1974	39.0	2.6	39.4	1.0	40.3	2.3	42.4	5.2	42.7	0.7	42.9	0.5	43.1	0.5	42.2	-2.1	42.5	0.7	42.9	0.9	43.1	0.5	43.6	1.2
1975	45.3	3.9	45.8	1.1	46.0	0.4	46.1	0.2	46.2	0.2	46.2	0.0	46.3	0.2	46.3	0.0	46.6	0.6	45.5	-2.4	45.5	0.0	45.8	0.7
1976	46.0	0.4	45.9	-0.2	45.9	0.0	45.0	-2.0	45.0	0.0	45.7	1.6	45.0	-1.5	44.6	-0.9	44.7	0.2	44.8	0.2	44.8	0.0	45.1	0.7
1977	47.4	5.1	47.6	0.4	47.9	0.6	49.4	3.1	49.4	0.0	49.4	0.0	49.4	0.0	49.5	0.2	49.6	0.2	51.2	3.2	51.5	0.6	51.7	0.4
1978	52.5	1.5	51.5	-1.9	52.5	1.9	61.0	16.2	62.3	2.1	62.4	0.2	66.9	7.2	68.1	1.8	69.3	1.8	66.6	-3.9	64.6	-3.0	69.4	7.4
1979	70.3	1.3	72.1	2.6	72.6	0.7	72.7	0.1	74.1	1.9	75.6	2.0	76.8	1.6	77.3	0.7	80.5	4.1	85.2	5.8	86.7	1.8	91.3	5.3
1980	103.9	13.8	111.8	7.6	103.8	-7.2	100.8	-2.9	100.6	-0.2	106.5	5.9	109.6	2.9	107.8	-1.6	112.9	4.7	113.3	0.4	108.5	-4.2	109.5	0.9
1981	107.4	-1.9	105.9	-1.4	103.8	-2.0	103.2	-0.6	103.3	0.1	102.6	-0.7	98.5	-4.0	98.9	0.4	102.1	3.2	103.0	0.9	101.9	-1.1	101.8	-0.1
1982	101.2	-0.6	100.8	-0.4	98.9	-1.9	98.7	-0.2	97.9	-0.8	97.1	-0.8	98.6	1.5	96.7	-1.9	102.0	5.5	102.0	0.0	102.0	0.0	103.9	1.9
1983	103.7	-0.2	106.4	2.6	103.6	-2.6	103.6	0.0	103.2	-0.4	104.5	1.3	104.5	0.0	104.3	-0.2	103.3	-1.0	103.2	-0.1	103.2	0.0	104.4	1.2
1984	103.7	-0.7	103.6	-0.1	104.7	1.1	104.0	-0.7	103.6	-0.4	103.5	-0.1	103.5	0.0	104.4	0.9	102.6	-1.7	103.0	0.4	103.4	0.4	103.5	0.1
1985	102.6	-0.9	103.7	1.1	103.0	-0.7	104.2	1.2	103.9	-0.3	103.7	-0.2	103.5	-0.2	103.4	-0.1	103.3	-0.1	103.4	0.1	103.5	0.1	103.1	-0.4
1986	103.7	0.6	103.9	0.2	104.2	0.3	104.4	0.2	104.5	0.1	104.5	0.0	104.6	0.1	105.1	0.5	105.5	0.4	106.1	0.6	106.0	-0.1	105.8	-0.2
1987	106.4	0.6	106.5	0.1	106.8	0.3	107.2	0.4	107.6	0.4	107.9	0.3	108.1	0.2	108.5	0.4	108.5	0.0	109.0	0.5	109.4	0.4	109.5	0.1
1988	110.0	0.5	109.8	-0.2	109.9	0.1	110.3	0.4	110.6	0.3	110.9	0.3	111.4	0.5	111.6	0.2	111.7	0.1	111.6	-0.1	111.9	0.3	112.1	0.2
1989	112.6	0.4	112.9	0.3	113.3	0.4	113.6	0.3	113.8	0.2	113.9	0.1	114.2	0.3	114.5	0.3	114.6	0.1	114.7	0.1	115.0	0.3	115.4	0.3
1990	116.5	1.0	117.0	0.4	117.4	0.3	117.2	-0.2	117.3	0.1	117.6	0.3	117.6	0.0	118.1	0.4	118.1	0.0	118.5	0.3	118.6	0.1	118.5	-0.1
1991	119.7	1.0	119.8	0.1	120.2	0.3	120.4	0.2	120.5	0.1	120.8	0.2	120.9	0.1	120.6	-0.2	120.4	-0.2	120.6	0.2	120.7	0.1	120.9	0.2

[Continued]

Other Miscellaneous Products
Producer Price Index
Base 1982 = 100
[Continued]

For 1947-1997. Columns headed % show percentile change in the index from the previous period for which an index is available.

Year	Jan Index	%	Feb Index	%	Mar Index	%	Apr Index	%	May Index	%	Jun Index	%	Jul Index	%	Aug Index	%	Sep Index	%	Oct Index	%	Nov Index	%	Dec Index	%
1992	121.6	0.6	121.6	0.0	121.7	0.1	122.2	0.4	122.3	0.1	122.4	0.1	122.5	0.1	122.7	0.2	122.6	-0.1	122.8	0.2	123.1	0.2	123.5	0.3
1993	123.9	0.3	124.2	0.2	124.2	0.0	124.9	0.6	125.3	0.3	125.3	0.0	125.8	0.4	126.0	0.2	125.8	-0.2	125.9	0.1	126.1	0.2	126.6	0.4
1994	126.8	0.2	126.6	-0.2	126.5	-0.1	127.0	0.4	127.3	0.2	127.4	0.1	127.7	0.2	127.7	0.0	127.8	0.1	128.0	0.2	128.4	0.3	128.9	0.4
1995	129.8	0.7	130.3	0.4	130.6	0.2	131.4	0.6	132.0	0.5	132.3	0.2	132.5	0.2	132.6	0.1	132.6	0.0	132.7	0.1	133.1	0.3	132.9	-0.2
1996	133.4	0.4	133.3	-0.1	132.6	-0.5	132.6	0.0	132.5	-0.1	132.7	0.2	132.7	0.0	132.9	0.2	132.6	-0.2	132.8	0.2	132.8	0.0	133.1	0.2
1997	133.3	0.2	133.2	-0.1	133.4	0.2	133.7	0.2	133.4	-0.2	133.5	0.1	133.2	-0.2	133.3	0.1	133.3	0.0	133.8	0.4	133.8	0.0	133.7	-0.1

Source: U.S. Department of Labor, Bureau of Labor Statistics, Division of Industry Prices and Price Indexes. n.e.c. stands for not elsewhere classified. - indicates no data collected for period or unavailable.

CHAPTER 8

SELECTED STOCK MARKET
PRICE INDEXES

SELECTED STOCK MARKET PRICE INDEXES

This chapter presents stock market index data for the American Stock Exchange, the NASDAQ Stock Market, and the New York Stock Exchange. The Standard & Poors composite index, used by the Conference Board as a component of the composite index of leading indicators, is shown in Chapter 3.

General Concepts

Stock indexes measure the value of stocks traded on exchanges or in the over-the-counter (OTC) market.

Index Weightings. All the indexes presented here are so-called "market-value weighted" indexes, also called "capitalization-weighted" indexes. This means that the contribution of any one stock to the index is weighted by the stock's overall value—its price multiplied by the number of its shares outstanding.

A stock (Stock A) with a price of $100 per share and 50,000 shares outstanding has a capitalization of $5 million; another stock (Stock B), with a price of $50 and 30,000 shares outstanding has a capitalization of $1.5 million. If only these two stocks were present in a market, the total market would be valued at $6.5 million. Stock A's contribution to index changes would be 77% ($5 million as a percent of $6.5 million); Stock B's contribution would be 23%. Since prices and the number of shares outstanding are constantly changing—and the number of stocks traded is large—any one stock's contribution to an index is continuously in flux and relatively small.

Indexes are calculated so that the distorting effect of stock splits, mergers, and similar changes in corporate capitalization are eliminated.

Alternatives to the market-value weighted indexes are price-weighted indexes (none is shown in *EIH*). In these indexes, for example, in the American Stock Exchange's Major Market Index and the Dow Jones Industrial Average, high-priced stocks have a greater influence on the index than low-priced issues.

Market-value weighted indexes reflect overall market performance; price-weighted indexes tend to reflect the performance of important, leading stocks.

Index Basing. Index values are expressed in relation to a base—the value of the market on a given date. The *base index* may be any value but is 50, 100, or 550 for the data shown here. Index values are calculated using the following formula:

(Market Today / Base Period Market) x Base Index

We can apply this formula to a situation where the base period market was $1,000, today's market is $1,050, and the base index is 100. The new index will be 105 (1,050 / 1,000 x 100). If a different base index is used, 50, for example, the same formula and values would yield a new index of 52.5.

The total market values ("market today" and "base period market") are obtained by adding, for each period, the capital value of all stocks: each stock's price multiplied by the number of shares of that stock outstanding. This, in effect, produces a market-value weighting of each stock.

Analytical Uses

The most common use of stock market indexes is to measure the performance of a given market or, by combining various indexes, measuring the performance of stocks as a whole. Investors can use stock market indexes to measure how well their portfolios are doing. The indexes included in this chapter are all broad composites; therefore, portfolios that under-perform these indexes may be overdue for review. Stock markets are sensitive indicators of anticipated economic conditions; the sustained rise or fall of composite indexes, therefore, can be used to forecast the future—the future as it is seen by all those buying and selling stocks.

Presentation

The composite indexes for the NASDAQ and the New York stock exchanges are presented for 1984-1997 side by side in the first table. The new American Stock Exchange Composite Index (see below) is included in the table as well beginning in December 1995, the basing period of the index. All other tables in this chapter are specific to one of these three stock markets.

American Stock Exchange. The AMEX Market Value Index was replaced, in early 1996, by a new AMEX Composite Index with a base of 550 on December 1995. The revision was made to bring the AMEX Composite more in line with other stock indexes. The old Market Value Index, unlike others, included the value of stock dividends paid. The new index is a market capitalization-weighed, price appreciation index. It is not comparable to the old Market Value Index, which no longer appears in *EIH*. A single table highlights the new AMEX Composite. The table shows monthly performance of the Composite and its 5 sub-indices.

NASDAQ Stock Market. NASDAQ stands for the National Association of Security Dealers Automated Quotation System; NASDAQ reports the prices of more than 5,000 stocks traded over-the-counter (OTC); this is a relatively small subset of the more than 40 million OTC stock issues traded. The base period for the NASDAQ Price Index is February 5, 1971; the base index is 100. Two tables are included for the NASDAQ index; the first shows high, low, and close data for the 1971 to 1995 period; the second shows quarterly data for 1980 through 1997. In addition to the composite index, data for six sub-indices are also included.

New York Stock Exchange. The New York Stock Exchange (NYSE) is the largest U.S. stock exchange, and the NYSE Composite Index reflects the share prices of more than 1,600 stocks traded on the exchange. The index base period is December 31, 1965 and the base index is 50. Two tables are included to summarize the NYSE's performance. The first shows the index from 1990 to 1997 by quarters. Sub-indices are included. The second shows annual high, low, and close data from 1966 through 1997.

Bibliography

1. Berlin, Howard M. *The Handbook of Financial Market Indexes, Averages, and Indicators*. Dow Jones-Irwin, Homewood, IL, 1990.

2. Downes, John and Jordan Elliot Goodman. *Dictionary of Finance and Investment Terms*. Barron's, New York, 1991.

3. *1997 Amex Fact Book*. American Stock Exchange, New York, 1997.

AMEX, NASD, and NYSE Indexes
1984-1997

For 1984-1997. Index is the closing value at month end. Columns headed % show percentile change in each index from the previous period. The acronyms AMEX, NASD, and NYSE stand for American Stock Exchange, National Association of Securities Dealers (over the counter market), and New York Stock Exchange. The American Stock Exchanged introduced a new index in 1996. The old Market Value Index is not shown. For an explanation of the index and related matters, please see the text.

Year	Month	AMEX		NASD		NYSE	
		Index	%	Index	%	Index	%
1984	JAN		-	268.43	-3.7	94.32	-0.9
	FEB		-	252.57	-5.9	90.44	-4.1
	MAR		-	250.78	-0.7	91.67	1.4
	APR		-	247.44	-1.3	91.98	0.3
	MAY		-	232.82	-5.9	86.71	-5.7
	JUN		-	239.65	2.9	88.38	1.9
	JUL		-	229.70	-4.2	86.73	-1.9
	AUG		-	254.64	10.9	95.86	10.5
	SEP		-	249.94	-1.8	95.77	-0.1
	OCT		-	247.03	-1.2	95.74	-0.0
	NOV		-	242.53	-1.8	94.30	-1.5
	DEC		-	247.35	2.0	96.38	2.2
1985	JAN		-	278.70	12.7	103.75	7.6
	FEB		-	284.17	2.0	104.93	1.1
	MAR		-	279.20	-1.7	104.60	-0.3
	APR		-	280.56	0.5	104.12	-0.5
	MAY		-	290.80	3.6	109.63	5.3
	JUN		-	296.20	1.9	111.11	1.3
	JUL		-	301.29	1.7	110.47	-0.6
	AUG		-	297.31	-1.3	109.47	-0.9
	SEP		-	280.33	-5.7	105.19	-3.9
	OCT		-	292.54	4.4	109.65	4.2
	NOV		-	313.95	7.3	116.55	6.3
	DEC		-	324.93	3.5	121.58	4.3
1986	JAN		-	335.77	3.3	122.13	0.5
	FEB		-	359.53	7.1	130.74	7.0
	MAR		-	374.72	4.2	137.71	5.3
	APR		-	383.24	2.3	135.75	-1.4
	MAY		-	400.16	4.4	142.06	4.6
	JUN		-	405.51	1.3	143.96	1.3
	JUL		-	371.37	-8.4	135.89	-5.6
	AUG		-	382.86	3.1	145.32	6.9
	SEP		-	350.67	-8.4	133.44	-8.2
	OCT		-	360.77	2.9	140.42	5.2
	NOV		-	359.57	-0.3	142.57	1.5
	DEC		-	348.83	-3.0	138.58	-2.8
1987	JAN		-	392.06	12.4	156.11	12.6
	FEB		-	424.97	8.4	162.01	3.8
	MAR		-	430.05	1.2	165.89	2.4
	APR		-	417.81	-2.8	162.86	-1.8
	MAY		-	416.54	-0.3	163.48	0.4
	JUN		-	424.67	2.0	171.07	4.6
	JUL		-	434.93	2.4	178.63	4.4
	AUG		-	454.97	4.6	184.45	3.3
	SEP		-	444.29	-2.3	180.24	-2.3
	OCT		-	323.30	-27.2	140.80	-21.9
	NOV		-	305.16	-5.6	129.69	-7.9
	DEC		-	330.47	8.3	138.23	6.6

[Continued]

AMEX, NASD, and NYSE Indexes
1984-1997
[Continued]

Year	Month	AMEX		NASD		NYSE	
		Index	%	Index	%	Index	%
1988	JAN		-	344.66	4.3	144.13	4.3
	FEB		-	366.94	6.5	150.46	4.4
	MAR		-	374.64	2.1	146.60	-2.6
	APR		-	379.23	1.2	147.87	0.9
	MAY		-	370.34	-2.3	148.04	0.1
	JUN		-	394.66	6.6	154.47	4.3
	JUL		-	387.33	-1.9	153.35	-0.7
	AUG		-	376.55	-2.8	148.29	-3.3
	SEP		-	387.71	3.0	153.57	3.6
	OCT		-	382.46	-1.4	156.94	2.2
	NOV		-	371.45	-2.9	153.90	-1.9
	DEC		-	381.38	2.7	156.26	1.5
1989	JAN		-	401.30	5.2	166.63	6.6
	FEB		-	399.71	-0.4	162.49	-2.5
	MAR		-	406.73	1.8	165.63	1.9
	APR		-	427.55	5.1	173.13	4.5
	MAY		-	446.17	4.4	178.85	3.3
	JUN		-	435.29	-2.4	177.90	-0.5
	JUL		-	453.84	4.3	192.41	8.2
	AUG		-	469.33	3.4	195.27	1.5
	SEP		-	472.92	0.8	193.97	-0.7
	OCT		-	455.63	-3.7	188.24	-3.0
	NOV		-	456.09	0.1	191.30	1.6
	DEC		-	454.82	-0.3	195.04	2.0
1990	JAN		-	415.81	-8.6	181.50	-6.9
	FEB		-	425.83	2.4	183.07	0.9
	MAR		-	435.54	2.3	186.84	2.1
	APR		-	420.07	-3.6	181.49	-2.9
	MAY		-	458.97	9.3	196.94	8.5
	JUN		-	462.29	0.7	195.48	-0.7
	JUL		-	438.24	-5.2	194.60	-0.5
	AUG		-	381.21	-13.0	176.97	-9.1
	SEP		-	344.51	-9.6	167.85	-5.2
	OCT		-	329.84	-4.3	166.17	-1.0
	NOV		-	359.06	8.9	176.06	6.0
	DEC		-	373.84	4.1	180.49	2.5
1991	JAN		-	414.20	10.8	187.59	3.9
	FEB		-	453.05	9.4	200.70	7.0
	MAR		-	482.30	6.5	205.30	2.3
	APR		-	484.72	0.5	205.37	0.0
	MAY		-	506.11	4.4	212.99	3.7
	JUN		-	475.92	-6.0	203.47	-4.5
	JUL		-	502.04	5.5	212.34	4.4
	AUG		-	525.68	4.7	216.69	2.0
	SEP		-	526.88	0.2	213.34	-1.5
	OCT		-	542.98	3.1	216.54	1.5
	NOV		-	523.90	-3.5	207.75	-4.1
	DEC		-	586.34	11.9	229.44	10.4

[Continued]

AMEX, NASD, and NYSE Indexes
1984-1997
[Continued]

Year	Month	AMEX		NASD		NYSE	
		Index	%	Index	%	Index	%
1992	JAN		-	620.21	5.8	226.20	-1.4
	FEB		-	633.47	2.1	228.21	0.9
	MAR		-	603.77	-4.7	223.25	-2.2
	APR		-	578.68	-4.2	228.30	2.3
	MAY		-	585.31	1.1	228.87	0.2
	JUN		-	563.60	-3.7	224.33	-2.0
	JUL		-	580.83	3.1	233.15	3.9
	AUG		-	563.12	-3.0	228.03	-2.2
	SEP		-	583.27	3.6	229.46	0.6
	OCT		-	605.17	3.8	230.57	0.5
	NOV		-	652.73	7.9	237.45	3.0
	DEC		-	676.95	3.7	240.21	1.2
1993	JAN		-	696.34	2.9	241.92	0.7
	FEB		-	670.77	-3.7	244.08	0.9
	MAR		-	690.13	2.9	249.42	2.2
	APR		-	661.42	-4.2	243.46	-2.4
	MAY		-	700.53	5.9	248.60	2.1
	JUN		-	703.95	0.5	249.10	0.2
	JUL		-	704.70	0.1	248.49	-0.2
	AUG		-	742.84	5.4	256.88	3.4
	SEP		-	762.78	2.7	255.23	-0.6
	OCT		-	779.26	2.2	259.38	1.6
	NOV		-	754.39	-3.2	254.79	-1.8
	DEC		-	776.80	3.0	259.08	1.7
1994	JAN		-	800.47	3.0	267.10	3.1
	FEB		-	792.50	-1.0	259.23	-2.9
	MAR		-	743.46	-6.2	247.06	-4.7
	APR		-	733.84	-1.3	250.36	1.3
	MAY		-	735.19	0.2	252.24	0.8
	JUN		-	705.96	-4.0	245.15	-2.8
	JUL		-	722.16	2.3	252.62	3.0
	AUG		-	765.62	6.0	261.99	3.7
	SEP		-	764.29	-0.2	255.52	-2.5
	OCT		-	777.49	1.7	258.61	1.2
	NOV		-	750.32	-3.5	248.41	-3.9
	DEC		-	751.96	0.2	250.94	1.0
1995	JAN		-	755.20	0.4	255.93	2.0
	FEB		-	793.73	5.1	264.65	3.4
	MAR		-	817.21	3.0	271.04	2.4
	APR		-	843.98	3.3	277.31	2.3
	MAY		-	864.58	2.4	286.44	3.3
	JUN		-	933.45	8.0	291.84	1.9
	JUL		-	1001.21	7.3	301.32	3.2
	AUG		-	1020.11	1.9	302.00	0.2
	SEP		-	1043.54	2.3	313.26	3.7
	OCT		-	1036.06	-0.7	309.61	-1.2
	NOV		-	1059.20	2.2	323.59	4.5
	DEC	550.00	-	1052.13	-0.7	329.51	1.8

[Continued]

AMEX, NASD, and NYSE Indexes
1984-1997

[Continued]

Year	Month	AMEX		NASD		NYSE	
		Index	%	Index	%	Index	%
1996	JAN	554.51	0.8	1059.79	0.7	340.03	3.2
	FEB	564.61	1.8	1100.05	3.8	342.80	0.8
	MAR	573.76	1.6	1101.40	0.1	346.92	1.2
	APR	592.94	3.3	1190.52	8.1	351.24	1.2
	MAY	613.15	3.4	1243.43	4.4	358.83	2.2
	JUN	576.28	-6.0	1185.02	-4.7	359.20	0.1
	JUL	537.15	-6.8	1080.59	-8.8	342.70	-4.6
	AUG	556.88	3.7	1141.50	5.6	350.99	2.4
	SEP	568.17	2.0	1226.92	7.5	367.33	4.7
	OCT	561.56	-1.2	1221.51	-0.4	374.50	2.0
	NOV	582.73	3.8	1292.61	5.8	398.43	6.4
	DEC	572.34	-1.8	1291.03	-0.1	392.30	-1.5
1997	JAN	588.77	2.9	1379.85	6.9	411.98	5.0
	FEB	594.24	0.9	1309.00	-5.1	415.51	0.9
	MAR	568.71	-4.3	1221.70	-6.7	398.55	-4.1
	APR	552.91	-2.8	1260.76	3.2	416.94	4.6
	MAY	605.38	9.5	1400.32	11.1	441.78	6.0
	JUN	622.57	2.8	1442.07	3.0	462.44	4.7
	JUL	646.30	3.8	1593.81	10.5	494.50	6.9
	AUG	650.16	0.6	1587.32	-0.4	470.48	-4.9
	SEP	699.26	7.6	1685.69	6.2	497.23	5.7
	OCT	675.75	-3.4	1593.61	-5.5	481.14	-3.2
	NOV	662.11	-2.0	1600.55	0.4	499.10	3.7
	DEC	684.61	3.4	1570.35	-1.9	511.19	2.4

Source: Data obtained from each of the exchanges shown.

American Stock Exchange Index
Composite Index and Sub-Indices

For 1996-1997 by month. Index base for the Composite Index is 550 for December 1995. Subindex bases are 100 for December 1995.

Year	Month	Composite Index	Financial sub-index	Healthcare sub-index	Industrial sub-index	Information technologies sub-index	Natural resources sub-index
1996	January	554.51	103.17	102.66	104.97	93.28	104.08
	February	564.61	104.62	105.94	105.78	96.33	105.11
	March	573.76	105.09	100.97	107.79	95.41	111.51
	April	592.94	106.09	109.54	113.09	98.92	116.05
	May	613.15	106.99	110.13	119.52	101.65	120.80
	June	576.28	105.48	94.66	113.13	95.67	113.99
	July	537.15	104.66	80.30	105.26	86.11	111.34
	August	556.88	106.87	89.32	110.40	84.22	118.24
	September	568.17	107.12	92.00	111.07	90.33	116.87
	October	561.56	109.97	87.68	107.65	85.98	121.87
	November	582.73	114.45	83.65	111.36	94.88	124.76
	December	572.34	116.14	80.54	110.31	90.00	126.47
1997	January	588.77	119.67	86.50	112.81	90.17	128.63
	February	594.24	122.88	85.76	115.39	90.19	127.86
	March	568.71	119.45	76.24	109.68	84.89	127.20
	April	552.91	121.65	74.85	107.20	77.36	124.42
	May	605.38	128.81	84.78	117.77	86.00	135.68
	June	622.57	136.43	88.02	120.44	87.31	136.54
	July	646.30	139.03	86.13	127.19	91.62	142.57
	August	650.16	138.78	86.73	128.94	90.25	145.20
	September	699.26	148.73	96.47	137.19	98.61	154.73
	October	675.75	148.86	90.49	130.97	94.20	151.51
	November	662.11	150.99	88.02	130.75	100.11	131.85
	December	684.61	156.71	90.18	132.84	109.62	132.07

Source: 1997 *Amex Fact Book*. American Stock Exchange, 1997 and *FactSet Research Systems*, the American Stock Exchange, February 1998.

NASDAQ Composite Index
Yearly High, Low, and Close
1971-1997

For 1971 through 1997. Dates indicate the date of high and low values reached in the year. Close is the last day of the year. Percent change is from previous year-end. The NASDAQ index began on February 5, 1971.

Year	High Index	High Date	Low Index	Low Date	Close Index	% Change
1971	114.12	12/31	99.68	2/22	114.12	-
1972	135.15	12/8	113.65	1/3	133.73	17.2
1973	136.84	1/11	88.67	12/24	92.19	-31.1
1974	96.53	3/15	54.87	10/3	59.82	-35.1
1975	88.00	7/15	60.70	1/2	77.62	29.8
1976	97.88	12/31	78.06	1/2	97.88	26.1
1977	105.05	12/30	93.66	4/5	105.05	7.3
1978	139.25	9/13	99.09	1/11	117.98	12.3
1979	152.29	10/5	117.84	1/2	151.14	28.1
1980	208.15	11/28	124.09	3/27	202.34	33.9
1981	223.47	5/29	175.03	9/28	195.84	-3.2
1982	240.70	12/8	159.14	8/13	232.41	18.7
1983	328.91	6/24	230.59	1/3	278.60	19.9
1984	287.90	1/6	225.30	7/25	247.35	-11.2
1985	325.22	12/31	245.91	1/2	325.22	31.5
1986	411.16	7/3	323.01	1/9	348.83	7.3
1987	455.26	8/26	291.88	10/28	330.47	-5.3
1988	396.11	7/5	331.97	1/12	381.38	15.4
1989	485.73	10/9	378.56	1/3	454.82	19.3
1990	469.60	7/16	325.44	10/16	373.84	-17.8
1991	586.34	12/31	355.75	1/14	586.34	56.8
1992	676.95	12/31	547.84	6/26	676.95	15.5
1993	787.42	10/15	645.87	4/26	776.80	14.7
1994	803.93	3/18	693.79	6/24	751.96	-3.2
1995	1069.79	12/4	743.58	1/3	1052.13	40.0
1996	1316.27	12/9	988.57	1/15	1291.03	22.7
1997	1745.85	10/9	1201.00	4/2	1570.35	21.6

Source: The NASDAQ Stock Market, Historical Data Services.

NASDAQ Stock Market Index
Quarterly Index and Sub-Indices

For 1980-1997 by Quarters. Data show closing index for each period.

QTR	Year	Composite Index	Industrials	Banks	Insurance	Financials	Trans-portation	Computers
1	1980	131.00	155.70	93.29	133.26	109.84	105.28	-
2		157.78	185.74	108.34	158.94	136.35	125.10	-
3		187.76	233.90	114.87	176.90	148.74	160.17	-
4		202.34	261.36	118.39	166.81	154.07	164.19	-
1	1981	210.18	264.85	126.96	184.80	168.44	171.81	-
2		215.75	265.68	138.92	198.44	178.53	193.04	-
3		180.03	212.22	128.86	177.56	160.41	166.15	-
4		195.84	229.29	143.13	194.31	176.20	167.77	-
1	1982	175.65	199.05	136.66	188.09	165.00	148.10	-
2		171.30	196.33	130.61	172.49	158.52	151.46	-
3		187.65	213.35	134.16	201.84	177.31	172.50	-
4		232.41	273.58	156.37	226.40	207.50	195.48	-
1	1983	270.80	323.52	169.58	259.19	235.16	230.82	-
2		318.70	392.90	186.70	268.63	269.96	259.46	-
3		296.65	353.52	201.06	262.89	280.58	277.99	-
4		278.60	323.68	203.75	257.63	277.53	280.80	-
1	1984	250.78	283.34	204.09	254.19	270.20	228.19	-
2		239.65	270.65	194.48	244.26	258.28	203.71	-
3		249.94	275.16	209.23	271.59	281.23	224.99	-
4		247.35	260.73	229.77	283.11	298.62	239.29	-
1	1985	279.20	297.37	253.43	326.29	330.37	255.54	-
2		296.20	303.82	290.49	350.14	377.06	261.79	-
3		280.33	284.39	296.10	329.77	365.53	256.52	-
4		325.22	330.17	349.36	382.07	423.49	291.59	-
1	1986	374.72	375.91	403.25	455.06	499.73	340.56	-
2		405.51	409.96	450.45	452.72	543.95	362.92	-
3		350.67	344.16	403.70	425.20	482.84	322.95	-
4		348.83	349.33	412.53	404.14	460.64	348.84	-
1	1987	430.05	454.21	506.19	446.17	527.82	398.87	-
2		424.67	450.71	475.48	433.04	511.97	406.13	-
3		444.29	475.25	489.82	457.39	520.74	418.38	-
4		330.47	338.94	390.66	351.06	406.96	319.21	-
1	1988	374.64	383.67	448.77	397.65	456.39	373.51	-
2		394.66	411.48	455.91	398.36	468.43	374.07	-
3		387.71	388.19	456.94	435.45	473.20	390.74	-
4		381.38	378.95	435.31	429.14	459.34	395.81	-
1	1989	406.73	398.63	458.57	470.56	487.75	412.84	-
2		435.29	421.71	466.03	505.05	513.14	421.25	-
3		472.92	458.97	478.84	533.63	559.54	476.97	-
4		454.82	447.99	391.02	546.01	505.64	498.20	-
1	1990	435.54	450.51	366.25	502.65	466.36	476.70	-
2		462.29	499.01	335.71	506.31	446.61	488.28	-
3		344.51	368.46	249.25	406.56	340.34	389.31	-
4		373.84	406.05	254.91	451.84	359.13	417.07	-
1	1991	482.30	545.03	310.15	548.98	437.31	509.21	-
2		475.92	527.10	327.30	534.39	472.42	513.80	-
3		526.88	590.19	343.52	534.10	521.94	530.73	-
4		586.34	668.95	350.56	601.09	560.79	571.39	-

[Continued]

NASDAQ Stock Market Index
Quarterly Index and Sub-Indices
[Continued]

QTR	Year	Composite Index	Industrials	Banks	Insurance	Financials	Trans-portation	Computers
1	1992	603.77	676.05	396.32	617.46	621.85	604.09	-
2		563.60	601.65	442.93	623.26	666.02	551.92	-
3		583.27	620.85	462.50	705.60	687.31	567.47	-
4		676.95	724.94	532.93	803.91	788.81	634.10	-
1	1993	690.13	713.55	627.47	861.30	860.92	672.01	-
2		703.95	729.52	607.88	853.02	834.96	673.48	-
3		762.78	780.13	698.81	946.00	907.00	701.78	-
4		776.80	805.84	689.43	920.59	892.64	746.26	-
1	1994	727.41	760.80	662.57	864.59	860.68	734.19	201.48
2		706.85	715.83	761.83	880.94	931.59	690.03	188.43
3		760.88	773.25	767.81	942.65	931.93	706.39	212.27
4		743.58	743.47	702.95	921.12	861.99	657.00	229.99
1	1995	818.05	801.44	769.10	1021.77	944.26	701.26	269.10
2		934.53	886.49	849.88	1057.38	1033.25	777.65	336.69
3		1027.57	966.32	962.09	1171.88	1166.12	795.36	360.03
4		1052.13	964.68	1009.41	1292.64	1240.87	816.36	366.13
1	1996	1106.57	1029.59	1056.39	1295.38	1296.98	882.14	382.40
2		1197.45	1119.92	1079.18	1319.56	1306.18	892.01	438.37
3		1221.51	1099.02	1150.46	1340.68	1434.97	844.62	465.99
4		1291.03	1109.63	1273.46	1465.43	1595.10	907.43	518.79
1	1997	1216.93	1010.52	1371.10	1425.24	1661.43	848.54	484.98
2		1438.25	1181.41	1629.86	1655.45	1917.56	969.70	589.21
3		1690.30	1376.36	1903.18	1822.97	2256.92	1118.17	702.79
4		1570.35	1221.03	2083.22	1797.95	2503.68	1064.77	618.66

Source: The NASDAQ Stock Market, Historical Data Services.

New York Stock Exchange Composite Index
Yearly High, Low, and Close
1966-1997

For 1966 through 1997. Dates indicate the date of high and low values reached in the year. Close is the last day of the year. Percent change is from previous year-end.

Year	High		Low		Close	% Change
	Index	Date	Index	Date	Index	
1966	51.06	9/2	39.37	7/10	43.72	-12.6
1967	54.16	9/10	43.74	3/1	53.83	23.1
1968	61.27	29/11	48.70	5/3	58.90	9.4
1969	59.32	14/5	49.31	29/7	51.53	-12.5
1970	52.36	5/1	37.69	26/5	50.23	-2.5
1971	57.76	28/4	49.60	23/11	56.43	12.3
1972	65.14	11/12	56.23	3/1	64.48	14.3
1973	65.48	11/1	49.05	5/12	51.82	-19.6
1974	53.37	13/3	32.89	3/10	36.13	-30.3
1975	51.24	15/7	37.06	2/1	47.64	31.9
1976	57.88	31/12	48.04	2/1	57.88	21.5
1977	57.69	3/1	49.78	2/11	52.50	-9.3
1978	60.38	11/9	48.37	6/3	53.62	2.1
1979	63.39	5/10	53.88	27/2	61.95	15.5
1980	81.02	28/11	55.30	27/3	77.86	25.7
1981	79.14	6/1	64.96	25/9	71.11	-8.7
1982	82.35	9/11	58.80	12/8	81.03	14.0
1983	99.63	10/10	79.79	3/1	95.18	17.5
1984	98.12	6/11	85.13	24/7	96.38	1.3
1985	121.90	16/12	94.60	4/1	121.58	26.1
1986	145.75	4/9	117.75	22/1	138.58	14.0
1987	187.99	25/8	125.91	4/12	138.23	-0.3
1988	159.42	21/10	136.72	20/1	156.26	13.0
1989	199.34	9/10	154.98	3/1	195.04	24.8
1990	201.13	16/7	162.20	11/10	180.49	-7.5
1991	229.44	31/12	170.97	9/1	229.44	27.1
1992	242.08	18/12	217.92	8/4	240.21	4.7
1993	260.67	29/12	236.21	8/1	259.08	7.9
1994	267.71	2/2	243.14	4/4	250.94	-3.1
1995	331.17	12/13	250.73	1/3	329.51	31.3
1996	398.86	11/25	321.41	1/10	392.30	19.1
1997	514.31	12/5	389.47	4/11	511.19	30.3

Source: New York Stock Exchange Data Services.

New York Stock Exchange Index
Quarterly Index and Sub-Indices

Data show closing values for the New York Stock Exchange composite index and sub-indices for 1990-1997 by quarters.

Quarter	Year	Composite	Industrial	Transportation	Utility	Finance
1	1990	186.85	227.42	177.41	93.48	140.75
2		195.48	242.35	172.56	91.87	144.75
3		167.85	209.19	130.38	84.41	110.78
4		180.49	223.60	141.49	91.30	122.07
1	1991	205.30	256.82	164.05	93.53	148.94
2		203.47	256.02	169.75	89.19	147.69
3		213.34	266.08	179.93	95.50	159.54
4		229.44	285.82	201.87	102.13	172.68
1	1992	223.25	279.66	200.93	93.70	172.33
2		224.33	277.98	199.68	97.31	178.36
3		229.46	283.52	190.86	102.89	180.96
4		240.21	294.39	214.72	104.83	200.83
1	1993	249.42	299.62	232.00	114.30	218.31
2		249.10	298.44	238.08	231.03	217.33
3		255.23	301.11	251.75	242.72	231.56
4		259.08	315.26	270.48	229.92	216.82
1	1994	247.06	304.56	252.48	208.35	204.19
2		245.16	301.49	242.06	202.68	208.91
3		255.52	320.63	231.66	205.26	205.94
4		250.94	318.10	222.46	198.41	195.80
1	1995	271.04	344.26	252.43	205.07	215.33
2		291.84	370.63	262.99	216.94	235.86
3		313.26	392.66	294.59	234.90	264.89
4		329.51	413.29	301.96	252.90	274.25
1	1996	346.92	439.26	323.40	245.68	292.39
2		359.20	457.35	329.80	254.55	295.83
3		367.33	467.90	327.90	244.28	315.08
4		392.30	494.38	352.30	259.91	351.17
1	1997	398.55	502.88	358.40	257.21	360.32
2		462.44	586.33	414.70	284.53	421.02
3		497.23	626.04	459.79	297.35	469.59
4		511.19	630.38	466.25	335.19	495.96

Source: New York Stock Exchange. Obtained from the NYSE Web page at www.nyse.com in February 1998.

KEYWORD INDEX

The *Keyword Index* is an alphabetical arrangement of the topics covered in the text and tables of *Economic Indicators Handbook*, 4th edition. The table of contents (page v) provides an alternative means of locating tables. The primary reference numbers that follow subject index terms are page numbers. Cities cited in this index are metropolitan statistical areas (MSAs). The abbreviation 'n.e.c.' stands for 'not elsewhere classified.'

Numbers following p. or pp. are page references.

Numbers following p. or pp. are page references.

Numbers following p. or pp. are page references.

Numbers following p. or pp. are page references.

Numbers following p. or pp. are page references.